D0467671

THE COMPLETE

New York Yankees

THE TOTAL ENCYCLOPEDIA OF THE TEAM

THE COMPLETE
New York
Yankees

THE TOTAL ENCYCLOPEDIA OF THE TEAM

With text by Derek Gentile

BLACK DOG
& LEVENTHAL
PUBLISHERS
NEW YORK

HOUSTON PUBLIC LIBRARY

R01251 13823

Copyright © 2001 Black Dog & Leventhal Publishers, Inc.

All rights reserved. No part of this book may be reproduced in any form or by any electronic or mechanical means including information storage and retrieval systems without written permission of the publisher.

Published by Black Dog & Leventhal Publishers, Inc.
151 West 19th Street, New York, NY 10011

Distributed by Workman Publishing Company
708 Broadway, New York, NY 10003

Statistics courtesy of Baseball Oracle by Lucid Software Engineering

Additional statistical consultation provided by David Chandler

Designed by Martin Lubin Graphic Design

Printed in the United States of America

ISBN 1-57912-152-7

h g f e d c

Library of Congress Cataloging-in-Publication Data

Gentile, Derek.
 The Complete New York Yankees : the total encyclopedia of the team / by Derek Gentile.
  p. cm.
  ISBN 1-57912-152-7
   1. New York Yankees (Baseball team)—History. 2. New York Yankees (Baseball team)—Statistics. 3. Baseball players—United States—Biography. I. Title
GV875.N4 G45 2000
796.357'09747'1—dc21   00-044481

Acknowledgments

Thanks are in order to a number of people who helped put together this book. This would include my two research assistants, *Berkshire Eagle* sports editor Brian Sullivan and radio station WSBS sports announcer Jack Passetto. Both men, die-hard Yankee fans, were enthusiastic about the project, and the only time they pestered me was to ask if they could do any more. They were the kind of associates of which one could only dream.

Thanks, too, go out to several colleagues at the *Berkshire Eagle,* who encouraged me throughout the length of this effort. These would include Donna Mattoon, now a big shot at IBM, and my fellow news-gatherer Tim Cebula.

Much gratitude goes to Lisi de Bourbon, now a big shot at the Associated Press in New York City, who provided spiritual sustenance when things looked difficult and a sense of humor at all times.

Thanks, too, to my mother and father, and my four sisters and their families, who have put up with me for years now, with nary a whimper. I owe them more than they could imagine.

Finally, thanks to my editor, Michael Driscoll and publisher, J.P. Leventhal, for giving me a chance to tackle this in the first place. They are true professionals and gentlemen.

CONTENTS

The Story of the New York Yankees

The History of the Yankees

1 IN THE BEGINNING

Even 100 years ago, there was no getting around the fact that if a consortium of sports teams wanted to be known as "big league," they needed to have a team in New York City. When the American League (AL) was hatched at the turn of the last century, however, it did not include a team in New York. And that was a problem.

The president of the American League at the time was also its founder: Byron "Ban" Johnson, a former sportswriter from Cincinnati who had revitalized the old Western Association, expanded it and renamed it the American League.

The league officially began operations in 1901. It had teams in Baltimore, Boston, Chicago, Cleveland, Detroit, Milwaukee, Philadelphia and Washington, D.C. But Johnson, at least, believed that a team in New York would solidify the

chances for the survival of the new league. Johnson also wanted badly to have a team in New York to compete against his old nemesis, John McGraw of the Giants.

So Johnson spent almost two years rectifying that problem. After a slew of legal maneuvers, principally against the politically connected New York Giants of the National League (NL), Johnson managed to move the original Baltimore Orioles north.

Thus was born the American League Base Ball Club of New York. They played at the northern end of Manhattan, at a hastily constructed park on Broadway between 165th and 168th streets in the Washington Heights neighborhood. It was about ten blocks north of the Polo Grounds, the home of the Giants. The park was located on what was then deemed the highest point in Manhattan and was dubbed Hilltop Park or Highland Park.

The Highlanders (later dubbed "Yankees") played at Hilltop Park from 1903 until 1913, when they moved to the Polo Grounds.

The team was nicknamed the Highlanders, but sportswriters of the time hated it because there was no way of shortening the name on second reference. So reporters dubbed the team the Americans, the Hilltoppers, the Kilties (as in Highlanders) and the Invaders. The latter name referred to the "invasion" of an American League team into what some deemed National League turf.

It was a major league operation, but there were a lot of not-so–major league components to the Highlanders. Highland Park, for example, was built in part on a ledge. The ball field was rocky and the infield pocked with holes and ruts. The ballplayers called it "the Rockpile." There was no clubhouse at the park for many years, forcing players to dress for the game in a hotel.

The park itself was basically a wooden structure thrown together for about $15,000. It seated 15,000 patrons. It looked old and rickety a few months after it was built.

The owners of the team were a pair of characters. Frank Farrell was a well-known New York City gambler. William "Big Bill" Devery was the former chief of the New York Police Department. Devery often bragged that he had never read a book in his life. Farrell had made a habit of keeping a host of local politicians on his payroll.

Johnson and sportswriter Joe Vila arranged for Farrell and Devery to purchase the Baltimore franchise for $18,000, and Johnson oversaw the construction of the ballpark in Manhattan. Well aware of the oddball reputations of his two New York owners, Johnson arranged for Joseph W. Gordon, a former New York assemblyman and the former owner of the New York Metropolitans of the American Association, to act as team president and front man.

One thing he didn't have to do was find better players for the team. Farrell and Devery, like most American League owners, found some of their best players by raiding the rosters of rival National League teams.

Outfielder "Wee Willie" Keeler, an 11-year National League veteran, was plucked from the Brooklyn Superbas, and veteran shortstop Herman Long came from the Boston Braves. But the Highlanders really stuck it to Pittsburgh. Pitcher Jack Chesbro came from the defending National

League champions, as did second-year third baseman Wid Conroy, 16-year veteran catcher John "Peach Pie" O'Connor, utility outfielder Alfonzo "Lefty" Davis and lefthander Jesse Tannehill, Chesbro's bullpen mate, a 20-game winner for the Pirates in 1902.

The New York consortium also hired Clark Griffith from the Chicago White Sox to manage. Griffith pitched as well.

New York did okay in its inaugural season, going 72-62 and finishing fourth, 17 games behind the eventual World Champion Boston Pilgrims. Keeler was fifth in the league in hitting, at .318, Chesbro's 21 wins were third and Conroy stole 33 bases, also fifth in the circuit. New York lost their opener, 3-1 at Washington on April 22. Harry Howell picked up the first win in franchise history the next day, a 7-2 decision at Washington. The Yankees also won their first-ever home opener, 6-2, also against Washington, on April 30. Ban Johnson threw out the first ball, and with an overflow crowd of 16,000 fans watching, Chesbro picked up the win.

But the team was not a success at the gate. The Highlanders drew only 211,808 on the year, the fewest fans the franchise would ever draw. (The Pirates, despite the loss of all those ballplayers, still finished first in the NL.)

Chesbro's 33 complete games were second in the league that year. He was a spitballer, and throwing the pitch didn't take a lot out of his arm. That was a good thing, because he carried the team on his back the next year.

In 1904, the Highlanders and Boston Pilgrims engaged in a thrilling pennant race that saw Boston win the American League flag by 1½ games.

The Pilgrims had a superb pitching staff led by the immortal Cy Young and the pretty-darn-good-in-his-own-right Bill Dineen, not to mention Tannehill, who had been traded to Boston for the promising but ultimately mediocre "Long" Tom Hughes just before the season began. Young, Dineen and Tannehill all won 20 games for Boston that year.

New York could only counter with Chesbro, Jake Powell and a staff that was mostly journeymen. Keeler hit .343 to lead the league, and New York used a 48-28 June, July and August to go from four games over .500 to 24 games above the break-even mark and propel them into the hunt.

Chesbro was a horse that year, starting 51 games, completing 48 and winning 41, numbers that are all still American League marks. His 454⅔ innings is second all-time to Ed Walsh's 464 in 1908. But with Chesbro and Powell (23 wins) combining for 64 of New York's 92 wins and 85 of their 123 complete games, New York fans rooted for "Jack and Jake and a rainout, for gosh sake" for most of the year.

The key series of the season was in Hilltop Park, the last day of the season, before a huge crowd of 25,584. Boston was 94-58, 1½ games ahead of New York at 91-58. If New York won both games, the Highlanders would win the pennant on the basis of a superior winning percentage. No provisions were made for making up rained-out games in those days, which was why New York had played three fewer contests.

But Chesbro, who had been almost flawless until that point, uncorked a wild pitch with the game tied, 2-2, in the ninth inning, scoring Boston base runner Lou Criger. The New Yorkers failed to score in their half of the inning and Boston won the flag.

In retrospect, although Chesbro's wild pitch probably cost the Highlanders the pennant, what really killed them was the Tannehill trade. Tannehill won 21 games for Boston, while Hughes won seven for New York. The Manhattanites wouldn't get as close for 16 more years.

The next season saw a radical backslide. Spitballs generally didn't take much out of a pitcher's arm, but Chesbro still probably shouldn't have thrown 450-plus innings in 1904. The next year, he became human again, winning 19 games and completing "only" 24 games. New York fell to 71-78.

Chesbro bounced back in 1906, and so did New York. The Highlanders, behind Chesbro and veteran Al "the Curveless Wonder" Orth, won 90 games and lost 61 to finish only 3 games behind the White Sox for the American League flag.

Orth was a strapping righty (6 feet, 195 pounds)

with a minimum of finesse. His principal pitch was a fastball, but he was a master at changing speeds. (He never did learn how to throw a good curveball, though, hence his nickname.) Picked up in mid season in 1904, he would go on to win 27 games in the 1906 campaign, with Chesbro winning 24.

But once again, the Highlanders would fall short in 1906 because of their thin pitching. Chicago won the pennant with 20-game winners Nick Altrock and Frank "Yip" Owen, as well as fastballers Eddie Walsh and Doc White. New York just couldn't match that, with only one other starter, journeyman "Buffalo Billy" Hogg, winning more than ten games, despite the fact that Keeler hit .304 and first baseman Hal Chase hit .323. The Highlanders were in first place in mid-September, but a 3-7 slump the last week of the month killed their chances.

The Highlanders' up-and-down fortunes began to curve downward. They were 70-78 in 1907, 21 games out of first, and 51-103 in 1908, 39½ games out and dead last in the league. The 1908 season saw Orth fall to 14-21, Chesbro to 10-10. Farrell fired Gordon, who was reportedly not unhappy to leave, and took over as president. Griffith was also fired as manager, and veteran shortstop Norman "the Tabasco Kid" Elberfeld took over the managerial duties. He didn't fare too well, either.

In 1909, Chase contracted smallpox in spring training. That was about the highlight of the season, as New York went 74-77, finishing 23½ games out of first place. The entire team was vaccinated and quarantined as the team headed north. George Stallings was hired to manage the team, replacing Elberfeld. Pitcher Jack Quinn was signed.

Chase would replace Stallings late in the 1910 season, as the team finished a respectable 88-63, 14½ games behind the powerful Athletics. Quinn won 18 games and rookie Russ Ford had a career year, with 26 wins and 8 shutouts. Diminutive (5 feet 6 inches, 155 pounds) outfielder William Franklin "Birdie" Cree was also a key, hitting .287 and, with Chase, leading the team in home runs (4) and RBI (73).

But with Chase running the show in 1911, things went terribly sour. In 1910, Stallings had complained to Farrell that Chase was throwing ballgames. Stallings was shown the door for his efforts, with Chase being elevated to coach. The team showed its support for that move in 1911 by dropping to 76-76, good for sixth place, 25½ games out of first.

Chase may or may not have been throwing games, but with Farrell's shady gambling connections, it was a suspect relationship at best, and even Farrell realized it. Farrell replaced Chase as manager with Harry Wolverton, who promptly drove the team into the cellar in 1912.

The 1912 Highlanders were 50-102, 55 games out of first place. There are few arguments that this was the worst team in franchise history. Chase, supposedly the best fielding first baseman in the game, led the league with 27 errors, so who knows whether he was trying to win games or bets. Ford, who had won 26 and 22 games in his first two years, managed a 13-21 season with 30 complete games. On April 20, the Boston Red Sox christened Fenway Park with a 7-6 win over the Highlanders before a crowd of 26,000. New York also unveiled its new pinstripe look that year.

Wolverton was fired before the 1913 season and Frank "the Peerless Leader" Chance was hired to run the club. Chance had been the premier first baseman in the National League with the Cubs, and had managed Chicago to four National League pennants and two World Championships. Farrell and Devery figured that Chance would pull some of the headlines away from New York Giant manager John McGraw.

Chance might have, if he had more than a handful of decent ballplayers. Pitcher Ray Caldwell was coming into his own, Cree was still good and rookie shortstop Roger "Peck" Peckinpaugh looked like he could play.

But that was about it. Chance moved players in and out of New York all year. A total of 45 players wore the pinstripes in 1913. One of Chance's moves was to trade Chase to the White Sox. Even though he was almost certainly betting on games, Chase was a popular player in New York. Chance was ripped in the papers and the team, now commonly called "The Yankees" by sportswriters, finished 57-94, one game ahead of last-place St. Louis.

The team also moved out of Hilltop Park that year. It was beginning to get pretty seedy-looking, and Farrell and Devery had no interest in paying for maintenance of the facility. They struck a deal with the Giants to rent the Polo Grounds when the Giants were out of town, and in 1914, Hilltop Park was razed.

Chance lasted for most of the 1914 season, but it was obvious to him that neither Farrell nor Devery had any intention of spending more than was necessary to keep the club afloat. So about two weeks from the end of the year, Chance quit and returned to his native California. Peckinpaugh was named manager.

Peck became, at 23, the youngest manager in major league history. New York finished 9-8 under him and 70-84 overall, 30 games behind the Athletics. Third baseman Fritz Maisel was the lone bright spot on offense, stealing a franchise record 74 bases, while Caldwell somehow won 17 games.

But by the end of 1914, the Yankees were a franchise in utter disarray. The team averaged well under 350,000 in attendance for its first 12 years, and Devery and Farrell were losing money hand over fist, each blaming the other for the whole fiasco.

They explained their plight to Giants' coach John McGraw, and told him they wanted to sell the team to whoever would take it. McGraw told Devery and Farrell he would see what he could do.

McGraw and his wife were good friends with Col. Tillinghast L'Hommedieu Huston, an engineer who had made his fortune in Cuba following the Spanish-American War. McGraw also knew Colonel Jacob Ruppert, a wealthy New York brewer and sportsman. Both men, ironically, were Giants fans. They were looking to purchase a baseball team, and initially they wanted to buy the Giants. McGraw told them that the team was not for sale. But, he said, he knew of a team that was.

On January 11, 1915, Ruppert and Huston bought the Yankees for $460,000. Immediately they set about upgrading the team, to show fans they were serious about turning it into a winner. Peckinpaugh was retired as manager to enable him to concentrate on playing, and "Wild Bill"

In the early days at the Polo Grounds, fans often parked their buggies and watched the game from beyond the outfield line.

Donovan was named to the post. Donovan's previous experience as manager was as honcho of the pennant-winning Providence Grays the year before. His star player had been a rookie named Babe Ruth.

The team stayed in better hotels, had their uniforms washed daily and slept in upgraded railroad cars. But in 1915–17 they never finished higher than fourth, and averaged a little more than 358,000 fans per year. Not exactly a tremendous improvement.

But they were making progress. First baseman Wally Pipp was purchased from Detroit. Pitcher Bob Shawkey was signed. And in 1916, the Yankees picked up Frank "Home Run" Baker, a bona fide star. These Yankees could hit, and in fact the Yanks of this era were dubbed "Murderers' Row" long before Babe Ruth or Lou Gehrig was on the roster.

On April 24, 1917, lefty George Mogridge no-hit the Red Sox in Fenway Park, winning 2-1 for the first no-hit game in Yankee history.

But Ruppert, in particular, was not happy with Donovan. The Yankees were getting players, but they weren't winning. Ruppert, more than anything, wanted to win. Without consulting Huston, he hired Miller Huggins, the St. Louis "Mighty Mite," to replace Donovan just before the beginning of the 1918 season.

Huggins had a couple strikes against him before he stepped to the managerial plate. His previous stint as a head man had been with the St. Louis Cardinals, who had had two winning seasons in St. Louis in his five years at the helm, never finishing better than third.

Plus, of course, Huston was furious at Ruppert for the decision. He had wanted his pal, former Brooklyn Dodger coach Wilbert Robinson, to take the helm. In addition, Donovan had been popular with the press, while Huggins was more reserved. Ruppert eventually made up with Huston, but Huston and Huggins never trusted each other.

In 1918, second baseman Del Pratt was picked up in a trade. The Yankees went 60-63 in a season shortened by World War I. In 1919, the Yankees traded for Red Sox pitchers Carl Mays and Ernie Shore and outfielder Duffy Lewis. New York's record improved to 80-59, 7½ games out of first place. The team set an attendance record with 619,000 fans. That year, rumor had it that the Yankees were looking to purchase Ty Cobb from the Tigers. But Huggins believed Cobb was getting a little old. He had his eye on another player from Boston. A big, strapping pitcher.

His name was Ruth.

2 THE BIG BAMBINO AND IRON HORSE LOU

The Red Sox were the dominating franchise in the American League at the time, and George Herman "Babe" Ruth was their best player. For the first five years of his career in Boston, he had made himself into the best lefthander in baseball. The Red Sox had won three World Championships in that span and five since the beginning of the American League.

Ruth was also a powerful hitter. In 1919, he hit a league-record 29 home runs. Baseball fans across the country argued whether the Babe was a better outfielder or pitcher.

At Huggins's suggestion, Ruppert and Huston made Sox owner Harry Frazee an offer he couldn't refuse: $125,000 for Ruth's contract and a $350,000 loan against the mortgage on Fenway Park. Frazee, whose principal interest was producing Broadway shows, needed money. Huston and Ruppert, whose principal interest was winning baseball games, needed players. It was a good situation for both sides—unless one happened to be a Red Sox fan.

At the time, it was the largest deal ever made for a ballplayer. But in light of what it did to the Yankees, Red Sox, the American League and the city of New York, it was one of the greatest bargains in the history of sport for New York.

The Babe Ruth deal restructured the American League forever. The Yankees, until that point a second-division franchise, became the premier ballclub in baseball within seven years. The Red Sox, up until then the most successful team in the league, went into a tailspin that lasted well beyond Ruth's career. And in terms of popularity within the city limits of New York, the deal propelled the Yankees past the Giants and Dodgers within the year.

Attendance at the Polo Grounds for the Yankees more than doubled, and in 1920, the team drew over 1 million fans for the first time in history. They came to see a thrilling pennant race between the Yankees, White Sox and eventual champion Cleveland Browns, of course. But most of all, they came to see Ruth.

Fans loved Ruth. They loved to see him hit home runs, and he obliged, ripping 54 of them that year, easily a new record and more than any other team in the American League. But sportswriters and baseball observers soon realized something else. The fans loved to see Babe Ruth do anything! They loved to see him hit high pop flies. They oohed and aahed when he would swing and miss at a ball so hard that his body would twist around like a corkscrew. When he bunted, they would laugh at his cleverness. When he stole a base, they would cheer his audacity. He was the most consistent gate attraction in professional sports.

Did he love the high life in those days? Yes. And New York was the perfect place for him. That first year, searching for yet another angle on Ruth to write about, a sportswriter approached the affable Francesco "Ping" Bodie, Ruth's roommate on the road. What was it like, the sporting writer asked, to room with a fellow like Ruth? Ruth, in his autobiography, replied that he stayed away from his room so much because Ping snored horribly.

"I don't room with Ruth," said Bodie. "I room with his suitcase."

The Yankees didn't win in 1920, finishing third to Cleveland. The other milestone that year was the hiring of another former Red Sox, Ed Barrow, to manage the club's finances.

But in 1921, Ruth had one of the greatest seasons an everyday ballplayer has ever enjoyed, hitting 59 home runs, hitting .378 with 171 RBI and a slugging average of .846. He also tied for the team lead in stolen bases with 17. Mays, Shawkey and newcomer Waite Hoyt solidified the pitching staff, veteran Wally Schang upgraded the Yankee catching and second-year outfielder Bob Meusel began showing promise. The Yankees finished 98-55, 4½ games ahead of the Indians.

That set up the first World Series between two New York teams, as the National League champs were the Giants. In fact, the entire series was played on the Polo Grounds. The teams alternated being the home squads.

The Yankees got excellent pitching performances from Mays and Hoyt in the first two games to take a 2-0 lead. But an elbow injury to Ruth relegated him to part-time status the rest of the Series. The Giants took five of the next six games to win the World Championship, five games to three. (This was the last year of a three-year experiment that expanded the World Series to the best five wins in nine games. The next year, the format returned to the best four wins in seven games.)

Although Yankee fans were heartened by the team's finish in 1921, the Yankees continued to trade or buy players for the 1922 season.

And amid the wheeling and dealing, Ruppert bought out Huston for $1.5 million in May 1922. It was a staggering sum at the time, but Ruppert believed he had to have complete control of the club. Huston did not think Huggins was a good manager, and blamed him for the World Series loss to the Giants. After buying out Huston, Ruppert went to the sportswriters and declared that Huggins would be his manager until Huggins no longer wanted the job.

"It was the longest five years of my life," admitted Huggins of the years under Huston.

Raiding the Red Sox continued, as the Yankees picked up pitchers "Bullet" Joe Bush and "Sad" Sam Jones, as well as third baseman "Jumping" Joe Dugan. This translated into another pennant and another shot at the Giants in the 1922 World Series.

Much was made of this Series in which the Giants swept the Yankees in four games, with one tie in the second game of the Series. The tie was a 3-3 game called on account of darkness. Ruth hit only .118 with no hits in the final three games.

Giant rooters crowed that masterful Giants manager John McGraw had called every pitch of every game, which, in fact, he probably did. But even McGraw himself later admitted that "we caught the big fellow in a slump." According to Giants hurler "Handsome Hugh" McQuillan, McGraw called for "slow curves in the dirt" against Ruth the entire Series.

That was clearly not the answer to Ruth all the time. In 1923, the Yankees and Giants once again met for the World Championship. This World Series was won by the Yankees, with Ruth hitting

.368 with one home run. Hustling second baseman Aaron Ward was actually the hitting star of the Series, with ten hits and a .417 average. It was the first World Championship in Yankee history.

The Yankees dominated the American League that year, finishing ahead of Detroit by 16 games. Interestingly, the team's strong showing generated at least a few stories about the 1923 squad being one of the best ever.

Statistically, the squad was pretty darn good. In addition to another solid year from Ruth, the pitching staff of Bush, Shawkey, Jones, Hoyt and another Red Sox newcomer, Herb Pennock, was judged one of the deepest staffs ever, at least to that point. Jones no-hit Philadelphia 2-0 on September 4 for the second no-hitter in team history.

Ruth again dominated and was the unanimous MVP of the league. He hit 41 home runs, batted .393 with 205 hits. Four more hits would have given him a .400 average. But Ruth didn't get much of a chance at the plate that year. He was walked 170 times, still an all-time record. His on-base percentage was an amazing .545. There have been arguments whether 1921 or 1927 was Ruth's best year. He felt 1923 was his peak.

And it all came together in a new ballpark. Ruppert no longer wanted to be a tenant of the Giants, so in 1922, he purchased some land in the Bronx and began building Yankee Stadium. On Opening Day in 1923, Ruth, of course, hit the first home run in the joint.

But as quickly as the Yankees had moved into the penthouse in 1923, they tumbled in 1924 and 1925. The Washington Senators, with veteran Walter Johnson heading a talented pitching staff, edged the Yankees in a close pennant race in 1924. In 1925, Ruth began the season with an intestinal problem and was never right. He hit an un-Ruthian 25 home runs and the Yankees finished seventh.

But two key players were inserted into the starting lineup that year. On June 1, Lou Gehrig took Pipp's place at first base. And following a strong spring, Earle Combs took over the center field job. Meanwhile, Huggins had also reacquired canny veteran Urban Shocker for the pitching staff.

With a healthy Ruth, the Yankees bounced

back in 1926. The Babe hit .372, second in the league, and led the circuit in home runs with 47, RBI with 139 and runs scored with 145. Meanwhile, Pennock, Shocker, Hoyt and Jones anchored the pitching staff.

Barrow also picked up two rookie phenoms from out west: second baseman Tony Lazzeri and shortstop Mark Koenig. Both started and made an immediate impact. New York won the pennant over Cleveland by three games.

The World Series was another story. The upstart St. Louis Cardinals beat the Yankees four games to three to win the 1926 championship. What was galling was that St. Louis won the final two games in Yankee Stadium. Still more galling was that Grover Cleveland Alexander—who didn't even get to the game until the third inning— pitched the final 2½ innings of Game 7 to clinch a 3-2 win. And most galling of all, the game ended when Ruth was thrown out trying to steal second base by Cardinal catcher Bobby O'Farrell. A few months later, when O'Farrell asked him in spring training what he was thinking of, Ruth was philosophical: With Alexander pitching well, Ruth said, "I wasn't doing a hell of a lot of good on first base."

It was, for New York fans, a bitter defeat. But the 1927 edition of the Yankees bounced back in an unforgettable way. They dominated the league as few other teams have before or since, winning 110 games and losing only 44. Ruth hit 60 home runs. Gehrig hit 47 with a league-record 175 RBI. Lazzeri hit 18 home runs, drove in 102 and played every position in the infield but first base. Dugan was a solid third baseman, Koenig was steady at shortstop. Only the catching was ordinary, but Pat Collins and Johnny Grabowski hit a combined .276 with 7 home runs and 61 RBI.

Ruth, Meusel and Combs were the best outfield in the majors, and one of the best ever. Hoyt led the league in wins (22) and ERA (2.63). Pennock won 19 games, Shocker 18. A 30-year-old rookie from Oklahoma named Wilcy Moore won 19 games, including 13 in relief.

The team shot out of the gate that spring and had the pennant in hand by July 4. The only suspense over the last few months of the season was whether Ruth or Gehrig would win the home run title.

That went to Ruth, who hit 17 home runs in September, the last off Washington pitcher Tom Zachary. His 60 round-trippers were more than any other team in the league. Ruth's milestone came in the next-to-last game of the season. As he hit it to right field, the ball began curving away and looked as if it might carry into foul territory. Zachary jumped off the mound and began crying, "Foul ball! Foul ball!" Ruth and the Yankees laughed. Many years later, Zachary attended Babe Ruth Day in Yankee Stadium. Ruth, wracked with the throat cancer that would soon kill him, leaned over to shake Zachary's hand and croaked, "You crooked-armed son of a bitch. You still think that ball was foul?"

Gehrig was MVP, but only because at the time there was a goofy rule prohibiting players from winning the MVP award more than once, which eliminated Ruth. After the Series, baseball sportswriters feted Ruth at a dinner and gave him a plaque as player of the year.

The Yankees swept the Pirates in the 1927 World Series. Sportswriters and observers believe that the home run–hitting exhibition by Ruth and Gehrig in batting practice the day before the first game of the Series may have won the Series then and there. But it was the Yankee pitching that stifled Pittsburgh. The Pirates scored only ten runs in the Series and hit .223. In Game 3, Pennock carried a perfect game into the eighth inning before Pirate third baseman Pie Traynor singled.

"Our outfield was marvelous, our infield great, our pitching fine," said Pennock many years later. "Our catching was secondary, but it was the best ball club ever."

If 1927 was a magic year, 1928 was a struggle. The pitching staff was beginning to show its age and the team battled injuries during the season's second half. But the Yankees had burst out of the blocks that year, going 24-5 in May, and were 50-16 by the end of June. That start enabled them to hold off the hard-charging Athletics. New York finished 101-53.

Still, Ruth socked 54 home runs and he and Gehrig tied for the RBI title with 142. Ruth, Gehrig and Meusel were 1-2-3 in RBI in the league. Newcomer George Pipgras won 24 games to lead the league, and he, Pennock and Hoyt were among the best pitchers in the game.

The Yanks swept the World Series again, this time against the hated Cardinals. It was all Ruth and Gehrig this time. Babe hit an astonishing .625 with three home runs, while Gehrig hit .545 with four home runs. St. Louis never had a chance.

The next three years belonged to Connie Mack's Athletics. In 1929, the Yankees could still hit, but the pitching staff had only one pitcher, Tom Zachary, with an ERA under 3.00. New York had to outscore teams to win, never an easy proposition. Catcher Bill Dickey joined the team that year, hitting .324. The Yankees also became the first team to wear numbers on the back of their uniforms.

In September of that year, Huggins died of blood poisoning. The Mighty Mite was never a healthy man, beset with stomach, head and tooth ailments. He entered St. Vincent's Hospital in New York on September 22 and died three days later. He was 49. Assistant coach Art Fletcher finished out the year.

In 1930, the Yankees acquired pitcher Red Ruffing and the fleet Ben Chapman, a third baseman at the time who eventually become a fine outfielder. Ruth's 49 homers led the league, while the ever-steady Gehrig led the league with 174 RBI. Shawkey was now the manager, but he tried to run the club as everybody's best friend. It didn't work and New York fell to third.

Barrow fired Shawkey after the season and hired former Cubs manager Joe McCarthy soon after. Ruth was more than a little annoyed. With Huggins' death, he began lobbying to manage. Ruppert and Barrow were appalled. To them, it was like giving the fox the keys to the henhouse. McCarthy would be the manager.

The 1931 season was another second-place finish, but the Yankees were rebuilding their pitching staff. Lefty Gomez and Ruffing were now the Yankees' two best hurlers. Ruth and Gehrig tied for the home run championship with 46 home runs, but Gehrig drove in a record 184 runs. As a team, the Yankees scored a record 1,067 runs. Six Yankees scored 100 runs or more. But the A's had two 20-game winners and a 30-game winner in Lefty Grove.

The Yankees finally passed Philadelphia in 1932, winning 107 games behind a strong pitching staff and timely hitting. Rookie Frankie Crosetti, who could play three infield positions, was clearly going to be a good one.

The Yankees-Athletics rivalry of 1926–32 was perhaps the fiercest in baseball history. In that span, New York won four American League pennants, Philadelphia three. The Yankees won three World Series, the Athletics, two. The Yankees were 82-72 against Philadelphia over those years.

The 1932 World Series was another sweep. This time, it was McCarthy's old team, the Chicago Cubs, and it was a particularly bitter matchup. In Game 3, with the Yankees leading the World Series two games to none, Ruth got into it with the Cub bench and Cub pitcher Charlie Root. At one point, he pointed at Root and reminded him that he, Ruth, needed only one pitch to hit the ball out of the park. Root sneered and tried to push a curveball past Ruth. Babe snapped his bat around and jerked the ball into right-center field, 436 feet away. It was his 15th and last World Series home run.

Ruth probably didn't predict a home run, as legend has indicated. But he certainly intended to make a hit, and he clearly told Root, at least, that he would do so. And he did. The reality is no less dramatic.

The Yankees finished off the Cubs the next day, giving New York three consecutive World championships and 12 consecutive World Series wins.

The Senators finished first in 1933, and the Tigers claimed the pennant in 1934 and '35. Ruth was slowing down, and when he retired after the 1934 season, McCarthy began retooling the club. George Selkirk surprised everyone by very capably handling Ruth's right field position in 1935, while Dickey, Crosetti and Chapman were coming into their own, and veterans Lazzeri and Gehrig were still strong. Lou won the Triple Crown in 1934, hitting 49 home runs, batting .363 and making 165 RBI. Gomez and Ruffing anchored the pitching staff.

By now, his consecutive game streak was getting attention. Writers were calling him "Iron Horse Lou," a powerful locomotive that never seemed to need a rest.

But more important than any of these players was the hiring of George Weiss to build the Yankees' farm system. Ruppert had spent more than $500,000 purchasing players and their contracts in the 1920s, and it had reaped benefits: six pennants and three World Championships. But Ruppert and Barrow believed there had to be a better, cheaper way.

They noticed that Branch Rickey had begun a system in St. Louis whereby the Cardinals purchased several minor league teams to form a sort of feeding system for the Cardinals. Although the purchase of several teams might be initially expensive, Ruppert and Barrow believed it would pay off sooner or later. Weiss, the former general manager of the Baltimore franchise in the International League, was hired to begin the process.

Weiss was a shrewd judge of talent, but more importantly, he was a fanatically hard worker. He and his small crew of scouts spread out over the country, evaluating prospects and signing talent. Within a few years the formula began to pay off, and the Yankee dynasty grew.

In 1936, one of Weiss's greatest finds made the big club. The era of DiMaggio had begun.

3 JOLTIN' JOE, THE WAR YEARS AND THE COMING OF CASEY

He was graceful, athletic and one of the smartest players in the game. It was, for Yankee opponents, too much to overcome. "Joltin'" Joe DiMaggio was signed by the Yankees for the 1936 season. This was a team with a solid pitching staff, anchored by "Red" Ruffing, Lefty Gomez and newcomer Monte Pearson. The veterans included all-time all-star Gehrig, who would lead the league in home runs and win his second league MVP, clutch hitter Lazzeri, the great Bill Dickey and infield stars Crosetti and Red Rolfe.

The 1936 Yankees, then, were pretty good already. Adding DiMaggio made them overwhelming. They scored 1,065 runs and allowed only 731. The team batted .300, with a .483 slugging average. New York was 20-8 by the end of May, 47-22 by June 30. They finished 102-51, 19½ games

ahead of second-place Detroit. Even the 1927 Yankees weren't as dominating during the regular season.

The 1936 team beat the Giants in the World Series, four games to two. In the first game, Giant ace Carl Hubbell dominated the Yankees, 6-1. But the Yankees' talent and depth overwhelmed the Giants in four of the next five games for the championship.

DiMaggio had been wonderful, hitting .346 with three doubles in his first World Series. And the Yankees, with Joltin' Joe showing the way, dominated baseball for the next three years. They beat the Giants again in 1937, four games to one. In 1938 and 1939, neither the Cubs nor the Reds could win a game in the World Series. It was the most overpowering four-year stint in World Series history.

The regular seasons were also pretty predictable. In 1937, the Yankees added outfielder Tommy Henrich and pitcher Johnny Murphy. They finished 13 games ahead of Detroit. Pitcher Spurgeon "Spud" Chandler came aboard in 1938, and the margin over the Red Sox was 11 games.

Gehrig was slowing down in 1938, and by early 1939, it was clear something was wrong. He sat out his first game in 15 years on May 2, and would never play again. Two years later, he was dead at the age of 37.

One would expect that with Gehrig out in 1939, some cracks might have shown in the Yankee machine. Fat chance. Second baseman Joe Gordon beat out Lazzeri for that position, and outfielder Charlie "King Kong" Keller became a regular as well. The talent well of George Weiss seemed bottomless. The Yankees thrashed the rest of the American League in 1939, going 106-45 and finishing 17 games ahead of the Tigers. DiMaggio won his first batting title with a .381 average and his first MVP award.

One other event took place on January 18, 1939. Colonel Ruppert died at age 71. His family took over ownership of the team, and Barrow took over as president.

The Yankees became merely good in 1940, as the Tigers held them off by two games in the pennant race. DiMaggio became the first (and so far only) Yankee to win two consecutive batting

For four seasons in the late '30s, Yankee heroes Lou Gehrig and Joe DiMaggio shared the same field.

crowns, hitting .352. Rookie Ernest "Tiny" Bonham's pitching kept the Yankees in the race the latter half of the year, but it was not enough to take the team into the postseason.

But 1941 was another one of those magic years, like 1927. Early in that year, DiMaggio's first-inning single off Edgar Smith on May 15 generated little comment, mostly because the Yankees were in the process of being whacked, 13-1 by the White Sox. It was New York's fifth consecutive loss, and 11th in 16 games. The Yankees, with a 14-15 record to that point, were looking worse than the 1940 team. More than a few boos were rolling out of the stands at the stadium.

But with DiMaggio hitting consistently, the team began to turn around. Over the next few weeks, DiMaggio hit safely in 20 games in a row as the Yankees went 10-8 with two ties. (In those days, games that couldn't be made up, that went five or more innings, and ended with the score knotted were declared tie games.) New York then won

eight of its next ten, and the DiMaggio hitting streak was 30, breaking the team record shared by Peckinpaugh and Earle Combs.

Ironically, one of the most interested players in DiMaggio's streak was Ted Williams of the Red Sox, a man who could well appreciate how difficult DiMaggio's feat was. Williams, playing left field, would often get information about DiMaggio's streak from the Fenway Park scoreboard operator. He would then relay it to Joe's brother, Williams's teammate, Dominic DiMaggio, who played center field. "Joe got one, Dom," Williams would say excitedly. Williams did okay that year, too, hitting .406 on the season.

DiMaggio tied Wee Willie Keeler on July 1 by hitting safely in both games of a doubleheader against Boston at Yankee Stadium. The next day, July 2, DiMaggio belted a fly ball to deep center field in his second at-bat. Brother Dominic tracked it down and just snagged it. In the next at-bat, DiMaggio made sure Dominic wouldn't have any more chances to snap the streak, drilling a long home run to break the record.

The streak continued. Forty-eight, fifty, fifty-six games. Finally, on July 17, before a sellout crowd in Cleveland's Municipal Stadium, the streak (now written as The Streak) came to an end. But it took two great plays by Indian third basemen Ken Keltner and another tough play by second baseman Lou Boudreau in the eighth inning to stop DiMaggio. He promptly began a 16-game streak the next day.

The Yankees? They were 41-13, with two ties over that span. Not only had Joe D. set an unbreakable record and clinched his second league MVP; he had righted the ship. New York won the pennant with a 101-53 record. They whipped the Dodgers in five games in the World Series. Keller and Gordon were the Series heroes, hitting .389 and .500, respectively.

That victory started another run of three consecutive pennants. The Yankees won the 1942 American League flag by ten games over the Red Sox. The hitting was timely, but not overpowering. The defense was superb, with Crosetti at third, Gordon at second and second-year shortstop Phil Rizzuto. The pitching was strong, too—Bonham won 21 games and five other pitchers won 8 or more. Gordon's all-around excellence won him the league MVP award that year.

The 1942 World Series was a bit of a shocker, however. The Yankees were stunned by the Cardinals, four games to one. Ruffing won the first game in St. Louis, but two journeymen pitchers, Johnny Beazley and Ed White, combined for three complete-game wins over New York to send the Yankees down to defeat in a World Series for the first time since 1926.

World War II began taking players away from all the clubs in baseball, including Rizzuto and DiMaggio in New York, but the Yankees still won the pennant in 1943 by 14 games over the Senators. And despite being the underdogs that year against the Cardinals and National League batting champion Stan Musial, New York won this series in five games. Third baseman Billy Johnson was the hitting star with a .300 average in a very low-scoring series that saw New York hit .220 and the

Cardinals .224. The Yankees pitching gave them the edge, with Chandler winning two games and Marius Russo and Hank Boroway winning one each. Murphy, by now the best relief pitcher in the game, also picked up a save.

The next two war years saw the New Yorkers finish third and fourth, respectively. George "Snuffy" Sternweiss tore up the league offensively and had help from first baseman Nick Etten and outfielder Johnny Lindell, but the pitching was inconsistent.

But the real news in 1945 was the purchase of the Yankees from the Ruppert family by Larry MacPhail, Dan Topping and Del Webb for $2.8 million. MacPhail was made president, replacing Barrow.

With the war over, the Yankees got back DiMaggio, Rizzuto, Keller and Henrich. But McCarthy had trouble getting along with the new owners. Poor health compounded his problems, and he resigned early in the 1946 season. Bill Dickey took over for most of the year, but gave way to Johnny Neun—longtime coach of the Yankees' farm team in Newark—in the last month of the season. The Yankees finished third.

The new owners settled on Bucky Harris as the team's manager in 1947, and with newcomer Allie Reynolds (acquired from Cleveland), Spec Shea and reliever Joe Page, the Yankees' retooled pitching staff was the foundation for a 97-57 record and another pennant. DiMaggio won his third and final MVP award and the Yankees narrowly edged the Brooklyn Dodgers four games to three in the World Series. Henrich earned his "Old Reliable" nickname in this Fall Classic, delivering several key hits, including the game-winner in the seventh game.

The 1948 season was a bad one. The Yankees finished third, Harris was fired, and on August 16, Babe Ruth died of throat cancer. He had been ailing for some time, and at a ceremony on June 13, his number was retired. Two months later, he was gone.

Topping and Webb (MacPhail's share of the team had been bought in 1947) began casting about for a replacement for Harris. Weiss, promoted to general manager in 1945, had not gotten along with the laid-back Harris and wanted a harder-working manager. His eventual choice, Charles "Casey" Stengel, seemed at first an odd one. Stengel had managed for nine years in the National League with the Boston Braves and Brooklyn Dodgers, and only once had he even had a winning record. He had never finished higher than fifth.

But Weiss, who had known Casey for many years, was impressed with how Stengel worked with younger players. Webb and Stengel were both West Coast residents, so that was their connection. A week after Harris was fired, Stengel was hired.

His 1949 team was a squad in transition. DiMaggio, Keller and Henrich, the offensive core of the team, were aging. The pitching staff was still strong, with Reynolds, second-year man Vic Raschi, Page, Ed Lopat and Tommy Byrne.

But by now, the talent stream provided by Weiss was becoming a river. Stengel had been provided with some superior young ballplayers, including infielders Bobby Brown and Jerry Coleman, and outfielders Hank Bauer, Cliff Mapes and Gene Woodling, not to mention outfielder-catcher Lawrence Peter "Yogi" Berra, who was in his fourth year with the team.

The pennant race with the Red Sox was a tight one all year. But Page turned out to be the key, saving a then-Yankee record 27 games. Berra was another key. Harris had been cool to the idea of the somewhat awkward-looking Yogi behind the plate. But Stengel realized that Berra was a tremendous weapon and started him at catcher on Opening Day. DiMaggio was injured for much of the year, but Mapes, Bauer and Woodling filled in very well and New York won 97 games, and then beat Brooklyn in five games in the World Series. Woodling (.400) and Brown (.500) were the hitting stars of the series.

That was the first of five consecutive pennants and five consecutive World Series championships for New York. This five-year run wasn't as dominating a span as the 1936–39 era of double-figure pennant margins and four-game World Series sweeps. The 1949–53 Yankees won their consecutive pennants by one, three, five, two and seven games this time around, and never once won

more than 100 games. Their World Series wins were mostly battles as well. The 1951 and 1953 series went six games and the 1952 Fall Classic was a seven-game war with the Dodgers.

But the bottom line is, they won.

4 MICKEY, WHITEY AND YOGI

The best of several players the Yankees would acquire as the team reloaded, former National League star Johnny Mize was picked up in 1949. In 1950, Rizzuto won the MVP award and the Yankees edged the Tigers by three games and then swept the Phillies in the World Series. A young left-hander, Edward "Whitey" Ford came up late in the season and won all nine of his starts. Ford was so cocky he was hard to believe. But he could back it up. First baseman Joe Collins began a regular turn at that position in 1950. Stengel also brought up infielder Billy Martin.

Yogi Berra rewarded Stengel's confidence in him by winning the MVP award in 1951 as the Yankees edged Cleveland by five games in the American League. Yogi hit .294 with 27 home runs and 88 RBI. That was also the year Stengel brought up Mickey Mantle, "the Commerce Comet." Mantle was a power-hitting switch-hitter who could run like a cheetah. His tremendous home runs begat the tradition of measuring their length, which begat the term "tape measure" home runs.

The Mick wasn't overpowering that first year, and in fact was sent down to Kansas City for a spell. But his raw ability was too impressive to keep him in the minors. The 1951 season was also infielder Gil McDougald's first year. He would prove to be another keeper.

The 1951 World Series was an exciting affair. The New York Giants took a one-game to none lead and then, after the Yankees tied the series at one win each, took a two games to one lead. But DiMaggio, hitless in his first three games, belted a two-run homer and a single to key a 6-2 win in Game 4. On October 9, rookie McDougald crushed a grand slam in Game 5 to give the Yankees a 13-1 win. The next day, a three-run triple by

Bauer keyed a 4-3 win and another World Championship.

It was DiMaggio's last. He could still play, but not at the high level of which he was formerly capable. "I don't want the fans to see me struggling," he said when asked about his decision. So he retired, believed by some to have been the greatest all-round ballplayer ever.

Were this any team but the Yankees, the departure of an all-time great might have been cause for some concern. But the 1952 squad was solid defensively, with Collins at first, Martin at second, Rizzuto at shortstop, McDougald at third and Berra behind the plate. Mantle, Bauer and Woodling were in the outfield most of the year, and Coleman, Bobby Brown and Mize were available on the bench. The pitching was flush, with Reynolds, Raschi, Lopat and Johnny Sain.

The Yankees held off the hopeful Cleveland Indians by winning 13 of their last 15 games to claim the pennant. The World Series was another dogfight, a seven-game thriller over the Brooklyn Dodgers.

With Pee Wee Reese and Duke Snider both hitting .345 in the series, the Dodgers seemed to have the edge in this matchup. Brooklyn took a three games to two lead back to Ebbets Field on October 6 and needed to win only one of the last two games at home to clinch the title.

But it didn't happen. Mantle and Berra hit home runs in the sixth game to give Raschi his second victory of the series, 3-2. In the seventh game, Mantle's sixth-inning home run was the game winner, as New York took home its 15th World Championship. Mantle hit .345 and the first two of his World Series-record 18 home runs. Woodling hit .348 and Mize socked .400 with 3 home runs and 6 RBI.

The 1953 season saw Stengel's fifth consecutive American League championship as the Yankees again edged the Indians, this time by 8½ games. The Yankees' pitching was once again the cornerstone of the squad, with five pitchers winning 13 or more games, led by Ford's 18 wins. Martin was the unquestioned star of the 1953 World Series, a four games to two win over the Dodgers. Billy hit .500 with 2 home runs, 8 RBI

and 5 runs scored as New York won its fifth straight World Series, an all-time record.

In 1954, the Cleveland Indians won the American League pennant, but it required a tremendous effort. The Yankees went 103-51—their best record to date under Stengel. But the Indians were 111-43 to set an American League record for wins. Early Wynn and Bob Lemon each won 23 games for the Indians. Bob Grim's 20 wins and Johnny Sain's 22 saves topped the Yankees. Berra was named MVP of the league, his second such award.

Although the team won more than 100 games for the first time in 12 years, Weiss wasted little time retooling the squad, acquiring Don Larsen, "Bullet" Bob Turley, Johnny Kucks and Tommy Byrne for the pitching staff and moving Moose Skowron into the starting lineup at first base. The Yankees nicked the Indians by three games for the 1955 American League crown behind another stellar season by Yogi, who won back-to-back MVP awards.

This was the eighth year of a heated Indians-Yankees rivalry. Although one team or the other (mostly the Yankees) had finished first since Cleveland won the pennant in 1948, the Yankees had won most of the battles during the season. New York held a 96-80 edge over the Indians in this span, and had won five season series, lost one and tied two.

By now, the tradition of the Yankees was clearly a factor in these pennant races and World Series matchups. There were, sportswriters and other players noticed, an abundance of "red asses," or "R.A.'s" on the team. (Though vague in its origins, the term "red ass" referred to a particularly gung ho player who hated to lose.) Making an honest effort, giving it "the old college try," was not acceptable if a player wanted to wear the pinstripes for any length of time. A Yankee made the play or he stepped aside for the next fellow. That was the unwritten rule.

New York once again faced the Dodgers in the 1955 World Series, a close battle the Dodgers won, four games to three. Dodger pitcher Johnny Podres threw an eight-hit shutout in the seventh and final game. Berra hit .417 in a losing cause.

The Yankees and the Dodgers met again in the 1956 Series, the seventh time in 16 years the two teams had met. New York turned the tables on Brooklyn this year, winning the Series in another seven-game squeaker. The Series was notable for Don Larsen's perfect game, but Berra was once again the offensive star, with a .360 average and 10 RBI.

The 1956 season was Mickey Mantle's from start to finish, and he went on to win the Triple Crown by leading the league in batting average (.353), homers (52) and RBI (130).

From 1956 through 1958, the Yankees once again dominated the American League with brutal efficiency, winning pennants each year. Their farm system had provided them with tremendous depth, which the Yankees either used themselves or traded, usually for pitching. Ford was the core of this staff, but solid performers like Kucks, Tom Sturdivant, Turley, Byrne, Grim, Art Ditmar, Ryne Duren and Bobby Shantz consistently produced. Turley won the Cy Young Award in 1958.

The infield seemed to be an endless parade of strong-fielding ballplayers who were tough outs in the clutch: Rizzuto, Martin, Coleman, Brown, Gordon, McDougald, Johnson, Andy Carey, Skowron, Collins and on and on.

Mantle continued to be the star of the show. He won his second MVP in 1957.

New York won two of the three World Series in which they played in this span, over the Dodgers in 1956 and the Milwaukee Braves in 1958. In an exciting seven-game Series in 1957, the Braves brought the city of Milwaukee its first major professional championship by beating New York. The next year, with his Braves up three games to one, pitcher Lew Burdette reported that the Yankees would have barely finished fifth in the National League.

Bad move. Turley was absolutely brilliant in the aftermath of Burdette's speech, winning Game 5 with a complete-game shutout, pitching the last third of the tenth inning in Game 6 to save Ryne Duren's 2-1 win and throwing 6⅔ innings of relief to win Game 7, 6-2. "I guess," said Stengel in the clubhouse, "we could play in the National League after all."

The White Sox, who had finished second the

A vendor hawks programs for the 1956 Subway Series pitting the Yankees against the Brooklyn Dodgers.

three previous years, made their move in 1959, winning the American League championship by five games over Cleveland. The Yankees never did get untracked and finished a very uncharacteristic 79-75.

It was time for Weiss to uncork another great trade, so he sent an aging Hank Bauer to Kansas City with several other players for Roger Maris. Bauer was a part-time player for the Athletics for two more years. Maris was one of the best players in baseball into the mid-1960s.

That trade, among other things, pushed the Yankees back to the top in 1960, when they finished eight games ahead of the Baltimore Orioles. The superb infield tandem of shortstop Tony Kubek and second baseman Bobby Richardson was also a factor, as was versatile utilityman Hector Lopez, third baseman Clete Boyer and talented catcher Elston Howard. Big Dale Long was a valuable man off the bench. And the pitching was still the best in baseball, with Ford, Ditmar, Turley, Ralph Terry and Jim Coates.

With MVP Maris and teammate Mantle dominating the hitting stats, the Yankees broke open a close American League race by winning their last 15 games.

But the World Series was a huge disappointment. New York was stunned by the Pittsburgh Pirates in seven games, despite outscoring the Pirates 55-27. The Yankees hit well, but the Pirates seemed to make the plays when they needed to, winning a wild 10-9 seventh game on second baseman Bill Mazeroski's home run. Lopez, Johnny Blanchard, Mantle and Elston Howard all hit over .400 for New York. Richardson's 12 World Series RBI are still a record.

The Yankee loss gave Topping and Webb an excuse to fire Stengel, who had won ten pennants —a record—and seven World Championships, which tied him with McCarthy. At a press conference two days after the World Series, new manager Ralph Houk, who had been a popular assistant coach, was introduced. Rather than insist that they wanted to keep Houk in the organization, Webb and Topping noted Stengel's advancing age as the principal factor for his release. "I'll never

make the mistake of being seventy again," said Casey bitterly.

But a more fateful leave-taking was announced on November 2 of the same year. Weiss, after 29 years with the Yankees, announced his retirement. Unlike Stengel, he had seen the writing on the wall and sensed that Topping and Webb also thought he was too old at 65. Weiss handed out a brief statement at his press conference and walked away.

It took several years, but the loss of Weiss's uncanny ability to appraise talent would cost the Yankees dearly. Meanwhile, he would be hired by the crosstown Mets and be responsible for the initial success of that squad in the late 1960s. Weiss's successor as general manager for the Yankees was his longtime assistant Roy Hamey. Hamey was a good executive, but Weiss was one of the best ever. It was the beginning of the end of the Yankee dominance.

But not right away. In 1961, Maris once again won the MVP award, hitting 61 home runs in the process.

In this media-savvy age, it is difficult to convey what Maris went through during the final weeks of the season. The Yankees, like every other team in pro sports, had little understanding of the burgeoning presence the media was becoming. As a consequence, when they came to a new town on the road, Roger was on his own. His locker room was staked out by hordes of reporters, all desperate to get his opinions on whether or not he could break Babe Ruth's record.

It would have been unnerving for any professional. For the self-conscious, team-oriented Maris, the whole thing was murder. At one point, with a few weeks left in the season, he begged Houk to take him out of the lineup. Houk, who realized that making such a move would open him to crucifixion by the press, told Roger to just hang in there.

And he did. He didn't sock 61 homers in Commissioner Ford Frick's arbitrarily imposed deadline of 154 games (the number of games in which Ruth hit 60), but he came into the last game of the year against Boston needing one dinger to break the record. And when he did it, in the fourth inning, a roar of joy exploded out of Yankee Stadium. It was from fans who understood, a little, what Maris had gone through. He trotted the bases as he always did, head down, but when he got to the dugout, his teammates were waiting for him. Gleefully they pushed him back out onto the field, again and again, as the multitudes roared.

Red Sox pitcher Tracy Stallard, who gave up the historic blast, was philosophical. "He hit sixty others, didn't he?" said Stallard after the game. "I have nothing to be ashamed of."

The 1961 Yankees were more than just Maris, however. Mantle, despite injuries, ripped 54 home runs with 134 RBI. The infield of Skowron, Richardson, Kubek and Boyer had become the best defensive infield in baseball. In time, it would be recognized as one of the best ever.

The pitching staff featured Cy Young–winner Ford, who was overwhelming that year with 25 wins, newcomer Bill Stafford, who won 16 games, Terry, Coates and Rollie Sheldon. Luis Arroyo became the bullpen ace with a league-leading 29 saves. The Yankees were 109-53 that year and finished eight games ahead of Detroit. They beat the Cincinnati Reds in five games, with Ford tossing two shutouts and Lopez hitting .400.

The Yankees won it all again in 1962, but needed seven games to beat Willie Mays and the San Francisco Giants in the World Series. Maris, of course, was excoriated in the press for hitting "only" 33 home runs (fifth best in the league) and making a mere 100 RBI (seventh in the league). Terry had a solid year, with a league-leading 23 wins, Ford had 17 and Stafford, who looked like he was going to be a good one, had 14. Marshall Bridges, picked up from the Reds, had 18 saves.

Mantle, meanwhile, was still a force, winning the MVP award by hitting .321 with 30 homers and 89 RBI.

In 1963, the Yankees won 104 games under Houk and unveiled a number of new young stars: pitcher Jim Bouton was second in the league in wins, winning percentage and shutouts, and fourth in ERA. Another hurler, Al Downing, won 13 games and was fifth in ERA. First baseman Joe

Pepitone, playing his first full season, hit 27 home runs and drove in 89 runs. Outfielder Tom Tresh was clearly going to be a star. Catcher Elston Howard was the MVP of the league, hitting .287 with 28 home runs. Even with Weiss gone the team seemed to be as good and as deep as ever.

But the Dodgers, now in Los Angeles, swept the Yankees behind pitchers Sandy Koufax and Don Drysdale. The Yankees and their fans were stung, but they believed they had been victimized by two outstanding pitchers and remained convinced that their team was as good as ever.

The 1964 season was the last hurrah. Yankee attendance had been declining, and Webb and Topping believed that the team needed a less dour image than Houk's at the helm. They hired Berra, who had just retired, and kicked Houk upstairs to the general manager's post.

Yogi's goofy-guy reputation hurt him all year. Sportswriters (and worse, his players), had difficulty taking him seriously. But Berra's Yankees won a three-way race for the pennant ahead of Chicago and Baltimore, and by September, Yogi was looking pretty smart. Bouton anchored the staff with Ford, and rookie Mel Stottlemyer picked up nine wins down the stretch, which was another key. Late-season pickup Pete Ramos saved several big games. The Yankees' bench strength was another plus, with Lopez, Phil Linz and Johnny Blanchard playing well.

The team lost in seven taut games to the Cardinals that fall. During the season, Topping and Webb began negotiating with the Columbia Broadcasting System (CBS) to buy the Yankees, a move that was finally consummated in November. CBS paid $11.2 million for 80 percent of the team and later purchased the remaining 20 percent.

The day after the World Series, Yogi was fired by Houk. The press, who had begun the year by making sport of Berra, ripped Houk. The hiring of Johnny Keane, the former manager of the World Champion Cardinals, did little to appease many fans. And, of course, it all got much worse the next year.

5 LOSING SEASONS, LOTS OF THEM

From 1965 to 1971, the Yankees never finished closer than 15 games to first place, and were, most of the time, a lot closer to last place than the top spot. They had three winning seasons in seven years. In that span, only two of their players, Bobby Murcer and Bobby Richardson, made the *Sporting News* All-Star team.

There were a number of explanations for this precipitous slide, but the basic reason for it was simple: no talent. Webb and Topping had been thinking about selling the team for several years before they actually did so. With that in mind, they began pulling back on the team's investment in its farm system to save money. The flow of good players began to dry up. By the early 1960s, the farm system was producing only a handful of players a year who could even be considered prospects.

To be sure, injury played a part, particularly in 1965. Bouton had arm trouble, Kubek's back was killing him, and Mantle was banged up in several spots. But in prior years, when a Mantle went down, a Gene Woodling or a Hank Bauer stepped in and produced. In this span, there were simply no players who could shoulder the burden effectively.

Another factor was the institution of the free agent draft in 1965. Now, the new players were placed in a pool and each club had a chance to draft them. No longer could New York scout and sign players independently.

Keane was the initial scapegoat for the situation. The Yankees had won before 1965, they were not winning now. To the untrained eye, the only difference was Keane, a hardworking, decent man who inherited a dynasty on the downswing. By mid-1966, Keane was gone, and Houk was reinstated. It didn't help.

The Yankees traded Blanchard in 1965, Maris and Boyer in 1966, and Howard in 1967. But instead of a couple of solid pitching prospects, or perhaps a young player with potential, the Yankees were now getting journeymen ballplayers at best.

The team had a few good players. Murcer and Horace Clarke came up in 1965, Fritz Peterson in 1966, and Roy White became a regular in 1968. But it wasn't anything like the old days.

Ford retired after 1967 as the best Yankee pitcher of all time. Mantle hit his 500th home run in 1968, and that quest kept the team in the papers for a while, but at the end of the season, he, too, was gone. His number was retired in a special ceremony at Yankee Stadium the next year.

In 1970, a slow turnaround began with Rookie of the Year Thurman Munson's solid season. Reliever Sparky Lyle came to New York via a trade for first baseman Danny Cater.

In January 1973, a syndicate headed by Cleveland shipping magnate George Steinbrenner purchased the team from CBS. At the press conference announcing the sale, Steinbrenner explained that his shipping business kept him pretty busy and he probably wouldn't have a lot of input with the team. The media, unaware of what was coming down the road, dutifully quoted him.

In 1973, general manager Gabe Paul picked up Lou Piniella from Kansas City, as well as first baseman Chris Chambliss, pitcher Dick Tidrow and Cecil Upshaw. The 1974 pennant race was a thriller, with the Yankees finishing in second place, just two games behind division champion Baltimore. New manager Bill Virdon, who had taken over from Houk, won Manager of the Year.

There were more deals in 1975, including the signing of Catfish Hunter and Bobby Bonds. The Yankees finished third, but they were clearly back in the hunt for more championships.

6 REGGIE, BILLY AND GEORGE

The 1976 season saw New York back on top, running away with the American League East championship. The team had been almost totally rebuilt. The infield of Graig Nettles at third, Fred Stanley at shortstop, rookie Willie Randolph at second base, Chambliss at first, was solid defensively and consistent at the plate. Munson was, with Boston's Carlton Fisk, the premier catcher in the American League. He won the MVP award that year, hitting .321, with 30 home runs and 89 RBI.

Willie Randolph attempts a diving catch while Rod Carew slides into second, as the Yankees battle the Minnesota Twins in 1976.

In the outfield, Mickey Rivers, Oscar Gamble and White were a strong combination. Hunter won 17 games, Ed Figueroa won 19, Dock Ellis 17, and Lyle led the league in saves with 23.

Also being rebuilt was Yankee Stadium. In 1972, after much debate, the Yankees signed a 30-year lease with the city of New York. The lease called for Yankee Stadium to be completely renovated for the 1976 season. While this was being done, the Yankees moved into Shea Stadium, leasing it from the Mets.

Virdon had been fired by Steinbrenner in 1975 and replaced with the combative Martin. Billy was an excellent manager, smart and outspoken. Unfortunately, as the years went on, Martin was clearly a little *too* smart and a little *too* outspoken for his own well-being.

Chambliss's ninth-inning home run in Yankee Stadium off Royals' pitcher Mark Littell in the fifth game of the American League championship series was the highlight of the Yankees' 1976 postseason. During New York's fallow years, major league baseball had instituted a two-tier playoff system. In addition to league champions playing in the World Series, each league now had an eastern and western division. Those divisional champions now played a five-game series for the American or National League titles, respectively.

Munson was the highlight of the 1976 World Series, in which the Yankees were swept by a very efficient Cincinnati Reds team. Thurman batted .529, while Chambliss hit .333.

Prior to the 1977 season, Steinbrenner signed superstar outfielder Reggie Jackson to a five-year contract and also picked up pitcher Don Gullett. Mike Torrez and Ron Guidry strengthened the pitching staff, and the Yankees added depth with Bucky Dent, Carlos May, Paul Blair and Cliff Johnson. New York won a very exciting three-way race with the Orioles and Red Sox for the American League East championship. Lyle, with 13 wins and 26 saves, was one of the big keys. His performance won him the Cy Young Award, the first time a reliever had earned the honor.

The American League championship series was another dogfight, with the Yankees coming from behind in the fifth and final game to beat Kansas City, 5-3. Rivers's single in the ninth inning was the gamewinner, and Lyle picked up his second win of the series in relief.

The Yankees returned to the winner's circle with a four games to two win over the Los Angeles Dodgers in the 1977 World Series. Guidry and Torrez were the pitching stars, but Jackson justified his hefty free-agent salary with a spectacular exhibition of home run hitting in the sixth and final game. He hit home runs off three different pitchers in the game, each on the first pitch. The final shot brought a roar of awe from the stadium crowd as the ball sailed into the night.

Steinbrenner made it clear that winning the championship was not going to change his tactics with regard to acquiring talent. In 1978, he picked up relievers Goose Gossage and Rawley Eastwick, as well as first baseman Jim Spencer and outfielder Gary Thomasson.

But this was Guidry's year. He won 25 games, lost 3, and kept the Yankees together even as they were being battered by injuries and torn apart by dissension. To be fair, a majority of the Yankees, such as Nettles, Guidry, Lyle, Randoph, Chambliss, White, Hunter and Gossage, tended to play the games and stay out of the limelight. It was Martin, Jackson, Steinbrenner and Munson who seemed to get on each other's nerves.

Things looked bad in mid-July, with the Red Sox taking a 14½ game lead on the field. But the Yankee pitching staff, the deepest in baseball, kept coming up with big performances and New York kept battling back. A mid-September sweep of the Red Sox pushed New York into first place, but the Sox came up with a late-season streak of their own to tie New York at the end of the season.

In the playoff game at Fenway Park, Dent's three-run homer (which was helped by winds that kept the ball from straying into foul territory), coupled with a strong relief effort from Gossage, finally settled the American League eastern division race.

Martin, alas, was not around to see it. He had been popping off about the Steinbrenner-Jackson situation, and finally, after calling Jackson a "born

liar" and Steinbrenner a "convicted" one, he was fired. Bob Lemon took his place.

The Yankees once again beat the Royals in the American League championship series, then matched up against the Dodgers in the World Series. After dropping the first two games, Guidry pitched Game 3. Aided by some spectacular defensive play at third base by Nettles, New York won the game, 5-1. The Yankees went on to take four straight wins and clinched the Series on a tidy seven-inning, six-hit performance by Hunter.

The Yankees picked up pitchers Tommy John, Ron Davis and Luis Tiant in 1979, which figured to improve the team. But Lyle had been traded, along with Rivers, to Texas. Gossage was injured wrestling with Johnson early in the season and Munson was killed in a tragic plane crash in mid-season. The Yankees slumped behind the Orioles and even Steinbrenner's firing of Lemon and replacing him with Martin didn't help.

Dick Howser took over from Martin in 1980, and the Yankees, with a healthy Gossage, a productive Jackson and the additions of catcher Rick Cerone and first baseman Bob Watson, won 103 games, New York's best record in 17 years. But New York was swept in three games by the hungry Royals and their leader, George Brett. Steinbrenner, who didn't get along with Howser, used the sweep as an excuse to fire the manager and hire Gene "the Stick" Michael, a former Yankee shortstop.

Under The Stick, the Yankees won the first half of the American League East title. This was a strike-shortened year, with the strike coming in midseason. Trying to salvage some interest in the latter half of the season, the owners declared that the division winners of the "first half" of the season would be awarded automatic playoff berths and would battle the winners of the "second half" of the season in an added playoff round. The winners of those series would then compete in the American League Championship Series, with the victor moving on to the World Series.

The Yankees acquired big Dave Winfield prior to the 1981 season, and he played well. But after gaining an automatic playoff berth, the Yankees started to coast. Michael wasn't worried, but it drove Steinbrenner crazy. About a month into the second half of the year, he fired Michael and brought Lemon back.

Piniella, hitting .438, and Gamble, hitting .556, sparked the Yankees past the Milwaukee Brewers in the first round of the playoffs. Gossage saved all three New York wins. New York swept the American League championship series against Oakland with Nettles and Jerry Mumphrey both hitting .500. The A's were managed, by the way, by Billy Martin.

The World Series was another matter. The Dodger pitching, led by Fernando Valenzuela, Burt Hooten and Jerry Reuss, shut down the Yankee bats. The Dodgers won the series, four games to two. Unlike Jackson, who made his money in playoff games, Winfield's first taste of the postseason was sour. He was 1 for 22 in the series—a .043 average.

7 THE ERA OF MEDIOCRITY

The 1982 season began a decade of close-but-no-cigar finishes interspersed with never-got-out-of-the-gate years. From 1982 to 1993, the Yankees never finished higher than second. The merry-go-round of managers began spinning faster and faster. Martin would have five separate stints as manager, Michael, Lemon and Piniella two each with Clyde King, Berra, Dallas Green, Dent and Stump Merrill also in the mix at one time or another. In all, there were 15 managerial changes from 1977 to 1989.

It was distracting and embarrassing. Steinbrenner was now the Yankees' main attraction, but for New York fans, this was not a positive thing. The Yankees roster was a revolving door of free agents, draft picks and traded players. New York went through 47 different players in 1982, 48 different players in 1987 and 50 different players in 1989.

All the publicity surrounding the Yankees seemed negative. Winfield was arrested in 1983 for accidentally killing a seagull in Toronto with a thrown ball. In that same year, Brett hit a ninth-inning, two-out two-run home run off Gossage at Yankee Stadium to give the Royals an apparent 5-4 lead.

But Martin, in his third managerial stint, pointed out to the umpire than the amount of pine tar on Brett's bat exceeded the legal limit. The home run was nullified, the Yankees given a 4-3 win and Brett sprinted from the dugout, ready to kill the umpire. He didn't, but the Royals did protest the game.

Eventually the game was ordered to be replayed at the point of the protest with Kansas City back in the lead, 5-4, as the home run was allowed to stand. Royal reliever Dan Quisenberry retired the Yankees in order in the bottom of the inning to preserve the restored 5-4 win. In the top of the ninth, in a typically cryptic Martinesque protest to the "travesty" of having to replay the game at all, the manager placed Guidry in the outfield and left-handed infielder Don Mattingly at second base.

But the team's championship chances never seemed very solid, even when they were playing well. Good players like Ricky Henderson, Tommy John, Roy Smalley, Bob Watson, Don Baylor, Jack Clark and Ken Griffey Sr. all came and went.

Through it all, Mattingly played with dignity and professionalism, as difficult as that was in those seasons. In 1985, he was MVP of the league, hitting .324, with 35 home runs and 145 RBI.

As the dark years dragged on, the fans began to revolt. *Steinbrenner Must Go* signs began appearing in Yankee Stadium. The ever-popular "Steinbrenner sucks!" chant was heard more and more often as well. But changes were in the offing.

8 BACK ON TOP

After a 1993 season that saw the Yankees under Buck Showalter finish in second place, seven games off the pace, the Yankees put it together in 1994. They went 70-43 to capture first place. But in an agonizing twist, another strike wiped out the postseason.

"We've failed the fans," said a disgusted Don Mattingly.

Mattingly and the Yankees got back to the postseason in 1995, but were knocked out in the first round by Seattle and their coach, Lou Piniella. It was Mattingly's last hurrah, and he retired soon after. A second playoff tier, a "divisional championship series" had been added to the American League championship series and the World Series to enable more teams to make the postseason cut.

Once again, the Yankees lost a great player but rallied to become champions. In 1996, New York finally returned to the World Series after running up a 92-70 record during the season. There were new stars in the Yankee pantheon. Third baseman Wade Boggs was brought over from Boston. Derek Jeter, a young shortstop, showed great promise. First baseman Tino Martinez and outfielders Bernie Williams, Paul O'Neill and Tim Raines became a potent hitting tandem. Cecil Fielder and Darryl Strawberry came off the bench.

The pitching staff came around, too. Old pros David Cone, Jimmy Key and Kenny Rogers teamed up well with newcomers John Wetteland,

Graeme Lloyd, Andy Pettitte and Jeff Nelson. On May 14, cast-off Dwight Gooden, who had sat out parts of the previous two seasons for drug violations, pitched a no-hitter for New York over Seattle.

The Yankees disposed of the Texas Rangers in the first round of the playoffs, then defeated the Baltimore Orioles in the American League championship series as Bernie Williams, Strawberry and Jeter all hit over .400 for the series.

The Yankees were underdogs against the Atlanta Braves, and played like it, dropping the first two games of the series by a combined score of 16-1 in New York. Things looked bleak.

But old pro Cone pitched a strong Game 3 and New York beat the Braves 5-2. The next night, trailing 6-0, the Yankees got key hits from Jeter and Jim Leyritz to tie the game and went ahead when Wade Boggs drew a bases-loaded walk. The final was 8-6. Andy Pettitte won Game 5 in

Don Mattingly, shown here sliding clear of a tag at home, lead the Yankee charge for much of the '80s and '90s.

Atlanta, 1-0 and Key won Game 6. Boggs made all the papers by jumping onto a police horse moments after the final out in the final game. Overseeing it all was new manager Joe Torre, whose zen-like confidence was apparently infectious.

After a frustrating 1997 season that saw New York beaten in the first round of the playoffs by the eventual American League champion Cleveland Indians, it all came together in 1998.

The Yankees led from wire to wire that year, racking up an American League–record 114 wins. Unlike 1927, or 1941, or 1961, there were no super-duper, record-setting offensive performances. Jeter, O'Neill, Williams and Martinez were the team's most productive hitters, but several other players had near-career years.

The pitching was outstanding, with Cone, Pettitte, David Wells, Lloyd and Orlando "El Duque"

A jubilant Mariano Rivera is mobbed by teammates after saving Game 4 of the 1998 World Series for a Yankee Sweep.

Hernandez starring. Hernandez is a Cuban refugee and one of that country's legendary hurlers. He soon became a key starter. Bullpen ace Mariano Rivera, meanwhile, came into his own. Rivera amassed 36 saves in 1998 and had three more, with an ERA of 0.00, in the postseason.

On May 17, Wells pitched the 13th perfect game in modern history against Minnesota. It was the first regular-season perfect game in Yankee history.

The Yankees swept the Rangers, defeated Cleveland four games to two in the American League championship series and swept the San Diego Padres. Their final 3-0 win gave New York a total of 125 wins in the regular and postseason.

New York showed no signs of slowing down in 1999. Wells was shipped to Toronto for all-time all-star Roger Clemens. On July 18, Cone pitched the 16th perfect game in modern history by shutting down Montreal in an interleague contest. The Yankees became the first team to have pitchers throw perfect games in back-to-back years.

After compiling a 98-64 regular season record, the best in the American League, New York swept the hapless Rangers again, beat the Red Sox in five games and swept the Atlanta Braves in one of the most impressive postseason performances in several years.

Rivera was once again almost unhittable in the playoffs and World Series. Against Atlanta, Third baseman Scott Brosius hit .375 against the Braves to take Series MVP honors. The win gave New York 12 consecutive World Series wins, tying them with the 1927, '28 and '32 squads.

The 2000 season saw the Yankees once again win the American League East, but the squad that year didn't exactly run away with the division. General Manager Brian Cashman had added some key performers, including David Justice from the Indians, Deanny Neagle from the Reds, Glenallen Hill from the Cubs, Jose Vizcaino from the Dodgers and Luis Sojo from the Pirates. Jose Canseco was plucked from the waiver wire and Luis Polonia was signed after being released by the Tigers.

In addition, Steinbrenner pushed for the signing of Dwight Gooden. Amazingly, all these moves panned out in some way, especially Justice, who completely revived the Yankee offense and was probably the team MVP of the second half of the season.

The Yankees pulled far enough ahead of the Red Sox to clinch the AL East despite a dismal 3-15 record to end the season. They finished with 87 wins, and the worst record of the four AL play-off teams

But the ever-confident Jeter assured Yankee fans and the media that the ship would be righted come playoff time. He was right, of course. New York beat a tough Oakland team 3-2 in the divisional series, stopped the Mariners in six in the ALCS and faced the Mets in the first Subway Series in 44 years.

After the Yankees defeated Bobby Valentine's squad 4 games to 1 in the World Series, Jeter admitted that the Mets were the toughest team the Yankees had beaten in the four World Series in which he had participated. He was probably right. Every game was tough. The Yankees won Game 1, 4-3, in twelve innings on Jose Vizcaino's two-out, bases-loaded single to left. In Game 2, Roger Clemens threw a 2-hitter over 8 innings, but after being yanked, the Mets roared back, only to lose, 6-5. (This game was perhaps more famous, however, for an incident in the second-inning. When Mike Piazza shattered his bat on a Clemens fast-ball, Clemens grabbed a chunk of the broken bat and flung it in the direction of the first base line—not far from Piazza. Benches cleared but cooler heads prevailed, and most attributed the outburst to nerves.) John Franco defeated the heretofore unbeatable Orlando Hernandez in the third contest, 4-2, ending at 14 the Yankees record streak of victories in World Series games. But the Yankees won another squeaker in Game 4, 3-2, and clinched in the fifth game, 4-2, on Luis Sojo's 2-out single in the ninth inning. Though he proved himself human with struggles earlier in the series, Mariano Rivera saved the clinching game for the third year in a row, another record. The Yankees became the first team since the 1972-74 Oakland A's to win three World Series in a row.

THE YANKEE STADIUM STORY

Former Yankee owner Jacob Ruppert was always fond of pointing out that Yankee Stadium was a mistake. Not his mistake of course—the New York Giants'.

Beginning in the 1913 season and running until 1922, the Yankees and the Giants shared the Polo Grounds, which was located on the west side of Eighth Avenue between 157th and 159th Streets in Manhattan. The Giants owned the facility and leased it to the Yankees.

For most of that ten-year span, the New York Giants of John McGraw were the kings of baseball in New York. But if fans in Boston thought Babe Ruth's leaving was disastrous for them, the management of the New York Giants soon discovered that Ruth's arrival in the Big Apple was no less hurtful to McGraw's team.

Ruth's first year in New York was 1920. The year before, the Yankees had finished third in the American League and drew 619,164, the team's best gate in its history. With Ruth's arrival, the Yankees still finished third. But they drew an astonishing 1,289,422 fans, becoming the first team ever to draw more than one million fans. That was impressive enough, but it was also more than 350,000 paying customers than the Giants. Clearly, from the point of view of the Giants, something had to be done.

So the Giants announced a few months later that the Yankees' lease would not be renewed. For the sake of publicity, the Giants drew no lines in the sand. The Yankees, they said, would have all the time they needed to find a new home. Just leave. As soon as possible.

Giants management, including McGraw, believed (probably correctly) that there was no real estate in Manhattan large enough to accommodate a second major league ballpark. Thus, the Yankees, like the Dodgers, would likely be exiled to one of the outer boroughs where (hopefully) their popularity would wane.

But Ruppert had a solid working knowledge of

Fans arriving for the grand opening of Yankee Stadium on April 18, 1923.

New York City real estate. He found a lot in the Bronx, less than a half mile away from the Polo Grounds, and proceeded to construct his own facility. And what a facility it would be.

The Osborne Engineering Company of Cleveland, Ohio, was hired to design the stadium. Ground for the $2.5 million complex was broken on May 5, 1922, on the 10-acre site, formerly a part of the estate of millionaire William Waldorf Astor. Thus, two years after Ruppert had invested $420,000 for Babe Ruth (including the purchase price and Ruth's salary), he invested another $3.2 million (the land acquisition costs were about $680,000) for a place to put him. And the whole thing would pay off handsomely, just as Ruppert anticipated.

Opening Day in the new Yankee Stadium was April 18, 1923. The announced attendance was reported to be 72,217. It was probably closer to 62,000, which was the actual number of seats in Yankee Stadium. Ever in competition with the Giants, Ruppert and his partner, Colonel Tillinghast L'Hommedieu Huston, were fond of inflating attendance figures in those early days, and, in fact, for many years, fans believed the stadium's official capacity was 70,000.

Regardless, Ruth accepted the challenge of christening the new stadium and socked a home run in the third inning against Howard Ehmke of the Red Sox. With two Yankees on base, Ehmke tried a slow curve. Ruth drilled it over the right field wall. The Yankees won, 4-1.

It was Ruppert who insisted the ballpark be named Yankee "Stadium," thus conferring on the facility a bit more grandeur than any of its major league brethren. In those days, you had Ebbets Field, Fenway Park and the Polo Grounds, all of which sounded homey and quaint. Ruppert decided that his ballpark would have the largest capacity of any complex in major league baseball. And it would be a stadium, not a park or a field. It would be bigger, and it would be better.

Sportswriters struggled to find a second reference. One called the place "Colonel Ruppert's Concrete Cashbox." But sportswriter Fred Lieb dubbed it "The House That Ruth Built." And so it was.

One of the ironies of The House That Ruth Built was that the builder wasn't initially all that happy about its construction.

"I cried when I found out we were moving out of the Polo Grounds," admitted Ruth several years later. It wasn't hard to see why. He hit 54 and 59 home runs during his first two years in New York, when the team played its home games at the Polo Grounds. He clearly loved the place.

But Yankee Stadium had some pretty inviting fences as well. The original dimensions of the stadium were 281 feet from home plate down the left-field line, a vast 490 feet to dead center field and 295 feet down the right-field line.

Over the years, these dimensions have been evened out somewhat, and in 1988, the date of the latest renovations, the distance down the line to left field is now 318 feet, to dead center field is 408 feet and down the right field line is 314 feet.

The relatively short right-field fence was inviting to lefty sluggers Ruth and Gehrig. And, in fact, the right field stands were dubbed "Ruthville," both from the number of home runs struck by Ruth into that area, and because Ruth himself patrolled right field for much of his Yankee career. In fact, Ruppert made no secret of the fact that Yankee Stadium was as much The House Built For Ruth as it was The House That Ruth Built. The Babe hit quite a few shots onto that short right-field porch.

The park was remodeled and refurbished over the years. Lights were added in 1946, the same

year the dugouts were switched, putting the Yankees' dugout on the first base side and the visitors' dugout on the third base side.

In 1974, the Yankees remodeled the stadium, giving it a $160 million facelift. The biggest change was the removal of the steel columns that obstructed views in the second and third decks. The stadium was reengineered to safely accommodate that change, fans were presented with better sight lines.

In addition, three escalator towers were added at the three entrances. The historic monuments and plaques that had been part of the playing field were enclosed and moved into "Monument Park" between the Yankee and visiting bullpens. The seats were enlarged to accommodate the bigger Americans that were occupying them, and as a result, the seating capacity dropped to 54,200.

And the Giants? Oh yeah—they left town.

HOME RUN DERBY

So far, no one has ever hit a ball out of Yankee Stadium, although Philadelphia Athletics first baseman Jimmy Foxx, Negro Leagues catcher Josh Gibson and Washington Senators outfielder Frank Howard have all come close. But experts agree that Mickey Mantle's blast off Kansas City's Bill Fischer on May 22, 1963, came closest of all. The ball hit the rooftop facade over the third deck in right field, only about three feet shy of going completely over the roof. The ball struck the facade at a point measured 106 feet above the playing field, and was still rising when it hit. Mantle himself said it was the "hardest ball I ever hit." The Yankees won the game, 8-7 in 11 innings. Mantle also holds the record for the longest home run hit in the stadium. On August 12, 1964, Mantle hit a ball that traveled 502 feet from home plate into the center field bleachers. The ball cleared the 22-foot-high fence in front of the bleachers with ease. Chicago pitcher Ray Herbert was the pitcher, and the Yankees won the game, 7-3.

OPENING DAY

The Yankees were among the first teams to turn opening day into Opening Day, especially after Yankee Stadium opened in 1923. Here are a few highlights.

1923 The first opening day at Yankee Stadium. Governor Al Smith throws out the first ball. Ruth hits the first-ever home run there, and the Yankees beat the Red Sox, 4-1.

1929 The first rain delay in 20 years pushes Opening Day back two days. Mayor Jimmy Walker, who is supposed to throw out the first ball, has another appointment, and names Joseph McKee, president of the New York Board of Alderman, as his pinch tosser. The Yankees beat the Red Sox, 7-3.

1930 Mayor Walker, stung by comments in local papers that he ducked throwing out the first ball last year because he threw poorly, is seen practicing tosses with longtime Yankee batboy Eddie Bennett before the ceremonies. Walker's throw is judged as adequate. The Yankees lose to the A's, 7-6.

1934 Mayor Fiorello LaGuardia, in his first Opening Day appearance, eschews the tradition of throwing out the first ball from the owners box and strides to the pitcher's mound for his pre-game toss. He reportedly throws a strike to catcher Bill Dickey. The Yankees beat the A's, 1-0. In subsequent years, LaGuardia stays in the owners' box to toss the first ball.

1942 Fans entering Yankee Stadium on Opening Day find large signs directing them to shelters under Yankee Stadium in case of an enemy air raid. There is no air raid, and the Yankees beat the Red Sox, 1-0.

1943 The Yankees introduce the tradition of lining up the starters from both teams along the foul lines. The Yankees beat the Senators, 5-4.

1949 Gary Simpson, captain of the baseball team at St. Mary's Industrial School in Baltimore, throws out the first ball as part of Babe Ruth Memorial Day. Ruth, who had died in August 1948, was a star ballplayer at St. Mary's as a boy. Simpson and his teammates were guests of the Yankees, who beat the A's, 3-2.

1954 Major Francis Sutherland's 7th Regiment Band, who played the national anthem for 31 Opening Days in a row, declines to play this year as part of a musicians' strike against a local radio station. Bronx Borough president James J. Lyons throws out the first ball. The Yankees beat the A's, 3-0.

1956 A rain delay of several hours prevents Opening Day ceremonies. However, photographers must have a shot of somebody throwing out the first ball somewhere. Mayor Wagner obliges by throwing a ball to an aide under the stands. The game is eventually played, and the Yankees beat the Red Sox, 7-1.

1962 Claire Hodgson Ruth, wife of the late Babe Ruth, becomes the first woman to throw out the first ball at the Stadium. The Yankees beat Baltimore, 7-6.

1967 Red Sox lefty Billy Rohr no-hits the Yankees for 8⅔ innings, before Elston Howard finally singles to break up the no-no. The Sox won, 3-0. Rohr goes on to win two more games in the major leagues. The Yankees finish ninth in 1967. Mayor John Lindsey throws out the first ball.

1973 Bob Shawkey, who pitched the first game ever at Yankee Stadium in 1923, throws out the first ball on the 50th anniversary of the opening of the Stadium. The Yankees beat Minnesota, 11-4.

1982 After four consecutive rainouts, the Yankees play the first-ever Opening Day doubleheader with the White Sox and lose both games, 7-6 and 2-0. Head groundskeeper Jimmy Esposito throws out the first ball in recognition of the efforts he and his crew made in keeping the field playable.

1994 Joe DiMaggio begins a tradition of throwing out the first ball that will continue until his death several months after the 1998 season. The Yankees beat the Rangers, 5-3.

GREAT NON-YANKEE EVENTS AT YANKEE STADIUM

Since its early days, Yankee Stadium has housed numerous other events besides Yankee games. Here are some of the more memorable:

December 12, 1928 Notre Dame defeats heavily favored Army, 12-6, as coach Knute Rockne gives his famous "win one for the Gipper" speech to the boys at halftime.

December 28, 1958 "The Greatest NFL Game Ever Played." The Baltimore Colts, behind a touchdown by Alan "the Horse" Ameche, defeat the New York Giants, 24-17 in over time, to win the NFL Championship. Yankee manager Joe Torre, then a Brooklyn teenager, watches the game from the stands. "It was freezing," he recalled. "And the Colts weren't even thinking about a field goal (in overtime). They just sent that big horse, Ameche, into the line for the touch-down."

June 22, 1938 Joe Louis knocks out Max Schmeling in the first round to retain his heavy-weight championship. With the victory, Louis avenged a bitter 1936 defeat at the hands of Schmeling in a nontitle fight. That 1936 fight served as a propaganda victory for the Nazi Party in Germany, and Louis burned for two years to avenge it. To many fight fans, this match remains the most dramatic boxing match in the history of the sport.

October 4, 1965 Pope Paul VI, in the first visit of a Pope to North America, celebrates Mass at Yankee Stadium for a crowd of more than 82,000.

September 9, 1974 Muhammad Ali narrowly defeats Ken Norton for the second time in one of the closest, hardest fights of Ali's long career. The win enables Ali to retain his heavyweight crown.

October 2, 1979 Pope John Paul II celebrates Mass at Yankee Stadium.

June 21, 1990 Nelson Mandela welcomed to the United States.

August 29-30, 1992 U2 plays two sold-out shows at Yankee Stadium.

THE ORIGIN OF THE YANKEE LOGO

Famed jeweler Louis B. Tiffany is reportedly the author of the Yankees' well-known interlocking "NY" logo. Tiffany was commissioned in 1877 to strike a commemorative medal to be presented by the New York City Police Department to Officer John McDowell, the first New York officer to be shot on duty. The logo appeared as part of the medal.

The NY logo first appeared on the uniforms of the New York Highlanders in 1909, on both the cap and the player's left sleeve. That logo replaced the former design, which featured the same letters separated on the left and right front breast area of a player's shirt.

How the logo was transferred from a police-man's medal to a baseball team is the subject of some speculation. Club officials believe the con-nection was established because one of the New York owners at the time, Bill Devery, was a former New York City police chief.

THE ORIGIN OF THE YANKEE PINSTRIPES

Legend has it that Colonel Jacob Ruppert approved a uniform change to pinstripes so as to make Babe Ruth, his portly right fielder, look a lit-tle slimmer. But, in fact, the Yankees unveiled their pinstripe look many years prior to Ruth's—or Rup-pert's—arrival. On April 11, 1912, the then-Highlanders took the field on Opening Day with their traditional white home uniforms that are now trimmed with snazzy black pinstripes—a look sev-eral big league teams were sporting at that time. The team abandoned the look for the next three seasons, but in 1915, the pinstripes returned for good. In 1917, the double monogrammed NY was removed from the front of the uniform and replaced with plain pinstripes for the next 20 years. In 1936, the interlocking Yankee logo was added to the front of the uniform. That look has remained unchanged ever since.

The Yankees were the first team in major league baseball to add numbers to the backs of their uniforms. On opening day in 1929, the Yankees took the field with numerals on their backs. The original numbers merely corresponded with the players' place in the batting order. Thus, leadoff batter Earle Combs was number 1, Mark Koenig number 2, Babe Ruth number 3, Lou Gehrig number 4, Bob Meusel number 5, Tony Lazzeri number 6, Leo Durocher number 7, and Johnny Grabowski number 8.

"It is hoped," wrote John Drebinger of the *New York Times* that day, "that some day Ruth will make the number three perhaps as famous as Red Grange made the number seventy-seven."

TRADES

YANKEE TOP PICKS THAT GOT AWAY

Since the advent of the major league draft in 1964, the Yankees have seen several number one picks (Ron Blomberg, 1967; Thurman Munson, 1968; Derek Jeter, 1992) mature into all-stars, or at least fairly solid players. But the Yankees have also had top picks that either didn't make the major league grade or blossomed elsewhere. Here are three in particular that got away:

1 John Elway, cf

The hard-hitting Elway was also a quarterback for the Stanford Cardinals. He was the Yankees first pick of 1981, coming in the second round, but the 6-foot 3-inch, 208-pound Elway eventually opted for the NFL. He was drafted in 1983 by the Denver Broncos and played pro football for 15 years,

winning Super Bowl championships in 1997 and 1998.

2 Bo Jackson, ss

Bo was a 6-foot 1-inch, 210-pound shortstop with overwhelming speed and considerable power when the Yankees drafted him 22nd out of Bessemer High School in Alabama in 1982. However, Jackson opted to attend Auburn University on a football scholarship. Jackson's dream by the time he was a senior was to play both baseball and football and this he did for several years, doubling as a halfback for the Oakland Raiders and an outfielder for the Kansas City Royals.

3 Scott McGregor, lhp

McGregor, along with catcher Rick Dempsey and pitchers Rudy May and Tippy Martinez, was traded to Baltimore in a multi-player deal for Doyle Alexander and Ken Holzman. He would eventually post a 138-108 record with the Orioles before retiring in 1988.

THE CURSE OF THE BAMBINO

The Curse of the Bambino? Well, it's more like the Curse of Many Dumb Red Sox Executives. Some Red Sox fans claim that Babe Ruth's purchase by the Yankees precipitated their 82 years (and counting) of misery. Possibly, but the reality is, the Red Sox have made some pretty bad business decisions over the past eight decades, and the Ruth sale was just one of them. The following are just the ones that benefited the Yankees.

1918 Boston owner Harry Frazee trades all-star pitcher Carl Mays to the Yankees for pitchers Bob McGraw (0-2 lifetime with Sox), Allen Russell (28-28) and $40,000. Mays will be 75-39 with New York.

1919 Ruth goes to New York for $100,000, plus a $300,000 loan.

1921 In a big multi-player deal, the Sox send eventual Hall of Famer Waite Hoyt, veteran catcher Wally Schang (.284 career, .278 with New York), backup infielder Mike McNally and journeyman pitcher Harry Harper to the Yankees for veteran Del Pratt (.292 career, .312 for the Sox), veteran catcher Muddy Ruel (.275 career, .266 with the Sox), journeyman outfielder Sammy Vick (.260 for the Sox) and lefty Hank Thormahlen (29-30 for his career, but 1-7 for Boston). This was a pretty even trade initially. In fact, until Hoyt clearly began to blossom with New York, nobody thought of it as a steal for the Yankees. Ruel and Pratt were quality players and Vick was a pretty good utility man.

1922 The Red Sox trade star third baseman Joe Dugan to New York, along with utility outfielder Elmer Smith in exchange for outfielder Elmer Miller (career .243 average), shortstop Chick Fewster (.258), shortstop Johnny Mitchell (.245) and pitcher Lefty O'Doul (career 1-1). The Sox eventually traded O'Doul to the Giants, where John McGraw converted him to an outfielder (for other conversions of Red Sox pitchers to outfielders, see: Ruth, Babe). O'Doul ended up hitting .349 in his career with the Giants. Dugan anchored the hot corner for several years in New York and was a key member of the 1927 team.

1923 The Red Sox trade Herb Pennock to New York for Camp Skinner (career .196 hitter), Norm McMillian (.260), pitcher George Murray (20-26, 5.38 ERA) and $50,000. Pennock, a future Hall of Famer, is 162-90 with New York.

1930 The Sox trade Red Ruffing to the Yankees for outfielder Cedric Durst (.244). Ruffing is a very bad 39-94 when the Sox make the trade. He goes 231-136 with the Yankees and is eventually elected to the Hall of Fame.

1972 The Red Sox trade veteran reliever Albert "Sparky" Lyle to New York for first baseman Danny Cater. Cater had hit .290 and averaged 63 RBI in a two-year stint for the Yankees, but he didn't put up those numbers for the Sox in his three years in Boston, hitting .262 and averaging only 29 RBI in a three-year span. Lyle, meanwhile, was the premier reliever in the league from 1972 to 1977, with 132 saves, twice leading the league in that span. He won the Cy Young Award in 1977.

The Yankees also pried several key free agents away from Boston. They include the following.

1978 Luis Tiant. El Tiante, as he was called in Boston, was a three-time 20-game winner for the Red Sox, performing there from 1971–78. New York signed him to a two-year deal (Boston only offered one year) and he turned in a respectable 21-17 mark for New York in those two seasons. In 1980, he helped the Yankees win the AL East.

1980 First baseman-designated hitter Bob Watson was a midseason pickup by the Sox in 1979, and hit .337 for Boston in that dual capacity. The Yankees signed him to a two-year deal in 1980, and Watson was not as productive in pinstripes, hitting .307 and then .212 in 1981. But he was another key cog in the Yankees 1980 AL East championship team.

1992 Perennial all-star third baseman Wade Boggs was thought by Sox management to be somewhat over the hill at the end of the 1992 season. Finishing his 11th season in Boston, Boggs had slumped to .259, a career low by 33 points. Signed by the Yankees later that year, Boggs jumped back to .302 the next year and turned in four .300-plus seasons from 1993-96, not to mention four All-Star game appearances.

NOTABLE ACCOMPLISHMENTS BY UN-NOTABLE YANKEES

Great players are players who play well when they're supposed to. When not-so-great players do it, that's news. Here are the top ten performances by non-all-stars in New York Yankee history.

1 Don Larsen's perfect game in 1956. Larsen was a good, but far from great, pitcher when he came to the Yankees in 1955. In fact, there was some debate about his goodness, let alone his greatness. In 1953, with St. Louis, he was 7-12. The next year, he was 3-21, one of the worst pitching records of all time. He improved somewhat when he got to New York, going 9-2 in 1955 and 11-5 in the 1956 regular season.

The zeroes on the scoreboard tell the story of Don Larsen's perfect game in the 1956 World Series.

But that afternoon in 1956, Larsen was perfect. He faced 27 batters and retired them all, breaking a 2-2 Series tie with the Dodgers in a pivotal game for New York. They went on to win the Series, 4-2.

2 Bucky Dent's home run in 1978. The Yankees were trailing, 3-0, when shortstop Bucky Dent stepped to the plate in the sixth inning of a one-game playoff for the AL East title between the Red Sox and the Yankees on October 2. Both teams were 99-63. Dent fouled the first pitch off his foot and sent the second pitch, from Boston starter Mike Torrez, into the net atop the Green Monster to tie it up. The Yankees went on to win the game and the World Series, and Red Sox fans still call the Yankee shortstop "Bucky bleeping Dent."

3 Mark Koenig hits .500 in the 1927 Series. While the National League champion Pittsburgh Pirates were worrying about Babe Ruth and his 60 home runs and Lou Gehrig and his 174 RBI, it was shortstop Koenig that ruined them, smacking nine hits in 18 at-bats and scoring five runs to spark a 4-0 sweep.

4 Brian Doyle ruins the Dodgers in 1978. The Yankees won the World Series in six games over the Dodgers in 1978, primarily because of some unexpected offense from backup second baseman Brian Doyle, who simply pummeled Dodger pitching. Doyle, filling in for the injured Willie Randoph, socked .438 with four runs scored.

5 Jim Leyritz turns the 1996 Series around. Backup dh-catcher Jim Leyritz stepped to the plate in Game 4 of the 1996 World Series against

Atlanta with two on and the Yankees trailing by three runs, 6-3. Leyritz admitted later that he just wanted to put the ball in play somewhere, particularly against the Braves' formidable closer, Mark Wohlers. But Leyritz homered, and suddenly the game was deadlocked, 6-6. In the tenth inning, the Yankees scored to complete the biggest comeback in Yankee World Series history. More importantly, the home run turned the game around, and in turn the entire World Series. Atlanta had been ahead, two games to one. A loss in Game 4 would have probably shut the door on New York. Instead, Leyritz threw it wide open.

6 Danny MacFayden makes the difference. On June 5, 1932, the Boston Red Sox traded right-hander "Deacon" Danny MacFayden, who had been 36-66 with the Sox over seven years, to New York for righty Hank Johnson 45-36 in seven seasons for the Yankees, righty Ivy Andrews (4-1 in two years) and cash. Johnson went 16-15 for the Sox over the next three years, Andrews was 15-19, while MacFayden was 14-10 for New York, giving the Red Sox a slight overall advantage in the trade in that Andrews and Johnson were more productive, if not more successful, than MacFayden.

Except that seven of MacFayden's 14 Yankee wins came in the latter part of the 1932 season, when the Yankees were trying to hold off the Philadelphia A's for the pennant. MacFayden's clutch effort was a key in the Yankees surge that year. He would win only seven more games in the next two years before he was shipped to the Reds in 1935.

7 Ricky Ledee sparks the Yankees in the 1998 World Series. Outfielder Ricky Ledee, who had not even been activiated for the first-round playoff series with the Texas Rangers, made up for that omission by smoking the San Diego Padres in the 1998 World Series. Ledee had six hits in 10 at-bats, including three doubles and 4 RBI.

8 Shane Spencer murders September. At the end of his stunning September in 1998, Shane Spencer told a reporter, "If this is a dream, please don't wake me." It was no dream. Spencer, called up from Columbus in late August, socked ten home runs in 67 at-bats. The Yankees didn't necessarily need this output (they were already 20 or so games up on the Red Sox), but Spencer's performance is one of the more memorable late-season drives in Yankee history.

9 Pedro Ramos saves the 1964 pennant. With the Yankees battling the Orioles and the White Sox in 1964, New York acquired veteran righty Pedro Ramos from the Indians. Ramos, who had pitched for ten years for second division squads, was 104-142 prior to his acquisition by New York on September 5, 1964. And, in fact, he would win only one game for the Yankees that year. But he also collected eight saves in September, which put the Yankees in the World Series for the last time in the 1960s.

10 Jim Beattie's postseason heroics. Rookie Jim Beattie had an unremarkable 6-9 record in 1978, and, in fact, was sent back to New York's Tacoma farm club after a poor performance against the Red Sox on June 20 of that year. But Beattie was recalled a few weeks later and was activated for the playoffs. In the American League championship series against Kansas City, he threw a two-hitter for five innings as the Yankees won the opening game 7-1 en route to a 3-1 series win. In the World Series, Beattie came through again, tossing a complete-game win over the Dodgers in Game 5, which gave New York a 3-2 lead in games en route to a 4-2 win. Beattie pitched for nine years in the majors and had one winning season. He was 52-87 for his career.

TEN PLAYERS YOU DIDN'T KNOW WERE YANKEES

Okay, we all know that Bobby Bonds played with New York for one year (1975) and that Deion Sanders played 56 games in the outfield in pinstripes in 1989-90. But here are ten guys who are the answers to some very good trivia questions.

1 Branch Rickey, 1907

Rickey, who would of course make a name for himself as an executive years later, played 52 games with the old Highlanders, hitting .182. He was released in spring training the next year.

2 Rocky Colavito, 1968

The six-time all-star outfielder for the Indians and Tigers played 39 games for the Yankees in his 14th and last year. This included one game as a relief pitcher, which he won for his only victory in the major leagues.

3 George Halas, 1919

Papa Bear, several years before he would help found the National Football League, played the outfield briefly for the Yankees, hitting .091 in 12 games.

4 Butch Hobson, 1982

The former Red Sox third baseman was a shadow of his former self by 1982, beset as he was by numerous injuries. But owner George Steinbrenner couldn't resist a chance to tweak the Red Sox, and Hobson was obtained in a trade with the Angels. He played 11 games at first base and was a designated hitter for 15 more. He hit .172 and was gone the next year.

5 Dave Kingman, 1977

The 1977 season was a tumultuous time for Kingman, who played for the Mets, Padres, Angels and, finally, the Yankees that year. New York acquired him in the last two weeks of September to hold off the Red Sox in a tight pennant race.

Kingman had six hits in eight games, but four of those hits were home runs. The Yankees went 6-2 in games in which Kingman appeared, and edged Boston by 2½ games. The next year, Kingman was off again, this time to the Cubs.

6 Fred Merkle, 1925–26

After 14 years in the National League, including 10 years with the crosstown Giants, the 37-year-old Merkle signed with the Yankees in 1925. He was a solid pinch hitter, batting .385 in seven games. He played one game in 1926 for the Yankees before retiring.

7 Paul "Big Poison" Waner, 1944–45

Seventeen years after his Pittsburgh Pirates were swept by Babe Ruth's Yankees in the World Series, future Hall of Famer Paul Waner was signed by New York. He was a pinch hitter, but he didn't get too many hits in a pinch, batting .143 in a ten-game stint. He retired in 1945.

8 Ralph Branca, 1954

Following a ten-year career with the Brooklyn Dodgers, Branca was released in 1953. After a brief stint with the Tigers, he was signed by the Yankees in 1954. He got three starts and two relief appearances and was 1-0 with a 2.54 ERA. Not bad, but Yankee management released him anyway. He was later signed by the Dodgers for one more year.

9 Sal "The Barber" Maglie, 1957–58

After 7½ years with the Giants and stints with the Dodgers and Indians, Maglie was picked up by the Yankees for the waiver price in 1957. He went 3-1 with three saves for New York in two years. In 1958, the Yankees traded Maglie to St. Louis.

10 Dazzy Vance, 1915, 1918

Hall of Famer Arthur "Dazzy" Vance had a brief, unsuccessful tryout with the Yankees in 1915 and again in 1918 before going on to glory in Brooklyn. The hard-throwing Vance had problems getting people out in those early days, as his 15.45 ERA with the Yankees in 1918 would attest. But when he returned to the major leagues in 1922 with the Dodgers, he had it all worked out. Vance would lead the National League in strikeouts for seven consecutive years with Brooklyn, and became one of the great pitchers of that era.

YANKEE BAD BOYS

These Yankees made headlines for activities on and off the ball field.

1 Hal Chase

When it came to betting on ballgames, Chase made Pete Rose look like a rank amateur. Again and again throughout his career, Chase was accused of either trying to throw games himself, or of bribing other players or officials to do it for him. While he played for the Highlanders, he was accused by his manager, George Stallings, of trying to lose games on purpose. Chase denied it. In 1917, he was accused by the venerable Christy Mathewson, then managing the Cincinnati Reds, of trying to throw games. Chase was also said to have had inside knowledge of the 1919 Black Sox scandal. He was finally thrown out of major league baseball that year because of that scandal and numerous others, and went back to his home state of California. But he couldn't stay away from trouble and he was banned in 1920 from the Pacific Coast League for trying to bribe an umpire. Baseball historian Bill James believes Chase holds the all-time record for "games fixed."

2 Babe Ruth

The fact is, during his career, and for a good time after, George Herman Ruth was in the headlines just about every day. Most of it was benign stuff. The Babe takes a trip. The Babe eats a big dinner. The Babe visits a hospital or orphanage. Sometimes it was a little naughty. In June of 1921, he was arrested for speeding in New York and he actually spent a few hours in jail. The newspapermen found out and had a field day with it, but it

was all in good fun. The Babe took his medicine like a man and that was it.

But he had some headline-grabbing spats. The first as a Yankee came against Judge Kenesaw Mountain Landis, the commissioner of baseball, when Ruth wanted to head up a barnstorming team after the 1922 World Series. Baseball had a rule that World Series players couldn't barnstorm. It was a silly rule and the Babe said so, and added that Landis should go jump in a lake. Landis was not amused. That spat kept reporters busy for a few months. Babe was eventually suspended and fined.

In 1925, Yankee manager Miller Huggins, tired of Ruth's off-the-field antics, suspended him and fined him $5,000, more than many players at the time were making in a season. Ruth, to put it mildly, did not take that very well. The two men had words. Huggins suspended Babe. Ruth finally calmed down and apologized to Huggins, but that brouhaha lasted several weeks.

Ruth also had a temper that landed him in hot water. In 1922, he was thrown out of a game for throwing dirt in an umpire's face. A fan started heckling him and Ruth almost went into the stands after the man. He snapped at teammate Wally Pipp that same year after Pipp had made an error, and the big, rawboned Pipp mopped the dugout floor with him.

Most of Ruth's exploits with women were ignored or covered up by the sporting press of the time. But in 1925, they could not ignore a $50,000 paternity suit filed against Ruth by a young woman who claimed Ruth was the father of her child. The suit was eventually dropped.

Ruth had a few other lawsuits with which to deal, among them an odd courtroom scuffle in which he was arrested in San Diego for violation of the child-labor laws in California in 1927. It turned out to be nothing more than a headline-grabbing stunt by a local official. Ruth's offense was inviting children onto the stage during his vaudeville act and joshing with them. A local judge ruled that any kid invited onstage with Babe Ruth was not about to complain about being exploited.

He was a lousy driver, and that precipitated several accidents. In 1920, he and several others, including his first wife, Helen, were driving to Philadelphia when the Babe's touring sedan failed to negotiate a curve in the road. No one was badly hurt in the ensuing accident but the vehicle was totaled. Ruth left it at a garage outside of Philadelphia in disgust and hired a cab for himself and his party. A newspaperman heard about the accident, and, being unable to track down Ruth for comment, relied instead on at least one third-hand story about the incident, then wrote his story accordingly. Ruth and his party were startled the next day in Philadelphia to read the headline Babe Ruth Dead! in the local papers. It took a day or so to assure everyone that he was all right.

3   Billy Martin

Bad Boy Billy spent most of his career dealing with lurid headlines. His first controversial exploit came when he beat up troubled Red Sox outfielder Jimmy Piersall in 1952. This fight wasn't all Martin's fault. Piersall called him "Pinocchio" and suggested the fight in the first place. Martin obliged, popping Piersall twice in the face under the stands in Boston before Yankee coach Bill Dickey broke it up.

Martin had several other fights in his major league career, including a pair with St. Louis Brown catcher Clint Courtney, in 1952 and 1953. Both times, Martin was victorious, and it made his reputation as a fighter. After that, few players would challenge him.

But in 1957, Martin lost his job as a Yankee because of a fight that never happened, according to police and virtually every witness in attendance. It was May 16 and Martin and several Yankee pals and their wives were out on the town celebrating Billy's 29th birthday. They ended up at the Copacabana, watching Sammy Davis Jr. perform.

Unfortunately, a rowdy drunk at the next table began heckling Davis, and then cussing out the Yankees. Martin turned to the man and told him that he was spoiling everyone's evening. Harsh words followed and Martin invited the man outside. The two got up, as did Yankees Hank Bauer and Mickey Mantle.

Billy Martin was a source of excitement on the field—and off it—during his tenure with the Yankees in the '50s.

At that point, cooler heads began prevailing, and people stepped between the two men. There was some pushing but no punches—at least not in the club. But during the confusion, two Copa bouncers reportedly followed the drunk into the men's room and beat the heck out of him. He was lying on the floor of the bathroom in a pool of blood, with a broken nose.

The Yankees' first reaction, after seeing that tableau, was to get out of there, and they left via a back door. But the rumor flew around New York that night that several Yankees had been in a barroom brawl and at least one New York paper reported it the next day.

As the story got out, Yankee general manager George Weiss was furious. Weiss was convinced it was all somehow Martin's fault, even after he had interviewed every Yankee who had been there and a grand jury investigation found no wrongdoing on any Yankee's part. His teammates, Weiss believed, were all covering for Martin. A month later, Billy was gone, to Kansas City.

It didn't end there, of course. Martin played for several other teams, got into a few more fights. He retired in 1961. He stayed in baseball and became a manager, and was as fiery in that incarnation as he was as a player.

During the 1980s, when he worked as a Yankee manager on several different occasions, Martin made headlines by tangling with, in order, a marshmallow salesman in a bar in 1979, another bar patron in Anaheim in 1983, yet another barfly in a bar in Baltimore in 1985, Yankee pitcher Ed Whitson in the same bar the next night and a bouncer at the Lace Topless Bar in Arlington, Texas, in 1988. Some he won, some he lost. But it didn't much help his relationship with Yankee management, principally owner George Steinbrenner.

4 Mike Kekich and Fritz Peterson

In 1972, pitchers Mike Kekich and Fritz Peterson moved in with each other's families, and, for all practical purposes, traded lives. Both were left-handed pitchers, and thus expected to be a little eccentric. But this was more than eccentric. This was about as un-Yankee-like as anyone could imagine. Their respective wives seemed to go along with it, at least for a while. But the Yankees swiftly traded Kekich to Cleveland, where he pitched for one year and retired. The next year, Peterson was also sent to Cleveland.

All along the pitchers insisted it was not a "wife swap" but a "lifestyle swap." As of 2000, Fritz Peterson and Susanne Kekich are still married. Mike Kekich and Marilyn Peterson only lasted three months.

5 The Bronx Zoo

The 1977 and 1978 seasons in New York were probably the two most tumultuous in team history. Billy Martin, Thurman Munson, Reggie Jackson,

George Steinbrenner, Mickey Rivers and several other Yankee personalities were in the headlines constantly. The most memorable controversy in 1977 came in the infamous Martin-Jackson dugout brawl in Boston.

The two men did not get along, and Jackson made matters worse by going to Steinbrenner every time he and Billy had an argument. It came to a head in June 1977, in Fenway Park. Martin believed Jackson had not tried hard enough to catch a fly ball. (Billy later admitted that Jackson almost certainly couldn't have gotten to it even if he had hustled.) Moments later, he sent Paul Blair out to replace Jackson in right field in front of a national television audience. Every fan in Fenway saw Jackson's astonished face as he watched Blair trot out to the outfield. For a second, Jackson couldn't believe it, and pointed to his chest, saying, "Me?" Blair nodded and Reggie ran to the Yankee dugout.

That's when the fur flew. Jackson and Martin had words. Some of Billy's were swear words. Suddenly, Martin flew at Jackson like a terrier. Several Yankee coaches broke it up, but it was great television.

The team won the World Series that year, and Billy and Reggie seemed to bury the hatchet after the final game.

But the next year was crazy. Pitcher Sparky Lyle, upset about his contract, once left the dugout in the middle of a game. Martin and Munson got into a shoving match on a plane. Centerfielder Mickey Rivers tried to choke a Yankee clubhouse official. A drunken Martin called Jackson a "born liar" and Steinbrenner a "convicted" one. That was enough for George, who fired him a few days later. But in the end, the Yankees came back, under more sedate manager Bob Lemon, to win the World Series.

6 George Steinbrenner

Steinbrenner has now owned the Yankees longer than any other individual. He has also generated more headlines than probably all the other owners combined. After the tumultuous 1978 season, Steinbrenner remained the focus of controversy throughout the 1980s and early 1990s.

There are too many individual incidents to recount here. The highlights include his 1981 alleged "fight" with two Dodgers fans in an elevator during the World Series; the "public apology" to New York fans after the Yankees lost the 1981 World Series to the Dodgers; his one-week suspension in 1983 for criticizing umpires; his decision to fire manager Yogi Berra 16 games into the 1985 season after promising that Berra would manage the club all year "win or lose"; his ongoing battle with manager Dallas Green during the 1989 season. Green, of course, was fired.

Steinbrenner fired a lot of people, and that often made headlines, too. Mostly it was his managers. He fired Martin five times and Bob Lemon, Gene Michael and Lou Piniella twice each. He fired Dick Howser, who won 103 games for him in 1980. He fired Bucky Dent in 1990, 12 years after Dent saved the Yankees with a three-run home run in Fenway Park to help beat the Red Sox and cap the most amazing season in Yankee history.

In 1990, Steinbrenner made more headlines when he was ordered by Commissioner Fay Vincent to give up control of the Yankees because of alleged payments to a New York City gambler for information about slugger Dave Winfield. That suspension was in effect for three years. Since that time, Steinbrenner has been much more low-key. It hasn't hurt that the Yankees are winning again.

SUPERSTITIONS AND RITUALS

Ballplayers at the turn of the 20th century were thought to be a superstitious lot, but they probably weren't a heck of a lot more superstitious than players these days, who would drink motor oil if they knew it would snap them out of a slump. Here are some Yankee superstitions and other eccentricities and rituals.

Gum on the cap button: Highlander first baseman Hal Chase was one of the early players to try this good-luck charm, but the Athletics' Eddie Collins quickly picked it up, as did many other ballplayers at the turn of the 20th century.

Gum under the bench: When Yankee manager Joe McCarthy was finished chewing a piece of gum, he would stick it under the bench on which he sat for luck.

Totems and charms: Babe Ruth was big on any kind of good-luck charm, including four-leaf clovers, horseshoes and a silver dollar he got as a present when he was with the Red Sox. He considered a white or yellow butterfly a good omen, and his biggest good-luck charm was batboy/mascot Eddie Bennett. Bennett had a hunched back, and Ruth and many other Yankees liked to rub his hump for good luck.

When he was a rookie with the Yankees, Leo Durocher got into the habit of touching the crucifix medal he wore for good luck during games, although he was probably not the first player to do so.

Pitcher Bob Shawkey had a lucky red sweater he would wear during starts.

Catcher Rick Cerone wore his lucky college long johns during games.

For many years, the only glove Phil Rizzuto would use was the one he bought for $10 as a Yankee rookie. Year after year, Rizzuto would have his lucky glove repaired by a representative from Rawlings instead of getting a new glove. He wore it until it literally fell apart late in his career.

When he pitched, "Sad" Sam Jones wore his cap pulled down almost over his eyes. One New York sportswriter thought it made Jones look "dour," and conferred upon Jones his famous nickname. Jones replied that pulling his cap down over his forehead made it easier to concentrate.

Markings: Third baseman Joe Dugan would draw an "X" in the dirt next to third base and plant his feet exactly equidistant from each side of the "X."

Messengers: For several years, utility infielder Mike Gazella kept his job as a Yankee in part because of his fielding and in part because manager Miller Huggins believed that when he sent Gazella to the bullpen to summon a relief pitcher, the pitcher would have a good outing.

Seating arrangements: Yankee reliever Johnny Murphy would sit in the same spot on the bench during games he pitched.

When Ruth would hit a home run, Huggins would find the man he sat next to during Ruth's homer and sit next to him again during Ruth's next at-bat.

Food: Wade Boggs ate chicken before every game he ever played in the major leagues. His wife bought several cookbooks to find different ways to prepare it.

In 1961, Roger Maris's lucky pre-game dish was scrambled eggs and baloney, which he insisted his friend Julius "Julie" Isaacson partake of also. Despite the fact that Isaacson was Jewish and baloney wasn't exactly kosher, for the good of the team, he ate it.

Rituals: Boggs made it a point to run wind sprints at exactly 7:17 pm every day. He also walked to and from the dugout from home plate and third base by taking the same number of steps each time.

Prior to a game, Joe Dugan would find a church and light a candle, in hopes of getting a base hit.

When he was working as a reliever, Wilcy Moore made sure that his first warm-up pitch was to disabled mascot Eddie Bennett. Moore apparently did not let Bennett warm him up when he was tabbed to start a game.

Catfish Hunter, in his biography, explained that when he was in the minor leagues, he noticed that every time he bowled the day before a start, he would pitch well. That became his good-luck ritual for a few seasons. Unfortunately, Hunter said, he began to have problems finding bowling alleys in some of the more out-of-the-way towns in which he pitched in the minors, so he finally, reluctantly, gave it up.

When Joe DiMaggio used to doff his civilian clothes before a game, Billy Martin (who for a few years dressed in the locker next to Joe) noticed that, after his shoes, the first item of clothing DiMaggio removed would be his pants—before his suitcoat, socks or anything else.

Sparky Lyle, when he was on the mound, chewed tobacco, as did (and do) many ballplayers. The difference with Lyle was that he would add to his chaw at the beginning of each inning in which he would pitch. If he went three or four innings, or more, Lyle would sometimes have a chaw so large he would have trouble getting it out of his cheek after the game.

Vic Raschi demanded to be left alone before he pitched a game, preferring to focus on the team he would face. He was also very superstitious about news photographers taking his picture prior to a start. He felt it ruined his concentration.

YANKEES ON THE SILVER SCREEN

ACTORS WHO HAVE PLAYED BABE RUTH IN THE MOVIES

The biggest star in the history of the game has been the subject of several cinematic efforts, including, alas, the worst baseball movie ever made, *The Babe Ruth Story.* The following is a list of actors who have played the Bambino.

William Bendix *The Babe Ruth Story* (1948). Bendix was a solid actor in the 1940s and '50s, but this was one of his stinkers. Or maybe it was director Roy Del Ruth. Or maybe it was the writers. Anyway, casting the 42-year-old Bendix as a teenaged Ruth was only the first of several brutally bad decisions in making this bomb. Ruth reportedly attended the opening in Manhattan and walked out halfway through.

Joe Don Baker *The Natural* (1984). This adaptation of Bernard Malamud's novel stars Robert

Redford in the title role, but there is a scene in which a young Redford, a pitcher, strikes out The Whammer, who is clearly supposed to be Babe Ruth. Baker's Ruth is a little too cranky to be given very high marks.

Stephen Lang *Babe Ruth* (1991). This made-for-television movie was surprisingly saccharine for the 1990s, but Lang isn't bad as the Babe.

John Goodman *The Babe* (1992). Goodman's portrayal of Ruth is a little over the top, but director Arthur Hiller's attempt to portray Babe Ruth realistically gets the job done.

ACTORS WHO HAVE PLAYED LOU GEHRIG IN THE MOVIES

Unlike the Babe Ruth legend, the Lou Gehrig story seems to have translated better to the screen. At least so far.

Gary Cooper *The Pride of the Yankees* (1942). Well, Gary Cooper didn't look too athletic, and he's certainly no Lou Gehrig in terms of physique, but this was a helluva movie. Superb performances by Cooper and Teresa Wright as wife Eleanor, Oscar-winning editing by Daniel Mandell. In fact, Ruth's cameo as himself is a better job than any of the actors who tried to portray him.

Edward Hermann *A Love Affair: The Eleanor and Lou Gehrig Story* (1978). Another excellent job, this time by Hermann, as well as a strong performance by Blythe Danner as Eleanor in this made-for-television movie.

MOVIES IN WHICH YANKEE PLAYERS APPEAR

Babe Ruth *Headin' Home* (1920); *The Babe Comes Home* (1927); *Speedy* (1927). The first two movies are baseball-flavored shorts; *Speedy* is a Hal Lloyd comedy in which the Babe has a cameo.

Lou Gehrig *Rawhide* (1938). Gehrig plays himself in a story that has the ballplayer running a ranch in the offseason. Not bad, actually, and

Gehrig's husky good looks make up for his wooden performance.

Tony Lazzeri *Slide, Kelly, Slide* (1927). Another contrived baseball movie that is relatively uneventful, except for the number of big-leaguers in it.

Bob Meusel *Slide, Kelly, Slide* (1927); *Pride of the Yankees* (1942). The Yankee outfielder makes cameo appearances in both.

Bill Dickey *Pride of the Yankees* (1942); *The Stratton Story* (1949). Dickey plays himself in *Pride* and in *Stratton*. He turns in a pretty good performance in the latter film, the story of Monty Stratton, the minor-leaguer who loses a leg but refuses to let it halt his career. (Jimmy Stewart plays Stratton.)

Mark Koenig *Pride of the Yankees* (1942). *The Babe Ruth Story* (1948). Koenig makes brief appearances in both.

Joe DiMaggio *Manhattan Merry-Go-Round* (1937); *Angels In The Outfield* (1951). DiMaggio makes a singing (!) cameo in *Manhattan,* a thin melodrama about a radio station taken over by a gangster. The movie is notable because it was on this set that he met his first wife, actress Dorothy Arnold, who is also in the movie. *Angels* stars Paul Douglas as a crusty manager whose Pittsburgh Pirates team goes on a winning streak with some heavenly intervention in the form of DiMaggio and, believe it or not, Ty Cobb.

Mickey Mantle *Safe At Home!* (1962); *That Touch of Mink* (1962). In *Safe*, Roger and Mickey star as themselves as they help a little kid out of a jam. Ralph Houk and Whitey Ford cameo as themselves. In *Touch,* the boys and Yogi have a clever cameo in this Cary Grant–Doris Day vehicle.

Roger Maris *Safe At Home!* (1962); *That Touch of Mink* (1962)

Whitey Ford *Safe At Home!* (1962)

Ralph Houk *Safe At Home!* (1962)

Yogi Berra *That Touch of Mink* (1962)

Bill Virdon *The Bad News Bears In Breaking Training* (1977). Ex-Yankee skipper Virdon is one of several big leaguers who appear in this tepid sequel.

Reggie Jackson *The Naked Gun: From The Files*

of *Police Squad* (1988); *BASEketball* (1998). Reggie is playing for the Angels in *Naked Gun,* but delivers a funny performance as an automaton murderer. He also cameos in *BASEketball,* a poorly-written comedy about the invention of a game that combines baseball and basketball.

Bobby Murcer *The Scout* (1994). Fair baseball yarn stars Albert Brooks as a baseball scout who discovers a great ballplayer with serious psychological problems. Murcer and George Steinbrenner appear as themselves.

George Steinbrenner *The Scout* (1994)

Lou Piniella *Little Big League* (1994). Youngster inherits the Minnesota Twins from his grandfather and decides to manage them himself. And it's two hours long. Lou and Paul O'Neill cameo along with several other major league stars.

Paul O'Neill *Little Big League* (1994)

FOR THE AGES

THE 20 MOST DRAMATIC EVENTS IN YANKEE HISTORY

1 Lou Gehrig Appreciation Day, July 4, 1939

It was a day of deep emotion for both Gehrig and his fans. For Lou, it was the end of his playing days. For the fans, it was end of the career of an all-time Yankee great, well before his time. As the man sportswriters once called Iron Horse Lou shuffled to the microphone that day, only one thing was certain: There would be no comfortable retirement for Lou Gehrig, and everybody in Yankee Stadium knew it.

Lou Gehrig's moving farewell to the game in 1939 is one of baseball's most lasting and powerful images.

2 Don Larsen's perfect game, October 8, 1956

Late in the game, with seven perfect innings to his credit against the Brooklyn Dodgers in the World Series, Larsen turned to Mickey Mantle and said, "Hey, do you think I'll make it?" Mantle said nothing, because although Larsen didn't seem to know it, ballplayers never talked about no-hitters or perfect games. Larsen did make it, of course, and his effort remains the only perfect postseason game in history.

3 Babe Ruth's called shot home run, October 1, 1932

No, Ruth didn't step out of the batter's box in the fifth inning of the third game of the World Series and point to right field, as William Bendix did in *The Babe Ruth Story,* because if he had, pitcher Charlie Root would have likely knocked him on his big can. But with the count at 2-2, the Chicago dugout calling him every name they could think of, and the Chicago fans hooting and booing, Ruth pointed to Root and said, "It only takes one to hit it, kid!" It does and he did.

4 Babe Ruth Day, April 4, 1947

By 1947, most people realized that the greatest player of all was not the man he once was. When he stepped to the microphone that day, his voice an awful croak, it was clear the end was near. Ruth died 16 months later.

5 Reggie Jackson's three home runs, October 18, 1977

It was an awesome display of power and an amazing exclamation point to a turbulent Yankee season.

6 Joe DiMaggio's 56-game hitting streak, 1941

Not a moment, but the last 30 games were a daily drama for Joe, the Yankees and their fans.

7 Bucky Dent's home run in the AL playoff, October 2, 1978

The Yankees cap off the most exciting pennant comeback in their history with a 5-4 win over the Red Sox in the 163rd game of the season—a one-game do-or-die playoff—at Fenway Park.

8 Roger Maris's 61st home run, October 1, 1961

Others had been here before: Jimmie Foxx of the Athletics, Hank Greenberg of the Tigers. They had chased Babe Ruth but fell short, for one reason or another. Maris, in a fine display of grace under pressure, came through.

9 Chris Chambliss' ninth-inning home run, October 14, 1976

It was the fifth and deciding game of the American League championship series, and the game was tied in the bottom of the ninth inning. Chambliss swung on Royal pitcher Mark Littell's first offering and deposited it into the seats, putting the Yankees in the World Series for the first time in 12 years.

10 Allie Reynolds second no-hitter of the season, September 28, 1951

By the ninth inning, the lead was 8-0 and the pennant was clinched. But Reynolds was working on his second no-hitter of the year. With two outs, he faced the Red Sox's Ted Williams. Allie jammed Williams into popping up a foul behind home plate, but Yogi Berra couldn't get to the ball. "You had your chance," Williams told Yogi when he got back to the batter's box. But on the next pitch, Williams hit another pop-up, and this time, Yogi grabbed it.

11 The Yankees sweep Boston to win the 1949 pennant, October 1-2, 1949

The Red Sox have a one-game lead on New York with the final two games of the year in Yankee Stadium. Reliever Joe Page wins the October 1 game, 5-4 on a home run by Johnny Lindell. Vic Raschi wins the October 2 game, 5-3, helped along by rookie Jerry Coleman's three-run single.

12 Bobby Murcer wins one for Thurman, August 6, 1979

Earlier in the day, catcher Thurman Munson had been buried following a fatal plane crash a few days prior, and his good friend Bobby Murcer had delivered a stirring eulogy. That night, the Yankees trailed the Baltimore Orioles, 4-0. Early in the game, Murcer socked a three-run home run to close the game to 4-3. Then, in the ninth inning, he drilled a two-run single to win the game, and was mobbed by his teammates at first base.

13 Bobby Richardson makes the play, October 16, 1962

Seventh game of the World Series. Two on, two out, and the Yankees leading by the slimmest of margins, 1-0, in the bottom of the ninth over the San Francisco Giants. Yankee pitcher Ralph Terry is facing Willie McCovey. Second pitch, and McCovey drills the ball right at second baseman Bobby Richardson. Bobby fields the bullet and the series is over. Years later, McCovey admits he never hit a harder ball.

14 Jim Leyritz fuels a comeback, October 23, 1996

The Atlanta Braves had won the first two World Series games in Yankees Stadium by a combined margin of 16-1. Going back to Atlanta, there was little talk of a Yankee victory. Instead, New York fans were hoping to avoid a sweep. The Yankees won Game 3, 5-2, behind David Cone, but the Braves seemed to be in control the next day, taking a 6-0 lead in Game 4. And that's when the Yankees began chipping away. By the eighth inning, the lead was down to 6-3. Yankee catcher Jim Leyritz then homered off Brave closer Mark Wohlers to tie the game. Wade Boggs's bases-loaded walk gave New York the lead for good. It was the biggest comeback for the Yankees in their long World Series history. New York wins the next two games for their 23rd World Championship.

15 Nettles and Guidry save the day, October 13, 1978

The Yankees are in a pickle, trailing the steamrolling Los Angeles Dodgers two games to none going into the third game at Yankee Stadium. But Ron Guidry, their ace, is ready to go. Unfortunately, the Dodgers show him little respect, drilling line drives all over the place. But the Yan-

kees still win, 5-1, thanks to some stunning glovework by third baseman Graig Nettles, who makes at least three incredible plays to help Guidry win the game. The Yankees sweep the next three games to win the Series.

16 Lou Gehrig's four home runs, June 3, 1932

Larrupin' Lou (another nickname; what's a larrup?) blasted home runs in the first, fourth and fifth innings off Philadelphia's George Earnshaw before A's manager Connie Mack took George out. Earnshaw was a power pitcher, and Mack put in veteran Roy "Popeye" Mahaffey to try to finesse Gehrig. Some finesse. Gehrig crushed a Mahaffey pitch into the right field stands for his fourth homer of the day in the seventh. Lou grounded out in the eighth, but in the ninth, ripped another Mahaffey pitch to center field that the A's Al Simmons had to hustle to catch. The Yankees, by the way, won this one, 20-13.

17 The Babe hits home run number 700, July 13, 1933

How amazing was this? The second place career home run hitter at the time was Gehrig, with 348, and third place was Rogers Hornsby, with 299. In 1933, 700 home runs was hard for many to conceive, and since then only Hank Aaron has reached that milestone.

18 David Wells's perfect game, May 17, 1998

Wells, in the midst of his best year, throws the first regular-season perfect game in New York Yankee history.

19 David Cone's perfect game, July 18, 1999

On "Yogi Berra Day," Cone throws only the second regular-season perfect game in Yankee history.

20 Bill Mazeroski's home run, October 13, 1960

Well, it didn't always work out for the Yankees. The Mazeroski home run caps a stunning World Series win by the Pirates over New York.

THE MAGIC YEARS

Over the course of a team's history, fans of the franchise have fond memories of a special year, usually a year that is somewhat out of the ordinary and results in a happy ending. For the Red Sox, for example, it would be 1967, "The Impossible Dream" year. For Pittsburgh, it's probably 1960 and for the Dodgers, it is 1955.

The Yankees, because of their storied history, have actually had several "special seasons." Here are five memorable ones.

1927 Babe Ruth hits 60 home runs and Lou Gehrig wins the Most Valuable Player award. The Yankees win 110 games and defeat the Pittsburgh Pirates in four games in the World Series.

Most memorable moment: Ruth's 60th homer.

Best line of the year: "Sixty, count 'em sixty! Let's see some son-of-a-bitch match that!"—Ruth, on hitting the record-setting dinger.

Fast fact: Ruth actually hit 66 home runs during the regular season that year. The Yankees, ever eager to capitalize on Ruth's popularity, played a

Babe Ruth hammers his 60th homerun in 1927, a record that would stand for nearly three-quarters of a century.

total of 12 exhibitions throughout the country during the regular season. Ruth was one of the few players who played virtually every inning of every exhibition game. He hit six home runs in those contests. (An ambitious exhibition slate was nothing new for the Yankees. For most of Ruth's career, New York played 12 to 14 exhibitions a year during the regular season to make money on the side. As far as can be determined, no other teams played nearly this many exhibitions during the season, although it was not unusual for major league teams to play two or three exhibitions near season's end.)

Key stat: Center fielder Earle Combs's 23 triples is still a team record.

1941 Joe DiMaggio hits for 56 games in a row, the Yankees win the American League pennant and win the World Series over the Brooklyn Dodgers in five games.

Most memorable moment: Joe D's hitting streak, going on and on and on.

Best line of the year: "I can't say I'm glad it's over. I would have liked to see it continue."—DiMaggio, moments after his streak was stopped in Cleveland. He went out and began a 16-game hitting streak the next day.

Fast fact: By walking in that Cleveland game, DiMaggio kept his getting-on-base streak alive. That streak ran to 74 games, finally ending on August 3.

Key stat: DiMaggio struck out only 13 times in 541 times at-bat that year.

1961 Roger Maris hits 61 home runs to break Babe Ruth's record. The Yankees go on to win 109 games and the World Series in five games over the Reds.

Most memorable moment: Maris's 61st homer on the last game of the year.

Best Line: "Holy Cow! He did it!"—Yankee broadcaster Phil Rizzuto watching Roger's 61st.

Fast fact: In 1903, the Chicago Cubs' famed infield of Joe Tinker, Johnny Evers, Frank Chance

and Harry Steinfeldt completed 100 double plays. The 1961 infield of Clete Boyer, Tony Kubek, Bobby Richardson and Moose Skowron completed 180.

Key stat: The Yankees hit 240 home runs as a team that year, still a franchise record.

1978 Trailing by 14½ games in July, the Yankees come back to win the American League pennant by edging the hated Red Sox in a playoff game in Fenway Park. After beating the Kansas City Royals in the American League Championship Series, they beat the Dodgers in the World Series.

Most memorable moment: Bucky Dent's home run in the playoff against the Red Sox.

Best Line: "One's a born liar, the other's convicted."—Yankee manager Billy Martin, referring to outfielder Reggie Jackson and owner George Steinbrenner. Martin was fired soon after that.

Fast fact: Pitcher Ron Guidry lost only three games that year, all to pitchers named Mike: Mike Caldwell of Milwaukee, Mike Flanagan of Baltimore and Mike Willis of Toronto.

Key stat: The Yankees were 22-8 in September of that year, which tied them for the most wins in September in team history.

1998 The Yankees dominate the American League, winning 114 games in the regular season and sweeping the San Diego Padres in the World Series. The 114 wins are an American League record, while the 125 total wins (an 11-2 postseason) are a major league record. Pitcher David Wells throws the first regular-season perfect game in Yankee history.

Most memorable moment: Wells' perfect game.

Best Line: "*Yo amo a Nueva York!*"—Orlando "El Duque" Hernandez, the Yankees' Cuban-born pitcher, yelling to a New York crowd at the Yankees' World Series parade. Nine months previously, Hernandez had defected from Cuba with seven other Cubans, landing on a small island, where they were picked up by the U.S. Coast Guard.

Fast fact: Outfielder Shane Spencer was called

up in midyear from Columbus and hit 10 home runs with 27 RBI in 27 games with the Yankees after spending nine years in the minor leagues.

Key stat: The Yankees finished 22 games ahead of the Boston Red Sox, who had the second-best record in the American League.

THE GREATEST TEAMS

No franchise in professional sports history has had as many World Champions as the New York Yankees—which makes picking the best of the best a fun, but very difficult, task. Champions, by definition, have that little something extra, and the Yankees have produced 26 such squads.

Interestingly, this effort of trying to identify the "Greatest Team Ever" has been around since the first half of the 20th century. It certainly did not start with the 1927 Yankees, although it may seem that way because this is the team that has gotten the most attention. The 1906 Cubs, the 1912 Red Sox and the 1923 Yankees were all squads generally conceded to be a cut above your average pennant winners.

There may well be a host of stats, numbers, charts, comparative graphs and formulae that have been concocted over the years, but a definitive way to measure "greatness" between teams of different eras has been elusive.

This section cobbled together its own ranking to line up the best of the Yankee championship nines. The formula includes wins, losses, runs scored, runs allowed, team ERA, team fielding and double plays turned to give the reader a rough picture of how each team stood against its contemporaries. Also a part of the formula are managerial changes, possible distractions, greatest player (you can't have a great team without a great player), intangibles and key facts to illustrate the pluses and minuses of each squad.

Call the whole thing the GFI, or Gut Feeling Index, because in the end, the only number that mattered was the score of the last World Series game of the year. And the Yankees almost always won that one.

1 THE 1927 YANKEES

Won-lost: 110-44.
Runs scored: 975 (1st)
Runs allowed: 599 (1st)
Team ERA: 3.20 (1st)
Team fielding: .969 (3rd)
Double plays turned: 123 (8th)
Managerial changes: none

Distractions: Babe Ruth's quest for 60 home runs was only a distraction after the Yankees had clinched the pennant.

Greatest player(s): Babe Ruth was the star of the Yankees, the American League and baseball in general in 1927, but Lou Gehrig was voted the league's best player that year. It was a bogus vote, because the league had a rule that said a player couldn't win the MVP more than once, and The Babe had already won it in an earlier season. Still, Larrupin' Lou was second in homers with 47, first in RBI with 174, second in hits with 218, first in total bases with 447, first in doubles with 52 and second in triples with 18. They were both pretty great that year.

Intangibles: One of the myths of the 1927 Yankees was that their starting lineup played most of the year. That was true of the outfield, where Babe Ruth missed three games, Earle Combs two and Bob Meusel 19. Gehrig, of course, played them all. But aside from Lou, the Yankee infield was pretty beat up for a large chunk of the season. At one point in the season, the Yankees went 38 consecutive games with a different lineup than their opening day starters. Mark Koenig was out for 31 games with various injuries and Joe Dugan sat for 42 games, mostly with knee problems. The bench wasn't deep, but it didn't really have to be. Manager Miller Huggins started Tony Lazzeri at third when Dugan was out, and at shortstop when Koenig was out. Ray Morehart would fill in at second base when Lazzeri was elsewhere. Mike Gazella was also an option at third base. A healthier Dugan and Koenig would have made this team that much better. But the unsettled infield situation was a big reason the Yankees were the worst team in the league in turning the double play.

Key facts: The Yankees pitching staff, not its hitters, is the reason this team was the best of the best. Waite Hoyt (.759), Urban Shocker (.750), Wilcy Moore (.731) and Herb Pennock (.704) were numbers 1-4 in winning percentage in the American League, the only time it's ever been done in major league baseball history. Moore (2.28), Hoyt (2.63) and Shocker (2.84) were 1-3 in earned run average in the league, only the second time this was ever done. (The 1906 Cubs did it, also.) Moore led the league in allowing the fewest hits per game with 7.82, while George Pipgras was third with 8.01. Shocker, with 1.85 and Hoyt with 1.90 were second and third in the league in fewest walks allowed. Hoyt and Walter Ruether led the team with three shutouts each. Moore led the league in saves. That's six pitchers that were key contributors to the championship season. This unit was not only good, they were very deep and very consistent.

And incidentally, the story of Ruth and Gehrig intimidating the Pirates with a show of home run hitting prior to the first game of the World Series doesn't hold much water. For one thing, the day before the Series, Pittsburgh stars Lloyd and Paul Waner visited with Ruth in his hotel room, introducing themselves and wishing Ruth luck. The reporter who witnessed the meeting didn't detect any sweating or shaking on the part of the Waners. For another, the Pirates probably didn't get to the World Series by doubting their ability. There was no intimidation involved. The Yankees were just a lot better.

2   THE 1939 YANKEES

Won-lost: 106-45
Runs scored: 967 (1st)
Runs allowed: 556 (1st)
Team ERA: 3.31 (1st)
Team fielding: .978 (1st)
Double plays turned: 159 (2nd)
Managerial changes: None

Distractions: Two big ones. On May 2, frustrated by his lack of production, Lou Gehrig took himself out of the lineup. He was replaced by Babe Dahlgren. Gehrig of course, was racked by the disease that would soon bear his name. He never played another game and died a few years later. And prior to the season, Col. Jacob Ruppert died, leaving the team to be run by Ed Barrow.

Greatest player: Joe DiMaggio won the first of three MVP awards this year. He led the league with a .381 batting average, his career best, and added 30 homers, 126 RBI and a slugging percentage of .671. All this, despite being out for about six weeks with a leg injury.

Intangibles: This team is often overlooked as one of the "best ever" because the 1939 Yankees didn't appear to have a very strong pitching staff. Red Ruffing won 21 games and led the league in shutouts, but no one else on the staff won more than 13 games, although reliever Johnny Murphy led the league in saves with 19.

This was somewhat deceiving. Manager Joe McCarthy had a very deep pitching staff that year. Five pitchers—Ruffing, Lefty Gomez, Bump Hadley, Atley Donald and Monte Pearson—got between 20 and 28 starts and represented the regular rotation. But McCarthy was not afraid to use the other pitchers on his staff, and frankly, they produced as well. Oral Hildebrand, who was 10-4 with a 3.06 ERA, got 15 starts. Steve Sundra and Marius Russo, who combined for 19 wins and an ERA under 3.00, each got 11 starts. Hard to imagine too many other teams that got such superb top-to-bottom production as the 1939 Yankees.

Key facts: The Yankees outscored their opponents 967-556, the widest margin (411 runs) of the 20th century. Three times they scored 20 or more runs in a game, a team record. They also turned 159 double plays and made only 128 errors as a team, the only team in the American League to have fewer errors than double plays in 1939. This team was also exceptionally tough on the road, winning a franchise-record 54 games away from Yankee Stadium.

The perception was that with Gehrig gone, the team would slump. But it's difficult to imagine a team with DiMaggio in his prime "slumping." Plus, there were other guys like Bill Dickey, Red Rolfe, Frankie Crosetti and Joe Gordon more than willing to pick up the slack. The Yankees swept the Reds in the World Series.

3 THE 1998 NEW YORK YANKEES

Won-lost: 114-48
Runs scored: 965 (1st)
Runs allowed: 656 (1st)
Team ERA: 3.82 (1st)
Team fielding: .987 (2nd)
Double plays turned: 146 (6th)
Managerial changes: none

Distractions: Days before the post-season was to begin, DH Darryl Strawberry was diagnosed with colon cancer. His absence did not particularly derail the Yankee juggernaut, however. Strawberry underwent a successful operation a few days later, although in 2000, the cancer resurfaced.

Greatest players: Although there seems to be a consensus that the 1998 Yankees had no "superstars," few Yankee fans would be willing to part with either shortstop Derek Jeter or center fielder Bernie Williams. If neither can be called "superstar," well, it's all a matter of opinion anyhow. Both are excellent players, and are the two greatest on this squad.

Intangibles: The Yankees led the league in bases on balls with 653. They may or may not all have read Ted Williams's book, *The Science of Hitting,* but they understood the concept of waiting for the right pitch. A patient ball club forces a pitcher to throw strikes or walk people, and high pitch counts wear a pitcher down faster. It made the 1998 Yankees just that much tougher to beat.

But patience at the plate has been a Yankee trademark since the days of Babe Ruth. Since the Yankees acquired the Big Bambino in 1920, the team was first or second in walks drawn 32 times over the next 80 years. In contrast, the stat that has jumped considerably is the number of strikeouts a team incurs. In 1927, the Philadelphia Ath-

letics struck out, as a team, only 326 times. In 1998, the Baltimore Orioles struck out 903 times, which was the lowest mark, by far, in the majors. The 1998 Yankees whiffed 1,025 times. So while the Yankees are extremely patient at the plate for a late-20th century team, they are bat-swinging wild men compared to the Ruth era.

The other, most intangible of intangibles, is the "dirty uniform" factor. The 1998 Yankees were a bunch of very intense players. This was typified by players like outfielders Paul O'Neill, second baseman Chuck Knobloch, Jeter, Williams, third baseman Scott Brosius and several others. Having an edge, if you will, gave them an edge. Does this mean the Yankees cornered the market on such ballplayers? Not at all. But as announcer John Madden regularly notes, the more guys you have who are willing to get their uniforms dirty, the better chance you have to win.

Key facts: While expansion may have diluted the pitching on most major league teams, the Yankees actually had six solid starters in David Cone (20-7), David Wells (18-4), Andy Pettitte (16-11), Hideki Irabu (13-9), Ramiro Mendoza (10-2) and Orlando Hernandez (12-4). Dissidents have implied that Irabu was inconsistent, and while it's true that he had the second-highest ERA and lowest winning percentage of the six aforementioned hurlers, he was also third in the league in allowing the fewest hits per start and third in the league in opponents batting average.

New York swept San Diego in the World Series.

4 THE 1961 YANKEES

Won-lost: 109-53
Runs scored: 827 (2nd)
Runs allowed: 612 (2nd)
Team ERA: 3.46 (2nd)
Team fielding: .980 (1st)
Double plays turned: 180 (1st)

Managerial changes: Before the start of the season, Casey Stengel was not rehired, and was replaced by Ralph "The Major" Houk. It was a move welcomed by the players, who were a little

Kubek and Boyer were part of a solid infield that turned 180 double plays during the season of '61.

tired of Casey's coziness with reporters, which sometimes seemed to be at the expense of players. They were also wary of his platooning schemes.

Distractions: The home run race between Mickey Mantle and Roger Maris didn't seem to be a major distraction to anyone but Roger. But for him, the final few weeks were incredibly tough.

Greatest player: Mantle, by an eyelash over eventual MVP Maris and Cy Young Award winner Whitey Ford. No reason to fault the baseball writers (Hey, would *you* have voted against the guy who broke Babe Ruth's home run record?), but Mantle had a slightly better year at the plate than Roger, believe it or not. Maris had 61 homers to Mickey's 54, had 142 RBI to Mickey's 128 and both men scored 132 runs. But Mickey batted .317 to Roger's .269, slugged .687 to Roger's .620, walked 126 times to Roger's 94, had 163

hits to Roger's 159 and stole 12 bases to Roger's none. Mantle's home run percentage (54 homers in 517 at bats, or .105) was even a hair better than Maris's (61 homers in 590 at-bats, or .103). Mantle was also healthy enough to be as good a defensive center fielder as there was in the American League that year. Maris was an excellent right fielder, but he was no Al Kaline. Ford easily won the Cy Young Award and had the best year of his career.

Intangibles: The Yankees have had some very strong defensive infields in their history, but it is difficult to argue against the one that played together this year. First baseman Bill Skowron, second baseman Bobby Richardson, shortstop Tony Kubek and third baseman Clete Boyer were all excellent fielders. They turned 180 double plays that year to lead the American League. Boyer led third basemen in both leagues with 353 assists, while Richardson was second only to Pittsburgh's peerless Bill Mazeroski in putouts for second basemen with 413. The pitching staff was anchored by Ford, who, at 25-4, was 21 games over .500, a mark reached by only a handful of pitchers this century. Luis Arroyo saved a league-leading 29 games and won 15 more. Ford, Ralph Terry (16-3) and Arroyo (15-5), were 1-2-3 in the American League in winning percentage.

Key facts: The Yankees did not run. Mantle's 12 stolen bases led the team, which swiped 28, the league low. But of course, they really didn't have to run. The Yankees hit 240 home runs, still an American League record, and 51 more than runnerup Los Angeles's 189. The team had six players, including Mantle, Maris, Ford, Kubek, Richardson and Elston Howard on *The Sporting News'* annual major-league all-star team, a Yankee record. As mentioned before, Ford's 25-4 led the league. More interestingly, he started 39 games and did not make a relief appearance. This was something of a switch for Whitey, who was used to getting five or six relief appearances a year under Stengel. Did it make him a better pitcher? Well, from 1961-63, when Houk managed the Yankees, Ford was 76-19, the most successful three-year span in his career. The Yankees beat the Reds in five games in the World Series.

5 THE 1978 NEW YORK YANKEES

Won-lost: 100-63
Runs scored: 735 (4th)
Runs allowed: 582 (1st)
Team ERA: 3.18 (1st)
Fielding average: .982 (1st)
Double plays turned: 134 (13th)

Managerial changes: After 94 games and countless headaches, George Steinbrenner fired Billy Martin. Dick Howser took over as interim manager for one game (a loss) and Bob Lemon was hired. Lemon's principal strength was as a calming factor in the clubhouse, although he was certainly a solid manager in his own right.

Distractions: See above for starters. In addition, reliever Sparky Lyle was unhappy with his contract

and at one point jumped the club for one game. Of course, Thurman Munson and Reggie Jackson didn't get along, and Catfish Hunter had shoulder problems. Mickey Rivers was always a pretty high-strung sort of fellow, and at one point, he was fined for lateness and ordered to meet with a Yankee official. He was late for the meeting. A number of the benchwarmers complained that they should play more, shortstop Bucky Dent was annoyed when he had to sit down for a pinch hitter and pitcher Ed Figueroa thought he should get more starts.

Greatest player: Pitcher Ron Guidry's 25-3, 1.74 ERA was one of the great pitching years of the 20th century. It's difficult to explain just how intimidating he was in 1978. At times, his slider was simply unhittable, and that is not an exaggeration. There were a few lapses, but very few.

Intangibles: Several members of the team spent most of the year battling injuries. Willie Randolph, Dent, Lou Piniella, Reggie Jackson and Catfish Hunter all lost major chunks of the season due to injury. Yet Guidry, Goose Gossage, Figueroa, Dick Tidrow and Sparky Lyle pitched well enough to keep the Yankees relatively close to first place for most of the year. Graig Nettles won the second of his two Gold Glove awards with the Yankees and, along with Chris Chambliss, anchored an, at times, very green infield corps.

Still, this was a team that, when all its part returned, was very tough to beat. They got hot in September because just about everyone was back. Grace under pressure doesn't show up in the box scores, but Munson, Piniella, Nettles, Jackson, Chambliss, Roy White and Paul Blair were all exceptional hitters in tight games. Hunter was the best money pitcher in the 1970s, and Lyle one of the best relievers. Gossage and Guidry could be unhittable. Numbers can't really measure this team, but it scores well in our mythical GFI.

Key facts: Chris Chambliss's team-leading 90 RBI was the lowest total for a World Champion in a non-strike year since the Mets' Tommy Agee's 76 in 1969. New York had only two players in the top five of any of the major offensive categories on the year, including runs, hits, doubles, triples, home runs, total bases, RBI, walks, batting average, slugging average and stolen bases. Thurman Munson was third in hits with 183 and Lou Piniella was fourth in batting average at .314.

This dearth of dominating stats would seem to indicate a team that didn't overpower anyone, perhaps a team that was lucky to win it all. Yet the 1978 Yankees, when healthy, were a most intimidating crew. Their lineup was packed with tough outs and on any given day, their pitching was very deep and consistent. After the All-Star break, the Yankees won 11 of 15 one-run games. In their battle to take over first place from the Red Sox, in a four-game series in Fenway Park, they won all four games by convincing margins. They had the best record in baseball and won seven of 10 postseason contests. Numbers don't always measure champions, and this was the case in 1978. The Yankees beat the Los Angeles Dodgers in six games in the World Series.

THE NEXT 10

6 The 1953 Yankees. This team was the best of the five consecutive pennant winners with Casey Stengel at the helm. They had the best record (99-52) of the 1949–53 champions and had the deepest pitching staff, including Whitey Ford, Johnny Sain, Vic Raschi, Allie Reynolds and Eddie Lopat. The Yankees were supposed to finally succumb to the Cleveland Indians, but New York broke out to a big lead early in the year and easily fought off Cleveland and the White Sox for the American League flag. New York beat a very tough Dodger team in six games in the World Series.

7 The 1936 Yankees. DiMaggio's first year, but let's face it: Joe DiMaggio was never a rookie. Lou Gehrig won the MVP award and the team scored an amazing 1,065 runs on the year. The pennant race is over by June, as the Yankees have a 47-22 mark at that juncture. They beat the second-place Tigers by a then-record 19½ games. The 1927 Yankees won the AL title by 19 games, then beat the crosstown Giants in six to win the World Series.

8 The 1941 Yankees. This was another team that made a shambles of the pennant race, albeit after a slow start. The Yankees were 67-30 by the end of July and finished ahead of Boston by 17 games. The infield of third baseman Red Rolfe, Joe Gordon, Phil Rizzuto and one-year wonder Johnny Sturm turned 196 double plays, which was an American League record up to that time. DiMaggio hit in 56 straight games, which is still a record. The team beat Brooklyn in a tough five-game series that year.

9 The 1923 Yankees. This was a team that went 19-4 on the road in May to run its record to a nearly uncatchable 29-10 after just two months. The Tigers and Indians made belated efforts to catch the Yankees, but it was a long, boring season for non-Yankee fans. Ruth won the League Award, as the MVP was called, for a year in which he hit .393 and led the league with 41 home runs, 151 runs scored, 131 RBI, a stunning 170 walks, a .545 on-base percentage, a .764 slugging percentage and 399 total bases. Ruth lost out to the Tigers' Harry Heilmann in the batting race when Heilmann hit .403. Pitchers "Sad" Sam Jones, "Bullet" Joe Bush, "Sailor" Bob Shawkey, Waite Hoyt and Herb Pennock anchored the staff. Second baseman Aaron Ward, shortstop Everett Scott, third baseman Joe Dugan, center fielder Whitey Witt and Ruth all led their respective positions in fielding average, while first baseman Wally Pipp was second. The Yankees beat the Giants in the World Series for their first-ever world championship.

10 The 1932 Yankees. This seems to be an overlooked team in the New York pantheon, and it's hard to picture why. The 1932 Yankees scored 1,002 runs and had a team on-base percentage of .376. Their team ERA was 3.98, the only ERA below 4.00 in the American League. The pitching staff of Lefty Gomez, Red Ruffing, George Pipgras, Johnny Allen and Herb Pennock struck out a league-leading 780 batters, which was 195 whiffs ahead of second-place Philadelphia. Ruth was the team's elder statesman, but in terms of production, with 41 home runs, 137 RBI, 130 walks, a .341 batting average, a .661 slugging average and a .489 on base percentage, he was probably second only to Jimmie Foxx that year. The Yankees were 48-19 at the end of June, effectively ending the pennant race. They swept the Cubs in the World Series.

11 **The 1928 Yankees.** Another team that shows that when you have so many winners, success is relative. Yes, they edged the A's by only 2½ games. But they were 65-23 on July 20 and beat the A's in seven of the eight series in which the two teams played. The Athletics got hot enough to actually take first place briefly at the end of August, but Connie Mack's lads simply couldn't beat New York. Ruth was, well, Ruthian, with a league-leading 54 home runs, 163 runs scored, 142 RBI, 135 walks and 380 total bases. George Pipgras led the pitching staff along with Pennock and Waite Hoyt. The Yankees also avenged them-

selves against the St. Louis Cardinals this year, sweeping them in the World Series to atone for the 1926 defeat.

12 **The 1937 Yankees.** Basically, another outstanding team in that four-year Yankee juggernaut that demolished the American League from 1936-39. This squad led the American League in runs scored with 979 and in fewest runs allowed with 671. Joe DiMaggio (with 151), Red Rolfe (143) and Lou Gehrig (138) are 1-2-3 in runs scored, and DiMaggio (167), Gehrig (159) and Bill Dickey (133) are 2-3-4 in RBI. Lefty Gomez and Red Ruffing lead the pitching staff, both in the top five in wins, winning percentage, shutouts, ERA and complete games. Johnny Murphy is second in the league in saves. The team finished 50 games over .500, at 102-52, 13 games ahead of the Tigers.

Mickey Mantle smashes a home-run off the scoreboard at Griffith Stadium in Washington, in April 1953.

13 The 1947 Yankees. The Bucky Harris champions. Boston's Ted Williams dominated virtually every offensive category, but Tommy Henrich and DiMaggio were usually right behind him. DiMaggio wins his third and final MVP, although Williams wins the Triple Crown. This is the year one of the Boston sportswriters left Ted completely off his ballot. Had he listed Williams 10th, Williams would have edged Joe D. for MVP. The Yankees win a franchise-record 19 games in a row from June 29 to July 17. They finished 12 games ahead of the Tigers in the AL race. Allie Reynolds, Spec Shea and Bill Bevan are the key starters, while Joe Page leads the AL with 17 saves. A total of nine Yankees are named to play in the All-Star game, which ties a team record. The Yankees edge Brooklyn in seven games to win the World Series.

14 The 1958 Yankees. Mantle has a great year, leading the league with 127 runs scored, 42 home runs, 307 total bases and 129 walks. The Yankee infield is superb, turning a league-leading 182 double plays. Whitey Ford, Bob Turley and Art Ditmar anchor the starting pitching staff, while Ryne Duren's 20 saves lead the league. The Yankees opened the year 25-6 and won the flag by 10 games over the White Sox. This was a tremendously deep team, with Bobby Richardson, Elston Howard, Jerry Lumpe, Enos Slaughter and yes, Marv Throneberry on the bench. All contributed at some point. New York beat Milwaukee in seven games in the Series.

15 The 1949 Yankees. Another team that statistically did not dominate. In fact, the Yankees came in second (or worse) to the Red Sox in runs scored, hits, doubles, home runs, bases on balls, team batting average, and team slugging average. The Cleveland Indians dominated the pitching stats. Joe DiMaggio missed half the season. On paper, there is no way this team wins anything. But that, as they say, is why they play the games. After going 97-57 and edging the Red Sox by one game, New York beat the Dodgers in five.

THE WORLD SERIES TEAMS

The New York Yankees have made 37 appearances in the World Series, winning 26 times as of 1999. Both are major league records that won't be broken for many years, if ever. Here is a capsule review of all 36 teams.

1921 (Regular season record, 98-55)

Manager: Miller Huggins
First place by: 4½ games
World Series opponent: New York Giants
Result: Lost, 3-5

Comments: Though this was the year of Babe Ruth's 59 home runs, he sustained an elbow injury in Game 3 of the Series and played only sparingly after that. Pitcher Waite Hoyt pitched three complete games without allowing a run, but his record was 2-1 in the Series, as he allowed an unearned run in Game 8 and lost, 1-0, to Art Nehf. The best Meusel in the Series was Emil "Irish" Meusel of the Giants, who hit .345 with a Series-leading 7 RBI. Brother Bob hit .200.

What you might not have known: Ruth nabbed two of the Yankees' six stolen bases in the Series.

1922 (94-60)

Manager: Miller Huggins
First place by: 1 game
World Series opponent: New York Giants
Result: Lost, 0-4 (with one tie)

Comments: Another bad Series for Ruth, who was 2-17 with a batting average of .118. This was the Series in which Giants fans trumpeted the pitching strategy of manager John McGraw for keeping the powerful Ruth in check. The big story was actually the Giants' pitching, with "Handsome" Hugh McQuillan, veteran Jack Scott and Artie Nehf all tossing complete game victories for the Giants. Nehf's five-hitter in Game 5 represented the second consecutive year he had clinched the Series for the Giants over the Yankees.

What you might not have known: In July of that year, pitcher Jack Scott was released by the Cincinnati Reds with a sore arm. He came to New York and begged McGraw for a tryout. They went out to the Polo Grounds and McGraw liked what he saw. Scott was 8-2 for the Giants during the regular season, then won Game 3 of the World Series, 3-0, allowing only four Yankee hits.

1923 (98-54)

Manager: Miller Huggins
First place by: 16 games
World Series opponent: New York Giants
Result: Won, 4-2

Comments: The Yankees finally got untracked offensively, hitting .293 as a team. Second baseman Aaron Ward hit .417, while Ruth hit .368 with three home runs and a series-high eight runs

scored. McGraw pitched Nehf in the sixth game, hoping to forestall the end, but the Yankees' Herb Pennock scattered ten hits and won, 6-4. Outfielder Casey Stengel was the hitting star for the Giants, with a .417 average and two home runs.

What you might not have known: Ruth belted two home runs in Game 2 and almost made it three. His blast to deep center field was caught by Stengel.

1926 (91-63)

Manager: Miller Huggins
First place by: 3 games
World Series opponent: St. Louis Cardinals
Result: Lost, 3-4

Comments: One of the more frustrating Series losses for New York. Pennock scattered seven hits in a 3-2, ten-inning win in Game 5 that gave the Yankees a three games to two edge in the

A packed house watches the World Series at Yankee Stadium in 1926.

Series. They needed to win only one of the final two games in Yankees Stadium. But they couldn't do it. Cardinal pitcher Grover Cleveland Alexander shut down the Yankees in Game 6, winning 10-2. And in the deciding game, Alexander, despite a long night celebrating his Game 6 win, pitched 2⅓ solid innings of relief to save the win for Jesse "Pop" Haines.

What you might not have known: The name of the speakeasy in which Alexander celebrated his Game 6 win was Billy LaHiff's Tavern on 158 West 48th St.

1927 (110-44)

Manager: Miller Huggins
First place by: 19 games
World Series opponent: Pittsburgh Pirates
Result: Won, 4-0

Comments: The Yankees had a banner year from Opening Day. Ruth hit 60 home runs, Gehrig won the MVP and the pitching staff was overpowering. The Pirates were not huge underdogs, and, in fact, several National League loyalists predicted a Pittsburgh win. Well, we all know what happened: Ruth hit .400, shortstop Mark Koenig hit .500 and the Pirates scored a total of 10 runs. Oklahoma rookie Wilcy Moore, the unexpected star of the season with 19 wins and 13 saves, won Game 4, 4-3.

What you might not have known: Following the World Series, Ruth and Gehrig went barnstorming across the country. Ruth paid Lou $10,000 for 22 games on the tour. Lou's salary that year for the Yankees was $8,000 for 154 games. (For his part, Ruth made about $25,000 on the barnstorming tour.)

1928 (101-53)

Manager: Miller Huggins
First place by: 2½ games
World Series opponent: St. Louis Cardinals
Result: Won, 4-0

Comments: Unlike the previous year, 1928 was a struggle. The Yankees jumped out to a big lead, but their pitching and hitting faltered, and they barely held off the Athletics. In the Series, oddsmakers had the Cardinals as 5-3 favorites. But in the World Series, Ruth and Gehrig pummeled the National League champs. Ruth hit .625 (10-16) with three home runs, nine runs scored and 4 RBI. Gehrig hit .545 (6-11) with four home runs and 9 RBI. Waite Hoyt was 2-0, with a 1.50 ERA, and George Pipgras and Tom Zachery both tossed complete game wins.

What you might not have known: Huggins used only three pitchers in the Series, the last time it was done in the 20th century. It had been done seven times previously in the World Series. (In 1910, Athletics manager Connie Mack only used two pitchers, Jack Coombs and Chief Bender, to beat the Cubs in five games.)

1932 (107-47)

Manager: Joe McCarthy
First place by: 13 games
World Series opponent: Chicago Cubs
Result: Won, 4-0

Comments: The Yankees rode complete-game victories by Red Ruffing and Lefty Gomez in the first two games of the Series, then rocked the Cubs in Game 3 with four home runs, two each by Ruth and Gehrig. Wilcy Moore and Herb Pennock benefited from a 19-hit attack in Game 4 to sweep the Series.

What you might not have known: Pennock had a 5-0 World Series record as a starter. But McCarthy had begun using him in relief, and the Knight of Kennett Square saved the third and fourth games of the Series to clinch it for the Yankees.

1936 (102-51)

Manager: Joe McCarthy
First place by: 19½ games
World Series opponent: New York Giants
Result: Won, 4-2

Comments: The Giants took a one game to none lead in the Series, as Carl Hubbell bamboozled the Yankees with his masterful screwball, tossing a seven-hitter for a 6-1 win. But the Yankees thumped five Giant pitchers in Game 2, winning 18-4. The Yankees then got two well-pitched games by Monte Pearson and Bump Hadley to put them up, three games to one. After a 5-4 Giant win in Game 5, the Yankees exploded again for 13 runs and 17 hits to annex the championship the next day.

What you might not have known: Outfielder Jake Powell played 4½ seasons with the Yankees and in three World Series. But 1936 was his year. While he didn't get a hit in part-time work in the 1937 and 1938 World Series, Powell hit .455 in the 1936 Series, going 10 for 22.

1937 (102-52)

Manager: Joe McCarthy
First place by: 13 games
World Series opponent: New York Giants
Result: Won, 4-1

Comments: The Yankees got complete-game victories from Lefty Gomez and Red Ruffing in the first two games of the Series, then got another strong (8⅔ innings, five hits, one run) performance from Monte Pearson to take an insurmountable three games to none lead. The Giants took Game 4 behind Hubbell's six-hitter, but Gomez clinched the series the next day with a 4-2 win, and Gehrig hit his 10th and last World Series home run.

What you might not have known: This was second baseman Tony Lazzeri's last World Series in a Yankee uniform, and he went out in style, drilling a triple in the top of the fifth inning of Game 5 and scoring the Series-clinching run on a Gomez single.

1938 (99-53)

Manager: Joe McCarthy
First place by: 9½ games
World Series opponent: Chicago Cubs
Result: Won, 4-0

Comments: Once again, Ruffing, Gomez and Pearson were too much for the opposition. Ruffing went first, tossing a complete-game nine-hitter in a 3-1 win. Next up was Gomez, who shut down the Cubs 6-3 with the help of Johnny Murphy's two innings of relief. Pearson's five-hitter in Game 3 put the Cubs in a 0-3 hole and Ruffing finished Chicago off, 8-3, in Game 4. Joe Gordon and Bill Dickey hit .400 to lead the way offensively. Lou Gehrig hit .286 in his last World Series.

What you might not have known: This was the fourth time in his career that Gehrig played on a team that swept its opponent in the World Series, a major league record.

1939 (106-45)

Manager: Joe McCarthy
First place by: 17 games
World Series opponent: Cincinnati Reds
Result: Won, 4-0

Comments: Bill Dickey's RBI single snapped a 1-1 tie in the ninth inning of Game 1 in New York to give the Yankees a 2-1 victory. In Game 2, Pearson carried a no-hitter into the seventh inning before Reds catcher Ernie Lombardi's single broke it up. Monte still won the game, 4-0. Charlie Keller belted two home runs and Joe DiMaggio one to give New York a 7-3 win in Game 3. In Game 4, three Red errors in the tenth inning enabled the Yankees to score three runs and snap a 4-4 tie to win their fourth consecutive World Series, 7-4. It was a feat no one thought could ever be duplicated.

What you might not have known: Lou Gehrig, in the last vestiges of his disease, traveled with the Yankees during the regular season and the World Series. After sweeping the Reds, the train ride home was a raucous celebration, except for Gehrig and his wife, Eleanor. Several weeks before the World Series, Yankee officials had informed Lou that he should think about finding a job after the season was over, as the Yankees had nothing for him. It was a sore spot for Mrs. Gehrig for many years afterward.

1941 (101-53)

Manager: Joe McCarthy
First place by: 17 games
World Series opponent: Brooklyn Dodgers
Result: Won, 4-1

Comments: This was a closer Series than it looked. The Yankees eked out a 3-2 victory in Game 1, but Brooklyn came right back in Game 2 behind Whitlow Wyatt to win 3-2 and tie the Series, with the next three games at Ebbets Field. But the Yankees won Game 3, 2-1 with two runs in the eighth inning. Game 4 was the key game. That was the game where Dodger pitcher Hugh Casey fired strike three past the Yankees' Tommy Henrich. Brooklyn was ahead, 4-3 with two outs in the top of the ninth inning. But the ball got away from Brooklyn catcher Mickey Owen, and Henrich scampered to first. New York then pushed across four runs to clinch a 7-4 victory. Tiny Bonham fired a four-hitter in Game 5 to clinch the championship.

What you might not have known: Johnny Sturm was a tall (6 feet 1 inches) drink of water who was born in St. Louis and was a rookie with the Yankees in 1941. McCarthy made him the regular first baseman that year, and he didn't hit well, wasn't particularly fast on the bases and was an average fielder. Still, he came back with a strong World Series, hitting .286, driving in a couple of runs and nabbing one of New York's two stolen bases as the Yankees won in five games. Sturm enlisted in the Army after the 1941 season, however, and never returned to the major leagues after the war.

1942 (103-51)

Manager: Joe McCarthy
First place by: 9 games
World Series opponents: St. Louis Cardinals
Result: Lost, 1-4

Comments: The Yankees jumped out to a 7-0 lead in Game 1, but the Cardinals came back with four runs in the top of the ninth to make it a game, eventually losing, 7-4. That proved to be an omen for the rest of the series, as the relentless Cardinals swept the next four contests. Musial's RBI single was the key hit in Game 2, while Enos Slaughter's RBI hit in the ninth inning was the key blow in Game 3. Game 4 went back and forth, but a Walker Cooper RBI single and a Marty Marion sacrifice fly in the seventh inning gave St. Louis another win. Whitey Kurowski's two-run homer in the ninth inning put the Yankees out in Game 5.

What you might not have known: Ernie White's six-hit shutout of New York in Game 3 was the first time the Yankees had been shut out in the World Series since Jesse "Pop" Haines, also of the Cardinals, did it in 1926.

1943 (98-56)

Manager: Joe McCarthy
First place by: 13½ games
World Series opponent: St. Louis Cardinals
Result: Won, 4-1

Comments: With Joe DiMaggio and Phil Rizzuto already in the service, no one gave this Yankee team much of a chance. But the Yankees had better pitching with Spurgeon "Spud" Chandler, who threw complete-game wins in Games 1 and 5; and reliever Johnny Murphy who collected a save in Game 3. The Cardinals scored only nine runs in five games. Billy Johnson hit .300 and Bill Dickey hit .278 with 4 RBI to lead the Yankees' attack. Stan Musial was limited to five singles in 18 at-bats.

What you might not have known: This was Johnny Murphy's final World Series with the Yankees. He had a perfect record in relief for the team in six postseason series, with two wins and four saves. He never lost a lead when he came into a World Series game.

1947 (97-57)

Manager: Bucky Harris
First place by: 12 games
World Series opponent: Brooklyn Dodgers
Result: Won, 4-3

Comments: The Yankees jumped out to a two games to none lead with a 5-3 win in Game 1 and a 10-3 romp in Game 2. But the Dodgers came back and thumped Yankee starter Bobo Newsome and reliever Vic Raschi to take a 7-2 lead after three innings in Game 3. Brooklyn won that game, 9-8 and tied the Series the next day with a 3-2 win. This was the game where the Yankees' Bill Bevens, leading 2-1, was one out away from a no-hitter when the Dodgers' Cookie Lavagetto doubled home two runs to give Brooklyn the win. New York's Spec Shea came back with a complete-game four-hitter to win Game 5, 2-1. But back in Yankee Stadium, a four-run sixth inning helped Brooklyn square the Series, 8-6. This was the game in which Dodger outfielder Al Gionfriddo snagged DiMaggio's 415-foot blast to kill a Yankee rally. In Game 7, Tommy Henrich's RBI single in the fourth was the key hit as the Yankees finally won the Series with a 5-2 win.

What you might not have known: Yogi Berra's pinch-hit home run in Game 3 was the first such homer in World Series history.

1949 (97-57)

Manager: Casey Stengel
First place by: 1 game
World Series opponent: Brooklyn Dodgers
Result: Won, 4-1

Comments: Another taut Series in which every game was close. Henrich blasted a leadoff home run in the bottom of the ninth to win Game 1, 1-0. Brooklyn reversed the score the next day, as Jackie Robinson scored on Gil Hodges's single in the tenth inning. In Game 3, National League pickup Johnny Mize cracked a two-run single in the top of the ninth, which broke a 1-1 tie. New York scored three runs in the inning to take a 4-1 lead. But the Dodgers got home runs from Campy Campanella and Robinson to fall just short, 4-3. New York took a three games to one lead in the Series when Allie Reynolds came in to pitch 3⅓ innings of relief and save the win for Eddie Lopat, 6-4. The Yankees wrapped up the Series the next day with a 10-6 victory.

What you might not have known: Allie Reynolds picked up the first of his four World Series saves in Game 4, a 6-4 Yankee win. It was the beginning of Reynolds's stint as a reliever in between starts, although he had performed the chore in Cleveland and a few times in New York prior to this outing. In his eight years with the Yankees, he collected 41 saves.

1950 (98-56)

Manager: Casey Stengel
First place by: 3 games
World Series opponent: Philadelphia Phillies
Result: Won, 4-0

Comments: The Yankees won the first three games by one run, 1-0, 2-1, 3-2, to place themselves in the driver's seat of this Fall Classic. That lead enabled Stengel to start rookie Ed "Whitey" Ford, a move he would ordinarily have avoided, in Game 4. But Ford didn't disappoint anyone, scattering seven hits in 8⅔ innings for an eventual 5-2 win. The Phillies, named the Whiz Kids for the youth and hustle, scored only five runs in the Series.

What you might not have known: The Yankees' team ERA in the Series was 0.73, the lowest ERA since the 1905 World Series, when the New York Giants' team ERA was 0.00. (These were the Giants of Christy Mathewson's three shutouts.)

1951 (98-56)

Manager: Casey Stengel
First place by: 5 games
World Series opponent: New York Giants
Result: Won, 4-2

Comments: The Giants took a one game to none Series lead with a 5-1 win in Yankee Stadium in the Series opener. Then, after the Yankees squared the Series with a 3-1 win behind Ed Lopat's five-hitter in Game 2, the Giants bounced back again, winning Game 3, 6-2. But the Yankees moved into a commanding position in the next two contests, as Allie Reynolds and Lopat each turned in tidy complete games. Hank Bauer's three-run triple in the sixth inning of Game 6 keyed the Yankees' 4-3 win in Yankee Stadium.

What you might not have known: In the battle of all-time great outfielders, this was the only World Series in which Joe DiMaggio, Mickey Mantle and Willie Mays all participated. DiMaggio hit .261, Mays hit .182, Mantle .200.

1952 (95-59)

Manager: Casey Stengel
First place by: 2 games
World Series opponent: Brooklyn Dodgers
Result: Won, 4-3

This put the "classic" in the Fall Classic. The Dodgers won Games 1, 3 and 5 to take one-game leads over the Yankees on three different occasions. Carl Erskine's 11-inning, five-hit gem in Game 5 was one of the great pitching performances in Series history. But each time, the Yankees came back, winning Games 2, 4 and 6. Game 7 was at Ebbets Field. Mantle's homer in the sixth inning put New York ahead to stay. Bob Kuzava saved the final win.

What you might not have known: Veteran Bob Kuzava saved the final game of both the 1951 and 1952 World Series. His ten-year career included stops in Cleveland, in Chicago with the White Sox, Washington, Baltimore, in Philadelphia with the Phillies, Pittsburgh and St. Louis, as well as his time with the Yankees. He pitched a total of 4⅓ innings in three World Series for New York, and also appeared in a game in the 1953 World Series.

1953 (99-52)

Manager: Casey Stengel
First place by: 9 games
World Series opponent: Brooklyn Dodgers
Result: Won, 4-2

Comments: With a record of 105-49, this might have been the best Brooklyn team ever, probably a little better than the team that won it all in 1955. Still, after all was said and done, the Yankees had

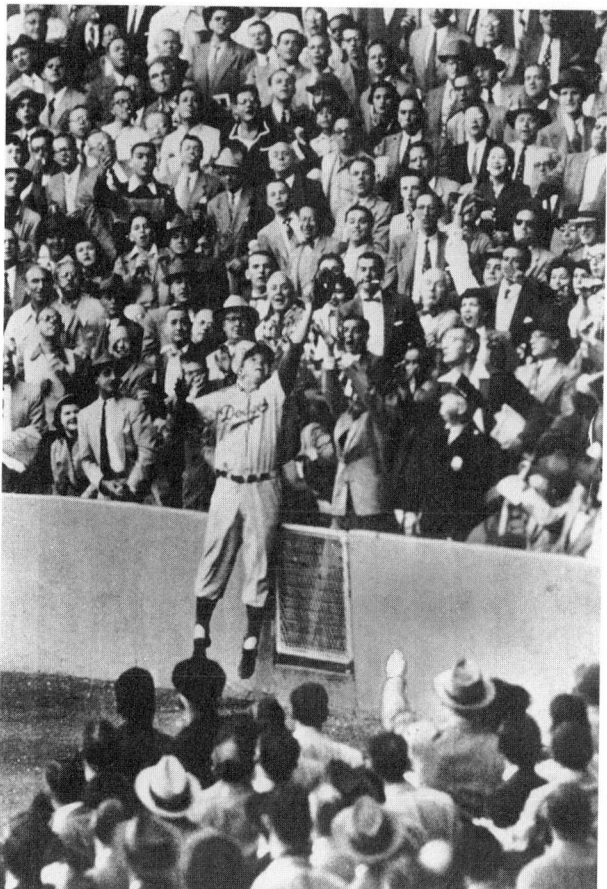

The Dodger's Andy Pafko makes a leaping catch in the '52 World Series—another Yankee victory.

accomplished what no one thought possible: five consecutive pennants and five consecutive World Series championships. New York jumped out to a two games to none lead with a 9-5 win in Game 1 and a 4-2 victory in Game 2. The series shifted to Ebbets Field, and the Dodgers rebounded with a 3-2 win in Game 3 and a 7-3 triumph in Game 4. Erskine submitted a 14-strikeout, six-hitter in Game 3 for Brooklyn. The 14 strikeouts were a World Series record to that point. The pivotal fifth game was a slugfest, with both teams combining for six home runs and 47 total bases as the Yankees won, 11-7. Ford and Reynolds held off Brooklyn in Game 6, 4-3, and New York had won the championship again.

What you might not have known: Whitey Ford and Billy Loes, the starting pitchers for Game 4, were New Yorkers who grew up ten blocks from each other in Astoria, Queens.

1955 (96-58)

Manager: Casey Stengel
First place by: 3 games
World Series opponent: Brooklyn Dodgers
Result: Lost, 3-4

Comments: When the Yankees won the first game of the Series, 6-5 and the second game, 4-2, no one was thinking about a Dodger championship. But Brooklyn did what it had been unable to do in prior Series against the Yankees: win all their home games. The Dodgers got a big win from Johnny Podres in Game 3. Podres scattered seven hits in the win. Brooklyn swept the next two games as well, as Clem Labine picked up a win and a save in relief. Trailing three games to two, the Yankees forced a seventh game with a 5-1 win in Game 6 behind Ford's four-hitter. But Podres scattered eight hits in a 2-0 shutout in Game 7, and the championship was Brooklyn's at last.

What you might not have known: The Cleveland Indians had won the American League championship in 1954, and throughout most of 1955, they, not the Yankees, were in first place. Confident of repeating, the Indians printed and sold tens of thousands of World Series tickets for the 1955 Series. But with only a few games left in the season, New York spurted, caught the Indians and clinched the pennant. Cleveland had to refund more than $2 million in tickets to their saddened fans.

1956 (97-57)

Manager: Casey Stengel
First place by: 9 games
World Series opponent: Brooklyn Dodgers
Result: Won, 4-3

Comments: Brooklyn turned the tables on the Yankees in 1956, winning the first two games at home, 6-3 (behind Sal "the Barber" Maglie), and 13-8. But the Yankees held serve in their three games in Yankee Stadium. Whitey Ford won Game 3, 5-3, by scattering eight hits. Tommy Sturdivant turned in another strong pitching performance for the Yankees in Game 4, allowing just six Dodger hits in a 6-2 Yankee victory. And, of course, Don Larsen faced the minimum 27 batters in Game 5, a perfect 2-0 Yankee win. Brooklyn came back with a 1-0 win in Game 6, as Clem Labine scattered six hits over 11 innings. Jackie Robinson's RBI single won it. Game 7 was anticlimactic, however, as Berra smacked two home runs, Moose Skowron belted a grand slam and Elston Howard had a four-bagger as well in a 9-0 Yankee win.

What you might not have known: Don Larsen's perfect game was home plate umpire Ralph A. "Babe" Pinelli's last major league game.

1957 (98-56)

Manager: Casey Stengel
First place by: 8 games
World Series opponent: Milwaukee Braves.
Result: Lost, 3-4.

Comments: The Yankees won Game 1, 3-1, as Whitey Ford outpitched Warren Spahn. But Milwaukee gained a split at Yankee Stadium, 4-2, behind Lew Burdette's seven-hitter. Game 3 was a blowout in Milwaukee, as the Yankees pounded six Brave pitchers for 12 runs. Game 4 was the key contest. Trailing 4-1, the Yankees tied the game in the top of the ninth inning on a three-run homer by Elston Howard. A triple by Hank Bauer scored Tony Kubek in the top of the tenth and New York led, 5-4. But in the bottom of the inning, Yankee pitcher Tommy Byrne hit Brave rookie Nippy Jones on the foot, Johnny Logan doubled and Eddie Matthews homered to give the Braves a 7-5 win. This was the famous game in which Jones proved he had been hit on the foot by pointing out a speck of black shoe polish on the ball after the Yankees protested that Byrne had missed him. Burdette edged Ford, 1-0 in

Game 5, but the Yankees came back and won Game 6, 3-2, on a home run by Hank Bauer. Burdette pitched Game 7 against Don Larsen, and Milwaukee won going away, 5-0. "We'd sure like to play them again next year," said Burdette.

What you might not have known: Burdette's pitching performance (3-0, 0.67 ERA, 3 complete games, 2 shutouts, 13 strikeouts, 4 walks) is considered the second-greatest pitching performance in World Series history behind Christy Matthewson's three shutouts of the Athletics in 1905 for the Giants. Burdette pitched Game 7 on only two days' rest.

1958 (92-62)

Manager: Casey Stengel
First place by: 10 games
World Series opponent: Milwaukee Braves
Result: Won, 4-3

Comments: This pretty much started out as a repeat of 1957. The Braves won Games 1, 3 and 4 to take a commanding three games to one lead in the Series. It looked to be a lock, and several Milwaukee players said so. Hank Bauer's home run in Game 3 gave him a hit in 17 consecutive World Series games, a record. (He went hitless the next day against Warren Spahn.) Only once, in 1925, when the Pittsburgh Pirates had taken three games in a row from the Washington Senators, had a team rallied from such a deficit. But the Yankees got a strong game from "Bullet" Bob Turley to win Game 5, 7-0. In Game 6, the Yankees scored two runs in the top of the tenth on a homer by Gil McDougald and RBI single by Moose Skowron. Milwaukee scored once, but with men on second and third and two outs, Turley, the Yankees' fourth pitcher of the day, jammed Frank Torre into flying out to McDougald to end the game. Don Larsen started Game 7. It was the fourth consecutive Game 7 for the Yankees in four years. But when Larsen faltered, Stengel came back with Turley for the third day in a row. Bullet Bob pitched 6⅔ innings of superb relief. The Yankees, behind a three-run homer by Skowron,

broke the game open in the eighth for a 6-2 win.

What you might not have known: The three winning pitchers for the Yankees were Larsen, Turley and Ryne Duren, all former St. Louis Browns.

1960 (97-57)

Manager: Casey Stengel
First place by: 8 games
World Series opponent: Pittsburgh Pirates
Result: Lost, 3-4

Comments: The strangest World Series ever saw the Yankees win Game 2 by 16-3, Game 3 by 10-0 and Game 6 by a score of 12-0. Meanwhile the Pirates, when the contests were close, won Game 1 by 6-4, Game 4 by 3-2 and Game 5 by 5-2. Game 7 was a doozy. Pittsburgh took a 4-0 lead after two innings, fell behind 5-4 after six and used a five-run eighth to lead, 9-7. The Yankees tied the game at 9-9 in the top of the ninth but lost the contest in the bottom of the inning on Bill Mazeroski's home run. New York had hit .338 for the series. Bobby Richardson had driven in a record 12 runs. Whitey Ford had pitched two complete-game shutouts. Yet the Yankees had somehow lost.

What you might not have known: Bobby Richardson's grand slam in Game 3 matched his home run total for the regular season.

1961 (109-53)

Manager: Ralph Houk
First place by: 8 games
World Series opponent: Cincinnati Reds
Result: Won, 4-1

Comments: This was the most prolific home-run-hitting Yankee team in history, with a team record 240 round-trippers. But as it often is in championship play, the Yankees' pitching was the key to this relatively easy win over the Reds. Whitey Ford shut the Reds out 2-0 in Game 1. The Reds knotted things up with a 6-2 win in Game 2. But home runs by Maris and Johnny Blanchard gave the

After scoring the series-winning homerun, Bill Mazeroski gallops back to the plate at Forbes Field in 1960—a rare instance of World Series defeat for the Yankees.

Yankees a 3-2 win in Game 3 and Ford and Jim Coates combined for a five-hitter to shut out the Reds in Game 4, 7-0. That win put the Yankees in the drivers' seat, and the Yankees pounded out 15 hits in the final contest to eliminate the Reds, 13-5. Ford extended his scoreless streak to 32 innings, a World Series record, before an ankle injury in the fifth inning of Game 4 forced him to sit down. The old record was Babe Ruth's 29⅔ innings.

What you might not have known: Maris was not the only player to have a career year in 1961. Third-string catcher Johnny Blanchard also had by far his best year as a pro. He hit 21 home runs in 1961, almost a third of his career total of 67 round-trippers over eight years. His career batting average was .239, but Blanchard hit .305 in 1961.

In the 1961 World Series, Blanchard hit the only two home runs in his postseason career, and got 4 of the 10 hits he would make in his 5-year, 15-game World Series career.

1962 (96-56)

Manager: Ralph Houk
First place by: 5 games
World Series opponent: San Francisco Giants
Result: Won, 4-3

Comments: This was another seven-game war, and Yankee pitching and defense tipped the scales—barely—in New York's favor. Ford once again gave his team a one game to none advantage with a 6-2 win in Game 1, sparked by Clete Boyer's seventh inning home run. It was Ford's tenth and last Series win. Jim Sanford's three-hitter knotted things up for the Giants, 2-0 in Game 2, but a complete-game four-hitter by New York's Bill Stafford in Game 3 put the Yankees up a game again with a 3-2 win. Back came the Giants, winning Game 4 by 7-3 behind Chuck Hiller's seventh-inning grand slam. Ralph Terry picked up the 5-3 win in Game 5, behind a three-run homer by Tom Tresh, but the Giants won Game 6 after a three-day rain delay, 5-2. Houk tabbed Terry to start Game 7 against Sanford. Both pitchers were outstanding, but the Yankees loaded the bases in the fifth inning with two outs. Giants manager Alvin Dark played his infield in, conceding a run to cut off the big inning and Tony Kubek obliged, hitting into a double play as Moose Skowron scored. That was the only run of the game. Terry scattered four hits in the game and picked up the win when Bobby Richardson caught Willie McCovey's screaming line drive in the bottom of the ninth. It was a sweet redemption for Terry, who had given up Bill Mazeroski's ninth-inning home run in 1960.

What you might not have known: Former Yankee Don Larsen made his final World Series appearances with the Giants in 1962. Larsen had been converted into a reliever, and he appeared in three games in 1962 for San Francisco, getting credit for a win in Game 4.

1963 (104-57)

Manager: Ralph Houk
First place by: 10½ games
World Series opponents: Los Angeles Dodgers
Result: Lost, 0-4

Comments: The Dodgers came back to Yankee Stadium and took no prisoners in Game 1 as pitcher Sandy Koufax struck out a Series-record 15 batters in a 5-2 win over Whitey Ford. The Yankees would have been shocked to learn that those two runs would represent half their total output for the series. The Dodgers won Game 2, 4-1 behind Johnny Podres, and Game 3 by 1-0, behind Don Drysdale. Jim Bouton's four-hitter was wasted.

Los Angeles completed only the second World Series sweep of the Yankees with another Koufax gem, this one a six-hitter.

What you might not have known: The last time the Yankees and Dodgers met in the World Series, 1956, Don "Big D" Drysdale was rookie Donnie Drysdale, a big, hard-throwing righty with potential but not much else. Drysdale pitched in Game 4 of the 1956 Series, giving up a long home run to Hank Bauer in a 6-2 Dodger loss. But Drysdale made up for that outing in 1963, firing a three-hit shutout and striking out nine in Game 3. That win essentially clinched the title for the Dodgers.

1964 (99-63)

Manager: Yogi Berra
First place by: 1 game
World Series opponent: St. Louis Cardinals
Result: Lost, 3-4

Comments: The Cardinals drew first blood in the series, as Ray Sadecki beat Whitey Ford, 9-5. But New York took the next two games, 8-3 and 2-1, to take a two games to one lead in the series. Ken Boyer's fifth inning grand slam was the big hit in the Cardinals' 4-3 win in Game 4, and Bob Gibson's 13-strikeout performance in Game 5 was the key to that 5-2 win. Jim Bouton scattered 10 hits, while Roger Maris, Mickey Mantle and Joe Pepitone all hit homers in Game 6, as New York tied up the series, 8-3. But in Game 7, it was Gibson who came through, striking out nine and holding off the Yankees inning after inning for a 7-5 win. Bobby Richardson set a Series record with 13 hits, and Mantle's homer in the sixth game was his 18th and last.

What you might not have known: Whitey Ford pitched his eighth opening World Series game out of the 11 World Series in which he participated, a major-league record. Ford was 4-3 with one no decision in the eight games. The Yankees were 2-2 in Series when Ford won the first game, and were 1-2 when he lost. New York also won the Series in which Ford earned his no decision.

1976 (97-62)

Manager: Billy Martin
First place by: 10½ games
World Series opponent: Cincinnati Reds
Result: Lost, 0-4

Comments: The Reds' Don Gullett tossed a five-hitter to spoil the Yankees' first World Series in 12 years, 5-1. Things didn't get much better than that, as Ken Griffey scored on a Tony Perez single in the bottom of the ninth in Game 2 to give the Reds a 4-3 win. Back in New York, the Reds swept to victory, winning Game 3 by a score of 6-2 and clinching the Series in Game 4 behind Johnny Bench's two homers, 7-2.

What you might not have known: Only nine men batted for the Reds in the World Series, a record low. Reds manager Sparky Anderson made no substitutions and used no pinch hitters, and designated hitter Dan Driessen hit for the seven pitchers who appeared in the series.

1977 (100-62)

Manager: Billy Martin
First place by: 2½ games
World Series opponent: Los Angeles Dodgers
Result: Won, 4-2

Comments: New York won the first game, 4-3 in 12 innings, when Willie Randolph scored on an RBI single by Paul Blair. The Dodgers tied the series at a win each, 6-1, behind a five-hitter by Burt Hooten. But New York won the next two games, 5-3 and 4-2, behind strong pitching performances from Mike Torrez and Ron Guidry. The Dodgers staved off elimination, 10-4 in Game 5, but back in Yankee Stadium, Reggie Jackson put on a Ruthian three–home run effort to clinch New York's first championship in 15 years.

What you might not have known: In addition to a record five home runs and 8 RBI, Jackson also scored ten runs in the Series, a feat accomplished only one other time in World Series play, in 1993 by the Blue Jays' Paul Molitor.

1978 (100-63)

Managers: Billy Martin, Bob Lemon
First place by: 1 game
World Series opponent: Los Angeles Dodgers
Result: Won, 4-2

Comments: The Dodgers swept to victory in the first two games, 11-5 in Game 1 and 4-3 in Game 2, and seemed to be in the driver's seat. But Yankee pitcher Ron Guidry scattered eight hits in Game 3 for a 5-1 win, and an extra-inning, 4-3, win in Game 4 abruptly squared the series. Game 5 was pivotal, and the Yankees exploded for 18 hits in a 12-2 rout. Old pro Catfish Hunter finished the Dodgers off, 7-2 in Game 6, with a little help from relief specialist Goose Gossage. Shortstop Bucky Dent, who started the championship run with a three-run homer in the playoff game at Fenway Park, hit .417 with 7 RBI in the series.

What you might not have known: Brian Doyle had two hits in the league championship series and seven more in the World Series. His World Series batting average of .438 led both teams. During the regular season, he had just ten hits all year. His double in the World Series was his only extra base hit that year, and his two RBI in the World Series were two more than he had in the regular season.

1981 (59-48)

Managers: Gene Michael, Bob Lemon
First place by: 2 games (in the first half of the season)
World Series opponent: Los Angeles Dodgers
Result: Lost, 2-4

Comments: In a reversal of the 1978 World Series, the Yankees won the first two games of the Series: 5-3 behind Ron Guidry and 3-0 behind ex-Dodger Tommy John. Dodgers' rookie sensation Fernando Valenzuela won Game 3, by a 5-4 count, although he had a rough outing, giving up nine hits and seven walks. The Dodgers trailed in Game 4 by three runs after 5½ innings, but Los

Angeles scored three runs in the bottom of the sixth and two more in the bottom of the seventh to win the contest by an 8-7 score. With the Series tied, the Dodgers took control with a 2-1 win in Game 5. Mario Guerrero and Steve Yeager drilled back-to-back home runs in the eighth inning off Ron Guidry to win the game. Los Angeles won Game 6 by a 9-2 score as Guerrero had a home run and 5 RBI.

What you might not have known: Yankee pitcher George Frazier was credited with three losses in the Series. In World Series history, only Claude "Lefty" Williams of the 1919 Chicago Black Sox lost as many. (Williams, however, was reportedly *trying* to do so.)

1996 (92-70)

Manager: Joe Torre
First place by: 4 games
World Series opponent: Atlanta Braves
Result: Won, 4-2

Comments: This was a turnaround to end all turnarounds. The Braves won the first game in Yankee Stadium by a stunning score of 12-1, and Atlanta's Andruw Jones became the youngest player, at 19, to hit a home run in the World Series. The next game wasn't much better, as the Braves' Greg Maddux and Mark Wohlers shackled the Yankees on seven hits in a 4-0 win. But New York crawled back into the Series; David Cone gave the Yankees six strong innings and New York bounced back with a 5-2 win. The next night was the turning point. Trailing 6-0 after five innings, New York climbed back into the game with three runs in the top of the sixth and three more in the top of the eighth on a three-run homer by Jim Leyritz. The Yankees capped the comeback by scoring two more runs in the top of the tenth. With the Series tied, Andy Pettitte threw a masterful eight innings and John Wetteland saved a 1-0 win in Game 5. Cecil Fielder's RBI double in the fourth was the key hit. The Yankees finished the Braves off, 3-2, before a delirious crowd of 56,375 in Game 6 for their first World Championship in 18

years. Wetteland's four saves made him the easy MVP choice.

What you might not have known: Cecil Fielder, a midseason pickup from the Tigers, made his lone World Series appearance a memorable one. Fielder had nine hits to lead the Yankees in hitting that year. No other Yankee had more than five hits.

1998 (114-48)

Manager: Joe Torre
First place by: 22 games (major league record)
World Series opponent: San Diego Padres
Result: Won, 4-0

Comments: New York established its dominance in Game 1, exploding for seven runs in the seventh inning, after Padres pitching star Kevin Brown was taken out. The attack was capped by a home run by Chuck Knoblauch and a grand slam by Tino Martinez. The final was 9-6. Home runs by Jorge Posada and Bernie Williams keyed a 9-3 Yankee win in Game 2, while a pair of home runs by Scott Brosius were the difference for New York in Game 3. Andy Pettite combined with Jeff Nelson and Mariano Rivera to blank the Padres in the final contest, 3-0.

What you might not have known: Outfielder Ricky Ledee, who spent virtually the entire year on the Yankees' farm team in Columbus, had a breakout Series against the Padres, hitting .600 with three doubles and 4 RBI. He started three of the four games, becoming the first rookie outfielder since Tom Tresh in 1962 to start in a World Series.

1999 (98-64)

Manager: Joe Torre
First place by: 4 games
World Series opponent: Atlanta Braves
Result: Won, 4-0

Comments: This was billed as the Series to settle which franchise, Atlanta or New York, was the dominant team of the 1990s. The Yankee sweep gave them the title emphatically. Game 1 was a marquee matchup: Orlando "El Duque" Hernandez against Greg Maddux of Atlanta. Hernandez left the game in the eighth inning trailing 1-0, but the Yankees had the last laugh as Derek Jeter struck an RBI single and Paul O'Neill drilled a two-run double to take the lead in the eighth inning. The final was 4-1. Game 2 was another strong effort by Cone, who allowed but one hit as the Yankees won, 7-2. The Braves led for most of Game 3, jumping out to a 5-1 lead after four innings and chasing starter Andy Pettitte. But as they had in 1996, the Yankees kept chipping away, and in the eighth inning, Chuck Knoblauch's two-run home run tied the game. In the tenth inning, Chad Curtis, who had hit five home runs all year, stepped up and blasted a home run off Brave reliever Mike Remlinger to win the game. Game 4 was the Roger Clemens show. The Rocket had been picked up from Toronto for David Wells on the first day of spring training in a blockbuster deal. Clemens had been 14-10 in the regular season but had had a shaky postseason, beating Texas 3-0 in the first round but getting blasted by his old team, the Red Sox, in the American League championship series. In Game 4 of the World Series, however, Roger was the Rocket again, giving up only four hits and anchoring the final 4-1 win. It was the Yankees' 25th World Championship.

What you might not have known: Mariano Rivera, in just two seasons, has become one of the dominant postseason closers of all time. He is 4-0 with 12 saves in 1998 and 1999. He has made 18 appearances in six playoff series and has an ERA of 0.00. He has been as close to an automatic win as there has ever been in baseball.

2000 (87-75)

Manager: Joe Torre
First place by: 2 games
World Series Opponent: New York Mets
Result: Won, 4-1

Comments: The first Subway Series since 1954 was closer than it appeared at first look. The Yan-

The Yankees celebrate after defeating the cross-town Mets in the 2000 World Series.

kees had struggled to beat Oakland in the Divisional Series, but looked better against Lou Piniella's Mariners in the ALCS. Still, the Mets, with their solid pitching corps, appeared to have a slight edge going into the Series. The Yankees drew first blood in Yankee Stadium, winning 4-3 in twelve innings as ex-Met Jose Vizcaino slapped an RBI single, his fourth hit of the night, to snap the tie. The Yanks held off the Mets, 6-5, in the second game, but most of the headlines concerned pitcher Roger Clemens' toss of a broken bat at Met catcher Mike Piazza. Clemens said he thought the bat chunk was the ball. Piazza said he thought Clemens was nutty. The game went on and the Yankees won. Mets reliever (and Brooklyn native) John Franco gave the Mets hope in Game 3 with a 4-2 win, but the Yankees came right back in Game 4 to pull out a 3-2 decision. Derek Jeter's leadoff homer was a key hit. Luis Sojo borrowed Clay Bellinger's bat in Game 5 to smack the game-winner in the ninth for a 4-2 Yanks win. Mariano Rivera saved the game—again.

What you might not have known: Derek Jeter was the first player ever to be named both the All-Star Game MVP and World Series MVP in the same year.

MR. ANNOUNCER: BOB SHEPPARD

The 2000 season was Yankee announcer Bob Sheppard's 50th year behind the microphone. The Voice of the Yankees (or in New York, "the voice of God") is now by far the most recognizable announcer in baseball.

Sheppard's career began in the 1940s, when he volunteered his services for a charity football game in Long Island. Soon after, he landed a job working weekends for the Brooklyn Dodgers football team in the old All-America Conference. When the Dodgers folded, Sheppard was hired by the New York football Yankees. The baseball Yankees liked what they heard and Sheppard was asked in 1950 to work for them. But his work as a high school speech teacher would not allow him to do so, and he turned the offer down.

The next year, the Yankees came back with an offer that would allow Sheppard to use a replacement for any games he would miss. So he agreed. The rest, as they say, is history.

Sheppard has a distinctive style, a sonorous delivery that oozes dignity. But to hear him speak in person, one realizes that he does not deepen or change his voice for effect when announcing. He speaks into a microphone the way he speaks to someone on the street.

Sheppard has announced more than 4,000 Yankee games, including 84 postseason contests.

Sheppard has been announcing for the New York Giants since 1956, and worked for the New York Titans of the old American Football League, the New York Stars of the former World Football League, the New York Cosmos of the old North American Soccer League, as well as baseball and football games for St. John's University.

In several interviews, he recalled that his favorite Yankee name was the alliterative Mickey Mantle.

Sheppard has been honored several times by the Yankees and has won several public-service awards. But early in the 2000 season, Sheppard was honored as few other individuals have been when the Yankees unveiled a plaque honoring Sheppard for his years of service to the team.

THE YANKEE MANAGERS: A LOOK AT THE GREATS

Miller Huggins
Years as manager: 1918-29
Record: 1,067-719 (.597)
Pennants: 6
World Championships: 3

At 5 feet 6 inches, 140 pounds, the Mighty Mite had been a switch-hitting second baseman for the St. Louis Cardinals and the Cincinnati Reds in his playing days. He was also known as Little Everywhere and Rabbit.

Miller Huggins batted from a crouch that produced a tiny strike zone. In 13 years, he walked 1,002 times and struck out only 312 times.

He managed the Cardinals for five years, but never finished higher than fourth. After Yankee owners Jacob Ruppert and T.L. Huston fired Yankee manager "Wild Bill" Donovan, Huston wanted to hire his drinking buddy, Wilbert Robinson, formerly of the Dodgers. But Ruppert interviewed Robinson and decided to look around a little more. At the urging of American League president Byron "Ban" Johnson, he interviewed Huggins.

Ruppert eventually offered Huggins the job, but made the offer while Huston was away in Europe. Huggins accepted the post, which infuriated Huston, who felt Ruppert went behind his back. Huston made life miserable for the Mighty Mite for several years. When a player, usually Babe Ruth, had a beef with Huggins, he would make a beeline to Huston's office.

Huggins took it all, mostly because Ruppert always backed him. But he was a man who was rarely at peace with himself. He had chronic neuritis, stomach miseries and very bad teeth that ached constantly.

Huggins had an excellent baseball mind, but it took him several years to learn to lead the Yankees, rather than try to control them. Ruth, of course, was uncontrollable, but the Yankees of the early 1920s had a couple of other bad actors, notably Carl Mays, Wally Pipp and Bob Meusel. They all delighted in mocking Huggins in the dugout and in front of baseball writers.

But Huggins eventually got rid of most of the pains in the neck, except Ruth and Meusel, and replaced them with more subdued ballplayers, like Lou Gehrig, Herb Pennock, Urban Shocker, Earle Combs and Tony Lazzeri. Huston was bought out by Ruppert in 1922, which made things a lot better for Huggins. And after he fined Ruth $5,000 in 1925 for a spate of carousing, the Babe realized Huggins meant business.

He was a private man, a lifelong bachelor who lived with his sister. His only other interest was the stock market, which he knew very well. Lazzeri once recalled Huggins taking him aside after his first World Series in 1926 and advising him to invest his World Series check and not spend it.

Huggins twice coached three consecutive pennant winners and his 1927 team is still considered by many to be the greatest team of all time. In September of 1929, he died of blood poisoning, and even Ruth cried when he heard the news.

Huggins was elected to the Hall of Fame in 1964. He is also memorialized in "Monument Park" in Yankee Stadium.

Joe McCarthy

Years as manager: 1931-46
Record: 1,460-867, (.627)
Pennants: 8
World Championships: 7

Joe McCarthy joined the Yankees in 1931 under difficult circumstances. The former manager of the Chicago Cubs had played 15 years in the minor leagues, but had never made it to the big club. For some of his players, this lack of big league experience was problematic. For another thing, he had been hired over Babe Ruth's objections. By 1931, Ruth himself had wanted to manage the Yankees and, in fact, went to Yankee owner Jacob Ruppert and team president Edward Barrow to lobby for his cause.

Ruppert and Barrow were none too keen on it, believing that Ruth the manager would have little success toning down Ruth the player's extracurricular activities. In addition, Barrow had long admired McCarthy's style, and when he was fired by the Cubs, Barrow sent Paul Kritchell to Chicago to sound McCarthy out. Joe was willing, and the Yankees signed him.

Ruth was not pleased. McCarthy realized this, but he also realized that in a popularity contest with New York's greatest player, he would come in a distant second. So he let Ruth alone and the Babe, who was more of a professional than Ruppert or Barrow gave him credit for, had a great season, hitting .373 with 46 home runs and 163 RBI. In fact, he was near .400 for much of the season, but injured his hand on the outfield fence late in the year and ended up second to Al Simmons's .390.

And except for Ruth, most of the rest of the team got along very well with McCarthy. He was a stickler for discipline, not just during the game, but all the time. He demanded that the players wear suits and ties after 8 pm. He forbade them to shave in the clubhouse and banned the clubhouse poker games, believing they generated dissension.

He was old school. He liked toughness, he liked players who played hurt. He loved Gehrig, who would never even consider sitting out the second game of a doubleheader on a hot August afternoon. He did not suffer fools well. At the start of each season, he would warn the younger players not to try to trick him on the road by staying out late and sneaking back to the hotel. "I know every trick you'll try, because I've tried them all myself," he would say.

During his first five years in New York, from 1931-35, the Yankees finished first once (in 1932) and second the other four years. The New York sportswriters dubbed him "Second Place Joe" and began pointing out that in Chicago, he never could win the big game, either.

But in 1936, Joe DiMaggio came to New York and ended all such talk. The Yankees won seven of the next eight pennants. Five times in those eight years, they won more than 100 games. More importantly, of the eight World Series in which his Yankee teams were involved, McCarthy's teams won seven.

The war years diluted the Yankees' talent, and McCarthy, uncomfortable with new owners Del Webb and Dan Topping, and battling an ailing gallbladder, resigned early in the 1943 season. He would resurface a few years later to manage the Red Sox to a pair of second-place finishes in three years before retiring for good. He lived a good long time before dying in Buffalo, in 1978, at age 90. He was elected to the Hall of Fame in 1957 and is still the all-time leader in managerial wins with the Yankees.'

Charles Dillon "Casey" Stengel

Years as manager: 1949–1960
Record: 1,149-696, (.623)
Pennants: 10
World Championships: 7

Casey Stengel came to the Yankees after a decidedly unremarkable nine-year managerial career with the Brooklyn Dodgers and Boston Braves. His highest finish with either team had been fifth, and he had had only one winning season in that nine-season span.

Moreover, he was considered something of a clown by his new players. During his 14-year playing career he was most remembered for first thumbing his nose, then blowing a kiss at the Yankees while rounding the bases during the 1923 World Series after he had hit a home run for his Giants team. Another time, while playing the outfield for Brooklyn, he caught a bird and hid it under his hat. Soon after, he made a fairly difficult catch. As the crowd applauded, he tipped his cap and the bird flew out.

He was nicknamed the Old Perfesser after a stint as a college teacher in Mississippi during his playing days.

His biggest transgression in New York was being hired on the heels of fired Yankee manager Bucky Harris. The Yankee players loved Harris's laid-back style and were concerned about what kind of manager Stengel would be, particularly since he was endorsed by the very unpopular George Weiss.

Stengel, however, had allies: the sportswriters, who appreciated Stengel's availability and quotability. He would respond to virtually any question, sometimes in such a roundabout way that reporters would ask questions about the answer. If a photographer needed Stengel to make a funny face, or look pensive, or wistful, Stengel happily obliged.

The players, early on, didn't know what to make of him. In spring training in 1949, his first year, he was duly respectful of the veterans, particularly DiMaggio. He understood that in the pecking order of the New York Yankees, he fell somewhere well below Joltin' Joe.

His list of rules was very short: Don't drink in the hotel bar (because he did) and be ready to play. The players who were smart enough to understand those two rules stuck around. Those who abused them were released. It was pretty much as simple as that.

Stengel had a tough first year. DiMaggio, battling a debilitating heel injury, would play in only 76 games. Tommy Henrich, the club's best clutch hitter after DiMaggio, played in only 61 games in the outfield and was also out for several weeks because of a bad back. But Stengel realized that

The legendary Casey Stengel (shown here with, from left, Gil McDougald, Jerry Coleman and Joe Collins) won more pennants than any other major league manager before or since.

this team had some things many other teams did not have: great pitching and tremendous depth. He cleverly platooned his outfielders and his infielders throughout the season, always seeming to get a key performance from a benchwarmer.

His decision to have Yogi Berra as his regular catcher was another big factor, not just in 1949, but throughout Stengel's career. Yogi was an awkward-looking player and Harris had not been confident using him behind the plate, alternating him in the outfield his first three years. But Stengel realized that Berra was just too good a hitter to keep on the bench. Berra was his catcher from Opening Day.

The Yankees won the 1949 pennant by edging the Red Sox (and former Yankee manager Joe McCarthy) by one game. They followed up by beating the Dodgers in five games in the World Series. It was the first of five consecutive pennants and five consecutive World Series championships for the Yankees. In 1954, New York won 103 games, but the Cleveland Indians won 111 to claim the American League flag. The 1955 season kicked off four more American League championships and two World Series championships.

But in 1959, the Yankees fell to third place amid whispers that the Old Perfesser had lost it. New York bounced back to win the 1960 American League championship, but was stunned in the World Series by the Pittsburgh Pirates.

This was apparently a worse finish than 1959's third place, and the Yankee owners, Del Webb and Dan Topping, were convinced that Stengel was just too old. A few days after the World Series, Stengel was forced to resign and Webb and Topping elevated coach Ralph "The Major" Houk.

The primary reason for Webb and Topping's decision was because Houk had proven to be a good coach and the Yankees were eager to keep him in their organization. But perversely, they opted to gloss over that and told the press that Stengel was being let go because he was too old. Casey was deeply hurt.

But he would bounce back a few years later. The upstart New York Mets needed a manager in 1962 and Stengel was hired. He never finished out of the cellar with the Mets, but he constantly made headlines with his interviews and observations, much to the chagrin of the Yankee administration.

In 1966, he was enshrined in the Hall of Fame. No manager has ever won more pennants or been as quotable. He died in California in 1975.

Ralph George "The Major" Houk

Years as manager: 1961–63
Record: (944-806, (.539)
Pennants: 3
World Championships: 2

The announcement that Ralph Houk would be the new manager of the Yankees was greeted with relief by many players in the Yankee organization.

Houk was an ex-Marine who had risen to the rank of major during World War II, winning several medals for bravery. He was part of the D-Day invasion of Normandy. He was not a subtle man and was known for his gruff manner. But he reserved that gruffness for the media and other denizens of the outside world. With his players and coaches, he was invariably upbeat.

The players took to him quickly. Unlike Stengel, who believed in using as much of the roster as possible, Houk almost immediately named Clete Boyer his third baseman, Bobby Richardson his second baseman and Tony Kubek his shortstop. Elston Howard would catch and Yogi Berra would

be in the outfield. He was not a platooner, and the players appreciated knowing their status, even when it was obvious some of them wouldn't be regulars.

Houk's philosophy was to make sure that every player on the roster knew their role. He made sure the players all understood that he believed in them. While Stengel had often pointed out his players' deficiencies, Houk told them all they were terrific.

Houk also went to work on Mickey Mantle. Stengel had been tough on Mantle, believing that making Mickey work was the only way to draw out his considerable talent. Houk took the opposite tack. He praised Mantle, and told him that he was the leader of the team. In addition, rather than trying to save him for big games as Stengel often did, Houk told Whitey Ford he would pitch every fourth day. The result, in 1961, was spectacular: Ford had his best year, 25-4.

In fact, the Yankees of 1961 were all pretty spectacular. They won 109 games and easily beat the Reds in the World Series. This, of course, was the year Roger Maris and Mickey Mantle engaged in their yearlong quest for Babe Ruth's home run title. But the entire Yankee lineup was a killer. Kubek and Richardson weren't power hitters, but they knew how to get on base. After Maris and Mantle, Moose Skowron could hit. Howard, Berra and Clete Boyer were all sluggers, and even Johnny Blanchard could sock the ball. In one double-header that year, Blanchard hit four consecutive home runs! The Major's first team was one of the best ever.

He coached two more pennant winners in 1962 and 1963, but after the 1963 team was swept by the Dodgers, owners Dan Topping and Del Webb believed it was time for another change. General manager Roy Hamey was retiring, and Webb and Topping needed Houk as general manager. He was sent upstairs, and Berra took the helm.

Houk stayed as GM for Yogi's one year as manager and through 1½ years of the disastrous Johnny Keane tenure before taking over again. Keane had been fired early in the 1966 season, with the Yankees at 4-16 in tenth place. With Houk back at the helm, the Yankees did a little better, percentagewise, but still finished tenth. Houk remained manager for the next several years and helped rebuild the team.

He ended his Yankee career with 944 wins, fourth all-time with the Yankees.

Alfred Manuel "Billy" Martin

Years as manager: 1975-78, 1979, 1983, 1985, 1988
Record: 556-385, (.576)
Pennants: 2
World Championships: 1

Billy Martin loved to manage the Yankees. How else to explain the five managerial stints, each one more humiliating than the last?

Martin was a feisty infielder with Casey Stengel's Yankees in the 1950s. Following his playing career he remained in baseball, and by the early 1970s he was known as one of the smartest managers in the game. This was no real surprise, because he had been known as one of the smartest players in the game during his days on the field.

Martin won a divisional title with the Minnesota Twins in 1969, but he was fired in the offseason after several brushes with management. He was hired by the Tigers in 1971 and won the American League East title with them in 1972. But in 1973, he was canned again.

In 1974, he was hired by Texas, and the Rangers finished second.

Yankee owner George Steinbrenner had his eye on Martin, and when Billy was fired as manager of the Rangers late in the 1975 season, George snapped him up.

Martin the manager was a lot like Martin the player, a man who paid attention to detail. He had studied that game under Stengel and his teams played an aggressive style of baseball that sportswriters dubbed "Billy Ball." His players stole bases, they bunted, they hustled.

Martin was also not afraid to criticize a player when he believed the player needed it. Unfortunately, he was also unafraid to criticize Steinbrenner, which was often ill-advised.

But the simple fact was that George Steinbrenner obviously had a soft spot for Martin, because he kept hiring him back. That Martin kept taking the job was his downfall.

The first stint as manager, from 1975 to late in 1978, was Billy's most productive: two American League championships, and a World Series win in 1977. The subsequent four times Martin managed the Yankees just seemed to evolve into more and more of a soap opera. By the third term, the question in everyone's minds was no longer if he would be fired, but when.

Martin didn't seem to cope with the situation well. His drinking got worse and his attention span toward his job got shorter. Each time he was rehired, he and Steinbrenner would speak in conciliatory tones and everything would be fine for a few months, or weeks, or days.

Steinbrenner's rationalization was that the fans loved Billy and that he would help fill Yankee Stadium. But sooner or later, Martin would get into a bar fight, or say something outrageous, or attack an umpire, and a mortified Steinbrenner would let him go.

What neither he nor Martin seemed to see was how demoralizing the hiring-and-firing cycle was for players. Like everyone else, they knew that Martin's hiring would inevitably lead to his firing, and it was hard to take Martin seriously after a while.

The situation resolved itself tragically. In 1989, on Christmas Day, Martin was killed in a car accident near his home in Fenton, New York. He was 61.

Joseph Paul Torre

Years as manager: 1996-present
Record: 487-323, (.603)
Pennants: 4
World Championships: 4

The 1971 National League MVP never played in a postseason game, and after his retirement, Torre

Joe Torre has made posing with the World Series trophy an annual habit.

managed the Mets from 1977–81. He followed that with stints in Atlanta and St. Louis, and in November 1995, Torre became the first New York-–born manager in Yankee history.

Since he has become manager, Torre has led the Yankees into the postseason five consecutive years and to the World Series in 1996, 1998, 1999 and 2000. After dropping the first two games to the Atlanta Braves, the Yankees won 14 World Series games in a row before losing one game to the Mets in 2000.

Torre is also the first to manage 14 consecutive World Series wins. (The Yankees of the '20s and '30s won 8 of their 12 wins in 1927 and 1928 with Miller Huggins, while the final 4 in 1932 came under Joe McCarthy.)

If nothing else, the gentlemanly Torre brings an air of professionalism and dignity to the organization. Controversies are rare. He and his coaches go about their business and go home. There are no bar fights, no critical back-and-forth with owner George Steinbrenner. More than that, he is a player's manager. Torre never criticizes one of his guys. If there is a problem, it's settled internally. But, like Stengel, he also understands the voracious nature of the media. He is honest and accessible, and he is unafraid to admit his mistakes. This combination of forthrightness and good baseball instincts mesh superbly.

He takes care of the details, too. In the 2000 World Series, for example, he pinch hit Luis Sojo in the ninth inning of Game 5. Torre pulled a "double switch," putting Sojo in the pitcher's spot, or ninth in the order, and moving the pitcher to the leadoff slot. He wanted Sojo to have a chance to bat in the ninth and, of course, it all paid off.

During spring training in 1999, Torre was diagnosed with prostate cancer, which required surgery. He missed the first 36 games of the season, as coach Don Zimmer took over the club. He returned to the team on May 18.

Like several other Yankee skippers before him, Torre's previous managerial stints were fairly unsuccessful. But, like many of these same managers, once Torre had the material, he proved he could do the job. He was Manager of the Year in 1996 and in 1998. His present all-time record is 1,294-1,251.

The Players

COMPLETE YANKEE PLAYER CAREER STATISTICS

WITH BIOGRAPHIES OF THE 100 BEST YANKEES

Key to Statistics

TEAM ABBREVIATIONS:

Atl	Atlanta
Ari	Arizona
Bal	Baltimore
Bos	Boston
Bro	Brooklyn
Buf	Buffalo
Cal	California
Chi	Chicago
Cin	Cincinnati
Cle	Cleveland
Col	Colorado
Clm	Columbus
Det	Detroit

Fla	Florida
Hou	Houston
Ind	Indianapolis
KC	Kansas City
LA	Los Angeles
Lou	Louisville
Mil	Milwaukee
Min	Minnesota
Mon	Montreal
NY	New York
Oak	Oakland
Phi	Philadelphia
Pit	Pittsburgh
Roc	Rochester
SD	San Diego

Sea	Seattle
SF	San Francisco
StL	St. Louis
Tex	Texas
Tor	Toronto
Was	Washington

LEAGUE ABBREVIATIONS:

N	National League
A	American League
F	Federal League (1914-15)
AA	American Association (1882–91)

STATISTICAL ABBREVIATIONS:

YEAR	Year
TEAM	Team
STARTS	Games started by a pitcher
GAMES	Pitching appearances (pitchers) Games played (position players)
WON	Games won by a pitcher
LOST	Games lost by a pitcher
PCT	Pitcher's winning percentage (Wins / (Wins + Losses))
ER	Earned Runs
ERA	Earned Run Average ((Earned Runs/Innings Pitched) x 9)
INNINGS PITCHED	Innings Pitched
STRIKEOUTS	Strikeouts
WALKS	Total Bases-on-Balls
HITS ALLOWED	Hits Allowed
HRS ALLOWED	Homeruns Allowed
COMP. GAMES	Complete Games
SHUTOUTS	Shutouts
SAVES	Saves
AB	At-bats
RUNS	Runs
HITS	Hits

2B	Doubles
3B	Triples
HR	Homeruns
RBI	Runs Batted In
BB	Bases-on-Balls
IBB	Intentional Bases-on-Balls
SO	Strikeouts
HBP	Hit by Pitch
SH	Sacrifice Hits
SF	Sacrifice Flies
SB	Stolen Bases
CS	Caught Stealing
BA	Batting Average (Hits / At-bats)
OBA	On-Base Average ((Hits + Total Bases-on-Balls +Hit-by-Pitch) / (At-bats + Total Bases-on-Balls + Hit-by-Pitch + Sacrifice Flies))
SA	Slugging Average (Total Bases / At-bats)
FA	Fielding Average ((Put-Outs + Assists) / (Put-Outs + Assists + Errors))

Knoblauch, Edward Charles (Chuck)

HEIGHT: 5'9" THROWS: RIGHT BATS: RIGHT BORN: 7/7/1968, HOUSTON, TEXAS POSITIONS PLAYED: SS, 2B, DH

YEAR	TEAM	GAMES	AB	RUNS	HITS	2B	3B	HR	RBI	BB	IBB	SO	HBP	SH	SF	SB	CS	BA	OBA	SA	FA
1991	Min-A	151	565	78	159	24	6	1	50	59	0	40	4	1	5	25	5	.281	.351	.350	.975
1992	Min-A	155	600	104	178	19	6	2		88			5	2	12	34	13	.297	.384	.358	.992
	NY-A								64	76							12	.292	.34		.963
1999	NY-A	150	603	120	176	36	4	18	68	83	0	57	0	3	5	28	9	.292	.375	.454	.963
2000	NY-A	102	400	75	113	22	2	5	26	46	0	45	8	1	2	15	7	.282	.366	.385	.958
Career average		142	555	103	165	29	6	8	55	72	2	63	8	1	5	35	11	.297	.382	.417	.989
Yankee average		134	535	104	150	28	3	13	53	68	0	57	3	2	5	25	9	.280	.361	.418	.972
Career total		1415	5545	1025	1646	293	61	83	549	718	20	625	82	13	52	350	105	.297	.382	.417	.989
Yankee total		402	1606	312	449	83	10	40	158	205	1	172	8	6	14	74	28	.280	.361	.418	.972

Sample position player entry

Hunter, James Augustus (Jim *or* Catfish)

HEIGHT: 6'0" RIGHTHANDER BORN: 4/8/1946 HERTFORD, NORTH CAROLINA DIED: 9/9/1999 HERTFORD, NORTH CAROLINA

YEAR	TEAM	STARTS	GAMES	WON	LOST	PCT	ER	ERA	INNINGS PITCHED	STRIKE-OUTS	WALKS	HITS ALLOWED	HRS ALLOWED	COMP. GAMES	SHUT-OUTS	SAVES
1965	KC-A	20	32	8	8	.500	63	4.26	133	82	46	124	21	3	2	0
1966	A	25	30	9	11	.450	79		176				17	4	0	0
	NY-A	20	21					3.58	118	35	34	128	16	1	0	0
1979	NY-A	19	19	2	9	.182	62	5.31	105	34	34	128	15	1	0	0
Career Average		32	33	15	11	.574	83	3.26	230	134	64	197	25	12	3	0
Yankee Average		27	27	13	11	.543	79	3.58	199	98	53	176	23	13	2	0
Career Total		476	500	224	166	.574	1248	3.26	3449	2012	954	2958	374	181	42	1
Yankee Total		136	137	63	53	.543	395	3.58	993	492	267	879	113	65	11	0

Sample pitcher entry

A NOTE ABOUT THE STATISTICS

Statisticians have yet to find a perfect system for quantifying a player's performance through numbers, and they probably never will.

Of course, that hasn't stopped generations of baseball fans from poring over numbers.

Though interpretation is subjective, numbers *in themselves* do not lie or exaggerate, and they are the best method we have comparing a pitcher who played in 1900 with one who played in 2000.

The statistics included here are presented for that purpose and for one very specific other: to compare how a player performed during his career with his performance while a member of the New York Yankees. To that end, we've calculated two sets of totals and averages, one looking at a player's performance across his career, and the other looking at his results in Yankee pinstripes.

But numbers are not perfect. Some categories (*Sacrifice Hits*, for example) aren't available for every year for every player. We've provided them where available. And while averages can help gauge a player's overall performance across many years, they can also muddy the picture by placing equal weight on each season—whether an individual appeared in 1 game or 100.

We present these statistics, therefore, not as the definitive measure of a player's worth but as a numerical standard upon which to build an interpretation, one way of looking at things. From there, readers are free to decide for themselves.

Position Players

Adams, Spencer Dewey

HEIGHT: 5'9"   THROWS: RIGHT   BATS: LEFT   BORN: 6/21/1898 LAYTON, UTAH   DIED: 11/24/1970 SALT LAKE CITY, UTAH   POSITIONS PLAYED: 2B, 3B, SS

YEAR	TEAM	GAMES	AB	RUNS	HITS	2B	3B	HR	RBI	BB	IBB	SO	HBP	SH	SF	SB	CS	BA	OBA	SA	FA
1923	Pit-N	25	56	11	14	0	1	0	4	6	—	6	0	0	—	2	1	.250	.323	.286	.879
1925	Was-A	39	55	11	15	4	1	0	4	5	—	4	0	3	—	1	1	.273	.333	.382	.941
1926	**NY-A**	**28**	**25**	**7**	**3**	**1**	**0**	**0**	**1**	**3**	**—**	**7**	**0**	**0**	**—**	**1**	**0**	**.120**	**.214**	**.160**	**1.000**
1927	StL-A	88	259	32	69	11	3	0	29	24	—	33	2	9	—	1	8	.266	.333	.332	.948
Career average		45	99	15	25	4	1	0	10	10	—	13	1	3	—	1	3	.256	.324	.322	.942
Yankee average		**28**	**25**	**7**	**3**	**1**	**0**	**0**	**1**	**3**	**—**	**7**	**0**	**0**	**—**	**1**	**0**	**.120**	**.214**	**.160**	**1.000**
Career total		180	395	61	101	16	5	0	38	38	—	50	2	12	—	5	10	.256	.324	.322	.942
Yankee total		**28**	**25**	**7**	**3**	**1**	**0**	**0**	**1**	**3**	**—**	**7**	**0**	**0**	**—**	**1**	**0**	**.120**	**.214**	**.160**	**1.000**

Aguayo, Luis (Muriel) BORN LUIS AGUAYO (MURIEL)

HEIGHT: 5'9"   THROWS: RIGHT   BATS: RIGHT   BORN: 3/13/1959, VEGA BAJA, PUERTO RICO   POSITIONS PLAYED: 2B, 3B, SS

YEAR	TEAM	GAMES	AB	RUNS	HITS	2B	3B	HR	RBI	BB	IBB	SO	HBP	SH	SF	SB	CS	BA	OBA	SA	FA
1980	Phi-N	20	47	7	13	1	2	1	8	2	0	3	0	0	1	1	1	.277	.300	.447	.962
1981	Phi-N	45	84	11	18	4	0	1	7	6	0	15	2	2	0	1	0	.214	.283	.298	.938
1982	Phi-N	50	56	11	15	1	2	3	7	5	1	7	1	1	0	1	1	.268	.339	.518	.966
1983	Phi-N	2	4	1	1	0	0	0	0	1	0	2	0	0	0	0	0	.250	.400	.250	1.000
1984	Phi-N	58	72	15	20	4	0	3	11	8	2	16	0	0	0	0	0	.278	.350	.458	.909
1985	Phi-N	91	165	27	46	7	3	6	21	22	5	26	6	4	3	1	0	.279	.378	.467	.957
1986	Phi-N	62	133	17	28	6	1	4	13	8	0	26	3	0	2	1	1	.211	.267	.361	.967
1987	Phi-N	94	209	25	43	9	1	12	21	15	1	56	5	3	2	0	0	.206	.273	.431	.971
1988	Phi-N	49	97	9	24	3	0	3	5	13	2	17	0	1	0	2	0	.247	.336	.371	.961
1988	**NY-A**	**50**	**140**	**12**	**35**	**4**	**0**	**3**	**8**	**7**	**1**	**33**	**1**	**0**	**1**	**0**	**2**	**.250**	**.289**	**.343**	**.967**
1989	Cle-A	47	97	7	17	4	1	1	8	7	0	19	2	3	3	0	0	.175	.239	.268	.950
Career average		52	100	13	24	4	1	3	10	9	1	20	2	1	1	1	1	.236	.304	.393	.959
Yankee average		**50**	**140**	**12**	**35**	**4**	**0**	**3**	**8**	**7**	**1**	**33**	**1**	**0**	**1**	**0**	**2**	**.250**	**.289**	**.343**	**.967**
Career total		568	1104	142	260	43	10	37	109	94	12	220	20	14	12	7	5	.236	.304	.393	.959
Yankee total		**50**	**140**	**12**	**35**	**4**	**0**	**3**	**8**	**7**	**1**	**33**	**1**	**0**	**1**	**0**	**2**	**.250**	**.289**	**.343**	**.967**

Aldrete, Michael Peter

HEIGHT: 5'11"   THROWS: LEFT   BATS: LEFT   BORN: 1/29/1961 CARMEL, CALIFORNIA   POSITIONS PLAYED: 1B, OF, DH

YEAR	TEAM	GAMES	AB	RUNS	HITS	2B	3B	HR	RBI	BB	IBB	SO	HBP	SH	SF	SB	CS	BA	OBA	SA	FA
1986	SF-N	84	216	27	54	18	3	2	25	33	4	34	2	4	1	1	3	.250	.353	.389	1.000
1987	SF-N	126	357	50	116	18	2	9	51	43	5	50	0	4	2	6	0	.325	.396	.462	.995
1988	SF-N	139	389	44	104	15	0	3	50	56	13	65	0	1	3	6	5	.267	.357	.329	1.000
1989	Mon-N	76	136	12	30	8	1	1	12	19	0	30	1	1	2	1	3	.221	.316	.316	1.000
1990	Mon-N	96	161	22	39	7	1	1	18	37	2	31	1	0	1	1	2	.242	.385	.317	.982
1991	SD-N	12	15	2	0	0	0	0	1	3	0	4	0	0	0	0	1	.000	.167	.000	1.000
1991	Cle-A	85	183	22	48	6	1	1	19	36	1	37	0	1	2	1	2	.262	.384	.322	.994
1993	Oak-A	95	255	40	68	13	1	10	33	34	2	45	0	3	0	1	1	.267	.353	.443	.995
1994	Oak-A	76	178	23	43	5	0	4	18	20	1	35	0	0	3	2	0	.242	.313	.337	.995
1995	Oak-A	60	125	18	34	8	0	4	21	19	1	23	1	0	2	0	0	.272	.367	.432	.941
1995	Cal-A	18	24	1	6	0	0	0	3	0	0	8	0	0	1	0	0	.250	.240	.250	1.000
1996	Cal-A	31	40	5	6	1	0	3	8	5	0	4	0	0	1	0	0	.150	.239	.400	.750
1996	**NY-A**	**32**	**68**	**11**	**17**	**5**	**0**	**3**	**12**	**9**	**0**	**15**	**0**	**0**	**0**	**0**	**1**	**.250**	**.338**	**.456**	**1.000**
Career average		72	165	21	44	8	1	3	21	24	2	29	0	1	1	2	1	.263	.356	.377	.973
Yankee average		**32**	**68**	**11**	**17**	**5**	**0**	**3**	**12**	**9**	**0**	**15**	**0**	**0**	**0**	**0**	**1**	**.250**	**.338**	**.456**	**1.000**
Career total		930	2147	277	565	104	9	41	271	314	29	381	5	14	18	19	18	.263	.356	.377	.973
Yankee total		**32**	**68**	**11**	**17**	**5**	**0**	**3**	**12**	**9**	**0**	**15**	**0**	**0**	**0**	**0**	**1**	**.250**	**.338**	**.456**	**1.000**

Alexander, Walter Ernest

HEIGHT: 5'10"   THROWS: RIGHT   BATS: RIGHT   BORN: 3/5/1891 ATLANTA, GEORGIA   DIED: 12/29/1978 FORT WORTH, TEXAS   POSITIONS PLAYED: C

YEAR	TEAM	GAMES	AB	RUNS	HITS	2B	3B	HR	RBI	BB	IBB	SO	HBP	SH	SF	SB	CS	BA	OBA	SA	FA
1912	StL-A	37	97	5	17	4	0	0	5	8	—	—	1	5	—	1	0	.175	.245	.216	.969
1913	StL-A	43	110	5	15	2	1	0	7	4	—	36	1	3	—	1	0	.136	.174	.173	.947
1915	StL-A	1	1	0	0	0	0	0	0	0	—	0	0	0	—	0	0	.000	.000	.000	.000
1915	**NY-A**	**25**	**68**	**7**	**17**	**4**	**0**	**1**	**5**	**13**	**—**	**16**	**0**	**4**	**—**	**2**	**1**	**.250**	**.370**	**.353**	**.967**
1916	**NY-A**	**36**	**78**	**8**	**20**	**6**	**1**	**0**	**3**	**13**	**—**	**20**	**2**	**0**	**—**	**0**	**0**	**.256**	**.376**	**.359**	**.960**
1917	**NY-A**	**20**	**51**	**1**	**7**	**2**	**1**	**0**	**4**	**4**	**—**	**11**	**0**	**4**	**—**	**1**	**0**	**.137**	**.200**	**.216**	**.951**

(continued)

(continued)

																	BA	OBA	SA	FA
Career average	27	68	4	13	3	1	0	4	7	—	—	1	3	—	1	0	.188	.271	.254	.799
Yankee average	**27**	**66**	**5**	**15**	**4**	**1**	**0**	**4**	**10**	**—**	**16**	**1**	**3**	**—**	**1**	**0**	**.223**	**.332**	**.320**	**.959**
Career total	162	405	26	76	18	3	1	24	42	—	83	4	16	—	5	1	.188	.271	.254	.799
Yankee total	**81**	**197**	**16**	**44**	**12**	**2**	**1**	**12**	**30**	**—**	**47**	**2**	**8**	**—**	**3**	**1**	**.223**	**.332**	**.320**	**.959**

Allen, Bernard Keith (Bernie)

HEIGHT: 6'0"   THROWS: RIGHT   BATS: LEFT   BORN: 4/16/1939, E. LIVERPOOL, OHIO   POSITIONS PLAYED: 2B, 3B

YEAR	TEAM	GAMES	AB	RUNS	HITS	2B	3B	HR	RBI	BB	IBB	SO	HBP	SH	SF	SB	CS	BA	OBA	SA	FA
1962	Min-A	159	573	79	154	27	7	12	64	62	10	82	0	7	4	0	1	.269	.338	.403	.983
1963	Min-A	139	421	52	101	20	1	9	43	38	8	52	1	3	3	0	0	.240	.302	.356	.976
1964	Min-A	74	243	28	52	8	1	6	20	33	7	30	1	3	1	1	2	.214	.309	.329	.979
1965	Min-A	19	39	2	9	2	0	0	6	6	2	8	0	0	1	0	0	.231	.326	.282	1.000
1966	Min-A	101	319	34	76	18	1	5	30	26	5	40	2	2	1	2	3	.238	.299	.348	.974
1967	Was-A	87	254	13	49	5	1	3	18	18	1	43	0	4	3	1	2	.193	.244	.256	.990
1968	Was-A	120	373	31	90	12	4	6	40	28	5	35	4	0	0	2	0	.241	.301	.343	.991
1969	Was-A	122	365	33	90	17	4	9	45	50	3	35	0	2	0	5	4	.247	.337	.389	.974
1970	Was-A	104	261	31	61	7	1	8	29	43	4	21	0	1	0	0	2	.234	.342	.360	.969
1971	Was-A	97	229	18	61	11	1	4	22	33	1	27	0	0	0	2	1	.266	.359	.376	.961
1972	**NY-A**	**84**	**220**	**26**	**50**	**9**	**0**	**9**	**21**	**23**	**4**	**42**	**0**	**1**	**4**	**0**	**1**	**.227**	**.296**	**.391**	**.980**
1973	**NY-A**	**17**	**57**	**5**	**13**	**3**	**0**	**0**	**4**	**5**	**1**	**5**	**0**	**0**	**0**	**0**	**0**	**.228**	**.290**	**.281**	**.985**
1973	Mon-N	16	50	5	9	1	0	2	9	5	1	4	0	1	0	0	0	.180	.255	.320	.947
Career average	88	262	28	63	11	2	6	27	29	4	33	1	2	1	1	1	.239	.314	.357	.978
Yankee average	**51**	**139**	**16**	**32**	**6**	**0**	**5**	**13**	**14**	**3**	**24**	**0**	**1**	**2**	**0**	**1**	**.227**	**.294**	**.368**	**.983**
Career total	1139	3404	357	815	140	21	73	351	370	52	424	8	24	17	13	16	.239	.314	.357	.978
Yankee total	**101**	**277**	**31**	**63**	**12**	**0**	**9**	**25**	**28**	**5**	**47**	**0**	**1**	**4**	**0**	**1**	**.227**	**.294**	**.368**	**.983**

Alomar, Santos Sr. (Sandy *or* Iron Pony) BORN SANDY ALOMAR (CONDE)

HEIGHT: 5'9"   THROWS: RIGHT   BATS: BOTH   BORN: 10/19/1943 SALINAS, PUERTO RICO   POSITIONS PLAYED: 1B, 2B, 3B, SS

YEAR	TEAM	GAMES	AB	RUNS	HITS	2B	3B	HR	RBI	BB	IBB	SO	HBP	SH	SF	SB	CS	BA	OBA	SA	FA
1964	Mil-N	19	53	3	13	1	0	0	6	0	0	11	0	0	0	1	0	.245	.245	.264	.967
1965	Mil-N	67	108	16	26	1	1	0	8	4	1	12	0	4	0	12	5	.241	.268	.269	.964
1966	Atl-N	31	44	4	4	1	0	0	2	1	1	10	0	0	0	0	0	.091	.111	.114	.981
1967	NY-N	15	22	1	0	0	0	0	0	0	0	6	0	0	0	0	0	.000	.000	.000	1.000
1967	Chi-A	12	15	4	3	0	0	0	0	2	0	0	0	1	0	2	0	.200	.294	.200	.952
1968	Chi-A	133	363	41	92	8	2	0	12	20	1	42	1	8	3	21	8	.253	.292	.287	.958
1969	Chi-A	22	58	8	13	2	0	0	4	4	0	6	0	2	0	2	0	.224	.274	.259	.980
1969	Cal-A	134	559	60	140	10	2	1	30	36	2	48	0	3	0	18	3	.250	.296	.281	.969
1970	Cal-A	162	672	82	169	18	2	2	36	49	2	65	1	11	2	35	12	.251	.302	.293	.978
1971	Cal-A	162	689	77	179	24	3	4	42	41	4	60	0	7	2	39	10	.260	.301	.321	.989
1972	Cal-A	155	610	65	146	20	3	1	25	47	5	55	0	6	3	20	12	.239	.292	.287	1.000
1973	Cal-A	136	470	45	112	7	1	0	28	34	1	44	0	12	3	25	10	.238	.288	.257	.979
1974	Cal-A	46	54	12	12	0	1	0	1	2	0	8	0	1	0	2	0	.222	.250	.259	1.000
1974	**NY-A**	**76**	**279**	**35**	**75**	**8**	**0**	**1**	**27**	**14**	**0**	**25**	**0**	**4**	**2**	**6**	**4**	**.269**	**.304**	**.308**	**.977**
1975	**NY-A**	**151**	**489**	**61**	**117**	**18**	**4**	**2**	**39**	**26**	**0**	**58**	**0**	**11**	**2**	**28**	**6**	**.239**	**.277**	**.305**	**1.000**
1976	**NY-A**	**67**	**163**	**20**	**39**	**4**	**0**	**1**	**10**	**13**	**0**	**12**	**0**	**2**	**0**	**12**	**7**	**.239**	**.295**	**.282**	**.800**
1977	Tex-A	69	83	21	22	3	0	1	11	8	0	13	1	4	1	4	3	.265	.333	.337	1.000
1978	Tex-A	24	29	3	6	1	0	0	1	1	0	7	0	1	0	0	0	.207	.233	.241	.975
Career average	82	264	31	65	7	1	1	16	17	1	27	0	4	1	13	4	.245	.290	.288	.971
Yankee average	**98**	**310**	**39**	**77**	**10**	**1**	**1**	**25**	**18**	**0**	**32**	**0**	**6**	**1**	**15**	**6**	**.248**	**.287**	**.302**	**.926**
Career total	1481	4760	558	1168	126	19	13	282	302	17	482	3	77	18	227	80	.245	.290	.288	.971
Yankee total	**294**	**931**	**116**	**231**	**30**	**4**	**4**	**76**	**53**	**0**	**95**	**0**	**17**	**4**	**46**	**17**	**.248**	**.287**	**.302**	**.926**

Alou, Felipe Rojas BORN FELIPE ROJAS (ALOU)

HEIGHT: 6'0"   THROWS: RIGHT   BATS: RIGHT   BORN: 5/12/1935 HAINA, DOMINICAN REPUBLIC   POSITIONS PLAYED: 1B, 3B, SS, OF

YEAR	TEAM	GAMES	AB	RUNS	HITS	2B	3B	HR	RBI	BB	IBB	SO	HBP	SH	SF	SB	CS	BA	OBA	SA	FA
1958	SF-N	75	182	21	46	9	2	4	16	19	2	34	1	1	1	4	2	.253	.325	.390	.985
1959	SF-N	95	247	38	68	13	2	10	33	17	1	38	0	1	3	5	3	.275	.318	.466	.974
1960	SF-N	106	322	48	85	17	3	8	44	16	1	42	2	3	4	10	2	.264	.299	.410	.958
1961	SF-N	132	415	59	120	19	0	18	52	26	2	41	2	2	2	11	4	.289	.333	.465	.990

(continued)

(continued)

YEAR	TEAM	GAMES	AB	RUNS	HITS	2B	3B	HR	RBI	BB	IBB	SO	HBP	SH	SF	SB	CS	BA	OBA	SA	FA
1962	SF-N	154	561	96	177	30	3	25	98	33	2	66	5	2	5	10	7	.316	.356	.513	.971
1963	SF-N	157	565	75	159	31	9	20	82	27	3	87	6	5	4	11	2	.281	.319	.474	.986
1964	Mil-N	121	415	60	105	26	3	9	51	30	5	41	4	1	5	5	2	.253	.306	.395	.975
1965	Mil-N	143	555	80	165	29	2	23	78	31	4	63	5	4	4	8	4	.297	.338	.481	1.000
1966	Atl-N	154	666	122	218	32	6	31	74	24	6	51	12	2	2	5	7	.327	.361	.533	1.000
1967	Atl-N	140	574	76	157	26	3	15	43	32	7	50	7	1	3	6	5	.274	.318	.408	.993
1968	Atl-N	160	662	72	210	37	5	11	57	48	14	56	4	0	4	12	11	.317	.365	.438	.980
1969	Atl-N	123	476	54	134	13	1	5	32	23	4	23	4	4	2	4	6	.282	.319	.345	.989
1970	Oak-A	154	575	70	156	25	3	8	55	32	6	31	1	4	6	10	5	.271	.308	.367	1.000
1971	Oak-A	2	8	0	2	1	0	0	0	0	0	1	0	1	0	0	0	.250	.250	.375	1.000
1971	**NY-A**	**131**	**461**	**52**	**133**	**20**	**6**	**8**	**69**	**32**	**3**	**24**	**2**	**1**	**5**	**5**	**5**	**.289**	**.337**	**.410**	**.985**
1972	**NY-A**	**120**	**324**	**33**	**90**	**18**	**1**	**6**	**37**	**22**	**1**	**27**	**2**	**1**	**2**	**1**	**0**	**.278**	**.326**	**.395**	**1.000**
1973	**NY-A**	**93**	**280**	**25**	**66**	**12**	**0**	**4**	**27**	**9**	**5**	**25**	**0**	**0**	**4**	**0**	**1**	**.236**	**.256**	**.321**	**.988**
1973	Mon-N	19	48	4	10	1	0	1	4	2	1	4	0	0	0	0	1	.208	.240	.292	1.000
1974	Mil-A	3	3	0	0	0	0	0	0	0	0	2	0	0	0	0	0	.000	.000	.000	.000
Career average		110	386	52	111	19	3	11	45	22	4	37	3	2	3	6	4	.286	.328	.433	.935
Yankee average		**115**	**355**	**37**	**96**	**17**	**2**	**6**	**44**	**21**	**3**	**25**	**1**	**1**	**4**	**2**	**2**	**.271**	**.311**	**.382**	**.991**
Career total		2082	7339	985	2101	359	49	206	852	423	67	706	57	33	56	107	67	.286	.328	.433	.935
Yankee total		**344**	**1065**	**110**	**289**	**50**	**7**	**18**	**133**	**63**	**9**	**76**	**4**	**2**	**11**	**6**	**6**	**.271**	**.311**	**.382**	**.991**

Alou, Mateo (Matty) BORN MATEO ROJAS (ALOU)

HEIGHT: 5'9"   THROWS: LEFT   BATS: LEFT   BORN: 12/22/1938 HAINA, DOMINICAN REPUBLIC   POSITIONS PLAYED: 1B, OF

YEAR	TEAM	GAMES	AB	RUNS	HITS	2B	3B	HR	RBI	BB	IBB	SO	HBP	SH	SF	SB	CS	BA	OBA	SA	FA
1960	SF-N	4	3	1	1	0	0	0	0	0	0	0	0	0	0	0	0	.333	.333	.333	1.000
1961	SF-N	81	200	38	62	7	2	6	24	15	2	18	0	1	1	3	2	.310	.356	.455	.978
1962	SF-N	78	195	28	57	8	1	3	14	14	0	17	3	1	0	3	1	.292	.349	.390	.976
1963	SF-N	63	76	4	11	1	0	0	2	2	0	13	1	1	0	0	1	.145	.177	.158	.952
1964	SF-N	110	250	28	66	4	2	1	14	11	3	25	3	2	1	5	3	.264	.302	.308	.976
1965	SF-N	117	324	37	75	12	2	2	18	17	2	28	2	8	0	10	2	.231	.274	.299	.986
1966	Pit-N	141	535	86	183	18	9	2	27	24	4	44	4	12	3	23	15	.342	.373	.421	.972
1967	Pit-N	139	550	87	186	21	7	2	28	24	1	42	6	3	1	16	10	.338	.372	.413	.989
1968	Pit-N	146	558	59	185	28	4	0	52	27	6	26	2	7	4	18	10	.332	.362	.396	.984
1969	Pit-N	162	698	105	231	41	6	1	48	42	9	35	2	1	3	22	8	.331	.369	.411	.977
1970	Pit-N	155	677	97	201	21	8	1	47	30	3	18	4	4	3	19	11	.297	.329	.356	.975
1971	StL-N	149	609	85	192	28	6	7	74	34	3	27	4	6	7	19	10	.315	.352	.415	.981
1972	StL-N	108	404	46	127	17	2	3	31	24	2	23	1	1	1	11	4	.314	.353	.389	1.000
1972	Oak-A	32	121	11	34	5	0	1	16	11	1	12	1	1	1	2	1	.281	.346	.347	1.000
1973	**NY-A**	**123**	**497**	**59**	**147**	**22**	**1**	**2**	**28**	**30**	**0**	**43**	**3**	**6**	**2**	**5**	**2**	**.296**	**.338**	**.356**	**.974**
1973	StL-N	11	11	1	3	0	0	0	1	1	1	0	0	0	0	0	0	.273	.333	.273	1.000
1974	SD-N	48	81	8	16	3	0	0	3	5	1	6	0	1	1	0	0	.198	.241	.235	1.000
Career average		98	341	46	105	14	3	2	25	18	2	22	2	3	2	9	5	.307	.345	.381	.984
Yankee average		**123**	**497**	**59**	**147**	**22**	**1**	**2**	**28**	**30**	**0**	**43**	**3**	**6**	**2**	**5**	**2**	**.296**	**.338**	**.356**	**.974**
Career total		1667	5789	780	1777	236	50	31	427	311	38	377	36	55	28	156	80	.307	.345	.381	.984
Yankee total		**123**	**497**	**59**	**147**	**22**	**1**	**2**	**28**	**30**	**0**	**43**	**3**	**6**	**2**	**5**	**2**	**.296**	**.338**	**.356**	**.974**

Alston, Wendell (Dell)

HEIGHT: 6'0"   THROWS: RIGHT   BATS: LEFT   BORN: 9/22/1952 VALHALLA, NEW YORK   POSITIONS PLAYED: OF

YEAR	TEAM	GAMES	AB	RUNS	HITS	2B	3B	HR	RBI	BB	IBB	SO	HBP	SH	SF	SB	CS	BA	OBA	SA	FA
1977	**NY-A**	**22**	**40**	**10**	**13**	**4**	**0**	**1**	**4**	**3**	**0**	**4**	**0**	**1**	**1**	**3**	**3**	**.325**	**.364**	**.500**	**1.000**
1978	**NY-A**	**3**	**3**	**0**	**0**	**0**	**0**	**0**	**0**	**0**	**0**	**2**	**0**	**0**	**0**	**0**	**0**	**.000**	**.000**	**.000**	**.000**
1978	Oak-A	58	173	17	36	2	0	1	10	10	0	21	0	4	1	11	10	.208	.250	.237	.956
1979	Cle-A	54	62	10	18	0	2	1	12	10	1	10	0	1	1	4	4	.290	.384	.403	.969
1980	Cle-A	52	54	11	12	1	2	0	9	5	2	7	2	1	2	2	4	.222	.302	.315	.947
Career average		38	66	10	16	1	1	1	7	6	1	9	0	1	1	4	4	.238	.297	.310	.774
Yankee average		**13**	**22**	**5**	**7**	**2**	**0**	**1**	**2**	**2**	**0**	**3**	**0**	**1**	**1**	**2**	**2**	**.302**	**.340**	**.465**	**.500**
Career total		189	332	48	79	7	4	3	35	28	3	44	2	7	5	20	21	.238	.297	.310	.774
Yankee total		**25**	**43**	**10**	**13**	**4**	**0**	**1**	**4**	**3**	**0**	**6**	**0**	**1**	**1**	**3**	**3**	**.302**	**.340**	**.465**	**.500**

Amaro, Ruben BORN RUBEN AMARO (MORA)

HEIGHT: 5'11" THROWS: RIGHT BATS: RIGHT BORN: 1/6/1936 VERACRUZ, MEXICO POSITIONS PLAYED: 1B, SS

YEAR	TEAM	GAMES	AB	RUNS	HITS	2B	3B	HR	RBI	BB	IBB	SO	HBP	SH	SF	SB	CS	BA	OBA	SA	FA
1958	StL-N	40	76	8	17	2	1	0	0	5	1	8	0	1	0	0	1	.224	.272	.276	.948
1960	Phi-N	92	264	25	61	9	1	0	16	21	2	32	2	4	1	0	1	.231	.292	.273	.965
1961	Phi-N	135	381	34	98	14	9	1	32	53	2	59	2	11	0	1	0	.257	.351	.349	.970
1962	Phi-N	79	226	24	55	10	0	0	19	30	4	28	1	4	4	5	2	.243	.330	.288	.968
1963	Phi-N	115	217	25	47	9	2	2	19	19	6	31	0	6	3	0	1	.217	.276	.304	.950
1964	Phi-N	129	299	31	79	11	0	4	34	16	2	37	3	4	1	1	6	.264	.307	.341	1.000
1965	Phi-N	118	184	26	39	7	0	0	15	27	3	22	1	3	3	1	1	.212	.312	.250	.957
1966	**NY-A**	**14**	**23**	**0**	**5**	**0**	**0**	**0**	**3**	**0**	**0**	**2**	**0**	**0**	**0**	**0**	**0**	**.217**	**.217**	**.217**	**.977**
1967	**NY-A**	**130**	**417**	**31**	**93**	**12**	**0**	**1**	**17**	**43**	**4**	**49**	**1**	**9**	**0**	**3**	**2**	**.223**	**.297**	**.259**	**1.000**
1968	**NY-A**	**47**	**41**	**3**	**5**	**1**	**0**	**0**	**0**	**9**	**0**	**6**	**0**	**0**	**0**	**0**	**0**	**.122**	**.280**	**.146**	**1.000**
1969	Cal-A	41	27	4	6	0	0	0	1	4	0	6	0	5	0	0	0	.222	.323	.222	1.000
Career average		86	196	19	46	7	1	1	14	21	2	26	1	4	1	1	1	.234	.309	.292	.976
Yankee average		**64**	**160**	**11**	**34**	**4**	**0**	**0**	**7**	**17**	**1**	**19**	**0**	**3**	**0**	**1**	**1**	**.214**	**.292**	**.247**	**.992**
Career total		940	2155	211	505	75	13	8	156	227	24	280	10	47	12	11	14	.234	.309	.292	.976
Yankee total		**191**	**481**	**34**	**103**	**13**	**0**	**1**	**20**	**52**	**4**	**57**	**1**	**9**	**0**	**3**	**2**	**.214**	**.292**	**.247**	**.992**

Anderson, John Joseph (Honest John)

HEIGHT: 6'2" THROWS: RIGHT BATS: BOTH BORN: 12/14/1873 SARPSBORG, NORWAY DIED: 7/23/1949, WORCESTER, MASS. POSITIONS PLAYED: 1B, OF

YEAR	TEAM	GAMES	AB	RUNS	HITS	2B	3B	HR	RBI	BB	IBB	SO	HBP	SH	SF	SB	CS	BA	OBA	SA	FA
1894	Bro-N	17	63	14	19	1	3	1	19	3	—	3	0	1	—	7	—	.302	.333	.460	.778
1895	Bro-N	102	419	76	120	11	14	9	87	12	—	29	5	1	—	24	—	.286	.314	.444	.882
1896	Bro-N	108	430	70	135	23	17	1	55	18	—	23	2	1	—	37	—	.314	.344	.453	.942
1897	Bro-N	117	492	93	160	28	12	4	85	17	—	—	7	11	—	29	—	.325	.357	.455	.936
1898	Bro-N	6	21	1	3	2	0	0	2	1	—	—	1	0	—	0	—	.143	.217	.238	1.000
1898	Was-N	110	430	70	131	28	18	9	71	23	—	—	12	6	—	18	—	.305	.357	.516	.948
1898	Bro-N	19	69	11	19	3	4	0	8	5	—	—	1	0	—	2	—	.275	.333	.435	.966
1899	Bro-N	117	439	65	118	18	7	4	92	27	—	—	4	2	—	25	—	.269	.317	.369	.933
1901	Mil-A	138	576	90	190	46	7	8	99	24	—	—	3	4	—	35	—	.330	.360	.476	.976
1902	StL-A	126	524	60	149	29	6	4	85	21	—	—	3	3	—	15	—	.284	.316	.385	.985
1903	StL-A	138	550	65	156	34	8	2	78	23	—	—	0	4	—	16	—	.284	.312	.385	.986
1904	**NY-A**	**143**	**558**	**62**	**155**	**27**	**12**	**3**	**82**	**23**	**—**	**—**	**6**	**11**	**—**	**20**	**—**	**.278**	**.313**	**.385**	**.985**
1905	**NY-A**	**32**	**99**	**12**	**23**	**3**	**1**	**0**	**14**	**8**	**—**	**—**	**1**	**0**	**—**	**9**	**—**	**.232**	**.296**	**.283**	**1.000**
1905	Was-A	101	400	50	116	21	6	1	38	22	—	—	2	4	—	22	—	.290	.330	.380	.960
1906	Was-A	151	583	62	158	25	4	3	70	19	—	—	2	3	—	39	—	.271	.296	.343	.953
1907	Was-A	87	333	33	96	12	4	0	44	34	—	—	3	1	—	19	—	.288	.359	.348	.983
1908	Chi-A	123	355	36	93	17	1	0	47	30	—	—	1	13	—	21	—	.262	.321	.315	.988
Career average		96	373	51	108	19	7	3	57	18	—	—	3	4	—	20	—	.290	.329	.404	.953
Yankee average		**88**	**329**	**37**	**89**	**15**	**7**	**2**	**48**	**16**	**—**	**—**	**4**	**6**	**—**	**15**	**—**	**.271**	**.311**	**.370**	**.993**
Career total		1635	6341	870	1841	328	124	49	976	310	—	55	53	65	—	338	—	.290	.329	.404	.953
Yankee total		**175**	**657**	**74**	**178**	**30**	**13**	**3**	**96**	**31**	**—**	**—**	**7**	**11**	**—**	**29**	**—**	**.271**	**.311**	**.370**	**.993**

Aragon, Angel (Pete) BORN ANGEL ARAGON (VALDES)

HEIGHT: 5'5" THROWS: RIGHT BATS: RIGHT BORN: 8/2/1890 HAVANA, CUBA DIED: 1/24/1952 NEW YORK, NEW YORK POSITIONS PLAYED: 3B, SS, OF

YEAR	TEAM	GAMES	AB	RUNS	HITS	2B	3B	HR	RBI	BB	IBB	SO	HBP	SH	SF	SB	CS	BA	OBA	SA	FA
1914	**NY-A**	**6**	**7**	**1**	**1**	**0**	**0**	**0**	**0**	**1**	**—**	**2**	**1**	**1**	**—**	**0**	**0**	**.143**	**.333**	**.143**	**.000**
1916	**NY-A**	**12**	**24**	**1**	**5**	**0**	**0**	**0**	**3**	**2**	**—**	**2**	**0**	**1**	**—**	**2**	**—**	**.208**	**.269**	**.208**	**.864**
1917	**NY-A**	**14**	**45**	**2**	**3**	**1**	**0**	**0**	**2**	**2**	**—**	**2**	**0**	**3**	**—**	**0**	**—**	**.067**	**.106**	**.089**	**.933**
Career average		11	25	1	3	0	0	0	2	2	—	2	0	2	—	1	—	.118	.183	.132	.599
Yankee average		**11**	**25**	**1**	**3**	**0**	**0**	**0**	**2**	**2**	**—**	**2**	**0**	**2**	**—**	**1**	**—**	**.118**	**.183**	**.132**	**.599**
Career total		32	76	4	9	1	0	0	5	5	—	6	1	5	—	2	0	.118	.183	.132	.599
Yankee total		**32**	**76**	**4**	**9**	**1**	**0**	**0**	**5**	**5**	**—**	**6**	**1**	**5**	**—**	**2**	**0**	**.118**	**.183**	**.132**	**.599**

Ashford, Thomas Steven (Tucker)

HEIGHT: 6'1"   THROWS: RIGHT   BATS: RIGHT   BORN: 12/4/1954 MEMPHIS, TENNESSEE   POSITIONS PLAYED: 1B, 3B, SS

YEAR	TEAM	GAMES	AB	RUNS	HITS	2B	3B	HR	RBI	BB	IBB	SO	HBP	SH	SF	SB	CS	BA	OBA	SA	FA
1976	SD-N	4	5	0	3	1	0	0	0	1	0	0	0	0	0	2	0	.600	.667	.800	1.000
1977	SD-N	81	249	25	54	18	0	3	24	21	4	35	1	4	2	2	3	.217	.278	.325	.929
1978	SD-N	75	155	11	38	11	0	3	26	14	1	31	0	1	4	1	0	.245	.301	.374	.984
1980	Tex-A	15	32	2	4	0	0	0	3	3	0	3	0	0	0	0	0	.125	.200	.125	1.000
1981	**NY-A**	**3**	**0**	**0**	**0**	**0**	**0**	**0**	**0**	**0**	**0**	**0**	**0**	**0**	**0**	**0**	**0**	**—**	**—**	**—**	**.000**
1983	NY-N	35	56	3	10	0	1	0	2	7	1	4	0	0	0	0	0	.179	.270	.214	.957
1984	KC-A	9	13	1	2	1	0	0	0	1	0	2	0	0	0	0	0	.154	.214	.231	.909
Career average		32	73	6	16	4	0	1	8	7	1	11	0	1	1	1	0	.218	.282	.318	.963
Yankee average		**3**	**0**	**0**	**0**	**0**	**0**	**0**	**0**	**0**	**0**	**0**	**0**	**0**	**0**	**0**	**0**	**—**	**—**	**—**	**.000**
Career total		222	510	42	111	31	1	6	55	47	6	75	1	5	6	5	3	.218	.282	.318	.963
Yankee total		**3**	**0**	**0**	**0**	**0**	**0**	**0**	**0**	**0**	**0**	**0**	**0**	**0**	**0**	**0**	**0**	**—**	**—**	**—**	**.000**

Austin, James Philip (Jimmy *or* Pepper)

HEIGHT: 5'7"   THROWS: RIGHT   BATS: BOTH   BORN: 12/08/1879 SWANSEA, WALES   DIED: 3/6/1965 LAGUNA BEACH, CAL.   POSITIONS PLAYED: 2B, 3B, SS

YEAR	TEAM	GAMES	AB	RUNS	HITS	2B	3B	HR	RBI	BB	IBB	SO	HBP	SH	SF	SB	CS	BA	OBA	SA	FA
1909	**NY-A**	**136**	**437**	**37**	**101**	**11**	**5**	**1**	**39**	**32**	**—**	**—**	**1**	**30**	**—**	**30**	**—**	**.231**	**.285**	**.286**	**.928**
1910	**NY-A**	**133**	**432**	**46**	**94**	**11**	**4**	**2**	**36**	**47**	**—**	**—**	**7**	**25**	**—**	**22**	**—**	**.218**	**.305**	**.275**	**.942**
1911	StL-A	148	541	84	141	25	11	2	45	69	—	—	6	34	—	26	—	.261	.351	.359	.931
1912	StL-A	149	536	57	135	14	8	2	44	38	—	—	4	26	—	28	—	.252	.306	.319	.911
1913	StL-A	142	489	56	130	18	6	0	42	45	—	51	8	17	—	37	—	.266	.338	.339	.944
1914	StL-A	130	466	55	111	16	4	0	30	40	—	59	1	16	—	20	23	.238	.300	.290	.935
1915	StL-A	141	477	61	127	6	6	1	30	64	—	60	2	35	—	18	15	.266	.355	.310	.917
1916	StL-A	129	411	55	85	15	6	1	28	74	—	59	4	19	—	19	—	.207	.333	.280	.939
1917	StL-A	127	455	61	109	18	8	0	19	50	—	46	3	26	—	13	—	.240	.319	.314	.947
1918	StL-A	110	367	42	97	14	4	0	20	53	—	32	1	21	—	18	—	.264	.359	.324	.939
1919	StL-A	106	396	54	94	9	9	1	21	42	—	31	2	10	—	8	—	.237	.314	.313	.939
1920	StL-A	83	280	38	76	11	3	1	32	31	—	15	4	15	—	2	4	.271	.352	.343	.943
1921	StL-A	27	66	8	18	2	1	0	2	4	—	7	1	4	—	2	1	.273	.324	.333	.938
1922	StL-A	15	31	6	9	3	1	0	1	3	—	2	0	0	—	0	0	.290	.353	.452	.957
1923	StL-A	1	0	0	0	0	0	0	0	0	—	0	0	0	—	0	0	—	—	—	.000
1925	StL-A	1	1	0	0	0	0	0	0	0	—	0	0	0	—	0	0	.000	.000	.000	1.000
1926	StL-A	1	2	1	1	1	0	0	1	0	—	0	0	0	—	1	0	.500	.500	1.000	1.000
1929	StL-A	1	1	0	0	0	0	0	0	0	—	1	0	0	—	0	0	.000	.000	.000	1.000
Career average		88	299	37	74	10	4	1	22	33	—	—	2	15	—	14	—	.246	.326	.314	.948
Yankee average		**135**	**435**	**42**	**98**	**11**	**5**	**2**	**38**	**40**	**—**	**—**	**4**	**28**	**—**	**26**	**—**	**.224**	**.295**	**.281**	**.935**
Career total		1580	5388	661	1328	174	76	13	390	592	—	363	44	278	—	244	43	.246	.326	.314	.948
Yankee total		**269**	**869**	**83**	**195**	**22**	**9**	**3**	**75**	**79**	**—**	**—**	**8**	**55**	**—**	**52**	**—**	**.224**	**.295**	**.281**	**.935**

Autry, Martin Gordon (Chick)

HEIGHT: 6'0"   THROWS: RIGHT   BATS: RIGHT   BORN: 3/5/1903 MARTINDALE, TEXAS   DIED: 1/26/1950 SAVANNAH, GEORGIA   POSITIONS PLAYED: C

YEAR	TEAM	GAMES	AB	RUNS	HITS	2B	3B	HR	RBI	BB	IBB	SO	HBP	SH	SF	SB	CS	BA	OBA	SA	FA
1924	**NY-A**	**2**	**0**	**1**	**0**	**0**	**0**	**0**	**0**	**0**	**—**	**0**	**1**	**0**	**—**	**0**	**0**	**—**	**1.000**	**—**	**1.000**
1926	Cle-A	3	7	1	1	0	0	0	0	1	—	0	0	0	—	0	0	.143	.250	.143	1.000
1927	Cle-A	16	43	5	11	4	1	0	7	0	—	6	0	3	—	0	0	.256	.256	.395	.933
1928	Cle-A	22	60	6	18	6	1	1	9	1	—	7	0	2	—	0	0	.300	.311	.483	.972
1929	Chi-A	43	96	7	20	6	0	1	12	1	—	8	1	2	—	0	0	.208	.224	.302	.940
1930	Chi-A	34	71	1	18	1	1	0	5	4	—	8	0	3	—	0	0	.254	.293	.296	.992
Career average		20	46	4	11	3	1	0	6	1	—	5	0	2	—	0	0	.245	.269	.350	.973
Yankee average		**2**	**0**	**1**	**0**	**0**	**0**	**0**	**0**	**0**	**—**	**0**	**1**	**0**	**—**	**0**	**0**	**—**	**1.000**	**—**	**1.000**
Career total		120	277	21	68	17	3	2	33	7	—	29	2	10	—	0	0	.245	.269	.350	.973
Yankee total		**2**	**0**	**1**	**0**	**0**	**0**	**0**	**0**	**0**	**—**	**0**	**1**	**0**	**—**	**0**	**0**	**—**	**1.000**	**—**	**1.000**

Azocar, Oscar Gregorio

HEIGHT: 6'1"   THROWS: LEFT   BATS: LEFT   BORN: 2/21/1965 CARACAS, VENEZUELA   POSITIONS PLAYED: OF

YEAR	TEAM	GAMES	AB	RUNS	HITS	2B	3B	HR	RBI	BB	IBB	SO	HBP	SH	SF	SB	CS	BA	OBA	SA	FA
1990	**NY-A**	**65**	**214**	**18**	**53**	**8**	**0**	**5**	**19**	**2**	**0**	**15**	**1**	**0**	**1**	**7**	**0**	**.248**	**.257**	**.355**	**.991**
1991	SD-N	38	57	5	14	2	0	0	9	1	1	9	1	0	1	2	0	.246	.267	.281	.875
1992	SD-N	99	168	15	32	6	0	0	8	9	1	12	0	4	1	1	0	.190	.230	.226	.942
Career average		67	146	13	33	5	0	2	12	4	1	12	1	1	1	3	0	.226	.248	.296	.936
Yankee average		**65**	**214**	**18**	**53**	**8**	**0**	**5**	**19**	**2**	**0**	**15**	**1**	**0**	**1**	**7**	**0**	**.248**	**.257**	**.355**	**.991**
Career total		202	439	38	99	16	0	5	36	12	2	36	2	4	3	10	0	.226	.248	.296	.936
Yankee total		**65**	**214**	**18**	**53**	**8**	**0**	**5**	**19**	**2**	**0**	**15**	**1**	**0**	**1**	**7**	**0**	**.248**	**.257**	**.355**	**.991**

Babe, Loren Rolland (Bee Bee)

HEIGHT: 5'10"   THROWS: RIGHT   BATS: LEFT   BORN: 1/11/1928 PISGAH, IOWA   DIED: 2/14/1984 OMAHA, NEBRASKA   POSITIONS PLAYED: 3B, SS

YEAR	TEAM	GAMES	AB	RUNS	HITS	2B	3B	HR	RBI	BB	IBB	SO	HBP	SH	SF	SB	CS	BA	OBA	SA	FA
1952	**NY-A**	**12**	**21**	**1**	**2**	**1**	**0**	**0**	**0**	**4**	**—**	**4**	**0**	**0**	**—**	**1**	**0**	**.095**	**.240**	**.143**	**.909**
1953	**NY-A**	**5**	**18**	**2**	**6**	**1**	**0**	**2**	**6**	**0**	**—**	**2**	**0**	**0**	**—**	**0**	**0**	**.333**	**.333**	**.722**	**.920**
1953	Phi-A	103	343	34	77	16	2	0	20	35	—	20	2	3	—	0	1	.224	.300	.283	.950
Career average		40	127	12	28	6	1	1	9	13	—	9	1	1	—	0	0	.223	.298	.296	.926
Yankee average		**9**	**20**	**2**	**4**	**1**	**0**	**1**	**3**	**2**	**—**	**3**	**0**	**0**	**—**	**1**	**0**	**.205**	**.279**	**.410**	**.915**
Career total		120	382	37	85	18	2	2	26	39	—	26	2	3	—	1	1	.223	.298	.296	.926
Yankee total		**17**	**39**	**3**	**8**	**2**	**0**	**2**	**6**	**4**	**—**	**6**	**0**	**0**	**—**	**1**	**0**	**.205**	**.279**	**.410**	**.915**

Bailey, Harry Lewis (Bill)

HEIGHT: 5'10"   THROWS: RIGHT   BATS: LEFT   BORN: 11/19/1881 SHAWNEE, OHIO   DIED: 10/27/1967 SEATTLE, WASHINGTON   POSITIONS PLAYED: 3B, OF

YEAR	TEAM	GAMES	AB	RUNS	HITS	2B	3B	HR	RBI	BB	IBB	SO	HBP	SH	SF	SB	CS	BA	OBA	SA	FA
1911	**NY-A**	**5**	**9**	**1**	**1**	**0**	**0**	**0**	**0**	**0**	**—**	**—**	**0**	**0**	**—**	**0**	**0**	**.111**	**.111**	**.111**	**.111**
Career average		5	9	1	1	0	0	0	0	0	—	—	0	0	—	0	0	.111	.111	.111	.111
Yankee average		**5**	**9**	**1**	**1**	**0**	**0**	**0**	**0**	**0**	**—**	**—**	**0**	**0**	**—**	**0**	**0**	**.111**	**.111**	**.111**	**.111**
Career total		5	9	1	1	0	0	0	0	0	—	—	0	0	—	0	0	.111	.111	.111	.111
Yankee total		**5**	**9**	**1**	**1**	**0**	**0**	**0**	**0**	**0**	**—**	**—**	**0**	**0**	**—**	**0**	**0**	**.111**	**.111**	**.111**	**.111**

Baker, John Franklin (Home Run)

HEIGHT: 5'11"   THROWS: RIGHT   BATS: LEFT   BORN: 3/13/1886 TRAPPE, MARYLAND   DIED: 6/28/1963 TRAPPE, MARYLAND   POSITIONS PLAYED: 3B

YEAR	TEAM	GAMES	AB	RUNS	HITS	2B	3B	HR	RBI	BB	IBB	SO	HBP	SH	SF	SB	CS	BA	OBA	SA	FA
1908	Phi-A	9	31	5	9	3	0	0	2	0	—	—	0	2	—	0	—	.290	.290	.387	1.000
1909	Phi-A	148	541	73	165	27	19	4	85	26	—	—	5	34	—	20	—	.305	.343	.447	.920
1910	Phi-A	146	561	83	159	25	15	2	74	34	—	—	4	21	—	21	—	.283	.329	.392	.920
1911	Phi-A	148	592	96	198	42	14	11	115	40	—	—	2	25	—	38	—	.334	.379	.508	.942
1912	Phi-A	149	577	116	200	40	21	10	130	50	—	—	6	11	—	40	—	.347	.404	.541	.941
1913	Phi-A	149	564	116	190	34	9	12	117	63	—	31	10	7	—	34	—	.337	.413	.493	.921
1914	Phi-A	150	570	84	182	23	10	9	89	53	—	37	3	8	—	19	20	.319	.380	.442	.955
1916	**NY-A**	**100**	**360**	**46**	**97**	**23**	**2**	**10**	**52**	**36**	**—**	**30**	**5**	**1**	**—**	**15**	**—**	**.269**	**.344**	**.428**	**.940**
1917	**NY-A**	**146**	**553**	**57**	**156**	**24**	**2**	**6**	**71**	**48**	**—**	**27**	**5**	**7**	**—**	**18**	**—**	**.282**	**.345**	**.365**	**.949**
1918	**NY-A**	**126**	**504**	**65**	**154**	**24**	**5**	**6**	**62**	**38**	**—**	**13**	**2**	**12**	**—**	**8**	**—**	**.306**	**.357**	**.409**	**.972**
1919	**NY-A**	**141**	**567**	**70**	**166**	**22**	**1**	**10**	**83**	**44**	**—**	**18**	**2**	**9**	**—**	**13**	**—**	**.293**	**.346**	**.388**	**.955**
1921	**NY-A**	**94**	**330**	**46**	**97**	**16**	**2**	**9**	**71**	**26**	**—**	**12**	**4**	**9**	**—**	**8**	**5**	**.294**	**.353**	**.436**	**.959**
1922	**NY-A**	**69**	**234**	**30**	**65**	**12**	**3**	**7**	**36**	**15**	**—**	**14**	**2**	**7**	**—**	**1**	**3**	**.278**	**.327**	**.444**	**.962**
Career average		121	460	68	141	24	8	7	76	36	—	—	4	12	—	18	—	.307	.363	.442	.949
Yankee average		**113**	**425**	**52**	**123**	**20**	**3**	**8**	**63**	**36**	**—**	**19**	**3**	**8**	**—**	**11**	**—**	**.288**	**.347**	**.404**	**.956**
Career total		1575	5984	887	1838	315	103	96	987	473	—	182	50	153	—	235	28	.307	.363	.442	.949
Yankee total		**676**	**2548**	**314**	**735**	**121**	**15**	**48**	**375**	**207**	**—**	**114**	**20**	**45**	**—**	**63**	**8**	**.288**	**.347**	**.404**	**.956**

John Franklin "Home Run" Baker, 3b, 1916–22

Frank Baker was the most feared slugger of the Dead Ball Era, and was actually known as the first real home-run hitter in the American League—long before a certain Yankee rightfielder ever stepped into the longball limelight.

Prior to his stint with the Yankees, Baker was a star for the Philadelphia Athletics from 1908 to 1914. In fact, the 1911 World Series was where his nickname originated. He drilled a two-run home run in the second game of the Series to give the Athletics a 3-1 win over the Giants on October 16, 1911. The next day, he belted a solo shot in the top of the ninth inning to tie the game with the Giants at 2-2. The A's went on to win that game 3-2 in 11 innings.

The A's went on to win that Series from Johnny McGraw's favored New York Giants, four games to two, and "Home Run" Baker was born.

Raised on a farm in Trappe, Maryland, Baker was signed by the Athletics in 1908 and had a stellar career with Philadelphia. He led or tied the league in home runs four straight years with the A's. But this was, of course, the Dead Ball Era. Baker's longball totals over that span were 11, 10, 12 and 9.

He was, initially, a fair to poor third baseman, plagued by a tendency to overthrow first base in his early years. But with hours of daily practice, Baker eventually shed that problem.

Baker was a part of Connie Mack's "$100,000 infield," along with first baseman Stuffy McInnis, second baseman Eddie "Cocky" Collins and shortstop Jack Barry.

But $100,000 was evidently as much as Mack was willing to pay his stars. When the newly minted Federal League began raiding both the National and American Leagues in 1914 and 1915, Mack began selling off his best players rather than get into a bidding war with what he and the rest of the baseball establishment at the time believed was an outlaw league.

Baker, however, was one of the players Mack wanted to hang onto. But rather than play for what he considered a lower salary, Baker held out in 1915 and eventually missed the entire season in the salary dispute. He made some money playing in a semi-pro league.

Mack finally sold him to the Yankees in 1916 for $37,500. This purchase was made at the beginning of the Jacob Ruppert years: The wealthy Ruppert wanted a winning team, and was more than willing to pay for it.

Baker was exactly the kind of player the Yankees needed at the time: a tough, savvy veteran who knew how to win and who knew how to help his team win as well.

Baker picked up in 1916 in New York where he left off in Philadelphia two years earlier. He was second in the league in home runs with ten, led the league in home run percentage and was fifth in slugging. He combined with Yankee first baseman Wally Pipp to give New York a fearful hitting duo. The Yankees, on the rise for the first time in their history, finished fourth in 1916 and third in 1919.

But in 1920, Baker was forced to put aside baseball again, this time to care for his ailing wife in the months prior to her death. He returned to the Yankees in 1921 and helped them win the American League pennant with a 98-56 record. Baker struck nine home runs in the 1921 campaign, but a Yankee outfielder by the name of Ruth led the league with 59.

The Yankees dropped the Series to the Giants that year, and again in 1922. But Baker was a solid performer for New York at third base throughout his Yankee career, averaging over 120 hits a year and regularly hitting about ten home runs a season (although, ironically, such production was no longer notable).

Interestingly, the King of the Deadball Homer, in his 13-year career, ended up with only 96 home runs.

Upon retirement, Baker managed briefly in the Eastern Shore League in 1924–25. He then returned to his farm in Trappe until his retirement. He was elected to the Hall of Fame in 1955 and died in 1963.

Balboni, Stephen Charles (Bones *or* Bye-Bye)

HEIGHT: 6'3" THROWS: RIGHT BATS: RIGHT BORN: 1/16/1957 BROCKTON, MASSACHUSETTS POSITIONS PLAYED: 1B

YEAR	TEAM	GAMES	AB	RUNS	HITS	2B	3B	HR	RBI	BB	IBB	SO	HBP	SH	SF	SB	CS	BA	OBA	SA	FA
1981	NY-A	4	7	2	2	1	1	0	2	1	0	4	0	0	0	0	0	.286	.375	.714	1.000
1982	NY-A	33	107	8	20	2	1	2	4	6	0	34	0	0	1	0	0	.187	.228	.280	.990
1983	NY-A	32	86	8	20	2	0	5	17	8	0	23	0	0	1	0	0	.233	.295	.430	.984
1984	KC-A	126	438	58	107	23	2	28	77	45	5	139	4	0	1	0	0	.244	.320	.498	.987
1985	KC-A	160	600	74	146	28	2	36	88	52	4	166	5	0	5	1	1	.243	.307	.477	.993
1986	KC-A	138	512	54	117	25	1	29	88	43	2	146	1	0	6	0	0	.229	.286	.451	.987
1987	KC-A	121	386	44	80	11	1	24	60	34	2	97	1	0	3	0	0	.207	.273	.427	.989
1988	KC-A	21	63	2	9	2	0	2	5	1	0	20	2	0	0	0	0	.143	.156	.270	.980
1988	Sea-A	97	350	44	88	15	1	21	61	23	2	67	1	0	2	0	1	.251	.299	.480	.994
1989	NY-A	110	300	33	71	12	2	17	59	25	2	67	3	0	6	0	0	.237	.296	.460	.994
1990	NY-A	116	266	24	51	6	0	17	34	35	2	91	3	1	2	0	0	.192	.291	.406	.984
1993	Tex-A	2	5	0	3	0	0	0	0	0	0	2	0	0	0	0	0	.600	.600	.600	.000
Career average		80	260	29	60	11	1	15	41	23	2	71	2	0	2	0	0	.229	.293	.451	.907
Yankee average		59	153	15	33	5	1	8	23	15	1	44	1	0	2	0	0	.214	.286	.415	.990
Career total		960	3120	351	714	127	11	181	495	273	21	856	19	1	27	1	2	.229	.293	.451	.907
Yankee total		295	766	75	164	23	4	41	116	75	7	219	6	1	10	0	0	.214	.286	.415	.990

Ball, Cornelius (Neal)

HEIGHT: 5'7" THROWS: RIGHT BATS: RIGHT BORN: 4/22/1881 GRAND HAVEN, MICH. DIED: 10/15/1957 BRIDGEPORT, CONN. POSITIONS PLAYED: 2B, 3B, SS

YEAR	TEAM	GAMES	AB	RUNS	HITS	2B	3B	HR	RBI	BB	IBB	SO	HBP	SH	SF	SB	CS	BA	OBA	SA	FA
1907	NY-A	15	44	5	9	1	1	0	4	1	—	—	0	2	—	1	—	.205	.222	.273	.817
1908	NY-A	132	446	34	110	16	2	0	38	21	—	—	2	15	—	32	—	.247	.284	.291	.898
1909	NY-A	8	29	5	6	1	1	0	3	3	—	—	0	2	—	2	—	.207	.281	.310	.917
1909	Cle-A	96	324	29	83	13	2	1	25	17	—	—	1	15	—	17	—	.256	.295	.318	.914
1910	Cle-A	53	119	13	25	3	1	0	12	9	—	—	0	6	—	4	—	.210	.266	.252	.927
1911	Cle-A	116	412	45	122	14	9	3	45	27	—	—	0	13	—	21	—	.296	.339	.396	.891
1912	Cle-A	40	132	12	30	4	1	0	14	9	—	—	0	4	—	7	—	.227	.277	.273	.938
1912	Bos-A	18	45	10	9	2	0	0	6	3	—	—	0	1	—	5	—	.200	.250	.244	.927
1913	Bos-A	23	58	9	10	2	0	0	4	9	—	13	1	2	—	3	—	.172	.294	.207	.902
Career average		56	179	18	45	6	2	0	17	11	—	—	0	7	—	10	—	.251	.296	.314	.903
Yankee average		52	173	15	42	6	1	0	15	8	—	—	1	6	—	12	—	.241	.278	.291	.877
Career total		501	1609	162	404	56	17	4	151	99	—	13	4	60	—	92	—	.251	.296	.314	.903
Yankee total		155	519	44	125	18	4	0	45	25	—	—	2	19	—	35	—	.241	.278	.291	.877

Barfield, Jesse Lee

HEIGHT: 6'1" THROWS: RIGHT BATS: RIGHT BORN: 10/29/1959, JOLIET, ILLINOIS POSITIONS PLAYED: OF

YEAR	TEAM	GAMES	AB	RUNS	HITS	2B	3B	HR	RBI	BB	IBB	SO	HBP	SH	SF	SB	CS	BA	OBA	SA	FA
1981	Tor-A	25	95	7	22	3	2	2	9	4	0	19	1	0	0	4	3	.232	.270	.368	1.000
1982	Tor-A	139	394	54	97	13	2	18	58	42	3	79	3	6	1	1	4	.246	.323	.426	.963
1983	Tor-A	128	388	58	98	13	3	27	68	22	0	110	4	1	3	2	5	.253	.300	.510	.966
1984	Tor-A	110	320	51	91	14	1	14	49	35	5	81	2	1	2	8	2	.284	.357	.466	.952
1985	Tor-A	155	539	94	156	34	9	27	84	66	5	143	4	0	3	22	8	.289	.369	.536	.989
1986	Tor-A	158	589	107	170	35	2	40	108	69	5	146	8	0	5	8	8	.289	.368	.559	.992
1987	Tor-A	159	590	89	155	25	3	28	84	58	7	141	3	1	2	3	5	.263	.331	.458	.992
1988	Tor-A	137	468	62	114	21	5	18	56	41	6	108	1	4	6	7	3	.244	.302	.425	.988
1989	Tor-A	21	80	8	16	4	0	5	11	5	0	28	1	0	0	0	2	.200	.256	.438	.979
1989	NY-A	129	441	71	106	19	1	18	56	82	6	122	2	1	3	5	3	.240	.362	.410	.972
1990	NY-A	153	476	69	117	21	2	25	78	82	4	150	5	2	5	4	3	.246	.359	.456	.973
1991	NY-A	84	284	37	64	12	0	17	48	36	6	80	0	0	1	1	0	.225	.312	.447	1.000
1992	NY-A	30	95	8	13	2	0	2	7	9	2	27	0	0	1	1	1	.137	.210	.221	.966
Career average		110	366	55	94	17	2	19	55	42	4	95	3	1	3	5	4	.256	.336	.466	.979
Yankee average		99	324	46	75	14	1	16	47	52	5	95	2	1	3	3	2	.231	.339	.421	.978
Career total		1428	4759	715	1219	216	30	241	716	551	49	1234	34	16	32	66	47	.256	.336	.466	.979
Yankee total		396	1296	185	300	54	3	62	189	209	18	379	7	3	10	11	7	.231	.339	.421	.978

Barker, Raymond Herrell (Buddy)

HEIGHT: 6'0"   THROWS: RIGHT   BATS: LEFT   BORN: 3/12/1936 MARTINSBURG, WEST VIRGINIA   POSITIONS PLAYED: 1B, 3B, OF

YEAR	TEAM	GAMES	AB	RUNS	HITS	2B	3B	HR	RBI	BB	IBB	SO	HBP	SH	SF	SB	CS	BA	OBA	SA	FA
1960	Bal-A	5	6	0	0	0	0	0	0	0	0	3	0	0	0	0	0	.000	.000	.000	.000
1965	Cle-A	11	6	0	0	0	0	0	2	1	1	2	0	0	0	0	0	.000	.250	.000	1.000
1965	NY-A	98	205	21	52	11	0	7	31	20	5	46	3	1	2	1	0	.254	.326	.410	.987
1966	NY-A	61	75	11	14	5	0	3	13	4	0	20	0	2	1	0	0	.187	.225	.373	.987
1967	NY-A	17	26	2	2	0	0	0	0	3	0	5	0	0	0	0	0	.077	.172	.077	.961
Career average		38	64	7	14	3	0	2	9	6	1	15	1	1	1	0	0	.214	.283	.358	.790
Yankee average		59	102	11	23	5	0	3	15	9	2	24	1	1	1	0	0	.222	.289	.373	.983
Career total		192	318	34	68	16	0	10	44	29	6	76	3	3	3	1	0	.214	.283	.358	.790
Yankee total		176	306	34	68	16	0	10	44	27	5	71	3	3	3	1	0	.222	.289	.373	.983

Barnes, John Francis (Honey)

HEIGHT: 5'10"   THROWS: RIGHT   BATS: LEFT   BORN: 1/30/1900 FULTON, NEW YORK   DIED: 6/18/1981 LOCKPORT, NEW YORK   POSITIONS PLAYED: C

YEAR	TEAM	GAMES	AB	RUNS	HITS	2B	3B	HR	RBI	BB	IBB	SO	HBP	SH	SF	SB	CS	BA	OBA	SA	FA
1926	NY-A	1	0	0	0	0	0	0	0	1	0	0	0	0	0	0	0	.000	1.000	.000	.000
Career average		1	0	0	0	0	0	0	0	1	0	0	0	0	0	0	0	.000	1.000	.000	.000
Yankee average		1	0	0	0	0	0	0	0	1	0	0	0	0	0	0	0	.000	1.000	.000	.000
Career total		1	0	0	0	0	0	0	0	1	0	0	0	0	0	0	0	.000	1.000	.000	.000
Yankee total		1	0	0	0	0	0	0	0	1	0	0	0	0	0	0	0	.000	1.000	.000	.000

Barney, Edmund J.

HEIGHT: 5'10"   THROWS: RIGHT   BATS: LEFT   BORN: 1/23/1890 AMERY, WISCONSIN   DIED: 10/4/1967 RICE LAKE, WISCONSIN   POSITIONS PLAYED: OF

YEAR	TEAM	GAMES	AB	RUNS	HITS	2B	3B	HR	RBI	BB	IBB	SO	HBP	SH	SF	SB	CS	BA	OBA	SA	FA
1915	NY-A	11	36	1	7	0	0	0	8	3	—	6	0	1	—	2	1	.194	.256	.194	1.000
1915	Pit-N	32	99	16	27	1	2	0	5	11	—	12	3	4	—	7	3	.273	.363	.323	.972
1916	Pit-N	45	137	16	27	4	0	0	9	23	—	15	0	6	—	8	—	.197	.313	.226	.964
Career average		29	91	11	20	2	1	0	7	12	—	11	1	4	—	6	—	.224	.324	.257	.979
Yankee average		11	36	1	7	0	0	0	8	3	—	6	0	1	—	2	1	.194	.256	.194	1.000
Career total		88	272	33	61	5	2	0	22	37	—	33	3	11	—	17	4	.224	.324	.257	.979
Yankee total		11	36	1	7	0	0	0	8	3	—	6	0	1	—	2	1	.194	.256	.194	1.000

Batten, George Burnett

HEIGHT: 5'11"   THROWS: RIGHT   BATS: RIGHT   BORN: 10/7/1891 HADDONFIELD, NEW JERSEY   DIED: 8/4/1972 NEW PORT RICHEY, FLORIDA   POSITIONS PLAYED: 2B

YEAR	TEAM	GAMES	AB	RUNS	HITS	2B	3B	HR	RBI	BB	IBB	SO	HBP	SH	SF	SB	CS	BA	OBA	SA	FA
1912	NY-A	1	3	0	0	0	0	0	0	0	0	0	0	0	0	0	0	.000	.000	.000	1.000
Career average		1	3	0	0	0	0	0	0	0	0	0	0	0	0	0	0	.000	.000	.000	1.000
Yankee average		1	3	0	0	0	0	0	0	0	0	0	0	0	0	0	0	.000	.000	.000	1.000
Career total		1	3	0	0	0	0	0	0	0	0	0	0	0	0	0	0	.000	.000	.000	1.000
Yankee total		1	3	0	0	0	0	0	0	0	0	0	0	0	0	0	0	.000	.000	.000	1.000

Bauer, Henry Albert (Hank)

HEIGHT: 6'0"   THROWS: RIGHT   BATS: RIGHT   BORN: 7/31/1922 E. ST. LOUIS, ILLINOIS   POSITIONS PLAYED: OF

YEAR	TEAM	GAMES	AB	RUNS	HITS	2B	3B	HR	RBI	BB	IBB	SO	HBP	SH	SF	SB	CS	BA	OBA	SA	FA
1948	NY-A	19	50	6	9	1	1	1	9	6	—	13	0	0	—	1	0	.180	.268	.300	.964
1949	NY-A	103	301	56	82	6	6	10	45	37	—	42	1	5	—	2	2	.272	.354	.432	.977
1950	NY-A	113	415	72	133	16	2	10	70	35	—	41	5	3	—	2	3	.320	.380	.463	.987
1951	NY-A	118	348	53	103	19	3	10	54	42	—	39	1	3	—	5	2	.296	.373	.454	.990
1952	NY-A	141	553	86	162	31	6	17	74	50	—	61	3	9	—	6	7	.293	.355	.446	.992
1953	NY-A	133	437	77	133	20	6	10	57	59	—	45	6	1	—	2	3	.304	.394	.446	.992
1954	NY-A	114	377	73	111	16	5	12	54	40	—	42	0	3	3	4	4	.294	.360	.459	.989
1955	NY-A	139	492	97	137	20	5	20	53	56	1	65	8	4	3	8	4	.278	.360	.461	.981

(continued)

Henry Albert "Hank" Bauer, of, 1948–59

When Hank Bauer drew a walk, he would run to first base. He, more than Pete Rose (who would not be in the majors for 20 more years), was the original "Charlie Hustle."

Bauer, born in East St. Louis, Missouri, in 1922, was a gruff, tough ballplayer whose game face, according to sportswriter Jim Murray, "resembled a clenched fist." Yet Bauer, despite his ferocious look, was a cool customer in close games. More often than not, he would make the big hit in a big game.

He became a Yankee in 1948 and spent 12 of his 14 years in the bigs in New York City. A tremendously sound fundamental player, Bauer rarely made a mistake, particularly on defense. In the Yankees' astonishing five-year World Series streak from 1949–53, Bauer totaled 15 errors in 578 games in the outfield.

Offensively he hit over .290 five times as a Yankee, and led the team in hitting in 1953 with a .304 average. He was not overwhelmingly fast, but adjudged by most observers to be a smart base runner. Four times in his career he led the Yankees in triples, and he led the league in that category in 1958. He also led the

Yankees in doubles in 1958.

His career was solid enough to earn him three appearances in the annual All-Star game during his Yankees years: 1952–54.

Bauer played in nine World Series with the Yankees, and was on the winning side in seven of them. His best Series was in 1958, when he smacked four home runs in the Yankees' thrilling, come-from-behind 4-3 win over Hank Aaron's Milwaukee Braves. It was the first time since 1925 that a team had rallied from a 3-1 deficit in games to win the Series.

He was one of the Yankees' money players, and in fact, at the beginning of each World Series, he would remind his teammates to play well, because "it's my money you're playing with," referring to a potential World Series winning share. They usually did. No one liked to mess with Bauer.

In December 1959, he, Norman Siebern and the immortal Marvin Throneberry were traded to Kansas City for several players, among them Roger Maris. He played two more years with the A's before retiring to manage. His managerial career lasted eight years with the Orioles, Royals and Athletics. In 1966, he managed the Orioles to a World Series Championship.

(continued)

Year	Team	G	AB	R	H	2B	3B	HR	RBI	BB	HBP	SO	SB	CS	SH	SF	GDP	AVG	OBP	SLG	OPS
1956	NY-A	147	539	96	130	18	7	26	84	59	3	72	2	7	5	4	2	.241	.316	.445	.969
1957	NY-A	137	479	70	124	22	9	18	65	42	4	64	4	6	4	7	2	.259	.321	.455	.986
1958	NY-A	128	452	62	121	22	6	12	50	32	1	56	1	3	2	3	2	.268	.316	.423	.980
1959	NY-A	114	341	44	81	20	0	9	39	33	1	54	2	2	2	4	2	.238	.307	.375	.972
1960	KC-A	95	255	30	70	15	0	3	31	21	1	36	1	3	5	1	0	.275	.326	.369	.978
1961	KC-A	43	106	11	28	3	1	3	18	9	0	8	0	2	1	1	0	.264	.319	.396	.958
Career average		110	368	60	102	16	4	12	50	37	1	46	2	4	2	4	2	.277	.346	.439	.979
Yankee average		**117**	**399**	**66**	**111**	**18**	**5**	**13**	**55**	**41**	**1**	**50**	**3**	**4**	**2**	**4**	**3**	**.277**	**.347**	**.444**	**.981**
Career total		1544	5145	833	1424	229	57	164	703	521	11	638	34	51	25	50	33	.277	.346	.439	.979
Yankee total		**1406**	**4784**	**792**	**1326**	**211**	**56**	**158**	**654**	**491**	**10**	**594**	**33**	**46**	**19**	**48**	**33**	**.277**	**.347**	**.444**	**.981**

Baumann, Charles John (Paddy)

HEIGHT: 5'9"   THROWS: RIGHT   BATS: RIGHT   BORN: 12/20/1885 INDIANAPOLIS, IND.   DIED: 11/20/1969 INDIANAPOLIS, IND.   POSITIONS PLAYED: 2B, 3B, OF

YEAR	TEAM	GAMES	AB	RUNS	HITS	2B	3B	HR	RBI	BB	IBB	SO	HBP	SH	SF	SB	CS	BA	OBA	SA	FA
1911	Det-A	26	94	8	24	2	4	0	11	6	—	—	1	4	—	1	—	.255	.307	.362	1.000
1912	Det-A	16	42	3	11	1	0	0	7	6	—	—	0	0	—	4	—	.262	.354	.286	.786
1913	Det-A	50	191	31	57	7	4	1	22	16	—	18	0	10	—	4	—	.298	.353	.393	.943
1914	Det-A	3	11	1	0	0	0	0	0	2	—	1	0	1	—	0	0	.000	.154	.000	1.000
1915	**NY-A**	**76**	**219**	**30**	**64**	**13**	**1**	**2**	**28**	**28**	**—**	**32**	**3**	**10**	**—**	**9**	**10**	**.292**	**.380**	**.388**	**.980**
1916	**NY-A**	**79**	**237**	**35**	**68**	**5**	**3**	**1**	**25**	**19**	**—**	**16**	**5**	**5**	**—**	**10**	**—**	**.287**	**.352**	**.346**	**.933**
1917	**NY-A**	**49**	**110**	**10**	**24**	**2**	**1**	**0**	**8**	**4**	**—**	**9**	**0**	**1**	**—**	**2**	**—**	**.218**	**.246**	**.255**	**.941**
Career average		43	129	17	35	4	2	1	14	12	—	11	1	4	—	4	—	.274	.340	.350	.940
Yankee average		**68**	**189**	**25**	**52**	**7**	**2**	**1**	**20**	**17**	**—**	**19**	**3**	**5**	**—**	**7**	**—**	**.276**	**.344**	**.345**	**.951**
Career total		299	904	118	248	30	13	4	101	81	—	76	9	31	—	30	10	.274	.340	.350	.940
Yankee total		**204**	**566**	**75**	**156**	**20**	**5**	**3**	**61**	**51**	**—**	**57**	**8**	**16**	**—**	**21**	**10**	**.276**	**.344**	**.345**	**.951**

Baylor, Don Edward

HEIGHT: 6'1"   THROWS: RIGHT   BATS: RIGHT   BORN: 6/28/1949, AUSTIN, TEXAS   POSITIONS PLAYED: 1B, OF, DH

YEAR	TEAM	GAMES	AB	RUNS	HITS	2B	3B	HR	RBI	BB	IBB	SO	HBP	SH	SF	SB	CS	BA	OBA	SA	FA
1970	Bal-A	8	17	4	4	0	0	0	4	2	0	3	0	0	1	1	1	.235	.300	.235	1.000
1971	Bal-A	1	2	0	0	0	0	0	1	2	0	1	1	0	0	0	0	.000	.600	.000	1.000
1972	Bal-A	102	320	33	81	13	3	11	38	29	0	50	9	2	3	24	2	.253	.330	.416	.982
1973	Bal-A	118	405	64	116	20	4	11	51	35	3	48	13	0	6	32	9	.286	.357	.437	.981
1974	Bal-A	137	489	66	133	22	1	10	59	43	6	56	10	3	4	29	12	.272	.341	.382	.978
1975	Bal-A	145	524	79	148	21	6	25	76	53	8	64	13	4	4	32	17	.282	.360	.489	1.000
1976	Oak-A	157	595	85	147	25	1	15	68	58	4	72	20	1	11	52	12	.247	.329	.368	.981
1977	Cal-A	154	561	87	141	27	0	25	75	62	7	76	12	2	8	26	12	.251	.334	.433	.966
1978	Cal-A	158	591	103	151	26	0	34	99	56	9	71	18	0	12	22	9	.255	.332	.472	.974
1979	Cal-A	162	628	120	186	33	3	36	139	71	6	51	11	0	12	22	12	.296	.371	.530	.976
1980	Cal-A	90	340	39	85	12	2	5	51	24	4	32	11	0	5	6	6	.250	.316	.341	.969
1981	Cal-A	103	377	52	90	18	1	17	66	42	1	51	7	0	6	3	3	.239	.322	.427	1.000
1982	Cal-A	157	608	80	160	24	1	24	93	57	7	69	7	0	8	10	4	.263	.329	.424	.000
1983	**NY-A**	**144**	**534**	**82**	**162**	**33**	**3**	**21**	**85**	**40**	**11**	**53**	**13**	**2**	**8**	**17**	**7**	**.303**	**.361**	**.494**	**.938**
1984	**NY-A**	**134**	**493**	**84**	**129**	**29**	**1**	**27**	**89**	**38**	**6**	**68**	**23**	**1**	**3**	**1**	**1**	**.262**	**.341**	**.489**	**.889**
1985	**NY-A**	**142**	**477**	**70**	**110**	**24**	**1**	**23**	**91**	**52**	**6**	**90**	**24**	**1**	**10**	**0**	**4**	**.231**	**.330**	**.430**	**.000**
1986	Bos-A	160	585	93	139	23	1	31	94	62	8	111	35	0	5	3	5	.238	.344	.439	1.000
1987	Bos-A	108	339	64	81	8	0	16	57	40	3	47	24	0	6	5	2	.239	.360	.404	.000
1987	Min-A	20	49	3	14	1	0	0	6	5	0	12	4	0	0	0	1	.286	.397	.306	.000
1988	Oak-A	92	264	28	58	7	0	7	34	34	2	44	12	0	3	0	1	.220	.335	.326	.000
Career average		115	410	62	107	18	1	17	64	40	5	54	13	1	6	14	6	.260	.342	.436	.732
Yankee average		**140**	**501**	**79**	**134**	**29**	**2**	**24**	**88**	**43**	**8**	**70**	**20**	**1**	**7**	**6**	**4**	**.267**	**.345**	**.472**	**.609**
Career total		2292	8198	1236	2135	366	28	338	1276	805	91	1069	267	16	115	285	120	.260	.342	.436	.732
Yankee total		**420**	**1504**	**236**	**401**	**86**	**5**	**71**	**265**	**130**	**23**	**211**	**60**	**4**	**21**	**18**	**12**	**.267**	**.345**	**.472**	**.609**

Beck, Zinn Bertram

HEIGHT: 5'10"   THROWS: RIGHT   BATS: RIGHT   BORN: 9/30/1885 STEUBENVILLE, OHIO   DIED: 3/19/1981 W. PALM BEACH, FLORIDA   POSITIONS PLAYED: 1B, 2B, 3B, SS

YEAR	TEAM	GAMES	AB	RUNS	HITS	2B	3B	HR	RBI	BB	IBB	SO	HBP	SH	SF	SB	CS	BA	OBA	SA	FA
1913	StL-N	10	30	4	5	1	0	0	2	4	—	10	0	2	—	1	—	.167	.265	.200	.833
1914	StL-N	137	457	42	106	15	11	3	45	28	—	32	4	15	—	14	—	.232	.282	.333	.935
1915	StL-N	70	223	21	52	9	4	0	15	12	—	31	3	7	—	3	10	.233	.282	.309	.935
1916	StL-N	62	184	8	41	7	1	0	10	14	—	21	1	2	—	3	—	.223	.281	.272	.910
1918	**NY-A**	**11**	**8**	**0**	**0**	**0**	**0**	**0**	**1**	**0**	**—**	**1**	**0**	**3**	**—**	**0**	**—**	**.000**	**.000**	**.000**	**1.000**
Career average		58	180	15	41	6	3	1	15	12	—	19	2	6	—	4	—	.226	.279	.307	.923
Yankee average		**11**	**8**	**0**	**0**	**0**	**0**	**0**	**1**	**0**	**—**	**1**	**0**	**3**	**—**	**0**	**—**	**.000**	**.000**	**.000**	**1.000**
Career total		290	902	75	204	32	16	3	73	58	—	95	8	29	—	21	10	.226	.279	.307	.923
Yankee total		**11**	**8**	**0**	**0**	**0**	**0**	**0**	**1**	**0**	**—**	**1**	**0**	**3**	**—**	**0**	**—**	**.000**	**.000**	**.000**	**1.000**

Bell, John (Rudy) BORN RUDOLPH FRED BAERWALD
HEIGHT: 5'8" THROWS: RIGHT BATS: RIGHT BORN: 1/1/1881 WAUSAU, WISCONSIN DIED: 7/28/1955 ALBUQUERQUE, NEW MEXICO POSITIONS PLAYED: OF

YEAR	TEAM	GAMES	AB	RUNS	HITS	2B	3B	HR	RBI	BB	IBB	SO	HBP	SH	SF	SB	CS	BA	OBA	SA	FA
1907	NY-A	17	52	4	11	2	1	0	3	3	—	—	1	3	—	4	—	.212	.268	.288	.897
Career average		17	52	4	11	2	1	0	3	3	—	—	1	3	—	4	—	.212	.268	.288	.897
Yankee average		17	52	4	11	2	1	0	3	3	—	—	1	3	—	4	—	.212	.268	.288	.897
Career total		17	52	4	11	2	1	0	3	3	—	—	1	3	—	4	—	.212	.268	.288	.897
Yankee total		17	52	4	11	2	1	0	3	3	—	—	1	3	—	4	—	.212	.268	.288	.897

Bella, John (Zeke)
HEIGHT: 5'11" THROWS: LEFT BATS: RIGHT BORN: 8/23/1930 GREENWICH, CONNECTICUT POSITIONS PLAYED: OF

YEAR	TEAM	GAMES	AB	RUNS	HITS	2B	3B	HR	RBI	BB	IBB	SO	HBP	SH	SF	SB	CS	BA	OBA	SA	FA
1957	NY-A	5	10	0	1	0	0	0	0	1	0	2	0	0	0	0	0	.100	.182	.100	1.000
1959	KC-A	47	82	10	17	2	1	1	9	9	0	14	1	1	0	0	0	.207	.293	.293	1.000
Career average		26	46	5	9	1	1	1	5	5	0	8	1	1	0	0	0	.196	.282	.272	1.000
Yankee average		5	10	0	1	0	0	0	0	1	0	2	0	0	0	0	0	.100	.182	.100	1.000
Career total		52	92	10	18	2	1	1	9	10	0	16	1	1	0	0	0	.196	.282	.272	1.000
Yankee total		5	10	0	1	0	0	0	0	1	0	2	0	0	0	0	0	.100	.182	.100	1.000

Bellinger, Clayton Daniel (Clay)
HEIGHT: 6'3" THROWS: RIGHT BATS: RIGHT BORN: 11/18/1968 ONEONTA, NEW YORK POSITIONS PLAYED: 1B, OF

YEAR	TEAM	GAMES	AB	RUNS	HITS	2B	3B	HR	RBI	BB	IBB	SO	HBP	SH	SF	SB	CS	BA	OBA	SA	FA
1999	NY-A	32	45	12	9	2	0	1	2	1	0	10	0	0	0	1	0	.200	.217	.311	1.000
2000	NY-A	98	184	33	38	8	2	6	21	17	1	48	5	1	2	6	0	.207	.288	.370	.968
Career average		65	115	23	24	5	1	4	12	9	1	29	3	1	1	4	0	.205	.276	.358	.984
Yankee average		65	115	23	24	5	1	4	12	9	1	29	3	1	1	4	0	.205	.276	.358	.984
Career total		130	229	45	47	10	2	7	23	18	1	58	5	1	2	7	0	.205	.276	.358	.984
Yankee total		130	229	45	47	10	2	7	23	18	1	58	5	1	2	7	0	.205	.276	.358	.984

Bengough, Bernard Oliver (Benny)
HEIGHT: 5'7" THROWS: RIGHT BATS: RIGHT BORN: 7/27/1898 NIAGARA FALLS, NEW YORK DIED: 12/22/1968 PHILADELPHIA, PENNSYLVANIA POSITIONS PLAYED: C

YEAR	TEAM	GAMES	AB	RUNS	HITS	2B	3B	HR	RBI	BB	IBB	SO	HBP	SH	SF	SB	CS	BA	OBA	SA	FA
1923	NY-A	19	53	1	7	2	0	0	3	4	—	2	0	1	—	0	0	.132	.193	.170	.973
1924	NY-A	11	16	4	5	1	1	0	3	2	—	0	0	1	—	0	0	.313	.389	.500	1.000
1925	NY-A	95	283	17	73	14	2	0	23	19	—	9	0	6	—	0	2	.258	.305	.322	.993
1926	NY-A	36	84	9	32	6	0	0	14	7	—	4	1	3	—	1	0	.381	.435	.452	.973
1927	NY-A	31	85	6	21	3	3	0	10	4	—	4	0	1	—	0	3	.247	.281	.353	.986
1928	NY-A	58	161	12	43	3	1	0	9	7	—	8	1	1	—	0	0	.267	.302	.298	.992
1929	NY-A	23	62	5	12	2	1	0	7	0	—	2	0	0	—	0	0	.194	.194	.258	.982
1930	NY-A	44	102	10	24	4	2	0	12	3	—	8	0	4	—	1	0	.235	.257	.314	.990
1931	StL-A	40	140	6	35	4	1	0	12	4	—	4	0	0	—	0	3	.250	.271	.293	.986
1932	StL-A	54	139	13	35	7	1	0	15	12	—	4	0	0	—	0	1	.252	.311	.317	.989
Career average		41	113	8	29	5	1	0	11	6	—	5	0	2	—	0	1	.255	.295	.317	.986
Yankee average		40	106	8	27	4	1	0	11	6	—	5	0	2	—	0	1	.257	.296	.322	.986
Career total		411	1125	83	287	46	12	0	108	62	—	45	2	17	—	2	9	.255	.295	.317	.986
Yankee total		317	846	64	217	35	10	0	81	46	—	37	2	17	—	2	5	.257	.296	.322	.986

Beniquez, Juan Jose BORN JUAN JOSE BENIQUEZ (TORRES)
HEIGHT: 5'11" THROWS: RIGHT BATS: RIGHT BORN: 5/13/1950 SAN SEBASTIAN, PUERTO RICO POSITIONS PLAYED: 1B, 2B, SS, OF

YEAR	TEAM	GAMES	AB	RUNS	HITS	2B	3B	HR	RBI	BB	IBB	SO	HBP	SH	SF	SB	CS	BA	OBA	SA	FA
1971	Bos-A	16	57	8	17	2	0	0	4	3	0	4	0	3	0	3	1	.298	.333	.333	.895
1972	Bos-A	33	99	10	24	4	1	1	8	7	0	11	0	0	2	2	0	.242	.287	.333	.900
1974	Bos-A	106	389	60	104	14	3	5	33	25	2	61	1	7	1	19	11	.267	.313	.357	.978
1975	Bos-A	78	254	43	74	14	4	2	17	25	1	26	2	6	1	7	10	.291	.358	.402	.991

(continued)

(continued)

YEAR	TEAM	GAMES	AB	RUNS	HITS	2B	3B	HR	RBI	BB	IBB	SO	HBP	SH	SF	SB	CS	BA	OBA	SA	FA
1976	Tex-A	145	478	49	122	14	4	0	33	39	1	56	3	5	1	17	6	.255	.315	.301	.500
1977	Tex-A	123	424	56	114	19	6	10	50	43	0	43	1	8	2	26	18	.269	.336	.413	.988
1978	Tex-A	127	473	61	123	17	3	11	50	20	1	59	1	10	4	10	12	.260	.292	.378	.972
1979	**NY-A**	**62**	**142**	**19**	**36**	**6**	**1**	**4**	**17**	**9**	**0**	**17**	**2**	**1**	**4**	**3**	**3**	**.254**	**.299**	**.394**	**1.000**
1980	Sea-A	70	237	26	54	10	0	6	21	17	0	25	0	3	1	2	3	.228	.278	.346	.957
1981	Cal-A	58	166	18	30	5	0	3	13	15	0	16	1	4	1	2	1	.181	.251	.265	.959
1982	Cal-A	112	196	25	52	11	2	3	24	15	1	21	1	16	0	3	0	.265	.321	.388	.983
1983	Cal-A	92	315	44	96	15	0	3	34	15	0	29	4	6	1	4	2	.305	.343	.381	.968
1984	Cal-A	110	354	60	119	17	0	8	39	18	0	43	3	4	3	0	3	.336	.370	.452	.971
1985	Cal-A	132	411	54	125	13	5	8	42	34	3	46	5	9	1	4	3	.304	.364	.418	.988
1986	Bal-A	113	343	48	103	15	0	6	36	40	1	49	3	2	6	2	3	.300	.372	.397	.990
1987	KC-A	57	174	14	41	7	0	3	26	11	1	26	1	2	2	0	0	.236	.282	.328	.875
1987	Tor-A	39	81	6	23	5	1	5	21	5	0	13	1	0	1	0	0	.284	.333	.556	.000
1988	Tor-A	27	58	9	17	2	0	1	8	8	0	6	0	1	1	0	0	.293	.373	.379	
Career average		83	258	34	71	11	2	4	26	19	1	31	2	5	2	6	4	.274	.327	.379	.884
Yankee average		**62**	**142**	**19**	**36**	**6**	**1**	**4**	**17**	**9**	**0**	**17**	**2**	**1**	**4**	**3**	**3**	**.254**	**.299**	**.394**	**1.000**
Career total		1500	4651	610	1274	190	30	79	476	349	11	551	31	87	32	104	76	.274	.327	.379	.884
Yankee total		**62**	**142**	**19**	**36**	**6**	**1**	**4**	**17**	**9**	**0**	**17**	**2**	**1**	**4**	**3**	**3**	**.254**	**.299**	**.394**	**1.000**

Berberet, Louis Joseph

HEIGHT: 5'11"   THROWS: RIGHT   BATS: LEFT   BORN: 11/20/1929, LONG BEACH, CALIFORNIA   POSITIONS PLAYED: C

YEAR	TEAM	GAMES	AB	RUNS	HITS	2B	3B	HR	RBI	BB	IBB	SO	HBP	SH	SF	SB	CS	BA	OBA	SA	FA
1954	**NY-A**	**5**	**5**	**1**	**2**	**0**	**0**	**0**	**3**	**1**	**0**	**1**	**0**	**0**	**0**	**0**	**0**	**.400**	**.500**	**.400**	**1.000**
1955	**NY-A**	**2**	**5**	**1**	**2**	**0**	**0**	**0**	**2**	**1**	**0**	**0**	**0**	**0**	**0**	**0**	**0**	**.400**	**.500**	**.400**	**1.000**
1956	Was-A	95	207	25	54	6	3	4	27	46	9	33	3	0	0	0	0	.261	.402	.377	.997
1957	Was-A	99	264	24	69	11	2	7	36	41	5	38	2	1	5	0	1	.261	.359	.398	1.000
1958	Was-A	5	6	0	1	0	0	0	0	4	0	1	0	0	0	0	0	.167	.500	.167	.917
1958	Bos-A	57	167	11	35	5	3	2	18	31	1	32	1	1	0	0	2	.210	.337	.311	.984
1959	Det-A	100	338	38	73	8	2	13	44	35	1	59	0	0	7	0	0	.216	.284	.367	.989
1960	Det-A	85	232	18	45	4	0	5	23	41	4	31	1	0	4	2	0	.194	.313	.276	.993
Career average		56	153	15	35	4	1	4	19	25	3	24	1	0	2	0	0	.230	.337	.350	.985
Yankee average		**4**	**5**	**1**	**2**	**0**	**0**	**0**	**3**	**1**	**0**	**1**	**0**	**0**	**0**	**0**	**0**	**.400**	**.500**	**.400**	**1.000**
Career total		448	1224	118	281	34	10	31	153	200	20	195	7	2	16	2	3	.230	.337	.350	.985
Yankee total		**7**	**10**	**2**	**4**	**0**	**0**	**0**	**5**	**2**	**0**	**1**	**0**	**0**	**0**	**0**	**0**	**.400**	**.500**	**.400**	**1.000**

Bergman, David Bruce

HEIGHT: 6'1"   THROWS: LEFT   BATS: LEFT   BORN: 6/6/1953 EVANSTON, ILLINOIS   POSITIONS PLAYED: 1B, OF

YEAR	TEAM	GAMES	AB	RUNS	HITS	2B	3B	HR	RBI	BB	IBB	SO	HBP	SH	SF	SB	CS	BA	OBA	SA	FA
1975	**NY-A**	**7**	**17**	**0**	**0**	**0**	**0**	**0**	**0**	**2**	**0**	**4**	**0**	**0**	**0**	**0**	**0**	**.000**	**.105**	**.000**	**.917**
1977	**NY-A**	**5**	**4**	**1**	**1**	**0**	**0**	**0**	**1**	**0**	**0**	**0**	**0**	**1**	**0**	**0**	**0**	**.250**	**.200**	**.250**	**1.000**
1978	Hou-N	104	186	15	43	5	1	0	12	39	9	32	0	1	2	2	0	.231	.361	.269	.993
1979	Hou-N	13	15	4	6	0	1	1	2	0	0	3	0	0	0	0	0	.400	.400	.600	1.000
1980	Hou-N	90	78	12	20	6	1	0	3	10	2	10	0	3	0	1	0	.256	.341	.359	1.000
1981	Hou-N	6	6	1	1	0	0	1	1	0	0	0	0	0	0	0	0	.167	.167	.667	1.000
1981	SF-N	63	145	16	37	9	0	3	13	19	3	18	0	2	1	2	0	.255	.339	.379	.952
1982	SF-N	100	121	22	33	3	1	4	14	18	3	11	0	0	1	3	0	.273	.364	.413	.991
1983	SF-N	90	140	16	40	4	1	6	24	24	2	21	1	2	0	2	1	.286	.394	.457	.994
1984	Det-A	120	271	42	74	8	5	7	44	33	2	40	3	3	6	3	4	.273	.351	.417	.989
1985	Det-A	69	140	8	25	2	0	3	7	14	0	15	0	1	2	0	0	.179	.257	.257	.991
1986	Det-A	65	130	14	30	6	1	1	9	21	0	16	0	0	0	0	0	.231	.338	.315	.986
1987	Det-A	91	172	25	47	7	3	6	22	30	4	23	1	1	3	0	1	.273	.379	.453	1.000
1988	Det-A	116	289	37	85	14	0	5	35	38	2	34	0	2	4	0	2	.294	.372	.394	1.000
1989	Det-A	137	385	38	103	13	1	7	37	44	3	44	2	4	1	1	3	.268	.345	.361	.993
1990	Det-A	100	205	21	57	10	1	2	26	33	3	17	0	1	2	3	2	.278	.375	.366	.995
1991	Det-A	86	194	23	46	10	1	7	29	35	2	40	0	0	2	1	1	.237	.351	.407	1.000
1992	Det-A	87	181	17	42	3	0	1	10	20	1	19	0	1	2	1	0	.232	.305	.265	.986
Career average		75	149	17	38	6	1	3	16	21	2	19	0	1	2	1	1	.258	.348	.367	.988
Yankee average		**6**	**11**	**1**	**1**	**0**	**0**	**0**	**1**	**1**	**0**	**2**	**0**	**0**	**1**	**0**	**0**	**.048**	**.125**	**.048**	**.959**
Career total		1349	2679	312	690	100	16	54	289	380	36	347	7	21	27	19	14	.258	.348	.367	.988
Yankee total		**12**	**21**	**1**	**1**	**0**	**0**	**0**	**1**	**2**	**0**	**4**	**0**	**0**	**1**	**0**	**0**	**.048**	**.125**	**.048**	**.959**

Bernhardt, Juan Ramon   BORN JUAN RAMON BERNHARDT (CORADIN)

HEIGHT: 5'11"   THROWS: RIGHT   BATS: RIGHT   BORN: 8/31/1953 SAN PEDRO DE MACORIS, DOMINICAN REPUBLIC   POSITIONS PLAYED: 1B, 3B, DH

YEAR	TEAM	GAMES	AB	RUNS	HITS	2B	3B	HR	RBI	BB	IBB	SO	HBP	SH	SF	SB	CS	BA	OBA	SA	FA
1976	**NY-A**	**10**	**21**	**1**	**4**	**1**	**0**	**0**	**1**	**0**	**0**	**4**	**0**	**0**	**0**	**0**	**0**	**.190**	**.190**	**.238**	**.800**
1977	Sea-A	89	305	32	74	9	2	7	30	5	0	26	2	4	1	2	3	.243	.259	.354	.982
1978	Sea-A	54	165	13	38	9	0	2	12	9	1	10	1	4	3	1	1	.230	.270	.321	.989
1979	Sea-A	1	1	0	1	0	0	0	0	0	0	0	0	0	0	0	0	1.000	1.000	1.000	.000
Career average		39	123	12	29	5	1	2	11	4	0	10	1	2	1	1	1	.238	.261	.339	.693
Yankee average		**10**	**21**	**1**	**4**	**1**	**0**	**0**	**1**	**0**	**0**	**4**	**0**	**0**	**0**	**0**	**0**	**.190**	**.190**	**.238**	**.800**
Career total		154	492	46	117	19	2	9	43	14	1	40	3	8	4	3	4	.238	.261	.339	.693
Yankee total		**10**	**21**	**1**	**4**	**1**	**0**	**0**	**1**	**0**	**0**	**4**	**0**	**0**	**0**	**0**	**0**	**.190**	**.190**	**.238**	**.800**

Berra, Dale Anthony

HEIGHT: 6'0"   THROWS: RIGHT   BATS: RIGHT   BORN: 12/13/1956 RIDGEWOOD, NEW JERSEY   POSITIONS PLAYED: 2B, 3B, SS

YEAR	TEAM	GAMES	AB	RUNS	HITS	2B	3B	HR	RBI	BB	IBB	SO	HBP	SH	SF	SB	CS	BA	OBA	SA	FA
1977	Pit-N	17	40	0	7	1	0	0	3	1	0	8	0	0	0	0	0	.195	.175	.200	.973
1978	Pit-N	56	135	16	28	2	0	6	14	13	3	20	2	0	1	3	1	.285	.207	.356	1.000
1979	Pit-N	44	123	11	26	5	0	3	15	11	2	17	0	2	2	0	0	.272	.211	.325	.879
1980	Pit-N	93	245	21	54	8	2	6	31	16	6	52	1	4	2	2		.269	.220	.343	1.000
1981	Pit-N	81	232	21	56	12	0	2	27	17	4	34	3	2	0	11	1	.302	.241	.319	1.000
1982	Pit-N	156	529	64	139	25	5	10	61	33	12	83	4	8	9	6	6	.306	.263	.386	1.000
1983	Pit-N	161	537	51	135	25	1	10	52	61	19	84	0	7	2	8	5	.327	.251	.358	.963
1984	Pit-N	136	450	31	100	16	0	9	52	34	8	78	1	6	9	1	3	.273	.222	.318	.955
1985	**NY-A**	**48**	**109**	**8**	**25**	**5**	**1**	**1**	**8**	**7**	**0**	**20**	**0**	**2**	**0**	**1**	**1**	**.276**	**.229**	**.321**	**.889**
1986	**NY-A**	**42**	**108**	**10**	**25**	**7**	**0**	**2**	**13**	**9**	**0**	**14**	**1**	**2**	**1**	**0**	**0**	**.294**	**.231**	**.352**	**.950**
1987	Hou-N	19	45	3	8	3	0	0	2	8	3	12	0	0	1	0	0	.296	.178	.244	1.000
Career average		78	232	22	55	10	1	5	25	19	5	38	1	3	3	3	2	.236	.294	.344	.964
Yankee average		**45**	**109**	**9**	**25**	**6**	**1**	**2**	**11**	**8**	**0**	**17**	**1**	**2**	**1**	**1**	**1**	**.230**	**.285**	**.336**	**.920**
Career total		853	2553	236	603	109	9	49	278	210	57	422	12	33	27	32	17	.236	.294	.344	.964
Yankee total		**90**	**217**	**18**	**50**	**12**	**1**	**3**	**21**	**16**	**0**	**34**	**1**	**4**	**1**	**1**	**1**	**.230**	**.285**	**.336**	**.920**

Berra, Lawrence Peter (Yogi)

HEIGHT: 5'8"   THROWS: RIGHT   BATS: LEFT   BORN: 5/12/1925 ST. LOUIS, MISSOURI   POSITIONS PLAYED: C, 1B, OF

YEAR	TEAM	GAMES	AB	RUNS	HITS	2B	3B	HR	RBI	BB	IBB	SO	HBP	SH	SF	SB	CS	BA	OBA	SA	FA
1946	**NY-A**	**7**	**22**	**3**	**8**	**1**	**0**	**2**	**4**	**1**	**0**	**1**	**0**	**0**	**0**	**0**	**0**	**.364**	**.391**	**.682**	**1.000**
1947	**NY-A**	**83**	**293**	**41**	**82**	**15**	**3**	**11**	**54**	**13**	**0**	**12**	**0**	**0**	**0**	**0**	**1**	**.280**	**.310**	**.464**	**.980**
1948	**NY-A**	**125**	**469**	**70**	**143**	**24**	**10**	**14**	**98**	**25**	**0**	**24**	**1**	**2**	**0**	**3**	**3**	**.305**	**.341**	**.488**	**.979**
1949	**NY-A**	**116**	**415**	**59**	**115**	**20**	**2**	**20**	**91**	**22**	**0**	**25**	**6**	**0**	**0**	**2**	**1**	**.277**	**.323**	**.480**	**.989**
1950	**NY-A**	**151**	**597**	**116**	**192**	**30**	**6**	**28**	**124**	**55**	**0**	**12**	**4**	**0**	**0**	**4**	**2**	**.322**	**.383**	**.533**	**.985**
1951	**NY-A**	**141**	**547**	**92**	**161**	**19**	**4**	**27**	**88**	**44**	**0**	**20**	**3**	**0**	**0**	**5**	**4**	**.294**	**.350**	**.492**	**.984**
1952	**NY-A**	**142**	**534**	**97**	**146**	**17**	**1**	**30**	**98**	**66**	**0**	**24**	**4**	**1**	**0**	**2**	**3**	**.273**	**.358**	**.478**	**.992**
1953	**NY-A**	**137**	**503**	**80**	**149**	**23**	**5**	**27**	**108**	**50**	**0**	**32**	**3**	**1**	**0**	**0**	**3**	**.296**	**.363**	**.523**	**.986**
1954	**NY-A**	**151**	**584**	**88**	**179**	**28**	**6**	**22**	**125**	**56**	**0**	**29**	**4**	**1**	**7**	**0**	**1**	**.307**	**.367**	**.488**	**.990**
1955	**NY-A**	**147**	**541**	**84**	**147**	**20**	**3**	**27**	**108**	**60**	**6**	**20**	**7**	**2**	**5**	**1**	**0**	**.272**	**.349**	**.470**	**.984**
1956	**NY-A**	**140**	**521**	**93**	**155**	**29**	**2**	**30**	**105**	**65**	**7**	**29**	**5**	**1**	**5**	**3**	**2**	**.298**	**.378**	**.534**	**1.000**
1957	**NY-A**	**134**	**482**	**74**	**121**	**14**	**2**	**24**	**82**	**57**	**10**	**24**	**1**	**1**	**4**	**1**	**2**	**.251**	**.329**	**.438**	**.995**
1958	**NY-A**	**122**	**433**	**60**	**115**	**17**	**3**	**22**	**90**	**35**	**5**	**35**	**2**	**0**	**6**	**3**	**0**	**.266**	**.319**	**.471**	**1.000**
1959	**NY-A**	**131**	**472**	**64**	**134**	**25**	**1**	**19**	**69**	**43**	**5**	**38**	**4**	**0**	**2**	**1**	**2**	**.284**	**.347**	**.462**	**.997**
1960	**NY-A**	**120**	**359**	**46**	**99**	**14**	**1**	**15**	**62**	**38**	**6**	**23**	**3**	**0**	**4**	**2**	**1**	**.276**	**.347**	**.446**	**.989**
1961	**NY-A**	**119**	**395**	**62**	**107**	**11**	**0**	**22**	**61**	**35**	**4**	**28**	**2**	**0**	**5**	**2**	**0**	**.271**	**.330**	**.466**	**1.000**
1962	**NY-A**	**86**	**232**	**25**	**52**	**8**	**0**	**10**	**35**	**24**	**4**	**18**	**2**	**0**	**5**	**0**	**1**	**.224**	**.297**	**.388**	**.990**
1963	**NY-A**	**64**	**147**	**20**	**43**	**6**	**0**	**8**	**28**	**15**	**2**	**17**	**1**	**0**	**1**	**1**	**0**	**.293**	**.360**	**.497**	**.988**
1965	NY-N	4	9	1	2	0	0	0	0	0	0	3	0	0	0	0	0	.222	.222	.222	.941
Career average		112	398	62	113	17	3	19	75	37	3	22	3	1	2	2	1	.285	.348	.482	.988
Yankee average		**118**	**419**	**65**	**119**	**18**	**3**	**20**	**79**	**39**	**3**	**23**	**3**	**1**	**2**	**2**	**1**	**.285**	**.348**	**.483**	**.990**
Career total		2120	7555	1175	2150	321	49	358	1430	704	49	414	52	9	44	30	26	.285	.348	.482	.988
Yankee total		**2116**	**7546**	**1174**	**2148**	**321**	**49**	**358**	**1430**	**704**	**49**	**411**	**52**	**9**	**44**	**30**	**26**	**.285**	**.348**	**.483**	**.990**

Lawrence Peter "Yogi" Berra, c-of, 1946–63

The first time Branch Rickey, then of the St. Louis Cardinals, took a look at the young catching prospect from The Hill section of St. Louis, he wasn't impressed. The sloping shoulders, the cartoon-character face, the big ears, fooled Rickey as they had fooled everyone else. This Berra kid, said Rickey, will be a Triple-A ballplayer at best.

But Lawrence Peter Berra fooled them all, parlaying his abilities into a career in which he would amass a stunning array of personal and team accomplishments. Fifteen All-Star Game appearances. Three Most Valuable Player Awards. Fourteen American League championships. Ten World Championships, more than any player in history. In fact, in all of professional sports, only Bill Russell of basketball's Boston Celtics has played on more winners.

He was born in 1925, the son of Italian immigrants. English was the second language in his home, and a language his mother never learned. He played baseball in high school and in the sandlots, and got his nickname when he and some of his friends saw a fortune-teller, or "Yogi," at a carnival and the man's cross-legged way of sitting reminded Berra's pals of the way he sat on a baseball bench.

Yogi's father, Pietro Berra, hated the whole baseball thing. It seemed to interfere with his son's education, and for a bricklayer from the old country, the educational opportunities here in this country were the most important thing of all for his family.

But Lawrence persevered and won a tryout with several big league teams. The Cardinals eventually offered him a contract, but he wanted to play for the Yankees, and he signed with them.

He was a lefthanded hitter, and a good one, but there was some initial doubt as to where he would play. The Yankees tried him in both the outfield and behind the plate in 1947. Former Yankee great Bill Dickey was eventually brought in to help him learn the catching position. Gradually, Berra got better.

The press enjoyed him right away. He had difficulty expressing himself and was remarkably unguarded in his dealings with newspapermen. It was a promising combination for the New York dailies and thus began what are known now as Yogi-isms. A bar was so crowded that "nobody goes there anymore." Inflation was such that "a nickel ain't worth a dime anymore." A recurring event was "Déjà vu all over again." And, of course, "It ain't over till it's over."

But over the past few years, Berra's greatness as a player has begun to be more appreciated. And his teammates and opponents have been more emphatic about explaining that these Berra blunders were more the invention of a simplistic media than reality. Mickey Mantle once estimated that Berra actually said only about a third of the quotes attributed to him.

And clearly, Berra was far more than jumbled

Beville, Henry Monte

HEIGHT: 5'11"   THROWS: RIGHT   BATS: LEFT   BORN: 2/24/1875 DUBLIN, INDIANA   DIED: 1/24/1955 GRAND RAPIDS, MICHIGAN   POSITIONS PLAYED: C, 1B

YEAR	TEAM	GAMES	AB	RUNS	HITS	2B	3B	HR	RBI	BB	IBB	SO	HBP	SH	SF	SB	CS	BA	OBA	SA	FA
1903	NY-A	82	258	23	50	14	1	0	29	16	—	—	4	5	—	4	—	.194	.252	.256	.960
1904	NY-A	9	22	2	6	2	0	0	2	2	—	—	0	0	—	0	—	.273	.333	.364	.882
Career average		46	140	13	28	8	1	0	16	9	—	—	2	3	—	2	—	.200	.258	.264	.921
Yankee average		46	140	13	28	8	1	0	16	9	—	—	2	3	—	2	—	.200	.258	.264	.921
Career total		91	280	25	56	16	1	0	31	18	—	—	4	5	—	4	—	.200	.258	.264	.921
Yankee total		91	280	25	56	16	1	0	31	18	—	—	4	5	—	4	—	.200	.258	.264	.921

quotes. He was a terrific bad-ball hitter, and his batting eye was such that he rarely struck out. Casey Stengel, his longtime manager, knew exactly how good his catcher was. He referred to Berra as "Mr. Berra, my assistant manager," and said that of all the players he ever coached, Berra was second only to Joe DiMaggio in ability.

But more than that, he was a major offensive force at the position, not unlike Johnny Bench for the Reds several decades later. He hit with power (358 home runs) and led the Yankees in RBI for seven consecutive years.

He was a tremendous clutch hitter, twice hitting over .400 in the World Series. He remains the team leader in pinch-hit home runs with nine. Ralph Houk, another of his managers, said Berra was the best clutch hitter he ever saw, ahead of Ted Williams, Mickey Mantle, Willie Mays and Stan Musial, among others. Williams himself wrote in one of his books that Berra's hitting prowess in the later innings was the best he has ever seen.

In the 1950 Series, for example, his sixth-inning home run was the winning score in a 5-2 victory over the Philadelphia Phillies in Game 4, which was a Yankee sweep. In 1952, his solo home run in the seventh put the Yankees ahead to stay in a 3-2 Game 6 win over the Dodgers. New York won the Series the next day. In 1953, he and Billy Martin combined for 21 hits in another six-game win over the Dodgers. His two Game 7 home runs in 1956 clinched another Series win against Brooklyn.

The 1956 Series featured, of course, the Don Larsen Game. Larsen (a good but not great pitcher for the Yankees that year) started Game 5 with the

Series tied, 2-2. Ninety-seven pitches later, Berra was jumping into his arms after Larsen completed his perfect game.

Perhaps this game is the most telling factor in the Berra legend. He ranks it as a greater thrill than his winning three MVP awards. Partly, he once said, because it was unique. But partly because it was a team effort, not an individual accomplishment.

Berra's post-player career has been successful as well. Upon his retirement in 1963, he was named manager of the Yankees, and he led the team to the 1964 American League pennant. In 1972, he was named manager of the New York Mets, and in 1973, the Mets won the National League flag before losing the World Series in seven games to Oakland, despite outhitting and outscoring the A's over the seven games.

In 1984, he was rehired as manager of the Yankees, during the George Steinbrenner revolving-door years. Steinbrenner fired Berra the next year, and the situation stung Berra to the point where he would not return to Yankee Stadium for Old-Timers games or other commemorative events. It wasn't until 1998 that he and Steinbrenner made amends, and Berra was welcomed back.

Berra was elected to the Hall of Fame in 1972, the same year the Yankees retired his number eight. In 1988, he and his former mentor, Dickey, were immortalized further when plaques bearing their names were unveiled in Memorial Park in Yankee Stadium.

Bladt, Richard Alan
HEIGHT: 6'1"   THROWS: RIGHT   BATS: RIGHT   BORN: 12/9/1946 SANTA CRUZ, CALIFORNIA   POSITIONS PLAYED: OF

YEAR	TEAM	GAMES	AB	RUNS	HITS	2B	3B	HR	RBI	BB	IBB	SO	HBP	SH	SF	SB	CS	BA	OBA	SA	FA
1969	Chi-N	10	13	1	2	0	0	0	1	0	0	5	0	0	0	0	0	.154	.154	.154	1.000
1975	**NY-A**	**52**	**117**	**13**	**26**	**3**	**1**	**1**	**11**	**11**	**0**	**8**	**1**	**3**	**1**	**6**	**2**	**.222**	**.292**	**.291**	**.973**
Career average		31	65	7	14	2	1	1	6	6	0	7	1	2	1	3	1	.215	.280	.277	.987
Yankee average		**52**	**117**	**13**	**26**	**3**	**1**	**1**	**11**	**11**	**0**	**8**	**1**	**3**	**1**	**6**	**2**	**.222**	**.292**	**.291**	**.973**
Career total		62	130	14	28	3	1	1	12	11	0	13	1	3	1	6	2	.215	.280	.277	.987
Yankee total		**52**	**117**	**13**	**26**	**3**	**1**	**1**	**11**	**11**	**0**	**8**	**1**	**3**	**1**	**6**	**2**	**.222**	**.292**	**.291**	**.973**

Blair, Paul L. D. (Motormouth)
HEIGHT: 6'0"   THROWS: RIGHT   BATS: RIGHT   BORN: 2/1/1944 CUSHING, OKLAHOMA   POSITIONS PLAYED: 2B, 3B, SS, OF, DH

YEAR	TEAM	GAMES	AB	RUNS	HITS	2B	3B	HR	RBI	BB	IBB	SO	HBP	SH	SF	SB	CS	BA	OBA	SA	FA
1964	Bal-A	8	1	0	0	0	0	0	0	0	0	1	0	0	0	0	1	.000	.000	.000	1.000
1965	Bal-A	119	364	49	85	19	2	5	25	32	3	52	4	8	1	8	5	.234	.302	.338	.992
1966	Bal-A	133	303	35	84	20	2	6	33	15	0	36	0	5	2	5	6	.277	.309	.416	.990
1967	Bal-A	151	552	72	162	27	12	11	64	50	3	68	5	5	7	8	6	.293	.353	.446	.985
1968	Bal-A	141	421	48	89	22	1	7	38	37	4	60	2	5	2	4	2	.211	.277	.318	.667
1969	Bal-A	150	625	102	178	32	5	26	76	40	1	72	2	13	5	20	6	.285	.327	.477	.988
1970	Bal-A	133	480	79	128	24	2	18	65	56	1	93	3	5	4	24	11	.267	.344	.438	.990
1971	Bal-A	141	516	75	135	24	8	10	44	32	2	94	1	6	0	14	11	.262	.306	.397	.991
1972	Bal-A	142	477	47	111	20	8	8	49	25	0	78	0	5	7	7	8	.233	.287	.358	.991
1973	Bal-A	146	500	73	140	25	3	10	64	43	4	72	0	6	5	18	8	.280	.334	.402	.990
1974	Bal-A	151	552	77	144	27	4	17	62	43	0	59	2	11	7	27	9	.261	.313	.417	.985
1975	Bal-A	140	440	51	96	13	4	5	31	25	0	82	0	17	5	17	11	.218	.257	.300	.991
1976	Bal-A	145	375	29	74	16	0	3	16	22	2	49	2	13	1	15	6	.197	.245	.264	.979
1977	**NY-A**	**83**	**164**	**20**	**43**	**4**	**3**	**4**	**25**	**9**	**1**	**16**	**2**	**5**	**3**	**3**	**2**	**.262**	**.303**	**.396**	**.969**
1978	**NY-A**	**75**	**125**	**10**	**22**	**5**	**0**	**2**	**13**	**9**	**0**	**17**	**0**	**2**	**0**	**1**	**1**	**.176**	**.231**	**.264**	**1.000**
1979	**NY-A**	**2**	**5**	**0**	**1**	**0**	**0**	**0**	**0**	**0**	**0**	**1**	**0**	**0**	**0**	**0**	**0**	**.200**	**.200**	**.200**	**1.000**
1979	Cin-N	75	140	7	21	4	1	2	12	11	3	27	0	2	2	0	0	.150	.212	.236	.992
1980	**NY-A**	**12**	**2**	**2**	**0**	**0**	**0**	**0**	**0**	**0**	**0**	**0**	**0**	**0**	**0**	**0**	**0**	**.000**	**.000**	**.000**	**1.000**
Career average		108	336	43	84	16	3	7	34	25	1	49	1	6	3	10	5	.250	.302	.382	.972
Yankee average		**43**	**74**	**8**	**17**	**2**	**1**	**2**	**10**	**5**	**0**	**9**	**1**	**2**	**1**	**1**	**1**	**.223**	**.270**	**.334**	**.992**
Career total		1947	6042	776	1513	282	55	134	617	449	23	877	23	108	51	171	93	.250	.302	.382	.972
Yankee total		**172**	**296**	**32**	**66**	**9**	**3**	**6**	**38**	**18**	**1**	**34**	**2**	**7**	**3**	**4**	**3**	**.223**	**.270**	**.334**	**.992**

Blair, Walter Allen (Heavy)
HEIGHT: 6'0"   THROWS: RIGHT   BATS: RIGHT   BORN: 10/13/1883 LANDRUS, PENNSYLVANIA   DIED: 8/20/1948 LEWISBURG, PENNSYLVANIA   POSITIONS PLAYED: C

YEAR	TEAM	GAMES	AB	RUNS	HITS	2B	3B	HR	RBI	BB	IBB	SO	HBP	SH	SF	SB	CS	BA	OBA	SA	FA
1907	**NY-A**	**7**	**22**	**1**	**4**	**0**	**0**	**0**	**1**	**2**	—	—	**0**	**0**	—	**0**	—	**.182**	**.250**	**.182**	**.922**
1908	**NY-A**	**76**	**211**	**9**	**40**	**5**	**1**	**1**	**13**	**11**	—	—	**2**	**6**	—	**4**	—	**.190**	**.237**	**.237**	**.956**
1909	**NY-A**	**42**	**110**	**5**	**23**	**2**	**2**	**0**	**11**	**7**	—	—	**2**	**2**	—	**2**	—	**.209**	**.269**	**.264**	**.964**
1910	**NY-A**	**6**	**22**	**2**	**5**	**0**	**1**	**0**	**2**	**0**	—	—	**0**	**1**	—	**0**	—	**.227**	**.227**	**.318**	**.970**
1911	**NY-A**	**85**	**222**	**18**	**43**	**9**	**2**	**0**	**26**	**16**	—	—	**3**	**13**	—	**2**	—	**.194**	**.257**	**.252**	**.970**
1914	Buf-F	128	378	22	92	11	2	0	33	32	—	64	1	5	—	6	—	.243	.304	.283	.984
1915	Buf-F	98	290	23	65	15	3	2	20	18	—	32	2	2	—	4	—	.224	.274	.317	.981
Career average		63	179	11	39	6	2	0	15	12	—	—	1	4	—	3	—	.217	.272	.275	.964
Yankee average		**43**	**117**	**7**	**23**	**3**	**1**	**0**	**11**	**7**	—	—	**1**	**4**	—	**2**	—	**.196**	**.251**	**.249**	**.956**
Career total		442	1255	80	272	42	11	3	106	86	—	96	10	29	—	18	—	.217	.272	.275	.964
Yankee total		**216**	**587**	**35**	**115**	**16**	**6**	**1**	**53**	**36**	—	—	**7**	**22**	—	**8**	—	**.196**	**.251**	**.249**	**.956**

Blanchard, John Edwin
HEIGHT: 6'1"   THROWS: RIGHT   BATS: LEFT   BORN: 2/26/1933 MINNEAPOLIS, MINNESOTA   POSITIONS PLAYED: C, 1B, OF

YEAR	TEAM	GAMES	AB	RUNS	HITS	2B	3B	HR	RBI	BB	IBB	SO	HBP	SH	SF	SB	CS	BA	OBA	SA	FA
1955	**NY-A**	**1**	**3**	**0**	**0**	**0**	**0**	**0**	**0**	**1**	**0**	**0**	**0**	**0**	**0**	**0**	**0**	**.000**	**.250**	**.000**	**1.000**
1959	**NY-A**	**49**	**59**	**6**	**10**	**1**	**0**	**2**	**4**	**7**	**0**	**12**	**0**	**0**	**0**	**0**	**0**	**.169**	**.258**	**.288**	**1.000**
1960	**NY-A**	**53**	**99**	**8**	**24**	**3**	**1**	**4**	**14**	**6**	**1**	**17**	**1**	**1**	**0**	**0**	**0**	**.242**	**.292**	**.414**	**.988**
1961	**NY-A**	**93**	**243**	**38**	**74**	**10**	**1**	**21**	**54**	**27**	**9**	**28**	**4**	**0**	**1**	**1**	**0**	**.305**	**.382**	**.613**	**1.000**
1962	**NY-A**	**93**	**246**	**33**	**57**	**7**	**0**	**13**	**39**	**28**	**0**	**32**	**1**	**0**	**3**	**0**	**0**	**.232**	**.309**	**.419**	**.923**
1963	**NY-A**	**76**	**218**	**22**	**49**	**4**	**0**	**16**	**45**	**26**	**3**	**30**	**0**	**1**	**2**	**0**	**0**	**.225**	**.305**	**.463**	**.987**
1964	**NY-A**	**77**	**161**	**18**	**41**	**8**	**0**	**7**	**28**	**24**	**4**	**24**	**0**	**0**	**4**	**1**	**0**	**.255**	**.344**	**.435**	**1.000**
1965	**NY-A**	**12**	**34**	**1**	**5**	**1**	**0**	**1**	**3**	**7**	**2**	**3**	**0**	**0**	**1**	**0**	**0**	**.147**	**.293**	**.265**	**.961**
1965	KC-A	52	120	10	24	2	0	2	11	8	1	16	1	0	3	0	0	.200	.256	.267	1.000
1965	Mil-N	10	10	1	1	0	0	1	2	2	0	1	0	0	0	0	0	.100	.250	.400	.000
Career average		52	119	14	29	4	0	7	20	14	2	16	1	0	1	0	0	.239	.317	.441	.886
Yankee average		**57**	**133**	**16**	**33**	**4**	**0**	**8**	**23**	**16**	**2**	**18**	**1**	**0**	**1**	**0**	**0**	**.245**	**.325**	**.461**	**.982**
Career total		516	1193	137	285	36	2	67	200	136	20	163	7	2	14	2	0	.239	.317	.441	.886
Yankee total		**454**	**1063**	**126**	**260**	**34**	**2**	**64**	**187**	**126**	**19**	**146**	**6**	**2**	**11**	**2**	**0**	**.245**	**.325**	**.461**	**.982**

Blefary, Curtis Le Roy

HEIGHT: 6'2"   THROWS: RIGHT   BATS: LEFT   BORN: 7/5/1943 BROOKLYN, NEW YORK   POSITIONS PLAYED: C, 1B, 3B, OF

YEAR	TEAM	GAMES	AB	RUNS	HITS	2B	3B	HR	RBI	BB	IBB	SO	HBP	SH	SF	SB	CS	BA	OBA	SA	FA
1965	Bal-A	144	462	72	120	23	4	22	70	88	4	73	3	7	1	4	2	.260	.381	.470	.979
1966	Bal-A	131	419	73	107	14	3	23	64	73	3	56	6	7	3	1	4	.255	.371	.468	.976
1967	Bal-A	155	554	69	134	19	5	22	81	73	11	94	8	7	3	4	4	.242	.337	.413	.989
1968	Bal-A	137	451	50	90	8	1	15	39	65	11	66	4	7	8	6	3	.200	.301	.322	.988
1969	Hou-N	155	542	66	137	26	7	12	67	77	10	79	4	4	5	8	7	.253	.347	.393	.987
1970	**NY-A**	**99**	**269**	**34**	**57**	**6**	**0**	**9**	**37**	**43**	**3**	**37**	**3**	**0**	**3**	**1**	**3**	**.212**	**.324**	**.335**	**1.000**
1971	**NY-A**	**21**	**36**	**4**	**7**	**1**	**0**	**1**	**2**	**3**	**0**	**5**	**0**	**0**	**0**	**0**	**0**	**.194**	**.256**	**.306**	**.875**
1971	Oak-A	50	101	15	22	2	0	5	12	15	2	15	1	1	0	0	1	.218	.325	.386	.929
1972	Oak-A	8	11	1	5	2	0	0	1	0	0	1	0	0	1	0	0	.455	.417	.636	.000
1972	SD-N	74	102	10	20	3	0	3	9	19	3	18	0	0	1	0	0	.196	.320	.314	.982
Career average		97	295	39	70	10	2	11	38	46	5	44	3	3	3	2	2	.237	.342	.400	.871
Yankee average		**60**	**153**	**19**	**32**	**4**	**0**	**5**	**20**	**23**	**2**	**21**	**2**	**0**	**2**	**1**	**2**	**.210**	**.317**	**.331**	**.938**
Career total		974	2947	394	699	104	20	112	382	456	47	444	29	33	25	24	24	.237	.342	.400	.871
Yankee total		**120**	**305**	**38**	**64**	**7**	**0**	**10**	**39**	**46**	**3**	**42**	**3**	**0**	**3**	**1**	**3**	**.210**	**.317**	**.331**	**.938**

Bliss, Elmer Ward

HEIGHT: 6'0"   THROWS: RIGHT   BATS: LEFT   BORN: 3/9/1875 PENFIELD, PENNSYLVANIA   DIED: 3/18/1962 BRADFORD, PENNSYLVANIA   POSITIONS PLAYED: P, OF

YEAR	TEAM	GAMES	AB	RUNS	HITS	2B	3B	HR	RBI	BB	IBB	SO	HBP	SH	SF	SB	CS	BA	OBA	SA	FA
1903	**NY-A**	**1**	**3**	**0**	**0**	**0**	**0**	**0**	**0**	**0**	**—**	**—**	**0**	**0**	**—**	**0**	**—**	**.000**	**.000**	**.000**	**.000**
1904	**NY-A**	**1**	**1**	**0**	**0**	**0**	**0**	**0**	**0**	**0**	**—**	**—**	**0**	**0**	**—**	**0**	**—**	**.000**	**.000**	**.000**	**.000**
Career average		1	2	0	0	0	0	0	0	0	—	—	0	0	—	0	—	.000	.000	.000	.000
Yankee average		**1**	**2**	**0**	**0**	**0**	**0**	**0**	**0**	**0**	**—**	**—**	**0**	**0**	**—**	**0**	**—**	**.000**	**.000**	**.000**	**.000**
Career total		2	4	0	0	0	0	0	0	0	—	—	0	0	—	0	—	.000	.000	.000	.000
Yankee total		**2**	**4**	**0**	**0**	**0**	**0**	**0**	**0**	**0**	**—**	**—**	**0**	**0**	**—**	**0**	**—**	**.000**	**.000**	**.000**	**.000**

Blomberg, Ronald Mark (Boomer)

HEIGHT: 6'1"   THROWS: RIGHT   BATS: LEFT   BORN: 8/23/1948 ATLANTA, GEORGIA   POSITIONS PLAYED: 1B, OF

YEAR	TEAM	GAMES	AB	RUNS	HITS	2B	3B	HR	RBI	BB	IBB	SO	HBP	SH	SF	SB	CS	BA	OBA	SA	FA
1969	**NY-A**	**4**	**6**	**0**	**3**	**0**	**0**	**0**	**0**	**1**	**0**	**0**	**0**	**0**	**0**	**0**	**0**	**.500**	**.571**	**.500**	**1.000**
1971	**NY-A**	**64**	**199**	**30**	**64**	**6**	**2**	**7**	**31**	**14**	**3**	**23**	**0**	**1**	**2**	**2**	**4**	**.322**	**.363**	**.477**	**.970**
1972	**NY-A**	**107**	**299**	**36**	**80**	**22**	**1**	**14**	**49**	**38**	**4**	**26**	**3**	**0**	**1**	**0**	**2**	**.268**	**.355**	**.488**	**.985**
1973	**NY-A**	**100**	**301**	**45**	**99**	**13**	**1**	**12**	**57**	**34**	**4**	**25**	**0**	**1**	**2**	**2**	**0**	**.329**	**.395**	**.498**	**.980**
1974	**NY-A**	**90**	**264**	**39**	**82**	**11**	**2**	**10**	**48**	**29**	**2**	**33**	**2**	**0**	**6**	**2**	**1**	**.311**	**.375**	**.481**	**1.000**
1975	**NY-A**	**34**	**106**	**18**	**27**	**8**	**2**	**4**	**17**	**13**	**1**	**10**	**0**	**0**	**0**	**0**	**0**	**.255**	**.336**	**.481**	**1.000**
1976	**NY-A**	**1**	**2**	**0**	**0**	**0**	**0**	**0**	**0**	**0**	**0**	**0**	**0**	**0**	**0**	**0**	**0**	**.000**	**.000**	**.000**	**.000**
1978	Chi-A	61	156	16	36	7	0	5	22	11	2	17	0	1	1	0	0	.231	.280	.372	.986
Career average		58	167	23	49	8	1	7	28	18	2	17	1	0	2	1	1	.293	.360	.473	.865
Yankee average		**57**	**168**	**24**	**51**	**9**	**1**	**7**	**29**	**18**	**2**	**17**	**1**	**0**	**2**	**1**	**1**	**.302**	**.370**	**.487**	**.848**
Career total		461	1333	184	391	67	8	52	224	140	16	134	5	3	12	6	7	.293	.360	.473	.865
Yankee total		**400**	**1177**	**168**	**355**	**60**	**8**	**47**	**202**	**129**	**14**	**117**	**5**	**2**	**11**	**6**	**7**	**.302**	**.370**	**.486**	**.848**

Blowers, Michael Roy

HEIGHT: 6'2"   THROWS: RIGHT   BATS: RIGHT   BORN: 4/24/1965 WURZBURG, GERMANY   POSITIONS PLAYED: 1B, 3B, SS, OF, DH

YEAR	TEAM	GAMES	AB	RUNS	HITS	2B	3B	HR	RBI	BB	IBB	SO	HBP	SH	SF	SB	CS	BA	OBA	SA	FA
1989	**NY-A**	**13**	**38**	**2**	**10**	**0**	**0**	**0**	**3**	**3**	**0**	**13**	**0**	**0**	**0**	**0**	**0**	**.263**	**.317**	**.263**	**.852**
1990	**NY-A**	**48**	**144**	**16**	**27**	**4**	**0**	**5**	**21**	**12**	**1**	**50**	**0**	**1**	**0**	**1**	**0**	**.188**	**.255**	**.319**	**.899**
1991	**NY-A**	**15**	**35**	**3**	**7**	**0**	**0**	**1**	**1**	**4**	**0**	**3**	**0**	**1**	**0**	**0**	**0**	**.200**	**.282**	**.286**	**.870**
1992	Sea-A	31	73	7	14	3	0	1	2	6	0	20	0	1	0	0	0	.192	.253	.274	1.000
1993	Sea-A	127	379	55	106	23	3	15	57	44	3	98	2	3	1	1	5	.280	.357	.475	.951
1994	Sea-A	85	270	37	78	13	0	9	49	25	2	60	1	1	3	2	2	.289	.348	.437	.939
1995	Sea-A	134	439	59	113	24	1	23	96	53	0	128	0	3	3	2	1	.257	.335	.474	.947
1996	LA-N	92	317	31	84	19	2	6	38	37	2	77	1	0	3	0	0	.265	.344	.394	.951
1997	Sea-A	68	150	22	44	5	0	5	20	21	1	33	0	4	2	0	0	.293	.376	.427	1.000
1998	Oak-A	129	409	56	97	24	2	11	71	39	1	116	0	2	4	1	0	.237	.301	.386	.927
1999	Sea-A	19	46	2	11	1	0	2	7	4	0	12	0	0	0	0	0	.239	.300	.391	.959
Career average		69	209	26	54	11	1	7	33	23	1	56	0	1	2	0	1	.257	.329	.416	.934
Yankee average		**25**	**72**	**7**	**15**	**1**	**0**	**2**	**8**	**6**	**0**	**22**	**0**	**0**	**0**	**0**	**0**	**.203**	**.270**	**.304**	**.874**
Career total		761	2300	290	591	116	8	78	365	248	10	610	5	15	16	7	8	.257	.329	.416	.934
Yankee total		**76**	**217**	**21**	**44**	**4**	**0**	**6**	**25**	**19**	**1**	**66**	**1**	**1**	**0**	**1**	**0**	**.203**	**.270**	**.304**	**.874**

Bockman, Joseph Edward (Eddie)
HEIGHT: 5'9" THROWS: RIGHT BATS: RIGHT BORN: 7/26/1920 SANTA ANA, CALIFORNIA POSITIONS PLAYED: 3B, SS

YEAR	TEAM	GAMES	AB	RUNS	HITS	2B	3B	HR	RBI	BB	IBB	SO	HBP	SH	SF	SB	CS	BA	OBA	SA	FA
1946	NY-A	4	12	2	1	1	0	0	0	1	—	4	0	0	—	0	0	.083	.154	.167	.933
1947	Cle-A	46	66	8	17	2	2	1	14	5	—	17	0	0	—	0	0	.258	.310	.394	.946
1948	Pit-N	70	176	23	42	7	1	4	23	17	—	35	1	2	—	2	—	.239	.309	.358	.962
1949	Pit-N	79	220	21	49	6	1	6	19	23	—	31	0	2	—	3	—	.223	.296	.341	.959
Career average		50	119	14	27	4	1	3	14	12	—	22	0	1	—	1	—	.230	.299	.350	.950
Yankee average		4	12	2	1	1	0	0	0	1	—	4	0	0	—	0	0	.083	.154	.167	.950
Career total		199	474	54	109	16	4	11	56	46	—	87	1	4	—	5	0	.230	.299	.350	.950
Yankee total		4	12	2	1	1	0	0	0	1	—	4	0	0	—	0	0	.083	.154	.167	.950

Bodie, Francesco Stephano Pezzolo (Ping)
HEIGHT: 5'8" THROWS: RIGHT BATS: RIGHT BORN: 10/8/1887 SAN FRANCISCO, CALIF. DIED: 12/17/1961 SAN FRANCISCO, CALIF. POSITIONS PLAYED: OF

YEAR	TEAM	GAMES	AB	RUNS	HITS	2B	3B	HR	RBI	BB	IBB	SO	HBP	SH	SF	SB	CS	BA	OBA	SA	FA
1911	Chi-A	145	551	75	159	27	13	4	97	49	—	—	1	17	—	14	—	.289	.348	.407	.969
1912	Chi-A	138	472	58	139	24	7	5	72	43	—	—	4	18	—	12	—	.294	.358	.407	.969
1913	Chi-A	127	406	39	107	14	8	8	48	35	—	57	2	21	—	5	—	.264	.325	.397	.968
1914	Chi-A	107	327	21	75	9	5	3	29	21	—	35	1	34	—	12	11	.229	.278	.315	.959
1917	Phi-A	148	557	51	162	28	11	7	74	53	—	40	3	22	—	13	—	.291	.356	.418	.959
1918	NY-A	91	324	36	83	12	6	3	46	27	—	24	3	17	—	6	—	.256	.319	.358	.971
1919	NY-A	134	475	45	132	27	8	6	59	36	—	46	4	17	—	15	—	.278	.334	.406	.959
1920	NY-A	129	471	63	139	26	12	7	79	40	—	30	0	12	—	6	14	.295	.350	.446	.968
1921	NY-A	31	87	5	15	2	2	0	12	8	—	8	0	2	—	0	1	.172	.242	.241	.944
Career average		117	408	44	112	19	8	5	57	35	—	27	2	18	—	9	—	.275	.335	.396	.963
Yankee average		96	339	37	92	17	7	4	49	28	—	27	2	12	—	7	—	.272	.330	.398	.961
Career total		1050	3670	393	1011	169	72	43	516	312	—	240	18	160	—	83	26	.275	.335	.396	.963
Yankee total		385	1357	149	369	67	28	16	196	111	—	108	7	48	—	27	15	.272	.330	.398	.961

Boehmer, Leonard Joseph Stephen
HEIGHT: 6'1" THROWS: RIGHT BATS: RIGHT BORN: 6/28/1941 FLINTHILL, MISSOURI POSITIONS PLAYED: 1B, 3B

YEAR	TEAM	GAMES	AB	RUNS	HITS	2B	3B	HR	RBI	BB	IBB	SO	HBP	SH	SF	SB	CS	BA	OBA	SA	FA
1967	Cin-N	2	3	0	0	0	0	0	0	0	0	0	0	0	0	0	0	.000	.000	.000	1.000
1969	NY-A	45	108	5	19	4	0	0	7	8	2	10	0	0	0	0	1	.233	.176	.213	.995
1971	NY-A	3	5	0	0	0	0	0	0	0	0	0	0	0	0	0	0	.000	.000	.000	1.000
Career average		17	39	2	6	1	0	0	2	3	1	3	0	0	0	0	0	.164	.218	.198	.998
Yankee average		24	57	3	10	2	0	0	4	4	1	5	0	0	0	0	1	.168	.223	.204	.998
Career total		50	116	5	19	4	0	0	7	8	2	10	0	0	0	0	1	.164	.218	.198	.998
Yankee total		48	113	5	19	4	0	0	7	8	2	10	0	0	0	0	1	.168	.223	.204	.998

Boggs, Wade Anthony
HEIGHT: 6'2" THROWS: RIGHT BATS: LEFT BORN: 6/15/1958 OMAHA, NEBRASKA POSITIONS PLAYED: 1B, 3B

YEAR	TEAM	GAMES	AB	RUNS	HITS	2B	3B	HR	RBI	BB	IBB	SO	HBP	SH	SF	SB	CS	BA	OBA	SA	FA
1982	Bos-A	104	338	51	118	14	1	5	44	35	4	21	0	4	4	1	0	.349	.406	.441	.994
1983	Bos-A	153	582	100	210	44	7	5	74	92	2	36	1	3	7	3	3	.361	.444	.486	.947
1984	Bos-A	158	625	109	203	31	4	6	55	89	6	44	0	8	4	3	2	.325	.407	.416	.959
1985	Bos-A	161	653	107	240	42	3	8	78	96	5	61	4	3	2	2	1	.368	.450	.478	.965
1986	Bos-A	149	580	107	207	47	2	8	71	105	14	44	0	4	4	0	4	.357	.453	.486	.953
1987	Bos-A	147	551	108	200	40	6	24	89	105	19	48	2	1	8	1	3	.363	.461	.588	.965
1988	Bos-A	155	584	128	214	45	6	5	58	125	18	34	3	0	7	2	3	.366	.476	.490	.971
1989	Bos-A	156	621	113	205	51	7	3	54	107	19	51	7	0	7	2	6	.330	.430	.449	.958
1990	Bos-A	155	619	89	187	44	5	6	63	87	19	68	1	0	6	0	0	.302	.386	.418	.946
1991	Bos-A	144	546	93	181	42	2	8	51	89	25	32	0	0	6	1	2	.332	.421	.460	.968
1992	Bos-A	143	514	62	133	22	4	7	50	74	19	31	4	0	6	1	3	.259	.353	.358	.952
1993	NY-A	143	560	83	169	26	1	2	59	74	4	49	0	1	9	0	1	.302	.378	.363	.970
1994	NY-A	97	366	61	125	19	1	11	55	61	3	29	1	2	4	2	1	.342	.433	.489	.962

(continued)

Wade Anthony Boggs, 3b-dh, 1993–97

For many Yankees, there is one indelible memory that New York fans will always have of them in pinstripes. For Babe Ruth, it is the eternal picture of him connecting for his 60th home run. For Lou Gehrig, it is the tragic scene of him trying to control his grief on "Lou Gehrig Day."

For Wade Boggs, it's that picture of him riding the damn horse in Yankee Stadium after the 1996 World Series.

Born in Omaha, Nebraska (not Florida, as many think), in 1958, Boggs spent an unusually long time in the minor leagues before being brought up to the Red Sox in 1982. This was primarily because the Sox were not happy with his fielding, although even as a minor league ballplayer, Boggs was a hitter.

He would lead the league in hitting five times with Boston, and collect more than 200 hits seven years in a row from 1984 to 1989. In Boston, he was called "The Chicken Man" for his unwavering habit of eating chicken before every game.

Boggs was, for the most part, a popular player in Boston. Even after his infamous affair with Margo Adams in the mid-1980s, he was appreciated by the Sox fans.

But by the end of the 1992 season, Boggs's average had dropped to an unheard-of (for Boggs) .259. The media in Boston began carping about Boggs's obsession with statistics. And his slump scared the Red Sox management out of re-signing him to a long-term contract. So Boggs moved on.

He signed a three-year contract with the Yankees on December 15, 1992 and told New York fans that he had "a lot left." He did.

Whatever malaise he had contracted in Boston he shook off in New York, batting .302 with 169 hits. He appeared in his ninth consecutive All-Star Game and helped lead the Yankees to a second-place finish behind the eventual World Champion Toronto Blue Jays.

Boggs hit .300 or better in four consecutive seasons with the Yankees, from 1993–96, and was an All-Star Game participant each of those seasons. His best year overall was 1994, when he hit .324 with 149 hits. But more interestingly, Boggs, long considered an indifferent fielder, won the first of two consecutive Gold Glove awards. In fact, his .981 fielding percentage at third base that year is a Yankee team record.

In 1996, Boggs did with New York what he had never done in Boston: win a World Championship. In the first two rounds of the expanded playoff series, with Texas and Baltimore, respectively, Boggs was relatively quiet, making only three hits in 27 at-bats.

But Boggs bounced back somewhat in the Series, hitting .273. His greatest contribution was not a hit, but a walk; his bases-loaded walk in Game 4 in Atlanta capped an 8-6 win for New York. The Yankees had rallied from six runs down to the victory.

That sparked a Yankee victory in six games. When Atlanta's Mark Lemke popped up to third baseman Charlie Hayes to end the game, the play touched off a spontaneous celebration. Boggs hopped up on the back of one of the mounted police officers and took a lap around the stadium. He looked goofy, but he was a winner at last.

In 1998, Boggs signed with the expansion Tampa Bay Marlins and in 1999, collected his 3,000th hit—and he did it in style with a home run. Boggs retired after the 1999 season.

(continued)

Year	Team	G	AB	R	H	2B	3B	HR	RBI	BB	SB	SO						AVG	OBP	SLG	FLD
1995	NY-A	126	460	76	149	22	4	5	63	74	5	50	0	0	7	1	1	.324	.412	.422	.981
1996	NY-A	132	501	80	156	29	2	2	41	67	7	32	0	1	5	1	2	.311	.389	.389	.974
1997	NY-A	103	353	55	103	23	1	4	28	48	3	38	0	2	4	0	1	.292	.373	.397	.979
1998	TB-A	123	435	51	122	23	4	7	52	46	6	54	0	0	2	3	2	.280	.348	.400	.973
1999	TB-A	90	292	40	88	14	1	2	29	38	0	23	0	0	4	1	0	.301	.377	.377	1.000
Career average		136	510	84	167	32	3	7	56	78	10	41	1	2	5	1	2	.328	.415	.443	.968
Yankee average		**120**	**448**	**71**	**140**	**24**	**2**	**5**	**49**	**65**	**4**	**40**	**0**	**1**	**6**	**1**	**1**	**.313**	**.396**	**.407**	**.973**
Career total		2439	9180	1513	3010	578	61	118	1014	1412	178	745	23	29	96	24	35	.328	.415	.443	.968
Yankee total		**458**	**1680**	**272**	**533**	**93**	**8**	**22**	**187**	**250**	**18**	**149**	**1**	**5**	**20**	**4**	**5**	**.317**	**.402**	**.421**	**.973**

Bollweg, Donald Raymond

HEIGHT: 6'1"　THROWS: LEFT　BATS: LEFT　BORN: 2/12/1921 WHEATON, ILLINOIS　DIED: 5/26/1996 WHEATON, ILLINOIS　POSITIONS PLAYED: 1B

YEAR	TEAM	GAMES	AB	RUNS	HITS	2B	3B	HR	RBI	BB	IBB	SO	HBP	SH	SF	SB	CS	BA	OBA	SA	FA
1950	StL-N	4	11	1	2	0	0	0	1	1	—	1	0	0	—	0	—	.182	.250	.182	1.000
1951	StL-N	6	9	1	1	1	0	0	2	0	—	1	0	0	—	0	0	.111	.111	.222	.941
1953	**NY-A**	**70**	**155**	**24**	**46**	**6**	**4**	**6**	**24**	**21**	**—**	**31**	**1**	**1**	**—**	**1**	**0**	**.297**	**.384**	**.503**	**.983**
1954	Phi-A	103	268	35	60	15	3	5	24	35	—	33	3	0	1	1	0	.224	.319	.358	.978
1955	KC-A	12	9	1	1	0	0	0	2	3	2	2	0	0	0	0	0	.111	.333	.111	1.000
Career average		39	90	12	22	4	1	2	11	12	—	14	1	0	—	0	—	.243	.337	.396	.980
Yankee average		**70**	**155**	**24**	**46**	**6**	**4**	**6**	**24**	**21**	**—**	**31**	**1**	**1**	**—**	**1**	**0**	**.297**	**.384**	**.503**	**.983**
Career total		195	452	62	110	22	7	11	53	60	2	68	4	1	1	2	0	.243	.337	.396	.980
Yankee total		**70**	**155**	**24**	**46**	**6**	**4**	**6**	**24**	**21**	**—**	**31**	**1**	**1**	**—**	**1**	**0**	**.297**	**.384**	**.503**	**.983**

Bonds, Bobby Lee

HEIGHT: 6'1"　THROWS: RIGHT　BATS: RIGHT　BORN: 3/15/1946 RIVERSIDE, CALIFORNIA　POSITIONS PLAYED: OF

YEAR	TEAM	GAMES	AB	RUNS	HITS	2B	3B	HR	RBI	BB	IBB	SO	HBP	SH	SF	SB	CS	BA	OBA	SA	FA
1968	SF-N	81	307	55	78	10	5	9	35	38	0	84	1	1	2	16	7	.254	.336	.407	.978
1969	SF-N	158	622	120	161	25	6	32	90	81	3	187	10	3	4	45	4	.259	.351	.473	.978
1970	SF-N	157	663	134	200	36	10	26	78	77	7	189	2	1	2	48	10	.302	.375	.504	.969
1971	SF-N	155	619	110	178	32	4	33	102	62	6	137	5	0	5	26	8	.288	.355	.512	.994
1972	SF-N	153	626	118	162	29	5	26	80	60	4	137	5	1	5	44	6	.259	.326	.446	.978
1973	SF-N	160	643	131	182	34	4	39	96	87	9	148	4	0	4	43	17	.283	.370	.530	.970
1974	SF-N	150	567	97	145	22	8	21	71	95	8	134	4	0	4	41	11	.256	.364	.434	.966
1975	**NY-A**	**145**	**529**	**93**	**143**	**26**	**3**	**32**	**85**	**89**	**8**	**137**	**3**	**0**	**5**	**30**	**17**	**.270**	**.375**	**.512**	**.987**
1976	Cal-A	99	378	48	100	10	3	10	54	41	6	90	3	0	5	30	15	.265	.337	.386	.977
1977	Cal-A	158	592	103	156	23	9	37	115	74	5	141	2	1	10	41	18	.264	.342	.520	.986
1978	Chi-A	26	90	8	25	4	0	2	8	10	1	10	0	1	1	6	2	.278	.347	.389	.956
1978	Tex-A	130	475	85	126	15	4	29	82	69	6	110	2	2	7	37	20	.265	.361	.497	.970
1979	Cle-A	146	538	93	148	24	1	25	85	74	4	135	8	4	7	34	23	.275	.367	.463	.979
1980	StL-N	86	231	37	47	5	3	5	24	33	3	74	2	1	3	15	5	.203	.305	.316	.967
1981	Chi-N	45	163	26	35	7	1	6	19	24	5	44	2	1	0	5	6	.215	.323	.380	.982
Career average		123	470	84	126	20	4	22	68	61	5	117	4	1	4	31	11	.268	.353	.471	.976
Yankee average		**145**	**529**	**93**	**143**	**26**	**3**	**32**	**85**	**89**	**8**	**137**	**3**	**0**	**5**	**30**	**17**	**.270**	**.375**	**.512**	**.987**
Career total		1849	7043	1258	1886	302	66	332	1024	914	75	1757	53	16	64	461	169	.268	.353	.471	.976
Yankee total		**145**	**529**	**93**	**143**	**26**	**3**	**32**	**85**	**89**	**8**	**137**	**3**	**0**	**5**	**30**	**17**	**.270**	**.375**	**.512**	**.987**

Bonilla, Juan Guillermo BORN JUAN GUILLERMO BONILLA (URANIA)

HEIGHT: 5'9"　THROWS: RIGHT　BATS: RIGHT　BORN: 2/12/1955 SANTURCE, PUERTO RICO　POSITIONS PLAYED: 2B, 3B

YEAR	TEAM	GAMES	AB	RUNS	HITS	2B	3B	HR	RBI	BB	IBB	SO	HBP	SH	SF	SB	CS	BA	OBA	SA	FA
1981	SD-N	99	369	30	107	13	2	1	25	25	5	23	2	9	2	4	9	.290	.337	.344	.976
1982	SD-N	45	182	21	51	6	2	0	8	11	0	15	1	3	0	0	1	.280	.325	.335	.975
1983	SD-N	152	556	55	132	17	4	4	45	50	11	40	3	3	5	3	0	.237	.301	.304	.986
1985	**NY-A**	**8**	**16**	**0**	**2**	**1**	**0**	**0**	**2**	**0**	**0**	**3**	**0**	**0**	**0**	**0**	**0**	**.125**	**.125**	**.188**	**.955**
1986	Bal-A	102	284	33	69	10	1	1	18	25	0	21	3	4	0	0	0	.243	.311	.296	.918
1987	**NY-A**	**23**	**55**	**6**	**14**	**3**	**0**	**1**	**3**	**5**	**0**	**6**	**0**	**3**	**0**	**0**	**0**	**.255**	**.317**	**.364**	**.965**
Career average		72	244	24	63	8	2	1	17	19	3	18	2	4	1	1	2	.256	.314	.317	.963
Yankee average		**16**	**36**	**3**	**8**	**2**	**0**	**1**	**3**	**3**	**0**	**5**	**0**	**2**	**0**	**0**	**0**	**.225**	**.276**	**.324**	**.960**
Career total		429	1462	145	375	50	9	7	101	116	16	108	9	22	7	7	10	.256	.314	.317	.963
Yankee total		**31**	**71**	**6**	**16**	**4**	**0**	**1**	**5**	**5**	**0**	**9**	**0**	**3**	**0**	**0**	**0**	**.225**	**.276**	**.324**	**.960**

Boone, Lute Joseph (Luke *or* Danny)

HEIGHT: 5'9"　THROWS: RIGHT　BATS: RIGHT　BORN: 5/6/1890 PITTSBURGH, PENNSYLVANIA　DIED: 8/1/1958　POSITIONS PLAYED: 2B, 3B, SS

YEAR	TEAM	GAMES	AB	RUNS	HITS	2B	3B	HR	RBI	BB	IBB	SO	HBP	SH	SF	SB	CS	BA	OBA	SA	FA
1913	**NY-A**	**6**	**12**	**3**	**4**	**0**	**0**	**0**	**1**	**3**	**—**	**1**	**0**	**0**	**—**	**0**	**—**	**.333**	**.467**	**.333**	**.857**
1914	**NY-A**	**106**	**370**	**34**	**82**	**8**	**2**	**0**	**21**	**31**	**—**	**41**	**2**	**10**	**—**	**10**	**18**	**.222**	**.285**	**.254**	**.960**
1915	**NY-A**	**130**	**431**	**44**	**88**	**12**	**2**	**5**	**43**	**41**	**—**	**53**	**8**	**14**	**—**	**14**	**17**	**.204**	**.285**	**.276**	**1.000**
1916	**NY-A**	**46**	**124**	**14**	**23**	**4**	**0**	**1**	**8**	**8**	**—**	**10**	**3**	**7**	**—**	**7**	**—**	**.185**	**.252**	**.242**	**1.000**
1918	Pit-N	27	91	7	18	3	0	0	3	8	—	6	0	6	—	1	—	.198	.263	.231	1.000

(continued)

(continued)

Career average	63	206	20	43	5	1	1	15	18	—	22	3	7	—	6	—	.209	.282	.261	.963
Yankee average	**72**	**234**	**24**	**49**	**6**	**1**	**2**	**18**	**21**	**—**	**26**	**3**	**8**	**—**	**8**	**—**	**.210**	**.284**	**.264**	**.954**
Career total	315	1028	102	215	27	4	6	76	91	—	111	13	37	—	32	35	.209	.282	.261	.963
Yankee total	**288**	**937**	**95**	**197**	**24**	**4**	**6**	**73**	**83**	**—**	**105**	**13**	**31**	**—**	**31**	**35**	**.210**	**.284**	**.264**	**.954**

Bordagaray, Stanley George (Frenchy)

HEIGHT: 5'7" THROWS: RIGHT BATS: RIGHT BORN: 1/3/1910 COALINGA, CALIFORNIA POSITIONS PLAYED: 2B, 3B, OF

YEAR	TEAM	GAMES	AB	RUNS	HITS	2B	3B	HR	RBI	BB	IBB	SO	HBP	SH	SF	SB	CS	BA	OBA	SA	FA
1934	Chi-A	29	87	12	28	3	1	0	2	3	—	8	0	1	—	1	2	.322	.344	.379	.938
1935	Bro-N	120	422	69	119	19	6	1	39	17	—	29	6	8	—	18	—	.282	.319	.363	.980
1936	Bro-N	125	372	63	117	21	3	4	31	17	—	42	1	11	—	12	—	.315	.346	.419	.991
1937	StL-N	96	300	43	88	11	4	1	37	15	—	25	2	4	—	11	—	.293	.331	.367	.942
1938	StL-N	81	156	19	44	5	1	0	21	8	—	9	2	3	—	2	—	.282	.325	.327	.959
1939	Cin-N	63	122	19	24	5	1	0	12	9	—	10	0	5	—	3	—	.197	.252	.254	.929
1941	**NY-A**	**36**	**73**	**10**	**19**	**1**	**0**	**0**	**4**	**6**	**—**	**8**	**1**	**1**	**—**	**1**	**0**	**.260**	**.325**	**.274**	**.967**
1942	Bro-N	48	58	11	14	2	0	0	5	3	—	3	0	1	—	2	—	.241	.279	.276	1.000
1943	Bro-N	89	268	47	81	18	2	0	19	30	—	15	3	1	—	6	—	.302	.379	.384	.885
1944	Bro-N	130	501	85	141	26	4	6	51	36	—	22	1	10	—	3	—	.281	.331	.385	.945
1945	Bro-N	113	273	32	70	9	6	2	49	29	—	15	1	3	—	7	—	.256	.328	.355	1.000
Career average	85	239	37	68	11	3	1	25	16	—	17	2	4	—	6	—	.283	.331	.366	.958
Yankee average	**36**	**73**	**10**	**19**	**1**	**0**	**0**	**4**	**6**	**—**	**8**	**1**	**1**	**—**	**1**	**0**	**.260**	**.325**	**.274**	**.967**
Career total	930	2632	410	745	120	28	14	270	173	—	186	16	48	—	66	2	.283	.331	.366	.958
Yankee total	**36**	**73**	**10**	**19**	**1**	**0**	**0**	**4**	**6**	**—**	**8**	**1**	**1**	**—**	**1**	**0**	**.260**	**.325**	**.274**	**.967**

Borton, William Baker (Babe)

HEIGHT: 6'0" THROWS: LEFT BATS: LEFT BORN: 8/14/1888 MARION, ILLINOIS DIED: 7/29/1954 BERKELEY, CALIFORNIA POSITIONS PLAYED: 1B

YEAR	TEAM	GAMES	AB	RUNS	HITS	2B	3B	HR	RBI	BB	IBB	SO	HBP	SH	SF	SB	CS	BA	OBA	SA	FA
1912	Chi-A	31	105	15	39	3	1	0	17	8	—	—	0	5	—	1	—	.371	.416	.419	.997
1913	Chi-A	28	80	9	22	5	0	0	13	23	—	5	1	2	—	1	—	.275	.442	.338	.991
1913	**NY-A**	**33**	**108**	**8**	**14**	**2**	**0**	**0**	**11**	**18**	**—**	**19**	**1**	**4**	**—**	**1**	**—**	**.130**	**.260**	**.148**	**.978**
1915	StL-F	159	549	97	157	20	14	3	83	92	—	64	7	20	—	17	—	.286	.395	.390	.993
1916	StL-A	66	98	10	22	1	2	1	12	19	—	13	0	2	—	1	—	.224	.350	.306	.991
Career average	63	188	28	51	6	3	1	27	32	—	—	2	7	—	4	—	.270	.381	.352	.990
Yankee average	**33**	**108**	**8**	**14**	**2**	**0**	**0**	**11**	**18**	**—**	**19**	**1**	**4**	**—**	**1**	**—**	**.130**	**.260**	**.148**	**.978**
Career total	317	940	139	254	31	17	4	136	160	—	101	9	33	—	21	—	.270	.381	.352	.990
Yankee total	**33**	**108**	**8**	**14**	**2**	**0**	**0**	**11**	**18**	**—**	**19**	**1**	**4**	**—**	**1**	**—**	**.130**	**.260**	**.148**	**.978**

Boston, Daryl Lamont

HEIGHT: 6'3" THROWS: LEFT BATS: LEFT BORN: 1/4/1963 CINCINNATI, OHIO POSITIONS PLAYED: OF

YEAR	TEAM	GAMES	AB	RUNS	HITS	2B	3B	HR	RBI	BB	IBB	SO	HBP	SH	SF	SB	CS	BA	OBA	SA	FA
1984	Chi-A	35	83	8	14	3	1	0	3	4	0	20	0	0	0	6	0	.169	.207	.229	.910
1985	Chi-A	95	232	20	53	13	1	3	15	14	1	44	0	1	1	8	6	.228	.271	.332	.989
1986	Chi-A	56	199	29	53	11	3	5	22	21	3	33	0	3	1	9	5	.266	.348	.419	.969
1987	Chi-A	103	337	51	87	21	2	10	29	25	2	68	0	4	3	12	6	.258	.307	.421	.991
1988	Chi-A	105	281	37	61	12	2	15	31	21	5	44	0	2	1	9	3	.217	.271	.434	.951
1989	Chi-A	101	218	34	55	3	4	5	23	24	3	31	0	4	1	7	2	.252	.325	.372	.971
1990	Chi-A	5	1	0	0	0	0	0	0	0	0	0	0	0	0	1	0	.000	.000	.000	.000
1990	NY-N	115	366	65	100	21	2	12	45	28	2	50	2	0	0	18	7	.273	.328	.440	.986
1991	NY-N	137	255	40	70	16	4	4	21	30	0	42	0	0	1	15	8	.275	.344	.424	.981
1992	NY-N	130	289	37	72	14	2	11	35	38	6	60	3	0	4	12	6	.249	.338	.426	.993
1993	Col-N	124	291	46	76	15	1	14	40	26	1	57	2	0	1	1	6	.261	.325	.464	.985
1994	**NY-A**	**52**	**77**	**11**	**14**	**2**	**0**	**4**	**14**	**6**	**0**	**20**	**1**	**0**	**0**	**0**	**1**	**.182**	**.250**	**.364**	**1.000**
Career average	88	219	32	55	11	2	7	23	20	2	39	1	1	1	8	4	.249	.312	.410	.894
Yankee average	**52**	**77**	**11**	**14**	**2**	**0**	**4**	**14**	**6**	**0**	**20**	**1**	**0**	**0**	**0**	**1**	**.182**	**.250**	**.364**	**.990**
Career total	1058	2629	378	655	131	22	83	278	237	23	469	8	14	13	98	50	.249	.312	.410	.894
Yankee total	**52**	**77**	**11**	**14**	**2**	**0**	**4**	**14**	**6**	**0**	**20**	**1**	**0**	**0**	**0**	**1**	**.182**	**.250**	**.364**	**.990**

Boyer, Cletis Leroy (Clete)
HEIGHT: 6'0"   THROWS: RIGHT   BATS: RIGHT   BORN: 2/9/1937 CASSVILLE, MISSOURI   POSITIONS PLAYED: 2B, 3B, SS, OF

YEAR	TEAM	GAMES	AB	RUNS	HITS	2B	3B	HR	RBI	BB	IBB	SO	HBP	SH	SF	SB	CS	BA	OBA	SA	FA
1955	KC-A	47	79	3	19	1	0	0	6	3	0	17	0	0	0	0	0	.241	.268	.253	.920
1956	KC-A	67	129	15	28	3	1	1	4	11	1	24	1	2	0	1	1	.217	.284	.279	1.000
1957	KC-A	10	0	0	0	0	0	0	0	0	0	0	0	0	0	0	0	—	—	—	.000
1959	NY-A	47	114	4	20	2	0	0	3	6	2	23	0	3	1	1	0	.175	.215	.193	.990
1960	NY-A	124	393	54	95	20	1	14	46	23	1	85	3	7	5	2	3	.242	.285	.405	.957
1961	NY-A	148	504	61	113	19	5	11	55	63	4	83	2	1	8	1	3	.224	.308	.347	.967
1962	NY-A	158	566	85	154	24	1	18	68	51	8	106	3	5	8	3	2	.272	.331	.413	.964
1963	NY-A	152	557	59	140	20	3	12	54	33	11	91	2	2	2	4	2	.251	.295	.363	.954
1964	NY-A	147	510	43	111	10	5	8	52	36	11	93	1	3	4	6	1	.218	.269	.304	.968
1965	NY-A	148	514	69	129	23	6	18	58	39	10	79	2	2	4	4	1	.251	.304	.424	.968
1966	NY-A	144	500	59	120	22	4	14	57	46	4	48	2	4	6	6	0	.240	.303	.384	.976
1967	Atl-N	154	572	63	140	18	3	26	96	39	3	81	2	0	6	6	3	.245	.292	.311	.981
1968	Atl-N	71	273	19	62	7	2	4	17	16	3	32	2	0	0	2	0	.227	.275	.371	.965
1969	Atl-N	144	496	57	124	16	1	14	57	55	6	87	4	4	3	3	7	.250	.328	.371	.947
1970	Atl-N	134	475	44	117	14	1	16	62	41	8	71	1	3	5	2	5	.246	.305	.439	.961
1971	Atl-N	30	98	10	24	1	0	6	19	8	2	11	0	1	1	0	0	.245	.299	.372	.905
Career average		108	361	40	87	13	2	10	41	29	5	58	2	2	3	3	2	.242	.299	.372	.905
Yankee average		134	457	54	110	18	3	12	49	37	6	76	2	3	5	3	2	.241	.298	.371	.968
Career total		1725	5780	645	1396	200	33	162	654	470	74	931	25	37	53	41	28	.242	.299	.372	.905
Yankee total		1068	3658	434	882	140	25	95	393	297	51	608	15	27	38	27	12	.241	.298	.371	.968

Bradley, Scott William
HEIGHT: 5'11"   THROWS: RIGHT   BATS: LEFT   BORN: 3/22/1960 GLEN RIDGE, NEW JERSEY   POSITIONS PLAYED: C, 1B, OF

YEAR	TEAM	GAMES	AB	RUNS	HITS	2B	3B	HR	RBI	BB	IBB	SO	HBP	SH	SF	SB	CS	BA	OBA	SA	FA
1984	**NY-A**	9	21	3	6	1	0	0	2	1	0	1	0	0	0	0	0	.286	.318	.333	1.000
1985	**NY-A**	19	49	4	8	2	1	0	1	1	0	5	1	0	0	0	2	.163	.196	.245	.923
1986	Chi-A	9	21	3	6	0	0	0	0	1	0	0	2	0	0	0	0	.286	.375	.286	.000
1986	Sea-A	68	199	17	60	8	3	5	28	12	1	7	2	2	2	0	1	.302	.344	.447	.990
1987	Sea-A	102	342	34	95	15	1	5	43	15	1	18	3	2	4	1	1	.278	.310	.371	.990
1988	Sea-A	103	335	45	86	17	1	4	33	17	1	16	2	3	2	1	1	.257	.295	.349	1.000
1989	Sea-A	103	270	21	74	16	0	3	37	21	4	23	1	1	6	1	1	.274	.322	.367	1.000
1990	Sea-A	101	233	11	52	9	0	1	28	15	2	20	0	3	6	0	1	.223	.264	.275	1.000
1991	Sea-A	83	172	10	35	7	0	0	11	19	2	19	0	5	2	0	0	.203	.280	.244	.993
1992	Sea-A	2	1	0	0	0	0	0	0	1	0	1	0	0	0	0	0	.000	.500	.000	1.000
1992	Cin-N	5	5	1	2	0	0	0	1	1	0	0	0	0	0	0	0	.400	.500	.400	1.000
Career average		55	150	14	39	7	1	2	17	10	1	10	1	2	2	0	1	.257	.302	.343	.900
Yankee average		14	35	4	7	2	1	0	2	1	0	3	1	0	0	0	0	.200	.233	.271	.962
Career total		604	1648	149	424	75	6	18	184	104	14	110	11	16	22	3	6	.257	.302	.343	.900
Yankee total		28	70	7	14	3	1	0	3	2	0	6	1	0	0	0	0	.200	.233	.271	.962

Brant, Marshall Lee
HEIGHT: 6'5"   THROWS: RIGHT   BATS: RIGHT   BORN: 9/17/1955 GARBERVILLE, CALIFORNIA   POSITIONS PLAYED: 1B, DH

YEAR	TEAM	GAMES	AB	RUNS	HITS	2B	3B	HR	RBI	BB	IBB	SO	HBP	SH	SF	SB	CS	BA	OBA	SA	FA
1980	**NY-A**	3	6	0	0	0	0	0	0	0	0	3	0	0	0	0	0	.000	.000	.000	1.000
1983	Oak-A	5	14	2	2	0	0	0	2	0	0	3	0	0	0	0	0	.143	.143	.143	.905
Career average		4	10	1	1	0	0	0	1	0	0	3	0	0	0	0	0	.100	.100	.100	.953
Yankee average		3	6	0	0	0	0	0	0	0	0	3	0	0	0	0	0	.000	.000	.000	1.000
Career total		8	20	2	2	0	0	0	2	0	0	6	0	0	0	0	0	.100	.100	.100	.953
Yankee total		8	20	2	2	0	0	0	2	0	0	6	0	0	0	0	0	.100	.100	.100	1.000

Cletus Leroy "Clete" Boyer, 3b-ss, 1959–66

Primarily a third baseman like his older brother, Ken, Clete Boyer anchored the hot corner in New York for eight years, including five Yankee pennant winners from 1960–64.

Clete Boyer, born on February 9, 1937, was the youngest of three Boyers to make it to the major leagues. Older brother Ken played 15 years for the Cardinals, Mets, White Sox and Dodgers. Oldest brother Cloyd, a pitcher, played five years with the Cardinals and Royals.

Ken was the All-Star of the family, but Clete won more championships: five pennants and two World Series championships in 1961 and 1962.

Clete was one of 14 children born in a tiny house in a very rural part of Missouri, with no electricity and no plumbing. His father, Vern Boyer, worked as a carpenter and stone cutter.

Baseball was a very large part of the Boyers' existence, and growing up, the Boyer boys, as well as virtually all the other boys in the area, played on town teams.

Ken and Cloyd signed with the St. Louis Cardinals, while Clete eventually ended up with the Kansas City Athletics in 1955. The A's had moved from Philadelphia to Kansas City that year, and while the crowds were enthusiastic, the team was only fair, winning 63 of 155 games and finishing 33 games behind the first-place Yankees.

Clete Boyer split his time between second base, third base and shortstop in his three years with the Athletics, who finished sixth, eighth and seventh. But in 1958, the A's and Yankees transacted a massive 12-player deal that sent Boyer and five A's teammates to New York.

By 1960, Boyer was the starting third baseman for the Yankees. He was not a great hitter, but was considered in Brooks Robinson's league, defensively. He played well in World Series games both at bat and in the field.

His best Series was in 1962. His seventh inning homer in Game 1 of the Series against the Giants broke a 2-2 tie and won the game for the Yankees. Overall, he hit .318 in the seven-game Series won by New York.

He and brother Ken met on the field in the 1964 World Series when the Yankees faced the Cardinals. Statistically they were about even, with Ken making six hits, Clete five. In Game 7, Ken struck a home run in the seventh and Clete bashed one in the ninth, the only time in World Series competition that brothers on different teams have each hit home runs. St. Louis won that series, 4-3.

But the Yankees began to decline after that, and Boyer was traded in 1966 to Atlanta, where he played his last five big league seasons. He played a year in the minors upon his retirement from the big leagues, and went over to Japan to play briefly as well.

In the 1980s he worked as a coach for the Yankees and Athletics, often working under his friend Billy Martin.

Brickell, Fritz Darrell

HEIGHT: 5'5"   THROWS: RIGHT   BATS: RIGHT   BORN: 3/19/1935 WICHITA, KANSAS   DIED: 10/15/1965 WICHITA, KANSAS   POSITIONS PLAYED: 2B, SS

YEAR	TEAM	GAMES	AB	RUNS	HITS	2B	3B	HR	RBI	BB	IBB	SO	HBP	SH	SF	SB	CS	BA	OBA	SA	FA
1958	NY-A	2	0	0	0	0	0	0	0	0	0	0	0	0	0	0	0	.000	.000	.000	1.000
1959	NY-A	18	39	4	10	1	0	1	4	1	0	10	0	1	0	0	0	.256	.275	.359	.925
1961	LA-A	21	49	3	6	0	0	0	3	6	0	9	0	0	0	0	0	.122	.218	.122	.901
Career average		20	44	4	8	1	0	1	4	4	0	10	0	1	0	0	0	.182	.242	.227	.942
Yankee average		**18**	**39**	**4**	**10**	**1**	**0**	**1**	**4**	**1**	**0**	**10**	**0**	**1**	**0**	**0**	**0**	**.256**	**.275**	**.359**	**.963**
Career total		39	88	7	16	1	0	1	7	7	0	19	0	1	0	0	0	.182	.242	.227	.942
Yankee total		**18**	**39**	**4**	**10**	**1**	**0**	**1**	**4**	**1**	**0**	**10**	**0**	**1**	**0**	**0**	**0**	**.256**	**.275**	**.359**	**.963**

Brideweser, James Ehrenfeld
HEIGHT: 6'0"   THROWS: RIGHT   BATS: RIGHT   BORN: 2/13/1927 LANCASTER, OHIO   DIED: 8/25/1989, EL TORO, CALIFORNIA   POSITIONS PLAYED: 3B, SS

YEAR	TEAM	GAMES	AB	RUNS	HITS	2B	3B	HR	RBI	BB	IBB	SO	HBP	SH	SF	SB	CS	BA	OBA	SA	FA
1951	**NY-A**	**2**	**8**	**1**	**3**	**0**	**0**	**0**	**0**	**0**	**—**	**1**	**0**	**0**	**—**	**0**	**0**	**.375**	**.375**	**.375**	**.818**
1952	**NY-A**	**42**	**38**	**12**	**10**	**0**	**0**	**0**	**2**	**3**	**—**	**5**	**0**	**0**	**—**	**0**	**0**	**.263**	**.317**	**.263**	**.000**
1953	**NY-A**	**7**	**3**	**3**	**3**	**0**	**1**	**0**	**3**	**1**	**—**	**0**	**0**	**0**	**—**	**0**	**0**	**1.000**	**1.000**	**1.667**	**.833**
1954	Bal-A	73	204	18	54	7	2	0	12	15	—	27	1	1	1	1	1	.265	.317	.319	.944
1955	Chi-A	34	58	6	12	3	2	0	4	3	0	7	0	2	0	0	0	.207	.246	.328	1.000
1956	Chi-A	10	11	0	2	1	0	0	1	0	0	3	1	0	0	0	0	.182	.250	.273	.938
1956	Det-A	70	156	23	34	4	0	0	10	20	2	19	0	4	0	3	1	.218	.307	.244	1.000
1957	Bal-A	91	142	16	38	7	1	1	18	21	2	15	0	4	0	2	0	.268	.362	.352	1.000
Career average		41	78	10	20	3	1	0	6	8	—	10	0	1	—	1	0	.252	.323	.311	.817
Yankee average		**17**	**16**	**5**	**5**	**0**	**0**	**0**	**2**	**1**	**—**	**2**	**0**	**0**	**—**	**0**	**0**	**.327**	**.377**	**.367**	**.550**
Career total		329	620	79	156	22	6	1	50	63	4	77	2	11	1	6	2	.252	.322	.311	.817
Yankee total		**51**	**49**	**16**	**16**	**0**	**1**	**0**	**5**	**4**	**—**	**6**	**0**	**0**	**—**	**0**	**0**	**.327**	**.377**	**.367**	**.550**

Bright, Harry James
HEIGHT: 6'0"   THROWS: RIGHT   BATS: RIGHT   BORN: 9/22/1929, KANSAS CITY, MISSOURI   POSITIONS PLAYED: 1B, 2B, 3B

YEAR	TEAM	GAMES	AB	RUNS	HITS	2B	3B	HR	RBI	BB	IBB	SO	HBP	SH	SF	SB	CS	BA	OBA	SA	FA
1958	Pit-N	15	24	4	6	1	0	1	3	1	0	6	0	0	1	0	0	.250	.269	.417	1.000
1959	Pit-N	40	48	4	12	1	0	3	8	5	0	10	0	1	0	0	0	.250	.321	.458	1.000
1960	Pit-N	4	4	0	0	0	0	0	0	0	0	2	0	0	0	0	0	.000	.000	.000	.000
1961	Was-A	72	183	20	44	6	0	4	21	19	1	23	0	1	1	0	2	.240	.310	.339	.928
1962	Was-A	113	392	55	107	15	4	17	67	26	0	51	2	2	3	2	1	.273	.319	.464	.989
1963	Cin-N	1	1	0	0	0	0	0	0	0	0	1	0	0	0	0	0	.000	.000	.000	1.000
1963	**NY-A**	**60**	**157**	**15**	**37**	**7**	**0**	**7**	**23**	**13**	**1**	**31**	**1**	**1**	**1**	**0**	**0**	**.236**	**.297**	**.414**	**.952**
1964	**NY-A**	**4**	**5**	**0**	**1**	**0**	**0**	**0**	**0**	**1**	**0**	**1**	**0**	**0**	**0**	**0**	**0**	**.200**	**.333**	**.200**	**1.000**
1965	Chi-N	27	25	1	7	1	0	0	4	0	0	8	0	0	1	0	0	.280	.280	.320	.000
Career average		7	8	1	2	0	0	0	1	1	0	2	0	0	0	0	0	.237	.289	.421	.763
Yankee average		**32**	**81**	**8**	**19**	**4**	**0**	**4**	**12**	**7**	**1**	**16**	**1**	**1**	**1**	**0**	**0**	**.235**	**.298**	**.407**	**.976**
Career total		336	839	99	214	31	4	32	126	65	2	133	3	5	7	2	3	.255	.309	.416	.763
Yankee total		**64**	**162**	**15**	**38**	**7**	**0**	**7**	**23**	**14**	**1**	**32**	**1**	**1**	**1**	**0**	**0**	**.235**	**.298**	**.407**	**.976**

Brinkman, Edwin Albert
HEIGHT: 6'0"   THROWS: RIGHT   BATS: RIGHT   BORN: 12/8/1941 CINCINNATI, OHIO   POSITIONS PLAYED: 2B, 3B, SS

YEAR	TEAM	GAMES	AB	RUNS	HITS	2B	3B	HR	RBI	BB	IBB	SO	HBP	SH	SF	SB	CS	BA	OBA	SA	FA
1961	Was-A	4	11	0	1	0	0	0	0	1	0	1	0	0	0	0	0	.091	.167	.091	.889
1962	Was-A	54	133	8	22	7	1	0	4	11	0	28	0	0	1	1	0	.165	.228	.233	.942
1963	Was-A	145	514	44	117	20	3	7	45	31	4	86	4	4	2	5	3	.228	.276	.319	.950
1964	Was-A	132	447	54	100	20	3	8	34	26	1	99	4	2	3	2	2	.224	.271	.336	.969
1965	Was-A	154	444	35	82	13	2	5	35	38	7	82	2	5	2	1	2	.185	.251	.257	.964
1966	Was-A	158	582	42	133	18	9	7	48	29	4	105	0	9	5	7	9	.229	.263	.326	.965
1967	Was-A	109	320	21	60	9	2	1	18	24	1	58	4	5	1	1	3	.188	.252	.238	.979
1968	Was-A	77	193	12	36	3	0	0	6	19	5	31	0	3	0	0	0	.187	.259	.202	.500
1969	Was-A	151	576	71	153	18	5	2	43	50	3	42	5	5	3	2	2	.266	.328	.325	.976
1970	Was-A	158	625	63	164	17	2	1	40	60	0	41	5	1	4	8	9	.262	.300	.301	.974
1971	Det-A	159	527	40	120	18	2	1	37	44	7	54	7	6	5	1	4	.228	.293	.275	.980
1972	Det-A	156	516	42	105	19	1	6	49	38	9	51	3	7	7	0	0	.203	.259	.279	.990
1973	Det-A	162	515	55	122	16	4	7	40	34	1	79	1	14	2	0	1	.237	.284	.324	.968
1974	Det-A	153	502	55	111	15	3	14	54	29	0	71	3	9	3	2	0	.221	.266	.347	.972
1975	StL-N	28	75	6	18	4	0	1	6	7	2	10	1	0	2	0	0	.240	.306	.333	.948
1975	Tex-A	1	2	0	0	0	0	0	0	0	0	1	0	0	0	0	0	.000	.000	.000	1.000
1975	**NY-A**	**44**	**63**	**2**	**11**	**4**	**1**	**0**	**2**	**3**	**0**	**6**	**1**	**1**	**0**	**0**	**0**	**.175**	**.224**	**.270**	**1.000**
Career average		109	356	32	80	12	2	4	27	26	3	50	2	4	2	2	2	.224	.280	.300	.939
Yankee average		**44**	**63**	**2**	**11**	**4**	**1**	**0**	**2**	**3**	**0**	**6**	**1**	**1**	**0**	**0**	**0**	**.175**	**.224**	**.270**	**1.000**
Career total		1845	6045	550	1355	201	38	60	461	444	44	845	40	71	40	30	35	.224	.280	.300	.939
Yankee total		**44**	**63**	**2**	**11**	**4**	**1**	**0**	**2**	**3**	**0**	**6**	**1**	**1**	**0**	**0**	**0**	**.175**	**.224**	**.270**	**1.000**

Brookens, Thomas Dale (Tom)

HEIGHT: 5'10" THROWS: RIGHT BATS: RIGHT BORN: 8/10/1953 CHAMBERSBURG, PENNSYLVANIA POSITIONS PLAYED: 2B, 3B, SS

YEAR	TEAM	GAMES	AB	RUNS	HITS	2B	3B	HR	RBI	BB	IBB	SO	HBP	SH	SF	SB	CS	BA	OBA	SA	FA
1979	Det-A	60	190	23	50	5	2	4	21	11	0	40	2	4	1	10	3	.263	.309	.374	.963
1980	Det-A	151	509	64	140	25	9	10	66	32	3	71	1	2	7	13	11	.275	.315	.418	1.000
1981	Det-A	71	239	19	58	10	1	4	25	14	0	43	2	4	6	5	3	.243	.284	.343	.952
1982	Det-A	140	398	40	92	15	3	9	58	27	0	63	0	2	5	5	9	.231	.277	.352	.939
1983	Det-A	138	332	50	71	13	3	6	32	29	2	46	2	5	6	10	6	.214	.276	.325	.960
1984	Det-A	113	224	32	55	11	4	5	26	19	0	33	1	8	1	6	6	.246	.306	.397	.950
1985	Det-A	156	485	54	115	34	6	7	47	27	0	78	0	9	1	14	5	.237	.277	.375	.943
1986	Det-A	98	281	42	76	11	2	3	25	20	0	42	1	6	2	11	8	.270	.319	.356	.955
1987	Det-A	143	444	59	107	15	3	13	59	33	3	63	2	9	2	7	4	.241	.295	.376	.930
1988	Det-A	136	441	62	107	23	5	5	38	44	2	74	3	6	4	4	4	.243	.313	.351	.952
1989	**NY-A**	**66**	**168**	**14**	**38**	**6**	**0**	**4**	**14**	**11**	**1**	**27**	**0**	**3**	**1**	**1**	**3**	**.226**	**.272**	**.333**	**1.000**
1990	Cle-A	64	154	18	41	7	2	1	20	14	1	25	0	1	3	0	0	.266	.322	.357	.989
Career average		111	322	40	79	15	3	6	36	23	1	50	1	5	3	7	5	.246	.296	.367	.961
Yankee average		**66**	**168**	**14**	**38**	**6**	**0**	**4**	**14**	**11**	**1**	**27**	**0**	**3**	**1**	**1**	**3**	**.226**	**.272**	**.333**	**1.000**
Career total		1336	3865	477	950	175	40	71	431	281	12	605	14	59	39	86	60	.246	.296	.367	.961
Yankee total		**66**	**168**	**14**	**38**	**6**	**0**	**4**	**14**	**11**	**1**	**27**	**0**	**3**	**1**	**1**	**3**	**.226**	**.272**	**.333**	**1.000**

Brosius, Scott David

HEIGHT: 6'1" THROWS: RIGHT BATS: RIGHT BORN: 8/15/1966 HILLSBORO, OREGON POSITIONS PLAYED: 1B, 2B, 3B, SS, OF

YEAR	TEAM	GAMES	AB	RUNS	HITS	2B	3B	HR	RBI	BB	IBB	SO	HBP	SH	SF	SB	CS	BA	OBA	SA	FA
1991	Oak-A	36	68	9	16	5	0	2	4	3	0	11	0	1	0	3	1	.235	.268	.397	1.000
1992	Oak-A	38	87	13	19	2	0	4	13	3	1	13	2	0	1	3	0	.218	.258	.379	1.000
1993	Oak-A	70	213	26	53	10	1	6	25	14	0	37	1	3	2	6	0	.249	.296	.390	.991
1994	Oak-A	96	324	31	77	14	1	14	49	24	0	57	2	4	6	2	6	.238	.289	.417	.946
1995	Oak-A	123	389	69	102	19	2	17	46	41	0	67	8	1	4	4	2	.262	.342	.452	.918
1996	Oak-A	114	428	73	130	25	0	22	71	59	4	85	7	1	5	7	2	.304	.393	.516	1.000
1997	Oak-A	129	479	59	97	20	1	11	41	34	1	102	4	5	4	9	4	.203	.259	.317	.977
1998	**NY-A**	**152**	**530**	**86**	**159**	**34**	**0**	**19**	**98**	**52**	**1**	**97**	**0**	**5**	**4**	**11**	**8**	**.300**	**.361**	**.472**	**1.000**
1999	**NY-A**	**133**	**473**	**64**	**117**	**26**	**1**	**17**	**71**	**39**	**0**	**74**	**0**	**2**	**9**	**9**	**3**	**.247**	**.299**	**.414**	**.962**
2000	**NY-A**	**135**	**470**	**57**	**108**	**20**	**0**	**16**	**64**	**45**	**1**	**73**	**2**	**0**	**2**	**0**	**3**	**.230**	**.299**	**.374**	**.968**
Career average		103	346	49	88	18	1	13	48	31	1	62	3	3	4	5	3	.254	.317	.419	.976
Yankee average		**140**	**491**	**69**	**128**	**27**	**0**	**17**	**78**	**45**	**1**	**81**	**1**	**3**	**5**	**7**	**5**	**.261**	**.321**	**.422**	**.977**
Career total		1026	3461	487	878	175	6	128	482	314	8	616	26	25	36	54	29	.254	.317	.419	.976
Yankee total		**420**	**1473**	**207**	**384**	**80**	**1**	**52**	**233**	**136**	**2**	**244**	**2**	**10**	**14**	**20**	**14**	**.261**	**.321**	**.422**	**.977**

Brower, Robert Richard

HEIGHT: 6'0" THROWS: RIGHT BATS: RIGHT BORN: 1/10/1960 JAMAICA, NEW YORK POSITIONS PLAYED: OF, DH

YEAR	TEAM	GAMES	AB	RUNS	HITS	2B	3B	HR	RBI	BB	IBB	SO	HBP	SH	SF	SB	CS	BA	OBA	SA	FA
1986	Tex-A	21	9	3	1	1	0	0	0	0	0	3	0	0	0	1	2	.111	.111	.222	1.000
1987	Tex-A	127	303	63	79	10	3	14	46	36	0	66	0	9	1	15	9	.261	.338	.452	.964
1988	Tex-A	82	201	29	45	7	0	1	11	27	0	38	0	6	0	10	5	.224	.316	.274	.972
1989	**NY-A**	**26**	**69**	**9**	**16**	**3**	**0**	**2**	**3**	**6**	**0**	**11**	**0**	**0**	**0**	**3**	**1**	**.232**	**.293**	**.362**	**.970**
Career average		64	146	26	35	5	1	4	15	17	0	30	0	4	0	7	4	.242	.322	.376	.977
Yankee average		**26**	**69**	**9**	**16**	**3**	**0**	**2**	**3**	**6**	**0**	**11**	**0**	**0**	**0**	**3**	**1**	**.232**	**.293**	**.362**	**.970**
Career total		256	582	104	141	21	3	17	60	69	0	118	0	15	1	29	17	.242	.322	.376	.977
Yankee total		**26**	**69**	**9**	**16**	**3**	**0**	**2**	**3**	**6**	**0**	**11**	**0**	**0**	**0**	**3**	**1**	**.232**	**.293**	**.362**	**.970**

Robert William "Bobby" "Doc" Brown, 3b-ss-2b-of, 1946–52, '54

At the press conference to announce the signing of Bobby Brown to a Yankee contract in 1945, then-Yankee owner Larry MacPhail waxed eloquent about Brown's talents as a player, as a person and, since he was going to medical school, as a potential physician. Finally, one of the sportswriters could not resist, and asked, "Larry, are you signing him as a player or as a doctor?"

Brown, born in Seattle, Washington, on October 25, 1924, was one of the Yankees' first "bonus babies." New York's ownership was not thrilled to be getting into the practice of giving players big money before they had swung a bat in a Yankee uniform, but it was either compete in that manner or fall behind.

Brown, then, faced considerable pressure his first few years, but he came through admirably, hitting .300 with a league-leading nine pinch hits in 1947, then hitting .300 again in 1948.

Yankee skipper Joe McCarthy loved Brown's bat, but he didn't think much of his fielding ability. As a result, McCarthy tried him at several positions in the infield in 1947 and '48. But by 1949, Brown was the team's starting third baseman, where he would stay for several years.

As good a hitter as Brown was during the regular season, he was a holy terror in the four World Series in which he played. He had three pinch hits in three at-bats in the 1947 Series, a 4-3 Yankee win over the Dodgers. In 1949, he hit .500, with a team-leading 5 RBI and a team-best four runs scored to lead the Yankees over the Dodgers again, this time in five games. He hit .333 in the 1950 Fall Classic and .357 in 1951, both Yankee victories.

Brown served in the military for part of 1952 and all of 1953. He came back to the Yankees in 1954 as a part-time player and had the worst year of his career, hitting only .217. He retired that year to practice medicine.

Throughout his early career with the Yankees, Brown also attended medical school with an eye toward a physician's practice after his playing days. Yogi Berra, his one-time roommate, once said that he appreciated doctors more because of all the time Brown spent in his room, studying.

Brown retired from medicine in 1984 at the age of 60. But that year, he returned to baseball—he was elected President of the American League, succeeding Lee MacPhail.

Brown, Robert William (Bobby *or* Doc)

HEIGHT: 6'1"   THROWS: RIGHT   BATS: LEFT   BORN: 10/25/1924 SEATTLE, WASHINGTON   POSITIONS PLAYED: 2B, 3B, SS, OF

YEAR	TEAM	GAMES	AB	RUNS	HITS	2B	3B	HR	RBI	BB	IBB	SO	HBP	SH	SF	SB	CS	BA	OBA	SA	FA
1946	NY-A	7	24	1	8	1	0	0	1	4	—	0	0	1	—	0	0	.333	.429	.375	1.000
1947	NY-A	69	150	21	45	6	1	1	18	21	—	9	1	3	—	0	2	.300	.390	.373	.932
1948	NY-A	113	363	62	109	19	5	3	48	48	—	16	1	4	—	0	1	.300	.383	.405	.931
1949	NY-A	104	343	61	97	14	4	6	61	38	—	18	3	0	—	4	3	.283	.359	.399	1.000
1950	NY-A	95	277	33	74	4	2	4	37	39	—	18	1	3	—	3	1	.267	.360	.339	.958
1951	NY-A	103	313	44	84	15	2	6	51	47	—	18	3	6	—	1	1	.268	.369	.387	.955
1952	NY-A	29	89	6	22	2	0	1	14	9	—	6	1	1	—	1	1	.247	.323	.303	.894
1954	NY-A	28	60	5	13	1	0	1	7	8	—	3	0	0	1	0	1	.217	.304	.283	1.000
Career average		69	202	29	57	8	2	3	30	27	—	11	1	2	—	1	1	.279	.367	.376	.959
Yankee average		69	202	29	57	8	2	3	30	27	—	11	1	2	—	1	1	.279	.367	.376	.959
Career total		548	1619	233	452	62	14	22	237	214	—	88	10	18	1	9	10	.279	.367	.376	.959
Yankee total		548	1619	233	452	62	14	22	237	214	—	88	10	18	1	9	10	.279	.367	.376	.959

Brown, Rogers Lee (Bobby)

HEIGHT: 6'2" THROWS: RIGHT BATS: BOTH BORN: 5/24/1954 NORFOLK, VIRGINIA POSITIONS PLAYED: OF, DH

YEAR	TEAM	GAMES	AB	RUNS	HITS	2B	3B	HR	RBI	BB	IBB	SO	HBP	SH	SF	SB	CS	BA	OBA	SA	FA
1979	Tor-A	4	10	1	0	0	0	0	0	2	0	1	0	0	0	0	0	.000	.167	.000	1.000
1979	**NY-A**	**30**	**68**	**7**	**17**	**3**	**1**	**0**	**3**	**2**	**0**	**17**	**0**	**1**	**0**	**2**	**1**	**.250**	**.271**	**.324**	**.949**
1980	**NY-A**	**137**	**412**	**65**	**107**	**12**	**5**	**14**	**47**	**29**	**4**	**82**	**0**	**2**	**3**	**27**	**8**	**.260**	**.306**	**.415**	**.972**
1981	**NY-A**	**31**	**62**	**5**	**14**	**1**	**0**	**0**	**6**	**5**	**0**	**15**	**0**	**1**	**1**	**4**	**2**	**.226**	**.279**	**.242**	**.949**
1982	Sea-A	79	245	29	59	7	1	4	17	17	2	32	0	3	2	28	6	.241	.288	.327	.968
1983	SD-N	57	225	40	60	5	3	5	22	23	0	38	0	1	1	27	9	.267	.333	.382	.963
1984	SD-N	85	171	28	43	7	2	3	29	11	0	33	0	2	3	16	4	.251	.292	.368	.971
1985	SD-N	79	84	8	13	3	0	0	6	5	0	20	0	1	1	6	4	.155	.200	.190	1.000
Career average		152	436	63	119	16	4	7	60	53	0	35	2	5	1	9	4	.273	.353	.371	.972
Yankee average		**72**	**209**	**30**	**57**	**8**	**2**	**4**	**29**	**25**	**1**	**19**	**1**	**2**	**1**	**4**	**2**	**.274**	**.351**	**.379**	**.957**
Career total		2283	6539	940	1782	240	58	98	900	790	6	524	33	70	14	139	67	.273	.353	.371	.972
Yankee total		**716**	**2093**	**303**	**573**	**75**	**19**	**36**	**290**	**248**	**4**	**185**	**10**	**21**	**4**	**40**	**20**	**.274**	**.351**	**.379**	**.957**

Bryan, William Ronald (Billy)

HEIGHT: 6'4" THROWS: RIGHT BATS: LEFT BORN: 12/4/1938 MORGAN, GEORGIA POSITIONS PLAYED: C, 1B

YEAR	TEAM	GAMES	AB	RUNS	HITS	2B	3B	HR	RBI	BB	IBB	SO	HBP	SH	SF	SB	CS	BA	OBA	SA	FA
1961	KC-A	9	19	2	3	0	0	1	2	2	0	7	0	0	0	0	0	.158	.238	.316	1.000
1962	KC-A	25	74	5	11	2	1	2	7	5	0	32	0	0	0	0	0	.149	.203	.284	.976
1963	KC-A	24	65	11	11	1	1	3	7	9	5	22	0	0	0	0	0	.169	.270	.354	.981
1964	KC-A	93	220	19	53	9	2	13	36	16	1	69	0	2	2	0	0	.241	.290	.477	.991
1965	KC-A	108	325	36	82	11	5	14	51	29	5	87	2	0	3	0	0	.252	.315	.446	.984
1966	KC-A	32	76	0	10	4	0	0	7	6	0	17	0	0	1	0	0	.132	.193	.184	1.000
1966	**NY-A**	**27**	**69**	**5**	**15**	**2**	**0**	**4**	**5**	**5**	**0**	**19**	**0**	**0**	**0**	**0**	**0**	**.217**	**.270**	**.420**	**.988**
1967	**NY-A**	**16**	**12**	**1**	**2**	**0**	**0**	**1**	**2**	**5**	**0**	**3**	**0**	**0**	**0**	**0**	**0**	**.167**	**.412**	**.417**	**1.000**
1968	Was-A	40	108	7	22	3	0	3	8	14	2	27	1	0	0	0	1	.204	.301	.315	.983
Career average		47	121	11	26	4	1	5	16	11	2	35	0	0	1	0	0	.216	.284	.395	.989
Yankee average		**16**	**12**	**1**	**2**	**0**	**0**	**1**	**2**	**5**	**0**	**3**	**0**	**0**	**0**	**0**	**0**	**.167**	**.412**	**.417**	**.994**
Career total		374	968	86	209	32	9	41	125	91	13	283	3	2	6	0	1	.216	.284	.395	.989
Yankee total		**16**	**12**	**1**	**2**	**0**	**0**	**1**	**2**	**5**	**0**	**3**	**0**	**0**	**0**	**0**	**0**	**.167**	**.412**	**.417**	**.994**

Buhner, Jay Campbell

HEIGHT: 6'3" THROWS: RIGHT BATS: RIGHT BORN: 8/13/1964 LOUISVILLE, KENTUCKY POSITIONS PLAYED: OF, DH

YEAR	TEAM	GAMES	AB	RUNS	HITS	2B	3B	HR	RBI	BB	IBB	SO	HBP	SH	SF	SB	CS	BA	OBA	SA	FA
1987	**NY-A**	**7**	**22**	**0**	**5**	**2**	**0**	**0**	**1**	**1**	**0**	**6**	**0**	**0**	**0**	**0**	**0**	**.227**	**.261**	**.318**	**1.000**
1988	**NY-A**	**25**	**69**	**8**	**13**	**0**	**0**	**3**	**13**	**3**	**0**	**25**	**3**	**0**	**1**	**0**	**0**	**.188**	**.250**	**.319**	**.964**
1988	Sea-A	60	192	28	43	13	1	10	25	25	1	68	3	1	2	1	1	.224	.323	.458	.993
1989	Sea-A	58	204	27	56	15	1	9	33	19	0	55	2	0	1	1	4	.275	.341	.490	.966
1990	Sea-A	51	163	16	45	12	0	7	33	17	1	50	4	0	1	2	2	.276	.357	.479	.966
1991	Sea-A	137	406	64	99	14	4	27	77	53	5	117	6	2	4	0	1	.244	.337	.498	.981
1992	Sea-A	152	543	69	132	16	3	25	79	71	2	146	6	1	8	0	0	.243	.333	.422	.994
1993	Sea-A	158	563	91	153	28	3	27	98	100	11	144	2	2	8	2	5	.272	.379	.476	.978
1994	Sea-A	101	358	74	100	23	4	21	68	66	3	63	5	2	5	0	1	.279	.394	.542	.990
1995	Sea-A	126	470	86	123	23	0	40	121	60	7	120	1	2	6	0	1	.262	.343	.566	.989
1996	Sea-A	150	564	107	153	29	0	44	138	84	5	159	9	0	10	0	1	.271	.369	.557	.989
1997	Sea-A	157	540	104	131	18	2	40	109	119	3	175	5	0	1	0	0	.243	.383	.506	.997
1998	Sea-A	72	244	33	59	7	1	15	45	38	0	71	0	1	2	0	0	.242	.342	.463	.985
1999	Sea-A	87	266	37	59	11	0	14	38	69	0	100	0	0	3	0	0	.222	.379	.421	.986
2000	Sea-A	112	364	50	92	20	0	26	82	59	3	98	4	1	2	0	2	.253	.361	.522	1.000
Career average		97	331	53	84	15	1	21	64	52	3	93	3	1	4	0	2	.254	.358	.494	.985
Yankee average		**16**	**46**	**4**	**9**	**1**	**0**	**2**	**7**	**2**	**0**	**16**	**2**	**0**	**1**	**0**	**0**	**.198**	**.253**	**.319**	**.982**
Career total		1453	4968	794	1263	231	19	308	960	784	41	1397	50	12	54	6	24	.254	.358	.494	.985
Yankee total		**32**	**91**	**8**	**18**	**2**	**0**	**3**	**14**	**4**	**0**	**31**	**3**	**0**	**1**	**0**	**0**	**.198**	**.253**	**.319**	**.982**

Burns, George Henry (Tioga George)
HEIGHT: 6'1"   THROWS: RIGHT   BATS: RIGHT   BORN: 1/31/1893 NILES, OHIO   DIED: 1/7/1978 KIRKLAND, WASHINGTON   POSITIONS PLAYED: 1B, OF

YEAR	TEAM	GAMES	AB	RUNS	HITS	2B	3B	HR	RBI	BB	IBB	SO	HBP	SH	SF	SB	CS	BA	OBA	SA	FA
1914	Det-A	137	478	55	139	22	5	5	57	32	—	56	12	22	—	23	13	.291	.351	.389	.982
1915	Det-A	105	392	49	99	18	3	5	50	22	—	51	5	17	—	9	3	.253	.301	.352	.986
1916	Det-A	135	479	60	137	22	6	4	73	22	—	30	7	19	—	12	—	.286	.327	.382	.985
1917	Det-A	119	407	42	92	14	10	1	40	15	—	33	6	14	—	3	—	.226	.264	.317	.990
1918	Phi-A	130	505	61	178	22	9	6	70	23	—	25	8	8	—	8	—	.352	.390	.467	.833
1919	Phi-A	126	470	63	139	29	9	8	57	19	—	18	12	6	—	15	—	.296	.339	.447	.934
1920	Phi-A	22	60	1	14	3	0	1	7	6	—	7	1	1	—	4	0	.233	.313	.333	.958
1920	Cle-A	44	56	7	15	4	1	0	13	4	—	3	2	2	—	1	0	.268	.339	.375	.979
1921	Cle-A	84	244	52	88	21	4	0	49	13	—	19	2	6	—	3	1	.361	.398	.480	.990
1922	Bos-A	147	558	71	171	32	5	12	73	20	—	28	9	15	—	8	2	.306	.341	.446	.987
1923	Bos-A	146	551	91	181	47	5	7	82	45	—	33	7	12	—	9	7	.328	.386	.470	.990
1924	Cle-A	129	462	64	143	37	5	4	68	29	—	27	15	23	—	14	5	.310	.370	.437	.987
1925	Cle-A	127	488	69	164	41	4	6	79	24	—	24	3	8	—	16	11	.336	.371	.473	.989
1926	Cle-A	151	603	97	216	64	3	4	114	28	—	33	8	18	—	13	7	.358	.394	.494	.988
1927	Cle-A	140	549	84	175	51	2	3	78	42	—	27	7	9	—	13	11	.319	.354	.435	.990
1928	Cle-A	82	209	29	52	12	1	5	30	17	—	11	6	6	—	2	3	.249	.323	.388	.984
1928	**NY-A**	**4**	**4**	**1**	**2**	**0**	**0**	**0**	**0**	**0**	**—**	**1**	**0**	**0**	**—**	**0**	**0**	**.500**	**.500**	**.500**	**1.000**
1929	**NY-A**	**9**	**9**	**0**	**0**	**0**	**0**	**0**	**0**	**0**	**—**	**4**	**0**	**0**	**—**	**0**	**0**	**.000**	**.000**	**.000**	**.000**
1929	Phi-A	29	49	5	13	5	0	1	11	2	—	3	0	1	—	1	0	.265	.294	.429	
Career average		98	346	47	106	23	4	4	50	19	—	23	6	10	—	8	—	.307	.354	.429	.924
Yankee average		**7**	**7**	**1**	**1**	**0**	**0**	**0**	**0**	**0**	**—**	**3**	**0**	**0**	**—**	**0**	**0**	**.154**	**.154**	**.154**	**.500**
Career total		1866	6573	901	2018	444	72	72	951	363	—	433	110	187	—	154	63	.307	.354	.429	.924
Yankee total		**13**	**13**	**1**	**2**	**0**	**0**	**0**	**0**	**0**	**—**	**5**	**0**	**0**	**—**	**0**	**0**	**.154**	**.154**	**.154**	**.500**

Burr, Alexander Thomson
HEIGHT: 6'3"   THROWS: RIGHT   BATS: RIGHT   BORN: 11/1/1893 CHICAGO, ILLINOIS   DIED: 11/12/1918 CAZAUX, FRANCE   POSITIONS PLAYED: OF

YEAR	TEAM	GAMES	AB	RUNS	HITS	2B	3B	HR	RBI	BB	IBB	SO	HBP	SH	SF	SB	CS	BA	OBA	SA	FA
1914	**NY-A**	**1**	**0**	**0**	**0**	**0**	**0**	**0**	**0**	**0**	**—**	**0**	**0**	**0**	**0**	**0**	**—**	**.000**	**.000**	**.000**	**.000**
Career average		1	0	0	0	0	0	0	0	0	0	0	0	0	0	0	0	.000	.000	.000	.000
Yankee average		**1**	**0**	**0**	**0**	**0**	**0**	**0**	**0**	**0**	**0**	**0**	**0**	**0**	**0**	**0**	**0**	**.000**	**.000**	**.000**	**.000**
Career total		1	0	0	0	0	0	0	0	0	0	0	0	0	0	0	0	.000	.000	.000	.000
Yankee total		**1**	**0**	**0**	**0**	**0**	**0**	**0**	**0**	**0**	**0**	**0**	**0**	**0**	**0**	**0**	**0**	**.000**	**.000**	**.000**	**.000**

Bush, Homer Giles
HEIGHT: 5'11"   THROWS: RIGHT   BATS: RIGHT   BORN: 11/12/1972 EAST ST. LOUIS, ILLINOIS   POSITIONS PLAYED: 2B, 3B, SS, DH

YEAR	TEAM	GAMES	AB	RUNS	HITS	2B	3B	HR	RBI	BB	IBB	SO	HBP	SH	SF	SB	CS	BA	OBA	SA	FA
1997	**NY-A**	**10**	**11**	**2**	**4**	**0**	**0**	**0**	**3**	**0**	**0**	**0**	**0**	**0**	**0**	**0**	**0**	**.364**	**.364**	**.364**	**.913**
1998	**NY-A**	**45**	**71**	**17**	**27**	**3**	**0**	**1**	**5**	**5**	**0**	**19**	**0**	**2**	**0**	**6**	**3**	**.380**	**.421**	**.465**	**.970**
1999	Tor-A	128	485	69	155	26	4	5	55	21	0	82	0	8	3	32	8	.320	.346	.421	.920
2000	Tor-A	76	297	38	64	8	0	1	18	18	0	60	5	4	1	9	4	.215	.271	.253	.986
Career average		65	216	32	63	9	1	2	20	11	0	40	1	4	1	12	4	.289	.326	.366	.947
Yankee average		**28**	**41**	**10**	**16**	**2**	**0**	**1**	**4**	**3**	**0**	**10**	**0**	**1**	**0**	**3**	**2**	**.378**	**.414**	**.451**	**.942**
Career total		259	864	126	250	37	4	7	81	44	0	161	5	14	4	47	15	.289	.326	.366	.947
Yankee total		**55**	**82**	**19**	**31**	**3**	**0**	**1**	**8**	**5**	**0**	**19**	**0**	**2**	**0**	**6**	**3**	**.378**	**.414**	**.451**	**.942**

Buzas, Joseph John
HEIGHT: 6'1"   THROWS: RIGHT   BATS: RIGHT   BORN: 10/2/1919, ALPHA, NEW JERSEY   POSITIONS PLAYED: SS

YEAR	TEAM	GAMES	AB	RUNS	HITS	2B	3B	HR	RBI	BB	IBB	SO	HBP	SH	SF	SB	CS	BA	OBA	SA	FA
1945	**NY-A**	**30**	**65**	**8**	**17**	**2**	**1**	**0**	**6**	**2**	**—**	**5**	**0**	**0**	**—**	**2**	**0**	**.262**	**.284**	**.323**	**.898**
Career average		30	65	8	17	2	1	0	6	2	—	5	0	0	—	2	0	.262	.284	.323	.898
Yankee average		**30**	**65**	**8**	**17**	**2**	**1**	**0**	**6**	**2**	**—**	**5**	**0**	**0**	**—**	**2**	**0**	**.262**	**.284**	**.323**	**.898**
Career total		30	65	8	17	2	1	0	6	2	—	5	0	0	—	2	0	.262	.284	.323	.898
Yankee total		**30**	**65**	**8**	**17**	**2**	**1**	**0**	**6**	**2**	**—**	**5**	**0**	**0**	**—**	**2**	**0**	**.262**	**.284**	**.323**	**.898**

Byrd, Samuel Dewey (Babe Ruth's Legs)

HEIGHT: 5'10"   THROWS: RIGHT   BATS: RIGHT   BORN: 10/15/1907 BREMEN, GEORGIA   DIED: 5/11/1981 MESA, ARIZONA   POSITIONS PLAYED: OF

YEAR	TEAM	GAMES	AB	RUNS	HITS	2B	3B	HR	RBI	BB	IBB	SO	HBP	SH	SF	SB	CS	BA	OBA	SA	FA
1929	NY-A	62	170	32	53	12	0	5	28	28	—	18	0	4	—	1	4	.312	.409	.471	.950
1930	NY-A	92	218	46	62	12	2	6	31	30	—	18	0	6	—	5	1	.284	.371	.440	.992
1931	NY-A	115	248	51	67	18	2	3	32	29	—	26	1	3	—	5	0	.270	.349	.395	.974
1932	NY-A	105	209	49	62	12	1	8	30	30	—	20	0	4	—	1	2	.297	.385	.478	.964
1933	NY-A	85	107	26	30	6	1	2	11	15	—	12	0	0	—	0	1	.280	.369	.411	.987
1934	NY-A	106	191	32	47	8	0	3	23	18	—	22	2	7	—	1	2	.246	.318	.335	.988
1935	Cin-N	121	416	51	109	25	4	9	52	37	—	51	0	7	—	4	—	.262	.322	.406	.970
1936	Cin-N	59	141	17	35	8	0	2	13	11	—	11	0	1	—	0	—	.248	.303	.348	.989
Career average		93	213	38	58	13	1	5	28	25	—	22	0	4	—	2	—	.274	.350	.412	.977
Yankee average		**94**	**191**	**39**	**54**	**11**	**1**	**5**	**26**	**25**	**—**	**19**	**1**	**4**	**—**	**2**	**2**	**.281**	**.366**	**.422**	**.976**
Career total		745	1700	304	465	101	10	38	220	198	—	178	3	32	—	17	10	.274	.350	.412	.977
Yankee total		**565**	**1143**	**236**	**321**	**68**	**6**	**27**	**155**	**150**	**—**	**116**	**3**	**24**	**—**	**13**	**10**	**.281**	**.366**	**.422**	**.976**

Byrne, Thomas Joseph

HEIGHT: 6'1"   THROWS: LEFT   BATS: LEFT   BORN: 12/31/1919, BALTIMORE, MARYLAND   POSITIONS PLAYED: —

YEAR	TEAM	GAMES	AB	RUNS	HITS	2B	3B	HR	RBI	BB	IBB	SO	HBP	SH	SF	SB	CS	BA	OBA	SA	FA
1943	NY-A	13	11	0	1	0	0	0	0	2	—	3	0	1	—	0	0	.091	.231	.091	.909
1946	NY-A	14	9	2	2	0	0	0	0	1	—	0	0	0	—	0	0	.222	.300	.222	1.000
1947	NY-A	4	0	0	0	0	0	0	0	1	—	0	0	0	—	0	0	—	1.000	—	1.000
1948	NY-A	31	46	8	15	3	1	1	7	1	—	7	1	4	—	0	0	.326	.354	.500	1.000
1949	NY-A	35	83	8	16	4	2	0	13	2	—	20	0	1	—	0	0	.193	.212	.289	1.000
1950	NY-A	34	81	14	22	3	1	2	16	4	—	15	2	0	—	1	0	.272	.322	.407	.897
1951	NY-A	9	9	2	2	0	0	1	3	0	—	2	0	0	—	0	0	.222	.222	.556	1.000
1951	StL-A	34	57	7	16	3	0	1	12	4	—	8	0	2	—	0	0	.281	.328	.386	.958
1952	StL-A	40	84	9	21	5	1	1	12	5	—	18	0	0	—	0	0	.250	.292	.369	.926
1953	Chi-A	18	18	2	3	0	0	1	5	2	—	6	0	0	—	0	0	.167	.250	.333	1.000
1953	Was-A	14	17	0	1	0	0	0	0	3	—	7	0	0	—	0	0	.059	.200	.059	.818
1954	NY-A	7	19	2	7	4	1	0	6	0	—	3	0	0	0	0	0	.368	.368	.684	.889
1955	NY-A	45	78	6	16	1	1	1	6	8	0	15	0	1	2	0	0	.205	.273	.282	.929
1956	NY-A	44	52	8	14	1	1	3	10	2	1	11	0	2	0	0	0	.269	.296	.500	.963
1957	NY-A	35	37	5	7	2	0	3	8	3	0	11	0	0	0	0	0	.189	.250	.486	.938
Career average		25	40	5	10	2	1	1	7	3	0	8	0	1	0	0	0	.238	.286	.378	.948
Yankee average		**25**	**39**	**5**	**9**	**2**	**1**	**1**	**6**	**2**	**0**	**8**	**0**	**1**	**0**	**0**	**0**	**.240**	**.284**	**.393**	**.957**
Career total		377	601	73	143	26	8	14	98	38	1	126	3	11	2	1	0	.238	.286	.378	.948
Yankee total		**271**	**425**	**55**	**102**	**18**	**7**	**11**	**69**	**24**	**1**	**87**	**3**	**9**	**2**	**1**	**0**	**.240**	**.284**	**.393**	**.957**

Caldwell, Raymond Benjamin (Rube *or* Slim)

HEIGHT: 6'2"   THROWS: RIGHT   BATS: LEFT   BORN: 4/26/1888 CORYDON, PENNSYLVANIA   DIED: 8/17/1967 SALAMANCA, NEW YORK   POSITIONS PLAYED: P, OF

YEAR	TEAM	GAMES	AB	RUNS	HITS	2B	3B	HR	RBI	BB	IBB	SO	HBP	SH	SF	SB	CS	BA	OBA	SA	FA
1910	NY-A	6	6	0	0	0	0	0	0	0	—	—	0	0	—	0	—	.000	.000	.000	1.000
1911	NY-A	59	147	14	40	4	1	0	17	11	—	—	0	1	—	5	—	.272	.323	.313	.953
1912	NY-A	44	76	18	18	1	2	0	6	5	—	—	0	1	—	4	—	.237	.284	.303	.938
1913	NY-A	59	97	10	28	3	2	0	11	3	—	15	0	2	—	3	—	.289	.310	.361	1.000
1914	NY-A	59	113	9	22	4	0	0	10	7	—	24	1	5	—	2	1	.195	.248	.230	.967
1915	NY-A	72	144	27	35	4	1	4	20	9	—	32	0	2	—	4	3	.243	.288	.368	.988
1916	NY-A	45	93	6	19	2	0	0	4	2	—	17	0	0	—	1	0	.204	.221	.226	.960
1917	NY-A	63	124	12	32	6	1	2	12	16	—	16	0	0	—	2	0	.258	.343	.371	.973
1918	NY-A	65	151	14	44	10	0	1	18	13	—	23	1	4	—	2	0	.291	.352	.377	.977
1919	Bos-A	33	48	5	13	1	1	0	4	0	—	9	0	3	—	0	0	.271	.271	.333	.950
1919	Cle-A	6	23	4	8	4	0	0	2	0	—	4	0	0	—	0	0	.348	.348	.522	.900
1920	Cle-A	41	89	17	19	3	0	0	7	10	—	13	1	5	—	0	2	.213	.300	.247	.917
1921	Cle-A	38	53	2	11	4	0	1	3	2	—	5	0	1	—	0	0	.208	.236	.340	.930
Career average		45	90	11	22	4	1	1	9	6	0	—	0	2	—	2	—	.248	.297	.322	.958
Yankee average		**61**	**125**	**14**	**30**	**5**	**0**	**1**	**13**	**9**	**—**	**—**	**0**	**2**	**—**	**2**	**—**	**.243**	**.298**	**.325**	**.973**
Career total		590	1164	138	289	46	8	8	114	78	—	158	3	24	—	23	6	.248	.297	.322	.958
Yankee total		**304**	**625**	**68**	**152**	**26**	**2**	**7**	**64**	**47**	**—**	**112**	**2**	**11**	**—**	**11**	**4**	**.243**	**.298**	**.325**	**.973**

Callison, John Wesley

HEIGHT: 5'10"   THROWS: RIGHT   BATS: LEFT   BORN: 3/12/1939, QUALLS, OKLAHOMA   POSITIONS PLAYED: OF

YEAR	TEAM	GAMES	AB	RUNS	HITS	2B	3B	HR	RBI	BB	IBB	SO	HBP	SH	SF	SB	CS	BA	OBA	SA	FA
1958	Chi-A	18	64	10	19	4	2	1	12	6	0	14	0	0	1	1	0	.297	.352	.469	.976
1959	Chi-A	49	104	12	18	3	0	3	12	13	0	20	1	0	0	0	1	.173	.271	.288	.983
1960	Phi-N	99	288	36	75	11	5	9	30	45	2	70	0	2	0	0	4	.260	.360	.427	.989
1961	Phi-N	138	455	74	121	20	11	9	47	69	5	76	3	6	5	10	4	.266	.363	.418	.967
1962	Phi-N	157	603	107	181	26	10	23	83	54	1	96	6	8	1	10	3	.300	.363	.491	.980
1963	Phi-N	157	626	96	178	36	11	26	78	50	4	111	2	13	1	8	3	.284	.339	.502	.994
1964	Phi-N	162	654	101	179	30	10	31	104	36	3	95	6	6	3	6	3	.274	.316	.492	.988
1965	Phi-N	160	619	93	162	25	16	32	101	57	2	117	6	4	5	6	5	.262	.328	.509	.982
1966	Phi-N	155	612	93	169	40	7	11	55	56	4	83	3	2	4	8	8	.276	.338	.418	.990
1967	Phi-N	149	556	62	145	30	5	14	64	55	17	63	3	3	3	6	12	.261	.329	.408	.977
1968	Phi-N	121	398	46	97	18	4	14	40	42	4	70	3	3	2	4	3	.244	.319	.415	1.000
1969	Phi-N	134	495	66	131	29	5	16	64	49	11	73	3	1	4	2	1	.265	.332	.440	.990
1970	Chi-N	147	477	65	126	23	2	19	68	60	11	63	3	0	3	7	2	.264	.348	.440	.973
1971	Chi-N	103	290	27	61	12	1	8	38	36	8	55	2	1	4	2	1	.210	.298	.341	.982
1972	**NY-A**	**92**	**275**	**28**	**71**	**10**	**0**	**9**	**34**	**18**	**1**	**34**	**0**	**2**	**5**	**3**	**0**	**.258**	**.299**	**.393**	**.992**
1973	**NY-A**	**45**	**136**	**10**	**24**	**4**	**0**	**1**	**10**	**4**	**0**	**24**	**0**	**0**	**2**	**1**	**1**	**.176**	**.197**	**.228**	**.960**
Career average		118	416	58	110	20	6	14	53	41	5	67	3	3	3	5	3	.264	.331	.441	.983
Yankee average		**69**	**206**	**19**	**48**	**7**	**0**	**5**	**22**	**11**	**1**	**29**	**0**	**1**	**4**	**2**	**1**	**.231**	**.266**	**.338**	**.976**
Career total		1886	6652	926	1757	321	89	226	840	650	73	1064	41	51	43	74	51	.264	.331	.441	.983
Yankee total		**137**	**411**	**38**	**95**	**14**	**0**	**10**	**44**	**22**	**1**	**58**	**0**	**2**	**7**	**4**	**1**	**.231**	**.266**	**.338**	**.976**

Camp, Howard Lee (Howie *or* Red)

HEIGHT: 5'9"   THROWS: RIGHT   BATS: LEFT   BORN: 7/1/1893 MUNFORD, ALABAMA   DIED: 5/8/1960 EASTABOGA, ALABAMA   POSITIONS PLAYED: OF

YEAR	TEAM	GAMES	AB	RUNS	HITS	2B	3B	HR	RBI	BB	IBB	SO	HBP	SH	SF	SB	CS	BA	OBA	SA	FA
1917	**NY-A**	**5**	**21**	**3**	**6**	**1**	**0**	**0**	**0**	**1**	—	**2**	**0**	**0**	—	**0**	—	**.286**	**.318**	**.333**	**.857**
Career average		5	21	3	6	1	0	0	0	1	—	2	0	0	—	0	—	.286	.318	.333	.857
Yankee average		**5**	**21**	**3**	**6**	**1**	**0**	**0**	**0**	**1**	—	**2**	**0**	**0**	—	**0**	—	**.286**	**.318**	**.333**	**.857**
Career total		5	21	3	6	1	0	0	0	1	—	2	0	0	—	0	—	.286	.318	.333	.857
Yankee total		**5**	**21**	**3**	**6**	**1**	**0**	**0**	**0**	**1**	—	**2**	**0**	**0**	—	**0**	—	**.286**	**.318**	**.333**	**.857**

Campaneris, Dagoberto (Blanco *or* Bert *or* Campy)

HEIGHT: 5'10"   THROWS: RIGHT   BATS: RIGHT   BORN: 3/9/1942 PUEBLO NUEVO, CUBA   POSITIONS PLAYED: 3B, SS

YEAR	TEAM	GAMES	AB	RUNS	HITS	2B	3B	HR	RBI	BB	IBB	SO	HBP	SH	SF	SB	CS	BA	OBA	SA	FA
1964	KC-A	67	269	27	69	14	3	4	22	15	0	41	4	2	0	10	2	.257	.306	.375	.953
1965	KC-A	144	578	67	156	23	12	6	42	41	0	71	9	3	3	51	19	.270	.326	.382	1.000
1966	KC-A	142	573	82	153	29	10	5	42	25	1	72	5	1	2	52	10	.267	.302	.379	.971
1967	KC-A	147	601	85	149	29	6	3	32	36	2	82	7	3	2	55	16	.248	.297	.331	.954
1968	Oak-A	159	642	87	177	25	9	4	38	50	2	69	4	8	3	62	22	.276	.330	.361	.956
1969	Oak-A	135	547	71	142	15	2	2	25	30	2	62	4	10	1	62	8	.260	.302	.305	.967
1970	Oak-A	147	603	97	168	28	4	22	64	36	1	73	4	3	4	42	10	.279	.321	.448	.973
1971	Oak-A	134	569	80	143	18	4	5	47	29	1	64	2	3	6	34	7	.251	.287	.323	.960
1972	Oak-A	149	625	85	150	25	2	8	32	32	0	88	2	20	2	52	14	.240	.278	.325	.977
1973	Oak-A	151	601	89	150	17	6	4	46	50	1	79	4	9	7	34	10	.250	.308	.318	.969
1974	Oak-A	134	527	77	153	18	8	2	41	47	2	81	0	11	2	34	15	.290	.347	.366	.966
1975	Oak-A	137	509	69	135	15	3	4	46	50	2	71	7	19	3	24	12	.265	.337	.330	.962
1976	Oak-A	149	536	67	137	14	1	1	52	63	0	80	3	18	11	54	12	.256	.331	.291	.969
1977	Tex-A	150	552	77	140	19	7	5	46	47	1	86	4	40	5	27	20	.254	.314	.341	.968
1978	Tex-A	98	269	30	50	5	3	1	17	20	0	36	2	25	3	22	4	.186	.245	.238	.954
1979	Tex-A	8	9	2	1	0	0	0	0	1	0	3	0	0	0	1	0	.111	.200	.111	.962
1979	Cal-A	85	239	27	56	4	4	0	15	19	0	32	2	11	2	12	4	.234	.296	.285	.957
1980	Cal-A	77	210	32	53	8	1	2	18	14	0	33	1	7	2	10	5	.252	.300	.329	.957
1981	Cal-A	55	82	11	21	2	1	1	10	5	0	10	0	3	1	5	2	.256	.295	.341	.900
1983	**NY-A**	**60**	**143**	**19**	**46**	**5**	**0**	**0**	**11**	**8**	**0**	**9**	**0**	**3**	**1**	**6**	**7**	**.322**	**.355**	**.357**	**.932**
Career average		123	457	62	118	17	5	4	34	33	1	60	3	11	3	34	11	.259	.311	.342	.960
Yankee average		**60**	**143**	**19**	**46**	**5**	**0**	**0**	**11**	**8**	**0**	**9**	**0**	**3**	**1**	**6**	**7**	**.322**	**.355**	**.357**	**.932**
Career total		2328	8684	1181	2249	313	86	79	646	618	15	1142	64	199	60	649	199	.259	.311	.342	.960
Yankee total		**60**	**143**	**19**	**46**	**5**	**0**	**0**	**11**	**8**	**0**	**9**	**0**	**3**	**1**	**6**	**7**	**.322**	**.355**	**.357**	**.932**

Canseco, Jose BORN JOSE CANSECO (CAPAS)
HEIGHT: 6'4" THROWS: RIGHT BATS: RIGHT BORN: 7/2/1964 HAVANA, CUBA POSITIONS PLAYED: OF, DH

YEAR	TEAM	GAMES	AB	RUNS	HITS	2B	3B	HR	RBI	BB	IBB	SO	HBP	SH	SF	SB	CS	BA	OBA	SA	FA
1985	Oak-A	29	96	16	29	3	0	5	13	4	0	31	0	0	0	1	1	.302	.330	.490	.951
1986	Oak-A	157	600	85	144	29	1	33	117	65	1	175	8	0	9	15	7	.240	.318	.457	.958
1987	Oak-A	159	630	81	162	35	3	31	113	50	2	157	2	0	9	15	3	.257	.310	.470	.975
1988	Oak-A	158	610	120	187	34	0	42	124	78	10	128	10	1	6	40	16	.307	.391	.569	.978
1989	Oak-A	65	227	40	61	9	1	17	57	23	4	69	2	0	6	6	3	.269	.333	.542	.976
1990	Oak-A	131	481	83	132	14	2	37	101	72	8	158	5	0	5	19	10	.274	.371	.543	.995
1991	Oak-A	154	572	115	152	32	1	44	122	78	8	152	9	0	6	26	6	.266	.359	.556	.965
1992	Oak-A	97	366	66	90	11	0	22	72	48	1	104	3	0	4	5	7	.246	.335	.456	.988
1992	Tex-A	22	73	8	17	4	0	4	15	15	1	24	0	0	0	1	0	.233	.385	.452	.970
1993	Tex-A	60	231	30	59	14	1	10	46	16	2	62	3	0	3	6	6	.255	.308	.455	.985
1994	Tex-A	111	429	88	121	19	2	31	90	69	8	114	5	0	2	15	8	.282	.386	.552	.818
1995	Bos-A	102	396	64	121	25	1	24	81	42	4	93	7	0	5	4	0	.306	.378	.556	1.000
1996	Bos-A	96	360	68	104	22	1	28	82	63	3	82	6	0	3	3	1	.289	.400	.589	1.000
1997	Oak-A	108	388	56	91	19	0	23	74	51	1	122	3	0	4	8	2	.235	.325	.461	.938
1998	Tor-A	151	583	98	138	26	0	46	107	65	5	159	6	0	4	29	17	.237	.311	.518	.960
1999	TB-A	113	430	75	120	18	1	34	95	58	3	135	7	0	7	3	0	.279	.360	.563	1.000
2000	TB-A	61	218	31	56	15	0	9	30	41	1	65	4	0	1	2	0	.257	.383	.450	.818
2000	**NY-A**	**37**	**111**	**16**	**27**	**3**	**0**	**6**	**19**	**23**	**1**	**37**	**0**	**0**	**0**	**3**	**0**	**.243**	**.365**	**.432**	**1.000**
Career average		101	378	63	101	18	1	25	75	48	4	104	5	0	4	11	5	.266	.352	.516	.960
Yankee average		**37**	**111**	**16**	**27**	**3**	**0**	**6**	**19**	**23**	**1**	**37**	**0**	**0**	**3**	**0**	**0**	**.243**	**.365**	**.432**	**1.000**
Career total		1811	6801	1140	1811	332	14	446	1358	861	63	1867	83	1	77	198	87	.266	.352	.516	.960
Yankee total		**37**	**111**	**16**	**27**	**3**	**0**	**6**	**19**	**23**	**1**	**37**	**0**	**0**	**3**	**0**	**0**	**.243**	**.365**	**.432**	**1.000**

Carey, Andrew Arthur
HEIGHT: 6'1" THROWS: RIGHT BATS: RIGHT BORN: 10/18/1931 OAKLAND, CALIFORNIA POSITIONS PLAYED: 3B

YEAR	TEAM	GAMES	AB	RUNS	HITS	2B	3B	HR	RBI	BB	IBB	SO	HBP	SH	SF	SB	CS	BA	OBA	SA	FA
1952	NY-A	16	40	6	6	0	0	0	1	3	—	10	0	2	—	0	0	.150	.209	.150	.889
1953	NY-A	51	81	14	26	5	0	4	8	9	—	12	0	1	—	2	1	.321	.389	.531	.988
1954	NY-A	122	411	60	124	14	6	8	65	43	—	38	7	5	5	5	5	.302	.373	.423	.967
1955	NY-A	135	510	73	131	19	11	7	47	44	6	51	1	8	7	3	3	.257	.313	.378	.954
1956	NY-A	132	422	54	100	18	2	7	50	45	4	53	2	6	5	9	6	.237	.310	.339	.948
1957	NY-A	85	247	30	63	6	5	6	33	15	3	42	5	4	2	2	2	.255	.309	.393	.977
1958	NY-A	102	315	39	90	19	4	12	45	34	4	43	6	7	3	1	2	.286	.363	.486	.961
1959	NY-A	41	101	11	26	1	0	3	9	7	0	17	0	1	0	1	1	.257	.306	.356	.916
1960	**NY-A**	**4**	**3**	**1**	**1**	**0**	**0**	**0**	**1**	**0**	**0**	**1**	**0**	**0**	**0**	**0**	**0**	**.333**	**.333**	**.333**	**1.000**
1960	KC-A	102	343	30	80	14	4	12	53	26	0	52	1	3	3	0	0	.233	.289	.402	.975
1961	KC-A	39	123	20	30	6	2	3	11	15	0	23	2	2	0	0	0	.244	.336	.398	.944
1961	Chi-N	56	143	21	38	12	3	0	14	11	0	24	2	4	2	0	1	.266	.327	.392	.961
1962	LA-N	53	111	12	26	5	1	2	13	16	1	23	1	1	1	0	0	.234	.333	.351	.932
Career average		85	259	34	67	11	4	6	32	24	—	35	3	4	—	2	2	.260	.329	.396	.955
Yankee average		**76**	**237**	**32**	**63**	**9**	**3**	**5**	**29**	**22**	**—**	**30**	**2**	**4**	**—**	**3**	**2**	**.266**	**.335**	**.397**	**.956**
Career total		938	2850	371	741	119	38	64	350	268	18	389	27	44	28	23	21	.260	.327	.396	.955
Yankee total		**688**	**2130**	**288**	**567**	**82**	**28**	**47**	**259**	**200**	**17**	**267**	**21**	**34**	**22**	**23**	**20**	**.266**	**.332**	**.397**	**.956**

Carlyle, Roy Edward (Dizzy)
HEIGHT: 6'2" THROWS: RIGHT BATS: LEFT BORN: 12/10/1900 BUFORD, GEORGIA DIED: 11/22/1956 NORCROSS, GEORGIA POSITIONS PLAYED: OF

YEAR	TEAM	GAMES	AB	RUNS	HITS	2B	3B	HR	RBI	BB	IBB	SO	HBP	SH	SF	SB	CS	BA	OBA	SA	FA
1925	Was-A	1	1	0	0	0	0	0	0	0	—	1	0	0	—	0	0	.000	.000	.000	.000
1925	Bos-A	93	276	36	90	20	3	7	49	16	—	28	1	7	—	1	1	.326	.365	.496	.909
1926	Bos-A	45	165	22	47	6	2	2	16	4	—	18	2	0	—	0	0	.285	.310	.382	.904
1926	**NY-A**	**35**	**52**	**3**	**20**	**5**	**1**	**0**	**11**	**4**	**—**	**9**	**1**	**0**	**—**	**0**	**0**	**.385**	**.439**	**.519**	**.941**
Career average		44	124	15	39	8	2	2	19	6	—	14	1	2	—	0	0	.318	.354	.460	.689
Yankee average		**35**	**52**	**3**	**20**	**5**	**1**	**0**	**11**	**4**	**—**	**9**	**1**	**0**	**—**	**0**	**0**	**.385**	**.439**	**.519**	**.941**
Career total		174	494	61	157	31	6	9	76	24	—	56	4	7	—	1	1	.318	.354	.460	.689
Yankee total		**35**	**52**	**3**	**20**	**5**	**1**	**0**	**11**	**4**	**—**	**9**	**1**	**0**	**—**	**0**	**0**	**.385**	**.439**	**.519**	**.941**

Carmel, Leon James (Duke)
HEIGHT: 6'3" THROWS: LEFT BATS: LEFT BORN: 4/23/1937 NEW YORK, NEW YORK POSITIONS PLAYED: 1B, OF

YEAR	TEAM	GAMES	AB	RUNS	HITS	2B	3B	HR	RBI	BB	IBB	SO	HBP	SH	SF	SB	CS	BA	OBA	SA	FA
1959	StL-N	10	23	2	3	1	0	0	3	1	0	6	0	0	0	0	1	.130	.167	.174	1.000
1960	StL-N	4	3	0	0	0	0	0	0	1	0	1	0	0	0	1	1	.000	.250	.000	1.000
1963	StL-N	57	44	9	10	1	0	1	2	9	0	11	0	0	0	0	0	.227	.358	.318	.974
1963	NY-N	47	149	11	35	5	3	3	18	16	2	37	0	1	1	2	2	.235	.307	.369	.980
1965	**NY-A**	**6**	**8**	**0**	**0**	**0**	**0**	**0**	**0**	**0**	**0**	**5**	**0**	**0**	**0**	**0**	**0**	**.000**	**.000**	**.000**	**1.000**
Career average		25	45	4	10	1	1	1	5	5	0	12	0	0	0	1	1	.211	.294	.322	.991
Yankee average		**6**	**8**	**0**	**0**	**0**	**0**	**0**	**0**	**0**	**0**	**5**	**0**	**0**	**0**	**0**	**0**	**.000**	**.000**	**.000**	**.990**
Career total		124	227	22	48	7	3	4	23	27	2	60	0	1	1	3	4	.211	.294	.322	.991
Yankee total		**6**	**8**	**0**	**0**	**0**	**0**	**0**	**0**	**0**	**0**	**5**	**0**	**0**	**0**	**0**	**0**	**.000**	**.000**	**.000**	**.990**

Carroll, Thomas Edward
HEIGHT: 6'3" THROWS: RIGHT BATS: RIGHT BORN: 9/17/1936 JAMAICA, NEW YORK POSITIONS PLAYED: 3B, SS

YEAR	TEAM	GAMES	AB	RUNS	HITS	2B	3B	HR	RBI	BB	IBB	SO	HBP	SH	SF	SB	CS	BA	OBA	SA	FA
1955	**NY-A**	**14**	**6**	**3**	**2**	**0**	**0**	**0**	**0**	**0**	**0**	**2**	**0**	**0**	**0**	**0**	**0**	**.333**	**.333**	**.333**	**.875**
1956	**NY-A**	**36**	**17**	**11**	**6**	**0**	**0**	**0**	**0**	**1**	**0**	**3**	**0**	**0**	**0**	**1**	**0**	**.353**	**.389**	**.353**	**.857**
1959	KC-A	14	7	1	1	0	0	0	1	0	0	1	0	0	0	0	0	.143	.143	.143	1.000
Career average		21	10	5	3	0	0	0	0	0	0	2	0	0	0	0	0	.300	.323	.300	.911
Yankee average		**25**	**12**	**7**	**4**	**0**	**0**	**0**	**0**	**1**	**0**	**3**	**0**	**0**	**0**	**1**	**0**	**.348**	**.375**	**.348**	**.866**
Career total		64	30	15	9	0	0	0	1	1	0	6	0	0	0	1	0	.300	.323	.300	.911
Yankee total		**50**	**23**	**14**	**8**	**0**	**0**	**0**	**0**	**1**	**0**	**5**	**0**	**0**	**0**	**1**	**0**	**.348**	**.375**	**.348**	**.866**

Cater, Danny Anderson
HEIGHT: 6'0" THROWS: RIGHT BATS: RIGHT BORN: 2/25/1940 AUSTIN, TEXAS POSITIONS PLAYED: 1B, 2B, 3B, OF

YEAR	TEAM	GAMES	AB	RUNS	HITS	2B	3B	HR	RBI	BB	IBB	SO	HBP	SH	SF	SB	CS	BA	OBA	SA	FA
1964	Phi-N	60	152	13	45	9	1	1	13	7	1	15	0	0	1	1	0	.296	.325	.388	.981
1965	Chi-A	142	514	74	139	18	4	14	55	33	0	65	3	2	3	3	3	.270	.316	.403	.933
1966	Chi-A	21	60	3	11	1	1	0	4	0	0	10	1	3	1	3	1	.183	.194	.233	.909
1966	KC-A	116	425	47	124	16	3	7	52	28	2	37	1	1	4	1	4	.292	.334	.393	.994
1967	KC-A	142	529	55	143	17	4	4	46	34	9	56	4	2	4	4	5	.270	.317	.340	.997
1968	Oak-A	147	504	53	146	28	3	6	62	35	3	43	2	5	4	8	7	.290	.336	.393	1.000
1969	Oak-A	152	584	64	153	24	2	10	76	28	3	40	2	1	5	1	4	.262	.296	.361	.992
1970	**NY-A**	**155**	**582**	**64**	**175**	**26**	**5**	**6**	**76**	**34**	**6**	**44**	**2**	**1**	**2**	**4**	**2**	**.301**	**.340**	**.393**	**.930**
1971	**NY-A**	**121**	**428**	**39**	**118**	**16**	**5**	**4**	**50**	**19**	**4**	**25**	**2**	**4**	**3**	**0**	**3**	**.276**	**.308**	**.364**	**.995**
1972	Bos-A	92	317	32	75	17	1	8	39	15	2	33	2	1	7	0	1	.237	.270	.372	.993
1973	Bos-A	63	195	30	61	12	0	1	24	10	1	22	1	1	1	0	0	.313	.348	.390	.917
1974	Bos-A	56	126	14	31	5	0	5	20	10	1	13	2	1	1	1	0	.246	.309	.405	1.000
1975	StL-N	22	35	3	8	2	0	0	2	1	1	3	0	0	0	0	0	.229	.250	.286	.981
Career average		99	342	38	95	15	2	5	40	20	3	31	2	2	3	2	2	.276	.316	.377	.971
Yankee average		**138**	**505**	**52**	**147**	**21**	**5**	**5**	**63**	**27**	**5**	**35**	**2**	**3**	**3**	**2**	**3**	**.290**	**.326**	**.381**	**.963**
Career total		1289	4451	491	1229	191	29	66	519	254	33	406	22	22	36	26	30	.276	.316	.377	.971
Yankee total		**276**	**1010**	**103**	**293**	**42**	**10**	**10**	**126**	**53**	**10**	**69**	**4**	**5**	**5**	**4**	**5**	**.290**	**.326**	**.381**	**.963**

Cerone, Richard Aldo (Rick)
HEIGHT: 5'11" THROWS: RIGHT BATS: RIGHT BORN: 5/19/1954 NEWARK, NEW JERSEY POSITIONS PLAYED: P, C, 1B, 2B, 3B, OF

YEAR	TEAM	GAMES	AB	RUNS	HITS	2B	3B	HR	RBI	BB	IBB	SO	HBP	SH	SF	SB	CS	BA	OBA	SA	FA
1975	Cle-A	7	12	1	3	1	0	0	0	1	0	0	0	1	0	0	0	.250	.308	.333	1.000
1976	Cle-A	7	16	1	2	0	0	0	1	0	0	2	0	0	0	0	0	.125	.125	.125	.963
1977	Tor-A	31	100	7	20	4	0	1	10	6	0	12	0	1	0	0	0	.200	.245	.270	.994
1978	Tor-A	88	282	25	63	8	2	3	20	23	0	32	1	4	0	0	3	.223	.284	.298	.992
1979	Tor-A	136	469	47	112	27	4	7	61	37	1	40	1	3	4	1	4	.239	.294	.358	.980
1980	**NY-A**	**147**	**519**	**70**	**144**	**30**	**4**	**14**	**85**	**32**	**2**	**56**	**6**	**8**	**10**	**1**	**3**	**.277**	**.321**	**.432**	**.990**
1981	**NY-A**	**71**	**234**	**23**	**57**	**13**	**2**	**2**	**21**	**12**	**0**	**24**	**0**	**4**	**4**	**0**	**2**	**.244**	**.276**	**.342**	**.992**
1982	**NY-A**	**89**	**300**	**29**	**68**	**10**	**0**	**5**	**28**	**19**	**1**	**27**	**1**	**4**	**5**	**0**	**2**	**.227**	**.271**	**.310**	**.989**
1983	**NY-A**	**80**	**246**	**18**	**54**	**7**	**0**	**2**	**22**	**15**	**1**	**29**	**1**	**4**	**0**	**0**	**0**	**.220**	**.267**	**.272**	**.991**

(continued)

Richard Aldo "Rick" Cerone, c, 1980–84, 1987, 1990

He was, to many New Yorkers, "The Guy Who Came After Thurman," but his talent and his New Jersey origins made Rick Cerone a popular Yankee in the 1980s.

Cerone, born in Newark, New Jersey, in 1954, came into the major leagues as a part-time player for the Cleveland Indians in 1975 and 1976. He and John Lowenstein were traded to Toronto in 1977 for Rico Carty, but it wasn't until 1979 that Cerone became the Blue Jays' full-time catcher.

The 1979 season was, of course, the year Yankee captain Thurman Munson was killed in a plane crash. The Yankee powers-that-be assumed correctly that they needed a replacement for Munson. They sent first baseman Chris Chambliss, second baseman Damaso Garcia and lefthanded pitcher Paul Mirabella to the Blue Jays for the up-and-coming Cerone, lefty Tom Underwood and utility outfielder Ted Wilborn.

Cerone hit the ground running in New York. He wasn't Munson and he knew it. But he hit a career-high .277 in 1980 with a career-best 14 home runs and 85 RBI. He finished seventh in the voting for MVP that year with a work ethic that made him a popular player.

The Yankees made the playoffs in 1980 and in 1981, and Cerone's hitting in the 1981 American League East playoff win over the Brewers was the difference for New York. (This was the strike-shortened split season. New York won the first half of the season, Milwaukee the second half.) Cerone singled and homered in the decisive fifth game, a 7-3 New York win.

He played well in the Yankees' 4-0 sweep of Oakland in the 1981 League championship series, but he and most of the rest of the Yankees were shackled by the Dodgers' pitching staff in the 1981 World Series.

Injuries hampered Cerone over the next three seasons, and he was traded to Atlanta before the start of the 1985 season. From there, Cerone was traded again, this time to Milwaukee in 1986. He returned to the Yankees in 1987, and had his best year since 1980, playing in 113 games and leading the American League in fielding percentage with .998.

The Yankees released the 33-year-old Cerone the next year, and he was picked up by the Red Sox, where he had two solid years. In 1988, he caught 83 games without making an error for Boston. He had one more tour of duty in the 1990 season, hitting a more-than-respectable .302 in 49 games. Cerone finished out his career with the Mets in 1991 and Montreal in 1992.

(continued)

Year	Team	G	AB	R	H	2B	3B	HR	RBI	BB	IBB	SO	HBP	SH	SF	GDP	SB	BA	OBP	SLG	FA
1984	NY-A	38	120	8	25	3	0	2	13	9	0	15	1	2	0	1	0	.208	.269	.283	.996
1985	Atl-N	96	282	15	61	9	0	3	25	29	1	25	1	0	4	0	3	.216	.288	.280	.986
1986	Mil-A	68	216	22	56	14	0	4	18	15	0	28	1	5	5	1	1	.259	.304	.380	.991
1987	**NY-A**	**113**	**284**	**28**	**69**	**12**	**1**	**4**	**23**	**30**	**0**	**46**	**4**	**5**	**4**	**0**	**1**	**.243**	**.320**	**.335**	**.998**
1988	Bos-A	84	264	31	71	13	1	3	27	20	0	32	3	1	1	0	0	.269	.326	.360	1.000
1989	Bos-A	102	296	28	72	16	1	4	48	34	1	40	2	4	5	0	0	.243	.320	.345	.984
1990	**NY-A**	**49**	**139**	**12**	**42**	**6**	**0**	**2**	**11**	**5**	**0**	**13**	**0**	**1**	**1**	**0**	**0**	**.302**	**.324**	**.388**	**.995**
1991	NY-N	90	227	18	62	13	0	2	16	30	2	24	1	0	0	1	1	.273	.360	.357	.987
1992	Mon-N	33	63	10	17	4	0	1	7	3	0	5	1	1	0	1	2	.270	.313	.381	1.000
Career average		74	226	22	55	11	1	3	24	18	1	25	1	3	2	0	1	.245	.301	.343	.990
Yankee average		**84**	**263**	**27**	**66**	**12**	**1**	**4**	**29**	**17**	**1**	**30**	**2**	**4**	**3**	**0**	**1**	**.249**	**.297**	**.351**	**.993**
Career total		1329	4069	393	998	190	15	59	436	320	9	450	24	48	43	6	22	.245	.301	.343	.990
Yankee total		**587**	**1842**	**188**	**459**	**81**	**7**	**31**	**203**	**122**	**4**	**210**	**13**	**28**	**24**	**2**	**8**	**.249**	**.297**	**.351**	**.993**

Cerv, Robert Henry

HEIGHT: 6'0"   THROWS: RIGHT   BATS: RIGHT   BORN: 5/5/1926 WESTON, NEBRASKA   POSITIONS PLAYED: 1B, OF

YEAR	TEAM	GAMES	AB	RUNS	HITS	2B	3B	HR	RBI	BB	IBB	SO	HBP	SH	SF	SB	CS	BA	OBA	SA	FA
1951	**NY-A**	**12**	**28**	**4**	**6**	**1**	**0**	**0**	**2**	**4**	**0**	**6**	**0**	**0**	**0**	**0**	**0**	**.214**	**.313**	**.250**	**.875**
1952	**NY-A**	**36**	**87**	**11**	**21**	**3**	**2**	**1**	**8**	**9**	**0**	**22**	**0**	**0**	**0**	**0**	**1**	**.241**	**.313**	**.356**	**1.000**
1953	**NY-A**	**8**	**6**	**0**	**0**	**0**	**0**	**0**	**0**	**0**	**—**	**1**	**0**	**0**	**—**	**0**	**0**	**.000**	**.143**	**.000**	**.000**
1954	**NY-A**	**56**	**100**	**14**	**26**	**6**	**0**	**5**	**13**	**11**	**0**	**17**	**0**	**0**	**1**	**0**	**2**	**.260**	**.330**	**.470**	**.897**
1955	**NY-A**	**55**	**85**	**17**	**29**	**4**	**2**	**3**	**22**	**7**	**0**	**16**	**3**	**1**	**0**	**4**	**0**	**.341**	**.411**	**.541**	**1.000**
1956	**NY-A**	**54**	**115**	**16**	**35**	**5**	**6**	**3**	**25**	**18**	**0**	**13**	**0**	**1**	**1**	**0**	**1**	**.304**	**.396**	**.530**	**.984**
1957	KC-A	124	345	35	94	14	2	11	44	20	1	57	1	2	3	1	1	.272	.312	.420	.964
1958	KC-A	141	515	93	157	20	7	38	104	50	10	82	5	0	2	3	3	.305	.371	.592	.985
1959	KC-A	125	463	61	132	22	4	20	87	35	5	87	3	1	11	3	2	.285	.332	.479	.980
1960	KC-A	23	78	14	20	1	1	6	12	10	1	17	0	0	1	0	0	.256	.337	.526	.977
1960	**NY-A**	**87**	**216**	**32**	**54**	**11**	**1**	**8**	**28**	**30**	**2**	**36**	**3**	**0**	**0**	**0**	**0**	**.250**	**.349**	**.421**	**.960**
1961	LA-A	18	57	3	9	3	0	2	6	1	0	8	0	1	1	0	0	.158	.169	.316	.944
1961	**NY-A**	**57**	**118**	**17**	**32**	**5**	**1**	**6**	**20**	**12**	**0**	**17**	**1**	**0**	**0**	**1**	**0**	**.271**	**.344**	**.483**	**1.000**
1962	**NY-A**	**14**	**17**	**1**	**2**	**1**	**0**	**0**	**0**	**2**	**0**	**3**	**1**	**0**	**0**	**0**	**0**	**.118**	**.250**	**.176**	**1.000**
1962	Hou-N	19	31	2	7	0	0	2	3	2	0	10	0	0	0	0	0	.226	.273	.419	.833
Career average		54	151	21	42	6	2	7	25	14	1	26	1	0	1	1	1	.276	.340	.481	.893
Yankee average		**42**	**86**	**12**	**23**	**4**	**1**	**3**	**13**	**10**	**0**	**15**	**1**	**0**	**0**	**1**	**0**	**.266**	**.350**	**.444**	**.857**
Career total		829	2261	320	624	96	26	105	374	212	19	392	17	6	20	12	10	.276	.340	.481	.893
Yankee total		**379**	**772**	**112**	**205**	**36**	**12**	**26**	**118**	**94**	**2**	**131**	**8**	**2**	**2**	**5**	**4**	**.266**	**.350**	**.444**	**.857**

Chambliss, Carroll Christopher

HEIGHT: 6'1"   THROWS: RIGHT   BATS: LEFT   BORN: 12/26/1948 DAYTON, OHIO   POSITIONS PLAYED: 1B

YEAR	TEAM	GAMES	AB	RUNS	HITS	2B	3B	HR	RBI	BB	IBB	SO	HBP	SH	SF	SB	CS	BA	OBA	SA	FA
1971	Cle-A	111	415	49	114	20	4	9	48	40	1	83	2	2	0	2	0	.275	.341	.407	.992
1972	Cle-A	121	466	51	136	27	2	6	44	26	2	63	0	3	4	3	4	.292	.327	.397	.993
1973	Cle-A	155	572	70	156	30	2	11	53	58	8	76	3	1	2	4	8	.273	.342	.390	.991
1974	Cle-A	17	67	8	22	4	0	0	7	5	1	5	0	0	0	0	1	.328	.375	.388	.982
1974	**NY-A**	**110**	**400**	**38**	**97**	**16**	**3**	**6**	**43**	**23**	**1**	**43**	**0**	**2**	**2**	**0**	**0**	**.243**	**.284**	**.343**	**.992**
1975	**NY-A**	**150**	**562**	**66**	**171**	**38**	**4**	**9**	**72**	**29**	**9**	**50**	**1**	**4**	**6**	**0**	**1**	**.304**	**.336**	**.434**	**.991**
1976	**NY-A**	**156**	**641**	**79**	**188**	**32**	**6**	**17**	**96**	**27**	**1**	**80**	**3**	**1**	**3**	**1**	**0**	**.293**	**.323**	**.441**	**.994**
1977	**NY-A**	**157**	**600**	**90**	**172**	**32**	**6**	**17**	**90**	**45**	**5**	**73**	**2**	**0**	**5**	**4**	**0**	**.287**	**.336**	**.445**	**.989**
1978	**NY-A**	**162**	**625**	**81**	**171**	**26**	**3**	**12**	**90**	**41**	**3**	**60**	**5**	**1**	**5**	**2**	**1**	**.274**	**.321**	**.382**	**.997**
1979	**NY-A**	**149**	**554**	**61**	**155**	**27**	**3**	**18**	**63**	**34**	**4**	**53**	**5**	**1**	**5**	**3**	**2**	**.280**	**.324**	**.437**	**.995**
1980	Atl-N	158	602	83	170	37	2	18	72	49	6	73	4	2	4	7	3	.282	.338	.440	.993
1981	Atl-N	107	404	44	110	25	2	8	51	44	10	41	1	2	3	4	1	.272	.343	.403	.997
1982	Atl-N	157	534	57	144	25	2	20	86	57	13	57	0	0	6	7	3	.270	.337	.436	.993
1983	Atl-N	131	447	59	125	24	3	20	78	63	15	68	0	0	3	2	7	.280	.366	.481	.996
1984	Atl-N	135	389	47	100	14	0	9	44	58	12	54	1	0	6	1	2	.257	.350	.362	.993
1985	Atl-N	101	170	16	40	7	0	3	21	18	4	22	0	0	1	0	0	.235	.307	.329	.997
1986	Atl-N	97	122	13	38	8	0	2	14	15	4	24	0	0	1	0	2	.311	.384	.426	.993
1988	**NY-A**	**1**	**1**	**0**	**0**	**0**	**0**	**0**	**0**	**0**	**0**	**1**	**0**	**0**	**0**	**0**	**0**	**.000**	**.000**	**.000**	**.000**
Career average		121	421	51	117	22	2	10	54	35	6	51	2	1	3	2	2	.279	.334	.415	.938
Yankee average		**126**	**483**	**59**	**136**	**24**	**4**	**11**	**65**	**28**	**3**	**51**	**2**	**1**	**4**	**1**	**1**	**.282**	**.323**	**.417**	**.851**
Career total		2175	7571	912	2109	392	42	185	972	632	99	926	27	19	56	40	35	.279	.334	.415	.938
Yankee total		**885**	**3383**	**415**	**954**	**171**	**25**	**79**	**454**	**199**	**23**	**360**	**16**	**9**	**26**	**10**	**4**	**.282**	**.323**	**.417**	**.851**

Chance, Frank Leroy (Husk *or* The Peerless Leader)

HEIGHT: 6'0"   THROWS: RIGHT   BATS: RIGHT   BORN: 9/9/1877 FRESNO, CALIFORNIA   DIED: 9/15/1924 LOS ANGELES, CALIFORNIA   POSITIONS PLAYED: C, 1B

YEAR	TEAM	GAMES	AB	RUNS	HITS	2B	3B	HR	RBI	BB	IBB	SO	HBP	SH	SF	SB	CS	BA	OBA	SA	FA
1898	Chi-N	53	147	32	41	4	3	1	14	7	—	—	3	2	—	7	—	.279	.338	.367	.950
1899	Chi-N	64	192	37	55	6	2	1	22	15	—	—	4	2	—	10	—	.286	.351	.354	.950
1900	Chi-N	56	149	26	44	9	3	0	13	15	—	—	15	8	—	8	—	.295	.413	.396	.932
1901	Chi-N	69	241	38	67	12	4	0	36	29	—	—	9	4	—	27	—	.278	.376	.361	.882
1902	Chi-N	75	240	39	69	9	4	1	31	35	—	—	8	2	—	27	—	.288	.396	.371	.972
1903	Chi-N	125	441	83	144	24	10	2	81	78	—	—	10	2	—	67	—	.327	.439	.440	.889
1904	Chi-N	124	451	89	140	16	10	6	49	36	—	—	16	11	—	42	—	.310	.382	.430	1.000
1905	Chi-N	118	392	92	124	16	12	2	70	78	—	—	17	15	—	38	—	.316	.450	.434	.990
1906	Chi-N	136	474	103	151	24	10	3	71	70	—	—	12	18	—	57	—	.319	.419	.430	.989
1907	Chi-N	111	382	58	112	19	2	1	49	51	—	—	13	5	—	35	—	.293	.395	.361	.992
1908	Chi-N	129	452	65	123	27	4	2	55	37	—	—	8	16	—	27	—	.272	.338	.363	.989
1909	Chi-N	93	324	53	88	16	4	0	46	30	—	—	4	12	—	29	—	.272	.341	.346	.994
1910	Chi-N	88	295	54	88	12	8	0	36	37	—	15	10	6	—	16	—	.298	.395	.393	.996

(continued)

Carroll Christopher "Chris" Chambliss, 1b, 1974–79, 1988

To the casual baseball fan, Chris Chambliss is known for basically one event in his career: a ninth-inning home run in the fifth game of the 1976 American League Championship Series, a hit that put the Yankees back in the World Series for the first time in 12 long years.

But to Yankee fans, Chambliss's stint in New York in the 1970s represented something more: a solid, two-way first baseman, something New York had not had since Joe Pepitone 11 years before.

Chambliss is a midwesterner by birth, having been born in Dayton, Ohio, in 1948. After a record-setting year at UCLA (15 hr, 45 rbi) in 1967, Chambliss spent four years in the minors before moving up to the big leagues in 1971 with Cleveland. He was an immediate starter for the Indians and was later voted Rookie of the Year. He hit around .280 in his 3 1/2 years there.

The Yankees acquired Chambliss midway through the 1974 season in a trade that some people believed, at least initially, was a bad one for New York. The Yankees sent veteran pitchers Fritz Peterson and Steve Kline, both solid starters, as well as journeyman hurler Fred Beene and second-year pitcher Tommy Busky, to the Indians for Chambliss, starter Dick Tidrow and journeyman righty Cecil Upshaw.

Chambliss didn't pay off immediately, but by 1976, the year he was named to the American League All-Star Game, he was driving in 90 runs or more and hitting around .290.

He was a solid performer who rarely chased bad balls at the plate and who made few errors in the field. He won a Gold Glove at first base in 1978.

His day in the spotlight came on that fateful evening in 1976 against Kansas City pitcher Mark Littel. It was a cold night, and Chambliss swung at the first pitch Littel threw. The ball bounded off his bat and into the right field seats, and the Yankees were back in the World Series.

Chambliss made it around first and past second, but between second and third base he was tripped by an overenthusiastic Yankee fan. As he got up, someone tried to steal his helmet. Making third base was a battle. Getting home was out of the question.

So Chambliss tucked his helmet under his arm, and like a football player, charged back to the Yankee dugout, shoulder-blocking another group of fans massing in front of it.

Later, with a police escort, he came out and trotted home, just to make it all official.

Chambliss's numbers dipped slightly in 1979, and in those days, with impatient owner George Steinbrenner at the helm, that was a bad sign. He was shipped to Atlanta prior to the 1980 season, and he spent seven years there until 1986. He was signed as a coach by the Yankees in 1988 and batted in one game that year.

After his big league career, Chambliss worked as a coach in both the major and minor leagues. He was hired by the Yankees in 1996 as a hitting coach.

(continued)

1911	Chi-N	31	88	23	21	6	3	1	17	25	—	13	5	6	—	9	—	.239	.432	.409	.990
1912	Chi-N	2	5	2	1	0	0	0	0	3	—	0	0	1	—	1	—	.200	.500	.200	1.000
1913	**NY-A**	**12**	**24**	**3**	**5**	**0**	**0**	**0**	**6**	**8**	—	**1**	**0**	**1**	—	**1**	—	**.208**	**.406**	**.208**	**1.000**
1914	**NY-A**	**1**	**1**	**0**	**0**	**0**	**0**	**0**	**0**	**0**	—	**0**	**0**	**0**	—	**0**	**0**	—	—	—	**1.000**
Career average		76	253	47	75	12	5	1	35	33	—	—	8	7	—	24	—	.296	.393	.393	.971
Yankee average		**7**	**13**	**2**	**3**	**0**	**0**	**0**	**3**	**4**	—	**1**	**0**	**1**	—	**1**	—	**.200**	**.394**	**.200**	**1.000**
Career total		1287	4298	797	1273	200	79	20	596	554	—	29	134	111	—	401	0	.296	.393	.393	.971
Yankee total		**13**	**25**	**3**	**5**	**0**	**0**	**0**	**6**	**8**	—	**1**	**0**	**1**	—	**1**	**0**	**.200**	**.394**	**.200**	**1.000**

William Benjamin "Ben" "Chappy" Chapman, of-2b-3b, 1930–36

The versatile Chapman was one of the Yankees best utility men in the early 1930s, first filling in at second and third base and later becoming a regular in the outfield for New York.

Chapman was born on Christmas Day 1908 in Nashville, Tennessee. He was signed by the Yankees at the age of 20 and began his career in New York in 1930.

Yankee manager Bob Shawkey liked the speedy Chapman at the plate that first year, where he had 162 hits and 31 doubles in 138 games. But in the field, Ben was no Joe Dugan, who had retired two years before. Shawkey tried him at third base, and at one point in 1930, he moved All-Star second baseman Tony Lazzeri to third and placed Chapman at second. But neither move was particularly successful. (Chapman's 24 errors at third base led the league.)

In 1931, Joe McCarthy took over the team, and he, too, liked Chapman. But McCarthy moved Chapman into the outfield where his speed would help him track down fly balls. Chapman played left field for three years and took over center field in 1935 when aging Earle Combs stepped aside.

Chapman had a tremendous year in 1931, hitting .315 with 122 RBI. He also stole a team-record 61 bases, a record until Rickey Henderson broke it in 1985.

From 1931 to 1933, he led the American League in stolen bases and scored 100 or more runs each of those years as well. He remains in fifth place on the Yankees' all-time stolen base list with 184.

Chapman's only World Series appearance was a memorable one. He was the Yankees' starting left fielder in the 1932 Series, a Yankee sweep. This was the Series when Babe Ruth supposedly called his home run in the fifth inning of the third game. Chapman had five hits in 17 at-bats for a .294 average. He also had two doubles and 6 RBI.

In 1933, Major League Baseball began having the All-Stars from the American and National Leagues play each other in an "All-Star game." Chapman, Lou Gehrig and Lefty Gomez were the only Yankees to be named to the first three AL All-Star teams.

But for all his talent, Chapman was also something of a hothead. In 1936, Chapman staged a holdout, to try and squeeze more money out of Yankee management. He eventually reported to the team on April 4, but it was clear that his days in New York were numbered. In July, the Yankees swapped Chapman to Washington even-up for the less talented but more compliant Jake Powell, who played less than two years with New York.

Chapman played the next eight years with several teams, including the Senators, Red Sox, White Sox and Dodgers, and finished his career as a player-manager for the Philadelphia Phillies. It was in Philadelphia that the world also learned that Chapman was something of a racist. Chapman was one of Jackie Robinson's cruelest tormentors in the early days of Robinson's career. He died in 1993 in Hoover, Alabama.

Channell, Lester Clark (Goat *or* Gint)

HEIGHT: 6'0" THROWS: LEFT BATS: LEFT BORN: 3/3/1886 CRESTLINE, OHIO DIED: 5/7/1954 DENVER, COLORADO POSITIONS PLAYED: OF

YEAR	TEAM	GAMES	AB	RUNS	HITS	2B	3B	HR	RBI	BB	IBB	SO	HBP	SH	SF	SB	CS	BA	OBA	SA	FA
1910	NY-A	6	19	3	6	0	0	0	3	2	—	—	0	0	—	2	—	.316	.381	.316	1.000
1914	NY-A	1	1	0	1	1	0	0	0	0	—	0	0	0	—	0	0	1.000	1.000	2.000	.000
Career average		4	10	2	4	1	0	0	2	1	—	—	0	0	—	1	—	.350	.409	.400	.500
Yankee average		**4**	**10**	**2**	**4**	**1**	**0**	**0**	**2**	**1**	**—**	**—**	**0**	**0**	**—**	**1**	**—**	**.350**	**.409**	**.400**	**.500**
Career total		7	20	3	7	1	0	0	3	2	—	0	0	0	—	2	0	.350	.409	.400	.500
Yankee total		**7**	**20**	**3**	**7**	**1**	**0**	**0**	**3**	**2**	**—**	**0**	**0**	**0**	**—**	**2**	**0**	**.350**	**.409**	**.400**	**.500**

Chapman, William Benjamin (Ben *or* Chappy)

HEIGHT: 6'0"   THROWS: RIGHT   BATS: RIGHT   BORN: 12/25/1908 NASHVILLE, TENNESSEE   DIED: 7/9/1993 HOOVER, ALABAMA   POSITIONS PLAYED: P, 2B, 3B, OF

YEAR	TEAM	GAMES	AB	RUNS	HITS	2B	3B	HR	RBI	BB	IBB	SO	HBP	SH	SF	SB	CS	BA	OBA	SA	FA
1930	NY-A	138	513	74	162	31	10	10	81	43	—	58	2	6	—	14	6	.316	.371	.474	.939
1931	NY-A	149	600	120	189	28	11	17	122	75	—	77	5	6	—	61	23	.315	.396	.483	.963
1932	NY-A	151	581	101	174	41	15	10	107	71	—	55	5	5	—	38	18	.299	.381	.473	.949
1933	NY-A	147	565	112	176	36	4	9	98	72	—	45	4	10	—	27	18	.312	.393	.437	.975
1934	NY-A	149	588	82	181	21	13	5	86	67	—	68	3	8	—	26	16	.308	.381	.413	.967
1935	NY-A	140	553	118	160	38	8	8	74	61	—	39	1	14	—	17	10	.289	.361	.430	.964
1936	NY-A	36	139	19	37	14	3	1	21	15	—	20	0	2	—	1	2	.266	.338	.432	.965
1936	Was-A	97	401	91	133	36	7	4	60	69	—	18	1	1	—	19	7	.332	.431	.486	.959
1937	Was-A	35	130	23	34	7	1	0	12	26	—	7	0	0	—	8	0	.262	.385	.331	.957
1937	Bos-A	113	423	76	130	23	11	7	57	57	—	35	1	6	—	27	12	.307	.391	.463	.750
1938	Bos-A	127	480	92	163	40	8	6	80	65	—	33	0	8	—	13	6	.340	.418	.494	1.000
1939	Cle-A	149	545	101	158	31	9	6	82	87	—	30	2	20	—	18	6	.290	.390	.413	.971
1940	Cle-A	143	548	82	157	40	6	4	50	78	—	45	2	3	—	13	7	.286	.377	.403	.964
1941	Was-A	28	110	9	28	6	0	1	10	10	—	6	0	1	—	2	2	.255	.317	.336	.983
1941	Chi-A	57	190	26	43	9	1	2	19	19	—	14	0	1	—	2	2	.226	.297	.316	.992
1944	Bro-N	20	38	11	14	4	0	0	11	5	—	4	0	1	—	1	0	.368	.442	.474	.900
1945	Bro-N	13	22	2	3	0	0	0	3	2	—	1	0	0	—	0	0	.136	.208	.136	.938
1945	Phi-N	24	51	4	16	2	0	0	4	2	—	1	0	0	—	0	0	.314	.340	.353	.933
1946	Phi-N	1	1	1	0	0	0	0	0	0	—	0	0	0	—	0	0	.000	.000	.000	.000
Career average		101	381	67	115	24	6	5	58	49	—	33	2	5	—	17	8	.302	.383	.440	.898
Yankee average		**130**	**506**	**89**	**154**	**30**	**9**	**9**	**84**	**58**	—	**52**	**3**	**7**	—	**26**	**13**	**.305**	**.379**	**.451**	**.960**
Career total		1717	6478	1144	1958	407	107	90	977	824	—	556	26	92	—	287	135	.302	.383	.440	.898
Yankee total		**910**	**3539**	**626**	**1079**	**209**	**64**	**60**	**589**	**404**	—	**362**	**20**	**51**	—	**184**	**93**	**.305**	**.379**	**.451**	**.960**

Chartak, Michael George (Shotgun)

HEIGHT: 6'2"   THROWS: LEFT   BATS: LEFT   BORN: 4/28/1916 BROOKLYN, NEW YORK   DIED: 7/25/1967 CEDAR RAPIDS, IOWA   POSITIONS PLAYED: 1B, OF

YEAR	TEAM	GAMES	AB	RUNS	HITS	2B	3B	HR	RBI	BB	IBB	SO	HBP	SH	SF	SB	CS	BA	OBA	SA	FA
1940	NY-A	11	15	2	2	1	0	0	3	5	—	5	0	0	—	0	0	.133	.350	.200	1.000
1942	NY-A	5	5	0	0	0	0	0	0	0	—	0	0	0	—	0	0	.000	.000	.000	.000
1942	Was-A	24	92	11	20	4	2	1	8	14	—	16	0	0	—	0	1	.217	.321	.337	.926
1942	StL-A	73	237	37	59	11	2	9	43	40	—	27	2	1	—	3	3	.249	.362	.426	.974
1943	StL-A	108	344	38	88	16	2	10	37	39	—	55	1	3	—	1	3	.256	.333	.401	.970
1944	StL-A	35	72	8	17	2	1	1	7	6	—	9	1	1	—	0	0	.236	.304	.333	1.000
Career average		64	191	24	47	9	2	5	25	26	—	28	1	1	—	1	2	.243	.337	.388	.812
Yankee average		**11**	**15**	**2**	**2**	**1**	**0**	**0**	**3**	**5**	—	**5**	**0**	**0**	—	**0**	**0**	**.133**	**.350**	**.200**	**.500**
Career total		256	765	96	186	34	7	21	98	104	—	112	4	5	—	4	7	.243	.337	.388	.812
Yankee total		**11**	**15**	**2**	**2**	**1**	**0**	**0**	**3**	**5**	—	**5**	**0**	**0**	—	**0**	**0**	**.133**	**.350**	**.200**	**.500**

Chase, Harold Homer (Prince Hal)

HEIGHT: 6'0"   THROWS: LEFT   BATS: RIGHT   BORN: 2/13/1883 LOS GATOS, CALIFORNIA   DIED: 5/18/1947 COLUSA, CALIFORNIA   POSITIONS PLAYED: 1B, 2B, OF

YEAR	TEAM	GAMES	AB	RUNS	HITS	2B	3B	HR	RBI	BB	IBB	SO	HBP	SH	SF	SB	CS	BA	OBA	SA	FA
1905	NY-A	128	465	60	116	16	6	3	49	15	—	0	3	18	—	22	—	.249	.277	.329	.976
1906	NY-A	151	597	84	193	23	10	0	76	13	—	0	3	24	—	28	—	.323	.341	.395	.980
1907	NY-A	125	498	72	143	23	3	2	68	19	—	0	1	10	—	32	—	.287	.315	.357	1.000
1908	NY-A	106	405	50	104	11	3	1	36	15	—	0	1	9	—	27	—	.257	.285	.306	.980
1909	NY-A	118	474	60	134	17	3	4	63	20	—	0	4	15	—	25	—	.283	.317	.357	.978
1910	NY-A	130	524	67	152	20	5	3	73	16	—	0	1	19	—	40	—	.290	.312	.365	.981
1911	NY-A	133	527	82	166	32	7	3	62	21	—	0	1	22	—	36	—	.315	.342	.419	1.000
1912	NY-A	131	522	61	143	21	9	4	58	17	—	0	2	25	—	33	—	.274	.299	.372	.979
1913	NY-A	39	146	15	31	2	4	0	9	11	—	13	0	3	—	5	—	.212	.268	.281	.765
1913	Chi-A	102	384	49	110	11	10	2	39	16	—	41	3	11	—	9	—	.286	.320	.383	.976
1914	Chi-A	58	206	27	55	10	5	0	20	23	—	19	1	6	—	9	4	.267	.343	.364	.981
1914	Buf-F	75	291	43	101	19	9	3	48	6	—	31	2	5	—	10	—	.347	.365	.505	.980
1915	Buf-F	145	567	85	165	31	10	17	89	20	—	50	1	8	—	23	—	.291	.316	.471	.983
1916	Cin-N	142	542	66	184	29	12	4	82	19	—	48	1	9	—	22	11	.339	.363	.459	.937
1917	Cin-N	152	602	71	167	28	15	4	86	15	—	49	1	10	—	21	—	.277	.296	.394	.983
1918	Cin-N	74	259	30	78	12	6	2	38	13	—	15	2	7	—	5	—	.301	.341	.417	.980
1919	NY-N	110	408	58	116	17	7	5	45	17	—	40	3	15	—	16	—	.284	.318	.397	.984
Career average		113	436	58	127	19	7	3	55	16	—	18	2	13	—	21	—	.291	.319	.391	.967
Yankee average		**118**	**462**	**61**	**131**	**18**	**6**	**2**	**55**	**16**	—	**1**	**2**	**16**	—	**28**	—	**.284**	**.311**	**.362**	**.960**
Career total		1919	7417	980	2158	322	124	57	941	276	—	306	30	216	—	363	15	.291	.319	.391	.967
Yankee total		**1061**	**4158**	**551**	**1182**	**165**	**50**	**20**	**494**	**147**	—	**13**	**16**	**145**	—	**248**	—	**.284**	**.311**	**.362**	**.960**

Harold Homer "Prince Hal" Chase, 1b, 1905–13

Babe Ruth thought he was one of the best first basemen ever. A lot of other people thought the sweet-fielding "Prince Hal" was a crook who fixed games.

He was a little of both. Chase was born in 1883 in Los Gatos, California. A minor league sensation in the Los Angeles area at the turn of the century, he came east to play for the New York Highlanders in 1905.

By the end of 1906, Chase was a certifiable star in the American League. He led the team with a .323 average, which was third in the league, and his fielding at first base was, by all accounts, terrific. Chase would often play several feet "in" on the infield grass on a bunting batter. There he could quickly field a bunt and make the throw to second base, nullifying a sacrifice. And if a batter tried to hit the ball over his head, Chase was reportedly so quick he often stabbed the ball as it came off the bat. In addition, newspaper accounts tell of Chase fielding bunts on the third-base side of the grass between home plate and the pitcher's mound and throwing to first, second or third base as was needed. There is not a modern player in either league with that ability.

The New Yorkers, after a sluggish start in 1906, were neck and neck with the Chicago White Sox for the pennant. Chicago eventually pulled out the flag by three games.

The Highlanders slumped in 1907, but Chase's play remained at a high level. He led the team again in batting average, RBI and hits, and was considered one of the top drawing cards in the league.

Chase was well aware of his prominence, and he desired compensation for it. He went to the papers and indicated he would like to be better paid. The Highlander management flatly refused. By 1908, things had become so strained between Chase and the Highlanders that he jumped the team and went back to California. There he played semipro ball under an assumed name.

He returned in 1909, but by now, there were whispers that Chase was at times "laying down," or trying to throw certain contests, to make a little extra money. Still, the Highlanders improved their record in 1909 and again in 1910.

There was little hard evidence of Chase cheating beyond the complaints of his teammates. Meanwhile, Chase had another angle, pressuring ownership to allow him to be the Highlanders' manager. At the end of the 1910 season, Chase went to the New York management and told them that manager George Stallings was incompetent. He offered to take over the squad. Stallings replied that Chase was throwing games to get him fired. Clearly unwilling to upset their star, the Highlanders agreed to fire Stallings and installed Chase for the last 11 games. The Highlanders went 9-2, which, New York papers hoped, might be a harbinger of things next year.

It wasn't. Chase managed the squad to a 76-76 record, 25 games behind the A's. Chase hit .315 and led the team in doubles, but the rumors persisted that something wasn't right. Some stories had Chase striking out at key moments in specified games, or muffing balls tossed to him at first to keep opponents' rallies alive. In 1912, his 36 errors were 13 more than any other first baseman in the American League. And this from a man who was supposedly the slickest first baseman in the majors.

His team's poor performance did move the Highlanders to remove his managerial hat and turn over the reins to Harry Wolverton in 1912, and then to Frank Chance a year later. Neither man had much use for Chase, and Chance, like Stallings, felt something wasn't on the up and up. He finally got Chase out of New York by trading him to Chicago in 1913.

Chase played six more years in the majors, and the "fixing" rumors seemed to follow him wherever he went. He was in Cincinnati in 1918, where he butted heads with legend-turned-manager Christy Mathewson, who began telling writers that Chase was throwing games. On he went to the Giants in 1919, where coach John MGraw throught he could rehabilitate him.

But that stop turned sour as well. Chase was one of several men indicted for helping fix the 1919 World Series. He was never tried, but he was finally banned from baseball. Chase bounced around in semipro leagues for several more years before returning to the West Coast. He died on May 8, 1947, in Colusa, California.

Clark, Alfred Aloysius (Allie)

HEIGHT: 6'0"   THROWS: RIGHT   BATS: RIGHT   BORN: 6/16/1923 S. AMBOY, NEW JERSEY   POSITIONS PLAYED: 1B, 3B, OF

YEAR	TEAM	GAMES	AB	RUNS	HITS	2B	3B	HR	RBI	BB	IBB	SO	HBP	SH	SF	SB	CS	BA	OBA	SA	FA
1947	**NY-A**	**24**	**67**	**9**	**25**	**5**	**0**	**1**	**14**	**5**	**—**	**2**	**0**	**1**	**—**	**0**	**0**	**.373**	**.417**	**.493**	**1.000**
1948	Cle-A	81	271	43	84	5	2	9	38	23	—	13	0	4	—	0	2	.310	.364	.443	.875
1949	Cle-A	35	74	8	13	4	0	1	9	4	—	7	0	0	—	0	0	.176	.218	.270	1.000
1950	Cle-A	59	163	19	35	6	1	6	21	11	—	10	0	1	—	0	1	.215	.264	.374	.987
1951	Cle-A	3	10	3	3	2	0	1	3	1	—	2	0	0	—	0	0	.300	.364	.800	1.000
1951	Phi-A	56	161	20	40	10	1	4	22	15	—	7	2	1	—	2	0	.248	.320	.398	.984
1952	Phi-A	71	186	23	51	12	0	7	29	10	—	19	1	3	—	0	2	.274	.315	.452	1.000
1953	Phi-A	20	74	6	15	4	0	3	13	3	—	5	0	1	—	0	0	.203	.234	.378	1.000
1953	Chi-A	9	15	0	1	0	0	0	0	0	—	5	0	0	—	0	0	.067	.067	.067	1.000
Career average		45	128	16	33	6	1	4	19	9	—	9	0	1	—	0	1	.262	.312	.410	.983
Yankee average		**24**	**67**	**9**	**25**	**5**	**0**	**1**	**14**	**5**	**—**	**2**	**0**	**1**	**—**	**0**	**0**	**.373**	**.417**	**.493**	**1.000**
Career total		358	1021	131	267	48	4	32	149	72	—	70	3	11	—	2	5	.262	.312	.410	.983
Yankee total		**24**	**67**	**9**	**25**	**5**	**0**	**1**	**14**	**5**	**—**	**2**	**0**	**1**	**—**	**0**	**0**	**.373**	**.417**	**.493**	**1.000**

Clark, Jack Anthony (The Ripper)

HEIGHT: 6'2"   THROWS: RIGHT   BATS: RIGHT   BORN: 11/10/1955 NEW BRIGHTON, PENNSYLVANIA   POSITIONS PLAYED: 1B, 3B, OF

YEAR	TEAM	GAMES	AB	RUNS	HITS	2B	3B	HR	RBI	BB	IBB	SO	HBP	SH	SF	SB	CS	BA	OBA	SA	FA
1975	SF-N	8	17	3	4	0	0	0	2	1	0	2	0	0	1	1	0	.235	.263	.235	1.000
1976	SF-N	26	102	14	23	6	2	2	10	8	0	18	0	3	2	6	2	.225	.277	.382	.987
1977	SF-N	136	413	64	104	17	4	13	51	49	2	73	2	1	3	12	4	.252	.332	.407	.975
1978	SF-N	156	592	90	181	46	8	25	98	50	8	72	3	3	9	15	11	.306	.358	.537	.982
1979	SF-N	143	527	84	144	25	2	26	86	63	6	95	1	1	6	11	8	.273	.348	.476	.982
1980	SF-N	127	437	77	124	20	8	22	82	74	13	52	2	1	10	2	5	.284	.382	.517	.967
1981	SF-N	99	385	60	103	19	2	17	53	45	6	45	1	0	6	1	1	.268	.341	.460	.981
1982	SF-N	157	563	90	154	30	3	27	103	90	7	91	1	0	5	6	9	.274	.372	.481	.980
1983	SF-N	135	492	82	132	25	0	20	66	74	6	79	1	0	7	5	3	.268	.361	.441	.967
1984	SF-N	57	203	33	65	9	1	11	44	43	7	29	0	0	3	1	1	.320	.434	.537	.970
1985	StL-N	126	442	71	124	26	3	22	87	83	14	88	2	0	5	1	4	.281	.393	.502	.988
1986	StL-N	65	232	34	55	12	2	9	23	45	4	61	1	0	1	1	1	.237	.362	.422	.995
1987	StL-N	131	419	93	120	23	1	35	106	136	13	139	0	0	3	1	2	.286	.459	.597	.989
1988	**NY-A**	**150**	**496**	**81**	**120**	**14**	**0**	**27**	**93**	**113**	**6**	**141**	**2**	**0**	**5**	**3**	**2**	**.242**	**.381**	**.433**	**.951**
1989	SD-N	142	455	76	110	19	1	26	94	132	18	145	1	0	5	6	2	.242	.410	.459	1.000
1990	SD-N	115	334	59	89	12	1	25	62	104	11	91	2	0	2	4	3	.266	.441	.533	.994
1991	Bos-A	140	481	75	120	18	1	28	87	96	3	133	3	0	5	0	2	.249	.374	.466	.000
1992	Bos-A	81	257	32	54	11	0	5	33	56	3	87	2	0	5	1	1	.210	.350	.311	.992
Career average		111	380	62	101	18	2	19	66	70	7	80	1	1	5	4	3	.267	.379	.476	.928
Yankee average		**150**	**496**	**81**	**120**	**14**	**0**	**27**	**93**	**113**	**6**	**141**	**2**	**0**	**5**	**3**	**2**	**.242**	**.381**	**.433**	**.951**
Career total		1994	6847	1118	1826	332	39	340	1180	1262	127	1441	24	9	83	77	61	.267	.379	.476	.928
Yankee total		**150**	**496**	**81**	**120**	**14**	**0**	**27**	**93**	**113**	**6**	**141**	**2**	**0**	**5**	**3**	**2**	**.242**	**.381**	**.433**	**.951**

Clarke, Horace Meredith (Hoss)

HEIGHT: 5'9"   THROWS: RIGHT   BATS: BOTH   BORN: 6/2/1940 FREDERIKSTED, ST. CROIX, VIRGIN ISLANDS   POSITIONS PLAYED: 2B, 3B, SS

YEAR	TEAM	GAMES	AB	RUNS	HITS	2B	3B	HR	RBI	BB	IBB	SO	HBP	SH	SF	SB	CS	BA	OBA	SA	FA
1965	**NY-A**	**51**	**108**	**13**	**28**	**1**	**0**	**1**	**9**	**6**	**0**	**6**	**0**	**1**	**1**	**2**	**1**	**.259**	**.296**	**.296**	**.923**
1966	**NY-A**	**96**	**312**	**37**	**83**	**10**	**4**	**6**	**28**	**27**	**4**	**24**	**1**	**1**	**3**	**5**	**3**	**.266**	**.324**	**.381**	**.970**
1967	**NY-A**	**143**	**588**	**74**	**160**	**17**	**0**	**3**	**29**	**42**	**2**	**64**	**0**	**3**	**0**	**21**	**4**	**.272**	**.321**	**.316**	**.990**
1968	**NY-A**	**148**	**579**	**52**	**133**	**6**	**1**	**2**	**26**	**23**	**0**	**46**	**0**	**3**	**2**	**20**	**7**	**.230**	**.258**	**.254**	**.984**
1969	**NY-A**	**156**	**641**	**82**	**183**	**26**	**7**	**4**	**48**	**53**	**1**	**41**	**0**	**3**	**2**	**33**	**13**	**.285**	**.339**	**.367**	**.982**
1970	**NY-A**	**158**	**686**	**81**	**172**	**24**	**2**	**4**	**46**	**35**	**5**	**35**	**2**	**2**	**7**	**23**	**7**	**.251**	**.286**	**.309**	**.979**
1971	**NY-A**	**159**	**625**	**76**	**156**	**23**	**7**	**2**	**41**	**64**	**2**	**43**	**2**	**4**	**1**	**17**	**7**	**.250**	**.321**	**.318**	**.981**
1972	**NY-A**	**147**	**547**	**65**	**132**	**20**	**2**	**3**	**37**	**56**	**4**	**44**	**4**	**3**	**3**	**18**	**6**	**.241**	**.315**	**.302**	**.985**
1973	**NY-A**	**148**	**590**	**60**	**155**	**21**	**0**	**2**	**35**	**47**	**0**	**48**	**2**	**6**	**5**	**11**	**10**	**.263**	**.317**	**.308**	**.979**
1974	**NY-A**	**24**	**47**	**3**	**11**	**1**	**0**	**0**	**1**	**4**	**0**	**5**	**0**	**2**	**0**	**1**	**0**	**.234**	**.294**	**.255**	**1.000**
1974	SD-N	42	90	5	17	0	0	0	4	8	0	6	0	1	0	0	0	.189	.255	.200	.978
Career average		116	438	50	112	14	2	3	28	33	2	33	1	3	2	14	5	.256	.308	.313	.977
Yankee average		**123**	**472**	**54**	**121**	**15**	**2**	**3**	**30**	**36**	**2**	**36**	**1**	**3**	**2**	**15**	**6**	**.257**	**.309**	**.315**	**.977**
Career total		1272	4813	548	1230	150	23	27	304	365	18	362	11	29	24	151	58	.256	.308	.313	.977
Yankee total		**1230**	**4723**	**543**	**1213**	**149**	**23**	**27**	**300**	**357**	**18**	**356**	**11**	**28**	**24**	**151**	**58**	**.257**	**.309**	**.315**	**.977**

Horace "Hoss" Meredith Clarke 2b-3b-ss, 1965–74

Horace Clarke's ascension to the big leagues coincides with the New York Yankees' decline of the 1960s, but the switch-hitting Clarke was one of the team's bright spots in those dark years.

Born on June 2, 1940 in St. Croix, the Virgin Islands, Clarke debuted as a Yankee in May 1965. The Yankees were the defending American League champions, but were clearly a team in disarray. Roger Maris, battling injuries, played in only 46 games. A banged-up Mickey Mantle hit only .255, his worst year to date. Eighteen-game winner Jim Bouton, fighting arm trouble, won only four games.

Clarke hit .259 as a backup infielder in 1965. In 1966, upon the retirement of All-Star shortstop Tony Kubek, Clarke was one of several players Yankee manager Johnny Keane tried out in Kubek's position. Clarke hit .266 and impressed the Yankees with his fielding.

Clarke improved his personal statistics in 1967, even as the Yankees themselves were sliding into the cellar. He hit .272 with 17 doubles and was 5th in the league with 21 stolen bases. Clarke was moved over to second base by the Yankees' new manager, Ralph Houk, and led the American League in assists and fielding percentage. But the Yankees finished tenth in 1966 and ninth in 1967.

Clarke continued his strong play in 1968, committing only 13 errors at second base and leading the league in putouts and assists as the Yankees improved to 83-79, good enough for fifth place in the league.

Clarke's best season was 1969. He was second in the American League in hits with 183 and triples with seven. He stole 33 bases to lead the team for the third year in a row. He was once again the best fielding second baseman in the league, and topped the league in assists and putouts. Clarke was the American League leader in assists at second base from 1967–72.

In 1973, Clarke had another good year, hitting .263, but the team seemed to be running in place. In 1974, George Steinbrenner of Cleveland purchased the team and began making changes. Clarke was sent to San Diego and Sandy Alomar was purchased from the California Angels. Clarke finished out the season with the Padres, hitting .189, and retired.

Clarke remains the tenth all-time basestealer for the Yankees.

Clinton, Luciean Louis (Ponca City Lou)

HEIGHT: 6'1"   THROWS: RIGHT   BATS: RIGHT   BORN: 10/13/1937 PONCA CITY, OKLAHOMA   DIED: 12/6/1997 POSITIONS PLAYED: OF

YEAR	TEAM	GAMES	AB	RUNS	HITS	2B	3B	HR	RBI	BB	IBB	SO	HBP	SH	SF	SB	CS	BA	OBA	SA	FA
1960	Bos-A	96	298	37	68	17	5	6	37	20	1	66	3	5	6	4	3	.228	.278	.379	.966
1961	Bos-A	17	51	4	13	2	1	0	3	2	0	10	0	1	0	0	0	.255	.283	.333	1.000
1962	Bos-A	114	398	63	117	24	10	18	75	34	3	79	1	1	2	2	1	.294	.349	.540	.979
1963	Bos-A	148	560	71	130	23	7	22	77	49	6	118	1	0	2	0	0	.232	.294	.416	.982
1964	Bos-A	37	120	15	31	4	3	3	6	9	1	33	0	1	0	1	0	.258	.310	.417	1.000
1964	LA-A	91	306	30	76	18	0	9	38	31	0	40	1	3	3	3	0	.248	.320	.395	.985
1965	Cal-A	89	222	29	54	12	3	1	8	23	1	37	1	2	1	2	3	.243	.316	.338	.983
1965	KC-A	1	1	0	0	0	0	0	0	0	0	0	0	0	0	0	0	.000	.000	.000	.000
1965	Cle-A	12	34	2	6	1	0	1	2	3	0	7	0	0	0	0	0	.176	.243	.294	.941
1966	**NY-A**	**80**	**159**	**18**	**35**	**10**	**2**	**5**	**21**	**16**	**1**	**27**	**0**	**2**	**2**	**0**	**0**	**.220**	**.288**	**.403**	**.976**
1967	**NY-A**	**6**	**4**	**1**	**2**	**1**	**0**	**0**	**2**	**1**	**1**	**1**	**0**	**0**	**0**	**0**	**0**	**.500**	**.600**	**.750**	**.000**
Career average		86	269	34	67	14	4	8	34	24	2	52	1	2	2	2	1	.247	.308	.418	.801
Yankee average		**43**	**82**	**10**	**19**	**6**	**1**	**3**	**12**	**9**	**1**	**14**	**0**	**1**	**1**	**0**	**0**	**.227**	**.297**	**.411**	**.488**
Career total		691	2153	270	532	112	31	65	269	188	14	418	7	15	16	12	7	.247	.308	.418	.801
Yankee total		**86**	**163**	**19**	**37**	**11**	**2**	**5**	**23**	**17**	**2**	**28**	**0**	**2**	**2**	**0**	**0**	**.227**	**.297**	**.411**	**.488**

Cockman, James
HEIGHT: 5'6"   THROWS: RIGHT   BATS: RIGHT   BORN: 4/26/1873 GUELPH, ONTARIO, CANADA   DIED: 9/28/1947 GUELPH, ONTARIO, CANADA   POSITIONS PLAYED: 3B

YEAR	TEAM	GAMES	AB	RUNS	HITS	2B	3B	HR	RBI	BB	IBB	SO	HBP	SH	SF	SB	CS	BA	OBA	SA	FA
1905	NY-A	13	38	5	4	0	0	0	2	4	—	—	0	0	—	2	—	.105	.190	.105	.875
Career average		13	38	5	4	0	0	0	2	4	—	—	0	0	—	2	—	.105	.190	.105	.875
Yankee average		**13**	**38**	**5**	**4**	**0**	**0**	**0**	**2**	**4**	**—**	**—**	**0**	**0**	**—**	**2**	**—**	**.105**	**.190**	**.105**	**.875**
Career total		13	38	5	4	0	0	0	2	4	—	—	0	0	—	2	—	.105	.190	.105	.875
Yankee total		**13**	**38**	**5**	**4**	**0**	**0**	**0**	**2**	**4**	**—**	**—**	**0**	**0**	**—**	**2**	**—**	**.105**	**.190**	**.105**	**.875**

Coggins, Richard Allen
HEIGHT: 5'8"   THROWS: LEFT   BATS: LEFT   BORN: 12/7/1950 INDIANAPOLIS, INDIANA   POSITIONS PLAYED: OF

YEAR	TEAM	GAMES	AB	RUNS	HITS	2B	3B	HR	RBI	BB	IBB	SO	HBP	SH	SF	SB	CS	BA	OBA	SA	FA
1972	Bal-A	16	39	5	13	4	0	0	1	1	0	6	0	3	0	0	2	.333	.350	.436	1.000
1973	Bal-A	110	389	54	124	19	9	7	41	28	2	24	0	7	2	17	9	.319	.363	.468	.987
1974	Bal-A	113	411	53	100	13	3	4	32	29	3	31	5	7	3	26	6	.243	.299	.319	.984
1975	Mon-N	13	37	1	10	3	1	0	4	1	0	7	0	2	0	0	0	.270	.289	.405	1.000
1975	NY-A	51	107	7	24	1	0	1	6	7	0	16	0	5	0	3	3	.224	.272	.262	.970
1976	NY-A	7	4	1	1	0	0	0	1	0	0	1	0	0	0	1	0	.250	.250	.250	1.000
1976	Chi-A	32	96	4	15	2	0	0	5	6	0	15	0	2	0	3	1	.156	.206	.177	1.000
Career average		68	217	25	57	8	3	2	18	14	1	20	1	5	1	10	4	.265	.312	.361	.992
Yankee average		**7**	**4**	**1**	**1**	**0**	**0**	**0**	**1**	**0**	**0**	**1**	**0**	**0**	**0**	**1**	**0**	**.250**	**.250**	**.250**	**.985**
Career total		342	1083	125	287	42	13	12	90	72	5	100	5	26	5	50	21	.265	.312	.361	.992
Yankee total		**7**	**4**	**1**	**1**	**0**	**0**	**0**	**1**	**0**	**0**	**1**	**0**	**0**	**0**	**1**	**0**	**.250**	**.250**	**.250**	**.985**

Colavito, Rocco Domenico (Rocky)
HEIGHT: 6'3"   THROWS: RIGHT   BATS: RIGHT   BORN: 8/10/1933 NEW YORK, NEW YORK   POSITIONS PLAYED: P, OF

YEAR	TEAM	GAMES	AB	RUNS	HITS	2B	3B	HR	RBI	BB	IBB	SO	HBP	SH	SF	SB	CS	BA	OBA	SA	FA
1955	Cle-A	5	9	3	4	2	0	0	0	0	0	2	0	0	0	0	0	.444	.444	.667	1.000
1956	Cle-A	101	322	55	89	11	4	21	65	49	0	46	2	4	3	0	1	.276	.372	.531	.968
1957	Cle-A	134	461	66	116	26	0	25	84	71	0	80	1	4	7	1	6	.252	.348	.471	.962
1958	Cle-A	143	489	80	148	26	3	41	113	84	6	89	2	0	3	0	2	.303	.405	.620	.981
1959	Cle-A	154	588	90	151	24	0	42	111	71	8	86	2	0	3	3	3	.257	.337	.512	.985
1960	Det-A	145	555	67	138	18	1	35	87	53	4	80	4	1	3	3	6	.249	.317	.474	.976
1961	Det-A	163	583	129	169	30	2	45	140	113	2	75	2	2	8	1	2	.290	.402	.580	.975
1962	Det-A	161	601	90	164	30	2	37	112	96	7	68	2	1	7	2	0	.273	.371	.514	.992
1963	Det-A	160	597	91	162	29	2	22	91	84	9	78	1	2	8	0	0	.271	.358	.437	.988
1964	KC-A	160	588	89	161	31	2	34	102	83	4	56	5	1	4	3	1	.274	.366	.507	.973
1965	Cle-A	162	592	92	170	25	2	26	108	93	11	63	3	0	7	1	1	.287	.383	.468	1.000
1966	Cle-A	151	533	68	127	13	0	30	72	76	4	81	3	0	2	2	1	.238	.336	.432	.982
1967	Cle-A	63	191	10	46	9	0	5	21	24	0	31	1	0	0	2	2	.241	.329	.366	.963
1967	Chi-A	60	190	20	42	4	1	3	29	25	2	10	0	1	4	1	1	.221	.312	.300	.977
1968	LA-N	40	113	8	23	3	0	3	11	15	1	18	0	1	0	1	1	.204	.295	.310	1.000
1968	**NY-A**	**39**	**91**	**13**	**20**	**2**	**2**	**5**	**13**	**14**	**0**	**17**	**1**	**0**	**0**	**0**	**0**	**.220**	**.330**	**.451**	**.933**
Career average		123	434	65	115	19	1	25	77	63	4	59	2	1	4	1	2	.266	.359	.489	.978
Yankee average		**39**	**91**	**13**	**20**	**2**	**2**	**5**	**13**	**14**	**0**	**17**	**1**	**0**	**0**	**0**	**0**	**.220**	**.330**	**.451**	**.933**
Career total		1841	6503	971	1730	283	21	374	1159	951	58	880	29	16	60	19	27	.266	.359	.489	.978
Yankee total		**39**	**91**	**13**	**20**	**2**	**2**	**5**	**13**	**14**	**0**	**17**	**1**	**0**	**0**	**0**	**0**	**.220**	**.330**	**.451**	**.933**

Coleman, Curtis Hancock
HEIGHT: 5'11"   THROWS: RIGHT   BATS: LEFT   BORN: 2/18/1887 SALEM, OREGON   DIED: 7/1/1980 NEWPORT, OREGON   POSITIONS PLAYED: 3B

YEAR	TEAM	GAMES	AB	RUNS	HITS	2B	3B	HR	RBI	BB	IBB	SO	HBP	SH	SF	SB	CS	BA	OBA	SA	FA
1912	NY-A	12	37	8	9	4	0	0	4	7	—	—	0	0	—	0	—	.243	.364	.351	.865
Career average		12	37	8	9	4	0	0	4	7	—	—	0	0	—	0	—	.243	.364	.351	.865
Yankee average		**12**	**37**	**8**	**9**	**4**	**0**	**0**	**4**	**7**	**—**	**—**	**0**	**0**	**—**	**0**	**—**	**.243**	**.364**	**.351**	**.865**
Career total		12	37	8	9	4	0	0	4	7	—	—	0	0	—	0	—	.243	.364	.351	.865
Yankee total		**12**	**37**	**8**	**9**	**4**	**0**	**0**	**4**	**7**	**—**	**—**	**0**	**0**	**—**	**0**	**—**	**.243**	**.364**	**.351**	**.865**

Coleman, Gerald Francis (Jerry)

HEIGHT: 6'0" THROWS: RIGHT BATS: RIGHT BORN: 9/14/1924 SAN JOSE, CALIFORNIA POSITIONS PLAYED: 2B, 3B, SS

YEAR	TEAM	GAMES	AB	RUNS	HITS	2B	3B	HR	RBI	BB	IBB	SO	HBP	SH	SF	SB	CS	BA	OBA	SA	FA
1949	NY-A	128	447	54	123	21	5	2	42	63	—	44	2	11	—	8	6	.275	.367	.358	.981
1950	NY-A	153	522	69	150	19	6	6	69	67	—	38	3	10	—	3	2	.287	.372	.381	.977
1951	NY-A	121	362	48	90	11	2	3	43	31	—	36	4	8	—	6	1	.249	.315	.315	.968
1952	NY-A	11	42	6	17	2	1	0	4	5	—	4	0	0	—	0	1	.405	.468	.500	.971
1953	NY-A	8	10	1	2	0	0	0	0	0	—	2	0	1	—	0	0	.200	.200	.200	1.000
1954	NY-A	107	300	39	65	7	1	3	21	26	—	29	0	5	1	3	0	.217	.278	.277	.977
1955	NY-A	43	96	12	22	5	0	0	8	11	0	11	2	3	0	0	2	.229	.321	.281	.500
1956	NY-A	80	183	15	47	5	1	0	18	12	2	33	1	6	1	1	2	.257	.305	.295	.979
1957	NY-A	72	157	23	42	7	2	2	12	20	0	21	1	2	0	1	1	.268	.354	.376	.750
Career average		62	149	18	36	5	1	1	12	14	—	19	1	3	—	1	1	.239	.306	.302	.900
Yankee average		62	149	18	36	5	1	1	12	14	—	19	1	3	—	1	1	.239	.306	.302	.900
Career total		310	746	90	178	24	4	5	59	69	2	96	4	17	2	5	5	.239	.306	.302	.900
Yankee total		310	746	90	178	24	4	5	59	69	2	96	4	17	2	5	5	.239	.306	.302	.900

Gerald Francis "Jerry" Coleman, 2b-ss-3b, 1949–57

This smooth-fielding, acrobatic utility man played in the World Series in six of his nine seasons with the Yankees.

Coleman was born in San Jose, California, on September 14, 1924. He was a sandlot star on the West Coast in the late 1930s and early 1940s. In 1944, he joined the service and flew bombing missions in the Pacific theater during World War II.

Coleman was back in baseball after the war, playing for the Yankees farm club in Newark, New Jersey. In 1949, the Yankees brought him up.

He was a shortstop for most of his career. But the Yankees already had a great shortstop in Phil Rizzuto, so manager Casey Stengel moved Coleman over to second base.

Initially, Coleman wasn't sure he could do the job. He spent hours with Rizzuto and infield coach Frank Crosetti working on his footwork. Eventually he became so smooth at second base that his teammates called him "Fancy Dan." He hit .275 with 128 hits in 123 games his first year, earning him the league's Rookie of the Year award.

Coleman was never a particularly acute offensive threat, but then, he wasn't supposed to be. The Yankees had made it clear to him very early on that his job was to make plays defensively. This he did with a consistency that reminded some Yankee old-timers of former All-Star Joe Gordon.

Coleman's best year was 1950, when he hit .287 and made the All-Star team. That was the year he was also voted the Most Valuable Player in the World Series. The Yankees swept the Philadelphia Phillies, but each contest was low-scoring and close. Coleman batted .286 with a team-leading 3 RBI (the Yankees scored only ten runs in the four games). In the first game, he drove in the game's only run with a sacrifice fly. In the pivotal third game, his RBI single drove in the winning run of a 3-2 contest.

Coleman's career was interrupted again by the Korean War in 1952–53. He returned in 1954 and played until 1957 as a backup infielder.

Following his retirement, Coleman worked and announced for the Yankees and then briefly managed the San Diego Padres in 1980 before becoming a broadcaster for the team.

Collins, David Scott

HEIGHT: 5'11" THROWS: LEFT BATS: BOTH BORN: 10/20/1952 RAPID CITY, SOUTH DAKOTA POSITIONS PLAYED: 1B, OF, DH

YEAR	TEAM	GAMES	AB	RUNS	HITS	2B	3B	HR	RBI	BB	IBB	SO	HBP	SH	SF	SB	CS	BA	OBA	SA	FA
1975	Cal-A	93	319	41	85	13	4	3	29	36	1	55	1	3	3	24	10	.266	.340	.361	.988
1976	Cal-A	99	365	45	96	12	1	4	28	40	2	55	0	7	1	32	19	.263	.335	.334	.994
1977	Sea-A	120	402	46	96	9	3	5	28	33	0	66	3	6	3	25	10	.239	.299	.313	.985
1978	Cin-N	102	102	13	22	1	0	0	7	15	0	18	0	1	2	7	7	.216	.311	.225	.969
1979	Cin-N	122	396	59	126	16	4	3	35	27	2	48	2	3	1	16	9	.318	.364	.402	.976
1980	Cin-N	144	551	94	167	20	4	3	35	53	2	68	3	3	3	79	21	.303	.366	.370	.986
1981	Cin-N	95	360	63	98	18	6	3	23	41	1	41	6	3	2	26	10	.272	.355	.381	.977
1982	**NY-A**	**111**	**348**	**41**	**88**	**12**	**3**	**3**	**25**	**28**	**3**	**49**	**5**	**9**	**3**	**13**	**8**	**.253**	**.315**	**.330**	**.992**
1983	Tor-A	118	402	55	109	12	4	1	34	43	1	67	2	2	2	31	7	.271	.343	.328	.989
1984	Tor-A	128	441	59	136	24	15	2	44	33	0	41	9	6	3	60	14	.308	.366	.444	.991
1985	Oak-A	112	379	52	95	16	4	4	29	29	2	37	1	5	4	29	8	.251	.303	.346	.978
1986	Det-A	124	419	44	113	18	2	1	27	44	0	49	2	9	2	27	12	.270	.340	.329	.995
1987	Cin-N	57	85	19	25	5	0	0	5	11	0	12	2	2	0	9	0	.294	.388	.353	1.000
1988	Cin-N	99	174	12	41	6	2	0	14	11	0	27	2	0	2	7	2	.236	.286	.293	.965
1989	Cin-N	78	106	12	25	4	0	0	7	10	0	17	0	2	0	3	1	.236	.302	.274	1.000
1990	StL-N	99	58	12	13	1	0	0	3	13	2	10	0	3	0	7	1	.224	.366	.241	1.000
Career average		106	307	42	83	12	3	2	23	29	1	41	2	4	2	25	9	.272	.338	.351	.987
Yankee average		**111**	**348**	**41**	**88**	**12**	**3**	**3**	**25**	**28**	**3**	**49**	**5**	**9**	**3**	**13**	**8**	**.253**	**.315**	**.330**	**.992**
Career total		1701	4907	667	1335	187	52	32	373	467	16	660	38	64	31	395	139	.272	.338	.351	.987
Yankee total		**111**	**348**	**41**	**88**	**12**	**3**	**3**	**25**	**28**	**3**	**49**	**5**	**9**	**3**	**13**	**8**	**.253**	**.315**	**.330**	**.992**

Collins, Joseph Edward BORN JOSEPH EDWARD KOLLONIGE

HEIGHT: 6'0" THROWS: LEFT BATS: LEFT BORN: 12/3/1922 SCRANTON, PENNSYLVANIA DIED: 8/30/1989 UNION, NEW JERSEY POSITIONS PLAYED: 1B, OF

YEAR	TEAM	GAMES	AB	RUNS	HITS	2B	3B	HR	RBI	BB	IBB	SO	HBP	SH	SF	SB	CS	BA	OBA	SA	FA
1948	NY-A	5	5	0	1	1	0	0	2	0	—	1	0	0	—	0	0	.200	.200	.400	.000
1949	NY-A	7	10	2	1	0	0	0	4	6	—	2	0	0	—	0	0	.100	.438	.100	.920
1950	NY-A	108	205	47	48	8	3	8	28	31	—	34	0	3	—	5	0	.234	.335	.420	1.000
1951	NY-A	125	262	52	75	8	5	9	48	34	—	23	0	2	—	9	7	.286	.368	.458	.987
1952	NY-A	122	428	69	120	16	8	18	59	55	—	47	1	5	—	4	2	.280	.364	.481	.990
1953	NY-A	127	387	72	104	11	2	17	44	59	—	36	0	4	—	2	6	.269	.365	.439	.917
1954	NY-A	130	343	67	93	20	2	12	46	51	—	37	0	4	0	2	2	.271	.365	.446	.992
1955	NY-A	105	278	40	65	9	1	13	45	44	2	32	2	3	3	0	2	.234	.339	.414	.981
1956	NY-A	100	262	38	59	5	3	7	43	34	2	33	1	1	3	3	1	.225	.313	.347	1.000
1957	NY-A	79	149	17	30	1	0	2	10	24	2	18	0	0	1	2	1	.201	.310	.248	.987
Career average		91	233	40	60	8	2	9	33	34	1	26	0	2	1	3	2	.256	.350	.421	.877
Yankee average		**91**	**233**	**40**	**60**	**8**	**2**	**9**	**33**	**34**	**1**	**26**	**0**	**2**	**1**	**3**	**2**	**.256**	**.350**	**.421**	**.877**
Career total		908	2329	404	596	79	24	86	329	338	6	263	4	22	7	27	21	.256	.350	.421	.877
Yankee total		**908**	**2329**	**404**	**596**	**79**	**24**	**86**	**329**	**338**	**6**	**263**	**4**	**22**	**7**	**27**	**21**	**.256**	**.350**	**.421**	**.877**

Collins, Orth Stein (Buck)

HEIGHT: 6'0" THROWS: RIGHT BATS: LEFT BORN: 4/27/1880 LAFAYETTE, INDIANA DIED: 12/13/1949 FT. LAUDERDALE, FLORIDA POSITIONS PLAYED: OF

YEAR	TEAM	GAMES	AB	RUNS	HITS	2B	3B	HR	RBI	BB	IBB	SO	HBP	SH	SF	SB	CS	BA	OBA	SA	FA
1904	**NY-A**	**5**	**17**	**3**	**6**	**1**	**1**	**0**	**1**	**1**	**—**	**—**	**0**	**0**	**—**	**0**	**—**	**.353**	**.389**	**.529**	**1.000**
1909	Was-A	8	7	0	0	0	0	0	0	0	—	—	0	0	—	0	—	.000	.000	.000	1.000
Career average		7	12	2	3	1	1	0	1	1	—	—	0	0	—	0	—	.250	.280	.375	1.000
Yankee average		**5**	**17**	**3**	**6**	**1**	**1**	**0**	**1**	**1**	**—**	**—**	**0**	**0**	**—**	**0**	**—**	**.353**	**.389**	**.529**	**1.000**
Career total		13	24	3	6	1	1	0	1	1	—	—	0	0	—	0	—	.250	.280	.375	1.000
Yankee total		**5**	**17**	**3**	**6**	**1**	**1**	**0**	**1**	**1**	**—**	**—**	**0**	**0**	**—**	**0**	**—**	**.353**	**.389**	**.529**	**1.000**

Collins, Robert Joseph (Rip)

HEIGHT: 5'11" THROWS: RIGHT BATS: RIGHT BORN: 9/18/1909 PITTSBURGH, PENNSYLVANIA DIED: 4/19/1969 PITTSBURGH, PENNSYLVANIA POSITIONS PLAYED: C

YEAR	TEAM	GAMES	AB	RUNS	HITS	2B	3B	HR	RBI	BB	IBB	SO	HBP	SH	SF	SB	CS	BA	OBA	SA	FA
1940	Chi-N	47	120	11	25	3	0	1	14	14	0	18	1	1	—	4	—	.208	.296	.258	.951
1944	**NY-A**	**3**	**3**	**0**	**1**	**0**	**0**	**0**	**0**	**1**	**0**	**0**	**0**	**0**	**—**	**0**	**0**	**.333**	**.500**	**.333**	**1.000**
Career average		25	62	6	13	2	0	1	7	8	0	9	1	1	—	2	—	.211	.302	.260	.976
Yankee average		**3**	**3**	**0**	**1**	**0**	**0**	**0**	**0**	**1**	**0**	**0**	**0**	**0**	**—**	**0**	**0**	**.333**	**.500**	**.333**	**1.000**
Career total		50	123	11	26	3	0	1	14	15	0	18	1	1	—	4	—	.211	.302	.260	.976
Yankee total		**3**	**3**	**0**	**1**	**0**	**0**	**0**	**0**	**1**	**0**	**0**	**0**	**0**	**—**	**0**	**0**	**.333**	**.500**	**.333**	**1.000**

Joseph Edward Collins, 1b-of, 1948–57

In the 11 years between the retirement of Lou Gehrig in 1939 and the ascension of Joe Collins to the position in 1950, the New York Yankees had five different first basemen. Collins, who played all of his ten years in a New York uniform, finally stabilized the position in the early 1950s.

Collins was born in Scranton, Pennsylvania, on December 3, 1922. Toward the end of a relatively extended minor league career, he was twice called up to the Yankees, in the latter part of the 1948 and 1949 seasons.

He was called up for good in 1950 at age 28. The Yankees had used outfielder Tommy Heinrich at first in 1949, but Heinrich, beset with knee problems, was clearly not going to be the answer at that position.

Manager Casey Stengel moved Collins into the first base slot almost immediately in 1950. Collins was a mediocre hitter throughout his career. His best year was 1952 when he hit

.280. But he was strong defensively.

In 1950, he made only seven errors at first base, the fewest in the American League, and throughout his career he would be among the league leaders in fewest miscues at first.

He had several big World Series games. In 1951, his home run in Game 2 against the Giants scored the winning run in a 3-1 victory and evened the series at 1-1. In 1953, his home run in the seventh inning of Game 1 against the Brooklyn Dodgers snapped a 5-5 tie. The Yankees went on to win the game, 9-5, and the Series in six games. In 1955, Collins smacked two home runs, including the game-winner, as the Yankees took the first game in that series, 6-5. The Dodgers, however, would go on to win that Series in seven games.

By 1955, Stengel had found a better first baseman in William "Moose" Skowron. Skowron was not the fielder Collins was, but he was a better hitter, and that was what the Yankees were looking for. Skowron and Collins platooned in 1955 and in 1956, but by 1957, Skowron took over first base for good. Collins, 37, decided to retire. He died in 1989 in Union, New Jersey.

Collins, Tharon Patrick

HEIGHT: 5'9"   THROWS: RIGHT   BATS: RIGHT   BORN: 9/13/1896 SWEET SPRINGS, MISSOURI   DIED: 5/20/1960, KANSAS CITY, KANSAS   POSITIONS PLAYED: C, 1B

YEAR	TEAM	GAMES	AB	RUNS	HITS	2B	3B	HR	RBI	BB	IBB	SO	HBP	SH	SF	SB	CS	BA	OBA	SA	FA
1919	StL-A	11	21	2	3	1	0	0	1	4	—	2	0	0	—	0	—	.143	.280	.190	.929
1920	StL-A	23	28	5	6	1	0	0	6	3	—	5	0	0	—	0	0	.214	.290	.250	1.000
1921	StL-A	58	111	9	27	3	0	1	10	16	—	17	0	3	—	1	0	.243	.339	.297	.961
1922	StL-A	63	127	14	39	6	0	8	23	21	—	21	0	1	—	0	1	.307	.405	.543	.980
1923	StL-A	85	181	9	32	8	0	3	30	15	—	45	0	8	—	0	0	.177	.240	.271	.980
1924	StL-A	32	54	9	17	2	0	1	11	11	—	14	0	2	—	0	1	.315	.431	.407	.969
1926	**NY-A**	102	290	41	83	11	3	7	35	73	—	57	2	8	—	3	2	**.286**	**.433**	**.417**	**.971**
1927	**NY-A**	92	251	38	69	9	3	7	36	54	—	24	2	4	—	0	1	**.275**	**.407**	**.418**	**.976**
1928	**NY-A**	70	136	18	30	5	0	6	14	35	—	16	0	3	—	0	0	**.221**	**.380**	**.390**	**.977**
1929	Bos-N	7	5	1	0	0	0	0	2	3	—	1	0	3	—	0	—	.000	.375	.000	1.000
Career average		54	120	15	31	5	1	3	17	24	—	20	0	3	—	0	1	.254	.378	.385	.974
Yankee average		88	226	32	61	8	2	7	28	54	—	32	1	5	—	1	1	**.269**	**.413**	**.412**	**.975**
Career total		543	1204	146	306	46	6	33	168	235	—	202	4	32	—	4	5	.254	.378	.385	.974
Yankee total		264	677	97	182	25	6	20	85	162	—	97	4	15	—	3	3	**.269**	**.413**	**.412**	**.975**

Colman, Frank Lloyd

HEIGHT: 5'11"   THROWS: LEFT   BATS: LEFT   BORN: 3/2/1918 LONDON, ONT., CANADA   DIED: 2/19/1983 LONDON, ONT., CANADA   POSITIONS PLAYED: 1B, OF

YEAR	TEAM	GAMES	AB	RUNS	HITS	2B	3B	HR	RBI	BB	IBB	SO	HBP	SH	SF	SB	CS	BA	OBA	SA	FA
1942	Pit-N	10	37	2	5	0	0	1	2	2	—	2	0	1	—	0	—	.135	.179	.216	1.000
1943	Pit-N	32	59	9	16	2	2	0	4	8	—	7	0	1	—	0	—	.271	.358	.373	1.000
1944	Pit-N	99	226	30	61	9	5	6	53	25	—	27	1	0	—	0	—	.270	.345	.434	.964
1945	Pit-N	77	153	18	32	11	1	4	30	9	—	16	0	0	—	0	—	.209	.253	.373	.993
1946	Pit-N	26	53	3	9	3	0	1	6	2	—	7	1	0	—	0	—	.170	.214	.283	1.000
1946	**NY-A**	**5**	**15**	**2**	**4**	**0**	**0**	**1**	**5**	**1**	**—**	**1**	**—**	**—**	**—**	**0**	**—**	**.267**	**.313**	**.467**	**1.000**
1947	**NY-A**	**22**	**28**	**2**	**3**	**0**	**0**	**2**	**6**	**2**	**—**	**6**	**0**	**0**	**—**	**0**	**0**	**.107**	**.167**	**.321**	**1.000**
Career average		39	82	9	19	4	1	2	15	7	—	9	0	0	—	0	0	.228	.291	.378	.994
Yankee average		**14**	**22**	**2**	**4**	**0**	**0**	**2**	**6**	**2**	**—**	**4**	**0**	**0**	**—**	**0**	**0**	**.163**	**.217**	**.372**	**1.000**
Career total		271	571	66	130	25	8	15	106	49	—	66	2	2	—	0	0	.228	.291	.378	.994
Yankee total		**27**	**43**	**4**	**7**	**0**	**0**	**3**	**11**	**3**	**—**	**7**	**0**	**0**	**—**	**0**	**0**	**.163**	**.217**	**.372**	**1.000**

Combs, Earle Bryan

HEIGHT: 6'0"   THROWS: RIGHT   BATS: LEFT   BORN: 05/14/1899 PEBWORTH, KENTUCKY   DIED: 7/21/1976 RICHMOND, VIRGINIA   POSITIONS PLAYED: OF

YEAR	TEAM	GAMES	AB	RUNS	HITS	2B	3B	HR	RBI	BB	IBB	SO	HBP	SH	SF	SB	CS	BA	OBA	SA	FA
1924	NY-A	24	35	10	14	5	0	0	2	4	—	2	0	0	—	0	1	.400	.462	.543	1.000
1925	NY-A	150	593	117	203	36	13	3	61	65	—	43	4	11	—	12	13	.342	.411	.462	.979
1926	NY-A	145	606	113	181	31	12	8	55	47	—	23	3	14	—	8	6	.299	.352	.429	.970
1927	NY-A	152	648	137	231	36	23	6	64	62	—	31	2	12	—	15	6	.356	.414	.511	.968
1928	NY-A	149	626	118	194	33	21	7	56	77	—	33	2	4	—	10	8	.310	.387	.463	.980
1929	NY-A	142	586	119	202	33	15	3	65	69	—	32	0	11	—	11	7	.345	.414	.468	.966
1930	NY-A	137	532	129	183	30	22	7	82	74	—	26	0	11	—	16	10	.344	.424	.523	.969
1931	NY-A	138	563	120	179	31	13	5	58	68	—	34	3	2	—	11	3	.318	.394	.446	.974
1932	NY-A	144	591	143	190	32	10	9	65	81	—	16	2	1	—	3	9	.321	.405	.455	.967
1933	NY-A	122	417	86	125	22	16	5	64	47	—	19	1	3	—	6	4	.300	.372	.465	.975
1934	NY-A	63	251	47	80	13	5	2	25	40	—	9	0	4	—	3	1	.319	.412	.434	.993
1935	NY-A	89	298	47	84	7	4	3	35	36	—	10	0	1	—	1	3	.282	.359	.362	.993
Career average		121	479	99	156	26	13	5	53	56	—	23	1	6	—	8	6	.325	.397	.462	.974
Yankee average		**121**	**479**	**99**	**156**	**26**	**13**	**5**	**53**	**56**	**—**	**23**	**1**	**6**	**—**	**8**	**6**	**.325**	**.397**	**.462**	**.974**
Career total		1455	5746	1186	1866	309	154	58	632	670	—	278	17	74	—	96	71	.325	.397	.462	.974
Yankee total		**1455**	**5746**	**1186**	**1866**	**309**	**154**	**58**	**632**	**670**	**—**	**278**	**17**	**74**	**—**	**96**	**71**	**.325**	**.397**	**.462**	**.974**

Connelly, Thomas Martin

HEIGHT: 6'0"   THROWS: RIGHT   BATS: LEFT   BORN: 10/20/1897 CHICAGO, ILLINOIS   DIED: 2/18/1941 HINES, ILLINOIS   POSITIONS PLAYED: OF

YEAR	TEAM	GAMES	AB	RUNS	HITS	2B	3B	HR	RBI	BB	IBB	SO	HBP	SH	SF	SB	CS	BA	OBA	SA	FA
1920	**NY-A**	**1**	**1**	**0**	**0**	**0**	**0**	**0**	**0**	**0**	**—**	**0**	**0**	**0**	**—**	**0**	**0**	**.000**	**.000**	**.000**	**.000**
1921	**NY-A**	**4**	**5**	**0**	**1**	**0**	**0**	**0**	**0**	**1**	**—**	**0**	**0**	**0**	**—**	**0**	**0**	**.200**	**.333**	**.200**	**.000**
Career average		3	3	0	1	0	0	0	0	1	—	0	0	0	—	0	0	.167	.286	.167	.500
Yankee average		**3**	**3**	**0**	**1**	**0**	**0**	**0**	**0**	**1**	**—**	**0**	**0**	**0**	**—**	**0**	**0**	**.167**	**.286**	**.167**	**.500**
Career total		5	6	0	1	0	0	0	0	1	—	0	0	0	—	0	0	.167	.286	.167	.500
Yankee total		**5**	**6**	**0**	**1**	**0**	**0**	**0**	**0**	**1**	**—**	**0**	**0**	**0**	**—**	**0**	**0**	**.167**	**.286**	**.167**	**.500**

Connor, Joseph Francis (Joe)

HEIGHT: 6'2"   THROWS: RIGHT   BATS: RIGHT   BORN: 12/8/1874 WATERBURY, CONN.   DIED: 11/8/1957 WATERBURY, CONN.   POSITIONS PLAYED: C, 1B, 2B, 3B, OF

YEAR	TEAM	GAMES	AB	RUNS	HITS	2B	3B	HR	RBI	BB	IBB	SO	HBP	SH	SF	SB	CS	BA	OBA	SA	FA
1895	StL-N	2	7	0	0	0	0	0	1	0	—	2	0	0	—	0	—	.000	.000	.000	1.000
1900	Bos-N	7	19	2	4	0	0	0	4	2	—	—	0	0	—	1	—	.211	.286	.211	.971
1901	Mil-A	38	102	10	28	3	1	1	9	6	—	—	1	3	—	4	—	.275	.321	.353	.949
1901	Cle-A	37	121	13	17	3	1	0	6	7	—	—	2	3	—	2	—	.140	.200	.182	.942
1905	**NY-A**	**8**	**22**	**4**	**5**	**1**	**0**	**0**	**2**	**3**	**—**	**—**	**0**	**2**	**—**	**1**	**—**	**.227**	**.320**	**.273**	**.978**
Career average		18	54	6	11	1	0	0	4	4	0	0	1	2	0	2	0	.199	.257	.251	.968
Yankee average		**8**	**22**	**4**	**5**	**1**	**0**	**0**	**2**	**3**	**—**	**—**	**0**	**2**	**0**	**1**	**—**	**.227**	**.320**	**.273**	**.978**
Career total		92	271	29	54	7	2	1	22	18	—	2	3	8	0	8	—	.199	.257	.251	.968
Yankee total		**8**	**22**	**4**	**5**	**1**	**0**	**0**	**2**	**3**	**—**	**—**	**0**	**2**	**0**	**1**	**—**	**.227**	**.320**	**.273**	**.978**

Earle Bryan Combs, of, 1924–35

The story goes that when Earle Combs joined the Yankees from Louisville, he told manager Miller Huggins, "Where I come from, they call me the Table-Setter." This was in reference to Combs's exceptional abilities as a lead-off hitter. Huggins, however, was less than overwhelmed. "Up, here," he told Combs, "you'll be known as the Waiter, because that's what you'll be doing on base until Ruth and Gehrig come to bat."

Contrary to these brash rumors, Earle Combs, born on May 14, 1899 in Pebworth, Kentucky, was often described as the quiet, digni-fied fellow on the Yankees of the Roaring Twenties and early 1930s. For the most part, he lived up to that billing.

Combs, a handsome, prematurely graying, devout Southerner, played baseball in the sandlots of Kentucky as a young boy. He once admitted modestly that the only reason he got to play in those games was that he often furnished the ball, which his father would make by winding string around an old rubber ball and sewing the whole

thing up. But it seems unlikely that the athletic Combs would not have been welcome on a ball field, even as a youngster.

Combs was well-educated. After high school, he graduated from the former Eastern Kentucky State Teachers' College in 1922, and soon went to work as a teacher and part-time ballplayer.

But he was good, and before long, scouts began attending his games in Louisville. The Yankees bought his contract for $65,000 and he joined the Yankees at the tail end of the 1924 season.

The initial assessment from the New York writers was that Combs was good, but probably not good enough to displace the veteran Whitey Witt in center field.

But he began hitting almost immediately, playing in 24 games and batting .400 that first year. By 1926, Witt was gone, sold to the A's, and Combs was a staple in the outfield.

Huggins loved his speed on both the base paths and in the outfield. In Louisville, in 1924, he was timed at 11 seconds flat in the 100-yard dash—wearing spikes and a floppy baseball uniform, not running shoes or track shorts. The world record for the 100 in 1924 was 10.9 seconds.

Conroy, William Edward (Wid)

HEIGHT: 5'9"   THROWS: RIGHT   BATS: RIGHT   BORN: 4/5/1877 CAMDEN, NEW JERSEY   DIED: 12/6/1959 MT. HOLLY, NEW JERSEY   POSITIONS PLAYED: 2B, 3B, SS, OF

YEAR	TEAM	GAMES	AB	RUNS	HITS	2B	3B	HR	RBI	BB	IBB	SO	HBP	SH	SF	SB	CS	BA	OBA	SA	FA
1901	Mil-A	131	503	74	129	20	6	5	64	36	—	—	8	21	—	21	—	.256	.316	.350	.868
1902	Pit-N	99	365	55	89	10	6	1	47	24	—	—	5	10	—	10	—	.244	.299	.312	.925
1903	NY-A	126	503	74	137	23	12	1	45	32	—	—	5	8	—	33	—	.272	.322	.372	.919
1904	NY-A	140	489	58	119	18	12	1	52	43	—	—	7	17	—	30	—	.243	.314	.335	.947
1905	NY-A	102	385	55	105	19	11	2	25	32	—	—	0	7	—	25	—	.273	.329	.395	.928
1906	NY-A	148	567	67	139	17	10	4	54	47	—	—	1	18	—	32	—	.245	.303	.332	.968
1907	NY-A	140	530	58	124	12	11	3	51	30	—	—	3	9	—	41	—	.234	.279	.315	.955
1908	NY-A	141	531	44	126	22	3	1	39	14	—	—	1	22	—	23	—	.237	.258	.296	.963
1909	Was-A	139	488	44	119	13	4	1	20	37	—	—	1	23	—	24	—	.244	.298	.293	.950
1910	Was-A	103	351	36	89	11	3	1	27	30	—	—	1	13	—	11	—	.254	.314	.311	.961
1911	Was-A	106	349	40	81	11	4	2	28	20	—	—	4	11	—	12	—	.232	.282	.304	1.000
Career average		125	460	55	114	16	7	2	41	31	—	—	3	14	—	24	—	.248	.301	.329	.944
Yankee average		133	501	59	125	19	10	2	44	33	—	—	3	14	—	31	—	.250	.300	.338	.947
Career total		1375	5061	605	1257	176	82	22	452	345	—	—	36	159	—	262	—	.248	.301	.329	.944
Yankee total		797	3005	356	750	111	59	12	266	198	—	—	17	81	—	184	—	.250	.300	.338	.947

At the plate, Combs batted from a deep crouch, which narrowed his strike zone. Only once in his career did he strike out more than 34 times in a full season.

As a leadoff hitter, the Yankees could not have found a better man. He hit .325 for his career, and three times led the league in triples. And Combs could steal bases, though Huggins didn't often need him to do so.

In the field, Combs used his tremendous speed to cover the enormous center field of Yankee Stadium. His arm strength was average, but he compensated for that somewhat by getting the ball out of his glove as quickly as possible. Due to his speed (and due also to their relative lack of it), left fielder Meusel and right fielder Ruth gave Combs plenty of room out there.

Defensively, Cleveland's Fred Shaute was probably slightly better, but by 1927, "The Kentucky Colonel," as the newsmen dubbed Combs, was clearly the best overall center fielder in the American League.

He was consistent and durable. His worst year as a regular was .298, his best as a regular was .356. That was in 1927 when he made 231 hits, far and away the best in the American League until that time, and a Yankee team record until 1986 when Don Mattingly had 238.

In the three World Series in which he appeared, Combs scored 17 runs in 16 games and batted .350.

He was a gentleman, who refrained from smoking or strong drink. He was a vocal man on the bench, but he would not cuss. He never stayed out late, but he was certainly not averse to eating dinner with his teammates and spinning a yarn or two. As the evening grew late, however, Combs would rise from the table, excuse himself, and return to his room.

The consistency ended in 1934, when his career was cut short. He fractured his skull running into a wall in the outfield, and retired the next year.

But he remained in baseball for several more years, working as a coach for the Yankees from 1936 to 1944, and following that with stints with the St. Louis Browns, the Red Sox and the Phillies. He died in 1976 in Kentucky. In 1970, he was elected to the Hall of Fame.

Combs remains in the top echelon of all-time Yankees, offensively. He is second all-time in triples with 154, and his 23 in 1927 is still the team record. He is tenth in doubles with 309, seventh in hits with 1,866, fifth in runs with 1,186 and third in batting average with his .325.

Cook, Luther Almus (Doc)

HEIGHT: 6'0"   THROWS: RIGHT   BATS: LEFT   BORN: 6/24/1886 WITT, TEXAS   DIED: 6/30/1973 LAWRENCEBURG, TENNESSEE   POSITIONS PLAYED: OF

YEAR	TEAM	GAMES	AB	RUNS	HITS	2B	3B	HR	RBI	BB	IBB	SO	HBP	SH	SF	SB	CS	BA	OBA	SA	FA
1913	NY-A	20	72	9	19	2	1	0	1	10	—	4	2	3	—	1	—	.264	.369	.319	.939
1914	NY-A	131	470	59	133	11	3	1	40	44	—	60	9	11	—	26	32	.283	.356	.326	.949
1915	NY-A	132	476	70	129	16	5	2	33	62	—	43	8	8	—	29	18	.271	.364	.338	.959
1916	NY-A	4	10	0	1	0	0	0	1	0	—	2	0	0	—	0	—	.100	.100	.100	1.000
Career average		72	257	35	71	7	2	1	19	29	—	27	5	6	—	14	13	.274	.359	.329	.953
Yankee average		**72**	**257**	**35**	**71**	**7**	**2**	**1**	**19**	**29**	**—**	**27**	**5**	**6**	**—**	**14**	**13**	**.274**	**.359**	**.329**	**.953**
Career total		287	1028	138	282	29	9	3	75	116	—	109	19	22	—	56	50	.274	.359	.329	.953
Yankee total		**287**	**1028**	**138**	**282**	**29**	**9**	**3**	**75**	**116**	**—**	**109**	**19**	**22**	**—**	**56**	**50**	**.274**	**.359**	**.329**	**.953**

Cooke, Allen Lindsey (Dusty)

HEIGHT: 6'1"   THROWS: RIGHT   BATS: LEFT   BORN: 6/23/1907 SWEPSONVILLE, N.C.   DIED: 11/21/1987 RALEIGH, N.C.   POSITIONS PLAYED: OF

YEAR	TEAM	GAMES	AB	RUNS	HITS	2B	3B	HR	RBI	BB	IBB	SO	HBP	SH	SF	SB	CS	BA	OBA	SA	FA
1930	NY-A	92	216	43	55	12	3	6	29	32	—	61	1	2	—	4	6	.255	.353	.421	.978
1931	NY-A	27	39	10	13	1	0	1	6	8	—	11	0	0	—	4	1	.333	.447	.436	1.000
1932	NY-A	3	0	1	0	0	0	0	0	1	—	0	0	0	—	0	0	.000	1.000	.000	.000
1933	Bos-A	119	454	86	133	35	10	5	54	67	—	71	2	8	—	7	5	.293	.386	.447	.956
1934	Bos-A	74	168	34	41	8	5	1	26	36	—	25	0	0	—	7	2	.244	.377	.369	.976
1935	Bos-A	100	294	51	90	18	6	3	34	46	—	24	0	6	—	6	8	.306	.400	.439	.972
1936	Bos-A	111	341	58	93	20	3	6	47	72	—	48	1	0	—	4	3	.273	.401	.402	.972
1938	Cin-N	82	233	41	64	15	1	2	33	28	—	36	1	2	—	0	0	.275	.355	.373	.963
Career average		76	218	41	61	14	4	3	29	36	—	35	1	2	—	4	3	.280	.384	.416	.852
Yankee average		41	85	18	23	4	1	2	12	14	—	24	0	1	—	3	2	.267	.370	.424	.659
Career total		608	1745	324	489	109	28	24	229	290	—	276	5	18	—	32	25	.280	.384	.416	.852
Yankee total		122	255	54	68	13	3	7	35	41	—	72	1	2	—	8	7	.267	.370	.424	.659

Cooney, John Walter

HEIGHT: 5'10"   THROWS: LEFT   BATS: RIGHT   BORN: 3/18/1901 CRANSTON, RHODE ISLAND   DIED: 7/8/1986 SARASOTA, FLORIDA   POSITIONS PLAYED: P, 1B, OF

YEAR	TEAM	GAMES	AB	RUNS	HITS	2B	3B	HR	RBI	BB	IBB	SO	HBP	SH	SF	SB	CS	BA	OBA	SA	FA
1921	Bos-N	8	5	0	1	0	0	0	0	0	—	1	0	0	—	0	—	.200	.200	.200	1.000
1922	Bos-N	4	8	0	0	0	0	0	0	0	—	1	0	0	—	0	—	.000	.000	.000	1.000
1923	Bos-N	42	66	7	25	1	0	0	3	4	—	2	0	3	—	0	1	.379	.414	.394	1.000
1924	Bos-N	55	130	10	33	2	1	0	4	9	—	5	0	5	—	0	4	.254	.302	.285	1.000
1925	Bos-N	54	103	17	33	7	0	0	13	3	—	6	1	5	—	1		.320	.346	.388	.000
1926	Bos-N	64	126	17	38	3	2	0	18	13	—	7	0	8	—	6		.302	.367	.357	.996
1927	Bos-N	10	1	3	0	0	0	0	0	0	—	0	0	0	—	0		.000	.000	.000	1.000
1928	Bos-N	33	41	2	7	0	0	0	2	4	—	3	0	1	—	0		.171	.244	.171	1.000
1929	Bos-N	41	72	10	23	4	1	0	6	3	—	3	1	0	—	1		.319	.355	.403	.952
1930	Bos-N	4	3	0	0	0	0	0	0	0	—	0	0	0	—	0		.000	.000	.000	1.000
1935	Bro-N	10	29	3	9	0	1	0	1	3	—	2	0	0	—	0		.310	.375	.379	1.000
1936	Bro-N	130	507	71	143	17	5	0	30	24	—	15	0	10	—	3		.282	.315	.335	.994
1937	Bro-N	120	430	61	126	18	5	0	37	22	—	10	0	6	—	5		.293	.327	.358	1.000
1938	Bos-N	120	432	45	117	25	5	0	17	22	—	12	1	11	—	2		.271	.308	.352	1.000
1939	Bos-N	118	368	39	101	8	1	2	27	21	—	8	2	11	—	2		.274	.317	.318	1.000
1940	Bos-N	108	365	40	116	14	3	0	21	25	—	9	1	13	—	4		.318	.363	.373	1.000
1941	Bos-N	123	442	52	141	25	2	0	29	27	—	15	0	9	—	3		.319	.358	.385	.996
1942	Bos-N	74	198	23	41	6	0	0	7	23	—	5	0	5	—	2	0	.207	.290	.237	.984
1943	Bro-N	37	34	7	7	0	0	0	2	4	—	3	0	1	—	1	0	.206	.289	.206	1.000
1944	Bro-N	7	4	0	3	0	0	0	1	0	—	0	0	1	—	0	0	.750	.750	.750	1.000
1944	NY-A	10	8	1	1	0	0	0	1	1	—	0	0	0	—	0	—	.125	.233	.125	1.000
Career average		56	161	19	46	6	1	0	10	10	—	5	0	4	0	1	0	.286	.329	.342	.996
Yankee average		10	8	1	1	0	0	0	1	1	—	0	0	0	0	0	0	.125	.233	.125	.000
Career total		1172	3372	408	965	130	26	2	219	208	—	107	6	89	—	30	5	.286	.329	.342	.996
Yankee total		10	8	1	1	0	0	0	1	1	—	0	0	0	—	0	0	.125	.233	.125	.000

Cooney, Philip Clarence Cohen BORN PHILIP CLARENCE COHEN

HEIGHT:5'8"   THROWS: RIGHT   BATS: LEFT   BORN: 9/14/1882 NEW YORK, NEW YORK   DIED: 10/6/1957 NEW YORK, NEW YORK   POSITIONS PLAYED: 3B

YEAR	TEAM	GAMES	AB	RUNS	HITS	2B	3B	HR	RBI	BB	IBB	SO	HBP	SH	SF	SB	CS	BA	OBA	SA	FA
1905	NY-A	1	3	0	0	0	0	0	0	0	0	0	0	0	0	0	0	.000	.000	.000	1.000
Career average		1	3	0	0	0	0	0	0	0	0	0	0	0	0	0	0	.000	.000	.000	1.000
Yankee average		1	3	0	0	0	0	0	0	0	0	0	0	0	0	0	0	.000	.000	.000	1.000
Career total		1	3	0	0	0	0	0	0	0	0	0	0	0	0	0	0	.000	.000	.000	1.000
Yankee total		1	3	0	0	0	0	0	0	0	0	0	0	0	0	0	0	.000	.000	.000	1.000

Costello, Daniel Francis (Dashing Dan)

HEIGHT: 6'1" THROWS: RIGHT BATS: LEFT BORN: 9/9/1891 JESSUP, PENNSYLVANIA DIED: 3/26/1936 PITTSBURGH, PENNSYLVANIA POSITIONS PLAYED: OF

YEAR	TEAM	GAMES	AB	RUNS	HITS	2B	3B	HR	RBI	BB	IBB	SO	HBP	SH	SF	SB	CS	BA	OBA	SA	FA
1913	**NY-A**	**2**	**2**	**1**	**1**	**0**	**0**	**0**	**0**	**0**	**—**	**0**	**0**	**0**	**0**	**0**	**—**	**.500**	**.500**	**.500**	**.000**
1914	Pit-N	21	64	7	19	1	0	0	5	8	—	16	0	1	0	2	1	.297	.375	.313	.970
1915	Pit-N	71	125	16	27	4	1	0	11	7	—	23	0	1	0	7	1	.216	.258	.264	.893
1916	Pit-N	60	159	11	38	1	3	0	8	6	—	23	0	4	0	3	—	.239	.267	.283	.976
Career average		39	88	9	21	2	1	0	6	5	—	16	0	2	0	3	1	.243	.286	.283	.710
Yankee average		**2**	**2**	**1**	**1**	**0**	**0**	**0**	**0**	**0**	**—**	**0**	**0**	**0**	**0**	**0**	**0**	**.500**	**.500**	**.500**	**.000**
Career total		154	350	35	85	6	4	0	24	21	—	62	0	6	0	12	2	.243	.286	.283	.710
Yankee total		**2**	**2**	**1**	**1**	**0**	**0**	**0**	**0**	**0**	**—**	**0**	**0**	**0**	**0**	**0**	**0**	**.500**	**.500**	**.500**	**.000**

Cotto, Henry

HEIGHT: 6'2" THROWS: RIGHT BATS: RIGHT BORN: 1/5/1961 NEW YORK, NEW YORK POSITIONS PLAYED: OF

YEAR	TEAM	GAMES	AB	RUNS	HITS	2B	3B	HR	RBI	BB	IBB	SO	HBP	SH	SF	SB	CS	BA	OBA	SA	FA
1984	Chi-N	105	146	24	40	5	0	0	8	10	2	23	1	3	0	9	3	.274	.325	.308	.984
1985	**NY-A**	**34**	**56**	**4**	**17**	**1**	**0**	**1**	**6**	**3**	**0**	**12**	**0**	**1**	**0**	**1**	**1**	**.304**	**.339**	**.375**	**.977**
1986	**NY-A**	**35**	**80**	**11**	**17**	**3**	**0**	**1**	**6**	**2**	**0**	**17**	**0**	**0**	**1**	**3**	**0**	**.213**	**.229**	**.288**	**1.000**
1987	**NY-A**	**68**	**149**	**21**	**35**	**10**	**0**	**5**	**20**	**6**	**0**	**35**	**1**	**0**	**0**	**4**	**2**	**.235**	**.269**	**.403**	**.989**
1988	Sea-A	133	386	50	100	18	1	8	33	23	0	53	2	4	3	27	3	.259	.302	.373	.992
1989	Sea-A	100	295	44	78	11	2	9	33	12	3	44	3	0	0	10	4	.264	.300	.407	.988
1990	Sea-A	127	355	40	92	14	3	4	33	22	2	52	4	6	3	21	3	.259	.307	.349	.990
1991	Sea-A	66	177	35	54	6	2	6	23	10	0	27	2	2	1	16	3	.305	.347	.463	.981
1992	Sea-A	108	294	42	76	11	1	5	27	14	3	49	1	3	1	23	2	.259	.294	.354	1.000
1993	Sea-A	54	105	10	20	1	0	2	7	2	0	22	1	1	0	5	4	.190	.213	.257	.983
1993	Fla-N	54	135	15	40	7	0	3	14	3	0	18	1	1	2	11	1	.296	.312	.415	.977
Career average		80	198	27	52	8	1	4	19	10	1	32	1	2	1	12	2	.261	.299	.370	.988
Yankee average		**46**	**95**	**12**	**23**	**5**	**0**	**2**	**11**	**4**	**0**	**21**	**0**	**0**	**0**	**3**	**1**	**.242**	**.272**	**.365**	**.989**
Career total		884	2178	296	569	87	9	44	210	107	10	352	16	21	11	130	26	.261	.299	.370	.989
Yankee total		**137**	**285**	**36**	**69**	**14**	**0**	**7**	**32**	**11**	**0**	**64**	**1**	**1**	**1**	**8**	**3**	**.242**	**.272**	**.365**	**.989**

Courtney, Clinton Dawson (Scrap Iron *or* The Toy Bulldog)

HEIGHT: 5'8" THROWS: RIGHT BATS: LEFT BORN: 3/16/1927 HALL SUMMIT, LOUISIANA DIED: 6/16/1975 ROCHESTER, NEW YORK POSITIONS PLAYED: OF

YEAR	TEAM	GAMES	AB	RUNS	HITS	2B	3B	HR	RBI	BB	IBB	SO	HBP	SH	SF	SB	CS	BA	OBA	SA	FA
1951	**NY-A**	**1**	**2**	**0**	**0**	**0**	**0**	**0**	**0**	**0**	**—**	**1**	**0**	**0**	**0**	**0**	**0**	**.000**	**.000**	**.000**	**.800**
1952	StL-A	119	413	38	118	24	3	5	50	39	—	26	1	5	0	0	2	.286	.349	.395	.996
1953	StL-A	106	355	28	89	12	2	4	19	25	—	20	1	3	0	0	1	.251	.302	.330	.980
1954	Bal-A	122	397	25	107	18	3	4	37	30	—	7	3	4	3	2	1	.270	.323	.360	.990
1955	Chi-A	19	37	7	14	3	0	1	10	7	2	0	0	0	1	0	0	.378	.467	.541	1.000
1955	Was-A	75	238	26	71	8	4	2	30	19	4	9	1	3	3	0	0	.298	.349	.391	.983
1956	Was-A	101	283	31	85	20	3	5	44	20	4	10	9	1	3	0	5	.300	.362	.445	.979
1957	Was-A	91	232	23	62	14	1	6	27	16	5	11	12	0	0	0	5	.267	.346	.414	.994
1958	Was-A	134	450	46	113	18	0	8	62	48	3	23	9	3	5	1	5	.251	.332	.344	.991
1959	Was-A	72	189	19	44	4	1	2	18	20	1	19	1	2	1	0	1	.233	.308	.296	.987
1960	Bal-A	83	154	14	35	3	0	1	12	30	3	14	8	1	3	0	1	.227	.374	.266	.975
1961	KC-A	1	1	0	0	0	0	0	0	0	0	0	0	0	0	0	0	.000	.000	.000	.000
1961	Bal-A	22	45	3	12	2	0	0	4	10	0	3	0	0	0	0	0	.267	.400	.311	1.000
Career average		73	215	20	58	10	1	3	24	20	2	11	3	2	1	0	1	.268	.339	.366	.987
Yankee average		**1**	**2**	**0**	**0**	**0**	**0**	**0**	**0**	**0**	**—**	**1**	**0**	**0**	**0**	**0**	**0**	**.000**	**.000**	**.000**	**.800**
Career total		946	2796	260	750	126	17	38	313	264	22	143	45	22	19	3	16	.268	.339	.366	.987
Yankee total		**1**	**2**	**0**	**0**	**0**	**0**	**0**	**0**	**0**	**0**	**1**	**0**	**0**	**0**	**0**	**0**	**.000**	**.000**	**.000**	**.800**

Courtney, Edward Ernest
HEIGHT: 5'10" THROWS: RIGHT BATS: LEFT BORN: 01/20/1875 DES MOINES, IOWA   DIED: 2/29/1920 BUFFALO, NEW YORK   POSITIONS PLAYED: 1B, 2B, 3B, SS, OF

YEAR	TEAM	GAMES	AB	RUNS	HITS	2B	3B	HR	RBI	BB	IBB	SO	HBP	SH	SF	SB	CS	BA	OBA	SA	FA
1902	Bos-N	48	165	23	36	3	0	0	17	13	—	—	4	1	—	3	—	.218	.291	.236	.974
1902	Bal-A	1	4	3	2	0	1	0	1	1	—	—	0	0	—	0	—	.500	.600	1.000	1.000
1903	**NY-A**	**25**	**79**	**7**	**21**	**3**	**3**	**1**	**8**	**7**	**—**	**—**	**2**	**3**	**—**	**1**	**—**	**.266**	**.341**	**.418**	**.916**
1903	Det-A	23	74	7	17	0	0	0	6	5	—	—	3	1	—	1	—	.230	.305	.230	.938
1905	Phi-N	155	601	77	165	14	7	2	77	47	—	—	7	26	—	17	—	.275	.334	.331	.923
1906	Phi-N	116	398	53	94	12	2	0	42	45	—	—	1	5	—	6	—	.236	.315	.276	.923
1907	Phi-N	130	440	42	107	17	4	2	43	55	—	—	6	7	—	6	—	.243	.335	.314	.978
1908	Phi-N	60	160	14	29	3	0	0	6	15	—	—	2	5	—	1	—	.181	.260	.200	1.000
Career average		70	240	28	59	7	2	1	25	24	—	—	3	6	—	4	—	.245	.321	.298	.961
Yankee average		**25**	**79**	**7**	**21**	**3**	**3**	**1**	**8**	**7**	**—**	**—**	**2**	**3**	**—**	**1**	**—**	**.266**	**.341**	**.418**	**.916**
Career total		558	1921	226	471	52	17	5	200	188	—	—	25	48	—	35	—	.245	.321	.298	.961
Yankee total		**25**	**79**	**7**	**21**	**3**	**3**	**1**	**8**	**7**	**—**	**—**	**2**	**3**	**—**	**1**	**—**	**.266**	**.341**	**.418**	**.916**

Cowan, Billy Rolland
HEIGHT: 6'0" THROWS: RIGHT B: RIGHT   BORN: 8/28/1938 CALHOUN CITY, MISSISSIPPI   POSITIONS PLAYED: 1B, 2B, 3B, SS, OF

YEAR	TEAM	GAMES	AB	RUNS	HITS	2B	3B	HR	RBI	BB	IBB	SO	HBP	SH	SF	SB	CS	BA	OBA	SA	FA
1963	Chi-N	14	36	1	9	1	1	1	2	0	0	11	0	0	0	0	1	.250	.250	.417	.917
1964	Chi-N	139	497	52	120	16	4	19	50	18	5	128	1	2	2	12	3	.241	.268	.404	.968
1965	NY-N	82	156	16	28	8	2	3	9	4	1	45	1	1	0	3	2	.179	.205	.314	1.000
1965	Mil-N	19	27	4	5	1	0	0	0	0	0	9	0	0	0	0	0	.185	.185	.222	1.000
1967	Phi-N	34	59	11	9	0	0	3	6	4	0	14	0	2	1	1	0	.153	.203	.305	1.000
1969	**NY-A**	**32**	**48**	**5**	**8**	**0**	**0**	**1**	**3**	**3**	**0**	**9**	**0**	**0**	**0**	**0**	**0**	**.167**	**.216**	**.229**	**1.000**
1969	Cal-A	28	56	10	17	1	0	4	10	3	1	9	1	0	0	0	0	.304	.350	.536	1.000
1970	Cal-A	68	134	20	37	9	1	5	25	11	2	29	1	0	0	0	1	.276	.336	.470	1.000
1971	Cal-A	74	174	12	48	9	0	4	20	7	1	41	0	1	0	1	1	.276	.304	.391	1.000
1972	Cal-A	3	3	0	0	0	0	0	0	0	0	2	0	0	0	0	0	.000	.000	.000	.000
Career average		49	119	13	28	4	1	4	13	5	1	30	0	1	0	2	1	.236	.269	.387	.977
Yankee average		**32**	**48**	**5**	**8**	**0**	**0**	**1**	**3**	**3**	**0**	**9**	**0**	**0**	**0**	**0**	**0**	**.167**	**.216**	**.229**	**1.000**
Career total		493	1190	131	281	44	8	40	125	50	10	297	4	6	3	17	8	.236	.269	.387	.977
Yankee total		**32**	**48**	**5**	**8**	**0**	**0**	**1**	**3**	**3**	**0**	**9**	**0**	**0**	**0**	**0**	**0**	**.167**	**.216**	**.229**	**1.000**

Cox, Robert Joe
HEIGHT: 5'11" THROWS: RIGHT BATS: RIGHT   BORN: 5/21/1941 TULSA, OKLAHOMA   POSITIONS PLAYED: 3B

YEAR	TEAM	GAMES	AB	RUNS	HITS	2B	3B	HR	RBI	BB	IBB	SO	HBP	SH	SF	SB	CS	BA	OBA	SA	FA
1968	**NY-A**	**135**	**437**	**33**	**100**	**15**	**1**	**7**	**41**	**41**	**7**	**85**	**5**	**3**	**4**	**3**	**2**	**.229**	**.300**	**.316**	**.957**
1969	**NY-A**	**85**	**191**	**17**	**41**	**7**	**1**	**2**	**17**	**34**	**7**	**41**	**1**	**0**	**3**	**0**	**1**	**.215**	**.332**	**.293**	**.935**
Career average		110	314	25	71	11	1	5	29	38	7	63	3	2	4	2	2	.225	.310	.309	.946
Yankee average		**110**	**314**	**25**	**71**	**11**	**1**	**5**	**29**	**38**	**7**	**63**	**3**	**2**	**4**	**2**	**2**	**.225**	**.310**	**.309**	**.946**
Career total		220	628	50	141	22	2	9	58	75	14	126	6	3	7	3	3	.225	.310	.309	.946
Yankee total		**220**	**628**	**50**	**141**	**22**	**2**	**9**	**58**	**75**	**14**	**126**	**6**	**3**	**7**	**3**	**3**	**.225**	**.310**	**.309**	**.946**

Cree, William Franklin (Birdie)
HEIGHT: 5'6" THROWS: RIGHT BATS: RIGHT   BORN: 10/23/1882 KHEDIVE, PENN.   DIED: 11/8/1942 SUNBURY, PENN.   POSITIONS PLAYED: 2B, 3B, SS, OF

YEAR	TEAM	GAMES	AB	RUNS	HITS	2B	3B	HR	RBI	BB	IBB	SO	HBP	SH	SF	SB	CS	BA	OBA	SA	FA
1908	**NY-A**	**21**	**78**	**5**	**21**	**0**	**2**	**0**	**4**	**7**	**—**	**—**	**2**	**1**	**0**	**1**	**—**	**.269**	**.345**	**.321**	**1.000**
1909	**NY-A**	**104**	**343**	**48**	**90**	**6**	**3**	**2**	**27**	**30**	**—**	**—**	**9**	**13**	**0**	**10**	**—**	**.262**	**.338**	**.315**	**.933**
1910	**NY-A**	**134**	**467**	**58**	**134**	**19**	**16**	**4**	**73**	**40**	**—**	**—**	**8**	**12**	**0**	**28**	**—**	**.287**	**.353**	**.422**	**.955**
1911	**NY-A**	**137**	**520**	**90**	**181**	**30**	**22**	**4**	**88**	**56**	**—**	**—**	**3**	**9**	**0**	**48**	**—**	**.348**	**.415**	**.513**	**.964**
1912	**NY-A**	**50**	**190**	**25**	**63**	**11**	**6**	**0**	**22**	**20**	**—**	**—**	**5**	**1**	**0**	**12**	**—**	**.332**	**.409**	**.453**	**.948**
1913	**NY-A**	**145**	**534**	**51**	**145**	**25**	**6**	**1**	**63**	**50**	**—**	**51**	**4**	**18**	**0**	**22**	**0**	**.272**	**.338**	**.346**	**.988**
1914	**NY-A**	**77**	**275**	**45**	**85**	**18**	**5**	**0**	**40**	**30**	**—**	**24**	**6**	**9**	**0**	**4**	**9**	**.309**	**.389**	**.411**	**.976**
1915	**NY-A**	**74**	**196**	**23**	**42**	**8**	**2**	**0**	**15**	**36**	**—**	**22**	**6**	**5**	**0**	**7**	**8**	**.214**	**.353**	**.276**	**.945**
Career average		93	325	43	95	15	8	1	42	34	—	12	5	9	0	17	2	.292	.368	.398	.965
Yankee average		**93**	**325**	**43**	**95**	**15**	**8**	**1**	**42**	**34**	**—**	**12**	**5**	**9**	**0**	**17**	**2**	**.292**	**.368**	**.398**	**.965**
Career total		742	2603	345	761	117	62	11	332	269	—	97	43	68	0	132	17	.292	.368	.398	.965
Yankee total		**742**	**2603**	**345**	**761**	**117**	**62**	**11**	**332**	**269**	**—**	**97**	**43**	**68**	**0**	**132**	**17**	**.292**	**.368**	**.398**	**.965**

Criger, Louis

HEIGHT: 5'10"   THROWS: RIGHT   BATS: RIGHT   BORN: 2/3/1872 ELKHART, INDIANA   DIED: 5/14/1934 TUCSON, ARIZONA   POSITIONS PLAYED: C, 1B, 3B, OF

YEAR	TEAM	GAMES	AB	RUNS	HITS	2B	3B	HR	RBI	BB	IBB	SO	HBP	SH	SF	SB	CS	BA	OBA	SA	FA
1896	Cle-N	2	5	0	0	0	0	0	0	1	—	—	0	0	—	1	—	.000	.167	.000	1.000
1897	Cle-N	39	138	15	31	4	1	0	22	23	—	—	1	3	—	5	—	.225	.340	.340	.937
1898	Cle-N	84	287	43	80	13	4	1	32	40	—	—	5	6	—	2	—	.279	.377	.362	.957
1899	Stl-N	77	258	39	66	4	5	2	44	28	—	—	2	6	—	14	—	.256	.333	.333	.949
1900	Stl-N	80	288	31	78	8	6	2	38	4	—	—	2	0	—	5	—	.271	.286	.361	.953
1901	Bos-A	76	268	26	62	6	3	0	24	11	—	—	3	6	—	7	—	.231	.270	.276	.967
1902	Bos-A	83	266	32	68	16	6	0	28	27	—	—	0	5	—	7	—	.256	.324	.361	.965
1903	Bos-A	96	317	41	61	7	10	3	31	26	—	—	1	14	—	5	—	.192	.256	.306	.979
1904	Bos-A	98	299	34	63	10	5	2	34	27	—	—	3	8	—	1	—	.211	.283	.298	.981
1905	Bos-A	109	313	33	62	6	7	1	36	54	—	—	3	7	—	5	—	.198	.322	.272	.972
1906	Bos-A	7	17	0	3	1	0	0	1	1	—	—	0	1	—	1	—	.176	.222	.235	.981
1907	Bos-A	75	226	12	41	4	0	0	14	19	—	—	2	10	—	2	—	.181	.251	.199	.978
1908	Bos-A	84	237	12	45	4	2	0	25	13	—	—	0	7	—	1	—	.190	.232	.224	.980
1909	StL-A	74	212	15	36	1	1	0	9	25	—	—	1	12	—	2	—	.170	.261	.184	.986
1910	**NY-A**	**27**	**69**	**3**	**13**	**2**	**0**	**0**	**4**	**10**	**—**	**—**	**0**	**0**	**—**	**0**	**—**	**.188**	**.291**	**.217**	**.993**
1912	StL-A	1	2	1	0	0	0	0	0	0	—	—	0	0	—	0	—	.000	.000	.000	1.000
Career average		63	200	21	44	5	3	1	21	19	—	—	1	5	0	4	0	.221	.295	.290	.971
Yankee average		**27**	**69**	**3**	**13**	**2**	**0**	**0**	**4**	**10**	**—**	**—**	**0**	**0**	**0**	**0**	**0**	**.188**	**.291**	**.217**	**.993**
Career total		1012	3202	337	709	86	50	11	342	309	—	—	23	85	0	58	0	.221	.295	.290	.971
Yankee total		**27**	**69**	**3**	**13**	**2**	**0**	**0**	**4**	**10**	**—**	**—**	**0**	**0**	**0**	**0**	**0**	**.188**	**.291**	**.217**	**.993**

Crompton, Herbert Bryan (Workhorse)

HEIGHT: 6'0"   THROWS: RIGHT   BATS: RIGHT   BORN: 11/7/1911 TAYLOR RIDGE, ILLINOIS   DIED: 8/5/1963 MOLINE, ILLINOIS

YEAR	TEAM	GAMES	AB	RUNS	HITS	2B	3B	HR	RBI	BB	IBB	SO	HBP	SH	SF	SB	CS	BA	OBA	SA	FA
1937	Was-A	2	3	0	1	0	0	0	0	0	—	0	0	0	—	0	0	.333	.333	.333	1.000
1945	**NY-A**	**36**	**99**	**6**	**19**	**3**	**0**	**0**	**12**	**2**	**—**	**7**	**0**	**3**	**—**	**0**	**0**	**.192**	**.208**	**.222**	**.984**
Career average		19	51	3	10	2	0	0	6	1	—	4	0	2	—	0	0	.196	.212	.225	.984
Yankee average		**36**	**99**	**6**	**19**	**3**	**0**	**0**	**12**	**2**	**—**	**7**	**0**	**3**	**—**	**0**	**0**	**.192**	**.208**	**.222**	**.992**
Career total		38	102	6	20	3	0	0	12	2	—	7	0	3	—	0	0	.196	.212	.225	.984
Yankee total		**36**	**99**	**6**	**19**	**3**	**0**	**0**	**12**	**2**	**—**	**7**	**0**	**3**	**—**	**0**	**0**	**.192**	**.208**	**.222**	**.992**

Crosetti, Frank Peter Joseph (Frankie)

HEIGHT: 5'10"   THROWS: RIGHT   BATS: RIGHT   BORN: 10/4/1910 SAN FRANCISCO, CALIFORNIA   POSITIONS PLAYED: 2B, 3B, SS

YEAR	TEAM	GAMES	AB	RUNS	HITS	2B	3B	HR	RBI	BB	IBB	SO	HBP	SH	SF	SB	CS	BA	OBA	SA	FA
1932	NY-A	116	398	47	96	20	9	5	57	51	—	51	5	7	—	3	2	.241	.335	.374	1.000
1933	NY-A	136	451	71	114	20	5	9	60	55	—	40	2	5	—	4	1	.253	.337	.379	.936
1934	NY-A	138	554	85	147	22	10	11	67	61	—	58	5	12	—	5	6	.265	.344	.401	.930
1935	NY-A	87	305	49	78	17	6	8	50	41	—	27	4	1	—	3	1	.256	.351	.430	.963
1936	NY-A	151	632	137	182	35	7	15	78	90	—	83	12	6	—	18	5	.288	.387	.437	.948
1937	NY-A	149	611	127	143	29	5	11	49	86	—	105	12	12	—	13	7	.234	.340	.352	.948
1938	NY-A	157	631	113	166	35	3	9	55	106	—	97	15	5	—	27	12	.263	.382	.371	.948
1939	NY-A	152	656	109	153	25	5	10	56	65	—	81	13	9	—	11	7	.233	.315	.332	.968
1940	NY-A	145	546	84	106	23	4	4	31	72	—	77	10	5	—	14	8	.194	.299	.273	.954
1941	NY-A	50	148	13	33	2	2	1	22	18	—	14	3	0	—	0	2	.223	.320	.284	.950
1942	NY-A	74	285	50	69	5	5	4	23	31	—	31	9	3	—	1	1	.242	.335	.337	1.000
1943	NY-A	95	348	36	81	8	1	2	20	36	—	47	7	4	—	4	4	.233	.317	.279	.946
1944	NY-A	55	197	20	47	4	2	5	30	11	—	21	6	6	—	3	0	.239	.299	.355	.960
1945	NY-A	130	441	57	105	12	0	4	48	59	—	65	10	14	—	7	1	.238	.341	.293	.946
1946	NY-A	28	59	4	17	3	0	0	3	8	—	2	1	1	—	0	3	.288	.382	.339	.940
1947	NY-A	3	1	0	0	0	0	0	0	0	—	0	0	0	—	0	0	.000	.000	.000	.000
1948	NY-A	17	14	4	4	0	1	0	0	2	—	0	0	0	—	0	0	.286	.375	.429	1.000
Career average		99	369	59	91	15	4	6	38	47	—	47	7	5	—	7	4	.245	.341	.354	.949
Yankee average		**99**	**369**	**59**	**91**	**15**	**4**	**6**	**38**	**47**	**—**	**47**	**7**	**5**	**—**	**7**	**4**	**.245**	**.341**	**.354**	**.949**
Career total		1683	6277	1006	1541	260	65	98	649	792	—	799	114	90	—	113	62	.245	.341	.354	.949
Yankee total		**1683**	**6277**	**1006**	**1541**	**260**	**65**	**98**	**649**	**792**	**—**	**799**	**114**	**90**	**—**	**113**	**62**	**.245**	**.341**	**.354**	**.949**

Frank Peter Joseph "Frankie" Crosetti, 2b-3b-ss, 1932–48

Consistency and durability were Crosetti's calling cards in his 17-year stint with the Yankees.

Crosetti was born on October 4, 1910 in San Francisco, California. Like Tony Lazzeri, he was a star on the baseball-mad West Coast in the late 1920s. The Yankees brought him up in 1932, and he contributed immediately.

New York had finished behind the Philadelphia Athletics for three consecutive years. But with a revitalized Babe Ruth, the ever-steady Lou Gehrig, and star players like Lazzeri, Bill Dickey and Ben Chapman providing the offense, New York finished ahead of the A's by 13 games. Their 107-47 record was only three games off their 110-44 mark of 1927.

Crosetti played in 115 games that year, including 83 at shortstop and 33 at third base, hitting .241.

He was not initially a great fielder, but he was an aggressive and hard-working one. He would lead the league in assists and errors on more than one occasion. Crosetti was not as talented as some of his teammates, but he worked at maximizing his contributions to the team.

He was, for example, a master at stealing signs from the opposing team. He was also well-known in the American League as an expert at the hidden ball trick.

In 1936 and 1939, Crosetti was a member of the American League All-Star team. He led the team in stolen bases three years in a row, from 1936–39. His 27 stolen bases in 1939 led the league.

But Crosetti always considered himself a team man who disdained personal statistics in favor of the bottom line, winning. His teams won nine pennants in his 17 years, and Crosetti appeared in seven World Series. He never hit better than .278 in the Fall Classic, but his teams won 25 World Series games and lost only eight.

His best World Series was in 1943. He hit .278 and had an RBI single to snap a 2-2 tie in Game 1 of the Series against the Cardinals, which the Yankees won, 4-2.

Following his retirement, Crosetti worked as a coach for the Yankees from 1947–68. Coaching stints in Seattle and Minnesota followed.

Crosetti is one of only nine Yankees to score 1,000 runs, his 1,006 places him ninth. He is tenth all-time in games played with New York at 1,682, and tenth in at-bats with 6,277. Crosetti is also 16th on the Yankees' all-time list with 1,541 hits, and 13th in doubles with 260.

Cruz, Jose Sr. (Cheo) BORN JOSE CRUZ (DILAN)
HEIGHT: 6'0"   THROWS: LEFT   BATS: LEFT   BORN: 8/8/1947 ARROYO, PUERTO RICO   POSITIONS PLAYED: 1B, OF

YEAR	TEAM	GAMES	AB	RUNS	HITS	2B	3B	HR	RBI	BB	IBB	SO	HBP	SH	SF	SB	CS	BA	OBA	SA	FA
1970	StL-N	6	17	2	6	1	0	0	1	4	0	0	1	0	0	0	0	.353	.500	.412	1.000
1971	StL-N	83	292	46	80	13	2	9	27	49	6	35	1	1	3	6	3	.274	.377	.425	.975
1972	StL-N	117	332	33	78	14	4	2	23	36	3	54	1	2	3	9	3	.235	.309	.319	.979
1973	StL-N	132	406	51	92	22	5	10	57	51	4	66	1	6	7	10	4	.227	.310	.379	.979
1974	StL-N	107	161	24	42	4	3	5	20	20	5	27	0	0	1	4	2	.261	.341	.416	1.000
1975	Hou-N	120	315	44	81	15	2	9	49	52	6	44	1	3	6	6	3	.257	.377	.401	.980
1976	Hou-N	133	439	49	133	21	5	4	61	53	5	46	0	2	2	28	11	.299	.368	.475	.972
1977	Hou-N	157	579	87	173	31	10	17	87	69	13	67	0	3	10	44	23	.315	.376	.460	.973
1978	Hou-N	153	565	79	178	34	9	10	83	57	9	57	0	2	3	37	9	.289	.367	.421	.959
1979	Hou-N	157	558	73	161	33	7	9	72	72	16	66	0	1	5	36	14	.302	.360	.426	.969
1980	Hou-N	160	612	79	185	29	7	11	91	60	13	66	0	0	8	36	11	.267	.319	.425	.984
1981	Hou-N	107	409	53	109	16	5	13	55	35	4	49	0	0	7	5	7	.267	.319	.425	.984
1982	Hou-N	155	570	62	157	27	2	9	68	60	12	67	1	3	6	21	11	.275	.342	.377	.964

YEAR	TEAM	GAMES	AB	RUNS	HITS	2B	3B	HR	RBI	BB	IBB	SO	HBP	SH	SF	SB	CS	BA	OBA	SA	FA
1983	Hou-N	160	594	85	189	28	8	14	92	65	10	86	1	1	3	30	16	.318	.385	.463	.979
1984	Hou-N	160	600	96	187	28	13	12	95	73	10	68	0	2	10	22	8	.312	.381	.462	.976
1985	Hou-N	141	544	69	163	34	4	9	79	43	10	74	0	0	3	16	5	.300	.349	.426	.971
1986	Hou-N	141	479	48	133	22	4	10	72	55	12	86	0	0	2	3	4	.278	.351	.403	.984
1987	Hou-N	126	365	47	88	17	4	11	38	36	3	65	0	1	3	4	1	.241	.307	.400	.984
1988	**NY-A**	**38**	**80**	**9**	**16**	**2**	**0**	**1**	**7**	**8**	**1**	**8**	**0**	**0**	**0**	**0**	**1**	**.200**	**.273**	**.263**	**.889**
Career average		124	417	55	118	21	5	9	57	47	7	54	0	1	4	17	7	.284	.354	.420	.973
Yankee average		**38**	**80**	**9**	**16**	**2**	**0**	**1**	**7**	**8**	**1**	**8**	**0**	**0**	**0**	**0**	**1**	**.200**	**.273**	**.263**	**.889**
Career total		2353	7917	1036	2251	391	94	165	1077	898	142	1031	7	27	82	317	136	.284	.354	.420	.973
Yankee total		**38**	**80**	**9**	**16**	**2**	**0**	**1**	**7**	**8**	**1**	**8**	**0**	**0**	**0**	**0**	**1**	**.200**	**.273**	**.263**	**.889**

Cruz, Luis Ivan

HEIGHT: 6'3"　THROWS: LEFT　BATS: LEFT　BORN: 5/3/1968 FAJARDO, PUERTO RICO　POSITIONS PLAYED: 1B, OF

YEAR	TEAM	GAMES	AB	RUNS	HITS	2B	3B	HR	RBI	BB	IBB	SO	HBP	SH	SF	SB	CS	BA	OBA	SA	FA
1997	**NY-A**	**11**	**20**	**0**	**5**	**1**	**0**	**0**	**3**	**2**	**0**	**4**	**0**	**0**	**0**	**0**	**0**	**.250**	**.318**	**.300**	**1.000**
1999	Pit-N	5	10	3	4	0	0	1	2	0	0	2	0	0	0	0	0	.400	.400	.700	.000
2000	Pit-N	8	11	0	1	0	0	0	0	0	0	8	0	0	0	0	0	.091	.091	.091	1.000
Career average		8	14	1	3	0	0	0	2	1	0	5	0	0	0	0	0	.244	.279	.341	.667
Yankee average		**11**	**20**	**0**	**5**	**1**	**0**	**0**	**3**	**2**	**0**	**4**	**0**	**0**	**0**	**0**	**0**	**.250**	**.318**	**.300**	**1.000**
Career total		24	41	3	10	1	0	1	5	2	0	14	0	0	0	0	0	.244	.279	.341	.667
Yankee total		**11**	**20**	**0**	**5**	**1**	**0**	**0**	**3**	**2**	**0**	**4**	**0**	**0**	**0**	**0**	**0**	**.250**	**.318**	**.300**	**1.000**

Cullenbine, Roy Joseph

HEIGHT: 6'1"　THROWS: RIGHT　BATS: BOTH　BORN: 10/18/1913 NASHVILLE, TENN.　DIED: 5/28/1991 MT. CLEMENS, MICHIGAN　POSITIONS PLAYED: 1B, 3B, OF

YEAR	TEAM	GAMES	AB	RUNS	HITS	2B	3B	HR	RBI	BB	IBB	SO	HBP	SH	SF	SB	CS	BA	OBA	SA	FA
1938	Det-A	25	67	12	19	1	3	0	9	12	—	9	0	0	—	2	0	.284	.392	.388	1.000
1939	Det-A	75	179	31	43	9	2	6	23	34	—	29	0	1	—	0	1	.240	.362	.413	1.000
1940	Bro-N	22	61	8	11	1	0	1	9	23	—	11	0	0	—	2	—	.180	.405	.246	1.000
1940	StL-A	86	257	41	59	11	2	7	31	50	—	34	2	1	—	0	1	.230	.359	.370	1.000
1941	StL-A	149	501	82	159	29	9	9	98	121	—	43	2	5	—	6	4	.317	.452	.465	.964
1942	StL-A	38	109	15	21	7	1	2	14	30	—	20	0	3	—	0	1	.193	.367	.330	.930
1942	Was-A	64	241	30	69	19	2	2	35	44	—	18	0	0	—	1	2	.286	.396	.390	.931
1942	**NY-A**	**21**	**77**	**16**	**28**	**7**	**0**	**2**	**17**	**18**	**—**	**2**	**0**	**2**	**—**	**0**	**1**	**.364**	**.484**	**.532**	**.980**
1943	Cle-A	138	488	66	141	24	4	8	56	96	—	58	1	13	—	3	4	.289	.407	.404	.986
1944	Cle-A	154	571	98	162	34	5	16	80	87	—	49	2	6	—	4	4	.284	.380	.445	.967
1945	Cle-A	8	13	3	1	1	0	0	0	11	—	0	0	0	—	0	0	.077	.500	.154	1.000
1945	Det-A	146	523	80	145	27	5	18	93	101	—	36	3	5	—	2	0	.277	.397	.451	.980
1946	Det-A	113	328	63	110	21	0	15	56	88	—	39	1	2	—	3	0	.335	.477	.537	.984
1947	Det-A	142	464	82	104	18	1	24	78	137	—	51	0	6	—	3	2	.224	.401	.422	.989
Career average		84	277	45	77	15	2	8	43	61	—	29	1	3	—	2	1	.276	.408	.432	.979
Yankee average		**21**	**77**	**16**	**28**	**7**	**0**	**2**	**17**	**18**	**—**	**2**	**0**	**2**	**—**	**0**	**1**	**.364**	**.484**	**.532**	**.980**
Career total		1181	3879	627	1072	209	32	110	599	852	—	399	11	44	—	26	20	.276	.408	.432	.979
Yankee total		**21**	**77**	**16**	**28**	**7**	**0**	**2**	**17**	**18**	**—**	**2**	**0**	**2**	**—**	**0**	**1**	**.364**	**.484**	**.532**	**.980**

Cullop, Heinrich Nicholas Kolop (Nick *or* Tomato Face)

HEIGHT: 6'0"　THROWS: RIGHT　BATS: RIGHT　BORN: 10/16/1900 ST. LOUIS, MISSOURI　DIED: 12/1/1978 WESTERVILLE, OHIO　POSITIONS PLAYED: P, 1B, OF

YEAR	TEAM	GAMES	AB	RUNS	HITS	2B	3B	HR	RBI	BB	IBB	SO	HBP	SH	SF	SB	CS	BA	OBA	SA	FA
1926	**NY-A**	**2**	**2**	**0**	**1**	**0**	**0**	**0**	**0**	**0**	**—**	**1**	**0**	**0**	**—**	**0**	**0**	**.500**	**.500**	**.500**	**.000**
1927	Was-A	15	23	2	5	2	0	0	1	1	—	6	0	0	—	0	0	.217	.250	.304	1.000
1927	Cle-A	32	68	9	16	2	3	1	8	9	—	19	1	2	—	0	4	.235	.333	.397	.982
1929	Bro-N	13	41	7	8	2	2	1	5	8	—	7	0	1	—	0	—	.195	.327	.415	1.000
1930	Cin-N	7	22	2	4	0	0	1	5	1	—	9	0	0	—	0	—	.182	.217	.318	1.000
1931	Cin-N	104	334	29	88	23	7	8	48	21	—	86	1	3	—	1	—	.263	.309	.446	.968
Career average		29	82	8	20	5	2	2	11	7	—	21	0	1	—	0	1	.249	.308	.424	.992
Yankee average		**2**	**2**	**0**	**1**	**0**	**0**	**0**	**0**	**0**	**—**	**1**	**0**	**0**	**—**	**0**	**0**	**.500**	**.500**	**.500**	**.000**
Career total		173	490	49	122	29	12	11	67	40	—	128	2	6	—	1	4	.249	.308	.424	.992
Yankee total		**2**	**2**	**0**	**1**	**0**	**0**	**0**	**0**	**0**	**—**	**1**	**0**	**0**	**—**	**0**	**0**	**.500**	**.500**	**.500**	**.000**

Curry, James E.

HEIGHT: 5'11" THROWS: RIGHT BATS: RIGHT BORN: 3/10/1893 CAMDEN, NEW JERSEY DIED: 8/2/1938 LAKELAND, NEW JERSEY POSITIONS PLAYED: 2B

YEAR	TEAM	GAMES	AB	RUNS	HITS	2B	3B	HR	RBI	BB	IBB	SO	HBP	SH	SF	SB	CS	BA	OBA	SA	FA
1909	Phi-A	1	4	1	1	0	0	0	0	0	—	—	0	0	0	0	—	.250	.250	.250	1.000
1911	**NY-A**	**4**	**11**	**3**	**2**	**0**	**0**	**0**	**0**	**1**	—	—	**0**	**1**	**0**	**0**	—	**.182**	**.250**	**.182**	**.773**
1918	Det-A	5	20	1	5	1	0	0	0	0	—	0	1	0	0	0	—	.250	.286	.300	.952
Career average		3	12	2	3	0	0	0	0	0	—	0	0	0	0	0	—	.229	.270	.257	.867
Yankee average		**4**	**11**	**3**	**2**	**0**	**0**	**0**	**0**	**1**	—	**0**	**0**	**1**	**0**	**0**	—	**.182**	**.250**	**.182**	**.773**
Career total		10	35	5	8	1	0	0	0	1	—	0	1	1	0	0	—	.229	.270	.257	.867
Yankee total		**4**	**11**	**3**	**2**	**0**	**0**	**0**	**0**	**1**	—	**0**	**0**	**1**	**0**	**0**	—	**.182**	**.250**	**.182**	**.773**

Curtis, Chad David

HEIGHT: 5'10" THROWS: RIGHT BATS: RIGHT BORN: 11/6/1968 MARION, INDIANA POSITIONS PLAYED: 2B, OF

YEAR	TEAM	GAMES	AB	RUNS	HITS	2B	3B	HR	RBI	BB	IBB	SO	HBP	SH	SF	SB	CS	BA	OBA	SA	FA
1992	Cal-A	139	441	59	114	16	2	10	46	51	2	71	6	5	4	43	18	.259	.341	.372	.978
1993	Cal-A	152	583	94	166	25	3	6	59	70	2	89	4	7	7	48	24	.285	.361	.369	1.000
1994	Cal-A	114	453	67	116	23	4	11	50	37	0	69	5	7	4	25	11	.256	.317	.397	.988
1995	Det-A	144	586	96	157	29	3	21	67	70	3	93	7	0	7	27	15	.268	.349	.435	.992
1996	Det-A	104	400	65	105	20	1	10	37	53	0	73	1	6	6	16	10	.263	.346	.393	.964
1996	LA-N	43	104	20	22	5	0	2	9	17	0	15	0	0	0	2	1	.212	.322	.317	.985
1997	Cle-A	22	29	8	6	1	0	3	5	7	0	10	0	0	0	0	0	.207	.361	.552	.980
1997	**NY-A**	**93**	**320**	**51**	**93**	**21**	**1**	**12**	**50**	**36**	**1**	**49**	**5**	**2**	**9**	**12**	**6**	**.284**	**.370**	**.481**	**.980**
1998	**NY-A**	**151**	**456**	**79**	**111**	**21**	**1**	**10**	**56**	**75**	**3**	**80**	**0**	**1**	**6**	**21**	**5**	**.243**	**.346**	**.360**	**.984**
1999	**NY-A**	**96**	**195**	**37**	**51**	**6**	**0**	**5**	**24**	**43**	**0**	**35**	**0**	**1**	**3**	**8**	**4**	**.262**	**.390**	**.369**	**.990**
2000	Tex-A	108	335	48	91	25	1	8	48	37	0	71	1	5	3	3	3	.272	.343	.424	.965
Career average		106	355	57	94	17	1	9	41	45	1	60	3	3	4	19	9	.264	.348	.397	.844
Yankee average		**113**	**324**	**56**	**85**	**16**	**1**	**9**	**43**	**51**	**1**	**55**	**2**	**1**	**6**	**14**	**5**	**.263**	**.361**	**.400**	**.000**
Career total		1166	3902	624	1032	192	16	98	451	496	11	655	29	34	49	205	97	.264	.348	.397	.844
Yankee total		**340**	**971**	**167**	**255**	**48**	**2**	**27**	**130**	**154**	**4**	**164**	**5**	**4**	**18**	**41**	**15**	**.263**	**.361**	**.400**	**.000**

Curtis, Frederick Marion

HEIGHT: 6'1" THROWS: RIGHT BATS: RIGHT BORN: 10/30/1880 BEAVER LAKE, MICHIGAN DIED: 4/5/1939 MINNEAPOLIS, MINNESOTA

YEAR	TEAM	GAMES	AB	RUNS	HITS	2B	3B	HR	RBI	BB	IBB	SO	HBP	SH	SF	SB	CS	BA	OBA	SA	FA
1905	**NY-A**	**2**	**9**	**0**	**2**	**1**	**0**	**0**	**2**	**1**	—	—	**0**	**0**	—	**1**	—	**.222**	**.300**	**.333**	**1.000**
Career average		2	9	0	2	1	0	0	2	1	—	—	0	0	—	1	—	.222	.300	.333	1.000
Yankee average		**2**	**9**	**0**	**2**	**1**	**0**	**0**	**2**	**1**	—	—	**0**	**0**	—	**1**	—	**.222**	**.300**	**.333**	**1.000**
Career total		2	9	0	2	1	0	0	2	1	—	—	0	0	—	1	—	.222	.300	.333	1.000
Yankee total		**2**	**9**	**0**	**2**	**1**	**0**	**0**	**2**	**1**	—	—	**0**	**0**	—	**1**	—	**.222**	**.300**	**.333**	**1.000**

Dahlgren, Ellsworth Tenney (Babe)

HEIGHT: 6'0" THROWS: RIGHT BATS: RIGHT BORN: 6/15/1912 SAN FRANCISCO, CALIFORNIA DIED: 9/4/1996 POSITIONS PLAYED: C, 1B, 3B, SS

YEAR	TEAM	GAMES	AB	RUNS	HITS	2B	3B	HR	RBI	BB	IBB	SO	HBP	SH	SF	SB	CS	BA	OBA	SA	FA
1935	Bos-A	149	525	77	138	27	7	9	63	56	—	67	3	12	—	6	5	.263	.337	.392	.988
1936	Bos-A	16	57	6	16	3	1	1	7	7	—	1	0	1	—	2	1	.281	.359	.421	.980
1937	**NY-A**	**1**	**1**	**0**	**0**	**0**	**0**	**0**	**0**	**0**	—	**0**	**0**	**0**	—	**0**	**0**	**.000**	**.000**	**.000**	**.000**
1938	**NY-A**	**27**	**43**	**8**	**8**	**1**	**0**	**0**	**1**	**1**	—	**7**	**0**	**0**	—	**0**	**0**	**.186**	**.205**	**.209**	**1.000**
1939	**NY-A**	**144**	**531**	**71**	**125**	**18**	**6**	**15**	**89**	**57**	—	**54**	**2**	**13**	—	**2**	**3**	**.235**	**.312**	**.377**	**.991**
1940	**NY-A**	**155**	**568**	**51**	**150**	**24**	**4**	**12**	**73**	**46**	—	**54**	**5**	**3**	—	**1**	**1**	**.264**	**.325**	**.384**	**.990**
1941	Bos-N	44	166	20	39	8	1	7	30	16	—	13	1	0	—	0	—	.235	.306	.422	.993
1941	Chi-N	99	359	50	101	20	1	16	59	43	—	39	1	0	—	2	—	.281	.360	.476	.991
1942	Chi-N	17	56	4	12	1	0	0	6	4	—	2	0	0	—	0	—	.214	.267	.232	.986
1942	Stl-A	2	2	0	0	0	0	0	0	0	—	0	0	0	—	0	—	.000	.000	.000	.990
1942	Bro-N	17	19	2	1	0	0	0	0	4	—	5	0	0	—	—	—	.053	.217	.053	1.000
1943	Phi-N	136	508	55	146	19	2	5	56	50	—	39	2	5	—	2	0	.287	.354	.362	.988
1944	Pit-N	158	599	67	173	28	7	12	101	47	—	56	6	7	—	2	—	.289	.347	.419	.987
1945	Pit-N	144	531	57	133	24	8	5	75	51	—	51	2	7	—	1	—	.250	.318	.354	.996
1946	StL-A	28	80	2	14	1	0	0	9	8	—	13	0	1	—	0	1	.175	.250	.188	.981
Career average		76	270	31	70	12	2	5	38	26	—	27	1	3	—	1	1	.261	.329	.383	.989
Yankee average		**82**	**286**	**33**	**71**	**11**	**3**	**7**	**41**	**26**	—	**29**	**2**	**4**	—	**1**	**1**	**.248**	**.314**	**.374**	**.994**
Career total		1137	4045	470	1056	174	37	82	569	390	—	401	21	49	—	18	11	.261	.329	.383	.989
Yankee total		**327**	**1143**	**130**	**283**	**43**	**10**	**27**	**163**	**104**	—	**115**	**7**	**16**	—	**3**	**4**	**.248**	**.314**	**.374**	**.994**

Daley, Thomas Francis (Pete)
HEIGHT: 5'5"   THROWS: RIGHT   BATS: LEFT   BORN: 11/13/1884 DU BOIS, PENNSYLVANIA   DIED: 12/2/1934 LOS ANGELES, CALIFORNIA   POSITIONS PLAYED: OF

YEAR	TEAM	GAMES	AB	RUNS	HITS	2B	3B	HR	RBI	BB	IBB	SO	HBP	SH	SF	SB	CS	BA	OBA	SA	FA
1908	Cin-N	14	46	5	5	0	0	0	1	3	—	0	2	0	—	1	—	.109	.180	.109	1.000
1913	Phi-A	62	141	13	36	2	1	0	11	13	—	28	2	5	—	4	—	.255	.327	.284	.963
1914	Phi-A	28	86	17	22	1	3	0	7	12	—	14	0	4	—	4	7	.256	.347	.337	1.000
1914	**NY-A**	**67**	**191**	**36**	**48**	**6**	**4**	**0**	**9**	**38**	**—**	**13**	**1**	**8**	**—**	**8**	**8**	**.251**	**.378**	**.325**	**.958**
1915	**NY-A**	**10**	**8**	**2**	**2**	**0**	**0**	**0**	**1**	**2**	**—**	**2**	**0**	**0**	**—**	**1**	**0**	**.250**	**.400**	**.250**	**1.000**
Career average		36	94	15	23	2	2	0	6	14	—	11	1	3	—	4	3	.239	.341	.292	.956
Yankee average		**39**	**100**	**19**	**25**	**3**	**2**	**0**	**5**	**20**	**—**	**8**	**1**	**4**	**—**	**5**	**4**	**.251**	**.379**	**.322**	**.979**
Career total		181	472	73	113	9	8	0	29	68	—	57	5	17	—	18	15	.239	.341	.292	.956
Yankee total		**77**	**199**	**38**	**50**	**6**	**4**	**0**	**10**	**40**	**—**	**15**	**1**	**8**	**—**	**9**	**8**	**.251**	**.379**	**.322**	**.979**

Daniels, Bernard Elmer (Bert)
HEIGHT: 5'9"   THROWS: RIGHT   BATS: RIGHT   BORN: 10/31/1882 DANVILLE, ILLINOIS   DIED: 6/6/1958 CEDAR GROVE, NEW JERSEY   POSITIONS PLAYED: 1B, 3B, OF

YEAR	TEAM	GAMES	AB	RUNS	HITS	2B	3B	HR	RBI	BB	IBB	SO	HBP	SH	SF	SB	CS	BA	OBA	SA	FA
1910	NY-A	95	356	68	90	13	8	1	17	41	—	—	16	8	—	41	—	.253	.356	.343	.917
1911	NY-A	131	462	74	132	16	9	2	31	48	—	—	18	19	—	40	—	.286	.375	.372	.941
1912	NY-A	133	496	72	136	25	11	2	41	51	—	—	18	19	—	37	—	.274	.363	.381	.945
1913	NY-A	93	320	52	69	13	5	0	22	44	—	36	18	5	—	27	—	.216	.343	.288	.966
1914	Cin-N	71	269	29	59	9	7	0	19	19	—	40	2	8	—	14	—	.219	.276	.305	.974
Career average		105	381	59	97	15	8	1	26	41	—	15	14	12	—	32	—	.255	.349	.345	.953
Yankee average		**113**	**409**	**67**	**107**	**17**	**8**	**1**	**28**	**46**	**—**	**9**	**18**	**13**	**—**	**36**	**—**	**.261**	**.361**	**.352**	**.949**
Career total		523	1903	295	486	76	40	5	130	203	—	76	72	59	—	159	—	.255	.349	.345	.953
Yankee total		**452**	**1634**	**266**	**427**	**67**	**33**	**5**	**111**	**184**	**—**	**36**	**70**	**51**	**—**	**145**	**—**	**.261**	**.361**	**.352**	**.949**

Davis, Alfonzo DeFord (Lefty)
HEIGHT: 5'10"   THROWS: LEFT   BATS: LEFT   BORN: 2/4/1875 NASHVILLE, TENNESSEE   DIED: 2/7/1919 COLLINS, NEW YORK   POSITIONS PLAYED: 2B, SS, OF

YEAR	TEAM	GAMES	AB	RUNS	HITS	2B	3B	HR	RBI	BB	IBB	SO	HBP	SH	SF	SB	CS	BA	OBA	SA	FA
1901	Bro-N	25	91	11	19	2	0	0	7	10	—	—	0	1	—	4	—	.209	.287	.231	.822
1901	Pit-N	87	335	87	105	8	11	2	33	56	—	—	2	8	—	22	—	.313	.415	.421	.943
1902	Pit-N	59	232	52	65	7	3	0	20	35	—	—	1	6	—	19	—	.280	.377	.336	.945
1903	**NY-A**	**104**	**372**	**54**	**88**	**10**	**0**	**0**	**25**	**43**	**—**	**—**	**2**	**18**	**—**	**11**	**—**	**.237**	**.319**	**.263**	**.906**
1907	Cin-N	73	266	28	61	5	5	1	25	23	—	—	1	8	—	9	—	.229	.293	.297	.972
Career average		70	259	46	68	6	4	1	22	33	—	—	1	8	—	13	—	.261	.348	.322	.921
Yankee average		**104**	**372**	**54**	**88**	**10**	**0**	**0**	**25**	**43**	**—**	**—**	**2**	**18**	**—**	**11**	**—**	**.237**	**.319**	**.263**	**.906**
Career total		348	1296	232	338	32	19	3	110	167	—	—	6	41	—	65	—	.261	.348	.322	.921
Yankee total		**104**	**372**	**54**	**88**	**10**	**0**	**0**	**25**	**43**	**—**	**—**	**2**	**18**	**—**	**11**	**—**	**.237**	**.319**	**.263**	**.906**

Davis, Charles Theodore (Chili)
HEIGHT: 6'3"   THROWS: RIGHT   BATS: BOTH   BORN: 1/17/1960 KINGSTON, JAMAICA   POSITIONS PLAYED: P, 1B, OF

YEAR	TEAM	GAMES	AB	RUNS	HITS	2B	3B	HR	RBI	BB	IBB	SO	HBP	SH	SF	SB	CS	BA	OBA	SA	FA
1981	SF-N	8	15	1	2	0	0	0	0	1	0	2	0	0	0	2	0	.133	.188	.133	1.000
1982	SF-N	154	641	86	167	27	6	19	76	45	2	115	2	7	6	24	13	.261	.308	.410	.972
1983	SF-N	137	486	54	113	21	2	11	59	55	6	108	0	3	9	10	12	.233	.305	.352	.976
1984	SF-N	137	499	87	157	21	6	21	81	42	6	74	1	2	2	12	8	.315	.368	.507	.971
1985	SF-N	136	481	53	130	25	2	13	56	62	12	74	0	1	7	15	7	.270	.349	.412	.980
1986	SF-N	153	526	71	146	28	3	13	70	84	23	96	1	2	5	16	13	.278	.375	.416	.972
1987	SF-N	149	500	80	125	22	1	24	76	72	15	109	2	0	4	16	9	.250	.344	.442	.975
1988	Cal-A	158	600	81	161	29	3	21	93	56	14	118	0	1	10	9	10	.268	.326	.432	.942
1989	Cal-A	154	560	81	152	24	1	22	90	61	12	109	0	3	6	3	0	.271	.340	.436	.979
1990	Cal-A	113	412	58	109	17	1	12	58	61	4	89	0	0	3	1	2	.265	.357	.398	.965
1991	Min-A	153	534	84	148	34	1	29	93	95	13	117	1	0	4	5	6	.277	.385	.507	1.000
1992	Min-A	138	444	63	128	27	2	12	66	73	11	76	3	0	9	4	5	.288	.386	.439	1.000
1993	Cal-A	153	573	74	139	32	0	27	112	71	12	135	1	0	4	4	1	.243	.327	.440	.000
1994	Cal-A	108	392	72	122	18	1	26	84	69	11	84	1	0	6	3	2	.311	.410	.561	1.000
1995	Cal-A	119	424	81	135	23	0	20	86	89	12	79	0	0	9	3	3	.318	.429	.514	.000

(continued)

(continued)

YEAR	TEAM	GAMES	AB	RUNS	HITS	2B	3B	HR	RBI	BB	IBB	SO	HBP	SH	SF	SB	CS	BA	OBA	SA	FA
1996	Cal-A	145	530	73	155	24	0	28	95	86	11	99	0	1	6	5	2	.292	.387	.496	.000
1997	KC-A	140	477	71	133	20	0	30	90	85	16	96	1	0	4	6	3	.279	.386	.509	.000
1998	**NY-A**	**35**	**103**	**11**	**30**	**7**	**0**	**3**	**9**	**14**	**1**	**18**	**0**	**0**	**1**	**0**	**1**	**.291**	**.373**	**.447**	**.000**
1999	**NY-A**	**146**	**476**	**59**	**128**	**25**	**1**	**19**	**78**	**73**	**0**	**100**	**0**	**0**	**3**	**4**	**1**	**.269**	**.364**	**.445**	**.000**
Career average		128	456	65	125	22	2	18	72	63	10	89	1	1	5	7	5	.274	.360	.451	.909
Yankee average		**91**	**290**	**35**	**79**	**16**	**1**	**11**	**44**	**44**	**1**	**59**	**0**	**0**	**2**	**2**	**1**	**.273**	**.366**	**.446**	**.000**
Career total		2436	8673	1240	2380	424	30	350	1372	1194	181	1698	13	20	94	142	98	.274	.360	.451	.909
Yankee total		**181**	**579**	**70**	**158**	**32**	**1**	**22**	**87**	**87**	**1**	**118**	**0**	**0**	**4**	**4**	**2**	**.273**	**.366**	**.446**	**.000**

Davis, George Willis (Kiddo)

HEIGHT: 5'11" THROWS: RIGHT BATS: RIGHT BORN: 2/12/1902 BRIDGEPORT, CONNECTICUT DIED: 3/4/1983 BRIDGEPORT, CONNECTICUT POSITIONS PLAYED: OF

YEAR	TEAM	GAMES	AB	RUNS	HITS	2B	3B	HR	RBI	BB	IBB	SO	HBP	SH	SF	SB	CS	BA	OBA	SA	FA
1926	**NY-A**	**1**	**0**	**0**	**0**	**0**	**0**	**0**	**0**	**0**	—	**0**	**0**	**0**	—	**0**	**0**	—	—	—	**.000**
1932	Phi-N	137	576	100	178	39	6	5	57	44	—	56	1	8	—	16	—	.309	.359	.424	.975
1933	NY-N	126	434	61	112	20	4	7	37	25	—	30	0	5	—	10	—	.258	.298	.371	.988
1934	StL-N	16	33	6	10	3	0	1	4	3	—	1	0	0	—	1	—	.303	.361	.485	.960
1934	Phi-N	100	393	50	115	25	5	3	48	27	—	28	0	0	—	1	—	.293	.338	.405	.951
1935	NY-N	47	91	16	24	7	1	2	6	10	—	4	1	3	—	2	—	.264	.343	.429	.977
1936	NY-N	47	67	6	16	1	0	0	5	6	—	5	0	1	—	0	—	.239	.301	.254	1.000
1937	NY-N	56	76	20	20	10	0	0	9	10	—	7	1	1	—	1	—	.263	.356	.395	.932
1937	Cin-N	40	136	19	35	6	0	1	16	5	—	6	1	0	—	1	—	.257	.340	.324	.951
1938	Cin-N	5	18	3	5	1	0	0	0	1	—	4	0	1	—	0	—	.278	.316	.333	1.000
Career average		58	182	28	52	11	2	2	18	13	—	14	1	2	0	3	0	.282	.336	.393	.873
Yankee average		**1**	**0**	**0**	**0**	**0**	**0**	**0**	**0**	**0**	—	**0**	**0**	**0**	—	**0**	**0**	—	—	—	**.000**
Career total		575	1824	281	515	112	16	19	182	131	—	141	4	19	0	32	0	.282	.336	.393	.872
Yankee total		**1**	**0**	**0**	**0**	**0**	**0**	**0**	**0**	**0**	—	**0**	**0**	**0**	—	**0**	**0**	—	—	—	**.000**

Davis, Russell Stuart

HEIGHT: 6'0" THROWS: RIGHT BATS: RIGHT BORN: 9/13/1969 BIRMINGHAM, ALABAMA POSITIONS PLAYED: 1B, 3B, SS, OF

YEAR	TEAM	GAMES	AB	RUNS	HITS	2B	3B	HR	RBI	BB	IBB	SO	HBP	SH	SF	SB	CS	BA	OBA	SA	FA
1994	**NY-A**	**4**	**14**	**0**	**2**	**0**	**0**	**0**	**1**	**0**	**0**	**4**	**0**	**0**	**0**	**0**	**0**	**.143**	**.143**	**.143**	**1.000**
1995	**NY-A**	**40**	**98**	**14**	**27**	**5**	**2**	**2**	**12**	**10**	**0**	**26**	**1**	**0**	**0**	**0**	**0**	**.276**	**.349**	**.429**	**.968**
1996	Sea-A	51	167	24	39	9	0	5	18	17	1	50	2	4	0	2	0	.234	.312	.377	.933
1997	Sea-A	119	420	57	114	29	1	20	63	27	2	100	2	3	2	6	2	.271	.317	.488	.939
1998	Sea-A	141	502	68	130	30	1	20	82	34	1	134	3	2	9	4	3	.259	.305	.442	.905
1999	Sea-A	124	432	55	106	17	1	21	59	32	1	111	5	7	2	3	3	.245	.296	.435	.959
2000	SF-N	80	180	27	47	5	0	9	24	9	0	29	2	0	1	0	3	.261	.302	.439	.928
Career average		80	259	35	66	14	1	11	37	18	1	65	2	2	2	2	2	.256	.309	.442	.952
Yankee average		**22**	**56**	**7**	**15**	**3**	**1**	**1**	**7**	**5**	**0**	**15**	**1**	**0**	**0**	**0**	**0**	**.259**	**.325**	**.393**	**.984**
Career total		559	1813	245	465	95	5	77	259	129	5	454	15	16	14	15	11	.256	.309	.442	.952
Yankee total		**44**	**112**	**14**	**29**	**5**	**2**	**2**	**13**	**10**	**0**	**30**	**1**	**0**	**0**	**0**	**0**	**.259**	**.325**	**.393**	**.984**

Dayett, Brian Kelly

HEIGHT: 5'10" THROWS: RIGHT BATS: RIGHT BORN: 1/22/1957 NEW LONDON, CONNECTICUT POSITIONS PLAYED: OF

YEAR	TEAM	GAMES	AB	RUNS	HITS	2B	3B	HR	RBI	BB	IBB	SO	HBP	SH	SF	SB	CS	BA	OBA	SA	FA
1983	**NY-A**	**11**	**29**	**3**	**6**	**0**	**1**	**0**	**5**	**2**	**0**	**4**	**0**	**1**	**0**	**0**	**0**	**.207**	**.258**	**.276**	**1.000**
1984	**NY-A**	**64**	**127**	**14**	**31**	**8**	**0**	**4**	**23**	**9**	**0**	**14**	**1**	**0**	**2**	**0**	**0**	**.244**	**.295**	**.402**	**.988**
1985	Chi-N	22	26	1	6	0	0	1	4	0	0	6	1	0	0	0	0	.231	.259	.346	1.000
1986	Chi-N	24	67	7	18	4	0	4	11	6	0	10	0	0	3	0	1	.269	.316	.507	1.000
1987	Chi-N	97	177	20	49	14	1	5	25	20	0	37	0	0	1	0	0	.277	.348	.452	1.000
Career average		44	85	9	22	5	0	3	14	7	0	14	0	0	1	0	0	.258	.316	.427	.995
Yankee average		**38**	**78**	**9**	**19**	**4**	**1**	**2**	**14**	**6**	**0**	**9**	**1**	**1**	**1**	**0**	**0**	**.237**	**.288**	**.378**	**.991**
Career total		218	426	45	110	26	2	14	68	37	0	71	2	1	6	0	1	.258	.316	.427	.995
Yankee total		**75**	**156**	**17**	**37**	**8**	**1**	**4**	**28**	**11**	**0**	**18**	**1**	**1**	**2**	**0**	**0**	**.237**	**.288**	**.378**	**.991**

Deidel, James Lawrence

HEIGHT: 6'2"   THROWS: RIGHT   BATS: RIGHT   BORN: 6/6/1949 DENVER, COLORADO   POSITIONS PLAYED: C

YEAR	TEAM	GAMES	AB	RUNS	HITS	2B	3B	HR	RBI	BB	IBB	SO	HBP	SH	SF	SB	CS	BA	OBA	SA	FA
1974	NY-A	2	2	0	0	0	0	0	0	0	0	0	0	0	0	0	0	.000	.000	.000	1.000
Career average		2	2	0	0	0	0	0	0	0	0	0	0	0	0	0	0	.000	.000	.000	1.000
Yankee average		**2**	**2**	**0**	**0**	**0**	**0**	**0**	**0**	**0**	**0**	**0**	**0**	**0**	**0**	**0**	**0**	**.000**	**.000**	**.000**	**1.000**
Career total		2	2	0	0	0	0	0	0	0	0	0	0	0	0	0	0	.000	.000	.000	1.000
Yankee total		**2**	**2**	**0**	**0**	**0**	**0**	**0**	**0**	**0**	**0**	**0**	**0**	**0**	**0**	**0**	**0**	**.000**	**.000**	**.000**	**1.000**

DeJesus, Ivan BORN IVAN DeJESUS (ALVAREZ)

HEIGHT: 5'11"   THROWS: RIGHT   BATS: RIGHT   BORN: 1/9/1953 SANTURCE, PUERTO RICO   POSITIONS PLAYED: 3B, SS

YEAR	TEAM	GAMES	AB	RUNS	HITS	2B	3B	HR	RBI	BB	IBB	SO	HBP	SH	SF	SB	CS	BA	OBA	SA	FA
1974	LA-N	3	3	1	1	0	0	0	0	0	0	2	0	0	0	0	0	.333	.333	.333	1.000
1975	LA-N	63	87	10	16	2	1	0	2	11	0	15	0	1	0	1	2	.184	.276	.230	.974
1976	LA-N	22	41	4	7	2	1	0	2	4	0	9	0	2	0	0	1	.171	.244	.268	.950
1977	Chi-N	155	624	91	166	31	7	3	40	56	4	90	4	7	4	24	12	.266	.328	.353	.962
1978	Chi-N	160	619	104	172	24	7	3	35	74	5	78	2	15	2	41	12	.278	.356	.354	.967
1979	Chi-N	160	636	92	180	26	10	3	52	59	1	82	2	17	2	24	20	.283	.345	.379	.959
1980	Chi-N	157	618	78	160	26	3	3	33	60	2	81	4	8	2	44	16	.259	.327	.325	.969
1981	Chi-N	106	403	49	78	8	4	0	13	46	2	61	0	10	1	21	9	.194	.276	.233	.959
1982	Phi-N	161	536	53	128	21	5	3	59	54	9	70	2	11	3	14	4	.239	.309	.313	.973
1983	Phi-N	158	497	60	126	15	7	4	45	53	18	77	0	11	4	11	4	.254	.323	.336	.966
1984	Phi-N	144	435	40	112	15	3	0	35	43	7	76	2	1	3	12	5	.257	.325	.306	.951
1985	StL-N	59	72	11	16	5	0	0	7	4	0	16	0	1	1	2	2	.222	.260	.292	1.000
1986	**NY-A**	**7**	**4**	**1**	**0**	**0**	**0**	**0**	**0**	**1**	**0**	**1**	**0**	**0**	**0**	**0**	**0**	**.000**	**.200**	**.000**	**.900**
1987	SF-N	9	10	0	2	0	0	0	1	0	0	2	0	0	0	0	1	.200	.200	.200	.840
1988	Det-A	7	17	1	3	0	0	0	0	1	0	4	0	3	0	0	0	.176	.222	.176	.893
Career average		91	307	40	78	12	3	1	22	31	3	44	1	6	1	13	6	.254	.323	.326	.951
Yankee average		**7**	**4**	**1**	**0**	**0**	**0**	**0**	**0**	**1**	**0**	**1**	**0**	**0**	**0**	**0**	**0**	**.000**	**.200**	**.000**	**.900**
Career total		1371	4602	595	1167	175	48	21	324	466	48	664	16	87	22	194	88	.254	.323	.326	.951
Yankee total		**7**	**4**	**1**	**0**	**0**	**0**	**0**	**0**	**1**	**0**	**1**	**0**	**0**	**0**	**0**	**0**	**.000**	**.200**	**.000**	**.900**

Del Greco, Robert George

HEIGHT: 5'11"   THROWS: RIGHT   BATS: RIGHT   BORN: 4/7/1933 PITTSBURGH, PENNSYLVANIA   POSITIONS PLAYED: 2B, 3B, OF

YEAR	TEAM	GAMES	AB	RUNS	HITS	2B	3B	HR	RBI	BB	IBB	SO	HBP	SH	SF	SB	CS	BA	OBA	SA	FA
1952	Pit-N	99	341	34	74	14	2	1	20	38	—	70	3	3	—	6	5	.217	.301	.279	.977
1956	Pit-N	14	20	4	4	0	0	2	3	3	0	3	0	1	0	0	0	.200	.304	.500	1.000
1956	Stl-N	102	270	29	58	16	2	5	18	32	3	50	6	3	4	1	1	.215	.308	.344	.987
1957	Chi-N	20	40	2	8	2	0	0	3	10	0	17	0	1	0	1	1	.200	.360	.250	.967
1957	**NY-A**	**8**	**7**	**3**	**3**	**0**	**0**	**0**	**0**	**2**	**0**	**2**	**0**	**0**	**0**	**1**	**0**	**.429**	**.556**	**.429**	**.971**
1958	**NY-A**	**12**	**5**	**1**	**1**	**0**	**0**	**0**	**0**	**1**	**0**	**1**	**0**	**0**	**0**	**0**	**1**	**.200**	**.333**	**.200**	**1.000**
1960	Phi-N	100	300	48	71	16	4	10	26	54	0	64	1	8	0	1	5	.237	.355	.417	.970
1961	Phi-N	41	112	14	29	5	0	2	11	12	1	17	3	1	1	0	0	.239	.326	.359	1.000
1961	KC-A	74	239	34	55	14	1	5	21	30	2	31	1	5	1	1	0	.230	.319	.360	.983
1962	KC-A	132	338	61	86	21	1	9	38	49	0	62	13	3	0	4	1	.254	.370	.402	.984
1963	KC-A	121	306	40	65	7	1	8	29	40	1	52	5	4	3	1	2	.212	.311	.320	.981
1965	Phi-N	8	4	1	0	0	0	0	0	0	0	3	0	0	0	0	0	.000	.000	.000	.000
Career average		61	165	23	38	8	1	4	14	23	1	31	3	2	1	1	1	.229	.330	.352	.982
Yankee average		**10**	**6**	**2**	**2**	**0**	**0**	**0**	**0**	**2**	**0**	**2**	**0**	**0**	**0**	**1**	**1**	**.333**	**.467**	**.333**	**.986**
Career total		731	1982	271	454	95	11	42	169	271	7	372	32	29	9	16	15	.229	.330	.352	.982
Yankee total		**20**	**12**	**4**	**4**	**0**	**0**	**0**	**0**	**3**	**0**	**3**	**0**	**0**	**0**	**1**	**1**	**.333**	**.467**	**.333**	**.986**

Delahanty, Frank George (Pudgie)

HEIGHT: 5'9"   THROWS: RIGHT   BATS: RIGHT   BORN: 1/29/1883 CLEVELAND, OHIO   DIED: 7/22/1966 CLEVELAND, OHIO   POSITIONS PLAYED: 1B, 2B, OF

YEAR	TEAM	GAMES	AB	RUNS	HITS	2B	3B	HR	RBI	BB	IBB	SO	HBP	SH	SF	SB	CS	BA	OBA	SA	FA
1905	**NY-A**	**9**	**27**	**0**	**6**	**1**	**0**	**0**	**2**	**1**	**—**	**—**	**0**	**1**	**—**	**0**	**—**	**.222**	**.250**	**.259**	**1.000**
1906	**NY-A**	**92**	**307**	**37**	**73**	**11**	**8**	**2**	**41**	**16**	**—**	**—**	**3**	**15**	**—**	**11**	**—**	**.238**	**.282**	**.345**	**.954**
1907	Cle-A	15	52	3	9	0	1	0	4	4	—	—	0	0	—	2	—	.173	.232	.212	.917
1908	**NY-A**	**37**	**125**	**12**	**32**	**1**	**2**	**0**	**10**	**10**	**—**	**—**	**1**	**1**	**—**	**9**	**—**	**.256**	**.316**	**.296**	**.957**
1914	Buf-F	79	274	29	55	4	7	2	27	23	—	19	1	11	—	21	—	.201	.265	.288	.976
1914	Pit-F	41	159	25	38	4	4	1	7	11	—	11	2	4	—	7	—	.239	.297	.333	.810
1915	Pit-F	14	42	3	10	1	0	0	3	1	—	0	1	—	0	—	.238	.256	.262	1.000

(continued)

(continued)

	GAMES	AB	RUNS	HITS	2B	3B	HR	RBI	BB	IBB	SO	HBP	SH	SF	SB	CS	BA	OBA	SA	FA
Career average	41	141	16	32	3	3	1	13	9	—	4	1	5	—	7	—	.226	.280	.308	.945
Yankee average	46	153	16	37	4	3	1	18	9	—	0	1	6	—	7	—	.242	.290	.327	.970
Career total	287	986	109	223	22	22	5	94	66	—	30	7	33	—	50	—	.226	.280	.308	.945
Yankee total	138	459	49	111	13	10	2	53	27	—	0	4	17	—	20	—	.242	.290	.327	.970

Delgado, Wilson BORN WILSON DELGADO (DURAN)
HEIGHT: 5'11" THROWS: RIGHT BATS: BOTH BORN: 7/15/1975 SAN CRISTOBAL, DOMINICAN REPUBLIC POSITIONS PLAYED: 2B, SS

YEAR	TEAM	GAMES	AB	RUNS	HITS	2B	3B	HR	RBI	BB	IBB	SO	HBP	SH	SF	SB	CS	BA	OBA	SA	FA
1996	SF-N	6	22	3	8	0	0	0	2	1	0	5	2	0	0	1	0	.364	.440	.364	.960
1997	SF-N	8	7	1	1	1	0	0	0	0	0	2	0	1	0	0	0	.143	.143	.286	1.000
1998	SF-N	10	12	1	2	1	0	0	1	1	0	3	0	0	0	0	0	.167	.231	.250	1.000
1999	SF-N	35	71	7	18	2	1	0	3	5	0	9	1	1	0	1	0	.254	.312	.310	.948
2000	**NY-A**	**31**	**45**	**6**	**11**	**1**	**0**	**1**	**4**	**5**	**0**	**9**	**0**	**0**	**1**	**1**	**0**	**.244**	**.314**	**.333**	**.954**
2000	KC-A	33	83	15	22	1	0	0	7	6	0	17	0	0	1	1	1	.265	.311	.277	.944
Career average		21	40	6	1	1	0	0	3	3	0	8	1	0	0	1	0	.258	.316	.304	.968
Yankee average		31	45	6	11	1	0	1	4	5	0	9	0	0	1	1	0	.244	.314	.333	.954
Career total		123	240	33	62	6	1	1	17	18	0	45	3	2	2	4	1	.258	.316	.304	.968
Yankee total		31	45	6	11	1	0	1	4	5	0	9	0	0	1	1	0	.244	.314	.333	.954

Delsing, James Henry
HEIGHT: 5'10" THROWS: RIGHT BATS: LEFT BORN: 11/13/1925 RUDOLPH, WISCONSIN POSITIONS PLAYED: OF

YEAR	TEAM	GAMES	AB	RUNS	HITS	2B	3B	HR	RBI	BB	IBB	SO	HBP	SH	SF	SB	CS	BA	OBA	SA	FA
1948	Chi-A	20	63	5	12	0	0	0	5	5	—	12	1	1	—	0	0	.190	.261	.190	1.000
1949	**NY-A**	**9**	**20**	**5**	**7**	**1**	**0**	**1**	**3**	**1**	**—**	**2**	**0**	**0**	**—**	**0**	**0**	**.350**	**.381**	**.550**	**1.000**
1950	**NY-A**	**12**	**10**	**2**	**4**	**0**	**0**	**0**	**2**	**2**	**—**	**0**	**0**	**0**	**—**	**0**	**0**	**.400**	**.500**	**.400**	**.994**
1950	StL-A	69	209	25	55	5	2	0	15	20	—	23	0	1	—	1	4	.263	.328	.306	.994
1951	StL-A	131	449	59	112	20	2	8	45	56	—	39	4	3	—	2	9	.249	.338	.356	.983
1952	StL-A	93	298	34	76	13	6	1	34	25	—	29	5	4	—	3	3	.255	.323	.349	.986
1952	Det-A	33	113	14	31	2	1	3	15	11	—	8	1	2	—	1	0	.274	.344	.389	.958
1953	Det-A	138	479	77	138	26	6	11	62	66	—	39	5	2	—	1	3	.288	.380	.436	.992
1954	Det-A	122	371	39	92	24	2	6	38	49	—	38	1	3	2	4	4	.248	.336	.372	.996
1955	Det-A	114	356	49	85	15	2	10	60	48	2	40	1	0	4	2	0	.239	.328	.376	.995
1956	Det-A	10	12	0	0	0	0	0	0	3	0	3	1	0	0	0	0	.000	.250	.000	1.000
1956	Chi-A	55	41	11	5	3	0	0	2	10	0	13	0	1	0	1	0	.122	.294	.195	.958
1960	KC-A	16	40	2	10	3	0	0	5	3	0	5	0	0	0	0	0	.250	.302	.325	1.000
Career average		75	189	25	48	9	2	3	22	23	0	19	1	1	0	1	2	.255	.339	.366	.147
Yankee average		11	15	4	6	1	0	1	3	2	0	1	0	0	0	0	0	.367	.424	.500	.000
Career total		822	2461	322	627	112	21	40	286	299	2	251	19	17	6	15	23	.255	.339	.366	1.916
Yankee total		21	30	7	11	1	0	1	5	3	0	2	0	0	0	0	0	.367	.424	.500	.000

DeMaestri, Joseph Paul (Oats)
HEIGHT: 6'0" THROWS: RIGHT BATS: RIGHT BORN: 12/9/1928 SAN FRANCISCO, CALIFORNIA POSITIONS PLAYED: 2B, 3B, SS

YEAR	TEAM	GAMES	AB	RUNS	HITS	2B	3B	HR	RBI	BB	IBB	SO	HBP	SH	SF	SB	CS	BA	OBA	SA	FA
1951	Chi-A	56	74	8	15	0	2	1	3	5	—	11	0	0	—	0	4	.203	.253	.297	.968
1952	StL-A	81	186	13	42	9	1	1	18	8	—	25	0	4	—	0	1	.226	.258	.301	1.000
1953	Phi-A	111	420	53	107	17	3	6	35	24	—	39	1	7	—	0	1	.255	.297	.352	.964
1954	Phi-A	146	539	49	124	16	3	8	40	20	—	63	3	3	7	1	4	.230	.258	.315	1.000
1955	KC-A	123	457	42	114	14	1	6	37	20	1	47	3	4	2	3	5	.249	.284	.324	.964
1956	KC-A	133	434	41	101	16	1	6	39	25	2	73	3	3	3	3	3	.233	.277	.316	.964
1957	KC-A	135	461	44	113	14	6	9	33	22	1	82	2	3	4	6	1	.245	.280	.360	.980
1958	KC-A	139	442	32	97	11	1	6	38	16	1	84	1	6	3	1	0	.219	.247	.290	.980
1959	KC-A	118	352	31	86	16	5	6	34	28	8	65	4	0	3	1	0	.244	.305	.369	.957
1960	**NY-A**	**49**	**35**	**8**	**8**	**1**	**0**	**0**	**2**	**0**	**0**	**9**	**0**	**0**	**0**	**0**	**0**	**.229**	**.229**	**.257**	**.952**
1961	**NY-A**	**30**	**41**	**1**	**6**	**0**	**0**	**0**	**2**	**0**	**0**	**13**	**0**	**0**	**0**	**0**	**0**	**.146**	**.146**	**.146**	**1.000**
Career average		102	313	29	74	10	2	4	26	15	1	46	2	3	2	1	2	.236	.274	.325	.000
Yankee average		40	38	5	7	1	0	0	2	0	0	11	0	0	0	0	0	.184	.184	.197	.000
Career total		1121	3441	322	813	114	23	49	281	168	13	511	17	30	22	15	19	.236	.274	.325	.000
Yankee total		79	76	9	14	1	0	0	4	0	0	22	0	0	0	0	0	.184	.184	.197	.000

Demmitt, Charles Raymond

HEIGHT: 5'8" THROWS: RIGHT BATS: LEFT BORN: 2/2/1884 ILLIOPOLIS, ILLINOIS ILLIOPOLIS, ILL. DIED: 2/19/1956 GLEN ELLYN, ILL. POSITIONS PLAYED: OF

YEAR	TEAM	GAMES	AB	RUNS	HITS	2B	3B	HR	RBI	BB	IBB	SO	HBP	SH	SF	SB	CS	BA	OBA	SA	FA
1909	**NY-A**	**123**	**427**	**68**	**105**	**12**	**12**	**4**	**30**	**55**	—	—	**6**	**10**	**0**	**16**	**0**	**.246**	**.340**	**.358**	**.908**
1910	StL-A	10	23	4	4	1	0	0	2	3	—	—	1	2	0	0	0	.174	.296	.217	1.000
1914	Det-A	1	0	0	0	0	0	0	0	0	—	0	0	0	0	0	0	—	—	—	.000
1914	Chi-A	146	515	63	133	13	12	2	46	61	—	48	6	15	0	12	20	.258	.344	.342	.953
1915	Chi-A	9	6	0	0	0	0	0	0	1	—	2	0	0	0	0	0	.000	.143	.000	1.000
1917	StL-A	14	53	6	15	1	2	0	7	0	—	8	1	0	0	1	0	.283	.296	.377	1.000
1918	StL-A	116	405	45	114	23	5	1	61	38	—	35	2	19	0	10	0	.281	.346	.370	.951
1919	StL-A	79	202	19	48	11	2	1	19	14	—	27	1	4	0	3	0	.238	.290	.327	.868
Career average		62	204	26	52	8	4	1	21	22	—	15	2	6	0	5	3	.257	.334	.349	.934
Yankee average		**123**	**427**	**68**	**105**	**12**	**12**	**4**	**30**	**55**	—	**0**	**6**	**10**	**0**	**16**	**0**	**.246**	**.340**	**.358**	**.908**
Career total		498	1631	205	419	61	33	8	165	172	—	120	17	50	0	42	20	.257	.334	.349	.934
Yankee total		**123**	**427**	**68**	**105**	**12**	**12**	**4**	**30**	**55**	—	**0**	**6**	**10**	**0**	**16**	**0**	**.246**	**.340**	**.358**	**.908**

Dempsey, John Rikard

HEIGHT: 6'0" THROWS: RIGHT BATS: RIGHT BORN: 9/13/1949 FAYETTEVILLE, TENNESSEE POSITIONS PLAYED: C, P, 1B, 3B, OF

YEAR	TEAM	GAMES	AB	RUNS	HITS	2B	3B	HR	RBI	BB	IBB	SO	HBP	SH	SF	SB	CS	BA	OBA	SA	FA
1969	Min-A	5	6	1	3	1	0	0	0	1	0	0	0	0	0	0	0	.500	.571	.667	.833
1970	Min-A	5	7	1	0	0	0	0	0	1	0	1	0	0	0	0	0	.000	.125	.000	.923
1971	Min-A	6	13	2	4	1	0	0	0	1	0	1	0	0	0	0	0	.308	.357	.385	.944
1972	Min-A	25	40	0	8	1	0	0	0	6	0	8	0	1	0	0	0	.200	.304	.225	.986
1973	**NY-A**	**6**	**11**	**0**	**2**	**0**	**0**	**0**	**0**	**1**	**0**	**3**	**0**	**1**	**0**	**0**	**0**	**.182**	**.250**	**.182**	**.818**
1974	**NY-A**	**43**	**109**	**12**	**26**	**3**	**0**	**2**	**12**	**8**	**0**	**7**	**0**	**1**	**1**	**0**	**0**	**.239**	**.288**	**.321**	**.978**
1975	**NY-A**	**71**	**145**	**18**	**38**	**8**	**0**	**1**	**11**	**21**	**1**	**15**	**0**	**3**	**1**	**0**	**0**	**.262**	**.353**	**.338**	**.977**
1976	**NY-A**	**21**	**42**	**1**	**5**	**0**	**0**	**0**	**2**	**5**	**0**	**4**	**0**	**1**	**0**	**0**	**0**	**.119**	**.213**	**.119**	**1.000**
1976	Bal-A	59	174	11	37	2	0	0	10	13	0	17	2	3	0	1	1	.213	.275	.224	.987
1977	Bal-A	91	270	27	61	7	4	3	34	34	1	34	2	5	3	2	3	.226	.314	.315	.977
1978	Bal-A	136	441	41	114	25	0	6	32	48	2	54	2	3	6	7	3	.259	.327	.315	.985
1979	Bal-A	124	368	48	88	23	0	6	41	38	1	37	0	3	4	0	1	.239	.307	.351	.990
1980	Bal-A	119	362	51	95	26	3	9	40	36	1	45	3	3	1	3	1	.262	.333	.425	1.000
1981	Bal-A	92	251	24	54	10	1	6	15	32	1	36	1	3	0	0	1	.215	.306	.335	.998
1982	Bal-A	125	344	35	88	15	1	5	36	46	1	37	0	7	5	0	3	.256	.339	.349	.991
1983	Bal-A	128	347	33	80	16	2	4	32	40	1	54	3	5	5	1	1	.231	.311	.323	.997
1984	Bal-A	109	330	37	76	11	0	11	34	40	0	58	1	5	4	1	2	.230	.311	.364	.992
1985	Bal-A	132	362	54	92	19	0	12	52	50	1	87	1	5	2	0	1	.254	.345	.406	.987
1986	Bal-A	122	327	42	68	15	1	13	29	45	0	78	3	7	0	1	0	.208	.309	.379	.990
1987	Cle-A	60	141	16	25	10	0	1	9	23	0	29	1	4	1	0	0	.177	.295	.270	.984
1988	LA-N	77	167	25	42	13	0	7	30	25	0	44	0	0	6	1	0	.251	.338	.455	.989
1989	LA-N	79	151	16	27	7	0	4	16	30	3	37	1	1	0	1	0	.179	.319	.305	.984
1990	Mil-A	62	128	13	25	5	0	2	15	23	0	29	0	0	1	0	0	.195	.318	.281	.992
1991	Mil-A	61	147	15	34	5	0	4	21	23	1	20	0	1	3	0	2	.231	.329	.347	.993
1992	Bal-A	8	9	2	1	0	0	0	0	2	0	1	0	0	0	0	0	.111	.273	.111	1.000
Career average		71	188	21	44	9	0	4	19	24	1	29	1	3	2	1	1	.233	.319	.347	.970
Yankee average		**35**	**77**	**8**	**18**	**3**	**0**	**1**	**6**	**9**	**0**	**7**	**0**	**2**	**1**	**0**	**0**	**.233**	**.319**	**.347**	**.970**
Career total		1766	4692	525	1093	223	12	96	471	592	13	736	18	63	42	20	19	.233	.308	.296	.932
Yankee total		**141**	**307**	**31**	**71**	**11**	**0**	**3**	**25**	**35**	**1**	**29**	**0**	**6**	**2**	**1**	**0**	**.231**	**.308**	**.296**	**.932**

Dent, Russell Earl (Bucky) BORN RUSSELL EARL O'DEY

HEIGHT: 5'11" THROWS: RIGHT BATS: RIGHT BORN: 11/25/1951 SAVANNAH, GEORGIA POSITIONS PLAYED: 2B, 3B, SS

YEAR	TEAM	GAMES	AB	RUNS	HITS	2B	3B	HR	RBI	BB	IBB	SO	HBP	SH	SF	SB	CS	BA	OBA	SA	FA
1973	Chi-A	40	117	17	29	2	0	0	10	10	0	18	1	2	2	2	3	.248	.308	.265	.903
1974	Chi-A	154	496	55	136	15	3	5	45	28	0	48	3	23	2	3	3	.274	.316	.347	.972
1975	Chi-A	157	602	52	159	29	4	3	58	36	3	48	0	15	9	2	4	.264	.301	.341	.981
1976	Chi-A	158	562	44	138	18	4	2	52	43	3	45	2	17	2	2	5	.246	.300	.302	.976
1977	**NY-A**	**158**	**477**	**54**	**118**	**18**	**4**	**8**	**49**	**39**	**0**	**28**	**1**	**14**	**9**	**1**	**1**	**.247**	**.300**	**.352**	**.974**
1978	**NY-A**	**123**	**379**	**40**	**92**	**11**	**1**	**5**	**40**	**23**	**1**	**24**	**2**	**6**	**5**	**3**	**1**	**.243**	**.286**	**.317**	**.981**
1979	**NY-A**	**141**	**431**	**47**	**99**	**14**	**2**	**2**	**32**	**37**	**1**	**30**	**1**	**13**	**8**	**0**	**0**	**.230**	**.287**	**.285**	**.977**
1980	**NY-A**	**141**	**489**	**57**	**128**	**26**	**2**	**5**	**52**	**48**	**1**	**37**	**2**	**9**	**5**	**0**	**3**	**.262**	**.327**	**.354**	**.982**
1981	**NY-A**	**73**	**227**	**20**	**54**	**11**	**0**	**7**	**27**	**19**	**0**	**17**	**2**	**8**	**2**	**0**	**1**	**.238**	**.300**	**.379**	**.970**
1982	**NY-A**	**59**	**160**	**11**	**27**	**1**	**1**	**0**	**9**	**8**	**0**	**11**	**0**	**4**	**1**	**0**	**0**	**.169**	**.207**	**.188**	**.962**
1982	Tex-A	46	146	16	32	9	0	1	14	13	0	10	0	3	2	0	0	.219	.280	.301	.980
1983	Tex-A	131	417	36	99	15	2	2	34	23	0	31	1	7	2	3	7	.237	.278	.297	.979
1984	KC-A	11	9	2	3	0	0	0	1	1	0	2	0	0	0	0	0	.333	.400	.333	1.000

(continued)

(continued)

	GAMES	AB	RUNS	HITS	2B	3B	HR	RBI	BB	IBB	SO	HBP	SH	SF	SB	CS	BA	OBA	SA	FA
Career average	107	347	35	86	13	2	3	33	25	1	27	1	9	4	1	2	.247	.297	.321	.978
Yankee average	**116**	**361**	**38**	**86**	**14**	**2**	**5**	**35**	**29**	**1**	**25**	**1**	**9**	**5**	**1**	**1**	**.239**	**.295**	**.324**	**.974**
Career total	1392	4512	451	1114	169	23	40	423	328	9	349	15	121	49	17	29	.247	.297	.321	.978
Yankee total	**695**	**2163**	**229**	**518**	**81**	**10**	**27**	**209**	**174**	**3**	**147**	**8**	**54**	**30**	**4**	**6**	**.239**	**.295**	**.324**	**.974**

Derrick, Claud Lester (Deek)
HEIGHT: 6'0" THROWS: RIGHT BATS: RIGHT BORN: 6/11/1886 BURTON, GEORGIA DIED: 7/15/1974 CLAYTON, GEORGIA POSITIONS PLAYED: 1B, 2B, 3B, SS

YEAR	TEAM	GAMES	AB	RUNS	HITS	2B	3B	HR	RBI	BB	IBB	SO	HBP	SH	SF	SB	CS	BA	OBA	SA	FA
1910	Phi-A	2	1	0	0	0	0	0	0	0	—	—	0	0	—	0	—	.000	.000	.000	.500
1911	Phi-A	36	100	14	23	1	2	0	5	7	—	—	2	7	—	7	—	.230	.294	.280	.960
1912	Phi-A	21	58	7	14	0	1	0	7	5	—	—	1	3	—	1	—	.241	.313	.276	.884
1913	**NY-A**	22	65	7	19	1	0	1	7	5	—	8	1	0	—	2	—	.292	.352	.354	.874
1914	Cin-N	3	6	2	2	1	0	0	1	0	—	0	0	0	—	1	—	.333	.333	.500	.889
1914	Chi-N	28	96	5	21	3	1	0	13	5	—	13	0	3	—	2	—	.219	.257	.271	.895
Career average		19	54.	6	13	1	1	0	6	4	—	4	1	2	—	2	—	.242	.298	.294	.834
Yankee average		**22**	**65**	**7**	**19**	**1**	**0**	**1**	**7**	**5**	**—**	**8**	**1**	**0**	**—**	**2**	**—**	**.292**	**.352**	**.354**	**.874**
Career total		112	326	35	79	6	4	1	33	22	—	21	4	13	—	13	—	.242	.298	.294	.834
Yankee total		**22**	**65**	**7**	**19**	**1**	**0**	**1**	**7**	**5**	**—**	**8**	**1**	**0**	**—**	**2**	**—**	**.292**	**.352**	**.354**	**.874**

Derry, Alva Russell (Russ)
HEIGHT: 6'1" THROWS: RIGHT BATS: LEFT BORN: 10/7/1916 PRINCETON, MISSOURI POSITIONS PLAYED: OF

YEAR	TEAM	GAMES	AB	RUNS	HITS	2B	3B	HR	RBI	BB	IBB	SO	HBP	SH	SF	SB	CS	BA	OBA	SA	FA
1944	**NY-A**	**38**	**114**	**14**	**29**	**3**	**0**	**4**	**14**	**20**	**—**	**19**	**0**	**1**	**—**	**1**	**0**	**.254**	**.366**	**.386**	**.949**
1945	**NY-A**	**78**	**253**	**37**	**57**	**6**	**2**	**13**	**45**	**31**	**—**	**49**	**1**	**1**	**—**	**1**	**0**	**.225**	**.312**	**.419**	**.978**
1946	Phi-A	69	184	17	38	8	5	0	14	27	—	54	1	2	—	0	0	.207	.311	.304	.985
1949	StL-N	2	2	0	0	0	0	0	0	0	—	2	0	0	—	0	—	.000	.000	.000	.000
Career average		47	138	17	31	4	2	4	18	20	—	31	1	1	—	1	0	.224	.322	.373	.728
Yankee average		**58**	**184**	**26**	**43**	**5**	**1**	**9**	**30**	**26**	**—**	**34**	**1**	**1**	**—**	**1**	**0**	**.234**	**.329**	**.409**	**.964**
Career total		187	553	68	124	17	7	17	73	78	—	124	2	4	—	2	0	.224	.322	.373	.728
Yankee total		**116**	**367**	**51**	**86**	**9**	**2**	**17**	**59**	**51**	**—**	**68**	**1**	**2**	**—**	**2**	**0**	**.234**	**.329**	**.409**	**.964**

Destrade, Orestes BORN ORESTES DESTRADE (CUCUAS)
HEIGHT: 6'4" THROWS: RIGHT BATS: BOTH BORN: 5/8/1962 SANTIAGO DE CUBA POSITIONS PLAYED: 1B

YEAR	TEAM	GAMES	AB	RUNS	HITS	2B	3B	HR	RBI	BB	IBB	SO	HBP	SH	SF	SB	CS	BA	OBA	SA	FA
1987	**NY-A**	**9**	**19**	**5**	**5**	**0**	**0**	**0**	**1**	**5**	**0**	**5**	**0**	**0**	**0**	**0**	**0**	**.263**	**.417**	**.263**	**1.000**
1988	Pit-N	36	47	2	7	1	0	1	3	5	0	17	0	0	1	0	0	.149	.226	.234	1.000
1993	Fla-N	153	569	61	145	20	3	20	87	58	8	130	3	1	6	0	2	.255	.324	.406	.987
1994	Fla-N	39	130	12	27	4	0	5	15	19	1	32	2	0	1	1	0	.208	.316	.354	.983
Career average		59	191	20	46	6	1	7	27	22	2	46	1	0	2	0	1	.241	.319	.383	.987
Yankee average		**9**	**19**	**5**	**5**	**0**	**0**	**0**	**1**	**5**	**0**	**5**	**0**	**0**	**0**	**0**	**0**	**.263**	**.417**	**.263**	**1.000**
Career total		237	765	80	184	25	3	26	106	87	9	184	5	1	8	1	2	.241	.319	.383	.987
Yankee total		**9**	**19**	**5**	**5**	**0**	**0**	**0**	**1**	**5**	**0**	**5**	**0**	**0**	**0**	**0**	**0**	**.263**	**.417**	**.263**	**1.000**

DeVormer, Albert E.
HEIGHT: 6'1" THROWS: RIGHT BATS: RIGHT BORN: 8/19/1891 GRAND RAPIDS, MICHI. DIED: 8/29/1966 GRAND RAPIDS, MICH. POSITIONS PLAYED: C, 1B, OF

YEAR	TEAM	GAMES	AB	RUNS	HITS	2B	3B	HR	RBI	BB	IBB	SO	HBP	SH	SF	SB	CS	BA	OBA	SA	FA
1918	Chi-A	8	19	2	5	2	0	0	0	0	—	4	0	0	—	1	—	.263	.263	.368	1.000
1921	**NY-A**	**22**	**49**	**6**	**17**	**4**	**0**	**0**	**7**	**2**	**—**	**4**	**0**	**2**	**—**	**2**	**0**	**.347**	**.373**	**.429**	**.950**
1922	**NY-A**	**24**	**59**	**8**	**12**	**4**	**1**	**0**	**11**	**1**	**—**	**6**	**0**	**4**	**—**	**0**	**0**	**.203**	**.217**	**.305**	**.968**
1923	Bos-A	74	209	20	54	7	3	0	18	6	—	21	1	6	—	3	0	.258	.282	.321	.979
1927	NY-N	68	141	14	35	3	1	2	21	11	—	11	2	4	—	1	—	.248	.312	.326	.953
Career average		39	95	10	25	4	1	0	11	4	0	9	1	3	0	1	0	.258	.292	.333	.970
Yankee average		**23**	**54**	**7**	**15**	**4**	**1**	**0**	**9**	**2**	**0**	**5**	**0**	**3**	**0**	**1**	**0**	**.269**	**.288**	**.361**	**.959**
Career total		196	477	50	123	20	5	2	57	20	0	46	3	16	0	7	0	.258	.292	.333	.970
Yankee total		**46**	**108**	**14**	**29**	**8**	**1**	**0**	**18**	**3**	**0**	**10**	**0**	**6**	**0**	**2**	**0**	**.269**	**.288**	**.361**	**.959**

William Malcolm Dickey, c, 1928–46

The numbers, as they say, speak for themselves.

In the latter part of the 20th century, Bill Dickey's stature as the best catcher of all time seems to be slowly receding as the memory of his abilities wanes. But make no mistake—Bill Dickey was one of the great ones.

Born in 1907 in Bastrop, Louisiana, Dickey signed with the Yankees in December 1927. Manager Miller Huggins may have boasted that the 1927 Yankees were the best team ever, but he knew they could use some help behind the plate.

The tall (6 foot 1 inch), soft-spoken Dickey was called up to the big club in August of 1928, and he caught ten of the Yankees' final 42 games. He was not overpowering at-bat, but neither were the two men ahead of him, Johnny Grabowski and Benny Bengough. Behind the plate, Dickey showed promise. In 1929, he was the regular catcher, and would continue to be until 1943, when he went into the service during World War II.

Dickey struck up an immediate friendship with Babe Ruth, with whom he shared a passion for hunting birds. Ruth's nickname for Dickey was "Pittridge," which was Ruth's word for partridge.

Lou Gehrig liked him, too, and the men were roommates for several years. It was to Dickey that Gehrig first confided that he had a serious muscular illness.

But it was, in fact, hard not to like Dickey, a fanatically hard worker who never shirked his catching duties, the consummate team man.

Dickey was a tremendous hitter, even in those years of high batting averages. His .362 batting average in 1936 was a record for catchers. He hit .313 lifetime with 202 home runs and 1,209 RBI.

He was a difficult man to strike out. The most he ever whiffed in his career was 37 times in 1939. But that was a lot for him; usually he would strike out closer to 20 times a year.

And he caught a lot of games. He caught 100 or more games for 13 consecutive seasons, from 1928 to 1941. That wasn't an easy thing to do. Mickey Cochrane caught 100 or more 11 times. Yogi Berra did it ten times. Luke Sewell, a contemporary of Dickey's, caught 100 games or more in a season, only nine times in 20 years. Wally Schang, a 19-year veteran, did it five times. It was a tough position to play in the '20s and '30s. Heck, it's a tough position nowadays.

And Dickey was a tough man. In 1932, he broke Washington outfielder Carl Reynolds's jaw with one punch after Reynolds tried to bowl him over in a rundown. In Dickey's defense, he had been smashed by a Washington base runner in a similar play the day before, and he was clearly trying to show the Senators that he would not be intimidated.

It worked, although Dickey was fined $1,000 and suspended for 30 days as a result of the incident. He had made his point, and opponents laid off him after that.

Dickey played in eight World Series and turned in several clutch performances. In 1932, he hit .438. His ninth-inning single won the first game of the 1939 Series and his home run in the fifth game of the 1943 Series won the game and the Series. His 24 RBI are eighth-best in Series play.

Dickey played on 11 American League All-Star teams, and his stats pepper the Yankee record book. He is 7th in hits with 1,969, 13th in runs scored with 930, 6th in doubles with 343, 10th in triples with 72, 10th in home runs with 202 and 6th in RBI with 1,209.

Following a brief comeback after World War II, Dickey retired as a player. He returned to the Yankees as manager in 1946 and later worked for the team as a scout. He was named to the Hall of Fame in 1954. He died in Little Rock, Arkansas, in 1993.

Dickey, William Malcolm

HEIGHT: 6'2"   THROWS: RIGHT   BATS: LEFT   BORN: 6/6/1907 BASTROP, LOUISIANA   DIED: 11/12/1993 LITTLE ROCK, ARKANSAS   POSITIONS PLAYED: C

YEAR	TEAM	GAMES	AB	RUNS	HITS	2B	3B	HR	RBI	BB	IBB	SO	HBP	SH	SF	SB	CS	BA	OBA	SA	FA
1928	NY-A	10	15	1	3	1	1	0	2	0	—	2	0	0	—	0	0	.200	.200	.400	1.000
1929	NY-A	130	447	60	145	30	6	10	65	14	—	16	1	11	—	4	3	.324	.346	.485	.979
1930	NY-A	109	366	55	124	25	7	5	65	21	—	14	0	9	—	7	1	.339	.375	.486	.977
1931	NY-A	130	477	65	156	17	10	6	78	39	—	20	0	7	—	2	1	.327	.378	.442	.996
1932	NY-A	108	423	66	131	20	4	15	84	34	—	13	0	2	—	2	4	.310	.361	.482	.987

(continued)

(continued)

YEAR	TEAM	GAMES	AB	RUNS	HITS	2B	3B	HR	RBI	BB	IBB	SO	HBP	SH	SF	SB	CS	BA	OBA	SA	FA
1933	NY-A	130	478	58	152	24	8	14	97	47	—	14	2	5	—	3	4	.318	.381	.490	.993
1934	NY-A	104	395	56	127	24	4	12	72	38	—	18	2	3	—	0	3	.322	.384	.494	.986
1935	NY-A	120	448	54	125	26	6	14	81	35	—	11	6	2	—	1	1	.279	.339	.458	.995
1936	NY-A	112	423	99	153	26	8	22	107	46	—	16	3	0	—	0	2	.362	.428	.617	.976
1937	NY-A	140	530	87	176	35	2	29	133	73	—	22	4	1	—	3	2	.332	.417	.570	.991
1938	NY-A	132	454	84	142	27	4	27	115	75	—	22	2	1	—	3	0	.313	.412	.568	.987
1939	NY-A	128	480	98	145	23	3	24	105	77	—	37	4	4	—	5	0	.302	.403	.513	.989
1940	NY-A	106	372	45	92	11	1	9	54	48	—	32	2	2	—	0	3	.247	.336	.355	.994
1941	NY-A	109	348	35	99	15	5	7	71	45	—	17	3	1	—	2	1	.284	.371	.417	.994
1942	NY-A	82	268	28	79	13	1	2	37	26	—	11	1	0	—	2	2	.295	.359	.373	.976
1943	NY-A	85	242	29	85	18	2	4	33	41	—	12	0	1	—	2	1	.351	.445	.492	.994
1946	NY-A	54	134	10	35	8	0	2	10	19	—	12	1	2	—	0	1	.261	.357	.366	.987
Career average		105	371	55	116	20	4	12	71	40	—	17	2	3	—	2	2	.313	.382	.486	.988
Yankee average		**105**	**371**	**55**	**116**	**20**	**4**	**12**	**71**	**40**	**—**	**17**	**2**	**3**	**—**	**2**	**2**	**.313**	**.382**	**.486**	**.988**
Career total		1789	6300	930	1969	343	72	202	1209	678	—	289	31	51	—	36	29	.313	.382	.486	.988
Yankee total		**1789**	**6300**	**930**	**1969**	**343**	**72**	**202**	**1209**	**678**	**—**	**289**	**31**	**51**	**—**	**36**	**29**	**.313**	**.382**	**.486**	**.988**

DiMaggio, Joseph Paul (Joltin' Joe *or* The Yankee Clipper)

HEIGHT: 6'2"   THROWS: RIGHT   BATS: RIGHT   BORN: 11/25/1914 MARTINEZ, CALIFORNIA   DIED: 3/8/1999   POSITIONS PLAYED: 1B, OF

YEAR	TEAM	GAMES	AB	RUNS	HITS	2B	3B	HR	RBI	BB	IBB	SO	HBP	SH	SF	SB	CS	BA	OBA	SA	FA
1936	NY-A	138	637	132	206	44	15	29	125	24	—	39	4	3	—	4	0	.323	.352	.576	.978
1937	NY-A	151	621	151	215	35	15	46	167	64	—	37	5	2	—	3	0	.346	.412	.673	.962
1938	NY-A	145	599	129	194	32	13	32	140	59	—	21	2	0	—	6	1	.324	.386	.581	.963
1939	NY-A	120	462	108	176	32	6	30	126	52	—	20	4	6	—	3	0	.381	.448	.671	.986
1940	NY-A	132	508	93	179	28	9	31	133	61	—	30	3	0	—	1	2	.352	.425	.626	.978
1941	NY-A	139	541	122	193	43	11	30	125	76	—	13	4	0	—	4	2	.357	.440	.643	.978
1942	NY-A	154	610	123	186	29	13	21	114	68	—	36	2	0	—	4	2	.305	.376	.498	.981
1946	NY-A	132	503	81	146	20	8	25	95	59	—	24	2	3	—	1	0	.290	.367	.511	.982
1947	NY-A	141	534	97	168	31	10	20	97	64	—	32	3	0	—	3	0	.315	.391	.522	.997
1948	NY-A	153	594	110	190	26	11	39	155	67	—	30	8	0	—	1	1	.320	.396	.598	.972
1949	NY-A	76	272	58	94	14	6	14	67	55	—	18	2	0	—	0	1	.346	.459	.596	.985
1950	NY-A	139	525	114	158	33	10	32	122	80	—	33	1	0	—	0	0	.301	.394	.585	.976
1951	NY-A	116	415	72	109	22	4	12	71	61	—	36	6	0	—	0	0	.263	.365	.422	.990
Career average		134	525	107	170	30	10	28	118	61	—	28	4	1	—	2	1	.325	.398	.579	.978
Yankee average		**134**	**525**	**107**	**170**	**30**	**10**	**28**	**118**	**61**	**—**	**28**	**4**	**1**	**—**	**2**	**1**	**.325**	**.398**	**.579**	**.978**
Career total		1736	6821	1390	2214	389	131	361	1537	790	—	369	46	14	—	30	9	.325	.398	.579	.978
Yankee total		**1736**	**6821**	**1390**	**2214**	**389**	**131**	**361**	**1537**	**790**	**—**	**369**	**46**	**14**	**—**	**30**	**9**	**.325**	**.398**	**.579**	**.978**

Dineen, Kerry Michael

HEIGHT: 5'11"   THROWS: LEFT   BATS: LEFT   BORN: 7/1/1952 ENGLEWOOD, NEW JERSEY   POSITIONS PLAYED: OF

YEAR	TEAM	GAMES	AB	RUNS	HITS	2B	3B	HR	RBI	BB	IBB	SO	HBP	SH	SF	SB	CS	BA	OBA	SA	FA
1975	NY-A	7	22	3	8	1	0	0	1	2	0	1	0	0	0	0	0	.364	.417	.409	1.000
1976	NY-A	4	7	0	2	0	0	0	1	1	0	2	0	0	0	1	1	.286	.375	.286	.900
1978	Phi-N	5	8	0	2	1	0	0	0	1	0	0	0	0	0	0	0	.250	.333	.375	1.000
Career average		5	12	1	4	1	0	0	1	1	0	1	0	0	0	0	0	.324	.390	.378	.967
Yankee average		**6**	**15**	**2**	**5**	**1**	**0**	**0**	**1**	**2**	**0**	**2**	**0**	**0**	**0**	**1**	**1**	**.345**	**.406**	**.379**	**.966**
Career total		16	37	3	12	2	0	0	2	4	0	3	0	0	0	1	1	.324	.390	.378	.967
Yankee total		**11**	**29**	**3**	**10**	**1**	**0**	**0**	**2**	**3**	**0**	**3**	**0**	**0**	**0**	**1**	**1**	**.345**	**.406**	**.379**	**.966**

Dolan, Patrick Henry (Cozy)

HEIGHT: 5'10"   THROWS: LEFT   BATS: LEFT   BORN: 12/3/1872 CAMBRIDGE, MASSACHUSETTS   DIED: 3/29/1907 LOUISVILLE, KENTUCKY   POSITIONS PLAYED: OF

YEAR	TEAM	GAMES	AB	RUNS	HITS	2B	3B	HR	RBI	BB	IBB	SO	HBP	SH	SF	SB	CS	BA	OBA	SA	FA
1909	Cin-N	3	6	2	1	0	0	0	0	2	—	—	0	1	—	0	—	.167	.375	.167	.750
1911	NY-A	19	69	19	21	1	2	0	6	8	—	—	1	4	—	12	—	.304	.385	.377	.947
1912	NY-A	18	60	15	12	1	3	0	11	5	—	—	1	0	—	5	—	.200	.273	.317	.768
1912	Phi-N	11	50	8	14	2	2	0	7	1	—	10	2	2	—	3	—	.280	.294	.400	.872
1913	Phi-N	55	126	15	33	4	0	0	8	1	—	21	1	2	—	9	—	.262	.273	.294	.905

(continued)

Joseph Paul "Joe" DiMaggio, of, 1936–42, 1946–51

Had his career not been shortened by World War II, there would surely be more people making a case for Joe DiMaggio as the greatest player of all time.

As it is, "Joltin' Joe" has his admirers. Certainly the man whom most regard as the greatest of all knew who he was. In DiMaggio's first year, Babe Ruth, newly retired, made his way into the Yankee locker room for a visit. Most of the players, even those he knew fairly well, Ruth called "Keed," which was Ruth's common nickname for just about anybody with whom he came in contact.

When he came to DiMaggio, Ruth stuck out his hand and said, "Hiya, Joe."

There was a very simple reason why DiMaggio seemed always able to master the game at every level: The man was a tremendous athlete. He was a very good tennis player in his younger days before he discovered he could make money as a baseball player. And after joining the Yankees in the mid-1930s, he barnstormed with a semi-professional basketball team for a year or two until the Yankees finally asked him to cut it out.

DiMaggio was born on November 25, 1914 in Martinez, California, just south of San Francisco, the fourth son of Giuseppe and Rosalie DiMaggio. Giuseppe, a native of Italy, worked as a fisherman in the Old Country and continued to do so after he and his family came to America.

Giuseppe expected his sons to follow him into the fishing trade. But while the waters of the Bay Area were fertile grounds for making a living, so, too, were the baseball fields. The Bay Area did not have a major league baseball team, but a host of minor league nines were headquartered there.

And Joe, along with older brother Vincent and younger brother Dominic, were better ballplayers than fishermen. Joe took a turn on

the boat, but admitted it often made him seasick.

Giuseppe didn't mind. He soon came to understand that fine sums of money could be made playing the game professionally, and in interviews over the years, none of the DiMaggio brothers could ever remember him discrediting the idea of his sons as baseball players.

Joe was a star on the sandlots around San Francisco almost as soon as he picked up a bat. In 1932, he was asked to join his brother Vincent's team, the San Francisco Seals, late in the season in a kind of unpaid tryout. He didn't overwhelm anyone, hitting .222 in the last three games of the season, as a shortstop.

But the Seals liked him, and after negotiations with the family, he was signed in 1933 as an 18-year-old rookie for $225 a month, twice the going rate for first-year players.

He came out of the blocks like a racehorse, playing in 187 games, hitting .340 with 45 doubles, 13 triples and 28 home runs, as well as a league-leading 169 RBI. And he hit in 61 consecutive games. He had already developed his wide-legged stance with his bat straight up in the air. He had a big swing that generated enormous power, but his reflexes were so sharp that he rarely struck out. In his major league career, he hit 361 home runs and struck out only 369 times. For power hitters, a 3-1 ratio of strikeouts to home runs is exceptional. A 1-1 ratio is amazing.

So he was immediately one of the best, if not the best, player in the Pacific Coast League. And in the depths of the Depression, the owners of the Seals thought more about selling his contract to a big league club than keeping the player.

All 16 major league teams were initially interested. But in his second year in the minors, DiMaggio injured his left knee. In the 1930s, the prescription for rehabilitating knee injuries was simple rest and hope. And the hope was that the ballplayer would play again at all. Suddenly the interest was drying up. Big league teams in those days simply did not want to deal with such a problem.

Still, DiMaggio was just a teenager, and a teenager with tremendous potential. The Yankees, coming off their powerhouse 1932 finish, were still interested, and they could afford to wait. After some tests on the knee, DiMaggio's contract was purchased for $25,000. The Yankees also agreed to allow him to play for San Francisco in 1935, for "seasoning," and bring him up in 1936.

He hit .398 for San Francisco in 1935, easily winning the MVP award as the Seals won the pennant.

Nothing changed in spring training the next year. DiMaggio, who had faced great pitching in the PCl, admitted many years later that he wasn't particularly worried about "making it" in the big leagues.

The veteran Yankees cast a skeptical eye toward the rookie. Big Red Ruffing, one of the Yanks' star pitchers, mocked his .398 average in the Pacific Coast League by sarcastically estimating that DiMaggio would probably hit .800 in the bigs. DiMaggio said nothing and then proceeded to tear up the league in spring training, hitting .400 before a foot injury slowed him down.

That injury delayed his debut in New York by about a month, but it was worth waiting for. DiMaggio had three hits in six at-bats in his first game against the Browns, and hit .420 in his first few weeks in the league.

He was already one of the most fundamentally sound players in the majors. He had tremendous patience. He waited for his pitch and swung at it. He was almost never fooled. He ran the bases well. He played a shallow center field, but was rarely out of position on a hit.

New York fans, their interest stoked by an almost embarrassingly adoring New York press, ate it up. The Yankees drew more than 300,000 more fans in 1936 than in 1935.

And when DiMaggio added his talents to those of MVP first baseman Lou Gehrig, who hit .354 with 49 home runs, catcher Bill Dickey, who hit .362, second baseman Tony Lazzeri, who hit .287 with 109 RBI and third baseman Red Rolfe, who hit .362, the Yankees blitzed the league. They won 102 games and finished 19 1/2 games ahead of second-place Detroit. (By contrast, the 1927 Yankees finished 19 games ahead of Philadelphia.)

And it only got better in the World Series that year. The Yankees once again faced the crosstown Giants of Bill Terry and Mel Ott. The Giants won the first game, 6-1, but the Yankees swept to four wins in five games after that, and won their fifth world title. That set the Yankees on a path of seven pennants in eight years, including six World Series wins. Dickey later admitted that he never believed that one player could make such a difference in a team, but after he saw DiMaggio play, he realized he was wrong.

In 1941 DiMaggio set a record many believe will never be topped, hitting in 56 consecutive games. That broke "Wee Willie" Keeler's decades-old record of 44.

But DiMaggio's consistency was nothing new to his teammates. He had hit in 61 straight with the Seals, and in his rookie year, he hit in 18 straight games. The next year, he had a 22-game streak, and in 1938, a 23-game streak.

Interestingly, DiMaggio was initially aiming at the "modern" streak of former All-Star first baseman George Sisler, who hit in 41 consecutive games in 1922, the year Sisler hit .420. But when DiMaggio

(continued)

1913	Pit-N	35	133	22	27	5	2	0	9	15	—	14	1	4	—	14	—	.203	.289	.271	.937
1914	StL-N	126	421	76	101	16	3	4	32	55	—	74	5	18	—	42	—	.240	.335	.321	.955
1915	StL-N	111	322	53	90	14	9	2	38	34	—	37	4	20	—	17	11	.280	.356	.398	.929
1922	NY-N	1	0	0	0	0	0	0	0	0	—	0	0	0	—	0	0	—	—	—	.000
Career average		42	132	23	33	5	2	1	12	13	0	17	2	6	0	11	1	.252	.329	.339	.785
Yankee average		**19**	**65**	**17**	**17**	**1**	**3**	**0**	**9**	**7**	**0**	**0**	**1**	**2**	**0**	**9**	**0**	**.256**	**.333**	**.349**	**.858**
Career total		379	1187	210	299	43	21	6	111	121	0	156	15	51	0	102	11	.252	.329	.339	.785
Yankee total		**37**	**129**	**34**	**33**	**2**	**5**	**0**	**17**	**13**	**0**	**0**	**2**	**4**	**0**	**17**	**0**	**.256**	**.333**	**.349**	**.858**

topped that on June 29, 1941, historians rummaged around and found Keeler's 1897 streak. When DiMaggio topped that one on July 1, he was on his own.

It ended on July 17. But in that span, DiMaggio had hit .408, and more importantly, had pushed his team from fourth place to first, a position they held for the rest of the year.

There was some controversy, manufactured in part by newspapermen, about who would be the Most Valuable Player in 1941. After all, Boston's Ted Williams hit .406 that year, the last year a major-leaguer would do so. But even Williams conceded that DiMaggio was the league MVP.

Like many healthy American males, DiMaggio went into the service after the 1942 season ended with another American League pennant for the Yankees. He spent three years in the Navy before returning to the Yankees for the 1946 season. DiMaggio picked up where he left off before the war, and led New York to four World Championships in his final six years.

But it was beginning to be a struggle. More often than not, he battled injuries. More often that not, he came through. Still, it was becoming harder and harder.

In 1949, a bone spur in his left heel forced him to miss 66 games. Yet he still managed to come through in the clutch, helping the Yankees hold off the surging Red Sox and playing a key role in New York's win over the Brooklyn Dodgers in the World Series.

He retired in 1951, telling the Yankee ownership that he didn't want his fans to see him on the downside of his career.

That awareness of his image shaped the rest of his life. After his very public—and very brief—

marriage to Marilyn Monroe, he lived privately. He was elected to the Hall of Fame in 1955. He appeared in 13 All-Star Games in his 13 years in the Majors. He led the American League in batting average twice, in home runs twice, in RBI twice. He was the Most Valuable Player in the league three times, in 1939, 1941 and 1947.

DiMaggio still holds the team record for most home runs by a righthanded hitter— 46 in 1937. His .381 batting average in 1939 is second only to Ruth's .393 in 1923. But numbers don't necessarily define DiMaggio. Writers wax eloquent on his grace afield and at the plate. Teammates spoke of his leadership. Managers always lauded his intelligent play. If he was not the greatest ever, he was the greatest player when measured against the players whom he played against.

After retirement, there was the unfortunate nine-month marriage to Monroe, and a series of mostly successful business ventures. His decision to retain his privacy intrigued many and, ironically, contributed to his status as an American icon, although he certainly had no interest in such a title.

Toward the end of his life, DiMaggio seemed to relax more. He was inevitably a favorite at Old-Timers' games. In the mid-1990s, the Yankees made an Opening Day ritual of DiMaggio throwing out the first ball of the season, and he seemed to have fun with it. He became more outgoing and socialized more with former teammates and their wives.

But he was still a private man. He died in 1998 of complications from cancer, and the baseball world mourned.

Donovan, Michael Berchman (Mike)

HEIGHT: 5'8"   THROWS: RIGHT   BATS: RIGHT   BORN: 10/18/1881 BROOKLYN, NEW YORK   DIED: 2/3/1938 NEW YORK, NEW YORK   POSITIONS PLAYED: 3B, SS

YEAR	TEAM	GAMES	AB	RUNS	HITS	2B	3B	HR	RBI	BB	IBB	SO	HBP	SH	SF	SB	CS	BA	OBA	SA	FA
1904	Cle-A	2	2	0	0	0	0	0	0	0	—	—	0	0	—	0	—	.000	.000	.000	.000
1908	**NY-A**	**5**	**19**	**2**	**5**	**1**	**0**	**0**	**2**	**0**	—	—	**0**	**0**	—	**0**	—	**.263**	**.263**	**.316**	**1.000**
Career average		4	11	1	3	1	0	0	1	0	—	—	0	0	—	0	—	.238	.238	.286	.500
Yankee average		**5**	**19**	**2**	**5**	**1**	**0**	**0**	**2**	**0**	—	—	**0**	**0**	—	**0**	—	**.263**	**.263**	**.316**	**1.000**
Career total		7	21	2	5	1	0	0	2	0	—	—	0	0	—	0	—	.238	.238	.286	.500
Yankee total		**5**	**19**	**2**	**5**	**1**	**0**	**0**	**2**	**0**	—	—	**0**	**0**	—	**0**	—	**.263**	**.263**	**.316**	**1.000**

Dorsett, Brian Richard

HEIGHT: 6'4" THROWS: RIGHT BATS: RIGHT BORN: 4/9/1961 TERRE HAUTE, INDIANA POSITIONS PLAYED: C, 1B

YEAR	TEAM	GAMES	AB	RUNS	HITS	2B	3B	HR	RBI	BB	IBB	SO	HBP	SH	SF	SB	CS	BA	OBA	SA	FA
1987	Cle-A	5	11	2	3	0	0	1	3	0	0	3	1	0	0	0	0	.273	.333	.545	1.000
1988	Cal-A	7	11	0	1	0	0	0	2	1	0	5	0	0	0	0	0	.091	.167	.091	1.000
1989	**NY-A**	**8**	**22**	**3**	**8**	**1**	**0**	**0**	**4**	**1**	**0**	**3**	**0**	**0**	**0**	**0**	**0**	**.364**	**.391**	**.409**	**1.000**
1990	**NY-A**	**14**	**35**	**2**	**5**	**2**	**0**	**0**	**0**	**2**	**0**	**4**	**0**	**0**	**0**	**0**	**0**	**.143**	**.189**	**.200**	**1.000**
1991	SD-N	11	12	0	1	0	0	0	1	0	0	3	0	0	0	0	0	.083	.083	.083	1.000
1993	Cin-N	25	63	7	16	4	0	2	12	3	0	14	0	0	0	0	0	.254	.288	.413	1.000
1994	Cin-N	76	216	21	53	8	0	5	26	21	7	33	1	1	2	0	0	.245	.313	.352	.991
1996	Chi-N	17	41	3	5	0	0	1	3	4	0	8	0	0	1	0	0	.122	.196	.195	1.000
Career average		20	51	5	12	2	0	1	6	4	1	9	0	0	0	0	0	.224	.281	.326	.995
Yankee average		**11**	**29**	**3**	**7**	**2**	**0**	**0**	**2**	**2**	**0**	**4**	**0**	**0**	**0**	**0**	**0**	**.228**	**.267**	**.281**	**1.000**
Career total		163	411	38	92	15	0	9	51	32	7	73	2	1	3	0	0	.224	.281	.326	.995
Yankee total		**22**	**57**	**5**	**13**	**3**	**0**	**0**	**4**	**3**	**0**	**7**	**0**	**0**	**0**	**0**	**0**	**.228**	**.267**	**.281**	**2.000**

Dougherty, Patrick Henry (Patsy)

HEIGHT: 6'2" THROWS: RIGHT BATS: LEFT BORN: 10/27/1876 ANDOVER, NEW YORK   DIED: 4/30/1940 BOLIVAR, NEW YORK   POSITIONS PLAYED: 3B, OF

YEAR	TEAM	GAMES	AB	RUNS	HITS	2B	3B	HR	RBI	BB	IBB	SO	HBP	SH	SF	SB	CS	BA	OBA	SA	FA
1902	Bos-A	108	438	77	150	12	6	0	34	42	—	—	6	3	—	20	—	.342	.407	.397	.899
1903	Bos-A	139	590	107	195	19	12	4	59	33	—	—	6	18	—	35	—	.331	.372	.424	.952
1904	Bos-A	49	195	33	53	5	4	0	4	25	—	—	0	3	—	10	—	.272	.355	.338	.925
1904	**NY-A**	**106**	**452**	**80**	**128**	**13**	**10**	**6**	**22**	**19**	**—**	**—**	**3**	**4**	**—**	**11**	**—**	**.283**	**.316**	**.396**	**.925**
1905	**NY-A**	**116**	**418**	**56**	**110**	**9**	**6**	**3**	**29**	**28**	**—**	**—**	**6**	**7**	**—**	**17**	**—**	**.263**	**.319**	**.335**	**.898**
1906	**NY-A**	**12**	**52**	**3**	**10**	**2**	**0**	**0**	**4**	**0**	**—**	**—**	**0**	**0**	**—**	**0**	**—**	**.192**	**.192**	**.231**	**1.000**
1906	Chi-A	75	253	30	59	9	4	1	27	19	—	—	3	18	—	11	—	.233	.295	.312	.985
1907	Chi-A	148	533	69	144	17	2	1	59	36	—	—	5	17	—	33	—	.270	.322	.315	.946
1908	Chi-A	138	482	68	134	11	6	0	45	58	—	—	10	19	—	47	—	.278	.367	.326	.947
1909	Chi-A	139	491	71	140	23	13	1	55	51	—	—	6	21	—	36	—	.285	.359	.391	.942
1910	Chi-A	127	443	45	110	8	6	1	43	41	—	—	4	4	—	22	—	.248	.318	.300	.923
1911	Chi-A	76	211	39	61	10	9	0	32	26	—	—	5	10	—	19	—	.289	.380	.422	.933
Career average		103	380	57	108	12	7	1	34	32	—	—	5	10	—	22	—	.284	.346	.360	.935
Yankee average		**78**	**307**	**46**	**83**	**8**	**5**	**3**	**18**	**16**	**—**	**—**	**3**	**4**	**—**	**9**	**—**	**.269**	**.311**	**.359**	**1.000**
Career total		1233	4558	678	1294	138	78	17	413	378	—	—	54	124	—	261	—	.284	.346	.360	.935
Yankee total		**234**	**922**	**139**	**248**	**24**	**16**	**9**	**55**	**47**	**—**	**—**	**9**	**11**	**—**	**28**	**—**	**.269**	**.311**	**.359**	**1.000**

Dowd, John Leo

HEIGHT: 5'8" THROWS: RIGHT BATS: RIGHT BORN: 1/3/1891 WEYMOUTH, MASS.   DIED: 1/31/1981 FT. LAUDERDALE, FLA.   POSITIONS PLAYED: SS

YEAR	TEAM	GAMES	AB	RUNS	HITS	2B	3B	HR	RBI	BB	IBB	SO	HBP	SH	SF	SB	CS	BA	OBA	SA	FA
1912	**NY-A**	**10**	**31**	**1**	**6**	**1**	**0**	**0**	**0**	**6**	**—**	**—**	**1**	**0**	**—**	**0**	**—**	**.194**	**.342**	**.226**	**.840**
Career average		10	31	1	6	1	0	0	0	6	—	—	1	0	—	0	—	.194	.342	.226	.840
Yankee average		**10**	**31**	**1**	**6**	**1**	**0**	**0**	**0**	**6**	**—**	**—**	**1**	**0**	**—**	**0**	**—**	**.194**	**.342**	**.226**	**.840**
Career total		10	31	1	6	1	0	0	0	6	—	—	1	0	—	0	—	.194	.342	.226	.840
Yankee total		**10**	**31**	**1**	**6**	**1**	**0**	**0**	**0**	**6**	**—**	**—**	**1**	**0**	**—**	**0**	**—**	**.194**	**.342**	**.226**	**.840**

Doyle, Brian Reed

HEIGHT: 5'10" THROWS: RIGHT BATS: LEFT BORN: 1/26/1955 GLASGOW, KENTUCKY POSITIONS PLAYED: 2B, 3B, SS

YEAR	TEAM	GAMES	AB	RUNS	HITS	2B	3B	HR	RBI	BB	IBB	SO	HBP	SH	SF	SB	CS	BA	OBA	SA	FA
1978	**NY-A**	**39**	**52**	**6**	**10**	**0**	**0**	**0**	**0**	**0**	**0**	**3**	**0**	**2**	**0**	**0**	**3**	**.192**	**.192**	**.192**	**.984**
1979	**NY-A**	**20**	**32**	**2**	**4**	**2**	**0**	**0**	**5**	**3**	**0**	**1**	**0**	**1**	**0**	**0**	**0**	**.125**	**.200**	**.188**	**.944**
1980	**NY-A**	**34**	**75**	**8**	**13**	**1**	**0**	**1**	**5**	**6**	**0**	**7**	**0**	**0**	**0**	**1**	**1**	**.173**	**.235**	**.227**	**.953**
1981	Oak-A	17	40	2	5	0	0	0	3	1	0	2	0	2	0	0	1	.125	.146	.125	1.000
Career average		28	50	5	8	1	0	0	3	3	0	3	0	1	0	0	1	.161	.201	.191	.970
Yankee average		**31**	**53**	**5**	**9**	**1**	**0**	**0**	**3**	**3**	**0**	**4**	**0**	**1**	**0**	**0**	**1**	**.170**	**.214**	**.208**	**.960**
Career total		110	199	18	32	3	0	1	13	10	0	13	0	5	0	1	5	.161	.201	.191	.970
Yankee total		**93**	**159**	**16**	**27**	**3**	**0**	**1**	**10**	**9**	**0**	**11**	**0**	**3**	**0**	**1**	**4**	**.170**	**.214**	**.208**	**.960**

Doyle, John Joseph (Dirty Jack)

HEIGHT: 5'9" THROWS: RIGHT BATS: RIGHT BORN: 10/25/1869 KILLORGLIN, IRL. DIED: 12/31/1958 HOLYOKE, MASS. POSITIONS PLAYED: C, 1B, 2B, 3B, SS, OF

YEAR	TEAM	GAMES	AB	RUNS	HITS	2B	3B	HR	RBI	BB	IBB	SO	HBP	SH	SF	SB	CS	BA	OBA	SA	FA
1889	Clm-AA	11	36	6	10	1	1	0	3	6	—	6	0	—	—	9	—	.278	.381	.361	.897
1890	Clm-AA	77	298	47	80	17	7	2	44	13	—	—	0	—	—	27	—	.268	.299	.393	.887
1891	Cle-N	69	250	43	69	14	4	0	43	26	—	44	3	—	—	24	—	.276	.351	.364	.897
1892	Cle-N	24	88	17	26	4	1	1	14	6	—	10	0	—	—	5	—	.295	.340	.398	.875
1892	NY-N	90	366	61	109	22	1	5	55	18	—	30	3	—	—	42	—	.298	.336	.404	.864
1893	NY-N	82	318	56	102	17	5	1	51	27	—	12	5	—	—	40	—	.321	.383	.415	.919
1894	NY-N	105	422	90	155	30	8	3	100	35	—	3	3	4	—	42	—	.367	.420	.498	.965
1895	NY-N	82	319	52	100	21	3	1	66	24	—	12	2	0	—	35	—	.313	.365	.408	.968
1896	Bal-N	118	487	116	165	29	4	1	101	42	—	15	8	9	—	73	—	.339	.400	.421	.974
1897	Bal-N	114	460	91	163	29	4	2	87	29	—	—	1	2	—	62	—	.354	.394	.448	.979
1898	Was-A	43	177	26	54	2	2	2	26	7	—	—	1	0	—	9	—	.305	.335	.373	.963
1898	NY-N	82	297	42	84	15	3	1	43	12	—	—	3	4	—	14	—	.283	.317	.364	.860
1899	NY-N	118	448	55	134	15	7	3	76	33	—	—	4	3	—	35	—	.299	.353	.384	.976
1900	NY-N	133	505	69	135	24	1	1	66	34	—	—	3	2	—	34	—	.267	.317	.325	.971
1901	Chi-N	75	285	21	66	9	2	0	39	7	—	0	5	2	—	8	—	.232	.263	.277	.973
1902	NY-N	49	186	21	56	13	0	1	19	10	—	—	1	2	—	12	—	.301	.340	.387	.929
1902	Was-A	78	312	52	77	15	2	1	20	29	—	0	0	5	—	6	—	.247	.311	.317	.991
1903	Bro-N	139	524	84	164	27	6	0	91	54	—	0	5	9	—	34	—	.313	.383	.387	.981
1904	Bro-N	8	22	2	5	1	0	0	2	6	—	0	1	0	—	1	—	.227	.414	.273	1.000
1904	Phi-N	66	236	20	52	10	3	1	22	19	—	0	1	3	—	4	—	.220	.281	.301	.977
1905	**NY-A**	**1**	**3**	**0**	**0**	**0**	**0**	**0**	**0**	**0**	**—**	**0**	**0**	**0**	**—**	**0**	**—**	**.000**	**.000**	**.000**	**.833**
Career average		74	288	46	86	15	3	1	46	21	—	6	2	2	—	25	—	.299	.351	.385	.000
Yankee average		**1**	**3**	**0**	**0**	**0**	**0**	**0**	**0**	**0**	**—**	**0**	**0**	**0**	**—**	**0**	**—**	**.000**	**.000**	**.000**	**.833**
Career total		1564	6039	971	1806	315	64	26	968	437	—	132	49	45	—	516	—	.299	.351	.385	.000
Yankee total		**1**	**3**	**0**	**0**	**0**	**0**	**0**	**0**	**0**	**—**	**0**	**0**	**0**	**—**	**0**	**—**	**.000**	**.000**	**.000**	**.833**

Drescher, William Clayton (Dutch *or* Moose)

HEIGHT: 6'2" THROWS: RIGHT BATS: LEFT BORN: 5/23/1921 CONGERS, NEW YORK DIED: 5/15/1968 HAVERSTRAW, NEW YORK POSITIONS PLAYED: C

YEAR	TEAM	GAMES	AB	RUNS	HITS	2B	3B	HR	RBI	BB	IBB	SO	HBP	SH	SF	SB	CS	BA	OBA	SA	FA
1944	NY-A	4	7	0	1	0	0	0	0	0	—	0	0	0	—	0	0	.143	.143	.143	.875
1945	NY-A	48	126	10	34	3	1	0	15	8	—	5	0	4	—	0	2	.270	.313	.310	.991
1946	NY-A	5	6	0	2	1	0	0	1	0	—	0	0	0	—	0	0	.333	.333	.500	1.000
Career average		19	46	3	12	1	0	0	5	3	—	2	0	1	—	0	1	.266	.306	.309	.955
Yankee average		**19**	**46**	**3**	**12**	**1**	**0**	**0**	**5**	**3**	**—**	**2**	**0**	**1**	**—**	**0**	**1**	**.266**	**.306**	**.309**	**.955**
Career total		57	139	10	37	4	1	0	16	8	—	5	0	4	—	0	2	.266	.306	.309	.955
Yankee total		**57**	**139**	**10**	**37**	**4**	**1**	**0**	**16**	**8**	**—**	**5**	**0**	**4**	**—**	**0**	**2**	**.266**	**.306**	**.309**	**.955**

Dugan, Joseph Anthony (Jumpin' Joe)

HEIGHT: 5'11" THROWS: RIGHT BATS: RIGHT BORN: 05/12/1897 MAHANOY CITY, PENN. DIED: 7/7/1982 NORWOOD, MASS. POSITIONS PLAYED: 2B, 3B, SS, OF

YEAR	TEAM	GAMES	AB	RUNS	HITS	2B	3B	HR	RBI	BB	IBB	SO	HBP	SH	SF	SB	CS	BA	OBA	SA	FA
1917	Phi-A	43	134	9	26	8	0	0	16	3	—	16	3	7	—	0	—	.194	.229	.254	.917
1918	Phi-A	121	411	26	80	11	3	3	34	16	—	55	3	17	—	4	—	.195	.230	.258	.930
1919	Phi-A	104	387	25	105	17	2	1	30	11	—	30	5	9	—	9	—	.271	.300	.333	.889
1920	Phi-A	123	491	65	158	40	5	3	60	19	—	51	3	8	—	5	8	.322	.351	.442	.956
1921	Phi-A	119	461	54	136	22	6	10	58	28	—	45	5	13	—	5	1	.295	.342	.434	.953
1922	Bos-A	84	341	45	98	22	3	3	38	9	—	28	1	10	—	2	3	.287	.308	.396	.943
1922	**NY-A**	**60**	**252**	**44**	**72**	**9**	**1**	**3**	**25**	**13**	**—**	**21**	**4**	**12**	**—**	**1**	**0**	**.286**	**.331**	**.365**	**.907**
1923	**NY-A**	**146**	**644**	**111**	**182**	**30**	**7**	**7**	**67**	**25**	**—**	**41**	**2**	**13**	**—**	**4**	**2**	**.283**	**.311**	**.384**	**.974**
1924	**NY-A**	**148**	**610**	**105**	**184**	**31**	**7**	**3**	**56**	**31**	**—**	**33**	**5**	**25**	**—**	**1**	**2**	**.302**	**.341**	**.390**	**.962**
1925	**NY-A**	**102**	**404**	**50**	**118**	**19**	**4**	**0**	**31**	**19**	**—**	**20**	**4**	**14**	**—**	**2**	**4**	**.292**	**.330**	**.359**	**.970**
1926	**NY-A**	**123**	**434**	**39**	**125**	**19**	**5**	**1**	**64**	**25**	**—**	**16**	**1**	**23**	**—**	**2**	**4**	**.288**	**.328**	**.362**	**.955**
1927	**NY-A**	**112**	**387**	**44**	**104**	**24**	**3**	**2**	**43**	**27**	**—**	**37**	**3**	**12**	**—**	**1**	**4**	**.269**	**.321**	**.362**	**.938**
1928	**NY-A**	**94**	**312**	**33**	**86**	**15**	**0**	**6**	**34**	**16**	**—**	**15**	**3**	**8**	**—**	**1**	**0**	**.276**	**.317**	**.381**	**.952**
1929	Bos-N	60	125	14	38	10	0	0	15	8	—	8	0	6	—	0	—	.304	.346	.384	.813
1931	Det-A	8	17	1	4	0	0	0	0	0	—	3	0	0	—	0	—	.235	.235	.235	.900
Career average		96	361	44	101	18	3	3	38	17	—	28	3	12	—	2	2	.280	.317	.372	.931
Yankee average		**112**	**435**	**61**	**124**	**21**	**4**	**3**	**46**	**22**	**—**	**26**	**3**	**15**	**—**	**2**	**2**	**.286**	**.326**	**.374**	**.960**
Career total		1447	5410	665	1516	277	46	42	571	250	—	419	42	177	—	37	28	.280	.317	.372	.931
Yankee total		**785**	**3043**	**426**	**871**	**147**	**27**	**22**	**320**	**156**	**—**	**183**	**22**	**107**	**—**	**12**	**16**	**.286**	**.326**	**.374**	**.960**

Joseph Anthony "Jumpin' Joe" Dugan, 3b-2b-ss, 1922–28

As acrobatic as he often was around third base, Joe Dugan picked up his nickname more for his abrupt and unannounced leaves of absence from the Philadelphia A's in his early years than his abilities afield.

Dugan, born on May 12, 1897, in Mahanoy City, Pennsylvania, was still in high school when the A's manager, Connie Mack, offered him a contract in 1916. His family wanted him to go to college, and Dugan tried Holy Cross College in Worcester for a while. But the prospect of making money playing baseball was too attractive. He reported to the A's in 1917.

He was a shortstop for his first three years before Mack moved him to third base in 1920. Dugan did fairly well, but by his own admission, he didn't like Philadelphia, and he didn't like losing, which is what the A's were doing a lot of in those days. He jumped the team about a dozen times in five years.

Mack tired of his act by 1921 and shipped him over to Boston. The same year, the Red Sox sent him to the Yankees, who needed to replace aging star Frank "Home Run" Baker.

Dugan stepped in immediately for Baker and hit .286. His best year offensively came in 1924 when he hit .302 with 31 doubles.

Baker was a great hitter, better by far than Dugan, but Jumpin' Joe earned his paycheck defensively. He was tops among third basemen in fielding percentage in 1923 and among the league leaders for the rest of his career with the Yankees.

Dugan was a gregarious sort who made friends quickly. Babe Ruth reportedly liked him immediately. Along with outfielder Bob Meusel, he became one of Ruth's early pals.

In 1921 or 1922, Dugan tore cartilage in his left knee while sliding into second base at the Polo Grounds. He had had an operation to repair it (or to repair it as much as it could be repaired in the 1920s), but the knee bothered him throughout the rest of his career.

By 1928, the knee was becoming a problem. He played in only 94 games, and the Yankees began looking for his replacement. He was waived by the Yankees in 1929 and picked up by the Boston Braves, as a part-time player. He retired for good in 1931 after a brief stint with the Tigers. He died in Norwood, Massachusetts, in 1982.

Duncan, Mariano BORN MARIANO DUNCAN (NALASCO)

HEIGHT: 6'0"   THROWS: RIGHT   BATS: RIGHT   BORN: 3/13/1963 SAN PEDRO DE MACORIS, DOMINICAN REPUBLIC   POSITIONS PLAYED: 1B, 2B, 3B, SS, OF

YEAR	TEAM	GAMES	AB	RUNS	HITS	2B	3B	HR	RBI	BB	IBB	SO	HBP	SH	SF	SB	CS	BA	OBA	SA	FA
1985	LA-N	142	562	74	137	24	6	6	39	38	4	113	3	13	4	38	8	.244	.293	.340	.969
1986	LA-N	109	407	47	93	7	0	8	30	30	1	78	2	5	1	48	13	.229	.284	.305	.951
1987	LA-N	76	261	31	56	8	1	6	18	17	1	62	2	6	1	11	1	.215	.267	.322	1.000
1989	LA-N	49	84	9	21	5	1	0	8	0	0	15	2	1	0	3	3	.250	.267	.333	.800
1989	Cin-N	45	174	23	43	10	1	3	13	8	0	36	3	1	0	6	2	.247	.292	.368	.943
1990	Cin-N	125	435	67	133	22	11	10	55	24	4	67	4	4	4	13	7	.306	.345	.476	.914
1991	Cin-N	100	333	46	86	7	4	12	40	12	0	57	3	5	3	5	4	.258	.288	.411	1.000
1992	Phi-N	142	574	71	153	40	3	8	50	17	0	108	5	5	4	23	3	.267	.292	.389	.969
1993	Phi-N	124	496	68	140	26	4	11	73	12	0	88	4	4	2	6	5	.282	.304	.417	.969
1994	Phi-N	88	347	49	93	22	1	8	48	17	1	72	4	2	4	10	2	.268	.306	.406	1.000
1995	Phi-N	52	196	20	56	12	1	3	23	0	0	43	1	1	3	1	2	.286	.285	.403	.980
1995	Cin-N	29	69	16	20	2	1	3	13	5	0	19	0	0	2	0	1	.290	.329	.478	1.000
1996	**NY-A**	**109**	**400**	**62**	**136**	**34**	**3**	**8**	**56**	**9**	**1**	**77**	**0**	**1**	**5**	**2**	**1**	**.340**	**.352**	**.500**	**1.000**
1997	**NY-A**	**50**	**172**	**16**	**42**	**8**	**0**	**1**	**13**	**6**	**0**	**39**	**0**	**1**	**0**	**2**	**1**	**.244**	**.270**	**.308**	**.976**
1997	Tor-A	39	167	20	38	6	0	0	12	6	0	39	3	0	0	4	2	.228	.267	.263	.984
Career average		85	312	41	83	16	2	6	33	13	1	61	2	3	2	12	4	.267	.300	.388	.964
Yankee average		**80**	**286**	**39**	**89**	**21**	**2**	**5**	**35**	**8**	**1**	**58**	**1**	**2**	**3**	**3**	**2**	**.311**	**.327**	**.442**	**.988**
Career total		1279	4677	619	1247	233	37	87	491	201	12	913	37	50	33	174	57	.267	.300	.388	.964
Yankee total		**159**	**572**	**78**	**178**	**42**	**3**	**9**	**69**	**15**	**1**	**116**	**1**	**3**	**5**	**6**	**4**	**.311**	**.327**	**.442**	**.988**

Durocher, Leo Ernest (The Lip)

HEIGHT: 5'10"   THROWS: RIGHT   BATS: RIGHT   BORN: 7/27/1905 W.SPRINGFIELD, MASS.   DIED: 10/7/1991 PALM SPRINGS, CALIF.   POSITIONS PLAYED: 2B, 3B, SS

YEAR	TEAM	GAMES	AB	RUNS	HITS	2B	3B	HR	RBI	BB	IBB	SO	HBP	SH	SF	SB	CS	BA	OBA	SA	FA
1925	**NY-A**	**2**	**1**	**1**	**0**	**0**	**0**	**0**	**0**	**0**	—	**0**	**0**	**0**	—	**0**	**0**	**.000**	**.000**	**.000**	**.000**
1928	**NY-A**	**102**	**296**	**46**	**80**	**8**	**6**	**0**	**31**	**22**	—	**52**	**3**	**7**	—	**1**	**4**	**.270**	**.327**	**.338**	**.940**
1929	**NY-A**	**106**	**341**	**53**	**84**	**4**	**5**	**0**	**32**	**34**	—	**33**	**3**	**7**	—	**3**	**1**	**.246**	**.320**	**.287**	**.984**
1930	Cin-N	119	354	31	86	15	3	3	32	20	—	45	2	9	—	0	0	.243	.287	.328	1.000
1931	Cin-N	121	361	26	82	11	5	1	29	18	—	32	0	6	—	0	0	.227	.264	.294	.965
1932	Cin-N	143	457	43	99	22	5	1	33	36	—	40	1	10	—	3	0	.217	.275	.293	.960
1933	Cin-N	16	51	6	11	1	0	1	3	4	—	5	0	3	—	0	0	.216	.273	.294	.953
1933	StL-N	123	395	45	102	18	4	2	41	26	—	32	1	8	—	3	0	.258	.306	.339	.961
1934	StL-N	146	500	62	130	26	5	3	70	33	—	40	2	6	—	2	0	.260	.308	.350	.957
1935	StL-N	143	513	62	136	23	5	8	78	29	—	46	0	4	—	4	0	.265	.304	.376	.963
1936	StL-N	136	510	57	146	22	3	1	58	29	—	47	2	8	—	3	0	.286	.327	.347	.971
1937	StL-N	135	477	46	97	11	3	1	47	38	—	36	0	5	—	6	0	.203	.262	.245	.959
1938	Bro-N	141	479	41	105	18	5	1	56	47	—	30	3	3	—	3	0	.219	.293	.284	.966
1939	Bro-N	116	390	42	108	21	6	1	34	27	—	24	1	3	—	2	0	.277	.325	.369	1.000
1940	Bro-N	62	160	10	37	9	1	1	14	12	—	13	0	3	—	1	0	.231	.285	.319	.929
1941	Bro-N	18	42	2	12	1	0	0	6	1	—	3	0	1	—	0	0	.286	.302	.310	.917
1943	Bro-N	6	18	1	4	0	0	0	1	1	—	2	0	0	—	0	0	.222	.263	.222	1.000
1945	Bro-N	2	5	1	1	0	0	0	2	0	—	0	0	0	—	0	0	.200	.200	.200	1.000
Career average		91	297	32	73	12	3	1	32	21	0	27	1	5	0	2	0	.247	.299	.320	.967
Yankee average		**70**	**213**	**33**	**55**	**4**	**4**	**0**	**21**	**19**	**0**	**28**	**2**	**5**	**0**	**1**	**2**	**.257**	**.323**	**.310**	**.962**
Career total		1637	5350	575	1320	210	56	24	567	377	0	480	18	82	0	31	5	.247	.299	.320	.967
Yankee total		**210**	**638**	**100**	**164**	**12**	**11**	**0**	**63**	**56**	**0**	**85**	**6**	**14**	**0**	**4**	**5**	**.257**	**.323**	**.310**	**.962**

Durst, Cedric Montgomery

HEIGHT: 5'11"   THROWS: LEFT   BATS: LEFT   BORN: 08/23/1896 AUSTIN, TEXAS   DIED: 2/16/1971 SAN DIEGO, CALIFORNIA   POSITIONS PLAYED: 1B, OF

YEAR	TEAM	GAMES	AB	RUNS	HITS	2B	3B	HR	RBI	BB	IBB	SO	HBP	SH	SF	SB	CS	BA	OBA	SA	FA
1922	StL-A	15	12	5	4	1	0	0	0	0	—	1	0	1	—	0	0	.333	.333	.417	.857
1923	StL-A	45	85	12	18	2	0	5	11	8	—	14	0	2	—	0	0	.212	.280	.412	.955
1926	StL-A	80	219	32	52	7	5	3	16	22	—	19	1	10	—	0	5	.237	.310	.356	.980
1927	**NY-A**	**65**	**129**	**18**	**32**	**4**	**3**	**0**	**25**	**6**	—	**7**	**0**	**7**	—	**0**	**3**	**.248**	**.281**	**.326**	**.980**
1928	**NY-A**	**74**	**135**	**18**	**34**	**2**	**1**	**2**	**10**	**7**	—	**9**	**0**	**4**	—	**1**	**0**	**.252**	**.289**	**.326**	**1.000**
1929	**NY-A**	**92**	**202**	**32**	**52**	**3**	**3**	**4**	**31**	**15**	—	**25**	**0**	**5**	—	**3**	**2**	**.257**	**.309**	**.361**	**1.000**
1930	**NY-A**	**8**	**19**	**0**	**3**	**1**	**0**	**0**	**5**	**0**	—	**1**	**0**	**0**	—	**0**	**0**	**.158**	**.158**	**.211**	**1.000**
1930	Bos-A	102	302	29	74	19	5	1	24	17	—	24	2	9	—	3	1	.245	.290	.351	.968
Career average		60	138	18	34	5	2	2	15	9	—	13	0	5	—	1	1	.244	.294	.351	.000
Yankee average		**60**	**121**	**17**	**30**	**3**	**2**	**2**	**18**	**7**	—	**11**	**0**	**4**	—	**1**	**1**	**.249**	**.290**	**.336**	**.000**
Career total		481	1103	146	269	39	17	15	122	75	—	100	3	38	—	7	11	.244	.294	.351	.000
Yankee total		**239**	**485**	**68**	**121**	**10**	**7**	**6**	**71**	**28**	—	**42**	**0**	**16**	—	**4**	**5**	**.249**	**.290**	**.336**	**.000**

Easler, Michael Anthony (The Hit Man)

HEIGHT: 6'1"   THROWS: RIGHT   BATS: LEFT   BORN: 11/29/1950 CLEVELAND, OHIO   POSITIONS PLAYED: 1B, OF

YEAR	TEAM	GAMES	AB	RUNS	HITS	2B	3B	HR	RBI	BB	IBB	SO	HBP	SH	SF	SB	CS	BA	OBA	SA	FA
1973	Hou-N	6	7	1	0	0	0	0	0	2	1	4	0	0	0	0	0	.000	.222	.000	.500
1974	Hou-N	15	15	0	1	0	0	0	0	0	0	5	0	0	0	0	0	.067	.067	.067	.000
1975	Hou-N	5	5	0	0	0	0	0	0	0	0	1	0	0	0	0	0	.000	.000	.000	.000
1976	Cal-A	21	54	6	13	1	1	0	4	2	1	11	0	1	2	1	1	.241	.259	.296	.000
1977	Pit-N	10	18	3	8	2	0	1	5	0	0	1	0	0	1	0	0	.444	.421	.722	1.000
1979	Pit-N	55	54	8	15	1	1	2	11	8	0	13	0	0	0	0	1	.278	.371	.444	.000
1980	Pit-N	132	393	66	133	27	3	21	74	43	6	65	0	0	9	5	9	.338	.396	.583	.986
1981	Pit-N	95	339	43	97	18	5	7	42	24	7	45	0	0	6	4	1	.286	.328	.431	.980
1982	Pit-N	142	475	52	131	27	2	15	58	40	12	85	6	1	4	1	1	.276	.337	.436	.973
1983	Pit-N	115	381	44	117	17	2	10	54	22	1	64	3	1	1	4	2	.307	.349	.441	.965
1984	Bos-A	156	601	87	188	31	5	27	91	58	4	134	4	1	2	1	1	.313	.376	.516	.976
1985	Bos-A	155	568	71	149	29	4	16	74	53	1	129	3	0	7	0	1	.262	.325	.412	.914
1986	**NY-A**	**146**	**490**	**64**	**148**	**26**	**2**	**14**	**78**	**49**	**13**	**87**	**0**	**2**	**5**	**3**	**2**	**.302**	**.362**	**.449**	**.958**
1987	Phi-N	33	110	7	31	4	0	1	10	6	0	20	0	0	1	0	1	.282	.316	.345	.981
1987	**NY-A**	**65**	**167**	**13**	**47**	**6**	**0**	**4**	**21**	**14**	**0**	**32**	**1**	**0**	**2**	**1**	**0**	**.281**	**.341**	**.389**	**1.000**
Career average		77	245	31	72	13	2	8	35	21	3	46	1	0	3	1	2	.293	.349	.454	.923
Yankee average		**106**	**329**	**39**	**98**	**16**	**1**	**9**	**50**	**32**	**7**	**60**	**1**	**1**	**4**	**2**	**1**	**.297**	**.356**	**.434**	**.958**
Career total		1151	3677	465	1078	189	25	118	522	321	46	696	17	6	40	20	26	.293	.349	.454	.923
Yankee total		**211**	**657**	**77**	**195**	**32**	**2**	**18**	**99**	**63**	**13**	**119**	**1**	**2**	**7**	**4**	**2**	**.297**	**.356**	**.434**	**.958**

Edwards, Howard Rodney (Doc)

HEIGHT: 6'2" THROWS: RIGHT BATS: RIGHT BORN: 12/10/1936 RED JACKET, WEST VIRGINIA POSITIONS PLAYED: C, 1B

YEAR	TEAM	GAMES	AB	RUNS	HITS	2B	3B	HR	RBI	BB	IBB	SO	HBP	SH	SF	SB	CS	BA	OBA	SA	FA
1962	Cle-A	53	143	13	39	6	0	3	9	9	0	14	2	0	0	0	0	.273	.325	.378	.992
1963	Cle-A	10	31	6	8	2	0	0	0	2	2	6	0	0	0	0	0	.258	.303	.323	.988
1963	KC-A	71	240	16	60	12	0	6	35	11	6	23	2	1	1	0	1	.250	.289	.375	.987
1964	KC-A	97	294	25	66	10	0	5	28	13	0	40	3	0	0	0	1	.224	.265	.310	.983
1965	KC-A	6	20	1	3	0	0	0	0	1	0	2	0	0	0	0	0	.150	.190	.150	1.000
1965	**NY-A**	**45**	**100**	**3**	**19**	**3**	**0**	**1**	**9**	**13**	**6**	**14**	**1**	**0**	**0**	**1**	**2**	**.190**	**.289**	**.250**	**.986**
1970	Phi-N	35	78	5	21	0	0	0	6	4	3	10	1	3	0	0	0	.269	.313	.269	.970
Career average		45	129	10	31	5	0	2	12	8	2	16	1	1	0	0	1	.238	.287	.325	.987
Yankee average		**45**	**100**	**3**	**19**	**3**	**0**	**1**	**9**	**13**	**6**	**14**	**1**	**0**	**0**	**1**	**2**	**.190**	**.289**	**.250**	**.986**
Career total		317	906	69	216	33	0	15	87	53	17	109	9	4	1	1	4	.238	.287	.325	.987
Yankee total		**45**	**100**	**3**	**19**	**3**	**0**	**1**	**9**	**13**	**6**	**14**	**1**	**0**	**0**	**1**	**2**	**.190**	**.289**	**.250**	**.986**

Eenhoorn, Robert Franciscus

HEIGHT: 6'3" THROWS: RIGHT BATS: RIGHT BORN: 2/9/1968 ROTTERDAM, THE NETHERLANDS POSITIONS PLAYED: 2B, 3B, SS

YEAR	TEAM	GAMES	AB	RUNS	HITS	2B	3B	HR	RBI	BB	IBB	SO	HBP	SH	SF	SB	CS	BA	OBA	SA	FA
1994	**NY-A**	**3**	**4**	**1**	**2**	**1**	**0**	**0**	**0**	**0**	**0**	**0**	**0**	**0**	**0**	**0**	**0**	**.500**	**.500**	**.750**	**1.000**
1995	**NY-A**	**5**	**14**	**1**	**2**	**1**	**0**	**0**	**2**	**1**	**0**	**3**	**0**	**0**	**0**	**0**	**0**	**.143**	**.200**	**.214**	**1.000**
1996	**NY-A**	**12**	**14**	**2**	**1**	**0**	**0**	**0**	**2**	**2**	**0**	**3**	**0**	**1**	**2**	**0**	**0**	**.071**	**.167**	**.071**	**1.000**
1996	Cal-A	6	15	1	4	0	0	0	0	0	0	2	0	0	0	0	0	.267	.267	.267	.889
1997	Ana-A	11	20	2	7	1	0	1	6	0	0	2	0	0	1	0	0	.350	.333	.550	.833
Career average		7	13	1	3	1	0	0	2	1	0	2	0	0	1	0	0	.239	.260	.328	.944
Yankee average		**7**	**11**	**1**	**2**	**1**	**0**	**0**	**1**	**1**	**0**	**2**	**0**	**0**	**1**	**0**	**0**	**.156**	**.216**	**.219**	**1.000**
Career total		37	67	7	16	3	0	1	10	3	0	10	0	1	3	0	0	.239	.260	.328	.944
Yankee total		**20**	**32**	**4**	**5**	**2**	**0**	**0**	**4**	**3**	**0**	**6**	**0**	**1**	**2**	**0**	**0**	**.156**	**.216**	**.219**	**1.000**

Elberfeld, Norman Arthur (The Tabasco Kid)

HEIGHT: 5'7" THROWS: RIGHT BATS: RIGHT BORN: 04/13/1875 POMEROY, OHIO DIED: 1/13/1944 CHATTANOOGA, TENNESSEE POSITIONS PLAYED: SS, 2B, 3B

YEAR	TEAM	GAMES	AB	RUNS	HITS	2B	3B	HR	RBI	BB	IBB	SO	HBP	SH	SF	SB	CS	BA	OBA	SA	FA
1898	Phi-R	14	38	1	9	4	0	0	7	5	—	—	7	2	—	0	—	.237	.420	.342	.795
1899	Cin-R	41	138	23	36	4	2	0	22	15	—	—	11	2	—	5	—	.261	.319	.319	.882
1901	Det-A	121	432	76	133	21	11	3	76	57	—	—	7	12	—	23	—	.308	.397	.428	.907
1902	Det-A	130	488	70	127	17	6	1	64	55	—	—	11	8	—	6	—	.260	.348	.326	.921
1903	Det-A	35	132	29	45	5	3	0	19	11	—	—	5	1	—	6	—	.341	.412	.424	1.000
1903	**NY-A**	**90**	**349**	**49**	**100**	**18**	**5**	**0**	**45**	**22**	**—**	**—**	**10**	**4**	**—**	**16**	**—**	**.287**	**.346**	**.367**	**.919**
1904	**NY-A**	**122**	**445**	**55**	**117**	**13**	**5**	**2**	**46**	**37**	**—**	**—**	**13**	**16**	**—**	**18**	**—**	**.263**	**.337**	**.328**	**.933**
1905	**NY-A**	**111**	**390**	**48**	**102**	**18**	**2**	**0**	**53**	**23**	**—**	**—**	**16**	**20**	**—**	**18**	**—**	**.262**	**.329**	**.318**	**.908**
1906	**NY-A**	**99**	**346**	**59**	**106**	**11**	**5**	**2**	**31**	**30**	**—**	**—**	**10**	**7**	**—**	**19**	**—**	**.306**	**.378**	**.384**	**.925**
1907	**NY-A**	**120**	**447**	**61**	**121**	**17**	**6**	**0**	**51**	**36**	**—**	**—**	**13**	**9**	**—**	**22**	**—**	**.271**	**.343**	**.336**	**.930**
1908	**NY-A**	**19**	**56**	**11**	**11**	**3**	**0**	**0**	**5**	**6**	**—**	**—**	**5**	**2**	**—**	**1**	**—**	**.196**	**.328**	**.250**	**.916**
1909	**NY-A**	**106**	**379**	**47**	**90**	**9**	**5**	**0**	**26**	**28**	**—**	**—**	**14**	**10**	**—**	**23**	**—**	**.237**	**.314**	**.288**	**.956**
1910	Was-A	127	455	53	114	9	5	0	42	35	—	—	13	12	—	19	—	.251	.322	.292	.943
1911	Was-A	127	404	58	110	19	4	0	47	65	—	—	25	13	—	24	—	.272	.405	.339	.927
1914	Bro-N	30	62	7	14	1	0	0	1	2	—	4	5	1	—	0	—	.226	.304	.242	1.000
Career average		86	304	43	82	11	4	1	36	28	—	—	11	8	0	14	—	.271	.355	.339	.924
Yankee average		**95**	**345**	**47**	**92**	**13**	**4**	**1**	**37**	**26**	**—**	**—**	**12**	**10**	**—**	**17**	**—**	**.268**	**.340**	**.333**	**.927**
Career total		1292	4561	647	1235	169	56	10	535	427	—	4	165	119	0	213	—	.271	.355	.339	.924
Yankee total		**667**	**2412**	**330**	**647**	**89**	**28**	**4**	**257**	**182**	**—**	**—**	**81**	**68**	**—**	**117**	**—**	**.268**	**.340**	**.333**	**.927**

Elliott, Eugene Birminghouse

HEIGHT: 5'7" THROWS: RIGHT BATS: LEFT BORN: 2/08/1889 FAYETTE CITY, PENN. DIED: 1/5/1976 HUNTINGDON, PENN. POSITIONS PLAYED: 3B, OF

YEAR	TEAM	GAMES	AB	RUNS	HITS	2B	3B	HR	RBI	BB	IBB	SO	HBP	SH	SF	SB	CS	BA	OBA	SA	FA
1911	**NY-A**	**5**	**13**	**1**	**1**	**1**	**0**	**0**	**1**	**2**	**—**	**—**	**0**	**1**	**—**	**0**	**—**	**.077**	**.200**	**.154**	**.000**
Career average		5	13	1	1	1	0	0	1	2	—	—	0	1	—	0	—	.077	.200	.154	.000
Yankee average		**5**	**13**	**1**	**1**	**1**	**0**	**0**	**1**	**2**	**—**	**—**	**0**	**1**	**—**	**0**	**—**	**.077**	**.200**	**.154**	**.000**
Career total		5	13	1	1	1	0	0	1	2	—	—	0	1	—	0	—	.077	.200	.154	.000
Yankee total		**5**	**13**	**1**	**1**	**1**	**0**	**0**	**1**	**2**	**—**	**—**	**0**	**1**	**—**	**0**	**—**	**.077**	**.200**	**.154**	**.000**

Norman Arthur "The Tabasco Kid" Elberfeld, ss-3b-2b, 1903–09

The 5 foot 5 inch Elberfeld was one of the toughest players in baseball at the turn of the century. How tough? Well, he once stopped Ty Cobb from stealing second base by smashing his knee into Cobb's neck and then shoving Cobb's face into the dirt as Cobb slid toward him.

Elberfeld, dubbed "The Tabasco Kid" for his hot temper, was born in 1875 in Pomeroy, Ohio. He debuted in the major leagues with the Philadelphia Phillies in 1898. After a stint with the Cincinnati Reds, he became a regular with the Tigers in 1901, hitting .308 with 21 doubles and 23 stolen bases. He also led the Tigers in putouts by a shortstop. For their part, the Tigers led the league in ballplayers with "Kid" as their nickname—as Elberfeld's infield partner at second base was William "Kid" Gleason.

Elberfeld was traded early in the 1903 season to the New York Highlanders, where he led the league's third basemen in total chances that year.

He was becoming well-known for his feistiness and his toughness. He took great pride in never (well, rarely, anyway) shying away from a high-sliding base runner at second base, especially while trying to turn a double play. And after the game, he was known for cauterizing his spike wounds with straight whiskey.

He also perfected the art of leaning into a pitch to be hit by it and therefore reach base.

In 1906 the Highlanders came within three games of the first-place Chicago White Sox, and Elberfeld had his best year, hitting .306, which was second on the team behind first baseman Hal Chase.

An injury in 1908 limited him to only 19 games, and the Highlanders had one of their worst years ever. He played one more year in New York, hitting .237 in a part-time role at both shortstop and third base. But knowing he was on his way out, he worked patiently with the rookie third baseman, Jimmy Austin, to groom him for the position.

Elberfeld had stints with the Senators and Boston Braves before retiring in 1914. He died in 1944 in Tennessee.

Ellis, John Charles

HEIGHT: 6'2" THROWS: RIGHT BATS: RIGHT BORN: 8/21/1948 NEW LONDON, CONNECTICUT POSITIONS PLAYED: C, 1B

YEAR	TEAM	GAMES	AB	RUNS	HITS	2B	3B	HR	RBI	BB	IBB	SO	HBP	SH	SF	SB	CS	BA	OBA	SA	FA
1969	**NY-A**	**22**	**62**	**2**	**18**	**4**	**0**	**1**	**8**	**1**	**0**	**11**	**1**	**0**	**1**	**0**	**2**	**.290**	**.308**	**.403**	**.978**
1970	**NY-A**	**78**	**226**	**24**	**56**	**12**	**1**	**7**	**29**	**18**	**0**	**47**	**2**	**0**	**3**	**0**	**1**	**.248**	**.305**	**.403**	**.992**
1971	**NY-A**	**83**	**238**	**16**	**58**	**12**	**1**	**3**	**34**	**23**	**5**	**42**	**6**	**1**	**3**	**0**	**0**	**.244**	**.322**	**.340**	**.990**
1972	**NY-A**	**52**	**136**	**13**	**40**	**5**	**1**	**5**	**25**	**8**	**0**	**22**	**0**	**0**	**0**	**0**	**0**	**.294**	**.333**	**.456**	**.965**
1973	Cle-A	127	437	59	118	12	2	14	68	46	2	57	3	1	7	0	0	.270	.339	.403	.984
1974	Cle-A	128	477	58	136	23	6	10	64	32	3	53	1	1	2	1	2	.285	.330	.421	.992
1975	Cle-A	92	296	22	68	11	1	7	32	14	2	33	2	0	4	0	1	.230	.266	.345	.976
1976	Tex-A	11	31	4	13	2	0	1	8	0	0	4	0	0	0	0	0	.419	.419	.581	1.000
1977	Tex-A	49	119	7	28	7	0	4	15	8	2	26	0	0	0	0	0	.235	.283	.395	1.000
1978	Tex-A	34	94	7	23	4	0	3	17	6	0	20	0	1	3	0	1	.245	.282	.383	.958
1979	Tex-A	111	316	33	90	12	0	12	61	15	1	55	2	0	4	2	2	.285	.318	.437	1.000
1980	Tex-A	73	182	12	43	9	1	1	23	14	1	23	1	0	3	3	0	.236	.290	.313	1.000
1981	Tex-A	23	58	2	8	3	0	1	7	5	1	10	1	0	0	0	1	.138	.219	.241	.993
Career average		68	206	20	54	9	1	5	30	15	1	31	1	0	2	0	1	.262	.312	.392	.987
Yankee average		**59**	**166**	**14**	**43**	**8**	**1**	**4**	**24**	**13**	**1**	**31**	**2**	**0**	**2**	**0**	**1**	**.260**	**.317**	**.391**	**.981**
Career total		883	2672	259	699	116	13	69	391	190	17	403	19	4	30	6	10	.262	.312	.392	.987
Yankee total		**235**	**662**	**55**	**172**	**33**	**3**	**16**	**96**	**50**	**5**	**122**	**9**	**1**	**7**	**0**	**3**	**.260**	**.317**	**.391**	**.981**

Elster, Kevin Daniel

HEIGHT: 6'2" THROWS: RIGHT BATS: RIGHT BORN: 8/3/1964 SAN PEDRO, CALIFORNIA POSITIONS PLAYED: SS

YEAR	TEAM	GAMES	AB	RUNS	HITS	2B	3B	HR	RBI	BB	IBB	SO	HBP	SH	SF	SB	CS	BA	OBA	SA	FA
1986	NY-N	19	30	3	5	1	0	0	0	3	1	8	0	0	0	0	0	.167	.242	.200	.962
1987	NY-N	5	10	1	4	2	0	0	1	0	0	1	0	0	0	0	0	.400	.400	.600	.909
1988	NY-N	149	406	41	87	11	1	9	37	35	12	47	3	6	0	2	0	.214	.282	.313	.977
1989	NY-N	151	458	52	106	25	2	10	55	34	11	77	2	6	8	4	3	.231	.283	.360	.976
1990	NY-N	92	314	36	65	20	1	9	45	30	2	54	1	1	6	2	0	.207	.274	.363	.960
1991	NY-N	115	348	33	84	16	2	6	36	40	6	53	1	1	4	2	3	.241	.318	.351	.970
1992	NY-N	6	18	0	4	0	0	0	0	0	0	2	0	0	0	0	0	.222	.222	.222	1.000
1994	**NY-A**	**7**	**20**	**0**	**0**	**0**	**0**	**0**	**0**	**1**	**0**	**6**	**0**	**0**	**0**	**0**	**0**	**.000**	**.048**	**.000**	**1.000**
1995	**NY-A**	**10**	**17**	**1**	**2**	**1**	**0**	**0**	**0**	**1**	**0**	**5**	**0**	**0**	**0**	**0**	**0**	**.118**	**.167**	**.176**	**1.000**
1995	Phi-N	26	53	10	11	4	1	1	9	7	1	14	1	2	2	0	0	.208	.302	.377	1.000
1996	Tex-A	157	515	79	130	32	2	24	99	52	1	138	2	16	11	4	1	.252	.317	.462	.981
1997	Pit-N	39	138	14	31	6	2	7	25	21	0	39	1	2	2	0	2	.225	.327	.449	.994
1998	Tex-A	84	297	33	69	10	1	8	37	33	0	66	0	2	2	0	2	.232	.307	.354	.976
Career average		66	202	23	46	10	1	6	26	20	3	39	1	3	3	1	1	.228	.296	.370	.977
Yankee average		**9**	**19**	**1**	**1**	**1**	**0**	**0**	**0**	**1**	**0**	**6**	**0**	**0**	**0**	**0**	**0**	**.054**	**.103**	**.081**	**1.000**
Career total		860	2624	303	598	128	12	74	344	257	34	510	11	37	35	14	11	.228	.296	.370	.977
Yankee total		**17**	**37**	**1**	**2**	**1**	**0**	**0**	**0**	**2**	**0**	**11**	**0**	**1**	**0**	**0**	**0**	**.054**	**.103**	**.081**	**1.000**

Engle, Arthur Clyde (Hack)

HEIGHT: 5'10" THROWS: RIGHT BATS: RIGHT BORN: 03/19/1884 DAYTON, OHIO DIED: 12/26/1939 BOSTON, MASSACHUSETTS POSITIONS PLAYED: 1B, 2B, SS

YEAR	TEAM	GAMES	AB	RUNS	HITS	2B	3B	HR	RBI	BB	IBB	SO	HBP	SH	SF	SB	CS	BA	OBA	SA	FA
1909	**NY-A**	**135**	**492**	**66**	**137**	**20**	**5**	**3**	**71**	**47**	**—**	**—**	**5**	**19**	**—**	**18**	**—**	**.278**	**.347**	**.358**	**.946**
1910	**NY-A**	**5**	**13**	**0**	**3**	**0**	**0**	**0**	**0**	**2**	**—**	**—**	**0**	**0**	**—**	**1**	**—**	**.231**	**.333**	**.231**	**.857**
1910	Bos-A	106	363	59	96	18	7	2	38	31	—	—	2	12	—	12	—	.264	.326	.369	.915
1911	Bos-A	146	514	58	139	13	3	2	48	51	—	—	6	16	—	24	—	.270	.343	.319	1.000
1912	Bos-A	58	171	32	40	5	3	0	18	28	—	—	2	6	—	12	—	.234	.348	.298	.912
1913	Bos-A	143	498	75	144	17	12	2	50	53	—	41	5	13	—	28	—	.289	.363	.384	.987
1914	Bos-A	59	134	14	26	2	0	0	9	14	—	11	1	2	—	4	9	.194	.275	.209	1.000
1914	Buf-F	32	110	12	28	4	1	0	12	11	—	18	1	5	—	5	—	.255	.328	.309	.889
1915	Buf-F	141	501	56	131	22	8	3	71	34	—	43	3	13	—	24	—	.261	.312	.355	.969
1916	Cle-A	11	26	1	4	0	0	0	1	0	—	6	0	2	—	0	—	.154	.154	.154	1.000
Career average		84	282	37	75	10	4	1	32	27	—	—	3	9	—	13	—	.265	.335	.341	.948
Yankee average		**70**	**253**	**33**	**70**	**10**	**3**	**2**	**36**	**25**	**—**	**—**	**3**	**10**	**—**	**10**	**—**	**.277**	**.347**	**.354**	**.902**
Career total		836	2822	373	748	101	39	12	318	271	—	119	25	88	—	128	9	.265	.335	.341	.948
Yankee total		**140**	**505**	**66**	**140**	**20**	**5**	**3**	**71**	**49**	**—**	**—**	**5**	**19**	**—**	**19**	**—**	**.277**	**.347**	**.354**	**.902**

Espino, Juan BORN JUAN ESPINO (REYES)

HEIGHT: 6'1" THROWS: RIGHT BATS: RIGHT BORN: 3/16/1956 BONAO, DOMINICAN REPUBLIC

YEAR	TEAM	GAMES	AB	RUNS	HITS	2B	3B	HR	RBI	BB	IBB	SO	HBP	SH	SF	SB	CS	BA	OBA	SA	FA
1982	**NY-A**	**3**	**2**	**0**	**0**	**0**	**0**	**0**	**0**	**0**	**0**	**1**	**0**	**0**	**0**	**0**	**0**	**.000**	**.000**	**.000**	**1.000**
1983	**NY-A**	**10**	**23**	**1**	**6**	**0**	**0**	**1**	**3**	**1**	**0**	**5**	**0**	**0**	**1**	**0**	**0**	**.261**	**.280**	**.391**	**1.000**
1985	**NY-A**	**9**	**11**	**0**	**4**	**0**	**0**	**0**	**0**	**0**	**0**	**0**	**0**	**0**	**0**	**0**	**0**	**.364**	**.364**	**.364**	**1.000**
1986	**NY-A**	**27**	**37**	**1**	**6**	**2**	**0**	**0**	**5**	**2**	**0**	**9**	**0**	**0**	**1**	**0**	**0**	**.162**	**.200**	**.216**	**.987**
Career average		12.25	18.25	0.5	4	0.5	0	0.25	2	0.75	0	3.75	0	0	0.5	0	0	.219	.244	.288	.997
Yankee average		**12.25**	**18.25**	**0.5**	**4**	**0.5**	**0**	**0.25**	**2**	**0.75**	**0**	**3.75**	**0**	**0**	**0.5**	**0**	**0**	**.219**	**.244**	**.288**	**.997**
Career total		49	73	2	16	2	0	1	8	3	0	15	0	0	2	0	0	.219	.244	.288	.997
Yankee total		**49**	**73**	**2**	**16**	**2**	**0**	**1**	**8**	**3**	**0**	**15**	**0**	**0**	**2**	**0**	**0**	**.219**	**.244**	**.288**	**.997**

Espinoza, Alvaro Alberto BORN ALVARA ALBERTO ESPINOZA (RAMIREZ)

HEIGHT: 6'0" THROWS: RIGHT BATS: RIGHT BORN: 2/19/1962 VALENCIA, VENEZUELA POSITIONS PLAYED: 1B, 2B, 3B, SS

YEAR	TEAM	GAMES	AB	RUNS	HITS	2B	3B	HR	RBI	BB	IBB	SO	HBP	SH	SF	SB	CS	BA	OBA	SA	FA
1984	Min-A	1	0	0	0	0	0	0	0	0	0	0	0	0	0	0	0	—	—	—	.000
1985	Min-A	32	57	5	15	2	0	0	9	1	0	9	1	3	0	0	1	.263	.288	.298	.949
1986	Min-A	37	42	4	9	1	0	0	1	1	0	10	0	2	0	0	1	.214	.233	.238	.964
1988	**NY-A**	**3**	**3**	**0**	**0**	**0**	**0**	**0**	**0**	**0**	**0**	**0**	**0**	**0**	**0**	**0**	**0**	**.000**	**.000**	**.000**	**1.000**
1989	**NY-A**	**146**	**503**	**51**	**142**	**23**	**1**	**0**	**41**	**14**	**1**	**60**	**1**	**23**	**3**	**3**	**3**	**.282**	**.301**	**.332**	**.970**
1990	**NY-A**	**150**	**438**	**31**	**98**	**12**	**2**	**2**	**20**	**16**	**0**	**54**	**5**	**11**	**2**	**1**	**2**	**.224**	**.258**	**.274**	**.977**
1991	**NY-A**	**148**	**480**	**51**	**123**	**23**	**2**	**5**	**33**	**16**	**0**	**57**	**2**	**9**	**2**	**4**	**1**	**.256**	**.282**	**.344**	**1.000**

(continued)

(continued)

YEAR	TEAM	GAMES	AB	RUNS	HITS	2B	3B	HR	RBI	BB	IBB	SO	HBP	SH	SF	SB	CS	BA	OBA	SA	FA
1993	Cle-A	129	263	34	73	15	0	4	27	8	0	36	1	8	3	2	2	.278	.298	.380	.900
1994	Cle-A	90	231	27	55	13	0	1	19	6	0	33	1	4	2	1	3	.238	.258	.307	.915
1995	Cle-A	66	143	15	36	4	0	2	17	2	0	16	1	2	2	0	2	.252	.264	.322	1.000
1996	Cle-A	59	112	12	25	4	2	4	11	6	0	18	3	3	1	1	1	.223	.279	.402	.947
1996	NY-N	48	134	19	41	7	2	4	16	4	0	19	0	5	1	0	2	.306	.324	.478	1.000
1997	Sea-A	33	72	3	13	1	0	0	7	2	0	12	1	3	0	1	1	.181	.213	.194	.965
Career average		72	191	19	48	8	1	2	15	6	0	25	1	6	1	1	1	.254	.279	.331	.891
Yankee average		**112**	**356**	**33**	**91**	**15**	**1**	**2**	**24**	**12**	**0**	**43**	**2**	**11**	**2**	**2**	**2**	**.255**	**.281**	**.317**	**.987**
Career total		942	2478	252	630	105	9	22	201	76	1	324	16	73	16	13	19	.254	.279	.331	.891
Yankee total		**447**	**1424**	**133**	**363**	**58**	**5**	**7**	**94**	**46**	**1**	**171**	**8**	**43**	**7**	**8**	**6**	**.255**	**.281**	**.317**	**.987**

Etten, Nicholas Raymond Thomas
HEIGHT: 6'2" THROWS: LEFT BATS: LEFT BORN: 9/19/1913 SPRING GROVE, ILLINOIS DIED: 10/18/1990 HINSDALE, ILLINOIS POSITIONS PLAYED: 1B

YEAR	TEAM	GAMES	AB	RUNS	HITS	2B	3B	HR	RBI	BB	IBB	SO	HBP	SH	SF	SB	CS	BA	OBA	SA	FA
1938	Phi-A	22	81	6	21	6	2	0	11	9	—	7	0	0	—	1	0	.259	.333	.383	.987
1939	Phi-A	43	155	20	39	11	2	3	29	16	—	11	0	3	—	0	0	.252	.322	.406	.990
1941	Phi-N	151	540	78	168	27	4	14	79	82	—	33	3	2	—	9	—	.311	.405	.454	.984
1942	Phi-N	139	459	37	121	21	3	8	41	67	—	26	0	5	—	3	—	.264	.357	.375	.985
1943	**NY-A**	**154**	**583**	**78**	**158**	**35**	**5**	**14**	**107**	**76**	**—**	**31**	**0**	**6**	**—**	**3**	**7**	**.271**	**.355**	**.420**	**.989**
1944	**NY-A**	**154**	**573**	**88**	**168**	**25**	**4**	**22**	**91**	**97**	**—**	**29**	**4**	**6**	**—**	**4**	**2**	**.293**	**.399**	**.466**	**.989**
1945	**NY-A**	**152**	**565**	**77**	**161**	**24**	**4**	**18**	**111**	**90**	**—**	**23**	**4**	**4**	**—**	**2**	**3**	**.285**	**.387**	**.437**	**.989**
1946	**NY-A**	**108**	**323**	**37**	**75**	**14**	**1**	**9**	**49**	**38**	**—**	**35**	**1**	**2**	**—**	**0**	**1**	**.232**	**.315**	**.365**	**.991**
1947	Phi-N	14	41	5	10	4	0	1	8	5	—	4	0	0	—	0	—	.244	.326	.415	.990
Career average		104	369	47	102	19	3	10	58	53	—	22	1	3	—	2	—	.277	.371	.423	.988
Yankee average		**142**	**511**	**70**	**141**	**25**	**4**	**16**	**90**	**75**	**—**	**30**	**2**	**5**	**—**	**2**	**3**	**.275**	**.370**	**.429**	**.990**
Career total		937	3320	426	921	167	25	89	526	480	—	199	12	28	—	22	13	.277	.371	.423	.988
Yankee total		**568**	**2044**	**280**	**562**	**98**	**14**	**63**	**358**	**301**	**—**	**118**	**9**	**18**	**—**	**9**	**13**	**.275**	**.370**	**.429**	**.990**

Evans, Barry Steven
HEIGHT: 6'1" THROWS: RIGHT BATS: RIGHT BORN: 11/30/1955 ATLANTA, GEORGIA POSITIONS PLAYED: 2B, 3B, SS

YEAR	TEAM	GAMES	AB	RUNS	HITS	2B	3B	HR	RBI	BB	IBB	SO	HBP	SH	SF	SB	CS	BA	OBA	SA	FA
1978	SD-N	24	90	7	24	1	1	0	4	4	1	10	0	0	1	0	0	.267	.295	.300	.947
1979	SD-N	56	162	9	35	5	0	1	14	5	0	16	0	5	2	0	2	.216	.237	.265	1.000
1980	SD-N	73	125	11	29	3	2	1	14	17	1	21	0	2	3	1	1	.232	.317	.312	.983
1981	SD-N	54	93	11	30	5	0	0	7	9	2	9	0	1	3	2	2	.323	.371	.376	1.000
1982	**NY-A**	**17**	**31**	**2**	**8**	**3**	**0**	**0**	**2**	**6**	**0**	**6**	**1**	**0**	**0**	**0**	**0**	**.258**	**.395**	**.355**	**1.000**
Career average		45	100	8	25	3	1	0	8	8	1	12	0	2	2	1	1	.251	.304	.309	.986
Yankee average		**17**	**31**	**2**	**8**	**3**	**0**	**0**	**2**	**6**	**0**	**6**	**1**	**0**	**0**	**0**	**0**	**.258**	**.395**	**.355**	**1.000**
Career total		224	501	40	126	17	3	2	41	41	4	62	1	8	9	3	5	.251	.304	.309	.986
Yankee total		**17**	**31**	**2**	**8**	**3**	**0**	**0**	**2**	**6**	**0**	**6**	**1**	**0**	**0**	**0**	**0**	**.258**	**.395**	**.355**	**1.000**

Farrell, Edward Stephen (Doc)
HEIGHT: 5'8" THROWS: RIGHT BATS: RIGHT BORN: 12/26/1901 JOHNSON CITY, N.Y. DIED: 12/20/1966 LIVINGSTON, N.J. POSITIONS PLAYED: 2B, 3B, SS

YEAR	TEAM	GAMES	AB	RUNS	HITS	2B	3B	HR	RBI	BB	IBB	SO	HBP	SH	SF	SB	CS	BA	OBA	SA	FA
1925	NY-N	27	56	6	12	1	0	0	4	4	—	6	0	2	—	0	1	.214	.267	.232	1.000
1926	NY-N	67	171	19	49	10	1	2	23	12	—	17	2	5	—	4	—	.287	.341	.392	1.000
1927	NY-N	42	142	13	55	10	1	3	34	12	—	11	2	3	—	0	—	.387	.442	.535	.919
1927	Bos-N	110	424	44	124	13	2	1	58	14	—	21	0	19	—	4	—	.292	.315	.340	.952
1928	Bos-N	134	483	36	104	14	2	3	43	26	—	26	5	19	—	3	—	.215	.263	.271	.933
1929	Bos-N	5	8	0	1	0	0	0	2	0	—	1	0	0	—	0	—	.125	.125	.125	1.000
1929	NY-N	63	178	18	38	6	0	0	16	9	—	17	0	5	—	2	—	.213	.251	.247	.925
1930	StL-N	23	61	3	13	1	1	0	6	4	—	2	0	1	—	1	—	.213	.262	.262	1.000
1930	Chi-N	46	113	21	33	6	0	1	16	9	—	5	0	3	—	0	—	.292	.344	.372	.937
1932	**NY-A**	**26**	**63**	**4**	**11**	**1**	**1**	**0**	**4**	**2**	**—**	**8**	**1**	**1**	**—**	**0**	**0**	**.175**	**.212**	**.222**	**.963**
1933	**NY-A**	**44**	**93**	**16**	**25**	**0**	**0**	**0**	**6**	**16**	**—**	**6**	**0**	**3**	**—**	**0**	**0**	**.269**	**.376**	**.269**	**.947**
1935	Bos-A	4	7	1	2	1	0	0	1	1	—	0	0	0	—	0	—	.286	.375	.429	.917
Career average		49	150	15	39	5	1	1	18	9	—	10	1	5	—	1	—	.260	.306	.320	.958
Yankee average		**35**	**78**	**10**	**18**	**1**	**1**	**0**	**5**	**9**	**—**	**7**	**1**	**2**	**—**	**0**	**0**	**.231**	**.314**	**.250**	**.955**
Career total		591	1799	181	467	63	8	10	213	109	—	120	10	61	—	14	1	.260	.306	.320	.958
Yankee total		**70**	**156**	**20**	**36**	**1**	**1**	**0**	**10**	**18**	**—**	**14**	**1**	**4**	**—**	**0**	**0**	**.231**	**.314**	**.250**	**.955**

Fernandez, Frank

HEIGHT: 6'0" THROWS: RIGHT BATS: RIGHT BORN: 4/16/1943 STATEN ISLAND, NEW YORK POSITIONS PLAYED: C, OF

YEAR	TEAM	GAMES	AB	RUNS	HITS	2B	3B	HR	RBI	BB	IBB	SO	HBP	SH	SF	SB	CS	BA	OBA	SA	FA
1967	NY-A	9	28	1	6	2	0	1	4	2	0	7	1	0	1	1	1	.214	.281	.393	1.000
1968	NY-A	51	135	15	23	6	1	7	30	35	2	50	0	0	0	1	0	.170	.341	.385	.989
1969	NY-A	89	229	34	51	6	1	12	29	65	3	68	3	0	1	1	3	.223	.399	.415	.994
1970	Oak-A	94	252	30	54	5	0	15	44	40	4	76	2	0	0	0	0	.214	.327	.413	.993
1971	Oak-A	4	9	1	1	1	0	0	1	1	0	3	0	0	0	0	0	.111	.200	.222	1.000
1971	Was-A	18	30	0	3	0	0	0	4	4	0	10	0	1	2	0	0	.100	.194	.100	1.000
1971	Chi-N	17	41	11	7	1	0	4	4	17	0	15	0	0	0	0	0	.171	.414	.488	.980
1972	Chi-N	3	3	0	0	0	0	0	0	0	0	2	0	0	0	0	0	.000	.000	.000	1.000
Career average		36	91	12	18	3	0	5	15	21	1	29	1	0	1	1	1	.199	.350	.395	.995
Yankee average		**50**	**131**	**17**	**27**	**5**	**1**	**7**	**21**	**34**	**2**	**42**	**1**	**0**	**1**	**1**	**1**	**.204**	**.372**	**.403**	**.994**
Career total		285	727	92	145	21	2	39	116	164	9	231	6	1	4	4	4	.199	.350	.395	.995
Yankee total		**149**	**392**	**50**	**80**	**14**	**2**	**20**	**63**	**102**	**5**	**125**	**4**	**0**	**2**	**3**	**4**	**.204**	**.372**	**.403**	**.994**

Fernandez, Octavio Antonio (Tony) BORN OCTAVIO ANTONIO FERNANDEZ (CASTRO)

HEIGHT: 6'2" THROWS: RIGHT BATS: BOTH BORN: 6/30/1962 SAN PEDRO DE MACORIS, DOMINICAN REPUBLIC POSITIONS PLAYED: 2B, 3B, SS, DH

YEAR	TEAM	GAMES	AB	RUNS	HITS	2B	3B	HR	RBI	BB	IBB	SO	HBP	SH	SF	SB	CS	BA	OBA	SA	FA
1983	Tor-A	15	34	5	9	1	1	0	2	2	0	2	1	1	0	0	1	.265	.324	.353	1.000
1984	Tor-A	88	233	29	63	5	3	3	19	17	0	15	1	2	2	5	7	.270	.317	.356	.952
1985	Tor-A	161	564	71	163	31	10	2	51	43	2	41	2	7	2	13	6	.289	.340	.390	.962
1986	Tor-A	163	687	91	213	33	9	10	65	27	3	52	4	5	4	25	12	.310	.338	.428	.983
1987	Tor-A	146	578	90	186	29	8	5	67	51	3	48	5	4	4	32	12	.322	.379	.426	.979
1988	Tor-A	154	648	76	186	41	4	5	70	45	3	65	4	3	4	15	5	.287	.335	.386	.981
1989	Tor-A	140	573	64	147	25	9	11	64	29	1	51	3	2	10	22	6	.257	.291	.389	.992
1990	Tor-A	161	635	84	175	27	17	4	66	71	0	70	7	2	6	26	13	.276	.352	.391	.989
1991	SD-N	145	558	81	152	27	5	4	38	55	0	74	0	7	1	23	9	.272	.337	.360	.972
1992	SD-N	155	622	84	171	32	4	4	37	56	0	62	1	3	2	20	20	.275	.337	.359	.983
1993	NY-N	48	173	20	39	5	2	1	14	25	0	19	1	3	3	6	2	.225	.323	.295	.975
1993	Tor-A	94	353	45	108	18	9	4	50	31	3	26	0	5	1	15	8	.306	.362	.442	.985
1994	Cin-N	104	366	50	102	18	6	8	50	44	8	40	5	4	3	12	7	.279	.361	.426	.920
1995	**NY-A**	**108**	**384**	**57**	**94**	**20**	**2**	**5**	**45**	**42**	**0**	**47**	**2**	**6**	**3**	**6**	**6**	**.245**	**.322**	**.346**	**1.000**
1997	Cle-A	120	409	55	117	21	1	11	44	22	0	53	2	6	3	13	6	.286	.323	.423	.974
1998	Tor-A	138	486	71	156	36	2	9	72	45	5	62	0	3	6	6	7	.321	.374	.459	.975
1999	Tor-A	142	485	73	159	41	0	6	75	77	0	62	4	0	4	14	8	.328	.417	.449	.951
Career average		122	458	62	128	29	6	6	46	40	2	45	2	4	4	14	8	.280	.338	.407	.975
Yankee average		**108**	**384**	**57**	**94**	**20**	**2**	**5**	**45**	**42**	**0**	**47**	**2**	**6**	**3**	**6**	**6**	**.245**	**.322**	**.346**	**1.000**
Career total		2082	7788	1046	2177	500	101	97	783	682	37	767	42	66	60	245	135	.280	.338	.407	.975
Yankee total		**108**	**384**	**57**	**94**	**20**	**2**	**5**	**45**	**42**	**0**	**47**	**2**	**6**	**3**	**6**	**6**	**.245**	**.322**	**.346**	**1.000**

Ferraro, Michael Dennis

HEIGHT: 5'11" THROWS: RIGHT BATS: RIGHT BORN: 8/18/1944 KINGSTON, NEW YORK POSITIONS PLAYED: 3B

YEAR	TEAM	GAMES	AB	RUNS	HITS	2B	3B	HR	RBI	BB	IBB	SO	HBP	SH	SF	SB	CS	BA	OBA	SA	FA
1966	NY-A	10	28	4	5	0	0	0	0	3	0	3	1	0	0	0	0	.179	.281	.179	.926
1968	NY-A	23	87	5	14	0	1	0	1	2	1	17	0	0	0	0	0	.161	.180	.184	.975
1969	Sea-A	5	4	0	0	0	0	0	0	1	0	0	0	0	0	0	0	.000	.200	.000	.950
1972	Mil-A	124	381	19	97	18	1	2	29	17	1	41	0	4	4	0	5	.255	.284	.323	.950
Career average		41	125	7	29	5	1	1	8	6	1	15	0	1	1	0	1	.232	.265	.288	.950
Yankee average		**17**	**58**	**5**	**10**	**0**	**1**	**0**	**1**	**3**	**1**	**10**	**1**	**0**	**0**	**0**	**0**	**.165**	**.207**	**.183**	**.951**
Career total		162	500	28	116	18	2	2	30	23	2	61	1	4	4	0	5	.232	.265	.288	.950
Yankee total		**33**	**115**	**9**	**19**	**0**	**1**	**0**	**1**	**5**	**1**	**20**	**1**	**0**	**0**	**0**	**0**	**.165**	**.207**	**.183**	**.951**

Fewster, Wilson Lloyd (Chick)

HEIGHT: 5'11"   THROWS: RIGHT   BATS: RIGHT   BORN: 11/10/1895 BALTIMORE, MD.   DIED: 4/16/1945 BALTIMORE, MD.   POSITIONS PLAYED: 2B, 3B, SS, OF

YEAR	TEAM	GAMES	AB	RUNS	HITS	2B	3B	HR	RBI	BB	IBB	SO	HBP	SH	SF	SB	CS	BA	OBA	SA	FA
1917	**NY-A**	**11**	**36**	**2**	**8**	**0**	**0**	**0**	**1**	**5**	**—**	**5**	**0**	**0**	**—**	**1**	**—**	**.222**	**.317**	**.222**	**.919**
1918	**NY-A**	**5**	**2**	**1**	**1**	**0**	**0**	**0**	**0**	**0**	**—**	**0**	**0**	**0**	**—**	**0**	**—**	**.500**	**.500**	**.500**	**.000**
1919	**NY-A**	**81**	**244**	**38**	**69**	**9**	**3**	**1**	**15**	**34**	**—**	**36**	**7**	**8**	**—**	**8**	**—**	**.283**	**.386**	**.357**	**.901**
1920	**NY-A**	**21**	**21**	**8**	**6**	**1**	**0**	**0**	**1**	**7**	**—**	**2**	**0**	**1**	**—**	**0**	**1**	**.286**	**.464**	**.333**	**1.000**
1921	**NY-A**	**66**	**207**	**44**	**58**	**19**	**0**	**1**	**19**	**28**	**—**	**43**	**6**	**7**	**—**	**4**	**4**	**.280**	**.382**	**.386**	**.974**
1922	**NY-A**	**44**	**132**	**20**	**32**	**4**	**1**	**1**	**9**	**16**	**—**	**23**	**0**	**11**	**—**	**2**	**4**	**.242**	**.324**	**.311**	**.975**
1922	Bos-A	23	83	8	24	4	1	0	9	6	—	10	1	3	—	8	3	.289	.344	.361	.959
1923	Bos-A	90	284	32	67	10	1	0	15	39	—	35	3	5	—	7	14	.236	.334	.278	.938
1924	Cle-A	101	322	36	86	12	2	0	36	24	—	36	3	8	—	12	12	.267	.324	.317	.909
1925	Cle-A	93	294	39	73	16	1	1	38	36	—	25	0	13	—	6	9	.248	.330	.320	1.000
1926	Bro-N	105	337	53	82	16	3	2	24	45	—	49	5	9	—	9	—	.243	.341	.326	.953
1927	Bro-N	4	1	1	0	0	0	0	0	0	—	0	0	0	—	0	—	.000	.000	.000	.000
Career average		54	164	24	42	8	1	1	14	20	—	22	2	5	—	5	—	.258	.346	.326	.794
Yankee average		**38**	**107**	**19**	**29**	**6**	**1**	**1**	**8**	**15**	**—**	**18**	**2**	**5**	**—**	**3**	**—**	**.271**	**.372**	**.349**	**.795**
Career total		644	1963	282	506	91	12	6	167	240	—	264	25	65	—	57	47	.258	.346	.326	.794
Yankee total		**228**	**642**	**113**	**174**	**33**	**4**	**3**	**45**	**90**	**—**	**109**	**13**	**27**	**—**	**15**	**9**	**.271**	**.372**	**.349**	**.795**

Fielder, Cecil Grant

HEIGHT: 6'3"   THROWS: RIGHT   BATS: RIGHT   BORN: 9/21/1963 LOS ANGELES, CALIFORNIA   POSITIONS PLAYED: 1B

YEAR	TEAM	GAMES	AB	RUNS	HITS	2B	3B	HR	RBI	BB	IBB	SO	HBP	SH	SF	SB	CS	BA	OBA	SA	FA
1985	Tor-A	30	74	6	23	4	0	4	16	6	0	16	0	0	1	0	0	.311	.358	.527	.979
1986	Tor-A	34	83	7	13	2	0	4	13	6	0	27	1	0	0	0	0	.157	.222	.325	1.000
1987	Tor-A	82	175	30	47	7	1	14	32	20	2	48	1	0	1	0	1	.269	.345	.560	1.000
1988	Tor-A	74	174	24	40	6	1	9	23	14	0	53	1	0	1	0	1	.230	.289	.431	1.000
1990	Det-A	159	573	104	159	25	1	51	132	90	11	182	5	0	5	0	1	.277	.377	.592	.989
1991	Det-A	162	624	102	163	25	0	44	133	78	12	151	6	0	4	0	0	.261	.347	.513	.993
1992	Det-A	155	594	80	145	22	0	35	124	73	8	151	2	0	7	0	0	.244	.325	.458	.991
1993	Det-A	154	573	80	153	23	0	30	117	90	15	125	4	0	5	0	1	.267	.368	.464	.991
1994	Det-A	109	425	67	110	16	2	28	90	50	4	110	2	0	4	0	0	.259	.337	.504	.993
1995	Det-A	136	494	70	120	18	1	31	82	75	8	116	5	0	4	0	1	.243	.346	.472	.993
1996	Det-A	107	391	55	97	12	0	26	80	63	8	91	3	0	3	2	0	.248	.354	.478	.989
1996	**NY-A**	**53**	**200**	**30**	**52**	**8**	**0**	**13**	**37**	**24**	**4**	**48**	**2**	**0**	**2**	**0**	**0**	**.260**	**.342**	**.495**	**1.000**
1997	**NY-A**	**98**	**361**	**40**	**94**	**15**	**0**	**13**	**61**	**51**	**3**	**87**	**7**	**0**	**6**	**0**	**0**	**.260**	**.358**	**.410**	**1.000**
1998	Ana-A	103	381	48	92	16	1	17	68	52	1	98	0	0	3	0	1	.241	.330	.423	.997
1998	Cle-A	14	35	1	5	1	0	0	0	1	0	13	0	0	0	0	0	.143	.167	.171	.933
Career average		98	344	50	88	13	0	21	67	46	5	88	3	0	3	0	0	.255	.345	.482	.990
Yankee average		**76**	**281**	**35**	**73**	**12**	**0**	**13**	**49**	**38**	**4**	**68**	**5**	**0**	**4**	**0**	**0**	**.260**	**.352**	**.440**	**1.000**
Career total		1470	5157	744	1313	200	7	319	1008	693	76	1316	39	0	46	2	6	.255	.345	.482	.990
Yankee total		**151**	**561**	**70**	**146**	**23**	**0**	**26**	**98**	**75**	**7**	**135**	**9**	**0**	**8**	**0**	**0**	**.260**	**.352**	**.440**	**1.000**

Figga, Michael Anthony

HEIGHT: 6'0"   THROWS: RIGHT   BATS: RIGHT   BORN: 7/31/1970 TAMPA, FLORIDA   POSITIONS PLAYED: C

YEAR	TEAM	GAMES	AB	RUNS	HITS	2B	3B	HR	RBI	BB	IBB	SO	HBP	SH	SF	SB	CS	BA	OBA	SA	FA
1997	**NY-A**	**2**	**4**	**0**	**0**	**0**	**0**	**0**	**0**	**0**	**0**	**3**	**0**	**0**	**0**	**0**	**0**	**.000**	**.000**	**.000**	**1.000**
1998	**NY-A**	**1**	**4**	**1**	**1**	**0**	**0**	**0**	**0**	**0**	**0**	**1**	**0**	**0**	**0**	**0**	**0**	**.250**	**.250**	**.250**	**1.000**
1999	**NY-A**	**2**	**0**	**0**	**0**	**0**	**0**	**0**	**0**	**0**	**0**	**0**	**0**	**0**	**0**	**0**	**0**	**—**	**—**	**—**	**1.000**
1999	Bal-A	41	86	12	19	4	0	1	5	2	0	27	0	2	1	0	2	.221	.236	.302	.973
Career average		12	24	3	5	1	0	0	1	1	0	8	0	1	0	0	1	.213	.227	.287	.993
Yankee average		**2**	**3**	**0**	**0**	**0**	**0**	**0**	**0**	**0**	**0**	**1**	**0**	**0**	**0**	**0**	**0**	**.125**	**.125**	**.125**	**1.000**
Career total		46	94	13	20	4	0	1	5	2	0	31	0	2	1	0	2	.213	.227	.287	.993
Yankee total		**5**	**8**	**1**	**1**	**0**	**0**	**0**	**0**	**0**	**0**	**4**	**0**	**0**	**0**	**0**	**0**	**.125**	**.125**	**.125**	**1.000**

Fischlin, Michael Thomas
HEIGHT: 6'1"   THROWS: RIGHT   BATS: RIGHT   BORN: 9/13/1955 SACRAMENTO, CALIFORNIA   POSITIONS PLAYED: 2B, 3B, SS

YEAR	TEAM	GAMES	AB	RUNS	HITS	2B	3B	HR	RBI	BB	IBB	SO	HBP	SH	SF	SB	CS	BA	OBA	SA	FA
1977	Hou-N	13	15	0	3	0	0	0	0	0	0	2	0	0	0	0	0	.200	.200	.200	1.000
1978	Hou-N	44	86	3	10	1	0	0	0	4	1	9	1	4	0	1	0	.116	.165	.128	.928
1980	Hou-N	1	1	0	0	0	0	0	0	0	0	1	0	0	0	0	0	.000	.000	.000	1.000
1981	Cle-A	22	43	3	10	1	0	0	5	3	0	6	0	1	1	3	2	.233	.277	.256	.889
1982	Cle-A	112	276	34	74	12	1	0	21	34	0	36	2	9	1	9	5	.268	.351	.319	.750
1983	Cle-A	95	225	31	47	5	2	2	23	26	0	32	2	11	2	9	2	.209	.294	.276	.889
1984	Cle-A	85	133	17	30	4	2	1	14	12	0	20	0	5	0	2	2	.226	.290	.308	.981
1985	Cle-A	73	60	12	12	4	1	0	2	5	0	7	0	4	0	0	1	.200	.262	.300	.941
1986	**NY-A**	**71**	**102**	**9**	**21**	**2**	**0**	**0**	**3**	**8**	**0**	**29**	**0**	**5**	**1**	**0**	**1**	**.206**	**.261**	**.225**	**.955**
1987	Atl-N	1	0	0	0	0	0	0	0	0	0	0	0	0	0	0	0	.000	.000	.000	.000
Career average		52	94	11	21	3	1	0	7	9	0	14	1	4	1	2	1	.220	.291	.273	.926
Yankee average		**71**	**102**	**9**	**21**	**2**	**0**	**0**	**3**	**8**	**0**	**29**	**0**	**5**	**1**	**0**	**1**	**.206**	**.261**	**.225**	**.955**
Career total		517	941	109	207	29	6	3	68	92	1	142	5	39	5	24	13	.220	.291	.273	.926
Yankee total		**71**	**102**	**9**	**21**	**2**	**0**	**0**	**3**	**8**	**0**	**29**	**0**	**5**	**1**	**0**	**1**	**.206**	**.261**	**.225**	**.955**

Fisher, August Harris
HEIGHT: 5'10"   THROWS: RIGHT   BATS: LEFT   BORN: 10/21/1885 POTTSBOROUGH, TEXAS   DIED: 4/8/1972 PORTLAND, OREGON

YEAR	TEAM	GAMES	AB	RUNS	HITS	2B	3B	HR	RBI	BB	IBB	SO	HBP	SH	SF	SB	CS	BA	OBA	SA	FA
1911	Cle-A	70	203	20	53	6	3	0	12	7	0	0	5	5	0	6	0	.261	.302	.320	.956
1912	**NY-A**	**4**	**10**	**1**	**1**	**0**	**0**	**0**	**0**	**0**	**0**	**0**	**0**	**0**	**0**	**0**	**0**	**.100**	**.100**	**.100**	**1.000**
Career average		37	107	11	27	3	2	0	6	4	0	0	3	3	0	3	0	.254	.293	.310	.978
Yankee average		**4**	**10**	**1**	**1**	**0**	**0**	**0**	**0**	**0**	**0**	**0**	**0**	**0**	**0**	**0**	**0**	**.100**	**.100**	**.100**	**1.000**
Career total		74	213	21	54	6	3	0	12	7	0	0	5	5	0	6	0	.254	.293	.310	.978
Yankee total		**4**	**10**	**1**	**1**	**0**	**0**	**0**	**0**	**0**	**0**	**0**	**0**	**0**	**0**	**0**	**0**	**.100**	**.100**	**.100**	**1.000**

Fitzgerald, Justin Howard
HEIGHT: 5'8"   THROWS: RIGHT   BATS: LEFT   BORN: 6/22/1890 SAN MATEO, CALIFORNIA   DIED: 1/17/1945 SAN MATEO, CALIFORNIA

YEAR	TEAM	GAMES	AB	RUNS	HITS	2B	3B	HR	RBI	BB	IBB	SO	HBP	SH	SF	SB	CS	BA	OBA	SA	FA
1911	**NY-A**	**16**	**37**	**6**	**10**	**1**	**0**	**0**	**6**	**4**	**0**	**0**	**0**	**2**	**0**	**4**	**0**	**.270**	**.341**	**.297**	**1.000**
1918	Phi-N	66	133	21	39	8	0	0	6	13	0	6	1	5	0	3	0	.293	.361	.353	.966
Career average		41	85	14	25	5	0	0	6	9	0	3	1	4	0	4	0	.288	.356	.341	.983
Yankee average		**16**	**37**	**6**	**10**	**1**	**0**	**0**	**6**	**4**	**0**	**0**	**0**	**2**	**0**	**4**	**0**	**.270**	**.341**	**.297**	**1.000**
Career total		82	170	27	49	9	0	0	12	17	0	6	1	7	0	7	0	.288	.356	.341	.983
Yankee total		**16**	**37**	**6**	**10**	**1**	**0**	**0**	**6**	**4**	**0**	**0**	**0**	**2**	**0**	**4**	**0**	**.270**	**.341**	**.297**	**1.000**

Foli, Timothy John (Crazy Horse)
HEIGHT: 6'0"   THROWS: RIGHT   BATS: RIGHT   BORN: 12/8/1950 CULVER CITY, CALIFORNIA   POSITIONS PLAYED: 2B, 3B, SS, OF

YEAR	TEAM	GAMES	AB	RUNS	HITS	2B	3B	HR	RBI	BB	IBB	SO	HBP	SH	SF	SB	CS	BA	OBA	SA	FA
1970	NY-N	5	11	0	4	0	0	0	1	0	0	2	0	0	0	0	0	.364	.364	.364	1.000
1971	NY-N	97	288	32	65	12	2	0	24	18	4	50	1	3	2	5	0	.226	.272	.281	1.000
1972	Mon-N	149	540	45	130	12	2	2	35	25	2	43	6	16	5	11	7	.241	.280	.281	.966
1973	Mon-N	126	458	37	110	11	0	2	36	28	11	40	1	10	3	6	3	.240	.284	.277	1.000
1974	Mon-N	121	441	41	112	10	3	0	39	28	0	27	3	17	4	8	2	.254	.300	.290	.971
1975	Mon-N	152	572	64	136	25	2	1	29	36	5	49	2	17	3	13	3	.238	.284	.294	.975
1976	Mon-N	149	546	41	144	36	1	6	54	16	1	33	0	2	8	6	5	.264	.281	.366	.975
1977	Mon-N	13	57	2	10	5	1	0	3	0	0	4	0	0	1	0	0	.175	.172	.298	1.000
1977	SF-N	104	368	30	84	17	3	4	27	11	1	16	0	3	5	2	4	.228	.247	.323	.974
1978	NY-N	113	413	37	106	21	1	1	27	14	1	30	2	12	2	2	5	.257	.283	.320	.966
1979	NY-N	3	7	0	0	0	0	0	0	0	0	0	0	0	0	0	0	.000	.000	.000	1.000
1979	Pit-N	133	525	70	153	23	1	1	65	28	0	14	9	19	6	6	5	.291	.388	.345	.978
1980	Pit-N	127	495	61	131	22	0	3	38	19	1	23	6	13	7	11	7	.265	.296	.327	.981
1981	Pit-N	86	316	32	78	12	2	0	20	17	0	10	1	14	3	7	7	.247	.285	.297	.965
1982	Cal-A	150	480	46	121	14	2	3	56	14	1	22	2	26	6	2	4	.252	.273	.308	1.000
1983	Cal-A	88	330	29	83	10	0	2	29	5	1	18	1	11	2	2	3	.252	.263	.300	.930
1984	**NY-A**	**61**	**163**	**8**	**41**	**11**	**0**	**0**	**16**	**2**	**0**	**16**	**1**	**6**	**0**	**0**	**0**	**.252**	**.265**	**.319**	**.950**
1985	Pit-N	19	37	1	7	0	0	0	2	4	1	2	0	0	0	0	0	.189	.268	.189	.980

(continued)

(continued)

	GAMES	AB	RUNS	HITS	2B	3B	HR	RBI	BB	IBB	SO	HBP	SH	SF	SB	CS	BA	OBA	SA	FA
Career average	94	336	32	84	13	1	1	28	15	2	22	2	9	3	5	3	.251	.283	.309	.980
Yankee average	**61**	**163**	**8**	**41**	**11**	**0**	**0**	**16**	**2**	**0**	**16**	**1**	**6**	**0**	**0**	**0**	**.252**	**.265**	**.319**	**.950**
Career total	1696	6047	576	1515	241	20	25	501	265	29	399	35	169	57	81	55	.251	.283	.309	.980
Yankee total	**61**	**163**	**8**	**41**	**11**	**0**	**0**	**16**	**2**	**0**	**16**	**1**	**6**	**0**	**0**	**0**	**.252**	**.265**	**.319**	**.950**

Foote, Barry Clifton
HEIGHT: 6'3"   THROWS: RIGHT   BATS: RIGHT   BORN: 2/16/1952 SMITHFIELD, NORTH CAROLINA   POSITIONS PLAYED: C

YEAR	TEAM	GAMES	AB	RUNS	HITS	2B	3B	HR	RBI	BB	IBB	SO	HBP	SH	SF	SB	CS	BA	OBA	SA	FA
1973	Mon-N																				
1974	Mon-N	125	420	44	110	23	4	11	60	35	11	74	3	2	12	2	1	.262	.315	.414	.984
1975	Mon-N	118	387	25	75	16	1	7	30	17	6	48	1	4	1	0	1	.194	.229	.295	.985
1976	Mon-N	105	350	32	82	12	2	7	27	17	3	32	1	0	0	2	1	.234	.272	.340	.989
1977	Mon-N	15	49	4	12	3	1	2	8	4	0	10	0	0	0	0	0	.245	.302	.469	.988
1977	Phi-N	18	32	3	7	1	0	1	3	3	0	60	0	0	0	0	0	.219	.286	.344	.980
1978	Phi-N	39	57	4	9	0	0	1	4	1	0	11	0	0	0	0	0	.158	.172	.211	1.000
1979	Chi-N	132	429	47	109	26	0	16	56	34	7	49	5	0	1	5	2	.254	.316	.427	.979
1980	Chi-N	63	202	16	48	13	1	6	28	13	2	18	0	1	1	1	1	.238	.282	.401	.992
1981	Chi-N	9	22	0	0	0	0	0	1	3	0	7	0	1	0	0	0	.000	.115	.000	1.000
1981	**NY-A**	**40**	**125**	**12**	**26**	**4**	**0**	**6**	**10**	**8**	**0**	**21**	**0**	**4**	**0**	**0**	**0**	**.208**	**.256**	**.384**	**1.000**
1982	**NY-A**	**17**	**48**	**4**	**7**	**5**	**0**	**0**	**2**	**1**	**0**	**11**	**0**	**0**	**1**	**0**	**0**	**.146**	**.160**	**.250**	**.973**
Career average	57	177	16	40	9	1	5	19	11	2	28	1	1	1	1	1	.229	.276	.366	.988
Yankee average	**29**	**87**	**8**	**17**	**5**	**0**	**3**	**6**	**5**	**0**	**16**	**0**	**2**	**1**	**0**	**0**	**.191**	**.230**	**.347**	**.987**
Career total	681	2121	191	485	103	9	57	229	136	29	341	10	10	17	10	6	.229	.276	.366	.988
Yankee total	**57**	**173**	**16**	**33**	**9**	**0**	**6**	**12**	**9**	**0**	**32**	**0**	**4**	**1**	**0**	**0**	**.191**	**.230**	**.347**	**.987**

Foster, Edward Cunningham (Kid)
HEIGHT: 5'6"   THROWS: RIGHT   BATS: RIGHT   BORN: 02/13/1887 CHICAGO, ILLINOIS   DIED: 1/15/1937 WASHINGTON   POSITIONS PLAYED: SS, 2B, 3B

YEAR	TEAM	GAMES	AB	RUNS	HITS	2B	3B	HR	RBI	BB	IBB	SO	HBP	SH	SF	SB	CS	BA	OBA	SA	FA
1910	**NY-A**	**30**	**83**	**5**	**11**	**2**	**0**	**0**	**1**	**8**	**—**	**—**	**1**	**0**	**—**	**2**	**—**	**.133**	**.217**	**.157**	**.909**
1912	Was-A	154	618	98	176	34	9	2	70	53	—	—	4	3	—	27	—	.285	.345	.379	.920
1913	Was-A	106	409	56	101	11	5	1	41	36	—	31	1	3	—	22	—	.247	.309	.306	.901
1914	Was-A	157	616	82	174	16	10	2	50	60	—	47	2	6	—	31	18	.282	.348	.351	.929
1915	Was-A	154	618	75	170	25	10	0	52	48	—	30	2	8	—	20	6	.275	.329	.348	.953
1916	Was-A	158	606	75	153	18	9	1	44	68	—	26	4	7	—	23	16	.252	.332	.317	.960
1917	Was-A	143	554	66	130	16	8	0	43	46	—	23	0	18	—	11	—	.235	.293	.292	.935
1918	Was-A	129	519	70	147	13	3	0	29	41	—	20	3	12	—	12	—	.283	.339	.320	.936
1919	Was-A	120	478	57	126	12	5	0	26	33	—	21	2	13	—	20	—	.264	.314	.310	.946
1920	Bos-A	117	386	48	100	17	6	0	41	42	—	17	3	11	—	10	4	.259	.336	.334	.949
1921	Bos-A	120	412	51	117	18	6	0	35	57	—	15	0	16	—	13	7	.284	.371	.357	.954
1922	Bos-A	48	109	11	23	3	0	0	3	9	—	10	1	3	—	1	1	.211	.277	.239	1.000
1922	StL-A	37	144	29	44	4	0	0	12	20	—	8	1	5	—	3	1	.306	.394	.333	.886
1923	StL-A	27	100	9	18	2	0	0	4	7	—	7	1	7	—	0	0	.180	.241	.200	.913
Career average	107	404	52	106	14	5	0	32	38	—	—	2	8	—	14	—	.264	.329	.326	.935
Yankee average	**30**	**83**	**5**	**11**	**2**	**0**	**0**	**1**	**8**	**—**	**—**	**1**	**0**	**—**	**2**	**—**	**.133**	**.217**	**.157**	**.909**
Career total	1500	5652	732	1490	191	71	6	451	528	—	255	25	112	—	195	53	.264	.329	.326	.935
Yankee total	**30**	**83**	**5**	**11**	**2**	**0**	**0**	**1**	**8**	**—**	**—**	**1**	**0**	**—**	**2**	**—**	**.133**	**.217**	**.157**	**.909**

Fournier, John Frank
HEIGHT: 6'0"   THROWS: RIGHT   BATS: LEFT   BORN: 09/28/1889 AUSABLE, MICHIGAN   DIED: 9/5/1973 TACOMA, WASHINGTON   POSITIONS PLAYED: 1B, OF

YEAR	TEAM	GAMES	AB	RUNS	HITS	2B	3B	HR	RBI	BB	IBB	SO	HBP	SH	SF	SB	CS	BA	OBA	SA	FA
1912	Chi-A	35	73	6	14	5	2	0	2	4	—	—	3	1	—	1	—	.192	.263	.315	.988
1913	Chi-A	68	172	20	40	8	5	1	23	21	—	23	2	3	—	9	—	.233	.323	.355	.990
1914	Chi-A	109	379	44	118	14	9	6	44	31	—	44	3	14	—	10	13	.311	.368	.443	.833
1915	Chi-A	126	422	86	136	20	18	5	77	64	—	37	15	13	—	21	16	.322	.429	.491	.986
1916	Chi-A	105	313	36	75	13	9	3	44	36	—	40	5	8	—	19	—	.240	.328	.367	.976
1917	Chi-A	1	1	0	0	0	0	0	0	0	—	1	0	0	—	0	—	.000	.000	.000	.000
1918	**NY-A**	**27**	**100**	**9**	**35**	**6**	**1**	**0**	**12**	**7**	**—**	**7**	**0**	**3**	**—**	**7**	**—**	**.350**	**.393**	**.430**	**.976**
1920	StL-N	141	530	77	162	33	14	3	61	42	—	42	12	24	—	26	20	.306	.370	.438	.983
1921	StL-N	149	574	103	197	27	9	16	86	56	—	48	8	23	—	20	22	.343	.409	.505	.987
1922	StL-N	128	404	64	119	23	9	10	61	40	—	21	7	11	—	6	8	.295	.368	.470	.982

(continued)

(continued)

YEAR	TEAM	GAMES	AB	RUNS	HITS	2B	3B	HR	RBI	BB	IBB	SO	HBP	SH	SF	SB	CS	BA	OBA	SA	FA
1923	Bro-N	133	515	91	181	30	13	22	102	43	—	28	9	11	—	11	4	.351	.411	.588	.985
1924	Bro-N	154	563	93	188	25	4	27	116	83	—	46	10	13	—	7	5	.334	.428	.536	.985
1925	Bro-N	145	545	99	191	21	16	22	130	86	—	39	8	10	—	4	6	.350	.446	.569	.989
1926	Bro-N	87	243	39	69	9	2	11	48	30	—	16	1	6	—	0	—	.284	.365	.473	.986
1927	Bos-N	122	374	55	106	18	2	10	53	44	—	16	6	9	—	4	—	.283	.368	.422	.989
Career average		102	347	55	109	17	8	9	57	39	—	27	6	10	—	10	—	.313	.392	.483	.909
Yankee average		**27**	**100**	**9**	**35**	**6**	**1**	**0**	**12**	**7**	**—**	**7**	**0**	**3**	**—**	**7**	**—**	**.350**	**.393**	**.430**	**.976**
Career total		1530	5208	822	1631	252	113	136	859	587	—	408	89	149	—	145	94	.313	.392	.483	.909
Yankee total		**27**	**100**	**9**	**35**	**6**	**1**	**0**	**12**	**7**	**—**	**7**	**0**	**3**	**—**	**7**	**—**	**.350**	**.393**	**.430**	**.976**

Fox, Andrew Junipero

HEIGHT: 6'4" THROWS: RIGHT BATS: LEFT BORN: 1/12/1971 SACRAMENTO, CALIFORNIA POSITIONS PLAYED: 2B, 3B, SS

YEAR	TEAM	GAMES	AB	RUNS	HITS	2B	3B	HR	RBI	BB	IBB	SO	HBP	SH	SF	SB	CS	BA	OBA	SA	FA
1996	**NY-A**	**113**	**189**	**26**	**37**	**4**	**0**	**3**	**13**	**20**	**0**	**28**	**1**	**9**	**0**	**11**	**3**	**.196**	**.276**	**.265**	**.889**
1997	**NY-A**	**22**	**31**	**13**	**7**	**1**	**0**	**0**	**1**	**7**	**0**	**9**	**0**	**2**	**0**	**2**	**1**	**.226**	**.368**	**.258**	**1.000**
1998	Ari-N	139	502	67	139	21	6	9	44	43	0	97	18	0	1	14	7	.277	.355	.396	1.000
1999	Ari-N	99	274	34	70	12	2	6	33	33	0	61	0	1	3	4	1	.255	.332	.380	.945
2000	Ari-N	31	86	10	18	4	0	1	10	4	1	16	0	0	0	2	1	.209	.244	.291	.945
2000	Fla-N	69	104	19	40	4	2	3	10	18	3	37	3	0	0	8	3	.244	.330	.348	.942
Career average		79	198	28	52	8	2	4	19	21	1	41	4	2	1	7	3	.262	.343	.374	.954
Yankee average		**68**	**110**	**20**	**22**	**3**	**0**	**2**	**7**	**14**	**0**	**19**	**1**	**6**	**0**	**7**	**2**	**.200**	**.290**	**.264**	**.945**
Career total		473	1186	169	311	46	10	22	111	125	4	248	22	12	4	41	16	.262	.343	.374	.954
Yankee total		**135**	**220**	**39**	**44**	**5**	**0**	**3**	**14**	**27**	**0**	**37**	**1**	**11**	**0**	**13**	**4**	**.200**	**.290**	**.264**	**.945**

Frey, Linus Reinhard (Lonny *or* Junior)

HEIGHT: 5'10" THROWS: RIGHT BATS: LEFT BORN: 8/23/1910 ST.LOUIS, MISSOURI POSITIONS PLAYED: 2B, 3B, SS

YEAR	TEAM	GAMES	AB	RUNS	HITS	2B	3B	HR	RBI	BB	IBB	SO	HBP	SH	SF	SB	CS	BA	OBA	SA	FA
1933	Bro-N	34	135	25	43	5	3	0	12	13	—	13	0	2	—	4	—	.319	.378	.400	.896
1934	Bro-N	125	490	77	139	24	5	8	57	52	—	54	5	9	—	11	—	.284	.358	.402	.884
1935	Bro-N	131	515	88	135	35	11	11	77	66	—	68	5	2	—	6	—	.262	.352	.437	.937
1936	Bro-N	148	524	63	146	29	4	4	60	71	—	56	4	8	—	7	—	.279	.369	.372	.918
1937	Chi-N	78	198	33	55	9	3	1	22	33	—	15	0	7	—	6	—	.278	.381	.369	.889
1938	Cin-N	124	501	76	133	26	6	4	36	49	—	50	0	7	—	4	—	.265	.331	.365	.964
1939	Cin-N	125	484	95	141	27	9	11	55	72	—	46	4	25	—	5	—	.291	.388	.452	.976
1940	Cin-N	150	563	102	150	23	6	8	54	80	—	48	3	17	—	22	—	.266	.361	.371	.977
1941	Cin-N	146	543	78	138	29	5	6	59	72	—	37	3	11	—	16	—	.254	.345	.359	.970
1942	Cin-N	141	523	66	139	23	6	2	39	87	—	38	2	8	—	9	—	.266	.373	.344	.977
1943	Cin-N	144	586	78	154	20	8	2	43	76	—	56	0	5	—	7	—	.263	.347	.334	.985
1946	Cin-N	111	333	46	82	10	3	3	24	63	—	31	1	3	—	5	—	.246	.368	.321	.957
1947	Chi-N	24	43	4	9	0	0	0	3	4	—	6	0	0	—	0	—	.209	.277	.209	1.000
1947	**NY-A**	**24**	**28**	**10**	**5**	**2**	**0**	**0**	**2**	**10**	**—**	**1**	**1**	**1**	**—**	**3**	**0**	**.179**	**.410**	**.250**	**.923**
1948	**NY-A**	**1**	**0**	**1**	**0**	**0**	**0**	**0**	**0**	**0**	**—**	**0**	**0**	**0**	**—**	**0**	**0**	**—**	**—**	**—**	**.000**
1948	NY-N	29	51	6	13	1	0	1	6	4	—	6	0	0	—	0	—	.255	.309	.333	.920
Career average		96	345	53	93	16	4	4	34	47	—	33	2	7	—	7	—	.269	.359	.374	.886
Yankee average		**13**	**14**	**6**	**3**	**1**	**0**	**0**	**1**	**5**	**—**	**1**	**1**	**1**	**—**	**2**	**0**	**.179**	**.410**	**.250**	**.462**
Career total		1535	5517	848	1482	263	69	61	549	752	—	525	28	105	—	105	0	.269	.359	.374	.886
Yankee total		**25**	**28**	**11**	**5**	**2**	**0**	**0**	**2**	**10**	**—**	**1**	**1**	**1**	**—**	**3**	**0**	**.179**	**.410**	**.250**	**.462**

Fultz, David Lewis (Swarthy Dane)

HEIGHT: 5'11" THROWS: RIGHT BATS: RIGHT BORN: 05/29/1875 STAUNTON, VIRGINIA DIED: 10/29/1959 DELAND, FLORIDA POSITIONS PLAYED: 2B, 3B, SS, OF

YEAR	TEAM	GAMES	AB	RUNS	HITS	2B	3B	HR	RBI	BB	IBB	SO	HBP	SH	SF	SB	CS	BA	OBA	SA	FA
1898	Phi-N	19	55	7	10	2	2	0	5	6	—	—	0	0	—	1	—	.182	.262	.231	.871
1899	Phi-N	2	5	0	2	0	0	0	0	0	—	—	0	0	—	1	—	.400	.400	.400	.750
1899	Bal-N	57	210	31	62	3	2	0	18	13	—	—	2	6	—	17	—	.295	.342	.329	.940
1901	Phi-A	132	561	95	164	17	9	0	52	32	—	—	3	16	—	36	—	.292	.334	.355	.818
1902	Phi-A	129	506	109	153	20	5	1	49	62	—	—	2	35	—	44	—	.302	.381	.368	.911
1903	**NY-A**	**79**	**295**	**39**	**66**	**12**	**1**	**0**	**25**	**25**	**—**	**—**	**5**	**10**	**—**	**29**	**—**	**.224**	**.295**	**.271**	**.727**
1904	**NY-A**	**97**	**339**	**39**	**93**	**17**	**4**	**2**	**32**	**24**	**—**	**—**	**1**	**18**	**—**	**17**	**—**	**.274**	**.324**	**.366**	**.976**
1905	**NY-A**	**129**	**422**	**49**	**98**	**13**	**3**	**0**	**42**	**39**	**—**	**—**	**7**	**14**	**—**	**44**	**—**	**.232**	**.308**	**.277**	**.966**

(continued)

(continued)

	GAMES	AB	RUNS	HITS	2B	3B	HR	RBI	BB	IBB	SO	HBP	SH	SF	SB	CS	BA	OBA	SA	FA
Career average	81	299	46	81	11	3	0	28	25	—	—	3	12	—	24	—	.271	.332	.331	.870
Yankee average	**102**	**352**	**42**	**86**	**14**	**3**	**1**	**33**	**29**	**—**	**—**	**4**	**14**	**—**	**30**	**—**	**.243**	**.309**	**.304**	**.890**
Career total	644	2393	369	648	84	26	3	223	201	—	—	20	99	—	189	—	.271	.332	.331	.890
Yankee total	**305**	**1056**	**127**	**257**	**42**	**8**	**2**	**99**	**88**	**—**	**—**	**13**	**42**	**—**	**90**	**—**	**.243**	**.309**	**.304**	**.890**

Funk, Elias Calvin (Liz)

HEIGHT: 5'8" THROWS: LEFT BATS: LEFT BORN: 10/28/1904 LACYGNE, KANSAS DIED: 1/16/1968 NORMAN, OKLAHOMA POSITIONS PLAYED: OF

YEAR	TEAM	GAMES	AB	RUNS	HITS	2B	3B	HR	RBI	BB	IBB	SO	HBP	SH	SF	SB	CS	BA	OBA	SA	FA
1929	**NY-A**	**1**	**0**	**0**	**0**	**0**	**0**	**0**	**0**	**0**	**—**	**0**	**0**	**0**		**0**	**0**	**—**	**—**	**—**	**.000**
1930	Det-A	140	527	74	145	26	11	4	65	29	—	39	5	23	—	12	6	.275	.319	.389	.965
1932	Chi-A	122	440	59	114	21	5	2	40	43	—	19	0	11	—	17	15	.259	.325	.343	.979
1933	Chi-A	10	9	1	2	0	0	0	0	1	—	0	0	0	—	0	0	.222	.300	.222	.000
Career average		68	244	34	65	12	4	2	26	18	—	15	1	9	—	7	5	.267	.322	.367	.486
Yankee average		**1**	**0**	**0**	**0**	**0**	**0**	**0**	**0**	**0**	**—**	**0**	**0**	**0**		**0**	**0**	**—**	**—**	**—**	**.000**
Career total		273	976	134	261	47	16	6	105	73	—	58	5	34	—	29	21	.267	.322	.367	.486
Yankee total		**1**	**0**	**0**	**0**	**0**	**0**	**0**	**0**	**0**	**—**	**0**	**0**	**0**		**0**	**0**	**—**	**—**	**—**	**.000**

Gallagher, Joseph Emmett (Muscles)

HEIGHT: 6'2" THROWS: RIGHT BATS: RIGHT BORN: 3/7/1914 BUFFALO, NEW YORK DIED: 2/25/1998 POSITIONS PLAYED: OF

YEAR	TEAM	GAMES	AB	RUNS	HITS	2B	3B	HR	RBI	BB	IBB	SO	HBP	SH	SF	SB	CS	BA	OBA	SA	FA
1939	**NY-A**	**14**	**41**	**8**	**10**	**0**	**1**	**2**	**9**	**3**	**—**	**8**	**1**	**2**	**—**	**1**	**0**	**.244**	**.311**	**.439**	**1.000**
1939	StL-A	71	266	41	75	17	2	9	40	17	—	42	1	6	—	0	1	.282	.327	.462	.944
1940	StL-A	23	70	14	19	3	1	2	8	4	—	12	0	1	—	2	0	.271	.311	.429	.966
1940	Bro-N	57	110	10	29	6	1	3	16	2	—	14	1	0	—	1	—	.264	.283	.418	.941
Career average		41	121	18	33	7	1	4	18	7	—	19	1	2	—	1	0	.273	.314	.446	.963
Yankee average		**14**	**41**	**8**	**10**	**0**	**1**	**2**	**9**	**3**	**—**	**8**	**1**	**2**	**—**	**1**	**0**	**.244**	**.311**	**.439**	**1.000**
Career total		165	487	73	133	26	5	16	73	26	—	76	3	9	—	4	1	.273	.314	.446	.963
Yankee total		**14**	**41**	**8**	**10**	**0**	**1**	**2**	**9**	**3**	**—**	**8**	**1**	**2**	**—**	**1**	**0**	**.244**	**.311**	**.439**	**1.000**

Gallego, Michael Anthony

HEIGHT: 5'8" THROWS: RIGHT BATS: RIGHT BORN: 10/31/1960 WHITTIER, CALIFORNIA POSITIONS PLAYED: 2B, 3B, SS

YEAR	TEAM	GAMES	AB	RUNS	HITS	2B	3B	HR	RBI	BB	IBB	SO	HBP	SH	SF	SB	CS	BA	OBA	SA	FA
1985	Oak-A	76	77	13	16	5	1	1	9	12	0	14	1	2	1	1	1	.208	.319	.338	1.000
1986	Oak-A	20	37	2	10	2	0	0	4	1	0	6	0	2	0	0	2	.270	.289	.324	.986
1987	Oak-A	72	124	18	31	6	0	2	14	12	0	21	1	5	1	0	1	.250	.319	.347	.920
1988	Oak-A	129	277	38	58	8	0	2	20	34	0	53	1	8	0	2	3	.209	.298	.260	1.000
1989	Oak-A	133	357	45	90	14	2	3	30	35	0	43	6	8	3	7	5	.252	.327	.328	.967
1990	Oak-A	140	389	36	80	13	2	3	34	35	0	50	4	17	2	5	5	.206	.277	.272	1.000
1991	Oak-A	159	482	67	119	15	4	12	49	67	3	84	5	10	3	6	9	.247	.343	.369	.989
1992	**NY-A**	**53**	**173**	**24**	**44**	**7**	**1**	**3**	**14**	**20**	**0**	**22**	**4**	**3**	**1**	**0**	**1**	**.254**	**.343**	**.358**	**.990**
1993	**NY-A**	**119**	**403**	**63**	**114**	**20**	**1**	**10**	**54**	**50**	**0**	**65**	**4**	**3**	**5**	**3**	**2**	**.283**	**.364**	**.412**	**.976**
1994	**NY-A**	**89**	**306**	**39**	**73**	**17**	**1**	**6**	**41**	**38**	**1**	**46**	**4**	**5**	**4**	**0**	**1**	**.239**	**.327**	**.359**	**1.000**
1995	Oak-N	43	120	11	28	0	0	0	8	9	0	24	1	2	0	0	1	.233	.292	.233	.882
1996	StL-N	51	143	12	30	2	0	0	4	12	1	31	1	3	0	0	0	.210	.276	.224	.985
1997	StL-N	27	43	6	7	2	0	0	1	1	0	6	0	1	1	0	0	.163	.178	.209	1.000
Career average		85	225	29	54	9	1	3	22	25	0	36	2	5	2	2	2	.239	.320	.328	.977
Yankee average		**87**	**294**	**42**	**77**	**15**	**1**	**6**	**36**	**36**	**0**	**44**	**4**	**4**	**3**	**1**	**1**	**.262**	**.347**	**.383**	**.989**
Career total		1111	2931	374	700	111	12	42	282	326	5	465	32	69	21	24	31	.239	.320	.328	.977
Yankee total		**261**	**882**	**126**	**231**	**44**	**3**	**19**	**109**	**108**	**1**	**133**	**12**	**11**	**10**	**3**	**4**	**.262**	**.347**	**.383**	**.989**

Gamble, Oscar Charles
HEIGHT: 5'11" THROWS: RIGHT BATS: LEFT BORN: 12/20/1949 RAMER, ALABAMA POSITIONS PLAYED: OF

YEAR	TEAM	GAMES	AB	RUNS	HITS	2B	3B	HR	RBI	BB	IBB	SO	HBP	SH	SF	SB	CS	BA	OBA	SA	FA
1969	Chi-N	24	71	6	16	1	1	1	5	10	1	12	0	0	0	0	2	.225	.321	.310	.913
1970	Phi-N	88	275	31	72	12	4	1	19	27	3	37	1	2	0	5	4	.262	.330	.345	.956
1971	Phi-N	92	280	24	62	11	1	6	23	21	2	35	1	3	4	5	2	.237	.331	.326	1.000
1972	Phi-N	74	135	17	32	5	2	1	13	19	0	16	1	0	2	0	1	.267	.329	.464	.971
1973	Cle-A	113	390	56	104	11	3	20	44	34	1	37	3	3	2	3	6	.291	.363	.469	1.000
1974	Cle-A	135	454	74	132	16	4	19	59	48	10	51	5	0	1	11	5	.261	.361	.454	.987
1975	Cle-A	121	348	60	91	16	3	15	45	53	4	39	2	1	1	5	3	.232	.317	.426	.981
1976	**NY-A**	110	340	43	79	13	1	17	57	38	4	38	4	2	0	5	2	.297	.386	.588	.987
1977	Chi-A	137	408	75	121	22	2	31	83	54	2	54	6	1	1	1	2	.275	.366	.387	.979
1978	SD-N	126	375	46	103	15	3	7	47	51	11	45	6	0	5	1	2	.335	.458	.522	1.000
1979	Tex-A	64	161	27	54	6	0	8	32	37	11	15	1	0	2	2	1	.389	.452	.735	.943
1979	**NY-A**	36	113	21	44	4	1	11	32	13	1	13	0	0	0	2	0	.278	.376	.567	1.000
1980	**NY-A**	78	194	40	54	10	2	14	50	28	4	21	4	0	3	2	0	.238	.357	.439	1.000
1981	**NY-A**	80	189	24	45	8	0	10	27	35	2	23	1	0	2	0	2	.272	.387	.522	1.000
1982	**NY-A**	108	316	49	86	21	2	18	57	58	2	47	4	0	4	6	3	.261	.361	.456	.942
1983	**NY-A**	74	180	26	47	10	2	7	26	25	1	23	3	0	0	0	0	.184	.318	.440	1.000
1984	**NY-A**	54	125	17	23	2	0	10	27	25	0	18	0	0	1	1	0	.203	.355	.318	.000
1985	Chi-A	70	148	20	30	5	0	4	20	34	3	22	1	0	0	3	2	.265	.356	.454	.924
Career average		88	250	36	66	10	2	11	37	34	3	30	2	1	2	3	2	.259	.361	.496	.981
Yankee average		77	208	31	54	10	1	12	39	32	2	26	2	0	1	2	1				
Career total		1584	4502	656	1195	188	31	200	666	610	62	546	43	12	30	47	37	.265	.356	.454	.924
Yankee total		540	1457	220	378	68	8	87	276	222	14	183	16	2	10	14	8	.259	.361	.496	.981

Ganzel, John Henry
HEIGHT: 6'0" THROWS: RIGHT BATS: RIGHT BORN: 04/07/1874 KALAMAZOO, MICHIGAN DIED: 1/14/1959 ORLANDO, FLORIDA POSITIONS PLAYED: 1B

YEAR	TEAM	GAMES	AB	RUNS	HITS	2B	3B	HR	RBI	BB	IBB	SO	HBP	SH	SF	SB	CS	BA	OBA	SA	FA
1898	Pit-N	15	45	5	6	0	0	0	2	4	—	—	1	0	—	0	—	.133	.220	.133	.963
1900	Chi-N	78	284	29	78	14	4	4	32	10	—	—	7	7	—	5	—	.275	.316	.394	.980
1901	NY-N	138	526	42	113	13	3	2	66	20	—	—	9	7	—	6	—	.215	.256	.262	.986
1903	**NY-A**	129	476	62	132	25	7	3	71	30	—	—	12	15	—	9	—	.277	.336	.378	.988
1904	**NY-A**	130	465	50	121	16	10	6	48	24	—	—	9	4	—	13	—	.260	.309	.376	.952
1907	Cin-N	145	531	61	135	20	16	2	64	29	—	—	3	12	—	9	—	.254	.297	.363	.990
1908	Cin-N	112	388	32	97	16	10	1	53	19	—	—	2	18	—	6	—	.250	.289	.351	.990
Career average		107	388	40	97	15	7	3	48	19	—	—	6	9	—	7	—	.251	.298	.346	.978
Yankee average		130	471	56	127	21	9	5	60	27	—	—	11	10	—	11	—	.269	.323	.377	.970
Career total		747	2715	281	682	104	50	18	336	136	—	—	21	19	—	22	—	.251	.298	.346	.978
Yankee total		259	941	112	253	41	17	9	119	54	—	—	21	19	—	22	—	.269	.323	.377	.970

Garbark, Michael Nathaniel BORN MICHAEL NATHANIEL GARBACH
HEIGHT: 6'0' THROWS: RIGHT BATS: RIGHT BORN: 2/2/1916 HOUSTON, TEXAS DIED: 8/31/1994 POSITIONS PLAYED: C

YEAR	TEAM	GAMES	AB	RUNS	HITS	2B	3B	HR	RBI	BB	IBB	SO	HBP	SH	SF	SB	CS	BA	OBA	SA	FA
1944	NY-A	89	299	23	78	9	4	1	33	25	—	27	1	2	—	—	1	.261	.320	.328	.988
1945	NY-A	60	176	23	38	5	3	1	26	23	—	12	1	1	—	—	1	.216	.310	.295	.972
Career average		75	238	23	58	7	4	1	30	24	—	20	1	2	—	—	1	.244	.316	.316	.980
Yankee average		75	238	23	58	7	4	1	30	24	—	20	1	2	—	—	1	.244	.316	.316	.980
Career total		149	475	46	116	14	7	2	59	48	—	39	2	3	—	—	2	.244	.316	.316	.980
Yankee total		149	475	46	116	14	7	2	59	48	—	39	2	3	—	—	2	.244	.316	.316	.980

Garcia, Damaso Domingo BORN DAMASO DOMINGO GARCIA (SANCHEZ)
HEIGHT: 6'1" THROWS: RIGHT BATS: RIGHT BORN: 2/7/1957 MOCA, DOMINICAN REPUBLIC POSITIONS PLAYED: 1B, 2B, 3B, SS

YEAR	TEAM	GAMES	AB	RUNS	HITS	2B	3B	HR	RBI	BB	IBB	SO	HBP	SH	SF	SB	CS	BA	OBA	SA	FA
1978	**NY-A**	18	41	5	8	0	0	0	1	2	0	6	0	0	1	1	0	.195	.227	.195	.959
1979	**NY-A**	11	38	3	10	1	0	0	4	0	0	2	0	0	0	2	0	.263	.263	.289	.902
1980	Tor-A	140	543	50	151	30	7	4	46	12	2	55	3	4	3	13	13	.278	.296	.381	.980
1981	Tor-A	64	250	24	63	8	1	1	13	9	1	32	0	3	1	13	3	.252	.277	.304	.972
1982	Tor-A	147	597	89	185	32	3	5	42	21	1	44	5	5	1	54	20	.310	.338	.399	.980

(continued)

(continued)

YEAR	TEAM	GAMES	AB	RUNS	HITS	2B	3B	HR	RBI	BB	IBB	SO	HBP	SH	SF	SB	CS	BA	OBA	SA	FA
1983	Tor-A	131	525	84	161	23	6	3	38	24	3	34	2	5	5	31	17	.307	.336	.390	.981
1984	Tor-A	152	633	79	180	32	5	5	46	16	1	46	9	3	4	46	12	.284	.310	.374	.980
1985	Tor-A	146	600	70	169	25	4	8	65	15	2	41	4	5	3	28	15	.282	.302	.377	.981
1986	Tor-A	122	424	57	119	22	0	6	46	13	0	32	4	2	3	9	6	.281	.306	.375	1.000
1988	Atl-N	21	60	3	7	1	0	1	4	3	0	10	0	1	0	1	0	.117	.159	.183	.984
1989	Mon-N	80	203	26	55	9	1	3	18	15	1	20	0	1	3	5	4	.271	.317	.369	.972
Career average		94	356	45	101	17	2	3	29	12	1	29	2	3	2	18	8	.283	.309	.371	.972
Yankee average		**15**	**40**	**4**	**9**	**1**	**0**	**0**	**3**	**1**	**0**	**4**	**0**	**0**	**1**	**2**	**0**	**.228**	**.244**	**.241**	**.931**
Career total		1032	3914	490	1108	183	27	36	323	130	11	322	27	29	24	203	90	.283	.309	.371	.972
Yankee total		**29**	**79**	**8**	**18**	**1**	**0**	**0**	**5**	**2**	**0**	**8**	**0**	**0**	**1**	**3**	**0**	**.228**	**.244**	**.241**	**.931**

Gardner, Earle McClurkin

HEIGHT: 5'11"   THROWS: RIGHT   BATS: RIGHT   BORN: 01/24/1884 SPARTA, ILLINOIS   DIED: 3/2/1943 SPARTA, ILLINOIS   POSITIONS PLAYED: 2B

YEAR	TEAM	GAMES	AB	RUNS	HITS	2B	3B	HR	RBI	BB	IBB	SO	HBP	SH	SF	SB	CS	BA	OBA	SA	FA
1908	NY-A	20	75	7	16	2	0	0	4	1	—	—	1	3	0	0	—	.213	.234	.240	.947
1909	NY-A	22	85	12	28	4	0	0	15	3	—	—	0	1	0	4	—	.329	.352	.376	.945
1910	NY-A	86	271	36	66	4	2	1	24	21	—	—	2	9	0	9	—	.244	.303	.284	.936
1911	NY-A	102	357	36	94	13	2	0	39	20	—	—	5	13	0	14	—	.263	.312	.311	.959
1912	NY-A	43	160	14	45	3	1	0	26	5	—	—	0	5	0	11	—	.281	.303	.313	.922
Career average		55	190	21	50	5	1	0	22	10	—	—	2	6	0	8	—	.263	.305	.304	.942
Yankee average		**55**	**190**	**21**	**50**	**5**	**1**	**0**	**22**	**10**	**—**	**—**	**2**	**6**	**0**	**8**	**—**	**.263**	**.305**	**.304**	**.942**
Career total		273	948	105	249	26	5	1	108	50	—	—	8	31	0	38	—	.263	.305	.304	.942
Yankee total		**273**	**948**	**105**	**249**	**26**	**5**	**1**	**108**	**50**	**—**	**—**	**8**	**31**	**0**	**38**	**—**	**.263**	**.305**	**.304**	**.942**

Gardner, William Frederick (Billy *or* Shotgun *or* Goofball)

HEIGHT: 6'0"   THROWS: RIGHT   BATS: RIGHT   BORN: 7/19/1927 WATERFORD, CONNECTICUT   POSITIONS PLAYED: 2B, 3B, SS

YEAR	TEAM	GAMES	AB	RUNS	HITS	2B	3B	HR	RBI	BB	IBB	SO	HBP	SH	SF	SB	CS	BA	OBA	SA	FA
1954	NY-N	62	108	10	23	5	0	1	7	6	—	19	1	0	0	0	1	.213	.261	.287	.987
1955	NY-N	59	187	26	38	10	1	3	17	13	0	19	2	4	1	0	0	.203	.261	.316	.889
1956	Bal-A	144	515	53	119	16	2	11	50	29	1	53	7	8	1	5	5	.231	.281	.356	1.000
1957	Bal-A	154	644	79	169	36	3	6	55	53	2	67	8	11	2	10	7	.262	.325	.356	.987
1958	Bal-A	151	560	32	126	28	2	3	33	34	4	53	3	6	4	2	3	.225	.271	.298	1.000
1959	Bal-A	140	401	34	87	13	2	6	27	38	9	61	1	8	3	2	1	.217	.284	.304	1.000
1960	Was-A	145	592	71	152	26	5	9	56	43	0	76	6	7	1	0	4	.257	.313	.363	1.000
1961	Min-A	45	154	13	36	9	0	1	11	10	1	14	0	7	0	0	0	.234	.280	.312	.973
1961	**NY-A**	**41**	**99**	**11**	**21**	**5**	**0**	**1**	**2**	**16**	**0**	**32**	**3**	**1**	**0**	**0**	**0**	**.225**	**.279**	**.304**	**.952**
1962	**NY-A**	**4**	**1**	**0**	**0**	**0**	**0**	**0**	**0**	**0**	**0**	**1**	**0**	**0**	**0**	**0**	**0**	**.000**	**.000**	**.000**	**1.000**
1962	Bos-A	53	199	22	54	9	2	0	12	10	0	39	1	2	0	0	1	.271	.310	.337	.955
1963	Bos-A	36	84	4	16	2	1	0	1	4	1	19	1	0	0	0	0	.190	.236	.238	1.000
Career average		86	295	30	70	13	2	3	23	21	—	38	3	5	1	2	2	.237	.294	.327	.979
Yankee average		**23**	**50**	**6**	**11**	**3**	**0**	**1**	**1**	**8**	**0**	**17**	**2**	**1**	**0**	**0**	**0**	**.210**	**.336**	**.290**	**.976**
Career total		1034	3544	356	841	159	18	41	271	256	18	453	33	54	12	19	22	.237	.294	.327	.979
Yankee total		**45**	**100**	**12**	**21**	**5**	**0**	**1**	**2**	**16**	**0**	**33**	**3**	**1**	**0**	**0**	**0**	**.210**	**.336**	**.290**	**.976**

Gazella, Michael

HEIGHT: 5'7"   THROWS: RIGHT   BATS: RIGHT   BORN: 10/13/1896 OLYPHANT, PENNSYLVANIA   DIED: 9/11/1978 ODESSA, TEXAS   POSITIONS PLAYED: 3B, SS

YEAR	TEAM	GAMES	AB	RUNS	HITS	2B	3B	HR	RBI	BB	IBB	SO	HBP	SH	SF	SB	CS	BA	OBA	SA	FA
1923	NY-A	8	13	2	1	0	0	0	1	2	—	3	0	0	—	0	0	.077	.200	.077	1.000
1926	NY-A	66	168	21	39	6	0	0	20	25	—	24	1	10	—	2	2	.232	.335	.268	.913
1927	NY-A	54	115	17	32	8	4	0	9	23	—	16	1	9	—	4	1	.278	.403	.417	.961
1928	NY-A	32	56	11	13	0	0	0	2	6	—	7	1	1	—	2	1	.232	.317	.232	.969
Career average		40	88	13	21	4	1	0	8	14	—	13	1	5	—	2	1	.241	.350	.304	.961
Yankee average		**40**	**88**	**13**	**21**	**4**	**1**	**0**	**8**	**14**	**—**	**13**	**1**	**5**	**—**	**2**	**1**	**.241**	**.350**	**.304**	**.961**
Career total		160	352	51	85	14	4	0	32	56	—	50	3	20	—	8	4	.241	.350	.304	.961
Yankee total		**160**	**352**	**51**	**85**	**14**	**4**	**0**	**32**	**56**	**—**	**50**	**3**	**20**	**—**	**8**	**4**	**.241**	**.350**	**.304**	**.961**

Gedeon, Elmer Joseph

HEIGHT: 6'0"   THROWS: RIGHT   BATS: RIGHT   BORN: 12/05/1893 SACRAMENTO, CALIFORNIA   DIED: 5/19/1941 SAN FRANCISCO, CALIFORNIA
POSITIONS PLAYED: 2B, 3B, SS, OF

YEAR	TEAM	GAMES	AB	RUNS	HITS	2B	3B	HR	RBI	BB	IBB	SO	HBP	SH	SF	SB	CS	BA	OBA	SA	FA
1913	Was-A	29	71	3	13	1	3	0	6	1	—	6	1	1	—	3	—	.183	.205	.282	1.000
1914	Was-A	4	2	0	0	0	0	0	1	0	—	1	1	1	—	0	0	.000	.333	.000	.667
1916	NY-A	122	435	50	92	14	4	0	27	40	—	61	3	13	—	14	—	.211	.282	.262	.955
1917	NY-A	33	117	15	28	7	0	0	8	7	—	13	1	6	—	4	—	.239	.288	.299	.983
1918	StL-A	123	441	39	94	14	3	1	41	27	—	29	8	23	—	7	—	.213	.271	.265	.977
1919	StL-A	120	437	57	111	13	4	0	27	50	—	35	7	40	—	4	—	.254	.340	.302	.975
1920	StL-A	153	606	95	177	33	6	0	61	55	—	36	4	48	—	1	3	.292	.355	.366	.964
Career average		83	301	37	74	12	3	0	24	26	—	26	4	19	—	5	—	.244	.311	.303	.932
Yankee average		78	276	33	60	11	2	0	18	24	—	37	2	10	—	9	—	.217	.284	.270	.969
Career total		584	2109	259	515	82	20	1	171	180	—	181	25	132	—	33	3	.244	.311	.303	.932
Yankee total		155	552	65	120	21	4	0	35	47	—	74	4	19	—	18	—	.217	.284	.270	.969

Gehrig, Henry Louis (Lou)

HEIGHT: 6'0"   THROWS: LEFT   BATS: LEFT   BORN: 6/19/1903 NEW YORK, NEW YORK   DIED: 6/2/1941 RIVERDALE, NEW YORK   POSITIONS PLAYED: 1B

YEAR	TEAM	GAMES	AB	RUNS	HITS	2B	3B	HR	RBI	BB	IBB	SO	HBP	SH	SF	SB	CS	BA	OBA	SA	FA
1923	NY-A	13	26	6	11	4	1	1	9	2	—	5	0	1	—	0	0	.423	.464	.769	.933
1924	NY-A	10	12	2	6	1	0	0	5	1	—	3	0	0	—	0	0	.500	.538	.583	1.000
1925	NY-A	126	437	73	129	23	10	20	68	46	—	49	2	12	—	6	3	.295	.365	.531	.818
1926	NY-A	155	572	135	179	47	20	16	112	105	—	73	1	18	—	6	5	.313	.420	.549	.991
1927	NY-A	155	584	149	218	52	18	47	175	109	—	84	3	21	—	10	8	.373	.474	.765	.992
1928	NY-A	154	562	139	210	47	13	27	142	95	—	69	4	16	—	4	11	.374	.467	.648	.989
1929	NY-A	154	553	127	166	32	10	35	126	122	—	68	5	12	—	4	4	.300	.431	.584	.994
1930	NY-A	154	581	143	220	42	17	41	174	101	—	63	3	18	—	12	14	.379	.473	.721	1.000
1931	NY-A	155	619	163	211	31	15	46	184	117	—	56	0	2	—	17	12	.341	.446	.662	.991
1932	NY-A	156	596	138	208	42	9	34	151	108	—	38	3	1	—	4	11	.349	.451	.621	.987
1933	NY-A	152	593	138	198	41	12	32	139	92	—	42	1	1	—	9	13	.334	.424	.605	.993
1934	NY-A	154	579	128	210	40	6	49	165	109	—	31	2	0	—	9	5	.363	.465	.706	.994
1935	NY-A	149	535	125	176	26	10	30	119	132	—	38	5	0	—	8	7	.329	.466	.583	.990
1936	NY-A	155	579	167	205	37	7	49	152	130	—	46	7	3	—	3	4	.354	.478	.696	.994
1937	NY-A	157	569	138	200	37	9	37	159	127	—	49	4	0	—	4	3	.351	.473	.643	.989
1938	NY-A	157	576	115	170	32	6	29	114	107	—	75	5	1	—	6	1	.295	.410	.523	.991
1939	NY-A	8	28	2	4	0	0	0	1	5	—	1	0	0	—	0	0	.143	.273	.143	.971
Career average		127	471	111	160	31	10	29	117	89	—	46	3	6	—	6	6	.340	.447	.632	.977
Yankee average		127	471	111	160	31	10	29	117	89	—	46	3	6	—	6	6	.340	.447	.632	.977
Career total		2164	8001	1888	2721	534	163	493	1995	1508	—	790	45	106	—	102	101	.340	.447	.632	.977
Yankee total		2164	8001	1888	2721	534	163	493	1995	1508	—	790	45	106	—	102	101	.340	.447	.632	.977

Geren, Robert Peter

HEIGHT: 6'3"   THROWS: RIGHT   BATS: RIGHT   BORN: 9/22/1961 SAN DIEGO, CALIFORNIA   POSITIONS PLAYED: C

YEAR	TEAM	GAMES	AB	RUNS	HITS	2B	3B	HR	RBI	BB	IBB	SO	HBP	SH	SF	SB	CS	BA	OBA	SA	FA
1988	NY-A	10	10	0	1	0	0	0	0	2	0	3	0	0	0	0	0	.100	.250	.100	1.000
1989	NY-A	65	205	26	59	5	1	9	27	12	0	44	1	6	1	0	0	.288	.329	.454	.991
1990	NY-A	110	277	21	59	7	0	8	31	13	1	73	5	6	2	0	0	.213	.259	.325	.993
1991	NY-A	64	128	7	28	3	0	2	12	9	0	31	0	3	0	0	1	.219	.270	.289	.989
1993	SD-N	58	145	8	31	6	0	3	6	13	4	28	0	4	0	0	0	.214	.278	.317	1.000
Career average		61	153	12	36	4	0	4	15	10	1	36	1	4	1	0	0	.233	.283	.349	.995
Yankee average		62	155	14	37	4	0	5	18	9	0	38	2	4	1	0	0	.237	.284	.356	.993
Career total		307	765	62	178	21	1	22	76	49	5	179	6	19	3	0	1	.233	.283	.349	.995
Yankee total		249	620	54	147	15	1	19	70	36	1	151	6	15	3	0	1	.237	.284	.356	.993

Gibbs, Jerry Dean (Jake)

HEIGHT: 6'0"   THROWS: RIGHT   BATS: LEFT   BORN: 11/7/1938 GRENADA, MISSISSIPPI   POSITIONS PLAYED: C

YEAR	TEAM	GAMES	AB	RUNS	HITS	2B	3B	HR	RBI	BB	IBB	SO	HBP	SH	SF	SB	CS	BA	OBA	SA	FA
1962	NY-A	2	0	2	0	0	0	0	0	0	0	0	0	0	0	0	0	—	—	—	.000
1963	NY-A	4	8	1	2	0	0	0	0	0	0	1	0	0	0	0	0	.250	.250	.250	1.000
1964	NY-A	3	6	1	1	0	0	0	0	0	0	2	0	0	0	0	0	.167	.167	.167	1.000

(continued)

Henry Louis "Lou" Gehrig, 1b, 1923–39

Henry Louis Gehrig was a man who was driven to succeed. Throughout his too-short life, hard work was his mantra.

And it paid off. Over his career, Gehrig was one of the most feared hitters in the history of baseball. He led the American League in RBI five times, in runs scored four times, in home runs three times, in doubles twice. Five times he had over 400 total bases in a season, a stunning statistic that denotes a hitter of unusual power. Babe Ruth, for example, went over 400 total bases twice, Hank Aaron once. Hank Greenberg never did it.

Gehrig was MVP in 1927, the year Ruth hit 60 home runs, and again in 1936. He hit four home runs in a game in 1932 and hit more grand slams than anyone in baseball history—23.

And while he was not as graceful afield as, say, a Hal Chase, Gehrig was a focused athlete who made himself into a great defensive first baseman.

The end of his life was more of a tragedy than anyone knew. The man who thrived on hard work was victimized by a disease that left him immobile and unable to do anything as his body slowly shut down. It was a terrible way for Gehrig to die.

Lou Gehrig was born June 19, 1903, on Second Avenue in the Yorkville section of Manhattan. His parents, Christina and Heinrich, were German immigrants. Gehrig was one of four children, but he was the only one who lived past infancy. Two sisters and a brother all died within a year of their respective births.

Lou enrolled at the Manhattan High School of Commerce in 1917. He was a baseball and football star at Commerce, and following graduation, he attended Columbia on a football scholarship. Gehrig played both on the line and in the backfield at Columbia. In baseball, he pitched and played the outfield.

Gehrig was on the Columbia varsity only one year, but he made his mark, hitting .444 with seven home runs and five stolen bases. On the mound, he was 6-4 and set a school record that has yet to be broken with 17 strikeouts against Williams College.

The hitting attracted scouts, including Yankee scout Paul Krichell. The first time Krichell saw Gehrig, Lou smashed two home runs against Rutgers. Krichell was impressed, and the Yankees eventually signed Gehrig for $1,500 for the remainder of 1923, plus a $2,000 bonus.

Gehrig was up and down with the Yankees for his first two years and the accepted reason was for "seasoning" in the minor leagues. But another reason was that Yankee manager Miller Huggins didn't know where the heck to put him. The starting first baseman at the time, Wally Pipp, was a solid defensive player and one of the best clutch hitters in the league. The outfield had Babe Ruth, Bob Meusel and Whitey Witt, all strong hitters.

But on June 2, 1925, Pipp was in the batting cage against a prospect from Princeton named Charlie Caldwell, Jr. Caldwell unleashed a wild pitch that bounced off Pipp's temple and laid him out on home plate. The popular story is that Huggins saw Pipp reaching for aspirin tablets later that day and decided to start Gehrig in his place. Never happened. Pipp was hospitalized for almost two weeks after the incident. And Gehrig, who had pinch-hit the day before, began his long career at first base.

By 1926, the Yankees were back on top of the American League, and Gehrig, hitting .313 with a league-leading 20 triples and 107 RBI, good for seventh in the league, was hitting his stride. With the Browns' George Sisler and the Indians' George Burns both in their mid-30s, Gehrig was already considered one of the top first basemen in the league. By 1927, his first MVP year, he was in a class by himself.

That year, he hit .373, with a league-leading 52 doubles and a then-record 172 RBI. And, of course, his 47 home runs gave Ruth a run for first place in the home run chase.

He was stunningly consistent over the next 11 years. There were no down years, no slumps. Rather, he made more than 100 RBI 14 years in a row, more than 20 doubles 15 years in a row and more than 27 homers 13 years in a row. His 184 RBI in 1931 is an American League mark. In 1932, when he hit four home runs in one game, it should have been five, but he got under the ball just a hair, and the drive fell about five feet short of the right field fence.

He was also a smart base runner, stealing home 15 times in his career, usually as the scoring end of a double steal. In contrast, Jackie Robinson, a renowned stealer of home, did it 19 times.

He was more of a line-drive hitter than Ruth, and Huggins once pointed out that Gehrig's strength enabled him to get more hits off good pitches than Ruth. He was a great clutch player, hitting .500 in two different World Series, 1928 and 1932. He hit ten Series homers in his career.

And while it was always in the shadow of Ruth at first and later Joe DiMaggio, it was unclear if he really resented it. He was always a team player, and one who was never comfortable in the spotlight. He was a lunch pail type of guy.

By 1933, the consecutive-game streak was his. He passed former Yankee Everett Scott's mark of 1,307 in August. When he finally sat down in 1939, he had played in 2,130 games, a mark not broken for 46 years, until Cal Ripkin, Jr., would eventually play in 2,632 straight games.

He won the triple crown in 1934, hitting .363 with 49 homers and 165 RBI, the same year he married the former Eleanor Twichell of Chicago, who would be his wife and best friend for the rest of his short life.

That final, dramatic, sad chapter began in fits and starts. He was MVP again in 1936, with 49 home runs and 152 RBI, but by 1938, he seemed to be failing. Critics pointed to the

streak and the rigor of playing every day, but it seemed to be more than that. His production wasn't dropping, it was plummeting. In the first few weeks of 1939, Gehrig looked bad at the plate and in the field, and he knew it.

Finally, in early May, he asked manager Joe McCarthy to sit him down. Frankly, with the pressure of the streak bearing down on him, McCarthy admitted later that he was grateful the decision was Lou's. McCarthy had no intention of being known as the man who sat the Iron Horse down. In an interview that year with the Associated Press, Gehrig noted that it was the first time since he was 15 years old that he had not started in an athletic contest, including baseball, football, soccer and basketball games. He never played in another big league game.

But while his career might have been over, there was still no real information as to what exactly was ailing Gehrig. Finally, a few weeks later, after a trip to the Mayo Clinic, the verdict was in: amyotrophic lateral sclerosis, a degenerative illness of the body's central nervous system. The diagnosis was not good: perhaps three to four years to live.

In July of 1939, the Yankees held Lou Gehrig Appreciation Day, which is, of course, the afternoon during which Gehrig gave his "luckiest man on the face of the Earth" speech, probably the most memorable speech in baseball history. Ironically, Gehrig was initally so overcome by emotion that he didn't think he'd be able to speak. Later that year, by special dispensation, the Baseball Writers of America waived the five-year waiting period and elected Gehrig into the Hall of Fame immediately. If doctors hadn't told him how serious his illness was, Gehrig probably knew by now. Everyone wanted to see him elected to the Hall of Fame before he died.

With his playing days over, Gehrig worked as a parole officer for the city of New York for a few years, but the ALS eventually slowed him so much he could no longer get to work. On June 2, 1941, Lou Gehrig, 37 years old, died, much too young, in his sleep.

(continued)

YEAR	TEAM	GAMES	AB	RUNS	HITS	2B	3B	HR	RBI	BB	IBB	SO	HBP	SH	SF	SB	CS	BA	OBA	SA	FA
1965	NY-A	37	68	6	15	1	0	2	7	4	0	20	1	1	2	0	0	.221	.267	.324	.991
1966	NY-A	62	182	19	47	6	0	3	20	19	2	16	0	0	1	5	2	.258	.327	.341	.988
1967	NY-A	116	374	33	87	7	1	4	25	28	1	57	4	2	3	7	6	.233	.291	.289	.975
1968	NY-A	124	423	31	90	12	3	3	29	27	5	68	6	4	0	9	8	.213	.270	.277	.991
1969	NY-A	71	219	18	49	9	2	0	18	23	9	30	0	0	3	3	4	.224	.294	.283	.990
1970	NY-A	49	153	23	46	9	2	8	26	7	1	14	1	0	2	2	0	.301	.331	.542	.987
1971	NY-A	70	206	23	45	9	0	5	21	12	1	23	3	2	1	2	2	.218	.270	.335	.988
Career average		54	164	16	38	5	1	3	15	12	2	23	2	1	1	3	2	.233	.289	.321	.891
Yankee average		54	164	16	38	5	1	3	15	12	2	23	2	1	1	3	2	.233	.289	.321	.891
Career total		538	1639	157	382	53	8	25	146	120	19	231	15	9	12	28	22	.233	.289	.321	.891
Yankee total		538	1639	157	382	53	8	25	146	120	19	231	15	9	12	28	22	.233	.289	.321	.891

Gilhooley, Frank Patrick (Flash)
HEIGHT: 5'8"   THROWS: RIGHT   BATS: LEFT   BORN: 06/10/1892 TOLEDO, OHIO   DIED: 7/11/1959 TOLEDO, OHIO   POSITIONS PLAYED: OF

YEAR	TEAM	GAMES	AB	RUNS	HITS	2B	3B	HR	RBI	BB	IBB	SO	HBP	SH	SF	SB	CS	BA	OBA	SA	FA
1911	StL-N	1	0	0	0	0	0	0	0	0	—	0	0	0	—	0	—	—	—	—	.000
1912	StL-N	13	49	5	11	0	0	0	2	3	—	8	0	0	—	0	—	.224	.269	.224	1.000
1913	NY-A	24	85	10	29	2	1	0	14	4	—	9	1	3	—	6	—	.341	.378	.388	.977
1914	NY-A	1	3	0	2	0	0	0	0	1	—	0	0	0	—	0	—	.667	.750	.667	.000
1915	NY-A	1	4	0	0	0	0	0	0	0	—	1	0	0	—	0	0	.000	.000	.000	1.000
1916	NY-A	58	223	40	62	5	3	1	10	37	—	17	1	2	—	16	0	.278	.383	.341	.971
1917	NY-A	54	165	14	40	6	1	0	8	30	—	13	1	5	—	6	—	.242	.362	.291	.933
1918	NY-A	112	427	59	118	13	5	1	23	53	—	24	1	12	—	7	—	.276	.358	.337	.961
1919	Bos-A	48	112	14	27	4	0	0	1	12	—	8	0	3	—	2	—	.241	.315	.277	.922
Career average		35	119	16	32	3	1	0	6	16	—	9	0	3	—	4	—	.271	.357	.323	.752
Yankee average		42	151	21	42	4	2	0	9	21	—	11	1	4	—	6	—	.277	.367	.334	.807
Career total		312	1068	142	289	30	10	2	58	140	—	80	4	25	—	37	0	.271	.357	.323	.752
Yankee total		250	907	123	251	26	10	2	55	125	—	64	4	22	—	35	0	.277	.367	.334	.807

Girardi, Joseph Elliott
HEIGHT: 5'11"   THROWS: RIGHT   BATS: RIGHT   BORN: 10/14/1964 PEORIA, ILLINOIS   POSITIONS PLAYED: C

YEAR	TEAM	GAMES	AB	RUNS	HITS	2B	3B	HR	RBI	BB	IBB	SO	HBP	SH	SF	SB	CS	BA	OBA	SA	FA
1989	Chi-N	59	157	15	39	10	0	1	14	11	5	26	2	1	1	2	1	.248	.304	.331	.981
1990	Chi-N	133	419	36	113	24	2	1	38	17	11	50	3	4	4	8	3	.270	.300	.344	.985
1991	Chi-N	21	47	3	9	2	0	0	6	6	1	6	0	1	0	0	0	.191	.283	.234	.972
1992	Chi-N	91	270	19	73	3	1	1	12	19	3	38	1	0	1	0	2	.270	.320	.300	.991
1993	Col-N	86	310	35	90	14	5	3	31	24	0	41	3	12	1	6	6	.290	.346	.397	.989
1994	Col-N	93	330	47	91	9	4	4	34	21	1	48	2	6	2	3	3	.276	.321	.364	.992
1995	Col-N	125	462	63	121	17	2	8	55	29	0	76	2	12	1	3	3	.262	.308	.359	.988
1996	NY-A	124	422	55	124	22	3	2	45	30	1	55	5	11	3	13	4	.294	.346	.374	.996
1997	NY-A	112	398	38	105	23	1	1	50	26	1	53	2	5	2	2	3	.264	.311	.334	.994
1998	NY-A	78	254	31	70	11	4	3	31	14	1	38	0	8	1	2	4	.276	.312	.386	.995
1999	NY-A	65	209	23	50	16	1	2	27	10	0	26	0	8	2	3	1	.239	.271	.354	.984
2000	Chi-N	106	363	47	101	15	1	6	40	32	3	61	3	6	3	1	0	.278	.339	.375	.993
Career average		91	303	34	82	14	2	3	32	20	2	43	2	6	2	4	3	.271	.318	.356	.988
Yankee average		95	321	37	87	18	2	2	38	20	1	43	2	8	2	5	3	.272	.316	.361	.992
Career total		1093	3641	412	986	166	24	32	383	239	27	518	23	74	21	43	30	.271	.318	.356	.988
Yankee total		379	1283	147	349	72	9	8	153	80	3	172	7	32	8	20	12	.272	.316	.361	.992

Gleich, Frank Elmer (Inch)
HEIGHT: 5'11"   THROWS: RIGHT   BATS: LEFT   BORN: 3/7/1894 COLUMBUS, OHIO   DIED: 3/27/1949 COLUMBUS, OHIO

YEAR	TEAM	GAMES	AB	RUNS	HITS	2B	3B	HR	RBI	BB	IBB	SO	HBP	SH	SF	SB	CS	BA	OBA	SA	FA
1919	NY-A	5	4	0	1	0	0	0	1	1	—	0	0	0	—	0	—	.250	.400	.250	.000
1920	NY-A	24	41	6	5	0	0	0	3	6	—	10	0	1	—	0	—	.122	.234	.122	.864
Career average		15	23	3	3	0	0	0	2	4	—	5	0	1	—	0	—	.133	.250	.133	.432
Yankee average		15	23	3	3	0	0	0	2	4	—	5	0	1	—	0	—	.133	.250	.133	.432
Career total		29	45	6	6	0	0	0	4	7	—	10	0	1	—	0	0	.133	.250	.133	.432
Yankee total		29	45	6	6	0	0	0	4	7	—	10	0	1	—	0	0	.133	.250	.133	.432

Glenn, Joseph Charles (Gabby)
HEIGHT: 5'11" THROWS: RIGHT BATS: RIGHT BORN: 11/19/1908 DICKSON CITY, PENN. DIED: 5/6/1985 TUNKHANNOCK, PENN. POSITIONS PLAYED: C

YEAR	TEAM	GAMES	AB	RUNS	HITS	2B	3B	HR	RBI	BB	IBB	SO	HBP	SH	SF	SB	CS	BA	OBA	SA	FA
1932	**NY-A**	**6**	**16**	**0**	**2**	**0**	**0**	**0**	**0**	**1**	**—**	**5**	**1**	**0**	**—**	**0**	**0**	**.125**	**.222**	**.125**	**1.000**
1933	**NY-A**	**5**	**21**	**1**	**3**	**0**	**0**	**0**	**1**	**0**	**—**	**3**	**0**	**0**	**—**	**0**	**0**	**.143**	**.143**	**.143**	**1.000**
1935	**NY-A**	**17**	**43**	**7**	**10**	**4**	**0**	**0**	**6**	**4**	**—**	**1**	**0**	**2**	**—**	**0**	**0**	**.233**	**.298**	**.326**	**.984**
1936	**NY-A**	**44**	**129**	**21**	**35**	**7**	**0**	**1**	**20**	**20**	**—**	**10**	**1**	**0**	**—**	**1**	**1**	**.271**	**.373**	**.349**	**.970**
1937	**NY-A**	**25**	**53**	**6**	**15**	**2**	**2**	**0**	**4**	**10**	**—**	**11**	**0**	**1**	**—**	**0**	**0**	**.283**	**.397**	**.396**	**.978**
1938	**NY-A**	**41**	**123**	**10**	**32**	**7**	**2**	**0**	**25**	**10**	**—**	**14**	**0**	**0**	**—**	**1**	**0**	**.260**	**.316**	**.350**	**.974**
1939	StL-A	88	286	29	78	13	1	4	29	31	—	40	0	3	—	4	4	.273	.344	.367	.968
1940	Bos-A	22	47	3	6	1	0	0	4	5	—	7	0	1	—	0	0	.128	.212	.149	.961
Career average		31	90	10	23	4	1	1	11	10	—	11	0	1	—	1	1	.252	.330	.334	.979
Yankee average		**23**	**64**	**8**	**16**	**3**	**1**	**0**	**9**	**8**	**—**	**7**	**0**	**1**	**—**	**0**	**0**	**.252**	**.333**	**.332**	**.984**
Career total		248	718	77	181	34	5	5	89	81	—	91	2	7	—	6	5	.252	.330	.334	.979
Yankee total		**138**	**385**	**45**	**97**	**20**	**4**	**1**	**56**	**45**	**—**	**44**	**2**	**3**	**—**	**2**	**1**	**.252**	**.333**	**.332**	**.984**

Gonder, Jesse Lemar
HEIGHT: 5'10" THROWS: RIGHT BATS: LEFT BORN: 1/20/1936 MONTICELLO, ARKANSAS POSITIONS PLAYED: C

YEAR	TEAM	GAMES	AB	RUNS	HITS	2B	3B	HR	RBI	BB	IBB	SO	HBP	SH	SF	SB	CS	BA	OBA	SA	FA
1960	**NY-A**	**7**	**7**	**1**	**2**	**0**	**0**	**1**	**3**	**1**	**0**	**1**	**0**	**0**	**1**	**0**	**0**	**.286**	**.333**	**.714**	**1.000**
1961	**NY-A**	**15**	**12**	**2**	**4**	**1**	**0**	**0**	**3**	**3**	**1**	**1**	**0**	**0**	**0**	**0**	**0**	**.333**	**.467**	**.417**	**.000**
1962	Cin-N	4	4	0	0	0	0	0	0	0	0	3	0	0	0	0	0	.000	.000	.000	.000
1963	Cin-N	31	32	5	10	2	0	3	5	1	0	12	0	0	0	0	0	.313	.333	.656	1.000
1963	NY-N	42	126	12	38	4	0	3	15	6	0	25	0	0	2	1	2	.302	.333	.405	.978
1964	NY-N	131	341	28	92	11	1	7	35	29	5	65	2	0	2	0	0	.270	.329	.370	.979
1965	NY-N	53	105	6	25	4	0	4	9	11	4	20	0	0	1	0	0	.238	.308	.390	.992
1965	Mil-N	31	53	2	8	2	0	1	5	4	0	9	0	0	0	0	0	.151	.211	.245	.989
1966	Pit-N	59	160	13	36	3	1	7	16	12	7	39	2	0	0	0	0	.225	.287	.388	.978
1967	Pit-N	22	36	4	5	1	0	0	3	5	3	9	2	2	0	0	0	.139	.279	.167	.971
Career average		40	88	7	22	3	0	3	9	7	2	18	1	0	1	0	0	.251	.310	.377	.789
Yankee average		**11**	**10**	**2**	**3**	**1**	**0**	**1**	**3**	**2**	**1**	**1**	**0**	**0**	**1**	**0**	**0**	**.316**	**.417**	**.526**	**.500**
Career total		395	876	73	220	28	2	26	94	72	20	184	6	2	6	1	2	.251	.310	.377	.789
Yankee total		**22**	**19**	**3**	**6**	**1**	**0**	**1**	**6**	**4**	**1**	**2**	**0**	**0**	**1**	**0**	**0**	**.316**	**.417**	**.526**	**.500**

Gonzalez, Jose Fernando BORN JOSE FERNANDO GONZALEZ (QUINONES)
HEIGHT: 5'10" THROWS: RIGHT BATS: RIGHT BORN: 6/19/1950 ARECIBO, PUERTO RICO POSITIONS PLAYED: 2B, 3B, SS, OF

YEAR	TEAM	GAMES	AB	RUNS	HITS	2B	3B	HR	RBI	BB	IBB	SO	HBP	SH	SF	SB	CS	BA	OBA	SA	FA
1972	Pit-N	3	2	0	0	0	0	0	0	0	0	2	0	0	0	0	0	.000	.000	.000	.500
1973	Pit-N	37	49	5	11	0	1	1	5	1	0	11	1	0	0	0	0	.224	.255	.327	.923
1974	KC-A	9	21	1	3	1	0	0	2	0	0	4	0	0	0	1	0	.143	.143	.190	1.000
1974	**NY-A**	**51**	**121**	**11**	**26**	**5**	**1**	**1**	**7**	**7**	**0**	**7**	**0**	**2**	**0**	**0**	**0**	**.215**	**.258**	**.298**	**1.000**
1977	Pit-N	80	181	17	50	10	0	4	27	13	6	21	0	3	3	3	3	.276	.320	.398	1.000
1978	Pit-N	9	21	2	4	1	0	0	0	1	0	3	0	0	0	0	0	.190	.227	.238	.500
1978	SD-N	101	320	27	80	10	2	2	29	18	3	32	0	7	5	4	4	.250	.286	.313	.982
1979	SD-N	114	323	22	70	13	3	9	34	18	11	34	0	0	0	0	0	.217	.258	.359	.976
Career average		51	130	11	31	5	1	2	13	7	3	14	0	1	1	1	1	.235	.274	.336	.860
Yankee average		**51**	**121**	**11**	**26**	**5**	**1**	**1**	**7**	**7**	**0**	**7**	**0**	**2**	**0**	**0**	**0**	**.215**	**.258**	**.298**	**1.000**
Career total		404	1038	85	244	40	7	17	104	58	20	114	1	9	8	8	7	.235	.274	.336	.860
Yankee total		**51**	**121**	**11**	**26**	**5**	**1**	**1**	**7**	**7**	**0**	**7**	**0**	**2**	**0**	**0**	**0**	**.215**	**.258**	**.298**	**1.000**

Gonzalez, Pedro BORN PEDRO GONZALES (OLIVARES)
HEIGHT: 6'0" THROWS: RIGHT BATS: RIGHT BORN: 12/12/1937 SAN PEDRO DE MACORIS, DOMINICAN REPUBLIC POSITIONS PLAYED: 1B, 2B, OF

YEAR	TEAM	GAMES	AB	RUNS	HITS	2B	3B	HR	RBI	BB	IBB	SO	HBP	SH	SF	SB	CS	BA	OBA	SA	FA
1963	**NY-A**	**14**	**26**	**3**	**5**	**1**	**0**	**0**	**1**	**0**	**0**	**5**	**0**	**2**	**0**	**0**	**1**	**.192**	**.192**	**.231**	**.963**
1964	**NY-A**	**80**	**112**	**18**	**31**	**8**	**1**	**0**	**5**	**7**	**0**	**22**	**2**	**2**	**0**	**3**	**4**	**.277**	**.331**	**.366**	**1.000**
1965	**NY-A**	**7**	**5**	**0**	**2**	**1**	**0**	**0**	**0**	**0**	**0**	**2**	**0**	**1**	**0**	**0**	**0**	**.400**	**.400**	**.400**	**.000**
1965	Cle-A	116	400	38	101	14	3	5	39	18	7	57	3	8	3	7	4	.253	.288	.340	.980
1966	Cle-A	110	352	21	82	9	2	2	17	15	1	54	2	4	1	8	5	.233	.268	.287	.984
1967	Cle-A	80	189	19	43	6	0	1	8	12	0	36	1	4	2	4	6	.228	.275	.275	.971

(continued)

(continued)

																	BA	OBA	SA	FA
Career average	68	181	17	44	7	1	1	12	9	1	29	1	4	1	4	3	.244	.282	.313	.816
Yankee average	34	48	7	13	3	0	0	2	2	0	10	1	2	0	1	2	.266	.309	.350	.654
Career total	407	1084	99	264	39	6	8	70	52	8	176	8	21	6	22	20	.244	.282	.313	.816
Yankee total	101	143	21	38	10	1	0	6	7	0	29	2	5	0	3	5	.266	.309	.350	.654

Good, Wilbur David (Lefty)

HEIGHT: 5'6"   THROWS: LEFT   BATS: LEFT   BORN: 09/28/1885 PUNXSUTAWNEY, PENNSYLVANIA   DIED: 12/30/1963 BROOKSVILLE, FLORIDA   POSITIONS PLAYED: OF

YEAR	TEAM	GAMES	AB	RUNS	HITS	2B	3B	HR	RBI	BB	IBB	SO	HBP	SH	SF	SB	CS	BA	OBA	SA	FA
1905	**NY-A**	5	8	2	3	0	0	0	0	0	—	—	0	0	—	0	—	.375	.375	.375	.889
1908	Cle-A	46	154	23	43	1	3	1	14	13	—	—	4	4	—	7	—	.279	.351	.344	.845
1909	Cle-A	94	318	33	68	6	5	0	17	28	—	—	9	5	—	13	—	.214	.296	.264	.953
1910	Bos-N	23	86	15	29	5	4	0	11	6	—	13	2	4	—	5	—	.337	.394	.488	.969
1911	Bos-N	43	165	21	44	9	3	0	15	12	—	22	0	4	—	3	—	.267	.316	.358	.945
1911	Chi-N	54	145	27	39	5	4	2	21	11	—	17	2	5	—	10	—	.269	.329	.400	.928
1912	Chi-N	39	35	7	5	0	0	0	1	3	—	7	0	0	—	3	—	.143	.211	.143	1.000
1913	Chi-N	49	91	11	23	3	2	1	12	11	—	16	1	0	—	5	—	.253	.340	.363	.974
1914	Chi-N	154	580	70	158	24	7	2	43	53	—	74	7	24	—	31	—	.272	.341	.348	.930
1915	Chi-N	128	498	66	126	18	9	2	27	34	—	65	5	8	—	19	17	.253	.307	.337	.936
1916	Phi-N	75	136	25	34	4	3	1	15	8	—	13	3	5	—	7	—	.250	.306	.346	.983
1918	Chi-A	35	148	24	37	9	4	0	11	11	—	16	3	1	—	1	—	.250	.315	.365	.982
Career average	62	197	27	51	7	4	1	16	16	—	—	3	5	—	9	—	.258	.322	.342	.945
Yankee average	5	8	2	3	0	0	0	0	0	—	—	0	0	—	0	—	.375	.375	.375	.889
Career total	745	2364	324	609	84	44	9	187	190	—	243	36	60	—	104	17	.258	.322	.342	.945
Yankee total	5	8	2	3	0	0	0	0	0	—	—	0	0	—	0	—	.375	.375	.375	.889

Gordon, Joseph Lowell (Flash)

HEIGHT: 5'10"   THROWS: RIGHT   BATS: RIGHT   BORN: 2/18/1915 LOS ANGELES, CAL.   DIED: 4/14/1978 SACRAMENTO, CAL.   POSITIONS PLAYED: 1,B, 2B, SS

YEAR	TEAM	GAMES	AB	RUNS	HITS	2B	3B	HR	RBI	BB	IBB	SO	HBP	SH	SF	SB	CS	BA	OBA	SA	FA
1938	**NY-A**	127	458	83	117	24	7	25	97	56	—	72	3	3	—	11	3	.255	.340	.502	.960
1939	**NY-A**	151	567	92	161	32	5	28	111	75	—	57	2	4	—	11	10	.284	.370	.506	.967
1940	**NY-A**	155	616	112	173	32	10	30	103	52	—	57	3	6	—	18	8	.281	.340	.511	.975
1941	**NY-A**	156	588	104	162	26	7	24	87	72	—	80	4	1	—	10	9	.276	.358	.466	.958
1942	**NY-A**	147	538	88	173	29	4	18	103	79	—	95	1	7	—	12	6	.322	.409	.491	.966
1943	**NY-A**	152	543	82	135	28	5	17	69	98	—	75	2	7	—	4	7	.249	.365	.413	.969
1946	**NY-A**	112	376	35	79	15	0	11	47	49	—	72	4	2	—	2	5	.210	.308	.338	.974
1947	Cle-A	155	562	89	153	27	6	29	93	62	—	49	1	1	—	7	3	.272	.346	.496	.978
1948	Cle-A	144	550	96	154	21	4	32	124	77	—	68	3	3	—	5	2	.280	.371	.507	1.000
1949	Cle-A	148	541	74	136	18	3	20	84	83	—	33	4	4	—	5	6	.251	.355	.407	.980
1950	Cle-A	119	368	59	87	12	1	19	57	56	—	44	2	3	—	4	1	.236	.340	.429	.969
Career average	142	519	83	139	24	5	23	89	69	—	64	3	4	—	8	5	.268	.357	.466	.972
Yankee average	143	527	85	143	27	5	22	88	69	—	73	3	4	—	10	7	.271	.358	.467	.967
Career total	1566	5707	914	1530	264	52	253	975	759	—	702	29	41	—	89	60	.268	.357	.466	.972
Yankee total	1000	3686	596	1000	186	38	153	617	481	—	508	19	30	—	68	48	.271	.358	.467	.967

Gossett, John Star (Dick)

HEIGHT: 5'11"   THROWS: RIGHT   BATS: RIGHT   BORN: 8/21/1891 DENNISON, OHIO   DIED: 10/6/1962 MASSILLON   POSITIONS PLAYED: C

YEAR	TEAM	GAMES	AB	RUNS	HITS	2B	3B	HR	RBI	BB	IBB	SO	HBP	SH	SF	SB	CS	BA	OBA	SA	FA
1913	**NY-A**	39	105	9	17	2	0	0	9	10	—	22	3	4	—	1	—	.162	.254	.181	.966
1914	**NY-A**	10	21	3	3	0	0	0	1	5	—	5	1	0	—	0	0	.143	.333	.143	.977
Career average	24.5	63	6	10	1	0	0	5	7.5	—	13.5	2	2	—	0.5	—	.159	.269	.175	.972
Yankee average	24.5	63	6	10	1	0	0	5	7.5	—	13.5	2	2	—	0.5	—	.159	.269	.175	.972
Career total	49	126	12	20	2	0	0	10	15	—	27	4	4	—	1	0	.159	.269	.175	.972
Yankee total	49	126	12	20	2	0	0	10	15	—	27	4	4	—	1	0	.159	.269	.175	.972

Joseph Lowell "Flash" Gordon, 2b-1b-ss, 1938–46

The athletic Gordon was the successor to Hall of Fame second baseman Tony Lazzeri, and for the seven years he spent there, he proved to be a worthy replacement.

Gordon was born on February 18, 1915, in Los Angeles, California. He was brought up by the Yankees as a 21-year-old rookie who had starred, along with outfielder Charlie Keller, on the 1937 Newark Bears.

Gordon was expected to fill Lazzeri's large shoes, and he did not disappoint. In his first year, he had 25 home runs, 97 RBI and scored 83 runs. He fit in perfectly with the veteran infield of third baseman Red Rolfe, shortstop Frankie Crosetti and first baseman Lou Gehrig.

But Gordon was downright amazing in the 1938 World Series. His .400 batting average was a team high, as were his six RBI. He won the third game of the Series by himself with a solo home run in the fifth and a two-run single in the sixth. The Yankees swept the Cubs in four games.

The next season, Gordon began a run of nine consecutive appearances in the All-Star Game, including six in a row for the Yankees.

He was a solid defensive player with great range. But he was also a very good hitter. He had 110 or more hits for six of his seven years with the Yankees. He averaged 22 home runs and 88 RBI for his Yankee career. In 1942, he hit in 29 straight games. That was also the year he was awarded the MVP of the American League. He hit .322 with 173 hits.

Gordon was a tough out in the World Series. In addition to hitting .400 in 1938, he led the Yankees with a .500 average in the 1941 Series, a win over Brooklyn.

In 1946, the Yankees were in need of pitching, and they sent Gordon to Cleveland for Allie Reynolds. Gordon continued his high level of play for the Indians, helping them to the 1948 World Series championship over the Boston Braves.

Following his playing career, Gordon managed the Indians from 1958 to 1960, and followed that up with managerial stints in Detroit and Kansas City. Gordon died in 1978 in Sacramento, California.

Grabowski, John Patrick (Nig)

HEIGHT: 5'10"   THROWS: RIGHT   BATS: RIGHT   BORN: 1/7/1900 WARE, MASSACHUSETTS   DIED: 5/23/1946 ALBANY, NEW YORK   POSITIONS PLAYED: C

YEAR	TEAM	GAMES	AB	RUNS	HITS	2B	3B	HR	RBI	BB	IBB	SO	HBP	SH	SF	SB	CS	BA	OBA	SA	FA
1924	Chi-A	20	56	10	14	3	0	0	3	2	—	4	0	4	—	0	0	.250	.276	.304	.972
1925	Chi-A	21	46	5	14	4	1	0	10	2	—	4	0	0	—	0	1	.304	.333	.435	.983
1926	Chi-A	48	122	6	32	1	1	1	11	4	—	15	0	3	—	0	1	.262	.286	.311	1.000
1927	**NY-A**	**70**	**195**	**29**	**54**	**2**	**4**	**0**	**25**	**20**	**—**	**15**	**2**	**6**	**—**	**0**	**0**	**.277**	**.350**	**.328**	**.984**
1928	**NY-A**	**75**	**202**	**21**	**48**	**7**	**1**	**1**	**21**	**10**	**—**	**21**	**0**	**3**	**—**	**0**	**0**	**.238**	**.274**	**.297**	**.987**
1929	**NY-A**	**22**	**59**	**4**	**12**	**1**	**0**	**0**	**2**	**3**	**—**	**6**	**0**	**2**	**—**	**1**	**0**	**.203**	**.242**	**.220**	**.943**
1931	Det-A	40	136	9	32	7	1	1	14	6	—	19	0	2	—	0	0	.235	.268	.324	.984
Career average		42	117	12	29	4	1	0	12	7	—	12	0	3	—	0	0	.252	.295	.314	.979
Yankee average		**56**	**152**	**18**	**38**	**3**	**2**	**0**	**16**	**11**	**—**	**14**	**1**	**4**	**—**	**0**	**0**	**.250**	**.303**	**.300**	**.971**
Career total		296	816	84	206	25	8	3	86	47	—	84	2	20	—	1	2	.252	.295	.314	.979
Yankee total		**167**	**456**	**54**	**114**	**10**	**5**	**1**	**48**	**33**	**—**	**42**	**2**	**11**	**—**	**1**	**0**	**.250**	**.303**	**.300**	**.971**

Greene, Patrick Joseph (Paddy *or* Patsy *or* Willie)

HEIGHT: 5'8" THROWS: RIGHT BATS: RIGHT BORN: 3/20/1875 PROVIDENCE, R.I. DIED: 10/20/1934 PROVIDENCE, R.I. POSITIONS PLAYED: OF

YEAR	TEAM	GAMES	AB	RUNS	HITS	2B	3B	HR	RBI	BB	IBB	SO	HBP	SH	SF	SB	CS	BA	OBA	SA	FA
1902	Phi-N	19	65	6	11	1	0	0	1	2	—	—	1	2	—	2	—	.169	.206	.185	.912
1903	**NY-A**	4	13	1	4	1	0	0	0	0	—	—	0	0	—	0	—	.308	.309	.385	1.000
1903	Det-A	1	3	0	0	0	0	0	0	0	—	—	0	0	—	0	—	.000	.000	.000	.750
Career average		8	27	2	5	1	0	0	0	1	—	—	0	1	—	1	—	.185	.214	.210	.887
Yankee average		**4**	**13**	**1**	**4**	**1**	**0**	**0**	**0**	**0**	**—**	**—**	**0**	**0**	**—**	**0**	**—**	**.308**	**.308**	**.385**	**1.000**
Career total		24	81	7	15	2	0	0	1	2	—	—	1	2	—	2	—	.185	.214	.210	.887
Yankee total		**4**	**13**	**1**	**4**	**1**	**0**	**0**	**0**	**0**	**—**	**—**	**0**	**0**	**—**	**0**	**—**	**.308**	**.308**	**.385**	**1.000**

Griffey, George Kenneth Sr.

HEIGHT: 6'0" THROWS: LEFT BATS: LEFT BORN: 4/10/1950 DONORA, PENNSYLVANIA POSITIONS PLAYED: OF

YEAR	TEAM	GAMES	AB	RUNS	HITS	2B	3B	HR	RBI	BB	IBB	SO	HBP	SH	SF	SB	CS	BA	OBA	SA	FA
1973	Cin-N	25	86	19	33	5	1	3	14	6	0	10	0	0	0	4	2	.384	.424	.570	1.000
1974	Cin-N	88	227	24	57	9	5	2	19	27	2	43	1	1	0	9	4	.251	.333	.361	1.000
1975	Cin-N	132	463	95	141	15	9	4	46	67	2	67	1	6	3	16	7	.305	.391	.402	.967
1976	Cin-N	148	562	111	189	28	9	6	74	62	0	65	1	0	3	34	11	.336	.401	.450	.979
1977	Cin-N	154	585	117	186	35	8	12	57	69	2	84	0	1	2	17	8	.318	.389	.467	.990
1978	Cin-N	158	614	90	177	33	8	10	63	54	1	70	0	9	3	23	5	.288	.344	.417	.969
1979	Cin-N	95	380	62	120	27	4	8	32	36	3	39	1	0	3	12	5	.316	.374	.471	.984
1980	Cin-N	146	544	89	160	28	10	13	85	62	4	77	1	3	5	23	1	.294	.364	.454	.978
1981	Cin-N	101	396	65	123	21	6	2	34	39	6	42	1	2	4	12	4	.311	.370	.409	.989
1982	**NY-A**	127	484	70	134	23	2	12	54	39	1	58	0	1	3	10	4	.277	.329	.407	.983
1983	**NY-A**	118	458	60	140	21	3	11	46	34	3	45	2	3	2	6	1	.306	.355	.437	.992
1984	**NY-A**	120	399	44	109	20	1	7	56	29	2	32	1	3	4	2	2	.273	.321	.381	.959
1985	**NY-A**	127	438	68	120	28	4	10	69	41	4	51	0	0	8	7	7	.274	.331	.425	1.000
1986	**NY-A**	59	198	33	60	7	0	9	26	15	0	24	1	1	4	2	2	.303	.349	.475	.971
1986	Atl-N	80	292	36	90	15	3	12	32	20	4	43	0	0	1	12	7	.308	.351	.503	1.000
1987	Atl-N	122	399	65	114	24	1	14	64	46	11	54	1	1	4	4	7	.286	.358	.456	.995
1988	Atl-N	69	193	21	48	5	0	2	19	17	2	26	0	0	2	1	3	.249	.307	.306	.969
1988	Cin-N	25	50	5	14	1	0	2	4	2	1	5	0	0	0	0	0	.280	.308	.420	.986
1989	Cin-N	106	236	26	62	8	3	8	30	29	3	42	1	0	0	4	2	.263	.346	.424	.979
1990	Cin-N	46	63	6	13	2	0	1	8	2	0	5	1	0	2	2	1	.206	.235	.286	.979
1990	Sea-A	21	77	13	29	2	0	3	18	13	0	3	0	0	1	0	0	.282	.384	.400	.963
1991	Sea-A	30	85	10	24	7	0	1	9	13	0	13	1	0	1	0	0	.282	.380	.400	1.000
Career average		95	329	51	97	17	4	7	39	33	2	41	1	1	3	9	4	.296	.359	.431	.983
Yankee average		**110**	**395**	**55**	**113**	**20**	**2**	**10**	**50**	**32**	**2**	**42**	**1**	**2**	**4**	**5**	**3**	**.285**	**.336**	**.419**	**.981**
Career total		2097	7229	1129	2143	364	77	152	859	722	51	898	14	31	55	200	83	.296	.359	.431	.983
Yankee total		**551**	**1977**	**275**	**563**	**99**	**10**	**49**	**251**	**158**	**10**	**210**	**4**	**8**	**21**	**27**	**16**	**.285**	**.336**	**.419**	**.981**

Grimes, Oscar Ray Jr.

HEIGHT: 5'11" THROWS: RIGHT BATS: RIGHT BORN: 4/13/1915 MINERVA, OHIO DIED: 5/19/1993 WESTLAKE, OHIO POSITIONS PLAYED: 3B, 2B, 1B, SS

YEAR	TEAM	GAMES	AB	RUNS	HITS	2B	3B	HR	RBI	BB	IBB	SO	HBP	SH	SF	SB	CS	BA	OBA	SA	FA
1938	Cle-A	4	10	2	2	0	1	0	2	2	0	0	0	0	0	0	0	.200	.333	.400	1.000
1939	Cle-A	119	364	51	98	20	5	4	56	56	0	61	1	11	0	8	3	.269	.368	.385	.968
1940	Cle-A	11	13	3	0	0	0	0	0	0	0	5	0	0	0	0	0	.000	.000	.000	.958
1941	Cle-A	77	244	28	58	9	3	4	24	39	0	47	1	7	0	4	0	.238	.345	.348	.995
1942	Cle-A	51	84	10	15	2	0	0	2	13	0	17	0	3	0	3	2	.179	.289	.202	.944
1943	**NY-A**	9	20	4	3	0	0	0	1	3	0	7	0	0	0	0	0	.150	.261	.150	1.000
1944	**NY-A**	116	387	44	108	17	8	5	46	59	0	57	2	8	0	6	0	.279	.377	.403	.945
1945	**NY-A**	142	480	64	127	19	7	4	45	97	0	73	6	12	0	7	6	.265	.395	.358	.937
1946	**NY-A**	14	39	1	8	1	0	0	4	1	0	7	0	1	0	0	1	.205	.225	.231	.958
1946	Phi-A	59	191	28	50	5	0	1	20	27	0	29	1	11	0	2	0	.262	.356	.304	.895
Career average		60	183	24	47	7	2	2	20	30	0	30	1	5	0	3	1	.256	.363	.352	.960
Yankee average		**70**	**232**	**28**	**62**	**9**	**4**	**2**	**24**	**40**	**0**	**36**	**2**	**5**	**0**	**3**	**2**	**.266**	**.378**	**.367**	**.960**
Career total		602	1832	235	469	73	24	18	200	297	0	303	11	53	0	30	12	.256	.363	.352	.960
Yankee total		**281**	**926**	**113**	**246**	**37**	**15**	**9**	**96**	**160**	**0**	**144**	**8**	**21**	**0**	**13**	**7**	**.266**	**.378**	**.367**	**.960**

Gulden, Bradley Lee
HEIGHT: 5'11"   THROWS: RIGHTBATS: LEFT   BORN: 6/10/1956 NEW ULM, MINNESOTA   PRIMARY POSTIONS: C

YEAR	TEAM	GAMES	AB	RUNS	HITS	2B	3B	HR	RBI	BB	IBB	SO	HBP	SH	SF	SB	CS	BA	OBA	SA	FA
1978	LA-N	3	4	0	0	0	0	0	0	0	0	2	0	0	0	0	0	.000	.000	.000	1.000
1979	**NY-A**	40	92	10	15	4	0	0	6	9	0	16	0	4	0	0	1	.163	.238	.207	.995
1980	**NY-A**	2	3	1	1	0	0	1	2	0	0	0	0	0	0	0	0	.333	.333	1.333	1.000
1981	Sea-A	8	16	0	3	2	0	0	1	0	0	2	0	0	0	0	0	.188	.188	.313	1.000
1982	Mon-N	5	6	1	0	0	0	0	0	1	0	1	0	0	0	0	0	.000	.143	.000	1.000
1984	Cin-N	107	292	31	66	8	2	4	33	33	2	35	2	3	2	2	2	.226	.307	.308	.975
1986	SF-N	17	22	2	2	0	0	0	1	2	2	5	0	0	0	0	0	.091	.167	.091	1.000
Career average		26	62	6	12	2	0	1	6	6	1	9	0	1	0	0	0	.200	.277	.276	.996
Yankee average		**21**	**48**	**6**	**8**	**2**	**0**	**1**	**4**	**5**	**0**	**8**	**0**	**2**	**0**	**0**	**1**	**.168**	**.240**	**.242**	**.998**
Career total		182	435	45	87	14	2	5	43	45	4	61	2	7	2	2	3	.200	.277	.276	.996
Yankee total		**42**	**95**	**11**	**16**	**4**	**0**	**1**	**8**	**9**	**0**	**16**	**0**	**4**	**0**	**0**	**1**	**.168**	**.240**	**.242**	**.998**

Hadley, Kent William
HEIGHT: 6'3"   THROWS: LEFT   BATS: LEFT   BORN: 12/17/1934 POCATELLO, IDAHO   POSITIONS PLAYED: 1B

YEAR	TEAM	GAMES	AB	RUNS	HITS	2B	3B	HR	RBI	BB	IBB	SO	HBP	SH	SF	SB	CS	BA	OBA	SA	FA
1958	KC-A	3	11	1	2	0	0	0	0	0	0	4	0	0	0	0	0	.182	.182	.182	1.000
1959	KC-A	113	288	40	73	11	1	10	39	24	0	74	1	2	3	1	2	.253	.310	.403	.989
1960	**NY-A**	55	64	8	13	2	0	4	11	6	0	19	0	0	0	0	0	.203	.271	.422	.991
Career average		57	121	16	29	4	0	5	17	10	0	32	0	1	1	0	1	.242	.300	.399	.993
Yankee average		**55**	**64**	**8**	**13**	**2**	**0**	**4**	**11**	**6**	**0**	**19**	**0**	**0**	**0**	**0**	**0**	**.203**	**.271**	**.422**	**.991**
Career total		171	363	49	88	13	1	14	50	30	0	97	1	2	3	1	2	.242	.300	.399	.993
Yankee total		**55**	**64**	**8**	**13**	**2**	**0**	**4**	**11**	**6**	**0**	**19**	**0**	**0**	**0**	**0**	**0**	**.203**	**.271**	**.422**	**.991**

Hahn, William Edgar
HEIGHT: UNAVAILABLE   THROWS: RIGHT   BATS: LEFT   BORN: 8/27/1875 NEVADA, OHIO   DIED: 11/29/1941 DES MOINES, IOWA   POSITIONS PLAYED: OF

YEAR	TEAM	GAMES	AB	RUNS	HITS	2B	3B	HR	RBI	BB	IBB	SO	HBP	SH	SF	SB	CS	BA	OBA	SA	FA
1905	**NY-A**	43	160	32	51	5	0	0	11	25	0	0	5	4	0	1	0	.319	.426	.350	.957
1906	**NY-A**	11	22	2	2	1	0	0	1	3	0	0	2	2	0	2	0	.091	.259	.136	1.000
1906	Chi-A	130	484	80	110	7	5	0	27	69	0	69	0	0	0	19	0	.227	.335	.262	.949
1907	Chi-A	156	592	87	151	9	7	0	45	84	0	0	12	10	0	17	0	.255	.359	.294	.990
1908	Chi-A	122	447	58	112	12	8	0	21	39	0	0	13	13	0	11	0	.251	.329	.313	.965
1909	Chi-A	76	287	30	52	6	0	1	16	31	0	0	3	8	0	9	0	.181	.268	.213	.990
1910	Chi-A	15	53	2	6	2	0	0	1	7	0	0	0	7	0	0	0	.113	.217	.151	.933
Career average		79	292	42	69	6	3	0	17	37	0	10	5	6	0	8	0	.237	.332	.278	.969
Yankee average		**27**	**91**	**17**	**27**	**3**	**0**	**0**	**6**	**14**	**0**	**0**	**4**	**3**	**0**	**2**	**0**	**.291**	**.406**	**.324**	**.979**
Career total		553	2045	291	484	42	20	1	122	258	0	69	35	44	0	59	0	.237	.332	.278	.969
Yankee total		**54**	**182**	**34**	**53**	**6**	**0**	**0**	**12**	**28**	**0**	**0**	**7**	**6**	**0**	**3**	**0**	**.291**	**.406**	**.324**	**.979**

Haines, Henry Luther (Hinkey)
HEIGHT: 5'10"   THROWS: RIGHT   BATS: RIGHT   BORN: 12/23/1898, RED LION, PENN.   DIED: 1/9/1979 SHARON HILL, PENN.   POSITIONS PLAYED: OF

YEAR	TEAM	GAMES	AB	RUNS	HITS	2B	3B	HR	RBI	BB	IBB	SO	HBP	SH	SF	SB	CS	BA	OBA	SA	FA
1923	**NY-A**	28	25	9	4	2	0	0	3	4	0	5	0	1	0	3	1	.160	.276	.240	1.000
Career average		28	25	9	4	2	0	0	3	4	0	5	0	1	0	3	1	.160	.276	.240	1.000
Yankee average		**28**	**25**	**9**	**4**	**2**	**0**	**0**	**3**	**4**	**0**	**5**	**0**	**1**	**0**	**3**	**1**	**.160**	**.276**	**.240**	**1.000**
Career total		28	25	9	4	2	0	0	3	4	0	5	0	1	0	3	1	.160	.276	.240	1.000
Yankee total		**28**	**25**	**9**	**4**	**2**	**0**	**0**	**3**	**4**	**0**	**5**	**0**	**1**	**0**	**3**	**1**	**.160**	**.276**	**.240**	**1.000**

Halas, George Stanley

HEIGHT: 6'0" THROWS: RIGHT BATS: B BORN: 2/2/1895, CHICAGO, ILLINOIS DIED: 10/31/1983, CHICAGO, ILLINOIS POSITIONS PLAYED: OF

YEAR	TEAM	GAMES	AB	RUNS	HITS	2B	3B	HR	RBI	BB	IBB	SO	HBP	SH	SF	SB	CS	BA	OBA	SA	FA
1919	NY-A	12	22	0	2	0	0	0	0	0	0	8	0	0	0	0	0	.091	.091	.091	1.000
Career average		12	22	0	2	0	0	0	0	0	0	8	0	0	0	0	0	.091	.091	.091	1.000
Yankee average		**12**	**22**	**0**	**2**	**0**	**0**	**0**	**0**	**0**	**0**	**8**	**0**	**0**	**0**	**0**	**0**	**.091**	**.091**	**.091**	**1.000**
Career total		12	22	0	2	0	0	0	0	0	0	8	0	0	0	0	0	.091	.091	.091	1.000
Yankee total		**12**	**22**	**0**	**2**	**0**	**0**	**0**	**0**	**0**	**0**	**8**	**0**	**0**	**0**	**0**	**0**	**.091**	**.091**	**.091**	**1.000**

Hale, Robert Houston

HEIGHT: 5'10" THROWS: LEFT BATS: LEFT BORN: 11/7/1933 SARASOTA, FLORIDA POSITIONS PLAYED: 1B

YEAR	TEAM	GAMES	AB	RUNS	HITS	2B	3B	HR	RBI	BB	IBB	SO	HBP	SH	SF	SB	CS	BA	OBA	SA	FA
1955	Bal-A	67	182	13	65	7	1	0	29	5	0	19	1	1	1	0	2	.357	.376	.407	.974
1956	Bal-A	85	207	18	49	10	1	1	24	11	0	10	1	0	4	0	2	.237	.274	.309	.975
1957	Bal-A	42	44	2	11	0	0	0	7	2	1	2	0	1	0	0	0	.250	.265	.250	1.000
1958	Bal-A	19	20	2	7	2	0	0	3	2	0	1	0	0	0	0	0	.350	.409	.450	1.000
1959	Bal-A	40	54	2	10	3	0	0	7	2	1	6	0	0	0	0	0	.185	.214	.241	1.000
1960	Cle-A	70	70	2	21	7	0	0	12	3	1	6	0	0	4	0	0	.300	.312	.400	.944
1961	Cle-A	42	36	0	6	0	0	0	6	1	0	7	1	0	2	0	0	.167	.200	.167	.000
1961	**NY-A**	**11**	**13**	**2**	**2**	**0**	**0**	**1**	**1**	**0**	**0**	**0**	**0**	**0**	**0**	**0**	**0**	**.154**	**.154**	**.385**	**1.000**
Career average		47	78	5	21	4	0	0	11	3	0	6	0	0	2	0	1	.273	.299	.335	.862
Yankee average		**11**	**13**	**2**	**2**	**0**	**0**	**1**	**1**	**0**	**0**	**0**	**0**	**0**	**0**	**0**	**0**	**.154**	**.154**	**.385**	**1.000**
Career total		376	626	41	171	29	2	2	89	26	3	51	3	1	14	0	4	.273	.302	.335	.862
Yankee total		**11**	**13**	**2**	**2**	**0**	**0**	**1**	**1**	**0**	**0**	**0**	**0**	**0**	**0**	**0**	**0**	**.154**	**.154**	**.385**	**1.000**

Hall, Jimmie Randolph

HEIGHT: 6'0" THROWS: RIGHT BATS: LEFT BORN: 3/17/1938 MT.HOLLY, NORTH CAROLINA POSITIONS PLAYED: 1B, OF

YEAR	TEAM	GAMES	AB	RUNS	HITS	2B	3B	HR	RBI	BB	IBB	SO	HBP	SH	SF	SB	CS	BA	OBA	SA	FA
1963	Min-A	156	497	88	129	21	5	33	80	63	4	101	0	9	2	3	3	.260	.342	.521	.982
1964	Min-A	149	510	61	144	20	3	25	75	44	3	112	1	2	5	5	2	.282	.338	.480	.985
1965	Min-A	148	522	81	149	25	4	20	86	51	6	79	1	0	6	14	7	.285	.347	.464	.976
1966	Min-A	120	356	52	85	7	4	20	47	33	5	66	0	0	2	1	2	.239	.302	.449	.978
1967	Cal-A	129	401	54	100	8	3	16	55	42	7	65	0	1	3	4	1	.249	.318	.404	.990
1968	Cal-A	46	126	15	27	3	0	1	8	16	3	19	0	0	0	1	0	.214	.303	.262	.981
1968	Cle-A	53	111	4	22	4	0	1	8	10	3	19	0	0	0	1	0	.198	.264	.261	.983
1969	Cle-A	4	10	1	0	0	0	0	0	2	1	3	0	0	0	1	0	.000	.167	.000	1.000
1969	**NY-A**	**80**	**212**	**21**	**50**	**8**	**5**	**3**	**26**	**19**	**1**	**34**	**0**	**0**	**2**	**8**	**3**	**.236**	**.296**	**.363**	**.968**
1969	Chi-N	11	24	1	5	1	0	0	1	1	0	5	0	0	0	0	0	.208	.240	.250	1.000
1970	Chi-N	28	32	2	3	1	0	0	1	4	1	12	0	0	0	0	0	.094	.194	.125	1.000
1970	Atl-N	39	47	7	10	2	0	2	4	2	1	14	0	0	0	0	0	.213	.245	.383	1.000
Career average		80	237	32	60	8	2	10	33	24	3	44	0	1	2	3	2	.254	.321	.434	.987
Yankee average		**80**	**212**	**21**	**50**	**8**	**5**	**3**	**26**	**19**	**1**	**34**	**0**	**0**	**2**	**8**	**3**	**.236**	**.296**	**.363**	**.968**
Career total		963	2848	387	724	100	24	121	391	287	35	529	2	12	20	38	18	.254	.321	.434	.987
Yankee total		**80**	**212**	**21**	**50**	**8**	**5**	**3**	**26**	**19**	**1**	**34**	**0**	**0**	**2**	**8**	**3**	**.236**	**.296**	**.363**	**.968**

Hall, Melvin

HEIGHT: 6'1" THROWS: LEFT BATS: LEFT BORN: 9/16/1960, LYONS, NEW YORK POSITIONS PLAYED: OF

YEAR	TEAM	GAMES	AB	RUNS	HITS	2B	3B	HR	RBI	BB	IBB	SO	HBP	SH	SF	SB	CS	BA	OBA	SA	FA
1981	Chi-N	10	11	1	1	0	0	1	2	1	0	4	0	0	0	0	0	.091	.167	.364	.000
1982	Chi-N	24	80	6	21	3	2	0	4	5	1	17	2	0	1	0	1	.263	.318	.350	.939
1983	Chi-N	112	410	60	116	23	5	17	56	42	6	101	3	1	2	6	6	.283	.352	.488	.988
1984	Chi-N	48	150	25	42	11	3	4	22	12	3	23	0	0	2	2	1	.280	.329	.473	.961
1984	Cle-A	83	257	43	66	13	1	7	30	35	5	55	2	0	5	1	1	.257	.344	.397	.993
1985	Cle-A	23	66	7	21	6	0	0	12	6	0	12	0	0	1	0	1	.318	.387	.409	1.000
1986	Cle-A	140	442	68	131	29	2	18	77	33	8	65	2	0	3	6	2	.296	.346	.493	.972
1987	Cle-A	142	485	57	136	21	1	18	76	20	6	68	1	0	2	5	4	.280	.309	.439	.989
1988	Cle-A	150	515	69	144	32	4	6	71	28	12	50	0	2	8	7	3	.280	.312	.392	.967
1989	**NY-A**	**113**	**361**	**54**	**94**	**9**	**0**	**17**	**58**	**21**	**4**	**37**	**0**	**1**	**8**	**0**	**0**	**.260**	**.295**	**.427**	**.993**

(continued)

(continued)

YEAR	TEAM	GAMES	AB	RUNS	HITS	2B	3B	HR	RBI	BB	IBB	SO	HBP	SH	SF	SB	CS	BA	OBA	SA	FA
1990	NY-A	113	360	41	93	23	2	12	46	6	2	46	2	0	3	0	0	.258	.272	.433	.973
1991	NY-A	141	492	67	140	23	2	19	80	26	6	40	3	0	6	0	1	.285	.321	.455	.987
1992	NY-A	152	583	67	163	36	3	15	81	29	4	53	1	0	9	4	2	.280	.310	.429	.990
1996	SF-N	25	25	3	3	0	0	0	5	1	0	4	0	0	1	0	0	.120	.148	.120	.981
Career average		91	303	41	84	16	2	10	44	19	4	41	1	0	4	2	2	.276	.318	.437	.910
Yankee average		130	449	57	123	23	2	16	66	21	4	44	2	0	7	1	1	.273	.303	.437	.986
Career total		1276	4237	568	1171	229	25	134	620	267	57	575	16	4	51	31	22	.276	.318	.437	.910
Yankee total		519	1796	229	490	91	7	63	265	82	16	176	6	1	26	4	3	.273	.303	.437	.986

Handiboe, Aloysius James (Coalyard Mike)
HEIGHT: 5'10" THROWS: LEFT BATS: LEFT BORN: 7/21/1887, WASHINGTON, D.C. DIED: 1/31/1953, SAVANNAH, GEORGIA POSITIONS PLAYED: OF

YEAR	TEAM	GAMES	AB	RUNS	HITS	2B	3B	HR	RBI	BB	IBB	SO	HBP	SH	SF	SB	CS	BA	OBA	SA	FA
1911	NY-A	5	15	0	1	0	0	0	0	2	0	0	0	1	0	0	0	.067	.176	.067	1.000
Career average		5	15	0	1	0	0	0	0	2	0	0	0	1	0	0	0	.067	.176	.067	1.000
Yankee average		5	15	0	1	0	0	0	0	2	0	0	0	1	0	0	0	.067	.176	.067	1.000
Career total		5	15	0	1	0	0	0	0	2	0	0	0	1	0	0	0	.067	.176	.067	1.000
Yankee total		5	15	0	1	0	0	0	0	2	0	0	0	1	0	0	0	.067	.176	.067	1.000

Hannah, James Harrison (Truck)
HEIGHT: 6'1" THROWS: RIGHT BATS: RIGHT BORN: 6/5/1889, LARIMORE, NORTH DAKOTA DIED: 4/27/1982, FOUNTAIN VALLEY, CALIFORNIA POSITIONS PLAYED: C, 1B

YEAR	TEAM	GAMES	AB	RUNS	HITS	2B	3B	HR	RBI	BB	IBB	SO	HBP	SH	SF	SB	CS	BA	OBA	SA	FA
1918	NY-A	90	250	24	55	6	0	2	21	51	0	25	4	7	0	5	0	.220	.361	.268	.974
1919	NY-A	75	227	14	54	8	3	1	20	22	0	19	3	8	0	0	0	.238	.313	.313	.500
1920	NY-A	79	259	24	64	11	1	2	25	24	0	35	1	8	0	2	0	.247	.313	.320	.961
Career average		81	245	21	58	8	1	2	22	32	0	26	3	8	0	2	0	.235	.331	.300	.812
Yankee average		81	245	21	58	8	1	2	22	32	0	26	3	8	0	2	0	.235	.331	.300	.812
Career total		244	736	62	173	25	4	5	66	97	0	79	8	23	0	7	0	.235	.331	.300	.812
Yankee total		244	736	62	173	25	4	5	66	97	0	79	8	23	0	7	0	.235	.331	.300	.812

Hansen, Ronald Lavern
HEIGHT: 6'3" THROWS: RIGHT BATS: RIGHT BORN: 4/5/1938, OXFORD, NEBRASKA POSITIONS PLAYED: SS, 2B

YEAR	TEAM	GAMES	AB	RUNS	HITS	2B	3B	HR	RBI	BB	IBB	SO	HBP	SH	SF	SB	CS	BA	OBA	SA	FA
1958	Bal-A	12	19	1	0	0	0	0	1	0	0	7	1	1	1	0	0	.000	.048	.000	.943
1959	Bal-A	2	4	0	0	0	0	0	0	1	0	1	0	0	0	0	0	.000	.200	.000	.889
1960	Bal-A	153	530	72	135	22	5	22	86	69	5	94	2	1	2	3	3	.255	.342	.440	.964
1961	Bal-A	155	533	51	132	13	2	12	51	66	2	96	1	3	4	1	3	.248	.329	.347	.975
1962	Bal-A	71	196	12	34	7	0	3	17	30	3	36	2	1	0	0	1	.173	.289	.255	.965
1963	Chi-A	144	482	55	109	17	2	13	67	78	2	74	0	5	6	1	1	.226	.330	.351	.983
1964	Chi-A	158	575	85	150	25	3	20	68	73	7	73	6	5	6	1	0	.261	.347	.419	.975
1965	Chi-A	162	587	61	138	23	4	11	66	60	8	73	2	5	8	1	1	.235	.304	.344	.969
1966	Chi-A	23	74	3	13	1	0	0	4	15	3	10	1	5	0	0	1	.176	.322	.189	.946
1967	Chi-A	157	498	35	116	20	0	8	51	64	11	51	0	7	6	0	3	.233	.317	.321	.964
1968	Was-A	86	275	28	51	12	0	8	28	35	5	49	2	2	1	0	0	.185	.281	.316	.905
1968	Chi-A	40	87	7	20	3	0	1	4	11	0	12	0	1	0	0	0	.230	.316	.299	1.000
1969	Chi-A	85	185	15	48	6	1	2	22	18	0	25	1	2	1	2	0	.259	.327	.335	.967
1970	**NY-A**	59	91	13	27	4	0	4	14	19	0	9	1	1	1	0	1	.297	.420	.473	1.000
1971	**NY-A**	61	145	6	30	3	0	2	20	9	2	27	0	0	5	0	0	.207	.245	.269	.957
1972	KC-A	16	30	2	4	0	0	0	2	3	1	6	0	0	0	0	0	.133	.212	.133	.944
Career average		87	269	28	63	10	1	7	31	34	3	40	1	2	3	1	1	.234	.320	.351	.959
Yankee average		60	118	10	29	4	0	3	17	14	1	18	1	1	3	0	1	.242	.317	.347	.979
Career total		1384	4311	446	1007	156	17	106	501	551	49	643	19	39	41	9	14	.234	.320	.351	.959
Yankee total		120	236	19	57	7	0	6	34	28	2	36	1	1	6	0	1	.242	.317	.347	.979

Hanson, Harry Francis (Joe)

HEIGHT: 5'11"   THROWS: RIGHT   BATS: RIGHT   BORN: 1/17/1896, ELGIN, ILLINOIS   DIED: 10/5/1966, SAVANNAH, GEORGIA   POSITIONS PLAYED: C

YEAR	TEAM	GAMES	AB	RUNS	HITS	2B	3B	HR	RBI	BB	IBB	SO	HBP	SH	SF	SB	CS	BA	OBA	SA	FA
1913	NY-A	1	2	0	0	0	0	0	0	0	0	0	0	0	0	0	0	.000	.000	.000	.000
Career average		1	2	0	0	0	0	0	0	0	0	0	0	0	0	0	0	.000	.000	.000	.000
Yankee average		**1**	**2**	**0**	**0**	**0**	**0**	**0**	**0**	**0**	**0**	**0**	**0**	**0**	**0**	**0**	**0**	**.000**	**.000**	**.000**	**.000**
Career total		1	2	0	0	0	0	0	0	0	0	0	0	0	0	0	0	.000	.000	.000	.000
Yankee total		**1**	**2**	**0**	**0**	**0**	**0**	**0**	**0**	**0**	**0**	**0**	**0**	**0**	**0**	**0**	**0**	**.000**	**.000**	**.000**	**.000**

Hargrave, Eugene Franklin (Bubbles)

HEIGHT: 5'11"   THROWS: RIGHT   BATS: RIGHT   BORN: 7/15/1892, NEW HAVEN, INDIANA   DIED: 2/23/1969, CINCINNATI, OHIO   POSITIONS PLAYED: C

YEAR	TEAM	GAMES	AB	RUNS	HITS	2B	3B	HR	RBI	BB	IBB	SO	HBP	SH	SF	SB	CS	BA	OBA	SA	FA
1913	Chi-N	3	3	0	1	0	0	0	1	0	0	0	0	0	0	0	0	.333	.333	.333	1.000
1914	Chi-N	23	36	3	8	2	0	0	2	0	0	4	0	1	0	0	0	.222	.222	.278	.930
1915	Chi-N	15	19	2	3	0	1	0	2	1	0	5	0	0	0	2	0	.158	.200	.263	1.000
1921	Cin-N	93	263	28	76	17	8	1	38	12	0	15	3	6	0	4	2	.289	.327	.426	.973
1922	Cin-N	98	320	49	101	22	10	7	57	26	0	18	2	10	0	7	4	.316	.371	.513	.982
1923	Cin-N	118	378	54	126	23	9	10	78	44	0	22	12	10	0	4	5	.333	.419	.521	.988
1924	Cin-N	98	312	42	94	19	10	3	33	30	0	20	4	8	0	2	2	.301	.370	.455	.983
1925	Cin-N	87	273	28	82	13	6	2	33	25	0	23	1	3	0	4	3	.300	.361	.414	.979
1926	Cin-N	105	326	42	115	22	8	6	62	25	0	17	4	10	0	2	0	.353	.406	.525	.988
1927	Cin-N	102	305	36	94	18	3	0	35	31	0	18	2	11	0	0	0	.308	.376	.387	.988
1928	Cin-N	65	190	19	56	12	3	0	23	13	0	14	4	8	0	0	0	.295	.353	.389	.991
1930	**NY-A**	**45**	**108**	**11**	**30**	**7**	**0**	**0**	**12**	**10**	**0**	**9**	**0**	**3**	**0**	**0**	**0**	**.278**	**.339**	**.343**	**.992**
Career average		71	211	26	66	13	5	2	31	18	0	14	3	6	0	2	1	.310	.372	.452	.983
Yankee average		**45**	**108**	**11**	**30**	**7**	**0**	**0**	**12**	**10**	**0**	**9**	**0**	**3**	**0**	**0**	**0**	**.278**	**.339**	**.343**	**.992**
Career total		852	2533	314	786	155	58	29	376	217	0	165	32	70	0	29	16	.310	.372	.452	.983
Yankee total		**45**	**108**	**11**	**30**	**7**	**0**	**0**	**12**	**10**	**0**	**9**	**0**	**3**	**0**	**0**	**0**	**.278**	**.339**	**.343**	**.992**

Harrah, Colbert Dale (Toby)

HEIGHT: 6'0"   THROWS: RIGHT   BATS: RIGHT   BORN: 10/26/1948, SISSONVILLE, WEST VIRGINIA   POSITIONS PLAYED: SS, 3B

YEAR	TEAM	GAMES	AB	RUNS	HITS	2B	3B	HR	RBI	BB	IBB	SO	HBP	SH	SF	SB	CS	BA	OBA	SA	FA
1969	Was-A	8	1	4	0	0	0	0	0	0	0	0	0	0	0	0	0	.000	.000	.000	.000
1971	Was-A	127	383	45	88	11	3	2	22	40	3	48	0	2	3	10	9	.230	.300	.290	.955
1972	Tex-A	116	374	47	97	14	3	1	31	34	1	31	0	5	6	16	7	.259	.316	.321	.960
1973	Tex-A	118	461	64	120	16	1	10	50	46	2	49	2	7	3	10	3	.260	.328	.364	.951
1974	Tex-A	161	573	79	149	23	2	21	74	50	2	65	2	8	6	15	14	.260	.319	.417	1.000
1975	Tex-A	151	522	81	153	24	1	20	93	98	3	71	1	6	4	23	9	.293	.403	.458	.949
1976	Tex-A	155	584	64	152	21	1	15	67	91	5	59	3	5	5	8	5	.260	.360	.377	.955
1977	Tex-A	159	539	90	142	25	5	27	87	109	7	73	10	9	6	27	5	.263	.393	.479	.955
1978	Tex-A	139	450	56	103	17	3	12	59	83	3	66	2	9	3	31	8	.229	.349	.360	.988
1979	Cle-A	149	527	99	147	25	1	20	77	89	2	60	8	7	4	20	9	.279	.389	.444	.940
1980	Cle-A	160	561	100	150	22	4	11	72	98	3	60	7	2	7	17	2	.267	.379	.380	.971
1981	Cle-A	103	361	64	105	12	4	5	44	57	8	44	1	0	8	12	1	.291	.382	.388	.949
1982	Cle-A	162	602	100	183	29	4	25	78	84	7	52	12	7	3	17	3	.304	.398	.490	.971
1983	Cle-A	138	526	81	140	23	1	9	53	75	1	49	7	4	3	16	10	.266	.363	.365	.971
1984	**NY-A**	**88**	**253**	**40**	**55**	**9**	**4**	**1**	**26**	**42**	**2**	**28**	**2**	**0**	**2**	**3**	**0**	**.217**	**.331**	**.296**	**.968**
1985	Tex-A	126	396	65	107	18	1	9	44	113	2	60	4	2	6	11	4	.270	.432	.389	.989
1986	Tex-A	95	289	36	63	18	2	7	41	44	0	53	2	3	3	2	5	.218	.322	.367	.982
Career average		127	435	66	115	18	2	12	54	68	3	51	4	5	4	14	6	.264	.365	.395	.909
Yankee average		**88**	**253**	**40**	**55**	**9**	**4**	**1**	**26**	**42**	**2**	**28**	**2**	**0**	**2**	**3**	**0**	**.217**	**.331**	**.296**	**.909**
Career total		2155	7402	1115	1954	307	40	195	918	1153	51	868	63	76	72	238	94	.264	.365	.395	.968
Yankee total		**88**	**253**	**40**	**55**	**9**	**4**	**1**	**26**	**42**	**2**	**28**	**2**	**0**	**2**	**3**	**0**	**.217**	**.331**	**.296**	**.968**

Harris, Joseph (Moon)
HEIGHT: 5'9" THROWS: RIGHT BATS: RIGHT BORN: 5/20/1891, COULTERS, PENNSYLVANIA DIED: 12/10/1959, RENTON, PENNSYLVANIA POSITIONS PLAYED: OF, 1B

YEAR	TEAM	GAMES	AB	RUNS	HITS	2B	3B	HR	RBI	BB	IBB	SO	HBP	SH	SF	SB	CS	BA	OBA	SA	FA
1914	NY-A	2	1	0	0	0	0	0	0	3	0	1	1	1	0	0	0	.000	.800	.000	1.000
1917	Cle-A	112	369	40	112	22	4	0	65	55	0	32	3	8	0	11	0	.304	.398	.385	.985
1919	Cle-A	62	184	30	69	16	1	1	46	33	0	21	1	9	0	2	6	.375	.472	.489	1.000
1922	Bos-A	119	408	53	129	30	9	6	54	30	0	15	1	9	0	7	3	.316	.364	.478	.953
1923	Bos-A	142	483	82	162	28	11	13	76	52	0	27	5	13	0	6	1	.335	.406	.520	.968
1924	Bos-A	133	491	82	148	36	9	3	77	81	0	25	5	15	0	0	0	.301	.406	.430	1.000
1925	Bos-A	8	19	4	3	0	1	1	2	5	0	5	0	1	0	6	3	.158	.333	.421	.986
1925	Was-A	100	300	60	97	21	9	12	59	51	0	28	5	7	0	2	3	.323	.430	.573	.985
1926	Was-A	92	257	43	79	13	9	5	55	37	0	9	5	8	0	0	0	.307	.405	.486	.990
1927	Pit-N	129	411	57	134	27	9	5	73	48	0	19	4	23	0	0	0	.326	.402	.472	1.000
1928	Pit-N	16	23	2	9	2	1	0	2	4	0	2	1	0	0	0	0	.391	.500	.565	.958
1928	Bro-N	55	89	8	21	6	1	1	8	14	0	4	0	1	0	0	0	.236	.340	.360	.985
Career average		81	253	38	80	17	5	4	43	34	0	16	3	8	0	3	1	.317	.404	.472	.985
Yankee average		2	1	0	0	0	0	0	0	3	0	1	1	1	0	0	0	.000	.800	.000	1.000
Career total		970	3035	461	963	201	64	47	517	413	0	188	31	95	0	36	16	.317	.404	.472	.985
Yankee total		2	1	0	0	0	0	0	0	3	0	1	1	1	0	0	0	.000	.800	.000	1.000

Hart, James Ray (Jim Ray)
HEIGHT: 5'11" THROWS: RIGHT BATS: RIGHT BORN: 10/30/1941 HOOKERTON, NORTH CAROLINA POSITIONS PLAYED: 3B, OF

YEAR	TEAM	GAMES	AB	RUNS	HITS	2B	3B	HR	RBI	BB	IBB	SO	HBP	SH	SF	SB	CS	BA	OBA	SA	FA
1963	SF-N	7	20	1	4	1	0	0	2	3	1	6	2	0	0	0	0	.200	.360	.250	1.000
1964	SF-N	153	566	71	162	15	6	31	81	47	4	94	4	2	6	5	2	.286	.342	.498	.937
1965	SF-N	160	591	91	177	30	6	23	96	47	3	75	2	2	7	6	4	.299	.349	.487	.919
1966	SF-N	156	578	88	165	23	4	33	93	48	6	75	4	2	5	2	1	.285	.342	.510	.941
1967	SF-N	158	578	98	167	26	7	29	99	77	11	100	3	1	6	3	1	.289	.373	.509	.977
1968	SF-N	136	480	67	124	14	3	23	78	46	10	74	5	0	2	0	0	.258	.323	.444	.925
1969	SF-N	95	236	27	60	9	0	3	26	28	1	49	3	0	4	1	0	.254	.343	.331	.833
1970	SF-N	76	255	30	72	12	1	8	37	30	6	29	3	0	2	0	0	.282	.360	.431	.958
1971	SF-N	31	39	5	10	0	0	2	5	6	0	8	1	0	0	0	1	.256	.356	.410	.833
1972	SF-N	24	79	10	24	5	0	5	8	6	0	10	1	0	1	0	1	.304	.356	.557	.886
1973	SF-N	5	3	0	0	0	0	0	1	3	0	1	0	0	2	0	0	.000	.429	.000	.600
1973	**NY-A**	**114**	**339**	**29**	**86**	**13**	**2**	**13**	**52**	**36**	**7**	**45**	**0**	**1**	**2**	**0**	**2**	**.254**	**.324**	**.419**	**.000**
1974	**NY-A**	**10**	**19**	**1**	**1**	**0**	**0**	**0**	**0**	**3**	**0**	**7**	**0**	**0**	**0**	**0**	**0**	**.053**	**.182**	**.053**	**.000**
Career average		87	291	40	81	11	2	13	44	29	4	44	2	1	3	1	1	.278	.345	.467	.755
Yankee average		**62**	**179**	**15**	**44**	**7**	**1**	**7**	**26**	**20**	**4**	**26**	**0**	**1**	**1**	**0**	**1**	**.243**	**.316**	**.399**	**.000**
Career total		1125	3783	518	1052	148	29	170	578	380	49	573	28	8	37	17	17	.278	.345	.467	.755
Yankee total		**124**	**358**	**30**	**87**	**13**	**2**	**13**	**52**	**39**	**7**	**52**	**0**	**1**	**2**	**0**	**2**	**.243**	**.316**	**.399**	**.000**

Hartzell, Roy Allen
HEIGHT: 5'9" THROWS: RIGHT BATS: LEFT BORN: 7/6/1881, GOLDEN, COLORADO DIED: 11/6/1961, GOLDEN, COLORADO POSITIONS PLAYED: OF, 2, 3BB

YEAR	TEAM	GAMES	AB	RUNS	HITS	2B	3B	HR	RBI	BB	IBB	SO	HBP	SH	SF	SB	CS	BA	OBA	SA	FA
1906	StL-A	113	404	43	86	7	0	0	24	19	0	0	10	10	0	21	0	.213	.266	.230	1.000
1907	StL-A	60	220	20	52	3	5	0	13	11	0	0	4	7	0	24	0	.236	.285	.295	.911
1908	StL-A	115	422	41	112	5	6	2	32	19	0	0	3	23	0	14	0	.265	.302	.320	.878
1909	StL-A	152	595	64	161	12	5	2	32	29	0	0	7	16	0	14	0	.271	.312	.308	.940
1910	StL-A	151	542	52	118	13	5	2	30	49	0	0	6	18	0	18	0	.218	.290	.271	.935
1911	**NY-A**	**144**	**527**	**67**	**156**	**17**	**11**	**3**	**91**	**63**	**0**	**0**	**4**	**22**	**0**	**22**	**0**	**.296**	**.375**	**.387**	**.936**
1912	**NY-A**	**125**	**416**	**50**	**113**	**10**	**11**	**1**	**38**	**64**	**0**	**40**	**1**	**14**	**0**	**20**	**0**	**.272**	**.370**	**.356**	**.889**
1913	**NY-A**	**141**	**490**	**60**	**127**	**18**	**1**	**0**	**38**	**67**	**0**	**38**	**4**	**16**	**0**	**26**	**25**	**.259**	**.353**	**.300**	**1.000**
1914	**NY-A**	**137**	**481**	**55**	**112**	**15**	**9**	**1**	**32**	**68**	**0**	**37**	**6**	**22**	**0**	**22**	**19**	**.233**	**.335**	**.308**	**.905**
1915	**NY-A**	**119**	**387**	**39**	**97**	**11**	**2**	**3**	**60**	**57**	**0**	**3**	**3**	**19**	**0**	**7**	**0**	**.251**	**.351**	**.313**	**.833**
1916	**NY-A**	**33**	**64**	**12**	**12**	**1**	**0**	**0**	**7**	**9**	**0**	**1**	**1**	**2**	**0**	**1**	**0**	**.188**	**.297**	**.203**	**1.000**
Career average		117	414	46	104	10	5	1	36	41	0	11	5	15	0	16	7	.261	.355	.330	.927
Yankee average		**117**	**394**	**47**	**103**	**12**	**6**	**1**	**44**	**55**	**0**	**20**	**3**	**16**	**0**	**16**	**4**	**.252**	**.327**	**.309**	**.930**
Career total		1290	4548	503	1146	112	55	12	397	455	0	118	49	169	0	182	44	.261	.355	.330	.927
Yankee total		**699**	**2365**	**283**	**617**	**72**	**34**	**8**	**266**	**328**	**0**	**118**	**19**	**95**	**0**	**98**	**44**	**.252**	**.327**	**.309**	**.930**

Hassett, John Aloysius (Buddy)

HEIGHT: 5'11" THROWS: LEFT BATS: LEFT BORN: 9/5/1911, NEW YORK, NEW YORK NEW YORK DIED: 8/23/1997, WESTWOOD, NJ POSITIONS PLAYED: 1B

YEAR	TEAM	GAMES	AB	RUNS	HITS	2B	3B	HR	RBI	BB	IBB	SO	HBP	SH	SF	SB	CS	BA	OBA	SA	FA
1936	Bro-N	156	635	79	197	29	11	3	82	35	0	17	4	9	0	5	0	.310	.350	.405	.983
1937	Bro-N	137	556	71	169	31	6	1	53	20	0	19	5	14	0	13	0	.304	.334	.387	.984
1938	Bro-N	115	335	49	98	11	6	0	40	32	0	19	1	8	0	3	0	.293	.356	.361	.974
1939	Bos-N	147	590	72	182	15	3	2	60	29	0	14	1	18	0	13	0	.308	.342	.354	.985
1940	Bos-N	124	458	59	107	19	4	0	27	25	0	16	0	2	0	4	0	.234	.273	.293	.979
1941	Bos-N	118	405	59	120	9	4	1	33	36	0	15	0	8	0	10	0	.296	.354	.346	.991
1942	**NY-A**	**132**	**538**	**80**	**153**	**16**	**6**	**5**	**48**	**32**	**0**	**16**	**0**	**11**	**0**	**5**	**5**	**.284**	**.325**	**.364**	**.991**
Career average		133	502	67	147	19	6	2	49	30	0	17	2	10	0	8	1	.292	.333	.362	.984
Yankee average		**132**	**538**	**80**	**153**	**16**	**6**	**5**	**48**	**32**	**0**	**16**	**0**	**11**	**0**	**5**	**5**	**.284**	**.325**	**.364**	**.991**
Career total		929	3517	469	1026	130	40	12	343	209	0	116	11	70	0	53	5	.292	.333	.362	.984
Yankee total		**132**	**538**	**80**	**153**	**16**	**6**	**5**	**48**	**32**	**0**	**16**	**0**	**11**	**0**	**5**	**5**	**.284**	**.325**	**.364**	**.991**

Hassey, Ronald William

HEIGHT: 6'2" THROWS: RIGHT BATS: LEFT BORN: 2/27/1953, TUCSON, ARIZONA POSITIONS PLAYED: C, 1B

YEAR	TEAM	GAMES	AB	RUNS	HITS	2B	3B	HR	RBI	BB	IBB	SO	HBP	SH	SF	SB	CS	BA	OBA	SA	FA
1978	Cle-A	25	74	5	15	0	0	2	9	5	0	7	1	1	2	2	0	.203	.256	.284	.993
1979	Cle-A	75	223	20	64	14	0	4	32	19	2	19	0	4	3	1	0	.287	.339	.404	.992
1980	Cle-A	130	390	43	124	18	4	8	65	49	3	51	1	1	6	0	2	.318	.390	.446	.993
1981	Cle-A	61	190	8	44	4	0	1	25	17	0	11	2	3	3	0	1	.232	.297	.268	1.000
1982	Cle-A	113	323	33	81	18	0	5	34	53	5	32	1	3	2	3	2	.251	.356	.353	1.000
1983	Cle-A	117	341	48	92	21	0	6	42	38	2	35	2	2	5	2	2	.270	.342	.384	.995
1984	Cle-A	48	149	11	38	5	1	0	19	15	2	26	0	0	1	1	0	.255	.321	.302	1.000
1984	Chi-N	19	33	5	11	0	0	2	5	4	1	6	0	0	0	0	0	.333	.405	.515	1.000
1985	**NY-A**	**92**	**267**	**31**	**79**	**16**	**1**	**13**	**42**	**28**	**4**	**21**	**3**	**0**	**0**	**0**	**0**	**.296**	**.369**	**.509**	**.984**
1986	**NY-A**	**64**	**191**	**23**	**57**	**14**	**0**	**6**	**29**	**24**	**1**	**16**	**2**	**1**	**1**	**1**	**1**	**.298**	**.381**	**.466**	**.985**
1986	Chi-A	49	150	22	53	11	1	3	20	22	2	11	1	0	1	0	0	.353	.437	.500	1.000
1987	Chi-A	49	145	15	31	9	0	3	12	17	2	11	2	0	1	0	0	.214	.303	.338	1.000
1988	Oak-A	107	323	32	83	15	0	7	45	30	1	42	4	3	5	2	0	.257	.323	.368	.994
1989	Oak-A	97	268	29	61	12	0	5	23	24	2	45	1	1	4	1	0	.228	.290	.328	.991
1990	Oak-A	94	254	18	54	7	0	5	22	27	3	29	1	1	3	0	0	.213	.288	.299	.997
1991	Mon-N	52	119	5	27	8	0	1	14	13	1	16	0	2	1	1	1	.227	.301	.319	.989
Career average		75	215	22	57	11	0	4	27	24	2	24	1	1	2	1	1	.266	.340	.382	.995
Yankee average		**78**	**229**	**27**	**68**	**15**	**1**	**10**	**36**	**26**	**3**	**19**	**3**	**1**	**1**	**1**	**1**	**.297**	**.374**	**.491**	**.985**
Career total		1192	3440	348	914	172	7	71	438	385	31	378	21	22	38	14	10	.266	.340	.382	.995
Yankee total		**156**	**458**	**54**	**136**	**30**	**1**	**19**	**71**	**52**	**5**	**37**	**5**	**1**	**1**	**1**	**1**	**.297**	**.374**	**.491**	**.985**

Hawks, Nelson Louis (Chicken)

HEIGHT: 5'11" THROWS: LEFT BATS: LEFT BORN: 2/3/1896, SAN FRANCISCO, CALIFORNIA DIED: 5/26/1973, SAN RAFAEL, CALIFORNIA POSITIONS PLAYED: 1B

YEAR	TEAM	GAMES	AB	RUNS	HITS	2B	3B	HR	RBI	BB	IBB	SO	HBP	SH	SF	SB	CS	BA	OBA	SA	FA
1921	NY-A	41	73	16	21	2	3	2	15	5	0	12	0	1	0	0	1	.288	.333	.479	.970
1925	Phi-N	105	320	52	103	15	5	5	45	32	0	33	2	12	0	3	6	.322	.387	.447	.986
Career average		73	197	34	62	9	4	4	30	19	0	23	1	7	0	2	4	.316	.377	.453	.978
Yankee average		**41**	**73**	**16**	**21**	**2**	**3**	**2**	**15**	**5**	**0**	**12**	**0**	**1**	**0**	**0**	**1**	**.288**	**.333**	**.479**	**.970**
Career total		146	393	68	124	17	8	7	60	37	0	45	2	13	0	3	7	.316	.377	.453	.978
Yankee total		**41**	**73**	**16**	**21**	**2**	**3**	**2**	**15**	**5**	**0**	**12**	**0**	**1**	**0**	**0**	**1**	**.288**	**.333**	**.479**	**.970**

Hayes, Charles Dewayne

HEIGHT: 6'0" THROWS: RIGHT BATS: RIGHT BORN: 5/29/1965, HATTIESBURG, MISSISSIPPI POSITIONS PLAYED: 1B, 2B, 3B, SS, OF

YEAR	TEAM	GAMES	AB	RUNS	HITS	2B	3B	HR	RBI	BB	IBB	SO	HBP	SH	SF	SB	CS	BA	OBA	SA	FA
1988	SF-N	7	11	0	1	0	0	0	0	0	0	3	0	0	0	0	0	.091	.091	.091	1.000
1989	SF-N	3	5	0	1	0	0	0	0	0	0	1	0	0	0	0	0	.200	.200	.200	1.000
1989	Phi-N	84	299	26	77	15	1	8	43	11	1	49	0	2	3	3	1	.258	.281	.395	.910
1990	Phi-N	152	561	56	145	20	0	10	57	28	3	91	2	0	6	4	4	.258	.293	.348	.957
1991	Phi-N	142	460	34	106	23	1	12	53	16	3	75	1	2	1	3	3	.230	.257	.363	.857
1992	**NY-A**	**142**	**509**	**52**	**131**	**19**	**2**	**18**	**66**	**28**	**0**	**100**	**3**	**3**	**6**	**3**	**5**	**.257**	**.297**	**.409**	**.963**

(continued)

(continued)

YEAR	TEAM	GAMES	AB	RUNS	HITS	2B	3B	HR	RBI	BB	IBB	SO	HBP	SH	SF	SB	CS	BA	OBA	SA	FA
1993	Col-N	157	573	89	175	45	2	25	98	43	6	82	5	1	8	11	6	.305	.355	.522	.954
1994	Col-N	113	423	46	122	23	4	10	50	36	4	71	3	0	1	3	6	.288	.348	.433	.944
1995	Phi-N	141	529	58	146	30	3	11	85	50	2	88	4	0	6	5	1	.276	.340	.406	.963
1996	Pit-N	128	459	51	114	21	2	10	62	36	4	78	0	2	3	6	0	.248	.301	.368	.950
1996	**NY-A**	**20**	**67**	**7**	**19**	**3**	**0**	**2**	**13**	**1**	**0**	**12**	**0**	**1**	**0**	**0**	**0**	**.284**	**.294**	**.418**	**1.000**
1997	**NY-A**	**100**	**353**	**39**	**91**	**16**	**0**	**11**	**53**	**40**	**2**	**66**	**1**	**0**	**4**	**3**	**2**	**.258**	**.332**	**.397**	**.947**
1998	SF-N	111	329	39	94	8	0	12	62	34	0	61	0	1	2	2	1	.286	.351	.419	.989
1999	SF-N	95	264	33	54	9	1	6	48	33	0	41	1	0	3	3	1	.205	.292	.314	.960
2000	Mil-N	121	370	46	93	17	0	9	46	57	4	84	1	0	6	1	1	.251	.348	.370	.983
Career average		101	348	38	91	17	1	10	49	28	2	60	1	1	3	3	2	.263	.317	.399	.958
Yankee average		**87**	**310**	**33**	**80**	**13**	**1**	**10**	**44**	**23**	**1**	**59**	**1**	**1**	**3**	**2**	**2**	**.259**	**.310**	**.405**	**.970**
Career total		1516	5212	576	1369	249	16	144	736	413	29	902	21	12	49	47	31	.263	.317	.399	.958
Yankee total		**262**	**929**	**98**	**241**	**38**	**2**	**31**	**132**	**69**	**2**	**178**	**4**	**4**	**10**	**6**	**7**	**.259**	**.310**	**.405**	**.970**

Healy, Francis Xavier

HEIGHT: 6'5"   THROWS: RIGHT   BATS: RIGHT   BORN: 9/6/1946, HOLYOKE, MASSACHUSETTS   POSITIONS PLAYED: C

YEAR	TEAM	GAMES	AB	RUNS	HITS	2B	3B	HR	RBI	BB	IBB	SO	HBP	SH	SF	SB	CS	BA	OBA	SA	FA
1969	KC-A	6	10	0	4	1	0	0	0	0	0	5	0	0	0	0	0	.400	.400	.500	1.000
1971	SF-N	47	93	10	26	3	0	2	11	15	0	24	0	0	0	1	0	.280	.380	.376	.966
1972	SF-N	45	99	12	15	4	0	1	8	13	2	24	1	0	0	0	1	.152	.257	.222	.995
1973	KC-A	95	279	25	77	15	2	6	34	31	0	56	0	5	0	3	4	.276	.348	.409	.979
1974	KC-A	139	445	59	112	24	2	9	53	62	1	73	1	4	2	16	8	.252	.343	.375	.977
1975	KC-A	56	188	16	48	5	2	2	18	14	1	19	0	1	0	4	3	.255	.307	.335	.982
1976	KC-A	8	24	2	3	0	0	0	1	4	0	10	0	0	0	2	0	.125	.250	.125	1.000
1976	**NY-A**	**46**	**120**	**10**	**32**	**3**	**0**	**0**	**9**	**9**	**0**	**17**	**0**	**0**	**0**	**3**	**1**	**.267**	**.318**	**.292**	**.983**
1977	**NY-A**	**27**	**67**	**10**	**15**	**5**	**0**	**0**	**7**	**6**	**0**	**13**	**0**	**2**	**0**	**1**	**0**	**.224**	**.288**	**.299**	**.971**
1978	**NY-A**	**1**	**1**	**0**	**0**	**0**	**0**	**0**	**0**	**0**	**0**	**1**	**0**	**0**	**0**	**0**	**0**	**.000**	**.000**	**.000**	**.000**
Career average		47	133	14	33	6	1	2	14	15	0	24	0	1	0	3	2	.250	.329	.350	.885
Yankee average		**25**	**63**	**7**	**16**	**3**	**0**	**0**	**5**	**5**	**0**	**10**	**0**	**1**	**0**	**1**	**0**	**.250**	**.305**	**.293**	**.651**
Career total		470	1326	144	332	60	6	20	141	154	4	242	2	12	2	30	17	.250	.329	.350	.885
Yankee total		**74**	**188**	**20**	**47**	**8**	**0**	**0**	**16**	**15**	**0**	**31**	**0**	**2**	**0**	**4**	**1**	**.250**	**.305**	**.293**	**.651**

Heath, Michael Thomas

HEIGHT: 5'11"   THROWS: RIGHT   BATS: RIGHT   BORN: 2/5/1955, TAMPA, FLORIDA   POSITIONS PLAYED: OF, C, 3B

YEAR	TEAM	GAMES	AB	RUNS	HITS	2B	3B	HR	RBI	BB	IBB	SO	HBP	SH	SF	SB	CS	BA	OBA	SA	FA
1978	**NY-A**	**33**	**92**	**6**	**21**	**3**	**1**	**0**	**8**	**4**	**0**	**9**	**1**	**1**	**1**	**0**	**0**	**.228**	**.268**	**.283**	**.970**
1979	Oak-A	74	258	19	66	8	0	3	27	17	1	18	3	3	5	1	0	.256	.304	.322	1.000
1980	Oak-A	92	305	27	74	10	2	1	33	16	2	28	0	7	1	3	3	.243	.280	.298	.986
1981	Oak-A	84	301	26	71	7	1	8	30	13	1	36	1	5	1	3	3	.236	.269	.346	1.000
1982	Oak-A	101	318	43	77	18	4	3	39	27	3	36	0	2	4	8	3	.242	.298	.352	.973
1983	Oak-A	96	345	45	97	17	0	6	33	18	4	59	1	1	1	3	4	.281	.318	.383	1.000
1984	Oak-A	140	475	49	118	21	5	13	64	26	2	72	1	2	4	7	4	.248	.287	.396	.986
1985	Oak-A	138	436	71	109	18	6	13	55	41	0	63	1	10	4	7	7	.250	.313	.408	.982
1986	StL-N	65	190	19	39	8	1	4	25	23	4	36	1	1	1	2	3	.205	.293	.321	1.000
1986	Det-A	30	98	11	26	3	0	4	11	4	0	17	0	0	1	4	1	.265	.291	.418	.000
1987	Det-A	93	270	34	76	16	0	8	33	21	0	42	3	1	1	1	5	.281	.339	.430	.750
1988	Det-A	86	219	24	54	7	2	5	18	18	0	32	1	3	0	1	0	.247	.307	.365	.984
1989	Det-A	122	396	38	104	16	2	10	43	24	2	71	4	1	4	7	1	.263	.308	.389	1.000
1990	Det-A	122	370	46	100	18	2	7	38	19	0	71	4	2	3	7	6	.270	.311	.386	1.000
1991	Atl-N	49	139	4	29	3	1	1	12	7	5	26	1	2	1	0	0	.209	.250	.266	.991
Career average		92	294	33	74	12	2	6	33	20	2	43	2	3	2	4	3	.252	.300	.369	.908
Yankee average		**33**	**92**	**6**	**21**	**3**	**1**	**0**	**8**	**4**	**0**	**9**	**0**	**0**	**0**	**0**	**0**	**.228**	**.260**	**.283**	**.970**
Career total		1292	4120	456	1040	170	26	86	461	274	24	607	21	40	31	54	40	.252	.300	.369	.908
Yankee total		**33**	**92**	**6**	**21**	**3**	**1**	**0**	**8**	**4**	**0**	**9**	**0**	**0**	**0**	**0**	**0**	**.228**	**.260**	**.283**	**.970**

Heffner, Donald Henry (Jeep)

HEIGHT: 5'10" THROWS: RIGHT BATS: RIGHT BORN: 2/8/1911, ROUZERVILLE, PENN. DIED: 8/1/1989, PASADENA, CALIF. POSITIONS PLAYED: 1B, 2B, 3B, SS, OF

YEAR	TEAM	GAMES	AB	RUNS	HITS	2B	3B	HR	RBI	BB	IBB	SO	HBP	SH	SF	SB	CS	BA	OBA	SA	FA
1934	NY-A	72	241	29	63	8	3	0	25	25	—	18	0	4	—	1	1	.261	.331	.320	.971
1935	NY-A	10	36	3	11	3	1	0	8	4	—	1	0	0	—	0	0	.306	.375	.444	.980
1936	NY-A	19	48	7	11	2	1	0	6	6	—	5	0	1	—	0	0	.229	.315	.313	.971
1937	NY-A	60	201	23	50	6	5	0	21	19	—	19	0	1	—	0	0	.249	.314	.328	1.000
1938	StL-A	141	473	47	116	23	3	2	69	65	—	53	4	12	—	1	4	.245	.341	.319	.971
1939	StL-A	110	375	45	100	10	2	1	35	48	—	39	0	11	—	1	7	.267	.350	.312	.944
1940	StL-A	126	487	52	115	23	2	3	53	39	—	37	2	2	—	5	5	.236	.295	.310	.977
1941	StL-A	110	399	48	93	14	2	0	17	38	—	27	2	7	—	5	6	.233	.303	.278	.974
1942	StL-A	19	36	2	6	2	0	0	3	1	—	4	0	1	—	1	0	.167	.189	.222	1.000
1943	StL-A	18	33	2	4	1	0	0	2	2	—	2	0	2	—	0	0	.121	.171	.152	1.000
1943	Phi-A	52	178	17	37	6	0	0	8	18	—	12	1	1	—	3	2	.208	.284	.242	.978
1944	Det-A	6	19	0	4	1	0	0	1	5	—	1	0	0	—	0	0	.211	.375	.263	.962
Career average		62	211	23	51	8	2	1	21	23	—	18	1	3	—	2	2	.241	.317	.303	.977
Yankee average		40	132	16	34	5	3	0	15	14	—	11	0	2	—	1	1	.257	.326	.331	.981
Career total		743	2526	275	610	99	19	6	248	270	—	218	9	41	—	18	26	.241	.317	.303	.977
Yankee total		161	526	62	135	19	10	0	60	54	—	43	0	6	—	2	5	.257	.326	.331	.981

Hegan, James Michael

HEIGHT: 6'1" THROWS: LEFT BATS: LEFT BORN: 7/21/1942, CLEVELAND, OHIO POSITIONS PLAYED: 1B, OF

YEAR	TEAM	GAMES	AB	RUNS	HITS	2B	3B	HR	RBI	BB	IBB	SO	HBP	SH	SF	SB	CS	BA	OBA	SA	FA
1964	NY-A	5	5	0	0	0	0	0	0	1	0	2	0	0	0	0	0	.000	.167	.000	1.000
1966	NY-A	13	39	7	8	0	1	0	2	7	0	11	0	2	0	1	0	.205	.326	.256	.991
1967	NY-A	68	118	12	16	4	1	1	3	20	1	40	1	1	0	1	1	.136	.266	.212	1.000
1969	Sea-A	95	267	54	78	9	6	8	37	62	1	61	1	3	0	6	5	.292	.427	.461	.993
1970	Mil-A	148	476	70	116	21	2	11	52	67	3	116	1	8	4	9	7	.244	.336	.366	1.000
1971	Mil-A	46	122	19	27	4	1	4	11	26	2	19	0	5	1	1	1	.221	.356	.369	1.000
1971	Oak-A	65	55	5	13	3	0	0	3	5	0	13	0	1	2	1	0	.236	.300	.291	.667
1972	Oak-A	98	79	13	26	3	1	1	5	7	1	20	0	2	2	1	0	.329	.375	.430	1.000
1973	Oak-A	75	71	8	13	2	0	1	5	5	1	17	0	1	0	0	0	.183	.237	.254	.988
1973	NY-A	37	131	12	36	3	2	6	14	7	1	34	0	4	1	0	0	.275	.309	.466	.992
1974	NY-A	18	53	3	12	2	0	2	9	5	0	9	2	2	0	1	1	.226	.317	.377	1.000
1974	Mil-A	89	190	21	45	7	1	7	32	33	4	34	0	1	2	0	1	.237	.347	.395	1.000
1975	Mil-A	93	203	19	51	11	0	5	22	31	3	42	0	1	2	1	1	.251	.347	.379	.995
1976	Mil-A	80	218	30	54	4	3	5	31	25	1	54	1	1	3	1	1	.248	.324	.362	.969
1977	Mil-A	35	53	8	9	0	0	2	3	10	1	17	1	0	3	0	0	.170	.313	.283	.980
Career average		64	139	19	34	5	1	4	15	21	1	33	1	2	1	2	1	.242	.341	.371	.972
Yankee average		28	69	7	14	2	1	2	6	8	0	19	1	2	0	2	1	.208	.295	.335	.997
Career total		965	2080	281	504	73	18	53	229	311	19	489	7	31	15	28	21	.242	.341	.371	.972
Yankee total		141	346	34	72	9	4	9	28	40	2	96	3	9	1	9	3	.208	.295	.335	.997

Held, Woodson George (Woodie)

HEIGHT: 5'10" THROWS: RIGHT BATS: RIGHT BORN: 3/25/1932, SACRAMENTO, CALIFORNIA POSITIONS PLAYED: 2B, 3B, SS, OF

YEAR	TEAM	GAMES	AB	RUNS	HITS	2B	3B	HR	RBI	BB	IBB	SO	HBP	SH	SF	SB	CS	BA	OBA	SA	FA
1954	NY-A	4	3	2	0	0	0	0	0	2	—	1	0	0	0	0	0	.000	.400	.000	1.000
1957	NY-A	1	1	0	0	0	0	0	0	0	—	0	0	0	0	0	0	.000	.000	.000	.000
1957	KC-A	92	326	48	78	14	3	20	50	37	1	81	3	3	2	4	0	.239	.321	.485	.996
1958	KC-A	47	131	13	28	2	0	4	16	10	0	28	2	2	2	0	1	.214	.276	.321	1.000
1958	Cle-A	67	144	12	28	4	1	3	17	15	0	36	4	1	2	1	2	.194	.285	.299	.966
1959	Cle-A	143	525	82	132	19	3	29	71	46	1	118	2	2	2	1	2	.251	.305	.465	.984
1960	Cle-A	109	376	45	97	15	1	21	67	44	1	73	2	2	2	1	2	.258	.342	.471	.967
1961	Cle-A	146	509	67	136	23	5	23	78	69	11	111	5	3	2	0	1	.267	.354	.468	.960
1962	Cle-A	139	466	55	116	12	2	19	58	73	5	107	3	3	6	0	0	.249	.362	.406	1.000
1963	Cle-A	133	416	61	103	19	4	17	61	61	10	96	8	4	4	2	2	.248	.352	.435	.982
1964	Cle-A	118	364	50	86	13	0	18	49	43	8	88	7	0	1	1	0	.236	.328	.420	.953
1965	Was-A	122	332	46	82	16	0	16	54	49	1	74	3	2	4	0	0	.247	.352	.452	1.000
1966	Bal-A	56	82	6	17	3	1	1	7	12	0	30	0	1	0	0	0	.207	.309	.305	1.000
1967	Bal-A	26	41	6	6	3	0	1	6	6	0	12	0	1	0	0	0	.146	.286	.293	.974
1967	Cal-A	58	141	15	31	3	0	4	17	18	0	41	2	5	0	0	2	.220	.317	.326	1.000
1968	Cal-A	33	45	4	5	1	0	0	0	5	0	15	2	1	0	0	0	.111	.231	.133	1.000
1968	Chi-A	40	54	5	9	1	0	0	2	5	0	14	1	1	1	0	0	.167	.246	.185	1.000
1969	Chi-A	56	63	9	9	1	0	3	6	13	3	19	1	2	1	0	0	.143	.299	.317	1.000

(continued)

(continued)

	GAMES	AB	RUNS	HITS	2B	3B	HR	RBI	BB	IBB	SO	HBP	SH	SF	SB	CS	BA	OBA	SA	FA
Career average	77	223	29	54	8	1	10	31	28	—	52	3	2	2	1	1	.240	.331	.421	.928
Yankee average	**3**	**2**	**1**	**0**	**0**	**0**	**0**	**0**	**0**	**1**	**—**	**1**	**0**	**0**	**0**	**0**	**0**	**.000**	**.333**	**.000**	**.500**
Career total	1390	4019	524	963	150	22	179	559	508	45	944	56	34	28	14	11	.240	.331	.421	.928
Yankee total	**5**	**4**	**2**	**0**	**0**	**0**	**0**	**0**	**0**	**2**	**0**	**1**	**0**	**0**	**0**	**0**	**0**	**.000**	**.333**	**.000**	**.500**

Hemphill, Charles Judson (Eagle Eye)
HEIGHT: 5'9" THROWS: LEFT BATS: LEFT BORN: 4/20/1876, GREENVILLE, MICHIGAN DIED: 6/22/1953, DETROIT, MICHIGAN POSITIONS PLAYED: 2B, OF

YEAR	TEAM	GAMES	AB	RUNS	HITS	2B	3B	HR	RBI	BB	IBB	SO	HBP	SH	SF	SB	CS	BA	OBA	SA	FA
1899	StL-N	11	37	4	9	0	0	1	3	6	—	—	0	0	—	0	—	.243	.364	.324	.750
1899	Cle-N	55	202	23	56	3	5	2	23	6	—	—	1	0	—	3	—	.277	.301	.371	.859
1901	Bos-A	136	545	71	142	10	10	3	62	39	—	—	2	9	—	11	—	.261	.312	.332	.925
1902	Cle-A	25	94	14	25	2	0	0	11	5	—	—	0	3	—	4	—	.266	.303	.287	.860
1902	StL-A	103	416	67	132	14	11	6	58	44	—	—	0	3	—	23	—	.317	.383	.447	.875
1903	StL-A	105	383	36	94	6	3	3	29	23	—	—	2	7	—	16	—	.245	.292	.300	.961
1904	StL-A	114	438	47	112	13	2	2	45	35	—	—	0	10	—	23	—	.256	.311	.308	.926
1906	StL-A	154	585	90	169	19	12	4	62	43	—	—	0	18	—	33	—	.289	.338	.383	.961
1907	StL-A	153	603	66	156	20	9	0	38	51	—	—	2	19	—	14	—	.259	.319	.322	.957
1908	**NY-A**	**142**	**505**	**62**	**150**	**12**	**9**	**0**	**44**	**59**	**—**	**—**	**3**	**14**	**—**	**42**	**—**	**.297**	**.374**	**.356**	**.937**
1909	**NY-A**	**73**	**181**	**23**	**44**	**5**	**1**	**0**	**10**	**32**	**—**	**—**	**0**	**3**	**—**	**10**	**—**	**.243**	**.357**	**.282**	**.976**
1910	**NY-A**	**102**	**351**	**45**	**84**	**9**	**4**	**0**	**21**	**55**	**—**	**—**	**5**	**8**	**—**	**19**	**—**	**.239**	**.350**	**.288**	**.971**
1911	**NY-A**	**69**	**201**	**32**	**57**	**4**	**2**	**1**	**15**	**37**	**—**	**—**	**1**	**5**	**—**	**9**	**—**	**.284**	**.397**	**.338**	**.952**
Career average	96	349	45	95	9	5	2	32	34	—	—	1	8	—	16	—	.271	.337	.341	.916
Yankee average	**97**	**310**	**41**	**84**	**8**	**4**	**0**	**23**	**46**	**—**	**—**	**2**	**8**	**—**	**20**	**—**	**.271**	**.369**	**.323**	**.959**
Career total	1242	4541	580	1230	117	68	22	421	435	—	—	16	99	—	207	—	.271	.337	.341	.916
Yankee total	**386**	**1238**	**162**	**335**	**30**	**16**	**1**	**90**	**183**	**—**	**—**	**9**	**30**	**—**	**80**	**—**	**.271**	**.369**	**.323**	**.959**

Hemsley, Ralston Burdett (Rollie)
HEIGHT: 5'10" THROWS: RIGHT BATS: RIGHT BORN: 6/24/1907, SYRACUSE, OHIO DIED: 7/31/1972, WASHINGTON, D.C. POSITIONS PLAYED: C, 1B, OF

YEAR	TEAM	GAMES	AB	RUNS	HITS	2B	3B	HR	RBI	BB	IBB	SO	HBP	SH	SF	SB	CS	BA	OBA	SA	FA
1928	Pit-N	50	133	14	36	2	3	0	18	4	—	10	0	3	—	1	—	.271	.292	.331	.962
1929	Pit-N	88	235	31	68	13	7	0	37	11	—	22	0	9	—	1	—	.289	.321	.404	.954
1930	Pit-N	104	324	45	82	19	6	2	45	22	—	21	0	10	—	3	—	.253	.301	.367	.979
1931	Pit-N	10	35	3	6	3	0	0	1	3	—	3	0	0	—	0	—	.171	.237	.257	1.000
1931	Chi-N	66	204	28	63	17	4	3	31	17	—	30	0	3	—	4	—	.309	.362	.475	.975
1932	Chi-N	60	151	27	36	10	3	4	20	10	—	16	0	4	—	2	—	.238	.286	.424	1.000
1933	Cin-N	49	116	9	22	8	0	0	7	6	—	8	0	0	—	0	—	.190	.230	.259	.970
1933	StL-A	32	95	7	23	2	1	1	15	11	—	12	0	1	—	0	0	.242	.321	.316	.965
1934	StL-A	123	431	47	133	31	7	2	52	29	—	37	2	11	—	6	2	.309	.355	.427	.973
1935	StL-A	144	504	57	146	32	7	0	48	44	—	41	2	10	—	3	2	.290	.349	.381	.979
1936	StL-A	116	377	43	99	24	2	2	39	46	—	30	0	4	—	2	3	.263	.343	.353	.969
1937	StL-A	100	334	30	74	12	3	3	28	25	—	29	0	5	—	0	0	.222	.276	.302	1.000
1938	Cle-A	66	203	27	60	11	3	2	28	23	—	14	0	4	—	1	1	.296	.367	.409	.980
1939	Cle-A	107	395	58	104	17	4	2	36	26	—	26	0	11	—	2	4	.263	.309	.342	.984
1940	Cle-A	119	416	46	111	20	5	4	42	22	—	25	0	5	—	1	3	.267	.304	.368	.994
1941	Cle-A	98	288	29	69	10	5	2	24	18	—	19	0	3	—	2	0	.240	.284	.330	.980
1942	Cin-N	36	115	7	13	1	2	0	7	4	—	11	0	0	—	0	—	.113	.143	.157	.982
1942	**NY-A**	**31**	**85**	**12**	**25**	**3**	**1**	**0**	**15**	**5**	**—**	**9**	**0**	**2**	**—**	**1**	**0**	**.294**	**.333**	**.353**	**.991**
1943	**NY-A**	**62**	**180**	**12**	**43**	**6**	**3**	**2**	**24**	**13**	**—**	**9**	**0**	**6**	**—**	**0**	**1**	**.239**	**.290**	**.339**	**.981**
1944	**NY-A**	**81**	**284**	**23**	**76**	**12**	**5**	**2**	**26**	**9**	**—**	**13**	**0**	**6**	**—**	**0**	**2**	**.268**	**.290**	**.366**	**.983**
1946	Phi-N	49	139	7	31	4	1	0	11	9	—	10	0	4	—	0	0	.223	.270	.266	.977
1947	Phi-N	2	3	0	1	0	0	0	1	0	—	0	0	0	—	0	0	.333	.333	.333	1.000
Career average	72	229	26	60	12	3	1	25	16	—	18	0	5	—	1	—	.262	.311	.360	.981
Yankee average	**58**	**183**	**16**	**48**	**7**	**3**	**1**	**22**	**9**	**—**	**10**	**0**	**5**	**—**	**0**	**1**	**.262**	**.297**	**.355**	**.985**
Career total	1593	5047	562	1321	257	72	31	555	357	—	395	4	101	—	29	18	.262	.311	.360	.981
Yankee total	**174**	**549**	**47**	**144**	**21**	**9**	**4**	**65**	**27**	**—**	**31**	**0**	**14**	**—**	**1**	**3**	**.262**	**.297**	**.355**	**.985**

Rickey Henley Henderson, of-dh, 1985–89

Rickey Henderson does two things on a ball field about as well as anyone who has ever played: steal bases and score runs.

Henderson, born on Christmas Day 1958 in Chicago, debuted as a rookie with the Oakland Athletics in 1979. After six seasons with the A's, he was traded to the Yankees in 1985.

By then, Henderson had established an impressive resume. He had already led the American League in stolen bases five times, including a record 130 swipes in 1982. He went over 100 steals in 1980 and 1983, too. In five full years with the A's, Henderson averaged 107 runs scored. He also showed some power, hitting ten or more home runs 12 times in his career.

Little changed when he came to the Yankees. He led the league in stolen bases and runs scored in 1985 and 1986. He was named to the All-Star team every year he was in New York and remains the all-time leader in stolen bases for the Yankees with 326.

But Henderson always seemed to be at odds with whichever Yankee manager was at the helm at the time, with the exception of Billy Martin. Henderson had played for Martin in Oakland and the two men always got along well. Things were less copacetic with Yankee skippers Lou Piniella and Dallas Green, both of whom felt Henderson was not always a team player.

Still, the Yankees were never out of the running as long as Henderson was in pinstripes. They finished second in the American League East in 1985 and 1986, and finished 3 1/2 games out of first place in 1988.

But while Henderson probably wasn't as bad a guy as Piniella and especially Green made him out to be, he had a hard time keeping his mouth shut. In 1988, he told two New York reporters that the reason the Yankees lost the pennant was because they were a team of alcohol abusers. Maybe that was true and maybe it wasn't, but the problem was that Henderson wasn't above having a few snootfuls himself.

Anyway, by 1989, he was gone, traded back to Oakland. Since then, he has gone from Oakland to Toronto back to Oakland to San Diego to Anaheim to Oakland once again and in 1999 to the New York Mets. In 2000 he switched teams again, this time signing-up with the Seattle Mariners.

Henderson, Rickey Henley

HEIGHT: 5'10"　THROWS: LEFT　BATS: RIGHT　BORN: 12/25/1958, CHICAGO, ILLINOIS　POSITIONS PLAYED: OF

YEAR	TEAM	GAMES	AB	RUNS	HITS	2B	3B	HR	RBI	BB	IBB	SO	HBP	SH	SF	SB	CS	BA	OBA	SA	FA
1979	Oak-A	89	351	49	96	13	3	1	26	34	0	39	2	8	3	33	11	.274	.338	.336	.973
1980	Oak-A	158	591	111	179	22	4	9	53	117	7	54	5	6	3	100	26	.303	.420	.399	.984
1981	Oak-A	108	423	89	135	18	7	6	35	64	4	68	2	0	4	56	22	.319	.408	.437	.979
1982	Oak-A	149	536	119	143	24	4	10	51	116	1	94	2	0	2	130	42	.267	.398	.382	.977
1983	Oak-A	145	513	105	150	25	7	9	48	103	8	80	4	1	1	108	19	.292	.414	.421	.992
1984	Oak-A	142	502	113	147	27	4	16	58	86	1	81	5	1	3	66	18	.293	.399	.458	.969
1985	**NY-A**	**143**	**547**	**146**	**172**	**28**	**5**	**24**	**72**	**99**	**1**	**65**	**3**	**0**	**5**	**80**	**10**	**.314**	**.419**	**.516**	**.980**
1986	**NY-A**	**153**	**608**	**130**	**160**	**31**	**5**	**28**	**74**	**89**	**2**	**81**	**2**	**0**	**2**	**87**	**18**	**.263**	**.358**	**.469**	**.986**
1987	**NY-A**	**95**	**358**	**78**	**104**	**17**	**3**	**17**	**37**	**80**	**1**	**52**	**2**	**0**	**0**	**41**	**8**	**.291**	**.423**	**.497**	**.980**
1988	**NY-A**	**140**	**554**	**118**	**169**	**30**	**2**	**6**	**50**	**82**	**1**	**54**	**3**	**2**	**6**	**93**	**13**	**.305**	**.394**	**.399**	**.965**
1989	**NY-A**	**65**	**235**	**41**	**58**	**13**	**1**	**3**	**22**	**56**	**0**	**29**	**1**	**0**	**1**	**25**	**8**	**.247**	**.392**	**.349**	**.993**
1989	Oak-A	85	306	72	90	13	2	9	35	70	5	39	2	0	3	52	6	.294	.425	.438	.985
1990	Oak-A	136	489	119	159	33	3	28	61	97	2	60	4	2	2	65	10	.325	.439	.577	.983
1991	Oak-A	134	470	105	126	17	1	18	57	98	7	73	7	0	3	58	18	.268	.400	.423	.970
1992	Oak-A	117	396	77	112	18	3	15	46	95	5	56	6	0	3	48	11	.283	.426	.457	.984
1993	Oak-A	90	318	77	104	19	1	17	47	85	6	46	2	0	2	31	6	.327	.469	.553	.974
1993	Tor-A	44	163	37	35	3	1	4	12	35	1	19	2	1	2	22	2	.215	.356	.319	.975
1994	Oak-A	87	296	66	77	13	0	6	20	72	1	45	5	1	2	22	7	.260	.411	.365	.977
1995	Oak-A	112	407	67	122	31	1	9	54	72	2	66	4	1	3	32	10	.300	.407	.447	.988
1996	SD-N	148	465	110	112	17	2	9	29	125	2	90	10	0	2	37	15	.241	.410	.344	.917

(continued)

(continued)

YEAR	TEAM	GAMES	AB	RUNS	HITS	2B	3B	HR	RBI	BB	IBB	SO	HBP	SH	SF	SB	CS	BA	OBA	SA	FA
1997	SD-N	88	288	63	79	11	0	6	27	71	2	62	4	0	2	29	4	.274	.422	.375	.959
1997	Ana-A	32	115	21	21	3	0	2	7	26	0	23	2	1	0	16	4	.183	.343	.261	1.000
1998	Oak-A	152	542	101	128	16	1	14	57	118	0	114	0	2	3	66	13	.236	.371	.347	.987
1999	NY-A	121	438	89	138	30	0	12	42	82	0	82	0	1	3	37	14	.315	.421	.466	.988
2000	NY-N	31	96	17	21	1	0	0	2	25	1	20	2	0	1	5	2	.219	.387	.229	.977
2000	Sea-A	92	324	58	77	13	2	4	30	63	0	55	2	3	3	31	9	.238	.362	.327	.977
Career average		110	397	84	112	19	2	11	41	79	2	60	3	1	3	53	13	.282	.403	.423	.978
Yankee average		**119**	**460**	**103**	**133**	**24**	**3**	**16**	**51**	**81**	**1**	**56**	**2**	**0**	**3**	**65**	**11**	**.288**	**.395**	**.455**	**.981**
Career total		2856	10331	2178	2914	486	62	282	1052	2060	60	1547	83	30	64	1370	326	.282	.403	.423	.978
Yankee total		**596**	**2302**	**513**	**663**	**119**	**16**	**78**	**255**	**406**	**5**	**281**	**11**	**2**	**14**	**326**	**57**	**.288**	**.395**	**.455**	**.981**

Hendrick, Harvey (Gink)

HEIGHT: 6'2"   THROWS: RIGHT   BATS: LEFT   BORN: 11/9/1897, MASON, TENN.   DIED: 10/29/1941, COVINGTON, TENN.   POSITIONS PLAYED: 1B, 2B, 3B, SS, OF

YEAR	TEAM	GAMES	AB	RUNS	HITS	2B	3B	HR	RBI	BB	IBB	SO	HBP	SH	SF	SB	CS	BA	OBA	SA	FA
1923	**NY-A**	**37**	**66**	**9**	**18**	**3**	**1**	**3**	**12**	**2**	—	**8**	**0**	**1**	—	**3**	**0**	**.273**	**.294**	**.485**	**.947**
1924	**NY-A**	**40**	**76**	**7**	**20**	**0**	**0**	**1**	**11**	**2**	—	**7**	**1**	**1**	—	**1**	**0**	**.263**	**.291**	**.303**	**.975**
1925	Cle-A	25	28	2	8	1	2	0	9	3	—	5	0	2	—	0	0	.286	.355	.464	1.000
1927	Bro-N	128	458	55	142	18	11	4	50	24	—	40	4	9	—	29	—	.310	.350	.424	.875
1928	Bro-N	126	425	83	135	15	10	11	59	54	—	34	2	12	—	16	—	.318	.397	.478	.913
1929	Bro-N	110	384	69	136	25	6	14	82	31	—	20	1	8	—	14	—	.354	.404	.560	.824
1930	Bro-N	68	167	29	43	10	1	5	28	20	—	19	2	3	—	2	—	.257	.344	.419	1.000
1931	Bro-N	1	1	0	0	0	0	0	0	0	—	0	0	0	—	0	—	.000	.000	.000	.000
1931	Cin-N	137	530	74	167	32	9	1	75	53	—	40	2	8	—	3	—	.315	.379	.415	.987
1932	StL-N	28	72	8	18	2	0	1	5	5	—	9	0	0	—	0	—	.250	.299	.319	1.000
1932	Cin-N	94	398	56	120	30	3	4	40	23	—	29	1	6	—	3	—	.302	.341	.422	.986
1933	Chi-N	69	189	30	55	13	3	4	23	13	—	17	3	3	—	4	—	.291	.346	.455	.895
1934	Phi-N	59	116	12	34	8	0	0	19	9	—	15	0	2	—	0	—	.293	.344	.362	.978
Career average		71	224	33	69	12	4	4	32	18	—	19	1	4	—	6	—	.308	.364	.443	.875
Yankee average		**39**	**71**	**8**	**19**	**2**	**1**	**2**	**12**	**2**	—	**8**	**1**	**1**	—	**2**	**0**	**.268**	**.293**	**.387**	**.961**
Career total		922	2910	434	896	157	46	48	413	239	—	243	16	55	—	75	0	.308	.364	.443	.875
Yankee total		**77**	**142**	**16**	**38**	**3**	**1**	**4**	**23**	**4**	—	**15**	**1**	**2**	—	**4**	**0**	**.268**	**.293**	**.387**	**.961**

Hendricks, Elrod Jerome (Ellie)

HEIGHT: 6'1"   THROWS: RIGHT   BATS: LEFT   BORN: 12/22/1940, CHARLOTTE AMALIE, VIRGIN ISLANDS   POSITIONS PLAYED: C, 1B

YEAR	TEAM	GAMES	AB	RUNS	HITS	2B	3B	HR	RBI	BB	IBB	SO	HBP	SH	SF	SB	CS	BA	OBA	SA	FA
1968	Bal-A	79	183	19	37	8	1	7	23	19	2	51	1	0	1	0	0	.202	.279	.372	.991
1969	Bal-A	105	295	36	72	5	0	12	38	39	5	44	2	0	3	0	1	.244	.333	.383	1.000
1970	Bal-A	106	322	32	78	9	0	12	41	33	4	44	4	2	4	1	0	.242	.317	.382	.986
1971	Bal-A	101	316	33	79	14	1	9	42	39	5	38	2	2	2	0	0	.250	.334	.386	.985
1972	Bal-A	33	84	6	13	4	0	0	4	12	2	19	0	1	1	0	1	.155	.258	.202	.986
1972	Chi-N	17	43	7	5	1	0	2	6	13	6	8	0	1	1	0	0	.116	.321	.279	.978
1973	Bal-A	41	101	9	18	5	1	3	15	10	4	22	1	1	1	0	0	.178	.257	.337	.994
1974	Bal-A	66	159	18	33	8	2	3	8	17	4	25	1	0	3	0	0	.208	.283	.340	1.000
1975	Bal-A	85	223	32	48	8	2	8	38	34	5	40	1	2	2	0	1	.215	.319	.377	.995
1976	Bal-A	28	79	2	11	1	0	1	4	7	1	13	0	0	0	0	0	.139	.209	.190	.971
1976	**NY-A**	**26**	**53**	**6**	**12**	**1**	**0**	**3**	**5**	**3**	**0**	**10**	**0**	**0**	**1**	**0**	**0**	**.226**	**.263**	**.415**	**1.000**
1977	**NY-A**	**10**	**11**	**1**	**3**	**1**	**0**	**1**	**5**	**0**	**0**	**2**	**0**	**0**	**0**	**0**	**0**	**.273**	**.273**	**.636**	**1.000**
1978	Bal-A	13	18	4	6	1	0	1	1	3	2	3	0	0	0	0	0	.333	.429	.556	.955
1979	Bal-A	1	1	0	0	0	0	0	0	0	0	0	0	0	0	0	0	.000	.000	.000	.500
Career average		51	135	15	30	5	1	4	16	16	3	23	1	1	1	0	0	.220	.306	.361	.953
Yankee average		**18**	**32**	**4**	**8**	**1**	**0**	**2**	**5**	**2**	**0**	**6**	**0**	**0**	**1**	**0**	**0**	**.234**	**.265**	**.453**	**1.000**
Career total		711	1888	205	415	66	7	62	230	229	40	319	12	8	18	1	5	.220	.306	.361	.953
Yankee total		**36**	**64**	**7**	**15**	**2**	**0**	**4**	**10**	**3**	**0**	**12**	**0**	**0**	**1**	**0**	**0**	**.234**	**.265**	**.453**	**1.000**

Hendryx, Timothy Green

HEIGHT: 5'9"   THROWS: RIGHT   BATS: RIGHT   BORN: 1/31/1891, LEROY, ILLINOIS   DIED: 8/14/1957, CORPUS CHRISTI, TEXAS   POSITIONS PLAYED: OF

YEAR	TEAM	GAMES	AB	RUNS	HITS	2B	3B	HR	RBI	BB	IBB	SO	HBP	SH	SF	SB	CS	BA	OBA	SA	FA
1911	Cle-A	4	7	0	2	0	0	0	0	0	0	0	0	1	0	0	0	.286	.286	.286	1.000
1912	Cle-A	23	70	9	17	2	4	1	14	8	0	0	1	7	0	3	0	.243	.329	.429	1.000
1915	**NY-A**	**13**	**40**	**4**	**8**	**2**	**0**	**0**	**1**	**4**	**0**	**2**	**1**	**1**	**0**	**4**	**3**	**.200**	**.289**	**.250**	**.968**
1916	**NY-A**	**15**	**62**	**10**	**18**	**7**	**1**	**0**	**5**	**8**	**0**	**6**	**1**	**1**	**0**	**6**	**0**	**.290**	**.380**	**.435**	**1.000**
1917	**NY-A**	**125**	**393**	**43**	**98**	**14**	**7**	**5**	**44**	**62**	**0**	**45**	**5**	**16**	**0**	**0**	**0**	**.249**	**.359**	**.359**	**.955**

(continued)

Thomas David "Old Reliable" Henrich, of-1b, 1937–50

It is said that of all the individual statistics throughout Yankee history, Tommy Henrich's lifetime mark of .282 is the most misleading of all.

He was one of the best clutch players in Yankee history, a hard man to get out with men on base, harder to retire in the late innings and hardest of all with the game on the line.

Henrich was born February 20, 1913 in Massillon, Ohio. He was playing ball in a sandlot in Massillon when he was approached by a scout from Cleveland. Much to Henrich's surprise, a contract was offered. Henrich signed in 1933.

But there were some problems with the way the Indians had signed him, and he was consequently declared a free agent. The Yankees signed him for a $25,000 bonus in 1937 and brought him up that year.

He played with great concentration. He studied opposing hitters to determine how they would strike the ball. He studied opposing pitchers to see how they delivered. It was Mel Allen, the Yankee broadcaster, who named him Old Reliable for his knack of delivering in the clutch.

In 1949, he was the MVP of the Yankees, and probably the league. Although no real statistics were kept of such feats, Henrich had 24 home runs that year, and at least 12 of them won or tied a ballgame for the Yankees in the late innings. Seeing as the Yankees won the pennant by one game over the Red Sox, every game-winning hit Henrich made that year was big.

He was involved in two of the most famous plays in Yankee World Series history. In 1941, he swung at a pitch delivered by Dodger reliever Hugh Casey with two outs in the top of the ninth inning. It was strike three, but Brooklyn catcher Mickey Owen dropped the ball, and Henrich raced to first base.

The Yankees were trailing, 4-3 at that point, but the miscue opened the floodgates. The Yankees scored four runs in the inning to win, 7-4. They went on to win the Series, 4-1.

In 1949, Henrich struck again, smacking a dramatic home run in the bottom of the ninth inning to snap a scoreless tie and give New York a 1-0 victory in another Series win over Brooklyn.

Henrich, a five-time All-Star, is among the all-time Yankee leaders in several offensive categories, including 14th in runs scored with 901, 12th in doubles with 269, 8th in triples with 73, 12th in home runs with 183 and 13th in RBI with 795. Following his retirement in 1950, he coached with several teams, including the Yankees, Giants and Tigers.

(continued)

YEAR	TEAM																				
1918	StL-A	88	219	22	61	14	3	0	33	37	0	35	2	11	0	5	0	.279	.388	.370	.982
1920	Bos-A	99	363	54	119	21	5	0	73	42	0	27	2	13	0	7	9	.328	.400	.413	.964
1921	Bos-A	49	137	10	33	8	2	0	22	24	0	13	2	6	0	1	1	.241	.362	.328	.958
Career average		52	161	19	45	9	3	1	24	23	0	16	2	7	0	3	2	.276	.372	.376	.978
Yankee average		**51**	**165**	**19**	**41**	**8**	**3**	**2**	**17**	**25**	**0**	**18**	**2**	**6**	**0**	**3**	**1**	**.251**	**.356**	**.360**	**.974**
Career total		416	1291	152	356	68	22	6	192	185	0	128	14	56	0	26	13	.276	.372	.376	.978
Yankee total		**153**	**495**	**57**	**124**	**23**	**8**	**5**	**50**	**74**	**0**	**53**	**7**	**18**	**0**	**10**	**3**	**.251**	**.356**	**.360**	**.974**

Henrich, Thomas David (Old Reliable)

HEIGHT: 6'0"   THROWS: LEFT   BATS: LEFT   BORN: 2/20/1913, MASSILLON, OHIO   POSITIONS PLAYED: OF

YEAR	TEAM	GAMES	AB	RUNS	HITS	2B	3B	HR	RBI	BB	IBB	SO	HBP	SH	SF	SB	CS	BA	OBA	SA	FA
1937	NY-A	67	206	39	66	14	5	8	42	35	0	17	0	1	0	4	0	.320	.419	.553	.970
1938	NY-A	131	471	109	127	24	7	22	91	92	0	32	2	10	0	6	2	.270	.391	.490	.984
1939	NY-A	99	347	64	96	18	4	9	57	51	0	23	1	7	0	7	0	.277	.371	.429	1.000
1940	NY-A	90	293	57	90	28	5	10	53	48	0	30	2	3	0	1	2	.307	.408	.539	.969

(continued)

(continued)

YEAR	TEAM	GAMES	AB	RUNS	HITS	2B	3B	HR	RBI	BB	IBB	SO	HBP	SH	SF	SB	CS	BA	OBA	SA	FA
1941	NY-A	144	538	106	149	27	5	31	85	81	0	40	5	8	0	3	1	.277	.377	.519	.980
1942	NY-A	127	483	77	129	30	5	13	67	58	0	42	5	9	0	4	4	.267	.352	.431	.987
1946	NY-A	150	565	92	142	25	4	19	83	87	0	63	7	12	0	5	2	.251	.358	.411	.987
1947	NY-A	142	550	109	158	35	13	16	98	71	0	54	3	5	0	3	2	.287	.372	.485	1.000
1948	NY-A	146	588	138	181	42	14	25	100	76	0	42	4	5	0	2	3	.308	.391	.554	.984
1949	NY-A	115	411	90	118	20	3	24	85	86	0	34	5	0	0	2	2	.287	.416	.526	.958
1950	NY-A	73	151	20	41	6	8	6	34	27	0	6	0	0	0	0	1	.272	.382	.536	.987
Career average		117	419	82	118	25	7	17	72	65	0	35	3	6	0	3	2	.282	.382	.491	.982
Yankee average		117	419	82	118	25	7	17	72	65	0	35	3	6	0	3	2	.282	.382	.491	.982
Career total		1284	4603	901	1297	269	73	183	795	712	0	383	34	60	0	37	19	.282	.382	.491	.982
Yankee total		1284	4603	901	1297	269	73	183	795	712	0	383	34	60	0	37	19	.282	.382	.491	.982

Hernandez, Leonardo Jesus BORN LEONARDO JESUS ANTIAH (HERNANDEZ)
HEIGHT: 5'11"   THROWS: RIGHT   BATS: RIGHT   BORN: 11/6/1959, SANTA LUCIA, VENEZUELA   POSITIONS PLAYED: OF

YEAR	TEAM	GAMES	AB	RUNS	HITS	2B	3B	HR	RBI	BB	IBB	SO	HBP	SH	SF	SB	CS	BA	OBA	SA	FA
1982	Bal-A	2	2	0	0	0	0	0	0	0	0	2	0	0	0	0	0	.000	.000	.000	.000
1983	Bal-A	64	203	21	50	6	1	6	26	12	1	19	0	0	1	1	0	.246	.287	.374	.922
1985	Bal-A	12	21	0	1	0	0	0	0	0	0	4	0	0	0	0	0	.048	.048	.048	1.000
1986	NY-A	7	22	2	5	2	0	1	4	1	0	8	0	0	0	0	0	.227	.261	.455	1.000
Career average		21	62	6	14	2	0	2	8	3	0	8	0	0	0	0	0	.226	.263	.351	.731
Yankee average		7	22	2	5	2	0	1	4	1	0	8	0	0	0	0	0	.227	.261	.455	1.000
Career total		85	248	23	56	8	1	7	30	13	1	33	0	0	1	1	0	.226	.263	.351	.731
Yankee total		7	22	2	5	2	0	1	4	1	0	8	0	0	0	0	0	.227	.261	.455	1.000

Herrmann, Edward Martin
HEIGHT: 6'1"   THROWS: RIGHT   BATS: LEFT   BORN: 8/27/1946, SAN DIEGO, CALIFORNIA   POSITIONS PLAYED: C

YEAR	TEAM	GAMES	AB	RUNS	HITS	2B	3B	HR	RBI	BB	IBB	SO	HBP	SH	SF	SB	CS	BA	OBA	SA	FA
1967	Chi-A	2	3	1	2	1	0	0	1	1	1	0	0	0	0	0	0	.667	.750	1.000	1.000
1969	Chi-A	102	290	31	67	8	0	8	31	30	0	35	8	0	1	0	2	.231	.319	.341	.983
1970	Chi-A	96	297	42	84	9	0	19	52	31	3	41	3	2	0	0	1	.283	.356	.505	.988
1971	Chi-A	101	294	32	63	6	0	11	35	44	12	48	2	0	4	2	0	.214	.317	.347	.995
1972	Chi-A	116	354	23	88	9	0	10	40	43	19	37	4	0	4	0	0	.249	.333	.359	.989
1973	Chi-A	119	379	42	85	17	1	10	39	31	3	55	7	2	6	2	4	.224	.291	.354	.984
1974	Chi-A	107	367	32	95	13	1	10	39	16	6	49	0	2	3	1	0	.259	.288	.381	.987
1975	NY-A	80	200	16	51	9	2	6	30	16	5	23	0	0	1	0	0	.255	.309	.410	.979
1976	Cal-A	29	46	5	8	3	0	2	8	7	2	8	0	2	1	0	0	.174	.278	.370	.954
1976	Hou-N	79	265	14	54	8	0	3	25	22	2	40	4	3	2	0	0	.204	.273	.268	.987
1977	Hou-N	56	158	7	46	7	0	1	17	15	1	18	1	3	2	1	1	.291	.352	.354	.990
1978	Hou-N	16	36	1	4	1	0	0	0	3	1	3	0	1	0	0	0	.111	.179	.139	1.000
1978	Mon-N	19	40	1	7	1	0	0	3	1	0	4	0	0	0	0	0	.175	.195	.200	.977
Career average		71	210	19	50	7	0	6	25	20	4	28	2	1	2	1	1	.240	.310	.364	.986
Yankee average		80	200	16	51	9	2	6	30	16	5	23	0	0	1	0	0	.255	.309	.410	.979
Career total		922	2729	247	654	92	4	80	320	260	55	361	29	15	24	6	8	.240	.310	.364	.986
Yankee total		80	200	16	51	9	2	6	30	16	5	23	0	0	1	0	0	.255	.309	.410	.979

High, Hugh Jenken (Bunny)
HEIGHT: 5'8"   THROWS: LEFT   BATS: LEFT   BORN: 10/24/1887, POTTSTOWN, PENNSYLVANIA   DIED: 11/16/1962, ST.LOUIS, MISSOURI   POSITIONS PLAYED: OF

YEAR	TEAM	GAMES	AB	RUNS	HITS	2B	3B	HR	RBI	BB	IBB	SO	HBP	SH	SF	SB	CS	BA	OBA	SA	FA
1913	Det-A	87	183	18	42	6	1	0	16	28	0	24	1	4	0	6	0	.230	.335	.273	.982
1914	Det-A	84	184	25	49	5	3	0	17	26	0	21	2	9	0	7	6	.266	.363	.326	.959
1915	NY-A	119	427	51	110	19	7	1	43	62	0	47	3	13	0	22	13	.258	.356	.342	.981
1916	NY-A	116	377	44	99	13	4	1	28	47	0	44	3	24	0	13	0	.263	.349	.326	.950
1917	NY-A	103	365	37	86	11	6	1	19	48	0	31	3	14	0	8	0	.236	.329	.307	.986
1918	NY-A	7	10	1	0	0	0	0	0	1	0	1	0	0	0	0	0	.000	.091	.000	1.000
Career average		86	258	29	64	9	4	1	21	35	0	28	2	11	0	9	3	.250	.345	.318	.976
Yankee average		86	295	33	74	11	4	1	23	40	0	31	2	13	0	11	3	.250	.343	.323	.979
Career total		516	1546	176	386	54	21	3	123	212	0	168	12	64	0	56	19	.250	.345	.318	.976
Yankee total		345	1179	133	295	43	17	3	90	158	0	123	9	51	0	43	13	.250	.343	.323	.979

Hill, Glenallen

HEIGHT: 6'3" THROWS: RIGHT BATS: RIGHT BORN: 3/22/1965, SANTA CRUZ, CALIFORNIA POSITIONS PLAYED: OF, DH

YEAR	TEAM	GAMES	AB	RUNS	HITS	2B	3B	HR	RBI	BB	IBB	SO	HBP	SH	SF	SB	CS	BA	OBA	SA	FA
1989	Tor-A	19	52	4	15	0	0	1	7	3	0	12	0	0	0	2	1	.288	.327	.346	.964
1990	Tor-A	84	260	47	60	11	3	12	32	18	0	62	0	0	0	8	3	.231	.281	.435	.983
1991	Tor-A	35	99	14	25	5	2	3	11	7	0	24	0	0	2	2	2	.253	.296	.434	.967
1991	Cle-A	37	122	15	32	3	0	5	14	16	0	30	0	1	1	4	2	.262	.345	.410	.978
1992	Cle-A	102	369	38	89	16	1	18	49	20	0	73	4	1	1	2	6	.241	.287	.436	.956
1993	Cle-A	66	174	19	39	7	2	5	25	11	1	50	1	1	4	9	3	.224	.268	.374	.940
1993	Chi-N	31	87	14	30	7	0	10	22	6	0	21	0	0	1	7	3	.345	.387	.770	.957
1994	Chi-N	89	269	48	80	12	1	10	38	29	0	57	0	0	1	19	6	.297	.365	.461	.987
1995	SF-N	132	497	71	131	29	4	24	86	39	4	98	1	0	2	25	5	.264	.317	.483	.959
1996	SF-N	98	379	56	106	26	0	19	67	33	3	95	6	0	3	6	3	.280	.344	.499	.959
1997	SF-N	128	398	47	104	28	4	11	64	19	0	87	4	0	7	7	4	.261	.297	.435	.947
1998	Sea-A	74	259	37	75	20	2	12	33	14	1	45	0	0	1	1	1	.290	.325	.521	.964
1998	Chi-N	48	131	26	46	5	0	8	23	14	1	34	0	0	0	0	0	.351	.414	.573	1.000
1999	Chi-N	99	253	43	76	9	1	20	55	22	0	61	0	0	3	5	1	.300	.353	.581	.958
2000	Chi-N	64	168	23	44	4	1	11	29	10	2	43	0	0	0	0	1	.262	.303	.494	.000
2000	**NY-A**	**40**	**132**	**22**	**44**	**5**	**0**	**16**	**29**	**9**	**0**	**33**	**1**	**0**	**1**	**0**	**0**	**.333**	**.378**	**.735**	**.000**
Career average		72	228	33	62	12	1	12	37	17	1	52	1	0	2	6	2	.273	.324	.488	.845
Yankee average		**40**	**132**	**22**	**44**	**5**	**0**	**16**	**29**	**9**	**0**	**33**	**1**	**0**	**1**	**0**	**0**	**.333**	**.378**	**.735**	**.000**
Career total		1146	3649	524	996	187	21	185	584	270	12	825	17	2	26	96	38	.273	.324	.488	.845
Yankee total		**40**	**132**	**22**	**44**	**5**	**0**	**16**	**29**	**9**	**0**	**33**	**1**	**0**	**1**	**0**	**0**	**.333**	**.378**	**.735**	**.000**

Hill, Jesse Terrill

HEIGHT: 5'9" THROWS: RIGHT BATS: RIGHT BORN: 1/20/1907, YATES, MISSOURI DIED: 8/31/1993, PASADENA, CALIFORNIA POSITIONS PLAYED: OF

YEAR	TEAM	GAMES	AB	RUNS	HITS	2B	3B	HR	RBI	BB	IBB	SO	HBP	SH	SF	SB	CS	BA	OBA	SA	FA
1935	**NY-A**	**107**	**392**	**69**	**115**	**20**	**3**	**4**	**33**	**42**	**—**	**32**	**0**	**10**	**—**	**14**	**4**	**.293**	**.362**	**.390**	**.951**
1936	Was-A	85	233	50	71	19	5	0	34	29	—	23	1	2	—	14	0	.305	.384	.429	.967
1937	Was-A	33	92	24	20	2	1	1	4	13	—	11	0	2	—	2	1	.217	.314	.293	.986
1937	Phi-A	70	242	32	71	12	3	1	37	31	—	20	0	2	—	16	3	.293	.374	.380	.954
Career average		74	240	44	69	13	3	2	27	29	—	23	0	4	—	11	2	.289	.366	.388	.965
Yankee average		**107**	**392**	**69**	**115**	**20**	**3**	**4**	**33**	**42**	**—**	**32**	**0**	**10**	**—**	**14**	**4**	**.293**	**.362**	**.390**	**.951**
Career total		295	959	175	277	53	12	6	108	115	—	91	1	16	—	43	8	.289	.366	.388	.965
Yankee total		**107**	**392**	**69**	**115**	**20**	**3**	**4**	**33**	**42**	**—**	**32**	**0**	**10**	**—**	**14**	**4**	**.293**	**.362**	**.390**	**.951**

Hillis, Malcolm David (Mack)

HEIGHT: 5'10" THROWS: RIGHT BATS: RIGHT BORN: 7/23/1901, CAMBRIDGE, MASS. DIED: 6/16/1961, CAMBRIDGE, MASS. POSITIONS PLAYED: 2B

YEAR	TEAM	GAMES	AB	RUNS	HITS	2B	3B	HR	RBI	BB	IBB	SO	HBP	SH	SF	SB	CS	BA	OBA	SA	FA
1924	**NY-A**	**1**	**1**	**1**	**0**	**0**	**0**	**0**	**0**	**0**	**0**	**0**	**0**	**0**	**0**	**0**	**0**	**.000**	**.000**	**.000**	**.000**
1928	Pit-N	11	36	6	9	2	3	1	7	0	0	6	0	2	0	1	0	.250	.250	.556	.973
Career average		6	19	4	5	1	2	1	4	0	0	3	0	1	0	1	0	.243	.243	.541	.487
Yankee average		**1**	**1**	**1**	**0**	**0**	**0**	**0**	**0**	**0**	**0**	**0**	**0**	**0**	**0**	**0**	**0**	**.000**	**.000**	**.000**	**.000**
Career total		12	37	7	9	2	3	1	7	0	0	6	0	2	0	1	0	.243	.243	.541	.487
Yankee total		**1**	**1**	**1**	**0**	**0**	**0**	**0**	**0**	**0**	**0**	**0**	**0**	**0**	**0**	**0**	**0**	**.000**	**.000**	**.000**	**.000**

Hoag, Myril Oliver

HEIGHT: 5'11" THROWS: RIGHT BATS: RIGHT BORN: 3/9/1908, DAVIS, CALIFORNIA DIED: 7/28/1971, HIGH SPRINGS, FLORIDA POSITIONS PLAYED: P, 1B, 3B, OF

YEAR	TEAM	GAMES	AB	RUNS	HITS	2B	3B	HR	RBI	BB	IBB	SO	HBP	SH	SF	SB	CS	BA	OBA	SA	FA
1931	**NY-A**	**44**	**28**	**6**	**4**	**2**	**0**	**0**	**3**	**1**	**—**	**8**	**0**	**0**	**—**	**0**	**0**	**.143**	**.172**	**.214**	**1.000**
1932	**NY-A**	**46**	**54**	**18**	**20**	**5**	**0**	**1**	**7**	**7**	**—**	**13**	**0**	**0**	**—**	**1**	**1**	**.370**	**.443**	**.519**	**.962**
1934	**NY-A**	**97**	**251**	**45**	**67**	**8**	**2**	**3**	**34**	**21**	**—**	**21**	**0**	**3**	**—**	**1**	**3**	**.267**	**.324**	**.351**	**.974**
1935	**NY-A**	**48**	**110**	**13**	**28**	**4**	**1**	**1**	**13**	**12**	**—**	**19**	**0**	**2**	**—**	**4**	**2**	**.255**	**.328**	**.336**	**.986**
1936	**NY-A**	**45**	**156**	**23**	**47**	**9**	**4**	**3**	**34**	**7**	**—**	**16**	**3**	**3**	**—**	**3**	**1**	**.301**	**.343**	**.468**	**.955**
1937	**NY-A**	**106**	**362**	**48**	**109**	**19**	**8**	**3**	**46**	**33**	**—**	**33**	**3**	**6**	**—**	**4**	**7**	**.301**	**.364**	**.423**	**.955**
1938	**NY-A**	**85**	**267**	**28**	**74**	**14**	**3**	**0**	**48**	**25**	**—**	**31**	**2**	**4**	**—**	**4**	**3**	**.277**	**.344**	**.352**	**.965**
1939	StL-A	129	482	58	142	23	4	10	75	24	—	35	1	8	—	9	5	.295	.329	.421	.971
1940	StL-A	76	191	20	50	11	0	3	26	13	—	30	0	3	—	2	0	.262	.309	.366	.971
1941	StL-A	1	1	0	0	0	0	0	0	0	—	0	0	0	—	0	0	.000	.000	.000	.000

(continued)

(continued)

YEAR	TEAM	GAMES	AB	RUNS	HITS	2B	3B	HR	RBI	BB	IBB	SO	HBP	SH	SF	SB	CS	BA	OBA	SA	FA
1941	Chi-A	106	380	30	97	13	3	1	44	27	—	29	1	3	—	6	10	.255	.306	.313	.957
1942	Chi-A	113	412	47	99	18	2	2	37	36	—	21	0	9	—	17	8	.240	.301	.308	.972
1944	Chi-A	17	48	5	11	1	0	0	4	10	—	1	0	1	—	1	3	.229	.362	.250	.969
1944	Cle-A	67	277	33	79	9	3	1	27	25	—	23	1	5	—	6	4	.285	.347	.350	.947
1945	Cle-A	40	128	10	27	5	3	0	3	11	—	18	1	3	—	1	2	.211	.279	.297	.987
Career average		68	210	26	57	9	2	2	27	17	—	20	1	3	—	4	3	.271	.328	.364	.905
Yankee average		**67**	**175**	**26**	**50**	**9**	**3**	**2**	**26**	**15**	**—**	**20**	**1**	**3**	**—**	**2**	**2**	**.284**	**.345**	**.390**	**.971**
Career total		1020	3147	384	854	141	33	28	401	252	—	298	12	50	—	59	49	.271	.328	.364	.905
Yankee total		**471**	**1228**	**181**	**349**	**61**	**18**	**11**	**185**	**106**	**—**	**141**	**8**	**18**	**—**	**17**	**17**	**.284**	**.345**	**.390**	**.971**

Hobson, Clell Lavern (Butch)

HEIGHT: 6'1"   THROWS: RIGHT   BATS: RIGHT   BORN: 8/17/1951, TUSCALOOSA, ALABAMA   POSITIONS PLAYED: 3B

YEAR	TEAM	GAMES	AB	RUNS	HITS	2B	3B	HR	RBI	BB	IBB	SO	HBP	SH	SF	SB	CS	BA	OBA	SA	FA
1975	Bos-A	2	4	0	1	0	0	0	0	0	0	2	0	0	0	0	0	.250	.250	.250	1.000
1976	Bos-A	76	269	34	63	7	5	8	34	15	1	62	0	5	3	0	1	.234	.272	.387	.936
1977	Bos-A	159	593	77	157	33	5	30	112	27	4	162	4	10	3	5	4	.265	.300	.489	.946
1978	Bos-A	147	512	65	128	26	2	17	80	50	3	122	0	4	8	1	0	.250	.312	.408	.899
1979	Bos-A	146	528	74	138	26	7	28	93	30	2	78	0	6	6	3	2	.261	.298	.496	.935
1980	Bos-A	93	324	35	74	6	0	11	39	25	2	69	0	0	3	1	1	.228	.281	.349	.910
1981	Cal-A	85	268	27	63	7	4	4	36	35	0	60	1	2	4	1	1	.235	.321	.336	.929
1982	**NY-A**	**30**	**58**	**2**	**10**	**2**	**0**	**0**	**3**	**1**	**0**	**14**	**0**	**0**	**1**	**0**	**0**	**.172**	**.183**	**.207**	**.951**
Career average		92	320	39	79	13	3	12	50	23	2	71	1	3	4	1	1	.248	.297	.423	.938
Yankee average		**30**	**58**	**2**	**10**	**2**	**0**	**0**	**3**	**1**	**0**	**14**	**0**	**0**	**1**	**0**	**0**	**.172**	**.183**	**.207**	**.951**
Career total		738	2556	314	634	107	23	98	397	183	12	569	5	27	28	11	9	.248	.297	.423	.938
Yankee total		**30**	**58**	**2**	**10**	**2**	**0**	**0**	**3**	**1**	**0**	**14**	**0**	**0**	**1**	**0**	**0**	**.172**	**.183**	**.207**	**.951**

Hoffman, Daniel John

HEIGHT: 5'9"   THROWS: LEFT   BATS: LEFT   BORN: 3/2/1880, CANTON, CONNECTICUT   DIED: 3/14/1922, MANCHESTER, CONNECTICUT   POSITIONS PLAYED: P, OF

YEAR	TEAM	GAMES	AB	RUNS	HITS	2B	3B	HR	RBI	BB	IBB	SO	HBP	SH	SF	SB	CS	BA	OBA	SA	FA
1903	Phi-A	74	248	29	61	5	7	2	22	6	—	—	1	4	—	7	—	.246	.267	.347	.950
1904	Phi-A	53	204	31	61	7	5	3	24	5	—	—	4	5	—	9	—	.299	.329	.426	.936
1905	Phi-A	120	459	66	120	10	10	1	35	33	—	—	1	18	—	46	—	.261	.312	.333	.942
1906	Phi-A	7	22	4	5	0	0	0	0	3	—	—	0	4	—	1	—	.227	.320	.227	1.000
1906	NY-A	100	320	34	82	10	6	0	23	27	—	—	2	10	—	32	—	.256	.318	.325	.938
1907	**NY-A**	**136**	**517**	**81**	**131**	**10**	**3**	**5**	**46**	**42**	**—**	**—**	**13**	**11**	**—**	**30**	**—**	**.253**	**.325**	**.313**	**.953**
1908	StL-A	99	363	41	91	9	7	1	25	23	—	—	5	11	—	17	—	.251	.304	.322	.962
1909	StL-A	110	387	44	104	6	7	2	26	41	—	—	7	5	—	24	—	.269	.349	.336	.968
1910	StL-A	106	380	20	90	11	5	0	27	34	—	—	4	7	—	16	—	.237	.306	.292	.960
1911	StL-A	24	81	11	17	3	2	0	7	12	—	—	2	4	—	3	—	.210	.326	.296	.908
Career average		83	298	36	76	7	5	1	24	23	—	—	4	8	—	19	—	.256	.316	.328	.952
Yankee average		**118**	**419**	**58**	**107**	**10**	**5**	**3**	**35**	**35**	**—**	**—**	**8**	**11**	**—**	**31**	**—**	**.254**	**.322**	**.318**	**.946**
Career total		829	2981	361	762	71	52	14	235	226	—	—	39	79	—	185	—	.256	.316	.328	.952
Yankee total		**236**	**837**	**115**	**213**	**20**	**9**	**5**	**69**	**69**	**—**	**—**	**15**	**21**	**—**	**62**	**—**	**.254**	**.322**	**.318**	**.946**

Hofman, Arthur Frederick (Solly or Circus Solly)

HEIGHT: 6'0"   THROWS: RIGHT   BATS: RIGHT   BORN: 10/29/1882, ST. LOUIS, MISSOURI   DIED: 3/10/1956, ST.LOUIS, MISSOURI   POSITIONS PLAYED: 1B, 2B, 3B, SS, OF

YEAR	TEAM	GAMES	AB	RUNS	HITS	2B	3B	HR	RBI	BB	IBB	SO	HBP	SH	SF	SB	CS	BA	OBA	SA	FA
1903	Pit-N	3	2	1	0	0	0	0	0	0	—	—	0	0	—	0	—	.000	.000	.000	.000
1904	Chi-N	7	26	7	7	0	0	1	4	1	—	—	0	0	—	2	—	.269	.296	.385	1.000
1905	Chi-N	86	287	43	68	14	4	1	38	20	—	—	1	8	—	15	—	.237	.289	.324	.846
1906	Chi-N	64	195	30	50	2	3	2	20	20	—	—	0	6	—	13	—	.256	.326	.328	.976
1907	Chi-N	134	470	67	126	11	3	1	36	41	—	—	1	24	—	29	—	.268	.328	.311	.990
1908	Chi-N	120	411	55	100	15	5	2	42	33	—	—	6	28	—	15	—	.243	.309	.319	.955
1909	Chi-N	153	527	60	150	21	4	2	58	53	—	—	1	32	—	20	—	.285	.351	.351	.965
1910	Chi-N	136	477	83	155	24	16	3	86	65	—	34	0	30	—	29	—	.325	.406	.461	.978
1911	Chi-N	143	512	66	129	17	2	2	70	66	—	40	3	24	—	30	—	.252	.341	.305	.984

(continued)

(continued)

YEAR	TEAM	GAMES	AB	RUNS	HITS	2B	3B	HR	RBI	BB	IBB	SO	HBP	SH	SF	SB	CS	BA	OBA	SA	FA
1912	Chi-N	36	125	28	34	11	0	0	18	22	—	13	1	2	—	5	—	.272	.385	.360	.987
1912	Pit-N	17	53	7	15	4	1	0	2	5	—	6	0	2	—	0	—	.283	.345	.396	1.000
1913	Pit-N	28	83	11	19	5	2	0	7	8	—	6	0	4	—	3	—	.229	.297	.337	.964
1914	Bro-F	147	515	65	148	25	12	5	83	54	—	41	2	12	—	34	—	.287	.357	.412	1.000
1915	Buf-F	109	346	29	81	10	6	0	27	30	—	28	0	10	—	12	—	.234	.295	.298	1.000
1916	**NY-A**	**6**	**27**	**0**	**8**	**1**	**1**	**0**	**2**	**1**	**—**	**1**	**0**	**1**	**—**	**1**	**—**	**.296**	**.321**	**.407**	**1.000**
1916	Chi-N	5	16	2	5	2	1	0	2	2	—	2	0	0	—	0	—	.313	.389	.563	1.000
Career average		75	255	35	68	10	4	1	31	26	—	—	1	11	—	13	—	.269	.340	.352	.915
Yankee average		6	27	0	8	1	1	0	2	1	—	1	0	1	—	1	—	.296	.321	.407	1.000
Career total		1194	4072	554	1095	162	60	19	495	421	—	171	15	183	—	208	—	.269	.340	.352	.915
Yankee total		6	27	0	8	1	1	0	2	1	—	1	0	1	—	1	—	.296	.321	.407	1.000

Hofmann, Fred (Bootnose)

HEIGHT: 5'11 1/2" THROWS: RIGHT BATS: RIGHT BORN: 6/10/1894, ST.LOUIS, MISSOURI DIED: 11/19/1964, ST. HELENA, CALIFORNIA POSITIONS PLAYED: C

YEAR	TEAM	GAMES	AB	RUNS	HITS	2B	3B	HR	RBI	BB	IBB	SO	HBP	SH	SF	SB	CS	BA	OBA	SA	FA
1919	NY-A	1	1	0	0	0	0	0	0	0	0	0	0	0	0	0	0	.000	.000	.000	1.000
1920	NY-A	15	24	3	7	0	0	0	1	1	0	2	1	0	0	0	0	.292	.346	.292	.905
1921	NY-A	23	62	7	11	1	1	1	5	5	0	13	1	0	0	0	0	.177	.250	.274	.952
1922	NY-A	37	91	13	27	5	3	2	10	9	0	12	0	1	0	0	0	.297	.360	.484	.962
1923	NY-A	72	238	24	69	10	4	3	26	18	0	27	4	3	0	2	1	.290	.350	.403	.979
1924	NY-A	62	166	17	29	6	1	1	11	12	0	15	2	5	0	2	1	.175	.239	.241	.991
1925	NY-A	3	2	0	0	0	0	0	0	0	0	0	0	0	0	0	0	.000	.000	.000	1.000
1927	Bos-A	87	217	20	59	19	1	0	24	21	0	26	2	9	0	2	0	.272	.342	.369	.943
1928	Bos-A	78	199	14	45	8	1	0	16	11	0	25	1	2	0	0	1	.226	.270	.276	.982
Career average		42	111	11	27	5	1	1	10	9	0	13	1	2	0	1	0	.247	.308	.339	.968
Yankee average		30	83	9	20	3	1	1	8	6	0	10	1	1	0	1	0	.245	.308	.349	.970
Career total		378	1000	98	247	49	11	7	93	77	0	120	11	20	0	6	3	.247	.308	.339	.968
Yankee total		213	584	64	143	22	9	7	53	45	0	69	8	9	0	4	2	.245	.308	.349	.970

Holden, William Paul

HEIGHT: 6'0" THROWS: RIGHT BATS: RIGHT BORN: 9/7/1889, BIRMINGHAM, ALABAMA DIED: 9/14/1971, PENSACOLA, FLORIDA POSITIONS PLAYED: OF

YEAR	TEAM	GAMES	AB	RUNS	HITS	2B	3B	HR	RBI	BB	IBB	SO	HBP	SH	SF	SB	CS	BA	OBA	SA	FA
1913	NY-A	18	53	6	16	3	1	0	8	8	0	5	0	4	0	0	0	.302	.393	.396	.977
1914	NY-A	50	165	12	30	3	2	0	12	16	0	26	0	3	0	2	4	.182	.254	.224	.981
1914	Cin-N	11	28	2	6	0	0	0	1	3	0	5	0	0	0	0	0	.214	.290	.214	1.000
Career average		26	82	7	17	2	1	0	7	9	0	12	0	2	0	1	1	.211	.289	.260	.986
Yankee average		34	109	9	23	3	2	0	10	12	0	16	0	4	0	1	1	.211	.289	.266	.979
Career total		79	246	20	52	6	3	0	21	27	0	36	0	7	0	2	4	.211	.289	.260	.986
Yankee total		68	218	18	46	6	3	0	20	24	0	31	0	7	0	2	4	.211	.289	.266	.979

Holmes, Frederick C.

HEIGHT. — THROWS: RIGHT BATS: RIGHT BORN: 7/1/1878, CHICAGO, ILLINOIS DIED: 2/13/1956, NORWOOD PARK, ILLINOIS POSITIONS PLAYED: C, 1B

YEAR	TEAM	GAMES	AB	RUNS	HITS	2B	3B	HR	RBI	BB	IBB	SO	HBP	SH	SF	SB	CS	BA	OBA	SA	FA
1903	NY-A	1	0	0	0	0	0	0	0	1	0	0	0	0	0	0	0	—	1.000	—	.833
1904	Chi-N	1	3	1	1	1	0	0	0	0	0	0	0	0	0	0	0	.333	.333	.667	1.000
Career average		1	2	1	1	1	0	0	0	1	0	0	0	0	0	0	0	.333	.500	.667	.917
Yankee average		1	0	0	0	0	0	0	0	1	0	0	0	0	0	0	0	—	1.000	—	.833
Career total		2	3	1	1	1	0	0	0	1	0	0	0	0	0	0	0	.333	.500	.667	.917
Yankee total		1	0	0	0	0	0	0	0	1	0	0	0	0	0	0	0	—	1.000	—	.833

Holt, Roger Boyd
HEIGHT: 5'11" THROWS: RIGHT BATS: B BORN: 4/8/1956, DAYTONA BEACH, FLORIDA POSITIONS PLAYED: 2B

YEAR	TEAM	GAMES	AB	RUNS	HITS	2B	3B	HR	RBI	BB	IBB	SO	HBP	SH	SF	SB	CS	BA	OBA	SA	FA
1980	NY-A	2	6	0	1	0	0	0	1	1	0	2	0	0	0	0	0	.167	.286	.167	1.000
Career average		2	6	0	1	0	0	0	1	1	0	2	0	0	0	0	0	.167	.286	.167	1.000
Yankee average		**2**	**6**	**0**	**1**	**0**	**0**	**0**	**1**	**1**	**0**	**2**	**0**	**0**	**0**	**0**	**0**	**.167**	**.286**	**.167**	**1.000**
Career total		2	6	0	1	0	0	0	1	1	0	2	0	0	0	0	0	.167	.286	.167	1.000
Yankee total		**2**	**6**	**0**	**1**	**0**	**0**	**0**	**1**	**1**	**0**	**2**	**0**	**0**	**0**	**0**	**0**	**.167**	**.286**	**.167**	**1.000**

Hopp, John Leonard (Hippity *or* Cotney)
HEIGHT: 5'10" THROWS: LEFT BATS: LEFT BORN: 7/18/1916, HASTINGS, NEBRASKA POSITIONS PLAYED: 1B, OF

YEAR	TEAM	GAMES	AB	RUNS	HITS	2B	3B	HR	RBI	BB	IBB	SO	HBP	SH	SF	SB	CS	BA	OBA	SA	FA
1939	StL-N	6	4	1	2	1	0	0	2	1	—	1	0	0	—	0	—	.500	.600	.750	1.000
1940	StL-N	80	152	24	41	7	4	1	14	9	—	21	1	1	—	3	—	.270	.315	.388	.967
1941	StL-N	134	445	83	135	25	11	4	50	50	—	63	3	11	—	15	—	.303	.378	.436	.989
1942	StL-N	95	314	41	81	16	7	3	37	36	—	40	0	4	—	14	—	.258	.334	.382	.983
1943	StL-N	91	241	33	54	10	2	2	25	24	—	22	1	6	—	8	—	.224	.297	.307	.950
1944	StL-N	139	527	106	177	35	9	11	72	58	—	47	2	4	—	15	—	.336	.404	.499	.997
1945	StL-N	124	446	67	129	22	8	3	44	49	—	24	3	7	—	14	—	.289	.363	.395	.980
1946	Bos-N	129	445	71	148	23	8	3	48	34	—	34	5	8	—	21	—	.333	.386	.440	1.000
1947	Bos-N	134	430	74	124	20	2	2	32	58	—	30	2	12	—	13	—	.288	.376	.358	.980
1948	Pit-N	120	392	64	109	15	12	1	31	40	—	25	0	3	—	5	—	.278	.345	.385	.996
1949	Pit-N	20	55	5	12	3	1	0	3	7	—	3	0	0	—	0	0	.218	.306	.309	.994
1949	Bro-N	8	14	0	0	0	0	0	0	0	—	3	0	0	—	0	0	.000	.000	.000	1.000
1949	Pit-N	85	316	50	106	11	4	5	36	30	—	26	0	0	—	9	—	.335	.393	.443	.946
1950	Pit-N	106	318	51	108	24	5	8	47	43	—	17	1	0	—	7	—	.340	.420	.522	1.000
1950	**NY-A**	**19**	**27**	**9**	**9**	**2**	**1**	**1**	**8**	**8**	—	**1**	**0**	**0**	—	**0**	**1**	**.333**	**.486**	**.593**	**1.000**
1951	**NY-A**	**46**	**63**	**10**	**13**	**1**	**0**	**2**	**4**	**9**	—	**11**	**0**	**1**	—	**2**	**0**	**.206**	**.306**	**.317**	**.992**
1952	**NY-A**	**15**	**25**	**4**	**4**	**0**	**0**	**0**	**2**	**2**	—	**3**	**1**	**0**	—	**2**	**0**	**.160**	**.250**	**.160**	**1.000**
1952	Det-A	42	46	5	10	1	0	0	3	6	—	7	0	1	—	0	0	.217	.308	.239	1.000
Career average		77	237	39	70	12	4	3	25	26	—	21	1	3	—	7	—	.296	.368	.414	.987
Yankee average		**27**	**38**	**8**	**9**	**1**	**0**	**1**	**5**	**6**	—	**5**	**0**	**0**	—	**1**	**0**	**.226**	**.341**	**.348**	**.997**
Career total		1393	4260	698	1262	216	74	46	458	464	—	378	19	58	—	128	1	.296	.368	.414	.987
Yankee total		**80**	**115**	**23**	**26**	**3**	**1**	**3**	**14**	**19**	—	**15**	**1**	**1**	—	**4**	**1**	**.226**	**.341**	**.348**	**.997**

Horan, Joseph Patrick (Shags)
HEIGHT: 5'10" THROWS: RIGHT BATS: RIGHT BORN: 9/6/1895, ST. LOUIS, MISSOURI DIED: 2/13/1969, TORRANCE, CALIFORNIA POSITIONS PLAYED: OF

YEAR	TEAM	GAMES	AB	RUNS	HITS	2B	3B	HR	RBI	BB	IBB	SO	HBP	SH	SF	SB	CS	BA	OBA	SA	FA
1924	NY-A	22	31	4	9	1	0	0	7	1	0	5	0	1	0	0	0	.290	.313	.323	1.000
Career average		22	31	4	9	1	0	0	7	1	0	5	0	1	0	0	0	.290	.313	.323	1.000
Yankee average		**22**	**31**	**4**	**9**	**1**	**0**	**0**	**7**	**1**	**0**	**5**	**0**	**1**	**0**	**0**	**0**	**.290**	**.313**	**.323**	**1.000**
Career total		22	31	4	9	1	0	0	7	1	0	5	0	1	0	0	0	.290	.313	.323	1.000
Yankee total		**22**	**31**	**4**	**9**	**1**	**0**	**0**	**7**	**1**	**0**	**5**	**0**	**1**	**0**	**0**	**0**	**.290**	**.313**	**.323**	**1.000**

Houk, Ralph George (Major)
HEIGHT: 5'11" THROWS: RIGHT BATS: RIGHT BORN: 8/9/1919, LAWRENCE, KANSAS POSITIONS PLAYED: C

YEAR	TEAM	GAMES	AB	RUNS	HITS	2B	3B	HR	RBI	BB	IBB	SO	HBP	SH	SF	SB	CS	BA	OBA	SA	FA
1947	NY-A	41	92	7	25	3	1	0	12	11	0	5	1	0	0	0	0	.272	.356	.326	.987
1948	NY-A	14	29	3	8	2	0	0	3	0	0	0	0	0	0	0	0	.276	.276	.345	1.000
1949	NY-A	5	7	0	4	0	0	0	1	0	0	1	0	0	0	0	0	.571	.571	.571	.889
1950	NY-A	10	9	0	1	1	0	0	1	0	0	2	0	0	0	0	0	.111	.111	.222	.929
1951	NY-A	3	5	0	1	0	0	0	2	0	0	1	0	0	0	0	0	.200	.200	.200	1.000
1952	NY-A	9	6	0	2	0	0	0	0	1	0	0	0	0	0	0	0	.333	.429	.333	.917
1953	NY-A	8	9	2	2	0	0	0	1	0	0	1	0	0	0	0	0	.222	.222	.222	1.000
1954	NY-A	1	1	0	0	0	0	0	0	0	0	0	0	0	0	0	0	.000	.000	.000	.000
Career average		11	20	2	5	1	0	0	3	2	0	1	0	0	0	0	0	.272	.327	.323	.840
Yankee average		**11**	**20**	**2**	**5**	**1**	**0**	**0**	**3**	**2**	**0**	**1**	**0**	**0**	**0**	**0**	**0**	**.272**	**.327**	**.323**	**.840**
Career total		91	158	12	43	6	1	0	20	12	0	10	1	0	0	0	0	.272	.327	.323	.840
Yankee total		**91**	**158**	**12**	**43**	**6**	**1**	**0**	**20**	**12**	**0**	**10**	**1**	**0**	**0**	**0**	**0**	**.272**	**.327**	**.323**	**.840**

Elston Gene Howard, c-of-1b, 1955–67

As the first black player to play for the Yankees, Elston Howard's tenure in New York may not have been as difficult as, say, Jackie Robinson's time with the Brooklyn Dodgers a decade earlier, but surely Howard was a man who had a long, hard road in his own right.

Born on February 23, 1929, Howard was a star athlete at Vashon High School in St. Louis, Missouri. In the late 1940s, he was signed by the Kansas City Monarchs of the Negro Leagues, and he quickly became one of the best players on the team.

Soon, as athletes like Robinson and others made it clear to the major leagues that blacks were in the bigs to stay, teams began to show an interest in Howard. Even the Yankees, dominated by a racist management that did not think white fans would root for black players, began making inquiries.

Howard eventually signed with New York, and after an unusually long stint in the minor leagues, he was brought up in 1955. That wasn't an easy time for him. For several years, he was not allowed to stay in the same hotel in St. Petersburg as his Yankee teammates during spring training.

Unfortunately, Yankee management did not seem to see this as much of a problem. Nor were there any particular concerns when Howard and his family had difficulty finding housing in the New York area. Throughout these years, Howard endured the slights stoically. There was, he believed, great honor in being the first black Yankee. His wife, Arlene,

hated the situation and hated that Elston wouldn't complain.

He was an outfielder by trade, but Yankee management turned him into a catcher. That put him behind Yogi Berra on the depth chart in New York, but when he came up to the Yankees, he was so good he went to the outfield for most of his first five years there. Three of those years, from 1957 to 1959, he was named to the American League All-Star team.

By 1960, Berra was being platooned into the outfield, and Yankee manager Casey Stengel gave the catching job to Howard. He responded by once again making the All-Star team, this time as a catcher. It was the first of six consecutive All-Star Games behind the plate for Howard.

His most productive years were from 1961 to 1964, when he hit in the high .200s, averaged about 20 home runs and 84 RBI per season. In 1963, he was the MVP of the league, hitting .287 with 28 home runs and 85 RBI.

He hit over .400 in two different World Series, in 1956 when the Yankees beat the Dodgers, and in 1960, when the Yankees were defeated by the Pittsburgh Pirates.

He was the most consistent Yankee in the down years of 1965–67. Midway through that season, he was traded to the Red Sox, and helped Boston win their lone pennant in the 1960s.

After he retired, he coached for the Yankees for several years, until his death in 1980. In 1985, his number 22 was retired by the Yankees. His 161 home runs place him 18th all time with the Yankees, as do his 1,405 hits, and his 732 RBI rank 15th.

Howard, Elston Gene

HEIGHT: 6'2" THROWS: RIGHT BATS: RIGHT BORN: 2/23/1929, ST.LOUIS, MISSOURI DIED: 12/14/1980, NEW YORK, NEW YORK POSITIONS PLAYED: C, 1B, OF

YEAR	TEAM	GAMES	AB	RUNS	HITS	2B	3B	HR	RBI	BB	IBB	SO	HBP	SH	SF	SB	CS	BA	OBA	SA	FA
1955	NY-A	97	279	33	81	8	7	10	43	20	5	36	1	1	4	0	0	.290	.336	.477	.978
1956	NY-A	98	290	35	76	8	3	5	34	21	6	30	1	2	2	0	1	.262	.312	.362	.990
1957	NY-A	110	356	33	90	13	4	8	44	16	6	43	0	6	2	2	5	.253	.283	.379	.984
1958	NY-A	103	376	45	118	19	5	11	66	22	6	60	0	4	4	1	1	.314	.348	.479	1.000
1959	NY-A	125	443	59	121	24	6	18	73	20	4	57	3	4	4	0	1	.273	.306	.476	.992
1960	NY-A	107	323	29	79	11	3	6	39	28	7	43	0	2	8	3	0	.245	.298	.353	.987
1961	NY-A	129	446	64	155	17	5	21	77	28	6	65	3	1	4	0	3	.348	.387	.549	.989
1962	NY-A	136	494	63	138	23	5	21	91	31	1	76	1	3	9	1	1	.279	.318	.474	.995
1963	NY-A	135	487	75	140	21	6	28	85	35	4	68	6	1	2	0	0	.287	.342	.528	.994

(continued)

(continued)

YEAR	TEAM	GAMES	AB	RUNS	HITS	2B	3B	HR	RBI	BB	IBB	SO	HBP	SH	SF	SB	CS	BA	OBA	SA	FA
1964	NY-A	150	550	63	172	27	3	15	84	48	12	73	5	0	4	1	1	.313	.371	.455	.998
1965	NY-A	110	391	38	91	15	1	9	45	24	3	65	1	1	1	0	0	.233	.278	.345	.991
1966	NY-A	126	410	38	105	19	2	6	35	37	9	65	1	0	3	0	0	.256	.317	.356	.985
1967	NY-A	66	199	13	39	6	0	3	17	12	3	36	2	1	2	0	0	.196	.247	.271	.984
1967	Bos-A	42	116	9	17	3	0	1	11	9	3	24	1	1	2	0	0	.147	.211	.198	.996
1968	Bos-A	71	203	22	49	4	0	5	18	22	7	45	1	2	1	1	1	.241	.317	.335	.995
Career average		107	358	41	98	15	3	11	51	25	6	52	2	2	4	1	1	.274	.322	.427	.991
Yankee average		115	388	45	108	16	4	12	56	26	6	55	2	2	4	1	1	.279	.324	.436	.990
Career total		1605	5363	619	1471	218	50	167	762	373	82	786	26	29	52	9	14	.274	.322	.427	.991
Yankee total		1492	5044	588	1405	211	50	161	733	342	72	717	24	26	49	8	13	.279	.324	.436	.990

Howell, Henry Harry

HEIGHT: 5' 9" THROWS: RIGHT BATS: RIGHT BORN: 11/14/1876, NEW JERSEY DIED: 5/22/1956, SPOKANE, WASHINGTON POSITIONS PLAYED: P, OF

YEAR	TEAM	GAMES	AB	RUNS	HITS	2B	3B	HR	RBI	BB	IBB	SO	HBP	SH	SF	SB	CS	BA	OBA	SA	FA
1898	Bro-N	2	8	1	2	0	0	0	1	1	0	0	0	0	0	0	0	.250	.333	.250	1.000
1899	Bal-N	28	82	4	12	2	2	0	3	3	0	0	0	0	0	0	0	.146	.176	.220	.940
1900	Bro-N	22	42	6	12	2	0	1	6	6	0	0	1	0	0	1	0	.286	.388	.405	.949
1901	Bal-A	53	188	26	41	10	5	2	26	5	0	0	1	4	0	6	0	.218	.242	.356	.905
1902	Bal-A	96	347	42	93	16	11	2	42	18	0	0	4	8	0	7	0	.268	.312	.395	.951
1903	**NY-A**	40	106	14	23	3	2	1	12	5	0	0	1	3	0	1	0	.217	.259	.311	1.000
1904	StL-A	36	113	9	25	5	2	1	6	4	0	0	2	4	0	0	0	.221	.261	.327	.971
1905	StL-A	42	135	9	26	6	2	1	10	3	0	0	1	1	0	0	0	.193	.216	.289	.966
1906	StL-A	35	103	5	13	3	1	0	6	6	0	0	0	3	0	2	0	.126	.174	.175	.934
1907	StL-A	44	114	12	27	5	0	2	7	7	0	0	0	9	0	2	0	.237	.281	.333	.982
1908	StL-A	41	120	10	22	7	0	1	9	4	0	0	0	1	0	0	0	.183	.210	.267	.961
1909	StL-A	18	34	5	6	1	0	0	3	2	0	0	0	3	0	0	0	.176	.222	.206	.938
1910	StL-A	1	2	0	0	0	0	0	0	0	0	0	0	0	0	0	0	.000	.000	.000	1.000
Career average		35	107	11	23	5	2	1	10	5	0	0	1	3	0	2	0	.217	.256	.319	.961
Yankee average		40	106	14	23	3	2	1	12	5	0	0	1	3	0	1	0	.217	.259	.311	1.000
Career total		458	1394	143	302	60	25	11	131	64	0	0	10	36	0	19	0	.217	.256	.319	.961
Yankee total		40	106	14	23	3	2	1	12	5	0	0	1	3	0	1	0	.217	.259	.311	1.000

Howser, Richard Dalton

HEIGHT: 5'8" THROWS: RIGHT BATS: RIGHT BORN: 5/14/1936, MIAMI, FLORIDA DIED: 6/17/1987, KANSAS CITY, MISSOURI POSITIONS PLAYED: 2B, 3B, SS

YEAR	TEAM	GAMES	AB	RUNS	HITS	2B	3B	HR	RBI	BB	IBB	SO	HBP	SH	SF	SB	CS	BA	OBA	SA	FA
1961	KC-A	158	611	108	171	29	6	3	45	92	0	38	5	8	3	37	9	.280	.377	.362	.950
1962	KC-A	83	286	53	68	8	3	6	34	38	0	8	1	9	3	19	2	.238	.326	.350	.962
1963	KC-A	15	41	4	8	0	0	0	1	7	1	3	0	1	0	0	0	.195	.313	.195	.957
1963	Cle-A	49	162	25	40	5	0	1	10	22	0	18	0	4	2	9	3	.247	.333	.296	.950
1964	Cle-A	162	637	101	163	23	4	3	52	76	1	39	2	16	4	20	7	.256	.335	.319	.974
1965	Cle-A	107	307	47	72	8	2	1	6	57	0	25	1	10	2	17	4	.235	.354	.283	.977
1966	Cle-A	67	140	18	32	9	1	2	4	15	0	23	0	4	2	2	4	.229	.299	.350	.986
1967	**NY-A**	63	149	18	40	6	0	0	10	25	0	15	2	3	0	1	4	.268	.381	.309	.939
1968	**NY-A**	85	150	24	23	2	1	0	3	35	0	17	2	3	0	0	1	.153	.321	.180	1.000
Career average		88	276	44	69	10	2	2	18	41	0	21	1	6	2	12	4	.248	.346	.318	.966
Yankee average		74	150	21	32	4	1	0	7	30	0	16	2	3	0	1	3	.211	.350	.244	.970
Career total		789	2483	398	617	90	17	16	165	367	2	186	13	58	16	105	34	.248	.346	.318	.966
Yankee total		148	299	42	63	8	1	0	13	60	0	32	4	6	0	1	5	.211	.350	.244	.970

Hudler, Rex Allen

HEIGHT: 6'0" THROWS: RIGHT BATS: RIGHT BORN: 9/2/1960, TEMPE, ARIZONA POSITIONS PLAYED: 1B, 2B, 3B, SS, OF

YEAR	TEAM	GAMES	AB	RUNS	HITS	2B	3B	HR	RBI	BB	IBB	SO	HBP	SH	SF	SB	CS	BA	OBA	SA	FA
1984	**NY-A**	9	7	2	1	1	0	0	0	1	0	5	1	0	0	0	0	.143	.333	.286	1.000
1985	**NY-A**	20	51	4	8	0	1	0	1	1	0	9	0	5	0	0	1	.157	.173	.196	1.000
1986	Bal-A	14	1	1	0	0	0	0	0	0	0	0	0	0	0	1	0	.000	.000	.000	.800
1988	Mon-N	77	216	38	59	14	2	4	14	10	6	34	0	1	2	29	7	.273	.303	.412	.944
1989	Mon-N	92	155	21	38	7	0	6	13	6	2	23	1	0	0	15	4	.245	.278	.406	.958
1990	Mon-N	4	3	1	1	0	0	0	0	0	0	1	0	0	0	0	0	.333	.333	.333	.000

(continued)

(continued)

YEAR	TEAM	GAMES	AB	RUNS	HITS	2B	3B	HR	RBI	BB	IBB	SO	HBP	SH	SF	SB	CS	BA	OBA	SA	FA
1990	StL-N	89	217	30	61	11	2	7	22	12	1	31	2	2	1	18	10	.281	.323	.447	.979
1991	StL-N	101	207	21	47	10	2	1	15	10	1	29	0	2	2	12	8	.227	.260	.309	1.000
1992	StL-N	61	98	17	24	4	0	3	5	2	0	23	1	1	1	2	6	.245	.265	.378	1.000
1994	Cal-A	56	124	17	37	8	0	8	20	6	0	28	0	4	2	2	2	.298	.326	.556	1.000
1995	Cal-A	84	223	30	59	16	0	6	27	10	1	48	5	2	1	13	0	.265	.310	.417	.955
1996	Cal-A	92	302	60	94	20	3	16	40	9	0	54	3	2	1	14	5	.311	.337	.556	.981
1997	Phi-N	50	122	17	27	4	0	5	10	6	1	28	1	1	0	1	0	.221	.264	.377	1.000
1998	Phi-N	25	41	2	5	1	0	0	2	4	0	12	0	0	0	0	0	.122	.200	.146	1.000
Career average		55	126	19	33	7	1	4	12	6	1	23	1	1	1	8	3	.261	.296	.422	.901
Yankee average		**15**	**29**	**3**	**5**	**1**	**1**	**0**	**1**	**1**	**0**	**7**	**1**	**3**	**0**	**0**	**1**	**.155**	**.197**	**.207**	**1.000**
Career total		774	1767	261	461	96	10	56	169	77	12	325	14	20	10	107	43	.261	.296	.422	.901
Yankee total		**29**	**58**	**6**	**9**	**1**	**1**	**0**	**1**	**2**	**0**	**14**	**1**	**5**	**0**	**0**	**1**	**.155**	**.197**	**.207**	**1.000**

Hughes, Keith Wills

HEIGHT: 6' 3" THROWS: LEFT BATS: LEFT BORN: 9/12/1963, BRYN MAWR, PENNSYLVANIA POSITIONS PLAYED: OF

YEAR	TEAM	GAMES	AB	RUNS	HITS	2B	3B	HR	RBI	BB	IBB	SO	HBP	SH	SF	SB	CS	BA	OBA	SA	FA
1987	**NY-A**	**4**	**4**	**0**	**0**	**0**	**0**	**0**	**0**	**0**	**0**	**2**	**0**	**0**	**0**	**0**	**0**	**.000**	**.000**	**.000**	**.000**
1987	Phi-N	37	76	8	20	2	0	0	10	7	0	11	1	0	0	0	0	.263	.333	.289	.963
1988	Bal-A	41	108	10	21	4	2	2	14	16	1	27	0	0	2	1	0	.194	.294	.324	.969
1990	NY-N	8	9	0	0	0	0	0	0	0	0	4	0	0	0	0	0	.000	.000	.000	1.000
1993	Cin-N	3	4	0	0	0	0	0	0	0	0	0	0	0	0	0	0	.000	.000	.000	.000
Career average		19	40	4	8	1	0	0	5	5	0	9	0	0	0	0	0	.204	.286	.284	.586
Yankee average		**4**	**4**	**0**	**0**	**0**	**0**	**0**	**0**	**0**	**0**	**2**	**0**	**0**	**0**	**0**	**0**	**.000**	**.000**	**.000**	**.000**
Career total		93	201	18	41	6	2	2	24	23	1	44	1	0	2	1	0	.204	.286	.284	.586
Yankee total		**4**	**4**	**0**	**0**	**0**	**0**	**0**	**0**	**0**	**0**	**2**	**0**	**0**	**0**	**0**	**0**	**.000**	**.000**	**.000**	**.000**

Hummel, John Edwin (Silent John)

HEIGHT: 5'11" THROWS: RIGHT BATS: RIGHT BORN: 4/4/1883, BLOOMSBURG, PENN. DIED: 5/18/1959, SPRINGFIELD, MASS. POSITIONS PLAYED: 2B, OF

YEAR	TEAM	GAMES	AB	RUNS	HITS	2B	3B	HR	RBI	BB	IBB	SO	HBP	SH	SF	SB	CS	BA	OBA	SA	FA
1905	Bro-N	30	109	19	29	3	4	0	7	9	0	0	0	3	0	6	0	.266	.322	.367	.962
1906	Bro-N	97	286	20	57	6	4	1	21	36	0	0	0	4	0	10	0	.199	.289	.259	.952
1907	Bro-N	107	342	41	80	12	3	3	31	26	0	0	3	15	0	8	0	.234	.294	.313	.985
1908	Bro-N	154	594	51	143	11	12	4	41	34	0	0	2	12	0	20	0	.241	.284	.320	.938
1909	Bro-N	146	542	54	152	15	9	4	52	22	0	0	2	31	0	16	0	.280	.311	.363	.950
1910	Bro-N	153	578	67	141	21	13	5	74	57	0	81	2	14	0	21	0	.244	.314	.351	.965
1911	Bro-N	137	477	54	129	21	11	5	58	67	0	66	0	12	0	16	0	.270	.360	.392	1.000
1912	Bro-N	122	411	55	116	21	7	5	54	49	0	55	0	10	0	7	0	.282	.359	.404	.969
1913	Bro-N	67	198	20	48	7	7	2	24	13	0	23	1	1	0	4	0	.242	.292	.379	.953
1914	Bro-N	73	208	25	55	8	9	0	20	16	0	25	0	6	0	5	0	.264	.317	.389	.982
1915	Bro-N	53	100	6	23	2	3	0	8	6	0	11	0	5	0	1	1	.230	.274	.310	1.000
1918	**NY-A**	**22**	**61**	**9**	**18**	**1**	**2**	**0**	**4**	**11**	**0**	**8**	**1**	**1**	**0**	**3**	**0**	**.295**	**.411**	**.377**	**1.000**
Career average		97	326	35	83	11	7	2	33	29	0	22	1	10	0	10	0	.254	.316	.352	.971
Yankee average		**22**	**61**	**9**	**18**	**1**	**2**	**0**	**4**	**11**	**0**	**8**	**1**	**1**	**0**	**3**	**0**	**.295**	**.411**	**.377**	**1.000**
Career total		1161	3906	421	991	128	84	29	394	346	0	269	11	114	0	117	1	.254	.316	.352	.971
Yankee total		**22**	**61**	**9**	**18**	**1**	**2**	**0**	**4**	**11**	**0**	**8**	**1**	**1**	**0**	**3**	**0**	**.295**	**.411**	**.377**	**1.000**

Humphreys, Michael Butler

HEIGHT: 6'0" THROWS: RIGHT BATS: RIGHT BORN: 4/10/1967, DALLAS, TEXAS POSITIONS PLAYED: OF, DH

YEAR	TEAM	GAMES	AB	RUNS	HITS	2B	3B	HR	RBI	BB	IBB	SO	HBP	SH	SF	SB	CS	BA	OBA	SA	FA
1991	**NY-A**	**25**	**40**	**9**	**8**	**0**	**0**	**0**	**3**	**9**	**0**	**7**	**0**	**1**	**0**	**2**	**0**	**.200**	**.347**	**.200**	**1.000**
1992	**NY-A**	**4**	**10**	**0**	**1**	**0**	**0**	**0**	**0**	**0**	**0**	**1**	**0**	**0**	**0**	**0**	**0**	**.100**	**.100**	**.100**	**1.000**
1993	**NY-A**	**25**	**35**	**6**	**6**	**2**	**1**	**1**	**6**	**4**	**0**	**11**	**0**	**0**	**1**	**2**	**1**	**.171**	**.250**	**.371**	**1.000**
Career average		18	28	5	5	1	0	0	3	4	0	6	0	0	0	1	0	.176	.283	.259	1.000
Yankee average		**18**	**28**	**5**	**5**	**1**	**0**	**0**	**3**	**4**	**0**	**6**	**0**	**0**	**0**	**1**	**0**	**.176**	**.283**	**.259**	**1.000**
Career total		54	85	15	15	2	1	1	9	13	0	19	0	1	1	4	1	.176	.283	.259	1.000
Yankee total		**54**	**85**	**15**	**15**	**2**	**1**	**1**	**9**	**13**	**0**	**19**	**0**	**1**	**1**	**4**	**1**	**.176**	**.283**	**.259**	**1.000**

Hunt, Kenneth Lawrence

HEIGHT: 6'1" THROWS: RIGHT BATS: RIGHT BORN: 7/13/1934, GRAND FORKS, NORTH DAKOTA DIED: 6/8/1997 POSITIONS PLAYED: 1B, 2B, OF

YEAR	TEAM	GAMES	AB	RUNS	HITS	2B	3B	HR	RBI	BB	IBB	SO	HBP	SH	SF	SB	CS	BA	OBA	SA	FA
1959	NY-A	6	12	2	4	1	0	0	1	0	0	3	0	0	1	0	0	.333	.308	.417	1.000
1960	NY-A	25	22	4	6	2	0	0	1	4	0	4	1	2	0	0	0	.273	.407	.364	.957
1961	LA-A	149	479	70	122	29	3	25	84	49	1	120	4	3	6	8	2	.255	.325	.484	.950
1962	LA-A	13	11	4	2	0	0	1	1	1	0	5	0	0	0	1	0	.182	.250	.455	.867
1963	LA-A	59	142	17	26	6	1	5	16	15	2	49	0	0	0	0	0	.183	.261	.345	.972
1963	Was-A	7	20	1	4	0	0	1	4	2	1	6	0	0	0	0	0	.200	.273	.350	1.000
1964	Was-A	51	96	9	13	4	0	1	4	14	0	35	0	2	1	0	1	.135	.243	.208	1.000
Career average		44	112	15	25	6	1	5	16	12	1	32	1	1	1	1	1	.226	.303	.417	.964
Yankee average		16	17	3	5	2	0	0	1	2	0	4	1	1	1	0	0	.294	.375	.382	.979
Career total		310	782	107	177	42	4	33	111	85	4	222	5	9	8	9	4	.226	.303	.417	.964
Yankee total		31	34	6	10	3	0	0	2	4	0	7	1	2	1	0	0	.294	.375	.382	.979

Hunter, Gordon William (Billy)

HEIGHT: 6'0" THROWS: RIGHT BATS: RIGHT BORN: 6/4/1928, PUNXSUTAWNEY, PENNSYLVANIA POSITIONS PLAYED: 2B, 3B, SS

YEAR	TEAM	GAMES	AB	RUNS	HITS	2B	3B	HR	RBI	BB	IBB	SO	HBP	SH	SF	SB	CS	BA	OBA	SA	FA
1953	StL-A	154	567	50	124	18	1	1	37	24	—	45	2	11	—	3	1	.219	.253	.259	.970
1954	Bal-A	125	411	28	100	9	5	2	27	21	—	38	2	13	4	5	4	.243	.281	.304	.948
1955	NY-A	98	255	14	58	7	1	3	20	15	2	18	0	8	1	9	2	.227	.269	.298	.958
1956	NY-A	39	75	8	21	3	4	0	11	2	0	4	0	2	0	0	1	.280	.299	.427	1.000
1957	KC-A	116	319	39	61	10	4	8	29	27	2	43	3	7	3	1	1	.191	.259	.323	.952
1958	KC-A	22	58	6	9	1	1	2	11	5	0	7	0	3	0	1	1	.155	.222	.310	1.000
1958	Cle-A	76	190	21	37	10	2	0	9	17	1	37	1	5	1	4	1	.195	.263	.268	.948
Career average		90	268	24	59	8	3	2	21	16	—	27	1	7	—	3	2	.219	.264	.294	.968
Yankee average		69	165	11	40	5	3	2	16	9	1	11	0	5	1	5	2	.239	.276	.327	.979
Career total		630	1875	166	410	58	18	16	144	111	5	192	8	49	9	23	12	.219	.264	.294	.968
Yankee total		137	330	22	79	10	5	3	31	17	2	22	0	10	1	9	3	.239	.276	.327	.979

Hyatt, Robert Hamilton (Ham)

HEIGHT: 6'1" THROWS: RIGHT BATS: LEFT BORN: 11/1/1884, BUNCOMBE CO., N.C. DIED: 9/11/1963, LIBERTY LAKE, WASH. POSITIONS PLAYED: 1B, OF

YEAR	TEAM	GAMES	AB	RUNS	HITS	2B	3B	HR	RBI	BB	IBB	SO	HBP	SH	SF	SB	CS	BA	OBA	SA	FA
1909	Pit-N	49	67	9	20	3	4	0	7	3	0	0	0	1	0	1	0	.299	.329	.463	.933
1910	Pit-N	74	175	19	46	5	6	1	30	8	0	14	3	0	0	3	0	.263	.306	.377	.986
1912	Pit-N	46	97	13	28	3	1	0	22	6	0	8	0	2	0	2	0	.289	.330	.340	.875
1913	Pit-N	63	81	8	27	6	2	0	16	3	0	8	2	2	0	0	0	.333	.372	.605	1.000
1914	Pit-N	74	79	2	17	3	1	1	15	7	0	14	2	2	0	1	0	.215	.295	.316	1.000
1915	StL-N	106	295	23	79	8	9	2	46	28	0	24	3	4	0	3	0	.268	.337	.376	.933
1918	NY-A	53	131	11	30	8	0	2	10	8	0	8	0	3	0	1	0	.229	.273	.336	1.000
Career average		66	132	12	35	5	3	1	21	9	0	11	1	2	0	2	0	.267	.321	.388	.961
Yankee average		53	131	11	30	8	0	2	10	8	0	8	0	3	0	1	0	.229	.273	.336	1.000
Career total		465	925	85	247	36	23	10	146	63	0	76	10	14	0	11	3	.267	.321	.388	.961
Yankee total		53	131	11	30	8	0	2	10	8	0	8	0	3	0	1	0	.229	.273	.336	1.000

Incaviglia, Peter Joseph

HEIGHT: 6'1" THROWS: RIGHT BATS: RIGHT BORN: 4/2/1964, PEBBLE BEACH, CALIFORNIA POSITIONS PLAYED: OF

YEAR	TEAM	GAMES	AB	RUNS	HITS	2B	3B	HR	RBI	BB	IBB	SO	HBP	SH	SF	SB	CS	BA	OBA	SA	FA
1986	Tex-A	153	540	82	135	21	2	30	88	55	2	185	4	0	7	3	2	.250	.320	.463	.921
1987	Tex-A	139	509	85	138	26	4	27	80	48	1	168	1	0	5	9	3	.271	.332	.497	.945
1988	Tex-A	116	418	59	104	19	3	22	54	39	3	153	7	0	3	6	4	.249	.321	.467	.989
1989	Tex-A	133	453	48	107	27	4	21	81	32	0	136	6	0	4	5	7	.236	.293	.453	.973
1990	Tex-A	153	529	59	123	27	0	24	85	45	5	146	9	0	4	3	4	.233	.302	.420	.974
1991	Det-A	97	337	38	72	12	1	11	38	36	0	92	1	1	2	1	3	.214	.290	.353	.973
1992	Hou-N	113	349	31	93	22	1	11	44	25	2	99	3	0	2	2	2	.266	.319	.430	.970
1993	Phi-N	116	368	60	101	16	3	24	89	21	1	82	6	0	7	1	1	.274	.318	.530	.971

(continued)

(continued)

YEAR	TEAM	GAMES	AB	RUNS	HITS	2B	3B	HR	RBI	BB	IBB	SO	HBP	SH	SF	SB	CS	BA	OBA	SA	FA
1994	Phi-N	80	244	28	56	10	1	13	32	16	3	71	1	0	2	1	0	.230	.278	.439	.979
1996	Phi-N	99	269	33	63	7	2	16	42	30	2	82	3	0	0	2	0	.234	.318	.454	1.000
1996	Bal-A	12	33	4	10	2	0	2	8	0	0	7	1	0	1	0	0	.303	.314	.545	1.000
1997	Bal-A	48	138	18	34	4	0	5	12	11	2	43	3	0	1	0	0	.246	.314	.384	.952
1997	**NY-A**	**5**	**16**	**1**	**4**	**0**	**0**	**0**	**0**	**0**	**0**	**3**	**0**	**0**	**0**	**0**	**0**	**.250**	**.250**	**.250**	**.947**
1998	Det-A	7	14	0	1	0	0	0	0	1	0	6	0	0	0	0	0	.071	.133	.071	.000
1998	Hou-N	13	16	0	2	1	0	0	2	1	0	4	0	0	0	0	0	.125	.176	.188	1.000
Career average		86	282	36	70	13	1	14	44	24	1	85	3	0	3	2	2	.246	.310	.448	.906
Yankee average		**5**	**16**	**1**	**4**	**0**	**0**	**0**	**0**	**0**	**0**	**3**	**0**	**0**	**0**	**0**	**0**	**.250**	**.250**	**.250**	**.947**
Career total		1284	4233	546	1043	194	21	206	655	360	21	1277	45	1	38	33	26	.246	.310	.448	.906
Yankee total		**5**	**16**	**1**	**4**	**0**	**0**	**0**	**0**	**0**	**0**	**3**	**0**	**0**	**0**	**0**	**0**	**.250**	**.250**	**.250**	**.947**

Jacklitsch, Frederick Lawrence

HEIGHT: 5'9"   THROWS: RIGHT   BATS: RIGHT   BORN: 5/24/1876, BROOKLYN, NEW YORK   DIED: 7/18/1937, BROOKLYN, NEW YORK   POSITIONS PLAYED: C

YEAR	TEAM	GAMES	AB	RUNS	HITS	2B	3B	HR	RBI	BB	IBB	SO	HBP	SH	SF	SB	CS	BA	OBA	SA	FA
1901	Phi-N	33	120	14	30	4	3	0	24	12	0	0	2	0	0	2	0	.250	.328	.333	1.000
1902	Phi-N	38	114	8	23	4	0	0	8	9	0	0	3	1	0	2	0	.202	.278	.237	.927
1903	Bro-N	60	176	31	47	8	3	1	21	33	0	0	2	1	0	4	0	.267	.389	.364	.600
1904	Bro-N	26	77	8	18	3	1	0	8	7	0	0	3	1	0	7	0	.234	.322	.299	.848
1905	**NY-A**	**1**	**3**	**1**	**0**	**0**	**0**	**0**	**1**	**1**	**0**	**0**	**0**	**0**	**0**	**0**	**0**	**.000**	**.250**	**.000**	**1.000**
1907	Phi-N	73	202	19	43	7	0	0	17	27	0	0	2	1	0	7	0	.213	.312	.248	.984
1908	Phi-N	37	86	6	19	3	0	0	7	14	0	0	1	4	0	3	0	.221	.337	.256	.976
1909	Phi-N	20	32	6	10	1	1	0	1	10	0	0	0	0	0	1	0	.313	.476	.406	.964
1910	Phi-N	25	51	7	10	3	0	0	2	5	0	9	0	1	0	0	0	.196	.268	.255	1.000
1914	Bal-F	122	337	40	93	21	4	2	48	52	0	66	2	5	0	7	0	.276	.376	.380	.988
1915	Bal-F	49	135	20	32	9	0	2	13	31	0	25	2	2	0	2	0	.237	.387	.348	.992
Career average		44	121	15	30	6	1	1	14	18	0	9	2	2	0	3	0	.244	.350	.320	.934
Yankee average		**1**	**3**	**1**	**0**	**0**	**0**	**0**	**1**	**1**	**0**	**0**	**0**	**0**	**0**	**0**	**0**	**.000**	**.250**	**.000**	**1.000**
Career total		484	1333	160	325	63	12	5	150	201	0	100	17	16	0	35	0	.244	.350	.320	.934
Yankee total		**1**	**3**	**1**	**0**	**0**	**0**	**0**	**1**	**1**	**0**	**0**	**0**	**0**	**0**	**0**	**0**	**.000**	**.250**	**.000**	**1.000**

Jackson, Reginald Martinez (Reggie)

HEIGHT: 6'0"   THROWS: LEFT   BATS: LEFT   BORN: 5/18/1946, WYNCOTE, PENNSYLVANIA   POSITIONS PLAYED: OF

YEAR	TEAM	GAMES	AB	RUNS	HITS	2B	3B	HR	RBI	BB	IBB	SO	HBP	SH	SF	SB	CS	BA	OBA	SA	FA
1967	KC-A	35	118	13	21	4	4	1	6	10	0	46	5	1	1	1	1	.178	.269	.305	.933
1968	Oak-A	154	553	82	138	13	6	29	74	50	5	171	5	4	2	14	4	.250	.316	.452	.959
1969	Oak-A	152	549	123	151	36	3	47	118	114	20	142	12	1	1	13	5	.275	.410	.608	.964
1970	Oak-A	149	426	57	101	21	2	23	66	75	11	135	8	2	3	26	17	.237	.359	.458	.956
1971	Oak-A	150	567	87	157	29	3	32	80	63	5	161	6	0	6	16	10	.277	.352	.508	.977
1972	Oak-A	135	499	72	132	25	2	25	75	59	7	125	8	4	2	9	8	.265	.350	.473	.971
1973	Oak-A	151	539	99	158	28	2	32	117	76	11	111	7	0	7	22	8	.293	.383	.531	.971
1974	Oak-A	148	506	90	146	25	1	29	93	86	20	105	4	0	8	25	5	.289	.391	.514	.968
1975	Oak-A	157	593	91	150	39	3	36	104	67	5	133	3	0	6	17	8	.253	.329	.511	.965
1976	Bal-A	134	498	84	138	27	2	27	91	54	7	108	4	0	2	28	7	.277	.351	.502	.964
1977	**NY-A**	**146**	**525**	**93**	**150**	**39**	**2**	**32**	**110**	**74**	**4**	**129**	**3**	**0**	**4**	**17**	**3**	**.286**	**.375**	**.550**	**.949**
1978	**NY-A**	**139**	**511**	**82**	**140**	**13**	**5**	**27**	**97**	**58**	**2**	**133**	**9**	**0**	**3**	**14**	**11**	**.274**	**.356**	**.477**	**.986**
1979	**NY-A**	**131**	**465**	**78**	**138**	**24**	**2**	**29**	**89**	**65**	**3**	**107**	**2**	**0**	**5**	**9**	**8**	**.297**	**.382**	**.544**	**.986**
1980	**NY-A**	**143**	**514**	**94**	**154**	**22**	**4**	**41**	**111**	**83**	**15**	**122**	**2**	**0**	**2**	**1**	**2**	**.300**	**.398**	**.597**	**.962**
1981	**NY-A**	**94**	**334**	**33**	**79**	**17**	**1**	**15**	**54**	**46**	**2**	**82**	**1**	**0**	**1**	**0**	**3**	**.237**	**.330**	**.428**	**.974**
1982	Cal-A	153	530	92	146	17	1	39	101	85	12	156	2	0	4	4	5	.275	.375	.532	.972
1983	Cal-A	116	397	43	77	14	1	14	49	52	5	140	4	0	5	0	2	.194	.290	.340	.986
1984	Cal-A	143	525	67	117	17	2	25	81	55	7	141	3	1	0	8	4	.223	.300	.406	1.000
1985	Cal-A	143	460	64	116	27	0	27	85	78	12	138	1	0	2	1	2	.252	.360	.487	.944
1986	Cal-A	132	419	65	101	12	2	18	58	92	11	115	3	0	3	1	1	.241	.379	.408	.833
1987	Oak-A	115	336	42	74	14	1	15	43	33	0	97	4	0	1	2	1	.220	.297	.402	1.000
Career average		134	470	74	123	22	2	27	81	66	8	124	5	1	3	11	6	.262	.356	.490	.963
Yankee average		**131**	**470**	**76**	**132**	**23**	**3**	**29**	**92**	**65**	**5**	**115**	**3**	**0**	**3**	**11**	**5**	**.281**	**.371**	**.526**	**.971**
Career total		2820	9864	1551	2584	463	49	563	1702	1375	164	2597	96	13	68	228	115	.262	.356	.490	.963
Yankee total		**653**	**2349**	**380**	**661**	**115**	**14**	**144**	**461**	**326**	**26**	**573**	**17**	**0**	**15**	**41**	**27**	**.281**	**.371**	**.526**	**.971**

Reginald Martinez "Reggie" Jackson, of, 1977–81

If ever there was a ballplayer who seemed to thrive in the looney bin that was the New York Yankees of the late 1970s and 1980s, it was Reggie Jackson. Surely, Reggie was the only player who actually seemed to enjoy it—at least most of the time.

Jackson was born on May 18, 1946, in Wyncote, Pennsylvania. As a rookie in 1967, he was a part-time outfielder for the up-and-coming Kansas City Athletics, playing in 35 games. But by 1969, he was a bona fide star, leading the league with 123 runs scored and a .608 slugging average.

Along with Catfish Hunter, Jackson was a linchpin on the Oakland A's teams that won three consecutive World Series from 1972–74. In 1973, he was the unanimous MVP of the American League.

Following the 1976 season, Jackson became a free agent. The Yankees quickly moved in to sign him, giving him $3.3 million for five years.

That's when the real craziness began. Jackson came to a Yankee team that had won the 1976 American League pennant, a team with several established stars and led by quiet veterans Thurman Munson and Hunter, who had been signed the year before. They were managed by Billy Martin, the Yankees' fiery former second baseman.

Jackson saw himself as, in his own words, "the straw that stirred the drink." And perhaps he was. But to the veteran Yankees, he was a player who had yet to prove himself to them. When he did not show what was deemed by them the proper respect, he had problems.

However, Jackson had, for most of his New York career, the ultimate trump card: Owner George Steinbrenner would almost always support his flamboyant star, because Reggie, more than any of the Yankees of that era, always put people in the stands.

The bottom line was that Munson and Jackson didn't get along. Jackson and Martin didn't get along. And Martin and Steinbrenner didn't get along. Despite all this, the 1977 season was a personal triumph for Jackson, who starred in the postseason as the Yankees won their first World Series since 1962.

It was in the sixth game of that Series that Jackson hit three consecutive home runs on three consecutive pitches off three different Dodger pitchers to anchor the Yankees' 5-3 win. The final home run, off reliever Charlie Hough, generated a roar of wonder and disbelief from the 56,407 people in Yankee Stadium that night. Only Babe Ruth had ever hit three home runs in a game in a World Series, and no one had ever hit five home runs, as Jackson did, over the course of the Series. His reputation as Mr. October was made that night.

"I can't relate to Babe Ruth," said Jackson after the final game. "He's too far above me."

But Munson and Martin still didn't like him.

Things came to a head in 1978. The Yankees struggled in the early going and no one got along that year, either. Finally, Martin, who was by now drinking far too much, told a handful of New York sportswriters in July that Jackson was a "born liar" and Steinbrenner was a "convicted" liar, referring to Steinbrenner's conviction on making illegal campaign contributions to the Nixon campaign in the early 1970s. The New York writers weren't sure they should use the quote. Martin insisted. When Steinbrenner found out, Billy was gone and Reggie stayed.

And the Yankees, with Jackson hitting .462 in the league championship series against the Royals, and .391 in the 1987 World Series, won it again.

The Yankees returned to the postseason in 1980 and to the World Series in 1981, and Jackson continued to have great statistics. But 1978 was his day in the sun while in pinstripes.

His five-year contract expired in 1981 and Jackson signed with California for the final three years of his 18-year career. The Angels won the AL East in 1984 with Jackson as a part-time player. The four-time home run champ was elected to the Hall of Fame in 1993.

In his relatively brief career, Jackson did not crack any of the Yankees' all-time lists. But his slugging percentage of .755 is tops for World Series players and his .357 batting average is ninth best. He remains one of the most exciting and controversial players ever to play in New York—and that is exactly how he wants it.

James, Dion

HEIGHT: 6'1" THROWS: LEFT BATS: LEFT BORN: 11/9/1962, PHILADELPHIA, PENNSYLVANIA POSITIONS PLAYED: 1B, OF

YEAR	TEAM	GAMES	AB	RUNS	HITS	2B	3B	HR	RBI	BB	IBB	SO	HBP	SH	SF	SB	CS	BA	OBA	SA	FA
1983	Mil-A	11	20	1	2	0	0	0	1	2	0	2	0	0	0	1	0	.100	.182	.100	1.000
1984	Mil-A	128	387	52	114	19	5	1	30	32	1	41	3	6	3	10	10	.295	.351	.377	.989
1985	Mil-A	18	49	5	11	1	0	0	3	6	0	6	0	0	0	0	0	.224	.309	.245	1.000
1987	Atl-N	134	494	80	154	37	6	10	61	70	2	63	2	5	3	10	8	.312	.397	.472	.996
1988	Atl-N	132	386	46	99	17	5	3	30	58	5	59	1	2	2	9	9	.256	.353	.350	.987
1989	Atl-N	63	170	15	44	7	0	1	11	25	2	23	1	3	1	1	3	.259	.355	.318	1.000
1989	Cle-A	71	245	26	75	11	0	4	29	24	4	26	0	2	0	1	4	.306	.368	.400	.976
1990	Cle-A	87	248	28	68	15	2	1	22	27	3	23	1	3	1	5	3	.274	.347	.363	.947
1992	**NY-A**	**67**	**145**	**24**	**38**	**8**	**0**	**3**	**17**	**22**	**0**	**15**	**1**	**0**	**2**	**1**	**0**	**.262**	**.359**	**.379**	**1.000**
1993	**NY-A**	**115**	**343**	**62**	**114**	**21**	**2**	**7**	**36**	**31**	**1**	**31**	**2**	**1**	**1**	**0**	**0**	**.332**	**.390**	**.466**	**.966**
1995	**NY-A**	**85**	**209**	**22**	**60**	**6**	**1**	**2**	**26**	**20**	**2**	**16**	**0**	**0**	**2**	**4**	**1**	**.287**	**.346**	**.354**	**1.000**
1996	**NY-A**	**6**	**12**	**1**	**2**	**0**	**0**	**0**	**0**	**1**	**0**	**2**	**0**	**0**	**0**	**1**	**0**	**.167**	**.231**	**.167**	**1.000**
Career average		76	226	30	65	12	2	3	22	27	2	26	1	2	1	4	3	.288	.364	.392	.988
Yankee average		**68**	**177**	**27**	**54**	**9**	**1**	**3**	**20**	**19**	**1**	**16**	**1**	**0**	**1**	**2**	**0**	**.302**	**.364**	**.392**	**.992**
Career total		917	2708	362	781	142	21	32	266	318	20	307	11	22	15	43	38	.288	.364	.392	.988
Yankee total		**273**	**709**	**109**	**214**	**35**	**3**	**12**	**79**	**74**	**3**	**64**	**3**	**1**	**5**	**6**	**1**	**.302**	**.368**	**.410**	**.992**

Javier, Stanley Julian BORN STANLEY JULIAN JAVIER (DeJAVIER)

HEIGHT: 6'0" THROWS: RIGHT BATS: B BORN: 1/9/1964, SAN FRANCISCO DE MACORIS, DOMINICAN REPUBLIC POSITIONS PLAYED: OF

YEAR	TEAM	GAMES	AB	RUNS	HITS	2B	3B	HR	RBI	BB	IBB	SO	HBP	SH	SF	SB	CS	BA	OBA	SA	FA
1984	**NY-A**	**7**	**7**	**1**	**1**	**0**	**0**	**0**	**0**	**0**	**0**	**1**	**0**	**0**	**0**	**0**	**0**	**.143**	**.143**	**.143**	**1.000**
1986	Oak-A	59	114	13	23	8	0	0	8	16	0	27	1	0	0	8	0	.202	.305	.272	1.000
1987	Oak-A	81	151	22	28	3	1	2	9	19	3	33	0	6	0	3	2	.185	.276	.258	.976
1988	Oak-A	125	397	49	102	13	3	2	35	32	1	63	2	6	3	20	1	.257	.313	.320	1.000
1989	Oak-A	112	310	42	77	12	3	1	28	31	1	45	1	4	2	12	2	.248	.317	.316	.991
1990	Oak-A	19	33	4	8	0	2	0	3	3	0	6	0	0	0	0	0	.242	.306	.364	1.000
1990	LA-N	104	276	56	84	9	4	3	24	37	2	44	0	6	2	15	7	.304	.384	.399	1.000
1991	LA-N	121	176	21	36	5	3	1	11	16	0	36	0	3	2	7	1	.205	.268	.284	.986
1992	LA-N	56	58	6	11	3	0	1	5	6	2	11	1	1	0	1	2	.190	.277	.293	1.000
1992	Phi-N	74	276	36	72	14	1	0	24	31	0	43	2	2	2	17	1	.261	.338	.319	.986
1993	Cal-A	92	237	33	69	10	4	3	28	27	1	33	1	1	3	12	2	.291	.362	.405	.981
1994	Oak-A	109	419	75	114	23	0	10	44	49	1	76	2	7	3	24	7	.272	.349	.399	1.000
1995	Oak-A	130	442	81	123	20	2	8	56	49	3	63	4	5	4	36	5	.278	.353	.387	.986
1996	SF-N	71	274	44	74	25	0	2	22	25	0	51	2	5	0	14	2	.270	.336	.383	.993
1997	SF-N	142	440	69	126	16	4	8	50	56	1	70	5	2	7	25	3	.286	.368	.395	.971
1998	SF-N	135	417	63	121	13	5	4	49	65	4	63	0	4	3	21	5	.290	.384	.374	.980
1999	SF-N	112	333	49	92	15	1	3	30	29	0	55	0	0	0	13	6	.276	.334	.354	.974
1999	Hou-N	20	64	12	21	4	1	0	4	9	0	8	0	0	0	3	1	.328	.411	.422	1.000
2000	Sea-A	105	342	61	94	18	5	5	40	42	2	64	0	4	4	4	3	.275	.351	.401	.000
Career average		88	251	39	67	11	2	3	25	29	1	42	1	3	2	12	3	.268	.343	.362	.938
Yankee average		**7**	**7**	**1**	**1**	**0**	**0**	**0**	**0**	**0**	**0**	**1**	**0**	**0**	**0**	**0**	**0**	**.143**	**.143**	**.143**	**1.000**
Career total		1674	4766	737	1276	211	39	53	470	542	21	792	21	56	35	235	50	.268	.343	.362	.938
Yankee total		**7**	**7**	**1**	**1**	**0**	**0**	**0**	**0**	**0**	**0**	**1**	**0**	**0**	**0**	**0**	**0**	**.143**	**.143**	**.143**	**1.000**

Jefferson, Stanley

HEIGHT: 5'11" THROWS: RIGHT BATS: B BORN: 12/4/1962, NEW YORK, NEW YORK POSITIONS PLAYED: OF

YEAR	TEAM	GAMES	AB	RUNS	HITS	2B	3B	HR	RBI	BB	IBB	SO	HBP	SH	SF	SB	CS	BA	OBA	SA	FA
1986	NY-N	14	24	6	5	1	0	1	3	2	0	8	1	0	0	0	0	.208	.296	.375	1.000
1987	SD-N	116	422	59	97	8	7	8	29	39	2	92	2	3	3	34	11	.230	.296	.339	.987
1988	SD-N	49	111	16	16	1	2	1	4	9	0	22	1	2	2	5	1	.144	.211	.216	1.000
1989	**NY-A**	**10**	**12**	**1**	**1**	**0**	**0**	**0**	**1**	**0**	**0**	**4**	**0**	**0**	**0**	**1**	**1**	**.083**	**.083**	**.083**	**1.000**
1989	Bal-A	35	127	19	33	7	0	4	20	4	0	22	1	0	2	9	3	.260	.284	.409	.988
1990	Bal-A	10	19	1	0	0	0	0	0	2	0	8	0	0	0	1	0	.000	.095	.000	1.000
1990	Cle-A	49	98	21	27	8	0	2	10	8	0	18	2	1	3	8	4	.276	.333	.418	.985
1991	Cin-N	13	19	2	1	0	0	0	0	1	0	3	0	0	0	2	0	.053	.100	.053	1.000
Career average		37	104	16	23	3	1	2	8	8	0	22	1	1	1	8	3	.216	.276	.326	.995
Yankee average		**10**	**12**	**1**	**1**	**0**	**0**	**0**	**1**	**0**	**0**	**4**	**0**	**0**	**0**	**1**	**1**	**.083**	**.083**	**.083**	**1.000**
Career total		296	832	125	180	25	9	16	67	65	2	177	7	6	10	60	20	.216	.276	.326	.995
Yankee total		**10**	**12**	**1**	**1**	**0**	**0**	**0**	**1**	**0**	**0**	**4**	**0**	**0**	**0**	**1**	**1**	**.083**	**.083**	**.083**	**1.000**

Jensen, Jack Eugene (Jackie)

HEIGHT: 5'11" THROWS: RIGHT BATS: RIGHT BORN: 3/9/1927, SAN FRANCISCO, CALIF. DIED: 7/14/1982, CHARLOTTESVILLE, VA. POSITIONS PLAYED: OF

YEAR	TEAM	GAMES	AB	RUNS	HITS	2B	3B	HR	RBI	BB	IBB	SO	HBP	SH	SF	SB	CS	BA	OBA	SA	FA
1950	NY-A	45	70	13	12	2	2	1	5	7	—	8	0	1	—	4	0	.171	.247	.300	.947
1951	NY-A	56	168	30	50	8	1	8	25	18	—	18	1	1	—	8	2	.298	.369	.500	.974
1952	NY-A	7	19	3	2	1	1	0	2	4	—	4	0	0	—	1	0	.105	.261	.263	1.000
1952	Was-A	144	570	80	163	29	5	10	80	63	—	40	3	5	—	17	6	.286	.360	.407	.977
1953	Was-A	147	552	87	147	32	8	10	84	73	—	51	5	1	—	18	8	.266	.357	.408	.983
1954	Bos-A	152	580	92	160	25	7	25	117	79	—	52	2	1	11	22	7	.276	.359	.472	.986
1955	Bos-A	152	574	95	158	27	6	26	116	89	8	63	3	3	12	16	7	.275	.369	.479	.977
1956	Bos-A	151	578	80	182	23	11	20	97	89	5	43	1	1	4	11	3	.315	.405	.497	.962
1957	Bos-A	145	544	82	153	29	2	23	103	75	3	66	2	1	5	8	5	.281	.367	.469	.960
1958	Bos-A	154	548	83	157	31	0	35	122	99	7	65	3	1	4	9	4	.286	.396	.535	.981
1959	Bos-A	148	535	101	148	31	0	28	112	88	3	67	0	1	12	20	5	.277	.372	.492	.982
1961	Bos-A	137	498	64	131	21	2	13	66	66	2	69	3	2	4	9	8	.263	.350	.392	.986
Career average		120	436	68	122	22	4	17	77	63	—	46	2	2	—	12	5	.279	.372	.460	.976
Yankee average		36	86	15	21	4	1	3	11	10	—	10	0	1	—	4	1	.249	.328	.428	.974
Career total		1438	5236	810	1463	259	45	199	929	750	28	546	23	18	52	143	55	.279	.369	.460	.976
Yankee total		108	257	46	64	11	4	9	32	29	0	30	1	2	0	13	2	.249	.328	.428	.974

Jeter, Derek Sanderson

HEIGHT: 6'3" THROWS: RIGHT BATS: RIGHT BORN: 6/26/1974, KALAMAZOO, MICHIGAN POSITIONS PLAYED: SS

YEAR	TEAM	GAMES	AB	RUNS	HITS	2B	3B	HR	RBI	BB	IBB	SO	HBP	SH	SF	SB	CS	BA	OBA	SA	FA
1995	NY-A	15	48	5	12	4	1	0	7	3	0	11	0	0	0	0	0	.250	.294	.375	.962
1996	NY-A	157	582	104	183	25	6	10	78	48	1	102	9	6	9	14	7	.314	.370	.430	.969
1997	NY-A	159	654	116	190	31	7	10	70	74	0	125	10	8	2	23	12	.291	.370	.405	.975
1998	NY-A	149	626	127	203	25	8	19	84	57	1	119	5	3	3	30	6	.324	.384	.481	.986
1999	NY-A	158	627	134	219	37	9	24	102	91	0	116	0	3	6	19	8	.349	.428	.552	.978
2000	NY-A	148	593	119	201	31	4	15	73	68	4	99	12	3	3	22	4	.339	.416	.481	.961
Career average		131	522	101	168	26	6	13	69	57	1	95	6	4	4	18	6	.322	.392	.468	.974
Yankee average		131	522	101	168	26	6	13	69	57	1	95	6	4	4	18	6	.322	.392	.468	.974
Career total		786	3130	605	1008	153	35	78	414	341	6	572	36	23	23	108	37	.322	.392	.468	.974
Yankee total		786	3130	605	1008	153	35	78	414	341	6	572	36	23	23	108	37	.322	.392	.468	.974

Johnson, Alexander

HEIGHT: 6'0" THROWS: RIGHT BATS: RIGHT BORN: 12/7/1942, HELENA, ARKANSAS POSITIONS PLAYED: OF

YEAR	TEAM	GAMES	AB	RUNS	HITS	2B	3B	HR	RBI	BB	IBB	SO	HBP	SH	SF	SB	CS	BA	OBA	SA	FA
1964	Phi-N	43	109	18	33	7	1	4	18	6	1	26	1	0	0	1	2	.303	.345	.495	.980
1965	Phi-N	97	262	27	77	9	3	8	28	15	3	60	2	1	0	4	4	.294	.337	.443	.966
1966	StL-N	25	86	7	16	0	1	2	6	5	1	18	0	0	0	1	1	.186	.231	.279	.962
1967	StL-N	81	175	20	39	9	2	1	12	9	0	26	3	1	1	6	3	.223	.271	.314	.970
1968	Cin-N	149	603	79	188	32	6	2	58	26	4	71	3	0	2	16	6	.312	.342	.395	.947
1969	Cin-N	139	523	86	165	18	4	17	88	25	1	69	9	4	11	11	8	.315	.350	.463	.927
1970	Cal-A	156	614	85	202	26	6	14	86	35	9	68	7	0	3	17	2	.329	.370	.459	.959
1971	Cal-A	65	242	19	63	8	0	2	21	15	3	34	2	1	1	5	2	.260	.308	.318	.926
1972	Cle-A	108	356	31	85	10	1	8	37	22	10	40	1	2	3	6	8	.239	.283	.340	.955
1973	Tex-A	158	624	62	179	26	3	8	68	32	5	82	2	1	4	10	5	.287	.322	.377	.987
1974	Tex-A	114	453	57	132	14	3	4	41	28	4	59	4	1	0	20	9	.291	.338	.362	.956
1975	**NY-A**	52	119	15	31	5	1	1	15	7	1	21	0	0	2	2	3	.261	.297	.345	1.000
1976	Det-A	125	429	41	115	15	2	6	45	19	1	49	2	1	6	14	10	.268	.298	.354	.954
Career average		101	354	42	102	14	3	6	40	19	3	48	3	1	3	9	5	.288	.327	.392	.961
Yankee average		52	119	15	31	5	1	1	15	7	1	21	0	0	2	2	3	.261	.297	.345	1.000
Career total		1312	4595	547	1325	179	33	77	523	244	43	623	36	12	33	113	63	.288	.327	.392	.961
Yankee total		52	119	15	31	5	1	1	15	7	1	21	0	0	2	2	3	.261	.297	.345	1.000

Derek Sanderson Jeter, ss, 1995–2000

Derek Jeter has been in the major leagues since 1995. He has already been a Rookie of the Year, a four-time All-Star and a four-time World Champion. Wow.

Born June 26, 1974, in Pequannock, New Jersey, Jeter was a first-round pick of the Yankees in 1992 right out of Kalamazoo Central High School, where he hit .508 as a senior.

After three years in the minor leagues, Jeter was called up briefly by the Yankees in 1995. He became the team's everyday shortstop by 1996 and was Rookie of the Year that season.

He is one of the American League's best players. He has always hit for average, but in 1999, he hit 24 home runs. And think about this: Only one player in Yankees' history scored more than 100 runs in his first four seasons besides Jeter, and that is Joe DiMaggio. And this: Jeter's 17-game hitting streak as a rookie was the longest hitting streak by a first-year player since DiMaggio's 18-game streak in 1936. Double wow.

And like DiMaggio, Jeter has been a consistent performer in the postseason. He hit .412 in his first postseason series against Texas, which the Yankees won, three games to one. Then, as the Yankees knocked off the Orioles, four games to one in the American League championship series, Jeter hit .417. He tailed off a bit against the Braves in the 1996 World Series, but his team came out on top in six games.

In fact, Jeter's team has usually come out on top. In thirteen postseason series so far, Jeter has been on the losing team only once. His Yankee teams won fourteen consecutive World Series games. For a while, Jeter has been lumped in with Seattle's Alex Rodriguez and Boston's Nomar Garciaparra as three of the best shortstops in the league. That is a reasonable point.

But in the postseason, Jeter has clearly been the best of the three. His home run in Game 4 of the 2000 World Series—on the first pitch of the game—stole the momentum from the Mets, who had won Game 3, with one swing. His defense and base running throughout the 2000 postseason was confident and error-free. He is a known playoff quantity, in the Ruth-DiMaggio-Munson-Jackson mold (a player who plays better as the games become more important).

Jeter has been consistently excellent in both the regular season and playoffs. He has dated singer-diva Mariah Carey. And he's a nice guy. As Waite Hoyt said many years before, it's great to be young and a Yankee.

If Derek Jeter retired tomorrow, he will have had a career most players would envy. But the good news for Yankee fans is that such a thing probably won't happen for a long time.

Johnson, Clifford Jr.

HEIGHT: 6'4"   THROWS: RIGHT   BATS: RIGHT   BORN: 7/22/1947, SAN ANTONIO, TEXAS   POSITIONS PLAYED: C, 1B, OF

YEAR	TEAM	GAMES	AB	RUNS	HITS	2B	3B	HR	RBI	BB	IBB	SO	HBP	SH	SF	SB	CS	BA	OBA	SA	FA
1972	Hou-N	5	4	0	1	0	0	0	0	2	0	0	0	0	0	0	0	.250	.500	.250	1.000
1973	Hou-N	7	20	6	6	2	0	2	6	1	0	7	1	0	0	0	0	.300	.364	.700	1.000
1974	Hou-N	83	171	26	39	4	1	10	29	33	1	45	3	0	3	0	1	.228	.357	.439	.994
1975	Hou-N	122	340	52	94	16	1	20	65	46	5	64	5	1	1	1	0	.276	.370	.506	.991
1976	Hou-N	108	318	36	72	21	2	10	49	62	6	59	4	0	0	0	0	.226	.359	.399	1.000
1977	Hou-N	51	144	22	43	8	0	10	23	23	2	30	4	0	0	0	1	.299	.409	.563	.946
1977	**NY-A**	**56**	**142**	**24**	**42**	**8**	**0**	**12**	**31**	**20**	**0**	**23**	**6**	**0**	**0**	**0**	**1**	**.296**	**.405**	**.606**	**1.000**
1978	**NY-A**	**76**	**174**	**20**	**32**	**9**	**1**	**6**	**19**	**30**	**5**	**32**	**1**	**0**	**0**	**0**	**0**	**.184**	**.307**	**.351**	**.975**
1979	**NY-A**	**28**	**64**	**11**	**17**	**6**	**0**	**2**	**6**	**10**	**4**	**7**	**0**	**1**	**1**	**0**	**0**	**.266**	**.360**	**.453**	**1.000**

(continued)

(continued)

YEAR	TEAM	GAMES	AB	RUNS	HITS	2B	3B	HR	RBI	BB	IBB	SO	HBP	SH	SF	SB	CS	BA	OBA	SA	FA
1979	Cle-A	72	240	37	65	10	0	18	61	24	1	39	5	0	5	2	0	.271	.343	.538	.000
1980	Cle-A	54	174	25	40	3	1	6	28	25	5	30	0	0	4	0	1	.230	.320	.362	.000
1980	Chi-N	68	196	28	46	8	0	10	34	29	5	35	1	0	1	0	0	.235	.335	.429	.992
1981	Oak-A	84	273	40	71	8	0	17	59	28	2	60	3	0	6	5	3	.260	.329	.476	1.000
1982	Oak-A	73	214	19	51	10	0	7	31	26	2	41	2	0	2	1	2	.238	.324	.383	.987
1983	Tor-A	142	407	59	108	23	1	22	76	67	8	69	5	1	4	0	1	.265	.373	.489	1.000
1984	Tor-A	127	359	51	109	23	1	16	61	50	4	62	3	0	3	0	1	.304	.390	.507	1.000
1985	Tex-A	82	296	31	76	17	1	12	56	31	2	44	3	1	3	0	0	.257	.330	.443	.000
1985	Tor-A	24	73	4	20	0	0	1	10	9	0	15	0	0	1	0	0	.274	.349	.315	.947
1986	Tor-A	107	336	48	84	12	1	15	55	52	1	57	4	0	2	0	1	.250	.355	.426	1.000
Career average		72	208	28	54	10	1	10	37	30	3	38	3	0	2	1	1	.258	.355	.459	.833
Yankee average		**53**	**127**	**18**	**30**	**8**	**0**	**7**	**19**	**20**	**3**	**21**	**2**	**0**	**0**	**0**	**0**	**.239**	**.353**	**.463**	**.992**
Career total		1369	3945	539	1016	188	10	196	699	568	53	719	50	4	36	9	12	.258	.355	.459	.833
Yankee total		**160**	**380**	**55**	**91**	**23**	**1**	**20**	**56**	**60**	**9**	**62**	**7**	**1**	**1**	**0**	**1**	**.239**	**.353**	**.463**	**.992**

Johnson, Darrell Dean

HEIGHT: 6'1"   THROWS: RIGHT   BATS: RIGHT   BORN: 8/25/1928, HORACE, NEBRASKA   POSITIONS PLAYED: C

YEAR	TEAM	GAMES	AB	RUNS	HITS	2B	3B	HR	RBI	BB	IBB	SO	HBP	SH	SF	SB	CS	BA	OBA	SA	FA
1952	StL-A	29	78	9	22	2	1	0	9	11	—	4	0	0	—	0	0	.282	.371	.333	.990
1952	Chi-A	22	37	3	4	0	0	0	1	5	—	9	0	1	—	1	0	.108	.214	.108	.955
1957	**NY-A**	**21**	**46**	**4**	**10**	**1**	**0**	**1**	**8**	**3**	**0**	**10**	**1**	**0**	**1**	**0**	**0**	**.217**	**.275**	**.304**	**1.000**
1958	**NY-A**	**5**	**16**	**1**	**4**	**0**	**0**	**0**	**0**	**0**	**0**	**2**	**0**	**0**	**0**	**0**	**0**	**.250**	**.250**	**.250**	**1.000**
1960	StL-N	8	2	0	0	0	0	0	0	1	0	0	0	0	0	0	0	.000	.333	.000	1.000
1961	Phi-N	21	61	4	14	1	0	0	3	3	0	8	1	0	0	0	0	.230	.277	.246	.982
1961	Cin-N	20	54	3	17	2	0	1	6	1	0	2	0	0	1	0	0	.315	.321	.407	1.000
1962	Cin-N	2	4	0	0	0	0	0	0	2	1	0	0	0	0	0	0	.000	.333	.000	1.000
1962	Bal-A	6	22	0	4	0	0	0	1	0	0	4	0	0	0	0	0	.182	.182	.182	1.000
Career average		15	36	3	8	1	0	0	3	3	—	4	0	0	—	0	0	.234	.296	.278	.992
Yankee average		**13**	**31**	**3**	**7**	**1**	**0**	**1**	**4**	**2**	**0**	**6**	**1**	**0**	**1**	**0**	**0**	**.226**	**.269**	**.290**	**1.000**
Career total		134	320	24	75	6	1	2	28	26	1	39	2	1	2	1	0	.234	.294	.278	.992
Yankee total		**26**	**62**	**5**	**14**	**1**	**0**	**1**	**8**	**3**	**0**	**12**	**1**	**0**	**1**	**0**	**0**	**.226**	**.269**	**.290**	**1.000**

Johnson, Deron Roger

HEIGHT: 6'2"   THROWS: RIGHT   BATS: RIGHT   BORN: 7/17/1938, SAN DIEGO, CALIFORNIA   DIED: 4/23/1992, POWAY, CALIFORNIA   POSITIONS PLAYED: 1B, 3B, OF

YEAR	TEAM	GAMES	AB	RUNS	HITS	2B	3B	HR	RBI	BB	IBB	SO	HBP	SH	SF	SB	CS	BA	OBA	SA	FA
1960	**NY-A**	**6**	**4**	**0**	**2**	**1**	**0**	**0**	**0**	**0**	**0**	**0**	**0**	**0**	**0**	**0**	**0**	**.500**	**.500**	**.750**	**.750**
1961	**NY-A**	**13**	**19**	**1**	**2**	**0**	**0**	**0**	**2**	**2**	**0**	**5**	**0**	**0**	**1**	**0**	**0**	**.105**	**.182**	**.105**	**1.000**
1961	KC-A	83	283	31	61	11	3	8	42	14	1	44	1	1	4	0	1	.216	.252	.360	.948
1962	KC-A	17	19	1	2	1	0	0	0	3	0	8	0	0	0	0	0	.105	.227	.158	1.000
1964	Cin-N	140	477	63	130	24	4	21	79	37	0	98	2	1	2	4	3	.273	.326	.472	1.000
1965	Cin-N	159	616	92	177	30	7	32	130	52	9	97	2	0	10	0	4	.287	.340	.515	.948
1966	Cin-N	142	505	75	130	25	3	24	81	39	5	87	2	1	7	1	2	.257	.309	.461	.980
1967	Cin-N	108	361	39	81	18	1	13	53	22	2	104	2	0	4	0	1	.224	.270	.388	.997
1968	Atl-N	127	342	29	71	11	1	8	33	35	2	79	3	0	3	0	1	.208	.285	.316	.981
1969	Phi-N	138	475	51	121	19	4	17	80	60	4	111	0	1	9	4	2	.255	.333	.419	.993
1970	Phi-N	159	574	66	147	28	3	27	93	72	7	132	0	2	2	0	0	.256	.338	.456	1.000
1971	Phi-N	158	582	74	154	29	0	34	95	72	8	146	2	2	2	0	1	.265	.347	.490	.907
1972	Phi-N	96	230	19	49	4	1	9	31	26	4	69	3	0	3	0	1	.213	.298	.357	.982
1973	Phi-N	12	36	3	6	2	0	1	5	5	0	10	1	1	1	0	0	.167	.279	.306	.976
1973	Oak-A	131	464	61	114	14	2	19	81	59	7	116	1	3	3	0	1	.246	.330	.407	.994
1974	Oak-A	50	174	16	34	1	2	7	23	11	2	37	0	0	3	1	0	.195	.239	.345	.991
1974	Mil-A	49	152	14	23	3	0	6	18	21	2	41	0	0	1	1	0	.151	.253	.289	.833
1974	Bos-A	11	25	0	3	0	0	0	2	0	0	6	0	1	1	0	0	.120	.115	.120	.000
1975	Chi-A	148	555	66	129	25	1	18	72	48	0	117	1	0	5	0	1	.232	.292	.378	.994
1975	Bos-A	3	10	2	6	0	0	1	3	2	0	0	0	0	0	0	0	.600	.667	.900	1.000
1976	Bos-A	15	38	3	5	1	1	0	0	5	1	11	0	0	0	0	0	.132	.233	.211	1.000
Career average		84	283	34	69	12	2	12	44	28	3	63	1	1	3	1	1	.244	.311	.420	.918
Yankee average		**10**	**12**	**1**	**2**	**1**	**0**	**0**	**1**	**1**	**0**	**3**	**0**	**0**	**1**	**0**	**0**	**.174**	**.231**	**.217**	**.875**
Career total		1765	5941	706	1447	247	33	245	923	585	54	1318	20	13	61	11	18	.244	.311	.420	.918
Yankee total		**19**	**23**	**1**	**4**	**1**	**0**	**0**	**2**	**2**	**0**	**5**	**0**	**0**	**1**	**0**	**0**	**.174**	**.231**	**.217**	**.875**

Johnson, Ernest Rudolph

HEIGHT: 5'9"   THROWS: RIGHT   BATS: LEFT   BORN: 4/29/1888, CHICAGO, ILLINOIS   DIED: 5/1/1952, MONROVIA, CALIFORNIA   POSITIONS PLAYED: SS, 3B

YEAR	TEAM	GAMES	AB	RUNS	HITS	2B	3B	HR	RBI	BB	IBB	SO	HBP	SH	SF	SB	CS	BA	OBA	SA	FA
1912	Chi-A	21	42	7	11	0	1	0	5	1	0	0	0	1	0	0	0	.262	.279	.310	.984
1915	StL-F	152	512	58	123	18	10	7	67	46	0	35	2	23	0	32	0	.240	.305	.355	.942
1916	StL-A	74	236	29	54	9	3	0	19	30	0	23	3	9	0	13	0	.229	.323	.292	.936
1917	StL-A	80	199	28	49	6	2	2	20	12	0	16	2	11	0	13	0	.246	.296	.327	.981
1918	StL-A	29	34	7	9	1	0	0	0	0	0	2	1	0	0	4	0	.265	.286	.294	.821
1921	Chi-A	142	613	93	181	28	7	1	51	29	0	24	1	21	0	22	13	.295	.328	.369	.947
1922	Chi-A	144	603	85	153	17	3	0	56	40	0	30	4	26	0	21	18	.254	.304	.292	.952
1923	Chi-A	12	53	5	10	2	0	0	1	3	0	5	1	1	0	2	1	.189	.246	.226	.922
1923	**NY-A**	**19**	**38**	**6**	**17**	**1**	**1**	**1**	**8**	**1**	**0**	**1**	**0**	**1**	**0**	**0**	**0**	**.447**	**.462**	**.605**	**1.000**
1924	**NY-A**	**64**	**119**	**24**	**42**	**4**	**8**	**3**	**12**	**11**	**0**	**7**	**1**	**3**	**0**	**1**	**6**	**.353**	**.412**	**.597**	**1.000**
1925	**NY-A**	**76**	**170**	**30**	**48**	**5**	**1**	**5**	**17**	**8**	**0**	**10**	**0**	**4**	**0**	**6**	**3**	**.282**	**.315**	**.412**	**.955**
Career average		74	238	34	63	8	3	2	23	17	0	14	1	9	0	10	4	.266	.317	.350	.949
Yankee average		**53**	**109**	**20**	**36**	**3**	**3**	**3**	**12**	**7**	**0**	**6**	**0**	**3**	**0**	**2**	**3**	**.327**	**.368**	**.502**	**.985**
Career total		813	2619	372	697	91	36	19	256	181	0	153	15	100	0	114	41	.266	.317	.350	.949
Yankee total		**159**	**327**	**60**	**107**	**10**	**10**	**9**	**37**	**20**	**0**	**18**	**1**	**8**	**0**	**7**	**9**	**.327**	**.368**	**.502**	**.985**

Johnson, Kenneth Lance

HEIGHT: 5'11"   THROWS: LEFT   BATS: LEFT   BORN: 7/6/1963, LINCOLN HEIGHTS, OHIO   POSITIONS PLAYED: OF

YEAR	TEAM	GAMES	AB	RUNS	HITS	2B	3B	HR	RBI	BB	IBB	SO	HBP	SH	SF	SB	CS	BA	OBA	SA	FA
1987	StL-N	33	59	4	13	2	1	0	7	4	1	6	0	0	0	6	1	.220	.270	.288	.931
1988	Chi-A	33	124	11	23	4	1	0	6	6	0	11	0	2	0	6	2	.185	.223	.234	.970
1989	Chi-A	50	180	28	54	8	2	0	16	17	0	24	0	2	0	16	3	.300	.360	.367	.983
1990	Chi-A	151	541	76	154	18	9	1	51	33	2	45	1	8	4	36	22	.285	.325	.357	.973
1991	Chi-A	159	588	72	161	14	13	0	49	26	2	58	1	6	3	26	11	.274	.304	.342	.995
1992	Chi-A	157	567	67	158	15	12	3	47	34	4	33	1	4	5	41	14	.279	.318	.363	.987
1993	Chi-A	147	540	75	168	18	14	0	47	36	1	33	0	3	0	35	7	.311	.354	.396	.980
1994	Chi-A	106	412	56	114	11	14	3	54	26	5	23	2	0	3	26	6	.277	.321	.393	1.000
1995	Chi-A	142	607	98	186	18	12	10	57	32	2	31	1	2	3	40	6	.306	.341	.425	.991
1996	NY-N	160	682	117	227	31	21	9	69	33	8	40	1	3	5	50	12	.333	.362	.479	.971
1997	NY-N	72	265	43	82	10	6	1	24	33	2	21	0	0	1	15	10	.309	.385	.404	.975
1997	Chi-N	39	145	17	44	6	2	4	15	9	1	10	0	0	1	5	2	.303	.342	.455	.971
1998	Chi-N	85	304	51	85	8	4	2	21	26	1	22	0	1	1	10	6	.280	.335	.352	.975
1999	Chi-N	95	335	46	87	11	6	1	21	37	0	20	0	4	0	13	3	.260	.332	.337	.988
2000	**NY-A**	**18**	**30**	**6**	**9**	**1**	**0**	**0**	**2**	**0**	**0**	**7**	**0**	**0**	**0**	**2**	**0**	**.300**	**.300**	**.333**	**1.000**
Career average		97	359	51	104	12	8	2	32	24	2	26	1	2	2	22	7	.291	.334	.386	.979
Yankee average		**18**	**30**	**6**	**9**	**1**	**0**	**0**	**2**	**0**	**0**	**7**	**0**	**0**	**0**	**2**	**0**	**.300**	**.300**	**.333**	**1.000**
Career total		1447	5379	767	1565	175	117	34	486	352	29	384	7	35	27	327	105	.291	.334	.386	.979
Yankee total		**18**	**30**	**6**	**9**	**1**	**0**	**0**	**2**	**0**	**0**	**7**	**0**	**0**	**0**	**2**	**0**	**.300**	**.300**	**.333**	**1.000**

Johnson, Otis L.

HEIGHT: 5'9"   THROWS: RIGHT   BATS: B   BORN: 11/5/1883, FOWLER, INDIANA   DIED: 11/9/1915, JOHNSON CITY, NEW YORK   POSITIONS PLAYED: SS, 3B

YEAR	TEAM	GAMES	AB	RUNS	HITS	2B	3B	HR	RBI	BB	IBB	SO	HBP	SH	SF	SB	CS	BA	OBA	SA	FA
1911	**NY-A**	**71**	**209**	**21**	**49**	**9**	**6**	**3**	**36**	**39**	**0**	**0**	**3**	**11**	**0**	**12**	**0**	**.234**	**.363**	**.378**	**.907**
Career average		71	209	21	49	9	6	3	36	39	0	0	3	11	0	12	0	.234	.363	.378	.907
Yankee average		**71**	**209**	**21**	**49**	**9**	**6**	**3**	**36**	**39**	**0**	**0**	**3**	**11**	**0**	**12**	**0**	**.234**	**.363**	**.378**	**.907**
Career total		71	209	21	49	9	6	3	36	39	0	0	3	11	0	12	0	.234	.363	.378	.907
Yankee total		**71**	**209**	**21**	**49**	**9**	**6**	**3**	**36**	**39**	**0**	**0**	**3**	**11**	**0**	**12**	**0**	**.234**	**.363**	**.378**	**.907**

Johnson, Roy Cleveland

HEIGHT: 5'9"   THROWS: RIGHT   BATS: LEFT   BORN: 2/23/1903, PRYOR, OKLAHOMA   DIED: 9/10/1973, TACOMA, WASHINGTON   POSITIONS PLAYED: OF

YEAR	TEAM	GAMES	AB	RUNS	HITS	2B	3B	HR	RBI	BB	IBB	SO	HBP	SH	SF	SB	CS	BA	OBA	SA	FA
1929	Det-A	148	640	128	201	45	14	10	69	67	—	60	0	6	—	20	15	.314	.379	.475	.928
1930	Det-A	125	462	84	127	30	13	2	35	40	—	46	0	3	—	17	10	.275	.333	.409	.936
1931	Det-A	151	621	107	173	37	19	8	55	72	—	51	2	2	—	33	21	.279	.355	.438	.960
1932	Det-A	49	195	33	49	14	2	3	22	20	—	26	1	0	—	7	2	.251	.324	.390	.929

(continued)

(continued)

YEAR	TEAM	GAMES	AB	RUNS	HITS	2B	3B	HR	RBI	BB	IBB	SO	HBP	SH	SF	SB	CS	BA	OBA	SA	FA
1932	Bos-A	94	349	70	104	24	4	11	47	44	—	41	1	0	—	13	4	.298	.378	.484	.930
1933	Bos-A	133	483	88	151	30	7	10	95	55	—	36	4	5	—	13	10	.313	.387	.466	.922
1934	Bos-A	143	569	85	182	43	10	7	119	54	—	36	0	3	—	11	5	.320	.379	.467	.948
1935	Bos-A	145	553	70	174	33	9	3	66	74	—	34	3	5	—	11	12	.315	.398	.423	.944
1936	**NY-A**	**63**	**147**	**21**	**39**	**8**	**2**	**1**	**19**	**21**	**—**	**14**	**1**	**1**	**—**	**3**	**1**	**.265**	**.361**	**.367**	**.944**
1937	**NY-A**	**12**	**51**	**5**	**15**	**3**	**0**	**0**	**6**	**3**	**—**	**2**	**0**	**0**	**—**	**1**	**0**	**.294**	**.333**	**.353**	**.840**
1937	Bos-N	85	260	24	72	8	3	3	22	38	—	29	0	1	—	5	—	.277	.369	.365	.965
1938	Bos-N	7	29	2	5	0	0	0	1	1	—	5	0	0	—	1	—	.172	.200	.172	.769
Career average		96	363	60	108	23	7	5	46	41	—	32	1	2	—	11	—	.296	.369	.437	.918
Yankee average		**38**	**99**	**13**	**27**	**6**	**1**	**1**	**13**	**12**	**—**	**8**	**1**	**1**	**—**	**2**	**1**	**.273**	**.354**	**.364**	**.892**
Career total		1155	4359	717	1292	275	83	58	556	489	—	380	12	26	—	135	80	.296	.369	.437	.918
Yankee total		**75**	**198**	**26**	**54**	**11**	**2**	**1**	**25**	**24**	**—**	**16**	**1**	**1**	**—**	**4**	**1**	**.273**	**.354**	**.364**	**.892**

Johnson, William Russell (Billy *or* Bull)

HEIGHT: 5'10" THROWS: RIGHT BATS: RIGHT BORN: 8/30/1918, MONTCLAIR, NEW JERSEY POSITIONS PLAYED: 1B, 2B, 3B

YEAR	TEAM	GAMES	AB	RUNS	HITS	2B	3B	HR	RBI	BB	IBB	SO	HBP	SH	SF	SB	CS	BA	OBA	SA	FA
1943	**NY-A**	**155**	**592**	**70**	**166**	**24**	**6**	**5**	**94**	**53**	**—**	**30**	**4**	**6**	**—**		**3**	**5**	**.280**	**.344**	**.367**	**.966**
1946	**NY-A**	**85**	**296**	**51**	**77**	**14**	**5**	**4**	**35**	**31**	**—**	**42**	**2**	**5**	**—**		**1**	**0**	**.260**	**.334**	**.382**	**.955**
1947	**NY-A**	**132**	**494**	**67**	**141**	**19**	**8**	**10**	**95**	**44**	**—**	**43**	**6**	**3**	**—**		**1**	**2**	**.285**	**.351**	**.417**	**.952**
1948	**NY-A**	**127**	**446**	**59**	**131**	**20**	**6**	**12**	**64**	**41**	**—**	**30**	**4**	**1**	**—**		**0**	**0**	**.294**	**.358**	**.446**	**.947**
1949	**NY-A**	**113**	**329**	**48**	**82**	**11**	**3**	**8**	**56**	**48**	**—**	**44**	**2**	**4**	**—**		**1**	**0**	**.249**	**.348**	**.374**	**.951**
1950	**NY-A**	**108**	**327**	**44**	**85**	**16**	**2**	**6**	**40**	**42**	**—**	**30**	**1**	**2**	**—**		**1**	**0**	**.260**	**.346**	**.376**	**.958**
1951	**NY-A**	**15**	**40**	**5**	**12**	**3**	**0**	**0**	**4**	**7**	**—**	**0**	**0**	**1**	**—**		**0**	**1**	**.300**	**.404**	**.375**	**.960**
1951	StL-N	124	442	52	116	23	1	14	64	46	—	49	6	8	—		5	3	.262	.340	.414	.976
1952	StL-N	94	282	23	71	10	2	2	34	34	—	21	3	1	—		1	0	.252	.339	.351	.951
1953	StL-N	11	5	0	1	1	0	0	1	1	—	1	0	0	—		0	0	.200	.333	.400	1.000
Career average		96	325	42	88	14	3	6	49	35	—	29	3	3	—		1	1	.271	.346	.391	.962
Yankee average		**105**	**361**	**49**	**99**	**15**	**4**	**6**	**55**	**38**	**—**	**31**	**3**	**3**	**—**		**1**	**1**	**.275**	**.349**	**.395**	**.956**
Career total		964	3253	419	882	141	33	61	487	347	—	290	28	31	—		13	11	.271	.346	.391	.962
Yankee total		**735**	**2524**	**344**	**694**	**107**	**30**	**45**	**388**	**266**	**—**	**219**	**19**	**22**	**—**		**7**	**8**	**.275**	**.349**	**.395**	**.956**

Johnstone, John William (Jay)

HEIGHT: 6'1" THROWS: RIGHT BATS: LEFT BORN: 11/20/1945, MANCHESTER, CONNECTICUT POSITIONS PLAYED: 1B, 2B, OF

YEAR	TEAM	GAMES	AB	RUNS	HITS	2B	3B	HR	RBI	BB	IBB	SO	HBP	SH	SF	SB	CS	BA	OBA	SA	FA
1966	Cal-A	61	254	35	67	12	4	3	17	11	1	36	1	2	0	3	3	.264	.297	.378	.975
1967	Cal-A	79	230	18	48	7	1	2	10	5	0	37	0	2	0	3	2	.209	.226	.274	.973
1968	Cal-A	41	115	11	30	4	1	0	3	7	0	15	0	2	0	2	1	.261	.303	.313	.984
1969	Cal-A	148	540	64	146	20	5	10	59	38	5	75	5	8	6	3	9	.270	.321	.381	.983
1970	Cal-A	119	320	34	76	10	5	11	39	24	6	53	1	3	3	1	0	.238	.290	.403	.981
1971	Chi-A	124	388	53	101	14	1	16	40	38	4	50	3	5	2	10	5	.260	.329	.425	.968
1972	Chi-A	113	261	27	49	9	0	4	17	25	2	42	0	4	0	2	1	.188	.259	.268	.988
1973	Oak-A	23	28	1	3	1	0	0	3	2	0	4	0	0	0	0	1	.107	.167	.143	1.000
1974	Phi-N	64	200	30	59	10	4	6	30	24	4	28	0	0	0	5	5	.295	.371	.475	.968
1975	Phi-N	122	350	50	115	19	2	7	54	42	7	39	0	3	3	7	3	.329	.397	.454	.976
1976	Phi-N	129	440	62	140	38	4	5	53	41	5	39	2	1	7	5	5	.318	.373	.457	.906
1977	Phi-N	112	363	64	103	18	4	15	59	38	3	38	2	1	7	3	7	.284	.349	.479	1.000
1978	Phi-N	35	56	3	10	2	0	0	4	6	0	9	0	0	0	0	2	.179	.258	.214	1.000
1978	**NY-A**	**36**	**65**	**6**	**17**	**0**	**0**	**1**	**6**	**4**	**0**	**10**	**3**	**0**	**1**	**0**	**1**	**.262**	**.329**	**.308**	**1.000**
1979	**NY-A**	**23**	**48**	**7**	**10**	**1**	**0**	**1**	**7**	**2**	**0**	**7**	**0**	**0**	**1**	**1**	**0**	**.208**	**.240**	**.292**	**1.000**
1979	SD-N	75	201	10	59	8	2	0	32	18	3	21	0	4	2	1	3	.294	.348	.353	.979
1980	LA-N	109	251	31	77	15	2	2	20	24	1	29	2	2	0	3	2	.307	.372	.406	.965
1981	LA-N	61	83	8	17	3	0	3	6	7	0	13	0	0	0	0	1	.205	.267	.349	1.000
1982	LA-N	21	13	1	1	1	0	0	2	5	1	2	0	1	0	0	0	.077	.316	.154	.000
1982	Chi-N	98	269	39	67	13	1	10	43	40	8	41	0	1	3	0	2	.249	.343	.416	.982
1983	Chi-N	86	140	16	36	7	0	6	22	20	6	24	3	2	0	1	1	.257	.362	.436	.935
1984	Chi-N	52	73	8	21	2	2	0	3	7	4	18	0	0	0	1	0	.288	.350	.370	1.000
1985	LA-N	17	15	0	2	1	0	0	2	1	1	2	0	0	0	0	0	.133	.188	.200	.000
Career average		76	205	25	55	9	2	4	23	19	3	28	1	2	2	2	2	.267	.329	.394	.894
Yankee average		**30**	**57**	**7**	**14**	**1**	**0**	**1**	**7**	**3**	**0**	**9**	**2**	**0**	**1**	**1**	**1**	**.239**	**.293**	**.301**	**1.000**
Career total		1748	4703	578	1254	215	38	102	531	429	61	632	22	40	35	50	54	.267	.329	.394	.894
Yankee total		**59**	**113**	**13**	**27**	**1**	**0**	**2**	**13**	**6**	**0**	**17**	**3**	**0**	**1**	**1**	**1**	**.239**	**.293**	**.301**	**1.000**

William Russell Johnson, 3b-1b-2b, 1943–51

Billy Johnson was one of the strong, silent leaders in the Yankee clubhouse in the late 1940s who, like many players, lost several years to World War II.

Born on August 30, 1918, in Montclair, New Jersey, Johnson was signed by the Yankees in 1937 for $100. Johnson spent six years in the minor leagues, slowly working his way up to the big club. He finally made it in 1943 as the Yankees' regular third baseman and played very well, hitting .280 with 94 RBI.

But Johnson spent the next two years in the military, and when he returned in 1946, he was platooned at third with Snuffy Stirnweiss. By 1947, he had won his job back, and he had his best year, hitting .285 with a career-high 95 RBI. He was named to the All-Star team that year.

In 1948, he hit a career-high .294 and played 118 games at third base. But Johnson was being pressed hard by Bobby Brown—who had received a fat bonus for signing. Brown, who was faster on the base paths than

Johnson, was actually the choice of the Yankee front office to play third that year. But an early-season injury to Brown enabled Johnson to keep his spot.

By 1949, however, manager Casey Stengel was platooning the righthanded Johnson against lefthanded pitchers and the lefthanded Brown against righthanded pitchers. Both men hated the setup, believing that they would be more productive if they played more. But together they were an effective combination over the next two years.

Johnson was one of the Yankee "R.A.s," or "red asses," a man who demanded his teammates play hard at all times, even when far ahead or far behind. Johnson was not afraid to challenge even Joe DiMaggio to do better.

In 1951, Stengel traded Johnson to the Cardinals for first baseman Don Bollweg and cash. Johnson played for St. Louis for 2 1/2 years before retiring.

Jones, Darryl Lee

HEIGHT: 5'10" THROWS: RIGHT BATS: RIGHT BORN: 6/5/1951, MEADVILLE, PENNSYLVANIA POSITIONS PLAYED: DH

YEAR	TEAM	GAMES	AB	RUNS	HITS	2B	3B	HR	RBI	BB	IBB	SO	HBP	SH	SF	SB	CS	BA	OBA	SA	FA
1979	NY-A	18	47	6	12	5	1	0	6	2	0	7	0	2	0	0	0	.255	.286	.404	1.000
Career average		18	47	6	12	5	1	0	6	2	0	7	0	2	0	0	0	.255	.286	.404	1.000
Yankee average		18	47	6	12	5	1	0	6	2	0	7	0	2	0	0	0	.255	.286	.404	1.000
Career total		18	47	6	12	5	1	0	6	2	0	7	0	2	0	0	0	.255	.286	.404	1.000
Yankee total		18	47	6	12	5	1	0	6	2	0	7	0	2	0	0	0	.255	.286	.404	1.000

Jones, Ruppert Sanderson

HEIGHT: 5'10" THROWS: LEFT BATS: LEFT BORN: 3/12/1955, DALLAS, TEXAS POSITIONS PLAYED: OF

YEAR	TEAM	GAMES	AB	RUNS	HITS	2B	3B	HR	RBI	BB	IBB	SO	HBP	SH	SF	SB	CS	BA	OBA	SA	FA
1976	KC-A	28	51	9	11	1	1	1	7	3	0	16	0	0	0	0	2	.216	.259	.333	1.000
1977	Sea-A	160	597	85	157	26	8	24	76	55	3	120	2	3	6	13	9	.263	.324	.454	.981
1978	Sea-A	129	472	48	111	24	3	6	46	55	2	85	0	8	5	22	6	.235	.312	.337	.985
1979	Sea-A	162	622	109	166	29	9	21	78	85	4	78	3	2	4	33	12	.267	.356	.444	.989
1980	**NY-A**	**83**	**328**	**38**	**73**	**11**	**3**	**9**	**42**	**34**	**3**	**50**	**3**	**5**	**3**	**18**	**8**	**.223**	**.299**	**.357**	**.988**
1981	SD-N	105	397	53	99	34	1	4	39	43	2	66	0	4	7	7	9	.249	.318	.370	.993
1982	SD-N	116	424	69	120	20	2	12	61	62	11	90	1	3	3	18	15	.283	.373	.425	.984
1983	SD-N	133	335	42	78	12	3	12	49	35	4	58	0	2	0	11	11	.233	.305	.394	.981
1984	Det-A	79	215	26	61	12	1	12	37	21	0	47	0	0	1	2	4	.284	.346	.516	1.000

(continued)

(continued)

YEAR	TEAM	GAMES	AB	RUNS	HITS	2B	3B	HR	RBI	BB	IBB	SO	HBP	SH	SF	SB	CS	BA	OBA	SA	FA
1985	Cal-A	125	389	66	90	17	2	21	67	57	2	82	0	8	2	7	4	.231	.328	.447	.995
1986	Cal-A	126	393	73	90	21	3	17	49	64	5	87	3	7	3	10	3	.229	.339	.427	.981
1987	Cal-A	85	192	25	47	8	2	8	28	20	2	38	0	1	0	2	1	.245	.316	.432	.965
Career average		111	368	54	92	18	3	12	48	45	3	68	1	4	3	12	7	.250	.330	.416	.987
Yankee average		**83**	**328**	**38**	**73**	**11**	**3**	**9**	**42**	**34**	**3**	**50**	**3**	**5**	**3**	**18**	**8**	**.223**	**.299**	**.357**	**.988**
Career total		1331	4415	643	1103	215	38	147	579	534	38	817	12	43	34	143	84	.250	.330	.416	.987
Yankee total		**83**	**328**	**38**	**73**	**11**	**3**	**9**	**42**	**34**	**3**	**50**	**3**	**5**	**3**	**18**	**8**	**.223**	**.299**	**.357**	**.988**

Jordan, Timothy Joseph (Hoboken)

HEIGHT: 6'1"   THROWS: LEFT   BATS: LEFT   BORN: 2/14/1879, NEW YORK, NEW YORK   DIED: 9/13/1949, BRONX, NEW YORK   POSITIONS PLAYED: 1B

YEAR	TEAM	GAMES	AB	RUNS	HITS	2B	3B	HR	RBI	BB	IBB	SO	HBP	SH	SF	SB	CS	BA	OBA	SA	FA
1901	Was-A	6	20	2	4	1	0	0	2	3	0	0	0	0	0	0	0	.200	.304	.250	.941
1903	**NY-A**	**2**	**8**	**2**	**1**	**0**	**0**	**0**	**0**	**0**	**0**	**0**	**0**	**0**	**0**	**0**	**0**	**.125**	**.125**	**.125**	**.889**
1906	Bro-N	129	450	67	118	20	8	12	78	59	0	0	3	10	0	16	0	.262	.352	.422	.978
1907	Bro-N	147	485	43	133	15	8	4	53	74	0	0	1	15	0	10	0	.274	.371	.363	.980
1908	Bro-N	148	515	58	127	18	5	12	60	59	0	0	3	11	0	9	0	.247	.328	.371	.982
1909	Bro-N	103	330	47	90	20	3	3	36	59	0	0	2	12	0	13	0	.273	.386	.379	.983
Career average		89	301	37	79	12	4	5	38	42	0	0	2	8	0	8	0	.262	.355	.381	.959
Yankee average		**2**	**8**	**2**	**1**	**0**	**0**	**0**	**0**	**0**	**0**	**0**	**0**	**0**	**0**	**0**	**0**	**.125**	**.125**	**.125**	**.889**
Career total		535	1808	219	473	74	24	31	229	254	0	0	9	48	0	48	0	.262	.355	.381	.959
Yankee total		**2**	**8**	**2**	**1**	**0**	**0**	**0**	**0**	**0**	**0**	**0**	**0**	**0**	**0**	**0**	**0**	**.125**	**.125**	**.125**	**.889**

Jorgens, Arndt Ludwig

HEIGHT: 5'9"   THROWS: RIGHT   BATS: RIGHT   BORN: 5/18/1905, MODUM, NORWAY   DIED: 3/1/1980, WILMETTE, ILLINOIS   POSITIONS PLAYED: C

YEAR	TEAM	GAMES	AB	RUNS	HITS	2B	3B	HR	RBI	BB	IBB	SO	HBP	SH	SF	SB	CS	BA	OBA	SA	FA
1929	NY-A	18	34	6	11	3	0	0	4	6	0	7	0	1	0	0	2	.324	.425	.412	.979
1930	NY-A	16	30	7	11	3	0	0	1	2	0	4	0	3	0	0	0	.367	.406	.467	.960
1931	NY-A	46	100	12	27	1	2	0	14	9	0	3	0	2	0	0	1	.270	.330	.320	.963
1932	NY-A	56	151	13	33	7	1	2	19	14	0	11	0	1	0	0	0	.219	.285	.318	.967
1933	NY-A	21	50	9	11	3	0	2	13	12	0	3	0	0	0	1	0	.220	.371	.400	.982
1934	NY-A	58	183	14	38	6	1	0	20	23	0	24	0	1	0	2	0	.208	.296	.251	.984
1935	NY-A	36	84	6	20	2	0	0	8	12	0	10	0	2	0	0	0	.238	.333	.262	1.000
1936	NY-A	31	66	5	18	3	1	0	5	2	0	3	0	1	0	0	0	.273	.294	.348	.990
1937	NY-A	13	23	3	3	1	0	0	3	2	0	5	0	0	0	0	0	.130	.200	.174	1.000
1938	NY-A	9	17	3	4	2	0	0	2	3	0	3	0	1	0	0	0	.235	.350	.353	.923
1939	NY-A	3	0	1	0	0	0	0	0	0	0	0	0	0	0	0	0	—	—	—	1.000
Career average		28	67	7	16	3	1	0	8	8	0	7	0	1	0	0	0	.238	.317	.310	.977
Yankee average		**28**	**67**	**7**	**16**	**3**	**1**	**0**	**8**	**8**	**0**	**7**	**0**	**1**	**0**	**0**	**0**	**.238**	**.317**	**.310**	**.977**
Career total		307	738	79	176	31	5	4	89	85	0	73	0	12	0	3	3	.238	.317	.310	.977
Yankee total		**307**	**738**	**79**	**176**	**31**	**5**	**4**	**89**	**85**	**0**	**73**	**0**	**12**	**0**	**3**	**3**	**.238**	**.317**	**.310**	**.977**

Jose, Domingo Felix BORN DOMINGO FELIX ANDUJAR (JOSE)

HEIGHT: 6'1"   THROWS: RIGHT   BATS: B   BORN: 5/2/1965, SANTO DOMINGO, DOMINICAN REPUBLIC   POSITIONS PLAYED: OF

YEAR	TEAM	GAMES	AB	RUNS	HITS	2B	3B	HR	RBI	BB	IBB	SO	HBP	SH	SF	SB	CS	BA	OBA	SA	FA
1988	Oak-A	8	6	2	2	1	0	0	1	0	0	1	0	0	0	1	0	.333	.333	.500	1.000
1989	Oak-A	20	57	3	11	2	0	0	5	4	0	13	0	0	0	0	1	.193	.246	.228	.974
1990	Oak-A	101	341	42	90	12	0	8	39	16	0	65	5	2	1	8	2	.264	.306	.370	.977
1990	StL-N	25	85	12	23	4	1	3	13	8	0	16	0	0	0	4	4	.271	.333	.447	1.000
1991	StL-N	154	568	69	173	40	6	8	77	50	8	113	2	0	5	20	12	.305	.360	.438	.990
1992	StL-N	131	509	62	150	22	3	14	75	40	8	100	1	0	1	28	12	.295	.347	.432	.979
1993	KC-A	149	499	64	126	24	3	6	43	36	5	95	1	1	2	31	13	.253	.303	.349	.972
1994	KC-A	99	366	56	111	28	1	11	55	35	6	75	0	0	2	10	12	.303	.362	.475	.980
1995	KC-A	9	30	2	4	1	0	0	1	2	0	9	0	0	0	0	0	.133	.188	.167	1.000
2000	**NY-A**	**20**	**29**	**4**	**7**	**0**	**0**	**1**	**5**	**2**	**0**	**9**	**0**	**0**	**0**	**1**	**1**	**.241**	**.281**	**.345**	**.982**
Career average		72	249	32	70	13	1	5	31	19	3	50	1	0	1	10	6	.280	.332	.406	.985
Yankee average		**20**	**29**	**4**	**7**	**0**	**0**	**1**	**5**	**2**	**0**	**9**	**0**	**0**	**0**	**1**	**1**	**.241**	**.281**	**.345**	**.982**
Career total		716	2490	316	697	134	14	51	314	193	27	496	9	3	12	102	57	.280	.332	.406	.985
Yankee total		**20**	**29**	**4**	**7**	**0**	**0**	**1**	**5**	**2**	**0**	**9**	**0**	**0**	**0**	**1**	**1**	**.241**	**.281**	**.345**	**.982**

Justice, David Christopher

HEIGHT: 6'3"   THROWS: LEFT   BATS: LEFT   BORN: 4/14/1966, CINCINNATI, OHIO   POSITIONS PLAYED: OF

YEAR	TEAM	GAMES	AB	RUNS	HITS	2B	3B	HR	RBI	BB	IBB	SO	HBP	SH	SF	SB	CS	BA	OBA	SA	FA
1989	Atl-N	16	51	7	12	3	0	1	3	3	1	9	1	1	0	2	1	.235	.291	.353	1.000
1990	Atl-N	127	439	76	124	23	2	28	78	64	4	92	0	0	1	11	6	.282	.373	.535	.968
1991	Atl-N	109	396	67	109	25	1	21	87	65	9	81	3	0	5	8	8	.275	.377	.503	.968
1992	Atl-N	144	484	78	124	19	5	21	72	79	8	85	2	0	6	2	4	.256	.359	.446	.976
1993	Atl-N	157	585	90	158	15	4	40	120	78	12	90	3	0	4	3	5	.270	.357	.515	.985
1994	Atl-N	104	352	61	110	16	2	19	59	69	5	45	2	0	1	2	4	.313	.427	.531	.947
1995	Atl-N	120	411	73	104	17	2	24	78	73	5	68	2	0	5	4	2	.253	.365	.479	.984
1996	Atl-N	40	140	23	45	9	0	6	25	21	1	22	1	0	2	1	1	.321	.409	.514	1.000
1997	Cle-A	139	495	84	163	31	1	33	101	80	11	79	0	0	7	3	5	.329	.418	.596	.983
1998	Cle-A	146	540	94	151	39	2	21	88	76	7	98	0	0	9	9	3	.280	.363	.476	1.000
1999	Cle-A	133	429	75	123	18	0	21	88	94	0	90	0	0	5	1	3	.287	.411	.476	.977
2000	CLE-A	68	249	46	66	14	1	21	58	38	2	49	0	0	1	1	1	.265	.361	.582	.983
2000	**NY-A**	**78**	**275**	**43**	**84**	**17**	**0**	**20**	**60**	**39**	**1**	**42**	**1**	**0**	**2**	**1**	**0**	**.305**	**.391**	**.585**	**.981**
Career average		106	373	63	106	19	2	21	71	60	5	65	1	0	4	4	3	.283	.381	.513	.981
Yankee average		**78**	**275**	**43**	**84**	**17**	**0**	**20**	**60**	**39**	**1**	**42**	**1**	**0**	**2**	**1**	**0**	**.305**	**.391**	**.585**	**.981**
Career total		1381	4846	817	1373	246	20	276	917	779	66	850	15	1	48	48	43	.283	.381	.513	.981
Yankee total		**78**	**275**	**43**	**84**	**17**	**0**	**20**	**60**	**39**	**1**	**42**	**1**	**0**	**2**	**1**	**0**	**.305**	**.391**	**.585**	**.981**

Kane, Francis Thomas (Sugar)

HEIGHT: 5'11 1/2"   THROWS: RIGHT   BATS: LEFT   BORN: 3/9/1895, WHITMAN, MASS.   DIED: 12/2/1962, BROCKTON, MASS.   POSITIONS PLAYED: OF

YEAR	TEAM	GAMES	AB	RUNS	HITS	2B	3B	HR	RBI	BB	IBB	SO	HBP	SH	SF	SB	CS	BA	OBA	SA	FA
1915	Bro-F	3	10	2	2	0	1	0	2	0	0	0	0	0	0	0	0	.200	.200	.400	1.000
1919	**NY-A**	**1**	**1**	**0**	**0**	**0**	**0**	**0**	**0**	**0**	**0**	**0**	**0**	**0**	**0**	**0**	**0**	**.000**	**.000**	**.000**	**.000**
Career average		2	6	1	1	0	1	0	1	0	0	0	0	0	0	0	0	.182	.182	.364	.500
Yankee average		**1**	**0**	**0**	**0**	**0**	**0**	**0**	**0**	**0**	**0**	**0**	**0**	**0**	**0**	**0**	**0**	**.000**	**.000**	**.000**	**.000**
Career total		4	11	2	2	0	1	0	2	0	0	0	0	0	0	0	0	.182	.182	.364	.500
Yankee total		**1**	**0**	**0**	**0**	**0**	**0**	**0**	**0**	**0**	**0**	**0**	**0**	**0**	**0**	**0**	**0**	**.000**	**.000**	**.000**	**.000**

Karlon, William John (Hank)

HEIGHT: 6'1"   THROWS: RIGHT   BATS: RIGHT   BORN: 1/21/1909, PALMER, MASSACHUSETTS   DIED: 12/7/1964, WARE, MASSACHUSETTS   POSITIONS PLAYED: OF

YEAR	TEAM	GAMES	AB	RUNS	HITS	2B	3B	HR	RBI	BB	IBB	SO	HBP	SH	SF	SB	CS	BA	OBA	SA	FA
1930	**NY-A**	**2**	**5**	**0**	**0**	**0**	**0**	**0**	**0**	**0**	**0**	**1**	**0**	**0**	**0**	**0**	**0**	**.000**	**.000**	**.000**	**1.000**
Career average		2	5	0	0	0	0	0	0	0	0	1	0	0	0	0	0	.000	.000	.000	1.000
Yankee average		**2**	**5**	**0**	**0**	**0**	**0**	**0**	**0**	**0**	**0**	**1**	**0**	**0**	**0**	**0**	**0**	**.000**	**.000**	**.000**	**1.000**
Career total		2	5	0	0	0	0	0	0	0	0	1	0	0	0	0	0	.000	.000	.000	1.000
Yankee total		**2**	**5**	**0**	**0**	**0**	**0**	**0**	**0**	**0**	**0**	**1**	**0**	**0**	**0**	**0**	**0**	**.000**	**.000**	**.000**	**1.000**

Kauff, Benjamin Michael (Benny)

HEIGHT: 5'8"   THROWS: LEFT   BATS: LEFT   BORN: 1/5/1890, POMEROY, OHIO   DIED: 11/17/1961, COLUMBUS, OHIO   POSITIONS PLAYED: OF

YEAR	TEAM	GAMES	AB	RUNS	HITS	2B	3B	HR	RBI	BB	IBB	SO	HBP	SH	SF	SB	CS	BA	OBA	SA	FA
1912	**NY-A**	**5**	**11**	**4**	**3**	**0**	**0**	**0**	**2**	**3**	**0**	**0**	**0**	**0**	**0**	**1**	**0**	**.273**	**.429**	**.273**	**1.000**
1914	Ind-F	154	571	120	211	44	13	8	95	72	0	55	8	16	0	75	0	.370	.447	.534	.953
1915	Bro-F	136	483	92	165	23	11	12	83	85	0	50	6	7	0	55	0	.342	.446	.509	.959
1916	NY-N	154	552	71	146	22	15	9	74	68	0	65	3	9	0	40	26	.264	.348	.408	.962
1917	NY-N	153	559	89	172	22	4	5	68	59	0	54	5	21	0	30	0	.308	.379	.388	.976
1918	NY-N	67	270	41	85	19	4	2	39	16	0	30	1	7	0	9	0	.315	.355	.437	.952
1919	NY-N	135	491	73	136	27	7	10	67	39	0	45	3	11	0	21	0	.277	.334	.422	.950
1920	NY-N	55	157	31	43	12	3	3	26	25	0	14	2	4	0	3	7	.274	.380	.446	.960
Career average		107	387	65	120	21	7	6	57	46	0	39	4	9	0	29	4	.311	.389	.450	.964
Yankee average		**5**	**11**	**4**	**3**	**0**	**0**	**0**	**2**	**3**	**0**	**0**	**0**	**0**	**0**	**1**	**0**	**.273**	**.429**	**.273**	**1.000**
Career total		859	3094	521	961	169	57	49	454	367	0	313	28	75	0	234	33	.311	.389	.450	.964
Yankee total		**5**	**11**	**4**	**3**	**0**	**0**	**0**	**2**	**3**	**0**	**0**	**0**	**0**	**0**	**1**	**0**	**.273**	**.429**	**.273**	**1.000**

William Henry "Wee Willie" Keeler, of-2b-3b, 1903–09

One of the greatest hitters of the 19th and 20th centuries, Keeler came to the Yankees as a 31-year-old outfielder who had played in the National League his entire career.

Keeler, born William Henry O'Kelleher on March 3, 1872, in Brooklyn, New York, was 5 feet 4 inches and weighed 140 pounds. He was a terrific bunter and one of the fastest players in baseball. He began his career with the New York Giants in 1892, but was quickly picked up by Jack Dunn's Baltimore Orioles in 1894.

Baltimore is where Keeler made his reputation. He made 200 or more hits for eight consecutive years in Baltimore. In 1897, he had a league-leading 239 hits, good for a .424 batting average, the second best of all time.

He choked up almost a foot on his 30-inch bat, the smallest in the league. He was known for his famous "Baltimore chop," in which he would slap down at the ball and make it bounce high off the infield grass. By the time it came down, Keeler was on first base.

In fact, Keeler was certainly one of the players for whom the foul-strike rule was changed in the 19th century. Keeler could bunt a pitched ball almost at will, making his at-bats last for 20 or 30 pitches, because under the rule at the time, batters could not strike out on a bunted foul ball. Batters like Keeler forced the powers-that-be to adjust the rule so that batters who bunted a foul ball after two strikes would be out.

The 1897 season was the year Keeler hit in 44 consecutive games. Asked by a sportswriter what his secret was, Keeler thought about it and said, "Keep a clear eye, and hit 'em where they ain't." It became the most well-known baseball quote from the 19th century.

In 1903, the fledgling American League announced its intention to have a team in New York. Keeler, realizing that his career was winding down, signed with the New York Highlanders along with pitcher Jack Chesbro.

He led the team in batting average his first three years in New York, with a high of .343 in 1904. That was the year the Highlanders and the Boston Pilgrims went down to the wire for the American League pennant, with Boston winning. That was also the year Keeler collected two inside-the-park home runs in one game in a 9-1 win over the St. Louis Browns in New York.

Keeler was still productive through the 1907 season, but by 1908, he was relegated to part-time outfielder with the Highlanders. Nonetheless, young players praised Keeler for his willingness to help them out and give them advice to help their careers.

Keeler retired in 1910 after one last year with the New York Giants. He was elected to the Hall of Fame in 1939.

Kearse, Edward Paul (Truck)

HEIGHT: 6'3" THROWS: LEFT BATS: LEFT BORN: 4/14/1966, CINCINNATI, OHIO POSITIONS PLAYED: OF

YEAR	TEAM	GAMES	AB	RUNS	HITS	2B	3B	HR	RBI	BB	IBB	SO	HBP	SH	SF	SB	CS	BA	OBA	SA	FA
1942	NY-A	11	26	2	5	0	0	0	2	3	0	1	0	1	0	1	0	.192	.276	.192	1.000
Career average		11	26	2	5	0	0	0	2	3	0	1	0	1	0	1	0	.192	.276	.192	1.000
Yankee average		**11**	**26**	**2**	**5**	**0**	**0**	**0**	**2**	**3**	**0**	**1**	**0**	**1**	**0**	**1**	**0**	**.192**	**.276**	**.192**	**1.000**
Career total		11	26	2	5	0	0	0	2	3	0	1	0	1	0	1	0	.192	.276	.192	1.000
Yankee total		**11**	**26**	**2**	**5**	**0**	**0**	**0**	**2**	**3**	**0**	**1**	**0**	**1**	**0**	**1**	**0**	**.192**	**.276**	**.192**	**1.000**

Keeler, Willie Henry (Wee Willie)
HEIGHT: 5'5"   THROWS: LEFT   BATS: LEFT   BORN: 3/3/1872 BROOKLYN, NEW YORK   DIED: 1/1/1923 BROOKLYN, NEW YORK   POSITIONS PLAYED: 2B, 3B, OF

YEAR	TEAM	GAMES	AB	RUNS	HITS	2B	3B	HR	RBI	BB	IBB	SO	HBP	SH	SF	SB	CS	BA	OBA	SA	FA
1892	NY-N	14	53	7	17	3	0	0	6	3	0	3	0	0	0	5	0	.321	.357	.377	.878
1893	NY-N	7	24	5	8	2	1	1	7	5	0	1	0	0	0	3	0	.333	.448	.625	.750
1893	Bro-N	20	80	14	25	1	1	1	9	4	0	4	0	0	0	2	0	.313	.345	.388	.833
1894	Bal-N	129	590	165	219	27	22	5	94	40	0	6	18	16	0	32	0	.371	.427	.517	1.000
1895	Bal-N	131	565	162	213	24	15	4	78	37	0	12	14	21	0	47	0	.377	.429	.494	.964
1896	Bal-N	126	544	153	210	22	13	4	82	37	0	9	7	13	0	67	0	.386	.432	.496	.969
1897	Bal-N	129	564	145	239	27	19	0	74	35	0	0	7	12	0	64	0	.424	.464	.539	.970
1898	Bal-N	129	561	126	216	7	2	1	44	31	0	0	0	0	0	28	0	.385	.417	.410	.961
1899	Bro-N	141	570	140	216	12	13	1	61	37	0	0	9	17	0	45	0	.379	.425	.451	.969
1900	Bro-N	136	563	106	204	13	12	4	68	30	0	0	7	19	0	41	0	.362	.402	.449	1.000
1901	Bro-N	136	595	123	202	18	12	2	43	21	0	0	7	22	0	23	0	.339	.369	.420	1.000
1901	Bro-N	136	595	123	202	18	12	2	43	21	0	0	7	22	0	23	0	.339	.369	.420	.985
1902	Bro-N	133	559	86	186	20	5	0	38	21	0	0	7	25	0	19	0	.333	.365	.386	.978
1903	**NY-A**	**132**	**512**	**95**	**160**	**14**	**7**	**0**	**32**	**32**	**0**	**0**	**13**	**27**	**0**	**24**	**0**	**.313**	**.368**	**.367**	**.935**
1904	**NY-A**	**143**	**543**	**78**	**186**	**14**	**8**	**2**	**40**	**35**	**0**	**0**	**7**	**21**	**0**	**21**	**0**	**.343**	**.390**	**.409**	**.935**
1905	**NY-A**	**149**	**560**	**81**	**169**	**14**	**4**	**4**	**38**	**43**	**0**	**0**	**5**	**42**	**0**	**19**	**0**	**.302**	**.357**	**.363**	**.750**
1906	**NY-A**	**152**	**592**	**96**	**180**	**8**	**3**	**2**	**33**	**40**	**0**	**0**	**5**	**35**	**0**	**23**	**0**	**.304**	**.353**	**.338**	**.987**
1907	**NY-A**	**107**	**423**	**50**	**99**	**5**	**2**	**0**	**17**	**15**	**0**	**0**	**3**	**26**	**0**	**7**	**0**	**.234**	**.265**	**.255**	**.969**
1908	**NY-A**	**91**	**323**	**38**	**85**	**3**	**1**	**1**	**14**	**31**	**0**	**0**	**5**	**21**	**0**	**14**	**0**	**.263**	**.337**	**.288**	**.936**
1909	**NY-A**	**99**	**360**	**44**	**95**	**7**	**5**	**1**	**32**	**24**	**0**	**0**	**10**	**33**	**0**	**10**	**0**	**.264**	**.327**	**.319**	**.968**
1910	NY-N	19	10	5	3	0	0	0	0	3	0	1	0	1	0	1	0	.300	.462	.300	1.000
Career average		108	437	88	149	12	7	2	41	26	0	2	6	18	0	25	0	.341	.386	.415	.940
Yankee average		**125**	**473**	**69**	**139**	**9**	**4**	**1**	**29**	**31**	**0**	**0**	**7**	**30**	**0**	**17**	**0**	**.294**	**.347**	**.341**	**.926**
Career total		2259	9186	1842	3134	259	157	35	853	545	0	36	131	379	0	518	0	.341	.386	.415	.940
Yankee total		**873**	**3313**	**482**	**974**	**65**	**30**	**10**	**206**	**220**	**0**	**0**	**48**	**211**	**0**	**118**	**0**	**.294**	**.347**	**.341**	**.926**

Keller, Charles Ernest (King Kong)
HEIGHT: 5'10"   THROWS: RIGHT   BATS: LEFT   BORN: 9/12/1916, MIDDLETOWN, MARYLAND   DIED: 5/23/1990, FREDERICK, MARYLAND   POSITIONS PLAYED: OF

YEAR	TEAM	GAMES	AB	RUNS	HITS	2B	3B	HR	RBI	BB	IBB	SO	HBP	SH	SF	SB	CS	BA	OBA	SA	FA
1939	**NY-A**	**111**	**398**	**87**	**133**	**21**	**6**	**11**	**83**	**81**	**0**	**49**	**0**	**11**	**0**	**6**	**3**	**.334**	**.447**	**.500**	**.969**
1940	**NY-A**	**138**	**500**	**102**	**143**	**18**	**15**	**21**	**93**	**106**	**0**	**65**	**0**	**3**	**0**	**8**	**2**	**.286**	**.411**	**.508**	**.967**
1941	**NY-A**	**140**	**507**	**102**	**151**	**24**	**10**	**33**	**122**	**102**	**0**	**65**	**1**	**0**	**0**	**6**	**4**	**.298**	**.416**	**.580**	**.980**
1942	**NY-A**	**152**	**544**	**106**	**159**	**24**	**9**	**26**	**108**	**114**	**0**	**61**	**2**	**1**	**0**	**14**	**2**	**.292**	**.417**	**.513**	**.985**
1943	**NY-A**	**141**	**512**	**97**	**139**	**15**	**11**	**31**	**86**	**106**	**0**	**60**	**0**	**2**	**0**	**7**	**5**	**.271**	**.396**	**.525**	**.994**
1945	**NY-A**	**44**	**163**	**26**	**49**	**7**	**4**	**10**	**34**	**31**	**0**	**21**	**0**	**0**	**0**	**0**	**2**	**.301**	**.412**	**.577**	**1.000**
1946	**NY-A**	**150**	**538**	**98**	**148**	**29**	**10**	**30**	**101**	**113**	**0**	**101**	**4**	**0**	**0**	**1**	**4**	**.275**	**.405**	**.533**	**.979**
1947	**NY-A**	**45**	**151**	**36**	**36**	**6**	**1**	**13**	**36**	**41**	**0**	**18**	**1**	**0**	**0**	**0**	**0**	**.238**	**.404**	**.550**	**.967**
1948	**NY-A**	**83**	**247**	**41**	**66**	**15**	**2**	**6**	**44**	**41**	**0**	**25**	**0**	**1**	**0**	**1**	**1**	**.267**	**.372**	**.417**	**.977**
1949	**NY-A**	**60**	**116**	**17**	**29**	**4**	**1**	**3**	**16**	**25**	**0**	**15**	**2**	**1**	**0**	**2**	**0**	**.250**	**.392**	**.379**	**.976**
1950	Det-A	50	51	7	16	1	3	2	16	13	0	6	0	0	0	0	0	.314	.453	.569	1.000
1951	Det-A	54	62	6	16	2	0	3	21	11	0	12	0	1	0	0	0	.258	.370	.435	1.000
1952	**NY-A**	**2**	**1**	**0**	**0**	**0**	**0**	**0**	**0**	**0**	**0**	**1**	**0**	**0**	**0**	**0**	**0**	**.000**	**.000**	**.000**	**.000**
Career average		90	292	56	84	13	6	15	59	60	0	38	1	2	0	4	2	.286	.410	.518	.907
Yankee average		**97**	**334**	**65**	**96**	**15**	**6**	**17**	**66**	**69**	**0**	**44**	**1**	**2**	**0**	**4**	**2**	**.286**	**.410**	**.518**	**.890**
Career total		1170	3790	725	1085	166	72	189	760	784	0	499	10	20	0	45	23	.286	.410	.518	.907
Yankee total		**1066**	**3677**	**712**	**1053**	**163**	**69**	**184**	**723**	**760**	**0**	**481**	**10**	**19**	**0**	**45**	**23**	**.286**	**.410**	**.518**	**.890**

Kelly, Patrick Franklin
HEIGHT: 6'0"   THROWS: RIGHT   BATS: RIGHT   BORN: 10/14/1967, PHILADELPHIA, PENNSYLVANIA   POSITIONS PLAYED: OF

YEAR	TEAM	GAMES	AB	RUNS	HITS	2B	3B	HR	RBI	BB	IBB	SO	HBP	SH	SF	SB	CS	BA	OBA	SA	FA
1991	**NY-A**	**96**	**298**	**35**	**72**	**12**	**4**	**3**	**23**	**15**	**0**	**52**	**5**	**2**	**2**	**12**	**1**	**.242**	**.288**	**.339**	**.926**
1992	**NY-A**	**106**	**318**	**38**	**72**	**22**	**2**	**7**	**27**	**25**	**1**	**72**	**10**	**6**	**3**	**8**	**5**	**.226**	**.301**	**.374**	**.978**
1993	**NY-A**	**127**	**406**	**49**	**111**	**24**	**1**	**7**	**51**	**24**	**0**	**68**	**5**	**10**	**6**	**14**	**11**	**.273**	**.317**	**.389**	**.978**
1994	**NY-A**	**93**	**286**	**35**	**80**	**21**	**2**	**3**	**41**	**19**	**1**	**51**	**5**	**14**	**5**	**6**	**5**	**.280**	**.330**	**.399**	**.978**
1995	**NY-A**	**89**	**270**	**32**	**64**	**12**	**1**	**4**	**29**	**23**	**0**	**65**	**5**	**10**	**2**	**8**	**3**	**.237**	**.330**	**.333**	**.983**
1996	**NY-A**	**13**	**21**	**4**	**3**	**0**	**0**	**0**	**2**	**2**	**0**	**9**	**0**	**0**	**0**	**0**	**1**	**.143**	**.217**	**.143**	**.970**
1997	**NY-A**	**67**	**120**	**25**	**29**	**6**	**1**	**2**	**10**	**14**	**1**	**37**	**1**	**2**	**1**	**8**	**1**	**.242**	**.324**	**.358**	**.981**
1998	StL-N	53	153	18	33	5	0	4	14	13	0	48	0	1	1	5	1	.216	.275	.327	1.000
1999	Tor-A	37	116	17	31	7	0	6	20	10	0	23	0	1	3	0	1	.267	.318	.483	.962
Career average		76	221	28	55	12	1	4	24	16	0	47	3	5	3	7	3	.249	.307	.369	.973
Yankee average		**84**	**246**	**31**	**62**	**14**	**2**	**4**	**26**	**17**	**0**	**51**	**4**	**6**	**3**	**8**	**4**	**.251**	**.309**	**.365**	**.971**
Career total		681	1988	253	495	109	11	36	217	145	3	425	31	46	23	61	29	.249	.307	.369	.973
Yankee total		**591**	**1719**	**218**	**431**	**97**	**11**	**26**	**183**	**122**	**3**	**354**	**31**	**44**	**19**	**56**	**27**	**.251**	**.309**	**.365**	**.971**

Charles Ernest "King Kong" Keller, of, 1939–43

Keller was nicknamed "King Kong" because of his great strength and hairy body. He was a quiet man in the Yankee clubhouse but one of the team's leaders almost from the start of his career.

Born September 19, 1916, in Middletown, Maryland, Keller was a baseball and football star at the University of Maryland. He was courted by several major league teams following his senior season, and eventually signed with the Yankees for a $2,500 bonus.

He moved up quickly in the Yankees' farm system. He played for the Newark Bears in 1937 and 1938, leading them to the championship both years. Keller was Minor League Player of the Year in 1937.

The Yankees brought him up in 1939, and he hit .334, fifth in the league. In the World Series, Keller tore up the Cincinnati Reds, hitting .438 with three home runs, 6 RBI and eight runs scored. He was part of an outfield considered among the best ever, with Joe DiMaggio and Tommy Henrich.

He was never afraid to openly criticize a teammate, and his size made it unlikely that a teammate would retort. Only the diminutive shortstop Phil Rizzuto could sometimes get away with needling Keller. But if he went too far, Rizzuto knew that Keller would simply pick him up and stuff him in a nearby locker.

Keller was not as fearsome a hitter as DiMaggio, and perhaps not as deadly in the clutch as Henrich, but he was tremendously consistent. He drew over 100 walks 5 times in his 11-year Yankee career, leading the league in 1940 and 1943. He had over 130 hits six times. He was not a formidable home run hitter, but he struck 20 or more five times.

By 1947, a degenerative disc problem in his back began to limit his playing time. At the end of the 1949 season, with several other outfield prospects in the wings, Keller was released. He eventually retired to his horse farm, Yankeeland, in Maryland, for good in 1952. He died in 1990.

A five-time All-Star with New York, Keller is 11th on both the Yankees home run list with 184 and triples with 69.

Kelly, Roberto Conrado   BORN ROBERTO CONRADO KELLY (GRAY)

HEIGHT: 6'2"   THROWS: RIGHT   BATS: RIGHT   BORN: 10/1/1964, PANAMA CITY, PANAMA   POSITIONS PLAYED: OF

YEAR	TEAM	GAMES	AB	RUNS	HITS	2B	3B	HR	RBI	BB	IBB	SO	HBP	SH	SF	SB	CS	BA	OBA	SA	FA
1987	NY-A	23	52	12	14	3	0	1	7	5	0	15	0	1	1	9	3	.269	.328	.385	.955
1988	NY-A	38	77	9	19	4	1	1	7	3	0	15	0	3	1	5	2	.247	.272	.364	.986
1989	NY-A	137	441	65	133	18	3	9	48	41	3	89	6	8	0	35	12	.285	.323	.418	.988
1990	NY-A	162	641	85	183	32	4	9	61	33	0	148	4	4	4	42	17	.285	.323	.418	.988
1991	NY-A	126	486	68	130	22	2	20	69	45	2	77	5	2	5	32	9	.267	.333	.444	.986
1992	NY-A	152	580	81	158	31	2	10	66	41	4	96	4	1	6	28	5	.272	.322	.384	.983
1993	Cin-N	78	320	44	102	17	3	9	35	17	0	43	2	0	3	21	5	.319	.354	.475	.992
1994	Cin-N	47	179	29	54	8	0	3	21	11	1	35	3	0	1	9	8	.302	.351	.397	.992
1994	Atl-N	63	255	44	73	15	3	6	24	24	0	36	0	0	2	10	3	.286	.345	.439	1.000
1995	Mon-N	24	95	11	26	4	0	1	9	7	1	14	2	0	0	4	3	.274	.337	.347	.985
1995	LA-N	112	409	47	114	19	2	6	48	15	5	65	4	0	7	15	7	.279	.306	.379	.969
1996	Min-A	98	322	41	104	17	4	6	47	23	0	53	7	0	5	10	2	.323	.375	.457	1.000
1997	Min-A	75	247	39	71	19	2	5	37	17	0	50	2	1	2	7	4	.287	.336	.441	1.000
1997	Sea-A	30	121	19	36	7	0	7	22	5	0	17	1	1	1	2	1	.298	.328	.529	1.000
1998	Tex-A	75	257	48	83	7	3	16	46	8	0	46	0	1	1	0	2	.323	.342	.560	1.000
1999	Tex-A	87	290	41	87	17	1	8	37	21	0	57	0	0	2	6	1	.300	.345	.448	.981
2000	NY-A	10	25	4	3	1	0	1	1	1	0	6	1	0	0	0	0	.120	.185	.280	1.000
Career average		79	282	40	82	14	2	7	34	19	1	51	2	1	2	14	5	.290	.336	.430	.988
Yankee average		93	329	46	91	16	2	8	37	24	1	64	3	3	2	22	7	.278	.331	.411	.983
Career total		1337	4797	687	1390	241	30	124	585	317	16	862	41	22	41	235	84	.290	.336	.430	.988
Yankee total		648	2302	324	640	111	12	57	259	169	9	446	20	19	17	151	48	.278	.331	.411	.983

Kemp, Steven F.

HEIGHT: 6'0" THROWS: LEFT BATS: LEFT BORN: 8/7/1954, SAN ANGELO, TEXAS POSITIONS PLAYED: OF

YEAR	TEAM	GAMES	AB	RUNS	HITS	2B	3B	HR	RBI	BB	IBB	SO	HBP	SH	SF	SB	CS	BA	OBA	SA	FA
1977	Det-A	151	552	75	142	29	4	18	88	71	0	93	5	1	7	3	3	.257	.343	.422	.981
1978	Det-A	159	582	75	161	18	4	15	79	97	3	87	1	3	3	2	3	.277	.379	.399	.977
1979	Det-A	134	490	88	156	26	3	26	105	68	2	70	2	2	8	5	6	.318	.398	.543	.976
1980	Det-A	135	508	88	149	23	3	21	101	69	3	64	4	1	9	5	1	.293	.376	.474	.995
1981	Det-A	105	372	52	103	18	4	9	49	70	5	48	1	0	4	9	3	.277	.389	.419	.986
1982	Chi-A	160	580	91	166	23	1	19	98	89	8	83	3	1	6	7	7	.286	.381	.428	.976
1983	**NY-A**	**109**	**373**	**53**	**90**	**17**	**3**	**12**	**49**	**41**	**3**	**37**	**2**	**1**	**2**	**1**	**0**	**.241**	**.318**	**.399**	**.987**
1984	**NY-A**	**94**	**313**	**37**	**91**	**12**	**1**	**7**	**41**	**40**	**0**	**54**	**1**	**3**	**4**	**4**	**1**	**.291**	**.369**	**.403**	**.972**
1985	Pit-N	92	236	19	59	13	2	2	21	25	1	54	0	1	4	1	0	.250	.317	.347	1.000
1986	Pit-N	13	16	1	3	0	0	1	1	4	0	6	0	0	0	1	0	.188	.350	.375	1.000
1988	Tex-A	16	36	2	8	0	0	0	2	2	0	9	0	0	1	1	0	.222	.256	.222	1.000
Career average		106	369	53	103	16	2	12	58	52	2	55	2	1	4	4	2	.278	.367	.431	.986
Yankee average		**102**	**343**	**45**	**91**	**15**	**2**	**10**	**45**	**41**	**2**	**46**	**2**	**2**	**3**	**3**	**1**	**.264**	**.341**	**.401**	**.980**
Career total		1168	4058	581	1128	179	25	130	634	576	25	605	19	13	48	39	24	.278	.367	.431	.986
Yankee total		**203**	**686**	**90**	**181**	**29**	**4**	**19**	**90**	**81**	**3**	**91**	**3**	**4**	**6**	**5**	**1**	**.264**	**.341**	**.401**	**.980**

Kennedy, John Edward

HEIGHT: 6'0" THROWS: RIGHT BATS: RIGHT BORN: 5/29/1941, CHICAGO, ILLINOIS POSITIONS PLAYED: 1B, 2B, 3B, SS

YEAR	TEAM	GAMES	AB	RUNS	HITS	2B	3B	HR	RBI	BB	IBB	SO	HBP	SH	SF	SB	CS	BA	OBA	SA	FA
1962	Was-A	14	42	6	11	0	1	1	2	2	0	7	0	0	0	0	1	.262	.295	.381	.974
1963	Was-A	36	62	3	11	1	1	0	4	6	0	22	1	0	0	2	0	.177	.261	.226	.954
1964	Was-A	148	482	55	111	16	4	7	35	29	2	119	5	4	1	3	3	.230	.280	.324	1.000
1965	LA-N	104	105	12	18	3	0	1	5	8	1	33	2	5	0	1	0	.171	.243	.229	.971
1966	LA-N	125	274	15	55	9	2	3	24	10	1	64	5	4	1	1	2	.201	.241	.281	1.000
1967	**NY-A**	**78**	**179**	**22**	**35**	**4**	**0**	**1**	**17**	**17**	**0**	**35**	**1**	**8**	**3**	**2**	**1**	**.196**	**.265**	**.235**	**.960**
1969	Sea-A	61	128	18	30	3	1	4	14	14	1	25	1	2	0	4	0	.234	.315	.367	.967
1970	Mil-A	25	55	8	14	2	0	2	6	5	0	9	0	2	0	0	1	.255	.317	.400	.921
1970	Bos-A	43	129	15	33	7	1	4	17	6	1	14	1	1	1	0	0	.256	.292	.419	.960
1971	Bos-A	74	272	41	75	12	5	5	22	14	0	42	4	5	1	1	1	.276	.320	.412	.974
1972	Bos-A	71	212	22	52	11	1	2	22	18	4	40	3	2	2	0	1	.245	.311	.335	.824
1973	Bos-A	67	155	17	28	9	1	1	16	12	0	45	2	3	2	0	0	.181	.246	.271	.946
1974	Bos-A	10	15	3	2	0	0	1	1	1	0	6	0	0	0	0	0	.133	.188	.333	1.000
Career average		66	162	18	37	6	1	3	14	11	1	36	2	3	1	1	1	.225	.281	.323	.958
Yankee average		**78**	**179**	**22**	**35**	**4**	**0**	**1**	**17**	**17**	**0**	**35**	**1**	**8**	**3**	**2**	**1**	**.196**	**.265**	**.235**	**.960**
Career total		856	2110	237	475	77	17	32	185	142	10	461	25	36	11	14	10	.225	.281	.323	.958
Yankee total		**78**	**179**	**22**	**35**	**4**	**0**	**1**	**17**	**17**	**0**	**35**	**1**	**8**	**3**	**2**	**1**	**.196**	**.265**	**.235**	**.960**

Kenney, Gerald Tennyson Jr. (Jerry)

HEIGHT: 6'1" THROWS: RIGHT BATS: LEFT BORN: 6/30/1945, ST. LOUIS, MISSOURI POSITIONS PLAYED: SS, 2B, 3B

YEAR	TEAM	GAMES	AB	RUNS	HITS	2B	3B	HR	RBI	BB	IBB	SO	HBP	SH	SF	SB	CS	BA	OBA	SA	FA
1967	**NY-A**	**20**	**58**	**4**	**18**	**2**	**0**	**1**	**5**	**10**	**0**	**8**	**0**	**6**	**0**	**2**	**1**	**.310**	**.412**	**.397**	**.952**
1969	**NY-A**	**130**	**447**	**49**	**115**	**14**	**2**	**2**	**34**	**48**	**2**	**36**	**1**	**9**	**4**	**25**	**14**	**.257**	**.328**	**.311**	**.975**
1970	**NY-A**	**140**	**404**	**46**	**78**	**10**	**7**	**4**	**35**	**52**	**2**	**44**	**0**	**3**	**2**	**20**	**6**	**.193**	**.284**	**.282**	**1.000**
1971	**NY-A**	**120**	**325**	**50**	**85**	**10**	**3**	**0**	**20**	**56**	**3**	**38**	**1**	**9**	**4**	**9**	**8**	**.262**	**.368**	**.311**	**1.000**
1972	**NY-A**	**50**	**119**	**16**	**25**	**2**	**0**	**0**	**7**	**16**	**2**	**13**	**0**	**1**	**0**	**3**	**0**	**.210**	**.304**	**.227**	**1.000**
1973	Cle-A	5	16	0	4	0	1	0	2	2	0	0	0	0	1	0	0	.250	.316	.375	1.000
Career average		78	228	28	54	6	2	1	17	31	2	23	0	5	2	10	5	.237	.326	.299	.988
Yankee average		**92**	**271**	**33**	**64**	**8**	**2**	**1**	**20**	**36**	**2**	**28**	**0**	**6**	**2**	**12**	**6**	**.237**	**.326**	**.299**	**.985**
Career total		465	1369	165	325	38	13	7	103	184	9	139	2	28	11	59	29	.237	.326	.299	.988
Yankee total		**460**	**1353**	**165**	**321**	**38**	**12**	**7**	**101**	**182**	**9**	**139**	**2**	**28**	**10**	**59**	**29**	**.237**	**.326**	**.299**	**.985**

Kingman, David Arthur (Kong)
HEIGHT: 6'6"   THROWS: RIGHT   BATS: RIGHT   BORN: 12/21/1948, PENDLETON, OREGON   POSITIONS PLAYED: 1B, OF, 3B

YEAR	TEAM	GAMES	AB	RUNS	HITS	2B	3B	HR	RBI	BB	IBB	SO	HBP	SH	SF	SB	CS	BA	OBA	SA	FA
1971	SF-N	41	115	17	32	10	2	6	24	9	0	35	1	0	3	5	0	.278	.328	.557	.950
1972	SF-N	135	472	65	106	17	4	29	83	51	2	140	4	0	4	16	6	.225	.303	.462	.932
1973	SF-N	112	305	54	62	10	1	24	55	41	3	122	2	1	2	8	5	.203	.300	.479	.910
1974	SF-N	121	350	41	78	18	2	18	55	37	2	125	3	2	1	8	8	.223	.302	.440	.983
1975	NY-N	134	502	65	116	22	1	36	88	34	5	153	4	1	2	7	5	.231	.284	.494	.919
1976	NY-N	123	474	70	113	14	1	37	86	28	4	135	5	0	3	7	4	.238	.286	.506	1.000
1977	NY-N	58	211	22	44	7	0	9	28	13	3	66	3	0	1	3	2	.209	.263	.370	.992
1977	SD-N	56	168	16	40	9	0	11	39	12	1	48	2	2	3	2	3	.238	.292	.488	.833
1977	Cal-A	10	36	4	7	2	0	2	4	1	0	16	1	1	0	0	0	.194	.237	.417	.974
1977	**NY-A**	**8**	**24**	**5**	**6**	**2**	**0**	**4**	**7**	**2**	**0**	**13**	**1**	**0**	**0**	**0**	**1**	**.250**	**.333**	**.833**	**.000**
1978	Chi-N	119	395	65	105	17	4	28	79	39	8	111	6	2	6	3	4	.266	.336	.542	.978
1979	Chi-N	145	532	97	153	19	5	48	115	45	7	131	4	0	8	4	2	.288	.343	.613	.954
1980	Chi-N	81	255	31	71	8	0	18	57	21	3	44	0	0	4	2	2	.278	.329	.522	.941
1981	NY-N	100	353	40	78	11	3	22	59	55	7	105	1	1	2	6	0	.221	.326	.456	.974
1982	NY-N	149	535	80	109	9	1	37	99	59	9	156	4	3	6	4	0	.204	.285	.432	.986
1983	NY-N	100	248	25	49	7	0	13	29	22	1	57	1	1	1	2	1	.198	.265	.383	1.000
1984	Oak-A	147	549	68	147	23	1	35	118	44	8	119	6	0	14	2	1	.268	.321	.505	1.000
1985	Oak-A	158	592	66	141	16	0	30	91	62	6	114	2	2	8	3	2	.238	.309	.417	1.000
1986	Oak-A	144	561	70	118	19	0	35	94	33	3	126	3	0	7	3	3	.210	.255	.431	.895

		GAMES	AB	RUNS	HITS	2B	3B	HR	RBI	BB	IBB	SO	HBP	SH	SF	SB	CS	BA	OBA	SA	FA
Career average		102	351	47	83	13	1	23	64	32	4	96	3	1	4	5	3	.236	.302	.478	.906
Yankee average		**8**	**24**	**5**	**6**	**2**	**0**	**4**	**7**	**2**	**0**	**13**	**1**	**0**	**0**	**0**	**1**	**.250**	**.333**	**.833**	**.000**
Career total		1941	6677	901	1575	240	25	442	1210	608	72	1816	53	16	75	85	49	.236	.302	.478	.906
Yankee total		**8**	**24**	**5**	**6**	**2**	**0**	**4**	**7**	**2**	**0**	**13**	**1**	**0**	**0**	**0**	**1**	**.250**	**.333**	**.833**	**.000**

Kingman, Henry Lees
HEIGHT: 6'2"   THROWS: LEFT   BATS: LEFT   BORN: 4/3/1892, TIENTSIN, CHINA   DIED: 12/27/1982, OAKLAND, CALIFORNIA   POSITIONS PLAYED: 1B

YEAR	TEAM	GAMES	AB	RUNS	HITS	2B	3B	HR	RBI	BB	IBB	SO	HBP	SH	SF	SB	CS	BA	OBA	SA	FA
1914	**NY-A**	**4**	**3**	**0**	**0**	**0**	**0**	**0**	**0**	**1**	**0**	**2**	**0**	**0**	**0**	**0**	**0**	**.000**	**.250**	**.000**	**1.000**
Career average		4	3	0	0	0	0	0	0	1	0	2	0	0	0	0	0	.000	.250	.000	1.000
Yankee average		**4**	**3**	**0**	**0**	**0**	**0**	**0**	**0**	**1**	**0**	**2**	**0**	**0**	**0**	**0**	**0**	**.000**	**.250**	**.000**	**1.000**
Career total		4	3	0	0	0	0	0	0	1	0	2	0	0	0	0	0	.000	.250	.000	1.000
Yankee total		**4**	**3**	**0**	**0**	**0**	**0**	**0**	**0**	**1**	**0**	**2**	**0**	**0**	**0**	**0**	**0**	**.000**	**.250**	**.000**	**1.000**

Kittle, Ronald Dale (Kitty)
HEIGHT: 6'4"   THROWS: RIGHT   BATS: RIGHT   BORN: 1/5/1958, GARY, INDIANA   POSITIONS PLAYED: OF, DH

YEAR	TEAM	GAMES	AB	RUNS	HITS	2B	3B	HR	RBI	BB	IBB	SO	HBP	SH	SF	SB	CS	BA	OBA	SA	FA
1982	Chi-A	20	29	3	7	2	0	1	7	3	0	12	0	0	0	0	0	.241	.313	.414	1.000
1983	Chi-A	145	520	75	132	19	3	35	100	39	8	150	8	0	3	8	3	.254	.314	.504	.964
1984	Chi-A	139	466	67	100	15	0	32	74	49	5	137	6	0	4	3	6	.215	.295	.453	.972
1985	Chi-A	116	379	51	87	12	0	26	58	31	1	92	5	0	2	1	4	.230	.295	.467	.989
1986	Chi-A	86	296	34	63	11	0	17	48	28	0	87	3	0	6	2	1	.213	.282	.422	1.000
1986	**NY-A**	**30**	**80**	**8**	**19**	**2**	**0**	**4**	**12**	**7**	**1**	**23**	**0**	**0**	**2**	**2**	**0**	**.238**	**.292**	**.413**	**1.000**
1987	**NY-A**	**59**	**159**	**21**	**44**	**5**	**0**	**12**	**28**	**10**	**1**	**36**	**1**	**0**	**3**	**0**	**1**	**.277**	**.318**	**.535**	**1.000**
1988	Cle-A	75	225	31	58	8	0	18	43	16	1	65	8	0	5	0	0	.258	.323	.533	.000
1989	Chi-A	51	169	26	51	10	0	11	37	22	1	42	1	0	4	0	1	.302	.378	.556	.982
1990	Chi-A	83	277	29	68	14	0	16	43	24	2	77	3	0	1	0	0	.245	.311	.469	.987
1990	Bal-A	22	61	4	10	2	0	2	3	2	0	14	1	0	0	0	0	.164	.203	.295	1.000
1991	Chi-A	17	47	7	9	0	0	2	7	5	0	9	2	0	1	0	0	.191	.291	.319	.982

		GAMES	AB	RUNS	HITS	2B	3B	HR	RBI	BB	IBB	SO	HBP	SH	SF	SB	CS	BA	OBA	SA	FA
Career average		44	143	19	34	5	0	9	24	12	1	39	2	0	2	1	1	.239	.306	.473	.906
Yankee average		**30**	**80**	**10**	**21**	**2**	**0**	**5**	**13**	**6**	**1**	**20**	**0**	**0**	**2**	**1**	**0**	**.264**	**.309**	**.494**	**1.000**
Career total		843	2708	356	648	100	3	176	460	236	20	744	38	0	31	16	16	.239	.306	.473	.906
Yankee total		**89**	**239**	**29**	**63**	**7**	**0**	**16**	**40**	**17**	**2**	**59**	**1**	**0**	**5**	**2**	**1**	**.264**	**.309**	**.494**	**1.000**

Kleinow, John Peter (Red)

HEIGHT: 5'10" THROWS: RIGHT BATS: RIGHT BORN: 7/20/1879, MILWAUKEE, WIS. DIED: 10/9/1929, NEW YORK, N.Y. POSITIONS PLAYED: C, 1B, 2B, 3B, OF

YEAR	TEAM	GAMES	AB	RUNS	HITS	2B	3B	HR	RBI	BB	IBB	SO	HBP	SH	SF	SB	CS	BA	OBA	SA	FA
1904	**NY-A**	**68**	**209**	**12**	**43**	**8**	**4**	**0**	**16**	**15**	—	—	**0**	**6**	—	**4**	—	**.206**	**.259**	**.282**	**.966**
1905	**NY-A**	**88**	**253**	**23**	**56**	**6**	**3**	**1**	**24**	**20**	—	—	**2**	**3**	—	**7**	—	**.221**	**.284**	**.281**	**.978**
1906	**NY-A**	**96**	**268**	**30**	**59**	**9**	**3**	**0**	**31**	**24**	—	—	**1**	**13**	—	**8**	—	**.220**	**.287**	**.276**	**.972**
1907	**NY-A**	**90**	**269**	**30**	**71**	**6**	**4**	**0**	**26**	**24**	—	—	**1**	**7**	—	**5**	—	**.264**	**.327**	**.316**	**1.000**
1908	**NY-A**	**96**	**279**	**16**	**47**	**3**	**2**	**1**	**13**	**22**	—	—	**3**	**8**	—	**5**	—	**.168**	**.237**	**.204**	**.800**
1909	**NY-A**	**78**	**206**	**24**	**47**	**11**	**4**	**0**	**15**	**25**	—	—	**1**	**9**	—	**7**	—	**.228**	**.315**	**.320**	**.966**
1910	**NY-A**	**6**	**12**	**2**	**5**	**0**	**0**	**0**	**2**	**1**	—	—	**0**	**0**	—	**2**	—	**.417**	**.462**	**.417**	**1.000**
1910	Bos-A	50	147	9	22	1	0	1	8	20	—	—	0	2	—	3	—	.150	.251	.177	.968
1911	Bos-A	8	14	0	3	0	0	0	0	2	—	—	0	1	—	1	—	.214	.313	.214	1.000
1911	Phi-N	4	8	0	1	1	0	0	0	0	—	1	0	0	—	0	—	.125	.125	.250	1.000
Career average	58	167	15	35	5	2	0	14	15	—	—	1	5	—	4	—	.213	.282	.269	.965
Yankee average	**75**	**214**	**20**	**47**	**6**	**3**	**0**	**18**	**19**	—	—	**1**	**7**	—	**5**	—	**.219**	**.286**	**.279**	**.955**
Career total	584	1665	146	354	45	20	3	135	153	—	1	8	49	—	42	—	.213	.282	.269	.965
Yankee total	**522**	**1496**	**137**	**328**	**43**	**20**	**2**	**127**	**131**	—	—	**8**	**46**	—	**38**	—	**.219**	**.286**	**.279**	**.955**

Klutts, Gene Ellis (Mickey)

HEIGHT: 5'11" THROWS: RIGHT BATS: RIGHT BORN: 9/20/1954, MONTEBELLO, CALIFORNIA POSITIONS PLAYED: 3B

YEAR	TEAM	GAMES	AB	RUNS	HITS	2B	3B	HR	RBI	BB	IBB	SO	HBP	SH	SF	SB	CS	BA	OBA	SA	FA
1976	**NY-A**	**2**	**3**	**0**	**0**	**0**	**0**	**0**	**0**	**0**	**0**	**1**	**0**	**0**	**0**	**0**	**0**	**.000**	**.000**	**.000**	**.875**
1977	**NY-A**	**5**	**15**	**3**	**4**	**1**	**0**	**1**	**4**	**2**	**0**	**1**	**1**	**0**	**0**	**0**	**1**	**.267**	**.389**	**.533**	**1.000**
1978	**NY-A**	**1**	**2**	**1**	**2**	**1**	**0**	**0**	**0**	**0**	**0**	**0**	**1**	**0**	**0**	**0**	**0**	**1.000**	**1.000**	**1.500**	**.750**
1979	Oak-A	24	73	3	14	2	1	1	4	7	0	20	0	0	0	0	1	.192	.263	.288	.882
1980	Oak-A	75	197	20	53	14	0	4	21	13	1	41	0	1	1	1	4	.269	.313	.401	.950
1981	Oak-A	15	46	9	17	0	0	5	11	2	1	9	0	0	0	0	0	.370	.396	.696	.957
1982	Oak-A	55	157	10	28	8	0	0	14	9	1	18	0	3	1	0	0	.178	.222	.229	.946
1983	Tor-A	22	43	3	11	0	0	3	5	1	1	11	1	0	0	0	1	.256	.289	.465	1.000
Career average	25	67	6	16	3	0	2	7	4	0	13	0	1	0	0	1	.241	.289	.371	.920
Yankee average	**3**	**7**	**1**	**2**	**1**	**0**	**0**	**1**	**1**	**0**	**1**	**1**	**0**	**0**	**0**	**0**	**.300**	**.417**	**.550**	**.875**
Career total	199	536	49	129	26	1	14	59	34	3	101	3	4	2	1	7	.241	.289	.371	.920
Yankee total	**8**	**20**	**4**	**6**	**2**	**0**	**1**	**4**	**2**	**0**	**2**	**2**	**0**	**0**	**0**	**1**	**.300**	**.417**	**.550**	**.875**

Knickerbocker, William Hart

HEIGHT: 5'11" THROWS: RIGHT BATS: RIGHT BORN: 12/29/1911, LOS ANGELES, CALIFORNIA DIED: 9/8/1963, SEBASTOPOL, CALIFORNIA POSITIONS PLAYED: SS

YEAR	TEAM	GAMES	AB	RUNS	HITS	2B	3B	HR	RBI	BB	IBB	SO	HBP	SH	SF	SB	CS	BA	OBA	SA	FA
1933	Cle-A	80	279	20	63	16	3	2	32	11	0	30	0	13	0	1	4	.226	.255	.326	.939
1934	Cle-A	146	593	82	188	32	5	4	67	25	0	40	2	12	0	6	6	.317	.347	.408	.962
1935	Cle-A	132	540	77	161	34	5	0	55	27	0	31	0	10	0	2	12	.298	.332	.380	.956
1936	Cle-A	155	618	81	182	35	3	8	73	56	0	30	1	11	0	5	14	.294	.354	.400	.952
1937	StL-A	121	491	53	128	29	5	4	61	30	0	32	0	9	0	3	2	.261	.303	.365	.963
1938	**NY-A**	**46**	**128**	**15**	**32**	**8**	**3**	**1**	**21**	**11**	**0**	**10**	**0**	**4**	**0**	**0**	**0**	**.250**	**.309**	**.383**	**1.000**
1939	**NY-A**	**6**	**13**	**2**	**2**	**1**	**0**	**0**	**1**	**0**	**0**	**0**	**0**	**0**	**0**	**0**	**0**	**.154**	**.154**	**.231**	**1.000**
1940	**NY-A**	**45**	**124**	**17**	**30**	**8**	**1**	**1**	**10**	**14**	**0**	**8**	**3**	**4**	**0**	**1**	**1**	**.242**	**.333**	**.347**	**.985**
1941	Chi-A	89	343	51	84	23	2	7	29	41	0	27	2	10	0	6	5	.245	.329	.385	.970
1942	Phi-A	87	289	25	73	12	0	1	19	29	0	30	1	9	0	1	2	.253	.323	.304	.000
Career average	91	342	42	94	20	3	3	37	24	0	24	1	8	0	3	5	.276	.326	.374	.873
Yankee average	**32**	**88**	**11**	**21**	**6**	**1**	**1**	**11**	**8**	**0**	**6**	**1**	**3**	**0**	**0**	**0**	**.242**	**.314**	**.358**	**.995**
Career total	907	3418	423	943	198	27	28	368	244	0	238	9	82	0	25	46	.276	.326	.374	.873
Yankee total	**97**	**265**	**34**	**64**	**17**	**4**	**2**	**32**	**25**	**0**	**18**	**3**	**8**	**0**	**1**	**1**	**.242**	**.314**	**.358**	**.995**

Knight, John Wesley (Schoolboy)

HEIGHT: 6'3" THROWS: RIGHT BATS: RIGHT BORN: 10/6/1885, PHILADELPHIA, PENN. DIED: 12/19/1965, WALNUT CREEK, CALIF. POSITIONS PLAYED: SS, 3B

YEAR	TEAM	GAMES	AB	RUNS	HITS	2B	3B	HR	RBI	BB	IBB	SO	HBP	SH	SF	SB	CS	BA	OBA	SA	FA
1905	Phi-A	88	325	28	66	12	1	3	29	9	0	0	1	11	0	4	0	.203	.227	.274	.895
1906	Phi-A	74	253	29	49	7	2	3	20	19	0	0	0	5	0	6	0	.194	.250	.273	.922
1907	Phi-A	40	139	6	29	7	1	0	12	10	0	0	2	2	0	1	0	.209	.272	.273	.862
1907	Bos-A	98	360	31	78	9	3	2	29	19	0	0	0	3	0	8	0	.217	.256	.275	.846
1909	**NY-A**	**116**	**360**	**46**	**85**	**8**	**5**	**0**	**40**	**37**	**0**	**0**	**2**	**17**	**0**	**15**	**0**	**.236**	**.311**	**.286**	**.986**
1910	**NY-A**	**117**	**414**	**58**	**129**	**25**	**4**	**3**	**45**	**34**	**0**	**0**	**6**	**19**	**0**	**23**	**0**	**.312**	**.372**	**.413**	**.938**
1911	**NY-A**	**132**	**470**	**69**	**126**	**16**	**7**	**3**	**62**	**42**	**0**	**0**	**11**	**19**	**0**	**18**	**0**	**.268**	**.342**	**.351**	**.907**
1912	Was-A	32	93	10	15	2	1	0	9	16	0	0	0	7	0	4	0	.161	.284	.204	.926
1913	**NY-A**	**70**	**250**	**24**	**59**	**10**	**0**	**0**	**24**	**25**	**0**	**27**	**2**	**6**	**0**	**7**	**0**	**.236**	**.310**	**.276**	**.952**
Career average		85	296	33	71	11	3	2	30	23	0	3	3	10	0	10	0	.239	.300	.309	.915
Yankee average		**109**	**374**	**49**	**99.8**	**15**	**4**	**2**	**43**	**35**	**0**	**7**	**5**	**15**	**0**	**16**	**0**	**.267**	**.338**	**.340**	**.946**
Career total		767	2664	301	636	96	24	14	270	211	0	27	24	89	0	86	0	.239	.300	.309	.915
Yankee total		**435**	**1494**	**197**	**399**	**59**	**16**	**6**	**171**	**138**	**0**	**27**	**21**	**61**	**0**	**63**	**0**	**.267**	**.338**	**.340**	**.946**

Knoblauch, Edward Charles (Chuck)

HEIGHT: 5'9" THROWS: RIGHT BATS: RIGHT BORN: 7/7/1968, HOUSTON, TEXAS POSITIONS PLAYED: SS, 2B, DH

YEAR	TEAM	GAMES	AB	RUNS	HITS	2B	3B	HR	RBI	BB	IBB	SO	HBP	SH	SF	SB	CS	BA	OBA	SA	FA
1991	Min-A	151	565	78	159	24	6	1	50	59	0	40	4	1	5	25	5	.281	.351	.350	.975
1992	Min-A	155	600	104	178	19	6	2	56	88	1	60	5	2	12	34	13	.297	.384	.358	.992
1993	Min-A	153	602	82	167	27	4	2	41	65	1	44	9	4	5	29	11	.277	.354	.346	1.000
1994	Min-A	109	445	85	139	45	3	5	51	41	2	56	10	0	3	35	6	.312	.381	.461	1.000
1995	Min-A	136	538	107	179	34	8	11	63	78	3	95	10	0	3	46	18	.333	.424	.487	1.000
1996	Min-A	153	578	140	197	35	14	13	72	98	6	74	19	0	6	45	14	.341	.448	.517	.988
1997	Min-A	156	611	117	178	26	10	9	58	84	6	84	17	0	4	62	10	.291	.390	.411	.985
1998	**NY-A**	**150**	**603**	**117**	**160**	**25**	**4**	**17**	**64**	**76**	**1**	**70**	**0**	**2**	**7**	**31**	**12**	**.265**	**.344**	**.405**	**.963**
1999	**NY-A**	**150**	**603**	**120**	**176**	**36**	**4**	**18**	**68**	**83**	**0**	**57**	**0**	**3**	**5**	**28**	**9**	**.292**	**.375**	**.454**	**.963**
2000	**NY-A**	**102**	**400**	**75**	**113**	**22**	**2**	**5**	**26**	**46**	**0**	**45**	**8**	**1**	**2**	**15**	**7**	**.282**	**.366**	**.385**	**.958**
Career average		142	555	103	165	29	6	8	55	72	2	63	8	1	5	35	11	.297	.382	.417	.989
Yankee average		**134**	**535**	**104**	**150**	**28**	**3**	**13**	**53**	**68**	**0**	**57**	**3**	**2**	**5**	**25**	**9**	**.280**	**.361**	**.418**	**.972**
Career total		1415	5545	1025	1646	293	61	83	549	718	20	625	82	13	52	350	105	.297	.382	.417	.989
Yankee total		**402**	**1606**	**312**	**449**	**83**	**10**	**40**	**158**	**205**	**1**	**172**	**8**	**6**	**14**	**74**	**28**	**.280**	**.361**	**.418**	**.972**

Koenig, Mark Anthony

HEIGHT: 6'0" THROWS: RIGHT BATS: B BORN: 7/19/1904, SAN FRANCISCO, CALIFORNIA DIED: 4/22/1993, WILLOWS, CALIFORNIA POSITIONS PLAYED: SS, 3B

YEAR	TEAM	GAMES	AB	RUNS	HITS	2B	3B	HR	RBI	BB	IBB	SO	HBP	SH	SF	SB	CS	BA	OBA	SA	FA
1925	**NY-A**	**28**	**110**	**14**	**23**	**6**	**1**	**0**	**4**	**5**	**0**	**4**	**0**	**2**	**0**	**0**	**1**	**.209**	**.243**	**.282**	**.944**
1926	**NY-A**	**147**	**617**	**93**	**167**	**26**	**8**	**5**	**62**	**43**	**0**	**37**	**1**	**17**	**0**	**4**	**3**	**.271**	**.319**	**.363**	**.931**
1927	**NY-A**	**123**	**526**	**99**	**150**	**20**	**11**	**3**	**62**	**25**	**0**	**21**	**2**	**15**	**0**	**3**	**2**	**.285**	**.320**	**.382**	**.936**
1928	**NY-A**	**132**	**533**	**89**	**170**	**19**	**10**	**4**	**63**	**32**	**0**	**19**	**2**	**11**	**0**	**3**	**5**	**.319**	**.360**	**.415**	**.923**
1929	**NY-A**	**116**	**373**	**44**	**109**	**27**	**5**	**3**	**41**	**23**	**0**	**17**	**1**	**3**	**0**	**1**	**1**	**.292**	**.335**	**.416**	**.916**
1930	**NY-A**	**21**	**74**	**9**	**17**	**5**	**0**	**0**	**9**	**6**	**0**	**5**	**1**	**5**	**0**	**0**	**0**	**.230**	**.296**	**.297**	**.905**
1930	Det-A	76	267	37	64	9	2	1	16	20	0	15	1	13	0	2	0	.240	.295	.300	1.000
1931	Det-A	106	364	33	92	24	4	1	39	14	0	12	1	2	0	8	2	.253	.282	.349	.909
1932	Chi-N	33	102	15	36	5	1	3	11	3	0	5	1	0	0	0	0	.353	.377	.510	.932
1933	Chi-N	80	218	32	62	12	1	3	25	15	0	9	0	6	0	5	0	.284	.330	.390	1.000
1934	Cin-N	151	633	60	172	26	6	1	67	15	0	24	0	13	0	5	0	.272	.289	.336	1.000
1935	NY-N	107	396	40	112	12	0	3	37	13	0	18	0	11	0	0	0	.283	.306	.336	.935
1936	NY-N	42	58	7	16	4	0	1	7	8	0	4	1	1	0	0	0	.276	.373	.397	.905
Career average		89	329	44	92	15	4	2	34	17	0	15	1	8	0	2	1	.279	.316	.367	.936
Yankee average		**95**	**372**	**58**	**106**	**17**	**6**	**3**	**40**	**22**	**0**	**17**	**1**	**9**	**0**	**2**	**2**	**.285**	**.327**	**.382**	**.926**
Career total		1162	4271	572	1190	195	49	28	443	222	0	190	11	99	0	31	14	.279	.316	.367	.936
Yankee total		**567**	**2233**	**348**	**636**	**103**	**35**	**15**	**241**	**134**	**0**	**103**	**7**	**53**	**0**	**11**	**12**	**.285**	**.327**	**.382**	**.926**

Kosco, Andrew John

HEIGHT: 6'3"   THROWS: RIGHT   BATS: RIGHT   BORN: 10/5/1941, YOUNGSTOWN, OHIO   POSITIONS PLAYED: 1B, 3B, OF

YEAR	TEAM	GAMES	AB	RUNS	HITS	2B	3B	HR	RBI	BB	IBB	SO	HBP	SH	SF	SB	CS	BA	OBA	SA	FA
1965	Min-A	23	55	3	13	4	0	1	6	1	0	15	0	0	2	0	0	.236	.241	.364	1.000
1966	Min-A	57	158	11	35	5	0	2	13	7	1	31	0	3	2	0	1	.222	.251	.291	.986
1967	Min-A	9	28	4	4	1	0	0	4	2	0	4	0	0	0	0	0	.143	.200	.179	.923
1968	**NY-A**	**131**	**466**	**47**	**112**	**19**	**1**	**15**	**59**	**16**	**2**	**71**	**3**	**3**	**4**	**2**	**2**	**.240**	**.268**	**.382**	**.992**
1969	LA-N	120	424	51	105	13	2	19	74	21	2	66	1	3	4	0	1	.248	.282	.422	1.000
1970	LA-N	74	224	21	51	12	0	8	27	1	0	40	0	2	1	1	1	.228	.230	.388	1.000
1971	Mil-A	98	264	27	60	6	2	10	39	24	5	57	0	1	1	1	3	.227	.291	.379	.952
1972	Cal-A	49	142	15	34	4	2	6	13	5	1	23	1	1	2	1	0	.239	.267	.423	.985
1972	Bos-A	17	47	5	10	2	1	3	6	2	0	9	1	0	0	0	0	.213	.260	.489	1.000
1973	Cin-N	47	118	17	33	7	0	9	21	13	6	26	0	2	2	0	0	.280	.346	.568	1.000
1974	Cin-N	33	37	3	7	2	0	0	5	7	1	8	0	0	1	0	0	.189	.311	.243	.846
Career average		60	179	19	42	7	1	7	24	9	2	32	1	1	2	1	1	.236	.273	.394	.971
Yankee average		**131**	**466**	**47**	**112**	**19**	**1**	**15**	**59**	**16**	**2**	**71**	**3**	**3**	**4**	**2**	**2**	**.240**	**.268**	**.382**	**.992**
Career total		658	1963	204	464	75	8	73	267	99	18	350	6	15	19	5	8	.236	.273	.394	.971
Yankee total		**131**	**466**	**47**	**112**	**19**	**1**	**15**	**59**	**16**	**2**	**71**	**3**	**3**	**4**	**2**	**2**	**.240**	**.268**	**.382**	**.992**

Krueger, Ernest George

HEIGHT: 5'10"   THROWS: RIGHT   BATS: RIGHT   BORN: 12/27/1890, CHICAGO, ILLINOIS   DIED: 4/22/1976, WAUKEGAN, ILLINOIS   POSITIONS PLAYED: 1B, OF

YEAR	TEAM	GAMES	AB	RUNS	HITS	2B	3B	HR	RBI	BB	IBB	SO	HBP	SH	SF	SB	CS	BA	OBA	SA	FA
1913	Cle-A	5	6	0	0	0	0	0	0	0	—	2	0	0	—	0	—	.000	.000	.000	1.000
1915	**NY-A**	**10**	**29**	**3**	**5**	**1**	**0**	**0**	**0**	**0**	**—**	**5**	**1**	**1**	**—**	**0**	**1**	**.172**	**.200**	**.207**	**.905**
1917	NY-N	8	10	0	0	0	0	0	0	0	—	4	0	0	—	0	—	.000	.000	.000	.857
1917	Bro-N	31	81	10	22	2	2	1	6	5	—	7	2	1	—	1	—	.272	.330	.383	.979
1918	Bro-N	30	87	4	25	4	2	0	7	4	—	9	0	0	—	2	—	.287	.319	.379	.986
1919	Bro-N	80	226	24	56	7	4	5	36	19	—	25	2	3	—	4	—	.248	.312	.381	.963
1920	Bro-N	52	146	21	42	4	2	1	17	16	—	13	0	0	—	2	0	.288	.358	.363	.959
1921	Bro-N	65	163	18	43	11	4	3	20	14	—	12	0	1	—	2	2	.264	.322	.436	.969
1925	Cin-N	37	88	7	27	4	0	1	7	6	—	8	0	2	—	1	2	.307	.351	.386	.946
Career average		35	93	10	24	4	2	1	10	7	—	9	1	1	—	1	—	.263	.319	.376	.952
Yankee average		**10**	**29**	**3**	**5**	**1**	**0**	**0**	**0**	**0**	**—**	**5**	**1**	**1**	**—**	**0**	**1**	**.172**	**.200**	**.207**	**.905**
Career total		318	836	87	220	33	14	11	93	64	—	85	5	8	—	12	5	.263	.319	.376	.952
Yankee total		**10**	**29**	**3**	**5**	**1**	**0**	**0**	**0**	**0**	**—**	**5**	**1**	**1**	**—**	**0**	**1**	**.172**	**.200**	**.207**	**.905**

Kryhoski, Richard David

HEIGHT: 6'2"   THROWS: LEFT   BATS: LEFT   BORN: 3/24/1925, LEONIA, NEW JERSEY   POSITIONS PLAYED: 1B

YEAR	TEAM	GAMES	AB	RUNS	HITS	2B	3B	HR	RBI	BB	IBB	SO	HBP	SH	SF	SB	CS	BA	OBA	SA	FA
1949	**NY-A**	**54**	**177**	**18**	**52**	**10**	**3**	**1**	**27**	**9**	**0**	**17**	**2**	**0**	**0**	**2**	**4**	**.294**	**.335**	**.401**	**.983**
1950	Det-A	53	169	20	37	10	0	4	19	8	0	11	1	1	0	0	1	.219	.258	.349	.991
1951	Det-A	119	421	58	121	19	4	12	57	28	0	29	2	4	0	1	2	.287	.335	.437	.991
1952	StL-A	111	342	38	83	13	1	11	42	23	0	42	3	4	0	2	0	.243	.296	.383	.989
1953	StL-A	104	338	35	94	18	4	16	50	26	0	33	2	3	0	0	5	.278	.333	.497	.992
1954	Bal-A	100	300	32	78	13	2	1	34	19	0	24	2	5	4	0	0	.260	.305	.327	.992
1955	KC-A	28	47	2	10	2	0	0	2	6	0	7	0	0	0	0	1	.213	.302	.255	.988
Career average		81	256	29	68	12	2	6	33	17	0	23	2	2	1	1	2	.265	.314	.403	.989
Yankee average		**54**	**177**	**18**	**52**	**10**	**3**	**1**	**27**	**9**	**0**	**17**	**2**	**0**	**0**	**2**	**4**	**.294**	**.335**	**.401**	**.983**
Career total		569	1794	203	475	85	14	45	231	119	0	163	12	17	4	5	13	.265	.314	.403	.989
Yankee total		**54**	**177**	**18**	**52**	**10**	**3**	**1**	**27**	**9**	**0**	**17**	**2**	**0**	**0**	**2**	**4**	**.294**	**.335**	**.401**	**.983**

Anthony Christopher "Tony" Kubek, ss-2b-3b-1b-of, 1957–65

Tony Kubek was one of the most versatile infielders the Yankees ever had, and also one of the toughest.

Born October 12, 1936, in Milwaukee, Wisconsin, Kubek joined New York as a 21-year-old rookie who had starred for the Yankees' formidable farm club in Denver the year before.

In New York, Kubek seemed not to lose a step in 1957, hitting .297, while playing virtually everywhere on the field but pitcher and catcher. Of the 127 games Kubek played, he spent 50 of them in the outfield, 41 at shortstop, 38 at third base and one at second base. He was an easy choice for rookie of the year in the American League.

Manager Casey Stengel simply loved his versatility, but by 1958, he had Kubek at short-stop for most of the season and most of the rest of his career.

Kubek was not as graceful afield as a Luis Aparicio, but he played hitters extremely well, and from 1958–64, he was either second or

third in fielding percentage at his position. He was not a great hitter, certainly not in the class of a Mantle or a Maris, but he could get the big hit when his team needed it.

He was a three-time All-Star, but those years, 1958, 1959 and 1961, were not appre-ciably different from the rest of his career. He was, simply, a consistently solid fundamental player. And he was tough. He gave no quarter and asked for none on the field. Kubek never hesitated to take out an opposing player on the base paths if he thought the player deserved it.

In 1962, he injured his back while playing a touch football game, and by 1964, the pain was beginning to seriously limit his playing time. He appeared in only 106 games that year, only 99 in the field.

By the next year, he was told there was a possibility that the injury to his back could result in permanent damage, and at age 29, at the height of his abilities, he retired. He caught on quickly as a broadcaster of major league baseball games, and proved to be as honest and forthright in the broadcast booth as he was on the field.

Kubek, Anthony Christopher (Tony)

HEIGHT: 6'3"   THROWS: RIGHT   BATS: LEFT   BORN: 10/12/1936, MILWAUKEE, WISCONSIN   POSITIONS PLAYED: 1B, 2B, 3B, SS, OF

YEAR	TEAM	GAMES	AB	RUNS	HITS	2B	3B	HR	RBI	BB	IBB	SO	HBP	SH	SF	SB	CS	BA	OBA	SA	FA
1957	NY-A	127	431	56	128	21	3	3	39	24	3	48	3	13	4	6	6	.297	.335	.381	1.000
1958	NY-A	138	559	66	148	21	1	2	48	25	3	57	1	8	4	5	4	.265	.295	.317	1.000
1959	NY-A	132	512	67	143	25	7	6	51	24	3	46	2	13	2	3	3	.279	.313	.391	.968
1960	NY-A	147	568	77	155	25	3	14	62	31	5	42	3	12	4	3	0	.273	.312	.401	1.000
1961	NY-A	153	617	84	170	38	6	8	46	27	1	60	1	10	3	1	3	.276	.306	.395	.959
1962	NY-A	45	169	28	53	6	1	4	17	12	0	17	0	2	1	2	1	.314	.357	.432	1.000
1963	NY-A	135	557	72	143	21	3	7	44	28	3	68	2	3	2	4	2	.257	.294	.343	.980
1964	NY-A	106	415	46	95	16	3	8	31	26	3	55	1	4	1	4	1	.229	.275	.340	.978
1965	NY-A	109	339	26	74	5	3	5	35	20	0	48	0	6	5	1	3	.218	.258	.295	.964
Career average		121	463	58	123	20	3	6	41	24	3	49	1	8	3	3	3	.266	.303	.364	.983
Yankee average		121	463	58	123	20	3	6	41	24	3	49	1	8	3	3	3	.266	.303	.364	.983
Career total		1092	4167	522	1109	178	30	57	373	217	24	441	13	71	26	29	23	.266	.303	.364	.983
Yankee total		1092	4167	522	1109	178	30	57	373	217	24	441	13	71	26	29	23	.266	.303	.364	.983

Lamar, William Harmong (Good Time Bill)

HEIGHT: 6'1" THROWS: RIGHT BATS: LEFT BORN: 3/21/1897 ROCKVILLE, MARYLAND DIED: 5/24/1970 ROCKPORT, MASS. POSITIONS PLAYED: 1B, OF

YEAR	TEAM	GAMES	AB	RUNS	HITS	2B	3B	HR	RBI	BB	IBB	SO	HBP	SH	SF	SB	CS	BA	OBA	SA	FA
1917	**NY-A**	**11**	**41**	**2**	**10**	**0**	**0**	**0**	**3**	**0**	**—**	**2**	**0**	**1**	**—**	**1**	**—**	**.244**	**.244**	**.244**	**1.000**
1918	**NY-A**	**28**	**110**	**12**	**25**	**3**	**0**	**0**	**2**	**6**	**—**	**2**	**0**	**3**	**—**	**2**	**—**	**.227**	**.267**	**.255**	**.884**
1919	**NY-A**	**11**	**16**	**1**	**3**	**1**	**0**	**0**	**0**	**2**	**—**	**1**	**0**	**0**	**—**	**1**	**—**	**.188**	**.278**	**.250**	**1.000**
1919	Bos-A	48	148	18	43	5	1	0	14	5	—	9	0	0	—	3	—	.291	.314	.338	.922
1920	Bro-N	24	44	5	12	4	0	0	4	0	—	1	0	0	—	0	0	.273	.273	.364	1.000
1921	Bro-N	3	3	2	1	0	0	0	0	0	—	0	0	0	—	0	0	.333	.333	.333	1.000
1924	Phi-A	87	367	68	121	22	5	7	48	18	—	21	0	11	—	8	8	.330	.361	.474	.971
1925	Phi-A	138	568	85	202	39	8	3	77	21	—	17	0	15	—	2	6	.356	.379	.468	.953
1926	Phi-A	116	419	62	119	17	6	5	50	18	—	15	1	19	—	4	5	.284	.315	.389	.954
1927	Phi-A	84	324	48	97	23	3	4	47	16	—	10	1	14	—	4	8	.299	.334	.426	.952
Career average		55	204	30	63	11	2	2	25	9	—	8	0	6	—	3	—	.310	.339	.417	.864
Yankee average		**17**	**56**	**5**	**13**	**1**	**0**	**0**	**2**	**3**	**—**	**2**	**0**	**1**	**—**	**1**	**—**	**.228**	**.263**	**.251**	**.961**
Career total		550	2040	303	633	114	23	19	245	86	—	78	2	63	—	25	27	.310	.339	.417	.864
Yankee total		**50**	**167**	**15**	**38**	**4**	**0**	**0**	**5**	**8**	**—**	**5**	**0**	**4**	**—**	**4**	**—**	**.228**	**.263**	**.251**	**.961**

Lanier, Harold Clifton (Hal)

HEIGHT: 6'2" THROWS: RIGHT BATS: RIGHT BORN: 7/4/1942 DENTON, NORTH CAROLINA POSITIONS PLAYED: 1B, 2B, 3B, SS

YEAR	TEAM	GAMES	AB	RUNS	HITS	2B	3B	HR	RBI	BB	IBB	SO	HBP	SH	SF	SB	CS	BA	OBA	SA	FA
1964	SF-N	98	383	40	105	16	3	2	28	5	0	44	0	12	1	2	1	.274	.283	.347	1.000
1965	SF-N	159	522	41	118	15	9	0	39	21	4	67	0	12	1	2	1	.226	.256	.289	.976
1966	SF-N	149	459	37	106	14	2	3	37	16	7	49	0	8	1	1	0	.231	.256	.290	.952
1967	SF-N	151	525	37	112	16	3	0	42	16	2	61	2	13	1	2	2	.213	.239	.255	.974
1968	SF-N	151	486	37	100	14	1	0	27	12	0	57	0	14	6	2	2	.206	.222	.239	.979
1969	SF-N	150	495	37	113	9	1	0	35	25	5	68	0	13	4	0	1	.228	.263	.251	.969
1970	SF-N	134	438	33	101	13	1	2	41	21	4	41	0	2	2	1	2	.231	.265	.279	1.000
1971	SF-N	109	206	21	48	8	0	1	13	15	3	26	0	4	2	0	0	.233	.283	.286	1.000
1972	**NY-A**	**60**	**103**	**5**	**22**	**3**	**0**	**0**	**6**	**2**	**0**	**13**	**1**	**0**	**1**	**1**	**2**	**.214**	**.234**	**.243**	**1.000**
1973	**NY-A**	**35**	**86**	**9**	**18**	**3**	**0**	**0**	**5**	**3**	**0**	**10**	**1**	**0**	**0**	**0**	**0**	**.209**	**.244**	**.244**	**1.000**
Career average		120	370	30	84	11	2	1	27	14	3	44	0	8	2	1	1	.228	.255	.275	.985
Yankee average		**48**	**95**	**7**	**20**	**3**	**0**	**0**	**6**	**3**	**0**	**12**	**1**	**0**	**1**	**1**	**1**	**.212**	**.239**	**.243**	**1.000**
Career total		1196	3703	297	843	111	20	8	273	136	25	436	4	78	19	11	11	.228	.255	.275	.985
Yankee total		**95**	**189**	**14**	**40**	**6**	**0**	**0**	**11**	**5**	**0**	**23**	**2**	**0**	**1**	**1**	**2**	**.212**	**.239**	**.243**	**1.000**

LaPorte, Frank Breyfogle (Pot)

HEIGHT: 5'8" THROWS: RIGHT BATS: RIGHT BORN: 2/6/1880 UHRICHSVILLE, OH. DIED: 9/25/1939 NEWCOMERSTOWN, OH. POSITIONS PLAYED: 1B, 2B, 3B, OF

YEAR	TEAM	GAMES	AB	RUNS	HITS	2B	3B	HR	RBI	BB	IBB	SO	HBP	SH	SF	SB	CS	BA	OBA	SA	FA
1905	**NY-A**	**11**	**40**	**4**	**16**	**1**	**0**	**1**	**12**	**1**	**—**		**0**	**0**	**—**	**1**	**—**	**.400**	**.415**	**.500**	**.918**
1906	**NY-A**	**123**	**454**	**60**	**120**	**23**	**9**	**2**	**54**	**22**	**—**		**1**	**6**	**—**	**10**	**—**	**.264**	**.300**	**.368**	**.904**
1907	**NY-A**	**130**	**470**	**56**	**127**	**20**	**11**	**0**	**48**	**27**	**—**		**5**	**9**	**—**	**10**	**—**	**.270**	**.317**	**.360**	**.896**
1908	Bos-A	62	156	14	37	1	3	0	15	12	—		1	5	—	3	—	.237	.296	.282	.950
1908	**NY-A**	**39**	**145**	**7**	**38**	**3**	**4**	**1**	**15**	**8**	**—**		**0**	**5**	**—**	**3**	**—**	**.262**	**.301**	**.359**	**.934**
1909	**NY-A**	**89**	**309**	**35**	**92**	**19**	**3**	**0**	**31**	**18**	**—**		**2**	**8**	**—**	**5**	**—**	**.298**	**.340**	**.379**	**.938**
1910	**NY-A**	**124**	**432**	**43**	**114**	**14**	**6**	**2**	**67**	**33**	**—**		**3**	**19**	**—**	**16**	**—**	**.264**	**.321**	**.338**	**.959**
1911	StL-A	136	507	71	159	37	12	2	82	34	—		4	18	—	4	—	.314	.361	.446	.950
1912	StL-A	80	266	32	83	11	4	1	38	20	—		3	10	—	7	—	.312	.367	.395	.944
1912	Was-A	40	136	13	42	9	1	0	17	12	—		0	4	—	3	—	.309	.365	.390	.939
1913	Was-A	79	242	25	61	5	4	0	18	17	—	16	3	3	—	10	—	.252	.309	.306	.952
1914	Ind-F	133	505	86	157	27	12	4	107	36	—	36	4	21	—	15	—	.311	.361	.436	.956
1915	New-F	148	550	55	139	28	10	2	56	48	—	33	1	17	—	14	—	.253	.314	.351	.960
Career average		92	324	38	91	15	6	1	43	22	—		2	10	—	8	—	.281	.331	.377	.938
Yankee average		**86**	**308**	**34**	**85**	**13**	**6**	**1**	**38**	**18**	**—**		**2**	**8**	**—**	**8**	**—**	**.274**	**.318**	**.363**	**.925**
Career total		1194	4212	501	1185	198	79	15	560	288	—	85	27	125	—	101	—	.281	.331	.377	.938
Yankee total		**516**	**1850**	**205**	**507**	**80**	**33**	**6**	**227**	**109**	**—**		**11**	**47**	**—**	**45**	**—**	**.274**	**.318**	**.363**	**.925**

Larsen, Don James

HEIGHT: 6'4" THROWS: RIGHT BATS: RIGHT BORN: 8/7/1929 MICHIGAN CITY, INDIANA POSITIONS PLAYED: P, OF

YEAR	TEAM	GAMES	AB	RUNS	HITS	2B	3B	HR	RBI	BB	IBB	SO	HBP	SH	SF	SB	CS	BA	OBA	SA	FA
1953	StL-A	50	81	11	23	3	1	3	10	4	—	14	0	0	—	0	0	.284	.318	.457	.949
1954	Bal-A	44	88	6	22	5	3	1	4	5	—	15	0	2	0	0	0	.250	.290	.409	.980
1955	**NY-A**	**21**	**41**	**4**	**6**	**1**	**0**	**2**	**7**	**4**	**0**	**13**	**0**	**0**	**0**	**0**	**0**	**.146**	**.222**	**.317**	**.947**
1956	**NY-A**	**45**	**79**	**10**	**19**	**5**	**0**	**2**	**12**	**6**	**0**	**17**	**0**	**1**	**0**	**0**	**0**	**.241**	**.294**	**.380**	**.923**
1957	**NY-A**	**31**	**56**	**6**	**14**	**5**	**0**	**0**	**5**	**6**	**0**	**11**	**0**	**0**	**1**	**0**	**1**	**.250**	**.317**	**.339**	**.938**
1958	**NY-A**	**28**	**49**	**9**	**15**	**1**	**0**	**4**	**13**	**5**	**0**	**9**	**0**	**2**	**1**	**0**	**2**	**.306**	**.364**	**.571**	**.905**
1959	**NY-A**	**29**	**47**	**8**	**12**	**2**	**0**	**0**	**8**	**7**	**0**	**15**	**0**	**1**	**1**	**0**	**0**	**.255**	**.345**	**.298**	**.931**
1960	KC-A	23	29	3	6	1	0	0	3	0	0	11	0	0	0	0	0	.207	.207	.241	.923
1961	KC-A	18	20	2	6	0	0	1	4	1	0	5	0	1	0	0	0	.300	.333	.450	1.000
1961	Chi-A	25	25	2	8	0	0	1	4	0	0	5	0	1	0	0	0	.320	.320	.440	1.000
1962	SF-N	52	25	3	5	0	1	0	1	0	0	7	0	1	0	0	0	.200	.200	.280	1.000
1963	SF-N	46	11	1	2	0	0	0	0	1	0	1	0	1	0	0	0	.182	.250	.182	.941
1964	SF-N	6	1	0	0	0	0	0	0	0	0	0	0	0	0	0	0	.000	.000	.000	1.000
1964	Hou-N	31	31	0	3	1	0	0	0	4	0	10	0	1	0	0	0	.097	.200	.129	.966
1965	Hou-N	1	2	0	0	0	0	0	0	0	0	1	0	0	0	0	0	.000	.000	.000	.957
1965	Bal-A	27	11	0	3	1	0	0	1	0	0	4	0	0	0	0	0	.273	.273	.364	1.000
1967	Chi-N	3	0	0	0	0	0	0	0	0	0	0	0	0	0	0	0	—	—	—	.000
Career average	28	35	4	9	2	0	1	4	3	—	8	0	1	—	0	0	.242	.293	.371	.962
Yankee average	**31**	**54**	**7**	**13**	**3**	**0**	**2**	**9**	**6**	**0**	**13**	**0**	**1**	**1**	**0**	**1**	**.243**	**.310**	**.382**	**.929**
Career total	480	596	65	144	25	5	14	72	43	0	138	0	11	3	0	3	.242	.291	.371	.962
Yankee total	**154**	**272**	**37**	**66**	**14**	**0**	**8**	**45**	**28**	**0**	**65**	**0**	**4**	**3**	**0**	**3**	**.243**	**.310**	**.382**	**.929**

Lary, Lynford Hobart (Lyn)

HEIGHT: 6'0" THROWS: RIGHT BATS: RIGHT BORN: 1/28/1906 ARMONA, CALIFORNIA DIED: 1/9/1973 DOWNEY, CAL. POSITIONS PLAYED: 1B, 2B, 3B, SS, OF

YEAR	TEAM	GAMES	AB	RUNS	HITS	2B	3B	HR	RBI	BB	IBB	SO	HBP	SH	SF	SB	CS	BA	OBA	SA	FA
1929	**NY-A**	**80**	**236**	**48**	**73**	**9**	**2**	**5**	**26**	**24**	**—**	**15**	**3**	**5**	**—**	**4**	**1**	**.309**	**.380**	**.428**	**1.000**
1930	**NY-A**	**117**	**464**	**93**	**134**	**20**	**8**	**3**	**52**	**45**	**—**	**40**	**4**	**19**	**—**	**14**	**2**	**.289**	**.357**	**.386**	**.940**
1931	**NY-A**	**155**	**610**	**100**	**171**	**35**	**9**	**10**	**107**	**88**	**—**	**54**	**6**	**8**	**—**	**13**	**10**	**.280**	**.376**	**.416**	**.946**
1932	**NY-A**	**91**	**280**	**56**	**65**	**14**	**4**	**3**	**39**	**52**	**—**	**28**	**3**	**4**	**—**	**9**	**3**	**.232**	**.358**	**.343**	**.941**
1933	**NY-A**	**52**	**127**	**25**	**28**	**3**	**3**	**0**	**13**	**28**	**—**	**17**	**0**	**3**	**—**	**2**	**1**	**.220**	**.361**	**.291**	**1.000**
1934	**NY-A**	**1**	**0**	**0**	**0**	**0**	**0**	**0**	**0**	**1**	**—**	**0**	**0**	**0**	**—**	**0**	**0**	**—**	**1.000**	**—**	**.800**
1934	Bos-A	129	419	58	101	20	4	2	54	66	—	51	0	15	—	12	5	.241	.344	.322	.965
1935	Was-A	39	103	8	20	4	0	0	7	12	—	10	0	7	—	3	0	.194	.278	.233	.953
1935	StL-A	93	371	78	17	25	7	2	35	64	—	43	2	3	—	25	4	.288	.396	.410	.962
1936	StL-A	155	619	112	179	30	6	2	52	117	—	54	2	7	—	37	9	.289	.404	.367	.956
1937	Cle-A	156	644	110	187	46	7	8	77	88	—	64	3	6	—	18	8	.290	.378	.421	.963
1938	Cle-A	141	568	94	152	36	4	3	51	88	—	65	0	5	—	23	6	.268	.366	.361	.964
1939	Cle-A	3	2	0	0	0	0	0	0	0	—	1	0	0	—	0	0	.000	.000	.000	.000
1939	Bro-N	29	31	7	5	1	1	0	1	12	—	6	1	2	—	1	—	.161	.409	.258	.867
1939	StL-A	34	75	11	14	3	0	0	9	16	—	15	0	5	—	1	—	.187	.330	.227	.961
1940	StL-A	27	54	5	3	1	1	0	3	4	—	7	1	2	—	0	0	.056	.136	.111	.952
Career average	81	288	50	72	15	4	2	33	44	—	29	2	6	—	10	—	.250	.352	.352	.886
Yankee average	**83**	**286**	**54**	**79**	**14**	**4**	**4**	**40**	**40**	**—**	**26**	**3**	**7**	**—**	**7**	**3**	**.274**	**.368**	**.388**	**.938**
Career total	1302	4603	805	1149	247	56	38	526	705	—	470	25	91	—	162	49	.250	.352	.352	.886
Yankee total	**496**	**1717**	**322**	**471**	**81**	**26**	**21**	**237**	**238**	**—**	**154**	**16**	**39**	**—**	**42**	**17**	**.274**	**.368**	**.388**	**.938**

Lawton, Marcus Dwayne

HEIGHT: 6'1" THROWS: RIGHT BATS: BOTH BORN: 8/18/1965 GULFPORT, MISSISSIPPI POSITIONS PLAYED: OF

YEAR	TEAM	GAMES	AB	RUNS	HITS	2B	3B	HR	RBI	BB	IBB	SO	HBP	SH	SF	SB	CS	BA	OBA	SA	FA
1989	**NY-A**	**10**	**14**	**1**	**3**	**0**	**0**	**0**	**0**	**0**	**0**	**3**	**0**	**0**	**0**	**1**	**0**	**.214**	**.214**	**.214**	**.818**
Career average	10	14	1	3	0	0	0	0	0	0	3	0	0	0	1	0	.214	.214	.214	.818
Yankee average	**10**	**14**	**1**	**3**	**0**	**0**	**0**	**0**	**0**	**0**	**3**	**0**	**0**	**0**	**1**	**0**	**.214**	**.214**	**.214**	**.818**
Career total	10	14	1	3	0	0	0	0	0	0	3	0	0	0	1	0	.214	.214	.214	.818
Yankee total	**10**	**14**	**1**	**3**	**0**	**0**	**0**	**0**	**0**	**0**	**3**	**0**	**0**	**0**	**1**	**0**	**.214**	**.214**	**.214**	**.818**

Layden, Eugene Francis (Gene)
HEIGHT: 5'10"   THROWS: LEFT BATS: LEFT   BORN: 3/14/1894 PITTSBURGH, PENNSYLVANIA   DIED: 12/12/1984 PITTSBURGH, PENN.   POSITIONS PLAYED: OF

YEAR	TEAM	GAMES	AB	RUNS	HITS	2B	3B	HR	RBI	BB	IBB	SO	HBP	SH	SF	SB	CS	BA	OBA	SA	FA
1915	NY-A	3	7	2	2	0	0	0	0	0	—	1	0	0	—	0	1	.286	.286	.286	.750
Career average		3	7	2	2	0	0	0	0	0	—	1	0	0	—	0	1	.286	.286	.286	.750
Yankee average		**3**	**7**	**2**	**2**	**0**	**0**	**0**	**0**	**0**	**—**	**1**	**0**	**0**	**—**	**0**	**1**	**.286**	**.286**	**.286**	**.750**
Career total		3	7	2	2	0	0	0	0	0	—	1	0	0	—	0	1	.286	.286	.286	.750
Yankee total		**3**	**7**	**2**	**2**	**0**	**0**	**0**	**0**	**0**	**—**	**1**	**0**	**0**	**—**	**0**	**1**	**.286**	**.286**	**.286**	**.750**

Lazzeri, Anthony Michael (Poosh 'Em Up Tony)
HEIGHT: 5'1"   THROWS: RIGHT   BATS: RIGHT   BORN: 12/6/1903 SAN FRANCISCO, CAL.   DIED: 8/6/1946 SAN FRANCISCO, CAL.   POSITIONS PLAYED: 1B, 2B, 3B, SS, OF

YEAR	TEAM	GAMES	AB	RUNS	HITS	2B	3B	HR	RBI	BB	IBB	SO	HBP	SH	SF	SB	CS	BA	OBA	SA	FA
1926	NY-A	155	589	79	162	28	14	18	114	54	—	96	2	20	—	16	7	.275	.338	.462	.961
1927	NY-A	153	570	92	176	29	8	18	102	69	—	82	0	21	—	22	14	.309	.383	.482	.971
1928	NY-A	116	404	62	134	30	11	10	82	43	—	50	1	15	—	15	5	.332	.397	.535	.956
1929	NY-A	147	545	101	193	37	11	18	106	68	—	45	4	18	—	9	10	.354	.429	.561	.969
1930	NY-A	143	571	109	173	34	15	9	121	60	—	62	3	16	—	4	4	.303	.372	.462	.952
1931	NY-A	135	484	67	129	27	7	8	83	79	—	80	1	4	—	18	9	.267	.371	.401	.958
1932	NY-A	142	510	79	153	28	16	15	113	82	—	64	2	7	—	11	11	.300	.399	.506	1.000
1933	NY-A	139	523	94	154	22	12	18	104	73	—	62	2	4	—	15	7	.294	.383	.486	.968
1934	NY-A	123	438	59	117	24	6	14	67	71	—	64	0	5	—	11	1	.267	.369	.445	.976
1935	NY-A	130	477	72	130	18	6	13	83	63	—	75	3	1	—	11	5	.273	.361	.417	.935
1936	NY-A	150	537	82	154	29	6	14	109	97	—	65	1	3	—	8	5	.287	.397	.441	1.000
1937	NY-A	126	446	56	109	21	3	14	70	71	—	76	0	1	—	7	1	.244	.348	.399	.966
1938	Chi-N	54	120	21	32	5	0	5	23	22	—	30	0	1	—	0	—	.267	.380	.433	.946
1939	Bro-N	14	39	6	11	2	0	3	6	10	—	7	2	0	—	1	—	.282	.451	.564	1.000
1939	NY-N	13	44	7	13	0	0	1	8	7	—	6	2	0	—	0	—	.295	.382	.364	.889
Career average		116	420	66	123	22	8	12	79	58	—	58	2	8	—	10	—	.292	.380	.467	.963
Yankee average		**138**	**508**	**79**	**149**	**27**	**10**	**14**	**96**	**69**	**—**	**68**	**2**	**10**	**—**	**12**	**7**	**.293**	**.379**	**.467**	**.968**
Career total		1740	6297	986	1840	334	115	178	1191	869	—	864	23	116	—	148	79	.292	.380	.467	.963
Yankee total		**1659**	**6094**	**952**	**1784**	**327**	**115**	**169**	**1154**	**830**	**—**	**821**	**19**	**115**	**—**	**147**	**79**	**.293**	**.379**	**.467**	**.968**

Ledee, Ricardo Alberto (Ricky)
HEIGHT: 6'1"   THROWS: LEFT BATS: LEFT   BORN: 11/22/1973 PONCE, PUERTO RICO   POSITIONS PLAYED: OF

YEAR	TEAM	GAMES	AB	RUNS	HITS	2B	3B	HR	RBI	BB	IBB	SO	HBP	SH	SF	SB	CS	BA	OBA	SA	FA
1998	NY-A	42	79	13	19	5	2	1	12	7	0	29	0	0	1	3	1	.241	.299	.392	.979
1999	NY-A	88	250	45	69	13	5	9	40	28	5	73	0	0	2	4	3	.276	.346	.476	.942
2000	NY-A	62	191	23	46	11	1	7	31	26	2	39	1	0	2	7	3	.241	.332	.419	.981
2000	Cle-A	17	63	13	14	2	1	2	8	8	0	9	0	0	0	0	0	.222	.310	.381	.981
2000	Tex-A	58	213	23	50	6	3	4	38	25	2	50	1	0	1	6	3	.235	.317	.347	.981
Career average		53	159	23	40	7	2	5	26	19	2	40	0	0	1	4	2	.249	.327	.412	.973
Yankee average		**64**	**173**	**27**	**45**	**10**	**3**	**6**	**28**	**20**	**2**	**47**	**0**	**0**	**2**	**5**	**2**	**.258**	**.334**	**.442**	**.967**
Career total		267	796	117	198	37	12	23	129	94	9	200	2	0	6	20	10	.249	.327	.412	.973
Yankee total		**192**	**520**	**81**	**134**	**29**	**8**	**17**	**83**	**61**	**7**	**141**	**1**	**0**	**5**	**14**	**7**	**.258**	**.334**	**.442**	**.967**

Lefebvre, Joseph Henry
HEIGHT: 5'10"   THROWS: RIGHT   BATS: LEFT   BORN: 2/22/1956 CONCORD, NEW HAMPSHIRE   POSITIONS PLAYED: C, 3B, OF

YEAR	TEAM	GAMES	AB	RUNS	HITS	2B	3B	HR	RBI	BB	IBB	SO	HBP	SH	SF	SB	CS	BA	OBA	SA	FA
1980	NY-A	74	150	26	34	1	1	8	21	27	3	30	0	1	0	0	0	.227	.345	.407	.975
1981	SD-N	86	246	31	63	13	4	8	31	35	7	33	2	2	1	6	4	.256	.352	.439	.994
1982	SD-N	102	239	25	57	9	0	4	21	18	2	50	1	4	2	0	0	.238	.292	.326	1.000
1983	SD-N	18	20	1	5	0	0	0	1	2	0	3	0	0	0	0	0	.250	.318	.250	1.000
1983	Phi-N	101	258	34	80	20	8	8	38	31	6	46	3	1	2	5	3	.310	.388	.543	.990
1984	Phi-N	52	160	22	40	9	0	3	18	23	4	37	0	0	2	0	2	.250	.348	.363	1.000
1986	Phi-N	14	18	0	2	0	0	0	0	3	0	5	0	0	0	0	0	.111	.238	.111	1.000
Career average		64	156	20	40	7	2	4	19	20	3	29	1	1	1	2	1	.258	.344	.414	.994
Yankee average		**74**	**150**	**26**	**34**	**1**	**1**	**8**	**21**	**27**	**3**	**30**	**0**	**1**	**0**	**0**	**0**	**.227**	**.345**	**.407**	**.975**
Career total		447	1091	139	281	52	13	31	130	139	22	204	8	8	7	11	9	.258	.344	.414	.994
Yankee total		**74**	**150**	**26**	**34**	**1**	**1**	**8**	**21**	**27**	**3**	**30**	**0**	**1**	**0**	**0**	**0**	**.227**	**.345**	**.407**	**.975**

Anthony Michael "Poosh 'Em Up Tony" Lazzeri, 2b-ss-3b, 1926–37

Tony Lazzeri was the first in a long line of "utility infielders" in the Joe Gordon, Gil McDougald, Frankie Crosetti mold that has made the Yankees so stong over the years.

Born on December 6, 1903, in San Francisco, California, Lazzeri came from a tough Italian neighborhood. He was quick with his fists, once explaining that "it was fight or get licked, and I never got licked."

Lazzeri, the son of a blacksmith, became interested in baseball at an early age in baseball-crazy San Francisco. He eventually signed with the San Francisco Seals. In 1925, he had one of the greatest minor league seasons in the history of the Pacific Coast League—or any league for that matter—hitting 60 home runs and making an incredible 222 RBI.

In 1926, his contract was purchased by the Yankees. He replaced the light-hitting Aaron Ward at second base and was an immediate star, finishing third in the league in home runs with 18, and second only to Babe Ruth in RBI with 114.

And Tony was also second only to Ruth in popularity with the New York fans. Lazzeri's success drew a large Italian contingent to Yankee Stadium. They urged him to "Poosh 'em up!," or hit a home run, when Lazzeri came to the plate.

Lazzeri was quiet and confident in the Yankee clubhouse and became a team leader shortly after he came to New York. The "Wondrous Wop," as politically incorrect sportswriters of the time named him, was a smart defensive player, extremely tough in the clutch and yet another home run threat along with Ruth and Gehrig.

He was also an epileptic, which some writers believed was in part responsible for Lazzeri's extreme shyness. Lazzeri never had a seizure on the field, and teammates say that other than perhaps one or two episodes in spring training, he never seemed to have any problems in the clubhouse during the regular season, either. But he kept to himself when strangers were around.

Although Lazzeri is long remembered as a great clutch player, he was also one of the most well-known strikeout victims in baseball history in 1926.

It was in the famous seventh game that St. Louis Cardinal pitcher Grover Cleveland Alexander fanned Lazzeri in the seventh inning and held off the Yankees the rest of the way for a stunning victory. That win gave the Cardinals an upset win in the 1926 World Series, four games to three.

But Lazzeri and the entire Yankee team came back in 1927, winning a then-record 110 games and annexing the World Series from the Pittsburgh Pirates in a four-game sweep. Lazzeri hit .309 and finished third to Ruth and Gehrig in home runs with 18 and was seventh in the league in RBI with 102. On June 8, he bashed three home runs in a game against the Chicago White Sox, the first time in the history of the franchise that it had been done.

He was a consistent .300 hitter for the Yankees in five of his first seven years in New York. After 1933, his average began to dip, but he remained a very versatile defensive player. His primary position was second base, but manager Miller Huggins was never afraid to play him at third base or shortstop. Joe McCarthy, who managed Lazzeri in the early 1930s, was also prone to using Tony in the outfield.

By 1937, Lazzeri's numbers were down, and the Yankees had a young pheenom, Joe Gordon, waiting in the wings. Lazzeri went to the Chicago Cubs in 1938 as a player-coach. He also had stints with the Dodgers and the Giants in 1939 before retiring.

Lazzeri is 7th on the all-time Yankees' list for RBI with 1,154, 10th in hits with 1,784, 11th in runs scored with 952, 8th in doubles with 327 and 14th in home runs with 169. In 1991, he was inducted by the Veterans' Committee into the Baseball Hall of Fame.

Leja, Frank John

HEIGHT: 6'4" THROWS: LEFT BATS: LEFT BORN: 2/7/1936 HOLYOKE, MASSACHUSETTS DIED: 5/3/1991 BOSTON, MASSACHUSETTS POSITIONS PLAYED: 1B

YEAR	TEAM	GAMES	AB	RUNS	HITS	2B	3B	HR	RBI	BB	IBB	SO	HBP	SH	SF	SB	CS	BA	OBA	SA	FA
1954	NY-A	12	5	2	1	0	0	0	0	0	—	1	0	0	0	0	0	.200	.200	.200	1.000
1955	NY-A	7	2	1	0	0	0	0	0	0	0	1	0	0	0	0	0	.000	.000	.000	1.000
1962	LA-A	7	16	0	0	0	0	0	0	1	0	6	0	1	0	0	0	.000	.059	.000	.953
Career average		9	8	1	0	0	0	0	0	0	—	3	0	0	0	0	0	.043	.083	.043	.984
Yankee average		10	4	2	1	0	0	0	0	0	—	1	0	0	0	0	0	.143	.143	.143	1.000
Career total		26	23	3	1	0	0	0	0	1	0	8	0	1	0	0	0	.043	.083	.043	.984
Yankee total		19	7	3	1	0	0	0	0	0	0	2	0	0	0	0	0	.143	.143	.143	1.000

Lelivelt, John Frank (Jack)

HEIGHT: 5'11" THROWS: LEFT BATS: LEFT BORN: 11/14/1885 CHICAGO, ILLINOIS DIED: 1/20/1941 SEATTLE, WASHINGTON POSITIONS PLAYED: 1B, OF

YEAR	TEAM	GAMES	AB	RUNS	HITS	2B	3B	HR	RBI	BB	IBB	SO	HBP	SH	SF	SB	CS	BA	OBA	SA	FA
1909	Was-A	91	318	25	93	8	6	0	24	19	—	—	1	7	—	8	—	.292	.334	.355	.970
1910	Was-A	110	347	40	92	10	3	0	33	40	—	—	1	17	—	20	—	.265	.343	.311	.947
1911	Was-A	72	225	29	72	12	4	0	22	22	—	—	2	6	—	7	—	.320	.386	.409	.939
1912	NY-A	36	149	12	54	6	7	2	23	4	—	—	1	0	—	7	—	.362	.383	.537	.963
1913	NY-A	18	28	2	6	0	1	0	4	2	—	2	0	0	—	1	—	.214	.267	.286	1.000
1913	Cle-A	23	23	0	9	2	0	0	7	0	—	3	0	0	—	1	—	.391	.391	.478	.000
1914	Cle-A	34	64	6	21	5	1	0	13	2	—	10	0	1	—	2	3	.328	.348	.438	.933
Career average		55	165	16	50	6	3	0	18	13	—	—	1	4	—	7	—	.301	.353	.381	.822
Yankee average		27	89	7	30	3	4	1	14	3	—	—	1	0	—	4	—	.339	.364	.497	.982
Career total		384	1154	114	347	43	22	2	126	89	—	15	5	31	—	46	3	.301	.353	.381	.822
Yankee total		54	177	14	60	6	8	2	27	6	—	2	1	0	—	8	—	.339	.364	.497	.982

Leon, Eduardo Antonio (Eddie)

HEIGHT: 6'0" THROWS: RIGHT BATS: RIGHT BORN: 8/11/1946 TUCSON, ARIZONA POSITIONS PLAYED: 2B, 3B, SS

YEAR	TEAM	GAMES	AB	RUNS	HITS	2B	3B	HR	RBI	BB	IBB	SO	HBP	SH	SF	SB	CS	BA	OBA	SA	FA
1968	Cle-A	6	1	0	0	0	0	0	0	0	0	1	0	0	0	0	0	.000	.000	.000	1.000
1969	Cle-A	64	213	20	51	6	0	3	19	19	3	37	0	3	1	2	2	.239	.300	.310	.952
1970	Cle-A	152	549	58	136	20	4	10	56	47	2	89	2	23	3	1	2	.248	.308	.353	.978
1971	Cle-A	131	429	35	112	12	2	4	35	34	5	69	1	12	0	3	5	.261	.317	.326	.980
1972	Cle-A	89	225	14	45	2	1	4	16	20	1	47	1	2	3	0	2	.200	.265	.271	.979
1973	Chi-A	127	399	37	91	10	3	3	30	34	0	103	3	11	4	1	5	.228	.291	.291	.972
1974	Chi-A	31	46	1	5	1	0	0	3	2	0	12	0	4	1	0	0	.109	.143	.130	.966
1975	NY-A	1	0	0	0	0	0	0	0	0	0	0	0	0	0	0	0	—	—	—	1.000
Career average		75	233	21	55	6	1	3	20	20	1	45	1	7	2	1	2	.236	.296	.313	.853
Yankee average		1	0	0	0	0	0	0	0	0	0	0	0	0	0	0	0	—	—	—	1.000
Career total		601	1862	165	440	51	10	24	159	156	11	358	7	55	12	7	16	.236	.296	.313	.853
Yankee total		1	0	0	0	0	0	0	0	0	0	0	0	0	0	0	0	—	—	—	1.000

Levy, Edward Clarence Whitner

HEIGHT: 6'5" THROWS: RIGHT BATS: RIGHT BORN: 10/28/1916 BIRMINGHAM, ALABAMA POSITIONS PLAYED: 1B, OF

YEAR	TEAM	GAMES	AB	RUNS	HITS	2B	3B	HR	RBI	BB	IBB	SO	HBP	SH	SF	SB	CS	BA	OBA	SA	FA
1940	Phi-N	1	1	0	0	0	0	0	0	0	—	0	0	0	—	0	—	.000	.000	.000	.000
1942	NY-A	13	41	5	5	0	0	0	3	4	—	5	0	0	—	1	0	.122	.200	.122	.992
1944	NY-A	40	153	12	37	11	2	4	29	6	—	19	0	4	—	1	1	.242	.270	.418	.963
Career average		18	65	6	14	4	1	1	11	3	—	8	0	1	—	1	—	.215	.254	.354	.652
Yankee average		27	97	9	21	6	1	2	16	5	—	12	0	2	—	1	1	.216	.255	.356	.978
Career total		54	195	17	42	11	2	4	32	10	—	24	0	4	—	2	1	.215	.254	.354	.652
Yankee total		53	194	17	42	11	2	4	32	10	—	24	0	4	—	2	1	.216	.255	.356	.978

Lewis, George Edward (Duffy)

HEIGHT: 5'10"   THROWS: RIGHT   BATS: RIGHT   BORN: 04/18/1888 SAN FRANCISCO, CAL.   DIED: 6/17/1979 SALEM, NEW HAMPSHIRE   POSITIONS PLAYED: P, 3B, OF

YEAR	TEAM	GAMES	AB	RUNS	HITS	2B	3B	HR	RBI	BB	IBB	SO	HBP	SH	SF	SB	CS	BA	OBA	SA	FA
1910	Bos-A	151	541	64	153	29	7	8	68	32	—	—	4	27	—	10	—	.283	.328	.407	.944
1911	Bos-A	130	469	64	144	32	4	7	86	25	—	—	10	23	—	11	—	.307	.355	.437	.939
1912	Bos-A	154	581	85	165	36	9	6	109	52	—	—	3	31	—	9	—	.284	.346	.408	.947
1913	Bos-A	149	551	54	164	31	12	0	90	30	—	55	2	29	—	12	—	.298	.336	.397	.960
1914	Bos-A	146	510	53	142	37	9	2	79	57	—	41	5	24	—	22	31	.278	.357	.398	.952
1915	Bos-A	152	557	69	162	31	7	2	76	45	—	63	4	28	—	14	7	.291	.348	.382	.952
1916	Bos-A	152	563	56	151	29	5	1	56	33	—	56	4	24	—	16	—	.268	.313	.343	.970
1917	Bos-A	150	553	55	167	29	9	1	65	29	—	54	5	33	—	8	—	.302	.342	.392	.972
1919	**NY-A**	**141**	**559**	**67**	**152**	**23**	**4**	**7**	**89**	**17**	**—**	**42**	**0**	**26**	**—**	**8**	**—**	**.272**	**.293**	**.365**	**.985**
1920	**NY-A**	**107**	**365**	**34**	**99**	**8**	**1**	**4**	**61**	**24**	**—**	**32**	**2**	**16**	**—**	**2**	**8**	**.271**	**.320**	**.332**	**.961**
1921	Was-A	27	102	11	19	4	1	0	14	8	—	10	1	3	—	1	1	.186	.252	.245	.980
Career average		133	487	56	138	26	6	4	72	32	—	—	4	24	—	10	—	.284	.333	.384	.960
Yankee average		**124**	**462**	**51**	**126**	**16**	**3**	**6**	**75**	**21**	**—**	**37**	**1**	**21**	**—**	**5**	**—**	**.272**	**.304**	**.352**	**.973**
Career total		1459	5351	612	1518	289	68	38	793	352	—	353	40	264	—	113	47	.284	.333	.384	.960
Yankee total		**248**	**924**	**101**	**251**	**31**	**5**	**11**	**150**	**41**	**—**	**74**	**2**	**42**	**—**	**10**	**8**	**.272**	**.304**	**.352**	**.973**

Leyritz, James Joseph

HEIGHT: 5'11"   THROWS: RIGHT   BATS: RIGHT   BORN: 12/27/1963 LAKEWOOD, OHIO   POSITIONS PLAYED: C, 1B, 2B, 3B, OF, DH

YEAR	TEAM	GAMES	AB	RUNS	HITS	2B	3B	HR	RBI	BB	IBB	SO	HBP	SH	SF	SB	CS	BA	OBA	SA	FA
1990	**NY-A**	**92**	**303**	**28**	**78**	**13**	**1**	**5**	**25**	**27**	**1**	**51**	**7**	**1**	**1**	**2**	**0**	**.257**	**.331**	**.356**	**.929**
1991	**NY-A**	**32**	**77**	**8**	**14**	**3**	**0**	**0**	**4**	**13**	**0**	**15**	**0**	**1**	**0**	**0**	**1**	**.182**	**.300**	**.221**	**.909**
1992	**NY-A**	**63**	**144**	**17**	**37**	**6**	**0**	**7**	**26**	**14**	**1**	**22**	**6**	**0**	**3**	**0**	**0**	**.257**	**.341**	**.444**	**.998**
1993	**NY-A**	**95**	**259**	**43**	**80**	**14**	**0**	**14**	**53**	**37**	**3**	**59**	**8**	**0**	**1**	**0**	**1**	**.309**	**.410**	**.525**	**.993**
1994	**NY-A**	**75**	**249**	**47**	**66**	**12**	**0**	**17**	**58**	**35**	**1**	**61**	**6**	**0**	**3**	**0**	**0**	**.265**	**.365**	**.518**	**1.000**
1995	**NY-A**	**77**	**264**	**37**	**71**	**12**	**0**	**7**	**37**	**37**	**2**	**73**	**8**	**0**	**1**	**1**	**1**	**.269**	**.374**	**.394**	**.993**
1996	**NY-A**	**88**	**265**	**23**	**70**	**10**	**0**	**7**	**40**	**30**	**3**	**68**	**9**	**2**	**3**	**2**	**0**	**.264**	**.355**	**.381**	**1.000**
1997	Ana-A	84	294	47	81	7	0	11	50	37	2	56	3	3	5	1	1	.276	.357	.412	1.000
1997	Tex-A	37	85	11	24	4	0	0	14	23	0	22	3	1	1	1	1	.282	.446	.329	.984
1998	Bos-A	52	129	17	37	6	0	8	24	21	1	34	0	0	4	0	0	.287	.377	.519	1.000
1998	SD-N	62	143	17	38	10	0	4	18	21	0	40	0	0	1	0	0	.266	.358	.420	1.000
1999	SD-N	50	134	17	32	5	0	8	21	15	0	37	0	0	0	0	0	.239	.315	.455	.994
1999	**NY-A**	**31**	**66**	**8**	**15**	**4**	**1**	**0**	**5**	**13**	**0**	**17**	**0**	**0**	**1**	**0**	**0**	**.227**	**.350**	**.318**	**.985**
2000	**NY-A**	**24**	**55**	**2**	**12**	**0**	**0**	**1**	**4**	**7**	**0**	**14**	**1**	**0**	**0**	**0**	**0**	**.218**	**.317**	**.273**	**1.000**
2000	LA-N	41	60	3	12	1	0	1	8	7	0	12	1	0	0	0	0	.200	.294	.267	1.000
Career average		60	169	22	45	7	0	6	26	23	1	39	4	1	2	1	0	.264	.359	.415	.986
Yankee average		**64**	**187**	**24**	**49**	**8**	**0**	**6**	**28**	**24**	**1**	**42**	**5**	**0**	**1**	**1**	**0**	**.263**	**.359**	**.413**	**.979**
Career total		903	2527	325	667	107	2	90	387	337	14	581	52	8	24	7	4	.264	.359	.415	.986
Yankee total		**577**	**1682**	**213**	**443**	**74**	**2**	**58**	**252**	**213**	**11**	**380**	**45**	**4**	**13**	**5**	**3**	**.263**	**.359**	**.413**	**.979**

Lindell, John Harlan

HEIGHT: 6'4"   THROWS: RIGHT   BATS: RIGHT   BORN: 8/30/1916 GREELEY, COLORADO   DIED: 8/27/1985 NEWPORT BEACH, CAL.   POSITIONS PLAYED: P, 1B, OF

YEAR	TEAM	GAMES	AB	RUNS	HITS	2B	3B	HR	RBI	BB	IBB	SO	HBP	SH	SF	SB	CS	BA	OBA	SA	FA
1941	**NY-A**	**1**	**1**	**0**	**0**	**0**	**0**	**0**	**0**	**0**	**—**	**0**	**0**	**0**	**—**	**0**	**0**	**.000**	**.000**	**.000**	**.000**
1942	**NY-A**	**27**	**24**	**1**	**6**	**1**	**0**	**0**	**4**	**0**	**—**	**5**	**0**	**0**	**—**	**0**	**0**	**.250**	**.250**	**.292**	**.923**
1943	**NY-A**	**122**	**441**	**53**	**108**	**17**	**12**	**4**	**51**	**51**	**—**	**55**	**4**	**4**	**—**	**2**	**5**	**.245**	**.329**	**.365**	**.966**
1944	**NY-A**	**149**	**594**	**91**	**178**	**33**	**16**	**18**	**103**	**44**	**—**	**56**	**3**	**5**	**—**	**5**	**4**	**.300**	**.351**	**.500**	**.986**
1945	**NY-A**	**41**	**159**	**26**	**45**	**6**	**3**	**1**	**20**	**17**	**—**	**10**	**3**	**2**	**—**	**2**	**1**	**.283**	**.363**	**.382**	**.982**
1946	**NY-A**	**102**	**332**	**41**	**86**	**10**	**5**	**10**	**40**	**32**	**—**	**47**	**2**	**3**	**—**	**4**	**1**	**.259**	**.328**	**.410**	**.976**
1947	**NY-A**	**127**	**476**	**66**	**131**	**18**	**7**	**11**	**67**	**32**	**—**	**70**	**1**	**4**	**—**	**1**	**2**	**.275**	**.322**	**.412**	**.978**
1948	**NY-A**	**88**	**309**	**58**	**98**	**17**	**2**	**13**	**55**	**35**	**—**	**50**	**0**	**1**	**—**	**0**	**0**	**.317**	**.387**	**.511**	**.994**
1949	**NY-A**	**78**	**211**	**33**	**51**	**10**	**0**	**6**	**27**	**35**	**—**	**27**	**0**	**0**	**—**	**3**	**0**	**.242**	**.350**	**.374**	**.983**
1950	**NY-A**	**7**	**21**	**2**	**4**	**0**	**0**	**0**	**2**	**4**	**—**	**2**	**0**	**0**	**—**	**0**	**0**	**.190**	**.320**	**.190**	**.857**
1950	StL-N	36	113	16	21	5	2	5	16	15	—	24	1	3	—	0	0	.186	.287	.398	.984
1953	Pit-N	58	91	11	26	6	1	4	15	16	—	15	2	0	—	0	0	.286	.404	.505	.923
1953	Phi-N	11	18	3	7	1	0	0	2	6	—	2	0	0	—	0	0	.389	.542	.444	.667
1954	Phi-N	7	5	0	1	0	0	0	2	2	—	3	0	0	0	0	0	.200	.429	.200	.000
Career average		61	200	29	54	9	3	5	29	21	—	26	1	2	—	1	1	.273	.344	.429	.801
Yankee average		**74**	**257**	**37**	**71**	**11**	**5**	**6**	**37**	**25**	**—**	**32**	**1**	**2**	**—**	**2**	**1**	**.275**	**.343**	**.428**	**.865**
Career total		854	2795	401	762	124	48	72	404	289	—	366	16	22	0	17	13	.273	.344	.429	.801
Yankee total		**742**	**2568**	**371**	**707**	**112**	**45**	**63**	**369**	**250**	**—**	**322**	**13**	**19**	**—**	**17**	**13**	**.275**	**.343**	**.428**	**.865**

Linz, Philip Francis (Super Sub)

HEIGHT: 6'1"   THROWS: RIGHT   BATS: RIGHT   BORN: 6/4/1939 BALTIMORE, MARYLAND   POSITIONS PLAYED: 2B, 3B, SS, OF

YEAR	TEAM	GAMES	AB	RUNS	HITS	2B	3B	HR	RBI	BB	IBB	SO	HBP	SH	SF	SB	CS	BA	OBA	SA	FA
1962	NY-A	71	129	28	37	8	0	1	14	6	2	17	0	0	1	6	2	.287	.316	.372	.937
1963	NY-A	72	186	22	50	9	0	2	12	15	0	18	2	5	1	1	6	.269	.328	.349	1.000
1964	NY-A	112	368	63	92	21	3	5	25	43	2	61	2	4	0	3	4	.250	.332	.364	.952
1965	NY-A	99	285	37	59	12	1	2	16	30	1	33	0	7	2	2	1	.207	.281	.277	1.000
1966	Phi-N	40	70	4	14	3	0	0	6	2	0	14	0	0	0	0	0	.200	.222	.243	.971
1967	Phi-N	23	18	4	4	2	0	1	5	2	0	1	0	0	0	0	0	.222	.300	.500	.833
1967	NY-N	24	58	8	12	2	0	0	1	4	0	10	1	2	0	0	0	.207	.270	.241	.964
1968	NY-N	78	258	19	54	7	0	0	17	10	0	41	2	3	2	1	0	.209	.243	.236	.968
Career average		65	172	23	40	8	1	1	12	14	1	24	1	3	1	2	2	.235	.295	.311	.953
Yankee average		**88**	**242**	**38**	**60**	**13**	**1**	**3**	**17**	**24**	**1**	**32**	**1**	**4**	**1**	**3**	**3**	**.246**	**.314**	**.337**	**.972**
Career total		519	1372	185	322	64	4	11	96	112	5	195	7	21	6	13	13	.235	.295	.311	.953
Yankee total		**354**	**968**	**150**	**238**	**50**	**4**	**10**	**67**	**94**	**5**	**129**	**4**	**16**	**4**	**12**	**13**	**.246**	**.314**	**.337**	**.972**

Little, Richard Bryan

HEIGHT: 5'10"   THROWS: RIGHT   BATS: BOTH   BORN: 10/8/1959 HOUSTON, TEXAS   POSITIONS PLAYED: 2B, 3B, SS

YEAR	TEAM	GAMES	AB	RUNS	HITS	2B	3B	HR	RBI	BB	IBB	SO	HBP	SH	SF	SB	CS	BA	OBA	SA	FA
1982	Mon-N	29	42	6	9	0	0	0	3	4	0	6	0	0	1	2	1	.214	.277	.214	1.000
1983	Mon-N	106	350	48	91	15	3	1	36	50	1	22	2	5	4	4	5	.260	.352	.329	.968
1984	Mon-N	85	266	31	65	11	1	0	9	34	0	19	1	8	0	2	3	.244	.332	.293	.982
1985	Chi-A	73	188	35	47	9	1	2	27	26	0	21	3	3	3	0	1	.250	.345	.340	.000
1986	Chi-A	20	35	3	6	1	0	0	2	4	0	4	0	0	0	0	0	.171	.256	.200	1.000
1986	NY-A	14	41	3	8	1	0	0	0	2	0	7	0	0	0	0	0	.195	.233	.220	.975
Career average		55	154	21	38	6	1	1	13	20	0	13	1	3	1	1	2	.245	.333	.306	.821
Yankee average		**14**	**41**	**3**	**8**	**1**	**0**	**0**	**0**	**2**	**0**	**7**	**0**	**0**	**0**	**0**	**0**	**.195**	**.233**	**.220**	**.975**
Career total		327	922	126	226	37	5	3	77	120	1	79	6	16	8	8	10	.245	.333	.306	.821
Yankee total		**14**	**41**	**3**	**8**	**1**	**0**	**0**	**0**	**2**	**0**	**7**	**0**	**0**	**0**	**0**	**0**	**.195**	**.233**	**.220**	**.975**

Little, William Arthur (Jack)

HEIGHT: 5'11"   THROWS: RIGHT   BATS: RIGHT   BORN: 3/12/1891 MART, TEXAS   DIED: 7/27/1961 DALLAS, TEXAS   POSITIONS PLAYED: OF

YEAR	TEAM	GAMES	AB	RUNS	HITS	2B	3B	HR	RBI	BB	IBB	SO	HBP	SH	SF	SB	CS	BA	OBA	SA	FA
1912	NY-A	3	12	2	3	0	0	0	0	1	—	—	1	0	—	2	—	.250	.357	.250	1.000
Career average		3	12	2	3	0	0	0	0	1	—	—	1	0	—	2	—	.250	.357	.250	1.000
Yankee average		**3**	**12**	**2**	**3**	**0**	**0**	**0**	**0**	**1**	**—**	**—**	**1**	**0**	**—**	**2**	**—**	**.250**	**.357**	**.250**	**1.000**
Career total		3	12	2	3	0	0	0	0	1	—	—	1	0	—	2	—	.250	.357	.250	1.000
Yankee total		**3**	**12**	**2**	**3**	**0**	**0**	**0**	**0**	**1**	**—**	**—**	**1**	**0**	**—**	**2**	**—**	**.250**	**.357**	**.250**	**1.000**

Locklear, Gene

HEIGHT: 5'10"   THROWS: RIGHT   BATS: LEFT   BORN: 7/19/1949 LUMBERTON, NORTH CAROLINA   POSITIONS PLAYED: OF

YEAR	TEAM	GAMES	AB	RUNS	HITS	2B	3B	HR	RBI	BB	IBB	SO	HBP	SH	SF	SB	CS	BA	OBA	SA	FA
1973	Cin-N	29	26	6	5	0	0	0	0	2	0	5	1	0	0	0	0	.192	.276	.192	1.000
1973	SD-N	67	154	20	37	6	1	3	25	21	1	22	0	1	1	9	4	.240	.330	.351	.952
1974	SD-N	39	74	7	20	3	2	1	3	4	0	12	0	1	0	0	1	.270	.308	.405	1.000
1975	SD-N	100	237	31	76	11	1	5	27	22	4	26	1	1	2	4	2	.321	.378	.439	.970
1976	SD-N	43	67	9	15	3	0	0	8	4	1	15	0	2	1	0	0	.224	.264	.269	.952
1976	NY-A	13	32	2	7	1	0	0	1	2	0	7	0	0	0	0	0	.219	.265	.250	1.000
1977	NY-A	1	5	1	3	0	0	0	2	0	0	0	0	0	0	0	0	.600	.600	.600	.667
Career average		42	85	11	23	3	1	1	9	8	1	12	0	1	1	2	1	.274	.335	.373	.934
Yankee average		**7**	**19**	**2**	**5**	**1**	**0**	**0**	**2**	**1**	**0**	**4**	**0**	**0**	**0**	**0**	**0**	**.270**	**.308**	**.297**	**.834**
Career total		292	595	76	163	24	4	9	66	55	6	87	2	5	4	13	7	.274	.335	.373	.934
Yankee total		**14**	**37**	**3**	**10**	**1**	**0**	**0**	**3**	**2**	**0**	**7**	**0**	**0**	**0**	**0**	**0**	**.270**	**.308**	**.297**	**.834**

Lollar, John Sherman (Sherm)

HEIGHT: 6'1" THROWS: RIGHT BATS: RIGHT BORN: 8/23/1924 DURHAM, ARKANSAS DIED: 9/24/1977 SPRINGFIELD, MISSOURI POSITIONS PLAYED: C, 1B, 3B

YEAR	TEAM	GAMES	AB	RUNS	HITS	2B	3B	HR	RBI	BB	IBB	SO	HBP	SH	SF	SB	CS	BA	OBA	SA	FA
1946	Cle-A	28	62	7	15	6	0	1	9	5	—	9	0	3	—	0	1	.242	.299	.387	.990
1947	**NY-A**	**11**	**32**	**4**	**7**	**0**	**1**	**1**	**6**	**1**	—	**5**	**0**	**0**	—	**0**	**1**	**.219**	**.242**	**.375**	**1.000**
1948	**NY-A**	**22**	**38**	**0**	**8**	**0**	**0**	**0**	**4**	**1**	—	**6**	**0**	**0**	—	**0**	**0**	**.211**	**.231**	**.211**	**.976**
1949	StL-A	109	284	28	74	9	1	8	49	32	—	22	2	3	—	0	1	.261	.340	.384	.988
1950	StL-A	126	396	55	111	22	3	13	65	64	—	25	8	6	—	2	0	.280	.391	.449	.981
1951	StL-A	98	310	44	78	21	0	8	44	43	—	26	4	2	—	1	0	.252	.350	.397	.995
1952	Chi-A	132	375	35	90	15	0	13	50	54	—	34	12	6	—	1	0	.240	.354	.384	.989
1953	Chi-A	113	334	46	96	19	0	8	54	47	—	29	8	7	—	1	0	.287	.388	.416	.994
1954	Chi-A	107	316	31	77	13	0	7	34	37	—	28	7	3	2	0	1	.244	.334	.351	.993
1955	Chi-A	138	426	67	111	13	1	16	61	68	12	34	10	4	2	2	2	.261	.374	.408	.995
1956	Chi-A	136	450	55	132	28	2	11	75	53	4	34	16	2	6	2	0	.293	.383	.438	.993
1957	Chi-A	101	351	33	90	11	2	11	70	35	2	24	13	0	4	2	0	.256	.342	.393	.998
1958	Chi-A	127	421	53	115	16	0	20	84	57	3	37	8	1	4	2	1	.273	.367	.454	.987
1959	Chi-A	140	505	63	134	22	3	22	84	55	6	49	9	2	5	4	3	.265	.345	.451	.993
1960	Chi-A	129	421	43	106	23	0	7	46	42	3	39	8	5	8	2	0	.252	.326	.356	.995
1961	Chi-A	116	337	38	95	10	1	7	41	37	10	22	6	1	3	0	0	.282	.360	.380	.998
1962	Chi-A	84	220	17	59	12	0	2	26	32	9	23	3	1	0	1	0	.268	.369	.350	.991
1963	Chi-A	35	73	4	17	4	0	0	6	8	0	7	1	1	0	0	0	.233	.317	.288	1.000
Career average		97	297	35	79	14	1	9	45	37	—	25	6	3	—	1	1	.264	.359	.402	.992
Yankee average		**17**	**35**	**2**	**8**	**0**	**1**	**1**	**5**	**1**	—	**6**	**0**	**0**	—	**0**	**1**	**.214**	**.236**	**.286**	**.988**
Career total		1752	5351	623	1415	244	14	155	808	671	49	453	115	47	34	20	10	.264	.357	.402	.992
Yankee total		**33**	**70**	**4**	**15**	**0**	**1**	**1**	**10**	**2**	—	**11**	**0**	**0**	—	**0**	**1**	**.214**	**.236**	**.286**	**.988**

Lombardi, Phillip Arden

HEIGHT: 6'2" THROWS: RIGHT BATS: RIGHT BORN: 2/20/1963 ABILENE, TEXAS POSITIONS PLAYED: C, 1B, OF

YEAR	TEAM	GAMES	AB	RUNS	HITS	2B	3B	HR	RBI	BB	IBB	SO	HBP	SH	SF	SB	CS	BA	OBA	SA	FA
1986	**NY-A**	**20**	**36**	**6**	**10**	**3**	**0**	**2**	**6**	**4**	**0**	**7**	**1**	**0**	**0**	**0**	**0**	**.278**	**.366**	**.528**	**.893**
1987	**NY-A**	**5**	**8**	**0**	**1**	**0**	**0**	**0**	**0**	**0**	**0**	**2**	**0**	**0**	**0**	**0**	**0**	**.125**	**.125**	**.125**	**1.000**
1989	NY-N	18	48	4	11	1	0	1	3	5	0	8	0	0	0	0	0	.229	.302	.313	.980
Career average		14	31	3	7	1	0	1	3	3	0	6	0	0	0	0	0	.239	.314	.380	.958
Yankee average		**13**	**22**	**3**	**6**	**2**	**0**	**1**	**3**	**2**	**0**	**5**	**1**	**0**	**0**	**0**	**0**	**.250**	**.327**	**.455**	**.947**
Career total		43	92	10	22	4	0	3	9	9	0	17	1	0	0	0	0	.239	.314	.380	.958
Yankee total		**25**	**44**	**6**	**11**	**3**	**0**	**2**	**6**	**4**	**0**	**9**	**1**	**0**	**0**	**0**	**0**	**.250**	**.327**	**.455**	**.947**

Long, Herman C. (Germany *or* The Flying Dutchman)

HEIGHT: 5'8" THROWS: RIGHT BATS: LEFT BORN: 4/13/1866 CHICAGO, ILLINOIS DIED: 9/17/1909 DENVER, COLORADO POSITIONS PLAYED: 1B, 2B, 3B, SS, OF

YEAR	TEAM	GAMES	AB	RUNS	HITS	2B	3B	HR	RBI	BB	IBB	SO	HBP	SH	SF	SB	CS	BA	OBA	SA	FA
1889	KC-AA	136	574	137	158	32	6	3	60	64	—	63	10	—	—	89	—	.275	.358	.368	.874
1890	Bos-N	101	431	95	108	15	3	8	52	40	—	34	0	—	—	49	—	.251	.314	.355	.898
1891	Bos-N	139	577	129	163	21	12	9	76	80	—	51	0	—	—	60	—	.282	.370	.407	.902
1892	Bos-N	151	646	115	181	33	6	6	78	44	—	36	0	—	—	57	—	.280	.326	.378	.889
1893	Bos-N	128	552	149	159	22	6	6	58	73	—	32	0	—	—	38	—	.288	.371	.382	.883
1894	Bos-N	104	475	136	154	28	11	12	79	35	—	17	0	8	—	24	—	.324	.371	.505	.920
1895	Bos-N	124	535	109	169	23	10	9	75	31	—	12	3	21	—	35	—	.316	.357	.447	.891
1896	Bos-N	120	501	105	172	26	8	6	100	26	—	16	5	12	—	36	—	.343	.382	.463	.897
1897	Bos-N	107	450	89	145	32	7	3	69	23	—	—	2	17	—	22	—	.322	.358	.444	.905
1898	Bos-N	144	589	99	156	21	10	6	99	39	—	—	0	17	—	20	—	.265	.311	.365	1.000
1899	Bos-N	145	578	91	153	30	8	6	100	45	—	—	3	25	—	20	—	.265	.321	.375	.929
1900	Bos-N	125	486	80	127	19	4	12	66	44	—	—	2	18	—	26	—	.261	.325	.391	.937
1901	Bos-N	138	518	54	112	14	6	3	68	25	—	—	1	15	—	20	—	.216	.254	.284	.946
1902	Bos-N	120	439	40	101	11	0	2	44	31	—	—	1	13	—	24	—	.230	.282	.269	.916
1903	**NY-A**	**22**	**80**	**6**	**15**	**3**	**0**	**0**	**8**	**2**	—	—	**0**	**6**	—	**3**	—	**.188**	**.207**	**.225**	**.889**
1903	Det-A	69	239	21	53	12	0	0	23	10	—	—	1	6	—	11	—	.222	.256	.272	.970
1904	Phi-N	1	4	0	1	0	0	0	0	0	—	—	0	0	—	0	—	.250	.250	.250	.889
Career average		110	451	86	125	20	6	5	62	36	—	—	2	—	—	31	—	.277	.333	.383	.914
Yankee average		**22**	**80**	**6**	**15**	**3**	**0**	**0**	**8**	**2**	—	—	**0**	**6**	—	**3**	—	**.188**	**.207**	**.225**	**.889**
Career total		1874	7674	1455	2127	342	97	91	1055	612	—	261	28	158	—	534	—	.277	.333	.383	.914
Yankee total		**22**	**80**	**6**	**15**	**3**	**0**	**0**	**8**	**2**	—	—	**0**	**6**	—	**3**	—	**.188**	**.207**	**.225**	**.889**

Long, Richard Dale

HEIGHT: 6'4"   THROWS: LEFT   BATS: LEFT   BORN: 2/6/1926 SPRINGFIELD, MISSOURI   DIED: 1/27/1991 PALM COAST, FLORIDA   POSITIONS PLAYED: C, 1B, OF

YEAR	TEAM	GAMES	AB	RUNS	HITS	2B	3B	HR	RBI	BB	IBB	SO	HBP	SH	SF	SB	CS	BA	OBA	SA	FA
1951	Pit-N	10	12	1	2	0	0	1	1	0	—	3	0	0	—	0	0	.167	.167	.417	1.000
1951	StL-A	34	105	11	25	5	1	2	11	10	—	22	1	0	—	0	0	.238	.310	.362	.988
1955	Pit-N	131	419	59	122	19	13	16	79	48	6	72	1	6	4	0	1	.291	.362	.513	.988
1956	Pit-N	148	517	64	136	20	7	27	91	54	11	85	0	0	11	1	0	.263	.326	.485	.982
1957	Pit-N	7	22	0	4	1	0	0	5	4	0	10	0	0	1	0	0	.182	.296	.227	1.000
1957	Chi-N	123	397	55	121	19	0	21	62	52	4	63	1	1	4	1	1	.305	.383	.511	.995
1958	Chi-N	142	480	68	130	26	4	20	75	66	9	64	2	0	6	2	0	.271	.357	.467	.992
1959	Chi-N	110	296	34	70	10	3	14	37	31	2	53	0	0	3	0	0	.236	.306	.432	.985
1960	SF-N	37	54	4	9	0	0	3	6	7	1	7	0	0	0	0	0	.167	.262	.333	1.000
1960	**NY-A**	**26**	**41**	**6**	**15**	**3**	**1**	**3**	**10**	**5**	**1**	**6**	**0**	**0**	**0**	**0**	**0**	**.366**	**.435**	**.707**	**.988**
1961	Was-A	123	377	52	94	20	4	17	49	39	5	41	1	0	0	0	0	.249	.317	.459	.983
1962	Was-A	67	191	17	46	8	0	4	24	18	0	22	1	0	6	0	0	.241	.307	.346	.996
1962	**NY-A**	**41**	**94**	**12**	**28**	**4**	**0**	**4**	**17**	**18**	**0**	**9**	**0**	**0**	**2**	**5**	**1**	**.298**	**.404**	**.468**	**.992**
1963	**NY-A**	**14**	**15**	**1**	**3**	**0**	**0**	**0**	**0**	**1**	**0**	**3**	**0**	**0**	**2**	**1**	**0**	**.200**	**.250**	**.200**	**.917**
Career average		72	216	27	58	10	2	9	33	25	—	33	1	1	—	1	0	.267	.345	.464	.986
Yankee average		**27**	**50**	**6**	**15**	**2**	**0**	**2**	**9**	**8**	**0**	**6**	**0**	**0**	—	**1**	**0**	**.307**	**.398**	**.507**	**.966**
Career total		1013	3020	384	805	135	33	132	467	353	39	460	7	7	39	10	3	.267	.341	.464	.986
Yankee total		**81**	**150**	**19**	**46**	**7**	**1**	**7**	**27**	**24**	**1**	**18**	**0**	**0**	**2**	**1**	**0**	**.307**	**.398**	**.507**	**.966**

Lopez, Arturo BORN ARTURO LOPEZ (RODRIGUEZ)

HEIGHT: 5'9"   THROWS: LEFT   BATS: LEFT   BORN: 6/8/1937 MAYAGUEZ, PUERTO RICO   POSITIONS PLAYED: OF

YEAR	TEAM	GAMES	AB	RUNS	HITS	2B	3B	HR	RBI	BB	IBB	SO	HBP	SH	SF	SB	CS	BA	OBA	SA	FA
1965	**NY-A**	**38**	**49**	**5**	**7**	**0**	**0**	**0**	**0**	**1**	**0**	**6**	**0**	**1**	**0**	**0**	**0**	**.143**	**.160**	**.143**	**.958**
Career average		38	49	5	7	0	0	0	0	1	0	6	0	1	0	0	0	.143	.160	.143	.958
Yankee average		**38**	**49**	**5**	**7**	**0**	**0**	**0**	**0**	**1**	**0**	**6**	**0**	**1**	**0**	**0**	**0**	**.143**	**.160**	**.143**	**.958**
Career total		38	49	5	7	0	0	0	0	1	0	6	0	1	0	0	0	.143	.160	.143	.958
Yankee total		**38**	**49**	**5**	**7**	**0**	**0**	**0**	**0**	**1**	**0**	**6**	**0**	**1**	**0**	**0**	**0**	**.143**	**.160**	**.143**	**.958**

Lopez, Hector Headley BORN HECTOR HEADLEY LOPEZ (SWAINSON)

HEIGHT: 5'11"   THROWS: RIGHT   BATS: RIGHT   BORN: 7/8/1929 COLON, PANAMA   POSITIONS PLAYED: 1B, 2B, 3B, SS, OF

YEAR	TEAM	GAMES	AB	RUNS	HITS	2B	3B	HR	RBI	BB	IBB	SO	HBP	SH	SF	SB	CS	BA	OBA	SA	FA
1955	KC-A	128	483	50	140	15	2	15	68	33	1	58	3	4	4	1	4	.290	.337	.422	.970
1956	KC-A	151	561	91	153	27	3	18	69	63	3	73	3	8	4	4	5	.273	.347	.428	.940
1957	KC-A	121	391	51	115	19	4	11	35	41	5	66	0	4	5	1	6	.294	.357	.448	.937
1958	KC-A	151	564	84	147	28	4	17	73	49	2	61	2	7	9	2	2	.261	.317	.415	.974
1959	KC-A	35	135	22	38	10	3	6	24	8	0	23	1	1	1	1	0	.281	.324	.533	.933
1959	**NY-A**	**112**	**406**	**60**	**115**	**16**	**2**	**16**	**69**	**28**	**1**	**54**	**6**	**3**	**4**	**3**	**1**	**.283**	**.336**	**.451**	**.955**
1960	**NY-A**	**131**	**408**	**66**	**116**	**14**	**6**	**9**	**42**	**46**	**0**	**64**	**4**	**9**	**2**	**1**	**1**	**.284**	**.361**	**.414**	**1.000**
1961	**NY-A**	**93**	**243**	**27**	**54**	**7**	**2**	**3**	**22**	**24**	**1**	**38**	**1**	**2**	**3**	**1**	**0**	**.222**	**.292**	**.305**	**.977**
1962	**NY-A**	**106**	**335**	**45**	**92**	**19**	**1**	**6**	**48**	**33**	**2**	**53**	**0**	**2**	**2**	**0**	**1**	**.275**	**.338**	**.391**	**1.000**
1963	**NY-A**	**130**	**433**	**54**	**108**	**13**	**4**	**14**	**52**	**35**	**5**	**71**	**0**	**2**	**3**	**1**	**2**	**.249**	**.304**	**.395**	**1.000**
1964	**NY-A**	**127**	**285**	**34**	**74**	**9**	**3**	**10**	**34**	**24**	**2**	**54**	**1**	**1**	**2**	**1**	**1**	**.260**	**.317**	**.418**	**.971**
1965	**NY-A**	**111**	**283**	**25**	**74**	**12**	**2**	**7**	**39**	**26**	**2**	**61**	**1**	**3**	**4**	**0**	**0**	**.261**	**.322**	**.392**	**.942**
1966	**NY-A**	**54**	**117**	**14**	**25**	**4**	**1**	**4**	**16**	**8**	**0**	**20**	**1**	**2**	**1**	**0**	**0**	**.214**	**.268**	**.368**	**.936**
Career average		112	357	48	96	15	3	11	46	32	2	54	2	4	3	1	2	.269	.330	.415	.887
Yankee average		**108**	**314**	**41**	**82**	**12**	**3**	**9**	**40**	**28**	**2**	**52**	**2**	**3**	**3**	**1**	**1**	**.262**	**.324**	**.399**	**.848**
Career total		1450	4644	623	1251	193	37	136	591	418	24	696	23	48	44	16	23	.269	.330	.415	.887
Yankee total		**864**	**2510**	**325**	**658**	**94**	**21**	**69**	**322**	**224**	**13**	**415**	**14**	**24**	**21**	**7**	**6**	**.262**	**.324**	**.399**	**.848**

Louden, William P. (Baldy)

HEIGHT: 5'11"   THROWS: RIGHT   BATS: RIGHT   BORN: 08/27/1885 PIEDMONT, WEST VA.   DIED: 12/8/1935 PIEDMONT, WEST VA.   POSITIONS PLAYED: 2B, 3B, SS, OF

YEAR	TEAM	GAMES	AB	RUNS	HITS	2B	3B	HR	RBI	BB	IBB	SO	HBP	SH	SF	SB	CS	BA	OBA	SA	FA
1907	**NY-A**	**4**	**9**	**4**	**1**	**0**	**0**	**0**	**0**	**2**	—	—	**0**	**0**	—	**1**	—	**.111**	**.273**	**.111**	**.750**
1912	Det-A	122	403	57	97	12	4	1	36	58	—	—	11	17	—	28	—	.241	.352	.298	.951
1913	Det-A	76	191	28	46	4	5	0	23	24	—	22	6	10	—	6	—	.241	.344	.314	.906
1914	Buf-F	126	431	73	135	11	4	6	63	52	—	41	3	18	—	35	—	.313	.391	.399	.931

(continued)

(continued)

YEAR	TEAM	GAMES	AB	RUNS	HITS	2B	3B	HR	RBI	BB	IBB	SO	HBP	SH	SF	SB	CS	BA	OBA	SA	FA
1915	Buf-F	141	469	67	132	18	5	4	48	64	—	45	4	20	—	30	—	.281	.372	.367	.978
1916	Cin-N	134	439	38	96	16	4	1	32	54	—	54	6	4	—	12	—	.219	.313	.280	.968
Career average		101	324	45	85	10	4	2	34	42	—	—	5	12	—	19	—	.261	.355	.334	.914
Yankee average		**4**	**9**	**4**	**1**	**0**	**0**	**0**	**0**	**2**	**—**	**—**	**0**	**0**	**—**	**1**	**—**	**.111**	**.273**	**.111**	**.750**
Career total		603	1942	267	507	61	22	12	202	254	—	162	30	69	—	112	—	.261	.355	.334	.914
Yankee total		**4**	**9**	**4**	**1**	**0**	**0**	**0**	**0**	**2**	**—**	**—**	**0**	**0**	**—**	**1**	**—**	**.111**	**.273**	**.111**	**.750**

Lovullo, Salvatore Anthony (Torey)

HEIGHT: 6'0"   THROWS: RIGHT   BATS: BOTH   BORN: 7/25/1965 SANTA MONICA, CALIFORNIA   POSITIONS PLAYED: 1B, 2B, 3B, SS, OF

YEAR	TEAM	GAMES	AB	RUNS	HITS	2B	3B	HR	RBI	BB	IBB	SO	HBP	SH	SF	SB	CS	BA	OBA	SA	FA
1988	Det-A	12	21	2	8	1	1	1	2	1	0	2	0	1	0	0	0	.381	.409	.667	1.000
1989	Det-A	29	87	8	10	2	0	1	4	14	0	20	0	1	2	0	0	.115	.233	.172	.963
1991	**NY-A**	**22**	**51**	**0**	**9**	**2**	**0**	**0**	**2**	**5**	**1**	**7**	**0**	**3**	**0**	**0**	**0**	**.176**	**.250**	**.216**	**.940**
1993	Cal-A	116	367	42	92	20	0	6	30	36	1	49	1	3	2	7	6	.251	.318	.354	1.000
1994	Sea-A	36	72	9	16	5	0	2	7	9	1	13	0	0	0	1	0	.222	.309	.375	1.000
1996	Oak-A	65	82	15	18	4	0	3	9	11	0	17	2	3	1	1	2	.220	.323	.378	.955
1998	Cle-A	6	19	1	4	1	0	0	1	1	0	2	0	1	0	0	0	.211	.250	.263	.947
1999	Phi-N	17	38	3	8	0	0	2	5	3	0	11	0	0	0	0	0	.211	.268	.368	1.000
Career average		38	92	10	21	4	0	2	8	10	0	15	0	2	1	1	1	.224	.301	.335	.976
Yankee average		**22**	**51**	**0**	**9**	**2**	**0**	**0**	**2**	**5**	**1**	**7**	**0**	**3**	**0**	**0**	**0**	**.176**	**.250**	**.216**	**.940**
Career total		303	737	80	165	35	1	15	60	80	3	121	3	12	5	9	8	.224	.301	.335	.976
Yankee total		**22**	**51**	**0**	**9**	**2**	**0**	**0**	**2**	**5**	**1**	**7**	**0**	**3**	**0**	**0**	**0**	**.176**	**.250**	**.216**	**.940**

Lucadello, John (Johnny)

HEIGHT: 5'11"   THROWS: RIGHT   BATS: BOTH   BORN: 2/22/1919 THURBER, TEXAS   POSITIONS PLAYED: 2B, 3B, SS, OF

YEAR	TEAM	GAMES	AB	RUNS	HITS	2B	3B	HR	RBI	BB	IBB	SO	HBP	SH	SF	SB	CS	BA	OBA	SA	FA
1938	StL-A	7	20	1	3	1	0	0	0	0	—	0	0	0	—	0	0	.150	.150	.200	.909
1939	StL-A	9	30	0	7	2	0	0	4	2	—	4	0	1	—	0	0	.233	.281	.300	.912
1940	StL-A	17	63	15	20	4	2	2	10	6	—	4	2	0	—	1	0	.317	.394	.540	.968
1941	StL-A	107	351	58	98	22	4	2	31	48	—	23	0	1	—	5	2	.279	.366	.382	.855
1946	StL-A	87	210	21	52	7	1	1	15	36	—	20	0	3	—	0	1	.248	.358	.305	.989
1947	**NY-A**	**12**	**12**	**0**	**1**	**0**	**0**	**0**	**0**	**1**	**—**	**5**	**0**	**0**	**—**	**0**	**0**	**.083**	**.154**	**.083**	**1.000**
Career average		40	114	16	30	6	1	1	10	16	—	9	0	1	—	1	1	.264	.353	.359	.939
Yankee average		**12**	**12**	**0**	**1**	**0**	**0**	**0**	**0**	**1**	**—**	**5**	**0**	**0**	**—**	**0**	**0**	**.083**	**.154**	**.083**	**1.000**
Career total		239	686	95	181	36	7	5	60	93	—	56	2	5	—	6	3	.264	.353	.359	.939
Yankee total		**12**	**12**	**0**	**1**	**0**	**0**	**0**	**0**	**1**	**—**	**5**	**0**	**0**	**—**	**0**	**0**	**.083**	**.154**	**.083**	**1.000**

Lucey, Joseph Earl (Joe *or* Scootch)

HEIGHT: 6'0"   THROWS: RIGHT   BATS: RIGHT   BORN: 3/27/1897 HOLYOKE, MASSACHUSETTS   DIED: 7/30/1980 HOLYOKE, MASS.   POSITIONS PLAYED: P, 2B, SS

YEAR	TEAM	GAMES	AB	RUNS	HITS	2B	3B	HR	RBI	BB	IBB	SO	HBP	SH	SF	SB	CS	BA	OBA	SA	FA
1920	**NY-A**	**3**	**3**	**0**	**0**	**0**	**0**	**0**	**0**	**0**	**—**	**0**	**0**	**0**	**—**	**0**	**0**	**.000**	**.000**	**.000**	**1.000**
1925	Bos-A	10	15	0	2	0	0	0	0	0	—	4	0	0	—	0	0	.133	.133	.133	.889
Career average		7	9	0	1	0	0	0	0	0	—	2	0	0	—	0	0	.111	.111	.111	.945
Yankee average		**3**	**3**	**0**	**0**	**0**	**0**	**0**	**0**	**0**	**—**	**0**	**0**	**0**	**—**	**0**	**0**	**.000**	**.000**	**.000**	**1.000**
Career total		13	18	0	2	0	0	0	0	0	—	4	0	0	—	0	0	.111	.111	.111	.945
Yankee total		**3**	**3**	**0**	**0**	**0**	**0**	**0**	**0**	**0**	**—**	**0**	**0**	**0**	**—**	**0**	**0**	**.000**	**.000**	**.000**	**1.000**

Luebbe, Roy John

HEIGHT: 6'0"   THROWS: RIGHT   BATS: BOTH   BORN: 9/17/1900 PARKERSBURG, IOWA   DIED: 8/21/1985 PAPILLION, NEBRASKA   POSITIONS PLAYED: C

YEAR	TEAM	GAMES	AB	RUNS	HITS	2B	3B	HR	RBI	BB	IBB	SO	HBP	SH	SF	SB	CS	BA	OBA	SA	FA
1925	**NY-A**	**8**	**15**	**1**	**0**	**0**	**0**	**0**	**3**	**2**	**—**	**6**	**0**	**1**	**—**	**0**	**0**	**.000**	**.118**	**.000**	**1.000**
Career average		8	15	1	0	0	0	0	3	2	—	6	0	1	—	0	0	.000	.118	.000	1.000
Yankee average		**8**	**15**	**1**	**0**	**0**	**0**	**0**	**3**	**2**	**—**	**6**	**0**	**1**	**—**	**0**	**0**	**.000**	**.118**	**.000**	**1.000**
Career total		8	15	1	0	0	0	0	3	2	—	6	0	1	—	0	0	.000	.118	.000	1.000
Yankee total		**8**	**15**	**1**	**0**	**0**	**0**	**0**	**3**	**2**	**—**	**6**	**0**	**1**	**—**	**0**	**0**	**.000**	**.118**	**.000**	**1.000**

Lumpe, Jerry Dean

HEIGHT: 6'2" THROWS: RIGHT BATS: LEFT BORN: 6/2/1933 LINCOLN, MISSOURI POSITIONS PLAYED: 2B, 3B, SS

YEAR	TEAM	GAMES	AB	RUNS	HITS	2B	3B	HR	RBI	BB	IBB	SO	HBP	SH	SF	SB	CS	BA	OBA	SA	FA
1956	**NY-A**	**20**	**62**	**12**	**16**	**3**	**0**	**0**	**4**	**5**	**2**	**11**	**0**	**1**	**0**	**1**	**1**	**.258**	**.313**	**.306**	**.916**
1957	**NY-A**	**40**	**103**	**15**	**35**	**6**	**2**	**0**	**11**	**9**	**0**	**13**	**0**	**0**	**1**	**2**	**2**	**.340**	**.389**	**.437**	**.956**
1958	**NY-A**	**81**	**232**	**34**	**59**	**8**	**4**	**3**	**32**	**23**	**2**	**21**	**1**	**2**	**4**	**1**	**2**	**.254**	**.319**	**.362**	**.943**
1959	**NY-A**	**18**	**45**	**2**	**10**	**0**	**0**	**0**	**2**	**6**	**5**	**7**	**0**	**2**	**0**	**0**	**0**	**.222**	**.314**	**.222**	**1.000**
1959	KC-A	108	403	47	98	11	5	3	28	41	1	32	0	7	0	2	1	.243	.313	.318	.986
1960	KC-A	146	574	69	156	19	3	8	53	48	1	49	0	4	4	1	1	.272	.326	.357	.960
1961	KC-A	148	569	81	167	29	9	3	54	48	0	39	2	4	4	1	0	.293	.348	.392	.979
1962	KC-A	156	641	89	193	34	10	10	83	44	0	38	0	6	9	0	2	.301	.341	.432	1.000
1963	KC-A	157	595	75	161	26	7	5	59	58	3	44	0	6	4	3	2	.271	.333	.363	.988
1964	Det-A	158	624	75	160	21	6	6	46	50	3	61	2	8	4	2	1	.256	.312	.338	.983
1965	Det-A	145	502	72	129	15	3	4	39	56	1	34	3	10	4	7	0	.257	.333	.323	.985
1966	Det-A	113	385	30	89	14	3	1	26	24	1	44	0	7	2	0	3	.231	.275	.291	.991
1967	Det-A	81	177	19	41	4	0	4	17	16	2	18	0	0	0	0	0	.232	.295	.322	.917
Career average		106	378	48	101	15	4	4	35	33	2	32	1	4	3	2	1	.268	.325	.356	.970
Yankee average		**40**	**111**	**16**	**30**	**4**	**2**	**1**	**12**	**11**	**2**	**13**	**0**	**1**	**1**	**1**	**1**	**.271**	**.334**	**.357**	**.954**
Career total		1371	4912	620	1314	190	52	47	454	428	21	411	8	57	36	20	15	.268	.325	.356	.970
Yankee total		**159**	**442**	**63**	**120**	**17**	**6**	**3**	**49**	**43**	**9**	**52**	**1**	**5**	**5**	**4**	**5**	**.271**	**.334**	**.357**	**.954**

Lusader, Scott Edward

HEIGHT: 5'10" THROWS: LEFT BATS: LEFT BORN: 9/30/1964 CHICAGO, ILLINOIS POSITIONS PLAYED: OF

YEAR	TEAM	GAMES	AB	RUNS	HITS	2B	3B	HR	RBI	BB	IBB	SO	HBP	SH	SF	SB	CS	BA	OBA	SA	FA
1987	Det-A	23	47	8	15	3	1	1	8	5	1	7	0	1	1	1	0	.319	.377	.489	.967
1988	Det-A	16	16	3	1	0	0	1	3	1	0	4	0	0	1	0	0	.063	.111	.250	1.000
1989	Det-A	40	103	15	26	4	0	1	8	9	0	21	0	0	1	3	0	.252	.310	.320	.933
1990	Det-A	45	87	13	21	2	0	2	16	12	0	8	0	0	3	0	0	.241	.324	.333	.982
1991	**NY-A**	**11**	**7**	**2**	**1**	**0**	**0**	**0**	**1**	**1**	**0**	**3**	**0**	**0**	**0**	**0**	**1**	**.143**	**.250**	**.143**	**1.000**
Career average		27	52	8	13	2	0	1	7	6	0	9	0	0	1	1	0	.246	.313	.346	.976
Yankee average		**11**	**7**	**2**	**1**	**0**	**0**	**0**	**1**	**1**	**0**	**3**	**0**	**0**	**0**	**0**	**1**	**.143**	**.250**	**.143**	**1.000**
Career total		135	260	41	64	9	1	5	36	28	1	43	0	1	6	4	1	.246	.313	.346	.976
Yankee total		**11**	**7**	**2**	**1**	**0**	**0**	**0**	**1**	**1**	**0**	**3**	**0**	**0**	**0**	**0**	**1**	**.143**	**.250**	**.143**	**1.000**

Lyttle, James Lawrence

HEIGHT: 6'0" THROWS: RIGHT BATS: LEFT BORN: 5/20/1946 HAMILTON, OHIO POSITIONS PLAYED: OF

YEAR	TEAM	GAMES	AB	RUNS	HITS	2B	3B	HR	RBI	BB	IBB	SO	HBP	SH	SF	SB	CS	BA	OBA	SA	FA
1969	**NY-A**	**28**	**83**	**7**	**15**	**4**	**0**	**0**	**4**	**4**	**0**	**19**	**0**	**0**	**0**	**1**	**2**	**.181**	**.218**	**.229**	**.983**
1970	**NY-A**	**87**	**126**	**20**	**39**	**7**	**1**	**3**	**14**	**10**	**1**	**26**	**0**	**2**	**2**	**3**	**6**	**.310**	**.355**	**.452**	**.989**
1971	**NY-A**	**49**	**86**	**7**	**17**	**5**	**0**	**1**	**7**	**8**	**2**	**18**	**1**	**1**	**1**	**0**	**2**	**.198**	**.271**	**.291**	**1.000**
1972	Chi-A	44	82	8	19	5	2	0	5	1	0	28	0	1	0	0	1	.232	.241	.341	1.000
1973	Mon-N	49	116	12	30	5	1	4	19	9	2	14	0	2	3	0	0	.259	.305	.422	.974
1974	Mon-N	25	9	1	3	0	0	0	2	1	1	3	0	0	1	0	0	.333	.364	.333	1.000
1975	Mon-N	44	55	7	15	4	0	0	6	13	3	6	0	1	1	0	1	.273	.406	.345	1.000
1976	Mon-N	42	85	6	23	4	1	1	8	7	1	13	0	1	0	0	0	.271	.326	.376	.977
1976	LA-N	23	68	3	15	3	0	0	5	8	4	12	0	0	0	0	1	.221	.303	.265	1.000
Career average		43	79	8	20	4	1	1	8	7	2	15	0	1	1	0	2	.248	.305	.352	.991
Yankee average		**55**	**98**	**11**	**24**	**5**	**0**	**1**	**8**	**7**	**1**	**21**	**0**	**1**	**1**	**1**	**3**	**.241**	**.293**	**.342**	**.991**
Career total		391	710	71	176	37	5	9	70	61	14	139	1	8	8	4	15	.248	.305	.352	.991
Yankee total		**164**	**295**	**34**	**71**	**16**	**1**	**4**	**25**	**22**	**3**	**63**	**1**	**3**	**3**	**4**	**10**	**.241**	**.293**	**.342**	**.991**

Maas, Kevin Christian

HEIGHT: 6'3" THROWS: LEFT BATS: LEFT BORN: 1/20/1965 CASTRO VALLEY, CALIFORNIA POSITIONS PLAYED: 1B

YEAR	TEAM	GAMES	AB	RUNS	HITS	2B	3B	HR	RBI	BB	IBB	SO	HBP	SH	SF	SB	CS	BA	OBA	SA	FA
1990	**NY-A**	**79**	**254**	**42**	**64**	**9**	**0**	**21**	**41**	**43**	**10**	**76**	**3**	**0**	**0**	**1**	**2**	**.252**	**.367**	**.535**	**.983**
1991	**NY-A**	**148**	**500**	**69**	**110**	**14**	**1**	**23**	**63**	**83**	**3**	**128**	**4**	**0**	**5**	**5**	**1**	**.220**	**.333**	**.390**	**.983**
1992	**NY-A**	**98**	**286**	**35**	**71**	**12**	**0**	**11**	**35**	**25**	**4**	**63**	**0**	**0**	**4**	**3**	**1**	**.248**	**.305**	**.406**	**.986**
1993	**NY-A**	**59**	**151**	**20**	**31**	**4**	**0**	**9**	**25**	**24**	**2**	**32**	**1**	**0**	**1**	**1**	**1**	**.205**	**.316**	**.411**	**.984**
1995	Min-A	22	57	5	11	4	0	1	5	7	2	11	0	0	0	0	0	.193	.281	.316	.936
Career average		81	250	34	57	9	0	13	34	36	4	62	2	0	2	2	1	.230	.329	.422	.974
Yankee average		**96**	**298**	**42**	**69**	**10**	**0**	**16**	**41**	**44**	**5**	**75**	**2**	**0**	**3**	**3**	**1**	**.232**	**.332**	**.427**	**.984**
Career total		406	1248	171	287	43	1	65	169	182	21	310	8	0	10	10	5	.230	.329	.422	.974
Yankee total		**384**	**1191**	**166**	**276**	**39**	**1**	**64**	**164**	**175**	**19**	**299**	**8**	**0**	**10**	**10**	**5**	**.232**	**.332**	**.427**	**.984**

Mack, Raymond James BORN RAYMOND JAY MICKOVSKY
HEIGHT: 6'0" THROWS: RIGHT BATS: RIGHT BORN: 8/31/1916, CLEVELAND, OHIO DIED: 5/7/1969 BUCYRUS, OHIO POSITIONS PLAYED: 2B, 3B

YEAR	TEAM	GAMES	AB	RUNS	HITS	2B	3B	HR	RBI	BB	IBB	SO	HBP	SH	SF	SB	CS	BA	OBA	SA	FA
1938	Cle-A	2	6	2	2	0	1	0	2	0	—	1	0	0	—	0	0	.333	.333	.667	1.000
1939	Cle-A	36	112	12	17	4	1	1	6	12	—	19	1	1	—	0	2	.152	.240	.232	.976
1940	Cle-A	146	530	60	150	21	5	12	69	51	—	77	0	2	—	4	2	.283	.346	.409	.965
1941	Cle-A	145	500	54	114	22	4	9	44	54	—	69	0	11	—	8	4	.228	.303	.342	.970
1942	Cle-A	143	481	43	108	14	6	2	45	41	—	51	2	7	—	9	3	.225	.288	.291	.969
1943	Cle-A	153	545	56	120	25	2	7	62	47	—	61	2	14	—	8	3	.220	.285	.312	.967
1944	Cle-A	83	284	24	66	15	3	0	29	28	—	45	0	7	—	4	1	.232	.301	.306	.951
1946	Cle-A	61	171	13	35	6	2	1	9	23	—	27	0	0	—	2	2	.205	.299	.281	.970
1947	**NY-A**	**1**	**0**	**0**	**0**	**0**	**0**	**0**	**0**	**0**	**—**	**0**	**0**	**0**	**—**	**0**	**0**	**—**	**—**	**—**	**1.000**
1947	Chi-N	21	78	9	17	6	0	2	12	5	—	15	1	0	—	0	0	.218	.274	.372	.965
Career average		79	271	27	63	11	2	3	28	26	—	37	1	4	—	4	2	.232	.301	.330	.873
Yankee average		**1**	**0**	**0**	**0**	**0**	**0**	**0**	**0**	**0**	**—**	**0**	**0**	**0**	**—**	**0**	**0**	**—**	**—**	**—**	**1.000**
Career total		791	2707	273	629	113	24	34	278	261	—	365	6	42	—	35	17	.232	.301	.330	.873
Yankee total		**1**	**0**	**0**	**0**	**0**	**0**	**0**	**0**	**0**	**—**	**0**	**0**	**0**	**—**	**0**	**0**	**—**	**—**	**—**	**1.000**

Madden, Thomas Joseph
HEIGHT: 5'11" THROWS: LEFT BATS: LEFT BORN: 7/31/1883 PHILADELPHIA, PENNSYLVANIA DIED: 7/26/1930 PHILADELPHIA, PENN. POSITIONS PLAYED: OF

YEAR	TEAM	GAMES	AB	RUNS	HITS	2B	3B	HR	RBI	BB	IBB	SO	HBP	SH	SF	SB	CS	BA	OBA	SA	FA
1906	Bos-N	4	15	1	4	0	0	0	0	1	—	—	0	0	—	0	—	.267	.313	.267	1.000
1910	**NY-A**	**1**	**1**	**0**	**0**	**0**	**0**	**0**	**0**	**0**	**—**	**—**	**0**	**0**	**—**	**0**	**—**	**.000**	**.000**	**.000**	**.000**
Career average		3	8	1	2	0	0	0	0	1	—	—	0	0	—	0	—	.250	.294	.250	.500
Yankee average		**1**	**1**	**0**	**0**	**0**	**0**	**0**	**0**	**0**	**—**	**—**	**0**	**0**	**—**	**0**	**—**	**.000**	**.000**	**.000**	**.000**
Career total		5	16	1	4	0	0	0	0	1	—	—	0	0	—	0	—	.250	.294	.250	.500
Yankee total		**1**	**1**	**0**	**0**	**0**	**0**	**0**	**0**	**0**	**—**	**—**	**0**	**0**	**—**	**0**	**—**	**.000**	**.000**	**.000**	**.000**

Maddox, Elliott
HEIGHT: 5'11" THROWS: RIGHT BATS: RIGHT BORN: 12/21/1947 EAST ORANGE, NEW JERSEY POSITIONS PLAYED: 1B, 2B, 3B, SS, OF

YEAR	TEAM	GAMES	AB	RUNS	HITS	2B	3B	HR	RBI	BB	IBB	SO	HBP	SH	SF	SB	CS	BA	OBA	SA	FA
1970	Det-A	109	258	30	64	13	4	3	24	30	1	42	3	1	1	2	3	.248	.332	.364	.909
1971	Was-A	128	258	38	56	8	2	1	18	51	3	42	0	1	2	10	4	.217	.344	.275	.990
1972	Tex-A	98	294	40	74	7	2	0	10	49	4	53	2	3	1	20	10	.252	.361	.289	.990
1973	Tex-A	100	172	24	41	1	0	1	17	29	2	28	3	5	1	5	4	.238	.356	.262	1.000
1974	**NY-A**	**137**	**466**	**75**	**141**	**26**	**2**	**3**	**45**	**69**	**4**	**48**	**4**	**8**	**3**	**6**	**5**	**.303**	**.395**	**.386**	**1.000**
1975	**NY-A**	**55**	**218**	**36**	**67**	**10**	**3**	**1**	**23**	**21**	**0**	**24**	**7**	**2**	**3**	**9**	**3**	**.307**	**.382**	**.394**	**1.000**
1976	**NY-A**	**18**	**46**	**4**	**10**	**2**	**0**	**0**	**3**	**4**	**1**	**3**	**0**	**0**	**1**	**0**	**1**	**.217**	**.275**	**.261**	**1.000**
1977	Bal-A	49	107	14	28	7	0	2	9	13	0	9	4	2	2	2	2	.262	.357	.383	.990
1978	NY-N	119	389	43	100	18	2	2	39	71	1	38	2	2	5	2	11	.257	.370	.329	.500
1979	NY-N	86	224	21	60	13	0	1	12	20	0	27	3	1	1	3	2	.268	.335	.339	.950
1980	NY-N	130	411	35	101	16	1	4	34	52	5	44	6	5	4	1	9	.246	.336	.319	1.000
Career average		94	259	33	68	11	2	2	21	37	2	33	3	3	2	6	5	.261	.358	.334	.939
Yankee average		**70**	**243**	**38**	**73**	**13**	**2**	**1**	**24**	**31**	**2**	**25**	**4**	**3**	**2**	**5**	**3**	**.299**	**.384**	**.381**	**1.000**
Career total		1029	2843	360	742	121	16	18	234	409	21	358	34	30	24	60	54	.261	.358	.334	.939
Yankee total		**210**	**730**	**115**	**218**	**38**	**5**	**4**	**71**	**94**	**5**	**75**	**11**	**10**	**7**	**15**	**9**	**.299**	**.384**	**.381**	**1.000**

Magee, Leo Christopher BORN LEOPOLD CHRISTOPHER HOERNSCHEMEYER
HEIGHT: 5'11" THROWS: RIGHT BATS: BOTH BORN: 6/4/1889 CINCINNATI, OHIO DIED: 3/14/1966 COLUMBUS, OHIO POSITIONS PLAYED: 1B, 2B, 3B, SS, OF

YEAR	TEAM	GAMES	AB	RUNS	HITS	2B	3B	HR	RBI	BB	IBB	SO	HBP	SH	SF	SB	CS	BA	OBA	SA	FA
1911	StL-N	26	69	9	18	1	1	0	8	8	—	8	0	0	—	4	—	.261	.338	.304	.800
1912	StL-N	128	458	60	133	13	8	0	40	39	—	29	1	25	—	16	33	.290	.347	.354	.942
1913	StL-N	137	531	54	142	13	7	2	31	34	—	30	2	22	—	23	—	.267	.314	.330	1.000
1914	StL-N	142	529	59	150	23	4	2	40	42	—	24	1	35	—	36	—	.284	.337	.353	1.000
1915	Bro-F	121	452	87	146	19	10	4	49	22	—	19	1	19	—	34	—	.323	.356	.436	.952

(continued)

(continued)

YEAR	TEAM	GAMES	AB	RUNS	HITS	2B	3B	HR	RBI	BB	IBB	SO	HBP	SH	SF	SB	CS	BA	OBA	SA	FA
1916	NY-A	131	510	57	131	18	4	3	45	50	—	31	1	20	—	29	25	.257	.324	.325	.975
1917	NY-A	51	173	17	38	4	1	0	8	13	—	18	1	13	—	3	—	.220	.278	.254	.938
1917	StL-A	36	112	11	19	1	0	0	4	6	—	6	0	7	—	3	—	.170	.212	.179	1.000
1918	Cin-N	119	459	61	133	22	13	0	28	28	—	19	0	27	—	19	—	.290	.331	.394	.956
1919	Bro-N	45	181	16	43	7	2	0	7	5	—	8	1	13	—	5	—	.238	.262	.298	.938
1919	Chi-N	79	267	36	78	12	4	1	17	18	—	16	1	13	—	14	—	.292	.339	.378	.978
Career average		92	340	43	94	12	5	1	25	24	—	19	1	18	—	17	—	.276	.325	.350	.953
Yankee average		**91**	**342**	**37**	**85**	**11**	**3**	**2**	**27**	**32**	—	**25**	**1**	**17**	—	**16**	—	**.247**	**.313**	**.307**	**.957**
Career total		1015	3741	467	1031	133	54	12	277	265	—	208	9	194	—	186	58	.276	.325	.350	.953
Yankee total		**182**	**683**	**74**	**169**	**22**	**5**	**3**	**53**	**63**	—	**49**	**2**	**33**	—	**32**	**25**	**.247**	**.313**	**.307**	**.957**

Magner, Edmund Burke (Stubby)

HEIGHT: 5'3"   THROWS: RIGHT   BATS: RIGHT   BORN: 2/20/1888 KALAMAZOO, MICHIGAN   DIED: 9/6/1956 CHILLICOTHE, OHIO

YEAR	TEAM	GAMES	AB	RUNS	HITS	2B	3B	HR	RBI	BB	IBB	SO	HBP	SH	SF	SB	CS	BA	OBA	SA	FA
1911	NY-A	13	33	3	7	0	0	0	4	4	—	0	0	4	—	1	—	.212	.297	.212	.959
Career average		13	33	3	7	0	0	0	4	4	—	—	0	4	—	1	—	.212	.297	.212	.959
Yankee average		**13**	**33**	**3**	**7**	**0**	**0**	**0**	**4**	**4**	—	—	**0**	**4**	—	**1**	—	**.212**	**.297**	**.212**	**.959**
Career total		13	33	3	7	0	0	0	4	4	—	—	0	4	—	1	—	.212	.297	.212	.959
Yankee total		**13**	**33**	**3**	**7**	**0**	**0**	**0**	**4**	**4**	—	—	**0**	**4**	—	**1**	—	**.212**	**.297**	**.212**	**.959**

Maisel, Frederick Charles (Fritz *or* Flash)

HEIGHT: 5'7"   THROWS: RIGHT   BATS: RIGHT   BORN: 12/23/1889 CATONSVILLE, MARYLAND   DIED: 4/22/1967 BALTIMORE, MARYLAND   POSITIONS PLAYED: 2B, 3B, OF

YEAR	TEAM	GAMES	AB	RUNS	HITS	2B	3B	HR	RBI	BB	IBB	SO	HBP	SH	SF	SB	CS	BA	OBA	SA	FA
1913	NY-A	51	187	33	48	4	3	0	12	34	—	20	0	3	—	25	—	.257	.371	.310	.950
1914	NY-A	150	548	78	131	23	9	2	47	76	—	69	2	4	—	74	17	.239	.334	.325	.928
1915	NY-A	135	530	77	149	16	6	4	46	48	—	35	1	13	—	51	12	.281	.342	.357	.940
1916	NY-A	53	158	18	36	5	0	0	7	20	—	18	1	4	—	4	—	.228	.318	.259	1.000
1917	NY-A	113	404	46	80	4	4	0	20	36	—	18	2	24	—	29	—	.198	.267	.228	.967
1918	StL-A	90	284	43	66	4	2	0	16	46	—	17	1	23	—	11	—	.232	.341	.261	.949
Career average		99	352	49	85	9	4	1	25	43	—	30	1	12	—	32	—	.242	.327	.299	.956
Yankee average		**100**	**365**	**50**	**89**	**10**	**4**	**1**	**26**	**43**	—	**32**	**1**	**10**	—	**37**	—	**.243**	**.324**	**.305**	**.957**
Career total		592	2111	295	510	56	24	6	148	260	—	177	7	71	—	194	29	.242	.327	.299	.956
Yankee total		**502**	**1827**	**252**	**444**	**52**	**22**	**6**	**132**	**214**	—	**160**	**6**	**48**	—	**183**	**29**	**.243**	**.324**	**.305**	**.957**

Majeski, Henry (Hank *or* Heeney)

HEIGHT: 5'9"   THROWS: RIGHT   BATS: RIGHT   BORN: 12/13/1916 STATEN ISLAND, NY.   DIED: 8/9/1991 STATEN ISLAND, NY.   POSITIONS PLAYED: 2B, 3B, SS, OF

YEAR	TEAM	GAMES	AB	RUNS	HITS	2B	3B	HR	RBI	BB	IBB	SO	HBP	SH	SF	SB	CS	BA	OBA	SA	FA
1939	Bos-N	106	367	35	100	16	1	7	54	18	—	30	2	7	—	2	—	.272	.310	.379	.945
1940	Bos-N	3	3	0	0	0	0	0	0	0	—	0	0	0	—	0	—	.000	.000	.000	.000
1941	Bos-N	19	55	5	8	5	0	0	3	1	—	13	0	0	—	0	—	.145	.161	.236	.911
1946	NY-A	8	12	1	1	0	1	0	0	0	—	3	0	0	—	0	0	.083	.083	.250	.750
1946	Phi-A	78	264	25	66	14	3	1	25	26	—	13	1	2	—	3	2	.250	.320	.337	.967
1947	Phi-A	141	479	54	134	26	5	8	72	53	—	31	5	8	—	1	0	.280	.358	.405	.988
1948	Phi-A	148	590	88	183	41	4	12	120	48	—	43	6	2	—	2	1	.310	.368	.454	.975
1949	Phi-A	114	448	62	124	26	5	9	67	29	—	23	4	6	—	0	1	.277	.326	.417	.957
1950	Chi-A	122	414	47	128	18	2	6	46	42	—	34	3	8	—	1	4	.309	.377	.406	.970
1951	Chi-A	12	35	4	9	4	0	0	6	1	—	0	0	0	—	0	0	.257	.278	.371	.950
1951	Phi-A	89	323	41	92	19	4	5	42	35	—	24	2	4	—	1	2	.285	.358	.415	.974
1952	Phi-A	34	117	14	30	2	2	2	20	19	—	10	1	2	—	0	1	.256	.365	.359	.976
1952	Cle-A	36	54	7	16	2	0	0	9	7	—	7	0	1	—	0	0	.296	.377	.333	1.000
1953	Cle-A	50	50	6	15	1	0	2	12	3	—	8	1	1	—	0	0	.300	.352	.440	1.000
1954	Cle-A	57	121	10	34	4	0	3	17	7	—	14	0	1	0	0	0	.281	.320	.388	.943
1955	Cle-A	36	48	3	9	2	0	2	6	8	—	3	2	0	1	0	0	.188	.322	.354	1.000
1955	Bal-A	16	41	2	7	1	0	0	2	2	1	4	0	0	0	0	0	.171	.209	.195	1.000
Career average		63	201	24	56	11	2	3	30	18	—	15	2	3	—	1	—	.279	.342	.398	.900
Yankee average		**8**	**12**	**1**	**1**	**0**	**1**	**0**	**0**	**0**	—	**3**	**0**	**0**	—	**0**	**0**	**.083**	**.083**	**.250**	**.750**
Career total		1069	3421	404	956	181	27	57	501	299	1	260	27	42	1	10	11	.279	.342	.398	.900
Yankee total		**8**	**12**	**1**	**1**	**0**	**1**	**0**	**0**	**0**	—	**3**	**0**	**0**	—	**0**	**0**	**.083**	**.083**	**.250**	**.750**

Mickey Charles Mantle, of, 1951-68

There is a story, told in Mickey Mantle's first biography, written in 1953, about several Yankee coaches and sportswriters sitting around in spring training in 1950 musing about the professional demise of center fielder Joe DiMaggio and what that would mean to the New York franchise. Joltin' Joe was beset by injuries and no one expected him to play much longer.

At that point, Yankee scout Tom Greenwade sauntered in (at least that's how the story goes) and said softly, "I think I've seen the man who can replace DiMaggio. His name is Mantle. Like the shelf over your fireplace. Remember that name."

Within two years, of course, no one would forget it. And bless him, but Tom Greenwade was essentially right. Mickey Mantle might not have replaced Joe DiMaggio—no one could—but he helped people get over Joe D's retirement pretty fast.

Mickey Mantle was born on October 30, 1931, in Spavinaw, Oklahoma. His father, Elven "Mutt" Mantle, named Mickey after his favorite player, All-Star catcher Mickey Cochrane. Mutt, who had toiled in the lead and zinc mines throughout Oklahoma, wanted fervently for his son to be a ballplayer. Or at least do something that would take him out of the mines.

Thus, Mickey got his first baseball cap at two years old, his first uniform (sewed by his mom) at six and his first glove a few years later.

Mutt had all the angles figured out. When Mantle was five, he and Mickey's grandfather, Charley Mantle, began teaching Mickey to switch-hit. Mantle was a natural righty. But switch-hitters, Mutt reasoned, would have a better shot at making the pros.

By the time Mickey graduated from Commerce High School in 1949, he was pretty hot stuff. Greenwade had scouted him several times, as had scouts from the St. Louis Cardinals. But it was the Yankees who signed Mantle to a contract, offering him a bonus of $1,150. The Cardinals had a contract ready, too, but there was no bonus money available.

After a brief stint in the minors, where he was playing shortstop, he was invited to the Yankees spring training camp in 1951.

To term his stint there "sensational" is actually an understatement. By this time, Mantle was 5 feet 10 inches, about 190, with tremendous upper-body strength. He also had terrific foot speed, and was winning the spring training base running races so easily that Yankee coaches thought he was somehow jumping the starting whistle. He wasn't.

He would step into the batting cage and drill thunderous home runs—from either side of the plate. Veteran players would stop to watch. And crowds gathered everywhere the Yankees played. That first spring training, he hit .402.

His first year included one more stint in the minors. Mantle had a problem with high fastballs: He swung at them. He began striking out in bunches in the early part of the season. Satchel Paige, then pitching for the St. Louis Browns, once laughed out loud as Mantle flailed away at his offerings.

Mickey spent 40 games with the Kansas City Blues and hit .361. He was called back up in August and stayed there for the next 17 years.

Maloney, Patrick William (Pat)

HEIGHT: 6'0" THROWS: RIGHT BATS: RIGHT BORN: 1/9/1888 GROSVENOR DALE, CONN. DIED: 6/27/1979 PAWTUCKET, RHODE ISLAND POSITIONS PLAYED: OF

YEAR	TEAM	GAMES	AB	RUNS	HITS	2B	3B	HR	RBI	BB	IBB	SO	HBP	SH	SF	SB	CS	BA	OBA	SA	FA
1912	NY-A	25	79	9	17	1	0	0	4	6	—	—	1	4	—	3	—	.215	.279	.228	.926
Career average		25	79	9	17	1	0	0	4	6	—	—	1	4	—	3	—	.215	.279	.228	.926
Yankee average		25	79	9	17	1	0	0	4	6	—	—	1	4	—	3	—	.215	.279	.228	.926
Career total		25	79	9	17	1	0	0	4	6	—	—	1	4	—	3	—	.215	.279	.228	.926
Yankee total		25	79	9	17	1	0	0	4	6	—	—	1	4	—	3	—	.215	.279	.228	.926

Mantle was in right field that year, as DiMaggio was still the Yankees starting center fielder when he wasn't injured. In the 1951 World Series against the Giants, the two men both went after a ball hit by Willie Mays. DiMaggio called him off it, and Mantle pulled up. Mantle's foot snagged in the cover of a storm drain in the field, and he tore ligaments in his knee. He was out for the Series.

After that, Mantle rarely went through a season without some kind of injury, usually to his legs. Yet he remained a dominant player in the American League for the next ten years and a certified star until he retired.

He was MVP three times, in 1956, 1957 and 1962. But beyond that, he was second in the voting three times, third once and fifth two other times in his career.

In 1956, he won the triple crown with 52 home runs, 130 RBI and a .353 batting average, numbers that not only topped the American League but were better than anyone put up in the National League, too. He also led the league in runs scored with 132. It was one of the great individual performances in baseball history. He also won the Hickock Belt as the best professional athlete in the world.

He hit .345 in the 1952 World Series, .400 in the 1960 Fall Classic. He was a 17-time All-Star and the all-time leader for the Yankees in inside-the-park home runs with nine.

In addition to the numbers, Mantle's other strength was as a clubhouse leader. He loved playing the game and he understood that it was a team effort, first and foremost. Yankee rookies in the Mantle era usually have a story about how Mickey made their transition easier, or helped them in some way or another.

Some believe he may have taken things a little too far when it came to loosening up after the games. Mutt Mantle was in his 40s when he died, as was grandfather Charley Mantle. Mickey believed the whole thing was hereditary, and that his days were numbered as well. Years later, he would admit to a major problem with alcohol. But in his playing days, getting the job done while badly hungover was just part of the job.

This was coupled with a disregard for any kind of conditioning program. Many players of that era preferred to "play themselves into shape" in the spring. But the oft-injured Mantle, in particular, would have benefited from off-season training.

But he got it done, somehow. He took a silly pride in belting long home runs. Five times, one of his power blasts hit the facade overhang in Yankee Stadium. In Washington, D.C.'s, Griffith Park, in 1963, he smacked one of the longest home runs in the history of the game: the ball traveled more than 565 feet.

He stayed on as a player a little too long. His last two years, he hit .245 and .237. It stung him, because that dropped his lifetime average below .300. When he finally retired in 1968, he was the all-time Yankee leader in games and at-bats—and strikeouts. He was second in home runs with 536, third in hits with 2,415, third in runs with 1,677, fourth all-time in RBI with 1,509 and eighth in stolen bases with 153. He had hit 18 home runs in World Series competition, another record.

In 1969, the Yankees retired his number and in 1972, he was elected to the Hall of Fame.

Mantle's final years were not easy. His early alcohol abuse led to many health problems, and despite a liver transplant, he died in 1995 in Texas.

Mantle, Mickey Charles (The Commerce Comet)

HEIGHT: 5'11"   THROWS: RIGHT   BATS: BOTH   BORN: 10/20/1931 SPAVINAW, OKLAHOMA   DIED: 8/13/1995   POSITIONS PLAYED: 1B, 2B, 3B, SS, OF

YEAR	TEAM	GAMES	AB	RUNS	HITS	2B	3B	HR	RBI	BB	IBB	SO	HBP	SH	SF	SB	CS	BA	OBA	SA	FA
1951	NY-A	96	341	61	91	11	5	13	65	43	—	74	0	2	—	8	7	.267	.349	.443	.959
1952	NY-A	142	549	94	171	37	7	23	87	75	—	111	0	2	—	4	1	.311	.394	.530	.500
1953	NY-A	127	461	105	136	24	3	21	92	79	—	90	0	0	—	8	4	.295	.398	.497	.982
1954	NY-A	146	543	129	163	17	12	27	102	102	—	107	0	2	4	5	2	.300	.408	.525	1.000
1955	NY-A	147	517	121	158	25	11	37	99	113	6	97	3	2	3	8	1	.306	.431	.611	1.000
1956	NY-A	150	533	132	188	22	5	52	130	112	6	99	2	1	4	10	1	.353	.464	.705	.990
1957	NY-A	144	474	121	173	28	6	34	94	146	23	75	0	0	3	16	3	.365	.512	.665	.979
1958	NY-A	150	519	127	158	21	1	42	97	129	13	120	2	2	2	18	3	.304	.443	.592	.977
1959	NY-A	144	541	104	154	23	4	31	75	93	6	126	2	1	2	21	3	.285	.390	.514	.995
1960	NY-A	153	527	119	145	17	6	40	94	111	6	125	1	0	5	14	3	.275	.399	.558	.991
1961	NY-A	153	514	132	163	16	6	54	128	126	9	112	0	1	5	12	1	.317	.448	.687	.983
1962	NY-A	123	377	96	121	15	1	30	89	122	9	78	1	0	2	9	0	.321	.486	.605	.978
1963	NY-A	65	172	40	54	8	0	15	35	40	4	32	0	0	1	2	1	.314	.441	.622	.990

continued)

YEAR	TEAM																		BA	OBA	SA	FA
1964	NY-A	143	465	92	141	25	2	35	111	99	18	102	0	0	3	6	3		.303	.423	.591	.978
1965	NY-A	122	361	44	92	12	1	19	46	73	7	76	0	0	1	4	1		.255	.379	.452	.966
1966	NY-A	108	333	40	96	12	1	23	56	57	5	76	0	0	3	1	1		.288	.389	.538	1.000
1967	NY-A	144	440	63	108	17	0	22	55	107	7	113	1	0	5	1	1		.245	.391	.434	.993
1968	NY-A	144	435	57	103	14	1	18	54	106	7	97	1	1	4	6	2		.237	.385	.398	.988
Career average		133	450	93	134	19	4	30	84	96	—	95	1	1	—	9	2		.298	.423	.557	.958
Yankee average		**133**	**450**	**93**	**134**	**19**	**4**	**30**	**84**	**96**	**—**	**95**	**1**	**1**	**—**	**9**	**2**		**.298**	**.423**	**.557**	**.958**
Career total		2401	8102	1677	2415	344	72	536	1509	1733	126	1710	13	14	47	153	38		.298	.421	.557	.958
Yankee total		**2401**	**8102**	**1677**	**2415**	**344**	**72**	**536**	**1509**	**1733**	**126**	**1710**	**13**	**14**	**47**	**153**	**38**		**.298**	**.421**	**.557**	**.958**

Manto, Jeffrey Paul

HEIGHT: 6'3" THROWS: RIGHT BATS: RIGHT BORN: 8/23/1964 BRISTOL, PENNSYLVANIA POSITIONS PLAYED: C, 1B, 2B, 3B, SS, OF

YEAR	TEAM	GAMES	AB	RUNS	HITS	2B	3B	HR	RBI	BB	IBB	SO	HBP	SH	SF	SB	CS	BA	OBA	SA	FA
1990	Cle-A	30	76	12	17	5	1	2	14	21	1	18	0	0	0	0	1	.224	.392	.395	.990
1991	Cle-A	47	128	15	27	7	0	2	13	14	0	22	4	1	1	2	0	.211	.306	.313	.929
1993	Phi-N	8	18	0	1	0	0	0	0	0	0	3	1	0	0	0	0	.056	.105	.056	1.000
1995	Bal-A	89	254	31	65	9	0	17	38	24	0	69	2	0	0	0	3	.256	.325	.492	1.000
1996	Bos-A	10	30	5	8	3	1	3	4	3	0	6	1	0	0	0	0	—	—	—	.963
1996	Sea-A	21	54	7	10	3	0	1	4	9	0	12	0	0	0	0	1	.185	.302	.296	.971
1996	Bos-A	12	18	3	2	0	0	0	2	5	0	6	0	0	0	0	0	.111	.304	.111	.913
1997	Cle-A	16	30	3	8	3	0	2	7	1	0	10	0	0	0	0	1	.267	.290	.567	1.000
1998	Cle-A	15	37	8	8	1	0	2	6	2	0	10	0	0	0	0	1	.216	.256	.405	.981
1998	Det-A	16	30	6	8	2	0	1	3	3	0	11	0	0	0	1	0	.267	.333	.433	1.000
1999	Cle-A	12	25	5	5	0	0	1	2	11	0	11	0	1	0	0	0	.200	.444	.320	1.000
1999	**NY-A**	**6**	**8**	**0**	**1**	**0**	**0**	**0**	**0**	**2**	**0**	**4**	**0**	**1**	**0**	**0**	**0**	**.125**	**.300**	**.125**	**1.000**
2000	Col-N	7	5	2	4	2	0	1	4	2	0	0	0	0	0	0	0	.800	.857	1.800	1.000
Career average		22	55	8	13	3	0	3	8	8	0	14	1	0	0	0	1	.230	.328	.419	.981
Yankee average		**6**	**8**	**0**	**1**	**0**	**0**	**0**	**0**	**2**	**0**	**4**	**0**	**1**	**0**	**0**	**0**	**.125**	**.300**	**.125**	**1.000**
Career total		289	713	97	164	35	2	32	97	97	1	182	8	3	1	3	6	.230	.328	.419	.981
Yankee total		**6**	**8**	**0**	**1**	**0**	**0**	**0**	**0**	**2**	**0**	**4**	**0**	**1**	**0**	**0**	**0**	**.125**	**.300**	**.125**	**1.000**

Mapes, Clifford Franklin

HEIGHT: 6'3" THROWS: RIGHT BATS: LEFT BORN: 3/13/1922 SUTHERLAND, NEBRASKA DIED: 12/5/1996 POSITIONS PLAYED: OF

YEAR	TEAM	GAMES	AB	RUNS	HITS	2B	3B	HR	RBI	BB	IBB	SO	HBP	SH	SF	SB	CS	BA	OBA	SA	FA
1948	NY-A	53	88	19	22	11	1	1	12	6	—	13	0	0	—	1	1	.250	.298	.432	.958
1949	NY-A	111	304	56	75	13	3	7	38	58	—	50	1	6	—	6	0	.247	.369	.378	.976
1950	NY-A	108	356	60	88	14	6	12	61	47	—	61	2	9	—	1	6	.247	.338	.421	.950
1951	NY-A	45	51	6	11	3	1	2	8	4	—	14	0	0	—	0	0	.216	.273	.431	1.000
1951	StL-A	56	201	32	55	7	2	7	30	26	—	33	1	1	—	0	1	.274	.360	.433	1.000
1952	Det-A	86	193	26	38	7	0	9	23	27	—	42	0	1	—	0	1	.197	.295	.373	.967
Career average		77	199	33	48	9	2	6	29	28	—	36	1	3	—	1	2	.242	.338	.406	.975
Yankee average		**79**	**200**	**35**	**49**	**10**	**3**	**6**	**30**	**29**	**—**	**35**	**1**	**4**	**—**	**2**	**2**	**.245**	**.342**	**.407**	**.971**
Career total		459	1193	199	289	55	13	38	172	168	—	213	4	17	—	8	9	.242	.338	.406	.975
Yankee total		**317**	**799**	**141**	**196**	**41**	**11**	**22**	**119**	**115**	**—**	**138**	**3**	**15**	**—**	**8**	**7**	**.245**	**.342**	**.407**	**.971**

Maris, Roger Eugene

HEIGHT: 6'0" THROWS: RIGHT BATS: LEFT BORN: 9/10/1934 HIBBING, MINNESOTA DIED: 12/14/1985 HOUSTON, TEXAS POSITIONS PLAYED: OF

YEAR	TEAM	GAMES	AB	RUNS	HITS	2B	3B	HR	RBI	BB	IBB	SO	HBP	SH	SF	SB	CS	BA	OBA	SA	FA
1957	Cle-A	116	358	61	84	9	5	14	51	60	5	79	1	3	2	8	4	.235	.344	.405	.975
1958	Cle-A	51	182	26	41	5	1	9	27	17	2	33	0	0	3	4	2	.225	.287	.412	.967
1958	KC-A	99	401	61	99	14	3	19	53	28	1	52	2	2	2	0	0	.247	.298	.439	.975
1959	KC-A	122	433	69	118	21	7	16	72	58	5	53	3	0	4	2	1	.273	.359	.464	.975
1960	NY-A	136	499	98	141	18	7	39	112	70	4	65	3	1	5	2	2	.283	.371	.581	.985
1961	NY-A	161	590	132	159	16	4	61	142	94	0	67	7	0	7	0	0	.269	.372	.620	.968
1962	NY-A	157	590	92	151	34	1	33	100	87	11	78	6	1	3	1	0	.256	.356	.485	.991
1963	NY-A	90	312	53	84	14	1	23	53	35	3	40	2	1	1	1	0	.269	.346	.542	.988
1964	NY-A	141	513	86	144	12	2	26	71	62	1	78	6	1	2	3	0	.281	.364	.464	.996
1965	NY-A	46	155	22	37	7	0	8	27	29	1	29	0	1	1	0	0	.239	.357	.439	.971

(continued)

Roger Eugene Maris, of, 1960–66

Roger Maris is remembered, of course, for his 61 home runs in 1961. It is the ultimate irony, because Maris was as great an all-around ballplayer as the Yankees have ever had. But for the rest of his career, he struggled against the "one-year wonder" tag writers hung on him that season.

Maris was born in Hibbing, Minnesota, on September 10, 1934. His family moved to North Dakota, where Maris became a local legend, enjoying record-setting years as a high school football player.

He began his major league career in 1957 as the regular right fielder with the Cleveland Indians. In 1958, he was traded to Kansas City. The Yankees acquired him in a seven-player deal with the Athletics in late 1959.

Maris had shown decent power with the Indians and Athletics, but he really began popping the ball with the Yankees. He hit 39 home runs in 1960, and added a league-leading 112 RBI and 98 runs scored. Those numbers, as well as the legitimate designation as the best defensive right fielder in baseball, earned him the 1960 MVP award.

In 1961, helped by 15 home runs in June, Maris got off to a hot start and drilled 61 round-trippers. The problem was, in the eyes of some fans—and writers—the wrong guy was breaking Babe Ruth's record.

The low-key Maris was doing something everyone thought his lovable, quotable, affable teammate Mickey Mantle should be doing. And somehow, that was Maris's fault. In fact, Commissioner Ford Frick, a former ghostwriter for Ruth, decreed midway through the 1961 season that the Maris record wouldn't really count unless Roger hit 61 homers in 154 games. If it took 162 games, ruled Frick, the record would have an asterisk.

Thus, under excruciating conditions, particularly at the end of the season when everybody wanted a piece of him, Maris went ahead and broke Babe Ruth's home run record as the Yankees won the pennant. In 162 games, by the way.

The whole thing took its toll. Maris's hair began to fall out and he complained of ulcers. Instead of looking forward to the 1961 World Series, he admitted that he just wanted to see the season over. He had two hits in 19 at-bats in that 1961 victory over the Cincinnati Reds.

Yet Maris won his second consecutive MVP award that year, something only a handful of players have ever done. He was also awarded the Hickock Belt as the best professional athlete in the world.

In 1962, he hit 33 home runs, and that seemed to confirm in the eyes of some that Maris was already a has-been. But as he pointed out to a sportswriter, he also hit a career-high 34 doubles, drove in 100 runs and scored 92 and committed only 3 errors in right field. He was hardly a bust. And the Yankees once again won the pennant and the World Series, this time over the San Francisco Giants.

In 1963 and again in 1965, he was hampered by injuries, and the booing in Yankee Stadium began to get louder. He was traded to the Cardinals in 1966 and the new venue revitalized him. He helped St. Louis to pennants in 1967 and 1968 before retiring.

Maris stayed away from New York for ten years after his retirement. But he was finally invited back to Opening Day by George Steinbrenner in 1978 and received a huge ovation from the New York fans. He died in 1985 of complications from cancer only a few months before the Yankees retired his uniform number nine.

Maris still ranks 9th all-time in home runs for New York, with 203.

(continued)

Year	Team	G	AB	R	H	2B	3B	HR	RBI	BB	SH	SO	SB	CS	GDP	HBP	AVG	OBP	SLG	OPS
1966	NY-A	119	348	37	81	9	2	13	43	36	3	60	3	0	4	0	0	.233	.307	.382	.993
1967	StL-N	125	410	64	107	18	7	9	55	52	3	61	4	1	5	0	0	.261	.346	.405	.991
1968	StL-N	100	310	25	79	18	2	5	45	24	3	38	1	1	4	0	0	.255	.307	.374	.983
Career average		113	392	64	102	15	3	21	66	50	3	56	3	1	3	2	1	.260	.345	.476	.981
Yankee average		**121**	**430**	**74**	**114**	**16**	**2**	**29**	**78**	**59**	**3**	**60**	**4**	**1**	**3**	**1**	**0**	**.265**	**.356**	**.515**	**.985**
Career total		1463	5101	826	1325	195	42	275	851	652	42	733	38	12	43	21	9	.260	.345	.476	.981
Yankee total		**850**	**3007**	**520**	**797**	**110**	**17**	**203**	**548**	**413**	**23**	**417**	**27**	**5**	**23**	**7**	**2**	**.265**	**.356**	**.515**	**.985**

Marsans, Armando

HEIGHT: 5'10" THROWS: RIGHT BATS: RIGHT BORN: 10/3/1887 MATANZAS, CUBA DIED: 9/3/1960 HAVANA, CUBA POSITIONS PLAYED: 1B, 2B, 3B, SS, OF

YEAR	TEAM	GAMES	AB	RUNS	HITS	2B	3B	HR	RBI	BB	IBB	SO	HBP	SH	SF	SB	CS	BA	OBA	SA	FA
1911	Cin-N	58	138	17	36	2	2	0	11	15	—	11	3	5	—	11	—	.261	.346	.304	1.000
1912	Cin-N	110	416	59	132	19	7	1	38	20	—	17	3	9	—	35	—	.317	.353	.404	.957
1913	Cin-N	118	435	49	129	7	6	0	38	17	—	25	3	15	—	37	—	.297	.327	.340	1.000
1914	Cin-N	36	124	16	37	3	0	0	22	14	—	6	1	6	—	13	—	.298	.374	.323	.916
1914	StL-F	9	40	5	14	0	2	0	2	3	—	0	0	0	—	4	—	.350	.395	.450	.857
1915	StL-F	36	124	16	22	3	0	0	6	14	—	5	0	7	—	5	—	.177	.261	.202	.975
1916	StL-A	151	528	51	134	12	1	1	60	57	—	41	6	23	—	46	26	.254	.333	.286	.977
1917	StL-A	75	257	31	59	12	0	0	20	20	—	6	0	9	—	11	—	.230	.285	.276	.750
1917	**NY-A**	**25**	**88**	**10**	**20**	**4**	**0**	**0**	**15**	**8**	**—**	**3**	**0**	**4**	**—**	**6**	**—**	**.227**	**.292**	**.273**	**.974**
1918	**NY-A**	**37**	**123**	**13**	**29**	**5**	**1**	**0**	**9**	**5**	**—**	**3**	**0**	**4**	**—**	**3**	**—**	**.236**	**.266**	**.293**	**.943**
Career average		66	227	27	61	7	2	0	22	17	—	12	2	8	—	17	—	.269	.325	.318	.935
Yankee average		**31**	**106**	**12**	**25**	**5**	**1**	**0**	**12**	**7**	**—**	**3**	**0**	**4**	**—**	**5**	**—**	**.232**	**.277**	**.284**	**.959**
Career total		655	2273	267	612	67	19	2	221	173	—	117	16	82	—	171	26	.269	.325	.318	.935
Yankee total		**62**	**211**	**23**	**49**	**9**	**1**	**0**	**24**	**13**	**—**	**6**	**0**	**8**	**—**	**9**	**—**	**.232**	**.277**	**.284**	**.959**

Alfred Manuel "Billy" Martin, 2b-3b-ss-of, 1950–57

Billy Martin was combative and tough, traits that endeared him to manager Casey Stengel, but which caused him trouble with the Yankee front office throughout his career.

Martin, born May 16, 1928, in Berkeley, California, was an excellent all-around athlete in high school and in fact won a basketball scholarship to the University of Santa Clara. But baseball was his first love.

He played under Stengel in 1948 with the Oakland Oaks of the Pacific Coast League. When Stengel was hired by the Yankees in 1949, he brought Martin to the club in 1950. Billy was a part-time player his first two years, filling in mostly at second base. But by 1952, he won the second baseman's job.

He only hit .267, but that batting average was only a number. Martin was a great hit-and-run batter, ran the base paths with a chip on his shoulder and always seemed to make the right decision in a tight situation.

"My one for four would kill 'em," he once said, meaning that he may only get one hit in a game, but it was more than likely the key one. That was usually true.

His World Series performances were legendary. He won Game 2 of the 1952 series against the Dodgers with a double, homer and 4 RBI. His catch of Jackie Robinson's pop fly in Game 7 won the game and the series for the Yankees. In 1953, he hit .500 with 12 hits, including a single in the bottom of the ninth inning in Game 7 to win the game, 4-3, again over the Dodgers.

After a stint in the service, he returned to the Yankees in 1955 and sparked them to the pennant, hitting .300 in September. He hit .320 in the 1955 Series, a loss to the Dodgers, and .296 in the 1956 Series, a win over Brooklyn.

But Yankee general manager George Weiss was not a Martin fan, believing the combative player was un-Yankee-like. A 1957 nightclub incident at the Copacabana in New York sealed Martin's fate. Weiss, believing Martin to be the instigator, traded him to Kansas City soon after. He played for five teams in the next four years before retiring in 1961.

Martin then became a successful coach and manager, eventually returning to the Yankees in 1975. He had several stints with the Yankees and a stormy relationship with owner George Steinbrenner before his death on Christmas Day 1989, in a car accident.

Martin, Alfred Manuel (Billy)

HEIGHT: 5'1"   THROWS: RIGHT   BATS: RIGHT   BORN: 5/16/1928 BERKELEY, CAL.   DIED: 12/25/1989 JOHNSON CITY, NY.   POSITIONS PLAYED: 2B, 3B, SS, OF

YEAR	TEAM	GAMES	AB	RUNS	HITS	2B	3B	HR	RBI	BB	IBB	SO	HBP	SH	SF	SB	CS	BA	OBA	SA	FA
1950	NY-A	34	36	10	9	1	0	1	8	3	—	3	0	0	—	0	0	.250	.308	.361	.976
1951	NY-A	51	58	10	15	1	2	0	2	4	—	9	2	1	—	0	1	.259	.328	.345	.988
1952	NY-A	109	363	32	97	13	3	3	33	22	—	31	8	8	—	3	6	.267	.323	.344	.984
1953	NY-A	149	587	72	151	24	6	15	75	43	—	56	6	9	—	6	7	.257	.314	.395	.985
1955	NY-A	20	70	8	21	2	0	1	9	7	1	9	0	1	2	1	2	.300	.354	.371	.977
1956	NY-A	121	458	76	121	24	5	9	49	30	0	56	3	8	5	7	3	.264	.310	.397	.889
1957	NY-A	43	145	12	35	5	2	1	12	3	0	14	1	2	3	2	1	.241	.257	.324	.973
1957	KC-A	73	265	33	68	9	3	9	27	12	0	20	3	2	1	7	1	.257	.295	.415	1.000
1958	Det-A	131	498	56	127	19	1	7	42	16	0	62	3	13	6	5	3	.255	.279	.339	.958
1959	Cle-A	73	242	37	63	7	0	9	24	8	2	18	3	4	2	0	2	.260	.290	.401	.997
1960	Cin-N	103	317	34	78	17	1	3	16	27	5	34	0	2	1	0	0	.246	.304	.334	.975
1961	Mil-N	6	6	1	0	0	0	0	0	0	0	1	0	0	0	0	0	.000	.000	.000	.000
1961	Min-A	108	374	44	92	15	5	6	36	13	0	42	3	5	3	3	2	.246	.275	.361	.963
Career average		79	263	33	68	11	2	5	26	15	—	27	3	4	—	3	2	.257	.301	.369	.897
Yankee average		**75**	**245**	**31**	**64**	**10**	**3**	**4**	**27**	**16**	**—**	**25**	**3**	**4**	**—**	**3**	**3**	**.262**	**.314**	**.376**	**.967**
Career total		1021	3419	425	877	137	28	64	333	188	8	355	32	55	23	34	29	.257	.300	.369	.897
Yankee total		**527**	**1717**	**220**	**449**	**70**	**18**	**30**	**188**	**112**	**1**	**178**	**20**	**29**	**10**	**19**	**20**	**.262**	**.313**	**.376**	**.967**

Martin, Hershel Ray (Hersh)

HEIGHT: 6'2"   THROWS: RIGHT   BATS: BOTH   BORN: 9/19/1909 BIRMINGHAM, ALABAMA   DIED: 11/17/1980 CUBA, MISSOURI   POSITIONS PLAYED: OF

YEAR	TEAM	GAMES	AB	RUNS	HITS	2B	3B	HR	RBI	BB	IBB	SO	HBP	SH	SF	SB	CS	BA	OBA	SA	FA
1937	Phi-N	141	579	102	164	35	7	8	49	69	—	66	2	4	—	11	—	.283	.362	.409	.978
1938	Phi-N	120	466	58	139	36	6	3	39	34	—	48	1	7	—	8	—	.298	.347	.421	.965
1939	Phi-N	111	393	59	111	28	5	1	22	42	—	27	2	5	—	4	—	.282	.355	.387	.976
1940	Phi-N	33	83	10	21	6	1	0	5	9	—	9	0	4	—	1	—	.253	.326	.349	.979
1944	NY-A	85	328	49	99	12	4	9	47	34	—	26	2	4	—	5	2	.302	.371	.445	.964
1945	NY-A	117	408	53	109	18	6	7	53	65	—	31	0	6	—	4	1	.267	.368	.392	.984
Career average		101	376	55	107	23	5	5	36	42	—	35	1	5	—	6	—	.285	.359	.408	.974
Yankee average		**101**	**368**	**51**	**104**	**15**	**5**	**8**	**50**	**50**	**—**	**29**	**1**	**5**	**—**	**5**	**2**	**.283**	**.369**	**.416**	**.974**
Career total		607	2257	331	643	135	29	28	215	253	—	207	7	30	—	33	3	.285	.359	.408	.974
Yankee total		**202**	**736**	**102**	**208**	**30**	**10**	**16**	**100**	**99**	**—**	**57**	**2**	**10**	**—**	**9**	**3**	**.283**	**.369**	**.416**	**.974**

Martin, John Christopher (Jack)

HEIGHT: 5'9"   THROWS: RIGHT   BATS: RIGHT   BORN: 4/19/1887 PLAINFIELD, NEW JERSEY   DIED: 7/4/1980 PLAINFIELD, NJ.   POSITIONS PLAYED: 1B, 2B, 3B, SS

YEAR	TEAM	GAMES	AB	RUNS	HITS	2B	3B	HR	RBI	BB	IBB	SO	HBP	SH	SF	SB	CS	BA	OBA	SA	FA
1912	NY-A	71	231	30	52	6	1	0	17	37	—	—	6	7	—	14	—	.225	.347	.260	.842
1914	Bos-N	33	85	10	18	2	0	0	5	6	—	7	0	3	—	0	—	.212	.264	.235	.500
1914	Phi-N	83	292	26	74	5	3	0	21	27	—	29	1	14	—	6	—	.253	.319	.291	.930
Career average		62	203	22	48	4	1	0	14	23	—	—	2	8	—	7	—	.237	.323	.271	.757
Yankee average		**71**	**231**	**30**	**52**	**6**	**1**	**0**	**17**	**37**	**—**	**—**	**6**	**7**	**—**	**14**	**—**	**.225**	**.347**	**.260**	**.842**
Career total		187	608	66	144	13	4	0	43	70	—	36	7	24	—	20	—	.237	.323	.271	.757
Yankee total		**71**	**231**	**30**	**52**	**6**	**1**	**0**	**17**	**37**	**—**	**—**	**6**	**7**	**—**	**14**	**—**	**.225**	**.347**	**.260**	**.842**

Martinez, Constantino (Tino)

HEIGHT: 6'2"   THROWS: RIGHT   BATS: LEFT   BORN: 12/7/1967 TAMPA, FLORIDA   POSITIONS PLAYED: 1B

YEAR	TEAM	GAMES	AB	RUNS	HITS	2B	3B	HR	RBI	BB	IBB	SO	HBP	SH	SF	SB	CS	BA	OBA	SA	FA
1990	Sea-A	24	68	4	15	4	0	0	5	9	0	9	0	0	1	0	0	.221	.308	.279	1.000
1991	Sea-A	36	112	11	23	2	0	4	9	11	0	24	0	0	2	0	0	.205	.272	.330	.993
1992	Sea-A	136	460	53	118	19	2	16	66	42	9	77	2	1	8	2	1	.257	.316	.411	.995
1993	Sea-A	109	408	48	108	25	1	17	60	45	9	56	5	3	3	0	3	.265	.343	.456	.997
1994	Sea-A	97	329	42	86	21	0	20	61	29	2	52	1	4	3	1	2	.261	.320	.508	.997
1995	Sea-A	141	519	92	152	35	3	31	111	62	15	91	4	2	6	0	0	.293	.369	.551	.993
1996	NY-A	155	595	82	174	28	0	25	117	68	4	85	2	1	5	2	1	.292	.364	.466	.996
1997	NY-A	158	594	96	176	31	2	44	141	75	14	75	3	0	13	3	1	.296	.371	.577	.994
1998	NY-A	142	531	92	149	33	1	28	123	61	3	83	0	0	10	2	1	.281	.349	.505	.992
1999	NY-A	159	589	95	155	27	2	28	105	69	0	86	0	0	4	3	4	.263	.338	.458	.995
2000	NY-A	155	569	69	147	37	4	16	91	52	9	74	8	0	3	4	1	.258	.328	.422	.994

(continued)

Constantino "Tino" Martinez, 1b, 1996–2000

Despite the extra pressure of replacing a popular and talented player, Tino Martinez has been a very good first baseman for the Yankees in the last half of the 1990s and into the year 2000.

Martinez, born December 7, 1967 in Tampa, Florida, was acquired from the Seattle Mariners in 1996. The Yankees had lost the services of longtime All-Star first baseman Don Mattingly, who retired, and New York badly needed some lefthanded power.

Tino was a good candidate. In 1995, the 28-year-old Martinez had had his best year ever in the big leagues, with 31 home runs and 111 RBIs and making the All-Star team. In the Mariners' divisional playoff series with the Yankees in 1995, he hit .409 as Seattle beat New York, three games to two.

New York acquired him in 1996, and he has been a tremendously consistent player, hitting .280 in his five years with the Yankees and averaging more than 25 home runs and 100 RBI in those five years.

In May 1999, he played his 500th game with the Yankees. At that point, he had 407 RBI, exactly matching the number reached by Hall-of-Famer Lou Gehrig in 500 Yankees games.

His best World Series was in 1998, when he hit .385 as New York swept the San Diego Padres. Martinez hit what may well have been the decisive blow in that series, cracking a a 2-out grand slam against Mark Langston that capped a 7-run seventh inning in the Yankees' 9-6 Game 1 win. He had another strong Series in 2000, with eight hits and his usual flawless defensive play.

(continued)

	GAMES	AB	RUNS	HITS	2B	3B	HR	RBI	BB	IBB	SO	HBP	SH	SF	SB	CS	BA	OBA	SA	FA
Career average	119	434	62	119	24	1	21	81	48	6	65	2	1	5	2	1	.273	.344	.478	.995
Yankee average	**154**	**576**	**87**	**160**	**31**	**2**	**28**	**115**	**65**	**6**	**81**	**3**	**0**	**7**	**3**	**2**	**.278**	**.350**	**.486**	**.994**
Career total	1312	4774	684	1303	262	15	229	889	523	65	712	25	11	58	17	14	.273	.344	.478	.995
Yankee total	**769**	**2878**	**434**	**801**	**156**	**9**	**141**	**577**	**325**	**30**	**403**	**13**	**1**	**35**	**14**	**8**	**.278**	**.350**	**.486**	**.994**

Mason, James Percy (Jim)

HEIGHT: 6'2" THROWS: RIGHT BATS: LEFT BORN: 8/14/1950 MOBILE, ALABAMA POSITIONS PLAYED: 2B, 3B, SS

YEAR	TEAM	GAMES	AB	RUNS	HITS	2B	3B	HR	RBI	BB	IBB	SO	HBP	SH	SF	SB	CS	BA	OBA	SA	FA
1971	Was-A	3	9	0	3	0	0	0	0	1	0	3	0	0	0	0	0	.333	.400	.333	.955
1972	Tex-A	46	147	10	29	3	0	0	10	9	0	39	1	1	1	0	0	.197	.247	.218	.905
1973	Tex-A	92	238	23	49	7	2	3	19	23	0	48	0	2	3	0	1	.206	.273	.290	.947
1974	**NY-A**	**152**	**440**	**41**	**110**	**18**	**6**	**5**	**37**	**35**	**1**	**87**	**0**	**7**	**5**	**1**	**2**	**.250**	**.302**	**.352**	**.964**
1975	**NY-A**	**94**	**223**	**17**	**34**	**3**	**2**	**2**	**16**	**22**	**0**	**49**	**0**	**5**	**1**	**0**	**2**	**.152**	**.228**	**.211**	**.955**
1976	**NY-A**	**93**	**217**	**17**	**39**	**7**	**1**	**1**	**14**	**9**	**0**	**37**	**0**	**7**	**3**	**0**	**0**	**.180**	**.210**	**.235**	**.966**
1977	Tor-A	22	79	10	13	3	0	0	2	7	0	10	0	2	0	1	1	.165	.233	.203	.971
1977	Tex-A	36	55	9	12	3	0	1	7	6	0	10	0	3	1	0	0	.218	.290	.327	.000
1978	Tex-A	55	105	10	20	4	0	0	3	5	0	17	0	6	0	0	0	.190	.227	.229	.905
1979	Mon-N	40	71	3	13	5	1	0	6	7	1	16	0	0	0	0	2	.183	.256	.282	.966
Career average	63	158	14	32	5	1	1	11	12	0	32	0	3	1	0	1	.203	.259	.275	.853
Yankee average	**113**	**293**	**25**	**61**	**9**	**3**	**3**	**22**	**22**	**0**	**58**	**0**	**6**	**3**	**0**	**1**	**.208**	**.261**	**.288**	**.962**
Career total	633	1584	140	322	53	12	12	114	124	2	316	1	33	14	2	8	.203	.259	.275	.853
Yankee total	**339**	**880**	**75**	**183**	**28**	**9**	**8**	**67**	**66**	**1**	**173**	**0**	**19**	**9**	**1**	**4**	**.208**	**.261**	**.288**	**.962**

Mata, Victor Jose BORN VICTOR JOSE MATA (ABREAU)

HEIGHT: 6'1" THROWS: RIGHT BATS: RIGHT BORN: 6/17/1961 SANTIAGO, DOMINICAN REPUBLIC POSITIONS PLAYED: OF

YEAR	TEAM	GAMES	AB	RUNS	HITS	2B	3B	HR	RBI	BB	IBB	SO	HBP	SH	SF	SB	CS	BA	OBA	SA	FA
1984	NY-A	30	70	8	23	5	0	1	6	0	0	12	1	4	1	1	1	.329	.333	.443	.942
1985	NY-A	6	7	1	1	0	0	0	0	0	0	0	0	0	0	0	0	.143	.143	.143	1.000
Career average	18	39	5	12	3	0	1	3	0	0	6	1	2	1	1	1	.312	.316	.416	.971
Yankee average	**18**	**39**	**5**	**12**	**3**	**0**	**1**	**3**	**0**	**0**	**6**	**1**	**2**	**1**	**1**	**1**	**.312**	**.316**	**.416**	**.971**
Career total	36	77	9	24	5	0	1	6	0	0	12	1	4	1	1	1	.312	.316	.416	.971
Yankee total	**36**	**77**	**9**	**24**	**5**	**0**	**1**	**6**	**0**	**0**	**12**	**1**	**4**	**1**	**1**	**1**	**.312**	**.316**	**.416**	**.971**

Mattingly, Donald Arthur

HEIGHT: 6'0"   THROWS: LEFT   BATS: LEFT   BORN: 4/20/1961 EVANSVILLE, INDIANA   POSITIONS PLAYED: 1B, 2B, 3B, OF

YEAR	TEAM	GAMES	AB	RUNS	HITS	2B	3B	HR	RBI	BB	IBB	SO	HBP	SH	SF	SB	CS	BA	OBA	SA	FA
1982	NY-A	7	12	0	2	0	0	0	1	0	0	1	0	0	1	0	0	.167	.154	.167	1.000
1983	NY-A	91	279	34	79	15	4	4	32	21	5	31	1	2	2	0	0	.283	.333	.409	.974
1984	NY-A	153	603	91	207	44	2	23	110	41	8	33	1	8	9	1	1	.343	.381	.537	.974
1985	NY-A	159	652	107	211	48	3	35	145	56	13	41	2	2	15	2	2	.324	.371	.567	.995
1986	NY-A	162	677	117	238	53	2	31	113	53	11	35	1	1	10	0	0	.352	.394	.573	.923

(continued)

Donald Arthur Mattingly, 1b-of-dh, 1982–95

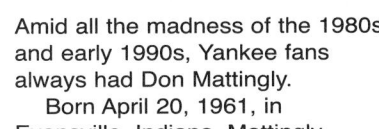

Amid all the madness of the 1980s and early 1990s, Yankee fans always had Don Mattingly.

Born April 20, 1961, in Evansville, Indiana, Mattingly played in New York for 14 years. And no matter how odd or weird things got, New York fans knew that day in and day out, they could count on a professional effort from "Donnie Baseball" every single day of those 14 years.

Mattingly was a late-round pick of the Yankees in the 1979 free agent draft. He was caught in the New York-to-Columbus turnstile in 1982 and 1983, shuttling back and forth from the Yankees to their Ohio farm team.

In 1984, Yankee manager Yogi Berra made Mattingly his starting first baseman. Mattingly responded by winning the batting title, edging teammate Dave Winfield by three percentage points with a .343 average.

He became the first Yankee to win a batting crown since Mickey Mantle in 1956 and the first lefthander to hit over .340 since Lou Gehrig in 1936.

Mattingly was one of the greatest players of the 1980s. He was a superb defensive player, winning nine of his ten Gold Glove Awards between 1985 and 1994, a major league record for first basemen. At the plate, Mattingly could hit for power and average. He led the Yankees in batting average five times over his career, led the team in home runs three times and in RBI six times.

In 1985, he was the MVP of the American League, with 35 home runs, a .324 batting average and a league-leading 145 RBI. But 1986, when he finished second in the MVP voting, was actually his best year. He belted 238 hits, easily topping a team record set 59 years before by Earle Combs. Among those hits were 53 doubles, which led the league and broke Lou Gehrig's team record, also set in 1927. He also had a 24-game hitting streak, which was seventh all-time for the Yankees.

Mattingly was steady, he was tough, he was consistent. He was a leader in a clubhouse that in the late 1980s and early 1990s often seemed chaotic. In 1991, he was named the tenth captain in Yankee history, a title he would keep until his retirement.

A chronic back problem began to limit his effectiveness in the 1990s, but that is speaking relatively. Mattingly still hit in the .290s and fielded his position better than any other first baseman in the league.

In 1995, after 13 years of frustration, Mattingly and the Yankees finally made it into the postseason. New York lost a five-game series to the Mariners, but Mattingly's last hurrah was an individual triumph, as he hit .417 with 6 RBI, four doubles and three runs scored. A few weeks after that series, Mattingly retired.

He remains 5th all-time on the Yankee's list for hits with 2,153, 2nd all-time on the list with 442 doubles, 7th in home runs with 222, 8th in RBI with 1,099, 9th in batting average with .307 and 8th in runs scored with 1,007. He also shares a major league record of eight consecutive games hitting a home run in 1987. He also set a team record with six grand slams that same year.

(continued)

YEAR	TEAM	GAMES	AB	RUNS	HITS	2B	3B	HR	RBI	BB	IBB	SO	HBP	SH	SF	SB	CS	BA	OBA	SA	FA
1987	NY-A	141	569	93	186	38	2	30	115	51	13	38	1	0	8	1	4	.327	.378	.559	.996
1988	NY-A	144	599	94	186	37	0	18	88	41	14	29	3	0	8	1	0	.311	.353	.462	.993
1989	NY-A	158	631	79	191	37	2	23	113	51	18	30	1	0	10	3	0	.303	.351	.477	1.000
1990	NY-A	102	394	40	101	16	0	5	42	28	13	20	3	0	3	1	0	.256	.308	.335	.997
1991	NY-A	152	587	64	169	35	0	9	68	46	11	42	4	0	9	2	0	.288	.339	.394	.996
1992	NY-A	157	640	89	184	40	0	14	86	39	7	43	1	0	6	3	0	.288	.327	.416	.997
1993	NY-A	134	530	78	154	27	2	17	86	61	9	42	2	0	3	0	0	.291	.364	.445	.998
1994	NY-A	97	372	62	113	20	1	6	51	60	7	24	0	0	4	0	0	.304	.397	.411	.998
1995	NY-A	128	458	59	132	32	2	7	49	40	7	35	1	0	8	0	2	.288	.341	.413	.994
Career average		128	500	72	154	32	1	16	79	42	10	32	2	1	7	1	1	.307	.358	.471	.988
Yankee average		128	500	72	154	32	1	16	79	42	10	32	2	1	7	1	1	.307	.358	.471	.988
Career total		1785	7003	1007	2153	442	20	222	1099	588	136	444	21	13	96	14	9	.307	.358	.471	.988
Yankee total		1785	7003	1007	2153	442	20	222	1099	588	136	444	21	13	96	14	9	.307	.358	.471	.988

May, Carlos

HEIGHT: 5'11"   THROWS: RIGHT   BATS: LEFT   BORN: 5/17/1948 BIRMINGHAM, ALABAMA   POSITIONS PLAYED: 1B, OF

YEAR	TEAM	GAMES	AB	RUNS	HITS	2B	3B	HR	RBI	BB	IBB	SO	HBP	SH	SF	SB	CS	BA	OBA	SA	FA
1968	Chi-A	17	67	4	12	1	0	0	1	3	1	15	0	1	0	0	0	.179	.214	.194	.960
1969	Chi-A	100	367	62	103	18	2	18	62	58	7	66	6	0	3	1	4	.281	.385	.488	.982
1970	Chi-A	150	555	83	158	28	4	12	68	79	9	96	3	0	6	12	5	.285	.373	.414	.977
1971	Chi-A	141	500	64	147	21	7	7	·70	62	5	61	6	1	5	16	7	.294	.375	.406	.986
1972	Chi-A	148	523	83	161	26	3	12	68	79	14	70	9	0	4	23	14	.308	.405	.438	.983
1973	Chi-A	149	553	62	148	20	0	20	96	53	5	73	5	1	5	8	6	.268	.334	.412	.992
1974	Chi-A	149	551	66	137	19	2	8	58	46	3	76	1	2	4	8	9	.249	.306	.334	.988
1975	Chi-A	128	454	55	123	19	2	8	53	67	13	46	9	0	4	12	7	.271	.373	.374	.989
1976	Chi-A	20	63	7	11	2	0	0	3	9	0	5	0	0	0	4	0	.175	.278	.206	1.000
1976	**NY-A**	**87**	**288**	**38**	**80**	**11**	**2**	**3**	**40**	**34**	**2**	**32**	**5**	**1**	**5**	**1**	**1**	**.278**	**.358**	**.361**	**1.000**
1977	**NY-A**	**65**	**181**	**21**	**41**	**7**	**1**	**2**	**16**	**17**	**4**	**24**	**1**	**1**	**3**	**0**	**0**	**.227**	**.292**	**.309**	**1.000**
1977	Cal-A	11	18	0	6	0	0	0	1	5	0	1	0	0	0	0	0	.333	.478	.333	1.000
Career average		97	343	45	94	14	2	8	45	43	5	47	4	1	3	7	4	.274	.357	.392	.988
Yankee average		76	235	30	61	9	2	3	28	26	3	28	3	1	4	1	1	.258	.333	.341	1.000
Career total		1165	4120	545	1127	172	23	90	536	512	63	565	45	7	39	85	53	.274	.357	.392	.988
Yankee total		152	469	59	121	18	3	5	56	51	6	56	6	2	8	1	1	.258	.333	.341	1.000

Mayberry, John Claiborn (Big John)

HEIGHT: 6'3"   THROWS: LEFT   BATS: LEFT   BORN: 2/18/1949 DETROIT, MICHIGAN   POSITIONS PLAYED: 1B

YEAR	TEAM	GAMES	AB	RUNS	HITS	2B	3B	HR	RBI	BB	IBB	SO	HBP	SH	SF	SB	CS	BA	OBA	SA	FA
1968	Hou-N	4	9	0	0	0	0	0	0	0	0	2	1	0	0	0	0	.000	.100	.000	1.000
1969	Hou-N	5	4	0	0	0	0	0	0	1	0	1	0	0	0	0	0	.000	.200	.000	.000
1970	Hou-N	50	148	23	32	3	2	5	14	21	6	33	2	1	2	1	1	.216	.318	.365	.995
1971	Hou-N	46	137	16	25	0	1	7	14	13	2	32	2	0	2	0	0	.182	.260	.350	.997
1972	KC-A	149	503	65	150	24	3	25	100	78	13	74	3	1	3	0	2	.298	.394	.507	.995
1973	KC-A	152	510	87	142	20	2	26	100	122	17	79	2	0	4	3	0	.278	.417	.478	.994
1974	KC-A	126	427	63	100	13	1	22	69	77	11	72	6	1	1	4	2	.234	.358	.424	.990
1975	KC-A	156	554	95	161	38	1	34	106	119	16	73	4	1	5	5	3	.291	.416	.547	.988
1976	KC-A	161	594	76	138	22	2	13	95	82	7	73	2	0	12	3	2	.232	.322	.342	.996
1977	KC-A	153	543	73	125	22	1	23	82	83	9	86	7	1	7	1	3	.230	.336	.401	.995
1978	Tor-A	152	515	51	129	15	2	22	70	60	2	57	4	1	7	1	2	.250	.329	.416	.993
1979	Tor-A	137	464	61	127	22	1	21	74	69	7	60	5	1	2	1	1	.274	.372	.461	.995
1980	Tor-A	149	501	62	124	19	2	30	82	77	9	80	3	3	4	0	0	.248	.349	.473	.994
1981	Tor-A	94	290	34	72	6	1	17	43	44	4	45	8	0	2	1	1	.248	.360	.452	.993
1982	Tor-A	17	33	7	9	0	0	2	3	7	1	5	1	0	1	0	0	.273	.405	.455	1.000
1982	**NY-A**	**69**	**215**	**20**	**45**	**7**	**0**	**8**	**27**	**28**	**2**	**38**	**5**	**0**	**1**	**0**	**0**	**.209**	**.313**	**.353**	**.996**
Career average		101	340	46	86	13	1	16	55	55	7	51	3	1	3	1	1	.253	.360	.439	.933
Yankee average		69	215	20	45	7	0	8	27	28	2	38	5	0	1	0	1	.209	.313	.353	.996
Career total		1620	5447	733	1379	211	19	255	879	881	106	810	55	10	53	20	17	.253	.360	.439	.933
Yankee total		69	215	20	45	7	0	8	27	28	2	38	5	0	1	0	0	.209	.313	.353	.996

Mazzilli, Lee Louis

HEIGHT: 6'1" THROWS: RIGHT BATS: BOTH BORN: 3/25/1955 NEW YORK, NEW YORK POSITIONS PLAYED: 1B, OF

YEAR	TEAM	GAMES	AB	RUNS	HITS	2B	3B	HR	RBI	BB	IBB	SO	HBP	SH	SF	SB	CS	BA	OBA	SA	FA
1976	NY-N	24	77	9	15	2	0	2	7	14	0	10	1	0	1	5	4	.195	.323	.299	.983
1977	NY-N	159	537	66	134	24	3	6	46	72	6	72	3	4	2	22	15	.250	.340	.339	.992
1978	NY-N	148	542	78	148	28	5	16	61	69	6	82	1	2	5	20	13	.273	.353	.432	.987
1979	NY-N	158	597	78	181	34	4	15	79	93	5	74	0	0	3	34	12	.303	.395	.449	.993
1980	NY-N	152	578	82	162	31	4	16	76	82	11	92	3	0	5	41	15	.280	.370	.431	.983
1981	NY-N	95	324	36	74	14	5	6	34	46	3	53	2	0	4	17	7	.228	.324	.358	.970
1982	Tex-A	58	195	23	47	8	0	4	17	28	0	26	1	0	0	11	6	.241	.339	.344	.945
1982	**NY-A**	**37**	**128**	**20**	**34**	**2**	**0**	**6**	**17**	**15**	**0**	**15**	**1**	**0**	**0**	**2**	**3**	**.266**	**.347**	**.422**	**.995**
1983	Pit-N	109	246	37	59	9	0	5	24	49	1	43	2	4	4	15	5	.240	.365	.337	.956
1984	Pit-N	111	266	37	63	11	1	4	21	40	2	42	1	1	1	8	1	.237	.338	.331	1.000
1985	Pit-N	92	117	20	33	8	0	1	9	29	1	17	0	1	0	4	1	.282	.425	.376	.929
1986	Pit-N	61	93	18	21	2	1	1	8	26	1	25	0	0	1	3	3	.226	.392	.301	1.000
1986	NY-N	39	58	10	16	3	0	2	7	12	1	11	2	0	0	1	1	.276	.417	.431	1.000
1987	NY-N	88	124	26	38	8	1	3	24	21	3	14	0	0	3	5	3	.306	.399	.460	1.000
1988	NY-N	68	116	9	17	2	0	0	12	12	0	16	1	0	3	4	1	.147	.227	.164	1.000
1989	NY-N	48	60	10	11	2	0	2	7	17	0	19	0	0	0	3	0	.183	.364	.317	1.000
1989	Tor-A	28	66	12	15	3	0	4	11	17	1	16	2	0	1	2	0	.227	.395	.455	.944
Career average		87	243	34	63	11	1	6	27	38	2	37	1	1	2	12	5	.259	.359	.385	.981
Yankee average		**37**	**128**	**20**	**34**	**2**	**0**	**6**	**17**	**15**	**0**	**15**	**1**	**0**	**0**	**2**	**3**	**.266**	**.347**	**.422**	**.995**
Career total		1475	4124	571	1068	191	24	93	460	642	41	627	20	12	33	197	90	.259	.359	.385	.981
Yankee total		**37**	**128**	**20**	**34**	**2**	**0**	**6**	**17**	**15**	**0**	**15**	**1**	**0**	**0**	**2**	**3**	**.266**	**.347**	**.422**	**.995**

McCarthy, Joseph N. (Joe)

HEIGHT: 6' 1" THROWS: RIGHT BATS: RIGHT BORN: 12/25/1881 SYRACUSE, NEW YORK DIED: 1/12/1937 SYRACUSE, NEW YORK POSITIONS PLAYED: C

YEAR	TEAM	GAMES	AB	RUNS	HITS	2B	3B	HR	RBI	BB	IBB	SO	HBP	SH	SF	SB	CS	BA	OBA	SA	FA
1905	**NY-A**	**1**	**2**	**0**	**0**	**0**	**0**	**0**	**0**	**0**	**—**	**—**	**0**	**0**	**—**	**0**	**—**	**.000**	**.000**	**.000**	**1.000**
1906	StL-N	15	37	3	9	2	0	0	2	2	—	—	0	0	—	0	—	.243	.282	.297	.984
Career average		8	20	2	5	1	0	0	1	1	—	—	0	0	—	0	—	.231	.268	.282	.992
Yankee average		**1**	**2**	**0**	**0**	**0**	**0**	**0**	**0**	**0**	**—**	**—**	**0**	**0**	**—**	**0**	**—**	**.000**	**.000**	**.000**	**1.000**
Career total		16	39	3	9	2	0	0	2	2	—	—	0	0	—	0	—	.231	.268	.282	.992
Yankee total		**1**	**2**	**0**	**0**	**0**	**0**	**0**	**0**	**0**	**—**	**—**	**0**	**0**	**—**	**0**	**—**	**.000**	**.000**	**.000**	**1.000**

McCauley, Patrick M.

HEIGHT: 5'11" THROWS: RIGHT BATS: — BORN: 6/10/1870 WARE, MASSACHUSETTS DIED: 1/23/1917 NEWARK, NEW JERSEY POSITIONS PLAYED: C, OF

YEAR	TEAM	GAMES	AB	RUNS	HITS	2B	3B	HR	RBI	BB	IBB	SO	HBP	SH	SF	SB	CS	BA	OBA	SA	FA
1893	StL-N	5	16	0	1	0	0	0	0	0	—	1	0	—	—	0	—	.063	.063	.063	.808
1896	Was-N	26	84	14	21	3	0	3	11	7	—	8	1	3	—	3	—	.250	.308	.393	.917
1903	**NY-A**	**6**	**19**	**0**	**1**	**0**	**0**	**0**	**1**	**0**	**—**	**0**	**0**	**0**	**—**	**0**	**—**	**.053**	**.053**	**.053**	**.920**
Career average		12	40	5	8	1	0	1	4	2	—	3	0	—	—	1	—	.193	.244	.294	.882
Yankee average		**6**	**19**	**0**	**1**	**0**	**0**	**0**	**1**	**0**	**—**	**0**	**0**	**0**	**—**	**0**	**—**	**.053**	**.053**	**.053**	**.920**
Career total		37	119	14	23	3	0	3	12	7	—	9	1	3	—	3	—	.193	.244	.294	.882
Yankee total		**6**	**19**	**0**	**1**	**0**	**0**	**0**	**1**	**0**	**—**	**0**	**0**	**0**	**—**	**0**	**—**	**.053**	**.053**	**.053**	**.920**

McClure, Lawrence Ledwith (Larry)

HEIGHT: 5'6" THROWS: RIGHT BATS: RIGHT BORN: 10/3/1885 WAYNE, WEST VIRGINIA DIED: 8/31/1949 HUNTINGTON, WEST VIRGINIA POSITIONS PLAYED: OF

YEAR	TEAM	GAMES	AB	RUNS	HITS	2B	3B	HR	RBI	BB	IBB	SO	HBP	SH	SF	SB	CS	BA	OBA	SA	FA
1910	**NY-A**	**1**	**1**	**0**	**0**	**0**	**0**	**0**	**0**	**0**	**0**	**0**	**0**	**0**	**0**	**0**	**0**	**.000**	**.000**	**.000**	**.000**
Career average		1	1	0	0	0	0	0	0	0	0	0	0	0	0	0	0	.000	.000	.000	.000
Yankee average		**1**	**1**	**0**	**0**	**0**	**0**	**0**	**0**	**0**	**0**	**0**	**0**	**0**	**0**	**0**	**0**	**.000**	**.000**	**.000**	**.000**
Career total		1	1	0	0	0	0	0	0	0	0	0	0	0	0	0	0	.000	.000	.000	.000
Yankee total		**1**	**1**	**0**	**0**	**0**	**0**	**0**	**0**	**0**	**0**	**0**	**0**	**0**	**0**	**0**	**0**	**.000**	**.000**	**.000**	**.000**

McConnell, George Neely

HEIGHT: 6'3" THROWS: RIGHT BATS: RIGHT BORN: 9/16/1877 SHELBYVILLE, TENNESSEE DIED: 5/10/1964 CHATTANOOGA, TENN. POSITIONS PLAYED: P, 1B

YEAR	TEAM	GAMES	AB	RUNS	HITS	2B	3B	HR	RBI	BB	IBB	SO	HBP	SH	SF	SB	CS	BA	OBA	SA	FA
1909	NY-A	13	43	4	9	0	1	0	5	1	—	—	0	1	—	1	—	.209	.227	.256	.965
1912	NY-A	42	91	11	27	4	2	0	8	4	—	—	1	1	—	0	—	.297	.333	.385	.925
1913	NY-A	39	67	4	12	2	0	0	2	0	—	11	0	3	—	0	—	.179	.179	.209	.966
1914	Chi-N	1	2	0	0	0	0	0	0	0	—	1	0	0	—	0	—	.000	.000	.000	1.000
1915	Chi-F	53	125	14	31	6	2	1	18	0	—	16	1	3	—	2	—	.248	.254	.352	.974
1916	Chi-N	28	57	2	9	0	0	0	0	2	—	4	1	2	—	0	—	.158	.200	.158	.952
Career average		29	64	6	15	2	1	0	6	1	—	—	1	2	—	1	—	.229	.248	.294	.964
Yankee average		**31**	**67**	**6**	**16**	**2**	**1**	**0**	**5**	**2**	**—**	**—**	**0**	**2**	**—**	**0**	**—**	**.239**	**.261**	**.299**	**.952**
Career total		176	385	35	88	12	5	1	33	7	—	32	3	10	—	3	—	.229	.248	.294	.964
Yankee total		**94**	**201**	**19**	**48**	**6**	**3**	**0**	**15**	**5**	**—**	**11**	**1**	**5**	**—**	**1**	**—**	**.239**	**.261**	**.299**	**.952**

McDermott, Maurice Joseph (Mickey)

HEIGHT: 6'2" THROWS: LEFT BATS: LEFT BORN: 4/29/1928 POUGHKEEPSIE, NEW YORK POSITIONS PLAYED: P, 1B

YEAR	TEAM	GAMES	AB	RUNS	HITS	2B	3B	HR	RBI	BB	IBB	SO	HBP	SH	SF	SB	CS	BA	OBA	SA	FA
1948	Bos-A	7	8	2	3	1	0	0	0	0	—	0	0	0	—	0	0	.375	.375	.500	1.000
1949	Bos-A	12	33	3	7	3	0	0	6	3	—	6	0	0	—	0	0	.212	.278	.303	.941
1950	Bos-A	39	44	11	16	5	0	0	12	9	—	3	0	0	—	0	0	.364	.472	.477	.938
1951	Bos-A	43	66	8	18	1	1	1	6	3	—	14	1	1	—	0	1	.273	.314	.364	.950
1952	Bos-A	36	62	10	14	1	1	1	7	4	—	11	0	3	—	0	0	.226	.273	.323	.944
1953	Bos-A	45	93	9	28	8	0	1	13	2	—	13	0	0	—	0	1	.301	.316	.419	.953
1954	Was-A	54	95	7	19	3	0	0	4	7	—	12	0	2	0	0	0	.200	.255	.232	.955
1955	Was-A	70	95	10	25	4	0	1	10	6	0	16	1	1	1	1	0	.263	.311	.337	.943
1956	**NY-A**	**46**	**52**	**4**	**11**	**0**	**0**	**1**	**4**	**8**	**0**	**13**	**0**	**1**	**0**	**0**	**0**	**.212**	**.317**	**.269**	**1.000**
1957	KC-A	58	49	6	12	1	0	4	7	9	2	16	0	0	0	0	0	.245	.362	.510	.935
1958	Det-A	4	3	0	1	0	0	0	1	0	0	2	0	0	0	0	0	.333	.333	.333	.000
1961	StL-N	22	14	1	1	1	0	0	3	0	0	4	0	0	0	0	0	.071	.071	.143	1.000
1961	KC-A	7	5	0	1	1	0	0	1	1	0	2	0	0	0	0	0	.200	.333	.400	.500
Career average		34	48	6	12	2	0	1	6	4	—	9	0	1	—	0	0	.252	.312	.349	.851
Yankee average		**46**	**52**	**4**	**11**	**0**	**0**	**1**	**4**	**8**	**0**	**13**	**0**	**1**	**0**	**0**	**0**	**.212**	**.317**	**.269**	**1.000**
Career total		443	619	71	156	29	2	9	74	52	2	112	2	8	1	1	2	.252	.312	.349	.851
Yankee total		**46**	**52**	**4**	**11**	**0**	**0**	**1**	**4**	**8**	**0**	**13**	**0**	**1**	**0**	**0**	**0**	**.212**	**.317**	**.269**	**1.000**

McDonald, David Bruce

HEIGHT: 6'3" THROWS: RIGHT BATS: LEFT BORN: 5/20/1943 NEW ALBANY, INDIANA POSITIONS PLAYED: 1B, OF

YEAR	TEAM	GAMES	AB	RUNS	HITS	2B	3B	HR	RBI	BB	IBB	SO	HBP	SH	SF	SB	CS	BA	OBA	SA	FA
1969	**NY-A**	**9**	**23**	**0**	**5**	**1**	**0**	**0**	**2**	**2**	**0**	**5**	**0**	**0**	**0**	**0**	**1**	**.217**	**.280**	**.261**	**.960**
1971	Mon-N	24	39	3	4	2	0	1	4	4	0	14	0	0	2	0	0	.103	.178	.231	.983
Career average		17	31	2	5	2	0	1	3	3	0	10	0	0	1	0	1	.145	.214	.242	.972
Yankee average		**9**	**23**	**0**	**5**	**1**	**0**	**0**	**2**	**2**	**0**	**5**	**0**	**0**	**0**	**0**	**1**	**.217**	**.280**	**.261**	**.960**
Career total		33	62	3	9	3	0	1	6	6	0	19	0	0	2	0	1	.145	.214	.242	.972
Yankee total		**9**	**23**	**0**	**5**	**1**	**0**	**0**	**2**	**2**	**0**	**5**	**0**	**0**	**0**	**0**	**1**	**.217**	**.280**	**.261**	**.960**

McDougald, Gilbert James (Gil)

HEIGHT: 6'0" THROWS: RIGHT BATS: RIGHT BORN: 5/19/1928 SAN FRANCISCO, CALIFORNIA POSITIONS PLAYED: 2B, 3B, SS

YEAR	TEAM	GAMES	AB	RUNS	HITS	2B	3B	HR	RBI	BB	IBB	SO	HBP	SH	SF	SB	CS	BA	OBA	SA	FA
1951	NY-A	131	402	72	123	23	4	14	63	56	—	54	4	11	—	14	5	.306	.396	.488	.949
1952	NY-A	152	555	65	146	16	5	11	78	57	—	73	4	16	—	6	5	.263	.336	.369	.968
1953	NY-A	141	541	82	154	27	7	10	83	60	—	65	5	8	—	3	4	.285	.361	.416	.953
1954	NY-A	126	394	66	102	22	2	12	48	62	—	64	5	9	3	3	4	.259	.364	.416	.989
1955	NY-A	141	533	79	152	10	8	13	53	65	2	77	2	8	7	6	4	.285	.361	.407	.985
1956	NY-A	120	438	79	136	13	3	13	56	68	1	59	3	7	2	3	8	.311	.405	.443	.985
1957	NY-A	141	539	87	156	25	9	13	62	59	1	71	4	19	3	2	5	.289	.362	.442	.991
1958	NY-A	138	503	69	126	19	1	14	65	59	1	75	3	7	6	6	2	.250	.329	.376	.977
1959	NY-A	127	434	44	109	16	8	4	34	35	3	40	3	5	4	0	3	.251	.309	.353	.989
1960	NY-A	119	337	54	87	16	4	8	34	38	0	45	3	7	2	2	4	.258	.337	.401	.994

(continued)

Gilbert James "Gil" McDougald, 2b-3b-ss, 1951–60

Gil McDougald was perhaps the most versatile player the Yankees ever had. But because he played in the shadow of Mickey Mantle, Whitey Ford and Yogi Berra, he was also one of the most underrated.

McDougald was born in San Francisco, California, on May 19, 1928. When he came to the Yankees in 1951, he was a second baseman. Manager Casey Stengel approached him with the idea of using him at shortstop and third base as well. McDougald had never played third base but told Stengel he thought he could handle it.

He could. He played 55 games at second base, 82 games at third, hit .306 and was the Rookie of the Year in 1951.

He was simply an amazing athlete. In 1952, he led the league's third basemen in double plays. In 1955, he led American League second basemen in double plays and in 1957, he led American League shortstops in double plays. It was an unprecedented show of versatility.

He was tough and combative, which Stengel loved. His teammates called him "Smash," for his hell-bent-for-leather style. When the major leagues began requiring players to wear helmets, McDougald looked at the measure less for protection than as another way to get on base: All he had to do was stick his head in the way of the pitch.

But in 1957, he drilled a line drive up the middle that struck Cleveland Indian pitcher Herb Score in the face, injuring him badly. McDougald was deeply affected by the incident, admitting years later that he had considered retiring. He didn't, but he began to be a bit more cautious at the plate, and his effectiveness was lessened. "It took the starch out of me," he admitted once.

The next three years, McDougald hit .250, .251 and .258. In 1960, at the relatively young age of 32, McDougald retired, turning down a lucrative offer from the Los Angeles Angels to become a player-manager.

Following his retirement from baseball, McDougald became a businessman in the New York City area and coached the Fordham University baseball team for several years.

(continued)

																		BA	OBA	SA	FA
Career average	134	468	70	129	19	5	11	58	56	—	62	4	10	—	5	4	.276	.358	.410	.978
Yankee average	**134**	**468**	**70**	**129**	**19**	**5**	**11**	**58**	**56**	**—**	**62**	**4**	**10**	**—**	**5**	**4**	**.276**	**.358**	**.410**	**.978**
Career total	1336	4676	697	1291	187	51	112	576	559	8	623	36	97	27	45	44	.276	.356	.410	.978
Yankee total	**1336**	**4676**	**697**	**1291**	**187**	**51**	**112**	**576**	**559**	**8**	**623**	**36**	**97**	**27**	**45**	**44**	**.276**	**.356**	**.410**	**.978**

McFarland, Hermas Walter

HEIGHT: 5'6"   THROWS: RIGHT   BATS: LEFT   BORN: 3/11/1870 DES MOINES, IOWA   DIED: 9/21/1935 RICHMOND, VIRGINIA   POSITIONS PLAYED: C, OF

YEAR	TEAM	GAMES	AB	RUNS	HITS	2B	3B	HR	RBI	BB	IBB	SO	HBP	SH	SF	SB	CS	BA	OBA	SA	FA
1896	Lou-N	30	110	11	21	4	1	1	12	9	—	14	0	0	—	4	—	.191	.252	.273	.833
1898	Cin-N	19	64	10	18	1	3	0	11	7	—	—	0	0	—	3	—	.281	.352	.391	.968
1901	Chi-A	132	473	83	130	21	9	4	59	75	—	—	9	11	—	33	—	.275	.384	.383	.946
1902	Chi-A	7	27	5	5	0	0	0	4	2	—	—	0	1	—	1	—	.185	.241	.185	1.000
1902	Bal-A	61	242	54	78	19	6	3	36	36	—	—	4	0	—	10	—	.322	.418	.488	.965
1903	**NY-A**	**103**	**362**	**41**	**88**	**16**	**9**	**5**	**45**	**46**	**—**	**—**	**4**	**0**	**—**	**10**	**—**	**.322**	**.418**	**.488**	**.965**
Career average	59	213	34	57	10	5	2	28	29	—	—	3	4	—	11	—	.266	.361	.388	.942
Yankee average	**103**	**362**	**41**	**88**	**16**	**9**	**5**	**45**	**46**	**—**	**—**	**3**	**12**	**—**	**13**	**—**	**.243**	**.333**	**.378**	**.939**
Career total	352	1278	204	340	61	28	13	167	175	—	14	16	24	—	64	—	.266	.361	.388	.942
Yankee total	**103**	**362**	**41**	**88**	**16**	**9**	**5**	**45**	**46**	**—**	**—**	**3**	**12**	**—**	**13**	**—**	**.243**	**.333**	**.378**	**.939**

McGuire, James Thomas (Deacon)

HEIGHT: 6'1" THROWS: RIGHT BATS: RIGHT BORN: 11/18/1863 YOUNGSTOWN, OH. DIED: 10/31/1936 ALBION, MICH. POSITIONS PLAYED: P, C, 1B, 3B, SS, OF

YEAR	TEAM	GAMES	AB	RUNS	HITS	2B	3B	HR	RBI	BB	IBB	SO	HBP	SH	SF	SB	CS	BA	OBA	SA	FA
1884	Tol-AA	45	151	12	28	7	0	1	—	5	—	—	1	—	—	—	—	.185	.212	.252	.906
1885	Det-N	34	121	11	23	4	2	0	9	5	—	23	—	—	—	—	—	.190	.222	.256	.920
1886	Phi-N	50	167	25	33	7	1	2	18	19	—	25	—	—	—	2	—	.198	.280	.287	.899
1887	Phi-N	41	150	22	46	6	6	2	23	11	—	8	2	—	—	3	—	.307	.354	.467	.884
1888	Phi-N	12	51	7	17	4	2	0	11	4	—	9	0	—	—	0	—	.333	.382	.490	.800
1888	Det-N	3	13	0	0	0	0	0	0	0	—	4	0	—	—	0	—	.000	.000	.000	.000
1888	Cle-AA	26	94	15	24	1	3	1	13	7	—	—	4	—	—	2	—	.255	.307	.362	.750
1890	Roc-AA	87	331	46	99	16	4	4	53	21	—	—	8	—	—	8	—	.299	.341	.408	1.000
1891	Was-AA	114	413	55	125	22	10	3	66	43	—	34	10	—	—	10	—	.303	.382	.426	1.000
1892	Was-N	97	315	46	73	14	4	4	43	61	—	48	2	—	—	7	—	.232	.356	.340	1.000
1893	Was-N	63	237	29	61	14	3	1	26	26	—	12	3	—	—	3	—	.257	.331	.354	.889
1894	Was-N	104	425	67	130	18	6	6	78	33	—	19	7	4	—	11	—	.306	.356	.419	.918
1895	Was-N	132	533	89	179	30	8	10	97	40	—	18	5	5	—	16	—	.336	.382	.478	.667
1896	Was-N	108	389	60	125	25	3	2	70	30	—	14	6	6	—	12	—	.321	.370	.416	1.000
1897	Was-N	93	327	51	112	17	7	4	53	21	—	—	2	1	—	9	—	.343	.382	.474	.947
1898	Was-N	131	489	59	131	18	3	1	57	24	—	—	6	10	—	10	—	.268	.310	.323	.965
1899	Was-N	59	199	25	54	3	1	1	12	16	—	—	3	1	—	3	—	.271	.326	.312	.973
1899	Bro-N	46	157	22	50	12	4	0	23	12	—	—	5	1	—	4	—	.318	.385	.446	.971
1900	Bro-N	71	241	20	69	15	2	0	34	19	—	—	4	1	—	2	—	.286	.348	.365	.952
1901	Bro-N	85	301	28	89	16	4	0	40	18	—	—	3	4	—	4	—	.296	.342	.375	.960
1902	Det-A	73	229	27	52	14	1	2	23	24	—	—	0	5	—	0	—	.227	.300	.323	.952
1903	Det-A	72	248	15	62	12	1	0	21	19	—	—	1	1	—	3	—	.250	.306	.306	.500
1904	**NY-A**	**101**	**322**	**17**	**67**	**12**	**2**	**0**	**20**	**27**	—	—	**3**	**5**	—	**2**	—	**.208**	**.276**	**.258**	**1.000**
1905	**NY-A**	**72**	**228**	**17**	**67**	**12**	**2**	**0**	**33**	**18**	—	—	**5**	**3**	—	**3**	—	**.219**	**.291**	**.268**	**.975**
1906	**NY-A**	**51**	**144**	**9**	**50**	**7**	**2**	**0**	**14**	**12**	—	—	**3**	**0**	—	**3**	—	**.299**	**.365**	**.333**	**.962**
1907	**NY-A**	**1**	**1**	**11**	**43**	**5**	**0**	**0**	**0**	**0**	—	—	**0**	**0**	—	**0**	—	**.000**	**.000**	**.000**	**1.000**
1907	Bos-A	6	4	0	0	0	0	0	0	0	—	—	0	0	—	0	—	.750	.750	1.500	.000
1908	Bos-A	1	1	1	3	0	0	1	1	0	—	—	0	0	—	0	—	.000	.000	.000	.000
1908	Cle-A	1	4	0	0	0	0	0	0	0	—	—	0	0	—	0	—	.250	.250	.500	1.000
1910	Cle-A	1	3	0	1	1	0	0	2	0	—	—	1	0	—	0	—	.333	.500	.333	1.000
1912	Det-A	1	2	1	1	0	0	0	0	0	—	—	0	0	—	0	—	.500	.500	.500	.714
Career average		58	203	25	56	10	3	2	27	17	—	—	3	—	—	4	—	.278	.341	.372	.849
Yankee average		**56**	**174**	**9**	**40**	**6**	**1**	**0**	**17**	**14**	—	—	**3**	**2**	—	**2**	—	**.230**	**.299**	**.276**	**.984**
Career total		1781	6290	770	1748	300	79	45	840	515	—	214	84	47	—	117	—	.278	.341	.372	.849
Yankee total		**225**	**695**	**37**	**160**	**24**	**4**	**0**	**67**	**57**	—	—	**11**	**8**	—	**8**	—	**.230**	**.299**	**.276**	**.984**

McIlveen, Henry Cooke (Irish)

HEIGHT: 5'1" THROWS: LEFT BATS: LEFT BORN: 7/27/1880 BELFAST, IRELAND DIED: 10/18/1960 LORAIN, OHIO POSITIONS PLAYED: P, OF

YEAR	TEAM	GAMES	AB	RUNS	HITS	2B	3B	HR	RBI	BB	IBB	SO	HBP	SH	SF	SB	CS	BA	OBA	SA	FA
1906	Pit-N	5	5	1	2	0	0	0	0	0	—	—	0	0	—	0	—	.400	.400	.400	1.000
1908	**NY-A**	**44**	**169**	**17**	**36**	**3**	**3**	**0**	**8**	**14**	—	—	**1**	**4**	—	**6**	—	**.213**	**.277**	**.266**	**.949**
1909	**NY-A**	**4**	**3**	**0**	**0**	**0**	**0**	**0**	**0**	**1**	—	—	**0**	**0**	—	**0**	—	**.000**	**.250**	**.000**	**.000**
Career average		18	59	6	13	1	1	0	3	5	—	—	0	1	—	2	—	.215	.280	.266	.650
Yankee average		**24**	**86**	**9**	**18**	**2**	**2**	**0**	**4**	**8**	—	—	**1**	**2**	—	**3**	—	**.209**	**.277**	**.262**	**.475**
Career total		53	177	18	38	3	3	0	8	15	—	—	1	4	—	6	—	.215	.280	.266	.650
Yankee total		**48**	**172**	**17**	**36**	**3**	**3**	**0**	**8**	**15**	—	—	**1**	**4**	—	**6**	—	**.209**	**.277**	**.262**	**.475**

McIntosh, Timothy Alan

HEIGHT: 5'11" THROWS: RIGHT BATS: RIGHT BORN: 3/21/1965 MINNEAPOLIS, MINNESOTA POSITIONS PLAYED: C, 1B, 3B, OF

YEAR	TEAM	GAMES	AB	RUNS	HITS	2B	3B	HR	RBI	BB	IBB	SO	HBP	SH	SF	SB	CS	BA	OBA	SA	FA
1990	Mil-A	5	5	1	1	0	0	1	1	0	0	2	0	0	0	0	0	.200	.200	.800	.875
1991	Mil-A	7	11	2	4	1	0	1	1	0	0	4	0	0	0	0	0	.364	.364	.727	.000
1992	Mil-A	35	77	7	14	3	0	0	6	3	0	9	2	1	1	3	0	.182	.229	.221	.983
1993	Mil-A	1	0	0	0	0	0	0	0	0	0	0	0	0	0	0	0	—	—	—	.000
1993	Mon-N	20	21	2	2	1	0	0	2	0	0	7	0	0	0	0	0	.095	.095	.143	1.000
1996	**NY-A**	**3**	**3**	**0**	**0**	**0**	**0**	**0**	**0**	**0**	**0**	**0**	**0**	**0**	**0**	**0**	**0**	**.000**	**.000**	**.000**	**.000**
Career average		12	20	2	4	1	0	0	2	1	0	4	0	0	0	1	0	.179	.211	.274	.476
Yankee average		**3**	**3**	**3**	**3**	**3**	**3**	**3**	**3**	**3**	**3**	**3**	**3**	**3**	**3**	**3**	**3**	**1.000**	**.750**	**7.000**	**.000**
Career total		71	117	12	21	5	0	2	10	3	0	22	2	1	1	3	3	.179	.211	.274	.476
Yankee total		**3**	**3**	**3**	**3**	**3**	**3**	**3**	**3**	**3**	**3**	**3**	**3**	**3**	**3**	**3**	**3**	**1.000**	**.750**	**7.000**	**.000**

McKechnie, William Boyd (Deacon)

HEIGHT: 5'10" THROWS: RIGHT BATS: BOTH BORN: 8/7/1886 WILKINSBURG, PENN. DIED: 10/29/1965 BRADENTON, FLA. POSITIONS PLAYED: 1B, 2B, 3B, SS, OF

YEAR	TEAM	GAMES	AB	RUNS	HITS	2B	3B	HR	RBI	BB	IBB	SO	HBP	SH	SF	SB	CS	BA	OBA	SA	FA
1907	Pit-N	3	8	0	1	0	0	0	0	0	—	—	0	0	—	0	—	.125	.125	.125	1.000
1910	Pit-N	71	212	23	46	1	2	0	12	11	—	23	0	8	—	4	—	.217	.256	.241	.928
1911	Pit-N	104	321	40	73	8	7	2	37	28	—	18	2	25	—	9	—	.227	.293	.315	.900
1912	Pit-N	24	73	8	18	0	1	0	4	4	—	5	0	2	—	2	—	.247	.286	.274	.917
1913	Bos-N	1	4	1	0	0	0	0	0	0	—	1	1	0	—	0	—	.000	.200	.000	1.000
1913	**NY-A**	**45**	**112**	**7**	**15**	**0**	**0**	**0**	**8**	**8**	**—**	**17**	**1**	**3**	**—**	**2**	**—**	**.134**	**.198**	**.134**	**.750**
1914	Ind-F	149	570	107	173	24	6	2	38	53	—	36	5	36	—	47	—	.304	.368	.377	.939
1915	New-F	127	451	49	113	22	5	1	43	41	—	31	2	21	—	28	—	.251	.316	.328	.956
1916	NY-N	71	260	22	64	9	1	0	17	7	—	20	1	5	—	7	—	.246	.269	.288	.940
1916	Cin-N	37	130	4	36	3	0	0	10	3	—	12	0	7	—	4	—	.277	.293	.300	.960
1917	Cin-N	48	134	11	34	3	1	0	15	7	—	7	1	3	—	5	—	.254	.296	.291	1.000
1918	Pit-N	126	435	34	111	13	9	2	43	24	—	22	2	19	—	12	—	.255	.297	.340	.966
1920	Pit-N	40	133	13	29	3	1	1	13	4	—	7	0	3	—	7	4	.218	.241	.278	1.000
Career average		65	219	25	55	7	3	1	19	15	—	—	1	10	—	10	—	.251	.301	.313	.943
Yankee average		**45**	**112**	**7**	**15**	**0**	**0**	**0**	**8**	**8**	**—**	**17**	**1**	**3**	**—**	**2**	**—**	**.134**	**.198**	**.134**	**.750**
Career total		846	2843	319	713	86	33	8	240	190	—	199	15	132	—	127	4	.251	.301	.313	.943
Yankee total		**45**	**112**	**7**	**15**	**0**	**0**	**0**	**8**	**8**	**—**	**17**	**1**	**3**	**—**	**2**	**—**	**.134**	**.198**	**.134**	**.750**

McKinney, Charles Richard (Rich)

HEIGHT: 5'11" •THROWS: RIGHT BATS: RIGHT BORN: 11/22/1946 PIQUA, OHIO POSITIONS PLAYED: 1B, 2B, 3B, SS, OF

YEAR	TEAM	GAMES	AB	RUNS	HITS	2B	3B	HR	RBI	BB	IBB	SO	HBP	SH	SF	SB	CS	BA	OBA	SA	FA
1970	Chi-A	43	119	12	20	5	0	4	17	11	0	25	1	0	1	3	2	.168	.242	.311	.950
1971	Chi-A	114	369	35	100	11	2	8	46	35	1	37	2	4	4	0	0	.271	.334	.377	.971
1972	**NY-A**	**37**	**121**	**10**	**26**	**2**	**0**	**1**	**7**	**7**	**0**	**13**	**0**	**0**	**0**	**1**	**0**	**.215**	**.258**	**.256**	**.917**
1973	Oak-A	48	65	9	16	3	0	1	7	7	0	4	0	0	0	0	0	.246	.319	.338	.941
1974	Oak-A	5	7	0	1	0	0	0	0	0	0	0	0	0	0	0	0	.143	.143	.143	1.000
1975	Oak-A	8	7	0	1	0	0	0	2	1	0	2	0	0	2	0	0	.143	.200	.143	1.000
1977	Oak-A	86	198	13	35	7	0	6	21	16	0	43	0	0	2	0	1	.177	.236	.303	.964
Career average		49	127	11	28	4	0	3	14	11	0	18	0	1	1	1	0	.225	.286	.328	.963
Yankee average		**37**	**121**	**10**	**26**	**2**	**0**	**1**	**7**	**7**	**0**	**13**	**0**	**0**	**0**	**1**	**0**	**.215**	**.258**	**.256**	**.917**
Career total		341	886	79	199	28	2	20	100	77	1	124	3	4	9	4	3	.225	.286	.328	.963
Yankee total		**37**	**121**	**10**	**26**	**2**	**0**	**1**	**7**	**7**	**0**	**13**	**0**	**0**	**0**	**1**	**0**	**.215**	**.258**	**.256**	**.917**

McManus, Francis E.

HEIGHT: 5'7" THROWS: RIGHT BATS: — BORN: 9/21/1875 LAWRENCE, MASSACHUSETTS DIED: 9/1/1923 SYRACUSE, NEW YORK POSITIONS PLAYED: C

YEAR	TEAM	GAMES	AB	RUNS	HITS	2B	3B	HR	RBI	BB	IBB	SO	HBP	SH	SF	SB	CS	BA	OBA	SA	FA
1899	Was-N	7	21	3	8	1	0	0	2	2	—	—	0	0	—	3	—	.381	.435	.429	.931
1903	Bro-N	2	7	0	0	0	0	0	0	0	—	—	0	0	—	0	—	.000	.000	.000	.929
1904	Det	1	0	0	0	0	0	0	0	0	—	—	0	0	—	0	—	—	—	—	.000
1904	**NY-A**	**4**	**7**	**0**	**0**	**0**	**0**	**0**	**0**	**0**	**—**	**—**	**0**	**0**	**—**	**0**	**—**	**.000**	**.000**	**.000**	**.900**
Career average		4	9	1	2	0	0	0	1	1	—	—	0	0	—	1	—	.229	.270	.257	.690
Yankee average		**4**	**7**	**0**	**0**	**0**	**0**	**0**	**0**	**0**	**—**	**—**	**0**	**0**	**—**	**0**	**—**	**.000**	**.000**	**.000**	**.900**
Career total		14	35	3	8	1	0	0	2	2	—	—	0	0	—	3	—	.229	.270	.257	.690
Yankee total		**4**	**7**	**0**	**0**	**0**	**0**	**0**	**0**	**0**	**—**	**—**	**0**	**0**	**—**	**0**	**—**	**.000**	**.000**	**.000**	**.900**

McMillan, Norman Alexis (Bub)

HEIGHT: 6'0"   THROWS: RIGHT   BATS: RIGHT   BORN: 10/5/1895 LATTA, S. CAROLINA   DIED: 9/28/1969 MARION, S. CAROLINA   POSITIONS PLAYED: 2B, 3B, SS, OF

YEAR	TEAM	GAMES	AB	RUNS	HITS	2B	3B	HR	RBI	BB	IBB	SO	HBP	SH	SF	SB	CS	BA	OBA	SA	FA
1922	**NY-A**	**33**	**78**	**7**	**20**	**1**	**2**	**0**	**11**	**6**	—	**10**	**0**	**5**	—	**4**	**1**	**.256**	**.310**	**.321**	**1.000**
1923	Bos-A	131	459	37	116	24	5	0	42	28	—	44	2	10	—	13	5	.253	.299	.327	.942
1924	StL-A	76	201	25	56	12	2	0	27	12	—	17	4	9	—	6	4	.279	.332	.358	.909
1928	Chi-N	49	123	11	27	2	2	1	12	13	—	19	1	6	—	0	—	.220	.299	.293	.977
1929	Chi-N	124	495	77	134	35	5	5	55	36	—	43	3	7	—	13	—	.271	.324	.392	.944
Career average		83	271	31	71	15	3	1	29	19	—	27	2	7	—	7	—	.260	.313	.352	.954
Yankee average		**33**	**78**	**7**	**20**	**1**	**2**	**0**	**11**	**6**	—	**10**	**0**	**5**	—	**4**	**1**	**.256**	**.310**	**.321**	**1.000**
Career total		413	1356	157	353	74	16	6	147	95	—	133	10	37	—	36	10	.260	.313	.352	.954
Yankee total		**33**	**78**	**7**	**20**	**1**	**2**	**0**	**11**	**6**	—	**10**	**0**	**5**	—	**4**	**1**	**.256**	**.310**	**.321**	**1.000**

McMillan, Thomas Law (Rebel)

HEIGHT: 5'5"   THROWS: RIGHT   BATS: RIGHT   BORN: 4/18/1888 PITTSTON, PENNSYLVANIA   DIED: 7/15/1966 ORLANDO, FLA.   POSITIONS PLAYED: 2B, 3B, SS, OF

YEAR	TEAM	GAMES	AB	RUNS	HITS	2B	3B	HR	RBI	BB	IBB	SO	HBP	SH	SF	SB	CS	BA	OBA	SA	FA
1908	Bro-N	43	147	9	35	3	0	0	3	9	—	—	3	5	—	5	—	.238	.296	.259	.938
1909	Bro-N	108	373	18	79	15	1	0	24	20	—	—	1	6	—	11	—	.212	.254	.257	.914
1910	Bro-N	23	74	2	13	1	0	0	2	6	—	10	0	3	—	4	—	.176	.238	.189	.898
1910	Cin-N	82	248	20	46	0	3	0	13	31	—	23	2	12	—	7	—	.185	.281	.210	.927
1912	**NY-A**	**41**	**149**	**24**	**34**	**2**	**0**	**0**	**12**	**15**	—	—	**1**	**9**	—	**18**	—	**.228**	**.303**	**.242**	**.948**
Career average		59	198	15	41	4	1	0	11	16	—	—	1	7	—	9	—	.209	.273	.238	.925
Yankee average		**41**	**149**	**24**	**34**	**2**	**0**	**0**	**12**	**15**	—	—	**1**	**9**	—	**18**	—	**.228**	**.303**	**.242**	**.948**
Career total		297	991	73	207	21	4	0	54	81	—	33	7	35	—	45	—	.209	.273	.238	.925
Yankee total		**41**	**149**	**24**	**34**	**2**	**0**	**0**	**12**	**15**	—	—	**1**	**9**	—	**18**	—	**.228**	**.303**	**.242**	**.948**

McNally, Michael Joseph

HEIGHT: 5'11"   THROWS: RIGHT   BATS: RIGHT   BORN: 9/9/1892 MINOOKA, PENN.   DIED: 5/29/1965 BETHLEHEM, PENN.   POSITIONS PLAYED: 1B, 2B, 3B, SS, OF

YEAR	TEAM	GAMES	AB	RUNS	HITS	2B	3B	HR	RBI	BB	IBB	SO	HBP	SH	SF	SB	CS	BA	OBA	SA	FA
1915	Bos-A	23	53	7	8	0	1	0	0	3	—	7	0	0	—	0	2	.151	.196	.189	1.000
1916	Bos-A	87	135	28	23	0	0	0	9	10	—	19	0	6	—	9	—	.170	.228	.170	.964
1917	Bos-A	42	50	9	15	1	0	0	2	6	—	3	0	7	—	3	—	.300	.375	.320	1.000
1919	Bos-A	33	42	10	11	4	0	0	6	1	—	2	0	4	—	4	—	.262	.279	.357	1.000
1920	Bos-A	93	312	42	80	5	1	0	23	31	—	24	1	20	—	13	10	.256	.326	.279	.930
1921	**NY-A**	**71**	**215**	**36**	**56**	**4**	**2**	**1**	**24**	**14**	—	**15**	**0**	**11**	—	**5**	**6**	**.260**	**.306**	**.312**	**.974**
1922	**NY-A**	**52**	**143**	**20**	**36**	**2**	**2**	**0**	**18**	**16**	—	**14**	**1**	**17**	—	**3**	**0**	**.252**	**.331**	**.294**	**1.000**
1923	**NY-A**	**30**	**38**	**5**	**8**	**0**	**0**	**0**	**1**	**3**	—	**4**	**0**	**3**	—	**2**	**0**	**.211**	**.268**	**.211**	**.895**
1924	**NY-A**	**49**	**69**	**11**	**17**	**0**	**0**	**0**	**2**	**7**	—	**5**	**0**	**3**	—	**1**	**1**	**.246**	**.316**	**.246**	**.970**
1925	Was-A	12	21	1	3	0	0	0	0	1	—	4	0	0	—	0	0	.143	.182	.143	1.000
Career average		49	108	17	26	2	1	0	9	9	—	10	0	7	—	4	—	.238	.299	.267	.973
Yankee average		**51**	**116**	**18**	**29**	**2**	**1**	**0**	**11**	**10**	—	**10**	**0**	**9**	—	**3**	**2**	**.252**	**.312**	**.288**	**.960**
Career total		492	1078	169	257	16	6	1	85	92	—	97	2	71	—	40	19	.238	.299	.267	.973
Yankee total		**202**	**465**	**72**	**117**	**6**	**4**	**1**	**45**	**40**	—	**38**	**1**	**34**	—	**11**	**7**	**.252**	**.312**	**.288**	**.960**

McQuinn, George Hartley

HEIGHT: 5'11"   THROWS: LEFT   BATS: LEFT   BORN: 5/29/1910 ARLINGTON, VIRGINIA   DIED: 12/24/1978 ALEXANDRIA, VIRGINIA   POSITIONS PLAYED: 1B

YEAR	TEAM	GAMES	AB	RUNS	HITS	2B	3B	HR	RBI	BB	IBB	SO	HBP	SH	SF	SB	CS	BA	OBA	SA	FA
1936	Cin-N	38	134	5	27	3	4	0	13	10	—	22	1	1	—	0	—	.201	.262	.284	.992
1938	StL-A	148	602	100	195	42	7	12	82	58	—	49	1	13	—	4	5	.324	.384	.477	.992
1939	StL-A	154	617	101	195	37	13	20	94	65	—	42	2	18	—	6	5	.316	.383	.515	.993
1940	StL-A	151	594	78	166	39	10	16	84	57	—	58	0	8	—	3	3	.279	.343	.460	.992
1941	StL-A	130	495	93	147	28	4	18	80	74	—	30	0	5	—	5	4	.297	.388	.479	.995
1942	StL-A	145	554	86	145	32	5	12	78	60	—	77	1	16	—	1	1	.262	.335	.403	.991
1943	StL-A	125	449	53	109	19	2	12	74	56	—	65	0	11	—	4	3	.243	.327	.374	.992
1944	StL-A	146	516	83	129	26	3	11	72	85	—	74	1	21	—	4	3	.250	.357	.376	.994
1945	StL-A	139	483	69	134	31	3	7	61	65	—	51	1	12	—	1	1	.277	.364	.398	.991
1946	Phi-A	136	484	47	109	23	6	3	35	64	—	62	1	7	—	4	2	.225	.317	.316	.988
1947	**NY-A**	**144**	**517**	**84**	**157**	**24**	**3**	**13**	**80**	**78**	—	**66**	**0**	**14**	—	**0**	**2**	**.304**	**.395**	**.437**	**.994**
1948	**NY-A**	**94**	**302**	**33**	**75**	**11**	**4**	**11**	**41**	**40**	—	**38**	**0**	**4**	—	**0**	**2**	**.248**	**.336**	**.421**	**.993**

(continued)

(continued)

	GAMES	AB	RUNS	HITS	2B	3B	HR	RBI	BB	IBB	SO	HBP	SH	SF	SB	CS	BA	OBA	SA	FA
Career average	129	479	69	132	26	5	11	66	59	—	53	1	11	—	3	—	.276	.357	.424	.992
Yankee average	**119**	**410**	**59**	**116**	**18**	**4**	**12**	**61**	**59**	**—**	**52**	**0**	**9**	**—**	**0**	**2**	**.283**	**.374**	**.431**	**.994**
Career total	1550	5747	832	1588	315	64	135	794	712	—	634	8	130	—	32	31	.276	.357	.424	.992
Yankee total	**238**	**819**	**117**	**232**	**35**	**7**	**24**	**121**	**118**	**—**	**104**	**0**	**18**	**—**	**0**	**4**	**.283**	**.374**	**.431**	**.994**

Meacham, Robert Andrew (Bobby)

HEIGHT: 6'1" THROWS: RIGHT BATS: BOTH BORN: 8/25/1960 LOS ANGELES, CALIFORNIA POSITIONS PLAYED: 2B, 3B, SS

YEAR	TEAM	GAMES	AB	RUNS	HITS	2B	3B	HR	RBI	BB	IBB	SO	HBP	SH	SF	SB	CS	BA	OBA	SA	FA
1983	NY-A	22	51	5	12	2	0	0	4	4	0	10	1	0	0	8	0	.235	.304	.275	.929
1984	NY-A	99	360	62	91	13	4	2	25	32	0	70	3	14	9	9	5	.253	.312	.328	1.000
1985	NY-A	156	481	70	105	16	2	1	47	54	1	102	5	23	3	25	7	.218	.302	.266	.963
1986	NY-A	56	161	19	36	7	1	0	10	17	0	39	3	4	0	3	6	.224	.309	.280	.948
1987	NY-A	77	203	28	55	11	1	5	21	19	0	33	6	3	1	6	5	.271	.349	.409	.980
1988	NY-A	47	115	18	25	9	0	0	7	14	0	22	2	1	2	7	1	.217	.308	.296	.959
Career average		76	229	34	54	10	1	1	19	23	0	46	3	8	3	10	4	.236	.313	.308	.963
Yankee average		**76**	**229**	**34**	**54**	**10**	**1**	**1**	**19**	**23**	**0**	**46**	**3**	**8**	**3**	**10**	**4**	**.236**	**.313**	**.308**	**.963**
Career total		457	1371	202	324	58	8	8	114	140	1	276	20	45	15	58	24	.236	.313	.308	.963
Yankee total		**457**	**1371**	**202**	**324**	**58**	**8**	**8**	**114**	**140**	**1**	**276**	**20**	**45**	**15**	**58**	**24**	**.236**	**.313**	**.308**	**.963**

Meara, Charles Edward (Goggy)

HEIGHT: 5'10" THROWS: RIGHT BATS: LEFT BORN: 4/16/1891, NEW YORK, NEW YORK DIED: 2/8/1962 BRONX, NEW YORK POSITIONS PLAYED: OF

YEAR	TEAM	GAMES	AB	RUNS	HITS	2B	3B	HR	RBI	BB	IBB	SO	HBP	SH	SF	SB	CS	BA	OBA	SA	FA
1914	NY-A	4	7	2	2	0	0	0	1	2	—	2	0	0	—	0	1	.286	.444	.286	1.000
Career average		4	7	2	2	0	0	0	1	2	—	2	0	0	—	0	1	.286	.444	.286	1.000
Yankee average		**4**	**7**	**2**	**2**	**0**	**0**	**0**	**1**	**2**	**—**	**2**	**0**	**0**	**—**	**0**	**1**	**.286**	**.444**	**.286**	**1.000**
Career total		4	7	2	2	0	0	0	1	2	—	2	0	0	—	0	1	.286	.444	.286	1.000
Yankee total		**4**	**7**	**2**	**2**	**0**	**0**	**0**	**1**	**2**	**—**	**2**	**0**	**0**	**—**	**0**	**1**	**.286**	**.444**	**.286**	**1.000**

Melvin, Robert Paul

HEIGHT: 6'4" THROWS: RIGHT BATS: RIGHT BORN: 10/28/1961 PALO ALTO, CALIFORNIA POSITIONS PLAYED: C, 1B, 3B

YEAR	TEAM	GAMES	AB	RUNS	HITS	2B	3B	HR	RBI	BB	IBB	SO	HBP	SH	SF	SB	CS	BA	OBA	SA	FA
1985	Det-A	41	82	10	18	4	1	0	4	3	0	21	0	2	0	0	0	.220	.247	.293	.989
1986	SF-N	89	268	24	60	14	2	5	25	15	1	69	0	3	3	3	2	.224	.262	.347	.988
1987	SF-N	84	246	31	49	8	0	11	31	17	3	44	0	0	2	0	4	.199	.249	.366	.988
1988	SF-N	92	273	23	64	13	1	8	27	13	0	46	0	1	1	0	2	.234	.268	.377	.984
1989	Bal-A	85	278	22	67	10	1	1	32	15	3	53	0	7	1	1	4	.241	.279	.295	.991
1990	Bal-A	93	301	30	73	14	1	5	37	11	1	53	0	3	3	0	1	.243	.267	.346	.997
1991	Bal-A	79	228	11	57	10	0	1	23	11	2	46	0	1	5	0	0	.250	.279	.307	.998
1992	KC-A	32	70	5	22	5	0	0	6	5	0	13	0	0	2	0	0	.314	.351	.386	1.000
1993	Bos-A	77	176	13	39	7	0	3	23	7	0	44	1	3	0	0	0	.222	.251	.313	.994
1994	**NY-A**	**9**	**14**	**2**	**4**	**0**	**0**	**1**	**3**	**0**	**0**	**3**	**0**	**0**	**0**	**0**	**0**	**.286**	**.286**	**.500**	**1.000**
1994	Chi-A	11	19	3	3	0	0	0	1	1	0	4	0	1	0	0	0	.158	.200	.158	1.000
Career average		63	178	16	42	8	1	3	19	9	1	36	0	2	2	0	1	.233	.268	.337	.994
Yankee average		**9**	**14**	**2**	**4**	**0**	**0**	**1**	**3**	**0**	**0**	**3**	**0**	**0**	**0**	**0**	**0**	**.286**	**.286**	**.500**	**1.000**
Career total		692	1955	174	456	85	6	35	212	98	10	396	1	21	20	4	13	.233	.268	.337	.994
Yankee total		**9**	**14**	**2**	**4**	**0**	**0**	**1**	**3**	**0**	**0**	**3**	**0**	**0**	**0**	**0**	**0**	**.286**	**.286**	**.500**	**1.000**

Merkle, Carl Frederick Rudolf

HEIGHT: 6'1" THROWS: RIGHT BATS: RIGHT BORN: 12/20/1888 WATERTOWN, WIS. DIED: 3/2/1956 DAYTONA BEACH, FLA. POSITIONS PLAYED: 1B, 2B, 3B, OF

YEAR	TEAM	GAMES	AB	RUNS	HITS	2B	3B	HR	RBI	BB	IBB	SO	HBP	SH	SF	SB	CS	BA	OBA	SA	FA
1907	NY-N	15	47	0	12	1	0	0	5	1	—	—	0	1	—	0	—	.255	.271	.277	.949
1908	NY-N	38	41	6	11	2	1	1	7	4	—	—	0	2	—	0	—	.268	.333	.439	1.000
1909	NY-N	79	236	15	45	9	1	0	20	16	—	—	1	4	—	8	—	.191	.245	.237	1.000
1910	NY-N	144	506	75	148	35	14	4	70	44	—	59	3	19	—	23	—	.292	.353	.441	.981
1911	NY-N	149	541	80	153	24	10	12	84	43	—	60	6	14	—	49	—	.283	.342	.431	.985

(continued)

(continued)

YEAR	TEAM	GAMES	AB	RUNS	HITS	2B	3B	HR	RBI	BB	IBB	SO	HBP	SH	SF	SB	CS	BA	OBA	SA	FA
1912	NY-N	129	479	82	148	22	6	11	84	42	—	70	8	8	—	37	—	.309	.374	.449	.980
1913	NY-N	153	563	78	147	30	13	2	69	41	—	60	3	10	—	35	—	.261	.315	.371	.986
1914	NY-N	146	512	71	132	25	7	7	63	52	—	80	1	7	—	23	—	.258	.327	.375	.990
1915	NY-N	140	505	52	151	25	3	4	62	36	—	39	2	14	—	20	15	.299	.348	.384	.973
1916	NY-N	112	401	45	95	19	3	7	44	33	—	46	8	7	—	17	—	.237	.308	.352	.984
1916	Bro-N	23	69	6	16	1	0	0	2	7	—	4	1	1	—	2	—	.232	.312	.246	1.000
1917	Bro-N	2	8	1	1	1	0	0	0	0	—	1	0	0	—	0	—	.125	.125	.250	1.000
1917	Chi-N	146	549	65	146	30	9	3	57	42	—	60	4	13	—	13	—	.266	.323	.370	1.000
1918	Chi-N	129	482	55	143	25	5	3	65	35	—	36	4	20	—	21	—	.297	.349	.388	.990
1919	Chi-N	133	498	52	133	20	6	3	62	33	—	35	2	12	—	20	—	.267	.315	.349	.985
1920	Chi-N	92	330	33	94	20	4	3	38	24	—	32	1	12	—	3	5	.285	.335	.397	.985
1925	**NY-A**	**7**	**13**	**4**	**5**	**1**	**0**	**0**	**1**	**1**	—	**1**	**0**	**2**	—	**1**	**0**	**.385**	**.429**	**.462**	**1.000**
1926	**NY-A**	**1**	**2**	**0**	**0**	**0**	**0**	**0**	**0**	**0**	—	**0**	**0**	**0**	—	**0**	**0**	**.000**	**.000**	**.000**	**1.000**
Career average		91	321	40	88	16	5	3	41	25	—	—	2	8	—	15	—	.273	.331	.383	.988
Yankee average		**4**	**8**	**2**	**3**	**1**	**0**	**0**	**1**	**1**	—	**1**	**0**	**1**	—	**1**	**0**	**.333**	**.375**	**.400**	**1.000**
Career total		1638	5782	720	1580	290	82	60	733	454	—	583	44	146	—	272	20	.273	.331	.383	.988
Yankee total		**8**	**15**	**4**	**5**	**1**	**0**	**0**	**1**	**1**	—	**1**	**0**	**2**	—	**1**	**0**	**.333**	**.375**	**.400**	**1.000**

Metheny, Arthur Beauregard (Bud)

HEIGHT: 5'11"   THROWS: LEFT   BATS: LEFT   BORN: 6/1/1915 ST.LOUIS, MISSOURI   POSITIONS PLAYED: OF

YEAR	TEAM	GAMES	AB	RUNS	HITS	2B	3B	HR	RBI	BB	IBB	SO	HBP	SH	SF	SB	CS	BA	OBA	SA	FA
1943	NY-A	103	360	51	94	18	2	9	36	39	—	34	0	9	—	2	3	.261	.333	.397	.963
1944	NY-A	137	518	72	124	16	1	14	67	56	—	57	2	14	—	5	5	.239	.316	.355	.956
1945	NY-A	133	509	64	126	18	2	8	53	54	—	31	4	12	—	5	2	.248	.325	.338	.984
1946	NY-A	3	3	0	0	0	0	0	0	0	—	0	0	0	—	0	0	.000	.000	.000	.000
Career average		94	348	47	86	13	1	8	39	37	—	31	2	9	—	3	3	.247	.323	.359	.726
Yankee average		**94**	**348**	**47**	**86**	**13**	**1**	**8**	**39**	**37**	—	**31**	**2**	**9**	—	**3**	**3**	**.247**	**.323**	**.359**	**.726**
Career total		376	1390	187	344	52	5	31	156	149	—	122	6	35	—	12	10	.247	.323	.359	.726
Yankee total		**376**	**1390**	**187**	**344**	**52**	**5**	**31**	**156**	**149**	—	**122**	**6**	**35**	—	**12**	**10**	**.247**	**.323**	**.359**	**.726**

Meulens, Hensley Filemon Acasio (Bam-Bam)

HEIGHT: 6'3"   THROWS: RIGHT   BATS: RIGHT   BORN: 6/23/1967 WILLEMSTAD, CURACAO   POSITIONS PLAYED: 1B, 3B, OF

YEAR	TEAM	GAMES	AB	RUNS	HITS	2B	3B	HR	RBI	BB	IBB	SO	HBP	SH	SF	SB	CS	BA	OBA	SA	FA
1989	NY-A	8	28	2	5	0	0	0	1	2	0	8	0	0	0	0	1	.179	.233	.179	.875
1990	NY-A	23	83	12	20	7	0	3	10	9	0	25	3	0	0	1	0	.241	.337	.434	.963
1991	NY-A	96	288	37	64	8	1	6	29	18	1	97	4	1	2	3	0	.222	.276	.319	.967
1992	NY-A	2	5	1	3	0	0	1	1	1	0	0	0	0	0	0	0	.600	.667	1.200	1.000
1993	NY-A	30	53	8	9	1	1	2	5	8	0	19	0	0	0	0	1	.170	.279	.340	1.000
1997	Mon-N	16	24	6	7	1	0	2	6	4	0	10	0	0	1	0	0	.292	.379	.583	1.000
1998	Ari-N	7	15	1	1	0	0	1	1	0	0	6	0	0	0	0	0	.067	.067	.267	1.000
Career average		26	71	10	16	2	0	2	8	6	0	24	1	0	0	1	0	.220	.288	.353	.972
Yankee average		**32**	**91**	**12**	**20**	**3**	**0**	**2**	**9**	**8**	**0**	**30**	**1**	**0**	**0**	**1**	**0**	**.221**	**.290**	**.344**	**.961**
Career total		182	496	67	109	17	2	15	53	42	1	165	7	1	3	4	3	.220	.288	.353	.972
Yankee total		**159**	**457**	**60**	**101**	**16**	**2**	**12**	**46**	**38**	**1**	**149**	**7**	**1**	**2**	**4**	**2**	**.221**	**.290**	**.344**	**.961**

Meusel, Robert William (Long Bob)

HEIGHT: 6'3"   THROWS: RIGHT   BATS: RIGHT   BORN: 7/19/1896 SAN JOSE, CALIFORNIA   DIED: 11/28/1977 DOWNEY, CAL.   POSITIONS PLAYED: 1B, 3B, OF

YEAR	TEAM	GAMES	AB	RUNS	HITS	2B	3B	HR	RBI	BB	IBB	SO	HBP	SH	SF	SB	CS	BA	OBA	SA	FA
1920	NY-A	119	460	75	151	40	7	11	83	20	—	72	2	12	—	4	4	.328	.359	.517	.947
1921	NY-A	149	598	104	190	40	16	24	135	34	—	88	2	12	—	17	6	.318	.356	.559	.934
1922	NY-A	121	473	61	151	26	11	16	84	40	—	58	3	11	—	13	8	.319	.376	.522	.950
1923	NY-A	132	460	59	144	29	10	9	91	31	—	52	2	10	—	13	15	.313	.359	.478	.953
1924	NY-A	143	579	93	188	40	11	12	120	32	—	43	5	14	—	26	14	.325	.365	.494	.951
1925	NY-A	156	624	101	181	34	12	33	138	54	—	55	1	17	—	13	14	.290	.348	.542	.985
1926	NY-A	108	413	73	130	22	3	12	81	37	—	32	1	23	—	16	17	.315	.373	.470	.960
1927	NY-A	135	516	75	174	47	9	8	103	45	—	58	2	21	—	24	10	.337	.393	.510	.950
1928	NY-A	131	518	77	154	45	5	11	113	39	—	56	2	18	—	6	9	.297	.349	.467	.975
1929	NY-A	100	391	46	102	15	3	10	57	17	—	42	0	5	—	1	5	.261	.292	.391	.968
1930	Cin-N	113	443	62	128	30	8	10	62	26	—	63	1	14	—	9	0	.289	.330	.460	.963

(continued)

Robert William "Long Bob" Meusel, of-3b, 1920–29

Bob Meusel had the misfortune of being a very good outfielder on a team with two other Hall of Fame outfielders. He was also, in the early part of his career, overshadowed by his older brother, Emil "Irish" Meusel. The players who played with him and against him, however, have always affirmed that Bob Meusel was as good as anybody in that era.

Born on July 19, 1896, in San Jose, California, Meusel signed with the Yankees in 1920. At 6 foot 3 inches, he was a gangly fellow with a rocket arm. Yankee manager Miller Huggins used Meusel as much at third base as he did in the outfield that year. Meusel played in 119 games in 1920, alternating at those positions. He hit .328 with 11 home runs and 83 RBI.

But by 1921, veteran Duffy Lewis was traded, opening up a slot for Meusel in the outfield. Meusel responded by hitting .318 with 24 home runs and 124 RBI, both third in the league. From 1921 to 1928, Meusel was one of the most consistent and hardest hitters in baseball.

He was also evolving into the best defensive outfielder in the league. By 1924 he had, without question, the best outfield arm in the American League, perhaps in either league.

Old-timers tell of the moments when Ty Cobb would be on third base when a fly ball was hit to Meusel in left field. Meusel, holding the ball, would dare Cobb to tag up and try to score. Ty usually stayed put where he was.

He was a quiet man, a sharp contrast to his close pal Babe Ruth. Sportswriters mistook his laid-back approach to the game as apathy. But, when aroused, he could be formidable. He was usually the man who broke up fights between his Yankee teammates and players on other teams.

In 1925, with Ruth laid up with several injuries, Meusel led the American League in home runs with 33, and RBI with 135. When Ruth came back in 1925, the two men were joined in the outfield by the swift Earle Combs. From 1926–29, this was the best outfield in baseball.

But by 1929, injuries began slowing Meusel down. He was waived by New York before the 1930 season and picked up by Cincinnati. He played one more season with the Reds before retiring. He died on November 28, 1977 in Downey, California.

He hit for the cycle three times in his Yankee career, a team record. His .311 batting average is 8th all-time with the Yankees, while his 1,565 hits are 14th all-time and his 1,005 RBI 9th all-time.

(continued)

Career average	128	498	75	154	34	9	14	97	34	—	56	2	14	—	13	9	.309	.356	.497	.958
Yankee average	**129**	**503**	**76**	**157**	**34**	**9**	**15**	**101**	**35**	**—**	**56**	**2**	**14**	**—**	**13**	**10**	**.311**	**.358**	**.500**	**.957**
Career total	1407	5475	826	1693	368	95	156	1067	375	—	619	21	157	—	142	102	.309	.356	.497	.958
Yankee total	**1294**	**5032**	**764**	**1565**	**338**	**87**	**146**	**1005**	**349**	**—**	**556**	**20**	**143**	**—**	**133**	**102**	**.311**	**.358**	**.500**	**.957**

Michael, Eugene Richard (Gene *or* Stick)

HEIGHT: 6'2"   THROWS: RIGHT   BATS: BOTH   BORN: 6/2/1938 KENT, OHIO   POSITIONS PLAYED: P, 2B, 3B, SS

YEAR	TEAM	GAMES	AB	RUNS	HITS	2B	3B	HR	RBI	BB	IBB	SO	HBP	SH	SF	SB	CS	BA	OBA	SA	FA
1966	Pit-N	30	33	9	5	2	1	0	2	0	0	7	0	0	0	0	0	.152	.152	.273	.903
1967	LA-N	98	223	20	45	3	1	0	7	11	0	30	2	9	0	1	3	.202	.246	.224	.950
1968	**NY-A**	**61**	**116**	**8**	**23**	**3**	**0**	**1**	**8**	**2**	**0**	**23**	**1**	**0**	**0**	**3**	**2**	**.198**	**.218**	**.250**	**1.000**
1969	**NY-A**	**119**	**412**	**41**	**112**	**24**	**4**	**2**	**31**	**43**	**1**	**56**	**1**	**6**	**2**	**7**	**4**	**.272**	**.341**	**.364**	**.968**
1970	**NY-A**	**134**	**435**	**42**	**93**	**10**	**1**	**2**	**38**	**50**	**5**	**93**	**0**	**4**	**4**	**3**	**1**	**.214**	**.292**	**.255**	**1.000**
1971	**NY-A**	**139**	**456**	**36**	**102**	**15**	**0**	**3**	**35**	**48**	**8**	**64**	**3**	**3**	**4**	**3**	**3**	**.224**	**.299**	**.276**	**.973**
1972	**NY-A**	**126**	**391**	**29**	**91**	**7**	**4**	**1**	**32**	**32**	**4**	**45**	**1**	**2**	**4**	**4**	**2**	**.233**	**.290**	**.279**	**.969**

(continued)

(continued)

YEAR	TEAM	GAMES	AB	RUNS	HITS	2B	3B	HR	RBI	BB	IBB	SO	HBP	SH	SF	SB	CS	BA	OBA	SA	FA
1973	NY-A	129	418	30	94	11	1	3	47	26	0	51	0	1	1	1	3	.225	.270	.278	.965
1974	NY-A	81	177	19	46	9	0	0	13	14	0	24	0	1	1	0	0	.260	.313	.311	1.000
1975	Det-A	56	145	15	31	2	0	3	13	8	0	28	0	4	1	0	0	.214	.253	.290	1.000
Career average		97	281	25	64	9	1	2	23	23	2	42	1	3	2	2	2	.229	.288	.284	.973
Yankee average		**113**	**344**	**29**	**80**	**11**	**1**	**2**	**29**	**31**	**3**	**51**	**1**	**2**	**2**	**3**	**2**	**.233**	**.296**	**.289**	**.982**
Career total		973	2806	249	642	86	12	15	226	234	18	421	8	30	17	22	18	.229	.288	.284	.973
Yankee total		**789**	**2405**	**205**	**561**	**79**	**10**	**12**	**204**	**215**	**18**	**356**	**6**	**17**	**16**	**21**	**15**	**.233**	**.296**	**.289**	**.982**

Midkiff, Ezra Millington (Salt Rock)

HEIGHT: 5'10" THROWS: RIGHT BATS: LEFT BORN: 11/13/1882 SALT ROCK, W. VIRGINIA DIED: 3/20/1957 HUNTINGTON, W. VA POSITIONS PLAYED: 2B, 3B, SS

YEAR	TEAM	GAMES	AB	RUNS	HITS	2B	3B	HR	RBI	BB	IBB	SO	HBP	SH	SF	SB	CS	BA	OBA	SA	FA
1909	Cin-N	1	2	0	0	0	0	0	0	0	—	—	0	0	—	0	—	.000	.000	.000	.000
1912	NY-A	21	86	9	21	1	0	0	9	7	—	—	0	4	—	4	—	.244	.301	.256	.901
1913	NY-A	83	284	22	56	9	1	0	14	12	—	33	1	8	—	9	—	.197	.232	.236	.959
Career average		35	124	10	26	3	0	0	8	6	—	—	0	4	—	4	—	.207	.247	.239	.620
Yankee average		**52**	**185**	**16**	**39**	**5**	**1**	**0**	**12**	**10**	—	—	**1**	**6**	—	**7**	—	**.208**	**.249**	**.241**	**.930**
Career total		105	372	31	77	10	1	0	23	19	—	33	1	12	—	13	—	.207	.247	.239	.620
Yankee total		**104**	**370**	**31**	**77**	**10**	**1**	**0**	**23**	**19**	—	**33**	**1**	**12**	—	**13**	—	**.208**	**.249**	**.241**	**.930**

Milbourne, Lawrence William

HEIGHT: 6'0" THROWS: RIGHT BATS: BOTH BORN: 2/14/1951 PORT NORRIS, NEW JERSEY POSITIONS PLAYED: 2B, 3B, SS

YEAR	TEAM	GAMES	AB	RUNS	HITS	2B	3B	HR	RBI	BB	IBB	SO	HBP	SH	SF	SB	CS	BA	OBA	SA	FA
1974	Hou-N	112	136	31	38	2	1	0	9	10	0	14	0	2	0	6	2	.279	.329	.309	1.000
1975	Hou-N	73	151	17	32	1	2	1	9	6	1	14	1	4	1	1	2	.212	.245	.265	.968
1976	Hou-N	59	145	22	36	4	0	0	7	14	0	10	1	1	0	6	1	.248	.319	.276	.965
1977	Sea-A	86	242	24	53	10	0	2	21	6	0	20	2	8	5	3	1	.219	.239	.285	.000
1978	Sea-A	93	234	31	53	6	2	2	20	9	1	6	0	3	1	5	7	.226	.254	.295	.989
1979	Sea-A	123	356	40	99	13	4	2	26	19	2	20	0	2	2	5	3	.278	.313	.354	.967
1980	Sea-A	106	258	31	68	6	6	0	26	19	4	13	1	15	3	7	6	.264	.313	.333	.889
1981	NY-A	61	163	24	51	7	2	1	12	9	2	14	1	3	1	2	0	.313	.351	.399	.970
1982	NY-A	14	27	2	4	1	0	0	0	1	0	4	0	0	0	0	1	.148	.179	.185	1.000
1982	MIN	29	98	9	23	1	1	0	1	7	0	8	0	0	1	1	1	.235	.283	.265	.981
1982	Cle-A	82	291	29	80	11	4	2	25	12	0	20	2	7	7	2	5	.275	.301	.361	.981
1983	Phi-N	41	66	3	16	0	1	0	4	4	0	7	0	2	1	2	1	.242	.282	.273	.963
1983	NY-A	31	70	5	14	4	0	0	2	5	0	10	1	0	0	1	1	.200	.263	.257	1.000
1984	Sea-A	79	211	22	56	5	1	1	22	12	0	16	0	11	1	0	2	.265	.304	.313	.867
Career average		71	175	21	45	5	2	1	13	10	1	13	1	4	2	3	2	.254	.293	.317	.896
Yankee average		**35**	**87**	**10**	**23**	**4**	**1**	**0**	**5**	**5**	**1**	**9**	**1**	**1**	**0**	**1**	**1**	**.265**	**.309**	**.338**	**.990**
Career total		989	2448	290	623	71	24	11	184	133	10	176	9	58	23	41	33	.254	.293	.317	.896
Yankee total		**106**	**260**	**31**	**69**	**12**	**2**	**1**	**14**	**15**	**2**	**28**	**2**	**3**	**1**	**3**	**2**	**.265**	**.309**	**.338**	**.990**

Miller, Elmer

HEIGHT: 6'0" THROWS: RIGHT BATS: RIGHT BORN: 7/28/1890 SANDUSKY, OHIO DIED: 11/28/1944 BELOIT, WISCONSIN POSITIONS PLAYED: OF

YEAR	TEAM	GAMES	AB	RUNS	HITS	2B	3B	HR	RBI	BB	IBB	SO	HBP	SH	SF	SB	CS	BA	OBA	SA	FA
1912	StL-N	12	37	5	7	1	0	0	3	4	—	9	0	0	—	1	—	.189	.268	.216	1.000
1915	NY-A	26	83	4	12	1	0	0	3	4	—	14	1	2	—	0	0	.145	.193	.157	.955
1916	NY-A	43	152	12	34	3	2	1	18	11	—	18	1	6	—	8	—	.224	.280	.289	.969
1917	NY-A	114	379	43	95	11	3	3	35	40	—	44	9	21	—	11	—	.251	.336	.319	.961
1918	NY-A	67	202	18	49	9	2	1	22	19	—	17	3	14	—	2	—	.243	.317	.322	.947
1921	NY-A	56	242	41	72	9	8	4	36	19	—	16	3	6	—	2	2	.298	.356	.450	.947
1922	NY-A	51	172	31	46	7	2	3	18	11	—	12	0	5	—	2	3	.267	.311	.384	.982
1922	Bos-A	44	147	16	28	2	3	4	16	5	—	10	1	3	—	3	1	.190	.222	.327	.957
Career average		52	177	21	43	5	3	2	19	14	—	18	2	7	—	4	—	.243	.307	.335	.965
Yankee average		**60**	**205**	**25**	**51**	**7**	**3**	**2**	**22**	**17**	—	**20**	**3**	**9**	—	**4**	—	**.250**	**.318**	**.340**	**.960**
Career total		413	1414	170	343	43	20	16	151	113	—	140	18	57	—	29	6	.243	.307	.335	.965
Yankee total		**357**	**1230**	**149**	**308**	**40**	**17**	**12**	**132**	**104**	—	**121**	**17**	**54**	—	**25**	**5**	**.250**	**.318**	**.340**	**.960**

Miller, John Allen

HEIGHT: 5'11" THROWS: RIGHT BATS: RIGHT BORN: 3/14/1944 ALHAMBRA, CALIFORNIA POSITIONS PLAYED: 1B, OF

YEAR	TEAM	GAMES	AB	RUNS	HITS	2B	3B	HR	RBI	BB	IBB	SO	HBP	SH	SF	SB	CS	BA	OBA	SA	FA
1966	NY-A	6	23	1	2	0	0	1	2	0	0	9	0	0	0	0	0	.087	.087	.217	1.000
1969	LA-N	26	38	3	8	1	0	1	1	2	0	9	0	0	0	0	0	.211	.250	.316	1.000
Career average		16	31	2	5	1	0	1	2	1	0	9	0	0	0	0	0	.164	.190	.279	1.000
Yankee average		6	23	1	2	0	0	1	2	0	0	9	0	0	0	0	0	.087	.087	.217	1.000
Career total		32	61	4	10	1	0	2	3	2	0	18	0	0	0	0	0	.164	.190	.279	1.000
Yankee total		6	23	1	2	0	0	1	2	0	0	9	0	0	0	0	0	.087	.087	.217	1.000

Mills, Colonel Buster

HEIGHT: 5'11" THROWS: RIGHT BATS: RIGHT BORN: 9/16/1908 RANGER, TEXAS DIED: 12/1/1991 ARLINGTON, TEXAS POSITIONS PLAYED: OF

YEAR	TEAM	GAMES	AB	RUNS	HITS	2B	3B	HR	RBI	BB	IBB	SO	HBP	SH	SF	SB	CS	BA	OBA	SA	FA
1934	StL-N	29	72	7	17	4	1	1	8	4	—	11	2	2	—	0	—	.236	.295	.361	1.000
1935	Bro-N	17	56	12	12	2	1	1	7	5	—	11	4	0	—	0	—	.214	.323	.339	.971
1937	Bos-A	123	505	85	149	25	8	7	58	46	—	41	6	9	—	11	8	.295	.361	.418	.946
1938	StL-A	123	466	66	133	24	4	3	46	43	—	46	3	8	—	7	8	.285	.350	.373	.964
1940	**NY-A**	**34**	**63**	**10**	**25**	**3**	**3**	**1**	**15**	**7**	**—**	**5**	**0**	**0**	**—**	**0**	**0**	**.397**	**.457**	**.587**	**1.000**
1942	Cle-A	80	195	19	54	4	2	1	26	23	—	18	0	2	—	5	4	.277	.353	.333	.973
1946	Cle-A	9	22	1	6	0	0	0	3	3	—	5	0	0	—	0	1	.273	.360	.273	1.000
Career average		59	197	29	57	9	3	2	23	19	—	20	2	3	—	3	—	.287	.355	.390	.979
Yankee average		**34**	**63**	**10**	**25**	**3**	**3**	**1**	**15**	**7**	**—**	**5**	**0**	**0**	**—**	**0**	**0**	**.397**	**.457**	**.587**	**1.000**
Career total		415	1379	200	396	62	19	14	163	131	—	137	15	21	—	23	21	.287	.355	.390	.979
Yankee total		**34**	**63**	**10**	**25**	**3**	**3**	**1**	**15**	**7**	**—**	**5**	**0**	**0**	**—**	**0**	**0**	**.397**	**.457**	**.587**	**1.000**

Milosevich, Michael (Mollie)

HEIGHT: 5'11" THROWS: RIGHT BATS: RIGHT 1/13/1915 ZEIGLER, ILLINOIS DIED: 2/3/1966 E.CHICAGO, INDIANA POSITIONS PLAYED: SS

YEAR	TEAM	GAMES	AB	RUNS	HITS	2B	3B	HR	RBI	BB	IBB	SO	HBP	SH	SF	SB	CS	BA	OBA	SA	FA
1944	**NY-A**	**94**	**312**	**27**	**77**	**11**	**4**	**0**	**32**	**30**	**—**	**37**	**0**	**3**	**—**	**1**	**2**	**.247**	**.313**	**.308**	**.954**
1945	**NY-A**	**30**	**69**	**5**	**15**	**2**	**0**	**0**	**7**	**6**	**—**	**6**	**1**	**2**	**—**	**0**	**0**	**.217**	**.289**	**.246**	**.957**
Career average		62	191	16	46	7	2	0	20	18	—	22	1	3	—	1	1	.241	.309	.297	.956
Yankee average		**62**	**191**	**16**	**46**	**7**	**2**	**0**	**20**	**18**	**—**	**22**	**1**	**3**	**—**	**1**	**1**	**.241**	**.309**	**.297**	**.956**
Career total		124	381	32	92	13	4	0	39	36	—	43	1	5	—	1	2	.241	.309	.297	.956
Yankee total		**124**	**381**	**32**	**92**	**13**	**4**	**0**	**39**	**36**	**—**	**43**	**1**	**5**	**—**	**1**	**2**	**.241**	**.309**	**.297**	**.956**

Miranda, Guillermo (Willie) BORN GUILLERMO MIRANDA (PEREZ)

HEIGHT: 5'9" THROWS: RIGHT BATS: BOTH BORN: 5/24/1926 VELASCO, CUBA DIED: 9/7/1996 POSITIONS PLAYED: SS

YEAR	TEAM	GAMES	AB	RUNS	HITS	2B	3B	HR	RBI	BB	IBB	SO	HBP	SH	SF	SB	CS	BA	OBA	SA	FA
1951	Was-A	7	9	2	4	0	0	0	0	0	—	0	0	0	—	0	0	.444	.444	.444	1.000
1952	Chi-A	12	8	1	2	1	0	0	0	3	—	0	1	6	—	2	0	.250	.500	.375	1.000
1952	StL-A	7	11	2	1	0	1	0	1	3	—	1	0	1	—	0	0	.091	.286	.273	.900
1952	Chi-A	58	142	13	31	3	1	0	7	10	—	14	1	6	—	1	0	.218	.287	.254	.975
1953	StL-A	17	6	2	1	0	0	0	0	1	—	1	0	0	—	1	1	.167	.286	.167	1.000
1953	**NY-A**	**48**	**58**	**12**	**13**	**0**	**0**	**1**	**5**	**5**	**—**	**10**	**0**	**0**	**—**	**1**	**1**	**.224**	**.286**	**.276**	**.984**
1954	**NY-A**	**92**	**116**	**12**	**29**	**4**	**2**	**1**	**12**	**10**	**—**	**10**	**0**	**1**	**4**	**0**	**3**	**.250**	**.300**	**.345**	**.962**
1955	Bal-A	153	487	42	124	12	6	1	38	42	4	58	1	3	3	4	3	.255	.313	.310	1.000
1956	Bal-A	148	461	38	100	16	4	2	34	46	3	73	0	5	1	3	6	.217	.287	.282	.962
1957	Bal-A	115	314	29	61	3	0	0	20	24	2	42	0	8	3	2	1	.194	.249	.204	.966
1958	Bal-A	102	214	15	43	6	0	1	8	14	2	25	0	2	0	1	1	.201	.250	.243	.962
1959	Bal-A	65	88	8	14	5	0	0	7	7	0	16	0	1	0	0	0	.159	.221	.216	1.000
Career average		69	160	15	35	4	1	1	11	14	—	21	0	3	—	1	1	.221	.284	.271	.979
Yankee average		**70**	**87**	**12**	**21**	**2**	**1**	**1**	**9**	**8**	**—**	**10**	**0**	**1**	**—**	**1**	**2**	**.241**	**.302**	**.322**	**.992**
Career total		824	1914	176	423	50	14	6	132	165	11	250	3	33	11	15	16	.221	.282	.271	.979
Yankee total		**140**	**174**	**24**	**42**	**4**	**2**	**2**	**17**	**15**	**—**	**20**	**0**	**1**	**4**	**1**	**4**	**.241**	**.295**	**.322**	**.992**

Mitchell, Frederick Francis (Fred)

HEIGHT: 5'9" THROWS: RIGHT BATS: RIGHT 6/5/1878 CAMBRIDGE, MASSACHUSETTS 10/13/1970 NEWTON, MASSACHUSETTS POSITIONS PLAYED: P, C, 1B

YEAR	TEAM	GAMES	AB	RUNS	HITS	2B	3B	HR	RBI	BB	IBB	SO	HBP	SH	SF	SB	CS	BA	OBA	SA	FA
1901	Bos-A	20	44	5	7	0	2	0	4	2	—	—	0	0	—	0	—	.159	.196	.250	.857
1902	Bos-A	1	1	0	0	0	0	0	0	0	—	—	0	0	—	0	—	.000	.000	.000	.667
1902	Phi-A	19	48	7	9	1	1	0	3	1	—	—	0	3	—	1	—	.188	.204	.250	.942
1903	Phi-N	29	95	11	19	4	0	0	10	0	—	—	0	2	—	0	—	.200	.200	.242	.857
1904	Phi-N	25	82	9	17	3	1	0	3	5	—	—	0	3	—	1	—	.207	.253	.268	.981
1904	Bro-N	8	24	3	7	1	1	0	6	1	—	—	1	1	—	0	—	.292	.346	.417	.906
1905	Bro-N	27	79	4	15	0	0	0	8	4	—	—	1	1	—	0	—	.190	.238	.190	.898
1910	**NY-A**	**68**	**196**	**16**	**45**	**7**	**2**	**0**	**18**	**9**	**—**	**—**	**3**	**0**	**—**	**6**	**—**	**.230**	**.274**	**.286**	**.968**
1913	Bos-N	4	3	0	1	0	0	0	0	0	—	2	0	1	—	0	—	.333	.333	.333	.000
Career average		22	64	6	13	2	1	0	6	2	—	—	1	1	—	1	—	.210	.245	.262	.786
Yankee average		**68**	**196**	**16**	**45**	**7**	**2**	**0**	**18**	**9**	**—**	**—**	**3**	**0**	**—**	**6**	**—**	**.230**	**.274**	**.286**	**.968**
Career total		201	572	55	120	16	7	0	52	22	—	2	5	11	—	8	—	.210	.245	.262	.786
Yankee total		**68**	**196**	**16**	**45**	**7**	**2**	**0**	**18**	**9**	**—**	**—**	**3**	**0**	**—**	**6**	**—**	**.230**	**.274**	**.286**	**.968**

Mitchell, John Franklin

HEIGHT: 5'8" THROWS: RIGHT BATS: BOTH 8/9/1894 DETROIT, MICHIGAN DIED: 11/4/1965 BIRMINGHAM, MICHIGAN POSITIONS PLAYED: 2B, SS

YEAR	TEAM	GAMES	AB	RUNS	HITS	2B	3B	HR	RBI	BB	IBB	SO	HBP	SH	SF	SB	CS	BA	OBA	SA	FA
1921	**NY-A**	**13**	**42**	**4**	**11**	**1**	**0**	**0**	**2**	**4**	**—**	**4**	**0**	**1**	**—**	**1**	**0**	**.262**	**.326**	**.286**	**.958**
1922	**NY-A**	**4**	**4**	**1**	**0**	**0**	**0**	**0**	**0**	**0**	**—**	**1**	**0**	**0**	**—**	**0**	**0**	**.000**	**.000**	**.000**	**1.000**
1922	Bos-A	59	203	20	51	4	1	1	8	16	—	17	4	15	—	1	2	.251	.318	.296	.962
1923	Bos-A	92	347	40	78	15	4	0	19	34	—	18	1	3	—	7	11	.225	.296	.291	1.000
1924	Bro-N	64	243	42	64	10	0	1	16	37	—	22	0	16	—	3	1	.263	.361	.317	.951
1925	Bro-N	97	336	45	84	8	3	0	18	28	—	19	0	4	—	2	0	.250	.308	.292	.947
Career average		55	196	25	48	6	1	0	11	20	—	14	1	7	—	2	2	.245	.317	.296	.970
Yankee average		**9**	**23**	**3**	**6**	**1**	**0**	**0**	**1**	**2**	**—**	**3**	**0**	**1**	**—**	**1**	**0**	**.239**	**.300**	**.261**	**.979**
Career total		329	1175	152	288	38	8	2	63	119	—	81	5	39	—	14	14	.245	.317	.296	.970
Yankee total		**17**	**46**	**5**	**11**	**1**	**0**	**0**	**2**	**4**	**—**	**5**	**0**	**1**	**—**	**1**	**0**	**.239**	**.300**	**.261**	**.979**

Mitchell, Robert Van

HEIGHT: 5'10" THROWS: LEFT BATS: LEFT BORN: 4/7/1955 SALT LAKE CITY, UTAH POSITIONS PLAYED: OF

YEAR	TEAM	GAMES	AB	RUNS	HITS	2B	3B	HR	RBI	BB	IBB	SO	HBP	SH	SF	SB	CS	BA	OBA	SA	FA
1970	**NY-A**	**10**	**22**	**1**	**5**	**2**	**0**	**0**	**4**	**2**	**0**	**3**	**1**	**0**	**0**	**0**	**2**	**.227**	**.320**	**.318**	**1.000**
1971	Mil-A	35	55	7	10	1	1	2	6	6	1	18	0	0	0	2	2	.182	.262	.345	.974
1973	Mil-A	47	130	12	29	6	0	5	20	5	1	32	0	0	1	4	1	.223	.250	.385	.960
1974	Mil-A	88	173	27	42	6	2	5	20	18	1	46	1	0	2	7	6	.243	.314	.387	.969
1975	Mil-A	93	229	39	57	14	3	9	41	25	1	69	0	3	2	3	4	.249	.320	.454	.992
Career average		30	68	10	16	3	1	2	10	6	0	19	0	0	1	2	2	.235	.299	.406	.979
Yankee average		**10**	**22**	**1**	**5**	**2**	**0**	**0**	**4**	**2**	**0**	**3**	**1**	**0**	**0**	**0**	**2**	**.227**	**.320**	**.318**	**1.000**
Career total		273	609	86	143	29	6	21	91	56	4	168	2	3	5	14	15	.235	.299	.406	.979
Yankee total		**10**	**22**	**1**	**5**	**2**	**0**	**0**	**4**	**2**	**0**	**3**	**1**	**0**	**0**	**0**	**2**	**.227**	**.320**	**.318**	**1.000**

Mize, John Robert (The Big Cat)

HEIGHT: 6'2" THROWS: RIGHT BATS: LEFT BORN: 1/7/1913 DEMOREST, GEORGIA DIED: 6/2/1993 DEMOREST, GEORGIA POSITIONS PLAYED: 1B

YEAR	TEAM	GAMES	AB	RUNS	HITS	2B	3B	HR	RBI	BB	IBB	SO	HBP	SH	SF	SB	CS	BA	OBA	SA	FA
1936	StL-N	126	414	76	136	30	8	19	93	50	—	32	1	4	—	1	—	.329	.402	.577	1.000
1937	StL-N	145	560	103	204	40	7	25	113	56	—	57	5	0	—	2	—	.364	.427	.595	.988
1938	StL-N	149	531	85	179	34	16	27	102	74	—	47	4	0	—	0	—	.337	.422	.614	.989
1939	StL-N	153	564	104	197	44	14	28	108	92	—	49	4	10	—	0	—	.349	.444	.626	.987
1940	StL-N	155	579	111	182	31	13	43	137	82	—	49	5	0	—	7	—	.314	.404	.636	.990
1941	StL-N	126	473	67	150	39	8	16	100	70	—	45	1	3	—	4	—	.317	.406	.535	.994
1942	NY-N	142	541	97	165	25	7	26	110	60	—	39	5	1	—	3	—	.305	.380	.521	.995
1946	NY-N	101	377	70	127	18	3	22	70	62	—	26	5	1	—	3	0	.337	.437	.576	.989
1947	NY-N	154	586	137	177	26	2	51	138	74	—	42	4	0	—	2	0	.302	.384	.614	.996

(continued)

Johnny Robert "The Big Cat" Mize, 1b, 1949–53

Johnny Mize was a star in the National League for ten years. But he didn't become a World Champion until he came to the Yankees in 1949.

Mize, born on January 7, 1913, in Demorest, Georgia, was a star in the National League with the St. Louis Cardinals and the New York Giants. From 1936 to 1948, the 6 foot 2 inch first baseman led the league in home runs four times and in RBI three times.

But the nine-time All-Star was 36 years old in 1949, and the new manager of the Giants, Leo Durocher, preferred speed and finesse over power. Mize began to sit on the bench more than he played.

Mize ran into Yankee manager Casey Stengel in mid-1949 at the annual Mayor's Trophy Game. Stengel asked Mize how he was doing. Not too well, admitted Mize. He told Stengel he was not playing much. You'd be playing for me, said Stengel, who instructed Yankee manager George Weiss to acquire Mize. This Weiss did, for $40,000.

It was a steal. Mize won two games for the Yankees with clutch hits in 1949, a year New York won the pennant by one game. In 1950, he hit 25 home runs and had 72 RBI, both third on the team. From 1951–53, he led the league in pinch hits. In the 1952 World Series, he hit .400.

In 1950, he had 76 hits and 72 RBI. He was a smart hitter who could produce in the clutch. He tended to second-guess his teammates, particularly after they had had a bad at-bat, but his observations about hitting were usually on the money.

By 1953, the 40-year-old Mize was slowing down considerably. Stengel was using him more and more as a pinch hitter and not as a regular. He retired at the end of the season with 359 lifetime home runs, and was named to the Hall of Fame in 1981. He died in his hometown in 1993.

(continued)

1948	NY-N	152	560	110	162	26	4	40	125	94	—	37	4	0	—	4	—	.289	.395	.564	.991
1949	NY-N	106	388	59	102	15	0	18	62	50	—	19	3	1	—	1	1	.263	.351	.441	.994
1949	**NY-A**	**13**	**23**	**4**	**6**	**1**	**0**	**1**	**2**	**4**	—	**2**	**1**	**0**	—	**0**	**0**	**.261**	**.393**	**.435**	**.980**
1950	**NY-A**	**90**	**274**	**43**	**76**	**12**	**0**	**25**	**72**	**29**	—	**24**	**2**	**0**	—	**0**	**1**	**.277**	**.351**	**.595**	**.996**
1951	**NY-A**	**113**	**332**	**37**	**86**	**14**	**1**	**10**	**49**	**36**	—	**24**	**4**	**0**	—	**1**	**0**	**.259**	**.339**	**.398**	**.994**
1952	**NY-A**	**78**	**137**	**9**	**36**	**9**	**0**	**4**	**29**	**11**	—	**15**	**2**	**0**	—	**0**	**0**	**.263**	**.327**	**.416**	**.987**
1953	**NY-A**	**81**	**104**	**6**	**26**	**3**	**0**	**4**	**27**	**12**	—	**17**	**2**	**0**	—	**0**	**0**	**.250**	**.339**	**.394**	**1.000**
Career average		118	403	70	126	23	5	22	84	54	—	33	3	1	—	2	—	.312	.397	.562	.992
Yankee average		**75**	**174**	**20**	**46**	**8**	**0**	**9**	**36**	**18**	—	**16**	**2**	**0**	—	**0**	**0**	**.264**	**.342**	**.463**	**.991**
Career total		1884	6443	1118	2011	367	83	359	1337	856	—	524	52	20	—	28	2	.312	.397	.562	.992
Yankee total		**375**	**870**	**99**	**230**	**39**	**1**	**44**	**179**	**92**	—	**82**	**11**	**0**	—	**1**	**1**	**.264**	**.342**	**.463**	**.991**

Mole, Fenton Le Roy (Muscles)

HEIGHT: 6'1" BATS: LEFT THROWS: LEFT BORN: 6/14/1925 SAN LEANDRO, CALIFORNIA POSITIONS PLAYED: 1B

YEAR	TEAM	GAMES	AB	RUNS	HITS	2B	3B	HR	RBI	BB	IBB	SO	HBP	SH	SF	SB	CS	BA	OBA	SA	FA
1949	**NY-A**	**10**	**27**	**2**	**5**	**2**	**1**	**0**	**2**	**3**	—	**5**	**0**	**0**	—	**0**	**0**	**.185**	**.267**	**.333**	**1.000**
Career average		10	27	2	5	2	1	0	2	3	—	5	0	0	—	0	0	.185	.267	.333	1.000
Yankee average		**10**	**27**	**2**	**5**	**2**	**1**	**0**	**2**	**3**	—	**5**	**0**	**0**	—	**0**	**0**	**.185**	**.267**	**.333**	**1.000**
Career total		10	27	2	5	2	1	0	2	3	—	5	0	0	—	0	0	.185	.267	.333	1.000
Yankee total		**10**	**27**	**2**	**5**	**2**	**1**	**0**	**2**	**3**	—	**5**	**0**	**0**	—	**0**	**0**	**.185**	**.267**	**.333**	**1.000**

Moore, Archie Francis

HEIGHT: 6'2"   THROWS: LEFT   BATS: LEFT   BORN: 8/30/1941 UPPER DARBY, PENNSYLVANIA   POSITIONS PLAYED: 1B, OF

YEAR	TEAM	GAMES	AB	RUNS	HITS	2B	3B	HR	RBI	BB	IBB	SO	HBP	SH	SF	SB	CS	BA	OBA	SA	FA
1964	NY-A	31	23	4	4	2	0	0	1	2	0	9	0	0	0	0	0	.174	.240	.261	1.000
1965	NY-A	9	17	1	7	2	0	1	4	4	1	4	0	0	0	0	0	.412	.524	.706	.889
Career average		20	20	3	6	2	0	1	3	3	1	7	0	0	0	0	0	.275	.370	.450	.945
Yankee average		20	20	3	6	2	0	1	3	3	1	7	0	0	0	0	0	.275	.370	.450	.945
Career total		40	40	5	11	4	0	1	5	6	1	13	0	0	0	0	0	.275	.370	.450	.945
Yankee total		40	40	5	11	4	0	1	5	6	1	13	0	0	0	0	0	.275	.370	.450	.945

Morehart, Raymond Anderson

HEIGHT: 5'9"   THROWS: RIGHT   BATS: LEFT   BORN: 12/2/1899 NEAR ABNER, TEXAS   DIED: 1/13/1989 DALLAS, TEXAS   POSITIONS PLAYED: 2B, SS

YEAR	TEAM	GAMES	AB	RUNS	HITS	2B	3B	HR	RBI	BB	IBB	SO	HBP	SH	SF	SB	CS	BA	OBA	SA	FA
1924	Chi-A	31	100	10	20	4	2	0	8	17	—	7	0	3	—	3	1	.200	.316	.280	.873
1926	Chi-A	73	192	27	61	10	3	0	21	11	—	15	1	4	—	3	11	.318	.358	.401	.950
1927	NY-A	73	195	45	50	7	2	1	20	29	—	18	0	6	—	4	4	.256	.353	.328	.945
Career average		59	162	27	44	7	2	0	16	19	—	13	0	4	—	3	5	.269	.347	.347	.923
Yankee average		73	195	45	50	7	2	1	20	29	—	18	0	6	—	4	4	.256	.353	.328	.945
Career total		177	487	82	131	21	7	1	49	57	—	40	1	13	—	10	16	.269	.347	.347	.923
Yankee total		73	195	45	50	7	2	1	20	29	—	18	0	6	—	4	4	.256	.353	.328	.945

Moreno, Omar Renan (Quintero) BORN OMAR RENAN MORENO (QUINTERO)

HEIGHT: 6'2"   THROWS: LEFT   BATS: LEFT   BORN: 10/24/1952 PUERTO ARMUELLES, PANAMA   POSITIONS PLAYED: OF

YEAR	TEAM	GAMES	AB	RUNS	HITS	2B	3B	HR	RBI	BB	IBB	SO	HBP	SH	SF	SB	CS	BA	OBA	SA	FA
1975	Pit-N	6	6	1	1	0	0	0	0	1	0	1	0	0	0	1	0	.167	.286	.167	.000
1976	Pit-N	48	122	24	33	4	1	2	12	16	0	24	1	1	1	15	5	.270	.357	.369	.960
1977	Pit-N	150	492	69	118	19	9	7	34	38	5	102	1	0	2	53	16	.240	.295	.358	.977
1978	Pit-N	155	515	95	121	15	7	2	33	81	4	104	3	17	5	71	22	.235	.339	.303	.984
1979	Pit-N	162	695	110	196	21	12	8	69	51	9	104	3	6	2	77	21	.282	.333	.381	.975
1980	Pit-N	162	676	87	168	20	13	2	36	57	11	101	2	3	7	96	33	.249	.306	.325	.990
1981	Pit-N	103	434	62	120	18	8	1	35	26	4	76	3	1	4	39	14	.276	.319	.362	.997
1982	Pit-N	158	645	82	158	18	9	3	44	44	2	121	1	10	6	60	26	.245	.292	.315	.983
1983	Hou-N	97	405	48	98	12	11	0	25	22	3	72	1	0	1	30	13	.242	.282	.326	.977
1983	NY-A	48	152	17	38	9	1	1	17	8	0	31	0	3	0	7	3	.250	.288	.342	.982
1984	NY-A	117	355	37	92	12	6	4	38	18	1	48	1	4	4	20	11	.259	.294	.361	.985
1985	NY-A	34	66	12	13	4	1	1	4	1	0	16	0	1	0	1	1	.197	.209	.333	1.000
1985	KC-A	24	70	9	17	1	3	2	12	3	0	8	1	0	1	0	1	.243	.280	.429	1.000
1986	Atl-N	118	359	46	84	18	6	4	27	21	2	77	0	6	0	17	16	.234	.276	.351	.970
Career average		99	357	50	90	12	6	3	28	28	3	63	1	4	2	35	13	.252	.306	.343	.913
Yankee average		66	191	22	48	8	3	2	20	9	0	32	0	3	1	9	5	.250	.283	.353	.989
Career total		1382	4992	699	1257	171	87	37	386	387	41	885	17	52	33	487	182	.252	.306	.343	.913
Yankee total		199	573	66	143	25	8	6	59	27	1	95	1	8	4	28	15	.250	.283	.353	.989

Moriarty, George Joseph

HEIGHT: 6'0"   THROWS: RIGHT   BATS: RIGHT   BORN: 6/7/1884 CHICAGO, ILLINOIS   DIED: 4/8/1964 MIAMI, FLORIDA   POSITIONS PLAYED: 1B, 2B, 3B, SS, OF

YEAR	TEAM	GAMES	AB	RUNS	HITS	2B	3B	HR	RBI	BB	IBB	SO	HBP	SH	SF	SB	CS	BA	OBA	SA	FA
1903	Chi-N	1	5	1	0	0	0	0	0	0	—	—	0	0	—	0	—	.000	.000	.000	1.000
1904	Chi-N	4	13	0	0	0	0	0	0	1	—	—	0	0	—	0	—	.000	.071	.000	.800
1906	NY-A	65	197	22	46	7	7	0	23	17	—	—	1	14	—	8	—	.234	.298	.340	1.000
1907	NY-A	126	437	51	121	16	5	0	43	25	—	—	3	9	—	28	—	.277	.320	.336	.667
1908	NY-A	101	348	25	82	12	1	0	27	11	—	—	5	8	—	22	—	.236	.269	.276	1.000
1909	Det-A	133	473	43	129	20	4	1	39	24	—	—	1	17	—	34	—	.273	.309	.338	.990
1910	Det-A	136	490	53	123	24	3	2	60	33	—	—	7	14	—	33	—	.251	.308	.324	.927
1911	Det-A	130	478	51	116	20	4	1	60	27	—	—	3	28	—	28	—	.243	.287	.308	.929
1912	Det-A	105	375	38	93	23	1	0	54	26	—	—	11	20	—	27	—	.248	.316	.315	.933
1913	Det-A	105	347	29	83	5	2	0	30	24	—	25	7	15	—	33	—	.239	.302	.265	.933
1914	Det-A	132	465	56	118	19	5	1	40	39	—	27	5	25	—	34	15	.254	.318	.323	.956
1915	Det-A	31	38	2	8	1	0	0	0	5	—	7	1	2	—	1	1	.211	.318	.237	1.000
1916	Chi-A	7	5	1	1	0	0	0	2	0	—	0	0	0	—	0	0	.200	.429	.200	1.000

(continued)

(continued)

	GAMES	AB	RUNS	HITS	2B	3B	HR	RBI	BB	IBB	SO	HBP	SH	SF	SB	CS	BA	OBA	SA	FA
Career average	83	282	29	71	11	2	0	29	18	—	—	3	12	—	19	—	.251	.303	.312	.933
Yankee average	**97**	**327**	**33**	**83**	**12**	**4**	**0**	**31**	**18**	**—**	**—**	**3**	**10**	**—**	**19**	**—**	**.254**	**.298**	**.316**	**.889**
Career total	1076	3671	372	920	147	32	5	376	234	—	59	44	152	—	248	16	.251	.303	.312	.933
Yankee total	**292**	**982**	**98**	**249**	**35**	**13**	**0**	**93**	**53**	**—**	**—**	**9**	**31**	**—**	**58**	**—**	**.254**	**.298**	**.316**	**.889**

Moronko, Jeffrey Robert

HEIGHT: 6'2" THROWS: RIGHT BATS: RIGHT BORN: 8/17/1959 HOUSTON, TEXAS POSITIONS PLAYED: 3B, SS, OF

YEAR	TEAM	GAMES	AB	RUNS	HITS	2B	3B	HR	RBI	BB	IBB	SO	HBP	SH	SF	SB	CS	BA	OBA	SA	FA
1984	Cle-A	7	19	1	3	1	0	0	3	3	0	5	0	1	0	0	0	.158	.273	.211	.895
1987	**NY-A**	**7**	**11**	**0**	**1**	**0**	**0**	**0**	**0**	**0**	**0**	**2**	**1**	**0**	**0**	**0**	**0**	**.091**	**.167**	**.091**	**1.000**
Career average		7	15	1	2	1	0	0	2	2	0	4	1	1	0	0	0	.133	.235	.167	.948
Yankee average		**7**	**11**	**0**	**1**	**0**	**0**	**0**	**0**	**0**	**0**	**2**	**1**	**0**	**0**	**0**	**0**	**.091**	**.167**	**.091**	**1.000**
Career total		14	30	1	4	1	0	0	3	3	0	7	1	1	0	0	0	.133	.235	.167	.948
Yankee total		**7**	**11**	**0**	**1**	**0**	**0**	**0**	**0**	**0**	**0**	**2**	**1**	**0**	**0**	**0**	**0**	**.091**	**.167**	**.091**	**1.000**

Morris, William Harold (Hal)

HEIGHT: 6'2" THROWS: LEFT BATS: LEFT BORN: 4/9/1965 FORT RUCKER, ALABAMA POSITIONS PLAYED: 1B, OF

YEAR	TEAM	GAMES	AB	RUNS	HITS	2B	3B	HR	RBI	BB	IBB	SO	HBP	SH	SF	SB	CS	BA	OBA	SA	FA
1988	**NY-A**	**15**	**20**	**1**	**2**	**0**	**0**	**0**	**0**	**0**	**0**	**9**	**0**	**0**	**0**	**0**	**0**	**.100**	**.100**	**.100**	**1.000**
1989	**NY-A**	**15**	**18**	**2**	**5**	**0**	**0**	**0**	**4**	**1**	**0**	**4**	**0**	**0**	**0**	**0**	**0**	**.278**	**.316**	**.278**	**1.000**
1990	Cin-N	107	309	50	105	22	3	7	36	21	4	32	1	3	2	9	3	.340	.381	.498	.857
1991	Cin-N	136	478	72	152	33	1	14	59	46	7	61	1	5	7	10	4	.318	.374	.479	.992
1992	Cin-N	115	395	41	107	21	3	6	53	45	8	53	2	5	2	6	6	.271	.347	.385	.999
1993	Cin-N	101	379	48	120	18	0	7	49	34	4	51	2	0	6	2	2	.317	.371	.420	.994
1994	Cin-N	112	436	60	146	30	4	10	78	34	8	62	5	2	6	6	2	.335	.385	.491	.994
1995	Cin-N	101	359	53	100	25	2	11	51	29	7	58	1	1	1	1	1	.279	.333	.451	.994
1996	Cin-N	142	528	82	165	32	4	16	80	50	5	76	5	5	6	7	5	.313	.374	.479	.993
1997	Cin-N	96	333	42	92	20	1	1	33	23	2	43	5	5	6	7	5	.276	.328	.351	.990
1998	KC-A	127	472	50	146	27	2	1	40	32	6	52	3	4	7	1	0	.309	.350	.381	1.000
1999	Cin-N	80	102	10	29	9	0	0	16	10	0	21	0	0	0	0	0	.284	.348	.373	.992
2000	Cin-N	59	63	9	14	2	1	2	6	12	3	10	1	1	1	0	0	.222	.351	.381	.992
2000	Det-A	40	106	15	33	7	0	1	8	19	1	16	0	1	0	0	0	.311	.416	.406	.992
Career average		89	286	38	87	18	2	5	37	25	4	39	2	2	3	3	2	.304	.361	.433	.985
Yankee average		**15**	**19**	**2**	**4**	**0**	**0**	**0**	**2**	**1**	**0**	**7**	**0**	**0**	**0**	**0**	**0**	**.184**	**.205**	**.184**	**1.000**
Career total		1246	3998	535	1216	246	21	76	513	356	55	548	21	28	39	45	24	.304	.361	.433	.985
Yankee total		**30**	**38**	**3**	**7**	**0**	**0**	**0**	**4**	**1**	**0**	**13**	**0**	**0**	**0**	**0**	**0**	**.184**	**.205**	**.184**	**1.000**

Moschitto, Rosaire Allen (Ross)

HEIGHT: 6'2" THROWS: RIGHT BATS: RIGHT BORN: 2/15/1945 FRESNO, CALIFORNIA POSITIONS PLAYED: OF

YEAR	TEAM	GAMES	AB	RUNS	HITS	2B	3B	HR	RBI	BB	IBB	SO	HBP	SH	SF	SB	CS	BA	OBA	SA	FA
1965	**NY-A**	**96**	**27**	**12**	**5**	**0**	**0**	**1**	**3**	**0**	**0**	**12**	**0**	**0**	**1**	**0**	**0**	**.185**	**.179**	**.296**	**.941**
1967	**NY-A**	**14**	**9**	**1**	**1**	**0**	**0**	**0**	**0**	**1**	**0**	**2**	**0**	**1**	**0**	**0**	**0**	**.111**	**.200**	**.111**	**1.000**
Career average		55	18	7	3	0	0	1	2	1	0	7	0	1	1	0	0	.167	.184	.250	.971
Yankee average		**55**	**18**	**7**	**3**	**0**	**0**	**1**	**2**	**1**	**0**	**7**	**0**	**1**	**1**	**0**	**0**	**.167**	**.184**	**.250**	**.971**
Career total		110	36	13	6	0	0	1	3	1	0	14	0	1	1	0	0	.167	.184	.250	.971
Yankee total		**110**	**36**	**13**	**6**	**0**	**0**	**1**	**3**	**1**	**0**	**14**	**0**	**1**	**1**	**0**	**0**	**.167**	**.184**	**.250**	**.971**

Moses, Gerald Braheen (Jerry)

HEIGHT: 6'3" THROWS: RIGHT BATS: RIGHT BORN: 8/9/1946 YAZOO CITY, MISSISSIPPI POSITIONS PLAYED: C

YEAR	TEAM	GAMES	AB	RUNS	HITS	2B	3B	HR	RBI	BB	IBB	SO	HBP	SH	SF	SB	CS	BA	OBA	SA	FA
1965	Bos-A	4	4	1	1	0	0	1	1	0	0	2	0	0	0	0	0	.250	.250	1.000	.000
1968	Bos-A	6	18	2	6	0	0	2	4	1	0	4	0	0	0	0	0	.333	.368	.667	.963
1969	Bos-A	53	135	13	41	9	1	4	17	5	1	23	1	0	0	0	1	.304	.326	.474	.981
1970	Bos-A	92	315	26	83	18	1	6	35	21	9	45	2	1	1	1	1	.263	.313	.384	.990
1971	Cal-A	69	181	12	41	8	2	4	15	10	4	34	0	1	1	0	1	.227	.266	.359	.971

(continued)

(continued)

YEAR	TEAM	GAMES	AB	RUNS	HITS	2B	3B	HR	RBI	BB	IBB	SO	HBP	SH	SF	SB	CS	BA	OBA	SA	FA
1972	Cle-A	52	141	9	31	3	0	4	14	11	3	29	3	2	0	0	0	.220	.290	.326	.982
1973	**NY-A**	**21**	**59**	**5**	**15**	**2**	**0**	**0**	**3**	**2**	**0**	**6**	**0**	**1**	**2**	**0**	**0**	**.254**	**.270**	**.288**	**1.000**
1974	Det-A	74	198	19	47	6	3	4	19	11	2	38	2	2	2	0	1	.237	.282	.359	.985
1975	Chi-A	2	2	1	1	0	1	0	0	0	0	0	0	0	0	0	0	.500	.500	1.500	1.000
1975	SD-N	13	19	1	3	2	0	0	1	2	0	3	0	0	0	0	0	.158	.238	.263	.900
Career average		43	119	10	30	5	1	3	12	7	2	20	1	1	1	0	0	.251	.295	.381	.877
Yankee average		**21**	**59**	**5**	**15**	**2**	**0**	**0**	**3**	**2**	**0**	**6**	**0**	**1**	**2**	**0**	**0**	**.254**	**.270**	**.288**	**1.000**
Career total		386	1072	89	269	48	8	25	109	63	19	184	8	7	9	1	4	.251	.295	.381	.877
Yankee total		**21**	**59**	**5**	**15**	**2**	**0**	**0**	**3**	**2**	**0**	**6**	**0**	**1**	**2**	**0**	**0**	**.254**	**.270**	**.288**	**1.000**

Mullen, Charles George

HEIGHT: 5'10"   THROWS: RIGHT   BATS: RIGHT   BORN: 3/15/1889 SEATTLE, WASHINGTON   DIED: 6/6/1963 SEATTLE, WASH.   POSITIONS PLAYED: 1B, 2B, OF

YEAR	TEAM	GAMES	AB	RUNS	HITS	2B	3B	HR	RBI	BB	IBB	SO	HBP	SH	SF	SB	CS	BA	OBA	SA	FA
1910	Chi-A	41	123	15	24	2	1	0	13	4	—	—	0	10	—	4	—	.195	.220	.228	1.000
1911	Chi-A	20	59	7	12	2	1	0	5	5	—	—	0	3	—	1	—	.203	.266	.271	.969
1914	NY-A	93	323	33	84	8	0	0	44	33	—	55	2	21	—	11	17	.260	.332	.285	.994
1915	NY-A	40	90	11	24	1	0	0	7	10	—	12	0	2	—	5	2	.267	.340	.278	.982
1916	NY-A	59	146	11	39	9	1	0	18	9	—	13	0	6	—	7	0	.267	.310	.342	.943
Career average		51	148	15	37	4	1	0	17	12	—	—	0	8	—	6	—	.247	.306	.285	.978
Yankee average		**64**	**186**	**18**	**49**	**6**	**0**	**0**	**23**	**17**	**—**	**27**	**1**	**10**	**—**	**8**	**6**	**.263**	**.328**	**.299**	**.973**
Career total		253	741	77	183	22	3	0	87	61	—	80	2	42	—	28	19	.247	.306	.285	.978
Yankee total		**192**	**559**	**55**	**147**	**18**	**1**	**0**	**69**	**52**	**—**	**80**	**2**	**29**	**—**	**23**	**19**	**.263**	**.328**	**.299**	**.973**

Mumphrey, Jerry Wayne

HEIGHT: 6'2"   THROWS: RIGHT   BATS: BOTH   BORN: 9/9/1952 TYLER, TEXAS   POSITIONS PLAYED: OF

YEAR	TEAM	GAMES	AB	RUNS	HITS	2B	3B	HR	RBI	BB	IBB	SO	HBP	SH	SF	SB	CS	BA	OBA	SA	FA
1974	StL-N	5	2	2	0	0	0	0	0	0	0	0	0	0	0	0	0	.000	.000	.000	.000
1975	StL-N	11	16	2	6	2	0	0	1	4	0	3	0	0	0	0	0	.375	.500	.500	1.000
1976	StL-N	112	384	51	99	15	5	1	26	37	0	53	1	2	3	22	6	.258	.322	.331	.993
1977	StL-N	145	463	73	133	20	10	2	38	47	6	70	1	1	0	22	15	.287	.354	.387	.971
1978	StL-N	125	367	41	96	13	4	2	37	30	0	40	1	2	3	14	10	.262	.317	.335	.995
1979	StL-N	124	339	53	100	10	3	3	32	26	2	39	0	6	4	8	11	.295	.341	.369	.984
1980	SD-N	160	564	61	168	24	3	4	59	49	4	90	0	5	4	52	5	.298	.352	.372	.974
1981	**NY-A**	**80**	**319**	**44**	**98**	**11**	**5**	**6**	**32**	**24**	**1**	**27**	**0**	**5**	**2**	**14**	**9**	**.307**	**.354**	**.429**	**.966**
1982	**NY-A**	**123**	**477**	**76**	**143**	**24**	**10**	**9**	**68**	**50**	**4**	**66**	**0**	**3**	**3**	**11**	**3**	**.300**	**.364**	**.449**	**.986**
1983	**NY-A**	**83**	**267**	**41**	**70**	**11**	**4**	**7**	**36**	**28**	**2**	**33**	**0**	**2**	**5**	**2**	**3**	**.262**	**.327**	**.412**	**.983**
1983	Hou-N	44	143	17	48	10	2	1	17	22	3	23	1	0	1	5	0	.336	.425	.455	.990
1984	Hou-N	151	524	66	152	20	3	9	83	56	7	79	0	0	6	15	7	.290	.355	.391	.988
1985	Hou-N	130	444	52	123	25	2	8	61	37	8	57	0	1	6	6	7	.277	.329	.396	.969
1986	Chi-N	111	309	37	94	11	2	5	32	26	4	45	0	1	3	2	3	.304	.355	.401	.982
1987	Chi-N	118	309	41	103	19	2	13	44	35	6	47	0	1	1	1	1	.333	.400	.534	.992
1988	Chi-N	63	66	3	9	2	0	0	9	7	2	16	0	0	0	0	0	.136	.219	.167	1.000
Career average		99	312	41	90	14	3	4	36	30	3	43	0	2	3	11	5	.289	.349	.396	.923
Yankee average		**95**	**354**	**54**	**104**	**15**	**6**	**7**	**45**	**34**	**2**	**42**	**0**	**3**	**3**	**9**	**5**	**.293**	**.351**	**.434**	**.978**
Career total		1585	4993	660	1442	217	55	70	575	478	49	688	4	29	41	174	80	.289	.349	.396	.923
Yankee total		**286**	**1063**	**161**	**311**	**46**	**19**	**22**	**136**	**102**	**7**	**126**	**0**	**10**	**10**	**27**	**15**	**.293**	**.351**	**.434**	**.978**

Munson, Thurman Lee

HEIGHT: 5'11"   THROWS: RIGHT   BATS: RIGHT   BORN: 6/7/1947 AKRON, OHIO   DIED: 8/2/1979 CANTON, OHIO   POSITIONS PLAYED: C, 1B, 3B, OF

YEAR	TEAM	GAMES	AB	RUNS	HITS	2B	3B	HR	RBI	BB	IBB	SO	HBP	SH	SF	SB	CS	BA	OBA	SA	FA
1969	**NY-A**	**26**	**86**	**6**	**22**	**1**	**2**	**1**	**9**	**10**	**1**	**10**	**0**	**0**	**1**	**0**	**1**	**.256**	**.330**	**.349**	**.986**
1970	**NY-A**	**132**	**453**	**59**	**137**	**25**	**4**	**6**	**53**	**57**	**6**	**56**	**7**	**5**	**4**	**5**	**7**	**.302**	**.386**	**.415**	**.989**
1971	**NY-A**	**125**	**451**	**71**	**113**	**15**	**4**	**10**	**42**	**52**	**1**	**65**	**7**	**4**	**3**	**6**	**5**	**.251**	**.335**	**.368**	**.998**
1972	**NY-A**	**140**	**511**	**54**	**143**	**16**	**3**	**7**	**46**	**47**	**5**	**58**	**3**	**4**	**2**	**6**	**7**	**.280**	**.343**	**.364**	**.977**
1973	**NY-A**	**147**	**519**	**80**	**156**	**29**	**4**	**20**	**74**	**48**	**4**	**64**	**4**	**1**	**4**	**4**	**6**	**.301**	**.362**	**.487**	**.984**
1974	**NY-A**	**144**	**517**	**64**	**135**	**19**	**2**	**13**	**60**	**44**	**12**	**66**	**1**	**1**	**8**	**2**	**0**	**.261**	**.316**	**.381**	**.974**
1975	**NY-A**	**157**	**597**	**83**	**190**	**24**	**3**	**12**	**102**	**45**	**8**	**52**	**6**	**3**	**10**	**3**	**2**	**.318**	**.366**	**.429**	**1.000**

(continued)

Thurman Lee Munson, c-of-dh, 1969–79

He was the unquestioned leader of the Yankees during their three-pennant run of 1976–78, and when he died tragically in 1979, the team was never the same.

Born on June 7, 1947, in Akron, Ohio, Munson was an All-American at Kent State University when he was drafted by the Yankees. He spent less than a year in the minors before being brought up by the big club in August 1969. He hit .256 in 26 games that summer.

The 1970 season was Munson's first full year and he was an immediate star, hitting .302 and leading all American League catchers in assists with 80. He was a near-unanimous choice for Rookie of the Year.

He was one of the principal building blocks on which the Yankees began their slow climb back to respectability in the early 1970s. For the next ten years, Munson never had fewer than 110 hits and his average hovered around .300 in that span. He also won three Gold Gloves.

Munson was powerfully built, but his wide body made him look shorter and squatter than he really was. He was one of the fastest catchers of all time, had a great throwing arm and was extremely quick in covering bunts. He was a most worthy successor to the long tradition of great Yankee catchers like Bill Dickey, Yogi Berra and Elston Howard.

His best year was 1976, when he won the Most Valuable Player Award. That year, he hit .302 and drove in 105 runs. In the World Series against Cincinnati, he hit .529, although the Yankees were swept by the Reds. That season, Munson became the fifth captain of the Yankees, and the first since the title had been more or less retired after Lou Gehrig's tenure.

A six-time All-Star, Munson was a proud man who played hurt and never complained. In 1977, the Yankees acquired outfielder Reggie Jackson. In a preseason interview with Sport magazine, Jackson characterized himself as "the straw that stirs the drink." Munson, said Jackson, thinks he is the straw, "but he can only stir it bad."

Much has been made of the rivalry between the two men in those years. Munson respected Jackson's ability, certainly, but was always troubled by Jackon's need to draw the spotlight to himself. Such a stance simply did not fit with Munson's midwestern ideals.

Regardless, the two men were the key factors in the Yankees' back-to-back championships. Munson hit .320 in both the 1977 and 1978 World Series wins, and his World Series average of .373 is the third best in history.

In addition to his exploits on the diamond, Munson was also a licensed pilot who enjoyed flying every chance he could. On August 2, 1979, Munson was practicing takeoffs and landings in a twin-engine Cessna when the plane crashed into a tree, killing the Yankee catcher at the too-young age of 32.

The next year, the Yankees unveiled a plaque dedicated to Munson at Yankee Stadium. His number 15 was retired, and his locker in the Yankee clubhouse remains empty in his memory.

Munson is 15th on the Yankees' all-time list in hits with 1,558.

(continued)

Year	Team	G	AB	R	H	2B	3B	HR	RBI	BB	HBP	SO	SB	CS				BA	OBP	SLG	
1976	NY-A	152	616	79	186	27	1	17	105	29	6	38	9	1	10	14	11	.302	.337	.432	.981
1977	NY-A	149	595	85	183	28	5	18	100	39	8	55	2	0	2	5	6	.308	.351	.462	.984
1978	NY-A	154	617	73	183	27	1	6	71	35	6	70	3	1	10	2	3	.297	.332	.373	.970
1979	NY-A	97	382	42	110	18	3	3	39	32	2	37	0	1	4	1	2	.288	.340	.374	1.000
Career average		129	486	63	142	21	3	10	64	40	5	52	4	2	5	4	5	.292	.346	.410	.986
Yankee average		**129**	**486**	**63**	**142**	**21**	**3**	**10**	**64**	**40**	**5**	**52**	**4**	**2**	**5**	**4**	**5**	**.292**	**.346**	**.410**	**.986**
Career total		1423	5344	696	1558	229	32	113	701	438	59	571	42	21	58	48	50	.292	.346	.410	.986
Yankee total		**1423**	**5344**	**696**	**1558**	**229**	**32**	**113**	**701**	**438**	**59**	**571**	**42**	**21**	**58**	**48**	**50**	**.292**	**.346**	**.410**	**.986**

Bobby Ray Murcer, of-ss-dh, 1965–66, 1969–74, 1979–83

A four-time All-Star with the Yankees in the early 1970s, Bobby Murcer was a slugging outfielder whom the Yankee brass at one point hoped would replace Mickey Mantle.

Murcer, born on May 20, 1946, in Oklahoma City, Oklahoma, was good, but neither he nor anyone else would turn out to be a replacement for the Mick.

Murcer was no slouch, however. He played parts of two seasons for the Yankees in 1965 and 1966 as a shortstop. When he came back up in 1969, it was as an outfielder, a position with which he was more comfortable.

Murcer was solid but unspectacular in 1969 and 1970. By 1971, however, he had worked his average up to .331 and led the American League in on base percentage. From 1971 to 1974, he was by far the Yankees' best hitter, and the only Yankee to make the All-Star team all four of those years.

He was not as prodigious a home run hitter as players like Babe Ruth or Mantle, but he was consistent, leading the team in that category four years in a row. He twice hit three home runs in one game, in 1970 against Cleveland and in 1973 against the Royals. He once hit four consecutive home runs in a doubleheader.

In 1975, he was traded to the San Francisco Giants. After stints with the Giants and Cubs, he was reacquired by the Yankees in 1979. In his final go-round, Murcer became a part-time player. He was not happy with the role, but again, he produced. In 1981, his three pinch-hit home runs led the league, and Murcer's seven pinch-hit homers with New York is third all-time.

He and former Yankee catcher Thurman Munson were good friends, having come up in the minor leagues together. On the evening of Munson's funeral, four days after his tragic death, Murcer had a home run and a dramatic, ninth-inning, two-RBI single to beat the Orioles. Somehow, it was a fitting tribute to the Yankee catcher.

Murcer, Bobby Ray

HEIGHT: 5'11" THROWS: RIGHT BATS: LEFT BORN: 5/20/1946, OKLAHOMA CITY, OKLAHOMA POSITIONS PLAYED: 2B, 3B, SS, OF

YEAR	TEAM	GAMES	AB	RUNS	HITS	2B	3B	HR	RBI	BB	IBB	SO	HBP	SH	SF	SB	CS	BA	OBA	SA	FA
1965	NY-A	11	37	2	9	0	1	1	4	5	0	12	0	0	0	0	0	.243	.333	.378	.932
1966	NY-A	21	69	3	12	1	1	0	5	4	0	5	0	0	0	2	2	.174	.219	.217	.931
1969	NY-A	152	564	82	146	24	4	26	82	50	2	103	3	2	6	7	5	.259	.319	.454	.964
1970	NY-A	159	581	95	146	23	3	23	78	87	5	100	2	4	6	15	10	.251	.348	.420	.992
1971	NY-A	146	529	94	175	25	6	25	94	91	13	60	0	1	3	14	8	.331	.427	.543	.985
1972	NY-A	153	585	102	171	30	7	33	96	63	7	67	2	0	4	11	9	.292	.361	.537	.992
1973	NY-A	160	616	83	187	29	2	22	95	50	6	67	3	0	3	6	7	.304	.357	.464	.985
1974	NY-A	156	606	69	166	25	4	10	88	57	10	59	2	2	12	14	5	.274	.332	.378	.978
1975	SF-N	147	526	80	157	29	4	11	91	91	6	45	2	1	12	9	5	.298	.396	.432	.981
1976	SF-N	147	533	73	138	20	2	23	90	84	10	78	4	0	3	12	7	.259	.362	.433	.961
1977	Chi-N	154	554	90	147	18	3	27	89	80	13	77	3	2	10	16	7	.265	.355	.455	.970
1978	Chi-N	146	499	66	140	22	6	9	64	80	15	57	0	0	6	14	5	.281	.376	.403	.979
1979	Chi-N	58	190	22	49	4	1	7	22	36	2	20	1	1	3	2	3	.258	.374	.400	1.000
1979	NY-A	74	264	42	72	12	0	8	33	25	2	32	2	2	1	1	1	.273	.339	.409	.983
1980	NY-A	100	297	41	80	9	1	13	57	34	2	28	2	3	9	2	0	.269	.339	.438	.955
1981	NY-A	50	117	14	31	6	0	6	24	12	1	15	0	0	1	0	0	.265	.331	.470	.000
1982	NY-A	65	141	12	32	6	0	7	30	12	2	15	1	0	2	2	1	.227	.288	.418	.000
1983	NY-A	9	22	2	4	2	0	1	1	1	0	1	0	0	0	0	0	.182	.217	.409	.000

(continued)

(continued)

Career average	106	374	54	103	16	3	14	58	48	5	47	2	1	5	7	4	.277	.357	.445	.810
Yankee average	**97**	**341**	**49**	**95**	**15**	**2**	**13**	**53**	**38**	**4**	**43**	**1**	**1**	**4**	**6**	**4**	**.278**	**.349**	**.453**	**.746**
Career total	1908	6730	972	1862	285	45	252	1043	862	96	841	27	18	81	127	75	.277	.357	.445	.810
Yankee total	**1256**	**4428**	**641**	**1231**	**192**	**29**	**175**	**687**	**491**	**50**	**564**	**17**	**14**	**47**	**74**	**48**	**.278**	**.349**	**.453**	**.746**

Murray, Larry
HEIGHT: 5'11" THROWS: RIGHT BATS: BOTH BORN: 4/1/1953 CHICAGO, ILLINOIS POSITIONS PLAYED: OF

YEAR	TEAM	GAMES	AB	RUNS	HITS	2B	3B	HR	RBI	BB	IBB	SO	HBP	SH	SF	SB	CS	BA	OBA	SA	FA
1974	**NY-A**	**6**	**1**	**1**	**0**	**0**	**0**	**0**	**0**	**0**	**0**	**0**	**0**	**0**	**0**	**0**	**0**	**.000**	**.000**	**.000**	**.000**
1975	**NY-A**	**6**	**1**	**1**	**0**	**0**	**0**	**0**	**0**	**0**	**0**	**0**	**0**	**0**	**0**	**0**	**0**	**.000**	**.000**	**.000**	**1.000**
1976	**NY-A**	**8**	**10**	**2**	**1**	**0**	**0**	**0**	**2**	**1**	**0**	**2**	**0**	**0**	**0**	**2**	**0**	**.100**	**.182**	**.100**	**1.000**
1977	Oak-A	90	162	19	29	5	2	1	9	17	2	36	0	3	0	12	3	.179	.257	.253	.992
1978	Oak-A	11	12	1	1	0	0	0	0	3	0	2	0	0	0	0	0	.083	.267	.083	1.000
1979	Oak-A	105	226	25	42	11	2	2	20	28	1	34	0	6	1	6	6	.186	.275	.279	.963
Career average	38	69	8	12	3	1	1	5	8	1	12	0	2	0	3	2	.177	.264	.257	.826
Yankee average	**7**	**4**	**1**	**0**	**0**	**0**	**0**	**1**	**0**	**0**	**1**	**0**	**0**	**0**	**1**	**0**	**.083**	**.154**	**.083**	**.667**
Career total	226	412	49	73	16	4	3	31	49	3	74	0	9	1	20	9	.177	.264	.257	.826
Yankee total	**20**	**12**	**4**	**1**	**0**	**0**	**0**	**2**	**1**	**0**	**2**	**0**	**0**	**0**	**2**	**0**	**.083**	**.154**	**.083**	**.667**

Narron, Jerry Austin
HEIGHT: 6'3" THROWS: RIGHT BATS: LEFT BORN: 1/15/1956 GOLDSBORO, NORTH CAROLINA POSITIONS PLAYED: C

YEAR	TEAM	GAMES	AB	RUNS	HITS	2B	3B	HR	RBI	BB	IBB	SO	HBP	SH	SF	SB	CS	BA	OBA	SA	FA
1979	**NY-A**	**61**	**123**	**17**	**21**	**3**	**1**	**4**	**18**	**9**	**0**	**26**	**0**	**3**	**1**	**0**	**0**	**.171**	**.226**	**.309**	**.973**
1980	Sea-A	48	107	7	21	3	0	4	18	13	2	18	0	1	2	0	0	.196	.279	.336	.992
1981	Sea-A	76	203	13	45	5	0	3	17	16	3	35	2	3	0	0	0	.222	.285	.291	.996
1983	Cal-A	10	22	1	3	0	0	1	4	1	0	3	0	0	0	0	0	.136	.174	.273	.895
1984	Cal-A	69	150	9	37	5	0	3	17	8	1	12	1	1	2	0	0	.247	.286	.340	.994
1985	Cal-A	67	132	12	29	4	0	5	14	11	2	17	0	0	0	0	0	.220	.280	.364	1.000
1986	Cal-A	57	95	5	21	3	1	1	8	9	0	14	1	1	1	0	0	.221	.292	.305	.988
1987	Sea-A	4	8	0	0	0	0	0	0	0	0	2	0	0	0	0	0	.000	.000	.000	1.000
Career average	49	105	8	22	3	0	3	12	8	1	16	1	1	1	0	0	.211	.270	.318	.980
Yankee average	**61**	**123**	**17**	**21**	**3**	**1**	**4**	**18**	**9**	**0**	**26**	**0**	**3**	**1**	**0**	**0**	**.171**	**.226**	**.309**	**.973**
Career total	392	840	64	177	23	2	21	96	67	8	127	4	9	6	0	0	.211	.270	.318	.980
Yankee total	**61**	**123**	**17**	**21**	**3**	**1**	**4**	**18**	**9**	**0**	**26**	**0**	**3**	**1**	**0**	**0**	**.171**	**.226**	**.309**	**.973**

Nettles, Graig
HEIGHT: 6'0" THROWS: RIGHT BATS: LEFT BORN: 8/20/1944 SAN DIEGO, CALIFORNIA POSITIONS PLAYED: 1B, 3B, SS, OF

YEAR	TEAM	GAMES	AB	RUNS	HITS	2B	3B	HR	RBI	BB	IBB	SO	HBP	SH	SF	SB	CS	BA	OBA	SA	FA
1967	Min-A	3	3	0	1	1	0	0	0	0	0	0	0	0	0	0	0	.333	.333	.667	.000
1968	Min-A	22	76	13	17	2	1	5	8	7	1	20	1	0	0	0	0	.224	.298	.474	1.000
1969	Min-A	96	225	27	50	9	2	7	26	32	1	47	1	1	2	1	2	.222	.319	.373	.982
1970	Cle-A	157	549	81	129	13	1	26	62	81	3	77	3	0	0	3	1	.235	.336	.404	1.000
1971	Cle-A	158	598	78	156	18	1	28	86	82	6	56	3	1	6	7	4	.261	.350	.435	.973
1972	Cle-A	150	557	65	141	28	0	17	70	57	5	50	4	2	3	2	3	.253	.325	.395	.956
1973	NY-A	160	552	65	129	18	0	22	81	78	3	76	7	0	4	0	0	.234	.334	.386	.953
1974	NY-A	155	566	74	139	21	1	22	75	59	8	75	3	1	9	1	0	.246	.316	.403	.961
1975	NY-A	157	581	71	155	24	4	21	91	51	3	88	2	2	11	1	3	.267	.322	.430	.964
1976	NY-A	158	583	88	148	29	2	32	93	62	6	94	4	2	5	11	6	.254	.327	.475	.965
1977	NY-A	158	589	99	150	23	4	37	107	68	8	79	3	0	4	2	5	.255	.333	.496	.974
1978	NY-A	159	587	81	162	23	2	27	93	59	6	69	6	1	9	1	1	.276	.343	.460	1.000
1979	NY-A	145	521	71	132	15	1	20	73	59	6	53	0	0	8	1	2	.253	.325	.401	.966
1980	NY-A	89	324	52	79	14	0	16	45	42	5	42	1	0	2	0	0	.244	.331	.435	.960
1981	NY-A	103	349	46	85	7	1	15	46	47	4	49	1	2	3	0	2	.244	.333	.398	.972
1982	NY-A	122	405	47	94	11	2	18	55	51	4	49	1	0	4	1	5	.232	.317	.402	.934
1983	NY-A	129	462	56	123	17	3	20	75	51	2	65	3	0	3	0	1	.266	.341	.446	.956
1984	SD-N	124	395	56	90	11	1	20	65	58	4	55	5	0	7	0	0	.228	.329	.413	.936
1985	SD-N	137	440	66	115	23	1	15	61	72	5	59	0	0	3	0	0	.261	.363	.420	.959
1986	SD-N	126	354	36	77	9	0	16	55	41	8	62	2	0	3	0	1	.218	.300	.379	.941
1987	Atl-N	112	177	16	37	8	1	5	33	22	4	25	0	0	2	1	0	.209	.294	.350	1.000
1988	Mon-N	80	93	5	16	4	0	1	14	9	2	19	0	0	2	0	0	.172	.240	.247	.966

(continued)

Graig Nettles, 3b-ss-dh, 1973–83

Graig Nettles only won two Gold Gloves when he was with the Yankees, but for most of his New York career, he was one of the best defensive third basemen in either league and one of the best all-around players in the 1970s.

Nettles, born in San Diego, California, on August 20, 1944, came to the majors in 1967 with the Minnesota Twins. After a stint with the Cleveland Indians from 1970–72, Nettles was acquired by the Yankees in a six-player deal.

Nettles stabilized third base for the Yankees, who had had three different players there over the previous five years. Nettles's 11 years at third base for New York was the longest such stint at that position in the history of the club.

His fielding was nearly without peer. In Game 3 of the 1978 World Series, he made three stunning plays in a 5-1 Yankee win that turned the Series around for New York. Dodgers' manager Tommy Lasorda said at the time that Nettles's play that day was the greatest exhibition of fielding he had ever witnessed.

He was also a terrific home run hitter. In 1976, he led the American League with 32 homers, and in 1977, he came back with a career-high 37 round-trippers. From 1973 to 1979, Nettles hit at least 20 home runs each year.

He was a five-time All-Star for New York, but by 1981, his average had dropped to .244 with only 15 home runs. In 1983, hinting that Nettles, at 39, was getting too old to play regularly, Steinbrenner traded him to the Padres. Nettles responded by leading the Padres to their first-ever World Series appearance in 1984.

Throughout his career, Nettles was the unquestioned master of the one-liner in the Yankee clubhouse. His quips were repeated almost as much as Yogi Berra's. "Some kids want to play in the big leagues when they grow up," he once observed. "Other kids want to join the circus. I'm lucky. When I came to the Yankees, I got to do both."

Nettles is 6th all-time on the Yankees' home run list with 250, and 10th all-time in RBI with 834.

(continued)

Career average	123	408	54	101	15	1	18	60	49	4	55	2	1	4	1	2	.248	.329	.421	.924
Yankee average	**140**	**502**	**68**	**127**	**18**	**2**	**23**	**76**	**57**	**5**	**67**	**3**	**1**	**6**	**2**	**2**	**.253**	**.329**	**.433**	**.964**
Career total	2700	8986	1193	2225	328	28	390	1314	1088	94	1209	50	12	90	32	36	.248	.329	.421	.924
Yankee total	**1535**	**5519**	**750**	**1396**	**202**	**20**	**250**	**834**	**627**	**55**	**739**	**31**	**8**	**62**	**18**	**25**	**.253**	**.329**	**.433**	**.964**

Niarhos, Constantine Gregory (Gus)

HEIGHT: 6'0" THROWS: RIGHT BATS: RIGHT   BORN: 12/6/1920 BIRMINGHAM, ALABAMA   POSITIONS PLAYED: C

YEAR	TEAM	GAMES	AB	RUNS	HITS	2B	3B	HR	RBI	BB	IBB	SO	HBP	SH	SF	SB	CS	BA	OBA	SA	FA
1946	NY-A	37	40	11	9	1	1	0	2	11	—	2	0	0	—	1	0	.225	.392	.300	.989
1948	NY-A	83	228	41	61	12	2	0	19	52	—	15	0	5	—	1	3	.268	.404	.338	.990
1949	NY-A	32	43	7	12	2	1	0	6	13	—	8	1	0	—	0	0	.279	.456	.372	1.000
1950	NY-A	1	0	0	0	0	0	0	0	0	—	0	0	0	—	0	0	—	—	—	.000
1950	Chi-A	41	105	17	34	4	0	0	16	14	—	6	1	1	—	0	0	.324	.408	.362	.978
1951	Chi-A	66	168	27	43	6	0	1	10	47	—	9	0	2	—	4	3	.256	.419	.310	.985
1952	Bos-A	29	58	4	6	0	0	0	4	12	—	9	1	1	—	0	0	.103	.268	.103	.992
1953	Bos-A	16	35	6	7	1	1	0	2	4	—	4	1	1	—	0	1	.200	.300	.286	.985
1954	Phi-N	3	5	0	1	0	0	0	0	0	—	1	0	0	—	0	0	.200	.200	.200	1.000
1955	Phi-N	7	9	1	1	0	0	0	0	0	0	2	0	0	0	0	0	.111	.111	.111	1.000
Career average		32	69	11	17	3	1	0	6	15	—	6	0	1	—	1	1	.252	.390	.308	.892
Yankee average		**38**	**78**	**15**	**21**	**4**	**1**	**0**	**7**	**19**	**—**	**6**	**0**	**1**	**—**	**1**	**1**	**.264**	**.410**	**.338**	**.745**
Career total		315	691	114	174	26	5	1	59	153	0	56	4	10	0	6	7	.252	.390	.308	.892
Yankee total		**153**	**311**	**59**	**82**	**15**	**4**	**0**	**27**	**76**	**—**	**25**	**1**	**5**	**—**	**2**	**3**	**.264**	**.410**	**.338**	**.745**

Niles, Herbert Clyde (Harry)

HEIGHT: 5'8" THROWS: RIGHT BATS: RIGHT BORN: 9/10/1880 BUCHANAN, MICHIGAN DIED: 4/18/1953 STURGIS, MICH. POSITIONS PLAYED: 2B, 3B, SS, OF

YEAR	TEAM	GAMES	AB	RUNS	HITS	2B	3B	HR	RBI	BB	IBB	SO	HBP	SH	SF	SB	CS	BA	OBA	SA	FA
1906	StL-A	142	541	71	124	14	4	2	31	46	—	—	6	15	—	30	—	.229	.297	.281	.912
1907	StL-A	120	492	65	142	9	5	2	35	28	—	—	3	9	—	19	—	.289	.331	.339	1.000
1908	**NY-A**	**96**	**362**	**43**	**90**	**14**	**6**	**4**	**24**	**25**	**—**	**—**	**4**	**10**	**—**	**18**	**—**	**.249**	**.304**	**.354**	**.928**
1908	Bos-A	17	32	4	8	0	0	1	3	6	—	—	1	4	—	3	—	.250	.385	.344	1.000
1909	Bos-A	145	546	64	134	12	5	1	38	39	—	—	13	18	—	27	—	.245	.311	.291	.957
1910	Bos-A	18	57	6	12	3	0	1	3	4	—	—	0	2	—	1	—	.211	.262	.316	.920
1910	Cle-A	70	240	25	51	6	4	1	18	15	—	—	3	3	—	9	—	.213	.267	.283	.829
Career average		87	324	40	80	8	3	2	22	23	—	—	4	9	—	15	—	.247	.306	.310	.935
Yankee average		**96**	**362**	**43**	**90**	**14**	**6**	**4**	**24**	**25**	**—**	**—**	**4**	**10**	**—**	**18**	**—**	**.249**	**.304**	**.354**	**.928**
Career total		608	2270	278	561	58	24	12	152	163	—	—	30	61	—	107	—	.247	.306	.310	.935
Yankee total		**96**	**362**	**43**	**90**	**14**	**6**	**4**	**24**	**25**	**—**	**—**	**4**	**10**	**—**	**18**	**—**	**.249**	**.304**	**.354**	**.928**

Nixon, Otis Junior

HEIGHT: 6'2" THROWS: RIGHT BATS: BOTH BORN: 1/9/1959 EVERGREEN, NORTH CAROLINA POSITIONS PLAYED: OF

YEAR	TEAM	GAMES	AB	RUNS	HITS	2B	3B	HR	RBI	BB	IBB	SO	HBP	SH	SF	SB	CS	BA	OBA	SA	FA
1983	**NY-A**	**13**	**14**	**2**	**2**	**0**	**0**	**0**	**0**	**1**	**0**	**5**	**0**	**0**	**0**	**2**	**0**	**.143**	**.200**	**.143**	**.938**
1984	Cle-A	49	91	16	14	0	0	0	1	8	0	11	0	3	1	12	6	.154	.220	.154	1.000
1985	Cle-A	104	162	34	38	4	0	3	9	8	0	27	0	4	0	20	11	.235	.271	.315	.971
1986	Cle-A	105	95	33	25	4	1	0	8	13	0	12	0	2	0	23	6	.263	.352	.326	.969
1987	Cle-A	19	17	2	1	0	0	0	1	3	0	4	0	0	0	2	3	.059	.200	.059	1.000
1988	Mon-N	90	271	47	66	8	2	0	15	28	0	42	0	4	2	46	13	.244	.312	.288	.994
1989	Mon-N	126	258	41	56	7	2	0	21	33	1	36	0	2	0	37	12	.217	.306	.260	.988
1990	Mon-N	119	231	46	58	6	2	1	20	28	0	33	0	3	1	50	13	.251	.331	.307	1.000
1991	Atl-N	124	401	81	119	10	1	0	26	47	3	40	2	7	3	72	21	.297	.371	.327	.987
1992	Atl-N	120	456	79	134	14	2	2	22	39	2	54	0	5	2	41	18	.294	.348	.346	.991
1993	Atl-N	134	461	77	124	12	3	1	24	61	2	63	0	5	5	47	13	.269	.351	.315	.990
1994	Bos-A	103	398	60	109	15	1	0	25	55	1	65	0	6	2	42	10	.274	.360	.317	.989
1995	Tex-A	139	589	87	174	21	2	0	45	58	1	85	0	6	3	50	21	.295	.357	.338	.989
1996	Tor-A	125	496	87	142	15	1	1	29	71	1	68	1	7	0	54	13	.286	.377	.327	.994
1997	Tor-A	103	401	54	105	12	1	1	26	52	0	54	0	6	5	47	10	.262	.343	.304	.996
1997	LA-N	42	175	30	48	6	2	1	18	13	0	24	0	2	1	12	2	.274	.323	.349	.990
1998	Min-A	110	448	71	133	6	6	1	20	44	0	56	0	4	2	37	7	.297	.358	.344	.989
1999	Atl-N	84	151	31	31	2	1	0	8	23	1	15	0	1	1	26	7	.205	.309	.232	.981
Career average		95	284	49	77	8	2	1	18	33	1	39	0	4	2	34	10	.270	.343	.314	.986
Yankee average		**13**	**14**	**2**	**2**	**0**	**0**	**0**	**0**	**1**	**0**	**5**	**0**	**0**	**0**	**2**	**0**	**.143**	**.200**	**.143**	**.938**
Career total		1709	5115	878	1379	142	27	11	318	585	10	694	3	67	28	620	186	.270	.343	.314	.986
Yankee total		**13**	**14**	**2**	**2**	**0**	**0**	**0**	**0**	**1**	**0**	**5**	**0**	**0**	**0**	**2**	**0**	**.143**	**.200**	**.143**	**.938**

Nokes, Matthew Dodge

HEIGHT: 6'1" THROWS: RIGHT BATS: LEFT BORN: 10/31/1963 SAN DIEGO, CALIFORNIA POSITIONS PLAYED: C

YEAR	TEAM	GAMES	AB	RUNS	HITS	2B	3B	HR	RBI	BB	IBB	SO	HBP	SH	SF	SB	CS	BA	OBA	SA	FA
1985	SF-N	19	53	3	11	2	0	2	5	1	0	9	1	0	0	0	0	.208	.236	.358	.977
1986	Det-A	7	24	2	8	1	0	1	2	1	1	1	0	0	0	0	0	.333	.360	.500	1.000
1987	Det-A	135	461	69	133	14	2	32	87	35	2	70	6	3	3	2	1	.289	.345	.536	.992
1988	Det-A	122	382	53	96	18	0	16	53	34	3	58	1	6	2	0	1	.251	.313	.424	.989
1989	Det-A	87	268	15	67	10	0	9	39	17	1	37	2	1	2	1	0	.250	.298	.388	.978
1990	Det-A	44	111	12	30	5	1	3	8	4	3	14	2	0	1	0	0	.270	.305	.414	.984
1990	**NY-A**	**92**	**240**	**21**	**57**	**4**	**0**	**8**	**32**	**20**	**3**	**33**	**4**	**0**	**0**	**2**	**2**	**.238**	**.307**	**.354**	**1.000**
1991	**NY-A**	**135**	**456**	**52**	**122**	**20**	**0**	**24**	**77**	**25**	**5**	**49**	**5**	**0**	**7**	**3**	**2**	**.268**	**.308**	**.469**	**.992**
1992	**NY-A**	**121**	**384**	**42**	**86**	**9**	**1**	**22**	**59**	**37**	**11**	**62**	**3**	**0**	**6**	**0**	**1**	**.224**	**.293**	**.424**	**.993**
1993	**NY-A**	**76**	**217**	**25**	**54**	**8**	**0**	**10**	**35**	**16**	**2**	**31**	**2**	**0**	**3**	**0**	**0**	**.249**	**.303**	**.424**	**.992**
1994	**NY-A**	**28**	**79**	**11**	**23**	**3**	**0**	**7**	**19**	**5**	**0**	**16**	**0**	**0**	**1**	**0**	**0**	**.291**	**.329**	**.595**	**.975**
1995	Bal-A	26	49	4	6	1	0	2	6	4	0	11	0	0	1	0	0	.122	.185	.265	.989
1995	Col-N	10	11	1	2	1	0	0	0	1	1	4	0	0	0	0	0	.182	.250	.273	.909
Career average		69	210	24	53	7	0	10	32	15	2	30	2	1	2	1	1	.254	.308	.441	.982
Yankee average		**90**	**275**	**30**	**68**	**9**	**0**	**14**	**44**	**21**	**4**	**38**	**3**	**0**	**3**	**1**	**1**	**.249**	**.304**	**.437**	**.990**
Career total		902	2735	310	695	96	4	136	422	200	32	395	26	10	26	8	7	.254	.308	.441	.982
Yankee total		**452**	**1376**	**151**	**342**	**44**	**1**	**71**	**222**	**103**	**21**	**191**	**14**	**0**	**17**	**5**	**5**	**.249**	**.304**	**.437**	**.990**

Noren, Irving Arnold (Irv)

HEIGHT: 6'0" THROWS: LEFT BATS: LEFT BORN: 11/29/1924 JAMESTOWN, NEW YORK POSITIONS PLAYED: 1B, OF

YEAR	TEAM	GAMES	AB	RUNS	HITS	2B	3B	HR	RBI	BB	IBB	SO	HBP	SH	SF	SB	CS	BA	OBA	SA	FA
1950	Was-A	138	542	80	160	27	10	14	98	67	—	77	2	4	—	5	2	.295	.375	.459	.957
1951	Was-A	129	509	82	142	33	5	8	86	51	—	35	0	4	—	10	7	.279	.345	.411	.978
1952	Was-A	12	49	4	12	3	1	0	2	6	—	3	0	1	—	1	0	.245	.327	.347	1.000
1952	**NY-A**	**93**	**272**	**36**	**64**	**13**	**2**	**5**	**21**	**26**	—	**34**	**6**	**2**	—	**4**	**2**	**.235**	**.316**	**.353**	**.986**
1953	**NY-A**	**109**	**345**	**55**	**92**	**12**	**6**	**6**	**46**	**42**	—	**39**	**2**	**2**	—	**3**	**3**	**.267**	**.350**	**.388**	**.991**
1954	**NY-A**	**125**	**426**	**70**	**136**	**21**	**6**	**12**	**66**	**43**	—	**38**	**1**	**3**	**7**	**4**	**6**	**.319**	**.377**	**.481**	**.980**
1955	**NY-A**	**132**	**371**	**49**	**94**	**19**	**1**	**8**	**59**	**43**	**5**	**33**	**3**	**0**	**6**	**5**	**2**	**.253**	**.331**	**.375**	**.980**
1956	**NY-A**	**29**	**37**	**4**	**8**	**1**	**0**	**0**	**6**	**12**	**2**	**7**	**0**	**0**	**0**	**0**	**0**	**.216**	**.408**	**.243**	**1.000**
1957	KC-A	81	160	8	34	8	0	2	16	11	2	19	1	0	0	0	0	.213	.267	.300	1.000
1957	StL-N	17	30	3	11	4	1	1	10	4	2	6	0	0	1	0	1	.367	.429	.667	1.000
1958	StL-N	117	178	24	47	9	1	4	22	13	2	21	4	0	1	0	1	.264	.327	.393	.974
1959	StL-N	8	8	0	1	1	0	0	0	0	0	2	0	0	0	0	0	.125	.125	.250	1.000
1959	Chi-N	65	156	27	50	6	2	4	19	13	1	24	3	0	0	2	0	.321	.384	.462	1.000
1960	Chi-N	12	11	0	1	0	0	0	1	3	0	4	0	0	0	0	0	.091	.286	.091	1.000
1960	LA-N	26	25	1	5	0	0	1	1	1	0	8	0	0	0	0	0	.200	.231	.320	1.000
Career average		73	208	30	57	10	2	4	30	22	—	23	1	1	—	2	2	.275	.349	.410	.990
Yankee average		**98**	**290**	**43**	**79**	**13**	**3**	**6**	**40**	**33**	—	**30**	**2**	**1**	—	**3**	**3**	**.272**	**.351**	**.402**	**.987**
Career total		1093	3119	443	857	157	35	65	453	335	14	350	22	16	15	34	24	.275	.348	.410	.990
Yankee total		**488**	**1451**	**214**	**394**	**66**	**15**	**31**	**198**	**166**	**7**	**151**	**12**	**7**	**13**	**16**	**13**	**.272**	**.348**	**.402**	**.987**

Nunamaker, Leslie Grant

HEIGHT: 6'2" THROWS: RIGHT BATS: RIGHT BORN: 1/25/1889 MALCOLM, NEBRASKA DIED: 11/14/1938 HASTINGS, NEBRASKA POSITIONS PLAYED: C, 1B

YEAR	TEAM	GAMES	AB	RUNS	HITS	2B	3B	HR	RBI	BB	IBB	SO	HBP	SH	SF	SB	CS	BA	OBA	SA	FA
1911	Bos-A	62	183	18	47	4	3	0	19	12	—	—	0	12	—	1	—	.257	.303	.311	.972
1912	Bos-A	35	103	15	26	5	2	0	6	6	—	—	3	3	—	2	—	.252	.313	.340	.971
1913	Bos-A	29	65	9	14	5	2	0	9	8	—	8	1	2	—	2	—	.215	.311	.354	.977
1914	Bos-A	5	5	0	1	0	0	0	0	1	—	0	0	0	—	0	—	.200	.333	.200	1.000
1914	**NY-A**	**87**	**257**	**19**	**68**	**10**	**3**	**2**	**29**	**22**	—	**34**	**2**	**3**	—	**11**	**9**	**.265**	**.327**	**.350**	**.971**
1915	**NY-A**	**87**	**249**	**24**	**56**	**6**	**3**	**0**	**17**	**23**	—	**24**	**1**	**4**	—	**3**	**2**	**.225**	**.293**	**.273**	**.964**
1916	**NY-A**	**91**	**260**	**25**	**77**	**14**	**7**	**0**	**28**	**34**	—	**21**	**1**	**1**	—	**4**	—	**.296**	**.380**	**.404**	**.983**
1917	**NY-A**	**104**	**310**	**22**	**81**	**9**	**2**	**0**	**33**	**21**	—	**25**	**1**	**6**	—	**5**	—	**.261**	**.310**	**.303**	**.976**
1918	StL-A	85	274	22	71	9	2	0	22	28	—	16	5	8	—	6	—	.259	.339	.307	.714
1919	Cle-A	26	56	6	14	1	1	0	7	2	—	6	0	1	—	0	—	.250	.276	.304	.927
1920	Cle-A	34	54	10	18	3	3	0	14	4	—	5	0	1	—	1	—	.333	.379	.500	.963
1921	Cle-A	46	131	16	47	7	2	0	25	11	—	8	0	6	—	1	1	.359	.408	.443	.970
1922	Cle-A	25	43	8	13	2	0	0	7	4	—	3	0	2	—	0	0	.302	.362	.349	.936
Career average		55	153	15	41	6	2	0	17	14	—	—	1	4	—	3	—	.268	.332	.339	.948
Yankee average		**92**	**269**	**23**	**71**	**10**	**4**	**1**	**27**	**25**	—	**26**	**1**	**4**	—	**6**	—	**.262**	**.328**	**.332**	**.974**
Career total		716	1990	194	533	75	30	2	216	176	—	150	14	49	—	36	12	.268	.332	.339	.948
Yankee total		**369**	**1076**	**90**	**282**	**39**	**15**	**2**	**107**	**100**	—	**104**	**5**	**14**	—	**23**	**11**	**.262**	**.328**	**.332**	**.974**

Oates, Johnny Lane

HEIGHT: 5'11" THROWS: RIGHT BATS: LEFT BORN: 1/21/1946 SYLVA, NORTH CAROLINA POSITIONS PLAYED: C

YEAR	TEAM	GAMES	AB	RUNS	HITS	2B	3B	HR	RBI	BB	IBB	SO	HBP	SH	SF	SB	CS	BA	OBA	SA	FA
1970	Bal-A	5	18	2	5	0	1	0	2	2	0	0	0	0	1	0	0	.278	.333	.389	.939
1972	Bal-A	85	253	20	66	12	1	4	21	28	8	31	0	5	2	5	7	.261	.332	.364	.995
1973	Atl-N	93	322	27	80	6	0	4	27	22	4	31	1	6	0	1	4	.248	.299	.304	.981
1974	Atl-N	100	291	22	65	10	0	1	21	23	10	24	0	11	2	2	3	.223	.278	.268	.992
1975	Atl-N	8	18	0	4	1	0	0	0	1	0	4	0	0	0	0	0	.222	.263	.278	1.000
1975	Phi-N	90	269	28	77	14	0	1	25	33	10	29	0	4	4	1	0	.286	.359	.349	.990
1976	Phi-N	37	99	10	25	2	0	0	8	8	0	12	0	0	0	0	1	.253	.308	.273	.994
1977	LA-N	60	156	18	42	4	0	3	11	11	4	11	0	2	2	1	0	.269	.314	.353	.987
1978	LA-N	40	75	5	23	1	0	0	6	5	1	3	0	0	0	1	1	.307	.350	.320	.956
1979	LA-N	26	46	4	6	2	0	0	2	4	1	1	0	1	0	0	1	.130	.200	.174	.975
1980	**NY-A**	**39**	**64**	**6**	**12**	**3**	**0**	**1**	**3**	**2**	**0**	**3**	**1**	**0**	**0**	**1**	**2**	**.188**	**.224**	**.281**	**.991**
1981	**NY-A**	**10**	**26**	**4**	**5**	**1**	**0**	**0**	**0**	**2**	**0**	**0**	**0**	**0**	**0**	**0**	**0**	**.192**	**.250**	**.231**	**.963**
Career average		49	136	12	34	5	0	1	11	12	3	12	0	2	1	1	2	.250	.309	.313	.980
Yankee average		**25**	**45**	**5**	**9**	**2**	**0**	**1**	**2**	**2**	**0**	**2**	**1**	**0**	**0**	**1**	**1**	**.189**	**.232**	**.267**	**.977**
Career total		593	1637	146	410	56	2	14	126	141	38	149	2	29	11	11	19	.250	.309	.313	.980
Yankee total		**49**	**90**	**10**	**17**	**4**	**0**	**1**	**3**	**4**	**0**	**3**	**1**	**0**	**0**	**1**	**2**	**.189**	**.232**	**.267**	**.977**

O'Berry, Preston Michael
HEIGHT: 6'2"   THROWS: RIGHT   BATS: RIGHT   BORN: 4/20/1954 BIRMINGHAM, ALABAMA   POSITIONS PLAYED: C

YEAR	TEAM	GAMES	AB	RUNS	HITS	2B	3B	HR	RBI	BB	IBB	SO	HBP	SH	SF	SB	CS	BA	OBA	SA	FA
1979	Bos-A	43	59	8	10	1	0	1	4	5	0	16	1	2	1	0	0	.169	.242	.237	.957
1980	Chi-N	19	48	7	10	1	0	0	5	5	0	13	0	2	2	0	0	.208	.273	.229	.982
1981	Cin-N	55	111	6	20	3	1	1	5	14	0	19	0	3	0	0	0	.180	.272	.252	.983
1982	Cin-N	21	45	5	10	2	0	0	3	10	0	13	0	0	0	0	0	.222	.364	.267	.990
1983	Cal-A	26	60	7	10	1	0	1	5	3	0	11	0	2	0	0	0	.167	.206	.233	1.000
1984	**NY-A**	**13**	**32**	**3**	**8**	**2**	**0**	**0**	**5**	**2**	**0**	**2**	**0**	**0**	**0**	**0**	**0**	**.250**	**.294**	**.313**	**1.000**
1985	Mon-N	20	21	2	4	0	0	0	0	4	0	3	0	1	0	1	0	.190	.320	.190	1.000
Career average		28	54	5	10	1	0	0	4	6	0	11	0	1	0	0	0	.191	.274	.247	.987
Yankee average		**13**	**32**	**3**	**8**	**2**	**0**	**0**	**5**	**2**	**0**	**2**	**0**	**0**	**0**	**0**	**0**	**.250**	**.294**	**.313**	**1.000**
Career total		197	376	38	72	10	1	3	27	43	0	77	1	10	3	1	0	.191	.274	.247	.987
Yankee total		**13**	**32**	**3**	**8**	**2**	**0**	**0**	**5**	**2**	**0**	**2**	**0**	**0**	**0**	**0**	**0**	**.250**	**.294**	**.313**	**1.000**

O'Connor, John Joseph (Jack *or* Peach Pie)
HEIGHT: 5'10"   THROWS: RIGHT   BATS: RIGHT   BORN: 6/2/1869 ST.LOUIS, MISSOURI   DIED: 11/14/1937 ST.LOUIS, MISSOURI   POSITIONS PLAYED: C, 1B, OF

YEAR	TEAM	GAMES	AB	RUNS	HITS	2B	3B	HR	RBI	BB	IBB	SO	HBP	SH	SF	SB	CS	BA	OBA	SA	FA
1887	Cin-AA	12	40	4	4	0	0	0	1	2	—	—	0	—	—	3	—	.100	.143	.100	.813
1888	Cin-AA	36	137	14	28	3	1	1	17	6	—	—	0	—	—	12	—	.204	.238	.263	.852
1889	Col-AA	107	398	69	107	17	7	4	60	33	—	37	0	—	—	26	—	.269	.325	.377	.964
1890	Col-AA	121	457	89	148	14	10	2	66	38	—	—	0	—	—	29	—	.324	.376	.411	.929
1891	Col-AA	56	229	28	61	12	3	0	37	11	—	14	0	—	—	10	—	.266	.300	.345	.878
1892	Cle-N	140	572	71	142	22	5	1	58	25	—	48	0	—	—	17	—	.248	.280	.309	.966
1893	Cle-N	96	384	72	110	23	1	4	75	29	—	12	0	—	—	29	—	.286	.337	.383	.949
1894	Cle-N	86	330	67	104	23	7	2	51	15	—	7	0	—	—	15	—	.315	.345	.445	.983
1895	Cle-N	89	340	51	99	14	10	0	58	30	—	22	3	12	—	11	—	.291	.354	.391	.995
1896	Cle-N	68	256	41	76	11	1	1	43	15	—	12	0	0	—	15	—	.297	.336	.359	.966
1897	Cle-N	103	397	49	115	21	4	2	69	26	—	—	0	0	—	20	—	.290	.333	.378	.940
1898	Cle-N	131	478	50	119	17	4	1	56	26	—	—	2	11	—	8	—	.249	.291	.308	.983
1899	StL-N	84	289	33	73	5	6	0	43	15	—	—	0	0	—	7	—	.253	.289	.311	.943
1900	StL-N	10	32	4	7	0	0	0	6	2	—	—	2	0	—	0	—	.219	.300	.219	.957
1900	Pit-N	43	147	15	35	4	1	0	19	3	—	—	2	1	—	5	—	.238	.263	.279	1.000
1901	Pit-N	61	202	16	39	7	3	0	22	10	—	—	2	6	—	2	—	.193	.238	.257	.978
1902	Pit-N	49	170	13	50	1	2	1	28	3	—	—	0	3	—	2	—	.294	.306	.341	.979
1903	**NY-A**	**64**	**212**	**13**	**43**	**4**	**1**	**0**	**12**	**8**	**—**	**—**	**1**	**3**	**—**	**4**	**—**	**.203**	**.235**	**.231**	**1.000**
1904	StL-A	14	47	4	10	1	0	0	2	2	—	—	0	1	—	0	—	.213	.245	.234	.943
1906	StL-A	55	174	8	33	0	0	0	11	2	—	—	0	8	—	4	—	.190	.199	.190	.990
1907	StL-A	25	89	2	14	2	0	0	4	0	—	—	2	1	—	0	—	.157	.176	.180	.991
1910	StL-A	1	0	0	0	0	0	0	0	0	—	0	0	0	—	0	—	—	—	—	1.000
Career average		66	245	32	64	9	3	1	34	14	—	—	1	—	—	10	—	.263	.304	.336	.955
Yankee average		**64**	**212**	**13**	**43**	**4**	**1**	**0**	**12**	**8**	**—**	**—**	**1**	**3**	**—**	**4**	**—**	**.203**	**.235**	**.231**	**1.000**
Career total		1451	5380	713	1417	201	66	19	738	301	—	152	14	46	—	219	—	.263	.304	.336	.955
Yankee total		**64**	**212**	**13**	**43**	**4**	**1**	**0**	**12**	**8**	**—**	**—**	**1**	**3**	**—**	**4**	**—**	**.203**	**.235**	**.231**	**1.000**

O'Connor, Patrick Francis (Paddy)
HEIGHT: 5'8"   THROWS: RIGHT   BATS: RIGHT   BORN: 8/4/1879 COUNTY KERRY, IRELAND   DIED: 8/17/1950 SPRINGFIELD, MASSACHUSETTS   POSITIONS PLAYED: C

YEAR	TEAM	GAMES	AB	RUNS	HITS	2B	3B	HR	RBI	BB	IBB	SO	HBP	SH	SF	SB	CS	BA	OBA	SA	FA
1908	Pit-N	12	16	1	3	0	0	0	2	0	—	—	0	1	—	0	—	.188	.188	.188	.889
1909	Pit-N	9	16	1	5	1	0	0	3	0	—	—	0	0	—	0	—	.313	.313	.375	.750
1910	Pit-N	6	4	0	1	0	0	0	0	1	—	1	0	0	—	0	—	.250	.400	.250	1.000
1914	StL-N	10	9	0	0	0	0	0	0	2	—	2	1	0	—	0	—	.000	.250	.000	1.000
1915	Pit-F	70	219	15	50	10	1	0	16	14	—	30	1	7	—	4	—	.228	.278	.283	.987
1918	**NY-A**	**1**	**3**	**0**	**1**	**0**	**0**	**0**	**0**	**0**	**—**	**1**	**0**	**0**	**—**	**0**	**—**	**.333**	**.333**	**.333**	**1.000**
Career average		18	45	3	10	2	0	0	4	3	—	—	0	1	—	1	—	.225	.276	.273	.938
Yankee average		**1**	**3**	**0**	**1**	**0**	**0**	**0**	**0**	**0**	**—**	**1**	**0**	**0**	**—**	**0**	**—**	**.333**	**.333**	**.333**	**1.000**
Career total		108	267	17	60	11	1	0	21	17	—	34	2	8	—	4	—	.225	.276	.273	.938
Yankee total		**1**	**3**	**0**	**1**	**0**	**0**	**0**	**0**	**0**	**—**	**1**	**0**	**0**	**—**	**0**	**—**	**.333**	**.333**	**.333**	**1.000**

Odom, Herman Boyd (Heinie)

HEIGHT: 6'0"   THROWS: RIGHT   BATS: BOTH   BORN: 10/13/1900 RUSK, TEXAS   DIED: 8/31/1970 RUSK, TEXAS   POSITIONS PLAYED: 3B

YEAR	TEAM	GAMES	AB	RUNS	HITS	2B	3B	HR	RBI	BB	IBB	SO	HBP	SH	SF	SB	CS	BA	OBA	SA	FA
1925	NY-A	1	1	0	1	0	0	0	0	0	—	0	0	0	—	0	0	1.000	1.000	1.000	1.000
Career average		1	1	0	1	0	0	0	0	0	—	0	0	0	—	0	0	1.000	1.000	1.000	1.000
Yankee average		1	1	0	1	0	0	0	0	0	—	0	0	0	—	0	0	1.000	1.000	1.000	1.000
Career total		1	1	0	1	0	0	0	0	0	—	0	0	0	—	0	0	1.000	1.000	1.000	1.000
Yankee total		1	1	0	1	0	0	0	0	0	—	0	0	0	—	0	0	1.000	1.000	1.000	1.000

O'Doul, Francis Joseph (Lefty)

HEIGHT: 6'0"   THROWS: LEFT   BATS: LEFT   BORN: 3/4/1897 SAN FRANCISCO, CALIFORNIA   DIED: 12/7/1969 SAN FRANCISCO, CAL.   POSITIONS PLAYED: P, OF

YEAR	TEAM	GAMES	AB	RUNS	HITS	2B	3B	HR	RBI	BB	IBB	SO	HBP	SH	SF	SB	CS	BA	OBA	SA	FA
1919	NY-A	19	16	2	4	0	0	0	1	1	—	2	0	0	—	1	—	.250	.294	.250	.500
1920	NY-A	13	12	2	2	1	0	0	1	1	—	1	0	0	—	0	0	.167	.231	.250	.000
1922	NY-A	8	9	0	3	1	0	0	4	0	—	2	0	0	—	0	0	.333	.333	.444	1.000
1923	Bos-A	36	35	2	5	0	0	0	4	2	—	3	0	2	—	0	0	.143	.189	.143	.958
1928	NY-N	114	354	67	113	19	4	8	46	30	—	8	0	6	—	9	—	.319	.372	.463	.962
1929	Phi-N	154	638	152	254	35	6	32	122	76	—	19	4	13	—	2	—	.398	.465	.622	.971
1930	Phi-N	140	528	122	202	37	7	22	97	63	—	21	5	10	—	3	—	.383	.453	.604	.953
1931	Bro-N	134	512	85	172	32	11	7	75	48	—	16	3	1	—	5	—	.336	.396	.482	.954
1932	Bro-N	148	595	120	219	32	8	21	90	50	—	20	7	5	—	11	—	.368	.423	.555	.979
1933	Bro-N	43	159	14	40	5	1	5	21	15	—	6	1	0	—	2	—	.252	.320	.390	.947
1933	NY-N	78	229	31	70	9	1	9	35	29	—	17	2	1	—	1	—	.306	.388	.472	.974
1934	NY-N	83	177	27	56	4	3	9	46	18	—	7	1	1	—	2	—	.316	.383	.525	.968
Career average		81	272	52	95	15	3	9	45	28	—	10	2	3	—	3	—	.349	.413	.532	.847
Yankee average		13	12	1	3	1	0	0	2	1	—	2	0	0	—	0	—	.243	.282	.297	.500
Career total		970	3264	624	1140	175	41	113	542	333	—	122	23	39	—	36	0	.349	.413	.532	.847
Yankee total		40	37	4	9	2	0	0	6	2	—	5	0	0	—	1	0	.243	.282	.297	.500

Office, Rowland Johnie

HEIGHT: 6'0"   THROWS: LEFT   BATS: LEFT   BORN: 10/25/1952 SACRAMENTO, CALIFORNIA   POSITIONS PLAYED: OF

YEAR	TEAM	GAMES	AB	RUNS	HITS	2B	3B	HR	RBI	BB	IBB	SO	HBP	SH	SF	SB	CS	BA	OBA	SA	FA
1972	Atl-N	2	5	1	2	0	0	0	0	1	0	2	0	0	0	0	0	.400	.500	.400	1.000
1974	Atl-N	131	248	20	61	16	1	3	31	16	2	30	0	1	3	5	3	.246	.288	.355	.994
1975	Atl-N	126	355	30	103	14	1	3	30	23	4	41	3	5	2	2	2	.290	.337	.361	.967
1976	Atl-N	99	359	51	101	17	1	4	34	37	3	49	2	5	4	2	8	.281	.348	.368	.986
1977	Atl-N	124	428	42	103	13	1	5	39	23	1	58	3	4	3	2	4	.241	.282	.311	.988
1978	Atl-N	146	404	40	101	13	1	9	40	22	2	52	6	4	3	8	6	.250	.297	.354	.990
1979	Atl-N	124	277	35	69	14	2	2	37	27	2	33	2	1	0	5	4	.249	.320	.336	.988
1980	Mon-N	116	292	36	78	13	4	6	30	36	1	39	0	3	4	3	3	.267	.343	.401	.987
1981	Mon-N	26	40	4	7	0	0	0	0	4	0	6	0	0	0	0	0	.175	.250	.175	.938
1982	Mon-N	3	3	0	1	1	0	0	0	0	0	1	0	0	0	0	0	.333	.333	.667	1.000
1983	NY-A	2	2	0	0	0	0	0	1	0	0	0	0	0	1	0	0	.000	.000	.000	1.000
Career average		82	219	24	57	9	1	3	22	17	1	28	1	2	2	2	3	.259	.315	.350	.985
Yankee average		2	2	0	0	0	0	0	1	0	0	0	0	0	1	0	0	.000	.000	.000	1.000
Career total		899	2413	259	626	101	11	32	242	189	15	311	16	23	20	27	30	.259	.315	.350	.985
Yankee total		2	2	0	0	0	0	0	1	0	0	0	0	0	1	0	0	.000	.000	.000	1.000

Oldring, Ruben Henry (Rube)

HEIGHT: 5'10"   THROWS: RIGHT   BATS: RIGHT   BORN: 5/30/1884 NEW YORK, NEW YORK   DIED: 9/9/1961 BRIDGETON, NJ.   POSITIONS PLAYED: 1B, 2B, 3B, SS, OF

YEAR	TEAM	GAMES	AB	RUNS	HITS	2B	3B	HR	RBI	BB	IBB	SO	HBP	SH	SF	SB	CS	BA	OBA	SA	FA
1905	NY-A	8	30	2	9	0	1	1	6	2	—	—	0	1	—	4	—	.300	.344	.467	.967
1906	Phi-A	59	174	15	42	10	1	0	19	2	—	—	3	1	—	7	—	.241	.263	.310	.800
1907	Phi-A	117	441	48	126	27	8	1	40	7	—	—	5	7	—	29	—	.286	.305	.390	.974
1908	Phi-A	116	434	38	96	14	2	1	39	18	—	—	9	19	—	13	—	.221	.267	.270	.941
1909	Phi-A	90	326	39	75	13	8	1	28	20	—	—	6	15	—	17	—	.230	.287	.328	.963
1910	Phi-A	134	546	79	168	27	14	4	57	23	—	—	4	21	—	17	—	.308	.340	.430	.978
1911	Phi-A	121	495	84	147	11	14	3	59	21	—	—	5	26	—	21	—	.297	.332	.394	.979
1912	Phi-A	98	395	61	119	14	5	1	24	10	—	—	3	18	—	17	—	.301	.324	.370	.974
1913	Phi-A	137	538	101	152	27	9	5	71	34	—	37	2	18	—	40	—	.283	.328	.394	.968
1914	Phi-A	119	466	68	129	21	7	3	49	18	—	35	3	13	—	14	16	.277	.308	.371	.965
1915	Phi-A	107	408	49	101	23	3	6	42	22	—	21	4	5	—	11	6	.248	.293	.363	.982
1916	Phi-A	40	146	10	36	8	3	0	14	9	—	9	0	2	—	1	—	.247	.290	.342	.897
1916	NY-A	43	158	17	37	8	0	1	12	12	—	13	0	3	—	6	—	.234	.288	.304	.926
1918	Phi-A	49	133	5	31	2	1	0	11	8	—	10	1	6	—	0	—	.233	.282	.263	.833
Career average		88	335	44	91	15	5	2	34	15	—	—	3	11	—	14	—	.270	.307	.364	.940
Yankee average		26	94	10	23	4	1	1	9	7	—	—	0	2	—	5	—	.245	.297	.330	.967
Career total		1238	4690	616	1268	205	76	27	471	206	—	125	45	155	—	197	22	.270	.307	.364	.940
Yankee total		51	188	19	46	8	1	2	18	14	—	13	0	4	—	10	—	.245	.297	.330	.967

Oliver, Nathaniel (Nate *or* Pee Wee)

HEIGHT: 5'10"   THROWS: RIGHT   BATS: RIGHT   BORN: 12/13/1940 ST. PETERSBURG, FLORIDA   POSITIONS PLAYED: 2B, 3B, SS, OF

YEAR	TEAM	GAMES	AB	RUNS	HITS	2B	3B	HR	RBI	BB	IBB	SO	HBP	SH	SF	SB	CS	BA	OBA	SA	FA
1963	LA-N	65	163	23	39	2	3	1	9	13	0	25	1	0	1	3	4	.239	.298	.307	1.000
1964	LA-N	99	321	28	78	9	0	0	21	31	6	57	0	4	1	7	4	.243	.309	.271	.967
1965	LA-N	8	1	3	1	0	0	0	0	0	0	0	0	1	0	1	0	1.000	1.000	1.000	1.000
1966	LA-N	80	119	17	23	2	0	0	3	13	2	17	1	4	1	3	3	.193	.276	.210	.977
1967	LA-N	77	232	18	55	6	2	0	7	13	0	50	2	2	0	3	2	.237	.283	.280	.973
1968	SF-N	36	73	3	13	2	0	0	1	1	0	13	0	2	0	0	1	.178	.189	.205	.950
1969	NY-A	1	1	0	0	0	0	0	0	0	0	0	0	0	0	0	0	.000	.000	.000	.000
1969	Chi-N	44	44	15	7	3	0	1	4	1	0	10	1	3	0	0	1	.159	.196	.295	1.000
Career average		59	136	15	31	3	1	0	6	10	1	25	1	2	0	2	2	.226	.283	.268	.858
Yankee average		1	1	0	0	0	0	0	0	0	0	0	0	0	0	0	0	.000	.000	.000	.000
Career total		410	954	107	216	24	5	2	45	72	8	172	5	16	3	17	15	.226	.283	.268	.858
Yankee total		1	1	0	0	0	0	0	0	0	0	0	0	0	0	0	0	.000	.000	.000	.000

Oliver, Robert Lee

HEIGHT: 6'3"   THROWS: RIGHT   BATS: RIGHT   BORN: 2/8/1943 SHREVEPORT, LOUISIANA   POSITIONS PLAYED: 1B, 3B, OF

YEAR	TEAM	GAMES	AB	RUNS	HITS	2B	3B	HR	RBI	BB	IBB	SO	HBP	SH	SF	SB	CS	BA	OBA	SA	FA
1965	Pit-N	3	2	1	0	0	0	0	0	0	0	0	0	0	0	0	0	.000	.000	.000	1.000
1969	KC-A	118	394	43	100	8	4	13	43	21	2	74	2	6	2	5	5	.254	.294	.393	1.000
1970	KC-A	160	612	83	159	24	6	27	99	42	4	126	3	2	3	3	3	.260	.309	.451	.958
1971	KC-A	128	373	35	91	12	2	8	52	14	3	88	5	1	5	0	0	.244	.277	.351	.990
1972	KC-A	16	63	7	17	2	1	1	6	2	0	12	0	0	0	1	0	.270	.292	.381	.979
1972	Cal-A	134	509	47	137	20	4	19	70	27	8	97	3	0	5	4	3	.269	.307	.436	.994
1973	Cal-A	151	544	51	144	24	1	18	89	33	7	100	5	0	4	1	1	.265	.311	.412	.987
1974	Cal-A	110	359	22	89	9	1	8	55	16	2	51	1	0	6	2	1	.248	.277	.345	.939
1974	Bal-A	9	20	1	3	2	0	0	4	0	0	5	0	0	0	1	1	.150	.150	.250	.974
1975	NY-A	18	38	3	5	1	0	0	1	1	0	9	0	0	0	0	0	.132	.154	.158	1.000
Career average		94	324	33	83	11	2	10	47	17	3	62	2	1	3	2	2	.256	.295	.400	.982
Yankee average		18	38	3	5	1	0	0	1	1	0	9	0	0	0	0	0	.132	.154	.158	1.000
Career total		847	2914	293	745	102	19	94	419	156	26	562	19	9	25	17	14	.256	.295	.400	.982
Yankee total		18	38	3	5	1	0	0	1	1	0	9	0	0	0	0	0	.132	.154	.158	1.000

Paul Andrew O'Neill, of, 1993-2000

The Yankees don't have an official captain these days, but they have Paul O'Neill.

O'Neill, born February 25, 1963, in Columbus, Ohio, is a throwback to the old days. It would not be difficult to envision O'Neill as a ballplayer at the turn of the century, sitting next to Norm "Kid" Elberfeld, the diminutive tough guy from the New York Highlanders, watching him pouring straight whiskey on his spike wounds, then borrowing the bottle for his own use.

The 6 foot 4 inch O'Neill was a three-sport athlete in high school. He spent six years in the minors before being brought up by the Cincinnati Reds in 1987. He performed well for the Reds, but was known there as a free-swinger who struck out too much.

At the end of the 1992 season, O'Neill was traded to the Yankees for Roberto Kelly. It turned out to be a pretty good deal for New York. O'Neill has since become a five-time All-Star for the Yankees, and has hit .300 all six years he has been on the Yankee roster. In 1994, he hit a league-leading .359 with 21 home runs and 83 RBI, and was fifth in the league's MVP voting.

And in a way, the Kelly/O'Neill trade was the foundation of this rebuilt Yankee team. Since then, the Yankees of the 1980s, the bickerers, the malingerers, the problem players, have been sent packing. These new Yankees are like Paul O'Neill—tough, fundamentally sound, hard to beat.

O'Neill has always been solid in the postseason. His best series was, ironically, the only one the Yankees have lost in the last four years, when he hit .421 in 1997. That was the year the Yankees lost the divisional series to the Cleveland Indians. In 1999, his RBI single in the seventh inning gave the Yankees a 3-2 win over the Red Sox in Game 2 of the American League championship series.

After battling a painful hip injury throughout the 2000 playoffs, he bounced back in the World Series to collect nine hits, though a base on balls he earned late in Game 1 was probably his most memorable contribution. After a ten-pitch battle against the Mets' Armando Benitez, O'Neill was walked to first, and he eventually scored the tying run. The Yankees won the game, 4-3, in twelve innings.

O'Neill's .317 batting average with the Yankees is 5th best all-time. He trails only Babe Ruth, Lou Gehrig, Earle Combs and Joe DiMaggio.

O'Neill, Paul Andrew

HEIGHT: 6'4"   THROWS: LEFT   BATS: LEFT   BORN: 2/25/1963 COLUMBUS, OHIO   POSITIONS PLAYED: P, 1B, OF

YEAR	TEAM	GAMES	AB	RUNS	HITS	2B	3B	HR	RBI	BB	IBB	SO	HBP	SH	SF	SB	CS	BA	OBA	SA	FA
1985	Cin-N	5	12	1	4	1	0	0	1	0	0	2	0	0	0	0	0	.333	.333	.417	1.000
1986	Cin-N	3	2	0	0	0	0	0	0	1	0	1	0	0	0	0	0	.000	.333	.000	.000
1987	Cin-N	84	160	24	41	14	1	7	28	18	1	29	0	0	0	2	1	.256	.331	.488	.949
1988	Cin-N	145	485	58	122	25	3	16	73	38	5	65	2	3	5	8	6	.252	.306	.414	.984
1989	Cin-N	117	428	49	118	24	2	15	74	46	8	64	2	0	4	20	5	.276	.346	.446	.983
1990	Cin-N	145	503	59	136	28	0	16	78	53	13	103	2	1	5	13	11	.270	.339	.421	.993
1991	Cin-N	152	532	71	136	36	0	28	91	73	14	107	1	0	1	12	7	.256	.346	.481	.994
1992	Cin-N	148	496	59	122	19	1	14	66	77	15	85	2	3	6	6	3	.246	.346	.373	.997
1993	**NY-A**	**141**	**498**	**71**	**155**	**34**	**1**	**20**	**75**	**44**	**5**	**69**	**2**	**0**	**3**	**2**	**4**	**.311**	**.367**	**.504**	**.992**
1994	**NY-A**	**103**	**368**	**68**	**132**	**25**	**1**	**21**	**83**	**72**	**13**	**56**	**0**	**0**	**3**	**5**	**4**	**.359**	**.460**	**.603**	**.995**
1995	**NY-A**	**127**	**460**	**82**	**138**	**30**	**4**	**22**	**96**	**71**	**8**	**76**	**1**	**0**	**11**	**1**	**2**	**.300**	**.387**	**.526**	**.987**
1996	**NY-A**	**150**	**546**	**89**	**165**	**35**	**1**	**19**	**91**	**102**	**8**	**76**	**4**	**0**	**8**	**0**	**1**	**.302**	**.411**	**.474**	**1.000**
1997	**NY-A**	**149**	**553**	**89**	**179**	**42**	**0**	**21**	**117**	**75**	**8**	**92**	**0**	**0**	**9**	**10**	**7**	**.324**	**.399**	**.514**	**1.000**
1998	**NY-A**	**152**	**602**	**95**	**191**	**40**	**2**	**24**	**116**	**57**	**2**	**103**	**2**	**0**	**11**	**15**	**1**	**.317**	**.372**	**.510**	**.987**
1999	**NY-A**	**153**	**597**	**70**	**170**	**39**	**4**	**19**	**110**	**66**	**1**	**89**	**2**	**0**	**10**	**11**	**9**	**.285**	**.353**	**.459**	**.974**
2000	**NY-A**	**142**	**566**	**79**	**160**	**26**	**0**	**18**	**100**	**51**	**2**	**90**	**0**	**0**	**11**	**14**	**9**	**.283**	**.336**	**.424**	**.993**
Career average		113	400	57	116	25	1	15	71	50	6	65	1	0	5	7	4	.289	.365	.471	.922
Yankee average		**140**	**524**	**8**	**161**	**34**	**2**	**21**	**99**	**67**	**6**	**81**	**1**	**0**	**8**	**7**	**5**	**.308**	**.383**	**.496**	**.991**
Career total		1916	6808	964	1969	418	20	260	1199	844	103	1107	20	7	87	119	70	.289	.365	.471	.922
Yankee total		**1117**	**4190**	**643**	**1290**	**271**	**13**	**164**	**788**	**538**	**47**	**651**	**11**	**0**	**66**	**58**	**37**	**.308**	**.383**	**.496**	**.991**

O'Neill, Stephen Francis

HEIGHT: 5'10" THROWS: RIGHT BATS: RIGHT BORN: 7/6/1891 MINOOKA, PENNSYLVANIA DIED: 1/26/1962 CLEVELAND, OHIO POSITIONS PLAYED: C, 1B

YEAR	TEAM	GAMES	AB	RUNS	HITS	2B	3B	HR	RBI	BB	IBB	SO	HBP	SH	SF	SB	CS	BA	OBA	SA	FA
1911	Cle-A	9	27	1	4	1	0	0	1	4	—	—	1	1	—	2	—	.148	.281	.185	.986
1912	Cle-A	68	215	17	49	4	0	0	14	12	—	—	1	5	—	2	—	.228	.272	.247	.961
1913	Cle-A	78	234	19	69	13	3	0	29	10	—	24	2	8	—	5	—	.295	.329	.376	.973
1914	Cle-A	86	269	28	68	12	2	0	20	15	—	35	0	2	—	1	3	.253	.292	.312	.956
1915	Cle-A	121	386	32	91	14	2	2	34	26	—	41	5	9	—	2	3	.236	.293	.298	.968
1916	Cle-A	130	378	30	89	23	0	0	29	24	—	33	4	11	—	2	—	.235	.288	.296	.971
1917	Cle-A	129	370	21	68	10	0	0	29	41	—	55	4	14	—	2	—	.184	.272	.222	.980
1918	Cle-A	114	359	34	87	8	7	1	35	48	—	22	7	6	—	5	—	.242	.343	.312	.983
1919	Cle-A	125	398	46	115	35	7	2	47	48	—	21	5	10	—	4	—	.289	.373	.427	.977
1920	Cle-A	149	489	63	157	39	5	3	55	69	—	39	3	15	—	3	5	.321	.408	.440	.976
1921	Cle-A	106	335	39	108	22	1	1	50	57	—	22	2	11	—	0	1	.322	.424	.403	.982
1922	Cle-A	133	392	33	122	27	4	2	65	73	—	25	3	9	—	2	2	.311	.423	.416	.974
1923	Cle-A	113	330	31	82	12	0	0	50	64	—	34	2	8	—	0	4	.248	.374	.285	.968
1924	Bos-A	106	307	29	73	15	1	0	38	63	—	23	2	5	—	0	2	.238	.371	.293	.970
1925	**NY-A**	**35**	**91**	**7**	**26**	**5**	**0**	**1**	**13**	**10**	**—**	**3**	**1**	**2**	**—**	**0**	**0**	**.286**	**.363**	**.374**	**.946**
1927	StL-A	74	191	14	44	7	0	1	22	20	—	6	0	13	—	0	3	.230	.303	.283	.983
1928	StL-A	10	24	4	7	1	0	0	6	8	—	0	1	2	—	0	0	.292	.485	.333	.958
Career average		93	282	26	74	15	2	1	32	35	—	—	3	8	—	2	—	.263	.349	.337	.971
Yankee average		**35**	**91**	**7**	**26**	**5**	**0**	**1**	**13**	**10**	**—**	**3**	**1**	**2**	**—**	**0**	**0**	**.286**	**.363**	**.374**	**.946**
Career total		1586	4795	448	1259	248	34	13	537	592	—	383	43	131	—	30	23	.263	.349	.337	.971
Yankee total		**35**	**91**	**7**	**26**	**5**	**0**	**1**	**13**	**10**	**—**	**3**	**1**	**2**	**—**	**0**	**0**	**.286**	**.363**	**.374**	**.946**

O'Rourke, James Stephen (Queenie)

HEIGHT: 5'7" THROWS: RIGHT BATS: RIGHT BORN: 12/26/1883 BRIDGEPORT, CONN. DIED: 12/22/1955 SPARROWS POINT, MD. POSITIONS PLAYED: 2B, 3B, SS, OF

YEAR	TEAM	GAMES	AB	RUNS	HITS	2B	3B	HR	RBI	BB	IBB	SO	HBP	SH	SF	SB	CS	BA	OBA	SA	FA
1908	**NY-A**	**34**	**108**	**5**	**25**	**1**	**0**	**0**	**3**	**4**	**—**	**—**	**0**	**3**	**—**	**4**	**—**	**.231**	**.259**	**.241**	**.938**
Career average		34	108	5	25	1	0	0	3	4	—	—	0	3	—	4	—	.231	.259	.241	.000
Yankee average		**34**	**108**	**5**	**25**	**1**	**0**	**0**	**3**	**4**	**—**	**—**	**0**	**3**	**—**	**4**	**—**	**.231**	**.259**	**.241**	**.000**
Career total		34	108	5	25	1	0	0	3	4	—	—	0	3	—	4	—	.231	.259	.241	.000
Yankee total		**34**	**108**	**5**	**25**	**1**	**0**	**0**	**3**	**4**	**—**	**—**	**0**	**3**	**—**	**4**	**—**	**.231**	**.259**	**.241**	**.000**

Orth, Albert Lewis (Smilin' Al *or* The Curveless Wonder)

HEIGHT: 6'0" THROWS: RIGHT BATS: LEFT BORN: 9/5/1872 TIPTON, INDIANA DIED: 10/8/1948 LYNCHBURG, VIRGINIA POSITIONS PLAYED: P, 1B, 2B, SS, OF

YEAR	TEAM	GAMES	AB	RUNS	HITS	2B	3B	HR	RBI	BB	IBB	SO	HBP	SH	SF	SB	CS	BA	OBA	SA	FA
1895	Phi-N	11	45	8	16	4	0	1	13	1	—	6	0	2	—	0	—	.356	.370	.511	.842
1896	Phi-N	25	82	12	21	3	3	1	13	3	—	11	0	0	—	2	—	.256	.282	.402	.901
1897	Phi-N	53	152	26	50	7	4	1	17	3	—	—	0	2	—	5	—	.329	.342	.447	.929
1898	Phi-N	39	123	17	36	6	4	1	14	3	—	—	0	7	—	1	—	.293	.310	.431	.959
1899	Phi-N	22	62	5	13	3	1	1	5	1	—	—	0	1	—	2	—	.210	.222	.339	.793
1900	Phi-N	39	129	6	40	4	1	1	21	2	—	—	1	0	—	2	—	.310	.326	.380	.943
1901	Phi-N	41	128	14	36	6	0	1	15	3	—	—	1	0	—	3	—	.281	.303	.352	.945
1902	Was-A	56	175	20	38	3	2	2	10	9	—	—	0	3	—	2	—	.217	.255	.291	.923
1903	Was-A	55	162	19	49	9	7	0	11	4	—	—	1	1	—	3	—	.302	.323	.444	.920
1904	Was-A	31	102	7	22	3	1	0	11	1	—	—	2	0	—	2	—	.216	.238	.265	.816
1904	**NY-A**	**26**	**64**	**6**	**19**	**1**	**1**	**0**	**7**	**0**	**—**	**—**	**1**	**1**	**—**	**2**	**—**	**.297**	**.308**	**.344**	**.968**
1905	**NY-A**	**55**	**131**	**13**	**24**	**3**	**1**	**1**	**8**	**4**	**—**	**—**	**1**	**3**	**—**	**2**	**—**	**.183**	**.213**	**.244**	**.940**
1906	**NY-A**	**47**	**135**	**12**	**37**	**2**	**2**	**1**	**17**	**6**	**—**	**—**	**0**	**3**	**—**	**2**	**—**	**.274**	**.305**	**.341**	**.934**
1907	**NY-A**	**44**	**105**	**11**	**34**	**6**	**0**	**1**	**13**	**4**	**—**	**—**	**1**	**2**	**—**	**1**	**—**	**.324**	**.355**	**.410**	**.920**
1908	**NY-A**	**38**	**69**	**4**	**20**	**1**	**2**	**0**	**4**	**2**	**—**	**—**	**0**	**2**	**—**	**0**	**—**	**.290**	**.310**	**.362**	**.980**
1909	**NY-A**	**22**	**34**	**3**	**9**	**0**	**1**	**0**	**5**	**5**	**—**	**—**	**0**	**1**	**—**	**1**	**—**	**.265**	**.359**	**.324**	**1.000**
Career average		38	106	11	29	4	2	1	12	3	—	—	1	2	—	2	—	.273	.298	.366	.920
Yankee average		**39**	**90**	**8**	**24**	**2**	**1**	**1**	**9**	**4**	**—**	**—**	**1**	**2**	**—**	**1**	**—**	**.266**	**.297**	**.333**	**.957**
Career total		604	1698	183	464	61	30	12	184	51	—	17	8	28	—	30	—	.273	.298	.366	.920
Yankee total		**232**	**538**	**49**	**143**	**13**	**7**	**3**	**54**	**21**	**—**	**—**	**3**	**12**	**—**	**8**	**—**	**.266**	**.297**	**.333**	**.957**

Osteen, James Champlin (Champ)

HEIGHT: 5'8" THROWS: RIGHT BATS: LEFT BORN: 2/24/1877 HENDERSONVILLE, N. CAR. DIED: 12/14/1962 GREENVILLE, S. CARO. POSITIONS PLAYED: 1B, 3B, SS

YEAR	TEAM	GAMES	AB	RUNS	HITS	2B	3B	HR	RBI	BB	IBB	SO	HBP	SH	SF	SB	CS	BA	OBA	SA	FA
1903	Was-A	10	40	4	8	0	2	0	4	2	—	—	1	0	—	0	—	.200	.256	.300	.938
1904	**NY-A**	**28**	**107**	**15**	**21**	**1**	**4**	**2**	**9**	**1**	—	—	**2**	**1**	—	**0**	—	**.196**	**.218**	**.336**	**.930**
1908	StL-N	29	112	2	22	4	0	0	11	0	—	—	1	2	—	0	—	.196	.204	.232	.847
1909	StL-N	16	45	6	9	1	0	0	7	7	—	—	0	2	—	1	—	.200	.308	.222	.879
Career average		21	76	7	15	2	2	1	8	3	—	—	1	1	—	0	—	.197	.233	.276	.899
Yankee average		**28**	**107**	**15**	**21**	**1**	**4**	**2**	**9**	**1**	—	—	**2**	**1**	—	**0**	—	**.196**	**.218**	**.336**	**.930**
Career total		83	304	27	60	6	6	2	31	10	—	—	4	5	—	1	—	.197	.233	.276	.899
Yankee total		**28**	**107**	**15**	**21**	**1**	**4**	**2**	**9**	**1**	—	—	**2**	**1**	—	**0**	—	**.196**	**.218**	**.336**	**.930**

Otis, Paul Franklin (Bill)

HEIGHT: 5'11" THROWS: RIGHT BATS: LEFT BORN: 12/24/1889 SCITUATE, MASSACHUSETTS DIED: 12/15/1990 DULUTH, MINNESOTA POSITIONS PLAYED: OF

YEAR	TEAM	GAMES	AB	RUNS	HITS	2B	3B	HR	RBI	BB	IBB	SO	HBP	SH	SF	SB	CS	BA	OBA	SA	FA
1912	**NY-A**	**4**	**17**	**1**	**1**	**0**	**0**	**0**	**2**	**3**	—	—	**0**	**0**	—	**0**	—	**.059**	**.200**	**.059**	**.917**
Career average		4	17	1	1	0	0	0	2	3	—	—	0	0	—	0	—	.059	.200	.059	.917
Yankee average		**4**	**17**	**1**	**1**	**0**	**0**	**0**	**2**	**3**	—	—	**0**	**0**	—	**0**	—	**.059**	**.200**	**.059**	**.917**
Career total		4	17	1	1	0	0	0	2	3	—	—	0	0	—	0	—	.059	.200	.059	.917
Yankee total		**4**	**17**	**1**	**1**	**0**	**0**	**0**	**2**	**3**	—	—	**0**	**0**	—	**0**	—	**.059**	**.200**	**.059**	**.917**

Owen, Spike Dee

HEIGHT: 5'10" THROWS: RIGHT BATS: BOTH BORN: 4/19/1961 CLEBURNE, TEXAS POSITIONS PLAYED: 1B, 2B, 3B, SS

YEAR	TEAM	GAMES	AB	RUNS	HITS	2B	3B	HR	RBI	BB	IBB	SO	HBP	SH	SF	SB	CS	BA	OBA	SA	FA
1983	Sea-A	80	306	36	60	11	3	2	21	24	0	44	2	5	3	10	6	.196	.257	.271	.970
1984	Sea-A	152	530	67	130	18	8	3	43	46	0	63	3	9	2	16	8	.245	.308	.326	.977
1985	Sea-A	118	352	41	91	10	6	6	37	34	0	27	0	5	2	11	5	.259	.322	.372	.975
1986	Sea-A	112	402	46	99	22	6	0	35	34	1	42	1	7	2	1	3	.246	.305	.331	.973
1986	Bos-A	42	126	21	23	2	1	1	10	17	0	9	1	2	1	3	1	.183	.283	.238	.976
1987	Bos-A	132	437	50	113	17	7	2	48	53	2	43	1	9	4	11	8	.259	.337	.343	.975
1988	Bos-A	89	257	40	64	14	1	5	18	27	0	27	2	7	1	0	1	.249	.324	.370	.967
1989	Mon-N	142	437	52	102	17	4	6	41	76	25	44	3	3	3	3	2	.233	.349	.332	.979
1990	Mon-N	149	453	55	106	24	5	5	35	70	12	60	0	5	5	8	6	.234	.333	.342	.989
1991	Mon-N	139	424	39	108	22	8	3	26	42	11	61	1	4	4	2	6	.255	.321	.366	.986
1992	Mon-N	122	386	52	104	16	3	7	40	50	3	30	0	4	6	9	4	.269	.348	.381	.982
1993	**NY-A**	**103**	**334**	**41**	**78**	**16**	**2**	**2**	**20**	**29**	**2**	**30**	**0**	**3**	**1**	**3**	**2**	**.234**	**.294**	**.311**	**.968**
1994	Cal-A	82	268	30	83	17	2	3	37	49	0	17	1	3	0	2	8	.310	.418	.422	1.000
1995	Cal-A	82	218	17	50	9	3	1	28	18	1	22	0	1	0	3	2	.229	.288	.312	.952
Career average		110	352	42	87	15	4	3	31	41	4	37	1	5	2	6	4	.246	.324	.341	.976
Yankee average		**103**	**334**	**41**	**78**	**16**	**2**	**2**	**20**	**29**	**2**	**30**	**0**	**3**	**1**	**3**	**2**	**.234**	**.294**	**.311**	**.968**
Career total		1544	4930	587	1211	215	59	46	439	569	57	519	15	67	34	82	62	.246	.324	.341	.976
Yankee total		**103**	**334**	**41**	**78**	**16**	**2**	**2**	**20**	**29**	**2**	**30**	**0**	**3**	**1**	**3**	**2**	**.234**	**.294**	**.311**	**.968**

Paddock, Delmer Harold

HEIGHT: 5'9" THROWS: RIGHT BATS: LEFT BORN: 6/8/1887 VOLGA, SOUTH DAKOTA DIED: 2/6/1952 REMER, MINNESOTA POSITIONS PLAYED: 2B, 3B, OF

YEAR	TEAM	GAMES	AB	RUNS	HITS	2B	3B	HR	RBI	BB	IBB	SO	HBP	SH	SF	SB	CS	BA	OBA	SA	FA
1912	Chi-A	1	1	0	0	0	0	0	0	0	—	—	0	0	—	0	—	.000	.000	.000	.000
1912	**NY-A**	**46**	**156**	**26**	**45**	**5**	**3**	**1**	**14**	**23**	—	—	**4**	**2**	—	**9**	—	**.288**	**.393**	**.378**	**.894**
Career average		24	79	13	23	3	2	1	7	12	—	—	2	1	—	5	—	.287	.391	.376	.447
Yankee average		**46**	**156**	**26**	**45**	**5**	**3**	**1**	**14**	**23**	—	—	**4**	**2**	—	**9**	—	**.288**	**.393**	**.378**	**.894**
Career total		47	157	26	45	5	3	1	14	23	—	—	4	2	—	9	—	.287	.391	.376	.447
Yankee total		**46**	**156**	**26**	**45**	**5**	**3**	**1**	**14**	**23**	—	—	**4**	**2**	—	**9**	—	**.288**	**.393**	**.378**	**.894**

Pagliarulo, Michael Timothy (Pags)

HEIGHT: 6'1"   THROWS: RIGHT   BATS: LEFT   BORN: 3/15/1960 MEDFORD, MASSACHUSETTS   POSITIONS PLAYED: 1B, 2B, 3B, SS

YEAR	TEAM	GAMES	AB	RUNS	HITS	2B	3B	HR	RBI	BB	IBB	SO	HBP	SH	SF	SB	CS	BA	OBA	SA	FA
1984	NY-A	67	201	24	48	15	3	7	34	15	0	46	0	0	3	0	0	.239	.288	.448	.955
1985	NY-A	138	380	55	91	16	2	19	62	45	4	86	4	3	3	0	0	.239	.324	.442	.951
1986	NY-A	149	504	71	120	24	3	28	71	54	10	120	4	1	2	4	1	.238	.316	.464	1.000
1987	NY-A	150	522	76	122	26	3	32	87	53	9	111	2	2	3	1	3	.234	.305	.479	.959
1988	NY-A	125	444	46	96	20	1	15	67	37	9	104	2	1	6	1	0	.216	.276	.367	.943
1989	NY-A	74	223	19	44	10	0	4	16	19	0	43	2	0	0	1	1	.197	.266	.296	.936
1989	SD-N	50	148	12	29	7	0	3	14	18	4	39	1	1	0	2	0	.196	.287	.304	.936
1990	SD-N	128	398	29	101	23	2	7	38	39	3	66	3	2	4	1	3	.254	.322	.374	.955
1991	Min-A	121	365	38	102	20	0	6	36	21	3	55	3	2	2	1	2	.279	.322	.384	.965
1992	Min-A	42	105	10	21	4	0	0	9	1	0	17	1	0	1	1	0	.200	.213	.238	.962
1993	Min-A	83	253	31	74	16	4	3	23	18	2	34	5	2	1	6	6	.292	.350	.423	.984
1993	Bal-A	33	117	24	38	9	0	6	21	8	0	15	1	0	0	0	0	.325	.373	.556	1.000
1995	Tex-A	86	241	27	56	16	0	4	27	15	2	49	1	2	3	0	0	.232	.277	.349	.963
Career average		96	300	36	72	16	1	10	39	26	4	60	2	1	2	1	1	.241	.306	.407	.962
Yankee average		117	379	49	87	19	2	18	56	37	5	85	2	1	3	1	1	.229	.300	.427	.957
Career total		1246	3901	462	942	206	18	134	505	343	46	785	29	16	28	18	16	.241	.306	.407	.962
Yankee total		703	2274	291	521	111	12	105	337	223	32	510	14	7	17	7	5	.229	.300	.427	.957

Paschal, Benjamin Edwin

HEIGHT: 5'11"   THROWS: RIGHT   BATS: RIGHT   BORN: 10/13/1895 ENTERPRISE, ALABAMA   DIED: 11/10/1974 CHARLOTTE, N. CAROLINA   POSITIONS PLAYED: OF

YEAR	TEAM	GAMES	AB	RUNS	HITS	2B	3B	HR	RBI	BB	IBB	SO	HBP	SH	SF	SB	CS	BA	OBA	SA	FA
1915	Cle-A	9	9	0	1	0	0	0	0	0	—	3	0	0	—	0	0	.111	.111	.111	.000
1920	Bos-A	9	28	5	10	0	0	0	5	5	—	2	0	0	—	1	0	.357	.455	.357	1.000
1924	NY-A	4	12	2	3	1	0	0	3	1	—	0	0	0	—	0	0	.250	.308	.333	1.000
1925	NY-A	89	247	49	89	16	5	12	56	22	—	29	2	4	—	14	9	.360	.417	.611	.953
1926	NY-A	96	258	46	74	12	3	7	32	26	—	35	1	11	—	7	6	.287	.354	.438	.935
1927	NY-A	50	82	16	26	9	2	2	16	4	—	10	0	1	—	0	2	.317	.349	.549	.976
1928	NY-A	65	79	12	25	6	1	1	15	8	—	11	0	3	—	1	0	.316	.379	.456	1.000
1929	NY-A	42	72	13	15	3	0	2	11	6	—	3	0	3	—	1	1	.208	.269	.333	.951
Career average		46	98	18	30	6	1	3	17	9	—	12	0	3	—	3	2	.309	.369	.488	.974
Yankee average		58	125	23	39	8	2	4	22	11	—	15	1	4	—	4	3	.309	.368	.497	.969
Career total		364	787	143	243	47	11	24	138	72	—	93	3	22	—	24	18	.309	.369	.488	.974
Yankee total		346	750	138	232	47	11	24	133	67	—	88	3	22	—	23	18	.309	.368	.497	.969

Pasqua, Daniel Anthony

HEIGHT: 6'0"   THROWS: LEFT   BATS: LEFT   BORN: 10/17/1961 YONKERS, NEW YORK   POSITIONS PLAYED: 1B, OF

YEAR	TEAM	GAMES	AB	RUNS	HITS	2B	3B	HR	RBI	BB	IBB	SO	HBP	SH	SF	SB	CS	BA	OBA	SA	FA
1985	NY-A	60	148	17	31	3	1	9	25	16	4	38	1	0	1	0	0	.209	.289	.426	1.000
1986	NY-A	102	280	44	82	17	0	16	45	47	3	78	3	1	1	2	0	.293	.399	.525	.987
1987	NY-A	113	318	42	74	7	1	17	42	40	3	99	1	2	1	0	2	.233	.319	.421	1.000
1988	Chi-A	129	422	48	96	16	2	20	50	46	5	100	3	2	2	1	0	.227	.307	.417	.996
1989	Chi-A	73	246	26	61	9	1	11	47	25	1	58	1	1	4	1	2	.248	.315	.427	.993
1990	Chi-A	112	325	43	89	27	3	13	58	37	7	66	2	0	5	1	1	.274	.347	.495	.962
1991	Chi-A	134	417	71	108	22	5	18	66	62	4	86	3	1	1	0	2	.259	.358	.465	.988
1992	Chi-A	93	265	26	56	16	1	6	33	36	1	57	1	1	3	0	1	.211	.305	.442	1.000
1993	Chi-A	78	176	22	36	10	1	5	20	26	1	51	0	1	3	2	2	.205	.302	.358	.984
1994	Chi-A	11	23	2	5	2	0	2	4	0	0	9	0	0	0	0	0	.217	.217	.565	.500
Career average		91	262	34	64	13	2	12	39	34	3	64	2	1	2	1	1	.244	.330	.438	.941
Yankee average		92	249	34	62	9	1	14	37	34	3	72	2	1	1	1	1	.251	.344	.461	.996
Career total		905	2620	341	638	129	15	117	390	335	29	642	15	9	21	7	10	.244	.330	.438	.941
Yankee total		275	746	103	187	27	2	42	112	103	10	215	5	3	3	2	2	.251	.344	.461	.996

Patterson, Michael Lee

HEIGHT: 5'10"   THROWS: RIGHT   BATS: LEFT   BORN: 1/26/1958 SANTA MONICA, CALIFORNIA   POSITIONS PLAYED: OF

YEAR	TEAM	GAMES	AB	RUNS	HITS	2B	3B	HR	RBI	BB	IBB	SO	HBP	SH	SF	SB	CS	BA	OBA	SA	FA
1981	Oak-A	12	23	4	8	1	1	0	1	2	1	5	0	0	0	0	1	.348	.400	.478	1.000
1981	NY-A	4	9	2	2	0	2	0	0	0	0	0	0	0	0	0	0	.222	.222	.667	1.000
1982	NY-A	11	16	3	3	1	0	1	1	2	0	6	0	0	0	1	0	.188	.278	.438	1.000
Career average		9	16	3	4	1	1	0	1	1	0	4	0	0	0	0	0	.271	.327	.500	1.000
Yankee average		8	13	3	3	1	1	1	1	1	0	3	0	0	0	1	0	.200	.259	.520	1.000
Career total		27	48	9	13	2	3	1	2	4	1	11	0	0	0	1	1	.271	.327	.500	1.000
Yankee total		15	25	5	5	1	2	1	1	2	0	6	0	0	0	1	0	.200	.259	.520	1.000

Roger Thorpe Peckinpaugh, ss, 1913–21

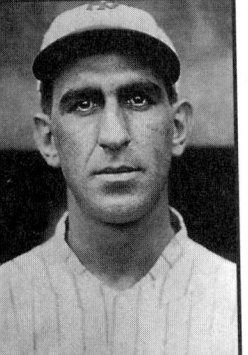

Roger Peckinpaugh is the answer to one of the more interesting trivia questions in New York Yankee history: He is the only shortstop to ever lead the team in home runs, and he did it twice, in 1914 and 1915.

Of course, Peckinpaugh, born on February 5, 1891, in Wooster, Ohio, hit five and three homers, respectively, to take team honors. But the smooth-fielding Peckinpaugh, along with Home Run Baker, was one of the building blocks on which Yankee management founded its first pennant-winner in 1921.

Peckinpaugh was a three-sport star at East Cleveland High School, who was signed by the Indians a few days after his graduation in 1910. After two so-so years in Cleveland, he was traded to New York in 1913. He became New York's regular shortstop almost immediately.

Peckinpaugh was quick, wide-ranging and had a good throwing arm. In his nine years with New York, he led American League shortstops in assists three times.

But he was also a very good hitter in the clutch. His batting average hovered around .260 throughout his Yankee career, but Peck was a good man in a pinch. Walter Johnson once admitted that if a home run could beat him, Babe Ruth was the toughest batter he ever faced. But if just a single was needed, Peckinpaugh was even tougher.

He was also a leader in the clubhouse. He was named captain of the Yankees in 1914 and also served as the team's manager for the last 20 games of that year. He was relieved of his managerial duties in 1915, but remained captain until he was traded in 1921. He was good friends with Ruth when the Babe came over from Boston, but that may have hurt Peckinpaugh in the long run. When Ruth and manager Miller Huggins were spatting in the early 1920s, Ruth suggested to the press several times that his buddy "Peck" would be a better manager.

By 1922, Huggins had begun solidifying his power base, and the 31-year-old Peckinpaugh was a casualty when the Yankees traded him to the Senators. Peckinpaugh played six more years with Washington and Cleveland, then worked for many years as a manager. He died on November 17, 1977, in Cleveland.

Peckinpaugh is 14th on the Yankees' all-time list with 143 stolen bases.

Peckinpaugh, Roger Thorpe

HEIGHT: 5'10" THROWS: RIGHT BATS: RIGHT BORN: 2/5/1891 WOOSTER, OHIO DIED: 11/17/1977 CLEVELAND, OHIO POSITIONS PLAYED: 1B, SS

YEAR	TEAM	GAMES	AB	RUNS	HITS	2B	3B	HR	RBI	BB	IBB	SO	HBP	SH	SF	SB	CS	BA	OBA	SA	FA
1910	Cle-A	15	45	1	9	0	0	0	6	1	—	—	1	3	—	3	—	.200	.234	.200	.906
1912	Cle-A	69	236	18	50	4	1	1	22	16	—	—	0	6	—	11	—	.212	.262	.250	.924
1913	Cle-A	1	0	1	0	0	0	0	0	0	—	0	0	0	—	0	—	—	—	—	.000
1913	NY-A	95	340	35	91	10	7	1	32	24	—	47	0	9	—	19	—	.268	.316	.347	.931
1914	NY-A	157	570	55	127	14	6	3	51	51	—	73	1	13	—	38	17	.223	.288	.284	.956
1915	NY-A	142	540	67	119	18	7	5	44	49	—	72	3	33	—	19	12	.220	.289	.307	.942
1916	NY-A	146	552	65	141	22	8	4	58	62	—	50	1	20	—	18	—	.255	.332	.346	.946
1917	NY-A	148	543	63	141	24	7	0	41	64	—	46	2	20	—	17	—	.260	.340	.330	.934
1918	NY-A	122	446	59	103	15	3	0	43	43	—	41	3	25	—	12	—	.231	.303	.278	.961
1919	NY-A	122	453	89	138	20	2	7	33	59	—	37	4	23	—	10	—	.305	.390	.404	.943
1920	NY-A	139	534	109	144	26	6	8	54	72	—	47	0	14	—	8	12	.270	.356	.386	.962
1921	NY-A	149	577	128	166	25	7	8	71	84	—	44	2	33	—	2	2	.288	.380	.397	.948
1922	Was-A	147	520	62	132	14	4	2	48	55	—	36	3	23	—	11	6	.254	.329	.308	.951
1923	Was-A	154	568	73	150	18	4	2	62	64	—	30	1	40	—	10	8	.264	.340	.320	.948
1924	Was-A	155	523	72	142	20	5	2	73	72	—	45	0	20	—	9	6	.272	.360	.340	.963
1925	Was-A	126	422	67	124	16	4	4	64	49	—	23	0	22	—	13	4	.294	.367	.379	1.000
1926	Was-A	57	147	19	35	4	1	0	14	28	—	12	0	3	—	3	0	.238	.360	.299	.875
1927	Chi-A	68	217	23	64	6	3	0	23	21	—	6	1	7	—	2	3	.295	.360	.350	.964
Career average		112	402	56	104	14	4	3	41	45	—	—	1	17	—	11	—	.259	.336	.335	.892
Yankee average		**136**	**506**	**74**	**130**	**19**	**6**	**4**	**47**	**56**	**—**	**51**	**2**	**21**	**—**	**16**	**—**	**.257**	**.334**	**.342**	**.947**
Career total		2012	7233	1006	1876	256	75	48	739	814	—	609	22	314	—	205	70	.259	.336	.335	.892
Yankee total		**1220**	**4555**	**670**	**1170**	**174**	**53**	**36**	**427**	**508**	**—**	**457**	**16**	**190**	**—**	**143**	**43**	**.257**	**.334**	**.342**	**.947**

Pepitone, Joseph Anthony (Pepi)

HEIGHT: 6'2"   THROWS: LEFT   BATS: LEFT   BORN: 10/9/1940 BROOKLYN, NEW YORK   POSITIONS PLAYED: 1B, OF

YEAR	TEAM	GAMES	AB	RUNS	HITS	2B	3B	HR	RBI	BB	IBB	SO	HBP	SH	SF	SB	CS	BA	OBA	SA	FA
1962	NY-A	63	138	14	33	3	2	7	17	3	0	21	0	0	0	1	1	.239	.255	.442	.982
1963	NY-A	157	580	79	157	16	3	27	89	23	2	63	7	0	5	3	5	.271	.304	.448	.931
1964	NY-A	160	613	71	154	12	3	28	100	24	7	63	3	2	5	2	1	.251	.281	.418	1.000
1965	NY-A	143	531	51	131	18	3	18	62	43	11	59	2	3	1	4	2	.247	.305	.394	.980
1966	NY-A	152	585	85	149	21	4	31	83	29	6	58	2	0	5	4	3	.255	.290	.463	.967
1967	NY-A	133	501	45	126	18	3	13	64	34	4	62	3	3	4	1	3	.251	.301	.377	.980
1968	NY-A	108	380	41	93	9	3	15	56	37	9	45	1	0	3	8	2	.245	.311	.403	1.000
1969	NY-A	135	513	49	124	16	3	27	70	30	11	42	1	0	2	8	6	.242	.284	.442	.995
1970	Hou-N	75	279	44	70	9	5	14	35	18	9	28	1	0	1	5	2	.251	.298	.470	.995
1970	Chi-N	56	213	38	57	9	2	12	44	15	2	15	0	4	2	0	2	.268	.313	.498	.992
1971	Chi-N	115	427	50	131	19	4	16	61	24	8	41	4	2	3	1	1	.307	.347	.482	.990
1972	Chi-N	66	214	23	56	5	0	8	21	13	4	22	3	0	3	1	2	.262	.309	.397	.997
1973	Chi-N	31	112	16	30	3	0	3	18	8	0	6	1	0	1	3	1	.268	.320	.375	.985
1973	Atl-N	3	11	0	4	0	0	0	1	1	0	1	0	0	0	0	0	.364	.417	.364	.983
Career average	100	364	43	94	11	3	16	52	22	5	38	2	1	3	3	2	.258	.301	.432	.984
Yankee average	**131**	**480**	**54**	**121**	**14**	**3**	**21**	**68**	**28**	**6**	**52**	**2**	**1**	**3**	**4**	**3**	**.252**	**.294**	**.423**	**.979**
Career total	1397	5097	606	1315	158	35	219	721	302	73	526	28	14	35	41	32	.258	.301	.432	.984
Yankee total	**1051**	**3841**	**435**	**967**	**113**	**24**	**166**	**541**	**223**	**50**	**413**	**19**	**8**	**25**	**31**	**23**	**.252**	**.294**	**.423**	**.979**

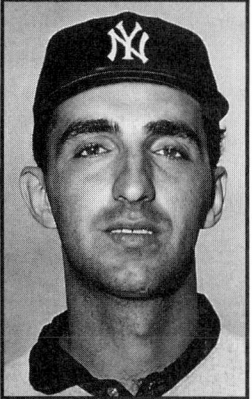

Joseph Anthony "Pepi" Pepitone, 1b-of, 1962–69

The fans loved him, as did most of his teammates, but it's safe to say that Joe Pepitone was never the darling of Yankee management.

Pepitone, born October 9, 1940, in Brooklyn, New York, was the unquestioned star of his high school baseball team in Brooklyn. The Yankees desired him greatly, even after he was involved in an accidental shooting. (He was shot just below the heart by a friend who was showing off his new .38 pistol.) New York signed him for $20,000 in 1958 and he immediately blew the money on a car and a speedboat.

He spent four years in the minors, moving quickly up the Yankee ladder. He was known almost as much for his late-night antics as for his hitting, which was considerable. In six of his final seven seasons with New York, Pepitone had at least 120 hits. From 1963–69, he averaged more than 23 home runs and 75 RBI.

Though he was a very good player and a three-time All-Star in New York, Pepitone was uncomfortable with convention. His teammates were aghast when he brought a hair-dryer with him on the road. He respected his teammates, but even as a first-year player, demanded respect himself, a position that did not necessarily endear him to some of the older players. He enjoyed the New York nightlife.

Pepi was a big fan favorite. He was an affable star, always available for autographs, always willing to stop and talk with an admirer, and he always played hard. He was an excellent fielder, winning three Gold Gloves with the Yankees at first base.

As the Yankees began their slow decline in the late 1960s, Pepitone was one of the few players for whom fans could root. But the Yankee front office was getting tired of his antics and traded him to the Houston Astros just before the 1970 season.

Pepitone spent four years playing for various National League teams before accepting an offer to play overseas in Japan.

Pepitone is 15th on the Yankees' all-time home run list with 166.

Perez, Martin Roman

HEIGHT: 5'11" THROWS: RIGHT BATS: RIGHT BORN: 2/28/1947 VISALIA, CALIFORNIA POSITIONS PLAYED: 2B, 3B, SS

YEAR	TEAM	GAMES	AB	RUNS	HITS	2B	3B	HR	RBI	BB	IBB	SO	HBP	SH	SF	SB	CS	BA	OBA	SA	FA
1969	Cal-A	13	13	3	3	0	0	0	0	2	0	1	0	0	0	0	0	.231	.333	.231	1.000
1970	Cal-A	3	3	0	0	0	0	0	1	0	0	0	0	0	0	0	0	.000	.000	.000	.833
1971	Atl-N	130	410	28	93	15	3	4	32	25	5	44	1	7	2	1	2	.227	.272	.307	.000
1972	Atl-N	141	479	33	109	13	1	1	28	30	1	55	3	3	3	0	3	.228	.276	.265	.957
1973	Atl-N	141	501	66	125	15	5	8	57	49	1	66	2	10	5	2	3	.250	.316	.347	.962
1974	Atl-N	127	447	51	116	20	5	2	34	35	1	51	1	7	1	2	0	.260	.314	.340	.985
1975	Atl-N	120	461	50	127	14	2	2	34	37	2	44	0	7	3	2	2	.275	.327	.328	.917
1976	Atl-N	31	96	12	24	4	0	1	6	8	0	9	0	4	1	0	0	.250	.305	.323	1.000
1976	SF-N	93	332	37	86	13	1	2	26	30	0	28	0	10	3	3	4	.259	.318	.322	.979
1977	**NY-A**	**1**	**4**	**0**	**2**	**0**	**0**	**0**	**0**	**0**	**0**	**1**	**0**	**0**	**0**	**0**	**0**	**.500**	**.500**	**.500**	**1.000**
1977	Oak-A	115	373	32	86	14	5	2	23	29	0	65	3	7	2	1	3	.231	.290	.311	.974
1978	Oak-A	16	12	1	0	0	0	0	0	0	0	5	0	1	0	0	0	.000	.000	.000	1.000
Career average		78	261	26	64	9	2	2	20	20	1	31	1	5	2	1	1	.246	.301	.316	.884
Yankee average		**1**	**4**	**0**	**2**	**0**	**0**	**0**	**0**	**0**	**0**	**1**	**0**	**0**	**0**	**0**	**0**	**.500**	**.500**	**.500**	**1.000**
Career total		931	3131	313	771	108	22	22	241	245	10	369	10	56	20	11	17	.246	.301	.316	.884
Yankee total		**1**	**4**	**0**	**2**	**0**	**0**	**0**	**0**	**0**	**0**	**1**	**0**	**0**	**0**	**0**	**0**	**.500**	**.500**	**.500**	**1.000**

Perkins, Ralph Foster (Cy)

HEIGHT: 5'10" THROWS: RIGHT BATS: RIGHT BORN: 2/27/1896, GLOUCESTER, MASS. DIED: 10/2/1963 PHILADELPHIA, PENN. POSITIONS PLAYED: C, 1B, 2B, 3B, SS

YEAR	TEAM	GAMES	AB	RUNS	HITS	2B	3B	HR	RBI	BB	IBB	SO	HBP	SH	SF	SB	CS	BA	OBA	SA	FA
1915	Phi-A	7	20	2	4	1	0	0	0	3	—	3	0	1	—	0	0	.200	.304	.250	.920
1917	Phi-A	6	18	1	3	0	0	0	2	2	—	1	0	1	—	0	—	.167	.250	.167	.978
1918	Phi-A	68	218	9	41	4	1	1	14	8	—	15	0	4	—	1	—	.188	.217	.229	.990
1919	Phi-A	101	305	22	77	12	7	2	29	27	—	22	0	4	—	2	—	.252	.313	.357	.971
1920	Phi-A	148	492	40	128	24	6	5	52	28	—	35	2	13	—	5	6	.260	.303	.364	1.000
1921	Phi-A	141	538	58	155	31	4	12	73	32	—	32	1	10	—	5	9	.288	.329	.428	.971
1922	Phi-A	148	505	58	135	20	6	6	69	40	—	30	1	14	—	1	7	.267	.322	.366	.984
1923	Phi-A	143	500	53	135	34	5	2	65	65	—	30	2	13	—	1	3	.270	.356	.370	.971
1924	Phi-A	128	392	31	95	19	4	0	32	31	—	20	4	5	—	3	4	.242	.304	.311	.983
1925	Phi-A	65	140	21	43	10	0	1	18	26	—	6	3	8	—	0	0	.307	.426	.400	.980
1926	Phi-A	63	148	14	43	6	0	0	19	18	—	7	1	14	—	0	2	.291	.371	.331	.984
1927	Phi-A	59	137	11	35	7	2	1	15	12	—	8	0	5	—	0	2	.255	.315	.358	.979
1928	Phi-A	19	29	1	5	0	0	0	1	1	—	1	0	1	—	0	1	.172	.200	.172	.982
1929	Phi-A	38	76	4	16	4	0	0	9	5	—	4	0	3	—	0	0	.211	.259	.263	.990
1930	Phi-A	20	38	1	6	2	0	0	4	2	—	3	0	0	—	0	0	.158	.200	.211	.964
1931	**NY-A**	**16**	**47**	**3**	**12**	**1**	**0**	**0**	**7**	**1**	**—**	**4**	**1**	**0**	**—**	**0**	**0**	**.255**	**.286**	**.277**	**1.000**
1934	Det-A	1	1	0	0	0	0	0	0	0	—	0	0	0	—	0	0	.000	.000	.000	.000
Career average		69	212	19	55	10	2	2	24	18	—	13	1	6	—	1	—	.259	.319	.352	.920
Yankee average		**16**	**47**	**3**	**12**	**1**	**0**	**0**	**7**	**1**	**—**	**4**	**1**	**0**	**—**	**0**	**0**	**.255**	**.286**	**.277**	**1.000**
Career total		1171	3604	329	933	175	35	30	409	301	—	221	15	96	—	18	34	.259	.319	.352	.920
Yankee total		**16**	**47**	**3**	**12**	**1**	**0**	**0**	**7**	**1**	**—**	**4**	**1**	**0**	**—**	**0**	**0**	**.255**	**.286**	**.277**	**1.000**

Phelps, Kenneth Allen

HEIGHT: 6'1" THROWS: LEFT BATS: LEFT BORN: 8/6/1954 SEATTLE, WASHINGTON POSITIONS PLAYED: 1B

YEAR	TEAM	GAMES	AB	RUNS	HITS	2B	3B	HR	RBI	BB	IBB	SO	HBP	SH	SF	SB	CS	BA	OBA	SA	FA
1980	KC-A	3	4	0	0	0	0	0	0	0	0	2	0	0	0	0	0	.000	.000	.000	1.000
1981	KC-A	21	22	1	3	0	1	0	1	1	0	13	0	0	0	0	0	.136	.174	.227	1.000
1982	Mon-N	10	8	0	2	0	0	0	0	0	0	3	1	0	0	0	0	.250	.333	.250	.000
1983	Sea-A	50	127	10	30	4	1	7	16	13	0	25	0	1	3	0	0	.236	.301	.449	1.000
1984	Sea-A	101	290	52	70	9	0	24	51	61	5	73	5	0	4	3	3	.241	.378	.521	.987
1985	Sea-A	61	116	18	24	3	0	9	24	24	2	33	0	0	0	2	0	.207	.343	.466	1.000
1986	Sea-A	125	344	69	85	16	4	24	64	88	6	96	6	0	3	2	3	.247	.406	.526	.983
1987	Sea-A	120	332	68	86	13	1	27	68	80	5	75	8	0	4	1	1	.259	.410	.548	1.000
1988	Sea-A	72	190	37	54	8	0	14	32	51	2	35	1	0	2	1	0	.284	.434	.547	.952
1988	**NY-A**	**45**	**107**	**17**	**24**	**5**	**0**	**10**	**22**	**19**	**3**	**26**	**0**	**0**	**1**	**0**	**0**	**.224**	**.339**	**.551**	**.980**
1989	**NY-A**	**86**	**185**	**26**	**46**	**3**	**0**	**7**	**29**	**27**	**2**	**47**	**0**	**0**	**3**	**0**	**0**	**.249**	**.340**	**.378**	**.983**
1989	Oak-A	11	9	0	1	1	0	0	0	4	0	4	0	0	0	0	0	.111	.385	.222	.000
1990	Oak-A	32	59	6	11	2	0	1	6	12	1	10	0	0	1	0	0	.186	.319	.271	.992
1990	Cle-A	24	61	4	7	0	0	0	10	2	0	11	0	0	0	1	0	.115	.239	.115	1.000

(continued)

(continued)

	GAMES	AB	RUNS	HITS	2B	3B	HR	RBI	BB	IBB	SO	HBP	SH	SF	SB	CS	BA	OBA	SA	FA
Career average	54	132	22	32	5	1	9	22	28	2	32	2	0	2	1	1	.239	.374	.480	.848
Yankee average	**66**	**146**	**22**	**35**	**4**	**0**	**9**	**26**	**23**	**3**	**37**	**0**	**0**	**2**	**0**	**0**	**.240**	**.339**	**.442**	**.982**
Career total	761	1854	308	443	64	7	123	313	390	28	449	21	1	21	10	7	.239	.374	.480	.848
Yankee total	**131**	**292**	**43**	**70**	**8**	**0**	**17**	**51**	**46**	**5**	**73**	**0**	**0**	**4**	**0**	**0**	**.240**	**.339**	**.442**	**.982**

Phillips, Edward David
HEIGHT: 6'0"   THROWS: RIGHT   BATS: RIGHT   BORN: 2/17/1901 WORCESTER, MASSACHUSETTS   DIED: 1/26/1968 BUFFALO, NEW YORK   POSITIONS PLAYED: C

YEAR	TEAM	GAMES	AB	RUNS	HITS	2B	3B	HR	RBI	BB	IBB	SO	HBP	SH	SF	SB	CS	BA	OBA	SA	FA
1924	Bos-N	3	3	0	0	0	0	0	0	0	—	2	0	0	—	0	0	.000	.000	.000	1.000
1929	Det-A	68	221	24	52	13	1	2	21	20	—	16	1	7	—	0	1	.235	.302	.330	.967
1931	Pit-N	106	353	30	82	18	3	7	44	41	—	49	3	4	—	1	—	.232	.317	.360	.986
1932	**NY-A**	**9**	**31**	**4**	**9**	**1**	**0**	**2**	**4**	**2**	**—**	**3**	**0**	**0**	**—**	**1**	**0**	**.290**	**.333**	**.516**	**1.000**
1934	Was-A	56	169	6	33	6	1	2	16	26	—	24	1	4	—	1	0	.195	.306	.278	.984
1935	Cle-A	70	220	18	60	16	1	1	41	15	—	21	0	0	—	0	0	.273	.319	.368	.980
Career average	52	166	14	39	9	1	2	21	17	—	19	1	3	—	1	—	.237	.312	.345	.986
Yankee average	**9**	**31**	**4**	**9**	**1**	**0**	**2**	**4**	**2**	**—**	**3**	**0**	**0**	**—**	**1**	**0**	**.290**	**.333**	**.516**	**1.000**
Career total	312	997	82	236	54	6	14	126	104	—	115	5	15	—	3	1	.237	.312	.345	.986
Yankee total	**9**	**31**	**4**	**9**	**1**	**0**	**2**	**4**	**2**	**—**	**3**	**0**	**0**	**—**	**1**	**0**	**.290**	**.333**	**.516**	**1.000**

Phillips, John Stephen
HEIGHT: 6'4"   THROWS: RIGHT   BATS: RIGHT   BORN: 9/6/1921 CLARENCE, NEW YORK   POSITIONS PLAYED: P, 1B, 2B, 3B, OF

YEAR	TEAM	GAMES	AB	RUNS	HITS	2B	3B	HR	RBI	BB	IBB	SO	HBP	SH	SF	SB	CS	BA	OBA	SA	FA
1947	**NY-A**	**16**	**36**	**5**	**10**	**0**	**1**	**1**	**2**	**3**	**—**	**5**	**0**	**0**	**—**	**0**	**0**	**.278**	**.333**	**.417**	**.986**
1948	**NY-A**	**1**	**2**	**0**	**0**	**0**	**0**	**0**	**0**	**0**	**—**	**1**	**0**	**0**	**—**	**0**	**0**	**.000**	**.000**	**.000**	**.889**
1949	**NY-A**	**45**	**91**	**16**	**28**	**4**	**1**	**1**	**10**	**12**	**—**	**9**	**0**	**2**	**—**	**1**	**0**	**.308**	**.388**	**.407**	**.977**
1949	Pit-N	18	56	6	13	3	1	0	3	4	—	6	0	0	—	1	—	.232	.283	.321	1.000
1950	Pit-N	69	208	25	61	7	6	5	34	20	—	17	0	1	—	1	—	.293	.355	.457	.986
1951	Pit-N	70	156	12	37	7	3	0	12	15	—	17	0	3	—	1	2	.237	.304	.321	.900
1952	Pit-N	1	1	0	0	0	0	0	0	0	—	0	0	0	—	0	0	.000	.000	.000	1.000
1955	Det-A	55	117	15	37	8	2	1	20	10	0	12	0	2	2	0	0	.316	.364	.444	.992
1956	Det-A	67	224	31	66	13	2	1	20	21	0	19	0	1	1	1	1	.295	.354	.384	.981
1957	Det-A	1	1	1	0	0	0	0	0	0	0	0	0	0	0	0	0	.000	.000	.000	.000
Career average	34	89	11	25	4	2	1	10	9	—	9	0	1	—	1	—	.283	.345	.396	.968
Yankee average	**21**	**43**	**7**	**13**	**1**	**1**	**1**	**4**	**5**	**—**	**5**	**0**	**1**	**—**	**0**	**0**	**.295**	**.368**	**.403**	**.951**
Career total	343	892	111	252	42	16	9	101	85	—	86	0	9	3	5	3	.283	.344	.396	.968
Yankee total	**62**	**129**	**21**	**38**	**4**	**2**	**2**	**12**	**15**	**—**	**15**	**0**	**2**	**0**	**1**	**0**	**.295**	**.368**	**.403**	**.951**

Piniella, Louis Victor (Sweet Lou)
HEIGHT: 6'0"   THROWS: RIGHT   BATS: RIGHT   BORN: 8/28/1943 TAMPA, FLORIDA   POSITIONS PLAYED: 1B, OF

YEAR	TEAM	GAMES	AB	RUNS	HITS	2B	3B	HR	RBI	BB	IBB	SO	HBP	SH	SF	SB	CS	BA	OBA	SA	FA
1964	Bal-A	4	1	0	0	0	0	0	0	0	0	0	0	0	0	0	0	.000	.000	.000	.000
1968	Cle-A	6	5	1	0	0	0	0	1	0	0	0	0	0	1	0	0	.000	.000	.000	1.000
1969	KC-A	135	493	43	139	21	6	11	68	33	2	56	3	1	9	2	4	.282	.325	.416	.977
1970	KC-A	144	542	54	163	24	5	11	88	35	6	42	2	2	5	3	6	.301	.342	.424	.984
1971	KC-A	126	448	43	125	21	5	3	51	21	4	43	2	0	5	5	3	.279	.311	.368	.986
1972	KC-A	151	574	65	179	33	4	11	72	34	9	59	8	4	4	7	2	.312	.356	.441	.976
1973	KC-A	144	513	53	128	28	1	9	69	30	7	65	2	3	5	5	7	.250	.291	.361	.986
1974	**NY-A**	**140**	**518**	**71**	**158**	**26**	**0**	**9**	**70**	**32**	**7**	**58**	**2**	**4**	**11**	**1**	**8**	**.305**	**.341**	**.407**	**.989**
1975	**NY-A**	**74**	**199**	**7**	**39**	**4**	**1**	**0**	**22**	**16**	**3**	**22**	**3**	**0**	**3**	**0**	**0**	**.196**	**.262**	**.226**	**.986**
1976	**NY-A**	**100**	**327**	**36**	**92**	**16**	**6**	**3**	**38**	**18**	**8**	**34**	**2**	**3**	**1**	**0**	**1**	**.281**	**.322**	**.394**	**.982**
1977	**NY-A**	**103**	**339**	**47**	**112**	**19**	**3**	**12**	**45**	**20**	**3**	**31**	**1**	**5**	**4**	**2**	**2**	**.330**	**.365**	**.510**	**.975**
1978	**NY-A**	**130**	**472**	**67**	**148**	**34**	**5**	**6**	**69**	**34**	**8**	**36**	**2**	**4**	**1**	**3**	**1**	**.314**	**.361**	**.445**	**.969**
1979	**NY-A**	**130**	**461**	**49**	**137**	**22**	**2**	**11**	**69**	**17**	**6**	**31**	**2**	**3**	**8**	**3**	**2**	**.297**	**.320**	**.425**	**.982**
1980	**NY-A**	**116**	**321**	**39**	**92**	**18**	**0**	**2**	**27**	**29**	**5**	**20**	**0**	**2**	**3**	**0**	**2**	**.287**	**.343**	**.361**	**.971**
1981	**NY-A**	**60**	**159**	**16**	**44**	**9**	**0**	**5**	**18**	**13**	**4**	**9**	**0**	**2**	**0**	**0**	**1**	**.277**	**.331**	**.428**	**.986**
1982	**NY-A**	**102**	**261**	**33**	**80**	**17**	**1**	**6**	**37**	**18**	**6**	**18**	**1**	**2**	**1**	**0**	**1**	**.307**	**.352**	**.448**	**1.000**
1983	**NY-A**	**53**	**148**	**19**	**43**	**9**	**1**	**2**	**16**	**11**	**3**	**12**	**1**	**0**	**0**	**1**	**1**	**.291**	**.344**	**.405**	**.959**
1984	**NY-A**	**29**	**86**	**8**	**26**	**4**	**1**	**1**	**6**	**7**	**1**	**5**	**0**	**0**	**0**	**0**	**0**	**.302**	**.355**	**.407**	**1.000**

(continued)

Louis Victor "Sweet Lou" Piniella, of-dh-1b, 1974–84

Lou Piniella was never a graceful athlete, but throughout his career, he has always seemed to come up with the big play when he needed to.

Born on August 28, 1943, in Tampa, Florida, Piniella played with the Orioles, Indians and Athletics for seven years before coming to the Yankees. New York had traded Lindy McDaniel to the A's for Piniella.

Lou was from Tampa, the adopted home-town of Yankee owner George Steinbrenner. As such, it was an open secret that Piniella was Steinbrenner's favorite Yankee. That helped sometimes and hurt sometimes, as George often felt the need to discipline the happy-go-lucky Piniella as much as he defended him. Given Piniella's hot temper, the two were often at odds.

Piniella may have been a night owl at times, but he was also what coaches now call a professional hitter. Five times in his 11 years with the Yankees, he hit over .300. He hit .305 in five league championship series, including a sizzling .600 in 1981. And he hit .319 in four World Series with New York, including .438 in 1981 and .333 in 1976.

But the play he may be best known for was a defensive play in the 1978 playoff game against the Red Sox at Fenway Park. In the bottom of the ninth inning, with the Yankees ahead 5-4, with one out and a man on base, Sox second baseman Jerry Remy drilled a line drive to Piniella in right field.

Piniella lost the ball in the sun, but he pretended he was going to catch it, pounding his glove. Rick Burleson had to hold at first. When the ball bounced in front of Piniella, Burleson could only get to second base. Jim Rice's fly ball was a harmless out instead of a game-tying sacrifice fly. Reliever Goose Gossage got Carl Yastrzemski for the final out.

"That play," said Sparky Lyle of Piniella's non-catch, "won the ball game for us."

Piniella split his time between the outfield and DH jobs with New York. In 1983 and 1984, he was slowing up a bit on the base paths, and was bothered by a shoulder injury, but he still hit .291 and .302 those two years. He finally retired in June of 1984 on a special Lou Piniella Day. His .295 batting average as a Yankee is 15th all-time.

After his retirement, Piniella was by no means finished with the Yankees. He returned to manage the team in 1986–87 and again in 1988, and was both times fired by Steinbrenner. He has since moved on to become the manager of the Seattle Mariners.

(continued)

																		BA	OBA	SA	FA
Career average	97	326	36	95	17	2	6	43	20	5	30	2	2	3	2	2		.291	.333	.409	.928
Yankee average	**94**	**299**	**36**	**88**	**16**	**2**	**5**	**38**	**20**	**5**	**25**	**1**	**2**	**3**	**1**	**2**		**.295**	**.338**	**.413**	**.982**
Career total	1747	5867	651	1705	305	41	102	766	368	82	541	31	35	61	32	41		.291	.333	.409	.928
Yankee total	**1037**	**3291**	**392**	**971**	**178**	**20**	**57**	**417**	**215**	**54**	**276**	**14**	**25**	**32**	**10**	**19**		**.295**	**.338**	**.413**	**.982**

Pipp, Walter Clement
HEIGHT: 6'1" THROWS: LEFT BATS: LEFT BORN: 2/17/1893 CHICAGO, ILLINOIS DIED: 1/11/1965 GRAND RAPIDS, MICHIGAN POSITIONS PLAYED: 1B

YEAR	TEAM	GAMES	AB	RUNS	HITS	2B	3B	HR	RBI	BB	IBB	SO	HBP	SH	SF	SB	CS	BA	OBA	SA	FA
1913	Det-A	12	31	3	5	0	3	0	5	2	—	6	1	0	—	0	—	.161	.235	.355	.977
1915	NY-A	136	479	59	118	20	13	4	60	66	—	81	1	14	—	18	7	.246	.339	.367	.992
1916	NY-A	151	545	70	143	20	14	12	93	54	—	82	2	16	—	16	—	.262	.331	.417	.992
1917	NY-A	155	587	82	143	29	12	9	70	60	—	66	6	15	—	11	—	.244	.320	.380	.990
1918	NY-A	91	349	48	106	15	9	2	44	22	—	34	0	14	—	11	—	.304	.345	.415	.988

(continued)

(continued)

Year	Team	G	AB	R	H	2B	3B	HR	RBI	BB		SO						BA	OBP	SLG	FA
1919	NY-A	138	523	74	144	23	10	7	50	39	—	42	4	30	—	9	—	.275	.330	.398	.991
1920	NY-A	153	610	109	171	30	14	11	76	48	—	54	6	23	—	4	10	.280	.339	.430	.991
1921	NY-A	153	588	96	174	35	9	8	97	45	—	28	1	33	—	17	10	.296	.347	.427	.991
1922	NY-A	152	577	96	190	32	10	9	90	56	—	32	4	27	—	7	12	.329	.392	.466	.993
1923	NY-A	144	569	79	173	19	8	6	108	36	—	28	6	22	—	6	13	.304	.352	.397	.992
1924	NY-A	153	589	88	174	30	19	9	114	51	—	36	0	23	—	12	5	.295	.352	.457	.994
1925	NY-A	62	178	19	41	6	3	3	24	13	—	12	1	8	—	3	3	.230	.286	.348	.991
1926	Cin-N	155	574	72	167	22	15	6	99	49	—	26	5	21	—	8	—	.291	.352	.413	.992
1927	Cin-N	122	443	49	115	19	6	2	41	32	—	11	0	14	—	2	—	.260	.309	.343	.996
1928	Cin-N	95	272	30	77	11	3	2	26	23	—	13	1	11	—	1	—	.283	.341	.368	.989
Career average		125	461	65	129	21	10	6	66	40	—	37	3	18	—	8	—	.281	.341	.408	.991
Yankee average		**135**	**509**	**75**	**143**	**24**	**11**	**7**	**75**	**45**	**—**	**45**	**3**	**20**	**—**	**10**	**—**	**.282**	**.343**	**.414**	**.991**
Career total		1872	6914	974	1941	311	148	90	997	596	—	551	38	271	—	125	60	.281	.341	.408	.991
Yankee total		**1488**	**5594**	**820**	**1577**	**259**	**121**	**80**	**826**	**490**	**—**	**495**	**31**	**225**	**—**	**114**	**60**	**.282**	**.343**	**.414**	**.991**

Walter Clement "Wally" Pipp, 1b, 1915–25

Before he became the most well-known benchwarmer in baseball history, Wally Pipp was one of the best first basemen in the American League.

Born on February 17, 1893, in Chicago, Pipp came to the Yankees in 1915 after a brief tour of duty with the Detroit Tigers in 1913. He was a terrific defensive player right off the bat, leading the league's first basemen in putouts, assists and fielding percentage in his rookie year.

Pipp led the American League in home runs in 1916 and 1917 and was second in RBI in 1916. He, Frank "Home Run" Baker, Del Pratt, Ping Bodie and Roger Peckinpaugh, among others, were dubbed the original "Murderers' Row" by New York sportswriters.

By 1919, Pipp was becoming one of the Yankees' leaders and a very good first baseman. Not as good a hitter as the Tigers' Harry Heilmann or the Browns' George Sisler, certainly, and not as good defensively as the White Sox Chick Gandil, but a solid all-around player.

In 1920, the Yankees added Babe Ruth and Bob Meusel to become a devastating offensive machine. Pipp was having another strong year, but he and the Yankees' latest manager, Miller Huggins, weren't always getting along. Wally was one of several Yankees who enjoyed a night out from time to time and was disdainful of Huggins's admonitions to stay in his room.

Pipp was a tough ballplayer. In 1923, with both legs taped from ankle to hip, he played all six games of the World Series, collected five singles and 2 RBI and played errorless ball as the Yankees won their first world title.

In 1925, Huggins was trying to figure out where to play this big kid from Columbia—Lou Gehrig—when fate intervened. Pipp was hit by a pitch in batting practice on June 2 and Huggins put Gehrig in his place. It wasn't a tough decision. Pipp and Huggins were never on good terms, and Huggins was only too glad to move Wally out. By the end of the season, Pipp was traded to the Reds, where he played three more years before retiring.

Pipp died in Michigan in 1965. He remains 13th on the Yankees' all-time list for hits with 1,577, 14th in doubles with 259 and 11th in RBI with 825.

Pisoni, James Pete

HEIGHT: 5'10" THROWS: RIGHT BATS: RIGHT BORN: 8/14/1929 ST. LOUIS, MISSOURI POSITIONS PLAYED: OF

YEAR	TEAM	GAMES	AB	RUNS	HITS	2B	3B	HR	RBI	BB	IBB	SO	HBP	SH	SF	SB	CS	BA	OBA	SA	FA
1953	StL-A	3	12	1	1	0	0	1	1	0	—	5	0	0	—	0	0	.083	.083	.333	1.000
1956	KC-A	10	30	4	8	0	0	2	5	2	0	8	0	0	1	0	0	.267	.303	.467	.966
1957	KC-A	44	97	14	23	2	2	3	12	10	1	17	2	1	1	0	0	.237	.318	.392	.989
1959	Mil-N	9	24	4	4	1	0	0	0	2	0	6	0	0	0	0	0	.167	.231	.208	.941
1959	**NY-A**	**17**	**17**	**2**	**3**	**0**	**1**	**0**	**1**	**1**	**0**	**9**	**0**	**2**	**0**	**0**	**0**	**.176**	**.222**	**.294**	**.971**
1960	**NY-A**	**20**	**9**	**1**	**1**	**0**	**0**	**0**	**1**	**1**	**0**	**2**	**0**	**0**	**0**	**0**	**0**	**.111**	**.200**	**.111**	**.938**
Career average		17	32	4	7	1	1	1	3	3	—	8	0	1	—	0	0	.212	.280	.354	.968
Yankee average		**19**	**13**	**2**	**2**	**0**	**1**	**0**	**1**	**1**	**0**	**6**	**0**	**1**	**0**	**0**	**0**	**.154**	**.214**	**.231**	**.955**
Career total		103	189	26	40	3	3	6	20	16	1	47	2	3	2	0	0	.212	.278	.354	.968
Yankee total		**37**	**26**	**3**	**4**	**0**	**1**	**0**	**2**	**2**	**0**	**11**	**0**	**2**	**0**	**0**	**0**	**.154**	**.214**	**.231**	**.955**

Polonia, Luis Andrew BORN LUIS ANDREW POLONIA (ALMONTE)

HEIGHT: 5'8" THROWS: LEFT BATS: LEFT BORN: 10/12/1964 SANTIAGO, DOMINICAN REPUBLIC POSITIONS PLAYED: OF, DH

YEAR	TEAM	GAMES	AB	RUNS	HITS	2B	3B	HR	RBI	BB	IBB	SO	HBP	SH	SF	SB	CS	BA	OBA	SA	FA
1987	Oak-A	125	435	78	125	16	10	4	49	32	1	64	0	1	1	29	7	.287	.335	.398	.979
1988	Oak-A	84	288	51	84	11	4	2	27	21	0	40	0	2	2	24	9	.292	.338	.378	.988
1989	Oak-A	59	206	31	59	6	4	1	17	9	0	15	0	2	1	13	4	.286	.315	.369	.984
1989	**NY-A**	**66**	**227**	**39**	**71**	**11**	**2**	**2**	**29**	**16**	**1**	**29**	**2**	**0**	**3**	**9**	**4**	**.313**	**.359**	**.405**	**.982**
1990	**NY-A**	**11**	**22**	**2**	**7**	**0**	**0**	**0**	**3**	**0**	**0**	**1**	**0**	**0**	**1**	**1**	**0**	**.318**	**.304**	**.318**	**.000**
1990	Cal-A	109	381	50	128	7	9	2	32	25	1	42	1	3	3	20	14	.336	.376	.417	.980
1991	Cal-A	150	604	92	179	28	8	2	50	52	4	74	1	2	3	48	23	.296	.352	.379	.981
1992	Cal-A	149	577	83	165	17	4	0	35	45	6	64	1	8	4	51	21	.286	.337	.329	.980
1993	Cal-A	152	576	75	156	17	6	1	32	48	7	53	2	8	3	55	24	.271	.328	.326	.983
1994	**NY-A**	**95**	**350**	**62**	**109**	**21**	**6**	**1**	**36**	**37**	**1**	**36**	**4**	**2**	**1**	**20**	**12**	**.311**	**.383**	**.414**	**.976**
1995	**NY-A**	**67**	**238**	**37**	**62**	**9**	**3**	**2**	**15**	**25**	**1**	**29**	**0**	**2**	**4**	**10**	**4**	**.261**	**.326**	**.349**	**1.000**
1995	Atl-N	28	53	6	14	7	0	0	2	3	0	9	0	1	0	3	0	.264	.304	.396	1.000
1996	Bal-A	58	175	25	42	4	1	2	14	10	0	20	1	1	0	8	6	.240	.285	.309	.968
1996	Atl-N	22	31	3	13	0	0	0	2	1	0	3	0	0	1	1	1	.419	.424	.419	8.000
1999	Det-A	87	333	46	108	21	8	10	32	16	0	32	2	2	2	17	9	.324	.357	.526	.986
2000	Det-A	80	267	37	73	10	5	6	25	22	1	25	1	3	5	8	5	.273	.325	.416	.971
2000	**NY-A**	**37**	**77**	**11**	**22**	**4**	**0**	**1**	**5**	**7**	**0**	**7**	**0**	**0**	**1**	**4**	**2**	**.286**	**.341**	**.377**	**1.000**
Career average		81	285	43	83	11	4	2	24	22	1	32	1	2	2	19	9	.293	.342	.383	1.339
Yankee average		**55**	**183**	**30**	**54**	**9**	**2**	**1**	**18**	**17**	**1**	**20**	**1**	**1**	**2**	**9**	**4**	**.296**	**.357**	**.389**	**.792**
Career total		1379	4840	728	1417	189	70	36	405	369	23	543	15	37	35	321	145	.293	.342	.383	1.339
Yankee total		**276**	**914**	**151**	**271**	**45**	**11**	**6**	**88**	**85**	**3**	**102**	**6**	**4**	**10**	**44**	**22**	**.296**	**.357**	**.389**	**.792**

Posada, Jorge Rafael BORN JOSE RAFAEL POSADA (VILLETA)

HEIGHT: 6'2" THROWS: RIGHT BATS: BOTH BORN: 8/17/1971 SANTURCE, PUERTO RICO POSITIONS PLAYED: CC, 1B

YEAR	TEAM	GAMES	AB	RUNS	HITS	2B	3B	HR	RBI	BB	IBB	SO	HBP	SH	SF	SB	CS	BA	OBA	SA	FA
1995	**NY-A**	**1**	**0**	**0**	**0**	**0**	**0**	**0**	**0**	**0**	**0**	**0**	**0**	**0**	**0**	**0**	**0**	**—**	**—**	**—**	**1.000**
1996	**NY-A**	**8**	**14**	**1**	**1**	**0**	**0**	**0**	**0**	**1**	**0**	**6**	**0**	**0**	**0**	**0**	**0**	**.071**	**.133**	**.071**	**1.000**
1997	**NY-A**	**60**	**188**	**29**	**47**	**12**	**0**	**6**	**25**	**30**	**2**	**33**	**3**	**1**	**2**	**1**	**2**	**.250**	**.359**	**.410**	**.992**
1998	**NY-A**	**111**	**358**	**56**	**96**	**23**	**0**	**17**	**63**	**47**	**7**	**92**	**0**	**0**	**4**	**0**	**1**	**.268**	**.350**	**.475**	**.994**
1999	**NY-A**	**112**	**379**	**50**	**93**	**19**	**2**	**12**	**57**	**53**	**2**	**91**	**3**	**0**	**2**	**1**	**0**	**.245**	**.341**	**.401**	**.995**
2000	**NY-A**	**151**	**505**	**92**	**145**	**35**	**1**	**28**	**86**	**107**	**10**	**151**	**8**	**0**	**4**	**2**	**2**	**.287**	**.417**	**.527**	**.994**
Career average		74	241	38	64	15	1	11	39	40	4	62	2	0	2	1	1	.265	.371	.461	.996
Yankee average		**74**	**241**	**38**	**64**	**15**	**1**	**11**	**39**	**40**	**4**	**62**	**2**	**0**	**2**	**1**	**1**	**.265**	**.371**	**.461**	**.996**
Career total		443	1444	228	382	89	3	63	231	238	21	373	14	1	12	4	5	.265	.371	.461	.996
Yankee total		**443**	**1444**	**228**	**382**	**89**	**3**	**63**	**231**	**238**	**21**	**373**	**14**	**1**	**12**	**4**	**5**	**.265**	**.371**	**.461**	**.996**

Pose, Scott Vernon

HEIGHT: 5'11" THROWS: RIGHT BATS: LEFT BORN: 2/11/67 DAVENPORT, IOWA POSITIONS PLAYED: OF

YEAR	TEAM	GAMES	AB	RUNS	HITS	2B	3B	HR	RBI	BB	IBB	SO	HBP	SH	SF	SB	CS	BA	OBA	SA	FA
1993	Fla-N	15	41	0	8	2	0	0	3	2	0	4	0	0	0	0	2	.195	.233	.244	1.000
1997	**NY-A**	**54**	**87**	**19**	**19**	**2**	**1**	**0**	**5**	**9**	**0**	**11**	**0**	**0**	**0**	**3**	**1**	**.218**	**.292**	**.264**	**1.000**
1999	KC-A	86	137	27	39	3	0	0	12	21	1	22	0	1	1	6	2	.285	.377	.307	.970
2000	KC-A	47	48	6	9	0	0	0	1	6	0	13	0	0	0	0	1	.188	.278	.188	.775
Career average		51	78	13	19	2	0	0	5	10	0	13	0	0	0	2	2	.240	.321	.268	.936
Yankee average		**54**	**87**	**19**	**19**	**2**	**1**	**0**	**5**	**9**	**0**	**11**	**0**	**0**	**0**	**3**	**1**	**.218**	**.292**	**.264**	**1.000**
Career total		202	313	52	75	7	1	0	21	38	1	50	0	1	1	9	6	.240	.321	.268	.936
Yankee total		**54**	**87**	**19**	**19**	**2**	**1**	**0**	**5**	**9**	**0**	**11**	**0**	**0**	**0**	**3**	**1**	**.218**	**.292**	**.264**	**1.000**

Powell, Alvin Jacob

HEIGHT: 5'11" THROWS: RIGHT BATS: RIGHT BORN: 7/15/1908 SILVER SPRING, MD. DIED: 11/4/1948 WASHINGTON, D.C. POSITIONS PLAYED: 2B, 3B, OF

YEAR	TEAM	GAMES	AB	RUNS	HITS	2B	3B	HR	RBI	BB	IBB	SO	HBP	SH	SF	SB	CS	BA	OBA	SA	FA
1930	Was-A	3	4	1	0	0	0	0	0	0	—	1	0	0	—	0	0	.000	.000	.000	1.000
1934	Was-A	9	35	6	10	2	0	0	1	4	—	2	0	1	—	1	1	.286	.359	.343	.955
1935	Was-A	139	551	88	172	26	10	6	98	37	—	37	4	12	—	15	7	.312	.360	.428	.976
1936	Was-A	53	210	40	62	11	5	1	30	18	—	21	0	1	—	10	4	.295	.351	.410	.967
1936	**NY-A**	**87**	**328**	**62**	**99**	**13**	**3**	**7**	**48**	**33**	**—**	**30**	**0**	**3**	**—**	**16**	**7**	**.302**	**.366**	**.424**	**.976**
1937	**NY-A**	**97**	**365**	**54**	**96**	**22**	**3**	**3**	**45**	**25**	**—**	**36**	**2**	**8**	**—**	**7**	**5**	**.263**	**.314**	**.364**	**.981**
1938	**NY-A**	**45**	**164**	**27**	**42**	**12**	**1**	**2**	**20**	**15**	**—**	**20**	**2**	**2**	**—**	**3**	**1**	**.256**	**.326**	**.378**	**.978**
1939	**NY-A**	**31**	**86**	**12**	**21**	**4**	**1**	**1**	**9**	**3**	**—**	**8**	**0**	**2**	**—**	**1**	**2**	**.244**	**.270**	**.349**	**.983**
1940	**NY-A**	**12**	**27**	**3**	**5**	**0**	**0**	**0**	**2**	**1**	**—**	**4**	**0**	**0**	**—**	**0**	**0**	**.185**	**.214**	**.185**	**1.000**
1943	Was-A	37	132	14	35	10	2	0	20	5	—	13	1	3	—	3	5	.265	.297	.371	.978
1944	Was-A	96	367	29	88	9	1	1	37	16	—	26	0	9	—	7	2	.240	.272	.278	.980
1945	Was-A	31	98	4	19	2	0	0	3	8	—	8	0	0	—	1	1	.194	.255	.214	.970
1945	Phi-N	48	173	13	40	5	0	1	14	8	—	13	0	2	—	1	—	.231	.265	.277	.986
Career average		53	195	27	53	9	2	2	25	13	—	17	1	3	—	5	—	.271	.320	.363	.979
Yankee average		**54**	**194**	**32**	**53**	**10**	**2**	**3**	**25**	**15**	**—**	**20**	**1**	**3**	**—**	**5**	**3**	**.271**	**.327**	**.380**	**.984**
Career total		688	2540	353	689	116	26	22	327	173	—	219	9	43	—	65	35	.271	.320	.363	.979
Yankee total		**272**	**970**	**158**	**263**	**51**	**8**	**13**	**124**	**77**	**—**	**98**	**4**	**15**	**—**	**27**	**15**	**.271**	**.327**	**.380**	**.984**

Powers, Michael Riley (Doc)

HEIGHT: 6'1" THROWS: RIGHT BATS: RIGHT BORN: 9/22/1870 PITTSFIELD, MASSACHUSETTS DIED: 4/26/1909 PHILADELPHIA, PENN. POSITIONS PLAYED: C, 1B, OF

YEAR	TEAM	GAMES	AB	RUNS	HITS	2B	3B	HR	RBI	BB	IBB	SO	HBP	SH	SF	SB	CS	BA	OBA	SA	FA
1898	Lou-N	34	99	13	27	4	3	1	19	5	—	—	0	3	—	1	—	.273	.308	.404	.962
1899	Lou-N	49	169	15	35	8	2	0	22	6	—	—	1	6	—	1	—	.207	.239	.278	.942
1899	Was-N	14	38	3	10	2	0	0	3	1	—	—	0	2	—	0	—	.263	.282	.316	.942
1901	Phi-A	116	431	53	108	26	5	1	47	18	—	—	7	1	—	10	—	.251	.292	.341	.938
1902	Phi-A	71	246	35	65	7	1	2	39	14	—	—	3	3	—	3	—	.264	.312	.325	1.000
1903	Phi-A	75	247	19	56	11	1	0	23	5	—	—	0	10	—	1	—	.227	.242	.279	.981
1904	Phi-A	57	184	11	35	3	0	0	11	6	—	—	1	5	—	3	—	.190	.220	.207	.965
1905	Phi-A	40	121	8	18	0	0	0	10	3	—	—	1	6	—	4	—	.149	.176	.149	.928
1905	**NY-A**	**11**	**33**	**3**	**6**	**1**	**0**	**0**	**2**	**1**	**—**	**—**	**0**	**0**	**—**	**0**	**—**	**.182**	**.206**	**.212**	**.975**
1906	Phi-A	58	185	5	29	1	0	0	7	1	—	—	2	4	—	2	—	.157	.170	.162	1.000
1907	Phi-A	59	159	9	29	3	0	0	9	7	—	—	0	14	—	1	—	.182	.217	.201	.983
1908	Phi-A	62	172	8	31	6	1	0	7	5	—	—	3	6	—	1	—	.180	.217	.227	.975
1909	Phi-A	1	4	1	1	0	0	0	0	0	—	—	0	0	—	0	—	.250	.250	.250	1.000
Career average		50	161	14	35	6	1	0	15	6	—	—	1	5	—	2	—	.216	.248	.268	.968
Yankee average		**11**	**33**	**3**	**6**	**1**	**0**	**0**	**2**	**1**	**—**	**—**	**0**	**0**	**—**	**0**	**—**	**.182**	**.206**	**.212**	**.975**
Career total		647	2088	183	450	72	13	4	199	72	—	—	18	60	—	27	—	.216	.248	.268	.968
Yankee total		**11**	**33**	**3**	**6**	**1**	**0**	**0**	**2**	**1**	**—**	**—**	**0**	**0**	**—**	**0**	**—**	**.182**	**.206**	**.212**	**.975**

Pratt, Derrill Burnham (Del)

HEIGHT: 5'11" THROWS: RIGHT BATS: RIGHT BORN: 1/10/1888 WALHALIA, S. CAROLINA DIED: 9/30/1977 TEXAS CITY, TEX. POSITIONS PLAYED: 1B, 2B, 3B, SS, OF

YEAR	TEAM	GAMES	AB	RUNS	HITS	2B	3B	HR	RBI	BB	IBB	SO	HBP	SH	SF	SB	CS	BA	OBA	SA	FA
1912	StL-A	151	570	76	172	26	15	5	69	36	—		4	12	—	24		.302	.348	.426	.896
1913	StL-A	155	592	60	175	31	13	2	87	40	—	57	1	18	—	37	—	.296	.341	.402	.951
1914	StL-A	158	584	85	165	34	13	5	65	50	—	45	2	18	—	37	28	.283	.341	.411	1.000
1915	StL-A	159	602	61	175	31	11	3	78	26	—	43	3	32	—	32	23	.291	.323	.394	.965
1916	StL-A	158	596	64	159	35	12	5	103	54	—	56	3	16	—	26	17	.267	.331	.391	.966
1917	StL-A	123	450	40	111	22	8	1	53	33	—	36	2	14	—	18	—	.247	.301	.338	1.000
1918	**NY-A**	**126**	**477**	**65**	**131**	**19**	**7**	**2**	**55**	**35**	**—**	**26**	**2**	**23**	**—**	**12**	**—**	**.275**	**.327**	**.356**	**.969**
1919	**NY-A**	**140**	**527**	**69**	**154**	**27**	**7**	**4**	**56**	**36**	**—**	**24**	**4**	**16**	**—**	**22**	**—**	**.292**	**.342**	**.393**	**.969**
1920	**NY-A**	**154**	**574**	**84**	**180**	**37**	**8**	**4**	**97**	**50**	**—**	**24**	**3**	**27**	**—**	**12**	**10**	**.314**	**.372**	**.427**	**.971**
1921	Bos-A	135	521	80	169	36	10	5	102	44	—	10	1	8	—	8	10	.324	.378	.461	.961
1922	Bos-A	154	607	73	183	44	7	6	86	53	—	20	4	9	—	7	10	.301	.361	.427	.966
1923	Det-A	101	297	43	92	18	3	0	40	25	—	9	6	14	—	6	1	.310	.375	.391	1.000
1924	Det-A	121	429	56	130	32	3	1	77	31	—	10	2	26	—	6	9	.303	.353	.399	.948
Career average		141	525	66	154	30	9	3	74	39	—		3	18	—	19		.292	.345	.403	.966
Yankee average		**140**	**526**	**73**	**155**	**28**	**7**	**3**	**69**	**40**	**—**	**—**	**3**	**22**	**—**	**15**	**—**	**.295**	**.348**	**.394**	**.970**
Career total		1835	6826	856	1996	392	117	43	968	513	—	360	37	233	—	247	108	.292	.345	.403	.966
Yankee total		**420**	**1578**	**218**	**465**	**83**	**22**	**10**	**208**	**121**	**—**	**74**	**9**	**66**	**—**	**46**	**10**	**.295**	**.348**	**.394**	**.970**

Priddy, Gerald Edward

HEIGHT: 5'11" THROWS: RIGHT BATS: RIGHT BORN: 11/9/1919 LOS ANGELES, CAL. DIED: 3/3/1980 HOLLYWOOD, CAL. POSITIONS PLAYED: 1B, 2B, 3B, SS

YEAR	TEAM	GAMES	AB	RUNS	HITS	2B	3B	HR	RBI	BB	IBB	SO	HBP	SH	SF	SB	CS	BA	OBA	SA	FA
1941	**NY-A**	**56**	**174**	**18**	**37**	**7**	**0**	**1**	**26**	**18**	**—**	**16**	**1**	**1**	**—**	**4**	**2**	**.213**	**.290**	**.270**	**.941**
1942	**NY-A**	**59**	**189**	**23**	**53**	**9**	**2**	**2**	**28**	**31**	**—**	**27**	**1**	**1**	**—**	**0**	**1**	**.280**	**.385**	**.381**	**.989**
1943	Was-A	149	560	68	152	31	3	4	62	67	—	76	1	7	—	5	5	.271	.350	.359	1.000
1946	Was-A	138	511	54	130	22	8	6	58	57	—	73	2	7	—	9	3	.254	.332	.364	.962
1947	Was-A	147	505	42	108	20	3	3	49	62	—	79	1	8	—	7	6	.214	.301	.283	.980
1948	StL-A	151	560	96	166	40	9	8	79	86	—	71	1	10	—	6	5	.296	.391	.443	.968
1949	StL-A	145	544	83	158	26	4	11	63	80	—	81	1	9	—	5	3	.290	.382	.414	.968
1950	Det-A	157	618	104	171	26	6	13	75	95	—	95	3	13	—	2	7	.277	.376	.401	.981
1951	Det-A	154	584	73	152	22	6	8	57	69	—	73	0	12	—	4	3	.260	.338	.360	.980
1952	Det-A	75	279	37	79	23	3	4	20	42	—	29	1	1	—	1	8	.283	.379	.430	.968
1953	Det-A	65	196	14	46	6	2	1	24	17	—	19	1	2	—	1	1	.235	.299	.301	.977
Career average		118	429	56	114	21	4	6	49	57	—	58	1	6	—	4	4	.265	.353	.373	.974
Yankee average		**58**	**182**	**21**	**45**	**8**	**1**	**2**	**27**	**25**	**—**	**22**	**1**	**1**	**—**	**2**	**2**	**.248**	**.341**	**.328**	**.965**
Career total		1296	4720	612	1252	232	46	61	541	624	—	639	13	71	—	44	44	.265	.353	.373	.974
Yankee total		**115**	**363**	**41**	**90**	**16**	**2**	**3**	**54**	**49**	**—**	**43**	**2**	**2**	**—**	**4**	**3**	**.248**	**.341**	**.328**	**.965**

Priest, John Gooding

HEIGHT: 5'11" THROWS: RIGHT BATS: RIGHT BORN: 6/23/1886 ST. JOSEPH, MISSOURI DIED: 11/4/1979 WASHINGTON, D.C. POSITIONS PLAYED: 2B, 3B, SS

YEAR	TEAM	GAMES	AB	RUNS	HITS	2B	3B	HR	RBI	BB	IBB	SO	HBP	SH	SF	SB	CS	BA	OBA	SA	FA
1911	**NY-A**	**7**	**21**	**2**	**3**	**0**	**0**	**0**	**2**	**2**	**—**	**—**	**1**	**0**	**—**	**3**	**—**	**.143**	**.250**	**.143**	**.813**
1912	**NY-A**	**2**	**2**	**1**	**1**	**0**	**0**	**0**	**1**	**0**	**—**	**—**	**0**	**0**	**—**	**0**	**—**	**.500**	**.500**	**.500**	**1.000**
Career average		5	12	2	2	0	0	0	2	1	—	—	1	0	—	2	—	.174	.269	.174	.907
Yankee average		**5**	**12**	**2**	**2**	**0**	**0**	**0**	**2**	**1**	**—**	**—**	**1**	**0**	**—**	**2**	**—**	**.174**	**.269**	**.174**	**.907**
Career total		9	23	3	4	0	0	0	3	2	—	—	1	0	—	3	—	.174	.269	.174	.907
Yankee total		**9**	**23**	**3**	**4**	**0**	**0**	**0**	**3**	**2**	**—**	**—**	**1**	**0**	**—**	**3**	**—**	**.174**	**.269**	**.174**	**.907**

Quirk, James Patrick

HEIGHT: 6'4" THROWS: RIGHT BATS: LEFT BORN: 10/22/1954 WHITTIER, CALIFORNIA POSITIONS PLAYED: C, 1B, 2B, 3B, SS, OF

YEAR	TEAM	GAMES	AB	RUNS	HITS	2B	3B	HR	RBI	BB	IBB	SO	HBP	SH	SF	SB	CS	BA	OBA	SA	FA
1975	KC-A	14	39	2	10	0	0	1	5	2	1	7	0	0	0	0	0	.256	.293	.333	1.000
1976	KC-A	64	114	11	28	6	0	1	15	2	0	22	0	0	3	0	0	.246	.252	.325	1.000
1977	Mil-A	93	221	16	48	14	1	3	13	8	2	47	2	2	0	0	1	.217	.251	.330	.950

(continued)

(continued)

YEAR	TEAM	GAMES	AB	RUNS	HITS	2B	3B	HR	RBI	BB	IBB	SO	HBP	SH	SF	SB	CS	BA	OBA	SA	FA
1978	KC-A	17	29	3	6	2	0	0	2	5	0	4	0	0	0	0	0	.207	.324	.276	1.000
1979	KC-A	51	79	8	24	6	1	1	11	5	0	13	1	0	0	0	0	.304	.353	.443	1.000
1980	KC-A	62	163	13	45	5	0	5	21	7	2	24	1	3	3	3	2	.276	.305	.399	1.000
1981	KC-A	46	100	8	25	7	0	0	10	6	1	17	1	0	0	0	2	.250	.299	.320	.985
1982	KC-A	36	78	8	18	3	0	1	5	3	0	15	0	0	1	0	0	.231	.256	.308	1.000
1983	StL-N	48	86	3	18	2	1	2	11	6	0	27	1	0	0	0	0	.209	.269	.326	.929
1984	Chi-A	3	2	0	0	0	0	0	1	0	0	2	0	0	1	0	0	.000	.000	.000	1.000
1984	Cle-A	1	1	1	1	0	0	1	1	0	0	0	0	0	0	0	0	1.000	1.000	4.000	.000
1985	KC-A	19	57	3	16	3	1	0	4	2	0	9	0	0	0	0	0	.281	.305	.368	1.000
1986	KC-A	80	219	24	47	10	0	8	26	17	3	41	1	0	1	0	1	.215	.273	.370	.989
1987	KC-A	109	296	24	70	17	0	5	33	28	1	56	4	2	4	1	0	.236	.307	.345	.986
1988	KC-A	84	196	22	47	7	1	8	25	28	2	41	1	4	3	1	5	.240	.333	.408	.982
1989	**NY-A**	**13**	**24**	**0**	**2**	**0**	**0**	**0**	**0**	**3**	**0**	**5**	**0**	**0**	**0**	**0**	**1**	**.083**	**.185**	**.083**	**1.000**
1989	Oak-A	9	10	1	2	0	0	1	1	0	0	4	0	0	0	0	0	.200	.200	.500	.500
1989	Bal-A	25	51	5	11	2	0	0	9	9	0	11	0	1	1	0	1	.216	.328	.255	1.000
1990	Oak-A	56	121	12	34	5	1	3	26	14	1	34	1	5	3	0	0	.281	.353	.413	1.000
1991	Oak-A	76	203	16	53	4	0	1	17	16	1	28	2	3	0	0	3	.261	.321	.296	.982
1992	Oak-A	78	177	13	39	7	1	2	11	16	3	28	3	5	1	0	0	.220	.294	.305	1.000
Career average		47	108	9	26	5	0	2	12	8	1	21	1	1	1	0	1	.240	.298	.347	.919
Yankee average		**13**	**24**	**0**	**2**	**0**	**0**	**0**	**0**	**3**	**0**	**5**	**0**	**0**	**0**	**0**	**1**	**.083**	**.185**	**.083**	**1.000**
Career total		984	2266	193	544	100	7	43	247	177	17	435	18	25	21	5	16	.240	.298	.347	.919
Yankee total		**13**	**24**	**0**	**2**	**0**	**0**	**0**	**0**	**3**	**0**	**5**	**0**	**0**	**0**	**0**	**1**	**.083**	**.185**	**.083**	**1.000**

Raines, Timothy (Rock)

HEIGHT: 5'8" THROWS: RIGHT BATS: BOTH BORN: 9/16/1959 SANFORD, FLORIDA POSITIONS PLAYED: 2B, OF

YEAR	TEAM	GAMES	AB	RUNS	HITS	2B	3B	HR	RBI	BB	IBB	SO	HBP	SH	SF	SB	CS	BA	OBA	SA	FA
1979	Mon-N	6	0	3	0	0	0	0	0	0	0	0	0	0	0	2	0	—	—	—	.000
1980	Mon-N	15	20	5	1	0	0	0	0	6	0	3	0	1	0	5	0	.050	.269	.050	1.000
1981	Mon-N	88	313	61	95	13	7	5	37	45	5	31	2	0	3	71	11	.304	.391	.438	.976
1982	Mon-N	156	647	90	179	32	8	4	43	75	9	83	2	6	1	78	16	.277	.353	.369	.968
1983	Mon-N	156	615	133	183	32	8	11	71	97	9	70	2	2	4	90	14	.298	.393	.429	1.000
1984	Mon-N	160	622	106	192	38	9	8	60	87	7	69	2	3	4	75	10	.309	.393	.437	.000
1985	Mon-N	150	575	115	184	30	13	11	41	81	13	60	3	3	3	70	9	.320	.405	.475	.993
1986	Mon-N	151	580	91	194	35	10	9	62	78	9	60	2	1	3	70	9	.334	.413	.476	.979
1987	Mon-N	139	530	123	175	34	8	18	68	90	26	52	4	0	3	50	5	.330	.429	.526	.987
1988	Mon-N	109	429	66	116	19	7	12	48	53	14	44	2	0	4	33	7	.270	.350	.431	.988
1989	Mon-N	145	517	76	148	29	6	9	60	93	18	48	3	0	5	41	9	.286	.395	.418	.996
1990	Mon-N	130	457	65	131	11	5	9	62	70	8	43	3	0	8	49	16	.287	.379	.392	.976
1991	Chi-A	155	609	102	163	20	6	5	50	83	9	68	5	9	3	51	15	.268	.359	.345	.990
1992	Chi-A	144	551	102	162	22	9	7	54	81	4	48	0	4	8	45	6	.294	.380	.405	.994
1993	Chi-A	115	415	75	127	16	4	16	54	64	4	35	3	2	2	21	7	.306	.401	.480	1.000
1994	Chi-A	101	384	80	102	15	5	10	52	61	3	43	1	4	3	13	0	.266	.365	.409	.981
1995	Chi-A	133	502	81	143	25	4	12	67	70	3	52	3	3	3	13	2	.285	.374	.422	.980
1996	**NY-A**	**59**	**201**	**45**	**57**	**10**	**0**	**9**	**33**	**34**	**1**	**29**	**1**	**0**	**4**	**10**	**1**	**.284**	**.383**	**.468**	**.988**
1997	**NY-A**	**74**	**271**	**56**	**87**	**20**	**2**	**4**	**38**	**41**	**0**	**34**	**0**	**0**	**6**	**8**	**5**	**.321**	**.403**	**.454**	**.988**
1998	**NY-A**	**109**	**321**	**53**	**93**	**13**	**1**	**5**	**47**	**55**	**1**	**49**	**3**	**0**	**3**	**8**	**3**	**.290**	**.395**	**.383**	**.985**
1999	Oak-A	58	135	20	29	5	0	4	17	26	1	17	0	1	2	4	1	.215	.337	.341	1.000
Career average		112	414	74	122	20	5	8	46	61	7	45	2	2	3	38	7	.295	.385	.427	.894
Yankee average		**81**	**264**	**51**	**79**	**14**	**1**	**6**	**39**	**43**	**1**	**37**	**1**	**0**	**4**	**9**	**3**	**.299**	**.395**	**.429**	**.987**
Career total		2353	8694	1548	2561	419	112	168	964	1290	144	938	41	39	72	807	146	.295	.385	.427	.894
Yankee total		**242**	**793**	**154**	**237**	**43**	**3**	**18**	**118**	**130**	**2**	**112**	**4**	**0**	**13**	**26**	**9**	**.299**	**.395**	**.429**	**.987**

Ramos, John Joseph

HEIGHT: 6'0" THROWS: RIGHT BATS: RIGHT BORN: 8/6/1965 TAMPA, FLORIDA POSITIONS PLAYED: C

YEAR	TEAM	GAMES	AB	RUNS	HITS	2B	3B	HR	RBI	BB	IBB	SO	HBP	SH	SF	SB	CS	BA	OBA	SA	FA
1991	**NY-A**	**10**	**26**	**4**	**8**	**1**	**0**	**0**	**3**	**1**	**0**	**3**	**0**	**0**	**2**	**0**	**0**	**.308**	**.310**	**.346**	**1.000**
Career average		10	26	4	8	1	0	0	3	1	0	3	0	0	2	0	0	.308	.310	.346	1.000
Yankee average		**10**	**26**	**4**	**8**	**1**	**0**	**0**	**3**	**1**	**0**	**3**	**0**	**0**	**2**	**0**	**0**	**.308**	**.310**	**.346**	**1.000**
Career total		10	26	4	8	1	0	0	3	1	0	3	0	0	2	0	0	.308	.310	.346	1.000
Yankee total		**10**	**26**	**4**	**8**	**1**	**0**	**0**	**3**	**1**	**0**	**3**	**0**	**0**	**2**	**0**	**0**	**.308**	**.310**	**.346**	**1.000**

Ramos, Pedro (Pete) BORN PEDRO RAMOS (GUERRA)

HEIGHT: 6'0" THROWS: RIGHT BATS: BOTH BORN: 4/28/1935 PINAR DEL RIO, CUBA POSITIONS PLAYED: P

YEAR	TEAM	GAMES	AB	RUNS	HITS	2B	3B	HR	RBI	BB	IBB	SO	HBP	SH	SF	SB	CS	BA	OBA	SA	FA
1955	Was-A	59	38	6	3	0	0	0	0	2	0	18	0	0	0	0	1	.079	.125	.079	.964
1956	Was-A	56	44	9	9	0	2	0	2	2	0	16	0	4	0	0	1	.205	.239	.295	1.000
1957	Was-A	56	76	6	13	0	0	1	10	2	0	27	0	3	0	0	0	.171	.192	.211	1.000
1958	Was-A	53	88	9	21	1	0	0	10	0	0	33	0	7	1	0	0	.239	.236	.250	.982
1959	Was-A	45	75	7	11	1	1	1	2	4	0	38	0	6	0	1	0	.147	.190	.227	1.000
1960	Was-A	53	86	6	10	3	0	2	4	1	0	36	0	7	0	0	0	.116	.126	.221	1.000
1961	Min-A	53	93	8	16	1	0	3	11	3	0	42	1	2	1	0	0	.172	.204	.280	.955
1962	Cle-A	39	68	6	10	3	0	3	8	1	0	29	1	2	0	0	0	.147	.171	.324	.962
1963	Cle-A	54	55	13	6	0	0	3	7	3	0	32	0	4	0	0	0	.109	.155	.273	.963
1964	Cle-A	44	39	6	7	0	0	2	2	2	0	22	0	1	0	0	0	.179	.220	.333	.960
1964	**NY-A**	**13**	**5**	**0**	**0**	**0**	**0**	**0**	**0**	**0**	**0**	**2**	**0**	**1**	**0**	**0**	**0**	**.000**	**.000**	**.000**	**.000**
1965	**NY-A**	**65**	**12**	**0**	**1**	**0**	**0**	**0**	**0**	**0**	**0**	**8**	**0**	**2**	**0**	**1**	**0**	**.083**	**.083**	**.083**	**.895**
1966	**NY-A**	**52**	**13**	**0**	**2**	**0**	**0**	**0**	**0**	**0**	**0**	**8**	**0**	**0**	**0**	**0**	**0**	**.154**	**.154**	**.154**	**.952**
1967	Phi-N	6	1	0	0	0	0	0	0	0	0	0	0	0	0	0	0	.000	.000	.000	1.000
1969	Pit-N	5	1	0	0	0	0	0	0	0	0	1	0	0	0	0	0	.000	.000	.000	1.000
1969	Cin-N	38	8	0	0	0	0	0	0	1	0	4	0	2	0	0	0	.000	.111	.000	1.000
1970	Was-A	5	1	0	0	0	0	0	0	1	0	0	0	0	0	0	0	.000	.500	.000	1.000
Career average		41	41	4	6	1	0	1	3	1	0	19	0	2	0	0	0	.155	.182	.240	.920
Yankee average		**43**	**10**	**0**	**1**	**0**	**0**	**0**	**0**	**0**	**0**	**6**	**0**	**1**	**0**	**0**	**0**	**.100**	**.100**	**.100**	**.616**
Career total		696	703	76	109	9	3	15	56	22	0	316	2	41	2	2	2	.155	.182	.240	.920
Yankee total		**130**	**30**	**0**	**3**	**0**	**0**	**0**	**0**	**0**	**0**	**18**	**0**	**3**	**0**	**1**	**0**	**.100**	**.100**	**.100**	**.616**

Ramos, Roberto

HEIGHT: 5'11" THROWS: RIGHT BATS: RIGHT BORN: 11/5/1955 CALABAZAR DE SAGUA, CUBA POSITIONS PLAYED: C

YEAR	TEAM	GAMES	AB	RUNS	HITS	2B	3B	HR	RBI	BB	IBB	SO	HBP	SH	SF	SB	CS	BA	OBA	SA	FA
1978	Mon-N	2	4	0	0	0	0	0	0	0	0	1	0	0	0	0	0	.000	.000	.000	1.000
1980	Mon-N	13	32	5	5	2	0	0	2	5	0	5	0	0	0	0	0	.156	.270	.219	.964
1981	Mon-N	26	41	4	8	1	0	1	3	3	0	5	0	0	0	0	0	.195	.250	.273	.974
1982	**NY-A**	**4**	**11**	**1**	**1**	**0**	**0**	**1**	**2**	**0**	**0**	**3**	**0**	**0**	**0**	**0**	**0**	**.091**	**.091**	**.364**	**1.000**
1983	Mon-N	27	61	2	14	3	1	0	5	8	1	11	1	0	0	0	0	.230	.329	.311	.984
1984	Mon-N	31	83	8	16	1	0	2	5	6	1	13	0	1	1	0	0	.193	.244	.277	.982
Career average		17	39	3	7	1	0	1	3	4	0	6	0	0	0	0	0	.190	.262	.280	.984
Yankee average		**4**	**11**	**1**	**1**	**0**	**0**	**1**	**2**	**0**	**0**	**3**	**0**	**0**	**0**	**0**	**0**	**.091**	**.091**	**.364**	**1.000**
Career total		103	232	20	44	7	1	4	17	22	2	38	1	1	1	0	0	.190	.262	.280	.984
Yankee total		**4**	**11**	**1**	**1**	**0**	**0**	**1**	**2**	**0**	**0**	**3**	**0**	**0**	**0**	**0**	**0**	**.091**	**.091**	**.364**	**1.000**

Randle, Leonard Shenoff

HEIGHT: 5'10" THROWS: RIGHT BATS: BOTH BORN: 2/12/1949 LONG BEACH, CALIFORNIA POSITIONS PLAYED: C, 2B, 3B, SS, OF

YEAR	TEAM	GAMES	AB	RUNS	HITS	2B	3B	HR	RBI	BB	IBB	SO	HBP	SH	SF	SB	CS	BA	OBA	SA	FA
1971	Was-A	75	215	27	47	11	0	2	13	24	2	56	1	7	2	1	1	.219	.298	.298	.967
1972	Tex-A	74	249	23	48	13	0	2	21	13	2	51	1	3	1	4	5	.193	.235	.269	.952
1973	Tex-A	10	29	3	6	1	1	1	1	0	0	2	0	1	0	0	2	.207	.207	.414	.500
1974	Tex-A	151	520	65	157	17	4	1	49	29	2	43	2	16	6	26	17	.302	.338	.356	.935
1975	Tex-A	156	601	85	166	24	7	4	57	57	3	80	4	10	4	16	19	.276	.341	.359	1.000
1976	Tex-A	142	539	53	121	11	6	1	51	46	2	63	2	6	4	30	15	.224	.286	.273	1.000
1977	NY-N	136	513	78	156	22	7	5	27	65	3	70	2	3	2	33	21	.304	.383	.404	.976
1978	NY-N	132	437	53	102	16	8	2	35	64	7	57	1	2	4	14	11	.233	.330	.320	1.000
1979	**NY-A**	**20**	**39**	**2**	**7**	**0**	**0**	**0**	**3**	**3**	**0**	**2**	**0**	**0**	**0**	**0**	**0**	**.179**	**.238**	**.179**	**1.000**
1980	Chi-N	130	489	67	135	19	6	5	39	50	2	55	1	7	2	19	13	.276	.343	.370	.978
1981	Sea-A	82	273	22	63	9	1	4	25	17	4	22	1	6	3	11	6	.231	.276	.315	.986
1982	Sea-A	30	46	10	8	2	0	0	1	4	0	4	0	1	0	2	2	.174	.240	.217	.964
Career average		95	329	41	85	12	3	2	27	31	2	42	1	5	2	13	9	.257	.321	.335	.938
Yankee average		**20**	**39**	**2**	**7**	**0**	**0**	**0**	**3**	**3**	**0**	**2**	**0**	**0**	**0**	**0**	**0**	**.179**	**.238**	**.179**	**1.000**
Career total		1138	3950	488	1016	145	40	27	322	372	27	505	15	62	28	156	112	.257	.321	.335	.938
Yankee total		**20**	**39**	**2**	**7**	**0**	**0**	**0**	**3**	**3**	**0**	**2**	**0**	**0**	**0**	**0**	**0**	**.179**	**.238**	**.179**	**1.000**

Randolph, Willie Larry

HEIGHT: 5'11"   THROWS: RIGHT   BATS: RIGHT   BORN: 7/6/1954 HOLLY HILL, SOUTH CAROLINA   POSITIONS PLAYED: 2B, 3B

YEAR	TEAM	GAMES	AB	RUNS	HITS	2B	3B	HR	RBI	BB	IBB	SO	HBP	SH	SF	SB	CS	BA	OBA	SA	FA
1975	Pit-N	30	61	9	10	1	0	0	3	7	1	6	0	1	1	1	0	.164	.246	.180	.500
1976	NY-A	125	430	59	115	15	4	1	40	58	5	39	3	6	3	37	12	.267	.356	.328	.974
1977	NY-A	147	551	91	151	28	11	4	40	64	1	53	1	2	6	13	6	.274	.347	.387	.980
1978	NY-A	134	499	87	139	18	6	3	42	82	1	51	4	6	5	36	7	.279	.381	.357	.978
1979	NY-A	153	574	98	155	15	13	5	61	95	5	39	3	5	5	33	12	.270	.374	.368	.985
1980	NY-A	138	513	99	151	23	7	7	46	119	4	45	2	5	3	30	5	.294	.427	.407	.976
1981	NY-A	93	357	59	83	14	3	2	24	57	0	24	0	5	3	14	5	.232	.336	.305	.977
1982	NY-A	144	553	85	155	21	4	3	36	75	3	35	3	10	2	16	9	.280	.368	.349	.981
1983	NY-A	104	420	73	117	21	1	2	38	53	0	32	1	3	0	12	4	.279	.361	.348	.979
1984	NY-A	142	564	86	162	24	2	2	31	86	4	42	0	7	7	10	6	.287	.377	.348	.983
1985	NY-A	143	497	75	137	21	2	5	40	85	3	39	4	5	6	16	9	.276	.382	.356	.985
1986	NY-A	141	492	76	136	15	2	5	50	94	0	49	3	8	4	15	2	.276	.393	.346	.972
1987	NY-A	120	449	96	137	24	2	7	67	82	1	25	2	5	5	11	1	.305	.411	.414	.981
1988	NY-A	110	404	43	93	20	1	2	34	55	2	39	2	8	5	8	4	.230	.322	.300	.988
1989	LA-N	145	549	62	155	18	0	2	36	71	2	51	4	4	5	7	6	.282	.366	.326	.987
1990	LA-N	26	96	15	26	4	0	1	9	13	0	9	1	3	0	1	0	.271	.364	.344	.979
1990	Oak-A	93	292	37	75	9	3	1	21	32	1	25	1	7	1	6	1	.257	.331	.318	.982
1991	Mil-A	124	431	60	141	14	3	0	54	75	3	38	0	3	3	4	2	.327	.424	.374	.968
1992	NY-N	90	286	29	72	11	1	2	15	40	1	34	4	6	0	1	3	.252	.352	.318	.977
Career average		116	422	65	116	17	3	3	36	65	2	36	2	5	3	14	5	.276	.373	.351	.954
Yankee average		**130**	**485**	**79**	**133**	**20**	**4**	**4**	**42**	**77**	**2**	**39**	**2**	**6**	**4**	**19**	**6**	**.275**	**.374**	**.357**	**.980**
Career total		2202	8018	1239	2210	316	65	54	687	1243	37	675	38	99	64	271	94	.276	.373	.351	.954
Yankee total		**1694**	**6303**	**1027**	**1731**	**259**	**58**	**48**	**549**	**1005**	**29**	**512**	**28**	**75**	**54**	**251**	**82**	**.275**	**.374**	**.357**	**.980**

Willie Larry Randolph, 2b, 1976–88

Willie Randolph was a rarity in the Yankee clubhouse of the mid-1970s and 1980s: a quiet, modest player who did his job and went home.

Born on July 6, 1954, in Holy Hill, South Carolina, Randolph and his family moved to Brooklyn when he was a baby. As a youngster, Randolph was a die-hard Dodgers fan. He was signed by the Pirates and began his career there. But he was traded to the Yankees in 1976. Such was his obvious potential that Randolph was the first rookie to be on the All-Star ballot.

He was a solid defensive player almost immediately, especially good at the double play. And Randolph was very consistent at the plate: In 10 of his 13 years with the Yankees, he hit .270 or better. In eight of those years, he had 20 or more doubles. He walked about twice as often as he struck out.

He played more games at second base than any other Yankee, a total of 1,688. In 1986, he and Ron Guidry were named co-captains of the Yankees.

He was a five-time All-Star with the Yankees, and his best year was 1987, when he was 33. That year, Randolph hit .305, with 96 runs scored and 67 RBI.

In 1989, Randolph was a free agent. He signed with the Dodgers and played four more years with Los Angeles, Oakland, Milwaukee and the Mets.

Randolph is 7th on the Yankees' all-time list in runs scored with 1,027, 11th in hits with 1,731, 14th in doubles with 259, 19th in triples with 58, 9th in games played with 1,694 and 2nd all-time in stolen bases with 251.

In 1993, Randolph was hired by the Yankees to be the team's third base coach.

Reed, John Burwell
HEIGHT: 6'0" THROWS: RIGHT BATS: RIGHT BORN: 2/2/1933 SILVER CITY, MISSISSIPPI POSITIONS PLAYED: OF

YEAR	TEAM	GAMES	AB	RUNS	HITS	2B	3B	HR	RBI	BB	IBB	SO	HBP	SH	SF	SB	CS	BA	OBA	SA	FA
1961	NY-A	28	13	4	2	0	0	0	1	1	0	1	0	0	0	0	0	.154	.214	.154	.933
1962	NY-A	88	43	17	13	2	1	1	4	4	1	7	0	1	0	2	1	.302	.362	.465	.941
1963	NY-A	106	73	18	15	3	1	0	1	9	0	14	0	0	0	5	1	.205	.293	.274	1.000
Career average		74	43	13	10	2	1	0	2	5	0	7	0	0	0	2	1	.233	.308	.326	.958
Yankee average		**74**	**43**	**13**	**10**	**2**	**1**	**0**	**2**	**5**	**0**	**7**	**0**	**0**	**0**	**2**	**1**	**.233**	**.308**	**.326**	**.958**
Career total		222	129	39	30	5	2	1	6	14	1	22	0	1	0	7	2	.233	.308	.326	.958
Yankee total		**222**	**129**	**39**	**30**	**5**	**2**	**1**	**6**	**14**	**1**	**22**	**0**	**1**	**0**	**7**	**2**	**.233**	**.308**	**.326**	**.958**

Reese, James Herman
HEIGHT: 5'11" THROWS: RIGHT BATS: LEFT BORN: 10/1/1901 NEW YORK, NEW YORK DIED: 7/13/1994 SANTA ANA, CALIFORNIA POSITIONS PLAYED: 2B, 3B

YEAR	TEAM	GAMES	AB	RUNS	HITS	2B	3B	HR	RBI	BB	IBB	SO	HBP	SH	SF	SB	CS	BA	OBA	SA	FA
1930	NY-A	77	188	44	65	14	2	3	18	11	—	8	0	4	—	1	1	.346	.382	.489	1.000
1931	NY-A	65	245	41	59	10	2	3	26	17	—	10	1	2	—	2	3	.241	.293	.335	.972
1932	StL-N	90	309	38	82	15	0	2	26	20	—	19	2	2	—	4	—	.265	.314	.333	.979
Career average		77	247	41	69	13	1	3	23	16	—	12	1	3	—	2	—	.278	.324	.373	.984
Yankee average		**71**	**217**	**43**	**62**	**12**	**2**	**3**	**22**	**14**	**—**	**9**	**1**	**3**	**—**	**2**	**2**	**.286**	**.331**	**.402**	**.986**
Career total		232	742	123	206	39	4	8	70	48	—	37	3	8	—	7	4	.278	.324	.373	.984
Yankee total		**142**	**433**	**85**	**124**	**24**	**4**	**6**	**44**	**28**	**—**	**18**	**1**	**6**	**—**	**3**	**4**	**.286**	**.331**	**.402**	**.986**

Renna, William Beneditto (Big Bill)
HEIGHT: 6'3" THROWS: RIGHT BATS: RIGHT BORN: 10/14/1924 HANFORD, CALIFORNIA POSITIONS PLAYED: OF

YEAR	TEAM	GAMES	AB	RUNS	HITS	2B	3B	HR	RBI	BB	IBB	SO	HBP	SH	SF	SB	CS	BA	OBA	SA	FA
1953	NY-A	61	121	19	38	6	3	2	13	13	—	31	1	2	—	0	1	.314	.385	.463	.983
1954	Phi-A	123	422	52	98	15	4	13	53	41	—	60	3	4	4	1	3	.232	.302	.379	.972
1955	KC-A	100	249	33	53	7	3	7	28	31	0	42	2	2	0	0	3	.213	.305	.349	.992
1956	KC-A	33	48	12	13	3	0	2	5	3	0	10	0	0	0	1	0	.271	.314	.458	.950
1958	Bos-A	39	56	5	15	5	0	4	18	6	1	14	0	0	0	0	0	.268	.339	.571	1.000
1959	Bos-A	14	22	2	2	0	0	0	2	5	0	9	0	0	0	0	0	.091	.259	.091	1.000
Career average		62	153	21	37	6	2	5	20	17	—	28	1	1	—	0	1	.239	.317	.391	.983
Yankee average		**61**	**121**	**19**	**38**	**6**	**3**	**2**	**13**	**13**	**—**	**31**	**1**	**2**	**—**	**0**	**1**	**.314**	**.385**	**.463**	**.983**
Career total		370	918	123	219	36	10	28	119	99	1	166	6	8	4	2	7	.239	.315	.391	.983
Yankee total		**61**	**121**	**19**	**38**	**6**	**3**	**2**	**13**	**13**	**—**	**31**	**1**	**2**	**—**	**0**	**1**	**.314**	**.385**	**.463**	**.983**

Rensa, George Anthony (Pug)
HEIGHT: 5'10" THROWS: RIGHT BATS: RIGHT BORN: 9/29/1901 PARSONS, PENNSYLVANIA DIED: 1/4/1987 WILKES-BARRE, PENN. POSITIONS PLAYED: C

YEAR	TEAM	GAMES	AB	RUNS	HITS	2B	3B	HR	RBI	BB	IBB	SO	HBP	SH	SF	SB	CS	BA	OBA	SA	FA
1930	Det-A	20	37	6	10	2	1	1	3	6	—	7	1	1	—	1	0	.270	.386	.459	.940
1930	Phi-N	54	172	31	49	11	2	3	31	10	—	18	1	2	—	0	—	.285	.328	.424	.932
1931	Phi-N	19	29	2	3	1	0	0	2	6	—	2	0	0	—	0	—	.103	.257	.138	.958
1933	**NY-A**	**8**	**29**	**4**	**9**	**2**	**1**	**0**	**3**	**1**	**—**	**3**	**0**	**1**	**—**	**0**	**1**	**.310**	**.333**	**.448**	**.977**
1937	Chi-A	26	57	10	17	5	1	0	5	8	—	6	0	0	—	3	0	.298	.385	.421	.975
1938	Chi-A	59	165	15	41	5	0	3	19	25	—	16	1	0	—	1	1	.248	.351	.333	.982
1939	Chi-A	14	25	3	5	0	0	0	2	1	—	2	0	1	—	0	0	.200	.231	.200	.972
Career average		29	73	10	19	4	1	1	9	8	—	8	0	1	—	1	—	.261	.338	.372	.962
Yankee average		**8**	**29**	**4**	**9**	**2**	**1**	**0**	**3**	**1**	**—**	**3**	**0**	**1**	**—**	**0**	**1**	**.310**	**.333**	**.448**	**.977**
Career total		200	514	71	134	26	5	7	65	57	—	54	3	5	—	5	2	.261	.338	.372	.962
Yankee total		**8**	**29**	**4**	**9**	**2**	**1**	**0**	**3**	**1**	**—**	**3**	**0**	**1**	**—**	**0**	**1**	**.310**	**.333**	**.448**	**.977**

Repoz, Roger Allen
HEIGHT: 6'3" THROWS: LEFT BATS: LEFT BORN: 8/3/1940 BELLINGHAM, WASHINGTON POSITIONS PLAYED: 1B, OF

YEAR	TEAM	GAMES	AB	RUNS	HITS	2B	3B	HR	RBI	BB	IBB	SO	HBP	SH	SF	SB	CS	BA	OBA	SA	FA
1964	**NY-A**	**11**	**1**	**1**	**0**	**0**	**0**	**0**	**0**	**1**	**0**	**1**	**0**	**0**	**0**	**0**	**0**	**.000**	**.500**	**.000**	**1.000**
1965	**NY-A**	**79**	**218**	**34**	**48**	**7**	**4**	**12**	**28**	**25**	**4**	**57**	**0**	**0**	**2**	**1**	**1**	**.220**	**.298**	**.454**	**.993**
1966	**NY-A**	**37**	**43**	**4**	**15**	**4**	**1**	**0**	**9**	**4**	**0**	**8**	**0**	**1**	**1**	**0**	**0**	**.349**	**.396**	**.488**	**1.000**
1966	KC-A	101	319	40	69	10	3	11	34	44	4	80	2	3	1	3	3	.216	.314	.370	.989
1967	KC-A	40	87	9	21	6	1	2	8	12	1	20	1	1	0	4	2	.241	.340	.402	.972
1967	Cal-A	74	176	25	44	9	1	5	20	19	1	37	0	0	3	2	2	.250	.318	.398	.959
1968	Cal-A	133	375	30	90	8	1	13	54	38	3	83	3	2	8	8	7	.240	.309	.371	.987
1969	Cal-A	103	219	25	36	1	1	8	19	32	2	52	0	3	1	1	3	.164	.270	.288	.985
1970	Cal-A	137	407	50	97	17	6	18	47	45	6	90	3	6	2	4	2	.238	.317	.442	.992
1971	Cal-A	113	297	39	59	11	1	13	41	60	6	69	1	0	2	3	5	.199	.333	.374	1.000
1972	Cal-A	3	3	0	1	0	0	0	0	0	0	2	0	0	0	0	0	.333	.333	.333	.000
Career average		76	195	23	44	7	2	7	24	25	2	45	1	1	2	2	2	.224	.314	.390	.898
Yankee average		**42**	**87**	**13**	**21**	**4**	**2**	**4**	**12**	**10**	**1**	**22**	**0**	**0**	**1**	**0**	**0**	**.240**	**.315**	**.458**	**.998**
Career total		831	2145	257	480	73	19	82	260	280	27	499	10	16	20	26	25	.224	.314	.390	.898
Yankee total		**127**	**262**	**39**	**63**	**11**	**5**	**12**	**37**	**30**	**4**	**66**	**0**	**1**	**3**	**1**	**1**	**.240**	**.315**	**.458**	**.998**

Revering, David Alvin
HEIGHT: 6'4" THROWS: RIGHT BATS: LEFT BORN: 2/12/1953 ROSEVILLE, CALIFORNIA POSITIONS PLAYED: 1B

YEAR	TEAM	GAMES	AB	RUNS	HITS	2B	3B	HR	RBI	BB	IBB	SO	HBP	SH	SF	SB	CS	BA	OBA	SA	FA
1978	Oak-A	152	521	49	141	21	3	16	46	26	5	55	0	2	4	0	1	.271	.303	.415	.989
1979	Oak-A	125	472	63	136	25	5	19	77	34	5	65	1	1	5	1	4	.288	.334	.492	.986
1980	Oak-A	106	376	48	109	21	5	15	62	32	6	37	0	2	2	1	0	.290	.344	.492	.989
1981	Oak-A	31	87	12	20	1	1	2	10	11	2	12	1	0	1	0	1	.230	.320	.333	.994
1981	**NY-A**	**45**	**119**	**8**	**28**	**4**	**1**	**2**	**7**	**11**	**5**	**20**	**0**	**0**	**0**	**0**	**1**	**.235**	**.300**	**.336**	**.995**
1982	**NY-A**	**14**	**40**	**2**	**6**	**2**	**0**	**0**	**2**	**3**	**2**	**4**	**0**	**0**	**1**	**0**	**0**	**.150**	**.205**	**.200**	**.992**
1982	Tor-A	55	135	15	29	6	0	5	18	22	1	30	0	0	2	0	3	.215	.321	.370	1.000
1982	Sea-A	29	82	8	17	3	1	3	12	9	0	17	0	0	0	0	0	.207	.283	.378	.986
Career average		70	229	26	61	10	2	8	29	19	3	30	0	1	2	0	1	.265	.318	.430	.991
Yankee average		**30**	**80**	**5**	**17**	**3**	**1**	**1**	**5**	**7**	**4**	**12**	**0**	**0**	**1**	**0**	**1**	**.214**	**.276**	**.302**	**.994**
Career total		557	1832	205	486	83	16	62	234	148	26	240	2	5	16	2	10	.265	.318	.430	.991
Yankee total		**59**	**159**	**10**	**34**	**6**	**1**	**2**	**9**	**14**	**7**	**24**	**0**	**0**	**1**	**0**	**1**	**.214**	**.276**	**.302**	**.994**

Reynolds, William Dee
HEIGHT: 6'0" THROWS: RIGHT BATS: RIGHT BORN: 8/14/1884 EASTLAND, TEXAS DIED: 6/5/1924 CARNEGIE, OKLAHOMA POSITIONS PLAYED: C

YEAR	TEAM	GAMES	AB	RUNS	HITS	2B	3B	HR	RBI	BB	IBB	SO	HBP	SH	SF	SB	CS	BA	OBA	SA	FA
1913	**NY-A**	**5**	**5**	**0**	**0**	**0**	**0**	**0**	**0**	**0**	**—**	**1**	**0**	**0**	**—**	**0**	**—**	**.000**	**.000**	**.000**	**.917**
1914	**NY-A**	**4**	**5**	**0**	**2**	**0**	**0**	**0**	**0**	**0**	**—**	**3**	**0**	**0**	**—**	**0**	**0**	**.400**	**.400**	**.400**	**1.000**
Career average		5	5	0	1	0	0	0	0	0	—	2	0	0	—	0	—	.200	.200	.200	.959
Yankee average		**5**	**5**	**0**	**1**	**0**	**0**	**0**	**0**	**0**	**—**	**2**	**0**	**0**	**—**	**0**	**—**	**.200**	**.200**	**.200**	**.959**
Career total		9	10	0	2	0	0	0	0	0	—	4	0	0	—	0	0	.200	.200	.200	.959
Yankee total		**9**	**10**	**0**	**2**	**0**	**0**	**0**	**0**	**0**	**—**	**4**	**0**	**0**	**—**	**0**	**0**	**.200**	**.200**	**.200**	**.959**

Rice, Harry Francis
HEIGHT: 5'9" THROWS: RIGHT BATS: LEFT BORN: 11/22/1901 WARE STATION, ILL. DIED: 1/1/1971 PORTLAND, ORE. POSITIONS PLAYED: C, 1B, 2B, 3B, SS, OF

YEAR	TEAM	GAMES	AB	RUNS	HITS	2B	3B	HR	RBI	BB	IBB	SO	HBP	SH	SF	SB	CS	BA	OBA	SA	FA
1923	StL-A	148	595	117	188	35	18	3	75	57	—	12	6	13	—	20	8	.316	.000	.450	.000
1924	StL-A	54	93	19	26	7	0	0	15	7	—	5	3	2	—	1	3	.280	.350	.355	.750
1925	StL-A	103	354	87	127	25	8	11	47	54	—	15	5	7	—	8	7	.359	.450	.568	.500
1926	StL-A	148	578	86	181	27	10	9	59	63	—	40	4	10	—	10	11	.313	.384	.441	1.000
1927	StL-A	137	520	90	149	26	9	7	68	50	—	21	2	16	—	5	4	.287	.351	.412	.833
1928	Det-A	131	510	87	154	21	12	6	81	44	—	27	2	17	—	20	13	.302	.360	.425	.962
1929	Det-A	130	536	97	163	33	7	6	69	61	—	23	4	12	—	6	10	.304	.379	.425	.960
1930	Det-A	37	138	16	39	6	0	2	24	19	—	8	2	4	—	0	3	.305	.403	.398	.944
1930	**NY-A**	**100**	**346**	**62**	**103**	**17**	**5**	**7**	**74**	**31**	**—**	**21**	**3**	**10**	**—**	**3**	**3**	**.298**	**.372**	**.436**	**.969**
1931	Was-A	47	162	32	43	5	6	0	15	12	—	10	1	4	—	2	1	.265	.320	.370	.968
1933	Cin-N	143	510	44	133	19	6	0	54	35	—	24	6	17	—	4	—	.261	.316	.322	.991

(continued)

(continued)

Career average	107	394	67	119	20	7	5	53	39	—	19	3	10	—	7	—	.301	.370	.425	.791
Yankee average	**100**	**346**	**62**	**103**	**17**	**5**	**7**	**74**	**31**	**—**	**21**	**3**	**10**	**—**	**3**	**3**	**.298**	**.361**	**.436**	**.969**
Career total	1178	4332	737	1306	221	81	51	581	433	—	206	38	112	—	79	63	.301	.370	.425	.791
Yankee total	**100**	**346**	**62**	**103**	**17**	**5**	**7**	**74**	**31**	**—**	**21**	**3**	**10**	**—**	**3**	**3**	**.298**	**.361**	**.436**	**.969**

Richardson, Clifford Nolen

HEIGHT: 6'1" THROWS: RIGHT BATS: RIGHT BORN: 1/18/1903 CHATTANOOGA, TENNESSEE DIED: 9/25/1951 ATHENS, GEORGIA POSITIONS PLAYED: 3B, SS

YEAR	TEAM	GAMES	AB	RUNS	HITS	2B	3B	HR	RBI	BB	IBB	SO	HBP	SH	SF	SB	CS	BA	OBA	SA	FA
1929	Det-A	13	21	2	4	0	0	0	2	2	—	1	0	1	—	1	1	.190	.261	.190	.839
1931	Det-A	38	148	13	40	9	2	0	16	6	—	3	0	4	—	2	1	.270	.299	.358	.946
1932	Det-A	69	155	13	34	5	2	0	12	9	—	13	0	5	—	5	2	.219	.262	.277	.938
1935	**NY-A**	**12**	**46**	**3**	**10**	**1**	**1**	**0**	**5**	**3**	**—**	**1**	**0**	**0**	**—**	**0**	**0**	**.217**	**.265**	**.283**	**.922**
1938	Cin-N	35	100	8	29	4	0	0	10	3	—	4	0	3	—	0	—	.290	.311	.330	.966
1939	Cin-N	1	3	0	0	0	0	0	0	0	—	0	0	0	—	0	—	.000	.000	.000	1.000
Career average		28	79	7	20	3	1	0	8	4	—	4	0	2	—	1	—	.247	.282	.309	.935
Yankee average		**12**	**46**	**3**	**10**	**1**	**1**	**0**	**5**	**3**	**—**	**1**	**0**	**0**	**—**	**0**	**0**	**.217**	**.265**	**.283**	**.922**
Career total		168	473	39	117	19	5	0	45	23	—	22	0	13	—	8	4	.247	.282	.309	.935
Yankee total		**12**	**46**	**3**	**10**	**1**	**1**	**0**	**5**	**3**	**—**	**1**	**0**	**0**	**—**	**0**	**0**	**.217**	**.265**	**.283**	**.922**

Robert Clinton "Bobby" Richardson, 2b-3b-ss, 1955–66

In addition to being one of the best second basemen of his era, Bobby Richardson was a deeply spiritual man and one of the leaders of the Yankee teams of the late 1950s and early 1960s.

Born on August 19, 1935, in Sumter, South Carolina, Richardson played parts of the 1955–56 seasons and came up for good in 1957. He played 93 games at second base and even made the All-Star team. But manager Casey Stengel was platooning him in 1957 and 1958 and Richardson admitted years later that he was often frustrated during this time.

In 1959, former Yankee great Bill Dickey began tutoring Richardson about hitting. Richardson began using a heavier bat and got more aggressive at the plate, and his average jumped from .247 to .301. He became an All-Star fixture in the Yankees' infield for the next eight seasons.

In 1960, his former manager from Denver, Ralph Houk, was named Yankee manager, and Richardson got even better. He won the Gold Glove from 1961–65, and with roommate Tony Kubek at shortstop, Moose Skowron at first base and Clete Boyer at third base, he anchored one of the best defensive infields ever.

His best year was 1962, when he hit .302, led the league in hits with 209 and finished second to Mickey Mantle in the MVP race. He had an amazing World Series in 1960 against Pittsburgh, with a Series-record 12 RBI and 11 hits. In 1964, he made 13 hits, another World Series record, against the Cardinals.

He was an extremely religious man throughout his life, and his teammates for the most part respected his faith. One story has Richardson's teammate Moose Skowron striking out in a crucial part of a game in the 1960s and returning to the dugout to unleash a stream of invectives. As he passed Richardson, sitting on the bench, he stopped, said, "Excuse me, Bobby," and continued on his way.

Although Richardson was only 31, he retired in 1966 because, for him, the game had ceased being fun. He went on to work as a baseball coach at the University of South Carolina and later Liberty College.

On the Yankees' all-time list, Richardson is 17th in hits with 1,432; 18th in games played with 1,412 and 16th in at-bats with 5,386.

Richardson, Robert Clinton (Bobby)

HEIGHT: 5'9"   THROWS: RIGHT   BATS: RIGHT   BORN: 8/19/1935 SUMTER, SOUTH CAROLINA   POSITIONS PLAYED: 2B, 3B, SS

YEAR	TEAM	GAMES	AB	RUNS	HITS	2B	3B	HR	RBI	BB	IBB	SO	HBP	SH	SF	SB	CS	BA	OBA	SA	FA
1955	NY-A	11	26	2	4	0	0	0	3	2	0	0	0	1	0	1	1	.154	.214	.154	1.000
1956	NY-A	5	7	1	1	0	0	0	0	0	0	1	0	0	0	0	0	.143	.143	.143	1.000
1957	NY-A	97	305	36	78	11	1	0	19	9	3	26	0	3	3	1	3	.256	.274	.298	.979
1958	NY-A	73	182	18	45	6	2	0	14	8	0	5	0	3	2	1	3	.247	.276	.302	.972
1959	NY-A	134	469	53	141	18	6	2	33	26	3	20	0	10	3	5	5	.301	.335	.377	.970
1960	NY-A	150	460	45	116	12	3	1	26	35	6	19	0	9	3	6	6	.252	.303	.298	1.000
1961	NY-A	162	662	80	173	17	5	3	49	30	1	23	2	10	2	9	7	.261	.295	.316	.978
1962	NY-A	161	692	99	209	38	5	8	59	37	1	24	1	20	4	11	9	.302	.337	.406	.982
1963	NY-A	151	630	72	167	20	6	3	48	25	0	22	2	8	3	15	1	.265	.294	.330	.984
1964	NY-A	159	679	90	181	25	4	4	50	28	1	36	0	16	5	11	2	.267	.294	.333	1.000
1965	NY-A	160	664	76	164	28	2	6	47	37	4	39	1	9	2	7	5	.247	.287	.322	.981
1966	NY-A	149	610	71	153	21	3	7	42	25	1	28	1	9	3	6	6	.251	.280	.330	.980
Career average		118	449	54	119	16	3	3	33	22	2	20	1	8	3	6	4	.266	.299	.335	.986
Yankee average		118	449	54	119	16	3	3	33	22	2	20	1	8	3	6	4	.266	.299	.335	.986
Career total		1412	5386	643	1432	196	37	34	390	262	20	243	7	98	30	73	48	.266	.299	.335	.986
Yankee total		1412	5386	643	1432	196	37	34	390	262	20	243	7	98	30	73	48	.266	.299	.335	.986

Rickey, Wesley Branch (The Mahatma)

HEIGHT: 5'9"   THROWS: RIGHT   BATS: LEFT   BORN: 12/20/1881 FLAT, OHIO   DIED: 12/9/1965 COLUMBIA, MISSOURI   POSITIONS PLAYED: C, 1B, OF

YEAR	TEAM	GAMES	AB	RUNS	HITS	2B	3B	HR	RBI	BB	IBB	SO	HBP	SH	SF	SB	CS	BA	OBA	SA	FA
1905	StL-A	1	3	0	0	0	0	0	0	0	—	—	0	0	—	0	0	.000	.000	.000	1.000
1906	StL-A	65	201	22	57	7	3	3	24	16	—	—	3	3	—	4	0	.284	.345	.393	.954
1907	**NY-A**	52	137	16	25	1	3	0	15	11	—	—	2	2	—	4	0	.182	.253	.234	.846
1914	StL-A	2	2	0	0	0	0	0	0	0	—	1	0	0	—	0	0	.000	.000	.000	.000
Career average		30	86	10	21	2	2	1	10	7	—	—	1	1	—	2	0	.239	.304	.324	.700
Yankee average		52	137	16	25	1	3	0	15	11	—	—	2	2	—	4	0	.182	.253	.234	.846
Career total		120	343	38	82	8	6	3	39	27	—	1	5	5	—	8	0	.239	.304	.324	.700
Yankee total		52	137	16	25	1	3	0	15	11	—	—	2	2	—	4	0	.182	.253	.234	.846

Rivera, Ruben BORN RUBEN RIVERA (MORENO)

HEIGHT: 6'3"   THROWS: RIGHT   BATS: RIGHT   BORN: 11/14/1973 LA CHORRERA, PANAMA   POSITIONS PLAYED: OF

YEAR	TEAM	GAMES	AB	RUNS	HITS	2B	3B	HR	RBI	BB	IBB	SO	HBP	SH	SF	SB	CS	BA	OBA	SA	FA
1995	**NY-A**	5	1	0	0	0	0	0	0	0	0	1	0	0	0	0	0	.000	.000	.000	1.000
1996	**NY-A**	46	88	17	25	6	1	2	16	13	0	26	2	1	2	6	2	.284	.381	.443	1.000
1997	SD-N	17	20	2	5	1	0	0	1	2	0	9	0	0	0	2	1	.250	.318	.300	1.000
1998	SD-N	95	172	31	36	7	2	6	29	28	0	52	2	1	1	5	1	.209	.325	.378	.973
1999	SD-N	147	411	65	80	16	1	23	48	55	0	143	0	0	4	18	7	.195	.287	.406	.976
2000	SD-N	135	423	62	88	18	6	17	57	44	1	137	10	0	2	8	4	.208	.296	.400	.984
Career average		74	186	30	39	8	2	8	25	24	0	61	2	0	2	7	3	.210	.305	.400	.989
Yankee average		26	45	9	13	3	1	1	8	7	0	14	1	1	1	3	1	.281	.377	.438	1.000
Career total		445	1115	177	234	48	10	48	151	142	1	368	14	2	9	39	15	.210	.305	.400	.989
Yankee total		51	89	17	25	6	1	2	16	13	0	27	2	1	2	6	2	.281	.377	.438	1.000

Rivers, John Milton (Mickey)

HEIGHT: 5'10"   THROWS: LEFT   BATS: LEFT   BORN: 10/31/1948 MIAMI, FLORIDA   POSITIONS PLAYED: OF

YEAR	TEAM	GAMES	AB	RUNS	HITS	2B	3B	HR	RBI	BB	IBB	SO	HBP	SH	SF	SB	CS	BA	OBA	SA	FA
1970	Cal-A	17	25	6	8	2	0	0	3	3	0	5	1	1	0	1	0	.320	.414	.400	1.000
1971	Cal-A	79	268	31	71	12	2	1	12	19	1	38	1	8	0	13	1	.265	.316	.336	.976
1972	Cal-A	58	159	18	34	6	2	0	7	8	1	26	1	8	0	4	3	.214	.256	.277	.981
1973	Cal-A	30	129	26	45	6	4	0	16	8	0	11	1	3	0	8	3	.349	.391	.457	.909
1974	Cal-A	118	466	69	133	19	11	3	31	39	0	47	1	11	1	30	13	.285	.341	.393	.994
1975	Cal-A	155	616	70	175	17	13	1	53	43	5	42	2	7	4	70	14	.284	.331	.359	.977
1976	**NY-A**	137	590	95	184	31	8	8	67	13	0	51	3	2	5	43	7	.312	.327	.432	.986
1977	**NY-A**	138	565	79	184	18	5	12	69	18	4	45	4	5	2	22	14	.326	.350	.439	.982
1978	**NY-A**	141	559	78	148	25	8	11	48	29	3	51	3	7	6	25	5	.265	.302	.397	.980

(continued)

John Milton "Mickey" Rivers, of, 1976–79

Mickey Rivers spent only four years with the New York Yankees, but the speedy centerfielder was one of the cornerstones of three pennant-winning squads.

Born on October 31, 1948 in Miami, Florida, Rivers was a star at Miami-Dade Junior College in the late 1960s. He began his big league career with the California Angels. The Yankees acquired Rivers and pitcher Ed Figueroa for Bobby Bonds in 1976.

Rivers became the best leadoff man for New York in years. In 1976, he hit .312 and stole 43 bases. He had intimidating speed on the base paths, which also helped him overcome a weak throwing arm in the outfield.

More than a few Yankees—and other observers—thought Rivers deserved the Most Valuable Player award given to teammate Thurman Munson in 1976. But frankly, as soon as the Yankees locked up the division, Rivers, as he often did throughout his career, took much of September off, which surely hurt his chances.

He was the most visible character on a team

of characters during those pennant-winning years from 1976–78. From his slow, old-man's walk to the plate, to his bat-twirling act when he missed a pitch, Rivers was the darling of Yankee fans and the target of opposing rooters.

He hit over .300 two of the three full years he was with the Yanks. He liked to play baseball, but he loved to play the horses. Because he didn't pick too many winners, he was constantly hitting management up for salary advances.

Rivers liked to play dumb, but he often displayed a quick wit. He almost always came out on top in his verbal duels with teammate Reggie Jackson. Once, during a bus trip, Jackson, who was in a batting slump, and Rivers began arguing. Why, declared Jackson, am I arguing with a man who can't read or write? To which Rivers replied, "Better stop readin' and writin' and start hittin'."

As good as Mick the Quick was, his eccentricities frustrated owner George Steinbrenner once too often and he was traded to Texas midway through the 1979 season. He played 5½ years for the Rangers before retiring in 1984.

(continued)

YEAR	TEAM	GAMES	AB	RUNS	HITS	2B	3B	HR	RBI	BB	IBB	SO	HBP	SH	SF	SB	CS	BA	OBA	SA	FA
1979	NY-A	74	286	37	82	18	5	3	25	13	2	21	1	2	5	3	7	.287	.315	.416	.978
1979	Tex-A	58	247	35	74	9	3	6	25	9	0	18	1	3	3	7	2	.300	.323	.433	.981
1980	Tex-A	147	630	96	210	32	6	7	60	20	1	34	1	6	4	18	7	.333	.353	.437	.978
1981	Tex-A	99	399	62	114	21	2	3	26	24	2	31	1	3	1	9	5	.286	.327	.371	.996
1982	Tex-A	19	68	6	16	1	1	1	4	0	0	7	0	0	1	0	0	.235	.232	.324	.000
1983	Tex-A	96	309	37	88	17	0	1	20	11	0	21	1	5	3	9	4	.285	.309	.350	.980
1984	Tex-A	102	313	40	94	13	1	4	33	9	1	23	0	4	0	5	5	.300	.320	.387	1.000
Career average		92	352	49	104	15	4	4	31	17	1	29	1	5	2	17	6	.295	.327	.397	.919
Yankee average		123	500	72	150	23	7	9	52	18	2	42	3	4	5	23	8	.299	.324	.422	.982
Career total		1468	5629	785	1660	247	71	61	499	266	20	471	22	75	35	267	90	.295	.327	.397	.919
Yankee total		490	2000	289	598	92	26	34	209	73	9	168	11	16	18	93	33	.299	.324	.422	.982

Rizzuto, Phillip Francis (Scooter)

HEIGHT: 5'6"   THROWS: RIGHT   BATS: RIGHT   BORN: 9/25/1917 BROOKLYN, NEW YORK   POSITIONS PLAYED: 2B, SS

YEAR	TEAM	GAMES	AB	RUNS	HITS	2B	3B	HR	RBI	BB	IBB	SO	HBP	SH	SF	SB	CS	BA	OBA	SA	FA
1941	NY-A	133	515	65	158	20	9	3	46	27	—	36	1	5	—	14	5	.307	.343	.398	.957
1942	NY-A	144	553	79	157	24	7	4	68	44	—	40	6	10	—	22	6	.284	.343	.374	.962
1946	NY-A	126	471	53	121	17	1	2	38	34	—	39	6	7	—	14	7	.257	.315	.310	.961
1947	NY-A	153	549	78	150	26	9	2	60	57	—	31	8	9	—	11	6	.273	.350	.364	.969
1948	NY-A	128	464	65	117	13	2	6	50	60	—	24	2	13	—	6	5	.252	.340	.328	.973
1949	NY-A	153	614	110	169	22	7	5	65	72	—	34	1	25	—	18	6	.275	.352	.358	.971
1950	NY-A	155	617	125	200	36	7	7	66	92	—	39	7	19	—	12	8	.324	.418	.439	.982

(continued)

Phillip Francis "Scooter" Rizzuto, ss-2b, 1941–56

During Phil Rizzuto's best years with the Yankees, the pitchers playing in front of him valued this diminutive shortstop and his defensive skills much more than they valued his slugging teammates.

Rizzuto was born September 25, 1917, in Brooklyn, NY. His parents were both immigrants from Italy and his father was not initially comfortable with Rizzuto's decision to try professional baseball over college. Rizzuto was an exceptional athlete and earned athletic scholarships from several local colleges, including Fordham University, to, ironically, play football as a 5 foot 6 inch quarterback. But Rizzuto was leaning toward baseball, which was where the money was in those days. After graduation from high school, he attended tryouts for the Giants, Dodgers and Yankees. Casey Stengel, then the manager of the Dodgers, suggested he buy a shoeshine box, a nasty insult Rizzuto never forgot. The Giants barely looked at him. Only the Yankees saw his potential, but even they were admittedly underwhelmed. New York offered him a contract with a $75 signing bonus.

He worked his way up the minor league ladder slowly but steadily. He was not a big man, obviously, but he had tremendous quickness, great anticipation and was usually the fastest player on the minor league teams on which he played. He seemed to swallow up ground balls easily, regardless of how hard they were hit. Pitchers for teams at every professional level in which Rizzuto played learned to love him.

In 1940, playing for Kansas City, Rizzuto was Minor League Player of the Year.

The Yankees brought him up in 1941. Rizzuto realized that he would never be a great slugger, but he worked to get on base for teammates who could park the long ball. He never hit more than seven home runs in a season, but from 1941 to 1953, Rizzuto averaged 135 hits a year.

On the base paths, there was virtually no disagreement: The Dodgers' Jackie Robinson was surely the smartest and most aggressive base runner of that era, but Rizzuto was not far behind. He would lead the Yankees in stolen bases eight times, a team record.

His numbers were never overwhelming. He

(continued)

YEAR	TEAM	GAMES	AB	RUNS	HITS	2B	3B	HR	RBI	BB	IBB	SO	HBP	SH	SF	SB	CS	BA	OBA	SA	FA
1951	NY-A	144	540	87	148	21	6	2	43	58	—	27	5	26	—	18	3	.274	.350	.346	.968
1952	NY-A	152	578	89	147	24	10	2	43	67	—	42	5	23	—	17	6	.254	.337	.341	.976
1953	NY-A	134	413	54	112	21	3	2	54	71	—	39	4	18	—	4	3	.271	.383	.351	.963
1954	NY-A	127	307	47	60	11	0	2	15	41	—	23	1	18	2	3	2	.195	.291	.251	1.000
1955	NY-A	81	143	19	37	4	1	1	9	22	1	18	3	13	0	7	1	.259	.369	.322	.957
1956	NY-A	31	52	6	12	0	0	0	6	6	0	6	0	7	0	3	0	.231	.310	.231	.934
Career average		128	447	67	122	18	5	3	43	50	—	31	4	15	—	11	4	.273	.351	.355	.967
Yankee average		**128**	**447**	**67**	**122**	**18**	**5**	**3**	**43**	**50**	**—**	**31**	**4**	**15**	**—**	**11**	**4**	**.273**	**.351**	**.355**	**.967**
Career total		1661	5816	877	1588	239	62	38	563	651	1	398	49	193	2	149	58	.273	.351	.355	.967
Yankee total		**1661**	**5816**	**877**	**1588**	**239**	**62**	**38**	**563**	**651**	**1**	**398**	**49**	**193**	**2**	**149**	**58**	**.273**	**.351**	**.355**	**.967**

Roach, Wilbur Charles (Roxey)

HEIGHT: 5'11" THROWS: RIGHT BATS: RIGHT BORN: 11/28/1882 ANITA, PENNSYLVANIA DIED: 12/26/1947 BAY CITY, MICHIGAN POSITIONS PLAYED: 2B, SS, OF

YEAR	TEAM	GAMES	AB	RUNS	HITS	2B	3B	HR	RBI	BB	IBB	SO	HBP	SH	SF	SB	CS	BA	OBA	SA	FA
1910	NY-A	70	220	27	47	9	2	0	20	29	—	—	3	8	—	15	—	.214	.313	.273	.913
1911	NY-A	13	40	4	10	2	1	0	2	6	—	—	0	2	—	0	—	.250	.348	.350	.880
1912	Was-A	2	2	1	1	0	0	1	1	0	—	—	0	0	—	0	—	.500	.500	2.000	.500
1915	Buf-F	92	346	35	93	20	3	2	31	17	—	34	0	7	—	11	—	.269	.303	.361	.959

(continued)

hit better than .300 only twice: in his rookie year, 1941, and in his MVP year, 1950. In 1950, he made 200 hits, second in the league, smacked 36 doubles, third in the league, and scored 125 runs, also third in the league. He also was the best fielding shortstop in the league that year and won the Hickock Belt as the best pro athlete in the world.

His play afield was something to watch. Yankee fans knew: Day in and day out, Rizzuto would make a difficult play look easy, and make a seemingly impossible play almost routine. Stengel, now one of the converted, called him the best all-around shortstop he had ever seen, better in many ways than the great Honus Wagner.

He was a tough player who would always stand up to a sliding baserunner when turning the double play. His teammates were aware of this and appreciated it. But they would not allow Yankee opponents to take liberties on the base paths when Rizzuto was involved. If Rizzuto was, in their opinion, the victim of a harsh play at second base, there would be retaliation.

He was city-born and bred, but Rizzuto enjoyed playing the rube to his Yankee teammates. He had a deathly fear (so he said) of things that crawled or flew, like reptiles or insects. His teammates would fill his glove with worms, or put a snake in his locker, and watch him recoil in horror.

In 1956, on Old-Timers Day in August, Rizzuto was released by the Yankees in a bizarre scene in which he was called into general manager George Weiss's office to look over the roster and determine who to release to make room for veteran outfielder Enos Slaughter. After a few moments of discussion, Weiss worked up the courage to explain to Rizzuto that the man the Yankees would be releasing was, in fact, Phil Rizzuto.

In tears, Rizzuto left the office. But he was smart enough not to criticize the Yankees, and the next year, he ascended to the broadcast booth. He was a Yankee broadcaster for many years, and his trademark "Holy Cow" is one of the most well-known expressions in radio.

A five-time All-Star, Rizzuto is 12th all-time on the Yankees in base hits with 1,588, 12th in at-bats with 5,816, 11th all-time in games played with 1,661, 16th in triples with 62, 11th in stolen bases with 149 and 15th in runs scored with 877. In 1984, the Yankees held a day in his honor and retired his number ten. In 1994, after several years of near-misses, he was elected to the Baseball Hall of Fame.

(continued)

	GAMES	AB	RUNS	HITS	2B	3B	HR	RBI	BB	IBB	SO	HBP	SH	SF	SB	CS	BA	OBA	SA	FA
Career average	44	152	17	38	8	2	1	14	13	—	—	1	4	—	7	—	.248	.311	.334	.813
Yankee average	**42**	**130**	**16**	**29**	**6**	**2**	**0**	**11**	**18**	**—**	**—**	**2**	**5**	**—**	**8**	**—**	**.219**	**.319**	**.285**	**.897**
Career total	177	608	67	151	31	6	3	54	52	—	34	3	17	—	26	—	.248	.311	.334	.813
Yankee total	**83**	**260**	**31**	**57**	**11**	**3**	**0**	**22**	**35**	**—**	**—**	**3**	**10**	**—**	**15**	**—**	**.219**	**.319**	**.285**	**.897**

Robertson, Andre Levett

HEIGHT: 5'10" THROWS: RIGHT BATS: RIGHT BORN: 10/2/1957 ORANGE, TEXAS POSITIONS PLAYED: 2B, 3B, SS

YEAR	TEAM	GAMES	AB	RUNS	HITS	2B	3B	HR	RBI	BB	IBB	SO	HBP	SH	SF	SB	CS	BA	OBA	SA	FA
1981	NY-A	10	19	1	5	1	0	0	0	0	0	3	0	0	0	1	1	.263	.263	.316	1.000
1982	NY-A	44	118	16	26	5	0	2	9	8	0	19	0	2	0	0	0	.220	.270	.314	.966
1983	NY-A	98	322	37	80	16	3	1	22	8	0	54	3	7	3	2	4	.248	.271	.326	.992
1984	NY-A	52	140	10	30	5	1	0	6	4	0	20	0	8	0	0	1	.214	.236	.264	.930
1985	NY-A	50	125	16	41	5	0	2	17	6	0	24	1	2	2	1	2	.328	.358	.416	.950
Career average		51	145	16	36	6	1	1	11	5	0	24	1	4	1	1	2	.251	.279	.327	.968
Yankee average		**51**	**145**	**16**	**36**	**6**	**1**	**1**	**11**	**5**	**0**	**24**	**1**	**4**	**1**	**1**	**2**	**.251**	**.279**	**.327**	**.968**
Career total		254	724	80	182	32	4	5	54	26	0	120	4	19	5	4	8	.251	.279	.327	.968
Yankee total		**254**	**724**	**80**	**182**	**32**	**4**	**5**	**54**	**26**	**0**	**120**	**4**	**19**	**5**	**4**	**8**	**.251**	**.279**	**.327**	**.968**

Robertson, Eugene Edward (Gene)

HEIGHT: 5'7" THROWS: RIGHT BATS: LEFT BORN: 12/25/1898 ST. LOUIS, MISSOURI DIED: 10/21/1981 FALLON, NEVADA POSITIONS PLAYED: 2B, 3B, SS

YEAR	TEAM	GAMES	AB	RUNS	HITS	2B	3B	HR	RBI	BB	IBB	SO	HBP	SH	SF	SB	CS	BA	OBA	SA	FA
1919	StL-A	5	7	1	1	0	0	0	0	1	—	2	0	0	—	0	—	.143	.250	.143	.750
1922	StL-A	18	27	2	8	2	1	0	1	1	—	1	0	0	—	1	0	.296	.321	.444	.875
1923	StL-A	78	251	36	62	10	1	0	17	21	—	7	2	18	—	4	2	.247	.310	.295	.935
1924	StL-A	121	439	70	140	25	4	4	52	36	—	14	2	6	—	3	5	.319	.373	.421	1.000
1925	StL-A	154	582	97	158	26	5	14	76	81	—	30	4	14	—	10	7	.271	.364	.405	1.000
1926	StL-A	78	247	23	62	12	6	1	19	17	—	10	1	9	—	5	1	.251	.302	.360	1.000
1928	**NY-A**	**83**	**251**	**29**	**73**	**9**	**0**	**1**	**36**	**14**	**—**	**6**	**0**	**11**	**—**	**2**	**4**	**.291**	**.328**	**.339**	**.926**
1929	**NY-A**	**90**	**309**	**45**	**92**	**15**	**6**	**0**	**35**	**28**	**—**	**6**	**1**	**9**	**—**	**3**	**3**	**.298**	**.358**	**.385**	**.966**
1929	Bos-N	8	28	1	8	0	0	0	6	1	—	0	0	2	—	1	—	.286	.310	.286	1.000
1930	Bos-N	21	59	7	11	1	0	0	7	5	—	3	0	3	—	0	—	.186	.250	.203	.949
Career average		66	220	31	62	10	2	2	25	21	—	8	1	7	—	3		.280	.344	.373	.940
Yankee average		**87**	**280**	**37**	**83**	**12**	**3**	**1**	**36**	**21**	**—**	**6**	**1**	**10**	**—**	**3**	**4**	**.295**	**.345**	**.364**	**.946**
Career total		656	2200	311	615	100	23	20	249	205	—	79	10	72	—	29	22	.280	.344	.373	.940
Yankee total		**173**	**560**	**74**	**165**	**24**	**6**	**1**	**71**	**42**	**—**	**12**	**1**	**20**	**—**	**5**	**7**	**.295**	**.345**	**.364**	**.946**

Robinson, Aaron Andrew

HEIGHT: 6'2" THROWS: RIGHT BATS: LEFT BORN: 6/23/1915 LANCASTER, S. CAROLINA DIED: 3/9/1966 LANCASTER, S. CAROLINA POSITIONS PLAYED: C

YEAR	TEAM	GAMES	AB	RUNS	HITS	2B	3B	HR	RBI	BB	IBB	SO	HBP	SH	SF	SB	CS	BA	OBA	SA	FA
1943	**NY-A**	**1**	**1**	**0**	**0**	**0**	**0**	**0**	**0**	**0**	**—**	**1**	**0**	**0**	**—**	**0**	**0**	**.000**	**.000**	**.000**	**.000**
1945	**NY-A**	**50**	**160**	**19**	**45**	**6**	**1**	**8**	**24**	**21**	**—**	**23**	**1**	**1**	**—**	**0**	**0**	**.281**	**.368**	**.481**	**1.000**
1946	**NY-A**	**100**	**330**	**32**	**98**	**17**	**2**	**16**	**64**	**48**	**—**	**39**	**1**	**2**	**—**	**0**	**1**	**.297**	**.388**	**.506**	**.983**
1947	**NY-A**	**82**	**252**	**23**	**68**	**11**	**5**	**5**	**36**	**40**	**—**	**26**	**0**	**0**	**—**	**0**	**1**	**.270**	**.370**	**.413**	**.997**
1948	Chi-A	98	326	47	82	14	2	8	39	46	—	30	0	1	—	0	1	.252	.344	.380	.989
1949	Det-A	110	331	38	89	12	0	13	56	73	—	21	1	6	—	0	2	.269	.402	.423	.986
1950	Det-A	107	283	37	64	7	0	9	37	75	—	35	0	0	—	0	1	.226	.388	.346	.993
1951	Det-A	36	82	3	17	6	0	0	9	17	—	9	0	0	—	0	0	.207	.343	.280	.991
1951	Bos-A	26	74	9	15	1	1	2	7	17	—	10	0	0	—	0	0	.203	.352	.324	.983
Career average		68	204	23	53	8	1	7	30	37	—	22	0	1	—	0	1	.260	.375	.412	.880
Yankee average		**58**	**186**	**19**	**53**	**9**	**2**	**7**	**31**	**27**	**—**	**22**	**1**	**1**	**—**	**0**	**1**	**.284**	**.377**	**.468**	**.745**
Career total		610	1839	208	478	74	11	61	272	337	—	194	3	10	—	0	6	.260	.375	.412	.880
Yankee total		**233**	**743**	**74**	**211**	**34**	**8**	**29**	**124**	**109**	**—**	**89**	**2**	**3**	**—**	**0**	**2**	**.284**	**.377**	**.468**	**.745**

Robinson, Bruce Philip

HEIGHT: 6'1" THROWS: RIGHT BATS: LEFT BORN: 4/16/1954 LA JOLLA, CALIFORNIA POSITIONS PLAYED: C

YEAR	TEAM	GAMES	AB	RUNS	HITS	2B	3B	HR	RBI	BB	IBB	SO	HBP	SH	SF	SB	CS	BA	OBA	SA	FA
1978	Oak-A	28	84	5	21	3	1	0	8	3	0	8	0	1	0	0	0	.250	.276	.310	.965
1979	**NY-A**	**6**	**12**	**0**	**2**	**0**	**0**	**0**	**2**	**1**	**0**	**0**	**0**	**0**	**0**	**0**	**0**	**.167**	**.231**	**.167**	**.943**
1980	**NY-A**	**4**	**5**	**0**	**0**	**0**	**0**	**0**	**0**	**0**	**0**	**4**	**0**	**0**	**0**	**0**	**0**	**.000**	**.000**	**.000**	**1.000**
Career average		13	34	2	8	1	0	0	3	1	0	4	0	0	0	0	0	.228	.257	.277	.969
Yankee average		**5**	**9**	**0**	**1**	**0**	**0**	**0**	**1**	**1**	**0**	**2**	**0**	**0**	**0**	**0**	**0**	**.118**	**.167**	**.118**	**.972**
Career total		38	101	5	23	3	1	0	10	4	0	12	0	1	0	0	0	.228	.257	.277	.969
Yankee total		**10**	**17**	**0**	**2**	**0**	**0**	**0**	**2**	**1**	**0**	**4**	**0**	**0**	**0**	**0**	**0**	**.118**	**.167**	**.118**	**.972**

Robinson, William Edward

HEIGHT: 6'2" THROWS: RIGHT BATS: LEFT BORN: 12/15/1920 PARIS, TEXAS POSITIONS PLAYED: 1B

YEAR	TEAM	GAMES	AB	RUNS	HITS	2B	3B	HR	RBI	BB	IBB	SO	HBP	SH	SF	SB	CS	BA	OBA	SA	FA
1942	Cle-A	8	8	1	1	0	0	0	2	1	—	0	0	0	—	0	0	.125	.222	.125	1.000
1946	Cle-A	8	30	6	12	1	0	3	4	2	—	4	0	2	—	0	0	.400	.438	.733	.988
1947	Cle-A	95	318	52	78	10	1	14	52	30	—	18	2	5	—	1	0	.245	.314	.415	.994
1948	Cle-A	134	493	53	125	18	5	16	83	36	—	42	2	9	—	1	0	.254	.307	.408	.995
1949	Was-A	143	527	66	155	27	3	18	78	67	—	30	7	2	—	3	4	.294	.381	.459	.987
1950	Was-A	36	129	21	30	4	2	1	13	25	—	4	2	0	—	0	0	.233	.365	.318	1.000
1950	Chi-A	119	424	62	133	11	2	20	73	60	—	28	5	2	—	0	0	.314	.405	.491	.987
1951	Chi-A	151	564	85	159	23	5	29	117	77	—	54	3	5	—	2	5	.282	.371	.495	.988
1952	Chi-A	155	594	79	176	33	4	22	104	70	—	49	12	5	—	2	0	.296	.382	.466	.990

(continued)

(continued)

YEAR	TEAM	GAMES	AB	RUNS	HITS	2B	3B	HR	RBI	BB	IBB	SO	HBP	SH	SF	SB	CS	BA	OBA	SA	FA
1953	Phi-A	156	615	64	152	28	4	22	102	63	—	56	5	2	—	1	2	.247	.322	.413	.988
1954	**NY-A**	**85**	**142**	**11**	**37**	**9**	**0**	**3**	**27**	**19**	**—**	**21**	**0**	**0**	**2**	**0**	**0**	**.261**	**.344**	**.387**	**.980**
1955	**NY-A**	**88**	**173**	**25**	**36**	**1**	**0**	**16**	**42**	**36**	**7**	**26**	**5**	**0**	**1**	**0**	**0**	**.208**	**.358**	**.491**	**.995**
1956	**NY-A**	**26**	**54**	**7**	**12**	**1**	**0**	**5**	**11**	**5**	**1**	**3**	**3**	**0**	**0**	**0**	**1**	**.222**	**.323**	**.519**	**1.000**
1956	KC-A	75	172	13	34	5	1	2	12	26	1	20	2	1	1	0	0	.198	.308	.273	.977
1957	Det-A	13	9	0	0	0	0	0	0	3	1	0	1	0	0	0	0	.000	.308	.000	1.000
1957	Cle-A	19	27	1	6	1	0	1	3	0	0	3	1	0	1	0	0	.222	.241	.370	1.000
1957	Bal-A	4	3	0	0	0	0	0	0	1	0	1	0	0	0	0	0	.000	.250	.000	.000
Career average		77	252	32	67	10	1	10	43	31	—	21	3	2	—	1	1	.268	.354	.440	.933
Yankee average		**66**	**123**	**14**	**28**	**4**	**0**	**8**	**27**	**20**	**—**	**17**	**3**	**0**	**1**	**0**	**0**	**.230**	**.348**	**.455**	**.992**
Career total		1315	4282	546	1146	172	24	172	723	521	10	359	50	33	5	10	12	.268	.353	.440	.933
Yankee total		**199**	**369**	**43**	**85**	**11**	**0**	**24**	**80**	**60**	**8**	**50**	**8**	**0**	**3**	**0**	**1**	**.230**	**.348**	**.455**	**.992**

Robinson, William Henry

HEIGHT: 6'2" THROWS: RIGHT BATS: RIGHT BORN: 6/26/1943 MCKEESPORT, PENNSYLVANIA POSITIONS PLAYED: 1B, 3B, OF

YEAR	TEAM	GAMES	AB	RUNS	HITS	2B	3B	HR	RBI	BB	IBB	SO	HBP	SH	SF	SB	CS	BA	OBA	SA	FA
1966	Atl-N	6	11	1	3	0	1	0	3	0	0	1	0	0	0	0	0	.273	.273	.455	.800
1967	**NY-A**	**116**	**342**	**31**	**67**	**6**	**1**	**7**	**29**	**28**	**4**	**56**	**2**	**5**	**3**	**2**	**2**	**.196**	**.259**	**.281**	**.968**
1968	**NY-A**	**107**	**342**	**34**	**82**	**16**	**7**	**6**	**40**	**26**	**3**	**54**	**2**	**4**	**4**	**7**	**6**	**.240**	**.294**	**.380**	**.985**
1969	**NY-A**	**87**	**222**	**23**	**38**	**11**	**2**	**3**	**21**	**16**	**3**	**39**	**0**	**0**	**1**	**3**	**1**	**.171**	**.226**	**.279**	**1.000**
1972	Phi-N	82	188	19	45	9	1	8	21	5	0	30	0	1	1	2	3	.239	.258	.426	.982
1973	Phi-N	124	452	62	130	32	1	25	65	27	1	91	1	3	4	5	4	.288	.326	.529	.850
1974	Phi-N	100	280	32	66	14	1	5	29	17	4	61	1	4	2	5	3	.236	.280	.346	.971
1975	Pit-N	92	200	26	56	12	2	6	33	11	4	36	0	3	3	3	1	.280	.313	.450	.991
1976	Pit-N	122	393	55	119	22	3	21	64	16	1	73	1	3	3	2	4	.303	.329	.534	.909
1977	Pit-N	137	507	74	154	32	1	26	104	25	3	92	3	4	5	12	6	.304	.337	.525	.992
1978	Pit-N	136	499	70	123	36	2	14	80	35	8	105	5	2	11	14	11	.246	.296	.411	.988
1979	Pit-N	148	421	59	111	17	6	24	75	24	11	81	1	4	5	13	2	.264	.302	.504	1.000
1980	Pit-N	100	272	28	78	10	1	12	36	15	2	45	0	3	4	1	4	.287	.320	.463	.979
1981	Pit-N	39	88	8	19	3	0	2	8	5	1	18	0	1	0	1	0	.216	.258	.318	.500
1982	Pit-N	31	71	8	17	3	0	4	12	5	3	19	0	0	1	0	1	.239	.286	.451	1.000
1982	Phi-N	35	69	6	18	6	0	3	19	7	1	15	0	0	2	1	1	.261	.321	.478	1.000
1983	Phi-N	10	7	0	1	0	0	0	2	1	0	4	0	0	0	0	0	.143	.250	.143	.000
Career average		87	257	32	66	13	2	10	38	15	3	48	1	2	3	4	3	.258	.300	.438	.877
Yankee average		**103**	**302**	**29**	**62**	**11**	**3**	**5**	**30**	**23**	**3**	**50**	**1**	**3**	**3**	**4**	**3**	**.206**	**.264**	**.318**	**.984**
Career total		1472	4364	536	1127	229	29	166	641	263	49	820	16	37	49	71	49	.258	.300	.438	.877
Yankee total		**310**	**906**	**88**	**187**	**33**	**10**	**16**	**90**	**70**	**10**	**149**	**4**	**9**	**8**	**12**	**9**	**.206**	**.264**	**.318**	**.984**

Rodriguez, Aurelio (Radio) BORN AURELIO RODRIGUEZ (ITUARTE)

HEIGHT: 5'10" THROWS: RIGHT BATS: RIGHT BORN: 12/28/1947 CANANEA, MEXICO POSITIONS PLAYED: 1B, 2B, 3B, SS

YEAR	TEAM	GAMES	AB	RUNS	HITS	2B	3B	HR	RBI	BB	IBB	SO	HBP	SH	SF	SB	CS	BA	OBA	SA	FA
1967	Cal-A	29	130	14	31	3	1	1	8	2	0	21	0	1	0	1	0	.238	.250	.300	.989
1968	Cal-A	76	223	14	54	10	1	1	16	17	2	36	1	1	0	0	2	.242	.299	.309	.921
1969	Cal-A	159	561	47	130	17	2	7	49	32	11	88	2	4	7	5	3	.232	.272	.307	.954
1970	Cal-A	17	63	6	17	2	2	0	7	3	0	6	1	0	0	0	1	.270	.313	.365	1.000
1970	Was-A	142	547	64	135	31	5	19	76	37	5	81	7	0	5	15	5	.247	.300	.426	1.000
1971	Det-A	154	604	68	153	30	7	15	39	27	6	93	3	3	2	4	6	.253	.288	.401	1.000
1972	Det-A	153	601	65	142	23	5	13	56	28	4	104	2	7	1	2	3	.236	.272	.356	.969
1973	Det-A	160	555	46	123	27	3	9	58	31	0	85	3	9	1	3	1	.222	.266	.330	1.000
1974	Det-A	159	571	54	127	23	5	5	49	26	2	70	1	5	5	2	0	.222	.255	.306	.961
1975	Det-A	151	507	47	124	20	6	13	60	30	1	63	0	8	1	1	1	.245	.286	.385	.953
1976	Det-A	128	480	40	115	13	2	8	50	19	3	61	1	9	5	0	4	.240	.267	.325	.978
1977	Det-A	96	306	30	67	14	1	10	32	16	1	36	0	1	1	1	1	.219	.257	.369	.972
1978	Det-A	134	385	40	102	25	2	7	43	19	1	37	3	5	2	0	1	.265	.303	.395	.987
1979	Det-A	106	343	27	87	18	0	5	36	11	0	40	1	5	3	0	2	.254	.277	.370	.956
1980	SD-N	89	175	7	35	7	2	2	13	6	0	26	0	2	0	1	1	.200	.227	.297	.965
1980	**NY-A**	**52**	**164**	**14**	**36**	**6**	**1**	**3**	**14**	**7**	**1**	**35**	**0**	**11**	**0**	**0**	**0**	**.220**	**.251**	**.323**	**.905**
1981	**NY-A**	**27**	**52**	**4**	**18**	**2**	**0**	**2**	**8**	**2**	**0**	**10**	**0**	**1**	**0**	**0**	**0**	**.346**	**.370**	**.500**	**1.000**
1982	Chi-A	118	257	24	62	15	1	3	31	11	0	35	1	8	0	0	0	.241	.275	.342	1.000
1983	Bal-A	45	67	0	8	0	0	0	2	0	0	13	1	1	0	0	0	.119	.130	.119	.978
1983	Chi-A	22	20	1	4	1	0	1	1	0	0	3	0	1	0	0	0	.200	.200	.400	.969
Career average		101	331	31	79	14	2	6	32	16	2	47	1	4	2	2	2	.237	.275	.351	.973
Yankee average		**40**	**108**	**9**	**27**	**4**	**1**	**3**	**11**	**5**	**1**	**23**	**0**	**6**	**0**	**0**	**0**	**.250**	**.280**	**.366**	**.953**
Career total		2017	6611	612	1570	287	46	124	648	324	37	943	27	82	34	35	31	.237	.275	.351	.973
Yankee total		**79**	**216**	**18**	**54**	**8**	**1**	**5**	**22**	**9**	**1**	**45**	**0**	**12**	**0**	**0**	**0**	**.250**	**.280**	**.366**	**.953**

Rodriguez, Carlos BORN CARLOS RODRIGUEZ (MARQUEZ)
HEIGHT: 5'9" THROWS: RIGHT BATS: BOTH BORN: 11/1/1967 MEXICO CITY, MEXICO POSITIONS PLAYED: 2B, 3B, SS

YEAR	TEAM	GAMES	AB	RUNS	HITS	2B	3B	HR	RBI	BB	IBB	SO	HBP	SH	SF	SB	CS	BA	OBA	SA	FA
1991	**NY-A**	**15**	**37**	**1**	**7**	**0**	**0**	**0**	**2**	**1**	**0**	**2**	**0**	**1**	**0**	**0**	**0**	**.189**	**.211**	**.189**	**.957**
1994	Bos-A	57	174	15	50	14	1	1	13	11	0	13	0	7	0	1	0	.287	.330	.397	.800
1995	Bos-A	13	30	5	10	2	0	0	5	2	0	2	1	3	0	0	0	.333	.394	.400	1.000
Career average		28	80	7	22	5	0	0	7	5	0	6	0	4	0	0	0	.278	.320	.365	.919
Yankee average		**15**	**37**	**1**	**7**	**0**	**0**	**0**	**2**	**1**	**0**	**2**	**0**	**1**	**0**	**0**	**0**	**.189**	**.211**	**.189**	**.957**
Career total		85	241	21	67	16	1	1	20	14	0	17	1	11	0	1	0	.278	.320	.365	.919
Yankee total		**15**	**37**	**1**	**7**	**0**	**0**	**0**	**2**	**1**	**0**	**2**	**0**	**1**	**0**	**0**	**0**	**.189**	**.211**	**.189**	**.957**

Rodriguez, Edwin BORN EDWIN RODRIGUEZ (MORALES)
HEIGHT: 5'11" THROWS: RIGHT BATS: RIGHT BORN: 8/14/1960 PONCE, PUERTO RICO POSITIONS PLAYED: 2B, 3B, SS

YEAR	TEAM	GAMES	AB	RUNS	HITS	2B	3B	HR	RBI	BB	IBB	SO	HBP	SH	SF	SB	CS	BA	OBA	SA	FA
1982	**NY-A**	**3**	**9**	**2**	**3**	**0**	**0**	**0**	**1**	**1**	**0**	**1**	**0**	**0**	**0**	**0**	**0**	**.333**	**.400**	**.333**	**.875**
1983	SD-N	7	12	1	2	1	0	0	0	1	0	3	0	1	0	0	0	.167	.231	.250	1.000
1985	SD-N	1	1	0	0	0	0	0	0	0	0	0	0	0	0	0	0	.000	.000	.000	.000
Career average		4	7	1	2	0	0	0	0	1	0	1	0	0	0	0	0	.227	.292	.273	.625
Yankee average		**3**	**9**	**2**	**3**	**0**	**0**	**0**	**1**	**1**	**0**	**1**	**0**	**0**	**0**	**0**	**0**	**.333**	**.400**	**.333**	**.875**
Career total		11	22	3	5	1	0	0	1	2	0	4	0	1	0	0	0	.227	.292	.273	.625
Yankee total		**3**	**9**	**2**	**3**	**0**	**0**	**0**	**1**	**1**	**0**	**1**	**0**	**0**	**0**	**0**	**0**	**.333**	**.400**	**.333**	**.875**

Rodriguez, Elisio (Ellie) BORN ELISIO RODRIGUEZ (DELGADO)
HEIGHT: 5'11" THROWS: RIGHT BATS: RIGHT BORN: 5/24/1946 FAJARDO, PUERTO RICO POSITIONS PLAYED: C

YEAR	TEAM	GAMES	AB	RUNS	HITS	2B	3B	HR	RBI	BB	IBB	SO	HBP	SH	SF	SB	CS	BA	OBA	SA	FA
1968	**NY-A**	**9**	**24**	**1**	**5**	**0**	**0**	**0**	**1**	**3**	**0**	**3**	**0**	**0**	**0**	**0**	**0**	**.208**	**.296**	**.208**	**1.000**
1969	KC-A	95	267	27	63	10	0	2	20	31	6	26	8	2	0	3	2	.236	.333	.296	.990
1970	KC-A	80	231	25	52	8	2	1	15	27	2	35	4	1	4	2	1	.225	.312	.290	.988
1971	Mil-A	115	319	28	67	10	1	1	30	41	5	51	8	7	5	1	1	.210	.311	.257	.992
1972	Mil-A	116	355	31	101	14	2	2	35	52	5	43	7	3	5	1	4	.285	.382	.352	.983
1973	Mil-A	94	290	30	78	8	1	0	30	41	3	28	10	7	2	4	3	.269	.376	.303	.986
1974	Cal-A	140	395	48	100	20	0	7	36	69	6	56	9	8	4	4	5	.253	.373	.357	.992
1975	Cal-A	90	226	20	53	6	0	3	27	49	0	37	6	9	3	2	2	.235	.380	.301	.991
1976	LA-N	36	66	10	14	0	0	0	9	19	2	12	3	0	2	0	0	.212	.400	.212	.986
Career average		86	241	24	59	8	1	2	23	37	3	32	6	4	3	2	2	.245	.356	.308	.990
Yankee average		**9**	**24**	**1**	**5**	**0**	**0**	**0**	**1**	**3**	**0**	**3**	**0**	**0**	**0**	**0**	**0**	**.208**	**.296**	**.208**	**1.000**
Career total		775	2173	220	533	76	6	16	203	332	29	291	55	37	25	17	18	.245	.356	.308	.990
Yankee total		**9**	**24**	**1**	**5**	**0**	**0**	**0**	**1**	**3**	**0**	**3**	**0**	**0**	**0**	**0**	**0**	**.208**	**.296**	**.208**	**1.000**

Roenicke, Gary Steven
HEIGHT: 6'3" THROWS: RIGHT BATS: RIGHT BORN: 12/5/1954 COVINA, CALIFORNIA POSITIONS PLAYED: 1B, 3B, OF

YEAR	TEAM	GAMES	AB	RUNS	HITS	2B	3B	HR	RBI	BB	IBB	SO	HBP	SH	SF	SB	CS	BA	OBA	SA	FA
1976	Mon-N	29	90	9	20	3	1	2	5	4	0	18	1	0	1	0	0	.222	.260	.344	.955
1978	Bal-A	27	58	5	15	3	0	3	15	8	0	3	1	1	2	0	1	.259	.348	.466	1.000
1979	Bal-A	133	376	60	98	16	1	25	64	61	4	74	12	1	3	1	3	.261	.378	.508	.981
1980	Bal-A	118	297	40	71	13	0	10	28	41	5	49	6	2	3	2	0	.239	.340	.384	1.000
1981	Bal-A	85	219	31	59	16	0	3	20	23	1	29	2	5	3	1	2	.269	.340	.384	.983
1982	Bal-A	137	393	58	106	25	1	21	74	70	2	73	9	5	0	6	7	.270	.392	.499	1.000
1983	Bal-A	115	323	45	84	13	0	19	64	30	2	35	4	4	5	2	2	.260	.326	.477	1.000
1984	Bal-A	121	326	36	73	19	1	10	44	58	1	43	4	3	2	1	2	.224	.346	.380	.995
1985	Bal-A	114	225	36	49	9	0	15	43	44	1	36	0	2	3	2	2	.218	.342	.458	.993
1986	**NY-A**	**69**	**136**	**11**	**36**	**5**	**0**	**3**	**18**	**27**	**0**	**30**	**1**	**0**	**1**	**1**	**1**	**.265**	**.388**	**.368**	**1.000**
1987	Atl-N	67	151	25	33	8	0	9	28	32	0	23	1	0	0	0	0	.219	.353	.450	.968
1988	Atl-N	49	114	11	26	5	0	1	7	8	0	15	0	0	0	0	0	.228	.279	.298	1.000
Career average		89	226	31	56	11	0	10	34	34	1	36	3	2	2	1	2	.247	.351	.434	.990
Yankee average		**69**	**136**	**11**	**36**	**5**	**0**	**3**	**18**	**27**	**0**	**30**	**1**	**0**	**1**	**1**	**1**	**.265**	**.388**	**.368**	**1.000**
Career total		1064	2708	367	670	135	4	121	410	406	16	428	41	23	26	16	20	.247	.351	.434	.990
Yankee total		**69**	**136**	**11**	**36**	**5**	**0**	**3**	**18**	**27**	**0**	**30**	**1**	**0**	**1**	**1**	**1**	**.265**	**.388**	**.368**	**1.000**

Roettger, Oscar Frederick Louis

HEIGHT: 6'0" THROWS: RIGHT BATS: RIGHT BORN: 2/9/1900 ST. LOUIS, MISSOURI DIED: 7/4/1986 ST. LOUIS, MISSOURI POSITIONS PLAYED: P, 1B, OF

YEAR	TEAM	GAMES	AB	RUNS	HITS	2B	3B	HR	RBI	BB	IBB	SO	HBP	SH	SF	SB	CS	BA	OBA	SA	FA
1923	NY-A	5	2	0	0	0	0	0	0	0	—	0	0	0	—	0	0	.000	.000	.000	1.000
1924	NY-A	1	0	0	0	0	0	0	0	0	—	0	0	0	—	0	0	—	—	—	.000
1927	Bro-N	5	4	0	0	0	0	0	0	1	—	1	1	0	—	0	—	.000	.333	.000	.000
1932	Phi-A	26	60	7	14	1	0	0	6	5	—	4	0	1	—	0	0	.233	.292	.250	.978
Career average		9	17	2	4	0	0	0	2	2	—	1	0	0	—	0	—	.212	.288	.227	.495
Yankee average		**3**	**1**	**0**	**0**	**0**	**0**	**0**	**0**	**0**	**—**	**0**	**0**	**0**	**—**	**0**	**0**	**.000**	**.000**	**.000**	**.500**
Career total		37	66	7	14	1	0	0	6	6	—	5	1	1	—	0	0	.212	.288	.227	.495
Yankee total		**6**	**2**	**0**	**0**	**0**	**0**	**0**	**0**	**0**	**—**	**0**	**0**	**0**	**—**	**0**	**0**	**.000**	**.000**	**.000**	**.500**

Rolfe, Robert Abial (Red)

HEIGHT: 5'11" THROWS: RIGHT BATS: LEFT BORN: 10/17/1908 PENACOOK, NEW HAMP. DIED: 7/8/1969 GILFORD, NEW HAMP. POSITIONS PLAYED: 3B, SS

YEAR	TEAM	GAMES	AB	RUNS	HITS	2B	3B	HR	RBI	BB	IBB	SO	HBP	SH	SF	SB	CS	BA	OBA	SA	FA
1931	NY-A	1	0	0	0	0	0	0	0	0	—	0	0	0	—	0	0	—	—	—	1.000
1934	NY-A	89	279	54	80	13	2	0	18	26	—	16	0	4	—	2	3	.287	.348	.348	.944
1935	NY-A	149	639	108	192	33	9	5	67	57	—	39	3	7	—	7	3	.300	.361	.404	.964
1936	NY-A	135	568	116	181	39	15	10	70	68	—	38	0	10	—	3	0	.319	.392	.493	.957
1937	NY-A	154	648	143	179	34	10	4	62	90	—	53	1	1	—	4	2	.276	.365	.378	.962
1938	NY-A	151	631	132	196	36	8	10	80	74	—	44	3	6	—	13	1	.311	.386	.441	.959
1939	NY-A	152	648	139	213	46	10	14	80	81	—	41	1	1	—	7	6	.329	.404	.495	.958
1940	NY-A	139	588	102	147	26	6	10	53	50	—	48	2	7	—	4	2	.250	.311	.366	.949
1941	NY-A	136	561	106	148	22	5	8	42	57	—	38	0	3	—	3	2	.264	.332	.364	.946
1942	NY-A	69	265	42	58	8	2	8	25	23	—	18	0	3	—	1	1	.219	.281	.355	.959
Career average		118	483	94	139	26	7	7	50	53	—	34	1	4	—	4	2	.289	.360	.413	.960
Yankee average		**118**	**483**	**94**	**139**	**26**	**7**	**7**	**50**	**53**	**—**	**34**	**1**	**4**	**—**	**4**	**2**	**.289**	**.360**	**.413**	**.960**
Career total		1175	4827	942	1394	257	67	69	497	526	—	335	10	42	—	44	20	.289	.360	.413	.960
Yankee total		**1175**	**4827**	**942**	**1394**	**257**	**67**	**69**	**497**	**526**	**—**	**335**	**10**	**42**	**—**	**44**	**20**	**.289**	**.360**	**.413**	**.960**

Rosar, Warren Vincent (Buddy)

HEIGHT: 5'9" THROWS: RIGHT BATS: RIGHT BORN: 7/3/1914 BUFFALO, NEW YORK DIED: 3/13/1994 ROCHESTER, NEW YORK POSITIONS PLAYED: C

YEAR	TEAM	GAMES	AB	RUNS	HITS	2B	3B	HR	RBI	BB	IBB	SO	HBP	SH	SF	SB	CS	BA	OBA	SA	FA
1939	NY-A	43	105	18	29	5	1	0	12	13	—	10	0	3	—	4	0	.276	.356	.343	.980
1940	NY-A	73	228	34	68	11	3	4	37	19	—	11	2	5	—	7	1	.298	.357	.425	.983
1941	NY-A	67	209	25	60	17	2	1	36	22	—	10	0	2	—	0	0	.287	.355	.402	.996
1942	NY-A	69	209	18	48	10	0	2	34	17	—	20	0	0	—	1	2	.230	.288	.306	.996
1943	Cle-A	115	382	53	108	17	1	1	41	33	—	12	0	4	—	0	4	.283	.340	.340	.983
1944	Cle-A	99	331	29	87	9	3	0	30	34	—	17	4	6	—	1	2	.263	.339	.308	.989
1945	Phi-A	92	300	23	63	12	1	1	25	20	—	16	1	4	—	2	1	.210	.262	.267	.987
1946	Phi-A	121	424	34	120	22	2	2	47	36	—	17	0	4	—	1	3	.283	.339	.358	1.000
1947	Phi-A	102	359	40	93	20	2	1	33	40	—	13	1	9	—	1	3	.259	.335	.334	.996
1948	Phi-A	90	302	30	77	13	0	4	41	39	—	12	2	6	—	0	2	.255	.344	.338	.997
1949	Phi-A	32	95	7	19	2	0	0	6	16	—	5	0	3	—	0	0	.200	.315	.221	.992
1950	Bos-A	27	84	13	25	2	0	1	12	7	—	4	0	0	—	0	0	.298	.352	.357	.991
1951	Bos-A	58	170	11	39	7	0	1	13	19	—	14	0	2	—	0	0	.229	.307	.288	.996
Career average		76	246	26	64	11	1	1	28	24	—	12	1	4	—	1	1	.261	.330	.334	.991
Yankee average		**63**	**188**	**24**	**51**	**11**	**2**	**2**	**30**	**18**	**—**	**13**	**1**	**3**	**—**	**3**	**1**	**.273**	**.337**	**.374**	**.989**
Career total		988	3198	335	836	147	15	18	367	315	—	161	10	48	—	17	18	.261	.330	.334	.991
Yankee total		**252**	**751**	**95**	**205**	**43**	**6**	**7**	**119**	**71**	**—**	**51**	**2**	**10**	**—**	**12**	**3**	**.273**	**.337**	**.374**	**.989**

Robert Abial "Red" Rolfe, 3b-ss, 1931, 1934–42

Unspectacular but steady, Red Rolfe was an anchor at third base for New York throughout the mid to late 1930s.

Born on October 17, 1908, in Penacook, New Hampshire, Rolfe initially split his time between shortstop and third base during his first two years in New York. But manager Joe McCarthy was looking for stability at third base and installed Rolfe there for good in 1935.

He was a very consistent and productive leadoff hitter, scoring 100 runs or more seven years in a row, from 1935–41. He hit .300 or more four times during that span. His best year was 1939, when he hit .329 and led the American League in runs scored, hits and doubles.

Rolfe was a four-time All-Star who played third base for six pennant winners and five World Champions. He played very well in World Series against the National League teams from New York. He hit .400 in the Yankees World Series win over the Giants in 1936, then .300 in the Yankees 1937 win over the Giants. He hit .300 in the Yanks' 1941 win over the Dodgers.

Rolfe, at 6 feet, 170 pounds, was a tall and lanky drink of water. He suffered from painful stomach ulcers, but he was durable. He rarely missed more than a handful of games during the seasons he was a regular, and only Graig Nettles played third base for the Yankees more years (11) than Rolfe did.

Rolfe twice led the American League in fielding, in 1935 and 1936.

Rolfe retired in 1942. He served as baseball coach at Yale for several years, then returned to the big leagues, managing the Tigers for 3 1/2 years from 1949–52. The Tigers finished second to the Yankees in 1950. Rolfe died in 1969 in New Hampshire.

Red Rolfe is 12th on the Yankees' all-time list in runs scored with 942, 20th in hits with 1,394, 16th in doubles with 257 and 12th in triples with 67.

Rosenthal, Lawrence John

HEIGHT: 6'0"   THROWS: LEFT   BATS: LEFT   BORN: 5/21/1910 ST. PAUL, MINNESOTA   DIED: 3/4/1992 WOODBURY, MINNESOTA   POSITIONS PLAYED: 1B, OF

YEAR	TEAM	GAMES	AB	RUNS	HITS	2B	3B	HR	RBI	BB	IBB	SO	HBP	SH	SF	SB	CS	BA	OBA	SA	FA
1936	Chi-A	85	317	71	89	15	8	3	46	59	—	37	0	5	—	2	0	.281	.394	.407	.977
1937	Chi-A	58	97	20	28	5	3	0	9	9	—	20	1	1	—	1	0	.289	.355	.402	.980
1938	Chi-A	61	105	14	30	5	1	1	12	12	—	13	0	1	—	0	1	.286	.359	.381	.959
1939	Chi-A	107	324	50	86	21	5	10	51	53	—	46	0	10	—	6	4	.265	.369	.454	.990
1940	Chi-A	107	276	46	83	14	5	6	42	64	—	32	0	6	—	2	3	.301	.432	.453	.977
1941	Chi-A	20	59	9	14	4	0	0	1	12	—	5	0	0	—	0	0	.237	.366	.305	.938
1941	Cle-A	45	75	10	14	3	1	1	8	9	—	10	0	2	—	1	0	.187	.274	.293	1.000
1944	**NY-A**	**36**	**101**	**9**	**20**	**3**	**0**	**0**	**9**	**19**	**—**	**15**	**0**	**0**	**—**	**1**	**0**	**.198**	**.325**	**.228**	**.986**
1944	Phi-A	32	54	5	11	2	0	1	6	5	—	9	0	3	—	0	0	.204	.271	.296	.960
1945	Phi-A	28	75	6	15	3	2	0	5	9	—	8	0	2	—	0	1	.200	.286	.293	1.000
Career average		58	148	24	39	8	3	2	19	25	—	20	0	3	—	1	1	.263	.370	.392	.977
Yankee average		**36**	**101**	**9**	**20**	**3**	**0**	**0**	**9**	**19**	**—**	**15**	**0**	**0**	**—**	**1**	**0**	**.198**	**.325**	**.228**	**.986**
Career total		579	1483	240	390	75	25	22	189	251	—	195	1	30	—	13	9	.263	.370	.392	.977
Yankee total		**36**	**101**	**9**	**20**	**3**	**0**	**0**	**9**	**19**	**—**	**15**	**0**	**0**	**—**	**1**	**0**	**.198**	**.325**	**.228**	**.986**

Roth, Robert Frank (Braggo)

HEIGHT: 5'7"   THROWS: RIGHT   BATS: RIGHT   BORN: 8/28/1892 BURLINGTON, WISCONSIN   DIED: 9/11/1936 CHICAGO, ILLINOIS   POSITIONS PLAYED: 3B, OF

YEAR	TEAM	GAMES	AB	RUNS	HITS	2B	3B	HR	RBI	BB	IBB	SO	HBP	SH	SF	SB	CS	BA	OBA	SA	FA
1914	Chi-A	34	126	14	37	4	6	1	10	8	—	25	4	3	—	3	3	.294	.355	.444	.924
1915	Chi-A	70	240	44	60	6	10	3	35	29	—	50	3	5	—	12	6	.250	.338	.396	.943
1915	Cle-A	39	144	23	43	4	7	4	20	22	—	22	2	5	—	14	4	.299	.399	.507	.878
1916	Cle-A	125	409	50	117	19	7	4	72	38	—	48	2	16	—	29	14	.286	.350	.396	.954
1917	Cle-A	145	495	69	141	30	9	1	72	52	—	73	2	20	—	51	—	.285	.355	.388	.957
1918	Cle-A	106	375	53	106	21	12	1	59	53	—	41	8	12	—	35	—	.283	.383	.411	.936
1919	Phi-A	48	195	33	63	13	8	5	29	15	—	21	2	2	—	11	—	.323	.377	.549	.975
1919	Bos-A	63	227	32	58	9	4	0	23	24	—	32	4	5	—	9	—	.256	.337	.330	.943
1920	Was-A	138	468	80	136	23	8	9	92	75	—	57	6	12	—	24	12	.291	.395	.432	.952
1921	**NY-A**	**43**	**152**	**29**	**43**	**9**	**2**	**2**	**10**	**19**	**—**	**20**	**2**	**3**	**—**	**1**	**2**	**.283**	**.370**	**.408**	**.923**
Career average		81	283	43	80	14	7	3	42	34	—	39	4	8	—	19	—	.284	.367	.416	.939
Yankee average		**43**	**152**	**29**	**43**	**9**	**2**	**2**	**10**	**19**	**—**	**20**	**2**	**3**	**—**	**1**	**2**	**.283**	**.370**	**.408**	**.923**
Career total		811	2831	427	804	138	73	30	422	335	—	389	35	83	—	189	41	.284	.367	.416	.939
Yankee total		**43**	**152**	**29**	**43**	**9**	**2**	**2**	**10**	**19**	**—**	**20**	**2**	**3**	**—**	**1**	**2**	**.283**	**.370**	**.408**	**.923**

Royster, Jeron Kennis (Jerry)

HEIGHT: 6'0"   THROWS: RIGHT   BATS: RIGHT   BORN: 10/18/1952 SACRAMENTO, CALIFORNIA   POSITIONS PLAYED: 2B, 3B, SS, OF

YEAR	TEAM	GAMES	AB	RUNS	HITS	2B	3B	HR	RBI	BB	IBB	SO	HBP	SH	SF	SB	CS	BA	OBA	SA	FA
1973	LA-N	10	19	1	4	0	0	0	2	0	0	5	0	0	0	1	0	.211	.211	.211	1.000
1974	LA-N	6	0	2	0	0	0	0	0	0	0	0	0	0	0	0	0	—	—	—	1.000
1975	LA-N	13	36	2	9	2	1	0	1	1	0	3	0	0	0	1	0	.250	.270	.361	1.000
1976	Atl-N	149	533	65	132	13	1	5	45	52	4	53	1	14	5	24	13	.248	.313	.304	.857
1977	Atl-N	140	445	64	96	10	2	6	28	38	3	67	1	6	1	28	10	.216	.278	.288	.958
1978	Atl-N	140	529	67	137	17	8	2	35	56	2	49	3	8	4	27	17	.259	.331	.333	.956
1979	Atl-N	154	601	103	164	25	6	3	51	62	0	59	0	6	7	35	8	.273	.337	.349	.948
1980	Atl-N	123	392	42	95	17	5	1	20	37	1	48	1	4	1	22	13	.242	.309	.319	.948
1981	Atl-N	64	93	13	19	4	1	0	9	7	0	14	0	4	1	7	5	.204	.257	.269	.960
1982	Atl-N	108	261	43	77	13	2	2	25	22	1	36	2	5	3	14	6	.295	.351	.383	.975
1983	Atl-N	91	268	32	63	10	3	3	30	28	2	35	0	5	2	11	7	.235	.305	.328	.989
1984	SD-N	81	227	22	47	13	2	1	21	15	1	41	1	2	2	6	4	.207	.257	.295	.957
1985	SD-N	90	249	31	70	13	2	5	31	32	1	31	1	3	2	6	5	.281	.363	.410	.975
1986	SD-N	118	257	31	66	12	0	5	26	32	3	45	0	6	3	3	5	.257	.336	.362	.970
1987	Chi-A	55	154	25	37	11	0	7	23	19	1	28	1	2	2	2	1	.240	.324	.448	1.000
1987	**NY-A**	**18**	**42**	**1**	**15**	**2**	**0**	**0**	**4**	**4**	**0**	**4**	**0**	**1**	**0**	**2**	**1**	**.357**	**.413**	**.405**	**1.000**
1988	Atl-N	68	102	8	18	3	0	0	1	6	1	16	0	3	0	0	0	.176	.222	.206	1.000
Career average		84	248	32	62	10	2	2	21	24	1	31	1	4	2	11	6	.249	.315	.333	.970
Yankee average		**18**	**42**	**1**	**15**	**2**	**0**	**0**	**4**	**4**	**0**	**4**	**0**	**1**	**0**	**2**	**1**	**.357**	**.413**	**.405**	**1.000**
Career total		1428	4208	552	1049	165	33	40	352	411	20	534	11	69	33	189	95	.249	.315	.333	.970
Yankee total		**18**	**42**	**1**	**15**	**2**	**0**	**0**	**4**	**4**	**0**	**4**	**0**	**1**	**0**	**2**	**1**	**.357**	**.413**	**.405**	**1.000**

Ruel, Harold Dominic (Muddy)

HEIGHT: 5'9"   THROWS: RIGHT   BATS: RIGHT   BORN: 2/20/1896 ST. LOUIS, MISSOURI   DIED: 11/13/1963 PALO ALTO, CALIFORNIA   POSITIONS PLAYED: C, 1B

YEAR	TEAM	GAMES	AB	RUNS	HITS	2B	3B	HR	RBI	BB	IBB	SO	HBP	SH	SF	SB	CS	BA	OBA	SA	FA
1915	StL-A	10	14	0	0	0	0	0	1	5	—	5	0	0	—	0	0	.000	.263	.000	.958
1917	**NY-A**	**6**	**17**	**1**	**2**	**0**	**0**	**0**	**1**	**2**	**—**	**2**	**0**	**1**	**—**	**1**	**—**	**.118**	**.211**	**.118**	**1.000**
1918	**NY-A**	**3**	**6**	**0**	**2**	**0**	**0**	**0**	**0**	**2**	**—**	**1**	**0**	**0**	**—**	**1**	**—**	**.333**	**.500**	**.333**	**1.000**
1919	**NY-A**	**79**	**233**	**18**	**56**	**6**	**0**	**0**	**31**	**34**	**—**	**26**	**1**	**5**	**—**	**4**	**—**	**.240**	**.340**	**.266**	**.975**
1920	**NY-A**	**82**	**261**	**30**	**70**	**14**	**1**	**1**	**15**	**15**	**—**	**18**	**1**	**7**	**—**	**4**	**2**	**.268**	**.310**	**.341**	**.984**
1921	Bos-A	113	358	41	99	21	1	1	45	41	—	15	1	12	—	2	7	.277	.353	.349	.977
1922	Bos-A	116	361	34	92	15	1	0	28	41	—	26	1	11	—	4	2	.255	.333	.302	.978
1923	Was-A	136	449	63	142	24	3	0	54	55	—	21	3	21	—	4	6	.316	.394	.383	.980
1924	Was-A	149	501	50	142	20	2	0	57	62	—	20	7	29	—	7	11	.283	.370	.331	.980
1925	Was-A	127	393	55	122	9	2	0	54	63	—	16	4	13	—	4	5	.310	.411	.344	1.000
1926	Was-A	117	368	42	110	22	4	1	53	61	—	14	2	13	—	7	6	.299	.401	.389	.989
1927	Was-A	131	428	61	132	16	5	1	52	63	—	18	5	8	—	9	6	.308	.403	.376	.988
1928	Was-A	108	350	31	90	18	2	0	55	44	—	14	1	9	—	12	10	.257	.342	.320	.989
1929	Was-A	69	188	16	46	4	2	0	20	31	—	7	0	5	—	0	4	.245	.352	.287	.990
1930	Was-A	66	198	18	50	3	4	0	26	24	—	13	3	4	—	1	0	.253	.342	.308	.986
1931	Bos-A	33	83	6	25	5	0	0	6	9	—	6	0	1	—	0	0	.301	.370	.361	.945

(continued)

(continued)

YEAR	TEAM																	BA	OBA	SA	FA
1931	Det-A	14	50	1	6	1	0	0	3	5	—	1	0	0	—	0	0	.120	.200	.140	.975
1932	Det-A	51	136	10	32	4	2	0	18	17	—	6	0	2	—	1	0	.235	.320	.294	.989
1933	StL-A	36	63	13	12	2	0	0	8	24	—	4	0	0	—	0	0	.190	.414	.222	1.000
1934	Chi-A	22	57	4	12	3	0	0	7	8	—	5	0	2	—	0	0	.211	.308	.263	.976
Career average		73	226	25	62	9	1	0	27	30	—	12	1	7	—	3	—	.275	.365	.332	.983
Yankee average		**43**	**129**	**12**	**33**	**5**	**0**	**0**	**12**	**13**	**—**	**12**	**1**	**3**	**—**	**3**	**—**	**.251**	**.323**	**.300**	**.990**
Career total		1468	4514	494	1242	187	29	4	534	606	—	238	29	143	—	61	59	.275	.365	.332	.983
Yankee total		**170**	**517**	**49**	**130**	**20**	**1**	**1**	**47**	**53**	**—**	**47**	**2**	**13**	**—**	**10**	**2**	**.251**	**.323**	**.300**	**.990**

Ruether, Walter Henry (Dutch)

HEIGHT: 6'1"   BATS: L   BORN: 9/13/1893 ALAMEDA, CALIFORNIA   DIED: 5/16/1970 PHOENIX, ARIZONA   POSITIONS PLAYED: P, 1B

YEAR	TEAM	GAMES	AB	RUNS	HITS	2B	3B	HR	RBI	BB	IBB	SO	HBP	SH	SF	SB	CS	BA	OBA	SA	FA
1917	Chi-N	31	44	3	12	1	3	0	11	8	—	11	0	1	—	0	—	.273	.385	.432	1.000
1917	Cin-N	19	24	1	5	2	0	0	1	3	—	6	0	0	—	1	—	.208	.296	.292	.833
1918	Cin-N	2	3	0	0	0	0	0	0	0	—	2	0	0	—	0	—	.000	.000	.000	1.000
1919	Cin-N	42	92	8	24	2	3	0	6	4	—	18	0	3	—	1	—	.261	.292	.348	.971
1920	Cin-N	45	104	3	20	4	0	0	10	5	—	24	0	2	—	0	0	.192	.229	.231	.952
1921	Bro-N	49	97	12	34	5	2	2	13	4	—	9	0	2	—	1	0	.351	.376	.505	.966
1922	Bro-N	67	125	12	26	6	1	2	20	12	—	11	1	5	—	0	0	.208	.283	.320	1.000
1923	Bro-N	49	117	6	32	1	0	0	10	12	—	12	0	2	—	0	0	.274	.341	.282	.968
1924	Bro-N	34	62	5	15	1	1	0	4	5	—	2	0	1	—	0	0	.242	.299	.290	.981
1925	Was-A	55	108	18	36	3	2	1	15	10	—	8	0	3	—	0	1	.333	.390	.426	.962
1926	Was-A	47	92	6	23	2	0	1	11	6	—	10	0	3	—	0	0	.250	.296	.304	.946
1926	**NY-A**	**13**	**21**	**2**	**2**	**0**	**0**	**0**	**0**	**0**	**—**	**1**	**1**	**0**	**—**	**0**	**0**	**.095**	**.136**	**.095**	**1.000**
1927	**NY-A**	**35**	**80**	**7**	**21**	**3**	**0**	**1**	**10**	**8**	**—**	**15**	**0**	**0**	**—**	**0**	**0**	**.263**	**.330**	**.338**	**1.000**
Career average		38	75	6	19	2	1	1	9	6	—	10	0	2	—	0	—	.258	.314	.335	.968
Yankee average		**24**	**51**	**5**	**12**	**2**	**0**	**1**	**5**	**4**	**—**	**8**	**1**	**0**	**—**	**0**	**0**	**.228**	**.291**	**.287**	**1.000**
Career total		488	969	83	250	30	12	7	111	77	—	129	2	22	—	3	1	.258	.314	.335	.968
Yankee total		**48**	**101**	**9**	**23**	**3**	**0**	**1**	**10**	**8**	**—**	**16**	**1**	**0**	**—**	**0**	**0**	**.228**	**.291**	**.287**	**1.000**

Ruffing, Charles Herbert (Red)

HEIGHT: 6'1"   THROWS: RIGHT   BATS: RIGHT   BORN: 5/3/1904 GRANVILLE, ILLINOIS   DIED: 2/17/1986 MAYFIELD HTS., OHIO   POSITIONS PLAYED: P, OF

YEAR	TEAM	GAMES	AB	RUNS	HITS	2B	3B	HR	RBI	BB	IBB	SO	HBP	SH	SF	SB	CS	BA	OBA	SA	FA
1924	Bos-A	8	7	0	1	0	1	0	0	0	—	1	0	0	—	0	0	.143	.143	.429	1.000
1925	Bos-A	37	79	6	17	4	2	0	11	1	—	22	1	2	—	0	0	.215	.235	.316	.983
1926	Bos-A	37	51	8	10	1	0	1	5	2	—	12	0	2	—	0	1	.196	.226	.275	1.000
1927	Bos-A	29	55	5	14	3	1	0	4	0	—	6	1	6	—	0	0	.255	.268	.345	.978
1928	Bos-A	60	121	12	38	13	1	2	19	3	—	12	0	7	—	0	0	.314	.331	.488	.951
1929	Bos-A	60	114	9	35	9	0	2	17	2	—	13	1	3	—	0	0	.307	.325	.439	.946
1930	Bos-A	6	11	2	3	2	0	0	1	0	—	1	0	0	—	0	0	.273	.273	.455	.914
1930	**NY-A**	**52**	**99**	**15**	**37**	**6**	**2**	**4**	**21**	**7**	**—**	**7**	**0**	**0**	**—**	**0**	**0**	**.374**	**.415**	**.596**	**.938**
1931	**NY-A**	**48**	**109**	**14**	**36**	**8**	**1**	**3**	**12**	**1**	**—**	**13**	**0**	**6**	**—**	**0**	**0**	**.330**	**.336**	**.505**	**1.000**
1932	**NY-A**	**55**	**124**	**20**	**38**	**6**	**1**	**3**	**19**	**6**	**—**	**10**	**0**	**2**	**—**	**0**	**0**	**.306**	**.338**	**.444**	**.955**
1933	**NY-A**	**55**	**115**	**10**	**29**	**3**	**1**	**2**	**13**	**7**	**—**	**15**	**0**	**2**	**—**	**0**	**0**	**.252**	**.295**	**.348**	**.964**
1934	**NY-A**	**45**	**113**	**11**	**28**	**3**	**0**	**2**	**13**	**3**	**—**	**17**	**1**	**0**	**—**	**0**	**0**	**.248**	**.274**	**.327**	**.933**
1935	**NY-A**	**50**	**109**	**13**	**37**	**10**	**0**	**2**	**18**	**3**	**—**	**9**	**1**	**1**	**—**	**0**	**0**	**.339**	**.363**	**.486**	**1.000**
1936	**NY-A**	**53**	**127**	**14**	**37**	**5**	**0**	**5**	**22**	**11**	**—**	**12**	**0**	**2**	**—**	**0**	**0**	**.291**	**.348**	**.449**	**.986**
1937	**NY-A**	**54**	**129**	**11**	**26**	**3**	**0**	**1**	**10**	**13**	**—**	**24**	**0**	**2**	**—**	**0**	**0**	**.202**	**.275**	**.248**	**.974**
1938	**NY-A**	**45**	**107**	**12**	**24**	**4**	**1**	**3**	**17**	**17**	**—**	**21**	**0**	**1**	**—**	**0**	**0**	**.224**	**.331**	**.364**	**1.000**
1939	**NY-A**	**44**	**114**	**12**	**35**	**1**	**0**	**1**	**20**	**7**	**—**	**18**	**0**	**3**	**—**	**1**	**0**	**.307**	**.347**	**.342**	**.952**
1940	**NY-A**	**33**	**89**	**8**	**11**	**4**	**0**	**1**	**7**	**3**	**—**	**9**	**0**	**1**	**—**	**0**	**0**	**.124**	**.152**	**.202**	**.947**
1941	**NY-A**	**38**	**89**	**10**	**27**	**8**	**1**	**2**	**22**	**4**	**—**	**12**	**0**	**1**	**—**	**0**	**0**	**.303**	**.333**	**.483**	**1.000**
1942	**NY-A**	**30**	**80**	**8**	**20**	**4**	**0**	**1**	**13**	**5**	**—**	**13**	**1**	**2**	**—**	**0**	**0**	**.250**	**.302**	**.338**	**.974**
1945	**NY-A**	**21**	**46**	**4**	**10**	**0**	**1**	**1**	**5**	**0**	**—**	**8**	**0**	**0**	**—**	**0**	**0**	**.217**	**.217**	**.326**	**.929**
1946	**NY-A**	**8**	**25**	**1**	**3**	**1**	**0**	**0**	**1**	**1**	**—**	**8**	**0**	**0**	**—**	**0**	**0**	**.120**	**.154**	**.160**	**1.000**
1947	Chi-A	14	24	2	5	0	0	0	3	1	—	3	0	0	—	0	0	.208	.240	.208	1.000
Career average		38	84	9	23	4	1	2	12	4	—	12	0	2	—	0	0	.269	.306	.389	.971
Yankee average		**42**	**98**	**11**	**27**	**4**	**1**	**2**	**14**	**6**	**—**	**13**	**0**	**2**	**—**	**0**	**0**	**.270**	**.312**	**.388**	**.970**
Career total		882	1937	207	521	98	13	36	273	97	—	266	6	43	—	1	1	.269	.306	.389	.971
Yankee total		**631**	**1475**	**163**	**398**	**66**	**8**	**31**	**213**	**88**	**—**	**196**	**3**	**23**	**—**	**1**	**0**	**.270**	**.312**	**.388**	**.970**

Ruth, George Herman (Babe *or* The Bambino *or* The Sultan Of Swat)
HEIGHT: 6'2"   THROWS: LEFT   BATS: LEFT   BORN: 2/6/1895 BALTIMORE, MARYLAND   DIED: 8/16/1948 NEW YORK, NEW YORK   POSITIONS PLAYED: P, 1B, OF

YEAR	TEAM	GAMES	AB	RUNS	HITS	2B	3B	HR	RBI	BB	IBB	SO	HBP	SH	SF	SB	CS	BA	OBA	SA	FA
1914	Bos-A	5	10	1	2	1	0	0	2	0	—	4	0	0	—	0	0	.200	.200	.300	1.000
1915	Bos-A	42	92	16	29	10	1	4	21	9	—	23	0	2	—	0	0	.315	.376	.576	.976
1916	Bos-A	67	136	18	37	5	3	3	15	10	—	23	0	4	—	0	—	.272	.322	.419	.973
1917	Bos-A	52	123	14	40	6	3	2	12	12	—	18	0	7	—	0	—	.325	.385	.472	.984
1918	Bos-A	95	317	50	95	26	11	11	66	57	—	58	2	3	—	6	—	.300	.410	.555	.928
1919	Bos-A	130	432	103	139	34	12	29	114	101	—	58	6	3	—	7	—	.322	.456	.657	.975
1920	NY-A	142	458	158	172	36	9	54	137	148	—	80	3	5	—	14	14	.376	.530	.847	.909
1921	NY-A	152	540	177	204	44	16	59	171	144	—	81	4	4	—	17	13	.378	.512	.846	.966
1922	NY-A	110	406	94	128	24	8	35	99	84	—	80	1	4	—	2	5	.315	.434	.672	.964
1923	NY-A	152	522	151	205	45	13	41	131	170	—	93	4	3	—	17	21	.393	.545	.764	.973
1924	NY-A	153	529	143	200	39	7	46	121	142	—	81	4	6	—	9	13	.378	.513	.739	.962
1925	NY-A	98	359	61	104	12	2	25	66	59	—	68	2	6	—	2	4	.290	.393	.543	.974
1926	NY-A	152	495	139	184	30	5	47	146	144	—	76	3	10	—	11	9	.372	.516	.737	1.000
1927	NY-A	151	540	158	192	29	8	60	164	138	—	89	0	14	—	7	6	.356	.487	.772	.963
1928	NY-A	154	536	163	173	29	8	54	142	135	—	87	3	8	—	4	5	.323	.461	.709	.975
1929	NY-A	135	499	121	172	26	6	46	154	72	—	60	3	13	—	5	3	.345	.430	.697	.984
1930	NY-A	145	518	150	186	28	9	49	153	136	—	61	1	21	—	10	10	.359	.493	.732	1.000
1931	NY-A	145	534	149	199	31	3	46	163	128	—	51	1	0	—	5	4	.373	.495	.700	1.000
1932	NY-A	133	457	120	156	13	5	41	137	130	—	62	2	0	—	2	2	.341	.489	.661	1.000
1933	NY-A	137	459	97	138	21	3	34	103	114	—	90	2	0	—	4	5	.301	.442	.582	1.000
1934	NY-A	125	365	78	105	17	4	22	84	103	—	63	2	0	—	1	3	.288	.447	.537	.962
1935	Bos-N	28	72	13	13	0	0	6	12	20	—	24	0	0	—	0	—	.181	.359	.431	.952
Career average		114	382	99	131	23	6	32	101	93	—	60	2	5	—	6	—	.342	.474	.690	.974
Yankee average		**139**	**481**	**131**	**168**	**28**	**7**	**44**	**131**	**123**	**—**	**75**	**2**	**6**	**—**	**7**	**8**	**.349**	**.484**	**.711**	**.975**
Career total		2503	8399	2174	2873	506	136	714	2213	2056	—	1330	43	113	—	123	117	.342	.474	.690	.974
Yankee total		**2084**	**7217**	**1959**	**2518**	**424**	**106**	**659**	**1971**	**1847**	**—**	**1122**	**35**	**94**	**—**	**110**	**117**	**.349**	**.484**	**.711**	**.975**

Ryan, John Collins (Blondy)
HEIGHT: 6'1"   THROWS: RIGHT   BATS: RIGHT   BORN: 1/4/1906 LYNN, MASSACHUSETTS   DIED: 11/28/1959 SWAMPSCOTT, MASS.   POSITIONS PLAYED: 2B, 3B, SS

YEAR	TEAM	GAMES	AB	RUNS	HITS	2B	3B	HR	RBI	BB	IBB	SO	HBP	SH	SF	SB	CS	BA	OBA	SA	FA
1930	Chi-A	28	87	9	18	0	4	1	10	6	—	13	0	1	—	2	0	.207	.258	.333	.833
1933	NY-N	146	525	47	125	10	5	3	48	15	—	62	0	3	—	0	—	.238	.259	.293	.950
1934	NY-N	110	385	35	93	19	0	2	41	19	—	68	0	12	—	3	—	.242	.277	.306	.953
1935	Phi-N	39	129	13	34	3	0	1	10	7	—	20	2	1	—	1	—	.264	.312	.310	.912
1935	**NY-A**	**30**	**105**	**12**	**25**	**1**	**3**	**0**	**11**	**3**	**—**	**10**	**0**	**1**	**—**	**0**	**0**	**.238**	**.259**	**.305**	**.908**
1937	NY-N	21	75	10	18	3	1	1	13	6	—	8	0	1	—	0	—	.240	.296	.347	.942
1938	NY-N	12	24	1	5	0	0	0	0	1	—	3	0	1	—	0	—	.208	.240	.208	1.000
Career average		55	190	18	45	5	2	1	19	8	—	26	0	3	—	1	—	.239	.271	.304	.928
Yankee average		**30**	**105**	**12**	**25**	**1**	**3**	**0**	**11**	**3**	**—**	**10**	**0**	**1**	**—**	**0**	**0**	**.238**	**.259**	**.305**	**.908**
Career total		386	1330	127	318	36	13	8	133	57	—	184	2	20	—	6	0	.239	.271	.304	.928
Yankee total		**30**	**105**	**12**	**25**	**1**	**3**	**0**	**11**	**3**	**—**	**10**	**0**	**1**	**—**	**0**	**0**	**.238**	**.259**	**.305**	**.908**

Sakata, Lenn Haruki
HEIGHT: 5'9"   THROWS: RIGHT   BATS: RIGHT   BORN: 6/8/1954 HONOLULU, HAWAII   POSITIONS PLAYED: C, 2B, 3B, SS, OF

YEAR	TEAM	GAMES	AB	RUNS	HITS	2B	3B	HR	RBI	BB	IBB	SO	HBP	SH	SF	SB	CS	BA	OBA	SA	FA
1977	Mil-A	53	154	13	25	2	0	2	12	9	0	22	0	6	0	1	3	.162	.209	.214	.985
1978	Mil-A	30	78	8	15	4	0	0	3	8	1	11	0	0	0	1	0	.192	.267	.244	.975
1979	Mil-A	4	14	1	7	2	0	0	1	0	0	1	0	0	0	0	0	.500	.500	.643	1.000
1980	Bal-A	43	83	12	16	3	2	1	9	6	0	10	0	0	1	2	1	.193	.244	.313	1.000
1981	Bal-A	61	150	19	34	4	0	5	15	11	0	18	1	1	1	4	0	.227	.282	.353	.963
1982	Bal-A	136	343	40	89	18	1	6	31	30	2	39	4	8	4	7	4	.259	.323	.370	.958
1983	Bal-A	66	134	23	34	7	0	3	12	16	0	17	1	1	0	8	4	.254	.338	.373	.990
1984	Bal-A	81	157	23	30	1	0	3	11	6	2	15	0	5	0	4	1	.191	.221	.255	.988
1985	Bal-A	55	97	15	22	3	0	3	6	6	0	15	1	1	0	3	2	.227	.279	.351	.960
1986	Oak-A	17	34	4	12	2	0	0	5	3	0	6	0	0	1	0	1	.353	.395	.412	.984
1987	**NY-A**	**19**	**45**	**5**	**12**	**0**	**1**	**2**	**4**	**2**	**0**	**4**	**1**	**0**	**0**	**0**	**1**	**.267**	**.313**	**.444**	**1.000**
Career average		51	117	15	27	4	0	2	10	9	0	14	1	2	1	3	2	.230	.286	.330	.982
Yankee average		**19**	**45**	**5**	**12**	**0**	**1**	**2**	**4**	**2**	**0**	**4**	**1**	**0**	**0**	**0**	**1**	**.267**	**.313**	**.444**	**1.000**
Career total		565	1289	163	296	46	4	25	109	97	5	158	8	22	7	30	17	.230	.286	.330	.982
Yankee total		**19**	**45**	**5**	**12**	**0**	**1**	**2**	**4**	**2**	**0**	**4**	**1**	**0**	**0**	**0**	**1**	**.267**	**.313**	**.444**	**1.000**

George Herman "Babe" Ruth, of, 1920–32

There is room for debate as to whether Babe Ruth was the greatest lefthanded pitcher of the years between 1910 and 1920. And in light of the accomplishments of sluggers like Mark McGwire and Sammy Sosa, there is also room for discussion on whether Ruth was the greatest home run hitter of all. But there is no doubt about one point: Babe Ruth was the greatest baseball player of the 20th century.

Seventy years after his retirement, 50 years after his death, it is difficult to assess the incredible impact Ruth had on baseball in particular and American sports in general, except in this way: He was, and remains, the yardstick by which all professional athletes must measure themselves.

George Ruth was born February 6, 1895, in Baltimore, Maryland. His father, George Herman Ruth, was a bartender. His mother, Kate, worked in the saloon with him. Kate Ruth bore her husband eight children. But only two, George Herman and Mary Margaret, called "Mamie" by her family, survived infancy.

In his autobiography, Ruth recalls that he was a "bad kid." He admitted to chewing tobacco before he was ten, often stole from relatives and could curse like a sailor. This last skill was not unusual, because he was often in their midst, particularly when they visited the saloon of his father, "Big George." The Babe was, at the time, known as "Little George."

But his problem was principally a lack of direction. His parents showed they understood the situation by enrolling him in St. Mary's Industrial School for Boys when he was seven. Although he was periodically paroled home, Ruth spent most of the next 12 years at St. Mary's, and it turned his life around.

He became a heck of a shirtmaker (his specialty was sewing the collars, the most difficult part of the process) and his penmanship became exquisite (his autograph is still one of

the most graceful around). But he quickly showed he had an aptitude for baseball.

Ruth was the star of the St. Mary's team, first as a catcher, then as a pitcher. His coach and surrogate father (although Ruth always insisted he was close to Big George as well) was Brother Matthias, a 6 foot 5 inch taskmaster, who commanded Ruth's respect and won his devotion. In fact, Ruth adopted Matthias's quirky, mincing gait as his own in later years.

The kid was a natural. In 1914, he was sold to the Baltimore Orioles of Jack Dunn, then a minor league team. At his first spring training, one veteran asked another who the big kid was. That, said the other fellow, is Jack Dunn's baby. The nickname stuck. In short order, Dunn turned Ruth over, selling him to the Red Sox for $2,000. The Sox sent him down to Providence of the International League, one of the best minor leagues in the country for seasoning. He quickly became the best pitcher there.

By 1915, he was on his way to becoming the best lefthander in baseball. By 1919, he had led the Red Sox to a trio of World Championships. He pitched 29 2/3 scoreless innings in World Series play, a record not topped until 43 years later by Whitey Ford. He pitched a 14-inning complete-game win with 13 consecutive scoreless innings in 1916, single-game feats that will most likely never be duplicated again in the World Series.

But he had always shown a preference for hitting, particularly home runs. In 1918, he won his first home run title, with 11. The Red Sox made him a regular outfielder in 1919, and he won the home run crown again, this time with a then-record 29.

In 1920, he was sold to the Yankees by Sox owner Harry Frazee, who was desperate for cash. New York gave Harry $125,000 for Ruth, plus a $300,000 loan. It became the most lopsided deal in the history of baseball.

It was more than the idea that the trade depleted the Red Sox and elevated the

Yankees to championship contenders in one sweep (although it did). The trade at once tipped the balance of power in the American League to New York. It also tipped the financial balance of power in New York irrevocably to the Yankees.

In his 15-year career with the Yankees, Babe Ruth simply rewrote the record book. But more than that, he did it as an everyday player, after being a pitcher his entire career. To render a parallel metaphor, it would be as if New York Giant Lawrence Taylor played his dominating brand of defensive football for the first six years of his career and then opted to become a quarterback, and consequently broke all of Dan Marino's records. Or if Wayne Gretzky decided, after several record-setting years as a scorer, to become a goalie, and led his team to championships that way.

Amazing.

He was the first player to hit 30 home runs, the first to hit 40, the first to hit 50 and the first to hit 60. He won 10 home run titles in New York, 5 RBI championships, 10 slugging percentage titles, topped the league in runs 7 times, in walks 11 times, in on-base percentage 9 times and in batting average once. His career slugging percentage of .690 is miles ahead of runner-up Ted Williams's .634 (consider that the number three man, Lou Gehrig, has a .632 career slugging average).

He walked a major-league high 2,056 times. He is second all-time in runs scored (2,174), home runs (714), runs batted in (2,213), on-base percentage (.474).

But that is only a part of his abilities. He was, according to Red Smith, the most complete player of his time, and maybe of all time. He was, for example, an excellent bunter. Consider this: In 1927, the year in which Ruth smacked 60 home runs, he also had 14 sacrifice bunts. In 1998, the year Mark McGwire hit 70 home runs, he had no sacrifice bunts.

He was a superb base runner. Three times, in 1920, 1921 and 1923, he led the Yankees in stolen bases. Twice he led the team in doubles and twice he led the Yankees in triples.

He terrorized pitchers. In 1923, he was walked a record 170 times. Three times that year, in order to dissuade them from walking him, Ruth stepped up to the plate and batted righthanded. Twice they walked him anyway. The other time, he switched after one pitch and hit a home run.

Defensively, Ruth was one of the best in the game. For four years, in 1923, 1924, 1927 and 1928, he led American League rightfielders in putouts, finishing second in 1927 and 1930. In the late 1920s, he was always among the leaders in assists, and in 1921 and 1926, he led all American League rightfielders in double plays.

He was, by acclamation of teammates and foes alike, one of the smartest, if not the smartest, player in the game at the time. Joe Dugan used to tell the story of the time the Yankees were locked in a tie game against an opponent with one out and a man on third. The opposing batter struck a long fly ball. Ruth backpedaled and suddenly stopped, waving his hand in disgust, as though the ball was out of the park.

The base runner on third, seeing him, began trotting home. Suddenly, Ruth took a few quick steps backward and caught the ball. He fired it to Dugan on one hop for an easy double play as the stunned base runner watched from halfway down the line.

Take all that and ratchet it up several notches for the World Series. The Fall Classic was Ruth's stage. In 1977, Reggie Jackson hit three home runs in a single World Series, a feat acclaimed as one of the great dramatic moments in baseball. Ruth did that in two separate Series, in 1926 and again in 1928.

In 1932, he took on the entire Chicago Cubs

team and their fans, smacking two home runs in Game 3 of the World Series to shut everybody up.

The first of those dingers was the famous "called shot" home run. Now, did he actually point to the right field stands to show everyone where he was going to park the next pitch and then follow through?

No. Waite Hoyt recalled that he was actually pointing at pitcher Charlie Root and yelling, "It only takes one to hit it, kid!" And Ruth was right. On the next pitch, he drilled a Root curve into the seats. With apologies to Reggie, that was the most dramatic moment in Series history.

His personal life was not settled until he married his second wife, Claire Hodgson. He met Claire while still married to his first wife, Helen Woodford. By the time of Helen's tragic death in a fire at her home in 1929, she and Babe had been separated for three years. Less than a year after Helen's death, Babe and Claire married.

Claire Hodgson, an actress and model, filled a void vacated by Brother Matthias years ago by giving her husband direction. The running around, which had been a hallmark of Ruth's life after St. Mary's and through most of the Roaring Twenties, stopped (for the most part, anyway). The diet was moderated. The drinking, though never as bad as many claimed, was cut back. This probably prolonged his career.

In fact, Yankee owner Colonel Jacob Ruppert very actively pushed for Claire to come on road trips with her husband soon after they were married. A domesticated Babe, he figured, would be a productive one.

The Yankees released Ruth in 1934. He caught on briefly with the Boston Braves in 1935, a publicity stunt that helped the Braves briefly at the gate but did nothing for Ruth's dignity. There had been a managerial job dangled before him, and that was

why he signed with Boston in the first place. But no job materialized, and he retired.

He waited by the phone for many years after, and it is hard to believe that no one had any interest in giving him a shot. The Yankees were never an option, mostly because Joe McCarthy was doing such a great job. But except for a brief fling with the Dodgers, the phone never rang. Many thought it was primarily because Ruth believed a managerial job was to be a reward for his illustrious career as opposed to a job to be taken seriously. In fact, he did field a few offers from minor league clubs, but he never considered them.

His later years were quiet. He played lots of golf and took part in endless civic and public ceremonies that benefited from the Babe's presence. By 1946, he began having headaches and his voice took on a raspy quality. He was hospitalized in early 1947 and had an operation and X-ray treatments for cancer.

On April 27, 1947, he was honored at Babe Ruth Day with speeches, gifts and applause. His own oratory was brief, impromptu and a little scary, because the operation had made his voice a hoarse croak. Later that year, he worked with Bob Considine on his autobiography. In June 1948, he returned once more to Yankee Stadium to see his number retired. Two months later, he was dead.

He was buried with all the hoopla of an international dignitary. Reams of mawkish praise followed, and in 1949, the Yankees erected a monument to Ruth in center field, to go with former teammate Gehrig and former manager Miller Huggins. With New York, Ruth is 1st in runs scored with 1,959, 1st in home runs with 659, 1st in batting average at .349, 2nd in RBI with 1,970, 2nd in hits with 2,518, 3rd in doubles with 424 and 6th in triples with 106.

Salas, Mark Bruce (Chief)

HEIGHT: 6'0" THROWS: RIGHT BATS: LEFT BORN: 3/8/1961 MONTEBELLO, CALIFORNIA POSITIONS PLAYED: C, 1B, 3B, OF

YEAR	TEAM	GAMES	AB	RUNS	HITS	2B	3B	HR	RBI	BB	IBB	SO	HBP	SH	SF	SB	CS	BA	OBA	SA	FA
1984	StL-N	14	20	1	2	1	0	0	1	0	0	3	0	1	0	0	0	.100	.100	.150	1.000
1985	Min-A	120	360	51	108	20	5	9	41	18	5	37	1	0	3	0	1	.300	.332	.458	.991
1986	Min-A	91	258	28	60	7	4	8	33	18	2	32	1	5	3	3	1	.233	.282	.384	.980
1987	Min-A	22	45	8	17	2	0	3	9	5	1	6	0	0	1	0	1	.378	.431	.622	.989
1987	**NY-A**	**50**	**115**	**13**	**23**	**4**	**0**	**3**	**12**	**10**	**0**	**17**	**3**	**1**	**1**	**0**	**0**	**.200**	**.279**	**.313**	**1.000**
1988	Chi-A	75	196	17	49	7	0	3	9	12	2	17	3	0	0	0	0	.250	.303	.332	.979
1989	Cle-A	30	77	4	17	4	1	2	7	5	1	13	1	0	0	0	0	.221	.277	.377	1.000
1990	Det-A	74	164	18	38	3	0	9	24	21	2	28	1	1	0	0	0	.232	.323	.415	.988
1991	Det-A	33	57	2	5	1	0	1	7	0	0	10	2	0	0	0	0	.088	.117	.158	1.000
Career average		57	144	16	35	5	1	4	16	10	1	18	1	1	1	0	0	.247	.300	.389	.992
Yankee average		**50**	**115**	**13**	**23**	**4**	**0**	**3**	**12**	**10**	**0**	**17**	**3**	**1**	**1**	**0**	**0**	**.200**	**.279**	**.313**	**1.000**
Career total		509	1292	142	319	49	10	38	143	89	13	163	12	8	9	3	3	.247	.300	.389	.992
Yankee total		**50**	**115**	**13**	**23**	**4**	**0**	**3**	**12**	**10**	**0**	**17**	**3**	**1**	**1**	**0**	**0**	**.200**	**.279**	**.313**	**1.000**

Saltzgaver, Otto Hamlin (Jack)

HEIGHT: 5'11" THROWS: RIGHT BATS: LEFT BORN: 1/23/1903 CROTON, IOWA DIED: 2/1/1978 KEOKUK, IOWA POSITIONS PLAYED: 1B, 2B, 3B

YEAR	TEAM	GAMES	AB	RUNS	HITS	2B	3B	HR	RBI	BB	IBB	SO	HBP	SH	SF	SB	CS	BA	OBA	SA	FA
1932	**NY-A**	**20**	**47**	**10**	**6**	**2**	**1**	**0**	**5**	**10**	**—**	**10**	**0**	**3**	**—**	**1**	**1**	**.128**	**.281**	**.213**	**.958**
1934	**NY-A**	**94**	**350**	**64**	**95**	**8**	**1**	**6**	**36**	**48**	**—**	**28**	**0**	**8**	**—**	**8**	**1**	**.271**	**.359**	**.351**	**.923**
1935	**NY-A**	**61**	**149**	**17**	**39**	**6**	**0**	**3**	**18**	**23**	**—**	**12**	**2**	**1**	**—**	**0**	**2**	**.262**	**.368**	**.362**	**1.000**
1936	**NY-A**	**34**	**90**	**14**	**19**	**5**	**0**	**1**	**13**	**13**	**—**	**18**	**0**	**2**	**—**	**0**	**0**	**.211**	**.311**	**.300**	**.964**
1937	**NY-A**	**17**	**11**	**6**	**2**	**0**	**0**	**0**	**0**	**3**	**—**	**4**	**0**	**0**	**—**	**0**	**0**	**.182**	**.357**	**.182**	**1.000**
1945	Pit-N	52	117	20	38	5	3	0	10	8	—	8	0	1	—	0	0	.325	.368	.419	.963
Career average		46	127	22	33	4	1	2	14	18	—	13	0	3	—	2	1	.260	.351	.347	.968
Yankee average		**45**	**129**	**22**	**32**	**4**	**0**	**2**	**14**	**19**	**—**	**14**	**0**	**3**	**—**	**2**	**1**	**.249**	**.349**	**.334**	**.969**
Career total		278	764	131	199	26	5	10	82	105	—	80	2	15	—	9	4	.260	.351	.347	.968
Yankee total		**226**	**647**	**111**	**161**	**21**	**2**	**10**	**72**	**97**	**—**	**72**	**2**	**14**	**—**	**9**	**4**	**.249**	**.349**	**.334**	**.969**

Sample, William Amos

HEIGHT: 5'9" THROWS: RIGHT BATS: RIGHT BORN: 4/2/1955 ROANOKE, VIRGINIA POSITIONS PLAYED: 2B, OF

YEAR	TEAM	GAMES	AB	RUNS	HITS	2B	3B	HR	RBI	BB	IBB	SO	HBP	SH	SF	SB	CS	BA	OBA	SA	FA
1978	Tex-A	8	15	2	7	2	0	0	3	0	0	3	0	0	0	0	0	.467	.467	.600	.000
1979	Tex-A	128	325	60	95	21	2	5	35	37	1	28	2	10	3	8	6	.292	.365	.415	1.000
1980	Tex-A	99	204	29	53	10	0	4	19	18	2	15	6	4	2	8	5	.260	.335	.368	.973
1981	Tex-A	66	230	36	65	16	0	3	25	17	1	21	7	3	3	4	1	.283	.346	.391	.993
1982	Tex-A	97	360	56	94	14	2	10	29	27	0	35	3	8	0	10	2	.261	.318	.394	.981
1983	Tex-A	147	554	80	152	28	3	12	57	44	2	46	5	4	4	44	8	.274	.331	.401	.988
1984	Tex-A	130	489	67	121	20	2	5	33	29	1	46	0	4	6	18	6	.247	.286	.327	.986
1985	**NY-A**	**59**	**139**	**18**	**40**	**5**	**0**	**1**	**15**	**9**	**0**	**10**	**2**	**2**	**2**	**2**	**1**	**.288**	**.336**	**.345**	**.989**
1986	Atl-N	92	200	23	57	11	0	6	14	14	1	26	3	2	2	4	2	.285	.338	.430	.986
Career average		92	280	41	76	14	1	5	26	22	1	26	3	4	2	11	3	.272	.329	.384	.877
Yankee average		**59**	**139**	**18**	**40**	**5**	**0**	**1**	**15**	**9**	**0**	**10**	**2**	**2**	**2**	**2**	**1**	**.288**	**.336**	**.345**	**.989**
Career total		826	2516	371	684	127	9	46	230	195	8	230	28	37	22	98	31	.272	.329	.384	.877
Yankee total		**59**	**139**	**18**	**40**	**5**	**0**	**1**	**15**	**9**	**0**	**10**	**2**	**2**	**2**	**2**	**1**	**.288**	**.336**	**.345**	**.989**

Sanchez, Celerino BORN CELERINO SANCHEZ (PEREZ)

HEIGHT: 5'11" THROWS: RIGHT BATS: RIGHT BORN: 2/3/1944 VERACRUZ, MEXICO DIED: 5/1/1992 LEON, MEXICO POSITIONS PLAYED: 3B, SS, OF

YEAR	TEAM	GAMES	AB	RUNS	HITS	2B	3B	HR	RBI	BB	IBB	SO	HBP	SH	SF	SB	CS	BA	OBA	SA	FA
1972	**NY-A**	**71**	**250**	**18**	**62**	**8**	**3**	**0**	**22**	**12**	**1**	**30**	**4**	**2**	**1**	**0**	**0**	**.248**	**.292**	**.304**	**.939**
1973	**NY-A**	**34**	**64**	**12**	**14**	**3**	**0**	**1**	**9**	**2**	**0**	**12**	**0**	**0**	**1**	**1**	**1**	**.219**	**.239**	**.313**	**1.000**
Career average		53	157	15	38	6	2	1	16	7	1	21	2	1	1	1	1	.242	.281	.306	.970
Yankee average		**53**	**157**	**15**	**38**	**6**	**2**	**1**	**16**	**7**	**1**	**21**	**2**	**1**	**1**	**1**	**1**	**.242**	**.281**	**.306**	**.970**
Career total		105	314	30	76	11	3	1	31	14	1	42	4	2	2	1	1	.242	.281	.306	.970
Yankee total		**105**	**314**	**30**	**76**	**11**	**3**	**1**	**31**	**14**	**1**	**42**	**4**	**2**	**2**	**1**	**1**	**.242**	**.281**	**.306**	**.970**

Sanchez, Rey Francisco BORN REY FRANCISCO SANCHEZ (GUADALUPE)

HEIGHT: 5'9"   THROWS: RIGHT   BATS: RIGHT   BORN: 10/5/1967 RIO PIEDRAS, PUERTO RICO   POSITIONS PLAYED: 2B, 3B, SS

YEAR	TEAM	GAMES	AB	RUNS	HITS	2B	3B	HR	RBI	BB	IBB	SO	HBP	SH	SF	SB	CS	BA	OBA	SA	FA
1991	Chi-N	13	23	1	6	0	0	0	2	4	0	3	0	0	0	0	0	.261	.370	.261	1.000
1992	Chi-N	74	255	24	64	14	3	1	19	10	1	17	3	5	2	2	1	.251	.285	.341	.974
1993	Chi-N	105	344	35	97	11	2	0	28	15	7	22	3	9	2	1	1	.282	.316	.326	.969
1994	Chi-N	96	291	26	83	13	1	0	24	20	4	29	7	4	1	2	5	.285	.345	.337	.960
1995	Chi-N	114	428	57	119	22	2	3	27	14	2	48	1	8	2	6	4	.278	.301	.360	1.000
1996	Chi-N	95	289	28	61	9	0	1	12	22	6	42	3	8	2	7	1	.211	.272	.253	.977
1997	Chi-N	97	205	14	51	9	0	1	12	11	2	26	0	4	0	4	2	.249	.287	.307	.964
1997	**NY-A**	**38**	**138**	**21**	**43**	**12**	**0**	**1**	**15**	**5**	**0**	**21**	**1**	**5**	**1**	**0**	**4**	**.312**	**.338**	**.420**	**1.000**
1998	SF-N	109	316	44	90	14	2	2	30	16	0	47	0	1	2	0	5	.285	.317	.361	.991
1999	KC-A	134	479	66	141	18	6	2	56	22	0	48	0	10	3	11	5	.294	.323	.370	.982
2000	KC-A	143	509	68	139	18	2	1	38	28	0	55	4	11	3	7	3	.273	.314	.322	.994
Career average		93	298	35	81	13	2	1	24	15	2	33	2	6	2	4	2	.273	.311	.338	.983
Yankee average		**38**	**138**	**21**	**43**	**12**	**0**	**1**	**15**	**5**	**0**	**21**	**1**	**5**	**1**	**0**	**4**	**.312**	**.338**	**.420**	**1.000**
Career total		1018	3277	384	894	140	18	12	263	167	22	358	22	65	18	40	26	.273	.311	.338	.983
Yankee total		**38**	**138**	**21**	**43**	**12**	**0**	**1**	**15**	**5**	**0**	**21**	**1**	**5**	**1**	**0**	**4**	**.312**	**.338**	**.420**	**1.000**

Sanders, Deion Luwynn (Neon Deion *or* Prime Time)

HEIGHT: 6'1"   THROWS: LEFT   BATS: LEFT   BORN: 8/9/1967 FORT MYERS, FLORIDA   POSITIONS PLAYED: OF

YEAR	TEAM	GAMES	AB	RUNS	HITS	2B	3B	HR	RBI	BB	IBB	SO	HBP	SH	SF	SB	CS	BA	OBA	SA	FA
1989	**NY-A**	**14**	**47**	**7**	**11**	**2**	**0**	**2**	**7**	**3**	**1**	**8**	**0**	**0**	**0**	**1**	**0**	**.234**	**.280**	**.404**	**.969**
1990	**NY-A**	**57**	**133**	**24**	**21**	**2**	**2**	**3**	**9**	**13**	**0**	**27**	**1**	**1**	**1**	**8**	**2**	**.158**	**.236**	**.271**	**.973**
1991	Atl-N	54	110	16	21	1	2	4	13	12	0	23	0	0	0	11	3	.191	.270	.345	.952
1992	Atl-N	97	303	54	92	6	14	8	28	18	0	52	2	1	1	26	9	.304	.346	.495	.983
1993	Atl-N	95	272	42	75	18	6	6	28	16	3	42	3	1	2	19	7	.276	.321	.452	.986
1994	Atl-N	46	191	32	55	10	0	4	21	16	1	28	1	1	2	19	7	.288	.343	.403	.980
1994	Cin-N	46	184	26	51	7	4	0	7	16	0	35	2	1	0	19	9	.277	.342	.359	1.000
1995	Cin-N	33	129	19	31	2	3	1	10	9	0	18	2	2	2	16	3	.240	.296	.326	.968
1995	SF-N	52	214	29	61	9	5	5	18	18	0	42	2	1	0	8	6	.285	.346	.444	.984
1997	Cin-N	115	465	53	127	13	7	5	23	34	2	67	6	2	2	56	13	.273	.329	.363	.984
Career average		61	205	30	55	7	4	4	16	16	1	34	2	1	1	18	6	.266	.322	.398	.978
Yankee average		**36**	**90**	**16**	**16**	**2**	**1**	**3**	**8**	**8**	**1**	**18**	**1**	**1**	**1**	**5**	**1**	**.178**	**.247**	**.306**	**.971**
Career total		609	2048	302	545	70	43	38	164	155	7	342	19	10	10	183	59	.266	.322	.398	.978
Yankee total		**71**	**180**	**31**	**32**	**4**	**2**	**5**	**16**	**16**	**1**	**35**	**1**	**1**	**1**	**9**	**2**	**.178**	**.247**	**.306**	**.971**

Sands, Charles Duane

HEIGHT: 6'2"   THROWS: RIGHT   BATS: LEFT   BORN: 12/17/1947 NEWPORT NEWS, VIRGINIA   POSITIONS PLAYED: C

YEAR	TEAM	GAMES	AB	RUNS	HITS	2B	3B	HR	RBI	BB	IBB	SO	HBP	SH	SF	SB	CS	BA	OBA	SA	FA
1967	**NY-A**	**1**	**1**	**0**	**0**	**0**	**0**	**0**	**0**	**0**	**0**	**1**	**0**	**0**	**0**	**0**	**0**	**.000**	**.000**	**.000**	**.000**
1971	Pit-N	28	25	4	5	2	0	1	5	7	1	6	0	0	0	0	0	.200	.375	.400	1.000
1972	Pit-N	1	1	0	0	0	0	0	0	0	0	0	0	0	0	0	0	.000	.000	.000	.000
1973	Cal-A	17	33	5	9	2	1	1	5	5	1	10	0	0	0	0	0	.273	.368	.485	.917
1974	Cal-A	43	83	6	16	2	0	4	13	23	2	17	1	0	1	0	0	.193	.370	.361	1.000
1975	Oak-A	3	2	0	1	0	0	0	0	1	0	1	0	0	0	0	0	.500	.667	.500	.000
Career average		19	29	3	6	1	0	1	5	7	1	7	0	0	0	0	0	.214	.372	.393	.486
Yankee average		**1**	**1**	**0**	**0**	**0**	**0**	**0**	**0**	**0**	**0**	**1**	**0**	**0**	**0**	**0**	**0**	**.000**	**.000**	**.000**	**.000**
Career total		93	145	15	31	6	1	6	23	36	4	35	1	0	1	0	0	.214	.372	.393	.486
Yankee total		**1**	**1**	**0**	**0**	**0**	**0**	**0**	**0**	**0**	**0**	**1**	**0**	**0**	**0**	**0**	**0**	**.000**	**.000**	**.000**	**.000**

Santana, Rafael Francisco (Ralph) BORN RAFAEL FRANCISCO SANTANA (DE LA CRUZ)

HEIGHT: 6'1"   THROWS: RIGHT   BATS: RIGHT   BORN: 1/31/1958 LA ROMANA, DOMINICAN REPUBLIC   POSITIONS PLAYED: 2B, 3B, SS

YEAR	TEAM	GAMES	AB	RUNS	HITS	2B	3B	HR	RBI	BB	IBB	SO	HBP	SH	SF	SB	CS	BA	OBA	SA	FA
1983	StL-N	30	14	1	3	0	0	0	2	2	0	2	1	0	0	0	1	.214	.353	.214	.500
1984	NY-N	51	152	14	42	11	1	1	12	9	0	17	0	1	0	0	3	.276	.317	.382	.970
1985	NY-N	154	529	41	136	19	1	1	29	29	12	54	0	4	2	1	0	.257	.295	.302	.965
1986	NY-N	139	394	38	86	11	0	1	28	36	12	43	2	1	3	0	0	.218	.285	.254	.973
1987	NY-N	139	439	41	112	21	2	5	44	29	10	57	1	0	1	1	1	.255	.302	.346	.973
1988	**NY-A**	**148**	**480**	**50**	**115**	**12**	**1**	**4**	**38**	**33**	**0**	**61**	**1**	**5**	**2**	**1**	**2**	**.240**	**.289**	**.294**	**.966**
1990	Cle-A	7	13	3	3	0	0	0	3	0	0	0	0	0	0	0	0	.231	.231	.462	1.000

(continued)

(continued)

																			BA	OBA	SA	FA
Career average	95	289	27	71	11	1	2	22	20	5	33	1	2	1	0	1	.246	.295	.307	.907
Yankee average	**148**	**480**	**50**	**115**	**12**	**1**	**4**	**38**	**33**	**0**	**61**	**1**	**5**	**2**	**1**	**2**	**.240**	**.289**	**.294**	**.969**
Career total	668	2021	188	497	74	5	13	156	138	34	234	5	11	8	3	7	.246	.295	.307	.907
Yankee total	**148**	**480**	**50**	**115**	**12**	**1**	**4**	**38**	**33**	**0**	**61**	**1**	**5**	**2**	**1**	**2**	**.240**	**.289**	**.294**	**.969**

Savage, Donald Anthony

HEIGHT: 6'0"   THROWS: RIGHT   BATS: RIGHT   BORN: 3/5/1919 BLOOMFIELD, NEW JERSEY   DIED: 12/25/1961 MONTCLAIR, NJ.   POSITIONS PLAYED: 3B, OF

YEAR	TEAM	GAMES	AB	RUNS	HITS	2B	3B	HR	RBI	BB	IBB	SO	HBP	SH	SF	SB	CS	BA	OBA	SA	FA
1944	NY-A	71	239	31	63	7	5	4	24	20	—	41	1	2	—	1	1	.264	.323	.385	.946
1945	NY-A	34	58	5	13	1	0	0	3	3	—	14	0	0	—	1	0	.224	.262	.241	.891
Career average		53	149	18	38	4	3	2	14	12	—	28	1	1	—	1	1	.256	.312	.357	.919
Yankee average		**53**	**149**	**18**	**38**	**4**	**3**	**2**	**14**	**12**	**—**	**28**	**1**	**1**	**—**	**1**	**1**	**.256**	**.312**	**.357**	**.919**
Career total		105	297	36	76	8	5	4	27	23	—	55	1	2	—	2	1	.256	.312	.357	.919
Yankee total		**105**	**297**	**36**	**76**	**8**	**5**	**4**	**27**	**23**	**—**	**55**	**1**	**2**	**—**	**2**	**1**	**.256**	**.312**	**.357**	**.919**

Sax, Stephen Louis

HEIGHT: 5'11"   THROWS: RIGHT   BATS: RIGHT   BORN: 1/29/1960 SACRAMENTO, CALIFORNIA   POSITIONS PLAYED: 2B, 3B, OF

YEAR	TEAM	GAMES	AB	RUNS	HITS	2B	3B	HR	RBI	BB	IBB	SO	HBP	SH	SF	SB	CS	BA	OBA	SA	FA
1981	LA-N	31	119	15	33	2	0	2	9	7	1	14	0	1	0	5	7	.277	.317	.345	.975
1982	LA-N	150	638	88	180	23	7	4	47	49	1	53	2	10	0	49	19	.282	.335	.359	.977
1983	LA-N	155	623	94	175	18	5	5	41	58	3	73	1	8	2	56	30	.281	.342	.350	.961
1984	LA-N	145	569	70	138	24	4	1	35	47	3	53	1	2	3	34	19	.243	.300	.304	.973
1985	LA-N	136	488	62	136	8	4	1	42	54	12	43	3	3	3	27	11	.279	.352	.318	.969
1986	LA-N	157	633	91	210	43	4	6	56	59	5	58	3	6	3	40	17	.332	.390	.441	.980
1987	LA-N	157	610	84	171	22	7	6	46	44	5	61	3	5	1	37	11	.280	.331	.369	.982
1988	LA-N	160	632	70	175	19	4	5	57	45	6	51	1	7	2	42	12	.277	.325	.343	.981
1989	**NY-A**	**158**	**651**	**88**	**205**	**26**	**3**	**5**	**63**	**52**	**2**	**44**	**1**	**8**	**5**	**43**	**17**	**.315**	**.364**	**.387**	**.987**
1990	**NY-A**	**155**	**615**	**70**	**160**	**24**	**2**	**4**	**42**	**49**	**3**	**46**	**4**	**6**	**6**	**43**	**9**	**.260**	**.316**	**.325**	**.987**
1991	**NY-A**	**158**	**652**	**85**	**198**	**38**	**2**	**10**	**56**	**41**	**2**	**38**	**3**	**5**	**6**	**31**	**11**	**.304**	**.345**	**.414**	**.824**
1992	Chi-A	143	567	74	134	26	4	4	47	43	4	42	2	12	6	30	12	.236	.290	.317	.972
1993	Chi-A	57	119	20	28	5	0	1	8	8	0	6	0	2	0	7	3	.235	.283	.303	1.000
1994	Oak-A	7	24	2	6	0	1	0	1	0	0	2	0	0	0	0	0	.250	.250	.333	1.000
Career average		126	496	65	139	20	3	4	39	40	3	42	2	5	3	32	13	.281	.335	.358	.969
Yankee average		**157**	**639**	**81**	**188**	**29**	**2**	**6**	**54**	**47**	**2**	**43**	**3**	**6**	**6**	**39**	**12**	**.294**	**.342**	**.376**	**.933**
Career total		1769	6940	913	1949	278	47	54	550	556	47	584	24	75	37	444	178	.281	.335	.358	.969
Yankee total		**471**	**1918**	**243**	**563**	**88**	**7**	**19**	**161**	**142**	**7**	**128**	**8**	**19**	**17**	**117**	**37**	**.294**	**.342**	**.376**	**.933**

Schaefer, Herman A. (Germany)

HEIGHT: 5'9"   THROWS: RIGHT   BATS: RIGHT   BORN: 2/4/1877 CHICAGO, ILLINOIS   DIED: 5/6/1919 SARANAC LAKE, NY.   POSITIONS PLAYED: P, 1B, 2B, 3B, SS, OF

YEAR	TEAM	GAMES	AB	RUNS	HITS	2B	3B	HR	RBI	BB	IBB	SO	HBP	SH	SF	SB	CS	BA	OBA	SA	FA
1901	Chi-N	2	5	0	3	1	0	0	0	2	—	—	0	0	—	0	—	.600	.714	.800	1.000
1902	Chi-N	81	291	32	57	2	3	0	14	19	—	—	2	11	—	12	—	.196	.250	.223	1.000
1905	Det-A	153	554	64	135	17	9	2	47	45	—	—	1	29	—	19	—	.244	.302	.318	.955
1906	Det-A	124	446	48	106	14	3	2	42	32	—	—	1	19	—	31	—	.238	.290	.296	.880
1907	Det-A	109	372	45	96	12	3	1	32	30	—	—	0	17	—	21	—	.258	.313	.315	.955
1908	Det-A	153	584	96	151	20	10	3	52	37	—	—	1	43	—	40	—	.259	.304	.342	.952
1909	Det-A	87	280	26	70	12	0	0	22	14	—	—	0	14	—	12	—	.250	.286	.293	.966
1909	Was-A	37	128	13	31	5	1	1	4	6	—	—	1	5	—	2	—	.242	.281	.320	.800
1910	Was-A	74	229	27	63	6	5	0	14	25	—	—	2	9	—	17	—	.275	.352	.345	1.000
1911	Was-A	125	440	74	147	14	7	0	45	57	—	—	1	18	—	22	—	.334	.412	.398	.980
1912	Was-A	60	166	21	41	7	3	0	19	23	—	—	1	4	—	11	—	.247	.342	.325	.900
1913	Was-A	54	100	17	32	1	1	0	7	15	—	12	2	2	—	6	—	.320	.419	.350	.967
1914	Was-A	30	29	6	7	1	0	0	2	3	—	5	0	1	—	4	1	.241	.313	.276	1.000
1915	New-F	59	154	26	33	5	3	0	8	25	—	11	1	3	—	3	—	.214	.328	.286	1.000
1916	**NY-A**	**1**	**1**	**0**	**0**	**0**	**0**	**0**	**0**	**0**	**—**	**0**	**0**	**0**	**—**	**0**	**—**	**.000**	**.000**	**.000**	**1.000**
1918	Cle-A	1	5	2	0	0	0	0	0	0	—	0	0	0	—	1	—	.000	.000	.000	1.000
Career average		72	237	31	61	7	3	1	19	21	—	—	1	11	—	13	—	.257	.319	.320	.897
Yankee average		**1**	**1**	**0**	**0**	**0**	**0**	**0**	**0**	**0**	**—**	**0**	**0**	**0**	**—**	**0**	**—**	**.000**	**.000**	**.000**	**.000**
Career total		1150	3784	497	972	117	48	9	308	333	—	28	13	175	—	201	1	.257	.319	.320	.897
Yankee total		**1**	**1**	**0**	**0**	**0**	**0**	**0**	**0**	**0**	**—**	**0**	**0**	**0**	**—**	**0**	**—**	**.000**	**.000**	**.000**	**.000**

Schalk, LeRoy John (Roy)

HEIGHT: 5'10" THROWS: RIGHT BATS: RIGHT BORN: 11/9/1908 CHICAGO, ILLINOIS DIED: 3/11/1990 GAINESVILLE, TEXAS POSITIONS PLAYED: 2B, SS

YEAR	TEAM	GAMES	AB	RUNS	HITS	2B	3B	HR	RBI	BB	IBB	SO	HBP	SH	SF	SB	CS	BA	OBA	SA	FA
1932	**NY-A**	**3**	**12**	**3**	**3**	**1**	**0**	**0**	**0**	**2**	—	**2**	**0**	**0**	—	**0**	**0**	**.250**	**.357**	**.333**	**.867**
1944	Chi-A	146	587	47	129	14	4	1	44	45	—	52	1	21	—	5	4	.220	.276	.262	.966
1945	Chi-A	133	513	50	127	23	1	1	65	32	—	41	1	24	—	3	6	.248	.293	.302	.977
Career average		94	371	33	86	13	2	1	36	26	—	32	1	15	—	3	3	.233	.285	.281	.937
Yankee average		**3**	**12**	**3**	**3**	**1**	**0**	**0**	**0**	**2**	—	**2**	**0**	**0**	—	**0**	**0**	**.250**	**.357**	**.333**	**.867**
Career total		282	1112	100	259	38	5	2	109	79	—	95	2	45	—	8	10	.233	.285	.281	.937
Yankee total		**3**	**12**	**3**	**3**	**1**	**0**	**0**	**0**	**2**	—	**2**	**0**	**0**	—	**0**	**0**	**.250**	**.357**	**.333**	**.867**

Schang, Walter Henry (Wally)

HEIGHT: 5'10" THROWS: RIGHT BATS: BOTH BORN: 8/22/1889 SOUTH WALES, NEW YORK DIED: 3/6/1965 ST. LOUIS, MISS. POSITIONS PLAYED: C, 3B, SS, OF

YEAR	TEAM	GAMES	AB	RUNS	HITS	2B	3B	HR	RBI	BB	IBB	SO	HBP	SH	SF	SB	CS	BA	OBA	SA	FA
1913	Phi-A	79	207	32	55	16	3	3	30	34	—	44	9	2	—	4	—	.266	.392	.415	.967
1914	Phi-A	107	307	44	88	11	8	3	45	32	—	33	9	7	—	7	7	.287	.371	.404	.956
1915	Phi-A	116	359	64	89	9	11	1	44	66	—	47	14	12	—	18	3	.248	.385	.343	.890
1916	Phi-A	110	338	41	90	15	8	7	38	38	—	44	10	13	—	14	—	.266	.358	.420	.935
1917	Phi-A	118	316	41	90	14	9	3	36	29	—	24	9	12	—	6	—	.285	.362	.415	1.000

(continued)

Walter Henry "Wally" Schang, c, 1921–25

Wally Schang was a winner everywhere he went, a talented catcher who was an asset to three American League squads, including the Yankees.

Schang was born August 22, 1889, in South Wales, New York. He was signed by the Philadelphia Athletics and began his big league career in 1913, splitting the catching duties with the light-hitting Jack Lapp.

The A's won the pennant that year, and manger Connie Mack started Schang over Lapp in the Series. There was no outcry at the decision: Schang was already clearly the better player.

Schang spent five years in Philadelphia, then three more in Boston before coming to the Yankees in 1921. Along with several other key veterans, including teammate Babe Ruth, Schang helped put the Yankees over the top. In all, Schang played for six pennant winners and three World Champions, one each for the A's, Red Sox and Yankees.

He was a solid hitter, hitting over .300 six times, including twice with New York, in 1921 and 1922. In the postseason, he was equally consistent, with a lifetime .287 average in 32 games. He is one of the few catchers to have stolen more than 100 bases (121) in his career.

Defensively, Schang was one of the best of his generation and was renowned for handling pitchers. He was also probably the strongest man in the majors in the teens and '20s, before Lou Gehrig came along.

In 1923, Schang was hit in the head by a pitch and suffered a serious injury, sidelining him for several weeks. Yet he returned to the New York lineup and hit .318 to help the Yankees win their first World Series. That win over the Giants made Schang the only man in major league history to win the World Championship with three different teams.

In 1925, he was 36 and the Yankees had (they thought) a young prospect in Benny Bengough, so Schang was shipped to the St. Louis Browns. He played six more years in the American League before retiring. Schang coached for the Indians in the 1930s. He died in 1965 in St. Louis.

(continued)

YEAR	TEAM	GAMES	AB	RUNS	HITS	2B	3B	HR	RBI	BB	IBB	SO	HBP	SH	SF	SB	CS	BA	OBA	SA	FA
1918	Bos-A	88	225	36	55	7	1	0	20	46	—	35	2	9	—	4	—	.244	.377	.284	.962
1919	Bos-A	113	330	43	101	16	3	0	55	71	—	42	5	7	—	15	—	.306	.436	.373	.972
1920	Bos-A	122	387	58	118	30	7	4	51	64	—	37	7	8	—	7	7	.305	.413	.450	.958
1921	**NY-A**	**134**	**424**	**77**	**134**	**30**	**5**	**6**	**55**	**78**	**—**	**35**	**5**	**6**	**—**	**7**	**4**	**.316**	**.428**	**.453**	**.969**
1922	**NY-A**	**124**	**408**	**46**	**130**	**21**	**7**	**1**	**53**	**53**	**—**	**36**	**6**	**23**	**—**	**12**	**6**	**.319**	**.405**	**.412**	**.976**
1923	**NY-A**	**84**	**272**	**39**	**75**	**8**	**2**	**2**	**29**	**27**	**—**	**17**	**9**	**7**	**—**	**5**	**2**	**.276**	**.360**	**.342**	**.970**
1924	**NY-A**	**114**	**356**	**46**	**104**	**19**	**7**	**5**	**52**	**48**	**—**	**43**	**4**	**13**	**—**	**2**	**6**	**.292**	**.382**	**.427**	**.972**
1925	**NY-A**	**73**	**167**	**17**	**40**	**8**	**1**	**2**	**24**	**17**	**—**	**9**	**0**	**7**	**—**	**2**	**1**	**.240**	**.310**	**.335**	**.974**
1926	StL-A	103	285	36	94	19	5	8	50	32	—	20	4	11	—	5	5	.330	.405	.516	.968
1927	StL-A	97	264	40	84	15	2	5	42	41	—	33	2	4	—	3	2	.318	.414	.447	.976
1928	StL-A	91	245	41	70	10	5	3	39	68	—	26	4	8	—	8	2	.286	.448	.464	.984
1929	StL-A	94	249	43	59	10	5	5	36	74	—	22	7	4	—	1	4	.237	.424	.378	.988
1930	Phi-A	45	92	16	16	4	1	1	9	17	—	15	1	6	—	0	0	.174	.309	.272	.973
1931	Det-A	30	76	9	14	2	0	0	2	14	—	11	0	1	—	1	0	.184	.311	.211	.965
Career average		97	279	40	79	14	5	3	37	45	—	30	6	8	—	6	—	.284	.393	.401	.966
Yankee average		**106**	**325**	**45**	**97**	**17**	**4**	**3**	**45**	**45**	**—**	**28**	**5**	**11**	**—**	**6**	**4**	**.297**	**.390**	**.406**	**.972**
Career total		1842	5307	769	1506	264	90	59	710	849	—	573	107	160	—	121	49	.284	.393	.401	.966
Yankee total		**529**	**1627**	**225**	**483**	**86**	**22**	**16**	**213**	**223**	**—**	**140**	**24**	**56**	**—**	**28**	**19**	**.297**	**.390**	**.406**	**.972**

Schmidt, Charles John (Butch)

HEIGHT: 6'1"   THROWS: LEFT   BATS: LEFT   BORN: 7/19/1886 BALTIMORE, MARYLAND   DIED: 9/4/1952 BALTIMORE, MARYLAND   POSITIONS PLAYED: P, 1B

YEAR	TEAM	GAMES	AB	RUNS	HITS	2B	3B	HR	RBI	BB	IBB	SO	HBP	SH	SF	SB	CS	BA	OBA	SA	FA
1909	**NY-A**	**1**	**2**	**0**	**0**	**0**	**0**	**0**	**0**	**0**	**—**	**—**	**0**	**0**	**—**	**0**	**—**	**.000**	**.000**	**.000**	**.500**
1913	Bos-N	22	78	6	24	2	2	1	14	2	—	5	1	1	—	1	—	.308	.333	.423	.983
1914	Bos-N	147	537	67	153	17	9	1	71	43	—	55	11	23	—	14	—	.285	.350	.356	.990
1915	Bos-N	127	458	46	115	26	7	2	60	36	—	59	9	21	—	3	10	.251	.318	.352	.987
Career average		74	269	30	73	11	5	1	36	20	—	—	5	11	—	5	—	.272	.335	.358	.865
Yankee average		**1**	**2**	**0**	**0**	**0**	**0**	**0**	**0**	**0**	**—**	**—**	**0**	**0**	**—**	**0**	**—**	**.000**	**.000**	**.000**	**.500**
Career total		297	1075	119	292	45	18	4	145	81	—	119	21	45	—	18	10	.272	.335	.358	.865
Yankee total		**1**	**2**	**0**	**0**	**0**	**0**	**0**	**0**	**0**	**—**	**—**	**0**	**0**	**—**	**0**	**—**	**.000**	**.000**	**.000**	**.500**

Schmidt, Robert Benjamin

HEIGHT: 6'2"   THROWS: RIGHT   BATS: RIGHT   BORN: 4/22/1933 ST. LOUIS, MISSOURI   POSITIONS PLAYED: C

YEAR	TEAM	GAMES	AB	RUNS	HITS	2B	3B	HR	RBI	BB	IBB	SO	HBP	SH	SF	SB	CS	BA	OBA	SA	FA
1958	SF-N	127	393	46	96	20	2	14	54	33	5	59	3	1	2	0	1	.244	.306	.412	.982
1959	SF-N	71	181	17	44	7	1	5	20	13	4	24	1	0	1	0	2	.243	.296	.376	1.000
1960	SF-N	110	344	31	92	12	1	8	37	26	4	51	0	3	2	0	3	.267	.317	.378	.981
1961	SF-N	2	6	0	1	0	0	0	1	0	0	1	0	0	1	0	0	.167	.143	.167	1.000
1961	Cin-N	27	70	4	9	0	0	1	4	8	1	14	0	1	0	0	0	.129	.218	.171	.994
1962	Was-A	88	256	28	62	14	0	10	31	14	2	37	1	0	3	0	0	.242	.281	.414	.997
1963	Was-A	9	15	3	3	1	0	0	0	3	0	5	0	0	0	0	0	.200	.333	.267	1.000
1965	**NY-A**	**20**	**40**	**4**	**10**	**1**	**0**	**1**	**3**	**3**	**1**	**8**	**0**	**2**	**0**	**0**	**0**	**.250**	**.302**	**.350**	**.990**
Career average		57	163	17	40	7	1	5	19	13	2	25	1	1	1	0	1	.243	.297	.381	.993
Yankee average		**20**	**40**	**4**	**10**	**1**	**0**	**1**	**3**	**3**	**1**	**8**	**0**	**2**	**0**	**0**	**0**	**.250**	**.302**	**.350**	**.990**
Career total		454	1305	133	317	55	4	39	150	100	17	199	5	7	9	0	6	.243	.297	.381	.993
Yankee total		**20**	**40**	**4**	**10**	**1**	**0**	**1**	**3**	**3**	**1**	**8**	**0**	**2**	**0**	**0**	**0**	**.250**	**.302**	**.350**	**.990**

Schofield, John Richard (Ducky)

HEIGHT: 5'9"   THROWS: RIGHT   BATS: BOTH   BORN: 1/7/1935 SPRINGFIELD, ILLINOIS   POSITIONS PLAYED: 2B, 3B, SS, OF

YEAR	TEAM	GAMES	AB	RUNS	HITS	2B	3B	HR	RBI	BB	IBB	SO	HBP	SH	SF	SB	CS	BA	OBA	SA	FA
1953	StL-N	33	39	9	7	0	0	2	4	2	—	11	0	0	—	0	0	.179	.220	.333	.917
1954	StL-N	43	7	17	1	0	1	0	1	0	—	3	0	0	0	1	1	.143	.143	.429	1.000
1955	StL-N	12	4	3	0	0	0	0	0	0	0	1	0	0	0	0	0	.000	.000	.000	1.000
1956	StL-N	16	30	3	3	2	0	0	1	0	0	6	0	0	0	0	0	.100	.100	.167	.923
1957	StL-N	65	56	10	9	0	0	0	1	7	0	13	0	1	0	1	3	.161	.254	.161	.948
1958	StL-N	39	108	16	23	4	0	1	8	23	0	15	0	1	1	0	2	.213	.348	.278	.932
1958	Pit-N	26	27	4	4	0	1	0	2	3	0	6	0	0	1	0	1	.148	.226	.222	1.000
1959	Pit-N	81	145	21	34	10	1	1	9	16	0	22	0	2	0	1	1	.234	.311	.338	1.000
1960	Pit-N	65	102	9	34	4	1	0	10	16	4	20	1	2	0	0	1	.333	.429	.392	1.000

(continued)

(continued)

YEAR	TEAM	GAMES	AB	RUNS	HITS	2B	3B	HR	RBI	BB	IBB	SO	HBP	SH	SF	SB	CS	BA	OBA	SA	FA
1961	Pit-N	60	78	16	15	2	1	0	2	10	0	19	0	2	0	0	1	.192	.284	.244	.975
1962	Pit-N	54	104	19	30	3	0	2	10	17	0	22	0	0	2	0	1	.288	.382	.375	1.000
1963	Pit-N	138	541	54	133	18	2	3	32	69	1	83	3	4	2	2	4	.246	.333	.303	.981
1964	Pit-N	121	398	50	98	22	5	3	36	54	3	60	7	3	2	1	2	.246	.345	.349	.950
1965	Pit-N	31	109	13	25	5	0	0	6	15	1	19	0	1	2	1	0	.229	.317	.275	.974
1965	SF-N	101	379	39	77	10	1	2	19	33	0	50	3	5	1	2	4	.203	.272	.251	.974
1966	SF-N	11	16	4	1	0	0	0	0	2	0	2	0	0	0	0	4	.063	.167	.063	1.000
1966	**NY-A**	**25**	**58**	**5**	**9**	**2**	**0**	**0**	**2**	**9**	**0**	**8**	**0**	**1**	**1**	**0**	**0**	**.155**	**.265**	**.190**	**.909**
1966	LA-N	20	70	10	18	0	0	0	4	8	0	8	2	3	0	1	1	.257	.350	.257	.923
1967	LA-N	84	232	23	50	10	1	2	15	31	4	40	0	4	1	1	2	.216	.307	.293	1.000
1968	StL-N	69	127	14	28	7	1	1	8	13	2	31	2	0	0	1	2	.220	.303	.315	.973
1969	Bos-A	94	226	30	58	9	3	2	20	29	1	44	4	0	2	0	2	.257	.349	.350	.981
1970	Bos-A	76	139	16	26	1	2	1	14	21	2	26	1	0	2	0	1	.187	.294	.245	.969
1971	Mil-A	23	28	2	3	2	0	0	1	2	0	8	1	0	0	0	0	.107	.194	.179	1.000
1971	StL-N	34	60	7	13	2	0	1	6	10	0	9	2	0	0	0	0	.217	.347	.300	.935
Career average		55	128	16	29	5	1	1	9	16	—	22	1	1	—	1	1	.227	.319	.297	.969
Yankee average		**25**	**58**	**5**	**9**	**2**	**0**	**0**	**2**	**9**	**0**	**8**	**0**	**1**	**1**	**0**	**0**	**.155**	**.265**	**.190**	**.909**
Career total		1321	3083	394	699	113	20	21	211	390	18	526	26	29	17	12	29	.227	.317	.297	.969
Yankee total		**25**	**58**	**5**	**9**	**2**	**0**	**0**	**2**	**9**	**0**	**8**	**0**	**1**	**1**	**0**	**0**	**.155**	**.265**	**.190**	**.909**

Schult, Arthur William (Dutch)

HEIGHT: 6'3" THROWS: RIGHT BATS: RIGHT BORN: 6/20/1928 BROOKLYN, NEW YORK POSITIONS PLAYED: 1B, OF

YEAR	TEAM	GAMES	AB	RUNS	HITS	2B	3B	HR	RBI	BB	IBB	SO	HBP	SH	SF	SB	CS	BA	OBA	SA	FA
1953	**NY-A**	**7**	**0**	**3**	**0**	**0**	**0**	**0**	**0**	**0**	**—**	**0**	**0**	**0**	**—**	**0**	**0**	**—**	**—**	**—**	**.000**
1956	Cin-N	5	7	3	3	0	0	0	2	1	0	1	0	0	0	0	0	.429	.500	.429	.000
1957	Cin-N	21	34	4	9	2	0	0	4	0	0	2	1	0	0	0	0	.265	.286	.324	1.000
1957	Was-N	77	247	30	65	14	0	4	35	14	0	30	1	1	2	0	1	.263	.303	.368	.987
1959	Chi-N	42	118	17	32	7	0	2	14	7	0	14	2	2	1	0	0	.271	.320	.381	.985
1960	Chi-N	12	15	1	2	1	0	0	1	1	1	3	0	0	0	0	0	.133	.188	.200	1.000
Career average		27	70	10	19	4	0	1	9	4	—	8	1	1	—	0	0	.264	.308	.363	.794
Yankee average		**7**	**0**	**3**	**0**	**0**	**0**	**0**	**0**	**0**	**—**	**0**	**0**	**0**	**—**	**0**	**0**	**—**	**—**	**—**	**.000**
Career total		164	421	58	111	24	0	6	56	23	1	50	4	3	3	0	1	.264	.306	.363	.794
Yankee total		**7**	**0**	**3**	**0**	**0**	**0**	**0**	**0**	**0**	**—**	**0**	**0**	**0**	**—**	**0**	**0**	**—**	**—**	**—**	**.000**

Schwarz, William DeWitt

HEIGHT: — THROWS: RIGHT BATS: — BORN: 1/30/1891 BIRMINGHAM, ALABAMA DIED: 6/24/1949 JACKSONVILLE, FLORIDA POSITIONS PLAYED: C

YEAR	TEAM	GAMES	AB	RUNS	HITS	2B	3B	HR	RBI	BB	IBB	SO	HBP	SH	SF	SB	CS	BA	OBA	SA	FA
1914	**NY-A**	**1**	**1**	**0**	**0**	**0**	**0**	**0**	**0**	**0**	**—**	**1**	**0**	**0**	**—**	**0**	**0**	**.000**	**.000**	**.000**	**.000**
Career average		1	1	0	0	0	0	0	0	0	—	1	0	0	—	0	0	.000	.000	.000	.000
Yankee average		**1**	**1**	**0**	**0**	**0**	**0**	**0**	**0**	**0**	**—**	**1**	**0**	**0**	**—**	**0**	**0**	**.000**	**.000**	**.000**	**.000**
Career total		1	1	0	0	0	0	0	0	0	—	1	0	0	—	0	0	.000	.000	.000	.000
Yankee total		**1**	**1**	**0**	**0**	**0**	**0**	**0**	**0**	**0**	**—**	**1**	**0**	**0**	**—**	**0**	**0**	**.000**	**.000**	**.000**	**.000**

Schwert, Pius Louis

HEIGHT: 5'10" THROWS: RIGHT BATS: RIGHT BORN: 11/22/1892 ANGOLA, NEW YORK DIED: 3/11/1941 WASHINGTON, D.C. POSITIONS PLAYED: C

YEAR	TEAM	GAMES	AB	RUNS	HITS	2B	3B	HR	RBI	BB	IBB	SO	HBP	SH	SF	SB	CS	BA	OBA	SA	FA
1914	**NY-A**	**2**	**5**	**0**	**0**	**0**	**0**	**0**	**0**	**2**	**—**	**2**	**0**	**0**	**—**	**0**	**0**	**.000**	**.286**	**.000**	**.909**
1915	**NY-A**	**9**	**18**	**6**	**5**	**3**	**0**	**0**	**6**	**1**	**—**	**6**	**0**	**0**	**—**	**0**	**0**	**.278**	**.316**	**.444**	**.972**
Career average		6	12	3	3	2	0	0	3	2	—	4	0	0	—	0	0	.217	.308	.348	.941
Yankee average		**6**	**12**	**3**	**3**	**2**	**0**	**0**	**3**	**2**	**—**	**4**	**0**	**0**	**—**	**0**	**0**	**.217**	**.308**	**.348**	**.941**
Career total		11	23	6	5	3	0	0	6	3	—	8	0	0	—	0	0	.217	.308	.348	.941
Yankee total		**11**	**23**	**6**	**5**	**3**	**0**	**0**	**6**	**3**	**—**	**8**	**0**	**0**	**—**	**0**	**0**	**.217**	**.308**	**.348**	**.941**

Scott, George Charles (Boomer)

HEIGHT: 6'2" THROWS: RIGHT BATS: RIGHT BORN: 3/23/1944 GREENVILLE, MISSISSIPPI POSITIONS PLAYED: 1B, 3B

YEAR	TEAM	GAMES	AB	RUNS	HITS	2B	3B	HR	RBI	BB	IBB	SO	HBP	SH	SF	SB	CS	BA	OBA	SA	FA
1966	Bos-A	162	601	73	147	18	7	27	90	65	13	152	8	2	5	4	0	.245	.324	.433	.818
1967	Bos-A	159	565	74	171	21	7	19	82	63	10	119	4	3	6	10	8	.303	.373	.465	.987
1968	Bos-A	124	350	23	60	14	0	3	25	26	3	88	5	1	5	3	5	.171	.236	.237	.987
1969	Bos-A	152	549	63	139	14	5	16	52	61	12	74	4	1	2	4	3	.253	.331	.384	.994
1970	Bos-A	127	480	50	142	24	5	16	63	44	5	95	2	0	4	4	11	.296	.355	.467	.990
1971	Bos-A	146	537	72	141	16	4	24	78	41	5	102	5	0	7	0	3	.263	.317	.441	.992
1972	Mil-A	152	578	71	154	24	4	20	88	43	4	130	4	2	2	16	4	.266	.321	.426	.992
1973	Mil-A	158	604	98	185	30	4	24	107	61	6	94	2	2	4	9	5	.306	.370	.488	.994
1974	Mil-A	158	604	74	170	36	2	17	82	59	5	90	3	0	6	9	9	.281	.345	.432	.992
1975	Mil-A	158	617	86	176	26	4	36	109	51	7	97	3	1	3	6	5	.285	.341	.515	.909
1976	Mil-A	156	606	73	166	21	5	18	77	53	6	118	5	0	7	0	1	.274	.334	.414	.991
1977	Bos-A	157	584	103	157	26	5	33	95	57	4	112	6	1	5	1	1	.269	.337	.500	.985
1978	Bos-A	120	412	51	96	16	4	12	54	44	3	86	0	7	3	1	1	.233	.305	.379	.991
1979	Bos-A	45	156	18	35	9	1	4	23	17	1	22	0	1	1	0	0	.224	.299	.372	.986
1979	KC-A	44	146	19	39	8	2	1	20	12	1	32	2	1	1	1	1	.267	.329	.370	.989
1979	**NY-A**	**16**	**44**	**9**	**14**	**3**	**1**	**1**	**6**	**2**	**0**	**7**	**0**	**0**	**1**	**1**	**0**	**.318**	**.340**	**.500**	**1.000**
Career average		127	465	60	125	19	4	17	66	44	5	89	3	1	4	4	4	.268	.333	.435	.975
Yankee average		**16**	**44**	**9**	**14**	**3**	**1**	**1**	**6**	**2**	**0**	**7**	**0**	**0**	**1**	**1**	**0**	**.318**	**.340**	**.500**	**1.000**
Career total		2034	7433	957	1992	306	60	271	1051	699	85	1418	53	22	62	69	57	.268	.333	.435	.975
Yankee total		**16**	**44**	**9**	**14**	**3**	**1**	**1**	**6**	**2**	**0**	**7**	**0**	**0**	**1**	**1**	**0**	**.318**	**.340**	**.500**	**1.000**

Scott, Lewis Everett (Deacon)

HEIGHT: 5'8" THROWS: RIGHT BATS: RIGHT BORN: 11/19/1892 BLUFFTON, INDIANA DIED: 11/2/1960 FT. WAYNE, INDIANA POSITIONS PLAYED: 2B, 3B, SS

YEAR	TEAM	GAMES	AB	RUNS	HITS	2B	3B	HR	RBI	BB	IBB	SO	HBP	SH	SF	SB	CS	BA	OBA	SA	FA
1914	Bos-A	144	539	66	129	15	6	2	37	32	—	43	3	26	—	9	14	.239	.286	.301	.949
1915	Bos-A	100	359	25	72	11	0	0	28	17	—	21	0	23	—	4	7	.201	.237	.231	.961
1916	Bos-A	123	366	37	85	19	2	0	27	23	—	24	3	30	—	8	—	.232	.283	.295	1.000
1917	Bos-A	157	528	40	127	24	7	0	50	20	—	46	0	41	—	12	—	.241	.268	.313	.953
1918	Bos-A	126	443	40	98	11	5	0	43	12	—	16	0	26	—	11	—	.221	.242	.269	.976
1919	Bos-A	138	507	41	141	19	0	0	38	19	—	26	1	13	—	8	—	.278	.306	.316	.976
1920	Bos-A	154	569	41	153	21	12	4	61	21	—	15	4	21	—	4	11	.269	.300	.369	.973
1921	Bos-A	154	576	65	151	21	9	1	62	27	—	21	0	17	—	5	9	.262	.295	.335	.972
1922	**NY-A**	**154**	**557**	**64**	**150**	**23**	**5**	**3**	**45**	**23**	**—**	**22**	**5**	**28**	**—**	**2**	**3**	**.269**	**.304**	**.345**	**.966**
1923	**NY-A**	**152**	**533**	**48**	**131**	**16**	**4**	**6**	**60**	**13**	**—**	**19**	**2**	**20**	**—**	**1**	**3**	**.246**	**.266**	**.325**	**.961**
1924	**NY-A**	**153**	**548**	**56**	**137**	**12**	**6**	**4**	**64**	**21**	**—**	**15**	**0**	**18**	**—**	**3**	**7**	**.250**	**.278**	**.316**	**.966**
1925	**NY-A**	**22**	**60**	**3**	**13**	**0**	**0**	**0**	**4**	**2**	**—**	**2**	**0**	**3**	**—**	**0**	**1**	**.217**	**.242**	**.217**	**.988**
1925	Was-A	33	103	10	28	6	1	0	18	4	—	4	0	3	—	1	2	.272	.299	.350	1.000
1926	Chi-A	40	143	15	36	10	1	0	13	9	—	8	0	6	—	1	3	.252	.296	.336	.949
1926	Cin-N	4	6	1	4	0	0	0	1	0	—	0	0	0	—	0	—	.667	.667	.667	.875
Career average		110	389	37	97	14	4	1	37	16	—	19	1	18	—	5	—	.249	.281	.315	.964
Yankee average		**120**	**425**	**43**	**108**	**13**	**4**	**3**	**43**	**15**	**—**	**15**	**2**	**17**	**—**	**2**	**4**	**.254**	**.282**	**.324**	**.970**
Career total		1654	5837	552	1455	208	58	20	551	243	—	282	18	275	—	69	60	.249	.281	.315	.964
Yankee total		**481**	**1698**	**171**	**431**	**51**	**15**	**13**	**173**	**59**	**—**	**58**	**7**	**69**	**—**	**6**	**14**	**.254**	**.282**	**.324**	**.970**

Scott, Rodney Darrell

HEIGHT: 6'0" THROWS: RIGHT BATS: BOTH BORN: 10/16/1953 INDIANAPOLIS, INDIANA POSITIONS PLAYED: 2B, 3B, SS, OF

YEAR	TEAM	GAMES	AB	RUNS	HITS	2B	3B	HR	RBI	BB	IBB	SO	HBP	SH	SF	SB	CS	BA	OBA	SA	FA
1975	KC-A	48	15	13	1	0	0	0	0	1	0	3	0	2	0	4	2	.067	.125	.067	.867
1976	Mon-N	7	10	3	4	0	0	0	0	1	0	1	0	0	0	2	0	.400	.455	.400	1.000
1977	Oak-A	133	364	56	95	4	4	0	20	43	0	50	3	5	2	33	18	.261	.342	.294	.945
1978	Chi-N	78	227	41	64	5	1	0	15	43	0	41	3	7	0	27	10	.282	.403	.313	.929
1979	Mon-N	151	562	69	134	12	5	3	42	66	2	82	2	12	3	39	12	.238	.319	.294	.952
1980	Mon-N	154	567	84	127	13	13	0	46	70	0	75	1	11	6	63	13	.224	.307	.293	.982
1981	Mon-N	95	336	43	69	9	3	0	26	50	0	35	1	13	2	30	7	.205	.308	.250	.983
1982	Mon-N	14	25	2	5	0	0	0	1	3	0	2	0	0	0	5	0	.200	.286	.200	.971
1982	**NY-A**	**10**	**26**	**5**	**5**	**0**	**0**	**0**	**0**	**4**	**0**	**2**	**0**	**1**	**0**	**2**	**0**	**.192**	**.300**	**.192**	**.963**
Career average		77	237	35	56	5	3	0	17	31	0	32	1	6	1	23	7	.236	.326	.285	.955
Yankee average		**10**	**26**	**5**	**5**	**0**	**0**	**0**	**0**	**4**	**0**	**2**	**0**	**1**	**0**	**2**	**0**	**.192**	**.300**	**.192**	**.963**
Career total		690	2132	316	504	43	26	3	150	281	2	291	10	51	13	205	62	.236	.326	.285	.955
Yankee total		**10**	**26**	**5**	**5**	**0**	**0**	**0**	**0**	**4**	**0**	**2**	**0**	**1**	**0**	**2**	**0**	**.192**	**.300**	**.192**	**.963**

Sears, Kenneth Eugene (Ziggy)

HEIGHT: 6'1" THROWS: RIGHT BATS: LEFT BORN: 7/6/1917 STREATOR, ILLINOIS DIED: 7/17/1968 BRIDGEPORT, TEXAS POSITIONS PLAYED: C

YEAR	TEAM	GAMES	AB	RUNS	HITS	2B	3B	HR	RBI	BB	IBB	SO	HBP	SH	SF	SB	CS	BA	OBA	SA	FA
1943	NY-A	60	187	22	52	7	0	2	22	11	—	18	3	0	—	1	3	.278	.328	.348	.974
1946	StL-A	7	15	1	5	0	0	0	1	3	—	0	0	0	—	0	0	.333	.444	.333	1.000
Career average		34	101	12	29	4	0	1	12	7	—	9	2	0	—	1	2	.282	.338	.347	.987
Yankee average		**60**	**187**	**22**	**52**	**7**	**0**	**2**	**22**	**11**	**—**	**18**	**3**	**0**	**—**	**1**	**3**	**.278**	**.328**	**.348**	**.974**
Career total		67	202	23	57	7	0	2	23	14	—	18	3	0	—	1	3	.282	.338	.347	.987
Yankee total		**60**	**187**	**22**	**52**	**7**	**0**	**2**	**22**	**11**	**—**	**18**	**3**	**0**	**—**	**1**	**3**	**.278**	**.328**	**.348**	**.974**

Seeds, Ira Robert (Suitcase Bob)

HEIGHT: 6'0" THROWS: RIGHT BATS: RIGHT BORN: 2/24/1907 RINGGOLD, TEXAS DIED: 10/28/1993 ERICK, OKLAHOMA POSITIONS PLAYED: 1B, 3B, OF

YEAR	TEAM	GAMES	AB	RUNS	HITS	2B	3B	HR	RBI	BB	IBB	SO	HBP	SH	SF	SB	CS	BA	OBA	SA	FA
1930	Cle-A	85	277	37	79	11	3	3	32	12	—	22	0	7	—	1	3	.285	.315	.379	.953
1931	Cle-A	48	134	26	41	4	1	1	10	11	—	11	0	1	—	1	0	.306	.359	.373	.966
1932	Cle-A	2	4	0	0	0	0	0	0	0	—	0	0	0	—	0	0	.000	.000	.000	.964
1932	Chi-A	116	434	53	126	18	6	2	45	31	—	37	3	7	—	5	7	.290	.340	.373	.964
1933	Bos-A	82	230	26	56	13	4	0	23	21	—	20	1	3	—	1	3	.243	.310	.335	.985
1934	Bos-A	8	6	0	1	0	0	0	1	0	—	1	0	0	—	0	0	.167	.167	.167	.977
1934	Cle-A	61	186	28	46	8	1	0	18	21	—	13	1	5	—	2	1	.247	.327	.301	.977
1936	**NY-A**	**13**	**42**	**12**	**11**	**1**	**0**	**4**	**10**	**5**	**—**	**3**	**0**	**0**	**—**	**3**	**1**	**.262**	**.340**	**.571**	**1.000**
1938	NY-N	81	296	35	86	12	3	9	52	20	—	33	1	3	—	0	—	.291	.338	.443	.987
1939	NY-N	63	173	33	46	5	1	5	26	22	—	31	1	2	—	1	—	.266	.352	.393	.975
1940	NY-N	56	155	18	45	5	2	4	16	17	—	19	3	2	—	0	—	.290	.371	.426	.985
Career average		56	176	24	49	7	2	3	21	15	—	17	1	3	—	1	—	.277	.336	.382	.976
Yankee average		**13**	**42**	**12**	**11**	**1**	**0**	**4**	**10**	**5**	**—**	**3**	**0**	**0**	**—**	**3**	**1**	**.262**	**.340**	**.571**	**1.000**
Career total		615	1937	268	537	77	21	28	233	160	—	190	10	30	—	14	15	.277	.336	.382	.976
Yankee total		**13**	**42**	**12**	**11**	**1**	**0**	**4**	**10**	**5**	**—**	**3**	**0**	**0**	**—**	**3**	**1**	**.262**	**.340**	**.571**	**1.000**

Segrist, Kal Hill

HEIGHT: 6'0" THROWS: RIGHT BATS: RIGHT BORN: 4/14/1931 GREENVILLE, TEXAS POSITIONS PLAYED: 1B, 2B, 3B

YEAR	TEAM	GAMES	AB	RUNS	HITS	2B	3B	HR	RBI	BB	IBB	SO	HBP	SH	SF	SB	CS	BA	OBA	SA	FA
1952	NY-A	13	23	3	1	0	0	0	1	3	—	1	0	1	—	0	0	.043	.154	.043	.971
1955	Bal-A	7	9	1	3	0	0	0	0	2	0	0	0	0	0	0	0	.333	.455	.333	1.000
Career average		10	16	2	2	0	0	0	1	3	—	1	0	1	—	0	0	.125	.243	.125	.986
Yankee average		**13**	**23**	**3**	**1**	**0**	**0**	**0**	**1**	**3**	**—**	**1**	**0**	**1**	**—**	**0**	**0**	**.043**	**.154**	**.043**	**.971**
Career total		20	32	4	4	0	0	0	1	5	0	1	0	1	0	0	0	.125	.243	.125	.986
Yankee total		**13**	**23**	**3**	**1**	**0**	**0**	**0**	**1**	**3**	**—**	**1**	**0**	**1**	**—**	**0**	**0**	**.043**	**.154**	**.043**	**.971**

Selkirk, George Alexander (Twinkletoes)

HEIGHT: 6'1" THROWS: RIGHT BATS: LEFT BORN: 1/4/1908 HUNTSVILLE, ONTARIO DIED: 1/19/1987 FT. LAUDERDALE, FLORIDA POSITIONS PLAYED: OF

YEAR	TEAM	GAMES	AB	RUNS	HITS	2B	3B	HR	RBI	BB	IBB	SO	HBP	SH	SF	SB	CS	BA	OBA	SA	FA
1934	NY-A	46	176	23	55	7	1	5	38	15	—	17	1	0	—	1	1	.313	.370	.449	.989
1935	NY-A	128	491	64	153	29	12	11	94	44	—	36	3	3	—	2	7	.312	.372	.487	.975
1936	NY-A	137	493	93	152	28	9	18	107	94	—	60	1	4	—	13	7	.308	.420	.511	.974
1937	NY-A	78	256	49	84	13	5	18	68	34	—	24	2	1	—	8	2	.328	.411	.629	.987
1938	NY-A	99	335	58	85	12	5	10	62	68	—	52	3	1	—	9	4	.254	.384	.409	.973
1939	NY-A	128	418	103	128	17	4	21	101	103	—	49	8	8	—	12	5	.306	.452	.517	.989
1940	NY-A	118	379	68	102	17	5	19	71	84	—	43	3	4	—	3	6	.269	.406	.491	.962
1941	NY-A	70	164	30	36	5	0	6	25	28	—	30	2	1	—	1	0	.220	.340	.360	.967
1942	NY-A	42	78	15	15	3	0	0	10	16	—	8	0	1	—	0	0	.192	.330	.231	1.000
Career average		94	310	56	90	15	5	12	64	54	—	35	3	3	—	5	4	.290	.400	.483	.980
Yankee average		**94**	**310**	**56**	**90**	**15**	**5**	**12**	**64**	**54**	**—**	**35**	**3**	**3**	**—**	**5**	**4**	**.290**	**.400**	**.483**	**.980**
Career total		846	2790	503	810	131	41	108	576	486	—	319	23	23	—	49	32	.290	.400	.483	.980
Yankee total		**846**	**2790**	**503**	**810**	**131**	**41**	**108**	**576**	**486**	**—**	**319**	**23**	**23**	**—**	**49**	**32**	**.290**	**.400**	**.483**	**.980**

George Alexander "Twinkletoes" Selkirk, of, 1934–42

The toughest job in the history of baseball? How about following Babe Ruth in right field for the New York Yankees?

That was George Selkirk's job, and it was, initially, not much fun. After Ruth was released in 1935 and Selkirk was announced as his replacement, the fans booed him unmercifully the first few games. Selkirk even wore Ruth's number three. But while he didn't approach Ruth's home run numbers, Selkirk was a solid hitter, batting over .300 five of the nine years he toiled for New York.

Selkirk was born on January 4, 1908, in Huntsville, Ontario, and he didn't make the big leagues until he was 26. In 1934, he played 46 games in the outfield. By 1935, he was a regular. He hit .312 that year and was second on the team with 94 RBI. The next year, the Yankees picked up rookie Joe DiMaggio and won the first of four straight World Championships.

In 1939, Selkirk was part of the most potent outfield in the history of the majors, as he, DiMaggio and Charlie Keller all hit over .300 and combined for 310 RBI.

Selkirk got the name "Twinkletoes" in the minor leagues for his habit of running on the balls of his feet.

After his retirement from the Yankees at age 34, Selkirk worked as minor league coordinator for both the Athletics and Orioles. He later became both general manager and vice president of the Senators in the 1960s. He returned to New York in 1970 as a scout. He died in 1987 in Fort Lauderdale.

Selkirk is 22nd on the Yankees' all-time list in batting average with a .290 mark.

Sepkowski, Theodore Walter

HEIGHT: 5'11"   THROWS: RIGHT   BATS: LEFT   BORN: 11/19/1923 BALTIMORE, MARYLAND   POSITIONS PLAYED: 2B, 3B, OF

YEAR	TEAM	GAMES	AB	RUNS	HITS	2B	3B	HR	RBI	BB	IBB	SO	HBP	SH	SF	SB	CS	BA	OBA	SA	FA
1942	Cle-A	5	10	0	1	0	0	0	0	0	—	3	0	0	—	0	0	.100	.100	.100	.824
1946	Cle-A	2	8	2	4	1	0	0	1	0	—	0	0	0	—	0	0	.500	.500	.625	.833
1947	Cle-A	10	8	0	1	1	0	0	0	1	—	1	0	0	—	0	0	.125	.222	.250	.000
1947	**NY-A**	**2**	**0**	**1**	**0**	**0**	**0**	**0**	**0**	**0**	**—**	**0**	**0**	**0**	**—**	**0**	**0**	**—**	**—**	**—**	**.000**
Career average		5	7	1	2	1	0	0	0	0	—	1	0	0	—	0	0	.231	.259	.308	.414
Yankee average		**2**	**0**	**1**	**0**	**0**	**0**	**0**	**0**	**0**	**—**	**0**	**0**	**0**	**—**	**0**	**0**	**—**	**—**	**—**	**.000**
Career total		19	26	3	6	2	0	0	1	1	—	4	0	0	—	0	0	.231	.259	.308	.414
Yankee total		**2**	**0**	**1**	**0**	**0**	**0**	**0**	**0**	**0**	**—**	**0**	**0**	**0**	**—**	**0**	**0**	**—**	**—**	**—**	**.000**

Severeid, Henry Levai (Hank)

HEIGHT: 6'0"   THROWS: RIGHT   BATS: RIGHT   BORN: 6/1/1891 STORY CITY, IOWA   DIED: 12/17/1968 SAN ANTONIO, TEXAS   POSITIONS PLAYED: C, 1B, 3B, OF

YEAR	TEAM	GAMES	AB	RUNS	HITS	2B	3B	HR	RBI	BB	IBB	SO	HBP	SH	SF	SB	CS	BA	OBA	SA	FA
1911	Cin-N	37	56	5	17	6	1	0	10	3	—	6	1	0	—	0	—	.304	.350	.446	.913
1912	Cin-N	50	114	10	27	0	3	0	13	8	—	11	0	4	—	0	—	.237	.287	.289	.889
1913	Cin-N	8	6	0	0	0	0	0	0	1	—	1	0	0	—	0	—	.000	.143	.000	1.000
1915	StL-A	80	203	12	45	6	1	1	22	16	—	25	0	1	—	2	1	.222	.279	.276	.966
1916	StL-A	100	293	23	80	8	2	0	34	26	—	17	4	5	—	3	—	.273	.341	.314	.976
1917	StL-A	143	501	45	133	23	4	1	57	28	—	20	1	14	—	6	—	.265	.306	.333	1.000
1918	StL-A	51	133	8	34	4	0	0	11	18	—	4	3	2	—	4	—	.256	.357	.286	.946
1919	StL-A	112	351	16	87	12	2	0	36	21	—	13	4	8	—	2	—	.248	.298	.293	.983
1920	StL-A	123	422	46	117	14	5	2	49	33	—	11	4	6	—	5	3	.277	.336	.348	.983

(continued)

(continued)

YEAR	TEAM	GAMES	AB	RUNS	HITS	2B	3B	HR	RBI	BB	IBB	SO	HBP	SH	SF	SB	CS	BA	OBA	SA	FA
1921	StL-A	143	472	66	153	23	7	2	78	42	—	9	0	17	—	7	2	.324	.379	.415	.972
1922	StL-A	137	517	49	166	32	7	3	78	28	—	12	0	14	—	1	4	.321	.356	.427	.984
1923	StL-A	122	432	50	133	27	6	3	51	31	—	11	1	16	—	3	0	.308	.356	.419	.993
1924	StL-A	137	432	37	133	23	2	4	48	36	—	15	1	31	—	1	6	.308	.362	.398	.990
1925	StL-A	34	109	15	40	9	0	1	21	11	—	2	0	3	—	0	2	.367	.425	.477	.990
1925	Was-A	34	109	15	40	9	0	1	21	11	—	2	0	3	—	0	2	.367	.423	.477	.986
1926	Was-A	22	34	2	7	1	0	0	4	3	—	2	0	0	—	0	0	.206	.270	.235	.985
1926	**NY-A**	**41**	**127**	**13**	**34**	**8**	**1**	**0**	**13**	**13**	**—**	**4**	**0**	**2**	**—**	**1**	**1**	**.268**	**.336**	**.346**	**.988**
Career average		81	254	24	73	12	2	1	32	19	—	10	1	7	—	2	—	.289	.342	.368	.973
Yankee average		**41**	**127**	**13**	**34**	**8**	**1**	**0**	**13**	**13**	**—**	**4**	**0**	**2**	**—**	**1**	**1**	**.268**	**.336**	**.346**	**.988**
Career total		1374	4311	412	1246	205	41	18	546	329	—	165	19	126	—	35	21	.289	.342	.368	.973
Yankee total		**41**	**127**	**13**	**34**	**8**	**1**	**0**	**13**	**13**	**—**	**4**	**0**	**2**	**—**	**1**	**1**	**.268**	**.336**	**.346**	**.988**

Sewell, Joseph Wheeler

HEIGHT: 5'6"   THROWS: RIGHT   BATS: LEFT   BORN: 10/9/1898, TITUS, ALABAMA   DIED: 3/6/1990, MOBILE, ALABAMA   POSITIONS PLAYED: 3B, SS

YEAR	TEAM	GAMES	AB	RUNS	HITS	2B	3B	HR	RBI	BB	IBB	SO	HBP	SH	SF	SB	CS	BA	OBA	SA	FA
1920	Cle-A	22	70	14	23	4	1	0	12	9	—	4	1	3	—	1	0	.329	.413	.414	.884
1921	Cle-A	154	572	101	182	36	12	4	93	80	—	17	11	20	—	7	6	.318	.412	.444	.944
1922	Cle-A	153	558	80	167	28	7	2	83	73	—	20	6	19	—	10	12	.299	.386	.385	.954
1923	Cle-A	153	553	98	195	41	10	3	109	98	—	12	7	24	—	9	6	.353	.456	.479	.930
1924	Cle-A	153	594	99	188	45	5	4	106	67	—	13	2	22	—	3	3	.316	.384	.429	.960
1925	Cle-A	155	608	78	204	37	7	1	98	64	—	4	4	23	—	7	6	.336	.402	.424	1.000
1926	Cle-A	154	578	91	187	41	5	4	85	65	—	6	8	21	—	17	7	.324	.399	.433	.955
1927	Cle-A	153	569	83	180	48	5	1	92	51	—	7	9	23	—	3	16	.316	.382	.424	.962
1928	Cle-A	155	588	79	190	40	2	4	70	58	—	9	7	25	—	7	1	.323	.391	.418	.943
1929	Cle-A	152	578	90	182	38	3	7	73	48	—	4	5	41	—	6	6	.315	.372	.427	.975
1930	Cle-A	109	353	44	102	17	6	0	48	41	—	3	7	13	—	1	4	.289	.374	.371	.950
1931	**NY-A**	**130**	**484**	**102**	**146**	**22**	**1**	**6**	**64**	**61**	**—**	**8**	**9**	**17**	**—**	**1**	**1**	**.302**	**.390**	**.388**	**.952**
1932	**NY-A**	**125**	**503**	**95**	**137**	**21**	**3**	**11**	**68**	**56**	**—**	**3**	**3**	**14**	**—**	**0**	**2**	**.272**	**.349**	**.392**	**.974**
1933	**NY-A**	**135**	**524**	**87**	**143**	**18**	**1**	**2**	**54**	**71**	**—**	**4**	**1**	**10**	**—**	**2**	**2**	**.273**	**.361**	**.323**	**.964**
Career average		136	509	82	159	31	5	4	75	60	—	8	6	20	—	5	5	.312	.391	.413	.953
Yankee average		**130**	**504**	**95**	**142**	**20**	**2**	**6**	**62**	**63**	**—**	**5**	**4**	**14**	**—**	**1**	**2**	**.282**	**.366**	**.367**	**.963**
Career total		1903	7132	1141	2226	436	68	49	1055	842	—	114	80	275	—	74	72	.312	.391	.413	.953
Yankee total		**390**	**1511**	**284**	**426**	**61**	**5**	**19**	**186**	**188**	**—**	**15**	**13**	**41**	**—**	**3**	**5**	**.282**	**.366**	**.367**	**.963**

Shanks, Howard Samuel (Hank)

HEIGHT: 5'11"   THROWS: RIGHT   BATS: RIGHT   BORN: 7/21/1890, CHICAGO, ILLINOIS   DIED: 7/30/1941, MONACA, PENNSYLVANIA   POSITIONS PLAYED: 2B, 3B, SS, OF

YEAR	TEAM	GAMES	AB	RUNS	HITS	2B	3B	HR	RBI	BB	IBB	SO	HBP	SH	SF	SB	CS	BA	OBA	SA	FA
1912	Was-A	116	399	52	92	14	7	1	48	40	—	—	3	19	—	21	—	.231	.305	.308	.962
1913	Was-A	109	390	38	99	11	5	1	37	15	—	40	3	8	—	24	—	.254	.287	.315	.978
1914	Was-A	143	500	44	112	22	10	4	64	29	—	51	2	30	—	18	16	.224	.269	.332	.954
1915	Was-A	141	492	52	123	19	8	0	47	30	—	42	3	21	—	12	14	.250	.297	.321	.982
1916	Was-A	140	471	51	119	15	7	1	48	41	—	34	3	25	—	23	12	.253	.317	.321	.933
1917	Was-A	126	430	45	87	15	5	0	28	33	—	37	6	27	—	15	—	.202	.269	.260	.977
1918	Was-A	120	436	42	112	19	4	1	56	31	—	21	4	17	—	23	—	.257	.312	.326	.950
1919	Was-A	135	491	33	122	8	7	1	54	25	—	48	3	32	—	13	—	.248	.289	.299	.922
1920	Was-A	128	444	56	119	16	7	4	37	29	—	43	2	14	—	11	6	.268	.316	.363	.951
1921	Was-A	154	562	81	170	24	18	7	69	57	—	38	3	24	—	11	10	.302	.370	.447	.960
1922	Was-A	84	272	35	77	10	9	1	32	25	—	25	4	13	—	6	0	.283	.352	.397	.971
1923	Bos-A	131	464	38	118	19	5	3	57	19	—	37	1	15	—	6	6	.254	.285	.336	.833
1924	Bos-A	72	193	22	50	16	3	0	25	21	—	12	0	9	—	1	0	.259	.332	.373	1.000
1925	**NY-A**	**66**	**155**	**15**	**40**	**3**	**1**	**1**	**18**	**20**	**—**	**15**	**0**	**9**	**—**	**1**	**0**	**.258**	**.343**	**.310**	**.938**
Career average		119	407	43	103	15	7	2	44	30	—	—	3	19	—	13	—	.253	.308	.337	.951
Yankee average		**66**	**155**	**15**	**40**	**3**	**1**	**1**	**18**	**20**	**—**	**15**	**0**	**9**	**—**	**1**	**0**	**.258**	**.343**	**.310**	**.938**
Career total		1665	5699	604	1440	211	96	25	620	415	—	443	37	263	—	185	64	.253	.308	.337	.951
Yankee total		**66**	**155**	**15**	**40**	**3**	**1**	**1**	**18**	**20**	**—**	**15**	**0**	**9**	**—**	**1**	**0**	**.258**	**.343**	**.310**	**.938**

Sheridan, Patrick Arthur

HEIGHT: 6'3" THROWS: RIGHT BATS: LEFT BORN: 12/4/1957 ANN ARBOR, MICHIGAN POSITIONS PLAYED: OF

YEAR	TEAM	GAMES	AB	RUNS	HITS	2B	3B	HR	RBI	BB	IBB	SO	HBP	SH	SF	SB	CS	BA	OBA	SA	FA
1981	KC-A	3	1	0	0	0	0	0	0	0	0	1	0	0	0	0	0	.000	.000	.000	1.000
1983	KC-A	109	333	43	90	12	2	7	36	20	0	64	0	4	0	12	3	.270	.312	.381	.988
1984	KC-A	138	481	64	136	24	4	8	53	41	3	91	1	5	3	19	6	.283	.338	.399	.986
1985	KC-A	78	206	18	47	9	2	3	17	23	2	38	1	3	1	11	3	.228	.307	.335	.983
1986	Det-A	98	236	41	56	9	1	6	19	21	4	57	1	2	2	9	2	.237	.300	.360	.977
1987	Det-A	141	421	57	109	19	3	6	49	44	4	90	1	2	5	18	13	.259	.327	.361	.976
1988	Det-A	127	347	47	88	9	5	11	47	44	4	64	2	7	2	8	6	.254	.339	.403	.982
1989	Det-A	50	120	16	29	3	0	3	15	17	0	21	0	1	1	4	0	.242	.333	.342	.982
1989	SF-N	70	161	20	33	3	4	3	14	13	1	45	0	0	0	4	1	.205	.264	.329	.983
1991	**NY-A**	**62**	**113**	**13**	**23**	**3**	**0**	**4**	**7**	**13**	**1**	**30**	**0**	**1**	**0**	**1**	**1**	**.204**	**.286**	**.336**	**1.000**
Career average		88	242	32	61	9	2	5	26	24	2	50	1	3	1	9	4	.253	.319	.371	.986
Yankee average		**62**	**113**	**13**	**23**	**3**	**0**	**4**	**7**	**13**	**1**	**30**	**0**	**1**	**0**	**1**	**1**	**.204**	**.286**	**.336**	**1.000**
Career total		876	2419	319	611	91	21	51	257	236	19	501	6	25	14	86	35	.253	.319	.371	.986
Yankee total		**62**	**113**	**13**	**23**	**3**	**0**	**4**	**7**	**13**	**1**	**30**	**0**	**1**	**0**	**1**	**1**	**.204**	**.286**	**.336**	**1.000**

Shopay, Thomas Michael

HEIGHT: 5'9" THROWS: RIGHT BATS: LEFT BORN: 2/21/1945 BRISTOL, CONNECTICUT POSITIONS PLAYED: OF

YEAR	TEAM	GAMES	AB	RUNS	HITS	2B	3B	HR	RBI	BB	IBB	SO	HBP	SH	SF	SB	CS	BA	OBA	SA	FA
1967	**NY-A**	**8**	**27**	**2**	**8**	**1**	**0**	**2**	**6**	**1**	**1**	**5**	**0**	**0**	**1**	**2**	**0**	**.296**	**.310**	**.556**	**.917**
1969	**NY-A**	**28**	**48**	**2**	**4**	**0**	**1**	**0**	**0**	**2**	**1**	**10**	**0**	**0**	**0**	**0**	**1**	**.083**	**.120**	**.125**	**1.000**
1971	Bal-A	47	74	10	19	2	0	0	5	3	1	7	0	2	0	2	1	.257	.286	.284	1.000
1972	Bal-A	49	40	3	9	0	0	0	2	5	0	12	0	0	0	0	0	.225	.311	.225	1.000
1975	Bal-A	40	31	4	5	1	0	0	2	4	0	7	0	1	0	3	0	.161	.257	.194	1.000
1976	Bal-A	14	20	4	4	0	0	0	1	3	0	3	0	0	0	1	0	.200	.304	.200	1.000
1977	Bal-A	67	69	15	13	3	0	1	4	8	0	7	0	2	0	3	3	.188	.273	.275	1.000
Career average		36	44	6	9	1	0	0	3	4	0	7	0	1	0	2	1	.201	.262	.259	.988
Yankee average		**18**	**38**	**2**	**6**	**1**	**1**	**1**	**3**	**2**	**1**	**8**	**0**	**0**	**1**	**1**	**1**	**.160**	**.190**	**.280**	**.959**
Career total		253	309	40	62	7	1	3	20	26	3	51	0	5	1	11	5	.201	.262	.259	.988
Yankee total		**36**	**75**	**4**	**12**	**1**	**1**	**2**	**6**	**3**	**2**	**15**	**0**	**0**	**1**	**2**	**1**	**.160**	**.190**	**.280**	**.959**

Siebern, Norman Leroy

HEIGHT: 6'2" THROWS: RIGHT BATS: LEFT BORN: 7/26/1933 ST.LOUIS, MISSOURI POSITIONS PLAYED: 1B, OF

YEAR	TEAM	GAMES	AB	RUNS	HITS	2B	3B	HR	RBI	BB	IBB	SO	HBP	SH	SF	SB	CS	BA	OBA	SA	FA
1956	**NY-A**	**54**	**162**	**27**	**33**	**1**	**4**	**4**	**21**	**19**	**0**	**38**	**0**	**2**	**1**	**1**	**1**	**.204**	**.286**	**.333**	**.971**
1958	**NY-A**	**134**	**460**	**79**	**138**	**19**	**5**	**14**	**55**	**66**	**3**	**87**	**1**	**4**	**2**	**5**	**8**	**.300**	**.388**	**.454**	**.982**
1959	**NY-A**	**120**	**380**	**52**	**103**	**17**	**0**	**11**	**53**	**41**	**2**	**71**	**2**	**3**	**5**	**3**	**1**	**.271**	**.341**	**.403**	**1.000**
1960	KC-A	144	520	69	145	31	6	19	69	72	6	68	2	4	4	0	0	.279	.366	.471	.987
1961	KC-A	153	560	68	166	36	5	18	98	82	3	91	1	0	6	2	4	.296	.384	.475	.989
1962	KC-A	162	600	114	185	25	6	25	117	110	9	88	1	1	7	3	1	.308	.412	.495	.994
1963	KC-A	152	556	80	151	25	2	16	83	79	6	82	0	1	8	1	4	.272	.358	.410	1.000
1964	Bal-A	150	478	92	117	24	2	12	56	106	3	87	2	3	7	2	3	.245	.379	.379	.995
1965	Bal-A	106	297	44	76	13	4	8	32	50	7	49	1	2	3	1	2	.256	.362	.407	.991
1966	Cal-A	125	336	29	83	14	1	5	41	63	7	61	0	0	5	0	1	.247	.361	.339	.992
1967	SF-N	46	58	6	9	1	1	0	4	14	0	13	0	0	0	0	0	.155	.319	.207	1.000
1967	Bos-A	33	44	2	9	0	2	0	7	6	1	8	0	0	0	0	0	.205	.300	.295	.981
1968	Bos-A	27	30	0	2	0	0	0	0	0	0	5	0	0	0	0	0	.067	.067	.067	1.000
Career average		108	345	51	94	16	3	10	49	55	4	58	1	2	4	1	2	.272	.369	.423	.991
Yankee average		**103**	**334**	**53**	**91**	**12**	**3**	**10**	**43**	**42**	**2**	**65**	**1**	**3**	**3**	**3**	**3**	**.273**	**.354**	**.415**	**.984**
Career total		1406	4481	662	1217	206	38	132	636	708	47	748	10	20	48	18	25	.272	.369	.423	.991
Yankee total		**308**	**1002**	**158**	**274**	**37**	**9**	**29**	**129**	**126**	**5**	**196**	**3**	**9**	**8**	**9**	**10**	**.273**	**.354**	**.415**	**.984**

Sierra, Ruben Angel BORN RUBEN ANGEL SIERRA (GARCIA)

HEIGHT: 6'1" THROWS: RIGHT BATS: BOTH BORN: 10/6/1965 RIO PIEDRAS, PUERTO RICO POSITIONS PLAYED: OF

YEAR	TEAM	GAMES	AB	RUNS	HITS	2B	3B	HR	RBI	BB	IBB	SO	HBP	SH	SF	SB	CS	BA	OBA	SA	FA
1986	Tex-A	113	382	50	101	13	10	16	55	22	3	65	1	1	5	7	8	.264	.302	.476	.972
1987	Tex-A	158	643	97	169	35	4	30	109	39	4	114	2	0	12	16	11	.263	.302	.470	.963
1988	Tex-A	156	615	77	156	32	2	23	91	44	10	91	1	0	8	18	4	.254	.301	.424	.979
1989	Tex-A	162	634	101	194	35	14	29	119	43	2	82	2	0	10	8	2	.306	.347	.543	.973
1990	Tex-A	159	608	70	170	37	2	16	96	49	13	86	1	0	8	9	0	.280	.330	.426	.967
1991	Tex-A	161	661	110	203	44	5	25	116	56	7	91	0	0	9	16	4	.307	.357	.502	.979
1992	Tex-A	124	500	66	139	30	6	14	70	31	6	59	0	0	8	12	4	.278	.315	.446	.970
1992	OAK	27	101	17	28	4	1	3	17	14	6	9	0	0	2	2	0	.277	.359	.426	1.000
1993	Oak-A	158	630	77	147	23	5	22	101	52	16	97	0	0	10	25	5	.233	.288	.390	.977
1994	Oak-A	110	426	71	114	21	1	23	92	23	4	64	0	1	11	8	5	.268	.298	.484	.948
1995	Oak-A	70	264	40	70	17	0	12	42	24	2	42	0	0	3	4	4	.265	.323	.466	.957
1995	**NY-A**	**56**	**215**	**33**	**56**	**15**	**0**	**7**	**44**	**22**	**2**	**34**	**0**	**0**	**5**	**1**	**0**	**.260**	**.322**	**.428**	**.950**
1996	**NY-A**	**96**	**360**	**39**	**93**	**17**	**1**	**11**	**52**	**40**	**11**	**58**	**0**	**0**	**7**	**1**	**3**	**.258**	**.327**	**.403**	**.983**
1996	Det-A	46	158	22	35	9	1	1	20	20	1	25	0	0	2	3	1	.222	.306	.310	.926
1997	Cin-N	25	90	6	22	5	1	2	7	6	1	21	0	0	0	0	0	.244	.292	.389	1.000
1997	Tor-A	14	48	4	10	0	2	1	5	3	1	13	0	0	1	0	0	.208	.250	.354	.923
1998	Chi-A	27	74	7	16	4	1	4	11	3	0	11	0	0	0	2	0	.216	.247	.459	1.000
2000	Tex-A	20	60	5	14	0	0	1	7	4	0	9	0	0	0	1	0	.233	.281	.283	.000
Career average		93	359	50	97	19	3	13	59	28	5	54	0	0	6	7	3	.269	.317	.450	.915
Yankee average		**76**	**288**	**36**	**75**	**16**	**1**	**9**	**48**	**31**	**7**	**46**	**0**	**0**	**6**	**1**	**2**	**.259**	**.325**	**.412**	**.967**
Career total		1682	6469	892	1737	341	56	240	1054	495	89	971	7	1	101	133	51	.269	.317	.450	.915
Yankee total		**152**	**575**	**72**	**149**	**32**	**1**	**18**	**96**	**62**	**13**	**92**	**0**	**0**	**12**	**2**	**3**	**.259**	**.325**	**.412**	**.967**

Silvera, Charles Anthony Ryan (Swede)

HEIGHT: 5'10" THROWS: RIGHT BATS: RIGHT BORN: 10/13/1924, SAN FRANCISCO, CALIFORNIA POSITIONS PLAYED: C

YEAR	TEAM	GAMES	AB	RUNS	HITS	2B	3B	HR	RBI	BB	IBB	SO	HBP	SH	SF	SB	CS	BA	OBA	SA	FA
1948	**NY-A**	**4**	**14**	**1**	**8**	**0**	**1**	**0**	**1**	**0**	**—**	**1**	**0**	**0**	**—**	**0**	**0**	**.571**	**.571**	**.714**	**1.000**
1949	**NY-A**	**58**	**130**	**8**	**41**	**2**	**0**	**0**	**13**	**18**	**—**	**5**	**1**	**0**	**—**	**2**	**1**	**.315**	**.403**	**.423**	**.985**
1950	**NY-A**	**18**	**25**	**2**	**4**	**0**	**0**	**0**	**1**	**1**	**—**	**2**	**0**	**0**	**—**	**0**	**0**	**.160**	**.192**	**.160**	**.959**
1951	**NY-A**	**18**	**51**	**5**	**14**	**3**	**0**	**1**	**7**	**5**	**—**	**3**	**0**	**0**	**—**	**0**	**0**	**.275**	**.339**	**.392**	**1.000**
1952	**NY-A**	**20**	**55**	**4**	**18**	**3**	**0**	**0**	**11**	**5**	**—**	**2**	**0**	**0**	**—**	**0**	**3**	**.327**	**.383**	**.382**	**1.000**
1953	**NY-A**	**42**	**82**	**11**	**23**	**3**	**1**	**0**	**12**	**9**	**—**	**5**	**0**	**3**	**—**	**0**	**1**	**.280**	**.352**	**.341**	**.992**
1954	**NY-A**	**20**	**37**	**1**	**10**	**1**	**0**	**0**	**4**	**3**	**—**	**2**	**1**	**1**	**0**	**0**	**1**	**.270**	**.341**	**.297**	**.963**
1955	**NY-A**	**14**	**26**	**1**	**5**	**0**	**0**	**0**	**1**	**6**	**0**	**4**	**0**	**0**	**0**	**0**	**0**	**.192**	**.344**	**.192**	**1.000**
1956	**NY-A**	**7**	**9**	**0**	**2**	**0**	**0**	**0**	**0**	**2**	**0**	**3**	**0**	**0**	**0**	**0**	**0**	**.222**	**.364**	**.222**	**.909**
1957	Chi-N	26	53	1	11	3	0	0	2	4	0	5	0	0	0	0	0	.208	.263	.264	.982
Career average		23	48	3	14	2	0	0	5	5	—	3	0	0	—	0	1	.282	.356	.328	.979
Yankee average		**22**	**48**	**4**	**14**	**1**	**0**	**0**	**6**	**5**	**—**	**3**	**0**	**0**	**—**	**0**	**1**	**.291**	**.367**	**.336**	**.979**
Career total		227	482	34	136	15	2	1	52	53	0	32	2	4	0	2	6	.282	.356	.328	.979
Yankee total		**201**	**429**	**33**	**125**	**12**	**2**	**1**	**50**	**49**	**0**	**27**	**2**	**4**	**0**	**2**	**6**	**.291**	**.367**	**.336**	**.979**

Silvestri, David Joseph

HEIGHT: 6'0" THROWS: RIGHT BATS: RIGHT BORN: 9/29/1967, ST.LOUIS, MISSOURI POSITIONS PLAYED: 1B, 3B, SS

YEAR	TEAM	GAMES	AB	RUNS	HITS	2B	3B	HR	RBI	BB	IBB	SO	HBP	SH	SF	SB	CS	BA	OBA	SA	FA
1992	**NY-A**	**7**	**13**	**3**	**4**	**0**	**2**	**0**	**1**	**0**	**0**	**3**	**0**	**0**	**0**	**0**	**0**	**.308**	**.308**	**.615**	**.889**
1993	**NY-A**	**7**	**21**	**4**	**6**	**1**	**0**	**1**	**4**	**5**	**0**	**3**	**0**	**0**	**0**	**0**	**0**	**.286**	**.423**	**.476**	**.873**
1994	**NY-A**	**12**	**18**	**3**	**2**	**0**	**1**	**1**	**2**	**4**	**0**	**9**	**0**	**0**	**1**	**0**	**1**	**.111**	**.261**	**.389**	**.857**
1995	**NY-A**	**17**	**21**	**4**	**2**	**0**	**0**	**1**	**4**	**4**	**0**	**9**	**1**	**0**	**1**	**0**	**0**	**.095**	**.259**	**.238**	**1.000**
1995	Mon-N	39	72	12	19	6	0	2	7	9	0	27	0	1	1	2	0	.264	.341	.431	1.000
1996	Mon-N	86	162	16	33	4	0	1	17	34	6	41	0	3	1	2	1	.204	.340	.247	1.000
1997	Tex-A	2	4	0	0	0	0	0	0	0	0	1	0	0	0	0	0	.000	.000	.000	.000
1998	TB-A	8	14	0	1	0	0	0	0	0	0	2	0	0	0	0	0	.071	.071	.071	1.000
1999	Ana-A	3	11	0	1	1	0	0	1	0	0	1	0	0	0	0	0	.091	.091	.182	1.000
Career average		20	37	5	8	1	0	1	4	6	1	11	0	0	0	0	0	.202	.315	.310	.847
Yankee average		**11**	**18**	**4**	**4**	**0**	**1**	**1**	**3**	**3**	**0**	**6**	**0**	**0**	**1**	**0**	**0**	**.192**	**.315**	**.411**	**.905**
Career total		181	336	42	68	12	3	6	36	56	6	96	1	4	4	4	2	.202	.315	.310	.847
Yankee total		**43**	**73**	**14**	**14**	**1**	**3**	**3**	**11**	**13**	**0**	**24**	**1**	**0**	**2**	**0**	**1**	**.192**	**.315**	**.411**	**.905**

Simmons, George Washington (Hack)

HEIGHT: 5'8" THROWS: RIGHT BATS: RIGHT BORN: 1/29/1885,BROOKLYN, NEW YORK DIED: 4/26/1942, ARVERNE, NY POSITIONS PLAYED: 1B, 2B, 3B, SS, OF

YEAR	TEAM	GAMES	AB	RUNS	HITS	2B	3B	HR	RBI	BB	IBB	SO	HBP	SH	SF	SB	CS	BA	OBA	SA	FA
1910	Det-A	42	110	12	25	3	1	0	9	10	—	—	2	4	—	1	—	.227	.303	.273	.923
1912	**NY-A**	**110**	**401**	**45**	**96**	**17**	**2**	**0**	**41**	**33**	**—**	**—**	**7**	**7**	**—**	**19**	**—**	**.239**	**.308**	**.292**	**.985**
1914	Bal-F	114	352	50	95	16	5	1	38	32	—	26	6	9	—	7	—	.270	.341	.352	1.000
1915	Bal-F	39	88	8	18	7	1	1	14	10	—	9	1	4	—	1	—	.205	.293	.341	.880
Career average		76	238	29	59	11	2	1	26	21	—	—	4	6	—	7	—	.246	.318	.317	.947
Yankee average		**110**	**401**	**45**	**96**	**17**	**2**	**0**	**41**	**33**	**—**	**—**	**7**	**7**	**—**	**19**	**—**	**.239**	**.308**	**.292**	**.985**
Career total		305	951	115	234	43	9	2	102	85	—	35	16	24	—	28	—	.246	.318	.317	.947
Yankee total		**110**	**401**	**45**	**96**	**17**	**2**	**0**	**41**	**33**	**—**	**—**	**7**	**7**	**—**	**19**	**—**	**.239**	**.308**	**.292**	**.985**

Simpson, Harry Leon (Suitcase)

HEIGHT: 6'1" THROWS: RIGHT BATS: LEFT BORN: 12/3/1925 ATLANTA, GEORGIA DIED: 4/3/1979 AKRON POSITIONS PLAYED: 1B, OF

YEAR	TEAM	GAMES	AB	RUNS	HITS	2B	3B	HR	RBI	BB	IBB	SO	HBP	SH	SF	SB	CS	BA	OBA	SA	FA
1951	Cle-A	122	332	51	76	7	0	7	24	45	—	48	2	2	—	6	4	.229	.325	.313	.988
1952	Cle-A	146	545	66	145	21	10	10	65	56	—	82	2	4	—	5	3	.266	.337	.396	.988
1953	Cle-A	82	242	25	55	3	1	7	22	18	—	27	1	3	—	0	0	.227	.284	.335	.968
1955	Cle-A	3	1	1	0	0	0	0	0	2	0	0	0	0	0	0	0	.000	.667	.000	.000
1955	KC-A	112	396	42	119	16	7	5	52	34	4	61	2	1	3	3	5	.301	.356	.414	.978
1956	KC-A	141	543	76	159	22	11	21	105	47	8	82	1	1	5	2	3	.293	.347	.490	.965
1957	KC-A	50	179	24	53	9	6	6	24	12	2	28	0	1	1	0	1	.296	.339	.514	.996
1957	NY-A	75	224	27	56	7	3	7	39	19	0	36	0	3	1	1	0	.250	.307	.402	.952
1958	**NY-A**	**24**	**51**	**1**	**11**	**2**	**1**	**0**	**6**	**6**	**0**	**12**	**1**	**0**	**0**	**0**	**0**	**.216**	**.310**	**.294**	**1.000**
1958	KC-A	78	212	21	56	7	1	7	27	26	3	33	0	1	0	0	2	.264	.345	.406	.990
1959	KC-A	8	14	1	4	0	0	1	2	2	0	4	1	0	1	0	0	.286	.389	.500	1.000
1959	Chi-A	38	75	5	14	5	1	2	13	4	0	14	0	0	0	0	0	.187	.228	.360	.947
1959	Pit-N	9	15	3	4	2	0	0	2	0	0	2	0	0	0	0	0	.267	.267	.400	1.000
Career average		68	218	26	58	8	3	6	29	21	1	33	1	1	1	1	1	.266	.331	.408	.906
Yankee average		**50**	**138**	**14**	**34**	**5**	**2**	**4**	**23**	**13**	**0**	**24**	**1**	**2**	**1**	**1**	**0**	**.244**	**.308**	**.382**	**.976**
Career total		888	2829	343	752	101	41	73	381	271	17	429	10	16	11	17	18	.266	.331	.408	.906
Yankee total		**99**	**275**	**28**	**67**	**9**	**4**	**7**	**45**	**25**	**0**	**48**	**1**	**3**	**1**	**1**	**0**	**.244**	**.308**	**.382**	**.976**

Simpson, Richard Charles

HEIGHT: 6'4" THROWS: RIGHT BATS: RIGHT BORN: 7/28/1943 WASHINGTON, D.C. POSITIONS PLAYED: OF

YEAR	TEAM	GAMES	AB	RUNS	HITS	2B	3B	HR	RBI	BB	IBB	SO	HBP	SH	SF	SB	CS	BA	OBA	SA	FA
1962	LA-A	6	8	1	2	1	0	0	1	2	0	3	0	0	0	0	0	.250	.400	.375	1.000
1964	LA-A	21	50	11	7	1	0	2	4	8	0	15	0	0	0	2	2	.140	.259	.280	1.000
1965	Cal-A	8	27	2	6	1	0	0	3	2	0	8	0	0	1	1	0	.222	.267	.259	.875
1966	Cin-N	92	84	26	20	2	0	4	14	10	0	32	2	3	0	0	1	.238	.333	.405	.921
1967	Cin-N	44	54	8	14	3	0	1	6	7	1	11	0	0	1	0	1	.259	.339	.370	.973
1968	StL-N	26	56	11	13	0	0	3	8	8	2	21	0	0	1	0	1	.232	.323	.393	1.000
1968	Hou-N	59	177	25	33	7	2	3	11	20	2	61	4	0	1	4	4	.186	.282	.299	.970
1969	**NY-A**	**6**	**11**	**2**	**3**	**2**	**0**	**0**	**4**	**3**	**0**	**6**	**0**	**0**	**0**	**0**	**0**	**.273**	**.429**	**.455**	**1.000**
1969	Sea-A	26	51	8	9	2	0	2	5	4	0	17	0	0	0	3	1	.176	.236	.333	1.000
Career average		32	58	10	12	2	0	2	6	7	1	19	1	0	0	1	1	.207	.299	.338	.971
Yankee average		**6**	**11**	**2**	**3**	**2**	**0**	**0**	**4**	**3**	**0**	**6**	**0**	**0**	**0**	**0**	**0**	**.273**	**.429**	**.455**	**1.000**
Career total		288	518	94	107	19	2	15	56	64	5	174	6	3	4	10	10	.207	.299	.338	.971
Yankee total		**6**	**11**	**2**	**3**	**2**	**0**	**0**	**4**	**3**	**0**	**6**	**0**	**0**	**0**	**0**	**0**	**.273**	**.429**	**.455**	**1.000**

Sims, Duane B. (Duke)

HEIGHT: 6'2" THROWS: RIGHT BATS: LEFT BORN: 6/5/1941 SALT LAKE CITY, UTAH POSITIONS PLAYED: C, 1B, OF

YEAR	TEAM	GAMES	AB	RUNS	HITS	2B	3B	HR	RBI	BB	IBB	SO	HBP	SH	SF	SB	CS	BA	OBA	SA	FA
1964	Cle-A	2	6	0	0	0	0	0	0	0	0	2	0	0	0	0	0	.000	.000	.000	1.000
1965	Cle-A	48	118	9	21	0	0	6	15	15	2	33	0	0	0	0	0	.178	.271	.331	.980
1966	Cle-A	52	133	12	35	2	2	6	19	11	1	31	4	0	0	0	1	.263	.338	.444	.975
1967	Cle-A	88	272	25	55	8	2	12	37	30	2	64	6	0	2	3	3	.202	.294	.379	.989
1968	Cle-A	122	361	48	90	21	0	11	44	62	11	68	5	0	1	1	3	.249	.366	.399	.983
1969	Cle-A	114	326	40	77	8	0	18	45	66	5	80	6	1	0	1	2	.236	.374	.426	1.000

(continued)

(continued)

YEAR	TEAM	GAMES	AB	RUNS	HITS	2B	3B	HR	RBI	BB	IBB	SO	HBP	SH	SF	SB	CS	BA	OBA	SA	FA
1970	Cle-A	110	345	46	91	12	0	23	56	46	1	59	6	1	0	0	4	.264	.360	.499	.944
1971	LA-N	90	230	23	63	7	2	6	25	30	7	39	1	0	2	0	1	.274	.357	.400	.992
1972	LA-N	51	151	7	29	7	0	2	11	17	3	23	1	0	0	0	0	.192	.278	.278	.989
1972	Det-A	38	98	11	31	4	0	4	19	19	0	18	1	3	0	0	0	.316	.432	.480	.750
1973	Det-A	80	252	31	61	10	0	8	30	30	1	36	2	1	3	1	2	.242	.324	.377	.979
1973	**NY-A**	**4**	**9**	**3**	**3**	**0**	**0**	**1**	**1**	**3**	**0**	**1**	**0**	**0**	**0**	**0**	**0**	**.333**	**.500**	**.667**	**1.000**
1974	**NY-A**	**5**	**15**	**1**	**2**	**1**	**0**	**0**	**2**	**1**	**0**	**5**	**0**	**0**	**0**	**0**	**0**	**.133**	**.188**	**.200**	**1.000**
1974	Tex-A	39	106	7	22	0	0	3	6	8	1	24	3	0	1	0	0	.208	.280	.292	.970
Career average		60	173	19	41	6	0	7	22	24	2	35	3	0	1	0	1	.239	.340	.401	.968
Yankee average		**5**	**12**	**2**	**3**	**1**	**0**	**1**	**2**	**2**	**0**	**3**	**0**	**0**	**0**	**0**	**0**	**.208**	**.321**	**.375**	**1.000**
Career total		843	2422	263	580	80	6	100	310	338	34	483	35	6	9	6	16	.239	.340	.401	.968
Yankee total		**9**	**24**	**4**	**5**	**1**	**0**	**1**	**3**	**4**	**0**	**6**	**0**	**0**	**0**	**0**	**0**	**.208**	**.321**	**.375**	**1.000**

Skinner, Joel Patrick

HEIGHT: 6'4" THROWS: RIGHT BATS: RIGHT BORN: 2/21/1961 LA JOLLA, CALIFORNIA POSITIONS PLAYED: C

YEAR	TEAM	GAMES	AB	RUNS	HITS	2B	3B	HR	RBI	BB	IBB	SO	HBP	SH	SF	SB	CS	BA	OBA	SA	FA
1983	Chi-A	6	11	2	3	0	0	0	1	0	0	1	0	0	0	0	0	.273	.273	.273	.960
1984	Chi-A	43	80	4	17	2	0	0	3	7	0	19	0	0	1	1	0	.213	.273	.238	.989
1985	Chi-A	22	44	9	15	4	1	1	5	5	0	13	0	1	0	0	0	.341	.408	.545	.971
1986	Chi-A	60	149	17	30	5	1	4	20	9	0	43	1	2	1	1	0	.201	.250	.329	.988
1986	NY-A	54	166	6	43	4	0	1	17	7	0	40	0	0	1	0	4	.259	.287	.301	.981
1987	**NY-A**	**64**	**139**	**9**	**19**	**4**	**0**	**3**	**14**	**8**	**0**	**46**	**1**	**4**	**2**	**0**	**0**	**.137**	**.187**	**.230**	**.984**
1988	**NY-A**	**88**	**251**	**23**	**57**	**15**	**0**	**4**	**23**	**14**	**0**	**72**	**0**	**6**	**1**	**0**	**0**	**.227**	**.267**	**.335**	**.990**
1989	Cle-A	79	178	10	41	10	0	1	13	9	0	42	1	1	0	1	1	.230	.271	.303	.990
1990	Cle-A	49	139	16	35	4	1	2	16	7	0	44	0	1	4	2	0	.252	.288	.338	.996
1991	Cle-A	99	284	23	69	14	0	1	24	14	1	67	1	4	2	0	2	.243	.279	.303	.991
Career average		56	144	12	33	6	0	2	14	8	0	39	0	2	1	0	1	.228	.269	.311	.984
Yankee average		**69**	**185**	**13**	**40**	**8**	**0**	**3**	**18**	**10**	**0**	**53**	**0**	**3**	**1**	**0**	**1**	**.214**	**.253**	**.299**	**.985**
Career total		564	1441	119	329	62	3	17	136	80	1	387	4	18	8	3	7	.228	.269	.311	.984
Yankee total		**206**	**556**	**38**	**119**	**23**	**0**	**8**	**54**	**29**	**0**	**158**	**1**	**10**	**4**	**0**	**4**	**.214**	**.253**	**.299**	**.985**

Skizas, Louis Peter (The Nervous Greek)

HEIGHT: 5'11" THROWS: RIGHT BATS: RIGHT BORN: 6/2/1932 CHICAGO, ILLINOIS POSITIONS PLAYED: 3B, OF

YEAR	TEAM	GAMES	AB	RUNS	HITS	2B	3B	HR	RBI	BB	IBB	SO	HBP	SH	SF	SB	CS	BA	OBA	SA	FA
1956	NY-A	6	6	0	1	0	0	0	1	0	0	2	0	0	0	0	0	.167	.167	.167	.000
1956	KC-A	83	297	39	94	11	3	11	39	15	1	17	0	2	3	3	1	.316	.346	.485	.975
1957	KC-A	119	376	34	92	14	1	18	44	27	1	15	2	3	3	5	2	.245	.297	.431	.945
1958	Det-A	23	33	4	8	2	0	1	2	5	1	1	0	0	0	0	0	.242	.342	.394	.800
1959	Chi-A	8	13	3	1	0	0	0	0	3	0	2	0	0	0	0	0	.077	.250	.077	1.000
Career average		48	145	16	39	5	1	6	17	10	1	7	0	1	1	2	1	.270	.317	.443	.744
Yankee average		**6**	**6**	**0**	**1**	**0**	**0**	**0**	**1**	**0**	**0**	**2**	**0**	**0**	**0**	**0**	**0**	**.167**	**.167**	**.167**	**.000**
Career total		239	725	80	196	27	4	30	86	50	3	37	2	5	6	8	3	.270	.317	.443	.744
Yankee total		**6**	**6**	**0**	**1**	**0**	**0**	**0**	**1**	**0**	**0**	**2**	**0**	**0**	**0**	**0**	**0**	**.167**	**.167**	**.167**	**.000**

Skowron, William Joseph (Moose)

HEIGHT: 5'11" THROWS: RIGHT BATS: RIGHT BORN: 12/18/1930 CHICAGO, ILLINOIS POSITIONS PLAYED: 1B, 2B, 3B

YEAR	TEAM	GAMES	AB	RUNS	HITS	2B	3B	HR	RBI	BB	IBB	SO	HBP	SH	SF	SB	CS	BA	OBA	SA	FA
1954	**NY-A**	**87**	**215**	**37**	**73**	**12**	**9**	**7**	**41**	**19**	**—**	**18**	**1**	**0**	**2**	**2**	**1**	**.340**	**.392**	**.577**	**1.000**
1955	**NY-A**	**108**	**288**	**46**	**92**	**17**	**3**	**12**	**61**	**21**	**4**	**32**	**3**	**0**	**2**	**1**	**1**	**.319**	**.369**	**.524**	**.989**
1956	**NY-A**	**134**	**464**	**78**	**143**	**21**	**6**	**23**	**90**	**50**	**3**	**60**	**6**	**2**	**1**	**4**	**4**	**.308**	**.382**	**.528**	**.993**
1957	**NY-A**	**122**	**457**	**54**	**139**	**15**	**5**	**17**	**88**	**31**	**6**	**60**	**3**	**3**	**7**	**3**	**2**	**.304**	**.347**	**.470**	**.992**
1958	**NY-A**	**126**	**465**	**61**	**127**	**22**	**3**	**14**	**73**	**28**	**1**	**69**	**4**	**1**	**5**	**1**	**1**	**.273**	**.317**	**.424**	**.286**
1959	**NY-A**	**74**	**282**	**39**	**84**	**13**	**5**	**15**	**59**	**20**	**0**	**47**	**3**	**2**	**2**	**1**	**0**	**.298**	**.349**	**.539**	**.991**
1960	**NY-A**	**146**	**538**	**63**	**166**	**34**	**3**	**26**	**91**	**38**	**2**	**95**	**2**	**0**	**6**	**2**	**3**	**.309**	**.353**	**.528**	**.991**
1961	**NY-A**	**150**	**561**	**76**	**150**	**23**	**4**	**28**	**89**	**35**	**9**	**108**	**8**	**0**	**3**	**0**	**0**	**.267**	**.318**	**.472**	**.993**
1962	**NY-A**	**140**	**478**	**63**	**129**	**16**	**6**	**23**	**80**	**36**	**1**	**99**	**5**	**1**	**4**	**0**	**1**	**.270**	**.325**	**.473**	**.991**
1963	LA-N	89	237	19	48	8	0	4	19	13	4	49	3	2	1	0	1	.203	.252	.287	.991
1964	Was-A	73	262	28	71	10	0	13	41	11	2	56	3	0	2	0	0	.271	.306	.458	.994
1964	Chi-A	73	273	19	80	11	3	4	38	19	4	36	1	0	4	0	0	.293	.337	.399	.998

(continued)

William Joseph "Moose" Skowron, 1b-2b-3b, 1954–62

As huge and intimidating-looking as Moose Skowron was, at heart, he was a man with a gentle soul and a relaxed personality.

Skowron was born on December 18, 1930, in Chicago, Illinois. A relative gave him the nickname, Mussolini as a joke, and it stuck, sort of.

Skowron was signed by New York in 1951 for $25,000 off the campus of Purdue University.

Purdue officials were hot about it, because Skowron, at 6 feet, 195 lbs., was the team's starting halfback. But manager Casey Stengel promised Skowron that he would be with the big club in three years. Sure enough, in 1954, Moose was brought up.

Skowron hit .340 in a part-time role, playing first, second and third base and pinch-hitting. By the 1956 season, he had won the first base-

man's job. That year, he hit .308 with 23 home runs and 90 RBI.

Moose was hard working but easy going. He was often hard on himself during stretches of poor play, but that wasn't too often: He hit over .300 five of the nine years he played in New York. As a Yankee he was five times an All-Star, played in seven World Series, and was one of their most consistent RBI men.

His biggest problems were injuries, particularly in the latter part of his career. Skowron was beset by leg, knee and back miseries. But he persevered.

In 1963, after nine years with the Yankees, Skowron was traded to Los Angeles, where he helped the Dodgers sweep New York in the World Series that year. But he was on the downside of his career and would play only four more years after that.

Skowron is 16th on the Yankees' all-time home run list with 165.

(continued)

YEAR	TEAM	GAMES	AB	RUNS	HITS	2B	3B	HR	RBI	BB	IBB	SO	HBP	SH	SF	SB	CS	BA	OBA	SA	FA
1965	Chi-A	146	559	63	153	24	3	18	78	32	4	77	5	4	5	1	3	.274	.316	.424	.994
1966	Chi-A	120	337	27	84	15	2	6	29	26	4	45	3	2	1	1	1	.249	.308	.359	.991
1967	Chi-A	8	8	0	0	0	0	0	1	0	0	1	0	0	0	0	0	.000	.000	.000	.000
1967	Cal-A	62	123	8	27	2	1	1	10	4	1	18	4	0	0	0	0	.220	.267	.276	.988
Career average		104	347	43	98	15	3	13	56	24	—	54	3	1	3	1	1	.282	.332	.459	.886
Yankee average		**121**	**416**	**57**	**123**	**19**	**5**	**18**	**75**	**31**	**—**	**65**	**4**	**1**	**4**	**2**	**1**	**.294**	**.346**	**.496**	**.914**
Career total		1658	5547	681	1566	243	53	211	888	383	48	870	54	17	45	16	18	.282	.332	.459	.886
Yankee total		**1087**	**3748**	**517**	**1103**	**173**	**44**	**165**	**672**	**278**	**29**	**588**	**35**	**9**	**32**	**14**	**13**	**.294**	**.346**	**.496**	**.914**

Slaught, Donald Martin (Sluggo)

HEIGHT: 6'1"   THROWS: RIGHT   BATS: RIGHT   BORN: 9/11/1958, LONG BEACH, CALIFORNIA   POSITIONS PLAYED: C

YEAR	TEAM	GAMES	AB	RUNS	HITS	2B	3B	HR	RBI	BB	IBB	SO	HBP	SH	SF	SB	CS	BA	OBA	SA	FA
1982	KC-A	43	115	14	32	6	0	3	8	9	0	12	0	2	0	0	0	.278	.331	.409	.994
1983	KC-A	83	276	21	86	13	4	0	28	11	0	27	0	1	2	3	1	.312	.336	.388	.964
1984	KC-A	124	409	48	108	27	4	4	42	20	4	55	2	8	7	0	0	.264	.297	.379	.982
1985	Tex-A	102	343	34	96	17	4	8	35	20	1	41	6	1	0	5	4	.280	.331	.423	.990
1986	Tex-A	95	314	39	83	17	1	13	46	16	0	59	5	3	3	3	2	.264	.308	.449	.993
1987	Tex-A	95	237	25	53	15	2	8	16	24	3	51	1	4	0	0	3	.224	.298	.405	.985
1988	**NY-A**	**97**	**322**	**33**	**91**	**25**	**1**	**9**	**43**	**24**	**3**	**54**	**3**	**5**	**4**	**1**	**0**	**.283**	**.334**	**.450**	**.979**
1989	**NY-A**	**117**	**350**	**34**	**88**	**21**	**3**	**5**	**38**	**30**	**3**	**57**	**5**	**2**	**5**	**1**	**1**	**.251**	**.315**	**.371**	**.991**
1990	Pit-N	84	230	27	69	18	3	4	29	27	2	27	3	3	4	0	1	.300	.375	.457	.979
1991	Pit-N	77	220	19	65	17	1	1	29	21	1	32	3	5	1	1	0	.295	.363	.395	.987
1992	Pit-N	87	255	26	88	17	3	4	37	17	5	23	2	6	5	2	2	.345	.384	.482	.988
1993	Pit-N	116	377	34	113	19	2	10	55	29	2	56	6	4	4	2	1	.300	.356	.440	.993
1994	Pit-N	76	240	21	69	7	0	2	21	34	2	31	3	1	1	0	0	.288	.381	.342	.994

(continued)

(continued)

YEAR	TEAM	GAMES	AB	RUNS	HITS	2B	3B	HR	RBI	BB	IBB	SO	HBP	SH	SF	SB	CS	BA	OBA	SA	FA
1995	Pit-N	35	112	13	34	6	0	0	13	9	2	8	1	1	0	0	0	.304	.361	.357	.996
1996	Cal-A	62	207	23	67	9	0	6	32	13	0	20	2	0	2	0	0	.324	.366	.454	.992
1996	Chi-A	14	36	2	9	1	0	0	4	2	0	2	0	1	0	0	0	.250	.289	.278	.986
1997	SD-N	20	20	2	0	0	0	0	0	5	0	4	0	1	0	0	0	.000	.200	.000	1.000
Career average		78	239	24	68	14	2	5	28	18	2	33	3	3	2	1	1	.283	.338	.412	.988
Yankee average		**107**	**336**	**34**	**90**	**23**	**2**	**7**	**41**	**27**	**3**	**56**	**4**	**4**	**5**	**1**	**1**	**.266**	**.324**	**.409**	**.985**
Career total		1327	4063	415	1151	235	28	77	476	311	28	559	42	48	38	18	15	.283	.338	.412	.988
Yankee total		**214**	**672**	**67**	**179**	**46**	**4**	**14**	**81**	**54**	**6**	**111**	**8**	**7**	**9**	**2**	**1**	**.266**	**.324**	**.409**	**.985**

Slaughter, Enos Bradsher (Country)

HEIGHT: 5'9"   THROWS: RIGHT   BATS: LEFT   BORN: 4/27/1916 ROXBORO, NORTH CAROLINA   POSITIONS PLAYED: OF

YEAR	TEAM	GAMES	AB	RUNS	HITS	2B	3B	HR	RBI	BB	IBB	SO	HBP	SH	SF	SB	CS	BA	OBA	SA	FA
1938	StL-N	112	395	59	109	20	10	8	58	32	—	38	0	4	—	1	—	.276	.330	.438	.970
1939	StL-N	149	604	95	193	52	5	12	86	44	—	53	5	11	—	2	—	.320	.371	.482	.968
1940	StL-N	140	516	96	158	25	13	17	73	50	—	35	2	1	—	8	—	.306	.370	.504	.989
1941	StL-N	113	425	71	132	22	9	13	76	53	—	28	2	4	—	4	—	.311	.390	.496	.947
1942	StL-N	152	591	100	188	31	17	13	98	88	—	30	6	2	—	9	—	.318	.412	.494	.987
1946	StL-N	156	609	100	183	30	8	18	130	69	—	41	2	5	—	9	—	.300	.374	.465	.981
1947	StL-N	147	551	100	162	31	13	10	86	59	—	27	4	5	—	4	—	.294	.366	.452	.982
1948	StL-N	146	549	91	176	27	11	11	90	81	—	29	1	6	—	4	—	.321	.409	.470	.971
1949	StL-N	151	568	92	191	34	13	13	96	79	—	37	1	6	—	3	—	.336	.418	.511	.983
1950	StL-N	148	556	82	161	26	7	10	101	66	—	33	2	8	—	3	—	.290	.367	.415	.978
1951	StL-N	123	409	48	115	17	8	4	64	67	—	25	3	4	—	7	2	.281	.386	.391	.995
1952	StL-N	140	510	73	153	17	12	11	101	70	—	25	1	6	—	6	1	.300	.386	.445	.989
1953	StL-N	143	492	64	143	34	9	6	89	80	—	28	5	1	—	4	4	.291	.395	.433	.996
1954	**NY-A**	**69**	**125**	**19**	**31**	**4**	**2**	**1**	**19**	**28**	**—**	**8**	**0**	**1**	**0**	**0**	**2**	**.248**	**.386**	**.336**	**.974**
1955	NY-A	10	9	1	1	0	0	0	1	1	—	1	0	0	0	0	0	.111	.200	.111	.000
1955	KC-A	108	267	49	86	12	4	5	34	40	4	17	2	1	5	2	3	.322	.408	.453	.985
1956	KC-A	91	223	37	62	14	3	2	23	29	1	20	1	1	1	1	0	.278	.362	.395	.981
1956	NY-A	24	83	15	24	4	2	0	4	5	0	6	0	1	0	1	1	.289	.330	.386	1.000
1957	**NY-A**	**96**	**209**	**24**	**53**	**7**	**1**	**5**	**34**	**40**	**5**	**19**	**0**	**4**	**3**	**0**	**2**	**.254**	**.369**	**.368**	**1.000**
1958	**NY-A**	**77**	**138**	**21**	**42**	**4**	**1**	**4**	**19**	**21**	**0**	**16**	**0**	**1**	**0**	**2**	**0**	**.304**	**.396**	**.435**	**.957**
1959	**NY-A**	**74**	**99**	**10**	**17**	**2**	**0**	**6**	**21**	**13**	**1**	**19**	**0**	**1**	**1**	**1**	**0**	**.172**	**.265**	**.374**	**.964**
1959	Mil-N	11	18	0	3	0	0	0	3	0	0	3	0	0	0	0	0	.167	.286	.167	1.000
Career average		108	361	57	108	19	7	8	59	46	—	25	2	3	—	3	—	.300	.382	.453	.936
Yankee average		**58**	**111**	**15**	**28**	**4**	**1**	**3**	**16**	**18**	**—**	**12**	**0**	**1**	**1**	**1**	**1**	**.253**	**.356**	**.376**	**.816**
Career total		2380	7946	1247	2383	413	148	169	1306	1015	11	538	37	73	10	71	15	.300	.381	.453	.936
Yankee total		**350**	**663**	**90**	**168**	**21**	**6**	**16**	**98**	**108**	**6**	**69**	**0**	**8**	**4**	**4**	**5**	**.253**	**.356**	**.376**	**.816**

Smalley, Roy Frederick III

HEIGHT: 6'1"   THROWS: RIGHT   BATS: BOTH   BORN: 10/25/1952 LOS ANGELES, CALIFORNIA   POSITIONS PLAYED: 1B, 2B, 3B, SS

YEAR	TEAM	GAMES	AB	RUNS	HITS	2B	3B	HR	RBI	BB	IBB	SO	HBP	SH	SF	SB	CS	BA	OBA	SA	FA
1975	Tex-A	78	250	22	57	8	0	3	33	30	1	42	0	4	2	4	0	.228	.309	.296	.941
1976	Tex-A	41	129	15	29	2	0	1	8	29	3	27	0	3	2	2	0	.225	.363	.264	.963
1976	Min-A	103	384	46	104	16	3	2	36	47	1	79	2	22	0	0	4	.271	.353	.344	.967
1977	Min-A	150	584	93	135	21	5	6	56	74	1	89	1	15	6	5	5	.231	.316	.315	.958
1978	Min-A	158	586	80	160	31	3	19	77	85	3	70	1	23	7	2	8	.273	.362	.433	.970
1979	Min-A	162	621	94	168	28	3	24	95	80	8	80	4	15	9	2	3	.271	.353	.441	1.000
1980	Min-A	133	486	64	135	24	1	12	63	65	4	63	2	2	9	3	3	.278	.359	.405	1.000
1981	Min-A	56	167	24	44	7	1	7	22	31	5	24	0	0	2	0	0	.263	.375	.443	1.000
1982	Min-A	4	13	2	2	1	0	0	0	3	1	4	0	0	0	0	0	.154	.313	.231	1.000
1982	**NY-A**	**142**	**486**	**55**	**125**	**14**	**2**	**20**	**67**	**68**	**7**	**100**	**0**	**7**	**4**	**0**	**1**	**.257**	**.346**	**.418**	**.953**
1983	**NY-A**	**130**	**451**	**70**	**124**	**24**	**1**	**18**	**62**	**58**	**2**	**68**	**2**	**5**	**4**	**3**	**3**	**.275**	**.357**	**.452**	**.959**
1984	**NY-A**	**67**	**209**	**17**	**50**	**8**	**1**	**7**	**26**	**15**	**2**	**35**	**0**	**0**	**3**	**2**	**1**	**.239**	**.286**	**.388**	**.978**
1984	Chi-A	47	135	15	23	4	0	4	13	22	1	30	0	0	1	1	1	.170	.285	.289	.947
1985	Min-A	129	388	57	100	20	0	12	45	60	3	65	1	1	2	0	2	.258	.357	.402	.987
1986	Min-A	143	459	59	113	20	4	20	57	68	4	80	1	1	2	1	3	.246	.342	.441	1.000
1987	Min-A	110	309	32	85	16	1	8	34	36	1	52	1	0	1	2	0	.275	.352	.411	.850
Career average		103	354	47	91	15	2	10	43	48	3	57	1	6	3	2	2	.257	.345	.395	.967
Yankee average		**113**	**382**	**47**	**100**	**15**	**1**	**15**	**52**	**47**	**4**	**68**	**1**	**4**	**4**	**2**	**2**	**.261**	**.340**	**.426**	**.963**
Career total		1653	5657	745	1454	244	25	163	694	771	47	908	14	98	54	27	34	.257	.345	.395	.967
Yankee total		**339**	**1146**	**142**	**299**	**46**	**4**	**45**	**155**	**141**	**11**	**203**	**2**	**12**	**11**	**5**	**5**	**.261**	**.340**	**.426**	**.963**

Smith, Charles William

HEIGHT: 6'1"   THROWS: RIGHT   BATS: RIGHT   BORN: 9/15/1937 CHARLESTON, SOUTH CAROLINA   DIED: 11/29/1994   POSITIONS PLAYED: 3B, SS

YEAR	TEAM	GAMES	AB	RUNS	HITS	2B	3B	HR	RBI	BB	IBB	SO	HBP	SH	SF	SB	CS	BA	OBA	SA	FA
1960	LA-N	18	60	2	10	1	1	0	5	1	0	15	0	2	3	0	0	.167	.172	.217	.953
1961	LA-N	9	24	4	6	1	0	2	3	1	0	6	0	0	0	0	0	.250	.280	.542	1.000
1961	Phi-A	112	411	43	102	13	4	9	47	23	3	76	5	10	3	3	4	.248	.294	.365	.924
1962	Chi-A	65	145	11	30	4	0	2	17	9	0	32	1	3	1	0	1	.207	.256	.276	.944
1963	Chi-A	4	7	0	2	0	1	0	1	0	0	2	0	0	0	0	0	.286	.286	.571	1.000
1964	Chi-A	2	7	1	1	0	1	0	0	1	0	1	0	0	0	0	0	.143	.250	.429	1.000
1964	NY-N	127	443	44	106	12	0	20	58	19	1	101	3	5	1	2	2	.239	.275	.402	.938
1965	NY-N	135	499	49	122	20	3	16	62	17	3	123	4	7	4	2	1	.244	.273	.393	1.000
1966	StL-N	116	391	34	104	13	4	10	43	22	4	81	0	5	5	0	2	.266	.301	.396	1.000
1967	**NY-A**	**135**	**425**	**38**	**95**	**15**	**3**	**9**	**38**	**32**	**6**	**110**	**1**	**4**	**3**	**0**	**2**	**.224**	**.278**	**.336**	**.947**
1968	**NY-A**	**46**	**70**	**2**	**16**	**4**	**1**	**1**	**7**	**5**	**2**	**18**	**0**	**2**	**0**	**0**	**0**	**.229**	**.280**	**.357**	**.961**
1969	Chi-N	2	2	0	0	0	0	0	0	0	0	0	0	0	0	0	0	.000	.000	.000	.000
Career average		64	207	19	50	7	2	6	23	11	2	47	1	3	2	1	1	.239	.279	.370	.889
Yankee average		**91**	**248**	**20**	**56**	**10**	**2**	**5**	**23**	**19**	**4**	**64**	**1**	**3**	**2**	**0**	**1**	**.224**	**.278**	**.339**	**.954**
Career total		771	2484	228	594	83	18	69	281	130	19	565	14	38	20	7	12	.239	.279	.370	.889
Yankee total		**181**	**495**	**40**	**111**	**19**	**4**	**10**	**45**	**37**	**8**	**128**	**1**	**6**	**3**	**0**	**2**	**.224**	**.278**	**.339**	**.954**

Smith, Elmer John

HEIGHT: 5'10"   THROWS: RIGHT   BATS: LEFT   BORN: 9/21/1892 SANDUSKY, OHIO   DIED: 8/3/1984 COLUMBIA, KENTUCKY   POSITIONS PLAYED: OF

YEAR	TEAM	GAMES	AB	RUNS	HITS	2B	3B	HR	RBI	BB	IBB	SO	HBP	SH	SF	SB	CS	BA	OBA	SA	FA
1914	Cle-A	13	53	5	17	3	0	0	8	2	—	11	0	1	—	1	1	.321	.345	.377	1.000
1915	Cle-A	144	476	37	118	23	12	3	67	36	—	75	0	16	—	10	11	.248	.301	.366	.923
1916	Cle-A	79	213	25	59	15	3	3	40	18	—	35	1	6	—	3	—	.277	.336	.418	.966
1916	Was-A	45	168	12	36	10	3	2	27	18	—	28	2	7	—	4	—	.214	.298	.345	.988
1917	Was-A	35	117	8	26	4	3	0	17	5	—	14	1	5	—	1	—	.222	.260	.308	.901
1917	Cle-A	64	161	21	42	5	1	3	22	13	—	18	0	7	—	6	—	.261	.316	.360	.986
1919	Cle-A	114	395	60	110	24	6	9	54	41	—	30	5	10	—	15	—	.278	.354	.438	.957
1920	Cle-A	129	456	82	144	37	10	12	103	53	—	35	3	13	—	5	4	.316	.391	.520	.970
1921	Cle-A	129	431	98	125	28	9	16	85	56	—	46	2	16	—	0	2	.290	.374	.508	.971
1922	Bos-A	73	231	43	66	13	6	6	32	25	—	21	1	6	—	0	3	.286	.358	.472	.947
1922	**NY-A**	**21**	**27**	**1**	**5**	**0**	**0**	**1**	**5**	**3**	**—**	**5**	**0**	**1**	**—**	**0**	**0**	**.185**	**.267**	**.296**	**.933**
1923	**NY-A**	**70**	**183**	**30**	**56**	**6**	**2**	**7**	**35**	**21**	**—**	**21**	**0**	**4**	**—**	**3**	**1**	**.306**	**.377**	**.475**	**.948**
1925	Cin-N	96	284	47	77	13	7	8	46	28	—	20	1	7	—	6	5	.271	.339	.451	.967
Career average		78	246	36	68	14	5	5	42	25	—	28	1	8	—	4	—	.276	.344	.437	.958
Yankee average		**46**	**105**	**16**	**31**	**3**	**1**	**4**	**20**	**12**	**—**	**13**	**0**	**3**	**—**	**2**	**1**	**.290**	**.363**	**.452**	**.941**
Career total		1012	3195	469	881	181	62	70	541	319	—	359	16	99	—	54	27	.276	.344	.437	.958
Yankee total		**91**	**210**	**31**	**61**	**6**	**2**	**8**	**40**	**24**	**—**	**26**	**0**	**5**	**—**	**3**	**1**	**.290**	**.363**	**.452**	**.941**

Snow, Jack Thomas (J.T.)

HEIGHT: 6'2"   THROWS: LEFT   BATS: LEFT   BORN: 2/26/1968 LONG BEACH, CALIFORNIA   POSITIONS PLAYED: 1B

YEAR	TEAM	GAMES	AB	RUNS	HITS	2B	3B	HR	RBI	BB	IBB	SO	HBP	SH	SF	SB	CS	BA	OBA	SA	FA
1992	**NY-A**	**7**	**14**	**1**	**2**	**1**	**0**	**0**	**2**	**5**	**1**	**5**	**0**	**0**	**0**	**0**	**0**	**.143**	**.368**	**.214**	**1.000**
1993	Cal-A	129	419	60	101	18	2	16	57	55	4	88	2	7	6	3	0	.241	.328	.408	.995
1994	Cal-A	61	223	22	49	4	0	8	30	19	1	48	3	2	1	0	1	.220	.289	.345	.996
1995	Cal-A	143	544	80	157	22	1	24	102	52	4	91	3	5	2	2	1	.289	.353	.465	.997
1996	Cal-A	155	575	69	148	20	1	17	67	56	6	96	5	2	3	1	6	.257	.327	.384	.993
1997	SF-N	157	531	81	149	36	1	28	104	96	13	124	1	2	7	6	4	.281	.387	.510	.995
1998	SF-N	138	435	65	108	29	1	15	79	58	3	84	0	0	7	1	2	.248	.332	.423	.999
1999	SF-N	161	570	93	156	25	2	24	98	86	7	121	5	1	6	0	4	.274	.370	.451	.996
2000	SF-N	155	536	82	152	33	2	19	96	66	6	129	11	0	14	1	3	.284	.365	.459	.995
Career average		158	550	79	146	27	1	22	91	70	6	112	4	3	7	2	3	.266	.350	.437	.996
Yankee average		**7**	**14**	**1**	**2**	**1**	**0**	**0**	**2**	**5**	**1**	**5**	**0**	**0**	**0**	**0**	**0**	**.143**	**.368**	**.214**	**1.000**
Career total		1106	3847	553	1022	188	10	151	635	493	45	786	30	19	46	14	21	.266	.350	.437	.996
Yankee total		**7**	**14**	**1**	**2**	**1**	**0**	**0**	**2**	**5**	**1**	**5**	**0**	**0**	**0**	**0**	**0**	**.143**	**.368**	**.214**	**1.000**

Soderholm, Eric Thane

HEIGHT: 5'11"   THROWS: RIGHT   BATS: RIGHT   BORN: 9/24/1948 CORTLAND, NEW YORK   POSITIONS PLAYED: 3B

YEAR	TEAM	GAMES	AB	RUNS	HITS	2B	3B	HR	RBI	BB	IBB	SO	HBP	SH	SF	SB	CS	BA	OBA	SA	FA
1971	Min-A	21	64	9	10	4	0	1	4	10	1	17	3	1	0	0	1	.156	.299	.266	.942
1972	Min-A	93	287	28	54	10	0	13	39	19	2	48	3	3	1	3	3	.188	.245	.359	.942
1973	Min-A	35	111	22	33	7	2	1	9	21	0	16	1	2	0	1	2	.297	.414	.423	.921
1974	Min-A	141	464	63	128	18	3	10	51	48	1	68	5	5	2	7	3	.276	.349	.392	.956
1975	Min-A	117	419	62	120	17	2	11	58	53	1	66	0	1	2	3	5	.286	.365	.415	.969
1977	Chi-A	130	460	77	129	20	3	25	67	47	5	47	4	2	3	2	2	.280	.350	.500	.978
1978	Chi-A	143	457	57	118	17	1	20	67	39	2	44	4	3	7	2	2	.258	.318	.431	.964
1979	Chi-A	56	210	31	53	8	2	6	34	19	1	19	0	1	1	0	1	.252	.313	.395	.986
1979	Tex-A	63	147	15	40	6	0	4	19	12	0	9	1	2	3	0	0	.272	.325	.395	.909
1980	**NY-A**	**95**	**275**	**38**	**79**	**13**	**1**	**11**	**35**	**27**	**2**	**25**	**1**	**1**	**0**	**0**	**0**	**.287**	**.353**	**.462**	**.952**
Career average		89	289	40	76	12	1	10	38	30	2	36	2	2	2	2	2	.264	.335	.421	.952
Yankee average		**95**	**275**	**38**	**79**	**13**	**1**	**11**	**35**	**27**	**2**	**25**	**1**	**1**	**0**	**0**	**0**	**.287**	**.353**	**.462**	**.952**
Career total		894	2894	402	764	120	14	102	383	295	15	359	22	21	19	18	21	.264	.335	.421	.952
Yankee total		**95**	**275**	**38**	**79**	**13**	**1**	**11**	**35**	**27**	**2**	**25**	**1**	**1**	**0**	**0**	**0**	**.287**	**.353**	**.462**	**.952**

Sojo, Luis Beltran

HEIGHT: 5'11"   THROWS: RIGHT   BATS: RIGHT   BORN: 1/3/1966 BARQUISIMETO, VENEZUELA   POSITIONS PLAYED: 1B, 2B, 3B, SS

YEAR	TEAM	GAMES	AB	RUNS	HITS	2B	3B	HR	RBI	BB	IBB	SO	HBP	SH	SF	SB	CS	BA	OBA	SA	FA
1990	Tor-A	33	80	14	18	3	0	1	9	5	0	5	0	0	0	1	1	.225	.271	.300	.842
1991	Cal-A	113	364	38	94	14	1	3	20	14	0	26	5	19	0	4	2	.258	.295	.327	.981
1992	Cal-A	106	368	37	100	12	3	7	43	14	0	24	1	7	1	7	11	.272	.299	.378	.917
1993	Tor-A	19	47	5	8	2	0	0	6	4	0	2	0	2	1	0	0	.170	.231	.213	1.000
1994	Sea-A	63	213	32	59	9	2	6	22	8	0	25	2	3	1	2	1	.277	.308	.423	.980
1995	Sea-A	102	339	50	98	18	2	7	39	23	0	19	1	6	1	4	2	.289	.335	.416	.957
1996	Sea-A	77	247	20	52	8	1	1	16	10	0	13	1	6	0	2	2	.211	.244	.263	.981
1996	**NY-A**	**18**	**40**	**3**	**11**	**2**	**0**	**0**	**5**	**1**	**0**	**4**	**0**	**2**	**1**	**0**	**0**	**.275**	**.286**	**.325**	**1.000**
1997	**NY-A**	**77**	**215**	**27**	**66**	**6**	**1**	**2**	**25**	**16**	**0**	**14**	**1**	**5**	**2**	**3**	**1**	**.307**	**.355**	**.372**	**1.000**
1998	**NY-A**	**54**	**147**	**16**	**34**	**3**	**1**	**0**	**14**	**4**	**0**	**15**	**0**	**1**	**1**	**1**	**0**	**.231**	**.250**	**.265**	**.991**
1999	**NY-A**	**49**	**127**	**20**	**32**	**6**	**0**	**2**	**16**	**4**	**0**	**17**	**0**	**2**	**0**	**1**	**0**	**.252**	**.275**	**.346**	**.988**
2000	Pit-N	61	176	14	50	11	0	5	20	11	3	16	1	0	1	1	0	.284	.328	.432	.975
2000	**NY-A**	**34**	**125**	**19**	**36**	**7**	**1**	**2**	**17**	**6**	**0**	**6**	**0**	**3**	**0**	**1**	**0**	**.288**	**.321**	**.408**	**.989**
Career average		62	191	23	51	8	1	3	19	9	0	14	1	4	1	2	2	.264	.300	.358	.969
Yankee average		**46**	**131**	**17**	**36**	**5**	**1**	**1**	**15**	**6**	**0**	**11**	**0**	**3**	**1**	**1**	**0**	**.274**	**.306**	**.347**	**.995**
Career total		806	2488	295	658	101	12	36	252	120	3	186	12	56	9	27	20	.264	.300	.358	.969
Yankee total		**46**	**131**	**17**	**36**	**5**	**1**	**1**	**15**	**6**	**0**	**11**	**0**	**3**	**1**	**1**	**0**	**.274**	**.306**	**.347**	**.995**

Solaita, Tolia (Tony)

HEIGHT: 6'0   THROWS: LEFT   BATS: LEFT   BORN: 1/15/1947 NUUYLI, AMERICAN SOMOA   DIED: 2/10/1990 TAFUNA, AMERICAN SOMOA   POSITIONS PLAYED: 1B

YEAR	TEAM	GAMES	AB	RUNS	HITS	2B	3B	HR	RBI	BB	IBB	SO	HBP	SH	SF	SB	CS	BA	OBA	SA	FA
1968	**NY-A**	**1**	**1**	**0**	**0**	**0**	**0**	**0**	**0**	**0**	**0**	**1**	**0**	**0**	**0**	**0**	**0**	**.000**	**.000**	**.000**	**1.000**
1974	KC-A	96	239	31	64	12	0	7	30	35	5	70	1	0	2	0	3	.268	.361	.406	.991
1975	KC-A	93	231	35	60	11	0	16	44	39	1	79	2	1	2	0	1	.260	.369	.515	.994
1976	KC-A	31	68	4	16	4	0	0	9	6	0	17	0	0	3	0	0	.235	.286	.294	.974
1976	Cal-A	63	215	25	58	9	0	9	33	34	3	44	0	1	2	1	1	.270	.367	.437	.998
1977	Cal-A	116	324	40	78	15	0	14	53	56	6	77	0	2	4	1	3	.241	.349	.417	.990
1978	Cal-A	60	94	10	21	3	0	1	14	16	3	25	0	0	0	0	0	.223	.336	.287	1.000
1979	Mon-N	29	42	5	12	4	0	1	7	11	0	16	0	0	0	0	0	.286	.434	.452	.989
1979	Tor-A	36	102	14	27	8	1	2	13	17	0	16	0	0	2	0	0	.265	.364	.422	1.000
Career average		58	146	18	37	7	0	6	23	24	2	38	0	0	2	0	1	.255	.357	.421	.993
Yankee average		**1**	**1**	**0**	**0**	**0**	**0**	**0**	**0**	**0**	**0**	**1**	**0**	**0**	**0**	**0**	**0**	**.000**	**.000**	**.000**	**1.000**
Career total		525	1316	164	336	66	1	50	203	214	18	345	3	4	15	2	8	.255	.357	.421	.993
Yankee total		**1**	**1**	**0**	**0**	**0**	**0**	**0**	**0**	**0**	**0**	**1**	**0**	**0**	**0**	**0**	**0**	**.000**	**.000**	**.000**	**1.000**

Soriano, Alfonso Guilleard
HEIGHT: 6'1"   THROWS: RIGHT   BATS: LEFT   BORN: 1/7/1978 SAN PEDRO DE MACORIS, DOMINICAN REPUBLIC   POSITIONS PLAYED: SS

YEAR	TEAM	GAMES	AB	RUNS	HITS	2B	3B	HR	RBI	BB	IBB	SO	HBP	SH	SF	SB	CS	BA	OBA	SA	FA
1999	NY-A	9	8	2	1	0	0	1	1	0	0	3	0	0	0	0	1	.125	.125	.500	.500
2000	NY-A	22	50	5	9	3	0	2	3	1	0	15	0	2	0	2	0	.180	.196	.360	.856
Career average		16	29	4	5	2	0	2	2	1	0	9	0	1	0	1	1	.172	.186	.379	.678
Yankee average		16	29	4	5	2	0	2	2	1	0	9	0	1	0	1	1	.172	.186	.379	.678
Career total		31	58	7	10	3	0	3	4	1	0	18	0	2	0	2	1	.172	.186	.379	.678
Yankee total		31	58	7	10	3	0	3	4	1	0	18	0	2	0	2	1	.172	.186	.379	.678

Souchock, Stephen (Bud)
HEIGHT: 6'3"   THROWS: RIGHT   BATS: RIGHT   BORN: 3/3/1919 YATESBORO, PENNSYLVANIA   POSITIONS PLAYED: 1B, OF

YEAR	TEAM	GAMES	AB	RUNS	HITS	2B	3B	HR	RBI	BB	IBB	SO	HBP	SH	SF	SB	CS	BA	OBA	SA	FA
1946	NY-A	47	86	15	26	3	3	2	10	7	—	13	1	0	—	0	3	.302	.362	.477	.964
1948	NY-A	44	118	11	24	3	1	3	11	7	—	13	0	1	—	3	0	.203	.248	.322	.988
1949	Chi-A	84	252	29	59	13	5	7	37	25	—	38	0	0	—	5	2	.234	.303	.409	.996
1951	Det-A	91	188	33	46	10	3	11	28	18	—	27	1	2	—	0	2	.245	.314	.505	.941
1952	Det-A	92	265	40	66	16	4	13	45	21	—	28	0	0	—	1	0	.249	.304	.487	.989
1953	Det-A	89	278	29	84	13	3	11	46	8	—	35	2	2	—	5	1	.302	.326	.489	.962
1954	Det-A	25	39	6	7	0	1	3	8	2	—	10	0	0	0	1	1	.179	.220	.462	1.000
1955	Det-A	1	1	0	1	0	0	0	1	0	0	0	0	0	0	0	0	1.000	1.000	1.000	.000
Career average		59	153	20	39	7	3	6	23	11	—	21	1	1	—	2	1	.255	.307	.457	.855
Yankee average		46	102	13	25	3	2	3	11	7	—	13	1	1	—	2	2	.245	.297	.387	.976
Career total		473	1227	163	313	58	20	50	186	88	0	164	4	5	0	15	9	.255	.307	.457	.855
Yankee total		91	204	26	50	6	4	5	21	14	—	26	1	1	—	3	3	.245	.297	.387	.976

Spencer, Michael Shane
HEIGHT: 5'11"   THROWS: RIGHT   BATS: RIGHT   BORN: 2/20/1972 KEY WEST, FLORIDA   POSITIONS PLAYED: 1B, OF

YEAR	TEAM	GAMES	AB	RUNS	HITS	2B	3B	HR	RBI	BB	IBB	SO	HBP	SH	SF	SB	CS	BA	OBA	SA	FA
1998	NY-A	27	67	18	25	6	0	10	27	5	0	12	0	0	1	0	1	.373	.411	.910	1.000
1999	NY-A	71	205	25	48	8	0	8	20	18	0	51	0	0	1	0	4	.234	.295	.390	1.000
2000	NY-A	73	248	33	70	11	3	9	40	19	0	45	2	0	7	1	2	.282	.330	.460	.989
Career average		57	173	25	48	8	1	9	29	14	0	36	1	0	3	0	2	.275	.326	.490	.996
Yankee average		57	173	25	48	8	1	9	29	14	0	36	1	0	3	0	2	.275	.326	.490	.996
Career total		171	520	76	143	25	3	27	87	42	0	108	2	0	9	1	7	.275	.326	.490	.996
Yankee total		171	520	76	143	25	3	27	87	42	0	108	2	0	9	1	7	.275	.326	.490	.996

Spencer, James Lloyd
HEIGHT: 6'2"   THROWS: LEFT   BATS: LEFT   BORN: 7/30/1946 HANOVER, PENNSYLVANIA   POSITIONS PLAYED: 1B

YEAR	TEAM	GAMES	AB	RUNS	HITS	2B	3B	HR	RBI	BB	IBB	SO	HBP	SH	SF	SB	CS	BA	OBA	SA	FA
1968	Cal-A	19	68	2	13	1	0	0	5	3	0	10	1	0	1	0	0	.191	.233	.206	.994
1969	Cal-A	113	386	39	98	14	3	10	31	26	6	53	2	8	0	1	0	.254	.304	.383	.991
1970	Cal-A	146	511	61	140	20	4	12	68	28	6	61	0	6	5	0	2	.274	.309	.399	.995
1971	Cal-A	148	510	50	121	21	2	18	59	48	7	63	3	6	5	0	1	.237	.304	.392	.994
1972	Cal-A	82	212	13	47	5	0	1	14	12	1	25	0	0	1	0	1	.222	.262	.259	1.000
1973	Cal-A	29	87	10	21	4	2	2	11	9	1	9	1	1	1	0	0	.241	.316	.402	1.000
1973	Tex-A	102	352	35	94	12	3	4	43	34	6	41	1	1	2	0	3	.267	.332	.352	.999
1974	Tex-A	118	352	36	98	11	4	7	44	22	3	27	3	3	4	1	2	.278	.323	.392	.998
1975	Tex-A	132	403	50	107	18	1	11	47	35	6	43	2	2	1	0	1	.266	.327	.397	.995
1976	Chi-A	150	518	53	131	13	2	14	70	49	19	52	1	4	7	6	4	.253	.315	.390	.998
1977	Chi-A	128	470	56	116	16	1	18	69	36	11	50	2	2	5	1	2	.247	.300	.400	.991
1978	NY-A	71	150	12	34	9	1	7	24	15	3	32	0	0	1	0	1	.227	.295	.440	1.000
1979	NY-A	106	295	60	85	15	3	23	53	38	11	25	0	1	2	0	2	.288	.367	.593	.992

(continued)

(continued)

YEAR	TEAM	G	AB	R	H	2B	3B	HR	RBI	BB	IBB	SO	HBP	SH	SF	SB	CS	BA	OBA	SA	FA
1980	**NY-A**	97	259	38	61	9	0	13	43	30	2	44	1	1	4	1	0	.236	.313	.421	.990
1981	**NY-A**	25	63	6	9	2	0	2	4	9	2	7	0	0	0	0	0	.143	.250	.270	1.000
1981	Oak-A	54	171	14	35	6	0	2	9	10	1	20	0	0	2	1	0	.205	.246	.275	.997
1982	Oak-A	33	101	6	17	3	1	2	5	3	1	20	0	0	1	0	0	.168	.190	.277	.992
Career average		91	289	32	72	11	2	9	35	24	5	34	1	2	3	1	1	.250	.307	.387	.996
Yankee average		**75**	**192**	**29**	**47**	**9**	**1**	**11**	**31**	**23**	**5**	**27**	**0**	**1**	**2**	**0**	**1**	**.246**	**.325**	**.478**	**.996**
Career total		1553	4908	541	1227	179	27	146	599	407	86	582	17	35	42	11	19	.250	.307	.387	.996
Yankee total		**299**	**767**	**116**	**189**	**35**	**4**	**45**	**124**	**92**	**18**	**108**	**1**	**2**	**7**	**1**	**3**	**.246**	**.325**	**.478**	**.996**

Spikes, Leslie Charles (Charlie)

HEIGHT: 6'3" THROWS: RIGHT BATS: RIGHT BORN: 1/23/1951 BOGALUSA, LOUISIANA POSITIONS PLAYED: OF

YEAR	TEAM	GAMES	AB	RUNS	HITS	2B	3B	HR	RBI	BB	IBB	SO	HBP	SH	SF	SB	CS	BA	OBA	SA	FA
1972	**NY-A**	14	34	2	5	1	0	0	3	1	0	13	0	0	0	0	1	.147	.171	.176	1.000
1973	Cle-A	140	506	68	120	12	3	23	73	45	1	103	5	0	5	5	3	.237	.303	.409	.964
1974	Cle-A	155	568	63	154	23	1	22	80	34	2	100	7	0	3	10	7	.271	.319	.431	.968
1975	Cle-A	111	345	41	79	13	3	11	33	30	3	51	0	3	0	7	6	.229	.291	.380	.974
1976	Cle-A	101	334	34	79	11	5	3	31	23	3	50	5	1	2	5	6	.237	.294	.326	.985
1977	Cle-A	32	95	13	22	2	0	3	11	11	0	17	2	0	1	0	2	.232	.321	.347	.972
1978	Det-A	10	28	1	7	1	0	0	2	2	1	6	2	0	0	0	0	.250	.344	.286	.909
1979	Atl-N	66	93	12	26	8	0	3	21	5	1	30	0	0	2	0	0	.280	.310	.462	.842
1980	Atl-N	41	36	6	10	1	0	0	2	3	2	18	1	0	0	0	0	.278	.350	.306	1.000
Career average		74	227	27	56	8	1	7	28	17	1	43	2	0	1	3	3	.246	.304	.389	.957
Yankee average		**14**	**34**	**2**	**5**	**1**	**0**	**0**	**3**	**1**	**0**	**13**	**0**	**0**	**0**	**0**	**1**	**.147**	**.171**	**.176**	**1.000**
Career total		670	2039	240	502	72	12	65	256	154	13	388	22	4	13	27	25	.246	.304	.389	.957
Yankee total		**14**	**34**	**2**	**5**	**1**	**0**	**0**	**3**	**1**	**0**	**13**	**0**	**0**	**0**	**0**	**1**	**.147**	**.171**	**.176**	**1.000**

Stahl, Garland (Jake)

HEIGHT: 6'2" THROWS: RIGHT BATS: RIGHT BORN: 4/13/1879 ELKHART, ILLINOIS DIED: 9/18/1922 MONROVIA, CALIFORNIA POSITIONS PLAYED: 1B, OF

YEAR	TEAM	GAMES	AB	RUNS	HITS	2B	3B	HR	RBI	BB	IBB	SO	HBP	SH	SF	SB	CS	BA	OBA	SA	FA
1903	Bos-A	40	92	14	22	3	5	2	8	4	—	—	2	0		1	—	.239	.286	.446	.956
1904	Was-A	142	520	54	136	29	12	3	50	21	—	—	15	10		25	—	.262	.309	.381	.978
1905	Was-A	141	501	66	125	22	12	5	66	28	—	—	17	14		41	—	.250	.311	.371	.986
1906	Was-A	137	482	38	107	9	8	0	51	21	—	—	8	15		30	—	.222	.266	.274	.983
1908	**NY-A**	75	274	34	70	18	5	2	42	11	—	—	8	9		17	—	.255	.304	.380	.933
1908	Bos-A	78	262	29	64	9	11	0	23	20	—	—	15	10		13	—	.244	.333	.363	.984
1909	Bos-A	127	435	62	128	19	12	6	60	43	—	—	15	12		16	—	.294	.377	.434	.986
1910	Bos-A	144	531	68	144	19	16	10	77	42	—	—	8	17		22	—	.271	.334	.424	.985
1912	Bos-A	95	326	40	98	21	6	3	60	31	—	—	6	17		13	—	.301	.372	.429	.980
1913	Bos-A	2	2	0	0	0	0	0	0	0	—	1	0	0		0	—	.000	.000	.000	.000
Career average		98	343	41	89	15	9	3	44	22	—	—	9	11		18	—	.261	.323	.382	.877
Yankee average		**75**	**274**	**34**	**70**	**18**	**5**	**2**	**42**	**11**	**—**	**—**	**8**	**9**		**17**	**—**	**.255**	**.304**	**.380**	**.933**
Career total		981	3425	405	894	149	87	31	437	221	—	1	94	105		178	—	.261	.323	.382	.877
Yankee total		**75**	**274**	**34**	**70**	**18**	**5**	**2**	**42**	**11**	**—**	**—**	**8**	**9**		**17**	**—**	**.255**	**.304**	**.380**	**.933**

Staiger, Roy Joseph (Linus)

HEIGHT: 6'0" THROWS: RIGHT BATS: RIGHT BORN: 1/6/1950 TULSA, OKLAHOMA POSITIONS PLAYED: 3B

YEAR	TEAM	GAMES	AB	RUNS	HITS	2B	3B	HR	RBI	BB	IBB	SO	HBP	SH	SF	SB	CS	BA	OBA	SA	FA
1975	NY-N	13	19	2	3	1	0	0	0	0	0	4	0	0	0	0	0	.158	.158	.211	1.000
1976	NY-N	95	304	23	67	8	1	2	26	25	6	35	1	1	4	3	3	.220	.278	.273	.967
1977	NY-N	40	123	16	31	9	0	2	11	4	0	20	0	2	0	1	0	.252	.276	.374	.934
1979	**NY-A**	4	11	1	3	1	0	0	1	1	0	0	0	0	0	1	0	.273	.308	.364	1.000
Career average		38	114	11	26	5	0	1	10	8	2	15	0	1	1	1	1	.228	.274	.300	.975
Yankee average		**4**	**11**	**1**	**3**	**1**	**0**	**0**	**1**	**1**	**0**	**0**	**0**	**0**	**0**	**1**	**0**	**.273**	**.308**	**.364**	**1.000**
Career total		152	457	42	104	19	1	4	38	30	6	59	1	3	5	4	3	.228	.274	.300	.975
Yankee total		**4**	**11**	**1**	**3**	**1**	**0**	**0**	**1**	**1**	**0**	**0**	**0**	**0**	**0**	**1**	**0**	**.273**	**.308**	**.364**	**1.000**

Stainback, George Tucker (Tuck)

HEIGHT: 5'11" THROWS: RIGHT BATS: RIGHT BORN: 8/4/1911 LOS ANGELES, CALIFORNIA DIED: 11/29/1992 CAMARILLO, CALIFORNIA POSITIONS PLAYED: OF

YEAR	TEAM	GAMES	AB	RUNS	HITS	2B	3B	HR	RBI	BB	IBB	SO	HBP	SH	SF	SB	CS	BA	OBA	SA	FA
1934	Chi-N	104	359	47	110	14	3	2	46	8	—	42	3	7	—	7	—	.306	.327	.379	1.000
1935	Chi-N	47	94	16	24	4	0	3	11	0	—	13	2	1	—	1	—	.255	.271	.394	.932
1936	Chi-N	44	75	13	13	3	0	1	5	6	—	14	0	1	—	1	—	.173	.235	.253	1.000
1937	Chi-N	72	160	18	37	7	1	0	14	7	—	16	1	3	—	3	—	.231	.268	.288	.981
1938	StL-N	6	10	2	0	0	0	0	0	0	—	3	0	1	—	0	—	.000	.000	.000	1.000
1938	Phi-A	30	81	9	21	3	0	1	11	3	—	3	1	0	—	1	—	.259	.294	.333	.980
1938	Bro-N	35	104	15	34	6	3	0	20	2	—	4	1	2	—	1	—	.327	.346	.442	.981
1939	Bro-N	68	201	22	54	7	0	3	19	4	—	23	2	2	—	0	—	.269	.290	.348	.938
1940	Det-A	15	40	4	9	2	0	0	1	1	—	9	1	2	—	0	0	.225	.262	.275	.968
1941	Det-A	94	200	19	49	8	1	2	10	3	—	21	1	7	—	6	3	.245	.260	.325	.948
1942	**NY-A**	**15**	**10**	**0**	**2**	**0**	**0**	**0**	**0**	**0**	**—**	**2**	**0**	**0**	**—**	**0**	**0**	**.200**	**.200**	**.200**	**1.000**
1943	**NY-A**	**71**	**231**	**31**	**60**	**11**	**2**	**0**	**10**	**7**	**—**	**16**	**1**	**4**	**—**	**3**	**3**	**.260**	**.285**	**.325**	**.993**
1944	**NY-A**	**30**	**78**	**13**	**17**	**3**	**0**	**0**	**5**	**3**	**—**	**7**	**0**	**4**	**—**	**1**	**0**	**.218**	**.247**	**.256**	**.957**
1945	**NY-A**	**95**	**327**	**40**	**84**	**12**	**2**	**5**	**32**	**13**	**—**	**20**	**2**	**7**	**—**	**0**	**4**	**.257**	**.289**	**.352**	**.968**
1946	Phi-A	91	291	35	71	10	2	0	20	7	—	20	1	1	—	3	2	.244	.264	.292	.963
Career average		55	151	19	39	6	1	1	14	4	—	14	1	3	—	2	—	.259	.284	.333	.974
Yankee average		**53**	**162**	**21**	**41**	**7**	**1**	**1**	**12**	**6**	**—**	**11**	**1**	**4**	**—**	**1**	**2**	**.252**	**.281**	**.328**	**.980**
Career total		817	2261	284	585	90	14	17	204	64	—	213	16	42	—	27	12	.259	.284	.333	.974
Yankee total		**211**	**646**	**84**	**163**	**26**	**4**	**5**	**47**	**23**	**—**	**45**	**3**	**15**	**—**	**4**	**7**	**.252**	**.281**	**.328**	**.980**

Stankiewicz, Andrew Neal (Andy)

HEIGHT: 5'9" THROWS: RIGHT BATS: RIGHT BORN: 8/10/1964 INGLEWOOD, CALIFORNIA POSITIONS PLAYED: 2B, 3B, SS

YEAR	TEAM	GAMES	AB	RUNS	HITS	2B	3B	HR	RBI	BB	IBB	SO	HBP	SH	SF	SB	CS	BA	OBA	SA	FA
1992	**NY-A**	**116**	**400**	**52**	**107**	**22**	**2**	**2**	**25**	**38**	**0**	**42**	**5**	**7**	**1**	**9**	**5**	**.268**	**.339**	**.348**	**.973**
1993	**NY-A**	**16**	**9**	**5**	**0**	**0**	**0**	**0**	**0**	**1**	**0**	**1**	**0**	**0**	**0**	**0**	**0**	**.000**	**.100**	**.000**	**1.000**
1994	Hou-N	37	54	10	14	3	0	1	5	12	0	12	1	2	0	1	1	.259	.403	.370	1.000
1995	Hou-N	43	52	6	6	1	0	0	7	12	2	19	0	1	0	4	2	.115	.281	.135	1.000
1996	Mon-N	64	77	12	22	5	1	0	9	6	1	12	3	1	1	1	0	.286	.356	.377	.964
1997	Mon-N	76	107	11	24	9	0	1	5	4	0	22	0	7	1	1	1	.224	.250	.336	1.000
1998	Ari-N	77	145	9	30	5	0	0	8	7	0	33	0	0	1	1	0	.207	.242	.241	.994
Career average		61	121	15	29	6	0	1	8	11	0	20	1	3	1	2	1	.241	.312	.315	.990
Yankee average		**66**	**205**	**29**	**54**	**11**	**1**	**1**	**13**	**20**	**0**	**22**	**3**	**4**	**1**	**5**	**3**	**.262**	**.333**	**.340**	**.987**
Career total		429	844	105	203	45	3	4	59	80	3	141	9	18	4	17	9	.241	.312	.315	.990
Yankee total		**132**	**409**	**57**	**107**	**22**	**2**	**2**	**25**	**39**	**0**	**43**	**5**	**7**	**1**	**9**	**5**	**.262**	**.333**	**.340**	**.987**

Stanley, Frederick Blair (Fred *or* Chicken)

HEIGHT: 5'10" THROWS: RIGHT BATS: RIGHT BORN: 8/13/1947, FARNHAMVILLE, IOWA POSITIONS PLAYED: 2B, 3B, SS

YEAR	TEAM	GAMES	AB	RUNS	HITS	2B	3B	HR	RBI	BB	IBB	SO	HBP	SH	SF	SB	CS	BA	OBA	SA	FA
1969	Sea-A	17	43	2	12	2	1	0	4	3	0	8	0	1	1	1	0	.279	.319	.372	1.000
1970	Mil-A	6	0	1	0	0	0	0	0	0	0	0	0	0	0	0	0	—	—	—	1.000
1971	Cle-A	60	129	14	29	4	0	2	12	27	3	25	1	2	1	1	0	.225	.361	.302	1.000
1972	Cle-A	6	12	1	2	1	0	0	0	2	0	3	0	1	0	0	0	.167	.286	.250	1.000
1972	SD-N	39	85	15	17	2	0	0	2	12	1	19	1	1	0	1	0	.200	.306	.224	1.000
1973	**NY-A**	**26**	**66**	**6**	**14**	**0**	**1**	**1**	**5**	**7**	**0**	**16**	**0**	**2**	**0**	**0**	**0**	**.212**	**.288**	**.288**	**1.000**
1974	**NY-A**	**33**	**38**	**2**	**7**	**0**	**0**	**0**	**3**	**3**	**0**	**2**	**0**	**1**	**0**	**1**	**2**	**.184**	**.244**	**.184**	**.973**
1975	**NY-A**	**117**	**252**	**34**	**56**	**5**	**1**	**0**	**15**	**21**	**0**	**27**	**1**	**8**	**2**	**3**	**1**	**.222**	**.283**	**.250**	**.982**
1976	**NY-A**	**110**	**260**	**32**	**62**	**2**	**2**	**1**	**20**	**34**	**0**	**29**	**1**	**11**	**0**	**1**	**0**	**.238**	**.329**	**.273**	**.800**
1977	**NY-A**	**48**	**46**	**6**	**12**	**0**	**0**	**1**	**7**	**8**	**0**	**6**	**0**	**2**	**0**	**1**	**1**	**.261**	**.370**	**.326**	**1.000**
1978	**NY-A**	**81**	**160**	**14**	**35**	**7**	**0**	**1**	**9**	**25**	**0**	**31**	**0**	**4**	**0**	**0**	**0**	**.219**	**.324**	**.281**	**1.000**
1979	**NY-A**	**57**	**100**	**9**	**20**	**1**	**0**	**2**	**14**	**5**	**0**	**17**	**0**	**4**	**1**	**0**	**1**	**.200**	**.236**	**.270**	**.978**
1980	**NY-A**	**49**	**86**	**13**	**18**	**3**	**0**	**0**	**5**	**5**	**0**	**5**	**2**	**1**	**1**	**0**	**0**	**.209**	**.266**	**.244**	**.980**
1981	Oak-A	66	145	15	28	4	0	0	7	15	0	23	0	8	0	2	0	.193	.269	.221	.986
1982	Oak-A	101	228	33	44	7	0	2	17	29	0	32	1	1	0	0	1	.193	.287	.250	1.000
Career average		54	110	13	24	3	0	1	8	13	0	16	1	3	0	1	0	.216	.301	.263	.980
Yankee average		**65**	**126**	**15**	**28**	**2**	**1**	**1**	**10**	**14**	**0**	**17**	**1**	**4**	**1**	**1**	**1**	**.222**	**.299**	**.266**	**.964**
Career total		816	1650	197	356	38	5	10	120	196	4	243	7	47	6	11	6	.216	.301	.263	.980
Yankee total		**521**	**1008**	**116**	**224**	**18**	**4**	**6**	**78**	**108**	**0**	**133**	**4**	**33**	**4**	**6**	**5**	**.222**	**.299**	**.266**	**.964**

Stanley, Robert Michael (Mike)

HEIGHT: 6'0" THROWS: RIGHT BATS: RIGHT BORN: 6/25/1963 FT.LAUDERDALE, FLORIDA POSITIONS PLAYED: C, 1B

YEAR	TEAM	GAMES	AB	RUNS	HITS	2B	3B	HR	RBI	BB	IBB	SO	HBP	SH	SF	SB	CS	BA	OBA	SA	FA
1986	Tex-A	15	30	4	10	3	0	1	1	3	0	7	0	0	0	1	0	.333	.394	.533	1.000
1987	Tex-A	78	216	34	59	8	1	6	37	31	0	48	1	1	4	3	0	.273	.361	.403	.980
1988	Tex-A	94	249	21	57	8	0	3	27	37	0	62	0	1	5	0	0	.229	.323	.297	.970
1989	Tex-A	67	122	9	30	3	1	1	11	12	1	29	2	1	0	1	0	.246	.324	.311	.978
1990	Tex-A	103	189	21	47	8	1	2	19	30	2	25	0	6	1	1	0	.249	.350	.333	.985
1991	Tex-A	95	181	25	45	13	1	3	25	34	0	44	2	5	1	0	0	.249	.372	.381	.833
1992	**NY-A**	**68**	**173**	**24**	**43**	**7**	**0**	**8**	**27**	**33**	**0**	**45**	**1**	**0**	**0**	**0**	**0**	**.249**	**.372**	**.428**	**1.000**
1993	**NY-A**	**130**	**423**	**70**	**129**	**17**	**1**	**26**	**84**	**57**	**4**	**85**	**5**	**0**	**6**	**1**	**1**	**.305**	**.389**	**.534**	**.996**
1994	**NY-A**	**82**	**290**	**54**	**87**	**20**	**0**	**17**	**57**	**39**	**2**	**56**	**2**	**0**	**2**	**0**	**0**	**.300**	**.384**	**.545**	**.966**
1995	**NY-A**	**118**	**399**	**63**	**107**	**29**	**1**	**18**	**83**	**57**	**1**	**106**	**5**	**0**	**9**	**1**	**1**	**.268**	**.360**	**.481**	**.993**
1996	Bos-A	121	397	73	107	20	1	24	69	69	3	62	5	0	2	2	0	.270	.383	.506	.985
1997	Bos-A	97	260	45	78	17	0	13	53	39	0	50	6	0	7	0	1	.300	.394	.515	.996
1997	**NY-A**	**28**	**87**	**16**	**25**	**8**	**0**	**3**	**12**	**15**	**4**	**22**	**0**	**0**	**1**	**0**	**0**	**.287**	**.388**	**.483**	**.997**
1998	Tor-A	98	341	49	82	13	0	22	47	56	3	86	0	0	3	2	1	.240	.345	.472	.995
1998	Bos-A	47	156	25	45	12	0	7	32	26	2	43	0	0	4	1	0	.288	.382	.500	1.000
1999	Bos-A	136	427	59	120	22	0	19	72	70	0	94	0	0	4	0	0	.281	.379	.466	.988
2000	Bos-A	58	185	22	41	5	0	10	28	30	0	44	0	1	2	0	0	.222	.327	.411	.933
2000	Oak-A	32	97	11	26	7	0	4	18	14	0	21	1	0	1	0	0	.268	.363	.464	.993
Career average		82	235	35	63	12	0	10	39	36	1	52	2	1	3	1	0	.270	.367	.458	.977
Yankee average		**85**	**274**	**45**	**78**	**16**	**0**	**14**	**53**	**40**	**2**	**63**	**3**	**0**	**4**	**0**	**0**	**.285**	**.377**	**.504**	**.990**
Career total		1467	4222	625	1138	220	7	187	702	652	22	929	30	15	52	13	4	.270	.367	.458	.977
Yankee total		**426**	**1372**	**227**	**391**	**81**	**2**	**72**	**263**	**201**	**11**	**314**	**13**	**0**	**18**	**2**	**2**	**.285**	**.377**	**.504**	**.990**

Stewart, Edward Perry (Bud)

HEIGHT: 5'11" THROWS: RIGHT BATS: LEFT BORN: 6/15/1916 SACRAMENTO, CALIFORNIA POSITIONS PLAYED: OF

YEAR	TEAM	GAMES	AB	RUNS	HITS	2B	3B	HR	RBI	BB	IBB	SO	HBP	SH	SF	SB	CS	BA	OBA	SA	FA
1941	Pit-N	73	172	27	46	7	0	0	10	12	—	17	0	3	—	3	—	.267	.315	.308	.962
1942	Pit-N	82	183	21	40	8	4	0	20	22	—	16	0	3	—	2	—	.219	.302	.306	1.000
1948	**NY-A**	**6**	**5**	**1**	**1**	**1**	**0**	**0**	**0**	**0**	**—**	**0**	**0**	**0**	**—**	**0**	**0**	**.200**	**.200**	**.400**	**.000**
1948	Was-A	118	401	56	112	17	13	7	69	49	—	27	2	8	—	8	9	.279	.361	.439	.975
1949	Was-A	118	388	58	110	23	4	8	43	49	—	33	3	7	—	6	4	.284	.368	.425	.982
1950	Was-A	118	378	46	101	15	6	4	35	46	—	33	1	3	—	5	4	.267	.348	.370	.991
1951	Chi-A	95	217	40	60	13	5	6	40	29	—	9	2	5	—	1	6	.276	.367	.465	.983
1952	Chi-A	92	225	23	60	10	0	5	30	28	—	17	1	4	—	3	0	.267	.350	.378	.982
1953	Chi-A	53	59	16	16	2	0	2	13	14	—	3	0	0	—	1	0	.271	.411	.407	1.000
1954	Chi-A	18	13	0	1	0	0	0	0	3	—	2	0	0	0	0	0	.077	.250	.077	1.000
Career average		77	204	29	55	10	3	3	26	25	—	16	1	3	—	3	—	.268	.351	.393	.888
Yankee average		**6**	**5**	**1**	**1**	**1**	**0**	**0**	**0**	**0**	**—**	**0**	**0**	**0**	**—**	**0**	**0**	**.200**	**.200**	**.400**	**.000**
Career total		773	2041	288	547	96	32	32	260	252	—	157	9	33	0	29	23	.268	.351	.393	.888
Yankee total		**6**	**5**	**1**	**1**	**1**	**0**	**0**	**0**	**0**	**—**	**0**	**0**	**0**	**—**	**0**	**0**	**.200**	**.200**	**.400**	**.000**

Stirnweiss, George Henry (Snuffy)

HEIGHT: 5'8" THROWS: RIGHT BATS: RIGHT BORN: 10/26/1918 NEW YORK, N.Y. DIED: 9/15/1958, NEWARK BAY, N.J. POSITIONS PLAYED: 2B, 3B, SS

YEAR	TEAM	GAMES	AB	RUNS	HITS	2B	3B	HR	RBI	BB	IBB	SO	HBP	SH	SF	SB	CS	BA	OBA	SA	FA
1943	**NY-A**	**83**	**274**	**34**	**60**	**8**	**4**	**1**	**25**	**47**	**—**	**37**	**0**	**4**	**—**	**11**	**9**	**.219**	**.333**	**.288**	**1.000**
1944	**NY-A**	**154**	**643**	**125**	**205**	**35**	**16**	**8**	**43**	**73**	**—**	**87**	**1**	**6**	**—**	**55**	**11**	**.319**	**.389**	**.460**	**.982**
1945	**NY-A**	**152**	**632**	**107**	**195**	**32**	**22**	**10**	**64**	**78**	**—**	**62**	**1**	**6**	**—**	**33**	**17**	**.309**	**.385**	**.476**	**.970**
1946	**NY-A**	**129**	**487**	**75**	**122**	**19**	**7**	**0**	**37**	**66**	**—**	**58**	**0**	**7**	**—**	**18**	**6**	**.251**	**.340**	**.318**	**.991**
1947	**NY-A**	**148**	**571**	**102**	**146**	**18**	**8**	**5**	**41**	**89**	**—**	**47**	**2**	**11**	**—**	**5**	**3**	**.256**	**.358**	**.342**	**.983**
1948	**NY-A**	**141**	**515**	**90**	**130**	**20**	**7**	**3**	**32**	**86**	**—**	**62**	**1**	**8**	**—**	**5**	**4**	**.252**	**.361**	**.336**	**.993**
1949	**NY-A**	**70**	**157**	**29**	**41**	**8**	**2**	**0**	**11**	**29**	**—**	**20**	**1**	**3**	**—**	**3**	**2**	**.261**	**.380**	**.338**	**.974**
1950	**NY-A**	**7**	**2**	**0**	**0**	**0**	**0**	**0**	**0**	**0**	**—**	**0**	**0**	**0**	**—**	**0**	**0**	**.000**	**.000**	**.000**	**1.000**
1950	StL-A	93	326	32	71	16	2	1	24	51	—	49	0	4	—	3	3	.218	.324	.288	.875
1951	Cle-A	50	88	10	19	1	0	1	4	22	—	25	0	1	—	1	0	.216	.373	.261	1.000
1952	Cle-A	1	0	0	0	0	0	0	0	0	—	0	0	0	—	0	0	—	—	—	.000
Career average		94	336	55	90	14	6	3	26	49	—	41	1	5	—	12	5	.268	.362	.371	.888
Yankee average		**111**	**410**	**70**	**112**	**18**	**8**	**3**	**32**	**59**	**—**	**47**	**1**	**6**	**—**	**16**	**7**	**.274**	**.366**	**.382**	**.987**
Career total		1028	3695	604	989	157	68	29	281	541	—	447	6	50	—	134	55	.268	.362	.371	.888
Yankee total		**884**	**3281**	**562**	**899**	**140**	**66**	**27**	**253**	**468**	**—**	**373**	**6**	**45**	**—**	**130**	**52**	**.274**	**.366**	**.382**	**.987**

George Henry "Snuffy" Stirnweiss, 2b-3b-ss, 1943–50

Snuffy Stirnweiss made the most of his chance with the Yankees during World War II, when he was exempted from the draft because of hay fever and allergies.

Stirnweiss, born October 26, 1918, in New York City, became a part-time player with the Yankees in 1943, backing up Joe Gordon at second base. But when Gordon went into the service the next year, Stirnweiss took over.

He was one of the best players in the war-thin American League in 1944, leading the American League in hits (205), triples (16), runs (125) and stolen bases (55). In fact, his stolen base total was the Yankees' third highest ever. He also had a stellar year defensively, leading the league's second basemen in putouts, assists, total chances per game and fielding average.

Stirnweiss came back with another explosive season the next year, again leading the

league in several categories, including the aforementioned four offensive categories. He also won the batting championship on the last day of the season with a .309 average.

The speedy Stirnweiss was shifted to third base in 1946, where he struggled. But Yankee manager Bucky Harris returned him to second in 1947, and he helped the Yankees win the pennant. Stirnweiss collected seven hits in the World Series that year, a Yankee win over Brooklyn.

Stirnweiss played well in 1948, but by 1949, he was being eased out by new manager Casey Stengel, who had several young infielders from which to choose. Stirnweiss held on for another year before being traded in 1950 to the Browns. He played two more years after that, retiring in 1952. He died in September 1958 in Newark, New Jersey

Stirnweiss remains 17th all-time in stolen bases with the Yankees with 130 swipes.

Strawberry, Darryl Eugene (Straw)

HEIGHT: 6'6" THROWS: LEFT BATS: LEFT BORN: 3/12/1962, LOS ANGELES, CALIFORNIA POSITIONS PLAYED: OF

YEAR	TEAM	GAMES	AB	RUNS	HITS	2B	3B	HR	RBI	BB	IBB	SO	HBP	SH	SF	SB	CS	BA	OBA	SA	FA
1983	NY-N	122	420	63	108	15	7	26	74	47	9	128	4	0	2	19	6	.257	.336	.512	.984
1984	NY-N	147	522	75	131	27	4	26	97	75	15	131	0	1	4	27	8	.251	.343	.467	.980
1985	NY-N	111	393	78	109	15	4	29	79	73	13	96	1	0	3	26	11	.277	.389	.557	.991
1986	NY-N	136	475	76	123	27	5	27	93	72	9	141	6	0	9	28	12	.259	.358	.507	.975
1987	NY-N	154	532	108	151	32	5	39	104	97	13	122	7	0	4	36	12	.284	.398	.583	.972
1988	NY-N	153	543	101	146	27	3	39	101	85	21	127	3	0	9	29	14	.269	.366	.545	.971
1989	NY-N	134	476	69	107	26	1	29	77	61	13	105	1	0	3	11	4	.225	.312	.466	.972
1990	NY-N	152	542	92	150	18	1	37	108	70	15	110	4	0	5	15	8	.277	.361	.518	.989
1991	LA-N	139	505	86	134	22	4	28	99	75	4	125	3	0	5	10	8	.265	.361	.491	.978
1992	LA-N	43	156	20	37	8	0	5	25	19	4	34	1	0	1	3	1	.237	.322	.385	.986
1993	LA-N	32	100	12	14	2	0	5	12	16	1	19	2	0	2	1	0	.140	.267	.310	.905
1994	SF-N	29	92	13	22	3	1	4	17	19	4	22	0	0	2	0	3	.239	.363	.424	.969
1995	**NY-A**	**32**	**87**	**15**	**24**	**4**	**1**	**3**	**13**	**10**	**1**	**22**	**2**	**0**	**0**	**0**	**0**	**.276**	**.364**	**.448**	**.909**
1996	**NY-A**	**63**	**202**	**35**	**53**	**13**	**0**	**11**	**36**	**31**	**5**	**55**	**1**	**0**	**3**	**6**	**5**	**.262**	**.359**	**.490**	**1.000**
1997	**NY-A**	**11**	**29**	**1**	**3**	**1**	**0**	**0**	**2**	**3**	**0**	**9**	**0**	**0**	**0**	**0**	**0**	**.103**	**.188**	**.138**	**1.000**
1998	**NY-A**	**101**	**295**	**44**	**73**	**11**	**2**	**24**	**57**	**46**	**4**	**90**	**0**	**0**	**1**	**8**	**7**	**.247**	**.348**	**.542**	**.905**
1999	**NY-A**	**24**	**49**	**10**	**16**	**5**	**0**	**3**	**6**	**17**	**0**	**16**	**0**	**0**	**0**	**2**	**0**	**.327**	**.500**	**.612**	**.000**
Career average		93	319	53	82	15	2	20	59	48	8	80	2	0	3	13	6	.259	.356	.505	.911
Yankee average		**46**	**132**	**21**	**34**	**7**	**1**	**8**	**23**	**21**	**2**	**38**	**1**	**0**	**1**	**3**	**2**	**.255**	**.360**	**.502**	**.763**
Career total		1583	5418	898	1401	256	38	335	1000	816	131	1352	35	1	53	221	99	.259	.356	.505	.911
Yankee total		**231**	**662**	**105**	**169**	**34**	**3**	**41**	**114**	**107**	**10**	**192**	**3**	**0**	**4**	**16**	**12**	**.255**	**.360**	**.502**	**.763**

Street, Charles Evard (Gabby *or* Old Sarge)
HEIGHT: 5'11" THROWS: RIGHT BATS: RIGHT BORN: 9/30/1882 HUNTSVILLE, ALABAMA DIED: 2/6/1951 JOPLIN, MISSOURI POSITIONS PLAYED: C

YEAR	TEAM	GAMES	AB	RUNS	HITS	2B	3B	HR	RBI	BB	IBB	SO	HBP	SH	SF	SB	CS	BA	OBA	SA	FA
1904	Cin-N	11	33	1	4	1	0	0	0	1	—	—	0	0	—	2	—	.121	.147	.152	.973
1905	Cin-N	2	2	0	0	0	0	0	0	2	—	—	1	0	—	0	—	.000	.600	.000	1.000
1905	Bos-N	3	12	0	2	0	0	0	0	0	—	—	0	0	—	1	—	.167	.167	.167	.778
1905	Cin-N	29	91	8	23	5	1	0	8	6	—	—	1	0	—	1	—	.253	.306	.330	.975
1908	Was-A	131	394	31	81	12	7	1	32	40	—	—	6	9	—	5	—	.206	.289	.279	.973
1909	Was-A	137	407	25	86	12	1	0	29	26	—	—	2	17	—	2	—	.211	.262	.246	.981
1910	Was-A	89	257	13	52	6	0	1	16	23	—	—	2	9	—	1	—	.202	.273	.237	.978
1911	Was-A	72	216	16	48	7	1	0	14	14	—	—	3	5	—	4	—	.222	.279	.264	.973
1912	**NY-A**	**29**	**88**	**4**	**16**	**1**	**1**	**0**	**6**	**7**	**—**	**—**	**2**	**1**	**—**	**1**	**—**	**.182**	**.258**	**.216**	**.958**
1931	StL-N	1	1	0	0	0	0	0	0	0	—	—	0	0	—	0	—	.000	.000	.000	1.000
Career average		50	150	10	31	4	1	0	11	12	—	—	2	4	—	2	—	.208	.274	.256	.959
Yankee average		**29**	**88**	**4**	**16**	**1**	**1**	**0**	**6**	**7**	**—**	**—**	**2**	**1**	**—**	**1**	**—**	**.182**	**.258**	**.216**	**.958**
Career total		504	1501	98	312	44	11	2	105	119	—	0	17	41	—	17	—	.208	.274	.256	.959
Yankee total		**29**	**88**	**4**	**16**	**1**	**1**	**0**	**6**	**7**	**—**	**—**	**2**	**1**	**—**	**1**	**—**	**.182**	**.258**	**.216**	**.958**

Sturm, John Peter Joseph
HEIGHT: 6'1" THROWS: LEFT BATS: LEFT BORN: 1/23/1916 ST.LOUIS, MISSOURI POSITIONS PLAYED: 1B

YEAR	TEAM	GAMES	AB	RUNS	HITS	2B	3B	HR	RBI	BB	IBB	SO	HBP	SH	SF	SB	CS	BA	OBA	SA	FA
1941	**NY-A**	**124**	**524**	**58**	**125**	**17**	**3**	**3**	**36**	**37**	**—**	**50**	**3**	**4**	**—**	**3**	**5**	**.239**	**.293**	**.300**	**.990**
Career average		124	524	58	125	17	3	3	36	37	—	50	3	4	—	3	5	.239	.293	.300	.990
Yankee average		**124**	**524**	**58**	**125**	**17**	**3**	**3**	**36**	**37**	**—**	**50**	**3**	**4**	**—**	**3**	**5**	**.239**	**.293**	**.300**	**.990**
Career total		124	524	58	125	17	3	3	36	37	—	50	3	4	—	3	5	.239	.293	.300	.990
Yankee total		**124**	**524**	**58**	**125**	**17**	**3**	**3**	**36**	**37**	**—**	**50**	**3**	**4**	**—**	**3**	**5**	**.239**	**.293**	**.300**	**.990**

Sudakis, William Paul (Suds)
HEIGHT: 6'1" THROWS: RIGHT BATS: BOTH BORN: 3/27/1946 JOLIET, ILLINOIS POSITIONS PLAYED: C, 1B, 3B

YEAR	TEAM	GAMES	AB	RUNS	HITS	2B	3B	HR	RBI	BB	IBB	SO	HBP	SH	SF	SB	CS	BA	OBA	SA	FA
1968	LA-N	24	87	11	24	4	2	3	12	15	1	14	0	0	0	1	0	.276	.382	.471	.953
1969	LA-N	132	462	50	108	17	5	14	53	40	5	94	1	1	3	3	2	.234	.294	.383	.946
1970	LA-N	94	269	37	71	11	0	14	44	35	4	46	3	1	3	4	0	.264	.352	.461	1.000
1971	LA-N	41	83	10	16	3	0	3	7	12	2	22	1	0	0	0	1	.193	.302	.337	1.000
1972	NY-N	18	49	3	7	0	0	1	7	6	0	14	0	1	0	0	0	.143	.236	.204	1.000
1973	Tex-A	82	235	32	60	11	0	15	43	23	1	53	0	4	1	0	1	.255	.320	.494	.994
1974	**NY-A**	**89**	**259**	**26**	**60**	**8**	**0**	**7**	**39**	**25**	**1**	**48**	**1**	**2**	**6**	**0**	**0**	**.232**	**.296**	**.344**	**.800**
1975	Cal-A	30	58	4	7	2	0	1	6	12	3	15	1	0	2	1	1	.121	.274	.207	.941
1975	Cle-A	20	46	4	9	0	0	1	3	4	1	7	0	0	0	0	1	.196	.260	.261	1.000
Career average		59	172	20	40	6	1	7	24	19	2	35	1	1	2	1	1	.234	.311	.393	.959
Yankee average		**89**	**259**	**26**	**60**	**8**	**0**	**7**	**39**	**25**	**1**	**48**	**1**	**2**	**6**	**0**	**0**	**.232**	**.296**	**.344**	**.800**
Career total		530	1548	177	362	56	7	59	214	172	18	313	7	9	15	9	6	.234	.311	.393	.959
Yankee total		**89**	**259**	**26**	**60**	**8**	**0**	**7**	**39**	**25**	**1**	**48**	**1**	**2**	**6**	**0**	**0**	**.232**	**.296**	**.344**	**.800**

Sveum, Dale Curtis
HEIGHT: 6'3" THROWS: RIGHT BATS: BOTH BORN: 11/23/1963 RICHMOND, CALIFORNIA POSITIONS PLAYED: 1B, 2B, 3B, SS

YEAR	TEAM	GAMES	AB	RUNS	HITS	2B	3B	HR	RBI	BB	IBB	SO	HBP	SH	SF	SB	CS	BA	OBA	SA	FA
1986	Mil-A	91	317	35	78	13	2	7	35	32	0	63	1	5	1	4	3	.246	.316	.366	.865
1987	Mil-A	153	535	86	135	27	3	25	95	40	4	133	1	5	5	2	6	.252	.303	.454	.966
1988	Mil-A	129	467	41	113	14	4	9	51	21	0	122	1	3	3	1	0	.242	.274	.347	.955
1990	Mil-A	48	117	15	23	7	0	1	12	12	0	30	2	0	2	0	1	.197	.278	.282	1.000
1991	Mil-A	90	266	33	64	19	1	4	43	32	0	78	1	5	4	2	4	.241	.320	.365	.957
1992	Phi-N	54	135	13	24	4	0	2	16	16	4	39	0	0	2	0	0	.178	.261	.252	.948
1992	Chi-A	40	114	15	25	9	0	2	12	12	0	29	0	2	3	1	1	.219	.287	.351	.954
1993	Oak-A	30	79	12	14	2	1	2	6	16	1	21	0	1	0	0	0	.177	.316	.304	1.000
1994	Sea-A	10	27	3	5	0	0	1	2	2	0	10	0	0	0	0	0	.185	.241	.296	.909
1996	Pit-N	12	34	9	12	5	0	1	5	6	0	6	0	0	0	0	0	.353	.450	.588	.913
1997	Pit-N	126	306	30	80	20	1	12	47	27	2	81	0	4	2	0	3	.261	.319	.451	.988
1998	**NY-A**	**30**	**58**	**6**	**9**	**0**	**0**	**0**	**3**	**4**	**0**	**16**	**0**	**0**	**2**	**0**	**0**	**.155**	**.203**	**.155**	**.909**
1999	Pit-N	49	71	7	15	5	1	3	13	7	0	28	0	1	1	0	0	.211	.278	.437	.956

(continued)

(continued)

	GAMES	AB	RUNS	HITS	2B	3B	HR	RBI	BB	IBB	SO	HBP	SH	SF	SB	CS	BA	OBA	SA	FA
Career average	66	194	24	46	10	1	5	26	18	1	51	1	2	2	1	1	.236	.298	.378	.947
Yankee average	**30**	**58**	**6**	**9**	**0**	**0**	**0**	**3**	**4**	**0**	**16**	**0**	**0**	**2**	**0**	**0**	**.155**	**.203**	**.155**	**.909**
Career total	862	2526	305	597	125	13	69	340	227	11	656	6	26	25	10	18	.236	.298	.378	.947
Yankee total	**30**	**58**	**6**	**9**	**0**	**0**	**0**	**3**	**4**	**0**	**16**	**0**	**0**	**2**	**0**	**0**	**.155**	**.203**	**.155**	**.909**

Sweeney, Edward Francis (Jeff)

HEIGHT: 6'1" THROWS: RIGHT BATS: RIGHT BORN: 7/19/1888, CHICAGO, ILLINOIS DIED: 7/4/1947 CHICAGO, ILLINOIS POSITIONS PLAYED: C, 1B

YEAR	TEAM	GAMES	AB	RUNS	HITS	2B	3B	HR	RBI	BB	IBB	SO	HBP	SH	SF	SB	CS	BA	OBA	SA	FA
1908	NY-A	32	82	4	12	2	0	0	2	5	—	—	0	2	—	0	—	.146	.195	.171	.923
1909	NY-A	67	176	19	47	3	0	0	21	16	—	—	0	8	—	3	—	.267	.328	.284	.947
1910	NY-A	78	215	25	43	4	4	0	13	17	—	—	4	10	—	12	—	.200	.271	.256	.974
1911	NY-A	83	229	17	53	6	5	0	18	14	—	—	8	14	—	8	—	.231	.299	.301	.964
1912	NY-A	110	351	37	94	12	1	0	30	27	—	—	3	7	—	6	—	.268	.325	.308	.955
1913	NY-A	117	351	35	93	10	2	2	40	37	—	41	8	9	—	11	—	.265	.348	.322	1.000
1914	NY-A	87	258	25	55	8	1	1	22	35	—	30	4	9	—	19	6	.213	.316	.264	.980
1915	NY-A	53	137	12	26	2	0	0	5	25	—	12	1	10	—	3	3	.190	.319	.204	.975
1919	Pit-N	17	42	0	4	1	0	0	0	5	—	6	0	0	—	1	—	.095	.191	.119	.944
Career average		72	205	19	47	5	1	0	17	20	—	—	3	8	—	7	—	.232	.310	.277	.962
Yankee average		**78**	**225**	**22**	**53**	**6**	**2**	**0**	**19**	**22**	**—**	**—**	**4**	**9**	**—**	**8**	**—**	**.235**	**.313**	**.281**	**.965**
Career total		644	1841	174	427	48	13	3	151	181	—	89	28	69	—	63	9	.232	.310	.277	.962
Yankee total		**627**	**1799**	**174**	**423**	**47**	**13**	**3**	**151**	**176**	**—**	**83**	**28**	**69**	**—**	**62**	**9**	**.235**	**.313**	**.281**	**.965**

Swoboda, Ronald Alan (Rocky)

HEIGHT: 6'2" THROWS: RIGHT BATS: RIGHT BORN: 6/30/1944 BALTIMORE, MARYLAND POSITIONS PLAYED: OF

YEAR	TEAM	GAMES	AB	RUNS	HITS	2B	3B	HR	RBI	BB	IBB	SO	HBP	SH	SF	SB	CS	BA	OBA	SA	FA
1965	NY-N	135	399	52	91	15	3	19	50	33	3	102	3	1	2	2	3	.228	.291	.424	.947
1966	NY-N	112	342	34	76	9	4	8	50	31	4	76	5	2	1	4	2	.222	.296	.342	.987
1967	NY-N	134	449	47	126	17	3	13	53	41	4	96	1	0	3	3	1	.281	.340	.419	.957
1968	NY-N	132	450	46	109	14	6	11	59	52	1	113	4	1	1	8	1	.242	.325	.373	.975
1969	NY-N	109	327	38	77	10	2	9	52	43	4	90	2	1	2	1	1	.235	.326	.361	.988
1970	NY-N	115	245	29	57	8	2	9	40	40	0	72	1	1	2	2	4	.233	.340	.392	.984
1971	Mon-N	39	75	7	19	4	3	0	6	11	0	16	2	1	0	0	1	.253	.364	.387	.977
1971	**NY-A**	**54**	**138**	**17**	**36**	**2**	**1**	**2**	**20**	**27**	**1**	**35**	**3**	**1**	**1**	**0**	**0**	**.261**	**.391**	**.333**	**.965**
1972	**NY-A**	**63**	**113**	**9**	**28**	**8**	**0**	**1**	**12**	**17**	**1**	**29**	**0**	**1**	**2**	**0**	**1**	**.248**	**.341**	**.345**	**1.000**
1973	**NY-A**	**35**	**43**	**6**	**5**	**0**	**0**	**1**	**2**	**4**	**0**	**18**	**0**	**0**	**0**	**0**	**0**	**.116**	**.191**	**.186**	**1.000**
Career average		93	258	29	62	9	2	7	34	30	2	65	2	1	1	2	1	.242	.324	.379	.978
Yankee average		**51**	**98**	**11**	**23**	**3**	**0**	**1**	**11**	**16**	**1**	**27**	**1**	**1**	**1**	**0**	**0**	**.235**	**.345**	**.316**	**.988**
Career total		928	2581	285	624	87	24	73	344	299	18	647	21	9	14	20	14	.242	.324	.379	.978
Yankee total		**152**	**294**	**32**	**69**	**10**	**1**	**4**	**34**	**48**	**2**	**82**	**3**	**2**	**3**	**0**	**1**	**.235**	**.345**	**.316**	**.988**

Tarasco, Antonio Giacinto (Tony)

HEIGHT: 6'0" THROWS: RIGHT BATS: LEFT BORN: 12/9/1970 NEW YORK, NEW YORK POSITIONS PLAYED: OF

YEAR	TEAM	GAMES	AB	RUNS	HITS	2B	3B	HR	RBI	BB	IBB	SO	HBP	SH	SF	SB	CS	BA	OBA	SA	FA
1993	Atl-N	24	35	6	8	2	0	0	2	0	0	5	1	0	1	0	1	.229	.250	.286	1.000
1994	Atl-N	87	132	16	36	6	0	5	19	9	1	17	0	0	3	5	0	.273	.313	.432	1.000
1995	Mon-N	126	438	64	109	18	4	14	40	51	12	78	2	3	1	24	3	.249	.329	.404	.979
1996	Bal-A	31	84	14	20	3	0	1	9	7	0	15	0	1	0	5	3	.238	.297	.310	1.000
1997	Bal-A	100	166	26	34	8	1	7	26	25	1	33	1	1	0	2	2	.205	.313	.392	.991
1998	Cin-N	15	24	5	5	2	0	1	4	3	0	5	0	1	0	0	0	.208	.296	.417	1.000
1999	**NY-A**	**14**	**31**	**5**	**5**	**2**	**0**	**0**	**3**	**3**	**0**	**5**	**0**	**0**	**1**	**1**	**0**	**.161**	**.229**	**.226**	**1.000**
Career average		62	146	22	35	7	1	5	17	16	2	26	1	1	1	6	1	.239	.316	.391	.996
Yankee average		**14**	**31**	**5**	**5**	**2**	**0**	**0**	**3**	**3**	**0**	**5**	**0**	**0**	**1**	**1**	**0**	**.161**	**.229**	**.226**	**1.000**
Career total		373	875	130	209	39	5	28	101	98	14	153	3	6	5	37	8	.239	.316	.391	.996
Yankee total		**14**	**31**	**5**	**5**	**2**	**0**	**0**	**3**	**3**	**0**	**5**	**0**	**0**	**1**	**1**	**0**	**.161**	**.229**	**.226**	**1.000**

Tartabull, Danilo (Danny)
HEIGHT: 6'1"   THROWS: RIGHT   BATS: RIGHT   BORN: 10/30/1962 SAN JUAN, FLORIDA   POSITIONS PLAYED: 2B, SS, OF

YEAR	TEAM	GAMES	AB	RUNS	HITS	2B	3B	HR	RBI	BB	IBB	SO	HBP	SH	SF	SB	CS	BA	OBA	SA	FA
1984	Sea-A	10	20	3	6	1	0	2	7	2	0	3	1	0	1	0	0	.300	.375	.650	1.000
1985	Sea-A	19	61	8	20	7	1	1	7	8	0	14	0	0	0	1	0	.328	.406	.525	1.000
1986	Sea-A	137	511	76	138	25	6	25	96	61	2	157	1	2	3	4	8	.270	.347	.489	.953
1987	KC-A	158	582	95	180	27	3	34	101	79	2	136	1	0	5	9	4	.309	.390	.541	.976
1988	KC-A	146	507	80	139	38	3	26	102	76	4	119	4	0	6	8	5	.274	.369	.515	.963
1989	KC-A	133	441	54	118	22	0	18	62	69	2	123	3	0	2	4	2	.268	.369	.440	.982
1990	KC-A	88	313	41	84	19	0	15	60	36	0	93	0	0	3	1	1	.268	.341	.473	.965
1991	KC-A	132	484	78	153	35	3	31	100	65	6	121	3	0	5	6	3	.316	.397	.593	.965
1992	**NY-A**	**123**	**421**	**72**	**112**	**19**	**0**	**25**	**85**	**103**	**14**	**115**	**0**	**0**	**2**	**2**	**2**	**.266**	**.409**	**.489**	**.980**
1993	**NY-A**	**138**	**513**	**87**	**128**	**33**	**2**	**31**	**102**	**92**	**9**	**156**	**2**	**0**	**4**	**0**	**0**	**.250**	**.363**	**.503**	**.978**
1994	**NY-A**	**104**	**399**	**68**	**102**	**24**	**1**	**19**	**67**	**66**	**3**	**111**	**1**	**0**	**4**	**1**	**1**	**.256**	**.360**	**.464**	**1.000**
1995	**NY-A**	**59**	**192**	**25**	**43**	**12**	**0**	**6**	**28**	**33**	**1**	**54**	**1**	**0**	**4**	**0**	**0**	**.224**	**.335**	**.380**	**1.000**
1995	Oak-A	24	88	9	23	4	0	2	7	10	0	28	0	0	0	0	2	.261	.337	.375	1.000
1996	Chi-A	132	472	58	120	23	3	27	101	64	4	128	0	0	5	1	2	.254	.340	.487	.973
1997	Phi-N	3	7	2	0	0	0	0	0	4	0	4	0	0	0	0	0	.000	.364	.000	1.000
Career average		94	334	50	91	19	2	18	62	51	3	91	1	0	3	3	2	.273	.368	.496	.982
Yankee average		**106**	**381**	**63**	**96**	**22**	**1**	**20**	**71**	**74**	**7**	**109**	**1**	**0**	**4**	**1**	**1**	**.252**	**.372**	**.473**	**.990**
Career total		1406	5011	756	1366	289	22	262	925	768	47	1362	17	2	44	37	30	.273	.368	.496	.982
Yankee total		**424**	**1525**	**252**	**385**	**88**	**3**	**81**	**282**	**294**	**27**	**436**	**4**	**0**	**14**	**3**	**3**	**.252**	**.372**	**.473**	**.990**

Taylor, James Wren (Zack)
HEIGHT: 5'11"   THROWS: RIGHT   BATS: RIGHT   BORN: 7/27/1898 YULEE, FLORIDA   DIED: 9/19/1974 ORLANDO, FLORIDA   POSITIONS PLAYED: C

YEAR	TEAM	GAMES	AB	RUNS	HITS	2B	3B	HR	RBI	BB	IBB	SO	HBP	SH	SF	SB	CS	BA	OBA	SA	FA
1920	Bro-N	9	13	3	5	2	0	0	5	0	—	2	0	0	—	0	1	.385	.385	.538	.882
1921	Bro-N	30	102	6	20	0	2	0	8	1	—	8	1	4	—	2	0	.196	.212	.235	.965
1922	Bro-N	7	14	0	3	0	0	0	2	1	—	1	0	1	—	0	0	.214	.267	.214	.950
1923	Bro-N	96	337	29	97	11	6	0	46	9	—	13	3	4	—	2	5	.288	.312	.356	.967
1924	Bro-N	99	345	36	100	9	4	1	39	14	—	14	1	8	—	0	1	.290	.319	.348	.988
1925	Bro-N	109	352	33	109	16	4	3	44	17	—	19	1	4	—	0	0	.310	.343	.403	.959
1926	Bos-N	125	432	36	110	22	3	0	42	28	—	27	2	8	—	1	—	.255	.303	.319	.985
1927	Bos-N	30	96	8	23	2	1	1	14	8	—	5	0	1	—	0	—	.240	.298	.313	.988
1927	NY-N	83	258	18	60	7	3	0	21	17	—	20	1	7	—	2	—	.233	.283	.283	.972
1928	Bos-N	125	399	36	100	15	1	2	30	33	—	29	3	7	—	2	—	.251	.313	.308	.985
1929	Bos-N	34	101	8	25	7	0	0	10	7	—	9	1	5	—	0	—	.248	.303	.317	.965
1929	Chi-N	64	215	29	59	16	3	1	31	19	—	18	1	3	—	0	—	.274	.336	.391	.979
1930	Chi-N	32	95	12	22	2	1	1	11	2	—	12	1	4	—	0	—	.232	.255	.305	1.000
1931	Chi-N	8	4	0	1	0	0	0	0	2	—	1	0	2	—	0	—	.250	.500	.250	1.000
1932	Chi-N	21	30	2	6	1	0	0	3	1	—	4	0	1	—	0	—	.200	.226	.233	1.000
1933	Chi-N	16	11	0	0	0	0	0	0	0	—	1	0	0	—	0	—	.000	.000	.000	1.000
1934	**NY-A**	**4**	**7**	**0**	**1**	**0**	**0**	**0**	**0**	**0**	**—**	**1**	**0**	**0**	**—**	**0**	**0**	**.143**	**.143**	**.143**	**1.000**
1935	Bro-N	26	54	2	7	3	0	0	5	2	—	8	1	0	—	0	—	.130	.175	.185	.970
Career average		51	159	14	42	6	2	1	17	9	—	11	1	3	—	1	—	.261	.304	.329	.975
Yankee average		**4**	**7**	**0**	**1**	**0**	**0**	**0**	**0**	**0**	**—**	**1**	**0**	**0**	**—**	**0**	**0**	**.143**	**.143**	**.143**	**1.000**
Career total		918	2865	258	748	113	28	9	311	161	—	192	16	59	—	9	7	.261	.304	.329	.975
Yankee total		**4**	**7**	**0**	**1**	**0**	**0**	**0**	**0**	**0**	**—**	**1**	**0**	**0**	**—**	**0**	**0**	**.143**	**.143**	**.143**	**1.000**

Tepedino, Frank Ronald
HEIGHT: 5'11"   THROWS: LEFT   BATS: LEFT   BORN: 11/23/1947 BROOKLYN, NEW YORK   POSITIONS PLAYED: 1B, OF

YEAR	TEAM	GAMES	AB	RUNS	HITS	2B	3B	HR	RBI	BB	IBB	SO	HBP	SH	SF	SB	CS	BA	OBA	SA	FA
1967	**NY-A**	**9**	**5**	**0**	**2**	**0**	**0**	**0**	**0**	**1**	**0**	**1**	**0**	**0**	**0**	**0**	**0**	**.400**	**.500**	**.400**	**1.000**
1969	**NY-A**	**13**	**39**	**6**	**9**	**0**	**0**	**0**	**4**	**4**	**0**	**4**	**0**	**0**	**0**	**1**	**0**	**.231**	**.302**	**.231**	**.950**
1970	**NY-A**	**16**	**19**	**2**	**6**	**2**	**0**	**0**	**2**	**1**	**0**	**2**	**0**	**0**	**0**	**0**	**1**	**.316**	**.350**	**.421**	**1.000**
1971	**NY-A**	**6**	**6**	**0**	**0**	**0**	**0**	**0**	**0**	**0**	**0**	**0**	**0**	**0**	**0**	**0**	**0**	**.000**	**.000**	**.000**	**1.000**
1971	Mil-A	53	106	11	21	1	0	2	7	4	0	17	1	1	0	2	2	.198	.234	.264	.986
1972	**NY-A**	**8**	**8**	**0**	**0**	**0**	**0**	**0**	**0**	**0**	**0**	**1**	**0**	**0**	**0**	**0**	**0**	**.000**	**.000**	**.000**	**.000**
1973	Atl-N	74	148	20	45	5	0	4	29	13	3	21	0	1	3	0	0	.304	.354	.419	.992
1974	Atl-N	78	169	11	39	5	1	0	16	9	2	13	1	1	1	1	2	.231	.272	.272	.988
1975	Atl-N	8	7	0	0	0	0	0	0	1	0	0	0	0	0	0	0	.000	.125	.000	.000
Career average		29	56	6	14	1	0	1	6	4	1	7	0	0	0	0	1	.241	.288	.306	.768
Yankee average		**10**	**15**	**2**	**3**	**0**	**0**	**0**	**1**	**1**	**0**	**2**	**0**	**0**	**0**	**0**	**0**	**.221**	**.277**	**.247**	**.790**
Career total		265	507	50	122	13	1	6	58	33	5	61	2	3	4	4	5	.241	.288	.306	.768
Yankee total		**52**	**77**	**8**	**17**	**2**	**0**	**0**	**6**	**6**	**0**	**8**	**0**	**0**	**0**	**1**	**1**	**.221**	**.277**	**.247**	**.790**

Thomas, Ira Felix

HEIGHT: 6'2" THROWS: RIGHT BATS: RIGHT BORN: 1/22/1881, BALLSTON SPA, NEW YORK DIED: 10/11/1958, PHILADELPHIA, PENN. POSITIONS PLAYED: C

YEAR	TEAM	GAMES	AB	RUNS	HITS	2B	3B	HR	RBI	BB	IBB	SO	HBP	SH	SF	SB	CS	BA	OBA	SA	FA
1906	**NY-A**	**44**	**115**	**12**	**23**	**1**	**2**	**0**	**15**	**8**	—	—	**1**	**2**	—	**2**	—	**.200**	**.258**	**.243**	**.938**
1907	**NY-A**	**80**	**208**	**20**	**40**	**5**	**4**	**1**	**24**	**10**	—	—	**3**	**3**	—	**5**	—	**.192**	**.240**	**.269**	**1.000**
1908	Det-A	40	101	6	31	1	0	0	8	5	—	—	1	1	—	0	—	.307	.346	.317	.972
1909	Phi-A	84	256	22	57	9	3	0	31	18	—	—	7	5	—	4	—	.223	.292	.281	.985
1910	Phi-A	60	180	14	50	8	2	1	19	6	—	—	0	3	—	2	—	.278	.301	.361	.967
1911	Phi-A	103	297	33	81	14	3	0	39	23	—	—	8	9	—	4	—	.273	.341	.340	.974
1912	Phi-A	48	139	14	30	4	2	1	13	8	—	—	2	5	—	3	—	.216	.268	.295	.971
1913	Phi-A	22	53	3	15	4	1	0	6	4	—	8	0	1	—	0	0	.283	.333	.396	.983
1914	Phi-A	2	3	0	0	0	0	0	0	0	—	0	0	0	—	0	0	.000	.000	.000	1.000
1915	Phi-A	1	0	0	0	0	0	0	0	0	—	0	0	0	—	0	0	—	—	—	1.000
Career average		48	135	12	33	5	2	0	16	8	—	—	2	3	—	2	—	.242	.296	.308	.979
Yankee average		**62**	**162**	**16**	**32**	**3**	**3**	**1**	**20**	**9**	—	—	**2**	**3**	—	**4**	—	**.195**	**.246**	**.260**	**.969**
Career total		484	1352	124	327	46	17	3	155	82	—	8	22	29	—	20	0	.242	.296	.308	.979
Yankee total		**124**	**323**	**32**	**63**	**6**	**6**	**1**	**39**	**18**	—	—	**4**	**5**	—	**7**	—	**.195**	**.246**	**.260**	**.969**

Thomas, James Leroy (Lee)

HEIGHT: 6'2" THROWS: LEFT BATS: LEFT BORN: 2/5/1936 PEORIA, ILLINOIS POSITIONS PLAYED: 1B, OF

YEAR	TEAM	GAMES	AB	RUNS	HITS	2B	3B	HR	RBI	BB	IBB	SO	HBP	SH	SF	SB	CS	BA	OBA	SA	FA
1961	**NY-A**	**2**	**2**	**0**	**1**	**0**	**0**	**0**	**0**	**0**	**0**	**0**	**0**	**0**	**0**	**0**	**0**	**.500**	**.500**	**.500**	**.000**
1961	LA-A	130	450	77	128	11	5	24	70	47	2	74	2	2	3	0	5	.284	.353	.491	.982
1962	LA-A	160	583	88	169	21	2	26	104	55	3	74	6	4	4	6	0	.290	.355	.467	.972
1963	LA-A	149	528	52	116	12	6	9	55	53	6	82	9	2	2	6	0	.220	.301	.316	.986
1964	LA-A	47	172	14	47	8	1	2	24	18	1	22	0	3	1	1	0	.273	.340	.366	.949
1964	Bos-A	107	401	44	103	19	2	13	42	34	4	29	4	0	3	2	1	.257	.361	.464	.968
1965	Bos-A	151	521	74	141	27	4	22	75	72	8	42	3	5	2	6	2	.271	.361	.464	.968
1966	Atl-N	39	126	11	25	1	1	6	15	10	1	15	1	1	1	0	1	.242	.319	.289	.992
1966	Chi-N	75	149	15	36	4	0	1	9	14	1	15	3	1	0	0	0	.220	.284	.283	1.000
1967	Chi-N	77	191	16	42	4	1	2	23	15	5	22	3	1	2	1	0	.194	.249	.229	1.000
1968	Hou-N	90	201	14	39	4	0	1	11	14	4	22	1	4	1	2	1	.194	.249	.229	1.000
Career average		93	302	37	77	10	2	10	39	30	3	36	3	2	2	2	1	.255	.327	.397	.894
Yankee average		**2**	**2**	**0**	**1**	**0**	**0**	**0**	**0**	**0**	**0**	**0**	**0**	**0**	**0**	**0**	**0**	**.500**	**.500**	**.500**	**.000**
Career total		1027	3324	405	847	111	22	106	428	332	35	397	32	23	19	25	11	.255	.327	.397	.894
Yankee total		**2**	**2**	**0**	**1**	**0**	**0**	**0**	**0**	**0**	**0**	**0**	**0**	**0**	**0**	**0**	**0**	**.500**	**.500**	**.500**	**.000**

Thomasson, Gary Leah

HEIGHT: 6'1" THROWS: LEFT BATS: LEFT BORN: 7/29/1951 SAN DIEGO, CALIFORNIA POSITIONS PLAYED: 1B, OF

YEAR	TEAM	GAMES	AB	RUNS	HITS	2B	3B	HR	RBI	BB	IBB	SO	HBP	SH	SF	SB	CS	BA	OBA	SA	FA
1972	SF-N	10	27	5	9	1	1	0	1	1	0	7	0	0	0	0	0	.333	.357	.444	1.000
1973	SF-N	112	235	35	67	10	4	4	30	22	2	43	0	3	1	2	0	.285	.345	.413	.992
1974	SF-N	120	315	41	77	14	3	2	29	38	2	56	0	3	1	7	1	.244	.325	.327	.981
1975	SF-N	114	326	44	74	12	3	7	32	37	1	48	1	0	5	9	3	.227	.304	.347	.978
1976	SF-N	103	328	45	85	20	5	8	38	30	7	45	1	0	2	8	3	.259	.321	.424	.980
1977	SF-N	145	446	63	114	24	6	17	71	75	8	102	1	4	8	16	4	.256	.358	.451	.981
1978	Oak-A	47	154	17	31	4	1	5	16	15	2	44	0	2	0	4	1	.201	.272	.338	.969
1978	**NY-A**	**55**	**116**	**20**	**32**	**4**	**1**	**3**	**20**	**13**	**0**	**22**	**0**	**0**	**1**	**0**	**2**	**.276**	**.339**	**.422**	**1.000**
1979	LA-N	115	315	39	78	11	1	14	45	43	4	70	1	2	1	4	2	.216	.326	.270	1.000
1980	LA-N	80	111	6	24	3	0	1	12	17	3	26	1	0	0	0	0	.216	.326	.270	1.000
Career average		90	237	32	59	10	3	6	29	29	3	46	1	1	2	5	2	.249	.330	.391	.985
Yankee average		**55**	**116**	**20**	**32**	**4**	**1**	**3**	**20**	**13**	**0**	**22**	**0**	**0**	**1**	**0**	**2**	**.276**	**.346**	**.405**	**.972**
Career total		901	2373	315	591	103	25	61	294	291	29	463	5	14	19	50	16	.249	.330	.391	.985
Yankee total		**55**	**116**	**20**	**32**	**4**	**1**	**3**	**20**	**13**	**0**	**22**	**0**	**0**	**1**	**0**	**2**	**.276**	**.346**	**.405**	**.972**

Thompson, Ryan Orlando
HEIGHT: 6'3" THROWS: RIGHT BATS: RIGHT BORN: 11/4/1967 CHESTERTOWN, MARYLAND POSITIONS PLAYED: OF

YEAR	TEAM	GAMES	AB	RUNS	HITS	2B	3B	HR	RBI	BB	IBB	SO	HBP	SH	SF	SB	CS	BA	OBA	SA	FA
1992	NY-N	30	108	15	24	7	1	3	10	8	0	24	0	0	1	2	2	.222	.274	.389	.988
1993	NY-N	80	288	34	72	19	2	11	26	19	4	81	3	5	1	2	7	.250	.302	.444	.987
1994	NY-N	98	334	39	75	14	1	18	59	28	7	94	10	3	4	1	1	.225	.301	.434	.992
1995	NY-N	75	267	39	67	13	0	7	31	19	1	77	4	0	0	4	3	.251	.306	.378	.985
1996	Cle-A	8	22	2	7	0	0	1	5	1	0	6	0	0	0	0	0	.318	.348	.455	1.000
1999	Hou-N	12	20	2	4	1	0	1	5	2	0	7	0	0	0	0	0	.200	.273	.400	.800
2000	**NY-A**	**33**	**50**	**12**	**13**	**3**	**0**	**3**	**14**	**5**	**0**	**12**	**1**	**0**	**0**	**0**	**1**	**.260**	**.339**	**.500**	**1.000**
Career average		48	156	20	37	8	1	6	21	12	2	43	3	1	1	1	2	.241	.302	.421	.965
Yankee average		**33**	**50**	**12**	**13**	**3**	**0**	**3**	**14**	**5**	**0**	**12**	**1**	**0**	**0**	**0**	**1**	**.260**	**.339**	**.500**	**1.000**
Career total		336	1089	143	262	57	4	44	150	82	12	301	18	8	10	8	12	.241	.302	.421	.965
Yankee total		**33**	**50**	**12**	**13**	**3**	**0**	**3**	**14**	**5**	**0**	**12**	**1**	**0**	**0**	**0**	**1**	**.260**	**.339**	**.500**	**1.000**

Thoney, John (Bullet Jack)
HEIGHT: 5'10" THROWS: RIGHT BATS: RIGHT BORN: 12/8/1879 FT. THOMAS, KENTUCKY DIED: 10/24/1948 COVINGTON, KENTUCKY POSITIONS PLAYED: 3B, OF

YEAR	TEAM	GAMES	AB	RUNS	HITS	2B	3B	HR	RBI	BB	IBB	SO	HBP	SH	SF	SB	CS	BA	OBA	SA	FA
1902	Cle-A	28	105	14	30	7	1	0	11	9	—	—	0	1	—	4	—	.286	.342	.371	.891
1902	Bal-A	3	11	1	0	0	0	0	0	1	—	—	0	0	—	1	—	.000	.083	.000	.778
1903	Cle-A	32	122	10	25	3	0	1	9	2	—	—	0	0	—	7	—	.205	.218	.254	.800
1904	Was-A	17	70	6	21	3	0	0	6	1	—	—	0	0	—	2	—	.300	.310	.343	.860
1904	**NY-A**	**36**	**128**	**17**	**24**	**4**	**2**	**0**	**12**	**8**	**—**	**—**	**1**	**3**	**—**	**9**	**—**	**.188**	**.241**	**.250**	**.826**
1908	Bos-A	109	416	58	106	5	9	2	30	13	—	—	3	9	—	16	—	.255	.282	.325	.948
1909	Bos-A	13	40	1	5	1	0	0	3	2	—	—	0	1	—	2	—	.125	.167	.150	.960
1911	Bos-A	26	20	5	5	0	0	0	2	0	—	—	0	0	—	1	—	.250	.250	.250	.000
Career average		33	114	14	27	3	2	0	9	5	—	—	1	2	—	5	—	.237	.269	.298	.758
Yankee average		**36**	**128**	**17**	**24**	**4**	**2**	**0**	**12**	**8**	**—**	**—**	**1**	**3**	**—**	**9**	**—**	**.188**	**.241**	**.250**	**.826**
Career total		264	912	112	216	23	12	3	73	36	—	—	4	14	—	42	—	.237	.269	.298	.758
Yankee total		**36**	**128**	**17**	**24**	**4**	**2**	**0**	**12**	**8**	**—**	**—**	**1**	**3**	**—**	**9**	**—**	**.188**	**.241**	**.250**	**.826**

Throneberry, Marvin Eugene (Marvelous Marv)
HEIGHT: 6'1" THROWS: LEFT BATS: LEFT BORN: 9/2/1933 COLLIERVILLE, TENNESSEE DIED: 6/23/1994 FISHERVILLE, TENN. POSITIONS PLAYED: 1B, OF

YEAR	TEAM	GAMES	AB	RUNS	HITS	2B	3B	HR	RBI	BB	IBB	SO	HBP	SH	SF	SB	CS	BA	OBA	SA	FA
1955	**NY-A**	**1**	**2**	**1**	**2**	**1**	**0**	**0**	**3**	**0**	**0**	**0**	**0**	**0**	**1**	**1**	**0**	**1.000**	**.667**	**1.500**	**1.000**
1958	**NY-A**	**60**	**150**	**30**	**34**	**5**	**2**	**7**	**19**	**19**	**0**	**40**	**1**	**1**	**1**	**0**	**1**	**.227**	**.316**	**.427**	**.991**
1959	**NY-A**	**80**	**192**	**27**	**46**	**5**	**0**	**8**	**22**	**18**	**1**	**51**	**0**	**2**	**2**	**0**	**0**	**.240**	**.302**	**.391**	**.989**
1960	KC-A	104	236	29	59	9	2	11	41	23	1	60	0	0	1	0	0	.250	.315	.445	.991
1961	KC-A	40	130	17	31	2	1	6	24	19	1	30	0	1	0	0	0	.238	.336	.408	1.000
1961	Bal-A	56	96	9	20	3	0	5	11	12	0	20	0	0	0	0	0	.208	.296	.396	.923
1962	Bal-A	9	9	1	0	0	0	0	0	4	0	6	0	0	0	0	0	.000	.308	.000	1.000
1962	NY-N	116	357	29	87	11	3	16	49	34	4	83	0	1	4	1	3	.244	.306	.426	.981
1963	NY-N	14	14	0	2	1	0	0	1	1	0	5	0	0	0	0	0	.143	.200	.214	1.000
Career average		53	132	16	31	4	1	6	19	14	1	33	0	1	1	0	0	.237	.311	.416	.986
Yankee average		**47**	**115**	**19**	**27**	**4**	**1**	**5**	**15**	**12**	**0**	**30**	**0**	**1**	**1**	**1**	**0**	**.238**	**.311**	**.413**	**.993**
Career total		480	1186	143	281	37	8	53	170	130	7	295	1	5	9	3	4	.237	.311	.416	.986
Yankee total		**141**	**344**	**58**	**82**	**11**	**2**	**15**	**44**	**37**	**1**	**91**	**1**	**3**	**4**	**2**	**1**	**.238**	**.311**	**.413**	**.993**

Tillman, John Robert (Bob)

HEIGHT: 6'4"   THROWS: RIGHT   BATS: RIGHT   BORN: 3/24/1937 NASHVILLE, TENNESSEE   POSITIONS PLAYED: C

YEAR	TEAM	GAMES	AB	RUNS	HITS	2B	3B	HR	RBI	BB	IBB	SO	HBP	SH	SF	SB	CS	BA	OBA	SA	FA
1962	Bos-A	81	249	28	57	6	4	14	38	19	0	65	1	0	3	0	0	.229	.283	.454	.983
1963	Bos-A	96	307	24	69	10	2	8	32	34	8	64	1	1	0	0	0	.225	.304	.349	.992
1964	Bos-A	131	425	43	118	18	1	17	61	49	11	74	0	4	1	0	0	.278	.352	.445	.989
1965	Bos-A	111	368	20	79	10	3	6	35	40	3	69	0	0	5	0	0	.215	.288	.307	.988
1966	Bos-A	78	204	12	47	8	0	3	24	22	3	35	0	1	2	0	0	.230	.303	.314	.990
1967	Bos-A	30	64	4	12	1	0	1	4	3	0	18	0	0	0	0	0	.188	.224	.250	.977
1967	**NY-A**	**22**	**63**	**5**	**16**	**1**	**0**	**2**	**9**	**7**	**1**	**17**	**0**	**0**	**1**	**0**	**0**	**.254**	**.324**	**.365**	**.970**
1968	Atl-N	86	236	16	52	4	0	5	20	16	2	55	3	2	0	1	0	.220	.278	.301	.990
1969	Atl-N	69	190	18	37	5	0	12	29	18	1	47	0	0	1	0	0	.195	.263	.411	.988
1970	Atl-N	71	223	19	53	5	0	11	30	20	4	66	0	1	1	0	0	.238	.299	.408	.988
Career average		78	233	19	54	7	1	8	28	23	3	51	1	1	1	0	0	.232	.300	.371	.986
Yankee average		**22**	**63**	**5**	**16**	**1**	**0**	**2**	**9**	**7**	**1**	**17**	**0**	**0**	**1**	**0**	**0**	**.254**	**.324**	**.365**	**.970**
Career total		775	2329	189	540	68	10	79	282	228	33	510	5	9	14	1	0	.232	.300	.371	.986
Yankee total		**22**	**63**	**5**	**16**	**1**	**0**	**2**	**9**	**7**	**1**	**17**	**0**	**0**	**1**	**0**	**0**	**.254**	**.324**	**.365**	**.970**

Tolleson, Jimmy Wayne

HEIGHT: 5'9"   THROWS: RIGHT   BATS: BOTH   BORN: 11/22/1955 SPARTANBURG, SOUTH CAROLINA   POSITIONS PLAYED: 2B, 3B, SS

YEAR	TEAM	GAMES	AB	RUNS	HITS	2B	3B	HR	RBI	BB	IBB	SO	HBP	SH	SF	SB	CS	BA	OBA	SA	FA
1981	Tex-A	14	24	6	4	0	0	0	1	1	0	5	0	0	0	2	0	.167	.200	.167	1.000
1982	Tex-A	38	70	6	8	1	0	0	2	5	0	14	0	3	0	1	1	.114	.173	.129	.958
1983	Tex-A	134	470	64	122	13	2	3	20	40	0	68	2	7	2	33	10	.260	.319	.315	.988
1984	Tex-A	118	338	35	72	9	2	0	9	27	0	47	3	9	1	22	4	.213	.276	.251	1.000
1985	Tex-A	123	323	45	101	9	5	1	18	21	0	46	0	9	2	21	12	.313	.353	.381	.972
1986	Chi-A	81	260	39	65	7	3	3	29	38	0	43	0	9	3	13	6	.250	.342	.335	.974
1986	**NY-A**	**60**	**215**	**22**	**61**	**9**	**2**	**0**	**14**	**14**	**0**	**33**	**2**	**4**	**1**	**4**	**4**	**.284**	**.332**	**.344**	**1.000**
1987	**NY-A**	**121**	**349**	**48**	**77**	**4**	**0**	**1**	**22**	**43**	**0**	**72**	**0**	**6**	**0**	**5**	**3**	**.221**	**.306**	**.241**	**1.000**
1988	**NY-A**	**21**	**59**	**8**	**15**	**2**	**0**	**0**	**5**	**8**	**0**	**12**	**0**	**1**	**1**	**1**	**0**	**.254**	**.338**	**.288**	**.981**
1989	**NY-A**	**80**	**140**	**16**	**23**	**5**	**2**	**1**	**9**	**16**	**0**	**23**	**1**	**3**	**0**	**5**	**1**	**.164**	**.255**	**.250**	**.975**
1990	**NY-A**	**73**	**74**	**12**	**11**	**1**	**1**	**0**	**4**	**6**	**0**	**21**	**0**	**2**	**1**	**1**	**0**	**.149**	**.210**	**.189**	**.983**
Career average		79	211	27	51	6	2	1	12	20	0	35	1	5	1	10	4	.241	.307	.293	.985
Yankee average		**71**	**167**	**21**	**37**	**4**	**1**	**0**	**11**	**17**	**0**	**32**	**1**	**3**	**1**	**3**	**2**	**.223**	**.298**	**.268**	**.988**
Career total		863	2322	301	559	60	17	9	133	219	0	384	8	53	11	108	41	.241	.307	.293	.985
Yankee total		**355**	**837**	**106**	**187**	**21**	**5**	**2**	**54**	**87**	**0**	**161**	**3**	**16**	**3**	**16**	**8**	**.223**	**.298**	**.268**	**.988**

Torgeson, Clifford Earl (The Earl Of Snohomish)

HEIGHT: 6'3"   THROWS: LEFT   BATS: LEFT   BORN: 1/1/1924 SNOHOMISH, WASHINGTON   DIED: 11/8/1990 EVERETT, WASHINGTON   POSITIONS PLAYED: 1B

YEAR	TEAM	GAMES	AB	RUNS	HITS	2B	3B	HR	RBI	BB	IBB	SO	HBP	SH	SF	SB	CS	BA	OBA	SA	FA
1947	Bos-N	128	399	73	112	20	6	16	78	82	—	59	0	3	—	11	—	.281	.403	.481	.984
1948	Bos-N	134	438	70	111	23	5	10	67	81	—	54	2	10	—	19	—	.253	.372	.397	.993
1949	Bos-N	25	100	17	26	5	1	4	19	13	—	4	0	0	—	4	—	.260	.345	.450	.988
1950	Bos-N	156	576	120	167	30	3	23	87	119	—	69	1	8	—	15	—	.290	.412	.472	.986
1951	Bos-N	155	581	99	153	21	4	24	92	102	—	70	2	5	—	20	11	.263	.375	.437	.988
1952	Bos-N	122	382	49	88	17	0	5	34	81	—	38	1	7	—	11	7	.230	.366	.314	.989
1953	Phi-N	111	379	58	104	25	8	11	64	53	—	57	2	3	—	7	1	.274	.366	.470	.987
1954	Phi-N	135	490	63	133	22	6	5	54	75	—	52	0	11	6	7	1	.271	.364	.371	.990
1955	Phi-N	47	150	29	40	5	3	1	17	32	1	20	0	1	1	2	3	.267	.393	.360	.995
1955	Det-A	89	300	58	85	10	1	9	50	61	2	29	0	1	7	9	0	.283	.397	.413	.992
1956	Det-A	117	318	61	84	9	3	12	42	78	0	47	0	1	3	6	4	.264	.406	.425	.992
1957	Det-A	30	50	5	12	2	1	1	5	12	0	10	0	0	0	0	0	.240	.387	.380	1.000
1957	Chi-A	86	251	53	74	11	2	7	46	49	0	44	0	4	3	7	3	.295	.406	.438	.998
1958	Chi-A	96	188	37	50	8	0	10	30	48	1	29	0	0	0	7	2	.266	.415	.468	.978
1959	Chi-A	127	277	40	61	5	3	9	45	62	1	55	0	1	4	7	6	.220	.359	.357	.983
1960	Chi-A	68	57	12	15	2	0	2	9	21	2	8	0	0	0	1	0	.263	.462	.404	.983
1961	Chi-A	20	15	1	1	0	0	0	1	3	0	5	0	0	1	1	0	.067	.211	.067	1.000
1961	**NY-A**	**22**	**18**	**3**	**2**	**0**	**0**	**0**	**0**	**8**	**0**	**3**	**0**	**0**	**0**	**0**	**1**	**.111**	**.385**	**.111**	**.969**
Career average		93	276	47	73	12	3	8	41	54	—	36	0	3	—	7	—	.265	.387	.417	.989
Yankee average		**22**	**18**	**3**	**2**	**0**	**0**	**0**	**0**	**8**	**0**	**3**	**0**	**0**	**0**	**0**	**1**	**.111**	**.385**	**.111**	**.969**
Career total		1668	4969	848	1318	215	46	149	740	980	7	653	8	55	25	133	39	.265	.385	.417	.989
Yankee total		**22**	**18**	**3**	**2**	**0**	**0**	**0**	**0**	**8**	**0**	**3**	**0**	**0**	**0**	**0**	**1**	**.111**	**.385**	**.111**	**.969**

Torres, Rosendo (Rusty) BORN ROSENDO TORRES (HERNANDEZ)

HEIGHT: 5'10" THROWS: RIGHT BATS: BOTH BORN: 9/30/1948 AQUADILLA, PUERTO RICO POSITIONS PLAYED: OF

YEAR	TEAM	GAMES	AB	RUNS	HITS	2B	3B	HR	RBI	BB	IBB	SO	HBP	SH	SF	SB	CS	BA	OBA	SA	FA
1971	NY-A	9	26	5	10	3	0	2	3	0	0	8	0	0	0	0	1	.385	.385	.731	1.000
1972	NY-A	80	199	15	42	7	0	3	13	18	3	44	1	1	0	0	4	.211	.280	.291	.978
1973	Cle-A	122	312	31	64	8	1	7	28	50	5	62	3	7	4	6	5	.205	.317	.304	.976
1974	Cle-A	108	150	19	28	2	0	3	12	13	1	24	0	4	2	2	1	.187	.248	.260	.959
1976	Cal-A	120	264	37	54	16	3	6	27	36	3	39	0	8	1	4	4	.205	.299	.356	.990
1977	Cal-A	58	77	9	12	1	1	3	10	10	0	18	0	1	1	0	1	.156	.250	.312	.984
1978	Chi-A	16	44	7	14	3	0	3	6	6	0	7	0	1	0	0	1	.318	.400	.591	.964
1979	Chi-A	90	170	26	43	5	0	8	24	23	1	37	2	8	0	0	0	.253	.349	.424	.976
1980	KC-A	51	72	10	12	0	0	0	3	8	0	7	0	0	0	1	3	.167	.250	.167	.973
Career average		73	146	18	31	5	1	4	14	18	1	27	1	3	1	1	2	.212	.301	.334	.978
Yankee average		**45**	**113**	**10**	**26**	**5**	**0**	**3**	**8**	**9**	**2**	**26**	**1**	**1**	**0**	**0**	**3**	**.231**	**.291**	**.342**	**.989**
Career total		654	1314	159	279	45	5	35	126	164	13	246	6	30	8	13	20	.212	.301	.334	.978
Yankee total		**89**	**225**	**20**	**52**	**10**	**0**	**5**	**16**	**18**	**3**	**52**	**1**	**1**	**0**	**0**	**5**	**.231**	**.291**	**.342**	**.989**

Tovar, Cesar Leonardo (Pepito) BORN CESAR LEONARDO PEREZ (TOVAR)

HEIGHT: 5'9" THROWS: RIGHT BATS: RIGHT BORN: 7/3/1940 CARACAS, VENEZUELA DIED: 7/14/1994 CARACAS, VENEZUELA POSITIONS PLAYED: 2B, 3B, OF

YEAR	TEAM	GAMES	AB	RUNS	HITS	2B	3B	HR	RBI	BB	IBB	SO	HBP	SH	SF	SB	CS	BA	OBA	SA	FA
1965	Min-A	18	25	3	5	1	0	0	2	2	0	3	0	0	0	2	0	.200	.259	.240	.800
1966	Min-A	134	465	57	121	19	5	2	41	44	1	50	4	7	7	16	6	.260	.325	.335	.978
1967	Min-A	164	649	98	173	32	7	6	47	46	0	51	13	13	5	19	11	.267	.335	.365	.875
1968	Min-A	157	613	89	167	31	6	6	47	34	0	41	17	5	4	35	13	.272	.326	.372	1.000
1969	Min-A	158	535	99	154	25	5	11	52	37	3	37	9	7	3	45	12	.288	.342	.415	.962
1970	Min-A	161	650	120	195	36	13	10	54	52	5	47	8	10	6	30	15	.300	.356	.442	.931
1971	Min-A	157	657	94	204	29	3	1	45	45	5	39	3	11	2	18	14	.311	.356	.368	.986
1972	Min-A	141	548	86	145	20	6	2	31	39	6	39	14	5	1	21	10	.265	.329	.334	.983
1973	Phi-N	97	328	49	88	18	4	1	21	29	2	35	5	0	2	6	4	.268	.335	.357	.928
1974	Tex-A	138	562	78	164	24	6	4	58	47	0	33	9	8	3	13	9	.292	.354	.377	.980
1975	Tex-A	102	427	53	110	16	0	3	28	27	0	25	3	5	1	16	11	.258	.306	.316	1.000
1975	Oak-A	19	26	5	6	1	0	0	3	3	0	3	0	0	0	4	0	.231	.310	.269	1.000
1976	Oak-A	29	45	1	8	0	0	0	4	4	0	4	2	1	0	1	2	.178	.275	.178	.958
1976	**NY-A**	**13**	**39**	**2**	**6**	**1**	**0**	**0**	**2**	**4**	**1**	**3**	**1**	**1**	**0**	**0**	**1**	**.154**	**.250**	**.179**	**1.000**
Career average		106	398	60	110	18	4	3	31	30	2	29	6	5	2	16	8	.278	.335	.368	.956
Yankee average		**13**	**39**	**2**	**6**	**1**	**0**	**0**	**2**	**4**	**1**	**3**	**1**	**1**	**0**	**0**	**1**	**.154**	**.250**	**.179**	**1.000**
Career total		1488	5569	834	1546	253	55	46	435	413	23	410	88	73	34	226	108	.278	.335	.368	.956
Yankee total		**13**	**39**	**2**	**6**	**1**	**0**	**0**	**2**	**4**	**1**	**3**	**1**	**1**	**0**	**0**	**1**	**.154**	**.250**	**.179**	**1.000**

Tresh, Thomas Michael

HEIGHT: 6'1" THROWS: RIGHT BATS: BOTH BORN: 9/20/1937 DETROIT, MICHIGAN POSITIONS PLAYED: SS, OF

YEAR	TEAM	GAMES	AB	RUNS	HITS	2B	3B	HR	RBI	BB	IBB	SO	HBP	SH	SF	SB	CS	BA	OBA	SA	FA
1961	NY-A	9	8	1	2	0	0	0	0	0	0	1	0	0	0	0	0	.250	.250	.250	1.000
1962	NY-A	157	622	94	178	26	5	20	93	67	3	74	8	8	7	4	8	.286	.359	.441	.970
1963	NY-A	145	520	91	140	28	5	25	71	83	5	79	4	2	5	3	3	.269	.371	.487	.981
1964	NY-A	153	533	75	131	25	5	16	73	73	3	110	7	3	4	13	0	.246	.342	.402	.996
1965	NY-A	156	602	94	168	29	6	26	74	59	4	92	5	2	0	5	2	.279	.348	.477	.970
1966	NY-A	151	537	76	125	12	4	27	68	86	5	89	6	1	7	5	4	.233	.341	.421	.985
1967	NY-A	130	448	45	98	23	3	14	53	50	0	86	4	3	3	1	0	.219	.301	.377	.972
1968	NY-A	152	507	60	99	18	3	11	52	76	8	97	4	1	2	10	5	.195	.304	.308	.951
1969	NY-A	45	143	13	26	5	2	1	9	17	2	23	0	1	0	2	1	.182	.269	.266	.980
1969	Det-A	94	331	46	74	13	1	13	37	39	0	47	2	0	5	2	2	.224	.305	.387	.955
Career average		110	392	55	97	17	3	14	49	51	3	65	4	2	3	4	2	.247	.337	.413	.976
Yankee average		**122**	**436**	**61**	**107**	**18**	**4**	**16**	**55**	**57**	**3**	**72**	**4**	**2**	**3**	**5**	**3**	**.247**	**.337**	**.413**	**.978**
Career total		1098	3920	549	967	166	33	140	493	511	30	651	38	21	28	43	23	.247	.337	.413	.976
Yankee total		**1098**	**3920**	**549**	**967**	**166**	**33**	**140**	**493**	**511**	**30**	**651**	**38**	**21**	**28**	**43**	**23**	**.247**	**.337**	**.413**	**.978**

Thomas Michael Tresh, of-ss, 1961–69

Tom Tresh was forced to shoulder the burden as the Yankees "can't miss" kid of the late 1950s and early 1960s. Not only did he accept it, he seemed to thrive on it.

Tresh, born September 30, 1937, in Detroit, Michigan, was an impressive minor league player almost from the start. The switch-hitting shortstop was the International League's Rookie of the Year in 1961 when he was first brought up by the Yankees.

Tresh earned back-to-back rookie awards by claiming the American League's version the next year. Hitting .286 with 20 home runs and 93 RBI for the Yankees, Tresh won the title by a wide margin.

Tresh had begun his career in New York as a power-hitting shortstop, but that was only because the Yankees' Tony Kubek was in the service for most of the season. When Kubek returned in August, the Yankees moved Tresh to the outfield, despite the fact that Tresh had made the All-Star team at shortstop.

In 1963, he was in the outfield, and he made the All-Star team again, hitting .269 with 25 home runs. He was a key performer in 1964 when the Yankees won their last pennant of the decade, and by 1965, he was the team's best player, leading New York in batting average, hits, doubles, triples, home runs, RBI and runs scored.

He was a power hitter. Three times in his career, he hit home runs from both sides of the plate in one game. In 1965, he hit three home runs in a game aganst the White Sox.

But 1966 was a bad year for Tresh. He injured his knee in spring training. The Yankee front office urged him to continue playing. Tresh obliged, and while he still hit with some power (27 home runs), his batting average dropped to .233.

Tresh battled injuries for the rest of his career after that. In 1969, he was traded to Detroit. When the Tigers released him in the spring of 1970, he retired. Following his retirement, Tresh worked as coach of Central Michigan University.

Triandos, Gus Constantine

HEIGHT: 6'3"   THROWS: RIGHT   BATS: RIGHT   BORN: 7/30/1930 SAN FRANCISCO, CALIFORNIA   POSITIONS PLAYED: C, 1B

YEAR	TEAM	GAMES	AB	RUNS	HITS	2B	3B	HR	RBI	BB	IBB	SO	HBP	SH	SF	SB	CS	BA	OBA	SA	FA
1953	NY-A	18	51	5	8	2	0	1	6	3	—	9	0	1	—	0	0	.157	.204	.255	.947
1954	NY-A	2	1	0	0	0	0	0	0	0	—	1	0	0	0	0	0	.000	.000	.000	.000
1955	Bal-A	140	481	47	133	17	3	12	65	40	4	55	2	3	3	0	0	.277	.333	.399	1.000
1956	Bal-A	131	452	47	126	18	1	21	88	48	4	73	2	3	4	0	0	.279	.348	.462	.983
1957	Bal-A	129	418	44	106	21	1	19	72	38	7	73	3	4	4	0	0	.254	.317	.445	.992
1958	Bal-A	137	474	59	116	10	0	30	79	60	4	65	1	2	7	1	0	.245	.327	.456	.987
1959	Bal-A	126	393	43	85	7	1	25	73	65	6	56	3	4	3	0	0	.216	.330	.430	.981
1960	Bal-A	109	364	36	98	18	0	12	54	41	5	62	1	5	2	0	0	.269	.343	.418	.989
1961	Bal-A	115	397	35	97	21	0	17	63	44	7	60	1	1	2	0	0	.244	.320	.426	.989
1962	Bal-A	66	207	20	33	7	0	6	23	29	2	43	0	0	1	0	0	.159	.262	.280	.985
1963	Det-A	106	327	28	78	13	0	14	41	32	4	67	6	1	3	0	0	.239	.315	.407	.998
1964	Phi-N	73	188	17	47	9	0	8	33	26	5	41	1	2	3	0	0	.250	.339	.426	.985
1965	Phi-N	30	82	3	14	2	0	0	4	9	1	17	0	0	0	0	0	.171	.253	.195	.975
1965	Hou-N	24	72	5	13	2	0	2	7	5	0	14	1	0	0	0	0	.181	.244	.292	.970
Career average		86	279	28	68	11	0	12	43	31	—	45	2	2	—	0	0	.244	.324	.413	.913
Yankee average		**10**	**26**	**3**	**4**	**1**	**0**	**1**	**3**	**2**	**—**	**5**	**0**	**1**	**—**	**0**	**0**	**.154**	**.200**	**.250**	**.474**
Career total		1206	3907	389	954	147	6	167	608	440	49	636	21	26	32	1	0	.244	.322	.413	.913
Yankee total		**20**	**52**	**5**	**8**	**2**	**0**	**1**	**6**	**3**	**—**	**10**	**0**	**1**	**0**	**0**	**0**	**.154**	**.200**	**.250**	**.474**

Truesdale, Frank Day

HEIGHT: 5'8" THROWS: RIGHT BATS: BOTH BORN: 3/31/1884, ST.LOUIS, MISSOURI DIED: 8/27/1943 ALBUQUERQUE, NEW MEXICO. POSITIONS PLAYED: 2B

YEAR	TEAM	GAMES	AB	RUNS	HITS	2B	3B	HR	RBI	BB	IBB	SO	HBP	SH	SF	SB	CS	BA	OBA	SA	FA
1910	StL-A	123	415	39	91	7	2	1	25	48	—	—	2	7	—	29	—	.219	.303	.253	.914
1911	StL-A	1	0	1	0	0	0	0	0	0	—	—	0	0	—	0	—	—	—	—	.000
1914	**NY-A**	**77**	**217**	**22**	**46**	**4**	**0**	**0**	**13**	**39**	**—**	**35**	**3**	**4**	**—**	**11**	**11**	**.212**	**.340**	**.230**	**.857**
1918	Bos-A	15	36	6	10	1	0	0	2	4	—	5	0	2	—	1	0	.278	.350	.306	.913
Career average		54	167	17	37	3	1	0	10	23	—	—	1	3	—	10	—	.220	.318	.249	.671
Yankee average		**77**	**217**	**22**	**46**	**4**	**0**	**0**	**13**	**39**	**—**	**35**	**3**	**4**	**—**	**11**	**11**	**.212**	**.340**	**.230**	**.857**
Career total		216	668	68	147	12	2	1	40	91	—	40	5	13	—	41	11	.220	.318	.249	.671
Yankee total		**77**	**217**	**22**	**46**	**4**	**0**	**0**	**13**	**39**	**—**	**35**	**3**	**4**	**—**	**11**	**11**	**.212**	**.340**	**.230**	**.857**

Turner, Christopher Wan

HEIGHT: 6'1" THROWS: RIGHT BATS: RIGHT BORN: 3/23/1969 BOWLING GREEN, KENTUCKY POSITIONS PLAYED: C

YEAR	TEAM	GAMES	AB	RUNS	HITS	2B	3B	HR	RBI	BB	IBB	SO	HBP	SH	SF	SB	CS	BA	OBA	SA	FA
1993	Cal-A	25	75	9	21	5	0	1	13	9	0	16	1	0	1	1	1	.280	.365	.387	.992
1994	Cal-A	58	149	23	36	7	1	1	12	10	0	29	1	1	2	3	0	.242	.290	.322	.997
1995	Cal-A	5	10	0	1	0	0	0	1	0	0	3	0	0	0	0	0	.100	.100	.100	1.000
1996	Cal-A	4	3	1	1	0	0	0	1	1	0	0	0	0	1	0	0	.333	.400	.333	1.000
1997	Ana-A	13	23	4	6	1	1	1	2	5	0	8	0	1	0	0	0	.261	.393	.522	1.000
1998	KC-A	4	9	0	0	0	0	0	0	0	0	4	0	0	0	0	0	.000	.000	.000	1.000
1999	Cle-A	12	21	3	4	0	0	0	0	1	0	8	0	0	0	1	0	.190	.227	.190	.964
2000	**NY-A**	**37**	**89**	**9**	**21**	**3**	**0**	**1**	**7**	**10**	**0**	**21**	**1**	**2**	**0**	**0**	**1**	**.236**	**.320**	**.303**	**1.000**
Career average		19	43	6	10	2	0	0	3	4	0	10	0	1	0	1	0	.227	.292	.306	.994
Yankee average		**37**	**89**	**9**	**21**	**3**	**0**	**1**	**7**	**10**	**0**	**21**	**1**	**2**	**0**	**0**	**1**	**.236**	**.320**	**.303**	**1.000**
Career total		133	304	40	69	11	2	3	23	27	0	73	2	4	3	4	1	.227	.292	.306	.994
Yankee total		**37**	**89**	**9**	**21**	**3**	**0**	**1**	**7**	**10**	**0**	**21**	**1**	**2**	**0**	**0**	**1**	**.236**	**.320**	**.303**	**1.000**

Valo, Elmer William

HEIGHT: 5'11" THROWS: RIGHT BATS: LEFT BORN: 3/5/1921 RIBNIK, CZECHOSLOVAKIA DIED: 7/19/1998 POSITIONS PLAYED: OF

YEAR	TEAM	GAMES	AB	RUNS	HITS	2B	3B	HR	RBI	BB	IBB	SO	HBP	SH	SF	SB	CS	BA	OBA	SA	FA
1940	Phi-A	6	23	6	8	0	0	0	0	3	—	0	0	0	—	2	0	.348	.423	.348	1.000
1941	Phi-A	15	50	13	21	0	1	2	6	4	—	2	0	0	—	0	0	.420	.463	.580	1.000
1942	Phi-A	133	459	64	115	13	10	2	40	70	—	21	4	9	—	13	8	.251	.355	.336	.964
1943	Phi-A	77	249	31	55	6	2	3	18	35	—	13	1	2	—	2	6	.221	.319	.297	.986
1946	Phi-A	108	348	59	107	21	6	1	31	60	—	18	1	2	—	9	8	.307	.411	.411	.974
1947	Phi-A	112	370	60	111	12	6	5	36	64	—	21	2	14	—	11	3	.300	.406	.405	.973
1948	Phi-A	113	383	72	117	17	4	3	46	81	—	13	4	7	—	10	6	.305	.432	.394	.983
1949	Phi-A	150	547	86	155	27	12	5	85	119	—	32	2	12	—	14	11	.283	.413	.404	.981
1950	Phi-A	129	446	62	125	16	5	10	46	82	—	22	7	7	—	12	7	.280	.400	.406	.982
1951	Phi-A	123	444	75	134	27	8	7	55	75	—	20	8	3	—	11	6	.302	.412	.446	.981
1952	Phi-A	129	388	69	109	26	4	5	47	101	—	16	2	4	—	12	11	.281	.432	.407	.962
1953	Phi-A	50	85	15	19	3	0	0	9	22	—	7	0	0	—	0	1	.224	.383	.259	1.000
1954	Phi-A	95	224	28	48	11	6	1	33	51	—	18	0	3	3	2	1	.214	.356	.330	.965
1955	KC-A	112	283	50	103	17	4	3	37	52	2	18	0	1	2	5	3	.364	.464	.484	.987
1956	KC-A	9	9	1	2	0	0	0	2	1	0	1	0	0	1	0	0	.222	.273	.222	.000
1956	Phi-N	98	291	40	84	13	3	5	37	48	6	21	3	1	2	7	6	.289	.392	.405	.966
1957	Bro-N	81	161	14	44	10	1	4	26	25	2	16	1	0	2	0	1	.273	.370	.422	1.000
1958	LA-N	65	101	9	25	2	1	1	14	12	0	11	0	0	2	0	1	.248	.322	.317	1.000
1959	Cle-A	34	24	3	7	0	0	0	5	7	1	0	0	0	2	0	0	.292	.424	.292	1.000
1960	**NY-A**	**8**	**5**	**1**	**0**	**0**	**0**	**0**	**0**	**2**	**0**	**1**	**0**	**0**	**0**	**0**	**0**	**.000**	**.286**	**.000**	**.000**
1960	Was-A	76	64	6	18	3	0	0	16	17	0	4	1	0	3	0	0	.281	.424	.328	1.000
1961	Min-A	33	32	0	5	2	0	0	4	3	1	3	1	0	0	0	0	.156	.250	.219	1.000
1961	Phi-N	50	43	4	8	2	0	1	8	8	—	6	1	0	0	0	0	.186	.327	.302	.000
Career average		79	219	33	62	10	3	3	26	41	—	12	2	3	—	5	3	.282	.399	.391	.857
Yankee average		**8**	**5**	**1**	**0**	**0**	**0**	**0**	**0**	**2**	**0**	**1**	**0**	**0**	**0**	**0**	**0**	**.000**	**.286**	**.000**	**.000**
Career total		1806	5029	768	1420	228	73	58	601	942	12	284	38	65	17	110	79	.282	.398	.391	.857
Yankee total		**8**	**5**	**1**	**0**	**0**	**0**	**0**	**0**	**2**	**0**	**1**	**0**	**0**	**0**	**0**	**0**	**.000**	**.286**	**.000**	**.000**

Vaughn, Robert

HEIGHT: 5'9"   THROWS: RIGHT   BATS: RIGHT   BORN: 6/4/1885 STAMFORD, NEW YORK   DIED: 4/11/1965, SEATTLE, WASH.   POSITIONS PLAYED: 2B, 3B, SS

YEAR	TEAM	GAMES	AB	RUNS	HITS	2B	3B	HR	RBI	BB	IBB	SO	HBP	SH	SF	SB	CS	BA	OBA	SA	FA
1909	**NY-A**	**5**	**14**	**1**	**2**	**0**	**0**	**0**	**0**	**1**	—	—	**0**	**0**	—	**1**	—	**.143**	**.200**	**.143**	**.882**
1915	StL-F	144	521	69	146	19	9	0	32	58	—	38	3	42	—	24	—	.280	.356	.351	.917
Career average		75	268	35	74	10	5	0	16	30	—	—	2	21	—	13	—	.277	.352	.346	.900
Yankee average		**5**	**14**	**1**	**2**	**0**	**0**	**0**	**0**	**1**	—	—	**0**	**0**	—	**1**	—	**.143**	**.200**	**.143**	**.882**
Career total		149	535	70	148	19	9	0	32	59	—	38	3	42	—	25	—	.277	.352	.346	.900
Yankee total		**5**	**14**	**1**	**2**	**0**	**0**	**0**	**0**	**1**	—	—	**0**	**0**	—	**1**	—	**.143**	**.200**	**.143**	**.882**

Veach, Robert Hayes

HEIGHT: 5'11"   THROWS: RIGHT   BATS: LEFT   BORN: 6/29/1888 ISLAND, KENTUCKY   DIED: 8/7/1945 DETROIT, MICHIGAN

YEAR	TEAM	GAMES	AB	RUNS	HITS	2B	3B	HR	RBI	BB	IBB	SO	HBP	SH	SF	SB	CS	BA	OBA	SA	FA
1912	Det-A	23	79	8	27	5	1	0	15	5	—	—	1	3	—	2	—	.342	.388	.430	.927
1913	Det-A	137	491	54	132	22	10	0	64	53	—	31	5	15	—	22	—	.269	.346	.354	.917
1914	Det-A	149	531	56	146	19	14	1	72	50	—	29	3	22	—	20	20	.275	.341	.369	.965
1915	Det-A	152	569	81	178	40	10	3	112	68	—	43	4	18	—	16	19	.313	.390	.434	.975
1916	Det-A	150	566	92	173	33	15	3	91	52	—	41	3	24	—	24	15	.306	.367	.433	.967
1917	Det-A	154	571	79	182	31	12	8	103	61	—	44	9	25	—	21	—	.319	.393	.457	.956
1918	Det-A	127	499	59	139	21	13	3	78	35	—	23	4	17	—	21	—	.279	.331	.391	.977
1919	Det-A	139	538	87	191	45	17	3	101	33	—	33	5	22	—	19	—	.355	.398	.519	.967
1920	Det-A	154	612	92	188	39	15	11	113	36	—	22	7	15	—	11	7	.307	.353	.474	.967
1921	Det-A	150	612	110	207	43	13	16	128	48	—	31	1	27	—	14	10	.338	.387	.529	.974
1922	Det-A	155	618	96	202	34	13	9	126	42	—	27	8	36	—	9	1	.327	.377	.468	.982
1923	Det-A	114	293	45	94	13	3	2	39	29	—	21	3	14	—	10	3	.321	.388	.406	.943
1924	Bos-A	142	519	77	153	35	9	5	99	47	—	18	5	28	—	5	5	.295	.359	.426	.956
1925	Bos-A	1	5	0	1	0	0	0	2	1	—	1	0	0	—	0	0	.200	.333	.200	1.000
1925	**NY-A**	**56**	**116**	**13**	**41**	**10**	**2**	**0**	**15**	**8**	—	**0**	**1**	**2**	—	**1**	**4**	**.353**	**.400**	**.474**	**.957**
1925	Was-A	18	37	4	9	3	0	0	8	3	—	3	0	3	—	0	0	.243	.300	.324	.923
Career average		114	416	60	129	25	9	4	73	36	—	—	4	17	—	12	—	.310	.370	.442	.960
Yankee average		**56**	**116**	**13**	**41**	**10**	**2**	**0**	**15**	**8**	—	**0**	**1**	**2**	—	**1**	**4**	**.353**	**.400**	**.474**	**.957**
Career total		1821	6656	953	2063	393	147	64	1166	571	—	367	59	271	—	195	84	.310	.370	.442	.960
Yankee total		**56**	**116**	**13**	**41**	**10**	**2**	**0**	**15**	**8**	—	**0**	**1**	**2**	—	**1**	**4**	**.353**	**.400**	**.474**	**.957**

Velarde, Randy Lee

HEIGHT: 6'0"   THROWS: RIGHT   BATS: RIGHT   BORN: 11/24/1962 MIDLAND, TEXAS   POSITIONS PLAYED: 2B, 3B, SS, OF

YEAR	TEAM	GAMES	AB	RUNS	HITS	2B	3B	HR	RBI	BB	IBB	SO	HBP	SH	SF	SB	CS	BA	OBA	SA	FA
1987	**NY-A**	**8**	**22**	**1**	**4**	**0**	**0**	**0**	**1**	**0**	**0**	**6**	**0**	**0**	**0**	**0**	**0**	**.182**	**.182**	**.182**	**.933**
1988	**NY-A**	**48**	**115**	**18**	**20**	**6**	**0**	**5**	**12**	**8**	**0**	**24**	**2**	**0**	**0**	**1**	**1**	**.174**	**.240**	**.357**	**.967**
1989	**NY-A**	**33**	**100**	**12**	**34**	**4**	**2**	**2**	**11**	**7**	**0**	**14**	**1**	**3**	**0**	**0**	**3**	**.340**	**.389**	**.480**	**.962**
1990	**NY-A**	**95**	**229**	**21**	**48**	**6**	**2**	**5**	**19**	**20**	**0**	**53**	**1**	**2**	**1**	**0**	**3**	**.210**	**.275**	**.319**	**.979**
1991	**NY-A**	**80**	**184**	**19**	**45**	**11**	**1**	**1**	**15**	**18**	**0**	**43**	**3**	**5**	**0**	**3**	**1**	**.245**	**.322**	**.332**	**1.000**
1992	**NY-A**	**121**	**412**	**57**	**112**	**24**	**1**	**7**	**46**	**38**	**1**	**78**	**4**	**2**	**4**	**7**	**2**	**.272**	**.333**	**.386**	**.974**
1993	**NY-A**	**85**	**226**	**28**	**68**	**13**	**2**	**7**	**24**	**18**	**2**	**39**	**4**	**3**	**2**	**2**	**2**	**.301**	**.360**	**.469**	**.932**
1994	**NY-A**	**77**	**280**	**47**	**78**	**16**	**1**	**9**	**34**	**22**	**0**	**61**	**4**	**2**	**2**	**4**	**2**	**.279**	**.338**	**.439**	**.944**
1995	**NY-A**	**111**	**367**	**60**	**102**	**19**	**1**	**7**	**46**	**55**	**0**	**64**	**4**	**3**	**3**	**5**	**1**	**.278**	**.375**	**.392**	**.977**
1996	Cal-A	136	530	82	151	27	3	14	54	70	0	118	5	4	2	7	7	.285	.372	.426	.906
1997	Ana-A	1	0	0	0	0	0	0	0	0	0	0	0	0	0	0	0	—	—	—	.000
1998	Ana-A	51	188	29	49	13	1	4	26	34	0	42	0	0	1	7	2	.261	.372	.404	.982
1999	Ana-A	95	376	57	115	15	4	9	48	43	0	56	0	0	0	13	4	.306	.377	.439	.986
1999	Oak-A	61	255	48	85	10	3	7	28	27	0	42	0	0	0	11	4	.333	.397	.478	.977
2000	Oak-A	122	485	82	135	23	0	12	41	54	0	95	3	3	1	9	3	.278	.354	.400	.982
Career average		87	290	43	81	14	2	7	31	32	0	57	2	2	1	5	3	.278	.352	.409	.900
Yankee average		**73**	**215**	**29**	**57**	**11**	**1**	**5**	**23**	**21**	**0**	**42**	**2**	**2**	**1**	**2**	**2**	**.264**	**.333**	**.392**	**.963**
Career total		1124	3769	561	1046	187	21	89	405	414	3	735	29	29	17	69	35	.278	.352	.409	.900
Yankee total		**658**	**1935**	**263**	**511**	**99**	**10**	**43**	**208**	**186**	**3**	**382**	**21**	**22**	**13**	**22**	**15**	**.264**	**.333**	**.392**	**.963**

Velez, Otoniel (Otto) BORN OTONIEL VELEZ (FRANCESCHI)

HEIGHT: 6'0" THROWS: RIGHT BATS: RIGHT BORN: 11/29/1950 PONCE, PUERTO RICO POSITIONS PLAYED: 1B, OF

YEAR	TEAM	GAMES	AB	RUNS	HITS	2B	3B	HR	RBI	BB	IBB	SO	HBP	SH	SF	SB	CS	BA	OBA	SA	FA
1973	**NY-A**	**23**	**77**	**9**	**15**	**4**	**0**	**2**	**7**	**15**	**0**	**24**	**0**	**0**	**0**	**0**	**1**	**.195**	**.326**	**.325**	**.959**
1974	**NY-A**	**27**	**67**	**9**	**14**	**1**	**1**	**2**	**10**	**15**	**1**	**24**	**0**	**0**	**2**	**0**	**0**	**.209**	**.345**	**.343**	**1.000**
1975	**NY-A**	**6**	**8**	**0**	**2**	**0**	**0**	**0**	**1**	**2**	**0**	**0**	**0**	**0**	**0**	**0**	**0**	**.250**	**.400**	**.250**	**1.000**
1976	**NY-A**	**49**	**94**	**11**	**25**	**6**	**0**	**2**	**10**	**23**	**1**	**26**	**0**	**0**	**0**	**0**	**0**	**.266**	**.410**	**.394**	**.978**
1977	Tor-A	120	360	50	92	19	3	16	62	65	1	87	1	2	6	4	2	.256	.366	.458	.973
1978	Tor-A	91	248	29	66	14	2	9	38	45	1	41	2	3	2	1	3	.266	.380	.448	1.000
1979	Tor-A	99	274	45	79	21	0	15	48	46	2	45	3	2	0	0	1	.288	.396	.529	1.000
1980	Tor-A	104	357	54	96	12	3	20	62	54	8	86	2	0	4	0	0	.269	.365	.487	.975
1981	Tor-A	80	240	32	51	9	2	11	28	55	3	60	3	2	2	0	3	.213	.363	.404	1.000
1982	Tor-A	28	52	4	10	1	0	1	5	13	0	15	0	0	0	1	0	.192	.354	.269	.000
1983	Cle-A	10	25	1	2	0	0	0	1	3	0	6	0	0	0	0	0	.080	.179	.080	.000
Career average		58	164	22	41	8	1	7	25	31	2	38	1	1	2	1	1	.251	.369	.441	.808
Yankee average		**26**	**62**	**7**	**14**	**3**	**0**	**2**	**7**	**14**	**1**	**19**	**0**	**0**	**1**	**0**	**0**	**.228**	**.366**	**.354**	**.984**
Career total		637	1802	244	452	87	11	78	272	336	17	414	11	9	16	6	10	.251	.369	.441	.808
Yankee total		**105**	**246**	**29**	**56**	**11**	**1**	**6**	**28**	**55**	**2**	**74**	**0**	**0**	**2**	**0**	**1**	**.228**	**.366**	**.354**	**.984**

Vick, Samuel Bruce

HEIGHT: 5'10" THROWS: RIGHT BATS: RIGHT BORN: 4/12/1895 BATESVILLE, MISSISSIPPI DIED: 8/17/1986 MEMPHIS, TENNESSEE POSITIONS PLAYED: OF

YEAR	TEAM	GAMES	AB	RUNS	HITS	2B	3B	HR	RBI	BB	IBB	SO	HBP	SH	SF	SB	CS	BA	OBA	SA	FA
1917	**NY-A**	**10**	**36**	**4**	**10**	**3**	**0**	**0**	**2**	**1**	**—**	**6**	**0**	**1**	**—**	**2**	**—**	**.278**	**.297**	**.361**	**.882**
1918	**NY-A**	**2**	**3**	**1**	**2**	**0**	**0**	**0**	**1**	**0**	**—**	**0**	**0**	**0**	**—**	**0**	**—**	**.667**	**.667**	**.667**	**.000**
1919	**NY-A**	**106**	**407**	**59**	**101**	**15**	**9**	**2**	**27**	**35**	**—**	**55**	**0**	**7**	**—**	**9**	**—**	**.248**	**.308**	**.344**	**.952**
1920	**NY-A**	**51**	**118**	**21**	**26**	**7**	**1**	**0**	**11**	**14**	**—**	**20**	**2**	**1**	**—**	**1**	**1**	**.220**	**.313**	**.297**	**.949**
1921	Bos-A	44	77	5	20	3	1	0	9	1	—	10	0	2	—	0	1	.260	.269	.325	1.000
Career average		43	128	18	32	6	2	0	10	10	—	18	0	2	—	2	—	.248	.305	.335	.757
Yankee average		**42**	**141**	**21**	**35**	**6**	**3**	**1**	**10**	**13**	**—**	**20**	**1**	**2**	**—**	**3**	**—**	**.246**	**.310**	**.337**	**.696**
Career total		213	641	90	159	28	11	2	50	51	—	91	2	11	—	12	2	.248	.305	.335	.757
Yankee total		**169**	**564**	**85**	**139**	**25**	**10**	**2**	**41**	**50**	**—**	**81**	**2**	**9**	**—**	**12**	**1**	**.246**	**.310**	**.337**	**.696**

Vizcaino, Jose Luis BORN JOSE LUIS VIZCAINO (PIMENTAL)

HEIGHT: 6'1" THROWS: RIGHT BATS: BOTH BORN: 3/26/1968 SAN CRISTOBAL, DOMINICAN REPUBLIC POSITIONS PLAYED: 2B, 3B, SS

YEAR	TEAM	GAMES	AB	RUNS	HITS	2B	3B	HR	RBI	BB	IBB	SO	HBP	SH	SF	SB	CS	BA	OBA	SA	FA
1989	LA-N	7	10	2	2	0	0	0	0	0	0	1	0	1	0	0	0	.200	.200	.200	.882
1990	LA-N	37	51	3	14	1	1	0	2	4	1	8	0	0	0	1	1	.275	.327	.333	1.000
1991	Chi-N	93	145	7	38	5	0	0	10	5	0	18	0	2	2	2	1	.262	.283	.297	.972
1992	Chi-N	86	285	25	64	10	4	1	17	14	2	35	0	5	1	3	0	.225	.260	.298	.969
1993	Chi-N	151	551	74	158	19	4	4	54	46	2	71	3	8	9	12	9	.287	.340	.358	.986
1994	NY-N	103	410	47	105	13	3	3	33	33	3	62	2	5	6	1	11	.256	.310	.324	.970
1995	NY-N	135	509	66	146	21	5	3	56	35	4	76	1	13	3	8	3	.287	.332	.365	1.000
1996	NY-N	96	363	47	110	12	6	1	32	28	0	58	3	6	2	9	5	.303	.356	.377	.986
1996	Cle-A	48	179	23	51	5	2	0	13	7	0	24	0	4	1	6	2	.285	.310	.335	.981
1997	SF-N	151	568	77	151	19	7	5	50	48	1	87	0	13	1	8	8	.266	.323	.350	1.000
1998	LA-N	67	237	30	62	9	0	3	29	17	0	35	0	10	2	7	3	.262	.309	.338	.985
1999	LA-N	94	266	27	67	9	0	1	29	20	0	23	0	9	2	2	1	.252	.302	.297	.988
2000	LA-N	40	93	9	19	2	1	0	4	10	3	15	1	2	0	0	0	.204	.288	.247	.000
2000	**NY-A**	**73**	**174**	**23**	**48**	**8**	**1**	**0**	**10**	**12**	**0**	**28**	**0**	**3**	**2**	**5**	**7**	**.276**	**.319**	**.333**	**1.000**
Career average		84	274	33	74	10	2	2	24	20	1	39	1	6	2	5	4	.269	.318	.338	.909
Yankee average		**73**	**174**	**23**	**48**	**8**	**1**	**0**	**10**	**12**	**0**	**28**	**0**	**3**	**2**	**5**	**7**	**.276**	**.319**	**.333**	**1.000**
Career total		1181	3841	460	1035	133	34	21	339	279	16	541	10	81	31	64	51	.269	.318	.338	.909
Yankee total		**73**	**174**	**23**	**48**	**8**	**1**	**0**	**10**	**12**	**0**	**28**	**0**	**3**	**2**	**5**	**7**	**.276**	**.319**	**.333**	**1.000**

Wakefield, Richard Cummings

HEIGHT: 6'4" THROWS: RIGHT BATS: LEFT BORN: 5/6/1921 CHICAGO, ILLINOIS DIED: 8/26/1985 REDFORD, MICHIGAN POSITIONS PLAYED: OF

YEAR	TEAM	GAMES	AB	RUNS	HITS	2B	3B	HR	RBI	BB	IBB	SO	HBP	SH	SF	SB	CS	BA	OBA	SA	FA
1941	Det-A	7	7	0	1	0	0	0	0	0	—	1	0	0	—	0	0	.143	.143	.143	1.000
1943	Det-A	155	633	91	200	38	8	7	79	62	—	60	0	2	—	4	5	.316	.377	.434	.959
1944	Det-A	78	276	53	98	15	5	12	53	55	—	29	1	0	—	2	2	.355	.464	.576	.963
1946	Det-A	111	396	64	106	11	5	12	59	59	—	55	1	2	—	3	5	.268	.364	.412	.964
1947	Det-A	112	368	59	104	15	5	8	51	80	—	44	1	4	—	1	4	.283	.412	.416	.950
1948	Det-A	110	322	50	89	20	5	11	53	70	—	55	0	1	—	0	1	.276	.406	.472	.948
1949	Det-A	59	126	17	26	3	1	6	19	32	—	24	0	1	—	0	0	.206	.367	.389	1.000
1950	**NY-A**	**3**	**2**	**0**	**1**	**0**	**0**	**0**	**1**	**1**	**—**	**1**	**0**	**0**	**—**	**0**	**0**	**.500**	**.667**	**.500**	**.000**
1952	NY-N	3	2	0	0	0	0	0	0	1	—	1	0	0	—	0	0	.000	.333	.000	.000
Career average		71	237	37	69	11	3	6	35	40	—	30	0	1	—	1	2	.293	.396	.447	.754
Yankee average		**3**	**2**	**0**	**1**	**0**	**0**	**0**	**1**	**1**	**—**	**1**	**0**	**0**	**—**	**0**	**0**	**.500**	**.667**	**.500**	**.000**
Career total		638	2132	334	625	102	29	56	315	360	—	270	3	10	—	10	17	.293	.396	.447	.754
Yankee total		**3**	**2**	**0**	**1**	**0**	**0**	**0**	**1**	**1**	**—**	**1**	**0**	**0**	**—**	**0**	**0**	**.500**	**.667**	**.500**	**.000**

Walker, Fred (Dixie *or* The People's Cherce)

HEIGHT: 6'1" THROWS: RIGHT BATS: LEFT BORN: 9/24/1910 VILLA RICA, GEORGIA DIED: 5/17/1982 BIRMINGHAM, ALABAMA POSITIONS PLAYED: OF

YEAR	TEAM	GAMES	AB	RUNS	HITS	2B	3B	HR	RBI	BB	IBB	SO	HBP	SH	SF	SB	CS	BA	OBA	SA	FA
1931	**NY-A**	**2**	**10**	**1**	**3**	**2**	**0**	**0**	**1**	**0**	**—**	**4**	**0**	**0**	**—**	**0**	**0**	**.300**	**.300**	**.500**	**1.000**
1933	**NY-A**	**98**	**328**	**68**	**90**	**15**	**7**	**15**	**51**	**26**	**—**	**28**	**1**	**4**	**—**	**2**	**2**	**.274**	**.330**	**.500**	**.962**
1934	**NY-A**	**17**	**17**	**2**	**2**	**0**	**0**	**0**	**0**	**1**	**—**	**3**	**0**	**1**	**—**	**0**	**0**	**.118**	**.167**	**.118**	**1.000**
1935	**NY-A**	**8**	**13**	**1**	**2**	**1**	**0**	**0**	**1**	**0**	**—**	**1**	**0**	**0**	**—**	**0**	**0**	**.154**	**.154**	**.231**	**.750**
1936	**NY-A**	**6**	**20**	**3**	**7**	**0**	**2**	**1**	**5**	**1**	**—**	**3**	**0**	**0**	**—**	**1**	**1**	**.350**	**.381**	**.700**	**1.000**
1936	Chi-A	26	70	12	19	2	0	0	11	14	—	6	1	0	—	1	0	.271	.400	.300	1.000
1937	Chi-A	154	593	105	179	28	16	9	95	78	—	26	0	17	—	1	2	.302	.383	.444	.950
1938	Det-A	127	454	84	140	27	6	6	43	65	—	32	1	6	—	5	4	.308	.396	.434	.979
1939	Det-A	43	154	30	47	4	5	4	19	15	—	8	0	8	—	4	—	.305	.367	.474	.970
1939	Bro-N	61	225	27	63	6	4	2	38	20	—	10	0	7	—	1	—	.280	.339	.369	.968
1940	Bro-N	143	556	75	171	37	8	6	66	42	—	21	1	6	—	3	—	.308	.357	.435	.973
1941	Bro-N	148	531	88	165	32	8	9	71	70	—	18	0	5	—	4	—	.311	.391	.452	.976
1942	Bro-N	118	393	57	114	28	1	6	54	47	—	15	1	10	—	1	—	.290	.367	.412	.986
1943	Bro-N	138	540	83	163	32	6	5	71	49	—	24	3	4	—	3	3	.302	.363	.411	.969
1944	Bro-N	147	535	77	191	37	8	13	91	72	—	27	1	3	—	6	0	.357	.434	.529	.962
1945	Bro-N	154	607	102	182	42	9	8	124	75	—	16	5	1	—	6	—	.300	.381	.438	.992
1946	Bro-N	150	576	80	184	29	9	9	116	67	—	28	1	2	—	14	5	.319	.391	.448	.969
1947	Bro-N	148	529	77	162	31	3	9	94	97	—	26	1	10	—	6	2	.306	.415	.427	.964
1948	Pit-N	129	408	39	129	19	3	2	54	52	—	18	0	5	—	1	—	.316	.393	.392	.977
1949	Pit-N	88	181	26	51	4	1	1	18	26	—	11	0	4	—	0	—	.282	.372	.331	.900
Career average		95	337	52	103	19	5	5	51	41	—	16	1	5	—	3	—	.306	.383	.437	.962
Yankee average		**26**	**78**	**15**	**21**	**4**	**2**	**3**	**12**	**6**	**—**	**8**	**0**	**1**	**—**	**1**	**1**	**.268**	**.319**	**.485**	**.942**
Career total		1905	6740	1037	2064	376	96	105	1023	817	—	325	16	93	—	59	19	.306	.383	.437	.962
Yankee total		**131**	**388**	**75**	**104**	**18**	**9**	**16**	**58**	**28**	**—**	**39**	**1**	**5**	**—**	**3**	**3**	**.268**	**.319**	**.485**	**.942**

Walker, William Curtis

HEIGHT: 5'9" THROWS: RIGHT BATS: LEFT BORN: 7/3/1896 BEEVILLE, TEXAS DIED: 12/9/1955 BEEVILLE, TEXAS POSITIONS PLAYED: OF

YEAR	TEAM	GAMES	AB	RUNS	HITS	2B	3B	HR	RBI	BB	IBB	SO	HBP	SH	SF	SB	CS	BA	OBA	SA	FA
1919	**NY-A**	**1**	**1**	**0**	**0**	**0**	**0**	**0**	**0**	**0**	**—**	**0**	**0**	**0**	**—**	**0**	**—**	**.000**	**.000**	**.000**	**.000**
1920	NY-N	8	14	0	1	0	0	0	0	1	—	3	0	0	—	0	—	.071	.133	.071	1.000
1921	NY-N	64	192	30	55	13	5	3	35	15	—	8	0	7	—	4	3	.286	.338	.453	.978
1921	Phi-N	21	77	11	26	2	1	0	8	5	—	5	0	3	—	0	2	.338	.378	.390	.970
1922	Phi-N	148	581	102	196	36	11	12	89	56	—	46	4	14	—	11	4	.337	.399	.499	.955
1923	Phi-N	140	527	66	148	26	5	5	66	45	—	31	0	8	—	12	12	.281	.337	.378	.947
1924	Phi-N	24	71	11	21	6	1	1	8	7	—	4	0	2	—	0	1	.296	.359	.451	.900
1924	Cin-N	109	397	55	119	21	10	4	46	44	—	15	1	10	—	7	5	.300	.371	.433	.978
1925	Cin-N	145	509	86	162	22	16	6	71	57	—	31	0	12	—	14	11	.318	.387	.460	.983
1926	Cin-N	155	571	83	175	24	20	6	78	60	—	31	0	30	—	3	—	.306	.372	.450	.961
1927	Cin-N	146	527	60	154	16	10	6	80	47	—	19	0	27	—	5	—	.292	.350	.395	.957
1928	Cin-N	123	427	64	119	15	12	6	73	49	—	14	1	25	—	19	—	.279	.354	.412	.955
1929	Cin-N	141	492	76	154	28	15	7	83	85	—	17	2	22	—	17	—	.313	.416	.474	.969
1930	Cin-N	134	472	74	145	26	11	8	51	64	—	30	1	10	—	4	—	.307	.391	.460	.965

(continued)

(continued)

																		BA	OBA	SA	FA
Career average	97	347	51	105	17	8	5	49	38	—	18	1	12	—	7	—	.304	.374	.440	.894
Yankee average	**1**	**1**	**0**	**0**	**0**	**0**	**0**	**0**	**0**	**—**	**0**	**0**	**0**	**—**	**0**	**—**	**.000**	**.000**	**.000**	**.000**
Career total	1359	4858	718	1475	235	117	64	688	535	—	254	9	170	—	96	38	.304	.374	.440	.894
Yankee total	**1**	**1**	**0**	**0**	**0**	**0**	**0**	**0**	**0**	**—**	**0**	**0**	**0**	**—**	**0**	**—**	**.000**	**.000**	**.000**	**.000**

Walsh, James Charles (Jimmy)

HEIGHT: 5'10" THROWS: RIGHT BATS: LEFT BORN: 9/22/1885 KALLILA, IRELAND DIED: 7/3/1962 SYRACUSE, NEW YORK POSITIONS PLAYED: 3B, OF

YEAR	TEAM	GAMES	AB	RUNS	HITS	2B	3B	HR	RBI	BB	IBB	SO	HBP	SH	SF	SB	CS	BA	OBA	SA	FA
1912	Phi-A	31	107	11	27	8	2	0	15	12	—	—	0	2	—	7	—	.252	.328	.364	.947
1913	Phi-A	97	303	56	77	16	5	0	27	38	—	40	2	12	—	15	—	.254	.341	.340	.961
1914	**NY-A**	**43**	**136**	**13**	**26**	**1**	**3**	**1**	**11**	**29**	**—**	**21**	**0**	**1**	**—**	**6**	**9**	**.191**	**.333**	**.265**	**.977**
1914	Phi-A	68	216	35	51	11	6	3	36	30	—	27	4	23	—	6	12	.236	.340	.384	.971
1915	Phi-A	117	417	48	86	15	6	1	20	57	—	64	3	11	—	22	12	.206	.306	.278	.976
1916	Phi-A	114	390	42	91	13	6	1	27	54	—	36	2	16	—	27	16	.233	.330	.305	1.000
1916	Bos-A	14	17	5	3	1	0	0	2	4	—	2	0	2	—	3	—	.176	.333	.235	1.000
1917	Bos-A	57	185	25	49	6	3	0	12	25	—	14	0	2	—	6	—	.265	.352	.330	.982
Career average	68	221	29	51	9	4	1	19	31	—	1	9	—	12	—	.232	.330	.317	.977
Yankee average	**43**	**136**	**13**	**26**	**1**	**3**	**1**	**11**	**29**	**—**	**21**	**0**	**1**	**—**	**6**	**9**	**.191**	**.333**	**.265**	**.977**
Career total	541	1771	235	410	71	31	6	150	249	—	204	11	69	—	92	49	.232	.330	.317	.977
Yankee total	**43**	**136**	**13**	**26**	**1**	**3**	**1**	**11**	**29**	**—**	**21**	**0**	**1**	**—**	**6**	**9**	**.191**	**.333**	**.265**	**.977**

Walters, Alfred John (Roxy)

HEIGHT: 5'8" THROWS: RIGHT BATS: RIGHT BORN: 11/5/1892 SAN FRANCISCO, CALIFORNIA DIED: 6/3/1956 ALAMEDA, CALIFORNIA POSITIONS PLAYED: C

YEAR	TEAM	GAMES	AB	RUNS	HITS	2B	3B	HR	RBI	BB	IBB	SO	HBP	SH	SF	SB	CS	BA	OBA	SA	FA
1915	**NY-A**	**2**	**3**	**0**	**1**	**0**	**0**	**0**	**0**	**0**	**—**	**0**	**0**	**0**	**—**	**0**	**0**	**.333**	**.333**	**.333**	**1.000**
1916	**NY-A**	**66**	**203**	**13**	**54**	**9**	**3**	**0**	**23**	**14**	**—**	**42**	**2**	**6**	**—**	**2**	**—**	**.266**	**.320**	**.340**	**.974**
1917	**NY-A**	**61**	**171**	**16**	**45**	**2**	**0**	**0**	**14**	**9**	**—**	**22**	**1**	**6**	**—**	**2**	**—**	**.263**	**.304**	**.275**	**.968**
1918	**NY-A**	**64**	**191**	**18**	**38**	**5**	**1**	**0**	**12**	**9**	**—**	**18**	**1**	**4**	**—**	**3**	**—**	**.199**	**.239**	**.236**	**.933**
1919	Bos-A	48	135	7	26	2	0	0	9	7	—	15	5	7	—	1	—	.193	.259	.207	.982
1920	Bos-A	88	258	25	51	11	1	0	28	30	—	21	9	11	—	2	2	.198	.303	.248	.980
1921	Bos-A	54	169	17	34	4	1	0	14	10	—	11	2	5	—	3	0	.201	.254	.237	.990
1922	Bos-A	38	98	4	19	2	0	0	6	6	—	8	0	5	—	0	0	.194	.244	.214	.967
1923	Bos-A	40	104	9	26	4	0	0	5	2	—	6	0	11	—	0	2	.250	.264	.288	1.000
1924	Cle-A	32	74	10	19	2	0	0	5	10	—	6	0	3	—	0	1	.257	.345	.284	1.000
1925	Cle-A	5	20	0	4	0	0	0	0	0	—	2	0	0	—	0	0	.200	.200	.200	1.000
Career average	45	130	11	29	4	1	0	11	9	—	14	2	5	—	1	—	.222	.281	.259	.981
Yankee average	**48**	**142**	**12**	**35**	**4**	**1**	**0**	**12**	**8**	**—**	**21**	**1**	**4**	**—**	**2**	**—**	**.243**	**.288**	**.285**	**.969**
Career total	498	1426	119	317	41	6	0	116	97	—	151	20	58	—	13	5	.222	.281	.259	.981
Yankee total	**193**	**568**	**47**	**138**	**16**	**4**	**0**	**49**	**32**	**—**	**82**	**4**	**16**	**—**	**7**	**0**	**.243**	**.288**	**.285**	**.969**

Walton, Daniel James (Danny *or* Mickey)

HEIGHT: 6'0 THROWS: RIGHT BATS: RIGHT BORN: 7/14/1947 LOS ANGELES, CALIFORNIA POSITIONS PLAYED: OF

YEAR	TEAM	GAMES	AB	RUNS	HITS	2B	3B	HR	RBI	BB	IBB	SO	HBP	SH	SF	SB	CS	BA	OBA	SA	FA
1968	Hou-N	2	2	0	0	0	0	0	0	0	0	1	0	0	0	0	0	.000	.000	.000	.000
1969	Sea-A	23	92	12	20	1	2	3	10	5	0	26	3	0	2	2	0	.217	.275	.370	.976
1970	Mil-A	117	397	32	102	20	1	17	66	51	4	126	6	0	1	2	3	.257	.349	.441	.965
1971	Mil-A	30	69	5	14	3	0	2	9	7	0	22	1	0	0	0	0	.203	.286	.333	.923
1971	**NY-A**	**5**	**14**	**1**	**2**	**0**	**0**	**1**	**2**	**0**	**0**	**7**	**0**	**0**	**0**	**0**	**0**	**.143**	**.143**	**.357**	**1.000**
1973	Min-A	37	96	13	17	1	1	4	8	17	0	28	0	0	0	0	0	.177	.301	.333	1.000
1975	Min-A	42	63	4	11	2	0	1	8	4	2	18	0	0	0	0	0	.175	.224	.254	1.000
1976	LA-N	18	15	0	2	0	0	0	2	1	0	2	0	0	1	0	0	.133	.176	.133	.000
1977	Hou-N	13	21	0	4	0	0	0	1	0	0	5	0	0	0	0	0	.190	.190	.190	.956
1980	Tex-A	10	10	2	2	0	0	0	1	3	0	5	0	0	0	0	0	.200	.385	.255	.000
Career average	30	78	7	17	3	0	3	11	9	1	24	1	0	0	0	0	.223	.309	.376	.682
Yankee average	**5**	**14**	**1**	**2**	**0**	**0**	**1**	**2**	**0**	**0**	**7**	**0**	**0**	**0**	**0**	**0**	**.143**	**.143**	**.357**	**1.000**
Career total	297	779	69	174	27	4	28	107	88	6	240	10	0	4	4	3	.223	.309	.376	.682
Yankee total	**5**	**14**	**1**	**2**	**0**	**0**	**1**	**2**	**0**	**0**	**7**	**0**	**0**	**0**	**0**	**0**	**.143**	**.143**	**.357**	**1.000**

Waner, Paul Glee (Big Poison)

HEIGHT: 5'8"   THROWS: LEFT   BATS: LEFT   BORN: 4/16/1903 HARRAH, OKLAHOMA   DIED: 8/29/1965 SARASOTA, FLORIDA   POSITIONS PLAYED: 1B, OF

YEAR	TEAM	GAMES	AB	RUNS	HITS	2B	3B	HR	RBI	BB	IBB	SO	HBP	SH	SF	SB	CS	BA	OBA	SA	FA
1926	Pit-N	144	536	101	180	35	22	8	79	66	—	19	4	12	—	11	—	.336	.413	.528	.976
1927	Pit-N	155	623	114	237	42	18	9	131	60	—	14	3	23	—	5	—	.380	.437	.549	.980
1928	Pit-N	152	602	142	223	50	19	6	86	77	—	16	5	13	—	6	—	.370	.446	.547	.984
1929	Pit-N	151	596	131	200	43	15	15	100	89	—	24	3	15	—	15	—	.336	.424	.534	1.000
1930	Pit-N	145	589	117	217	32	18	8	77	57	—	18	4	15	—	18	—	.368	.428	.525	.959
1931	Pit-N	150	559	88	180	35	10	6	70	73	—	21	4	10	—	6	—	.322	.404	.453	1.000
1932	Pit-N	154	630	107	215	62	10	8	82	56	—	24	2	9	—	13	—	.341	.397	.510	.974
1933	Pit-N	154	618	101	191	38	16	7	70	60	—	20	2	14	—	3	—	.309	.372	.456	.981
1934	Pit-N	146	599	122	217	32	16	14	90	68	—	24	2	8	—	8	—	.362	.429	.539	.985
1935	Pit-N	139	549	98	176	29	12	11	78	61	—	22	3	10	—	2	—	.321	.392	.477	.983
1936	Pit-N	148	585	107	218	53	9	5	94	74	—	29	3	4	—	7	—	.373	.446	.520	.960
1937	Pit-N	154	619	94	219	30	9	2	74	63	—	34	0	8	—	4	—	.354	.413	.441	.938
1938	Pit-N	148	625	77	175	31	6	6	69	47	—	28	1	7	—	2	—	.280	.331	.378	.977
1939	Pit-N	125	461	62	151	30	6	3	45	35	—	18	0	10	—	0	—	.328	.375	.438	.978
1940	Pit-N	89	238	32	69	16	1	1	32	23	—	14	0	0	—	0	—	.290	.352	.378	.985
1941	Bro-N	11	35	5	6	0	0	0	4	8	—	0	0	1	—	0	—	.171	.326	.171	.923
1941	Bos-N	95	294	40	82	10	2	2	46	47	—	14	0	0	—	1	—	.279	.378	.347	.909
1942	Bos-N	114	333	43	86	17	1	1	39	62	—	20	1	8	—	2	—	.258	.376	.324	.969
1943	Bro-N	82	225	29	70	16	0	1	26	35	—	9	1	6	—	0	1	.311	.406	.396	.960
1944	Bro-N	83	136	16	39	4	1	0	16	27	—	7	0	1	—	0	0	.287	.405	.331	.983
1944	**NY-A**	**9**	**7**	**1**	**1**	**0**	**0**	**0**	**1**	**2**	**—**	**1**	**0**	**0**	**—**	**1**	**0**	**.143**	**.333**	**.143**	**.000**
1945	**NY-A**	**1**	**0**	**0**	**0**	**0**	**0**	**0**	**0**	**1**	**—**	**0**	**0**	**0**	**—**	**0**	**0**	**—**	**1.000**	**—**	**.000**
Career average		116	430	74	143	28	9	5	60	50	—	17	2	8	—	5	—	.333	.404	.473	.882
Yankee average		**5**	**4**	**1**	**1**	**0**	**0**	**0**	**1**	**2**	**—**	**1**	**0**	**0**	**—**	**1**	**0**	**.143**	**.400**	**.143**	**.000**
Career total		2549	9459	1627	3152	605	191	113	1309	1091	—	376	38	174	—	104	1	.333	.404	.473	.882
Yankee total		**10**	**7**	**1**	**1**	**0**	**0**	**0**	**1**	**3**	**—**	**1**	**0**	**0**	**—**	**1**	**0**	**.143**	**.400**	**.143**	**.000**

Wanninger, Paul Louis (Pee Wee)

HEIGHT: 5'7"   THROWS: RIGHT   BATS: LEFT   BORN: 12/12/1902 BIRMINGHAM, ALABAMA   DIED: 3/7/1981 N.AUGUSTA, S. CAROLINA   POSITIONS PLAYED: 3B, SS

YEAR	TEAM	GAMES	AB	RUNS	HITS	2B	3B	HR	RBI	BB	IBB	SO	HBP	SH	SF	SB	CS	BA	OBA	SA	FA
1925	**NY-A**	**117**	**403**	**35**	**95**	**13**	**6**	**1**	**22**	**11**	**—**	**34**	**0**	**13**	**—**	**3**	**5**	**.236**	**.256**	**.305**	**1.000**
1927	Bos-A	18	60	4	12	0	0	0	1	6	—	2	1	0	—	2	4	.200	.284	.200	.890
1927	Cin-N	28	93	14	23	2	2	0	8	6	—	7	0	5	—	0	—	.247	.293	.312	.953
Career average		54	185	18	43	5	3	0	10	8	—	14	0	6	—	2	—	.234	.266	.295	.948
Yankee average		**117**	**403**	**35**	**95**	**13**	**6**	**1**	**22**	**11**	**—**	**34**	**0**	**13**	**—**	**3**	**5**	**.236**	**.256**	**.305**	**1.000**
Career total		163	556	53	130	15	8	1	31	23	—	43	1	18	—	5	9	.234	.266	.295	.948
Yankee total		**117**	**403**	**35**	**95**	**13**	**6**	**1**	**22**	**11**	**—**	**34**	**0**	**13**	**—**	**3**	**5**	**.236**	**.256**	**.305**	**1.000**

Ward, Aaron Lee

HEIGHT: 5'10"   THROWS: RIGHT   BATS: RIGHT   BORN: 8/28/1896 BOONEVILLE, ARKANSAS   DIED: 1/30/1961 NEW ORLEANS, LA.   POSITIONS PLAYED: 2B, 3B, SS

YEAR	TEAM	GAMES	AB	RUNS	HITS	2B	3B	HR	RBI	BB	IBB	SO	HBP	SH	SF	SB	CS	BA	OBA	SA	FA
1917	**NY-A**	**8**	**26**	**0**	**3**	**0**	**0**	**0**	**1**	**1**	**—**	**5**	**0**	**0**	**—**	**0**	**—**	**.115**	**.148**	**.115**	**.926**
1918	**NY-A**	**20**	**32**	**2**	**4**	**1**	**0**	**0**	**1**	**2**	**—**	**7**	**0**	**2**	**—**	**1**	**—**	**.125**	**.176**	**.156**	**1.000**
1919	**NY-A**	**27**	**34**	**5**	**7**	**2**	**0**	**0**	**2**	**5**	**—**	**6**	**0**	**1**	**—**	**0**	**—**	**.206**	**.308**	**.265**	**1.000**
1920	**NY-A**	**127**	**496**	**62**	**127**	**18**	**7**	**11**	**54**	**33**	**—**	**84**	**1**	**17**	**—**	**7**	**5**	**.256**	**.304**	**.387**	**.975**
1921	**NY-A**	**153**	**556**	**77**	**170**	**30**	**10**	**5**	**75**	**42**	**—**	**68**	**8**	**29**	**—**	**6**	**8**	**.306**	**.363**	**.423**	**.961**
1922	**NY-A**	**154**	**558**	**69**	**149**	**19**	**5**	**7**	**68**	**45**	**—**	**64**	**6**	**32**	**—**	**6**	**4**	**.267**	**.328**	**.357**	**1.000**
1923	**NY-A**	**152**	**567**	**79**	**161**	**26**	**11**	**10**	**82**	**56**	**—**	**65**	**3**	**14**	**—**	**8**	**8**	**.284**	**.351**	**.422**	**.980**
1924	**NY-A**	**120**	**400**	**42**	**101**	**13**	**10**	**8**	**66**	**40**	**—**	**45**	**2**	**23**	**—**	**1**	**4**	**.253**	**.324**	**.395**	**.973**
1925	**NY-A**	**125**	**439**	**41**	**108**	**22**	**3**	**4**	**38**	**49**	**—**	**49**	**3**	**9**	**—**	**1**	**4**	**.246**	**.326**	**.337**	**.966**
1926	**NY-A**	**22**	**31**	**5**	**10**	**2**	**0**	**0**	**3**	**2**	**—**	**6**	**0**	**1**	**—**	**0**	**0**	**.323**	**.364**	**.387**	**1.000**
1927	Chi-A	145	463	75	125	25	8	5	56	63	—	56	2	23	—	6	5	.270	.360	.391	.963
1928	Cle-A	6	9	0	1	0	0	0	0	1	—	2	0	1	—	0	0	.111	.200	.111	1.000
Career average		88	301	38	81	13	5	4	37	28	—	38	2	13	—	3	—	.268	.335	.383	.979
Yankee average		**91**	**314**	**38**	**84**	**13**	**5**	**5**	**39**	**28**	**—**	**40**	**2**	**13**	**—**	**3**	**—**	**.268**	**.331**	**.382**	**.978**
Career total		1059	3611	457	966	158	54	50	446	339	—	457	25	152	—	36	38	.268	.335	.383	.979
Yankee total		**908**	**3139**	**382**	**840**	**133**	**46**	**45**	**390**	**275**	**—**	**399**	**23**	**128**	**—**	**30**	**33**	**.268**	**.331**	**.382**	**.978**

Ward, Gary Lamell

HEIGHT: 6'2" THROWS: RIGHT BATS: RIGHT BORN: 12/6/1953 LOS ANGELES, CALIFORNIA POSITIONS PLAYED: 1B, OF

YEAR	TEAM	GAMES	AB	RUNS	HITS	2B	3B	HR	RBI	BB	IBB	SO	HBP	SH	SF	SB	CS	BA	OBA	SA	FA
1979	Min-A	10	14	2	4	0	0	0	1	3	0	3	0	0	0	0	1	.286	.412	.286	1.000
1980	Min-A	13	41	11	19	6	2	1	10	3	1	6	0	1	1	0	0	.463	.489	.780	1.000
1981	Min-A	85	295	42	78	7	6	3	29	28	4	48	0	1	1	0	0	.264	.325	.359	.975
1982	Min-A	152	570	85	165	33	7	28	91	37	4	105	1	1	7	5	2	.289	.330	.519	.989
1983	Min-A	157	623	76	173	34	5	19	88	44	2	98	3	1	5	13	1	.278	.326	.440	.978
1984	Tex-A	155	602	97	171	21	7	21	79	55	3	95	0	1	1	8	1	.284	.343	.447	.987
1985	Tex-A	154	593	77	170	28	7	15	70	39	3	97	1	0	5	7	5	.287	.329	.433	.969
1986	Tex-A	105	380	54	120	15	2	5	51	31	3	72	4	1	5	26	7	.316	.372	.405	.996
1987	**NY-A**	**146**	**529**	**65**	**131**	**22**	**1**	**16**	**78**	**33**	**2**	**101**	**1**	**2**	**4**	**12**	**8**	**.248**	**.291**	**.384**	**.985**
1988	**NY-A**	**91**	**231**	**26**	**52**	**8**	**0**	**4**	**24**	**24**	**4**	**41**	**2**	**4**	**1**	**9**	**1**	**.225**	**.302**	**.312**	**.992**
1989	**NY-A**	**8**	**17**	**3**	**5**	**1**	**0**	**0**	**1**	**3**	**1**	**5**	**0**	**0**	**0**	**0**	**1**	**.294**	**.400**	**.353**	**1.000**
1989	Det-A	105	275	24	69	10	2	9	29	21	1	54	0	0	0	0	0	.251	.300	.400	.986
1990	Det-A	106	309	32	79	11	2	9	46	30	0	50	1	2	2	1	3	.256	.322	.392	1.000
Career average		99	345	46	95	15	3	10	46	27	2	60	1	1	3	6	2	.276	.328	.425	.989
Yankee average		**82**	**259**	**31**	**63**	**10**	**0**	**7**	**34**	**20**	**2**	**49**	**1**	**2**	**2**	**3**	**1**	**.242**	**.297**	**.362**	**.992**
Career total		1287	4479	594	1236	196	41	130	597	351	28	775	13	14	35	83	30	.276	.328	.425	.989
Yankee total		**245**	**777**	**94**	**188**	**31**	**1**	**20**	**103**	**60**	**7**	**147**	**3**	**6**	**5**	**9**	**2**	**.242**	**.297**	**.362**	**.992**

Ward, Peter Thomas

HEIGHT: 6'1" THROWS: RIGHT BATS: LEFT BORN: 7/26/1939 MONTREAL, QUEBEC, CANADA POSITIONS PLAYED: 1B, 3B, OF

YEAR	TEAM	GAMES	AB	RUNS	HITS	2B	3B	HR	RBI	BB	IBB	SO	HBP	SH	SF	SB	CS	BA	OBA	SA	FA
1962	Bal-A	8	21	1	3	2	0	0	2	4	0	5	0	0	0	0	0	.143	.280	.238	1.000
1963	Chi-A	157	600	80	177	34	6	22	84	52	1	77	5	4	6	7	6	.295	.353	.482	1.000
1964	Chi-A	144	539	61	152	28	3	23	94	56	11	76	2	3	7	1	1	.282	.348	.473	.958
1965	Chi-A	138	507	62	125	25	3	10	57	56	11	83	6	2	3	2	4	.247	.327	.367	1.000
1966	Chi-A	84	251	22	55	7	1	3	28	24	0	49	3	1	5	3	1	.219	.290	.291	.978
1967	Chi-A	146	467	49	109	16	2	18	62	61	9	109	11	0	3	3	2	.233	.334	.392	.994
1968	Chi-A	125	399	43	86	15	0	15	50	76	8	85	10	1	1	4	3	.216	.354	.366	.946
1969	Chi-A	105	199	22	49	7	0	6	32	33	1	38	3	1	2	0	0	.246	.359	.372	.994
1970	**NY-A**	**66**	**77**	**5**	**20**	**2**	**2**	**1**	**18**	**9**	**1**	**17**	**0**	**0**	**1**	**0**	**0**	**.260**	**.359**	**.372**	**.994**
Career average		108	340	38	86	15	2	11	47	41	5	60	4	1	3	2	2	.254	.339	.405	.986
Yankee average		**66**	**77**	**5**	**20**	**2**	**2**	**1**	**18**	**9**	**0**	**17**	**0**	**0**	**1**	**0**	**0**	**.260**	**.333**	**.377**	**1.000**
Career total		973	3060	345	776	136	17	98	427	371	41	539	40	12	28	20	17	.254	.339	.405	.986
Yankee total		**66**	**77**	**5**	**20**	**2**	**2**	**1**	**18**	**9**	**0**	**17**	**0**	**0**	**1**	**0**	**0**	**.260**	**.333**	**.377**	**1.000**

Washington, Claudell

HEIGHT: 6'0 THROWS: LEFT BATS: LEFT BORN: 8/31/1954 LOS ANGELES, CALIFORNIA POSITIONS PLAYED: OF

YEAR	TEAM	GAMES	AB	RUNS	HITS	2B	3B	HR	RBI	BB	IBB	SO	HBP	SH	SF	SB	CS	BA	OBA	SA	FA
1974	Oak-A	73	221	16	63	10	5	0	19	13	1	44	1	1	1	6	8	.285	.326	.376	.985
1975	Oak-A	148	590	86	182	24	7	10	77	32	9	80	5	1	7	40	15	.308	.345	.424	.978
1976	Oak-A	134	490	65	126	20	6	5	53	30	1	90	3	3	4	37	20	.257	.302	.353	.963
1977	Tex-A	129	521	63	148	31	2	12	68	25	9	112	3	1	4	21	8	.284	.318	.420	.978
1978	Tex-A	12	42	1	7	0	0	0	2	1	0	12	0	0	0	0	1	.167	.186	.167	.917
1978	Chi-A	86	314	33	83	16	5	6	31	12	2	57	1	0	4	5	5	.264	.290	.404	.959
1979	Chi-A	131	471	79	132	33	5	13	66	28	7	93	3	2	4	19	11	.280	.322	.454	.974
1980	Chi-A	32	90	15	26	4	2	1	12	5	0	19	1	1	0	4	2	.289	.323	.411	.933
1980	NY-N	79	284	38	78	16	4	10	42	20	5	63	1	0	1	17	5	.275	.324	.465	.978
1981	Atl-N	85	320	37	93	22	3	5	37	15	1	47	4	8	2	12	6	.291	.328	.425	.993
1982	Atl-N	150	563	94	150	24	6	16	80	50	9	107	6	1	6	33	10	.266	.330	.416	.950
1983	Atl-N	134	496	75	138	24	8	9	44	35	6	103	0	1	6	31	9	.278	.322	.413	.974
1984	Atl-N	120	416	62	119	21	2	17	61	59	8	77	1	0	3	21	9	.286	.374	.469	.967
1985	Atl-N	122	398	62	110	14	6	15	43	40	11	66	1	0	2	14	4	.276	.342	.455	.962
1986	Atl-N	40	137	17	37	11	0	5	14	14	0	26	0	1	1	4	7	.270	.336	.460	.957
1986	**NY-A**	**54**	**135**	**19**	**32**	**5**	**0**	**6**	**16**	**7**	**0**	**33**	**2**	**0**	**0**	**6**	**1**	**.237**	**.285**	**.407**	**.985**
1987	**NY-A**	**102**	**312**	**42**	**87**	**17**	**0**	**9**	**44**	**27**	**2**	**54**	**2**	**0**	**0**	**10**	**1**	**.279**	**.336**	**.420**	**.988**
1988	**NY-A**	**126**	**455**	**62**	**140**	**22**	**3**	**11**	**64**	**24**	**2**	**74**	**2**	**0**	**4**	**15**	**6**	**.308**	**.342**	**.442**	**.984**
1989	Cal-A	110	418	53	114	18	4	13	42	27	3	84	2	3	1	13	5	.273	.319	.428	.975
1990	**NY-A**	**33**	**80**	**4**	**13**	**1**	**1**	**0**	**6**	**2**	**1**	**17**	**0**	**0**	**0**	**1**	**0**	**.176**	**.222**	**.294**	**1.000**
Career average		91	323	44	90	16	3	8	39	22	4	60	2	1	2	15	6	.278	.325	.420	.971
Yankee average		**79**	**246**	**32**	**68**	**11**	**1**	**7**	**33**	**15**	**1**	**45**	**1**	**0**	**1**	**9**	**2**	**.277**	**.320**	**.410**	**.989**
Career total		1912	6787	926	1884	334	69	164	824	468	77	1266	36	25	51	312	134	.278	.325	.420	.971
Yankee total		**315**	**982**	**127**	**272**	**45**	**4**	**26**	**130**	**60**	**5**	**178**	**4**	**0**	**5**	**34**	**9**	**.277**	**.320**	**.410**	**.989**

Watson, Robert Jose

HEIGHT: 6'0" THROWS: RIGHT BATS: RIGHT BORN: 4/10/1946 LOS ANGELES, CALIFORNIA POSITIONS PLAYED: 1B, OF

YEAR	TEAM	GAMES	AB	RUNS	HITS	2B	3B	HR	RBI	BB	IBB	SO	HBP	SH	SF	SB	CS	BA	OBA	SA	FA
1966	Hou-N	1	1	0	0	0	0	0	0	0	0	0	0	0	0	0	0	.000	.000	.000	.000
1967	Hou-N	6	14	1	3	0	0	1	2	0	0	3	0	0	0	0	0	.214	.214	.429	.958
1968	Hou-N	45	140	13	32	7	0	2	8	13	1	32	1	0	1	1	0	.229	.297	.321	.885
1969	Hou-N	20	40	3	11	3	0	0	3	6	0	5	2	0	0	0	0	.275	.396	.350	1.000
1970	Hou-N	97	327	48	89	19	2	11	61	24	1	59	4	1	6	1	1	.272	.324	.443	.992
1971	Hou-N	129	468	49	135	17	3	9	67	41	5	56	2	1	2	0	3	.288	.347	.395	.985
1972	Hou-N	147	548	74	171	27	4	16	86	53	5	83	8	2	5	1	1	.312	.378	.464	1.000
1973	Hou-N	158	573	97	179	24	3	16	94	85	8	73	4	1	3	1	4	.312	.403	.449	.929
1974	Hou-N	150	524	69	156	19	4	11	67	60	9	61	3	1	5	3	4	.298	.370	.412	1.000
1975	Hou-N	132	485	67	157	27	1	18	85	40	10	50	3	0	5	3	5	.324	.375	.495	.993
1976	Hou-N	157	585	76	183	31	3	16	102	62	10	64	4	2	9	3	3	.313	.377	.458	.990
1977	Hou-N	151	554	77	160	38	6	22	110	57	11	69	7	1	4	5	0	.289	.360	.498	.994
1978	Hou-N	139	461	51	133	25	4	14	79	51	16	57	4	0	11	3	1	.289	.357	.451	.992
1979	Hou-N	49	163	15	39	4	0	3	18	16	1	23	0	1	2	0	0	.239	.304	.319	.993
1979	Bos-A	84	312	48	105	19	4	13	53	29	7	33	5	0	1	3	2	.337	.401	.548	.988
1980	**NY-A**	**130**	**469**	**62**	**144**	**25**	**3**	**13**	**68**	**48**	**5**	**56**	**1**	**1**	**6**	**2**	**1**	**.307**	**.368**	**.456**	**.990**
1981	**NY-A**	**59**	**156**	**15**	**33**	**3**	**3**	**6**	**12**	**24**	**2**	**17**	**0**	**0**	**0**	**0**	**0**	**.212**	**.317**	**.385**	**.997**
1982	**NY-A**	**7**	**17**	**3**	**4**	**3**	**0**	**0**	**3**	**3**	**0**	**0**	**0**	**0**	**0**	**0**	**0**	**.235**	**.350**	**.412**	**1.000**
1982	Atl-N	57	114	16	28	3	1	5	22	14	2	20	0	0	2	1	1	.246	.323	.421	1.000
1983	Atl-N	65	149	14	46	9	0	6	37	18	3	23	0	0	3	0	2	.309	.376	.490	.984
1984	Atl-N	49	85	4	18	4	0	2	12	9	2	12	0	0	0	0	0	.212	.287	.329	.983
Career average		87	295	38	87	15	2	9	47	31	5	38	2	1	3	1	1	.295	.364	.447	.936
Yankee average		**65**	**214**	**27**	**60**	**10**	**2**	**6**	**28**	**25**	**2**	**24**	**0**	**0**	**2**	**1**	**0**	**.282**	**.355**	**.438**	**.996**
Career total		1832	6185	802	1826	307	41	184	989	653	98	796	48	11	65	27	28	.295	.364	.447	.936
Yankee total		**196**	**642**	**80**	**181**	**31**	**6**	**19**	**83**	**75**	**7**	**73**	**1**	**1**	**6**	**2**	**1**	**.282**	**.355**	**.438**	**.996**

Weatherly, Cyril Roy (Stormy)

HEIGHT: 5'6" THROWS: RIGHT BATS: LEFT BORN: 2/25/1915 WARREN, TEXAS DIED: 1/19/1991 WOODVILLE, TEXAS POSITIONS PLAYED: OF

YEAR	TEAM	GAMES	AB	RUNS	HITS	2B	3B	HR	RBI	BB	IBB	SO	HBP	SH	SF	SB	CS	BA	OBA	SA	FA
1936	Cle-A	84	349	64	117	28	6	8	53	16	—	29	0	1	—	3	8	.335	.364	.519	.973
1937	Cle-A	53	134	19	27	4	0	5	13	6	—	14	2	3	—	1	1	.201	.246	.343	.964
1938	Cle-A	83	210	32	55	14	3	2	18	14	—	14	0	4	—	8	5	.262	.308	.386	.975
1939	Cle-A	95	323	43	100	16	6	1	32	19	—	23	0	2	—	7	2	.310	.348	.406	.961
1940	Cle-A	135	578	90	175	35	11	12	59	27	—	26	1	9	—	9	8	.303	.335	.464	.969
1941	Cle-A	102	363	59	105	21	5	3	37	32	—	20	2	7	—	2	5	.289	.350	.399	.968
1942	Cle-A	128	473	61	122	23	7	5	39	35	—	25	1	5	—	8	13	.258	.310	.368	.991
1943	**NY-A**	**77**	**280**	**37**	**74**	**8**	**3**	**7**	**28**	**18**	**—**	**9**	**1**	**8**	**—**	**4**	**7**	**.264**	**.311**	**.389**	**.983**
1946	**NY-A**	**2**	**2**	**0**	**1**	**0**	**0**	**0**	**0**	**0**	**—**	**0**	**0**	**0**	**—**	**0**	**0**	**.500**	**.500**	**.500**	**.000**
1950	NY-N	52	69	10	18	3	3	0	11	13	—	10	0	1	—	0	0	.261	.378	.391	1.000
Career average		81	278	42	79	15	4	4	29	18	—	17	1	4	—	4	5	.286	.331	.418	.878
Yankee average		**40**	**141**	**19**	**38**	**4**	**2**	**4**	**14**	**9**	**—**	**5**	**1**	**4**	**—**	**2**	**4**	**.266**	**.312**	**.390**	**.492**
Career total		811	2781	415	794	152	44	43	290	180	—	170	7	40	—	42	49	.286	.331	.418	.878
Yankee total		**79**	**282**	**37**	**75**	**8**	**3**	**7**	**28**	**18**	**—**	**9**	**1**	**8**	**—**	**4**	**7**	**.266**	**.312**	**.390**	**.492**

Werber, William Murray

HEIGHT: 5'10" THROWS: RIGHT BATS: RIGHT BORN: 6/20/1908 BERWYN, MARYLAND POSITIONS PLAYED: 3B, SS

YEAR	TEAM	GAMES	AB	RUNS	HITS	2B	3B	HR	RBI	BB	IBB	SO	HBP	SH	SF	SB	CS	BA	OBA	SA	FA
1930	**NY-A**	**4**	**14**	**5**	**4**	**0**	**0**	**0**	**2**	**3**	**—**	**1**	**0**	**0**	**—**	**0**	**0**	**.286**	**.412**	**.286**	**.955**
1933	**NY-A**	**3**	**2**	**0**	**0**	**0**	**0**	**0**	**0**	**0**	**—**	**0**	**0**	**0**	**—**	**0**	**0**	**.000**	**.000**	**.000**	**.000**
1933	Bos-A	108	425	64	110	30	6	3	39	33	—	39	0	13	—	15	5	.259	.312	.379	.910
1934	Bos-A	152	623	129	200	41	10	11	67	77	—	37	1	15	—	40	15	.321	.397	.472	.889
1935	Bos-A	124	462	84	118	30	3	14	61	69	—	41	4	14	—	29	7	.255	.357	.424	.942
1936	Bos-A	145	535	89	147	29	6	10	67	89	—	37	4	11	—	23	13	.275	.382	.407	.942
1937	Phi-A	128	493	85	144	31	4	7	70	74	—	39	1	8	—	35	13	.292	.386	.414	1.000
1938	Phi-A	134	499	92	129	22	7	11	69	93	—	37	2	5	—	19	15	.259	.377	.397	.935
1939	Cin-N	147	599	115	173	35	5	5	57	91	—	46	6	11	—	15	—	.289	.388	.389	.933
1940	Cin-N	143	584	105	162	35	5	12	48	68	—	40	8	3	—	16	—	.277	.361	.416	.954
1941	Cin-N	109	418	56	100	9	2	4	46	53	—	24	2	4	—	14	—	.239	.328	.299	.959
1942	NY-N	98	370	51	76	9	2	1	13	51	—	22	4	4	—	9	—	.205	.308	.249	.927
Career average		108	419	73	114	23	4	7	45	58	—	30	3	7	—	18	—	.271	.364	.392	.863
Yankee average		**4**	**8**	**3**	**2**	**0**	**0**	**0**	**1**	**2**	**—**	**1**	**0**	**0**	**—**	**0**	**0**	**.250**	**.368**	**.250**	**.478**
Career total		1295	5024	875	1363	271	50	78	539	701	—	363	32	88	—	215	68	.271	.364	.392	.863
Yankee total		**7**	**16**	**5**	**4**	**0**	**0**	**0**	**2**	**3**	**—**	**1**	**0**	**0**	**—**	**0**	**0**	**.250**	**.368**	**.250**	**.478**

Whitaker, Stephen Edward
HEIGHT: 6'0" THROWS: RIGHT BATS: LEFT BORN: 5/7/1943 TACOMA, WASHINGTON POSITIONS PLAYED: OF

YEAR	TEAM	GAMES	AB	RUNS	HITS	2B	3B	HR	RBI	BB	IBB	SO	HBP	SH	SF	SB	CS	BA	OBA	SA	FA
1966	NY-A	31	114	15	28	3	2	7	15	9	0	24	1	0	0	0	0	.246	.306	.491	.955
1967	NY-A	122	441	37	107	12	3	11	50	23	2	89	3	2	3	2	5	.243	.283	.358	.982
1968	NY-A	28	60	3	7	2	0	0	3	8	0	18	0	0	0	0	1	.117	.221	.150	.917
1969	Sea-A	69	116	15	29	2	1	6	13	12	1	29	1	0	1	2	0	.250	.323	.440	.962
1970	SF-N	16	27	3	3	1	0	0	4	2	0	14	0	0	1	0	0	.111	.167	.148	.857
Career average		53	152	15	35	4	1	5	17	11	1	35	1	0	1	1	1	.230	.283	.367	.935
Yankee average		60	205	18	47	6	2	6	23	13	1	44	1	1	1	1	2	.231	.281	.363	.951
Career total		266	758	73	174	20	6	24	85	54	3	174	5	2	5	4	6	.230	.283	.367	.935
Yankee total		181	615	55	142	17	5	18	68	40	2	131	4	2	3	2	6	.231	.281	.363	.951

White, Roy Hilton
HEIGHT: 5'10" THROWS: RIGHT BATS: BOTH BORN: 12/27/1943 LOS ANGELES, CALIFORNIA POSITIONS PLAYED: 1B, 2B, 3B, OF

YEAR	TEAM	GAMES	AB	RUNS	HITS	2B	3B	HR	RBI	BB	IBB	SO	HBP	SH	SF	SB	CS	BA	OBA	SA	FA
1965	NY-A	14	42	7	14	2	0	0	3	4	0	7	1	0	0	2	1	.333	.404	.381	1.000
1966	NY-A	115	316	39	71	13	2	7	20	37	1	43	1	2	0	14	7	.225	.308	.345	.957
1967	NY-A	70	214	22	48	8	0	2	18	19	0	25	1	1	3	10	4	.224	.287	.290	.968
1968	NY-A	159	577	89	154	20	7	17	62	73	6	50	3	3	4	20	11	.267	.350	.414	.997
1969	NY-A	130	448	55	130	30	5	7	74	81	4	51	1	2	11	18	10	.290	.392	.426	.989
1970	NY-A	162	609	109	180	30	6	22	94	95	11	66	0	1	7	24	10	.296	.387	.473	.994
1971	NY-A	147	524	86	153	22	7	19	84	86	7	66	7	0	17	14	7	.292	.388	.469	1.000
1972	NY-A	155	556	76	150	29	0	10	54	99	10	59	5	4	2	23	7	.270	.384	.376	.994
1973	NY-A	162	639	88	157	22	3	18	60	78	3	81	2	3	1	16	9	.246	.329	.374	.977
1974	NY-A	136	473	68	130	19	8	7	43	67	5	44	4	8	3	15	6	.275	.367	.393	.993
1975	NY-A	148	556	81	161	32	5	12	59	72	1	50	2	4	2	16	15	.290	.372	.430	.983
1976	NY-A	156	626	104	179	29	3	14	65	83	1	52	0	10	9	31	13	.286	.365	.409	.987
1977	NY-A	143	519	72	139	25	2	14	52	75	9	58	0	8	4	18	11	.268	.358	.405	.981
1978	NY-A	103	346	44	93	13	3	8	43	42	7	35	2	2	3	10	4	.269	.349	.393	.992
1979	NY-A	81	205	24	44	6	0	3	27	23	1	21	0	5	3	2	2	.215	.290	.288	1.000
Career average		125	443	64	120	20	3	11	51	62	4	47	2	4	5	16	8	.271	.360	.404	.987
Yankee average		125	443	64	120	20	3	11	51	62	4	47	2	4	5	16	8	.271	.360	.404	.987
Career total		1881	6650	964	1803	300	51	160	758	934	66	708	29	53	69	233	117	.271	.360	.404	.987
Yankee total		1881	6650	964	1803	300	51	160	758	934	66	708	29	53	69	233	117	.271	.360	.404	.987

Whiten, Mark Anthony
HEIGHT: 6'3" THROWS: RIGHT BATS: BOTH BORN: 11/25/1966 PENSACOLA, FLORIDA POSITIONS PLAYED: OF

YEAR	TEAM	GAMES	AB	RUNS	HITS	2B	3B	HR	RBI	BB	IBB	SO	HBP	SH	SF	SB	CS	BA	OBA	SA	FA
1990	Tor-A	33	88	12	24	1	1	2	7	7	0	14	0	0	1	2	0	.273	.323	.375	1.000
1991	Tor-A	46	149	12	33	4	3	2	19	11	1	35	1	0	3	0	1	.221	.274	.329	1.000
1991	Cle-A	70	258	34	66	14	4	7	26	19	1	50	2	0	2	4	2	.256	.310	.422	.962
1992	Cle-A	148	508	73	129	19	4	9	43	72	10	102	2	3	3	16	12	.254	.347	.360	.980
1993	StL-N	152	562	81	142	13	4	25	99	58	9	110	2	0	4	15	8	.253	.323	.423	.971
1994	StL-N	92	334	57	98	18	2	14	53	37	9	75	1	0	2	10	5	.293	.364	.485	.964
1995	Bos-A	32	108	13	20	3	0	1	10	8	0	23	0	0	1	1	0	.185	.239	.241	1.000
1995	Phi-N	60	212	38	57	10	1	11	37	31	1	63	1	0	0	7	0	.269	.365	.481	.965
1996	Phi-N	60	182	33	43	8	0	7	21	33	2	62	1	0	0	13	3	.236	.356	.396	.949
1996	Atl-N	36	90	12	23	5	1	3	17	16	0	25	0	0	1	2	5	.256	.364	.433	.933
1996	Sea-A	40	140	31	42	7	0	12	33	21	4	40	2	0	0	2	1	.300	.399	.607	.750
1997	**NY-A**	**69**	**215**	**34**	**57**	**11**	**0**	**5**	**24**	**30**	**5**	**47**	**2**	**1**	**0**	**4**	**2**	**.265**	**.360**	**.386**	**.871**
1998	Cle-A	87	226	31	64	14	0	6	29	29	0	60	0	1	0	2	1	.283	.365	.425	.970
1999	Cle-A	8	25	2	4	1	0	1	4	3	0	4	0	0	0	0	0	.160	.250	.320	1.000
2000	Cle-A	6	7	2	2	1	0	0	1	3	0	2	0	0	0	2	1	.286	.500	.429	1.000
Career average		63	207	31	54	9	1	7	28	25	3	48	1	0	1	5	3	.259	.340	.415	.954
Yankee average		69	215	34	57	11	0	5	24	30	5	47	2	1	0	4	2	.265	.360	.386	.871
Career total		939	3104	465	804	129	20	105	423	378	42	712	14	5	17	80	41	.259	.340	.415	.954
Yankee total		69	215	34	57	11	0	5	24	30	5	47	2	1	0	4	2	.265	.360	.386	.871

Roy Hilton White, of-dh-1b-2b-3b, 1965–79

Though his birth certificate listed it as "Hilton," Roy White's middle name might as well have been "Professionalism."

Born on December 27, 1943, in Los Angeles, California, White was a star second baseman at Centennial High, where he teamed with future big-leaguer Reggie Smith. He came up to the Yankees in 1965. By 1966, he was the Yankees' fourth outfielder behind Mickey Mantle, Roger Maris and Tom Tresh. He still played enough to lead the team in stolen bases with 14.

By 1969, the Yankee dynasty had completely crumbled, leaving White as one of the team's few stars. He led the Yankees in virtually every offensive category through the early 1970s. Ironically, the 5 foot 10 inch, 165-pound White was almost certainly the slightest clean-up hitter in baseball.

His size made doubters of many coaches. But eventually, they all came around. White was a professional hitter from both sides of the plate. In 1970, he smacked both right- and left-handed triples in one game, one of only a handful of players in major league history to do so.

Defensively, he was a smart outfielder who learned to compensate for an average throwing arm by hitting the cutoff man and charging fly balls hit to him. In 1975, he played an entire season in the outfield without making an error, the first Yankee to accomplish that feat.

He was a thoughtful man who kept his dignity during the bad years and who kept his composure during the tumultuous late 1970s, when almost every Yankee was helping sell papers with outrageous quotes.

In the postseason, White proved he could make the grade. He tortured the Kansas City Royals in three consecutive league championship series, hitting .294 in 1976, .400 in 1977 and .313 in 1978. His best World Series was 1978, when White hit .333 and scored a Series-high nine runs. His home run in the first inning of the third game started the Yankees on their comeback that year, as New York swept the last four games of that matchup with the Dodgers to win the championship in six games.

White retired in 1979 after 15 years with New York, and he now works as a scout with the team. He is 5th all-time on the Yankees in games played with 1,881, 10th in runs scored with 964, 9th in hits with 1,803, 11th in doubles with 300, 18th in home runs with 160 and 14th in RBI with 758. He is 4th all-time in stolen bases with 233.

Whitfield, Terry Bertland

HEIGHT: 6'1" THROWS: RIGHT BATS: LEFT BORN: 1/12/1953 BLYTHE, CALIFORNIA POSITIONS PLAYED: OF

YEAR	TEAM	GAMES	AB	RUNS	HITS	2B	3B	HR	RBI	BB	IBB	SO	HBP	SH	SF	SB	CS	BA	OBA	SA	FA
1974	NY-A	2	5	0	1	0	0	0	0	0	0	1	0	0	0	0	0	.200	.200	.200	.000
1975	NY-A	28	81	9	22	1	1	0	7	1	0	17	0	0	2	1	0	.272	.274	.309	.978
1976	NY-A	1	0	0	0	0	0	0	0	0	0	0	0	0	0	0	0	—	—	—	.000
1977	SF-N	114	326	41	93	21	3	7	36	20	1	46	2	2	2	2	3	.285	.329	.433	.972
1978	SF-N	149	488	70	141	20	2	10	32	33	5	69	2	17	3	5	11	.289	.335	.400	.988
1979	SF-N	133	394	52	113	20	4	5	44	36	6	47	4	7	4	5	4	.287	.349	.396	.957
1980	SF-N	118	321	38	95	16	2	4	26	20	3	44	1	4	2	4	2	.296	.337	.396	.987
1984	LA-N	87	180	15	44	8	0	4	18	17	2	35	1	2	0	1	4	.244	.313	.356	.988
1985	LA-N	79	104	8	27	7	0	3	16	6	1	27	0	0	0	0	0	.260	.300	.413	.926
1986	LA-N	19	14	0	1	0	0	0	0	5	2	2	0	0	0	0	0	.071	.316	.071	1.000
Career average		73	191	23	54	9	1	3	18	14	2	29	1	3	1	2	2	.281	.330	.394	.780
Yankee average		**10**	**29**	**3**	**8**	**0**	**0**	**0**	**2**	**0**	**0**	**6**	**0**	**0**	**1**	**0**	**0**	**.267**	**.270**	**.302**	**.326**
Career total		730	1913	233	537	93	12	33	179	138	20	288	10	32	13	18	24	.281	.330	.394	.780
Yankee total		**31**	**86**	**9**	**23**	**1**	**1**	**0**	**7**	**1**	**0**	**18**	**0**	**0**	**2**	**1**	**0**	**.267**	**.270**	**.302**	**.326**

Bernabe Figueroa "Bernie" Williams, of, 1991–2000

Over the past five years, Bernie Williams has been one of the Yankees' most consistent performers at the plate and in the field.

Born on September 13, 1968, in San Juan, Puerto Rico, Williams was signed by the Yankees in 1986. A terrific athlete, Williams was a world-class middle-distance runner in his teens. He spent five full years in the minors, but after a pair of split seasons between New York and the Yankee Triple-A affiliate in Columbus, Ohio, Williams came to New York for good in 1993.

Williams showed he could hit in the bigs, embarking on a 21-game hitting streak that year. The 21-game streak was the tenth best such streak of all time.

But 1995 was Williams's breakout season. He hit .307 with 18 home runs and led the Yankees in runs (93), hits (173), total bases (274), triples (9) and walks (75). By 1997, he was one of the best players in the American League. That was the year he won the first of three consecutive Gold Glove awards.

He has worked to become a fearsome switch-hitter. Three times he has hit home runs from both sides of the plate in one game. In 1995, he hit home runs from both sides of the plate in the American League divisional series against Seattle, the only time that has been done in the postseason.

Williams won the batting title in 1998 with a .339 average. He became the first player in major league history to win a batting title, a Gold Glove and a World Series championship in the same year.

Williams came back strongly in 1999, hitting .342 with 25 home runs and career highs in hits (202) and RBI (115). Williams had over 100 RBI and 100 runs scored for the third time in four years.

Williams led the Yankees in home runs again in 2000 with 30. In the 2000 World Series, Bernie was mired in a hideous slump when he smacked a home run to lead off the second inning of Game 5. That gave New York a 1-0 lead in a game they would eventually win, 4-2, to clinch the Series.

Williams is already 19th on the Yankees' all-time list in runs scored with 754, 17th in doubles with 245 and 20th in RBI with 681.

Wickland, Albert

HEIGHT: 5'7" THROWS: LEFT BATS: LEFT BORN: 1/27/1888 CHICAGO, ILLINOIS DIED: 3/14/1980 PORT WASHINGTON, WISCONSIN POSITIONS PLAYED: OF

YEAR	TEAM	GAMES	AB	RUNS	HITS	2B	3B	HR	RBI	BB	IBB	SO	HBP	SH	SF	SB	CS	BA	OBA	SA	FA
1913	Cin-N	26	79	7	17	5	5	0	8	6	—	19	1	1	—	3	—	.215	.279	.405	.983
1914	Chi-F	157	536	74	148	31	10	6	68	81	—	58	4	27	—	17	—	.276	.375	.405	.962
1915	Chi-F	30	86	11	21	2	2	1	5	13	—	11	0	1	—	3	—	.244	.343	.349	.946
1915	Pit-F	110	389	63	117	12	8	1	30	52	—	47	2	30	—	23	—	.301	.386	.380	.968
1918	Bos-N	95	332	55	87	7	13	4	32	53	—	39	2	12	—	12	—	.262	.367	.398	.975
1919	**NY-A**	**26**	**46**	**2**	**7**	**1**	**0**	**0**	**1**	**2**	—	**10**	**0**	**1**	—	**0**	—	**.152**	**.188**	**.174**	**1.000**
Career average		74	245	35	66	10	6	2	24	35	—	31	2	12	—	10	—	.270	.364	.386	.972
Yankee average		**26**	**46**	**2**	**7**	**1**	**0**	**0**	**1**	**2**	—	**10**	**0**	**1**	—	**0**	—	**.152**	**.188**	**.174**	**1.000**
Career total		444	1468	212	397	58	38	12	144	207	—	184	9	72	—	58	—	.270	.364	.386	.972
Yankee total		**26**	**46**	**2**	**7**	**1**	**0**	**0**	**1**	**2**	—	**10**	**0**	**1**	—	**0**	—	**.152**	**.188**	**.174**	**1.000**

Williams, Bernabe (Bernie) BORN BERNABE WILLIAMS (FIGUEROA)

HEIGHT: 6'2" THROWS: RIGHT BATS: BOTH BORN: 9/13/1968 SAN JUAN, PUERTO RICO POSITIONS PLAYED: OF

YEAR	TEAM	GAMES	AB	RUNS	HITS	2B	3B	HR	RBI	BB	IBB	SO	HBP	SH	SF	SB	CS	BA	OBA	SA	FA
1991	NY-A	85	320	43	76	19	4	3	34	48	0	57	1	2	3	10	5	.238	.336	.350	.979
1992	NY-A	62	261	39	73	14	2	5	26	29	1	36	1	2	0	7	6	.280	.354	.406	.995
1993	NY-A	139	567	67	152	31	4	12	68	53	4	106	4	1	3	9	9	.268	.333	.400	.989
1994	NY-A	108	408	80	118	29	1	12	57	61	2	54	3	1	3	9	9	.289	.384	.453	.990
1995	NY-A	144	563	93	173	29	9	18	82	75	1	98	5	2	3	8	6	.307	.392	.487	.982
1996	NY-A	143	551	108	168	26	7	29	102	82	8	72	0	1	7	17	4	.305	.391	.535	.986
1997	NY-A	129	509	107	167	35	6	21	100	73	7	80	1	0	8	15	8	.328	.408	.544	.993

(continued)

(continued)

YEAR	TEAM	GAMES	AB	RUNS	HITS	2B	3B	HR	RBI	BB	IBB	SO	HBP	SH	SF	SB	CS	BA	OBA	SA	FA
1998	NY-A	128	499	101	169	30	5	26	97	74	9	81	0	0	4	15	9	.339	.421	.575	.990
1999	NY-A	158	591	116	202	28	6	25	115	100	0	95	0	0	5	9	10	.342	.434	.536	.987
2000	NY-A	141	537	108	165	37	6	30	121	71	11	84	5	0	3	13	5	.307	.391	.566	1.000
Career average		124	481	86	146	28	5	18	80	67	4	76	2	1	4	12	7	.304	.389	.496	.989
Yankee average		124	481	86	146	28	5	18	80	67	4	76	2	1	4	12	7	.304	.389	.496	.989
Career total		1237	4806	862	1463	278	50	181	802	666	43	763	20	9	38	119	71	.304	.389	.496	.989
Yankee total		1237	4806	862	1463	278	50	181	802	666	43	763	20	9	38	119	71	.304	.389	.496	.989

Williams, Gerald Floyd

HEIGHT: 6'2"   THROWS: RIGHT   BATS: RIGHT   BORN: 8/10/1966 NEW ORLEANS, LOUISIANA   POSITIONS PLAYED: OF

YEAR	TEAM	GAMES	AB	RUNS	HITS	2B	3B	HR	RBI	BB	IBB	SO	HBP	SH	SF	SB	CS	BA	OBA	SA	FA
1992	NY-A	15	27	7	8	2	0	3	6	0	0	3	0	0	0	2	0	.206	.296	.296	.913
1993	NY-A	42	67	11	10	2	3	0	6	1	0	14	2	0	1	2	0	.149	.183	.269	.956
1994	NY-A	57	86	19	25	8	0	4	13	4	0	17	0	0	1	1	3	.291	.319	.523	.957
1995	NY-A	100	182	33	45	18	2	6	28	22	1	34	1	0	3	4	2	.247	.327	.467	.993
1996	NY-A	99	233	37	63	15	4	5	30	15	2	39	4	1	5	7	8	.270	.319	.433	.917
1996	Mil-A	26	92	6	19	4	0	0	4	4	1	18	1	2	0	3	1	.207	.247	.250	.987
1997	Mil-A	155	566	73	143	32	2	10	41	19	1	90	6	5	5	23	9	.253	.282	.369	1.000
1998	Atl-N	129	266	46	81	19	2	10	44	17	1	48	0	2	1	11	5	.305	.345	.504	.971
1999	Atl-N	143	422	76	116	24	1	17	68	33	0	67	0	4	2	19	11	.275	.326	.457	.988
2000	TB-A	146	632	87	173	30	2	21	89	34	0	103	3	9	4	12	12	.274	.312	.427	.983
Career average		91	257	40	68	15	2	8	33	15	1	43	2	2	2	8	5	.265	.307	.426	.967
Yankee average		63	119	21	30	9	2	4	17	8	1	21	1	0	2	3	3	.254	.306	.450	.947
Career total		912	2573	395	683	154	16	76	329	149	6	433	17	23	22	84	51	.265	.307	.426	.967
Yankee total		313	595	107	151	45	9	18	83	42	3	107	7	1	10	16	13	.254	.306	.450	.947

Williams, James Thomas (Buttons)

HEIGHT: 5'9"   THROWS: RIGHT   BATS: RIGHT   BORN: 12/20/1876 ST.LOUIS, MISSOURI   DIED: 1/16/1965 ST.PETERSBURG, FLORIDA   POSITIONS PLAYED: 2B, 3B

YEAR	TEAM	GAMES	AB	RUNS	HITS	2B	3B	HR	RBI	BB	IBB	SO	HBP	SH	SF	SB	CS	BA	OBA	SA	FA
1899	Pit-N	152	617	126	219	28	27	9	116	60	—	—	6	6	—	26	—	.355	.417	.532	.902
1900	Pit-N	106	416	73	110	15	11	5	68	32	—	—	4	3	—	18	—	.264	.323	.389	.889
1901	Bal-A	130	501	113	159	26	21	7	96	56	—	—	2	9	—	21	—	.317	.388	.495	.935
1902	Bal-A	125	498	83	156	27	21	8	83	36	—	—	1	10	—	14	—	.313	.361	.500	.821
1903	NY-A	132	502	60	134	30	12	3	82	39	—	—	4	11	—	14	—	.263	.314	.354	.951
1904	NY-A	146	559	62	147	31	7	2	74	38	—	—	3	10	—	14	—	.228	.306	.343	.964
1905	NY-A	129	470	54	107	20	8	6	62	50	—	—	5	21	—	8	—	.277	.342	.373	.958
1906	NY-A	139	501	62	139	25	7	3	77	44	—	—	1	11	—	14	—	.270	.319	.359	.966
1907	NY-A	139	504	53	136	17	11	2	63	35	—	—	3	22	—	7	—	.236	.310	.321	.963
1908	StL-A	148	539	63	127	20	7	4	53	55	—	—	3	10	—	6	—	.195	.257	.235	.962
1909	StL-A	110	374	32	73	3	6	0	22	29	—	—	2	10	—		—	.275	.337	.396	.933
Career average		132	498	71	137	22	13	5	72	43	—	—	3	11	—	14	—	.275	.337	.396	.933
Yankee average		137	507	58	133	25	9	3	72	41	—	—	4	12	—	12	—	.261	.321	.364	.959
Career total		1456	5481	781	1507	242	138	49	796	474	—	—	36	121	—	151	—	.261	.321	.364	.959
Yankee total		685	2536	291	663	123	45	16	358	206	—	—	18	61	—	59	—	.261	.321	.364	.959

Williams, Walter Allen (No-Neck)

HEIGHT: 5'6"   THROWS: RIGHT   BATS: RIGHT   BORN: 12/19/1943 BROWNWOOD, TEXAS   POSITIONS PLAYED: OF

YEAR	TEAM	GAMES	AB	RUNS	HITS	2B	3B	HR	RBI	BB	IBB	SO	HBP	SH	SF	SB	CS	BA	OBA	SA	FA
1964	Hou-N	10	9	1	0	0	0	0	0	0	0	2	0	1	0	1	0	.000	.000	.000	1.000
1967	Chi-A	104	275	35	66	16	3	3	15	17	0	20	2	2	0	3	2	.240	.289	.353	.983
1968	Chi-A	63	133	6	32	6	0	1	8	4	1	17	2	2	1	0	1	.241	.271	.308	1.000
1969	Chi-A	135	471	59	143	22	1	3	32	26	1	33	3	5	2	6	2	.304	.343	.374	.985
1970	Chi-A	110	315	43	79	18	1	3	15	19	0	30	2	2	3	5	3	.251	.296	.343	.949
1971	Chi-A	114	361	43	106	17	3	8	35	24	1	27	5	4	3	5	5	.294	.344	.424	1.000
1972	Chi-A	77	221	22	55	7	1	2	11	13	1	20	0	1	1	6	1	.249	.289	.317	.990
1973	Cle-A	104	350	43	101	15	1	8	38	14	2	29	1	1	2	9	4	.289	.316	.406	.970
1974	**NY-A**	43	53	5	6	0	0	0	3	1	0	10	0	1	1	1	0	.113	.127	.113	.955
1975	**NY-A**	82	185	27	52	5	1	5	16	8	1	23	3	3	1	0	1	.281	.320	.400	.982
Career average		84	237	28	64	11	1	3	17	13	1	21	2	3	1	3	2	.270	.310	.365	.969
Yankee average		63	119	16	29	3	1	3	10	5	1	17	2	2	1	1	1	.244	.278	.336	.969
Career total		842	2373	284	640	106	11	33	173	126	7	211	18	25	13	34	19	.270	.310	.365	.981
Yankee total		125	238	32	58	5	1	5	19	9	1	33	3	4	2	1	1	.244	.278	.336	.969

David Mark Winfield, of-dh, 1981–90

Dave Winfield was one of the dominant ballplayers of the 1980s, a fearsome hitter with a tremendous arm from the outfield.

Winfield was born October 3, 1951, in St. Paul, Minnesota. After a stellar high school career, he played baseball and basketball at the University of Minnesota. He starred in both sports and was drafted by four professional teams in three leagues: the San Diego Padres, the NBA's Atlanta Hawks, the ABA's Utah Stars and the Minnesota Vikings of the NFL, even though he hadn't played football since high school.

The Padres signed him and he was a four-time All-Star in his eight years there. In 1981, he was signed by the Yankees to a ten-year $23 million contract. Winfield continued to put up big numbers in New York, but the Yankees only made the postseason once in the 1980s, in 1981.

That postseason proved to be an up-and-down experience for Big Dave. He hit .350 in a first-round win over the Milwaukee Brewers. (That was the year of the players' strike, and the resulting split season was resolved by adding an extra playoff tier.) But he hit only .154 in the American League championship series win over Oakland and a much-discussed .045 (1-22) in the Yankees' World Series loss to the Los Angeles Dodgers.

Still, Winfield was an eight-time All-Star in New York, winning four Gold Gloves in the outfield. He made 100 RBI five straight years, from 1982–86, the first Yankee to do so since Joe DiMaggio. As he often pointed out, he was "there with the numbers" at the end of the season more often than not.

Winfield missed the 1989 season with back surgery, and in 1990, he was traded to California. He played five more years for several American League teams before retiring in 1995.

Winfield is 8th on the Yankees' all-time list with 205 home runs and 12th in RBI with 818.

Winfield, David Mark

HEIGHT: 6'6"   THROWS: RIGHT   BATS: RIGHT   BORN: 10/3/1951 ST.PAUL, MINNESOTA   POSITIONS PLAYED: OF

YEAR	TEAM	GAMES	AB	RUNS	HITS	2B	3B	HR	RBI	BB	IBB	SO	HBP	SH	SF	SB	CS	BA	OBA	SA	FA
1973	SD-N	56	141	9	39	4	1	3	12	12	1	19	0	0	1	0	0	.277	.331	.383	.956
1974	SD-N	145	498	57	132	18	4	20	75	40	2	96	1	0	5	9	7	.265	.318	.438	.960
1975	SD-N	143	509	74	136	20	2	15	76	69	14	82	3	3	7	23	4	.267	.354	.403	.972
1976	SD-N	137	492	81	139	26	4	13	69	65	8	78	3	2	5	26	7	.283	.366	.431	.982
1977	SD-N	157	615	104	169	29	7	25	92	58	10	75	0	0	5	16	7	.275	.335	.467	.972
1978	SD-N	158	587	88	181	30	5	24	97	55	20	81	2	0	5	21	9	.308	.367	.499	.979
1979	SD-N	159	597	97	184	27	10	34	118	85	24	71	2	0	2	15	9	.308	.395	.558	.986
1980	SD-N	162	558	89	154	25	6	20	87	79	14	83	2	0	4	23	7	.276	.365	.450	.987
1981	**NY-A**	**105**	**388**	**52**	**114**	**25**	**1**	**13**	**68**	**43**	**3**	**41**	**1**	**1**	**7**	**11**	**1**	**.294**	**.360**	**.464**	**.985**
1982	**NY-A**	**140**	**539**	**84**	**151**	**24**	**8**	**37**	**106**	**45**	**7**	**64**	**0**	**5**	**8**	**5**	**3**	**.280**	**.331**	**.560**	**.974**
1983	**NY-A**	**152**	**598**	**99**	**169**	**26**	**8**	**32**	**116**	**58**	**2**	**77**	**2**	**0**	**6**	**15**	**6**	**.283**	**.345**	**.513**	**.978**
1984	**NY-A**	**141**	**567**	**106**	**193**	**34**	**4**	**19**	**100**	**53**	**9**	**71**	**0**	**0**	**6**	**6**	**4**	**.340**	**.393**	**.515**	**.994**
1985	**NY-A**	**155**	**633**	**105**	**174**	**34**	**6**	**26**	**114**	**52**	**8**	**96**	**0**	**0**	**4**	**19**	**7**	**.275**	**.328**	**.471**	**.991**
1986	**NY-A**	**154**	**565**	**90**	**148**	**31**	**5**	**24**	**104**	**77**	**9**	**106**	**2**	**2**	**6**	**6**	**5**	**.262**	**.349**	**.462**	**.984**
1987	**NY-A**	**156**	**575**	**83**	**158**	**22**	**1**	**27**	**97**	**76**	**5**	**96**	**0**	**1**	**3**	**5**	**6**	**.275**	**.358**	**.457**	**.989**
1988	**NY-A**	**149**	**559**	**96**	**180**	**37**	**2**	**25**	**107**	**69**	**10**	**88**	**2**	**0**	**1**	**9**	**4**	**.322**	**.398**	**.530**	**.989**
1990	**NY-A**	**20**	**61**	**7**	**13**	**3**	**0**	**2**	**6**	**4**	**0**	**13**	**1**	**0**	**1**	**0**	**0**	**.213**	**.269**	**.361**	**1.000**
1990	Cal-A	112	414	63	114	18	2	19	72	48	3	68	1	1	6	0	1	.275	.348	.466	.989
1991	Cal-A	150	568	75	149	27	4	28	86	56	4	109	1	2	6	7	2	.262	.326	.472	.990
1992	Tor-A	156	583	92	169	33	3	26	108	82	10	89	1	1	3	2	3	.290	.377	.491	1.000
1993	Min-A	143	547	72	148	27	2	21	76	45	2	106	0	0	2	2	3	.271	.325	.442	1.000
1994	Min-A	77	294	35	74	15	3	10	43	31	5	51	0	1	2	2	1	.252	.321	.425	1.000
Career average		133	495	75	140	24	4	21	83	55	8	76	1	1	4	10	4	.284	.353	.476	.984
Yankee average		**130**	**498**	**80**	**144**	**26**	**4**	**23**	**91**	**53**	**6**	**72**	**1**	**1**	**5**	**8**	**4**	**.290**	**.356**	**.495**	**.987**
Career total		2927	10888	1658	3088	535	88	463	1829	1202	170	1660	24	19	95	222	96	.284	.353	.476	.984
Yankee total		**1172**	**4485**	**722**	**1300**	**236**	**35**	**205**	**818**	**477**	**53**	**652**	**8**	**9**	**42**	**76**	**36**	**.290**	**.356**	**.495**	**.987**

Witek, Nicholas Joseph (Mickey)

HEIGHT: 5'10" THROWS: RIGHT BATS: RIGHT BORN: 12/19/1915 LUZERNE, PENNSYLVANIA DIED: 8/24/1990 KINGSTON, PENNSYLVANIA POSITIONS PLAYED: 2B

YEAR	TEAM	GAMES	AB	RUNS	HITS	2B	3B	HR	RBI	BB	IBB	SO	HBP	SH	SF	SB	CS	BA	OBA	SA	FA
1940	NY-N	119	433	34	111	7	0	3	31	24	—	17	0	4	—	2	—	.256	.295	.293	.960
1941	NY-N	26	94	11	34	5	0	1	16	4	—	2	0	2	—	0	—	.362	.388	.447	.933
1942	NY-N	148	553	72	144	19	6	5	48	36	—	20	0	14	—	2	—	.260	.306	.344	.978
1943	NY-N	153	622	68	195	17	0	6	55	41	—	23	0	9	—	1	7	.314	.356	.370	.967
1946	NY-N	82	284	32	75	13	2	4	29	28	—	10	0	1	—	1	0	.264	.330	.366	.878
1947	NY-N	51	160	22	35	4	1	3	17	15	—	12	0	0	—	1	0	.219	.286	.313	.983
1949	**NY-A**	**1**	**1**	**0**	**1**	**0**	**0**	**0**	**0**	**0**	**—**	**0**	**0**	**0**	**—**	**0**	**0**	**1.000**	**1.000**	**1.000**	**.000**
Career average		83	307	34	85	9	1	3	28	21	—	12	0	4	—	1		.277	.324	.347	.814
Yankee average		**1**	**1**	**0**	**1**	**0**	**0**	**0**	**0**	**0**	**—**	**0**	**0**	**0**	**—**	**0**	**0**	**1.000**	**1.000**	**1.000**	**.000**
Career total		580	2147	239	595	65	9	22	196	148	—	84	0	30	—	7	7	.277	.324	.347	.814
Yankee total		**1**	**1**	**0**	**1**	**0**	**0**	**0**	**0**	**0**	**—**	**0**	**0**	**0**	**—**	**0**	**0**	**1.000**	**1.000**	**1.000**	**.000**

Witt, Lawton Walter (Whitey) BORN LADISLAW WALDEMAR WITTKOWSKI

HEIGHT: 5'7" THROWS: RIGHT BATS: LEFT BORN: 9/28/1895 ORANGE, MASSACHUSETTS DIED: 7/14/1988 SALEM CO., NEW JERSEY POSITIONS PLAYED: SS, OF

YEAR	TEAM	GAMES	AB	RUNS	HITS	2B	3B	HR	RBI	BB	IBB	SO	HBP	SH	SF	SB	CS	BA	OBA	SA	FA
1916	Phi-A	143	563	64	138	16	15	2	36	55	—	71	2	6	—	19	—	.245	.315	.337	.903
1917	Phi-A	128	452	62	114	13	4	0	28	65	—	45	0	13	—	12	—	.252	.346	.299	.935
1919	Phi-A	122	460	56	123	15	6	0	33	46	—	26	0	12	—	11	—	.267	.334	.326	.951
1920	Phi-A	65	218	29	70	11	3	1	25	27	—	16	0	8	—	2	3	.321	.396	.413	1.000
1921	Phi-A	154	629	100	198	31	11	4	45	77	—	52	1	19	—	16	15	.315	.390	.418	.959
1922	**NY-A**	**140**	**528**	**98**	**157**	**11**	**6**	**4**	**40**	**89**	**—**	**29**	**1**	**10**	**—**	**5**	**8**	**.297**	**.400**	**.364**	**.976**
1923	**NY-A**	**146**	**596**	**113**	**187**	**18**	**10**	**6**	**56**	**67**	**—**	**42**	**3**	**19**	**—**	**2**	**7**	**.314**	**.386**	**.408**	**.979**
1924	**NY-A**	**147**	**600**	**88**	**178**	**26**	**5**	**1**	**36**	**45**	**—**	**20**	**0**	**15**	**—**	**9**	**7**	**.297**	**.346**	**.362**	**.976**
1925	**NY-A**	**31**	**40**	**9**	**8**	**2**	**1**	**0**	**0**	**6**	**—**	**2**	**0**	**0**	**—**	**1**	**1**	**.200**	**.304**	**.300**	**1.000**
1926	Bro-N	63	85	13	22	1	1	0	3	12	—	6	0	2	—	1	0	.259	.351	.294	.920
Career average		114	417	63	120	14	6	2	30	49	—	31	1	10	—	8	—	.287	.362	.364	.960
Yankee average		**116**	**441**	**77**	**133**	**14**	**6**	**3**	**33**	**52**	**—**	**23**	**1**	**11**	**—**	**4**	**6**	**.300**	**.375**	**.376**	**.983**
Career total		1139	4171	632	1195	144	62	18	302	489	—	309	7	104	—	78	41	.287	.362	.364	.960
Yankee total		**464**	**1764**	**308**	**530**	**57**	**22**	**11**	**132**	**207**	**—**	**93**	**4**	**44**	**—**	**17**	**23**	**.300**	**.375**	**.376**	**.983**

Wolter, Harry Meigs

HEIGHT: 5'10" THROWS: RIGHT BATS: LEFT BORN: 7/11/1884 MONTEREY, CALIFORNIA DIED: 7/7/1970 PALO ALTO, CALIFORNIA POSITIONS PLAYED: OF

YEAR	TEAM	GAMES	AB	RUNS	HITS	2B	3B	HR	RBI	BB	IBB	SO	HBP	SH	SF	SB	CS	BA	OBA	SA	FA
1907	Cin-N	4	15	1	2	0	0	0	1	0	—	—	0	0	—	0	—	.133	.133	.133	1.000
1907	Pit-N	1	1	0	0	0	0	0	0	0	—	—	0	0	—	0	—	.000	.000	.000	.000
1907	StL-N	16	47	4	16	0	0	0	6	3	—	—	0	0	—	1	—	.340	.380	.340	.962
1909	Bos-A	54	121	14	29	2	4	2	10	9	—	—	0	5	—	2	—	.240	.292	.372	1.000
1910	**NY-A**	**135**	**479**	**84**	**128**	**15**	**9**	**4**	**42**	**66**	**—**	**—**	**7**	**20**	**—**	**39**	**—**	**.267**	**.364**	**.361**	**.940**
1911	**NY-A**	**122**	**434**	**78**	**132**	**17**	**15**	**4**	**36**	**62**	**—**	**—**	**4**	**10**	**—**	**28**	**—**	**.304**	**.396**	**.440**	**.889**
1912	**NY-A**	**12**	**32**	**8**	**11**	**2**	**1**	**0**	**1**	**10**	**—**	**—**	**1**	**0**	**—**	**5**	**—**	**.344**	**.512**	**.469**	**.923**
1913	**NY-A**	**127**	**425**	**53**	**108**	**18**	**6**	**2**	**43**	**80**	**—**	**50**	**4**	**12**	**—**	**13**	**—**	**.254**	**.377**	**.339**	**.946**
1917	Chi-N	117	353	44	88	15	7	0	28	38	—	40	1	9	—	7	—	.249	.324	.331	1.000
Career average		65	212	32	57	8	5	1	19	30	—	—	2	6	—	11	—	.270	.365	.369	.851
Yankee average		**99**	**343**	**56**	**95**	**13**	**8**	**3**	**31**	**55**	**—**	**—**	**4**	**11**	**—**	**21**	**—**	**.277**	**.382**	**.382**	**.925**
Career total		588	1907	286	514	69	42	12	167	268	—	90	17	56	—	95	—	.270	.365	.369	.851
Yankee total		**396**	**1370**	**223**	**379**	**52**	**31**	**10**	**122**	**218**	**—**	**50**	**16**	**42**	**—**	**85**	**—**	**.277**	**.382**	**.382**	**.925**

Wolverton, Harry Sterling

HEIGHT: 5'11" THROWS: RIGHT BATS: LEFT BORN: 12/6/1873 MT.VERNON, OHIO DIED: 2/4/1937 OAKLAND, CALIFORNIA POSITIONS PLAYED: 3B

YEAR	TEAM	GAMES	AB	RUNS	HITS	2B	3B	HR	RBI	BB	IBB	SO	HBP	SH	SF	SB	CS	BA	OBA	SA	FA
1898	Chi-N	13	49	4	16	1	0	0	2	1	—	—	1	3	—	1	—	.327	.353	.347	.848
1899	Chi-N	99	389	50	111	14	11	1	49	30	—	—	9	14	—	14	—	.285	.350	.386	.860
1900	Chi-N	3	11	2	2	0	0	0	0	2	—	—	0	0	—	1	—	.182	.308	.182	.875
1900	Phi-N	101	383	42	108	10	8	3	58	20	—	—	3	8	—	4	—	.282	.323	.373	.881
1901	Phi-N	93	379	42	117	15	4	0	43	22	—	—	6	6	—	13	—	.309	.356	.369	.921
1902	Was-A	59	249	35	62	8	3	1	23	13	—	—	2	2	—	8	—	.249	.292	.317	.904
1902	Phi-N	34	136	12	40	3	2	0	16	9	—	—	2	5	—	3	—	.294	.347	.346	.931

(continued)

Eugene Richard "Gene" Woodling, of, 1949–54

Gene Woodling was another of Casey Stengel's platoon players (situational players who were placed in the game when circumstances favored their strengths). The difference was that Woodling handled sitting down worse than most.

Born August 16, 1922, in Akron, Ohio, Woodling began his major league career as a benchwarmer with the Cleveland Indians in 1943. After World War II, Woodling spent two frustrating years as a backup player in Cleveland and then Pittsburgh.

He played in the Pacific Coast League in 1948, where he led the league in hitting with a .385 average. That was where Stengel saw him and signed him for the Yankees for the 1949 season.

Stengel platooned Woodling and Hank Bauer. The two men were friends, but they were not happy with Stengel for not playing one or the other every day. Woodling, in particular, would check the lineup card daily. If his name was not on it, he would confront Stengel, much to the amusement of his teammates, and unleash a torrent of verbal abuse.

Stengel didn't mind. The two men invariably got more than 350 at-bats per season, and their competition kept them sharp.

Stengel loved Woodling because he was a better than average defensive player and a great clutch performer. He invariably had big games against the Cleveland Indians, who were the Yankees' principal opponents in the late 1940s and early 1950s. In the postseason, Woodling was tremendous. He hit over .400 in both the 1949 and 1950 series and hit over .300 in the 1952 and 1953 Fall Classics.

Woodling's Yankee career ended in 1954 when he was traded to the Orioles. But in 1962, Stengel, then with the Mets, picked him up from the Senators. That year, Casey finally let the 40-year-old Woodling play every game on the schedule.

(continued)

YEAR	TEAM	GAMES	AB	RUNS	HITS	2B	3B	HR	RBI	BB	IBB	SO	HBP	SH	SF	SB	CS	BA	OBA	SA	FA
1903	Phi-N	123	494	72	152	13	12	0	53	18	—	—	8	23	—	10	—	.308	.342	.383	.941
1904	Phi-N	102	398	43	106	15	5	0	49	26	—	—	6	10	—	18	—	.266	.321	.329	.925
1905	Bos-N	122	463	38	104	15	7	2	55	23	—	—	6	10	—	18	—	.225	.276	.300	.934
1912	**NY-A**	**34**	**50**	**6**	**15**	**1**	**1**	**0**	**4**	**2**	—	—	**10**	**9**	—	**10**	—	**.225**	**.276**	**.300**	**.934**
Career average		71	273	32	76	9	5	1	32	15	—	—	4	7	—	8	—	.278	.326	.352	.895
Yankee average		**34**	**50**	**6**	**15**	**1**	**1**	**0**	**4**	**2**	—	—	**1**	**1**	—	**1**	—	**.300**	**.340**	**.360**	**.821**
Career total		783	3001	346	833	95	53	7	352	166	—	—	48	81	—	83	—	.278	.326	.352	.895
Yankee total		**34**	**50**	**6**	**15**	**1**	**1**	**0**	**4**	**2**	—	—	**1**	**1**	—	**1**	—	**.300**	**.340**	**.360**	**.821**

Woodling, Eugene Richard (Gene)

HEIGHT: 5'9"   THROWS: RIGHT   BATS: LEFT   BORN: 8/16/1922 AKRON, OHIO   POSITIONS PLAYED: OF

YEAR	TEAM	GAMES	AB	RUNS	HITS	2B	3B	HR	RBI	BB	IBB	SO	HBP	SH	SF	SB	CS	BA	OBA	SA	FA
1943	Cle-A	8	25	5	8	2	1	1	5	1	—	5	0	1	—	0	0	.320	.346	.600	1.000
1946	Cle-A	61	133	8	25	1	4	0	9	16	—	13	1	5	—	1	2	.188	.280	.256	1.000
1947	Pit-N	22	79	7	21	2	2	0	10	7	—	5	0	1	—	0	—	.266	.326	.342	.968
1949	**NY-A**	**112**	**296**	**60**	**80**	**13**	**7**	**5**	**44**	**52**	—	**21**	**1**	**7**	—	**2**	**2**	**.270**	**.381**	**.412**	**.982**
1950	**NY-A**	**122**	**449**	**81**	**127**	**20**	**10**	**6**	**60**	**70**	—	**31**	**1**	**3**	—	**5**	**3**	**.283**	**.381**	**.412**	**.993**
1951	**NY-A**	**120**	**420**	**65**	**118**	**15**	**8**	**15**	**71**	**62**	—	**37**	**0**	**3**	—	**0**	**4**	**.281**	**.373**	**.462**	**.993**
1952	**NY-A**	**122**	**408**	**58**	**126**	**19**	**6**	**12**	**63**	**59**	—	**31**	**1**	**3**	—	**1**	**4**	**.309**	**.397**	**.473**	**.996**
1953	**NY-A**	**125**	**395**	**64**	**121**	**26**	**4**	**10**	**58**	**82**	—	**29**	**3**	**2**	—	**2**	**7**	**.306**	**.429**	**.468**	**.996**
1954	**NY-A**	**97**	**304**	**33**	**76**	**12**	**5**	**3**	**40**	**53**	—	**35**	**0**	**0**	**3**	**2**	**4**	**.250**	**.358**	**.352**	**.983**
1955	Bal-A	47	145	22	32	6	2	3	18	24	4	18	1	0	3	3	4	.250	.358	.352	.983
1955	Cle-A	79	259	33	72	15	1	5	35	36	2	15	3	1	4	1	1	.221	.329	.352	1.000
1956	Cle-A	100	317	56	83	17	0	8	38	69	2	29	3	7	3	2	4	.278	.368	.402	.993
1957	Cle-A	133	430	74	138	25	2	19	78	64	2	35	3	4	5	0	6	.262	.395	.391	.981
1958	Bal-A	133	413	57	114	16	1	15	65	66	3	49	2	4	5	4	2	.321	.408	.521	.992
1959	Bal-A	140	440	63	132	22	2	14	77	78	4	35	0	1	5	1	1	.276	.378	.429	.974
1960	Bal-A	140	435	68	123	18	3	11	62	84	7	40	4	3	3	3	0	.300	.402	.455	.981
1961	Was-A	110	342	39	107	16	4	10	57	50	3	24	2	1	1	1	0	.283	.401	.414	.995
1962	Was-A	44	107	19	30	4	0	5	16	24	4	5	2	1	0	1	0	.313	.403	.471	.988
1962	NY-N	81	190	18	52	8	1	5	24	24	3	22	1	0	3	0	0	.280	.421	.458	.953
																		.274	.353	.405	.986

(continued)

(continued)

	GAMES	AB	RUNS	HITS	2B	3B	HR	RBI	BB	IBB	SO	HBP	SH	SF	SB	CS	BA	OBA	SA	FA
Career average	95	294	44	83	14	3	8	44	49	—	25	2	2	—	2	—	.284	.388	.431	.987
Yankee average	116	379	60	108	18	7	9	56	63	—	31	1	3	—	2	4	.285	.389	.434	.991
Career total	1796	5587	830	1585	257	63	147	830	921	34	479	28	46	31	29	45	.284	.386	.431	.987
Yankee total	698	2272	361	648	105	40	51	336	378	—	184	6	18	3	13	24	.285	.388	.434	.991

Woods, Ronald Lawrence (Ron)

HEIGHT: 5'10"   THROWS: RIGHT   BATS: RIGHT   BORN: 2/1/1943 HAMILTON, OHIO   POSITIONS PLAYED: OF

YEAR	TEAM	GAMES	AB	RUNS	HITS	2B	3B	HR	RBI	BB	IBB	SO	HBP	SH	SF	SB	CS	BA	OBA	SA	FA
1969	Det-A	17	15	3	4	0	0	1	3	2	0	3	0	0	0	0	0	.267	.353	.467	1.000
1969	NY-A	72	171	18	30	5	2	1	7	22	1	29	1	6	0	2	0	.175	.273	.246	1.000
1970	NY-A	95	225	30	51	5	3	8	27	33	3	35	0	3	1	4	2	.227	.324	.382	.974
1971	NY-A	25	32	4	8	1	0	1	2	4	0	2	0	0	0	0	0	.250	.333	.375	.929
1971	Mon-N	51	138	26	41	7	3	1	17	19	0	18	0	2	0	0	2	.297	.382	.413	.989
1972	Mon-N	97	221	21	57	5	1	10	31	22	2	33	0	3	3	3	3	.258	.344	.425	.991
1973	Mon-N	135	318	45	73	11	3	3	31	56	3	34	0	10	1	12	6	.230	.344	.311	.977
1974	Mon-N	90	127	15	26	0	0	1	12	17	1	17	1	4	2	6	5	.205	.299	.228	.987
Career average		73	156	20	36	4	2	3	16	22	1	21	0	4	1	3	2	.233	.326	.342	.981
Yankee average		64	143	17	30	4	2	3	12	20	1	22	0	3	0	2	1	.208	.305	.327	.968
Career total		582	1247	162	290	34	12	26	130	175	10	171	2	28	7	27	18	.233	.326	.342	.981
Yankee total		192	428	52	89	11	5	10	36	59	4	66	1	9	1	6	2	.208	.305	.327	.968

Wynegar, Harold Delano (Butch)

HEIGHT: 6'1"   THROWS: RIGHT   BATS: BOTH   BORN: 3/14/1956 YORK, PENNSYLVANIA   POSITIONS PLAYED: C

YEAR	TEAM	GAMES	AB	RUNS	HITS	2B	3B	HR	RBI	BB	IBB	SO	HBP	SH	SF	SB	CS	BA	OBA	SA	FA
1976	Min-A	149	534	58	139	21	2	10	69	79	7	63	2	4	3	0	0	.260	.356	.363	.978
1977	Min-A	144	532	76	139	22	3	10	79	68	5	61	2	10	5	2	3	.261	.344	.370	.993
1978	Min-A	135	454	36	104	22	1	4	45	47	2	42	6	11	4	1	0	.229	.307	.308	.988
1979	Min-A	149	504	74	136	20	0	7	57	74	5	36	2	11	4	2	2	.270	.363	.351	.992
1980	Min-A	146	486	61	124	18	3	5	57	63	6	36	2	7	6	3	1	.255	.335	.335	.988
1981	Min-A	47	150	11	37	5	0	0	10	17	2	9	1	1	3	0	0	.247	.322	.280	.995
1982	Min-A	24	86	9	18	4	0	1	8	10	1	12	0	0	0	0	1	.209	.292	.291	.986
1982	NY-A	63	191	27	56	8	1	3	20	40	1	21	1	7	3	0	1	.293	.413	.393	.993
1983	NY-A	94	301	40	89	18	2	6	42	52	1	29	1	1	2	1	4	.296	.399	.429	.985
1984	NY-A	129	442	48	118	13	1	6	45	65	6	35	0	4	1	0	0	.267	.360	.342	.993
1985	NY-A	102	309	27	69	15	0	5	32	64	2	43	0	1	0	0	0	.223	.336	.320	.990
1986	NY-A	61	194	19	40	4	1	7	29	30	2	21	0	0	2	0	0	.206	.310	.345	.994
1987	Cal-A	31	92	4	19	2	0	0	5	9	0	13	0	1	0	0	0	.207	.277	.228	.994
1988	Cal-A	27	55	8	14	4	1	1	8	8	1	7	0	0	2	0	0	.255	.338	.418	.981
Career average		93	309	36	79	13	1	5	36	45	3	31	1	4	3	1	1	.255	.348	.347	.989
Yankee average		90	287	32	74	12	1	5	34	50	2	30	0	3	2	0	1	.259	.368	.363	.991
Career total		1301	4330	498	1102	176	15	65	506	626	41	428	17	58	36	10	13	.255	.348	.347	.989
Yankee total		449	1437	161	372	58	5	27	168	251	12	149	2	13	9	2	6	.259	.368	.363	.991

Wynn, James Sherman (Jimmy *or* The Toy Cannon)

HEIGHT: 5'10"   THROWS: RIGHT   BATS: RIGHT   BORN: 3/12/1942 HAMILTON, OHIO   POSITIONS PLAYED: OF

YEAR	TEAM	GAMES	AB	RUNS	HITS	2B	3B	HR	RBI	BB	IBB	SO	HBP	SH	SF	SB	CS	BA	OBA	SA	FA
1963	Hou-N	70	250	31	61	10	5	4	27	30	4	53	0	1	5	4	2	.244	.319	.372	.926
1964	Hou-N	67	219	19	49	7	0	5	18	24	2	58	1	2	2	5	5	.224	.301	.324	.958
1965	Hou-N	157	564	90	155	30	7	22	73	84	3	126	5	5	5	43	4	.275	.371	.470	.978
1966	Hou-N	105	418	62	107	21	1	18	62	41	4	81	1	3	4	13	10	.256	.321	.474	.978
1967	Hou-N	158	594	102	148	29	3	37	107	74	7	137	2	6	7	16	4	.249	.331	.495	.968
1968	Hou-N	156	542	85	146	23	5	26	67	90	9	131	5	5	4	23	7	.269	.376	.474	.988
1969	Hou-N	149	495	113	133	17	1	33	87	148	14	142	3	2	5	24	5	.269	.436	.507	.985
1970	Hou-N	157	554	82	156	32	2	27	88	106	12	96	1	0	7	10	5	.282	.394	.493	.987
1971	Hou-N	123	404	38	82	16	0	7	45	56	6	63	2	2	3	17	7	.203	.302	.295	.988
1972	Hou-N	145	542	117	148	29	3	24	90	103	6	99	2	2	3	14	11	.273	.389	.470	.986
1973	Hou-N	139	481	90	106	14	5	20	55	91	9	102	4	1	4	18	15	.220	.347	.395	.992
1974	LA-N	150	535	104	145	17	4	32	108	108	4	104	0	2	11	7	3	.271	.403	.497	.983
1975	LA-N	130	412	80	102	16	0	18	58	110	2	77	1	1	5	16	6	.248	.403	.417	.971
1976	Atl-N	148	449	75	93	19	1	17	66	127	1	111	0	0	8	16	6	.207	.377	.367	1.000
1977	NY-A	30	77	7	11	2	1	0	10	17	0	31	0	0	2	3	0	.143	.283	.234	.967
1977	Mil-A	36	117	10	23	3	1	0	10	17	0	31	0	0	2	3	0	.197	.294	.239	.967

(continued)

(continued)

	GAMES	AB	RUNS	HITS	2B	3B	HR	RBI	BB	IBB	SO	HBP	SH	SF	SB	CS	BA	OBA	SA	FA
Career average	120	416	69	104	18	2	18	60	77	5	89	2	2	5	14	6	.250	.366	.436	.977
Yankee average	**30**	**77**	**7**	**11**	**2**	**1**	**1**	**3**	**15**	**1**	**16**	**0**	**0**	**0**	**1**	**0**	**.143**	**.283**	**.234**	**1.000**
Career total	1920	6653	1105	1665	285	39	291	964	1224	84	1427	27	32	74	225	101	.250	.366	.436	.977
Yankee total	**30**	**77**	**7**	**11**	**2**	**1**	**1**	**3**	**15**	**1**	**16**	**0**	**0**	**0**	**1**	**0**	**.143**	**.283**	**.234**	**1.000**

Yeager, Joseph F. (Little Joe)

HEIGHT: 5'10"   THROWS: RIGHT   BATS: RIGHT   BORN: 8/28/1875 PHILADELPHIA, PENN.   DIED: 7/2/1937 DETROIT, MICH.   POSITIONS PLAYED: P, 2B, 3B, SS

YEAR	TEAM	GAMES	AB	RUNS	HITS	2B	3B	HR	RBI	BB	IBB	SO	HBP	SH	SF	SB	CS	BA	OBA	SA	FA
1898	Bro-N	43	134	12	23	5	1	0	15	7	—	—	1	3	—	1	—	.172	.218	.224	.908
1899	Bro-N	23	47	12	9	0	1	0	4	6	—	—	4	2	—	0	—	.191	.333	.234	.914
1900	Bro-N	3	9	0	3	0	0	0	0	0	—	—	0	0	—	0	—	.333	.333	.333	1.000
1901	Det-A	41	125	18	37	7	1	2	17	4	—	—	5	2	—	3	—	.296	.343	.416	.919
1902	Det-A	50	161	17	39	6	5	1	23	5	—	—	4	1	—	0	—	.242	.282	.360	.875
1903	Det-A	109	402	36	103	15	6	1	43	18	—	—	9	9	—	9	—	.256	.303	.323	.921
1905	**NY-A**	**115**	**401**	**54**	**107**	**16**	**7**	**0**	**42**	**25**	—	—	**13**	**10**	—	**8**	—	**.267**	**.330**	**.342**	**.934**
1906	**NY-A**	**57**	**123**	**20**	**37**	**6**	**1**	**0**	**12**	**13**	—	—	**9**	**7**	—	**3**	—	**.301**	**.407**	**.366**	**1.000**
1907	StL-A	123	436	32	104	21	7	1	44	31	—	—	3	8	—	11	—	.239	.294	.326	.934
1908	StL-A	10	15	3	5	1	0	0	1	1	—	—	3	1	—	2	—	.333	.474	.400	1.000
Career average		57	185	20	47	8	3	0	20	11	—	—	5	4	—	4	—	.252	.312	.331	.941
Yankee average		**86**	**262**	**37**	**72**	**11**	**4**	**0**	**27**	**19**	—	—	**11**	**9**	—	**6**	—	**.275**	**.349**	**.347**	**.967**
Career total		574	1853	204	467	77	29	4	201	110	—	—	51	43	—	37	—	.252	.312	.331	.941
Yankee total		**172**	**524**	**74**	**144**	**22**	**8**	**0**	**54**	**38**	—	—	**22**	**17**	—	**11**	—	**.275**	**.349**	**.347**	**.967**

Young, Ralph Stuart

HEIGHT: 5'5"   THROWS: RIGHT   BATS: BOTH   BORN: 9/19/1889 PHILADELPHIA, PENN.   DIED: 1/24/1965 PHILADELPHIA, PENN.   POSITIONS PLAYED: 2B, SS

YEAR	TEAM	GAMES	AB	RUNS	HITS	2B	3B	HR	RBI	BB	IBB	SO	HBP	SH	SF	SB	CS	BA	OBA	SA	FA
1913	**NY-A**	**7**	**15**	**2**	**1**	**0**	**0**	**0**	**0**	**3**	—	**3**	**0**	**0**	—	**2**	—	**.067**	**.222**	**.067**	**.857**
1915	Det-A	123	378	44	92	6	5	0	31	53	—	31	2	22	—	12	11	.243	.339	.286	.950
1916	Det-A	153	528	60	139	16	6	1	45	62	—	43	1	23	—	20	20	.263	.342	.322	1.000
1917	Det-A	141	503	64	116	18	2	1	35	61	—	35	3	31	—	8	—	.231	.317	.280	.958
1918	Det-A	91	298	31	56	7	1	0	21	54	—	17	0	16	—	15	—	.188	.313	.218	.939
1919	Det-A	125	456	63	96	13	5	1	25	53	—	32	1	46	—	8	—	.211	.294	.268	.943
1920	Det-A	150	594	84	173	21	6	0	33	85	—	30	2	22	—	8	13	.291	.382	.347	.969
1921	Det-A	107	401	70	120	8	3	0	29	69	—	23	3	13	—	11	9	.299	.406	.334	.947
1922	Phi-A	125	470	62	105	19	2	1	35	55	—	21	3	10	—	8	6	.223	.309	.279	.960
Career average		114	405	53	100	12	3	0	28	55	—	26	2	20	—	10	—	.247	.339	.296	.947
Yankee average		**7**	**15**	**2**	**1**	**0**	**0**	**0**	**0**	**3**	—	**3**	**0**	**0**	—	**2**	—	**.067**	**.222**	**.067**	**.857**
Career total		1022	3643	480	898	108	30	4	254	495	—	235	15	183	—	92	59	.247	.339	.296	.947
Yankee total		**7**	**15**	**2**	**1**	**0**	**0**	**0**	**0**	**3**	—	**3**	**0**	**0**	—	**2**	—	**.067**	**.222**	**.067**	**.857**

Zeider, Rollie Hubert (Bunions)

HEIGHT: 5'10"   THROWS: RIGHT   BATS: RIGHT   BORN: 11/16/1883 AUBURN, INDIANA   DIED: 9/12/1967 GARRETT, INDIANA   POSITIONS PLAYED: 1B, 2B, 3B, SS

YEAR	TEAM	GAMES	AB	RUNS	HITS	2B	3B	HR	RBI	BB	IBB	SO	HBP	SH	SF	SB	CS	BA	OBA	SA	FA
1910	Chi-A	136	498	57	108	9	2	0	31	62	—	—	1	20	—	49	—	.217	.305	.243	.900
1911	Chi-A	73	217	39	55	3	0	2	21	29	—	—	2	12	—	28	—	.253	.347	.295	.886
1912	Chi-A	130	420	57	103	12	10	1	42	50	—	—	3	24	—	47	—	.245	.330	.329	.979
1913	Chi-A	16	20	4	7	0	0	0	2	4	—	1	0	1	—	3	—	.350	.458	.350	1.000
1913	**NY-A**	**50**	**159**	**15**	**37**	**2**	**0**	**0**	**12**	**25**	—	**9**	**1**	**4**	—	**3**	—	**.233**	**.341**	**.245**	**.901**
1914	Chi-F	119	452	60	124	13	2	1	36	44	—	28	4	18	—	35	—	.274	.344	.319	.936
1915	Chi-F	129	494	65	112	22	2	0	34	43	—	24	6	15	—	16	—	.227	.297	.279	.960
1916	Chi-N	98	345	29	81	11	2	1	22	26	—	26	3	5	—	9	—	.235	.294	.287	1.000
1917	Chi-N	108	354	36	86	14	2	0	27	28	—	30	2	9	—	17	—	.243	.302	.294	.926
1918	Chi-N	82	251	31	56	3	2	0	26	23	—	20	0	14	—	16	—	.223	.288	.251	1.000
Career average		94	321	39	77	9	2	1	25	33	—	—	2	12	—	22	—	.240	.315	.286	.949
Yankee average		**50**	**159**	**15**	**37**	**2**	**0**	**0**	**12**	**25**	—	**9**	**1**	**4**	—	**3**	—	**.233**	**.341**	**.245**	**.901**
Career total		941	3210	393	769	89	22	5	253	334	—	138	22	122	—	223	—	.240	.315	.286	.949
Yankee total		**50**	**159**	**15**	**37**	**2**	**0**	**0**	**12**	**25**	—	**9**	**1**	**4**	—	**3**	—	**.233**	**.341**	**.245**	**.901**

Zinn, Guy
HEIGHT: 5'10"   THROWS: RIGHT   BATS: LEFT   BORN: 2/13/1887 HALLBROOK, W. VIRGINIA   DIED: 10/6/1949 CLARKSBURG, W. VIRGINIA   POSITIONS PLAYED: OF

YEAR	TEAM	GAMES	AB	RUNS	HITS	2B	3B	HR	RBI	BB	IBB	SO	HBP	SH	SF	SB	CS	BA	OBA	SA	FA
1911	NY-A	9	27	5	4	0	2	0	1	4	—	—	1	0	—	0	—	.148	.281	.296	.923
1912	NY-A	106	401	56	105	15	10	6	55	50	—	—	1	10	—	3	—	.262	.345	.394	.893
1913	Bos-N	36	138	15	41	8	2	1	15	4	—	23	1	4	—	6	—	.297	.322	.406	.948
1914	Bal-F	61	225	30	63	10	6	3	25	16	—	26	3	3	—	6	—	.280	.336	.418	.935
1915	Bal-F	102	312	30	84	18	3	5	43	35	—	28	0	12	—	2	—	.269	.343	.394	.949
Career average		63	221	27	59	10	5	3	28	22	—	—	1	6	—	6	—	.269	.338	.398	.930
Yankee average		58	214	31	55	8	6	3	28	27	—	—	1	5	—	9	—	.255	.341	.388	.908
Career total		314	1103	136	297	51	23	15	139	109	—	77	6	29	—	28	—	.269	.338	.398	.930
Yankee total		115	428	61	109	15	12	6	56	54	—	—	2	10	—	17	—	.255	.341	.388	.908

Zuvella, Paul
HEIGHT: 6'0"   THROWS: RIGHT   BATS: RIGHT   BORN: 10/31/1958 SAN MATEO, CALIFORNIA   POSITIONS PLAYED: 2B, 3B, SS

YEAR	TEAM	GAMES	AB	RUNS	HITS	2B	3B	HR	RBI	BB	IBB	SO	HBP	SH	SF	SB	CS	BA	OBA	SA	FA
1982	Atl-N	2	1	0	0	0	0	0	0	0	0	0	0	0	0	0	0	.000	.000	.000	.800
1983	Atl-N	3	5	0	0	0	0	0	0	2	0	1	1	0	0	0	0	.000	.375	.000	.750
1984	Atl-N	11	25	2	5	1	0	0	1	2	0	3	0	0	0	0	0	.200	.259	.240	1.000
1985	Atl-N	81	190	16	48	8	1	0	4	16	1	14	0	4	0	2	0	.253	.311	.305	1.000
1986	NY-A	21	48	2	4	1	0	0	2	5	0	4	0	4	0	0	0	.083	.170	.104	.966
1987	NY-A	14	34	2	6	0	0	0	0	0	0	4	0	2	0	0	0	.176	.176	.176	1.000
1988	Cle-A	51	130	9	30	5	1	0	7	8	0	13	0	8	0	0	0	.231	.275	.285	.959
1989	Cle-A	24	58	10	16	2	0	2	6	1	0	11	1	0	0	0	0	.276	.300	.414	.923
1991	KC-A	2	0	0	0	0	0	0	0	0	0	0	0	0	0	0	0	—	—	—	.000
Career average		23	55	5	12	2	0	0	2	4	0	6	0	2	0	0	0	.222	.275	.277	.822
Yankee average		18	41	2	5	1	0	0	1	3	0	4	0	3	0	0	0	.122	.172	.134	.983
Career total		209	491	41	109	17	2	2	20	34	1	50	2	18	0	2	0	.222	.275	.277	.822
Yankee total		35	82	4	10	1	0	0	2	5	0	8	0	6	0	0	0	.122	.172	.134	.983

Pitchers

Abbott, James Anthony (Jim)

HEIGHT: 6'3"   LEFTHANDER   BORN: 9/9/1967 FLINT, MICHIGAN

YEAR	TEAM	STARTS	GAMES	WON	LOST	PCT	ER	ERA	INNINGS PITCHED	STRIKE-OUTS	WALKS	HITS ALLOWED	HRS ALLOWED	COMP. GAMES	SHUT-OUTS	SAVES
1989	Cal-A	29	29	12	12	.500	79	3.92	181 1/3	115	74	190	13	4	2	0
1990	Cal-A	33	33	10	14	.417	106	4.51	211 2/3	105	72	246	16	4	1	0
1991	Cal-A	34	34	18	11	.621	78	2.89	243	158	73	222	14	5	1	0
1992	Cal-A	29	29	7	15	.318	65	2.77	211	130	68	208	12	7	0	0
1993	**NY-A**	**32**	**32**	**11**	**14**	**.440**	**104**	**4.37**	**214**	**95**	**73**	**221**	**22**	**4**	**1**	**0**
1994	**NY-A**	**24**	**24**	**9**	**8**	**.529**	**81**	**4.55**	**160 1/3**	**90**	**64**	**167**	**24**	**2**	**0**	**0**
1995	Chi-A	17	17	6	4	.600	42	3.36	112 1/3	45	35	116	10	3	1	0
1995	Cal-A	13	13	5	4	.556	39	4.15	84 2/3	41	29	93	4	1	0	0
1996	Cal-A	23	27	2	18	.100	118	7.48	142	58	78	171	23	1	0	0
1998	Chi-A	5	5	5	0	1.000	16	4.55	31 2/3	14	12	35	2	0	0	0
1999	Mil-N	15	20	2	8	.200	63	6.91	82	37	42	110	14	0	0	0
Career Average		23.1	24	8	10	.446	72	4.25	152	81	56	162	14	3	0	0
Yankee Average		**28**	**28**	**10**	**11**	**.476**	**93**	**4.45**	**187**	**93**	**69**	**194**	**23**	**3**	**1**	**0**
Career Total		254	263	87	108	.446	791	4.25	1674	888	620	1779	154	31	6	0
Yankee Total		**56**	**56**	**20**	**22**	**.476**	**185**	**4.45**	**374**	**185**	**137**	**388**	**46**	**6**	**1**	**0**

Ables, Harry Terrell (Hans)

HEIGHT: 6'2"   LEFTHANDER   BORN: 10/4/1884 TERRELL, TEXAS   DIED: 2/8/1951 SAN ANTONIO, TEXAS

YEAR	TEAM	STARTS	GAMES	WON	LOST	PCT	ER	ERA	INNINGS PITCHED	STRIKE-OUTS	WALKS	HITS ALLOWED	HRS ALLOWED	COMP. GAMES	SHUT-OUTS	SAVES
1905	StL-A	3	6	0	3	.000	13	3.82	30 2/3	11	13	37	0	1	0	0
1909	Cle-A	3	5	1	1	.500	7	2.12	29 2/3	24	10	26	1	3	0	0
1911	**NY-A**	**2**	**3**	**0**	**1**	**.000**	**12**	**9.82**	**11**	**6**	**7**	**16**	**0**	**0**	**0**	**0**
Career Average		8	5	0	2	.167	11	4.04	24	14	10	26	0	1	0	0
Yankee Average		**2**	**3**	**0**	**1**	**.000**	**12**	**9.82**	**11**	**6**	**7**	**16**	**0**	**0**	**0**	**0**
Career Total		8	14	1	5	.167	32	4.04	71 1/3	41	30	79	1	4	0	0
Yankee Total		**2**	**3**	**0**	**1**	**.000**	**12**	**9.82**	**11**	**6**	**7**	**16**	**0**	**0**	**0**	**0**

Adkins, Merle Theron (Doc)

HEIGHT: 5'10"   RIGHTHANDER   BORN: 8/5/1872 TROY, WINSCONSIN   DIED: 2/21/1934 DURHAM, NORTH CAROLINA

YEAR	TEAM	STARTS	GAMES	WON	LOST	PCT	ER	ERA	INNINGS PITCHED	STRIKE-OUTS	WALKS	HITS ALLOWED	HRS ALLOWED	COMP. GAMES	SHUT-OUTS	SAVES
1902	Bos-A	2	4	1	1	.500	9	4.05	20	3	7	30	2	1	0	0
1903	**NY-A**	**1**	**2**	**0**	**0**	**—**	**6**	**7.71**	**7**	**0**	**5**	**10**	**0**	**0**	**0**	**1**
Career Average		2	3	1	1	.500	8	5.00	14	2	6	20	1	1	0	1
Yankee Average		**1**	**2**	**0**	**0**	**—**	**6**	**7.71**	**7**	**0**	**5**	**10**	**0**	**0**	**0**	**1**
Career Total		3	6	1	1	.500	15	5.00	27	3	12	40	2	1	0	1
Yankee Total		**1**	**2**	**0**	**0**	**—**	**6**	**7.71**	**7**	**0**	**5**	**10**	**0**	**0**	**0**	**1**

Adkins, Steven Thomas

HEIGHT: 6'6"   LEFTHANDER   BORN: 10/26/1964 CHICAGO, ILLINOIS

YEAR	TEAM	STARTS	GAMES	WON	LOST	PCT	ER	ERA	INNINGS PITCHED	STRIKE-OUTS	WALKS	HITS ALLOWED	HRS ALLOWED	COMP. GAMES	SHUT-OUTS	SAVES
1990	**NY-A**	**5**	**5**	**1**	**2**	**.333**	**17**	**6.38**	**24**	**14**	**29**	**19**	**4**	**0**	**0**	**0**
Career Average		5	5	1	2	.333	17	6.38	24	14	29	19	4	0	0	0
Yankee Average		**5**	**5**	**1**	**2**	**.333**	**17**	**6.38**	**24**	**14**	**29**	**19**	**4**	**0**	**0**	**0**
Career Total		5	5	1	2	.333	17	6.38	24	14	29	19	4	0	0	0
Yankee Total		**5**	**5**	**1**	**2**	**.333**	**17**	**6.38**	**24**	**14**	**29**	**19**	**4**	**0**	**0**	**0**

Aker, Jackie Delane (Jack)
HEIGHT: 6'2" RIGHTHANDER BORN: 7/13/1940 TULARE, CALIFORNIA

YEAR	TEAM	STARTS	GAMES	WON	LOST	PCT	ER	ERA	INNINGS PITCHED	STRIKE-OUTS	WALKS	HITS ALLOWED	HRS ALLOWED	COMP. GAMES	SHUT-OUTS	SAVES
1964	KC-A	0	9	0	1	.000	16	8.82	16 1/3	7	10	17	6	0	0	0
1965	KC-A	0	34	4	3	.571	18	3.16	51 1/3	26	18	45	3	0	0	3
1966	KC-A	0	66	8	4	.667	25	1.99	113	68	28	81	7	0	0	32
1967	KC-A	0	57	3	8	273	42	4.30	88	65	32	87	9	0	0	12
1968	Oak-A	0	54	4	4	.500	34	4.10	74 2/3	44	33	72	6	0	0	11
1969	Sea-A	0	15	0	2	.000	14	7.56	16 2/3	7	13	25	4	0	0	3
1969	**NY-A**	**0**	**38**	**8**	**4**	**.667**	**15**	**2.06**	**65 2/3**	**40**	**22**	**51**	**4**	**0**	**0**	**11**
1970	**NY-A**	**0**	**41**	**4**	**2**	**.667**	**16**	**2.06**	**70**	**36**	**20**	**57**	**3**	**0**	**0**	**16**
1971	**NY-A**	**0**	**41**	**4**	**4**	**.500**	**16**	**2.59**	**55 1/3**	**24**	**26**	**48**	**3**	**0**	**0**	**4**
1972	Chi-N	0	48	6	6	.500	22	2.96	67	36	23	65	4	0	0	17
1972	**NY-A**	**0**	**4**	**0**	**0**	**—**	**2**	**3.00**	**6**	**1**	**3**	**5**	**0**	**0**	**0**	**0**
1973	Chi-N	0	47	4	5	.444	29	4.10	63 2/3	25	23	76	8	0	0	12
1974	NY-N	0	24	2	1	.667	16	3.48	41 1/3	18	14	33	4	0	0	2
1974	Atl-N	0	17	0	1	.000	7	3.78	16 2/3	7	9	17	3	0	0	0
Career Average		0	35	3	3	.511	19	3.28	53	29	20	49	5	0	0	9
Yankee Average		**0**	**31**	**4**	**3**	**.615**	**12**	**2.23**	**49**	**25**	**18**	**40**	**3**	**0**	**0**	**8**
Career Total		0	495	47	45	.511	272	3.28	746	404	274	679	64	0	0	123
Yankee Total		**0**	**124**	**16**	**10**	**.615**	**49**	**2.23**	**197**	**101**	**71**	**161**	**10**	**0**	**0**	**31**

Aldrete, Michael Peter
HEIGHT: 5'11" LEFTHANDER BORN: 1/29/1961 CARMEL, CALIFORNIA

YEAR	TEAM	STARTS	GAMES	WON	LOST	PCT	ER	ERA	INNINGS PITCHED	STRIKE-OUTS	WALKS	HITS ALLOWED	HRS ALLOWED	COMP. GAMES	SHUT-OUTS	SAVES
1996	**NY-A**	**0**	**1**	**0**	**0**	**—**	**0**	**0.00**	**1**	**0**	**0**	**1**	**0**	**0**	**0**	**0**
Career Average		0	1	0	0	—	0	0.00	1	0	0	1	0	0	0	0
Yankee Average		**0**	**1**	**0**	**0**	**—**	**0**	**0.00**	**1**	**0**	**0**	**1**	**0**	**0**	**0**	**0**
Career Total		0	1	0	0	—	0	0.00	1	0	0	1	0	0	0	0
Yankee Total		**0**	**1**	**0**	**0**	**—**	**0**	**0.00**	**1**	**0**	**0**	**1**	**0**	**0**	**0**	**0**

Alexander, Doyle Lafayette
HEIGHT: 6'3" RIGHTHANDER BORN: 9/4/1950 CORDOVA, ALABAMA

YEAR	TEAM	STARTS	GAMES	WON	LOST	PCT	ER	ERA	INNINGS PITCHED	STRIKE-OUTS	WALKS	HITS ALLOWED	HRS ALLOWED	COMP. GAMES	SHUT-OUTS	SAVES
1971	LA-N	12	17	6	6	.500	39	3.80	92 1/3	30	18	105	6	4	0	0
1972	Bal-A	9	35	6	8	.429	29	2.45	106 1/3	49	30	78	5	2	2	2
1973	Bal-A	26	29	12	8	.600	75	3.86	174 2/3	63	52	169	19	10	0	0
1974	Bal-A	12	30	6	9	.400	51	4.01	114 1/3	40	43	127	7	2	0	0
1975	Bal-A	11	32	8	8	.500	45	3.04	133 1/3	46	47	127	7	3	1	1
1976	Bal-A	6	11	3	4	.429	25	3.50	58	17	24	58	3	2	1	0
1976	**NY-A**	**19**	**19**	**10**	**5**	**.667**	**50**	**3.29**	**136 2/3**	**41**	**39**	**114**	**9**	**5**	**2**	**0**
1977	Tex-A	34	34	17	11	.607	96	3.65	237	82	82	221	24	12	1	0
1978	Tex-A	28	31	9	10	.474	82	3.86	191	81	71	198	18	7	1	0
1979	Tex-A	18	23	5	7	.417	56	4.45	113 1/3	50	69	114	3	0	0	0
1980	Atl-N	35	35	14	11	.560	108	4.20	231 2/3	114	74	227	20	7	1	0
1981	SF-N	24	24	11	7	.611	49	2.89	152 1/3	77	44	156	11	1	1	0
1982	**NY-A**	**11**	**16**	**1**	**7**	**.125**	**45**	**6.08**	**66 2/3**	**26**	**14**	**81**	**14**	**0**	**0**	**0**
1983	**NY-A**	**5**	**8**	**0**	**2**	**.000**	**20**	**6.35**	**28 1/3**	**17**	**7**	**31**	**6**	**0**	**0**	**0**
1983	Tor-A	15	17	7	6	.538	51	3.93	116 2/3	46	26	126	14	5	0	0
1984	Tor-A	35	36	17	6	.739	91	3.13	261 2/3	139	59	238	21	11	2	0
1985	Tor-A	36	36	17	10	.630	100	3.45	260 2/3	142	67	268	28	6	1	0
1986	Tor-A	17	17	5	4	.556	55	4.46	111	65	20	120	18	3	0	0
1986	Atl-N	17	17	6	6	.500	50	3.84	117 1/3	74	17	135	9	2	0	0
1987	Atl-N	16	16	5	10	.333	54	4.13	117 2/3	64	27	115	21	3	0	0
1987	Det-A	11	11	9	0	1.000	15	1.53	88 1/3	44	26	63	3	3	3	0
1988	Det-A	34	34	14	11	.560	110	4.32	229	126	46	260	30	5	1	0
1989	Det-A	33	33	6	18	.250	110	4.44	223	95	76	245	28	5	1	0
Career Average		20	24	8	8	.527	61	3.76	146	66	43	147	14	4	1	0
Yankee Average		**12**	**14**	**4**	**5**	**.440**	**38**	**4.47**	**77**	**28**	**20**	**75**	**10**	**2**	**1**	**0**
Career Total		464	561	194	174	.527	1406	3.76	3367 2/3	1528	978	3376	324	98	18	3
Yankee Total		**35**	**43**	**11**	**14**	**.440**	**115**	**4.47**	**232**	**84**	**60**	**226**	**29**	**5**	**2**	**0**

Allen, John Thomas

HEIGHT: 6'0"   RIGHTHANDER   BORN: 9/30/1905 LENOIR, NORTH CAROLINA   DIED: 5/29/1959 ST. PETERSBURG, FLORIDA

YEAR	TEAM	STARTS	GAMES	WON	LOST	PCT	ER	ERA	INNINGS PITCHED	STRIKE-OUTS	WALKS	HITS ALLOWED	HRS ALLOWED	COMP. GAMES	SHUT-OUTS	SAVES
1932	**NY-A**	**21**	**33**	**17**	**4**	**.810**	**79**	**3.70**	**192**	**109**	**76**	**162**	**10**	**13**	**3**	**4**
1933	**NY-A**	**24**	**25**	**15**	**7**	**.682**	**90**	**4.39**	**184 2/3**	**119**	**87**	**171**	**9**	**10**	**1**	**1**
1934	**NY-A**	**10**	**13**	**5**	**2**	**.714**	**23**	**2.89**	**71 2/3**	**54**	**32**	**62**	**3**	**4**	**0**	**0**
1935	**NY-A**	**23**	**23**	**13**	**6**	**.684**	**67**	**3.61**	**167**	**113**	**58**	**149**	**11**	**12**	**2**	**0**
1936	Cle-A	31	36	20	10	.667	93	3.44	243	165	97	234	5	19	4	1
1937	Cle-A	20	24	15	1	.938	49	2.55	173	87	60	157	4	14	0	0
1938	Cle-A	27	30	14	8	.636	93	4.19	200	112	81	189	15	13	0	0
1939	Cle-A	26	28	9	7	.563	89	4.58	175	79	56	199	9	9	2	0
1940	Cle-A	17	32	9	8	.529	53	3.44	138 2/3	62	48	126	3	5	3	5
1941	StL-A	9	20	2	5	.286	49	6.58	67	27	29	89	4	2	0	1
1941	Bro-N	4	11	3	0	1.000	16	2.51	57 1/3	21	12	38	6	1	0	0
1942	Bro-N	15	27	10	6	.625	42	3.20	118	50	39	106	11	5	1	3
1943	Bro-N	1	17	5	1	.833	18	4.26	38	15	25	42	3	0	0	1
1943	NY-N	0	15	1	3	.250	14	3.07	41	24	14	37	4	0	0	2
1944	NY-N	13	18	4	7	.364	38	4.07	84	33	24	88	7	2	1	0
Career Average		16	23	9	5	.654	54	3.75	130	71	49	123	7	7	1	1
Yankee Average		**20**	**24**	**13**	**5**	**.725**	**65**	**3.79**	**154**	**99**	**63**	**136**	**8**	**10**	**2**	**1**
Career Total		241	352	142	75	.654	813	3.75	1950 1/3	1070	738	1849	104	109	17	18
Yankee Total		**78**	**94**	**50**	**19**	**.725**	**259**	**3.79**	**615**	**395**	**253**	**544**	**33**	**39**	**6**	**5**

Allen, Neil Patrick

HEIGHT: 6'2"   RIGHTHANDER   BORN: 1/24/1958 KANSAS CITY, KANSAS

YEAR	TEAM	STARTS	GAMES	WON	LOST	PCT	ER	ERA	INNINGS PITCHED	STRIKE-OUTS	WALKS	HITS ALLOWED	HRS ALLOWED	COMP. GAMES	SHUT-OUTS	SAVES
1979	NY-N	5	50	6	10	.375	39	3.55	99	65	47	100	4	0	0	8
1980	NY-N	0	59	7	10	.412	40	3.70	97 1/3	79	40	87	7	0	0	22
1981	NY-N	0	43	7	6	.538	22	2.97	66 2/3	50	26	64	4	0	0	18
1982	NY-N	0	50	3	7	.300	22	3.06	64 2/3	59	30	65	5	0	0	19
1983	NY-N	4	21	2	7	.222	27	4.50	54	32	36	57	6	1	1	2
1983	StL-N	18	25	10	6	.625	50	3.70	121 2/3	74	48	122	6	4	2	0
1984	StL-N	1	57	9	6	.600	47	3.55	119	66	49	105	6	0	0	3
1985	StL-N	1	23	1	4	.200	18	5.59	29	10	17	32	3	0	0	2
1985	**NY-A**	**0**	**17**	**1**	**0**	**1.000**	**9**	**2.76**	**29 1/3**	**16**	**13**	**26**	**1**	**0**	**0**	**1**
1986	Chi-A	17	22	7	2	.778	48	3.82	113	57	38	101	8	2	2	0
1987	Chi-A	10	15	0	7	.000	39	7.07	49 2/3	26	26	74	6	0	0	0
1987	**NY-A**	**1**	**8**	**0**	**1**	**.000**	**10**	**3.65**	**24 2/3**	**16**	**10**	**23**	**2**	**0**	**0**	**0**
1988	**NY-A**	**2**	**41**	**5**	**3**	**.625**	**50**	**3.84**	**117 1/3**	**61**	**37**	**121**	**14**	**0**	**1**	**0**
1989	Cle-A	0	3	0	1	.000	5	15.00	3	0	0	8	1	0	0	0
Career Average		4	31	4	5	.453	30	3.88	71	44	30	70	5	1	0	5
Yankee Average		**1**	**22**	**2**	**1**	**.600**	**23**	**3.62**	**57**	**31**	**20**	**57**	**6**	**0**	**0**	**0**
Career Total		59	434	58	70	.453	426	3.88	988 1/3	611	417	985	73	7	6	75
Yankee Total		**3**	**66**	**6**	**4**	**.600**	**69**	**3.62**	**171**	**93**	**60**	**170**	**17**	**0**	**1**	**1**

Anderson, Richard Lee

HEIGHT: 6'2"   RIGHTHANDER   BORN: 12/25/1953 INGLEWOOD, CALIFORNIA   DIED: 6/23/1989 WILMINGTON, CALIFORNIA

YEAR	TEAM	STARTS	GAMES	WON	LOST	PCT	ER	ERA	INNINGS PITCHED	STRIKE-OUTS	WALKS	HITS ALLOWED	HRS ALLOWED	COMP. GAMES	SHUT-OUTS	SAVES
1979	**NY-A**	**0**	**1**	**0**	**0**	**—**	**1**	**3.86**	**2 1/3**	**0**	**4**	**1**	**0**	**0**	**0**	**0**
1980	Sea-A	2	5	0	0	—	4	3.72	9 2/3	7	10	8	1	0	0	0
Career Average		1	3	0	0	—	3	3.75	6	4	7	5	1	0	0	0
Yankee Average		**0**	**1**	**0**	**0**	**—**	**1**	**3.86**	**2 1/3**	**0**	**4**	**1**	**0**	**0**	**0**	**0**
Career Total		2	6	0	0	—	5	3.75	12	7	14	9	1	0	0	0
Yankee Total		**0**	**1**	**0**	**0**	**—**	**1**	**3.86**	**2 1/3**	**0**	**4**	**1**	**0**	**0**	**0**	**0**

Andrews, Ivy Paul (Poison)

HEIGHT: 6'1" RIGHTHANDER BORN: 5/6/1907 DORA, ALABAMA DIED: 11/24/1970 BIRMINGHAM, ALABAMA

YEAR	TEAM	STARTS	GAMES	WON	LOST	PCT	ER	ERA	INNINGS PITCHED	STRIKE-OUTS	WALKS	HITS ALLOWED	HRS ALLOWED	COMP. GAMES	SHUT-OUTS	SAVES
1931	**NY-A**	**3**	**7**	**2**	**0**	**1.000**	**16**	**4.19**	**34 1/3**	**10**	**8**	**36**	**3**	**1**	**0**	**0**
1932	**NY-A**	**1**	**4**	**2**	**1**	**.667**	**5**	**1.82**	**24 2/3**	**7**	**9**	**20**	**0**	**1**	**0**	**0**
1932	Bos-A	19	25	8	6	.571	60	3.81	141 2/3	30	53	144	4	8	0	0
1933	Bos-A	17	34	7	13	.350	77	4.95	140	37	61	157	8	5	0	1
1934	StL-A	13	43	4	11	.267	72	4.66	139	51	65	166	7	2	0	3
1935	StL-A	20	50	13	7	.650	84	3.54	213 1/3	43	53	231	10	10	0	1
1936	StL-A	25	36	7	12	.368	103	4.84	191 1/3	33	50	221	19	11	0	1
1937	Cle-A	4	20	3	4	.429	29	4.37	59 2/3	16	9	76	3	1	1	0
1937	**NY-A**	**5**	**11**	**3**	**2**	**.600**	**17**	**3.12**	**49**	**17**	**17**	**49**	**2**	**3**	**1**	**1**
1938	**NY-A**	**1**	**19**	**1**	**3**	**.250**	**16**	**3.00**	**48**	**13**	**17**	**51**	**3**	**1**	**0**	**1**
Career Average		11	25	5	6	.459	48	4.14	104	26	34	115	6	4	0	1
Yankee Average		**3**	**10**	**2**	**2**	**.571**	**14**	**3.12**	**39**	**12**	**13**	**39**	**2**	**2**	**0**	**1**
Career Total		108	249	50	59	.459	479	4.14	1041	257	342	1151	59	43	2	8
Yankee Total		**10**	**41**	**8**	**6**	**.571**	**54**	**3.12**	**156**	**47**	**51**	**156**	**8**	**6**	**1**	**2**

Appleton, Peter William (Jake)

HEIGHT: 5'11" RIGHTHANDER BORN: 5/20/1904 TERRYVILLE, CONNECTICUT DIED: 1/18/1974 TRENTON, NEW JERSEY

YEAR	TEAM	STARTS	GAMES	WON	LOST	PCT	ER	ERA	INNINGS PITCHED	STRIKE-OUTS	WALKS	HITS ALLOWED	HRS ALLOWED	COMP. GAMES	SHUT-OUTS	SAVES
1927	Cin-N	2	6	2	1	.667	6	1.82	29 2/3	3	17	29	0	2	1	0
1928	Cin-N	1	31	3	4	.429	43	4.68	82 2/3	20	22	101	7	0	0	0
1930	Cle-A	7	39	8	7	.533	53	4.02	118 2/3	45	53	122	8	2	0	1
1931	Cle-A	4	29	4	4	.500	41	4.63	79 2/3	25	29	100	2	3	0	0
1932	Cle-A	0	4	0	0	—	9	16.20	5	1	3	11	1	0	0	0
1932	Bos-A	3	11	0	3	.000	21	4.11	46	15	26	49	2	0	0	0
1933	**NY-A**	**0**	**1**	**0**	**0**	**—**	**0**	**0.00**	**2**	**0**	**1**	**3**	**0**	**0**	**0**	**0**
1936	Was-A	20	38	14	9	.609	79	3.53	201 2/3	77	77	199	7	12	1	3
1937	Was-A	18	35	8	15	.348	83	4.45	168	62	72	167	16	7	4	2
1938	Was-A	10	43	7	9	.438	84	4.60	164 1/3	62	61	175	12	5	0	5
1939	Was-A	4	40	5	10	.333	52	4.56	102 2/3	50	48	104	7	2	0	6
1940	Chi-A	0	25	4	0	1.000	36	5.62	57 2/3	21	28	54	8	0	0	5
1941	Chi-A	0	13	0	3	.000	16	5.27	27 1/3	12	17	27	4	0	0	1
1942	Chi-A	0	4	0	0	—	2	3.86	4 2/3	2	3	2	0	0	0	0
1942	StL-A	0	14	1	1	.500	9	2.96	27 1/3	12	11	25	1	0	0	2
1945	StL-A	0	2	0	0	—	4	15.43	2 1/3	1	7	3	0	0	0	0
1945	Was-A	2	6	1	0	1.000	8	3.38	21 1/3	12	11	16	1	1	0	1
Career Average		4	20	3	4	.463	32	4.30	67	25	29	70	4	2	0	2
Yankee Average		**0**	**1**	**0**	**0**	**—**	**0**	**0.00**	**2**	**0**	**1**	**3**	**0**	**0**	**0**	**0**
Career Total		71	341	57	66	.463	546	4.31	1141	420	486	1187	76	34	6	26
Yankee Total		**0**	**1**	**0**	**0**	**—**	**0**	**0.00**	**2**	**0**	**1**	**3**	**0**	**0**	**0**	**0**

Ardizoia, Rinaldo Joseph (Rugger)

HEIGHT: 5'11" RIGHTHANDER BORN: 11/20/1919 OLEGGIO, ITALY

YEAR	TEAM	STARTS	GAMES	WON	LOST	PCT	ER	ERA	INNINGS PITCHED	STRIKE-OUTS	WALKS	HITS ALLOWED	HRS ALLOWED	COMP. GAMES	SHUT-OUTS	SAVES
1947	**NY-A**	**0**	**1**	**0**	**0**	**—**	**2**	**9.00**	**2**	**0**	**1**	**4**	**1**	**0**	**0**	**0**
Career Average		0	1	0	0	—	2	9.00	2	0	1	4	1	0	0	0
Yankee Average		**0**	**1**	**0**	**0**	**—**	**2**	**9.00**	**2**	**0**	**1**	**4**	**1**	**0**	**0**	**0**
Career Total		0	1	0	0	—	2	9.00	2	0	1	4	1	0	0	0
Yankee Total		**0**	**1**	**0**	**0**	**—**	**2**	**9.00**	**2**	**0**	**1**	**4**	**1**	**0**	**0**	**0**

Armstrong, Michael Dennis
HEIGHT: 6′3″   RIGHTHANDER   BORN: 3/7/1954 GLEN COVE, NEW YORK

YEAR	TEAM	STARTS	GAMES	WON	LOST	PCT	ER	ERA	INNINGS PITCHED	STRIKE-OUTS	WALKS	HITS ALLOWED	HRS ALLOWED	COMP. GAMES	SHUT-OUTS	SAVES
1980	SD-N	0	11	0	0	—	9	5.65	14 1/3	14	13	16	3	0	0	0
1981	SD-N	0	10	0	2	.000	8	6.00	12	9	11	14	1	0	0	0
1982	KC-A	0	52	5	5	.500	40	3.20	112 2/3	75	43	88	9	0	0	6
1983	KC-A	0	58	10	7	.588	44	3.86	102 2/3	52	45	86	11	0	0	3
1984	**NY-A**	**0**	**36**	**3**	**2**	**.600**	**21**	**3.48**	**54 1/3**	**43**	**26**	**47**	**6**	**0**	**0**	**1**
1985	**NY-A**	**0**	**9**	**0**	**0**	**—**	**5**	**3.07**	**14 2/3**	**11**	**2**	**9**	**4**	**0**	**0**	**0**
1986	**NY-A**	**1**	**7**	**0**	**1**	**.000**	**9**	**9.35**	**8 2/3**	**8**	**5**	**13**	**4**	**0**	**0**	**0**
1987	Cle-A	0	14	1	0	1.000	18	8.68	18 2/3	9	10	27	4	0	0	1
Career Average		0	25	2	2	.528	19	4.10	42	28	19	38	5	0	0	1
Yankee Average		**0**	**17**	**1**	**1**	**.500**	**12**	**4.06**	**26**	**21**	**11**	**23**	**5**	**0**	**0**	**0**
Career Total		1	197	19	17	.528	154	4.10	338	221	155	300	42	0	0	11
Yankee Total		**1**	**52**	**3**	**3**	**.500**	**35**	**4.06**	**78**	**62**	**33**	**69**	**14**	**0**	**0**	**1**

Arnsberg, Bradley James
HEIGHT: 6′4″   RIGHTHANDER   BORN: 8/20/1963 SEATTLE, WASHINGTON

YEAR	TEAM	STARTS	GAMES	WON	LOST	PCT	ER	ERA	INNINGS PITCHED	STRIKE-OUTS	WALKS	HITS ALLOWED	HRS ALLOWED	COMP. GAMES	SHUT-OUTS	SAVES
1986	**NY-A**	**1**	**2**	**0**	**0**	**—**	**3**	**3.38**	**8**	**3**	**1**	**13**	**1**	**0**	**0**	**0**
1987	**NY-A**	**2**	**6**	**1**	**3**	**.250**	**12**	**5.59**	**19 1/3**	**14**	**13**	**22**	**5**	**0**	**0**	**0**
1989	Tex-A	1	16	2	1	.667	22	4.13	48	26	22	45	6	0	0	1
1990	Tex-A	0	53	6	1	.857	15	2.15	62 2/3	44	33	56	4	0	0	5
1991	Tex-A	0	9	0	1	.000	9	8.38	9 2/3	8	5	10	5	0	0	0
1992	Cle-A	0	8	0	0	—	14	11.81	10 2/3	5	11	13	6	0	0	0
Career Average		1	16	2	1	.600	13	4.26	26	17	14	27	5	0	0	1
Yankee Average		**2**	**4**	**1**	**2**	**.250**	**8**	**4.94**	**14**	**9**	**7**	**18**	**3**	**0**	**0**	**0**
Career Total		4	94	9	6	.600	75	4.26	158 1/3	100	85	159	27	0	0	6
Yankee Total		**3**	**8**	**1**	**3**	**.250**	**15**	**4.94**	**27**	**17**	**14**	**35**	**6**	**0**	**0**	**0**

Arroyo, Luis Enrique
HEIGHT: 5′8″   LEFTHANDER   BORN: 2/18/1927 PENUELAS, PUERTO RICO

YEAR	TEAM	STARTS	GAMES	WON	LOST	PCT	ER	ERA	INNINGS PITCHED	STRIKE-OUTS	WALKS	HITS ALLOWED	HRS ALLOWED	COMP. GAMES	SHUT-OUTS	SAVES
1955	StL-N	24	35	11	8	.579	74	4.19	159	68	63	162	22	9	1	0
1956	Pit-N	2	18	3	3	.500	15	4.71	28 2/3	17	12	36	5	1	0	0
1957	Pit-N	10	54	3	11	.214	68	4.68	130 2/3	101	31	151	19	0	0	1
1959	Cin-N	0	10	1	0	1.000	6	3.95	13 2/3	8	11	17	0	0	0	0
1960	**NY-A**	**0**	**29**	**5**	**1**	**.833**	**13**	**2.88**	**40 2/3**	**29**	**22**	**30**	**2**	**0**	**0**	**7**
1961	**NY-A**	**0**	**65**	**15**	**5**	**.750**	**29**	**2.19**	**119**	**87**	**49**	**83**	**5**	**0**	**0**	**29**
1962	**NY-A**	**0**	**27**	**1**	**3**	**.250**	**18**	**4.81**	**33 2/3**	**21**	**17**	**33**	**5**	**0**	**0**	**7**
1963	**NY-A**	**0**	**6**	**1**	**1**	**.500**	**9**	**13.50**	**6**	**5**	**3**	**12**	**0**	**0**	**0**	**0**
Career Average		5	31	5	4	.556	29	3.93	66	42	26	66	7	1	0	6
Yankee Average		**0**	**32**	**6**	**3**	**.688**	**17**	**3.12**	**50**	**36**	**23**	**40**	**3**	**0**	**0**	**11**
Career Total		36	244	40	32	.556	232	3.93	531 1/3	336	208	524	58	10	1	44
Yankee Total		**0**	**127**	**22**	**10**	**.688**	**69**	**3.12**	**199**	**142**	**91**	**158**	**12**	**0**	**0**	**43**

Assenmacher, Paul Andre
HEIGHT: 6′3″   LEFTHANDER   BORN: 12/10/1960 DETROIT, MICHIGAN

YEAR	TEAM	STARTS	GAMES	WON	LOST	PCT	ER	ERA	INNINGS PITCHED	STRIKE-OUTS	WALKS	HITS ALLOWED	HRS ALLOWED	COMP. GAMES	SHUT-OUTS	SAVES
1986	Atl-N	0	61	7	3	.700	19	2.50	68 1/3	56	26	61	5	0	0	7
1987	Atl-N	0	52	1	1	.500	31	5.10	54 2/3	39	24	58	8	0	0	2
1988	Atl-N	0	64	8	7	.533	27	3.06	79 1/3	71	32	72	4	0	0	5
1989	Atl-N	0	49	1	3	.250	23	3.59	57 2/3	64	16	55	2	0	0	0
1989	Chi-N	0	14	2	1	.667	11	5.21	19	15	12	19	1	0	0	0
1990	Chi-N	1	74	7	2	.778	32	2.80	103	95	36	90	10	0	0	10

(continued)

(continued)

YEAR	TEAM	STARTS	GAMES	WON	LOST	PCT	ER	ERA	INNINGS PITCHED	STRIKE-OUTS	WALKS	HITS ALLOWED	HRS ALLOWED	COMP. GAMES	SHUT-OUTS	SAVES
1991	Chi-N	0	75	7	8	.467	37	3.24	$102\frac{2}{3}$	117	31	85	10	0	0	15
1992	Chi-N	0	70	4	4	.500	31	4.10	68	67	26	72	6	0	0	8
1993	Chi-N	0	46	2	1	.667	15	3.49	$38\frac{2}{3}$	34	13	44	5	0	0	0
1993	**NY-A**	**0**	**26**	**2**	**2**	**.500**	**6**	**3.12**	**$17\frac{1}{3}$**	**11**	**9**	**10**	**0**	**0**	**0**	**0**
1994	Chi-A	0	44	1	2	.333	13	3.55	33	29	13	26	2	0	0	1
1995	Cle-A	0	47	6	2	.750	12	2.82	$38\frac{1}{3}$	40	12	32	3	0	0	0
1996	Cle-A	0	63	4	2	.667	16	3.09	$46\frac{2}{3}$	44	14	46	1	0	0	1
1997	Cle-A	0	75	5	0	1.000	16	2.94	49	53	15	43	5	0	0	4
1998	Cle-A	0	69	2	5	.286	17	3.26	47	43	19	54	5	0	0	3
1999	Cle-A	0	55	2	1	.667	30	8.18	33	29	17	50	6	0	0	0
Career Average		0	55	4	3	.581	21	3.54	53	50	20	51	5	0	0	4
Yankee Average		**0**	**26**	**2**	**2**	**.500**	**6**	**3.12**	**$17\frac{1}{3}$**	**11**	**9**	**10**	**0**	**0**	**0**	**0**
Career Total		1	884	61	44	.581	336	3.53	$855\frac{2}{3}$	807	315	817	73	0	0	56
Yankee Total		**0**	**26**	**2**	**2**	**.500**	**6**	**3.12**	**$17\frac{1}{3}$**	**11**	**9**	**10**	**0**	**0**	**0**	**0**

Ausanio, Joseph John

HEIGHT: 6'1"   RIGHTHANDER   BORN: 12/9/1965 KINGSTON, NEW YORK

YEAR	TEAM	STARTS	GAMES	WON	LOST	PCT	ER	ERA	INNINGS PITCHED	STRIKE-OUTS	WALKS	HITS ALLOWED	HRS ALLOWED	COMP. GAMES	SHUT-OUTS	SAVES
1994	**NY-A**	**0**	**13**	**2**	**1**	**.667**	**9**	**5.17**	**$15\frac{2}{3}$**	**15**	**6**	**16**	**3**	**0**	**0**	**0**
1995	**NY-A**	**0**	**28**	**2**	**0**	**1.000**	**24**	**5.73**	**$37\frac{2}{3}$**	**36**	**23**	**42**	**9**	**0**	**0**	**1**
Career Average		0	21	2	1	.800	17	5.57	27	26	15	29	6	0	0	1
Yankee Average		**0**	**21**	**2**	**1**	**.800**	**17**	**5.57**	**27**	**26**	**15**	**29**	**6**	**0**	**0**	**1**
Career Total		0	41	4	1	.800	33	5.57	$53\frac{1}{3}$	51	29	58	12	0	0	1
Yankee Total		**0**	**41**	**4**	**1**	**.800**	**33**	**5.57**	**53**	**51**	**29**	**58**	**12**	**0**	**0**	**1**

Bahnsen, Stanley Raymond

HEIGHT: 6'2"   RIGHTHANDER   BORN: 12/15/1944 COUNCIL BLUFFS, IOWA

YEAR	TEAM	STARTS	GAMES	WON	LOST	PCT	ER	ERA	INNINGS PITCHED	STRIKE-OUTS	WALKS	HITS ALLOWED	HRS ALLOWED	COMP. GAMES	SHUT-OUTS	SAVES
1966	**NY-A**	**3**	**4**	**1**	**1**	**.500**	**9**	**3.52**	**23**	**16**	**7**	**15**	**3**	**1**	**0**	**1**
1968	**NY-A**	**34**	**37**	**17**	**12**	**.586**	**61**	**2.05**	**$162\frac{1}{3}$**	**162**	**68**	**216**	**14**	**10**	**1**	**0**
1969	**NY-A**	**33**	**40**	**9**	**16**	**.360**	**94**	**3.83**	**$220\frac{2}{3}$**	**130**	**90**	**222**	**28**	**5**	**2**	**1**
1970	**NY-A**	**35**	**36**	**14**	**11**	**.560**	**86**	**3.33**	**$232\frac{2}{3}$**	**116**	**75**	**227**	**23**	**6**	**2**	**0**
1971	**NY-A**	**34**	**36**	**14**	**12**	**.538**	**90**	**3.35**	**221**	**110**	**72**	**221**	**20**	**14**	**3**	**0**
1972	Chi-A	41	43	21	16	.568	101	3.60	$252\frac{1}{3}$	157	73	263	22	5	1	0
1973	Chi-A	42	42	18	21	.462	112	3.57	$282\frac{1}{3}$	120	117	290	20	14	4	0
1974	Chi-A	35	38	12	15	.444	113	4.70	$216\frac{1}{3}$	102	110	230	17	10	1	0
1975	Chi-A	12	12	4	6	.400	45	6.01	$67\frac{1}{3}$	31	40	78	9	2	0	0
1975	Oak-A	16	21	6	7	.462	36	3.24	100	49	37	88	2	2	0	0
1976	Oak-A	14	35	8	7	.533	53	3.34	143	82	43	124	13	1	1	0
1977	Oak-A	2	11	1	2	.333	15	6.14	22	21	13	24	5	0	0	1
1977	Mon-N	22	23	8	9	.471	68	4.81	$127\frac{1}{3}$	58	38	142	14	3	1	0
1978	Mon-N	1	44	1	5	.167	32	3.84	75	44	31	74	9	0	0	7
1979	Mon-N	0	55	3	1	.750	33	3.15	$94\frac{1}{3}$	71	42	80	10	0	0	5
1980	Mon-N	0	57	7	6	.538	31	3.05	$91\frac{1}{3}$	48	33	80	7	0	0	4
1981	Mon-N	3	25	2	1	.667	27	4.96	49	28	24	45	7	0	0	1
1982	Cal-A	0	7	0	1	.000	5	4.66	$9\frac{2}{3}$	5	8	13	0	0	0	0
1982	Phi-N	0	8	0	0	—	2	1.35	$13\frac{1}{3}$	9	3	8	0	0	0	0
Career Average		17	30	8	8	.495	53	3.60	133	72	49	128	12	4	1	1
Yankee Average		**28**	**31**	**11**	**10**	**.514**	**68**	**3.10**	**197**	**107**	**62**	**180**	**18**	**7**	**2**	**0**
Career Total		327	574	146	149	.495	1013	3.60	2529	1359	924	2440	223	73	16	20
Yankee Total		**139**	**153**	**55**	**52**	**.514**	**340**	**3.10**	**986**	**534**	**312**	**901**	**88**	**36**	**8**	**2**

Bankhead, Michael Scott

HEIGHT: 5'10" RIGHTHANDER BORN: 7/31/1963 RALEIGH, NORTH CAROLINA

YEAR	TEAM	STARTS	GAMES	WON	LOST	PCT	ER	ERA	INNINGS PITCHED	STRIKE-OUTS	WALKS	HITS ALLOWED	HRS ALLOWED	COMP. GAMES	SHUT-OUTS	SAVES
1986	KC-A	17	24	8	9	.471	62	4.61	121	94	37	121	14	0	0	0
1987	Sea-A	25	27	9	8	.529	90	5.42	149 1/3	95	37	168	35	2	0	0
1988	Sea-A	21	21	7	9	.438	46	3.07	135	102	38	115	8	2	1	0
1989	Sea-A	33	33	14	6	.700	78	3.34	210 1/3	140	63	187	19	3	2	0
1990	Sea-A	4	4	0	2	.000	16	11.08	13	10	7	18	2	0	0	0
1991	Sea-A	9	17	3	6	.333	33	4.90	60 2/3	28	21	73	8	0	0	0
1992	Cin-N	0	54	10	4	.714	23	2.93	70 2/3	53	29	57	4	0	0	1
1993	Bos-A	0	40	2	1	.667	25	3.50	64 1/3	47	29	59	7	0	0	0
1994	Bos-A	0	27	3	2	.600	19	4.62	37	25	12	34	5	0	0	0
1995	**NY-A**	**1**	**20**	**1**	**1**	**.500**	**26**	**6.00**	**39**	**20**	**16**	**44**	**9**	**0**	**0**	**0**
Career Average		11	27	6	5	.543	42	4.18	90	61	29	88	11	1	0	0
Yankee Average		**1**	**20**	**1**	**1**	**.500**	**26**	**6.00**	**39**	**20**	**16**	**44**	**9**	**0**	**0**	**0**
Career Total		110	267	57	48	.543	418	4.18	900	614	289	876	111	7	3	1
Yankee Total		**1**	**20**	**1**	**1**	**.500**	**26**	**6.00**	**39**	**20**	**16**	**44**	**9**	**0**	**0**	**0**

Banks, Willie Anthony

HEIGHT: 6'1" RIGHTHANDER BORN: 2/27/1969 JERSEY CITY, NEW JERSEY

YEAR	TEAM	STARTS	GAMES	WON	LOST	PCT	ER	ERA	INNINGS PITCHED	STRIKE-OUTS	WALKS	HITS ALLOWED	HRS ALLOWED	COMP. GAMES	SHUT-OUTS	SAVES
1991	Min-A	3	5	1	1	.500	11	5.71	17 1/3	16	12	21	1	0	0	0
1992	Min-A	12	16	4	4	.500	45	5.70	71	37	37	80	6	0	0	0
1993	Min-A	30	31	11	12	.478	77	4.04	171 1/3	138	78	186	17	0	0	0
1994	Chi-N	23	23	8	12	.400	83	5.41	138	91	56	139	16	1	0	0
1995	Chi-N	0	10	0	1	.000	20	16.36	11 2/3	9	12	27	5	0	0	0
1995	LA-N	6	6	0	2	.000	13	4.03	29	23	16	36	2	0	0	0
1995	Fla-N	9	9	2	3	.400	24	4.32	50	30	30	43	7	0	0	0
1997	**NY-A**	**1**	**5**	**3**	**0**	**1.000**	**3**	**1.93**	**14**	**8**	**6**	**9**	**0**	**0**	**0**	**0**
1998	**NY-A**	**0**	**9**	**1**	**1**	**.500**	**16**	**10.29**	**14 1/3**	**8**	**12**	**20**	**4**	**0**	**0**	**0**
1998	Ari-N	0	33	1	2	.333	15	3.14	43 2/3	32	25	34	2	0	0	1
Career Average		8	15	3	4	.449	31	4.95	56	39	28	60	6	0	0	0
Yankee Average		**1**	**7**	**2**	**1**	**.800**	**10**	**6.11**	**14**	**8**	**9**	**15**	**2**	**0**	**0**	**0**
Career Total		84	147	31	38	.449	307	4.95	559	392	284	595	60	1	0	1
Yankee Total		**1**	**14**	**4**	**1**	**.800**	**19**	**6.11**	**28**	**16**	**18**	**29**	**4**	**0**	**0**	**0**

Barber, Stephen David

HEIGHT: 6'0" LEFTHANDER BORN: 2/22/1939 TAKOMA PARK, MARYLAND

YEAR	TEAM	STARTS	GAMES	WON	LOST	PCT	ER	ERA	INNINGS PITCHED	STRIKE-OUTS	WALKS	HITS ALLOWED	HRS ALLOWED	COMP. GAMES	SHUT-OUTS	SAVES
1960	Bal-A	27	36	10	7	.588	65	3.22	181 2/3	112	113	148	10	6	1	2
1961	Bal-A	34	37	18	12	.600	92	3.33	248 1/3	150	130	194	13	14	8	1
1962	Bal-A	19	28	9	6	.600	54	3.46	140 1/3	89	61	145	9	5	2	0
1963	Bal-A	36	39	20	13	.606	79	2.75	258 2/3	180	92	253	12	11	2	0
1964	Bal-A	26	36	9	13	.409	67	3.84	157	118	81	144	15	4	0	1
1965	Bal-A	32	37	15	10	.600	66	2.69	220 2/3	130	81	177	16	7	2	0
1966	Bal-A	22	25	10	5	.667	34	2.30	133 1/3	91	49	104	6	5	3	0
1967	Bal-A	15	15	4	9	.308	34	4.10	74 2/3	48	61	47	5	1	1	0
1967	**NY-A**	**17**	**17**	**6**	**9**	**.400**	**44**	**4.05**	**97 2/3**	**70**	**54**	**103**	**4**	**3**	**1**	**0**
1968	**NY-A**	**19**	**20**	**6**	**5**	**.545**	**46**	**3.23**	**128 1/3**	**87**	**64**	**127**	**7**	**3**	**1**	**0**
1969	Sea-A	16	25	4	7	.364	46	4.80	86 1/3	69	48	99	9	0	0	0
1970	Chi-N	0	5	0	1	.000	6	9.53	5 2/3	3	6	10	0	0	0	0
1970	Atl-N	2	5	0	0	.000	8	4.91	14 2/3	11	5	17	3	0	0	0
1971	Atl-N	3	39	3	1	.750	40	4.80	75	40	25	92	6	0	0	2
1972	Atl-N	0	5	0	0	—	10	5.74	15 2/3	6	6	18	1	0	0	0
1972	Cal-A	3	34	4	4	.500	13	2.02	58	34	30	37	4	0	0	2
1973	Cal-A	1	50	3	2	.600	35	3.53	89 1/3	58	32	90	5	0	0	4
1974	SF-N	0	13	0	1	.000	8	5.27	13 2/3	13	12	13	0	0	0	1
Career Average		14	24	6	5	.535	38	3.40	102	66	49	93	6	3	1	1
Yankee Average		**18**	**19**	**6**	**7**	**.462**	**45**	**3.58**	**113**	**79**	**59**	**115**	**6**	**3**	**1**	**0**
Career Total		274	488	122	106	.535	769	3.40	2038	1327	981	1852	128	59	21	15
Yankee Total		**36**	**37**	**12**	**14**	**.462**	**90**	**3.58**	**226**	**157**	**118**	**230**	**11**	**6**	**2**	**0**

Barger, Eros Bolivar (Cy)

HEIGHT: 6'0" RIGHTHANDER BORN: 5/18/1885 JAMESTOWN, KENTUCKY DIED: 9/23/1964 COLUMBIA, KENTUCKY

YEAR	TEAM	STARTS	GAMES	WON	LOST	PCT	ER	ERA	INNINGS PITCHED	STRIKE-OUTS	WALKS	HITS ALLOWED	HRS ALLOWED	COMP. GAMES	SHUT-OUTS	SAVES
1906	**NY-A**	**1**	**2**	**0**	**0**	**—**	**6**	**10.13**	**5 1/3**	**3**	**3**	**7**	**0**	**0**	**0**	**1**
1907	**NY-A**	**0**	**1**	**0**	**0**	**—**	**2**	**3.00**	**6**	**0**	**1**	**10**	**0**	**0**	**0**	**0**
1910	Bro-N	30	35	15	15	.500	87	2.88	271 2/3	87	107	267	2	25	2	1
1911	Bro-N	30	30	11	15	.423	85	3.52	217 1/3	60	71	224	4	21	1	0
1912	Bro-N	11	16	1	9	.100	57	5.46	94	30	42	120	4	6	0	0
1914	Pit-F	26	33	10	16	.385	110	4.34	228 1/3	70	63	252	7	18	1	1
1915	Pit-F	13	34	9	8	.529	39	2.29	153	47	47	130	1	8	1	6
Career Average		16	22	7	9	.422	55	3.56	139	42	48	144	3	11	1	1
Yankee Average		**1**	**2**	**0**	**0**	**—**	**4**	**6.35**	**6**	**2**	**2**	**9**	**0**	**0**	**0**	**1**
Career Total		111	151	46	63	.422	386	3.56	976	297	334	1010	18	78	5	9
Yankee Total		**1**	**3**	**0**	**0**	**—**	**8**	**6.35**	**11**	**3**	**4**	**17**	**0**	**0**	**0**	**1**

Barnes, Frank Samuel (Lefty)

HEIGHT: 6'2" LEFTHANDER BORN: 1/9/1900 DALLAS, TEXAS DIED: 9/27/1967 HOUSTON, TEXAS

YEAR	TEAM	STARTS	GAMES	WON	LOST	PCT	ER	ERA	INNINGS PITCHED	STRIKE-OUTS	WALKS	HITS ALLOWED	HRS ALLOWED	COMP. GAMES	SHUT-OUTS	SAVES
1929	Det-A	1	4	0	1	.000	4	7.20	5	0	3	10	0	0	0	0
1930	**NY-A**	**2**	**2**	**0**	**1**	**.000**	**11**	**8.03**	**12 1/3**	**2**	**13**	**13**	**0**	**0**	**0**	**0**
Career Average		2	3	0	1	.000	8	7.79	9	1	8	12	0	0	0	0
Yankee Average		**2**	**2**	**0**	**1**	**.000**	**11**	**8.03**	**12 1/3**	**2**	**13**	**13**	**0**	**0**	**0**	**0**
Career Total		3	6	0	2	.000	15	7.79	17	2	16	23	0	0	0	0
Yankee Total		**2**	**2**	**0**	**1**	**.000**	**11**	**8.03**	**12 1/3**	**2**	**13**	**13**	**0**	**0**	**0**	**0**

Beall, Walter Esau

HEIGHT: 5'10" RIGHTHANDER BORN: 7/29/1899 WASHINGTON, D.C. DIED: 1/28/1959 SUITLAND, MARYLAND

YEAR	TEAM	STARTS	GAMES	WON	LOST	PCT	ER	ERA	INNINGS PITCHED	STRIKE-OUTS	WALKS	HITS ALLOWED	HRS ALLOWED	COMP. GAMES	SHUT-OUTS	SAVES
1924	**NY-A**	**2**	**4**	**2**	**0**	**1.000**	**9**	**3.52**	**23**	**18**	**17**	**19**	**2**	**0**	**0**	**0**
1925	**NY-A**	**1**	**8**	**0**	**1**	**.000**	**16**	**12.71**	**11 1/3**	**8**	**19**	**11**	**0**	**0**	**0**	**0**
1926	**NY-A**	**9**	**20**	**2**	**4**	**.333**	**32**	**3.53**	**81 2/3**	**56**	**68**	**71**	**2**	**1**	**0**	**1**
1927	**NY-A**	**0**	**1**	**0**	**0**	**—**	**1**	**9.00**	**1**	**0**	**0**	**1**	**0**	**0**	**0**	**0**
1929	Was-A	0	3	1	0	1.000	3	3.86	7	3	7	8	0	0	0	0
Career Average		2	7	1	1	.500	12	4.43	25	17	22	22	1	0	0	0
Yankee Average		**3**	**8**	**1**	**1**	**.444**	**15**	**4.46**	**29**	**21**	**26**	**26**	**1**	**0**	**0**	**0**
Career Total		12	36	5	5	.500	61	4.43	124	85	111	110	4	1	0	1
Yankee Total		**12**	**33**	**4**	**5**	**.444**	**58**	**4.46**	**117**	**82**	**104**	**102**	**4**	**1**	**0**	**1**

Beattie, James Louis (Jim)

HEIGHT: 6'5" RIGHTHANDER BORN: 7/4/1954 HAMPTON, VIRGINIA

YEAR	TEAM	STARTS	GAMES	WON	LOST	PCT	ER	ERA	INNINGS PITCHED	STRIKE-OUTS	WALKS	HITS ALLOWED	HRS ALLOWED	COMP. GAMES	SHUT-OUTS	SAVES
1978	**NY-A**	**22**	**25**	**6**	**9**	**.400**	**53**	**3.73**	**128**	**65**	**51**	**123**	**8**	**0**	**0**	**0**
1979	**NY-A**	**13**	**15**	**3**	**6**	**.333**	**44**	**5.21**	**76**	**32**	**41**	**85**	**5**	**1**	**1**	**0**
1980	Sea-A	29	33	5	15	.667	101	4.85	187 1/3	67	98	205	19	3	0	0
1981	Sea-A	9	13	3	2	.600	22	2.97	66 2/3	36	18	59	2	0	0	1
1982	Sea-A	26	28	8	12	.400	64	3.34	172 1/3	140	65	149	13	6	1	0
1983	Sea-A	29	30	10	15	.400	84	3.84	196 2/3	132	66	197	12	8	2	0
1984	Sea-A	32	32	12	16	.429	80	3.41	211	119	75	206	13	12	2	0
1985	Sea-A	15	18	5	6	.455	57	7.29	70 1/3	45	33	93	9	1	1	0
1986	Sea-A	7	9	0	6	.000	27	6.02	40 1/3	24	14	57	7	0	0	0
Career Average		20	23	6	10	.374	59	4.17	128	73	51	130	10	3	1	0
Yankee Average		**18**	**20**	**5**	**8**	**.375**	**49**	**4.28**	**102**	**49**	**46**	**104**	**7**	**1**	**1**	**0**
Career Total		182	203	52	87	.374	532	4.17	1149	660	461	1174	88	31	7	1
Yankee Total		**35**	**40**	**9**	**15**	**.375**	**97**	**4.28**	**204**	**97**	**92**	**208**	**13**	**1**	**1**	**0**

Beck, Richard Henry

HEIGHT: 6'3"   RIGHTHANDER   BORN: 1/21/1941 PASCO, WASHINGTON

YEAR	TEAM	STARTS	GAMES	WON	LOST	PCT	ER	ERA	INNINGS PITCHED	STRIKE-OUTS	WALKS	HITS ALLOWED	HRS ALLOWED	COMP. GAMES	SHUT-OUTS	SAVES
1965	NY-A	3	3	2	1	.667	5	2.14	21	10	7	22	1	1	1	0
Career Average		3	3	2	1	.667	5	2.14	21	10	7	22	1	1	1	0
Yankee Average		**3**	**3**	**2**	**1**	**.667**	**5**	**2.14**	**21**	**10**	**7**	**22**	**1**	**1**	**1**	**0**
Career Total		3	3	2	1	.667	5	2.14	21	10	7	22	1	1	1	0
Yankee Total		**3**	**3**	**2**	**1**	**.667**	**5**	**2.14**	**21**	**10**	**7**	**22**	**1**	**1**	**1**	**0**

Beene, Freddy Ray

HEIGHT: 5'9"   RIGHTHANDER   BORN: 11/24/1942 ANGLETON, TEXAS

YEAR	TEAM	STARTS	GAMES	WON	LOST	PCT	ER	ERA	INNINGS PITCHED	STRIKE-OUTS	WALKS	HITS ALLOWED	HRS ALLOWED	COMP. GAMES	SHUT-OUTS	SAVES
1968	Bal-A	0	1	0	0	—	1	9.00	1	1	1	2	0	0	0	0
1969	Bal-A	0	2	0	0	—	0	0.00	2 2/3	0	1	2	0	0	0	0
1970	Bal-A	0	4	0	0	—	4	6.00	6	4	5	8	1	0	0	0
1972	**NY-A**	**1**	**29**	**1**	**3**	**.667**	**15**	**2.34**	**57 2/3**	**37**	**24**	**55**	**3**	**0**	**0**	**3**
1973	**NY-A**	**4**	**19**	**6**	**0**	**1.000**	**17**	**1.68**	**91**	**49**	**27**	**67**	**5**	**0**	**0**	**1**
1974	**NY-A**	**0**	**6**	**0**	**0**	**—**	**3**	**2.70**	**10**	**10**	**2**	**9**	**1**	**0**	**0**	**1**
1974	Cle-A	0	32	4	4	.500	40	4.93	73	35	26	68	7	0	0	2
1975	Cle-A	1	19	1	0	1.000	36	6.94	46 2/3	20	25	63	4	0	0	1
Career Average		1	14	2	1	.632	15	3.63	36	20	14	34	3	0	0	1
Yankee Average		**2**	**18**	**2**	**1**	**.700**	**12**	**1.99**	**53**	**32**	**18**	**44**	**3**	**0**	**0**	**2**
Career Total		6	112	12	7	.632	116	3.63	288	156	111	274	21	0	0	8
Yankee Total		**5**	**54**	**7**	**3**	**.700**	**35**	**1.99**	**159**	**96**	**53**	**131**	**9**	**0**	**0**	**5**

Beggs, Joseph Stanley (Fireman)

HEIGHT: 6'1"   RIGHTHANDER   BORN: 11/4/1910 RANKIN, PENNSYLVANIA   DIED: 7/19/1983 INDIANAPOLIS, INDIANA

YEAR	TEAM	STARTS	GAMES	WON	LOST	PCT	ER	ERA	INNINGS PITCHED	STRIKE-OUTS	WALKS	HITS ALLOWED	HRS ALLOWED	COMP. GAMES	SHUT-OUTS	SAVES
1938	**NY-A**	**9**	**14**	**3**	**2**	**.600**	**35**	**5.40**	**58 1/3**	**8**	**20**	**69**	**7**	**4**	**0**	**0**
1940	Cin-N	1	37	12	3	.800	17	2.00	76 2/3	25	21	68	1	0	0	7
1941	Cin-N	0	37	4	3	.571	24	3.79	57	19	27	57	2	0	0	5
1942	Cin-N	0	38	6	5	.545	21	2.13	88 2/3	24	33	65	4	0	0	8
1943	Cin-N	4	39	7	6	.538	30	2.34	115 1/3	28	25	121	0	4	2	6
1944	Cin-N	1	1	1	0	1.000	2	2.00	9	2	0	8	0	1	0	0
1946	Cin-N	22	28	12	10	.545	49	2.32	190	38	39	175	15	14	2	1
1947	Cin-N	4	11	0	3	.000	19	5.29	32 1/3	11	6	42	4	0	0	0
1947	NY-N	0	32	3	3	.500	31	4.23	66	23	18	81	6	0	0	2
1948	NY-N	0	1	0	0	—	0	0.00	1/3	0	0	2	0	0	0	0
Career Average		4	24	5	4	.578	23	2.96	69	18	19	69	4	2	0	3
Yankee Average		**9**	**14**	**3**	**2**	**.600**	**35**	**5.40**	**58 1/3**	**8**	**20**	**69**	**7**	**4**	**0**	**0**
Career Total		41	238	48	35	.578	228	2.96	694	178	189	688	39	23	4	29
Yankee Total		**9**	**14**	**3**	**2**	**.600**	**35**	**5.40**	**58 1/3**	**8**	**20**	**69**	**7**	**4**	**0**	**0**

Bernhardt, Walter Jacob

HEIGHT: 6'2"   RIGHTHANDER   BORN: 5/20/1893 PLEASANT VILLAGE, PENNSYLVANIA   DIED: 7/26/1958 WATERTOWN, NEW YORK

YEAR	TEAM	STARTS	GAMES	WON	LOST	PCT	ER	ERA	INNINGS PITCHED	STRIKE-OUTS	WALKS	HITS ALLOWED	HRS ALLOWED	COMP. GAMES	SHUT-OUTS	SAVES
1918	NY-A	0	1	0	0	—	0	0.00	2/3	1	0	0	0	0	0	0
Career Average		0	1	0	0	—	0	0.00	2/3	1	0	0	0	0	0	0
Yankee Average		**0**	**1**	**0**	**0**	**—**	**0**	**0.00**	**2/3**	**1**	**0**	**0**	**0**	**0**	**0**	**0**
Career Total		0	1	0	0	—	0	0.00	2/3	1	0	0	0	0	0	0
Yankee Total		**0**	**1**	**0**	**0**	**—**	**0**	**0.00**	**2/3**	**1**	**0**	**0**	**0**	**0**	**0**	**0**

Bevens, Floyd Clifford (Bill)

HEIGHT: 6'3"   RIGHTHANDER   BORN: 10/21/1916 HUBBARD, OREGON   DIED: 10/26/1991 SALEM, OREGON

YEAR	TEAM	STARTS	GAMES	WON	LOST	PCT	ER	ERA	INNINGS PITCHED	STRIKE-OUTS	WALKS	HITS ALLOWED	HRS ALLOWED	COMP. GAMES	SHUT-OUTS	SAVES
1944	**NY-A**	**5**	**8**	**4**	**1**	**.800**	**13**	**2.68**	**43 2/3**	**16**	**13**	**44**	**4**	**3**	**0**	**0**
1945	**NY-A**	**25**	**29**	**13**	**9**	**.591**	**75**	**3.67**	**184**	**76**	**68**	**174**	**12**	**14**	**2**	**0**
1946	**NY-A**	**31**	**31**	**16**	**13**	**.552**	**62**	**2.23**	**249 2/3**	**120**	**78**	**213**	**11**	**18**	**3**	**0**
1947	**NY-A**	**23**	**28**	**7**	**13**	**.350**	**70**	**3.82**	**165**	**77**	**77**	**167**	**13**	**11**	**1**	**0**
Career Average		21	24	10	9	.526	55	3.08	161	72	59	150	10	12	2	0
Yankee Average		**21**	**24**	**10**	**9**	**.526**	**55**	**3.08**	**161**	**72**	**59**	**150**	**10**	**12**	**2**	**0**
Career Total		84	96	40	36	.526	220	3.08	642	289	236	598	40	46	6	0
Yankee Total		**84**	**96**	**40**	**36**	**.526**	**220**	**3.08**	**642**	**289**	**236**	**598**	**40**	**46**	**6**	**0**

Billiard, Harry Pree

HEIGHT 6'0"   RIGHTHANDER   BORN: 11/11/1893 MONROE, INDIANA   DIED: 6/3/1923 WOOSTER, OHIO

YEAR	TEAM	STARTS	GAMES	WON	LOST	PCT	ER	ERA	INNINGS PITCHED	STRIKE-OUTS	WALKS	HITS ALLOWED	HRS ALLOWED	COMP. GAMES	SHUT-OUTS	SAVES
1908	**NY-A**	**0**	**6**	**0**	**0**	**—**	**5**	**2.65**	**17**	**10**	**14**	**15**	**1**	**0**	**0**	**0**
1914	Ind-F	16	32	8	7	.533	52	3.72	125 2/3	45	63	117	4	5	0	2
1915	New-F	2	14	0	1	.000	18	5.72	28 1/3	7	28	32	0	0	0	1
Career Average		6	17	3	3	.500	25	3.95	57	21	35	55	2	2	0	1
Yankee Average		**0**	**6**	**0**	**0**	**—**	**5**	**2.65**	**17**	**10**	**14**	**15**	**1**	**0**	**0**	**0**
Career Total		18	52	8	8	.500	75	3.95	171	62	105	164	5	5	0	3
Yankee Total		**0**	**6**	**0**	**0**	**—**	**5**	**2.65**	**17**	**10**	**14**	**15**	**1**	**0**	**0**	**0**

Bird, James Douglas

HEIGHT: 6'4"   RIGHTHANDER   BORN: 3/15/1950 CORONA, CALIFORNIA

YEAR	TEAM	STARTS	GAMES	WON	LOST	PCT	ER	ERA	INNINGS PITCHED	STRIKE-OUTS	WALKS	HITS ALLOWED	HRS ALLOWED	COMP. GAMES	SHUT-OUTS	SAVES
1973	KC-A	0	54	4	4	.500	34	2.99	102 1/3	83	30	81	10	0	0	20
1974	KC-A	1	55	7	6	.538	28	2.73	92 1/3	62	27	100	6	1	0	10
1975	KC-A	4	51	9	6	.600	38	3.25	105 1/3	81	40	100	7	0	0	11
1976	KC-A	27	39	12	10	.545	74	3.37	197 2/3	107	31	191	17	2	1	2
1977	KC-A	5	53	11	4	.733	51	3.88	118 1/3	83	29	120	14	0	0	14
1978	KC-A	6	40	6	6	.500	58	5.29	98 2/3	48	31	110	8	0	0	1
1979	Phi-N	1	32	2	0	1.000	35	5.16	61	33	16	73	7	1	0	0
1980	**NY-A**	**1**	**22**	**3**	**0**	**1.000**	**15**	**2.66**	**50 2/3**	**17**	**14**	**47**	**3**	**0**	**0**	**1**
1981	**NY-A**	**4**	**17**	**5**	**1**	**.833**	**16**	**2.70**	**53 1/3**	**28**	**16**	**58**	**5**	**0**	**0**	**0**
1981	Chi-N	12	12	4	5	.444	30	3.58	75 1/3	34	16	72	5	2	1	0
1982	Chi-N	33	35	9	14	.391	109	5.14	191	71	30	230	26	2	1	0
1983	Bos-A	6	22	1	4	.666	50	6.65	67 2/3	33	16	91	14	0	0	1
Career Average		8	36	6	5	.549	45	3.99	101	57	25	106	10	1	0	5
Yankee Average		**3**	**20**	**4**	**1**	**.889**	**16**	**2.68**	**52**	**23**	**15**	**53**	**4**	**0**	**0**	**1**
Career Total		100	432	73	60	.549	538	3.99	1214	680	296	1273	122	8	3	60
Yankee Total		**5**	**39**	**8**	**1**	**.889**	**31**	**2.68**	**104**	**45**	**30**	**105**	**8**	**0**	**0**	**1**

Blackwell, Ewell (The Whip)

HEIGHT: 6'6"   RIGHTHANDER   BORN: 10/23/1922 FRESNO, CALIFORNIA DIED: 10/29/1996 RIVERSIDE, NJ

YEAR	TEAM	STARTS	GAMES	WON	LOST	PCT	ER	ERA	INNINGS PITCHED	STRIKE-OUTS	WALKS	HITS ALLOWED	HRS ALLOWED	COMP. GAMES	SHUT-OUTS	SAVES
1942	Cin-N	0	2	0	0	—	2	6.00	3	1	3	3	0	0	0	0
1946	Cin-N	25	33	9	13	.409	53	2.45	194 1/3	100	79	160	1	10	5	0
1947	Cin-N	33	33	22	8	.733	75	2.47	273	193	95	227	10	23	6	0
1948	Cin-N	20	22	7	9	.438	70	4.54	138 2/3	114	52	134	12	4	1	1
1949	Cin-N	4	30	5	5	.500	36	4.23	76 2/3	55	34	80	7	0	0	1
1950	Cin-N	32	40	17	15	.531	86	2.97	261	188	112	203	12	18	1	4
1951	Cin-N	32	38	16	15	.516	89	3.44	232 2/3	120	97	204	16	11	2	2
1952	Cin-N	17	23	3	12	.666	61	5.38	102	48	60	107	6	3	0	0

(continued)

(continued)

YEAR	TEAM				PCT		ERA								
1952	NY-A	2	5	1	0	1.000	1	0.56	16	7	12	12	0	0	0	1
1953	NY-A	4	8	2	0	1.000	8	3.66	19 2/3	11	13	17	2	0	0	1
1955	KC-A	0	2	0	1	.000	3	6.75	4	2	5	3	1	0	0	0
Career Average		15	21	7	7	.513	44	3.30	120	76	51	105	6	6	1	1
Yankee Average		3	7	2	0	1.000	5	2.27	18	9	13	15	1	0	0	1
Career Total		169	236	82	78	.513	484	3.30	1321	839	562	1150	67	69	15	10
Yankee Total		6	13	3	0	1.000	9	2.27	36	18	25	29	2	0	0	2

Blanco, Gilbert Henry

HEIGHT: 6'5"   LEFTHANDER   BORN: 12/15/1945 PHOENIX, ARIZONA

YEAR	TEAM	STARTS	GAMES	WON	LOST	PCT	ER	ERA	INNINGS PITCHED	STRIKE-OUTS	WALKS	HITS ALLOWED	HRS ALLOWED	COMP. GAMES	SHUT-OUTS	SAVES
1965	NY-A	1	17	1	1	.500	9	3.98	20 1/3	14	12	16	1	0	0	0
1966	KC-A	8	11	2	4	.333	20	4.70	38 1/3	21	36	31	3	0	0	0
Career Average		5	14	2	3	.375	15	4.45	29	18	24	24	2	0	0	0
Yankee Average		1	17	1	1	.500	9	3.98	20 1/3	14	12	16	1	0	0	0
Career Total		9	28	3	5	.375	29	4.45	59	35	48	47	4	0	0	0
Yankee Total		1	17	1	1	.500	9	3.98	20 1/3	14	12	16	1	0	0	0

Blasingame, Wade Allen

HEIGHT: 6'1"   LEFTHANDER   BORN: 11/22/1943 DEMING, NEW MEXICO

YEAR	TEAM	STARTS	GAMES	WON	LOST	PCT	ER	ERA	INNINGS PITCHED	STRIKE-OUTS	WALKS	HITS ALLOWED	HRS ALLOWED	COMP. GAMES	SHUT-OUTS	SAVES
1963	Mil-N	0	2	0	0	—	4	12.00	3	6	2	7	0	0	0	0
1964	Mil-N	13	28	9	5	.643	55	4.24	116 2/3	70	51	113	15	3	1	2
1965	Mil-N	36	38	16	10	.615	94	3.77	224 2/3	117	116	200	17	10	1	1
1966	Atl-N	12	16	3	7	.300	40	5.32	67 2/3	34	25	71	5	0	0	0
1967	Atl-N	4	10	1	0	1.000	13	4.62	25 1/3	20	21	27	1	0	0	0
1967	Hou-N	14	15	4	7	.364	51	5.96	77	46	27	91	9	0	0	0
1968	Hou-N	2	22	1	2	.333	19	4.75	36	22	10	45	3	0	0	1
1969	Hou-N	5	26	0	5	.000	31	5.37	52	33	33	66	4	0	0	1
1970	Hou-N	13	13	3	3	.500	30	3.48	77 2/3	55	23	76	4	1	0	0
1971	Hou-N	28	30	9	11	.450	81	4.60	158 1/3	93	45	177	11	2	0	0
1972	Hou-N	0	10	0	0	—	8	8.64	8 1/3	9	8	4	1	0	0	0
1972	NY-A	1	12	0	1	.000	8	4.24	17	7	11	14	5	0	0	0
Career Average		11	19	4	4	.474	36	4.52	72	43	31	74	6	1	0	0
Yankee Average		1	12	0	1	.000	8	4.24	17	7	11	14	5	0	0	0
Career Total		128	222	46	51	.474	434	4.52	864	512	372	891	75	16	2	5
Yankee Total		1	12	0	1	.000	8	4.24	17	7	11	14	5	0	0	0

Blateric, Stephen Lawrence

HEIGHT: 6'3"   RIGHTHANDER   BORN: 3/20/1944 DENVER, COLORADO

YEAR	TEAM	STARTS	GAMES	WON	LOST	PCT	ER	ERA	INNINGS PITCHED	STRIKE-OUTS	WALKS	HITS ALLOWED	HRS ALLOWED	COMP. GAMES	SHUT-OUTS	SAVES
1971	Cin-N	0	2	0	0	—	4	13.50	2 2/3	4	0	5	2	0	0	0
1972	NY-A	0	1	0	0	—	0	0.00	4	4	0	2	0	0	0	0
1975	Cal-A	0	2	0	0	—	3	6.23	4 1/3	5	1	9	0	0	0	0
Career Average		0	2	0	0	—	2	5.73	4	4	0	5	1	0	0	0
Yankee Average		0	1	0	0	—	0	0.00	4	4	0	2	0	0	0	0
Career Total		0	5	0	0	—	7	5.73	11	13	1	16	2	0	0	0
Yankee Total		0	1	0	0	—	0	0.00	4	4	0	2	0	0	0	0

Blaylock, Gary Nelson

HEIGHT: 6'0" RIGHTHANDER BORN: 10/11/1931 CLARKTON, MISSOURI

YEAR	TEAM	STARTS	GAMES	WON	LOST	PCT	ER	ERA	INNINGS PITCHED	STRIKE-OUTS	WALKS	HITS ALLOWED	HRS ALLOWED	COMP. GAMES	SHUT-OUTS	SAVES
1959	StL-N	12	26	4	5	.444	57	5.13	100	61	43	117	14	3	0	0
1959	**NY-A**	**1**	**15**	**0**	**1**	**.000**	**10**	**3.51**	**25 2/3**	**20**	**15**	**30**	**0**	**0**	**0**	**0**
Career Average		7	21	2	3	.400	34	4.80	63	41	29	74	7	2	0	0
Yankee Average		**1**	**15**	**0**	**1**	**.000**	**10**	**3.51**	**25 2/3**	**20**	**15**	**30**	**0**	**0**	**0**	**0**
Career Total		13	41	4	6	.400	67	4.80	126	81	58	147	14	3	0	0
Yankee Total		**1**	**15**	**0**	**1**	**.000**	**10**	**3.51**	**25 2/3**	**20**	**15**	**30**	**0**	**0**	**0**	**0**

Bliss, Elmer Ward

HEIGHT: 6'0" RIGHTHANDER BORN: 3/9/1875 PENFIELD, PENNSYLVANIA DIED: 3/18/1962 BRADFORD, PENNSYLVANIA

YEAR	TEAM	STARTS	GAMES	WON	LOST	PCT	ER	ERA	INNINGS PITCHED	STRIKE-OUTS	WALKS	HITS ALLOWED	HRS ALLOWED	COMP. GAMES	SHUT-OUTS	SAVES
1903	NY-A	0	1	1	0	1.000	0	0.00	7	3	0	4	0	0	0	0
Career Average		0	1	1	0	1.000	0	0.00	7	3	0	4	0	0	0	0
Yankee Average		**0**	**1**	**1**	**0**	**1.000**	**0**	**0.00**	**7**	**3**	**0**	**4**	**0**	**0**	**0**	**0**
Career Total		0	1	1	0	1.000	0	0.00	7	3	0	4	0	0	0	0
Yankee Total		**0**	**1**	**1**	**0**	**1.000**	**0**	**0.00**	**7**	**3**	**0**	**4**	**0**	**0**	**0**	**0**

Boehringer, Brian Edward

HEIGHT: 6'2" RIGHTHANDER BORN: 1/8/1970 ST. LOUIS, MISSOURI

YEAR	TEAM	STARTS	GAMES	WON	LOST	PCT	ER	ERA	INNINGS PITCHED	STRIKE-OUTS	WALKS	HITS ALLOWED	HRS ALLOWED	COMP. GAMES	SHUT-OUTS	SAVES
1995	**NY-A**	**3**	**7**	**0**	**3**	**.000**	**27**	**13.76**	**17 2/3**	**10**	**22**	**24**	**5**	**0**	**0**	**0**
1996	**NY-A**	**3**	**15**	**2**	**4**	**.333**	**28**	**5.44**	**46 1/3**	**37**	**21**	**46**	**6**	**0**	**0**	**0**
1997	**NY-A**	**0**	**34**	**3**	**2**	**.600**	**14**	**2.63**	**48**	**53**	**32**	**39**	**4**	**0**	**0**	**0**
1998	SD-N	1	56	5	2	.714	37	4.36	76 1/3	67	45	75	10	0	0	0
1999	SD-N	11	33	6	5	.545	34	3.24	94	64	35	97	10	0	0	0
2000	SD-N	3	7	0	3	.000	10	5.74	15 2/3	9	0	18	4	0	0	0
Career Average		4	25	3	3	.457	25	4.53	50	40	26	50	7	0	0	0
Yankee Average		**2**	**19**	**2**	**3**	**.357**	**23**	**5.54**	**37**	**33**	**25**	**36**	**5**	**0**	**0**	**0**
Career Total		21	152	16	19	.457	150	4.53	298	240	155	299	39	0	0	0
Yankee Total		**6**	**56**	**5**	**9**	**.357**	**69**	**5.54**	**112**	**100**	**75**	**109**	**15**	**0**	**0**	**0**

Boggs, Wade Anthony

HEIGHT: 6'2" RIGHTHANDER BORN: 6/15/1958 OMAHA, NEBRASKA

YEAR	TEAM	STARTS	GAMES	WON	LOST	PCT	ER	ERA	INNINGS PITCHED	STRIKE-OUTS	WALKS	HITS ALLOWED	HRS ALLOWED	COMP. GAMES	SHUT-OUTS	SAVES
1997	**NY-A**	**0**	**1**	**0**	**0**	**—**	**0**	**0.00**	**1**	**1**	**1**	**0**	**0**	**0**	**0**	**0**
1999	TB-A	0	1	0	0	—	1	9.00	1	1	0	3	0	0	0	0
Career Average		0	1	0	0	—	1	4.50	1	1	1	2	0	0	0	0
Yankee Average		**0**	**1**	**0**	**0**	**—**	**0**	**0.00**	**1**	**1**	**1**	**0**	**0**	**0**	**0**	**0**
Career Total		0	2	0	0	—	1	4.50	2	2	1	3	0	0	0	0
Yankee Total		**0**	**1**	**0**	**0**	**—**	**0**	**0.00**	**1**	**1**	**1**	**0**	**0**	**0**	**0**

Bones, Ricardo (Ricky)

HEIGHT: 6'0" RIGHTHANDER BORN: 4/7/1969 SALINAS, PUERTO RICO

YEAR	TEAM	STARTS	GAMES	WON	LOST	PCT	ER	ERA	INNINGS PITCHED	STRIKE-OUTS	WALKS	HITS ALLOWED	HRS ALLOWED	COMP. GAMES	SHUT-OUTS	SAVES
1991	SD-N	11	11	4	6	.400	29	4.83	54	31	18	57	3	0	0	0
1992	Mil-A	28	31	9	10	.474	83	4.57	163 1/3	65	48	169	27	0	0	0
1993	Mil-A	31	32	11	11	.500	110	4.86	203 2/3	63	63	222	28	3	0	0

(continued)

(continued)

Year	Team														
1994	Mil-A	24	24	10	9	.526	65	3.44	170 2/3	57	45	166	17	4	0	0
1995	Mil-A	31	32	10	12	.455	103	4.64	200 1/3	77	83	218	26	3	0	0
1996	Mil-A	23	32	7	14	.333	94	5.83	145	59	62	170	28	0	0	0
1996	**NY-A**	**1**	**4**	**0**	**0**	**—**	**11**	**14.14**	**7**	**4**	**6**	**14**	**2**	**0**	**0**	**0**
1997	Cin-N	2	9	0	1	.000	20	10.59	17 2/3	8	11	31	2	0	0	0
1997	KC-A	11	21	4	7	.364	52	6.00	78 1/3	36	25	102	10	1	0	0
1998	KC-A	0	32	2	2	.500	18	3.06	53 1/3	38	24	49	4	0	0	1
1999	Bal-A	2	30	0	3	.000	29	6.07	43 2/3	26	19	59	7	0	0	0
2000	Fla-N	0	56	2	3	.400	39	4.54	77 1/3	59	27	94	6	0	0	0
Career Average		14	26	5	7	.431	54	4.84	101	44	36	113	13	1	0	0
Yankee Average		**1**	**4**	**0**	**0**	**—**	**11**	**14.14**	**7**	**4**	**6**	**14**	**2**	**0**	**0**	**0**
Career Total		164	314	59	78	.431	653	4.84	1214 1/3	523	431	1351	160	11	0	1
Yankee Total		**1**	**4**	**0**	**0**	**—**	**11**	**14.14**	**7**	**4**	**6**	**14**	**2**	**0**	**0**	**0**

Ernest Edward "Tiny" Bonham, rhp, 1940-46

Ernie Bonham's nickname was "Tiny," but of course he was anything but. At 6 foot 2 inches, 215 pounds, the hulking Bonham was a fierce presence with the war-time Yankees in the 1940s.

Bonham was born in 1913 in California. He was signed by the Yankees in 1940 and was brought up by the team on August 12.

Manager Joe McCarthy was not in the habit of throwing rookies into the breach, particularly during a pennant race, but with Bonham he had no choice. Starter Lefty Gomez, nursing a sore arm, wasn't producing and would start only five games that year.

Bonham, however, made an immediate splash, winning nine of 12 starts and leading the American League in ERA with a 1.90. But that shot in the arm didn't quite give the Yankees the pennant; they fell two games short in 1940.

But Bonham was not a one-year wonder. He won nine more games in 1941, and in 1942 went 21-5 with an .808 winning percentage, topping the league. He also had six shutouts and 22 complete games, both league highs.

He pitched in three World Series for the Yankees in 1941, 1942 and 1943. His four-hitter in Game 5 of the 1941 series clinched the championship for the Yankees over the Dodgers.

Bonham was possibly the first pitcher to use a forkball with any success, and he had great control throughout his career. In two of the seven years he pitched with the Yankees, he gave up fewer walks than games in which he started. His worst control year was 1943, when he gave up 52 walks in 225 2/3 innings.

Bonham's early career with the Yankees was a promising one. He was 57-28 in his first four years. But a back injury hindered his career the next two years. Over that span, he was only 13-19 for the Yankees.

He was traded to the Pirates for Arthur "Cookie" Cuccurullo in 1946. Bonham had modest success with Pittsburgh, going 24-22 from 1947-49.

Two weeks after he won what turned out to be his last game, Bonham contracted appendicitis. He died on September 15, 1949, in Pittsburgh, of complications from the disease.

His early demise has made Bonham somewhat of a forgotten man in Yankee history. But he is still in the Yankee record books. He remains 4th in career ERA for New York at 2.73, as well as 14th in shutouts with 17, 14th in winning percentage at .612 and 17th in complete games with 91.

Bonham, Ernest Edward (Tiny)

HEIGHT: 6'2" RIGHTHANDER BORN: 8/16/1913 IONE, CALIFORNIA DIED: 9/15/1949 PITTSBURGH, PENNSYLVANIA

YEAR	TEAM	STARTS	GAMES	WON	LOST	PCT	ER	ERA	INNINGS PITCHED	STRIKE-OUTS	WALKS	HITS ALLOWED	HRS ALLOWED	COMP. GAMES	SHUT-OUTS	SAVES
1940	NY-A	12	12	9	3	.750	21	1.90	99 1/3	37	13	83	4	10	3	0
1941	NY-A	14	23	9	6	.600	42	2.98	126 2/3	43	31	118	12	7	1	2
1942	NY-A	27	28	21	5	.808	57	2.27	226	71	24	199	11	22	6	0
1943	NY-A	26	28	15	8	.652	57	2.27	225 2/3	71	52	197	13	17	4	1
1944	NY-A	25	26	12	9	.571	71	2.99	213 2/3	54	41	228	14	17	1	0
1945	NY-A	23	23	8	11	.421	66	3.29	180 2/3	42	22	186	11	12	0	0
1946	NY-A	14	18	5	8	.385	43	3.70	104 2/3	30	23	97	6	6	2	3
1947	Pit-N	18	33	11	8	.579	64	3.85	149 2/3	63	35	167	17	7	3	3
1948	Pit-N	20	22	6	10	.375	65	4.31	135 2/3	42	23	145	18	7	0	0
1949	Pit-N	14	18	7	4	.636	42	4.25	89	25	23	81	11	5	1	0
Career Average		19	23	10	7	.589	53	3.06	155	48	29	150	12	11	2	1
Yankee Average		**20**	**23**	**11**	**7**	**.612**	**51**	**2.73**	**168**	**50**	**29**	**158**	**10**	**13**	**2**	**1**
Career Total		193	231	103	72	.589	528	3.06	1551	478	287	1501	117	110	21	9
Yankee Total		**141**	**158**	**79**	**50**	**.612**	**357**	**2.73**	**1177**	**348**	**206**	**1108**	**71**	**91**	**17**	**6**

Bordi, Richard Albert

HEIGHT: 6'7" RIGHTHANDER BORN: 4/18/1959 SAN FRANCISCO, CALIFORNIA

YEAR	TEAM	STARTS	GAMES	WON	LOST	PCT	ER	ERA	INNINGS PITCHED	STRIKE-OUTS	WALKS	HITS ALLOWED	HRS ALLOWED	COMP. GAMES	SHUT-OUTS	SAVES
1980	Oak-A	0	1	0	0	—	1	4.50	2	0	0	4	0	0	0	0
1981	Oak-A	0	2	0	0	—	0	0.00	2	0	1	1	0	0	0	0
1982	Sea-A	2	7	0	2	.000	12	8.31	13	10	1	18	4	0	0	0
1983	Chi-N	1	11	0	2	.000	14	4.97	25 1/3	20	12	34	2	0	0	1
1984	Chi-N	7	31	5	2	.714	32	3.46	83 1/3	41	20	78	11	0	0	4
1985	**NY-A**	**3**	**51**	**6**	**8**	**.429**	**35**	**3.21**	**98**	**64**	**29**	**95**	**5**	**0**	**0**	**2**
1986	Bal-A	1	52	6	4	.600	53	4.46	107	83	41	105	13	0	0	3
1987	**NY-A**	**1**	**16**	**3**	**1**	**.750**	**28**	**7.64**	**33**	**23**	**12**	**42**	**7**	**0**	**0**	**0**
1988	Oak-A	2	2	0	1	.000	4	4.70	7 2/3	6	5	6	0	0	0	0
Career Average		2	19	2	2	.500	20	4.34	41	27	13	43	5	0	0	1
Yankee Average		**2**	**34**	**5**	**5**	**.500**	**32**	**4.33**	**66**	**44**	**21**	**69**	**6**	**0**	**0**	**1**
Career Total		17	173	20	20	.500	179	4.34	371	247	121	383	42	0	0	10
Yankee Total		**4**	**67**	**9**	**9**	**.500**	**63**	**4.33**	**131**	**87**	**41**	**137**	**12**	**0**	**0**	**2**

Borowski, Joseph Thomas

HEIGHT: 6'2" RIGHTHANDER BORN: 5/4/1971 BAYONNE, NEW JERSEY

YEAR	TEAM	STARTS	GAMES	WON	LOST	PCT	ER	ERA	INNINGS PITCHED	STRIKE-OUTS	WALKS	HITS ALLOWED	HRS ALLOWED	COMP. GAMES	SHUT-OUTS	SAVES
1995	Bal-A	0	6	0	0	—	1	1.23	7 1/3	3	4	5	0	0	0	0
1996	Atl-N	0	22	2	4	.333	14	4.85	26	15	13	33	4	0	0	0
1997	Atl-N	0	20	2	2	.500	10	3.75	24	6	16	27	2	0	0	0
1997	**NY-A**	**0**	**1**	**0**	**1**	**.000**	**2**	**9.00**	**2**	**2**	**4**	**2**	**0**	**0**	**0**	**0**
1998	**NY-A**	**0**	**8**	**1**	**0**	**1.000**	**7**	**6.52**	**9 2/3**	**7**	**4**	**11**	**0**	**0**	**0**	**0**
Career Average		0	11	1	1	.417	7	4.43	14	7	8	16	1	0	0	0
Yankee Average		**0**	**5**	**1**	**1**	**.500**	**5**	**6.94**	**6**	**5**	**4**	**7**	**0**	**0**	**0**	**0**
Career Total		0	57	5	7	.417	34	4.43	69	33	41	78	6	0	0	0
Yankee Total		**0**	**9**	**1**	**1**	**.500**	**9**	**6.94**	**12**	**9**	**8**	**13**	**0**	**0**	**0**	**0**

Borowy, Henry Ludwig (Hank)

HEIGHT: 6'0" RIGHTHANDER BORN: 5/12/1916 BLOOMFIELD, NEW JERSEY

YEAR	TEAM	STARTS	GAMES	WON	LOST	PCT	ER	ERA	INNINGS PITCHED	STRIKE-OUTS	WALKS	HITS ALLOWED	HRS ALLOWED	COMP. GAMES	SHUT-OUTS	SAVES
1942	NY-A	21	25	15	4	.789	50	2.52	178 1/3	85	66	157	6	13	4	1
1943	NY-A	27	29	14	9	.609	68	2.82	217 1/3	113	72	195	11	14	3	0
1944	NY-A	30	35	17	12	.586	74	2.64	252 2/3	107	88	224	15	19	3	2
1945	NY-A	18	18	10	5	.667	46	3.13	132 1/3	35	58	107	6	7	1	0

(continued)

(continued)

YEAR	TEAM				PCT	ER	ERA	INNINGS PITCHED			HITS ALLOWED	HRS ALLOWED	COMP. GAMES	SHUT-OUTS	SAVES
1945	Chi-N	14	15	11	2	.846	29	2.13	122 1/3	47	47	105	2	11	1	1
1946	Chi-N	28	32	12	10	.545	84	3.76	201	95	61	220	9	8	1	0
1947	Chi-N	25	40	8	12	.400	89	4.38	183	75	63	190	19	7	1	2
1948	Chi-N	17	39	5	10	.333	69	4.89	127	50	49	156	9	2	1	1
1949	Phi-N	28	28	12	12	.500	90	4.19	193 1/3	43	63	188	19	12	1	0
1950	Phi-N	0	3	0	0	—	4	5.68	6 1/3	3	4	5	0	0	0	0
1950	Pit-N	3	11	1	3	.667	18	6.39	25 1/3	9	9	32	6	0	0	0
1950	Det-A	2	13	1	1	.500	12	3.31	32 2/3	12	16	23	3	1	0	0
1951	Det-A	1	26	2	2	.500	35	6.95	45 1/3	16	27	58	3	0	0	0
Career Average		17	24	8	6	.568	51	3.50	132	53	48	128	8	7	1	1
Yankee Average		**24**	**27**	**14**	**8**	**.651**	**60**	**2.74**	**195**	**85**	**71**	**171**	**10**	**13**	**3**	**1**
Career Total		214	314	108	82	.568	668	3.50	1717	690	623	1660	108	94	16	7
Yankee Total		**96**	**107**	**56**	**30**	**.651**	**238**	**2.74**	**781**	**340**	**284**	**683**	**38**	**53**	**11**	**3**

Bouton, James Alan (Jim)

HEIGHT: 6'0" RIGHTHANDER BORN: 3/8/1939 NEWARK, NEW JERSEY

YEAR	TEAM	STARTS	GAMES	WON	LOST	PCT	ER	ERA	INNINGS PITCHED	STRIKE-OUTS	WALKS	HITS ALLOWED	HRS ALLOWED	COMP. GAMES	SHUT-OUTS	SAVES
1962	**NY-A**	**16**	**36**	**7**	**7**	**.500**	**59**	**3.99**	**133**	**71**	**59**	**124**	**9**	**3**	**1**	**2**
1963	**NY-A**	**30**	**40**	**21**	**7**	**.750**	**70**	**2.53**	**249 1/3**	**148**	**87**	**191**	**18**	**12**	**6**	**1**
1964	**NY-A**	**37**	**38**	**18**	**13**	**.581**	**91**	**3.02**	**271 1/3**	**125**	**60**	**227**	**32**	**11**	**4**	**0**
1965	**NY-A**	**25**	**30**	**4**	**15**	**.666**	**81**	**4.82**	**151 1/3**	**97**	**60**	**158**	**23**	**2**	**0**	**0**
1966	**NY-A**	**19**	**24**	**3**	**8**	**.667**	**36**	**2.69**	**120 1/3**	**65**	**38**	**117**	**13**	**3**	**0**	**1**
1967	**NY-A**	**1**	**17**	**1**	**0**	**1.000**	**23**	**4.67**	**44 1/3**	**31**	**18**	**47**	**5**	**0**	**0**	**0**
1968	**NY-A**	**3**	**12**	**1**	**1**	**.500**	**18**	**3.68**	**44**	**24**	**9**	**49**	**5**	**1**	**0**	**0**
1969	Sea-A	1	57	2	1	.667	40	3.91	92	68	38	77	12	0	0	1
1969	Hou-N	1	16	0	2	.000	14	4.11	30 2/3	32	12	32	1	1	0	1
1970	Hou-N	6	29	4	6	.400	44	5.40	73 1/3	49	33	84	5	1	0	0
1978	Atl-N	5	5	1	3	.667	16	4.97	29	10	21	25	4	0	0	0
Career Average		13.	28	6	6	.496	45	3.57	113	65	40	103	12	3	1	1
Yankee Average		**19**	**28**	**8**	**7**	**.519**	**54**	**3.36**	**145**	**80**	**47**	**130**	**15**	**5**	**2**	**1**
Career Total		144	304	62	63	.496	492	3.57	1239	720	435	1131	127	34	11	6
Yankee Total		**131**	**197**	**55**	**51**	**.519**	**378**	**3.36**	**1014**	**561**	**331**	**913**	**105**	**32**	**11**	**4**

Bradley, Ryan James

HEIGHT: 6'4" RIGHTHANDER BORN: 10/26/1975 COVINA, CALIFORNIA

YEAR	TEAM	STARTS	GAMES	WON	LOST	PCT	ER	ERA	INNINGS PITCHED	STRIKE-OUTS	WALKS	HITS ALLOWED	HRS ALLOWED	COMP. GAMES	SHUT-OUTS	SAVES
1998	**NY-A**	**1**	**5**	**2**	**1**	**.667**	**8**	**5.68**	**12 2/3**	**13**	**9**	**12**	**2**	**0**	**0**	**0**
Career Average		1	5	2	1	.667	8	5.68	12 2/3	13	9	12	2	0	0	0
Yankee Average		**1**	**5**	**2**	**1**	**.667**	**8**	**5.68**	**12 2/3**	**13**	**9**	**12**	**2**	**0**	**0**	**0**
Career Total		1	5	2	1	.667	8	5.68	12 2/3	13	9	12	2	0	0	0
Yankee Total		**1**	**5**	**2**	**1**	**.667**	**8**	**5.68**	**12 2/3**	**13**	**9**	**12**	**2**	**0**	**0**	**0**

Brady, Cornelius Joseph (Neal)

HEIGHT: 6'0" RIGHTHANDER BORN: 3/4/1897 COVINGTON, KENTUCKY DIED: 6/19/1947 FORT MITCHELL, KENTUCKY

YEAR	TEAM	STARTS	GAMES	WON	LOST	PCT	ER	ERA	INNINGS PITCHED	STRIKE-OUTS	WALKS	HITS ALLOWED	HRS ALLOWED	COMP. GAMES	SHUT-OUTS	SAVES
1915	**NY-A**	**1**	**2**	**0**	**0**	**—**	**3**	**3.12**	**8 2/3**	**6**	**7**	**9**	**0**	**0**	**0**	**0**
1917	**NY-A**	**1**	**2**	**1**	**0**	**1.000**	**2**	**2.00**	**9**	**4**	**5**	**6**	**0**	**0**	**0**	**0**
1925	Cin-N	3	20	1	3	.667	33	4.66	63 2/3	12	20	73	4	2	0	1
Career Average		2	8	1	1	.400	13	4.20	27	7	11	29	1	1	0	0
Yankee Average		**1**	**2**	**1**	**0**	**1.000**	**3**	**2.55**	**9**	**5**	**6**	**8**	**0**	**0**	**0**	**0**
Career Total		5	24	2	3	.400	38	4.20	81	22	32	88	4	2	0	1
Yankee Total		**2**	**4**	**1**	**0**	**1.000**	**5**	**2.55**	**18**	**10**	**12**	**15**	**0**	**0**	**0**	**0**

Branca, Ralph Theodore Joseph (Hawk)
HEIGHT: 6'3"   RIGHTHANDER   BORN: 1/6/1926 MT. VERNON, NEW YORK

YEAR	TEAM	STARTS	GAMES	WON	LOST	PCT	ER	ERA	INNINGS PITCHED	STRIKE-OUTS	WALKS	HITS ALLOWED	HRS ALLOWED	COMP. GAMES	SHUT-OUTS	SAVES
1944	Bro-N	1	21	0	2	.000	35	7.05	44 2/3	16	32	46	2	0	0	1
1945	Bro-N	15	16	5	6	.455	37	3.04	109 2/3	69	79	73	4	7	0	1
1946	Bro-N	10	24	3	1	.750	29	3.88	67 1/3	42	41	62	4	2	2	3
1947	Bro-N	36	43	21	12	.636	83	2.67	280	148	98	251	22	15	4	1
1948	Bro-N	28	36	14	9	.609	84	3.51	215 2/3	122	80	189	24	11	1	1
1949	Bro-N	27	34	13	5	.722	91	4.39	186 2/3	109	91	181	21	9	2	1
1950	Bro-N	15	43	7	9	.438	74	4.69	142	100	55	152	24	5	0	7
1951	Bro-N	27	42	13	12	.520	74	3.26	204	118	85	180	19	13	3	3
1952	Bro-N	7	16	4	2	.667	26	3.84	61	26	21	52	8	2	0	0
1953	Bro-N	0	7	0	0	—	12	9.82	11	5	5	15	4	0	0	0
1953	Det-A	14	17	4	7	.364	47	4.15	102	50	31	98	7	7	0	1
1954	Det-A	5	17	3	3	.500	29	5.76	45 1/3	15	30	63	10	0	0	0
1954	**NY-A**	**3**	**5**	**1**	**0**	**1.000**	**4**	**2.84**	**12 2/3**	**7**	**13**	**9**	**0**	**0**	**0**	**0**
1956	Bro-N	0	1	0	0	—	0	0.00	2	2	2	1	0	0	0	0
Career Average		13	23	6	5	.564	45	3.79	106	59	47	98	11	5	1	1
Yankee Average		**3**	**5**	**1**	**0**	**1.000**	**4**	**2.84**	**12 2/3**	**7**	**13**	**9**	**0**	**0**	**0**	**0**
Career Total		188	322	88	68	.564	625	3.79	1484	829	663	1372	149	71	12	19
Yankee Total		**3**	**5**	**1**	**0**	**1.000**	**4**	**2.84**	**12 2/3**	**7**	**13**	**9**	**0**	**0**	**0**	**0**

Branch, Norman Downs (Red)
HEIGHT: 6'3"   RIGHTHANDER   BORN: 3/22/1915 SPOKANE, WASHINGTON   DIED: 11/21/1971 NAVASOTA, TEXAS

YEAR	TEAM	STARTS	GAMES	WON	LOST	PCT	ER	ERA	INNINGS PITCHED	STRIKE-OUTS	WALKS	HITS ALLOWED	HRS ALLOWED	COMP. GAMES	SHUT-OUTS	SAVES
1941	**NY-A**	**0**	**27**	**5**	**1**	**.833**	**15**	**2.87**	**47**	**28**	**26**	**37**	**2**	**0**	**0**	**2**
1942	**NY-A**	**0**	**10**	**0**	**1**	**.000**	**11**	**6.32**	**15 2/3**	**13**	**16**	**18**	**3**	**0**	**0**	**2**
Career Average		0	19	3	1	.714	13	3.73	31	21	21	28	3	0	0	2
Yankee Average		**0**	**19**	**3**	**1**	**.714**	**13**	**3.73**	**31**	**21**	**21**	**28**	**3**	**0**	**0**	**2**
Career Total		0	37	5	2	.714	26	3.73	63	41	42	55	5	0	0	4
Yankee Total		**0**	**37**	**5**	**2**	**.714**	**26**	**3.73**	**63**	**41**	**42**	**55**	**5**	**0**	**0**	**4**

Braxton, Edgar Garland
HEIGHT: 5'11"   LEFTHANDER   BORN: 6/10/1900 SNOW CAMP, NORTH CAROLINA   DIED: 2/26/1966 NORFOLK, VIRGINIA

YEAR	TEAM	STARTS	GAMES	WON	LOST	PCT	ER	ERA	INNINGS PITCHED	STRIKE-OUTS	WALKS	HITS ALLOWED	HRS ALLOWED	COMP. GAMES	SHUT-OUTS	SAVES
1921	Bos-N	2	17	1	3	.667	20	4.82	37 1/3	16	17	44	0	0	0	0
1922	Bos-N	4	25	1	2	.333	25	3.38	66 2/3	15	24	75	3	2	0	0
1925	**NY-A**	**2**	**3**	**1**	**1**	**.500**	**14**	**6.52**	**19 1/3**	**11**	**5**	**26**	**1**	**0**	**0**	**0**
1926	**NY-A**	**1**	**37**	**5**	**1**	**.833**	**20**	**2.67**	**67 1/3**	**30**	**19**	**71**	**1**	**0**	**0**	**2**
1927	Was-A	2	58	10	9	.526	51	2.95	155 1/3	96	33	144	5	0	0	13
1928	Was-A	24	38	13	11	.542	61	2.51	218 1/3	94	44	177	7	15	2	6
1929	Was-A	20	37	12	10	.545	98	4.85	182	59	51	219	6	9	0	4
1930	Was-A	0	15	3	2	.600	10	3.29	27 1/3	7	9	22	3	0	0	5
1930	Chi-A	10	19	4	10	.667	65	6.45	90 2/3	44	33	127	9	2	0	1
1931	Chi-A	3	17	0	3	.000	36	6.85	47 1/3	28	23	71	1	0	0	1
1931	StL-A	1	11	0	0	—	21	10.50	18	7	10	27	2	0	0	0
1933	StL-A	1	5	0	1	.000	9	9.72	8 1/3	5	8	11	0	0	0	0
Career Average		6	24	4	4	.485	36	4.13	78	34	23	85	3	2	0	3
Yankee Average		**2**	**20**	**3**	**1**	**.750**	**17**	**3.53**	**43**	**21**	**12**	**49**	**1**	**0**	**0**	**1**
Career Total		70	282	50	53	.485	430	4.13	938	412	276	1014	38	28	2	32
Yankee Total		**3**	**40**	**6**	**2**	**.750**	**34**	**3.53**	**87**	**41**	**24**	**97**	**2**	**0**	**0**	**2**

Brennan, James Donald

HEIGHT: 6'0" RIGHTHANDER BORN: 12/2/1903 AUGUSTA, MAINE DIED: 4/26/1953 BOSTON, MASSACHUSETTS

YEAR	TEAM	STARTS	GAMES	WON	LOST	PCT	ER	ERA	INNINGS PITCHED	STRIKE-OUTS	WALKS	HITS ALLOWED	HRS ALLOWED	COMP. GAMES	SHUT-OUTS	SAVES
1933	**NY-A**	**10**	**18**	**5**	**1**	**.833**	**47**	**4.98**	**85**	**46**	**47**	**92**	**4**	**3**	**0**	**3**
1934	Cin-N	7	28	4	3	.571	33	3.81	78	31	35	89	3	2	0	2
1935	Cin-N	5	38	5	5	.500	40	3.15	114 1/3	48	44	101	4	2	1	5
1936	Cin-N	4	41	5	2	.714	46	4.39	94 1/3	40	35	117	2	0	0	9
1937	Cin-N	0	10	1	1	.500	12	6.75	16	6	10	25	1	0	0	0
1937	NY-N	0	6	1	0	1.000	7	6.75	9 1/3	1	9	12	0	0	0	0
Career Average		4	24	4	2	.636	31	4.19	66	29	30	73	2	1	0	3
Yankee Average		**10**	**18**	**5**	**1**	**.833**	**47**	**4.98**	**85**	**46**	**47**	**92**	**4**	**3**	**0**	**3**
Career Total		26	141	21	12	.636	185	4.19	397	172	180	436	14	7	1	19
Yankee Total		**10**	**18**	**5**	**1**	**.833**	**47**	**4.98**	**85**	**46**	**47**	**92**	**4**	**3**	**0**	**3**

Brenneman, James Leroy

HEIGHT: 6'2" RIGHTHANDER BORN: 2/13/1941 SAN DIEGO, CALIFORNIA

YEAR	TEAM	STARTS	GAMES	WON	LOST	PCT	ER	ERA	INNINGS PITCHED	STRIKE-OUTS	WALKS	HITS ALLOWED	HRS ALLOWED	COMP. GAMES	SHUT-OUTS	SAVES
1965	**NY-A**	**0**	**3**	**0**	**0**	**—**	**4**	**18.00**	**2**	**2**	**3**	**5**	**1**	**0**	**0**	**0**
Career Average		0	3	0	0	—	4	18.00	2	2	3	5	1	0	0	0
Yankee Average		**0**	**3**	**0**	**0**	**—**	**4**	**18.00**	**2**	**2**	**3**	**5**	**1**	**0**	**0**	**0**
Career Total		0	3	0	0	—	4	18.00	2	2	3	5	1	0	0	0
Yankee Total		**0**	**3**	**0**	**0**	**—**	**4**	**18.00**	**2**	**2**	**3**	**5**	**1**	**0**	**0**	**0**

Brett, Kenneth Alven

HEIGHT 6'0" LEFTHANDER BORN: 9/18/1948 BROOKLYN, NEW YORK

YEAR	TEAM	STARTS	GAMES	WON	LOST	PCT	ER	ERA	INNINGS PITCHED	STRIKE-OUTS	WALKS	HITS ALLOWED	HRS ALLOWED	COMP. GAMES	SHUT-OUTS	SAVES
1967	Bos-A	0	1	0	0	—	1	4.50	2	2	0	3	0	0	0	0
1969	Bos-A	8	8	2	3	.400	23	5.26	39 1/3	23	22	41	6	0	0	0
1970	Bos-A	14	41	8	9	.471	63	4.07	139 1/3	155	79	118	17	1	0	2
1971	Bos-A	2	29	0	3	.000	35	5.34	59	57	35	57	7	0	0	1
1972	Mil-A	22	26	7	12	.368	67	4.53	133	74	49	121	13	2	1	0
1973	Phi-N	25	31	13	9	.591	81	3.44	211 2/3	111	74	206	19	10	1	0
1974	Pit-N	27	27	13	9	.591	70	3.30	191	96	52	192	9	10	3	0
1975	Pit-N	16	23	9	5	.643	44	3.36	118	47	43	110	10	4	1	0
1976	**NY-A**	**0**	**2**	**0**	**0**	**—**	**0**	**0.00**	**2 1/3**	**1**	**0**	**2**	**0**	**0**	**0**	**1**
1976	Chi-A	26	27	10	12	.455	74	3.32	200 2/3	91	76	171	5	16	1	1
1977	Chi-A	13	13	6	4	.600	46	5.01	82 2/3	39	15	101	10	2	0	0
1977	Cal-A	21	21	7	10	.412	67	4.25	142	41	38	157	15	5	1	1
1978	Cal-A	10	31	3	5	.375	55	4.95	100	43	42	100	12	1	1	0
1979	Min-A	0	9	0	0	—	7	4.97	12 2/3	3	6	16	1	0	0	2
1979	LA-N	0	30	4	3	.571	18	3.45	47	13	12	52	1	0	0	1
1980	KC-A	0	8	0	0	—	0	0.00	13 1/3	4	5	8	0	0	0	2
1981	KC-A	0	22	1	1	.500	15	4.18	32 1/3	7	14	35	2	0	0	1
Career Average		11	21	5	5	.494	39	3.93	90	47	33	88	7	3	0	1
Yankee Average		**0**	**2**	**0**	**0**	**—**	**0**	**0.00**	**2 1/3**	**1**	**0**	**2**	**0**	**0**	**0**	**1**
Career Total		184	349	83	85	.494	666	3.93	1526	807	562	1490	127	51	8	11
Yankee Total		**0**	**2**	**0**	**0**	**—**	**0**	**0.00**	**2 1/3**	**1**	**0**	**2**	**0**	**0**	**0**	**1**

Breuer, Marvin Howard (Baby Face)

HEIGHT: 6'2" RIGHTHANDER BORN: 4/29/1914 ROLLA, MISSOURI DIED: 1/17/1991 ROLLA, MISSOURI

YEAR	TEAM	STARTS	GAMES	WON	LOST	PCT	ER	ERA	INNINGS PITCHED	STRIKE-OUTS	WALKS	HITS ALLOWED	HRS ALLOWED	COMP. GAMES	SHUT-OUTS	SAVES
1939	**NY-A**	**0**	**1**	**0**	**0**	**—**	**1**	**9.00**	**1**	**0**	**1**	**2**	**0**	**0**	**0**	**0**
1940	**NY-A**	**22**	**27**	**8**	**9**	**.471**	**83**	**4.55**	**164**	**71**	**61**	**175**	**20**	**10**	**0**	**0**
1941	**NY-A**	**18**	**26**	**9**	**7**	**.563**	**64**	**4.09**	**141**	**77**	**49**	**131**	**10**	**7**	**1**	**2**
1942	**NY-A**	**19**	**27**	**8**	**9**	**.471**	**56**	**3.07**	**164 1/3**	**72**	**37**	**157**	**11**	**6**	**0**	**1**
1943	**NY-A**	**1**	**5**	**0**	**1**	**.000**	**13**	**8.36**	**14**	**6**	**6**	**22**	**0**	**0**	**0**	**0**

(continued)

(continued)

	STARTS	GAMES	WON	LOST	PCT	ER	ERA	INNINGS PITCHED	STRIKE-OUTS	WALKS	HITS ALLOWED	HRS ALLOWED	COMP. GAMES	SHUT-OUTS	SAVES
Career Average	30	43	13	13	.490	109	4.03	242	113	77	244	21	12	1	2
Yankee Average	**30**	**43**	**13**	**13**	**.490**	**109**	**4.03**	**242**	**113**	**77**	**244**	**21**	**12**	**1**	**2**
Career Total	60	86	25	26	.490	217	4.03	484	226	154	487	41	23	1	3
Yankee Total	**60**	**86**	**25**	**26**	**.490**	**217**	**4.03**	**484**	**226**	**154**	**487**	**41**	**23**	**1**	**3**

Brewer, William Robert

HEIGHT: 6'1" LEFTHANDER BORN: 4/15/1968 FORT WORTH, TEXAS

YEAR	TEAM	STARTS	GAMES	WON	LOST	PCT	ER	ERA	INNINGS PITCHED	STRIKE-OUTS	WALKS	HITS ALLOWED	HRS ALLOWED	COMP. GAMES	SHUT-OUTS	SAVES
1993	KC-A	0	46	2	2	.500	15	3.46	39	28	20	31	6	0	0	0
1994	KC-A	0	50	4	1	.800	11	2.56	38 2/3	25	16	28	4	0	0	3
1995	KC-A	0	48	2	4	.333	28	5.56	45 1/3	31	20	54	9	0	0	0
1996	**NY-A**	**0**	**4**	**1**	**0**	**1.000**	**6**	**9.53**	**5 2/3**	**8**	**8**	**7**	**0**	**0**	**0**	**0**
1997	Oak-A	0	3	0	0	—	3	13.50	2	1	2	4	1	0	0	0
1997	Phi-N	0	25	1	2	.333	8	3.27	22	16	11	15	2	0	0	0
1998	Phi-N	0	2	0	1	.000	4	108.00	1/3	0	2	3	0	0	0	0
1999	Phi-N	0	25	1	1	.500	20	7.01	25 2/3	28	14	30	4	0	0	2
Career Average	0	25	1	1	.500	12	4.79	22	17	12	22	3	0	0	1
Yankee Average	**0**	**4**	**1**	**0**	**1.000**	**6**	**9.53**	**5 2/3**	**8**	**8**	**7**	**0**	**0**	**0**	**0**
Career Total	0	203	11	11	.500	95	4.79	176	137	93	172	26	0	0	5
Yankee Total	**0**	**4**	**1**	**0**	**1.000**	**6**	**9.53**	**5 2/3**	**8**	**8**	**7**	**0**	**0**	**0**	**0**

Bridges, Marshall (Sheriff)

HEIGHT: 6'1" LEFTHANDER BORN: 6/2/1931 JACKSON, MISSISSIPPI DIED: 9/3/1990 JACKSON, MISSISSIPPI

YEAR	TEAM	STARTS	GAMES	WON	LOST	PCT	ER	ERA	INNINGS PITCHED	STRIKE-OUTS	WALKS	HITS ALLOWED	HRS ALLOWED	COMP. GAMES	SHUT-OUTS	SAVES
1959	StL-N	4	27	6	3	.667	36	4.26	76	76	37	67	10	1	0	1
1960	StL-N	1	20	2	2	.500	12	3.45	31 1/3	27	16	33	2	0	0	1
1960	Cin-N	0	14	4	0	1.000	3	1.07	25 1/3	26	9	14	1	0	0	2
1961	Cin-N	0	13	0	1	.000	18	7.84	20 2/3	17	11	26	4	0	0	0
1962	**NY-A**	**0**	**52**	**8**	**4**	**.667**	**25**	**3.14**	**71 2/3**	**66**	**48**	**49**	**4**	**0**	**0**	**18**
1963	**NY-A**	**0**	**23**	**2**	**0**	**1.000**	**14**	**3.82**	**33**	**35**	**30**	**27**	**2**	**0**	**0**	**1**
1964	Was-A	0	17	0	3	.000	19	5.70	30	16	17	37	3	0	0	2
1965	Was-A	0	40	1	2	.333	17	2.67	57 1/3	39	25	62	3	0	0	0
Career Average	1	26	3	2	.605	18	3.75	43	38	24	39	4	0	0	3
Yankee Average	**0**	**38**	**5**	**2**	**.714**	**20**	**3.35**	**52**	**51**	**39**	**38**	**3**	**0**	**0**	**10**
Career Total	5	206	23	15	.605	144	3.75	345	302	191	315	29	1	0	25
Yankee Total	**0**	**75**	**10**	**4**	**.714**	**39**	**3.35**	**105**	**101**	**78**	**76**	**6**	**0**	**0**	**19**

Broaca, John Joseph

HEIGHT: 5'11" RIGHTHANDER BORN: 10/3/1909 LAWRENCE, MASSACHUSETTS DIED: 5/16/1985 LAWRENCE, MASSACHUSETTS

YEAR	TEAM	STARTS	GAMES	WON	LOST	PCT	ER	ERA	INNINGS PITCHED	STRIKE-OUTS	WALKS	HITS ALLOWED	HRS ALLOWED	COMP. GAMES	SHUT-OUTS	SAVES
1934	NY-A	24	26	12	9	.571	82	4.16	177 1/3	74	65	203	9	13	1	0
1935	NY-A	27	29	15	7	.682	80	3.58	201	78	79	199	16	14	2	0
1936	NY-A	27	37	12	7	.632	97	4.24	206	84	66	235	16	12	1	3
1937	NY-A	6	7	1	4	.666	23	4.70	44	9	17	58	5	3	0	0
1939	Cle-A	2	22	4	2	.667	24	4.70	46	13	28	53	5	0	0	0
Career Average	17	24	9	6	.603	61	4.08	135	52	51	150	10	8	1	1
Yankee Average	**21**	**25**	**10**	**7**	**.597**	**71**	**4.04**	**157**	**61**	**57**	**174**	**12**	**11**	**1**	**1**
Career Total	86	121	44	29	.603	306	4.08	674	258	255	748	51	42	4	3
Yankee Total	**84**	**99**	**40**	**27**	**.597**	**282**	**4.04**	**628**	**245**	**227**	**695**	**46**	**42**	**4**	**3**

Brockett, Lewis Albert (King)
HEIGHT: 5'10" RIGHTHANDER BORN: 7/23/1980 BROWNSVILLE, ILLINOIS DIED: 9/19/1960 NORRIS CITY, ILLINOIS

YEAR	TEAM	STARTS	GAMES	WON	LOST	PCT	ER	ERA	INNINGS PITCHED	STRIKE-OUTS	WALKS	HITS ALLOWED	HRS ALLOWED	COMP. GAMES	SHUT-OUTS	SAVES
1907	NY-A	4	8	1	2	.333	32	6.22	46 1/3	13	26	58	1	1	0	0
1909	NY-A	18	26	10	8	.556	40	2.12	170	70	59	148	3	10	3	1
1911	NY-A	8	16	2	4	.333	39	4.66	75 1/3	25	39	73	3	2	0	0
Career Average		10	17	4	5	.481	37	3.43	97	36	41	93	2	4	1	0
Yankee Average		10	17	4	5	.481	37	3.43	97	36	41	93	2	4	1	0
Career Total		30	50	13	14	.481	111	3.43	292	108	124	279	7	13	3	1
Yankee Total		30	50	13	14	.481	111	3.43	292	108	124	279	7	13	3	1

Bronstad, James Warren
HEIGHT: 6'3" RIGHTHANDER BORN: 6/22/1936 FT. WORTH, TEXAS

YEAR	TEAM	STARTS	GAMES	WON	LOST	PCT	ER	ERA	INNINGS PITCHED	STRIKE-OUTS	WALKS	HITS ALLOWED	HRS ALLOWED	COMP. GAMES	SHUT-OUTS	SAVES
1959	NY-A	3	16	0	3	.000	17	5.22	29 1/3	14	13	34	2	0	0	2
1963	Was-A	0	25	1	3	.667	36	5.65	57 1/3	22	22	66	9	0	0	1
1964	Was-A	0	4	0	1	.000	4	5.14	7	9	2	10	0	0	0	0
Career Average		1	15	0	2	.125	19	5.48	31	15	12	37	4	0	0	1
Yankee Average		3	16	0	3	.000	17	5.22	29 1/3	14	13	34	2	0	0	2
Career Total		3	45	1	7	.125	57	5.48	94	45	37	110	11	0	0	3
Yankee Total		3	16	0	3	.000	17	5.22	29 1/3	14	13	34	2	0	0	2

Brown, Carroll William (Boardwalk)
HEIGHT: 6'1" RIGHTHANDER BORN: 2/20/1887 WOODBURY, NEW JERSEY DIED: 2/8/1977 BURLINGTON, NEW JERSEY

YEAR	TEAM	STARTS	GAMES	WON	LOST	PCT	ER	ERA	INNINGS PITCHED	STRIKE-OUTS	WALKS	HITS ALLOWED	HRS ALLOWED	COMP. GAMES	SHUT-OUTS	SAVES
1911	Phi-A	1	2	0	1	.000	6	4.50	12	6	2	12	0	1	0	0
1912	Phi-A	24	34	13	11	.542	81	3.66	199	64	87	204	2	15	3	0
1913	Phi-A	35	43	17	11	.607	77	2.94	235 1/3	70	87	200	6	11	3	1
1914	Phi-A	8	15	1	6	.143	30	4.09	66	20	26	64	1	2	0	0
1914	NY-A	14	20	5	5	.500	44	3.24	122 1/3	57	42	123	2	8	0	1
1915	NY-A	11	19	2	6	.667	44	4.10	96 2/3	34	47	95	4	5	0	1
Career Average		16	22	6	7	.487	47	3.47	122	42	49	116	3	7	1	1
Yankee Average		13	20	4	6	.389	44	3.62	109	46	45	109	3	7	0	1
Career Total		93	133	38	40	.487	282	3.47	731	251	291	698	15	42	6	3
Yankee Total		25	39	7	11	.389	88	3.62	219	91	89	218	6	13	0	2

Brown, Curtis Steven
HEIGHT: 6'5" RIGHTHANDER BORN: 1/15/1960 FT. LAUDERDALE, FLORIDA

YEAR	TEAM	STARTS	GAMES	WON	LOST	PCT	ER	ERA	INNINGS PITCHED	STRIKE-OUTS	WALKS	HITS ALLOWED	HRS ALLOWED	COMP. GAMES	SHUT-OUTS	SAVES
1983	Cal-A	0	10	1	1	.500	13	7.31	16	7	4	25	1	0	0	0
1984	NY-A	0	13	1	1	.500	5	2.70	16 2/3	10	4	18	1	0	0	0
1986	Mon-N	0	6	0	1	.000	4	3.00	12	4	2	15	0	0	0	0
1987	Mon-N	0	5	0	1	.000	6	7.71	7	6	4	10	2	0	0	0
Career Average		0	9	1	1	.333	7	4.88	13	7	4	17	1	0	0	0
Yankee Average		0	13	1	1	.500	5	2.70	16 2/3	10	4	18	1	0	0	0
Career Total		0	34	2	4	.333	28	4.88	52	27	14	68	4	0	0	0
Yankee Total		0	13	1	1	.500	5	2.70	16 2/3	10	4	18	1	0	0	0

Brown, Hector Harold (Skinny)
HEIGHT: 6'2"   RIGHTHANDER   BORN: 12/11/1924 GREENSBORO, NORTH CAROLINA

YEAR	TEAM	STARTS	GAMES	WON	LOST	PCT	ER	ERA	INNINGS PITCHED	STRIKE-OUTS	WALKS	HITS ALLOWED	HRS ALLOWED	COMP. GAMES	SHUT-OUTS	SAVES
1951	Chi-A	0	3	0	0	—	9	9.35	8 2/3	4	4	15	3	0	0	1
1952	Chi-A	8	24	2	3	.400	34	4.23	72 1/3	31	21	82	8	1	0	0
1953	Bos-A	25	30	11	6	.647	86	4.65	166 1/3	62	57	177	16	6	1	0
1954	Bos-A	5	40	1	8	.111	54	4.12	118	66	41	126	6	1	0	0
1955	Bos-A	0	2	1	0	1.000	1	2.25	4	2	2	2	0	0	0	0
1955	Bal-A	5	15	0	4	.000	26	4.11	57	26	26	51	5	1	0	0
1956	Bal-A	14	35	9	7	.563	68	4.04	151 2/3	57	37	142	18	4	1	2
1957	Bal-A	20	25	7	8	.467	65	3.90	150	62	37	132	17	7	2	1
1958	Bal-A	17	19	7	5	.583	33	3.07	96 2/3	44	20	96	9	4	2	1
1959	Bal-A	21	31	11	9	.550	69	3.79	164	81	32	158	16	2	0	3
1960	Bal-A	20	30	12	5	.706	54	3.06	159	66	22	155	14	6	1	0
1961	Bal-A	23	27	10	6	.625	59	3.19	166 2/3	61	33	153	14	6	3	1
1962	Bal-A	11	22	6	4	.600	39	4.10	85 2/3	25	21	88	12	0	0	1
1962	**NY-A**	**1**	**2**	**0**	**1**	**.000**	**5**	**6.75**	**6 2/3**	**2**	**2**	**9**	**3**	**0**	**0**	**0**
1963	Hou-N	20	26	5	11	.313	52	3.31	141 1/3	68	8	137	14	6	3	0
1964	Hou-N	21	27	3	15	.167	58	3.95	132	53	26	154	18	3	0	1
Career Average		13	22	5	6	.480	45	3.81	105	44	24	105	11	3	1	1
Yankee Average		**1**	**2**	**0**	**1**	**.000**	**5**	**6.75**	**6 2/3**	**2**	**2**	**9**	**3**	**0**	**0**	**0**
Career Total		211	358	85	92	.480	712	3.81	1680	710	389	1677	173	47	13	11
Yankee Total		**1**	**2**	**0**	**1**	**.000**	**5**	**6.75**	**6 2/3**	**2**	**2**	**9**	**3**	**0**	**0**	**0**

Brown, Walter George (Jumbo)
HEIGHT: 6'4"   RIGHTHANDER   BORN: 4/30/1907 GREENE, RHODE ISLAND   DIED: 10/2/1966 FREEPORT, NEW YORK

YEAR	TEAM	STARTS	GAMES	WON	LOST	PCT	ER	ERA	INNINGS PITCHED	STRIKE-OUTS	WALKS	HITS ALLOWED	HRS ALLOWED	COMP. GAMES	SHUT-OUTS	SAVES
1925	Chi-N	0	2	0	0	—	2	3.00	6	0	4	5	0	0	0	0
1927	Cle-A	0	8	0	2	.000	13	6.27	18 2/3	8	26	19	3	0	0	0
1928	Cle-A	0	5	0	1	.000	11	6.75	14 2/3	12	15	19	0	0	0	0
1932	**NY-A**	**3**	**19**	**5**	**2**	**.714**	**28**	**4.53**	**55 2/3**	**31**	**30**	**58**	**1**	**3**	**1**	**1**
1933	**NY-A**	**8**	**21**	**7**	**5**	**.583**	**43**	**5.23**	**74**	**55**	**52**	**78**	**3**	**1**	**0**	**0**
1935	**NY-A**	**8**	**20**	**6**	**5**	**.545**	**35**	**3.61**	**87 1/3**	**41**	**37**	**94**	**2**	**3**	**1**	**0**
1936	**NY-A**	**3**	**20**	**1**	**4**	**.666**	**42**	**5.91**	**64**	**19**	**29**	**93**	**4**	**0**	**0**	**1**
1937	Cin-N	1	4	1	0	1.000	9	8.38	9 2/3	4	3	16	0	0	0	0
1937	NY-N	0	4	1	0	1.000	1	1.04	8 2/3	4	5	5	0	0	0	0
1938	NY-N	0	43	5	3	.625	18	1.80	90	42	28	65	5	0	0	5
1939	NY-N	0	31	4	0	1.000	26	4.15	56 1/3	24	25	69	1	0	0	7
1940	NY-N	0	41	2	4	.333	21	3.42	55 1/3	31	25	49	5	0	0	7
1941	NY-N	0	31	1	5	.167	21	3.32	57	30	21	49	2	0	0	8
Career Average		2	19	3	2	.516	21	4.07	46	23	23	48	2	1	0	2
Yankee Average		**6**	**20**	**5**	**4**	**.543**	**37**	**4.74**	**70**	**37**	**37**	**81**	**3**	**2**	**1**	**1**
Career Total		23	249	33	31	.516	270	4.07	597	301	300	619	26	7	2	29
Yankee Total		**22**	**80**	**19**	**16**	**.543**	**148**	**4.74**	**281**	**146**	**148**	**323**	**10**	**7**	**2**	**2**

Bruske, James Scott
HEIGHT: 6'1"   RIGHTHANDER   BORN: 10/7/1964 EAST ST. LOUIS, ILLINOIS

YEAR	TEAM	STARTS	GAMES	WON	LOST	PCT	ER	ERA	INNINGS PITCHED	STRIKE-OUTS	WALKS	HITS ALLOWED	HRS ALLOWED	COMP. GAMES	SHUT-OUTS	SAVES
1995	LA-N	0	9	0	0	—	5	4.50	10	5	4	12	0	0	0	1
1996	LA-N	0	11	0	0	—	8	5.68	12 2/3	12	3	17	2	0	0	0
1997	SD-N	0	28	4	1	.800	18	3.63	44 2/3	32	25	37	4	0	0	0
1998	LA-N	0	35	3	0	1.000	17	3.48	44	31	19	47	2	0	0	1
1998	SD-N	0	4	0	0	—	3	3.86	7	4	4	10	1	0	0	0
1998	**NY-A**	**1**	**3**	**1**	**0**	**1.000**	**3**	**3.00**	**9**	**3**	**1**	**9**	**2**	**0**	**0**	**0**
2000	Mil-N	0	15	1	0	1.000	12	6.48	16 2/3	8	12	22	5	0	0	0
Career Average		0	15	1	0	.900	9	4.13	21	15	9	22	2	0	0	0
Yankee Average		**1**	**3**	**1**	**0**	**1.000**	**3**	**3.00**	**9**	**3**	**1**	**9**	**2**	**0**	**0**	**0**
Career Total		1	105	9	1	.900	66	4.13	144	68	56	152	16	0	0	2
Yankee Total		**1**	**3**	**1**	**0**	**1.000**	**3**	**3.00**	**9**	**3**	**1**	**9**	**2**	**0**	**0**	**0**

Buckles, Jesse Robert (Jim)

HEIGHT: 6'2"   LEFTHANDER   BORN: 5/20/1890 LAVERNE, CALIFORNIA   DIED: 8/2/1975 WESTMINSTER, CALIFORNIA

YEAR	TEAM	STARTS	GAMES	WON	LOST	PCT	ER	ERA	INNINGS PITCHED	STRIKE-OUTS	WALKS	HITS ALLOWED	HRS ALLOWED	COMP. GAMES	SHUT-OUTS	SAVES
1916	NY-A	0	2	0	0	—	1	2.25	4	2	1	3	0	0	0	0
Career Average		0	2	0	0	—	1	2.25	4	2	1	3	0	0	0	0
Yankee Average		**0**	**2**	**0**	**0**	**—**	**1**	**2.25**	**4**	**2**	**1**	**3**	**0**	**0**	**0**	**0**
Career Total		0	2	0	0	—	1	2.25	4	2	1	3	0	0	0	0
Yankee Total		**0**	**2**	**0**	**0**	**—**	**1**	**2.25**	**4**	**2**	**1**	**3**	**0**	**0**	**0**	**0**

Buddie, Michael J.

HEIGHT: 6'3"   RIGHTHANDER   BORN: 12/12/1970 BEREA, OHIO

YEAR	TEAM	STARTS	GAMES	WON	LOST	PCT	ER	ERA	INNINGS PITCHED	STRIKE-OUTS	WALKS	HITS ALLOWED	HRS ALLOWED	COMP. GAMES	SHUT-OUTS	SAVES
1998	NY-A	2	24	4	1	.800	26	5.62	41 2/3	20	13	46	5	0	0	0
1999	NY-A	0	2	0	0	—	1	4.50	2	1	0	3	1	0	0	0
2000	Mil-N	0	5	0	0	—	3	4.50	6	5	1	8	0	0	0	0
Career Average		1	10	1	0	.800	10	5.44	17	9	5	19	2	0	0	0
Yankee Average		**1**	**13**	**2**	**1**	**.800**	**14**	**5.56**	**22**	**11**	**7**	**25**	**3**	**0**	**0**	**0**
Career Total		2	31	4	1	.800	30	5.44	50	26	14	57	6	0	0	0
Yankee Total		**2**	**26**	**4**	**1**	**.800**	**27**	**5.56**	**44**	**21**	**13**	**49**	**6**	**0**	**0**	**0**

Burbach, William David

HEIGHT: 6'4"   RIGHTHANDER   BORN: 8/22/1947 DICKEYVILLE, WISCONSIN

YEAR	TEAM	STARTS	GAMES	WON	LOST	PCT	ER	ERA	INNINGS PITCHED	STRIKE-OUTS	WALKS	HITS ALLOWED	HRS ALLOWED	COMP. GAMES	SHUT-OUTS	SAVES
1969	NY-A	24	31	6	8	.429	57	3.65	140 2/3	82	102	112	15	2	1	0
1970	NY-A	4	4	0	2	.000	19	10.26	16 2/3	10	9	23	2	0	0	0
1971	NY-A	0	2	0	1	.000	4	10.80	3 1/3	3	5	6	0	0	0	0
Career Average		9	12	2	4	.353	27	4.48	54	32	39	47	6	1	0	0
Yankee Average		**9**	**12**	**2**	**4**	**.353**	**27**	**4.48**	**54**	**32**	**39**	**47**	**6**	**1**	**0**	**0**
Career Total		28	37	6	11	.353	80	4.48	161	95	116	141	17	2	1	0
Yankee Total		**28**	**37**	**6**	**11**	**.353**	**80**	**4.48**	**161**	**95**	**116**	**141**	**17**	**2**	**1**	**0**

Burdette, Selva Lewis

HEIGHT: 6'2"   RIGHTHANDER   BORN: 11/22/1926 NITRO, WEST VIRGINIA

YEAR	TEAM	STARTS	GAMES	WON	LOST	PCT	ER	ERA	INNINGS PITCHED	STRIKE-OUTS	WALKS	HITS ALLOWED	HRS ALLOWED	COMP. GAMES	SHUT-OUTS	SAVES
1950	**NY-A**	**0**	**2**	**0**	**0**	**—**	**1**	**6.75**	**1 1/3**	**0**	**0**	**3**	**0**	**0**	**0**	**0**
1951	Bos-N	0	3	0	0	—	3	6.23	4 1/3	1	5	6	0	0	0	0
1952	Bos-N	9	45	6	11	.353	55	3.61	137	47	47	138	8	5	0	7
1953	Mil-N	13	46	15	5	.750	63	3.24	175	58	56	177	7	6	1	8
1954	Mil-N	32	38	15	14	.517	73	2.76	238	79	62	224	17	13	4	0
1955	Mil-N	33	42	13	8	.619	103	4.03	230	70	73	253	25	11	2	0
1956	Mil-N	35	39	19	10	.655	77	2.70	256 1/3	110	52	234	22	16	6	1
1957	Mil-N	33	37	17	9	.654	106	3.72	256 2/3	78	59	260	25	14	1	0
1958	Mil-N	36	40	20	10	.667	89	2.91	275 1/3	113	50	279	18	19	3	0
1959	Mil-N	39	41	21	15	.583	131	4.07	289 2/3	105	38	312	38	20	4	1
1960	Mil-N	32	45	19	13	.594	103	3.36	275 2/3	83	35	277	19	18	4	4
1961	Mil-N	36	40	18	11	.621	121	4.00	272 1/3	92	33	295	31	14	3	0
1962	Mil-N	19	37	10	9	.526	78	4.89	143 2/3	59	23	172	26	6	1	2
1963	Mil-N	13	15	6	5	.545	34	3.64	84	28	24	71	15	4	1	0
1963	StL-N	14	21	3	8	.667	41	3.77	98	45	16	106	6	3	0	2
1964	StL-N	0	8	1	0	1.000	2	1.80	10	3	3	10	1	0	0	2

(continued)

(continued)

1964	Chi-N	17	28	9	9	.500	71	4.88	131	40	19	152	15	8	2	0
1965	Chi-N	3	7	0	2	.000	12	5.31	20 1/3	5	4	26	3	0	0	0
1965	Phi-N	9	19	3	3	.500	43	5.48	70 2/3	23	17	95	5	1	1	0
1966	Cal-A	0	54	7	2	.778	30	3.39	79 2/3	27	12	80	4	0	0	5
1967	Cal-A	0	19	1	0	1.000	10	4.91	18 1/3	8	0	16	4	0	0	1
Career Average		18	30	10	7	.585	59	3.66	146	51	30	152	14	8	2	1
Yankee Average		**0**	**2**	**0**	**0**	**—**	**1**	**6.75**	**1 1/3**	**0**	**0**	**3**	**0**	**0**	**0**	**0**
Career Total		373	626	203	144	.585	1246	3.66	3067	1074	628	3186	289	158	33	31
Yankee Total		**0**	**2**	**0**	**0**	**—**	**1**	**6.75**	**1 1/3**	**0**	**0**	**3**	**0**	**0**	**0**	**0**

Burke, Timothy Philip
HEIGHT: 6'3"   RIGHTHANDER   BORN: 2/19/1959 OMAHA, NEBRASKA

YEAR	TEAM	STARTS	GAMES	WON	LOST	PCT	ER	ERA	INNINGS PITCHED	STRIKE-OUTS	WALKS	HITS ALLOWED	HRS ALLOWED	COMP. GAMES	SHUT-OUTS	SAVES
1985	Mon-N	0	78	9	4	.692	32	2.39	120 1/3	87	44	86	9	0	0	8
1986	Mon-N	2	68	9	7	.563	33	2.93	101 1/3	82	46	103	7	0	0	4
1987	Mon-N	0	55	7	0	1.000	12	1.19	91	58	17	64	3	0	0	18
1988	Mon-N	0	61	3	5	.375	31	3.40	82	42	25	84	7	0	0	18
1989	Mon-N	0	68	9	3	.750	24	2.55	84 2/3	54	22	68	6	0	0	28
1990	Mon-N	0	58	3	3	.500	21	2.52	75	47	21	71	6	0	0	20
1991	Mon-N	0	37	3	4	.429	21	4.11	46	25	14	41	3	0	0	5
1991	NY-N	0	35	3	3	.500	17	2.75	55 2/3	34	12	55	5	0	0	1
1992	NY-N	0	15	1	2	.333	10	5.74	15 2/3	7	3	26	1	0	0	0
1992	**NY-A**	**0**	**23**	**2**	**2**	**.500**	**10**	**3.25**	**27 2/3**	**8**	**15**	**26**	**2**	**0**	**0**	**0**
Career Average		0	50	5	3	.598	21	2.72	70	44	22	62	5	0	0	10
Yankee Average		**0**	**23**	**2**	**2**	**.500**	**10**	**3.25**	**27 2/3**	**8**	**15**	**26**	**2**	**0**	**0**	**0**
Career Total		2	498	49	33	.598	211	2.72	699	444	219	624	49	0	0	102
Yankee Total		**0**	**23**	**2**	**2**	**.500**	**10**	**3.25**	**27 2/3**	**8**	**15**	**26**	**2**	**0**	**0**	**0**

Burris, Bertram Ray
HEIGHT: 6'5"   RIGHTHANDER   BORN: 8/22/1950 IDABEL, OKLAHOMA

YEAR	TEAM	STARTS	GAMES	WON	LOST	PCT	ER	ERA	INNINGS PITCHED	STRIKE-OUTS	WALKS	HITS ALLOWED	HRS ALLOWED	COMP. GAMES	SHUT-OUTS	SAVES
1973	Chi-N	1	31	1	1	.500	21	2.92	64 2/3	57	27	65	2	0	0	0
1974	Chi-N	5	40	3	5	.375	55	6.60	75	40	26	91	8	0	0	1
1975	Chi-N	35	36	15	10	.600	109	4.12	238 1/3	108	73	259	25	8	2	0
1976	Chi-N	36	37	15	13	.536	86	3.11	249	112	70	251	22	10	4	0
1977	Chi-N	39	39	14	16	.467	116	4.72	221	105	67	270	29	5	1	0
1978	Chi-N	32	40	7	13	.350	105	4.76	198 2/3	94	79	210	15	4	1	1
1979	Chi-N	0	14	0	0	—	15	6.23	21 2/3	14	15	23	0	0	0	0
1979	**NY-A**	**0**	**15**	**1**	**3**	**.667**	**19**	**6.18**	**27 2/3**	**19**	**10**	**40**	**5**	**0**	**0**	**0**
1979	NY-N	4	4	0	2	.000	8	3.32	21 2/3	10	6	21	2	0	0	0
1980	NY-N	29	29	7	13	.350	76	4.02	170 1/3	83	54	181	20	1	0	0
1981	Mon-N	21	22	9	7	.563	46	3.05	135 2/3	52	41	117	9	4	0	0
1982	Mon-N	15	37	4	14	.666	65	4.73	123 2/3	55	53	143	14	2	0	2
1983	Mon-N	17	40	4	7	.364	63	3.68	154	100	56	139	13	2	1	0
1984	Oak-A	28	34	13	10	.565	74	3.15	211 2/3	93	90	193	15	5	1	0
1985	Mil-A	28	29	9	13	.409	91	4.81	170 1/3	81	53	182	25	6	0	0
1986	StL-N	10	23	4	5	.444	51	5.60	82	34	32	92	13	0	0	0
1987	Mil-A	2	10	2	2	.500	15	5.87	23	8	12	33	4	0	0	0
Career Average		18	28	6	8	.446	60	4.17	129	63	45	136	13	3	1	0
Yankee Average		**0**	**15**	**1**	**3**	**.250**	**19**	**6.18**	**27 2/3**	**19**	**10**	**40**	**5**	**0**	**0**	**0**
Career Total		302	480	108	134	.446	1015	4.17	2188	1065	764	2310	221	47	10	4
Yankee Total		**0**	**15**	**1**	**3**	**.250**	**19**	**6.18**	**27 2/3**	**19**	**10**	**40**	**5**	**0**	**0**	**0**

Bush, Leslie Ambrose (Bullet Joe)

HEIGHT: 5'9"   RIGHTHANDER   BORN: 11/27/1892 BRAINERD, MINNESOTA   DIED: 11/1/1974 FT. LAUDERDALE, FLORIDA

YEAR	TEAM	STARTS	GAMES	WON	LOST	PCT	ER	ERA	INNINGS PITCHED	STRIKE-OUTS	WALKS	HITS ALLOWED	HRS ALLOWED	COMP. GAMES	SHUT-OUTS	SAVES
1912	Phi-A	1	1	0	0	—	7	7.88	8	3	4	14	0	0	0	0
1913	Phi-A	16	39	15	6	.714	85	3.82	200 1/3	81	66	199	3	6	1	3
1914	Phi-A	23	38	17	12	.586	70	3.06	206	109	81	184	2	14	2	2
1915	Phi-A	18	25	5	15	.667	67	4.14	145 2/3	89	89	137	3	8	0	0
1916	Phi-A	33	40	15	24	.385	82	2.57	286 2/3	157	130	222	3	25	8	0
1917	Phi-A	31	37	11	17	.393	64	2.47	233 1/3	121	111	207	3	17	4	2
1918	Bos-A	31	36	15	15	.500	64	2.11	272 2/3	125	91	241	3	26	7	2
1919	Bos-A	2	3	0	0	—	5	5.00	9	3	4	11	0	0	0	0
1920	Bos-A	32	35	15	15	.500	115	4.25	243 2/3	88	94	287	3	18	0	1
1921	Bos-A	32	37	16	9	.640	99	3.50	254 1/3	96	93	244	10	21	3	1
1922	**NY-A**	**30**	**39**	**26**	**7**	**.788**	**94**	**3.31**	**255 1/3**	**92**	**85**	**240**	**16**	**20**	**0**	**3**
1923	**NY-A**	**30**	**37**	**19**	**15**	**.559**	**105**	**3.43**	**275 2/3**	**125**	**117**	**263**	**7**	**22**	**3**	**0**
1924	**NY-A**	**31**	**39**	**17**	**16**	**.515**	**100**	**3.57**	**252**	**80**	**109**	**262**	**9**	**19**	**3**	**1**
1925	StL-A	28	33	14	14	.500	118	5.09	208 2/3	63	91	230	18	15	2	0
1926	Was-A	11	12	1	8	.111	53	6.69	71 1/3	27	35	83	6	3	0	0
1926	Pit-N	11	19	6	6	.500	37	3.01	110 2/3	38	35	97	7	9	2	3
1927	Pit-N	3	5	1	2	.333	10	13.50	6 2/3	1	5	14	1	0	0	0
1927	NY-A	2	3	1	1	.500	10	7.50	12	6	5	18	1	1	0	0
1928	Phi-A	2	11	2	1	.667	20	5.09	35 1/3	15	18	39	1	1	0	1
Career Average		19	26	10	10	.517	63	3.51	162	69	66	157	5	12	2	1
Yankee Average		30	38	21	13	.620	100	3.44	261	99	104	255	11	20	2	1
Career Total		367	489	196	183	.517	1205	3.51	3087	1319	1263	2992	96	225	35	19
Yankee Total		91	115	62	38	.620	299	3.44	783	297	311	765	32	61	6	4

Buskey, Thomas William

HEIGHT: 6'3"   RIGHTHANDER   BORN: 2/20/1947 HARRISBURG, PENNSYLVANIA

YEAR	TEAM	STARTS	GAMES	WON	LOST	PCT	ER	ERA	INNINGS PITCHED	STRIKE-OUTS	WALKS	HITS ALLOWED	HRS ALLOWED	COMP. GAMES	SHUT-OUTS	SAVES
1973	**NY-A**	**0**	**8**	**0**	**1**	**.000**	**10**	**5.40**	**16 2/3**	**8**	**4**	**18**	**2**	**0**	**0**	**1**
1974	**NY-A**	**0**	**4**	**0**	**1**	**.000**	**4**	**6.35**	**5 2/3**	**3**	**3**	**10**	**1**	**0**	**0**	**1**
1974	Cle-A	0	51	2	6	.667	33	3.19	93	40	33	93	10	0	0	17
1975	Cle-A	0	50	5	3	.625	22	2.57	77	29	29	69	7	0	0	7
1976	Cle-A	0	39	5	4	.556	38	3.63	94 1/3	32	34	88	9	0	0	1
1977	Cle-A	0	21	0	0	—	20	5.29	34	15	8	45	6	0	0	0
1978	Tor-A	0	8	0	1	.000	5	3.38	13 1/3	7	5	14	1	0	0	0
1979	Tor-A	0	44	6	10	.375	30	3.43	78 2/3	44	25	74	10	0	0	7
1980	Tor-A	0	33	3	1	.750	33	4.46	66 2/3	34	26	68	11	0	0	0
Career Average		0	29	2	3	.438	22	3.66	53	24	19	53	6	0	0	4
Yankee Average		0	6	0	1	.000	7	5.64	11	6	4	14	2	0	0	1
Career Total		0	258	21	27	.438	195	3.66	479	212	167	479	57	0	0	34
Yankee Total		0	12	0	2	.000	14	5.64	22	11	7	28	3	0	0	2

Buxton, Ralph Stanley (Buck)

HEIGHT: 5'11"   RIGHTHANDER   BORN: 6/7/1911 WEYBURN, SASKATCHEWAN, CANADA

YEAR	TEAM	STARTS	GAMES	WON	LOST	PCT	ER	ERA	INNINGS PITCHED	STRIKE-OUTS	WALKS	HITS ALLOWED	HRS ALLOWED	COMP. GAMES	SHUT-OUTS	SAVES
1938	Phi-A	0	5	0	1	.000	5	4.82	9 1/3	9	5	12	1	0	0	0
1949	**NY-A**	**0**	**14**	**0**	**1**	**.000**	**12**	**4.05**	**26 2/3**	**14**	**16**	**22**	**3**	**0**	**0**	**2**
Career Average		0	10	0	1	.000	9	4.25	18	12	11	17	2	0	0	1
Yankee Average		0	14	0	1	.000	12	4.05	26 2/3	14	16	22	3	0	0	2
Career Total		0	19	0	2	.000	17	4.25	36	23	21	34	4	0	0	2
Yankee Total		0	14	0	1	.000	12	4.05	26 2/3	14	16	22	3	0	0	2

Byrd, Harry Gladwin

HEIGHT: 6'1"   RIGHTHANDER   BORN: 2/3/1925 DARLINGTON, SOUTH CAROLINA   DIED: 5/14/1985 DARLINGTON, SOUTH CAROLINA

YEAR	TEAM	STARTS	GAMES	WON	LOST	PCT	ER	ERA	INNINGS PITCHED	STRIKE-OUTS	WALKS	HITS ALLOWED	HRS ALLOWED	COMP. GAMES	SHUT-OUTS	SAVES
1950	Phi-A	0	6	0	0	—	20	16.88	10 2/3	2	9	25	3	0	0	0
1952	Phi-A	28	37	15	15	.500	84	3.31	228 1/3	116	98	244	12	15	3	2
1953	Phi-A	37	40	11	20	.355	145	5.51	236 2/3	122	115	279	23	11	2	0
1954	**NY-A**	**21**	**25**	**9**	**7**	**.563**	**44**	**2.99**	**132 1/3**	**52**	**43**	**131**	**10**	**5**	**1**	**0**
1955	Bal-A	8	14	3	2	.600	33	4.55	65 1/3	25	28	64	7	1	1	1
1955	Chi-A	12	25	4	6	.400	47	4.65	91	44	30	85	10	1	1	1
1956	Chi-A	1	3	0	1	.000	5	10.39	4 1/3	0	4	9	0	0	0	0
1957	Det-A	1	37	4	3	.571	22	3.36	59	20	28	53	6	0	0	5
Career Average		14	23	6	7	.460	50	4.35	103	48	44	111	9	4	1	1
Yankee Average		**21**	**25**	**9**	**7**	**.563**	**44**	**2.99**	**132 1/3**	**52**	**43**	**131**	**10**	**5**	**1**	**0**
Career Total		108	187	46	54	.460	400	4.35	828	381	355	890	71	33	8	9
Yankee Total		**21**	**25**	**9**	**7**	**.563**	**44**	**2.99**	**132 1/3**	**52**	**43**	**131**	**10**	**5**	**1**	**0**

Byrne, Thomas Joseph (Tommy)

HEIGHT: 6'1"   LEFTHANDER   BORN: 12/31/1919 BALTIMORE, MARYLAND

YEAR	TEAM	STARTS	GAMES	WON	LOST	PCT	ER	ERA	INNINGS PITCHED	STRIKE-OUTS	WALKS	HITS ALLOWED	HRS ALLOWED	COMP. GAMES	SHUT-OUTS	SAVES
1943	**NY-A**	**2**	**11**	**2**	**1**	**.667**	**23**	**6.54**	**31 2/3**	**22**	**35**	**28**	**1**	**0**	**0**	**0**
1946	**NY-A**	**1**	**4**	**0**	**1**	**.000**	**6**	**5.79**	**9 1/3**	**5**	**8**	**7**	**1**	**0**	**0**	**0**
1947	**NY-A**	**1**	**4**	**0**	**0**	**—**	**2**	**4.15**	**4 1/3**	**2**	**6**	**5**	**0**	**0**	**0**	**0**
1948	**NY-A**	**11**	**31**	**8**	**5**	**.615**	**49**	**3.30**	**133 2/3**	**93**	**101**	**79**	**8**	**0**	**0**	**0**
1949	**NY-A**	**30**	**32**	**15**	**7**	**.682**	**81**	**3.72**	**196**	**129**	**179**	**125**	**11**	**5**	**1**	**2**
1950	**NY-A**	**31**	**31**	**15**	**9**	**.625**	**107**	**4.74**	**203 1/3**	**118**	**160**	**188**	**23**	**12**	**3**	**0**
1951	**NY-A**	**3**	**9**	**2**	**1**	**.667**	**16**	**6.86**	**21**	**14**	**36**	**16**	**0**	**10**	**2**	**0**
1951	StL-A	17	19	4	10	.667	52	3.82	122 2/3	57	114	104	5	0	0	0
1952	StL-A	24	29	7	14	.333	102	4.68	196	91	112	182	16	7	2	0
1953	Chi-A	6	6	2	0	1.000	18	10.13	16	4	26	18	3	14	0	0
1953	Was-A	5	6	0	5	.000	16	4.28	33 2/3	22	22	35	0	0	0	0
1954	**NY-A**	**5**	**5**	**3**	**2**	**.600**	**12**	**2.70**	**40**	**24**	**19**	**36**	**3**	**2**	**0**	**0**
1955	**NY-A**	**22**	**27**	**16**	**5**	**.762**	**56**	**3.15**	**160**	**76**	**87**	**137**	**6**	**4**	**1**	**0**
1956	**NY-A**	**8**	**37**	**7**	**3**	**.700**	**41**	**3.36**	**109 2/3**	**52**	**72**	**108**	**12**	**9**	**3**	**2**
1957	**NY-A**	**4**	**30**	**4**	**6**	**.400**	**41**	**4.36**	**84 2/3**	**57**	**60**	**70**	**9**	**1**	**0**	**6**
Career Average		11	19	6	5	.552	41	4.11	91	51	69	76	7	4	1	1
Yankee Average		**11**	**20**	**7**	**4**	**.643**	**39**	**3.93**	**90**	**54**	**69**	**73**	**7**	**4**	**1**	**1**
Career Total		170	281	85	69	.552	622	4.11	1362	766	1037	1138	98	65	12	12
Yankee Total		**118**	**221**	**72**	**40**	**.643**	**434**	**3.93**	**994**	**592**	**763**	**799**	**74**	**42**	**10**	**12**

Bystrom, Martin Eugene

HEIGHT: 6'5"   RIGHTHANDER   BORN: 7/26/1958 CORAL GABLES, FLORIDA

YEAR	TEAM	STARTS	GAMES	WON	LOST	PCT	ER	ERA	INNINGS PITCHED	STRIKE-OUTS	WALKS	HITS ALLOWED	HRS ALLOWED	COMP. GAMES	SHUT-OUTS	SAVES
1980	Phi-N	5	6	5	0	1.000	6	1.50	36	21	9	26	1	1	1	0
1981	Phi-N	9	9	4	3	.571	20	3.35	53 2/3	24	16	55	3	1	1	0
1982	Phi-N	16	19	5	6	.455	48	4.85	89	50	35	93	2	0	0	0
1983	Phi-N	23	24	6	9	.400	61	4.60	119 1/3	87	44	136	6	1	0	0
1984	Phi-N	11	11	4	4	.500	32	5.08	56 2/3	36	22	66	5	1	0	0
1984	**NY-A**	**7**	**7**	**2**	**2**	**.500**	**13**	**2.97**	**39 1/3**	**24**	**13**	**34**	**3**	**0**	**0**	**0**
1985	**NY-A**	**8**	**8**	**3**	**2**	**.600**	**26**	**5.71**	**41**	**16**	**19**	**44**	**8**	**0**	**0**	**0**
Career Average		11	12	4	4	.527	29	4.26	62	37	23	65	4	1	0	0
Yankee Average		**8**	**8**	**3**	**2**	**.556**	**20**	**4.37**	**40**	**20**	**16**	**39**	**6**	**0**	**0**	**0**
Career Total		79	84	29	26	.527	206	4.26	435	258	158	454	28	4	2	0
Yankee Total		**15**	**15**	**5**	**4**	**.556**	**39**	**4.37**	**80**	**40**	**32**	**78**	**11**	**0**	**0**	**0**

Thomas Joseph "Tommy" Byrne, lhp, 1943–51, 1954–57

A tall lefty with an overpowering fastball, Byrne's one weakness, which kept him from becoming a true star, was chronic wildness. From 1949 to 1951, he led the league in walks.

But Byrne, born in Baltimore, Maryland, on New Year's Eve 1919, was also sometimes overpowering. During the three years he led the league in bases on balls, he averaged almost 110 strikeouts a season and posted seven shutouts and 29 complete games.

Byrne was a Yankee bonus baby, getting $10,000 in 1940 to sign with the club—at the time one of the highest bonuses the Yankees gave out. When he was called up to the big leagues for good in 1946, he struggled early, going 8-6 in his first three years. Because of his penchant for walks (Byrne felt that, especially in his later years, this rep hurt him; umpires rarely gave him the benefit of the doubt in close pitches), his games tended to be long, drawn-out affairs.

But he was also a winner. His 72-40 record over his 11 years of service with the Yankees gave him a .643 winning percentage, tying for 10th overall on the Yankees all-time list with Hall Of Famer Herb Pennock. He is 20th on the all-time list for strikeouts with 592.

Byrne's two best years with New York were in 1949 and 1950. In the 1949 season, he was 15-7 with 129 strikeouts and 179 walks. He also had three shutouts and contributed several key wins as the Yankees edged the Boston Red Sox for the American League pennant.

In the 1950 season, he was 15-9, with 118 strikeouts and 160 walks. He was named to the All-Star Game that year.

But Yankee management, exasperated with Byrne's wildness, traded him to the Browns in 1951. Three years later, however, he was traded back to New York, where he had another strong season with a career-high record of 16-5. He had become less of a fireballing thrower and was relying more on skill. That strategy finally cut down on his walks—he issued only 87 free passes that year. And Byrne had a great World Series that fall. He pitched a complete-game victory over the Dodgers in Game 2, becoming the first lefthanded pitcher to win a complete game against them that year. He also won the game with a two-run single in the fourth, which was the winning blow.

Byrne was also a tremendous pinch-hitter in the majors, with 14 homers and 98 runs batted in for his career. In fact, the Yankees initially tried to make him a first baseman, a move he refused.

Byrne retired in 1957 and eventually entered politics. He was the mayor of Wake Forest, North Carolina, for several years.

Cadaret, Gregory James

HEIGHT: 6'3" LEFTHANDER BORN: 2/27/1962 DETROIT, MICHIGAN

YEAR	TEAM	STARTS	GAMES	WON	LOST	PCT	ER	ERA	INNINGS PITCHED	STRIKE-OUTS	WALKS	HITS ALLOWED	HRS ALLOWED	COMP. GAMES	SHUT-OUTS	SAVES
1987	Oak-A	0	29	6	2	.750	20	4.54	39 2/3	30	24	37	6	0	0	0
1988	Oak-A	0	58	5	2	.714	23	2.89	71 2/3	64	36	60	2	0	0	0
1989	Oak-A	0	26	0	0	—	7	2.28	27 2/3	14	19	21	0	0	0	0
1989	**NY-A**	**13**	**20**	**5**	**5**	**.500**	**47**	**4.58**	**92 1/3**	**66**	**38**	**109**	**7**	**3**	**1**	**3**
1990	**NY-A**	**6**	**54**	**5**	**4**	**.556**	**56**	**4.15**	**121 1/3**	**80**	**64**	**120**	**8**	**0**	**0**	**3**
1991	**NY-A**	**5**	**68**	**8**	**6**	**.571**	**49**	**3.62**	**121 2/3**	**105**	**59**	**110**	**8**	**0**	**0**	**1**
1992	**NY-A**	**11**	**46**	**4**	**8**	**.333**	**49**	**4.25**	**103 2/3**	**73**	**74**	**104**	**12**	**1**	**1**	**1**
1993	Cin-N	0	34	2	1	.667	18	4.96	32 2/3	23	23	40	3	0	0	0
1993	KC-A	0	13	1	1	.500	5	2.93	15 1/3	2	7	14	0	0	0	0
1994	Tor-A	0	21	0	1	.000	13	5.85	20	15	17	24	4	0	0	2
1994	Det-A	0	17	1	0	1.000	8	3.60	20	14	16	17	0	0	0	0
1997	Ana-A	0	15	0	0	—	5	3.46	13 2/3	11	8	11	1	0	0	1
1998	Ana-A	0	39	1	2	.333	17	4.14	37	37	15	38	6	0	0	0
1998	Tex-A	0	11	0	0		4	5.14	7 2/3	5	3	11	1	0	0	1
Career Average		3	32	3	2	.543	23	3.99	52	39	29	51	4	0	0	1
Yankee Average		**9**	**47**	**6**	**6**	**.489**	**50**	**4.12**	**110**	**81**	**59**	**111**	**9**	**1**	**1**	**2**
Career Total		35	451	38	32	.543	321	3.99	724 1/3	539	403	716	58	4	2	14
Yankee Total		**35**	**188**	**22**	**23**	**.489**	**201**	**4.12**	**439**	**324**	**235**	**443**	**35**	**4**	**2**	**7**

Caldwell, Charles William (Chuck)

HEIGHT: 5'10" RIGHTHANDER BORN: 8/2/1901 BRISTOL, VIRGINIA DIED: 11/1/1957 PRINCETON, NEW JERSEY

YEAR	TEAM	STARTS	GAMES	WON	LOST	PCT	ER	ERA	INNINGS PITCHED	STRIKE-OUTS	WALKS	HITS ALLOWED	HRS ALLOWED	COMP. GAMES	SHUT-OUTS	SAVES
1925	NY-A	0	3	0	0	—	5	16.88	2 2/3	1	3	7	0	0	0	0
Career Average		0	3	0	0	—	5	16.88	2 2/3	1	3	7	0	0	0	0
Yankee Average		0	3	0	0	—	5	16.88	2 2/3	1	3	7	0	0	0	0
Career Total		0	3	0	0	—	5	16.88	2 2/3	1	3	7	0	0	0	0
Yankee Total		0	3	0	0	—	5	16.88	2 2/3	1	3	7	0	0	0	0

Caldwell, Raymond Benjamin (Slim)

HEIGHT: 6'2" RIGHTHANDER BORN: 4/2/1888 CROYDON, PENNSYLVANIA DIED: 8/17/1967 SALAMANCA, NEW YORK

YEAR	TEAM	STARTS	GAMES	WON	LOST	PCT	ER	ERA	INNINGS PITCHED	STRIKE-OUTS	WALKS	HITS ALLOWED	HRS ALLOWED	COMP. GAMES	SHUT-OUTS	SAVES
1910	NY-A	2	6	1	0	1.000	8	3.72	19 1/3	17	9	19	1	1	0	1
1911	NY-A	27	41	14	14	.500	95	3.35	255	145	79	240	7	19	1	1
1912	NY-A	26	30	8	16	.333	91	4.47	183 1/3	95	67	196	1	13	3	0
1913	NY-A	16	27	9	8	.529	44	2.41	164 1/3	87	60	131	5	15	2	1
1914	NY-A	23	31	17	9	.654	46	1.94	213	92	51	153	5	22	5	1
1915	NY-A	35	36	19	16	.543	98	2.89	305	130	107	266	6	31	3	0
1916	NY-A	18	21	5	12	.667	55	2.99	165 2/3	76	65	142	6	14	1	0
1917	NY-A	29	32	13	16	.448	75	2.86	236	102	76	199	8	21	1	0
1918	NY-A	21	24	9	8	.529	60	3.06	176 2/3	59	62	173	2	14	1	1
1919	Bos-A	12	18	7	4	.636	38	3.96	86 1/3	23	31	92	1	6	1	0
1919	Cle-A	6	6	5	1	.833	10	1.71	52 2/3	24	19	33	1	4	1	0
1920	Cle-A	33	34	20	10	.667	102	3.86	237 2/3	80	63	286	9	20	1	0
1921	Cle-A	12	37	6	6	.500	80	4.90	147	76	49	159	7	4	1	4
Career Average		20	26	10	9	.526	62	3.22	172	77	57	161	5	14	2	1
Yankee Average		22	28	11	11	.490	64	3.00	191	89	64	169	5	17	2	1
Career Total		260	343	133	120	.526	802	3.22	2242	1006	738	2089	59	184	21	9
Yankee Total		197	248	95	99	.490	572	3.00	1718	803	576	1519	41	150	17	5

Campbell, Archibald Stewart (Iron Man)

HEIGHT: 6'0" RIGHTHANDER BORN: 10/20/1903 MAPLEWOOD, NEW JERSEY DIED: 12/22/1989 SPARKS, NEVADA

YEAR	TEAM	STARTS	GAMES	WON	LOST	PCT	ER	ERA	INNINGS PITCHED	STRIKE-OUTS	WALKS	HITS ALLOWED	HRS ALLOWED	COMP. GAMES	SHUT-OUTS	SAVES
1928	NY-A	1	13	0	1	.000	14	5.25	24	9	11	30	0	0	0	2
1929	Was-A	0	4	0	1	.000	7	15.75	4	1	5	10	1	0	0	0
1930	Cin-N	3	23	2	4	.333	35	5.43	58	19	31	71	2	1	0	4
Career Average		1	13	1	2	.250	19	5.86	29	10	16	37	1	0	0	2
Yankee Average		1	13	0	1	.000	14	5.25	24	9	11	30	0	0	0	2
Career Total		4	40	2	6	.250	56	5.86	86	29	47	111	3	1	0	6
Yankee Total		1	13	0	1	.000	14	5.25	24	9	11	30	0	0	0	2

Candelaria, John Robert (Candy Man)

HEIGHT: 6'6" LEFTHANDER BORN: 11/6/1953 NEW YORK, NEW YORK

YEAR	TEAM	STARTS	GAMES	WON	LOST	PCT	ER	ERA	INNINGS PITCHED	STRIKE-OUTS	WALKS	HITS ALLOWED	HRS ALLOWED	COMP. GAMES	SHUT-OUTS	SAVES
1975	Pit-N	18	18	8	6	.571	37	2.76	120 2/3	95	36	95	8	4	1	0
1976	Pit-N	31	32	16	7	.696	77	3.15	220	138	60	173	22	11	4	1
1977	Pit-N	33	33	20	5	.800	60	2.34	230 2/3	133	50	197	29	6	1	0
1978	Pit-N	29	30	12	11	.522	68	3.24	189	94	49	191	15	3	1	1
1979	Pit-N	30	33	14	9	.609	74	3.22	207	101	41	201	25	8	0	0
1980	Pit-N	34	35	11	14	.440	104	4.01	233 1/3	97	50	246	14	7	0	1
1981	Pit-N	6	6	2	2	.500	16	3.54	40 2/3	14	11	42	3	0	0	0
1982	Pit-N	30	31	12	7	.632	57	2.94	174 2/3	133	37	166	13	1	1	1
1983	Pit-N	32	33	15	8	.652	71	3.23	197 2/3	157	45	191	15	2	0	0
1984	Pit-N	28	33	12	11	.522	56	2.72	185 1/3	133	34	179	19	3	1	2

(continued)

Raymond Benjamin "Slim" Caldwell, rhp, 1910-1918

Caldwell was a good pitcher on a series of mediocre Yankee teams in the pre-Miller Huggins, pre-Babe Ruth era.

Caldwell, born in 1888 in Croyden, Pennsylvania, was a bright-eyed, 22-year-old rookie when he was signed by the Yankees in 1910. His principal pitch was a nasty spitball that hooked and weaved as well as any in the American League at the time.

Caldwell was 14-14 in 1911 with 145 strikeouts and only 79 walks for the 76-76 Yankees, then called the Highlanders. He dropped to 8-16 in 1912, but the Highlanders endured the worst season in their long history, winning only 50 of 152 games. Through this season, Caldwell was the team's most consistent pitcher. The New York pitching staff had only three shutouts in 1912, and Caldwell had them all.

He improved to 9-8 the next year, which was a fairly difficult feat, as the team was again awful, posting a record of 57-94. Caldwell was the only pitcher on the staff with a winning record and the only pitcher with an ERA under 2.50.

Caldwell became an All-Star the next two seasons. Pitching on a team that was clearly the most offensively incompetent squad in the big leagues, Caldwell somehow went 17-9 in 1914. He was second in the league that year in allowing the fewest hits per game, which was fortunate, because New York was shut out a league-leading 27 times that year. The team went 70-84.

In 1915, Caldwell won 19 games, was second in the American League in complete games, and again was clearly the ace of the staff with 130 strikeouts. But the Yankees didn't appear to be getting any better, ending up 69-85.

By this time, Caldwell was doing everything for the Highlanders but selling tickets. Manager "Wild Bill" Donovan was also using Caldwell as a pinch hitter, and Caldwell led the league with 33 pinch hit at-bats. He made nine hits for a .291 average. No New York regular hit better than .281. He also hit two consecutive pinch hit home runs in consecutive games, still a team record.

Caldwell slumped the next three years to 27-36, and the New York management traded him to the Red Sox in 1919. He was sent to Cleveland later that same year. In 1920, he had his best season, with a 20-10 record, as the Indians won the World Series that year over Brooklyn. Caldwell played one more season before retiring.

Despite playing on New York teams that averaged about 12.5 games under .500, Caldwell's name appears throughout the Yankee record book. He is 18th in games played with 248, 11th in innings pitched with 1,718, 15th in wins with 96, 14th in strikeouts with 803, 19th in shutouts with 13, 8th in complete games with 151 and 9th in ERA with 2.99.

He died in 1967 in Salamanca, New York.

(continued)

Year	Team														
1985	Pit-N	0	37	2	4	.333	22	3.64	54 1/3	47	14	57	7	0	0	9
1985	Cal-A	13	13	7	3	.700	30	3.80	71	53	24	70	7	1	1	0
1986	Cal-A	16	16	10	2	.833	26	2.55	91 2/3	81	26	68	4	1	1	0
1987	Cal-A	20	20	8	6	.571	61	4.71	116 2/3	74	20	127	17	0	0	0
1987	NY-N	3	3	2	0	1.000	8	5.84	12 1/3	10	3	17	1	0	0	0
1988	**NY-A**	**24**	**25**	**13**	**7**	**.650**	**59**	**3.38**	**157**	**121**	**23**	**150**	**18**	**6**	**2**	**1**
1989	**NY-A**	**6**	**10**	**3**	**3**	**.500**	**28**	**5.14**	**49**	**37**	**12**	**49**	**8**	**1**	**0**	**0**
1989	Mon-N	0	12	0	2	.000	6	3.31	16 1/3	14	4	17	3	0	0	0
1990	Min-A	1	34	7	3	.700	22	3.39	58 1/3	44	9	55	9	0	0	4
1990	Tor-A	2	13	0	3	.000	13	5.48	21 1/3	19	11	32	2	0	0	1
1991	LA-N	0	59	1	1	.500	14	3.74	33 2/3	38	11	31	3	0	0	2
1992	LA-N	0	50	2	5	.667	8	2.84	25 1/3	23	13	20	1	0	0	5
1993	Pit-N	0	24	0	3	.000	18	8.24	19 2/3	17	9	25	2	0	0	1
Career Average		16	26	8	5	.592	41	3.33	110	73	26	104	11	2	1	1
Yankee Average		**15**	**18**	**8**	**5**	**.615**	**44**	**3.80**	**103**	**79**	**18**	**100**	**13**	**4**	**1**	**1**
Career Total		356	600	177	122	.592	935	3.33	2526	1673	592	2399	245	54	13	29
Yankee Total		**30**	**35**	**16**	**10**	**.615**	**87**	**3.80**	**206**	**158**	**35**	**199**	**26**	**7**	**2**	**1**

Cantwell, Michael Joseph
HEIGHT: 6'0" LEFTHANDER BORN: 1/15/1896 WASHINGTON, D.C. DIED: 1/5/1953 OTEEN, NORTH CAROLINA

YEAR	TEAM	STARTS	GAMES	WON	LOST	PCT	ER	ERA	INNINGS PITCHED	STRIKE-OUTS	WALKS	HITS ALLOWED	HRS ALLOWED	COMP. GAMES	SHUT-OUTS	SAVES
1916	**NY-A**	**0**	**1**	**0**	**0**	**—**	**0**	**0.00**	**2**	**0**	**2**	**0**	**0**	**0**	**0**	**0**
1919	Phi-N	3	5	1	3	.667	17	5.60	27 1/3	6	9	36	1	2	0	0
1920	Phi-N	1	5	0	3	.000	10	3.86	23 1/3	8	15	25	1	0	0	0
Career Average		1	4	0	2	.143	9	4.61	18	5	9	20	1	1	0	0
Yankee Average		**0**	**1**	**0**	**0**	**—**	**0**	**0.00**	**2**	**0**	**2**	**0**	**0**	**0**	**0**	**0**
Career Total		4	11	1	6	.143	27	4.61	53	14	26	61	2	2	0	0
Yankee Total		**0**	**1**	**0**	**0**	**—**	**0**	**0.00**	**2**	**0**	**2**	**0**	**0**	**0**	**0**	**0**

Carroll, Owen Thomas (Ownie)
HEIGHT: 5'10" RIGHTHANDER BORN: 11/11/1902 KEARNY, NEW JERSEY DIED: 6/8/1975 ORANGE, NEW JERSEY

YEAR	TEAM	STARTS	GAMES	WON	LOST	PCT	ER	ERA	INNINGS PITCHED	STRIKE-OUTS	WALKS	HITS ALLOWED	HRS ALLOWED	COMP. GAMES	SHUT-OUTS	SAVES
1925	Det-A	4	10	2	2	.500	17	3.76	40 2/3	12	28	46	1	1	0	0
1927	Det-A	15	31	10	6	.625	76	3.98	172	41	73	186	5	8	0	0
1928	Det-A	28	34	16	12	.571	84	3.27	231	51	87	219	6	19	2	2
1929	Det-A	26	34	9	17	.346	104	4.63	202	54	86	249	10	12	0	1
1930	Det-A	3	6	0	5	.000	24	10.62	20 1/3	4	9	30	3	0	0	0
1930	**NY-A**	**1**	**10**	**0**	**1**	**.000**	**24**	**6.61**	**32 2/3**	**8**	**18**	**49**	**2**	**0**	**0**	**0**
1930	Cin-N	2	3	0	1	.000	7	4.50	14	0	3	17	3	1	0	0
1931	Cin-N	12	29	3	9	.667	66	5.53	107 1/3	24	51	135	6	4	0	0
1932	Cin-N	26	32	10	19	.345	105	4.50	210	55	44	245	7	15	0	1
1933	Bro-N	31	33	13	15	.464	95	3.78	226 1/3	45	54	248	9	11	0	0
1934	Bro-N	5	26	1	3	.667	53	6.42	74 1/3	17	33	108	9	0	0	1
Career Average		14	23	6	8	.416	60	4.43	121	28	44	139	6	6	0	0
Yankee Average		**1**	**10**	**0**	**1**	**.000**	**24**	**6.61**	**32 2/3**	**8**	**18**	**49**	**2**	**0**	**0**	**0**
Career Total		153	248	64	90	.416	655	4.43	1331	311	486	1532	61	71	2	5
Yankee Total		**1**	**10**	**0**	**1**	**.000**	**24**	**6.61**	**32 2/3**	**8**	**18**	**49**	**2**	**0**	**0**	**0**

Carroll, Richard Thomas (Shadow)
HEIGHT: 6'2" RIGHTHANDER BORN: 7/21/1884 CLEVELAND, OHIO DIED: 11/22/1945 CLEVELAND

YEAR	TEAM	STARTS	GAMES	WON	LOST	PCT	ER	ERA	INNINGS PITCHED	STRIKE-OUTS	WALKS	HITS ALLOWED	HRS ALLOWED	COMP. GAMES	SHUT-OUTS	SAVES
1909	**NY-A**	**1**	**2**	**0**	**0**	**—**	**2**	**3.60**	**5**	**1**	**1**	**7**	**1**	**0**	**0**	**0**
Career Average		1	2	0	0	—	2	3.60	5	1	1	7	1	0	0	0
Yankee Average		**1**	**2**	**0**	**0**	**—**	**2**	**3.60**	**5**	**1**	**1**	**7**	**1**	**0**	**0**	**0**
Career Total		1	2	0	0	—	2	3.60	5	1	1	7	1	0	0	0
Yankee Total		**1**	**2**	**0**	**0**	**—**	**2**	**3.60**	**5**	**1**	**1**	**7**	**1**	**0**	**0**	**0**

Cary, Charles Douglas (Chuck)
HEIGHT: 6'4" LEFTHANDER BORN: 3/3/1960 WHITTIER, CALIFORNIA

YEAR	TEAM	STARTS	GAMES	WON	LOST	PCT	ER	ERA	INNINGS PITCHED	STRIKE-OUTS	WALKS	HITS ALLOWED	HRS ALLOWED	COMP. GAMES	SHUT-OUTS	SAVES
1985	Det-A	0	16	0	1	.000	9	3.42	23 2/3	22	8	16	2	0	0	2
1986	Det-A	0	22	1	2	.333	12	3.41	31 2/3	21	15	33	3	0	0	0
1987	Atl-N	0	13	1	1	.500	7	3.78	16 2/3	15	4	17	3	0	0	1
1988	Atl-N	0	7	0	0	—	6	6.48	8 1/3	7	4	8	1	0	0	0
1989	**NY-A**	**11**	**22**	**4**	**4**	**.500**	**36**	**3.26**	**99 1/3**	**79**	**29**	**78**	**13**	**2**	**0**	**0**
1990	**NY-A**	**27**	**28**	**6**	**12**	**.333**	**73**	**4.19**	**156 2/3**	**134**	**55**	**155**	**21**	**2**	**0**	**0**
1991	**NY-A**	**9**	**10**	**1**	**6**	**.143**	**35**	**5.91**	**53 1/3**	**34**	**32**	**61**	**6**	**0**	**0**	**0**
1993	Chi-A	0	16	1	0	1.000	12	5.23	20 2/3	10	11	22	1	0	0	0
Career Average		6	17	2	3	.350	24	4.17	51	40	20	49	6	1	0	0
Yankee Average		**16**	**20**	**4**	**7**	**.333**	**48**	**4.19**	**103**	**82**	**39**	**98**	**13**	**1**	**0**	**0**
Career Total		47	134	14	26	.350	190	4.17	410	322	158	390	50	4	0	3
Yankee Total		**47**	**60**	**11**	**22**	**.333**	**144**	**4.19**	**309**	**247**	**116**	**294**	**40**	**4**	**0**	**0**

Casey, Hugh Thomas
HEIGHT: 6'1" RIGHTHANDER BORN: 10/14/1913 ATLANTA, GEORGIA DIED: 7/3/1951 ATLANTA, GEORGIA

YEAR	TEAM	STARTS	GAMES	WON	LOST	PCT	ER	ERA	INNINGS PITCHED	STRIKE-OUTS	WALKS	HITS ALLOWED	HRS ALLOWED	COMP. GAMES	SHUT-OUTS	SAVES
1935	Chi-N	0	13	0	0	—	11	3.86	25 2/3	10	14	29	2	0	0	0
1939	Bro-N	25	40	15	10	.600	74	2.93	227 1/3	79	54	228	13	15	0	1
1940	Bro-N	10	44	11	8	.579	62	3.62	154	53	51	136	13	5	2	2
1941	Bro-N	18	45	14	11	.560	70	3.89	162	61	57	155	8	4	1	7
1942	Bro-N	2	50	6	3	.667	28	2.25	112	54	44	91	3	0	0	13
1946	Bro-N	1	46	11	5	.688	22	1.99	99 2/3	31	33	101	2	0	0	5
1947	Bro-N	0	46	10	4	.714	34	3.99	76 2/3	40	29	75	7	0	0	18
1948	Bro-N	0	22	3	0	1.000	32	8.00	36	7	17	59	6	0	0	4
1949	Pit-N	0	33	4	1	.800	20	4.66	38 2/3	9	14	50	4	0	0	5
1949	**NY-A**	**0**	**4**	**1**	**0**	**1.000**	**7**	**8.22**	**7 2/3**	**5**	**8**	**11**	**0**	**0**	**0**	**0**
Career Average		6	34	8	4	.641	36	3.45	94	35	32	94	6	2	0	6
Yankee Average		**0**	**4**	**1**	**0**	**1.000**	**7**	**8.22**	**7 2/3**	**5**	**8**	**11**	**0**	**0**	**0**	**0**
Career Total		56	343	75	42	.641	360	3.45	940	349	321	935	58	24	3	55
Yankee Total		**0**	**4**	**1**	**0**	**1.000**	**7**	**8.22**	**7 2/3**	**5**	**8**	**11**	**0**	**0**	**0**	**0**

Castleton, Royal Eugene
HEIGHT: 5'11" LEFTHANDER BORN: 7/26/1885 SALT LAKE CITY, UTAH DIED: 6/24/1967 LOS ANGELES, CALIFORNIA

YEAR	TEAM	STARTS	GAMES	WON	LOST	PCT	ER	ERA	INNINGS PITCHED	STRIKE-OUTS	WALKS	HITS ALLOWED	HRS ALLOWED	COMP. GAMES	SHUT-OUTS	SAVES
1907	**NY-A**	**2**	**3**	**1**	**1**	**.500**	**5**	**2.81**	**16**	**3**	**3**	**11**	**1**	**1**	**0**	**0**
1909	Cin-N	1	4	1	1	.500	3	1.93	14	5	6	14	0	1	0	0
1910	Cin-N	2	4	1	2	.333	5	3.29	13 2/3	5	6	15	0	1	0	0
Career Average		2	4	1	1	.429	4	2.68	15	4	5	13	0	1	0	0
Yankee Average		**2**	**3**	**1**	**1**	**.500**	**5**	**2.81**	**16**	**3**	**3**	**11**	**1**	**1**	**0**	**0**
Career Total		5	11	3	4	.429	13	2.68	44	13	15	40	1	3	0	0
Yankee Total		**2**	**3**	**1**	**1**	**.500**	**5**	**2.81**	**16**	**3**	**3**	**11**	**1**	**1**	**0**	**0**

Castro, William Radhames (Checo)
HEIGHT: 5'11" RIGHTHANDER BORN: 12/13/1953 SANTIAGO, DOMINICAN REPUBLIC

YEAR	TEAM	STARTS	GAMES	WON	LOST	PCT	ER	ERA	INNINGS PITCHED	STRIKE-OUTS	WALKS	HITS ALLOWED	HRS ALLOWED	COMP. GAMES	SHUT-OUTS	SAVES
1974	Mil-A	0	8	0	0	—	9	4.50	18	10	5	19	2	0	0	0
1975	Mil-A	5	18	3	2	.600	21	2.52	75	25	17	78	3	0	0	1
1976	Mil-A	0	39	4	6	.400	27	3.45	70 1/3	23	19	70	4	0	0	8
1977	Mil-A	0	51	8	6	.571	32	4.15	69 1/3	28	23	76	7	0	0	13
1978	Mil-A	0	42	5	4	.556	10	1.81	49 2/3	17	14	43	2	0	0	8
1979	Mil-A	0	39	3	1	.750	10	2.03	44 1/3	10	13	40	2	0	0	6
1980	Mil-A	0	56	2	4	.333	26	2.77	84 1/3	32	17	89	2	0	0	8
1981	**NY-A**	**0**	**11**	**1**	**1**	**.500**	**8**	**3.79**	**19**	**4**	**5**	**26**	**2**	**0**	**0**	**0**
1982	KC-A	4	21	3	2	.600	29	3.45	75 2/3	37	20	72	8	0	0	1
1983	KC-A	0	18	2	0	1.000	30	6.64	40 2/3	17	12	51	4	0	0	0
Career Average		1	30	3	3	.544	20	3.33	55	20	15	56	4	0	0	5
Yankee Average		**0**	**11**	**1**	**1**	**.500**	**8**	**3.79**	**19**	**4**	**5**	**26**	**2**	**0**	**0**	**0**
Career Total		9	303	31	26	.544	202	3.33	546	203	145	564	36	0	0	45
Yankee Total		**0**	**11**	**1**	**1**	**.500**	**8**	**3.79**	**19**	**4**	**5**	**26**	**2**	**0**	**0**	**0**

Cerone, Richard Aldo
HEIGHT: 5'11" RIGHTHANDER BORN: 5/19/1954 NEWARK, NEW JERSEY

YEAR	TEAM	STARTS	GAMES	WON	LOST	PCT	ER	ERA	INNINGS PITCHED	STRIKE-OUTS	WALKS	HITS ALLOWED	HRS ALLOWED	COMP. GAMES	SHUT-OUTS	SAVES
1987	**NY-A**	**0**	**2**	**0**	**0**	**—**	**0**	**0.00**	**2**	**1**	**1**	**0**	**0**	**0**	**0**	**0**
Career Average		0	2	0	0	—	0	0.00	2	1	1	0	0	0	0	0
Yankee Average		**0**	**2**	**0**	**0**	**—**	**0**	**0.00**	**2**	**1**	**1**	**0**	**0**	**0**	**0**	**0**
Career Total		0	2	0	0	—	0	0.00	2	1	1	0	0	0	0	0
Yankee Total		**0**	**2**	**0**	**0**	**—**	**0**	**0.00**	**2**	**1**	**1**	**0**	**0**	**0**	**0**	**0**

Spurgeon Ferdinand "Spud" Chandler, rhp, 1937–47

"Spud" Chandler remains in the history books as the hardest pitcher to beat in the history of the major leagues. His 109-43 record averages out to a .717 winning percentage.

Chandler, born in Commerce, Georgia, in 1907, was a terrific all-around athlete who played football, basketball and baseball at the University of Georgia. But he always said that his first love was baseball.

The Cardinals (and later the Cubs) tried to sign Chandler when he was in college, but he took less money to play for the Yankees. Chandler spent some time in the minors, including a stint with the 1937 Newark Bears, a Yankee farm club thought by some to be one of the best minor league teams of all time.

He came up to the Yankees for good in 1938 and posted a 14-5 record. He didn't pitch in the World Series in either 1938 or 1939, and he admitted once that he didn't become overwhelmingly successful until the 1941 season when he learned to throw a slider.

He was 46-13 over the next three seasons, including a league-leading 20-4 in 1943. That was the year he threw two complete-game victories in the Yankees' 4-1 win over the St. Louis Cardinals. Chandler allowed only one earned run in the two games with three walks and ten strikeouts.

He played sparingly in 1944 and 1945 due to his military service. But he settled back in 1946 with a 20-8 record. In 1947, his last year, he was 9-5 as a spot starter.

Chandler was named to four All-Star Games during his Yankee career. In addition to his all-time position as the Yankees' number one winner, he is also 15th in innings pitched for New York with 1,485, 14th in wins with 109, 19th in strikeouts with 614, 6th in shutouts with 26, 10th in complete games with 109 and 6th in ERA with 2.84.

After his 11-year career, all with the Yankees, he worked briefly for the team as a scout. He retired to Florida and died in 1990 in South Pasadena, Florida.

Chandler, Spurgeon Ferdinand (Spud)

HEIGHT: 6'0" RIGHTHANDER BORN: 9/12/1907 COMMERCE, GEORGIA DIED: 1/9/1990 S. PASADENA, FLORIDA

YEAR	TEAM	STARTS	GAMES	WON	LOST	PCT	ER	ERA	INNINGS PITCHED	STRIKE-OUTS	WALKS	HITS ALLOWED	HRS ALLOWED	COMP. GAMES	SHUT-OUTS	SAVES
1937	NY-A	10	12	7	4	.636	26	2.84	82 1/3	31	20	79	8	6	2	0
1938	NY-A	23	23	14	5	.737	77	4.03	172	36	47	183	7	14	2	0
1939	NY-A	0	11	3	0	1.000	6	2.84	19	4	9	26	0	0	0	0
1940	NY-A	24	27	8	7	.533	88	4.60	172	56	60	184	12	6	1	0
1941	NY-A	20	28	10	4	.714	58	3.19	163 2/3	60	60	146	5	11	4	4
1942	NY-A	24	24	16	5	.762	53	2.38	200 2/3	74	74	176	13	17	3	0
1943	NY-A	30	30	20	4	.833	46	1.64	253	134	54	197	5	20	5	0
1944	NY-A	1	1	0	0	—	3	4.50	6	1	1	6	1	0	0	0
1945	NY-A	4	4	2	1	.667	16	4.65	31	12	7	30	2	2	1	0
1946	NY-A	32	34	20	8	.714	60	2.10	257 1/3	138	90	200	7	20	6	2
1947	NY-A	16	17	9	5	.643	35	2.46	128	68	41	100	4	13	2	0
Career Average		92	106	55	22	.717	234	2.84	742	307	232	664	32	55	13	3
Yankee Average		**92**	**106**	**55**	**22**	**.717**	**234**	**2.84**	**742**	**307**	**232**	**664**	**32**	**55**	**13**	**3**
Career Total		184	211	109	43	.717	468	2.84	1485	614	463	1327	64	109	26	6
Yankee Total		**184**	**211**	**109**	**43**	**.717**	**468**	**2.84**	**1485**	**614**	**463**	**1327**	**64**	**109**	**26**	**6**

Chapin, Darrin John

HEIGHT: 6'0"   RIGHTHANDER   BORN: 2/1/1966 WARREN, OHIO

YEAR	TEAM	STARTS	GAMES	WON	LOST	PCT	ER	ERA	INNINGS PITCHED	STRIKE-OUTS	WALKS	HITS ALLOWED	HRS ALLOWED	COMP. GAMES	SHUT-OUTS	SAVES
1991	NY-A	0	3	0	1	.000	3	5.06	5 1/3	5	6	3	0	0	0	0
1992	Phi-N	0	1	0	0	—	2	9.00	2	1	0	2	1	0	0	0
Career Average		0	2	0	1	.000	3	6.14	4	3	3	3	1	0	0	0
Yankee Average		**0**	**3**	**0**	**1**	**.000**	**3**	**5.06**	**5 1/3**	**5**	**6**	**3**	**0**	**0**	**0**	**0**
Career Total		0	4	0	1	.000	5	6.14	7	6	6	5	1	0	0	0
Yankee Total		**0**	**3**	**0**	**1**	**.000**	**3**	**5.06**	**5 1/3**	**5**	**6**	**3**	**0**	**0**	**0**	**0**

Chase, Harold Homer (Prince Hal)

HEIGHT: 6'0"   LEFTHANDER   BORN: 2/13/1883 LOS GATOS, CALIFORNIA   DIED: 5/18/1947 COLUSA, CALIFORNIA

YEAR	TEAM	STARTS	GAMES	WON	LOST	PCT	ER	ERA	INNINGS PITCHED	STRIKE-OUTS	WALKS	HITS ALLOWED	HRS ALLOWED	COMP. GAMES	SHUT-OUTS	SAVES
1908	NY-A	0	1	0	0	—	0	0.00	1/3	0	0	0	0	0	0	0
Career Average		0	1	0	0	—	0	0.00	1/3	0	0	0	0	0	0	0
Yankee Average		**0**	**1**	**0**	**0**	**—**	**0**	**0.00**	**1/3**	**0**	**0**	**0**	**0**	**0**	**0**	**0**
Career Total		0	1	0	0	—	0	0.00	1/3	0	0	0	0	0	0	0
Yankee Total		**0**	**1**	**0**	**0**	**—**	**0**	**0.00**	**1/3**	**0**	**0**	**0**	**0**	**0**	**0**	**0**

Chesbro, John Dwight (Happy Jack)

HEIGHT: 5'9"   RIGHTHANDER   BORN: 6/5/1874 N. ADAMS, MASSACHUSETTS   DIED: 11/6/1931 CONWAY, MASSACHUSETTS

YEAR	TEAM	STARTS	GAMES	WON	LOST	PCT	ER	ERA	INNINGS PITCHED	STRIKE-OUTS	WALKS	HITS ALLOWED	HRS ALLOWED	COMP. GAMES	SHUT-OUTS	SAVES
1899	Pit-N	17	19	6	9	.400	68	4.11	149	28	59	165	3	15	0	0
1900	Pit-N	26	32	15	13	.536	88	3.67	215 2/3	56	79	220	4	20	3	1
1901	Pit-N	28	36	21	10	.677	76	2.38	287 2/3	129	52	261	4	26	6	1
1902	Pit-N	33	35	28	6	.824	69	2.17	286 1/3	136	62	242	1	31	8	1
1903	**NY-A**	**36**	**40**	**21**	**15**	**.583**	**100**	**2.77**	**324 2/3**	**147**	**74**	**300**	**7**	**33**	**1**	**0**
1904	**NY-A**	**51**	**55**	**41**	**12**	**.774**	**92**	**1.82**	**454 2/3**	**239**	**88**	**338**	**4**	**48**	**6**	**0**
1905	**NY-A**	**38**	**41**	**19**	**15**	**.559**	**74**	**2.20**	**303 1/3**	**156**	**71**	**262**	**5**	**24**	**3**	**0**
1906	**NY-A**	**42**	**49**	**23**	**17**	**.575**	**107**	**2.96**	**325**	**152**	**75**	**314**	**2**	**24**	**4**	**1**
1907	**NY-A**	**25**	**30**	**10**	**10**	**.500**	**58**	**2.53**	**206**	**78**	**46**	**192**	**0**	**17**	**1**	**0**
1908	**NY-A**	**31**	**45**	**14**	**20**	**.412**	**94**	**2.93**	**288 2/3**	**124**	**67**	**271**	**6**	**20**	**3**	**1**
1909	**NY-A**	**4**	**9**	**0**	**4**	**.000**	**35**	**6.34**	**49 2/3**	**17**	**13**	**70**	**2**	**2**	**0**	**0**
1909	Bos-A	1	1	0	1	.000	3	4.50	6	3	4	7	1	0	0	0
Career Average		28	33	17	11	.600	72	2.68	241	105	58	220	3	22	3	0
Yankee Average		**32**	**38**	**18**	**13**	**.579**	**80**	**2.58**	**279**	**130**	**62**	**250**	**4**	**24**	**3**	**0**
Career Total		332	392	198	132	.600	864	2.68	2897	1265	690	2642	39	260	35	5
Yankee Total		**227**	**269**	**128**	**93**	**.579**	**560**	**2.58**	**1952**	**913**	**434**	**1747**	**26**	**168**	**18**	**2**

Choate, Randol Doyle (Randy)

HEIGHT: 6'3"   LEFTHANDER   BORN: 9/15/1975 SAN ANTONIO, TEXAS

YEAR	TEAM	STARTS	GAMES	WON	LOST	PCT	ER	ERA	INNINGS PITCHED	STRIKE-OUTS	WALKS	HITS ALLOWED	HRS ALLOWED	COMP. GAMES	SHUT-OUTS	SAVES
2000	NY-A	22	22	0	1	.000	9	4.76	17	12	8	14	3	0	0	0
Career Average		22	22	0	1	.000	9	4.76	17	12	8	14	3	0	0	0
Yankee Average		**22**	**22**	**0**	**1**	**.000**	**9**	**4.76**	**17**	**12**	**8**	**14**	**3**	**0**	**0**	**0**
Career Total		22	22	0	1	.000	9	4.76	17	12	8	14	3	0	0	0
Yankee Total		**22**	**22**	**0**	**1**	**.000**	**9**	**4.76**	**17**	**12**	**8**	**14**	**3**	**0**	**0**	**0**

John Dwight "Happy Jack" Chesbro, rhp, 1903–09

Many believe that Jack Chesbro, one of the Yankees' earliest stars, is a Hall of Famer primarily on the back of his amazing 41-win season in 1904. That may or may not be true, but few can argue that Chesbro was a valuable workhorse for New York and Pittsburgh throughout his career.

Born in North Adams, Massachusetts, on June 5, 1874, Chesbro was a sandlot star throughout western Massachusetts before being signed by Pittsburgh in 1899. Chesbro was known as Happy Jack for his dour demeanor, as well as for a stint as a janitor in a psychiatric ward in his younger days. He was a standout pitcher for the Pirates from 1899 to 1902, going 70-38 and twice winning 20 or more games.

Chesbro was one of the first pitchers in baseball to throw a spitball successfully. He had terrific control overall, averaging less than two walks a game throughout his career.

Over the next decade, the spitball (or shineball or emery ball) would be used with great success by many major league hurlers. But in the first years of the 20th century, Chesbro was probably one of the best practitioners of the pitch.

In 1903, he came to the newly former New York Americans, also known as the Highlanders. The Highlanders finished a respectable 72-62 that year, and Chesbro turned in a more than respectable 21-15, ending up third in wins and innings pitched and fourth in complete games.

But in 1904, Happy Jack turned in the greatest pitching season in modern baseball. He won 41 games and lost 12. He started 51 games and appeared in 4 others. He was involved in a decision in every game in which he appeared except one, a 3-3 tie at Chicago. His 48 complete games are a record. His 454⅔ innings pitched are second only to Chicago's Ed Walsh in 1908.

The Highlanders won 92 games and finished 1½ games behind Boston and their Hall-of-Famer, Cy Young, that year.

But the pennant race was close all summer. In fact, it came down to a big doubleheader in New York between the two teams on the final day of the season. The Pilgrims (as the Boston team was then called) had a 1 1/2-game lead over New York with a record of 94-58. The Highlanders were 91-58. Three of their games in September had ended in ties and were called on account of darkness. So New York needed to win both games to clinch the pennant.

Chesbro was pitching the first game of the doubleheader before the largest crowd in Highlander history, a total of 25,584 fans. The score was tied 2-2 in the top of the ninth. Pilgrim catcher Lou Criger singled and was sacrificed to second. A ground ball moved him to third.

Needing only one more out, Chesbro loaded a spitter and sent it homeward. But his catcher, Jack Kleinow, couldn't handle it. The ball got away and Criger scored. New York could not come up with a run in their half of the inning, and the Pilgrims were the AL champs.

It would be another 17 years before the New Yorkers would make that final step to the top in 1921.

Chesbro faded badly in 1905, posting a 19-15 record. The team faded, too, slumping to 71-78, good for only sixth place, 25 games out of first place. In fact, after his incredible season of pitching virtually every other day, Chesbro never seemed as strong. He followed the 41-12 year with a 66-67 record over the next five seasons.

In 1909, he was waived by the Highlanders in September and picked up by Boston, where he appeared in one game in a losing effort.

Chesbro retired to his hometown of North Adams after that, pitching for many years in semi-pro leagues and becoming a prosperous businessman. In 1911, he was hired as the baseball coach at nearby Amherst College. In 1924, he was hired to be an assistant with the Washington Senators. But that job lasted less than a season.

He finally returned to the Berkshires the next year. He died in 1931.

Chesbro remains a fixture in several categories on the Yankees' all-time list. He is eighth in innings pitched with 1,953, tenth in wins with 126, tenth in strikeouts with 913, third in complete games with 169 and second all-time in ERA with 2.58.

In 1946, Jack Chesbro was elected to the Hall of Fame.

Christiansen, Clay C.

HEIGHT: 6'5" RIGHTHANDER BORN: 6/28/1958 WICHITA, KANSAS

YEAR	TEAM	STARTS	GAMES	WON	LOST	PCT	ER	ERA	INNINGS PITCHED	STRIKE-OUTS	WALKS	HITS ALLOWED	HRS ALLOWED	COMP. GAMES	SHUT-OUTS	SAVES
1984	NY-A	1	24	2	4	.333	26	6.05	38 2/3	27	12	50	4	0	0	2
Career Average		1	24	2	4	.333	26	6.05	38 2/3	27	12	50	4	0	0	2
Yankee Average		**1**	**24**	**2**	**4**	**.333**	**26**	**6.05**	**38 2/3**	**27**	**12**	**50**	**4**	**0**	**0**	**2**
Career Total		1	24	2	4	.333	26	6.05	38 2/3	27	12	50	4	0	0	2
Yankee Total		**1**	**24**	**2**	**4**	**.333**	**26**	**6.05**	**38 2/3**	**27**	**12**	**50**	**4**	**0**	**0**	**2**

Cicotte, Alva Warren (Bozo)

HEIGHT: 6'3" RIGHTHANDER BORN: 12/23/1929 MELVINDALE, MICHIGAN DIED: 11/29/82 WESTLAND, MICHIGAN

YEAR	TEAM	STARTS	GAMES	WON	LOST	PCT	ER	ERA	INNINGS PITCHED	STRIKE-OUTS	WALKS	HITS ALLOWED	HRS ALLOWED	COMP. GAMES	SHUT-OUTS	SAVES
1957	NY-A	2	20	2	2	.500	22	3.03	65 1/3	36	30	57	5	0	0	2
1958	Was-A	4	8	0	3	.000	15	4.82	28	14	14	36	3	0	0	0
1958	Det-A	2	14	3	1	.750	17	3.56	43	21	15	50	1	0	0	0
1959	Cle-A	1	26	3	1	.750	26	5.32	44	23	25	46	4	0	0	1
1961	StL-N	7	29	2	6	.667	44	5.28	75	51	34	83	16	0	0	1
1962	Hou-N	0	5	0	0	—	2	3.86	4 2/3	4	1	8	1	0	0	0
Career Average		8	17	2	2	.435	21	4.36	43	25	20	47	5	0	0	1
Yankee Average		**2**	**20**	**2**	**2**	**.500**	**22**	**3.03**	**65 1/3**	**36**	**30**	**57**	**5**	**0**	**0**	**2**
Career Total		16	102	10	13	.435	126	4.36	260	149	119	280	30	0	0	4
Yankee Total		**2**	**20**	**2**	**2**	**.500**	**22**	**3.03**	**65 1/3**	**36**	**30**	**57**	**5**	**0**	**0**	**2**

Clark, George Myron

HEIGHT: 6'0" LEFTHANDER BORN: 5/19/1891 SMITHLAND, IOWA DIED: 11/14/1940 SIOUX CITY, IOWA

YEAR	TEAM	STARTS	GAMES	WON	LOST	PCT	ER	ERA	INNINGS PITCHED	STRIKE-OUTS	WALKS	HITS ALLOWED	HRS ALLOWED	COMP. GAMES	SHUT-OUTS	SAVES
1913	NY-A	1	11	0	1	.000	19	9.00	19	5	19	22	1	0	0	0
Career Average		1	11	0	1	.000	19	9.00	19	5	19	22	1	0	0	0
Yankee Average		**1**	**11**	**0**	**1**	**.000**	**19**	**9.00**	**19**	**5**	**19**	**22**	**1**	**0**	**0**	**0**
Career Total		1	11	0	1	.000	19	9.00	19	5	19	22	1	0	0	0
Yankee Total		**1**	**11**	**0**	**1**	**.000**	**19**	**9.00**	**19**	**5**	**19**	**22**	**1**	**0**	**0**	**0**

Clarkson, Walter Hamilton

HEIGHT: 5'10" RIGHTHANDER BORN: 11/3/1878 CAMBRIDGE, MASSACHUSETTS DIED:10/10/1946 CAMBRIDGE, MASSACHUSETTS

YEAR	TEAM	STARTS	GAMES	WON	LOST	PCT	ER	ERA	INNINGS PITCHED	STRIKE-OUTS	WALKS	HITS ALLOWED	HRS ALLOWED	COMP. GAMES	SHUT-OUTS	SAVES
1904	NY-A	4	13	1	2	.333	37	5.02	66 1/3	43	25	63	3	2	0	1
1905	NY-A	4	9	3	3	.500	20	3.91	46	35	13	40	1	3	0	0
1906	NY-A	16	32	9	4	.692	39	2.32	151	64	55	135	6	9	3	0
1907	NY-A	2	5	1	1	.500	12	6.23	17 1/3	3	8	19	1	0	0	0
1907	Cle-A	10	17	4	6	.400	20	1.99	90 2/3	32	29	77	1	9	1	0
1908	Cle-A	1	2	0	0	—	4	10.80	3 1/3	1	2	6	0	0	0	0
Career Average		6	13	3	3	.529	22	3.17	62	30	22	57	2	4	1	0
Yankee Average		**7**	**15**	**4**	**3**	**.583**	**27**	**3.46**	**70**	**36**	**25**	**64**	**3**	**4**	**1**	**0**
Career Total		37	78	18	16	.529	132	3.17	375	178	132	340	12	23	4	1
Yankee Total		**26**	**59**	**14**	**10**	**.583**	**108**	**3.46**	**281**	**145**	**101**	**257**	**11**	**14**	**3**	**1**

Clay, Kenneth Earl

HEIGHT: 6'3" RIGHTHANDER BORN: 4/6/1954 LYNCHBURG, VIRGINIA

YEAR	TEAM	STARTS	GAMES	WON	LOST	PCT	ER	ERA	INNINGS PITCHED	STRIKE-OUTS	WALKS	HITS ALLOWED	HRS ALLOWED	COMP. GAMES	SHUT-OUTS	SAVES
1977	NY-A	3	21	2	3	.400	27	4.37	55 2/3	20	24	53	6	0	0	1
1978	NY-A	6	28	3	4	.429	36	4.28	75 2/3	32	21	89	3	0	0	0
1979	NY-A	5	32	1	7	.125	47	5.40	78 1/3	28	25	88	12	0	0	2
1980	Tex-A	8	8	2	3	.400	22	4.60	43	17	29	43	4	0	0	0
1981	Sea-A	14	22	2	7	.666	52	4.63	101	32	42	116	10	0	0	0
Career Average		7	22	2	5	.294	37	4.68	71	26	28	78	7	0	0	1
Yankee Average		5	27	2	5	.300	37	4.72	70	27	23	77	7	0	0	1
Career Total		36	111	10	24	.294	184	4.68	354	129	141	389	35	0	0	3
Yankee Total		14	81	6	14	.300	110	4.72	210	80	70	230	21	0	0	3

Clemens, William Roger

HEIGHT: 6'4" RIGHTHANDER BORN: 8/4/1962 DAYTON, OHIO

YEAR	TEAM	STARTS	GAMES	WON	LOST	PCT	ER	ERA	INNINGS PITCHED	STRIKE-OUTS	WALKS	HITS ALLOWED	HRS ALLOWED	COMP. GAMES	SHUT-OUTS	SAVES
1984	Bos-A	20	21	9	4	.692	64	4.32	133 1/3	126	29	146	13	5	1	0
1985	Bos-A	15	15	7	5	.583	36	3.29	98 1/3	74	37	83	5	3	1	0
1986	Bos-A	33	33	24	4	.857	70	2.48	254	238	67	179	21	10	1	0
1987	Bos-A	36	36	20	9	.690	93	2.97	281 2/3	256	83	248	19	18	7	0
1988	Bos-A	35	35	18	12	.600	86	2.93	264	291	62	217	17	14	8	0
1989	Bos-A	35	35	17	11	.607	88	3.13	253 1/3	230	93	215	20	8	3	0
1990	Bos-A	31	31	21	6	.778	49	1.93	228 1/3	209	54	193	7	7	4	0
1991	Bos-A	35	35	18	10	.643	79	2.62	271 1/3	241	65	219	15	13	4	0
1992	Bos-A	32	32	18	11	.621	66	2.41	246 2/3	208	62	203	11	11	5	0
1993	Bos-A	29	29	11	14	.440	95	4.46	191 2/3	160	67	175	17	2	1	0
1994	Bos-A	24	24	9	7	.563	54	2.86	170 2/3	168	71	124	15	3	1	0
1995	Bos-A	23	23	10	5	.667	65	4.18	140	132	60	141	15	0	0	0
1996	Bos-A	34	34	10	13	.435	98	3.64	242 2/3	257	106	216	19	6	2	0
1997	Tor-A	34	34	21	7	.750	60	2.05	264	292	68	204	9	9	3	0
1998	Tor-A	33	33	20	6	.769	69	2.65	234 2/3	271	88	169	11	5	3	0
1999	NY-A	30	30	14	10	.583	96	4.62	187 2/3	163	90	185	20	1	1	0
2000	NY-A	32	32	13	8	.619	64	3.70	204 1/3	188	84	184	26	1	0	0
Career Average		30	30	15	8	.647	74	3.07	216	206	70	182	15	7	3	0
Yankee Average		31	31	14	9	.600	90	4.13	196	176	87	185	23	1	1	0
Career Total		511	512	260	142	.647	1252	3.07	3666 2/3	3504	1186	3101	260	116	45	0
Yankee Total		62	62	27	18	.600	180	4.13	392	351	174	369	46	2	1	0

Clements, Patrick Brian

HEIGHT: 6'0" LEFTHANDER BORN: 2/2/1962 McCLOUD, CALIFORNIA

YEAR	TEAM	STARTS	GAMES	WON	LOST	PCT	ER	ERA	INNINGS PITCHED	STRIKE-OUTS	WALKS	HITS ALLOWED	HRS ALLOWED	COMP. GAMES	SHUT-OUTS	SAVES
1985	Cal-A	0	41	5	0	1.000	23	3.34	62	19	25	47	4	0	0	1
1985	Pit-N	0	27	0	2	.000	14	3.67	34 1/3	17	15	39	2	0	0	2
1986	Pit-N	0	65	0	4	.000	19	2.80	61	31	32	53	1	0	0	2
1987	NY-A	0	55	3	3	.500	44	4.95	80	36	30	91	4	0	0	7
1988	NY-A	1	6	0	0	—	6	6.48	8 1/3	3	4	12	1	0	0	0
1989	SD-N	1	23	4	1	.800	17	3.92	39	18	15	39	4	0	0	0
1990	SD-N	0	9	0	0	—	6	4.15	13	6	7	20	1	0	0	0
1992	Bal-A	0	23	2	0	1.000	9	3.28	24 2/3	9	11	23	0	0	0	0
1991	SD-N	0	12	1	0	1.000	6	3.77	14 1/3	8	9	13	0	0	0	0
1992	SD-N	0	27	2	1	.667	7	2.66	23 2/3	11	12	25	0	0	0	0
Career Average		0	29	2	1	.607	15	3.77	36	16	16	36	2	0	0	1
Yankee Average		1	31	2	2	.500	25	5.09	44	20	17	52	3	0	0	4
Career Total		2	288	17	11	.607	151	3.77	360	158	160	362	17	0	0	12
Yankee Total		1	61	3	3	.500	50	5.09	88	39	34	103	5	0	0	7

Clevenger, Truman Eugene (Tex)
HEIGHT: 6'1" RIGHTHANDER BORN: 7/9/1932 VISALIA, CALIFORNIA

YEAR	TEAM	STARTS	GAMES	WON	LOST	PCT	ER	ERA	INNINGS PITCHED	STRIKE-OUTS	WALKS	HITS ALLOWED	HRS ALLOWED	COMP. GAMES	SHUT-OUTS	SAVES
1954	Bos-A	8	23	2	4	.333	36	4.79	67 2/3	43	29	67	9	1	0	0
1956	Was-A	1	20	0	0	—	19	5.40	31 2/3	17	21	33	4	0	0	0
1957	Was-A	9	52	7	6	.538	65	4.19	139 2/3	75	47	139	11	2	0	8
1958	Was-A	4	55	9	9	.500	60	4.35	124	70	50	119	12	0	0	6
1959	Was-A	7	50	8	5	.615	51	3.91	117 1/3	71	51	114	9	2	2	8
1960	Was-A	11	53	5	11	.313	60	4.20	128 2/3	49	49	150	10	1	0	7
1961	LA-A	0	12	2	1	.667	3	1.69	16	11	13	13	1	0	0	1
1961	**NY-A**	**0**	**21**	**1**	**1**	**.500**	**17**	**4.83**	**31 2/3**	**14**	**21**	**35**	**3**	**0**	**0**	**0**
1962	**NY-A**	**0**	**21**	**2**	**0**	**1.000**	**12**	**2.84**	**38**	**11**	**17**	**36**	**3**	**0**	**0**	**0**
Career Average		4	34	4	4	.493	36	4.18	77	40	33	78	7	1	0	3
Yankee Average		**0**	**21**	**2**	**1**	**.750**	**15**	**3.75**	**35**	**13**	**19**	**36**	**3**	**0**	**0**	**0**
Career Total		40	307	36	37	.493	323	4.18	695	361	298	706	62	6	2	30
Yankee Total		**0**	**42**	**3**	**1**	**.750**	**29**	**3.75**	**70**	**25**	**38**	**71**	**6**	**0**	**0**	**0**

Closter, Alan Edward
HEIGHT: 6'2" LEFTHANDER BORN: 6/15/1943 CREIGHTON, NEBRASKA

YEAR	TEAM	STARTS	GAMES	WON	LOST	PCT	ER	ERA	INNINGS PITCHED	STRIKE-OUTS	WALKS	HITS ALLOWED	HRS ALLOWED	COMP. GAMES	SHUT-OUTS	SAVES
1966	Was-A	0	1	0	0	—	0	0.00	.333	0	2	1	0	0	0	0
1971	**NY-A**	**1**	**14**	**2**	**2**	**.500**	**16**	**5.08**	**28 1/3**	**22**	**13**	**33**	**4**	**0**	**0**	**0**
1972	**NY-A**	**0**	**2**	**0**	**0**	**—**	**3**	**11.57**	**2 1/3**	**2**	**4**	**2**	**1**	**0**	**0**	**0**
1973	Atl-N	0	4	0	0	—	7	14.54	4 1/3	2	4	7	1	0	0	0
Career Average		0	5	1	1	.500	7	6.62	9	7	6	11	2	0	0	0
Yankee Average		**1**	**8**	**1**	**1**	**.500**	**10**	**5.58**	**15**	**12**	**9**	**18**	**3**	**0**	**0**	**0**
Career Total		1	21	2	2	.500	26	6.62	35	26	23	43	6	0	0	0
Yankee Total		**1**	**16**	**2**	**2**	**.500**	**19**	**5.58**	**31**	**24**	**17**	**35**	**5**	**0**	**0**	**0**

Coakley, Andrew James
HEIGHT: 6'0" RIGHTHANDER BORN: 11/20/1882 PROVIDENCE, RHODE ISLAND DIED: 9/27/1963 NEW YORK, NEW YORK

YEAR	TEAM	STARTS	GAMES	WON	LOST	PCT	ER	ERA	INNINGS PITCHED	STRIKE-OUTS	WALKS	HITS ALLOWED	HRS ALLOWED	COMP. GAMES	SHUT-OUTS	SAVES
1902	Phi-A	3	3	2	1	.667	8	2.67	27	9	9	25	0	3	0	0
1903	Phi-A	3	6	0	3	.000	23	5.50	37 2/3	20	11	48	2	2	0	0
1904	Phi-A	8	8	4	3	.571	13	1.89	62	33	23	48	1	7	2	0
1905	Phi-A	31	35	18	8	.692	52	1.84	255	145	73	227	2	21	3	0
1906	Phi-A	16	22	7	8	.467	52	3.14	149	59	44	144	0	10	0	0
1907	Cin-N	30	37	17	16	.515	69	2.34	265 1/3	89	79	269	1	21	1	1
1908	Cin-N	28	32	8	18	.308	50	1.86	242 1/3	61	64	219	3	20	4	2
1908	Chi-N	3	4	2	0	1.000	2	0.89	20 1/3	7	6	14	0	2	1	0
1909	Chi-N	1	1	0	1	.000	4	18.00	2	1	3	7	0	0	0	0
1911	**NY-A**	**1**	**2**	**0**	**1**	**.000**	**7**	**5.40**	**11 2/3**	**4**	**2**	**20**	**0**	**1**	**0**	**0**
Career Average		12.4	15	6	6	.496	28	2.35	107	43	31	102	1	9	1	0
Yankee Average		**1**	**2**	**0**	**1**	**.000**	**7**	**5.40**	**11 2/3**	**4**	**2**	**20**	**0**	**1**	**0**	**0**
Career Total		124	150	58	59	.496	280	2.35	1072	428	314	1021	9	87	11	3
Yankee Total		**1**	**2**	**0**	**1**	**.000**	**7**	**5.40**	**11 2/3**	**4**	**2**	**20**	**0**	**1**	**0**	**0**

Coates, James Alton
HEIGHT: 6'4" RIGHTHANDER BORN: 8/4/1932 FARNHAM, VIRGINIA

YEAR	TEAM	STARTS	GAMES	WON	LOST	PCT	ER	ERA	INNINGS PITCHED	STRIKE-OUTS	WALKS	HITS ALLOWED	HRS ALLOWED	COMP. GAMES	SHUT-OUTS	SAVES
1956	**NY-A**	**0**	**2**	**0**	**0**	**—**	**3**	**13.50**	**2**	**0**	**4**	**1**	**0**	**0**	**0**	**0**
1959	**NY-A**	**4**	**37**	**6**	**1**	**.857**	**32**	**2.87**	**100 1/3**	**64**	**36**	**89**	**10**	**2**	**0**	**0**
1960	**NY-A**	**18**	**35**	**13**	**3**	**.813**	**71**	**4.28**	**149 1/3**	**73**	**66**	**139**	**16**	**6**	**2**	**1**
1961	**NY-A**	**11**	**43**	**11**	**5**	**.688**	**54**	**3.44**	**141 1/3**	**80**	**53**	**128**	**15**	**4**	**1**	**5**
1962	**NY-A**	**6**	**50**	**7**	**6**	**.538**	**58**	**4.44**	**117 2/3**	**67**	**50**	**119**	**9**	**0**	**0**	**6**

(continued)

(continued)

YEAR	TEAM	STARTS	GAMES	WON	LOST	PCT	ER	ERA	INNINGS PITCHED	STRIKE-OUTS	WALKS	HITS ALLOWED	HRS ALLOWED	COMP. GAMES	SHUT-OUTS	SAVES
1963	Was-A	2	20	2	4	.333	26	5.28	44 1/3	31	21	51	4	0	0	0
1963	Cin-N	0	9	0	0	—	10	5.51	16 1/3	11	7	21	2	0	0	0
1965	Cal-A	0	17	2	0	1.000	11	3.54	28	15	16	23	1	0	0	3
1966	Cal-A	4	9	1	1	.500	14	3.98	31 2/3	16	10	32	3	1	1	0
1967	Cal-A	1	25	1	2	.333	25	4.30	52 1/3	39	23	47	5	0	0	0
Career Average		5	25	4	2	.662	30	4.00	68	40	29	65	7	1	0	2
Yankee Average		**8**	**33**	**7**	**3**	**.712**	**44**	**3.84**	**102**	**57**	**42**	**95**	**10**	**2**	**1**	**2**
Career Total		46	247	43	22	.662	304	4.00	683	396	286	650	65	13	4	15
Yankee Total		**39**	**167**	**37**	**15**	**.712**	**218**	**3.84**	**511**	**284**	**209**	**476**	**50**	**12**	**3**	**12**

Colavito, Rocco Domenico (Rocky)

HEIGHT: 6'3" RIGHTHANDER BORN: 8/10/1933 NEW YORK, NEW YORK

YEAR	TEAM	STARTS	GAMES	WON	LOST	PCT	ER	ERA	INNINGS PITCHED	STRIKE-OUTS	WALKS	HITS ALLOWED	HRS ALLOWED	COMP. GAMES	SHUT-OUTS	SAVES
1958	Cle-A	0	1	0	0	—	0	0.00	3	1	3	0	0	0	0	0
1968	**NY-A**	**0**	**1**	**1**	**0**	**1.000**	**0**	**0.00**	**2 2/3**	**1**	**2**	**1**	**0**	**0**	**0**	**0**
Career Average		0	1	1	0	1.000	0	0.00	3	1	3	1	0	0	0	0
Yankee Average		**0**	**1**	**1**	**0**	**1.000**	**0**	**0.00**	**2 2/3**	**1**	**2**	**1**	**0**	**0**	**0**	**0**
Career Total		0	2	1	0	1.000	0	0.00	6	2	5	1	0	0	0	0
Yankee Total		**0**	**1**	**1**	**0**	**1.000**	**0**	**0.00**	**2 2/3**	**1**	**2**	**1**	**0**	**0**	**0**	**0**

Cole, Leonard Leslie (King)

HEIGHT: 6'1" RIGHTHANDER BORN: 4/15/1886 TOLEDO, IOWA DIED: 1/6/1916 BAY CITY, MICHIGAN

YEAR	TEAM	STARTS	GAMES	WON	LOST	PCT	ER	ERA	INNINGS PITCHED	STRIKE-OUTS	WALKS	HITS ALLOWED	HRS ALLOWED	COMP. GAMES	SHUT-OUTS	SAVES
1909	Chi-N	1	1	1	0	1.000	0	0.00	9	1	3	6	0	1	1	0
1910	Chi-N	29	33	20	4	.833	48	1.80	239 2/3	114	130	174	2	21	4	1
1911	Chi-N	27	32	18	7	.720	77	3.13	221 1/3	101	99	188	3	13	2	0
1912	Chi-N	3	8	1	2	.333	23	10.89	19	9	8	36	2	0	0	0
1912	Pit-N	4	12	2	2	.500	35	6.43	49	11	18	61	1	2	0	0
1914	**NY-A**	**15**	**33**	**11**	**9**	**.550**	**52**	**3.30**	**141 2/3**	**43**	**51**	**151**	**3**	**8**	**2**	**0**
1915	**NY-A**	**6**	**10**	**3**	**3**	**.500**	**18**	**3.18**	**51**	**19**	**22**	**41**	**2**	**2**	**0**	**1**
Career Average		12	18	8	4	.675	36	3.12	104	43	47	94	2	7	1	0
Yankee Average		**11**	**22**	**7**	**6**	**.538**	**35**	**3.27**	**96**	**31**	**37**	**96**	**3**	**5**	**1**	**1**
Career Total		85	129	56	27	.675	253	3.12	731	298	331	657	13	47	9	2
Yankee Total		**21**	**43**	**14**	**12**	**.538**	**70**	**3.27**	**193**	**62**	**73**	**192**	**5**	**10**	**2**	**1**

Coleman, Walter Gary (Rip)

HEIGHT: 6'2" LEFTHANDER BORN: 7/31/1931 TROY, NEW YORK

YEAR	TEAM	STARTS	GAMES	WON	LOST	PCT	ER	ERA	INNINGS PITCHED	STRIKE-OUTS	WALKS	HITS ALLOWED	HRS ALLOWED	COMP. GAMES	SHUT-OUTS	SAVES
1955	**NY-A**	**6**	**10**	**2**	**1**	**.667**	**17**	**5.28**	**29**	**15**	**16**	**40**	**2**	**0**	**0**	**1**
1956	**NY-A**	**9**	**29**	**3**	**5**	**.375**	**36**	**3.67**	**88 1/3**	**42**	**42**	**97**	**6**	**0**	**0**	**2**
1957	KC-A	6	19	0	7	.000	27	5.93	41	15	25	53	5	1	1	0
1959	Bal-A	0	3	0	0	—	0	0.00	4	4	2	4	0	0	0	0
1959	KC-A	11	29	2	10	.167	41	4.56	81	54	34	85	8	2	0	2
1960	Bal-A	1	5	0	2	.000	5	11.25	4	0	5	8	0	0	0	0
Career Average		6	16	1	4	.219	21	4.58	41	22	21	48	4	1	0	1
Yankee Average		**8**	**20**	**3**	**3**	**.455**	**27**	**4.07**	**59**	**29**	**29**	**69**	**4**	**0**	**0**	**2**
Career Total		33	95	7	25	.219	126	4.58	247	130	124	287	21	3	1	5
Yankee Total		**15**	**39**	**5**	**6**	**.455**	**53**	**4.07**	**117**	**57**	**58**	**137**	**8**	**0**	**1**	**3**

David Brian "Coney" Cone, rhp, 1995–2000

David Cone was an All-Star with two teams prior to his stint with the Yankees, and, in fact, was a local hero with the crosstown Mets in the late 1980s and early 1990s. From 1996 through the 1999 season, he was a pillar of postseason consistency for New York.

Born January 2, 1963, in Kansas City, Missouri, Cone was the Royals' third-round pick in the 1981 June free-agent draft as an 18-year-old. He was signed that summer and compiled a 6-4 record with the Royals' farm club in Sarasota, Florida. He spent five years in the minors.

After a brief stint with the Royals, Cone was traded to the Mets in 1987. He was 80-48 with the Mets before stints in Toronto and Kansas City. In 1994, he edged the Blue Jays' Jimmy Key for the Cy Young Award. Cone was the first player in the history of the award to win it without leading the league in any major statistical category.

But Cone has rarely been a pitcher who overwhelms opponents statistically. Rather, he has been, particularly for the Yankees, the pitcher who wins big games. And that is why he was purchased by New York in the first place.

He was a key to the Yankees' World Championship teams in 1996, 1998 and 1999,

going 6-1 in the postseason for the Yankees in his four years in pinstripes. His World Series record as a Yankee is 2-0 in three years.

He slumped somewhat in 2000, falling to 4-14 on the year. But Yankee manager Joe Torre refused to give up on his 37-year-old righthander. In Game 4 of the World Series, Cone jammed the very dangerous Mike Piazza into a pop-up to preserve a 3-2 lead. New York won the game, 4-2.

He has turned in some very clutch performances. None, perhaps, more crucial than his six-inning, four-hit stint in Game 3 of the 1996 World Series. The Yankees were reeling after being knocked around in two games in Yankee Stadium, and being outscored 16-1. There was talk in both the Atlanta and New York newspapers about a Braves sweep.

But Cone cooly shut the Braves down long enough for the Yankee bats to wake up, and his 5-2 win in Atlanta fueled New York's turnaround and eventual 4-2 Series victory.

In 1999, Cone won Game 3 of the Series against the Atlanta Braves, essentially clinching that series as well.

A four-time All-Star, Cone's crowning personal moment came in 1999 when he pitched a perfect game in Yankee Stadium in June against the Montreal Expos. It was the second perfect game thrown by a Yankee in two years and the third all-time.

Collins, Harry Warren (Rip)

HEIGHT: 6'1"   RIGHTHANDER   BORN: 2/26/1896 WEATHERFORD, TEXAS   DIED: 5/27/1968 BRYAN, TEXAS

YEAR	TEAM	STARTS	GAMES	WON	LOST	PCT	ER	ERA	INNINGS PITCHED	STRIKE-OUTS	WALKS	HITS ALLOWED	HRS ALLOWED	COMP. GAMES	SHUT-OUTS	SAVES
1920	NY-A	18	36	14	8	.636	67	3.22	187 1/3	66	79	171	6	10	2	1
1921	NY-A	16	28	11	5	.688	83	5.44	137 1/3	64	78	158	6	7	2	0
1922	Bos-A	29	32	14	11	.560	88	3.76	210 2/3	69	103	219	4	15	3	0
1923	Det-A	14	17	3	7	.300	50	4.87	92 1/3	25	22	104	3	3	1	0
1924	Det-A	30	34	14	7	.667	77	3.21	216	75	63	199	6	11	1	0
1925	Det-A	20	26	6	11	.353	71	4.56	140	33	52	149	7	5	0	0
1926	Det-A	13	30	8	8	.500	37	2.73	122	44	44	128	4	5	3	1
1927	Det-A	25	30	13	7	.650	90	4.69	172 2/3	37	59	207	5	10	1	0
1929	StL-A	20	26	11	6	.647	69	4.00	155 1/3	47	73	162	16	10	1	1
1930	StL-A	20	35	9	7	.563	83	4.35	171 2/3	75	63	168	11	6	1	2
1931	StL-A	14	17	5	5	.500	45	3.79	107	34	38	130	5	2	0	0
Career Average		20	28	10	7	.568	69	3.99	156	52	61	163	7	8	1	0
Yankee Average		**17**	**32**	**13**	**7**	**.658**	**75**	**4.16**	**162**	**65**	**79**	**165**	**6**	**9**	**2**	**1**
Career Total		219	311	108	82	.568	760	3.99	1712	569	674	1795	73	84	15	5
Yankee Total		**34**	**64**	**25**	**13**	**.658**	**150**	**4.16**	**325**	**130**	**157**	**329**	**12**	**17**	**4**	**1**

Colson, Loyd Albert

HEIGHT: 6'1"   RIGHTHANDER   BORN: 11/4/1947 WELLINGTON, TEXAS

YEAR	TEAM	STARTS	GAMES	WON	LOST	PCT	ER	ERA	INNINGS PITCHED	STRIKE-OUTS	WALKS	HITS ALLOWED	HRS ALLOWED	COMP. GAMES	SHUT-OUTS	SAVES
1970	NY-A	0	1	0	0	—	1	4.50	2	3	0	3	0	0	0	0
Career Average		0	1	0	0	—	1	4.50	2	3	0	3	0	0	0	0
Yankee Average		**0**	**1**	**0**	**0**	**—**	**1**	**4.50**	**2**	**3**	**0**	**3**	**0**	**0**	**0**	**0**
Career Total		0	1	0	0	—	1	4.50	2	3	0	3	0	0	0	0
Yankee Total		**0**	**1**	**0**	**0**	**—**	**1**	**4.50**	**2**	**3**	**0**	**3**	**0**	**0**	**0**	**0**

Cone, David Brian (Coney)

HEIGHT: 6'1"   RIGHTHANDER   BORN: 1/2/1963 KANSAS CITY, MO

YEAR	TEAM	STARTS	GAMES	WON	LOST	PCT	ER	ERA	INNINGS PITCHED	STRIKE-OUTS	WALKS	HITS ALLOWED	HRS ALLOWED	COMP. GAMES	SHUT-OUTS	SAVES
1986	KC-A	0	11	0	0	—	14	5.56	22 2/3	21	13	29	2	0	0	0
1987	NY-N	13	21	5	6	.455	41	3.71	99 1/3	68	44	87	11	1	0	1
1988	NY-N	28	35	20	3	.870	57	2.22	231 1/3	213	80	178	10	8	4	0
1989	NY-N	33	34	14	8	.636	86	3.52	219 2/3	190	74	183	20	7	2	0
1990	NY-N	30	31	14	10	.583	76	3.23	211 2/3	233	65	177	21	6	2	0
1991	NY-N	34	34	14	14	.500	85	3.29	232 2/3	241	73	204	13	5	2	0
1992	NY-N	27	27	13	7	.650	63	2.88	196 2/3	214	82	162	12	7	5	0
1992	Tor-A	7	8	4	3	.571	15	2.55	53	47	29	39	3	0	0	0
1993	KC-A	34	34	11	14	.440	94	3.33	254	191	114	205	20	6	1	0
1994	KC-A	23	23	16	5	.762	56	2.95	171 2/3	132	54	130	15	4	3	0
1995	Tor-A	17	17	9	6	.600	49	3.39	130 1/3	102	41	113	12	5	2	0
1995	**NY-A**	**13**	**13**	**9**	**2**	**.818**	**42**	**3.82**	**99**	**89**	**47**	**82**	**12**	**1**	**0**	**0**
1996	**NY-A**	**11**	**11**	**7**	**2**	**.778**	**23**	**2.88**	**72**	**71**	**34**	**50**	**3**	**1**	**0**	**0**
1997	**NY-A**	**29**	**29**	**12**	**6**	**.667**	**61**	**2.82**	**195**	**222**	**86**	**155**	**17**	**1**	**0**	**0**
1998	**NY-A**	**31**	**31**	**20**	**7**	**.741**	**82**	**3.57**	**207 2/3**	**209**	**59**	**186**	**20**	**3**	**0**	**0**
1999	**NY-A**	**31**	**31**	**12**	**9**	**.571**	**74**	**3.45**	**193 1/3**	**177**	**90**	**164**	**21**	**1**	**1**	**0**
2000	**NY-A**	**29**	**30**	**4**	**14**	**.222**	**119**	**6.91**	**155**	**120**	**82**	**192**	**25**	**0**	**0**	**0**
Career Average		23	25	11	7	.613	61	3.40	161	149	63	137	14	3	1	0
Yankee Average		**24**	**24**	**11**	**7**	**.615**	**67**	**3.91**	**154**	**148**	**66**	**138**	**16**	**1**	**0**	**0**
Career Total		390	420	184	116	.613	1037	3.40	2745	2540	1067	2336	237	56	22	1
Yankee Total		**144**	**145**	**64**	**40**	**.615**	**401**	**3.91**	**922**	**888**	**398**	**829**	**98**	**7**	**1**	**0**

Cook, Andrew Bernard

HEIGHT: 6'5"   RIGHTHANDER   BORN: 8/30/1967 MEMPHIS, TENNESSEE

YEAR	TEAM	STARTS	GAMES	WON	LOST	PCT	ER	ERA	INNINGS PITCHED	STRIKE-OUTS	WALKS	HITS ALLOWED	HRS ALLOWED	COMP. GAMES	SHUT-OUTS	SAVES
1993	NY-A	0	4	0	1	.000	3	5.06	5 1/3	4	7	4	1	0	0	0
Career Average		0	4	0	1	.000	3	5.06	5 1/3	4	7	4	1	0	0	0
Yankee Average		**0**	**4**	**0**	**1**	**.000**	**3**	**5.06**	**5 1/3**	**4**	**7**	**4**	**1**	**0**	**0**	**0**
Career Total		0	4	0	1	.000	3	5.06	5 1/3	4	7	4	1	0	0	0
Yankee Total		**0**	**4**	**0**	**1**	**.000**	**3**	**5.06**	**5 1/3**	**4**	**7**	**4**	**1**	**0**	**0**	**0**

Cooper, Donald James

HEIGHT: 6'1"   RIGHTHANDER   BORN: 1/15/1957 NEW YORK, NEW YORK

YEAR	TEAM	STARTS	GAMES	WON	LOST	PCT	ER	ERA	INNINGS PITCHED	STRIKE-OUTS	WALKS	HITS ALLOWED	HRS ALLOWED	COMP. GAMES	SHUT-OUTS	SAVES
1981	Min-A	2	27	1	5	.167	28	4.30	58 2/3	33	32	61	9	0	0	0
1982	Min-A	1	6	0	1	.000	12	9.53	11 1/3	5	11	14	0	0	0	0
1983	Tor-A	0	4	0	0	—	4	6.75	5 1/3	5	0	8	3	0	0	0
1985	**NY-A**	**0**	**7**	**0**	**0**	**—**	**6**	**5.40**	**10**	**4**	**3**	**12**	**2**	**0**	**0**	**0**
Career Average		1	11	0	2	.143	13	5.27	21	12	12	24	4	0	0	0
Yankee Average		**0**	**7**	**0**	**0**	**—**	**6**	**5.40**	**10**	**4**	**3**	**12**	**2**	**0**	**0**	**0**
Career Total		3	44	1	6	.143	50	5.27	85	47	46	95	14	0	0	0
Yankee Total		**0**	**7**	**0**	**0**	**—**	**6**	**5.40**	**10**	**4**	**3**	**12**	**2**	**0**	**0**	**0**

Cooper, Guy Evans (Rebel)
HEIGHT: 6'1" RIGHTHANDER BORN: 1/28/1893 ROME, GEORGIA   DIED: 8/2/1951 SANTA MONICA, CALIFORNIA

YEAR	TEAM	STARTS	GAMES	WON	LOST	PCT	ER	ERA	INNINGS PITCHED	STRIKE-OUTS	WALKS	HITS ALLOWED	HRS ALLOWED	COMP. GAMES	SHUT-OUTS	SAVES
1914	**NY-A**	**0**	**1**	**0**	**0**	**—**	**3**	**9.00**	**3**	**3**	**2**	**3**	**0**	**0**	**0**	**0**
1914	Bos-A	1	9	1	0	1.000	13	5.32	22	5	9	23	1	0	0	0
1915	Bos-A	0	1	0	0	—	0	0.00	2	0	2	0	0	0	0	0
Career Average		0	4	0	0	1.000	5	5.33	9	3	4	9	0	0	0	0
Yankee Average		**0**	**1**	**0**	**0**	**—**	**3**	**9.00**	**3**	**3**	**2**	**3**	**0**	**0**	**0**	**0**
Career Total		1	11	1	0	1.000	16	5.33	27	8	13	26	1	0	0	0
Yankee Total		**0**	**1**	**0**	**0**	**—**	**3**	**9.00**	**3**	**3**	**2**	**3**	**0**	**0**	**0**	**0**

Cottrell, Ensign Stover
HEIGHT: 5'10" LEFTHANDER BORN: 7/13/1889 HOOSICK FALLS, NEW YORK   DIED: 2/27/1947 SYRACUSE, NEW YORK

YEAR	TEAM	STARTS	GAMES	WON	LOST	PCT	ER	ERA	INNINGS PITCHED	STRIKE-OUTS	WALKS	HITS ALLOWED	HRS ALLOWED	COMP. GAMES	SHUT-OUTS	SAVES
1911	Pit-N	0	1	0	0	—	1	9.00	1	0	1	4	0	0	0	0
1912	Chi-N	0	1	0	0	—	4	9.00	4	1	1	8	0	0	0	0
1913	Phi-A	1	2	1	0	1.000	6	5.40	10	3	2	15	0	1	0	0
1914	Bos-N	1	1	0	1	.000	1	9.00	1	1	3	2	0	0	0	0
1915	**NY-A**	**0**	**7**	**0**	**1**	**.000**	**8**	**3.38**	**21 1/3**	**7**	**7**	**29**	**2**	**0**	**0**	**0**
Career Average		0	2	0	0	.333	4	4.82	7	2	3	12	0	0	0	0
Yankee Average		**0**	**7**	**0**	**1**	**.000**	**8**	**3.38**	**21 1/3**	**7**	**7**	**29**	**2**	**0**	**0**	**0**
Career Total		2	12	1	2	.333	20	4.82	37	12	14	58	2	1	0	0
Yankee Total		**0**	**7**	**0**	**1**	**.000**	**8**	**3.38**	**21 1/3**	**7**	**7**	**29**	**2**	**0**	**0**	**0**

Coveleski, Stanley Anthony
HEIGHT: 5'11" RIGHTHANDER BORN: 8/15/1958 SHAMOKIN, PENNSYLVANIA   DIED: 3/20/1984 SOUTH BEND, INDIANA

YEAR	TEAM	STARTS	GAMES	WON	LOST	PCT	ER	ERA	INNINGS PITCHED	STRIKE-OUTS	WALKS	HITS ALLOWED	HRS ALLOWED	COMP. GAMES	SHUT-OUTS	SAVES
1912	Phi-A	2	5	2	1	.667	8	3.43	21	9	4	18	0	2	1	0
1916	Cle-A	27	45	15	13	.536	88	3.41	232	76	58	247	6	11	1	3
1917	Cle-A	36	45	19	14	.576	60	1.81	298 1/3	133	94	202	3	24	9	4
1918	Cle-A	33	38	22	13	.629	63	1.82	311	87	76	261	2	25	2	1
1919	Cle-A	34	43	24	12	.667	83	2.61	286	118	60	286	2	24	4	4
1920	Cle-A	38	41	24	14	.632	87	2.49	315	133	65	284	6	26	3	2
1921	Cle-A	40	43	23	13	.639	118	3.37	315	99	84	341	6	28	2	2
1922	Cle-A	33	35	17	14	.548	102	3.32	276 2/3	98	64	292	14	21	3	2
1923	Cle-A	31	33	13	14	.481	70	2.76	228	54	42	251	8	17	5	2
1924	Cle-A	33	37	15	16	.484	108	4.04	240 1/3	58	73	286	6	18	2	0
1925	Was-A	32	32	20	5	.800	76	2.84	241	58	73	230	7	15	3	0
1926	Was-A	34	36	14	11	.560	85	3.12	245 1/3	50	81	272	1	11	3	1
1927	Was-A	4	5	2	1	.667	5	3.14	14 1/3	3	8	13	0	0	0	0
1928	**NY-A**	**8**	**12**	**5**	**1**	**.833**	**37**	**5.74**	**58**	**5**	**20**	**72**	**5**	**2**	**0**	**0**
Career Average		28	32	15	10	.602	71	2.89	220	70	57	218	5	16	3	2
Yankee Average		**8**	**12**	**5**	**1**	**.833**	**37**	**5.74**	**58**	**5**	**20**	**72**	**5**	**2**	**0**	**0**
Career Total		385	450	215	142	.602	990	2.89	3082	981	802	3055	66	224	38	21
Yankee Total		**8**	**12**	**5**	**1**	**.833**	**37**	**5.74**	**58**	**5**	**20**	**72**	**5**	**2**	**0**	**0**

Cowley, Joseph Alan
HEIGHT: 6'5" RIGHTHANDER BORN: 8/15/1958 LEXINGTON, KENTUCKY

YEAR	TEAM	STARTS	GAMES	WON	LOST	PCT	ER	ERA	INNINGS PITCHED	STRIKE-OUTS	WALKS	HITS ALLOWED	HRS ALLOWED	COMP. GAMES	SHUT-OUTS	SAVES
1982	Atl-N	8	17	1	2	.333	26	4.47	52 1/3	27	16	53	6	0	0	0
1984	**NY-A**	**11**	**16**	**9**	**2**	**.818**	**33**	**3.56**	**83 1/3**	**71**	**31**	**75**	**12**	**3**	**1**	**0**
1985	**NY-A**	**26**	**30**	**12**	**6**	**.667**	**70**	**3.95**	**159 2/3**	**97**	**85**	**132**	**29**	**1**	**0**	**0**
1986	Chi-A	27	27	11	11	.500	70	3.88	162 1/3	132	83	133	20	4	0	0
1987	Phi-N	4	5	0	4	.000	20	15.43	11 2/3	5	17	21	2	0	0	0

(continued)

(continued)

	STARTS	GAMES	WON	LOST	PCT	ER	ERA	INNINGS PITCHED	STRIKE-OUTS	WALKS	HITS ALLOWED	HRS ALLOWED	COMP. GAMES	SHUT-OUTS	SAVES
Career Average	15	19	7	5	.569	44	4.20	94	66	46	83	14	2	0	0
Yankee Average	19	23	11	4	.724	52	3.81	121	84	58	104	21	2	0	0
Career Total	76	95	33	25	.569	219	4.20	469	332	232	414	69	8	1	0
Yankee Total	37	46	21	8	.724	103	3.81	243	168	116	207	41	4	1	0

Cox, Joseph Casey

HEIGHT: 6'5" RIGHTHANDER BORN: 7/3/1941 LONG BEACH, CALIFORNIA

YEAR	TEAM	STARTS	GAMES	WON	LOST	PCT	ER	ERA	INNINGS PITCHED	STRIKE-OUTS	WALKS	HITS ALLOWED	HRS ALLOWED	COMP. GAMES	SHUT-OUTS	SAVES
1966	Was-A	0	66	4	5	.444	44	3.50	113	46	35	104	6	0	0	7
1967	Was-A	0	54	7	4	.636	24	2.96	73	32	21	67	2	0	0	1
1968	Was-A	0	4	0	1	.000	2	2.35	7 2/3	4	0	7	0	0	0	0
1969	Was-A	13	52	12	7	.632	53	2.78	171 1/3	73	64	161	15	4	0	0
1970	Was-A	30	37	8	12	.400	95	4.45	192 1/3	68	44	211	27	1	0	0
1971	Was-A	11	54	5	7	.417	55	3.98	124 1/3	43	40	131	9	0	0	7
1972	Tex-A	4	35	3	5	.375	32	4.41	65 1/3	27	26	73	7	0	0	4
1972	NY-A	1	5	0	1	.000	6	4.63	11 2/3	4	3	13	0	0	0	0
1973	NY-A	0	1	0	0	—	2	6.00	3	0	1	5	0	0	0	0
Career Average		7	34	4	5	.481	35	3.70	85	33	26	86	7	1	0	2
Yankee Average		1	3	0	1	.000	4	4.91	7	2	2	9	0	0	0	0
Career Total		59	308	39	42	.481	313	3.70	762	297	234	772	66	5	0	20
Yankee Total		1	6	0	1	.000	8	4.91	15	4	4	18	0	0	0	0

Cullen, John Patrick (Jack)

HEIGHT: 5'11" RIGHTHANDER BORN: 10/6/1939 NEWARK, NEW JERSEY

YEAR	TEAM	STARTS	GAMES	WON	LOST	PCT	ER	ERA	INNINGS PITCHED	STRIKE-OUTS	WALKS	HITS ALLOWED	HRS ALLOWED	COMP. GAMES	SHUT-OUTS	SAVES
1962	NY-A	0	2	0	0	—	0	0.00	3	2	2	2	0	0	0	1
1965	NY-A	9	12	3	4	.429	20	3.05	59	25	21	59	2	0	0	0
1966	NY-A	0	5	1	0	1.000	5	3.97	11 1/3	7	5	11	0	2	1	0
Career Average		3	6	1	1	.500	8	3.07	24	11	9	24	1	1	0	0
Yankee Average		3	6	1	1	.500	8	3.07	24	11	9	24	1	1	0	0
Career Total		9	19	4	4	.500	25	3.07	73	34	28	72	2	2	1	1
Yankee Total		9	19	4	4	.500	25	3.07	73	34	28	72	2	2	1	1

Cullop, Norman Andrew (Nick)

HEIGHT: 5'11" LEFTHANDER BORN: 9/17/1887 CHILHOWIE, VIRGINIA DIED: 4/15/1961 TAZEWELL, VIRGINIA

YEAR	TEAM	STARTS	GAMES	WON	LOST	PCT	ER	ERA	INNINGS PITCHED	STRIKE-OUTS	WALKS	HITS ALLOWED	HRS ALLOWED	COMP. GAMES	SHUT-OUTS	SAVES
1913	Cle-A	8	23	3	7	.300	48	4.42	97 2/3	30	35	105	3	4	0	0
1914	Cle-A	0	1	0	1	.000	1	2.70	3 1/3	3	1	4	0	0	0	0
1914	KC-F	36	44	14	19	.424	77	2.34	295 2/3	149	87	256	6	22	4	1
1915	KC-F	36	44	22	11	.667	82	2.44	302 1/3	111	67	278	8	22	3	2
1916	NY-A	22	28	13	6	.684	38	2.05	167	77	32	151	4	9	0	1
1917	NY-A	18	30	5	9	.357	54	3.32	146 1/3	27	31	161	2	5	0	1
1921	StL-A	1	4	0	2	.000	11	8.49	11 2/3	3	6	18	1	0	0	0
Career Average		17	25	8	8	.509	44	2.73	146	57	37	139	3	9	1	1
Yankee Average		20	29	9	8	.545	46	2.64	157	52	32	156	3	7	1	1
Career Total		121	174	57	55	.509	311	2.73	1024	400	259	973	24	62	9	5
Yankee Total		40	58	18	15	.545	92	2.64	313	104	63	312	6	14	2	2

Cumberland, John Sheldon
HEIGHT: 6'0" LEFTHANDER BORN: 5/10/1947 WESTBROOK, MAINE

YEAR	TEAM	STARTS	GAMES	WON	LOST	PCT	ER	ERA	INNINGS PITCHED	STRIKE-OUTS	WALKS	HITS ALLOWED	HRS ALLOWED	COMP. GAMES	SHUT-OUTS	SAVES
1968	NY-A	0	1	0	0	—	2	9.00	2	1	1	3	1	0	0	0
1969	NY-A	0	2	0	0	—	2	4.50	4	0	4	3	0	0	0	0
1970	NY-A	8	15	3	4	.429	28	3.94	64	38	15	62	9	1	0	0
1970	SF-N	0	7	2	0	1.000	1	0.82	11	6	4	6	0	0	0	2
1971	SF-N	21	45	9	6	.600	60	2.92	185	65	55	153	22	5	2	2
1972	SF-N	6	9	0	4	.000	24	8.64	25	8	7	38	6	0	0	0
1972	StL-N	1	14	1	1	.500	16	6.65	21 2/3	7	7	23	6	0	0	0
1974	Cal-A	0	17	0	1	.000	9	3.74	21 2/3	12	10	24	2	0	0	0
Career Average		45	14	2	2	.484	18	3.82	42	17	13	39	6	1	0	0
Yankee Average		3	6	1	1	.429	11	4.11	23	13	7	23	3	0	0	0
Career Total		36	110	15	16	.484	142	3.82	334	137	103	312	46	6	2	2
Yankee Total		8	18	3	4	.429	32	4.11	70	39	20	68	10	1	0	0

Daley, Leavitt Leo (Bud)
HEIGHT: 6'1" LEFTHANDER BORN: 10/7/1932 ORANGE, CALIFORNIA

YEAR	TEAM	STARTS	GAMES	WON	LOST	PCT	ER	ERA	INNINGS PITCHED	STRIKE-OUTS	WALKS	HITS ALLOWED	HRS ALLOWED	COMP. GAMES	SHUT-OUTS	SAVES
1955	Cle-A	1	2	0	1	.000	5	6.43	7	2	1	10	1	0	0	0
1956	Cle-A	0	14	1	0	1.000	14	6.20	20 1/3	13	14	21	2	0	0	2
1957	Cle-A	10	34	2	8	.666	43	4.43	87 1/3	54	40	99	7	1	0	0
1958	KC-A	5	26	3	2	.600	26	3.31	70 2/3	39	19	67	5	1	0	0
1959	KC-A	29	39	16	13	.552	76	3.16	216 1/3	125	62	212	24	12	2	1
1960	KC-A	35	37	16	16	.500	117	4.56	231	126	96	234	27	13	1	0
1961	KC-A	10	16	4	8	.333	35	4.95	63 2/3	36	22	84	6	2	0	1
1961	NY-A	17	23	8	9	.471	57	3.96	129 2/3	83	51	127	17	7	0	4
1962	NY-A	6	43	7	5	.583	42	3.59	105 1/3	55	21	105	8	0	0	1
1963	NY-A	0	1	0	0	—	0	0.00	1	0	0	2	0	0	0	1
1964	NY-A	3	13	3	2	.600	18	4.63	35	16	25	37	3	0	0	1
Career Average		11	23	5	6	.484	39	4.03	88	50	32	91	9	3	0	2
Yankee Average		7	20	5	4	.529	29	3.89	68	39	24	68	7	2	0	2
Career Total		116	248	60	64	.484	433	4.03	967	549	351	998	100	36	3	10
Yankee Total		26	80	18	16	.529	117	3.89	271	154	97	271	28	7	0	6

Davidson, Robert Banks
HEIGHT: 6'0" RIGHTHANDER BORN: 1/6/1963 BAD KURZNACH, WEST GERMANY

YEAR	TEAM	STARTS	GAMES	WON	LOST	PCT	ER	ERA	INNINGS PITCHED	STRIKE-OUTS	WALKS	HITS ALLOWED	HRS ALLOWED	COMP. GAMES	SHUT-OUTS	SAVES
1989	NY-A	0	1	0	0	—	2	18.00	1	0	1	1	1	0	0	0
Career Average		0	1	0	0	—	2	18.00	1	0	1	1	1	0	0	0
Yankee Average		0	1	0	0	—	2	18.00	1	0	1	1	1	0	0	0
Career Total		0	1	0	0	—	2	18.00	1	0	1	1	1	0	0	0
Yankee Total		0	1	0	0	—	2	18.00	1	0	1	1	1	0	0	0

Davis, George Allen (Iron)
HEIGHT: 5'10" RIGHTHANDER BORN: 3/9/1890 LANCASTER, NEW YORK DIED: 6/4/1961 BUFFALO, NEW YORK

YEAR	TEAM	STARTS	GAMES	WON	LOST	PCT	ER	ERA	INNINGS PITCHED	STRIKE-OUTS	WALKS	HITS ALLOWED	HRS ALLOWED	COMP. GAMES	SHUT-OUTS	SAVES
1912	NY-A	7	10	1	4	.666	39	6.50	54	22	28	61	3	5	0	0
1913	Bos-N	0	2	0	0	—	4	4.50	8	3	5	7	1	0	0	0
1914	Bos-N	6	9	3	3	.500	21	3.40	55 2/3	26	26	42	1	4	1	0
1915	Bos-N	9	15	3	3	.500	31	3.80	73 1/3	26	19	85	2	4	0	0
Career Average		6	9	2	3	.412	24	4.48	48	19	20	49	2	3	0	0
Yankee Average		7	10	1	4	.200	39	6.50	54	22	28	61	3	5	0	0
Career Total		22	36	7	10	.412	95	4.48	191	77	78	195	7	13	1	0
Yankee Total		7	10	1	4	.200	39	6.50	54	22	28	61	3	5	0	0

Davis, Ronald Gene
HEIGHT: 6'4"   RIGHTHANDER   BORN: 8/6/1955 HOUSTON, TEXAS

YEAR	TEAM	STARTS	GAMES	WON	LOST	PCT	ER	ERA	INNINGS PITCHED	STRIKE-OUTS	WALKS	HITS ALLOWED	HRS ALLOWED	COMP. GAMES	SHUT-OUTS	SAVES
1978	**NY-A**	0	4	0	0	—	3	11.57	2 1/3	0	3	3	0	0	0	0
1979	**NY-A**	0	44	14	2	.875	27	2.85	85 1/3	43	28	84	5	0	0	9
1980	**NY-A**	0	53	9	3	.750	43	2.95	131	65	32	121	9	0	0	7
1981	**NY-A**	0	43	4	5	.444	22	2.71	73	83	25	47	6	0	0	6
1982	Min-A	0	63	3	9	.667	52	4.42	106	89	47	106	16	0	0	22
1983	Min-A	0	66	5	8	.385	33	3.34	89	84	33	89	6	0	0	30
1984	Min-A	0	64	7	11	.389	42	4.55	83	74	41	79	11	0	0	29
1985	Min-A	0	57	2	6	.667	25	3.48	64 2/3	72	35	55	7	0	0	25
1986	Min-A	0	36	2	6	.667	39	9.08	38 2/3	30	29	55	7	0	0	2
1986	Chi-N	0	17	0	2	.000	17	7.65	20	10	3	31	3	0	0	0
1987	Chi-N	0	21	0	0	—	21	5.85	32 1/3	31	12	43	8	0	0	0
1987	LA-N	0	4	0	0	—	3	6.75	4	1	6	7	0	0	0	0
1988	SF-N	0	9	1	1	.500	9	4.67	17 1/3	15	6	15	4	0	0	0
Career Average		0	37	4	4	.470	26	4.05	57	46	23	57	6	0	0	10
Yankee Average		**0**	**36**	**7**	**3**	**.730**	**24**	**2.93**	**73**	**48**	**22**	**64**	**5**	**0**	**0**	**6**
Career Total		0	481	47	53	.470	336	4.05	747	597	300	735	82	0	0	130
Yankee Total		**0**	**144**	**27**	**10**	**.730**	**95**	**2.93**	**292**	**191**	**88**	**255**	**20**	**0**	**0**	**22**

Deering, John Thomas
HEIGHT: 6'0"   RIGHTHANDER   BORN: 6/25/1878 LYNN, MASSACHUSETTS   DIED: 2/15/1943 BEVERLY, MASSACHUSETTS

YEAR	TEAM	STARTS	GAMES	WON	LOST	PCT	ER	ERA	INNINGS PITCHED	STRIKE-OUTS	WALKS	HITS ALLOWED	HRS ALLOWED	COMP. GAMES	SHUT-OUTS	SAVES
1903	Det-A	8	10	3	4	.429	26	3.86	60 2/3	14	24	77	3	5	0	0
1903	**NY-A**	7	9	4	3	.571	25	3.75	60	14	18	59	0	6	1	0
Career Average		8	10	4	4	.500	26	3.80	60	14	21	68	2	6	1	0
Yankee Average		**7**	**9**	**4**	**3**	**.571**	**25**	**3.75**	**60**	**14**	**18**	**59**	**0**	**6**	**1**	**0**
Career Total		15	19	7	7	.500	51	3.80	121	28	42	136	3	11	1	0
Yankee Total		**7**	**9**	**4**	**3**	**.571**	**25**	**3.75**	**60**	**14**	**18**	**59**	**0**	**6**	**1**	**0**

Deshaies, James Joseph
HEIGHT: 6'5"   LEFTHANDER   BORN: 6/23/1960 MASSENA, NEW YORK

YEAR	TEAM	STARTS	GAMES	WON	LOST	PCT	ER	ERA	INNINGS PITCHED	STRIKE-OUTS	WALKS	HITS ALLOWED	HRS ALLOWED	COMP. GAMES	SHUT-OUTS	SAVES
1984	**NY-A**	2	2	0	1	.000	9	11.57	7	5	7	14	1	0	0	0
1985	Hou-N	0	2	0	0	—	0	0.00	3	2	0	1	0	0	0	0
1986	Hou-N	26	26	12	5	.706	52	3.25	144	128	59	124	16	1	1	0
1987	Hou-N	25	26	11	6	.647	78	4.62	152	104	57	149	22	1	0	0
1988	Hou-N	31	31	11	14	.440	69	3.00	207	127	72	164	20	3	2	0
1989	Hou-N	34	34	15	10	.600	73	2.91	225 2/3	153	79	180	15	6	3	0
1990	Hou-N	34	34	7	12	.368	88	3.78	209 1/3	119	84	186	21	2	0	0
1991	Hou-N	28	28	5	12	.667	89	4.98	161	98	72	156	19	1	0	0
1992	SD-N	15	15	4	7	.364	35	3.28	96	46	33	92	6	0	0	0
1993	Min-A	27	27	11	13	.458	82	4.41	167 1/3	80	51	159	24	1	0	0
1993	SF-N	4	5	2	2	.500	8	4.24	17	5	6	24	2	0	0	0
1994	Min-A	25	25	6	12	.333	107	7.41	130	78	54	170	30	0	0	0
1995	Phi-N	2	2	0	1	.000	12	21.60	5	6	1	15	3	0	0	0
Career Average		20	20	6	7	.469	54	4.14	117	73	44	110	14	1	0	0
Yankee Average		**2**	**2**	**0**	**1**	**.000**	**9**	**11.57**	**7**	**5**	**7**	**14**	**1**	**0**	**0**	**0**
Career Total		253	257	84	95	.469	702	4.14	1524	951	575	1434	179	15	6	0
Yankee Total		**2**	**2**	**0**	**1**	**.000**	**9**	**11.57**	**7**	**5**	**7**	**14**	**1**	**0**	**0**	**0**

DeShong, James Brooklyn (Jimmie)
HEIGHT: 5'11"   RIGHTHANDER   BORN: 11/30/1909 HARRISBURG, PENNSYLVANIA

YEAR	TEAM	STARTS	GAMES	WON	LOST	PCT	ER	ERA	INNINGS PITCHED	STRIKE-OUTS	WALKS	HITS ALLOWED	HRS ALLOWED	COMP. GAMES	SHUT-OUTS	SAVES
1932	Phi-A	0	6	0	0	—	13	11.70	10	5	9	17	3	0	0	0
1934	**NY-A**	**12**	**31**	**6**	**7**	**.462**	**61**	**4.11**	**133 2/3**	**40**	**56**	**126**	**6**	**6**	**0**	**3**
1935	**NY-A**	**3**	**29**	**4**	**1**	**.800**	**25**	**3.26**	**69**	**30**	**33**	**64**	**6**	**0**	**0**	**3**
1936	Was-A	31	34	18	10	.643	115	4.63	223 2/3	59	96	255	11	16	2	2
1937	Was-A	34	37	14	15	.483	144	4.90	264 1/3	86	124	290	15	20	0	1
1938	Was-A	14	31	5	8	.385	96	6.58	131 1/3	41	83	160	11	1	0	0
1939	Was-A	6	7	0	3	.000	39	8.63	40 2/3	12	31	56	7	1	0	0
Career Average		14	25	7	6	.516	70	5.08	125	39	62	138	8	6	0	1
Yankee Average		**8**	**30**	**5**	**4**	**.556**	**43**	**3.82**	**101**	**35**	**45**	**95**	**6**	**3**	**0**	**3**
Career Total		100	175	47	44	.516	493	5.08	873	273	432	968	59	44	2	9
Yankee Total		**15**	**60**	**10**	**8**	**.556**	**86**	**3.82**	**203**	**70**	**89**	**190**	**12**	**6**	**0**	**6**

Devens, Charles
HEIGHT: 6'1"   RIGHTHANDER   BORN: 1/1/1910 MILTON, MASSACHUSETTS

YEAR	TEAM	STARTS	GAMES	WON	LOST	PCT	ER	ERA	INNINGS PITCHED	STRIKE-OUTS	WALKS	HITS ALLOWED	HRS ALLOWED	COMP. GAMES	SHUT-OUTS	SAVES
1932	NY-A	1	1	1	0	1.000	2	2.00	9	4	7	6	0	1	0	0
1933	NY-A	8	14	3	3	.500	30	4.35	62	23	50	59	1	2	0	0
1934	NY-A	1	1	1	0	1.000	2	1.64	11	4	5	9	0	1	0	0
Career Average		3	5	2	1	.625	11	3.73	27	10	21	25	0	1	0	0
Yankee Average		**3**	**5**	**2**	**1**	**.625**	**11**	**3.73**	**27**	**10**	**21**	**25**	**0**	**1**	**0**	**0**
Career Total		10	16	5	3	.625	34	3.73	82	31	62	74	1	4	0	0
Yankee Total		**10**	**16**	**5**	**3**	**.625**	**34**	**3.73**	**82**	**31**	**62**	**74**	**1**	**4**	**0**	**0**

Dickson, Murry Monroe
HEIGHT: 5'11"   RIGHTHANDER   BORN: 8/21/1916 TRACY, MISSOURI   DIED: 9/21/1989 KANSAS CITY, KANSAS

YEAR	TEAM	STARTS	GAMES	WON	LOST	PCT	ER	ERA	INNINGS PITCHED	STRIKE-OUTS	WALKS	HITS ALLOWED	HRS ALLOWED	COMP. GAMES	SHUT-OUTS	SAVES
1939	StL-N	0	1	0	0	—	0	0.00	3 2/3	2	1	1	0	0	0	0
1940	StL-N	1	1	0	0	—	3	16.21	1 2/3	0	1	5	0	0	0	0
1942	StL-N	7	36	6	3	.667	39	2.91	120 2/3	66	61	91	1	2	0	2
1943	StL-N	7	31	8	2	.800	46	3.58	115 2/3	44	49	119	4	2	0	0
1946	StL-N	19	47	15	6	.714	59	2.88	184 1/3	82	56	160	8	12	2	1
1947	StL-N	25	47	13	16	.448	79	3.07	231 2/3	111	88	211	16	11	4	3
1948	StL-N	29	42	12	16	.429	116	4.14	252 1/3	113	85	257	39	11	1	1
1949	Pit-N	20	44	12	14	.462	82	3.29	224 1/3	89	80	216	17	11	2	0
1950	Pit-N	22	51	10	15	.400	95	3.80	225	76	83	227	20	8	0	3
1951	Pit-N	35	45	20	16	.556	129	4.02	288 2/3	112	101	294	32	19	3	2
1952	Pit-N	34	43	14	21	.400	110	3.57	277 2/3	112	76	278	26	21	2	2
1953	Pit-N	26	45	10	19	.345	101	4.53	200 2/3	88	58	240	27	10	1	4
1954	Phi-N	31	40	10	20	.333	95	3.78	226 1/3	64	73	256	31	12	4	3
1955	Phi-N	28	36	12	11	.522	84	3.50	216	92	82	190	27	12	4	0
1956	Phi-N	3	3	0	3	.000	13	5.09	23	1	12	20	1	0	0	0
1956	StL-N	27	28	13	8	.619	67	3.07	196 1/3	109	57	175	20	12	3	0
1957	StL-N	13	14	5	3	.625	34	4.14	74	29	25	87	8	3	1	0
1958	KC-A	9	27	9	5	.643	36	3.27	99	46	31	99	12	3	0	1
1958	**NY-A**	**2**	**6**	**1**	**2**	**.333**	**13**	**5.75**	**20 1/3**	**9**	**12**	**18**	**4**	**0**	**0**	**1**
1959	KC-A	0	38	2	1	.667	39	4.94	71	36	27	85	9	0	0	0
Career Average		17	31	9	9	.487	62	3.66	153	64	53	151	15	7	1	1
Yankee Average		**2**	**6**	**1**	**2**	**.333**	**13**	**5.75**	**20 1/3**	**9**	**12**	**18**	**4**	**0**	**0**	**1**
Career Total		338	625	172	181	.487	1240	3.66	3052	1281	1058	3029	302	149	27	23
Yankee Total		**2**	**6**	**1**	**2**	**.333**	**13**	**5.75**	**20 1/3**	**9**	**12**	**18**	**4**	**0**	**0**	**1**

Dingman, Craig Allen
HEIGHT: 6'4" RIGHTHANDER BORN: 3/12/1974 WITCHITA, KANSAS

YEAR	TEAM	STARTS	GAMES	WON	LOST	PCT	ER	ERA	INNINGS PITCHED	STRIKE-OUTS	WALKS	HITS ALLOWED	HRS ALLOWED	COMP. GAMES	SHUT-OUTS	SAVES
2000	NY-A	0	10	0	0	—	8	6.55	11	8	3	18	1	0	0	0
Career Average		0	10	0	0	—	8	6.55	11	8	3	18	1	0	0	0
Yankee Average		**0**	**10**	**0**	**0**	**—**	**8**	**6.55**	**11**	**8**	**3**	**18**	**1**	**0**	**0**	**0**
Career Total		0	10	0	0	—	8	6.55	11	8	3	18	1	0	0	0
Yankee Total		**0**	**10**	**0**	**0**	**—**	**8**	**6.55**	**11**	**8**	**3**	**18**	**1**	**0**	**0**	**0**

Ditmar, Arthur John
HEIGHT: 6'2" RIGHTHANDER BORN: 4/3/1929 WINTHROP, MASSACHUSETTS

YEAR	TEAM	STARTS	GAMES	WON	LOST	PCT	ER	ERA	INNINGS PITCHED	STRIKE-OUTS	WALKS	HITS ALLOWED	HRS ALLOWED	COMP. GAMES	SHUT-OUTS	SAVES
1954	Phi-A	5	14	1	4	.666	28	6.41	39 1/3	14	36	50	4	0	0	0
1955	KC-A	22	35	12	12	.500	98	5.03	175 1/3	79	86	180	23	7	1	1
1956	KC-A	34	44	12	22	.353	125	4.42	254 1/3	126	108	254	30	14	2	1
1957	**NY-A**	**11**	**46**	**8**	**3**	**.727**	**46**	**3.25**	**127 1/3**	**64**	**35**	**128**	**9**	**0**	**0**	**6**
1958	**NY-A**	**13**	**38**	**9**	**8**	**.529**	**53**	**3.42**	**139 2/3**	**52**	**38**	**124**	**14**	**4**	**0**	**4**
1959	**NY-A**	**25**	**38**	**13**	**9**	**.591**	**65**	**2.90**	**202**	**96**	**52**	**156**	**17**	**7**	**1**	**1**
1960	**NY-A**	**28**	**34**	**15**	**9**	**.625**	**68**	**3.06**	**200**	**65**	**56**	**195**	**25**	**8**	**1**	**0**
1961	**NY-A**	**8**	**12**	**2**	**3**	**.400**	**28**	**4.64**	**54 1/3**	**24**	**14**	**59**	**9**	**1**	**0**	**0**
1961	KC-A	5	20	0	5	.000	34	5.67	54	19	23	60	6	0	0	1
1962	KC-A	5	6	0	2	.000	16	6.65	21 2/3	13	13	31	1	0	0	0
Career Average		15.6	29	7	8	.483	56	3.98	127	55	46	124	14	4	1	1
Yankee Average		**17**	**34**	**9**	**6**	**.595**	**52**	**3.24**	**145**	**60**	**39**	**132**	**15**	**4**	**0**	**2**
Career Total		156	287	72	77	.483	561	3.98	1268	552	461	1237	138	41	5	14
Yankee Total		**85**	**168**	**47**	**32**	**.595**	**260**	**3.24**	**723**	**301**	**195**	**662**	**74**	**20**	**2**	**11**

Dixon, John Craig (Sonny)
HEIGHT: 6'2" RIGHTHANDER BORN: 11/5/1924 CHARLOTTE, NORTH CAROLINA

YEAR	TEAM	STARTS	GAMES	WON	LOST	PCT	ER	ERA	INNINGS PITCHED	STRIKE-OUTS	WALKS	HITS ALLOWED	HRS ALLOWED	COMP. GAMES	SHUT-OUTS	SAVES
1953	Was-A	6	43	5	8	.385	50	3.75	120	40	31	123	13	3	0	3
1954	Was-A	0	16	1	2	.333	10	3.03	29 2/3	7	12	26	3	0	0	1
1954	Phi-A	6	38	5	7	.417	58	4.86	107 1/3	42	27	136	8	1	0	4
1955	KC-A	0	2	0	0	—	3	16.21	1 2/3	0	0	6	1	0	0	0
1956	**NY-A**	**0**	**3**	**0**	**1**	**.000**	**1**	**2.08**	**4 1/3**	**1**	**5**	**5**	**0**	**0**	**0**	**1**
Career Average		2	20	2	4	.379	24	4.17	53	18	15	59	5	1	0	2
Yankee Average		**0**	**3**	**0**	**1**	**.000**	**1**	**2.08**	**4 1/3**	**1**	**5**	**5**	**0**	**0**	**0**	**1**
Career Total		12	102	11	18	.379	122	4.17	263	90	75	296	25	4	0	9
Yankee Total		**0**	**3**	**0**	**1**	**.000**	**1**	**2.08**	**4 1/3**	**1**	**5**	**5**	**0**	**0**	**0**	**1**

Dobson, Patrick Edward
HEIGHT: 6'3" RIGHTHANDER BORN: 2/12/1942 DEPEW, NEW YORK

YEAR	TEAM	STARTS	GAMES	WON	LOST	PCT	ER	ERA	INNINGS PITCHED	STRIKE-OUTS	WALKS	HITS ALLOWED	HRS ALLOWED	COMP. GAMES	SHUT-OUTS	SAVES
1967	Det-A	1	28	1	2	.333	16	2.92	49 1/3	34	27	38	6	0	0	0
1968	Det-A	10	47	5	8	.385	37	2.66	125	93	48	89	13	2	1	7
1969	Det-A	9	49	5	10	.333	42	3.60	105	64	39	100	10	1	0	9
1970	SD-N	34	40	14	15	.483	105	3.76	251	185	78	257	28	8	1	1
1971	Bal-A	37	38	20	8	.714	91	2.90	282 1/3	187	63	248	24	18	4	1
1972	Bal-A	36	38	16	18	.471	79	2.65	268 1/3	161	69	220	13	13	3	0
1973	Atl-N	10	12	3	7	.300	32	4.99	57 2/3	23	19	73	1	1	1	0
1973	**NY-A**	**21**	**22**	**9**	**8**	**.529**	**66**	**4.17**	**142 1/3**	**70**	**34**	**150**	**22**	**6**	**1**	**0**
1974	**NY-A**	**39**	**39**	**19**	**15**	**.559**	**96**	**3.07**	**281**	**157**	**75**	**282**	**23**	**12**	**2**	**0**
1975	**NY-A**	**30**	**33**	**11**	**14**	**.440**	**94**	**4.07**	**207 2/3**	**129**	**83**	**205**	**21**	**7**	**1**	**0**
1976	Cle-A	35	35	16	12	.571	84	3.48	217 1/3	117	65	226	13	6	0	0
1977	Cle-A	17	33	3	12	.666	91	6.14	133 1/3	81	65	155	23	0	0	1

(continued)

(continued)

Career Average	24	35	10	11	.486	69	3.54	177	108	55	170	16	6	1	2
Yankee Average	30	31	13	12	.513	85	3.65	210	119	64	212	22	8	1	0
Career Total	279	414	122	129	.486	833	3.54	2120	1301	665	2043	197	74	14	19
Yankee Total	90	94	39	37	.513	256	3.65	631	356	192	637	66	25	4	0

Donald, Richard Atley (Swampy)

HEIGHT: 6'1" RIGHTHANDER BORN: 8/19/1910 MORTON, MISSISSIPPI DIED: 10/19/1992 WEST MONROE, LOUISIANA

YEAR	TEAM	STARTS	GAMES	WON	LOST	PCT	ER	ERA	INNINGS PITCHED	STRIKE-OUTS	WALKS	HITS ALLOWED	HRS ALLOWED	COMP. GAMES	SHUT-OUTS	SAVES
1938	NY-A	2	2	0	1	.000	7	5.25	12	6	14	7	0	0	0	0
1939	NY-A	20	24	13	3	.813	63	3.71	153	55	60	144	12	11	2	1
1940	NY-A	11	24	8	3	.727	40	3.03	118 2/3	60	59	113	11	6	1	0
1941	NY-A	20	22	9	5	.643	63	3.57	159	71	69	141	11	10	0	0
1942	NY-A	19	20	11	3	.786	51	3.11	147 2/3	53	45	133	6	10	1	0
1943	NY-A	15	22	6	4	.600	61	4.60	119 1/3	57	38	134	10	2	0	0
1944	NY-A	19	30	13	10	.565	59	3.34	159	48	59	173	13	9	0	0
1945	NY-A	9	9	5	4	.556	21	2.97	63 2/3	19	25	62	3	6	2	0
Career Average	14	19	8	4	.663	46	3.52	117	46	46	113	8	7	1	0
Yankee Average	14	19	8	4	.663	46	3.52	117	46	46	113	8	7	1	0
Career Total	115	153	65	33	.663	365	3.52	932	369	369	907	66	54	6	1
Yankee Total	115	153	65	33	.663	365	3.52	932	369	369	907	66	54	6	1

Donovan, William Edward (Wild Bill)

HEIGHT: 5'11" RIGHTHANDER BORN: 10/13/1876 LAWRENCE, MASSACHUSETTS DIED: 12/9/1923 FORSYTH, NEW YORK

YEAR	TEAM	STARTS	GAMES	WON	LOST	PCT	ER	ERA	INNINGS PITCHED	STRIKE-OUTS	WALKS	HITS ALLOWED	HRS ALLOWED	COMP. GAMES	SHUT-OUTS	SAVES
1898	Was-N	7	17	1	6	.143	42	4.30	88	36	69	88	0	6	0	0
1899	Bro-N	2	5	1	2	.333	12	4.32	25	11	13	35	0	2	0	1
1900	Bro-N	4	5	1	2	.333	23	6.68	31	13	18	36	1	2	0	0
1901	Bro-N	38	45	25	15	.625	108	2.77	351	226	152	324	1	36	2	3
1902	Bro-N	33	35	17	15	.531	92	2.78	297 2/3	170	111	250	1	30	4	1
1903	Det-A	34	35	17	16	.515	78	2.29	307	187	95	247	3	34	4	0
1904	Det-A	34	34	17	16	.515	80	2.46	293	137	94	251	5	30	3	0
1905	Det-A	32	34	18	15	.545	81	2.60	280 2/3	135	101	236	2	27	5	0
1906	Det-A	25	25	9	15	.375	74	3.15	211 2/3	85	72	221	4	22	0	0
1907	Det-A	28	32	25	4	.862	66	2.19	271	123	82	222	3	27	3	1
1908	Det-A	28	29	18	7	.720	56	2.08	242 2/3	141	53	210	2	25	6	0
1909	Det-A	17	21	8	7	.533	36	2.31	140 1/3	76	60	121	0	13	4	2
1910	Det-A	23	26	17	7	.708	56	2.44	206 2/3	107	61	184	4	20	3	0
1911	Det-A	19	20	10	9	.526	62	3.31	168 1/3	81	64	160	4	15	1	0
1912	Det-A	1	3	1	0	1.000	1	0.90	10	6	2	5	0	0	0	0
1915	**NY-A**	1	9	0	3	.000	18	4.81	33 2/3	17	10	35	1	0	0	0
1916	**NY-A**	0	1	0	0	—	0	0.00	1	0	1	1	0	0	0	0
1918	Det-A	1	2	1	0	1.000	1	1.50	6	1	1	5	0	0	0	0
Career Average	18	21	10	8	.572	49	2.69	165	86	59	146	2	16	2	0
Yankee Average	1	5	0	2	.000	9	4.67	17	9	6	18	1	0	0	0
Career Total	327	378	186	139	.572	886	2.69	2965	1552	1059	2631	31	289	35	8
Yankee Total	1	10	0	3	.000	18	4.67	35	17	11	36	1	0	0	0

Dotson, Richard Elliott

HEIGHT: 6'1" RIGHTHANDER BORN: 10/1/1959 CINCINNATI, OHIO

YEAR	TEAM	STARTS	GAMES	WON	LOST	PCT	ER	ERA	INNINGS PITCHED	STRIKE-OUTS	WALKS	HITS ALLOWED	HRS ALLOWED	COMP. GAMES	SHUT-OUTS	SAVES
1979	Chi-A	5	5	2	0	1.000	10	3.70	24 1/3	13	6	28	0	1	1	0
1980	Chi-A	32	33	12	10	.545	94	4.27	198	109	87	185	20	8	0	0
1981	Chi-A	24	24	9	8	.529	59	3.77	141	73	49	145	13	5	4	0
1982	Chi-A	31	34	11	15	.423	84	3.84	196 2/3	109	73	219	19	3	1	0
1983	Chi-A	35	35	22	7	.759	86	3.23	240	137	106	209	19	8	1	0
1984	Chi-A	32	32	14	15	.483	98	3.59	245 2/3	120	103	216	24	14	1	0
1985	Chi-A	9	9	3	4	.429	26	4.47	52 1/3	33	17	53	5	0	0	0

(continued)

(continued)

Year	Team														
1986	Chi-A	34	34	10	17	.370	120	5.48	197	110	69	226	24	3	1	0
1987	Chi-A	31	31	11	12	.478	98	4.17	211 1/3	114	86	201	24	7	2	0
1988	**NY-A**	**29**	**32**	**12**	**9**	**.571**	**95**	**5.00**	**171**	**77**	**72**	**178**	**27**	**4**	**0**	**0**
1989	**NY-A**	**9**	**11**	**2**	**5**	**.667**	**32**	**5.57**	**51 2/3**	**14**	**17**	**69**	**8**	**1**	**0**	**0**
1989	Chi-A	17	17	3	7	.300	43	3.88	99 2/3	55	41	112	8	1	0	0
1990	KC-A	7	8	0	4	.000	27	8.48	28 2/3	9	14	43	3	0	0	0
Career Average		23	23	9	9	.496	67	4.23	143	75	57	145	15	4	1	0
Yankee Average		**19**	**22**	**7**	**7**	**.500**	**64**	**5.13**	**111**	**46**	**45**	**124**	**18**	**3**	**0**	**0**
Career Total		295	305	111	113	.496	872	4.23	1857	973	740	1884	194	55	11	0
Yankee Total		**38**	**43**	**14**	**14**	**.500**	**127**	**5.13**	**223**	**91**	**89**	**247**	**35**	**5**	**0**	**0**

Downing, Alphonso Erwin

HEIGHT: 5'11" LEFTHANDER BORN: 6/28/1941 TRENTON, NEW JERSEY

YEAR	TEAM	STARTS	GAMES	WON	LOST	PCT	ER	ERA	INNINGS PITCHED	STRIKE-OUTS	WALKS	HITS ALLOWED	HRS ALLOWED	COMP. GAMES	SHUT-OUTS	SAVES
1961	NY-A	1	5	0	1	.000	8	8.00	9	12	12	7	0	0	0	0
1962	NY-A	0	1	0	0	—	0	0.00	1	1	0	0	0	0	0	0
1963	NY-A	22	24	13	5	.722	50	2.56	175 2/3	171	80	114	7	10	4	0
1964	NY-A	35	37	13	8	.619	94	3.47	244	217	120	201	18	11	1	2
1965	NY-A	32	35	12	14	.462	80	3.40	212	179	105	185	16	8	2	0
1966	NY-A	30	30	10	11	.476	79	3.56	200	152	79	178	23	1	0	0
1967	NY-A	28	31	14	10	.583	59	2.63	201 2/3	171	61	158	13	10	4	0
1968	NY-A	12	15	3	3	.500	24	3.52	61 1/3	40	20	54	7	1	0	0
1969	NY-A	15	30	7	5	.583	49	3.38	130 2/3	85	49	117	12	5	1	0

(continued)

Alphonso Erwin "Al" Downing, lhp, 1961–69

Compact and powerful, Al Downing was a mainstay for the Yankees' pitching staff in the last years of their dynasty in the 1960s and during the "down years" thereafter.

Born in Trenton, New Jersey, in 1941, Downing was also the first black pitcher for the Yankees when he was called up in 1961. For the publicity-concious Yankees, he was perfect for the role: soft-spoken, intelligent and handsome, with a wealth of ability.

Such a distinction was not necessarily a role Downing coveted; he wanted to be a good ballplayer, not score points with a race-conscious management.

The Yankees signed Downing in 1961 and gave him a $16,000 bonus. He spent most of the next two years in the minor leagues before coming up for good in 1963.

Downing hit the ground running in 1963 with a very strong year, going 13-5 with a 2.56 ERA and 171 strikeouts as New York won the American League pennant, before being defeated in the World Series by the Los Angeles Dodgers.

In 1964, Downing was even more overpowering, with a 13-8 record and a league-leading 217 strikeouts. The Yankees again won the American League pennant, and again lost in the Series, this time to the St. Louis Cardinals.

But by 1965, the Yankees were on a downward slope. Downing was fifth in the league in strikeouts in 1965 with 179, but he was only 12-14 and New York finished sixth. He was 10-11 in 1966 but rebounded to 14-10 in 1967, leading the team in ERA with 2.63.

But he battled injuries the next two years, and was eventually traded to Oakland for Danny Cater. He finished his career with the Dodgers.

Downing, who led the Yankees in strikeouts four consecutive years, is seventh on the all-time team list with 1,028. His 3.25 ERA is 17th all-time for New York.

(continued)

YEAR	TEAM	STARTS	GAMES	WON	LOST	PCT	ER	ERA	INNINGS PITCHED	STRIKE-OUTS	WALKS	HITS ALLOWED	HRS ALLOWED	COMP. GAMES	SHUT-OUTS	SAVES
1970	Oak-A	6	10	3	3	.500	18	3.95	41	26	22	39	5	1	0	0
1970	Mil-A	16	17	2	10	.167	35	3.34	94 1/3	53	59	79	8	1	0	0
1971	LA-N	36	37	20	9	.690	78	2.68	262 1/3	136	84	245	16	12	5	0
1972	LA-N	30	31	9	9	.500	67	2.98	202 2/3	117	67	196	13	7	4	0
1973	LA-N	28	30	9	9	.500	71	3.31	193	124	68	155	19	5	2	0
1974	LA-N	16	21	5	6	.455	40	3.66	98 1/3	63	45	94	7	1	1	0
1975	LA-N	6	22	2	1	.667	24	2.89	74 2/3	39	28	59	6	0	0	1
1976	LA-N	3	17	1	2	.333	20	3.86	46 2/3	30	18	43	3	0	0	0
1977	LA-N	1	12	0	1	.000	15	6.75	20	23	16	22	4	0	0	0
Career Average		17.6	23	7	6	.535	45	3.22	126	91	52	108	10	4	1	0
Yankee Average		**19.4**	**23**	**8**	**6**	**.558**	**49**	**3.23**	**137**	**114**	**58**	**113**	**11**	**5**	**1**	**0**
Career Total		317	405	123	107	.535	811	3.22	2268	1639	933	1946	177	73	24	3
Yankee Total		**175**	**208**	**72**	**57**	**.558**	**443**	**3.23**	**1235**	**1028**	**526**	**1014**	**96**	**46**	**12**	**2**

Doyle, Judd Bruce (Slow Joe)

HEIGHT: 5'8" RIGHTHANDER BORN: 9/15/1881 CLAY CENTER, KANSAS DIED: 11/21/1947 TANNERSVILLE, NEW YORK

YEAR	TEAM	STARTS	GAMES	WON	LOST	PCT	ER	ERA	INNINGS PITCHED	STRIKE-OUTS	WALKS	HITS ALLOWED	HRS ALLOWED	COMP. GAMES	SHUT-OUTS	SAVES
1906	NY-A	6	9	2	1	.667	12	2.38	45 1/3	28	13	34	1	3	2	0
1907	NY-A	23	29	11	11	.500	57	2.65	193 2/3	94	67	169	2	15	1	1
1908	NY-A	4	12	1	1	.500	14	2.63	48	20	14	42	1	2	1	0
1909	NY-A	15	17	8	6	.571	36	2.58	125 2/3	57	37	103	3	8	3	0
1910	NY-A	2	3	0	2	.000	11	8.03	12 1/3	6	5	19	0	1	0	0
1910	Cin-N	0	5	0	0	—	8	6.35	11 1/3	4	11	16	0	0	0	0
Career Average		8	13	4	4	.512	23	2.85	73	35	25	64	1	5	1	0
Yankee Average		**10**	**14**	**4**	**4**	**.512**	**26**	**2.75**	**85**	**41**	**27**	**73**	**1**	**6**	**1**	**0**
Career Total		50	75	22	21	.512	138	2.85	436	209	147	383	7	29	7	1
Yankee Total		**50**	**70**	**22**	**21**	**.512**	**130**	**2.75**	**425**	**205**	**136**	**367**	**7**	**29**	**7**	**1**

Drabek, Douglas Dean

HEIGHT: 6'1" RIGHTHANDER BORN: 7/25/1962 VICTORIA, TEXAS

YEAR	TEAM	STARTS	GAMES	WON	LOST	PCT	ER	ERA	INNINGS PITCHED	STRIKE-OUTS	WALKS	HITS ALLOWED	HRS ALLOWED	COMP. GAMES	SHUT-OUTS	SAVES
1986	**NY-A**	**21**	**27**	**7**	**8**	**.467**	**60**	**4.10**	**131 2/3**	**76**	**50**	**126**	**13**	**0**	**0**	**0**
1987	Pit-N	28	29	11	12	.478	76	3.88	176 1/3	120	46	165	22	1	1	0
1988	Pit-N	32	33	15	7	.682	75	3.08	219 1/3	127	50	194	21	3	1	0
1989	Pit-N	34	35	14	12	.538	76	2.80	244 1/3	123	69	215	21	8	5	0
1990	Pit-N	33	33	22	6	.786	71	2.76	231 1/3	131	56	190	15	9	3	0
1991	Pit-N	35	35	15	14	.517	80	3.07	234 2/3	142	62	245	16	5	2	0
1992	Pit-N	34	34	15	11	.577	79	2.77	256 2/3	177	54	218	17	10	4	0
1993	Hou-N	34	34	9	18	.333	100	3.79	237 2/3	157	60	242	18	7	2	0
1994	Hou-N	23	23	12	6	.667	52	2.85	164 2/3	121	45	132	14	6	0	0
1995	Hou-N	31	31	10	9	.526	98	4.77	185	143	54	205	18	2	0	0
1996	Hou-N	30	30	7	9	.438	89	4.58	175 1/3	137	60	208	21	1	0	0
1997	Chi-A	31	31	12	11	.522	108	5.75	169 1/3	85	69	170	30	0	0	0
1998	Bal-A	21	23	6	11	.353	88	7.33	108 2/3	55	29	138	20	1	0	0
Career Average		30	31	12	10	.536	81	3.74	195	123	54	188	19	4	1	0
Yankee Average		**21**	**27**	**7**	**8**	**.467**	**60**	**4.10**	**131 2/3**	**76**	**50**	**126**	**13**	**0**	**0**	**0**
Career Total		387	398	155	134	.536	1052	3.74	2533	1594	704	2448	246	53	18	0
Yankee Total		**21**	**27**	**7**	**8**	**.467**	**60**	**4.10**	**131 2/3**	**76**	**50**	**126**	**13**	**0**	**0**	**0**

Drews, Karl August

HEIGHT: 6'4" RIGHTHANDER BORN: 2/22/1920 STATEN ISLAND, NEW YORK DIED: 8/15/1963 DANIA, FLORIDA

YEAR	TEAM	STARTS	GAMES	WON	LOST	PCT	ER	ERA	INNINGS PITCHED	STRIKE-OUTS	WALKS	HITS ALLOWED	HRS ALLOWED	COMP. GAMES	SHUT-OUTS	SAVES
1946	**NY-A**	**1**	**3**	**0**	**1**	**.000**	**6**	**8.53**	**6 1/3**	**4**	**6**	**6**	**0**	**0**	**0**	**0**
1947	**NY-A**	**10**	**30**	**6**	**6**	**.500**	**50**	**4.91**	**91 2/3**	**45**	**55**	**92**	**6**	**0**	**0**	**1**
1948	**NY-A**	**2**	**19**	**2**	**3**	**.400**	**16**	**3.79**	**38**	**11**	**31**	**35**	**3**	**0**	**0**	**1**
1948	StL-A	2	20	3	2	.600	34	8.05	38	11	38	43	3	0	0	2
1949	StL-A	23	31	4	12	.667	103	6.64	139 2/3	35	66	180	11	3	1	0

(continued)

(continued)

1951	Phi-N	3	5	1	0	1.000	16	6.26	23	13	7	29	2	1	0	0
1952	Phi-N	30	33	14	15	.483	69	2.72	228 2/3	96	52	213	13	15	5	0
1953	Phi-N	27	47	9	10	.474	93	4.52	185 1/3	72	50	218	26	6	0	3
1954	Phi-N	0	8	1	0	1.000	10	5.63	16	6	8	18	2	0	0	0
1954	Cin-N	9	22	4	4	.500	40	6.00	60	29	19	79	6	1	1	0
Career Average		11	22	4	5	.454	44	4.76	83	32	33	91	7	3	1	1
Yankee Average		**5.5**	**17**	**3**	**4**	**.462**	**28**	**5.14**	**49**	**25**	**31**	**49**	**3**	**0**	**0**	**1**
Career Total		107	218	44	53	.454	437	4.76	827	322	332	913	72	26	7	7
Yankee Total		**11**	**33**	**6**	**7**	**.462**	**56**	**5.14**	**98**	**49**	**61**	**98**	**6**	**0**	**0**	**1**

Dubiel, Walter John (Monk)

HEIGHT: 6'0" RIGHTHANDER BORN: 2/12/1918 HARTFORD, CONNECTICUT DIED: 10/23/1969 HARTFORD, CONNECTICUT

YEAR	TEAM	STARTS	GAMES	WON	LOST	PCT	ER	ERA	INNINGS PITCHED	STRIKE-OUTS	WALKS	HITS ALLOWED	HRS ALLOWED	COMP. GAMES	SHUT-OUTS	SAVES
1944	**NY-A**	**28**	**30**	**13**	**13**	**.500**	**87**	**3.38**	**232**	**79**	**86**	**217**	**12**	**19**	**3**	**0**
1945	**NY-A**	**20**	**26**	**10**	**9**	**.526**	**78**	**4.64**	**151 1/3**	**45**	**62**	**157**	**9**	**9**	**1**	**0**
1948	Phi-N	17	37	8	10	.444	65	3.89	150 1/3	42	58	139	13	6	2	4
1949	Chi-N	20	32	6	9	.400	68	4.14	147 2/3	52	54	142	16	3	1	4
1950	Chi-N	12	39	6	10	.375	66	4.16	142 2/3	51	67	152	12	4	2	2
1951	Chi-N	0	22	2	2	.500	14	2.30	54 2/3	19	22	46	3	0	0	1
1952	Chi-N	0	1	0	0	—	0	0.00	2/3	1	0	1	0	0	0	0
Career Average		14	27	6	8	.459	54	3.87	126	41	50	122	9	6	1	2
Yankee Average		**24**	**28**	**12**	**11**	**.511**	**83**	**3.87**	**192**	**62**	**74**	**187**	**11**	**14**	**2**	**0**
Career Total		97	187	45	53	.459	378	3.87	879	289	349	854	65	41	9	11
Yankee Total		**48**	**56**	**23**	**22**	**.511**	**165**	**3.87**	**383**	**124**	**148**	**374**	**21**	**28**	**4**	**0**

Duren, Rinold George (Ryne)

HEIGHT: 6'2" RIGHTHANDER BORN: 2/22/1929 CAZENOVIA, WISCONSIN

YEAR	TEAM	STARTS	GAMES	WON	LOST	PCT	ER	ERA	INNINGS PITCHED	STRIKE-OUTS	WALKS	HITS ALLOWED	HRS ALLOWED	COMP. GAMES	SHUT-OUTS	SAVES
1954	Bal-A	0	1	0	0	—	2	9.00	2	2	1	3	0	0	0	0
1957	KC-A	6	14	0	3	.000	25	5.27	42 2/3	37	30	37	4	0	0	1
1958	**NY-A**	**1**	**44**	**6**	**4**	**.600**	**17**	**2.02**	**75 2/3**	**87**	**43**	**40**	**4**	**0**	**0**	**20**
1959	**NY-A**	**0**	**41**	**3**	**6**	**.333**	**16**	**1.88**	**76 2/3**	**96**	**43**	**49**	**6**	**0**	**0**	**14**
1960	**NY-A**	**1**	**42**	**3**	**4**	**.429**	**27**	**4.96**	**49**	**67**	**49**	**27**	**3**	**0**	**0**	**9**
1961	**NY-A**	**0**	**4**	**0**	**1**	**.000**	**3**	**5.40**	**5**	**7**	**4**	**2**	**2**	**0**	**0**	**0**
1961	LA-A	14	40	6	12	.333	57	5.18	99	108	75	87	13	1	1	2
1962	LA-A	3	42	2	9	.182	35	4.42	71 1/3	74	57	53	1	0	0	8
1963	Phi-N	7	33	6	2	.750	32	3.30	87 1/3	84	52	65	6	1	0	2
1964	Phi-N	0	2	0	0	—	2	6.00	3	5	1	5	0	0	0	0
1964	Cin-N	0	26	0	2	.000	14	2.89	43 2/3	39	15	41	1	0	0	1
1965	Phi-N	0	6	0	0	—	4	3.27	11	6	4	10	0	0	0	0
1965	Was-A	0	16	1	1	.500	17	6.65	23	18	18	24	0	0	0	0
Career Average		3	24	2	3	.380	19	3.83	45	48	30	34	3	0	0	4
Yankee Average		**1**	**33**	**3**	**4**	**.444**	**16**	**2.75**	**52**	**64**	**35**	**30**	**4**	**0**	**0**	**11**
Career Total		32	311	27	44	.380	251	3.83	589	630	392	443	40	2	1	57
Yankee Total		**2**	**131**	**12**	**15**	**.444**	**63**	**2.75**	**206**	**257**	**139**	**118**	**15**	**0**	**0**	**43**

Eastwick, Rawlins Jackson

HEIGHT: 6'3" RIGHTHANDER BORN: 10/24/1950 CAMDEN, NEW JERSEY

YEAR	TEAM	STARTS	GAMES	WON	LOST	PCT	ER	ERA	INNINGS PITCHED	STRIKE-OUTS	WALKS	HITS ALLOWED	HRS ALLOWED	COMP. GAMES	SHUT-OUTS	SAVES
1974	Cin-N	0	8	0	0	—	4	2.04	17 2/3	14	5	12	1	0	0	2
1975	Cin-N	0	58	5	3	.625	26	2.60	90	61	25	77	6	0	0	22
1976	Cin-N	0	71	11	5	.688	25	2.09	107 2/3	70	27	93	3	0	0	26
1977	Cin-N	0	23	2	2	.500	14	2.91	43 1/3	17	8	40	3	0	0	7
1977	StL-N	0	41	3	7	.300	28	4.70	53 2/3	30	21	74	6	0	0	4
1978	**NY-A**	**0**	**8**	**2**	**1**	**.667**	**9**	**3.28**	**24 2/3**	**13**	**4**	**22**	**2**	**0**	**0**	**0**
1978	Phi-N	0	22	2	1	.667	18	4.02	40 1/3	14	18	31	5	0	0	0

(continued)

(continued)

1979	Phi-N	0	51	3	6	.333	45	4.90	82 2/3	47	25	90	8	0	0	6
1980	KC-A	0	14	0	1	.000	13	5.32	22	5	8	37	2	0	0	0
1981	Chi-N	0	30	0	1	.000	11	2.28	43 1/3	24	15	43	2	0	0	1
Career Average		0	33	3	3	.509	19	3.31	53	30	16	52	4	0	0	7
Yankee Average		**0**	**8**	**2**	**1**	**.667**	**9**	**3.28**	**24 2/3**	**13**	**4**	**22**	**2**	**0**	**0**	**0**
Career Total		1	326	28	27	.509	193	3.31	525	295	156	519	38	0	0	68
Yankee Total		**0**	**8**	**2**	**1**	**.667**	**9**	**3.28**	**24 2/3**	**13**	**4**	**22**	**2**	**0**	**0**	**0**

Edwards, Foster Hamilton (Eddie)

HEIGHT: 6'3" RIGHTHANDER BORN: 9/1/1903 HOLSTEIN, IOWA DIED: 1/4/1980 ORLEANS, MASSACHUSETTS

YEAR	TEAM	STARTS	GAMES	WON	LOST	PCT	ER	ERA	INNINGS PITCHED	STRIKE-OUTS	WALKS	HITS ALLOWED	HRS ALLOWED	COMP. GAMES	SHUT-OUTS	SAVES
1925	Bos-N	0	1	0	0	—	2	9.00	2	1	1	6	0	0	0	0
1926	Bos-N	3	3	2	0	1.000	2	0.72	25	4	13	20	0	1	0	0
1927	Bos-N	11	29	2	8	.666	51	4.99	92	37	45	95	2	1	0	0
1928	Bos-N	3	21	2	1	.667	31	5.66	49 1/3	17	23	67	2	2	0	0
1930	**NY-A**	**0**	**2**	**0**	**0**	**—**	**4**	**21.61**	**1 2/3**	**1**	**2**	**5**	**0**	**0**	**0**	**0**
Career Average		3	11	1	2	.400	18	4.76	34	12	17	39	1	1	0	0
Yankee Average		**0**	**2**	**0**	**0**	**—**	**4**	**21.61**	**1 2/3**	**1**	**2**	**5**	**0**	**0**	**0**	**0**
Career Total		17	56	6	9	.400	90	4.76	170	60	84	193	4	4	0	0
Yankee Total		**0**	**2**	**0**	**0**	**—**	**4**	**21.61**	**1 2/3**	**1**	**2**	**5**	**0**	**0**	**0**	**0**

Eiland, David William

HEIGHT: 6'3" RIGHTHANDER BORN: 7/5/1966 DADE CITY, FLORIDA

YEAR	TEAM	STARTS	GAMES	WON	LOST	PCT	ER	ERA	INNINGS PITCHED	STRIKE-OUTS	WALKS	HITS ALLOWED	HRS ALLOWED	COMP. GAMES	SHUT-OUTS	SAVES
1988	**NY-A**	**3**	**3**	**0**	**0**	**—**	**9**	**6.40**	**12 2/3**	**7**	**4**	**15**	**6**	**0**	**0**	**0**
1989	**NY-A**	**6**	**6**	**1**	**3**	**.667**	**22**	**5.77**	**34 1/3**	**11**	**13**	**44**	**5**	**0**	**0**	**0**
1990	**NY-A**	**5**	**5**	**2**	**1**	**.667**	**12**	**3.56**	**30 1/3**	**16**	**5**	**31**	**2**	**0**	**0**	**0**
1991	**NY-A**	**13**	**18**	**2**	**5**	**.667**	**43**	**5.33**	**72 2/3**	**18**	**23**	**87**	**10**	**0**	**0**	**0**
1992	SD-N	7	7	0	2	.000	17	5.67	27	10	5	33	1	0	0	0
1993	SD-N	9	10	0	3	.000	28	5.21	48 1/3	14	17	58	5	0	0	0
1995	**NY-A**	**1**	**4**	**1**	**1**	**.500**	**7**	**6.30**	**10**	**6**	**3**	**16**	**1**	**0**	**0**	**0**
1998	TB-A	1	1	0	1	.000	6	27.00	2	1	3	6	0	0	0	0
1999	TB-A	15	21	4	8	.333	50	5.63	80	53	27	98	8	0	0	0
2000	TB-A	10	17	2	3	.400	44	7.24	54 2/3	17	18	77	8	0	0	0
Career Average		7	9	1	3	.308	24	5.74	37	15	12	47	5	0	0	0
Yankee Average		**6**	**7**	**1**	**2**	**.375**	**19**	**5.23**	**32**	**12**	**10**	**39**	**5**	**0**	**0**	**0**
Career Total		70	92	12	27	.308	238	5.74	373	153	118	465	46	0	0	0
Yankee Total		**28**	**36**	**6**	**10**	**.375**	**93**	**5.23**	**160**	**58**	**48**	**193**	**24**	**0**	**0**	**0**

Einerston, Darrell Lee

HEIGHT: 6'2" RIGHTHANDER BORN: 9/4/1972 RHINELANDER, WISCONSIN

YEAR	TEAM	STARTS	GAMES	WON	LOST	PCT	ER	ERA	INNINGS PITCHED	STRIKE-OUTS	WALKS	HITS ALLOWED	HRS ALLOWED	COMP. GAMES	SHUT-OUTS	SAVES
2000	**NY-Y**	**0**	**11**	**0**	**0**	**—**	**5**	**3.55**	**12 2/3**	**3**	**4**	**16**	**1**	**0**	**0**	**0**
Career Average		0	11	0	0	—	5	3.55	12 2/3	3	4	16	1	0	0	0
Yankee Average		**0**	**11**	**0**	**0**	**—**	**5**	**3.55**	**12 2/3**	**3**	**4**	**16**	**1**	**0**	**0**	**0**
Career Total		0	11	0	0	—	5	3.55	12 2/3	3	4	16	1	0	0	0
Yankee Total		**0**	**11**	**0**	**0**	**—**	**5**	**3.55**	**12 2/3**	**3**	**4**	**16**	**1**	**0**	**0**	**0**

Ellis, Dock Phillip

HEIGHT: 6'3" RIGHTHANDER BORN: 3/11/1945 LOS ANGELES, CALIFORNIA

YEAR	TEAM	STARTS	GAMES	WON	LOST	PCT	ER	ERA	INNINGS PITCHED	STRIKE-OUTS	WALKS	HITS ALLOWED	HRS ALLOWED	COMP. GAMES	SHUT-OUTS	SAVES
1968	Pit-N	10	26	6	5	.545	29	2.51	104	52	38	82	4	2	0	0
1969	Pit-N	33	35	11	17	.393	87	3.58	218 2/3	173	76	206	14	8	2	0
1970	Pit-N	30	30	13	10	.565	72	3.21	201 2/3	128	87	194	9	9	4	0

(continued)

(continued)

YEAR	TEAM	STARTS	GAMES	WON	LOST	PCT	ER	ERA	INNINGS PITCHED	STRIKE-OUTS	WALKS	HITS ALLOWED	HRS ALLOWED	COMP. GAMES	SHUT-OUTS	SAVES
1971	Pit-N	31	31	19	9	.679	77	3.06	226 2/3	137	63	207	15	11	2	0
1972	Pit-N	25	25	15	7	.682	49	2.70	163 1/3	96	33	156	6	4	1	0
1973	Pit-N	28	28	12	14	.462	65	3.05	192	122	55	176	7	3	1	0
1974	Pit-N	26	26	12	9	.571	62	3.16	176 2/3	91	41	163	13	9	0	0
1975	Pit-N	24	27	8	9	.471	59	3.79	140	69	43	163	9	5	2	0
1976	**NY-A**	**32**	**32**	**17**	**8**	**.680**	**75**	**3.19**	**211 2/3**	**65**	**76**	**195**	**14**	**8**	**1**	**0**
1977	**NY-A**	**3**	**3**	**1**	**1**	**.500**	**4**	**1.83**	**19 2/3**	**5**	**8**	**18**	**1**	**1**	**0**	**0**
1977	Oak-A	7	7	1	5	.167	28	9.69	26	11	14	35	5	1	0	0
1977	Tex-A	22	23	10	6	.625	54	2.90	167 1/3	96	42	158	13	7	1	1
1978	Tex-A	22	22	9	7	.563	66	4.20	141 1/3	45	46	131	15	3	0	1
1979	Tex-A	9	10	1	5	.167	31	5.98	46 2/3	10	16	64	15	3	0	0
1979	NY-N	14	17	3	7	.300	57	6.04	85	41	34	110	5	0	0	0
1979	Pit-N	1	3	0	0	—	2	2.57	7	1	2	9	1	0	0	0
Career Average		20	22	9	7	.537	51	3.46	133	71	42	129	9	4	1	0
Yankee Average		**18**	**18**	**9**	**5**	**.667**	**40**	**3.07**	**116**	**35**	**42**	**107**	**8**	**5**	**1**	**0**
Career Total		317	345	138	119	.537	817	3.46	2128	1136	674	2067	140	71	14	1
Yankee Total		**35**	**35**	**18**	**9**	**.667**	**79**	**3.07**	**231**	**70**	**84**	**213**	**15**	**9**	**1**	**0**

Embree, Charles Willard (Red)

HEIGHT: 6'0"   RIGHTHANDER   BORN: 8/30/1917 ELMONTE, CALIFORNIA   DIED: 9/24/1996 EUGENE, OREGON

YEAR	TEAM	STARTS	GAMES	WON	LOST	PCT	ER	ERA	INNINGS PITCHED	STRIKE-OUTS	WALKS	HITS ALLOWED	HRS ALLOWED	COMP. GAMES	SHUT-OUTS	SAVES
1941	Cle-A	1	1	0	1	.000	3	6.75	4	4	3	7	0	0	0	0
1942	Cle-A	6	19	3	4	.429	27	3.86	63	44	31	58	0	2	0	0
1944	Cle-A	1	3	0	1	.000	5	13.50	3 1/3	4	5	2	0	0	0	0
1945	Cle-A	8	8	4	4	.500	15	1.93	70	42	26	56	3	5	0	0
1946	Cle-A	26	28	8	12	.400	77	3.47	200	87	79	170	15	8	0	0
1947	Cle-A	21	27	8	10	.444	57	3.15	162 2/3	56	67	137	13	6	0	0
1948	**NY-A**	**8**	**20**	**5**	**3**	**.625**	**32**	**3.76**	**76 2/3**	**25**	**30**	**77**	**6**	**4**	**0**	**0**
1949	StL-A	19	35	3	13	.188	76	5.37	127 1/3	24	89	146	13	4	0	1
Career Average		11	18	4	6	.392	37	3.72	88	36	41	82	6	4	0	0
Yankee Average		**8**	**20**	**5**	**3**	**.625**	**32**	**3.76**	**76 2/3**	**25**	**30**	**77**	**6**	**4**	**0**	**0**
Career Total		90	141	31	48	.392	292	3.72	707	286	330	653	50	29	1	1
Yankee Total		**8**	**20**	**5**	**3**	**.625**	**32**	**3.76**	**76 2/3**	**25**	**30**	**77**	**6**	**4**	**0**	**0**

Enright, Jackson Percy

HEIGHT: 5'11"   RIGHTHANDER   BORN: 11/29/1895 FORT WORTH, TEXAS   DIED: 8/17/1975 POMPANO BEACH, FLORIDA

YEAR	TEAM	STARTS	GAMES	WON	LOST	PCT	ER	ERA	INNINGS PITCHED	STRIKE-OUTS	WALKS	HITS ALLOWED	HRS ALLOWED	COMP. GAMES	SHUT-OUTS	SAVES
1917	NY-A	1	1	0	1	.000	3	5.40	5	1	3	5	0	0	0	0
Career Average		1	1	0	1	.000	3	5.40	5	1	3	5	0	0	0	0
Yankee Average		**1**	**1**	**0**	**1**	**.000**	**3**	**5.40**	**5**	**1**	**3**	**5**	**0**	**0**	**0**	**0**
Career Total		1	1	0	1	.000	3	5.40	5	1	3	5	0	0	0	0
Yankee Total		**1**	**1**	**0**	**1**	**.000**	**3**	**5.40**	**5**	**1**	**3**	**5**	**0**	**0**	**0**	**0**

Erdos, Todd Michael

HEIGHT: 6'1"   RIGHTHANDER   BORN: 11/21/1973 WASHINGTON, PENNSYLVANIA

YEAR	TEAM	STARTS	GAMES	WON	LOST	PCT	ER	ERA	INNINGS PITCHED	STRIKE-OUTS	WALKS	HITS ALLOWED	HRS ALLOWED	COMP. GAMES	SHUT-OUTS	SAVES
1997	SD-N	0	11	2	0	1.000	8	5.27	13 2/3	13	4	17	1	0	0	0
1998	**NY-A**	**0**	**2**	**0**	**0**	**—**	**2**	**9.00**	**2**	**0**	**1**	**5**	**0**	**0**	**0**	**0**
1999	**NY-A**	**0**	**4**	**0**	**0**	**—**	**3**	**3.86**	**7**	**4**	**4**	**5**	**0**	**0**	**0**	**0**
2000	**NY-A**	**1**	**14**	**0**	**0**	**—**	**14**	**5.04**	**25**	**18**	**11**	**31**	**2**	**0**	**0**	**1**
2000	SD-N	0	22	0	0	—	22	6.67	29 2/3	16	17	32	5	0	0	1
Career Average		0	11	0	0	1.000	10	5.70	15	10	7	18	2	0	0	0
Yankee Average		**0**	**7**	**0**	**0**	**—**	**6**	**5.03**	**11**	**7**	**5**	**14**	**1**	**0**	**0**	**0**
Career Total		1	53	2	0	1.000	49	5.70	77	51	37	90	10	0	0	2
Yankee Total		**1**	**20**	**0**	**0**	**—**	**19**	**5.03**	**34**	**22**	**16**	**41**	**4**	**0**	**0**	**1**

Erickson, Roger Farrell

HEIGHT: 6'3" RIGHTHANDER BORN: 8/30/1956 °SPRINGFIELD, ILLINOIS

YEAR	TEAM	STARTS	GAMES	WON	LOST	PCT	ER	ERA	INNINGS PITCHED	STRIKE-OUTS	WALKS	HITS ALLOWED	HRS ALLOWED	COMP. GAMES	SHUT-OUTS	SAVES
1978	Min-A	37	37	14	13	.519	117	3.96	265 2/3	121	79	268	19	14	0	0
1979	Min-A	21	24	3	10	.666	77	5.63	123	47	48	154	17	7	0	0
1980	Min-A	27	32	7	13	.350	69	3.25	191 1/3	97	56	198	13	1	0	0
1981	Min-A	14	14	3	8	.667	39	3.84	91 1/3	44	31	93	7	2	0	0
1982	Min-A	7	7	4	3	.571	22	4.87	40 2/3	12	12	56	6	0	0	1
1982	**NY-A**	**11**	**16**	**4**	**5**	**.444**	**35**	**4.46**	**70 2/3**	**37**	**17**	**86**	**5**	**0**	**0**	**0**
1983	**NY-A**	**0**	**5**	**0**	**1**	**.000**	**8**	**4.32**	**16 2/3**	**7**	**8**	**13**	**1**	**0**	**0**	**0**
Career Average		17	19	5	8	.398	52	4.13	114	52	36	124	10	3	0	0
Yankee Average		**6**	**11**	**2**	**3**	**.400**	**22**	**4.43**	**44**	**22**	**13**	**50**	**3**	**0**	**0**	**1**
Career Total		117	135	35	53	.398	367	4.13	799	365	251	868	68	24	0	1
Yankee Total		**11**	**21**	**4**	**6**	**.400**	**43**	**4.43**	**87**	**44**	**25**	**99**	**6**	**0**	**0**	**1**

Espinoza, Alvaro Alberto

HEIGHT: 6'0" RIGHTHANDER BORN: 2/19/1962 VALENCIA, VENEZUELA

YEAR	TEAM	STARTS	GAMES	WON	LOST	PCT	ER	ERA	INNINGS PITCHED	STRIKE-OUTS	WALKS	HITS ALLOWED	HRS ALLOWED	COMP. GAMES	SHUT-OUTS	SAVES
1991	**NY-A**	**0**	**1**	**0**	**0**	**—**	**0**	**0.00**	**2/3**	**0**	**0**	**0**	**0**	**0**	**0**	**0**
Career Average		0	1	0	0	—	0	0.00	2/3	0	0	0	0	0	0	0
Yankee Average		**0**	**1**	**0**	**0**	**—**	**0**	**0.00**	**2/3**	**0**	**0**	**0**	**0**	**0**	**0**	**0**
Career Total		0	1	0	0	—	0	0.00	2/3	0	0	0	0	0	0	0
Yankee Total		**0**	**1**	**0**	**0**	**—**	**0**	**0.00**	**2/3**	**0**	**0**	**0**	**0**	**0**	**0**	**0**

Farr, Steven Michael

HEIGHT: 5'11" RIGHTHANDER BORN: 12/12/1956 CHEVERLY, MARYLAND

YEAR	TEAM	STARTS	GAMES	WON	LOST	PCT	ER	ERA	INNINGS PITCHED	STRIKE-OUTS	WALKS	HITS ALLOWED	HRS ALLOWED	COMP. GAMES	SHUT-OUTS	SAVES
1984	Cle-A	16	31	3	11	.666	59	4.58	116	83	46	106	14	0	0	1
1985	KC-A	3	16	2	1	.667	13	3.11	37 2/3	36	20	34	2	0	0	8
1986	KC-A	0	56	8	4	.667	38	3.13	109 1/3	83	39	90	10	0	0	1
1987	KC-A	0	47	4	3	.571	42	4.15	91	88	44	97	9	0	0	20
1988	KC-A	1	62	5	4	.556	23	2.50	82 2/3	72	30	74	5	0	0	18
1989	KC-A	2	51	2	5	.667	29	4.12	63 1/3	56	22	75	5	0	0	1
1990	KC-A	6	57	13	7	.650	28	1.98	127	94	48	99	6	1	1	23
1991	**NY-A**	**0**	**60**	**5**	**5**	**.500**	**17**	**2.19**	**70**	**60**	**20**	**57**	**4**	**0**	**0**	**30**
1992	**NY-A**	**0**	**50**	**2**	**2**	**.500**	**9**	**1.56**	**52**	**37**	**19**	**34**	**2**	**0**	**0**	**25**
1993	**NY-A**	**0**	**49**	**2**	**2**	**.500**	**22**	**4.21**	**47**	**39**	**28**	**44**	**8**	**0**	**0**	**4**
1994	Cle-A	0	19	1	1	.500	9	5.40	15 1/3	12	15	17	3	0	0	0
1994	Bos-A	0	11	1	0	1.000	9	6.23	13	8	3	24	2	0	0	11
Career Average		2	42	4	4	.516	25	3.25	69	56	28	63	6	0	0	26
Yankee Average		**0**	**53**	**3**	**3**	**.500**	**16**	**2.56**	**56**	**45**	**22**	**45**	**5**	**0**	**0**	**26**
Career Total		28	509	48	45	.516	298	3.25	824	668	334	751	70	1	1	132
Yankee Total		**0**	**159**	**9**	**9**	**.500**	**48**	**2.56**	**169**	**136**	**67**	**135**	**14**	**0**	**0**	**78**

Ferguson, James Alexander

HEIGHT: 6'0" RIGHTHANDER BORN: 2/16/1897 MONTCLAIR, NEW JERSEY DIED: 4/26/1976 SEPULVEDA, CALIFORNIA

YEAR	TEAM	STARTS	GAMES	WON	LOST	PCT	ER	ERA	INNINGS PITCHED	STRIKE-OUTS	WALKS	HITS ALLOWED	HRS ALLOWED	COMP. GAMES	SHUT-OUTS	SAVES
1918	**NY-A**	**0**	**1**	**0**	**0**	**—**	**0**	**0.00**	**1 2/3**	**1**	**2**	**2**	**0**	**0**	**0**	**0**
1921	**NY-A**	**4**	**17**	**3**	**1**	**.750**	**37**	**5.91**	**56 1/3**	**9**	**27**	**64**	**4**	**1**	**0**	**1**
1922	Bos-A	27	39	9	16	.360	95	4.31	198 1/3	44	62	201	5	10	1	2
1923	Bos-A	27	34	9	13	.409	89	4.04	198 1/3	72	67	229	5	11	0	2
1924	Bos-A	32	41	14	17	.452	100	3.79	237 2/3	78	108	259	6	15	0	1
1925	Bos-A	4	5	0	2	.000	19	10.92	15 2/3	5	5	22	6	0	0	1
1925	**NY-A**	**5**	**21**	**4**	**2**	**.667**	**47**	**7.79**	**54 1/3**	**20**	**42**	**83**	**2**	**3**	**0**	**0**
1925	Was-A	6	7	5	1	.833	20	3.25	55 1/3	24	23	52	2	3	0	1
1926	Was-A	4	19	3	4	.429	41	7.74	47 2/3	16	18	69	4	0	0	0
1927	Phi-N	31	31	8	16	.333	122	4.84	227	73	65	280	15	16	1	2
1928	Phi-N	19	34	5	10	.333	88	5.88	134 2/3	51	52	168	14	5	0	0
1929	Phi-N	4	5	1	2	.333	17	12.08	12 2/3	3	10	19	2	1	0	0
1929	Bro-N	3	3	0	1	.000	5	22.50	2	1	1	7	2	0	0	0

(continued)

(continued)

Career Average	13	20	5	7	.418	52	4.93	96	31	37	112	5	5	0	1
Yankee Average	**3**	**13**	**2**	**1**	**.700**	**28**	**6.73**	**37**	**10**	**24**	**50**	**2**	**0**	**0**	**1**
Career Total	166	257	61	85	.418	680	4.93	1242	397	482	1455	68	62	2	10
Yankee Total	**9**	**39**	**7**	**3**	**.700**	**84**	**6.73**	**112**	**30**	**71**	**149**	**7**	**1**	**0**	**2**

Ferrell, Wesley Cheek

HEIGHT: 6'2"   RIGHTHANDER   BORN: 2/2/1908 GREENSBORO, NORTH CAROLINA   DIED: 12/9/1976 SARASOTA, FLORIDA

YEAR	TEAM	STARTS	GAMES	WON	LOST	PCT	ER	ERA	INNINGS PITCHED	STRIKE-OUTS	WALKS	HITS ALLOWED	HRS ALLOWED	COMP. GAMES	SHUT-OUTS	SAVES
1927	Cle-A	0	1	0	0	—	3	27.00	1	0	2	3	0	0	0	0
1928	Cle-A	2	2	0	2	.000	4	2.25	16	4	5	15	0	1	0	0
1929	Cle-A	25	43	21	10	.677	97	3.60	242 2/3	100	109	256	7	18	1	5
1930	Cle-A	35	43	25	13	.658	109	3.31	296 2/3	143	106	299	14	25	1	3
1931	Cle-A	35	40	22	12	.647	115	3.75	276 1/3	123	130	276	9	27	2	3
1932	Cle-A	34	38	23	13	.639	117	3.66	287 2/3	105	104	299	17	26	3	1
1933	Cle-A	26	28	11	12	.478	94	4.21	201	41	70	225	8	16	1	0
1934	Bos-A	23	26	14	5	.737	73	3.63	181	67	49	205	4	17	3	1
1935	Bos-A	38	41	25	14	.641	126	3.52	322 1/3	110	108	336	16	31	3	0
1936	Bos-A	38	39	20	15	.571	140	4.19	301	106	119	330	11	28	3	0
1937	Was-A	24	25	11	13	.458	91	3.94	207 2/3	92	88	214	11	21	0	0
1937	Bos-A	11	12	3	6	.333	62	7.61	73 1/3	31	34	111	14	5	0	0
1938	**NY-A**	**4**	**5**	**2**	**2**	**.500**	**27**	**8.10**	**30**	**7**	**18**	**52**	**6**	**1**	**0**	**0**
1938	Was-A	22	23	13	8	.619	98	5.92	149	36	68	193	12	9	0	0
1939	**NY-A**	**3**	**3**	**1**	**2**	**.333**	**10**	**4.66**	**19 1/3**	**6**	**17**	**14**	**2**	**1**	**0**	**0**
1940	Bro-N	0	1	0	0	—	3	6.75	4	4	4	4	0	0	0	0
1941	Bos-N	3	4	2	1	.667	8	5.14	14	10	9	13	1	1	0	0
Career Average	19	22	11	8	.601	69	4.04	154	58	61	167	8	13	1	1
Yankee Average	**4**	**4**	**2**	**2**	**.429**	**19**	**6.75**	**25**	**7**	**18**	**33**	**4**	**1**	**0**	**0**
Career Total	323	374	193	128	.601	1177	4.04	2623	985	1040	2845	132	227	17	13
Yankee Total	**7**	**8**	**3**	**4**	**.429**	**37**	**6.75**	**49**	**13**	**35**	**66**	**8**	**2**	**0**	**0**

Ferrick, Thomas Jerome

HEIGHT: 6'2"   RIGHTHANDER   BORN: 1/6/1915 NEW YORK, NEW YORK   DIED: 10/15/1966 LIMA, PENNSYLVANIA

YEAR	TEAM	STARTS	GAMES	WON	LOST	PCT	ER	ERA	INNINGS PITCHED	STRIKE-OUTS	WALKS	HITS ALLOWED	HRS ALLOWED	COMP. GAMES	SHUT-OUTS	SAVES
1941	Phi-A	4	36	8	10	.444	50	3.77	119 1/3	30	33	130	8	2	1	7
1942	Cle-A	2	31	3	2	.600	18	1.99	81 1/3	28	32	56	3	2	0	3
1946	Cle-A	0	9	0	0	—	10	5.00	18	9	4	25	3	0	0	1
1946	StL-A	1	25	4	1	.800	10	2.78	32 1/3	13	5	26	1	0	0	5
1947	Was-A	0	31	1	7	.125	21	3.15	60	23	20	57	1	0	0	9
1948	Was-A	0	37	2	5	.667	34	4.15	73 2/3	34	38	75	3	0	0	10
1949	StL-A	0	50	6	4	.600	45	3.88	104 1/3	34	41	102	9	0	0	6
1950	StL-A	0	16	1	3	.667	11	4.13	24	6	7	24	2	0	0	2
1950	**NY-A**	**0**	**30**	**8**	**4**	**.667**	**23**	**3.65**	**56 2/3**	**20**	**22**	**49**	**5**	**0**	**0**	**9**
1951	**NY-A**	**0**	**9**	**1**	**1**	**.500**	**10**	**7.50**	**12**	**3**	**7**	**21**	**4**	**0**	**0**	**1**
1951	Was-A	0	22	2	0	1.000	11	2.38	41 2/3	17	7	36	3	0	0	2
1952	Was-A	0	27	4	3	.571	17	3.02	50 2/3	28	11	53	2	0	0	1
Career Average	1	27	3	3	.500	22	3.47	56	20	19	55	4	0	0	5
Yankee Average	**0**	**20**	**5**	**3**	**.643**	**17**	**4.33**	**34**	**12**	**15**	**35**	**5**	**0**	**0**	**5**
Career Total	7	323	40	40	.500	260	3.47	674	245	227	654	44	4	1	56
Yankee Total	**0**	**39**	**9**	**5**	**.643**	**33**	**4.33**	**69**	**23**	**29**	**70**	**9**	**0**	**0**	**10**

Figueroa, Eduardo BORN EDUARDO FIGUEROA (PADILLA)

HEIGHT: 6'1"   RIGHTHANDER   BORN: 10/14/1948 CIALES, PUERTO RICO

YEAR	TEAM	STARTS	GAMES	WON	LOST	PCT	ER	ERA	INNINGS PITCHED	STRIKE-OUTS	WALKS	HITS ALLOWED	HRS ALLOWED	COMP. GAMES	SHUT-OUTS	SAVES
1974	Cal-A	12	25	2	8	.666	43	3.67	105 1/3	49	36	119	3	5	1	0
1975	Cal-A	32	33	16	13	.552	79	2.91	244 2/3	139	84	213	14	16	2	0
1976	**NY-A**	**34**	**34**	**19**	**10**	**.655**	**86**	**3.02**	**256 2/3**	**119**	**94**	**237**	**13**	**14**	**4**	**0**
1977	**NY-A**	**32**	**32**	**16**	**11**	**.593**	**95**	**3.57**	**239 1/3**	**104**	**75**	**228**	**19**	**12**	**2**	**0**
1978	**NY-A**	**35**	**35**	**20**	**9**	**.690**	**84**	**2.99**	**253**	**92**	**77**	**233**	**22**	**12**	**2**	**0**
1979	**NY-A**	**16**	**16**	**4**	**6**	**.400**	**48**	**4.13**	**104 2/3**	**42**	**35**	**109**	**6**	**4**	**1**	**0**
1980	**NY-A**	**9**	**15**	**3**	**3**	**.500**	**45**	**6.98**	**58**	**16**	**24**	**90**	**3**	**0**	**0**	**1**
1980	Tex-A	8	8	0	7	.000	26	5.90	39 2/3	9	12	62	9	0	0	0
1981	Oak-A	1	2	0	0	—	5	5.40	8 1/3	1	6	8	1	0	0	0

(continued)

Eduardo "Ed" Figueroa, rhp, 1976–80

The temperamental Figueroa was an integral part of the Yankees' three championship teams in the late 1970s.

Born in Ciales, Puerto Rico, on October 14, 1948, Figueroa came up to the big leagues in 1974 as a spot starter for the California Angels. He struggled that year to a 2-8 record, but bounced back with a solid 16-13 season in 1975.

Figueroa and center fielder Mickey Rivers came over to the Yankees in a trade for outfielder Bobby Bonds in 1976.

From 1976 to 1978, Figueroa was New York's most consistent starting pitcher. He led the Yankee staff in wins with 19 in 1976 and with 16 in 1977. In the injury-riddled season of 1978, he and Ron Guidry started a combined 70 games and won 45 games between them. Although Guidry rightly gets considerable credit for keeping the Yankees at least within striking distance of the Red Sox in that comeback year, it is worth noting that Figueroa was also extremely durable that season.

In 1978, Figueroa also became the first native-born Puerto Rican to win 20 games in a season in the major leagues. He did so on the next-to-last game of the season, a 7-0 win over the Indians. He had had a chance to win 20 again in 1976 on the last day of the season, but a rainout canceled the game.

For all his consistency in the regular season, Figueroa was not as fortunate in the postseason. He was 0-2 for the Yankees in the league championship series over three years and 0-2 in the World Series.

In 1979, Figueroa underwent elbow surgery and his effectiveness declined. He was 7-9 for New York over the next two seasons, and was traded to Texas midway through 1980. There, he continued to struggle, going 0-7 for the Rangers.

Figueroa played briefly in Oakland the next year before retiring from the major leagues. However, he continued to pitch in Mexico for several years after that.

(continued)

Career Average	20	22	9	7	.544	57	3.51	146	63	49	144	10	7	1	0
Yankee Average	**25**	**26**	**12**	**8**	**.614**	**72**	**3.53**	**182**	**75**	**61**	**179**	**13**	**8**	**2**	**0**
Career Total	179	200	80	67	.544	511	3.51	1310	571	443	1299	90	63	12	1
Yankee Total	**126**	**132**	**62**	**39**	**.614**	**358**	**3.53**	**912**	**373**	**305**	**897**	**63**	**42**	**9**	**1**

Filson, William Peter

HEIGHT: 6'2" LEFTHANDER BORN: 9/28/1958 DARBY, PENNSYLVANIA

YEAR	TEAM	STARTS	GAMES	WON	LOST	PCT	ER	ERA	INNINGS PITCHED	STRIKE- OUTS	WALKS	HITS ALLOWED	HRS ALLOWED	COMP. GAMES	SHUT- OUTS	SAVES
1982	Min-A	3	5	0	2	.000	12	8.76	12 1/3	10	8	17	2	0	0	0
1983	Min-A	8	26	4	1	.800	34	3.40	90	49	29	87	9	0	0	1
1984	Min-A	7	55	6	5	.545	54	4.10	118 2/3	59	54	106	14	0	0	1
1985	Min-A	6	40	4	5	.444	39	3.67	95 1/3	42	30	93	13	1	0	2
1986	Min-A	0	4	0	0	—	4	5.68	6 1/3	4	2	13	1	0	0	0
1986	Chi-A	1	3	0	1	.000	8	6.17	11 2/3	4	5	14	4	0	0	0
1987	**NY-A**	**2**	**7**	**1**	**0**	**1.000**	**8**	**3.27**	**22**	**10**	**9**	**26**	**2**	**0**	**0**	**0**
1990	KC-A	7	8	0	4	.000	23	5.91	35	9	13	42	6	0	0	0
Career Average	4	19	2	2	.455	23	4.18	49	23	19	50	6	0	0	1
Yankee Average	**2**	**7**	**1**	**0**	**1.000**	**8**	**3.27**	**22**	**10**	**9**	**26**	**2**	**0**	**0**	**0**
Career Total	34	148	15	18	.455	182	4.18	392	187	150	398	51	1	0	4
Yankee Total	**2**	**7**	**1**	**0**	**1.000**	**8**	**3.27**	**22**	**10**	**9**	**26**	**2**	**0**	**0**	**0**

Finneran, Joseph Ignatius (Happy *or* Smokey Joe)

HEIGHT: 5'11" RIGHTHANDER BORN: 10/29/1891 E. ORANGE, NEW JERSEY DIED: 2/3/1942 ORANGE, NEW JERSEY

YEAR	TEAM	STARTS	GAMES	WON	LOST	PCT	ER	ERA	INNINGS PITCHED	STRIKE- OUTS	WALKS	HITS ALLOWED	HRS ALLOWED	COMP. GAMES	SHUT- OUTS	SAVES
1912	Phi-N	4	14	0	2	.000	13	2.53	46 1/3	10	10	50	2	0	0	1
1913	Phi-N	0	3	0	0	—	4	7.20	5	0	2	12	0	0	0	0

(continued)

(continued)

1914	Bro-F	23	27	12	11	.522	62	3.18	175 1/3	54	60	153	6	13	2	1
1915	Bro-F	24	37	10	12	.455	67	2.80	215 1/3	68	87	197	2	12	1	2
1918	Det-A	2	5	0	2	.000	15	9.88	13 2/3	2	8	22	0	0	0	1
1918	**NY-A**	**13**	**23**	**3**	**6**	**.333**	**48**	**3.78**	**114 1/3**	**34**	**35**	**134**	**0**	**0**	**0**	**0**

Career Average		11	18	4	6	.431	35	3.30	95	28	34	95	3	5	1	1
Yankee Average		**13**	**23**	**3**	**6**	**.333**	**48**	**3.78**	**114 1/3**	**34**	**35**	**134**	**7**	**4**	**0**	**0**

Career Total		66	109	25	33	.431	209	3.30	570	168	202	568	17	29	3	5
Yankee Total		**13**	**23**	**3**	**6**	**.333**	**48**	**3.78**	**114 1/3**	**34**	**35**	**134**	**7**	**4**	**0**	**0**

Fisher, Brian Kevin

HEIGHT: 6'4"   RIGHTHANDER   BORN: 3/18/1962 HONOLULU, HAWAII

YEAR	TEAM	STARTS	GAMES	WON	LOST	PCT	ER	ERA	INNINGS PITCHED	STRIKE-OUTS	WALKS	HITS ALLOWED	HRS ALLOWED	COMP. GAMES	SHUT-OUTS	SAVES
1985	NY-A	0	55	4	4	.500	26	2.38	98 1/3	85	29	77	4	0	0	14
1986	NY-A	0	62	9	5	.643	53	4.93	96 2/3	67	37	105	14	0	0	6
1987	Pit-N	26	37	11	9	.550	93	4.52	185 1/3	117	72	185	27	6	3	0
1988	Pit-N	22	33	8	10	.444	75	4.61	146 1/3	66	57	157	13	1	1	0
1989	Pit-N	3	9	0	3	.000	15	7.94	17	8	10	25	2	0	0	1
1990	Hou-N	0	4	0	0	—	4	7.20	5	1	0	9	1	0	0	1
1992	Sea-A	14	22	4	3	.571	46	4.53	91 1/3	26	47	80	9	0	0	1

Career Average		9	32	5	5	.514	45	4.39	91	53	36	91	10	1	1	3
Yankee Average		**0**	**59**	**7**	**5**	**.591**	**40**	**3.65**	**97**	**76**	**33**	**91**	**9**	**0**	**0**	**10**

Career Total		65	222	36	34	.514	312	4.39	640	370	252	638	70	7	4	23
Yankee Total		**0**	**117**	**13**	**9**	**.591**	**79**	**3.65**	**195**	**152**	**66**	**182**	**18**	**0**	**0**	**20**

Fisher, Ray Lyle (Chic)

HEIGHT: 6'0"   RIGHTHANDER   BORN: 10/4/1887 MIDDLEBURY, VERMONT   DIED: 11/3/1982 ANN ARBOR, MICHIGAN

YEAR	TEAM	STARTS	GAMES	WON	LOST	PCT	ER	ERA	INNINGS PITCHED	STRIKE-OUTS	WALKS	HITS ALLOWED	HRS ALLOWED	COMP. GAMES	SHUT-OUTS	SAVES
1910	NY-A	7	17	5	3	.625	30	2.92	92 1/3	42	18	95	0	3	0	1
1911	NY-A	22	29	10	11	.476	62	3.25	171 2/3	99	55	178	3	8	2	0
1912	NY-A	13	17	2	8	.666	59	5.88	90 1/3	47	32	107	2	5	0	0
1913	NY-A	31	43	12	16	.429	87	3.18	246 1/3	92	71	244	3	14	1	1
1914	NY-A	26	29	10	12	.455	53	2.28	209	86	61	177	2	17	2	1
1915	NY-A	28	30	18	11	.621	63	2.11	247 2/3	97	62	219	7	20	4	1
1916	NY-A	21	31	11	8	.579	63	3.17	179	56	51	191	4	9	1	2
1917	NY-A	18	23	8	9	.471	35	2.19	144	64	43	126	3	12	3	0
1919	Cin-N	20	26	14	5	.737	42	2.17	174 1/3	41	38	141	5	12	5	1
1920	Cin-N	22	33	10	11	.476	61	2.73	201	56	50	189	5	10	1	1

Career Average		21	28	10	9	.515	55	2.82	176	68	48	167	3	11	2	1
Yankee Average		**21**	**27**	**10**	**10**	**.494**	**56**	**2.91**	**173**	**73**	**49**	**167**	**3**	**11**	**2**	**1**

Career Total		208	278	100	94	.515	550	2.82	1756	680	481	1667	34	110	19	7
Yankee Total		**166**	**219**	**76**	**78**	**.494**	**447**	**2.91**	**1380**	**583**	**393**	**1337**	**24**	**88**	**13**	**5**

Fontenot, Silton Ray

HEIGHT: 6'0"   LEFTHANDER   BORN: 8/8/1957 LAKE CHARLES, LOUISIANA

YEAR	TEAM	STARTS	GAMES	WON	LOST	PCT	ER	ERA	INNINGS PITCHED	STRIKE-OUTS	WALKS	HITS ALLOWED	HRS ALLOWED	COMP. GAMES	SHUT-OUTS	SAVES
1983	NY-A	15	15	8	2	.800	36	3.33	97 1/3	27	25	101	3	3	1	0
1984	NY-A	24	35	8	9	.471	68	3.61	169 1/3	85	58	189	8	0	0	0
1985	Chi-N	23	38	6	10	.375	75	4.36	154 2/3	70	45	177	23	0	0	0
1986	Chi-N	0	42	3	5	.375	24	3.86	56	24	21	57	5	0	0	2
1986	Min-A	0	15	0	0	—	18	9.92	16 1/3	10	4	27	3	0	0	0

Career Average		12	29	5	5	.490	44	4.03	99	43	31	110	8	1	0	0
Yankee Average		**19**	**25**	**8**	**6**	**.593**	**52**	**3.51**	**133**	**56**	**42**	**145**	**6**	**2**	**1**	**0**

Career Total		62	145	25	26	.490	221	4.03	494	216	153	551	42	3	1	2
Yankee Total		**39**	**50**	**16**	**11**	**.593**	**104**	**3.51**	**267**	**112**	**83**	**290**	**11**	**3**	**1**	**0**

Edward Charles "Whitey" Ford, lhp, 1950-67

More than just about anyone else in the New York Yankee pantheon, Ed "Whitey" Ford was probably fated to be a Yankee.

He was born on October 21, 1928 in Manhattan, on East Sixty-Sixth Street, between First and Second Avenues. He can recall little of that initial portion of his life, aside from a few early stickball games, because the Ford family moved to the Astoria section of Queens when little Ed was about five years old. In Queens, his father worked as a bartender while his mother worked at a local grocery store.

Ford began his baseball career as an infielder, a first baseman for his high school team, although he did pitch a few ball games in his senior year. In 1946, he attended a tryout at Yankee Stadium as an infielder. Paul Kritchell, then one of the premier Yankee scouts, suggested that Ford might want to try pitching.

It wasn't a sarcastic suggestion. At 5 feet 10 inches, Ford wasn't big. And Kritchell had seen his arm, and thought he might make a better pitcher than an infielder.

Ford accepted the suggestion, and in the summer of 1946, he played in a local sandlot league alternating as a pitcher and a first baseman. He was surprised to learn that he had very good control, and he spent the rest of the summer working on his curveball.

Ford's Queens team won the city sandlot league championship that year, and in the championship game at the Polo Grounds, Ford struck out 16 men and scored the winning run in a 1-0 win over the team from the Bronx.

In September of the same year, Ford was pursued by several teams, including the Red Sox, Giants and Yankees. He admits that while the Yankees were his first choice, he signed with them because in the end they offered him the most money: a $7,000 signing bonus.

Ford stayed in the minors from 1946 to the middle of 1950. Former Yankee hurler Lefty Gomez, by then a minor league coach, gave him his nickname Whitey because of his blond hair.

Ford actually tried to move up to the big club in 1949 by contacting Kritchell (whom he knew better than new Yankee manager Casey Stengel) and urging him to induce Stengel to call him up. It didn't work, but Stengel was impressed by the kid's brass. Stengel was the one who tagged Ford with the nickname, Slick, which was a sarcastic reference to Ford's predilection for having a good time.

(Ford, Mantle and Billy Martin, as well as many other big-leaguers, were not averse to playing a day game and going out on the town afterwards. Stengel called them all "whiskey-slick," which was a term used to describe someone who is drunk but still thinks he's acting sober. Eventually, Mantle and Ford began calling each other "Slick," and the name stuck to Ford more than to Mantle.)

In 1950, Ford made his big-league debut when the Yankees brought him up in late June. After a few stints as a reliever, Stengel started him against the Chicago White Sox. Not only was he cool about his impending debut but Ford spent the morning of the game assuring Stengel that everything would be all right. And, of course, it was. Ford won the game, 4-3, and, in fact, won nine games in a row before dropping his final decision of the year in Philadelphia.

The Yankees won the pennant that year and would face the Philadelphia Phillies in the 1950 World Series.

Ford, Edward Charles (Whitey *or* Chairman of the Board)
HEIGHT: 5'10"   LEFTHANDER   BORN: 10/21/1928 NEW YORK, NEW YORK

YEAR	TEAM	STARTS	GAMES	WON	LOST	PCT	ER	ERA	INNINGS PITCHED	STRIKE-OUTS	WALKS	HITS ALLOWED	HRS ALLOWED	COMP. GAMES	SHUT-OUTS	SAVES
1950	NY-A	12	20	9	1	.900	35	2.81	112	59	52	87	7	7	2	1
1953	NY-A	30	32	18	6	.750	69	3.00	207	110	110	187	13	11	3	0
1954	NY-A	28	34	16	8	.667	66	2.82	210 2/3	125	101	170	10	11	3	1
1955	NY-A	33	39	18	7	.720	74	2.63	253 2/3	137	113	188	20	18	5	2
1956	NY-A	30	31	19	6	.760	62	2.47	225 2/3	141	84	187	13	18	2	1
1957	NY-A	17	24	11	5	.688	37	2.57	129 1/3	84	53	114	10	5	0	0
1958	NY-A	29	30	14	7	.667	49	2.01	219 1/3	145	62	174	14	15	7	1
1959	NY-A	29	35	16	10	.615	69	3.04	204	114	89	194	13	9	2	1

(continued)

The first three games were close, tense pitchers duels, but the Yankees won all three games, 1-0, 2-1 and 3-2. At that point, Stengel tagged Ford to pitch the fourth game. Whitey responded with the same calm, collected approach he brought to his games during the regular season, pitching 8⅔ innings to earn a 5-2 win.

It was an auspicious debut, but Ford's second year with the Yankees would have to wait. He was inducted into the military and missed the entire 1951 and 1952 seasons. His stint in the Army Signal Corps was doubly frustrating for Ford because he was stationed at Fort Monmouth, New Jersey, about 60 miles south of New York—so close he could almost hear the crowd. His one turn on the mound in that time was in April 1951, when the Yankees asked him to throw out the first ball on Opening Day. He did, in his uniform, and the sportswriters covering the game couldn't help but notice how good he looked on the hill.

But Ford was back in 1953, to begin a dozen years of dominance with the club. He projected a remarkable aura of calm. He was, said teammate Jerry Coleman, "the oldest young player I ever saw."

After some initial bouts of wildness in his first three full years he settled down, walking less than three men a game the rest of his career. His win totals in those first years were modest: from 1953 to 1960, he averaged only about 16 wins a year.

But that was because Stengel was careful with him, pitching him every fifth day, which limited his starts to between 32 and 35 annually. When Stengel was replaced by Ralph Houk in 1961, Houk told Ford prior to the season that he would be pitching him every fourth day.

Ford had no problem with it, and for the next five years, he won 99 games for the Yankees, including a league-leading 25 in 1961 and 24 in 1963.

He was not a particularly overpowering pitcher, but he had great control and changed the speeds of his pitches well. His cool manner on the mound moved sportswriters to tag him "the Chairman of the Board." Whitey always looked like he was in charge.

Toward the end of his career, he was very successful at scuffing a ball, or applying a foreign substance to it, to make the ball dance. Ford's justification was that he faced about 10,000 batters in his 16-year career and his job was to get out as many as he could.

He was very tough in the clutch. He won ten World Series games—still a record. He pitched 33 consecutive scoreless innings in the Fall Classic, another record. And Stengel was always quick to remind sportswriters that he saved Ford for the tougher teams in the league whenever he could. Ford never complained. He played in 11 World Series, and the Yankees won six.

In 1964, he began to have arm trouble, limiting his participation in the 1964 World Series to five innings. He was fairly effective in 1965, with a 16-13 record, but that was the last full year, the last good year. He retired in 1967. In 1974, he and teammate Mickey Mantle were elected to the Hall of Fame.

Ford's numbers are great. His 236-106 makes him the Yankees' winningest pitcher, and second in winning percentage (.690) behind Spud Chandler. He won the Cy Young Award in 1961, was the league leader in victories three times, shutouts twice and ERA twice. He leads the Yankees' all-time list in strikeouts with 1,956, shutouts with 45, and ERA with a 2.54 career mark.

Ford worked for several years as a pitching coach for the Yankees following retirement, and has also been a successful businessman.

(continued)

1960	NY-A	29	33	12	9	.571	66	3.08	192⅔	85	65	168	15	8	4	0
1961	NY-A	39	39	25	4	.862	101	3.21	283	209	92	242	23	11	3	0
1962	NY-A	37	38	17	8	.680	83	2.90	257⅔	160	69	243	22	7	0	0
1963	NY-A	37	38	24	7	.774	82	2.74	269⅓	189	56	240	26	13	3	1
1964	NY-A	36	39	17	6	.739	58	2.13	244⅔	172	57	212	10	12	8	1
1965	NY-A	36	37	16	13	.552	88	3.24	244⅓	162	50	241	22	9	2	1
1966	NY-A	9	22	2	5	.667	20	2.47	73	43	24	79	8	0	0	0
1967	NY-A	7	7	2	4	.333	8	1.64	44	21	9	40	2	2	1	0
Career Average		27	31	15	7	.690	60	2.75	198	122	68	173	14	10	3	1
Yankee Average		**27**	**31**	**15**	**7**	**.690**	**60**	**2.75**	**198**	**122**	**68**	**173**	**14**	**10**	**3**	**1**
Career Total		438	498	236	106	.690	967	2.75	3170	1956	1086	2766	228	156	45	10
Yankee Total		**438**	**498**	**236**	**106**	**.690**	**967**	**2.75**	**3170**	**1956**	**1086**	**2766**	**228**	**156**	**45**	**10**

Russell William Ford, rhp, 1909–1913

In his brief career with the Highlanders, Russ Ford was one of the best pitchers in baseball playing for one of the worst teams.

Born in Manitoba, Canada on April 25, 1883, Ford came to the Yankees for a one-game stint in 1909. He was brought up to the big club for good in 1910 and had a terrific year, going 26-6 with a 1.65 ERA. He struck out 209 batters and had eight shutouts.

It was one of the best statistical years any Yankee pitcher has ever had. Only Ron Guidry had more shutouts, nine, in 1978. Only Jack Chesbro's 41 wins in 1904, Al Orth's 27 wins in 1908 and Carl Mays's 27 wins in 1921 topped Ford in that category. And his ERA that year is second, by a hundredth of a point, to Spud Chandler's 1.64 in 1943 in team history.

Like many of his contemporaries, Ford was a master of the doctored pitch. In his case, it was what sportswriters called an "emery ball."

Ford determined, early in his career, that he could make a baseball dance like a snowflake if he scuffed it with emery paper. But while "loading up" baseballs was legal at the turn of last century, filing them into an egg-shaped sphere was not. So Ford explained the ball's English by telling everyone that he was throwing a spitball.

Ford was 22-11 for the Highlanders in 1911, but the New York team had begun to fade, falling to .500 that year. Over the next two years, Ford won 25 games and lost 37 as the Highlanders struggled to stay out of the cellar.

In 1914, Ford jumped to Buffalo of the Federal League. He became the best pitcher in that circuit, once again bewildering hitters with the emery pitch. But Ford began having arm troubles and when the Federal League folded the next year, Ford was one of the players who could not find a job in the major leagues. He played for several years in the minor leagues and died in 1960 in Rockingham, North Carolina.

Ford, Russell William

HEIGHT: 5'11" RIGHTHANDER BORN: 4/25/1883 BRANDON, MANITOBA, CANADA DIED: 1/24/1960 ROCKINGHAM, NORTH CAROLINA

YEAR	TEAM	STARTS	GAMES	WON	LOST	PCT	ER	ERA	INNINGS PITCHED	STRIKE-OUTS	WALKS	HITS ALLOWED	HRS ALLOWED	COMP. GAMES	SHUT-OUTS	SAVES
1909	NY-A	0	1	0	0	—	3	9.00	3	2	4	4	0	0	0	0
1910	NY-A	33	36	26	6	.813	55	1.65	299 2/3	209	70	194	4	29	8	1
1911	NY-A	33	37	22	11	.667	71	2.27	281 1/3	158	76	251	3	26	1	0
1912	NY-A	35	36	13	21	.382	115	3.55	291 2/3	112	79	317	10	30	0	0
1913	NY-A	28	33	12	18	.400	70	2.66	237	72	58	244	9	15	1	2
1914	Buf-F	26	35	21	6	.778	50	1.82	247 1/3	123	41	190	11	19	5	6
1915	Buf-F	15	21	5	9	.357	64	4.52	127 1/3	34	48	140	7	7	0	0
Career Average		24	28	14	10	.582	61	2.59	212	101	54	191	6	18	2	1
Yankee Average		**26**	**29**	**15**	**11**	**.566**	**63**	**2.54**	**223**	**111**	**57**	**202**	**5**	**20**	**2**	**1**
Career Total		170	199	99	71	.582	428	2.59	1487	710	376	1340	44	126	15	9
Yankee Total		**129**	**143**	**73**	**56**	**.566**	**314**	**2.54**	**1113**	**553**	**287**	**1010**	**26**	**100**	**10**	**3**

Fossas, Emilio Antonio (Tony) BORN EMILIO ANTONIO FOSSAS (MOREJON)

HEIGHT: 6'0" LEFTHANDER BORN: 9/23/1957 HAVANA, CUBA

YEAR	TEAM	STARTS	GAMES	WON	LOST	PCT	ER	ERA	INNINGS PITCHED	STRIKE-OUTS	WALKS	HITS ALLOWED	HRS ALLOWED	COMP. GAMES	SHUT-OUTS	SAVES
1988	Tex-A	0	5	0	0	—	3	4.77	5 2/3	0	2	11	0	0	0	0
1989	Mil-A	0	51	2	2	.500	24	3.54	61	42	22	57	3	0	0	1
1990	Mil-A	0	32	2	3	.400	21	6.44	29 1/3	24	10	44	5	0	0	0
1991	Bos-A	0	64	3	2	.600	22	3.47	57	29	28	49	3	0	0	1
1992	Bos-A	0	60	1	2	.333	8	2.43	29 2/3	19	14	31	1	0	0	2
1993	Bos-A	0	71	1	1	.500	23	5.18	40	39	15	38	4	0	0	0
1994	Bos-A	0	44	2	0	1.000	18	4.76	34	31	15	35	6	0	0	1
1995	StL-N	0	58	3	0	1.000	6	1.50	36 2/3	40	10	28	1	0	0	0
1996	StL-N	0	65	0	4	.000	14	2.68	47	36	21	43	7	0	0	2
1997	StL-N	0	71	2	7	.666	22	3.88	51 2/3	41	26	62	7	0	0	0
1998	Sea-A	0	23	0	3	.000	11	9.00	11 1/3	10	6	19	1	0	0	0
1998	Chi-N	0	8	0	0	—	4	9.00	4	4	6	8	0	0	0	0
1998	Tex-A	0	10	1	0	1.000	0	0.00	7 1/3	7	4	3	0	0	0	0
1999	**NY-A**	0	5	0	0	—	4	36.00	1	0	1	6	1	0	0	0
Career Average		0	41	1	2	.415	13	3.92	30	23	13	31	3	0	0	1
Yankee Average		**0**	**5**	**0**	**0**	**—**	**4**	**36.00**	**1**	**0**	**1**	**6**	**1**	**0**	**0**	**0**
Career Total		0	567	17	24	.415	180	3.92	414	324	180	434	39	0	0	7
Yankee Total		**0**	**5**	**0**	**0**	**—**	**4**	**36.00**	**1**	**0**	**1**	**6**	**1**	**0**	**0**	**0**

Francis, Ray James

HEIGHT: 6'1" LEFTHANDER BORN: 3/8/1893 SHERMAN, TEXAS DIED: 7/6/1934 ATLANTA, GEORGIA

YEAR	TEAM	STARTS	GAMES	WON	LOST	PCT	ER	ERA	INNINGS PITCHED	STRIKE-OUTS	WALKS	HITS ALLOWED	HRS ALLOWED	COMP. GAMES	SHUT-OUTS	SAVES
1922	Was-A	26	39	7	18	.667	107	4.28	225	64	66	265	7	15	2	2
1923	Det-A	6	33	5	8	.385	39	4.42	79 1/3	27	28	95	2	0	0	1
1925	**NY-A**	0	4	0	0	—	4	7.72	4 2/3	1	3	5	0	0	0	0
1925	Bos-A	4	6	0	2	.000	24	7.71	28	4	13	44	3	0	0	0
Career Average		9	21	3	7	.300	44	4.65	84	24	28	102	3	4	1	1
Yankee Average		**0**	**4**	**0**	**0**	**—**	**4**	**7.72**	**4 2/3**	**1**	**3**	**5**	**0**	**0**	**0**	**0**
Career Total		36	82	12	28	.300	174	4.65	337	96	110	409	12	15	2	3
Yankee Total		**0**	**4**	**0**	**0**	**—**	**4**	**7.72**	**4 2/3**	**1**	**3**	**5**	**0**	**0**	**0**	**0**

Frazier, George Allen

HEIGHT: 6'5" RIGHTHANDER BORN: 10/13/1954 OKLAHOMA CITY, OKLAHOMA

YEAR	TEAM	STARTS	GAMES	WON	LOST	PCT	ER	ERA	INNINGS PITCHED	STRIKE-OUTS	WALKS	HITS ALLOWED	HRS ALLOWED	COMP. GAMES	SHUT-OUTS	SAVES
1978	StL-N	0	14	0	3	.000	10	4.09	22	8	6	22	2	0	0	0
1979	StL-N	0	25	2	4	.333	16	4.45	32 1/3	14	12	35	3	0	0	0
1980	StL-N	0	22	1	4	.666	7	2.74	23	11	7	24	2	0	0	3
1981	**NY-A**	0	16	0	1	.000	5	1.63	27 2/3	17	11	26	1	0	0	3
1982	**NY-A**	0	63	4	4	.500	43	3.47	111 2/3	69	39	103	7	0	0	1
1983	**NY-A**	0	61	4	4	.500	44	3.43	115 1/3	78	45	94	5	0	0	8
1984	Cle-A	0	22	3	2	.600	18	3.65	44 1/3	24	14	45	3	0	0	1
1984	Chi-N	0	37	6	3	.667	29	4.10	63 2/3	58	26	53	4	0	0	3
1985	Chi-N	0	51	7	8	.467	54	6.39	76	46	52	88	11	0	0	2
1986	Chi-N	0	35	2	4	.333	31	5.40	51 2/3	41	34	63	5	0	0	0
1986	Min-A	0	15	1	1	.500	13	4.39	26 2/3	25	16	23	2	0	0	6
1987	Min-A	0	54	5	5	.500	45	4.98	81 1/3	58	51	77	9	0	0	2
Career Average		0	35	3	4	.449	26	4.20	56	37	26	54	5	0	0	2
Yankee Average		**0**	**47**	**3**	**3**	**.471**	**31**	**3.25**	**85**	**55**	**32**	**74**	**4**	**0**	**0**	**4**
Career Total		0	415	35	43	.449	315	4.20	676	449	313	653	54	0	0	29
Yankee Total		**0**	**140**	**8**	**9**	**.471**	**92**	**3.25**	**255**	**164**	**95**	**223**	**13**	**0**	**0**	**12**

Freeman, Mark Price
HEIGHT: 6'4" RIGHTHANDER BORN: 12/7/1930 MEMPHIS, TENNESSEE

YEAR	TEAM	STARTS	GAMES	WON	LOST	PCT	ER	ERA	INNINGS PITCHED	STRIKE-OUTS	WALKS	HITS ALLOWED	HRS ALLOWED	COMP. GAMES	SHUT-OUTS	SAVES
1959	**NY-A**	**1**	**1**	**0**	**0**	**—**	**2**	**2.57**	**7**	**4**	**2**	**6**	**0**	**0**	**0**	**0**
1959	KC-A	0	3	0	0	—	4	9.82	3 2/3	1	3	6	0	0	0	0
1960	Chi-N	8	30	3	3	.500	48	5.63	76 2/3	50	33	70	10	1	0	1
Career Average		3	11	1	1	.500	18	5.56	29	18	13	27	3	0	0	0
Yankee Average		**1**	**1**	**0**	**0**	**—**	**2**	**2.57**	**7**	**4**	**2**	**6**	**0**	**0**	**0**	**0**
Career Total		9	34	3	3	.500	54	5.56	87	55	38	82	10	1	0	1
Yankee Total		**1**	**1**	**0**	**0**	**—**	**2**	**2.57**	**7**	**4**	**2**	**6**	**0**	**0**	**0**	**0**

Friend, Robert Bartmess (Warrior)
HEIGHT: 6'0" RIGHTHANDER BORN: 11/24/1930 LAFAYETTE, INDIANA

YEAR	TEAM	STARTS	GAMES	WON	LOST	PCT	ER	ERA	INNINGS PITCHED	STRIKE-OUTS	WALKS	HITS ALLOWED	HRS ALLOWED	COMP. GAMES	SHUT-OUTS	SAVES
1951	Pit-N	22	34	6	10	.375	71	4.27	149 2/3	41	68	173	12	3	1	0
1952	Pit-N	23	35	7	17	.667	86	4.18	185	75	84	186	15	6	1	0
1953	Pit-N	24	32	8	11	.421	93	4.90	170 2/3	66	57	193	18	8	0	0
1954	Pit-N	20	35	7	12	.368	96	5.07	170 1/3	73	58	204	16	4	2	2
1955	Pit-N	20	44	14	9	.609	63	2.83	200 1/3	98	52	178	18	9	2	2
1956	Pit-N	42	49	17	17	.500	121	3.46	314 1/3	166	85	310	25	19	4	3
1957	Pit-N	38	40	14	18	.438	104	3.38	277	143	68	273	28	17	3	0
1958	Pit-N	38	38	22	14	.611	112	3.68	274	135	61	299	25	16	1	0
1959	Pit-N	35	35	8	19	.667	105	4.03	234 2/3	104	52	267	19	7	2	0
1960	Pit-N	37	38	18	12	.600	92	3.00	275 2/3	183	45	266	18	16	4	1
1961	Pit-N	35	41	14	19	.424	101	3.85	236	108	45	271	16	10	1	1
1962	Pit-N	36	39	18	14	.563	89	3.06	261 2/3	144	53	280	23	13	5	1
1963	Pit-N	38	39	17	16	.515	70	2.34	268 2/3	144	44	236	13	12	4	0
1964	Pit-N	35	35	13	18	.419	89	3.33	240 1/3	128	50	253	10	13	3	0
1965	Pit-N	34	34	8	12	.400	80	3.24	222	74	47	221	17	8	2	0
1966	**NY-A**	**8**	**12**	**1**	**4**	**.666**	**24**	**4.84**	**44 2/3**	**22**	**9**	**61**	**2**	**0**	**0**	**0**
1966	NY-N	12	22	5	8	.385	42	4.40	86	30	16	101	11	2	1	1
Career Average		29	35	12	14	.461	85	3.58	212	102	53	222	17	10	2	1
Yankee Average		**8**	**12**	**1**	**4**	**.200**	**24**	**4.84**	**44 2/3**	**22**	**9**	**61**	**2**	**0**	**0**	**0**
Career Total		497	602	197	230	.461	1438	3.58	3611	1734	894	3772	286	163	36	11
Yankee Total		**8**	**12**	**1**	**4**	**.200**	**24**	**4.84**	**44 2/3**	**22**	**9**	**61**	**2**	**0**	**0**	**0**

Frill, John Edmond
HEIGHT: 5'10" LEFTHANDER BORN: 4/3/1879 READING, PENNSYLVANIA DIED: 9/28/1918 WESTERLY, RHODE ISLAND

YEAR	TEAM	STARTS	GAMES	WON	LOST	PCT	ER	ERA	INNINGS PITCHED	STRIKE-OUTS	WALKS	HITS ALLOWED	HRS ALLOWED	COMP. GAMES	SHUT-OUTS	SAVES
1910	**NY-A**	**5**	**10**	**2**	**2**	**.500**	**24**	**4.47**	**48 1/3**	**27**	**5**	**55**	**1**	**3**	**1**	**1**
1912	StL-A	3	3	0	1	.000	10	20.77	4 1/3	2	1	16	1	0	0	0
1912	Cin-N	2	3	1	0	1.000	10	6.00	15	4	1	19	0	0	0	0
Career Average		3	5	1	1	.500	15	5.85	23	11	2	30	1	1	0	0
Yankee Average		**5**	**10**	**2**	**2**	**.500**	**24**	**4.47**	**48 1/3**	**27**	**5**	**55**	**1**	**3**	**1**	**1**
Career Total		10	16	3	3	.500	44	5.85	68	33	7	90	2	3	1	1
Yankee Total		**5**	**10**	**2**	**2**	**.500**	**24**	**4.47**	**48 1/3**	**27**	**5**	**55**	**1**	**3**	**1**	**1**

Fulton, William Davis
HEIGHT: 6'3" RIGHTHANDER BORN: 10/22/1963 PITTSBURGH, PENNSYLVANIA

YEAR	TEAM	STARTS	GAMES	WON	LOST	PCT	ER	ERA	INNINGS PITCHED	STRIKE-OUTS	WALKS	HITS ALLOWED	HRS ALLOWED	COMP. GAMES	SHUT-OUTS	SAVES
1987	**NY-A**	**0**	**3**	**1**	**0**	**1.000**	**6**	**11.57**	**4 2/3**	**2**	**1**	**9**	**4**	**0**	**0**	**0**
Career Average		0	3	1	0	1.000	6	11.57	4 2/3	2	1	9	4	0	0	0
Yankee Average		**0**	**3**	**1**	**0**	**1.000**	**6**	**11.57**	**4 2/3**	**2**	**1**	**9**	**4**	**0**	**0**	**0**
Career Total		0	3	1	0	1.000	6	11.57	4 2/3	2	1	9	4	0	0	0
Yankee Total		**0**	**3**	**1**	**0**	**1.000**	**6**	**11.57**	**4 2/3**	**2**	**1**	**9**	**4**	**0**	**0**	**0**

Gabler, John Richard (Gabe)
HEIGHT: 6'2" RIGHTHANDER BORN: 10/2/1930 KANSAS CITY, MISSOURI

YEAR	TEAM	STARTS	GAMES	WON	LOST	PCT	ER	ERA	INNINGS PITCHED	STRIKE-OUTS	WALKS	HITS ALLOWED	HRS ALLOWED	COMP. GAMES	SHUT-OUTS	SAVES
1959	NY-A	1	3	1	1	.500	6	2.79	19⅓	11	10	21	1	0	0	0
1960	NY-A	4	21	3	3	.500	24	4.15	52	19	32	46	2	0	0	0
1961	Was-A	9	29	3	8	.667	50	4.86	92⅔	33	37	104	5	0	0	1
Career Average		5	18	2	4	.368	27	4.39	55	21	26	57	3	0	0	2
Yankee Average		3	12	2	2	.500	15	3.79	36	15	21	34	2	0	0	1
Career Total		14	53	7	12	.368	80	4.39	164	63	79	171	8	0	0	5
Yankee Total		5	24	4	4	.500	30	3.79	71	30	42	67	3	0	0	1

Gardner, Richard Frank (Rob)
HEIGHT: 6'1" LEFTHANDER BORN: 12/19/1944 BINGHAMTON, NEW YORK

YEAR	TEAM	STARTS	GAMES	WON	LOST	PCT	ER	ERA	INNINGS PITCHED	STRIKE-OUTS	WALKS	HITS ALLOWED	HRS ALLOWED	COMP. GAMES	SHUT-OUTS	SAVES
1965	NY-N	4	5	0	2	.000	10	3.21	28	19	7	23	4	0	0	0
1966	NY-N	17	41	4	8	.333	76	5.12	133⅔	74	64	147	15	3	0	1
1967	Chi-N	5	18	0	2	.000	14	3.98	31⅓	16	6	33	2	0	0	0
1968	Cle-A	0	5	0	0	—	2	6.75	2⅔	6	2	5	0	0	0	0
1970	NY-A	1	1	1	0	1.000	4	4.91	7⅓	6	4	8	2	0	0	0
1971	Oak-A	1	4	0	0	—	2	2.35	7⅔	5	3	8	1	0	0	0
1971	NY-A	0	2	0	0	—	1	3.00	3	2	2	3	0	0	0	0
1972	NY-A	14	20	8	5	.615	33	3.06	97	58	28	91	9	1	0	0
1973	Mil-A	0	10	1	1	.500	14	9.95	12⅔	5	13	17	0	0	0	1
1973	Oak-A	0	3	0	0	—	4	4.91	7⅓	2	4	10	2	0	0	0
Career Average		4	11	1	2	.438	16	4.35	33	19	13	35	4	0	0	0
Yankee Average		5	8	3	2	.643	13	3.19	36	22	11	34	4	0	0	0
Career Total		42	109	14	18	.438	160	4.35	331	193	133	345	35	4	0	2
Yankee Total		15	23	9	5	.643	38	3.19	107	66	34	102	11	1	0	0

Garvin, Virgil Lee (Ned)
HEIGHT: 6'4" RIGHTHANDER BORN: 1/1/1874 NAVASOTA, TEXAS DIED: 6/16/1908 FRESNO, CALIFORNIA

YEAR	TEAM	STARTS	GAMES	WON	LOST	PCT	ER	ERA	INNINGS PITCHED	STRIKE-OUTS	WALKS	HITS ALLOWED	HRS ALLOWED	COMP. GAMES	SHUT-OUTS	SAVES
1896	Phi-N	1	2	0	2	.000	11	7.62	13	4	7	19	0	1	0	0
1899	ChN-N	23	24	9	13	.409	63	2.85	199	69	42	202	1	22	4	0
1900	ChN-N	28	30	10	18	.357	66	2.41	246⅓	107	63	225	1	25	4	0
1901	Mil-A	27	37	7	20	.667	99	3.46	257⅓	122	90	258	4	22	1	2
1902	Chi-A	19	23	10	10	.500	43	2.21	175⅓	55	43	169	3	16	2	0
1902	Bro-N	2	2	1	1	.500	2	1.00	18	7	4	15	0	2	1	0
1903	Bro-N	34	38	15	18	.455	102	3.08	298	154	84	277	2	30	2	2
1904	Bro-N	22	23	5	15	.667	34	1.68	181⅔	86	78	141	6	16	2	0
1904	NY-A	2	2	0	1	.000	3	2.25	12	8	2	14	0	0	0	0
Career Average		18	20	6	11	.368	47	2.72	156	68	46	147	2	15	1	0
Yankee Average		2	2	0	1	.000	3	2.25	12	8	2	14	0	0	0	0
Career Total		158	181	57	98	.368	423	2.72	1401	612	413	1320	20	134	13	4
Yankee Total		2	2	0	1	.000	3	2.25	12	8	2	14	0	0	0	0

Gaston, Nathaniel Milton
HEIGHT: 6'1" RIGHTHANDER BORN: 1/27/1896 RIDGEFIELD PARK, NEW JERSEY DIED: 4/26/1996 HYANNIS, MASSACHUSETTS

YEAR	TEAM	STARTS	GAMES	WON	LOST	PCT	ER	ERA	INNINGS PITCHED	STRIKE-OUTS	WALKS	HITS ALLOWED	HRS ALLOWED	COMP. GAMES	SHUT-OUTS	SAVES
1924	NY-A	2	29	5	3	.625	43	4.50	86	24	44	92	3	0	0	1
1925	StL-A	30	42	15	14	.517	117	4.41	238⅔	84	101	284	8	16	0	1
1926	StL-A	28	32	10	18	.357	103	4.33	214⅓	39	101	227	13	14	1	0
1927	StL-A	30	37	13	17	.433	141	5.00	254	77	100	275	18	21	0	1
1928	Was-A	22	28	6	12	.333	91	5.51	148⅔	45	53	179	3	8	3	0
1929	Bos-A	29	39	12	19	.387	101	3.73	243⅔	83	81	265	15	20	1	2
1930	Bos-A	34	38	13	20	.394	119	3.92	273	99	98	272	15	20	2	2
1931	Bos-A	18	23	2	13	.133	59	4.46	119	33	41	137	4	4	0	0

(continued)

(continued)

YEAR	TEAM	STARTS	GAMES	WON	LOST	PCT	ER	ERA	INNINGS PITCHED	STRIKE-OUTS	WALKS	HITS ALLOWED	HRS ALLOWED	COMP. GAMES	SHUT-OUTS	SAVES
1932	Chi-A	25	28	7	17	.667	74	4.00	166 2/3	44	73	183	10	7	1	1
1933	Chi-A	25	30	8	12	.400	90	4.85	167	39	60	177	9	7	1	0
1934	Chi-A	28	29	6	19	.666	126	5.85	194	48	84	247	16	10	1	0
Career Average		25	32	9	15	.372	97	4.55	191	56	76	213	10	12	1	1
Yankee Average		**2**	**29**	**5**	**3**	**.625**	**43**	**4.50**	**86**	**24**	**44**	**92**	**3**	**0**	**0**	**1**
Career Total		271	355	97	164	.372	1064	4.55	2105	615	836	2338	114	127	10	8
Yankee Total		**2**	**29**	**5**	**3**	**.625**	**43**	**4.50**	**86**	**24**	**44**	**92**	**3**	**0**	**0**	**1**

Gettel, Allen Jones

HEIGHT: 6'3"   RIGHTHANDER   BORN: 9/7/1917 NORFOLK, VIRGINIA

YEAR	TEAM	STARTS	GAMES	WON	LOST	PCT	ER	ERA	INNINGS PITCHED	STRIKE-OUTS	WALKS	HITS ALLOWED	HRS ALLOWED	COMP. GAMES	SHUT-OUTS	SAVES
1945	**NY-A**	17	27	9	8	.529	67	3.90	154 2/3	67	53	141	11	9	0	3
1946	**NY-A**	11	26	6	7	.462	34	2.97	103	54	40	89	6	5	2	0
1947	Cle-A	21	31	11	10	.524	53	3.20	149	64	62	122	12	9	2	0
1948	Cle-A	2	5	0	1	.000	15	17.61	7 2/3	4	10	15	2	0	0	0
1948	Chi-A	19	22	8	10	.444	66	4.01	148	49	60	154	7	7	0	1
1949	Chi-A	7	19	2	5	.667	45	6.43	63	22	26	69	12	1	1	1
1949	Was-A	1	16	0	2	.000	21	5.45	34 2/3	7	24	43	4	0	0	1
1951	NY-N	1	30	1	2	.333	31	4.87	57 1/3	36	25	52	12	0	0	0
1955	StL-N	0	8	1	0	1.000	17	9.00	17	7	10	26	6	0	0	0
Career Average		9	20	4	5	.458	39	4.28	82	34	34	79	8	3	1	1
Yankee Average		**14**	**27**	**8**	**8**	**.500**	**51**	**3.53**	**129**	**61**	**47**	**115**	**9**	**7**	**1**	**2**
Career Total		79	184	38	45	.458	349	4.28	734	310	310	711	72	31	5	6
Yankee Total		**28**	**53**	**15**	**15**	**.500**	**101**	**3.53**	**258**	**121**	**93**	**230**	**17**	**14**	**2**	**3**

Giard, Joseph Oscar (Peco)

HEIGHT: 5'10"   LEFTHANDER   BORN: 10/7/1898 WARE, MASSACHUSETTS   DIED: 7/10/1956 WORCESTER, MASSACHUSETTS

YEAR	TEAM	STARTS	GAMES	WON	LOST	PCT	ER	ERA	INNINGS PITCHED	STRIKE-OUTS	WALKS	HITS ALLOWED	HRS ALLOWED	COMP. GAMES	SHUT-OUTS	SAVES
1925	StL-A	21	30	10	5	.667	90	5.04	160 2/3	43	87	179	13	9	4	0
1926	StL-A	15	22	3	10	.666	70	7.00	90	18	67	113	7	2	0	0
1927	**NY-A**	0	16	0	0	—	24	8.00	27	10	19	38	1	0	0	0
Career Average		12	23	4	5	.464	61	5.96	93	24	58	110	7	4	1	0
Yankee Average		**0**	**16**	**0**	**0**	**—**	**24**	**8.00**	**27**	**10**	**19**	**38**	**1**	**0**	**0**	**0**
Career Total		36	68	13	15	.464	184	5.96	278	71	173	330	21	11	4	0
Yankee Total		**0**	**16**	**0**	**0**	**—**	**24**	**8.00**	**27**	**10**	**19**	**38**	**1**	**0**	**0**	**0**

Gibson, Paul Marshall

HEIGHT: 6'1"   LEFTHANDER   BORN: 1/4/1960 SOUTHAMPTON, NEW YORK

YEAR	TEAM	STARTS	GAMES	WON	LOST	PCT	ER	ERA	INNINGS PITCHED	STRIKE-OUTS	WALKS	HITS ALLOWED	HRS ALLOWED	COMP. GAMES	SHUT-OUTS	SAVES
1988	Det-A	1	40	4	2	.667	30	2.93	92	50	34	83	6	0	0	0
1989	Det-A	13	45	4	8	.333	68	4.64	132	77	57	129	11	0	0	3
1990	Det-A	0	61	5	4	.556	33	3.05	97 1/3	56	44	99	10	0	0	8
1991	Det-A	0	68	5	7	.417	49	4.59	96	52	48	112	10	0	0	0
1992	NY-N	1	43	0	1	.000	36	5.23	62	49	25	70	7	0	0	0
1993	NY-N	0	8	1	1	.500	5	5.19	8 2/3	12	2	14	1	0	0	0
1993	**NY-A**	0	20	2	0	1.000	12	3.06	35 1/3	25	9	31	4	0	0	0
1994	**NY-A**	0	30	1	1	.500	16	4.97	29	21	17	26	5	0	0	0
1996	**NY-A**	0	4	0	0	—	3	6.75	4	3	0	6	1	0	0	1
Career Average		2	35	2	3	.478	28	4.08	62	38	26	63	6	0	0	1
Yankee Average		**0**	**18**	**1**	**0**	**.750**	**10**	**4.08**	**23**	**16**	**9**	**21**	**3**	**0**	**0**	**0**
Career Total		15	319	22	24	.478	252	4.08	556	345	236	570	55	0	0	11
Yankee Total		**0**	**54**	**3**	**1**	**.750**	**31**	**4.08**	**68**	**49**	**26**	**63**	**10**	**0**	**0**	**0**

Gibson, Samuel Braxton
HEIGHT: 6'2" RIGHTHANDER BORN: 8/5/1899 KING, NORTH CAROLINA DIED: 1/31/1983 HIGH POINT, NORTH CAROLINA

YEAR	TEAM	STARTS	GAMES	WON	LOST	PCT	ER	ERA	INNINGS PITCHED	STRIKE-OUTS	WALKS	HITS ALLOWED	HRS ALLOWED	COMP. GAMES	SHUT-OUTS	SAVES
1926	Det-A	24	35	12	9	.571	76	3.48	196 1/3	61	75	199	6	16	2	2
1927	Det-A	26	33	11	12	.478	78	3.80	184 2/3	76	86	201	9	11	0	0
1928	Det-A	18	20	5	8	.385	72	5.42	119 2/3	29	53	155	4	5	1	0
1930	**NY-A**	**2**	**2**	**0**	**1**	**.000**	**10**	**15.00**	**6**	**3**	**6**	**14**	**1**	**0**	**0**	**0**
1932	NY-N	5	41	4	8	.333	44	4.85	81 2/3	39	30	107	7	1	1	3
Career Average		15	26	6	8	.457	56	4.28	118	42	50	135	5	7	1	1
Yankee Average		**2**	**2**	**0**	**1**	**.000**	**10**	**15.00**	**6**	**3**	**6**	**14**	**1**	**0**	**0**	**0**
Career Total		75	131	32	38	.457	280	4.28	588	208	250	676	27	33	4	5
Yankee Total		**2**	**2**	**0**	**1**	**.000**	**10**	**15.00**	**6**	**3**	**6**	**14**	**1**	**0**	**0**	**0**

Glade, Frederick Monroe (Lucky)
HEIGHT: 5'10" RIGHTHANDER BORN: 1/25/1876 DUBUQUE, IOWA DIED: 11/21/1934 GRAND ISLAND, NEBRASKA

YEAR	TEAM	STARTS	GAMES	WON	LOST	PCT	ER	ERA	INNINGS PITCHED	STRIKE-OUTS	WALKS	HITS ALLOWED	HRS ALLOWED	COMP. GAMES	SHUT-OUTS	SAVES
1902	Chi-N	1	1	0	1	.000	8	9.00	8	3	3	13	0	1	0	0
1904	StL-A	34	35	18	15	.545	73	2.27	289	156	58	248	2	30	6	1
1905	StL-A	32	32	6	25	.194	86	2.81	275	127	58	257	3	28	2	0
1906	StL-A	32	35	15	14	.517	70	2.36	266 2/3	96	59	215	4	28	4	1
1907	StL-A	22	24	13	9	.591	60	2.67	202	71	45	187	2	18	2	0
1908	**NY-A**	**5**	**5**	**0**	**4**	**.000**	**15**	**4.22**	**32**	**11**	**14**	**30**	**0**	**2**	**0**	**0**
Career Average		21	22	9	11	.433	52	2.62	179	77	40	158	2	18	2	0
Yankee Average		**5**	**5**	**0**	**4**	**.000**	**15**	**4.22**	**32**	**11**	**14**	**30**	**0**	**2**	**0**	**0**
Career Total		126	132	52	68	.433	312	2.62	1073	464	237	950	11	107	14	2
Yankee Total		**5**	**5**	**0**	**4**	**.000**	**15**	**4.22**	**32**	**11**	**14**	**30**	**0**	**2**	**0**	**0**

Gomez, Vernon Louis (Lefty)
HEIGHT: 6'2" LEFTHANDER BORN: 11/26/1908 RODEO, CALIFORNIA DIED: 2/17/1989 GREENBRAE, CALIFORNIA

YEAR	TEAM	STARTS	GAMES	WON	LOST	PCT	ER	ERA	INNINGS PITCHED	STRIKE-OUTS	WALKS	HITS ALLOWED	HRS ALLOWED	COMP. GAMES	SHUT-OUTS	SAVES
1930	NY-A	6	15	2	5	.667	37	5.55	60	22	28	66	12	2	0	1
1931	NY-A	26	40	21	9	.700	72	2.67	243	150	85	206	7	17	1	3
1932	NY-A	31	37	24	7	.774	124	4.21	265 1/3	176	105	266	23	21	1	1
1933	NY-A	30	35	16	10	.615	83	3.18	234 2/3	163	106	218	16	14	4	2
1934	NY-A	33	38	26	5	.839	73	2.33	281 2/3	158	96	223	12	25	6	1
1935	NY-A	30	34	12	15	.444	87	3.18	246	138	86	223	18	15	2	1
1936	NY-A	30	31	13	7	.650	92	4.39	188 2/3	105	122	184	6	10	0	0
1937	NY-A	34	34	21	11	.656	72	2.33	278 1/3	194	93	233	10	25	6	0
1938	NY-A	32	32	18	12	.600	89	3.35	239	129	99	239	7	20	4	0
1939	NY-A	26	26	12	8	.600	75	3.41	198	102	84	173	11	14	2	0
1940	NY-A	5	9	3	3	.500	20	6.59	27 1/3	14	18	37	2	0	0	0
1941	NY-A	23	23	15	5	.750	65	3.74	156 1/3	76	103	151	10	8	2	0
1942	NY-A	13	13	6	4	.600	38	4.28	80	41	65	67	4	2	0	0
1943	Was-A	1	1	0	1	.000	3	5.79	4 2/3	0	5	4	0	0	0	0
Career Average		23	26	14	7	.649	66	3.34	179	105	78	164	10	12	2	1
Yankee Average		**25**	**28**	**15**	**8**	**.652**	**71**	**3.34**	**192**	**113**	**84**	**176**	**11**	**13**	**2**	**1**
Career Total		320	368	189	102	.649	930	3.34	2503	1468	1095	2290	138	173	28	9
Yankee Total		**319**	**367**	**189**	**101**	**.652**	**927**	**3.34**	**2498**	**1468**	**1090**	**2286**	**138**	**173**	**28**	**9**

Vernon Louis "Lefty" Gomez, lhp, 1930-42

His nickname was Goofy, but on the field, there wasn't much about Vernon Gomez that was funny. He was one of the biggest "big game" pitchers in the history of a team that had an awful lot of them.

Well, perhaps he wasn't all-business all of the time. In one celebrated incident, facing Philadelphia A's slugger Jimmy "The Beast" Foxx, Gomez shook off every one of catcher Bill Dickey's signs. Dickey called time, went out to the mound and asked Gomez just what pitch he was looking for.

"None of 'em," said Gomez. "I don't like the way he's looking at me. If it's all the same to you, I'll just hold on to the ball."

But this is more an illustration of Gomez's confidence. History doesn't record just what happened to Foxx that day, but it's a safe bet that Gomez found a way to get Foxx out.

Born on November 26, 1908, in Rodeo, California, Gomez began his professional career in the old Pacific Coast League. He was 12-14 for Salt Lake City in 1928 and 18-11 the next year with the San Francisco Seals. The Yankees, who had a pipeline out west in those days, purchased his contract after the 1929 season for $50,000.

Gomez was invited to spring training with the Yankees in 1930 and made the club as a spot starter. He finished with a 2-5 record, but was eventually sent to the Yankees affiliate in St. Paul, Minnesota, for seasoning.

Lucky for Gomez, the Yankees were in the middle of one of their rare reloading efforts, and the next year, new manager Joe McCarthy moved him up to the starting rotation.

He responded with a tremendous year, going 21-9 with 150 strikeouts. His 2.67 ERA was the second best in the American League, behind another nicknamed lefthander, Lefty Grove of the Philadelphia Athletics. Gomez was on his way.

Gomez, at 6 feet 2 inches, was never much of a physical specimen. Early in his career, he was admonished by McCarthy to put on a little more weight. He weighed between 160 and 170 pounds over his career. But Gomez was concerned that such poundage would slow him down. "You don't fatten up a greyhound," was his usual rejoinder.

He made his point on the mound. In 1931, the Yankees were edged out of the pennant race by the Athletics for the third consecutive year, but by 1932, McCarthy had rebuilt the Yankees again, particularly the pitching staff. Gomez was 24-7, former Red Sox righty Red Ruffing was 18-7 and newcomer Johnny Allen was 17-4.

The Yankees won the American League pennant by 13 games over the A's and faced the Chicago Cubs in the World Series. The Yankees won the Series in four games, and Gomez won the second game at Yankee Stadium, 5-2, for the first of his six World Series victories.

After a 16-win "slump" in 1933, Gomez bounced back with a career year in 1934. He was 26-5, and led the majors in wins, complete games (25), shutouts (6), strikeouts (158) and ERA (2.33).

By 1936, the Yankees were back on top of the American League, sparked by a young center fielder named DiMaggio. Gomez was a veteran by then, and he went out of his way to make the young DiMaggio comfortable. The two men roomed together for a time, and Lefty was one of the few Yankees who could josh with the shy, proud DiMaggio.

The Yankees dominated the World Series from 1936-39 and Gomez was one of the main reasons. He was 5-0 in five starts, with a 3.46 ERA. He was on the mound when the Yankees clinched the Series in 1936 and 1937. He credited "clean living and a fast outfield" for his success, but another big reason was a remarkable coolness under fire.

The 1940s were not as good to Gomez. He had one good year, 1941, when he was 15-5. But arm troubles began to cut into his starts. He was 6-4 in 1942, his last year with New York. He played one more season with the Washington Senators, starting one game.

In 1972, Gomez was elected to the Hall of Fame.

Gomez, of course, is near the head of the Yankee pitching pantheon. He is third all-time in wins with 189, seventh in winning percentage with .652, fourth in strikeouts with 1,468, fourth in shutouts with 28 and second in complete games with 173.

Good, Wilbur David (Lefty)
HEIGHT: 5'6" LEFTHANDER BORN: 9/28/1885 PUNXSUTAWNEY, PENNSYLVANIA DIED: 12/30/1963 BROOKSVILLE, FLORIDA

YEAR	TEAM	STARTS	GAMES	WON	LOST	PCT	ER	ERA	INNINGS PITCHED	STRIKE-OUTS	WALKS	HITS ALLOWED	HRS ALLOWED	COMP. GAMES	SHUT-OUTS	SAVES
1905	NY-A	2	5	0	2	.000	10	4.74	19	13	14	18	1	0	0	0
Career Average		2	5	0	2	.000	10	4.74	19	13	14	18	1	0	0	0
Yankee Average		**2**	**5**	**0**	**2**	**.000**	**10**	**4.74**	**19**	**13**	**14**	**18**	**1**	**0**	**0**	**0**
Career Total		2	5	0	2	.000	10	4.74	19	13	14	18	1	0	0	0
Yankee Total		**2**	**5**	**0**	**2**	**.000**	**10**	**4.74**	**19**	**13**	**14**	**18**	**1**	**0**	**0**	**0**

Gooden, Dwight Eugene (Doc)
HEIGHT: 6'3" RIGHTHANDER BORN: 11/16/1964 TAMPA, FLORIDA

YEAR	TEAM	STARTS	GAMES	WON	LOST	PCT	ER	ERA	INNINGS PITCHED	STRIKE-OUTS	WALKS	HITS ALLOWED	HRS ALLOWED	COMP. GAMES	SHUT-OUTS	SAVES
1984	NY-N	31	31	17	9	.654	63	2.60	218	276	73	161	7	7	3	0
1985	NY-N	35	35	24	4	.857	47	1.53	276 2/3	268	69	198	13	16	8	0
1986	NY-N	33	33	17	6	.739	79	2.84	250	200	80	197	17	12	2	0
1987	NY-N	25	25	15	7	.682	64	3.21	179 2/3	148	53	162	11	7	3	0
1988	NY-N	34	34	18	9	.667	88	3.19	248 1/3	175	57	242	8	10	3	0
1989	NY-N	17	19	9	4	.692	38	2.89	118 1/3	101	47	93	9	0	0	1
1990	NY-N	34	34	19	7	.731	99	3.83	232 2/3	223	70	229	10	2	1	0
1991	NY-N	27	27	13	7	.650	76	3.60	190	150	56	185	12	3	1	0
1992	NY-N	31	31	10	13	.435	84	3.67	206	145	70	197	11	3	0	0
1993	NY-N	29	29	12	15	.444	80	3.45	208 2/3	149	61	188	16	7	2	0
1994	NY-N	7	7	3	4	.429	29	6.37	41	40	15	46	9	0	0	0
1996	**NY-A**	**29**	**29**	**11**	**7**	**.611**	**95**	**5.03**	**170**	**126**	**88**	**169**	**19**	**1**	**1**	**0**
1997	**NY-A**	**19**	**20**	**9**	**5**	**.643**	**58**	**4.92**	**106 1/3**	**66**	**53**	**116**	**14**	**0**	**0**	**0**
1998	Cle-A	23	23	8	6	.571	56	3.76	134	83	51	135	13	0	0	0
1999	Cle-A	22	26	3	4	.429	80	6.26	115	88	67	127	18	0	0	0
2000	Hou-N	1	1	0	0	—	4	9.00	4	1	3	6	1	0	0	0
2000	TB-A	8	8	2	3	.400	27	6.63	36 2/3	23	20	47	14	0	0	0
2000	**NY-A**	**5**	**18**	**4**	**2**	**.667**	**24**	**3.36**	**64 1/3**	**31**	**21**	**66**	**8**	**0**	**0**	**2**
Career Average		23	24	11	6	.634	61	3.51	156	127	53	142	12	4	1	0
Yankee Average		**5**	**18**	**4**	**2**	**.667**	**24**	**3.36**	**64 1/3**	**31**	**21**	**66**	**8**	**0**	**0**	**2**
Career Total		410	430	194	112	.634	1091	3.51	2800 2/3	2293	954	2564	210	68	23	3
Yankee Total		**5**	**18**	**4**	**2**	**.667**	**24**	**3.36**	**64 1/3**	**31**	**21**	**66**	**8**	**0**	**2**	

Goodwin, Arthur Ingram
HEIGHT: 5'8" RIGHTHANDER BORN: 2/27/1876 WHITELEY TWNSHP, PENNSYLVANIA DIED: 6/19/1943 FRANKLIN TOWNSHIP, PENNSYLVANIA

YEAR	TEAM	STARTS	GAMES	WON	LOST	PCT	ER	ERA	INNINGS PITCHED	STRIKE-OUTS	WALKS	HITS ALLOWED	HRS ALLOWED	COMP. GAMES	SHUT-OUTS	SAVES
1905	NY-A	0	1	0	0	—	3	81.08	1/3	0	2	2	0	0	0	0
Career Average		0	1	0	0	—	3	81.08	1/3	0	2	2	0	0	0	0
Yankee Average		**0**	**1**	**0**	**0**	**—**	**3**	**81.08**	**1/3**	**0**	**2**	**2**	**0**	**0**	**0**	**0**
Career Total		0	1	0	0	—	3	81.08	1/3	0	2	2	0	0	0	0
Yankee Total		**0**	**1**	**0**	**0**	**—**	**3**	**81.08**	**1/3**	**0**	**2**	**2**	**0**	**0**	**0**	**0**

Gorman, Thomas Aloysius
HEIGHT: 6'1" RIGHTHANDER BORN: 1/4/1925 NEW YORK, NEW YORK DIED: 12/26/1992 VALLEY STREAM, NEW YORK

YEAR	TEAM	STARTS	GAMES	WON	LOST	PCT	ER	ERA	INNINGS PITCHED	STRIKE-OUTS	WALKS	HITS ALLOWED	HRS ALLOWED	COMP. GAMES	SHUT-OUTS	SAVES
1952	**NY-A**	**6**	**12**	**6**	**2**	**.750**	**31**	**4.60**	**60 2/3**	**31**	**22**	**63**	**8**	**1**	**1**	**1**
1953	**NY-A**	**1**	**40**	**4**	**5**	**.444**	**29**	**3.39**	**77**	**38**	**32**	**65**	**5**	**0**	**0**	**6**
1954	**NY-A**	**0**	**23**	**0**	**0**	**—**	**9**	**2.21**	**36 2/3**	**31**	**14**	**30**	**1**	**0**	**0**	**2**
1955	KC-A	0	57	7	6	.538	43	3.55	109	46	36	98	11	0	0	18
1956	KC-A	13	52	9	10	.474	73	3.83	171 1/3	56	68	168	23	1	0	3
1957	KC-A	12	38	5	9	.357	53	3.83	124 2/3	66	33	125	18	3	1	3
1958	KC-A	1	50	4	4	.500	35	3.51	89 2/3	44	20	86	8	0	0	8
1959	KC-A	0	17	1	0	1.000	16	7.08	20 1/3	9	14	24	3	0	0	1
Career Average		4	36	5	5	.500	36	3.77	86	40	30	82	10	1	0	5
Yankee Average		**2**	**25**	**3**	**2**	**.588**	**23**	**3.56**	**58**	**33**	**23**	**53**	**5**	**0**	**0**	**3**
Career Total		33	289	36	36	.500	289	3.77	689	321	239	659	77	5	2	42
Yankee Total		**7**	**75**	**10**	**7**	**.588**	**69**	**3.56**	**174**	**100**	**68**	**158**	**14**	**1**	**1**	**9**

Richard Michael "Goose" Gossage, rhp, 1978–83, 1989

The fiery Gossage was the best short reliever of the late 1970s, and his work with the Yankees, particularly in 1978, is the stuff of legend for Yankees fans. His appearance on the mound was chilling for opposing players: a 6 foot 3 inch bear of a man with a huge "Fu Manchu" mustache. Imperiously, in warm-ups, Gossage would flick his glove at the catcher, rear back, and fire a white blur toward home plate. It was as intimidating a sight as any in baseball.

Born in Colorado Springs, Colorado, on July 5, 1951, Gossage was a Yankee fan as a young boy. But he was eventually signed by the Chicago White Sox, and he made his way to the majors in 1973.

Gossage was 7-1 with two saves that first year with Chicago. By 1975, he was 9-8 with a league-leading 26 saves.

In 1977, Gossage, now an All-Star, was traded to the Pittsburgh Pirates, a move he welcomed. Gossage was uncomfortable with the circus-like atmosphere in Chicago cultivated by White Sox owner Bill Veeck. His 1977 season with Pittsburgh generated an 11-9 record with another 26 saves. The next year he was a free agent, and he signed a six-year $2.75 million deal.

Of course, the atmosphere in New York—with owner George Steinbrenner battling coach Billy Martin battling outfielder Reggie Jackson—made Chicago look like kindergarten to Gossage. The big reliever admitted that first year that he had difficulty keeping a straight face when Steinbrenner would come into the locker room for one of his patented pep talks. Catcher Thurman Munson often made it worse for Gossage, sitting behind Steinbrenner, making faces.

But Gossage, possessor of a hellacious fastball and a devastating curve, was almost as unhittable as teammate Ron Guidry that year. After a shaky start, he ended up with 10 wins, 27 saves, a 2.01 ERA and 122 strikeouts in 144 innings. The season culminated with Gossage retiring Red Sox star Carl Yastrzemski to end the fabled Red Sox–Yankees playoff game.

He was also 2-0 with one save in the post-season against Kansas City in the league championship series and Los Angeles in the World Series.

But in 1979, Gossage was injured in a shower-room scuffle with catcher Cliff Johnson, tearing ligaments in the thumb of his pitching hand. He was out for 12 weeks, and the Yankees finished fourth.

Gossage still had several other tremendous years in New York, saving a league-leading 33 games in 1980 and 30 more in 1982. His ERA in the strike-shortened 1981 season was 0.77, with 48 strikeouts in 46 innings.

But he was tiring of the New York Yankee circus, and of Steinbrenner. By the end of his contract in 1983, he wanted out, though the Yankees did everything they could to re-sign him. Gossage was signed by San Diego in 1984 and helped take the Padres to their first-ever World Series. He pitched for nine years after that, including a brief stint in 1989 for the Yankees, before finally retiring in 1993.

Gossage is third all-time on the Yankees' save list with 151. His total of 310 saves is eighth all-time on the major league list.

Gossage, Richard Michael (Goose)
HEIGHT: 6'3" RIGHTHANDER BORN: 7/5/1952 COLORADO SPRINGS, COLORADO

YEAR	TEAM	STARTS	GAMES	WON	LOST	PCT	ER	ERA	INNINGS PITCHED	STRIKE-OUTS	WALKS	HITS ALLOWED	HRS ALLOWED	COMP. GAMES	SHUT-OUTS	SAVES
1972	Chi-A	1	36	7	1	.875	38	4.28	80	57	44	72	2	0	0	2
1973	Chi-A	4	20	0	4	.000	41	7.43	49 2/3	33	37	57	9	1	0	0
1974	Chi-A	3	39	4	6	.400	41	4.13	89 1/3	64	47	92	4	0	0	1
1975	Chi-A	0	62	9	8	.529	29	1.84	141 2/3	130	70	99	3	0	0	26
1976	Chi-A	29	31	9	17	.346	98	3.94	224	135	90	214	16	15	0	1
1977	Pit-N	0	72	11	9	.550	24	1.62	133	151	49	78	9	0	0	26
1978	**NY-A**	**0**	**63**	**10**	**11**	**.476**	**30**	**2.01**	**134 1/3**	**122**	**59**	**87**	**9**	**0**	**0**	**27**
1979	**NY-A**	**0**	**36**	**5**	**3**	**.625**	**17**	**2.62**	**58 1/3**	**41**	**19**	**48**	**5**	**0**	**0**	**18**
1980	**NY-A**	**0**	**64**	**6**	**2**	**.750**	**25**	**2.27**	**99**	**103**	**37**	**74**	**5**	**0**	**0**	**33**
1981	**NY-A**	**0**	**32**	**3**	**2**	**.600**	**4**	**0.77**	**46 2/3**	**48**	**14**	**22**	**2**	**0**	**0**	**20**
1982	**NY-A**	**0**	**56**	**4**	**5**	**.444**	**23**	**2.23**	**93**	**102**	**28**	**63**	**5**	**0**	**0**	**30**
1983	**NY-A**	**0**	**57**	**13**	**5**	**.722**	**22**	**2.27**	**87 1/3**	**90**	**25**	**82**	**5**	**0**	**0**	**22**
1984	SD-N	0	62	10	6	.625	33	2.90	102 1/3	84	36	75	6	0	0	25
1985	SD-N	0	50	5	3	.625	16	1.82	79	52	17	64	1	0	0	26
1986	SD-N	0	45	5	7	.417	32	4.45	64 2/3	63	20	69	8	0	0	21
1987	SD-N	0	40	5	4	.556	18	3.12	52	44	19	47	4	0	0	11
1988	Chi-N	0	46	4	4	.500	21	4.33	43 2/3	30	15	50	3	0	0	13
1989	SF-N	0	31	2	1	.667	13	2.68	43 2/3	24	27	32	2	0	0	4
1989	**NY-A**	**0**	**11**	**1**	**0**	**1.000**	**6**	**3.77**	**14 1/3**	**6**	**3**	**14**	**0**	**0**	**0**	**1**
1991	Tex-A	0	44	4	2	.667	16	3.57	40 1/3	28	16	33	4	0	0	1
1992	Oak-A	0	30	0	2	.000	12	2.84	38	26	19	32	5	0	0	0
1993	Oak-A	0	39	4	5	.444	24	4.53	47 2/3	40	26	49	6	0	0	1
1994	Sea-A	0	36	3	0	1.000	22	4.21	47	29	15	44	6	0	0	1
Career Average		2	44	5	5	.537	26	3.01	79	65	32	65	5	1	0	13
Yankee Average		**0**	**46**	**6**	**4**	**.600**	**18**	**2.14**	**76**	**73**	**26**	**56**	**4**	**0**	**0**	**22**
Career Total		37	1002	124	107	.537	605	3.01	1809	1502	732	1497	119	16	0	310
Yankee Total		**0**	**319**	**42**	**28**	**.600**	**127**	**2.14**	**533**	**512**	**185**	**390**	**31**	**0**	**0**	**151**

Gowell, Lawrence Clyde
HEIGHT: 6'2" RIGHTHANDER BORN: 5/2/1948 LEWISTON, MAINE

YEAR	TEAM	STARTS	GAMES	WON	LOST	PCT	ER	ERA	INNINGS PITCHED	STRIKE-OUTS	WALKS	HITS ALLOWED	HRS ALLOWED	COMP. GAMES	SHUT-OUTS	SAVES
1972	**NY-A**	**1**	**2**	**0**	**1**	**.000**	**1**	**1.29**	**7**	**7**	**2**	**3**	**0**	**0**	**0**	**0**
Career Average		1	2	0	1	.000	1	1.29	7	7	2	3	0	0	0	0
Yankee Average		**1**	**2**	**0**	**1**	**.000**	**1**	**1.29**	**7**	**7**	**2**	**3**	**0**	**0**	**0**	**0**
Career Total		1	2	0	1	.000	1	1.29	7	7	2	3	0	0	0	0
Yankee Total		**1**	**2**	**0**	**1**	**.000**	**1**	**1.29**	**7**	**7**	**2**	**3**	**0**	**0**	**0**	**0**

Granger, Wayne Allan
HEIGHT: 6'2" RIGHTHANDER BORN: 3/15/1944 SPRINGFIELD, MASSACHUSETTS

YEAR	TEAM	STARTS	GAMES	WON	LOST	PCT	ER	ERA	INNINGS PITCHED	STRIKE-OUTS	WALKS	HITS ALLOWED	HRS ALLOWED	COMP. GAMES	SHUT-OUTS	SAVES
1968	StL-N	0	34	4	2	.667	11	2.25	44	27	12	40	2	0	0	4
1969	Cin-N	0	90	9	6	.600	45	2.80	144 2/3	68	40	143	10	0	0	27
1970	Cin-N	0	67	6	5	.545	25	2.66	84 2/3	38	27	79	5	0	0	35
1971	Cin-N	0	70	7	6	.538	37	3.33	100	51	28	94	8	0	0	11
1972	Min-A	0	63	4	6	.400	30	3.01	89 2/3	45	28	83	7	0	0	19
1973	StL-N	0	33	2	4	.333	22	4.24	46 2/3	14	21	50	3	0	0	5
1973	**NY-A**	**0**	**7**	**0**	**1**	**.000**	**3**	**1.76**	**15 1/3**	**10**	**3**	**19**	**1**	**0**	**0**	**0**
1974	Chi-A	0	5	0	0	—	7	8.22	7 2/3	4	3	16	1	0	0	0
1975	Hou-N	0	55	2	5	.667	30	3.65	74	30	23	76	7	0	0	5
1976	Mon-N	0	27	1	0	1.000	13	3.66	32	16	16	32	3	0	0	2
Career Average		0	45	4	4	.500	22	3.14	64	30	20	63	5	0	0	11
Yankee Average		**0**	**7**	**0**	**1**	**.000**	**3**	**1.76**	**15 1/3**	**10**	**3**	**19**	**1**	**0**	**0**	**0**
Career Total		0	451	35	35	.500	223	3.14	639	303	201	632	47	0	0	108
Yankee Total		**0**	**7**	**0**	**1**	**.000**	**3**	**1.76**	**15 1/3**	**10**	**3**	**19**	**1**	**0**	**0**	**0**

Gray, Ted Glenn
HEIGHT: 5'11" LEFTHANDER BORN: 12/31/1924 DETROIT, MICHIGAN

YEAR	TEAM	STARTS	GAMES	WON	LOST	PCT	ER	ERA	INNINGS PITCHED	STRIKE-OUTS	WALKS	HITS ALLOWED	HRS ALLOWED	COMP. GAMES	SHUT-OUTS	SAVES
1946	Det-A	2	3	0	2	.000	11	8.49	11 2/3	5	5	17	4	0	0	1
1948	Det-A	11	26	6	2	.750	40	4.22	85 1/3	60	72	73	2	3	1	0
1949	Det-A	27	34	10	10	.500	76	3.51	195	96	103	163	11	8	3	1
1950	Det-A	21	27	10	7	.588	73	4.40	149 1/3	102	72	139	22	7	0	1
1951	Det-A	28	34	7	14	.333	89	4.06	197 1/3	131	95	194	17	9	1	1
1952	Det-A	32	35	12	17	.414	103	4.14	224	138	101	212	21	13	2	0
1953	Det-A	28	30	10	15	.400	90	4.60	176	115	76	166	25	8	0	0
1954	Det-A	10	19	3	5	.375	43	5.38	72	29	56	70	8	2	0	0
1955	Chi-A	1	2	0	0	—	6	18.00	3	1	2	9	0	0	0	0
1955	Cle-A	0	2	0	0	—	4	18.00	2	1	2	5	1	0	0	0
1955	**NY-A**	**1**	**1**	**0**	**0**	**—**	**1**	**3.00**	**3**	**1**	**0**	**3**	**0**	**0**	**0**	**0**
1955	Bal-A	1	9	1	2	.333	14	8.22	15 1/3	8	11	21	3	0	0	0
Career Average		14	19	5	6	.444	46	4.37	94	57	50	89	10	4	1	0
Yankee Average		**1**	**1**	**0**	**0**	**—**	**1**	**3.00**	**3**	**1**	**0**	**3**	**0**	**0**	**0**	**0**
Career Total		162	222	59	74	.444	550	4.37	1134	687	595	1072	114	50	7	4
Yankee Total		**1**	**1**	**0**	**0**	**—**	**1**	**3.00**	**3**	**1**	**0**	**3**	**0**	**0**	**0**	**0**

Grba, Eli
HEIGHT: 6'2" RIGHTHANDER BORN: 8/9/1934 CHICAGO, ILLINOIS

YEAR	TEAM	STARTS	GAMES	WON	LOST	PCT	ER	ERA	INNINGS PITCHED	STRIKE-OUTS	WALKS	HITS ALLOWED	HRS ALLOWED	COMP. GAMES	SHUT-OUTS	SAVES
1959	**NY-A**	**6**	**19**	**2**	**5**	**.667**	**36**	**6.44**	**50 1/3**	**23**	**39**	**52**	**6**	**0**	**0**	**0**
1960	**NY-A**	**9**	**24**	**6**	**4**	**.600**	**33**	**3.68**	**80 2/3**	**32**	**46**	**65**	**9**	**1**	**0**	**1**
1961	LA-A	30	40	11	13	.458	100	4.25	211 2/3	105	114	197	26	8	0	2
1962	LA-A	29	40	8	9	.471	89	4.54	176 1/3	90	75	185	19	1	0	1
1963	LA-A	1	12	1	2	.333	9	4.67	17 1/3	5	10	14	2	0	0	0
Career Average		15	27	6	7	.459	53	4.48	107	51	57	103	12	2	0	1
Yankee Average		**8**	**22**	**4**	**5**	**.471**	**35**	**4.74**	**65**	**28**	**43**	**59**	**8**	**1**	**0**	**1**
Career Total		75	135	28	33	.459	267	4.48	536	255	284	513	62	10	0	4
Yankee Total		**15**	**43**	**8**	**9**	**.471**	**69**	**4.74**	**131**	**55**	**85**	**117**	**15**	**1**	**0**	**1**

Griffin, Michael Leroy
HEIGHT: 6'4" RIGHTHANDER BORN: 6/26/1957 COLUSA, CALIFORNIA

YEAR	TEAM	STARTS	GAMES	WON	LOST	PCT	ER	ERA	INNINGS PITCHED	STRIKE-OUTS	WALKS	HITS ALLOWED	HRS ALLOWED	COMP. GAMES	SHUT-OUTS	SAVES
1979	**NY-A**	**0**	**3**	**0**	**0**	**—**	**2**	**4.15**	**4 1/3**	**5**	**2**	**5**	**0**	**0**	**0**	**1**
1980	**NY-A**	**9**	**13**	**2**	**4**	**.333**	**29**	**4.83**	**54**	**25**	**23**	**64**	**6**	**0**	**0**	**0**
1981	**NY-A**	**0**	**2**	**0**	**0**	**—**	**1**	**2.08**	**4 1/3**	**4**	**0**	**5**	**0**	**0**	**0**	**0**
1981	Chi-N	9	16	2	5	.667	26	4.50	52	20	9	64	4	0	0	1
1982	SD-N	0	7	0	1	.000	4	3.48	10 1/3	4	3	9	0	0	0	0
1987	Bal-A	6	23	3	5	.375	36	4.36	74 1/3	42	33	78	9	1	0	1
1989	Cin-N	0	3	0	0	—	6	12.46	4 1/3	1	3	10	0	0	0	0
Career Average		3	10	1	2	.318	15	4.60	29	14	10	34	3	0	0	0
Yankee Average		**3**	**6**	**1**	**1**	**.333**	**11**	**4.60**	**21**	**11**	**8**	**25**	**2**	**0**	**0**	**0**
Career Total		24	67	7	15	.318	104	4.60	204	101	73	235	19	1	0	3
Yankee Total		**9**	**18**	**2**	**4**	**.333**	**32**	**4.60**	**63**	**34**	**25**	**74**	**6**	**0**	**0**	**1**

Griffith, Clark Calvin (The Old Fox)

HEIGHT: 5'7"   RIGHTHANDER   BORN: 11/20/1869 CLEAR CREEK, MISSOURI   DIED: 10/27/1955 WASHINGTON, D.C.

YEAR	TEAM	STARTS	GAMES	WON	LOST	PCT	ER	ERA	INNINGS PITCHED	STRIKE-OUTS	WALKS	HITS ALLOWED	HRS ALLOWED	COMP. GAMES	SHUT-OUTS	SAVES
1891	StL-A	17	27	11	8	.579	69	3.33	186 1/3	68	58	195	8	12	0	0
1891	Bos-A	4	7	3	1	.750	25	5.62	40	20	15	47	3	3	0	0
1893	Chi-N	2	4	1	2	.333	11	5.03	19 2/3	9	5	24	1	2	0	0
1894	Chi-N	30	36	21	14	.600	143	4.92	261 1/3	71	85	328	12	28	0	0
1895	Chi-N	41	42	26	14	.650	154	3.93	353	79	91	434	11	39	0	0
1896	Chi-N	35	36	23	11	.676	125	3.54	317 2/3	81	70	370	3	35	0	0
1897	Chi-N	38	41	21	18	.538	142	3.72	343 2/3	102	86	410	3	38	1	1
1898	Chi-N	38	38	24	10	.706	68	1.88	325 2/3	97	64	305	1	38	4	0
1899	Chi-N	38	38	22	14	611	99	2.79	319 2/3	73	65	329	5	36	4	0
1900	Chi-N	30	30	14	13	.519	84	3.05	248	61	51	245	6	35	4	0
1901	Chi-A	30	35	24	7	.774	79	2.67	266 2/3	67	50	275	4	27	5	1
1902	Chi-A	24	28	15	9	.625	99	4.18	213	51	47	247	11	26	3	0
1903	**NY-A**	**24**	**25**	**14**	**11**	**.560**	**64**	**2.70**	**213**	**69**	**33**	**201**	**3**	**20**	**2**	**0**
1904	**NY-A**	**11**	**16**	**7**	**5**	**.583**	**32**	**2.87**	**100 1/3**	**36**	**16**	**91**	**3**	**22**	**1**	**0**
1905	**NY-A**	**7**	**25**	**9**	**6**	**.600**	**19**	**1.68**	**101 2/3**	**46**	**15**	**82**	**1**	**8**	**2**	**1**
1906	**NY-A**	**2**	**17**	**2**	**2**	**.500**	**20**	**3.02**	**59 2/3**	**16**	**15**	**58**	**0**	**4**	**2**	**2**
1907	**NY-A**	**0**	**4**	**0**	**0**	**—**	**8**	**8.64**	**8 1/3**	**5**	**6**	**15**	**0**	**0**	**0**	**0**
1909	Cin-N	1	1	0	1	.000	4	6.00	6	3	2	11	0	1	0	0
1912	Was-A	0	1	0	0	—	0	0.00	0	0	1	1	0	0	0	0
1913	Was-A	0	1	0	0	—	0	0.00	1	0	0	1	0	0	0	0
1914	Was-A	0	1	0	0	—	0	0.00	1	1	0	1	0	0	0	1
Career Average		18	22	11	7	.619	59	3.56	150	45	37	175	4	16	1	0
Yankee Average		**9**	**17**	**6**	**5**	**.571**	**29**	**2.66**	**97**	**34**	**17**	**89**	**1**	**7**	**1**	**1**
Career Total		372	453	237	146	.619	1245	3.56	3150	955	774	3670	76	337	22	6
Yankee Total		**44**	**87**	**32**	**24**	**.571**	**143**	**2.66**	**483**	**172**	**85**	**447**	**7**	**35**	**5**	**3**

Grim, Robert Anton

HEIGHT: 6'1"   RIGHTHANDER   BORN: 3/8/1930 NEW YORK, NEW YORK   DIED 1/23/1966 SHAWNEE, KANSAS

YEAR	TEAM	STARTS	GAMES	WON	LOST	PCT	ER	ERA	INNINGS PITCHED	STRIKE-OUTS	WALKS	HITS ALLOWED	HRS ALLOWED	COMP. GAMES	SHUT-OUTS	SAVES
1954	**NY-A**	**20**	**37**	**20**	**6**	**.769**	**72**	**3.26**	**199**	**108**	**85**	**175**	**9**	**8**	**1**	**0**
1955	**NY-A**	**11**	**26**	**7**	**5**	**.583**	**43**	**4.19**	**92 1/3**	**63**	**42**	**81**	**9**	**1**	**1**	**4**
1956	**NY-A**	**6**	**26**	**6**	**1**	**.857**	**23**	**2.77**	**74 2/3**	**48**	**31**	**64**	**3**	**1**	**0**	**5**
1957	**NY-A**	**0**	**46**	**12**	**8**	**.600**	**21**	**2.63**	**72**	**52**	**36**	**60**	**5**	**0**	**0**	**19**
1958	**NY-A**	**0**	**11**	**0**	**1**	**.000**	**10**	**5.51**	**16 1/3**	**11**	**10**	**12**	**3**	**0**	**0**	**0**
1958	KC-A	14	26	7	6	.538	45	3.56	113 2/3	54	41	118	7	5	1	0
1959	KC-A	9	40	6	10	.375	57	4.09	125 1/3	65	57	124	10	3	1	4
1960	Cle-A	0	3	0	1	.000	3	11.57	2 1/3	2	1	6	0	0	0	0
1960	Cin-N	0	26	2	2	.500	15	4.45	30 1/3	22	10	32	3	0	0	2
1960	StL-N	0	15	1	0	1.000	7	3.05	20 2/3	15	9	22	1	0	0	0
1962	KC-A	0	12	0	1	.000	9	6.23	13	3	8	14	0	0	0	3
Career Average		6	24	6	4	.598	28	3.61	69	40	30	64	5	2	0	3
Yankee Average		**7**	**29**	**9**	**4**	**.682**	**34**	**3.35**	**91**	**56**	**41**	**78**	**6**	**2**	**0**	**6**
Career Total		60	268	61	41	.598	305	3.61	760	443	330	708	50	18	4	37
Yankee Total		**37**	**146**	**45**	**21**	**.682**	**169**	**3.35**	**454**	**282**	**204**	**392**	**29**	**10**	**2**	**28**

Grimes, Burleigh Arland (Ol' Stubblebeard)

HEIGHT: 5'10"   RIGHTHANDER   BORN: 8/18/1893 EMERALD, WISCONSIN   DIED: 12/6/1985 CLEAR LAKE, WISCONSIN

YEAR	TEAM	STARTS	GAMES	WON	LOST	PCT	ER	ERA	INNINGS PITCHED	STRIKE-OUTS	WALKS	HITS ALLOWED	HRS ALLOWED	COMP. GAMES	SHUT-OUTS	SAVES
1916	Pit-N	5	6	2	3	.400	12	2.36	45 2/3	20	10	40	1	4	0	0
1917	Pit-N	17	37	3	16	.158	76	3.53	194	72	70	186	5	8	1	0
1918	Bro-N	30	40	19	9	.679	64	2.14	269 2/3	113	76	210	3	19	7	1
1919	Bro-N	21	25	10	11	.476	70	3.47	181 1/3	82	60	179	2	13	1	0
1920	Bro-N	33	40	23	11	.676	75	2.22	303 2/3	131	67	271	5	25	5	2
1921	Bro-N	35	37	22	13	.629	95	2.83	302 1/3	136	76	313	6	30	2	0
1922	Bro-N	34	36	17	14	.548	137	4.76	259	99	84	324	17	18	1	1
1923	Bro-N	38	39	21	18	.538	130	3.58	327	119	100	356	9	33	2	0
1924	Bro-N	36	38	22	13	.629	132	3.82	310 2/3	135	91	351	15	30	1	1
1925	Bro-N	31	33	12	19	.387	138	5.04	246 2/3	73	102	305	15	19	0	0

(continued)

(continued)

YEAR	TEAM	STARTS	GAMES	WON	LOST	PCT	ER	ERA	INNINGS PITCHED	STRIKE-OUTS	WALKS	HITS ALLOWED	HRS ALLOWED	COMP. GAMES	SHUT-OUTS	SAVES
1926	Bro-N	29	30	12	13	.480	93	3.71	225⅓	64	88	238	4	18	1	0
1927	NY-N	34	39	19	8	.704	102	3.54	259⅔	102	87	274	12	15	2	2
1928	Pit-N	37	48	25	14	.641	110	2.99	330⅔	97	77	311	11	28	4	3
1929	Pit-N	29	33	17	7	.708	81	3.13	232⅔	62	70	245	11	18	2	2
1930	Bos-N	9	11	3	5	.375	40	7.35	49	15	22	72	4	1	0	0
1930	StL-N	19	22	13	6	.684	51	3.01	152⅓	58	43	174	5	10	1	0
1931	StL-N	28	29	17	9	.654	86	3.65	212⅓	67	59	240	11	17	3	0
1932	Chi-N	18	30	6	11	.353	75	4.78	141⅓	36	50	174	8	5	1	1
1933	Chi-N	7	17	3	6	.333	27	3.49	69⅔	12	29	71	2	3	1	3
1933	StL-N	3	4	0	1	.000	8	5.27	13⅔	4	8	15	1	0	0	1
1934	StL-N	0	4	2	1	.667	3	3.52	7⅔	1	2	5	1	0	0	0
1934	Pit-N	4	8	1	2	.333	22	7.24	27⅓	9	10	36	0	0	0	1
1934	**NY-A**	**0**	**10**	**1**	**2**	**.333**	**11**	**5.50**	**18**	**5**	**14**	**22**	**0**	**0**	**0**	**1**
Career Average		22	27	12	9	.560	71	3.53	182	66	56	192	6	14	2	1
Yankee Average		**0**	**10**	**1**	**2**	**.333**	**11**	**5.50**	**18**	**5**	**14**	**22**	**0**	**0**	**0**	**1**
Career Total		497	616	270	212	.560	1638	3.53	4180	1512	1295	4412	148	314	35	18
Yankee Total		**0**	**10**	**1**	**2**	**.333**	**11**	**5.50**	**18**	**5**	**14**	**22**	**0**	**0**	**0**	**1**

Grimsley, Jason Alan

HEIGHT: 6'3"   RIGHTHANDER   BORN: 8/7/1967 CLEVELAND, TEXAS

YEAR	TEAM	STARTS	GAMES	WON	LOST	PCT	ER	ERA	INNINGS PITCHED	STRIKE-OUTS	WALKS	HITS ALLOWED	HRS ALLOWED	COMP. GAMES	SHUT-OUTS	SAVES
1989	Phi-N	4	4	1	3	.667	12	5.89	18⅓	7	19	19	2	0	0	0
1990	Phi-N	11	11	3	2	.600	21	3.30	57⅓	41	43	47	1	0	0	0
1991	Phi-N	12	12	1	7	.125	33	4.87	61	42	41	54	4	0	0	0
1993	Cle-A	6	10	3	4	.429	25	5.32	42⅓	27	20	52	3	1	0	0
1994	Cle-A	13	14	5	2	.714	42	4.61	82⅔	59	34	91	7	1	0	1
1995	Cle-A	2	15	0	0	—	23	6.09	34	25	32	37	4	0	0	0
1996	Cal-A	20	35	5	7	.417	99	6.85	130⅓	82	74	150	14	2	1	0
1999	**NY-A**	**0**	**55**	**7**	**2**	**.778**	**30**	**3.60**	**75**	**49**	**40**	**66**	**7**	**0**	**0**	**1**
2000	**NY-A**	**4**	**63**	**3**	**2**	**.600**	**54**	**5.05**	**96⅓**	**53**	**42**	**100**	**5**	**0**	**0**	**1**
Career Average		8	24	3	3	.491	38	5.11	63⅔	43	38	68	5	0	0	1
Yankee Average		**0**	**59**	**5**	**2**	**.714**	**42**	**4.41**	**86**	**51**	**41**	**83**	**6**	**0**	**0**	**1**
Career Total		72	219	28	29	.491	339	5.11	597	385	345	616	47	3	0	3
Yankee Total		**4**	**118**	**10**	**4**	**.714**	**84**	**4.41**	**171⅓**	**102**	**82**	**166**	**12**	**0**	**0**	**2**

Grissom, Lee Theo

HEIGHT: 6'3"   LEFTHANDER   BORN: 11/22/1958 SHERMAN, TEXAS

YEAR	TEAM	STARTS	GAMES	WON	LOST	PCT	ER	ERA	INNINGS PITCHED	STRIKE-OUTS	WALKS	HITS ALLOWED	HRS ALLOWED	COMP. GAMES	SHUT-OUTS	SAVES
1934	Cin-N	1	4	0	1	.000	12	15.43	7	4	7	13	0	0	0	0
1935	Cin-N	3	3	1	1	.500	9	3.86	21	13	4	31	0	1	0	0
1936	Cin-N	4	6	1	1	.500	17	6.29	24⅓	13	9	33	1	0	0	0
1937	Cin-N	30	50	12	17	.414	81	3.26	223⅔	149	93	193	7	14	5	6
1938	Cin-N	7	14	2	3	.400	30	5.29	51	16	22	60	4	0	0	0
1939	Cin-N	21	33	9	7	.563	70	4.10	153⅔	53	56	145	14	3	0	0
1940	**NY-A**	**0**	**5**	**0**	**0**	**—**	**0**	**0.00**	**4⅔**	**1**	**2**	**4**	**0**	**0**	**0**	**0**
1940	Bro-N	10	14	2	5	.667	23	2.81	73⅔	56	34	59	3	3	1	0
1941	Bro-N	1	4	0	0	—	3	2.38	11⅓	5	8	10	2	0	0	1
1941	Phi-N	18	29	2	13	.133	58	3.97	131⅓	74	70	120	4	2	1	1
Career Average		10	16	3	5	.377	30	3.89	70	38	31	67	4	2	0	0
Yankee Average		**0**	**5**	**0**	**0**	**—**	**0**	**0.00**	**4⅔**	**1**	**2**	**4**	**0**	**0**	**0**	**0**
Career Total		95	162	29	48	.377	303	3.89	702	384	305	668	35	23	6	7
Yankee Total		**0**	**5**	**0**	**0**	**—**	**0**	**0.00**	**4⅔**	**1**	**2**	**4**	**0**	**0**	**0**	**0**

Guante, Cecilio BORN CECILIO GUANTE (MAGALLANE)
HEIGHT: 6'3" RIGHTHANDER BORN: 2/1/1960 VILLA MELLA, DOMINICAN REPUBLIC

YEAR	TEAM	STARTS	GAMES	WON	LOST	PCT	ER	ERA	INNINGS PITCHED	STRIKE-OUTS	WALKS	HITS ALLOWED	HRS ALLOWED	COMP. GAMES	SHUT-OUTS	SAVES
1982	Pit-N	0	10	0	0	—	10	3.33	27	26	5	28	1	0	0	0
1983	Pit-N	0	49	2	6	.667	37	3.32	100 1/3	82	46	90	5	0	0	9
1984	Pit-N	0	27	2	3	.400	12	2.61	41 1/3	30	16	32	3	0	0	2
1985	Pit-N	0	63	4	6	.400	33	2.72	109	92	40	84	5	0	0	5
1986	Pit-N	0	52	5	2	.714	29	3.35	78	63	29	65	11	0	0	4
1987	**NY-A**	**0**	**23**	**3**	**2**	**.600**	**28**	**5.73**	**44**	**46**	**20**	**42**	**8**	**0**	**0**	**1**
1988	**NY-A**	**0**	**56**	**5**	**6**	**.455**	**24**	**2.88**	**75**	**61**	**22**	**59**	**10**	**0**	**0**	**11**
1988	Tex-A	0	7	0	0	—	1	1.93	4 2/3	4	4	8	1	0	0	1
1989	Tex-A	0	50	6	6	.500	30	3.91	69	69	36	66	7	0	0	2
1990	Cle-A	1	26	2	3	.400	26	5.01	46 2/3	30	18	38	10	0	0	0
Career Average		0	36	3	3	.460	23	3.48	59	50	24	51	6	0	0	4
Yankee Average		**0**	**40**	**4**	**4**	**.500**	**26**	**3.93**	**60**	**54**	**21**	**51**	**9**	**0**	**0**	**6**
Career Total		1	363	29	34	.460	230	3.48	595	503	236	512	61	0	0	35
Yankee Total		**0**	**79**	**8**	**8**	**.500**	**52**	**3.93**	**119**	**107**	**42**	**101**	**18**	**0**	**0**	**12**

Guetterman, Arthur Lee
HEIGHT: 6'8" LEFTHANDER BORN: 11/22/1958 CHATTANOOGA, TENNESSEE

YEAR	TEAM	STARTS	GAMES	WON	LOST	PCT	ER	ERA	INNINGS PITCHED	STRIKE-OUTS	WALKS	HITS ALLOWED	HRS ALLOWED	COMP. GAMES	SHUT-OUTS	SAVES
1984	Sea-A	0	3	0	0	—	2	4.15	4 1/3	2	2	9	0	0	0	0
1986	Sea-A	4	41	0	4	.000	62	7.34	76	38	30	108	7	1	0	0
1987	Sea-A	17	25	11	4	.733	48	3.81	113 1/3	42	35	117	13	2	1	0
1988	**NY-A**	**2**	**20**	**1**	**2**	**.333**	**21**	**4.65**	**40 2/3**	**15**	**14**	**49**	**2**	**0**	**0**	**0**
1989	**NY-A**	**0**	**70**	**5**	**5**	**.500**	**28**	**2.45**	**103**	**51**	**26**	**98**	**6**	**0**	**0**	**13**
1990	**NY-A**	**0**	**64**	**11**	**7**	**.611**	**35**	**3.39**	**93**	**48**	**26**	**80**	**6**	**0**	**0**	**2**
1991	**NY-A**	**0**	**64**	**3**	**4**	**.429**	**36**	**3.68**	**88**	**35**	**25**	**91**	**6**	**0**	**0**	**6**
1992	**NY-A**	**0**	**15**	**1**	**1**	**.500**	**24**	**9.53**	**22 2/3**	**5**	**13**	**35**	**5**	**0**	**0**	**0**
1992	NY-N	0	43	3	4	.429	28	5.82	43 1/3	15	14	57	5	0	0	2
1993	StL-N	0	40	3	3	.500	15	2.93	46	19	16	41	1	0	0	1
1995	Sea-A	0	23	0	0	—	13	6.88	17	11	11	21	1	0	0	1
1996	Sea-A	0	17	0	2	.000	5	4.09	11	6	10	11	0	0	0	0
Career Average		2	35	3	3	.514	26	4.33	55	24	19	60	4	0	0	2
Yankee Average		**0**	**47**	**4**	**4**	**.525**	**29**	**3.73**	**69**	**31**	**21**	**71**	**5**	**0**	**0**	**4**
Career Total		23	425	38	36	.514	317	4.33	658	287	222	717	52	3	1	25
Yankee Total		**2**	**233**	**21**	**19**	**.525**	**144**	**3.73**	**347**	**154**	**104**	**353**	**25**	**0**	**0**	**21**

Guidry, Ronald Ames (Gator)
HEIGHT: 5'11" LEFTHANDER BORN: 8/28/1950 LAFAYETTE, LOUISIANA

YEAR	TEAM	STARTS	GAMES	WON	LOST	PCT	ER	ERA	INNINGS PITCHED	STRIKE-OUTS	WALKS	HITS ALLOWED	HRS ALLOWED	COMP. GAMES	SHUT-OUTS	SAVES
1975	**NY-A**	**1**	**10**	**0**	**1**	**.000**	**6**	**3.45**	**15 2/3**	**15**	**9**	**15**	**0**	**0**	**0**	**0**
1976	**NY-A**	**0**	**7**	**0**	**0**	**—**	**10**	**5.63**	**16**	**12**	**4**	**20**	**1**	**0**	**0**	**0**
1977	**NY-A**	**25**	**31**	**16**	**7**	**.696**	**66**	**2.82**	**210 2/3**	**176**	**65**	**174**	**12**	**9**	**5**	**1**
1978	**NY-A**	**35**	**35**	**25**	**3**	**.893**	**53**	**1.74**	**273 2/3**	**248**	**72**	**187**	**13**	**16**	**9**	**0**
1979	**NY-A**	**30**	**33**	**18**	**8**	**.692**	**73**	**2.78**	**236 1/3**	**201**	**71**	**203**	**20**	**15**	**2**	**2**
1980	**NY-A**	**29**	**37**	**17**	**10**	**.630**	**87**	**3.56**	**219 2/3**	**166**	**80**	**215**	**19**	**5**	**3**	**1**
1981	**NY-A**	**21**	**23**	**11**	**5**	**.688**	**39**	**2.76**	**127**	**104**	**26**	**100**	**12**	**0**	**0**	**0**
1982	**NY-A**	**33**	**34**	**14**	**8**	**.636**	**94**	**3.81**	**222**	**162**	**69**	**216**	**22**	**6**	**1**	**0**
1983	**NY-A**	**31**	**31**	**21**	**9**	**.700**	**95**	**3.42**	**250 1/3**	**156**	**60**	**232**	**26**	**21**	**3**	**0**
1984	**NY-A**	**28**	**29**	**10**	**11**	**.476**	**98**	**4.51**	**195 2/3**	**127**	**44**	**223**	**24**	**5**	**1**	**0**
1985	**NY-A**	**33**	**34**	**22**	**6**	**.786**	**94**	**3.27**	**259**	**143**	**42**	**243**	**28**	**11**	**2**	**0**
1986	**NY-A**	**30**	**30**	**9**	**12**	**.429**	**85**	**3.98**	**192 1/3**	**140**	**38**	**202**	**28**	**5**	**0**	**0**
1987	**NY-A**	**17**	**22**	**5**	**8**	**.385**	**48**	**3.67**	**117 2/3**	**96**	**38**	**111**	**14**	**2**	**0**	**0**
1988	**NY-A**	**10**	**12**	**2**	**3**	**.400**	**26**	**4.18**	**56**	**32**	**15**	**57**	**7**	**0**	**0**	**0**
Career Average		23	26	12	7	.651	62	3.29	171	127	45	157	16	7	2	0
Yankee Average		**23**	**26**	**12**	**7**	**.651**	**62**	**3.29**	**171**	**127**	**45**	**157**	**16**	**7**	**2**	**0**
Career Total		323	368	170	91	.651	874	3.29	2392	1778	633	2198	226	95	26	4
Yankee Total		**323**	**368**	**170**	**91**	**.651**	**874**	**3.29**	**2392**	**1778**	**633**	**2198**	**226**	**95**	**26**	**4**

Ronald Ames "Gator" Guidry, lhp, 1975–88

There may have been more overpowering seasons by a pitcher in the history of baseball than Ron Guidry's 1978 year, but darned few.

Two years after he was dismissed by owner George Steinbrenner as "just another triple A pitcher," Ron Guidry dominated the American League with a 25-3 record and an ERA of 1.74, the second-lowest ERA for a lefthanded pitcher in American League history. Only Dutch Leonard's 1.01 ERA in 1914 was lower. The season included nine shutouts, tying a record for lefthanders set by Babe Ruth when he pitched for the Red Sox in 1917. The season included 248 strikeouts, which broke a team record of 239 set by Jack Chesbro in 1904, the year Chesbro won 41 games. Guidry's .893 winning percentage was the highest in baseball history by a 20-game winner.

"It was," admitted Guidry in his autobiography, "an awesome year."

Guidry was born on August 28, 1950, in Lafayette, Louisiana. He was a pitcher from his earliest days as a ballplayer and recalls that even as a young boy, he could throw hard. Following his high school career, Guidry pitched for two years at the University of Southwest Louisiana. He was drafted in the third round by the Yankees in 1971.

He spent six years in the minors, partly because, at the time, the Yankees were investing heavily in the free agent market, and partly because he only had one reliable pitch, his devastating fastball. He was brought up for brief stints in 1975 and 1976, and had only moderate success.

In 1977, Guidry was struggling again. In fact, he looked so bad that Martin asked him if he thought there was anyone in the majors Guidry thought he could get out. "If there is, tell me and I'll let you pitch to him," Martin told Guidry.

But Guidry was now working with teammate Sparky Lyle, who taught Guidry the mechanics of his slider. In the second half of 1977, Guidry mastered the pitch, and suddenly, he became a very good pitcher, helping the Yankees to win their first World Series in 13 years.

In 1978, Guidry took his ability to another level. He was nearly unbeatable, and unhittable. With a lively fastball and a sinking slider, he won his first 13 decisions. He also struck out a club-record 18 batters on June 17 against the Angels. He easily won the Cy Young Award.

His record stood out even more because the Yankees, beset with injuries, fell further and further behind the Red Sox, trailing Boston by 14½ games at one point, before eventually rallying. The two teams were tied at the end of the regular season, and Guidry pitched the one-game playoff at Fenway Park, "the tensest game I ever pitched." With a little help from Bucky Dent and Goose Gossage, Guidry won that game, and two more games in the postseason, as the Yankees won another world title.

Guidry had a number of solid seasons after that. He won 21 games in 1983 and 22 games in 1985. But the Yankees would win no more world championships with Guidry pitching. In 1986, he and second baseman Willie Randolph were named Yankee co-captains.

His last three years were frustrating ones. He battled injuries, but, always the professional, went out and tried to pitch through the pain; he would be only 16-23 in those seasons.

He remains in the Yankee record books with 1,778 strikeouts, second only to Whitey Ford, as well as a winning percentage of .651, eighth overall. He is also the best-fielding pitcher in Yankee history, with five consecutive Gold Glove awards from 1982-86.

Gullett, Donald Edward
HEIGHT: 6'0" LEFTHANDER BORN: 1/6/1951 LYNN, KENTUCKY

YEAR	TEAM	STARTS	GAMES	WON	LOST	PCT	ER	ERA	INNINGS PITCHED	STRIKE-OUTS	WALKS	HITS ALLOWED	HRS ALLOWED	COMP. GAMES	SHUT-OUTS	SAVES
1970	Cin-N	2	44	5	2	.714	21	2.43	77 2/3	76	44	54	4	0	0	6
1971	Cin-N	31	35	16	6	.727	64	2.65	217 2/3	107	64	196	14	4	3	0
1972	Cin-N	16	31	9	10	.474	59	3.94	134 2/3	96	43	127	15	2	0	2
1973	Cin-N	30	45	18	8	.692	89	3.51	228 1/3	153	69	198	24	7	4	2
1974	Cin-N	35	36	17	11	.607	82	3.04	243	183	88	201	22	10	3	0
1975	Cin-N	22	22	15	4	.789	43	2.42	159 2/3	98	56	127	11	8	3	0
1976	Cin-N	20	23	11	3	.786	42	3.00	126	64	48	119	8	4	0	1
1977	**NY-A**	**22**	**22**	**14**	**4**	**.778**	**63**	**3.58**	**158 1/3**	**116**	**69**	**137**	**14**	**7**	**1**	**0**
1978	**NY-A**	**8**	**8**	**4**	**2**	**.667**	**18**	**3.63**	**44 2/3**	**28**	**20**	**46**	**3**	**2**	**0**	**0**
Career Average		21	30	12	6	.686	53	3.11	154	102	56	134	13	5	2	1
Yankee Average		**15**	**15**	**9**	**3**	**.750**	**41**	**3.59**	**101**	**72**	**45**	**92**	**9**	**5**	**1**	**0**
Career Total		186	266	109	50	.686	481	3.11	1390	921	501	1205	115	44	14	11
Yankee Total		**30**	**30**	**18**	**6**	**.750**	**81**	**3.59**	**203**	**144**	**89**	**183**	**17**	**9**	**1**	**0**

Gullickson, William Lee
HEIGHT: 6'3" RIGHTHANDER BORN: 2/20/1959 MARSHALL, MINNESOTA

YEAR	TEAM	STARTS	GAMES	WON	LOST	PCT	ER	ERA	INNINGS PITCHED	STRIKE-OUTS	WALKS	HITS ALLOWED	HRS ALLOWED	COMP. GAMES	SHUT-OUTS	SAVES
1979	Mon-N	0	1	0	0	—	0	0.00	1	0	0	2	0	0	0	0
1980	Mon-N	19	24	10	5	.667	47	3.00	141	120	50	127	6	5	2	0
1981	Mon-N	22	22	7	9	.438	49	2.80	157 1/3	115	34	142	3	3	2	0
1982	Mon-N	34	34	12	14	.462	94	3.57	236 2/3	155	61	231	25	6	0	0
1983	Mon-N	34	34	17	12	.586	101	3.75	242 1/3	120	59	230	19	10	1	0
1984	Mon-N	32	32	12	9	.571	91	3.61	226 2/3	100	37	230	27	3	0	0
1985	Mon-N	29	29	14	12	.538	71	3.52	181 1/3	68	47	187	8	4	1	0
1986	Cin-N	37	37	15	12	.556	92	3.38	244 2/3	121	60	245	24	6	2	0
1987	Cin-N	27	27	10	11	.476	89	4.85	165	89	39	172	33	3	1	0
1987	**NY-A**	**8**	**8**	**4**	**2**	**.667**	**26**	**4.88**	**48**	**28**	**11**	**46**	**7**	**1**	**0**	**0**
1990	Hou-N	32	32	10	14	.417	82	3.82	193 1/3	73	61	221	21	2	1	0
1991	Det-A	35	35	20	9	.690	98	3.90	226 1/3	91	44	256	22	4	0	0
1992	Det-A	34	34	14	13	.519	107	4.34	221 2/3	64	50	228	35	4	1	0
1993	Det-A	28	28	13	9	.591	95	5.37	159 1/3	70	44	186	28	2	0	0
1994	Det-A	19	21	4	5	.444	76	5.95	115	65	25	156	24	1	0	0
Career Average		26	27	11	9	.544	75	3.93	171	85	41	177	19	4	1	0
Yankee Average		**8**	**8**	**4**	**2**	**.667**	**26**	**4.88**	**48**	**28**	**11**	**46**	**7**	**1**	**0**	**0**
Career Total		390	398	162	136	.544	1118	3.93	2560	1279	622	2659	282	54	11	0
Yankee Total		**8**	**8**	**4**	**2**	**.667**	**26**	**4.88**	**48**	**28**	**11**	**46**	**7**	**1**	**0**	**0**

Gumpert, Randall Pennington
HEIGHT: 6'3" RIGHTHANDER BORN: 1/23/1918 MONOCACY, PENNSYLVANIA

YEAR	TEAM	STARTS	GAMES	WON	LOST	PCT	ER	ERA	INNINGS PITCHED	STRIKE-OUTS	WALKS	HITS ALLOWED	HRS ALLOWED	COMP. GAMES	SHUT-OUTS	SAVES
1936	Phi-A	3	22	1	2	.333	33	4.76	62 1/3	9	32	74	2	2	0	2
1937	Phi-A	1	10	0	0	—	16	12.00	12	5	15	16	1	0	0	0
1938	Phi-A	2	4	0	2	.000	15	10.95	12 1/3	1	10	24	1	0	0	0
1946	**NY-A**	**12**	**33**	**11**	**3**	**.786**	**34**	**2.31**	**132 2/3**	**63**	**32**	**113**	**8**	**4**	**0**	**1**
1947	**NY-A**	**6**	**24**	**4**	**1**	**.800**	**34**	**5.43**	**56 1/3**	**25**	**28**	**71**	**4**	**2**	**0**	**0**
1948	**NY-A**	**0**	**15**	**1**	**0**	**1.000**	**8**	**2.88**	**25**	**12**	**6**	**27**	**0**	**0**	**0**	**0**
1948	Chi-A	11	16	2	6	.667	41	3.79	97 1/3	31	13	103	6	6	1	0
1949	Chi-A	32	34	13	16	.448	99	3.81	234	78	83	223	22	18	3	1
1950	Chi-A	17	40	5	12	.667	82	4.75	155 1/3	48	58	165	15	6	1	0
1951	Chi-A	16	33	9	8	.529	68	4.32	141 2/3	45	34	156	20	7	1	2
1952	Bos-A	1	10	1	0	1.000	9	4.12	19 2/3	6	5	15	1	0	0	1
1952	Was-A	12	20	4	9	.308	49	4.24	104	29	30	112	12	2	0	0
Career Average		9	22	4	5	.464	41	4.17	88	29	29	92	8	4	1	1
Yankee Average		**6**	**24**	**5**	**1**	**.800**	**25**	**3.20**	**71**	**33**	**22**	**70**	**4**	**2**	**0**	**0**
Career Total		113	261	51	59	.464	488	4.17	1053	352	346	1099	92	47	6	7
Yankee Total		**18**	**72**	**16**	**4**	**.800**	**76**	**3.20**	**214**	**100**	**66**	**211**	**12**	**6**	**0**	**1**

Gura, Lawrence Cyril

HEIGHT: 6'0"   LEFTHANDER   BORN: 11/26/1947 JOLIET, ILLINOIS

YEAR	TEAM	STARTS	GAMES	WON	LOST	PCT	ER	ERA	INNINGS PITCHED	STRIKE-OUTS	WALKS	HITS ALLOWED	HRS ALLOWED	COMP. GAMES	SHUT-OUTS	SAVES
1970	Chi-N	3	20	1	3	.667	16	3.79	38	21	23	35	6	1	0	1
1971	Chi-N	0	6	0	0	—	2	6.00	3	2	1	6	0	0	0	1
1972	Chi-N	0	7	0	0	—	5	3.65	12 1/3	13	3	11	3	0	0	0
1973	Chi-N	7	21	2	4	.333	35	4.87	64 2/3	43	11	79	10	0	0	0
1974	**NY-A**	**8**	**8**	**5**	**1**	**.833**	**15**	**2.41**	**56**	**17**	**12**	**54**	**2**	**4**	**2**	**0**
1975	**NY-A**	**20**	**26**	**7**	**8**	**.467**	**59**	**3.51**	**151 1/3**	**65**	**41**	**173**	**13**	**5**	**0**	**0**
1976	KC-A	2	20	4	0	1.000	16	2.30	62 2/3	22	20	47	4	1	1	1
1977	KC-A	6	52	8	5	.615	37	3.13	106 1/3	46	28	108	8	1	1	10
1978	KC-A	26	35	16	4	.800	67	2.72	221 2/3	81	60	183	13	8	2	0
1979	KC-A	33	39	13	12	.520	116	4.47	233 2/3	85	73	226	29	7	1	0
1980	KC-A	36	36	18	10	.643	93	2.95	283 2/3	113	76	272	20	16	4	0
1981	KC-A	23	23	11	8	.579	52	2.72	172 1/3	61	35	139	11	12	2	0
1982	KC-A	37	37	18	12	.600	111	4.03	248	98	64	251	31	8	3	0
1983	KC-A	31	34	11	18	.379	109	4.90	200 1/3	57	76	220	23	5	0	0
1984	KC-A	25	31	12	9	.571	97	5.18	168 2/3	68	67	175	26	3	0	0
1985	KC-A	0	3	0	0	—	6	12.46	4 1/3	2	4	7	1	0	0	1
1985	Chi-N	4	5	0	3	.000	19	8.41	20 1/3	7	6	34	4	0	0	0
Career Average		15	24	7	6	.565	50	3.76	120	47	35	119	12	4	1	1
Yankee Average		**14**	**17**	**6**	**5**	**.571**	**37**	**3.21**	**104**	**41**	**27**	**114**	**8**	**5**	**1**	**0**
Career Total		261	403	126	97	.565	855	3.76	2047	801	600	2020	204	71	16	14
Yankee Total		**28**	**34**	**12**	**9**	**.571**	**74**	**3.21**	**207**	**82**	**53**	**227**	**15**	**9**	**2**	**0**

Habyan, John Gabriel

HEIGHT: 6'2"   RIGHTHANDER   BORN: 1/29/1964 BAY SHORE, NEW YORK

YEAR	TEAM	STARTS	GAMES	WON	LOST	PCT	ER	ERA	INNINGS PITCHED	STRIKE-OUTS	WALKS	HITS ALLOWED	HRS ALLOWED	COMP. GAMES	SHUT-OUTS	SAVES
1985	Bal-A	0	2	1	0	1.000	0	0.00	2 2/3	2	0	3	0	0	0	0
1986	Bal-A	5	6	1	3	.667	13	4.44	26 1/3	14	18	24	3	0	0	0
1987	Bal-A	13	27	6	7	.462	62	4.80	116 1/3	64	40	110	20	0	0	1
1988	Bal-A	0	7	1	0	1.000	7	4.30	14 2/3	4	4	22	2	0	0	1
1990	**NY-A**	**0**	**6**	**0**	**0**	**—**	**2**	**2.08**	**8 2/3**	**4**	**2**	**10**	**0**	**0**	**0**	**0**
1991	**NY-A**	**0**	**66**	**4**	**2**	**.667**	**23**	**2.30**	**90**	**70**	**20**	**73**	**2**	**0**	**0**	**2**
1992	**NY-A**	**0**	**56**	**5**	**6**	**.455**	**31**	**3.84**	**72 2/3**	**44**	**21**	**84**	**6**	**0**	**0**	**7**
1993	**NY-A**	**0**	**36**	**2**	**1**	**.667**	**19**	**4.04**	**42 1/3**	**29**	**16**	**45**	**5**	**0**	**0**	**1**
1993	KC-A	0	12	0	0	—	7	4.50	14	14	4	14	1	0	0	0
1994	StL-N	0	52	1	0	1.000	17	3.26	47 1/3	46	20	50	2	0	0	1
1995	StL-N	0	31	3	2	.600	13	2.93	40 2/3	35	15	32	0	0	0	0
1995	Cal-A	0	28	1	2	.333	15	4.22	32 1/3	25	12	36	2	0	0	0
1996	Col-N	0	19	1	1	.500	19	7.13	24	25	14	34	4	0	0	0
Career Average		1	27	2	2	.520	18	3.87	41	29	14	41	4	0	0	1
Yankee Average		**0**	**41**	**3**	**2**	**.550**	**19**	**3.16**	**53**	**37**	**15**	**53**	**3**	**0**	**0**	**3**
Career Total		18	348	26	24	.520	228	3.87	531	372	186	537	47	0	0	12
Yankee Total		**0**	**164**	**11**	**9**	**.550**	**75**	**3.16**	**214**	**147**	**59**	**212**	**13**	**0**	**0**	**10**

Hadley, Irving Darius (Bump)

HEIGHT: 5'11"   RIGHTHANDER   BORN: 7/5/1904 LYNN, MASSACHUSETTS   DIED: 2/15/1963 LYNN, MASSACHUSETTS

YEAR	TEAM	STARTS	GAMES	WON	LOST	PCT	ER	ERA	INNINGS PITCHED	STRIKE-OUTS	WALKS	HITS ALLOWED	HRS ALLOWED	COMP. GAMES	SHUT-OUTS	SAVES
1926	Was-A	0	1	0	0	—	4	12.00	3	0	2	6	0	0	0	0
1927	Was-A	27	30	14	6	.700	63	2.85	198 2/3	60	86	177	2	13	0	0
1928	Was-A	31	33	12	13	.480	91	3.54	231 2/3	80	100	236	4	16	3	0
1929	Was-A	27	37	6	16	.667	122	5.62	195 1/3	98	85	196	10	7	1	0
1930	Was-A	34	42	15	11	.577	108	3.73	260 1/3	162	105	242	6	15	1	2
1931	Was-A	11	55	11	10	.524	61	3.06	179 2/3	124	92	145	4	2	1	8
1932	Chi-A	2	3	1	1	.500	8	3.86	18 2/3	13	8	17	2	1	0	1
1932	StL-A	33	40	13	20	.394	141	5.53	229 2/3	132	163	244	21	12	1	1
1933	StL-A	36	45	15	20	.429	138	3.92	316 2/3	149	141	309	17	19	2	3
1934	StL-A	32	39	10	16	.385	103	4.35	213	79	127	212	14	7	2	1
1935	Was-A	32	35	10	15	.400	126	4.92	230 1/3	77	102	268	18	13	0	0
1936	**NY-A**	**17**	**31**	**14**	**4**	**.778**	**84**	**4.35**	**173 2/3**	**74**	**89**	**194**	**12**	**8**	**1**	**1**
1937	**NY-A**	**25**	**29**	**11**	**8**	**.579**	**105**	**5.30**	**178 1/3**	**70**	**83**	**199**	**16**	**6**	**0**	**0**

(continued)

(continued)

YEAR	TEAM	STARTS	GAMES	WON	LOST	PCT	ER	ERA	INNINGS PITCHED	STRIKE-OUTS	WALKS	HITS ALLOWED	HRS ALLOWED	COMP. GAMES	SHUT-OUTS	SAVES
1938	NY-A	17	29	9	8	.529	67	3.60	167 ⅓	61	66	165	13	8	1	1
1939	NY-A	18	26	12	6	.667	51	2.98	154	65	85	132	10	7	1	2
1940	NY-A	2	25	3	5	.375	51	5.74	80	39	52	88	4	0	0	2
1941	NY-N	2	3	1	0	1.000	9	6.23	13	4	9	19	1	0	0	0
1941	Phi-A	9	25	4	6	.400	57	5.01	102 ⅓	31	47	131	13	1	0	3
Career Average		20	29	9	9	.494	77	4.24	164	73	80	166	9	8	1	1
Yankee Average		16	28	10	6	.613	72	4.28	151	62	75	156	11	6	1	1
Career Total		355	528	161	165	.494	1389	4.24	2946	1318	1442	2980	167	135	14	25
Yankee Total		79	140	49	31	.613	358	4.28	753	309	375	778	55	29	3	6

Hahn, Frank George (Noodles)

HEIGHT: 5'9"   LEFTHANDER   BORN: 4/29/1879 NASHVILLE, TENNESSEE   DIED: 2/6/1960 CANDLER, NORTH CAROLINA

YEAR	TEAM	STARTS	GAMES	WON	LOST	PCT	ER	ERA	INNINGS PITCHED	STRIKE-OUTS	WALKS	HITS ALLOWED	HRS ALLOWED	COMP. GAMES	SHUT-OUTS	SAVES
1899	Cin-N	34	38	23	8	742	92	2.68	309	145	68	280	3	32	4	0
1900	Cin-N	37	39	16	20	.444	113	3.27	311 ⅓	132	89	306	4	29	4	0
1901	Cin-N	42	42	22	19	.537	113	2.71	375 ⅓	239	69	370	12	41	2	0
1902	Cin-N	36	36	23	12	.657	63	1.77	321	142	58	282	2	35	6	0
1903	Cin-N	34	34	22	12	.647	83	2.52	296	127	47	297	3	34	5	0
1904	Cin-N	34	35	16	18	.471	68	2.06	297 ⅔	98	35	258	3	33	2	0
1905	Cin-N	8	13	5	3	.625	24	2.81	77	17	9	85	0	5	1	0
1906	NY-A	6	6	3	2	.600	18	3.86	42	17	6	38	0	3	1	0
Career Average		29	30	16	12	.580	72	2.55	254	115	48	240	3	27	3	0
Yankee Average		6	6	3	2	.600	18	3.86	42	17	6	38	0	3	1	0
Career Total		231	243	94	94	.580	574	2.55	2029	917	381	1916	27	212	25	0
Yankee Total		6	6	3	2	.600	18	3.86	42	17	6	38	0	3	1	0

Hambright, Roger Dee

HEIGHT: 5'10"   RIGHTHANDER   BORN: 3/26/1949 SUNNYSIDE, WASHINGTON

YEAR	TEAM	STARTS	GAMES	WON	LOST	PCT	ER	ERA	INNINGS PITCHED	STRIKE-OUTS	WALKS	HITS ALLOWED	HRS ALLOWED	COMP. GAMES	SHUT-OUTS	SAVES
1971	NY-A	0	18	3	1	.750	13	4.39	26 ⅔	14	10	22	5	0	0	2
Career Average		0	18	3	1	.750	13	4.39	26 ⅔	14	10	22	5	0	0	2
Yankee Average		0	18	3	1	.750	13	4.39	26 ⅔	14	10	22	5	0	0	2
Career Total		0	18	3	1	.750	13	4.39	26 ⅔	14	10	22	5	0	0	2
Yankee Total		0	18	3	1	.750	13	4.39	26 ⅔	14	10	22	5	0	0	2

Hamilton, Steve Abshe

HEIGHT: 6'6"   LEFTHANDER   BORN: 11/30/1935 COLUMBIA, KENTUCKY

YEAR	TEAM	STARTS	GAMES	WON	LOST	PCT	ER	ERA	INNINGS PITCHED	STRIKE-OUTS	WALKS	HITS ALLOWED	HRS ALLOWED	COMP. GAMES	SHUT-OUTS	SAVES
1961	Cle-A	0	2	0	0	—	1	3.00	3	4	3	2	0	0	0	0
1962	Was-A	10	41	3	8	.667	45	3.77	107 ⅓	83	39	103	10	1	0	2
1963	Was-A	0	3	0	1	.000	3	13.50	2	1	2	5	0	0	0	0
1963	NY-A	0	34	5	1	.833	18	2.60	62 ⅓	63	24	49	3	0	0	5
1964	NY-A	3	30	7	2	.778	22	3.28	60 ⅓	49	15	55	6	1	0	3
1965	NY-A	1	46	3	1	.750	9	1.39	58 ⅓	51	16	47	2	0	0	5
1966	NY-A	3	44	8	3	.727	30	3.00	90	57	22	69	8	1	1	3
1967	NY-A	0	44	2	4	.333	24	3.48	62	55	23	57	7	0	0	4
1968	NY-A	0	40	2	2	.500	12	2.13	50 ⅔	42	13	37	0	0	0	11
1969	NY-A	0	38	3	4	.429	21	3.32	57	39	21	39	7	0	0	2
1970	NY-A	0	35	4	3	.571	14	2.78	45 ⅓	33	16	36	3	0	0	3
1970	Chi-A	0	3	0	0	—	2	6.00	3	3	1	4	0	0	0	0
1971	SF-N	0	39	2	2	.500	15	3.02	44 ⅔	38	11	29	4	0	0	4
1972	Chi-N	0	22	1	0	1.000	9	4.76	17	13	8	24	1	0	0	0
Career Average		1	30	3	2	.563	16	3.05	47	38	15	40	4	0	0	3
Yankee Average		1	39	4	3	.630	19	2.78	61	49	19	49	5	0	0	5
Career Total		17	421	40	31	.563	225	3.05	663	531	214	556	51	3	1	42
Yankee Total		7	311	34	20	.630	150	2.78	486	389	150	389	36	2	1	36

Hanley, James Patrick

HEIGHT: 5'11"   LEFTHANDER   BORN: 10/13/1885 PROVIDENCE, RHODE ISLAND   DIED: 5/1/1961 ELMHURST, NEW YORK

YEAR	TEAM	STARTS	GAMES	WON	LOST	PCT	ER	ERA	INNINGS PITCHED	STRIKE-OUTS	WALKS	HITS ALLOWED	HRS ALLOWED	COMP. GAMES	SHUT-OUTS	SAVES
1913	NY-A	0	1	0	0	—	3	6.75	4	2	4	5	0	0	0	0
Career Average		0	1	0	0	—	3	6.75	4	2	4	5	0	0	0	0
Yankee Average		**0**	**1**	**0**	**0**	**—**	**3**	**6.75**	**4**	**2**	**4**	**5**	**0**	**0**	**0**	**0**
Career Total		0	1	0	0	—	3	6.75	4	2	4	5	0	0	0	0
Yankee Total		**0**	**1**	**0**	**0**	**—**	**3**	**6.75**	**4**	**2**	**4**	**5**	**0**	**0**	**0**	**0**

Hardin, James Warren

HEIGHT: 6'0"   RIGHTHANDER   BORN: 8/6/1943 MORRIS CHAPEL, TENNESSEE   DIED: 3/9/1991 KEY WEST, FLORIDA

YEAR	TEAM	STARTS	GAMES	WON	LOST	PCT	ER	ERA	INNINGS PITCHED	STRIKE-OUTS	WALKS	HITS ALLOWED	HRS ALLOWED	COMP. GAMES	SHUT-OUTS	SAVES
1967	Bal-A	14	19	8	3	.727	28	2.27	111	64	27	85	5	5	2	0
1968	Bal-A	35	35	18	13	.581	68	2.51	244	160	70	188	20	16	2	0
1969	Bal-A	20	30	6	7	.462	55	3.60	137 2/3	64	43	128	18	3	1	1
1970	Bal-A	19	36	6	5	.545	57	3.53	145 1/3	78	26	150	13	3	2	1
1971	Bal-A	0	6	0	0	—	3	4.77	5 2/3	3	3	12	0	0	0	0
1971	NY-A	3	12	0	2	.000	16	5.08	28 1/3	14	9	35	3	0	0	0
1972	Atl-N	9	26	5	2	.714	39	4.41	79 2/3	25	24	93	11	1	0	2
Career Average		14	23	6	5	.573	38	3.18	107	58	29	99	10	4	1	1
Yankee Average		**3**	**12**	**0**	**2**	**.000**	**16**	**5.08**	**28 1/3**	**14**	**9**	**35**	**3**	**0**	**0**	**0**
Career Total		100	164	43	32	.573	266	3.18	752	408	202	691	70	28	7	4
Yankee Total		**3**	**12**	**0**	**2**	**.000**	**16**	**5.08**	**28 1/3**	**14**	**9**	**35**	**3**	**0**	**0**	**0**

Harper, Harry Clayton

HEIGHT: 6'2"   LEFTHANDER   BORN: 4/24/1895 HACKENSACK, NEW JERSEY   DIED: 4/23/1963 NEW YORK, NEW YORK

YEAR	TEAM	STARTS	GAMES	WON	LOST	PCT	ER	ERA	INNINGS PITCHED	STRIKE-OUTS	WALKS	HITS ALLOWED	HRS ALLOWED	COMP. GAMES	SHUT-OUTS	SAVES
1913	Was-A	0	4	0	0	—	5	3.55	12 2/3	9	5	10	1	0	0	0
1914	Was-A	3	23	2	1	.667	22	3.47	57	50	35	45	1	1	0	2
1915	Was-A	10	19	4	4	.500	17	1.77	86 1/3	54	40	66	1	5	2	2
1916	Was-A	34	36	14	10	.583	68	2.45	249 2/3	149	101	209	4	13	2	0
1917	Was-A	31	31	11	12	.478	60	3.01	179 1/3	99	106	145	1	10	4	0
1918	Was-A	32	35	11	10	.524	59	2.18	244	78	104	182	1	14	3	1
1919	Was-A	31	35	6	21	.666	86	3.72	208	87	97	220	3	8	0	0
1920	Bos-A	22	27	5	14	.667	55	3.04	162 2/3	71	66	163	9	11	1	0
1921	NY-A	7	8	4	3	.571	22	3.76	52 2/3	22	25	52	3	4	0	0
1923	Bro-N	1	1	0	1	.000	6	14.73	3 2/3	4	3	8	2	0	0	0
Career Average		17	22	6	8	.429	40	2.87	126	62	58	110	3	7	1	1
Yankee Average		**7**	**8**	**4**	**3**	**.571**	**22**	**3.76**	**52 2/3**	**22**	**25**	**52**	**3**	**4**	**0**	**0**
Career Total		171	219	57	76	.429	400	2.87	1256	623	582	1100	26	66	12	5
Yankee Total		**7**	**8**	**4**	**3**	**.571**	**22**	**3.76**	**52 2/3**	**22**	**25**	**52**	**3**	**4**	**0**	**0**

Harris, Greg Allen

HEIGHT: 6'0"   RIGHTHANDER   BORN: 11/2/1955 LYNWOOD, CALIFORNIA

YEAR	TEAM	STARTS	GAMES	WON	LOST	PCT	ER	ERA	INNINGS PITCHED	STRIKE-OUTS	WALKS	HITS ALLOWED	HRS ALLOWED	COMP. GAMES	SHUT-OUTS	SAVES
1981	NY-N	14	16	3	5	.375	34	4.46	68 2/3	54	28	65	8	0	0	1
1982	Cin-N	10	34	2	6	.667	49	4.83	91 1/3	67	37	96	12	1	0	1
1983	Cin-N	0	1	0	0	—	3	27.00	1	1	3	2	0	0	0	0
1984	Mon-N	0	15	0	1	.000	4	2.04	17 2/3	15	7	10	0	0	0	2
1984	SD-N	1	19	2	1	.667	11	2.70	36 2/3	30	18	28	3	0	0	1
1985	Tex-A	0	58	5	4	.556	31	2.47	113	111	43	74	7	0	0	11
1986	Tex-A	0	73	10	8	.556	35	2.83	111 1/3	95	42	103	12	0	0	20
1987	Tex-A	19	42	5	10	.333	76	4.86	140 2/3	106	56	157	18	0	0	0
1988	Phi-N	1	66	4	6	.400	28	2.36	107	71	52	80	7	0	0	1

(continued)

(continued)

YEAR	TEAM	STARTS	GAMES	WON	LOST	PCT	ER	ERA	INNINGS PITCHED	STRIKE-OUTS	WALKS	HITS ALLOWED	HRS ALLOWED	COMP. GAMES	SHUT-OUTS	SAVES
1989	Phi-N	0	44	2	2	.500	30	3.58	75 1/3	51	43	64	7	0	0	1
1989	Bos-A	0	15	2	2	.500	8	2.57	28	25	15	21	1	0	0	0
1990	Bos-A	30	34	13	9	.591	82	4.00	184 1/3	117	77	186	13	1	0	0
1991	Bos-A	21	53	11	12	.478	74	3.85	173	127	69	157	13	1	0	2
1992	Bos-A	2	70	4	9	.308	30	2.51	107 2/3	73	60	82	6	1	0	4
1993	Bos-A	0	80	6	7	.462	47	3.77	112 1/3	103	60	95	7	0	0	8
1994	Bos-A	0	35	3	4	.429	42	8.40	45	44	23	60	8	0	0	2
1994	**NY-A**	**0**	**3**	**0**	**1**	**.000**	**3**	**5.40**	**5**	**4**	**3**	**4**	**1**	**0**	**0**	**0**
1995	Mon-N	0	45	2	3	.400	14	2.63	48	47	16	45	6	0	0	0
Career Average		5	39	4	5	.451	33	3.69	81	63	36	74	7	0	0	3
Yankee Average		**0**	**3**	**0**	**1**	**.000**	**3**	**5.40**	**5**	**4**	**3**	**4**	**1**	**0**	**0**	**0**
Career Total		98	703	74	90	.451	601	3.69	1466	1141	652	1329	129	4	0	54
Yankee Total		**0**	**3**	**0**	**1**	**.000**	**3**	**5.40**	**5**	**4**	**3**	**4**	**1**	**0**	**0**	**0**

Hawkins, Melton Andrew

HEIGHT: 6'4"   RIGHTHANDER   BORN: 1/21/1960 WACO, TEXAS

YEAR	TEAM	STARTS	GAMES	WON	LOST	PCT	ER	ERA	INNINGS PITCHED	STRIKE-OUTS	WALKS	HITS ALLOWED	HRS ALLOWED	COMP. GAMES	SHUT-OUTS	SAVES
1982	SD-N	10	15	2	5	.667	29	4.10	63 2/3	25	27	66	4	1	0	0
1983	SD-N	19	21	5	7	.417	39	2.93	119 2/3	59	48	106	8	4	1	0
1984	SD-N	22	36	8	9	.471	76	4.68	146	77	72	143	13	2	1	0
1985	SD-N	33	33	18	8	.692	80	3.15	228 2/3	69	65	229	18	5	2	0
1986	SD-N	35	37	10	8	.556	100	4.30	209 1/3	117	75	218	24	3	1	0
1987	SD-N	20	24	3	10	.666	66	5.05	117 2/3	51	49	131	16	0	0	0
1988	SD-N	33	33	14	11	.560	81	3.35	217 2/3	91	76	196	16	4	2	0
1989	**NY-A**	**34**	**34**	**15**	**15**	**.500**	**111**	**4.80**	**208 1/3**	**98**	**76**	**238**	**23**	**5**	**2**	**0**
1990	**NY-A**	**26**	**28**	**5**	**12**	**.667**	**94**	**5.37**	**157 2/3**	**74**	**82**	**156**	**20**	**2**	**1**	**0**
1991	**NY-A**	**3**	**4**	**0**	**2**	**.000**	**14**	**9.95**	**12 2/3**	**5**	**6**	**23**	**5**	**0**	**0**	**0**
1991	Oak-A	14	15	4	4	.500	41	4.79	77	40	36	68	5	1	0	0
Career Average		23	25	8	8	.480	66	4.22	142	64	56	143	14	2	1	0
Yankee Average		**21**	**22**	**7**	**10**	**.408**	**73**	**5.21**	**126**	**59**	**55**	**139**	**16**	**2**	**1**	**0**
Career Total		249	280	84	91	.480	731	4.22	1558	706	612	1574	152	27	10	0
Yankee Total		**63**	**66**	**20**	**29**	**.408**	**219**	**5.21**	**379**	**177**	**164**	**417**	**48**	**7**	**3**	**0**

Heaton, Neal

HEIGHT: 6'1"   LEFTHANDER   BORN: 3/3/1960 JAMAICA, NEW YORK

YEAR	TEAM	STARTS	GAMES	WON	LOST	PCT	ER	ERA	INNINGS PITCHED	STRIKE-OUTS	WALKS	HITS ALLOWED	HRS ALLOWED	COMP. GAMES	SHUT-OUTS	SAVES
1982	Cle-A	4	8	0	2	.000	18	5.23	31	14	16	32	1	0	0	0
1983	Cle-A	16	39	11	7	.611	69	4.16	149 1/3	75	44	157	11	4	3	7
1984	Cle-A	34	38	12	15	.444	115	5.21	198 2/3	75	75	231	21	4	1	0
1985	Cle-A	33	36	9	17	.346	113	4.90	207 2/3	82	80	244	19	5	1	0
1986	Cle-A	12	12	3	6	.333	35	4.24	74 1/3	24	34	73	8	2	0	0
1986	Min-A	17	21	4	9	.308	55	3.98	124 1/3	66	47	128	18	3	0	1
1987	Mon-N	32	32	13	10	.565	97	4.52	193 1/3	105	37	207	25	3	1	0
1988	Mon-N	11	32	3	10	.666	54	4.99	97 1/3	43	43	98	14	0	0	2
1989	Pit-N	18	42	6	7	.462	50	3.05	147 1/3	67	55	127	12	1	0	0
1990	Pit-N	24	30	12	9	.571	56	3.45	146	68	38	143	17	0	0	0
1991	Pit-N	1	42	3	3	.500	33	4.33	68 2/3	34	21	72	6	0	0	0
1992	KC-A	0	31	3	1	.750	19	4.17	41	29	22	43	5	0	0	0
1992	Mil-A	0	1	0	0	—	0	0.00	1	2	1	0	0	0	0	0
1993	**NY-A**	**0**	**18**	**1**	**0**	**1.000**	**18**	**6.00**	**27**	**15**	**11**	**34**	**6**	**0**	**0**	**0**
Career Average		14	27	6	7	.455	52	4.37	108	50	37	114	12	2	0	1
Yankee Average		**0**	**18**	**1**	**0**	**1.000**	**18**	**6.00**	**27**	**15**	**11**	**34**	**6**	**0**	**0**	**0**
Career Total		202	382	80	96	.455	732	4.37	1507	699	524	1589	163	22	6	10
Yankee Total		**0**	**18**	**1**	**0**	**1.000**	**18**	**6.00**	**27**	**15**	**11**	**34**	**6**	**0**	**0**	**0**

Heimach, Frederick Amos (Lefty)
HEIGHT: 6'0" LEFTHANDER BORN: 1/27/1901 CAMDEN, NEW JERSEY DIED: 6/1/1973 FT. MYERS, FLORIDA

YEAR	TEAM	STARTS	GAMES	WON	LOST	PCT	ER	ERA	INNINGS PITCHED	STRIKE-OUTS	WALKS	HITS ALLOWED	HRS ALLOWED	COMP. GAMES	SHUT-OUTS	SAVES
1920	Phi-A	1	1	0	1	.000	8	14.40	5	0	1	13	0	0	0	0
1921	Phi-A	1	1	1	0	1.000	0	0.00	9	1	1	7	0	1	1	0
1922	Phi-A	19	37	7	11	.389	96	5.03	171 2/3	47	63	220	18	7	0	1
1923	Phi-A	19	40	6	12	.333	100	4.32	208 1/3	63	69	238	14	10	0	0
1924	Phi-A	26	40	14	12	.538	104	4.73	198	60	60	243	2	10	0	0
1925	Phi-A	0	10	0	1	.000	9	3.98	20 1/3	6	9	24	2	0	0	0
1926	Phi-A	1	13	1	0	1.000	10	2.84	31 2/3	8	5	28	1	0	0	0
1926	Bos-A	13	20	2	9	.182	64	5.65	102	17	42	119	5	6	0	0
1928	**NY-A**	**9**	**13**	**2**	**3**	**.400**	**25**	**3.31**	**68**	**25**	**16**	**66**	**3**	**5**	**0**	**0**
1929	**NY-A**	**10**	**35**	**11**	**6**	**.647**	**60**	**4.01**	**134 2/3**	**26**	**29**	**141**	**4**	**3**	**3**	**4**
1930	Bro-N	0	9	0	2	.000	4	4.91	7 1/3	1	3	14	0	0	0	1
1931	Bro-N	10	31	9	7	.563	52	3.46	135 1/3	43	23	145	6	7	1	1
1932	Bro-N	15	36	9	4	.692	74	3.97	167 2/3	30	28	203	7	7	0	0
1933	Bro-N	3	10	0	1	.000	33	10.01	29 2/3	7	11	49	2	0	0	0
Career Average		9	21	4	5	.473	46	4.46	92	24	26	108	5	4	0	1
Yankee Average		**10**	**24**	**7**	**5**	**.591**	**43**	**3.77**	**101**	**26**	**23**	**104**	**4**	**4**	**2**	**2**
Career Total		127	296	62	69	.473	639	4.46	1289	334	360	1510	64	56	5	7
Yankee Total		**19**	**48**	**13**	**9**	**.591**	**85**	**3.77**	**203**	**51**	**45**	**207**	**7**	**8**	**3**	**4**

Henderson, William Maxwell
HEIGHT: 6'0" RIGHTHANDER BORN: 11/4/1901 PENSACOLA, FLORIDA DIED: 10/6/1966 PENSACOLA, FLORIDA

YEAR	TEAM	STARTS	GAMES	WON	LOST	PCT	ER	ERA	INNINGS PITCHED	STRIKE-OUTS	WALKS	HITS ALLOWED	HRS ALLOWED	COMP. GAMES	SHUT-OUTS	SAVES
1930	**NY-A**	**0**	**3**	**0**	**0**	**—**	**4**	**4.50**	**8**	**2**	**4**	**7**	**1**	**0**	**0**	**0**
Career Average		0	3	0	0	—	4	4.50	8	2	4	7	1	0	0	0
Yankee Average		**0**	**3**	**0**	**0**	**—**	**4**	**4.50**	**8**	**2**	**4**	**7**	**1**	**0**	**0**	**0**
Career Total		0	3	0	0	—	4	4.50	8	2	4	7	1	0	0	0
Yankee Total		**0**	**3**	**0**	**0**	**—**	**4**	**4.50**	**8**	**2**	**4**	**7**	**1**	**0**	**0**	**0**

Henry, William Francis
HEIGHT: 6'3" LEFTHANDER BORN: 2/15/1942 LONG BEACH, CALIFORNIA

YEAR	TEAM	STARTS	GAMES	WON	LOST	PCT	ER	ERA	INNINGS PITCHED	STRIKE-OUTS	WALKS	HITS ALLOWED	HRS ALLOWED	COMP. GAMES	SHUT-OUTS	SAVES
1966	**NY-A**	**0**	**2**	**0**	**0**	**—**	**0**	**0.00**	**3**	**3**	**2**	**0**	**0**	**0**	**0**	**0**
Career Average		0	2	0	0	—	0	0.00	3	3	2	0	0	0	0	0
Yankee Average		**0**	**2**	**0**	**0**	**—**	**0**	**0.00**	**3**	**3**	**2**	**0**	**0**	**0**	**0**	**0**
Career Total		0	2	0	0	—	0	0.00	3	3	2	0	0	0	0	0
Yankee Total		**0**	**2**	**0**	**0**	**—**	**0**	**0.00**	**3**	**3**	**2**	**0**	**0**	**0**	**0**	**0**

Hernandez, Francis Xavier
HEIGHT: 6'2" RIGHTHANDER BORN: 8/16/1965 PORT ARTHUR, TEXAS

YEAR	TEAM	STARTS	GAMES	WON	LOST	PCT	ER	ERA	INNINGS PITCHED	STRIKE-OUTS	WALKS	HITS ALLOWED	HRS ALLOWED	COMP. GAMES	SHUT-OUTS	SAVES
1989	Tor-A	0	7	1	0	1.000	12	4.76	22 2/3	7	8	25	2	0	0	0
1990	Hou-N	1	34	2	1	.667	32	4.62	62 1/3	24	24	60	8	0	0	0
1991	Hou-N	6	32	2	7	.666	33	4.71	63	55	32	66	6	0	0	3
1992	Hou-N	0	77	9	1	.900	26	2.11	111	96	42	81	5	0	0	7
1993	Hou-N	0	72	4	5	.444	28	2.61	96 2/3	101	28	75	6	0	0	9
1994	**NY-A**	**0**	**31**	**4**	**4**	**.500**	**26**	**5.85**	**40**	**37**	**21**	**48**	**7**	**0**	**0**	**6**
1995	Cin-N	0	59	7	2	.778	46	4.60	90	84	31	95	8	0	0	3
1996	Cin-N	0	3	0	0	—	5	15.00	3 1/3	3	2	8	2	0	0	0
1996	Hou-N	0	58	5	5	.500	35	4.26	74 2/3	78	26	69	11	0	0	6
1997	Tex-A	0	44	0	4	.000	25	4.59	49 1/3	36	22	51	7	0	0	0
1998	Tex-A	0	46	6	6	.500	23	3.57	58	41	30	43	5	0	0	1
Career Average		1	42	4	3	.533	26	3.91	61	51	24	56	6	0	0	3
Yankee Average		**0**	**31**	**4**	**4**	**.500**	**26**	**5.85**	**40**	**37**	**21**	**48**	**7**	**0**	**0**	**6**
Career Total		7	463	40	35	.533	291	3.91	670	562	266	621	67	0	0	35
Yankee Total		**0**	**31**	**4**	**4**	**.500**	**26**	**5.85**	**40**	**37**	**21**	**48**	**7**	**0**	**0**	**6**

Orlando "El Duque" Hernandez, rhp, 1998–2000

This is one guy who has had an interesting life.

Hernandez was born on October 11, 1969 in Villa Clara, Cuba. Or maybe it was October 11, 1965. No one's sure. But regardless of his age, Hernandez had, in three short years, become one of the great "money" pitchers in Yankee history.

El Duque, so named for his regal bearing and winning ways, had been the star of the Cuban national team, earning a record of 129-47 over several years.

But in October of 1996, he was banned from the team by Cuban sports officials after they heard he was trying to defect. Hernandez worked briefly in a psychiatric hospital, but on December 26, 1997, he and seven others left Cuba in a small boat. A few days later, he was picked up, along with the other defectors, by a U.S. Coast Guard ship after landing on a small island.

He established residency in Costa Rica, and became a free agent. The Yankees won the bidding war for him.

It paid off almost immediately. He was 6-0 at Columbus in 1998, and brought up to the big club in May. On June 3 he pitched his first major league game, filling in for fellow pitcher David Cone, who had injured his hand. He pitched a 5-hitter as the Yankees beat Tampa Bay 7-1.

He was 12-4 in that first regular season, and improved to 17-9 in 1999, before slumping to 12-13 in 2000.

But for El Duque, the regular season has been simply a warm-up. The postseason has been his showcase. He was 8-0 over three postseason starts before finally losing a game in the 2000 World Series.

Hernandez relishes big games. In the dream season of 1998, when the Yankees found themselves improbably trailing the Indians two games to one in the American League Championship Series, manager Joe Torre tapped El Duque to start Game 4. He threw 7 shutout innings in a 4-0 Yankee win.

In 1999, he shut down the Atlanta Braves on one run in seven innings, and threw ten strikeouts. It was the most strikeouts by a Yankee pitcher since "Bullet Bob" Turley in Game 5 of the 1988 Series.

Hernandez, Orlando (El Duque)
HEIGHT: 6'2"   RIGHTHANDER   BORN: 10/11/1965 VILLA CLARA, CUBA

YEAR	TEAM	STARTS	GAMES	WON	LOST	PCT	ER	ERA	INNINGS PITCHED	STRIKE-OUTS	WALKS	HITS ALLOWED	HRS ALLOWED	COMP. GAMES	SHUT-OUTS	SAVES
1998	NY-A	21	21	12	4	.750	49	3.13	141	131	52	113	11	3	1	0
1999	NY-A	33	33	17	9	.654	98	4.12	214 1/3	157	87	187	24	2	1	0
2000	NY-A	29	29	12	13	.480	98	4.51	195 2/3	141	51	186	34	3	0	0
Career Average		28	28	14	9	.612	82	4.00	184	143	63	162	23	3	0	0
Yankee Average		**28**	**28**	**14**	**9**	**.612**	**82**	**4.00**	**184**	**143**	**63**	**162**	**23**	**3**	**0**	**0**
Career Total		83	83	41	26	.612	245	4.00	550 2/3	429	190	486	69	8	1	0
Yankee Total		**83**	**83**	**41**	**26**	**.612**	**245**	**4.00**	**550 2/3**	**429**	**190**	**486**	**69**	**8**	**1**	**0**

Hildebrand, Oral Clyde
HEIGHT: 6'3"   RIGHTHANDER   BORN: 4/7/1907 INDIANAPOLIS, INDIANA   DIED: 9/8/1977 SOUTHPORT, INDIANA

YEAR	TEAM	STARTS	GAMES	WON	LOST	PCT	ER	ERA	INNINGS PITCHED	STRIKE-OUTS	WALKS	HITS ALLOWED	HRS ALLOWED	COMP. GAMES	SHUT-OUTS	SAVES
1931	Cle-A	2	5	2	1	.667	13	4.39	26 2/3	6	13	25	0	2	0	0
1932	Cle-A	15	27	8	6	.571	53	3.69	129 1/3	49	62	124	7	7	0	0
1933	Cle-A	31	36	16	11	.593	92	3.76	220 1/3	90	88	205	8	15	6	0
1934	Cle-A	28	33	11	9	.550	99	4.50	198	72	99	225	14	10	1	1
1935	Cle-A	20	34	9	8	.529	75	3.94	171 1/3	49	63	171	12	8	0	5
1936	Cle-A	21	36	10	11	.476	95	4.90	174 2/3	65	83	197	10	9	0	4
1937	StL-A	27	30	8	17	.320	115	5.14	201 1/3	75	87	228	18	12	1	1
1938	StL-A	23	23	8	10	.444	103	5.69	163	66	73	194	18	10	0	0
1939	**NY-A**	**15**	**21**	**10**	**4**	**.714**	**43**	**3.06**	**126 2/3**	**50**	**41**	**102**	**11**	**7**	**1**	**2**
1940	**NY-A**	**0**	**13**	**1**	**1**	**.500**	**4**	**1.86**	**19 1/3**	**5**	**14**	**19**	**1**	**0**	**0**	**0**
Career Average		18	26	8	8	.516	69	4.35	143	53	62	149	10	8	1	1
Yankee Average		**8**	**17**	**6**	**3**	**.688**	**24**	**2.90**	**73**	**28**	**28**	**61**	**6**	**4**	**1**	**1**
Career Total		182	258	83	78	.516	692	4.35	1431	527	623	1490	99	80	9	13
Yankee Total		**15**	**34**	**11**	**5**	**.688**	**47**	**2.90**	**146**	**55**	**55**	**121**	**12**	**7**	**1**	**2**

Hillegas, Shawn Patrick
HEIGHT: 6'3"   RIGHTHANDER   BORN: 8/21/1964 DOS PALOS, CALIFORNIA

YEAR	TEAM	STARTS	GAMES	WON	LOST	PCT	ER	ERA	INNINGS PITCHED	STRIKE-OUTS	WALKS	HITS ALLOWED	HRS ALLOWED	COMP. GAMES	SHUT-OUTS	SAVES
1987	LA-N	10	12	4	3	.571	23	3.57	58	51	31	52	5	0	0	0
1988	LA-N	10	11	3	4	.429	26	4.13	56 2/3	30	17	54	5	0	0	0
1988	Chi-A	6	6	3	2	.600	14	3.15	40	26	18	30	4	0	0	0
1989	Chi-A	13	50	7	11	.389	63	4.74	119 2/3	76	51	132	12	0	0	3
1990	Chi-A	0	7	0	0	—	1	0.79	11 1/3	5	5	4	0	0	0	0
1991	Cle-A	3	51	3	4	.429	40	4.34	83	66	46	67	7	0	0	7
1992	**NY-A**	**9**	**21**	**1**	**8**	**.111**	**48**	**5.51**	**78 1/3**	**46**	**33**	**96**	**12**	**1**	**1**	**0**
1992	Oak-A	0	5	0	0	—	2	2.35	7 2/3	3	4	8	1	0	0	0
1993	Oak-A	11	18	3	6	.333	47	6.97	60 2/3	29	33	78	8	0	0	0
Career Average		7	20	3	4	.387	29	4.61	57	37	26	58	6	0	0	1
Yankee Average		**9**	**21**	**1**	**8**	**.111**	**48**	**5.51**	**78 1/3**	**46**	**33**	**96**	**12**	**1**	**1**	**0**
Career Total		62	181	24	38	.387	264	4.61	515	332	238	521	54	1	1	10
Yankee Total		**9**	**21**	**1**	**8**	**.111**	**48**	**5.51**	**78 1/3**	**46**	**33**	**96**	**12**	**1**	**1**	**0**

Hiller, Frank Walter (Dutch)
HEIGHT: 6'0"   RIGHTHANDER   BORN: 7/13/1920 NEWARK, NEW JERSEY   DIED: 1/8/1987 WEST CHESTER, PENNSYLVANIA

YEAR	TEAM	STARTS	GAMES	WON	LOST	PCT	ER	ERA	INNINGS PITCHED	STRIKE-OUTS	WALKS	HITS ALLOWED	HRS ALLOWED	COMP. GAMES	SHUT-OUTS	SAVES
1946	**NY-A**	**1**	**3**	**0**	**2**	**.000**	**6**	**4.76**	**11 1/3**	**4**	**6**	**13**	**2**	**0**	**0**	**0**
1948	**NY-A**	**5**	**22**	**5**	**2**	**.714**	**28**	**4.04**	**62 1/3**	**25**	**30**	**59**	**8**	**1**	**0**	**0**
1949	**NY-A**	**0**	**4**	**0**	**2**	**.000**	**5**	**5.87**	**7 2/3**	**3**	**7**	**9**	**0**	**0**	**0**	**1**
1950	Chi-N	17	38	12	5	.706	60	3.53	153	55	32	153	16	9	2	1
1951	Chi-N	21	24	6	12	.333	76	4.84	141 1/3	50	31	147	17	6	2	1
1952	Cin-N	15	28	5	8	.385	64	4.63	124 1/3	50	37	129	7	6	1	1
1953	NY-N	1	19	2	1	.667	23	6.15	33 2/3	10	15	43	6	0	0	0
Career Average		9	20	4	5	.484	37	4.42	76	28	23	79	8	3	1	1
Yankee Average		**2**	**10**	**2**	**2**	**.455**	**13**	**4.32**	**27**	**11**	**14**	**27**	**3**	**0**	**0**	**0**
Career Total		60	138	30	32	.484	262	4.42	534	197	158	553	56	22	5	4
Yankee Total		**6**	**29**	**5**	**6**	**.455**	**39**	**4.32**	**81**	**32**	**43**	**81**	**10**	**1**	**0**	**1**

Hinton, Richard Michael

HEIGHT: 6'2" LEFTHANDER BORN: 5/22/1947 TUCSON, ARIZONA

YEAR	TEAM	STARTS	GAMES	WON	LOST	PCT	ER	ERA	INNINGS PITCHED	STRIKE-OUTS	WALKS	HITS ALLOWED	HRS ALLOWED	COMP. GAMES	SHUT-OUTS	SAVES
1971	Chi-A	2	18	3	4	.429	12	4.44	24 1/3	15	6	27	1	0	0	0
1972	**NY-A**	**3**	**7**	**1**	**0**	**1.000**	**9**	**4.86**	**16 2/3**	**13**	**8**	**20**	**2**	**0**	**0**	**0**
1972	Tex-A	0	5	0	1	.000	3	2.38	11 1/3	4	10	7	1	0	0	0
1975	Chi-A	0	15	1	0	1.000	20	4.82	37 1/3	30	15	41	3	0	0	0
1976	Cin-N	1	12	1	2	.333	15	7.64	17 2/3	8	11	30	4	0	0	0
1978	Chi-A	4	29	2	6	.667	36	4.02	80 2/3	48	28	78	5	2	0	1
1979	Chi-A	2	16	1	2	.333	28	6.05	41 2/3	27	8	57	4	0	0	2
1979	Sea-A	1	14	0	2	.000	12	5.40	20	7	5	23	4	0	0	0
Career Average		2	15	1	2	.346	17	4.87	31	19	11	35	3	0	0	0
Yankee Average		**3**	**7**	**1**	**0**	**1.000**	**9**	**4.86**	**16 2/3**	**13**	**8**	**20**	**2**	**0**	**0**	**0**
Career Total		13	116	9	17	.346	135	4.87	250	152	91	283	24	2	0	3
Yankee Total		**3**	**7**	**1**	**0**	**1.000**	**9**	**4.86**	**16 2/3**	**13**	**8**	**20**	**2**	**0**	**0**	**0**

Hitchcock, Sterling Alex

HEIGHT: 6'1" LEFTHANDER BORN: 4/29/1971 FAYETTEVILLE, NORTH CAROLINA

YEAR	TEAM	STARTS	GAMES	WON	LOST	PCT	ER	ERA	INNINGS PITCHED	STRIKE-OUTS	WALKS	HITS ALLOWED	HRS ALLOWED	COMP. GAMES	SHUT-OUTS	SAVES
1992	**NY-A**	**3**	**3**	**0**	**2**	**.000**	**12**	**8.31**	**13**	**6**	**6**	**23**	**2**	**0**	**0**	**0**
1993	**NY-A**	**6**	**6**	**1**	**2**	**.333**	**16**	**4.65**	**31**	**26**	**14**	**32**	**4**	**0**	**0**	**0**
1994	**NY-A**	**5**	**23**	**4**	**1**	**.800**	**23**	**4.22**	**49 1/3**	**37**	**29**	**48**	**3**	**1**	**0**	**2**
1995	**NY-A**	**27**	**27**	**11**	**10**	**.524**	**88**	**4.71**	**168 1/3**	**121**	**68**	**155**	**22**	**4**	**0**	**0**
1996	Sea-A	35	35	13	9	.591	117	5.37	196 2/3	132	73	245	27	0	0	0
1997	SD-N	28	32	10	11	.476	93	5.20	161	106	55	172	24	1	0	0
1998	SD-N	27	39	9	7	.563	77	3.94	176 1/3	158	48	169	29	2	0	1
1999	SD-N	33	33	12	14	.462	94	4.13	205	194	76	202	29	1	0	0
2000	SD-N	11	11	1	6	.143	36	4.93	65 2/3	61	26	69	12	0	0	0
Career Average		19	23	7	7	.496	62	4.69	118	93	44	124	17	1	0	0
Yankee Average		**10**	**15**	**4**	**4**	**.516**	**35**	**4.79**	**65**	**48**	**29**	**65**	**8**	**1**	**0**	**1**
Career Total		175	209	61	62	.496	556	4.69	1067	841	395	1115	152	9	0	3
Yankee Total		**41**	**59**	**16**	**15**	**.516**	**139**	**4.79**	**261**	**190**	**117**	**258**	**31**	**5**	**0**	**2**

Hoff, Chester Cornelius (Red)

HEIGHT: 5'9" LEFTHANDER BORN: 5/8/1891 OSSINING, NEW YORK DIED: 9/7/1998 DAYTONA BEACH, FLORIDA

YEAR	TEAM	STARTS	GAMES	WON	LOST	PCT	ER	ERA	INNINGS PITCHED	STRIKE-OUTS	WALKS	HITS ALLOWED	HRS ALLOWED	COMP. GAMES	SHUT-OUTS	SAVES
1911	**NY-A**	**1**	**5**	**0**	**1**	**.000**	**5**	**2.18**	**20 2/3**	**10**	**7**	**21**	**0**	**0**	**0**	**0**
1912	**NY-A**	**1**	**5**	**0**	**1**	**.000**	**12**	**6.89**	**15 2/3**	**14**	**6**	**20**	**0**	**0**	**0**	**0**
1913	**NY-A**	**0**	**2**	**0**	**0**	**—**	**0**	**0.00**	**3**	**2**	**1**	**0**	**0**	**0**	**0**	**0**
1915	StL-A	3	11	2	2	.500	6	1.24	43 2/3	23	24	26	0	2	0	0
Career Average		1	6	1	1	.333	6	2.49	21	12	10	17	0	1	0	0
Yankee Average		**1**	**4**	**0**	**1**	**.000**	**6**	**3.89**	**13**	**9**	**5**	**14**	**0**	**0**	**0**	**0**
Career Total		5	23	2	4	.333	23	2.49	83	49	38	67	0	2	0	0
Yankee Total		**2**	**12**	**0**	**2**	**.000**	**17**	**3.89**	**39**	**26**	**14**	**41**	**0**	**0**	**0**	**0**

Hogg, William Johnston (Buffalo Bill)

HEIGHT: 6'0" RIGHTHANDER BORN: 9/11/1881 PORT HURON, MICHIGAN DIED: 12/8/1909 NEW ORLEANS, LOUISIANA

YEAR	TEAM	STARTS	GAMES	WON	LOST	PCT	ER	ERA	INNINGS PITCHED	STRIKE-OUTS	WALKS	HITS ALLOWED	HRS ALLOWED	COMP. GAMES	SHUT-OUTS	SAVES
1905	**NY-A**	**22**	**39**	**9**	**13**	**.409**	**73**	**3.20**	**205**	**125**	**101**	**178**	**1**	**9**	**3**	**1**
1906	**NY-A**	**25**	**28**	**14**	**13**	**.519**	**67**	**2.93**	**206**	**107**	**72**	**171**	**5**	**15**	**3**	**0**
1907	**NY-A**	**21**	**25**	**10**	**8**	**.556**	**57**	**3.08**	**166 2/3**	**64**	**83**	**173**	**3**	**13**	**0**	**0**
1908	**NY-A**	**21**	**24**	**4**	**16**	**.666**	**51**	**3.01**	**152 1/3**	**72**	**63**	**155**	**4**	**6**	**0**	**0**
Career Average		22	29	9	13	.425	62	3.06	182	92	80	169	3	11	2	0
Yankee Average		**22**	**29**	**9**	**13**	**.425**	**62**	**3.06**	**182**	**92**	**80**	**169**	**3**	**11**	**2**	**0**
Career Total		89	116	37	50	.425	248	3.06	730	368	319	677	13	43	6	1
Yankee Total		**89**	**116**	**37**	**50**	**.425**	**248**	**3.06**	**730**	**368**	**319**	**677**	**13**	**43**	**6**	**1**

Hogue, Robert Clinton
HEIGHT: 5'10" RIGHTHANDER BORN: 4/15/1921 MIAMI, FLORIDA DIED: 12/22/1987 MIAMI, FLORIDA

YEAR	TEAM	STARTS	GAMES	WON	LOST	PCT	ER	ERA	INNINGS PITCHED	STRIKE-OUTS	WALKS	HITS ALLOWED	HRS ALLOWED	COMP. GAMES	SHUT-OUTS	SAVES
1948	Bos-N	1	40	8	2	.800	31	3.23	86 1/3	43	19	88	4	0	0	2
1949	Bos-N	0	33	2	2	.500	25	3.13	72	23	25	78	4	0	0	3
1950	Bos-N	1	36	3	5	.375	35	5.03	62 2/3	15	31	69	8	0	0	7
1951	Bos-N	0	3	0	0	—	3	5.40	5	0	3	4	1	0	0	0
1951	StL-A	0	18	1	1	.500	17	5.16	29 2/3	11	23	31	1	0	0	1
1951	**NY-A**	**0**	**7**	**1**	**0**	**1.000**	**0**	**0.00**	**7 1/3**	**2**	**3**	**4**	**0**	**0**	**0**	**0**
1952	**NY-A**	**0**	**27**	**3**	**5**	**.375**	**28**	**5.32**	**47 1/3**	**12**	**25**	**52**	**6**	**0**	**0**	**4**
1952	StL-A	1	8	0	1	.000	5	2.76	16 1/3	2	13	10	1	0	0	0
Career Average		0	22	2	2	.529	18	3.97	41	14	18	42	3	0	0	2
Yankee Average		**0**	**17**	**2**	**3**	**.444**	**14**	**4.61**	**27**	**7**	**14**	**28**	**3**	**0**	**0**	**2**
Career Total		3	172	18	16	.529	144	3.97	327	108	142	336	25	0	0	17
Yankee Total		**0**	**34**	**4**	**5**	**.444**	**28**	**4.61**	**55**	**14**	**28**	**56**	**6**	**0**	**0**	**4**

Holcombe, Kenneth Edward
HEIGHT: 5'11" RIGHTHANDER BORN: 8/23/1918 BURNSVILLE, NORTH CAROLINA

YEAR	TEAM	STARTS	GAMES	WON	LOST	PCT	ER	ERA	INNINGS PITCHED	STRIKE-OUTS	WALKS	HITS ALLOWED	HRS ALLOWED	COMP. GAMES	SHUT-OUTS	SAVES
1945	**NY-A**	**2**	**23**	**3**	**3**	**.500**	**11**	**1.79**	**55 1/3**	**20**	**27**	**43**	**2**	**0**	**0**	**0**
1948	Cin-N	0	2	0	0	—	2	7.72	2 1/3	2	0	3	0	0	0	0
1950	Chi-A	15	24	3	10	.666	49	4.59	96	37	45	122	10	5	0	1
1951	Chi-A	23	28	11	12	.478	67	3.78	159 1/3	39	68	142	9	12	2	0
1952	Chi-A	7	7	0	5	.000	24	6.17	35	12	18	38	3	1	0	0
1952	StL-A	1	12	0	2	.000	9	3.86	21	7	9	20	1	0	0	0
1953	Bos-A	0	3	1	0	1.000	4	6.00	6	1	3	9	0	0	0	1
Career Average		7	14	3	5	.360	24	3.98	54	17	24	54	4	3	0	0
Yankee Average		**2**	**23**	**3**	**3**	**.500**	**11**	**1.79**	**55 1/3**	**20**	**27**	**43**	**2**	**0**	**0**	**0**
Career Total		48	99	18	32	.360	166	3.98	375	118	170	377	25	18	2	2
Yankee Total		**2**	**23**	**3**	**3**	**.500**	**11**	**1.79**	**55 1/3**	**20**	**27**	**43**	**2**	**0**	**0**	**0**

Holland, Alfred Willis
HEIGHT: 5'11" LEFTHANDER BORN: 8/16/1952 ROANOKE, VIRGINIA

YEAR	TEAM	STARTS	GAMES	WON	LOST	PCT	ER	ERA	INNINGS PITCHED	STRIKE-OUTS	WALKS	HITS ALLOWED	HRS ALLOWED	COMP. GAMES	SHUT-OUTS	SAVES
1977	Pit-N	0	2	0	0	—	2	7.72	2 1/3	1	0	4	0	0	0	0
1979	SF-N	0	3	0	0	—	0	0.00	7	7	5	3	0	0	0	0
1980	SF-N	0	54	5	3	.625	16	1.75	82 1/3	65	34	71	2	0	0	7
1981	SF-N	3	47	7	5	.583	27	2.41	100 2/3	78	44	87	4	0	0	7
1982	SF-N	7	58	7	3	.700	48	3.33	129 2/3	97	40	115	12	0	0	5
1983	Phi-N	0	68	8	4	.667	23	2.26	91 2/3	100	30	63	8	0	0	25
1984	Phi-N	0	68	5	10	.333	37	3.39	98 1/3	61	30	82	14	0	0	29
1985	Phi-N	0	3	0	1	.000	2	4.50	4	1	4	5	0	0	0	1
1985	Pit-N	0	38	1	3	.667	22	3.38	58 2/3	47	17	48	5	0	0	4
1985	Cal-A	0	15	0	1	.000	4	1.48	24 1/3	14	10	17	4	0	0	0
1986	**NY-A**	**1**	**25**	**1**	**0**	**1.000**	**23**	**5.09**	**40 2/3**	**37**	**9**	**44**	**5**	**0**	**0**	**0**
1987	**NY-A**	**0**	**3**	**0**	**0**	**—**	**10**	**14.21**	**6 1/3**	**5**	**9**	**9**	**1**	**0**	**0**	**0**
Career Average		1	32	3	3	.531	18	2.98	54	43	19	46	5	0	0	7
Yankee Average		**1**	**14**	**1**	**0**	**1.000**	**17**	**6.32**	**23**	**21**	**9**	**27**	**3**	**0**	**0**	**0**
Career Total		11	384	34	30	.531	214	2.98	646	513	232	548	55	0	0	78
Yankee Total		**1**	**28**	**1**	**0**	**1.000**	**33**	**6.32**	**47**	**42**	**18**	**53**	**6**	**0**	**0**	**0**

Holloway, Kenneth Eugene
HEIGHT: 6'0" RIGHTHANDER BORN: 8/8/1897 THOMAS COUNTY, GEORGIA DIED: 9/25/1968 THOMASVILLE, GEORGIA

YEAR	TEAM	STARTS	GAMES	WON	LOST	PCT	ER	ERA	INNINGS PITCHED	STRIKE-OUTS	WALKS	HITS ALLOWED	HRS ALLOWED	COMP. GAMES	SHUT-OUTS	SAVES
1922	Det-A	0	1	0	0	—	0	0.00	1	1	0	1	0	0	0	0
1923	Det-A	24	42	11	10	.524	96	4.45	194	55	75	232	12	7	1	1
1924	Det-A	14	49	14	6	.700	82	4.07	181 1/3	46	61	209	6	5	0	3
1925	Det-A	14	38	13	4	.765	81	4.62	157 2/3	29	67	170	8	6	0	2
1926	Det-A	12	36	4	6	.400	79	5.12	139	43	42	192	2	3	0	2
1927	Det-A	23	36	11	12	.478	83	4.07	183 1/3	36	61	210	10	11	1	6
1928	Det-A	11	30	4	8	.333	58	4.34	120 1/3	32	32	137	2	5	0	2
1929	Cle-A	11	25	6	5	.545	40	3.03	119	32	37	118	2	6	2	0
1930	**NY-A**	**0**	**16**	**0**	**0**	**—**	**20**	**5.24**	**34 1/3**	**11**	**8**	**52**	**2**	**6**	**2**	**0**
1930	Cle-A	2	12	1	1	.500	28	8.40	30	8	14	49	5	0	0	2
Career Average		11	29	6	5	.552	57	4.40	116	29	40	137	5	4	0	2
Yankee Average		**0**	**16**	**0**	**0**	**—**	**20**	**5.24**	**34 1/3**	**11**	**8**	**52**	**3**	**0**	**0**	**0**
Career Total		111	285	64	52	.552	567	4.40	1160	293	397	1370	50	43	4	18
Yankee Total		**0**	**16**	**0**	**0**	**—**	**20**	**5.24**	**34 1/3**	**11**	**8**	**52**	**3**	**0**	**0**	**0**

Holmes, Darren Lee
HEIGHT: 6'0" RIGHTHANDER BORN: 4/25/1966 ASHEVILLE, NORTH CAROLINA

YEAR	TEAM	STARTS	GAMES	WON	LOST	PCT	ER	ERA	INNINGS PITCHED	STRIKE-OUTS	WALKS	HITS ALLOWED	HRS ALLOWED	COMP. GAMES	SHUT-OUTS	SAVES
1990	LA-N	0	14	0	1	.000	10	5.19	17 1/3	19	11	15	1	0	0	0
1991	Mil-A	0	40	1	4	.666	40	4.72	76 1/3	59	27	90	6	0	0	3
1992	Mil-A	0	41	4	4	.500	12	2.55	42 1/3	31	11	35	1	0	0	6
1993	Col-N	0	62	3	3	.500	30	4.05	66 2/3	60	20	56	6	0	0	25
1994	Col-N	0	29	0	3	.000	20	6.43	28 1/3	33	24	35	5	0	0	3
1995	Col-N	0	68	6	1	.857	24	3.27	66 2/3	61	28	59	3	0	0	14
1996	Col-N	0	62	5	4	.556	34	3.97	77	73	28	78	8	0	0	1
1997	Col-N	6	42	9	2	.818	53	5.36	89 1/3	70	36	113	12	0	0	3
1998	**NY-A**	**0**	**34**	**0**	**3**	**.000**	**19**	**3.35**	**51 1/3**	**31**	**14**	**53**	**4**	**0**	**0**	**2**
1999	Ari-N	0	44	4	3	.571	20	3.75	48 1/3	35	25	50	3	0	0	0
2000	Ari-N	0	8	0	0	—	6	8.53	6 1/3	5	1	12	1	0	0	1
2000	StL-N	0	5	0	1	—	9	9.72	8 1/3	5	3	12	2	0	0	0
2000	Bal-A	0	5	0	0	—	13	13.03	4 2/3	6	5	13	3	0	0	0
Career Average		0	35	2	2	.525	22	4.47	45	38	18	48	4	0	0	4
Yankee Average		**0**	**34**	**0**	**3**	**.000**	**19**	**3.35**	**51 1/3**	**31**	**14**	**53**	**4**	**0**	**0**	**2**
Career Total		6	454	32	29	.525	290	4.47	583 1/3	488	233	621	55	0	0	58
Yankee Total		**0**	**34**	**0**	**3**	**.000**	**19**	**3.35**	**51 1/3**	**31**	**14**	**53**	**4**	**0**	**0**	**2**

Holtzman, Kenneth Dale
HEIGHT: 6'2" LEFTHANDER BORN: 11/3/1945 ST.LOUIS, MISSOURI

YEAR	TEAM	STARTS	GAMES	WON	LOST	PCT	ER	ERA	INNINGS PITCHED	STRIKE-OUTS	WALKS	HITS ALLOWED	HRS ALLOWED	COMP. GAMES	SHUT-OUTS	SAVES
1965	Chi-N	0	3	0	0	—	1	2.25	4	3	3	2	1	0	0	0
1966	Chi-N	33	34	11	16	.407	93	3.79	220 2/3	171	68	194	27	9	0	0
1967	Chi-N	12	12	9	0	1.000	26	2.53	92 2/3	62	44	76	11	3	0	0
1968	Chi-N	32	34	11	14	.440	80	3.35	215	151	76	201	17	6	3	0
1969	Chi-N	39	39	17	13	.567	104	3.58	261 1/3	176	93	248	18	12	6	1
1970	Chi-N	38	39	17	11	.607	108	3.38	287 2/3	202	94	271	30	15	1	0
1971	Chi-N	29	30	9	15	.375	97	4.48	195	143	64	213	18	9	3	0
1972	Oak-A	37	39	19	11	.633	74	2.51	265 1/3	134	52	232	23	16	4	0
1973	Oak-A	40	40	21	13	.618	98	2.97	297 1/3	157	66	275	22	16	4	0
1974	Oak-A	38	39	19	17	.528	87	3.07	255 1/3	117	51	273	14	9	3	0
1975	Oak-A	38	39	18	14	.563	93	3.14	266 1/3	122	108	217	16	13	2	0
1976	Bal-A	13	13	5	4	.556	31	2.86	97 2/3	25	35	100	4	6	1	0
1976	**NY-A**	**21**	**21**	**9**	**7**	**.563**	**69**	**4.17**	**149**	**41**	**35**	**165**	**14**	**10**	**2**	**0**
1977	**NY-A**	**11**	**18**	**2**	**3**	**.400**	**46**	**5.78**	**71 2/3**	**14**	**24**	**105**	**7**	**0**	**0**	**0**
1978	**NY-A**	**3**	**5**	**1**	**0**	**1.000**	**8**	**4.08**	**17 2/3**	**3**	**9**	**21**	**2**	**0**	**0**	**0**
1978	Chi-N	6	23	0	3	.000	36	6.11	53	36	35	61	10	0	0	2
1979	Chi-N	20	23	6	9	.400	60	4.59	117 2/3	44	53	133	15	3	2	0
Career Average		24	27	10	9	.537	65	3.49	169	94	54	164	15	7	2	0
Yankee Average		**12**	**15**	**4**	**3**	**.545**	**41**	**4.64**	**79**	**19**	**23**	**97**	**8**	**3**	**1**	**0**
Career Total		410	451	174	150	.537	1111	3.49	2867	1601	910	2787	249	127	31	3
Yankee Total		**35**	**44**	**12**	**10**	**.545**	**123**	**4.64**	**238**	**58**	**68**	**291**	**23**	**10**	**2**	**0**

Honeycutt, Frederick Wayne (Rick)

HEIGHT: 6'1" LEFTHANDER BORN: 6/29/1954 CHATTANOOGA, TENNESSEE

YEAR	TEAM	STARTS	GAMES	WON	LOST	PCT	ER	ERA	INNINGS PITCHED	STRIKE-OUTS	WALKS	HITS ALLOWED	HRS ALLOWED	COMP. GAMES	SHUT-OUTS	SAVES
1977	Sea-A	3	10	0	1	.000	14	4.34	29	17	11	26	7	0	0	0
1978	Sea-A	24	26	5	11	.313	73	4.89	134 1/3	50	49	150	12	4	1	0
1979	Sea-A	28	33	11	12	.478	87	4.04	194	83	67	201	22	8	1	0
1980	Sea-A	30	30	10	17	.370	89	3.94	203 1/3	79	60	221	22	9	1	0
1981	Tex-A	20	20	11	6	.647	47	3.31	127 2/3	40	17	120	12	8	2	0
1982	Tex-A	26	30	5	17	.666	96	5.27	164	64	54	201	20	4	1	0
1983	Tex-A	25	25	14	8	.636	47	2.42	174 2/3	56	37	168	9	5	2	0
1983	LA-N	7	9	2	3	.400	25	5.77	39	18	13	46	6	1	0	0
1984	LA-N	28	29	10	9	.526	58	2.84	183 2/3	75	51	180	11	6	2	1
1985	LA-N	25	31	8	12	.400	54	3.42	142	67	49	141	9	1	0	0
1986	LA-N	28	32	11	9	.550	63	3.32	171	100	45	164	9	0	0	0
1987	LA-N	20	27	2	12	.143	59	4.59	115 2/3	92	45	133	10	1	1	0
1987	Oak-A	4	7	1	4	.666	14	5.32	23 2/3	10	9	25	3	0	0	7
1988	Oak-A	0	55	3	2	.600	31	3.50	79 2/3	47	25	74	6	0	0	12
1989	Oak-A	0	64	2	2	.500	20	2.35	76 2/3	52	26	56	5	0	0	7
1990	Oak-A	0	63	2	2	.500	19	2.70	63 1/3	38	22	46	2	0	0	0
1991	Oak-A	0	43	2	4	.333	15	3.58	37 2/3	26	20	37	3	0	0	3
1992	Oak-A	0	54	1	4	.666	16	3.69	39	32	10	41	2	0	0	1
1993	Oak-A	0	52	1	4	.666	13	2.81	41 2/3	21	20	30	4	0	0	1
1994	Tex-A	0	42	1	2	.333	20	7.20	25	18	9	37	5	0	0	2
1995	Oak-A	0	49	5	1	.833	12	2.45	44	21	9	37	5	0	0	2
1995	**NY-A**	**0**	**3**	**0**	**0**	**—**	**3**	**27.00**	**1**	**0**	**1**	**2**	**1**	**0**	**0**	**4**
1996	StL-N	0	61	2	1	.667	15	2.87	47	30	7	42	3	0	0	0
1997	StL-N	0	2	0	0	—	3	13.50	2	2	1	5	0	0	0	0
Career Average		11	33	5	6	.433	37	3.72	90	43	27	91	8	2	0	2
Yankee Average		**0**	**3**	**0**	**0**	**—**	**3**	**27.00**	**1**	**0**	**1**	**2**	**1**	**0**	**0**	**38**
Career Total		268	797	109	143	.433	893	3.72	2159	1038	657	2183	185	47	11	38
Yankee Total		**0**	**3**	**0**	**0**	**—**	**3**	**27.00**	**1**	**0**	**1**	**2**	**1**	**0**	**0**	**0**

Hood, Donald Harris

HEIGHT: 6'2" LEFTHANDER BORN: 10/16/1949 FLORENCE, SOUTH CAROLINA

YEAR	TEAM	STARTS	GAMES	WON	LOST	PCT	ER	ERA	INNINGS PITCHED	STRIKE-OUTS	WALKS	HITS ALLOWED	HRS ALLOWED	COMP. GAMES	SHUT-OUTS	SAVES
1973	Bal-A	4	8	3	2	.600	14	3.90	32 1/3	18	6	31	1	1	1	1
1974	Bal-A	2	20	1	1	.500	22	3.45	57 1/3	26	20	47	1	0	0	0
1975	Cle-A	19	29	6	10	.375	66	4.39	135 1/3	51	57	136	16	2	0	1
1976	Cle-A	6	33	3	5	.375	42	4.87	77 2/3	32	41	89	5	0	0	1
1977	Cle-A	5	41	2	1	.667	35	3.00	105	62	49	87	3	1	0	0
1978	Cle-A	19	36	5	6	.455	77	4.48	154 2/3	73	77	166	13	1	0	1
1979	Cle-A	0	13	1	0	1.000	9	3.68	22	7	14	13	1	0	0	1
1979	**NY-A**	**6**	**27**	**3**	**1**	**.750**	**23**	**3.07**	**67 1/3**	**22**	**30**	**62**	**3**	**0**	**0**	**1**
1980	StL-N	8	33	4	6	.400	31	3.39	82 1/3	35	34	90	2	1	0	1
1982	KC-A	3	30	4	0	1.000	26	3.51	66 2/3	31	22	71	7	0	0	0
1983	KC-A	0	27	2	3	.400	12	2.27	47 2/3	17	14	48	5	0	0	0
Career Average		7	27	3	3	.493	32	3.79	77	34	33	76	5	1	0	1
Yankee Average		**6**	**27**	**3**	**1**	**.750**	**23**	**3.07**	**67 1/3**	**22**	**30**	**62**	**3**	**0**	**0**	**1**
Career Total		72	297	34	35	.493	357	3.79	848	374	364	840	57	6	1	6
Yankee Total		**6**	**27**	**3**	**1**	**.750**	**23**	**3.07**	**67 1/3**	**22**	**30**	**62**	**3**	**0**	**0**	**1**

Hood, Wallace James Jr.

HEIGHT: 6'1" RIGHTHANDER BORN: 9/24/1925 LOS ANGELES, CALIFORNIA

YEAR	TEAM	STARTS	GAMES	WON	LOST	PCT	ER	ERA	INNINGS PITCHED	STRIKE-OUTS	WALKS	HITS ALLOWED	HRS ALLOWED	COMP. GAMES	SHUT-OUTS	SAVES
1949	**NY-A**	**0**	**2**	**0**	**0**	**—**	**0**	**0.00**	**2 1/3**	**2**	**1**	**0**	**0**	**0**	**0**	**0**
Career Average		0	2	0	0	—	0	0.00	2 1/3	2	1	0	0	0	0	0
Yankee Average		**0**	**2**	**0**	**0**	**—**	**0**	**0.00**	**2 1/3**	**2**	**1**	**0**	**0**	**0**	**0**	**0**
Career Total		0	2	0	0	—	0	0.00	2 1/3	2	1	0	0	0	0	0
Yankee Total		**0**	**2**	**0**	**0**	**—**	**0**	**0.00**	**2 1/3**	**2**	**1**	**0**	**0**	**0**	**0**	**0**

Howe, Steven Roy

HEIGHT: 6'2" LEFTHANDER BORN: 3/10/1958 PONTIAC, MICHIGAN

YEAR	TEAM	STARTS	GAMES	WON	LOST	PCT	ER	ERA	INNINGS PITCHED	STRIKE-OUTS	WALKS	HITS ALLOWED	HRS ALLOWED	COMP. GAMES	SHUT-OUTS	SAVES
1980	LA-N	0	59	7	9	.438	25	2.66	84 2/3	39	22	83	1	0	0	17
1981	LA-N	0	41	5	3	.625	15	2.50	54	32	18	51	2	0	0	8
1982	LA-N	0	66	7	5	.583	23	2.08	99 1/3	49	17	87	3	0	0	13
1983	LA-N	0	46	4	7	.364	11	1.44	68 2/3	52	12	55	2	0	0	18
1985	LA-N	0	19	1	1	.500	12	4.91	22	11	5	30	2	0	0	3
1985	Min-A	0	13	2	3	.400	13	6.16	19	10	7	28	1	0	0	0
1987	Tex-A	0	24	3	3	.500	15	4.31	31 1/3	19	8	33	2	0	0	1
1991	**NY-A**	**0**	**37**	**3**	**1**	**.750**	**9**	**1.68**	**48 1/3**	**34**	**7**	**39**	**1**	**0**	**0**	**3**
1992	**NY-A**	**0**	**20**	**3**	**0**	**1.000**	**6**	**2.45**	**22**	**12**	**3**	**9**	**1**	**0**	**0**	**6**
1993	**NY-A**	**0**	**51**	**3**	**5**	**.375**	**28**	**4.97**	**50 2/3**	**19**	**10**	**58**	**7**	**0**	**0**	**4**
1994	**NY-A**	**0**	**40**	**3**	**0**	**1.000**	**8**	**1.80**	**40**	**18**	**7**	**28**	**2**	**0**	**0**	**15**
1995	**NY-A**	**0**	**56**	**6**	**3**	**.667**	**27**	**4.96**	**49**	**28**	**17**	**66**	**7**	**0**	**0**	**2**
1996	**NY-A**	**0**	**25**	**0**	**1**	**.000**	**12**	**6.35**	**17**	**5**	**6**	**19**	**1**	**0**	**0**	**1**
Career Average		0	38	4	3	.534	16	3.03	47	25	11	45	2	0	0	7
Yankee Average		**0**	**38**	**3**	**2**	**.643**	**15**	**3.57**	**38**	**19**	**8**	**37**	**3**	**0**	**0**	**5**
Career Total		0	497	47	41	.534	204	3.03	606	328	139	586	32	0	0	91
Yankee Total		**0**	**229**	**18**	**10**	**.643**	**90**	**3.57**	**227**	**116**	**50**	**219**	**19**	**0**	**0**	**31**

Howell, Henry Harry

HEIGHT: 5'9" RIGHTHANDER BORN: 11/14/1876, NEW JERSEY DIED: 5/22/1956 SPOKANE, WASHINGTON

YEAR	TEAM	STARTS	GAMES	WON	LOST	PCT	ER	ERA	INNINGS PITCHED	STRIKE-OUTS	WALKS	HITS ALLOWED	HRS ALLOWED	COMP. GAMES	SHUT-OUTS	SAVES
1898	Bro-N	2	2	2	0	1.000	10	5.00	18	2	11	15	0	2	0	0
1899	Bro-N	25	28	13	8	.619	91	3.91	204	58	69	248	1	21	0	1
1900	Bro-N	10	21	6	5	.545	46	3.75	110	26	36	131	4	7	2	0
1901	Bal-A	34	37	14	21	.400	120	3.67	294 2/3	93	79	333	5	32	1	0
1902	Bal-A	23	26	9	14	.391	91	4.12	199	33	48	243	5	19	1	0
1903	**NY-A**	**15**	**25**	**9**	**6**	**.600**	**61**	**3.53**	**155 2/3**	**62**	**44**	**140**	**4**	**13**	**0**	**0**
1904	StL-A	33	34	13	21	.382	73	2.19	299 2/3	122	60	254	1	32	2	0
1905	StL-A	37	38	15	22	.405	71	1.98	323	198	101	252	2	35	4	0
1906	StL-A	33	35	15	14	.517	65	2.11	276 2/3	140	61	233	1	30	6	1
1907	StL-A	35	42	16	15	.516	68	1.93	316 1/3	118	88	258	3	26	2	3
1908	StL-A	32	41	18	18	.500	68	1.89	324 1/3	117	70	279	1	27	2	1
1909	StL-A	3	10	1	1	.500	13	3.13	37 1/3	16	8	42	0	0	0	0
1910	StL-A	0	1	0	0	—	4	10.80	3 1/3	1	2	7	0	0	0	0
Career Average		22	26	10	11	.475	60	2.74	198	76	52	187	2	19	2	0
Yankee Average		**15**	**25**	**9**	**6**	**.600**	**61**	**3.53**	**155 2/3**	**62**	**44**	**140**	**4**	**13**	**0**	**0**
Career Total		282	340	131	145	.475	781	2.74	2568	986	677	2435	27	244	20	6
Yankee Total		**15**	**25**	**9**	**6**	**.600**	**61**	**3.53**	**156 2/3**	**62**	**44**	**140**	**4**	**13**	**0**	**0**

Howell, Jay Canfield

HEIGHT: 6'3" RIGHTHANDER BORN: 11/26/1955 MIAMI, FLORIDA

YEAR	TEAM	STARTS	GAMES	WON	LOST	PCT	ER	ERA	INNINGS PITCHED	STRIKE-OUTS	WALKS	HITS ALLOWED	HRS ALLOWED	COMP. GAMES	SHUT-OUTS	SAVES
1980	Cin-N	0	5	0	0	—	5	13.50	3 1/3	1	0	8	0	0	0	0
1981	Chi-N	2	10	2	0	1.000	12	4.84	22 1/3	10	10	23	3	0	0	0
1982	**NY-A**	**6**	**6**	**2**	**3**	**.400**	**24**	**7.71**	**28**	**21**	**13**	**42**	**1**	**0**	**0**	**0**
1983	**NY-A**	**12**	**19**	**1**	**5**	**.167**	**49**	**5.38**	**82**	**61**	**35**	**89**	**7**	**2**	**0**	**0**
1984	**NY-A**	**1**	**61**	**9**	**4**	**.692**	**31**	**2.69**	**103 2/3**	**109**	**34**	**86**	**5**	**0**	**0**	**7**
1985	Oak-A	0	63	9	8	.529	31	2.85	98	68	31	98	5	0	0	29
1986	Oak-A	0	38	3	6	.333	20	3.38	53 1/3	42	23	53	3	0	0	16
1987	Oak-A	0	36	3	4	.429	29	5.89	44 1/3	35	21	48	6	0	0	16
1988	LA-N	0	50	5	3	.625	15	2.08	65	70	21	44	1	0	0	21
1989	LA-N	0	56	5	3	.625	14	1.58	79 2/3	55	22	60	3	0	0	28
1990	LA-N	0	45	5	5	.500	16	2.18	66	59	20	59	5	0	0	16
1991	LA-N	0	44	6	5	.545	18	3.18	51	40	11	39	3	0	0	16
1992	LA-N	0	41	1	3	.667	8	1.54	46 2/3	36	18	41	2	0	0	4
1993	Atl-N	0	54	3	3	.500	15	2.31	58 1/3	37	16	48	3	0	0	0
1994	Tex-A	0	40	4	1	.800	26	5.44	43	22	16	44	10	0	0	2
Career Average		1	38	4	4	.523	21	3.34	56	44	19	52	4	0	0	10
Yankee Average		**6**	**29**	**4**	**4**	**.500**	**35**	**4.38**	**71**	**64**	**27**	**72**	**4**	**1**	**0**	**2**
Career Total		21	568	58	53	.523	313	3.34	845	666	291	782	57	2	0	155
Yankee Total		**19**	**86**	**12**	**12**	**.500**	**104**	**4.38**	**214**	**191**	**82**	**217**	**13**	**2**	**0**	**7**

Waite Charles "Schoolboy" Hoyt, rhp, 1921–30

Waite Hoyt was, as a sportswriter of the time once noted, "a man of many parts." He was a vaudeville singer, an actor who appeared on Broadway, an artist, a part-time undertaker and, not incidentally, one of the best right handed pitchers the Yankees have ever had.

Born in Brooklyn, New York, on August 9, 1899, Hoyt was a star in New York City long before he donned Yankee pinstripes. At Erasmus High School in Brooklyn, he went 31-2 in three years, with six no-hitters. He signed a contract with the New York Giants before he got out of high school, but only pitched one game with the Giants in 1918 before being traded to the Red Sox in 1919.

The Giants' coach, John McGraw, was a friend of the Hoyt family and won permission to sign young Waite while he was still a minor. But after one appearance in July 1918, McGraw was of the opinion that Hoyt should be sent down to the minor leagues to gain more experience.

When informed of the decision, Hoyt disagreed. McGraw was not used to spats with ten-year veterans, let alone fuzzy-cheeked rookies, so Hoyt was soon sent to Boston.

Hoyt came back to New York in 1921 as a 20-year-old veteran, and he blossomed immediately, winning 55 games from 1921-23 as the Yankees won three consecutive American League pennants.

He liked Boston, but he loved being back in New York City. His father, Ad Hoyt, was an old showman, and at least once (and probably more than that), father and son took the vaudeville stage in New York during those years for a few songs and a little soft-shoe.

As a pitcher, he was a tough, no-nonsense kind of fellow. He wasn't a fireballer, but he had very good command of his pitches. During his stint with the Yankees, he was often among the league leaders in fewest hits and fewest walks allowed per game.

He was cool under pressure. In five World Series, he was 6-3, allowing just 14 earned runs in 77 2/3 innings. In the 1922 World Series against the Giants, he pitched three complete games and allowed no earned runs.

He was only 2-1 in that series, however, as he lost the final game of the Series, 1-0, on a run scored on an error.

He was a favorite son of New Yorkers, and particularly Brooklynites, who rooted for Hoyt as one of their own, even if he did play for the hated Yankees. "Hoyt Hoit!" was the headline in a Brooklyn paper above a story about an injury Hoyt sustained in a game with the Yankees in the 1920s.)

By 1927, Hoyt was the dominant pitcher on a dominant team. He led the league in wins in 1927 with 22, and was second in 1928 with 23. Hoyt slumped to 10 wins in 1929. When former teammate Bob Shawkey was named to manage the Yankees in 1930, he and Hoyt clashed.

Hoyt and Mark Koenig were traded to the Tigers midway through the 1930 season, in one of the worst trades ever made by the Yankees. In return, New York got pitcher Ownie Carroll, who was 0-1 with New York; infielder George "Yats" Wuestling, a career .190 hitter; and veteran outfielder Harry Rice, the only decent player of the three.

Hoyt played another nine years after he left New York. He had nowhere near the success he enjoyed as a Yankee, although he returned to the World Series in 1931 with the A's. He retired in 1938.

Following his retirement, he took a job as a broadcaster for the Cincinnati Reds for many years. Old-timers fondly recall the times when Hoyt was forced to fill air time during rain delays. Waite would spin yarns of his days with the Yankees and Babe Ruth. In fact, a record album, Waite Hoyt in the Rain, featuring many of his favorite stories, was cut during his stint in Cincinnati.

Hoyt, who died in 1984, was elected to the Hall of Fame in 1969. He remains in eighth place all-time with the Yankees in wins with 157, and is also seventh all-time in complete games with 156.

Hoyt, Waite Charles (Schoolboy)

HEIGHT: 6'0" RIGHTHANDER BORN: 9/9/1899 BROOKLYN, NEW YORK DIED: 8/25/1984 CINCINNATI, OHIO

YEAR	TEAM	STARTS	GAMES	WON	LOST	PCT	ER	ERA	INNINGS PITCHED	STRIKE-OUTS	WALKS	HITS ALLOWED	HRS ALLOWED	COMP. GAMES	SHUT-OUTS	SAVES
1918	NY-N	0	1	0	0	—	0	0.00	1	2	0	0	0	0	0	0
1919	Bos-A	11	13	4	6	.400	38	3.25	105 1/3	28	22	99	1	6	1	0
1920	Bos-A	11	22	6	6	.500	59	4.38	121 1/3	45	47	123	2	6	2	1
1921	**NY-A**	**32**	**43**	**19**	**13**	**.594**	**97**	**3.09**	**282 1/3**	**102**	**81**	**301**	**3**	**21**	**1**	**3**
1922	**NY-A**	**31**	**37**	**19**	**12**	**.613**	**101**	**3.43**	**265**	**95**	**76**	**271**	**13**	**17**	**3**	**0**
1923	**NY-A**	**28**	**37**	**17**	**9**	**.654**	**80**	**3.02**	**238 2/3**	**60**	**66**	**227**	**9**	**19**	**1**	**1**
1924	**NY-A**	**32**	**46**	**18**	**13**	**.581**	**104**	**3.79**	**247**	**71**	**76**	**295**	**8**	**14**	**2**	**4**
1925	**NY-A**	**30**	**46**	**11**	**14**	**.440**	**108**	**4.00**	**243**	**86**	**78**	**283**	**14**	**17**	**1**	**6**
1926	**NY-A**	**28**	**40**	**16**	**12**	**.571**	**93**	**3.85**	**217 2/3**	**79**	**62**	**224**	**4**	**12**	**1**	**4**
1927	**NY-A**	**32**	**36**	**22**	**7**	**.759**	**75**	**2.63**	**256 1/3**	**86**	**54**	**242**	**10**	**23**	**3**	**1**
1928	**NY-A**	**31**	**42**	**23**	**7**	**.767**	**102**	**3.36**	**273**	**67**	**60**	**279**	**16**	**19**	**3**	**8**
1929	**NY-A**	**25**	**30**	**10**	**9**	**.526**	**95**	**4.24**	**201 2/3**	**57**	**69**	**219**	**9**	**12**	**0**	**1**
1930	**NY-A**	**7**	**8**	**2**	**2**	**.500**	**24**	**4.53**	**47 2/3**	**10**	**9**	**64**	**7**	**2**	**0**	**0**
1930	Det-A	20	26	9	8	.529	72	4.78	135 2/3	25	47	176	7	8	1	4
1931	Det-A	12	16	3	8	.667	60	5.87	92	10	32	124	2	5	0	0
1931	Phi-A	14	16	10	5	.667	52	4.22	111	30	37	130	9	9	2	0
1932	Bro-N	4	8	1	3	.667	23	7.76	26 2/3	7	12	38	3	0	0	1
1932	NY-N	12	18	5	7	.417	37	3.42	97 1/3	29	25	103	6	3	0	0
1933	Pit-N	8	36	5	7	.417	38	2.92	117	44	19	118	3	4	1	4
1934	Pit-N	15	48	15	6	.714	62	2.93	190 2/3	105	43	184	6	8	3	5
1935	Pit-N	11	39	7	11	.389	62	3.40	164	63	27	187	8	5	0	6
1936	Pit-N	9	22	7	5	.583	35	2.70	116 2/3	37	20	115	5	6	0	1
1937	Pit-N	0	11	1	2	.333	14	4.50	28	21	6	31	5	0	0	2
1937	Bro-N	19	27	7	7	.500	60	3.23	167	44	30	180	5	10	1	0
1938	Bro-N	1	6	0	3	.000	9	4.96	16 1/3	3	5	24	1	0	0	0
Career Average		17	27	9	7	.566	60	3.59	150	48	40	161	6	9	1	2
Yankee Average		**28**	**37**	**16**	**10**	**.616**	**88**	**3.48**	**227**	**71**	**63**	**241**	**9**	**16**	**2**	**3**
Career Total		423	674	237	182	.566	1500	3.59	3762	1206	1003	4037	154	226	26	52
Yankee Total		**276**	**365**	**157**	**98**	**.616**	**879**	**3.48**	**2272**	**713**	**631**	**2405**	**93**	**156**	**15**	**28**

Hudson, Charles Lynn

HEIGHT: 6'3" RIGHTHANDER BORN: 3/13/1959 ENNIS, TEXAS

YEAR	TEAM	STARTS	GAMES	WON	LOST	PCT	ER	ERA	INNINGS PITCHED	STRIKE-OUTS	WALKS	HITS ALLOWED	HRS ALLOWED	COMP. GAMES	SHUT-OUTS	SAVES
1983	Phi-N	26	26	8	8	.500	63	3.35	169 1/3	101	53	158	13	3	0	0
1984	Phi-N	30	30	9	11	.450	78	4.04	173 2/3	94	52	181	12	1	1	0
1985	Phi-N	26	38	8	13	.381	81	3.78	193	122	74	188	23	3	0	0
1986	Phi-N	23	33	7	10	.412	79	4.94	144	82	58	165	20	0	0	0
1987	**NY-A**	**16**	**35**	**11**	**7**	**.611**	**62**	**3.61**	**154 2/3**	**100**	**57**	**137**	**19**	**6**	**2**	**0**
1988	**NY-A**	**12**	**28**	**6**	**6**	**.500**	**53**	**4.49**	**106 1/3**	**58**	**36**	**93**	**9**	**1**	**0**	**2**
1989	Det-A	7	18	1	5	.167	47	6.35	66 2/3	23	31	75	14	0	0	0
Career Average		20	30	7	9	.455	66	4.14	144	83	52	142	16	2	0	0
Yankee Average		**14**	**32**	**9**	**7**	**.567**	**58**	**3.97**	**130**	**79**	**47**	**115**	**14**	**4**	**1**	**1**
Career Total		140	208	50	60	.455	463	4.14	1008	580	361	997	110	14	3	2
Yankee Total		**28**	**63**	**17**	**13**	**.567**	**115**	**3.97**	**261**	**158**	**93**	**230**	**28**	**7**	**2**	**2**

Hughes, Thomas James (Long Tom)

HEIGHT: 6'1" RIGHTHANDER BORN: 11/29/1878 CHICAGO, ILLINOIS DIED: 2/8/1956 CHICAGO, ILLINOIS

YEAR	TEAM	STARTS	GAMES	WON	LOST	PCT	ER	ERA	INNINGS PITCHED	STRIKE-OUTS	WALKS	HITS ALLOWED	HRS ALLOWED	COMP. GAMES	SHUT-OUTS	SAVES
1900	Chi-N	3	3	1	1	.500	12	5.14	21	12	7	31	0	0	0	0
1901	Chi-N	35	37	10	23	.303	111	3.24	308 1/3	225	115	309	4	32	0	0
1902	Bos-A	8	9	3	3	.500	18	3.28	49 1/3	15	24	51	0	4	0	0
1902	Bal-A	13	13	7	6	.538	47	3.90	108 1/3	45	32	120	2	12	1	0
1903	Bos-A	31	33	20	7	.741	70	2.57	244 2/3	112	60	232	4	25	1	0
1904	Was-A	14	16	2	13	.133	48	3.47	124 1/3	48	34	133	4	14	0	1
1904	**NY-A**	**18**	**19**	**7**	**11**	**.389**	**56**	**3.70**	**136 1/3**	**75**	**48**	**141**	**3**	**12**	**1**	**0**
1905	Was-A	35	39	17	20	.459	76	2.35	291 1/3	149	79	239	3	26	6	0
1906	Was-A	24	30	7	17	.667	82	3.62	204	90	81	230	5	18	1	0
1907	Was-A	23	34	7	14	.333	73	3.11	211	102	47	206	1	18	2	4

(continued)

James Augustus "Catfish" Hunter, rhp, 1975–79

On New Year's Eve 1974, the Yankees signed Jim "Catfish" Hunter to a five-year contract worth $3.75 million, making him the highest paid ballplayer in the history of the game to that point. Not bad for a guy who started his big league career pitching batting practice.

Hunter was born on April 8, 1946, in Hertford, North Carolina. He was signed right out of high school by the Kansas City A's in 1964 for $50,000. Charlie Finley, the owner of the team, didn't like Hunter's name. Jim Hunter just sounded too pedestrian. So Finley himself gave Hunter a nickname: Catfish.

But a fancy nickname wasn't helping him get in games. Throughout all of 1964, Hunter pitched batting practice for the pretty awful A's, who finished last in the American League that year and who easily had the highest team ERA in the league.

In 1965, Hunter won a spot in the regular rotation and went 8-8. Hunter and teammate Rollie Sheldon were the only pitchers on the staff who did not have losing records for the cellar-dwelling A's.

But the A's began to get better, and Hunter began to get much better. He pitched a perfect game in 1968, beating the Minnesota Twins 3-0 and driving in all the team's runs.

Between 1971 and 1974, Hunter won 88 games for the A's while losing 35. He was 4-0 in World Series play during that span, as the A's became only the second American League franchise to win three consecutive World Series, behind the Yankees who had done it several times. Catfish Hunter had become Big Game Hunter.

In 1974, Hunter, who was tiring of Finley's antics, claimed that his contract had been voided because the penurious Finley had not paid off an insurance claim. An arbitrator ruled in his favor, and Hunter became one of baseball's first free agents.

He was signed by the Yankees before the 1975 season, and he picked right up where he left off, winning 23 and losing 14 as New York finished 12 games behind the hated Red Sox for the American League East pennant. His 30 complete games that year led the league, and were the most by a Yankee in 54 years.

But 1976 saw New York win the first of three consecutive American League championships and Hunter, with a 17-15 record, was a key contributor, as much for his leadership in the clubhouse as for his victory totals.

He was deeply respected by his teammates as a pitcher who demanded the ball in big games and who came out and delivered. Not since Whitey Ford did the Yankees have a pitcher with such confidence.

Unlike the cocky Ford, Catfish played it cool. He took the ball, went out and won. He was not an overpowering pitcher. Once, in 1978, outfielder Mickey Rivers told Hunter that he was going to start wearing catcher Thurman Munson's chest protector on his back to ensure he would not be injured chasing the long fly balls Hunter inevitably gave up.

And Hunter did give up long fly balls and home runs. But, more often than not, he won the game anyway. Hunter could change speeds beautifully, and he walked only about 1½ batters a game.

Ironically, Hunter began to struggle in New York, even as the Yankees ascended back onto the championship throne in 1977. He went 9-9 that year after being sidelined by getting hit in the foot by a line drive early in the season. He rebounded from major arm problems early in 1978 to finish 12-6, including several huge wins late in the year.

But by 1979, the last year of his contract, Hunter fell back to 2-9. Never one to hang on when he felt he wasn't contrbuting, at 33, he felt it was time to retire. So he did, back to his farm in North Carolina. He was elected to the Hall of Fame in 1987.

Hunter died in 1999 of complications from Lou Gehrig's disease.

(continued)

1908	Was-A	31	43	18	15	.545	68	2.21	276 1/3	165	77	224	3	24	3	4
1909	Was-A	13	22	4	7	.364	36	2.69	120 1/3	77	33	113	1	7	2	1
1911	Was-A	27	34	11	17	.393	86	3.47	223	86	77	251	7	17	2	0
1912	Was-A	26	31	13	10	.565	64	2.94	196	108	78	201	8	11	1	0
1913	Was-A	12	36	4	12	.667	62	4.30	129 2/3	59	61	129	6	4	0	6
Career Average		21	27	9	12	.427	61	3.09	176	91	57	174	3	15	2	1
Yankee Average		**18**	**19**	**7**	**11**	**.389**	**56**	**3.70**	**136 1/3**	**75**	**48**	**141**	**3**	**12**	**1**	**0**
Career Total		313	399	131	176	.427	909	3.09	2644	1368	853	2610	51	227	25	16
Yankee Total		**18**	**19**	**7**	**11**	**.389**	**56**	**3.70**	**136 1/3**	**75**	**48**	**141**	**3**	**12**	**1**	**0**

Hughes, Thomas L. (Salida Tom)

HEIGHT: 6'2"   RIGHTHANDER   BORN: 1/28/1884 COAL CREEK, COLORADO   DIED: 11/1/1961 LOS ANGELES, CALIFORNIA

YEAR	TEAM	STARTS	GAMES	WON	LOST	PCT	ER	ERA	INNINGS PITCHED	STRIKE-OUTS	WALKS	HITS ALLOWED	HRS ALLOWED	COMP. GAMES	SHUT-OUTS	SAVES
1906	**NY-A**	**1**	**3**	**1**	**0**	**1.000**	**7**	**4.20**	**15**	**5**	**1**	**11**	**2**	**1**	**0**	**0**
1907	**NY-A**	**3**	**4**	**2**	**0**	**1.000**	**8**	**2.67**	**27**	**10**	**11**	**16**	**0**	**2**	**0**	**0**
1909	**NY-A**	**16**	**24**	**7**	**8**	**.467**	**35**	**2.65**	**118 2/3**	**69**	**37**	**109**	**3**	**9**	**2**	**1**
1910	**NY-A**	**15**	**23**	**7**	**9**	**.438**	**59**	**3.50**	**151 2/3**	**64**	**37**	**153**	**2**	**11**	**0**	**1**
1914	Bos-N	2	2	2	0	1.000	5	2.65	17	11	4	14	0	1	0	0
1915	Bos-N	25	50	16	14	.533	66	2.12	280 1/3	171	58	208	4	17	4	9
1916	Bos-N	14	40	16	3	.842	42	2.35	161	97	51	121	2	7	1	5
1917	Bos-N	8	11	5	3	.625	16	1.95	74	40	30	54	1	6	2	0
1918	Bos-N	3	3	0	2	.000	7	3.44	18 1/3	9	6	17	0	1	0	0
Career Average		10	18	6	4	.589	27	2.56	96	53	26	78	2	6	1	2
Yankee Average		**9**	**14**	**4**	**4**	**.500**	**27**	**3.14**	**78**	**37**	**22**	**72**	**2**	**6**	**1**	**1**
Career Total		87	160	56	39	.589	245	2.56	863	476	235	703	14	55	9	16
Yankee Total		**35**	**54**	**17**	**17**	**.500**	**109**	**3.14**	**312**	**148**	**86**	**289**	**7**	**23**	**2**	**2**

Hunter, James Augustus (Catfish)

HEIGHT: 6'0"   RIGHTHANDER   BORN: 4/8/1946 HERTFORD, NORTH CAROLINA   DIED: 9/9/1999 HERTFORD, NORTH CAROLINA

YEAR	TEAM	STARTS	GAMES	WON	LOST	PCT	ER	ERA	INNINGS PITCHED	STRIKE-OUTS	WALKS	HITS ALLOWED	HRS ALLOWED	COMP. GAMES	SHUT-OUTS	SAVES
1965	KC-A	20	32	8	8	.500	63	4.26	133	82	46	124	21	3	2	0
1966	KC-A	25	30	9	11	.450	79	4.02	176 2/3	103	64	158	17	4	0	0
1967	KC-A	35	35	13	17	.433	81	2.81	259 2/3	196	84	209	16	13	5	0
1968	Oak-A	34	36	13	13	.500	87	3.35	234	172	69	210	29	11	2	1
1969	Oak-A	35	38	12	15	.444	92	3.35	247	150	85	210	34	10	3	0
1970	Oak-A	40	40	18	14	.563	111	3.81	262 1/3	178	74	253	32	9	1	0
1971	Oak-A	37	37	21	11	.656	90	2.96	273 2/3	181	80	225	27	16	4	0
1972	Oak-A	37	38	21	7	.750	67	2.04	295 1/3	191	70	200	21	16	5	0
1973	Oak-A	36	36	21	5	.808	95	3.34	256 1/3	124	69	222	39	11	3	0
1974	Oak-A	41	41	25	12	.676	88	2.49	318 1/3	143	46	268	25	23	6	0
1975	**NY-A**	**39**	**39**	**23**	**14**	**.622**	**94**	**2.58**	**328**	**177**	**83**	**248**	**25**	**30**	**7**	**0**
1976	**NY-A**	**36**	**36**	**17**	**15**	**.531**	**117**	**3.53**	**298 2/3**	**173**	**68**	**268**	**28**	**21**	**2**	**0**
1977	**NY-A**	**22**	**22**	**9**	**9**	**.500**	**75**	**4.71**	**143 1/3**	**52**	**47**	**137**	**29**	**8**	**1**	**0**
1978	**NY-A**	**20**	**21**	**12**	**6**	**.667**	**47**	**3.58**	**118**	**56**	**35**	**98**	**16**	**5**	**1**	**0**
1979	**NY-A**	**19**	**19**	**2**	**9**	**.182**	**62**	**5.31**	**105**	**34**	**34**	**128**	**15**	**1**	**0**	**0**
Career Average		32	33	15	11	.574	83	3.26	230	134	64	197	25	12	3	0
Yankee Average		**27**	**27**	**13**	**11**	**.543**	**79**	**3.58**	**199**	**98**	**53**	**176**	**23**	**13**	**2**	**0**
Career Total		476	500	224	166	.574	1248	3.26	3449	2012	954	2958	374	181	42	1
Yankee Total		**136**	**137**	**63**	**53**	**.543**	**395**	**3.58**	**993**	**492**	**267**	**879**	**113**	**65**	**11**	**0**

Hutton, Mark Steven
HEIGHT: 6′8″   RIGHTHANDER   BORN: 2/6/1970 SOUTH ADELAIDE, AUSTRALIA

YEAR	TEAM	STARTS	GAMES	WON	LOST	PCT	ER	ERA	INNINGS PITCHED	STRIKE-OUTS	WALKS	HITS ALLOWED	HRS ALLOWED	COMP. GAMES	SHUT-OUTS	SAVES
1993	NY-A	4	7	1	1	.500	14	5.73	22	12	17	24	2	0	0	0
1994	NY-A	0	2	0	0	—	2	6.00	3 2/3	1	0	4	0	0	0	0
1996	NY-A	2	12	0	2	.000	17	5.10	30 1/3	25	18	32	3	0	0	0
1996	Fla-N	9	13	5	1	.833	23	3.70	56 1/3	31	18	47	6	0	0	0
1997	Fla-N	0	32	3	1	.750	20	3.83	47 2/3	29	19	50	7	0	0	0
1997	Col-N	1	8	0	1	.000	10	7.50	12 2/3	10	7	22	3	0	0	0
1998	Cin-N	2	10	0	1	.000	14	7.41	17	3	17	24	2	0	0	0
Career Average		3	12	1	1	.563	14	4.81	27	16	14	29	3	0	0	0
Yankee Average		2	7	0	1	.250	11	5.40	18	13	12	20	2	0	0	0
Career Total		18	84	9	7	.563	100	4.81	187	111	96	203	23	0	0	0
Yankee Total		6	21	1	3	.250	33	5.40	55	38	35	60	5	0	0	0

Irabu, Hideki
HEIGHT: 6′4″   RIGHTHANDER   BORN: 5/5/1969 HYOGO, JAPAN

YEAR	TEAM	STARTS	GAMES	WON	LOST	PCT	ER	ERA	INNINGS PITCHED	STRIKE-OUTS	WALKS	HITS ALLOWED	HRS ALLOWED	COMP. GAMES	SHUT-OUTS	SAVES
1997	NY-A	9	13	5	4	.556	42	7.09	53 1/3	56	20	69	15	0	0	0
1998	NY-A	28	29	13	9	.591	78	4.06	173	126	76	148	27	2	0	0
1999	NY-A	27	32	11	7	.611	91	4.85	169	133	46	180	26	2	1	0
2000	Mon-N	11	11	2	5	.286	44	7.24	54 2/3	42	14	77	9	0	0	0
Career Average		19	21	8	6	.554	64	5.10	112	89	39	119	19	1	0	0
Yankee Average		21	25	10	7	.592	70	4.80	132	105	47	132	23	1	0	0
Career Total		75	85	31	25	.554	255	5.10	450	357	156	474	77	4	1	0
Yankee Total		64	74	29	20	.592	211	4.80	395	315	142	397	68	4	1	0

Jackson, Grant Dwight (Buck)
HEIGHT: 6′0″   LEFTHANDER   BORN: 9/28/1942 FOSTORIA, OHIO

YEAR	TEAM	STARTS	GAMES	WON	LOST	PCT	ER	ERA	INNINGS PITCHED	STRIKE-OUTS	WALKS	HITS ALLOWED	HRS ALLOWED	COMP. GAMES	SHUT-OUTS	SAVES
1965	Phi-N	2	6	1	1	.500	11	7.24	13 2/3	15	5	17	4	0	0	0
1966	Phi-N	0	2	0	0	—	1	5.40	1 2/3	0	3	2	0	0	0	0
1967	Phi-N	4	43	2	3	.400	36	3.84	84 1/3	83	43	86	3	0	0	1
1968	Phi-N	6	33	1	6	.143	20	2.95	61	49	20	59	4	1	0	1
1969	Phi-N	35	38	14	18	.438	94	3.34	253	180	92	237	16	13	4	1
1970	Phi-N	23	32	5	15	.667	88	5.29	149 2/3	104	61	170	17	1	0	0
1971	Bal-A	9	29	4	3	.571	27	3.13	77 2/3	51	20	72	7	0	0	0
1972	Bal-A	0	32	1	1	.500	12	2.63	41	34	9	33	1	0	0	8
1973	Bal-A	0	45	8	0	1.000	17	1.90	80 1/3	47	24	54	5	0	0	9
1974	Bal-A	0	49	6	4	.600	19	2.57	66 2/3	56	22	48	7	0	0	12
1975	Bal-A	0	41	4	3	.571	18	3.35	48 1/3	39	21	42	3	0	0	7
1976	Bal-A	0	13	1	1	.500	11	5.12	19 1/3	14	9	19	1	0	0	3
1976	NY-A	2	21	6	0	1.000	11	1.69	58 2/3	25	16	38	1	1	1	1
1977	Pit-N	2	49	5	3	.625	39	3.86	91	41	39	81	11	0	0	4
1978	Pit-N	0	60	7	5	.583	28	3.26	77 1/3	45	32	89	5	0	0	5
1979	Pit-N	0	72	8	5	.615	27	2.96	82	39	35	67	9	0	0	14
1980	Pit-N	0	61	8	4	.667	23	2.92	71	31	20	71	4	0	0	9
1981	Pit-N	0	35	1	2	.333	9	2.51	32 1/3	17	10	30	1	0	0	4
1981	Mon-N	0	10	1	0	1.000	9	7.59	10 2/3	4	9	14	2	0	0	0
1982	KC-A	0	20	3	1	.750	22	5.17	38 1/3	15	21	42	7	0	0	0
1982	Pit-N	0	1	0	0	—	1	13.51	.666	0	0	1	1	0	0	0
Career Average		4	33	4	4	.534	25	3.46	65	42	24	61	5	1	0	4
Yankee Average		2	21	6	0	1.000	11	1.69	58 2/3	25	16	38	1	1	1	1
Career Total		83	692	86	75	.534	523	3.46	1359	889	511	1272	109	16	5	79
Yankee Total		2	21	6	0	1.000	11	1.69	58 2/3	25	16	38	1	1	1	1

James, John Phillip
HEIGHT: 5'10" RIGHTHANDER BORN: 7/23/1933 BONNERS FERRY, IDAHO

YEAR	TEAM	STARTS	GAMES	WON	LOST	PCT	ER	ERA	INNINGS PITCHED	STRIKE-OUTS	WALKS	HITS ALLOWED	HRS ALLOWED	COMP. GAMES	SHUT-OUTS	SAVES
1958	NY-A	0	1	0	0	—	0	0.00	3	1	4	2	0	0	0	0
1960	NY-A	0	28	5	1	.833	21	4.36	43 1/3	29	26	38	3	0	0	2
1961	NY-A	0	1	0	0	—	0	0.00	1 1/3	2	0	1	0	0	0	0
1961	LA-A	3	36	0	2	.000	42	5.30	71 1/3	41	54	66	12	0	0	0
Career Average		1	17	1	1	.625	16	4.76	30	18	21	27	4	0	0	1
Yankee Average		0	10	2	0	.833	7	3.97	16	11	10	14	1	0	0	1
Career Total		3	66	5	3	.625	63	4.76	119	73	84	107	15	0	0	2
Yankee Total		0	30	5	1	.833	21	3.97	48	32	30	41	3	0	0	2

Jean, Domingo
HEIGHT: 6'2" RIGHTHANDER BORN: 1/9/1969 SAN PEDRO DE MACORIS, DOMINICAN REPUBLIC

YEAR	TEAM	STARTS	GAMES	WON	LOST	PCT	ER	ERA	INNINGS PITCHED	STRIKE-OUTS	WALKS	HITS ALLOWED	HRS ALLOWED	COMP. GAMES	SHUT-OUTS	SAVES
1993	NY-A	6	10	1	1	.500	20	4.46	40 1/3	20	19	37	7	0	0	0
Career Average		6	10	1	1	.500	20	4.46	40 1/3	20	19	37	7	0	0	0
Yankee Average		6	10	1	1	.500	20	4.46	40 1/3	20	19	37	7	0	0	0
Career Total		6	10	1	1	.500	20	4.46	40 1/3	20	19	37	7	0	0	0
Yankee Total		6	10	1	1	.500	20	4.46	40 1/3	20	19	37	7	0	0	0

Jerzembeck, Mike
HEIGHT: 6'1" RIGHTHANDER BORN: 5/18/1972 QUEENS, NEW YORK

YEAR	TEAM	STARTS	GAMES	WON	LOST	PCT	ER	ERA	INNINGS PITCHED	STRIKE-OUTS	WALKS	HITS ALLOWED	HRS ALLOWED	COMP. GAMES	SHUT-OUTS	SAVES
1998	NY-A	2	3	0	1	.000	9	12.79	6 1/3	1	4	9	2	0	0	0
Career Average		2	3	0	1	.000	9	12.79	6 1/3	1	4	9	2	0	0	0
Yankee Average		2	3	0	1	.000	9	12.79	6 1/3	1	4	9	2	0	0	0
Career Total		2	3	0	1	.000	9	12.79	6 1/3	1	4	9	2	0	0	0
Yankee Total		2	3	0	1	.000	9	12.79	6 1/3	1	4	9	2	0	0	0

John, Thomas Edward (Tommy)
HEIGHT: 6'3" LEFTHANDER BORN: 5/22/1943 TERRE HAUTE, INDIANA

YEAR	TEAM	STARTS	GAMES	WON	LOST	PCT	ER	ERA	INNINGS PITCHED	STRIKE-OUTS	WALKS	HITS ALLOWED	HRS ALLOWED	COMP. GAMES	SHUT-OUTS	SAVES
1963	Cle-A	3	6	0	2	.000	5	2.21	20 1/3	9	6	23	1	0	0	0
1964	Cle-A	14	25	2	9	.182	41	3.91	94 1/3	65	35	97	10	2	1	0
1965	Chi-A	27	39	14	7	.667	63	3.09	183 2/3	126	58	162	12	6	1	3
1966	Chi-A	33	34	14	11	.560	65	2.62	223	138	57	195	13	10	5	0
1967	Chi-A	29	31	10	13	.435	49	2.47	178 1/3	110	47	143	12	9	6	0
1968	Chi-A	25	25	10	5	.667	39	1.98	177 1/3	117	49	135	10	5	1	0
1969	Chi-A	33	33	9	11	.450	84	3.25	232 1/3	128	90	230	16	6	2	0
1970	Chi-A	37	37	12	17	.414	98	3.27	269 1/3	138	101	253	19	10	3	0
1971	Chi-A	35	38	13	16	.448	92	3.61	229 1/3	131	58	244	17	10	3	0
1972	LA-N	29	29	11	5	.688	60	2.89	186 2/3	117	40	172	14	4	1	0
1973	LA-N	31	36	16	7	.696	75	3.10	218	116	50	202	16	4	2	0
1974	LA-N	22	22	13	3	.813	44	2.59	153	78	42	133	4	5	3	0
1976	LA-N	31	31	10	10	.500	71	3.09	207	91	61	207	7	6	2	0
1977	LA-N	31	31	20	7	.741	68	2.78	220 1/3	123	50	225	12	11	3	0
1978	LA-N	30	33	17	10	.630	78	3.30	213	124	53	230	11	7	0	1
1979	**NY-A**	**36**	**37**	**21**	**9**	**.700**	**91**	**2.96**	**276 1/3**	**111**	**65**	**268**	**9**	**17**	**3**	**0**
1980	**NY-A**	**36**	**36**	**22**	**9**	**.710**	**101**	**3.43**	**265 1/3**	**78**	**56**	**270**	**13**	**16**	**6**	**0**
1981	**NY-A**	**20**	**20**	**9**	**8**	**.529**	**41**	**2.63**	**140 1/3**	**50**	**39**	**135**	**10**	**7**	**0**	**0**
1982	**NY-A**	**26**	**30**	**10**	**10**	**.500**	**76**	**3.66**	**186 2/3**	**54**	**34**	**190**	**11**	**9**	**2**	**0**
1982	Cal-A	7	7	4	2	.667	15	3.86	35	14	5	49	4	1	0	0
1983	Cal-A	34	34	11	13	.458	113	4.33	234 2/3	65	49	287	20	9	0	0

(continued)

Thomas Edward "Tommy" John, lhp, 1979–82, 1986–89

Yankee owner George Steinbrenner may have splurged on a lot of free agents who didn't work out in the 1970s and 1980s, but his acquisition of Tommy John was one of his best moves ever.

John, born May 22, 1943, in Terre Haute, Indiana, had been in the major leagues for 15 years when the Yankees signed him to a four-year $1.42 million contract in November 1978.

John was not supposed to be earning this kind of money at this stage in his career. In 1975, he tore a ligament in the elbow of his pitching arm. That, according to virtually every doctor with whom John spoke, would signal the end of John's career.

But Dr. Frank Jobe of California came up with a radical plan: He sewed in a ligament from John's right arm to replace the old one in the left. And it worked. Sportswriters called him "the bionic man," after the television chacter played by Lee Majors.

In 1976, he was 10-10 and was the comeback player of the year. In 1977, he was 20-7, and in 1978, he was 17-10 for back-to-back

Dodger National League champions. His ligament transplant had pretty much robbed John of his fastball, but he still knew how to pitch.

The Yankees signed him at the conclusion of the 1978 season, and John had an extremely productive four years in New York, going 62-37 with a 3.21 ERA. He was a two-time All-Star and won 21 games in 1979 and 20 games in 1980. He also led the American League with six shutouts that year.

The low-key, mature John was a breath of fresh air in the Bronx Bombers' controversial clubhouse of the late 1970s and early 1980s, and his superb pitching helped New York make the playoffs in 1980 and 1981. The latter year saw John win one game in the American League championship series over the A's and also beat his old team, the Dodgers, in Game 2 of the World Series. John allowed only one earned run in three appearances for the Yankees that year, but the Dodgers won the series, four games to two.

John was traded to the Angels in 1982, but returned to New York in 1986 for four more years. But the bionic man had finally begun to run down. His record with New York in those final years was 29-24. John retired in 1989.

(continued)

1984	Cal-A	29	32	7	13	.350	91	4.52	181 1/3	47	56	223	15	4	1	0
1985	Cal-A	6	12	2	4	.333	20	4.70	38 1/3	17	15	51	3	0	0	0
1985	Oak-A	11	11	2	6	.667	33	6.19	48	8	13	66	6	0	0	0
1986	**NY-A**	**10**	**13**	**5**	**3**	**.625**	**23**	**2.93**	**70 2/3**	**28**	**15**	**73**	**8**	**1**	**0**	**0**
1987	**NY-A**	**33**	**33**	**13**	**6**	**.684**	**84**	**4.03**	**187 2/3**	**63**	**47**	**212**	**12**	**3**	**1**	**0**
1988	**NY-A**	**32**	**35**	**9**	**8**	**.529**	**88**	**4.49**	**176 1/3**	**81**	**46**	**221**	**11**	**0**	**0**	**0**
1989	**NY-A**	**10**	**10**	**2**	**7**	**.666**	**41**	**5.80**	**63 2/3**	**18**	**22**	**87**	**6**	**0**	**0**	**0**
Career Average		25	27	10	8	.555	62	3.34	168	80	45	171	11	6	2	0
Yankee Average		**25**	**27**	**11**	**8**	**.603**	**68**	**3.59**	**171**	**60**	**41**	**182**	**10**	**7**	**2**	**0**
Career Total		700	760	288	231	.555	1749	3.34	4710	2245	1259	4783	302	162	46	4
Yankee Total		**203**	**214**	**91**	**60**	**.603**	**545**	**3.59**	**1367**	**483**	**324**	**1456**	**80**	**53**	**12**	**0**

Johnson, Donald Roy

HEIGHT: 6'3" RIGHTHANDER BORN: 11/12/1926 PORTLAND, OREGON

YEAR	TEAM	STARTS	GAMES	WON	LOST	PCT	ER	ERA	INNINGS PITCHED	STRIKE-OUTS	WALKS	HITS ALLOWED	HRS ALLOWED	COMP. GAMES	SHUT-OUTS	SAVES
1947	**NY-A**	**8**	**15**	**4**	**3**	**.571**	**22**	**3.64**	**54 1/3**	**16**	**23**	**57**	**2**	**2**	**0**	**0**
1950	**NY-A**	**0**	**8**	**1**	**0**	**1.000**	**20**	**10.00**	**18**	**9**	**12**	**35**	**2**	**0**	**0**	**0**
1950	StL-A	12	25	5	6	.455	65	6.09	96	31	55	126	14	4	1	1
1951	StL-A	3	6	0	1	.000	21	12.60	15	8	18	27	4	0	0	0
1951	Was-A	20	21	7	11	.389	63	3.95	143 2/3	52	58	138	9	8	1	0
1952	Was-A	6	29	0	5	.000	34	4.43	69	37	33	80	4	0	0	2
1954	Chi-A	16	46	8	7	.533	50	3.13	144	68	43	129	14	3	3	7
1955	Bal-A	5	31	2	4	.333	44	5.82	68	27	35	89	4	0	0	1
1958	SF-N	0	17	0	1	.000	16	6.26	23	14	8	31	2	0	0	1
Career Average		8	22	3	4	.415	37	4.78	70	29	32	79	6	2	1	1
Yankee Average		**4**	**12**	**3**	**2**	**.625**	**21**	**5.23**	**36**	**13**	**18**	**46**	**2**	**1**	**0**	**0**
Career Total		70	198	27	38	.415	335	4.78	631	262	285	712	55	17	5	12
Yankee Total		**8**	**23**	**5**	**3**	**.625**	**42**	**5.23**	**72**	**25**	**35**	**92**	**4**	**2**	**0**	**0**

Johnson, Henry Ward (Hank)

HEIGHT: 5'11" RIGHTHANDER BORN: 5/21/1906 BRADENTON, FLORIDA DIED: 8/20/1982 BRADENTON, FLORIDA

YEAR	TEAM	STARTS	GAMES	WON	LOST	PCT	ER	ERA	INNINGS PITCHED	STRIKE-OUTS	WALKS	HITS ALLOWED	HRS ALLOWED	COMP. GAMES	SHUT-OUTS	SAVES
1925	**NY-A**	**4**	**24**	**1**	**3**	**.667**	**51**	**6.85**	**67**	**25**	**37**	**88**	**3**	**2**	**1**	**0**
1926	**NY-A**	**0**	**1**	**0**	**0**	**—**	**2**	**18.00**	**1**	**0**	**2**	**2**	**0**	**0**	**0**	**1**
1928	**NY-A**	**22**	**31**	**14**	**9**	**.609**	**95**	**4.30**	**199**	**110**	**104**	**188**	**16**	**10**	**1**	**0**
1929	**NY-A**	**8**	**12**	**3**	**3**	**.500**	**24**	**5.06**	**42 2/3**	**24**	**39**	**37**	**5**	**2**	**0**	**0**
1930	**NY-A**	**15**	**44**	**14**	**11**	**.560**	**91**	**4.67**	**175 1/3**	**115**	**104**	**177**	**12**	**7**	**1**	**2**
1931	**NY-A**	**23**	**40**	**13**	**8**	**.619**	**103**	**4.72**	**196 1/3**	**106**	**102**	**176**	**13**	**8**	**0**	**4**
1932	**NY-A**	**4**	**5**	**2**	**2**	**.500**	**17**	**4.88**	**31 1/3**	**27**	**15**	**34**	**7**	**2**	**0**	**0**
1933	Bos-A	21	25	8	6	.571	70	4.06	155 1/3	65	74	156	13	7	0	1
1934	Bos-A	14	31	6	8	.429	74	5.36	124 1/3	66	53	162	12	7	1	1
1935	Bos-A	2	13	2	1	.667	19	5.52	31	14	14	41	3	0	0	1
1936	Phi-A	3	3	0	2	.000	10	7.71	11 2/3	6	10	16	4	0	0	0
1939	Cin-N	0	20	0	3	.000	7	2.01	31 1/3	10	13	30	1	0	0	1
Career Average		10	21	5	5	.529	47	4.75	89	47	47	92	7	4	0	1
Yankee Average		**11**	**22**	**7**	**5**	**.566**	**55**	**4.84**	**102**	**58**	**58**	**100**	**8**	**4**	**0**	**1**
Career Total		116	249	63	56	.529	563	4.75	1066	568	567	1107	89	45	4	11
Yankee Total		**76**	**157**	**47**	**36**	**.566**	**383**	**4.84**	**713**	**407**	**403**	**702**	**56**	**31**	**3**	**7**

Johnson, John Clifford (Swede)

HEIGHT: 6'0" LEFTHANDER BORN: 9/29/1914 BELMORE, OHIO DIED: 6/26/1991 IRON MOUNTAIN, MICHIGAN

YEAR	TEAM	STARTS	GAMES	WON	LOST	PCT	ER	ERA	INNINGS PITCHED	STRIKE-OUTS	WALKS	HITS ALLOWED	HRS ALLOWED	COMP. GAMES	SHUT-OUTS	SAVES
1944	**NY-A**	**1**	**22**	**0**	**2**	**.000**	**12**	**4.05**	**26 2/3**	**11**	**24**	**25**	**0**	**0**	**0**	**3**
1945	Chi-A	0	29	3	0	1.000	33	4.26	69 2/3	38	35	85	2	0	0	4
Career Average		1	26	2	1	.600	23	4.20	48	25	30	55	1	0	0	4
Yankee Average		**1**	**22**	**0**	**2**	**.000**	**12**	**4.05**	**26 2/3**	**11**	**24**	**25**	**0**	**0**	**0**	**3**
Career Total		1	51	3	2	.600	45	4.20	96	49	59	110	2	0	0	7
Yankee Total		**1**	**22**	**0**	**2**	**.000**	**12**	**4.05**	**26 2/3**	**11**	**24**	**25**	**0**	**0**	**0**	**3**

Johnson, Kenneth Travis

HEIGHT: 6'4" RIGHTHANDER BORN: 6/16/1933 W. PALM BEACH, FLORIDA

YEAR	TEAM	STARTS	GAMES	WON	LOST	PCT	ER	ERA	INNINGS PITCHED	STRIKE-OUTS	WALKS	HITS ALLOWED	HRS ALLOWED	COMP. GAMES	SHUT-OUTS	SAVES
1958	KC-A	0	2	0	0	—	7	27.00	2 1/3	1	3	6	1	0	0	0
1959	KC-A	2	2	1	1	.500	5	4.09	11	8	5	11	2	0	0	0
1960	KC-A	6	42	5	10	.333	57	4.26	120 1/3	83	45	120	16	2	0	3
1961	KC-A	1	6	0	4	.000	11	10.61	9 1/3	4	7	11	2	0	0	0

(continued)

(continued)

YEAR	TEAM	STARTS	GAMES	WON	LOST	PCT	ER	ERA	INNINGS PITCHED	STRIKE-OUTS	WALKS	HITS ALLOWED	HRS ALLOWED	COMP. GAMES	SHUT-OUTS	SAVES
1961	Cin-N	11	15	6	2	.750	30	3.25	83	42	22	71	11	3	1	1
1962	Hou-N	31	33	7	16	.304	84	3.84	197	178	46	195	18	5	1	0
1963	Hou-N	32	37	11	17	.393	66	2.65	224	148	50	204	12	6	1	1
1964	Hou-N	35	35	11	16	.407	88	3.63	218	117	44	209	15	7	1	0
1965	Hou-N	8	8	3	2	.600	24	4.18	51 2/3	28	11	52	4	1	0	0
1965	Mil-N	26	29	13	8	.619	64	3.21	179 2/3	123	37	165	15	8	1	2
1966	Atl-N	31	32	14	8	.636	79	3.30	215 2/3	105	46	213	24	11	2	0
1967	Atl-N	29	29	13	9	.591	64	2.74	210 1/3	85	38	191	19	6	0	0
1968	Atl-N	16	31	5	8	.385	52	3.47	135	57	25	145	10	1	0	0
1969	Atl-N	2	9	0	1	.000	16	4.97	29	20	9	32	4	0	0	1
1969	**NY-A**	**0**	**12**	**1**	**2**	**.333**	**10**	**3.46**	**26**	**21**	**11**	**19**	**1**	**0**	**0**	**0**
1969	Chi-N	1	9	1	2	.333	6	2.84	19	18	13	17	2	0	0	1
1970	Mon-N	0	3	0	0	—	5	7.50	6	4	1	9	1	0	0	0
Career Average		14	20	5	6	.462	39	3.46	102	61	24	98	9	3	0	1
Yankee Average		**0**	**12**	**1**	**2**	**.333**	**10**	**3.46**	**26**	**21**	**11**	**19**	**1**	**0**	**0**	**0**
Career Total		231	334	91	106	.462	668	3.46	1737	1042	413	1670	157	50	7	9
Yankee Total		**0**	**12**	**1**	**2**	**.333**	**10**	**3.46**	**26**	**21**	**11**	**19**	**1**	**0**	**0**	**0**

Johnson, William Jeffrey

HEIGHT: 6'3" LEFTHANDER BORN: 8/4/1966 DURHAM, NORTH CAROLINA

YEAR	TEAM	STARTS	GAMES	WON	LOST	PCT	ER	ERA	INNINGS PITCHED	STRIKE-OUTS	WALKS	HITS ALLOWED	HRS ALLOWED	COMP. GAMES	SHUT-OUTS	SAVES
1991	**NY-A**	**23**	**23**	**6**	**11**	**.353**	**84**	**5.95**	**127**	**62**	**33**	**156**	**15**	**0**	**0**	**0**
1992	**NY-A**	**8**	**13**	**2**	**3**	**.400**	**39**	**6.66**	**52 2/3**	**14**	**23**	**71**	**4**	**0**	**0**	**0**
1993	**NY-A**	**2**	**2**	**0**	**2**	**.000**	**9**	**30.38**	**2 2/3**	**0**	**2**	**12**	**1**	**0**	**0**	**0**
Career Average		11	13	3	5	.333	44	6.52	61	25	19	80	7	0	0	0
Yankee Average		**11**	**13**	**3**	**5**	**.333**	**44**	**6.52**	**61**	**25**	**19**	**80**	**7**	**0**	**0**	**0**
Career Total		33	38	8	16	.333	132	6.52	182	76	58	239	20	0	0	0
Yankee Total		**33**	**38**	**8**	**16**	**.333**	**132**	**6.52**	**182**	**76**	**58**	**239**	**20**	**0**	**0**	**0**

Jones, Gareth Howell (Gary)

HEIGHT: 6'0" LEFTHANDER BORN: 6/12/1945 HUNTINGTON PARK, CALIFORNIA

YEAR	TEAM	STARTS	GAMES	WON	LOST	PCT	ER	ERA	INNINGS PITCHED	STRIKE-OUTS	WALKS	HITS ALLOWED	HRS ALLOWED	COMP. GAMES	SHUT-OUTS	SAVES
1970	**NY-A**	**0**	**2**	**0**	**0**	**—**	**0**	**0.00**	**2**	**2**	**1**	**3**	**0**	**0**	**0**	**0**
1971	**NY-A**	**0**	**12**	**0**	**0**	**—**	**14**	**9.00**	**14**	**10**	**7**	**19**	**1**	**0**	**0**	**0**
Career Average		0	7	0	0	—	7	7.88	8	6	4	11	1	0	0	0
Yankee Average		**0**	**7**	**0**	**0**	**—**	**7**	**7.88**	**8**	**6**	**4**	**11**	**1**	**0**	**0**	**0**
Career Total		0	14	0	0	—	14	7.88	16	12	8	22	1	0	0	0
Yankee Total		**0**	**14**	**0**	**0**	**—**	**14**	**7.88**	**16**	**12**	**8**	**22**	**1**	**0**	**0**	**0**

Jones, James Condia

HEIGHT: 6'2" RIGHTHANDER BORN: 4/20/1964 DALLAS, TEXAS

YEAR	TEAM	STARTS	GAMES	WON	LOST	PCT	ER	ERA	INNINGS PITCHED	STRIKE-OUTS	WALKS	HITS ALLOWED	HRS ALLOWED	COMP. GAMES	SHUT-OUTS	SAVES
1986	SD-N	3	3	2	0	1.000	5	2.50	18	15	3	10	1	1	1	0
1987	SD-N	22	30	9	7	.563	67	4.14	145 2/3	51	54	154	14	2	1	0
1988	SD-N	29	29	9	14	.391	82	4.12	179	82	44	192	14	3	0	0
1989	**NY-A**	**6**	**11**	**2**	**1**	**.667**	**28**	**5.25**	**48**	**25**	**16**	**56**	**7**	**0**	**0**	**0**
1990	**NY-A**	**7**	**17**	**1**	**2**	**.333**	**35**	**6.30**	**50**	**25**	**23**	**72**	**8**	**0**	**0**	**0**
1991	Hou-N	22	26	6	8	.429	66	4.39	135 1/3	88	51	143	9	1	1	0
1992	Hou-N	23	25	10	6	.625	63	4.07	139 1/3	69	39	135	13	0	0	0
1993	Mon-N	6	12	4	1	.800	28	6.35	39 2/3	21	9	47	6	0	0	0
Career Average		15	19	5	5	.524	47	4.46	94	47	30	101	9	1	0	0
Yankee Average		**7**	**14**	**2**	**2**	**.500**	**32**	**5.79**	**49**	**25**	**20**	**64**	**8**	**0**	**0**	**0**
Career Total		118	153	43	39	.524	374	4.46	755	376	239	809	72	7	3	0
Yankee Total		**13**	**28**	**3**	**3**	**.500**	**63**	**5.79**	**98**	**50**	**39**	**128**	**15**	**0**	**0**	**0**

Jones, Samuel Pond (Sad Sam)
HEIGHT: 6'0"   RIGHTHANDER   BORN: 7/26/1892 WOODSFIELD, OHIO   DIED: 7/6/1966 BARNESVILLE, OHIO

YEAR	TEAM	STARTS	GAMES	WON	LOST	PCT	ER	ERA	INNINGS PITCHED	STRIKE-OUTS	WALKS	HITS ALLOWED	HRS ALLOWED	COMP. GAMES	SHUT-OUTS	SAVES
1914	Cle-A	0	1	0	0	—	1	2.70	3 1/3	0	2	2	0	0	0	0
1915	Cle-A	9	48	4	9	.308	59	3.65	145 2/3	42	63	131	0	2	0	4
1916	Bos-A	0	12	0	1	.000	11	3.67	27	7	10	25	0	0	0	1
1917	Bos-A	1	9	0	1	.000	8	4.41	16 1/3	5	6	15	1	0	0	1
1918	Bos-A	21	24	16	5	.762	46	2.25	184	44	70	151	1	16	5	0
1919	Bos-A	31	35	12	20	.375	102	3.75	245	67	95	258	4	21	5	1
1920	Bos-A	33	37	13	16	.448	120	3.94	274	86	79	302	9	21	3	0
1921	Bos-A	38	40	23	16	.590	107	3.22	298 2/3	98	78	318	1	25	5	1
1922	**NY-A**	**28**	**45**	**13**	**13**	**.500**	**106**	**3.67**	**260**	**81**	**76**	**270**	**16**	**20**	**0**	**8**
1923	**NY-A**	**27**	**39**	**21**	**8**	**.724**	**98**	**3.63**	**243**	**68**	**69**	**239**	**11**	**18**	**3**	**4**
1924	**NY-A**	**21**	**36**	**9**	**6**	**.600**	**72**	**3.63**	**178 2/3**	**53**	**76**	**187**	**6**	**8**	**3**	**3**
1925	**NY-A**	**31**	**43**	**15**	**21**	**.417**	**127**	**4.63**	**246 2/3**	**92**	**104**	**267**	**14**	**14**	**1**	**2**
1926	**NY-A**	**23**	**39**	**9**	**8**	**.529**	**89**	**4.98**	**161**	**69**	**80**	**186**	**6**	**6**	**1**	**5**
1927	StL-A	26	30	8	14	.364	91	4.32	189 2/3	72	102	211	13	11	0	0
1928	Was-A	27	30	17	7	.708	71	2.84	224 2/3	63	78	209	5	19	4	0
1929	Was-A	24	24	9	9	.500	67	3.92	153 2/3	36	49	156	5	8	1	0
1930	Was-A	25	25	15	7	.682	83	4.07	183 1/3	60	61	195	4	14	1	0
1931	Was-A	24	25	9	10	.474	71	4.32	148	58	47	185	10	8	1	1
1932	Chi-A	28	30	10	15	.400	94	4.22	200 1/3	64	75	217	9	10	0	0
1933	Chi-A	25	27	10	12	.455	66	3.36	176 2/3	60	65	181	13	11	2	0
1934	Chi-A	26	27	8	12	.400	104	5.11	183 1/3	60	60	217	16	11	1	0
1935	Chi-A	19	21	8	7	.533	63	4.05	140	38	51	162	8	7	0	0
Career Average		22	29	10	10	.513	75	3.84	176	56	63	186	7	11	2	1
Yankee Average		**26**	**40**	**13**	**11**	**.545**	**98**	**4.06**	**218**	**73**	**81**	**230**	**11**	**13**	**2**	**4**
Career Total		487	647	229	217	.513	1656	3.84	3883	1223	1396	4084	152	250	36	31
Yankee Total		**130**	**202**	**67**	**56**	**.545**	**492**	**4.06**	**1089**	**363**	**405**	**1149**	**53**	**66**	**8**	**22**

Juden, Jeffrey Daniel
HEIGHT: 6'8"   RIGHTHANDER   BORN: 1/19/1971 SALEM, MASSACHUSETTS

YEAR	TEAM	STARTS	GAMES	WON	LOST	PCT	ER	ERA	INNINGS PITCHED	STRIKE-OUTS	WALKS	HITS ALLOWED	HRS ALLOWED	COMP. GAMES	SHUT-OUTS	SAVES
1991	Hou-N	3	4	0	2	.000	12	6.00	18	11	7	19	3	0	0	0
1993	Hou-N	0	2	0	1	.000	3	5.40	5	5	4	4	1	0	0	0
1994	Phi-N	5	6	1	4	.666	19	6.33	27 2/3	22	12	29	4	0	0	0
1995	Phi-N	10	13	2	4	.333	28	4.06	62 2/3	47	31	53	6	1	0	0
1996	SF-N	0	36	4	0	1.000	19	4.17	41 2/3	35	20	39	7	0	0	0
1996	Mon-N	0	22	1	0	1.000	8	2.25	32 2/3	26	14	22	1	0	0	0
1997	Mon-N	22	22	11	5	.688	61	4.22	130	107	57	125	17	3	0	0
1997	Cle-A	5	8	0	1	.000	19	5.52	31 1/3	29	15	32	6	0	0	0
1998	Mil-N	24	24	7	11	.389	85	5.54	138 1/3	109	66	149	20	2	0	0
1998	Ana-A	6	8	1	3	.667	30	6.75	40	39	18	33	7	0	0	0
1999	**NY-A**	**1**	**2**	**0**	**1**	**.000**	**1**	**1.80**	**5**	**9**	**3**	**5**	**1**	**0**	**0**	**0**
Career Average		7	13	2	3	.458	26	4.85	48	40	22	46	7	1	0	0
Yankee Average		**1**	**2**	**0**	**1**	**.000**	**1**	**1.80**	**5**	**9**	**3**	**5**	**1**	**0**	**0**	**0**
Career Total		76	147	27	32	.458	285	4.85	531	441	247	510	73	6	0	0
Yankee Total		**1**	**2**	**0**	**1**	**.000**	**1**	**1.80**	**5**	**9**	**3**	**5**	**1**	**0**	**0**	**0**

Jurewicz, Michael Allen
HEIGHT: 6'3"   LEFTHANDER   BORN: 9/20/1945 BUFFALO, NEW YORK

YEAR	TEAM	STARTS	GAMES	WON	LOST	PCT	ER	ERA	INNINGS PITCHED	STRIKE-OUTS	WALKS	HITS ALLOWED	HRS ALLOWED	COMP. GAMES	SHUT-OUTS	SAVES
1965	NY-A	0	2	0	0	—	2	7.72	2 1/3	2	1	5	0	0	0	0
Career Average		0	2	0	0	—	2	7.72	2 1/3	2	1	5	0	0	0	0
Yankee Average		**0**	**2**	**0**	**0**	**—**	**2**	**7.72**	**2 1/3**	**2**	**1**	**5**	**0**	**0**	**0**	**0**
Career Total		0	2	0	0	—	2	7.72	2 1/3	2	1	5	0	0	0	0
Yankee Total		**0**	**2**	**0**	**0**	**—**	**2**	**7.72**	**2 1/3**	**2**	**1**	**5**	**0**	**0**	**0**	**0**

Kaat, James Lee (Kitty)

HEIGHT: 6'4" LEFTHANDER BORN: 11/7/1938 ZEELAND, MICHIGAN

YEAR	TEAM	STARTS	GAMES	WON	LOST	PCT	ER	ERA	INNINGS PITCHED	STRIKE-OUTS	WALKS	HITS ALLOWED	HRS ALLOWED	COMP. GAMES	SHUT-OUTS	SAVES
1959	Was-A	2	3	0	2	.000	7	12.60	5	2	4	7	1	0	0	0
1960	Was-A	9	13	1	5	.167	31	5.58	50	25	31	48	8	0	0	0
1961	Min-A	29	36	9	17	.346	87	3.90	200 2/3	122	82	188	12	8	1	0
1962	Min-A	35	39	18	14	.563	94	3.14	269	173	75	243	23	16	5	1
1963	Min-A	27	31	10	10	.500	83	4.19	178 1/3	105	38	195	24	7	1	1
1964	Min-A	34	36	17	11	.607	87	3.22	243	171	60	231	23	13	0	1
1965	Min-A	42	45	18	11	.621	83	2.83	264 1/3	154	63	267	25	7	2	2
1966	Min-A	41	41	25	13	.658	93	2.75	304 2/3	205	55	271	29	19	3	0
1967	Min-A	38	42	16	13	.552	89	3.04	263 1/3	211	42	269	21	13	2	0
1968	Min-A	29	30	14	12	.538	68	2.94	208	130	40	192	16	9	2	0
1969	Min-A	32	40	14	13	.519	94	3.49	242 1/3	139	75	252	23	10	0	1
1970	Min-A	34	45	14	10	.583	91	3.56	230 1/3	120	58	244	26	4	1	0
1971	Min-A	38	39	13	14	.481	96	3.32	260 1/3	137	47	275	16	15	4	0
1972	Min-A	15	15	10	2	.833	26	2.06	113 1/3	64	20	94	6	5	0	0
1973	Min-A	28	29	11	12	.478	89	4.41	181 2/3	93	39	206	26	7	2	0
1973	Chi-A	7	7	4	1	.800	20	4.22	42 2/3	16	4	44	4	3	1	0
1974	Chi-A	39	42	21	13	.618	90	2.92	277 1/3	142	63	263	18	15	3	0
1975	Chi-A	41	43	20	14	.588	105	3.11	303 2/3	142	77	321	20	12	1	0
1976	Phi-N	35	38	12	14	.462	88	3.48	227 2/3	83	32	241	21	7	1	0
1977	Phi-N	27	35	6	11	.353	96	5.39	160 1/3	55	40	211	20	2	0	0
1978	Phi-N	24	26	8	5	.615	64	4.10	140 1/3	48	32	150	9	2	1	0
1979	Phi-N	1	3	1	0	1.000	4	4.32	8 1/3	2	5	9	1	0	0	0
1979	**NY-A**	**1**	**40**	**2**	**3**	**.400**	**25**	**3.86**	**58 1/3**	**23**	**14**	**64**	**4**	**0**	**0**	**2**
1980	**NY-A**	**0**	**4**	**0**	**1**	**.000**	**4**	**7.20**	**5**	**1**	**4**	**8**	**0**	**0**	**0**	**0**
1980	StL-N	14	49	8	7	.533	55	3.82	129 2/3	36	33	140	6	6	1	4
1981	StL-N	1	41	6	6	.500	20	3.40	53	8	17	60	2	0	0	4
1982	StL-N	2	62	5	3	.625	34	4.08	75	35	23	79	6	0	0	2
1983	StL-N	0	24	0	0	—	15	3.89	34 2/3	19	10	48	5	0	0	0
Career Average		22	32	10	8	.544	62	3.45	162	88	39	165	14	6	1	1
Yankee Average		**1**	**22**	**1**	**2**	**.333**	**15**	**4.12**	**32**	**12**	**9**	**36**	**2**	**0**	**0**	**1**
Career Total		625	898	283	237	.544	1738	3.45	4530	2461	1083	4620	395	180	31	18
Yankee Total		**1**	**44**	**2**	**4**	**.333**	**29**	**4.12**	**63**	**24**	**18**	**72**	**4**	**0**	**0**	**2**

Kamieniecki, Scott Andrew

HEIGHT: 6'0" RIGHTHANDER BORN: 4/19/1964 MT. CLEMENS, MICHIGAN

YEAR	TEAM	STARTS	GAMES	WON	LOST	PCT	ER	ERA	INNINGS PITCHED	STRIKE-OUTS	WALKS	HITS ALLOWED	HRS ALLOWED	COMP. GAMES	SHUT-OUTS	SAVES
1991	**NY-A**	**9**	**9**	**4**	**4**	**.500**	**24**	**3.90**	**55 1/3**	**34**	**22**	**54**	**8**	**0**	**0**	**0**
1992	**NY-A**	**28**	**28**	**6**	**14**	**.300**	**91**	**4.36**	**188**	**88**	**74**	**193**	**13**	**4**	**0**	**0**
1993	**NY-A**	**20**	**30**	**10**	**7**	**.588**	**70**	**4.08**	**154 1/3**	**72**	**59**	**163**	**17**	**2**	**0**	**1**
1994	**NY-A**	**16**	**22**	**8**	**6**	**.571**	**49**	**3.77**	**117**	**71**	**59**	**115**	**13**	**1**	**0**	**0**
1995	**NY-A**	**16**	**17**	**7**	**6**	**.538**	**40**	**4.04**	**89**	**43**	**49**	**83**	**8**	**1**	**0**	**0**
1996	**NY-A**	**5**	**7**	**1**	**2**	**.333**	**28**	**11.45**	**22**	**15**	**19**	**36**	**6**	**0**	**0**	**0**
1997	Bal-A	30	30	10	6	.625	80	4.02	179	109	67	179	20	0	0	0
1998	Bal-A	11	12	2	6	.667	41	6.83	54	25	26	67	7	0	0	0
1999	Bal-A	3	43	2	4	.333	31	4.98	56	39	29	52	4	0	0	2
2000	Cle-A	0	26	1	3	.250	21	5.67	33 1/3	29	20	42	6	0	0	0
2000	Atl-N	0	26	2	1	.667	15	5.47	24 2/3	17	22	22	3	0	0	2
Career Average		13	23	5	5	.473	45	4.52	88	49	41	91	11	1	0	0
Yankee Average		**16**	**19**	**6**	**7**	**.480**	**50**	**4.34**	**104**	**54**	**47**	**107**	**11**	**1**	**0**	**0**
Career Total		138	250	53	59	.473	490	4.52	975 2/3	542	446	1006	96	8	0	5
Yankee Total		**94**	**113**	**36**	**39**	**.480**	**302**	**4.34**	**626**	**323**	**282**	**644**	**65**	**8**	**0**	**1**

Kammeyer, Robert Lynn

HEIGHT: 6'4" RIGHTHANDER BORN: 2/12/1950 KANSAS CITY, KANSAS

YEAR	TEAM	STARTS	GAMES	WON	LOST	PCT	ER	ERA	INNINGS PITCHED	STRIKE-OUTS	WALKS	HITS ALLOWED	HRS ALLOWED	COMP. GAMES	SHUT-OUTS	SAVES
1978	**NY-A**	**0**	**7**	**0**	**0**	**—**	**14**	**5.82**	**21 2/3**	**11**	**6**	**24**	**1**	**0**	**0**	**0**
1979	**NY-A**	**0**	**1**	**0**	**0**	**—**	**0**	**—**	**0**	**0**	**0**	**7**	**2**	**0**	**0**	**0**

(continued)

(continued)

	STARTS	GAMES	WON	LOST	PCT	ER	ERA	INNINGS PITCHED	STRIKE-OUTS	WALKS	HITS ALLOWED	HRS ALLOWED	COMP. GAMES	SHUT-OUTS	SAVES
Career Average	0	4	0	0	—	7	5.82	11	6	3	16	2	0	0	0
Yankee Average	0	4	0	0	—	7	5.82	11	6	3	16	2	0	0	0
Career Total	0	8	0	0	—	14	5.82	21 2/3	11	6	31	3	0	0	0
Yankee Total	0	8	0	0	—	14	5.82	21 2/3	11	6	31	3	0	0	0

Karpel, Herbert (Lefty)

HEIGHT: 5'9" LEFTHANDER BORN: 12/27/1917 BROOKLYN, NEW YORK

YEAR	TEAM	STARTS	GAMES	WON	LOST	PCT	ER	ERA	INNINGS PITCHED	STRIKE-OUTS	WALKS	HITS ALLOWED	HRS ALLOWED	COMP. GAMES	SHUT-OUTS	SAVES
1946	NY-A	0	2	0	0	—	2	10.80	1 2/3	0	0	4	0	0	0	0
Career Average		0	2	0	0	—	2	10.80	1 2/3	0	0	4	0	0	0	0
Yankee Average		0	2	0	0	—	2	10.80	1 2/3	0	0	4	0	0	0	0
Career Total		0	2	0	0	—	2	10.80	1 2/3	0	0	4	0	0	0	0
Yankee Total		0	2	0	0	—	2	10.80	1 2/3	0	0	4	0	0	0	0

Kaufman, Curt Gerrard

HEIGHT: 6'2" RIGHTHANDER BORN: 7/9/1957 OMAHA, NEBRASKA

YEAR	TEAM	STARTS	GAMES	WON	LOST	PCT	ER	ERA	INNINGS PITCHED	STRIKE-OUTS	WALKS	HITS ALLOWED	HRS ALLOWED	COMP. GAMES	SHUT-OUTS	SAVES
1982	NY-A	0	7	1	0	1.000	5	5.19	8 2/3	1	6	9	2	0	0	0
1983	NY-A	0	4	0	0	—	3	3.12	8 2/3	8	4	10	0	0	0	0
1984	Cal-A	1	29	2	3	.400	35	4.57	69	41	20	68	13	0	0	1
Career Average		0	13	1	1	.500	14	4.48	29	17	10	29	5	0	0	0
Yankee Average		0	6	1	0	1.000	4	4.15	9	5	5	10	1	0	0	0
Career Total		1	40	3	3	.500	43	4.48	86	50	30	87	15	0	0	1
Yankee Total		0	11	1	0	1.000	8	4.15	17	9	10	19	2	0	0	0

Keating, Raymond Herbert

HEIGHT: 5'11" RIGHTHANDER BORN: 7/21/1891 BRIDGEPORT, CONNECTICUT DIED: 12/28/1963 SACRAMENTO, CALIFORNIA

YEAR	TEAM	STARTS	GAMES	WON	LOST	PCT	ER	ERA	INNINGS PITCHED	STRIKE-OUTS	WALKS	HITS ALLOWED	HRS ALLOWED	COMP. GAMES	SHUT-OUTS	SAVES
1912	NY-A	5	6	0	3	.000	23	5.80	35 2/3	21	18	36	0	3	0	0
1913	NY-A	21	28	6	12	.333	54	3.21	151 1/3	83	51	147	3	9	2	0
1914	NY-A	25	34	7	11	.389	69	2.96	210	109	67	198	1	14	0	1
1915	NY-A	10	11	3	6	.333	32	3.63	79 1/3	37	45	66	3	8	1	0
1916	NY-A	12	14	5	6	.455	31	3.07	91	35	37	91	4	6	0	0
1918	NY-A	6	15	2	2	.500	21	3.91	48 1/3	16	30	39	0	1	0	0
1919	Bos-N	13	22	7	11	.389	45	2.98	136	48	45	129	2	9	1	0
Career Average		13	19	4	7	.370	39	3.29	107	50	42	101	2	7	1	0
Yankee Average		13	18	4	7	.365	38	3.36	103	50	41	96	2	7	1	0
Career Total		92	130	30	51	.370	275	3.29	752	349	293	706	13	50	4	1
Yankee Total		79	108	23	40	.365	230	3.36	616	301	248	577	11	41	3	1

Keefe, Robert Francis

HEIGHT: 5'11" RIGHTHANDER BORN: 6/16/1882 FOLSOM, CALIFORNIA DIED: 12/7/1964 SACRAMENTO, CALIFORNIA

YEAR	TEAM	STARTS	GAMES	WON	LOST	PCT	ER	ERA	INNINGS PITCHED	STRIKE-OUTS	WALKS	HITS ALLOWED	HRS ALLOWED	COMP. GAMES	SHUT-OUTS	SAVES
1907	NY-A	3	19	3	5	.375	16	2.50	57 2/3	20	20	60	1	0	0	3
1911	Cin-N	26	39	12	13	.480	70	2.69	234 1/3	105	76	196	7	15	0	3
1912	Cin-N	6	17	1	3	.667	40	5.24	68 2/3	29	33	78	0	0	0	2
Career Average		12	25	5	7	.432	42	3.14	120	51	43	111	3	5	0	3
Yankee Average		3	19	3	5	.375	16	2.50	57 2/3	20	20	60	1	0	0	3
Career Total		35	75	16	21	.432	126	3.14	361	154	129	334	8	15	0	8
Yankee Total		3	19	3	5	.375	16	2.50	57 2/3	20	20	60	1	0	0	3

Keisler, Randy Dean

HEIGHT: 6'3" LEFTHANDER BORN: 2/24/1976 RICARDS, TEXAS

YEAR	TEAM	STARTS	GAMES	WON	LOST	PCT	ER	ERA	INNINGS PITCHED	STRIKE-OUTS	WALKS	HITS ALLOWED	HRS ALLOWED	COMP. GAMES	SHUT-OUTS	SAVES
2000	NY-A	1	4	1	0	1.000	14	11.81	10 2/3	6	8	16	1	0	0	0
Career Average		1	4	1	0	1.000	14	11.81	10 2/3	6	8	16	1	0	0	0
Yankee Average		**1**	**4**	**1**	**0**	**1.000**	**14**	**11.81**	**10 2/3**	**6**	**8**	**16**	**1**	**0**	**0**	**0**
Career Total		1	4	1	0	1.000	14	11.81	10 2/3	6	8	16	1	0	0	0
Yankee Total		**1**	**4**	**1**	**0**	**1.000**	**14**	**11.81**	**10 2/3**	**6**	**8**	**16**	**1**	**0**	**0**	**0**

Kekich, Michael Dennis

HEIGHT: 6'1" LEFTHANDER BORN: 4/2/1945 SAN DIEGO, CALIFORNIA

YEAR	TEAM	STARTS	GAMES	WON	LOST	PCT	ER	ERA	INNINGS PITCHED	STRIKE-OUTS	WALKS	HITS ALLOWED	HRS ALLOWED	COMP. GAMES	SHUT-OUTS	SAVES
1965	LA-N	1	5	0	1	.000	11	9.58	10 1/3	9	13	10	2	0	0	0
1968	LA-N	20	25	2	10	.167	50	3.91	115	84	46	116	9	1	1	0
1969	**NY-A**	**13**	**28**	**4**	**6**	**.400**	**53**	**4.54**	**105**	**66**	**49**	**91**	**11**	**1**	**0**	**1**
1970	**NY-A**	**14**	**26**	**6**	**3**	**.667**	**53**	**4.83**	**98 2/3**	**63**	**55**	**103**	**12**	**1**	**0**	**0**
1971	**NY-A**	**24**	**37**	**10**	**9**	**.526**	**77**	**4.07**	**170 1/3**	**93**	**82**	**167**	**13**	**3**	**0**	**0**
1972	**NY-A**	**28**	**29**	**10**	**13**	**.435**	**72**	**3.70**	**175 1/3**	**78**	**76**	**172**	**13**	**2**	**0**	**0**
1973	**NY-A**	**4**	**5**	**1**	**1**	**.500**	**15**	**9.20**	**14 2/3**	**4**	**14**	**20**	**1**	**0**	**0**	**0**
1973	Cle-A	6	16	1	4	.666	39	7.02	50	26	35	73	6	0	0	0
1975	Tex-A	0	23	0	0	—	13	3.73	31 1/3	19	21	33	2	0	0	2
1977	Sea-A	2	41	5	4	.556	56	5.60	90	55	51	90	11	0	0	3
Career Average		11	24	4	5	.433	44	4.59	86	50	44	88	8	1	0	1
Yankee Average		**17**	**25**	**6**	**6**	**.492**	**54**	**4.31**	**113**	**61**	**55**	**111**	**10**	**1**	**0**	**0**
Career Total		112	235	39	51	.433	439	4.59	861	497	442	875	80	8	1	6
Yankee Total		**83**	**125**	**31**	**32**	**.492**	**270**	**4.31**	**564**	**304**	**276**	**553**	**50**	**7**	**0**	**1**

Keough, Matthew Lon

HEIGHT: 6'3" RIGHTHANDER BORN: 7/3/1955 POMONA, CALIFORNIA

YEAR	TEAM	STARTS	GAMES	WON	LOST	PCT	ER	ERA	INNINGS PITCHED	STRIKE-OUTS	WALKS	HITS ALLOWED	HRS ALLOWED	COMP. GAMES	SHUT-OUTS	SAVES
1977	Oak-A	6	7	1	3	.667	23	4.85	42 2/3	23	22	39	4	0	0	0
1978	Oak-A	32	32	8	15	.348	71	3.24	197 1/3	108	85	178	9	6	0	0
1979	Oak-A	28	30	2	17	.105	99	5.04	176 2/3	95	78	220	18	7	1	0
1980	Oak-A	32	34	16	13	.552	81	2.92	250	121	94	218	24	20	2	0
1981	Oak-A	19	19	10	6	.625	53	3.40	140 1/3	60	45	125	11	10	2	0
1982	Oak-A	34	34	11	18	.379	133	5.72	209 1/3	75	101	233	38	10	2	0
1983	Oak-A	4	14	2	3	.400	27	5.52	44	28	31	50	7	0	0	0
1983	**NY-A**	**12**	**12**	**3**	**4**	**.429**	**32**	**5.17**	**55 2/3**	**26**	**20**	**59**	**12**	**0**	**0**	**0**
1985	StL-N	1	4	0	1	.000	5	4.50	10	10	4	10	0	0	0	0
1986	Chi-N	2	19	2	2	.500	16	4.97	29	19	12	36	4	0	0	0
1986	Hou-N	5	10	3	2	.600	12	3.09	35	25	18	22	5	0	0	0
Career Average		16	20	5	8	.408	50	4.17	108	54	46	108	12	5	1	0
Yankee Average		**12**	**12**	**3**	**4**	**.429**	**32**	**5.17**	**55 2/3**	**26**	**20**	**59**	**12**	**0**	**0**	**0**
Career Total		175	215	58	84	.408	552	4.17	1190	590	510	1190	132	53	7	0
Yankee Total		**12**	**12**	**3**	**4**	**.429**	**32**	**5.17**	**55 2/3**	**26**	**20**	**59**	**12**	**0**	**0**	**0**

Key, James Edward

HEIGHT: 6'1" LEFTHANDER BORN: 4/22/1961 HUNTSVILLE, ALABAMA

YEAR	TEAM	STARTS	GAMES	WON	LOST	PCT	ER	ERA	INNINGS PITCHED	STRIKE-OUTS	WALKS	HITS ALLOWED	HRS ALLOWED	COMP. GAMES	SHUT-OUTS	SAVES
1984	Tor-A	0	63	4	5	.444	32	4.65	62	44	32	70	8	0	0	10
1985	Tor-A	32	35	14	6	.700	71	3.00	212 2/3	85	50	188	22	3	0	0
1986	Tor-A	35	36	14	11	.560	92	3.57	232	141	74	222	24	4	2	0
1987	Tor-A	36	36	17	8	.680	80	2.76	261	161	66	210	24	8	1	0

(continued)

(continued)

YEAR	TEAM	STARTS	GAMES	WON	LOST	PCT	ER	ERA	INNINGS PITCHED	STRIKE-OUTS	WALKS	HITS ALLOWED	HRS ALLOWED	COMP. GAMES	SHUT-OUTS	SAVES
1988	Tor-A	21	21	12	5	.706	48	3.29	131⅓	65	30	127	13	2	2	0
1989	Tor-A	33	33	13	14	.481	93	3.88	216	118	27	226	18	5	1	0
1990	Tor-A	27	27	13	7	.650	73	4.25	154⅔	88	22	169	20	0	0	0
1991	Tor-A	33	33	16	12	.571	71	3.05	209⅓	125	44	207	12	2	2	0
1992	Tor-A	33	33	13	13	.500	85	3.53	216⅔	117	59	205	24	4	2	0
1993	**NY-A**	**34**	**34**	**18**	**6**	**.750**	**79**	**3.00**	**236⅔**	**173**	**43**	**219**	**26**	**4**	**2**	**0**
1994	**NY-A**	**25**	**25**	**17**	**4**	**.810**	**61**	**3.27**	**168**	**97**	**52**	**177**	**10**	**1**	**0**	**0**
1995	**NY-A**	**5**	**5**	**1**	**2**	**.333**	**19**	**5.70**	**30⅓**	**14**	**6**	**40**	**3**	**0**	**0**	**0**
1996	**NY-A**	**30**	**30**	**12**	**11**	**.522**	**88**	**4.69**	**169⅓**	**116**	**58**	**171**	**21**	**0**	**0**	**0**
1997	Bal-A	34	34	16	10	.615	81	3.44	212⅓	141	82	210	24	1	0	0
1998	Bal-A	11	25	6	3	.667	37	4.22	79⅓	53	23	77	5	0	0	0
Career Average		26	31	12	8	.614	67	3.51	173	103	45	168	17	2	1	1
Yankee Average		**24**	**24**	**12**	**6**	**.676**	**62**	**3.68**	**151**	**100**	**40**	**152**	**15**	**1**	**1**	**0**
Career Total		389	470	186	117	.614	1010	3.51	2591	1538	668	2518	254	34	12	10
Yankee Total		**94**	**94**	**48**	**23**	**.676**	**247**	**3.68**	**604**	**400**	**159**	**607**	**60**	**5**	**2**	**0**

Kipp, Fred Leo

HEIGHT: 6'4" LEFTHANDER BORN: 10/1/1931 PIQUA, KANSAS

YEAR	TEAM	STARTS	GAMES	WON	LOST	PCT	ER	ERA	INNINGS PITCHED	STRIKE-OUTS	WALKS	HITS ALLOWED	HRS ALLOWED	COMP. GAMES	SHUT-OUTS	SAVES
1957	Bro-N	0	1	0	0	—	4	9.00	4	3	0	6	2	0	0	0
1958	LA-N	9	40	6	6	.500	57	5.01	102⅓	58	45	107	16	0	0	0
1959	LA-N	0	2	0	0	—	0	0.00	2⅔	1	3	2	0	0	0	0
1960	**NY-A**	**0**	**4**	**0**	**1**	**.000**	**3**	**6.23**	**4⅓**	**2**	**0**	**4**	**0**	**0**	**0**	**0**
Career Average		2	12	2	2	.462	16	5.08	28	16	12	30	5	0	0	0
Yankee Average		**0**	**4**	**0**	**1**	**.000**	**3**	**6.23**	**4⅓**	**2**	**0**	**4**	**0**	**0**	**0**	**0**
Career Total		9	47	6	7	.462	64	5.08	113	64	48	119	18	0	0	0
Yankee Total		**0**	**4**	**0**	**1**	**.000**	**3**	**6.23**	**4⅓**	**2**	**0**	**4**	**0**	**0**	**0**	**0**

Kitson, Frank R.

HEIGHT: 5'11" RIGHTHANDER BORN: 9/11/1869 HOPKINS, MICHIGAN DIED: 4/14/1930 ALLEGAN, MICHIGAN

YEAR	TEAM	STARTS	GAMES	WON	LOST	PCT	ER	ERA	INNINGS PITCHED	STRIKE-OUTS	WALKS	HITS ALLOWED	HRS ALLOWED	COMP. GAMES	SHUT-OUTS	SAVES
1898	Bal-N	13	17	8	5	.615	43	3.24	119⅓	32	35	123	0	13	1	0
1899	Bal-N	37	40	22	16	.579	101	2.78	326⅔	75	65	327	6	34	2	0
1900	Bro-N	30	40	15	13	.536	118	4.19	253⅓	55	56	283	12	21	2	4
1901	Bro-N	32	38	19	11	.633	93	2.98	280⅔	127	67	312	9	26	5	2
1902	Bro-N	30	31	19	12	.613	82	2.84	259⅓	107	48	251	4	28	3	0
1903	Det-A	28	31	15	16	.484	74	2.58	257⅔	102	38	277	8	28	2	0
1904	Det-A	24	26	8	13	.381	68	3.07	199⅔	69	38	211	7	19	0	1
1905	Det-A	27	33	12	14	.462	87	3.47	225⅔	78	57	230	3	21	3	1
1906	Was-A	21	30	6	14	.300	80	3.65	197	59	57	196	2	15	1	1
1907	**NY-A**	**4**	**12**	**4**	**0**	**1.000**	**21**	**3.10**	**61**	**14**	**17**	**75**	**0**	**3**	**0**	**0**
1907	Was-A	3	5	0	3	.000	14	3.94	32	11	9	41	1	2	0	0
Career Average		23	28	12	11	.522	71	3.18	201	66	44	211	5	19	2	1
Yankee Average		**4**	**12**	**4**	**0**	**1.000**	**21**	**3.10**	**61**	**14**	**17**	**75**	**0**	**3**	**0**	**0**
Career Total		249	303	128	117	.522	781	3.18	2213	729	487	2326	52	210	19	8
Yankee Total		**4**	**12**	**4**	**0**	**1.000**	**21**	**3.10**	**61**	**14**	**17**	**75**	**0**	**3**	**0**	**0**

Kleinhans, Theodore Otto (Ted)

HEIGHT: 6'0" LEFTHANDER BORN: 4/8/1899 DEER PARK, WISCONSIN DIED: 7/24/1985 REDINGTON BEACH, FLORIDA

YEAR	TEAM	STARTS	GAMES	WON	LOST	PCT	ER	ERA	INNINGS PITCHED	STRIKE-OUTS	WALKS	HITS ALLOWED	HRS ALLOWED	COMP. GAMES	SHUT-OUTS	SAVES
1934	Phi-N	0	5	0	0	—	6	9.00	6	2	3	11	1	0	0	0
1934	Cin-N	9	24	2	6	.667	51	5.74	80	23	38	107	2	0	0	0
1936	**NY-A**	**0**	**19**	**1**	**1**	**.500**	**19**	**5.83**	**29⅓**	**10**	**23**	**36**	**0**	**0**	**0**	**1**
1937	Cin-N	3	7	1	2	.333	7	2.30	27⅓	13	12	29	0	0	0	1
1938	Cin-N	0	1	0	0	—	1	9.00	1	0	0	2	1	0	0	0
Career Average		2	11	1	2	.308	17	5.26	29	10	15	37	1	0	0	0
Yankee Average		**0**	**19**	**1**	**1**	**.500**	**19**	**5.83**	**29⅓**	**10**	**23**	**36**	**0**	**0**	**0**	**1**
Career Total		12	56	4	9	.308	84	5.26	144	48	76	185	4	1	0	1
Yankee Total		**0**	**19**	**1**	**1**	**.500**	**19**	**5.83**	**29⅓**	**10**	**23**	**36**	**0**	**0**	**0**	**1**

Klepfer, Edward Lloyd (Big Ed)
HEIGHT: 6'0" RIGHTHANDER BORN: 3/17/1888 SUMMERVILLE, PENNSYLVANIA DIED: 8/9/1950 TULSA, OKLAHOMA

YEAR	TEAM	STARTS	GAMES	WON	LOST	PCT	ER	ERA	INNINGS PITCHED	STRIKE-OUTS	WALKS	HITS ALLOWED	HRS ALLOWED	COMP. GAMES	SHUT-OUTS	SAVES
1911	NY-A	0	2	0	0	—	3	6.75	4	4	2	5	0	0	0	0
1913	NY-A	1	8	0	1	.000	21	7.66	24 2/3	10	12	38	2	0	0	0
1915	Chi-A	2	3	1	0	1.000	4	2.84	12 2/3	3	5	11	0	1	0	0
1915	Cle-A	7	8	1	6	.143	10	2.09	43	13	11	47	0	4	1	2
1916	Cle-A	13	31	6	6	.500	40	2.52	143	62	46	136	0	9	0	1
1917	Cle-A	27	41	14	4	.778	56	2.37	213	66	55	208	0	9	0	0
1919	Cle-A	0	5	0	0	—	6	7.36	7 1/3	7	6	12	1	0	0	0
Career Average		7	14	3	2	.564	20	2.81	64	24	20	65	0	2	0	0
Yankee Average		1	5	0	1	.000	12	7.54	14	7	7	22	1	0	0	0
Career Total		50	98	22	17	.564	140	2.81	448	165	137	457	3	16	1	3
Yankee Total		1	10	0	1	.000	24	7.54	29	14	14	43	2	0	0	0

Klimkowski, Ronald Bernard
HEIGHT: 6'2" RIGHTHANDER BORN: 3/1/1944 JERSEY CITY, NEW JERSEY

YEAR	TEAM	STARTS	GAMES	WON	LOST	PCT	ER	ERA	INNINGS PITCHED	STRIKE-OUTS	WALKS	HITS ALLOWED	HRS ALLOWED	COMP. GAMES	SHUT-OUTS	SAVES
1969	NY-A	1	3	0	0	—	1	0.64	14	3	5	6	0	0	0	0
1970	NY-A	3	45	6	7	.462	29	2.65	98 1/3	40	33	80	7	1	1	1
1971	Oak-A	0	26	2	2	.500	17	3.38	45 1/3	25	23	37	3	0	0	2
1972	NY-A	2	16	0	3	.000	14	4.02	31 1/3	11	15	32	3	0	0	1
Career Average		2	30	3	4	.400	20	2.90	63	26	25	52	4	0	0	1
Yankee Average		2	21	2	3	.375	15	2.76	48	18	18	39	3	0	0	1
Career Total		6	90	8	12	.400	61	2.90	189	79	76	155	13	1	1	4
Yankee Total		6	64	6	10	.375	44	2.76	144	54	53	118	10	1	1	2

Kline, Steven Jack
HEIGHT: 6'3" RIGHTHANDER BORN: 10/6/1947 WENATCHEE, WASHINGTON

YEAR	TEAM	STARTS	GAMES	WON	LOST	PCT	ER	ERA	INNINGS PITCHED	STRIKE-OUTS	WALKS	HITS ALLOWED	HRS ALLOWED	COMP. GAMES	SHUT-OUTS	SAVES
1970	NY-A	15	16	6	6	.500	38	3.41	100 1/3	49	24	99	8	5	0	0
1971	NY-A	30	31	12	13	.480	73	2.96	222 1/3	81	37	206	21	15	1	0
1972	NY-A	32	32	16	9	.640	63	2.40	236 1/3	58	44	210	11	11	4	0
1973	NY-A	13	14	4	7	.364	33	4.01	74	19	31	76	5	2	1	0
1974	NY-A	4	4	2	2	.500	10	3.46	26	6	5	26	3	0	0	0
1974	Cle-A	11	16	3	8	.667	40	5.07	71	17	31	70	9	1	0	1
1977	Atl-N	0	16	0	0	—	15	6.64	20 1/3	10	12	21	4	0	0	1
Career Average		15	18	6	6	.489	39	3.26	107	34	26	101	9	5	1	0
Yankee Average		19	19	8	7	.519	43	2.96	132	43	28	123	10	7	1	0
Career Total		105	129	43	45	.489	272	3.26	750	240	184	708	61	34	6	1
Yankee Total		94	97	40	37	.519	217	2.96	659	213	141	617	48	33	6	0

Konstanty, Casimir James
HEIGHT: 6'1" RIGHTHANDER BORN: 3/12/1917 STRYKERSVILLE, NEW YORK DIED: 6/11/1976 ONEONTA, NEW YORK

YEAR	TEAM	STARTS	GAMES	WON	LOST	PCT	ER	ERA	INNINGS PITCHED	STRIKE-OUTS	WALKS	HITS ALLOWED	HRS ALLOWED	COMP. GAMES	SHUT-OUTS	SAVES
1944	Cin-N	12	20	6	4	.600	35	2.80	112 2/3	19	33	113	11	5	1	0
1946	Bos-N	1	10	0	1	.000	9	5.28	15 1/3	9	7	17	2	0	0	2
1948	Phi-N	0	6	1	0	1.000	1	0.93	9 2/3	7	2	7	0	0	0	7
1949	Phi-N	0	53	9	5	.643	35	3.25	97	43	29	98	9	0	0	22
1950	Phi-N	0	74	16	7	.696	45	2.66	152	56	50	108	11	0	0	9
1951	Phi-N	1	58	4	11	.667	52	4.05	115 2/3	27	31	127	9	0	1	6
1952	Phi-N	2	42	5	3	.625	35	3.94	80	16	21	87	18	7	0	5
1953	Phi-N	19	48	14	10	.583	84	4.43	170 2/3	45	42	198	18	7	0	3
1954	Phi-N	1	33	2	3	.400	21	3.75	50 1/3	11	12	62	7	0	0	2
1954	NY-A	0	9	1	1	.500	2	0.98	18 1/3	3	6	11	0	0	0	2

(continued)

(continued)

YEAR	TEAM	STARTS	GAMES	WON	LOST	PCT	ER	ERA	INNINGS PITCHED	STRIKE-OUTS	WALKS	HITS ALLOWED	HRS ALLOWED	COMP. GAMES	SHUT-OUTS	SAVES
1955	NY-A	0	45	7	2	.778	19	2.32	73⅔	19	24	68	5	0	0	11
1956	NY-A	0	8	0	0	—	6	4.91	11	6	6	15	3	0	0	2
1956	StL-N	0	27	1	1	.500	20	4.58	39⅓	7	6	46	4	0	0	5
Career Average		3	33	5	4	.579	28	3.46	73	21	21	74	7	1	0	6
Yankee Average		**0**	**21**	**3**	**1**	**.727**	**9**	**2.36**	**34**	**9**	**12**	**31**	**3**	**0**	**0**	**5**
Career Total		36	433	66	48	.579	364	3.46	946	268	269	957	88	14	2	74
Yankee Total		**0**	**62**	**8**	**3**	**.727**	**27**	**2.36**	**103**	**28**	**36**	**94**	**8**	**0**	**0**	**15**

Kraly, Steve Charles (Lefty)

HEIGHT: 5'10" LEFTHANDER BORN: 4/18/1929 WHITING, INDIANA

YEAR	TEAM	STARTS	GAMES	WON	LOST	PCT	ER	ERA	INNINGS PITCHED	STRIKE-OUTS	WALKS	HITS ALLOWED	HRS ALLOWED	COMP. GAMES	SHUT-OUTS	SAVES
1953	NY-A	3	5	0	2	.000	9	3.24	25	8	16	19	2	0	0	1
Career Average		3	5	0	2	.000	9	3.24	25	8	16	19	2	0	0	1
Yankee Average		**3**	**5**	**0**	**2**	**.000**	**9**	**3.24**	**25**	**8**	**16**	**19**	**2**	**0**	**0**	**1**
Career Total		3	5	0	2	.000	9	3.24	25	8	16	19	2	0	0	1
Yankee Total		**3**	**5**	**0**	**2**	**.000**	**9**	**3.24**	**25**	**8**	**16**	**19**	**2**	**0**	**0**	**1**

Kucks, John Charles

HEIGHT: 6'3" RIGHTHANDER BORN: 7/27/1933 HOBOKEN, NEW JERSEY

YEAR	TEAM	STARTS	GAMES	WON	LOST	PCT	ER	ERA	INNINGS PITCHED	STRIKE-OUTS	WALKS	HITS ALLOWED	HRS ALLOWED	COMP. GAMES	SHUT-OUTS	SAVES
1955	NY-A	13	29	8	7	.533	48	3.41	126⅔	49	44	122	8	3	1	0
1956	NY-A	31	34	18	9	.667	96	3.85	224⅓	67	72	223	19	12	3	0
1957	NY-A	23	37	8	10	.444	71	3.56	179⅓	78	59	169	13	4	1	2
1958	NY-A	15	34	8	8	.500	55	3.93	126	46	39	132	14	4	1	4
1959	NY-A	1	9	0	1	.000	16	8.64	16⅔	9	9	21	5	0	0	0
1959	KC-A	23	33	8	11	.421	65	3.87	151⅓	51	42	163	10	6	1	1
1960	KC-A	17	31	4	10	.667	76	6.00	114	38	43	140	22	1	0	0
Career Average		18	30	8	8	.491	61	4.10	134	48	44	139	13	4	1	1
Yankee Average		**17**	**29**	**8**	**7**	**.545**	**57**	**3.82**	**135**	**50**	**45**	**133**	**12**	**5**	**1**	**1**
Career Total		123	207	54	56	.491	427	4.10	938	338	308	970	91	30	7	7
Yankee Total		**83**	**143**	**42**	**35**	**.545**	**286**	**3.82**	**673**	**249**	**223**	**667**	**59**	**23**	**6**	**6**

Kunkel, William Gustave James

HEIGHT: 6'1" RIGHTHANDER BORN: 7/7/1936 HOBOKEN, NEW JERSEY DIED: 5/4/1985 RED BANK, NEW JERSEY

YEAR	TEAM	STARTS	GAMES	WON	LOST	PCT	ER	ERA	INNINGS PITCHED	STRIKE-OUTS	WALKS	HITS ALLOWED	HRS ALLOWED	COMP. GAMES	SHUT-OUTS	SAVES
1961	KC-A	2	58	3	4	.429	51	5.18	88⅔	46	32	103	11	0	0	4
1962	KC-A	0	9	0	0	—	3	3.52	7⅔	6	4	8	3	0	0	0
1963	**NY-A**	**0**	**22**	**3**	**2**	**.600**	**14**	**2.72**	**46⅓**	**31**	**13**	**42**	**3**	**0**	**0**	**0**
Career Average		1	30	2	2	.500	23	4.29	48	28	16	51	6	0	0	1
Yankee Average		**0**	**22**	**3**	**2**	**.600**	**14**	**2.72**	**46⅓**	**31**	**13**	**42**	**3**	**0**	**0**	**0**
Career Total		2	89	6	6	.500	68	4.29	143	83	49	153	17	0	0	4
Yankee Total		**0**	**22**	**3**	**2**	**.600**	**14**	**2.72**	**46⅓**	**31**	**13**	**42**	**3**	**0**	**0**	**0**

Kuzava, Robert Leroy (Sarge)

HEIGHT: 6'2" LEFTHANDER BORN: 5/28/1923 WYANDOTTE, MICHIGAN

YEAR	TEAM	STARTS	GAMES	WON	LOST	PCT	ER	ERA	INNINGS PITCHED	STRIKE-OUTS	WALKS	HITS ALLOWED	HRS ALLOWED	COMP. GAMES	SHUT-OUTS	SAVES
1946	Cle-A	2	2	1	0	1.000	4	3.00	12	4	11	9	0	0	0	0
1947	Cle-A	4	4	1	1	.500	10	4.15	21⅔	9	9	22	1	1	1	0
1949	Chi-A	18	29	10	6	.625	70	4.02	156⅔	83	91	139	6	9	1	0
1950	Chi-A	7	10	1	3	.667	28	5.68	44⅓	21	27	43	5	1	0	0
1950	Was-A	22	22	8	7	.533	68	3.95	155	84	75	156	8	8	1	0

(continued)

(continued)

YEAR	TEAM	STARTS	GAMES	WON	LOST	PCT	ER	ERA	INNINGS PITCHED	STRIKE-OUTS	WALKS	HITS ALLOWED	HRS ALLOWED	COMP. GAMES	SHUT-OUTS	SAVES
1951	Was-A	8	8	3	3	.500	32	5.50	52 1/3	22	28	57	5	3	0	0
1951	**NY-A**	**8**	**23**	**8**	**4**	**.667**	**22**	**2.40**	**82 1/3**	**50**	**27**	**76**	**5**	**4**	**1**	**5**
1952	**NY-A**	**12**	**28**	**8**	**8**	**.500**	**51**	**3.45**	**133**	**67**	**63**	**115**	**7**	**6**	**1**	**3**
1953	**NY-A**	**6**	**33**	**6**	**5**	**.545**	**34**	**3.31**	**92 1/3**	**48**	**34**	**92**	**9**	**2**	**2**	**4**
1954	**NY-A**	**3**	**20**	**1**	**3**	**.667**	**24**	**5.45**	**39 2/3**	**22**	**18**	**46**	**3**	**0**	**0**	**1**
1954	Bal-A	4	4	1	3	.667	11	4.18	23 2/3	15	11	30	0	0	0	0
1955	Bal-A	1	6	0	1	.000	5	3.65	12 1/3	5	4	10	0	0	0	0
1955	Phi-N	4	17	1	0	1.000	26	7.24	32 1/3	13	12	47	5	0	0	0
1957	Pit-N	0	4	0	0	—	2	9.00	2	1	3	3	0	0	0	0
1957	StL-N	0	3	0	0	—	1	3.86	2 1/3	2	2	4	0	0	0	0
Career Average		7	14	3	3	.527	26	4.05	57	30	28	57	4	2	0	1
Yankee Average		**7**	**26**	**6**	**5**	**.535**	**33**	**3.39**	**87**	**47**	**36**	**82**	**6**	**3**	**1**	**3**
Career Total		99	213	49	44	.527	388	4.05	862	446	415	849	54	34	7	13
Yankee Total		**29**	**104**	**23**	**20**	**.535**	**131**	**3.39**	**347**	**187**	**142**	**329**	**24**	**12**	**4**	**13**

Lake, Joseph Henry

HEIGHT: 6'0"   RIGHTHANDER   BORN: 1/6/1881 BROOKLYN, NEW YORK   DIED: 6/30/1950 BROOKLYN, NEW YORK

YEAR	TEAM	STARTS	GAMES	WON	LOST	PCT	ER	ERA	INNINGS PITCHED	STRIKE-OUTS	WALKS	HITS ALLOWED	HRS ALLOWED	COMP. GAMES	SHUT-OUTS	SAVES
1908	**NY-A**	**27**	**38**	**9**	**22**	**.667**	**95**	**3.17**	**269 1/3**	**118**	**77**	**252**	**6**	**19**	**2**	**0**
1909	**NY-A**	**26**	**31**	**14**	**11**	**.560**	**45**	**1.88**	**215 1/3**	**117**	**59**	**180**	**2**	**17**	**3**	**1**
1910	StL-A	29	35	11	17	.393	64	2.20	261 1/3	141	77	243	2	24	1	2
1911	StL-A	25	30	10	15	.400	79	3.30	215 1/3	69	40	245	3	14	2	0
1912	StL-A	6	11	1	7	.125	28	4.42	57	28	16	70	0	4	0	0
1912	Det-A	14	26	9	11	.450	56	3.10	162 2/3	86	39	190	3	11	0	1
1913	Det-A	12	28	8	7	.533	50	3.28	137	35	24	149	3	6	0	1
Career Average		20	28	9	13	.408	60	2.85	188	85	47	190	3	14	1	1
Yankee Average		**27**	**35**	**12**	**17**	**.411**	**70**	**2.60**	**242**	**118**	**68**	**216**	**4**	**18**	**3**	**1**
Career Total		139	199	62	90	.408	417	2.85	1318	594	332	1329	19	95	8	5
Yankee Total		**53**	**69**	**23**	**33**	**.411**	**140**	**2.60**	**485**	**235**	**136**	**432**	**8**	**36**	**5**	**1**

LaPoint, David Jeffrey

HEIGHT: 6'3"   LEFTHANDER   BORN: 7/29/1959 GLENS FALLS, NEW YORK

YEAR	TEAM	STARTS	GAMES	WON	LOST	PCT	ER	ERA	INNINGS PITCHED	STRIKE-OUTS	WALKS	HITS ALLOWED	HRS ALLOWED	COMP. GAMES	SHUT-OUTS	SAVES
1980	Mil-A	3	5	1	0	1.000	10	6.00	15	5	13	17	2	0	0	1
1981	StL-N	2	3	1	0	1.000	5	4.22	10 2/3	4	2	12	1	0	0	0
1982	StL-N	21	42	9	3	.750	58	3.42	152 2/3	81	52	170	8	0	0	0
1983	StL-N	29	37	12	9	.571	84	3.95	191 1/3	113	84	191	12	1	0	0
1984	StL-N	33	33	12	10	.545	85	3.96	193	130	77	205	9	2	1	0
1985	SF-N	31	31	7	17	.667	82	3.57	206 2/3	122	74	215	18	2	1	0
1986	Det-A	8	16	3	6	.333	43	5.72	67 2/3	36	32	85	11	0	0	0
1986	SD-N	4	24	1	4	.666	29	4.26	61 1/3	41	24	67	8	0	0	0
1987	StL-N	2	6	1	1	.500	12	6.75	16	8	5	26	4	0	0	0
1987	Chi-A	12	14	6	3	.667	27	2.94	82 2/3	43	31	69	7	2	1	0
1988	Chi-A	25	25	10	11	.476	61	3.40	161 1/3	79	47	151	10	1	1	0
1988	Pit-N	8	8	4	2	.667	16	2.77	52	19	10	54	4	1	0	0
1989	**NY-A**	**20**	**20**	**6**	**9**	**.400**	**71**	**5.62**	**113 2/3**	**51**	**45**	**146**	**12**	**0**	**0**	**0**
1990	**NY-A**	**27**	**28**	**7**	**10**	**.412**	**72**	**4.11**	**157 2/3**	**67**	**57**	**180**	**11**	**2**	**0**	**0**
1991	Phi-N	2	2	0	1	.000	9	16.20	5	3	6	10	0	0	0	0
Career Average		15	20	5	6	.482	44	4.02	99	53	37	107	8	1	0	0
Yankee Average		**24**	**24**	**7**	**10**	**.406**	**72**	**4.74**	**136**	**59**	**51**	**163**	**12**	**1**	**0**	**0**
Career Total		227	294	80	86	.482	664	4.02	1487	802	559	1598	117	11	4	1
Yankee Total		**47**	**48**	**13**	**19**	**.406**	**143**	**4.74**	**271**	**118**	**102**	**326**	**23**	**2**	**0**	**0**

LaRoche, David Eugene

HEIGHT: 6'2"   LEFTHANDER   BORN: 5/14/1948 COLORADO SPRINGS, COLORADO

YEAR	TEAM	STARTS	GAMES	WON	LOST	PCT	ER	ERA	INNINGS PITCHED	STRIKE-OUTS	WALKS	HITS ALLOWED	HRS ALLOWED	COMP. GAMES	SHUT-OUTS	SAVES
1970	Cal-A	0	38	4	1	.800	19	3.44	49 2/3	44	21	41	6	0	0	4
1971	Cal-A	0	56	5	1	.833	20	2.50	72	63	27	55	3	0	0	9

(continued)

(continued)

Year	Team														
1972	Min-A	0	62	5	7	.417	30	2.83	$95\frac{1}{3}$	79	39	72	9	0	0	10
1973	Chi-N	0	45	4	1	.800	35	5.80	$54\frac{1}{3}$	34	29	55	7	0	0	4
1974	Chi-N	4	49	5	6	.455	49	4.79	92	49	47	103	9	0	0	5
1975	Cle-A	0	61	5	3	.625	20	2.19	$82\frac{1}{3}$	94	57	61	5	0	0	17
1976	Cle-A	0	61	1	4	.666	24	2.24	$96\frac{1}{3}$	104	49	57	2	0	0	21
1977	Cle-A	0	13	2	2	.500	11	5.30	$18\frac{2}{3}$	18	7	15	3	0	0	4
1977	Cal-A	0	46	6	5	.545	28	3.10	$81\frac{1}{3}$	61	37	64	8	0	0	13
1978	Cal-A	0	59	10	9	.526	30	2.82	$95\frac{2}{3}$	70	48	73	7	0	0	25
1979	Cal-A	1	53	7	11	.389	53	5.57	$85\frac{2}{3}$	59	32	107	13	0	0	10
1980	Cal-A	9	52	3	5	.375	58	4.08	128	89	39	122	14	1	0	4
1981	**NY-A**	**1**	**26**	**4**	**1**	**.800**	**13**	**2.49**	**47**	**24**	**16**	**38**	**3**	**0**	**0**	**0**
1982	**NY-A**	**0**	**25**	**4**	**2**	**.667**	**19**	**3.42**	**50**	**31**	**11**	**54**	**4**	**0**	**0**	**0**
1983	**NY-A**	**0**	**1**	**0**	**0**	**—**	**2**	**18.00**	**1**	**0**	**0**	**2**	**1**	**0**	**0**	**0**
Career Average		1	43	4	4	.528	27	3.53	70	55	31	61	6	0	0	8
Yankee Average		**0**	**17**	**3**	**1**	**.727**	**11**	**3.12**	**33**	**18**	**9**	**31**	**3**	**0**	**0**	**0**
Career Total		15	647	65	58	.528	411	3.53	1049	819	459	919	94	1	0	126
Yankee Total		**1**	**52**	**8**	**3**	**.727**	**34**	**3.12**	**98**	**55**	**27**	**94**	**8**	**0**	**0**	**0**

Don James Larsen, rhp, 1955–59

Is it possible to enter the Yankee pantheon of all-time greats on the strength of, essentially, one game? It is if you are Don Larsen.

To be fair, Larsen, born August 7, 1929, in Michigan City, Indiana, had a solid five-year career with the Yankees and spent 14 years in the major leagues overall.

But one game, played on October 8, 1956, in front of a crowd of 64,519, has catapulted Don Larsen into baseball immortality. Larsen out pitched the Brooklyn Dodgers' Sal Maglie that day, throwing a perfect game to beat the National League champions 2-0 in the fifth game of the World Series. The Yankees would go on to win that series in seven games.

Larsen was a most unlikely hero. A few days earlier, he had been cuffed around in Game 2, a 13-8 Dodger win. But by the fifth game, he had recovered his composure. Using a no-windup motion that he had developed a few years before, Larsen threw 97 pitches, walked no one and allowed no hits. He caught pinch hitter Dale Mitchell looking for out number 27, and World Series perfect game number one.

The irony was that two years before, Larsen was the worst pitcher in baseball. He was 3-21 with the Baltimore Orioles in 1954, which is, in fact, one of the worst pitching records in the history of the game.

But two of those wins came against the Yankees. In 1955, Larsen was part of a massive 18-player deal between the Yankees and the Orioles. New York was looking for some pitching and infield help.

Playing for a better team, Larsen showed he could come through, going 9-2 for New York in 1955. In 1956, he was a solid 11-5 and allowed only 6.7 hits per nine innings, second in the league only to the Cleveland Indians' Herb Score.

In his five years with New York, he was dependable, with a 45-24 record and a 3.50 ERA. In the World Series, he was 3-2 lifetime with a 2.67 ERA. His lifetime numbers aren't as good, 81-91 with a 3.78 ERA. That 3-21 season didn't help much.

But he was a great athlete. He had 14 career home runs, and was used as a pinch hitter 66 times.

Larsen was traded to Kansas City in 1960 and bounced around a bit after that, playing for five more teams after his stint with the A's. He retired in 1967.

Larsen, Don James
HEIGHT: 6'4"   RIGHTHANDER   BORN: 8/7/1929 MICHIGAN CITY, INDIANA

YEAR	TEAM	STARTS	GAMES	WON	LOST	PCT	ER	ERA	INNINGS PITCHED	STRIKE-OUTS	WALKS	HITS ALLOWED	HRS ALLOWED	COMP. GAMES	SHUT-OUTS	SAVES
1953	StL-A	22	38	7	12	.368	89	4.16	192 2/3	96	64	201	11	7	2	2
1954	Bal-A	28	29	3	21	.125	98	4.37	201 2/3	80	89	213	18	12	1	0
1955	**NY-A**	**13**	**19**	**9**	**2**	**.818**	**33**	**3.06**	**97**	**44**	**51**	**81**	**8**	**5**	**1**	**2**
1956	**NY-A**	**20**	**38**	**11**	**5**	**.688**	**65**	**3.26**	**179 2/3**	**107**	**96**	**133**	**19**	**6**	**1**	**1**
1957	**NY-A**	**20**	**27**	**10**	**4**	**.714**	**58**	**3.74**	**139 2/3**	**81**	**87**	**113**	**12**	**4**	**1**	**0**
1958	**NY-A**	**19**	**19**	**9**	**6**	**.600**	**39**	**3.07**	**114 1/3**	**55**	**52**	**100**	**4**	**5**	**3**	**0**
1959	**NY-A**	**18**	**25**	**6**	**7**	**.462**	**60**	**4.33**	**124 2/3**	**69**	**76**	**122**	**14**	**3**	**1**	**3**
1960	KC-A	15	22	1	10	.091	50	5.38	83 2/3	43	42	97	11	0	0	0
1961	KC-A	1	8	1	0	1.000	7	4.20	15	13	11	21	2	0	0	0
1961	Chi-A	3	25	7	2	.778	34	4.12	74 1/3	53	29	64	5	0	0	2
1962	SF-N	0	49	5	4	.556	42	4.38	86 1/3	58	47	83	9	0	0	11
1963	SF-N	0	46	7	7	.500	21	3.05	62	44	30	46	8	0	0	3
1964	SF-N	0	6	0	1	.000	5	4.35	10 1/3	6	6	10	0	0	0	0
1964	Hou-N	10	30	4	8	.333	26	2.26	103 1/3	58	20	92	4	2	1	1
1965	Hou-N	1	1	0	0	—	3	5.06	5 1/3	1	3	8	0	0	0	0
1965	Bal-A	1	27	1	2	.333	16	2.67	54	40	20	53	4	0	0	1
1967	Chi-N	0	3	0	0	—	4	9.00	4	1	2	5	1	0	0	0
Career Average		17	41	8	9	.471	65	3.78	155	85	73	144	13	4	1	3
Yankee Average		**18**	**26**	**9**	**5**	**.652**	**51**	**3.50**	**131**	**71**	**72**	**110**	**11**	**5**	**1**	**1**
Career Total		171	412	81	91	.471	650	3.78	1548	849	725	1442	130	44	11	26
Yankee Total		**90**	**128**	**45**	**24**	**.652**	**255**	**3.50**	**655**	**356**	**362**	**549**	**57**	**23**	**7**	**6**

Leary, Timothy James
HEIGHT: 6'3"   RIGHTHANDER   BORN: 12/23/1958 SANTA MONICA, CALIFORNIA

YEAR	TEAM	STARTS	GAMES	WON	LOST	PCT	ER	ERA	INNINGS PITCHED	STRIKE-OUTS	WALKS	HITS ALLOWED	HRS ALLOWED	COMP. GAMES	SHUT-OUTS	SAVES
1981	NY-N	1	1	0	0	—	0	0.00	2	3	1	0	0	0	0	0
1983	NY-N	2	2	1	1	.500	4	3.38	10 2/3	9	4	15	0	1	0	0
1984	NY-N	7	20	3	3	.500	24	4.02	53 2/3	29	18	61	2	0	0	0
1985	Mil-A	5	5	1	4	.666	15	4.05	33 1/3	29	8	40	5	0	0	0
1986	Mil-A	30	33	12	12	.500	88	4.21	188 1/3	110	53	216	20	3	2	0
1987	LA-N	12	39	3	11	.666	57	4.76	107 2/3	61	36	121	15	0	0	1
1988	LA-N	34	35	17	11	.607	74	2.91	228 2/3	180	56	201	13	9	6	0
1989	LA-N	17	19	6	7	.462	44	3.38	117 1/3	59	37	107	9	2	0	0
1989	Cin-N	14	14	2	7	.666	37	3.71	89 2/3	64	31	98	8	0	0	0
1990	**NY-A**	**31**	**31**	**9**	**19**	**.321**	**95**	**4.11**	**208**	**138**	**78**	**202**	**18**	**6**	**1**	**0**
1991	**NY-A**	**18**	**28**	**4**	**10**	**.667**	**87**	**6.49**	**120 2/3**	**83**	**57**	**150**	**20**	**1**	**0**	**0**
1992	**NY-A**	**15**	**18**	**5**	**6**	**.455**	**60**	**5.57**	**97**	**34**	**57**	**84**	**9**	**2**	**0**	**0**
1992	Sea-A	8	8	3	4	.429	24	4.91	44	12	30	47	3	1	0	0
1993	Sea-A	27	33	11	9	.550	95	5.05	169 1/3	68	58	202	21	0	0	0
1994	Tex-A	3	6	1	1	.500	19	8.14	21	9	11	26	4	0	0	0
Career Average		15	19	5	7	.426	48	4.36	99	59	36	105	10	2	1	0
Yankee Average		**21**	**26**	**6**	**12**	**.340**	**81**	**5.12**	**142**	**85**	**64**	**145**	**16**	**3**	**0**	**0**
Career Total		224	292	78	105	.426	723	4.36	1491	888	535	1570	147	25	9	1
Yankee Total		**64**	**77**	**18**	**35**	**.340**	**242**	**5.12**	**426**	**255**	**192**	**436**	**47**	**9**	**1**	**0**

Leiter, Alois Terry
HEIGHT: 6'3"   LEFTHANDER   BORN: 10/23/1965 TOMS RIVER, NEW JERSEY

YEAR	TEAM	STARTS	GAMES	WON	LOST	PCT	ER	ERA	INNINGS PITCHED	STRIKE-OUTS	WALKS	HITS ALLOWED	HRS ALLOWED	COMP. GAMES	SHUT-OUTS	SAVES
1987	**NY-A**	**4**	**4**	**2**	**2**	**.500**	**16**	**6.35**	**22 2/3**	**28**	**15**	**24**	**2**	**0**	**0**	**0**
1988	**NY-A**	**14**	**14**	**4**	**4**	**.500**	**25**	**3.92**	**57 1/3**	**60**	**33**	**49**	**7**	**0**	**0**	**0**
1989	**NY-A**	**4**	**4**	**1**	**2**	**.333**	**18**	**6.08**	**26 2/3**	**22**	**21**	**23**	**1**	**0**	**0**	**0**
1989	Tor-A	1	1	0	0	—	3	4.05	6 2/3	4	2	9	1	0	0	0
1990	Tor-A	0	4	0	0	—	0	0.00	6 1/3	5	2	1	0	0	0	0
1991	Tor-A	0	3	0	0	—	5	27.01	1 2/3	1	5	3	0	0	0	0
1992	Tor-A	0	1	0	0	—	1	9.00	1	0	2	1	0	0	0	0
1993	Tor-A	12	34	9	6	.600	48	4.11	105	66	56	93	8	1	1	2
1994	Tor-A	20	20	6	7	.462	63	5.11	111 2/3	100	65	125	6	1	0	0
1995	Tor-A	28	28	11	11	.500	74	3.64	183	153	108	162	15	2	0	0

(continued)

(continued)

1996	Fla-N	33	33	16	12	.571	70	2.93	215 1/3	200	119	153	14	2	0	0
1997	Fla-N	27	27	11	9	.550	73	4.35	151 1/3	132	91	133	13	0	0	0
1998	NY-N	28	28	17	6	.739	53	2.47	193	174	71	151	8	4	0	0
1999	NY-N	32	32	13	12	.520	100	4.23	213	162	93	209	19	1	1	0
2000	NY-N	31	31	16	8	.667	74	3.20	208	200	76	176	19	2	1	0
Career Average		16	18	7	5	.573	42	3.73	100	87	51	87	8	1	0	0
Yankee Average		**7**	**7**	**2**	**3**	**.467**	**20**	**4.98**	**36**	**37**	**23**	**32**	**3**	**0**	**0**	**0**
Career Total		234	264	106	79	.573	623	3.73	1502 2/3	1307	759	1312	113	13	3	2
Yankee Total		**22**	**22**	**7**	**8**	**.467**	**59**	**4.98**	**107**	**110**	**69**	**96**	**10**	**0**	**0**	**0**

Leiter, Mark Edward

HEIGHT: 6'3" RIGHTHANDER BORN: 4/13/1963 JOLIET, ILLINOIS

YEAR	TEAM	STARTS	GAMES	WON	LOST	PCT	ER	ERA	INNINGS PITCHED	STRIKE-OUTS	WALKS	HITS ALLOWED	HRS ALLOWED	COMP. GAMES	SHUT-OUTS	SAVES
1990	**NY-A**	**3**	**8**	**1**	**1**	**.500**	**20**	**6.84**	**26 1/3**	**21**	**9**	**33**	**5**	**0**	**0**	**0**
1991	Det-A	15	38	9	7	.563	63	4.21	134 2/3	103	50	125	16	1	0	1
1992	Det-A	14	35	8	5	.615	52	4.18	112	75	43	116	9	1	0	0
1993	Det-A	13	27	6	6	.500	56	4.73	106 2/3	70	44	111	17	1	0	0
1994	Cal-A	7	40	4	7	.364	50	4.74	95 1/3	71	35	99	13	0	0	2
1995	SF-N	29	30	10	12	.455	83	3.83	195 1/3	129	55	185	19	7	0	0
1996	SF-N	22	23	4	10	.667	78	5.20	135 1/3	118	50	151	25	1	0	0
1996	Mon-N	12	12	4	2	.667	34	4.43	69 2/3	46	19	68	12	1	0	0
1997	Phi-N	31	31	10	17	.370	115	5.69	182 1/3	148	64	216	25	3	0	0
1998	Phi-N	0	69	7	5	.583	35	3.58	88 2/3	84	47	67	8	0	0	23
1999	Sea-A	0	2	0	0	—	1	9.00	1	1	0	2	0	0	0	0
Career Average		13	29	6	7	.467	53	4.62	104	79	38	107	14	1	0	2
Yankee Average		**3**	**8**	**1**	**1**	**.500**	**20**	**6.84**	**26 1/3**	**21**	**9**	**33**	**5**	**0**	**0**	**0**
Career Total		146	315	63	72	.467	587	4.62	1145	866	416	1173	149	15	0	26
Yankee Total		**3**	**8**	**1**	**1**	**.500**	**20**	**6.84**	**26 1/3**	**21**	**9**	**33**	**5**	**0**	**0**	**0**

LeRoy, Louis Paul (Chief)

HEIGHT: 5'10" RIGHTHANDER BORN: 2/18/1879 OMRO, WISCONSIN DIED: 10/10/1944 SHAWANO, WISCONSIN

YEAR	TEAM	STARTS	GAMES	WON	LOST	PCT	ER	ERA	INNINGS PITCHED	STRIKE-OUTS	WALKS	HITS ALLOWED	HRS ALLOWED	COMP. GAMES	SHUT-OUTS	SAVES
1905	**NY-A**	**3**	**3**	**1**	**1**	**.500**	**10**	**3.75**	**24**	**8**	**1**	**26**	**2**	**2**	**0**	**0**
1906	**NY-A**	**2**	**11**	**2**	**0**	**1.000**	**11**	**2.22**	**44 2/3**	**28**	**12**	**33**	**0**	**1**	**0**	**1**
1910	Bos-A	0	1	0	0	—	5	11.25	4	3	2	7	1	0	0	0
Career Average		2	5	1	0	.750	9	3.22	24	13	5	22	1	1	0	0
Yankee Average		**3**	**7**	**2**	**1**	**.750**	**11**	**2.75**	**34**	**18**	**7**	**30**	**1**	**2**	**0**	**1**
Career Total		5	15	3	1	.750	26	3.22	73	39	15	66	3	3	0	1
Yankee Total		**5**	**14**	**3**	**1**	**.750**	**21**	**2.75**	**69**	**36**	**13**	**59**	**2**	**3**	**0**	**1**

Lewis, James Martin

HEIGHT: 6'3" RIGHTHANDER BORN: 10/12/1955 MIAMI, FLORIDA

YEAR	TEAM	STARTS	GAMES	WON	LOST	PCT	ER	ERA	INNINGS PITCHED	STRIKE-OUTS	WALKS	HITS ALLOWED	HRS ALLOWED	COMP. GAMES	SHUT-OUTS	SAVES
1979	Sea-A	0	2	0	0	—	4	15.43	2 1/3	0	1	10	1	0	0	0
1982	**NY-A**	**0**	**1**	**0**	**0**	**—**	**4**	**54.05**	**2/3**	**0**	**3**	**3**	**0**	**0**	**0**	**0**
1983	Min-A	0	6	0	0	—	13	6.50	18	8	7	24	5	0	0	0
1985	Sea-A	1	2	0	1	.000	4	7.72	4 2/3	1	1	8	1	0	0	0
Career Average		0	3	0	0	—	6	8.77	6	2	3	11	2	0	0	0
Yankee Average		**0**	**1**	**0**	**0**	**—**	**4**	**54.05**	**2/3**	**0**	**3**	**3**	**0**	**0**	**0**	**0**
Career Total		1	11	0	1	.000	25	8.77	26	9	12	45	7	0	0	0
Yankee Total		**0**	**1**	**0**	**0**	**—**	**4**	**54.05**	**2/3**	**0**	**3**	**3**	**0**	**0**	**0**

Ley, Terrance Richard
HEIGHT: 6'0"   LEFTHANDER   BORN: 2/21/1947 PORTLAND, OREGON

YEAR	TEAM	STARTS	GAMES	WON	LOST	PCT	ER	ERA	INNINGS PITCHED	STRIKE-OUTS	WALKS	HITS ALLOWED	HRS ALLOWED	COMP. GAMES	SHUT-OUTS	SAVES
1971	NY-A	0	6	0	0	—	5	5.00	9	7	9	9	1	0	0	0
Career Average		0	6	0	0	—	5	5.00	9	7	9	9	1	0	0	0
Yankee Average		0	6	0	0	—	5	5.00	9	7	9	9	1	0	0	0
Career Total		0	6	0	0	—	5	5.00	9	7	9	9	1	0	0	0
Yankee Total		0	6	0	0	—	5	5.00	9	7	9	9	1	0	0	0

Lilly, Theodore Roosevelt (Ted)
HEIGHT: 6'"   LEFTHANDER   BORN: 1/4/1976 LAMETA, CALIFORNIA

YEAR	TEAM	STARTS	GAMES	WON	LOST	PCT	ER	ERA	INNINGS PITCHED	STRIKE-OUTS	WALKS	HITS ALLOWED	HRS ALLOWED	COMP. GAMES	SHUT-OUTS	SAVES
1999	Mon-N	3	9	0	1	.000	20	7.61	23 2/3	28	9	30	7	0	0	0
2000	NY-A	0	7	0	0	—	5	5.63	8	11	5	8	1	0	0	0
Career Average		2	8	0	1	.000	13	7.11	16	20	7	19	4	0	0	0
Yankee Average		0	7	0	0	—	5	5.63	8	11	5	8	1	0	0	0
Career Total		3	16	0	1	.000	25	7.11	32	39	14	38	8	0	0	0
Yankee Total		0	7	0	0	—	5	5.63	8	11	5	8	1	0	0	0

Lindblad, Paul Aaron
HEIGHT: 6'1"   LEFTHANDER   BORN: 8/9/1941 CHANUTE, KANSAS

YEAR	TEAM	STARTS	GAMES	WON	LOST	PCT	ER	ERA	INNINGS PITCHED	STRIKE-OUTS	WALKS	HITS ALLOWED	HRS ALLOWED	COMP. GAMES	SHUT-OUTS	SAVES
1965	KC-A	0	4	0	1	.000	9	11.05	7 1/3	12	0	12	3	0	0	0
1966	KC-A	14	38	5	10	.333	56	4.17	121	69	37	138	14	0	0	1
1967	KC-A	10	46	5	8	.385	46	3.58	115 2/3	83	35	106	15	1	1	6
1968	Oak-A	1	47	4	3	.571	15	2.40	56 1/3	42	14	51	6	0	0	2
1969	Oak-A	0	60	9	6	.600	36	4.14	78 1/3	64	33	72	8	0	0	9
1970	Oak-A	0	62	8	2	.800	19	2.70	63 1/3	42	28	52	7	0	0	3
1971	Oak-A	0	8	1	0	1.000	7	3.94	16	4	2	18	1	0	0	0
1971	Was-A	0	43	6	4	.600	24	2.58	83 2/3	50	29	58	6	0	0	8
1972	Tex-A	0	66	5	8	.385	29	2.62	99 2/3	51	29	95	7	0	0	9
1973	Oak-A	3	36	1	5	.167	32	3.69	78	33	28	89	8	0	0	2
1974	Oak-A	2	45	4	4	.500	23	2.06	100 2/3	46	30	85	4	0	0	6
1975	Oak-A	0	68	9	1	.900	37	2.72	122 1/3	58	43	105	6	0	0	7
1976	Oak-A	0	65	6	5	.545	39	3.06	114 2/3	37	24	111	5	0	0	5
1977	Tex-A	1	42	4	5	.444	46	4.20	98 2/3	46	29	103	16	0	0	4
1978	Tex-A	0	18	1	1	.500	16	3.63	39 2/3	25	15	41	2	0	0	2
1978	**NY-A**	1	7	0	0	—	9	4.42	18 1/3	9	8	21	4	0	0	0
Career Average		2	41	4	4	.519	28	3.29	76	42	24	72	7	0	0	0
Yankee Average		1	7	0	0	—	9	4.42	18 1/3	9	8	21	4	0	0	64
Career Total		32	655	68	63	.519	443	3.29	1214	671	384	1157	112	1	1	0
Yankee Total		1	7	0	0	—	9	4.42	18 1/3	9	8	21	4	0	0	0

Lindell, John Harlan
HEIGHT: 6'5"   RIGHTHANDER   BORN: 8/30/1916 GREELEY, COLORADO   DIED: 8/27/1985 NEWPORT BEACH, CALIFORNIA

YEAR	TEAM	STARTS	GAMES	WON	LOST	PCT	ER	ERA	INNINGS PITCHED	STRIKE-OUTS	WALKS	HITS ALLOWED	HRS ALLOWED	COMP. GAMES	SHUT-OUTS	SAVES
1942	NY-A	2	23	2	1	.667	22	3.76	52 2/3	28	22	52	3	0	0	1
1953	Pit-N	23	27	5	16	.666	92	4.71	175 1/3	102	116	173	17	13	1	0
1953	Phi-N	3	5	1	1	.500	11	4.24	23 1/3	16	23	22	0	2	0	0
Career Average		9	18	3	6	.308	42	4.47	84	49	54	82	7	5	0	1
Yankee Average		2	23	2	1	.667	22	3.76	52 2/3	28	22	52	3	0	0	1
Career Total		28	55	8	18	.308	125	4.47	252	146	161	247	20	15	1	1
Yankee Total		2	23	2	1	.667	22	3.76	52 2/3	28	22	52	3	0	0	1

Llewellyn, Clement Manley (Clem *or* Lew)
HEIGHT: 6'2" RIGHTHANDER BORN: 8/1/1895 DOBSON, NORTH CAROLINA DIED: 11/26/1969 CONCORD, NORTH CAROLINA

YEAR	TEAM	STARTS	GAMES	WON	LOST	PCT	ER	ERA	INNINGS PITCHED	STRIKE-OUTS	WALKS	HITS ALLOWED	HRS ALLOWED	COMP. GAMES	SHUT-OUTS	SAVES
1922	NY-A	0	1	0	0	—	0	0.00	1	0	0	1	0	0	0	0
Career Average		0	1	0	0	—	0	0.00	1	0	0	1	0	0	0	0
Yankee Average		0	1	0	0	—	0	0.00	1	0	0	1	0	0	0	0
Career Total		0	1	0	0	—	0	0.00	1	0	0	1	0	0	0	0
Yankee Total		0	1	0	0	—	0	0.00	1	0	0	1	0	0	0	0

Lloyd, Graeme John
HEIGHT: 6'7" LEFTHANDER BORN: 4/9/1967 GEELONG, VICTORIA, AUSTRALIA

YEAR	TEAM	STARTS	GAMES	WON	LOST	PCT	ER	ERA	INNINGS PITCHED	STRIKE-OUTS	WALKS	HITS ALLOWED	HRS ALLOWED	COMP. GAMES	SHUT-OUTS	SAVES
1993	Mil-A	0	55	3	4	.429	20	2.83	63 2/3	31	13	64	5	0	0	0
1994	Mil-A	0	43	2	3	.400	27	5.17	47	31	15	49	4	0	0	3
1995	Mil-A	0	33	0	5	.000	16	4.50	32	13	8	28	4	0	0	4
1996	Mil-A	0	52	2	4	.333	16	2.82	51	24	17	49	3	0	0	0
1996	NY-A	0	13	0	2	.000	11	19.80	5 2/3	6	5	12	1	0	0	1
1997	NY-A	0	46	1	1	.500	18	3.31	49	26	20	55	6	0	0	1
1998	NY-A	0	50	3	0	1.000	7	1.70	37 2/3	20	6	26	3	0	0	0
1999	Tor-A	0	74	5	3	.625	29	3.63	72	47	23	68	11	0	0	3
Career Average		0	46	2	3	.421	18	3.63	45	25	13	44	5	0	0	1
Yankee Average		0	36	1	1	.571	12	3.56	30	17	10	31	3	0	0	0
Career Total		0	366	16	22	.421	144	3.63	357	198	107	351	37	0	0	11
Yankee Total		0	109	4	3	.571	36	3.56	91	52	31	93	10	0	0	1

Lollar, William Timothy (Tim)
HEIGHT: 6'3" LEFTHANDER BORN: 3/17/1956 POPLAR BLUFF, MISSOURI

YEAR	TEAM	STARTS	GAMES	WON	LOST	PCT	ER	ERA	INNINGS PITCHED	STRIKE-OUTS	WALKS	HITS ALLOWED	HRS ALLOWED	COMP. GAMES	SHUT-OUTS	SAVES
1980	NY-A	1	14	1	0	1.000	12	3.34	32 1/3	13	20	33	3	0	0	2
1981	SD-N	11	24	2	8	.666	52	6.10	76 2/3	38	51	87	4	0	0	1
1982	SD-N	34	34	16	9	.640	81	3.13	232 2/3	150	87	192	20	4	2	0
1983	SD-N	30	30	7	12	.368	90	4.61	175 2/3	135	85	170	22	1	0	0
1984	SD-N	31	31	11	13	.458	85	3.91	195 2/3	131	105	168	18	3	2	0
1985	Chi-A	13	18	3	5	.375	43	4.66	83	61	58	83	10	0	0	0
1985	Bos-A	10	16	5	5	.500	34	4.57	67	44	40	57	9	1	0	1
1986	Bos-A	1	32	2	0	1.000	33	6.91	43	28	34	51	7	0	0	0
Career Average		16	25	6	7	.475	54	4.27	113	75	60	105	12	1	1	1
Yankee Average		1	14	1	0	1.000	12	3.34	32 1/3	13	20	33	3	0	0	2
Career Total		131	199	47	52	.475	430	4.27	906	600	480	841	93	9	4	4
Yankee Total		1	14	1	0	1.000	12	3.34	32 1/3	13	20	33	3	0	0	2

Lopat, Edmund Walter (Steady Eddie) BORN EDMUND WALTER LOPATYNSKI
HEIGHT: 5'10" LEFTHANDER BORN: 6/21/1918 NEW YORK, NEW YORK DIED: 6/15/1992 DARIEN, CONNECTICUT

YEAR	TEAM	STARTS	GAMES	WON	LOST	PCT	ER	ERA	INNINGS PITCHED	STRIKE-OUTS	WALKS	HITS ALLOWED	HRS ALLOWED	COMP. GAMES	SHUT-OUTS	SAVES
1944	Chi-A	25	27	11	10	.524	76	3.26	210	75	59	217	12	13	1	0
1945	Chi-A	24	26	10	13	.435	91	4.11	199 1/3	74	56	226	8	17	1	1
1946	Chi-A	29	29	13	13	.500	70	2.73	231	89	48	216	18	20	2	0
1947	Chi-A	31	31	16	13	.552	79	2.81	252 2/3	109	73	241	17	22	3	0
1948	NY-A	31	33	17	11	.607	92	3.65	226 2/3	83	66	246	16	13	3	0
1949	NY-A	30	31	15	10	.600	78	3.26	215 1/3	70	69	222	19	14	4	1
1950	NY-A	32	35	18	8	.692	91	3.47	236 1/3	72	65	244	19	15	3	1
1951	NY-A	31	31	21	9	.700	76	2.91	234 2/3	93	71	209	12	20	4	0
1952	NY-A	19	20	10	5	.667	42	2.53	149 1/3	56	53	127	11	10	2	0
1953	NY-A	24	25	16	4	.800	48	2.42	178 1/3	50	32	169	13	9	3	0
1954	NY-A	23	26	12	4	.750	67	3.55	170	54	33	189	14	7	0	0

(continued)

Edmund Walter "Steady Eddie" Lopat, lhp, 1948–55

Lopat was, in the opinion of many, the smartest pitcher in baseball in the 1950s. Whether that was true or not, one thing was certain: Lopat was the master of mixing his pitches and keeping a hitter off balance.

Lopat was born on June 21, 1918, in New York City. He began his baseball career as a first baseman, but eventually was converted to a pitcher in the early 1940s. Lopat was a smart pitcher even then, but he did not have that one overpowering pitch that has scouts nodding in appreciation and that might have hastened his major league career.

In fact, he spent six years in the minor leagues, bouncing around from team to team. He was finally brought up to the Chicago White Sox in 1944. He was 11-10 for the floundering White Sox that year. It was not a great record, but Lopat was one of only two pitchers on the staff who had a winning record.

That was essentially how it went for Lopat with the White Sox. He was 51-50 in four years there, for a team that was, on the average, ten games under the .500 mark every year. One of his managers with Chicago was Hall of Famer Teddy Lyons, who worked with Lopat to show him how to change speeds and become a more effective thrower.

In 1948, Lopat was traded to the Yankees. There was some concern on the part of Yankee management that Lopat could not pitch as well for a first-division team as he did with the White Sox. Lopat quickly disabused them of that notion, going 17-11 as New York won the pennant.

He became one of the keystones of the Yankees' powerful pitching staffs of the late 1940s and early 1950s, along with Vic Raschi and Allie Reynolds. Often manager Casey Stengel would throw the fireballing Raschi and Reynolds for the first two games of a series with a team, then come back on the third day with junkballer Lopat. Opposing teams often couldn't recover their timing. Lopat was 113-58 with the Yankees, including a 21-9 season in 1951. In five World Series, he was 4-1 with a 2.60 ERA.

But the only category in which he was consistently among the league leaders in that span was fewest walks allowed. Lopat was the most economical of pitchers.

In 1955, the Yankees traded Lopat to Baltimore, where he finished the year and retired. He managed the Kansas City Athletics for two years in the 1960s and has also worked for the Yankees as a scout. Lopat is 6th all-time in winning percentage for the Yankees at .657, 11th in shutouts for New York with 20 and 12th in wins with 113.

(continued)

1955	NY-A	12	16	4	8	.333	36	3.74	86 2/3	24	16	101	12	3	1	0
1955	Bal-A	7	10	3	4	.429	23	4.22	49	10	9	57	8	1	0	0
Career Average		25	26	13	9	.597	67	3.21	188	66	50	190	14	13	2	0
Yankee Average		**25**	**27**	**14**	**7**	**.657**	**66**	**3.19**	**187**	**63**	**51**	**188**	**15**	**11**	**3**	**0**
Career Total		318	340	166	112	.597	869	3.21	2439	859	650	2464	179	164	27	3
Yankee Total		**202**	**217**	**113**	**59**	**.657**	**530**	**3.19**	**1497**	**502**	**405**	**1507**	**116**	**91**	**20**	**2**

Love, Edward Haughton (Slim)

HEIGHT: 6'7"   LEFTHANDER   BORN: 8/1/1890 LOVE, MISSISSIPPI   DIED: 11/30/1942 MEMPHIS, TENNESSEE

YEAR	TEAM	STARTS	GAMES	WON	LOST	PCT	ER	ERA	INNINGS PITCHED	STRIKE-OUTS	WALKS	HITS ALLOWED	HRS ALLOWED	COMP. GAMES	SHUT-OUTS	SAVES
1913	Was-A	1	5	1	0	1.000	3	1.62	16 2/3	5	6	14	0	0	0	1
1916	**NY-A**	**1**	**20**	**2**	**0**	**1.000**	**26**	**4.91**	**47 2/3**	**21**	**23**	**46**	**2**	**0**	**0**	**0**
1917	**NY-A**	**9**	**33**	**6**	**5**	**.545**	**34**	**2.35**	**130 1/3**	**82**	**57**	**115**	**0**	**2**	**0**	**1**
1918	**NY-A**	**29**	**38**	**13**	**12**	**.520**	**78**	**3.07**	**228 2/3**	**95**	**116**	**207**	**3**	**13**	**1**	**1**
1919	Det-A	8	22	6	4	.600	30	3.01	89 2/3	46	40	92	3	4	0	1
1920	Det-A	0	1	0	0	—	4	8.31	4 1/3	2	4	6	0	0	0	0

(continued)

(continued)

Career Average	8	20	5	4	.571	29	3.04	86	42	41	80	1	3	0	1
Yankee Average	**13**	**30**	**7**	**6**	**.553**	**46**	**3.05**	**136**	**66**	**65**	**123**	**2**	**5**	**0**	**1**
Career Total	48	119	28	21	.571	175	3.04	517	251	246	480	8	19	1	4
Yankee Total	**39**	**91**	**21**	**17**	**.553**	**138**	**3.05**	**407**	**198**	**196**	**368**	**5**	**15**	**1**	**2**

Lyle, Albert Walter (Sparky)

HEIGHT: 6'1"   LEFTHANDER   BORN: 7/22/1944 DU BOIS, PENNSYLVANIA

YEAR	TEAM	STARTS	GAMES	WON	LOST	PCT	ER	ERA	INNINGS PITCHED	STRIKE-OUTS	WALKS	HITS ALLOWED	HRS ALLOWED	COMP. GAMES	SHUT-OUTS	SAVES
1967	Bos-A	0	27	1	2	.333	11	2.28	43 1/3	42	14	33	3	0	0	5
1968	Bos-A	0	49	6	1	.857	20	2.74	65 2/3	52	14	67	6	0	0	11
1969	Bos-A	0	71	8	3	.727	29	2.54	102 2/3	93	48	91	8	0	0	17
1970	Bos-A	0	63	1	7	.125	29	3.88	67 1/3	51	34	62	5	0	0	20
1971	Bos-A	0	50	6	4	.600	16	2.75	52 1/3	37	23	41	5	0	0	16
1972	**NY-A**	**0**	**59**	**9**	**5**	**.643**	**23**	**1.92**	**107 2/3**	**75**	**29**	**84**	**3**	**0**	**0**	**35**

(continued)

Albert Walter "Sparky" Lyle, lhp, 1972–78

There may have been pitchers who threw harder, but there were few who took the mound with as much confidence as Sparky Lyle in his salad days with the New York Yankees.

Lyle, born July 22, 1944, in Du Bois, Pennsylvania, was originally a part of the Red Sox farm system, and he was brought up to the big club in 1967. Lyle didn't pitch much that year, but he had a ringside seat as the Red Sox won their first American League championship in 21 years.

He was a prankster, and his nickname was a backhanded reference to his put-ons, some of which "sparked" the team, some of which ticked off his teammates.

Lyle was a part of the Red Sox organization until 1972, when the Yankees acquired him for Danny Cater. Confident, fearless and pragmatic, Lyle, armed with a tenacious slider, became the closer the Yankees so desperately needed to build around. He never started a major league game, but he finished quite a few.

In 1972 Lyle had a league-leading 35 saves, and kept New York in the pennant race almost by himself. Throughout the early 1970s, the Yankees continued to rebuild. Lyle was the best reliever in baseball over that span, with 28 wins and 83 saves. He was, to Yankee fans, the closest thing to a sure thing in baseball. He loved pitching in close games and admitted that pitching in blowouts bored him.

In 1976, he had 23 saves and the Yankees won the American League pennant. But in 1977, he was even better, with a 13-5 record and 26 saves as the Yankees won the World Championship.

That performance earned Lyle the Cy Young award and, in some ways, precipitated the end of his Yankee career. The next year, the Yankees acquired free agent Rich Gossage, another reliever, from the Pirates.

The plan was to alternate righthander Gossage and lefthander Lyle for an unbeatable closer combination. The reality, accurately forecast by Lyle, was that the Yankees fell in love with the 95-plus mile-an-hour fastball of Gossage over Lyle's 85 m.p.h slider. By the next season, Sparky was in Texas.

Lyle pitched in the majors for four more years with middling success. He retired in 1982 after a stint with the White Sox. He is 4th on the Yankees' list of all-time saves with 141 and 4th in appearances with 420.

(continued)

YEAR	TEAM	STARTS	GAMES	WON	LOST	PCT	ER	ERA	INNINGS PITCHED	STRIKE-OUTS	WALKS	HITS ALLOWED	HRS ALLOWED	COMP. GAMES	SHUT-OUTS	SAVES
1973	NY-A	0	51	5	9	.357	23	2.51	82 1/3	63	18	66	4	0	0	27
1974	NY-A	0	66	9	3	.750	21	1.66	114	89	43	93	6	0	0	15
1975	NY-A	0	49	5	7	.417	31	3.12	89 1/3	65	36	94	1	0	0	6
1976	NY-A	0	64	7	8	.467	26	2.26	103 2/3	61	42	82	5	0	0	23
1977	NY-A	0	72	13	5	.722	33	2.17	137	68	33	131	7	0	0	26
1978	NY-A	0	59	9	3	.750	43	3.47	111 2/3	33	33	116	6	0	0	9
1979	Tex-A	0	67	5	8	.385	33	3.13	95	48	28	78	9	0	0	13
1980	Tex-A	0	49	3	2	.600	42	4.69	80 2/3	43	28	97	9	0	0	8
1980	Phi-N	0	10	0	0	—	3	1.93	14	6	6	11	0	0	0	2
1981	Phi-N	0	48	9	6	.600	37	4.44	75	29	33	85	4	0	0	2
1982	Phi-N	0	34	3	3	.500	21	5.15	36 2/3	12	12	50	3	0	0	2
1982	Chi-A	0	11	0	0	—	4	3.00	12	6	7	11	0	0	0	1
Career Average		0	50	6	4	.566	25	2.88	77	49	27	72	5	0	0	13
Yankee Average		**0**	**60**	**8**	**6**	**.588**	**29**	**2.41**	**107**	**65**	**33**	**95**	**5**	**0**	**0**	**20**
Career Total		0	899	99	76	.566	445	2.88	1390 1/3	873	481	1292	84	0	0	238
Yankee Total		**0**	**420**	**57**	**40**	**.588**	**200**	**2.41**	**746**	**454**	**234**	**666**	**32**	**0**	**0**	**141**

Lyons, Albert Harold

HEIGHT: 6'2"   RIGHTHANDER   BORN: 7/18/1918 ST. JOSEPH, MISSOURI   DIED: 12/20/1965 INGLEWOOD, CALIFORNIA

YEAR	TEAM	STARTS	GAMES	WON	LOST	PCT	ER	ERA	INNINGS PITCHED	STRIKE-OUTS	WALKS	HITS ALLOWED	HRS ALLOWED	COMP. GAMES	SHUT-OUTS	SAVES
1944	NY-A	0	11	0	0	—	20	4.55	39 2/3	14	24	43	2	0	0	0
1946	NY-A	1	2	0	1	.000	5	5.40	8 1/3	4	6	11	0	0	0	0
1947	NY-A	0	6	1	0	1.000	11	9.00	11	7	9	18	2	0	0	0
1947	Pit-N	0	13	1	2	.333	23	7.31	28 1/3	16	12	36	4	0	0	0
1948	Bos-N	0	7	1	0	1.000	11	7.82	12 2/3	5	8	17	1	0	0	0
Career Average		0	8	1	1	.500	14	6.30	20	9	12	25	2	0	0	0
Yankee Average		**0**	**6**	**0**	**0**	**.500**	**12**	**5.50**	**20**	**8**	**13**	**24**	**1**	**0**	**0**	**0**
Career Total		1	39	3	3	.500	70	6.30	100	46	59	125	9	0	0	0
Yankee Total		**1**	**19**	**1**	**1**	**.500**	**36**	**5.50**	**59**	**25**	**39**	**72**	**4**	**0**	**0**	**0**

Maas, Duane Frederick (Duke)

HEIGHT: 5'10"   RIGHTHANDER   BORN: 1/31/1929 UTICA, MICHIGAN   DIED: 12/7/1976 MT. CLEMENS, MICHIGAN

YEAR	TEAM	STARTS	GAMES	WON	LOST	PCT	ER	ERA	INNINGS PITCHED	STRIKE-OUTS	WALKS	HITS ALLOWED	HRS ALLOWED	COMP. GAMES	SHUT-OUTS	SAVES
1955	Det-A	16	18	5	6	.455	47	4.88	86 2/3	42	50	91	7	5	2	0
1956	Det-A	7	26	0	7	.000	46	6.54	63 1/3	34	32	81	9	0	0	0
1957	Det-A	26	45	10	14	.417	80	3.28	219 1/3	116	65	210	23	8	2	6
1958	KC-A	7	10	4	5	.444	24	3.90	55 1/3	19	13	49	3	3	1	1
1958	NY-A	13	22	7	3	.700	43	3.82	101 1/3	50	36	93	9	2	1	0
1959	NY-A	21	38	14	8	.636	68	4.43	138	67	53	149	14	3	1	4
1960	NY-A	1	35	5	1	.833	32	4.09	70 1/3	28	35	70	6	0	0	4
1961	NY-A	0	1	0	0	—	2	54.00	1/3	0	0	2	0	0	0	0
Career Average		11	24	6	6	.506	43	4.19	92	45	36	93	9	3	1	2
Yankee Average		**9**	**24**	**7**	**3**	**.684**	**36**	**4.21**	**78**	**36**	**31**	**79**	**7**	**1**	**1**	**2**
Career Total		91	195	45	44	.506	342	4.19	734 2/3	356	284	745	71	21	7	15
Yankee Total		**35**	**96**	**26**	**12**	**.684**	**145**	**4.21**	**310**	**145**	**124**	**314**	**29**	**5**	**2**	**8**

MacDonald, Robert Joseph

HEIGHT: 6'3"   LEFTHANDER   BORN: 4/27/1965 EAST ORANGE, NEW JERSEY

YEAR	TEAM	STARTS	GAMES	WON	LOST	PCT	ER	ERA	INNINGS PITCHED	STRIKE-OUTS	WALKS	HITS ALLOWED	HRS ALLOWED	COMP. GAMES	SHUT-OUTS	SAVES
1990	Tor-A	0	4	0	0	—	0	0.00	2 1/3	0	2	0	0	0	0	0
1991	Tor-A	0	45	3	3	.500	17	2.85	53 2/3	24	25	51	5	0	0	0
1992	Tor-A	0	27	1	0	1.000	23	4.37	47 1/3	26	16	50	4	0	0	0
1993	Det-A	0	68	3	3	.500	39	5.35	65 2/3	39	33	67	8	0	0	3
1995	NY-A	0	33	1	1	.500	25	4.86	46 1/3	41	22	50	7	0	0	0
1996	NY-N	0	20	0	2	.000	9	4.26	19	12	9	16	2	0	0	0

(continued)

(continued)

	STARTS	GAMES	WON	LOST	PCT	ER	ERA	INNINGS PITCHED	STRIKE-OUTS	WALKS	HITS ALLOWED	HRS ALLOWED	COMP. GAMES	SHUT-OUTS	SAVES
Career Average	0	33	1	2	.471	19	4.35	39	24	18	39	4	0	0	1
Yankee Average	**0**	**33**	**1**	**1**	**.500**	**25**	**4.86**	**46 1/3**	**41**	**22**	**50**	**7**	**0**	**0**	**0**
Career Total	0	197	8	9	.471	113	4.34	234 1/3	142	107	234	26	0	0	3
Yankee Total	**0**	**33**	**1**	**1**	**.500**	**25**	**4.86**	**46**	**41**	**22**	**50**	**7**	**0**	**0**	**0**

MacFayden, Daniel Knowles (Deacon Danny)

HEIGHT: 5'11"   RIGHTHANDER   BORN: 6/10/1905 N. TRURO, MASSACHUSETTS   DIED: 8/26/1972 BRUNSWICK, MAINE

YEAR	TEAM	STARTS	GAMES	WON	LOST	PCT	ER	ERA	INNINGS PITCHED	STRIKE-OUTS	WALKS	HITS ALLOWED	HRS ALLOWED	COMP. GAMES	SHUT-OUTS	SAVES
1926	Bos-A	1	3	0	1	.000	7	4.85	13	1	7	10	0	1	0	0
1927	Bos-A	16	34	5	8	.385	76	4.27	160 1/3	42	59	176	9	6	1	2
1928	Bos-A	28	33	9	15	.375	103	4.75	195	61	78	215	12	9	4	0
1929	Bos-A	26	32	10	18	.357	89	3.62	221	61	81	225	8	14	4	0
1930	Bos-A	33	36	11	14	.440	126	4.21	269 1/3	76	93	293	9	18	1	2
1931	Bos-A	32	35	16	12	.571	103	4.02	230 2/3	74	79	263	4	17	2	0
1932	Bos-A	11	12	1	10	.091	44	5.10	77 2/3	29	33	91	3	6	0	0
1932	**NY-A**	**15**	**17**	**7**	**5**	**.583**	**53**	**3.93**	**121 1/3**	**33**	**37**	**137**	**11**	**9**	**0**	**1**
1933	**NY-A**	**6**	**25**	**3**	**2**	**.600**	**59**	**5.88**	**90 1/3**	**28**	**37**	**120**	**8**	**2**	**0**	**0**
1934	**NY-A**	**11**	**22**	**4**	**3**	**.571**	**48**	**4.50**	**96**	**41**	**31**	**110**	**5**	**4**	**0**	**0**
1935	Cin-N	4	7	1	2	.333	19	4.75	36	13	13	39	1	1	0	0
1935	Bos-N	20	28	5	13	.278	86	5.10	151 2/3	46	34	200	8	7	1	0
1936	Bos-N	31	37	17	13	.567	85	2.87	266 2/3	86	66	268	5	21	2	0
1937	Bos-N	32	32	14	14	.500	80	2.93	246	70	60	250	5	16	2	0
1938	Bos-N	29	29	14	9	.609	72	2.95	219 2/3	58	64	208	6	19	5	0
1939	Bos-N	28	33	8	14	.364	83	3.90	191 2/3	46	59	221	11	8	0	2
1940	Pit-N	8	35	5	4	.556	36	3.55	91 1/3	24	27	112	5	0	0	2
1941	Was-A	0	5	0	1	.000	8	10.29	7	3	5	12	1	0	0	0
1943	Bos-N	1	10	2	1	.667	14	5.91	21 1/3	5	9	31	1	0	0	0
Career Average	17	24	7	8	.454	63	3.96	142	42	46	157	6	8	1	0
Yankee Average	**11**	**21**	**5**	**3**	**.583**	**53**	**4.68**	**103**	**34**	**35**	**122**	**8**	**5**	**0**	**0**
Career Total	332	465	132	159	.454	1191	3.96	2706	797	872	2981	112	158	18	9
Yankee Total	**32**	**64**	**14**	**10**	**.583**	**160**	**4.68**	**307 2/3**	**102**	**105**	**367**	**24**	**15**	**0**	**1**

Madison, David Pledger

HEIGHT: 6'3"   RIGHTHANDER   BORN: 2/1/1921 BROOKSVILLE, MISSISSIPPI   DIED: 12/8/1985 MACON, MISSISSIPPI

YEAR	TEAM	STARTS	GAMES	WON	LOST	PCT	ER	ERA	INNINGS PITCHED	STRIKE-OUTS	WALKS	HITS ALLOWED	HRS ALLOWED	COMP. GAMES	SHUT-OUTS	SAVES
1950	**NY-A**	**0**	**1**	**0**	**0**	**—**	**2**	**6.00**	**3**	**1**	**1**	**3**	**1**	**0**	**0**	**0**
1952	StL-A	4	31	4	2	.667	38	4.38	78	35	48	78	7	0	0	0
1952	Det-A	1	10	1	1	.500	13	7.80	15	7	10	16	1	0	0	0
1953	Det-A	1	32	3	4	.429	47	6.82	62	27	44	76	7	0	0	0
Career Average	2	19	2	2	.533	25	5.70	40	18	26	43	4	0	0	0
Yankee Average	**0**	**1**	**0**	**0**	**—**	**2**	**6.00**	**3**	**1**	**1**	**3**	**1**	**0**	**0**	**0**
Career Total	6	74	8	7	.533	100	5.70	158	70	103	173	16	0	0	0
Yankee Total	**0**	**1**	**0**	**0**	**—**	**2**	**6.00**	**3**	**1**	**1**	**3**	**1**	**0**	**0**	**0**

Maglie, Salvatore Anthony (The Barber)

HEIGHT: 6'2"   RIGHTHANDER   BORN: 4/26/1917 NIAGARA FALLS, NEW YORK   DIED: 12/28/1992 NIAGARA FALLS, NEW YORK

YEAR	TEAM	STARTS	GAMES	WON	LOST	PCT	ER	ERA	INNINGS PITCHED	STRIKE-OUTS	WALKS	HITS ALLOWED	HRS ALLOWED	COMP. GAMES	SHUT-OUTS	SAVES
1945	NY-N	10	13	5	4	.556	22	2.35	84 1/3	32	22	72	2	7	3	0
1950	NY-N	16	47	18	4	.818	62	2.71	206	96	86	169	14	12	5	1
1951	NY-N	37	42	23	6	.793	97	2.93	298	146	86	254	27	22	3	4
1952	NY-N	31	35	18	8	.692	70	2.92	216	112	75	199	16	12	5	1
1953	NY-N	24	27	8	9	.471	67	4.15	145 1/3	80	47	158	19	9	3	0
1954	NY-N	32	34	14	6	.700	79	3.26	218 1/3	117	70	222	21	9	1	2
1955	NY-N	21	23	9	5	.643	54	3.75	129 2/3	71	48	142	18	6	0	0
1955	Cle-A	2	10	0	2	.000	11	3.86	25 2/3	11	7	26	0	0	0	2
1956	Cle-A	0	2	0	0	—	2	3.60	5	2	2	6	1	0	0	0
1956	Bro-N	26	28	13	5	.722	61	2.87	191	108	52	154	21	9	3	0

(continued)

(continued)

YEAR	TEAM	STARTS	GAMES	WON	LOST	PCT	ER	ERA	INNINGS PITCHED	STRIKE-OUTS	WALKS	HITS ALLOWED	HRS ALLOWED	COMP. GAMES	SHUT-OUTS	SAVES
1957	Bro-N	17	19	6	6	.500	33	2.93	101⅓	50	26	94	12	4	1	1
1957	**NY-A**	**3**	**6**	**2**	**0**	**1.000**	**5**	**1.73**	**26**	**9**	**7**	**22**	**1**	**1**	**1**	**3**
1958	**NY-A**	**3**	**7**	**1**	**1**	**.500**	**12**	**4.63**	**23⅓**	**7**	**9**	**27**	**3**	**0**	**0**	**0**
1958	StL-N	10	10	2	6	.250	28	4.75	53	21	25	46	14	2	0	0
Career Average		17	22	9	4	.657	43	3.15	123	62	40	114	12	7	2	1
Yankee Average		**3**	**7**	**2**	**1**	**.750**	**9**	**3.10**	**25**	**8**	**8**	**25**	**2**	**1**	**1**	**2**
Career Total		232	303	119	62	.657	603	3.15	1723	862	562	1591	169	93	25	14
Yankee Total		**6**	**13**	**3**	**1**	**.750**	**17**	**3.10**	**49⅓**	**16**	**16**	**49**	**4**	**1**	**1**	**3**

Magnuson, James Robert

HEIGHT: 6'2" LEFTHANDER BORN: 8/18/1946 MARINETTE, WISCONSIN DIED: 5/30/1991 GREEN BAY, WISCONSIN

YEAR	TEAM	STARTS	GAMES	WON	LOST	PCT	ER	ERA	INNINGS PITCHED	STRIKE-OUTS	WALKS	HITS ALLOWED	HRS ALLOWED	COMP. GAMES	SHUT-OUTS	SAVES
1970	Chi-A	6	13	1	5	.167	24	4.84	44⅔	20	16	45	7	0	0	0
1971	Chi-A	4	15	1	1	.500	15	4.50	30	11	16	30	0	0	0	0
1973	**NY-A**	**0**	**8**	**0**	**1**	**.000**	**13**	**4.28**	**27⅓**	**9**	**9**	**38**	**2**	**0**	**0**	**0**
Career Average		3	12	1	2	.222	17	4.59	34	13	14	38	3	0	0	0
Yankee Average		**0**	**8**	**0**	**1**	**.000**	**13**	**4.28**	**27**	**9**	**9**	**38**	**2**	**0**	**0**	**0**
Career Total		10	36	2	7	.222	52	4.59	102	40	41	113	9	0	0	0
Yankee Total		**0**	**8**	**0**	**1**	**.000**	**13**	**4.28**	**27⅓**	**9**	**9**	**38**	**2**	**0**	**0**	**0**

Makosky, Frank (Dins)

HEIGHT: 6'1" RIGHTHANDER BORN: 1/20/1910 BOONTON, NEW JERSEY DIED: 1/10/1987 STROUDSBURG, PENNSYLVANIA

YEAR	TEAM	STARTS	GAMES	WON	LOST	PCT	ER	ERA	INNINGS PITCHED	STRIKE-OUTS	WALKS	HITS ALLOWED	HRS ALLOWED	COMP. GAMES	SHUT-OUTS	SAVES
1937	**NY-A**	**1**	**26**	**5**	**2**	**.714**	**32**	**4.97**	**58**	**27**	**24**	**64**	**6**	**1**	**0**	**3**
Career Average		1	26	5	2	.714	32	4.97	58	27	24	64	6	1	0	3
Yankee Average		**1**	**26**	**5**	**2**	**.714**	**32**	**4.97**	**58**	**27**	**24**	**64**	**6**	**1**	**0**	**3**
Career Total		1	26	5	2	.714	32	4.97	58	27	24	64	6	1	0	3
Yankee Total		**1**	**26**	**5**	**2**	**.714**	**32**	**4.97**	**58**	**27**	**24**	**64**	**6**	**1**	**0**	**3**

Malone, Perce Liegh (Pat)

HEIGHT: 6'0" RIGHTHANDER BORN: 9/25/1902 ALTOONA, PENNSYLVANIA DIED: 5/13/1943 ALTOONA, PENNSYLVANIA

YEAR	TEAM	STARTS	GAMES	WON	LOST	PCT	ER	ERA	INNINGS PITCHED	STRIKE-OUTS	WALKS	HITS ALLOWED	HRS ALLOWED	COMP. GAMES	SHUT-OUTS	SAVES
1928	Chi-N	25	42	18	13	.581	79	2.84	250⅔	155	99	218	15	16	2	2
1929	Chi-N	30	40	22	10	.688	106	3.57	267	166	102	283	12	19	5	4
1930	Chi-N	35	45	20	9	.690	119	3.94	271⅔	142	96	290	14	22	2	0
1931	Chi-N	30	36	16	9	.640	99	3.90	228⅓	112	88	229	9	12	2	0
1932	Chi-N	32	37	15	17	.469	89	3.38	237	120	78	222	13	17	2	0
1933	Chi-N	26	31	10	14	.417	81	3.91	186⅓	72	59	186	10	13	2	0
1934	Chi-N	21	34	14	7	.667	75	3.53	191	111	55	200	14	8	1	0
1935	**NY-A**	**2**	**29**	**3**	**5**	**.375**	**34**	**5.43**	**56⅓**	**25**	**33**	**53**	**7**	**0**	**0**	**3**
1936	**NY-A**	**9**	**35**	**12**	**4**	**.750**	**57**	**3.81**	**134⅔**	**72**	**60**	**144**	**4**	**5**	**0**	**9**
1937	**NY-A**	**9**	**28**	**4**	**4**	**.500**	**56**	**5.48**	**92**	**49**	**35**	**109**	**5**	**3**	**0**	**6**
Career Average		22	36	13	9	.593	80	3.74	192	102	71	193	10	12	2	3
Yankee Average		**7**	**31**	**6**	**4**	**.594**	**49**	**4.67**	**94**	**49**	**43**	**102**	**5**	**3**	**0**	**6**
Career Total		219	357	134	92	.593	795	3.74	1915	1024	705	1934	103	115	16	26
Yankee Total		**20**	**92**	**19**	**13**	**.594**	**147**	**4.67**	**283**	**146**	**128**	**306**	**16**	**8**	**0**	**18**

Mamaux, Albert Leon

HEIGHT: 6'1" RIGHTHANDER BORN: 5/30/1894 PITTSBURGH, PENNSYLVANIA DIED: 1/2/1963 SANTA MONICA, CALIFORNIA

YEAR	TEAM	STARTS	GAMES	WON	LOST	PCT	ER	ERA	INNINGS PITCHED	STRIKE-OUTS	WALKS	HITS ALLOWED	HRS ALLOWED	COMP. GAMES	SHUT-OUTS	SAVES
1913	Pit-N	0	1	0	0	—	1	3.00	3	2	2	2	0	0	0	0
1914	Pit-N	6	13	5	2	.714	12	1.71	63	30	24	41	1	4	2	0
1915	Pit-N	31	38	21	8	.724	57	2.04	251 2/3	152	96	182	3	17	8	0
1916	Pit-N	37	45	21	15	.583	87	2.53	310	163	136	264	3	26	1	2
1917	Pit-N	13	16	2	11	.154	50	5.25	85 2/3	22	50	92	1	5	0	0
1918	Bro-N	1	2	0	1	.000	6	6.75	8	2	2	14	0	0	0	0
1919	Bro-N	22	30	10	12	.455	59	2.66	199 1/3	80	66	174	2	16	2	0
1920	Bro-N	18	41	12	8	.600	57	2.69	190 2/3	101	63	172	2	9	2	4
1921	Bro-N	1	12	3	3	.500	15	3.14	43	21	13	36	1	0	0	1
1922	Bro-N	7	37	1	4	.200	36	3.70	87 2/3	35	33	97	7	1	0	3
1923	Bro-N	1	5	0	2	.000	12	8.31	13	5	6	20	0	0	0	0
1924	NY-A	2	14	1	1	.500	24	5.68	38	12	20	44	2	0	0	0
Career Average		12	21	6	6	.531	35	2.90	108	52	43	95	2	7	1	1
Yankee Average		**2**	**14**	**1**	**1**	**.500**	**24**	**5.68**	**38**	**12**	**20**	**44**	**2**	**0**	**0**	**0**
Career Total		139	254	76	67	.531	416	2.90	1293	625	511	1138	22	78	15	10
Yankee Total		**2**	**14**	**1**	**1**	**.500**	**24**	**5.68**	**38**	**12**	**20**	**44**	**2**	**0**	**0**	**0**

Manning, Walter S. (Rube)

HEIGHT: 6'0" RIGHTHANDER BORN: 4/29/1883 CHAMBERSBURG, PENNSYLVANIA DIED: 4/23/1930 WILLIAMSPORT, PENNSYLVANIA

YEAR	TEAM	STARTS	GAMES	WON	LOST	PCT	ER	ERA	INNINGS PITCHED	STRIKE-OUTS	WALKS	HITS ALLOWED	HRS ALLOWED	COMP. GAMES	SHUT-OUTS	SAVES
1907	**NY-A**	**1**	**1**	**0**	**1**	**.000**	**3**	**3.00**	**9**	**3**	**3**	**8**	**0**	**1**	**0**	**0**
1908	**NY-A**	**26**	**41**	**13**	**16**	**.448**	**80**	**2.94**	**245**	**113**	**86**	**228**	**4**	**19**	**2**	**1**
1909	**NY-A**	**21**	**26**	**7**	**11**	**.389**	**61**	**3.17**	**173**	**71**	**48**	**167**	**2**	**11**	**2**	**1**
1910	**NY-A**	**9**	**16**	**2**	**4**	**.333**	**31**	**3.72**	**75**	**25**	**25**	**80**	**4**	**4**	**0**	**0**
Career Average		14	21	6	8	.407	44	3.14	126	53	41	121	3	9	1	1
Yankee Average		**14**	**21**	**6**	**8**	**.407**	**44**	**3.14**	**126**	**53**	**41**	**121**	**3**	**9**	**1**	**1**
Career Total		57	84	22	32	.407	175	3.14	502	212	162	483	10	35	4	2
Yankee Total		**57**	**84**	**22**	**32**	**.407**	**175**	**3.14**	**502**	**212**	**162**	**483**	**10**	**35**	**4**	**2**

Manzanillo, Josias BORN JOSIAS MANZANILLO (ADAMS)

HEIGHT: 6'0" RIGHTHANDER BORN: 10/16/1967 SAN PEDRO DE MACORIS, DOMINICAN REPUBLIC

YEAR	TEAM	STARTS	GAMES	WON	LOST	PCT	ER	ERA	INNINGS PITCHED	STRIKE-OUTS	WALKS	HITS ALLOWED	HRS ALLOWED	COMP. GAMES	SHUT-OUTS	SAVES
1991	Bos-A	0	1	0	0	—	2	18.00	1	1	3	2	0	0	0	0
1993	Mil-A	1	10	1	1	.500	18	9.53	17	10	10	22	1	0	0	1
1993	NY-N	0	6	0	0	—	4	3.00	12	11	9	8	1	0	0	0
1994	NY-N	0	37	3	2	.600	14	2.66	47 1/3	48	13	34	4	0	0	2
1995	NY-N	0	12	1	2	.333	14	7.88	16	14	6	18	3	0	0	0
1995	**NY-A**	**0**	**11**	**0**	**0**	**—**	**4**	**2.12**	**17 1/3**	**11**	**9**	**19**	**1**	**0**	**0**	**0**
1997	Sea-A	0	16	0	1	.000	11	5.50	18 1/3	18	17	19	3	0	0	0
1999	NY-N	0	12	0	0	—	12	6.00	18 1/3	25	4	19	5	0	0	0
2000	Pit-N	0	43	2	2	.500	22	3.38	58 2/3	39	32	50	6	0	0	0
Career Average		0	13	1	1	.467	10	4.41	18	17	9	18	2	0	0	0
Yankee Average		**0**	**11**	**0**	**0**	**—**	**4**	**2.12**	**17 1/3**	**11**	**9**	**19**	**1**	**0**	**0**	**0**
Career Total		1	148	7	8	.467	101	4.41	206 1/3	177	103	191	24	0	0	3
Yankee Total		**0**	**11**	**0**	**0**	**—**	**4**	**2.12**	**17 1/3**	**11**	**9**	**19**	**1**	**0**	**0**	**0**

Markle, Clifford Monroe

HEIGHT: 5'9"   RIGHTHANDER   BORN: 5/3/1894 DRAVOSBURG, PENNSYLVANIA   DIED: 5/24/1974 TEMPLE CITY, CALIFORNIA

YEAR	TEAM	STARTS	GAMES	WON	LOST	PCT	ER	ERA	INNINGS PITCHED	STRIKE-OUTS	WALKS	HITS ALLOWED	HRS ALLOWED	COMP. GAMES	SHUT-OUTS	SAVES
1915	NY-A	2	3	2	0	1.000	1	0.39	23	12	6	15	1	2	0	0
1916	NY-A	7	11	4	3	.571	23	4.53	45 2/3	14	31	41	0	3	1	0
1921	Cin-N	6	10	2	6	.250	28	3.76	67	23	20	75	0	5	0	0
1922	Cin-N	3	25	4	5	.444	32	3.81	75 2/3	34	33	75	3	2	1	0
1924	NY-A	3	7	0	3	.000	23	8.87	23 1/3	7	20	29	5	0	0	0
Career Average		4	11	2	3	.414	21	4.10	47	18	22	47	2	2	0	0
Yankee Average		4	7	2	2	.500	16	4.60	31	11	19	28	2	2	0	0
Career Total		21	56	12	17	.414	107	4.10	234 2/3	90	110	235	9	12	2	0
Yankee Total		12	21	6	6	.500	47	4.60	92	33	57	85	6	5	1	0

Marquis, James Milburn

HEIGHT: 5'11"   RIGHTHANDER   BORN: 11/18/1900 YOAKUM, TEXAS   DIED: 8/5/1992 JACKSON, CALIFORNIA

YEAR	TEAM	STARTS	GAMES	WON	LOST	PCT	ER	ERA	INNINGS PITCHED	STRIKE-OUTS	WALKS	HITS ALLOWED	HRS ALLOWED	COMP. GAMES	SHUT-OUTS	SAVES
1925	NY-A	0	2	0	0	—	8	9.82	7 1/3	0	6	12	1	0	0	0
Career Average		0	2	0	0	—	8	9.82	7 1/3	0	6	12	1	0	0	0
Yankee Average		0	2	0	0	—	8	9.82	7 1/3	0	6	12	1	0	0	0
Career Total		0	2	0	0	—	8	9.82	7 1/3	0	6	12	1	0	0	0
Yankee Total		0	2	0	0	—	8	9.82	7 1/3	0	6	12	1	0	0	0

Marshall, Clarence Westly (Cuddles)

HEIGHT: 6'3"   RIGHTHANDER   BORN: 4/28/1925 BELLINGHAM, WASHINGTON

YEAR	TEAM	STARTS	GAMES	WON	LOST	PCT	ER	ERA	INNINGS PITCHED	STRIKE-OUTS	WALKS	HITS ALLOWED	HRS ALLOWED	COMP. GAMES	SHUT-OUTS	SAVES
1946	NY-A	11	23	3	4	.429	48	5.33	81	32	56	96	4	1	0	0
1948	NY-A	0	1	0	0	—	0	0.00	1	0	3	0	0	0	0	0
1949	NY-A	2	21	3	0	1.000	28	5.11	49 1/3	13	48	48	3	0	0	3
1950	StL-A	2	28	1	3	.250	47	7.88	53 2/3	24	51	72	1	0	0	1
Career Average		4	18	2	2	.500	31	5.98	46	17	40	54	2	0	0	1
Yankee Average		4	15	2	1	.600	25	5.21	44	15	36	48	2	0	0	1
Career Total		15	73	7	7	.500	123	5.98	185	69	158	216	8	1	0	4
Yankee Total		13	45	6	4	.600	76	5.21	131 1/3	45	107	144	7	1	0	3

Martinez, Felix Anthony (Tippy)

HEIGHT: 5'10"   LEFTHANDER   BORN: 5/31/1950 LAJUNTA, COLORADO

YEAR	TEAM	STARTS	GAMES	WON	LOST	PCT	ER	ERA	INNINGS PITCHED	STRIKE-OUTS	WALKS	HITS ALLOWED	HRS ALLOWED	COMP. GAMES	SHUT-OUTS	SAVES
1974	NY-A	0	10	0	0	—	6	4.26	12 2/3	10	9	14	0	0	0	0
1975	NY-A	2	23	1	2	.333	11	2.68	37	20	32	27	2	0	0	8
1976	NY-A	0	11	2	0	1.000	6	1.93	28	14	14	18	1	0	0	2
1976	Bal-A	0	28	3	1	.750	12	2.59	41 2/3	31	28	32	0	0	0	8
1977	Bal-A	0	41	5	1	.833	15	2.70	50	29	27	47	2	0	0	9
1978	Bal-A	0	42	3	3	.500	37	4.83	69	57	40	77	4	0	0	5
1979	Bal-A	0	39	10	3	.769	25	2.88	78	61	31	59	0	0	0	3
1980	Bal-A	0	53	4	4	.500	27	3.01	80 2/3	68	34	69	5	0	0	10
1981	Bal-A	0	37	3	3	.500	19	2.90	59	50	32	48	4	0	0	11
1982	Bal-A	0	76	8	8	.500	36	3.41	95	78	37	81	6	0	0	16
1983	Bal-A	0	65	9	3	.750	27	2.35	103 1/3	81	37	76	10	0	0	21
1984	Bal-A	0	55	4	9	.308	39	3.91	89 2/3	72	51	88	9	0	0	17
1985	Bal-A	0	49	3	3	.500	42	5.40	70	47	37	70	8	0	0	4
1986	Bal-A	0	14	0	2	.000	10	5.63	16	11	12	18	1	0	0	1
1988	Min-A	0	3	0	0	—	8	18.00	4	3	4	8	1	0	0	0

(continued)

(continued)

Career Average	0	36	4	3	.567	21	3.45	56	42	28	49	4	0	0	8
Yankee Average	**1**	**15**	**1**	**1**	**.600**	**8**	**2.67**	**26**	**15**	**18**	**20**	**1**	**0**	**0**	**3**
Career Total	2	546	55	42	.567	320	3.45	834	632	425	732	53	0	0	115
Yankee Total	**2**	**44**	**3**	**2**	**.600**	**23**	**2.67**	**77 2/3**	**44**	**55**	**59**	**3**	**0**	**0**	**10**

May, Rudolph

HEIGHT: 6'3"   LEFTHANDER   BORN: 7/18/1944 COFFEYVILLE, KANSAS

YEAR	TEAM	STARTS	GAMES	WON	LOST	PCT	ER	ERA	INNINGS PITCHED	STRIKE-OUTS	WALKS	HITS ALLOWED	HRS ALLOWED	COMP. GAMES	SHUT-OUTS	SAVES
1965	Cal-A	19	30	4	9	.308	54	3.92	124	76	78	111	7	2	1	0
1969	Cal-A	25	43	10	13	.435	69	3.44	180 1/3	133	66	142	20	4	0	2
1970	Cal-A	34	38	7	13	.350	93	4.01	208 2/3	164	81	190	20	2	2	0
1971	Cal-A	31	32	11	12	.478	70	3.02	208 1/3	156	87	160	12	7	2	0
1972	Cal-A	30	35	12	11	.522	67	2.94	205 1/3	169	82	162	15	10	3	1
1973	Cal-A	28	34	7	17	.292	90	4.38	185	134	80	177	20	10	4	0
1974	Cal-A	3	18	0	1	.000	21	7.00	27	12	10	29	2	0	0	2
1974	**NY-A**	**15**	**17**	**8**	**4**	**.667**	**29**	**2.28**	**114 1/3**	**90**	**48**	**75**	**5**	**8**	**2**	**0**
1975	**NY-A**	**31**	**32**	**14**	**12**	**.538**	**72**	**3.06**	**212**	**145**	**99**	**179**	**9**	**13**	**1**	**0**
1976	**NY-A**	**11**	**11**	**4**	**3**	**.571**	**27**	**3.57**	**68**	**38**	**28**	**49**	**5**	**2**	**1**	**0**
1976	Bal-A	21	24	11	7	.611	64	3.78	152 1/3	71	42	156	11	5	1	0
1977	Bal-A	37	37	18	14	.563	101	3.61	251 2/3	105	78	243	25	11	4	0
1978	Mon-N	23	27	8	10	.444	62	3.88	144	87	42	141	15	4	1	0
1979	Mon-N	7	33	10	3	.769	24	2.31	93 2/3	67	31	88	4	2	1	0
1980	**NY-A**	**17**	**41**	**15**	**5**	**.750**	**48**	**2.46**	**175 1/3**	**133**	**39**	**144**	**14**	**3**	**1**	**3**
1981	**NY-A**	**22**	**27**	**6**	**11**	**.353**	**68**	**4.14**	**147 2/3**	**79**	**41**	**137**	**10**	**4**	**0**	**1**
1982	**NY-A**	**6**	**41**	**6**	**6**	**.500**	**34**	**2.89**	**106**	**85**	**14**	**109**	**4**	**0**	**0**	**3**
1983	**NY-A**	**0**	**15**	**1**	**5**	**.167**	**14**	**6.87**	**18 1/3**	**16**	**12**	**22**	**1**	**0**	**0**	**0**

Career Average	20	30	8	9	.494	56	3.46	146	98	53	129	11	5	1	1
Yankee Average	**15**	**26**	**8**	**7**	**.540**	**42**	**3.12**	**120**	**84**	**40**	**102**	**7**	**4**	**1**	**1**
Career Total	360	535	152	156	.494	1007	3.46	2622	1760	958	2314	199	87	24	12
Yankee Total	**102**	**184**	**54**	**46**	**.540**	**292**	**3.12**	**841 2/3**	**586**	**281**	**715**	**48**	**30**	**5**	**7**

Mays, Carl William (Sub)

HEIGHT: 5'11"   RIGHTHANDER   BORN: 11/12/1891 LIBERTY, KENTUCKY   DIED: 4/4/1971 ELCAJON, CALIFORNIA

YEAR	TEAM	STARTS	GAMES	WON	LOST	PCT	ER	ERA	INNINGS PITCHED	STRIKE-OUTS	WALKS	HITS ALLOWED	HRS ALLOWED	COMP. GAMES	SHUT-OUTS	SAVES
1915	Bos-A	6	38	6	5	.545	38	2.60	131 2/3	65	21	119	0	2	0	7
1916	Bos-A	24	44	18	13	.581	65	2.39	245	76	74	208	3	14	2	3
1917	Bos-A	33	35	22	9	.710	56	1.74	289	91	74	230	1	27	2	0
1918	Bos-A	33	35	21	13	.618	72	2.21	293 1/3	114	81	230	2	30	8	0
1919	Bos-A	16	21	5	11	.313	40	2.47	146	53	40	131	3	14	2	2
1919	**NY-A**	**13**	**13**	**9**	**3**	**.750**	**22**	**1.65**	**120**	**54**	**37**	**96**	**2**	**12**	**1**	**0**
1920	**NY-A**	**37**	**45**	**26**	**11**	**.703**	**106**	**3.06**	**312**	**92**	**84**	**310**	**13**	**26**	**6**	**2**
1921	**NY-A**	**38**	**49**	**27**	**9**	**.750**	**114**	**3.05**	**336 2/3**	**70**	**76**	**332**	**11**	**30**	**1**	**7**
1922	**NY-A**	**29**	**34**	**12**	**14**	**.462**	**96**	**3.60**	**240**	**41**	**50**	**257**	**12**	**21**	**1**	**2**
1923	**NY-A**	**7**	**23**	**5**	**2**	**.714**	**56**	**6.20**	**81 1/3**	**16**	**32**	**119**	**8**	**2**	**0**	**0**
1924	Cin-N	27	37	20	9	.690	79	3.15	226	63	36	238	3	15	2	0
1925	Cin-N	5	12	3	5	.375	19	3.31	51 2/3	10	13	60	0	3	0	2
1926	Cin-N	33	39	19	12	.613	98	3.14	281	58	53	286	3	24	3	1
1927	Cin-N	9	14	3	7	.300	32	3.51	82	17	10	89	1	6	0	0
1928	Cin-N	7	14	4	1	.800	27	3.88	62 2/3	10	22	67	3	4	1	1
1929	NY-N	8	37	7	2	.778	59	4.32	123	32	31	140	8	1	0	4

Career Average	20	31	13	8	.622	61	2.92	189	54	46	182	5	14	2	2
Yankee Average	**25**	**33**	**16**	**8**	**.669**	**79**	**3.25**	**218**	**55**	**56**	**223**	**9**	**18**	**2**	**2**
Career Total	325	490	207	126	.622	979	2.92	3021 1/3	862	734	2912	73	231	29	31
Yankee Total	**124**	**164**	**79**	**39**	**.669**	**394**	**3.25**	**1090**	**273**	**279**	**1114**	**46**	**91**	**9**	**11**

Carl William "Sub" Mays, rhp, 1919–1923

Carl Mays never denied that he enjoyed throwing at batters. But ironically, the beaning for which he became most notorious, in 1920, was probably an accident.

Mays, born November 12, 1891, in Liberty, Kentucky, was another of those Boston to New York robberies of the years just prior to 1920. After a stellar 4½ year career with the Red Sox, Mays was traded to New York for journeymen pitchers Allan Russell and Bobby McGraw and $40,000.

Mays picked up in New York where he left off in Boston in 1919, winning nine of his 13 starts and leading the staff with a 1.93 ERA.

In 1920, Mays was 26-11, with a league-leading six shutouts. Mays delivered the ball in what is called today a "submarine" throw. That is, the ball came to a batter from below his waist. Sometimes, Mays actually scraped his knuckles on the pitcher's mound when he threw.

On August 16, 1920, Mays was pitching to Cleveland shortstop Ray Chapman. Chapman, leading off the inning, was leaning over the plate, as was his habit. Mays's submarine curve ball, coming in at a different angle than Chapman expected, confused the shortstop and he froze. Chapman may have not even seen the pitch. The ball struck him in the temple. Chapman died twenty-four hours later.

Mays denied intentionally hitting Chapman, and he was probably telling the truth. The situation (leadoff batter, start of the inning) is not a scenario in which a pitcher would tend to throw at a batter. Still, Mays was roundly criticized for his action.

It didn't seem to affect him. He shut out Detroit, 10-0, in his next start, and was second in the league in wins. The next year, he won a league-leading 27 games. In all, Mays was 79-39 with New York, with 11 shutouts and nine saves.

But he was a dour man, a loner and quick to criticize his teammates for a fielding gaffe. In 1924, after an injury-filled season, Mays was sold to Cincinnati. Few Yankees mourned the deal. He retired in 1929 and died in 1971 in California. He remains fifth all-time on the Yankees in winning percentage at .669.

McCall, Larry Stephen
HEIGHT: 6'2" RIGHTHANDER BORN: 9/8/1952 ASHEVILLE, NORTH CAROLINA

YEAR	TEAM	STARTS	GAMES	WON	LOST	PCT	ER	ERA	INNINGS PITCHED	STRIKE-OUTS	WALKS	HITS ALLOWED	HRS ALLOWED	COMP. GAMES	SHUT-OUTS	SAVES
1977	NY-A	0	2	0	1	.000	5	7.50	6	0	1	12	1	0	0	0
1978	NY-A	1	5	1	1	.500	10	5.63	16	7	6	20	2	0	0	0
1979	Tex-A	1	2	1	0	1.000	2	2.16	8 ⅓	3	3	7	0	0	0	0
Career Average		1	3	1	1	.500	6	5.04	10	3	3	13	1	0	0	0
Yankee Average		**1**	**4**	**1**	**1**	**.333**	**8**	**6.14**	**11**	**4**	**4**	**16**	**2**	**0**	**0**	**0**
Career Total		2	9	2	2	.500	17	5.04	30 ⅓	10	10	39	3	0	0	0
Yankee Total		**1**	**7**	**1**	**2**	**.333**	**15**	**6.14**	**22**	**7**	**7**	**32**	**3**	**0**	**0**	**0**

McConnell, George Neely
HEIGHT: 6'3" RIGHTHANDER BORN: 9/16/1877 SHELBYVILLE, TENNESSEE DIED: 5/10/1964 CHATTANOOGA, TENNESSEE

YEAR	TEAM	STARTS	GAMES	WON	LOST	PCT	ER	ERA	INNINGS PITCHED	STRIKE-OUTS	WALKS	HITS ALLOWED	HRS ALLOWED	COMP. GAMES	SHUT-OUTS	SAVES
1909	NY-A	1	2	0	1	.000	1	2.25	4	4	3	3	0	0	0	0
1912	NY-A	20	23	8	12	.400	54	2.75	176 ⅔	91	52	172	3	19	0	0
1913	NY-A	20	35	4	15	.211	64	3.20	180	72	60	162	2	8	0	3
1914	Chi-N	1	1	0	1	.000	1	1.29	7	3	3	3	0	0	0	0

(continued)

(continued)

1915	Chi-F	35	44	25	10	.714	74	2.20	303	151	89	262	8	23	4	1
1916	Chi-N	21	28	4	12	.250	49	2.57	171 1/3	82	35	137	8	8	1	0
Career Average		16	22	7	9	.446	41	2.60	140	67	40	123	4	10	1	1
Yankee Average		**14**	**20**	**4**	**9**	**.300**	**40**	**2.97**	**120**	**56**	**38**	**112**	**2**	**9**	**0**	**1**
Career Total		98	133	41	51	.446	243	2.60	842	403	242	739	21	58	5	4
Yankee Total		**41**	**60**	**12**	**28**	**.300**	**119**	**2.97**	**360 2/3**	**167**	**115**	**337**	**5**	**27**	**0**	**3**

McCormick, Michael Francis

HEIGHT: 6'2"   LEFTHANDER   BORN: 9/29/1938 PASADENA, CALIFORNIA

YEAR	TEAM	STARTS	GAMES	WON	LOST	PCT	ER	ERA	INNINGS PITCHED	STRIKE-OUTS	WALKS	HITS ALLOWED	HRS ALLOWED	COMP. GAMES	SHUT-OUTS	SAVES
1956	NY-N	2	3	0	1	.000	7	9.45	6 2/3	4	10	7	1	0	0	0
1957	NY-N	5	24	3	1	.750	34	4.10	74 2/3	50	32	79	7	1	0	0
1958	SF-N	28	42	11	8	.579	91	4.59	178 1/3	82	60	192	19	8	2	1
1959	SF-N	31	47	12	16	.429	100	3.99	225 2/3	151	86	213	24	7	3	4
1960	SF-N	34	40	15	12	.556	76	2.70	253	154	65	228	15	15	4	3
1961	SF-N	35	40	13	16	.448	89	3.20	250	163	75	235	33	13	3	0
1962	SF-N	15	28	5	5	.500	59	5.38	98 2/3	42	45	112	18	1	0	0
1963	Bal-A	21	25	6	8	.429	65	4.30	136	75	66	132	18	2	0	0
1964	Bal-A	2	4	0	2	.000	10	5.19	17 1/3	13	8	21	1	0	0	0
1965	Was-A	21	44	8	8	.500	59	3.36	158	88	36	158	17	3	1	1
1966	Was-A	32	41	11	14	.440	83	3.46	216	101	51	193	23	8	3	0
1967	SF-N	35	40	22	10	.688	83	2.85	262 1/3	150	81	220	25	14	5	0
1968	SF-N	28	38	12	14	.462	79	3.58	198 1/3	121	49	196	17	9	2	1
1969	SF-N	28	32	11	9	.550	73	3.34	196 2/3	76	77	175	20	9	0	0
1970	SF-N	11	23	3	4	.429	54	6.20	78 1/3	37	36	80	15	1	0	2
1970	**NY-A**	**4**	**9**	**2**	**0**	**1.000**	**14**	**6.10**	**20 2/3**	**12**	**13**	**26**	**2**	**0**	**0**	**0**
1971	KC-A	1	4	0	0	—	10	9.31	9 2/3	2	5	14	0	0	0	0
Career Average		20	28	8	8	.511	58	3.73	140	78	47	134	15	5	1	1
Yankee Average		**4**	**9**	**2**	**0**	**1.000**	**14**	**6.10**	**20 2/3**	**12**	**13**	**26**	**2**	**0**	**0**	**0**
Career Total		333	484	134	128	.511	986	3.73	2380 1/3	1321	795	2281	255	91	23	12
Yankee Total		**4**	**9**	**2**	**0**	**1.000**	**14**	**6.10**	**20 2/3**	**12**	**13**	**26**	**2**	**0**	**0**	**0**

McCullers, Lance Graye

HEIGHT: 6'1"   RIGHTHANDER   BORN: 3/8/1964 TAMPA, FLORIDA

YEAR	TEAM	STARTS	GAMES	WON	LOST	PCT	ER	ERA	INNINGS PITCHED	STRIKE-OUTS	WALKS	HITS ALLOWED	HRS ALLOWED	COMP. GAMES	SHUT-OUTS	SAVES
1985	SD-N	0	21	0	2	.000	9	2.31	35	27	16	23	3	0	0	5
1986	SD-N	7	70	10	10	.500	42	2.78	136	92	58	103	12	0	0	5
1987	SD-N	0	78	8	10	.444	51	3.72	123 1/3	126	59	115	11	0	0	16
1988	SD-N	0	60	3	6	.333	27	2.49	97 2/3	81	55	70	8	0	0	10
1989	**NY-A**	**1**	**52**	**4**	**3**	**.571**	**43**	**4.57**	**84 2/3**	**82**	**37**	**83**	**9**	**0**	**0**	**3**
1990	**NY-A**	**0**	**11**	**1**	**0**	**1.000**	**6**	**3.60**	**15**	**11**	**6**	**14**	**2**	**0**	**0**	**0**
1990	Det-A	1	9	1	0	1.000	9	2.73	29 2/3	20	13	18	2	0	0	0
1992	Tex-A	0	5	1	0	1.000	3	5.40	5	3	8	1	0	0	0	0
Career Average		1	38	4	4	.475	24	3.25	66	55	32	53	6	0	0	5
Yankee Average		**1**	**32**	**3**	**2**	**.625**	**25**	**4.42**	**50**	**47**	**22**	**49**	**6**	**0**	**0**	**2**
Career Total		9	306	28	31	.475	190	3.25	526 1/3	442	252	427	47	0	0	39
Yankee Total		**1**	**63**	**5**	**3**	**.625**	**49**	**4.42**	**99 2/3**	**93**	**43**	**97**	**11**	**0**	**0**	**3**

McDaniel, Lyndall Dale (Lindy)

HEIGHT: 6'3"   RIGHTHANDER   BORN: 12/13/1935 HOLLIS, OKLAHOMA

YEAR	TEAM	STARTS	GAMES	WON	LOST	PCT	ER	ERA	INNINGS PITCHED	STRIKE-OUTS	WALKS	HITS ALLOWED	HRS ALLOWED	COMP. GAMES	SHUT-OUTS	SAVES
1955	StL-N	2	4	0	0	—	10	4.74	19	7	7	22	4	0	0	0
1956	StL-N	7	39	7	6	.538	44	3.40	116 1/3	59	42	121	7	1	0	0
1957	StL-N	26	30	15	9	.625	74	3.49	191	75	53	196	13	10	1	0
1958	StL-N	17	26	5	7	.417	70	5.80	108 2/3	47	31	139	17	2	1	0
1959	StL-N	7	62	14	12	.538	56	3.82	132	86	41	144	11	1	0	15

(continued)

(continued)

YEAR	TEAM	STARTS	GAMES	WON	LOST	PCT	ER	ERA	INNINGS PITCHED	STRIKE-OUTS	WALKS	HITS ALLOWED	HRS ALLOWED	COMP. GAMES	SHUT-OUTS	SAVES
1960	StL-N	2	65	12	4	.750	27	2.09	116⅓	105	24	85	8	1	0	26
1961	StL-N	0	55	10	6	.625	51	4.87	94⅓	65	31	117	11	0	0	9
1962	StL-N	2	55	3	10	.231	49	4.12	107	79	29	96	12	0	0	14
1963	Chi-N	0	57	13	7	.650	28	2.86	88	75	27	82	9	0	0	22
1964	Chi-N	0	63	1	7	.125	41	3.88	95	71	23	104	4	0	0	15
1965	Chi-N	0	71	5	6	.455	37	2.59	128⅔	92	47	115	12	0	0	2
1966	SF-N	0	64	10	5	.667	36	2.66	121⅔	93	35	103	5	0	0	6
1967	SF-N	3	41	2	6	.250	30	3.72	72⅔	48	24	69	5	0	0	3
1968	SF-N	0	12	0	0	—	16	7.45	19⅓	9	5	30	2	0	0	0
1968	**NY-A**	**0**	**24**	**4**	**1**	**.800**	**10**	**1.75**	**51⅓**	**43**	**12**	**30**	**5**	**0**	**0**	**10**
1969	**NY-A**	**0**	**51**	**5**	**6**	**.455**	**33**	**3.55**	**83⅔**	**60**	**23**	**84**	**4**	**0**	**0**	**5**
1970	**NY-A**	**0**	**62**	**9**	**5**	**.643**	**25**	**2.01**	**111⅔**	**81**	**23**	**88**	**7**	**0**	**0**	**29**
1971	**NY-A**	**0**	**44**	**5**	**10**	**.333**	**39**	**5.04**	**69⅔**	**39**	**24**	**82**	**12**	**0**	**0**	**4**
1972	**NY-A**	**0**	**37**	**3**	**1**	**.750**	**17**	**2.25**	**68**	**47**	**25**	**54**	**4**	**0**	**0**	**0**
1973	**NY-A**	**3**	**47**	**12**	**6**	**.667**	**51**	**2.86**	**160⅓**	**93**	**49**	**148**	**11**	**1**	**0**	**10**
1974	KC-A	5	38	1	4	.200	41	3.46	106⅔	47	24	109	6	2	0	1
1975	KC-A	0	40	5	1	.833	36	4.15	78	40	24	81	3	0	0	1
Career Average		3	45	6	5	.542	37	3.45	97	62	28	95	8	1	0	8
Yankee Average		**1**	**44**	**6**	**5**	**.567**	**29**	**2.89**	**90**	**61**	**26**	**81**	**7**	**0**	**0**	**10**
Career Total		74	987	141	119	.542	821	3.45	2139⅓	1361	623	2099	172	18	2	172
Yankee Total		**3**	**265**	**38**	**29**	**.567**	**175**	**2.89**	**544⅔**	**363**	**156**	**486**	**43**	**1**	**0**	**58**

McDermott, Maurice Joseph (Mickey)

HEIGHT: 6'2" LEFTHANDER BORN: 4/29/1928 POUGHKEEPSIE, NEW YORK

YEAR	TEAM	STARTS	GAMES	WON	LOST	PCT	ER	ERA	INNINGS PITCHED	STRIKE-OUTS	WALKS	HITS ALLOWED	HRS ALLOWED	COMP. GAMES	SHUT-OUTS	SAVES
1948	Bos-A	0	7	0	0	—	16	6.17	23⅓	17	35	16	2	0	0	0
1949	Bos-A	12	12	5	4	.556	36	4.05	80	50	52	63	5	6	2	0
1950	Bos-A	15	38	7	3	.700	75	5.19	130	96	124	119	8	4	0	5
1951	Bos-A	19	34	8	8	.500	64	3.35	172	127	92	141	10	9	1	3
1952	Bos-A	21	30	10	9	.526	67	3.72	162	117	92	139	14	7	2	0
1953	Bos-A	30	32	18	10	.643	69	3.01	206⅓	92	109	169	9	8	4	0
1954	Was-A	26	30	7	15	.318	75	3.44	196⅓	95	110	172	8	11	1	1
1955	Was-A	20	31	10	10	.500	65	3.75	156	78	100	140	9	8	1	1
1956	**NY-A**	**9**	**23**	**2**	**6**	**.250**	**41**	**4.24**	**87**	**38**	**47**	**85**	**10**	**1**	**0**	**0**
1957	KC-A	4	29	1	4	.200	42	5.48	69	29	50	68	9	0	0	0
1958	Det-A	0	2	0	0	—	2	9.00	2	0	2	6	0	0	0	0
1961	StL-N	0	19	1	0	1.000	11	3.67	27	15	15	29	3	0	0	4
1961	KC-A	0	4	0	0	—	9	14.29	5⅔	3	10	14	0	0	0	0
Career Average		12	22	5	5	.500	44	3.91	101	58	64	89	7	4	1	1
Yankee Average		**9**	**23**	**2**	**6**	**.250**	**41**	**4.24**	**87**	**38**	**47**	**85**	**10**	**1**	**0**	**0**
Career Total		156	291	69	69	.500	572	3.91	1316⅔	757	838	1161	87	54	11	14
Yankee Total		**9**	**23**	**2**	**6**	**.250**	**41**	**4.24**	**87**	**38**	**47**	**85**	**10**	**1**	**0**	**0**

McDevitt, Daniel Eugene

HEIGHT: 5'10" LEFTHANDER BORN: 11/18/1932 NEW YORK, NEW YORK

YEAR	TEAM	STARTS	GAMES	WON	LOST	PCT	ER	ERA	INNINGS PITCHED	STRIKE-OUTS	WALKS	HITS ALLOWED	HRS ALLOWED	COMP. GAMES	SHUT-OUTS	SAVES
1957	Bro-N	17	22	7	4	.636	43	3.25	119	90	72	105	5	5	2	0
1958	LA-N	10	13	2	6	.250	40	7.45	48⅓	26	31	71	6	2	0	0
1959	LA-N	22	39	10	8	.556	64	3.97	145	106	51	149	16	6	2	4
1960	LA-N	7	24	0	4	.000	25	4.25	53	30	42	51	7	0	0	0
1961	**NY-A**	**2**	**8**	**1**	**2**	**.333**	**11**	**7.62**	**13**	**8**	**8**	**18**	**2**	**0**	**0**	**1**
1961	Min-A	1	16	1	0	1.000	7	2.36	26⅔	15	19	20	1	0	0	0
1962	KC-A	1	33	0	3	.000	33	5.82	51	28	41	47	5	0	0	2
Career Average		9	22	3	4	.438	32	4.40	65	43	38	66	6	2	1	1
Yankee Average		**2**	**8**	**1**	**2**	**.333**	**11**	**7.62**	**13**	**8**	**8**	**18**	**2**	**0**	**0**	**1**
Career Total		60	155	21	27	.438	223	4.40	456	303	264	461	42	13	4	7
Yankee Total		**2**	**8**	**1**	**2**	**.333**	**11**	**7.62**	**13**	**8**	**8**	**18**	**2**	**0**	**0**	**1**

McDonald, Jimmie LeRoy (Hot Rod)

HEIGHT: 5'11" RIGHTHANDER BORN: 5/17/1927 GRANTS PASS, OREGON

YEAR	TEAM	STARTS	GAMES	WON	LOST	PCT	ER	ERA	INNINGS PITCHED	STRIKE-OUTS	WALKS	HITS ALLOWED	HRS ALLOWED	COMP. GAMES	SHUT-OUTS	SAVES
1950	Bos-A	0	9	1	0	1.000	8	3.79	19	5	10	23	1	0	0	0
1951	StL-A	11	16	4	7	.364	38	4.07	84	28	46	84	5	5	0	1
1952	**NY-A**	**5**	**26**	**3**	**4**	**.429**	**27**	**3.50**	**69 1/3**	**20**	**40**	**71**	**1**	**1**	**0**	**0**
1953	**NY-A**	**18**	**27**	**9**	**7**	**.563**	**55**	**3.82**	**129 2/3**	**43**	**39**	**128**	**4**	**6**	**2**	**0**
1954	**NY-A**	**10**	**16**	**4**	**1**	**.800**	**25**	**3.17**	**71**	**20**	**45**	**54**	**3**	**3**	**1**	**0**
1955	Bal-A	8	21	3	5	.375	41	7.14	51 2/3	20	30	76	5	0	0	0
1956	Chi-A	3	8	0	2	.000	18	8.68	18 2/3	10	7	29	2	0	0	0
1957	Chi-A	0	10	0	1	.000	5	2.01	22 1/3	12	10	18	2	0	0	0
1958	Chi-A	0	3	0	0	—	5	19.29	2 1/3	0	4	6	1	0	0	0
Career Average		6	15	3	3	.471	25	4.27	52	18	26	54	3	2	0	0
Yankee Average		**11**	**23**	**5**	**4**	**.571**	**36**	**3.57**	**90**	**28**	**41**	**84**	**3**	**3**	**1**	**0**
Career Total		55	136	24	27	.471	222	4.27	468	158	231	489	24	15	3	1
Yankee Total		**33**	**69**	**16**	**12**	**.571**	**107**	**3.57**	**270**	**83**	**124**	**253**	**8**	**10**	**3**	**0**

McDowell, Samuel Edward (Sudden Sam)

HEIGHT: 6'5" LEFTHANDER BORN: 9/21/1942 PITTSBURGH, PENNSYLVANIA

YEAR	TEAM	STARTS	GAMES	WON	LOST	PCT	ER	ERA	INNINGS PITCHED	STRIKE-OUTS	WALKS	HITS ALLOWED	HRS ALLOWED	COMP. GAMES	SHUT-OUTS	SAVES
1961	Cle-A	1	1	0	0	—	0	0.00	6 1/3	5	5	3	0	0	0	0
1962	Cle-A	13	25	3	7	.300	59	6.06	87 2/3	70	70	81	9	0	0	1
1963	Cle-A	12	14	3	5	.375	35	4.85	65	63	44	63	6	3	1	0
1964	Cle-A	24	31	11	6	.647	52	2.70	173 1/3	177	100	148	8	6	2	1
1965	Cle-A	35	42	17	11	.607	66	2.18	273	325	132	178	9	14	3	4
1966	Cle-A	28	35	9	8	.529	62	2.87	194 1/3	225	102	130	12	8	5	3
1967	Cle-A	37	37	13	15	.464	101	3.85	236 1/3	236	123	201	21	10	1	0
1968	Cle-A	37	38	15	14	.517	54	1.81	269	283	110	181	13	11	3	0
1969	Cle-A	38	39	18	14	.563	93	2.94	285	279	102	222	13	18	4	1
1970	Cle-A	39	39	20	12	.625	99	2.92	305	304	131	236	25	19	1	0
1971	Cle-A	31	35	13	17	.433	81	3.40	214 2/3	192	153	160	22	8	2	1
1972	SF-N	25	28	10	8	.556	79	4.33	164 1/3	122	86	155	12	4	0	0
1973	SF-N	3	18	1	2	.333	20	4.50	40	35	29	45	4	0	0	3
1973	**NY-A**	**15**	**16**	**5**	**8**	**.385**	**42**	**3.95**	**95 2/3**	**75**	**64**	**73**	**4**	**2**	**1**	**0**
1974	**NY-A**	**7**	**13**	**1**	**6**	**.143**	**25**	**4.69**	**48**	**33**	**41**	**42**	**6**	**0**	**0**	**0**
1975	Pit-N	1	14	2	1	.667	11	2.86	34 2/3	29	20	30	0	0	0	0
Career Average		22	27	9	8	.513	55	3.17	156	153	82	122	10	6	1	1
Yankee Average		**11**	**15**	**3**	**7**	**.300**	**34**	**4.20**	**72**	**54**	**53**	**58**	**5**	**1**	**1**	**0**
Career Total		346	425	141	134	.513	879	3.17	2492 1/3	2453	1312	1948	164	103	23	14
Yankee Total		**22**	**29**	**6**	**14**	**.300**	**67**	**4.20**	**143 2/3**	**108**	**105**	**115**	**10**	**2**	**1**	**0**

McEvoy, Louis Anthony

HEIGHT: 6'3" RIGHTHANDER BORN: 5/30/1902 WILLIAMSBURG, KANSAS DIED: 12/17/1953 WEBSTER GROVES, MISSOURI

YEAR	TEAM	STARTS	GAMES	WON	LOST	PCT	ER	ERA	INNINGS PITCHED	STRIKE-OUTS	WALKS	HITS ALLOWED	HRS ALLOWED	COMP. GAMES	SHUT-OUTS	SAVES
1930	**NY-A**	**1**	**28**	**1**	**3**	**.250**	**39**	**6.71**	**52 1/3**	**14**	**29**	**64**	**4**	**0**	**0**	**3**
1931	**NY-A**	**0**	**6**	**0**	**0**	**—**	**17**	**12.41**	**12 1/3**	**3**	**12**	**19**	**1**	**0**	**0**	**1**
Career Average		1	17	1	2	.250	28	7.79	32	9	21	42	3	0	0	2
Yankee Average		**1**	**17**	**1**	**2**	**.250**	**28**	**7.79**	**32**	**9**	**21**	**42**	**3**	**0**	**0**	**2**
Career Total		1	34	1	3	.250	56	7.79	64 2/3	17	41	83	5	0	0	4
Yankee Total		**1**	**34**	**1**	**3**	**.250**	**56**	**7.79**	**64 2/3**	**17**	**41**	**83**	**5**	**0**	**0**	**4**

McGaffigan, Andrew Joseph
HEIGHT: 6'3" RIGHTHANDER BORN: 10/25/1956 W. PALM BEACH, FLORIDA

YEAR	TEAM	STARTS	GAMES	WON	LOST	PCT	ER	ERA	INNINGS PITCHED	STRIKE-OUTS	WALKS	HITS ALLOWED	HRS ALLOWED	COMP. GAMES	SHUT-OUTS	SAVES
1981	**NY-A**	**0**	**2**	**0**	**0**	**—**	**2**	**2.57**	**7**	**2**	**3**	**5**	**1**	**0**	**0**	**0**
1982	SF-N	0	4	1	0	1.000	0	0.00	8	4	1	5	0	0	0	0
1983	SF-N	16	43	3	9	.250	64	4.29	134 1/3	93	39	131	17	0	0	2
1984	Mon-N	3	21	3	4	.429	13	2.54	46	39	15	37	2	0	0	1
1984	Cin-N	3	9	0	2	.000	14	5.48	23	18	8	23	2	0	0	0
1985	Cin-N	15	15	3	3	.500	39	3.72	94 1/3	83	30	88	4	2	0	0
1986	Mon-N	14	48	10	5	.667	42	2.65	142 2/3	104	55	114	9	1	1	2
1987	Mon-N	0	69	5	2	.714	32	2.39	120 1/3	100	42	105	5	0	0	12
1988	Mon-N	0	63	6	0	1.000	28	2.76	91 1/3	71	37	81	4	0	0	4
1989	Mon-N	0	57	3	5	.375	39	4.68	75	40	30	85	3	0	0	2
1990	SF-N	0	4	0	0	—	9	17.36	4 2/3	4	4	10	2	0	0	0
1990	KC-A	11	24	4	3	.571	27	3.09	78 2/3	49	28	75	6	0	0	1
1991	KC-A	0	4	0	0	—	4	4.50	8	3	2	14	0	0	0	0
Career Average		5	28	3	3	.535	24	3.38	64	47	23	59	4	0	0	2
Yankee Average		**0**	**2**	**0**	**0**	**—**	**2**	**2.57**	**7**	**2**	**3**	**5**	**1**	**0**	**0**	**0**
Career Total		62	363	38	33	.535	313	3.38	833 1/3	610	294	773	55	3	1	24
Yankee Total		**0**	**2**	**0**	**0**	**—**	**2**	**2.57**	**7**	**2**	**3**	**5**	**1**	**0**	**0**	**0**

McGlothen, Lynn Everett
HEIGHT: 6'2" RIGHTHANDER BORN: 3/27/1950 MONROE, LOUISIANA DIED: 8/14/1984 DUBACH, LOUISIANA

YEAR	TEAM	STARTS	GAMES	WON	LOST	PCT	ER	ERA	INNINGS PITCHED	STRIKE-OUTS	WALKS	HITS ALLOWED	HRS ALLOWED	COMP. GAMES	SHUT-OUTS	SAVES
1972	Bos-A	22	22	8	7	.533	55	3.41	145	112	59	135	9	4	1	0
1973	Bos-A	3	6	1	2	.333	21	8.22	23	16	8	39	6	0	0	0
1974	StL-N	31	31	16	12	.571	71	2.69	237 1/3	142	89	212	12	8	3	0
1975	StL-N	34	35	15	13	.536	104	3.92	239	146	97	231	21	9	2	0
1976	StL-N	32	33	13	15	.464	89	3.91	205	106	68	209	10	10	4	0
1977	SF-N	15	21	2	9	.182	50	5.63	80	42	52	94	9	2	0	0
1978	Chi-N	1	49	5	3	.625	27	3.04	80	60	39	77	7	0	0	0
1978	SF-N	1	5	0	0	—	7	4.97	12 2/3	9	4	15	0	0	0	0
1979	Chi-N	29	42	13	14	.481	97	4.12	212	147	55	236	27	6	1	2
1980	Chi-N	27	39	12	14	.462	97	4.79	182 1/3	119	64	211	24	2	2	0
1981	Chi-N	6	20	1	4	.200	29	4.77	54 2/3	26	28	71	1	0	0	0
1981	Chi-A	0	11	0	0	—	10	4.15	21 2/3	12	7	14	0	0	0	0
1982	**NY-A**	**0**	**4**	**0**	**0**	**—**	**6**	**10.80**	**5**	**2**	**2**	**9**	**1**	**0**	**0**	**0**
Career Average		15	24	7	7	.480	51	3.98	115	72	44	119	10	3	1	0
Yankee Average		**0**	**4**	**0**	**0**	**—**	**6**	**10.80**	**5**	**2**	**2**	**9**	**1**	**0**	**0**	**0**
Career Total		201	318	86	93	.480	663	3.98	1497 2/3	939	572	1553	127	41	13	2
Yankee Total		**0**	**4**	**0**	**0**	**—**	**6**	**10.80**	**5**	**2**	**2**	**9**	**1**	**0**	**0**	**0**

McGraw, Robert Emmett
HEIGHT: 6'2" RIGHTHANDER BORN: 4/10/1895 LAVETA, COLORADO DIED: 6/2/1978 BOISE, IDAHO

YEAR	TEAM	STARTS	GAMES	WON	LOST	PCT	ER	ERA	INNINGS PITCHED	STRIKE-OUTS	WALKS	HITS ALLOWED	HRS ALLOWED	COMP. GAMES	SHUT-OUTS	SAVES
1917	**NY-A**	**2**	**2**	**0**	**1**	**.000**	**1**	**0.82**	**11**	**3**	**3**	**9**	**0**	**1**	**0**	**0**
1918	**NY-A**	**1**	**1**	**0**	**1**	**.000**	**4**	**—**	**0**	**0**	**4**	**0**	**0**	**0**	**0**	**0**
1919	**NY-A**	**0**	**6**	**1**	**0**	**1.000**	**6**	**3.31**	**16 1/3**	**3**	**10**	**11**	**1**	**0**	**0**	**0**
1919	Bos-A	1	10	0	2	.000	20	6.75	26 2/3	6	17	33	0	0	0	0
1920	**NY-A**	**0**	**15**	**0**	**0**	**—**	**14**	**4.67**	**27**	**11**	**20**	**24**	**1**	**0**	**0**	**0**
1925	Bro-N	2	2	0	2	.000	7	3.20	19 2/3	3	13	14	0	2	0	0
1926	Bro-N	21	33	9	13	.409	89	4.59	174 1/3	49	67	197	12	10	0	1
1927	Bro-N	1	1	0	1	.000	4	9.00	4	2	2	5	1	0	0	0
1927	StL-N	12	18	4	5	.444	53	5.07	94	37	30	121	3	4	1	0
1928	Phi-N	3	39	7	8	.467	68	4.64	132	28	56	148	7	0	0	1
1929	Phi-N	4	41	5	5	.500	55	5.73	86 1/3	22	43	113	6	0	0	4
Career Average		4	15	2	3	.406	29	4.82	54	15	24	62	3	2	0	1
Yankee Average		**1**	**6**	**0**	**1**	**.333**	**5**	**3.48**	**14**	**4**	**9**	**11**	**1**	**0**	**0**	**0**
Career Total		47	168	26	38	.406	321	4.89	591 1/3	164	265	675	31	17	1	6
Yankee Total		**3**	**24**	**1**	**2**	**.333**	**21**	**3.48**	**54 1/3**	**17**	**37**	**44**	**2**	**1**	**0**	**0**

McHale, Martin Joseph

HEIGHT: 5'11"   RIGHTHANDER   BORN: 10/30/1888 STONEHAM, MASSACHUSETTS   DIED: 5/7/1979 HEMPSTEAD, NEW YORK

YEAR	TEAM	STARTS	GAMES	WON	LOST	PCT	ER	ERA	INNINGS PITCHED	STRIKE-OUTS	WALKS	HITS ALLOWED	HRS ALLOWED	COMP. GAMES	SHUT-OUTS	SAVES
1910	Bos-A	2	2	0	2	.000	7	4.61	13 2/3	14	6	15	0	1	0	0
1911	Bos-A	1	4	0	0	—	10	9.64	9 1/3	3	3	19	1	0	0	0
1913	**NY-A**	6	7	2	4	.333	16	2.96	48 2/3	11	10	49	1	4	1	0
1914	**NY-A**	23	31	7	16	.304	63	2.97	191	75	33	195	3	12	0	1
1915	**NY-A**	11	13	3	7	.300	37	4.25	78 1/3	25	19	86	1	6	0	0
1916	Bos-A	1	2	0	1	.000	2	3.00	6	1	4	7	0	0	0	0
1916	Cle-A	0	5	0	0	—	7	5.56	11 1/3	2	6	10	1	0	0	0
Career Average		6	9	2	4	.286	20	3.57	51	19	12	54	1	3	0	0
Yankee Average		13	17	4	9	.308	39	3.28	106	37	21	110	2	7	0	0
Career Total		44	64	12	30	.286	142	3.57	358 1/3	131	81	381	7	23	1	1
Yankee Total		40	51	12	27	.308	116	3.28	318	111	62	330	5	22	1	1

McQuaid, Herbert George

HEIGHT: 6'2"   RIGHTHANDER   BORN: 3/29/1899 SAN FRANCISCO, CALIFORNIA   DIED: 4/4/1966 RICHMOND, CALIFORNIA

YEAR	TEAM	STARTS	GAMES	WON	LOST	PCT	ER	ERA	INNINGS PITCHED	STRIKE-OUTS	WALKS	HITS ALLOWED	HRS ALLOWED	COMP. GAMES	SHUT-OUTS	SAVES
1923	Cin-N	1	12	1	0	1.000	9	2.36	34 1/3	9	10	31	0	0	0	0
1926	**NY-A**	1	17	1	0	1.000	26	6.10	38 1/3	6	13	48	5	0	0	0
Career Average		1	15	1	0	1.000	18	4.33	36	8	12	40	3	0	0	0
Yankee Average		1	17	1	0	1.000	26	6.10	38 1/3	6	13	48	5	0	0	0
Career Total		2	29	2	0	1.000	35	4.33	72 2/3	15	23	79	5	0	0	0
Yankee Total		1	17	1	0	1.000	26	6.10	38 1/3	6	13	48	5	0	0	0

Mecir, James Jason

HEIGHT: 6'1"   RIGHTHANDER   BORN: 5/16/1970 QUEENS, NEW YORK

YEAR	TEAM	STARTS	GAMES	WON	LOST	PCT	ER	ERA	INNINGS PITCHED	STRIKE-OUTS	WALKS	HITS ALLOWED	HRS ALLOWED	COMP. GAMES	SHUT-OUTS	SAVES
1995	Sea-A	0	2	0	0	—	0	0.00	4 2/3	3	2	5	0	0	0	0
1996	**NY-A**	0	26	1	1	.500	23	5.13	40 1/3	38	23	42	6	0	0	0
1997	**NY-A**	0	25	0	4	.000	22	5.88	33 2/3	25	10	36	5	0	0	0
1998	TB-A	0	68	7	2	.778	29	3.11	84	77	33	68	6	0	0	0
1999	TB-A	0	17	0	1	.000	6	2.61	20 2/3	15	14	15	0	0	0	0
2000	TB-A	0	38	7	2	.778	17	3.08	49 2/3	33	22	35	2	0	0	1
2000	Oak-A	0	25	3	1	.750	11	2.80	35 1/3	37	14	35	2	0	0	4
Career Average		0	29	3	2	.621	15	3.62	38	33	17	34	3	0	0	1
Yankee Average		0	26	1	3	.167	23	5.47	37	32	17	39	6	0	0	0
Career Total		0	201	18	11	.621	108	3.62	268 1/3	228	118	236	21	0	0	5
Yankee Total		0	51	1	5	.167	45	5.47	74	63	33	78	11	0	0	0

Medich, George Francis (Doc)

HEIGHT: 6'5"   RIGHTHANDER   BORN: 12/9/1948 ALIQUIPPA, PENNSYLVANIA

YEAR	TEAM	STARTS	GAMES	WON	LOST	PCT	ER	ERA	INNINGS PITCHED	STRIKE-OUTS	WALKS	HITS ALLOWED	HRS ALLOWED	COMP. GAMES	SHUT-OUTS	SAVES
1972	**NY-A**	1	1	0	0	—	2	—	0	0	2	2	0	0	0	0
1973	**NY-A**	32	34	14	9	.609	77	2.95	235	145	74	217	20	11	3	0
1974	**NY-A**	38	38	19	15	.559	112	3.60	279 2/3	154	91	275	24	17	4	0
1975	**NY-A**	37	38	16	16	.500	106	3.50	272 1/3	132	72	271	25	15	2	0
1976	Pit-N	26	29	8	11	.421	70	3.52	179	86	48	193	10	3	0	0
1977	Oak-A	25	26	10	6	.625	77	4.69	147 2/3	74	49	155	19	1	0	0
1977	Sea-A	3	3	2	0	1.000	9	3.63	22 1/3	3	4	26	1	1	0	0
1977	NY-N	1	1	0	1	.000	3	3.86	7	3	1	6	0	0	0	0
1978	Tex-A	22	28	9	8	.529	71	3.74	171	71	52	166	10	6	2	2
1979	Tex-A	19	29	10	7	.588	69	4.17	149	58	49	156	9	4	1	0
1980	Tex-A	32	34	14	11	.560	89	3.92	204 1/3	91	56	230	13	6	0	0
1981	Tex-A	20	20	10	6	.625	49	3.08	143 1/3	65	33	136	8	4	4	0

(continued)

(continued)

YEAR	TEAM	STARTS	GAMES	WON	LOST	PCT	ER	ERA	INNINGS PITCHED	STRIKE-OUTS	WALKS	HITS ALLOWED	HRS ALLOWED	COMP. GAMES	SHUT-OUTS	SAVES
1982	Tex-A	21	21	7	11	.389	69	5.06	122 2/3	37	61	146	8	2	0	0
1982	Mil-A	10	10	5	4	.556	35	5.00	63	36	32	57	4	1	0	0
Career Average		21	22	9	8	.541	60	3.77	143	68	45	145	11	5	1	0
Yankee Average		**27**	**28**	**12**	**10**	**.551**	**74**	**3.37**	**197**	**108**	**60**	**191**	**17**	**11**	**2**	**0**
Career Total		287	312	124	105	.541	838	3.78	1996 1/3	955	624	2036	151	71	16	2
Yankee Total		**108**	**111**	**49**	**40**	**.551**	**295**	**3.37**	**787**	**431**	**239**	**765**	**69**	**43**	**9**	**0**

Mendoza, Ramiro

HEIGHT: 6'2" RIGHTHANDER BORN: 6/15/1972 LOS SANTOS, PANAMA

YEAR	TEAM	STARTS	GAMES	WON	LOST	PCT	ER	ERA	INNINGS PITCHED	STRIKE-OUTS	WALKS	HITS ALLOWED	HRS ALLOWED	COMP. GAMES	SHUT-OUTS	SAVES
1996	NY-A	11	12	4	5	.444	40	6.79	53	34	10	80	5	0	0	0
1997	NY-A	15	39	8	6	.571	63	4.24	133 2/3	82	28	157	15	0	0	2
1998	NY-A	14	41	10	2	.833	47	3.25	130 1/3	56	30	131	9	1	1	1
1999	NY-A	6	53	9	9	.500	59	4.29	123 2/3	80	27	141	13	0	0	3
2000	NY-A	9	14	7	4	.636	31	4.25	65 2/3	30	20	66	9	1	1	0
Career Average		11	32	8	5	.594	48	4.27	101	56	23	115	10	0	0	1
Yankee Average		**11**	**32**	**8**	**5**	**.594**	**48**	**4.27**	**101**	**56**	**23**	**115**	**10**	**0**	**0**	**1**
Career Total		55	159	38	26	.594	240	4.27	506 1/3	282	115	575	51	2	2	0
Yankee Total		**55**	**159**	**38**	**26**	**.594**	**240**	**4.27**	**506 1/3**	**282**	**115**	**575**	**51**	**2**	**2**	**0**

Messersmith, John Alexander (Andy)

HEIGHT: 6'1" RIGHTHANDER BORN: 8/6/1945 TOMS RIVER, NEW JERSEY

YEAR	TEAM	STARTS	GAMES	WON	LOST	PCT	ER	ERA	INNINGS PITCHED	STRIKE-OUTS	WALKS	HITS ALLOWED	HRS ALLOWED	COMP. GAMES	SHUT-OUTS	SAVES
1968	Cal-A	5	28	4	2	.667	20	2.21	81 1/3	74	35	44	3	2	1	4
1969	Cal-A	33	40	16	11	.593	70	2.52	250	211	100	169	17	10	2	2
1970	Cal-A	26	37	11	10	.524	65	3.01	194 2/3	162	78	144	21	6	1	5
1971	Cal-A	38	38	20	13	.606	92	2.99	276 2/3	179	121	224	16	14	4	0
1972	Cal-A	21	25	8	11	.421	53	2.81	169 2/3	142	68	125	5	10	3	2
1973	LA-N	33	33	14	10	.583	75	2.70	249 2/3	177	77	196	24	10	3	0
1974	LA-N	39	39	20	6	.769	84	2.59	292 1/3	221	94	227	24	13	3	0
1975	LA-N	40	42	19	14	.576	82	2.29	321 2/3	213	96	244	22	19	7	1
1976	Atl-N	28	29	11	11	.500	70	3.04	207 1/3	135	74	166	14	12	3	1
1977	Atl-N	16	16	5	4	.556	50	4.40	102 1/3	69	39	101	12	1	0	0
1978	**NY-A**	**5**	**6**	**0**	**3**	**.000**	**14**	**5.64**	**22 1/3**	**16**	**15**	**24**	**7**	**0**	**0**	**0**
1979	LA-N	11	11	2	4	.333	34	4.91	62 1/3	26	34	55	9	1	0	0
Career Average		25	29	11	8	.568	59	2.86	186	135	69	143	15	8	2	1
Yankee Average		**5**	**6**	**0**	**3**	**.000**	**14**	**5.64**	**22 1/3**	**16**	**15**	**24**	**7**	**0**	**0**	**0**
Career Total		295	344	130	99	.568	709	2.86	2230 1/3	1625	831	1719	174	98	27	15
Yankee Total		**5**	**6**	**0**	**3**	**.000**	**14**	**5.64**	**22 1/3**	**16**	**15**	**24**	**7**	**0**	**0**	**0**

Metcalf, Thomas John

HEIGHT: 6'3" RIGHTHANDER BORN: 7/16/1940 AMHERST, WISCONSIN

YEAR	TEAM	STARTS	GAMES	WON	LOST	PCT	ER	ERA	INNINGS PITCHED	STRIKE-OUTS	WALKS	HITS ALLOWED	HRS ALLOWED	COMP. GAMES	SHUT-OUTS	SAVES
1963	**NY-A**	**0**	**8**	**1**	**0**	**1.000**	**4**	**2.77**	**13**	**3**	**3**	**12**	**1**	**0**	**0**	**0**
Career Average		0	8	1	0	1.000	4	2.77	13	3	3	12	1	0	0	0
Yankee Average		**0**	**8**	**1**	**0**	**1.000**	**4**	**2.77**	**13**	**3**	**3**	**12**	**1**	**0**	**0**	**0**
Career Total		0	8	1	0	1.000	4	2.77	13	3	3	12	1	0	0	0
Yankee Total		**0**	**8**	**1**	**0**	**1.000**	**4**	**2.77**	**13**	**3**	**3**	**12**	**1**	**0**	**0**	**0**

Meyer, Robert Bernard
HEIGHT: 6'2" LEFTHANDER BORN: 8/4/1939 TOLEDO, OHIO

YEAR	TEAM	STARTS	GAMES	WON	LOST	PCT	ER	ERA	INNINGS PITCHED	STRIKE-OUTS	WALKS	HITS ALLOWED	HRS ALLOWED	COMP. GAMES	SHUT-OUTS	SAVES
1964	**NY-A**	1	7	0	3	.000	10	4.91	18 1/3	12	12	16	1	0	0	0
1964	LA-A	5	6	1	1	.500	10	5.00	18	13	13	25	2	0	0	0
1964	KC-A	7	9	1	4	.200	18	3.86	42	30	33	37	2	2	0	0
1969	Sea-A	5	6	0	3	.000	12	3.31	32 2/3	17	10	30	4	1	0	0
1970	Mil-A	0	10	0	1	.000	13	6.38	18 1/3	20	12	24	3	0	0	0
Career Average		4	8	0	2	.143	13	4.38	26	18	16	26	2	1	0	0
Yankee Average		**1**	**7**	**0**	**3**	**.000**	**10**	**4.91**	**18 1/3**	**12**	**12**	**16**	**1**	**0**	**0**	**0**
Career Total		18	38	2	12	.143	63	4.38	129 1/3	92	80	132	12	3	0	0
Yankee Total		**1**	**7**	**0**	**3**	**.000**	**10**	**4.91**	**18 1/3**	**12**	**12**	**16**	**1**	**0**	**0**	**0**

Michael, Eugene Richard (Stick)
HEIGHT: 6'2" RIGHTHANDER BORN: 6/2/1938 KENT, OHIO

YEAR	TEAM	STARTS	GAMES	WON	LOST	PCT	ER	ERA	INNINGS PITCHED	STRIKE-OUTS	WALKS	HITS ALLOWED	HRS ALLOWED	COMP. GAMES	SHUT-OUTS	SAVES
1968	**NY-A**	0	1	0	0	—	0	0.00	3	3	0	5	0	0	0	0
Career Average		0	1	0	0	—	0	0.00	3	3	0	5	0	0	0	0
Yankee Average		**0**	**1**	**0**	**0**	**—**	**0**	**0.00**	**3**	**3**	**0**	**5**	**0**	**0**	**0**	**0**
Career Total		0	1	0	0	—	0	0.00	3	3	0	5	0	0	0	0
Yankee Total		**0**	**1**	**0**	**0**	**—**	**0**	**0.00**	**3**	**3**	**0**	**5**	**0**	**0**	**0**	**0**

Mikkelsen, Peter James
HEIGHT: 6'2" RIGHTHANDER BORN: 10/25/1939 STATEN ISLAND, NEW YORK

YEAR	TEAM	STARTS	GAMES	WON	LOST	PCT	ER	ERA	INNINGS PITCHED	STRIKE-OUTS	WALKS	HITS ALLOWED	HRS ALLOWED	COMP. GAMES	SHUT-OUTS	SAVES
1964	**NY-A**	0	50	7	4	.636	34	3.56	86	63	41	79	3	0	0	12
1965	**NY-A**	3	41	4	9	.308	30	3.28	82 1/3	69	36	78	10	0	0	1
1966	Pit-N	0	71	9	8	.529	43	3.07	126	76	51	106	8	0	0	14
1967	Pit-N	0	32	1	2	.333	27	4.31	56 1/3	30	19	50	7	0	0	2
1967	Chi-N	0	7	0	0	—	5	6.43	7	0	5	9	1	0	0	0
1968	Chi-N	0	3	0	0	—	4	7.71	4 2/3	5	1	7	3	0	0	0
1968	StL-N	0	5	0	0	—	2	1.13	16	8	7	10	0	0	0	0
1969	LA-N	0	48	7	5	.583	25	2.77	81 1/3	51	30	57	9	0	0	4
1970	LA-N	0	33	4	2	.667	19	2.76	62	47	20	48	5	0	0	6
1971	LA-N	0	41	8	5	.615	30	3.65	74	46	17	67	10	0	0	5
1972	LA-N	0	33	5	5	.500	26	4.06	57 2/3	41	23	65	3	0	0	5
Career Average		0	33	4	4	.529	22	3.38	59	40	23	52	5	0	0	4
Yankee Average		**2**	**46**	**6**	**7**	**.458**	**32**	**3.42**	**84**	**66**	**39**	**79**	**7**	**0**	**0**	**7**
Career Total		3	364	45	40	.529	245	3.38	653 1/3	436	250	576	59	0	0	49
Yankee Total		**3**	**91**	**11**	**13**	**.458**	**64**	**3.42**	**168 1/3**	**132**	**77**	**157**	**13**	**0**	**0**	**13**

Militello, Sam Salvatore
HEIGHT: 6'3" RIGHTHANDER BORN: 11/26/1969 TAMPA, FLORIDA

YEAR	TEAM	STARTS	GAMES	WON	LOST	PCT	ER	ERA	INNINGS PITCHED	STRIKE-OUTS	WALKS	HITS ALLOWED	HRS ALLOWED	COMP. GAMES	SHUT-OUTS	SAVES
1992	**NY-A**	9	9	3	3	.500	23	3.45	60	42	32	43	6	0	0	0
1993	**NY-A**	2	3	1	1	.500	7	6.75	9 1/3	5	7	10	1	0	0	0
Career Average		6	6	2	2	.500	15	3.89	35	24	20	27	4	0	0	0
Yankee Average		**6**	**6**	**2**	**2**	**.500**	**15**	**3.89**	**35**	**24**	**20**	**27**	**4**	**0**	**0**	**0**
Career Total		11	12	4	4	.500	30	3.89	69 1/3	47	39	53	7	0	0	0
Yankee Total		**11**	**12**	**4**	**4**	**.500**	**30**	**3.89**	**69 1/3**	**47**	**39**	**53**	**7**	**0**	**0**	**0**

Miller, William Paul (Hooks)

HEIGHT: 6'0"   LEFTHANDER   BORN: 7/26/1927 MINERSVILLE, PENNSYLVANIA

YEAR	TEAM	STARTS	GAMES	WON	LOST	PCT	ER	ERA	INNINGS PITCHED	STRIKE-OUTS	WALKS	HITS ALLOWED	HRS ALLOWED	COMP. GAMES	SHUT-OUTS	SAVES
1952	NY-A	13	21	4	6	.400	34	3.48	88	45	49	78	4	5	2	0
1953	NY-A	3	13	2	1	.667	18	4.76	34	17	19	46	3	0	0	1
1954	NY-A	1	2	0	1	.000	4	6.35	5 2/3	6	1	9	0	0	0	0
1955	Bal-A	1	5	0	1	.000	6	13.50	4	4	10	3	0	0	0	0
Career Average		5	10	2	2	.400	16	4.24	33	18	20	34	2	1	1	0
Yankee Average		6	12	2	3	.429	19	3.95	43	23	23	44	2	2	1	0
Career Total		18	41	6	9	.400	62	4.24	131 2/3	72	79	136	7	5	2	1
Yankee Total		17	36	6	8	.429	56	3.95	127 2/3	68	69	133	7	5	2	1

Mills, Alan Bernard

HEIGHT: 6'1"   RIGHTHANDER   BORN: 10/18/1966 LAKELAND, FLORIDA

YEAR	TEAM	STARTS	GAMES	WON	LOST	PCT	ER	ERA	INNINGS PITCHED	STRIKE-OUTS	WALKS	HITS ALLOWED	HRS ALLOWED	COMP. GAMES	SHUT-OUTS	SAVES
1990	NY-A	0	36	1	5	.167	19	4.10	41 2/3	24	33	48	4	0	0	0
1991	NY-A	2	6	1	1	.500	8	4.41	16 1/3	11	8	16	1	0	0	0
1992	Bal-A	3	35	10	4	.714	30	2.61	103 1/3	60	54	78	5	0	0	2
1993	Bal-A	0	45	5	4	.556	36	3.23	100 1/3	68	51	80	14	0	0	4
1994	Bal-A	0	47	3	3	.500	26	5.16	45 1/3	44	24	43	7	0	0	2
1995	Bal-A	0	21	3	0	1.000	19	7.43	23	16	18	30	4	0	0	0
1996	Bal-A	0	49	3	2	.600	26	4.28	54 2/3	50	35	40	10	0	0	3
1997	Bal-A	0	39	2	3	.400	21	4.89	38 2/3	32	33	41	5	0	0	0
1998	Bal-A	0	72	3	4	.429	32	3.73	77	57	50	55	8	0	0	2
1999	LA-N	0	68	3	4	.429	30	3.73	72 1/3	49	43	70	10	0	0	0
2000	LA-N	0	18	2	1	.667	12	4.21	25 2/3	18	16	31	3	0	0	1
2000	Bal-A	0	23	2	0	1.000	17	6.46	23 2/3	18	19	26	6	0	0	1
Career Average		0	38	3	3	.551	23	3.99	52	37	32	47	6	0	0	1
Yankee Average		1	21	1	3	.250	14	4.19	29	18	21	32	3	0	0	0
Career Total		5	459	38	31	.551	276	3.99	620	447	384	558	77	0	0	15
Yankee Total		2	42	2	6	.250	27	4.19	58	35	41	64	5	0	0	0

Mirabella, Paul Thomas

HEIGHT: 6'1"   LEFTHANDER   BORN: 3/20/1954 BELLEVILLE, NEW JERSEY

YEAR	TEAM	STARTS	GAMES	WON	LOST	PCT	ER	ERA	INNINGS PITCHED	STRIKE-OUTS	WALKS	HITS ALLOWED	HRS ALLOWED	COMP. GAMES	SHUT-OUTS	SAVES
1978	Tex-A	4	10	3	2	.600	18	5.79	28	23	17	30	2	0	0	1
1979	NY-A	1	10	0	4	.000	14	8.79	14 1/3	4	10	16	3	0	0	0
1980	Tor-A	22	33	5	12	.294	63	4.34	130 2/3	53	66	151	11	3	1	0
1981	Tor-A	1	8	0	0	—	12	7.36	14 2/3	9	7	20	2	0	0	0
1982	Tex-A	0	40	1	1	.500	27	4.80	50 2/3	29	22	46	4	0	0	3
1983	Bal-A	2	3	0	0	—	6	5.59	9 2/3	4	7	9	1	0	0	0
1984	Sea-A	1	52	2	5	.286	33	4.37	68	41	32	74	6	0	0	3
1985	Sea-A	0	10	0	0	—	2	1.32	13 2/3	8	4	9	0	0	0	0
1986	Sea-A	0	8	0	0	—	6	8.53	6 1/3	6	3	13	1	0	0	0
1987	Mil-A	0	29	2	1	.667	16	4.91	29 1/3	14	16	30	0	0	0	2
1988	Mil-A	0	38	2	2	.500	11	1.65	60	33	21	44	3	0	0	4
1989	Mil-A	0	13	0	0	—	13	7.63	15 1/3	6	7	18	1	0	0	0
1990	Mil-A	2	44	4	2	.667	26	3.97	59	28	27	66	9	0	0	0
Career Average		3	23	1	2	.396	19	4.45	38	20	18	40	3	0	0	1
Yankee Average		1	10	0	4	.000	14	8.79	14 1/3	4	10	16	3	0	0	0
Career Total		33	298	19	29	.396	247	4.45	499 2/3	258	239	526	43	3	1	13
Yankee Total		1	10	0	4	.000	14	8.79	14 1/3	4	10	16	3	0	0	0

Mmahat, Kevin Paul
HEIGHT: 6'5" LEFTHANDER BORN: 11/9/1964 MEMPHIS, TENNESSEE

YEAR	TEAM	STARTS	GAMES	WON	LOST	PCT	ER	ERA	INNINGS PITCHED	STRIKE-OUTS	WALKS	HITS ALLOWED	HRS ALLOWED	COMP. GAMES	SHUT-OUTS	SAVES
1989	NY-A	2	4	0	2	.000	11	12.91	7 2/3	3	8	13	2	0	0	0
Career Average		2	4	0	2	.000	11	12.91	7 2/3	3	8	13	2	0	0	0
Yankee Average		**2**	**4**	**0**	**2**	**.000**	**11**	**12.91**	**7 2/3**	**3**	**8**	**13**	**2**	**0**	**0**	**0**
Career Total		2	4	0	2	.000	11	12.91	7 2/3	3	8	13	2	0	0	0
Yankee Total		**2**	**4**	**0**	**2**	**.000**	**11**	**12.91**	**7 2/3**	**3**	**8**	**13**	**2**	**0**	**0**	**0**

Mogridge, George Anthony
HEIGHT: 6'2" LEFTHANDER BORN: 2/18/1889 ROCHESTER, NEW YORK DIED: 3/4/1962 ROCHESTER, NEW YORK

YEAR	TEAM	STARTS	GAMES	WON	LOST	PCT	ER	ERA	INNINGS PITCHED	STRIKE-OUTS	WALKS	HITS ALLOWED	HRS ALLOWED	COMP. GAMES	SHUT-OUTS	SAVES
1911	Chi-A	1	4	0	2	.000	8	5.68	12 2/3	5	1	12	1	0	0	0
1912	Chi-A	7	17	3	4	.429	29	4.04	64 2/3	31	15	69	2	2	0	3
1915	**NY-A**	**6**	**6**	**2**	**3**	**.400**	**8**	**1.76**	**41**	**11**	**11**	**33**	**0**	**3**	**1**	**0**
1916	**NY-A**	**21**	**30**	**6**	**12**	**.333**	**50**	**2.31**	**194 2/3**	**66**	**45**	**174**	**3**	**10**	**2**	**0**
1917	**NY-A**	**25**	**29**	**9**	**11**	**.450**	**65**	**2.98**	**196 1/3**	**46**	**39**	**185**	**5**	**15**	**1**	**0**
1918	**NY-A**	**19**	**45**	**16**	**13**	**.552**	**58**	**2.18**	**239 1/3**	**62**	**43**	**232**	**6**	**13**	**1**	**7**
1919	**NY-A**	**18**	**35**	**10**	**7**	**.588**	**53**	**2.82**	**169**	**58**	**46**	**159**	**6**	**13**	**3**	**0**
1920	**NY-A**	**15**	**26**	**5**	**9**	**.357**	**60**	**4.31**	**125 1/3**	**35**	**36**	**146**	**4**	**7**	**0**	**1**
1921	Was-A	36	38	18	14	.563	96	3.00	288	101	66	301	12	21	4	0
1922	Was-A	32	34	18	13	.581	100	3.58	251 2/3	61	72	300	12	18	3	0
1923	Was-A	30	33	13	13	.500	73	3.11	211	62	56	228	10	17	3	1
1924	Was-A	30	30	16	11	.593	89	3.76	213	48	61	217	2	13	2	0
1925	Was-A	8	10	4	3	.571	24	4.08	53	12	18	58	2	3	0	0
1925	StL-A	2	2	1	1	.500	10	5.87	15 1/3	8	5	17	2	1	0	0
1926	Bos-N	10	39	6	10	.375	71	4.50	142	46	36	173	6	2	0	3
1927	Bos-N	1	20	6	4	.600	20	3.70	48 2/3	26	15	48	4	0	0	5
Career Average		16	25	8	8	.502	51	3.23	142	42	35	147	5	9	1	1
Yankee Average		**17**	**29**	**8**	**9**	**.466**	**49**	**2.73**	**161**	**46**	**37**	**155**	**4**	**10**	**1**	**1**
Career Total		261	398	133	130	.506	814	3.23	2265 2/3	678	565	2352	77	138	20	20
Yankee Total		**103**	**171**	**48**	**55**	**.466**	**293**	**2.73**	**965 2/3**	**278**	**220**	**929**	**24**	**61**	**8**	**8**

Mohorcic, Dale Robert
HEIGHT: 6'3" LEFTHANDER BORN: 1/25/1956 CLEVELAND, OHIO

YEAR	TEAM	STARTS	GAMES	WON	LOST	PCT	ER	ERA	INNINGS PITCHED	STRIKE-OUTS	WALKS	HITS ALLOWED	HRS ALLOWED	COMP. GAMES	SHUT-OUTS	SAVES
1986	Tex-A	0	58	2	4	.333	22	2.51	79	29	15	86	5	0	0	7
1987	Tex-A	0	74	7	6	.538	33	2.99	99 1/3	48	19	88	11	0	0	16
1988	Tex-A	0	43	2	6	.250	28	4.85	52	25	20	62	6	0	0	5
1988	**NY-A**	**0**	**13**	**2**	**2**	**.500**	**7**	**2.78**	**22 2/3**	**19**	**9**	**21**	**1**	**0**	**0**	**1**
1989	**NY-A**	**0**	**32**	**2**	**1**	**.667**	**32**	**4.99**	**57 2/3**	**24**	**18**	**65**	**8**	**0**	**0**	**2**
1990	Mon-N	0	34	1	2	.333	19	3.23	53	29	18	56	6	0	0	2
Career Average		0	42	3	4	.432	24	3.49	61	29	17	63	6	0	0	6
Yankee Average		**0**	**23**	**2**	**2**	**.571**	**20**	**4.37**	**40**	**22**	**14**	**43**	**5**	**0**	**0**	**2**
Career Total		0	254	16	21	.432	141	3.49	363 2/3	174	99	378	37	0	0	33
Yankee Total		**0**	**45**	**4**	**3**	**.571**	**39**	**4.37**	**80 1/3**	**43**	**27**	**86**	**9**	**0**	**0**	**3**

Monbouquette, William Charles
HEIGHT: 5'11" RIGHTHANDER BORN: 8/11/1936 MEDFORD, MASSACHUSETTS

YEAR	TEAM	STARTS	GAMES	WON	LOST	PCT	ER	ERA	INNINGS PITCHED	STRIKE-OUTS	WALKS	HITS ALLOWED	HRS ALLOWED	COMP. GAMES	SHUT-OUTS	SAVES
1958	Bos-A	8	10	3	4	.429	20	3.31	54 1/3	30	20	52	4	3	0	0
1959	Bos-A	17	34	7	7	.500	70	4.15	151 2/3	87	33	165	15	4	0	0
1960	Bos-A	30	35	14	11	.560	87	3.64	215	134	68	217	18	12	3	0
1961	Bos-A	32	32	14	14	.500	89	3.39	236 1/3	161	100	233	24	12	1	0
1962	Bos-A	35	35	15	13	.536	87	3.33	235 1/3	153	65	227	22	11	4	0

(continued)

(continued)

YEAR	TEAM	STARTS	GAMES	WON	LOST	PCT	ER	ERA	INNINGS PITCHED	STRIKE-OUTS	WALKS	HITS ALLOWED	HRS ALLOWED	COMP. GAMES	SHUT-OUTS	SAVES
1963	Bos-A	36	37	20	10	.667	113	3.81	266⅔	174	42	258	31	13	1	0
1964	Bos-A	35	36	13	14	.481	105	4.04	234	120	40	258	34	7	5	1
1965	Bos-A	35	35	10	18	.357	94	3.70	228⅔	110	40	239	32	10	2	0
1966	Det-A	14	30	7	8	.467	54	4.73	102⅔	61	22	120	14	2	1	0
1967	Det-A	0	2	0	0	—	0	0.00	2	2	0	1	0	0	0	0
1967	**NY-A**	**10**	**33**	**6**	**5**	**.545**	**35**	**2.36**	**133⅓**	**53**	**17**	**122**	**6**	**2**	**1**	**1**
1968	**NY-A**	**11**	**17**	**5**	**7**	**.417**	**44**	**4.43**	**89⅓**	**32**	**13**	**92**	**7**	**2**	**0**	**0**
1968	SF-N	0	7	0	1	.000	5	3.65	12⅓	5	2	11	4	0	0	1
Career Average		20	26	9	9	.504	62	3.68	151	86	36	153	16	6	1	0
Yankee Average		**11**	**25**	**6**	**6**	**.478**	**40**	**3.19**	**111**	**43**	**15**	**107**	**7**	**2**	**1**	**1**
Career Total		263	343	114	112	.504	803	3.68	1961⅔	1122	462	1995	211	78	18	3
Yankee Total		**21**	**50**	**11**	**12**	**.478**	**79**	**3.19**	**222⅔**	**85**	**30**	**214**	**13**	**4**	**1**	**1**

Monroe, Edward Oliver (Peck)

HEIGHT: 6'5"   RIGHTHANDER   BORN: 2/22/1895 LOUISVILLE, KENTUCKY   DIED: 4/29/1969 LOUISVILLE, KENTUCKY

YEAR	TEAM	STARTS	GAMES	WON	LOST	PCT	ER	ERA	INNINGS PITCHED	STRIKE-OUTS	WALKS	HITS ALLOWED	HRS ALLOWED	COMP. GAMES	SHUT-OUTS	SAVES
1917	**NY-A**	**1**	**9**	**1**	**0**	**1.000**	**11**	**3.45**	**28⅔**	**12**	**6**	**35**	**1**	**1**	**0**	**1**
1918	**NY-A**	**0**	**1**	**0**	**0**	**—**	**1**	**4.50**	**2**	**1**	**2**	**1**	**0**	**0**	**0**	**0**
Career Average		1	5	1	0	1.000	6	3.52	15	7	4	18	1	1	0	1
Yankee Average		**1**	**5**	**1**	**0**	**1.000**	**6**	**3.52**	**15**	**7**	**4**	**18**	**1**	**1**	**0**	**1**
Career Total		1	10	1	0	1.000	12	3.52	30⅔	13	8	36	1	1	0	1
Yankee Total		**1**	**10**	**1**	**0**	**1.000**	**12**	**3.52**	**30⅔**	**13**	**8**	**36**	**1**	**1**	**0**	**1**

Monroe, Zachary Charles

HEIGHT: 6'0"   RIGHTHANDER   BORN: 7/8/1931 PEORIA, ILLINOIS

YEAR	TEAM	STARTS	GAMES	WON	LOST	PCT	ER	ERA	INNINGS PITCHED	STRIKE-OUTS	WALKS	HITS ALLOWED	HRS ALLOWED	COMP. GAMES	SHUT-OUTS	SAVES
1958	**NY-A**	**6**	**21**	**4**	**2**	**.667**	**21**	**3.26**	**58**	**18**	**27**	**57**	**8**	**1**	**0**	**1**
1959	**NY-A**	**0**	**3**	**0**	**0**	**—**	**2**	**5.40**	**3⅓**	**1**	**2**	**3**	**2**	**0**	**0**	**0**
Career Average		3	12	2	1	.667	12	3.38	31	10	15	30	5	1	0	1
Yankee Average		**3**	**12**	**2**	**1**	**.667**	**12**	**3.38**	**31**	**10**	**15**	**30**	**5**	**1**	**0**	**1**
Career Total		6	24	4	2	.667	23	3.38	61⅓	19	29	60	10	1	0	1
Yankee Total		**6**	**24**	**4**	**2**	**.667**	**23**	**3.38**	**61⅓**	**19**	**29**	**60**	**10**	**1**	**0**	**1**

Montefusco, John Joseph (Count)

HEIGHT: 6'1"   RIGHTHANDER   BORN: 5/25/1950 LONG BRANCH, NEW JERSEY

YEAR	TEAM	STARTS	GAMES	WON	LOST	PCT	ER	ERA	INNINGS PITCHED	STRIKE-OUTS	WALKS	HITS ALLOWED	HRS ALLOWED	COMP. GAMES	SHUT-OUTS	SAVES
1974	SF-N	5	7	3	2	.600	21	4.81	39⅓	34	19	41	3	1	1	0
1975	SF-N	34	35	15	9	.625	78	2.88	243⅔	215	86	210	11	10	4	0
1976	SF-N	36	37	16	14	.533	80	2.84	253⅓	172	74	224	11	11	6	0
1977	SF-N	25	26	7	12	.368	61	3.49	157⅓	110	46	170	10	4	0	0
1978	SF-N	36	36	11	9	.550	101	3.81	238⅔	177	68	233	25	3	0	0
1979	SF-N	22	22	3	8	.273	60	3.94	137	76	51	145	15	0	0	0
1980	SF-N	17	22	4	8	.333	55	4.37	113⅓	85	39	120	15	1	0	0
1981	Atl-N	9	26	2	3	.400	30	3.51	77	34	27	75	9	0	0	1
1982	SD-N	32	32	10	11	.476	82	4.00	184⅓	83	41	177	17	1	0	0
1983	SD-N	10	31	9	4	.692	35	3.30	95⅓	52	32	94	6	1	0	4
1983	**NY-A**	**6**	**6**	**5**	**0**	**1.000**	**14**	**3.32**	**38**	**15**	**10**	**39**	**3**	**0**	**0**	**0**
1984	**NY-A**	**11**	**11**	**5**	**3**	**.625**	**22**	**3.58**	**55⅓**	**23**	**13**	**55**	**5**	**0**	**0**	**0**
1985	**NY-A**	**1**	**3**	**0**	**0**	**—**	**8**	**10.29**	**7**	**2**	**2**	**12**	**3**	**0**	**0**	**0**
1986	**NY-A**	**0**	**4**	**0**	**0**	**—**	**3**	**2.19**	**12⅓**	**3**	**5**	**9**	**2**	**0**	**0**	**0**
Career Average		17	149	6	6	.520	325	3.54	826	541	257	802	68	16	6	3
Yankee Average		**5**	**12**	**5**	**2**	**.769**	**24**	**3.75**	**56**	**22**	**15**	**58**	**7**	**0**	**0**	**0**
Career Total		244	298	90	83	.520	650	3.54	1652⅓	1081	513	1604	135	32	11	5
Yankee Total		**18**	**24**	**10**	**3**	**.769**	**47**	**3.75**	**112⅔**	**43**	**30**	**115**	**13**	**0**	**0**	**0**

Monteleone, Richard
HEIGHT: 6'2" RIGHTHANDER BORN: 3/22/1963 TAMPA, FLORIDA

YEAR	TEAM	STARTS	GAMES	WON	LOST	PCT	ER	ERA	INNINGS PITCHED	STRIKE-OUTS	WALKS	HITS ALLOWED	HRS ALLOWED	COMP. GAMES	SHUT-OUTS	SAVES
1987	Sea-A	0	3	0	0	—	5	6.43	7	2	4	10	2	0	0	0
1988	Cal-A	0	3	0	0	—	0	0.00	4 1/3	3	1	4	0	0	0	0
1989	Cal-A	0	24	2	2	.500	14	3.18	39 2/3	27	13	39	3	0	0	0
1990	**NY-A**	**0**	**5**	**0**	**1**	**.000**	**5**	**6.14**	**7 1/3**	**8**	**2**	**8**	**0**	**0**	**0**	**0**
1991	**NY-A**	**0**	**26**	**3**	**1**	**.750**	**19**	**3.64**	**47**	**34**	**19**	**42**	**5**	**0**	**0**	**0**
1992	**NY-A**	**0**	**47**	**7**	**3**	**.700**	**34**	**3.30**	**92 2/3**	**62**	**27**	**82**	**7**	**0**	**0**	**0**
1993	**NY-A**	**0**	**42**	**7**	**4**	**.636**	**47**	**4.94**	**85 2/3**	**50**	**35**	**85**	**14**	**0**	**0**	**0**
1994	SF-N	0	39	4	3	.571	16	3.18	45 1/3	16	13	43	6	0	0	0
1995	Cal-A	0	9	1	0	1.000	2	2.00	9	5	3	8	1	0	0	0
1996	Cal-A	0	12	0	3	.000	10	5.87	15 1/3	5	2	23	5	0	0	0
Career Average		0	21	2	2	.585	15	3.88	35	21	12	34	4	0	0	0
Yankee Average		**0**	**30**	**4**	**2**	**.654**	**26**	**4.06**	**58**	**39**	**21**	**54**	**7**	**0**	**0**	**0**
Career Total		0	210	24	17	.585	152	3.87	353 1/3	212	119	344	43	0	0	0
Yankee Total		**0**	**120**	**17**	**9**	**.654**	**105**	**4.06**	**232 2/3**	**154**	**83**	**217**	**26**	**0**	**0**	**0**

Moore, Earl Alonzo (Steam Engine in Boots)
HEIGHT: 6'0" RIGHTHANDER BORN: 7/29/1879 PICKERINGTON, OHIO DIED: 11/28/1961 COLUMBUS, OHIO

YEAR	TEAM	STARTS	GAMES	WON	LOST	PCT	ER	ERA	INNINGS PITCHED	STRIKE-OUTS	WALKS	HITS ALLOWED	HRS ALLOWED	COMP. GAMES	SHUT-OUTS	SAVES
1901	Cle-A	30	31	16	14	.533	81	2.90	251 1/3	99	107	234	4	28	4	0
1902	Cle-A	34	36	17	17	.500	96	2.95	293	84	101	304	8	29	4	1
1903	Cle-A	27	29	19	9	.679	48	1.74	247 2/3	148	62	196	0	27	3	1
1904	Cle-A	24	26	12	11	.522	57	2.25	227 2/3	139	61	186	2	22	1	0
1905	Cle-A	30	31	15	15	.500	79	2.64	269	131	92	232	6	28	3	0
1906	Cle-A	4	5	1	1	.500	13	3.94	29 2/3	8	18	27	1	2	0	0
1907	Cle-A	2	3	1	1	.500	10	4.66	19 1/3	7	8	18	0	1	0	0
1907	**NY-A**	**9**	**12**	**2**	**6**	**.250**	**28**	**3.94**	**64**	**28**	**30**	**72**	**1**	**3**	**1**	**0**
1908	Phi-N	3	3	2	1	.667	0	0.00	26	16	8	20	0	3	1	0
1909	Phi-N	34	38	18	12	.600	70	2.10	299 2/3	173	108	238	7	24	4	0
1910	Phi-N	35	46	22	15	.595	81	2.58	283	185	121	228	5	18	6	0
1911	Phi-N	36	42	15	19	.441	90	2.63	308 1/3	174	164	265	11	21	5	1
1912	Phi-N	24	31	9	14	.391	67	3.31	182 1/3	79	77	186	3	10	1	0
1913	Phi-N	5	12	1	3	.250	29	5.02	52	24	40	50	3	0	0	1
1913	Chi-N	2	7	1	1	.500	14	4.45	28 1/3	12	12	34	3	0	0	0
1914	Buf-F	27	36	11	15	.423	93	4.30	194 2/3	96	99	184	3	14	2	2
Career Average		20	24	10	10	.513	54	2.78	174	88	69	155	4	14	2	1
Yankee Average		**9**	**12**	**2**	**6**	**.250**	**28**	**3.94**	**64**	**28**	**30**	**72**	**1**	**3**	**0**	**1**
Career Total		326	388	162	154	.513	856	2.78	2776	1403	1108	2474	57	230	34	7
Yankee Total		**9**	**12**	**2**	**6**	**.250**	**28**	**3.94**	**64**	**28**	**30**	**72**	**1**	**3**	**0**	**1**

Moore, William Wilcy (Cy)
HEIGHT: 6'0" RIGHTHANDER BORN: 5/20/1897 BONITA, TEXAS DIED: 3/29/1963 HOLLIS, OKLAHOMA

YEAR	TEAM	STARTS	GAMES	WON	LOST	PCT	ER	ERA	INNINGS PITCHED	STRIKE-OUTS	WALKS	HITS ALLOWED	HRS ALLOWED	COMP. GAMES	SHUT-OUTS	SAVES
1927	**NY-A**	**12**	**50**	**19**	**7**	**.731**	**54**	**2.28**	**213**	**75**	**59**	**185**	**3**	**6**	**1**	**13**
1928	**NY-A**	**2**	**35**	**4**	**4**	**.500**	**28**	**4.18**	**60 1/3**	**18**	**31**	**71**	**4**	**0**	**0**	**2**
1929	**NY-A**	**0**	**41**	**6**	**4**	**.600**	**28**	**4.13**	**61**	**21**	**19**	**64**	**4**	**0**	**0**	**8**
1931	Bos-A	15	53	11	13	.458	80	3.88	185 1/3	37	55	195	7	8	1	10
1932	Bos-A	2	37	4	10	.286	49	5.23	84 1/3	28	42	98	5	0	0	4
1932	**NY-A**	**1**	**10**	**2**	**0**	**1.000**	**7**	**2.52**	**25**	**8**	**6**	**27**	**1**	**0**	**0**	**4**
1933	**NY-A**	**0**	**35**	**5**	**6**	**.455**	**38**	**5.52**	**62**	**17**	**20**	**92**	**1**	**0**	**0**	**8**
Career Average		5	37	7	6	.537	41	3.70	99	29	33	105	3	2	0	7
Yankee Average		**3**	**34**	**7**	**4**	**.632**	**31**	**3.31**	**84**	**28**	**27**	**88**	**2**	**1**	**0**	**7**
Career Total		32	261	51	44	.537	284	3.70	691	204	232	732	25	14	2	49
Yankee Total		**15**	**171**	**36**	**21**	**.632**	**155**	**3.31**	**421 1/3**	**139**	**135**	**439**	**12**	**6**	**1**	**35**

Morgan, Michael Thomas
HEIGHT: 6′2″ RIGHTHANDER BORN: 10/8/1959 TULARE, CALIFORNIA

YEAR	TEAM	STARTS	GAMES	WON	LOST	PCT	ER	ERA	INNINGS PITCHED	STRIKE-OUTS	WALKS	HITS ALLOWED	HRS ALLOWED	COMP. GAMES	SHUT-OUTS	SAVES
1978	Oak-A	3	3	0	3	.000	10	7.30	12 1/3	0	8	19	1	1	0	0
1979	Oak-A	13	13	2	10	.167	51	5.94	77 1/3	17	50	102	7	2	0	0
1982	**NY-A**	**23**	**30**	**7**	**11**	**.389**	**73**	**4.37**	**150 1/3**	**71**	**67**	**167**	**15**	**2**	**0**	**0**
1983	Tor-A	4	16	0	3	.000	26	5.16	45 1/3	22	21	48	6	0	0	0
1985	Sea-A	2	2	1	1	.500	8	12.00	6	2	5	11	2	0	0	0
1986	Sea-A	33	37	11	17	.393	109	4.53	216 1/3	116	86	243	24	9	1	1
1987	Sea-A	31	34	12	17	.414	107	4.65	207	85	53	245	25	8	2	0
1988	Bal-A	10	22	1	6	.143	43	5.43	71 1/3	29	23	70	6	2	0	1
1989	LA-N	19	40	8	11	.421	43	2.53	152 2/3	72	33	130	6	0	0	0
1990	LA-N	33	33	11	15	.423	88	3.75	211	106	60	216	19	6	4	0
1991	LA-N	33	34	14	10	.583	73	2.78	236 1/3	140	61	197	12	5	1	1
1992	Chi-N	34	34	16	8	.667	68	2.55	240	123	79	203	14	6	1	0
1993	Chi-N	32	32	10	15	.400	93	4.03	207 2/3	111	74	206	15	1	1	0
1994	Chi-N	15	15	2	10	.167	60	6.75	80 2/3	57	35	111	12	1	0	0
1995	Chi-N	4	4	2	1	.667	6	2.19	24 2/3	15	9	19	2	0	0	0
1995	StL-N	17	17	5	6	.455	46	3.88	106 2/3	46	25	114	10	1	0	0
1996	StL-N	18	18	4	8	.333	60	5.24	103	55	40	118	14	0	0	0
1996	Cin-N	5	5	2	3	.400	7	2.30	27 1/3	19	7	28	2	0	0	0
1997	Cin-N	30	31	9	12	.429	86	4.78	162	103	49	165	13	1	0	0
1998	Min-A	17	18	4	2	.667	38	3.49	98	50	24	108	13	0	0	0
1998	Chi-N	5	5	0	1	.000	18	7.15	22 2/3	10	15	30	8	0	0	0
1999	Tex-A	25	34	13	10	.565	97	6.24	140	61	48	184	25	1	0	0
2000	Ari-N	4	60	5	5	.500	55	4.87	101 2/3	56	40	123	10	0	0	5
Career Average		18	23	6	8	.429	55	4.22	117	59	40	124	11	2	0	0
Yankee Average		**23**	**30**	**7**	**11**	**.389**	**73**	**4.37**	**150 1/3**	**71**	**67**	**167**	**15**	**2**	**0**	**0**
Career Total		410	547	139	185	.429	1265	4.22	2700 1/3	1366	912	2857	261	46	10	8
Yankee Total		**23**	**30**	**7**	**11**	**.389**	**73**	**4.37**	**150 1/3**	**71**	**67**	**167**	**15**	**2**	**0**	**0**

Morgan, Tom Stephen (Plowboy)
HEIGHT: 6′1″ RIGHTHANDER BORN: 5/20/1930 EL MONTE, CALIFORNIA DIED: 1/13/1987 ANAHEIM, CALIFORNIA

YEAR	TEAM	STARTS	GAMES	WON	LOST	PCT	ER	ERA	INNINGS PITCHED	STRIKE-OUTS	WALKS	HITS ALLOWED	HRS ALLOWED	COMP. GAMES	SHUT-OUTS	SAVES
1951	**NY-A**	**16**	**27**	**9**	**3**	**.750**	**51**	**3.68**	**124 2/3**	**57**	**36**	**119**	**11**	**4**	**2**	**2**
1952	**NY-A**	**12**	**16**	**5**	**4**	**.556**	**32**	**3.07**	**93 2/3**	**35**	**33**	**86**	**8**	**2**	**1**	**2**
1954	**NY-A**	**17**	**32**	**11**	**5**	**.688**	**53**	**3.34**	**143**	**34**	**40**	**149**	**8**	**7**	**4**	**1**
1955	**NY-A**	**1**	**40**	**7**	**3**	**.700**	**26**	**3.25**	**72**	**17**	**24**	**72**	**3**	**0**	**0**	**10**
1956	**NY-A**	**0**	**41**	**6**	**7**	**.462**	**33**	**4.16**	**71 1/3**	**20**	**27**	**74**	**2**	**0**	**0**	**11**
1957	KC-A	13	46	9	7	.563	74	4.64	143 2/3	32	61	160	19	5	0	7
1958	Det-A	1	39	2	5	.286	22	3.16	62 2/3	32	4	70	7	0	0	1
1959	Det-A	1	46	1	4	.200	41	3.98	92 2/3	39	18	94	11	0	0	9
1960	Det-A	0	22	3	2	.600	15	4.66	29	12	10	33	6	0	0	1
1960	Was-A	0	14	1	3	.250	10	3.75	24	11	5	36	6	0	0	0
1961	LA-A	0	59	8	2	.800	24	2.36	91 2/3	39	17	74	7	0	0	10
1962	LA-A	0	48	5	2	.714	19	2.91	58 2/3	29	19	53	6	0	0	9
1963	LA-A	0	13	0	0	—	10	5.51	16 1/3	7	6	20	1	0	0	1
Career Average		5	34	5	4	.588	32	3.61	78	28	23	80	7	1	1	5
Yankee Average		**9**	**31**	**8**	**4**	**.633**	**39**	**3.48**	**101**	**33**	**32**	**100**	**6**	**3**	**1**	**5**
Career Total		61	443	67	47	.588	410	3.61	1023 1/3	364	300	1040	95	18	7	64
Yankee Total		**46**	**156**	**38**	**22**	**.633**	**195**	**3.48**	**504 2/3**	**163**	**160**	**500**	**32**	**13**	**7**	**26**

Mulholland, Terence John
HEIGHT: 6′3″ LEFTHANDER BORN: 3/9/1963 UNIONTOWN, PENNSYLVANIA

YEAR	TEAM	STARTS	GAMES	WON	LOST	PCT	ER	ERA	INNINGS PITCHED	STRIKE-OUTS	WALKS	HITS ALLOWED	HRS ALLOWED	COMP. GAMES	SHUT-OUTS	SAVES
1986	SF-N	10	15	1	7	.125	30	4.94	54 2/3	27	35	51	3	0	0	0
1988	SF-N	6	9	2	1	.667	19	3.72	46	18	7	50	3	2	1	0
1989	SF-N	1	5	0	0	—	5	4.09	11	6	4	15	0	0	0	0
1989	Phi-N	17	20	4	7	.364	58	5.00	104 1/3	60	32	122	8	2	1	0

(continued)

(continued)

YEAR	TEAM	STARTS	GAMES	WON	LOST	PCT	ER	ERA	INNINGS PITCHED	STRIKE-OUTS	WALKS	HITS ALLOWED	HRS ALLOWED	COMP. GAMES	SHUT-OUTS	SAVES
1990	Phi-N	26	33	9	10	.474	67	3.34	180 2/3	75	42	172	15	6	1	0
1991	Phi-N	34	34	16	13	.552	93	3.61	232	142	49	231	15	8	3	0
1992	Phi-N	32	32	13	11	.542	97	3.81	229	125	46	227	14	12	2	0
1993	Phi-N	28	29	12	9	.571	69	3.25	191	116	40	177	20	7	2	0
1994	**NY-A**	**19**	**24**	**6**	**7**	**.462**	**87**	**6.49**	**120 2/3**	**72**	**37**	**150**	**24**	**2**	**0**	**0**
1995	SF-N	24	29	5	13	.278	96	5.80	149	65	38	190	25	2	0	0
1996	Phi-N	21	21	8	7	.533	69	4.66	133 1/3	52	21	157	17	3	0	0
1996	Sea-A	12	12	5	4	.556	36	4.67	69 1/3	34	28	75	5	0	0	0
1997	Chi-N	25	25	6	12	.333	71	4.07	157	74	45	162	20	1	0	0
1997	SF-N	2	15	0	1	.000	17	5.16	29 2/3	25	6	28	4	0	0	0
1998	Chi-N	6	70	6	5	.545	36	2.89	112	72	39	100	7	0	0	3
1999	Chi-N	16	26	6	6	.500	63	5.15	110	44	32	137	16	0	0	0
1999	Atl-N	8	16	4	2	.667	20	2.98	60 1/3	39	13	64	5	0	0	1
2000	Atl-N	20	54	9	9	.500	89	5.11	156 2/3	78	41	198	24	1	0	1
Career Average		17	24	6	7	.475	55	4.28	117	62	30	124	12	3	1	0
Yankee Average		**19**	**24**	**6**	**7**	**.462**	**87**	**6.49**	**120 2/3**	**72**	**37**	**150**	**24**	**2**	**0**	**0**
Career Total		307	469	112	124	.475	1022	4.28	2146 2/3	1124	555	2306	225	46	10	5
Yankee Total		**19**	**24**	**6**	**7**	**.462**	**87**	**6.49**	**120 2/3**	**72**	**37**	**150**	**24**	**2**	**0**	**0**

Muncrief, Robert Cleveland

HEIGHT: 6'2" RIGHTHANDER BORN: 1/28/1916 MADILL, OKLAHOMA DIED: 2/6/1996 DUNCANVILLE, TEXAS

YEAR	TEAM	STARTS	GAMES	WON	LOST	PCT	ER	ERA	INNINGS PITCHED	STRIKE-OUTS	WALKS	HITS ALLOWED	HRS ALLOWED	COMP. GAMES	SHUT-OUTS	SAVES
1937	StL-A	1	1	0	0	—	1	4.50	2	0	2	3	1	0	0	0
1939	StL-A	0	2	0	0	—	5	15.00	3	1	3	7	1	0	0	0
1941	StL-A	24	36	13	9	.591	87	3.65	214 1/3	67	53	221	18	12	2	1
1942	StL-A	18	24	6	8	.429	58	3.89	134 1/3	39	31	149	11	7	1	0
1943	StL-A	27	35	13	12	.520	64	2.81	205	80	48	211	13	12	3	1
1944	StL-A	27	33	13	8	.619	75	3.08	219 1/3	88	50	216	11	12	3	1
1945	StL-A	15	27	13	4	.765	44	2.72	145 2/3	54	44	132	8	10	0	1
1946	StL-A	14	29	3	12	.200	64	4.99	115 1/3	49	31	149	6	4	1	0
1947	StL-A	23	31	8	14	.364	96	4.90	176 1/3	74	51	210	14	7	0	0
1948	Cle-A	9	21	5	4	.556	32	3.98	72 1/3	24	31	76	8	1	1	3
1949	Pit-N	4	13	1	5	.167	25	6.31	35 2/3	11	13	44	8	1	0	3
1949	Chi-N	3	34	5	6	.455	38	4.56	75	36	31	80	9	1	0	2
1951	**NY-A**	**0**	**2**	**0**	**0**	**—**	**3**	**9.00**	**3**	**2**	**4**	**5**	**0**	**0**	**0**	**0**
Career Average		12	21	6	6	.494	42	3.80	100	38	28	107	8	5	1	1
Yankee Average		**0**	**2**	**0**	**0**	**—**	**3**	**9.00**	**3**	**2**	**4**	**5**	**0**	**0**	**0**	**0**
Career Total		165	288	80	82	.494	592	3.80	1401 1/3	525	392	1503	108	67	11	9
Yankee Total		**0**	**2**	**0**	**0**	**—**	**3**	**9.00**	**3**	**2**	**4**	**5**	**0**	**0**	**0**	**0**

Munoz, Roberto BORN ROBERTO MUNOZ (SBERT)

HEIGHT: 6'7" RIGHTHANDER BORN: 3/3/1968 RIO PIEDRAS, PUERTO RICO

YEAR	TEAM	STARTS	GAMES	WON	LOST	PCT	ER	ERA	INNINGS PITCHED	STRIKE-OUTS	WALKS	HITS ALLOWED	HRS ALLOWED	COMP. GAMES	SHUT-OUTS	SAVES
1993	**NY-A**	**0**	**38**	**3**	**3**	**.500**	**27**	**5.32**	**45 2/3**	**33**	**26**	**48**	**1**	**0**	**0**	**0**
1994	Phi-N	14	21	7	5	.583	31	2.67	104 1/3	59	35	101	8	1	0	1
1995	Phi-N	3	3	0	2	.000	10	5.74	15 2/3	6	9	15	2	0	0	0
1996	Phi-N	6	6	0	3	.000	22	7.82	25 1/3	8	7	42	5	0	0	0
1997	Phi-N	7	8	1	5	.167	33	8.91	33 1/3	20	15	47	4	0	0	0
1998	Bal-A	1	9	0	0	—	13	9.75	12	6	6	18	4	0	0	0
Career Average		5	14	2	3	.379	23	5.18	39	22	16	45	4	0	0	0
Yankee Average		**0**	**38**	**3**	**3**	**.500**	**27**	**5.32**	**45 2/3**	**33**	**26**	**48**	**1**	**0**	**0**	**0**
Career Total		31	85	11	18	.379	136	5.18	236	132	98	271	24	1	0	1
Yankee Total		**0**	**38**	**3**	**3**	**.500**	**27**	**5.32**	**45 2/3**	**33**	**26**	**48**	**1**	**0**	**0**	**0**

John Joseph Murphy, rhp, 1932, 1934–43, 1946

It is difficult to determine exactly who was the first "pure" relief pitcher in the major leagues, but Johnny Murphy is a good place to start.

Murphy, born July 14, 1908, had a brief, uneventful stint with the Yankees in 1932. In 1934, manager Joe McCarthy brought Murphy back up. Murphy was a starter in McCarthy's 1934 rotation. Marse Joe needed starters that year, and Murphy fit the bill pretty well. He went 14-10 for the Yankees, with four saves.

Murphy was, ironically, not the ideal man for the reliever's job, at least not by today's standards. He was a control pitcher, not a hard-throwing fireballer. But McCarthy liked his composure in tight situations, and began using him almost exclusively as a reliever beginning in the 1935 season. By 1937, he was 12-4 in relief, with 10 saves, both league bests as New York easily won the pennant.

He was certainly not the first pitcher to star as a reliever. Teams were using relievers as early as 1915. But McCarthy was using Murphy almost exclusively in relief, something few managers had done at that time. Even Wilcy Moore, the famous reliever of the 1927 Yankees, had 12 starts and six complete games that year.

Murphy, a two-time All-Star, would lead the American League in relief wins six times between 1935 and 1943, still a major league record. No other pitcher has ever done it more than four times in a career. Murphy would also lead the league in saves four times in that span.

Murphy's World Series record with the Yankees was outstanding: 2-0 with three saves in five appearances. Twice, in 1936 and again in 1939, he earned a save to clinch the Series for the Yankees.

Murphy was drafted in 1944. When he came back, he had lost two years and a large portion of his control. He pitched one more year in New York before going to Boston in 1947. He retired that year and worked for the Red Sox as a minor league coach for several seasons. He died on January 14, 1970, in New York City.

Murphy is 5th all-time on the Yankees' save list with 104, 5th in appearances with 383 and 12th in winning percentage with .637.

Murphy, John Joseph

HEIGHT: 6'2"   RIGHTHANDER   BORN: 7/14/1908 NEW YORK, NEW YORK   DIED: 1/14/1970 NEW YORK, NEW YORK

YEAR	TEAM	STARTS	GAMES	WON	LOST	PCT	ER	ERA	INNINGS PITCHED	STRIKE-OUTS	WALKS	HITS ALLOWED	HRS ALLOWED	COMP. GAMES	SHUT-OUTS	SAVES
1932	NY-A	0	2	0	0	—	6	16.20	3 1/3	2	3	7	0	0	0	0
1934	NY-A	20	40	14	10	.583	72	3.12	207 2/3	70	76	193	11	10	0	4
1935	NY-A	8	40	10	5	.667	53	4.08	117	28	55	110	7	4	0	5
1936	NY-A	5	27	9	3	.750	33	3.38	88	34	36	90	5	2	0	5
1937	NY-A	4	39	13	4	.765	51	4.17	110	36	50	121	7	0	0	10
1938	NY-A	2	32	8	2	.800	43	4.24	91 1/3	43	41	90	5	1	0	11
1939	NY-A	0	38	3	6	.333	30	4.40	61 1/3	30	28	57	2	0	0	19
1940	NY-A	1	35	8	4	.667	26	3.69	63 1/3	23	15	58	5	0	0	9
1941	NY-A	0	35	8	3	.727	17	1.98	77 1/3	29	40	68	1	0	0	15
1942	NY-A	0	31	4	10	.286	22	3.41	58	24	23	66	2	0	0	11
1943	NY-A	0	37	12	4	.750	19	2.51	68	31	30	44	2	0	0	8
1946	NY-A	0	27	4	2	.667	17	3.40	45	19	19	40	4	0	0	7
1947	Bos-A	0	32	0	0	—	17	2.80	54 2/3	9	28	41	1	0	0	3
Career Average		3	32	7	4	.637	31	3.50	80	29	34	76	4	1	0	8
Yankee Average		**3**	**32**	**8**	**4**	**.637**	**32**	**3.54**	**83**	**31**	**35**	**79**	**4**	**1**	**0**	**9**
Career Total		40	415	93	53	.637	406	3.50	1045	378	444	985	52	17	0	107
Yankee Total		**40**	**383**	**93**	**53**	**.637**	**389**	**3.54**	**990 1/3**	**369**	**416**	**944**	**51**	**17**	**0**	**104**

Murphy, Robert Albert

HEIGHT: 6'2" LEFTHANDER BORN: 5/26/1960 MIAMI, FLORIDA

YEAR	TEAM	STARTS	GAMES	WON	LOST	PCT	ER	ERA	INNINGS PITCHED	STRIKE-OUTS	WALKS	HITS ALLOWED	HRS ALLOWED	COMP. GAMES	SHUT-OUTS	SAVES
1985	Cin-N	0	2	0	0	—	2	6.00	3	1	2	2	1	0	0	0
1986	Cin-N	0	34	6	0	1.000	4	0.72	50 1/3	36	21	26	0	0	0	1
1987	Cin-N	0	87	8	5	.615	34	3.04	100 2/3	99	32	91	7	0	0	3
1988	Cin-N	0	76	0	6	.000	29	3.08	84 2/3	74	38	69	3	0	0	3
1989	Bos-A	0	74	5	7	.417	32	2.74	105	107	41	97	7	0	0	9
1990	Bos-A	0	68	0	6	.000	40	6.32	57	54	32	85	10	0	0	7
1991	Sea-A	0	57	0	1	.000	16	3.00	48	34	19	47	4	0	0	4
1992	Hou-N	0	59	3	1	.750	25	4.04	55 2/3	42	21	56	2	0	0	0
1993	StL-N	0	73	5	7	.417	35	4.87	64 2/3	41	20	73	8	0	0	1
1994	StL-N	0	50	4	3	.571	17	3.79	40 1/3	25	13	35	7	0	0	2
1994	**NY-A**	**0**	**3**	**0**	**0**	**—**	**3**	**16.20**	**1 2/3**	**0**	**0**	**3**	**2**	**0**	**0**	**0**
1995	LA-N	0	6	0	1	.000	7	12.60	5	2	3	6	2	0	0	0
1995	Fla-N	0	8	1	1	.500	8	9.82	7 1/3	5	5	8	1	0	0	0
Career Average		0	46	2	3	.457	19	3.64	48	40	19	46	4	0	0	2
Yankee Average		**0**	**3**	**0**	**0**	**—**	**3**	**16.20**	**1 2/3**	**0**	**0**	**3**	**2**	**0**	**0**	**0**
Career Total		0	597	32	38	.457	252	3.64	623 1/3	520	247	598	54	0	0	30
Yankee Total		**0**	**3**	**0**	**0**	**—**	**3**	**16.20**	**1 2/3**	**0**	**0**	**3**	**2**	**0**	**0**	**0**

Murray, Dale Albert

HEIGHT: 6'4" RIGHTHANDER BORN: 2/2/1950 CUERO, TEXAS

YEAR	TEAM	STARTS	GAMES	WON	LOST	PCT	ER	ERA	INNINGS PITCHED	STRIKE-OUTS	WALKS	HITS ALLOWED	HRS ALLOWED	COMP. GAMES	SHUT-OUTS	SAVES
1974	Mon-N	0	32	1	1	.500	8	1.03	69 2/3	31	23	46	1	0	0	10
1975	Mon-N	0	63	15	8	.652	49	3.96	111 1/3	43	39	134	0	0	0	9
1976	Mon-N	0	81	4	9	.308	41	3.26	113 1/3	35	37	117	1	0	0	13
1977	Cin-N	1	61	7	2	.778	56	4.94	102	42	46	125	13	0	0	4
1978	Cin-N	0	15	1	1	.500	15	4.13	32 2/3	25	17	34	1	0	0	2
1978	NY-N	0	53	8	5	.615	35	3.65	86 1/3	37	36	85	4	0	0	5
1979	NY-N	0	58	4	8	.333	52	4.82	97	37	52	105	6	0	0	4
1979	Mon-N	0	9	1	2	.333	4	2.70	13 1/3	4	3	14	1	0	0	1
1980	Mon-N	0	16	0	1	.000	20	6.14	29 1/3	16	12	39	3	0	0	0
1981	Tor-A	0	11	1	0	1.000	2	1.17	15 1/3	12	5	12	0	0	0	0
1982	Tor-A	0	56	8	7	.533	39	3.16	111	60	32	115	3	0	0	11
1983	**NY-A**	**0**	**40**	**2**	**4**	**.333**	**47**	**4.48**	**94 1/3**	**45**	**22**	**113**	**5**	**0**	**0**	**1**
1984	**NY-A**	**0**	**19**	**1**	**2**	**.333**	**13**	**4.94**	**23 2/3**	**13**	**5**	**30**	**2**	**0**	**0**	**0**
1985	**NY-A**	**0**	**3**	**0**	**0**	**—**	**3**	**13.50**	**2**	**0**	**0**	**4**	**0**	**0**	**0**	**0**
1985	Tex-A	0	1	0	0	—	2	18.00	1	0	0	3	0	0	0	0
Career Average		0	35	4	3	.515	26	3.85	60	27	22	65	3	0	0	4
Yankee Average		**0**	**21**	**1**	**2**	**.333**	**21**	**4.73**	**40**	**19**	**9**	**49**	**2**	**0**	**0**	**0**
Career Total		1	518	53	50	.515	386	3.85	902 1/3	400	329	976	40	0	0	60
Yankee Total		**0**	**62**	**3**	**6**	**.333**	**63**	**4.73**	**120**	**58**	**27**	**147**	**7**	**0**	**0**	**1**

Murray, George King (Smiler)

HEIGHT: 6'2" RIGHTHANDER BORN: 9/23/1898 CHARLOTTE, NORTH CAROLINA DIED: 10/18/1955 MEMPHIS, TENNESSEE

YEAR	TEAM	STARTS	GAMES	WON	LOST	PCT	ER	ERA	INNINGS PITCHED	STRIKE-OUTS	WALKS	HITS ALLOWED	HRS ALLOWED	COMP. GAMES	SHUT-OUTS	SAVES
1922	**NY-A**	**3**	**22**	**4**	**2**	**.667**	**25**	**3.97**	**56 2/3**	**14**	**26**	**53**	**0**	**0**	**0**	**0**
1923	Bos-A	18	39	7	11	.389	97	4.91	177 2/3	40	87	190	9	5	0	0
1924	Bos-A	7	28	2	9	.182	60	6.72	80 1/3	27	32	97	6	0	0	0
1926	Was-A	12	12	6	3	.667	51	5.64	81 1/3	28	37	89	1	5	0	0
1927	Was-A	3	7	1	1	.500	14	7.00	18	5	15	18	1	0	0	0
1933	Chi-A	0	2	0	0	—	2	7.71	2 1/3	0	2	3	0	0	0	0
Career Average		7	18	3	4	.435	42	5.38	69	19	33	75	3	2	0	0
Yankee Average		**3**	**22**	**4**	**2**	**.667**	**25**	**3.97**	**56 2/3**	**14**	**26**	**53**	**0**	**0**	**0**	**0**
Career Total		43	110	20	26	.435	249	5.38	416 1/3	114	199	450	17	10	0	0
Yankee Total		**3**	**22**	**4**	**2**	**.667**	**25**	**3.97**	**56 2/3**	**14**	**26**	**53**	**0**	**0**	**0**	**0**

Naulty, Daniel Donovan

HEIGHT: 6′6″ RIGHTHANDER   BORN: 1/6/1970 LOS ANGELES, CALIFORNIA

YEAR	TEAM	STARTS	GAMES	WON	LOST	PCT	ER	ERA	INNINGS PITCHED	STRIKE-OUTS	WALKS	HITS ALLOWED	HRS ALLOWED	COMP. GAMES	SHUT-OUTS	SAVES
1996	Min-A	0	49	3	2	.600	24	3.79	57	56	35	43	5	0	0	4
1997	Min-A	0	29	1	1	.500	20	5.87	30 2/3	23	10	29	8	0	0	1
1998	Min-A	0	19	0	2	.000	13	4.94	23 2/3	15	10	25	3	0	0	0
1999	**NY-A**	0	33	1	0	1.000	24	4.38	49 1/3	25	22	40	8	0	0	0
Career Average		0	33	1	1	.500	20	4.54	40	30	19	34	6	0	0	1
Yankee Average		**0**	**33**	**1**	**0**	**1.000**	**24**	**4.38**	**49 1/3**	**25**	**22**	**40**	**8**	**0**	**0**	**0**
Career Total		0	130	5	5	.500	81	4.54	160 2/3	119	77	137	24	0	0	5
Yankee Total		**0**	**33**	**1**	**0**	**1.000**	**24**	**4.38**	**49 1/3**	**25**	**22**	**40**	**8**	**0**	**0**	**0**

Neagle, Dennis Edward

HEIGHT: 6′3″ LEFTHANDER   BORN: 9/13/1968 GAMBRILLS, MARYLAND

YEAR	TEAM	STARTS	GAMES	WON	LOST	PCT	ER	ERA	INNINGS PITCHED	STRIKE-OUTS	WALKS	HITS ALLOWED	HRS ALLOWED	COMP. GAMES	SHUT-OUTS	SAVES
1991	Min-A	3	7	0	1	.000	9	4.05	20	14	7	28	3	0	0	0
1992	Pit-N	6	55	4	6	.400	43	4.48	86 1/3	77	43	81	9	0	0	2
1993	Pit-N	7	50	3	5	.375	48	5.31	81 1/3	73	37	82	10	0	0	1
1994	Pit-N	24	24	9	10	.474	78	5.12	137	122	49	135	18	2	0	0
1995	Pit-N	31	31	13	8	.619	80	3.43	209 2/3	150	45	221	20	5	1	0
1996	Pit-N	27	27	14	6	.700	62	3.05	182 1/3	131	34	186	21	1	0	0
1996	Atl-N	6	6	2	3	.400	24	5.59	38 2/3	18	14	40	5	1	0	0
1997	Atl-N	34	34	20	5	.800	77	2.97	233 1/3	172	49	204	18	4	4	0
1998	Atl-N	31	32	16	11	.593	83	3.55	210 1/3	165	60	196	25	5	0	0
1999	Cin-N	19	20	9	5	.643	53	4.27	111 2/3	76	40	95	23	0	0	0
2000	Cin-N	27	27	8	2	.800	46	3.52	117 2/3	88	50	11	15	0	0	0
2000	**NY-A**	15	16	7	7	.500	.59	5.81	91 1/3	58	31	99	16	1	0	0
Career Average		19	27	9	6	.603	55	3.92	126	95	38	115	15	2	0	0
Yankee Average		**15**	**16**	**7**	**7**	**.500**	**59**	**5.81**	**91 1/3**	**58**	**31**	**99**	**16**	**1**	**0**	**0**
Career Total		230	329	105	69	.603	662	3.92	1517	1144	459	1378	183	19	0	3
Yankee Total		**15**	**16**	**7**	**7**	**.500**	**.59**	**5.81**	**91 1/3**	**58**	**31**	**99**	**16**	**1**	**0**	**0**

Nekola, Francis Joseph (Bots)

HEIGHT: 6′0″ LEFTHANDER   BORN: 12/10/1906 NEW YORK, NEW YORK   DIED: 3/11/1987 ROCKVILLE, MARYLAND

YEAR	TEAM	STARTS	GAMES	WON	LOST	PCT	ER	ERA	INNINGS PITCHED	STRIKE-OUTS	WALKS	HITS ALLOWED	HRS ALLOWED	COMP. GAMES	SHUT-OUTS	SAVES
1929	**NY-A**	1	9	0	0	—	9	4.34	18 2/3	2	15	21	0	0	0	0
1933	Det-A	0	2	0	0	—	4	27.00	1 1/3	0	1	4	1	0	0	0
Career Average		1	6	0	0	—	7	5.85	10	1	8	13	1	0	0	0
Yankee Average		**1**	**9**	**0**	**0**	**—**	**9**	**4.34**	**18 2/3**	**2**	**15**	**21**	**0**	**0**	**0**	**0**
Career Total		1	11	0	0	—	13	5.85	20	2	16	25	1	0	0	0
Yankee Total		**1**	**9**	**0**	**0**	**—**	**9**	**4.34**	**18 2/3**	**2**	**15**	**21**	**0**	**0**	**0**	**0**

Nelson, Jeffrey Allan

HEIGHT: 6′8″ RIGHTHANDER   BORN: 11/17/1966 BALTIMORE, MARYLAND

YEAR	TEAM	STARTS	GAMES	WON	LOST	PCT	ER	ERA	INNINGS PITCHED	STRIKE-OUTS	WALKS	HITS ALLOWED	HRS ALLOWED	COMP. GAMES	SHUT-OUTS	SAVES
1992	Sea-A	0	66	1	7	.125	31	3.44	81	46	44	71	7	0	0	6
1993	Sea-A	0	71	5	3	.625	29	4.35	60	61	34	57	5	0	0	1
1994	Sea-A	0	28	0	0	—	13	2.76	42 1/3	44	20	35	3	0	0	0
1995	Sea-A	0	62	7	3	.700	19	2.17	78	96	27	58	4	0	0	2
1996	**NY-A**	0	73	4	4	.500	36	4.36	74 1/3	91	36	75	6	0	0	2
1997	**NY-A**	0	77	3	7	.300	25	2.86	78 2/3	81	37	53	7	0	0	2
1998	**NY-A**	0	45	5	3	.625	17	3.79	40 1/3	35	22	44	1	0	0	3
1999	**NY-A**	0	39	2	1	.667	14	4.15	30 1/3	35	22	27	2	0	0	1
2000	**NY-A**	0	73	8	4	.667	19	2.45	69 2/3	71	45	44	2	0	0	0
Career Average		0	59	4	4	.522	23	3.29	61	62	32	52	4	0	0	2
Yankee Average		**0**	**61**	**4**	**4**	**.537**	**22**	**3.43**	**58**	**63**	**32**	**49**	**4**	**0**	**0**	**2**
Career Total		0	534	35	32	.522	203	3.29	555 1/3	560	287	464	37	0	0	17
Yankee Total		**0**	**307**	**22**	**19**	**.537**	**111**	**3.43**	**293 1/3**	**313**	**162**	**243**	**18**	**0**	**0**	**8**

Nelson, Luther Martin (Luke)

HEIGHT: 6'0" RIGHTHANDER BORN: 12/4/1893 CABLE, ILLINOIS DIED: 11/24/1985 MOLINE, ILLINOIS

YEAR	TEAM	STARTS	GAMES	WON	LOST	PCT	ER	ERA	INNINGS PITCHED	STRIKE-OUTS	WALKS	HITS ALLOWED	HRS ALLOWED	COMP. GAMES	SHUT-OUTS	SAVES
1919	NY-A	1	9	3	0	1.000	8	2.96	24 1/3	11	11	22	1	0	0	0
Career Average		1	9	3	0	1.000	8	2.96	24 1/3	11	11	22	1	0	0	0
Yankee Average		**1**	**9**	**3**	**0**	**1.000**	**8**	**2.96**	**24 1/3**	**11**	**11**	**22**	**1**	**0**	**0**	**0**
Career Total		1	9	3	0	1.000	8	2.96	24 1/3	11	11	22	1	0	0	0
Yankee Total		**1**	**9**	**3**	**0**	**1.000**	**8**	**2.96**	**24 1/3**	**11**	**11**	**22**	**1**	**0**	**0**	**0**

Nelson, Wayland Eugene (Gene)

HEIGHT: 6'0" RIGHTHANDER BORN: 12/3/1960 TAMPA, FLORIDA

YEAR	TEAM	STARTS	GAMES	WON	LOST	PCT	ER	ERA	INNINGS PITCHED	STRIKE-OUTS	WALKS	HITS ALLOWED	HRS ALLOWED	COMP. GAMES	SHUT-OUTS	SAVES
1981	NY-A	7	8	3	1	.750	21	4.81	39 1/3	16	23	40	5	0	0	0
1982	Sea-A	19	22	6	9	.400	63	4.62	122 2/3	71	60	133	16	2	1	0
1983	Sea-A	5	10	0	3	.000	28	7.88	32	11	21	38	6	1	0	0
1984	Chi-A	9	20	3	5	.375	37	4.46	74 2/3	36	17	72	9	2	0	1
1985	Chi-A	18	46	10	10	.500	69	4.26	145 2/3	101	67	144	23	1	0	2
1986	Chi-A	1	54	6	6	.500	49	3.85	114 2/3	70	41	118	7	0	0	6
1987	Oak-A	6	54	6	5	.545	54	3.93	123 2/3	94	35	120	12	0	0	3
1988	Oak-A	1	54	9	6	.600	38	3.06	111 2/3	67	38	93	9	0	0	3
1989	Oak-A	0	50	3	5	.375	29	3.26	80	70	30	60	5	0	0	3
1990	Oak-A	0	51	3	3	.500	13	1.57	74 2/3	38	17	55	5	0	0	5
1991	Oak-A	0	44	1	5	.167	37	6.84	48 2/3	23	23	60	12	0	0	0
1992	Oak-A	2	28	3	1	.750	37	6.45	51 2/3	23	22	68	5	0	0	0
1993	Cal-A	0	46	0	5	.000	18	3.08	52 2/3	31	23	50	3	0	0	4
1993	Tex-A	0	6	0	0	—	3	3.38	8	4	1	10	0	0	0	1
Career Average		5	35	4	5	.453	35	4.13	77	47	30	76	8	0	0	2
Yankee Average		**7**	**8**	**3**	**1**	**.750**	**21**	**4.81**	**39 1/3**	**16**	**23**	**40**	**5**	**0**	**0**	**0**
Career Total		68	493	53	64	.453	496	4.13	1080	655	418	1061	117	6	1	28
Yankee Total		**7**	**8**	**3**	**1**	**.750**	**21**	**4.81**	**39 1/3**	**16**	**23**	**40**	**5**	**0**	**0**	**0**

Neuer, John S. (Tex)

HEIGHT: 6'0" LEFTHANDER BORN: 6/8/1877 FREMONT, OHIO DIED: 1/14/1966 NORTHUMBERLAND, PENNSYLVANIA

YEAR	TEAM	STARTS	GAMES	WON	LOST	PCT	ER	ERA	INNINGS PITCHED	STRIKE-OUTS	WALKS	HITS ALLOWED	HRS ALLOWED	COMP. GAMES	SHUT-OUTS	SAVES
1907	NY-A	6	7	4	2	.667	13	2.17	54	22	19	40	1	6	3	0
Career Average		6	7	4	2	.667	13	2.17	54	22	19	40	1	6	3	0
Yankee Average		**6**	**7**	**4**	**2**	**.667**	**13**	**2.17**	**54**	**22**	**19**	**40**	**1**	**6**	**3**	**0**
Career Total		6	7	4	2	.667	13	2.17	54	22	19	40	1	6	3	0
Yankee Total		**6**	**7**	**4**	**2**	**.667**	**13**	**2.17**	**54**	**22**	**19**	**40**	**1**	**6**	**3**	**0**

Nevel, Ernie Wyre

HEIGHT: 5'11" RIGHTHANDER BORN: 8/17/1919 CHARLESTON, MISSOURI DIED: 7/10/1988 SPRINGFIELD, MISSOURI

YEAR	TEAM	STARTS	GAMES	WON	LOST	PCT	ER	ERA	INNINGS PITCHED	STRIKE-OUTS	WALKS	HITS ALLOWED	HRS ALLOWED	COMP. GAMES	SHUT-OUTS	SAVES
1950	NY-A	1	3	0	1	.000	7	9.95	6 1/3	3	6	10	0	0	0	0
1951	NY-A	0	1	0	0	—	0	0.00	4	1	1	1	0	0	0	1
1953	Cin-N	0	10	0	0	—	7	6.10	10 1/3	5	1	16	0	0	0	0
Career Average		0	5	0	0	—	5	6.10	7	3	3	9	0	0	0	0
Yankee Average		**1**	**2**	**0**	**1**	**.000**	**4**	**6.10**	**5**	**2**	**4**	**6**	**0**	**0**	**0**	**1**
Career Total		1	14	0	1	.000	14	6.10	20 2/3	9	8	27	0	0	0	1
Yankee Total		**1**	**4**	**0**	**1**	**.000**	**7**	**6.10**	**10 1/3**	**4**	**7**	**11**	**0**	**0**	**0**	**1**

Newkirk, Floyd Elmo (Three-Finger)
HEIGHT: 5'11"   RIGHTHANDER   BORN: 7/16/1908 NORRIS CITY, ILLINOIS   DIED: 4/15/1976 CLAYTON, MISSOURI

YEAR	TEAM	STARTS	GAMES	WON	LOST	PCT	ER	ERA	INNINGS PITCHED	STRIKE-OUTS	WALKS	HITS ALLOWED	HRS ALLOWED	COMP. GAMES	SHUT-OUTS	SAVES
1934	NY-A	0	1	0	0	—	0	0.00	1	0	1	1	0	0	0	0
Career Average		0	1	0	0	—	0	0.00	1	0	1	1	0	0	0	0
Yankee Average		**0**	**1**	**0**	**0**	**—**	**0**	**0.00**	**1**	**0**	**1**	**1**	**0**	**0**	**0**	**0**
Career Total		0	1	0	0	—	0	0.00	1	0	1	1	0	0	0	0
Yankee Total		**0**	**1**	**0**	**0**	**—**	**0**	**0.00**	**1**	**0**	**1**	**1**	**0**	**0**	**0**	**0**

Newsom, Louis Norman (Bobo *or* Buck)
HEIGHT: 6'3"   RIGHTHANDER   BORN: 8/11/1907 HARTSVILLE, SOUTH CAROLINA   DIED: 12/7/1962 ORLANDO, FLORIDA

YEAR	TEAM	STARTS	GAMES	WON	LOST	PCT	ER	ERA	INNINGS PITCHED	STRIKE-OUTS	WALKS	HITS ALLOWED	HRS ALLOWED	COMP. GAMES	SHUT-OUTS	SAVES
1929	Bro-N	2	3	0	3	.000	11	10.61	9 1/3	6	5	15	0	0	0	0
1930	Bro-N	0	2	0	0	—	0	0.00	3	1	2	2	0	0	0	0
1932	Chi-N	0	1	0	0	—	0	0.00	1	0	0	1	0	0	0	0
1934	StL-A	32	47	16	20	.444	117	4.01	262 1/3	135	149	259	15	15	2	5
1935	StL-A	6	7	0	6	.000	23	4.85	42 2/3	22	13	54	2	1	0	1
1935	Was-A	23	28	11	12	.478	98	4.45	198 1/3	65	84	222	9	17	2	2
1936	Was-A	38	43	17	15	.531	137	4.32	285 2/3	156	146	294	13	24	4	2
1937	Was-A	10	11	3	4	.429	44	5.85	67 2/3	39	48	76	4	3	0	0
1937	Bos-A	27	30	13	10	.565	103	4.46	207 2/3	127	119	193	14	14	1	0
1938	StL-A	40	44	20	16	.556	186	5.08	329 2/3	226	192	334	30	31	0	1
1939	StL-A	6	6	3	1	.750	24	4.73	45 2/3	28	22	50	5	3	0	0
1939	Det-A	31	35	17	10	.630	92	3.37	246	164	104	222	14	21	3	2
1940	Det-A	34	36	21	5	.808	83	2.83	264	164	100	235	19	20	3	0
1941	Det-A	36	43	12	20	.375	128	4.60	250 1/3	175	118	265	15	12	2	2
1942	Was-A	29	30	11	17	.393	117	4.93	213 2/3	113	92	236	5	15	2	0
1942	Bro-N	5	6	2	2	.500	12	3.38	32	21	14	28	1	2	1	0
1943	Bro-N	12	22	9	4	.692	42	3.02	125	75	57	113	4	6	1	1
1943	StL-A	9	10	1	6	.143	43	7.39	52 1/3	37	35	69	7	0	0	0
1943	Was-A	6	6	3	3	.500	17	3.83	40	11	21	38	1	2	0	0
1944	Phi-A	33	37	13	15	.464	83	2.82	265	142	82	243	11	18	2	1
1945	Phi-A	34	36	8	20	.286	94	3.29	257 1/3	127	103	255	12	16	3	0
1946	Phi-A	9	10	3	5	.375	22	3.38	58 2/3	32	30	61	2	3	1	0
1946	Was-A	22	24	11	8	.579	55	2.78	178	82	60	163	5	14	2	1
1947	Was-A	13	14	4	6	.400	38	4.09	83 2/3	40	37	99	2	1	0	0
1947	**NY-A**	**15**	**17**	**7**	**5**	**.583**	**36**	**2.80**	**115 2/3**	**42**	**30**	**109**	**8**	**6**	**2**	**0**
1948	NY-N	4	11	0	4	.000	12	4.21	25 2/3	9	13	35	1	0	0	0
1952	Was-A	0	10	1	1	.500	7	4.97	12 2/3	5	9	16	2	0	0	2
1952	Phi-A	5	14	3	3	.500	19	3.59	47 2/3	22	23	38	2	1	0	1
1953	Phi-A	2	17	2	1	.667	21	4.89	38 2/3	16	24	44	3	1	0	0
Career Average		17	0	7	8	.487	57	3.98	130	72	60	130	7	8	0	0
Yankee Average		**15**	**17**	**7**	**5**	**.583**	**36**	**2.80**	**115 2/3**	**42**	**30**	**109**	**8**	**6**	**2**	**0**
Career Total		600	483	211	222	.487	1664	3.98	3759 1/3	2082	1732	3769	206	246	31	12
Yankee Total		**15**	**17**	**7**	**5**	**.583**	**36**	**2.80**	**115 2/3**	**42**	**30**	**109**	**8**	**6**	**2**	**0**

Newton, Eustace James (Doc)
HEIGHT: 6'0"   LEFTHANDER   BORN: 10/26/1877 INDIANAPOLIS, INDIANA   DIED: 5/14/1931 MEMPHIS, TENNESSEE

YEAR	TEAM	STARTS	GAMES	WON	LOST	PCT	ER	ERA	INNINGS PITCHED	STRIKE-OUTS	WALKS	HITS ALLOWED	HRS ALLOWED	COMP. GAMES	SHUT-OUTS	SAVES
1900	Cin-N	27	36	9	15	.375	108	4.14	234 2/3	88	100	255	4	22	1	0
1901	Cin-N	18	20	4	13	.235	77	4.12	168 1/3	65	59	190	6	17	0	0
1901	Bro-N	12	13	6	5	.545	33	2.83	105	45	30	110	1	9	0	0
1902	Bro-N	28	31	15	14	.517	71	2.42	264 1/3	107	87	208	2	26	4	2
1905	**NY-A**	**7**	**11**	**2**	**2**	**.500**	**14**	**2.11**	**59 2/3**	**15**	**24**	**61**	**1**	**2**	**0**	**0**
1906	**NY-A**	**15**	**21**	**7**	**5**	**.583**	**44**	**3.17**	**125**	**52**	**33**	**118**	**3**	**6**	**2**	**0**
1907	**NY-A**	**15**	**19**	**7**	**10**	**.412**	**47**	**3.18**	**133**	**70**	**31**	**132**	**0**	**10**	**0**	**0**
1908	**NY-A**	**13**	**23**	**4**	**5**	**.444**	**29**	**2.95**	**88 1/3**	**49**	**41**	**78**	**0**	**6**	**1**	**1**
1909	**NY-A**	**4**	**4**	**0**	**3**	**.000**	**7**	**2.82**	**22 1/3**	**11**	**11**	**27**	**0**	**1**	**0**	**0**
Career Average		15	20	6	8	.425	48	3.22	134	56	45	131	2	11	1	0
Yankee Average		**11**	**16**	**4**	**5**	**.444**	**28**	**2.96**	**86**	**39**	**28**	**83**	**1**	**5**	**1**	**0**
Career Total		139	178	54	73	.425	430	3.22	1202 2/3	502	406	1179	17	99	8	3
Yankee Total		**54**	**78**	**20**	**25**	**.444**	**141**	**2.96**	**428 1/3**	**197**	**140**	**416**	**4**	**25**	**3**	**1**

Niekro, Joseph Franklin

HEIGHT: 6'1" RIGHTHANDER BORN: 11/7/1944 MARTINS FERRY, OHIO

YEAR	TEAM	STARTS	GAMES	WON	LOST	PCT	ER	ERA	INNINGS PITCHED	STRIKE-OUTS	WALKS	HITS ALLOWED	HRS ALLOWED	COMP. GAMES	SHUT-OUTS	SAVES
1967	Chi-N	22	36	10	7	.588	63	3.34	169 2/3	77	32	171	15	7	2	0
1968	Chi-N	29	34	14	10	.583	85	4.32	177	65	59	204	18	2	1	2
1969	Chi-N	3	4	0	1	.000	8	3.72	19 1/3	7	6	24	3	0	0	0
1969	SD-N	31	37	8	17	.320	83	3.70	202	55	45	213	15	8	3	0
1970	Det-A	34	38	12	13	.480	96	4.06	213	101	72	221	28	6	2	0
1971	Det-A	15	31	6	7	.462	61	4.49	122 1/3	43	49	136	13	0	0	1
1972	Det-A	7	18	3	2	.600	20	3.83	47	24	8	62	3	1	0	1
1973	Atl-N	0	20	2	4	.333	11	4.13	24	12	11	23	2	0	0	3
1974	Atl-N	2	27	3	2	.600	17	3.56	43	31	18	36	5	0	0	0
1975	Hou-N	4	40	6	4	.600	30	3.07	88	54	39	79	3	1	1	4
1976	Hou-N	13	36	4	8	.333	44	3.36	118	77	56	107	8	0	0	0
1977	Hou-N	14	44	13	8	.619	61	3.04	180 2/3	101	64	155	14	9	2	5
1978	Hou-N	29	35	14	14	.500	87	3.86	202 2/3	97	73	190	13	10	1	0
1979	Hou-N	38	38	21	11	.656	88	3.00	263 2/3	119	107	221	17	11	5	0
1980	Hou-N	36	37	20	12	.625	101	3.55	256	127	79	268	12	11	2	0
1981	Hou-N	24	24	9	9	.500	52	2.82	166	77	47	150	8	5	2	0
1982	Hou-N	35	35	17	12	.586	74	2.47	270	130	64	224	12	16	5	0
1983	Hou-N	38	38	15	14	.517	102	3.48	263 2/3	152	101	238	15	9	1	0
1984	Hou-N	38	38	16	12	.571	84	3.04	248 1/3	127	89	223	16	6	1	0
1985	Hou-N	32	32	9	12	.429	88	3.72	213	117	99	197	21	4	1	0
1985	**NY-A**	**3**	**3**	**2**	**1**	**.667**	**8**	**5.84**	**12 1/3**	**4**	**8**	**14**	**3**	**0**	**0**	**0**
1986	**NY-A**	**25**	**25**	**9**	**10**	**.474**	**68**	**4.87**	**125 2/3**	**59**	**63**	**139**	**15**	**0**	**0**	**0**
1987	**NY-A**	**8**	**8**	**3**	**4**	**.429**	**20**	**3.55**	**50 2/3**	**30**	**19**	**40**	**4**	**1**	**0**	**0**
1987	Min-A	18	19	4	9	.308	67	6.26	96 1/3	54	45	115	11	0	0	0
1988	Min-A	2	5	1	1	.500	13	10.03	11 2/3	7	9	16	2	0	0	0
Career Average		20	28	9	8	.520	57	3.59	143	70	50	139	11	4	1	1
Yankee Average		**12**	**12**	**5**	**5**	**.483**	**32**	**4.58**	**63**	**31**	**30**	**64**	**7**	**0**	**0**	**0**
Career Total		500	702	221	204	.520	1431	3.59	3584	1747	1262	3466	276	107	29	16
Yankee Total		**36**	**36**	**14**	**15**	**.483**	**96**	**4.58**	**188 2/3**	**93**	**90**	**193**	**22**	**1**	**0**	**0**

Niekro, Philip Henry

HEIGHT: 6'1" RIGHTHANDER BORN: 4/1/1939 BLAINE, OHIO

YEAR	TEAM	STARTS	GAMES	WON	LOST	PCT	ER	ERA	INNINGS PITCHED	STRIKE-OUTS	WALKS	HITS ALLOWED	HRS ALLOWED	COMP. GAMES	SHUT-OUTS	SAVES
1964	Mil-N	0	10	0	0	—	8	4.80	15	8	7	15	1	0	0	0
1965	Mil-N	1	41	2	3	.400	24	2.89	74 2/3	49	26	73	5	0	0	6
1966	Atl-N	0	28	4	3	.571	23	4.11	50 1/3	17	23	48	4	0	0	2
1967	Atl-N	20	46	11	9	.550	43	1.87	207	129	55	164	9	10	1	9
1968	Atl-N	34	37	14	12	.538	74	2.59	257	140	45	228	16	15	5	2
1969	Atl-N	35	40	23	13	.639	81	2.56	284 1/3	193	57	235	21	21	4	1
1970	Atl-N	32	34	12	18	.400	109	4.27	229 2/3	168	68	222	40	10	3	0
1971	Atl-N	36	42	15	14	.517	89	2.98	268 2/3	173	70	248	27	18	4	2
1972	Atl-N	36	38	16	12	.571	96	3.06	282 1/3	164	53	254	22	17	1	0
1973	Atl-N	30	42	13	10	.565	90	3.31	245	131	89	214	21	9	1	4
1974	Atl-N	39	41	20	13	.606	80	2.38	302 1/3	195	88	249	19	18	6	1
1975	Atl-N	37	39	15	15	.500	98	3.20	275 2/3	144	72	285	29	13	1	0
1976	Atl-N	37	38	17	11	.607	99	3.29	270 2/3	173	101	249	18	10	2	0
1977	Atl-N	43	44	16	20	.444	148	4.03	330 1/3	262	164	315	26	20	2	0
1978	Atl-N	42	44	19	18	.514	107	2.88	334 1/3	248	102	295	16	22	4	1
1979	Atl-N	44	44	21	20	.512	129	3.39	342	208	113	311	41	23	1	0
1980	Atl-N	38	40	15	18	.455	111	3.63	275	176	85	256	30	11	3	1
1981	Atl-N	22	22	7	7	.500	48	3.10	139 1/3	62	56	120	6	3	3	0
1982	Atl-N	35	35	17	4	.810	94	3.61	234 1/3	144	73	225	23	4	2	0
1983	Atl-N	33	34	11	10	.524	89	3.97	201 1/3	128	105	212	18	2	0	0
1984	**NY-A**	**31**	**32**	**16**	**8**	**.667**	**74**	**3.09**	**215 2/3**	**136**	**76**	**219**	**15**	**5**	**1**	**0**
1985	**NY-A**	**33**	**33**	**16**	**12**	**.571**	**100**	**4.09**	**220**	**149**	**120**	**203**	**29**	**7**	**1**	**0**
1986	Cle-A	32	34	11	11	.500	101	4.32	210 1/3	81	95	241	24	5	0	0
1987	Cle-A	22	22	7	11	.389	81	5.89	123 2/3	57	53	142	18	2	0	0
1987	Tor-A	3	3	0	2	.000	11	8.25	12	7	7	15	4	0	0	0
1987	Atl-N	1	1	0	0	—	5	15.00	3	0	6	6	0	0	0	0
Career Average		28	33	12	11	.537	77	3.35	208	129	70	194	19	9	2	1
Yankee Average		**32**	**33**	**16**	**10**	**.615**	**87**	**3.59**	**218**	**143**	**98**	**211**	**22**	**6**	**1**	**0**
Career Total		716	864	318	274	.537	2012	3.35	5404 1/3	3342	1809	5044	482	245	45	29
Yankee Total		**64**	**65**	**32**	**20**	**.615**	**174**	**3.59**	**435 2/3**	**285**	**196**	**422**	**44**	**12**	**2**	**0**

Nielsen, Jeffrey Scott
HEIGHT: 6'1" RIGHTHANDER BORN: 12/18/1958 SALT LAKE CITY, UTAH

YEAR	TEAM	STARTS	GAMES	WON	LOST	PCT	ER	ERA	INNINGS PITCHED	STRIKE-OUTS	WALKS	HITS ALLOWED	HRS ALLOWED	COMP. GAMES	SHUT-OUTS	SAVES
1986	**NY-A**	**9**	**10**	**4**	**4**	**.500**	**25**	**4.02**	**56**	**20**	**12**	**66**	**12**	**2**	**2**	**0**
1987	Chi-A	7	19	3	5	.375	46	6.24	66⅓	23	25	83	9	1	1	2
1988	NY-A	2	7	1	2	.333	15	6.86	19⅔	4	13	27	5	0	0	0
1989	NY-A	0	2	1	0	1.000	1	13.51	⅔	0	1	2	0	0	0	0
Career Average		5	10	2	3	.450	22	5.49	36	12	13	45	7	1	1	1
Yankee Average		**4**	**6**	**2**	**2**	**.500**	**14**	**4.83**	**25**	**8**	**9**	**32**	**6**	**1**	**1**	**0**
Career Total		18	38	9	11	.450	87	5.49	142⅔	47	51	178	26	3	3	2
Yankee Total		**11**	**19**	**6**	**6**	**.500**	**41**	**4.83**	**76⅓**	**24**	**26**	**95**	**17**	**2**	**2**	**0**

Nottebart, Donald Edward
HEIGHT: 6'1" RIGHTHANDER BORN: 1/23/1936 WEST NEWTON, MASSACHUSETTS

YEAR	TEAM	STARTS	GAMES	WON	LOST	PCT	ER	ERA	INNINGS PITCHED	STRIKE-OUTS	WALKS	HITS ALLOWED	HRS ALLOWED	COMP. GAMES	SHUT-OUTS	SAVES
1960	Mil-N	1	5	1	0	1.000	7	4.11	15⅓	8	15	14	0	0	0	1
1961	Mil-N	11	38	6	7	.462	57	4.06	126⅓	66	48	117	11	2	0	3
1962	Mil-N	0	39	2	2	.500	23	3.23	64	36	20	64	4	0	0	2
1963	Hou-N	27	31	11	8	.579	68	3.17	193	118	39	170	10	9	2	0
1964	Hou-N	24	28	6	11	.353	68	3.90	157	90	37	165	12	2	0	0
1965	Hou-N	25	29	4	15	.211	82	4.67	158	77	55	166	14	3	0	0
1966	Cin-N	1	59	5	4	.556	38	3.07	111⅓	69	43	97	11	0	0	11
1967	Cin-N	0	47	0	3	.000	17	1.93	79⅓	48	19	75	4	0	0	4
1969	**NY-A**	**0**	**4**	**0**	**0**	**—**	**3**	**4.50**	**6**	**5**	**0**	**6**	**1**	**0**	**0**	**0**
1969	Chi-N	0	16	1	1	.500	14	7.00	18	8	7	28	2	0	0	0
Career Average		9	30	4	5	.414	38	3.65	93	53	28	90	7	2	0	2
Yankee Average		**0**	**4**	**0**	**0**	**—**	**3**	**4.50**	**6**	**5**	**0**	**6**	**1**	**0**	**0**	**0**
Career Total		89	296	36	51	.414	377	3.65	928⅓	525	283	902	69	16	2	21
Yankee Total		**0**	**4**	**0**	**0**	**—**	**3**	**4.50**	**6**	**5**	**0**	**6**	**1**	**0**	**0**	**0**

O'Connor, Andrew James
HEIGHT: 6'0" RIGHTHANDER BORN: 9/14/1884 ROXBURY, MASSACHUSETTS DIED: 9/26/1980 NORWOOD, MASSACHUSETTS

YEAR	TEAM	STARTS	GAMES	WON	LOST	PCT	ER	ERA	INNINGS PITCHED	STRIKE-OUTS	WALKS	HITS ALLOWED	HRS ALLOWED	COMP. GAMES	SHUT-OUTS	SAVES
1908	**NY-A**	**1**	**1**	**0**	**1**	**.000**	**9**	**10.13**	**8**	**5**	**7**	**15**	**0**	**1**	**0**	**0**
Career Average		1	1	0	1	.000	9	10.13	8	5	7	15	0	1	0	0
Yankee Average		**1**	**1**	**0**	**1**	**.000**	**9**	**10.13**	**8**	**5**	**7**	**15**	**0**	**1**	**0**	**0**
Career Total		1	1	0	1	.000	9	10.13	8	5	7	15	0	1	0	0
Yankee Total		**1**	**1**	**0**	**1**	**.000**	**9**	**10.13**	**8**	**5**	**7**	**15**	**0**	**1**	**0**	**0**

O'Doul, Francis Joseph (Lefty)
HEIGHT: 6'0" LEFTHANDER BORN: 3/4/1897 SAN FRANCISCO, CALIFORNIA DIED: 12/7/1969 SAN FRANCISCO, CALIFORNIA

YEAR	TEAM	STARTS	GAMES	WON	LOST	PCT	ER	ERA	INNINGS PITCHED	STRIKE-OUTS	WALKS	HITS ALLOWED	HRS ALLOWED	COMP. GAMES	SHUT-OUTS	SAVES
1919	**NY-A**	**0**	**3**	**0**	**0**	**—**	**2**	**3.60**	**5**	**2**	**4**	**7**	**0**	**0**	**0**	**0**
1920	**NY-A**	**0**	**2**	**0**	**0**	**—**	**2**	**4.91**	**3⅔**	**2**	**2**	**4**	**0**	**0**	**0**	**0**
1922	**NY-A**	**0**	**6**	**0**	**0**	**—**	**6**	**3.38**	**16**	**5**	**12**	**24**	**0**	**0**	**0**	**0**
1923	Bos-A	0	23	1	1	.500	32	5.43	53	10	31	69	2	0	0	0
Career Average		0	9	0	0	.500	11	4.87	19	5	12	26	1	0	0	0
Yankee Average		**0**	**4**	**0**	**0**	**—**	**3**	**3.65**	**8**	**3**	**6**	**12**	**0**	**0**	**0**	**0**
Career Total		0	34	1	1	.500	42	4.87	77⅔	19	49	104	2	0	0	0
Yankee Total		**0**	**11**	**0**	**0**	**—**	**10**	**3.65**	**24⅔**	**9**	**18**	**35**	**0**	**0**	**0**	**0**

Ojeda, Robert Michael

HEIGHT: 6'1"   LEFTHANDER   BORN: 12/17/1957 LOS ANGELES, CALIFORNIA

YEAR	TEAM	STARTS	GAMES	WON	LOST	PCT	ER	ERA	INNINGS PITCHED	STRIKE-OUTS	WALKS	HITS ALLOWED	HRS ALLOWED	COMP. GAMES	SHUT-OUTS	SAVES
1980	Bos-A	7	7	1	1	.500	20	6.92	26	12	14	39	2	0	0	0
1981	Bos-A	10	10	6	2	.750	23	3.12	66 1/3	28	25	50	6	2	0	0
1982	Bos-A	14	22	4	6	.400	49	5.63	78 1/3	52	29	95	13	0	0	0
1983	Bos-A	28	29	12	7	.632	78	4.04	173 2/3	94	73	173	15	5	0	0
1984	Bos-A	32	33	12	12	.500	96	3.99	216 2/3	137	96	211	17	8	5	0
1985	Bos-A	22	39	9	11	.450	70	4.00	157 2/3	102	48	166	11	5	0	1
1986	NY-N	30	32	18	5	.783	62	2.57	217 1/3	148	52	185	15	7	2	0
1987	NY-N	7	10	3	5	.375	20	3.88	46 1/3	21	10	45	5	0	0	0
1988	NY-N	29	29	10	13	.435	61	2.88	190 1/3	133	33	158	6	5	5	0
1989	NY-N	31	31	13	11	.542	74	3.47	192	95	78	179	16	5	2	0
1990	NY-N	12	38	7	6	.538	48	3.66	118	62	40	123	10	0	0	0
1991	LA-N	31	31	12	9	.571	67	3.18	189 1/3	120	70	181	15	2	1	0
1992	LA-N	29	29	6	9	.400	67	3.63	166 1/3	94	81	169	8	2	1	0
1993	Cle-A	7	9	2	1	.667	21	4.40	43	27	21	48	5	0	0	0
1994	**NY-A**	**2**	**2**	**0**	**0**	**—**	**8**	**24.00**	**3**	**3**	**6**	**11**	**1**	**0**	**0**	**0**
Career Average		19	23	8	7	.540	51	3.65	126	75	45	122	10	3	1	0
Yankee Average		**2**	**2**	**0**	**0**	**—**	**8**	**24.00**	**3**	**3**	**6**	**11**	**1**	**0**	**0**	**0**
Career Total		291	351	115	98	.540	764	3.65	1884 1/3	1128	676	1833	145	41	16	1
Yankee Total		**2**	**2**	**0**	**0**	**—**	**8**	**24.00**	**3**	**3**	**6**	**11**	**1**	**0**	**0**	**0**

Orth, Albert Lewis (Smiling Al *or* The Curveless Wonder)

HEIGHT: 6'0"   RIGHTHANDER   BORN: 9/5/1872 TIPTON, INDIANA   DIED: 10/8/1948 LYNCHBURG, VIRGINIA

YEAR	TEAM	STARTS	GAMES	WON	LOST	PCT	ER	ERA	INNINGS PITCHED	STRIKE-OUTS	WALKS	HITS ALLOWED	HRS ALLOWED	COMP. GAMES	SHUT-OUTS	SAVES
1895	Phi-N	10	11	8	1	.889	38	3.89	88	25	22	103	0	9	0	1
1896	Phi-N	23	25	14	8	.636	96	4.41	196	23	46	244	10	19	0	1
1897	Phi-N	34	36	8	1	.636	145	4.62	282 1/3	64	82	349	12	29	2	0
1898	Phi-N	28	32	15	11	.577	84	3.02	250	52	53	290	2	25	1	0
1899	Phi-N	15	21	13	3	.813	40	2.49	144 2/3	35	19	149	0	13	3	3
1900	Phi-N	30	33	14	14	.500	110	3.78	262	68	60	302	4	24	2	1
1901	Phi-N	33	35	20	12	.625	71	2.27	281 2/3	92	32	250	3	30	6	1
1902	Was-A	37	38	19	18	.514	143	3.97	324	76	40	367	18	36	1	0
1903	Was-A	32	36	11	22	.333	135	4.34	279 2/3	88	62	326	8	30	2	2
1904	Was-A	7	10	3	4	.429	39	4.76	73 2/3	23	15	88	2	7	0	0
1904	**NY-A**	**18**	**20**	**11**	**6**	**.647**	**41**	**2.68**	**137 2/3**	**47**	**19**	**122**	**0**	**11**	**2**	**0**
1905	**NY-A**	**37**	**40**	**18**	**16**	**.529**	**97**	**2.86**	**305 1/3**	**121**	**61**	**273**	**8**	**26**	**6**	**0**
1906	**NY-A**	**39**	**45**	**27**	**17**	**.614**	**88**	**2.34**	**338 2/3**	**133**	**66**	**317**	**2**	**36**	**3**	**0**
1907	**NY-A**	**33**	**36**	**14**	**21**	**.400**	**72**	**2.61**	**248 2/3**	**78**	**53**	**244**	**2**	**21**	**2**	**0**
1908	**NY-A**	**17**	**21**	**2**	**13**	**.133**	**53**	**3.42**	**139 1/3**	**22**	**30**	**134**	**4**	**8**	**1**	**0**
1909	**NY-A**	**1**	**1**	**0**	**0**	**—**	**4**	**12.00**	**3**	**1**	**1**	**6**	**0**	**0**	**0**	**0**
Career Average		25	28	12	10	.540	79	3.37	210	59	41	223	5	20	2	1
Yankee Average		**24**	**27**	**12**	**12**	**.497**	**59**	**2.72**	**195**	**67**	**38**	**183**	**3**	**17**	**2**	**0**
Career Total		394	440	203	184	.525	1256	3.37	3354 2/3	948	661	3564	75	324	31	9
Yankee Total		**145**	**163**	**72**	**73**	**.497**	**355**	**2.72**	**1172 2/3**	**402**	**230**	**1096**	**16**	**102**	**14**	**0**

Ostrowski, Joseph Paul (Professor)

HEIGHT: 6'0"   LEFTHANDER   BORN: 11/15/1916 W. WYOMING, PENNSYLVANIA

YEAR	TEAM	STARTS	GAMES	WON	LOST	PCT	ER	ERA	INNINGS PITCHED	STRIKE-OUTS	WALKS	HITS ALLOWED	HRS ALLOWED	COMP. GAMES	SHUT-OUTS	SAVES
1948	StL-A	9	26	4	6	.400	52	5.97	78 1/3	20	17	108	6	3	0	3
1949	StL-A	13	40	8	8	.500	75	4.79	141	34	27	185	16	4	0	2
1950	StL-A	7	9	2	4	.333	16	2.51	57 1/3	15	7	57	2	2	0	0
1950	**NY-A**	**4**	**21**	**1**	**1**	**.500**	**25**	**5.15**	**43 2/3**	**15**	**15**	**50**	**11**	**1**	**0**	**3**
1951	**NY-A**	**3**	**34**	**6**	**4**	**.600**	**37**	**3.49**	**95 1/3**	**30**	**18**	**103**	**4**	**2**	**0**	**5**
1952	**NY-A**	**1**	**20**	**2**	**2**	**.500**	**25**	**5.63**	**40**	**17**	**14**	**56**	**5**	**0**	**0**	**2**
Career Average		6	25	4	4	.479	38	4.54	76	22	16	93	7	2	0	3
Yankee Average		**3**	**25**	**3**	**2**	**.563**	**29**	**4.37**	**60**	**21**	**16**	**70**	**7**	**1**	**0**	**3**
Career Total		37	150	23	25	.479	230	4.54	455 2/3	131	98	559	44	12	0	15
Yankee Total		**8**	**75**	**9**	**7**	**.563**	**87**	**4.37**	**179**	**62**	**47**	**209**	**20**	**3**	**0**	**10**

Overmire, Frank W. (Stubby)

HEIGHT: 5'7"   LEFTHANDER   BORN: 5/16/1919 MOLINE, MICHIGAN   DIED: 3/3/1977 LAKELAND, FLORIDA

YEAR	TEAM	STARTS	GAMES	WON	LOST	PCT	ER	ERA	INNINGS PITCHED	STRIKE-OUTS	WALKS	HITS ALLOWED	HRS ALLOWED	COMP. GAMES	SHUT-OUTS	SAVES
1943	Det-A	18	29	7	6	.538	52	3.18	147	48	38	135	5	8	3	1
1944	Det-A	28	32	11	11	.500	68	3.07	199 2/3	57	41	214	2	11	3	1
1945	Det-A	22	31	9	9	.500	70	3.88	162 1/3	36	42	189	6	9	0	4
1946	Det-A	13	24	5	7	.417	50	4.62	97 1/3	34	29	106	6	3	0	1
1947	Det-A	17	28	11	5	.688	59	3.77	140 2/3	33	44	142	9	7	3	0
1948	Det-A	4	37	3	4	.429	44	5.97	66 1/3	14	31	89	5	0	0	3
1949	Det-A	1	14	1	3	.250	19	9.87	17 1/3	3	9	29	2	0	0	0
1950	StL-A	19	31	9	12	.429	75	4.19	161	39	45	200	11	8	2	0
1951	StL-A	7	8	1	6	.143	21	3.54	53 1/3	13	21	61	5	3	0	0
1951	**NY-A**	**4**	**15**	**1**	**1**	**.500**	**23**	**4.63**	**44 2/3**	**14**	**18**	**50**	**2**	**1**	**0**	**0**
1952	StL-A	4	17	0	3	.000	17	3.73	41	10	7	44	3	0	0	0
Career Average		12	24	5	6	.464	45	3.96	103	27	30	114	5	5	1	1
Yankee Average		**4**	**15**	**1**	**1**	**.500**	**23**	**4.63**	**44 2/3**	**14**	**18**	**50**	**2**	**1**	**0**	**0**
Career Total		137	266	58	67	.464	498	3.96	1130 2/3	301	325	1259	56	50	11	10
Yankee Total		**4**	**15**	**1**	**1**	**.500**	**23**	**4.63**	**44 2/3**	**14**	**18**	**50**	**2**	**1**	**0**	**0**

Pacella, John Lewis

HEIGHT: 6'3"   RIGHTHANDER   BORN: 9/15/1956 BROOKLYN, NEW YORK

YEAR	TEAM	STARTS	GAMES	WON	LOST	PCT	ER	ERA	INNINGS PITCHED	STRIKE-OUTS	WALKS	HITS ALLOWED	HRS ALLOWED	COMP. GAMES	SHUT-OUTS	SAVES
1977	NY-N	0	3	0	0	—	0	0.00	4	1	2	2	0	0	0	0
1979	NY-N	3	4	0	2	.000	8	4.41	16 1/3	12	4	16	0	0	0	0
1980	NY-N	15	32	3	4	.429	48	5.14	84	68	59	89	5	0	0	0
1982	**NY-A**	**1**	**3**	**0**	**1**	**.000**	**8**	**7.20**	**10**	**2**	**9**	**13**	**0**	**0**	**0**	**0**
1982	Min-A	1	21	1	2	.333	42	7.32	51 2/3	20	37	61	14	0	0	2
1984	Bal-A	1	6	0	1	.000	11	6.75	14 2/3	8	9	15	2	0	0	0
1986	Det-A	0	5	0	0	—	5	4.09	11	5	13	10	0	0	0	1
Career Average		3	11	1	1	.286	17	5.73	27	17	19	29	3	0	0	0
Yankee Average		**1**	**3**	**0**	**1**	**.000**	**8**	**7.20**	**10**	**2**	**9**	**13**	**0**	**0**	**0**	**0**
Career Total		21	74	4	10	.286	122	5.73	191 2/3	116	133	206	21	0	0	3
Yankee Total		**1**	**3**	**0**	**1**	**.000**	**8**	**7.20**	**10**	**2**	**9**	**13**	**0**	**0**	**0**	**0**

Pagan, David Percy

HEIGHT: 6'2"   RIGHTHANDER   BORN: 9/15/1949 NIPAWIN, SASKATCHEWAN, CANADA

YEAR	TEAM	STARTS	GAMES	WON	LOST	PCT	ER	ERA	INNINGS PITCHED	STRIKE-OUTS	WALKS	HITS ALLOWED	HRS ALLOWED	COMP. GAMES	SHUT-OUTS	SAVES
1973	**NY-A**	**1**	**4**	**0**	**0**	**—**	**4**	**3.82**	**12 2/3**	**9**	**1**	**16**	**1**	**0**	**0**	**0**
1974	**NY-A**	**6**	**16**	**1**	**3**	**.250**	**28**	**5.11**	**49 1/3**	**39**	**28**	**49**	**1**	**1**	**0**	**0**
1975	**NY-A**	**0**	**13**	**0**	**0**	**—**	**14**	**4.06**	**31**	**18**	**13**	**30**	**2**	**0**	**0**	**1**
1976	**NY-A**	**2**	**7**	**1**	**1**	**.500**	**6**	**2.28**	**23 2/3**	**13**	**4**	**18**	**0**	**1**	**0**	**0**
1976	Bal-A	5	20	1	4	.200	31	5.98	46 2/3	34	23	54	2	0	0	1
1977	Sea-A	4	24	1	1	.500	45	6.14	66	30	26	86	3	1	1	2
1977	Pit-N	0	1	0	0	—	0	0.00	3	4	0	1	0	0	0	0
Career Average		3	12	1	1	.308	18	5.24	31	21	14	36	1	0	0	1
Yankee Average		**3**	**12**	**1**	**1**	**.333**	**16**	**4.15**	**34**	**23**	**15**	**32**	**1**	**1**	**0**	**0**
Career Total		18	85	4	9	.308	128	5.24	219 2/3	147	95	254	9	3	1	4
Yankee Total		**8**	**36**	**2**	**4**	**.333**	**48**	**4.15**	**104**	**70**	**45**	**97**	**3**	**2**	**0**	**1**

Page, Joseph Francis (Fireman)

HEIGHT: 6'2"   LEFTHANDER   BORN: 10/28/1917 CHERRY VALLEY, PENNSYLVANIA   DIED: 4/21/1980 LATROBE, PENNSYLVANIA

YEAR	TEAM	STARTS	GAMES	WON	LOST	PCT	ER	ERA	INNINGS PITCHED	STRIKE-OUTS	WALKS	HITS ALLOWED	HRS ALLOWED	COMP. GAMES	SHUT-OUTS	SAVES
1944	**NY-A**	**16**	**19**	**5**	**7**	**.417**	**52**	**4.56**	**102 2/3**	**63**	**52**	**100**	**3**	**4**	**0**	**0**
1945	**NY-A**	**9**	**20**	**6**	**3**	**.667**	**32**	**2.82**	**102**	**50**	**46**	**95**	**1**	**4**	**0**	**0**
1946	**NY-A**	**17**	**31**	**9**	**8**	**.529**	**54**	**3.57**	**136**	**77**	**72**	**126**	**7**	**6**	**1**	**3**
1947	**NY-A**	**2**	**56**	**14**	**8**	**.636**	**39**	**2.48**	**141 1/3**	**116**	**72**	**105**	**5**	**0**	**0**	**17**
1948	**NY-A**	**1**	**55**	**7**	**8**	**.467**	**51**	**4.26**	**107 2/3**	**77**	**66**	**116**	**6**	**0**	**0**	**16**

(continued)

Joseph Francis "Fireman" Page, lhp, 1944–50

Joe Page possessed a lively fast-ball and a livelier sense of nighttime adventure. It was the latter trait that infuriated his managers and many of his teammates in the late 1940s.

Page was born on October 28, 1917, in the tiny town of Cherry Valley in the heart of Pennsylvania coal country. Cherry Valley was a shot-and-a-beer community in those days and Joe saw no reason to alter his lifestyle when he made it to the bigs. A beer or two or three after a game was simply no big deal to him. But this nonchalant attitude slowed his ascent within the Yankees organization—he didn't make it to the majors until 1944, when he was 27.

He was initially a starter and, in fact, came out of the blocks fast, winning five of his first six decisions and making the All-Star Game. But he slumped in the second half of the season, losing six decisions in a row, and the Yankees returned him to their Newark farm team.

Page was back in 1945 and remained in the starting rotation until 1946. But the Yankees, particularly manager Joe McCarthy, were becoming frustrated by his penchant for the

nightlife. Several times, McCarthy attempted to sit down with Page and explain that his extracurricular activities were not good for himself or the team. Page, who didn't see it that way, shrugged off the criticism.

When the more laid-back Bucky Harris took over the managerial reins in 1947, he switched Page to the bullpen. The results were dramatic. He won 14 games, all in relief, and saved 17 more, and was the key to the Yankees' pennant surge. In the World Series against the Dodgers, he was overpowering, winning Game 7 with a five-inning, one-hit masterpiece of relief pitching.

Page was even more overpowering in 1949, winning 13 and saving 27, as the Yankees edged the Red Sox by a game. In all, he won 41 and saved 76 games in relief for New York in seven years.

But in 1951, he slipped on the mound in spring training and injured his arm, putting him out for the year. The injury, in fact, destroyed his motion, and after a brief stint with Pittsburgh, he retired. Page ran a tavern in Pittsburgh after his ballplaying days were over and died in 1980. His 76 saves are sixth all-time with New York.

(continued)

YEAR	TEAM	STARTS	GAMES	WON	LOST	PCT	ER	ERA	INNINGS PITCHED	STRIKE-OUTS	WALKS	HITS ALLOWED	HRS ALLOWED	COMP. GAMES	SHUT-OUTS	SAVES
1949	NY-A	0	60	13	8	.619	39	2.59	135 1/3	99	75	103	8	0	0	27
1950	NY-A	0	37	3	7	.300	31	5.04	55 1/3	33	31	66	8	0	0	13
1954	Pit-N	0	7	0	0	—	12	11.17	9 2/3	4	7	16	4	0	0	0
Career Average		6	36	7	6	.538	39	3.53	99	65	53	91	5	2	0	10
Yankee Average		6	40	8	7	.538	43	3.44	112	74	59	102	5	2	0	11
Career Total		45	285	57	49	.538	310	3.53	790	519	421	727	42	14	1	76
Yankee Total		45	278	57	49	.538	298	3.44	780 1/3	515	414	711	38	14	1	76

Pall, Donn Steven
HEIGHT: 6'1"   RIGHTHANDER   BORN: 1/11/1962 CHICAGO, ILLINOIS

YEAR	TEAM	STARTS	GAMES	WON	LOST	PCT	ER	ERA	INNINGS PITCHED	STRIKE-OUTS	WALKS	HITS ALLOWED	HRS ALLOWED	COMP. GAMES	SHUT-OUTS	SAVES
1988	Chi-A	0	17	0	2	.000	11	3.45	28 2/3	16	8	39	1	0	0	0
1989	Chi-A	0	53	4	5	.444	32	3.31	87	58	19	90	9	0	0	6
1990	Chi-A	0	56	3	5	.375	28	3.32	76	39	24	63	7	0	0	2
1991	Chi-A	0	51	7	2	.778	19	2.41	71	40	20	59	7	0	0	0
1992	Chi-A	0	39	5	2	.714	40	4.93	73	27	27	79	9	0	0	1
1993	Chi-A	0	39	2	3	.400	21	3.22	58 2/3	29	11	62	5	0	0	1

(continued)

(continued)

YEAR	TEAM	STARTS	GAMES	WON	LOST	PCT	ER	ERA	INNINGS PITCHED	STRIKE-OUTS	WALKS	HITS ALLOWED	HRS ALLOWED	COMP. GAMES	SHUT-OUTS	SAVES
1993	Phi-N	0	8	1	0	1.000	5	2.55	17 2/3	11	3	15	1	0	0	0
1994	**NY-A**	0	26	1	2	.333	14	3.60	35	21	9	43	3	0	0	0
1994	Chi-N	0	2	0	0	—	2	4.50	4	2	1	8	1	0	0	0
1996	Fla-N	0	12	1	1	.500	12	5.79	18 2/3	9	9	16	3	0	0	0
1997	Fla-N	0	2	0	0	—	1	3.86	2 1/3	0	1	3	1	0	0	0
1998	Fla-N	0	23	0	1	.000	19	5.13	33 1/3	26	7	42	5	0	0	0
Career Average		0	27	2	2	.511	17	3.64	42	23	12	43	4	0	0	1
Yankee Average		**0**	**26**	**1**	**2**	**.333**	**14**	**3.60**	**35**	**21**	**9**	**43**	**3**	**0**	**0**	**0**
Career Total		0	328	24	23	.511	204	3.63	505 1/3	278	139	519	52	0	0	10
Yankee Total		**0**	**26**	**1**	**2**	**.333**	**14**	**3.60**	**35**	**21**	**9**	**43**	**3**	**0**	**0**	**0**

Parker, James Clayton (Clay)

HEIGHT: 6'1" RIGHTHANDER BORN: 12/19/1962 COLUMBIA, LOUISIANA

YEAR	TEAM	STARTS	GAMES	WON	LOST	PCT	ER	ERA	INNINGS PITCHED	STRIKE-OUTS	WALKS	HITS ALLOWED	HRS ALLOWED	COMP. GAMES	SHUT-OUTS	SAVES
1987	Sea-A	1	3	0	0	—	9	10.57	7 2/3	8	4	15	2	0	0	0
1989	**NY-A**	17	22	4	5	.444	49	3.68	120	53	31	123	12	2	0	0
1990	**NY-A**	2	5	1	1	.500	11	4.50	22	20	7	19	5	0	0	0
1990	Det-A	1	24	2	2	.500	18	3.18	51	20	25	45	6	0	0	0
1992	Sea-A	6	8	0	2	.000	28	7.56	33 1/3	20	11	47	6	0	0	0
Career Average		5	12	1	2	.412	23	4.42	47	24	16	50	6	0	0	0
Yankee Average		**10**	**14**	**3**	**3**	**.455**	**30**	**3.80**	**71**	**37**	**19**	**71**	**9**	**1**	**0**	**0**
Career Total		27	62	7	10	.412	115	4.42	234	121	78	249	31	2	0	0
Yankee Total		**19**	**27**	**5**	**6**	**.455**	**60**	**3.80**	**142**	**73**	**38**	**142**	**17**	**2**	**0**	**0**

Patterson, Gilbert Thomas

HEIGHT: 6'1" RIGHTHANDER BORN: 9/5/1955 PHILADELPHIA, PENNSYLVANIA

YEAR	TEAM	STARTS	GAMES	WON	LOST	PCT	ER	ERA	INNINGS PITCHED	STRIKE-OUTS	WALKS	HITS ALLOWED	HRS ALLOWED	COMP. GAMES	SHUT-OUTS	SAVES
1977	**NY-A**	6	10	1	2	.333	20	5.40	33 1/3	29	20	38	3	0	0	1
Career Average		6	10	1	2	.333	20	5.40	33 1/3	29	20	38	3	0	0	1
Yankee Average		**6**	**10**	**1**	**2**	**.333**	**20**	**5.40**	**33 1/3**	**29**	**20**	**38**	**3**	**0**	**0**	**1**
Career Total		6	10	1	2	.333	20	5.40	33 1/3	29	20	38	3	0	0	1
Yankee Total		**6**	**10**	**1**	**2**	**.333**	**20**	**5.40**	**33 1/3**	**29**	**20**	**38**	**3**	**0**	**0**	**1**

Patterson, Jeffrey Simmons

HEIGHT: 6'2" RIGHTHANDER BORN: 10/1/1968 ANAHEIM, CALIFORNIA

YEAR	TEAM	STARTS	GAMES	WON	LOST	PCT	ER	ERA	INNINGS PITCHED	STRIKE-OUTS	WALKS	HITS ALLOWED	HRS ALLOWED	COMP. GAMES	SHUT-OUTS	SAVES
1995	**NY-A**	0	3	0	0	—	1	2.70	3 1/3	3	3	3	1	0	0	0
Career Average		0	3	0	0	—	1	2.70	3 1/3	3	3	3	1	0	0	0
Yankee Average		**0**	**3**	**0**	**0**	**—**	**1**	**2.70**	**3 1/3**	**3**	**3**	**3**	**1**	**0**	**0**	**0**
Career Total		0	3	0	0	—	1	2.70	3 1/3	3	3	3	1	0	0	0
Yankee Total		**0**	**3**	**0**	**0**	**—**	**1**	**2.70**	**3 1/3**	**3**	**3**	**3**	**1**	**0**	**0**	**0**

Pavlas, David Lee

HEIGHT: 6'7" RIGHTHANDER BORN: 8/12/1962 FRANKFURT, WEST GERMANY

YEAR	TEAM	STARTS	GAMES	WON	LOST	PCT	ER	ERA	INNINGS PITCHED	STRIKE-OUTS	WALKS	HITS ALLOWED	HRS ALLOWED	COMP. GAMES	SHUT-OUTS	SAVES
1990	Chi-N	0	13	2	0	1.000	5	2.11	21 1/3	12	6	23	2	0	0	0
1991	Chi-N	0	1	0	0	—	2	18.00	1	0	0	3	1	0	0	0
1995	**NY-A**	0	4	0	0	—	2	3.18	5 2/3	3	0	8	0	0	0	0
1996	**NY-A**	0	16	0	0	—	6	2.35	23	18	7	23	0	0	0	1

(continued)

(continued)

Career Average	0	9	1	0	1.000	4	2.68	13	8	3	14	1	0	0	0
Yankee Average	**0**	**10**	**0**	**0**	**—**	**4**	**2.51**	**14**	**11**	**4**	**16**	**0**	**0**	**0**	**1**
Career Total	0	34	2	0	1.000	15	2.68	50 1/3	33	13	57	3	0	0	1
Yankee Total	**0**	**20**	**0**	**0**	**—**	**8**	**2.51**	**28 2/3**	**21**	**7**	**31**	**0**	**0**	**0**	**1**

Pearson, Montgomery Marcellus (Monte)

HEIGHT: 6'0"   RIGHTHANDER   BORN: 9/2/1909 OAKLAND, CALIFORNIA   DIED: 1/27/1978 FRESNO, CALIFORNIA

YEAR	TEAM	STARTS	GAMES	WON	LOST	PCT	ER	ERA	INNINGS PITCHED	STRIKE-OUTS	WALKS	HITS ALLOWED	HRS ALLOWED	COMP. GAMES	SHUT-OUTS	SAVES
1932	Cle-A	0	8	0	0	—	9	10.13	8	5	11	10	1	0	0	0
1933	Cle-A	16	19	10	5	.667	35	2.33	135 1/3	54	55	111	5	10	0	0
1934	Cle-A	33	39	18	13	.581	128	4.52	254 2/3	140	130	257	16	19	0	2
1935	Cle-A	24	30	8	13	.381	99	4.90	181 2/3	90	103	199	9	10	1	0
1936	**NY-A**	**31**	**33**	**19**	**7**	**.731**	**92**	**3.71**	**223**	**118**	**135**	**191**	**13**	**15**	**1**	**1**
1937	**NY-A**	**20**	**22**	**9**	**3**	**.750**	**51**	**3.17**	**144 2/3**	**71**	**64**	**145**	**6**	**7**	**1**	**1**
1938	**NY-A**	**27**	**28**	**16**	**7**	**.696**	**89**	**3.97**	**202**	**98**	**113**	**198**	**12**	**17**	**1**	**0**
1939	**NY-A**	**20**	**22**	**12**	**5**	**.706**	**73**	**4.49**	**146 1/3**	**76**	**70**	**151**	**9**	**8**	**0**	**0**
1940	**NY-A**	**16**	**16**	**7**	**5**	**.583**	**45**	**3.69**	**109 2/3**	**43**	**44**	**108**	**8**	**7**	**1**	**0**
1941	Cin-N	4	7	1	3	.250	14	5.18	24 1/3	8	15	22	3	1	0	0
Career Average	19	22	10	6	.621	64	4.00	143	70	74	139	8	9	1	0
Yankee Average	**23**	**24**	**13**	**5**	**.700**	**70**	**3.82**	**165**	**81**	**85**	**159**	**10**	**11**	**1**	**0**
Career Total	191	224	100	61	.621	635	4.00	1429 2/3	703	740	1392	82	94	5	4
Yankee Total	**114**	**121**	**63**	**27**	**.700**	**350**	**3.82**	**825 2/3**	**406**	**426**	**793**	**48**	**54**	**4**	**2**

Montgomery Marcellus "Monte" Pearson, rhp, 1936–40

Monte Pearson always seemed to save his best game for last, at least for four of the five years he pitched for the Yankees.

Pearson, born September 2, 1909, in Oakland, California, was a solid performer for New York throughout his career in the Big Apple. But when the World Series came around, Pearson was spectacular.

Pearson pitched in four World Series for New York. He pitched one game in each series, and every one was a superb piece of work. His ERA for the four games was a minuscule 1.01, the seventh best of all time, and his winning percentage of 1.000 is never going to be topped.

Pearson started out in the Cleveland Indians organization, and was brought up in 1932. He did well for the Indians, going 36-31 in four years. In 1936, he came to New York in exchange for Johnny Allen.

The Yankees benefited immediately. Pearson went 19-7 and led the league in win-ning percentage. Pearson had control problems throughout his career, and he walked 100 or more men three times in his five years with New York. But when October came around, he seemed to become a much better pitcher.

In the 1936 World Series against the Giants, he fired a complete-game, seven-hit gem to beat future Hall of Famer Carl Hubbell and give the Yankees a commanding three games to one lead. In 1937, he beat the Giants' ace Hal Schumacher with a five-hit, one-run outing in Game 3 of that Series.

He threw another five-hitter to beat the Cubs' Clay Bryant in Game 3 of the 1938 Fall Classic, and in 1939, Pearson had a no-hitter for 7 1/3 innings before the Reds' Ernie Lombardi singled to break it up. His two-hit shutout beat Cincinnati ace Bucky Walters.

Pearson threw a no-hitter against his old team, the Indians, in 1937. In 1940, his record dropped to 7-5, and Pearson was traded to the Reds, with whom he played one more year before retiring. Pearson died in 1978 in Fresno, California.

Peek, Stephen George

HEIGHT: 6'2"   RIGHTHANDER   BORN: 7/30/1914 SPRINGFIELD, MASSACHUSETTS   DIED: 9/20/1991 SYRACUSE, NEW YORK

YEAR	TEAM	STARTS	GAMES	WON	LOST	PCT	ER	ERA	INNINGS PITCHED	STRIKE-OUTS	WALKS	HITS ALLOWED	HRS ALLOWED	COMP. GAMES	SHUT-OUTS	SAVES
1941	NY-A	8	17	4	2	.667	45	5.06	80	18	39	85	6	2	0	0
Career Average		8	17	4	2	.667	45	5.06	80	18	39	85	6	2	0	0
Yankee Average		**8**	**17**	**4**	**2**	**.667**	**45**	**5.06**	**80**	**18**	**39**	**85**	**6**	**2**	**0**	**0**
Career Total		8	17	4	2	.667	45	5.06	80	18	39	85	6	2	0	0
Yankee Total		**8**	**17**	**4**	**2**	**.667**	**45**	**5.06**	**80**	**18**	**39**	**85**	**6**	**2**	**0**	**0**

Pena, Hipolito BORN HIPOLITO PENA (CONCEPCION)

HEIGHT: 6'3"   LEFTHANDER   BORN: 1/30/1964 FANTINO, DOMINICAN REPUBLIC

YEAR	TEAM	STARTS	GAMES	WON	LOST	PCT	ER	ERA	INNINGS PITCHED	STRIKE-OUTS	WALKS	HITS ALLOWED	HRS ALLOWED	COMP. GAMES	SHUT-OUTS	SAVES
1986	Pit-N	1	10	0	3	.000	8	8.64	8 1/3	6	3	7	3	0	0	1
1987	Pit-N	1	16	0	3	.000	13	4.56	25 2/3	16	26	16	2	0	0	1
1988	**NY-A**	**0**	**16**	**1**	**1**	**.500**	**5**	**3.14**	**14 1/3**	**10**	**9**	**10**	**1**	**0**	**0**	**0**
Career Average		1	14	0	2	.125	9	4.84	16	11	13	11	2	0	0	1
Yankee Average		**0**	**16**	**1**	**1**	**.500**	**5**	**3.14**	**14 1/3**	**10**	**9**	**10**	**1**	**0**	**0**	**0**
Career Total		2	42	1	7	.125	26	4.84	48 1/3	32	38	33	6	0	0	2
Yankee Total		**0**	**16**	**1**	**1**	**.500**	**5**	**3.14**	**14 1/3**	**10**	**9**	**10**	**1**	**0**	**0**	**0**

Pennock, Herbert Jeffries (The Knight of Kennett Square)

HEIGHT: 6'0"   LEFTHANDER   BORN: 2/10/1894 KENNETT SQUARE, PENNSYLVANIA   DIED: 1/30/1948 NEW YORK, NEW YORK

YEAR	TEAM	STARTS	GAMES	WON	LOST	PCT	ER	ERA	INNINGS PITCHED	STRIKE-OUTS	WALKS	HITS ALLOWED	HRS ALLOWED	COMP. GAMES	SHUT-OUTS	SAVES
1912	Phi-A	2	17	1	2	.333	25	4.50	50	38	30	48	1	1	0	2
1913	Phi-A	4	14	2	1	.667	19	5.13	33 1/3	17	22	30	4	1	0	0
1914	Phi-A	14	28	11	4	.733	47	2.79	151 2/3	90	65	136	1	8	3	3
1915	Phi-A	8	11	3	6	.333	26	5.32	44	24	29	46	2	3	1	1
1915	Bos-A	1	5	0	0	—	15	9.64	14	7	10	23	0	0	0	0
1916	Bos-A	2	9	0	2	.000	9	3.04	26 2/3	12	8	23	0	0	0	1
1917	Bos-A	5	24	5	5	.500	37	3.31	100 2/3	35	23	90	2	4	1	1
1919	Bos-A	26	32	16	8	.667	66	2.71	219	70	48	223	2	16	5	0
1920	Bos-A	31	37	16	13	.552	99	3.68	242 1/3	68	61	244	9	19	4	2
1921	Bos-A	32	32	12	14	.462	100	4.04	222 2/3	91	59	268	7	15	1	0
1922	Bos-A	26	32	10	17	.370	97	4.32	202	59	74	230	7	15	1	1
1923	**NY-A**	**27**	**35**	**19**	**6**	**.760**	**83**	**3.13**	**238 1/3**	**93**	**68**	**235**	**11**	**21**	**1**	**3**
1924	**NY-A**	**34**	**40**	**21**	**9**	**.700**	**90**	**2.83**	**286 1/3**	**101**	**64**	**302**	**13**	**25**	**4**	**3**
1925	**NY-A**	**31**	**47**	**16**	**17**	**.485**	**91**	**2.96**	**277**	**88**	**71**	**267**	**11**	**21**	**2**	**2**
1926	**NY-A**	**33**	**40**	**23**	**11**	**.676**	**107**	**3.62**	**266 1/3**	**78**	**43**	**294**	**11**	**19**	**1**	**2**
1927	**NY-A**	**26**	**34**	**19**	**8**	**.704**	**70**	**3.00**	**209 2/3**	**51**	**48**	**225**	**5**	**18**	**1**	**2**
1928	**NY-A**	**24**	**28**	**17**	**6**	**.739**	**60**	**2.56**	**211**	**53**	**40**	**215**	**2**	**18**	**5**	**3**
1929	**NY-A**	**23**	**27**	**9**	**11**	**.450**	**86**	**4.92**	**157 1/3**	**49**	**28**	**205**	**11**	**8**	**1**	**2**
1930	**NY-A**	**19**	**25**	**11**	**7**	**.611**	**75**	**4.32**	**156 1/3**	**46**	**20**	**194**	**8**	**11**	**1**	**0**
1931	**NY-A**	**25**	**25**	**11**	**6**	**.647**	**90**	**4.28**	**189 1/3**	**65**	**30**	**247**	**7**	**12**	**1**	**0**
1932	**NY-A**	**21**	**22**	**9**	**5**	**.643**	**75**	**4.60**	**146 2/3**	**54**	**38**	**191**	**8**	**9**	**1**	**0**
1933	**NY-A**	**5**	**23**	**7**	**4**	**.636**	**40**	**5.54**	**65**	**22**	**21**	**96**	**4**	**2**	**1**	**4**
1934	Bos-A	2	30	2	0	1.000	21	3.05	62	16	16	68	2	1	0	1
Career Average		18	27	10	7	.597	62	3.60	155	53	40	170	6	11	2	1
Yankee Average		**24**	**31**	**15**	**8**	**.643**	**79**	**3.54**	**200**	**64**	**43**	**225**	**8**	**15**	**2**	**2**
Career Total		421	617	240	162	.597	1428	3.60	3571 2/3	1227	916	3900	128	247	35	33
Yankee Total		**268**	**346**	**162**	**90**	**.643**	**867**	**3.54**	**2203 1/3**	**700**	**471**	**2471**	**91**	**164**	**19**	**21**

Perez, Melido Turpen BORN MELIDO TURPEN GROSS (PEREZ)

HEIGHT: 6'4"   RIGHTHANDER   BORN: 2/15/1966 SAN CRISTOBAL, DOMINICAN REPUBLIC

YEAR	TEAM	STARTS	GAMES	WON	LOST	PCT	ER	ERA	INNINGS PITCHED	STRIKE-OUTS	WALKS	HITS ALLOWED	HRS ALLOWED	COMP. GAMES	SHUT-OUTS	SAVES
1987	KC-A	3	3	1	1	.500	9	7.84	10 1/3	5	5	18	2	0	0	0
1988	Chi-A	32	32	12	10	.545	83	3.79	197	138	72	186	26	3	1	0
1989	Chi-A	31	31	11	14	.440	102	5.01	183 1/3	141	90	187	23	2	0	0

(continued)

Herbert Jeffries "The Knight of Kennett Square" Pennock, lhp, 1923–33

Herb Pennock was a "money pitcher" in the days before such a term was coined. But the cool lefthander was a mainstay for the Yankee staff for more than a decade.

Pennock was born February 10, 1894, in Kennett Square, Pennsylvania. A Quaker from one of the oldest families in the state, Pennock was a prep school pheenom. His family wanted him to attend the University of Pennsylvania, but Pennock wanted to play professional baseball. So at the tender age of 17, he was signed by Connie Mack's Philadelphia Athletics.

He made his debut in May 1912 and was a regular member of the A's staff by 1914, winning 11 games that year. He was traded to the Red Sox in 1915 and won 60 games for Boston in 5½ seasons.

In 1923, Pennock was sent to the Yankees for three relative unknowns, and, more importantly for the cash-strapped Sox, $50,000. His career, which to that point had been merely solid, took off.

He won 19 games for New York in 1923 and then two more in the World Series, as the Yankees clinched their first-ever World Championship. It was noted at the time by more than a few writers that while Babe Ruth packed the fans into the park, New York didn't become a champion until their frontline pitching was shored up.

Pennock raised silver foxes at his estate in Kennett Square, and in the offseason, headed fox hunts. One of his frequent guests was Ruth, who admitted once in spring training that riding a horse after a bunch of foxes was tougher than it looked.

Pennock was six feet tall and very slightly built. He had a beautiful, smooth delivery that Ruth, a fellow lefty, loved to watch. He didn't mow teams down with fastballs. Instead, Pennock's artful assortment of curves, off-speed pitches and change-ups bamboozled enemy hitters. When he began enjoying better offensive support from his hard-hitting Yankee teammates, he was a hard pitcher to beat.

He was 5-0 in World Series contests. His managers would often adjust the rotation to enable Pennock to pitch a crucial game. Not only did he rarely complain, he also often produced in these situations. Ruth and the rest of his Yankee teammates loved him for it.

He and Ruth were often social companions, dating back to the days when both were in Boston. They were an odd couple, to be sure, but they had more in common than one would think. Both played for the Red Sox in the glory days, then were traded. Both were pitchers, both were lefthanders. And both enjoyed the high life.

Pennock won 11 or more games for the Yankees 8 times in his 11 years in New York. He won 23 games in 1926 and 21 in 1924. He pitched 35 shutouts in his career. Ruth, his biggest booster, declared Pennock a "lefthanded Christy Mathewson."

He pitched well in 1932, winning nine games, and saving two more in the 1932 World Series. But his pitches had lost a little that year and they lost a little more in 1933, when he won only seven games. He was released at the end of the season and picked up by the Red Sox in 1934 before retiring for good. He worked as a coach for the Red Sox for several years in the late '30s.

Pennock is 7th all-time on the Yankees with 162 wins, 4th all-time in complete games with 165, 16th all-time in strikeouts with 656 and 10th in winning percentage with .643.

In 1948, just months after his death on January 30, Pennock was elected to the Hall of Fame.

(continued)

YEAR	TEAM	STARTS	GAMES	WON	LOST	PCT	ER	ERA	INNINGS PITCHED	STRIKE-OUTS	WALKS	HITS ALLOWED	HRS ALLOWED	COMP. GAMES	SHUT-OUTS	SAVES
1990	Chi-A	35	35	13	14	.481	101	4.61	197	161	86	177	14	3	3	0
1991	Chi-A	8	49	8	7	.533	47	3.12	135 2/3	128	52	111	15	0	0	1
1992	**NY-A**	**33**	**33**	**13**	**16**	**.448**	**79**	**2.87**	**247 2/3**	**218**	**93**	**212**	**16**	**10**	**1**	**0**
1993	**NY-A**	**25**	**25**	**6**	**14**	**.300**	**94**	**5.19**	**163**	**148**	**64**	**173**	**22**	**0**	**0**	**0**
1994	**NY-A**	**22**	**22**	**9**	**4**	**.692**	**69**	**4.10**	**151 1/3**	**109**	**58**	**134**	**16**	**1**	**0**	**0**
1995	**NY-A**	**12**	**13**	**5**	**5**	**.500**	**43**	**5.58**	**69 1/3**	**44**	**31**	**70**	**10**	**1**	**0**	**0**
Career Average		22	27	9	9	.479	70	4.17	151	121	61	141	16	2	1	0
Yankee Average		**23**	**23**	**8**	**10**	**.458**	**71**	**4.07**	**157**	**130**	**62**	**147**	**16**	**3**	**0**	**0**
Career Total		201	243	78	85	.479	627	4.17	1354 2/3	1092	551	1268	144	20	5	1
Yankee Total		**92**	**93**	**33**	**39**	**.458**	**285**	**4.07**	**631 1/3**	**519**	**246**	**589**	**64**	**12**	**1**	**0**

Perez, Pascual BORN PASCUAL GROSS (PEREZ)

HEIGHT: 6'2"   RIGHTHANDER   BORN: 5/17/1957 SAN CRISTOBAL, DOMINICAN REPUBLIC

YEAR	TEAM	STARTS	GAMES	WON	LOST	PCT	ER	ERA	INNINGS PITCHED	STRIKE-OUTS	WALKS	HITS ALLOWED	HRS ALLOWED	COMP. GAMES	SHUT-OUTS	SAVES
1980	Pit-N	2	2	0	1	.000	5	3.75	12	7	2	15	0	0	0	0
1981	Pit-N	13	17	2	7	.222	38	3.96	86 1/3	46	34	92	5	2	0	0
1982	Atl-N	11	16	4	4	.500	27	3.06	79 1/3	29	17	85	4	0	0	0
1983	Atl-N	33	33	15	8	.652	82	3.43	215 1/3	144	51	213	20	7	1	0
1984	Atl-N	30	30	14	8	.636	88	3.74	211 2/3	145	51	208	26	4	1	0
1985	Atl-N	22	22	1	13	.071	65	6.14	95 1/3	57	57	115	10	0	0	0
1987	Mon-N	10	10	7	0	1.000	18	2.30	70 1/3	58	16	52	5	2	0	0
1988	Mon-N	27	27	12	8	.600	51	2.44	188	131	44	133	15	4	2	0
1989	Mon-N	28	33	9	13	.409	73	3.31	198 1/3	152	45	178	15	2	0	0
1990	**NY-A**	**3**	**3**	**1**	**2**	**.333**	**2**	**1.29**	**14**	**12**	**3**	**8**	**0**	**0**	**0**	**0**
1991	**NY-A**	**14**	**14**	**2**	**4**	**.333**	**26**	**3.18**	**73 2/3**	**41**	**24**	**68**	**7**	**0**	**0**	**0**
Career Average		18	19	6	6	.496	43	3.44	113	75	31	106	10	2	0	0
Yankee Average		**9**	**9**	**2**	**3**	**.333**	**14**	**2.87**	**44**	**27**	**14**	**38**	**4**	**0**	**0**	**0**
Career Total		193	207	67	68	.496	475	3.44	1244 1/3	822	344	1167	107	21	4	0
Yankee Total		**17**	**17**	**3**	**6**	**.333**	**28**	**2.87**	**87 2/3**	**53**	**27**	**76**	**7**	**0**	**0**	**0**

Perkins, Cecil Boyce

HEIGHT: 6'0"   RIGHTHANDER   BORN: 12/1/1940 BALTIMORE, MARYLAND

YEAR	TEAM	STARTS	GAMES	WON	LOST	PCT	ER	ERA	INNINGS PITCHED	STRIKE-OUTS	WALKS	HITS ALLOWED	HRS ALLOWED	COMP. GAMES	SHUT-OUTS	SAVES
1967	**NY-A**	**1**	**2**	**0**	**1**	**.000**	**5**	**9.00**	**5**	**1**	**2**	**6**	**1**	**0**	**0**	**0**
Career Average		1	2	0	1	.000	5	9.00	5	1	2	6	1	0	0	0
Yankee Average		**1**	**2**	**0**	**1**	**.000**	**5**	**9.00**	**5**	**1**	**2**	**6**	**1**	**0**	**0**	**0**
Career Total		1	2	0	1	.000	5	9.00	5	1	2	6	1	0	0	0
Yankee Total		**1**	**2**	**0**	**1**	**.000**	**5**	**9.00**	**5**	**1**	**2**	**6**	**1**	**0**	**0**	**0**

Perry, Gaylord Jackson

HEIGHT: 6'4"   RIGHTHANDER   BORN: 9/15/1938 WILLIAMSTON, NORTH CAROLINA

YEAR	TEAM	STARTS	GAMES	WON	LOST	PCT	ER	ERA	INNINGS PITCHED	STRIKE-OUTS	WALKS	HITS ALLOWED	HRS ALLOWED	COMP. GAMES	SHUT-OUTS	SAVES
1962	SF-N	7	13	3	1	.750	25	5.23	43	20	14	54	3	1	0	0
1963	SF-N	4	31	1	6	.143	34	4.03	76	52	29	84	10	0	0	2
1964	SF-N	19	44	12	11	.522	63	2.75	206 1/3	155	43	179	16	5	2	5
1965	SF-N	26	47	8	12	.400	91	4.19	195 2/3	170	70	194	21	6	0	1
1966	SF-N	35	36	21	8	.724	85	2.99	255 2/3	201	40	242	15	13	3	0
1967	SF-N	37	39	15	17	.469	85	2.61	293	230	84	231	20	18	3	1
1968	SF-N	38	39	16	15	.516	79	2.44	291	173	59	240	10	19	3	0
1969	SF-N	39	40	19	14	.576	90	2.49	325 1/3	233	91	290	23	26	3	0
1970	SF-N	41	41	23	13	.639	117	3.20	328 2/3	214	84	292	27	23	5	0
1971	SF-N	37	37	16	12	.571	86	2.76	280	158	67	255	20	14	2	1
1972	Cle-A	40	41	24	16	.600	73	1.92	342 2/3	234	82	253	17	29	5	0
1973	Cle-A	41	41	19	19	.500	129	3.38	344	238	115	315	34	29	7	0
1974	Cle-A	37	37	21	13	.618	90	2.51	322 1/3	216	99	230	25	28	4	0
1975	Cle-A	15	15	6	9	.400	48	3.55	121 2/3	85	34	120	16	10	1	0

(continued)

(continued)

Year	Team															
1975	Tex-A	22	22	12	8	.600	62	3.03	184	148	36	157	12	15	4	0
1976	Tex-A	32	32	15	14	.517	90	3.24	250 1/3	143	52	232	14	21	2	0
1977	Tex-A	34	34	15	12	.556	89	3.37	238	177	56	239	21	13	4	0
1978	SD-N	37	37	21	6	.778	79	2.73	260 2/3	154	66	241	9	5	2	0
1979	SD-N	32	32	12	11	.522	79	3.06	232 2/3	140	67	225	12	10	0	0
1980	Tex-A	24	24	6	9	.400	59	3.43	155	107	46	159	12	6	2	0
1980	**NY-A**	**8**	**10**	**4**	**4**	**.500**	**25**	**4.44**	**50 2/3**	**28**	**18**	**65**	**2**	**0**	**0**	**0**
1981	Atl-N	23	23	8	9	.471	66	3.94	150 2/3	60	24	182	9	3	0	0
1982	Sea-A	32	32	10	12	.455	106	4.40	216 2/3	116	54	245	27	6	0	0
1983	Sea-A	16	16	3	10	.231	56	4.94	102	42	23	116	18	2	0	0
1983	KC-A	14	14	4	4	.500	40	4.27	84 1/3	40	26	98	6	1	1	0
Career Average		28	31	13	11	.542	74	3.11	214	141	55	198	16	12	2	0
Yankee Average		**8**	**10**	**4**	**4**	**.500**	**25**	**4.44**	**50 2/3**	**28**	**18**	**65**	**2**	**0**	**0**	**0**
Career Total		690	777	314	265	.542	1846	3.11	5350 1/3	3534	1379	4938	399	303	53	11
Yankee Total		**8**	**10**	**4**	**4**	**.500**	**25**	**4.44**	**50 2/3**	**28**	**18**	**65**	**2**	**0**	**0**	**0**

Peterson, Fred Ingles (Fritz)

HEIGHT: 6'0" LEFTHANDER BORN: 2/8/1942 CHICAGO, ILLINOIS

YEAR	TEAM	STARTS	GAMES	WON	LOST	PCT	ER	ERA	INNINGS PITCHED	STRIKE-OUTS	WALKS	HITS ALLOWED	HRS ALLOWED	COMP. GAMES	SHUT-OUTS	SAVES
1966	NY-A	32	34	12	11	.522	79	3.31	215	96	40	196	15	11	2	0
1967	NY-A	30	36	8	14	.364	70	3.47	181 1/3	102	43	179	11	6	1	0
1968	NY-A	27	36	12	11	.522	62	2.63	212 1/3	115	29	187	13	6	2	0

(continued)

Fred Ingles "Fritz" Peterson, lhp, 1966–74

In the late 1960s and early 1970s, Fritz Peterson was as consistent as any pitcher the Yankees had.

Peterson, born on February 8, 1942, in Chicago, Illinois, was a solid prospect when he was signed by the Yankees in 1963. He spent only a few years in the minor leagues before being brought up to the big club in 1966.

In prior years, the Yankees would have kept Peterson back perhaps a year or two more. But by the mid-1960s, the Yankee farm system was beginning to dry up and New York needed pitching.

The Yankees finished dead last in 1966, but Peterson was one of the team's bright spots, going 12-11 to tie Mel Stottlemyre for the team lead in wins, and pitching 215 innings, second best on the team.

Things didn't improve much over the next several years for the Yankees, but Peterson and Stottlemyre could be counted on to perform consistently on the mound. Peterson was 20-11 with a team-leading 2.91 ERA in 1970, his best year in the majors.

Peterson wasn't overpowering, but he was an excellent control pitcher who led the league in fewest walks per nine innings for five consecutive seasons from 1968-72, an American League record.

In 1973, he and fellow pitcher Mike Kekich made history of sorts by swapping "lives" and moving in with each other's families in spring training. The Yankees avoided a potentially bizarre regular season by sending Kekich to the Indians.

In 1974, Peterson followed Kekich, as Fritz was one of several players sent to Cleveland for Chris Chambliss. Peterson played for three more years before retiring. Peterson is 10th all-time in innings pitched for the Yankees with 1,856, 13th in wins with 109, 12th in strikeouts with 893 and 13th in shutouts with 18.

(continued)

YEAR	TEAM	STARTS	GAMES	WON	LOST	PCT	ER	ERA	INNINGS PITCHED	STRIKE-OUTS	WALKS	HITS ALLOWED	HRS ALLOWED	COMP. GAMES	SHUT-OUTS	SAVES
1969	NY-A	37	37	17	16	.515	77	2.55	272	150	43	228	15	16	4	0
1970	NY-A	37	39	20	11	.645	84	2.90	260 1/3	127	40	247	24	8	2	0
1971	NY-A	35	37	15	13	.536	93	3.05	274	139	42	269	25	16	4	1
1972	NY-A	35	35	17	15	.531	90	3.24	250 1/3	100	44	270	17	12	3	0
1973	NY-A	31	31	8	15	.348	81	3.95	184 1/3	59	49	207	18	6	0	0
1974	NY-A	1	3	0	0	—	4	4.70	7 2/3	5	2	13	1	0	0	0
1974	Cle-A	29	29	9	14	.391	74	4.36	152 2/3	52	37	187	16	3	0	0
1975	Cle-A	25	25	14	8	.636	64	3.94	146 1/3	47	40	154	15	6	2	0
1976	Cle-A	9	9	0	3	.000	29	5.55	47	19	10	59	3	0	0	0
1976	Tex-A	2	4	1	0	1.000	6	3.60	15	4	7	21	0	0	0	0
Career Average		25	27	10	10	.504	63	3.30	171	78	33	171	13	7	2	0
Yankee Average		29	32	12	12	.507	71	3.10	206	99	37	200	15	9	2	0
Career Total		330	355	133	131	.504	813	3.30	2218 1/3	1015	426	2217	173	90	20	1
Yankee Total		265	288	109	106	.507	640	3.10	1857 1/3	893	332	1796	139	81	18	1

Pettitte, Andrew Eugene

HEIGHT: 6'5"   LEFTHANDER   BORN: 6/15/1972 BATON ROUGE, LOUISIANA

YEAR	TEAM	STARTS	GAMES	WON	LOST	PCT	ER	ERA	INNINGS PITCHED	STRIKE-OUTS	WALKS	HITS ALLOWED	HRS ALLOWED	COMP. GAMES	SHUT-OUTS	SAVES
1995	NY-A	26	31	12	9	.571	81	4.17	175	114	63	183	15	3	0	0
1996	NY-A	34	35	21	8	.724	95	3.87	221	162	72	229	23	2	0	0
1997	NY-A	35	35	18	7	.720	77	2.88	240 1/3	166	65	233	7	4	1	0
1998	NY-A	32	33	16	11	.593	102	4.24	216 1/3	146	87	226	20	5	0	0
1999	NY-A	31	31	14	11	.560	100	4.70	191 2/3	121	89	216	20	0	0	0
2000	NY-A	32	32	19	9	.679	99	4.35	124 2/3	125	80	219	17	3	1	0
Career Average		32	17	17	9	.645	92	3.99	208	139	76	218	17	3	0	0
Yankee Average		32	17	17	9	.645	92	3.99	208	139	76	218	17	3	0	0
Career Total		190	197	100	55	.645	554	3.99	1249	834	456	1306	102	17	2	0
Yankee Total		190	197	100	55	.645	554	3.99	1249	834	456	1306	102	17	2	0

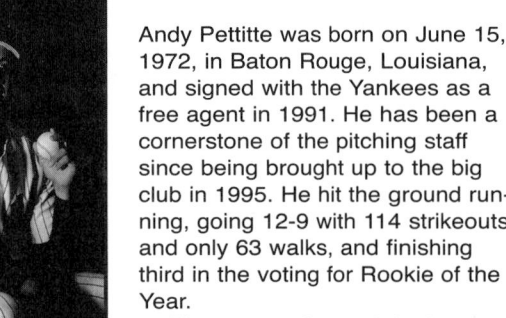

Andrew Eugene Pettitte, lhp, 1995–2000

Andy Pettitte was born on June 15, 1972, in Baton Rouge, Louisiana, and signed with the Yankees as a free agent in 1991. He has been a cornerstone of the pitching staff since being brought up to the big club in 1995. He hit the ground running, going 12-9 with 114 strikeouts and only 63 walks, and finishing third in the voting for Rookie of the Year.

The owner of one of the better change-ups in baseball, Pettitte had his best year to date in 1996, leading the American League with 21 wins and making the All-Star team. At 23, he was the youngest Yankee to start on Opening Day since James "Hippo" Vaughn in 1910.

He has become a solid performer for the Yankees in the postseason and is 3-1 in the World Series, including the clinching victory over the San Diego Padres in 1998.

In the 2000 playoffs, Pettitte turned in two strong performances in the AL Divisional series against the A's, going 2-0. He won another game against the Mariners in the ALCS and pitched two strong games in the World Series, though he didn't earn a decision.

The lanky (6 feet 5 inches) Pettitte has also become one of the best pickoff men in the league, nailing a league-leading 14 base runners in 1997.

Pieh, Edwin John (Cy)

HEIGHT: 6'2" RIGHTHANDER BORN: 9/29/1886 WAUNAKEE, WISCONSIN DIED: 9/12/1945 JACKSONVILLE, FLORIDA

YEAR	TEAM	STARTS	GAMES	WON	LOST	PCT	ER	ERA	INNINGS PITCHED	STRIKE-OUTS	WALKS	HITS ALLOWED	HRS ALLOWED	COMP. GAMES	SHUT-OUTS	SAVES
1913	NY-A	0	4	1	0	1.000	5	4.35	10 1/3	6	7	10	0	0	0	0
1914	NY-A	4	18	4	4	.500	35	5.05	62 1/3	24	29	68	6	1	0	0
1915	NY-A	8	21	4	5	.444	30	2.87	94	46	39	78	2	3	2	1
Career Average		4	14	3	3	.500	23	3.78	56	25	25	52	3	1	1	0
Yankee Average		4	14	3	3	.500	23	3.78	56	25	25	52	3	1	1	0
Career Total		12	43	9	9	.500	70	3.78	166 2/3	76	75	156	8	4	2	1
Yankee Total		12	43	9	9	.500	70	3.78	166 2/3	76	75	156	8	4	2	1

Piercy, William Benton (Wild Bill)

HEIGHT: 6'1" RIGHTHANDER BORN: 5/2/1896 EL MONTE, CALIFORNIA DIED: 8/28/1951 LONG BEACH, CALIFORNIA

YEAR	TEAM	STARTS	GAMES	WON	LOST	PCT	ER	ERA	INNINGS PITCHED	STRIKE-OUTS	WALKS	HITS ALLOWED	HRS ALLOWED	COMP. GAMES	SHUT-OUTS	SAVES
1917	NY-A	1	1	0	1	.000	3	3.00	9	4	2	9	0	1	0	0
1921	NY-A	10	14	5	4	.556	27	2.98	81 2/3	35	28	82	4	5	1	0
1922	Bos-A	12	29	3	9	.250	63	4.67	121 1/3	24	62	140	2	7	1	0
1923	Bos-A	24	30	8	17	.320	71	3.41	187 1/3	51	73	193	5	11	0	0
1924	Bos-A	18	23	5	7	.417	80	5.95	121	20	66	156	4	3	0	0
1926	Chi-N	5	19	6	5	.545	45	4.48	90 1/3	31	37	96	1	1	0	0
Career Average		12	19	5	7	.386	48	4.26	102	28	45	113	3	5	0	0
Yankee Average		6	8	3	3	.500	15	2.98	45	20	15	46	2	3	1	0
Career Total		70	116	27	43	.386	289	4.26	610 2/3	165	268	676	16	28	2	0
Yankee Total		11	15	5	5	.500	30	2.98	90 2/3	39	30	91	4	6	1	0

Pillette, Duane Xavier (Dee)

HEIGHT: 6'3" RIGHTHANDER BORN: 7/24/1922 DETROIT, MICHIGAN

YEAR	TEAM	STARTS	GAMES	WON	LOST	PCT	ER	ERA	INNINGS PITCHED	STRIKE-OUTS	WALKS	HITS ALLOWED	HRS ALLOWED	COMP. GAMES	SHUT-OUTS	SAVES
1949	NY-A	3	12	2	4	.333	18	4.34	37 1/3	9	19	43	6	2	0	0
1950	NY-A	0	4	0	0	—	1	1.29	7	4	3	9	0	0	0	0
1950	StL-A	7	24	3	5	.375	58	7.09	73 2/3	18	44	104	6	1	0	2
1951	StL-A	24	35	6	14	.300	106	4.99	191	65	115	205	14	6	1	0
1952	StL-A	30	30	10	13	.435	82	3.59	205 1/3	62	55	222	14	9	1	0
1953	StL-A	25	31	7	13	.350	83	4.48	166 2/3	58	62	181	16	5	1	0
1954	Bal-A	25	25	10	14	.417	62	3.12	179	66	67	158	9	11	1	0
1955	Bal-A	5	7	0	3	.000	15	6.53	20 2/3	13	14	31	0	0	0	0
1956	Phi-N	0	20	0	0	—	17	6.56	23 1/3	10	12	32	2	0	0	0
Career Average		13	21	4	7	.365	49	4.40	100	34	43	109	7	4	0	0
Yankee Average		2	8	1	2	.333	10	3.86	22	7	11	26	3	1	0	0
Career Total		119	188	38	66	.365	442	4.40	904	305	391	985	67	34	4	2
Yankee Total		3	16	2	4	.333	19	3.86	44 1/3	13	22	52	6	2	0	0

Pipgras, George William

HEIGHT: 6'1" RIGHTHANDER BORN: 12/20/1899 IDA GROVE, IOWA DIED: 10/19/1986 GAINESVILLE, FLORIDA

YEAR	TEAM	STARTS	GAMES	WON	LOST	PCT	ER	ERA	INNINGS PITCHED	STRIKE-OUTS	WALKS	HITS ALLOWED	HRS ALLOWED	COMP. GAMES	SHUT-OUTS	SAVES
1923	NY-A	2	8	1	3	.250	22	5.94	33 1/3	12	25	34	2	2	0	0
1924	NY-A	1	9	0	1	.000	17	9.98	15 1/3	4	18	20	0	0	0	1
1927	NY-A	21	29	10	3	.769	76	4.11	166 1/3	81	77	148	2	9	1	0
1928	NY-A	38	46	24	13	.649	113	3.38	300 2/3	139	103	314	4	22	4	3
1929	NY-A	33	39	18	12	.600	106	4.23	225 1/3	125	95	229	16	13	3	0
1930	NY-A	30	44	15	15	.500	101	4.11	221	111	70	230	9	15	3	4
1931	NY-A	14	36	7	6	.538	58	3.79	137 2/3	59	58	134	8	6	1	3
1932	NY-A	27	32	16	9	.640	102	4.19	219	111	87	235	15	14	2	0
1933	NY-A	4	4	2	2	.500	12	3.27	33	14	12	32	1	3	0	0

(continued)

George William Pipgras, rhp, 1923–33

George Pipgras was one of the aces of the great Yankee pitching staffs of the late 1920s and early '30s, before a freak arm injury ended his career.

Pipgras was born December 20, 1899, in Ida Grove, Iowa. After a stint in the Army, he pitched in several minor leagues and was brought up by the Yankees in 1923. Pipgras got a total of three starts in 1923-24 and didn't really start pitching regularly for the Yankees until 1927.

As the fifth starter for the 1927 Yankees, Pipgras was 10-3 that year. He also won a game in the 1927 World Series, which the Yankees swept from the Pittsburgh Pirates. Pipgras was a last-minute replacement for teammate Urban Shocker, who was already beginning to succumb to the heart disease that would kill him a year later.

His best year was 1928, when he won a league-high 24 games, pitching in a league-high 300⅔ innings. Pipgras also won a game

in that World Series, another Yankee sweep, this time over the Cardinals.

Pipgras won his third and final World Series decision in 1932, which was yet another Yankee whitewash, this time over the Cubs. The Series game in which Pipgras pitched was the occasion of Babe Ruth's "called shot" home run. Ruth's fifth-inning home run off the Cubs' Charley Root became the stuff of legend. Nowhere is it recorded what Pipgras thought of the historic poke. He was probably just glad the Babe hit it out.

Pipgras won 93 games for the Yankees when he was traded to the Red Sox in 1933. The next year, he broke his right arm throwing a pitch. Pipgras hadn't given much thought about a career after baseball, but at age 33, he realized he had to start. He attended umpiring school, and by 1938, he was back in the American League as an umpire. In one game, he ejected 17 players.

Pipgras umpired until 1946. He died on October 19, 1986, in Florida. He is 16th all-time with the Yankees in wins with 93, 17th in strikeouts with 652, 18th in shutouts with 13 and 17th in winning percentage at .595.

(continued)

1933	Bos-A	17	22	9	8	.529	58	4.07	128 ⅓	56	45	140	5	9	2	1
1934	Bos-A	1	2	0	0	—	3	8.10	3 ⅓	0	3	4	1	0	0	0
1935	Bos-A	1	5	0	1	.000	8	14.40	5	2	5	9	3	0	0	0
Career Average		16	23	9	6	.583	56	4.09	124	60	50	127	6	8	1	1
Yankee Average		**19**	**27**	**10**	**7**	**.592**	**67**	**4.04**	**150**	**73**	**61**	**153**	**6**	**9**	**2**	**1**
Career Total		189	276	102	73	.583	676	4.09	1488 ⅓	714	598	1529	66	93	16	12
Yankee Total		**170**	**247**	**93**	**64**	**.592**	**607**	**4.04**	**1351 ⅔**	**656**	**545**	**1376**	**57**	**84**	**14**	**11**

Plunk, Eric Vaughn

HEIGHT: 6'6"   RIGHTHANDER   BORN: 9/3/1963 WILMINGTON, CALIFORNIA

YEAR	TEAM	STARTS	GAMES	WON	LOST	PCT	ER	ERA	INNINGS PITCHED	STRIKE-OUTS	WALKS	HITS ALLOWED	HRS ALLOWED	COMP. GAMES	SHUT-OUTS	SAVES
1986	Oak-A	15	26	4	7	.364	71	5.31	120 ⅓	98	102	91	14	0	0	0
1987	Oak-A	11	32	4	6	.400	50	4.74	95	90	62	91	8	0	0	2
1988	Oak-A	0	49	7	2	.778	26	3.00	78	79	39	62	6	0	0	5
1989	Oak-A	0	23	1	1	.500	7	2.20	28 ⅔	24	12	17	1	0	0	1
1989	**NY-A**	**7**	**27**	**7**	**5**	**.583**	**31**	**3.69**	**75 ⅔**	**61**	**52**	**65**	**9**	**0**	**0**	**0**
1990	**NY-A**	**0**	**47**	**6**	**3**	**.667**	**22**	**2.72**	**72 ⅔**	**67**	**43**	**58**	**6**	**0**	**0**	**0**
1991	**NY-A**	**8**	**43**	**2**	**5**	**.286**	**59**	**4.76**	**111 ⅔**	**103**	**62**	**128**	**18**	**0**	**0**	**0**

(continued)

(continued)

YEAR	TEAM	STARTS	GAMES	WON	LOST	PCT	ER	ERA	INNINGS PITCHED	STRIKE-OUTS	WALKS	HITS ALLOWED	HRS ALLOWED	COMP. GAMES	SHUT-OUTS	SAVES
1992	Cle-A	0	58	9	6	.600	29	3.64	71 2/3	50	38	61	5	0	0	4
1993	Cle-A	0	70	4	5	.444	22	2.79	71	77	30	61	5	0	0	15
1994	Cle-A	0	41	7	2	.778	20	2.54	71	73	37	61	3	0	0	3
1995	Cle-A	0	56	6	2	.750	19	2.67	64	71	27	48	5	0	0	2
1996	Cle-A	0	56	3	2	.600	21	2.45	77 2/3	85	34	56	6	0	0	2
1997	Cle-A	0	56	4	5	.444	34	4.71	65 2/3	66	36	62	12	0	0	0
1998	Cle-A	0	37	3	1	.750	22	4.83	41	38	15	44	6	0	0	0
1998	Mil-N	0	26	1	2	.333	13	3.77	31 2/3	36	15	33	3	0	0	1
1999	Mil-N	0	68	4	4	.500	42	5.04	75 1/3	63	43	71	15	0	0	0
Career Average		3	45	5	4	.554	31	3.82	72	68	40	63	8	0	0	2
Yankee Average		**5**	**39**	**5**	**4**	**.536**	**37**	**3.88**	**87**	**77**	**52**	**84**	**11**	**0**	**0**	**0**
Career Total		41	715	72	58	.554	488	3.82	1151 2/3	1081	647	1009	122	0	0	35
Yankee Total		**15**	**117**	**15**	**13**	**.536**	**112**	**3.88**	**260**	**231**	**157**	**251**	**33**	**0**	**0**	**0**

Polley, Dale Ezra

HEIGHT: 6'0"   LEFTHANDER   BORN: 8/9/1965 GEORGETOWN, KENTUCKY

YEAR	TEAM	STARTS	GAMES	WON	LOST	PCT	ER	ERA	INNINGS PITCHED	STRIKE-OUTS	WALKS	HITS ALLOWED	HRS ALLOWED	COMP. GAMES	SHUT-OUTS	SAVES
1996	NY-A	0	32	1	3	.250	19	7.89	21 2/3	14	11	23	5	0	0	0
Career Average		0	32	1	3	.250	19	7.89	21 2/3	14	11	23	5	0	0	0
Yankee Average		**0**	**32**	**1**	**3**	**.250**	**19**	**7.89**	**21 2/3**	**14**	**11**	**23**	**5**	**0**	**0**	**0**
Career Total		0	32	1	3	.250	19	7.89	21 2/3	14	11	23	5	0	0	0
Yankee Total		**0**	**32**	**1**	**3**	**.250**	**19**	**7.89**	**21 2/3**	**14**	**11**	**23**	**5**	**0**	**0**	**0**

Porterfield, Erwin Coolidge (Bob)

HEIGHT: 6'0"   RIGHTHANDER   BORN: 8/10/1923 NEWPORT, VIRGINIA   DIED: 4/28/1980 SEALY, TEXAS

YEAR	TEAM	STARTS	GAMES	WON	LOST	PCT	ER	ERA	INNINGS PITCHED	STRIKE-OUTS	WALKS	HITS ALLOWED	HRS ALLOWED	COMP. GAMES	SHUT-OUTS	SAVES
1948	**NY-A**	**12**	**16**	**5**	**3**	**.625**	**39**	**4.50**	**78**	**30**	**34**	**85**	**5**	**2**	**1**	**0**
1949	**NY-A**	**8**	**12**	**2**	**5**	**.286**	**26**	**4.06**	**57 2/3**	**25**	**29**	**53**	**3**	**3**	**0**	**0**
1950	**NY-A**	**2**	**10**	**1**	**1**	**.500**	**19**	**8.70**	**19 2/3**	**9**	**8**	**28**	**3**	**0**	**0**	**0**
1951	Was-A	19	19	9	8	.529	48	3.24	133 1/3	53	54	109	8	10	3	1
1951	**NY-A**	**0**	**2**	**0**	**0**	**—**	**5**	**15.00**	**3**	**2**	**3**	**5**	**0**	**0**	**0**	**0**
1952	Was-A	29	31	13	14	.481	70	2.72	231 1/3	80	85	222	7	15	3	0
1953	Was-A	32	34	22	10	.688	95	3.35	255	77	73	243	19	24	9	0
1954	Was-A	31	32	13	15	.464	90	3.32	244	82	77	249	14	21	2	0
1955	Was-A	27	30	10	17	.370	88	4.45	178	74	54	197	14	8	2	0
1956	Bos-A	18	25	3	12	.200	72	5.14	126	53	64	127	21	4	1	0
1957	Bos-A	9	28	4	4	.500	46	4.05	102 1/3	28	30	107	8	3	1	1
1958	Bos-A	0	2	0	0	—	2	4.50	4	1	0	3	1	0	0	1
1958	Pit-N	6	37	4	6	.400	32	3.29	87 2/3	39	19	78	7	2	1	5
1959	Pit-N	0	30	1	2	.333	19	4.75	36	18	17	45	2	0	0	1
1959	Chi-N	0	4	0	0	—	8	11.37	6 1/3	0	3	14	1	0	0	0
Career Average		13	21	6	6	.473	44	3.80	104	38	37	104	7	6	2	1
Yankee Average		**6**	**10**	**2**	**2**	**.471**	**22**	**5.06**	**40**	**17**	**19**	**43**	**3**	**1**	**0**	**0**
Career Total		193	312	87	97	.473	659	3.80	1562	571	550	1565	112	92	23	8
Yankee Total		**22**	**40**	**8**	**9**	**.471**	**89**	**5.06**	**158 1/3**	**66**	**74**	**171**	**10**	**5**	**1**	**1**

Powell, John Joseph (Jack)

HEIGHT: 5'11"   RIGHTHANDER   BORN: 7/9/1874 BLOOMINGTON, ILLINOIS   DIED: 10/17/1944 CHICAGO, ILLINOIS

YEAR	TEAM	STARTS	GAMES	WON	LOST	PCT	ER	ERA	INNINGS PITCHED	STRIKE-OUTS	WALKS	HITS ALLOWED	HRS ALLOWED	COMP. GAMES	SHUT-OUTS	SAVES
1897	Cle-N	26	27	15	11	.557	79	3.16	225	61	62	245		24	2	0
1898	Cle-N	41	42	23	15	.605	114	3.00	342	93	112	328	2	36	6	0
1899	StL-N	43	48	22	18	.550	146	3.52	373	87	85	433	8	43	2	1
1900	StL.N	37	38	17	16	.515	142	4.44	287 2/3	77	77	325	15	33	3	0
1901	StL-N	37	45	19	19	.500	133	3.54	338 1/3	133	50	351	9	33	2	3
1902	StL-A	39	42	22	17	.564	117	3.21	328 1/3	137	93	320	14	33	3	2
1903	StL-A	34	38	15	19	.441	99	2.91	306 1/3	169	58	294	11	33	4	2

(continued)

(continued)

YEAR	TEAM	STARTS	GAMES	WON	LOST	PCT	ER	ERA	INNINGS PITCHED	STRIKE-OUTS	WALKS	HITS ALLOWED	HRS ALLOWED	COMP. GAMES	SHUT-OUTS	SAVES
1904	NY-A	45	47	23	19	.548	106	2.44	390 1/3	202	92	340	15	38	3	0
1905	NY-A	23	37	8	13	.381	79	3.50	203	84	57	214	4	13	1	1
1905	StL-A	3	3	2	1	.667	5	1.61	28	12	5	22	0	3	0	0
1906	StL-A	26	28	13	14	.481	48	1.77	244	132	55	196	2	25	3	1
1907	StL-A	31	32	13	16	.448	76	2.68	255 2/3	96	62	229	4	27	4	1
1908	StL-A	32	33	16	13	.552	60	2.11	256	85	47	208	1	23	5	1
1909	StL-A	27	34	12	16	.429	56	2.11	239	82	42	221	1	18	4	3
1910	StL-A	18	21	7	11	.389	33	2.30	129 1/3	52	28	121	0	8	3	0
1911	StL-A	27	31	8	19	.296	76	3.29	207 2/3	52	44	224	7	18	1	1
1912	StL-A	27	32	9	17	.346	81	3.10	235 1/3	67	52	248	5	19	0	0
1913	StL-A	0	2	0	0	—	0	0.00	2	0	2	1	0	0	0	0
Career Average		26	30	12	14	.463	69	2.76	226	93	49	214	5	21	2	1
Yankee Average		**34**	**42**	**16**	**16**	**.492**	**93**	**2.81**	**297**	**143**	**75**	**277**	**10**	**26**	**2**	**1**
Career Total		516	577	244	256	.488	1450	2.97	4389	1621	1021	4319	110	422	46	16
Yankee Total		**68**	**84**	**31**	**32**	**.492**	**185**	**2.81**	**593 1/3**	**286**	**149**	**554**	**19**	**51**	**4**	**1**

Pulido, Alfonso BORN ALFONSO PULIDO (MANZO)
HEIGHT: 5'11" LEFTHANDER BORN: 1/23/1957 VERACRUZ, MEXICO

YEAR	TEAM	STARTS	GAMES	WON	LOST	PCT	ER	ERA	INNINGS PITCHED	STRIKE-OUTS	WALKS	HITS ALLOWED	HRS ALLOWED	COMP. GAMES	SHUT-OUTS	SAVES
1983	Pit-N	1	1	0	0	—	2	9.00	2	1	1	4	2	0	0	0
1984	Pit-N	0	1	0	0	—	2	9.00	2	2	1	3	0	0	0	0
1986	NY-A	3	10	1	1	.500	16	4.70	30 2/3	13	9	38	8	0	0	1
Career Average		1	4	0	0	.500	7	5.19	12	5	4	15	3	0	0	0
Yankee Average		**3**	**10**	**1**	**1**	**.500**	**16**	**4.70**	**30 2/3**	**13**	**9**	**38**	**8**	**0**	**0**	**1**
Career Total		4	12	1	1	.500	20	5.19	34 2/3	16	11	45	10	0	0	1
Yankee Total		**3**	**10**	**1**	**1**	**.500**	**16**	**4.70**	**30 2/3**	**13**	**9**	**38**	**8**	**0**	**0**	**1**

Puttmann, Ambrose Nicholas (Putty)
HEIGHT: 6'4" LEFTHANDER BORN: 9/9/1880 CINCINNATI, OHIO DIED: 6/21/1936 JAMAICA, NEW YORK

YEAR	TEAM	STARTS	GAMES	WON	LOST	PCT	ER	ERA	INNINGS PITCHED	STRIKE-OUTS	WALKS	HITS ALLOWED	HRS ALLOWED	COMP. GAMES	SHUT-OUTS	SAVES
1903	NY-A	2	3	2	0	1.000	2	0.95	19	8	4	16	0	1	0	0
1904	NY-A	3	9	2	0	1.000	15	2.74	49 1/3	26	17	40	0	2	1	0
1905	NY-A	9	17	2	7	.222	41	4.27	86 1/3	39	37	79	2	5	1	1
1906	StL-N	4	4	2	2	.500	11	5.30	18 2/3	12	9	23	2	0	0	0
Career Average		5	8	2	2	.471	17	3.58	43	21	17	40	1	2	1	0
Yankee Average		**5**	**10**	**2**	**2**	**.462**	**19**	**3.38**	**52**	**24**	**19**	**45**	**1**	**3**	**1**	**0**
Career Total		18	33	8	9	.471	69	3.58	173 1/3	85	67	158	4	8	2	1
Yankee Total		**14**	**29**	**6**	**7**	**.462**	**58**	**3.38**	**154 2/3**	**73**	**58**	**135**	**2**	**8**	**2**	**1**

Queen, Melvin Joseph
HEIGHT: 6'0" RIGHTHANDER BORN: 3/4/1918 MAXWELL, PENNSYLVANIA DIED: 4/4/1982 FORT SMITH, ARKANSAS

YEAR	TEAM	STARTS	GAMES	WON	LOST	PCT	ER	ERA	INNINGS PITCHED	STRIKE-OUTS	WALKS	HITS ALLOWED	HRS ALLOWED	COMP. GAMES	SHUT-OUTS	SAVES
1942	NY-A	0	4	1	0	1.000	0	0.00	5 2/3	0	3	6	0	0	0	0
1944	NY-A	10	10	6	3	.667	30	3.31	81 2/3	30	34	68	7	4	1	0
1946	NY-A	3	14	1	1	.500	22	6.53	30 1/3	26	21	40	2	1	0	0
1947	NY-A	0	5	0	0	—	7	9.45	6 2/3	2	4	9	2	0	0	0
1947	Pit-N	12	14	3	7	.300	33	4.01	74	34	51	70	8	2	0	0
1948	Pit-N	8	25	4	4	.500	49	6.65	66 1/3	34	40	82	8	0	0	1
1950	Pit-N	21	33	5	14	.263	80	5.98	120 1/3	76	73	135	18	4	1	0
1951	Pit-N	21	39	7	9	.438	83	4.44	168 1/3	123	99	149	21	4	1	0
1952	Pit-N	2	2	0	2	.000	11	29.70	3 1/3	3	4	8	2	0	0	0
Career Average		9	16	3	4	.403	35	5.09	62	36	37	63	8	2	0	0
Yankee Average		**4**	**11**	**3**	**1**	**.667**	**20**	**4.27**	**41**	**19**	**21**	**41**	**4**	**2**	**0**	**0**
Career Total		77	146	27	40	.403	315	5.09	556 2/3	328	329	567	68	15	3	1
Yankee Total		**13**	**33**	**8**	**4**	**.667**	**59**	**4.27**	**124 1/3**	**58**	**62**	**123**	**11**	**5**	**1**	**0**

Quick, Edwin S.

HEIGHT: 5'11"   RIGHTHANDER   BORN: 12/1881   BALTIMORE, MARYLAND   DIED: 6/19/1913 ROCKY FORD, COLORADO

YEAR	TEAM	STARTS	GAMES	WON	LOST	PCT	ER	ERA	INNINGS PITCHED	STRIKE-OUTS	WALKS	HITS ALLOWED	HRS ALLOWED	COMP. GAMES	SHUT-OUTS	SAVES
1903	NY-A	1	1	0	0	—	2	9.00	2	0	1	5	0	0	0	0
Career Average		1	1	0	0	—	2	9.00	2	0	1	5	0	0	0	0
Yankee Average		**1**	**1**	**0**	**0**	**—**	**2**	**9.00**	**2**	**0**	**1**	**5**	**0**	**0**	**0**	**0**
Career Total		1	1	0	0	—	2	9.00	2	0	1	5	0	0	0	0
Yankee Total		**1**	**1**	**0**	**0**	**—**	**2**	**9.00**	**2**	**0**	**1**	**5**	**0**	**0**	**0**	**0**

Quinn, John Picus (Jack)

HEIGHT: 6'0"   RIGHTHANDER   BORN: 7/5/1883 JANESVILLE, PENNSYLVANIA   DIED: 4/17/1946 POTTSVILLE, PENNSYLVANIA

YEAR	TEAM	STARTS	GAMES	WON	LOST	PCT	ER	ERA	INNINGS PITCHED	STRIKE-OUTS	WALKS	HITS ALLOWED	HRS ALLOWED	COMP. GAMES	SHUT-OUTS	SAVES
1909	NY-A	11	23	9	5	.643	26	1.97	118 2/3	36	24	110	1	8	0	1
1910	NY-A	31	35	18	12	.600	62	2.37	235 2/3	82	58	214	2	20	0	0
1911	NY-A	16	40	8	10	.444	73	3.76	174 2/3	71	41	203	2	7	0	2
1912	NY-A	11	18	5	7	.417	66	5.79	102 2/3	47	23	139	4	7	0	0
1913	Bos-N	7	8	4	3	.571	15	2.40	56 1/3	33	7	55	1	6	1	0
1914	Bal-F	42	46	26	14	.650	99	2.60	342 2/3	164	65	335	3	27	4	1
1915	Bal-F	31	44	9	22	.290	105	3.45	273 2/3	118	63	289	9	21	0	1
1918	Chi-A	5	6	5	1	.833	13	2.29	51	22	7	38	0	5	0	0

(continued)

John Picus "Jack" Quinn, rhp, 1909–12, 1919–21

No one ever said Jack Quinn was one of the all-time greats; he was just a solid pitcher for a very long time.

Born John Quinn Picus on (probably) July 5, 1883, in Janesville, Pennsylvania, Quinn was looking at a short life in the Pennsylvania coal mines until baseball bailed him out. He was signed by the Highlanders in 1909. He was 9-5 that first year, which was fairly remarkable, since the Highlanders themselves were 74-77, 23½ games out of first place.

Quinn was a master spitballer with excellent control. During his first four years with the Highlanders, his winning percentage was .540. His team's was .450, with only one winning season and no pennants.

Quinn was traded to the Braves in 1913 and jumped to the Federal League in 1914. After the Federal League folded, he had a stint with the White Sox before coming back to New York in 1919. He went 15-14 that year, and then won 18 games in 1920 and led the team in saves with three.

He won several big games in 1921 when the Yankees won their first pennant. He was, at 37, a canny veteran pitcher who was cool under fire.

But by 1922, Yankee management decided he was too old and shipped him to the Red Sox. Quinn would play for 12 more years and win 135 more games before retiring. He would play with 31 Hall of Famers in his career.

Quinn was always pretty evasive on his birth year, but in 1933, at age 50 (or 51), he pitched in 14 games for the Cincinnati Reds, earning one save. He also hit a home run at age 46 (or 47), and won a World Series game with the Athletics at age 45 — or perhaps it was 46. Either way, he's the oldest player to do so.

Quinn is 15th all-time on the Yankees in ERA with a 3.12 mark and 20th in complete games with 82.

(continued)

YEAR	TEAM	STARTS	GAMES	WON	LOST	PCT	ER	ERA	INNINGS PITCHED	STRIKE-OUTS	WALKS	HITS ALLOWED	HRS ALLOWED	COMP. GAMES	SHUT-OUTS	SAVES
1919	**NY-A**	**31**	**38**	**15**	**14**	**.517**	**77**	**2.61**	**266**	**97**	**65**	**242**	**8**	**18**	**4**	**0**
1920	**NY-A**	**32**	**41**	**18**	**10**	**.643**	**90**	**3.20**	**253 1/3**	**101**	**48**	**271**	**8**	**17**	**2**	**3**
1921	**NY-A**	**13**	**33**	**8**	**7**	**.533**	**50**	**3.78**	**119**	**44**	**32**	**158**	**2**	**6**	**0**	**0**
1922	Bos-A	32	40	13	16	.448	99	3.48	256	67	59	263	9	16	4	0
1923	Bos-A	28	42	13	17	.433	105	3.89	243	71	53	302	6	16	1	7
1924	Bos-A	25	44	12	13	.480	83	3.27	228 2/3	64	52	241	10	13	2	7
1925	Bos-A	15	19	7	8	.467	51	4.37	105	24	26	140	3	8	0	0
1925	Phi-A	14	18	6	3	.667	43	3.88	99 2/3	19	16	119	3	4	0	0
1926	Phi-A	21	31	10	11	.476	62	3.41	163 2/3	58	36	191	4	8	3	1
1927	Phi-A	25	34	15	10	.600	73	3.26	201 1/3	43	37	211	8	11	3	1
1928	Phi-A	28	31	18	7	.720	68	2.90	211 1/3	43	34	239	3	18	4	1
1929	Phi-A	18	35	11	9	.550	71	3.97	161	41	39	182	8	7	0	2
1930	Phi-A	7	35	9	7	.563	44	4.42	89 2/3	28	22	109	6	0	0	6
1931	Bro-N	1	39	5	4	.556	19	2.66	64 1/3	25	24	65	1	0	0	15
1932	Bro-N	0	42	3	7	.300	32	3.30	87 1/3	28	24	102	1	0	0	8
1933	Cin-N	0	14	0	1	.000	7	4.02	15 2/3	3	5	20	0	0	0	1
Career Average		19	32	10	9	.531	60	3.29	163	55	36	177	4	10	1	2
Yankee Average		**21**	**33**	**12**	**9**	**.555**	**63**	**3.15**	**181**	**68**	**42**	**191**	**4**	**12**	**1**	**1**
Career Total		444	756	247	218	.531	1433	3.29	3920 1/3	1329	860	4238	102	243	28	57
Yankee Total		**145**	**228**	**81**	**65**	**.555**	**444**	**3.15**	**1270**	**478**	**291**	**1337**	**27**	**83**	**6**	**6**

Rajsich, David Christopher

HEIGHT: 6'5" LEFTHANDER BORN: 9/28/1951 YOUNGSTOWN, OHIO

YEAR	TEAM	STARTS	GAMES	WON	LOST	PCT	ER	ERA	INNINGS PITCHED	STRIKE-OUTS	WALKS	HITS ALLOWED	HRS ALLOWED	COMP. GAMES	SHUT-OUTS	SAVES
1978	**NY-A**	**2**	**4**	**0**	**0**	**—**	**6**	**4.05**	**13 1/3**	**9**	**6**	**16**	**0**	**0**	**0**	**0**
1979	Tex-A	3	27	1	3	.250	21	3.52	53 2/3	32	18	56	7	0	0	0
1980	Tex-A	1	24	2	1	.667	32	5.96	48 1/3	35	22	56	7	0	0	2
Career Average		3	28	2	2	.429	30	4.60	57	38	23	64	7	0	0	1
Yankee Average		**2**	**4**	**0**	**0**	**—**	**6**	**4.05**	**13 1/3**	**9**	**6**	**16**	**0**	**0**	**0**	**0**
Career Total		6	55	3	4	.429	59	4.60	115 1/3	76	46	128	14	0	0	2
Yankee Total		**2**	**4**	**0**	**0**	**—**	**6**	**4.05**	**13 1/3**	**9**	**6**	**16**	**0**	**0**	**0**	**0**

Ramos, Pedro (Pete) BORN PEDRO RAMOS (GUERRA)

HEIGHT: 6'0" RIGHTHANDER BORN: 4/28/1935 PINAR DEL RIO, CUBA

YEAR	TEAM	STARTS	GAMES	WON	LOST	PCT	ER	ERA	INNINGS PITCHED	STRIKE-OUTS	WALKS	HITS ALLOWED	HRS ALLOWED	COMP. GAMES	SHUT-OUTS	SAVES
1955	Was-A	9	45	5	11	.313	56	3.88	130	34	39	121	13	3	1	5
1956	Was-A	18	37	12	10	.545	89	5.27	152	54	76	178	23	4	0	0
1957	Was-A	30	43	12	16	.429	123	4.79	231	91	69	251	43	7	1	0
1958	Was-A	37	43	14	18	.438	122	4.23	259 1/3	132	77	277	38	10	4	3
1959	Was-A	35	37	13	19	.406	108	4.16	233 2/3	95	52	233	29	11	0	0
1960	Was-A	36	43	11	18	.379	105	3.45	274	160	99	254	24	14	1	2
1961	Min-A	34	42	11	20	.355	116	3.95	264 1/3	174	79	265	39	9	3	2
1962	Cle-A	27	37	10	12	.455	83	3.71	201 1/3	96	85	189	28	7	2	1
1963	Cle-A	22	36	9	8	.529	64	3.14	184 2/3	169	41	156	29	5	0	0
1964	Cle-A	19	36	7	10	.412	76	5.14	133	98	26	144	18	3	1	0
1964	**NY-A**	**0**	**13**	**1**	**0**	**1.000**	**3**	**1.25**	**21 2/3**	**21**	**0**	**13**	**1**	**0**	**0**	**8**
1965	**NY-A**	**0**	**65**	**5**	**5**	**.500**	**30**	**2.92**	**92 1/3**	**68**	**27**	**80**	**7**	**0**	**0**	**19**
1966	**NY-A**	**1**	**52**	**3**	**9**	**.250**	**36**	**3.61**	**89 2/3**	**58**	**18**	**98**	**10**	**0**	**0**	**13**
1967	Phi-N	0	6	0	0	—	8	9.00	8	1	8	14	1	0	0	0
1969	Pit-N	0	5	0	1	.000	4	6.00	6	4	0	8	2	0	0	0
1969	Cin-N	0	38	4	3	.571	38	5.16	66 1/3	40	24	73	8	0	0	2
1970	Was-A	0	4	0	0	—	7	7.56	8 1/3	10	4	10	2	0	0	0
Career Average		16	34	7	9	.422	63	4.08	138	77	43	139	19	4	1	3
Yankee Average		**0**	**43**	**3**	**5**	**.391**	**23**	**3.05**	**68**	**49**	**15**	**64**	**6**	**0**	**0**	**13**
Career Total		268	582	117	160	.422	1068	4.08	2355 2/3	1305	724	2364	315	73	13	55
Yankee Total		**1**	**130**	**9**	**14**	**.391**	**69**	**3.05**	**203 2/3**	**147**	**45**	**191**	**18**	**0**	**0**	**40**

Raschi, Victor John Angelo (Vic)

HEIGHT: 6'1"   RIGHTHANDER   BORN: 3/28/1919 W. SPRINGFIELD, MASSACHUSETTS   DIED: 10/14/1988 GROVELAND, NEW YORK

YEAR	TEAM	STARTS	GAMES	WON	LOST	PCT	ER	ERA	INNINGS PITCHED	STRIKE-OUTS	WALKS	HITS ALLOWED	HRS ALLOWED	COMP. GAMES	SHUT-OUTS	SAVES
1946	NY-A	2	2	2	0	1.000	7	3.94	16	11	5	14	0	2	0	0
1947	NY-A	14	15	7	2	.778	45	3.87	104 2/3	51	38	89	11	6	1	0
1948	NY-A	31	36	19	8	.704	95	3.84	222 2/3	124	74	208	15	18	6	1
1949	NY-A	37	38	21	10	.677	102	3.34	274 2/3	124	138	247	16	21	3	0
1950	NY-A	32	33	21	8	.724	114	4.00	256 2/3	116	116	232	19	17	2	1
1951	NY-A	34	35	21	10	.677	94	3.27	258 1/3	164	103	233	20	15	4	0
1952	NY-A	31	31	16	6	.727	69	2.78	223	127	91	174	13	13	4	0
1953	NY-A	26	28	13	6	.684	67	3.33	181	76	55	150	11	7	4	1
1954	StL-N	29	30	8	9	.471	94	4.73	179	73	71	182	24	6	2	0
1955	StL-N	1	1	0	1	.000	4	21.61	1 2/3	1	1	5	0	0	0	0
1955	KC-A	18	20	4	6	.400	61	5.42	101 1/3	38	35	132	10	1	0	0
Career Average		23	24	12	6	.667	68	3.72	165	86	66	151	13	10	2	0
Yankee Average		**26**	**27**	**15**	**6**	**.706**	**74**	**3.47**	**192**	**104**	**78**	**168**	**13**	**12**	**3**	**0**
Career Total		255	269	132	66	.667	752	3.72	1819	944	727	1666	139	106	26	3
Yankee Total		**207**	**218**	**120**	**50**	**.706**	**593**	**3.47**	**1537**	**832**	**620**	**1347**	**105**	**99**	**24**	**3**

Victor John Angelo "Vic" Raschi, rhp, 1946–53

On the days when Vic Raschi was scheduled to pitch, nobody came near him. The lean (6 feet 1 inch) Raschi sat by himself in the Yankee locker room, building up an overwhelming animosity toward his opponent, and he would brook no interruptions from teammates.

Born on March 28, 1919, in West Springfield, Massachusetts, Raschi was an outstanding three-sport athlete in high school. He spent a year at William and Mary College in Virginia, where his best sport was basketball.

But the Yankees had signed him, and after his freshman year, they vetoed basketball. He spent several years in the minors and was called up after the war.

By 1948, he had a devastating fastball and an improving curveball. He won 19, 21, 21 and 21 games over the next four years as the Yankees won three World Series. He would always have control problems, but inevitably, they would be in the earlier innings. As the game went on, Raschi's concentration seemed to intensify and he was nearly unbeatable. He is second all-time in winning percentage with New York, at .706, just behind Spud Chandler's .717.

As tough as he was in the clubhouse before the game, he was tougher on the mound. He disliked visits from coaches or catchers and would often tell them so. He completed 99 of his 207 starts as a Yankee, an unusually high percentage for a pitcher.

But because of World War II, he had been brought up relatively late in his career. In 1953, he was only 13-6, although he pitched well in the World Series. His 1954 contract called for a pay cut, and he was critical of the Yankee front office. He was soon traded to the Cardinals, where he played for two more years before retiring.

After his career in baseball, Raschi became a successful businessman. He died in 1988 in Groveland, New York. Raschi is 13th all-time with the Yankees in innings pitched with 1,537, 11th all-time in wins with 120, 13th in strikeouts with 832 and 14th in complete games with 99.

Rasmussen, Dennis Lee
HEIGHT: 6'7" LEFTHANDER BORN: 4/18/1959 LOS ANGELES, CALIFORNIA

YEAR	TEAM	STARTS	GAMES	WON	LOST	PCT	ER	ERA	INNINGS PITCHED	STRIKE-OUTS	WALKS	HITS ALLOWED	HRS ALLOWED	COMP. GAMES	SHUT-OUTS	SAVES
1983	SD-N	1	4	0	0	—	3	1.98	13 2/3	13	8	10	1	0	0	0
1984	NY-A	24	24	9	6	.600	75	4.57	147 2/3	110	60	127	16	1	0	0
1985	NY-A	16	22	3	5	.375	45	3.98	101 2/3	63	42	97	10	2	0	0
1986	NY-A	31	31	18	6	.750	87	3.88	202	131	74	160	28	3	1	0
1987	NY-A	25	26	9	7	.563	77	4.75	146	89	55	145	31	2	0	0
1987	Cin-N	7	7	4	1	.800	20	3.97	45 1/3	39	12	39	5	0	0	0
1988	Cin-N	11	11	2	6	.250	36	5.75	56 1/3	27	22	68	8	1	1	0
1988	SD-N	20	20	14	4	.778	42	2.55	148 1/3	85	36	131	9	6	0	0
1989	SD-N	33	33	10	10	.500	87	4.26	183 2/3	87	72	190	18	1	0	0
1990	SD-N	32	32	11	15	.423	94	4.51	187 2/3	86	62	217	28	3	1	0
1991	SD-N	24	24	6	13	.316	61	3.74	146 2/3	75	49	155	12	1	1	0
1992	Chi-N	1	3	0	0	—	6	10.80	5	0	2	7	2	0	0	0
1992	KC-A	5	5	4	1	.800	6	1.43	37 2/3	12	6	25	0	1	1	0
1993	KC-A	4	9	1	2	.333	24	7.45	29	12	14	40	4	0	0	0
1995	KC-A	1	5	0	1	.000	10	9.00	10	6	8	13	3	0	0	0
Career Average		16	17	6	5	.542	45	4.15	97	56	35	95	12	1	0	0
Yankee Average		24	26	10	6	.619	71	4.28	149	98	58	132	21	2	0	0
Career Total		235	256	91	77	.542	673	4.15	1460 2/3	835	522	1424	175	21	5	0
Yankee Total		96	103	39	24	.619	284	4.28	597 1/3	393	231	529	85	8	1	0

Rawley, Shane William
HEIGHT: 6'0" LEFTHANDER BORN: 7/27/1955 RACINE, WISCONSIN

YEAR	TEAM	STARTS	GAMES	WON	LOST	PCT	ER	ERA	INNINGS PITCHED	STRIKE-OUTS	WALKS	HITS ALLOWED	HRS ALLOWED	COMP. GAMES	SHUT-OUTS	SAVES
1978	Sea-A	2	52	4	9	.308	51	4.12	111 1/3	66	51	114	7	0	0	4
1979	Sea-A	3	48	5	9	.357	36	3.84	84 1/3	48	40	88	2	0	0	11
1980	Sea-A	0	59	7	7	.500	42	3.33	113 2/3	68	63	103	3	0	0	13
1981	Sea-A	0	46	4	6	.400	30	3.95	68 1/3	35	38	64	1	0	0	8
1982	NY-A	17	47	11	10	.524	74	4.06	164	111	54	165	10	3	0	3
1983	NY-A	33	34	14	14	.500	100	3.78	238 1/3	124	79	246	19	13	2	1
1984	NY-A	10	11	2	3	.400	29	6.21	42	24	27	46	0	0	0	0
1984	Phi-N	18	18	10	6	.625	51	3.81	120 1/3	58	27	117	13	3	0	0
1985	Phi-N	31	36	13	8	.619	73	3.31	198 2/3	106	81	188	16	6	2	0
1986	Phi-N	23	23	11	7	.611	62	3.54	157 2/3	73	50	166	13	7	1	0
1987	Phi-N	36	36	17	11	.607	112	4.39	229 2/3	123	86	250	23	4	1	0
1988	Phi-N	32	32	8	16	.333	92	4.18	198	87	78	220	27	4	1	0
1989	Min-A	25	27	5	12	.294	84	5.21	145	68	60	167	19	1	0	0
Career Average		18	36	9	9	.485	64	4.02	144	76	56	149	12	3	1	3
Yankee Average		20	31	9	9	.500	68	4.11	148	86	53	152	10	5	1	1
Career Total		230	469	111	118	.485	836	4.02	1871 1/3	991	734	1934	153	41	7	40
Yankee Total		60	92	27	27	.500	203	4.11	444 1/3	259	160	457	29	16	2	4

Reardon, Jeffrey James
HEIGHT: 6'0" RIGHTHANDER BORN: 10/1/1955 DALTON, MASSACHUSETTS

YEAR	TEAM	STARTS	GAMES	WON	LOST	PCT	ER	ERA	INNINGS PITCHED	STRIKE-OUTS	WALKS	HITS ALLOWED	HRS ALLOWED	COMP. GAMES	SHUT-OUTS	SAVES
1979	NY-N	0	18	1	2	.333	4	1.74	20 2/3	10	9	12	2	0	0	2
1980	NY-N	0	61	8	7	.533	32	2.61	110 1/3	101	47	96	10	0	0	6
1981	NY-N	0	18	1	0	1.000	11	3.45	28 2/3	28	12	27	2	0	0	2
1981	Mon-N	0	25	2	0	1.000	6	1.30	41 2/3	21	9	21	3	0	0	6
1982	Mon-N	0	75	7	4	.636	25	2.06	109	86	36	87	6	0	0	26
1983	Mon-N	0	66	7	9	.438	31	3.03	92	78	44	87	7	0	0	21
1984	Mon-N	0	68	7	7	.500	28	2.90	87	79	37	70	5	0	0	23
1985	Mon-N	0	63	2	8	.200	31	3.18	87 2/3	67	26	68	7	0	0	41
1986	Mon-N	0	62	7	9	.438	39	3.94	89	67	26	83	12	0	0	35
1987	Min-A	0	63	8	8	.500	40	4.48	80 1/3	83	28	70	14	0	0	31
1988	Min-A	0	63	2	4	.333	20	2.47	73	56	15	68	6	0	0	42
1989	Min-A	0	65	5	4	.556	33	4.07	73	46	12	68	8	0	0	31

(continued)

(continued)

YEAR	TEAM	STARTS	GAMES	WON	LOST	PCT	ER	ERA	INNINGS PITCHED	STRIKE-OUTS	WALKS	HITS ALLOWED	HRS ALLOWED	COMP. GAMES	SHUT-OUTS	SAVES
1990	Bos-A	0	47	5	3	.625	18	3.16	51 1/3	33	19	39	5	0	0	21
1991	Bos-A	0	57	1	4	.200	20	3.03	59 1/3	44	16	54	9	0	0	40
1992	Bos-A	0	46	2	2	.500	20	4.25	42 1/3	32	7	53	6	0	0	27
1992	Atl-N	0	14	3	0	1.000	2	1.15	15 2/3	7	2	14	0	0	0	3
1993	Cin-N	0	58	4	6	.400	28	4.09	61 2/3	35	10	66	4	0	0	8
1994	**NY-A**	**0**	**11**	**1**	**0**	**1.000**	**9**	**9.00**	**9**	**4**	**3**	**17**	**3**	**0**	**0**	**2**
Career Average		0	49	4	4	.487	22	3.16	63	49	20	56	6	0	0	20
Yankee Average		**0**	**11**	**1**	**0**	**1.000**	**9**	**9.00**	**9**	**4**	**3**	**17**	**3**	**0**	**0**	**2**
Career Total		0	880	73	77	.487	397	3.16	1131 2/3	877	358	1000	109	0	0	367
Yankee Total		**0**	**11**	**1**	**0**	**1.000**	**9**	**9.00**	**9**	**4**	**3**	**17**	**3**	**0**	**0**	**2**

Reniff, Harold Eugene (Hal *or* Porky)
HEIGHT: 6'0" RIGHTHANDER BORN: 7/2/1938 WARREN, OHIO

YEAR	TEAM	STARTS	GAMES	WON	LOST	PCT	ER	ERA	INNINGS PITCHED	STRIKE-OUTS	WALKS	HITS ALLOWED	HRS ALLOWED	COMP. GAMES	SHUT-OUTS	SAVES
1961	NY-A	0	25	2	0	1.000	13	2.58	45 1/3	21	31	31	1	0	0	2
1962	NY-A	0	2	0	0	—	3	7.36	3 2/3	1	5	6	0	0	0	0
1963	NY-A	0	48	4	3	.571	26	2.62	89 1/3	56	42	63	3	0	0	18
1964	NY-A	0	41	6	4	.600	24	3.12	69 1/3	38	30	47	3	0	0	9
1965	NY-A	0	51	3	4	.429	36	3.80	85 1/3	74	48	74	4	0	0	3
1966	NY-A	0	56	3	7	.300	34	3.21	95 1/3	79	49	80	2	0	0	9
1967	NY-A	0	24	0	2	.000	19	4.28	40	24	14	40	0	0	0	0
1967	NY-N	0	29	3	3	.500	16	3.35	43	21	23	42	1	0	0	4
Career Average		0	35	3	3	.477	21	3.27	59	39	30	48	2	0	0	6
Yankee Average		**0**	**35**	**3**	**3**	**.474**	**22**	**3.26**	**61**	**42**	**31**	**49**	**2**	**0**	**0**	**6**
Career Total		0	276	21	23	.477	171	3.27	471 1/3	314	242	383	14	0	0	45
Yankee Total		**0**	**247**	**18**	**20**	**.474**	**155**	**3.26**	**428**	**293**	**219**	**341**	**13**	**0**	**0**	**41**

Reuschel, Rickey Eugene (Big Daddy)
HEIGHT: 6'3" RIGHTHANDER BORN: 5/16/1949 QUINCY, ILLINOIS

YEAR	TEAM	STARTS	GAMES	WON	LOST	PCT	ER	ERA	INNINGS PITCHED	STRIKE-OUTS	WALKS	HITS ALLOWED	HRS ALLOWED	COMP. GAMES	SHUT-OUTS	SAVES
1972	Chi-N	18	21	10	8	.556	42	2.93	129	87	29	127	3	5	4	0
1973	Chi-N	36	36	14	15	.483	79	3.00	237	168	62	244	15	7	3	0
1974	Chi-N	38	41	13	12	.520	115	4.30	240 2/3	160	83	262	18	8	2	0
1975	Chi-N	37	38	11	17	.393	97	3.73	234	155	67	244	17	6	0	1
1976	Chi-N	37	38	14	12	.538	100	3.46	260	146	64	260	17	9	2	1
1977	Chi-N	37	39	20	10	.667	78	2.79	252	166	74	233	13	8	4	1
1978	Chi-N	35	35	14	15	.483	92	3.41	242 2/3	115	54	235	16	9	1	0
1979	Chi-N	36	36	18	12	.600	96	3.62	239	125	75	251	16	5	1	0
1980	Chi-N	38	38	11	13	.458	97	3.40	257	140	76	281	13	6	0	0
1981	Chi-N	13	13	4	7	.364	33	3.47	85 2/3	53	23	87	4	1	0	0
1981	**NY-A**	**11**	**12**	**4**	**4**	**.500**	**21**	**2.67**	**70 2/3**	**22**	**10**	**75**	**4**	**1**	**0**	**0**
1983	Chi-N	4	4	1	1	.500	9	3.92	20 2/3	9	10	18	1	3	0	0
1984	Chi-N	14	19	5	5	.500	53	5.17	92 1/3	43	23	123	7	0	0	0
1985	Pit-N	26	31	14	8	.636	49	2.27	194	138	52	153	7	1	0	0
1986	Pit-N	34	35	9	16	.360	95	3.96	215 2/3	125	57	232	20	9	1	1
1987	Pit-N	25	25	8	6	.571	54	2.75	177	80	35	163	12	4	2	0
1987	SF-N	8	9	5	3	.625	24	4.32	50	27	7	44	1	9	3	0
1988	SF-N	36	36	19	11	.633	85	3.12	245	92	42	242	11	3	1	0
1989	SF-N	32	32	17	8	.680	68	2.94	208 1/3	111	54	195	18	7	2	0
1990	SF-N	13	15	3	6	.333	38	3.93	87	49	31	102	8	2	0	0
1991	SF-N	1	4	0	2	.000	5	4.22	10 2/3	4	7	17	0	0	0	1
Career Average		25	27	10	9	.528	63	3.37	169	96	45	171	11	5	1	0
Yankee Average		**11**	**12**	**4**	**4**	**.500**	**21**	**2.67**	**70 2/3**	**22**	**10**	**75**	**4**	**3**	**0**	**0**
Career Total		529	557	214	191	.528	1330	3.37	3548 1/3	2015	935	3588	221	102	26	5
Yankee Total		**11**	**12**	**4**	**4**	**.500**	**21**	**2.67**	**70 2/3**	**22**	**10**	**75**	**4**	**3**	**0**	**0**

Allie Pierce "Superchief" Reynolds, rhp, 1947–54

Allie Reynolds was a Yankee mainstay in the late 1940s and early '50s, helping the team to six pennants in his eight years in New York.

Born in Bethany, Oklahoma, on February 10, 1910, Reynolds spent four average years in Cleveland before coming to New York in 1947 in a trade for Joe Gordon.

He had developed a bad reputation in Cleveland as a player who didn't pitch well in big games. Reynolds's problem was that he tried to overpower every batter he faced. He would often pitch very well for five or six innings and begin to tire, walking batters and throwing bad pitches.

But his arrival in New York changed all that. His roommate, Eddie Lopat, began working with him. Reynolds, many players believed, could throw as hard as the Indians' ace Bob Feller. Lopat taught him to control that velocity and change speeds on his pitches. In his eight years in New York, Reynolds was a five-time All-Star, with a record of 131-60 and 41 saves.

Reynolds soon became known as one of the best "big game" throwers in the major leagues. He was an impressive 7-2 with four saves for New York in World Series competition. He also worked willingly as a reliever in between starts.

Reynolds was one-quarter Creek Indian, which accounted for his Superchief nickname. He was also a tremendous athlete who could have played professional basketball or football had he opted to. And, unlike his friend, the intense Raschi, Reynolds rarely took a defeat home with him.

His most notable feat was pitching two no-hitters in 1951. The first was a tough 1-0 win over his old team, the Indians, and fellow star hurler Feller on July 12. The second came on September 28 against the Red Sox. New York, needing the win to clinch the pennant, was leading 8-0 with two outs in the bottom of the ninth. Reynolds was facing Teddy Ballgame himself, Red Sox star Ted Williams.

With an 0-1 count, Williams knocked a Reynolds fastball into foul territory. Reynolds and Berra raced for the ball, which just nicked off Yogi's glove. Berra admitted later that he was furious with himself for giving a hitter like Williams another chance. But he called for another heater and Williams swung again, fouling it again. This one, Yogi caught. That season, Reynolds was 17-8 and won the Hickock Belt as the best professional athlete in the world.

In 1953, Reynolds injured his back in a bus accident. The injury severely limited his pitching ability, and he retired after the season, going into business back in his native Oklahoma. He died on December 26, 1994 in Oklahoma City, Oklahoma. On the Yankees' all-time list, Reynolds is 12th all-time in innings pitched with 1,700, 9th in wins with 131, 4th in winning percentage at .686, 8th in strikeouts with 967, 5th in shutouts with 27, 15th in complete games with 96 and 12th in saves with 41.

Reynolds, Allie Pierce (Superchief)

HEIGHT: 6'0"   RIGHTHANDER   BORN: 2/10/1915 BETHANY, OKLAHOMA   DIED: 12/26/1994 OKLAHOMA CITY, OKLAHOMA

YEAR	TEAM	STARTS	GAMES	WON	LOST	PCT	ER	ERA	INNINGS PITCHED	STRIKE-OUTS	WALKS	HITS ALLOWED	HRS ALLOWED	COMP. GAMES	SHUT-OUTS	SAVES
1942	Cle-A	0	2	0	0	—	0	0.00	5	2	4	5	0	0	0	0
1943	Cle-A	21	34	11	12	.478	66	2.99	198 2/3	151	109	140	3	11	3	3
1944	Cle-A	21	28	11	8	.579	58	3.30	158	84	91	141	2	5	1	1
1945	Cle-A	30	44	18	12	.600	88	3.20	247 1/3	112	130	227	7	16	2	4
1946	Cle-A	28	31	11	15	.423	79	3.88	183 1/3	107	108	180	10	9	3	0

(continued)

(continued)

YEAR	TEAM	STARTS	GAMES	WON	LOST	PCT	ER	ERA	INNINGS PITCHED	STRIKE-OUTS	WALKS	HITS ALLOWED	HRS ALLOWED	COMP. GAMES	SHUT-OUTS	SAVES
1947	NY-A	30	34	19	8	.704	86	3.20	241 2/3	129	123	207	23	17	4	2
1948	NY-A	31	39	16	7	.696	99	3.77	236 1/3	101	111	240	17	11	1	3
1949	NY-A	31	35	17	6	.739	95	4.00	213 2/3	105	123	200	15	4	2	1
1950	NY-A	29	35	16	12	.571	100	3.74	240 2/3	160	138	215	12	14	2	2
1951	NY-A	26	40	17	8	.680	75	3.05	221	126	100	171	12	16	7	7
1952	NY-A	29	35	20	8	.714	56	2.06	244 1/3	160	97	194	10	24	6	6
1953	NY-A	15	41	13	7	.650	55	3.41	145	86	61	140	9	5	1	13
1954	NY-A	18	36	13	4	.765	58	3.32	157 1/3	100	66	133	13	5	4	7
Career Average		26	36	15	9	.630	76	3.30	208	119	105	183	11	11	3	4
Yankee Average		26	37	16	8	.686	78	3.30	212	121	102	188	14	12	3	5
Career Total		309	434	182	107	.630	915	3.30	2492 1/3	1423	1261	2193	133	137	36	49
Yankee Total		209	295	131	60	.686	624	3.30	1700	967	819	1500	111	96	27	41

Rhoden, Richard Alan (Rick)

HEIGHT: 6'4"   RIGHTHANDER   BORN: 5/16/1953 BOYNTON BEACH, FLORIDA

YEAR	TEAM	STARTS	GAMES	WON	LOST	PCT	ER	ERA	INNINGS PITCHED	STRIKE-OUTS	WALKS	HITS ALLOWED	HRS ALLOWED	COMP. GAMES	SHUT-OUTS	SAVES
1974	LA-N	0	4	1	0	1.000	2	2.00	9	7	4	5	1	0	0	0
1975	LA-N	11	26	3	3	.500	34	3.08	99 1/3	40	32	94	8	1	0	0
1976	LA-N	26	27	12	3	.800	60	2.98	181	77	53	165	17	10	3	0
1977	LA-N	31	31	16	10	.615	90	3.74	216 1/3	122	63	223	20	4	1	0
1978	LA-N	23	30	10	8	.556	67	3.66	164 2/3	79	51	160	13	6	3	0
1979	Pit-N	1	1	0	1	.000	4	7.20	5	2	2	5	0	0	0	0
1980	Pit-N	19	20	7	5	.583	54	3.84	126 2/3	70	40	133	9	2	0	0
1981	Pit-N	21	21	9	4	.692	59	3.89	136 1/3	76	53	147	6	4	2	0
1982	Pit-N	35	35	11	14	.440	106	4.14	230 1/3	128	70	239	14	6	1	0
1983	Pit-N	35	36	13	13	.500	84	3.09	244 1/3	153	68	256	13	7	2	1
1984	Pit-N	33	33	14	9	.609	72	2.72	238 1/3	136	62	216	13	6	3	0
1985	Pit-N	35	35	10	15	.400	106	4.47	213 1/3	128	69	254	18	2	0	0
1986	Pit-N	34	34	15	12	.556	80	2.84	253 2/3	159	76	211	17	12	1	0
1987	**NY-A**	**29**	**30**	**16**	**10**	**.615**	**78**	**3.86**	**181 2/3**	**107**	**61**	**184**	**22**	**4**	**0**	**0**
1988	**NY-A**	**30**	**30**	**12**	**12**	**.500**	**94**	**4.29**	**197**	**94**	**56**	**206**	**20**	**5**	**1**	**0**
1989	Hou-N	17	20	2	6	.250	46	4.28	96 2/3	41	41	108	7	0	0	0
Career Average		24	26	9	8	.547	65	3.59	162	89	50	163	12	4	1	0
Yankee Average		30	30	14	11	.560	86	4.09	189	101	59	195	21	5	1	0
Career Total		380	413	151	125	.547	1036	3.59	2593 2/3	1419	801	2606	198	69	17	1
Yankee Total		59	60	28	22	.560	172	4.09	378 2/3	201	117	390	42	9	1	0

Rhodes, John Gordon (Dusty)

HEIGHT: 6'0"   RIGHTHANDER   BORN: 8/11/1907 WINNEMUCCA, NEVADA   DIED: 3/24/1960 LONG BEACH, CALIFORNIA

YEAR	TEAM	STARTS	GAMES	WON	LOST	PCT	ER	ERA	INNINGS PITCHED	STRIKE-OUTS	WALKS	HITS ALLOWED	HRS ALLOWED	COMP. GAMES	SHUT-OUTS	SAVES
1929	**NY-A**	**4**	**10**	**0**	**4**	**.000**	**23**	**4.85**	**42 2/3**	**13**	**16**	**57**	**3**	**0**	**0**	**0**
1930	**NY-A**	**0**	**3**	**0**	**0**	**—**	**2**	**9.00**	**2**	**1**	**4**	**3**	**0**	**0**	**0**	**0**
1931	**NY-A**	**11**	**18**	**6**	**3**	**.667**	**33**	**3.41**	**87**	**36**	**52**	**82**	**3**	**4**	**0**	**0**
1932	**NY-A**	**2**	**10**	**1**	**2**	**.333**	**21**	**7.88**	**24**	**15**	**21**	**25**	**0**	**1**	**0**	**0**
1932	Bos-A	11	12	1	8	.111	45	5.11	79 1/3	22	31	79	5	4	0	0
1933	Bos-A	29	34	12	15	.444	104	4.03	232	85	93	242	13	14	0	0
1934	Bos-A	31	44	12	12	.500	111	4.56	219	79	98	247	10	10	0	2
1935	Bos-A	19	34	2	10	.167	88	5.41	146 1/3	44	60	195	14	1	0	2
1936	Phi-A	28	35	9	20	.310	138	5.74	216 1/3	61	102	266	26	13	1	1
Career Average		15	22	5	8	.368	63	4.85	116	40	53	133	8	5	0	1
Yankee Average		4	10	2	2	.438	20	4.57	39	16	23	42	2	1	0	0
Career Total		135	200	43	74	.368	565	4.85	1048 2/3	356	477	1196	74	47	1	5
Yankee Total		17	41	7	9	.438	79	4.57	155 2/3	65	93	167	6	5	0	0

Righetti, David Allan

HEIGHT: 6'4"   LEFTHANDER   BORN: 11/28/1958 SAN JOSE, CALIFORNIA

YEAR	TEAM	STARTS	GAMES	WON	LOST	PCT	ER	ERA	INNINGS PITCHED	STRIKE-OUTS	WALKS	HITS ALLOWED	HRS ALLOWED	COMP. GAMES	SHUT-OUTS	SAVES
1979	NY-A	3	3	0	1	.000	7	3.63	17 1/3	13	10	10	2	0	0	0
1981	NY-A	15	15	8	4	.667	24	2.05	105 1/3	89	38	75	1	2	0	0
1982	NY-A	27	33	11	10	.524	77	3.79	183	163	108	155	11	4	0	1
1983	NY-A	31	31	14	8	.636	83	3.44	217	169	67	194	12	7	2	0
1984	NY-A	0	64	5	6	.455	25	2.34	96 1/3	90	37	79	5	0	0	31
1985	NY-A	0	74	12	7	.632	33	2.78	107	92	45	96	5	0	0	29
1986	NY-A	0	74	8	8	.500	29	2.45	106 2/3	83	35	88	4	0	0	46
1987	NY-A	0	60	8	6	.571	37	3.51	95	77	44	95	9	0	0	31
1988	NY-A	0	60	5	4	.556	34	3.52	87	70	37	86	5	0	0	25
1989	NY-A	0	55	2	6	.250	23	3.00	69	51	26	73	3	0	0	25
1990	NY-A	0	53	1	1	.500	21	3.57	53	43	26	48	8	0	0	36
1991	SF-N	0	61	2	7	.222	27	3.39	71 2/3	51	28	64	4	0	0	24
1992	SF-N	4	54	2	7	.222	44	5.06	78 1/3	47	36	79	4	0	0	3
1993	SF-N	0	51	1	1	.500	30	5.70	47 1/3	31	17	58	11	0	0	1
1994	Oak-A	0	7	0	0	—	13	16.71	7	4	9	13	3	0	0	0
1994	Tor-A	0	13	0	1	.000	10	6.92	13	10	10	9	2	0	0	0
1995	Chi-A	9	10	3	2	.600	23	4.22	49	29	18	65	6	0	0	0
Career Average		5	42	5	5	.509	32	3.46	83	65	35	76	6	1	0	15
Yankee Average		**7**	**47**	**7**	**6**	**.548**	**36**	**3.11**	**103**	**85**	**43**	**91**	**6**	**1**	**0**	**20**
Career Total		89	718	82	79	.509	540	3.46	1403	1112	591	1287	95	13	2	252
Yankee Total		**76**	**522**	**74**	**61**	**.548**	**393**	**3.11**	**1136 2/3**	**940**	**473**	**999**	**65**	**13**	**2**	**224**

David Allan Righetti, lhp, 1979, 1981—90

He began his career as a starter, but within a few years, Dave Righetti became one of the great closers in Yankee history.

Righetti was born on November 28, 1958, in San Jose, California. While still in the minor leagues, he was part of a big ten-player deal between the Yankees and the Texas Rangers. He had a brief stint with the big club in 1979, and then became a regular at the start of the 1981 season.

It was not without considerable pressure. He was being dubbed the "next Ron Guidry," a hefty title to try to carry. Righetti wasn't the next Guidry, of course, although the big lefty did win eight of his 12 decisions in 1981, earning the Rookie of the Year award in the American League.

He won 11 and 14 games the next two years, and was a solid starter for New York, turning in a no-hitter against the Red Sox on July 4, 1983. But when reliever Goose Gossage signed with San Diego in 1984, the Yankees began casting about for someone to fill Gossage's shoes. Righetti, a hard-throwing lefty, was the natural choice.

Righetti didn't necessarily agree. He wanted to remain a starter. But the Yankee front office convinced him to try relieving, and Righetti was fabulous almost from the beginning. He had 31 saves in 1984, with 90 strikeouts in 96⅓ innings. He followed that up with 29 saves the next year, and a league-record 46 saves in 1986. From 1985-87, New York had the best bullpen in the American League. Righetti's 46 saves are still a Yankee single-season record.

He continued his excellent pitching during his last three years with the Yankees, averaging almost 27 saves a year from 1988-90. In 1991, he signed with the San Francisco Giants. He had one good year with San Francisco. Righetti retired in 1995, after stints with Oakland, Toronto and the White Sox.

He remains the Yankees' all-time save leader with 224, as well as the all-time Yankee leader in appearances with 522. Righetti is also 14th on the Yankees' ERA list with a 3.11 mark.

Rijo, Jose Antonio BORN JOSE ANTONIO RIJO (ABREU)
HEIGHT: 6'3" RIGHTHANDER BORN: 5/13/1965 SAN CRISTOBAL, DOMINICAN REPUBLIC

YEAR	TEAM	STARTS	GAMES	WON	LOST	PCT	ER	ERA	INNINGS PITCHED	STRIKE-OUTS	WALKS	HITS ALLOWED	HRS ALLOWED	COMP. GAMES	SHUT-OUTS	SAVES
1984	NY-A	5	24	2	8	.200	33	4.76	62 1/3	47	33	74	5	0	0	2
1985	Oak-A	9	12	6	4	.600	25	3.53	63 2/3	65	28	57	6	0	0	0
1986	Oak-A	26	39	9	11	.450	100	4.65	193 2/3	176	108	172	24	4	0	1
1987	Oak-A	14	21	2	7	.222	54	5.90	82 1/3	67	41	106	10	1	0	0
1988	Cin-N	19	49	13	8	.619	43	2.39	162	160	63	120	7	0	0	0
1989	Cin-N	19	19	7	6	.538	35	2.84	111	86	48	101	6	1	1	0
1990	Cin-N	29	29	14	8	.636	59	2.70	197	152	78	151	10	7	1	0
1991	Cin-N	30	30	15	6	.714	57	2.51	204 1/3	172	55	165	8	3	1	0
1992	Cin-N	33	33	15	10	.600	60	2.56	211	171	44	185	15	2	0	0
1993	Cin-N	36	36	14	9	.609	71	2.48	257 1/3	227	62	218	19	2	1	0
1994	Cin-N	26	26	9	6	.600	59	3.09	172	171	52	177	16	2	0	0
1995	Cin-N	14	14	5	4	.556	32	4.17	69	62	22	76	6	0	0	0
Career Average		22	28	9	7	.561	52	3.17	149	130	53	134	11	2	0	0
Yankee Average		**5**	**24**	**2**	**8**	**.200**	**33**	**4.76**	**62 1/3**	**47**	**33**	**74**	**5**	**0**	**0**	**2**
Career Total		260	332	111	87	.561	628	3.17	1785 2/3	1556	634	1602	132	22	4	3
Yankee Total		**5**	**24**	**2**	**8**	**.200**	**33**	**4.76**	**62 1/3**	**47**	**33**	**74**	**5**	**0**	**0**	**2**

Rios, Daniel
HEIGHT: 6'2" RIGHTHANDER BORN: 11/11/1972 MADRID, SPAIN

YEAR	TEAM	STARTS	GAMES	WON	LOST	PCT	ER	ERA	INNINGS PITCHED	STRIKE-OUTS	WALKS	HITS ALLOWED	HRS ALLOWED	COMP. GAMES	SHUT-OUTS	SAVES
1997	NY-A	0	2	0	0	—	5	19.29	2 1/3	1	2	9	3	0	0	0
1998	KC-A	0	5	0	1	.000	5	6.14	7 1/3	6	6	9	1	0	0	0
Career Average		0	4	0	1	.000	5	9.31	4	4	4	9	2	0	0	0
Yankee Average		**0**	**2**	**0**	**0**	**—**	**5**	**19.29**	**2 1/3**	**1**	**2**	**9**	**3**	**0**	**0**	**0**
Career Total		0	7	0	1	.000	10	9.31	9 2/3	7	8	18	4	0	0	0
Yankee Total		**0**	**2**	**0**	**0**	**—**	**5**	**19.29**	**2 1/3**	**1**	**2**	**9**	**3**	**0**	**0**	**0**

Rivera, Mariano
HEIGHT: 6'2" RIGHTHANDER BORN: 11/29/1969 PANAMA CITY, PANAMA

YEAR	TEAM	STARTS	GAMES	WON	LOST	PCT	ER	ERA	INNINGS PITCHED	STRIKE-OUTS	WALKS	HITS ALLOWED	HRS ALLOWED	COMP. GAMES	SHUT-OUTS	SAVES
1995	NY-A	10	19	5	3	.625	41	5.51	67	51	30	71	11	0	0	0
1996	NY-A	0	61	8	3	.727	25	2.09	107 2/3	130	34	73	1	0	0	5
1997	NY-A	0	66	6	4	.600	15	1.88	71 2/3	68	20	65	5	0	0	43
1998	NY-A	0	54	3	0	1.000	13	1.91	61 1/3	36	17	48	3	0	0	36
1999	NY-A	0	66	4	3	.571	14	1.83	69	52	18	43	2	0	0	45
2000	NY-A	0	66	7	4	.636	24	2.85	75 2/3	58	25	58	4	0	0	36
Career Average		2	55	6	3	.660	22	2.63	75	66	24	60	4	0	0	28
Yankee Average		**2**	**55**	**6**	**3**	**.660**	**22**	**2.63**	**75**	**66**	**24**	**60**	**4**	**0**	**0**	**28**
Career Total		10	332	33	17	.660	132	2.63	452 1/3	395	144	358	26	0	0	165
Yankee Total		**10**	**332**	**33**	**17**	**.660**	**132**	**2.63**	**452 1/3**	**395**	**144**	**358**	**26**	**0**	**0**	**165**

Roberts, Dale (Mountain Man)
HEIGHT: 6'4" LEFTHANDER BORN: 4/12/1942 OWENTON, KENTUCKY

YEAR	TEAM	STARTS	GAMES	WON	LOST	PCT	ER	ERA	INNINGS PITCHED	STRIKE-OUTS	WALKS	HITS ALLOWED	HRS ALLOWED	COMP. GAMES	SHUT-OUTS	SAVES
1967	NY-A	0	2	0	0	—	2	9.00	2	0	2	3	0	0	0	0
Career Average		0	2	0	0	—	2	9.00	2	0	2	3	0	0	0	0
Yankee Average		**0**	**2**	**0**	**0**	**—**	**2**	**9.00**	**2**	**0**	**2**	**3**	**0**	**0**	**0**	**0**
Career Total		0	2	0	0	—	2	9.00	2	0	2	3	0	0	0	0
Yankee Total		**0**	**2**	**0**	**0**	**—**	**2**	**9.00**	**2**	**0**	**2**	**3**	**0**	**0**	**0**	**0**

Mariano Rivera, rhp, 1995–2000

In a very short time, Mariano Rivera has established himself as the premier closer in the American League, and perhaps in all of baseball.

Rivera was born on November 29, 1969, in Panama City, Panama. He was signed by the Yankees in 1990, and spent five years in the Yankee farm system as a starter. He was a starter his first two years in New York and performed fairly well.

The Yankees were using Rivera as a starter and a reliever, with somewhat mixed results. He seemed to do well in both roles, but was not overpowering in either. He was, a few seasons into his career, somewhat of a question mark.

But in 1996, Yankee skipper Joe Torre converted the lanky righty into a full-time closer, and the results have been overwhelming.

During the 1997–2000 seasons, three of which resulted in World Championships for the Yankees, Rivera had 43, 36, 45 and 36 saves. His postseason work has been even more impressive.

Pitching in the World Series of 1998 and 1999, Rivera was virtually unhittable. He domi-nated both the Padres and the Atlanta Braves as the Yankees swept both clubs. As good as he was during the 1998 and 1999 regular seasons, his overpowering control and coolness on the mound in the playoffs and the World Series gave the Yankees an extraordinary advantage.

During the 2000 postseason, he was not as overpowering, and several Mets actually hit him. Still, his career postseason numbers make him the best closer ever: 4-0, 19 saves in 20 chances, 0.71 ERA and a conversion rate of 7 saves in 7 chances in the last three World Series. His 30⅔ scoreless innings in the play-offs pushed him ahead of former Yankee Whitey Ford that year.

Early in 2000, Rivera announced his plans to retire after the 2003 season and become an evangelical minister. After the 2000 World Series, he admitted he had changed his mind. He will no longer put time constraints on his career.

Rivera is already second on the Yankees' all-time save list with 155. During spring training in 1998–2000, he has worked with Goose Gossage, the former number two Yankee with 151 saves. Gossage admitted once that he loved Rivera's coolness on the mound.

"He's such an incredible weapon," said the Goose.

Robinson, Jeffrey Daniel

HEIGHT: 6'4"   RIGHTHANDER   BORN: 12/13/1960 SANTA ANA, CALIFORNIA

YEAR	TEAM	STARTS	GAMES	WON	LOST	PCT	ER	ERA	INNINGS PITCHED	STRIKE-OUTS	WALKS	HITS ALLOWED	HRS ALLOWED	COMP. GAMES	SHUT-OUTS	SAVES
1984	SF-N	33	34	7	15	.318	87	4.56	171 ⅔	102	52	195	12	1	1	0
1985	SF-N	0	8	0	0	—	7	5.11	12 ⅓	8	10	16	2	0	0	0
1986	SF-N	1	64	6	3	.667	39	3.36	104 ⅓	90	32	92	8	0	0	8
1987	SF-N	0	63	6	8	.429	30	2.79	96 ⅔	82	48	69	10	0	0	10
1987	Pit-N	0	18	2	1	.667	9	3.04	26 ⅔	19	6	20	1	0	0	4
1988	Pit-N	0	75	11	5	.688	42	3.03	124 ⅔	87	39	113	6	0	0	9
1989	Pit-N	19	50	7	13	.350	72	4.58	141 ⅓	95	59	161	14	0	0	4
1990	**NY-A**	4	54	3	6	.333	34	3.45	88 ⅔	43	34	82	8	1	0	0
1991	Cal-A	0	39	0	3	.000	34	5.37	57	57	29	56	9	0	0	3
1992	Chi-N	5	49	4	3	.571	26	3.00	78	46	40	76	5	0	0	1
Career Average		6	45	5	6	.447	38	3.79	90	63	35	88	8	0	0	4
Yankee Average		4	54	3	6	.333	34	3.45	88 ⅔	43	34	82	8	1	0	0
Career Total		62	454	46	57	.447	380	3.79	901 ⅓	629	349	880	75	2	1	39
Yankee Total		4	54	3	6	.333	34	3.45	88 ⅔	43	34	82	8	1	0	0

Robinson, John Henry (Hank *or* Rube)
HEIGHT: 5'11" LEFTHANDER BORN: 8/16/1889 FLOYD, ARKANSAS DIED: 7/3/1965 N. LITTLE ROCK, ARKANSAS

YEAR	TEAM	STARTS	GAMES	WON	LOST	PCT	ER	ERA	INNINGS PITCHED	STRIKE-OUTS	WALKS	HITS ALLOWED	HRS ALLOWED	COMP. GAMES	SHUT-OUTS	SAVES
1911	Pit-N	0	5	0	1	.000	4	2.77	13	8	5	13	0	0	0	0
1912	Pit-N	16	33	12	7	.632	44	2.26	175	79	30	146	3	11	0	2
1913	Pit-N	23	43	14	9	.609	52	2.38	196 1/3	50	41	184	1	8	1	0
1914	StL-N	16	26	7	8	.467	42	3.00	126	30	32	128	1	6	1	0
1915	StL-N	15	32	7	8	.467	39	2.45	143	57	35	128	1	6	1	0
1918	**NY-A**	**3**	**11**	**2**	**4**	**.333**	**16**	**3.00**	**48**	**14**	**16**	**47**	**0**	**1**	**0**	**0**
Career Average		12	25	7	6	.532	33	2.53	117	40	27	108	1	5	1	0
Yankee Average		**3**	**11**	**2**	**4**	**.333**	**16**	**3.00**	**48**	**14**	**16**	**47**	**0**	**1**	**0**	**0**
Career Total		73	150	42	37	.532	197	2.53	701 1/3	238	159	646	6	32	3	2
Yankee Total		**3**	**11**	**2**	**4**	**.333**	**16**	**3.00**	**48**	**14**	**16**	**47**	**0**	**1**	**0**	**0**

Roettger, Oscar Frederick Louis
HEIGHT: 6'0" RIGHTHANDER BORN: 2/19/1900 ST. LOUIS, MISSOURI DIED: 7/4/1986 ST. LOUIS, MISSOURI

YEAR	TEAM	STARTS	GAMES	WON	LOST	PCT	ER	ERA	INNINGS PITCHED	STRIKE-OUTS	WALKS	HITS ALLOWED	HRS ALLOWED	COMP. GAMES	SHUT-OUTS	SAVES
1923	NY-A	0	5	0	0	—	11	8.49	11 2/3	7	12	16	3	0	0	1
1924	NY-A	0	1	0	0	—	0	—	0	0	2	1	0	0	0	0
Career Average		0	3	0	0	—	6	8.49	5 5/6	4	7	9	2	0	0	1
Yankee Average		**0**	**3**	**0**	**0**	**—**	**6**	**8.49**	**5 5/6**	**4**	**7**	**9**	**2**	**0**	**0**	**1**
Career Total		0	6	0	0	—	11	8.49	11 2/3	7	14	17	3	0	0	1
Yankee Total		**0**	**6**	**0**	**0**	**—**	**11**	**8.49**	**11 2/3**	**7**	**14**	**17**	**3**	**0**	**0**	**1**

Rogers, Kenneth Scott
HEIGHT: 6'1" LEFTHANDER BORN: 11/10/1964 SAVANNAH, GEORGIA

YEAR	TEAM	STARTS	GAMES	WON	LOST	PCT	ER	ERA	INNINGS PITCHED	STRIKE-OUTS	WALKS	HITS ALLOWED	HRS ALLOWED	COMP. GAMES	SHUT-OUTS	SAVES
1989	Tex-A	0	73	3	4	.429	24	2.93	73 2/3	63	42	60	2	0	0	2
1990	Tex-A	3	69	10	6	.625	34	3.13	97 2/3	74	42	93	6	0	0	15
1991	Tex-A	9	63	10	10	.500	66	5.42	109 2/3	73	61	121	14	0	0	5
1992	Tex-A	0	81	3	6	.333	27	3.09	78 2/3	70	26	80	7	0	0	6
1993	Tex-A	33	35	16	10	.615	95	4.10	208 1/3	140	71	210	18	5	0	0
1994	Tex-A	24	24	11	8	.579	83	4.47	167 1/3	120	52	169	24	6	0	0
1995	Tex-A	31	31	17	7	.708	78	3.38	208	140	76	192	26	3	0	0
1996	**NY-A**	**30**	**30**	**12**	**8**	**.600**	**93**	**4.68**	**179**	**92**	**83**	**179**	**16**	**2**	**0**	**0**
1997	**NY-A**	**22**	**31**	**6**	**7**	**.462**	**91**	**5.65**	**145**	**78**	**62**	**161**	**18**	**1**	**0**	**0**
1998	Oak-A	34	34	16	8	.667	84	3.18	238 2/3	138	67	215	19	7	0	0
1999	Oak-A	19	19	5	3	.625	57	4.31	119 1/3	68	41	135	8	3	0	0
1999	NY-N	12	12	5	1	.833	34	4.03	76	58	28	71	8	2	1	0
2000	Tex-A	34	34	13	13	.500	115	4.55	227 1/3	127	78	257	20	2	0	0
Career Average		19	41	10	7	.583	68	4.11	148	95	56	149	14	2	0	2
Yankee Average		**26**	**31**	**9**	**8**	**.545**	**92**	**5.11**	**162**	**85**	**73**	**170**	**17**	**2**	**0**	**0**
Career Total		251	536	127	91	.583	881	4.11	1928 2/3	1241	729	1943	186	31	6	28
Yankee Total		**52**	**61**	**18**	**15**	**.545**	**184**	**5.11**	**324**	**170**	**145**	**340**	**34**	**3**	**0**	**0**

Rogers, Thomas Andrew (Shotgun)
HEIGHT: 6'1" RIGHTHANDER BORN: 2/12/1892 SPARTA, TENNESSEE DIED: 3/7/1936 NASHVILLE, TENNESSEE

YEAR	TEAM	STARTS	GAMES	WON	LOST	PCT	ER	ERA	INNINGS PITCHED	STRIKE-OUTS	WALKS	HITS ALLOWED	HRS ALLOWED	COMP. GAMES	SHUT-OUTS	SAVES
1917	StL-A	8	24	3	6	.333	47	3.89	108 2/3	27	44	112	2	3	0	0
1918	StL-A	16	29	8	10	.444	56	3.27	154	29	49	148	3	11	0	2
1919	StL-A	0	2	0	1	.000	3	27.00	1	1	0	7	0	0	0	0
1919	Phi-A	18	23	4	12	.250	67	4.31	140	37	60	152	9	7	1	0
1921	**NY-A**	**0**	**5**	**0**	**1**	**.000**	**9**	**7.36**	**11**	**0**	**9**	**12**	**1**	**0**	**0**	**1**
Career Average		8	17	3	6	.333	36	3.95	83	19	32	86	3	4	0	1
Yankee Average		**0**	**5**	**0**	**1**	**.000**	**9**	**7.36**	**11**	**0**	**9**	**12**	**1**	**0**	**0**	**1**
Career Total		42	83	15	30	.333	182	3.95	414 2/3	94	162	431	15	21	1	3
Yankee Total		**0**	**5**	**0**	**1**	**.000**	**9**	**7.36**	**11**	**0**	**9**	**12**	**1**	**0**	**0**	**1**

Roland, James Ivan
HEIGHT: 6'3"   LEFTHANDER   BORN: 12/14/1942 FRANKLIN, NORTH CAROLINA

YEAR	TEAM	STARTS	GAMES	WON	LOST	PCT	ER	ERA	INNINGS PITCHED	STRIKE-OUTS	WALKS	HITS ALLOWED	HRS ALLOWED	COMP. GAMES	SHUT-OUTS	SAVES
1962	Min-A	0	1	0	0	—	0	0.00	2	1	0	1	0	0	0	0
1963	Min-A	7	10	4	1	.800	14	2.57	49	34	27	32	4	2	1	0
1964	Min-A	13	30	2	6	.250	43	4.10	94 1/3	63	55	76	12	1	0	3
1966	Min-A	0	1	0	0	—	0	0.00	2	1	0	0	0	0	0	0
1967	Min-A	0	25	0	1	.000	12	3.03	35 2/3	16	17	33	3	0	0	2
1968	Min-A	4	28	4	1	.800	24	3.50	61 2/3	36	24	55	3	1	0	0
1969	Oak-A	3	39	5	1	.833	21	2.19	86 1/3	48	46	59	2	2	0	1
1970	Oak-A	2	28	3	3	.500	13	2.70	43 1/3	26	23	28	2	0	0	2
1971	Oak-A	0	31	1	3	.250	16	3.18	45 1/3	30	19	34	4	0	0	1
1972	Oak-A	0	2	0	0	—	1	3.86	2 1/3	0	0	5	0	0	0	0
1972	**NY-A**	**0**	**16**	**0**	**1**	**.000**	**14**	**5.04**	**25**	**13**	**16**	**27**	**3**	**0**	**0**	**0**
1972	Tex-A	0	5	0	0	—	3	8.10	3 1/3	4	2	7	1	0	0	0
Career Average		2	18	2	1	.528	13	3.22	37	23	19	30	3	1	0	1
Yankee Average		**0**	**16**	**0**	**1**	**.000**	**14**	**5.04**	**25**	**13**	**16**	**27**	**3**	**0**	**0**	**0**
Career Total		29	216	19	17	.528	161	3.22	450 1/3	272	229	357	34	6	1	9
Yankee Total		**0**	**16**	**0**	**1**	**.000**	**14**	**5.04**	**25**	**13**	**16**	**27**	**3**	**0**	**0**	**0**

Roser, Emerson Corey (Steve)
HEIGHT: 6'4"   RIGHTHANDER   BORN: 1/25/1918 ROME, NEW YORK

YEAR	TEAM	STARTS	GAMES	WON	LOST	PCT	ER	ERA	INNINGS PITCHED	STRIKE-OUTS	WALKS	HITS ALLOWED	HRS ALLOWED	COMP. GAMES	SHUT-OUTS	SAVES
1944	**NY-A**	**6**	**16**	**4**	**3**	**.571**	**36**	**3.86**	**84**	**34**	**34**	**80**	**3**	**1**	**0**	**1**
1945	**NY-A**	**0**	**11**	**0**	**0**	**—**	**11**	**3.67**	**27**	**11**	**8**	**27**	**1**	**0**	**0**	**0**
1946	**NY-A**	**1**	**4**	**1**	**1**	**.500**	**6**	**16.20**	**3 1/3**	**1**	**4**	**7**	**0**	**0**	**0**	**0**
1946	Bos-N	1	14	1	1	.500	14	3.60	35	18	18	33	1	0	0	1
Career Average		2	11	2	1	.545	17	4.04	37	16	16	37	1	0	0	1
Yankee Average		**2**	**10**	**2**	**1**	**.556**	**18**	**4.17**	**38**	**15**	**15**	**38**	**1**	**0**	**0**	**0**
Career Total		8	45	6	5	.545	67	4.04	149 1/3	64	64	147	5	1	0	2
Yankee Total		**7**	**31**	**5**	**4**	**.556**	**53**	**4.17**	**114 1/3**	**46**	**46**	**114**	**4**	**1**	**0**	**1**

Ruether, Walter Henry (Dutch)
HEIGHT: 6'2"   LEFTHANDER   BORN: 9/13/1893 ALAMEDA, CALIFORNIA   DIED: 5/16/1970 PHOENIX, ARIZONA

YEAR	TEAM	STARTS	GAMES	WON	LOST	PCT	ER	ERA	INNINGS PITCHED	STRIKE-OUTS	WALKS	HITS ALLOWED	HRS ALLOWED	COMP. GAMES	SHUT-OUTS	SAVES
1917	Chi-N	4	10	2	0	1.000	10	2.48	36 1/3	23	12	37	0	1	0	0
1917	Cin-N	4	7	1	2	.333	14	3.53	35 2/3	12	14	43	0	1	1	0
1918	Cin-N	2	2	0	1	.000	3	2.70	10	10	3	10	0	1	0	0
1919	Cin-N	29	33	19	6	.760	49	1.82	242 2/3	78	83	195	1	20	3	0
1920	Cin-N	33	37	16	12	.571	73	2.47	265 2/3	99	96	235	2	23	5	3
1921	Bro-N	27	36	10	13	.435	100	4.26	211 1/3	78	67	247	7	12	1	2
1922	Bro-N	35	35	21	12	.636	105	3.53	267 1/3	89	92	290	11	26	2	0
1923	Bro-N	34	34	15	14	.517	129	4.22	275	87	86	308	11	20	0	0
1924	Bro-N	21	30	8	13	.381	73	3.91	168	63	45	190	4	13	2	3
1925	Was-A	29	30	18	7	.720	96	3.87	223 1/3	68	105	241	5	16	1	0
1926	Was-A	23	23	12	6	.667	91	4.84	169 1/3	48	66	214	5	9	0	0
1926	**NY-A**	**5**	**5**	**2**	**3**	**.400**	**14**	**3.50**	**36**	**8**	**18**	**32**	**0**	**1**	**0**	**0**
1927	**NY-A**	**26**	**27**	**13**	**6**	**.684**	**69**	**3.38**	**184**	**45**	**52**	**202**	**9**	**12**	**3**	**0**
Career Average		21	24	11	7	.591	64	3.50	163	54	57	173	4	12	1	1
Yankee Average		**16**	**16**	**8**	**5**	**.625**	**42**	**3.40**	**110**	**27**	**35**	**117**	**5**	**7**	**2**	**0**
Career Total		272	309	137	95	.591	826	3.50	2124 2/3	708	739	2244	55	155	18	8
Yankee Total		**31**	**32**	**15**	**9**	**.625**	**83**	**3.40**	**220**	**53**	**70**	**234**	**9**	**13**	**3**	**0**

Ruffing, Charles Herbert (Red)

HEIGHT: 6'1"   RIGHTHANDER   BORN: 5/3/1904 GRANVILLE, ILLINOIS   DIED: 2/17/1986 MAYFIELD HEIGHTS, OHIO

YEAR	TEAM	STARTS	GAMES	WON	LOST	PCT	ER	ERA	INNINGS PITCHED	STRIKE-OUTS	WALKS	HITS ALLOWED	HRS ALLOWED	COMP. GAMES	SHUT-OUTS	SAVES
1924	Bos-A	2	8	0	0	—	17	6.65	23	10	9	29	0	0	0	0
1925	Bos-A	27	37	9	18	.333	121	5.01	217 1/3	64	75	253	10	13	3	1
1926	Bos-A	22	37	6	15	.286	81	4.39	166	58	68	169	4	6	0	2
1927	Bos-A	18	26	5	13	.278	82	4.66	158 1/3	77	87	160	7	10	0	2
1928	Bos-A	34	42	10	25	.286	125	3.89	289 1/3	96	118	303	8	25	1	2
1929	Bos-A	30	35	9	22	.290	132	4.86	244 1/3	109	118	280	17	18	1	1
1930	Bos-A	3	4	0	3	.000	17	6.38	24	14	6	32	1	1	0	0

(continued)

Charles Herbert "Red" Ruffing, rhp, 1930–42, 1945–46

In 1930, Red Ruffing's career was changed forever by his trade from Boston to New York.

Born on May 3, 1904, in Granville, Illinois, Ruffing started his career with the Red Sox in 1925. The Red Sox were struggling by then, and Ruffing took his lumps with the team, going a less than impressive 39-92 with the team. That included a 10-25 record in 1928 and a 9-22 mark in 1929.

But Ruffing had also led the American League in complete games in 1928 with 25, and was always among the league leaders in strikeouts in the late 1920s.

In New York, Yankee manager Miller Huggins was trying to rebuild his pitching staff following the death of ace Urban Shocker and with veterans Waite Hoyt and Herb Pennock getting older. Thus, in 1930, the Red Sox, desperate for cash, sold Ruffing to New York for $50,000 and utility outfielder Cedric Durst.

Ruffing turned his career around in New York. He was 15-5 his first year and 16-14 in 1931. In eight of his first nine years with the Yankees, Ruffing struck out more than 100 batters. For four consecutive years, from 1936-39, Ruffing won 20 games or more, including a league-leading 21 games in 1938.

He was equally successful in the post season. His World Series record was 7-2, tying him for second place in wins behind Whitey Ford.

Ruffing, for much of the 1930s, was a power pitcher. At 6 foot 1 inch, 205 lbs., he was an imposing presence who was not afraid to come inside on a batter. He hit 49 in his 22 years.

In addition to being a heck of a pitcher, Ruffing was perhaps the Yankees' best-hitting pitcher of all time. His lifetime batting average of .269 ranks him tenth all-time among pitchers, and his 36 career home runs place him third all-time. He has 30 of those home runs with New York; the next highest total by a Yankee pitcher is Spud Chandler's ten. Ruffing hit over .300 eight times in his career.

In 1942, the six-time All-Star was inducted into the Army in World War II. When he got out of the service, he lasted only three more years in the major leagues, including a final year in 1947 with the White Sox.

After retirement, Ruffing managed in the minors, scouted and worked as a pitching coach for the Mets in 1962. In 1967, he was admitted to the Baseball Hall of Fame. Ruffing died in 1986 in Mayfield Heights, Ohio.

Ruffing is among the leaders in most Yankee pitching categories. He is second to Ford in career wins with New York with 231, third in strikeouts with 1,526, second in shutouts with 40, third in games played with 426 and the runaway leader in complete games on the team with 261. In second place is Lefty Gomez, with 173.

(continued)

YEAR	TEAM	STARTS	GAMES	WON	LOST	PCT	ER	ERA	INNINGS PITCHED	STRIKE-OUTS	WALKS	HITS ALLOWED	HRS ALLOWED	COMP. GAMES	SHUT-OUTS	SAVES
1930	NY-A	25	34	15	5	.750	91	4.14	197 2/3	117	62	200	10	12	2	1
1931	NY-A	30	37	16	14	.533	116	4.41	237	132	87	240	11	19	1	2
1932	NY-A	29	35	18	7	.720	89	3.09	259	190	115	219	16	22	3	2
1933	NY-A	28	35	9	14	.391	102	3.91	235	122	93	230	7	18	0	3
1934	NY-A	31	36	19	11	.633	112	3.93	256 1/3	149	104	232	18	19	5	0
1935	NY-A	29	30	16	11	.593	77	3.12	222	81	76	201	17	19	2	0
1936	NY-A	33	33	20	12	.625	116	3.85	271	102	90	274	22	25	3	0
1937	NY-A	31	31	20	7	.741	85	2.98	256 1/3	131	68	242	17	22	4	0
1938	NY-A	31	31	21	7	.750	91	3.31	247 1/3	127	82	246	16	22	3	0
1939	NY-A	28	28	21	7	.750	76	2.93	233 1/3	95	75	211	15	22	5	0
1940	NY-A	30	30	15	12	.556	85	3.38	226	97	76	218	24	20	3	0
1941	NY-A	23	23	15	6	.714	73	3.54	185 2/3	60	54	177	13	13	2	0
1942	NY-A	24	24	14	7	.667	69	3.21	193 2/3	80	41	183	10	16	4	0
1945	NY-A	11	11	7	3	.700	28	2.89	87 1/3	24	20	85	2	8	1	0
1946	NY-A	8	8	5	1	.833	12	1.77	61	19	23	37	2	4	2	0
1947	Chi-A	9	9	3	5	.375	36	6.11	53	11	16	63	7	1	0	0
Career Average		23	27	12	10	.548	80	3.80	189	86	67	186	11	15	2	1
Yankee Average		26	28	15	8	.651	81	3.47	211	102	71	200	13	17	3	1
Career Total		536	624	273	225	.548	1833	3.80	4344	1987	1541	4284	254	335	45	16
Yankee Total		391	426	231	124	.651	1222	3.47	3168 2/3	1526	1066	2995	200	261	40	8

Russell, Allan E.

HEIGHT: 5'11" RIGHTHANDER BORN: 7/31/1893 BALTIMORE, MARYLAND DIED: 10/20/1972 BALTIMORE, MARYLAND

YEAR	TEAM	STARTS	GAMES	WON	LOST	PCT	ER	ERA	INNINGS PITCHED	STRIKE-OUTS	WALKS	HITS ALLOWED	HRS ALLOWED	COMP. GAMES	SHUT-OUTS	SAVES
1915	NY-A	3	5	1	2	.333	8	2.67	27	21	21	21	1	1	0	0
1916	NY-A	18	34	6	10	.375	61	3.20	171 1/3	104	75	138	8	8	1	6
1917	NY-A	10	25	7	8	.467	26	2.24	104 1/3	55	39	89	3	6	0	2
1918	NY-A	18	27	7	11	.389	51	3.26	141	54	73	139	6	7	2	4
1919	NY-A	9	23	5	5	.500	35	3.47	90 2/3	50	32	89	6	4	1	1
1919	Bos-A	11	21	10	4	.714	34	2.52	121 1/3	63	39	105	0	9	1	4
1920	Bos-A	10	16	5	6	.455	36	3.01	107 1/3	53	38	100	3	7	0	1
1921	Bos-A	13	39	7	11	.389	79	4.11	173	60	77	204	10	7	0	3
1922	Bos-A	11	34	6	7	.462	70	5.01	125 2/3	34	57	152	6	1	0	2
1923	Was-A	5	52	10	7	.588	61	3.03	181 1/3	67	77	177	9	4	0	9
1924	Was-A	0	37	5	1	.833	40	4.37	82 1/3	17	45	83	1	0	0	8
1925	Was-A	2	32	2	4	.333	44	5.77	68 2/3	25	37	85	6	0	0	2
Career Average		9	29	6	6	.483	45	3.52	116	50	51	115	5	5	0	4
Yankee Average		12	23	5	7	.419	36	3.05	107	57	48	95	5	5	1	3
Career Total		110	345	71	76	.483	545	3.52	1394 1/3	603	610	1382	59	54	5	42
Yankee Total		58	114	26	36	.419	181	3.05	534 1/3	284	240	476	24	26	4	13

Russo, Marius Ugo (Lefty)

HEIGHT: 6'1" LEFTHANDER BORN: 7/19/1914 BROOKLYN, NEW YORK

YEAR	TEAM	STARTS	GAMES	WON	LOST	PCT	ER	ERA	INNINGS PITCHED	STRIKE-OUTS	WALKS	HITS ALLOWED	HRS ALLOWED	COMP. GAMES	SHUT-OUTS	SAVES
1939	NY-A	11	21	8	3	.727	31	2.41	116	55	41	86	6	9	2	2
1940	NY-A	24	30	14	8	.636	69	3.28	189 1/3	87	55	181	17	15	0	1
1941	NY-A	27	28	14	10	.583	72	3.09	209 2/3	105	87	195	8	17	3	1
1942	NY-A	5	9	4	1	.800	14	2.78	45 1/3	15	14	41	2	2	0	0
1943	NY-A	14	24	5	10	.333	42	3.72	101 2/3	42	45	89	7	5	1	1
1946	NY-A	3	8	0	2	.000	9	4.34	18 2/3	7	11	26	1	0	0	0
Career Average		14	20	8	6	.570	40	3.13	113	52	42	103	7	8	1	1
Yankee Average		14	20	8	6	.570	40	3.13	113	52	42	103	7	8	1	1
Career Total		84	120	45	34	.570	237	3.13	680 2/3	311	253	618	41	48	6	5
Yankee Total		84	120	45	34	.570	237	3.13	680 2/3	311	253	618	41	48	6	5

Ruth, George Herman (Babe *or* The Bambino *or* The Sultan of Swat)

HEIGHT: 6'2"   LEFTHANDER   BORN: 2/6/1895 BALTIMORE, MARYLAND   DIED: 8/16/1948 NEW YORK, NEW YORK

YEAR	TEAM	STARTS	GAMES	WON	LOST	PCT	ER	ERA	INNINGS PITCHED	STRIKE-OUTS	WALKS	HITS ALLOWED	HRS ALLOWED	COMP. GAMES	SHUT-OUTS	SAVES
1914	Bos-A	3	4	2	1	.667	10	3.91	23	3	7	21	1	1	0	0
1915	Bos-A	28	32	18	8	.692	59	2.44	217 2/3	112	85	166	3	16	1	0
1916	Bos-A	41	44	23	12	.657	63	1.75	323 2/3	170	118	230	0	23	9	1
1917	Bos-A	38	41	24	13	.649	73	2.01	326 1/3	128	108	244	2	35	6	2
1918	Bos-A	19	20	13	7	.650	41	2.22	166 1/3	40	49	125	1	18	1	0
1919	Bos-A	15	17	9	5	.643	44	2.97	133 1/3	30	58	148	2	12	0	1
1920	**NY-A**	**1**	**1**	**1**	**0**	**1.000**	**2**	**4.50**	**4**	**0**	**2**	**3**	**0**	**0**	**0**	**0**
1921	**NY-A**	**1**	**2**	**2**	**0**	**1.000**	**9**	**9.00**	**9**	**2**	**9**	**14**	**1**	**0**	**0**	**0**
1930	**NY-A**	**1**	**1**	**1**	**0**	**1.000**	**3**	**3.00**	**9**	**3**	**2**	**11**	**0**	**1**	**0**	**0**
1933	**NY-A**	**1**	**1**	**1**	**0**	**1.000**	**5**	**5.00**	**9**	**0**	**3**	**12**	**0**	**1**	**0**	**0**
Career Average		15	16	9	5	.671	31	2.28	122	49	44	97	1	11	2	0
Yankee Average		**1**	**1**	**1**	**0**	**1.000**	**5**	**5.52**	**8**	**1**	**4**	**10**	**0**	**1**	**0**	**0**
Career Total		148	163	94	46	.671	309	2.28	1221 1/3	488	441	974	10	107	17	4
Yankee Total		**4**	**5**	**5**	**0**	**1.000**	**19**	**5.52**	**31**	**5**	**16**	**40**	**1**	**2**	**0**	**0**

Ryan, Wilfred Patrick Dolan (Rosy)

HEIGHT: 6'0"   RIGHTHANDER   BORN: 3/15/1898 WORCESTER, MASSACHUSETTS   DIED: 12/10/1980 SCOTTSDALE, ARIZONA

YEAR	TEAM	STARTS	GAMES	WON	LOST	PCT	ER	ERA	INNINGS PITCHED	STRIKE-OUTS	WALKS	HITS ALLOWED	HRS ALLOWED	COMP. GAMES	SHUT-OUTS	SAVES
1919	NY-N	3	4	1	2	.333	7	3.10	20 1/3	7	9	20	0	1	0	0
1920	NY-N	1	3	0	1	.000	3	1.76	15 1/3	5	4	14	1	1	0	0
1921	NY-N	16	36	7	10	.412	61	3.73	147 1/3	58	32	140	6	5	0	3
1922	NY-N	20	46	17	12	.586	64	3.01	191 2/3	75	74	194	5	12	1	3
1923	NY-N	15	45	16	5	.762	67	3.49	172 2/3	58	46	169	8	7	0	4
1924	NY-N	9	37	8	6	.571	59	4.26	124 2/3	36	37	137	1	2	0	5
1925	Bos-N	7	37	2	8	.200	86	6.31	122 2/3	48	52	152	7	1	0	2
1926	Bos-N	2	7	0	2	.000	16	7.58	19	1	7	29	1	0	0	0
1928	**NY-A**	**0**	**3**	**0**	**0**	**—**	**11**	**16.50**	**6**	**5**	**1**	**17**	**1**	**0**	**0**	**0**
1933	Bro-N	0	30	1	1	.500	31	4.55	61 1/3	22	16	69	3	0	0	2
Career Average		7	25	5	5	.525	41	4.14	88	32	28	94	3	3	0	2
Yankee Average		**0**	**3**	**0**	**0**	**—**	**11**	**16.50**	**6**	**5**	**1**	**17**	**1**	**0**	**0**	**0**
Career Total		73	248	52	47	.525	405	4.14	881	315	278	941	33	29	1	19
Yankee Total		**0**	**3**	**0**	**0**	**—**	**11**	**16.50**	**6**	**5**	**1**	**17**	**1**	**0**	**0**	**0**

Sain, John Franklin

HEIGHT: 6'2"   RIGHTHANDER   BORN: 9/25/1917 HAVANA, ARKANSAS

YEAR	TEAM	STARTS	GAMES	WON	LOST	PCT	ER	ERA	INNINGS PITCHED	STRIKE-OUTS	WALKS	HITS ALLOWED	HRS ALLOWED	COMP. GAMES	SHUT-OUTS	SAVES
1942	Bos-N	3	40	4	7	.364	42	3.90	97	68	63	79	8	0	0	6
1946	Bos-N	34	37	20	14	.588	65	2.21	265	129	87	225	8	24	3	2
1947	Bos-N	35	38	21	12	.636	104	3.52	266	132	79	265	19	22	3	1
1948	Bos-N	39	42	24	15	.615	91	2.60	314 2/3	137	83	297	19	28	4	1
1949	Bos-N	36	37	10	17	.370	130	4.81	243	73	75	285	15	16	1	0
1950	Bos-N	37	37	20	13	.606	122	3.94	278 1/3	96	70	294	34	25	3	0
1951	Bos-N	22	26	5	13	.278	75	4.21	160 1/3	63	45	195	16	6	1	0
1951	**NY-A**	**4**	**7**	**2**	**1**	**.667**	**17**	**4.14**	**37**	**21**	**8**	**41**	**5**	**1**	**0**	**1**
1952	**NY-A**	**16**	**35**	**11**	**6**	**.647**	**57**	**3.46**	**148 1/3**	**57**	**38**	**149**	**15**	**8**	**0**	**7**
1953	**NY-A**	**19**	**40**	**14**	**7**	**.667**	**63**	**3.00**	**189**	**84**	**45**	**189**	**16**	**10**	**1**	**9**
1954	**NY-A**	**0**	**45**	**6**	**6**	**.500**	**27**	**3.16**	**77**	**33**	**15**	**66**	**11**	**0**	**0**	**22**
1955	**NY-A**	**0**	**3**	**0**	**0**	**—**	**4**	**6.75**	**5 1/3**	**5**	**1**	**6**	**4**	**0**	**0**	**0**
1955	KC-A	0	25	2	5	.286	27	5.44	44 2/3	12	10	54	10	0	0	1
Career Average		19	32	11	9	.545	63	3.49	163	70	48	165	14	11	1	4
Yankee Average		**8**	**26**	**7**	**4**	**.623**	**34**	**3.31**	**91**	**40**	**21**	**90**	**10**	**4**	**0**	**8**
Career Total		245	412	139	116	.545	824	3.49	2125 2/3	910	619	2145	180	140	16	51
Yankee Total		**39**	**130**	**33**	**20**	**.623**	**168**	**3.31**	**456 2/3**	**200**	**107**	**451**	**51**	**19**	**1**	**39**

Sanders, Roy Lee (Simon)

HEIGHT: 6'0"   RIGHTHANDER   BORN: 6/10/1894, MISSOURI   DIED: 7/8/1963 LOUISVILLE, KENTUCKY

YEAR	TEAM	STARTS	GAMES	WON	LOST	PCT	ER	ERA	INNINGS PITCHED	STRIKE-OUTS	WALKS	HITS ALLOWED	HRS ALLOWED	COMP. GAMES	SHUT-OUTS	SAVES
1918	**NY-A**	**2**	**6**	**0**	**2**	**.000**	**12**	**4.21**	**25 2/3**	**8**	**16**	**28**	**0**	**0**	**0**	**0**
1920	StL-A	1	8	1	1	.500	10	5.19	17 1/3	2	17	20	1	0	0	0
Career Average		2	7	1	2	.250	11	4.60	21	5	17	24	1	0	0	0
Yankee Average		**2**	**6**	**0**	**2**	**.000**	**12**	**4.21**	**25 2/3**	**8**	**16**	**28**	**0**	**0**	**0**	**0**
Career Total		3	14	1	3	.250	22	4.60	43	10	33	48	1	0	0	0
Yankee Total		**2**	**6**	**0**	**2**	**.000**	**12**	**4.21**	**25 2/3**	**8**	**16**	**28**	**0**	**0**	**0**	**0**

Sanderson, Scott Douglas

HEIGHT: 6'5"   RIGHTHANDER   BORN: 7/22/1956 DEARBORN, MICHIGAN

YEAR	TEAM	STARTS	GAMES	WON	LOST	PCT	ER	ERA	INNINGS PITCHED	STRIKE-OUTS	WALKS	HITS ALLOWED	HRS ALLOWED	COMP. GAMES	SHUT-OUTS	SAVES
1978	Mon-N	9	10	4	2	.667	17	2.51	61	50	21	52	3	1	1	0
1979	Mon-N	24	34	9	8	.529	64	3.43	168	138	54	148	16	5	3	1
1980	Mon-N	33	33	16	11	.593	73	3.11	211 1/3	125	56	206	18	7	3	0
1981	Mon-N	22	22	9	7	.563	45	2.95	137 1/3	77	31	122	10	4	1	0
1982	Mon-N	32	32	12	12	.500	86	3.46	224	158	58	212	24	7	0	0
1983	Mon-N	16	18	6	7	.462	42	4.65	81 1/3	55	20	98	12	0	0	1
1984	Chi-N	24	24	8	5	.615	49	3.14	140 2/3	76	24	140	5	3	0	0
1985	Chi-N	19	19	5	6	.455	42	3.12	121	80	27	100	13	2	0	0
1986	Chi-N	28	37	9	11	.450	79	4.19	169 2/3	124	37	165	21	1	1	1
1987	Chi-N	22	32	8	9	.471	69	4.29	144 2/3	106	50	156	23	0	0	2
1988	Chi-N	0	11	1	2	.333	9	5.28	15 1/3	6	3	13	1	0	0	0
1989	Chi-N	23	37	11	9	.550	64	3.94	146 1/3	86	31	155	16	2	0	0
1990	Oak-A	34	34	17	11	.607	89	3.88	206 1/3	128	66	205	27	2	1	0
1991	**NY-A**	**34**	**34**	**16**	**10**	**.615**	**88**	**3.81**	**208**	**130**	**29**	**200**	**22**	**2**	**2**	**0**
1992	**NY-A**	**33**	**33**	**12**	**11**	**.522**	**106**	**4.93**	**193 1/3**	**104**	**64**	**220**	**28**	**2**	**1**	**0**
1993	Cal-A	21	21	7	11	.389	67	4.46	135 1/3	66	27	153	15	4	1	0
1993	SF-N	8	11	4	2	.667	19	3.51	48 2/3	36	7	48	12	0	0	0
1994	Chi-A	14	18	8	4	.667	52	5.09	92	36	12	110	20	1	0	0
1995	Cal-A	7	7	1	3	.250	18	4.15	39	23	4	48	6	0	0	0
1996	Cal-A	4	5	0	2	.000	15	7.50	18	7	4	39	5	0	0	0
Career Average		20	24	8	7	.533	55	3.84	128	81	31	130	15	2	1	0
Yankee Average		**34**	**34**	**14**	**11**	**.571**	**97**	**4.35**	**201**	**117**	**47**	**210**	**25**	**2**	**2**	**0**
Career Total		407	472	163	143	.533	1093	3.84	2561 1/3	1611	625	2590	297	43	14	5
Yankee Total		**67**	**67**	**28**	**21**	**.571**	**194**	**4.35**	**401 1/3**	**234**	**93**	**420**	**50**	**4**	**3**	**0**

Sanford, John Frederick (Fred)

HEIGHT: 6'1"   RIGHTHANDER   BORN: 8/9/1919 GARFIELD, UTAH

YEAR	TEAM	STARTS	GAMES	WON	LOST	PCT	ER	ERA	INNINGS PITCHED	STRIKE-OUTS	WALKS	HITS ALLOWED	HRS ALLOWED	COMP. GAMES	SHUT-OUTS	SAVES
1943	StL-A	0	3	0	0	—	2	1.93	9 1/3	2	4	7	0	0	0	0
1946	StL-A	3	3	2	1	.667	5	2.05	22	8	9	19	0	2	2	0
1947	StL-A	23	34	7	16	.304	77	3.71	186 2/3	62	76	186	17	9	0	4
1948	StL-A	33	42	12	21	.364	117	4.64	227	79	91	250	19	9	1	2
1949	**NY-A**	**11**	**29**	**7**	**3**	**.700**	**41**	**3.87**	**95 1/3**	**51**	**57**	**100**	**9**	**3**	**0**	**0**
1950	**NY-A**	**12**	**26**	**5**	**4**	**.556**	**57**	**4.55**	**112 2/3**	**54**	**79**	**103**	**9**	**2**	**0**	**0**
1951	**NY-A**	**2**	**11**	**0**	**3**	**.000**	**11**	**3.71**	**26 2/3**	**10**	**25**	**15**	**2**	**0**	**0**	**0**
1951	Was-A	7	7	2	3	.400	27	6.57	37	12	27	51	5	0	0	0
1951	StL-A	7	9	2	4	.333	31	10.21	27 1/3	7	23	37	6	1	0	0
Career Average		11	18	4	6	.402	41	4.45	83	32	43	85	7	3	0	1
Yankee Average		**8**	**22**	**4**	**3**	**.545**	**36**	**4.18**	**78**	**38**	**54**	**73**	**7**	**2**	**0**	**0**
Career Total		98	164	37	55	.402	368	4.45	744	285	391	768	67	26	3	6
Yankee Total		**25**	**66**	**12**	**10**	**.545**	**109**	**4.18**	**234 2/3**	**115**	**161**	**218**	**20**	**5**	**0**	**0**

Sawyer, Richard Clyde

HEIGHT: 6'2"   RIGHTHANDER   BORN: 4/7/1948 BAKERSFIELD, CALIFORNIA

YEAR	TEAM	STARTS	GAMES	WON	LOST	PCT	ER	ERA	INNINGS PITCHED	STRIKE-OUTS	WALKS	HITS ALLOWED	HRS ALLOWED	COMP. GAMES	SHUT-OUTS	SAVES
1974	**NY-A**	**0**	**1**	**0**	**0**	**—**	**3**	**16.21**	**1 2/3**	**1**	**1**	**2**	**0**	**0**	**0**	**0**
1975	**NY-A**	**0**	**4**	**0**	**0**	**—**	**2**	**3.00**	**6**	**3**	**2**	**7**	**0**	**0**	**0**	**0**
1976	SD-N	11	13	5	3	.625	23	2.53	81 2/3	33	38	84	2	4	2	0
1977	SD-N	9	56	7	6	.538	72	5.84	111	45	55	136	15	0	0	0
Career Average		5	19	3	2	.571	25	4.49	50	21	24	57	4	1	1	0
Yankee Average		**0**	**3**	**0**	**0**	**—**	**3**	**5.87**	**4**	**2**	**2**	**5**	**0**	**0**	**0**	**0**
Career Total		20	74	12	9	.571	100	4.49	200 1/3	82	96	229	17	4	2	0
Yankee Total		**0**	**5**	**0**	**0**	**—**	**5**	**5.87**	**7 2/3**	**4**	**3**	**9**	**0**	**0**	**0**	**0**

Scarborough, Rae Wilson (Ray)

HEIGHT: 6'0"   RIGHTHANDER   BORN: 7/23/1917 MOUNT GILEAD, NORTH CAROLINA   DIED: 7/1/1982 MOUNT OLIVE, NORTH CAROLINA

YEAR	TEAM	STARTS	GAMES	WON	LOST	PCT	ER	ERA	INNINGS PITCHED	STRIKE-OUTS	WALKS	HITS ALLOWED	HRS ALLOWED	COMP. GAMES	SHUT-OUTS	SAVES
1942	Was-A	5	17	2	1	.667	29	4.12	63 1/3	16	32	68	2	1	1	0
1943	Was-A	6	24	4	4	.500	27	2.83	86	43	46	93	2	2	0	3
1946	Was-A	20	32	7	11	.389	70	4.05	155 2/3	46	74	176	8	6	1	1
1947	Was-A	18	33	6	13	.316	61	3.41	161	63	67	165	5	8	2	0
1948	Was-A	26	31	15	8	.652	58	2.82	185 1/3	76	72	166	10	9	0	1
1949	Was-A	27	34	13	11	.542	102	4.60	199 2/3	81	88	204	10	11	1	0
1950	Was-A	8	8	3	5	.375	26	4.01	58 1/3	24	22	62	1	4	2	0
1950	Chi-A	23	27	10	13	.435	88	5.30	149 1/3	70	62	160	10	8	1	1
1951	Bos-A	22	37	12	9	.571	104	5.09	184	71	61	201	21	8	1	0
1952	Bos-A	8	28	1	5	.167	41	4.81	76 2/3	29	35	79	8	1	1	4
1952	**NY-A**	**4**	**9**	**5**	**1**	**.833**	**11**	**2.91**	**34**	**13**	**15**	**27**	**4**	**1**	**0**	**0**
1953	**NY-A**	**1**	**25**	**2**	**2**	**.500**	**20**	**3.29**	**54 2/3**	**20**	**26**	**52**	**4**	**0**	**0**	**0**
1953	Det-A	0	13	0	2	.000	19	8.27	20 2/3	12	11	34	3	0	0	2
Career Average		13	24	6	7	.485	50	4.13	110	43	47	114	7	5	1	1
Yankee Average		**3**	**17**	**4**	**2**	**.700**	**16**	**3.15**	**44**	**17**	**21**	**40**	**4**	**1**	**0**	**0**
Career Total		168	318	80	85	.485	656	4.13	1428 2/3	564	611	1487	88	59	9	12
Yankee Total		**5**	**34**	**7**	**3**	**.700**	**31**	**3.15**	**88 2/3**	**33**	**41**	**79**	**8**	**1**	**0**	**0**

Schallock, Arthur Lawrence

HEIGHT: 5'9"   LEFTHANDER   BORN: 4/25/1924 MILL VALLEY, CALIFORNIA

YEAR	TEAM	STARTS	GAMES	WON	LOST	PCT	ER	ERA	INNINGS PITCHED	STRIKE-OUTS	WALKS	HITS ALLOWED	HRS ALLOWED	COMP. GAMES	SHUT-OUTS	SAVES
1951	**NY-A**	**6**	**11**	**3**	**1**	**.750**	**20**	**3.88**	**46 1/3**	**19**	**20**	**50**	**3**	**1**	**0**	**0**
1952	**NY-A**	**0**	**2**	**0**	**0**	**—**	**2**	**9.00**	**2**	**1**	**2**	**3**	**0**	**0**	**0**	**0**
1953	**NY-A**	**1**	**7**	**0**	**0**	**—**	**7**	**2.95**	**21 1/3**	**13**	**15**	**30**	**2**	**0**	**0**	**1**
1954	**NY-A**	**1**	**6**	**0**	**1**	**.000**	**8**	**4.15**	**17 1/3**	**9**	**11**	**20**	**3**	**1**	**0**	**0**
1955	**NY-A**	**0**	**2**	**0**	**0**	**—**	**2**	**6.00**	**3**	**2**	**1**	**4**	**1**	**0**	**0**	**0**
1955	Bal-A	6	30	3	5	.375	37	4.15	80 1/3	33	42	92	2	1	0	0
Career Average		2	10	1	1	.462	13	4.02	28	13	15	33	2	1	0	0
Yankee Average		**2**	**6**	**1**	**0**	**.600**	**8**	**3.90**	**18**	**9**	**10**	**21**	**2**	**0**	**0**	**0**
Career Total		14	58	6	7	.462	76	4.02	170 1/3	77	91	199	11	3	0	1
Yankee Total		**8**	**28**	**3**	**2**	**.600**	**39**	**3.90**	**90**	**44**	**49**	**107**	**9**	**2**	**0**	**1**

Schmidt, Charles John Butch (Butcher Boy)

HEIGHT: 6'1"   LEFTHANDER   BORN: 7/19/1886 BALTIMORE, MARYLAND   DIED: 9/4/1952 BALTIMORE, MARYLAND

YEAR	TEAM	STARTS	GAMES	WON	LOST	PCT	ER	ERA	INNINGS PITCHED	STRIKE-OUTS	WALKS	HITS ALLOWED	HRS ALLOWED	COMP. GAMES	SHUT-OUTS	SAVES
1909	**NY-A**	**0**	**1**	**0**	**0**	**—**	**4**	**7.20**	**5**	**2**	**1**	**10**	**0**	**0**	**0**	**0**
Career Average		0	1	0	0	—	4	7.20	5	2	1	10	0	0	0	0
Yankee Average		**0**	**1**	**0**	**0**	**—**	**4**	**7.20**	**5**	**2**	**1**	**10**	**0**	**0**	**0**	**0**
Career Total		0	1	0	0	—	4	7.20	5	2	1	10	0	0	0	0
Yankee Total		**0**	**1**	**0**	**0**	**—**	**4**	**7.20**	**5**	**2**	**1**	**10**	**0**	**0**	**0**	**0**

Schmitz, John Albert (Bear Tracks)

HEIGHT: 6'0"   LEFTHANDER   BORN: 11/27/1920 WAUSAU, WISCONSIN

YEAR	TEAM	STARTS	GAMES	WON	LOST	PCT	ER	ERA	INNINGS PITCHED	STRIKE-OUTS	WALKS	HITS ALLOWED	HRS ALLOWED	COMP. GAMES	SHUT-OUTS	SAVES
1941	Chi-N	3	5	2	0	1.000	3	1.31	20 2/3	11	9	12	0	1	0	0
1942	Chi-N	10	23	3	7	.300	33	3.43	86 2/3	51	45	70	3	1	0	2
1946	Chi-N	31	41	11	11	.500	65	2.61	224 1/3	135	94	184	6	14	2	2
1947	Chi-N	28	38	13	18	.419	74	3.22	207	97	80	209	8	10	3	4
1948	Chi-N	30	34	18	13	.581	71	2.64	242	100	97	186	11	18	2	1
1949	Chi-N	31	36	11	13	.458	100	4.35	207	75	92	227	11	9	3	3
1950	Chi-N	27	39	10	16	.385	107	4.99	193	75	91	217	23	8	3	0
1951	Chi-N	3	8	1	2	.333	16	8.00	18	6	15	22	1	0	0	0
1951	Bro-N	7	16	1	4	.200	33	5.34	55 2/3	20	28	55	4	0	0	0
1952	Bro-N	3	10	1	1	.500	16	4.32	33 1/3	11	18	29	3	1	0	0
1952	**NY-A**	2	5	1	1	.500	6	3.60	15	3	9	15	0	1	0	1
1952	Cin-N	0	3	1	0	1.000	0	0.00	5	3	3	3	0	0	0	0
1953	**NY-A**	0	3	0	0	—	1	2.08	4 1/3	0	3	2	1	0	0	2
1953	Was-A	13	24	2	7	.222	44	3.68	107 2/3	39	37	118	9	5	0	4
1954	Was-A	23	29	11	8	.579	60	2.91	185 1/3	56	64	176	6	12	2	1
1955	Was-A	21	32	7	10	.412	68	3.71	165	49	54	187	8	6	1	1
1956	Bos-A	0	2	0	0	—	0	0.00	4 1/3	0	4	5	0	0	0	0
1956	Bal-A	3	18	0	3	.000	17	3.99	38 1/3	15	14	49	3	0	0	0
Career Average		13	20	5	6	.449	40	3.55	101	41	42	98	5	5	1	1
Yankee Average		**1**	**4**	**1**	**1**	**.500**	**4**	**3.26**	**10**	**2**	**6**	**9**	**1**	**1**	**0**	**2**
Career Total		235	366	93	114	.449	714	3.55	1812 2/3	746	757	1766	97	86	16	21
Yankee Total		**2**	**8**	**1**	**1**	**.500**	**7**	**3.26**	**19 1/3**	**3**	**12**	**17**	**1**	**1**	**0**	**3**

Schneider, Peter Joseph

HEIGHT: 6'1"   RIGHTHANDER   BORN: 8/20/1895 LOS ANGELES, CALIFORNIA   DIED: 6/1/1957 LOS ANGELES, CALIFORNIA

YEAR	TEAM	STARTS	GAMES	WON	LOST	PCT	ER	ERA	INNINGS PITCHED	STRIKE-OUTS	WALKS	HITS ALLOWED	HRS ALLOWED	COMP. GAMES	SHUT-OUTS	SAVES
1914	Cin-N	20	29	5	13	.278	45	2.81	144 1/3	62	56	143	1	11	1	1
1915	Cin-N	35	48	14	19	.424	76	2.48	275 2/3	108	104	254	4	16	5	2
1916	Cin-N	31	44	10	19	.345	82	2.69	274 1/3	117	82	259	4	16	2	1
1917	Cin-N	42	46	20	19	.513	78	2.10	333 2/3	138	117	311	4	24	0	0
1918	Cin-N	30	33	10	15	.400	85	3.53	217	51	117	213	2	17	2	0
1919	**NY-A**	4	7	0	1	.000	11	3.41	29	11	22	19	1	0	0	0
Career Average		27	35	10	14	.407	63	2.66	212	81	83	200	3	14	2	1.
Yankee Average		**4**	**7**	**0**	**1**	**.000**	**11**	**3.41**	**29**	**11**	**22**	**19**	**1**	**0**	**0**	**0**
Career Total		162	207	59	86	.407	377	2.66	1274	487	498	1199	16	84	10	4
Yankee Total		**4**	**7**	**0**	**1**	**.000**	**11**	**3.41**	**29**	**11**	**22**	**19**	**1**	**0**	**0**	**0**

Schreiber, Paul Frederick (Von)

HEIGHT: 6'2"   RIGHTHANDER   BORN: 10/8/1902 JACKSONVILLE, FLORIDA   DIED: 1/28/1982 SARASOTA, FLORIDA

YEAR	TEAM	STARTS	GAMES	WON	LOST	PCT	ER	ERA	INNINGS PITCHED	STRIKE-OUTS	WALKS	HITS ALLOWED	HRS ALLOWED	COMP. GAMES	SHUT-OUTS	SAVES
1922	Bro-N	0	1	0	0	—	0	0.00	1	0	0	2	0	0	0	0
1923	Bro-N	0	9	0	0	—	7	4.20	15	4	8	16	1	0	0	1
1945	**NY-A**	0	2	0	0	—	2	4.15	4 1/3	1	2	4	0	0	0	0
Career Average		0	4	0	0	—	3	3.98	7	2	3	7	0	0	0	0
Yankee Average		**0**	**2**	**0**	**0**	**—**	**2**	**4.15**	**4 1/3**	**1**	**2**	**4**	**0**	**0**	**0**	**0**
Career Total		0	12	0	0	—	9	3.98	20 1/3	5	10	22	1	0	0	1
Yankee Total		**0**	**2**	**0**	**0**	**—**	**2**	**4.15**	**4 1/3**	**1**	**2**	**4**	**0**	**0**	**0**	**0**

Schulz, Albert Christopher (Lefty)

HEIGHT: 6'0"   LEFTHANDER   BORN: 5/12/1889 TOLEDO, OHIO   DIED: 12/13/1931 GALLIPOLIS, OHIO

YEAR	TEAM	STARTS	GAMES	WON	LOST	PCT	ER	ERA	INNINGS PITCHED	STRIKE-OUTS	WALKS	HITS ALLOWED	HRS ALLOWED	COMP. GAMES	SHUT-OUTS	SAVES
1912	NY-A	1	3	1	1	.500	4	2.20	16 1/3	8	11	11	0	1	0	0
1913	NY-A	22	38	7	13	.350	80	3.73	193	77	69	197	4	9	0	0
1914	NY-A	4	6	1	3	.250	15	4.76	28 1/3	18	10	27	0	1	0	0

(continued)

(continued)

YEAR	TEAM	STARTS	GAMES	WON	LOST	PCT	ER	ERA	INNINGS PITCHED	STRIKE-OUTS	WALKS	HITS ALLOWED	HRS ALLOWED	COMP. GAMES	SHUT-OUTS	SAVES
1914	Buf-F	23	27	9	12	.429	64	3.37	171	87	77	160	3	10	0	2
1915	Buf-F	38	42	21	14	.600	106	3.08	309 2/3	160	149	264	8	25	5	0
1916	Cin-N	22	44	8	19	.296	75	3.14	215	95	93	208	4	10	0	2
Career Average		18	27	8	10	.431	57	3.32	156	74	68	145	3	9	1	1
Yankee Average		**9**	**16**	**3**	**6**	**.346**	**33**	**3.75**	**79**	**34**	**30**	**78**	**1**	**4**	**0**	**0**
Career Total		110	160	47	62	.431	344	3.32	933 1/3	445	409	867	19	56	5	4
Yankee Total		**27**	**47**	**9**	**17**	**.346**	**99**	**3.75**	**237 2/3**	**103**	**90**	**235**	**4**	**11**	**0**	**0**

Schulze, Donald Arthur

HEIGHT: 6'3"   RIGHTHANDER   BORN: 9/27/1962 ROSELLE, ILLINOIS

YEAR	TEAM	STARTS	GAMES	WON	LOST	PCT	ER	ERA	INNINGS PITCHED	STRIKE-OUTS	WALKS	HITS ALLOWED	HRS ALLOWED	COMP. GAMES	SHUT-OUTS	SAVES
1983	Chi-N	3	4	0	1	.000	11	7.07	14	8	7	19	1	0	0	0
1984	Chi-N	1	1	0	0	—	4	12.00	3	2	1	8	0	0	0	0
1984	Cle-A	14	19	3	6	.333	46	4.83	85 2/3	39	27	105	9	2	0	0
1985	Cle-A	18	19	4	10	.286	63	6.01	94 1/3	37	19	128	10	1	0	0
1986	Cle-A	13	19	4	4	.500	47	5.00	84 2/3	33	34	88	9	1	0	0
1987	NY-N	4	5	1	2	.333	15	6.23	21 2/3	5	6	24	4	0	0	0
1989	**NY-A**	**2**	**2**	**1**	**1**	**.500**	**5**	**4.09**	**11**	**5**	**5**	**12**	**1**	**0**	**0**	**0**
1989	SD-N	4	7	2	1	.667	15	5.55	24 1/3	15	6	38	6	0	0	0
Career Average		7	10	2	3	.375	26	5.47	42	18	13	53	5	1	0	0
Yankee Average		**2**	**2**	**1**	**1**	**.500**	**5**	**4.09**	**11**	**5**	**5**	**12**	**1**	**0**	**0**	**0**
Career Total		59	76	15	25	.375	206	5.47	338 2/3	144	105	422	40	4	0	0
Yankee Total		**2**	**2**	**1**	**1**	**.500**	**5**	**4.09**	**11**	**5**	**5**	**12**	**1**	**0**	**0**	**0**

Scurry, Rodney Grant

HEIGHT: 6'2"   LEFTHANDER   BORN: 3/17/1956 SACRAMENTO, CALIFORNIA   DIED: 11/5/1992 RENO, NEVADA

YEAR	TEAM	STARTS	GAMES	WON	LOST	PCT	ER	ERA	INNINGS PITCHED	STRIKE-OUTS	WALKS	HITS ALLOWED	HRS ALLOWED	COMP. GAMES	SHUT-OUTS	SAVES
1980	Pit-N	0	20	0	2	.000	9	2.15	37 2/3	28	17	23	2	0	0	0
1981	Pit-N	7	27	4	5	.444	31	3.77	74	65	40	74	6	0	0	7
1982	Pit-N	0	76	4	5	.444	20	1.74	103 2/3	94	64	79	3	0	0	14
1983	Pit-N	0	61	4	9	.308	42	5.56	68	67	53	63	6	0	0	7
1984	Pit-N	0	43	5	6	.455	13	2.53	46 1/3	48	22	28	1	0	0	4
1985	Pit-N	0	30	0	1	.000	17	3.21	47 2/3	43	28	42	4	0	0	2
1985	**NY-A**	**0**	**5**	**1**	**0**	**1.000**	**4**	**2.84**	**12 2/3**	**17**	**10**	**5**	**2**	**0**	**0**	**1**
1986	**NY-A**	**0**	**31**	**1**	**2**	**.333**	**16**	**3.66**	**39 1/3**	**36**	**22**	**38**	**1**	**0**	**0**	**2**
1988	Sea-A	0	39	0	2	.000	14	4.02	31 1/3	33	18	32	6	0	0	2
Career Average		1	37	2	4	.373	18	3.24	51	48	30	43	3	0	0	4
Yankee Average		**0**	**18**	**1**	**1**	**.500**	**10**	**3.46**	**26**	**27**	**16**	**22**	**2**	**0**	**0**	**2**
Career Total		7	332	19	32	.373	166	3.24	460 2/3	431	274	384	31	0	0	39
Yankee Total		**0**	**36**	**2**	**2**	**.500**	**20**	**3.46**	**52**	**53**	**32**	**43**	**3**	**0**	**0**	**3**

Shantz, Robert Clayton (Bobby)

HEIGHT: 5'6"   LEFTHANDER   BORN: 9/26/1925 POTTSTOWN, PENNSYLVANIA

YEAR	TEAM	STARTS	GAMES	WON	LOST	PCT	ER	ERA	INNINGS PITCHED	STRIKE-OUTS	WALKS	HITS ALLOWED	HRS ALLOWED	COMP. GAMES	SHUT-OUTS	SAVES
1949	Phi-A	7	33	6	8	.429	48	3.40	127	58	74	100	9	4	1	2
1950	Phi-A	23	36	8	14	.364	110	4.61	214 2/3	93	85	251	18	6	1	0
1951	Phi-A	25	32	18	10	.643	90	3.94	205 1/3	77	70	213	15	13	3	0
1952	Phi-A	33	33	24	7	.774	77	2.48	279 2/3	152	63	230	21	27	5	0
1953	Phi-A	16	16	5	9	.357	48	4.09	105 2/3	58	26	107	10	6	0	0
1954	Phi-A	1	2	1	0	1.000	7	7.88	8	3	3	12	2	0	0	0
1955	KC-A	17	23	5	10	.333	63	4.54	125	58	66	124	8	4	1	0
1956	KC-A	2	45	2	7	.222	49	4.35	101 1/3	67	37	95	12	1	0	9
1957	**NY-A**	**21**	**30**	**11**	**5**	**.688**	**47**	**2.45**	**173**	**72**	**40**	**157**	**15**	**9**	**1**	**5**
1958	**NY-A**	**13**	**33**	**7**	**6**	**.538**	**47**	**3.36**	**126**	**80**	**35**	**127**	**8**	**3**	**0**	**0**
1959	**NY-A**	**4**	**33**	**7**	**3**	**.700**	**25**	**2.38**	**94 2/3**	**66**	**33**	**64**	**4**	**2**	**2**	**3**
1960	**NY-A**	**0**	**42**	**5**	**4**	**.556**	**21**	**2.79**	**67 2/3**	**54**	**24**	**57**	**5**	**0**	**0**	**11**
1961	Pit-N	6	43	6	3	.667	33	3.32	89 1/3	61	26	91	5	2	1	2

(continued)

(continued)

YEAR	TEAM	STARTS	GAMES	WON	LOST	PCT	ER	ERA	INNINGS PITCHED	STRIKEOUTS	WALKS	HITS ALLOWED	HRS ALLOWED	COMP. GAMES	SHUT-OUTS	SAVES
1962	Hou-N	3	3	1	1	.500	3	1.31	20⅔	14	5	15	1	1	0	0
1962	StL-N	0	28	5	3	.625	14	2.18	57⅔	47	20	45	7	0	0	4
1963	StL-N	0	55	6	4	.600	23	2.61	79⅓	70	17	55	6	0	0	11
1964	StL-N	0	16	1	3	.250	6	3.12	17⅓	12	7	14	2	0	0	0
1964	Chi-N	0	20	0	1	.000	7	5.56	11⅓	12	6	15	2	0	0	1
1964	Phi-N	0	14	1	1	.500	8	2.25	32	18	6	23	1	0	0	0
Career Average		9	28	6	5	.546	38	3.38	102	56	34	94	8	4	1	3
Yankee Average		**10**	**35**	**8**	**5**	**.625**	**35**	**2.73**	**115**	**68**	**33**	**101**	**8**	**4**	**1**	**5**
Career Total		171	537	119	99	.546	726	3.38	1935⅔	1072	643	1795	151	78	15	48
Yankee Total		**38**	**138**	**30**	**18**	**.625**	**140**	**2.73**	**461⅓**	**272**	**132**	**405**	**32**	**14**	**3**	**19**

Shawkey, James Robert (Sailor Bob)

HEIGHT: 5'11" RIGHTHANDER BORN: 12/4/1890 SIGEL, PENNSYLVANIA 12/31/80 SYRACUSE, NEW YORK

YEAR	TEAM	STARTS	GAMES	WON	LOST	PCT	ER	ERA	INNINGS PITCHED	STRIKE-OUTS	WALKS	HITS ALLOWED	HRS ALLOWED	COMP. GAMES	SHUT-OUTS	SAVES
1913	Phi-A	15	18	6	5	.545	29	2.34	111⅓	52	50	92	2	8	1	0
1914	Phi-A	31	38	16	8	.667	72	2.73	237	89	75	223	4	18	5	2
1915	Phi-A	13	17	6	6	.500	45	4.05	100	56	38	103	3	7	1	0

(continued)

James Robert "Sailor Bob" Shawkey, rhp, 1915–27

Bob Shawkey was, for the majority of his career, the ace of the Yankee staff in the late 1910s and early '20s.

Born December 4, 1890, in Brookville, Pennsylvania, Shawkey spent 2½ years with the Philadelphia Athletics before coming to the Yankees in 1915. He was 4-7 that year, but in 1916, he exploded, winning 24 games, second only to Washington ace Walter Johnson. He also saved eight games for New York, tops in the league that year.

In 1918, he served in the U.S. Navy during World War I, giving rise to his nautical nickname. He won 20 games upon his return in 1919 and 20 more in 1920. By now, the Yankees had been building a pennant-winner for a few years, and populated their pitching staff with All-Stars Waite Hoyt, Bullet Joe Bush, Sad Sam Jones and Carl Mays.

Shawkey was not necessarily the best pitcher on the staff anymore, but he was still a consistent winner. From 1919 to 1924, he came out on top in 104 decisions, winning 20 games in a year three times in that span.

He was a deliberate pitcher, and a believer in knowing the habits of the hitters he faced. This was before ballplayers were videotaped, of course, so Shawkey spent most of his time at the near end of the Yankee dugout, intently watching the opposing batters and keeping a notebook on their tendencies.

He was superstitious, too. He would always take the mound wearing his lucky red sweater. It seems to have worked. His 168 wins are fifth on the Yankees' all-time list.

He retired from the Yankees in 1928. In 1930, the year after the death of Miller Huggins, Shawkey managed the team for a year, finishing third.

Shawkey became a baseball executive after retirement for several other organizations. In 1950, he became the coach at Dartmouth College. He died on New Year's Eve, 1981, in Syracuse. In addition to being 5th in wins, Shawkey is also 5th in innings with 2,489, 6th in strikeouts with 1,163, 8th in shutouts with 26 and 12th in career ERA with a mark of 3.10.

(continued)

YEAR	TEAM														
1915	NY-A	9	16	4	7	.364	31	3.26	85 2/3	31	35	78	2	5	1	0
1916	NY-A	27	53	24	14	.632	68	2.21	276 2/3	122	81	204	4	21	4	8
1917	NY-A	26	32	13	15	.464	64	2.44	236 1/3	97	72	207	2	16	2	0
1918	NY-A	2	3	1	1	.500	2	1.13	16	3	10	7	0	1	1	0
1919	NY-A	27	41	20	11	.645	79	2.72	261 1/3	122	92	218	7	22	3	5
1920	NY-A	31	38	20	13	.606	73	2.45	267 2/3	126	85	246	10	20	5	2
1921	NY-A	31	38	18	12	.600	111	4.08	245	126	86	245	15	18	3	2
1922	NY-A	34	39	20	12	.625	97	2.91	299 2/3	130	98	286	16	22	3	1
1923	NY-A	31	36	16	11	.593	101	3.51	258 2/3	125	102	232	17	17	1	1
1924	NY-A	25	38	16	11	.593	95	4.12	207 2/3	114	74	226	11	10	1	0
1925	NY-A	20	33	6	14	.300	85	4.11	186	81	67	209	12	9	1	0
1926	NY-A	10	29	8	7	.533	42	3.62	104 1/3	63	37	102	8	3	1	3
1927	NY-A	2	19	2	3	.400	14	2.89	43 2/3	23	16	44	1	0	0	4
Career Average		21	31	12	9	.566	63	3.09	184	85	64	170	7	12	2	2
Yankee Average		**21**	**32**	**13**	**10**	**.562**	**66**	**3.12**	**191**	**89**	**66**	**177**	**8**	**13**	**2**	**2**
Career Total		334	488	196	150	.566	1008	3.09	2937	1360	1018	2722	114	197	33	28
Yankee Total		**275**	**415**	**168**	**131**	**.562**	**862**	**3.12**	**2488 2/3**	**1163**	**855**	**2304**	**105**	**164**	**26**	**26**

Shea, Francis Joseph (Spec *or* The Naugatuck Nuggett)

HEIGHT: 6'0" BORN: 10/2/1920 NAUGATUCK, CONNECTICUT

YEAR	TEAM	STARTS	GAMES	WON	LOST	PCT	ER	ERA	INNINGS PITCHED	STRIKE-OUTS	WALKS	HITS ALLOWED	HRS ALLOWED	COMP. GAMES	SHUT-OUTS	SAVES
1947	NY-A	23	27	14	5	.737	61	3.07	178 2/3	89	89	127	10	13	3	1
1948	NY-A	22	28	9	10	.474	59	3.41	155 2/3	71	87	117	10	8	3	1
1949	NY-A	3	20	1	1	.500	31	5.33	52 1/3	22	43	48	5	0	0	1
1951	NY-A	11	25	5	5	.500	46	4.33	95 2/3	38	50	112	11	2	2	0
1952	Was-A	21	22	11	7	.611	55	2.93	169	65	92	144	6	12	2	0
1953	Was-A	23	23	12	7	.632	72	3.94	164 2/3	38	75	151	11	11	1	0
1954	Was-A	11	23	2	9	.182	49	6.18	71 1/3	22	34	97	9	1	0	0
1955	Was-A	4	27	2	2	.500	25	3.99	56 1/3	16	27	53	4	1	1	2
Career Average		15	24	7	6	.549	50	3.80	118	45	62	106	8	6	2	1
Yankee Average		**15**	**25**	**7**	**5**	**.580**	**49**	**3.68**	**118**	**55**	**67**	**101**	**9**	**6**	**2**	**1**
Career Total		118	195	56	46	.549	398	3.80	943 2/3	361	497	849	66	48	12	5
Yankee Total		**59**	**100**	**29**	**21**	**.580**	**197**	**3.68**	**482 1/3**	**220**	**269**	**404**	**36**	**23**	**8**	**3**

Shealy, Albert Berley

HEIGHT: 5'11" RIGHTHANDER BORN: 3/20/1900 CHAPIN, SOUTH CAROLINA DIED: 3/7/1967 HAGERSTOWN, MARYLAND

YEAR	TEAM	STARTS	GAMES	WON	LOST	PCT	ER	ERA	INNINGS PITCHED	STRIKE-OUTS	WALKS	HITS ALLOWED	HRS ALLOWED	COMP. GAMES	SHUT-OUTS	SAVES
1928	NY-A	12	23	8	6	.571	54	5.06	96	39	42	124	4	3	0	2
1930	Chi-N	0	24	0	0	—	24	8.00	27	14	14	37	2	0	0	0
Career Average		6	24	4	3	.571	39	5.71	62	27	28	81	3	2	0	1
Yankee Average		**12**	**23**	**8**	**6**	**.571**	**54**	**5.06**	**96**	**39**	**42**	**124**	**4**	**3**	**0**	**2**
Career Total		12	47	8	6	.571	78	5.71	123	53	56	161	6	3	0	2
Yankee Total		**12**	**23**	**8**	**6**	**.571**	**54**	**5.06**	**96**	**39**	**42**	**124**	**4**	**3**	**0**	**2**

Shears, George Penfield

HEIGHT: 6'3" LEFTHANDER BORN: 4/13/1890 MARSHALL, MISSOURI DIED: 11/12/1978 LOVELAND, COLORADO

YEAR	TEAM	STARTS	GAMES	WON	LOST	PCT	ER	ERA	INNINGS PITCHED	STRIKE-OUTS	WALKS	HITS ALLOWED	HRS ALLOWED	COMP. GAMES	SHUT-OUTS	SAVES
1912	NY-A	0	4	0	0	—	9	5.40	15	9	11	24	1	0	0	0
Career Average		0	4	0	0	—	9	5.40	15	9	11	24	1	0	0	0
Yankee Average		**0**	**4**	**0**	**0**	**—**	**9**	**5.40**	**15**	**9**	**11**	**24**	**1**	**0**	**0**	**0**
Career Total		0	4	0	0	—	9	5.40	15	9	11	24	1	0	0	0
Yankee Total		**0**	**4**	**0**	**0**	**—**	**9**	**5.40**	**15**	**9**	**11**	**24**	**1**	**0**	**0**	**0**

Sheehan, Thomas Clancy
HEIGHT: 6'2"   RIGHTHANDER   BORN: 3/31/1894 GRAND RIDGE, ILLINOIS   DIED: 10/29/1982 CHILLICOTHE, OHIO

YEAR	TEAM	STARTS	GAMES	WON	LOST	PCT	ER	ERA	INNINGS PITCHED	STRIKE-OUTS	WALKS	HITS ALLOWED	HRS ALLOWED	COMP. GAMES	SHUT-OUTS	SAVES
1915	Phi-A	13	15	4	9	.308	47	4.15	102	22	38	131	1	8	1	0
1916	Phi-A	17	38	1	16	.059	77	3.69	188	54	94	197	2	8	0	0
1921	**NY-A**	**1**	**12**	**1**	**0**	**1.000**	**20**	**5.45**	**33**	**7**	**19**	**43**	**1**	**0**	**0**	**1**
1924	Cin-N	16	39	9	11	.450	60	3.24	166 2/3	52	54	170	5	8	2	1
1925	Cin-N	3	10	1	0	1.000	26	8.07	29	5	12	37	3	1	0	1
1925	Pit-N	0	23	1	1	.500	17	2.67	57 1/3	13	13	63	2	0	0	2
1926	Pit-N	4	9	0	2	.000	23	6.68	31	16	12	36	0	1	0	0
Career Average		8	21	2	6	.304	39	4.00	87	24	35	97	2	4	0	1
Yankee Average		**1**	**12**	**1**	**0**	**1.000**	**20**	**5.45**	**33**	**7**	**19**	**43**	**1**	**0**	**0**	**1**
Career Total		54	146	17	39	.304	270	4.00	607	169	242	677	14	26	3	5
Yankee Total		**1**	**12**	**1**	**0**	**1.000**	**20**	**5.45**	**33**	**7**	**19**	**43**	**1**	**0**	**0**	**1**

Sheldon, Roland Frank (Rollie)
HEIGHT: 6'4"   RIGHTHANDER   BORN: 12/17/1936 PUTNAM, CONNECTICUT

YEAR	TEAM	STARTS	GAMES	WON	LOST	PCT	ER	ERA	INNINGS PITCHED	STRIKE-OUTS	WALKS	HITS ALLOWED	HRS ALLOWED	COMP. GAMES	SHUT-OUTS	SAVES
1961	**NY-A**	**21**	**35**	**11**	**5**	**.688**	**65**	**3.60**	**162 2/3**	**84**	**55**	**149**	**17**	**6**	**2**	**0**
1962	**NY-A**	**16**	**34**	**7**	**8**	**.467**	**72**	**5.49**	**118**	**54**	**28**	**136**	**12**	**2**	**0**	**1**
1964	**NY-A**	**12**	**19**	**5**	**2**	**.714**	**41**	**3.61**	**102 1/3**	**57**	**18**	**92**	**18**	**3**	**0**	**1**
1965	**NY-A**	**0**	**3**	**0**	**0**	**—**	**1**	**1.42**	**6 1/3**	**7**	**1**	**5**	**0**	**0**	**0**	**0**
1965	KC-A	29	32	10	8	.556	82	3.95	186 2/3	105	56	180	22	4	1	0
1966	KC-A	13	14	4	7	.364	24	3.13	69	26	26	73	3	1	1	0
1966	Bos-A	10	23	1	6	.143	44	4.97	79 2/3	38	23	106	15	1	0	0
Career Average		14	23	5	5	.514	47	4.09	104	53	30	106	12	2	1	0
Yankee Average		**12**	**23**	**6**	**4**	**.605**	**45**	**4.14**	**97**	**51**	**26**	**96**	**12**	**3**	**1**	**1**
Career Total		101	160	38	36	.514	329	4.09	724 2/3	371	207	741	87	17	4	2
Yankee Total		**49**	**91**	**23**	**15**	**.605**	**179**	**4.14**	**389 1/3**	**202**	**102**	**382**	**47**	**11**	**2**	**2**

Sherid, Royden Richard
HEIGHT: 6'2"   RIGHTHANDER   BORN: 1/25/1907 NORRISTOWN, PENNSYLVANIA   DIED: 2/28/1982 PARKER FORD, PENNSYLVANIA

YEAR	TEAM	STARTS	GAMES	WON	LOST	PCT	ER	ERA	INNINGS PITCHED	STRIKE-OUTS	WALKS	HITS ALLOWED	HRS ALLOWED	COMP. GAMES	SHUT-OUTS	SAVES
1929	**NY-A**	**15**	**33**	**6**	**6**	**.500**	**62**	**3.61**	**154 2/3**	**51**	**55**	**165**	**6**	**9**	**0**	**1**
1930	**NY-A**	**21**	**37**	**12**	**13**	**.480**	**107**	**5.23**	**184**	**59**	**87**	**214**	**13**	**8**	**0**	**4**
1931	**NY-A**	**8**	**17**	**5**	**5**	**.500**	**47**	**5.69**	**74 1/3**	**39**	**24**	**94**	**4**	**3**	**0**	**2**
Career Average		15	29	8	8	.489	72	4.71	138	50	55	158	8	7	0	2
Yankee Average		**15**	**29**	**8**	**8**	**.489**	**72**	**4.71**	**138**	**50**	**55**	**158**	**8**	**7**	**0**	**2**
Career Total		44	87	23	24	.489	216	4.71	413	149	166	473	23	20	0	7
Yankee Total		**44**	**87**	**23**	**24**	**.489**	**216**	**4.71**	**413**	**149**	**166**	**473**	**23**	**20**	**0**	**7**

Shields, Benjamin Cowan (Big Ben *or* Lefty)
HEIGHT: 6'1"   LEFTHANDER   BORN: 6/17/1903 HUNTERSVILLE, NORTH CAROLINA   DIED: 1/24/1982 WOODRUFF, SOUTH CAROLINA

YEAR	TEAM	STARTS	GAMES	WON	LOST	PCT	ER	ERA	INNINGS PITCHED	STRIKE-OUTS	WALKS	HITS ALLOWED	HRS ALLOWED	COMP. GAMES	SHUT-OUTS	SAVES
1924	**NY-A**	**0**	**2**	**0**	**0**	**—**	**6**	**27.00**	**2**	**3**	**2**	**6**	**0**	**0**	**0**	**0**
1925	**NY-A**	**2**	**4**	**3**	**0**	**1.000**	**13**	**4.88**	**24**	**5**	**12**	**24**	**2**	**2**	**0**	**0**
1930	Bos-A	0	3	0	0	—	10	9.00	10	1	6	16	0	0	0	0
1931	Phi-N	0	4	1	0	1.000	9	15.19	5 1/3	0	7	9	1	0	0	0
Career Average		1	3	1	0	1.000	10	8.27	10	2	7	14	1	1	0	0
Yankee Average		**1**	**3**	**2**	**0**	**1.000**	**10**	**6.58**	**13**	**4**	**7**	**15**	**1**	**1**	**0**	**0**
Career Total		2	13	4	0	1.000	38	8.27	41 1/3	9	27	55	3	2	0	0
Yankee Total		**2**	**6**	**3**	**0**	**1.000**	**19**	**6.58**	**26**	**8**	**14**	**30**	**2**	**2**	**0**	**0**

Shields, Stephen Mack
HEIGHT: 6'5" RIGHTHANDER BORN: 11/30/1958 GADSDEN, ALABAMA

YEAR	TEAM	STARTS	GAMES	WON	LOST	PCT	ER	ERA	INNINGS PITCHED	STRIKE-OUTS	WALKS	HITS ALLOWED	HRS ALLOWED	COMP. GAMES	SHUT-OUTS	SAVES
1985	Atl-N	6	23	1	2	.333	39	5.16	68	29	32	86	9	0	0	0
1986	KC-A	0	3	0	0	—	2	2.08	8 2/3	2	4	3	1	0	0	0
1986	Atl-N	0	6	0	0	—	10	7.11	12 2/3	6	7	13	4	0	0	0
1987	Sea-A	0	20	2	0	1.000	22	6.60	30	22	12	43	7	0	0	3
1988	**NY-A**	**0**	**39**	**5**	**5**	**.500**	**40**	**4.37**	**82 1/3**	**55**	**30**	**96**	**8**	**0**	**0**	**0**
1989	Min-A	0	11	0	1	.000	15	7.79	17 1/3	12	6	28	3	0	0	0
Career Average		1	17	1	1	.500	21	5.26	37	21	15	45	5	0	0	1
Yankee Average		**0**	**39**	**5**	**5**	**.500**	**40**	**4.37**	**82**	**55**	**30**	**96**	**8**	**0**	**0**	**0**
Career Total		6	102	8	8	.500	128	5.26	219	126	91	269	32	0	0	3
Yankee Total		**0**	**39**	**5**	**5**	**.500**	**40**	**4.37**	**82 1/3**	**55**	**30**	**96**	**8**	**0**	**0**	**0**

Shirley, Robert Charles
HEIGHT: 5'11" LEFTHANDER BORN: 6/25/1954 CUSHING, OKLAHOMA

YEAR	TEAM	STARTS	GAMES	WON	LOST	PCT	ER	ERA	INNINGS PITCHED	STRIKE-OUTS	WALKS	HITS ALLOWED	HRS ALLOWED	COMP. GAMES	SHUT-OUTS	SAVES
1977	SD-N	35	39	12	18	.400	88	3.70	214	146	100	215	22	1	0	0
1978	SD-N	20	50	8	11	.421	68	3.69	166	102	61	164	10	2	0	5
1979	SD-N	25	49	8	16	.333	77	3.38	205	117	59	196	15	4	1	0
1980	SD-N	12	59	11	12	.478	54	3.55	143	67	54	143	12	3	0	7
1981	StL-N	11	28	6	4	.600	36	4.08	79 1/3	36	34	78	6	1	0	1
1982	Cin-N	20	41	8	13	.381	61	3.60	152 2/3	89	73	138	17	1	0	0
1983	**NY-A**	**17**	**25**	**5**	**8**	**.385**	**61**	**5.08**	**108**	**53**	**36**	**122**	**10**	**1**	**1**	**0**
1984	**NY-A**	**7**	**41**	**3**	**3**	**.500**	**43**	**3.38**	**114 1/3**	**48**	**38**	**119**	**8**	**1**	**0**	**0**
1985	**NY-A**	**8**	**48**	**5**	**5**	**.500**	**32**	**2.64**	**109**	**55**	**26**	**103**	**5**	**2**	**0**	**2**
1986	**NY-A**	**6**	**39**	**0**	**4**	**.000**	**59**	**5.04**	**105 1/3**	**64**	**40**	**108**	**13**	**0**	**0**	**3**
1987	**NY-A**	**1**	**12**	**1**	**0**	**1.000**	**17**	**4.50**	**34**	**12**	**16**	**36**	**4**	**0**	**0**	**0**
1987	KC-A	0	3	0	0	—	12	14.73	7 1/3	1	6	10	5	0	0	0
Career Average		14	36	6	8	.416	51	3.82	119	66	45	119	11	1	0	2
Yankee Average		**8**	**33**	**3**	**4**	**.412**	**42**	**4.05**	**94**	**46**	**31**	**98**	**8**	**1**	**0**	**1**
Career Total		162	434	67	94	.416	608	3.82	1432	790	543	1432	127	16	2	18
Yankee Total		**39**	**165**	**14**	**20**	**.412**	**212**	**4.05**	**470 2/3**	**232**	**156**	**488**	**40**	**4**	**1**	**5**

Shocker, Urban James BORN URBAIN JACQUES SHOCKCOR
HEIGHT: 5'10" RIGHTHANDER BORN: 9/22/1892 CLEVELAND, OHIO DIED: 9/9/1928 DENVER, COLORADO

YEAR	TEAM	STARTS	GAMES	WON	LOST	PCT	ER	ERA	INNINGS PITCHED	STRIKE-OUTS	WALKS	HITS ALLOWED	HRS ALLOWED	COMP. GAMES	SHUT-OUTS	SAVES
1916	**NY-A**	**9**	**12**	**4**	**3**	**.571**	**24**	**2.62**	**82 1/3**	**43**	**32**	**67**	**2**	**4**	**1**	**0**
1917	**NY-A**	**13**	**26**	**8**	**5**	**.615**	**42**	**2.61**	**145**	**68**	**46**	**124**	**4**	**7**	**0**	**1**
1918	StL-A	9	14	6	5	.545	19	1.81	94 2/3	33	40	69	0	7	0	2
1919	StL-A	25	30	13	11	.542	63	2.69	211	86	55	193	6	14	5	0
1920	StL-A	28	38	20	10	.667	74	2.71	245 2/3	107	70	224	10	22	5	3
1921	StL-A	38	47	27	12	.692	129	3.55	326 2/3	132	86	345	21	30	4	4
1922	StL-A	38	48	24	17	.585	115	2.97	348	149	57	365	22	29	2	3
1923	StL-A	35	43	20	12	.625	105	3.41	277 1/3	109	49	292	12	24	3	5
1924	StL-A	33	40	16	13	.552	115	4.20	246 1/3	88	52	270	11	17	4	1
1925	**NY-A**	**30**	**41**	**12**	**12**	**.500**	**99**	**3.65**	**244 1/3**	**74**	**58**	**278**	**17**	**15**	**2**	**2**
1926	**NY-A**	**32**	**41**	**19**	**11**	**.633**	**97**	**3.38**	**258 1/3**	**59**	**71**	**272**	**13**	**18**	**0**	**2**
1927	**NY-A**	**27**	**31**	**18**	**6**	**.750**	**63**	**2.84**	**200**	**35**	**41**	**207**	**8**	**13**	**2**	**0**
1928	**NY-A**	**0**	**1**	**0**	**0**	**—**	**0**	**0.00**	**2**	**0**	**0**	**3**	**0**	**0**	**0**	**0**
Career Average		24	32	14	9	.615	73	3.17	206	76	51	208	10	15	2	2
Yankee Average		**19**	**25**	**10**	**6**	**.622**	**54**	**3.14**	**155**	**47**	**41**	**159**	**7**	**10**	**1**	**1**
Career Total		317	412	187	117	.615	945	3.17	2681 2/3	983	657	2709	126	200	28	25
Yankee Total		**111**	**152**	**61**	**37**	**.622**	**325**	**3.14**	**932**	**279**	**248**	**951**	**44**	**57**	**5**	**5**

Urban James Shocker, rhp, 1916–17, 1925–28

More than 70 years after his death, Urban Shocker has been all but forgotten by all but the most passionate Yankee fans. But in his time, Shocker was one of the great pitchers in the American League, and one of the veterans of the Yankee powerhouse teams of the late 1920s.

Born Urbain Jacques Shockcor on August 22, 1890, in Cleveland, Shocker began his career in New York in 1916 as a 26-year-old rookie. He was a spot starter for New York his first two years, winning 12 games and losing eight.

In 1918, he was traded to the Browns, a move manager Miller Huggins said many years later was one of his worst ever as a manager. Shocker, a master of the spitball and various other junk pitches, quickly became the ace of the St. Louis staff. He was a master at studying hitters and learning their weaknesses.

Shocker was a Brown for seven years, compiling a record of 120-75. But while Shocker was 45 games over .500 in that span, the Browns were 20 games over the break-even mark, with only two winning seasons. Worse, for the Yankees at least, Shocker seemed to have Babe Ruth's number, getting him out more consistently than any other pitcher in that time.

In 1925, Huggins sent rookie righties Milt Gaston and Joe Giard and veteran Bullet Joe Bush to the Browns to get Shocker back.

It was a trade that paid big dividends for New York. Over the next three years, Shocker would be one of the best pitchers in the American League, winning 49 games and losing 29. He would be runner-up in ERA (2.84) and winning percentage (.750) in the American League in 1927; 3rd in wins (19) and complete games (19) in 1926 and 7th in ERA (3.65) and 8th in innings (244) in 1925. In all three years, he was one of the leaders in fewest walks per nine innings.

But he was also carrying a dark secret: He had an enlarged heart. It was a dangerous condition that often caused him to sleep sitting up. Shocker refused treatment for his ailment and endured the dizzy spells and shortness of breath that accompanied the disease.

By the fall of 1927, he was having problems. He bowed out of the second game of the World Series against the Pirates, pleading exhaustion, a move that shocked his teammates. In 1928, he made one uninspired start for the Yankees before retiring to Denver to work at his burgeoning radio-shop business. By September, he was dead.

Shore, Ernest Grady
HEIGHT: 6'4" RIGHTHANDER BORN: 3/24/1891 EAST BEND, NORTH CAROLINA DIED: 9/24/1980 WINSTON-SALEM, NORTH CAROLINA

YEAR	TEAM	STARTS	GAMES	WON	LOST	PCT	ER	ERA	INNINGS PITCHED	STRIKE-OUTS	WALKS	HITS ALLOWED	HRS ALLOWED	COMP. GAMES	SHUT-OUTS	SAVES
1912	NY-N	0	1	0	0	—	3	27.00	1	1	1	8	1	0	0	1
1914	Bos-A	16	20	10	5	.667	31	2.00	139 2/3	51	34	103	1	10	1	1
1915	Bos-A	32	38	19	8	.704	45	1.64	247	102	66	207	3	17	4	0
1916	Bos-A	28	38	16	10	.615	66	2.63	225 2/3	62	49	221	1	10	3	1
1917	Bos-A	27	29	13	10	.565	56	2.22	226 2/3	57	55	201	1	14	1	1
1919	**NY-A**	**13**	**20**	**5**	**8**	**.385**	**44**	**4.17**	**95**	**24**	**44**	**105**	**4**	**3**	**0**	**0**
1920	**NY-A**	**5**	**14**	**2**	**2**	**.500**	**24**	**4.87**	**44 1/3**	**12**	**21**	**61**	**1**	**2**	**0**	**1**
Career Average		17	23	9	6	.602	38	2.47	140	44	39	129	2	8	1	1
Yankee Average		**9**	**17**	**4**	**5**	**.412**	**34**	**4.39**	**70**	**18**	**33**	**83**	**3**	**3**	**0**	**1**
Career Total		121	160	65	43	.602	269	2.47	979 1/3	309	270	906	12	56	9	5
Yankee Total		**18**	**34**	**7**	**10**	**.412**	**68**	**4.39**	**139 1/3**	**36**	**65**	**166**	**5**	**5**	**0**	**1**

Short, William Ross
HEIGHT: 5'9"   LEFTHANDER   BORN: 11/27/1937 KINGSTON, NEW YORK

YEAR	TEAM	STARTS	GAMES	WON	LOST	PCT	ER	ERA	INNINGS PITCHED	STRIKE-OUTS	WALKS	HITS ALLOWED	HRS ALLOWED	COMP. GAMES	SHUT-OUTS	SAVES
1960	**NY-A**	10	10	3	5	.375	25	4.79	47	14	30	49	5	2	0	0
1962	Bal-A	0	5	0	0	—	7	15.75	4	3	6	8	2	0	0	0
1966	Bal-A	6	6	2	3	.400	12	2.87	37⅔	27	10	34	1	1	1	0
1966	Bos-A	0	8	0	0	—	4	4.32	8⅓	2	2	10	0	0	0	0
1967	Pit-N	0	6	0	0	—	1	3.86	2⅓	1	1	1	0	0	0	0
1968	NY-N	0	34	0	3	.000	16	4.75	30⅓	24	14	24	0	0	0	1
1969	Cin-N	0	4	0	0	—	4	15.43	2⅓	0	1	4	0	0	0	1
Career Average		2	10	1	2	.313	10	4.70	19	10	9	19	1	0	0	0
Yankee Average		10	10	3	5	.375	25	4.79	47	14	30	49	5	2	0	0
Career Total		16	73	5	11	.313	69	4.70	132	71	64	130	8	3	1	2
Yankee Total		10	10	3	5	.375	25	4.79	47	14	30	49	5	2	0	0

Slagle, Roger Lee
HEIGHT: 6'3"   RIGHTHANDER   BORN: 11/4/1953 WICHITA, KANSAS

YEAR	TEAM	STARTS	GAMES	WON	LOST	PCT	ER	ERA	INNINGS PITCHED	STRIKE-OUTS	WALKS	HITS ALLOWED	HRS ALLOWED	COMP. GAMES	SHUT-OUTS	SAVES
1979	NY-A	0	1	0	0	—	0	0.00	2	2	0	0	0	0	0	0
Career Average		0	1	0	0	—	0	0.00	2	2	0	0	0	0	0	0
Yankee Average		0	1	0	0	—	0	0.00	2	2	0	0	0	0	0	0
Career Total		0	1	0	0	—	0	0.00	2	2	0	0	0	0	0	0
Yankee Total		0	1	0	0	—	0	0.00	2	2	0	0	0	0	0	0

Smallwood, Walter Clayton
HEIGHT: 6'2"   RIGHTHANDER   BORN: 4/24/1893 DAYTON, MARYLAND   DIED: 4/29/1967 BALTIMORE, MARYLAND

YEAR	TEAM	STARTS	GAMES	WON	LOST	PCT	ER	ERA	INNINGS PITCHED	STRIKE-OUTS	WALKS	HITS ALLOWED	HRS ALLOWED	COMP. GAMES	SHUT-OUTS	SAVES
1917	NY-A	0	2	0	0	—	0	0.00	2	1	1	1	0	0	0	0
1919	NY-A	0	6	0	0	—	12	4.98	21⅔	6	9	20	1	0	0	0
Career Average		0	4	0	0	—	6	4.56	12	4	5	11	1	0	0	0
Yankee Average		0	4	0	0	—	6	4.56	12	4	5	11	1	0	0	0
Career Total		0	8	0	0	—	12	4.56	23⅔	7	10	21	1	0	0	0
Yankee Total		0	8	0	0	—	12	4.56	23⅔	7	10	21	1	0	0	0

Smith, Lee Arthur
HEIGHT: 6'6"   RIGHTHANDER   BORN: 12/4/1957 SHREVEPORT, LOUISIANA

YEAR	TEAM	STARTS	GAMES	WON	LOST	PCT	ER	ERA	INNINGS PITCHED	STRIKE-OUTS	WALKS	HITS ALLOWED	HRS ALLOWED	COMP. GAMES	SHUT-OUTS	SAVES
1980	Chi-N	0	18	2	0	1.000	7	2.91	21⅔	17	14	21	0	0	0	0
1981	Chi-N	1	40	3	6	.333	26	3.51	66⅔	50	31	57	2	0	0	1
1982	Chi-N	5	72	2	5	.286	35	2.69	117	99	37	105	5	0	0	17
1983	Chi-N	0	66	4	10	.286	19	1.65	103⅓	91	41	70	5	0	0	29
1984	Chi-N	0	69	9	7	.563	41	3.65	101	86	35	98	6	0	0	33
1985	Chi-N	0	65	7	4	.636	33	3.04	97⅔	112	32	87	9	0	0	33
1986	Chi-N	0	66	9	9	.500	31	3.09	90⅓	93	42	69	7	0	0	31
1987	Chi-N	0	62	4	10	.286	29	3.12	83⅔	96	32	84	4	0	0	36
1988	Bos-A	0	64	4	5	.444	26	2.80	83⅔	96	37	72	7	0	0	29
1989	Bos-A	0	64	6	1	.857	28	3.57	70⅔	96	33	53	6	0	0	25
1990	Bos-A	0	11	2	1	.667	3	1.88	14⅓	17	9	13	0	0	0	4
1990	StL-N	0	53	3	4	.429	16	2.10	68⅔	70	20	58	3	0	0	27
1991	StL-N	0	67	6	3	.667	19	2.34	73	67	13	70	5	0	0	47
1992	StL-N	0	70	4	9	.308	26	3.12	75	60	26	62	4	0	0	43
1993	StL-N	0	55	2	4	.333	25	4.50	50	49	9	49	11	0	0	43
1993	**NY-A**	0	8	0	0	—	0	0.00	8	11	5	4	0	0	0	3
1994	Bal-A	0	41	1	4	.200	14	3.32	38	42	11	34	6	0	0	33

(continued)

(continued)

YEAR	TEAM	STARTS	GAMES	WON	LOST	PCT	ER	ERA	INNINGS PITCHED	STRIKE-OUTS	WALKS	HITS ALLOWED	HRS ALLOWED	COMP. GAMES	SHUT-OUTS	SAVES
1995	Cal-A	0	52	0	5	.000	19	3.49	49 1/3	43	25	42	3	0	0	37
1996	Cal-A	0	11	0	0	—	3	2.45	11	6	3	8	0	0	0	0
1996	Cin-N	0	43	3	4	.429	20	4.09	44 1/3	35	23	49	4	0	0	2
1997	Mon-N	0	25	0	1	.000	14	6.00	21 2/3	15	8	28	2	0	0	5
Career Average		0	49	3	4	.436	21	3.03	61	60	23	54	4	0	0	23
Yankee Average		0	8	0	0	—	0	0.00	8	11	5	4	0	0	0	3
Career Total		6	1022	71	92	.436	434	3.03	1288 2/3	1251	486	1133	89	0	0	478
Yankee Total		0	8	0	0	—	0	0.00	8	11	5	4	0	0	0	3

Smythe, William Henry (Harry)

HEIGHT: 5'10" LEFTHANDER BORN: 10/24/1904 AUGUSTA, GEORGIA DIED: 8/28/1980 AUGUSTA, GEORGIA

YEAR	TEAM	STARTS	GAMES	WON	LOST	PCT	ER	ERA	INNINGS PITCHED	STRIKE-OUTS	WALKS	HITS ALLOWED	HRS ALLOWED	COMP. GAMES	SHUT-OUTS	SAVES
1929	Phi-N	7	19	4	6	.400	40	5.24	68 2/3	12	15	94	3	2	0	1
1930	Phi-N	3	25	0	3	.000	43	7.79	49 2/3	9	31	84	3	0	0	2
1934	NY-A	0	8	0	2	.000	13	7.80	15	7	8	24	1	0	0	0
1934	Bro-N	0	8	1	1	.500	14	5.91	21 1/3	5	8	30	3	0	0	1
Career Average		3	15	1	3	.294	28	6.40	38	8	16	58	3	1	0	1
Yankee Average		0	8	0	2	.000	13	7.80	15	7	8	24	1	0	0	1
Career Total		10	60	5	12	.294	110	6.40	154 2/3	33	62	232	10	2	0	4
Yankee Total		0	8	0	2	.000	13	7.80	15	7	8	24	1	0	0	1

Springer, Russell Paul

HEIGHT: 6'4" RIGHTHANDER BORN: 11/7/1968 ALEXANDRIA, LOUISIANA

YEAR	TEAM	STARTS	GAMES	WON	LOST	PCT	ER	ERA	INNINGS PITCHED	STRIKE-OUTS	WALKS	HITS ALLOWED	HRS ALLOWED	COMP. GAMES	SHUT-OUTS	SAVES
1992	NY-A	0	14	0	0	—	11	6.19	16	12	10	18	0	1	0	0
1993	Cal-A	9	14	1	6	.143	48	7.20	60	31	32	73	11	1	0	0
1994	Cal-A	5	18	2	2	.500	28	5.60	45 2/3	28	14	53	9	0	0	2
1995	Cal-A	6	19	1	2	.333	35	6.18	51 2/3	38	25	60	11	0	0	1
1995	Phi-N	0	14	0	0	—	11	3.81	26 2/3	32	10	22	5	0	0	0
1996	Phi-N	7	51	3	10	.231	50	4.69	96 2/3	94	38	106	12	0	0	3
1997	Hou-N	0	54	3	3	.500	26	4.25	55 1/3	74	27	48	4	0	0	0
1998	Ari-N	0	26	4	3	.571	15	4.22	32 2/3	37	14	29	4	0	0	0
1998	Atl-N	0	22	1	1	.500	9	4.05	20	19	16	22	0	0	0	1
1999	Atl-N	0	49	2	1	.667	18	3.45	47 1/3	49	22	31	5	0	0	0
2000	Ari-N	0	52	2	4	.333	35	5.08	62	59	34	63	11	0	0	1
Career Average		2	30	2	3	.373	26	5.01	46	43	22	48	7	0	0	1
Yankee Average		0	14	0	0	—	11	6.19	16	12	10	18	0	0	0	0
Career Total		27	333	19	32	.373	514	5.01	517	473	242	525	72	1	0	7
Yankee Total		0	14	0	0	—	11	6.19	16	12	10	18	0	0	0	0

Stafford, William Charles

HEIGHT: 6'1" RIGHTHANDER BORN: 8/13/1939 CATSKILL, NEW YORK

YEAR	TEAM	STARTS	GAMES	WON	LOST	PCT	ER	ERA	INNINGS PITCHED	STRIKE-OUTS	WALKS	HITS ALLOWED	HRS ALLOWED	COMP. GAMES	SHUT-OUTS	SAVES
1960	NY-A	8	11	3	1	.750	15	2.25	60	36	18	50	3	2	1	0
1961	NY-A	25	36	14	9	.609	58	2.68	195	101	59	168	13	8	3	2
1962	NY-A	33	35	14	9	.609	87	3.67	213 1/3	109	77	188	23	7	2	0
1963	NY-A	14	28	4	8	.333	60	6.02	89 2/3	52	42	104	16	0	0	3
1964	NY-A	1	31	5	0	1.000	18	2.67	60 2/3	39	22	50	4	0	0	4
1965	NY-A	15	22	3	8	.273	44	3.56	111 1/3	71	31	93	16	1	0	0
1966	KC-A	8	9	0	4	.000	22	4.99	39 2/3	31	12	42	2	0	0	0
1967	KC-A	0	14	0	1	.000	3	1.69	16	10	9	12	0	0	0	1
Career Average		13	23	5	5	.518	38	3.52	98	56	34	88	10	2	1	2
Yankee Average		16	27	7	6	.551	47	3.48	122	68	42	109	13	3	1	2
Career Total		104	186	43	40	.518	307	3.52	785 2/3	449	270	707	77	18	6	9
Yankee Total		96	163	43	35	.551	282	3.48	730	408	249	653	75	18	6	9

Staley, Gerald Lee
HEIGHT: 6'0"   RIGHTHANDER   BORN: 8/21/1920 BRUSH PRAIRIE, WASHINGTON

YEAR	TEAM	STARTS	GAMES	WON	LOST	PCT	ER	ERA	INNINGS PITCHED	STRIKE-OUTS	WALKS	HITS ALLOWED	HRS ALLOWED	COMP. GAMES	SHUT-OUTS	SAVES
1947	StL-N	1	18	1	0	1.000	9	2.76	29 1/3	14	8	33	2	1	0	0
1948	StL-N	3	31	4	4	.500	40	6.92	52	23	21	61	5	0	0	0
1949	StL-N	17	45	10	10	.500	52	2.73	171 1/3	55	41	154	7	5	2	6
1950	StL-N	22	42	13	13	.500	94	4.99	169 2/3	62	61	201	14	7	1	3
1951	StL-N	30	42	19	13	.594	96	3.81	227	67	74	244	14	10	4	3
1952	StL-N	33	35	17	14	.548	87	3.27	239 2/3	93	52	238	21	15	0	0
1953	StL-N	32	40	18	9	.667	102	3.99	230	88	54	243	31	10	1	4
1954	StL-N	20	48	7	13	.350	91	5.26	155 2/3	50	47	198	21	3	1	2
1955	Cin-N	18	30	5	8	.385	62	4.66	119 2/3	40	28	146	22	2	0	0
1955	**NY-A**	**0**	**2**	**0**	**0**	**—**	**3**	**13.50**	**2**	**0**	**1**	**5**	**1**	**0**	**0**	**0**
1956	**NY-A**	**0**	**1**	**0**	**0**	**—**	**4**	**108.11**	**1/3**	**1**	**0**	**4**	**0**	**0**	**0**	**0**
1956	Chi-A	10	26	8	3	.727	33	2.92	101 2/3	25	20	98	11	5	0	0
1957	Chi-A	0	47	5	1	.833	24	2.06	105	44	27	95	7	0	0	7
1958	Chi-A	0	50	4	5	.444	30	3.16	85 1/3	27	24	81	10	0	0	8
1959	Chi-A	0	67	8	5	.615	29	2.24	116 1/3	54	25	111	5	0	0	14
1960	Chi-A	0	64	13	8	.619	31	2.42	115 1/3	52	25	94	8	0	0	10
1961	Chi-A	0	16	0	3	.000	10	5.00	18	8	5	17	3	0	0	0
1961	KC-A	0	23	1	1	.500	12	3.60	30	16	10	32	4	0	0	2
1961	Det-A	0	13	1	1	.500	5	3.38	13 1/3	8	6	15	1	0	0	2
Career Average		10	34	7	6	.547	43	3.70	104	38	28	109	10	3	0	3
Yankee Average		**0**	**2**	**0**	**0**	**—**	**4**	**27.00**	**1**	**1**	**1**	**5**	**1**	**0**	**0**	**0**
Career Total		186	640	134	111	.547	814	3.70	1981 2/3	727	529	2070	187	58	9	61
Yankee Total		**0**	**3**	**0**	**0**	**—**	**7**	**27.00**	**2 1/3**	**1**	**1**	**9**	**1**	**0**	**0**	**0**

Stanceu, Charles
HEIGHT: 6'2"   RIGHTHANDER   BORN: 1/9/1916 CANTON, OHIO   DIED: 4/3/1969 CANTON, OHIO

YEAR	TEAM	STARTS	GAMES	WON	LOST	PCT	ER	ERA	INNINGS PITCHED	STRIKE-OUTS	WALKS	HITS ALLOWED	HRS ALLOWED	COMP. GAMES	SHUT-OUTS	SAVES
1941	**NY-A**	**2**	**22**	**3**	**3**	**.500**	**30**	**5.63**	**48**	**21**	**35**	**58**	**3**	**0**	**0**	**0**
1946	**NY-A**	**0**	**3**	**0**	**0**	**—**	**4**	**9.00**	**4**	**3**	**5**	**6**	**0**	**0**	**0**	**0**
1946	Phi-N	11	14	2	4	.333	33	4.22	70 1/3	23	39	71	4	1	0	0
Career Average		4	13	2	2	.417	22	4.93	41	16	26	45	2	0	0	0
Yankee Average		**1**	**13**	**2**	**2**	**.500**	**17**	**5.88**	**26**	**12**	**20**	**32**	**2**	**0**	**0**	**0**
Career Total		13	39	5	7	.417	67	4.93	122 1/3	47	79	135	7	1	0	0
Yankee Total		**2**	**25**	**3**	**3**	**.500**	**34**	**5.88**	**52**	**24**	**40**	**64**	**3**	**0**	**0**	**0**

Stanton, William Michael
HEIGHT: 6'1"   LEFTHANDER   BORN: 6/2/1967 HOUSTON, TEXAS

YEAR	TEAM	STARTS	GAMES	WON	LOST	PCT	ER	ERA	INNINGS PITCHED	STRIKE-OUTS	WALKS	HITS ALLOWED	HRS ALLOWED	COMP. GAMES	SHUT-OUTS	SAVES
1989	Atl-N	0	20	0	1	.000	4	1.50	24	27	8	17	0	0	0	7
1990	Atl-N	0	7	0	3	.000	14	18.00	7	7	4	16	1	0	0	2
1991	Atl-N	0	74	5	5	.500	25	2.88	78	54	21	62	6	0	0	7
1992	Atl-N	0	65	5	4	.556	29	4.10	63 2/3	44	20	59	6	0	0	8
1993	Atl-N	0	63	4	6	.400	27	4.67	52	43	29	51	4	0	0	27
1994	Atl-N	0	49	3	1	.750	18	3.60	45 2/3	35	26	41	2	0	0	3
1995	Atl-N	0	26	1	1	.500	12	5.68	19 1/3	13	6	31	3	0	0	1
1995	Bos-A	0	22	1	0	1.000	7	3.00	21	10	8	17	3	0	0	0
1996	Bos-A	0	59	4	3	.571	24	3.86	56 1/3	46	23	58	9	0	0	1
1996	Tex-A	0	22	0	1	.000	8	3.27	22 1/3	14	4	20	2	0	0	0
1997	**NY-A**	**0**	**64**	**6**	**1**	**.857**	**19**	**2.59**	**66 2/3**	**70**	**34**	**50**	**3**	**0**	**0**	**3**
1998	**NY-A**	**0**	**67**	**4**	**1**	**.800**	**48**	**5.47**	**79**	**69**	**26**	**71**	**13**	**0**	**0**	**6**
1999	**NY-A**	**1**	**73**	**2**	**2**	**.500**	**30**	**4.35**	**62 1/3**	**59**	**18**	**71**	**5**	**0**	**0**	**0**
2000	**NY-A**	**0**	**69**	**2**	**3**	**.400**	**31**	**4.10**	**68**	**75**	**24**	**68**	**5**	**0**	**0**	**0**
Career Average		0	49	3	2	.536	21	4.00	47	40	18	45	4	0	0	5
Yankee Average		**0**	**68**	**4**	**2**	**.667**	**32**	**4.19**	**69**	**68**	**26**	**65**	**7**	**0**	**0**	**2**
Career Total		1	680	37	32	.536	296	4.00	665 1/3	566	251	632	62	0	0	65
Yankee Total		**1**	**273**	**14**	**7**	**.667**	**128**	**4.19**	**275**	**273**	**102**	**260**	**26**	**0**	**0**	**9**

Starr, Richard Eugene
HEIGHT: 6'3" RIGHTHANDER BORN: 3/2/1921 KITTANNING, PENNSYLVANIA

YEAR	TEAM	STARTS	GAMES	WON	LOST	PCT	ER	ERA	INNINGS PITCHED	STRIKE-OUTS	WALKS	HITS ALLOWED	HRS ALLOWED	COMP. GAMES	SHUT-OUTS	SAVES
1947	**NY-A**	1	4	1	0	1.000	2	1.46	12 1/3	1	8	12	1	1	0	0
1948	**NY-A**	0	1	0	0	—	1	4.50	2	2	2	0	0	0	0	0
1949	StL-A	8	30	1	7	.125	40	4.32	83 1/3	44	48	96	6	1	1	0
1950	StL-A	16	32	7	5	.583	69	5.02	123 2/3	30	74	140	11	4	1	2
1951	StL-A	9	15	2	5	.286	51	7.40	62	26	42	66	10	0	0	0
1951	Was-A	11	11	1	7	.125	38	5.58	61 1/3	17	24	76	12	1	0	0
Career Average		8	16	2	4	.333	34	5.25	57	20	33	65	7	1	0	0
Yankee Average		**1**	**3**	**1**	**0**	**1.000**	**2**	**1.88**	**7**	**2**	**5**	**6**	**1**	**1**	**0**	**0**
Career Total		45	93	12	24	.333	201	5.25	344 2/3	120	198	390	40	7	2	2
Yankee Total		**1**	**5**	**1**	**0**	**1.000**	**3**	**1.88**	**14 1/3**	**3**	**10**	**12**	**1**	**1**	**0**	**0**

Stine, Lee Elbert
HEIGHT: 5'11" RIGHTHANDER BORN: 11/17/1913 STILLWATER, OKLAHOMA

YEAR	TEAM	STARTS	GAMES	WON	LOST	PCT	ER	ERA	INNINGS PITCHED	STRIKE-OUTS	WALKS	HITS ALLOWED	HRS ALLOWED	COMP. GAMES	SHUT-OUTS	SAVES
1934	Chi-A	0	4	0	0	—	10	8.18	11	8	10	11	2	0	0	0
1935	Chi-A	0	1	0	0	—	2	9.00	2	1	3	2	1	0	0	0
1936	Cin-N	13	40	3	8	.273	68	5.03	121 2/3	26	41	157	6	5	1	2
1938	**NY-A**	0	4	0	0	—	1	1.04	8 2/3	4	1	9	0	0	0	0
Career Average		3	12	1	2	.273	20	5.09	36	10	14	45	2	1	0	1
Yankee Average		**0**	**4**	**0**	**0**	**—**	**1**	**1.04**	**8 2/3**	**4**	**1**	**9**	**0**	**0**	**0**	**0**
Career Total		13	49	3	8	.273	81	5.09	143 1/3	39	55	179	9	5	1	2
Yankee Total		**0**	**4**	**0**	**0**	**—**	**1**	**1.04**	**8 2/3**	**4**	**1**	**9**	**0**	**0**	**0**	**0**

Stoddard, Timothy Paul
HEIGHT: 6'7" RIGHTHANDER BORN: 1/24/1953 E. CHICAGO, INDIANA

YEAR	TEAM	STARTS	GAMES	WON	LOST	PCT	ER	ERA	INNINGS PITCHED	STRIKE-OUTS	WALKS	HITS ALLOWED	HRS ALLOWED	COMP. GAMES	SHUT-OUTS	SAVES
1975	Chi-A	0	1	0	0	—	1	9.00	1	0	0	2	1	0	0	0
1978	Bal-A	0	8	0	1	.000	12	6.00	18	14	8	22	3	0	0	0
1979	Bal-A	0	29	3	1	.750	11	1.71	58	47	19	44	3	0	0	3
1980	Bal-A	0	64	5	3	.625	24	2.51	86	64	38	72	2	0	0	26
1981	Bal-A	0	31	4	2	.667	16	3.86	37 1/3	32	18	38	6	0	0	7
1982	Bal-A	0	50	3	4	.429	25	4.02	56	42	29	53	4	0	0	12
1983	Bal-A	0	47	4	3	.571	39	6.09	57 2/3	50	29	65	10	0	0	9
1984	Chi-N	0	58	10	6	.625	39	3.82	92	87	57	77	9	0	0	7
1985	SD-N	0	44	1	6	.143	31	4.65	60	42	37	63	3	0	0	1
1986	SD-N	0	30	1	3	.250	19	3.77	45 1/3	47	34	33	6	0	0	0
1986	**NY-A**	0	24	4	1	.800	21	3.83	49 1/3	34	23	41	6	0	0	0
1987	**NY-A**	0	57	4	3	.571	36	3.50	92 2/3	78	30	83	13	0	0	8
1988	**NY-A**	0	28	2	2	.500	39	6.38	55	33	27	62	5	0	0	3
1989	Cle-A	0	14	0	0	—	7	2.95	21 1/3	12	7	25	1	0	0	0
Career Average		0	35	3	3	.539	23	3.95	52	42	25	49	5	0	0	5
Yankee Average		**0**	**55**	**5**	**3**	**.625**	**48**	**4.39**	**99**	**73**	**40**	**93**	**12**	**0**	**0**	**6**
Career Total		0	485	41	35	.539	320	3.95	729 2/3	582	356	680	72	0	0	76
Yankee Total		**0**	**109**	**10**	**6**	**.625**	**96**	**4.39**	**197**	**145**	**80**	**186**	**24**	**0**	**0**	**11**

Stottlemyre, Melvin Leon Sr.
HEIGHT: 6'1" RIGHTHANDER BORN: 11/13/1941 HAZELTON, MISSOURI

YEAR	TEAM	STARTS	GAMES	WON	LOST	PCT	ER	ERA	INNINGS PITCHED	STRIKE-OUTS	WALKS	HITS ALLOWED	HRS ALLOWED	COMP. GAMES	SHUT-OUTS	SAVES
1964	**NY-A**	12	13	9	3	.750	22	2.06	96	49	35	77	3	5	2	0
1965	**NY-A**	37	37	20	9	.690	85	2.63	291	155	88	250	18	18	4	0
1966	**NY-A**	35	37	12	20	.375	106	3.80	251	146	82	239	18	9	3	1

(continued)

Melvin Leon "Mel" Stottlemyre, rhp, 1964–74

Mel Stottlemyre was the best pitcher the Yankees had in the late 1960s and early '70s, when the team was at one of the lowest spots in franchise history.

Stottlemyre, born November 13, 1941, in Hazelton, Missouri, was called up to the Yankees in 1964, in the middle of a heated pennant race. Several members of Yankee management were against bringing up the 23-year-old righty, believing he needed another year of seasoning. But the Yankee pitching staff was battling injuries and inconsistency, and manager Yogi Berra believed a fresh, live arm would be a key to the race.

He was right. Stottlemyre went 9-3 down the stretch that year as the Yankees held off Baltimore and the White Sox for the pennant. His 2.06 ERA was the lowest on the Yankee staff.

Stottlemyre was terrific for New York right out of the minors. He was a cool customer with excellent control. He was not a power pitcher,

however. His strength was inducing batters to hit into ground outs.

He was a legendary workhorse. In a nine-year span from 1965 to 1973, he led the team in innings pitched eight times. He led the American League in complete games twice, in 1965 and in 1969. He started a stunning 272 games without missing a scheduled start.

But the Yankees of Stottlemyre's era were not always winners. In fact, though Mel won 20 games three times in his career, in 1965, 1968 and 1969, he also lost 20 in 1965 and lost 18 games in 1972. New York finished first only once during Stottlemyre's career, in 1964.

Stottlemyre retired after the 1974 season and is third among Yankee pitchers in innings pitched with 2,662, sixth in wins with 164, fifth in strikeouts with 1,257, second in shutouts behind Whitey Ford with 40 and ninth in complete games with 152 and ERA with a 2.97 mark.

Following his retirement, Stottlemyre has worked as a pitching coach for several teams. Since 1996, he has held that position with the Yankees.

(continued)

YEAR	TEAM	STARTS	GAMES	WON	LOST	PCT	ER	ERA	INNINGS PITCHED	STRIKE-OUTS	WALKS	HITS ALLOWED	HRS ALLOWED	COMP. GAMES	SHUT-OUTS	SAVES
1967	NY-A	36	36	15	15	.500	84	2.96	255	151	88	235	20	10	4	0
1968	NY-A	36	36	21	12	.636	76	2.45	278 2/3	140	65	243	21	19	6	0
1969	NY-A	39	39	20	14	.588	95	2.82	303	113	97	267	19	24	3	0
1970	NY-A	37	37	15	13	.536	93	3.09	271	126	84	262	23	14	0	0
1971	NY-A	35	35	16	12	.571	86	2.87	269 2/3	132	69	234	16	19	7	0
1972	NY-A	36	36	14	18	.438	93	3.22	260	110	85	250	13	9	7	0
1973	NY-A	38	38	16	16	.500	93	3.07	273	95	79	259	13	19	4	0
1974	NY-A	15	16	6	7	.462	45	3.58	113	40	37	119	7	6	0	0
Career Average		32	33	15	13	.541	80	2.97	242	114	74	221	16	14	4	0
Yankee Average		32	33	15	13	.541	80	2.97	242	114	74	221	16	14	4	0
Career Total		356	360	164	139	.541	878	2.97	2661 1/3	1257	809	2435	171	152	40	1
Yankee Total		356	360	164	139	.541	878	2.97	2661 1/3	1257	809	2435	171	152	40	1

Stowe, Harold Rudolph

HEIGHT: 6'0" LEFTHANDER BORN: 8/29/1937 GASTONIA, NORTH CAROLINA

YEAR	TEAM	STARTS	GAMES	WON	LOST	PCT	ER	ERA	INNINGS PITCHED	STRIKE-OUTS	WALKS	HITS ALLOWED	HRS ALLOWED	COMP. GAMES	SHUT-OUTS	SAVES
1960	NY-A	0	1	0	0	—	1	9.00	1	0	1	0	0	0	0	0
Career Average		0	1	0	0	—	1	9.00	1	0	1	0	0	0	0	0
Yankee Average		0	1	0	0	—	1	9.00	1	0	1	0	0	0	0	0
Career Total		0	1	0	0	—	1	9.00	1	0	1	0	0	0	0	0
Yankee Total		0	1	0	0	—	1	9.00	1	0	1	0	0	0	0	0

Stuart, Marlin Henry

HEIGHT: 6'2"   RIGHTHANDER   BORN: 8/8/1918 PARAGOULD, ARKANSAS   DIED: 6/16/1994 PARAGOULD, ARKANSAS

YEAR	TEAM	STARTS	GAMES	WON	LOST	PCT	ER	ERA	INNINGS PITCHED	STRIKE-OUTS	WALKS	HITS ALLOWED	HRS ALLOWED	COMP. GAMES	SHUT-OUTS	SAVES
1949	Det-A	2	14	0	2	.000	30	9.10	29 2/3	14	35	39	3	0	0	0
1950	Det-A	1	19	3	1	.750	27	5.56	43 2/3	19	22	59	6	0	0	2
1951	Det-A	15	29	4	6	.400	52	3.77	124	46	71	119	9	5	0	1
1952	Det-A	9	30	3	2	.600	50	4.93	91 1/3	32	48	91	8	2	0	1
1952	StL-A	2	12	1	2	.333	12	4.15	26	13	9	26	3	0	0	1
1953	StL-A	2	60	8	2	.800	50	3.94	114 1/3	46	44	136	6	0	0	7
1954	Bal-A	0	22	1	2	.333	19	4.46	38 1/3	13	15	46	2	0	0	2
1954	**NY-A**	**0**	**10**	**3**	**0**	**1.000**	**11**	**5.40**	**18 1/3**	**2**	**12**	**28**	**0**	**0**	**0**	**1**
Career Average		4	25	3	2	.575	31	4.65	61	23	32	68	5	1	0	2
Yankee Average		**0**	**10**	**3**	**0**	**1.000**	**11**	**5.40**	**18 1/3**	**2**	**12**	**28**	**0**	**0**	**0**	**1**
Career Total		31	196	23	17	.575	251	4.65	485 2/3	185	256	544	37	7	0	15
Yankee Total		**0**	**10**	**3**	**0**	**1.000**	**11**	**5.40**	**18 1/3**	**2**	**12**	**28**	**0**	**0**	**0**	**1**

Sturdivant, Thomas Virgil (Snake)

HEIGHT: 6'0"   RIGHTHANDER   BORN: 4/28/1930 GORDON, KANSAS

YEAR	TEAM	STARTS	GAMES	WON	LOST	PCT	ER	ERA	INNINGS PITCHED	STRIKE-OUTS	WALKS	HITS ALLOWED	HRS ALLOWED	COMP. GAMES	SHUT-OUTS	SAVES
1955	**NY-A**	**1**	**33**	**1**	**3**	**.250**	**24**	**3.16**	**68 1/3**	**48**	**42**	**48**	**6**	**0**	**0**	**0**
1956	**NY-A**	**17**	**32**	**16**	**8**	**.667**	**58**	**3.30**	**158 1/3**	**110**	**52**	**134**	**15**	**6**	**2**	**5**
1957	**NY-A**	**28**	**28**	**16**	**6**	**.727**	**57**	**2.54**	**201 2/3**	**118**	**80**	**170**	**14**	**7**	**2**	**0**
1958	**NY-A**	**10**	**15**	**3**	**6**	**.333**	**33**	**4.20**	**70 2/3**	**41**	**38**	**77**	**6**	**0**	**0**	**0**
1959	**NY-A**	**3**	**7**	**0**	**2**	**.000**	**14**	**4.97**	**25 1/3**	**16**	**9**	**20**	**4**	**0**	**0**	**0**
1959	KC-A	3	36	2	6	.250	37	4.65	71 2/3	57	34	70	9	0	0	5
1960	Bos-A	3	40	3	3	.500	56	4.97	101 1/3	67	45	106	16	0	0	1
1961	Was-A	10	15	2	6	.250	41	4.61	80	39	40	67	6	1	1	0
1961	Pit-N	11	13	5	2	.714	27	2.84	85 1/3	45	17	81	6	6	1	1
1962	Pit-N	12	49	9	5	.643	52	3.73	125 1/3	76	39	120	12	2	1	2
1963	Pit-N	0	3	0	0	—	6	6.48	8 1/3	6	4	8	1	0	0	0
1963	KC-A	3	17	1	2	.333	22	3.74	53	26	17	47	3	0	0	0
1963	Det-A	0	28	1	2	.333	23	3.76	55	36	24	43	7	0	0	2
1964	KC-A	0	3	0	0	—	4	9.82	3 2/3	1	1	4	0	0	0	0
1964	NY-N	0	16	0	0	—	19	5.97	28 2/3	18	7	34	2	0	0	1
Career Average		7	22	4	3	.536	32	3.74	76	47	30	69	7	1	0	1
Yankee Average		**12**	**23**	**7**	**5**	**.590**	**37**	**3.19**	**105**	**67**	**44**	**90**	**9**	**3**	**1**	**1**
Career Total		101	335	59	51	.536	473	3.74	1137	704	449	1029	107	22	7	17
Yankee Total		**59**	**115**	**36**	**25**	**.590**	**186**	**3.19**	**524 1/3**	**333**	**221**	**449**	**45**	**13**	**4**	**5**

Sundra, Stephen Richard (Smokey)

HEIGHT: 6'2"   RIGHTHANDER   BORN: 3/27/1910 LUXOR, PENNSYLVANIA   DIED: 3/23/1952 CLEVELAND, OHIO

YEAR	TEAM	STARTS	GAMES	WON	LOST	PCT	ER	ERA	INNINGS PITCHED	STRIKE-OUTS	WALKS	HITS ALLOWED	HRS ALLOWED	COMP. GAMES	SHUT-OUTS	SAVES
1936	**NY-A**	**0**	**1**	**0**	**0**	**—**	**0**	**0.00**	**2**	**1**	**2**	**2**	**0**	**0**	**0**	**0**
1938	**NY-A**	**8**	**25**	**6**	**4**	**.600**	**50**	**4.80**	**93 2/3**	**33**	**43**	**107**	**7**	**3**	**0**	**0**
1939	**NY-A**	**11**	**24**	**11**	**1**	**.917**	**37**	**2.76**	**120 2/3**	**27**	**56**	**110**	**7**	**8**	**1**	**0**
1940	**NY-A**	**8**	**27**	**4**	**6**	**.400**	**61**	**5.53**	**99 1/3**	**26**	**42**	**121**	**11**	**2**	**0**	**2**
1941	Was-A	23	28	9	13	.409	99	5.29	168 1/3	50	61	203	11	11	0	0
1942	Was-A	4	6	1	3	.250	21	5.61	33 2/3	5	15	43	1	2	0	0
1942	StL-A	13	20	8	3	.727	47	3.82	110 2/3	26	29	122	2	6	0	0
1943	StL-A	29	32	15	11	.577	75	3.25	208	44	66	212	10	13	3	0
1944	StL-A	3	3	2	0	1.000	3	1.42	19	1	4	15	1	2	0	0
1946	StL-A	0	2	0	0	—	5	11.25	4	1	3	9	0	0	0	0
Career Average		10	17	6	4	.577	40	4.17	86	21	32	94	5	5	0	0
Yankee Average		**7**	**19**	**5**	**3**	**.656**	**37**	**4.22**	**79**	**22**	**36**	**85**	**6**	**3**	**0**	**1**
Career Total		99	168	56	41	.577	398	4.17	859 1/3	214	321	944	50	47	4	2
Yankee Total		**27**	**77**	**21**	**11**	**.656**	**148**	**4.22**	**315 2/3**	**87**	**143**	**340**	**25**	**13**	**1**	**2**

Talbot, Frederick Lealand (Bubby)
HEIGHT: 6'2" RIGHTHANDER BORN: 6/28/1941 WASHINGTON, D.C.

YEAR	TEAM	STARTS	GAMES	WON	LOST	PCT	ER	ERA	INNINGS PITCHED	STRIKE-OUTS	WALKS	HITS ALLOWED	HRS ALLOWED	COMP. GAMES	SHUT-OUTS	SAVES
1963	Chi-A	0	1	0	0	—	1	3.00	3	2	4	2	0	0	0	0
1964	Chi-A	12	17	4	5	.444	31	3.70	75 1/3	34	20	83	7	3	2	0
1965	KC-A	33	39	10	12	.455	91	4.14	198	117	86	188	25	2	1	0
1966	KC-A	11	11	4	4	.500	36	4.79	67 2/3	37	28	65	6	0	0	0
1966	**NY-A**	**19**	**23**	**7**	**7**	**.500**	**57**	**4.13**	**124 1/3**	**48**	**45**	**123**	**16**	**3**	**0**	**0**
1967	**NY-A**	**22**	**29**	**6**	**8**	**.429**	**65**	**4.22**	**138 2/3**	**61**	**54**	**132**	**20**	**2**	**0**	**0**
1968	**NY-A**	**11**	**29**	**1**	**9**	**.100**	**37**	**3.36**	**99**	**67**	**42**	**89**	**6**	**1**	**0**	**0**
1969	**NY-A**	**0**	**8**	**0**	**0**	**—**	**7**	**5.11**	**12 1/3**	**7**	**6**	**13**	**1**	**0**	**0**	**0**
1969	Oak-A	2	12	1	2	.333	11	5.21	19	9	7	22	2	0	0	1
1969	Sea-A	16	25	5	8	.385	53	4.16	114 2/3	67	41	125	12	1	1	0
1970	Oak-A	0	1	0	1	.000	2	10.80	1 2/3	0	1	2	1	0	0	0
Career Average		11	18	3	5	.404	36	4.12	78	41	30	77	9	1	0	0
Yankee Average		**13**	**22**	**4**	**6**	**.368**	**42**	**3.99**	**93**	**46**	**37**	**89**	**11**	**2**	**0**	**0**
Career Total		126	195	38	56	.404	391	4.12	853 2/3	449	334	844	96	12	4	1
Yankee Total		**52**	**89**	**14**	**24**	**.368**	**166**	**3.99**	**374 1/3**	**183**	**147**	**357**	**43**	**6**	**0**	**0**

Tamulis, Vitautris Casimirus (Vito)
HEIGHT: 5'9" LEFTHANDER BORN: 7/11/1911 CAMBRIDGE, MASSACHUSETTS DIED: 5/5/1974 NASHVILLE, TENNESSEE

YEAR	TEAM	STARTS	GAMES	WON	LOST	PCT	ER	ERA	INNINGS PITCHED	STRIKE-OUTS	WALKS	HITS ALLOWED	HRS ALLOWED	COMP. GAMES	SHUT-OUTS	SAVES
1934	**NY-A**	**1**	**1**	**1**	**0**	**1.000**	**0**	**0.00**	**9**	**5**	**1**	**7**	**0**	**1**	**1**	**0**
1935	**NY-A**	**19**	**30**	**10**	**5**	**.667**	**73**	**4.09**	**160 2/3**	**57**	**55**	**178**	**7**	**9**	**3**	**1**
1938	StL-A	2	3	0	3	.000	13	7.63	15 1/3	11	10	26	2	0	0	0
1938	Bro-N	18	38	12	6	.667	68	3.83	159 2/3	70	40	181	11	9	0	2
1939	Bro-N	17	39	9	8	.529	77	4.37	158 2/3	83	45	177	10	8	1	4
1940	Bro-N	12	41	8	5	.615	53	3.09	154 1/3	55	34	147	5	4	1	2
1941	Bro-N	0	12	0	0	—	9	3.68	22	8	10	21	1	0	0	1
1941	Phi-N	1	6	0	1	.000	12	9.00	12	5	7	21	1	0	0	0
Career Average		9	21	5	4	.588	38	3.97	86	37	25	95	5	4	1	1
Yankee Average		**10**	**16**	**6**	**3**	**.688**	**37**	**3.87**	**85**	**31**	**28**	**93**	**4**	**5**	**2**	**1**
Career Total		70	170	40	28	.588	305	3.97	691 2/3	294	202	758	37	31	6	10
Yankee Total		**20**	**31**	**11**	**5**	**.688**	**73**	**3.87**	**169 2/3**	**62**	**56**	**185**	**7**	**10**	**4**	**1**

Tanana, Frank Daryl
HEIGHT: 6'2" LEFTHANDER BORN: 7/3/1953 DETROIT, MICHIGAN

YEAR	TEAM	STARTS	GAMES	WON	LOST	PCT	ER	ERA	INNINGS PITCHED	STRIKE-OUTS	WALKS	HITS ALLOWED	HRS ALLOWED	COMP. GAMES	SHUT-OUTS	SAVES
1973	Cal-A	4	4	2	2	.500	9	3.08	26 1/3	22	8	20	2	2	1	0
1974	Cal-A	35	39	14	19	.424	93	3.12	268 2/3	180	77	262	27	12	4	0
1975	Cal-A	33	34	16	9	.640	75	2.62	257 1/3	269	73	211	21	16	5	0
1976	Cal-A	34	34	19	10	.655	78	2.43	288 1/3	261	73	212	24	23	2	0
1977	Cal-A	31	31	15	9	.625	68	2.54	241 1/3	205	61	201	19	20	7	0
1978	Cal-A	33	33	18	12	.600	97	3.65	239	137	60	239	26	10	4	0
1979	Cal-A	17	18	7	5	.583	39	3.89	90 1/3	46	25	93	9	2	1	0
1980	Cal-A	31	32	11	12	.478	94	4.15	204	113	45	223	18	7	0	0
1981	Bos-A	23	24	4	10	.286	63	4.01	141 1/3	78	43	142	17	5	2	0
1982	Tex-A	30	30	7	18	.280	91	4.21	194 1/3	87	55	199	16	7	0	0
1983	Tex-A	22	29	7	9	.438	56	3.16	159 1/3	108	49	144	14	3	0	0
1984	Tex-A	35	35	15	15	.500	89	3.25	246 1/3	141	81	234	30	9	1	0
1985	Tex-A	13	13	2	7	.222	51	5.91	77 2/3	52	23	89	15	0	0	0
1985	Det-A	20	20	10	7	.588	51	3.34	137 1/3	107	34	131	13	4	0	0
1986	Det-A	31	32	12	9	.571	87	4.16	188 1/3	119	65	196	23	3	1	0
1987	Det-A	34	34	15	10	.600	95	3.91	218 2/3	146	56	216	27	5	3	0
1988	Det-A	32	32	14	11	.560	95	4.21	203	127	64	213	25	2	0	0
1989	Det-A	33	33	10	14	.417	89	3.58	223 2/3	147	74	227	21	6	1	0
1990	Det-A	29	34	9	8	.529	104	5.31	176 1/3	114	66	190	25	1	0	1
1991	Det-A	33	33	13	12	.520	91	3.77	217 1/3	107	78	217	26	3	2	0

(continued)

(continued)

1992	Det-A	31	32	13	11	.542	91	4.39	186 2/3	91	90	188	22	3	0	0
1993	NY-N	29	29	7	15	.318	91	4.48	183	104	48	198	26	0	0	0
1993	**NY-A**	**3**	**3**	**0**	**2**	**.000**	**7**	**3.20**	**19 2/3**	**12**	**7**	**18**	**2**	**0**	**0**	**0**
Career Average		27	28	10	10	.504	74	3.66	182	121	55	177	19	6	1	0
Yankee Average		**3**	**3**	**0**	**2**	**.000**	**7**	**3.20**	**19 2/3**	**12**	**7**	**18**	**2**	**0**	**0**	**0**
Career Total		616	638	240	236	.504	1704	3.66	4188 1/3	2773	1255	4063	448	143	34	1
Yankee Total		**3**	**3**	**0**	**2**	**.000**	**7**	**3.20**	**19 2/3**	**12**	**7**	**18**	**2**	**0**	**0**	**0**

Tannehill, Jesse Niles

HEIGHT: 5'8" LEFTHANDER BORN: 7/14/1874 DAYTON, KENTUCKY DIED: 9/22/1956 DAYTON, KENTUCKY

YEAR	TEAM	STARTS	GAMES	WON	LOST	PCT	ER	ERA	INNINGS PITCHED	STRIKE-OUTS	WALKS	HITS ALLOWED	HRS ALLOWED	COMP. GAMES	SHUT-OUTS	SAVES
1894	Cin-N	2	5	1	1	.500	23	7.14	29	7	16	37	1	1	0	1
1897	Pit-N	16	21	9	7	.563	67	4.25	142	40	24	172	1	11	1	1
1898	Pit-N	38	43	24	14	.632	107	2.95	326 2/3	93	63	338	2	34	5	2
1899	Pit-N	36	41	23	15	.605	95	2.73	313	61	51	354	4	33	3	2
1900	Pit-N	27	29	20	6	.769	75	2.88	234	50	43	247	3	23	2	0
1901	Pit-N	30	32	18	10	.643	61	2.18	252 1/3	118	36	240	1	25	4	1
1902	Pit-N	24	26	20	6	.769	50	1.95	231	100	25	203	0	23	2	0
1903	**NY-A**	**31**	**32**	**15**	**15**	**.500**	**87**	**3.27**	**239 2/3**	**106**	**34**	**258**	**3**	**22**	**2**	**0**
1904	Bos-A	31	33	21	11	.656	64	2.04	281 2/3	116	33	256	5	30	4	0
1905	Bos-A	32	37	22	9	.710	75	2.48	271 2/3	113	59	238	7	27	6	0
1906	Bos-A	26	27	13	11	.542	69	3.16	196 1/3	82	39	207	9	18	2	0
1907	Bos-A	16	18	6	7	.462	36	2.47	131	29	20	131	3	10	2	1
1908	Bos-A	1	1	0	0	—	2	3.60	5	2	3	4	0	0	0	0
1908	Was-A	9	10	2	4	.333	30	3.77	71 2/3	14	23	77	0	5	0	0
1909	Was-A	2	3	1	1	.500	8	3.43	21	8	5	19	1	2	1	0
1911	Cin-N	0	1	0	0	—	3	6.23	4 1/3	1	3	6	0	0	0	0
Career Average		20	22	12	7	.625	53	2.79	172	59	30	174	3	17	2	1
Yankee Average		**31**	**32**	**15**	**15**	**.500**	**87**	**3.27**	**239 2/3**	**106**	**34**	**258**	**3**	**22**	**2**	**0**
Career Total		321	359	195	117	.625	852	2.79	2750 1/3	940	477	2287	40	264	34	8
Yankee Total		**31**	**32**	**15**	**15**	**.500**	**87**	**3.27**	**239 2/3**	**106**	**34**	**258**	**3**	**22**	**2**	**0**

Taylor, Wade Eric

HEIGHT: 6'1" RIGHTHANDER BORN: 10/19/1965 MOBILE, ALABAMA

YEAR	TEAM	STARTS	GAMES	WON	LOST	PCT	ER	ERA	INNINGS PITCHED	STRIKE-OUTS	WALKS	HITS ALLOWED	HRS ALLOWED	COMP. GAMES	SHUT-OUTS	SAVES
1991	**NY-A**	**22**	**23**	**7**	**12**	**.368**	**81**	**6.27**	**116 1/3**	**72**	**53**	**144**	**13**	**0**	**0**	**0**
Career Average		22	23	7	12	.368	81	6.27	116 1/3	72	53	144	13	0	0	0
Yankee Average		**22**	**23**	**7**	**12**	**.368**	**81**	**6.27**	**116 1/3**	**72**	**53**	**144**	**13**	**0**	**0**	**0**
Career Total		22	23	7	12	.368	81	6.27	116 1/3	72	53	144	13	0	0	0
Yankee Total		**22**	**23**	**7**	**12**	**.368**	**81**	**6.27**	**116 1/3**	**72**	**53**	**144**	**13**	**0**	**0**	**0**

Terrell, Charles Walter (Walt)

HEIGHT: 6'2" RIGHTHANDER BORN: 5/11/1958 JEFFERSONVILLE, INDIANA

YEAR	TEAM	STARTS	GAMES	WON	LOST	PCT	ER	ERA	INNINGS PITCHED	STRIKE-OUTS	WALKS	HITS ALLOWED	HRS ALLOWED	COMP. GAMES	SHUT-OUTS	SAVES
1982	NY-N	3	3	0	3	.000	8	3.43	21	8	14	22	2	0	0	0
1983	NY-N	20	21	8	8	.500	53	3.57	133 2/3	59	55	123	7	4	2	0
1984	NY-N	33	33	11	12	.478	84	3.52	215	114	80	232	16	3	1	0
1985	Det-A	34	34	15	10	.600	98	3.85	229	130	95	221	9	5	3	0
1986	Det-A	33	34	15	12	.556	110	4.56	217 1/3	93	98	199	30	9	2	0
1987	Det-A	35	35	17	10	.630	110	4.05	244 2/3	143	94	254	30	10	1	0
1988	Det-A	29	29	7	16	.304	91	3.97	206 1/3	84	78	199	20	11	1	0
1989	SD-N	19	19	5	13	.278	55	4.01	123 1/3	63	26	134	14	4	1	0
1989	**NY-A**	**13**	**13**	**6**	**5**	**.545**	**48**	**5.20**	**83**	**30**	**24**	**102**	**9**	**1**	**1**	**0**
1990	Pit-N	16	16	2	7	.222	54	5.88	82 2/3	34	33	98	13	0	0	0

(continued)

(continued)

YEAR	TEAM	STARTS	GAMES	WON	LOST	PCT	ER	ERA	INNINGS PITCHED	STRIKE-OUTS	WALKS	HITS ALLOWED	HRS ALLOWED	COMP. GAMES	SHUT-OUTS	SAVES
1990	Det-A	12	13	6	4	.600	38	4.54	75 1/3	30	24	86	7	0	0	0
1991	Det-A	33	35	12	14	.462	103	4.24	218 2/3	80	79	257	16	8	2	0
1992	Det-A	14	36	7	10	.412	79	5.20	136 2/3	61	48	163	14	1	0	0
Career Average		23	25	9	10	.472	72	4.22	152	71	58	161	14	4	1	0
Yankee Average		**13**	**13**	**6**	**5**	**.545**	**48**	**5.20**	**83**	**30**	**24**	**102**	**9**	**1**	**1**	**0**
Career Total		294	321	111	124	.472	931	4.22	1986 2/3	929	748	2090	187	56	14	0
Yankee Total		**13**	**13**	**6**	**5**	**.545**	**48**	**5.20**	**83**	**30**	**24**	**102**	**9**	**1**	**1**	**0**

Terry, Ralph Willard

HEIGHT: 6'3" RIGHTHANDER BORN: 1/9/1936 BIG CABIN, OKLAHOMA

YEAR	TEAM	STARTS	GAMES	WON	LOST	PCT	ER	ERA	INNINGS PITCHED	STRIKE-OUTS	WALKS	HITS ALLOWED	HRS ALLOWED	COMP. GAMES	SHUT-OUTS	SAVES
1956	**NY-A**	**3**	**3**	**1**	**2**	**.333**	**14**	**9.45**	**13 1/3**	**8**	**11**	**17**	**2**	**0**	**0**	**0**
1957	**NY-A**	**2**	**7**	**1**	**1**	**.500**	**7**	**3.05**	**20 2/3**	**7**	**8**	**18**	**1**	**1**	**1**	**0**
1957	KC-A	19	21	4	11	.267	49	3.38	130 2/3	80	47	119	15	3	1	0
1958	KC-A	33	40	11	13	.458	102	4.24	216 2/3	134	61	217	29	8	3	2
1959	KC-A	7	9	2	4	.333	27	5.24	46 1/3	35	19	56	9	2	0	0
1959	**NY-A**	**16**	**24**	**3**	**7**	**.300**	**48**	**3.39**	**127 1/3**	**55**	**30**	**130**	**7**	**5**	**1**	**0**
1960	**NY-A**	**23**	**35**	**10**	**8**	**.556**	**63**	**3.40**	**166 2/3**	**92**	**52**	**149**	**15**	**7**	**3**	**1**
1961	**NY-A**	**27**	**31**	**16**	**3**	**.842**	**66**	**3.15**	**188 1/3**	**86**	**42**	**162**	**19**	**9**	**2**	**0**
1962	**NY-A**	**39**	**43**	**23**	**12**	**.657**	**106**	**3.19**	**298 2/3**	**176**	**57**	**257**	**40**	**14**	**3**	**2**
1963	**NY-A**	**37**	**40**	**17**	**15**	**.531**	**96**	**3.22**	**268**	**114**	**39**	**246**	**29**	**18**	**3**	**1**
1964	**NY-A**	**14**	**27**	**7**	**11**	**.389**	**58**	**4.54**	**115**	**77**	**31**	**130**	**20**	**2**	**1**	**4**
1965	Cle-A	26	30	11	6	.647	68	3.69	165 2/3	84	23	154	22	6	2	0
1966	NY-N	1	11	0	1	.000	13	4.74	24 2/3	14	11	27	1	0	0	1
1966	KC-A	10	15	1	5	.167	27	3.80	64	33	15	65	7	0	0	0
1967	NY-N	0	2	0	0	—	0	0.00	3 1/3	5	0	1	0	0	0	0
Career Average		17	23	7	7	.519	50	3.62	123	67	30	117	14	5	1	1
Yankee Average		**20**	**26**	**10**	**7**	**.569**	**57**	**3.44**	**150**	**77**	**34**	**139**	**17**	**7**	**2**	**1**
Career Total		257	338	107	99	.519	744	3.62	1849 1/3	1000	446	1748	216	75	20	11
Yankee Total		**161**	**210**	**78**	**59**	**.569**	**458**	**3.44**	**1198**	**615**	**270**	**1109**	**133**	**56**	**14**	**8**

Tessmer, Jay W.

HEIGHT: 6'3" RIGHTHANDER BORN: 12/26/1971 MEADVILLE, PENNSYLVANIA

YEAR	TEAM	STARTS	GAMES	WON	LOST	PCT	ER	ERA	INNINGS PITCHED	STRIKE-OUTS	WALKS	HITS ALLOWED	HRS ALLOWED	COMP. GAMES	SHUT-OUTS	SAVES
1998	**NY-A**	**0**	**7**	**1**	**0**	**1.000**	**3**	**3.12**	**8 2/3**	**6**	**4**	**4**	**1**	**0**	**0**	**0**
1999	**NY-A**	**0**	**6**	**0**	**0**	**—**	**11**	**16.50**	**6**	**3**	**4**	**16**	**1**	**0**	**0**	**0**
2000	**NY-A**	**0**	**7**	**0**	**0**	**—**	**5**	**6.75**	**6 2/3**	**5**	**1**	**73**	**5**	**0**	**0**	**0**
Career Average		0	7	0	0	1.000	6	7.77	7	5	3	31	2	0	0	0
Yankee Average		**0**	**7**	**0**	**0**	**1.000**	**6**	**7.77**	**7**	**5**	**3**	**31**	**2**	**0**	**0**	**0**
Career Total		0	20	1	0	1.000	19	7.77	22	14	9	93	7	0	0	0
Yankee Total		**0**	**20**	**1**	**0**	**1.000**	**19**	**7.77**	**22**	**14**	**9**	**93**	**7**	**0**	**0**	**0**

Tewksbury, Robert Alan

HEIGHT: 6'4" RIGHTHANDER BORN: 11/30/1960 CONCORD, NEW HAMPSHIRE

YEAR	TEAM	STARTS	GAMES	WON	LOST	PCT	ER	ERA	INNINGS PITCHED	STRIKE-OUTS	WALKS	HITS ALLOWED	HRS ALLOWED	COMP. GAMES	SHUT-OUTS	SAVES
1986	**NY-A**	**20**	**23**	**9**	**5**	**.643**	**48**	**3.31**	**130 1/3**	**49**	**31**	**144**	**8**	**2**	**0**	**0**
1987	**NY-A**	**6**	**8**	**1**	**4**	**.200**	**25**	**6.75**	**33 1/3**	**12**	**7**	**47**	**5**	**0**	**0**	**0**
1987	Chi-N	3	7	0	4	.000	13	6.50	18	10	13	32	1	0	0	0
1988	Chi-N	1	1	0	0	—	3	8.10	3 1/3	1	2	6	1	0	0	0
1989	StL-N	4	7	1	0	1.000	11	3.30	30	17	10	25	2	1	1	0
1990	StL-N	20	28	10	9	.526	56	3.47	145 1/3	50	15	151	7	3	2	1
1991	StL-N	30	30	11	12	.478	69	3.25	191	75	38	206	13	3	0	0
1992	StL-N	32	33	16	5	.762	56	2.16	233	91	20	217	15	5	0	0
1993	StL-N	32	32	17	10	.630	91	3.83	213 2/3	97	20	258	15	2	0	0
1994	StL-N	24	24	12	10	.545	92	5.34	155	79	22	190	19	4	0	0

(continued)

(continued)

1995	Tex-A	21	21	8	7	.533	66	4.60	129 ⅔	53	20	169	8	4	0	0
1996	SD-N	33	36	10	10	.500	99	4.33	206 ⅔	126	43	224	17	1	0	0
1997	Min-A	26	26	8	13	.381	79	4.23	168 ⅔	92	31	200	12	5	0	0
1998	Min-A	25	26	7	13	.350	79	4.80	148 ⅓	60	20	174	19	1	0	0
Career Average		20	22	8	7	.519	56	3.93	129	58	21	146	10	2	0	0
Yankee Average		**13**	**16**	**5**	**5**	**.526**	**37**	**4.01**	**82**	**31**	**19**	**96**	**7**	**1**	**0**	**0**
Career Total		277	302	110	102	.519	787	3.93	1806	812	292	2043	142	31	3	1
Yankee Total		**26**	**31**	**10**	**9**	**.526**	**73**	**4.01**	**163 ⅔**	**61**	**38**	**191**	**13**	**2**	**0**	**0**

Thomas, Myles Lewis (Duck Eye)

HEIGHT: 5'9"   RIGHTHANDER   BORN: 10/22/1897 STATE COLLEGE, PENNSYLVANIA   DIED: 12/12/1963 TOLEDO, OHIO

YEAR	TEAM	STARTS	GAMES	WON	LOST	PCT	ER	ERA	INNINGS PITCHED	STRIKE-OUTS	WALKS	HITS ALLOWED	HRS ALLOWED	COMP. GAMES	SHUT-OUTS	SAVES
1926	**NY-A**	**13**	**33**	**6**	**6**	**.500**	**66**	**4.23**	**140 ⅓**	**38**	**65**	**140**	**6**	**3**	**0**	**0**
1927	**NY-A**	**9**	**21**	**7**	**4**	**.636**	**48**	**4.87**	**88 ⅔**	**25**	**43**	**111**	**4**	**1**	**0**	**0**
1928	**NY-A**	**1**	**12**	**1**	**0**	**1.000**	**12**	**3.41**	**31 ⅔**	**10**	**9**	**33**	**3**	**0**	**0**	**0**
1929	**NY-A**	**1**	**5**	**0**	**2**	**.000**	**18**	**10.80**	**15**	**3**	**9**	**27**	**1**	**0**	**0**	**0**
1929	Was-A	14	22	7	8	.467	49	3.52	125 ⅓	33	48	139	3	7	0	2
1930	Was-A	2	12	2	2	.500	31	8.29	33 ⅔	12	15	49	3	0	0	0
Career Average		7	18	4	4	.511	37	4.64	72	20	32	83	3	2	0	0
Yankee Average		**6**	**18**	**4**	**3**	**.538**	**36**	**4.70**	**69**	**19**	**32**	**78**	**4**	**1**	**0**	**0**
Career Total		40	105	23	22	.511	224	4.64	434 ⅔	121	189	499	20	11	0	2
Yankee Total		**24**	**71**	**14**	**12**	**.538**	**144**	**4.70**	**275 ⅔**	**76**	**126**	**311**	**14**	**4**	**0**	**0**

Thomas, Stanley Brown

HEIGHT: 6'2"   RIGHTHANDER   BORN: 7/11/1949 RUMFORD, MAINE

YEAR	TEAM	STARTS	GAMES	WON	LOST	PCT	ER	ERA	INNINGS PITCHED	STRIKE-OUTS	WALKS	HITS ALLOWED	HRS ALLOWED	COMP. GAMES	SHUT-OUTS	SAVES
1974	Tex-A	0	12	0	0	—	10	6.59	13 ⅔	8	6	22	1	0	0	0
1975	Tex-A	1	46	4	4	.500	28	3.10	81 ⅓	46	34	72	2	0	0	3
1976	Cle-A	7	37	4	4	.500	27	2.30	105 ⅔	54	41	88	5	2	0	6
1977	Sea-A	9	13	2	6	.250	39	6.02	58 ⅓	14	25	74	8	1	0	0
1977	**NY-A**	**0**	**3**	**1**	**0**	**1.000**	**5**	**7.11**	**6 ⅓**	**1**	**4**	**7**	**0**	**0**	**0**	**0**
Career Average		3	22	2	3	.440	22	3.70	53	25	22	53	3	1	0	2
Yankee Average		**0**	**3**	**1**	**0**	**1.000**	**5**	**7.11**	**6 ⅓**	**1**	**4**	**7**	**0**	**0**	**0**	**0**
Career Total		17	111	11	14	.440	109	3.70	265 ⅓	123	110	263	16	3	0	9
Yankee Total		**0**	**3**	**1**	**0**	**1.000**	**5**	**7.11**	**6 ⅓**	**1**	**4**	**7**	**0**	**0**	**0**	**0**

Thompson, Thomas Carl

HEIGHT: 5'9"   RIGHTHANDER   BORN: 11/7/1889 SPRING CITY, TENNESSEE   DIED: 1/16/1963 LAJOLLA, CALIFORNIA

YEAR	TEAM	STARTS	GAMES	WON	LOST	PCT	ER	ERA	INNINGS PITCHED	STRIKE-OUTS	WALKS	HITS ALLOWED	HRS ALLOWED	COMP. GAMES	SHUT-OUTS	SAVES
1912	NY-A	2	7	0	2	.000	22	6.06	32 ⅔	15	13	43	0	1	0	0
Career Average		2	7	0	2	.000	22	6.06	32 ⅔	15	13	43	0	1	0	0
Yankee Average		**2**	**7**	**0**	**2**	**.000**	**22**	**6.06**	**32 ⅔**	**15**	**13**	**43**	**0**	**1**	**0**	**0**
Career Total		2	7	0	2	.000	22	6.06	32 ⅔	15	13	43	0	1	0	0
Yankee Total		**2**	**7**	**0**	**2**	**.000**	**22**	**6.06**	**32 ⅔**	**15**	**13**	**43**	**0**	**1**	**0**	**0**

Thormahlen, Herbert Ehler (Hank *or* Lefty)

HEIGHT: 6'0"   LEFTHANDER   BORN: 7/5/1896 JERSEY CITY, NEW JERSEY   DIED: 2/6/1955 LOS ANGELES, CALIFORNIA

YEAR	TEAM	STARTS	GAMES	WON	LOST	PCT	ER	ERA	INNINGS PITCHED	STRIKE-OUTS	WALKS	HITS ALLOWED	HRS ALLOWED	COMP. GAMES	SHUT-OUTS	SAVES
1917	**NY-A**	**1**	**1**	**0**	**1**	**.000**	**2**	**2.25**	**8**	**5**	**4**	**9**	**0**	**0**	**0**	**0**
1918	**NY-A**	**12**	**16**	**7**	**3**	**.700**	**31**	**2.48**	**112 ⅔**	**22**	**52**	**85**	**1**	**5**	**2**	**0**
1919	**NY-A**	**25**	**30**	**12**	**10**	**.545**	**55**	**2.62**	**188 ⅔**	**62**	**61**	**155**	**10**	**13**	**2**	**1**

(continued)

(continued)

YEAR	TEAM	STARTS	GAMES	WON	LOST	PCT	ER	ERA	INNINGS PITCHED	STRIKE-OUTS	WALKS	HITS ALLOWED	HRS ALLOWED	COMP. GAMES	SHUT-OUTS	SAVES
1920	NY-A	15	29	9	6	.600	66	4.14	143 1/3	35	43	178	5	6	0	1
1921	Bos-A	9	23	1	7	.125	48	4.48	96 1/3	17	34	101	3	3	0	0
1925	Bro-N	2	5	0	3	.000	7	3.94	16	7	9	22	0	0	0	0
Career Average		11	17	5	5	.492	35	3.33	94	25	34	92	3	5	1	0
Yankee Average		13	19	7	5	.583	39	3.06	113	31	40	107	4	6	1	1
Career Total		64	104	29	30	.492	209	3.33	565	148	203	550	19	27	4	2
Yankee Total		53	76	28	20	.583	154	3.06	452 2/3	124	160	427	16	24	4	2

Tiant, Luis Clemente BORN LUIS CLEMENTE TIANT (VEGA)
HEIGHT: 5'11" RIGHTHANDER BORN: 11/23/1940 MARIANO, CUBA

YEAR	TEAM	STARTS	GAMES	WON	LOST	PCT	ER	ERA	INNINGS PITCHED	STRIKE-OUTS	WALKS	HITS ALLOWED	HRS ALLOWED	COMP. GAMES	SHUT-OUTS	SAVES
1964	Cle-A	16	19	10	4	.714	40	2.83	127	105	47	94	13	9	3	1
1965	Cle-A	30	41	11	11	.500	77	3.53	196 1/3	152	66	166	20	10	2	1
1966	Cle-A	16	46	12	11	.522	48	2.79	155	145	50	121	16	7	5	8
1967	Cle-A	29	33	12	9	.571	65	2.74	213 2/3	219	67	177	24	9	1	2
1968	Cle-A	32	34	21	9	.700	46	1.60	258 1/3	264	73	152	16	19	9	0
1969	Cle-A	37	38	9	20	.310	103	3.71	249 2/3	156	129	229	37	9	1	0
1970	Min-A	17	18	7	3	.700	35	3.40	92 1/3	50	41	84	12	2	1	0
1971	Bos-A	10	21	1	7	.125	39	4.85	72 1/3	59	32	73	8	1	0	0
1972	Bos-A	19	43	15	6	.714	38	1.91	179	123	65	128	7	12	6	3
1973	Bos-A	35	35	20	13	.606	101	3.34	272	206	78	217	32	23	0	0
1974	Bos-A	38	38	22	13	.629	101	2.92	311 1/3	176	82	281	21	25	7	0
1975	Bos-A	35	35	18	14	.563	116	4.02	260	142	72	262	25	18	2	0
1976	Bos-A	38	38	21	12	.636	95	3.06	279	131	64	274	25	19	3	0
1977	Bos-A	32	32	12	8	.600	95	4.53	188 2/3	124	51	210	26	3	3	0
1978	Bos-A	31	32	13	8	.619	78	3.31	212 1/3	114	57	185	26	12	5	0
1979	**NY-A**	**30**	**30**	**13**	**8**	**.619**	**85**	**3.91**	**195 2/3**	**104**	**53**	**190**	**22**	**5**	**1**	**0**
1980	**NY-A**	**25**	**25**	**8**	**9**	**.471**	**74**	**4.89**	**136 1/3**	**84**	**50**	**139**	**10**	**3**	**0**	**0**
1981	Pit-N	9	9	2	5	.286	25	3.92	57 1/3	32	19	54	3	1	0	0
1982	Cal-A	5	6	2	2	.500	19	5.76	29 2/3	30	8	39	3	0	0	0
Career Average		25	30	12	9	.571	67	3.30	183	127	58	162	18	10	3	1
Yankee Average		28	28	11	9	.553	80	4.31	166	94	52	165	16	4	1	0
Career Total		484	573	229	172	.571	1280	3.30	3486 1/3	2416	1104	3075	346	187	49	15
Yankee Total		55	55	21	17	.553	159	4.31	332	188	103	329	32	8	1	0

Tidrow, Richard William (Dirt)
HEIGHT: 6'4" RIGHTHANDER BORN: 5/14/1947 SAN FRANCISCO, CALIFORNIA

YEAR	TEAM	STARTS	GAMES	WON	LOST	PCT	ER	ERA	INNINGS PITCHED	STRIKE-OUTS	WALKS	HITS ALLOWED	HRS ALLOWED	COMP. GAMES	SHUT-OUTS	SAVES
1972	Cle-A	34	39	14	15	.483	73	2.77	237 1/3	123	70	200	21	10	3	0
1973	Cle-A	40	42	14	16	.467	135	4.42	274 2/3	138	95	289	31	13	2	0
1974	Cle-A	4	4	1	3	.250	15	7.11	19	8	13	21	4	0	0	0
1974	**NY-A**	**25**	**33**	**11**	**9**	**.550**	**82**	**3.87**	**190 2/3**	**100**	**53**	**205**	**14**	**5**	**0**	**1**
1975	**NY-A**	**0**	**37**	**6**	**3**	**.667**	**24**	**3.12**	**69 1/3**	**38**	**31**	**65**	**5**	**0**	**0**	**5**
1976	**NY-A**	**2**	**47**	**4**	**5**	**.444**	**27**	**2.63**	**92 1/3**	**65**	**24**	**80**	**5**	**0**	**0**	**10**
1977	**NY-A**	**7**	**49**	**11**	**4**	**.733**	**53**	**3.16**	**151**	**83**	**41**	**143**	**20**	**0**	**0**	**5**
1978	**NY-A**	**25**	**31**	**7**	**11**	**.389**	**79**	**3.84**	**185 1/3**	**73**	**53**	**191**	**13**	**4**	**0**	**0**
1979	**NY-A**	**0**	**14**	**2**	**1**	**.667**	**20**	**7.94**	**22 2/3**	**7**	**4**	**38**	**5**	**0**	**0**	**2**
1979	Chi-N	0	63	11	5	.688	31	2.72	102 2/3	68	42	86	5	0	0	4
1980	Chi-N	0	84	6	5	.545	36	2.79	116	97	53	97	10	0	0	6
1981	Chi-N	0	51	3	10	.231	42	5.06	74 2/3	39	30	73	6	0	0	9
1982	Chi-N	0	65	8	3	.727	39	3.39	103 2/3	62	29	106	6	0	0	6
1983	Chi-A	1	50	2	4	.333	43	4.22	91 2/3	66	34	86	13	0	0	7
1984	NY-N	0	11	0	0	—	16	9.19	15 2/3	8	7	25	5	0	0	0
Career Average		9	41	7	6	.515	48	3.68	116	65	39	114	11	2	0	4
Yankee Average		10	35	7	6	.554	48	3.61	119	61	34	120	10	2	0	4
Career Total		138	620	100	94	.515	715	3.68	1746 2/3	975	579	1705	163	32	5	55
Yankee Total		59	211	41	33	.554	285	3.61	711 1/3	366	206	722	62	9	0	23

Tiefenauer, Bobby Gene
HEIGHT: 6'2" RIGHTHANDER BORN: 10/10/1929 DESLOGE, MISSOURI

YEAR	TEAM	STARTS	GAMES	WON	LOST	PCT	ER	ERA	INNINGS PITCHED	STRIKE-OUTS	WALKS	HITS ALLOWED	HRS ALLOWED	COMP. GAMES	SHUT-OUTS	SAVES
1952	StL-N	0	6	0	0	—	7	7.88	8	3	7	12	1	0	0	0
1955	StL-N	0	18	1	4	.200	16	4.41	32 2/3	16	10	31	6	0	0	0
1960	Cle-A	0	6	0	1	.000	2	2.00	9	2	3	8	0	0	0	0
1961	StL-N	0	3	0	0	—	3	6.23	4 1/3	3	4	9	0	0	0	0
1962	Hou-N	0	43	2	4	.333	41	4.34	85	60	21	91	6	0	0	1
1963	Mil-N	0	12	1	1	.500	4	1.21	29 2/3	22	4	20	1	0	0	2
1964	Mil-N	0	46	4	6	.400	26	3.21	73	48	15	61	6	0	0	13
1965	Mil-N	0	6	0	1	.000	6	7.71	7	7	3	8	1	0	0	0
1965	**NY-A**	**0**	**10**	**1**	**1**	**.500**	**8**	**3.54**	**20 1/3**	**15**	**5**	**19**	**3**	**0**	**0**	**2**
1965	Cle-A	0	15	0	5	.000	12	4.84	22 1/3	13	10	24	3	0	0	4
1967	Cle-A	0	5	0	1	.000	1	0.79	11 1/3	6	3	9	0	0	0	0
1968	Chi-N	0	9	0	1	.000	9	6.08	13 1/3	9	2	20	2	0	0	1
Career Average		0	15	1	2	.265	11	3.84	26	17	7	26	2	0	0	2
Yankee Average		**0**	**10**	**1**	**1**	**.500**	**8**	**3.54**	**20 1/3**	**15**	**5**	**19**	**3**	**0**	**0**	**2**
Career Total		0	179	9	25	.265	135	3.84	316	204	87	312	29	0	0	23
Yankee Total		**0**	**10**	**1**	**1**	**.500**	**8**	**3.54**	**20 1/3**	**15**	**5**	**19**	**3**	**0**	**0**	**2**

Tift, Raymond Frank
HEIGHT: — LEFTHANDER BORN: 6/21/1884 FITCHBURG, MASSACHUSETTS DIED: 3/29/1945 VERONA, NEW JERSEY

YEAR	TEAM	STARTS	GAMES	WON	LOST	PCT	ER	ERA	INNINGS PITCHED	STRIKE-OUTS	WALKS	HITS ALLOWED	HRS ALLOWED	COMP. GAMES	SHUT-OUTS	SAVES
1907	**NY-A**	**1**	**4**	**0**	**0**	**—**	**10**	**4.74**	**19**	**6**	**4**	**33**	**0**	**0**	**0**	**0**
Career Average		1	4	0	0	—	10	4.74	19	6	4	33	0	0	0	0
Yankee Average		**1**	**4**	**0**	**0**	**—**	**10**	**4.74**	**19**	**6**	**4**	**33**	**0**	**0**	**0**	**0**
Career Total		1	4	0	0	—	10	4.74	19	6	4	33	0	0	0	0
Yankee Total		**1**	**4**	**0**	**0**	**—**	**10**	**4.74**	**19**	**6**	**4**	**33**	**0**	**0**	**0**	**0**

Tillotson, Thaddeus Asa
HEIGHT: 6'2" RIGHTHANDER BORN: 12/20/1940 MERCED, CALIFORNIA

YEAR	TEAM	STARTS	GAMES	WON	LOST	PCT	ER	ERA	INNINGS PITCHED	STRIKE-OUTS	WALKS	HITS ALLOWED	HRS ALLOWED	COMP. GAMES	SHUT-OUTS	SAVES
1967	**NY-A**	**5**	**43**	**3**	**9**	**.250**	**44**	**4.03**	**98 1/3**	**62**	**39**	**99**	**9**	**1**	**0**	**2**
1968	**NY-A**	**0**	**7**	**1**	**0**	**1.000**	**5**	**4.35**	**10 1/3**	**1**	**7**	**11**	**0**	**0**	**0**	**0**
Career Average		3	25	2	5	.308	25	4.06	54	32	23	55	5	1	0	1
Yankee Average		**3**	**25**	**2**	**5**	**.308**	**25**	**4.06**	**54**	**32**	**23**	**55**	**5**	**1**	**0**	**1**
Career Total		5	50	4	9	.308	49	4.06	108 2/3	63	46	110	9	1	0	2
Yankee Total		**5**	**50**	**4**	**9**	**.308**	**49**	**4.06**	**108 2/3**	**63**	**46**	**110**	**9**	**1**	**0**	**2**

Tipple, Daniel E. (Big Dan *or* Rusty)
HEIGHT: 6'0" RIGHTHANDER BORN: 2/13/1890 ROCKFORD, ILLINOIS DIED: 3/26/1960 OMAHA, NEBRASKA

YEAR	TEAM	STARTS	GAMES	WON	LOST	PCT	ER	ERA	INNINGS PITCHED	STRIKE-OUTS	WALKS	HITS ALLOWED	HRS ALLOWED	COMP. GAMES	SHUT-OUTS	SAVES
1915	**NY-A**	**2**	**3**	**1**	**1**	**.500**	**2**	**0.95**	**19**	**14**	**11**	**14**	**1**	**2**	**0**	**0**
Career Average		2	3	1	1	.500	2	0.95	19	14	11	14	1	2	0	0
Yankee Average		**2**	**3**	**1**	**1**	**.500**	**2**	**0.95**	**19**	**14**	**11**	**14**	**1**	**2**	**0**	**0**
Career Total		2	3	1	1	.500	2	0.95	19	14	11	14	1	2	0	0
Yankee Total		**2**	**3**	**1**	**1**	**.500**	**2**	**0.95**	**19**	**14**	**11**	**14**	**1**	**2**	**0**	**0**

Torrez, Michael Augustine

HEIGHT: 6'5"   RIGHTHANDER   BORN: 8/28/1946 TOPEKA, KANSAS

YEAR	TEAM	STARTS	GAMES	WON	LOST	PCT	ER	ERA	INNINGS PITCHED	STRIKE-OUTS	WALKS	HITS ALLOWED	HRS ALLOWED	COMP. GAMES	SHUT-OUTS	SAVES
1967	StL-N	1	3	0	1	.000	2	3.18	5 2/3	5	1	5	0	0	0	0
1968	StL-N	2	5	2	1	.667	6	2.79	19 1/3	6	12	20	1	0	0	0
1969	StL-N	15	24	10	4	.714	43	3.59	107 2/3	61	62	96	7	3	0	0
1970	StL-N	28	30	8	10	.444	84	4.22	179 1/3	100	103	168	12	5	1	0
1971	StL-N	6	9	1	2	.333	24	6.00	36	8	30	41	2	0	0	0
1971	Mon-N	0	1	0	0	—	0	0.00	3	2	1	4	0	0	0	0
1972	Mon-N	33	34	16	12	.571	90	3.33	243 1/3	112	103	215	15	13	0	0
1973	Mon-N	34	35	9	12	.429	103	4.46	208	90	115	207	17	3	1	0
1974	Mon-N	30	32	15	8	.652	74	3.57	186 1/3	92	84	184	10	6	1	0
1975	Bal-A	36	36	20	9	.690	92	3.06	270 2/3	119	133	238	15	16	2	0
1976	Oak-A	39	39	16	12	.571	74	2.50	266 1/3	115	87	231	15	13	4	0
1977	Oak-A	4	4	3	1	.750	13	4.44	26 1/3	12	11	23	3	2	0	0
1977	**NY-A**	**31**	**31**	**14**	**12**	**.538**	**92**	**3.82**	**217**	**90**	**75**	**212**	**20**	**15**	**2**	**0**
1978	Bos-A	36	36	16	13	.552	110	3.96	250	120	99	272	19	15	2	0
1979	Bos-A	36	36	16	13	.552	126	4.49	252 1/3	125	121	254	20	12	1	0
1980	Bos-A	32	36	9	16	.360	117	5.08	207 1/3	97	75	256	18	6	1	0
1981	Bos-A	22	22	10	3	.769	52	3.68	127 1/3	54	51	130	10	2	0	0
1982	Bos-A	31	31	9	9	.500	102	5.23	175 2/3	84	74	196	20	1	0	0
1983	NY-N	34	39	10	17	.370	108	4.37	222 1/3	94	113	227	16	5	0	0
1984	NY-N	8	9	1	5	.167	21	5.02	37 2/3	16	18	55	3	0	0	0
1984	Oak-A	0	2	0	0	—	7	27.00	2 1/3	2	3	9	0	0	0	0
Career Average		22	24	9	8	.536	64	3.96	145	67	65	145	11	6	1	0
Yankee Average		**31**	**31**	**14**	**12**	**.538**	**92**	**3.82**	**217**	**90**	**75**	**212**	**20**	**15**	**2**	**0**
Career Total		458	494	185	160	.536	1340	3.96	3044	1404	1371	3043	223	117	15	0
Yankee Total		**31**	**31**	**14**	**12**	**.538**	**92**	**3.82**	**217**	**90**	**75**	**212**	**20**	**15**	**2**	**0**

Trout, Steven Russell (Rainbow)

HEIGHT: 6'4"   LEFTHANDER   BORN: 7/30/1957 DETROIT, MICHIGAN

YEAR	TEAM	STARTS	GAMES	WON	LOST	PCT	ER	ERA	INNINGS PITCHED	STRIKE-OUTS	WALKS	HITS ALLOWED	HRS ALLOWED	COMP. GAMES	SHUT-OUTS	SAVES
1978	Chi-A	3	4	3	0	1.000	10	4.03	22 1/3	11	11	19	0	1	0	0
1979	Chi-A	18	34	11	8	.579	67	3.89	155	76	59	165	10	6	2	4
1980	Chi-A	30	32	9	16	.360	82	3.70	199 2/3	89	49	229	14	7	2	0
1981	Chi-A	18	20	8	7	.533	48	3.47	124 2/3	54	38	122	7	3	0	0
1982	Chi-A	19	25	6	9	.400	57	4.26	120 1/3	62	50	130	9	2	0	0
1983	Chi-N	32	34	10	14	.417	93	4.65	180	80	59	217	13	1	0	0
1984	Chi-N	31	32	13	7	.650	72	3.41	190	81	59	205	7	6	2	0
1985	Chi-N	24	24	9	7	.563	53	3.39	140 2/3	44	63	142	8	3	1	0
1986	Chi-N	25	37	5	7	.417	85	4.75	161	69	78	184	6	0	0	0
1987	Chi-N	11	11	6	3	.667	25	3.00	75	32	27	72	3	3	2	0
1987	**NY-A**	**9**	**14**	**0**	**4**	**.000**	**34**	**6.60**	**46 1/3**	**27**	**37**	**51**	**4**	**0**	**0**	**0**
1988	Sea-A	13	15	4	7	.364	49	7.83	56 1/3	14	31	86	6	0	0	0
1989	Sea-A	3	19	4	3	.571	22	6.60	30	17	17	43	3	0	0	0
Career Average		18	23	7	7	.489	54	4.18	115	50	44	128	7	2	1	0
Yankee Average		**9**	**14**	**0**	**4**	**.000**	**34**	**6.60**	**46 1/3**	**27**	**37**	**51**	**4**	**0**	**0**	**0**
Career Total		236	301	88	92	.489	697	4.18	1501 1/3	656	578	1665	90	32	9	4
Yankee Total		**9**	**14**	**0**	**4**	**.000**	**34**	**6.60**	**46 1/3**	**27**	**37**	**51**	**4**	**0**	**0**	**0**

Trucks, Virgil Oliver (Fire)

HEIGHT: 5'11"   RIGHTHANDER   BORN: 4/26/1919 BIRMINGHAM, ALABAMA

YEAR	TEAM	STARTS	GAMES	WON	LOST	PCT	ER	ERA	INNINGS PITCHED	STRIKE-OUTS	WALKS	HITS ALLOWED	HRS ALLOWED	COMP. GAMES	SHUT-OUTS	SAVES
1941	Det-A	0	1	0	0	—	2	9.00	2	3	0	4	0	0	0	0
1942	Det-A	20	28	14	8	.636	51	2.74	167 2/3	91	74	147	3	8	2	0
1943	Det-A	25	33	16	10	.615	64	2.84	202 2/3	118	52	170	11	10	2	2
1945	Det-A	1	1	0	0	—	1	1.69	5 1/3	3	2	3	0	0	0	0
1946	Det-A	29	32	14	9	.609	85	3.23	236 2/3	161	75	217	23	15	2	0
1947	Det-A	26	36	10	12	.455	91	4.53	180 2/3	108	79	186	14	8	2	2
1948	Det-A	26	43	14	13	.519	89	3.78	211 2/3	123	85	190	14	7	0	2
1949	Det-A	32	41	19	11	.633	86	2.81	275	153	124	209	16	17	6	4

(continued)

(continued)

YEAR	TEAM				PCT		ERA	IP							
1950	Det-A	7	7	3	1	.750	19	3.54	48 1/3	25	21	45	6	2	1	0
1951	Det-A	18	37	13	8	.619	74	4.33	153 2/3	89	75	153	9	6	1	1
1952	Det-A	29	35	5	19	.208	87	3.97	197	129	82	190	12	8	3	1
1953	StL-A	12	16	5	4	.556	30	3.07	88	47	32	83	4	4	2	2
1953	Chi-A	21	24	15	6	.714	56	2.86	176 1/3	102	67	151	14	13	3	1
1954	Chi-A	33	40	19	12	.613	82	2.79	264 2/3	152	95	224	13	16	5	3
1955	Chi-A	26	32	13	8	.619	77	3.96	175	91	61	176	19	7	3	0
1956	Det-A	16	22	6	5	.545	51	3.83	120	43	63	104	15	3	1	1
1957	KC-A	7	48	9	7	.563	39	3.03	116	55	62	106	12	0	0	7
1958	**NY-A**	**0**	**25**	**2**	**1**	**.667**	**20**	**4.54**	**39 2/3**	**26**	**24**	**40**	**1**	**0**	**0**	**1**
1958	KC-A	0	16	0	1	.000	5	2.05	22	15	15	18	2	0	0	3
Career Average		17	27	9	7	.567	53	3.39	141	81	57	127	10	7	2	2
Yankee Average		**0**	**25**	**2**	**1**	**.667**	**20**	**4.54**	**39 2/3**	**26**	**24**	**40**	**1**	**0**	**0**	**1**
Career Total		328	517	177	135	.567	1009	3.39	2682 1/3	1534	1088	2416	188	124	33	30
Yankee Total		**0**	**25**	**2**	**1**	**.667**	**20**	**4.54**	**39 2/3**	**26**	**24**	**40**	**1**	**0**	**0**	**1**

Turley, Robert Lee (Bullet Bob)

HEIGHT: 6'2"   RIGHTHANDER   BORN: 9/19/1930 TROY, ILLINOIS

YEAR	TEAM	STARTS	GAMES	WON	LOST	PCT	ER	ERA	INNINGS PITCHED	STRIKE-OUTS	WALKS	HITS ALLOWED	HRS ALLOWED	COMP. GAMES	SHUT-OUTS	SAVES
1951	StL-A	1	1	0	1	.000	6	7.36	7 1/3	5	3	11	0	0	0	0
1953	StL-A	7	10	2	6	.250	22	3.28	60 1/3	61	44	39	4	3	1	0
1954	Bal-A	35	35	14	15	.483	95	3.46	247 1/3	185	181	178	7	14	0	0

(continued)

Robert Lee "Bullet Bob" Turley, rhp, 1955–62

Bob Turley was a gentleman on the mound throughout his career, which was a good thing in some ways, since he possessed a killer fastball.

Turley, born September 19, 1930, in Troy, Illinois., got his start in the big leagues with the St. Louis Browns in 1951. He was 16-22 in three years with that organization before coming to New York in 1954 with Don Larsen and Billy Hunter in a big 18-player deal.

In those early years, even after he came to New York, Turley just reared back and threw. He used a no-windup delivery and didn't try to pitch to spots or to a hitter's weakness. It was usually a one-on-one battle between Turley and the batsman.

But the opposition had an edge. Turley was a true gentleman both off and on the field. He refused to throw at opposing hitters, even those who dug in against him and crowded the plate.

Some years, it didn't matter. In 1958 he was easily the best pitcher in baseball, winning a league-high 21 games and striking out 168 batters, third in the league. That won him the Cy Young award.

That year, he was also the hero of the World Series, winning Game 5 against the Milwaukee Braves with a five-hit, complete-game shutout, saving Game 6 for Ryne Duren, and winning Game 7 in relief of Don Larsen.

The next two years saw Turley struggle, finishing 1959 with an 8-11 year and 1960 at 9-3. In 1961, he had arm problems, and by the end of next year, he had been sold to the Angels. He retired in 1963 after a stint with the Red Sox.

Turley is 19th on the Yankees' all-time list with 82 wins. His .612 winning percentage with New York is 14th all time, and he is 11th in strikeouts with 909 and 10th in shutouts with 20.

(continued)

YEAR	TEAM	STARTS	GAMES	WON	LOST	PCT	ER	ERA	INNINGS PITCHED	STRIKE-OUTS	WALKS	HITS ALLOWED	HRS ALLOWED	COMP. GAMES	SHUT-OUTS	SAVES
1955	NY-A	34	36	17	13	.567	84	3.06	246 2/3	210	177	168	16	13	6	1
1956	NY-A	21	27	8	4	.667	74	5.05	132	91	103	138	13	5	1	1
1957	NY-A	23	32	13	6	.684	53	2.71	176 1/3	152	85	120	17	9	4	3
1958	NY-A	31	33	21	7	.750	81	2.97	245 1/3	168	128	178	24	19	6	1
1959	NY-A	22	33	8	11	.421	74	4.32	154 1/3	111	83	141	15	7	3	0
1960	NY-A	24	34	9	3	.750	63	3.27	173 1/3	87	87	138	14	4	1	5
1961	NY-A	12	15	3	5	.375	46	5.75	72	48	51	74	11	1	0	0
1962	NY-A	8	24	3	3	.500	35	4.57	69	42	47	68	8	0	0	1
1963	LA-A	12	19	2	7	.222	32	3.30	87 1/3	70	51	71	5	3	2	0
1963	Bos-A	7	11	1	4	.200	28	6.10	41 1/3	35	28	42	6	0	0	0
Career Average		18	24	8	7	.543	53	3.64	132	97	82	105	11	6	2	1
Yankee Average		22	29	10	7	.612	64	3.62	159	114	95	128	15	7	3	2
Career Total		237	310	101	85	.543	693	3.64	1712 2/3	1265	1068	1366	140	78	24	12
Yankee Total		175	234	82	52	.612	510	3.62	1269	909	761	1025	118	58	21	12

Turner, James Riley (Milkman Jim)
HEIGHT: 6'0"   RIGHTHANDER   BORN: 8/6/1903 ANTIOCH, TENNESSEE

YEAR	TEAM	STARTS	GAMES	WON	LOST	PCT	ER	ERA	INNINGS PITCHED	STRIKE-OUTS	WALKS	HITS ALLOWED	HRS ALLOWED	COMP. GAMES	SHUT-OUTS	SAVES
1937	Bos-N	30	33	20	11	.645	68	2.38	256 2/3	69	52	228	13	24	5	1
1938	Bos-N	34	35	14	18	.438	103	3.46	268	71	54	267	21	22	3	0
1939	Bos-N	22	25	4	11	.267	75	4.28	157 2/3	50	51	181	10	9	0	0
1940	Cin-N	23	24	14	7	.667	60	2.89	187	53	32	187	9	11	0	0
1941	Cin-N	10	23	6	4	.600	39	3.11	113	34	24	120	5	3	0	0
1942	Cin-N	0	3	0	0	—	4	10.80	3 1/3	0	3	5	1	0	0	0
1942	NY-A	0	5	1	1	.500	1	1.29	7	2	1	4	0	0	0	1
1943	NY-A	0	18	3	0	1.000	17	3.53	43 1/3	15	13	44	1	0	0	1
1944	NY-A	0	35	4	4	.500	16	3.46	41 2/3	13	22	42	3	0	0	7
1945	NY-A	0	30	3	4	.429	22	3.64	54 1/3	22	31	45	4	0	0	10
Career Average		12	23	7	6	.535	41	3.22	113	33	28	112	7	7	1	2
Yankee Average		0	22	3	2	.550	14	3.44	37	13	17	34	2	0	0	5
Career Total		119	231	69	60	.535	405	3.22	1132	329	283	1123	67	69	8	20
Yankee Total		0	88	11	9	.550	56	3.44	146 1/3	52	67	135	8	0	0	19

Uhle, George Ernest (The Bull)
HEIGHT: 6'0"   RIGHTHANDER   BORN: 9/18/1898 CLEVELAND, OHIO   DIED: 2/26/1985 LAKEWOOD, NEW JERSEY

YEAR	TEAM	STARTS	GAMES	WON	LOST	PCT	ER	ERA	INNINGS PITCHED	STRIKE-OUTS	WALKS	HITS ALLOWED	HRS ALLOWED	COMP. GAMES	SHUT-OUTS	SAVES
1919	Cle-A	12	26	10	5	.667	41	2.91	127	50	43	129	1	7	1	0
1920	Cle-A	6	27	4	5	.444	49	5.21	84 2/3	27	29	98	3	2	0	1
1921	Cle-A	28	41	16	13	.552	106	4.01	238	63	63	288	9	13	2	2
1922	Cle-A	40	50	22	16	.579	130	4.07	287 1/3	82	89	328	6	23	5	3
1923	Cle-A	44	54	26	16	.619	150	3.77	357 2/3	109	102	378	8	29	1	5
1924	Cle-A	25	28	9	15	.375	104	4.77	196 1/3	57	75	238	6	15	0	1
1925	Cle-A	26	29	13	11	.542	96	4.10	210 2/3	68	78	218	5	17	1	0
1926	Cle-A	36	39	27	11	.711	100	2.83	318 1/3	159	118	300	7	32	3	1
1927	Cle-A	22	25	8	9	.471	74	4.34	153 1/3	69	59	187	3	10	1	1
1928	Cle-A	28	31	12	17	.414	97	4.07	214 1/3	74	48	252	8	18	2	1
1929	Det-A	30	32	15	11	.577	113	4.08	249	100	58	283	9	23	1	0
1930	Det-A	29	33	12	12	.500	97	3.65	239	117	75	239	18	18	1	3
1931	Det-A	18	29	11	12	.478	75	3.50	193	63	49	190	10	15	2	2
1932	Det-A	15	33	6	6	.500	73	4.48	146 2/3	51	42	152	15	6	1	5
1933	Det-A	0	1	0	0	—	2	27.03	2/3	1	0	2	1	0	0	0
1933	NY-N	1	6	1	1	.500	12	7.90	13 2/3	4	6	16	1	0	0	0
1933	NY-A	6	12	6	1	.857	35	5.16	61	26	20	63	4	4	0	0
1934	NY-A	2	10	2	4	.333	18	9.92	16 1/3	10	7	30	3	0	0	0
1936	Cle-A	0	7	0	1	.000	12	8.53	12 2/3	5	5	26	2	0	0	0
Career Average		19	27	11	9	.546	73	3.99	164	60	51	180	6	12	1	1
Yankee Average		4	11	4	3	.615	27	6.17	38	18	14	47	4	2	0	0
Career Total		368	513	200	166	.546	1384	3.99	3119 2/3	1135	966	3417	119	232	21	25
Yankee Total		8	22	8	5	.615	53	6.17	77 1/3	36	27	93	7	4	0	0

Underwood, Thomas Gerald
HEIGHT: 5'11" LEFTHANDER BORN: 12/22/1953 KOKOMO, INDIANA

YEAR	TEAM	STARTS	GAMES	WON	LOST	PCT	ER	ERA	INNINGS PITCHED	STRIKE-OUTS	WALKS	HITS ALLOWED	HRS ALLOWED	COMP. GAMES	SHUT-OUTS	SAVES
1974	Phi-N	0	7	1	0	1.000	7	4.85	13	8	5	15	1	0	0	0
1975	Phi-N	35	35	14	13	.519	101	4.14	219 1/3	123	84	221	12	7	2	0
1976	Phi-N	25	33	10	5	.667	61	3.53	155 2/3	94	63	154	9	3	0	2
1977	Phi-N	0	14	3	2	.600	19	5.13	33 1/3	20	18	44	2	0	0	1
1977	StL-N	17	19	6	9	.400	55	4.95	100	66	57	104	7	1	0	0
1978	Tor-A	30	31	6	14	.300	90	4.10	197 2/3	139	87	201	23	7	1	0
1979	Tor-A	32	33	9	16	.360	93	3.69	227	127	95	213	23	12	1	0
1980	**NY-A**	**27**	**38**	**13**	**9**	**.591**	**76**	**3.66**	**187**	**116**	**66**	**163**	**15**	**2**	**2**	**2**
1981	**NY-A**	**6**	**9**	**1**	**4**	**.200**	**16**	**4.41**	**32 2/3**	**29**	**13**	**32**	**2**	**0**	**0**	**0**
1981	Oak-A	5	16	3	2	.600	18	3.18	51	46	25	37	4	1	0	1
1982	Oak-A	10	56	10	6	.625	56	3.29	153	79	68	136	11	2	0	7
1983	Oak-A	15	51	9	7	.563	65	4.04	144 2/3	62	50	156	13	0	0	4
1984	Bal-A	1	37	1	0	1.000	28	3.52	71 2/3	39	31	78	8	0	0	1
Career Average		16	29	7	7	.497	53	3.89	122	73	51	120	10	3	0	1
Yankee Average		**17**	**24**	**7**	**7**	**.519**	**46**	**3.77**	**110**	**73**	**40**	**98**	**9**	**1**	**1**	**1**
Career Total		203	379	86	87	.497	685	3.89	1586	948	662	1554	130	35	6	18
Yankee Total		**33**	**47**	**14**	**13**	**.519**	**92**	**3.77**	**219 2/3**	**145**	**79**	**195**	**17**	**2**	**2**	**2**

Upshaw, Cecil Lee
HEIGHT: 6'6" RIGHTHANDER BORN: 10/22/1942 SPEARVILLE, LOUISIANA DIED: 2/7/1995

YEAR	TEAM	STARTS	GAMES	WON	LOST	PCT	ER	ERA	INNINGS PITCHED	STRIKE-OUTS	WALKS	HITS ALLOWED	HRS ALLOWED	COMP. GAMES	SHUT-OUTS	SAVES
1966	Atl-N	0	1	0	0	—	0	0.00	3	2	3	0	0	0	0	0
1967	Atl-N	0	30	2	3	.400	13	2.58	45 1/3	31	8	42	4	0	0	8
1968	Atl-N	0	52	8	7	.533	32	2.47	116 2/3	74	24	98	6	0	0	13
1969	Atl-N	0	62	6	4	.600	34	2.91	105 1/3	57	29	102	7	0	0	27
1971	Atl-N	0	49	11	6	.647	32	3.51	82	56	28	95	5	0	0	17
1972	Atl-N	0	42	3	5	.375	22	3.69	53 2/3	23	19	50	5	0	0	13
1973	Atl-N	0	5	0	1	.000	4	9.82	3 2/3	3	2	8	0	0	0	0
1973	Hou-N	0	35	2	3	.400	19	4.46	38 1/3	21	15	38	3	0	0	1
1974	Cle-A	0	7	0	1	.000	3	3.38	8	7	4	10	1	0	0	0
1974	**NY-A**	**0**	**36**	**1**	**5**	**.167**	**20**	**3.02**	**59 2/3**	**27**	**24**	**53**	**1**	**0**	**0**	**6**
1975	Chi-A	0	29	1	1	.500	17	3.23	47 1/3	22	21	49	5	0	0	1
Career Average		0	32	3	3	.486	18	3.13	51	29	16	50	3	0	0	8
Yankee Average		**0**	**36**	**1**	**5**	**.167**	**20**	**3.02**	**59 2/3**	**27**	**24**	**53**	**1**	**0**	**0**	**6**
Career Total		0	348	34	36	.486	196	3.13	563	323	177	545	37	0	0	86
Yankee Total		**0**	**36**	**1**	**5**	**.167**	**20**	**3.02**	**59 2/3**	**27**	**24**	**53**	**1**	**0**	**0**	**6**

Van Atta, Russell (Sheriff)
HEIGHT: 6'0" LEFTHANDER BORN: 6/21/1906 AUGUSTA, NEW JERSEY DIED: 10/10/1986 ANDOVER, NEW JERSEY

YEAR	TEAM	STARTS	GAMES	WON	LOST	PCT	ER	ERA	INNINGS PITCHED	STRIKE-OUTS	WALKS	HITS ALLOWED	HRS ALLOWED	COMP. GAMES	SHUT-OUTS	SAVES
1933	**NY-A**	**22**	**26**	**12**	**4**	**.750**	**73**	**4.18**	**157**	**76**	**63**	**160**	**8**	**10**	**2**	**1**
1934	**NY-A**	**9**	**28**	**3**	**5**	**.375**	**62**	**6.34**	**88**	**39**	**46**	**107**	**3**	**0**	**0**	**0**
1935	**NY-A**	**0**	**5**	**0**	**0**	**—**	**2**	**3.86**	**4 2/3**	**3**	**4**	**5**	**0**	**0**	**0**	**0**
1935	StL-A	17	53	9	16	.360	101	5.34	170 1/3	87	87	201	10	1	0	3
1936	StL-A	9	52	4	7	.364	90	6.60	122 2/3	59	68	164	9	2	0	2
1937	StL-A	6	16	1	2	.333	36	5.52	58 2/3	34	32	74	2	1	0	0
1938	StL-A	12	25	4	7	.364	70	6.06	104	35	61	118	7	3	1	0
1939	StL-A	1	2	0	0	—	9	11.57	7	6	7	9	0	0	0	0
Career Average		10	26	4	5	.446	55	5.60	89	42	46	105	5	2	0	1
Yankee Average		**10**	**20**	**5**	**3**	**.625**	**46**	**4.94**	**83**	**39**	**38**	**91**	**4**	**3**	**1**	**0**
Career Total		76	207	33	41	.446	443	5.60	712 1/3	339	368	838	39	17	3	6
Yankee Total		**31**	**59**	**15**	**9**	**.625**	**137**	**4.94**	**249 2/3**	**118**	**113**	**272**	**11**	**10**	**2**	**1**

Vance, Clarence Arthur (Dazzy)

HEIGHT: 6'2"   RIGHTHANDER   BORN: 3/4/1891 ORIENT, IOWA   DIED: 2/16/1961 HOMOSASSA SPRINGS, FLORIDA

YEAR	TEAM	STARTS	GAMES	WON	LOST	PCT	ER	ERA	INNINGS PITCHED	STRIKE-OUTS	WALKS	HITS ALLOWED	HRS ALLOWED	COMP. GAMES	SHUT-OUTS	SAVES
1915	Pit-N	1	1	0	1	.000	3	10.13	2 2/3	0	5	3	0	0	0	0
1915	**NY-A**	**3**	**8**	**0**	**3**	**.000**	**11**	**3.54**	**28**	**18**	**16**	**23**	**1**	**1**	**0**	**0**
1918	**NY-A**	**0**	**2**	**0**	**0**	**—**	**4**	**15.43**	**2 1/3**	**0**	**2**	**9**	**0**	**0**	**0**	**0**
1922	Bro-N	30	36	18	12	.600	101	3.70	245 2/3	134	94	259	9	16	5	0
1923	Bro-N	35	37	18	15	.545	109	3.50	280 1/3	197	100	263	10	21	3	0
1924	Bro-N	34	35	28	6	.824	74	2.16	308 1/3	262	77	238	11	30	3	0
1925	Bro-N	31	31	22	9	.710	104	3.53	265 1/3	221	66	247	8	26	4	0
1926	Bro-N	22	24	9	10	.474	73	3.89	169	140	58	172	7	12	0	1
1927	Bro-N	32	34	16	15	.516	82	2.70	273 1/3	184	69	242	12	25	2	1
1928	Bro-N	32	38	22	10	.688	65	2.09	280 1/3	200	72	226	11	24	4	2
1929	Bro-N	26	31	14	13	.519	100	3.89	231 1/3	126	47	244	15	17	1	0
1930	Bro-N	31	35	17	15	.531	75	2.61	258 2/3	173	55	241	15	20	4	0
1931	Bro-N	29	30	11	13	.458	82	3.38	218 2/3	150	53	221	12	12	2	0
1932	Bro-N	24	27	12	11	.522	82	4.20	175 2/3	103	57	171	10	9	1	1
1933	StL-N	11	28	6	2	.750	39	3.55	99	67	28	105	3	2	0	3
1934	Cin-N	2	6	0	2	.000	15	7.50	18	9	11	28	1	0	0	0
1934	StL-N	4	19	1	1	.500	24	3.66	59	33	14	62	4	1	0	1
1935	Bro-N	0	20	3	2	.600	25	4.41	51	28	16	55	3	0	0	2
Career Average		19	25	11	8	.585	59	3.24	165	114	47	156	7	12	2	1
Yankee Average		**2**	**5**	**0**	**2**	**.000**	**8**	**4.45**	**15**	**9**	**9**	**16**	**1**	**1**	**0**	**0**
Career Total		347	442	197	140	.585	1068	3.24	2966 2/3	2045	840	2809	132	216	29	11
Yankee Total		**3**	**10**	**0**	**3**	**.000**	**15**	**4.45**	**30 1/3**	**18**	**18**	**32**	**1**	**1**	**0**	**0**

Vance, Joseph Albert (Sandy)

HEIGHT: 6'1"   RIGHTHANDER   BORN: 9/16/1905 DEVINE, TEXAS   DIED: 7/4/1978 DEVINE, TEXAS

YEAR	TEAM	STARTS	GAMES	WON	LOST	PCT	ER	ERA	INNINGS PITCHED	STRIKE-OUTS	WALKS	HITS ALLOWED	HRS ALLOWED	COMP. GAMES	SHUT-OUTS	SAVES
1935	Chi-A	0	10	2	2	.500	23	6.68	31	12	21	36	1	0	0	0
1937	**NY-A**	**2**	**2**	**1**	**0**	**1.000**	**5**	**3.00**	**15**	**3**	**9**	**11**	**2**	**0**	**0**	**0**
1938	**NY-A**	**1**	**3**	**0**	**0**	**—**	**9**	**7.15**	**11 1/3**	**2**	**4**	**20**	**2**	**0**	**0**	**0**
Career Average		1	5	1	1	.600	12	5.81	19	6	11	22	2	0	0	0
Yankee Average		**2**	**3**	**1**	**0**	**1.000**	**7**	**4.78**	**13**	**3**	**7**	**16**	**2**	**0**	**0**	**0**
Career Total		3	15	3	2	.600	37	5.81	57 1/3	17	34	67	5	0	0	0
Yankee Total		**3**	**5**	**1**	**0**	**1.000**	**14**	**4.78**	**26 1/3**	**5**	**13**	**31**	**4**	**0**	**0**	**0**

Vaughn, James Leslie (Hippo)

HEIGHT: 6'4"   LEFTHANDER   BORN: 4/9/1888 WEATHERFORD, TEXAS   DIED: 5/29/1966 CHICAGO, ILLINOIS

YEAR	TEAM	STARTS	GAMES	WON	LOST	PCT	ER	ERA	INNINGS PITCHED	STRIKE-OUTS	WALKS	HITS ALLOWED	HRS ALLOWED	COMP. GAMES	SHUT-OUTS	SAVES
1908	**NY-A**	**0**	**2**	**0**	**0**	**—**	**1**	**3.86**	**2 1/3**	**2**	**4**	**1**	**0**	**0**	**0**	**0**
1910	**NY-A**	**25**	**30**	**13**	**11**	**.542**	**45**	**1.83**	**221 2/3**	**107**	**58**	**190**	**1**	**18**	**5**	**1**
1911	**NY-A**	**18**	**26**	**8**	**10**	**.444**	**71**	**4.39**	**145 2/3**	**74**	**54**	**158**	**2**	**11**	**0**	**0**
1912	**NY-A**	**10**	**15**	**2**	**8**	**.200**	**36**	**5.14**	**63**	**46**	**37**	**66**	**1**	**5**	**1**	**0**
1912	Was-A	8	12	4	3	.571	26	2.89	81	49	43	75	0	4	0	0
1913	Chi-N	6	7	5	1	.833	9	1.45	56	36	27	37	0	5	2	0
1914	Chi-N	35	42	21	13	.618	67	2.05	293 2/3	165	109	236	1	23	4	1
1915	Chi-N	34	41	20	12	.625	86	2.87	269 2/3	148	77	240	4	18	4	1
1916	Chi-N	35	44	17	15	.531	72	2.20	294	144	67	269	4	21	4	1
1917	Chi-N	39	41	23	13	.639	66	2.01	295 2/3	195	91	255	3	27	5	0
1918	Chi-N	33	35	22	10	.688	56	1.74	290 1/3	148	76	216	4	27	8	0
1919	Chi-N	37	38	21	14	.600	61	1.79	306 2/3	141	62	264	3	25	4	1
1920	Chi-N	38	40	19	16	.543	85	2.54	301	131	81	301	8	24	4	0
1921	Chi-N	14	17	3	11	.214	73	6.01	109 1/3	30	31	153	8	7	0	0
Career Average		24	28	13	10	.565	54	2.49	195	101	58	176	3	15	3	0
Yankee Average		**13**	**18**	**6**	**7**	**.442**	**38**	**3.18**	**108**	**57**	**38**	**104**	**1**	**9**	**2**	**0**
Career Total		332	390	178	137	.565	754	2.49	2730	1416	817	2461	39	215	41	5
Yankee Total		**53**	**73**	**23**	**29**	**.442**	**153**	**3.18**	**432 2/3**	**229**	**153**	**415**	**4**	**34**	**6**	**1**

Verbanic, Joseph Michael

HEIGHT: 6'0" RIGHTHANDER BORN: 4/24/1943 WASHINGTON, PENNSYLVANIA

YEAR	TEAM	STARTS	GAMES	WON	LOST	PCT	ER	ERA	INNINGS PITCHED	STRIKE-OUTS	WALKS	HITS ALLOWED	HRS ALLOWED	COMP. GAMES	SHUT-OUTS	SAVES
1966	Phi-N	0	17	1	1	.500	8	5.14	14	7	10	12	2	0	0	0
1967	**NY-A**	**6**	**28**	**4**	**3**	**.571**	**25**	**2.80**	**80 1/3**	**39**	**21**	**74**	**6**	**1**	**1**	**2**
1968	**NY-A**	**11**	**40**	**6**	**7**	**.462**	**34**	**3.15**	**97**	**40**	**41**	**104**	**6**	**2**	**1**	**4**
1970	**NY-A**	**0**	**7**	**1**	**0**	**1.000**	**8**	**4.60**	**15 2/3**	**8**	**12**	**20**	**1**	**0**	**0**	**0**
Career Average		4	23	3	3	.522	19	3.26	52	24	21	53	4	1	1	2
Yankee Average		**6**	**25**	**4**	**3**	**.524**	**22**	**3.12**	**64**	**29**	**25**	**66**	**4**	**1**	**1**	**2**
Career Total		17	92	12	11	.522	75	3.26	207	94	84	210	15	3	2	6
Yankee Total		**17**	**75**	**11**	**10**	**.524**	**67**	**3.12**	**193**	**87**	**74**	**198**	**13**	**3**	**2**	**6**

Wade, Jacob Fields (Whistlin' Jake)

HEIGHT: 6'2" LEFTHANDER BORN: 4/1/1912 MOREHEAD CITY, NORTH CAROLINA

YEAR	TEAM	STARTS	GAMES	WON	LOST	PCT	ER	ERA	INNINGS PITCHED	STRIKE-OUTS	WALKS	HITS ALLOWED	HRS ALLOWED	COMP. GAMES	SHUT-OUTS	SAVES
1936	Det-A	11	13	4	5	.444	46	5.29	78 1/3	30	52	93	7	4	1	0
1937	Det-A	25	33	7	10	.412	99	5.39	165 1/3	69	107	160	13	7	1	0
1938	Det-A	2	27	3	2	.600	51	6.56	70	23	48	73	9	0	0	0
1939	Bos-A	6	20	1	4	.200	33	6.23	47 2/3	21	37	68	1	1	0	0
1939	StL-A	2	4	0	2	.000	20	11.02	16 1/3	9	19	26	1	1	0	0
1942	Chi-A	10	15	5	5	.500	39	4.10	85 2/3	32	56	84	2	3	0	0
1943	Chi-A	9	21	3	7	.300	28	3.01	83 2/3	41	54	66	3	3	1	0
1944	Chi-A	5	19	2	4	.333	40	4.82	74 2/3	35	41	75	3	1	0	2
1946	**NY-A**	**1**	**13**	**2**	**1**	**.667**	**9**	**2.29**	**35 1/3**	**22**	**14**	**33**	**2**	**0**	**0**	**1**
1946	Was-A	0	6	0	0	—	6	4.76	11 1/3	9	12	12	1	0	0	0
Career Average		7	17	3	4	.403	37	5.00	67	29	44	69	4	2	0	0
Yankee Average		**1**	**13**	**2**	**1**	**.667**	**9**	**2.29**	**35 1/3**	**22**	**14**	**33**	**2**	**0**	**0**	**1**
Career Total		71	171	27	40	.403	371	5.00	668 1/3	291	440	690	42	20	3	3
Yankee Total		**1**	**13**	**2**	**1**	**.667**	**9**	**2.29**	**35 1/3**	**22**	**14**	**33**	**2**	**0**	**0**	**1**

Wallace, Michael Sherman

HEIGHT: 6'2" LEFTHANDER BORN: 2/3/1951 GASTONIA, NORTH CAROLINA

YEAR	TEAM	STARTS	GAMES	WON	LOST	PCT	ER	ERA	INNINGS PITCHED	STRIKE-OUTS	WALKS	HITS ALLOWED	HRS ALLOWED	COMP. GAMES	SHUT-OUTS	SAVES
1973	Phi-N	3	20	1	1	.500	14	3.78	33 1/3	20	15	38	1	1	0	1
1974	Phi-N	0	8	1	0	1.000	5	5.40	8 1/3	1	2	12	0	0	0	0
1974	**NY-A**	**1**	**23**	**6**	**0**	**1.000**	**14**	**2.41**	**52 1/3**	**34**	**35**	**42**	**3**	**0**	**0**	**0**
1975	**NY-A**	**0**	**3**	**0**	**0**	**—**	**7**	**14.54**	**4 1/3**	**2**	**1**	**11**	**1**	**0**	**0**	**0**
1975	StL-N	0	9	0	0	—	2	2.08	8 2/3	6	5	9	0	0	0	0
1976	StL-N	0	49	3	2	.600	30	4.07	66 1/3	40	39	66	3	0	0	2
1977	Tex-A	0	5	0	0	—	7	7.56	8 1/3	2	10	10	1	0	0	0
Career Average		1	17	2	0	.786	11	3.91	26	15	15	27	1	0	0	0
Yankee Average		**1**	**23**	**6**	**0**	**1.000**	**14**	**2.41**	**52**	**34**	**35**	**42**	**3**	**0**	**0**	**0**
Career Total		4	117	11	3	.786	79	3.91	181 2/3	105	107	188	9	1	0	3
Yankee Total		**1**	**23**	**6**	**0**	**1.000**	**14**	**2.41**	**58 2/3**	**34**	**35**	**42**	**3**	**0**	**0**	**0**

Warhop, John Milton (Chief *or* Crab)

HEIGHT: 5'10" RIGHTHANDER BORN: 7/4/1884 HINTON, WEST VIRGINIA DIED: 10/4/1960 FREEPORT, ILLINOIS

YEAR	TEAM	STARTS	GAMES	WON	LOST	PCT	ER	ERA	INNINGS PITCHED	STRIKE-OUTS	WALKS	HITS ALLOWED	HRS ALLOWED	COMP. GAMES	SHUT-OUTS	SAVES
1908	**NY-A**	**4**	**5**	**1**	**2**	**.333**	**18**	**4.46**	**36 1/3**	**11**	**8**	**40**	**0**	**3**	**0**	**0**
1909	**NY-A**	**23**	**36**	**13**	**15**	**.464**	**65**	**2.40**	**243 1/3**	**95**	**81**	**197**	**2**	**21**	**3**	**2**
1910	**NY-A**	**27**	**37**	**14**	**14**	**.500**	**81**	**3.00**	**243**	**75**	**79**	**219**	**1**	**20**	**0**	**2**
1911	**NY-A**	**25**	**31**	**12**	**13**	**.480**	**97**	**4.16**	**209 2/3**	**71**	**44**	**239**	**6**	**17**	**1**	**0**

(continued)

(continued)

YEAR	TEAM															
1912	NY-A	22	39	10	19	.345	82	2.86	258	110	59	256	3	16	0	3
1913	NY-A	7	15	4	6	.400	26	3.75	62 1/3	11	33	69	1	1	0	0
1914	NY-A	23	37	8	15	.348	57	2.37	216 2/3	56	44	182	8	15	0	0
1915	NY-A	19	21	7	9	.438	63	3.96	143 1/3	34	52	164	7	12	0	0
Career Average		19	28	9	12	.426	61	3.12	176	58	50	171	4	13	1	1
Yankee Average		**19**	**28**	**9**	**12**	**.426**	**61**	**3.12**	**176**	**58**	**50**	**171**	**4**	**13**	**1**	**1**
Career Total		150	221	69	93	.426	489	3.12	1412 2/3	463	400	1366	28	105	4	7
Yankee Total		**150**	**221**	**69**	**93**	**.426**	**489**	**3.12**	**1412 2/3**	**463**	**400**	**1366**	**28**	**105**	**4**	**7**

Washburn, George Edward
HEIGHT: 6′1″ RIGHTHANDER BORN: 10/6/1914 SOLON, MAINE DIED: 1/5/1979 BATON ROUGE, LOUISIANA

YEAR	TEAM	STARTS	GAMES	WON	LOST	PCT	ER	ERA	INNINGS PITCHED	STRIKE-OUTS	WALKS	HITS ALLOWED	HRS ALLOWED	COMP. GAMES	SHUT-OUTS	SAVES
1941	NY-A	1	1	0	1	.000	3	13.50	2	1	5	2	0	0	0	0
Career Average		1	1	0	1	.000	3	13.50	2	1	5	2	0	0	0	0
Yankee Average		**1**	**1**	**0**	**1**	**.000**	**3**	**13.50**	**2**	**1**	**5**	**2**	**0**	**0**	**0**	**0**
Career Total		1	1	0	1	.000	3	13.50	2	1	5	2	0	0	0	0
Yankee Total		**1**	**1**	**0**	**1**	**.000**	**3**	**13.50**	**2**	**1**	**5**	**2**	**0**	**0**	**0**	**0**

Waslewski, Gary Lee
HEIGHT: 6′4″ RIGHTHANDER BORN: 7/21/1941 MERIDEN, CONNECTICUT

YEAR	TEAM	STARTS	GAMES	WON	LOST	PCT	ER	ERA	INNINGS PITCHED	STRIKE-OUTS	WALKS	HITS ALLOWED	HRS ALLOWED	COMP. GAMES	SHUT-OUTS	SAVES
1967	Bos-A	8	12	2	2	.500	15	3.21	42	20	20	34	3	0	0	0
1968	Bos-A	11	34	4	7	.364	43	3.67	105 1/3	59	40	108	9	2	0	2
1969	StL-N	0	12	0	2	.000	9	3.92	20 2/3	16	8	19	3	0	0	1
1969	Mon-N	14	30	3	7	.300	40	3.29	109 1/3	63	63	102	5	3	1	1
1970	Mon-N	4	6	0	2	.000	14	5.11	24 2/3	19	15	23	3	0	0	0
1970	**NY-A**	5	26	2	2	.500	19	3.11	55	27	27	42	4	0	0	0
1971	**NY-A**	0	24	0	1	.000	13	3.28	35 2/3	17	16	28	2	0	0	1
1972	Oak-A	0	8	0	3	.000	4	2.04	17 2/3	8	8	12	3	0	0	0
Career Average		5	19	1	3	.297	20	3.44	51	29	25	46	4	1	0	1
Yankee Average		**3**	**25**	**1**	**2**	**.400**	**16**	**3.18**	**45**	**22**	**22**	**35**	**3**	**0**	**0**	**1**
Career Total		42	152	11	26	.297	157	3.44	410 1/3	229	197	368	32	5	1	5
Yankee Total		**5**	**50**	**2**	**3**	**.400**	**32**	**3.18**	**90 2/3**	**44**	**43**	**70**	**6**	**0**	**0**	**1**

Watson, Allen Kenneth
HEIGHT: 6′1″ LEFTHANDER BORN: 11/18/1970 JAMAICA, NEW YORK

YEAR	TEAM	STARTS	GAMES	WON	LOST	PCT	ER	ERA	INNINGS PITCHED	STRIKE-OUTS	WALKS	HITS ALLOWED	HRS ALLOWED	COMP. GAMES	SHUT-OUTS	SAVES
1993	StL-N	15	16	6	7	.462	44	4.60	86	49	28	90	11	0	0	0
1994	StL-N	22	22	6	5	.545	71	5.56	115 2/3	74	53	130	15	0	0	0
1995	StL-N	19	21	7	9	.438	63	4.97	114 1/3	49	41	126	17	0	0	0
1996	SF-N	29	29	8	12	.400	95	4.62	185 2/3	128	69	189	28	2	0	0
1997	Ana-A	34	35	12	12	.500	109	4.93	199	141	73	220	37	0	0	0
1998	Ana-A	14	28	6	7	.462	62	6.07	92 1/3	64	34	122	12	1	0	0
1999	Sea-A	0	3	0	1	.000	4	12.00	3	2	3	6	5	0	0	0
1999	NY-N	4	14	2	2	.500	18	4.15	39 2/3	32	22	36	5	0	0	1
1999	**NY-A**	0	21	4	0	1.000	8	2.12	34 1/3	30	10	30	3	0	0	0
2000	**NY-A**	0	17	0	0	—	25	10.23	22	22	20	18	30	3	0	0
Career Average		14	21	5	6	.481	50	5.03	87	59	35	97	16	1	0	0
Yankee Average		**0**	**19**	**2**	**0**	**1.000**	**17**	**7.30**	**20**	**26**	**15**	**24**	**17**	**2**	**0**	**0**
Career Total		137	206	51	55	.481	499	5.03	892	591	353	967	163	6	0	1
Yankee Total		**0**	**38**	**4**	**0**	**1.000**	**33**	**7.30**	**41**	**52**	**30**	**48**	**33**	**3**	**0**	**0**

Weathers, John David (Dave)
HEIGHT: 6'3" RIGHTHANDER BORN: 9/25/1969 LAWRENCEBURG, TENNESSEE

YEAR	TEAM	STARTS	GAMES	WON	LOST	PCT	ER	ERA	INNINGS PITCHED	STRIKE-OUTS	WALKS	HITS ALLOWED	HRS ALLOWED	COMP. GAMES	SHUT-OUTS	SAVES
1991	Tor-A	0	15	1	0	1.000	8	4.91	14 2/3	13	17	15	1	0	0	0
1992	Tor-A	0	2	0	0	—	3	8.10	3 1/3	3	2	5	1	0	0	0
1993	Fla-N	6	14	2	3	.400	26	5.12	45 2/3	34	13	57	3	0	0	0
1994	Fla-N	24	24	8	12	.400	79	5.27	135	72	59	166	13	0	0	0
1995	Fla-N	15	28	4	5	.444	60	6.00	90 1/3	60	52	104	8	0	0	0
1996	Fla-N	8	31	2	2	.500	36	4.56	71 1/3	40	28	85	7	0	0	0
1996	**NY-A**	**4**	**11**	**0**	**2**	**.000**	**18**	**9.53**	**17 1/3**	**13**	**14**	**23**	**1**	**0**	**0**	**0**
1997	**NY-A**	**0**	**10**	**0**	**1**	**.000**	**10**	**10.00**	**9**	**4**	**7**	**15**	**1**	**0**	**0**	**0**
1997	Cle-A	1	9	1	2	.333	14	7.88	16 2/3	14	8	23	2	0	0	0
1998	Cin-N	9	16	2	4	.333	43	6.24	62 1/3	51	27	86	3	0	0	0
1998	Mil-N	0	28	4	1	.800	17	3.26	47 2/3	43	14	44	3	0	0	0
1999	Mil-N	0	63	7	4	.636	48	4.65	93	74	38	102	14	0	0	2
2000	Mil-N	0	69	3	5	.375	26	3.07	76 1/3	50	32	73	7	0	0	1
Career Average		5	25	3	3	.453	30	5.12	52	36	24	61	5	0	0	0
Yankee Average		**2**	**11**	**0**	**2**	**.000**	**14**	**9.69**	**13**	**9**	**11**	**19**	**1**	**0**	**0**	**0**
Career Total		67	320	34	41	.453	388	5.12	682 2/3	471	311	798	64	0	0	3
Yankee Total		**4**	**21**	**0**	**3**	**.000**	**28**	**9.69**	**26**	**17**	**21**	**38**	**2**	**0**	**0**	**0**

Weaver, James Dement (Big Jim)
HEIGHT: 6'6" RIGHTHANDER BORN: 11/25/1903 OBION COUNTY, TENNESSEE DIED: 12/12/1983 LAKELAND, FLORIDA

YEAR	TEAM	STARTS	GAMES	WON	LOST	PCT	ER	ERA	INNINGS PITCHED	STRIKE-OUTS	WALKS	HITS ALLOWED	HRS ALLOWED	COMP. GAMES	SHUT-OUTS	SAVES
1928	Was-A	0	3	0	0	—	1	1.50	6	2	6	2	0	0	0	0
1931	**NY-A**	**5**	**17**	**2**	**1**	**.667**	**34**	**5.31**	**57 2/3**	**28**	**29**	**66**	**1**	**2**	**0**	**0**
1934	StL-A	5	5	2	0	1.000	14	6.41	19 2/3	11	20	17	3	2	0	0
1934	Chi-N	20	27	11	9	.550	69	3.91	159	98	54	163	5	8	1	0
1935	Pit-N	22	33	14	8	.636	67	3.42	176 1/3	87	58	177	9	11	4	0
1936	Pit-N	31	38	14	8	.636	108	4.31	225 2/3	108	74	239	12	11	1	0
1937	Pit-N	9	32	8	5	.615	39	3.20	109 2/3	44	31	106	2	2	1	0
1938	StL-A	1	1	0	1	.000	7	9.00	7	4	9	9	0	0	0	0
1938	Cin-N	15	30	6	4	.600	45	3.13	129 1/3	64	54	109	6	2	0	3
1939	Cin-N	0	3	0	0	—	1	3.00	3	3	1	3	0	0	0	0
Career Average		11	19	6	4	.613	39	3.88	89	45	34	89	4	4	1	0
Yankee Average		**5**	**17**	**2**	**1**	**.667**	**34**	**5.31**	**57 2/3**	**28**	**29**	**66**	**1**	**2**	**0**	**0**
Career Total		108	189	57	36	.613	385	3.88	893 1/3	449	336	891	38	38	7	3
Yankee Total		**5**	**17**	**2**	**1**	**.667**	**34**	**5.31**	**57 2/3**	**28**	**29**	**66**	**1**	**2**	**0**	**0**

Wehrmeister, David Thomas
HEIGHT: 6'4" RIGHTHANDER BORN: 11/9/1952 BERWYN, ILLINOIS

YEAR	TEAM	STARTS	GAMES	WON	LOST	PCT	ER	ERA	INNINGS PITCHED	STRIKE-OUTS	WALKS	HITS ALLOWED	HRS ALLOWED	COMP. GAMES	SHUT-OUTS	SAVES
1976	SD-N	4	7	0	4	.000	16	7.45	19 1/3	10	11	27	0	0	0	0
1977	SD-N	6	30	1	3	.250	47	6.07	69 2/3	32	44	81	8	0	0	0
1978	SD-N	0	4	1	0	1.000	5	6.14	7 1/3	2	5	8	1	0	0	0
1981	**NY-A**	**0**	**5**	**0**	**0**	**—**	**4**	**5.14**	**7**	**7**	**7**	**6**	**0**	**0**	**0**	**0**
1984	Phi-N	0	7	0	0	—	12	7.20	15	13	7	18	1	0	0	0
1985	Chi-A	0	23	2	2	.500	15	3.43	39 1/3	32	10	35	4	0	0	2
Career Average		2	13	1	2	.308	17	5.65	26	16	14	29	2	0	0	0
Yankee Average		**0**	**5**	**0**	**0**	**—**	**4**	**5.14**	**7**	**7**	**7**	**6**	**0**	**0**	**0**	**0**
Career Total		10	76	4	9	.308	99	5.65	157 2/3	96	84	175	14	0	0	2
Yankee Total		**0**	**5**	**0**	**0**	**—**	**4**	**5.14**	**7**	**7**	**7**	**6**	**0**	**0**	**0**	**0**

Weinert, Phillip Walter (Lefty)

HEIGHT: 6'1" LEFTHANDER BORN: 4/21/1902 PHILADELPHIA, PENNSYLVANIA DIED: 4/17/1973 ROCKLEDGE, FLORIDA

YEAR	TEAM	STARTS	GAMES	WON	LOST	PCT	ER	ERA	INNINGS PITCHED	STRIKE-OUTS	WALKS	HITS ALLOWED	HRS ALLOWED	COMP. GAMES	SHUT-OUTS	SAVES
1919	Phi-N	0	1	0	0	—	8	18.00	4	0	2	11	0	0	0	0
1920	Phi-N	2	10	1	1	.500	15	6.14	22	10	19	27	1	0	0	0
1921	Phi-N	0	8	1	0	1.000	2	1.46	12 1/3	2	5	8	1	0	0	0
1922	Phi-N	22	34	8	11	.421	63	3.40	166 2/3	58	70	189	10	10	0	1
1923	Phi-N	20	38	4	17	.190	94	5.42	156	46	81	207	10	8	0	1
1924	Phi-N	1	8	0	1	.000	4	2.45	14 2/3	7	11	10	0	0	0	0
1927	Chi-N	3	5	1	1	.500	10	4.58	19 2/3	5	6	21	2	1	0	0
1928	Chi-N	1	10	1	0	1.000	10	5.29	17	8	9	24	0	0	0	0
1931	**NY-A**	0	17	2	2	.500	17	6.20	24 2/3	24	19	31	2	0	0	0
Career Average		5	15	2	4	.353	25	4.59	49	18	25	59	3	2	0	0
Yankee Average		**0**	**17**	**2**	**2**	**.500**	**17**	**6.20**	**24 2/3**	**24**	**19**	**31**	**2**	**0**	**0**	**0**
Career Total		49	131	18	33	.353	223	4.59	437	160	222	528	26	19	0	2
Yankee Total		**0**	**17**	**2**	**2**	**.500**	**17**	**6.20**	**24 2/3**	**24**	**19**	**31**	**2**	**0**	**0**	**0**

Wells, David Lee

HEIGHT: 6'3" LEFTHANDER BORN: 5/20/1963 TORRANCE, CALIFORNIA

YEAR	TEAM	STARTS	GAMES	WON	LOST	PCT	ER	ERA	INNINGS PITCHED	STRIKE-OUTS	WALKS	HITS ALLOWED	HRS ALLOWED	COMP. GAMES	SHUT-OUTS	SAVES
1987	Tor-A	2	18	4	3	.571	13	3.99	29 1/3	32	12	37	0	0	0	1
1988	Tor-A	0	41	3	5	.375	33	4.62	64 1/3	56	31	65	12	0	0	4
1989	Tor-A	0	54	7	4	.636	23	2.40	86 1/3	78	28	66	5	0	0	2
1990	Tor-A	25	43	11	6	.647	66	3.14	189	115	45	165	14	0	0	3
1991	Tor-A	28	40	15	10	.600	82	3.72	198 1/3	106	49	188	24	2	0	1
1992	Tor-A	14	41	7	9	.438	72	5.40	120	62	36	138	16	0	0	2
1993	Det-A	30	32	11	9	.550	87	4.19	187	139	42	183	26	0	0	0
1994	Det-A	16	16	5	7	.417	49	3.97	111 1/3	71	24	113	13	5	0	0
1995	Det-A	18	18	10	3	.769	44	3.05	130	83	37	120	17	3	0	0
1995	Cin-N	11	11	6	5	.545	29	3.63	72	50	16	74	6	3	0	0
1996	Bal-A	34	34	11	14	.440	128	5.14	224 1/3	130	51	247	32	3	0	0
1997	**NY-A**	**32**	**32**	**16**	**10**	**.615**	**102**	**4.21**	**218**	**156**	**45**	**239**	**24**	**5**	**0**	**0**
1998	**NY-A**	**30**	**30**	**18**	**4**	**.818**	**83**	**3.49**	**214 1/3**	**163**	**29**	**195**	**29**	**8**	**0**	**0**
1999	Tor-A	34	34	17	10	.630	124	4.83	231 2/3	169	62	246	32	7	1	0
2000	Tor-A	35	35	20	8	.714	105	4.11	229 2/3	166	31	266	23	9	1	0
Career Average		21	32	11	7	.601	69	4.06	153	105	36	156	18	3	0	1
Yankee Average		**31**	**31**	**17**	**7**	**.708**	**93**	**3.85**	**216**	**160**	**37**	**217**	**27**	**7**	**0**	**0**
Career Total		309	479	161	107	.601	1040	4.06	2306 2/3	1576	538	2342	273	45	10	13
Yankee Total		**62**	**62**	**34**	**14**	**.708**	**185**	**3.85**	**432**	**319**	**74**	**434**	**53**	**13**	**0**	**0**

Wells, Edwin Lee (Satchelfoot)

HEIGHT: 6'1" LEFTHANDER BORN: 6/7/1900 ASHLAND, OHIO DIED: 5/1/1986 MONTGOMERY, ALABAMA

YEAR	TEAM	STARTS	GAMES	WON	LOST	PCT	ER	ERA	INNINGS PITCHED	STRIKE-OUTS	WALKS	HITS ALLOWED	HRS ALLOWED	COMP. GAMES	SHUT-OUTS	SAVES
1923	Det-A	0	7	0	0	—	6	5.40	10	6	6	11	0	0	0	0
1924	Det-A	15	29	6	8	.429	46	4.06	102	33	42	117	2	5	0	4
1925	Det-A	14	35	6	9	.400	93	6.23	134 1/3	45	62	190	8	5	0	2
1926	Det-A	26	36	12	10	.545	82	4.15	178	58	76	201	7	9	4	0
1927	Det-A	1	8	0	1	.000	15	6.75	20	5	5	28	3	0	0	1
1929	**NY-A**	**23**	**31**	**13**	**9**	**.591**	**93**	**4.33**	**193 1/3**	**78**	**81**	**179**	**19**	**10**	**3**	**0**
1930	**NY-A**	**21**	**27**	**12**	**3**	**.800**	**87**	**5.20**	**150 2/3**	**46**	**49**	**185**	**11**	**7**	**0**	**0**
1931	**NY-A**	**10**	**27**	**9**	**5**	**.643**	**56**	**4.32**	**116 2/3**	**34**	**37**	**130**	**7**	**6**	**0**	**2**
1932	**NY-A**	**0**	**22**	**3**	**3**	**.500**	**15**	**4.26**	**31 2/3**	**13**	**12**	**38**	**1**	**0**	**0**	**2**
1933	StL-A	22	36	6	14	.300	95	4.20	203 2/3	58	63	230	13	10	0	1
1934	StL-A	8	33	1	7	.125	49	4.79	92	27	35	108	7	2	0	1
Career Average		13	26	6	6	.496	58	4.65	112	37	43	129	7	5	1	1
Yankee Average		**14**	**27**	**9**	**5**	**.649**	**63**	**4.59**	**123**	**43**	**45**	**133**	**10**	**6**	**1**	**1**
Career Total		140	291	68	69	.496	637	4.65	1232 1/3	403	468	1417	78	54	7	13
Yankee Total		**54**	**107**	**37**	**20**	**.649**	**251**	**4.59**	**492 1/3**	**171**	**179**	**532**	**38**	**23**	**3**	**4**

Wensloff, Charles William (Butch)
HEIGHT: 5'11"   RIGHTHANDER   BORN: 12/3/1915 SAUSALITO, CALIFORNIA

YEAR	TEAM	STARTS	GAMES	WON	LOST	PCT	ER	ERA	INNINGS PITCHED	STRIKE-OUTS	WALKS	HITS ALLOWED	HRS ALLOWED	COMP. GAMES	SHUT-OUTS	SAVES
1943	NY-A	27	29	13	11	.542	63	2.54	223 1/3	105	70	179	7	18	1	1
1947	NY-A	5	11	3	1	.750	15	2.61	51 2/3	18	22	41	3	1	0	0
1948	Cle-A	0	1	0	1	.000	2	10.80	1 2/3	2	3	2	1	0	0	0
Career Average		11	14	5	4	.552	27	2.60	92	42	32	74	4	6	0	0
Yankee Average		**16**	**20**	**8**	**6**	**.571**	**39**	**2.55**	**138**	**62**	**46**	**110**	**5**	**10**	**1**	**1**
Career Total		32	41	16	13	.552	80	2.60	276 2/3	125	95	222	11	19	1	1
Yankee Total		**32**	**40**	**16**	**12**	**.571**	**78**	**2.55**	**275**	**123**	**92**	**220**	**10**	**19**	**1**	**1**

Wetteland, John Karl
HEIGHT: 6'2"   RIGHTHANDER   BORN: 8/21/1966 SAN MATEO, CALIFORNIA

YEAR	TEAM	STARTS	GAMES	WON	LOST	PCT	ER	ERA	INNINGS PITCHED	STRIKE-OUTS	WALKS	HITS ALLOWED	HRS ALLOWED	COMP. GAMES	SHUT-OUTS	SAVES
1989	LA-N	12	31	5	8	.385	43	3.77	102 2/3	96	34	81	8	0	0	1
1990	LA-N	5	22	2	4	.333	23	4.81	43	36	17	44	6	0	0	0
1991	LA-N	0	6	1	0	1.000	0	0.00	9	9	3	5	0	0	0	0
1992	Mon-N	0	67	4	4	.500	27	2.92	83 1/3	99	36	64	6	0	0	37
1993	Mon-N	0	70	9	3	.750	13	1.37	85 1/3	113	28	58	3	0	0	43
1994	Mon-N	0	52	4	6	.400	20	2.86	63 2/3	68	21	46	5	0	0	25
1995	**NY-A**	**0**	**60**	**1**	**5**	**.167**	**20**	**2.95**	**61 1/3**	**66**	**14**	**40**	**6**	**0**	**0**	**31**
1996	**NY-A**	**0**	**62**	**2**	**3**	**.400**	**20**	**2.86**	**63 2/3**	**69**	**21**	**54**	**9**	**0**	**0**	**43**
1997	Tex-A	0	61	7	2	.778	14	1.94	65	63	21	43	5	0	0	31
1998	Tex-A	0	63	3	1	.750	14	2.03	62	72	14	47	6	0	0	42
1999	Tex-A	0	62	4	4	.500	27	3.68	66	60	19	67	9	0	0	43
2000	Tex-A	0	62	6	5	.545	26	4.20	60	53	24	67	10	0	0	34
Career Average		1	52	4	4	.516	21	2.93	64	67	21	51	6	0	0	28
Yankee Average		**0**	**61**	**2**	**4**	**.273**	**20**	**2.90**	**62**	**68**	**18**	**47**	**8**	**0**	**0**	**37**
Career Total		17	618	48	45	.516	247	2.93	765	804	252	616	73	0	0	330
Yankee Total		**0**	**122**	**3**	**8**	**.273**	**40**	**2.90**	**124**	**135**	**35**	**94**	**15**	**0**	**0**	**74**

Wever, Stefan Matthew
HEIGHT: 6'8"   RIGHTHANDER   BORN: 4/22/1958 MARBURG, WEST GERMANY

YEAR	TEAM	STARTS	GAMES	WON	LOST	PCT	ER	ERA	INNINGS PITCHED	STRIKE-OUTS	WALKS	HITS ALLOWED	HRS ALLOWED	COMP. GAMES	SHUT-OUTS	SAVES
1982	NY-A	1	1	0	1	.000	8	27.01	2 2/3	2	3	6	1	0	0	0
Career Average		1	1	0	1	.000	8	27.01	2 2/3	2	3	6	1	0	0	0
Yankee Average		**1**	**1**	**0**	**1**	**.000**	**8**	**27.01**	**2 2/3**	**2**	**3**	**6**	**1**	**0**	**0**	**0**
Career Total		1	1	0	1	.000	8	27.01	2 2/3	2	3	6	1	0	0	0
Yankee Total		**1**	**1**	**0**	**1**	**.000**	**8**	**27.01**	**2 2/3**	**2**	**3**	**6**	**1**	**0**	**0**	**0**

Whitehurst, Walter Richard (Wally)
HEIGHT: 6'3"   RIGHTHANDER   BORN: 4/11/1964 SHREVEPORT, LOUISIANA

YEAR	TEAM	STARTS	GAMES	WON	LOST	PCT	ER	ERA	INNINGS PITCHED	STRIKE-OUTS	WALKS	HITS ALLOWED	HRS ALLOWED	COMP. GAMES	SHUT-OUTS	SAVES
1989	NY-N	1	9	0	1	.000	7	4.50	14	9	5	17	2	0	0	0
1990	NY-N	0	38	1	0	1.000	24	3.29	65 2/3	46	9	63	5	0	0	2
1991	NY-N	20	36	7	12	.368	62	4.19	133 1/3	87	25	142	12	0	0	1
1992	NY-N	11	44	3	9	.250	39	3.62	97	70	33	99	4	0	0	0
1993	SD-N	19	21	4	7	.364	45	3.83	105 2/3	57	30	109	11	0	0	0
1994	SD-N	13	13	4	7	.364	35	4.92	64	43	26	84	8	0	0	0
1996	NY-A	2	2	1	1	.500	6	6.75	8	1	2	11	1	0	0	0
Career Average		9	23	3	5	.351	31	4.02	69	45	19	75	6	0	0	0
Yankee Average		**2**	**2**	**1**	**1**	**.500**	**6**	**6.75**	**8**	**1**	**2**	**11**	**1**	**0**	**0**	**0**
Career Total		66	163	20	37	.351	218	4.02	487 2/3	313	130	525	43	0	0	3
Yankee Total		**2**	**2**	**1**	**1**	**.500**	**6**	**6.75**	**8**	**1**	**2**	**11**	**1**	**0**	**0**	**0**

Whitson, Eddie Lee

HEIGHT: 6'3" RIGHTHANDER BORN: 5/19/1955 JOHNSON CITY, TENNESSEE

YEAR	TEAM	STARTS	GAMES	WON	LOST	PCT	ER	ERA	INNINGS PITCHED	STRIKE-OUTS	WALKS	HITS ALLOWED	HRS ALLOWED	COMP. GAMES	SHUT-OUTS	SAVES
1977	Pit-N	2	5	1	0	1.000	6	3.45	15 2/3	10	9	11	0	0	0	0
1978	Pit-N	0	43	5	6	.455	27	3.27	74 1/3	64	37	66	5	0	0	4
1979	Pit-N	7	19	2	3	.400	28	4.37	57 2/3	31	36	53	6	0	0	1
1979	SF-N	17	18	5	8	.385	44	3.95	100 1/3	62	39	98	5	2	0	0
1980	SF-N	34	34	11	13	.458	73	3.10	211 2/3	90	56	222	7	6	2	0
1981	SF-N	22	22	6	9	.400	55	4.02	123	65	47	130	10	2	1	0
1982	Cle-A	9	40	4	2	.667	39	3.26	107 2/3	61	58	91	6	1	1	2
1983	SD-N	21	31	5	7	.417	69	4.30	144 1/3	81	50	143	23	2	0	1
1984	SD-N	31	31	14	8	.636	68	3.24	189	103	42	181	16	1	0	0
1985	**NY-A**	**30**	**30**	**10**	**8**	**.556**	**86**	**4.88**	**158 2/3**	**89**	**43**	**201**	**19**	**2**	**2**	**0**
1986	**NY-A**	**4**	**14**	**5**	**2**	**.714**	**31**	**7.54**	**37**	**27**	**23**	**54**	**5**	**0**	**0**	**0**
1986	SD-N	12	17	1	7	.125	47	5.59	75 2/3	46	37	85	8	0	0	0
1987	SD-N	34	36	10	13	.435	108	4.73	205 2/3	135	64	197	36	3	1	0
1988	SD-N	33	34	13	11	.542	86	3.77	205 1/3	118	45	202	17	3	1	0
1989	SD-N	33	33	16	11	.593	67	2.66	227	117	48	198	22	5	1	0
1990	SD-N	32	32	14	9	.609	66	2.60	228 2/3	127	47	215	13	6	3	0
1991	SD-N	12	13	4	6	.400	44	5.03	78 2/3	40	17	93	13	2	0	0
Career Average		20	27	7	7	.506	56	3.79	132	74	41	132	12	2	1	0
Yankee Average		**17**	**22**	**8**	**5**	**.600**	**59**	**5.38**	**98**	**58**	**33**	**128**	**12**	**1**	**1**	**0**
Career Total		333	452	126	123	.506	944	3.79	2240 1/3	1266	698	2240	211	35	12	8
Yankee Total		**34**	**44**	**15**	**10**	**.600**	**117**	**5.38**	**195 2/3**	**116**	**66**	**255**	**24**	**2**	**2**	**0**

Wicker, Kemp Caswell

HEIGHT: 5'11" LEFTHANDER BORN: 8/13/1906 KERNERSVILLE, NORTH CAROLINA DIED: 6/11/1973 KERNERSVILLE, NORTH CAROLINA

YEAR	TEAM	STARTS	GAMES	WON	LOST	PCT	ER	ERA	INNINGS PITCHED	STRIKE-OUTS	WALKS	HITS ALLOWED	HRS ALLOWED	COMP. GAMES	SHUT-OUTS	SAVES
1936	**NY-A**	**0**	**7**	**1**	**2**	**.333**	**17**	**7.65**	**20**	**5**	**11**	**31**	**2**	**0**	**0**	**0**
1937	**NY-A**	**10**	**16**	**7**	**3**	**.700**	**43**	**4.40**	**88**	**14**	**26**	**107**	**8**	**6**	**1**	**0**
1938	**NY-A**	**0**	**1**	**1**	**0**	**1.000**	**0**	**0.00**	**1**	**0**	**1**	**0**	**0**	**0**	**0**	**0**
1941	Bro-N	2	16	1	2	.333	13	3.66	32	8	14	30	3	0	0	1
Career Average		3	10	3	2	.588	18	4.66	35	7	13	42	3	2	0	0
Yankee Average		**3**	**8**	**3**	**2**	**.643**	**20**	**4.95**	**36**	**6**	**13**	**46**	**3**	**2**	**0**	**0**
Career Total		12	40	10	7	.588	73	4.66	141	27	52	168	13	6	1	1
Yankee Total		**10**	**24**	**9**	**5**	**.643**	**60**	**4.95**	**109**	**19**	**38**	**138**	**10**	**6**	**1**	**0**

Wickman, Robert Joe

HEIGHT: 6'1" RIGHTHANDER BORN: 2/6/1969 GREEN BAY, WISCONSIN

YEAR	TEAM	STARTS	GAMES	WON	LOST	PCT	ER	ERA	INNINGS PITCHED	STRIKE-OUTS	WALKS	HITS ALLOWED	HRS ALLOWED	COMP. GAMES	SHUT-OUTS	SAVES
1992	**NY-A**	**8**	**8**	**6**	**1**	**.857**	**23**	**4.11**	**50 1/3**	**21**	**20**	**51**	**2**	**0**	**0**	**0**
1993	**NY-A**	**19**	**41**	**14**	**4**	**.778**	**72**	**4.63**	**140**	**70**	**69**	**156**	**13**	**1**	**1**	**4**
1994	**NY-A**	**0**	**53**	**5**	**4**	**.556**	**24**	**3.09**	**70**	**56**	**27**	**54**	**3**	**0**	**0**	**6**
1995	**NY-A**	**1**	**63**	**2**	**4**	**.333**	**36**	**4.05**	**80**	**51**	**33**	**77**	**6**	**0**	**0**	**1**
1996	**NY-A**	**0**	**58**	**4**	**1**	**.800**	**41**	**4.67**	**79**	**61**	**34**	**94**	**7**	**0**	**0**	**0**
1996	Mil-A	0	12	3	0	1.000	6	3.38	16 2/3	14	10	12	3	0	0	0
1997	Mil-A	0	74	7	6	.538	29	2.75	95 2/3	78	41	89	8	0	0	1
1998	Mil-N	0	72	6	9	.400	34	3.73	82 1/3	71	39	79	5	0	0	25
1999	Mil-N	0	71	3	8	.273	28	3.41	74 1/3	60	38	75	6	0	0	37
2000	Mil-N	0	43	2	2	.500	15	2.93	46	44	20	37	1	0	0	16
2000	Cle-A	0	26	1	3	.250	10	3.38	26 2/3	11	12	27	0	0	0	14
Career Average		3	47	5	4	.558	29	3.76	69	49	31	68	5	0	0	9
Yankee Average		**6**	**45**	**6**	**3**	**.689**	**39**	**4.21**	**84**	**52**	**37**	**86**	**6**	**0**	**0**	**2**
Career Total		28	521	53	42	.558	318	3.76	761	537	343	751	54	1	1	104
Yankee Total		**28**	**223**	**31**	**14**	**.689**	**196**	**4.21**	**419 1/3**	**259**	**183**	**432**	**31**	**1**	**1**	**11**

Wiesler, Robert George
HEIGHT: 6'3" LEFTHANDER BORN: 8/13/1930 ST.LOUIS, MISSOURI

YEAR	TEAM	STARTS	GAMES	WON	LOST	PCT	ER	ERA	INNINGS PITCHED	STRIKE-OUTS	WALKS	HITS ALLOWED	HRS ALLOWED	COMP. GAMES	SHUT-OUTS	SAVES
1951	**NY-A**	**3**	**4**	**0**	**2**	**.000**	**14**	**13.50**	**9 1/3**	**3**	**11**	**13**	**0**	**0**	**0**	**0**
1954	**NY-A**	**5**	**6**	**3**	**2**	**.600**	**14**	**4.15**	**30 1/3**	**25**	**30**	**28**	**0**	**0**	**0**	**0**
1955	**NY-A**	**7**	**16**	**0**	**2**	**.000**	**23**	**3.91**	**53**	**22**	**49**	**39**	**1**	**0**	**0**	**0**
1956	Was-A	21	37	3	12	.200	88	6.44	123	49	112	141	11	3	0	0
1957	Was-A	2	3	1	1	.500	8	4.41	16 1/3	9	11	15	2	1	0	0
1958	Was-A	0	4	0	0	—	7	6.75	9 1/3	5	5	14	2	0	0	0
Career Average		6	12	1	3	.269	26	5.74	40	19	36	42	3	1	0	0
Yankee Average		**5**	**9**	**1**	**2**	**.333**	**17**	**4.95**	**31**	**17**	**30**	**27**	**0**	**0**	**0**	**0**
Career Total		38	70	7	19	.269	154	5.74	241 1/3	113	218	250	16	4	0	0
Yankee Total		**15**	**26**	**3**	**6**	**.333**	**51**	**4.95**	**92 2/3**	**50**	**90**	**80**	**1**	**0**	**0**	**0**

Wight, William Robert (Lefty)
HEIGHT: 6'1" LEFTHANDER BORN: 4/12/1922 RIO VISTA, CALIFORNIA

YEAR	TEAM	STARTS	GAMES	WON	LOST	PCT	ER	ERA	INNINGS PITCHED	STRIKE-OUTS	WALKS	HITS ALLOWED	HRS ALLOWED	COMP. GAMES	SHUT-OUTS	SAVES
1946	**NY-A**	**4**	**14**	**2**	**2**	**.500**	**20**	**4.46**	**40 1/3**	**11**	**30**	**44**	**1**	**1**	**0**	**0**
1947	**NY-A**	**1**	**1**	**1**	**0**	**1.000**	**1**	**1.00**	**9**	**3**	**2**	**8**	**0**	**1**	**0**	**0**
1948	Chi-A	32	34	9	20	.310	119	4.80	223 1/3	68	135	238	9	7	1	1
1949	Chi-A	33	35	15	13	.536	90	3.31	245	78	96	254	9	14	3	1
1950	Chi-A	28	30	10	16	.385	82	3.58	206	62	79	213	10	13	3	0
1951	Bos-A	17	34	7	7	.500	67	5.10	118 1/3	38	63	128	5	4	2	0
1952	Bos-A	2	10	2	1	.667	8	2.96	24 1/3	5	14	14	3	0	0	0
1952	Det-A	19	23	5	9	.357	62	3.88	143 2/3	65	55	167	7	8	3	0
1953	Det-A	4	13	0	3	.000	25	8.88	25 1/3	10	14	35	4	0	0	0
1953	Cle-A	0	20	2	1	.667	11	3.71	26 2/3	14	16	29	1	0	0	1
1955	Cle-A	0	17	0	0	—	7	2.63	24	9	9	24	0	0	0	1
1955	Bal-A	14	19	6	8	.429	32	2.45	117 1/3	54	39	111	6	8	2	2
1956	Bal-A	26	35	9	12	.429	78	4.02	174 2/3	84	72	198	7	7	1	0
1957	Bal-A	17	27	6	6	.500	49	3.64	121	50	54	122	4	2	0	0
1958	Cin-N	0	7	0	1	.000	3	4.05	6 2/3	5	4	7	1	0	0	0
1958	StL-N	1	28	3	0	1.000	32	5.02	57 1/3	18	32	64	7	1	0	2
Career Average		12	22	5	6	.438	43	3.95	98	36	45	104	5	4	1	1
Yankee Average		**3**	**8**	**2**	**1**	**.600**	**11**	**3.83**	**25**	**7**	**16**	**26**	**1**	**1**	**0**	**0**
Career Total		198	347	77	99	.438	686	3.95	1563	574	714	1656	74	66	15	8
Yankee Total		**5**	**15**	**3**	**2**	**.600**	**21**	**3.83**	**49 1/3**	**14**	**32**	**52**	**1**	**2**	**0**	**0**

Williams, Stanley Wilson
HEIGHT: 6'5" RIGHTHANDER BORN: 9/14/1936 ENFIELD, NEW HAMPSHIRE

YEAR	TEAM	STARTS	GAMES	WON	LOST	PCT	ER	ERA	INNINGS PITCHED	STRIKE-OUTS	WALKS	HITS ALLOWED	HRS ALLOWED	COMP. GAMES	SHUT-OUTS	SAVES
1958	LA-N	21	27	9	7	.563	53	4.01	119	80	65	99	10	3	2	0
1959	LA-N	15	35	5	5	.500	55	3.97	124 2/3	89	86	102	12	2	0	0
1960	LA-N	30	38	14	10	.583	69	3.00	207 1/3	175	72	162	26	9	2	1
1961	LA-N	35	41	15	12	.556	102	3.90	235 1/3	205	108	213	21	6	2	0
1962	LA-N	28	40	14	12	.538	92	4.46	185 2/3	108	98	184	16	4	1	1
1963	**NY-A**	**21**	**29**	**9**	**8**	**.529**	**52**	**3.21**	**146**	**98**	**57**	**137**	**7**	**6**	**1**	**0**
1964	**NY-A**	**10**	**21**	**1**	**5**	**.167**	**35**	**3.84**	**82**	**54**	**38**	**76**	**7**	**1**	**0**	**0**
1965	Cle-A	0	3	0	0	—	3	6.23	4 1/3	1	3	6	1	0	0	0
1967	Cle-A	8	16	6	4	.600	23	2.62	79	75	24	64	6	2	1	1
1968	Cle-A	24	44	13	11	.542	54	2.50	194 1/3	147	51	163	14	6	2	9
1969	Cle-A	15	61	6	14	.300	78	3.94	178 1/3	139	67	155	25	3	0	12
1970	Min-A	0	68	10	1	.909	25	1.99	113 1/3	76	32	85	8	0	0	15
1971	Min-A	1	46	4	5	.444	36	4.15	78	47	44	63	7	0	0	4
1971	StL-N	0	10	3	0	1.000	2	1.42	12 2/3	8	2	13	0	0	0	0
1972	Bos-A	0	3	0	0	—	3	6.23	4 1/3	3	1	5	0	0	0	0
Career Average		14	32	7	6	.537	45	3.48	118	87	50	102	11	3	1	3
Yankee Average		**16**	**25**	**5**	**7**	**.435**	**44**	**3.43**	**114**	**76**	**48**	**107**	**7**	**4**	**1**	**0**
Career Total		208	482	109	94	.537	682	3.48	1764 1/3	1305	748	1527	160	42	11	43
Yankee Total		**31**	**50**	**10**	**13**	**.435**	**87**	**3.43**	**228**	**152**	**95**	**213**	**14**	**7**	**1**	**0**

Wilson, Peter Alex

HEIGHT: — LEFTHANDER BORN: 10/9/1885 SPRINGFIELD, MASSACHUSETTS DIED: 6/5/1957 ST. PETERSBURG, FLORIDA

YEAR	TEAM	STARTS	GAMES	WON	LOST	PCT	ER	ERA	INNINGS PITCHED	STRIKE-OUTS	WALKS	HITS ALLOWED	HRS ALLOWED	COMP. GAMES	SHUT-OUTS	SAVES
1908	NY-A	6	6	3	3	.500	15	3.46	39	33	33	27	0	4	1	0
1909	NY-A	12	14	6	5	.545	33	3.17	93 2/3	44	43	82	2	7	1	0
Career Average		9	10	5	4	.529	24	3.26	66	36	38	55	1	6	1	0
Yankee Average		9	10	5	4	.529	24	3.26	66	36	38	55	1	6	1	0
Career Total		18	20	9	8	.529	48	3.26	132 2/3	72	76	109	2	11	2	0
Yankee Total		18	20	9	8	.529	48	3.26	132 2/3	72	76	109	2	11	2	0

Wiltse, Lewis De Witt (Snake)

HEIGHT: — LEFTHANDER BORN: 12/5/1871 BOUCKVILLE, NEW YORK DIED: 8/25/1928 HARRISBURG, PENNSYLVANIA

YEAR	TEAM	STARTS	GAMES	WON	LOST	PCT	ER	ERA	INNINGS PITCHED	STRIKE-OUTS	WALKS	HITS ALLOWED	HRS ALLOWED	COMP. GAMES	SHUT-OUTS	SAVES
1901	Pit-N	5	7	1	4	.200	21	4.26	44 1/3	10	13	57	2	3	0	0
1901	Phi-A	19	19	13	5	.722	66	3.58	166	40	35	185	1	18	2	0
1902	Phi-A	17	19	8	8	.500	79	5.15	138	28	41	182	7	13	0	1
1902	Bal-A	18	19	7	10	.412	93	5.10	164	37	51	215	4	18	0	0
1903	NY-A	3	4	0	3	.000	15	5.40	25	6	6	35	1	2	0	1
Career Average		12	14	6	6	.492	55	4.59	107	24	29	135	3	11	0	0
Yankee Average		3	4	0	3	.000	15	5.40	25	6	6	35	1	2	0	1
Career Total		62	68	29	30	.492	274	4.59	537 1/3	121	146	674	15	54	2	2
Yankee Total		3	4	0	3	.000	15	5.40	25	6	6	35	1	2	0	1

Witt, Michael Atwater

HEIGHT: 6'7" RIGHTHANDER BORN: 7/20/1960 FULLERTON, CALIFORNIA

YEAR	TEAM	STARTS	GAMES	WON	LOST	PCT	ER	ERA	INNINGS PITCHED	STRIKE-OUTS	WALKS	HITS ALLOWED	HRS ALLOWED	COMP. GAMES	SHUT-OUTS	SAVES
1981	Cal-A	21	22	8	9	.471	47	3.28	129	75	47	123	9	7	1	0
1982	Cal-A	26	33	8	6	.571	70	3.51	179 2/3	85	47	177	8	5	1	0
1983	Cal-A	19	43	7	14	.333	84	4.91	154	77	75	173	14	2	0	5
1984	Cal-A	34	34	15	11	.577	95	3.47	246 2/3	196	84	227	17	9	2	0
1985	Cal-A	35	35	15	9	.625	99	3.56	250	180	98	228	22	6	1	0
1986	Cal-A	34	34	18	10	.643	85	2.84	269	208	73	218	22	14	3	0
1987	Cal-A	36	36	16	14	.533	110	4.01	247	192	84	252	34	10	0	0
1988	Cal-A	34	34	13	16	.448	115	4.15	249 2/3	133	87	263	14	12	2	0
1989	Cal-A	33	33	9	15	.375	111	4.54	220	123	48	252	26	5	0	0
1990	Cal-A	0	10	0	3	.000	4	1.77	20 1/3	14	13	19	1	0	0	1
1990	NY-A	16	16	5	6	.455	48	4.47	96 2/3	60	34	87	8	2	1	0
1991	NY-A	2	2	0	1	.000	6	10.13	5 1/3	0	1	8	1	0	0	0
1993	NY-A	9	9	3	2	.600	24	5.27	41	30	22	39	7	0	0	0
Career Average		23	26	9	9	.502	69	3.83	162	106	55	159	14	6	1	0
Yankee Average		9	9	3	3	.471	26	4.91	48	30	19	45	5	1	0	0
Career Total		299	341	117	116	.502	898	3.83	2108 1/3	1373	713	2066	183	72	11	6
Yankee Total		27	27	8	9	.471	78	4.91	143	90	57	134	16	2	1	0

Wolfe, Wilbert Otto (Bill *or* Barney)

HEIGHT: 6'1" RIGHTHANDER BORN: 1/9/1876 INDEPENDENCE, PENNSYLVANIA 2/27/53 N. CHARLEROI, PENNSYLVANIA

YEAR	TEAM	STARTS	GAMES	WON	LOST	PCT	ER	ERA	INNINGS PITCHED	STRIKE-OUTS	WALKS	HITS ALLOWED	HRS ALLOWED	COMP. GAMES	SHUT-OUTS	SAVES
1903	NY-A	16	20	6	9	.400	49	2.97	148 1/3	48	26	143	1	12	1	0
1904	NY-A	3	7	0	3	.000	12	3.21	33 2/3	8	4	31	1	2	0	0
1904	Was-A	16	17	6	9	.400	46	3.27	126 2/3	44	22	131	0	13	2	0
1905	Was-A	23	28	9	13	.409	52	2.57	182	52	37	162	1	17	1	1
1906	Was-A	3	4	0	3	.000	9	4.05	20	8	10	17	0	2	0	0
Career Average		12	15	4	7	.362	34	2.96	102	32	20	97	1	9	1	0
Yankee Average		10	14	3	6	.333	31	3.02	91	28	15	87	1	7	1	0
Career Total		61	76	21	37	.362	168	2.96	510 2/3	160	99	484	3	46	4	1
Yankee Total		19	27	6	12	.333	61	3.02	182	56	30	174	2	14	1	0

Womack, Horace Guy (Dooley)

HEIGHT: 6'0"   RIGHTHANDER   BORN: 8/25/1939 COLUMBIA, SOUTH CAROLINA

YEAR	TEAM	STARTS	GAMES	WON	LOST	PCT	ER	ERA	INNINGS PITCHED	STRIKE-OUTS	WALKS	HITS ALLOWED	HRS ALLOWED	COMP. GAMES	SHUT-OUTS	SAVES
1966	NY-A	1	42	7	3	.700	22	2.64	75	50	23	52	6	0	0	4
1967	NY-A	0	65	5	6	.455	26	2.41	97	57	35	80	6	0	0	18
1968	NY-A	0	45	3	7	.300	22	3.21	61 2/3	27	29	53	6	0	0	2
1969	Hou-N	0	30	2	1	.667	20	3.51	51 1/3	32	20	49	1	0	0	0
1969	Sea-A	0	9	2	1	.667	4	2.51	14 1/3	8	3	15	0	0	0	0
1970	Oak-A	0	2	0	0	—	5	15.00	3	3	1	4	2	0	0	0
Career Average		0	32	3	3	.514	17	2.95	50	30	19	42	4	0	0	4
Yankee Average		0	51	5	5	.484	23	2.70	78	45	29	62	6	0	0	8
Career Total		1	193	19	18	.514	99	2.95	302 1/3	177	111	253	21	0	0	24
Yankee Total		1	152	15	16	.484	70	2.70	233 2/3	134	87	185	18	0	0	24

Woodson, Richard Lee

HEIGHT: 6'5"   RIGHTHANDER   BORN: 3/30/1945 OELWEIN, IOWA

YEAR	TEAM	STARTS	GAMES	WON	LOST	PCT	ER	ERA	INNINGS PITCHED	STRIKE-OUTS	WALKS	HITS ALLOWED	HRS ALLOWED	COMP. GAMES	SHUT-OUTS	SAVES
1969	Min-A	10	44	7	5	.583	45	3.67	110 1/3	66	49	99	11	2	0	1
1970	Min-A	0	21	1	2	.333	13	3.82	30 2/3	22	19	29	2	0	0	1
1972	Min-A	36	36	14	14	.500	76	2.72	251 2/3	150	101	193	19	9	3	0
1973	Min-A	23	23	10	8	.556	62	3.95	141 1/3	53	68	137	12	4	2	0
1974	Min-A	4	5	1	1	.500	13	4.33	27	12	4	30	5	0	0	0
1974	NY-A	3	8	1	2	.333	18	5.79	28	12	12	34	6	0	0	0
Career Average		13	23	6	5	.515	38	3.47	98	53	42	87	9	3	1	0
Yankee Average		3	8	1	2	.333	18	5.79	28	12	12	34	6	0	0	0
Career Total		76	137	34	32	.515	227	3.47	589	315	253	522	55	15	5	2
Yankee Total		3	8	1	2	.333	18	5.79	28	12	12	34	6	0	0	0

Wright, Kenneth Warren

HEIGHT: 6'2"   RIGHTHANDER   BORN: 9/4/1946 PENSACOLA, FLORIDA

YEAR	TEAM	STARTS	GAMES	WON	LOST	PCT	ER	ERA	INNINGS PITCHED	STRIKE-OUTS	WALKS	HITS ALLOWED	HRS ALLOWED	COMP. GAMES	SHUT-OUTS	SAVES
1970	KC-A	0	47	1	2	.333	31	5.23	53 1/3	30	29	49	2	0	0	3
1971	KC-A	12	21	3	6	.333	32	3.69	78	56	47	66	6	1	1	1
1972	KC-A	0	17	1	2	.333	10	4.91	18 1/3	18	15	15	0	0	0	4
1973	KC-A	12	25	6	5	.545	44	4.91	80 2/3	75	82	60	6	1	0	0
1974	NY-A	0	3	0	0	—	2	3.18	5 2/3	2	7	5	0	0	0	0
Career Average		5	23	2	3	.423	24	4.54	47	36	36	39	3	0	0	2
Yankee Average		0	3	0	0	—	2	3.18	5 2/3	2	7	5	0	0	0	0
Career Total		24	113	11	15	.423	119	4.54	236	181	180	195	14	2	1	8
Yankee Total		0	3	0	0	—	2	3.18	5 2/3	2	7	5	0	0	0	0

Wyatt, John Thomas

HEIGHT: 6'0"   RIGHTHANDER   BORN: 4/19/1935 CHICAGO, ILLINOIS

YEAR	TEAM	STARTS	GAMES	WON	LOST	PCT	ER	ERA	INNINGS PITCHED	STRIKE-OUTS	WALKS	HITS ALLOWED	HRS ALLOWED	COMP. GAMES	SHUT-OUTS	SAVES
1961	KC-A	0	5	0	0	—	2	2.45	7 1/3	6	4	8	0	0	0	1
1962	KC-A	9	59	10	7	.588	62	4.46	125	106	80	121	12	0	0	11
1963	KC-A	0	63	6	4	.600	32	3.13	92	81	43	83	12	0	0	21
1964	KC-A	0	81	9	8	.529	51	3.59	128	74	52	111	23	0	0	20
1965	KC-A	0	65	2	6	.250	32	3.25	88 2/3	70	53	78	8	0	0	18
1966	KC-A	0	19	0	3	.000	14	5.32	23 2/3	25	16	19	3	0	0	2
1966	Bos-A	0	42	3	4	.429	25	3.14	71 2/3	63	27	59	3	0	0	8
1967	Bos-A	0	60	10	7	.588	27	2.60	93 1/3	68	39	71	6	0	0	20
1968	Bos-A	0	8	1	2	.333	5	4.22	10 2/3	11	6	9	2	0	0	0

(continued)

(continued)

YEAR	TEAM	STARTS	GAMES	WON	LOST	PCT	ER	ERA	INNINGS PITCHED	STRIKE-OUTS	WALKS	HITS ALLOWED	HRS ALLOWED	COMP. GAMES	SHUT-OUTS	SAVES
1968	NY-A	0	7	0	2	.000	2	2.16	8 ⅓	6	9	7	1	0	0	0
1968	Det-A	0	22	1	0	1.000	8	2.37	30 ⅓	25	11	26	2	0	0	2
1969	Oak-A	0	4	0	1	.000	5	5.40	8 ⅓	5	6	8	0	0	0	0
Career Average		1	36	4	4	.488	22	3.47	57	45	29	50	6	0	0	9
Yankee Average		**0**	**7**	**0**	**2**	**.000**	**2**	**2.16**	**8 ⅓**	**6**	**9**	**7**	**1**	**0**	**0**	**0**
Career Total		9	435	42	44	.488	265	3.47	687 ⅓	540	346	600	72	0	0	103
Yankee Total		**0**	**7**	**0**	**2**	**.000**	**2**	**2.16**	**8 ⅓**	**6**	**9**	**7**	**1**	**0**	**0**	**0**

Yarnall, Harvey Edward

HEIGHT: 6'3"   LEFTHANDER   BORN: 12/4/1975 LIMA, PENNSYLVANIA

YEAR	TEAM	STARTS	GAMES	WON	LOST	PCT	ER	ERA	INNINGS PITCHED	STRIKE-OUTS	WALKS	HITS ALLOWED	HRS ALLOWED	COMP. GAMES	SHUT-OUTS	SAVES
1999	NY-A	2	5	1	0	1.000	7	3.71	17	13	10	17	1	0	0	0
Career Average		2	5	1	0	1.000	7	3.71	17	13	10	17	1	0	0	0
Yankee Average		**2**	**5**	**1**	**0**	**1.000**	**7**	**3.71**	**17**	**13**	**10**	**17**	**1**	**0**	**0**	**0**
Career Total		2	5	1	0	1.000	7	3.71	17	13	10	17	1	0	0	0
Yankee Total		**2**	**5**	**1**	**0**	**1.000**	**7**	**3.71**	**17**	**13**	**10**	**17**	**1**	**0**	**0**	**0**

York, James Harlan

HEIGHT: 6'3"   RIGHTHANDER   BORN: 8/27/1947 MAYWOOD, CALIFORNIA

YEAR	TEAM	STARTS	GAMES	WON	LOST	PCT	ER	ERA	INNINGS PITCHED	STRIKE-OUTS	WALKS	HITS ALLOWED	HRS ALLOWED	COMP. GAMES	SHUT-OUTS	SAVES
1970	KC-A	0	4	1	1	.500	3	3.38	8	6	2	5	2	0	0	0
1971	KC-A	0	53	5	5	.500	30	2.89	93 ⅓	103	44	70	7	0	0	3
1972	Hou-N	0	26	0	1	.000	21	5.25	36	25	18	45	3	0	0	0
1973	Hou-N	0	41	3	4	.429	26	4.42	53	22	20	65	4	0	0	6
1974	Hou-N	0	28	2	2	.500	14	3.29	38 ⅓	15	19	48	1	0	0	1
1975	Hou-N	4	19	4	4	.500	20	3.86	46 ⅔	17	25	43	1	0	0	0
1976	**NY-A**	**0**	**3**	**1**	**0**	**1.000**	**6**	**5.59**	**9 ⅔**	**6**	**4**	**14**	**1**	**0**	**0**	**0**
Career Average		1	25	2	2	.485	17	3.79	41	28	19	41	3	0	0	1
Yankee Average		**0**	**3**	**1**	**0**	**1.000**	**6**	**5.59**	**9 ⅔**	**6**	**4**	**14**	**1**	**0**	**0**	**0**
Career Total		4	174	16	17	.485	120	3.79	285	194	132	290	19	0	0	10
Yankee Total		**0**	**3**	**1**	**0**	**1.000**	**6**	**5.59**	**9 ⅔**	**6**	**4**	**14**	**1**	**0**	**0**	**0**

Young, Curtis Allen

HEIGHT: 6'1"   LEFTHANDER   BORN: 4/16/1960 SAGINAW, MICHIGAN

YEAR	TEAM	STARTS	GAMES	WON	LOST	PCT	ER	ERA	INNINGS PITCHED	STRIKE-OUTS	WALKS	HITS ALLOWED	HRS ALLOWED	COMP. GAMES	SHUT-OUTS	SAVES
1983	Oak-A	2	8	0	1	.000	16	16.00	9	5	5	17	1	0	0	0
1984	Oak-A	17	20	9	4	.692	49	4.06	108 ⅔	41	31	118	9	2	1	0
1985	Oak-A	7	19	0	4	.000	37	7.24	46	19	22	57	15	0	0	0
1986	Oak-A	27	29	13	9	.591	76	3.45	198	116	57	176	19	5	2	0
1987	Oak-A	31	31	13	7	.650	92	4.08	203	124	44	194	38	6	0	0
1988	Oak-A	26	26	11	8	.579	72	4.14	156 ⅓	69	50	162	23	1	0	0
1989	Oak-A	20	25	5	9	.357	46	3.73	111	55	47	117	10	1	0	0
1990	Oak-A	21	26	9	6	.600	67	4.85	124 ⅓	56	53	124	17	0	0	0
1991	Oak-A	1	41	4	2	.667	38	5.00	68 ⅓	27	34	74	8	0	0	0
1992	KC-A	2	10	1	2	.333	14	5.18	24 ⅓	7	7	29	1	0	0	0
1992	**NY-A**	**5**	**13**	**3**	**0**	**1.000**	**16**	**3.32**	**43 ⅓**	**13**	**10**	**51**	**1**	**0**	**0**	**0**
1993	Oak-A	3	3	1	1	.500	7	4.30	14 ⅔	4	6	14	5	0	0	0
Career Average		14	21	6	4	.566	44	4.31	92	45	31	94	12	1	0	0
Yankee Average		**5**	**13**	**3**	**0**	**1.000**	**16**	**3.32**	**43 ⅓**	**13**	**10**	**51**	**1**	**0**	**0**	**0**
Career Total		162	251	69	53	.566	530	4.31	1107	536	366	1133	147	15	3	0
Yankee Total		**5**	**13**	**3**	**0**	**1.000**	**16**	**3.32**	**43 ⅓**	**13**	**10**	**51**	**1**	**0**	**0**	**0**

Zachary, Jonathan Thompson Walton (Tom)
HEIGHT: 6'1" LEFTHANDER BORN: 5/7/1896 GRAHAM, NORTH CAROLINA DIED: 1/24/1969 BURLINGTON, NORTH CAROLINA

YEAR	TEAM	STARTS	GAMES	WON	LOST	PCT	ER	ERA	INNINGS PITCHED	STRIKE-OUTS	WALKS	HITS ALLOWED	HRS ALLOWED	COMP. GAMES	SHUT-OUTS	SAVES
1918	Phi-A	2	2	2	0	1.000	5	5.63	8	1	7	9	0	0	0	0
1919	Was-A	7	17	1	5	.167	20	2.92	61 2/3	9	20	68	0	0	0	0
1920	Was-A	31	44	15	16	.484	110	3.77	262 2/3	53	78	289	7	19	3	2
1921	Was-A	31	39	18	16	.529	110	3.96	250	53	59	314	10	17	2	1
1922	Was-A	25	32	15	10	.600	64	3.12	184 2/3	37	43	190	6	13	1	1
1923	Was-A	29	35	10	16	.385	102	4.49	204 1/3	40	63	270	9	10	0	0
1924	Was-A	27	33	15	9	.625	62	2.75	202 2/3	45	53	198	5	13	1	2
1925	Was-A	33	38	12	15	.444	93	3.85	217 2/3	58	74	247	10	11	1	2
1926	StL-A	31	34	14	15	.483	99	3.60	247 1/3	53	97	264	14	18	3	0
1927	StL-A	12	13	4	6	.400	38	4.37	78 1/3	13	27	110	4	6	0	0
1927	Was-A	14	15	4	7	.364	45	3.94	102 2/3	13	30	116	2	5	1	0
1928	Was-A	14	20	6	9	.400	62	5.44	102 1/3	19	40	130	5	5	1	0
1928	**NY-A**	**6**	**7**	**3**	**3**	**.500**	**20**	**3.94**	**45 2/3**	**7**	**15**	**54**	**1**	**3**	**0**	**1**
1929	**NY-A**	**11**	**26**	**12**	**0**	**1.000**	**33**	**2.48**	**119 2/3**	**35**	**30**	**131**	**5**	**7**	**2**	**2**
1930	**NY-A**	**3**	**3**	**1**	**1**	**.500**	**12**	**6.48**	**16 2/3**	**1**	**9**	**18**	**0**	**0**	**0**	**0**
1930	Bos-N	22	24	11	5	.688	77	4.58	151 1/3	57	50	192	9	10	1	0
1931	Bos-N	28	33	11	15	.423	79	3.10	229	64	53	243	8	16	3	2
1932	Bos-N	24	32	12	11	.522	73	3.10	212	67	55	231	5	12	1	0
1933	Bos-N	20	26	7	9	.438	49	3.53	125	22	35	134	1	6	2	2
1934	Bos-N	4	5	1	2	.333	9	3.38	24	4	8	27	1	2	1	0
1934	Bro-N	12	22	5	6	.455	50	4.43	101 1/3	28	21	122	5	4	0	2
1935	Bro-N	21	25	7	12	.368	63	3.59	158	33	35	193	10	9	1	4
1936	Bro-N	0	1	0	0	—	2	54.05	1/3	0	1	2	0	0	0	0
1936	Phi-N	2	7	0	3	.000	18	7.97	20 1/3	8	11	28	2	0	0	1
Career Average		17	22	8	8	.493	54	3.73	130	30	38	149	5	8	1	1
Yankee Average		**7**	**12**	**5**	**1**	**.800**	**22**	**3.21**	**61**	**14**	**18**	**68**	**2**	**3**	**1**	**1**
Career Total		409	533	186	191	.493	1295	3.73	3126 1/3	720	914	3580	119	186	24	22
Yankee Total		**20**	**36**	**16**	**4**	**.800**	**65**	**3.21**	**182**	**43**	**54**	**203**	**6**	**10**	**2**	**3**

Zuber, William Henry (Goober)
HEIGHT: 6'2" RIGHTHANDER BORN: 3/26/1913 MIDDLE AMANA, IOWA DIED: 11/2/1982 CEDAR RAPIDS, IOWA

YEAR	TEAM	STARTS	GAMES	WON	LOST	PCT	ER	ERA	INNINGS PITCHED	STRIKE-OUTS	WALKS	HITS ALLOWED	HRS ALLOWED	COMP. GAMES	SHUT-OUTS	SAVES
1936	Cle-A	2	2	1	1	.500	10	6.59	13 2/3	5	15	14	0	1	0	0
1938	Cle-A	0	15	0	3	.000	16	5.02	28 2/3	14	20	33	0	0	0	1
1939	Cle-A	1	16	2	0	1.000	21	5.97	31 2/3	16	19	41	2	0	0	0
1940	Cle-A	0	17	1	1	.500	15	5.63	24	12	14	25	3	0	0	0
1941	Was-A	7	36	6	4	.600	58	5.42	96 1/3	51	61	110	5	1	0	2
1942	Was-A	7	37	9	9	.500	54	3.84	126 2/3	64	82	115	5	3	1	1
1943	**NY-A**	**13**	**20**	**8**	**4**	**.667**	**51**	**3.89**	**118**	**57**	**74**	**100**	**3**	**7**	**0**	**1**
1944	**NY-A**	**13**	**22**	**5**	**7**	**.417**	**50**	**4.21**	**107**	**59**	**54**	**101**	**5**	**2**	**1**	**0**
1945	**NY-A**	**14**	**21**	**5**	**11**	**.313**	**45**	**3.19**	**127**	**50**	**56**	**121**	**2**	**7**	**0**	**1**
1946	**NY-A**	**0**	**3**	**0**	**1**	**.000**	**8**	**12.71**	**5 2/3**	**3**	**3**	**10**	**2**	**0**	**0**	**0**
1946	Bos-A	7	15	5	1	.833	16	2.54	56 2/3	29	39	37	4	2	1	0
1947	Bos-A	1	20	1	0	1.000	30	5.33	50 2/3	23	31	60	4	0	0	0
Career Average		5	19	4	4	.506	31	4.28	66	32	39	64	3	2	0	1
Yankee Average		**10**	**17**	**5**	**6**	**.439**	**39**	**3.88**	**89**	**42**	**47**	**83**	**3**	**4**	**0**	**1**
Career Total		65	224	43	42	.506	374	4.28	786	383	468	767	35	23	3	6
Yankee Total		**40**	**66**	**18**	**23**	**.439**	**154**	**3.88**	**357 2/3**	**169**	**187**	**332**	**12**	**16**	**1**	**2**

APPENDIX A:

Post-Season Play

1921 World Series

NEW YORK GIANTS (5) VS. NEW YORK YANKEES (3)

GAME 1
Wednesday, October 5
at the Polo Grounds, New York

	1	2	3	4	5	6	7	8	9	R	H	E
New York Yankees	1	0	0	0	1	1	0	0	0	3	7	0
New York Giants	0	0	0	0	0	0	0	0	0	0	5	0

WP - Carl Mays; LP - Phil Douglas

GAME 2
Thursday, October 6
at the Polo Grounds, New York

	1	2	3	4	5	6	7	8	9	R	H	E
New York Giants	0	0	0	0	0	0	0	0	0	0	2	3
New York Yankees	0	0	0	1	0	0	0	2	x	3	3	0

WP - Waite Hoyt; LP - Art Nehf

GAME 3
Friday, October 7
at the Polo Grounds, New York

	1	2	3	4	5	6	7	8	9	R	H	E
New York Yankees	0	0	4	0	0	0	0	1	0	5	8	0
New York Giants	0	0	4	0	0	0	8	1	x	13	20	0

WP - Jesse Barnes; LP - Jack Quinn

GAME 4
Sunday, October 9
at the Polo Grounds, New York

	1	2	3	4	5	6	7	8	9	R	H	E
New York Giants	0	0	0	0	0	0	0	3	1	4	9	1
New York Yankees	0	0	0	0	1	0	0	0	1	2	7	1

HR - NYY Babe Ruth

WP - Phil Douglas; LP - Carl Mays

GAME 5
Monday, October 10
at the Polo Grounds, New York

	1	2	3	4	5	6	7	8	9	R	H	E
New York Yankees	0	0	1	2	0	0	0	0	0	3	6	1
New York Giants	1	0	0	0	0	0	0	0	1	1	10	1

WP - Waite Hoyt; LP - Art Nehf

GAME 6
Tuesday, October 11
at the Polo Grounds, New York

	1	2	3	4	5	6	7	8	9	R	H	E
New York Giants	0	3	0	4	0	1	0	0	0	8	13	0
New York Yankees	3	2	0	0	0	0	0	0	0	5	7	2

HR - NYG Irish Meusel, Frank Snyder; NYY Chick Fewster

WP - Jesse Barnes; Bob Shawkey

GAME 7
Wednesday, October 12
at the Polo Grounds, New York

	1	2	3	4	5	6	7	8	9	R	H	E
New York Yankees	0	1	0	0	0	0	0	0	0	1	8	1
New York Giants	0	0	0	1	0	0	1	0	x	2	6	0

WP - Phil Douglas; LP - Carl Mays

GAME 8
Thursday, October 13
at the Polo Grounds, New York

	1	2	3	4	5	6	7	8	9	R	H	E
New York Giants	1	0	0	0	0	0	0	0	0	1	6	0
New York Yankees	0	0	0	0	0	0	0	0	0	4	4	1

WP - Art Nehf; LP - Waite Hoyt

BATTING STATISTICS

New York Giants	G	AB	R	H	2B	3B	HR	RBI	BB	SO	SB	CS	BA
Dave Bancroft	8	33	3	5	1	0	0	3	1	5	0	1	.152
Jesse Barnes	3	9	3	4	0	0	0	0	0	0	0	0	.444
George Burns	8	33	2	11	4	1	0	2	3	5	1	1	.333
Phil Douglas	3	7	0	0	0	0	0	0	0	2	0	0	.000
Frankie Frisch	8	30	5	9	0	1	0	1	4	3	3	0	.300
George Kelly	8	30	3	7	1	0	0	4	3	10	0	1	.233
Irish Meusel	8	29	4	10	2	1	1	7	2	3	1	2	.345
Art Nehf	3	9	0	0	0	0	0	0	1	3	0	0	.000
Johnny Rawlings	8	30	2	10	3	0	0	4	0	3	0	1	.333
Earl Smith	3	7	0	0	0	0	0	0	1	0	0	1	.000
Frank Snyder	7	22	4	8	1	0	1	3	0	2	0	1	.364
Ross Youngs	8	25	3	7	1	1	0	4	7	2	2	1	.280
Totals	8	264	29	71	13	4	2	28	22	38	7	9	**.269**

New York Yankees	G	AB	R	H	2B	3B	HR	RBI	BB	SO	SB	CS	BA
Home Run Baker	4	8	0	2	0	0	0	0	1	0	0	0	.250
Al DeVormer	2	1	0	0	0	0	0	0	0	0	0	0	.000
Chick Fewster	4	10	3	2	0	0	1	2	3	3	0	0	.200
Waite Hoyt	3	9	0	2	0	0	0	1	0	1	0	0	.222
Carl Mays	3	9	0	1	0	0	0	0	0	1	0	0	.111
Mike McNally	7	20	3	4	1	0	0	1	1	3	2	2	.200
Bob Meusel	8	30	3	6	2	0	0	3	2	5	1	2	.200
Elmer Miller	8	31	3	5	1	0	0	2	2	5	0	0	.161
Roger Peckinpaugh	8	28	2	5	1	0	0	0	4	3	0	1	.179
Wally Pipp	8	26	1	4	1	0	0	2	2	3	1	1	.154
Jack Quinn	1	2	0	0	0	0	0	0	0	1	0	0	.000
Babe Ruth	6	16	3	5	0	0	1	4	5	8	2	1	.313
Wally Schang	8	21	1	6	1	1	0	1	5	4	0	0	.286
Bob Shawkey	2	4	2	2	0	0	0	0	0	1	0	0	.500
Aaron Ward	8	26	1	6	0	0	0	4	2	6	0	0	.231
Totals	8	241	22	50	7	1	2	20	27	44	6	7	**.207**

PITCHING STATISTICS

New York Giants	G	GS	CG	IP	H	ER	BB	SO	W-L	Sv	ERA
Jesse Barnes	3	0	0	16 1/3	10	3	6	18	2-0	0	1.65
Phil Douglas	3	3	2	26	20	6	5	17	2-1	0	2.08
Art Nehf	3	3	3	26	13	4	13	8	1-2	0	1.38
Fred Toney	2	2	0	2 2/3	7	7	3	1	0-0	0	23.63
Totals	**8**	**8**	**5**	**71**	**50**	**20**	**27**	**44**	**5-3**	**0**	**2.54**

New York Yankees	G	GS	CG	IP	H	ER	BB	SO	W-L	Sv	ERA
Rip Collins	1	0	0	0 2/3	5	4	1	0	0-0	0	54.00
Harry Harper	1	1	0	1 1/3	3	3	2	1	0-0	0	20.25
Waite Hoyt	3	3	3	27	18	0	11	18	2-1	0	0.00
Carl Mays	3	3	3	26	20	5	0	9	1-2	0	1.73
Bill Piercy	1	0	0	1	2	0	0	2	0-0	0	0.00
Jack Quinn	1	0	0	3 2/3	8	4	2	2	0-1	0	9.82
Tom Rogers	1	0	0	1 1/3	3	1	0	1	0-0	0	6.75
Bob Shawkey	2	1	0	9	13	7	6	5	0-1	0	7.00
Totals	**8**	**8**	**6**	**70**	**72**	**24**	**22**	**38**	**3-5**	**0**	**3.09**

1922 World Series

NEW YORK GIANTS (4) VS. NEW YORK YANKEES (1)

GAME 1
Wednesday, October 4
at the Polo Grounds, New York

	1	2	3	4	5	6	7	8	9	R	H	E
New York Yankees	0	0	0	0	0	1	1	0	0	2	7	0
New York Giants	0	0	0	0	0	0	0	3	x	3	11	3

WP - Rosy Ryan; LP - Joe Bush

GAME 2
Thursday, October 5
at the Polo Grounds, New York

	1	2	3	4	5	6	7	8	9	10	R	H	E
New York Giants	3	0	0	0	0	0	0	0	0	0	3	8	1
New York Yankees	1	0	0	1	0	0	0	1	0	0	3	8	0

HR - NYG Irish Meusel; NYY Aaron Ward

Jsse Barnes (no decision) vs. Bob Shawkey (no decision)

GAME CALLED ON ACCOUNT OF DARKNESS

GAME 3
Friday, October 6
at the Polo Grounds, New York

	1	2	3	4	5	6	7	8	9	R	H	E
New York Yankees	0	0	0	0	0	0	0	0	0	0	4	1
New York Giants	0	0	2	0	0	0	1	0	x	3	12	1

WP - Jack Scott; LP - Waite Hoyt

GAME 4
Saturday, October 7
at the Polo Grounds, New York

	1	2	3	4	5	6	7	8	9	R	H	E
New York Giants	0	0	0	0	4	0	0	0	0	4	9	1
New York Yankees	2	0	0	0	0	0	1	0	0	3	8	0

HR - NYY Aaron Ward

WP - Hugh McQuillan; LP - Carl Mays

GAME 5
Sunday, October 8
at the Polo Grounds, New York

	1	2	3	4	5	6	7	8	9	R	H	E
New York Yankees	1	0	0	0	1	0	1	0	0	3	5	0
New York Giants	0	2	0	0	0	0	0	3	x	5	10	0

WP - Art Nehf; LP - Joe Bush

BATTING STATISTICS

New York Giants	G	AB	R	H	2B	3B	HR	RBI	BB	SO	SB	CS	BA
Dave Bancroft	5	19	4	4	0	0	0	2	2	1	0	0	.211
Jesse Barnes	1	4	0	0	0	0	0	0	0	1	0	0	.000
Bill Cunningham	4	10	0	2	0	0	0	2	2	1	0	0	.200
Frankie Frisch	5	17	3	8	1	0	0	2	1	0	1	1	.471
Heine Groh	5	19	4	9	0	1	0	0	2	1	0	1	.474
George Kelly	5	18	0	5	0	0	0	2	0	3	0	1	.278
Lee King	2	1	0	1	0	0	0	1	0	0	0	0	1.000
Hugh McQuillan	1	4	1	1	1	0	0	0	0	1	0	0	.250
Irish Meusel	5	20	3	5	0	0	1	7	0	1	0	0	.250
Art Nehf	2	3	0	0	0	0	0	0	2	0	0	0	.000
Jack Scott	1	4	0	1	0	0	0	0	0	1	0	0	.250
Earl Smith	4	7	0	1	0	0	0	0	0	2	0	0	.143
Frank Snyder	4	15	1	5	0	0	0	0	1	1	0	0	.333
Casey Stengel	2	5	0	2	0	0	0	0	0	1	0	0	.400
Ross Youngs	5	16	2	6	0	0	0	2	3	1	0	1	.375
Totals	**5**	**162**	**18**	**50**	**2**	**1**	**1**	**18**	**12**	**15**	**1**	**4**	**.309**

New York Yankees	G	AB	R	H	2B	3B	HR	RBI	BB	SO	SB	CS	BA
Home Run Baker	1	1	0	0	0	0	0	0	0	0	0	0	.000
Joe Bush	2	6	0	1	0	0	0	1	0	0	0	0	.167
Joe Dugan	5	20	4	5	1	0	0	0	0	1	0	0	.250
Waite Hoyt	2	2	0	1	0	0	0	0	0	0	0	0	.500
Carl Mays	1	2	0	0	0	0	0	0	0	0	0	0	.000
Norm McMillan	1	2	0	0	0	0	0	0	0	0	0	0	.000
Bob Meusel	5	20	2	6	1	0	0	2	1	3	1	0	.300
Wally Pipp	5	21	0	6	1	0	0	3	0	2	1	0	.286
Babe Ruth	5	17	1	2	1	0	0	1	2	3	0	1	.118
Wally Schang	5	16	0	3	1	0	0	0	0	3	0	0	.188
Everett Scott	5	14	0	2	0	0	0	1	1	0	0	0	.143
Bob Shawkey	1	4	0	0	0	0	0	0	0	1	0	0	.000
Elmer Smith	2	2	0	0	0	0	0	0	0	2	0	0	.000
Aaron Ward	5	13	3	2	0	0	2	3	3	3	0	0	.154
Whitey Witt	5	18	1	4	1	0	0	1	0	2	0	0	.222
Totals	**5**	**158**	**11**	**32**	**6**	**1**	**2**	**11**	**8**	**20**	**2**	**1**	**.203**

PITCHING STATISTICS

New York Giants	G	GS	CG	IP	H	ER	BB	SO	W-L	Sv	ERA
Jesse Barnes	1	1	1	10	8	2	2	6	0-0	0	1.80
Hugh McQuillan	1	1	1	9	8	3	2	4	1-0	0	3.00
Art Nehf	2	2	1	16	11	4	3	6	1-0	0	2.25
Rosy Ryan	1	0	0	2	1	0	0	2	1-0	0	0.00
Jack Scott	1	1	1	9	4	0	1	2	1-0	0	0.00
Totals	**5**	**5**	**4**	**46**	**32**	**9**	**8**	**20**	**4-0**	**0**	**1.76**

New York Yankees	G	GS	CG	IP	H	ER	BB	SO	W-L	Sv	ERA
Joe Bush	2	2	1	15	21	8	5	6	0-2	0	4.80
Waite Hoyt	2	1	0	8	11	1	2	4	0-1	0	1.13
Sad Sam Jones	2	0	0	2	1	0	1	0	0-0	0	0.00
Carl Mays	1	1	0	8	9	4	2	1	0-1	0	4.50
Bob Shawkey	1	1	1	10	8	3	2	4	0-0	0	2.70
Totals	**5**	**5**	**2**	**43**	**50**	**16**	**12**	**15**	**0-4**	**0**	**3.35**

1923 World Series

NEW YORK YANKEES (4) VS. NEW YORK GIANTS (2)

GAME 1
Wednesday, October 10
at Yankee Stadium, New York

	1	2	3	4	5	6	7	8	9	R	H	E
New York Giants	0	0	4	0	0	0	0	0	1	5	8	0
New York Yankees	1	2	0	0	0	0	1	0	0	4	12	1

HR - NYG Casey Stengel

WP - Rosy Ryan; **LP** - Joe Bush

GAME 2
Thursday, October 11
at the Polo Grounds, New York

	1	2	3	4	5	6	7	8	9	R	H	E
New York Yankees	0	1	0	2	1	0	0	0	0	4	10	0
New York Giants	0	1	0	0	0	1	0	0	0	2	9	2

HR - NYY Babe Ruth 2, Aaron Ward; NYG Irish Meusel

WP - Herb Pennock; **LP** - Hugh McQuillan

GAME 3
Friday, October 12
at Yankee Stadium, New York

	1	2	3	4	5	6	7	8	9	R	H	E
New York Giants	0	0	0	0	0	1	0	0	1	4	0	
New York Yankees	0	0	0	0	0	0	0	0	0	6	1	

HR - NYG Casey Stengel

WP - Art Nehf; **LP** - Sam Jones

GAME 4
Saturday, October 13
at the Polo Grounds, New York

	1	2	3	4	5	6	7	8	9	R	H	E
New York Yankees	0	6	1	1	0	0	0	0	8	13	1	
New York Giants	0	0	0	0	0	0	3	1	4	13	1	

HR - NYG Ross Youngs

WP - Bob Shawkey; **LP** - Jack Scott; **Sv** - Herb Pennock

GAME 5
Sunday, October 14
at Yankee Stadium, New York

	1	2	3	4	5	6	7	8	9	R	H	E
New York Giants	0	1	0	0	0	0	0	0	1	3	2	
New York Yankees	3	4	0	1	0	0	0	0	x	8	14	0

HR - NYY Joe Dugan

WP - Joe Bush; **LP** - Jack Bentley

GAME 6
Monday, October 15
at the Polo Grounds, New York

	1	2	3	4	5	6	7	8	9	R	H	E
New York Yankees	1	0	0	0	0	0	0	5	0	6	5	0
New York Giants	1	0	0	1	1	1	0	0	0	4	10	1

HR - NYY Babe Ruth; NYG Frank Snyder

WP - Herb Pennock; LP - Art Nehf; Sv - Sam Jones

BATTING STATISTICS

New York Yankees	G	AB	R	H	2B	3B	HR	RBI	BB	SO	SB	CS	BA
Joe Bush	4	7	2	3	1	0	0	1	1	1	0	0	.429
Joe Dugan	6	25	5	7	2	1	1	5	3	0	0	0	.280
Hinkey Haines	2	1	1	0	0	0	0	0	0	0	0	0	.000
Harvey Hendrick	1	1	0	0	0	0	0	0	0	0	0	0	.000
Fred Hofmann	2	1	0	0	0	0	0	0	1	0	0	0	.000
Waite Hoyt	1	1	0	0	0	0	0	0	0	1	0	0	.000
Ernie Johnson	2	0	1	0	0	0	0	0	0	0	0	0	—
Sad Sam Jones	2	2	0	0	0	0	0	0	0	1	0	0	.000
Bob Meusel	6	26	1	7	1	2	0	8	0	3	0	0	.269
Herb Pennock	3	6	0	0	0	0	0	0	0	2	0	0	.000
Wally Pipp	6	20	2	5	0	0	0	2	4	1	0	0	.250
Babe Ruth	6	19	8	7	1	1	3	3	8	6	0	1	.368
Wally Schang	6	22	3	7	1	0	0	0	1	2	0	0	.318
Everett Scott	6	22	2	7	0	0	0	3	0	1	0	0	.318
Bob Shawkey	1	3	0	1	0	0	0	1	0	0	0	0	.333
Aaron Ward	6	24	4	10	0	0	1	2	1	3	1	0	.417
Whitey Witt	6	25	1	6	2	0	0	4	1	1	0	0	.240
Totals	**6**	**205**	**30**	**60**	**8**	**4**	**5**	**29**	**20**	**22**	**1**	**1**	**.293**

New York Giants	G	AB	R	H	2B	3B	HR	RBI	BB	SO	SB	CS	BA
Dave Bancroft	6	24	1	2	0	0	0	1	1	2	1	0	.083
Jesse Barnes	2	1	0	0	0	0	0	0	0	1	0	0	.000
Jack Bentley	5	5	0	3	1	0	0	0	0	0	0	0	.600
Bill Cunningham	4	7	0	1	0	0	0	1	0	1	0	0	.143
Frankie Frisch	6	25	2	10	0	1	0	1	0	0	0	1	.400
Dinty Gearin	1	0	0	0	0	0	0	0	0	0	0	0	—
Hank Gowdy	3	4	0	0	0	0	0	0	1	0	0	0	.000
Heine Groh	6	22	3	4	0	1	0	2	3	1	0	0	.182
Travis Jackson	1	1	0	0	0	0	0	0	0	0	0	0	.000
George Kelly	6	22	1	4	0	0	0	1	1	2	0	0	.182
Freddie Maguire	2	0	1	0	0	0	0	0	0	0	0	0	—
Hugh McQuillan	2	3	0	0	0	0	0	0	0	1	0	0	.000
Irish Meusel	6	25	3	7	1	1	1	2	0	2	0	0	.280
Art Nehf	2	6	0	1	0	0	0	0	0	4	0	0	.167
Jimmy O'Connell	2	1	0	0	0	0	0	0	0	1	0	0	.000
Rosy Ryan	3	2	0	0	0	0	0	0	0	1	0	0	.000
Jack Scott	2	1	0	0	0	0	0	0	0	0	0	0	.000
Frank Snyder	5	17	1	2	0	0	1	2	0	2	0	0	.118
Casey Stengel	6	12	3	5	0	0	2	4	4	0	0	0	.417
Ross Youngs	6	23	2	8	0	0	1	3	2	0	0	1	.348
Totals	**6**	**201**	**17**	**47**	**2**	**3**	**5**	**17**	**12**	**18**	**1**	**2**	**.234**

PITCHING STATISTICS

New York Yankees	G	GS	CG	IP	H	ER	BB	SO	W-L	Sv	ERA
Joe Bush	3	1	1	16 2/3	7	2	4	5	1-1	0	1.08
Waite Hoyt	1	1	0	2 1/3	4	4	1	0	0-0	0	15.43
Sad Sam Jones	2	1	0	10	5	1	2	3	0-1	1	0.90
Herb Pennock	3	2	1	17 1/3	19	7	1	8	2-0	0	3.63
Bob Shawkey	1	1	0	7 2/3	12	3	4	2	1-0	0	3.52
Totals	**6**	**6**	**2**	**54**	**47**	**17**	**12**	**18**	**4-2**	**2**	**2.83**

New York Giants	G	GS	CG	IP	H	ER	BB	SO	W-L	Sv	ERA
Jesse Barnes	2	0	0	4 2/3	4	0	0	4	0-0	0	0.00
Jack Bentley	2	1	0	6 2/3	10	7	4	1	0-1	0	9.45
Claude Jonnard	2	0	0	2	1	0	1	1	0-0	0	0.00
Hugh McQuillan	2	1	0	9	11	5	4	3	0-1	0	5.00
Art Nehf	2	2	1	16 1/3	10	5	6	7	1-1	0	2.76
Rosy Ryan	3	0	0	9 1/3	11	1	3	3	1-0	0	0.96
Jack Scott	2	1	0	3	9	4	1	2	0-1	0	12.00
Mule Watson	1	1	0	2	4	3	1	1	0-0	0	13.50
Totals	**6**	**6**	**1**	**53**	**60**	**25**	**20**	**22**	**2-4**	**0**	**4.25**

1926 World Series

ST. LOUIS CARDINALS (4) VS. NEW YORK YANKEES (3)

GAME 1

Saturday, October 2
at Yankee Stadium, New York

	1	2	3	4	5	6	7	8	9	R	H	E
St. Louis Cardinals	1	0	0	0	0	0	0	0	0	1	3	1
New York Yankees	1	0	0	0	0	1	0	0	x	2	6	0

WP - Herb Pennock; LP - Bill Sherdel

GAME 2

Sunday, October 3
at Yankee Stadium, New York

	1	2	3	4	5	6	7	8	9	R	H	E
St. Louis Cardinals	0	0	2	0	0	0	3	0	1	6	12	1
New York Yankees	0	2	0	0	0	0	0	0	0	2	4	0

HR - STL Billy Southworth, Tommy Thevenow,

WP - Grover Alexander; LP - Urban Shocker

GAME 3

Tuesday, October 5
at Sportsman's Park, St. Louis

	1	2	3	4	5	6	7	8	9	R	H	E
New York Yankees	0	0	0	0	0	0	0	0	0	0	5	1
St. Louis Cardinals	0	0	3	1	0	0	0	x	4	8	0	

HR - STL Jesse Haines

WP - Jesse Haines; LP - Dutch Ruether

GAME 4

Wednesday, October 6
at Sportsman's Park, St. Louis

	1	2	3	4	5	6	7	8	9	R	H	E
New York Yankees	1	0	1	1	4	2	1	0	0	10	14	1
St. Louis Cardinals	1	0	0	3	0	0	0	1	5	14	0	

HR - NY Babe Ruth 3

WP - Waite Hoyt; LP - Art Reinhart

GAME 5

Thursday, October 7
at Sportsman's Park, St. Louis

	1	2	3	4	5	6	7	8	9	10	R	H	E
New York Yankees	0	0	0	0	0	1	0	0	1	1	3	9	1
St. Louis Cardinals	0	0	1	0	0	1	0	0	0	2	7	1	

WP - Herb Pennock; LP - Bill Sherdel

GAME 6

Saturday, October 9
at Yankee Stadium, New York

	1	2	3	4	5	6	7	8	9	R	H	E
St. Louis Cardinals	3	0	0	0	1	0	5	0	1	10	13	2
New York Yankees	0	0	0	1	0	0	1	0	0	2	8	1

HR - STL Hi Bell

WP - Grover Alexander; LP - Bob Shawkey

GAME 7

Sunday, October 10
at Yankee Stadium, New York

	1	2	3	4	5	6	7	8	9	R	H	E
St. Louis Cardinals	0	0	0	3	0	0	0	0	0	3	8	0
New York Yankees	0	0	1	0	0	1	0	0	0	2	8	3

HR - NY Babe Ruth

WP - Jesse Haines; LP - Waite Hoyt; Sv - Grover Alexander

BATTING STATISTICS

St. Louis Cardinals	G	AB	R	H	2B	3B	HR	RBI	BB	SO	SB	CS	BA
Grover Alexander	3	7	1	0	0	0	0	0	0	2	0	0	.000
Les Bell	7	27	4	7	1	0	1	6	2	5	0	2	.259
Jim Bottomley	7	29	4	10	3	0	0	5	1	2	0	1	.345
Taylor Douthit	4	15	3	4	2	0	0	1	3	2	0	0	.267
Jake Flowers	3	3	0	0	0	0	0	0	0	1	0	0	.000
Chick Hafey	7	27	2	5	2	0	0	0	0	7	0	1	.185
Jesse Haines	3	5	1	3	0	0	1	2	0	1	0	0	.600
Wattie Holm	5	16	1	2	0	0	0	1	1	2	0	0	.125
Rogers Hornsby	7	28	2	7	1	0	0	4	2	2	1	0	.250
Bob O'Farrell	7	23	2	7	1	0	0	2	2	2	0	0	.304
Flint Rhem	1	1	0	0	0	0	0	0	0	1	0	0	.000
Bill Sherdel	2	5	0	0	0	0	0	0	0	2	0	0	.000
Billy Southworth	7	29	6	10	1	1	1	4	0	0	0	1	.345
Tommy Thevenow	7	24	5	10	1	0	1	4	0	1	0	0	.417
Specs Toporcer	1	0	0	0	0	0	0	1	0	0	0	0	—
Totals	7	239	31	65	12	1	4	30	11	30	2	5	.272

New York Yankees	G	AB	R	H	2B	3B	HR	RBI	BB	SO	SB	CS	BA
Spencer Adams	2	0	0	0	0	0	0	0	0	0	0	0	—
Pat Collins	3	2	0	0	0	0	0	0	1	0	0	0	.000
Earle Combs	7	28	3	10	2	0	0	2	5	2	0	0	.357
Joe Dugan	7	24	2	8	1	0	0	2	1	1	0	1	.333
Mike Gazella	1	0	0	0	0	0	0	0	0	0	0	0	—
Lou Gehrig	7	23	1	8	2	0	0	4	5	4	0	0	.348
Waite Hoyt	2	6	0	0	0	0	0	0	0	1	0	0	.000
Mark Koenig	7	32	2	4	1	0	0	2	0	6	0	0	.125
Tony Lazzeri	7	26	2	5	1	0	0	3	1	6	0	1	.192
Bob Meusel	7	21	3	5	1	1	0	0	6	1	0	0	.238
Ben Paschal	5	4	0	1	0	0	0	1	1	2	0	0	.250
Herb Pennock	3	7	1	1	1	0	0	0	0	0	0	0	.143
Dutch Ruether	3	4	0	0	0	0	0	0	0	0	0	0	.000
Babe Ruth	7	20	6	6	0	0	4	5	11	2	1	1	.300
Hank Severeid	7	22	1	6	1	0	0	1	1	2	0	0	.273
Bob Shawkey	3	2	0	0	0	0	0	0	0	1	0	0	.000
Urban Shocker	2	2	0	0	0	0	0	0	0	2	0	0	.000
Totals	7	223	21	54	10	1	4	20	31	31	1	3	.242

PITCHING STATISTICS

St. Louis Cardinals	G	GS	CG	IP	H	ER	BB	SO	W-L	Sv	ERA
Grover Alexander	3	2	2	20 1/3	12	3	4	17	2-0	1	1.33
Hi Bell	1	0	0	2	4	2	1	1	0-0	0	9.00
Jesse Haines	3	2	1	16 2/3	13	2	9	5	2-0	0	1.08
Wild Bill Hallahan	1	0	0	2	2	1	3	1	0-0	0	4.50
Vic Keen	1	0	0	1	0	0	0	0	0-0	0	0.00
Art Reinhart	1	0	0	1	4	4	0	0	0-1	0	—
Flint Rhem	1	1	0	4	7	3	2	4	0-0	0	6.75
Bill Sherdel	2	2	1	17	15	4	8	3	0-2	0	2.12
Totals	**7**	**7**	**4**	**63**	**54**	**19**	**31**	**31**	**4-3**	**1**	**2.71**

New York Yankees	G	GS	CG	IP	H	ER	BB	SO	W-L	Sv	ERA
Waite Hoyt	2	2	1	15	19	2	1	10	1-1	0	1.20
Sad Sam Jones	1	0	0	1	2	1	2	1	0-0	0	9.00
Herb Pennock	3	2	2	22	13	3	4	8	2-0	0	1.23
Dutch Ruether	1	1	0	4 1/3	7	4	2	1	0-1	0	8.31
Bob Shawkey	3	1	0	10	8	6	2	7	0-1	0	5.40
Urban Shocker	2	1	0	7 2/3	13	5	0	3	0-1	0	5.87
Myles Thomas	2	0	0	3	3	1	0	0	0-0	0	3.00
Totals	**7**	**7**	**3**	**63**	**65**	**22**	**11**	**30**	**3-4**	**0**	**3.14**

1927 World Series

NEW YORK YANKEES (4) VS. PITTSBURGH PIRATES (0)

GAME 1

Wednesday, October 5
at Forbes Field, Pittsburgh

	1	2	3	4	5	6	7	8	9	R	H	E
New York Yankees	1	0	3	0	1	0	0	0	0	5	6	1
Pittsburgh Pirates	1	0	1	0	1	0	0	1	0	4	9	2

WP - Waite Hoyt; LP - Ray Kremer; Sv - Wilcy Moore

GAME 2

Thursday, October 6
at Forbes Field, Pittsburgh

	1	2	3	4	5	6	7	8	9	R	H	E
New York Yankees	0	0	3	0	0	0	0	3	0	6	11	0
Pittsburgh Pirates	1	0	0	0	0	0	1	0	2	7	2	

WP - George Pipgras; LP - Vic Aldridge

GAME 3

Friday, October 7
at Yankee Stadium, New York

	1	2	3	4	5	6	7	8	9	R	H	E
Pittsburgh Pirates	0	0	0	0	0	0	0	1	0	1	3	1
New York Yankees	2	0	0	0	0	6	0	x	8	9	0	

HR - NY Babe Ruth

WP - Herb Pennock; LP - Lee Meadows

GAME 4

Saturday, October 8
at Yankee Stadium, New York

	1	2	3	4	5	6	7	8	9	R	H	E
Pittsburgh Pirates	1	0	0	0	0	2	0	0	3	10	1	
New York Yankees	1	0	0	0	2	0	0	0	1	4	12	2

HR - NY Babe Ruth

WP - Wilcy Moore; LP - Johnny Miljus

BATTING STATISTICS

New York Yankees	G	AB	R	H	2B	3B	HR	RBI	BB	SO	SB	CS	BA
Benny Bengough	2	4	1	0	0	0	0	0	1	0	0	0	.000
Pat Collins	2	5	0	3	1	0	0	0	3	0	0	0	.600
Earle Combs	4	16	6	5	0	0	0	2	1	2	0	0	.313
Joe Dugan	4	15	2	3	0	0	0	0	0	0	0	0	.200
Cedric Durst	1	1	0	0	0	0	0	0	0	0	0	0	.000
Lou Gehrig	4	13	2	4	2	2	0	4	3	3	0	0	.308
Johnny Grabowski	1	2	0	0	0	0	0	0	0	0	0	0	.000
Waite Hoyt	1	3	0	0	0	0	0	0	0	0	0	0	.000
Mark Koenig	4	18	5	9	2	0	0	2	0	2	0	0	.500
Tony Lazzeri	4	15	1	4	1	0	0	2	1	4	0	0	.267
Bob Meusel	4	17	1	2	0	0	0	1	1	7	1	0	.118
Wilcy Moore	2	5	0	1	0	0	0	0	0	3	0	0	.200
Herb Pennock	1	4	1	0	0	0	0	1	0	1	0	0	.000
George Pipgras	1	3	0	1	0	0	0	0	1	1	0	0	.333
Babe Ruth	4	15	4	6	0	0	2	7	2	2	1	1	.400
Totals	**4**	**136**	**23**	**38**	**6**	**2**	**2**	**19**	**13**	**25**	**2**	**1**	**.279**

Pittsburgh Pirates	G	AB	R	H	2B	3B	HR	RBI	BB	SO	SB	CS	BA
Vic Aldridge	1	2	0	0	0	0	0	0	0	0	0	0	.000
Clyde Barnhart	4	16	0	5	1	0	0	4	0	0	0	0	.313
George Brickell	2	2	1	0	0	0	0	0	0	0	0	0	.000
Johnny Gooch	3	5	0	0	0	0	0	0	1	1	0	0	.000
George Grantham	3	11	0	4	1	0	0	0	1	1	0	0	.364
Heine Groh	1	1	0	0	0	0	0	0	0	0	0	0	.000
Joe Harris	4	15	0	3	0	0	0	1	0	0	0	0	.200
Carmen Hill	1	1	0	0	0	0	0	0	1	0	0	0	.000
Ray Kremer	1	2	1	1	1	0	0	0	0	1	0	0	.500
Lee Meadows	1	2	0	0	0	0	0	0	0	0	0	0	.000
Johnny Miljus	2	2	0	0	0	0	0	0	0	2	0	0	.000
Hal Rhyne	1	4	0	0	0	0	0	0	0	0	0	0	.000
Earl Smith	3	8	0	0	0	0	0	0	0	0	0	0	.000
Roy Spencer	1	1	0	0	0	0	0	0	0	0	0	0	.000
Pie Traynor	4	15	1	3	1	0	0	0	0	1	0	0	.200
Lloyd Waner	4	15	5	6	1	1	0	0	1	0	0	0	.400
Paul Waner	4	15	0	5	1	0	0	3	0	1	0	0	.333
Glenn Wright	4	13	1	2	0	0	0	2	0	0	0	0	.154
Emil Yde	1	0	1	0	0	0	0	0	0	0	0	0	—
Totals	**4**	**130**	**10**	**29**	**6**	**1**	**0**	**10**	**4**	**7**	**0**	**0**	**.223**

PITCHING STATISTICS

New York Yankees	G	GS	CG	IP	H	ER	BB	SO	W-L	Sv	ERA
Waite Hoyt	1	1	0	7 1/3	8	4	1	2	1-0	0	4.91
Wilcy Moore	2	1	1	10 2/3	11	1	2	2	1-0	1	0.84
Herb Pennock	1	1	1	9	3	1	0	1	1-0	0	1.00
George Pipgras	1	1	1	9	7	2	1	2	1-0	0	2.00
Totals	**4**	**4**	**3**	**36**	**29**	**8**	**4**	**7**	**4-0**	**1**	**2.00**

Pittsburgh Pirates	G	GS	CG	IP	H	ER	BB	SO	W-L	Sv	ERA
Vic Aldridge	1	1	0	7 1/3	10	6	4	4	0-1	0	7.36
Mike Cvengros	2	0	0	2 1/3	3	1	0	2	0-0	0	3.86
Joe Dawson	1	0	0	1	0	0	0	0	0-0	0	0.00
Carmen Hill	1	1	0	6	9	3	1	6	0-0	0	4.50
Ray Kremer	1	1	0	5	5	2	3	1	0-1	0	3.60
Lee Meadows	1	1	0	6 1/3	7	7	1	6	0-1	0	9.95
Johnny Mi1jus	2	0	0	6 2/3	4	1	4	6	0-1	0	1.35
Totals	**4**	**4**	**0**	**34 2/3**	**38**	**20**	**13**	**25**	**0-4**	**0**	**5.19**

1928 World Series

NEW YORK YANKEES (4) VS. ST. LOUIS CARDINALS (0)

GAME 1
Thursday, October 4
at Yankee Stadium, New York

	1	2	3	4	5	6	7	8	9	R	H	E
St. Louis Cardinals	0	0	0	0	0	0	1	0	0	1	3	1
New York Yankees	1	0	0	2	0	0	0	1	x	4	7	0

HR - STL Jim Bottomley; NY Bob Meusel

WP - Waite Hoyt; LP - Bill Sherdel

GAME 2
Friday, October 5
at Yankee Stadium, New York

	1	2	3	4	5	6	7	8	9	R	H	E
St. Louis Cardinals	0	3	0	0	0	0	0	0	0	3	4	1
New York Yankees	3	1	4	0	0	0	1	0	x	9	8	2

HR - NY Lou Gehrig

WP - George Pipgras; LP - Grover Alexander

GAME 3
Sunday, October 7
at Sportsman's Park, St. Louis

	1	2	3	4	5	6	7	8	9	R	H	E
New York Yankees	0	1	0	2	0	3	1	0	0	7	7	2
St. Louis Cardinals	2	0	0	0	1	0	0	0	0	3	9	3

HR - NY Lou Gehrig 2

WP - Tom Zachary; LP - Jesse Haines

GAME 4
Tuesday, October 9
at Sportsman's Park, St. Louis

	1	2	3	4	5	6	7	8	9	R	H	E
New York Yankees	0	0	0	1	0	0	4	2	0	7	15	2
St. Louis Cardinals	0	0	1	1	0	0	0	0	1	3	11	0

HR - NY Cedric Durst, Lou Gehrig, Babe Ruth 3

WP - Waite Hoyt; LP - Bill Sherdel

BATTING STATISTICS

New York Yankees	G	AB	R	H	2B	3B	HR	RBI	BB	SO	SB	CS	BA
Benny Bengough	4	13	1	3	0	0	0	1	1	1	0	0	.231
Pat Collins	1	1	0	1	1	0	0	0	0	0	0	0	1.000
Earle Combs	1	0	0	0	0	0	0	1	0	0	0	0	—
Joe Dugan	3	6	0	1	0	0	0	2	0	0	0	0	.167
Leo Durocher	4	2	0	0	0	0	0	0	0	1	0	0	.000
Cedric Durst	4	8	3	3	0	0	1	2	0	1	0	0	.375
Lou Gehrig	4	11	5	6	1	0	4	9	6	0	0	0	.545
Waite Hoyt	2	7	0	1	0	0	0	0	0	0	0	0	.143
Mark Koenig	4	19	1	3	0	0	0	0	0	1	0	0	.158
Tony Lazzeri	4	12	2	3	1	0	0	0	1	0	2	0	.250
Bob Meusel	4	15	5	3	1	0	1	3	2	5	2	0	.200
Ben Paschal	3	10	0	2	0	0	0	1	1	0	0	0	.200
George Pipgras	1	2	0	0	0	0	0	1	0	1	0	0	.000
Gene Robertson	3	8	1	1	0	0	0	2	1	0	0	0	.125
Babe Ruth	4	16	9	10	3	0	3	4	1	2	0	0	.625
Tom Zachary	1	4	0	0	0	0	0	0	0	1	0	0	.000
Totals	**4**	**134**	**27**	**37**	**7**	**0**	**8**	**25**	**13**	**13**	**4**	**0**	**.276**

St. Louis Cardinals	G	AB	R	H	2B	3B	HR	RBI	BB	SO	SB	CS	BA
Grover Alexander	2	1	0	0	0	0	0	1	0	0	0	0	.000
Ray Blades	1	1	0	0	0	0	0	0	0	1	0	0	.000
Jim Bottomley	4	14	1	3	0	1	1	3	2	6	0	0	.214
Taylor Douthit	3	11	1	1	0	0	0	1	1	1	0	0	.091
Frankie Frisch	4	13	1	3	0	0	0	1	2	2	2	0	.231
Chick Hafey	4	15	0	3	0	0	0	0	1	4	0	0	.200
Jesse Haines	1	2	0	0	0	0	0	0	0	0	0	0	.000
George Harper	3	9	1	1	0	0	0	0	2	2	0	0	.111
Andy High	4	17	1	5	2	0	0	1	1	3	0	0	.294
Wattie Holm	3	6	0	1	0	0	0	1	0	1	0	0	.167
Rabbit Maranville	4	13	2	4	1	0	0	0	1	1	1	0	.308
Pepper Martin	1	0	1	0	0	0	0	0	0	0	0	0	—
Clarence Mitchell	1	2	0	0	0	0	0	0	0	0	0	0	.000
Ernie Orsatti	4	7	1	2	1	0	0	0	1	3	0	0	.286
Bill Sherdel	2	5	0	0	0	0	0	0	0	2	0	0	.000
Earl Smith	1	4	0	3	0	0	0	0	0	0	0	1	.750
Jimmie Wilson	3	11	1	1	1	0	0	1	0	3	0	1	.091
Totals	**4**	**131**	**10**	**27**	**5**	**1**	**1**	**9**	**11**	**29**	**3**	**2**	**.206**

PITCHING STATISTICS

New York Yankees	G	GS	CG	IP	H	ER	BB	SO	W-L	Sv	ERA
Waite Hoyt	2	2	2	18	14	3	6	14	2-0	0	1.50
George Pipgras	1	1	1	9	4	2	4	8	1-0	0	2.00
Tom Zachary	1	1	1	9	9	3	1	7	1-0	0	3.00
Totals	**4**	**4**	**4**	**36**	**27**	**9**	**11**	**29**	**4-0**	**0**	**2.00**

St. Louis Cardinals	G	GS	CG	IP	H	ER	BB	SO	W-L	Sv	ERA
Grover Alexander	2	1	0	5	10	11	4	2	0-1	0	19.80
Jesse Haines	1	1	0	6	6	3	3	3	0-1	0	4.50
Syl Johnson	2	0	0	2	4	1	1	1	0-0	0	4.50
Clarence Mitchell	1	0	0	5 2/3	2	1	2	3	0-0	0	1.59
Flint Rhem	1	0	0	2	0	0	0	1	0-0	0	0.00
Bill Sherdel	2	2	0	13 1/3	15	7	3	3	0-2	0	4.72
Totals	**4**	**4**	**0**	**34**	**37**	**23**	**13**	**13**	**0-4**	**0**	**6.09**

1932 World Series

NEW YORK YANKEES (4) VS. CHICAGO CUBS (0)

GAME 1
Wednesday, September 28
at Yankee Stadium, New York

	1	2	3	4	5	6	7	8	9	R	H	E
Chicago Cubs	2	0	0	0	0	0	2	2	0	6	10	1
New York Yankees	0	0	0	3	0	5	3	1	x	12	8	2

HR - NY Lou Gehrig

WP - Red Ruffing; **LP** - Guy Bush

GAME 2
Thursday, September 29
at Yankee Stadium, New York

	1	2	3	4	5	6	7	8	9	R	H	E
Chicago Cubs	1	0	1	0	0	0	0	0	0	2	9	0
New York Yankees	2	0	2	0	1	0	0	0	x	5	10	1

WP - Lefty Gomez; **LP** - Lon Warneke

GAME 3
Saturday, October 1
at Wrigley Field, Chicago Cubs

	1	2	3	4	5	6	7	8	9	R	H	E
New York Yankees	3	0	1	0	2	0	0	0	1	7	8	1
Chicago Cubs	1	0	2	1	0	0	0	0	1	5	9	4

HR - NY Lou Gehrig 2, Babe Ruth 2; CHI Kiki Cuyler, Gabby Hartnett

WP - George Pipgras; **LP** - Charlie Root; **Sv** - Herb Pennock

GAME 4
Sunday, October 2
at Wrigley Field, Chicago

	1	2	3	4	5	6	7	8	9	R	H	E
New York Yankees	1	0	2	0	0	2	4	0	4	13	19	4
Chicago Cubs	4	0	0	0	1	0	0	1	0	6	9	1

HR - NY Earle Combs, Tony Lazzeri 2; CHI Frank Demaree

WP - Wilcy Moore; **LP** - Jakie May; **Sv** - Herb Pennock

BATTING STATISTICS

New York Yankees	G	AB	R	H	2B	3B	HR	RBI	BB	SO	SB	CS	BA
Ben Chapman	4	17	1	5	2	0	0	6	2	4	0	1	.294
Earle Combs	4	16	8	6	1	0	1	4	4	3	0	0	.375
Frankie Crosetti	4	15	2	2	1	0	0	0	2	3	0	0	.133
Bill Dickey	4	16	2	7	0	0	0	4	2	1	0	1	.438
Lou Gehrig	4	17	9	9	1	0	3	8	2	1	0	0	.529
Lefty Gomez	1	3	0	0	0	0	0	0	0	2	0	0	.000
Myril Hoag	1	0	1	0	0	0	0	0	0	0	0	0	—
Tony Lazzeri	4	17	4	5	0	0	2	5	2	1	0	0	.294
Wilcy Moore	1	3	0	1	0	0	0	0	0	2	0	0	.333
Herb Pennock	2	1	0	0	0	0	0	0	0	0	0	0	.000
George Pipgras	1	5	0	0	0	0	0	0	0	5	0	0	.000
Red Ruffing	2	4	0	0	0	0	0	0	1	1	0	0	.000
Babe Ruth	4	15	6	5	0	0	2	6	4	3	0	0	.333
Joe Sewell	4	15	4	5	1	0	0	3	4	0	0	0	.333
Totals	**4**	**144**	**37**	**45**	**6**	**0**	**8**	**36**	**23**	**26**	**0**	**2**	**.313**

Chicago Cubs	G	AB	R	H	2B	3B	HR	RBI	BB	SO	SB	CS	BA
Guy Bush	2	1	0	0	0	0	0	0	1	0	0	0	.000
Kiki Cuyler	4	18	2	5	1	1	1	2	0	3	1	0	.278
Frank Demaree	2	7	1	2	0	0	1	4	1	0	0	0	.286
Woody English	4	17	2	3	0	0	0	1	2	2	0	1	.176
Burleigh Grimes	2	1	0	0	0	0	0	0	0	1	0	0	.000
Charlie Grimm	4	15	2	5	2	0	0	1	2	2	0	0	.333
Marv Gudat	2	2	0	0	0	0	0	0	0	1	0	0	.000
Stan Hack	1	0	0	0	0	0	0	0	0	0	0	0	—
Gabby Hartnett	4	16	2	5	2	0	1	1	1	3	0	0	.313
Rollie Hemsley	3	3	0	0	0	0	0	0	0	3	0	0	.000
Billy Herman	4	18	5	4	1	0	0	1	1	3	0	0	.222
Billy Jurges	3	11	1	4	1	0	0	1	0	1	2	0	.364
Mark Koenig	2	4	1	1	0	1	0	1	1	0	0	0	.250
Jakie May	2	2	0	0	0	0	0	0	0	0	0	0	.000
Johnny Moore	2	7	1	0	0	0	0	0	2	1	0	0	.000
Charlie Root	1	2	0	0	0	0	0	0	0	1	0	0	.000
Riggs Stephenson	4	18	2	8	1	0	0	4	0	0	0	1	.444
Lon Warneke	2	4	0	0	0	0	0	0	0	3	0	0	.000
Totals	**4**	**146**	**19**	**37**	**8**	**2**	**3**	**16**	**11**	**24**	**3**	**1**	**.253**

PITCHING STATISTICS

New York Yankees	G	GS	CG	IP	H	ER	BB	SO	W-L	Sv	ERA
Johnny Allen	1	1	0	0 2/3	5	3	0	0	0-0	0	40.50
Lefty Gomez	1	1	1	9	9	1	1	8	1-0	0	1.00
Wilcy Moore	1	0	0	5 1/3	2	0	0	1	1-0	0	0.00
Herb Pennock	2	0	0	4	2	1	1	4	0-0	2	2.25
George Pipgras	1	1	0	8	9	4	3	1	1-0	0	4.50
Red Ruffing	1	1	1	9	10	3	6	10	1-0	0	3.00
Totals	**4**	**4**	**2**	**36**	**37**	**12**	**11**	**24**	**4-0**	**2**	**3.00**

Chicago Cubs	G	GS	CG	IP	H	ER	BB	SO	W-L	Sv	ERA
Guy Bush	2	2	0	5 2/3	5	9	6	2	0-1	0	14.29
Burleigh Grimes	2	0	0	2 2/3	7	7	2	0	0-0	0	23.63
Pat Malone	1	0	0	2 2/3	1	0	4	4	0-0	0	0.00
Jakie May	2	0	0	4 2/3	9	6	3	4	0-1	0	11.57
Charlie Root	1	1	0	4 1/3	6	5	3	4	0-1	0	10.38
Bob Smith	1	0	0	1	2	1	0	1	0-0	0	9.00
Bud Tinning	2	0	0	2 1/3	0	0	0	3	0-0	0	0.00
Lon Warneke	2	1	1	10 2/3	15	7	5	8	0-1	0	5.91
Totals	**4**	**4**	**1**	**34**	**45**	**35**	**23**	**26**	**0-4**	**0**	**9.26**

1936 World Series

NEW YORK YANKEES (4) VS. NEW YORK GIANTS (2)

GAME 1

Wednesday, September 30
at the Polo Grounds, New York

	1	2	3	4	5	6	7	8	9	R	H	E
New York Yankees	0	0	1	0	0	0	0	0	0	1	7	2
New York Giants	0	0	0	0	1	1	0	4	x	6	9	1

HR - NYY George Selkirk; NYG Dick Bartell.

WP - Carl Hubbell; **LP** - Red Ruffing

GAME 2

Friday, October 2
at the Polo Grounds, New York

	1	2	3	4	5	6	7	8	9	R	H	E
New York Yankees	2	0	7	0	0	1	2	0	6	18	17	0
New York Giants	0	1	0	3	0	0	0	0	0	4	6	1

HR - NYY Bill Dickey, Tony Lazzeri.

WP - Lefty Gomez; **LP** - Hal Schumacher

GAME 3

Saturday, October 3
at Yankee Stadium, New York

	1	2	3	4	5	6	7	8	9	R	H	E
New York Giants	0	0	0	0	1	0	0	0	1	1	11	0
New York Yankees	0	1	0	0	0	0	1	x	2	4	0	

HR - NYG Jimmy Ripple; NYY Lou Gehrig.

WP - Bump Hadley; **LP** - Freddie Fitzsimmons; **Sv** - Pat Malone

GAME 4

Sunday, October 4
at Yankee Stadium, New York

	1	2	3	4	5	6	7	8	9	R	H	E
New York Giants	0	0	0	1	0	0	0	1	0	2	7	1
New York Yankees	0	1	3	0	0	0	1	x	5	10	1	

HR - NYY Lou Gehrig

WP - Monte Pearson; **LP** - Carl Hubbell

GAME 5

Monday, October 5
at Yankee Stadium, New York

	1	2	3	4	5	6	7	8	9	10	R	H	E
New York Giants	3	0	0	0	0	1	0	0	1	5	8	3	
New York Yankees	0	1	1	0	0	2	0	0	0	4	10	1	

HR - NYY George Selkirk

WP - Hal Schumacher; **LP** - Pat Malone

GAME 6
Tuesday, October 6
at the Polo Grounds, New York

	1	2	3	4	5	6	7	8	9	R	H	E
New York Yankees	0	2	1	2	0	0	0	1	7	13	17	2
New York Giants	2	0	0	0	1	0	1	1	0	5	9	1

HR - NYY Jake Powell; NYG Jo-Jo Moore, Mel Ott.

WP - Lefty Gomez; LP - Freddie Fitzsimmons; Sv - Johnny Murphy

BATTING STATISTICS

New York Yankees	G	AB	R	H	2B	3B	HR	RBI	BB	SO	SB	CS	BA
Frankie Crosetti	6	26	5	7	2	0	0	3	3	5	0	0	.269
Bill Dickey	6	25	5	3	0	0	1	5	3	4	0	0	.120
Joe DiMaggio	6	26	3	9	3	0	0	3	1	3	0	0	.346
Lou Gehrig	6	24	5	7	1	0	2	7	3	2	0	1	.292
Lefty Gomez	2	8	1	2	0	0	0	3	0	3	0	0	.250
Bump Hadley	1	2	0	0	0	0	0	0	0	1	0	0	.000
Roy Johnson	2	1	0	0	0	0	0	0	0	1	0	0	.000
Tony Lazzeri	6	20	4	5	0	0	1	7	4	4	0	0	.250
Pat Malone	2	1	0	1	0	0	0	0	0	0	0	0	1.000
Johnny Murphy	1	2	1	1	0	0	0	1	0	1	0	0	.500
Monte Pearson	1	4	0	2	1	0	0	0	0	0	0	0	.500
Jake Powell	6	22	8	10	1	0	1	5	4	4	1	1	.455
Red Rolfe	6	25	5	10	0	0	0	4	3	1	0	1	.400
Red Ruffing	3	5	0	0	0	0	0	0	1	2	0	0	.000
Bob Seeds	1	0	0	0	0	0	0	0	0	0	0	1	—
George Selkirk	6	24	6	8	0	1	2	3	4	4	0	1	.333
Totals	**6**	**215**	**43**	**65**	**8**	**1**	**7**	**41**	**26**	**35**	**1**	**5**	**.302**

New York Giants	G	AB	R	H	2B	3B	HR	RBI	BB	SO	SB	CS	BA
Dick Bartell	6	21	5	8	3	0	1	3	4	4	0	0	.381
Slick Castleman	1	2	0	1	0	0	0	0	0	0	0	0	.500
Harry Danning	2	2	0	0	0	0	0	0	0	1	0	0	.000
Kiddo Davis	4	2	2	1	0	0	0	0	0	0	0	0	.500
Freddie Fitzsimmons	2	4	0	2	0	0	0	0	0	1	0	0	.500
Frank Gabler	2	0	0	0	0	0	0	0	1	0	0	0	—
Carl Hubbell	2	6	0	2	0	0	0	1	0	0	0	0	.333
Travis Jackson	6	21	1	4	0	0	0	1	1	3	0	0	.190
Mark Koenig	3	3	0	1	0	0	0	0	0	1	0	0	.333
Hank Leiber	2	6	0	0	0	0	0	0	2	2	0	0	.000
Sam Leslie	3	3	0	2	0	0	0	0	0	0	0	0	.667
Gus Mancuso	6	19	3	5	2	0	0	1	3	3	0	0	.263
Eddie Mayo	1	1	0	0	0	0	0	0	0	0	0	0	.000
Jo-Jo Moore	6	28	4	6	2	0	1	1	1	4	0	1	.214
Mel Ott	6	23	4	7	2	0	1	3	3	1	0	0	.304
Jimmy Ripple	5	12	2	4	0	0	1	3	3	3	0	1	.333
Hal Schumacher	2	4	0	0	0	0	0	0	1	3	0	0	.000
Bill Terry	6	25	1	6	0	0	0	5	1	4	0	0	.240
Burgess Whitehead	6	21	1	1	0	0	0	2	1	3	0	1	.048
Totals	**6**	**203**	**23**	**50**	**9**	**0**	**4**	**20**	**21**	**33**	**0**	**3**	**.246**

PITCHING STATISTICS

New York Yankees	G	GS	CG	IP	H	ER	BB	SO	W-L	Sv	ERA
Lefty Gomez	2	2	1	15 1/3	14	8	11	9	2-0	0	4.70
Bump Hadley	1	1	0	8	10	1	1	2	1-0	0	1.13
Pat Malone	2	0	0	5	2	1	1	2	0-1	1	1.80
Johnny Murphy	1	0	0	2 2/3	1	1	1	1	0-0	1	3.38
Monte Pearson	1	1	1	9	7	2	2	7	1-0	0	2.00
Red Ruffing	2	2	1	14	16	8	5	12	0-1	0	5.14
Totals	**6**	**6**	**3**	**54**	**50**	**21**	**21**	**33**	**4-2**	**2**	**3.50**

New York Giants	G	GS	CG	IP	H	ER	BB	SO	W-L	Sv	ERA
Slick Castleman	1	0	0	4 1/3	3	1	2	5	0-0	0	2.08
Dick Coffman	2	0	0	1 2/3	5	6	1	1	0-0	0	32.40
Freddie Fitzsimmons	2	2	1	11 2/3	13	7	2	6	0-2	0	5.40
Frank Gabler	2	0	0	5	7	4	4	0	0-0	0	7.20
Harry Gumbert	2	0	0	2	8	4	2	0	0-0	0	36.00
Carl Hubbell	2	2	1	16	15	4	2	10	1-1	0	2.25
Hal Schumacher	2	2	1	12	13	7	10	11	1-1	0	5.25
Al Smith	1	0	0	0 1/3	2	3	1	0	0-0	0	81.00
Totals	**6**	**6**	**3**	**53**	**65**	**40**	**26**	**35**	**2-4**	**0**	**6.79**

1937 World Series

NEW YORK YANKEES (4) VS. NEW YORK GIANTS (1)

GAME 1

Wednesday, October 6
at Yankee Stadium, New York

	1	2	3	4	5	6	7	8	9	R	H	E
New York Giants	0	0	0	0	1	0	0	0	0	1	6	2
New York Yankees	0	0	0	0	0	7	0	1	x	8	7	0

HR - NYY Tony Lazzeri

WP - Lefty Gomez; LP - Carl Hubbell

GAME 2

Thursday, October 7
at Yankee Stadium, New York

	1	2	3	4	5	6	7	8	9	R	H	E
New York Giants	1	0	0	0	0	0	0	0	0	1	7	0
New York Yankees	0	0	0	0	2	4	2	0	x	8	12	0

WP - Red Ruffing; LP - Cliff Melton

GAME 3

Friday, October 8
at the Polo Grounds, New York

	1	2	3	4	5	6	7	8	9	R	H	E
New York Yankees	0	1	2	1	1	0	0	0	0	5	9	0
New York Giants	0	0	0	0	0	0	1	0	0	1	5	4

WP - Monte Pearson; LP - Hal Schumacher; Sv - Johnny Murphy

GAME 4

Saturday, October 9
at the Polo Grounds, New York

	1	2	3	4	5	8	7	8	9	R	H	E
New York Yankees	1	0	1	0	0	0	0	0	1	3	6	0
New York Giants	0	6	0	0	0	0	1	0	x	7	12	3

HR - NYY Lou Gehrig

WP - Carl Hubbell; LP - Bump Hadley

GAME 5

Sunday, October 10
at the Polo Grounds, New York

	1	2	3	4	5	6	7	8	9	R	H	E
New York Yankees	0	1	1	0	2	0	0	0	0	4	8	0
New York Giants	0	0	2	0	0	0	0	0	0	2	10	0

HR - NYY Joe DiMaggio, Myril Hoag; NYG Mel Ott

WP - Lefty Gomez; LP - Cliff Melton

BATTING STATISTICS

New York Yankees	G	AB	R	H	2B	3B	HR	RBI	BB	SO	SB	CS	BA
Ivy Andrews	1	2	0	0	0	0	0	0	0	1	0	0	.000
Frankie Crosetti	5	21	2	1	0	0	0	0	3	2	0	0	.048
Bill Dickey	5	19	3	4	0	1	0	3	2	2	0	0	.211
Joe DiMaggio	5	22	2	6	0	0	1	4	0	3	0	0	.273
Lou Gehrig	5	17	4	5	1	1	1	3	5	4	0	0	.294
Lefty Gomez	2	6	2	1	0	0	0	1	2	1	0	0	.167
Myril Hoag	5	20	4	6	1	0	1	2	0	1	0	0	.300
Tony Lazzeri	5	15	3	6	0	1	1	2	3	3	0	0	.400
Monte Pearson	1	3	0	0	0	0	0	0	1	1	0	0	.000
Jake Powell	1	1	0	0	0	0	0	0	0	1	0	0	.000
Red Rolfe	5	20	3	6	2	1	0	1	3	2	0	0	.300
Red Ruffing	1	4	0	2	1	0	0	3	0	0	0	0	.500
George Selkirk	5	19	5	5	1	0	0	6	2	0	0	0	.263
Totals	5	169	28	42	6	4	4	25	21	21	0	0	.249

New York Giants	G	AB	R	H	2B	3B	HR	RBI	BB	SO	SB	CS	BA
Dick Bartell	5	21	3	5	1	0	0	1	0	3	0	0	.238
Wally Berger	3	3	0	0	0	0	0	0	0	1	0	0	.000
Lou Chiozza	2	7	0	2	0	0	0	0	1	1	0	0	.286
Dick Coffman	2	1	0	0	0	0	0	0	0	1	0	0	.000
Harry Danning	3	12	0	3	1	0	0	2	0	2	0	0	.250
Carl Hubbell	2	6	1	0	0	0	0	1	0	0	0	0	.000
Hank Leiber	3	11	2	4	0	0	0	2	1	1	0	0	.364
Sam Leslie	2	1	0	0	0	0	0	0	1	0	0	0	.000
Gus Mancuso	3	8	0	0	0	0	0	0	0	1	0	0	.000
Johnny McCarthy	5	19	1	4	1	0	0	1	1	2	0	0	.211
Cliff Melton	3	2	0	0	0	0	0	0	1	1	0	0	.000
Jo-Jo Moore	5	23	1	9	1	0	0	1	0	1	0	0	.391
Mel Ott	5	20	1	4	0	0	1	3	1	4	0	0	.200
Jimmy Ripple	5	17	2	5	0	0	0	0	3	1	0	1	.294
Blondy Ryan	1	1	0	0	0	0	0	0	0	1	0	0	.000
Hal Schumacher	1	1	0	0	0	0	0	0	0	1	0	0	.000
Burgess Whitehead	5	16	1	4	2	0	0	0	2	0	1	0	.250
Totals	5	169	12	40	6	0	1	11	11	21	1	1	.237

PITCHING STATISTICS

New York Yankees	G	GS	CG	IP	H	ER	BB	SO	W-L	Sv	ERA
Ivy Andrews	1	0	0	5 2/3	6	2	4	1	0-0	0	3.18
Lefty Gomez	2	2	2	18	16	3	2	8	2-0	0	1.50
Bump Hadley	1	1	0	1 1/3	6	5	0	0	0-1	0	33.75
Johnny Murphy	1	0	0	0 1/3	0	0	0	0	0-0	1	0.00
Monte Pearson	1	1	0	8 2/3	5	1	2	4	1-0	0	1.04
Red Ruffing	1	1	1	9	7	1	3	8	1-0	0	1.00
Kemp Wicker	1	0	0	1	0	0	0	0	0-0	0	0.00
Totals	5	5	3	44	40	12	11	21	4-1	1	2.45

New York Giants	G	GS	CG	IP	H	ER	BB	SO	W-L	Sv	ERA
Don Brennan	2	0	0	3	1	0	1	1	0-0	0	0.00
Dick Coffman	2	0	0	4 1/3	2	2	5	1	0-0	0	4.15
Harry Gumbert	2	0	0	1 1/3	4	4	1	1	0-0	0	27.00
Carl Hubbell	2	2	1	14 1/3	12	6	4	7	1-1	0	3.77
Cliff Melton	3	2	0	11	12	6	6	7	0-2	0	4.91
Hal Schumacher	1	1	0	6	9	4	4	3	0-1	0	6.00
Al Smith	2	0	0	3	2	1	0	1	0-0	0	3.00
Totals	5	5	1	43	42	23	21	21	1-4	0	4.81

1938 World Series

NEW YORK YANKEES (4) VS. CHICAGO CUBS (0)

GAME 1
Wednesday, October 5
at Wrigley Field, Chicago

	1	2	3	4	5	6	7	8	9	R	H	E
New York Yankees	0	2	0	0	0	1	0	0	0	3	12	1
Chicago Cubs	0	0	1	0	0	0	0	0	0	1	9	1

WP - Red Ruffing; LP - Bill Lee

GAME 2
Thursday, October 6
at Wrigley Field, Chicago

	1	2	3	4	5	6	7	8	9	R	H	E
New York Yankees	0	2	0	0	0	0	0	2	2	6	7	2
Chicago Cubs	1	0	2	0	0	0	0	0	0	3	11	0

HR - NY Frankie Crosetti, Joe DiMaggio

WP - Lefty Gomez; LP - Dizzy Dean; Sv - Johnny Murphy

GAME 3
Saturday, October 8
at Yankee Stadium, New York

	1	2	3	4	5	6	7	8	9	R	H	E
Chicago Cubs	0	0	0	0	1	0	0	1	0	2	5	1
New York Yankees	0	0	0	0	2	2	0	1	x	5	7	2

HR - CHI Joe Marty; NY Bill Dickey, Joe Gordon

WP - Monte Pearson; LP - Clay Bryant

GAME 4
Sunday, October 9
at Yankee Stadium, New York

	1	2	3	4	5	6	7	8	9	R	H	E
Chicago Cubs	0	0	0	1	0	0	0	2	0	3	8	1
New York Yankees	0	3	0	0	0	1	0	4	x	8	11	1

HR - CHI Ken O'Dea; NY Tommy Henrich

WP - Red Ruffing; LP - Bill Lee

BATTING STATISTICS

New York Yankees	G	AB	R	H	2B	3B	HR	RBI	BB	SO	SB	CS	BA
Frankie Crosetti	4	16	1	4	2	1	1	6	2	4	0	1	.250
Bill Dickey	4	15	2	6	0	0	1	2	1	0	0	0	.400
Joe DiMaggio	4	15	4	4	0	0	1	2	1	1	0	0	.267
Lou Gehrig	4	14	4	4	0	0	0	0	2	3	0	0	.286
Lefty Gomez	1	2	0	0	0	0	0	0	0	0	0	0	.000
Joe Gordon	4	15	3	6	2	0	1	6	1	3	1	0	.400
Tommy Henrich	4	16	3	4	1	0	1	1	0	1	0	1	.250
Myril Hoag	2	5	3	2	1	0	0	1	0	0	0	0	.400
Monte Pearson	1	3	1	1	0	0	0	0	1	0	0	0	.333
Red Rolfe	4	18	0	3	0	0	0	1	0	3	1	0	.167
Red Ruffing	2	6	1	1	0	0	0	1	1	0	0	0	.167
George Selkirk	3	10	0	2	0	0	0	1	2	1	0	0	.200
Totals	**4**	**135**	**22**	**37**	**6**	**1**	**5**	**21**	**11**	**16**	**3**	**2**	**.274**

Chicago Cubs	G	AB	R	H	2B	3B	HR	RBI	BB	SO	SB	CS	BA
Clay Bryant	1	2	0	0	0	0	0	0	0	1	0	0	.000
Phil Cavarretta	4	13	1	6	1	0	0	0	0	1	0	0	.462
Ripper Collins	4	15	1	2	0	0	0	0	0	3	0	0	.133
Dizzy Dean	2	3	0	2	0	0	0	0	0	0	0	1	.667
Frank Demaree	3	10	1	1	0	0	0	0	1	2	0	0	.100
Augie Galan	2	2	0	0	0	0	0	0	0	1	0	0	.000
Stan Hack	4	17	3	8	1	0	0	1	1	2	0	1	.471
Gabby Hartnett	3	11	0	1	0	1	0	0	0	2	0	0	.091
Billy Herman	4	16	1	3	0	0	0	0	1	4	0	0	.188
Billy Jurges	4	13	0	3	1	0	0	0	1	3	0	0	.231
Tony Lazzeri	2	2	0	0	0	0	0	0	1	0	0	0	.000
Bill Lee	2	3	0	0	0	0	0	0	0	1	0	0	.000
Joe Marty	3	12	1	6	1	0	1	5	0	2	0	1	.500
Ken O'Dea	3	5	1	1	0	0	1	2	1	0	0	0	.200
Carl Reynolds	4	12	0	0	0	0	0	0	1	3	0	0	.000
Totals	**4**	**136**	**9**	**33**	**4**	**1**	**2**	**8**	**6**	**26**	**0**	**3**	**.243**

PITCHING STATISTICS

New York Yankees	G	GS	CG	IP	H	ER	BB	SO	W-L	Sv	ERA
Lefty Gomez	1	1	0	7	9	3	1	5	1-0	0	3.86
Johnny Murphy	1	0	0	2	2	0	1	1	0-0	1	0.00
Monte Pearson	1	1	1	9	5	1	2	9	1-0	0	1.00
Red Ruffing	2	2	2	18	17	3	2	11	2-0	0	1.50
Totals	**4**	**4**	**3**	**36**	**33**	**7**	**6**	**26**	**4-0**	**1**	**1.75**

Chicago Cubs	G	GS	CG	IP	H	ER	BB	SO	W-L	Sv	ERA
Clay Bryant	1	1	0	5 1/3	6	4	5	3	0-1	0	6.75
Tex Carleton	1	0	0	1	2	2	2	0	0-0	0	—
Dizzy Dean	2	1	0	8 1/3	8	6	1	2	0-1	0	6.48
Larry French	3	0	0	3 1/3	1	1	1	2	0-0	0	2.70
Bill Lee	2	2	0	11	15	3	1	8	0-2	0	2.45
Vance Page	1	0	0	1 1/3	2	2	0	0	0-0	0	13.50
Charlie Root	1	0	0	3	3	1	0	1	0-0	0	3.00
Jack Russell	2	0	0	1 2/3	1	0	1	0	0-0	0	0.00
Totals	**4**	**4**	**0**	**34**	**37**	**19**	**11**	**16**	**0-4**	**0**	**5.03**

1939 World Series

NEW YORK YANKEES (4) VS. CINCINNATI REDS (0)

GAME 1
Wednesday, October 4
at Yankee Stadium, New York

	1	2	3	4	5	6	7	8	9	R	H	E
Cincinnati Reds	0	0	0	1	0	0	0	0	0	1	4	0
New York Yankees	0	0	0	0	1	0	0	0	1	2	6	0

WP - Red Ruffing; LP - Paul Derringer

GAME 2
Thursday, October 5
at Yankee Stadium, New York

	1	2	3	4	5	6	7	8	9	R	H	E
Cincinnati Reds	0	0	0	0	0	0	0	0	0	0	2	0
New York Yankees	0	0	3	1	0	0	0	0	x	4	9	0

HR - NY Babe Dahlgren

WP - Monte Pearson; LP - Bucky Walters

GAME 3
Saturday, October 7
at Crosley Field, Cincinnati

	1	2	3	4	5	6	7	8	9	R	H	E
New York Yankees	2	0	2	0	3	0	0	0	0	7	5	1
Cincinnati Reds	1	2	0	0	0	0	0	0	0	3	10	0

HR - NY Bill Dickey, Joe DiMaggio, Charlie Keller 2

WP - Bump Hadley; LP - Junior Thompson

GAME 4
Sunday, October 8
at Crosley Field, Cincinnati

	1	2	3	4	5	6	7	8	9	10	R	H	E
New York Yankees	0	0	0	0	0	0	2	0	2	3	7	7	1
Cincinnati Reds	0	0	0	0	0	0	3	1	0	0	4	11	4

HR - NY Bill Dickey, Charlie Keller

WP - Johnny Murphy; LP - Bucky Walters

BATTING STATISTICS

New York Yankees	G	AB	R	H	2B	3B	HR	RBI	BB	SO	SB	CS	BA
Frankie Crosetti	4	16	2	1	0	0	0	1	2	2	0	0	.063
Babe Dahlgren	4	14	2	3	2	0	1	2	0	4	0	0	.214
Bill Dickey	4	15	2	4	0	0	2	5	1	2	0	0	.267
Joe DiMaggio	4	16	3	5	0	0	1	3	1	1	0	0	.313
Lefty Gomez	1	1	0	0	0	0	0	0	0	1	0	0	.000
Joe Gordon	4	14	1	2	0	0	0	1	0	2	0	0	.143
Bump Hadley	1	3	0	0	0	0	0	0	0	0	0	0	.000
Oral Hildebrand	1	1	0	0	0	0	0	0	0	1	0	0	.000
Charlie Keller	4	16	8	7	1	1	3	6	1	2	0	0	.438
Johnny Murphy	1	2	0	0	0	0	0	0	0	1	0	0	.000
Monte Pearson	1	2	0	0	0	0	0	0	0	1	0	0	.000
Red Rolfe	4	16	2	2	0	0	0	0	0	0	0	0	.125
Red Ruffing	1	3	0	1	0	0	0	0	0	1	0	0	.333
George Selkirk	4	12	0	2	1	0	0	0	3	2	0	0	.167
Steve Sundra	1	0	0	0	0	0	0	0	0	1	0	0	—
Totals	**4**	**131**	**20**	**27**	**4**	**1**	**7**	**18**	**9**	**20**	**0**	**0**	**.206**

Reds	G	AB	R	H	2B	3B	HR	RBI	BB	SO	SB	CS	BA
Wally Berger	4	15	0	0	0	0	0	1	0	4	0	0	.000
Nino Bongiovanni	1	1	0	0	0	0	0	0	0	0	0	0	.000
Frenchy Bordagaray	2	0	0	0	0	0	0	0	0	0	0	0	—
Harry Craft	4	11	0	1	0	0	0	0	0	6	0	0	.091
Paul Derringer	2	5	0	1	0	0	0	0	0	0	0	0	.200
Lonny Frey	4	17	0	0	0	0	0	0	1	4	0	0	.000
Lee Gamble	1	1	0	0	0	0	0	0	0	1	0	0	.000
Ival Goodman	4	15	3	5	1	0	0	1	1	2	1	0	.333
Willard Hershberger	3	2	0	1	0	0	0	1	0	0	0	0	.500
Ernie Lombardi	4	14	0	3	0	0	0	2	0	1	0	0	.214
Frank McCormick	4	15	1	6	1	0	0	1	0	1	0	0	.400
Whitey Moore	1	1	0	0	0	0	0	0	0	0	0	0	.000
Billy Myers	4	12	2	4	0	1	0	0	2	3	0	0	.333
Al Simmons	1	4	1	1	1	0	0	0	0	0	0	0	.250
Junior Thompson	1	1	0	1	0	0	0	0	0	0	0	0	1.000
Bucky Walters	2	3	0	0	0	0	0	0	0	0	0	0	.000
Bill Werber	4	16	1	4	0	0	0	2	2	0	0	1	.250
Totals	**4**	**133**	**8**	**27**	**3**	**1**	**0**	**8**	**6**	**22**	**1**	**1**	**.203**

PITCHING STATISTICS

New York Yankees	G	GS	CG	IP	H	ER	BB	SO	W-L	Sv	ERA
Lefty Gomez	1	1	0	1	3	1	0	1	0-0	0	9.00
Bump Hadley	1	0	0	8	7	2	3	2	1-0	0	2.25
Oral Hildebrand	1	1	0	4	2	0	0	3	0-0	0	0.00
Johnny Murphy	1	0	0	3 1/3	5	1	0	2	1-0	0	2.70
Monte Pearson	1	1	1	9	2	0	1	8	1-0	0	0.00
Red Ruffing	1	1	1	9	4	1	1	4	1-0	0	1.00
Steve Sundra	1	0	0	2 2/3	4	0	1	2	0-0	0	0.00
Totals	**4**	**4**	**2**	**37**	**27**	**5**	**6**	**22**	**4-0**	**0**	**1.22**

Reds	G	GS	CG	IP	H	ER	BB	SO	W-L	Sv	ERA
Paul Derringer	2	2	1	15 1/3	9	4	3	9	0-1	0	2.35
Lee Grissom	1	0	0	1 1/3	0	0	1	0	0-0	0	0.00
Whitey Moore	1	0	0	3	0	0	0	2	0-0	0	0.00
Junior Thompson	1	1	0	4 2/3	5	7	4	3	0-1	0	13.50
Bucky Walters	2	1	1	11	13	6	1	6	0-2	0	4.91
Totals	**4**	**4**	**2**	**35 1/3**	**27**	**17**	**9**	**20**	**0-4**	**0**	**4.33**

1941 World Series

NEW YORK YANKEES (4) VS. BROOKLYN DODGERS (1)

GAME 1
Wednesday, October 1
at Yankee Stadium, New York

	1	2	3	4	5	6	7	8	9	R	H	E
Brooklyn Dodgers	0	0	0	0	1	0	1	0	0	2	6	0
New York Yankees	0	1	0	1	0	1	0	0	—	3	6	1

HR - NY Joe Gordon

WP - Red Ruffing; LP - Curt Davis

GAME 2
Thursday, October 2
at Yankee Stadium, New York

	1	2	3	4	5	6	7	8	9	R	H	E
Brooklyn Dodgers	0	0	0	0	2	1	0	0	0	3	6	2
New York Yankees	0	1	1	0	0	0	0	0	0	2	9	1

WP - Whit Wyatt; LP - Spud Chandler

GAME 3
Friday, October 3
at Ebbets Field, Brooklyn

	1	2	3	4	5	6	7	8	9	R	H	E
New York Yankees	0	0	0	0	0	0	0	2	0	2	8	0
Brooklyn Dodgers	0	0	0	0	0	0	0	1	0	1	4	0

WP - Marius Russo; LP - Hugh Casey

GAME 4
Sunday, October 5
at Ebbets Field, Brooklyn

	1	2	3	4	5	6	7	8	9	R	H	E
New York Yankees	1	0	0	2	0	0	0	4	7	12	0	
Brooklyn Dodgers	0	0	0	2	2	0	0	0	4	9	1	

HR - BRO Pete Reiser

WP - Johnny Murphy; LP - Hugh Casey

GAME 5
Monday, October 6
at Ebbets Field, Brooklyn

	1	2	3	4	5	6	7	8	9	R	H	E
New York Yankees	0	2	0	0	1	0	0	0	0	3	6	0
Brooklyn Dodgers	0	0	1	0	0	0	0	0	0	1	4	1

HR - NY Tommy Henrich

WP - Tiny Bonham; LP - Whit Wyatt

BATTING STATISTICS

New York Yankees	G	AB	R	H	2B	3B	HR	RBI	BB	SO	SB	CS	BA
Tiny Bonham	1	4	0	0	0	0	0	0	0	4	0	0	.000
Frenchy Bordagaray	1	0	0	0	0	0	0	0	0	0	0	0	—
Marv Breuer	1	1	0	0	0	0	0	0	0	0	0	0	.000
Spud Chandler	1	2	0	1	0	0	0	1	0	0	0	0	.500
Bill Dickey	5	18	3	3	1	0	0	1	3	1	0	0	.167
Joe DiMaggio	5	19	1	5	0	0	0	1	2	2	0	0	.263
Atley Donald	1	2	0	0	0	0	0	0	0	1	0	0	.000
Joe Gordon	5	14	2	7	1	1	1	5	7	0	0	0	.500
Tommy Henrich	5	18	4	3	1	0	1	1	3	3	0	0	.167
Charlie Keller	5	18	5	7	2	0	0	5	3	1	0	0	.389
Johnny Murphy	2	2	0	0	0	0	0	0	0	1	0	0	.000
Phil Rizzuto	5	18	0	2	0	0	0	0	3	1	1	0	.111
Red Rolfe	5	20	2	6	0	0	0	0	2	1	0	1	.300
Red Ruffing	1	3	0	0	0	0	0	0	0	0	0	0	.000
Marius Russo	1	4	0	0	0	0	0	0	0	1	0	0	.000
George Selkirk	2	2	0	1	0	0	0	0	0	0	0	0	.500
Johnny Sturm	5	21	0	6	0	0	0	2	0	2	1	1	.286
Totals	**5**	**166**	**17**	**41**	**5**	**1**	**2**	**16**	**23**	**18**	**2**	**2**	**.247**

Brooklyn Dodgers	G	AB	R	H	2B	3B	HR	RBI	BB	SO	SB	CS	BA
Dolph Camilli	5	18	1	3	1	0	0	1	1	6	0	0	.167
Hugh Casey	3	2	0	1	0	0	0	0	0	1	0	0	.500
Pete Coscarart	3	7	1	0	0	0	0	0	1	2	0	0	.000
Curt Davis	1	2	0	0	0	0	0	0	0	0	0	0	.000
Freddie Fitzsimmons	1	2	0	0	0	0	0	0	0	0	0	0	.000
Herman Franks	1	1	0	0	0	0	0	0	0	0	0	0	.000
Augie Galan	2	2	0	0	0	0	0	0	0	1	0	0	.000
Billy Herman	4	8	0	1	0	0	0	0	2	0	0	0	.125
Kirby Higbe	1	1	0	1	0	0	0	0	0	0	0	1	1.000
Cookie Lavagetto	3	10	1	1	0	0	0	0	2	0	0	0	.100
Joe Medwick	5	17	1	4	1	0	0	0	1	2	0	0	.235
Mickey Owen	5	12	1	2	0	1	0	2	3	0	0	1	.167
Pee Wee Reese	5	20	1	4	0	0	0	2	0	0	0	0	.200
Pete Reiser	5	20	1	4	1	1	1	3	1	6	0	0	.200
Lew Riggs	3	8	0	2	0	0	0	1	1	1	0	0	.250
Dixie Walker	5	18	3	4	2	0	0	0	2	1	0	0	.222
Jimmy Wasdell	3	5	0	1	1	0	0	0	0	0	0	0	.200
Whit Wyatt	2	6	1	1	1	0	0	0	0	1	0	0	.167
Totals	**5**	**159**	**11**	**29**	**7**	**2**	**1**	**11**	**14**	**21**	**0**	**1**	**.182**

PITCHING STATISTICS

New York Yankees	G	GS	CG	IP	H	ER	BB	SO	W-L	Sv	ERA
Tiny Bonham	1	1	1	9	4	1	2	2	1-0	0	1.00
Marv Breuer	1	0	0	3	3	0	1	2	0-0	0	0.00
Spud Chandler	1	1	0	5	4	2	2	2	0-1	0	3.60
Atley Donald	1	1	0	4	6	4	3	2	0-0	0	9.00
Johnny Murphy	2	0	0	6	2	0	1	3	1-0	0	0.00
Red Ruffing	1	1	1	9	6	1	3	5	1-0	0	1.00
Marius Russo	1	1	1	9	4	1	2	5	1-0	0	1.00
Totals	**5**	**5**	**3**	**45**	**29**	**9**	**14**	**21**	**4-1**	**0**	**1.80**

Brooklyn Dodgers	G	GS	CG	IP	H	ER	BB	SO	W-L	Sv	ERA
Johnny Allen	3	0	0	3 2/3	1	0	3	0	0-0	0	0.00
Hugh Casey	3	0	0	5 1/3	9	2	2	1	0-2	0	3.38
Curt Davis	1	1	0	5 1/3	6	3	3	1	0-1	0	5.06
Freddie Fitzsimmons	1	1	0	7	4	0	3	1	0-0	0	0.00
Larry French	2	0	0	1	0	0	0	0	0-0	0	0.00
Kirby Higbe	1	1	0	3 2/3	6	3	2	1	0-0	0	7.36
Whit Wyatt	2	2	2	18	15	5	10	14	1-1	0	2.50
Totals	**5**	**5**	**2**	**44**	**41**	**13**	**23**	**18**	**1-4**	**0**	**2.66**

1942 World Series

ST. LOUIS CARDINALS (4) VS. NEW YORK YANKEES (1)

GAME 1
Wednesday, September 30
at Sportsman's Park, St. Louis

	1	2	3	4	5	8	7	8	9	R	H	E
New York Yankees	0	0	0	1	1	0	0	3	2	7	11	0
St. Louis Cardinals	0	0	0	0	0	0	0	4	4	4	7	4

WP - Red Ruffing; LP - Mort Cooper; Sv - Spud Chandler

GAME 2
Thursday, October 1
at Sportsman's Park, St. Louis

	1	2	3	4	5	6	7	8	9	R	H	E
New York Yankees	0	0	0	0	0	0	3	0	3	10	2	
St. Louis Cardinals	2	0	0	0	0	0	1	1	x	4	6	0

HR - NY Charlie Keller

WP - Johnny Beazley; LP - Tiny Bonham

GAME 3
Saturday, October 3
at Yankee Stadium, New York

	1	2	3	4	5	6	7	8	9	R	H	E
St. Louis Cardinals	0	0	1	0	0	0	0	1		2	5	1
New York Yankees	0	0	0	0	0	0	0	0	0	6	1	

WP - Ernie White; LP - Spud Chandler

GAME 4
Sunday, October 4
at Yankee Stadium, New York

	1	2	3	4	5	6	7	8	9	R	H	E
St. Louis Cardinals	0	0	0	6	0	0	2	0	1	9	12	1
New York Yankees	1	0	0	0	5	0	0	0	6	10	1	

HR - NY Charlie Keller

WP - Howie Pollet; LP - Atley Donald; Sv - Max Lanier

GAME 5
Monday, October 5
at Yankee Stadium, New York

	1	2	3	4	5	6	7	8	9	R	H	E
St. Louis Cardinals	0	0	0	1	0	1	0	0	2	4	9	4
New York Yankees	1	0	0	1	0	0	0	0	0	2	7	1

HR - STL Whitey Kurowski, Enos Slaughter; NY Phil Rizzuto

WP - Johnny Beazley; LP - Red Ruffing

BATTING STATISTICS

St. Louis Cardinals	G	AB	R	H	2B	3B	HR	RBI	BB	SO	SS	CS	BA
Johnny Beazley	2	7	0	1	0	0	0	0	0	5	0	0	.143
Jimmy Brown	5	20	2	6	0	0	0	1	3	0	0	0	.300
Mort Cooper	2	5	1	1	0	0	0	2	0	1	0	0	.200
Walker Cooper	5	21	3	6	1	0	0	4	0	1	0	0	.286
Creepy Crespi	1	0	1	0	0	0	0	0	0	0	0	0	—
Johnny Hopp	5	17	3	3	0	0	0	0	1	1	0	0	.176
Whitey Kurowski	5	15	3	4	0	1	1	5	2	3	0	0	.267
Max Lanier	2	1	0	1	0	0	0	1	0	0	0	0	1.000
Marty Marion	5	18	2	2	0	1	0	3	1	2	0	0	.111
Terry Moore	5	17	2	5	1	0	0	2	2	3	0	0	.294
Stan Musial	5	18	2	4	1	0	0	2	4	0	0	1	.222
Ken O'Dea	1	1	0	1	0	0	0	1	0	0	0	0	1.000
Ray Sanders	2	1	1	0	0	0	0	0	1	0	0	0	.000
Enos Slaughter	5	19	3	5	1	0	1	2	3	2	0	0	.263
Harry Walker	1	1	0	0	0	0	0	0	0	1	0	0	.000
Ernie White	1	2	0	0	0	0	0	0	0	0	0	0	.000
Totals	5	163	23	39	4	2	2	23	17	19	0	1	.239

New York Yankees	G	AB	R	H	2B	3B	HR	RBI	BB	SO	SB	CS	BA
Tiny Bonham	2	2	0	0	0	0	0	0	1	0	0	0	.000
Hank Borowy	1	1	0	0	0	0	0	0	0	1	0	0	.000
Spud Chandler	2	2	0	0	0	0	0	0	0	1	0	0	.000
Frankie Crosetti	1	3	0	0	0	0	0	0	0	1	0	0	.000
Roy Cullenbine	5	19	3	5	1	0	0	2	1	2	1	0	.263
Bill Dickey	5	19	1	5	0	0	0	0	1	0	0	0	.263
Joe DiMaggio	5	21	3	7	0	0	0	3	0	1	0	0	.333
Atley Donald	1	2	0	0	0	0	0	0	0	0	0	0	.000
Joe Gordon	5	21	1	2	1	0	0	0	0	7	0	0	.095
Buddy Hassett	3	9	1	3	1	0	0	2	0	1	0	0	.333
Charlie Keller	5	20	2	4	0	0	2	5	1	3	0	0	.200
Jerry Priddy	3	10	0	1	1	0	0	1	1	0	0	0	.100
Phil Rizzuto	5	21	2	8	0	0	1	1	2	1	2	0	.381
Red Rolfe	4	17	5	6	2	0	0	0	1	2	0	0	.353
Buddy Rosar	1	1	0	1	0	0	0	0	0	0	0	0	1.000
Red Ruffing	4	9	0	2	0	0	0	0	0	2	0	0	.222
George Selkirk	1	1	0	0	0	0	0	0	0	0	0	0	.000
Tuck Stainback	2	0	0	0	0	0	0	0	0	0	0	0	—
Totals	5	178	18	44	6	0	3	14	8	22	3	0	.247

PITCHING STATISTICS

St. Louis Cardinals	G	GS	CG	IP	H	ER	BB	SO	W-L	Sv	ERA
Johnny Beazley	2	2	2	18	17	5	3	6	2-0	0	2.50
Mort Cooper	2	2	0	13	17	8	4	9	0-1	0	5.54
Harry Gumbert	2	0	0	0 2/3	1	0	0	0	0-0	0	0.00
Max Lanier	2	0	0	4	3	0	1	1	0-0	1	0.00
Howie Pollet	1	0	0	0 1/3	0	0	0	0	1-0	0	0.00
Ernie White	1	1	1	9	6	0	0	6	1-0	0	0.00
Totals	5	5	3	45	44	13	8	22	4-1	1	2.60

New York Yankees	G	GS	CG	IP	H	ER	BB	SO	W-L	Sv	ERA
Tiny Bonham	2	1	1	11	9	5	3	3	0-1	0	4.09
Hank Borowy	1	1	0	3	6	6	3	1	0-0	0	18.00
Marv Breuer	1	0	0	2	2	0	0	0	0-0	0	—
Spud Chandler	2	1	0	8 1/3	5	1	1	3	0-1	1	1.08
Atley Donald	1	0	0	3	3	2	2	1	0-0	0	6.00
Red Ruffing	2	2	1	17 2/3	14	8	7	11	1-1	0	4.08
Jim Turner	1	0	0	1	0	0	1	0	0-0	0	0.00
Totals	5	5	2	44	39	22	17	19	1-4	1	4.50

1943 World Series

NEW YORK YANKEES (4) VS. ST. LOUIS CARDINALS (1)

GAME 1

Tuesday, October 5
at Yankee Stadium, New York

```
                  1 2 3 4 5 6 7 8 9  R H E
St. Louis Cardinals 0 1 0 0 1 0 0 0 0  2 7 2
New York Yankees    0 0 0 2 0 2 0 0 x  4 8 2
```

HR - NY Joe Gordon

WP - Spud Chandler; **LP** - Max Lanier

GAME 2

Wednesday, October 6
at Yankee Stadium, New York

```
                  1 2 3 4 5 6 7 8 9  R H E
St. Louis Cardinals 0 0 1 3 0 0 0 0 0  4 7 2
New York Yankees    0 0 0 1 0 0 0 0 2  3 6 0
```

HR - STL Marty Marion, Ray Sanders

WP - Mort Cooper; **LP** - Tiny Bonham

GAME 3

Thursday, October 7
at Yankee Stadium, New York

```
                  1 2 3 4 5 6 7 8 9  R H E
St. Louis Cardinals 0 0 0 2 0 0 0 0 0  2 6 4
New York Yankees    0 0 0 0 0 1 0 5 x  6 8 0
```

WP - Hank Borowy; **LP** - Al Brazle; **Sv** - Johnny Murphy

GAME 4

Sunday, October 10
at Sportman's Park, St. Louis

```
                  1 2 3 4 5 6 7 8 9  R H E
New York Yankees    0 0 0 1 0 0 0 1 0  2 6 2
St. Louis Cardinals 0 0 0 0 0 0 1 0 0  1 7 1
```

WP - Marius Russo; **LP** - Harry Brecheen

GAME 5

Monday, October 11
at Sportsman's Park, St. Louis

```
                  1 2 3 4 5 6 7 8 9  R H E
New York Yankees    0 0 0 0 0 2 0 0 0  2 7 1
St. Louis Cardinals 0 0 0 0 0 0 0 0 0  1 0 1
```

HR - NY Bill Dickey

WP - Spud Chandler; **LP** - Mort Cooper

BATTING STATISTICS

New York Yankees	G	AB	R	H	2B	3B	HR	RBI	BB	SO	SB	CS	BA
Tiny Bonham	1	2	0	0	0	0	0	0	0	0	0	0	.000
Hank Borowy	1	2	1	1	1	0	0	0	0	1	0	0	.500
Spud Chandler	2	6	0	1	0	0	0	0	0	2	0	0	.167
Frankie Crosetti	5	18	4	5	0	0	0	1	2	3	1	0	.278
Bill Dickey	5	18	1	5	0	0	1	4	2	2	0	0	.278
Nick Etten	5	19	0	2	0	0	0	2	1	2	0	0	.105
Joe Gordon	5	17	2	4	1	0	1	2	3	3	0	0	.235
Bill Johnson	5	20	3	6	1	1	0	3	0	3	0	0	.300
Charlie Keller	5	18	3	4	0	1	0	2	2	5	1	0	.222
Johnny Lindell	4	9	1	1	0	0	0	0	1	4	0	0	.111
Bud Metheny	2	8	0	1	0	0	0	0	0	2	0	0	.125
Marius Russo	1	3	1	2	2	0	0	1	1	1	0	0	.667
Tuck Stainback	5	17	0	3	0	0	0	0	0	2	0	0	.176
Snuffy Stirnweiss	1	1	1	0	0	0	0	0	0	0	0	0	.000
Roy Weatherly	1	1	0	0	0	0	0	0	0	0	0	0	.000
Totals	**5**	**159**	**17**	**35**	**5**	**2**	**2**	**14**	**12**	**30**	**2**	**0**	**.220**

St. Louis Cardinals	G	AB	R	H	2B	3B	HR	RBI	BB	SO	SB	CS	BA
Al Brazle	1	3	0	0	0	0	0	0	0	1	0	0	.000
Mort Cooper	2	5	0	0	0	0	0	0	0	3	0	0	.000
Walker Cooper	5	17	1	5	0	0	0	0	0	1	0	1	.294
Frank Demaree	1	1	0	0	0	0	0	0	0	0	0	0	.000
Debs Garms	2	5	0	0	0	0	0	0	0	2	0	0	.000
Johnny Hopp	1	4	0	0	0	0	0	0	0	1	0	0	.000
Lou Klein	5	22	0	3	0	0	0	0	1	2	0	0	.136
Whitey Kurowski	5	18	2	4	1	0	0	1	0	3	0	0	.222
Max Lanier	3	4	0	1	0	0	0	1	0	0	0	0	.250
Danny Litwhiler	5	15	0	4	1	0	0	2	2	4	0	0	.267
Marty Marion	5	14	1	5	2	0	1	2	3	1	1	0	.357
Stan Musial	5	18	2	5	0	0	0	0	2	2	0	0	.278
Sam Narron	1	1	0	0	0	0	0	0	0	0	0	0	.000
Ken O'Dea	2	3	0	2	0	0	0	0	0	0	0	0	.667
Ray Sanders	5	17	3	5	0	0	1	2	3	4	0	0	.294
Harry Walker	5	18	0	3	1	0	0	0	0	2	0	0	.167
Ernie White	1	0	0	0	0	0	0	0	0	0	0	0	—
Totals	**5**	**185**	**9**	**37**	**5**	**0**	**2**	**8**	**11**	**26**	**1**	**1**	**.224**

PITCHING STATISTICS

New York Yankees	G	GS	CG	IP	H	ER	BB	SO	W-L	Sv	ERA
Tiny Bonham	1	1	0	8	6	4	3	9	0-1	0	4.50
Hank Borowy	1	1	0	8	6	2	3	4	1-0	0	2.25
Spud Chandler	2	2	2	18	17	1	3	10	2-0	0	0.50
Johnny Murphy	2	0	0	2	1	0	1	1	0-0	1	0.00
Marius Russo	1	1	1	9	7	0	1	2	1-0	0	0.00
Totals	**5**	**5**	**3**	**45**	**37**	**7**	**11**	**26**	**4-1**	**1**	**1.40**

St. Louis Cardinals	G	GS	CG	IP	H	ER	BB	SO	W-L	Sv	ERA
Al Brazle	1	1	0	7 1/3	5	3	2	4	0-1	0	3.68
Harry Brecheen	3	0	0	3 2/3	5	1	3	3	0-1	0	2.45
Mort Cooper	2	2	1	16	11	5	3	10	1-1	0	2.81
Murry Dickson	1	0	0	0 2/3	0	0	1	0	0-0	0	0.00
Howie Krist	1	0	0	0	1	0	0	0	0-0	0	—
Max Lanier	3	2	0	15 1/3	13	3	3	13	0-1	0	1.76
Totals	**5**	**5**	**1**	**43**	**35**	**12**	**12**	**30**	**1-4**	**0**	**2.51**

1947 World Series

NEW YORK YANKEES (4) VS. BROOKLYN DODGERS (3)

GAME 1
Tuesday, September 30
at Yankee Stadium, New York

	1	2	3	4	5	6	7	8	9	R	H	E
Brooklyn Dodgers	1	0	0	0	0	1	1	0	0	3	6	0
New York Yankees	0	0	0	0	5	0	0	0	x	5	4	0

WP - Spec Shea; LP - Ralph Branca; Sv - Joe Page

GAME 2
Wednesday, October 1
at Yankee Stadium, New York

	1	2	3	4	5	6	7	8	9	R	H	E
Brooklyn Dodgers	0	0	1	1	0	0	0	0	1	3	9	2
New York Yankees	1	0	1	1	2	1	4	0	x	10	15	1

HR - BRO Dixie Walker; NY Tommy Henrich

WP - Allie Reynolds; LP - Vic Lombardi

GAME 3
Thursday, October 2
at Ebbets Field, Brooklyn

	1	2	3	4	5	6	7	8	9	R	H	E
New York Yankees	0	0	2	2	2	1	1	0	0	8	13	0
Brooklyn Dodgers	0	6	1	2	0	0	0	x		9	13	1

HR - NY Yogi Berra, Joe DiMaggio

WP - Hugh Casey; LP - Bobo Newsom

GAME 4
Friday, October 3
at Ebbets Field, Brooklyn

	1	2	3	4	5	6	7	8	9	R	H	E
New York Yankees	1	0	0	1	0	0	0	0	0	2	8	1
Brooklyn Dodgers	0	0	0	0	1	0	0	0	2	3	1	3

WP - Hugh Casey; LP - Bill Bevens

GAME 5
Saturday, October 4
at Ebbets Field, Brooklyn

	1	2	3	4	5	6	7	8	9	R	H	E
New York Yankees	0	0	0	1	1	0	0	0	0	2	5	0
Brooklyn Dodgers	0	0	0	0	0	1	0	0	1	1	4	1

HR - NY Joe DiMaggio

WP - Spec Shea; LP - Rex Barney

GAME 6
Sunday, October 5
at Yankee Stadium, New York

	1	2	3	4	5	6	7	8	9	R	H	E
Brooklyn Dodgers	2	0	2	0	0	4	0	0	0	8	12	1
New York Yankees	0	0	4	1	0	0	0	0	1	6	15	2

WP - Ralph Branca; LP - Joe Page; Sv - Hugh Casey

GAME 7
Monday, October 6
at Yankee Stadium, New York

	1	2	3	4	5	6	7	8	9	R	H	E
Brooklyn Dodgers	0	2	0	0	0	0	0	0	0	2	7	0
New York Yankees	0	1	0	2	0	1	1	0	x	5	7	0

WP - Joe Page; LP - Hal Gregg

BATTING STATISTICS

New York Yankees	G	AB	R	H	2B	3B	HR	RBI	BB	SO	SB	CS	BA
Yogi Berra	6	19	2	3	0	0	1	2	1	2	0	0	.158
Bill Bevens	2	4	0	0	0	0	0	0	0	2	0	0	.000
Bobby Brown	4	3	2	3	2	0	0	3	1	0	0	0	1.000
Allie Clark	3	2	1	1	0	0	0	1	1	0	0	0	.500
Joe DiMaggio	7	26	4	6	0	0	2	5	6	2	0	0	.231
Karl Drews	2	2	0	0	0	0	0	0	0	2	0	0	.000
Lonny Frey	1	1	0	0	0	0	0	0	0	0	0	0	.000
Tommy Henrich	7	31	2	10	2	0	1	5	2	3	0	0	.323
Ralph Houk	1	1	0	1	0	0	0	0	0	0	0	0	1.000
Bill Johnson	7	26	8	7	0	3	0	2	3	4	0	0	.269
Johnny Lindell	6	18	3	9	3	1	0	7	5	2	0	0	.500
Sherm Lollar	2	4	3	3	2	0	0	1	0	0	0	0	.750
George McQuinn	7	23	3	3	0	0	0	1	5	8	0	0	.130
Joe Page	4	4	0	0	0	0	0	0	0	1	0	0	.000
Jack Phillips	2	2	0	0	0	0	0	0	0	0	0	0	.000
Allie Reynolds	2	4	2	2	0	0	0	1	0	0	0	0	.500
Phil Rizzuto	7	26	3	8	1	0	0	2	4	0	2	1	.308
Aaron Robinson	3	10	2	2	0	0	0	1	2	1	0	0	.200
Spec Shea	3	5	0	2	1	0	0	1	0	2	0	0	.400
Snuffy Stirnweiss	7	27	3	7	0	1	0	3	8	8	0	0	.259
Totals	7	238	38	67	11	5	4	36	38	37	2	1	.282

Brooklyn Dodgers	G	AB	R	H	2B	3B	HR	RBI	BB	SO	SB	CS	BA
Dan Bankhead	1	0	1	0	0	0	0	0	0	0	0	0	—
Rex Barney	3	1	0	0	0	0	0	0	0	0	0	0	.000
Bobby Bragan	1	1	0	1	1	0	0	1	0	0	0	0	1.000
Ralph Branca	3	4	0	0	0	0	0	0	0	1	0	0	.000
Hugh Casey	6	1	0	0	0	0	0	0	0	1	0	0	.000
Bruce Edwards	7	27	3	6	1	0	0	2	2	7	0	0	.222
Carl Furillo	6	17	2	6	2	0	0	3	3	0	0	0	.353
Al Gionfriddo	4	3	2	0	0	0	0	0	1	0	1	0	.000
Hal Gregg	3	3	0	0	0	0	0	0	1	1	0	0	.000
Joe Hatten	4	3	1	1	0	0	0	0	0	0	0	0	.333
Gene Hermanski	7	19	4	3	0	1	0	1	3	3	0	0	.158
Gil Hodges	1	1	0	0	0	0	0	0	0	1	0	0	.000
Spider Jorgensen	7	20	1	4	2	0	0	3	2	4	0	0	.200
Cookie Lavagetto	5	7	0	1	1	0	0	3	0	2	0	0	.143
Vic Lombardi	3	3	0	0	0	0	0	0	0	0	0	0	.000
Eddie Miksis	5	4	1	1	0	0	0	0	0	1	0	0	.250
Pee Wee Reese	7	23	5	7	1	0	0	4	6	3	3	2	.304
Pete Reiser	5	8	1	2	0	0	0	0	3	1	0	1	.250
Jackie Robinson	7	27	3	7	2	0	0	3	2	4	2	0	.259
Eddie Stanky	7	25	4	6	1	0	0	2	3	2	0	1	.240
Arky Vaughan	3	2	0	1	1	0	0	0	1	0	0	0	.500
Dixie Walker	7	27	1	6	1	0	1	4	3	1	1	0	.222
Totals	**7**	**226**	**29**	**52**	**13**	**1**	**1**	**26**	**30**	**32**	**7**	**4**	**.230**

PITCHING STATISTICS

New York Yankees	G	GS	CG	IP	H	ER	BB	SO	W-L	Sv	ERA
Bill Bevens	2	1	1	11 1/3	3	3	11	7	0-1	0	2.38
Spud Chandler	1	0	0	2	2	2	3	1	0-0	0	9.00
Karl Drews	2	0	0	3	2	1	1	0	0-0	0	3.00
Bobo Newsom	2	1	0	2 1/3	6	5	2	0	0-1	0	19.29
Joe Page	4	0	0	13	12	6	2	7	1-1	1	4.15
Vic Raschi	2	0	0	1 1/3	2	1	0	1	0-0	0	6.75
Allie Reynolds	2	2	1	11 1/3	15	6	3	6	1-0	0	4.76
Spec Shea	3	3	1	15 1/3	10	4	8	10	2-0	0	2.35
Butch Wensloff	1	0	0	2	0	0	0	0	0-0	0	0.00
Totals	**7**	**7**	**3**	**61 2/3**	**52**	**28**	**30**	**32**	**4-3**	**1**	**4.09**

Brooklyn Dodgers	G	GS	CG	IP	H	ER	BB	SO	W-L	Sv	ERA
Rex Barney	3	1	0	6 2/3	4	2	10	3	0-1	0	2.70
Hank Behrman	5	0	0	6 1/3	9	5	5	3	0-0	0	7.11
Ralph Branca	3	1	0	8 1/3	12	8	5	8	1-1	0	8.64
Hugh Casey	6	0	0	10 1/3	5	1	1	3	2-0	1	0.87
Hal Gregg	3	1	0	12 2/3	9	5	8	10	0-1	0	3.55
Joe Hatten	4	1	0	9	12	7	7	5	0-0	0	7.00
Vic Lombardi	2	2	0	6 2/3	14	9	1	5	0-1	0	12.15
Harry Taylor	1	1	0	0	2	0	1	0	0-0	0	—
Totals	**7**	**7**	**0**	**60**	**67**	**37**	**38**	**37**	**3-4**	**1**	**5.55**

1949 World Series

NEW YORK YANKEES (4) VS. BROOKLYN DODGERS (1)

GAME 1
Wednesday, October 5
at Yankee Stadium, New York

	1	2	3	4	5	6	7	8	9	R	H	E
Brooklyn Dodgers	0	0	0	0	0	0	0	0	0	0	2	0
New York Yankees	0	0	0	0	0	0	0	1	1	5	1

HR - NY Tommy Henrich

WP - Allie Reynolds; LP - Don Newcombe

GAME 2
Thursday, October 6
at Yankee Stadium, New York

	1	2	3	4	5	6	7	8	9	R	H	E
Brooklyn Dodgers	0	1	0	0	0	0	0	0	1	7	2
New York Yankees	0	0	0	0	0	0	0	0	0	6	1

WP - Preacher Roe; LP - Vic Raschi

GAME 3
Friday, October 7
at Ebbets Field, Brooklyn

	1	2	3	4	5	6	7	8	9	R	H	E
New York Yankees	0	0	0	0	0	0	0	3	4	5	0
Brooklyn Dodgers	0	0	0	1	0	0	0	0	2	3	5	0

HR - BRO Roy Campanella, Luis Olmo, Pee Wee Reese

WP - Joe Page; LP - Ralph Branca

GAME 4
Saturday, October 8
at Ebbets Field, Brooklyn

	1	2	3	4	5	6	7	8	9	R	H	E
New York Yankees	0	0	0	3	3	0	0	0	6	10	0
Brooklyn Dodgers	0	0	0	0	4	0	0	0	4	9	1

WP - Ed Lopat; LP - Don Newcombe; Sv - Allie Reynolds

GAME 5
Sunday, October 9
at Ebbets Field, Brooklyn

	1	2	3	4	5	6	7	8	9	R	H	E
New York Yankees	2	0	3	1	1	3	0	0	10	11	1
Brooklyn Dodgers	0	0	1	0	0	1	4	0	0	6	11	2

HR - NY Joe DiMaggio; BRO Gil Hodges

WP - Vic Raschi; LP - Rex Barney; Sv - Joe Page

BATTING STATISTICS

New York Yankees	G	AB	R	H	2B	3B	HR	RBI	BB	SO	SB	CS	BA
Hank Bauer	3	6	0	1	0	0	0	0	0	0	0	0	.167
Yogi Berra	4	16	2	1	0	0	0	1	1	3	0	0	.063
Bobby Brown	4	12	4	6	1	2	0	5	2	2	0	0	.500
Tommy Byrne	1	1	0	1	0	0	0	0	0	0	0	0	1.000
Jerry Coleman	5	20	0	5	3	0	0	4	0	4	0	0	.250
Joe DiMaggio	5	18	2	2	0	0	1	2	3	5	0	0	.111
Tommy Henrich	5	19	4	5	0	0	1	1	3	0	0	0	.263
Bill Johnson	2	7	0	1	0	0	0	0	0	2	1	0	.143
Johnny Lindell	2	7	0	1	0	0	0	0	0	2	0	0	.143
Ed Lopat	1	3	0	1	1	0	0	1	0	0	0	0	.333
Cliff Mapes	4	10	3	1	1	0	0	2	2	4	0	0	.100
Johnny Mize	2	2	0	2	0	0	0	2	0	0	0	0	1.000
Joe Page	3	4	0	0	0	0	0	0	0	2	0	0	.000
Vic Raschi	2	5	0	1	0	0	0	1	1	1	0	0	.200
Allie Reynolds	2	4	0	2	1	0	0	0	0	1	0	0	.500
Phil Rizzuto	5	18	2	3	0	0	0	1	3	1	1	0	.167
Charlie Silvera	1	2	0	0	0	0	0	0	0	0	0	0	.000
Snuffy Stirnweiss	1	0	0	0	0	0	0	0	0	0	0	0	—
Gene Woodling	3	10	4	4	3	0	0	0	3	0	0	0	.400
Totals	**5**	**164**	**21**	**37**	**10**	**2**	**2**	**20**	**18**	**27**	**2**	**0**	**.226**

Brooklyn Dodgers	G	AB	R	H	2B	3B	HR	RBI	BB	SO	SB	CS	BA
Jack Banta	3	1	0	0	0	0	0	0	0	0	0	0	.000
Ralph Branca	1	3	0	0	0	0	0	0	0	3	0	0	.000
Tommy Brown	2	2	0	0	0	0	0	0	0	1	0	0	.000
Roy Campanella	5	15	2	4	1	0	1	2	3	1	0	0	.267
Billy Cox	2	3	0	1	0	0	0	0	0	1	0	0	.333
Bruce Edwards	2	2	0	1	0	0	0	0	0	1	0	0	.500
Carl Furillo	3	8	0	1	0	0	0	0	1	0	0	0	.125
Gene Hermanski	4	13	1	4	0	1	0	2	3	3	0	0	.308
Gil Hodges	5	17	2	4	0	0	1	4	1	4	0	0	.235
Spider Jorgensen	4	11	1	2	2	0	0	0	2	2	0	0	.182
Eddie Miksis	3	7	0	2	1	0	0	0	0	1	0	0	.286
Don Newcombe	2	4	0	0	0	0	0	0	0	3	0	0	.000
Luis Olmo	4	11	3	3	0	0	1	2	0	2	0	0	.273
Marv Rackley	2	5	0	0	0	0	0	0	0	2	0	0	.000
Pee Wee Reese	5	19	2	6	1	0	1	2	1	0	1	0	.316
Jackie Robinson	5	16	2	3	1	0	0	2	4	2	0	0	.188
Preacher Roe	1	3	0	0	0	0	0	0	0	3	0	0	.000
Duke Snider	5	21	2	3	1	0	0	0	0	8	0	0	.143
Dick Whitman	1	1	0	0	0	0	0	0	0	1	0	0	.000
Totals	**5**	**162**	**14**	**34**	**7**	**1**	**4**	**14**	**15**	**38**	**1**	**0**	**.210**

PITCHING STATISTICS

New York Yankees	G	GS	CG	IP	H	ER	BB	SO	W-L	Sv	ERA
Tommy Byrne	1	1	0	3 1/3	2	1	2	1	0-0	0	2.70
Ed Lopat	1	1	0	5 2/3	9	4	1	4	1-0	0	6.35
Joe Page	3	0	0	9	6	2	3	8	1-0	1	2.00
Vic Raschi	2	2	0	14 2/3	15	7	5	11	1-1	0	4.30
Allie Reynolds	2	1	1	12 1/3	2	0	4	14	1-0	1	0.00
Totals	**5**	**5**	**1**	**45**	**34**	**14**	**15**	**38**	**4-1**	**2**	**2.80**

Brooklyn	G	GS	CG	IP	H	ER	BB	SO	W-L	Sv	ERA
Jack Banta	3	0	0	5 2/3	5	2	1	4	0-0	0	3.18
Rex Barney	1	1	0	2 2/3	3	5	6	2	0-1	0	16.88
Ralph Branca	1	1	0	8 2/3	4	4	4	6	0-1	0	4.15
Carl Erskine	2	0	0	1 2/3	3	3	1	0	0-0	0	16.20
Joe Hatten	2	0	0	1 2/3	4	3	2	0	0-0	0	16.20
Paul Minner	1	0	0	1	1	0	0	0	0-0	0	0.00
Don Newcombe	2	2	1	11 2/3	10	4	3	11	0-2	0	3.09
Erv Palica	1	0	0	2	1	0	1	1	0-0	0	0.00
Preacher Roe	1	1	1	9	6	0	0	3	1-0	0	0.00
Totals	**5**	**5**	**2**	**44**	**37**	**21**	**18**	**27**	**1-4**	**0**	**4.30**

1950 World Series

NEW YORK YANKEES (4) VS. PHILADELPHIA PHILLIES (0)

GAME 1
Wednesday, October 4
at Shibe Park, Philadelphia

	1	2	3	4	5	6	7	8	9	R	H	E
New York Yankees	0	0	0	1	0	0	0	0	0	1	5	0
Philadelphia Phillies	0	0	0	0	0	0	0	0	0	0	2	1

WP - Vic Raschi; LP - Jim Konstanty

GAME 2
Thursday, October 5
at Shibe Park, Philadelphia

	1	2	3	4	5	6	7	8	9	10	R	H	E
New York Yankees	0	1	0	0	0	0	0	0	1	2	10	0	
Philadelphia Phillies	0	0	0	1	0	0	0	0	0	1	7	0	

HR - NY Joe DiMaggio

WP - Allie Reynolds; LP - Robin Roberts

GAME 3
Friday, October 6
at Yankee Stadium, New York

	1	2	3	4	5	6	7	8	9	R	H	E
Philadelphia Phillies	0	0	0	0	0	1	1	0	0	2	10	2
New York Yankees	0	0	1	0	0	0	0	1	1	3	7	0

WP - Tom Ferrick; LP - Russ Meyer

GAME 4
Saturday, October 7
at Yankee Stadium, New York

	1	2	3	4	5	6	7	8	9	R	H	E
Philadelphia Phillies	0	0	0	0	0	0	0	2	2	7	1	
New York Yankees	2	0	0	0	3	0	0	x	5	8	2	

HR - NY Yogi Berra

WP - Whitey Ford; LP - Bob Miller; Sv - Allie Reynolds

BATTING STATISTICS

New York	G	AB	R	H	2B	3B	HR	RBI	BB	SO	SB	CS	BA
Hank Bauer	4	15	0	2	0	0	0	1	0	0	0	0	.133
Yogi Berra	4	15	2	3	0	0	1	2	2	1	0	0	.200
Bobby Brown	4	12	2	4	1	1	0	1	0	0	0	0	.333
Jerry Coleman	4	14	2	4	1	0	0	3	2	0	0	0	.286
Joe DiMaggio	4	13	2	4	1	0	1	2	3	1	0	0	.308
Whitey Ford	1	3	0	0	0	0	0	0	0	2	0	0	.000
Johnny Hopp	3	2	0	0	0	0	0	0	0	0	0	0	.000
Jackie Jensen	1	0	0	0	0	0	0	0	0	0	0	0	—
Bill Johnson	4	6	0	0	0	0	0	0	0	3	0	0	.000
Ed Lopat	1	2	0	1	0	0	0	0	0	1	0	0	.500
Cliff Mapes	1	4	0	0	0	0	0	0	0	1	0	0	.000
Johnny Mize	4	15	0	2	0	0	0	0	0	1	0	0	.133
Vic Raschi	1	3	0	1	0	0	0	0	0	0	0	0	.333
Allie Reynolds	2	3	0	1	0	0	0	0	1	2	0	0	.333
Phil Rizzuto	4	14	1	2	0	0	0	0	3	0	1	0	.143
Gene Woodling	4	14	2	6	0	0	1	2	1	2	0	1	.429
Totals	**4**	**135**	**11**	**30**	**3**	**1**	**2**	**10**	**13**	**12**	**1**	**1**	**.222**
Philadelphia	G	AB	R	H	2B	3B	HR	RBI	BB	SO	SB	CS	BA
Richie Ashburn	4	17	0	3	1	0	0	1	0	4	0	0	.176
Putsy Caballero	3	1	0	0	0	0	0	0	0	1	0	0	.000
Del Ennis	4	14	1	2	1	0	0	0	0	1	0	0	.143
Mike Goliat	4	14	1	3	0	0	0	1	1	2	0	0	.214
Granny Hamner	4	14	1	6	2	1	0	0	1	2	1	0	.429
Ken Heintzelman	1	2	0	0	0	0	0	0	0	0	0	0	.000
Ken Johnson	1	0	1	0	0	0	0	0	0	0	0	0	—
Willie Jones	4	14	1	4	1	0	0	0	0	3	0	0	.286
Jim Konstanty	3	4	0	1	0	0	0	0	0	1	0	0	.250
Stan Lopata	2	1	0	0	0	0	0	0	0	1	0	0	.000
Jackie Mayo	3	0	0	0	0	0	0	0	1	0	0	0	—
Robin Roberts	2	2	0	0	0	0	0	0	0	1	0	0	.000
Andy Seminick	4	11	0	2	0	0	0	0	1	3	0	0	.182
Dick Sisler	4	17	0	1	0	0	0	1	0	5	0	0	.059
Eddie Waitkus	4	15	0	4	1	0	0	0	2	0	0	0	.267
Dick Whitman	3	2	0	0	0	0	0	0	1	0	0	0	.000
Totals	**4**	**128**	**5**	**26**	**6**	**1**	**0**	**3**	**7**	**24**	**1**	**0**	**.203**

PITCHING STATISTICS

New York	G	GS	CG	IP	H	ER	BB	SO	W-L	Sv	ERA
Tom Ferrick	1	0	0	1	1	0	1	0	1-0	0	0.00
Whitey Ford	1	1	0	8 2/3	7	0	1	7	1-0	0	0.00
Ed Lopat	1	1	0	8	9	2	0	5	0-0	0	2.25
Vic Raschi	1	1	1	9	2	0	1	5	1-0	0	0.00
Allie Reynolds	2	1	1	10 1/3	7	1	4	7	1-0	1	0.87
Totals	**4**	**4**	**2**	**37**	**26**	**3**	**7**	**24**	**4-0**	**1**	**0.73**
Philadelphia	G	GS	CG	IP	H	ER	BB	SO	W-L	Sv	ERA
Ken Heintzelman	1	1	0	7 2/3	4	1	6	3	0-0	0	1.17
Jim Konstanty	3	1	0	15	9	4	4	3	0-1	0	2.40
Russ Meyer	2	0	0	1 2/3	4	1	0	1	0-1	0	5.40
Bob Miller	1	1	0	0 1/3	2	1	0	0	0-1	0	27.00
Robin Roberts	2	1	1	11	11	2	3	5	0-1	0	1.64
Totals	**4**	**4**	**1**	**35 2/3**	**30**	**9**	**13**	**12**	**0-4**	**0**	**2.27**

1951 World Series

NEW YORK YANKEES (4) VS. NEW YORK GIANTS (2)

GAME 1
Thursday, October 4
at Yankee Stadium, New York

	1	2	3	4	5	6	7	8	9	R	H	E
New York Giants	2	0	0	0	0	3	0	0	0	5	10	1
New York Yankees	0	1	0	0	0	0	0	0	0	1	7	1

HR - NYG Alvin Dark

WP - Dave Koslo; **LP** - Allie Reynolds

GAME 2
Friday, October 5
at Yankee Stadium, New York

	1	2	3	4	5	6	7	8	9	R	H	E
New York Giants	0	0	0	0	0	0	1	0	0	1	5	1
New York Yankees	1	1	0	0	0	0	0	1	x	3	6	0

HR - NYY Joe Collins

WP - Ed Lopat; **LP** - Larry Jansen

GAME 3
Saturday, October 6
at the Polo Grounds, New York

	1	2	3	4	5	6	7	8	9	R	H	E
New York Yankees	0	0	0	0	0	0	0	1	1	2	5	2
New York Giants	0	1	0	0	5	0	0	0	x	6	7	2

HR - NYY Gene Woodling; NYG Whitey Lockman

WP - Jim Hearn; **LP** - Vic Raschi; **Sv** - Sheldon Jones

GAME 4
Monday, October 8
at the Polo Grounds, New York

	1	2	3	4	5	6	7	8	9	R	H	E
New York Yankees	0	1	0	1	2	0	2	0	0	6	12	0
New York Giants	1	0	0	0	0	0	0	1	2	8	2

HR - NYY Joe DiMaggio

WP - Allie Reynolds; **LP** - Sal Maglie

GAME 5
Tuesday, October 9
at the Polo Grounds, New York

	1	2	3	4	5	6	7	8	9	R	H	E
New York Yankees	0	0	5	2	0	2	4	0	0	13	12	1
New York Giants	1	0	0	0	0	0	0	0	0	1	5	3

HR - NYY Gil McDougald, Phil Rizzuto

WP - Ed Lopat; LP - Larry Jansen

GAME 6
Wednesday, October 10
at Yankee Stadium, New York

	1	2	3	4	5	6	7	8	9	R	H	E
New York Giants	0	0	0	0	1	0	0	0	2	3	11	1
New York Yankees	1	0	0	0	0	3	0	0	x	4	7	0

WP - Vic Raschi; LP - Dave Koslo; Sv - Bob Kuzava

BATTING STATISTICS

New York Yankees	G	AB	R	H	2B	3B	HR	RBI	BB	SO	SB	CS	BA
Hank Bauer	6	18	0	3	0	1	0	3	1	1	0	0	.167
Yogi Berra	6	23	4	6	1	0	0	0	2	1	0	0	.261
Bobby Brown	5	14	1	5	1	0	0	0	2	1	0	0	.357
Jerry Coleman	5	8	2	2	0	0	0	0	1	2	0	0	.250
Joe Collins	6	18	2	4	0	0	1	3	2	1	0	0	.222
Joe DiMaggio	6	23	3	6	2	0	1	5	2	4	0	0	.261
Johnny Hopp	1	0	0	0	0	0	0	0	1	0	0	0	—
Ed Lopat	2	8	0	1	0	0	0	1	0	2	0	0	.125
Mickey Mantle	2	5	1	1	0	0	0	0	2	1	0	0	.200
Billy Martin	1	0	1	0	0	0	0	0	0	0	0	0	—
Gil McDougald	6	23	2	6	1	0	1	7	2	2	0	1	.261
Johnny Mize	4	7	2	2	1	0	0	1	2	0	0	0	.286
Vic Raschi	2	2	0	0	0	0	0	0	2	1	0	0	.000
Allie Reynolds	2	6	0	2	0	0	0	1	0	1	0	0	.333
Phil Rizzuto	6	25	5	8	0	0	1	3	2	3	0	1	.320
Johnny Sain	1	1	0	0	0	0	0	0	0	0	0	0	.000
Gene Woodling	6	18	6	3	1	1	1	1	5	3	0	0	.167
Totals	**6**	**199**	**29**	**49**	**7**	**2**	**5**	**25**	**26**	**23**	**0**	**2**	**.246**

New York Giants	G	AB	R	H	2B	3B	HR	RBI	BB	SO	SB	CS	BA
Alvin Dark	6	24	5	10	3	0	1	4	2	3	0	0	.417
Clint Hartung	2	4	0	0	0	0	0	0	0	0	0	0	.000
Jim Hearn	2	3	0	0	0	0	0	0	0	1	0	0	.000
Monte Irvin	6	24	3	11	0	1	0	2	2	1	2	1	.458
Larry Jansen	3	2	0	0	0	0	0	0	0	0	0	0	.000
Dave Koslo	2	5	0	0	0	0	0	0	0	2	0	0	.000
Whitey Lockman	6	25	1	6	2	0	1	4	1	2	0	0	.240
Jack Lohrke	2	2	0	0	0	0	0	0	0	1	0	0	.000
Sal Maglie	1	1	0	0	0	0	0	0	0	0	0	0	.000
Willie Mays	6	22	1	4	0	0	0	1	2	2	0	0	.182
Ray Noble	2	2	0	0	0	0	0	0	0	1	0	0	.000
Bill Rigney	4	4	0	1	0	0	0	0	1	0	1	0	.250
Hank Schenz	1	0	0	0	0	0	0	0	0	0	0	0	—
Eddie Stanky	6	22	3	3	0	0	0	1	3	2	0	1	.136
Hank Thompson	5	14	3	2	0	0	0	0	5	2	0	0	.143
Bobby Thomson	6	21	1	5	1	0	0	2	5	0	0	0	.238
Wes Westrum	6	17	1	4	1	0	0	0	5	3	0	0	.235
Davey Williams	2	1	0	0	0	0	0	0	0	0	0	0	.000
Sal Yvars	1	1	0	0	0	0	0	0	0	0	0	0	.000
Totals	**6**	**194**	**18**	**46**	**7**	**1**	**2**	**15**	**25**	**22**	**2**	**2**	**.237**

PITCHING STATISTICS

New York Yankees	G	GS	CG	IP	H	ER	BB	SO	W-L	Sv	ERA
Bobby Hogue	2	0	0	2 2/3	1	0	0	0	0-0	0	0.00
Bob Kuzava	1	0	0	1	0	0	0	0	0-0	1	0.00
Ed Lopat	2	2	2	18	10	1	3	4	2-0	0	0.50
Tom Morgan	1	0	0	2	2	0	1	3	0-0	0	0.00
Joe Ostrowski	1	0	0	2	1	0	0	1	0-0	0	0.00
Vic Raschi	2	2	0	10 1/3	12	1	8	4	1-1	0	0.87
Allie Reynolds	2	2	1	15	16	7	11	8	1-1	0	4.20
Johnny Sain	1	0	0	2	4	2	2	2	0-0	0	9.00
Totals	**6**	**6**	**3**	**53**	**46**	**11**	**25**	**22**	**4-2**	**1**	**1.87**

New York Giants	G	GS	CG	IP	H	ER	BB	SO	W-L	Sv	ERA
Al Corwin	1	0	0	1 2/3	1	0	0	1	0-0	0	0.00
Jim Hearn	2	1	0	8 2/3	5	1	8	1	1-0	0	1.04
Larry Jansen	3	2	0	10	8	7	4	6	0-2	0	6.30
Sheldon Jones	2	0	0	4 1/3	5	1	1	2	0-0	1	2.08
Monte Kennedy	2	0	0	3	3	2	1	4	0-0	0	6.00
Alex Konikowski	1	0	0	1	1	0	0	0	0-0	0	0.00
Dave Koslo	2	2	1	15	12	5	7	6	1-1	0	3.00
Sal Maglie	1	1	0	5	8	4	2	3	0-1	0	7.20
George Spencer	2	0	0	3 1/3	6	7	3	0	0-0	0	18.90
Totals	**6**	**6**	**1**	**52**	**49**	**27**	**26**	**23**	**2-4**	**1**	**4.67**

1952 World Series

NEW YORK YANKEES (4) VS. BROOKLYN DODGERS (3)

GAME 1
Wednesday, October 1
at Ebbets Field, Brooklyn

	1	2	3	4	5	6	7	8	9	R	H	E
New York Yankees	0	1	0	0	0	0	0	1	0	2	6	2
Brooklyn Dodgers	0	1	0	0	0	2	0	1	x	4	6	0

HR - NY Gil McDougald; BRO Pee Wee Reese, Jackie Robinson, Duke Snider

WP - Joe Black; LP - Allie Reynolds

GAME 2
Thursday, October 2
at Ebbets Field, Brooklyn

	1	2	3	4	5	6	7	8	9	R	H	E
New York Yankees	0	0	0	1	1	5	0	0	0	7	10	0
Brooklyn Dodgers	0	0	1	0	0	0	0	0	0	1	3	1

HR - NY Billy Martin

WP - Vic Raschi; LP - Carl Erskine

GAME 3
Friday, October 3
at Yankee Stadium, New York

	1	2	3	4	5	6	7	8	9	R	H	E
Brooklyn Dodgers	0	0	1	0	1	0	1	0	2	5	11	0
New York Yankees	1	0	0	0	0	0	1	1	3	6	2

HR - NY Yogi Berra, Johnny Mize

WP - Preacher Roe; LP - Ed Lopat

GAME 4
Saturday, October 4
at Yankee Stadium, New York

	1	2	3	4	5	6	7	8	9	R	H	E
Brooklyn Dodgers	0	0	0	0	0	0	0	0	0	0	4	1
New York Yankees	0	0	0	1	0	0	0	1	x	2	4	1

HR - NY Johnny Mize

WP - Allie Reynolds; LP - Joe Black

GAME 5
Sunday, October 5
at Yankee Stadium, New York

	1	2	3	4	5	6	7	8	9	10	11	R	H	E
Brooklyn Dodgers	0	1	0	0	3	0	1	0	0	0	1	6	10	0
New York Yankees	0	0	0	0	5	0	0	0	0	0	0	5	5	1

HR - BRO Duke Snider; NY Johnny Mize

WP - Carl Erskine; LP - Johnny Sain

GAME 6
Monday, October 6
at Ebbets Field, Brooklyn

	1	2	3	4	5	6	7	8	9	R	H	E
New York Yankees	0	0	0	0	0	0	2	1	0	3	9	0
Brooklyn Dodgers	0	0	0	0	0	1	0	1	0	2	8	1

HR - NY Yogi Berra, Mickey Mantle; BRO Duke Snider 2

WP - Vic Raschi; LP - Billy Loes; Sv - Allie Reynolds

GAME 7
Tuesday, October 7
at Ebbets Field, Brooklyn

	1	2	3	4	5	6	7	8	9	R	H	E
New York Yankees	0	0	0	1	1	1	1	0	0	4	10	4
Brooklyn Dodgers	0	0	0	1	1	0	0	0	0	2	8	1

HR - NY Mickey Mantle, Gene Woodling

WP - Allie Reynolds; LP - Joe Black; Sv - Bob Kuzava

BATTING STATISTICS

New York	G	AB	R	H	2B	3B	HR	RBI	BB	SO	SB	CS	BA
Hank Bauer	7	18	2	1	0	0	0	1	4	3	0	1	.056
Yogi Berra	7	28	2	6	1	0	2	3	2	4	0	0	.214
Ewell Blackwell	1	1	0	0	0	0	0	0	0	0	0	0	.000
Joe Collins	6	12	1	0	0	0	0	0	1	3	0	0	.000
Ralph Houk	1	1	0	0	0	0	0	0	0	0	0	0	.000
Bob Kuzava	1	1	0	0	0	0	0	0	0	0	0	0	.000
Ed Lopat	2	3	0	1	0	0	0	1	1	1	0	0	.333
Mickey Mantle	7	29	5	10	1	1	2	3	3	4	0	0	.345
Billy Martin	7	23	2	5	0	0	1	4	2	2	0	1	.217
Gil McDougald	7	25	5	5	0	0	1	3	5	2	1	0	.200
Johnny Mize	5	15	3	6	1	0	3	6	3	1	0	0	.400
Irv Noren	4	10	0	3	0	0	0	1	1	3	0	0	.300
Vic Raschi	3	6	0	1	0	0	0	1	1	2	0	0	.167
Allie Reynolds	4	7	0	0	0	0	0	0	0	2	0	0	.000
Phil Rizzuto	7	27	2	4	1	0	0	0	5	2	0	1	.148
Johnny Sain	2	3	0	0	0	0	0	0	0	0	0	0	.000
Gene Woodling	7	23	4	8	1	1	1	3	3	3	0	0	.348
Totals	**7**	**232**	**26**	**50**	**5**	**2**	**10**	**24**	**31**	**32**	**1**	**3**	**.216**

Brooklyn	G	AB	R	H	2B	3B	HR	RBI	BB	SO	SB	CS	BA
Sandy Amoros	1	0	0	0	0	0	0	0	0	0	0	0	—
Joe Black	3	6	0	0	0	0	0	0	1	6	0	0	.000
Roy Campanella	7	28	0	6	0	0	0	1	1	6	0	1	.214
Billy Cox	7	27	4	8	2	0	0	3	4	0	1	.296
Carl Erskine	3	6	1	0	0	0	0	0	0	1	0	0	.000
Carl Furillo	7	23	1	4	2	0	0	3	3	0	0	.174
Gil Hodges	7	21	1	0	0	0	1	5	6	0	0	.000
Tommy Holmes	3	1	0	0	0	0	0	0	0	0	0	.000
Billy Loes	2	3	0	1	0	0	0	0	1	1	0	.333
Bobby Morgan	2	1	0	0	0	0	0	0	0	0	0	.000
Rocky Nelson	4	3	0	0	0	0	0	1	2	0	0	.000
Andy Pafko	7	21	0	4	0	0	0	2	0	4	0	1	.190
Pee Wee Reese	7	29	4	10	0	0	1	4	2	2	1	1	.345
Jackie Robinson	7	23	4	4	0	0	1	2	7	5	2	0	.174
Preacher Roe	3	2	0	0	0	0	0	0	0	0	0	.000
George Shuba	4	10	0	3	1	0	0	0	0	4	0	0	.300
Duke Snider	7	29	5	10	2	0	4	8	1	5	1	0	.345
Totals	**7**	**233**	**20**	**50**	**7**	**0**	**6**	**18**	**24**	**49**	**5**	**4**	**.215**

PITCHING STATISTICS

New York	G	GS	CG	IP	H	ER	BB	SO	W-L	Sv	ERA
Ewell Blackwell	1	1	0	5	4	4	3	4	0-0	0	7.20
Tom Gorman	1	0	0	0 2/3	1	0	0	0	0-0	0	0.00
Bob Kuzava	1	0	0	2 2/3	0	0	0	2	0-0	1	0.00
Ed Lopat	2	2	0	11 1/3	14	6	4	3	0-1	0	4.76
Vic Raschi	3	2	1	17	12	3	8	18	2-0	0	1.59
Allie Reynolds	4	2	1	20 1/3	12	4	6	18	2-1	1	1.77
Johnny Sain	1	0	0	6	6	2	3	3	0-1	0	3.00
Ray Scarborough	1	0	0	1	1	1	0	1	0-0	0	9.00
Totals	**7**	**7**	**2**	**64**	**50**	**20**	**24**	**49**	**4-3**	**2**	**2.81**

Brooklyn	G	GS	CG	IP	H	ER	BB	SO	W-L	Sv	ERA
Joe Black	3	3	1	21 1/3	15	6	8	9	1-2	0	2.53
Carl Erskine	3	2	1	18	12	9	10	10	1-1	0	4.50
Ken Lehman	1	0	0	2	2	0	1	0	0-0	0	0.00
Billy Loes	2	1	0	10 1/3	11	5	5	5	0-1	0	4.35
Preacher Roe	3	1	1	11 1/3	9	4	6	7	1-0	0	3.18
Johnny Rutherford	1	0	0	1	1	1	1	1	0-0	0	9.00
Totals	**7**	**7**	**3**	**64**	**50**	**25**	**31**	**32**	**3-4**	**0**	**3.52**

1953 World Series

NEW YORK YANKEES (4) VS. BROOKLYN DODGERS (2)

GAME 1

Wednesday, September 30
at Yankee Stadium, New York

	1	2	3	4	5	8	7	8	9	R	H	E
Brooklyn Dodgers	0	0	0	1	3	1	0	0	5	12	2
New York Yankees	4	0	0	1	0	1	3	x	9	12	0

HR - BRO Jim Gilliam, Gil Hodges, George Shuba; NY Yogi Berra, Joe Collins

WP - Johnny Sain; LP - Clem Labine

GAME 2

Thursday, October 1
at Yankee Stadium, New York

	1	2	3	4	5	6	7	8	9	R	H	E
Brooklyn Dodgers	0	0	0	2	0	0	0	0	0	2	9	1
New York Yankees	1	0	0	0	0	0	1	2	x	4	5	0

HR - NY Mickey Mantle, Billy Martin

WP - Ed Lopat; LP - Preacher Roe

GAME 3

Friday, October 2
at Ebbets Field, Brooklyn

	1	2	3	4	5	6	7	8	9	R	H	E
New York Yankees	0	0	0	0	1	0	0	1	0	2	6	0
Brooklyn Dodgers	0	0	0	0	1	1	0	1	x	3	9	0

HR - BRO Roy Campanella

WP - Carl Erskine; LP - Vic Raschi

GAME 4

Saturday, October 3
at Ebbets Field, Brooklyn

	1	2	3	4	5	6	7	8	9	R	H	E
New York Yankees	0	0	0	0	2	0	0	0	1	3	9	0
Brooklyn Dodgers	3	0	0	1	0	2	1	0	x	7	12	0

HR - NY Gil McDougald; BRO Duke Snider

WP - Billy Loes; LP - Whitey Ford; Sv - Clem Labine

GAME 5

Sunday, October 4
at Ebbets Field, Brooklyn

	1	2	3	4	5	6	7	8	9	R	H	E
New York Yankees	1	0	5	0	0	0	3	1	1	11	11	1
Brooklyn Dodgers	0	1	0	0	1	0	0	4	1	7	14	1

HR - NY Mickey Mantle, Billy Martin, Gil McDougald, Gene Woodling; BRO Billy Cox, Jim Gilliam

WP - Jim McDonald; LP - Johnny Podres; Sv - Allie Reynolds

GAME 6
Monday, October 5
at Yankee Stadium, New York

	1	2	3	4	5	6	7	8	9	R	H	E
Brooklyn Dodgers	0	0	0	0	0	1	0	0	2	3	8	3
New York Yankees	2	1	0	0	0	0	0	0	1	4	13	0

HR - BRO Carl Furillo

WP - Allie Reynolds; **LP** - Clem Labine

BATTING STATISTICS

New York	G	AB	R	H	2B	3B	HR	RBI	BB	SO	SB	CS	BA
Hank Bauer	6	23	6	6	0	1	0	1	2	4	0	0	.261
Yogi Berra	6	21	3	9	1	0	1	4	3	3	0	1	.429
Don Bollweg	3	2	0	0	0	0	0	0	0	2	0	0	.000
Joe Collins	6	24	4	4	1	0	1	2	3	8	0	0	.167
Whitey Ford	2	3	0	1	0	0	0	0	0	0	0	0	.333
Tom Gorman	1	1	0	0	0	0	0	0	0	1	0	0	.000
Bob Kuzava	1	1	0	0	0	0	0	0	0	1	0	0	.000
Ed Lopat	1	3	0	0	0	0	0	0	0	2	0	0	.000
Mickey Mantle	6	24	3	5	0	0	2	7	3	8	0	1	.208
Billy Martin	6	24	5	12	1	2	2	8	1	2	1	2	.500
Jim McDonald	1	2	0	1	1	0	0	1	1	1	0	0	.500
Gil McDougald	6	24	2	4	0	1	2	4	1	3	0	0	.167
Johnny Mize	3	3	0	0	0	0	0	0	0	1	0	0	.000
Irv Noren	2	1	0	0	0	0	0	0	1	0	0	0	.000
Vic Raschi	1	2	0	0	0	0	0	0	0	1	0	0	.000
Allie Reynolds	3	2	0	1	0	0	0	0	1	1	0	0	.500
Phil Rizzuto	6	19	4	6	1	0	0	0	3	2	1	0	.316
Johnny Sain	2	2	1	1	1	0	0	2	0	1	0	0	.500
Gene Woodling	6	20	5	6	0	0	1	3	6	2	0	0	.300
Totals	**6**	**201**	**33**	**56**	**6**	**4**	**9**	**32**	**25**	**43**	**2**	**4**	**.279**

Brooklyn	G	AB	R	H	2B	3B	HR	RBI	BB	SO	SB	CS	BA
Wayne Belardi	2	2	0	0	0	0	0	0	0	1	0	0	.000
Roy Campanella	6	22	6	6	0	0	1	2	2	3	0	0	.273
Billy Cox	6	23	3	7	3	0	1	6	1	4	0	0	.304
Carl Erskine	3	4	0	1	0	0	0	0	0	1	0	0	.250
Carl Furillo	6	24	4	8	2	0	1	4	1	3	0	0	.333
Jim Gilliam	6	27	4	8	3	0	2	4	0	2	0	1	.296
Gil Hodges	6	22	3	8	0	0	1	1	3	3	1	0	.364
Jim Hughes	1	1	0	0	0	0	0	0	0	1	0	0	.000
Clem Labine	3	2	0	0	0	0	0	0	0	1	0	0	.000
Billy Loes	1	3	0	2	0	0	0	0	0	0	0	0	.667
Russ Meyer	1	1	0	0	0	0	0	0	0	1	0	0	.000
Bobby Morgan	1	1	0	0	0	0	0	0	0	0	0	0	.000
Johnny Podres	1	1	0	1	0	0	0	0	0	0	0	0	1.000
Pee Wee Reese	6	24	0	5	0	1	0	0	4	1	0	0	.208
Jackie Robinson	6	25	3	8	2	0	0	2	1	0	1	0	.320
Preacher Roe	1	3	0	0	0	0	0	0	0	2	0	0	.000
George Shuba	2	1	1	1	0	0	1	2	0	0	0	0	1.000
Duke Snider	6	25	3	8	3	0	1	5	2	6	0	0	.320
Dick Williams	3	2	0	1	0	0	0	0	1	1	0	0	.500
Totals	**6**	**213**	**27**	**64**	**13**	**1**	**8**	**26**	**15**	**30**	**2**	**1**	**.300**

PITCHING STATISTICS

New York	G	GS	CG	IP	H	ER	BB	SO	W-L	Sv	ERA
Whitey Ford	2	2	0	8	9	4	2	7	0-1	0	4.50
Tom Gorman	1	0	0	3	4	1	0	1	0-0	0	3.00
Bob Kuzava	1	0	0	0 2/3	2	1	0	1	0-0	0	13.50
Ed Lopat	1	1	1	9	9	2	4	3	1-0	0	2.00
Jim McDonald	1	1	0	7 2/3	12	5	0	3	1-0	0	5.87
Vic Raschi	1	1	1	8	9	3	3	4	0-1	0	3.38
Allie Reynolds	3	1	0	8	9	6	4	9	1-0	1	6.75
Johnny Sain	2	0	0	5 2/3	8	3	1	1	1-0	0	4.76
Art Schallock	1	0	0	2	2	1	1	1	0-0	0	4.50
Totals	**6**	**6**	**2**	**52**	**64**	**26**	**15**	**30**	**4-2**	**1**	**4.50**

Brooklyn	G	GS	CG	IP	H	ER	BB	SO	W-L	Sv	ERA
Joe Black	1	0	0	1	1	1	0	2	0-0	0	9.00
Carl Erskine	3	3	1	14	14	9	9	16	1-0	0	5.79
Jim Hughes	1	0	0	4	3	1	1	3	0-0	0	2.25
Clem Labine	3	0	0	5	10	2	1	3	0-2	1	3.60
Billy Loes	1	1	0	8	8	3	2	8	1-0	0	3.38
Russ Meyer	1	0	0	4 1/3	8	3	4	5	0-0	0	6.23
Bob Milliken	1	0	0	2	2	0	1	0	0-0	0	0.00
Johnny Podres	1	1	0	2 2/3	1	1	2	0	0-1	0	3.38
Preacher Roe	1	1	1	8	5	4	4	4	0-1	0	4.50
Ben Wade	2	0	0	2 1/3	4	4	1	2	0-0	0	15.43
Totals	**6**	**6**	**2**	**51 1/3**	**56**	**28**	**25**	**43**	**2-4**	**1**	**4.91**

1955 World Series

BROOKLYN DODGERS (4) VS. NEW YORK YANKEES (3)

GAME 1
Wednesday, September 28
at Yankee Stadium, New York

	1	2	3	4	5	6	7	8	9	R	H	E
Brooklyn Dodgers	0	2	1	0	0	0	0	2	0	5	10	0
New York Yankees	0	2	1	1	0	2	0	0	x	6	9	1

HR - BRO Carl Furillo, Duke Snider; NY Joe Collins 2, Elston Howard

WP - Whitey Ford; LP - Don Newcombe; Sv - Bob Grim

GAME 2
Thursday, September 29
at Yankee Stadium, New York

	1	2	3	4	5	6	7	8	9	R	H	E
Brooklyn Dodgers	0	0	0	1	1	0	0	0	0	2	5	2
New York Yankees	0	0	0	4	0	0	0	0	x	4	8	0

WP - Tommy Byrne; LP - Billy Loes

GAME 3
Friday, September 30
at Ebbets Field, Brooklyn

	1	2	3	4	5	6	7	8	9	R	H	E
New York Yankees	0	2	0	0	0	0	1	0	0	3	7	0
Brooklyn Dodgers	2	2	0	2	0	0	2	0	x	8	11	1

HR - NY Mickey Mantle; BRO Roy Campanella

WP - Johnny Podres; LP - Bob Turley

GAME 4
Saturday, October 1
at Ebbets Field, Brooklyn

	1	2	3	4	5	6	7	8	9	R	H	E
New York Yankees	1	1	0	1	0	2	0	0	0	5	9	0
Brooklyn Dodgers	0	0	1	3	3	0	1	0	x	8	14	0

HR - NY Gil McDougald; BRO Roy Campanella, Gil Hodges, Duke Snider

WP - Clem Labine; LP - Don Larsen

GAME 5
Sunday, October 2
at Ebbets Field, Brooklyn

	1	2	3	4	5	6	7	8	9	R	H	E
New York Yankees	0	0	0	1	0	0	1	1	0	3	6	0
Brooklyn Dodgers	0	2	1	0	1	0	0	1	x	5	9	2

HR - NY Yogi Berra, Bob Cerv; BRO Sandy Amoros, Duke Snider 2

WP - Roger Craig; LP - Bob Grim; Sv - Clem Labine

GAME 6
Monday, October 3
at Yankee Stadium, New York

	1	2	3	4	5	6	7	8	9	R	H	E
Brooklyn Dodgers	0	0	0	1	0	0	0	0	0	1	4	1
New York Yankees	5	0	0	0	0	0	0	0	x	5	8	0

HR - NY Bill Skowron

WP - Whitey Ford; LP - Karl Spooner

GAME 7
Tuesday, October 4
at Yankee Stadium, New York

	1	2	3	4	5	6	7	8	9	R	H	E
Brooklyn Dodgers	0	0	0	1	0	1	0	0	0	2	5	0
New York Yankees	0	0	0	0	0	0	0	0	0	0	8	1

WP - Johnny Podres; LP - Tommy Byrne

BATTING STATISTICS

Brooklyn Dodgers	G	AB	R	H	2B	3B	HR	RBI	BB	SO	SB	CS	BA
Sandy Amoros	5	12	3	4	0	0	1	3	4	4	0	0	.333
Don Bessent	3	1	0	0	0	0	0	0	0	1	0	0	.000
Roy Campanella	7	27	4	7	3	0	2	4	3	3	0	0	.259
Roger Craig	1	0	0	0	0	0	0	0	1	0	0	0	—
Carl Erskine	1	1	0	0	0	0	0	0	0	0	0	0	.000
Carl Furillo	7	27	4	8	1	0	1	3	3	5	0	0	.296
Jim Gilliam	7	24	2	7	1	0	0	3	8	1	1	1	.292
Don Hoak	3	3	0	1	0	0	0	0	2	0	0	0	.333
Gil Hodges	7	24	2	7	0	0	1	5	3	2	0	1	.292
Frank Kellert	3	3	0	1	0	0	0	0	0	0	0	0	.333
Clem Labine	4	4	0	0	0	0	0	0	0	3	0	0	.000
Billy Loes	1	1	0	0	0	0	0	0	0	0	0	0	.000
Russ Meyer	1	2	0	0	0	0	0	0	0	1	0	0	.000
Don Newcombe	1	3	0	0	0	0	0	0	0	0	0	0	.000
Johnny Podres	2	7	1	1	0	0	0	0	0	1	0	0	.143
Pee Wee Reese	7	27	5	8	1	0	0	2	3	5	0	0	.296
Jackie Robinson	6	22	5	4	1	1	0	1	2	1	1	0	.182
George Shuba	1	1	0	0	0	0	0	0	0	0	0	0	.000
Duke Snider	7	25	5	8	1	0	4	7	2	6	0	0	.320
Don Zimmer	4	9	0	2	0	0	0	2	2	5	0	0	.222
Totals	**7**	**223**	**31**	**58**	**8**	**1**	**9**	**30**	**33**	**38**	**2**	**2**	**.260**

New York Yankees	G	AB	R	H	RBI	2B	3B	HR	BB	SO	SB	CS	BA
Hank Bauer	6	14	1	6	0	0	0	1	0	1	0	1	.429
Yogi Berra	7	24	5	10	1	0	1	2	3	1	0	1	.417
Tommy Byrne	3	6	0	1	0	0	0	2	0	2	0	0	.167
Andy Carey	2	2	0	1	0	1	0	1	0	0	0	0	.500
Tom Carroll	2	0	0	0	0	0	0	0	0	0	0	0	—
Bob Cerv	5	16	1	2	0	0	1	1	0	4	0	0	.125
Jerry Coleman	3	3	0	0	0	0	0	0	0	1	0	0	.000
Joe Collins	5	12	6	2	0	0	2	3	6	4	1	0	.167
Whitey Ford	2	6	1	0	0	0	0	0	1	1	0	0	.000
Bob Grim	3	2	0	0	0	0	0	0	0	0	0	0	.000
Elston Howard	7	26	3	5	0	0	1	3	1	8	0	0	.192
Don Larsen	1	2	0	0	0	0	0	0	0	0	0	0	.000
Mickey Mantle	3	10	1	2	0	0	1	1	0	2	0	0	.200
Billy Martin	7	25	2	8	1	1	0	4	1	5	0	2	.320
Gil McDougald	7	27	2	7	0	0	1	1	2	6	0	0	.259
Irv Noren	5	16	0	1	0	0	0	1	1	1	0	0	.063
Phil Rizzuto	7	15	2	4	0	0	0	1	5	1	2	0	.267
Eddie Robinson	4	3	0	2	0	0	0	1	2	1	0	0	.667
Bill Skowron	5	12	2	4	2	0	1	3	0	1	0	0	.333
Bob Turley	3	1	0	0	0	0	0	0	0	0	0	0	.000
Totals	7	222	26	55	4	2	8	25	22	39	3	4	.248

PITCHING STATISTICS

Brooklyn Dodgers	G	GS	CG	IP	H	ER	BB	SO	W-L	Sv	ERA
Don Bessent	3	0	0	3 1/3	3	0	1	1	0-0	0	0.00
Roger Craig	1	1	0	6	4	2	5	4	1-0	0	3.00
Carl Erskine	1	1	0	3	3	3	2	3	0-0	0	9.00
Clem Labine	4	0	0	9 1/3	6	3	2	2	1-0	1	2.89
Billy Loes	1	1	0	3 2/3	7	4	1	5	0-1	0	9.82
Russ Meyer	1	0	0	5 2/3	4	0	2	4	0-0	0	0.00
Don Newcombe	1	1	0	5 2/3	8	6	2	4	0-1	0	9.53
Johnny Podres	2	2	2	18	15	2	4	10	2-0	0	1.00
Ed Roebuck	1	0	0	2	1	0	0	0	0-0	0	0.00
Karl Spooner	2	1	0	3 1/3	4	5	3	6	0-1	0	13.50
Totals	7	7	2	60	55	25	22	39	4-3	1	3.75

New York Yankees	G	GS	CG	IP	H	ER	BB	SO	W-L	Sv	ERA
Tommy Byrne	2	2	1	14 1/3	8	3	8	8	1-1	0	1.88
Rip Coleman	1	0	0	1	5	1	0	1	0-0	0	9.00
Whitey Ford	2	2	1	17	13	4	8	10	2-0	0	2.12
Bob Grim	3	1	0	8 2/3	8	4	5	8	0-1	1	4.15
Johnny Kucks	2	0	0	3	4	2	1	1	0-0	0	6.00
Don Larsen	1	1	0	4	5	5	2	2	0-1	0	11.25
Tom Morgan	2	0	0	3 2/3	3	2	3	1	0-0	0	4.91
Tom Sturdivant	2	0	0	3	5	2	2	0	0-0	0	6.00
Bob Turley	3	1	0	5 1/3	7	5	4	7	0-1	0	8.44
Totals	7	7	2	60	58	28	33	38	3-4	1	4.20

1956 World Series

NEW YORK YANKEES (4) VS. BROOKLYN DODGERS (3)

GAME 1
Wednesday, October 3
at Ebbets Field, Brooklyn

	1	2	3	4	5	6	7	8	9	R	H	E
New York Yankees	2	0	0	1	0	0	0	0	0	3	9	1
Brooklyn Dodgers	0	2	3	1	0	0	0	0	x	6	9	0

HR - NY Mickey Mantle, Billy Martin; BRO Gil Hodges, Jackie Robinson

WP - Sal Maglie; **LP** - Whitey Ford

GAME 2
Friday, October 5
at Ebbets Field, Brooklyn

	1	2	3	4	5	6	7	8	9	R	H	E
New York Yankees	1	5	0	1	0	0	0	0	1	8	12	2
Brooklyn Dodgers	0	6	1	2	2	0	0	2	x	13	12	0

HR - NY Yogi Berra; BRO Duke Snider

WP - Don Bessent; **LP** - Tom Morgan

GAME 3
Saturday, October 6
at Yankee Stadium, New York

	1	2	3	4	5	6	7	8	9	R	H	E
Brooklyn Dodgers	0	1	0	0	0	1	1	0	0	3	8	1
New York Yankees	0	1	0	0	0	3	0	1	x	5	8	1

HR - NY Billy Martin, Enos Slaughter

WP - Whitey Ford; **LP** - Roger Craig

GAME 4
Sunday, October 7
at Yankee Stadium, New York

	1	2	3	4	5	6	7	8	9	R	H	E
Brooklyn Dodgers	0	0	0	1	0	0	0	0	1	2	6	0
New York Yankees	1	0	0	2	0	1	2	0	x	6	7	2

HR - NY Hank Bauer, Mickey Mantle

WP - Tom Sturdivant; **LP** - Carl Erskine

GAME 5
Monday, October 8
at Yankee Stadium, New York

	1	2	3	4	5	6	7	8	9	R	H	E
Brooklyn Dodgers	0	0	0	0	0	0	0	0	0	0	0	0
New York Yankees	0	0	0	1	0	1	0	0	x	2	5	0

HR - NY Mickey Mantle

WP - Don Larsen; **LP** - Sal Maglie

GAME 6
Tuesday, October 9
at Ebbets Field, Brooklyn

	1	2	3	4	5	6	7	8	9	10	R	H	E
New York Yankees	0	0	0	0	0	0	0	0	0	0	0	7	0
Brooklyn Dodgers	0	0	0	0	0	0	0	0	0	1	1	4	0

WP - Clem Labine; LP - Bob Turley

GAME 7
Wednesday, October 10
at Ebbets Field, Brooklyn

	1	2	3	4	5	6	7	8	9	R	H	E
New York Yankees	2	0	2	1	0	0	4	0	0	9	10	0
Brooklyn Dodgers	0	0	0	0	0	0	0	0	0	0	3	1

HR - NY Yogi Berra 2, Elston Howard, Bill Skowron

WP - Johnny Kucks; LP - Don Newcombe

BATTING STATISTICS

New York	G	AB	R	H	2B	3B	HR	RBI	BB	SO	SB	CS	BA
Hank Bauer	7	32	3	9	0	0	1	3	0	5	1	0	.281
Yogi Berra	7	25	5	9	2	0	3	10	4	1	0	0	.360
Tommy Byrne	2	1	0	0	0	0	0	0	0	0	0	0	.000
Andy Carey	7	19	2	3	0	0	0	0	1	6	0	0	.158
Bob Cerv	1	1	0	1	0	0	0	0	0	0	0	0	1.000
Jerry Coleman	2	2	0	0	0	0	0	0	0	0	0	0	.000
Joe Collins	6	21	2	5	2	0	0	2	2	3	0	0	.238
Whitey Ford	2	4	0	0	0	0	0	0	0	3	0	0	.000
Elston Howard	1	5	1	2	1	0	1	1	0	0	0	0	.400
Johnny Kucks	3	3	0	0	0	0	0	0	0	1	0	0	.000
Don Larsen	2	3	1	1	0	0	0	1	0	1	0	0	.333
Mickey Mantle	7	24	6	6	1	0	3	4	6	5	1	0	.250
Billy Martin	7	27	5	8	0	0	2	3	1	6	0	0	.296
Mickey McDermott	1	1	0	1	0	0	0	0	0	0	0	0	1.000
Gil McDougald	7	21	0	3	0	0	0	1	3	6	0	0	.143
Tom Morgan	2	1	1	1	0	0	0	0	0	0	0	0	1.000
Norm Siebern	1	1	0	0	0	0	0	0	0	0	0	0	.000
Bill Skowron	3	10	1	1	0	0	1	4	0	3	0	0	.100
Enos Slaughter	6	20	6	7	0	0	1	4	4	0	0	0	.350
Tom Sturdivant	2	3	0	1	0	0	0	0	0	1	0	0	.333
Bob Turley	3	4	0	0	0	0	0	0	0	1	0	0	.000
George Wilson	1	1	0	0	0	0	0	0	0	1	0	0	.000
Totals	**7**	**229**	**33**	**58**	**6**	**0**	**12**	**33**	**21**	**43**	**2**	**0**	**.253**

Brooklyn	G	AB	R	H	2B	3B	HR	RBI	BB	SO	SB	CS	BA
Sandy Amoros	6	19	1	1	0	0	0	1	2	4	0	0	.053
Don Bessent	2	2	0	1	0	0	0	1	1	1	0	0	.500
Roy Campanella	7	22	2	4	1	0	0	3	3	7	0	1	.182
Roger Craig	2	2	0	1	0	0	0	0	0	0	0	0	.500
Carl Erskine	2	1	0	0	0	0	0	0	0	1	0	0	.000
Carl Furillo	7	25	2	6	2	0	0	1	2	3	0	0	.240
Jim Gilliam	7	24	2	2	0	0	0	2	7	3	1	1	.083
Gil Hodges	7	23	5	7	2	0	1	8	4	4	0	0	.304
Randy Jackson	3	3	0	0	0	0	0	0	0	2	0	0	.000
Clem Labine	2	4	0	1	1	0	0	0	0	2	0	0	.250
Sal Maglie	2	5	0	0	0	0	0	0	0	2	0	0	.000
Dale Mitchell	4	4	0	0	0	0	0	0	0	1	0	0	.000
Charlie Neal	1	4	0	0	0	0	0	0	0	1	0	0	.000
Don Newcombe	2	1	0	0	0	0	0	0	0	0	0	0	.000
Pee Wee Reese	7	27	3	6	0	1	0	2	2	6	0	0	.222
Jackie Robinson	7	24	5	6	1	0	1	2	5	2	0	0	.250
Duke Snider	7	23	5	7	1	0	1	4	6	8	0	0	.304
Rube Walker	2	2	0	0	0	0	0	0	0	0	0	0	.000
Totals	**7**	**215**	**25**	**42**	**8**	**1**	**3**	**24**	**32**	**47**	**1**	**2**	**.195**

PITCHING STATISTICS

New York	G	GS	CG	IP	H	ER	BB	SO	W-L	Sv	ERA
Tommy Byrne	1	0	0	0 1/3	1	0	0	1	0-0	0	0.00
Whitey Ford	2	2	1	12	14	7	2	8	1-1	0	5.25
Johnny Kucks	3	1	1	11	6	1	3	2	1-0	0	0.82
Don Larsen	2	2	1	10 2/3	1	0	4	7	1-0	0	0.00
Mickey McDermott	1	0	0	3	2	1	3	3	0-0	0	3.00
Tom Morgan	2	0	0	4	6	4	4	3	0-1	0	9.00
Tom Sturdivant	2	1	1	9 2/3	8	3	8	9	1-0	0	2.79
Bob Turley	3	1	1	11	4	1	8	14	0-1	0	0.82
Totals	**7**	**7**	**5**	**61 2/3**	**42**	**17**	**32**	**47**	**4-3**	**0**	**2.48**

Brooklyn	G	GS	CG	IP	H	ER	BB	SO	W-L	Sv	ERA
Don Bessent	2	0	0	10	8	2	3	5	1-0	0	1.80
Roger Craig	2	1	0	6	10	8	3	4	0-1	0	12.00
Don Drysdale	1	0	0	2	2	2	1	1	0-0	0	9.00
Carl Erskine	2	1	0	5	4	3	2	2	0-1	0	5.40
Clem Labine	2	1	1	12	8	0	3	7	1-0	0	0.00
Sal Maglie	2	2	2	17	14	5	6	15	1-1	0	2.65
Don Newcombe	2	2	0	4 2/3	11	11	3	4	0-1	0	21.21
Ed Roebuck	3	0	0	4 1/3	1	1	0	5	0-0	0	2.08
Totals	**7**	**7**	**3**	**61**	**58**	**32**	**21**	**43**	**3-4**	**0**	**4.72**

1957 World Series

MILWAUKEE BRAVES (4) VS. NEW YORK YANKEES (3)

GAME 1
Wednesday, October 2
at Yankee Stadium, New York

	1	2	3	4	5	6	7	8	9	R	H	E
Milwaukee Braves	0	0	0	0	0	0	1	0	0	1	5	0
New York Yankees	0	0	0	0	1	2	0	0	x	3	9	1

WP - Whitey Ford; LP - Warren Spahn

GAME 2
Thursday, October 3
at Yankee Stadium, New York

	1	2	3	4	5	6	7	8	9	R	H	E
Milwaukee Braves	0	1	1	2	0	0	0	0	0	4	8	0
New York Yankees	0	1	1	0	0	0	0	0	0	2	7	2

HR - MIL Johnny Logan; NY Hank Bauer

WP - Lew Burdette; LP - Bobby Shantz

GAME 3
Saturday, October 5
at County Stadium, Milwaukee

	1	2	3	4	5	6	7	8	9	R	H	E
New York Yankees	3	0	2	2	0	0	5	0	0	12	9	0
Milwaukee Braves	0	1	0	0	2	0	0	0	0	3	8	1

HR - NY Tony Kubek 2, Mickey Mantle; MIL Hank Aaron

WP - Don Larsen; LP - Bob Buhl

GAME 4
Sunday, October 6
at County Stadium, Milwaukee

	1	2	3	4	5	6	7	8	9	10	R	H	E
New York Yankees	1	0	0	0	0	0	0	0	3	1	5	11	0
Milwaukee Braves	0	0	4	0	0	0	0	0	3	7	7	0

HR - NY Elston Howard; MIL Hank Aaron, Eddie Mathews, Frank Torre

WP - Warren Spahn; LP - Bob Grim

GAME 5
Monday, October 7
at County Stadium, Milwuakee

	1	2	3	4	5	6	7	8	9	R	H	E
New York Yankees	0	0	0	0	0	0	0	0	0	0	7	0
Milwaukee Braves	0	0	0	0	0	1	0	0	x	1	6	1

WP - Lew Burdette; LP - Whitey Ford

GAME 6
Wednesday, October 9
at Yankee Stadium, New York

	1	2	3	4	5	6	7	8	9	R	H	E
Milwaukee Braves	0	0	0	0	1	0	1	0	0	2	4	0
New York Yankees	0	0	2	0	0	0	1	0	x	3	7	0

HR - MIL Hank Aaron, Frank Torre; NY Hank Bauer, Yogi Berra

WP - Bob Turley; LP - Ernie Johnson

GAME 7
Thursday, October 10
at Yankee Stadium, New York

	1	2	3	4	5	6	7	8	9	R	H	E
Milwaukee Braves	0	0	4	0	0	0	0	1	0	5	9	1
New York Yankees	0	0	0	0	0	0	0	0	0	0	7	3

HR - MIL Del Crandall

WP - Lew Burdette; LP - Don Larsen

BATTING STATISTICS

Milwaukee Braves	G	AB	R	H	2B	3B	HR	RBI	BB	SO	SB	CS	BA
Hank Aaron	7	28	5	11	0	1	3	7	1	6	0	0	.393
Joe Adcock	5	15	1	3	0	0	0	2	0	2	0	0	.200
Bob Buhl	2	1	0	0	0	0	0	0	0	1	0	0	.000
Lew Burdette	3	8	0	0	0	0	0	0	1	2	0	0	.000
Wes Covington	7	24	1	5	1	0	0	1	2	6	1	0	.208
Del Crandall	6	19	1	4	0	0	1	1	1	1	0	1	.211
John DeMerit	1	0	0	0	0	0	0	0	0	0	0	0	—
Bob Hazle	4	13	2	2	0	0	0	0	1	2	0	0	.154
Ernie Johnson	3	1	0	0	0	0	0	0	0	1	0	0	.000
Nippy Jones	3	2	0	0	0	0	0	0	0	0	0	0	.000
Johnny Logan	7	27	5	5	1	0	1	2	3	6	0	0	.185
Felix Mantilla	4	10	1'	0	0	0	0	0	1	0	0	0	.000
Eddie Mathews	7	22	4	5	3	0	1	4	8	5	0	0	.227
Andy Pafko	6	14	1	3	0	0	0	0	0	1	0	0	.214
Juan Pizarro	1	1	0	0	0	0	0	0	0	0	0	0	.000
Del Rice	2	6	0	1	0	0	0	0	1	2	0	0	.167
Carl Sawatski	2	2	0	0	0	0	0	0	0	2	0	0	.000
Red Schoendienst	5	18	0	5	1	0	0	2	0	1	0	0	.278
Warren Spahn	2	4	0	0	0	0	0	0	1	2	0	0	.000
Frank Torre	7	10	2	3	0	0	2	3	2	0	0	0	.300
Totals	**7**	**225**	**23**	**47**	**6**	**1**	**8**	**22**	**22**	**40**	**1**	**1**	**.209**

New York Yankees	G	AB	R	H	2B	3B	HR	RBI	BB	SO	SB	CS	BA
Hank Bauer	7	31	3	8	2	1	2	6	1	6	0	0	.258
Yogi Berra	7	25	5	8	1	0	1	2	4	0	0	0	.320
Tommy Byrne	2	2	0	1	0	0	0	0	0	1	0	0	.500
Andy Carey	2	7	0	2	1	0	0	1	1	0	0	0	.286
Jerry Coleman	7	22	2	8	2	0	0	2	3	1	0	0	.364
Joe Collins	6	5	0	0	0	0	0	0	0	3	0	0	.000
Art Ditmar	2	1	0	0	0	0	0	0	0	1	0	0	.000
Whitey Ford	2	5	0	0	0	0	0	0	0	1	0	0	.000
Elston Howard	6	11	2	3	0	0	1	3	1	3	0	0	.273
Tony Kubek	7	28	4	8	0	0	2	4	0	4	0	0	.286
Don Larsen	2	2	1	0	0	0	0	0	2	1	0	0	.000
Jerry Lumpe	6	14	0	4	0	0	0	2	1	1	0	1	.286
Mickey Mantle	6	19	3	5	0	0	1	2	3	1	0	2	.263
Gil McDougald	7	24	3	6	0	0	0	2	3	3	1	0	.250
Bobby Shantz	3	1	0	0	0	0	0	0	0	0	0	0	.000
Harry Simpson	5	12	0	1	0	0	0	1	0	4	0	0	.083
Bill Skowron	2	4	0	0	0	0	0	0	0	0	0	0	.000
Enos Slaughter	5	12	2	3	1	0	0	0	3	2	0	1	.250
Tom Sturdivant	2	1	0	0	0	0	0	0	0	0	0	0	.000
Bob Turley	3	4	0	0	0	0	0	0	0	2	0	0	.000
Totals	**7**	**230**	**25**	**57**	**7**	**1**	**7**	**25**	**22**	**34**	**1**	**4**	**.248**

PITCHING STATISTICS

Milwaukee Braves	G	GS	CG	IP	H	ER	BB	SO	W-L	Sv	ERA
Bob Buhl	2	2	0	3 1/3	6	4	6	4	0-1	0	10.80
Lew Burdette	3	3	3	27	21	2	4	13	3-0	0	0.67
Gene Conley	1	0	0	1 2/3	2	2	1	0	0-0	0	10.80
Ernie Johnson	3	0	0	7	2	1	1	8	0-1	0	1.29
Don McMahon	3	0	0	5	3	0	3	5	0-0	0	0.00
Juan Pizarro	1	0	0	1 2/3	3	2	2	1	0-0	0	10.80
Warren Spahn	2	2	1	15 1/3	18	8	2	2	1-1	0	4.70
Bob Trowbridge	1	0	0	1	2	5	3	1	0-0	0	45.00
Totals	**7**	**7**	**4**	**62**	**57**	**24**	**22**	**34**	**4-3**	**0**	**3.48**

New York Yankees	G	GS	CG	IP	H	ER	BB	SO	W-L	Sv	ERA
Tommy Byrne	2	0	0	3 1/3	1	2	2	1	0-0	0	5.40
Art Ditmar	2	0	0	6	2	0	0	2	0-0	0	0.00
Whitey Ford	2	2	1	16	11	2	5	7	1-1	0	1.13
Bob Grim	2	0	0	2 1/3	3	2	0	2	0-1	0	7.71
Johnny Kucks	1	0	0	2/3	1	0	1	1	0-0	0	0.00
Don Larsen	2	1	0	9 2/3	8	4	5	6	1-1	0	3.72
Bobby Shantz	3	1	0	6 2/3	8	3	2	7	0-1	0	4.05
Tom Sturdivant	2	1	0	6	6	4	1	2	0-0	0	6.00
Bob Turley	3	2	1	11 2/3	7	3	6	12	1-0	0	2.31
Totals	**7**	**7**	**2**	**62 1/3**	**47**	**20**	**22**	**40**	**3-4**	**0**	**2.89**

1958 World Series

NEW YORK YANKEES (4) VS MILWAUKEE BRAVES (3)

GAME 1
Wednesday, October 1
at County Stadium, Milwaukee

	1	2	3	4	5	6	7	8	9	10	R	H	E
New York Yankees	0	0	0	1	2	0	0	0	0	0	3	8	1
Milwaukee Braves	0	0	0	2	0	0	0	1	0	1	4	10	0

HR - NY Hank Bauer, Bill Skowron

WP - Warren Spahn; **LP** - Ryne Duren

GAME 2
Thursday, October 2
at County Stadium, Milwaukee

	1	2	3	4	5	6	7	8	9	R	H	E
New York Yankees	1	0	0	1	0	0	0	0	3	5	7	0
Milwaukee Braves	7	1	0	0	0	0	2	3	x	13	15	1

HR - NY Hank Bauer, Mickey Mantle 2; **MIL** Bill Bruton, Lew Burdette

WP - Lew Burdette; **LP** - Bob Turley

GAME 3
Saturday, October 4
at Yankee Stadium, New York

	1	2	3	4	5	6	7	8	9	R	H	E
Milwaukee Braves	0	0	0	0	0	0	0	0	0	0	6	0
New York Yankees	0	0	0	2	0	2	0	x		4	4	0

HR - NY Hank Bauer

WP - Don Larsen; **LP** - Bob Rush; **Sv** - Ryne Duren

GAME 4
Sunday, October 5
at Yankee Stadium, New York

	1	2	3	4	5	6	7	8	9	R	H	E
Milwaukee Braves	0	0	0	0	1	1	1	0		3	9	0
New York Yankees	0	0	0	0	0	0	0	0		0	2	1

WP - Warren Spahn; **LP** - Whitey Ford

GAME 5
Monday, October 6
at Yankee Stadium, New York

	1	2	3	4	5	6	7	8	9	R	H	E
Milwaukee Braves	0	0	0	0	0	0	0	0	0	5	0	
New York Yankees	0	0	1	0	0	6	0	0	x	7	10	0

HR - NY Gil McDougald

WP - Bob Turley; **LP** - Lew Burdette

GAME 6
Wednesday, October 8
at County Stadium, Milwaukee

	1	2	3	4	5	6	7	8	9	10	R	H	E
New York Yankees	1	0	0	0	0	1	0	0	0	2	4	10	1
Milwaukee Braves	1	1	0	0	0	0	0	0	0	1	3	10	4

HR - NY Hank Bauer, Gil McDougald

WP - Ryne Duren; **LP** - Warren Spahn; **Sv** - Bob Turley

GAME 7
Thursday, October 9
at County Stadium, Milwaukee

	1	2	3	4	5	6	7	8	9	R	H	E
New York Yankees	0	2	0	0	0	0	0	4	0	6	8	0
Milwaukee Braves	1	0	0	0	0	1	0	0	0	2	5	2

HR - NY Bill Skowron; MIL Del Crandall

WP - Bob Turley; **LP** - Lew Burdette

BATTING STATISTICS

New York Yankees	G	AB	R	H	2B	3B	HR	RBI	BB	SO	SB	CS	BA
Hank Bauer	7	31	6	10	0	0	4	8	0	5	0	1	.323
Yogi Berra	7	27	3	6	3	0	0	2	1	0	0	0	.222
Andy Carey	5	12	1	1	0	0	0	0	0	3	0	0	.083
Art Ditmar	1	1	0	0	0	0	0	0	0	0	0	0	.000
Ryne Duren	3	3	0	0	0	0	0	0	0	2	0	0	.000
Whitey Ford	3	4	1	0	0	0	0	0	2	2	0	0	.000
Elston Howard	6	18	4	4	0	0	0	2	1	4	1	0	.222
Tony Kubek	7	21	0	1	0	0	0	1	1	7	0	0	.048
Johnny Kucks	2	1	0	1	0	0	0	0	0	0	0	0	1.000
Don Larsen	2	2	0	0	0	0	0	0	1	0	0	0	.000
Jerry Lumpe	6	12	0	2	0	0	0	0	1	2	0	1	.167
Mickey Mantle	7	24	4	6	0	1	2	3	7	4	0	0	.250
Gil McDougald	7	28	5	9	2	0	2	4	2	4	0	0	.321
Bobby Richardson	4	5	0	0	0	0	0	0	0	0	0	0	.000
Norm Siebern	3	8	1	1	0	0	0	0	3	2	0	0	.125
Bill Skowron	7	27	3	7	0	0	2	7	1	4	0	0	.259
Enos Slaughter	4	3	1	0	0	0	0	0	1	1	0	0	.000
Marv Throneberry	1	1	0	0	0	0	0	0	0	1	0	0	.000
Bob Turley	4	5	0	1	0	0	0	2	0	1	0	0	.200
Totals	**7**	**233**	**29**	**49**	**5**	**1**	**10**	**29**	**21**	**42**	**1**	**2**	**.210**

Milwaukee Braves	G	AB	R	H	2B	3B	HR	RBI	BB	SO	SB	CS	BA
Hank Aaron	7	27	3	9	2	0	0	2	4	6	0	0	.333
Joe Adcock	4	13	1	4	0	0	0	0	1	3	0	0	.308
Bill Bruton	7	17	2	7	0	0	1	2	5	5	0	0	.412
Lew Burdette	3	9	1	1	0	0	1	3	0	3	0	0	.111
Wes Covington	7	26	2	7	0	0	0	4	2	4	0	0	.269
Del Crandall	7	25	4	6	0	0	1	3	3	10	0	0	.240
Harry Hanebrink	2	2	0	0	0	0	0	0	0	0	0	0	.000
Johnny Logan	7	25	3	3	2	0	0	2	2	4	0	0	.120
Felix Mantilla	4	0	1	0	0	0	0	0	0	0	0	0	—
Eddie Mathews	7	25	3	4	2	0	0	3	6	11	1	0	.160
Andy Pafko	4	9	0	3	1	0	0	1	0	0	0	0	.333
Bob Rush	1	2	0	0	0	0	0	0	0	2	0	0	.000
Red Schoendienst	7	30	5	9	3	1	0	0	2	1	0	0	.300
Warren Spahn	3	12	0	4	0	0	0	3	0	6	0	0	.333
Frank Torre	7	17	0	3	0	0	0	1	2	0	0	0	.176
Casey Wise	2	1	0	0	0	0	0	0	0	1	0	0	.000
Totals	**7**	**240**	**25**	**60**	**10**	**1**	**3**	**24**	**27**	**56**	**1**	**0**	**.250**

PITCHING STATISTICS

New York Yankees	G	GS	CG	IP	H	ER	BB	SO	W-L	Sv	ERA
Murry Dickson	2	0	0	4	4	2	0	1	0-0	0	4.50
Art Ditmar	1	0	0	3 2/3	2	0	0	2	0-0	0	0.00
Ryne Duren	3	0	0	9 1/3	7	2	6	14	1-1	1	1.93
Whitey Ford	3	3	0	15 1/3	19	7	5	16	0-1	0	4.11
Johnny Kucks	2	0	0	4 1/3	4	1	1	0	0-0	0	2.08
Don Larsen	2	2	0	9 1/3	9	1	6	9	1-0	0	0.96
Duke Maas	1	0	0	0 1/3	2	3	1	0	0-0	0	81.00
Zack Monroe	1	0	0	1	3	3	1	1	0-0	0	27.00
Bob Turley	4	2	1	16 1/3	10	5	7	13	2-1	1	2.76
Totals	**7**	**7**	**1**	**63 2/3**	**60**	**24**	**27**	**56**	**4-3**	**2**	**3.39**

Milwaukee Braves	G	GS	CG	IP	H	ER	BB	SO	W-L	Sv	ERA
Lew Burdette	3	3	1	22 1/3	22	14	4	12	1-2	0	5.64
Don McMahon	3	0	0	3 1/3	3	2	3	5	0-0	0	5.40
Juan Pizarro	1	0	0	1 2/3	2	1	1	3	0-0	0	5.40
Bob Rush	1	1	0	6	3	2	5	2	0-1	0	3.00
Warren Spahn	3	3	2	28 2/3	19	7	8	18	2-1	0	2.20
Carl Willey	1	0	0	1	0	0	0	2	0-0	0	0.00
Totals	**7**	**7**	**3**	**63**	**49**	**26**	**21**	**42**	**3-4**	**0**	**3.71**

1960 World Series

PITTSBURGH PIRATES (4) VS. NEW YORK YANKEES (3)

GAME 1
Wednesday, October 5
at Forbes Field, Pittsburgh

	1	2	3	4	5	6	7	8	9	R	H	E
New York Yankees	1	0	0	1	0	0	0	0	2	4	13	2
Pittsburgh Pirates	3	0	0	2	0	1	0	0	x	6	8	0

HR - NY Elston Howard, Roger Maris; PIT Bill Mazeroski

WP - Vern Law; **LP -** Art Ditmar; **Sv -** Roy Face

GAME 2
Thursday, October 6
at Forbes Field, Pittsburgh

	1	2	3	4	5	6	7	8	9	R	H	E
New York Yankees	0	0	2	1	2	7	3	0	1	16	19	1
Pittsburgh Pirates	0	0	0	1	0	0	0	0	2	3	13	1

HR - NY Mickey Mantle 2

WP - Bob Turley; **LP -** Bob Friend; **Sv -** Bobby Shantz

GAME 3
Saturday, October 8
at Yankee Stadium, New York

	1	2	3	4	5	6	7	8	9	R	H	E
Pittsburgh Pirates	0	0	0	0	0	0	0	0	0	0	4	0
New York Yankees	6	0	0	4	0	0	0	0	x	10	16	1

HR - NY Mickey Mantle, Bobby Richardson

WP - Whitey Ford; **LP -** Vinegar Bend Mizell

GAME 4
Sunday, October 9
at Yankee Stadium, New York

	1	2	3	4	5	6	7	8	9	R	H	E
Pittsburgh Pirates	0	0	0	0	3	0	0	0	0	3	7	0
New York Yankees	0	0	0	1	0	0	1	0	0	2	8	0

HR - NY Bill Skowron

WP - Vern Law; **LP -** Ralph Terry; **Sv -** Roy Face

GAME 5
Monday, October 10
at Yankee Stadium, New York

	1	2	3	4	5	6	7	8	9	R	H	E
Pittsburgh Pirates	0	3	1	0	0	0	0	1	5	10	2	
New York Yankees	0	1	1	0	0	0	0	0	2	5	2	

HR - NY Roger Maris

WP - Harvey Haddix; **LP -** Art Ditmar; **Sv -** Roy Face

GAME 6
Wednesday, October 12
at Forbes Field, Pittsburgh

	1	2	3	4	5	6	7	8	9	R	H	E
New York Yankees	0	1	5	0	0	2	2	2	0	12	17	1
Pittsburgh Pirates	0	0	0	0	0	0	0	0	0	0	7	1

WP - Whitey Ford; **LP -** Bob Friend

GAME 7
Wednesday, October 13
at Forbes Field, Pittsburgh

	1	2	3	4	5	6	7	8	9	R	H	E
New York Yankees	0	0	0	0	1	4	0	2	2	9	13	1
Pittsburgh Pirates	2	2	0	0	0	0	0	5	1	10	11	0

HR - NY Yogi Berra, Bill Skowron; PIT Bill Mazeroski, Rocky Nelson, Hal Smith

WP - Harvey Hadddix; **LP -** Ralph Terry

BATTING STATISTICS

Pittsburgh Pirates	G	AB	R	H	2B	3B	HR	RBI	BB	SO	SB	CS	BA
Gene Baker	3	3	0	0	0	0	0	0	0	1	0	0	.000
Smoky Burgess	5	18	2	6	1	0	0	0	2	1	0	0	.333
Joe Christopher	3	0	2	0	0	0	0	0	0	0	0	0	—
Gino Cimoli	7	20	4	5	0	0	0	1	2	4	0	0	.250
Roberto Clemente	7	29	1	9	0	0	0	3	0	4	0	0	.310
Roy Face	4	3	0	0	0	0	0	0	0	2	0	0	.000
Bob Friend	3	1	0	0	0	0	0	0	0	0	0	0	.000
Fred Green	3	1	0	0	0	0	0	0	0	0	0	0	.000
Dick Groat	7	28	3	6	2	0	0	2	0	1	0	0	.214
Harvey Haddix	2	3	0	1	0	0	0	0	0	1	0	0	.333
Don Hoak	7	23	3	5	2	0	0	3	4	1	0	1	.217
Vern Law	3	6	1	2	1	0	0	1	0	1	0	0	.333
Bill Mazeroski	7	25	4	8	2	0	2	5	0	3	0	0	.320
Rocky Nelson	4	9	2	3	0	0	1	2	1	1	0	0	.333
Dick Schofield	3	3	0	1	0	0	0	0	1	0	0	0	.333
Bob Skinner	2	5	2	1	0	0	0	1	1	0	1	0	.200
Hal Smith	3	8	1	3	0	0	1	3	0	0	0	0	.375
Dick Stuart	5	20	0	3	0	0	0	0	0	3	0	0	.150
Bill Virdon	7	29	2	7	3	0	0	5	1	3	1	0	.241
Totals	**7**	**234**	**27**	**60**	**11**	**0**	**4**	**26**	**12**	**26**	**2**	**1**	**.256**

New York Yankees	G	AB	R	H	2B	3B	HR	RBI	BB	SO	SB	CS	BA
Luis Arroyo	1	1	0	0	0	0	0	0	0	0	0	0	.000
Yogi Berra	7	22	6	7	0	0	1	8	2	0	0	0	.318
Johnny Blanchard	5	11	2	5	2	0	2	2	0	0	0	0	.455
Clete Boyer	4	12	1	3	2	1	0	1	0	1	0	0	.250
Bob Cerv	4	14	1	5	0	0	0	0	0	3	0	0	.357
Jim Coates	3	1	0	0	0	0	0	0	0	1	0	0	.000
Joe DeMaestri	4	2	1	1	0	0	0	0	0	1	0	0	.500
Whitey Ford	2	8	1	2	0	0	0	2	0	2	0	0	.250
Eli Grba	1	0	0	0	0	0	0	0	0	0	0	0	—
Elston Howard	5	13	4	6	1	1	1	4	1	4	0	0	.462
Tony Kubek	7	30	6	10	1	0	0	3	2	2	0	1	.333
Dale Long	3	3	0	1	0	0	0	0	0	0	0	0	.333
Hector Lopez	3	7	0	3	0	0	0	0	0	0	0	0	.429
Mickey Mantle	7	25	8	10	1	0	3	11	8	9	0	1	.400
Roger Maris	7	30	6	8	1	0	2	2	2	4	0	0	.267
Gil McDougald	6	18	4	5	1	0	0	2	2	3	0	0	.278
Bobby Richardson	7	30	8	11	2	2	1	12	1	1	0	0	.367
Bobby Shantz	3	3	0	1	0	0	0	0	0	0	0	0	.333
Bill Skowron	7	32	7	12	2	0	2	6	0	6	0	0	.375
Bill Stafford	2	1	0	0	0	0	0	0	0	1	0	0	.000
Ralph Terry	2	2	0	0	0	0	0	0	0	1	0	0	.000
Bob Turley	2	4	0	1	0	0	0	1	0	1	0	0	.250
Totals	**7**	**269**	**55**	**91**	**13**	**4**	**10**	**54**	**18**	**40**	**0**	**2**	**.338**

PITCHING STATISTICS

Pittsburgh Pirates	G	GS	CG	IP	H	ER	BB	SO	W-L	Sv	ERA
Tom Cheney	3	0	0	4	4	2	1	6	0-0	0	4.50
Roy Face	4	0	0	10 1/3	9	6	2	4	0-0	3	5.23
Bob Friend	3	2	0	6	13	9	3	7	0-2	0	13.50
Joe Gibbon	2	0	0	3	4	3	1	2	0-0	0	9.00
Fred Green	3	0	0	4	11	10	1	3	0-0	0	22.50
Harvey Haddix	2	1	0	7 1/3	6	2	2	6	2-0	0	2.45
Clem Labine	3	0	0	4	13	6	1	2	0-0	0	13.50
Vern Law	3	3	0	18 1/3	22	7	3	8	2-0	0	3.44
Vinegar Bend Mizell	2	1	0	2 1/3	4	4	2	1	0-1	0	15.43
George Witt	3	0	0	2 2/3	5	0	2	1	0-0	0	0.00
Totals	**7**	**7**	**0**	**62**	**91**	**49**	**18**	**40**	**4-3**	**3**	**7.11**

New York Yankees	G	GS	CG	IP	H	ER	BB	SO	W-L	Sv	ERA
Luis Arroyo	1	0	0	0 2/3	2	1	0	1	0-0	0	13.50
Jim Coates	3	0	0	6 1/3	6	4	1	3	0-0	0	5.68
Art Ditmar	2	2	0	1 2/3	6	4	1	0	0-2	0	21.60
Ryne Duren	2	0	0	4	2	1	1	5	0-0	0	2.25
Whitey Ford	2	2	2	18	11	0	2	8	2-0	0	0.00
Duke Maas	1	0	0	2	2	1	0	1	0-0	0	4.50
Bobby Shantz	3	0	0	6 1/3	4	3	1	1	0-0	0	4.26
Bill Stafford	2	0	0	6	5	1	1	2	0-0	0	1.50
Ralph Terry	2	1	0	6 2/3	7	4	1	5	0-2	0	5.40
Bob Turley	2	2	0	9 1/3	15	5	4	0	1-0	0	4.82
Totals	**7**	**7**	**2**	**61**	**60**	**24**	**12**	**26**	**3-4**	**0**	**3.54**

1961 World Series

NEW YORK YANKEES (4) VS. CINCINNATI REDS (1)

GAME 1

Wednesday, October 4
at Yankee Stadium, New York

	1	2	3	4	5	6	7	8	9	R	H	E
Cincinnati Reds	0	0	0	0	0	0	0	0	0	0	2	0
New York Yankees	0	0	1	0	1	0	0	x		2	6	0

HR - NY Elston Howard, Bill Skowron

WP - Whitey Ford; LP - Jim O'Toole

GAME 2

Thursday, October 5
at Yankee Stadium, New York

	1	2	3	4	5	6	7	8	9	R	H	E
Cincinnati Reds	0	0	0	2	1	1	0	2	0	6	9	0
New York Yankees	0	0	0	2	0	0	0	0	2	2	4	3

HR - CIN Gordy Coleman; NY Yogi Berra

WP - Joey Jay; LP - Ralph Terry

GAME 3

Saturday, October 7
at Crosley Field, Cincinnati

	1	2	3	4	5	6	7	8	9	R	H	E
New York Yankees	0	0	0	0	0	0	1	1	1	3	6	1
Cincinnati Reds	0	0	1	0	0	0	1	0	0	2	8	0

HR - NY Johnny Blanchard, Roger Maris

WP - Luis Arroyo; LP - Bob Purkey

GAME 4

Sunday, October 8
at Crosley Field, Cincinnati

	1	2	3	4	5	6	7	8	9	R	H	E
New York Yankees	0	0	0	1	1	2	3	0	0	7	11	0
Cincinnati Reds	0	0	0	0	0	0	0	0	0	0	5	1

WP - Whitey Ford; LP - Jim O'Toole; Sv - Jim Coates

GAME 5

Monday, October 9
at Crosley Field, Cincinnati

	1	2	3	4	5	6	7	8	9	R	H	E
New York Yankees	5	1	0	5	0	2	0	0	0	13	15	1
Cincinnati Reds	0	0	3	0	2	0	0	0	0	5	11	3

HR - NY Johnny Blanchard, Hector Lopez; CIN Wally Post, Frank Robinson

WP - Bud Daley; LP - Joey Jay

BATTING STATISTICS

New York	G	AB	R	H	2B	3B	HR	RBI	BB	SO	SB	CS	BA
Yogi Berra	4	11	2	3	0	0	1	3	5	1	0	0	.273
Johnny Blanchard	4	10	4	4	1	0	2	3	2	0	0	0	.400
Clete Boyer	5	15	0	4	2	0	0	3	4	0	0	0	.267
Jim Coates	1	1	0	0	0	0	0	0	0	1	0	0	.000
Bud Daley	2	1	0	0	0	0	0	1	0	0	0	0	.000
Whitey Ford	2	5	1	0	0	0	0	0	1	0	0	0	.000
Billy Gardner	1	1	0	0	0	0	0	0	0	0	0	0	.000
Elston Howard	5	20	5	5	3	0	1	1	2	3	0	0	.250
Tony Kubek	5	22	3	5	0	0	0	1	1	4	0	0	.227
Hector Lopez	4	9	3	3	0	1	1	7	2	3	0	0	.333
Mickey Mantle	2	6	0	1	0	0	0	0	0	2	0	0	.167
Roger Maris	5	19	4	2	1	0	1	2	4	6	0	0	.105
Bobby Richardson	5	23	2	9	1	0	0	0	0	1	1	1	.391
Bill Skowron	5	17	3	6	0	0	1	5	3	4	0	0	.353
Bill Stafford	1	2	0	0	0	0	0	0	0	0	0	0	.000
Ralph Terry	2	3	0	0	0	0	0	0	0	1	0	0	.000
Totals	**5**	**165**	**27**	**42**	**8**	**1**	**7**	**26**	**24**	**25**	**1**	**1**	**.255**

Cincinnati	G	AB	R	H	2B	3B	HR	RBI	BB	SO	SB	CS	BA
Gus Bell	3	3	0	0	0	0	0	0	0	0	0	0	.000
Don Blasingame	3	7	1	1	0	0	0	0	0	3	0	0	.143
Leo Cardenas	3	3	0	1	1	0	0	0	0	1	0	0	.333
Elio Chacon	4	12	2	3	0	0	0	0	1	2	0	0	.250
Gordy Coleman	5	20	2	5	0	0	1	2	0	1	0	0	.250
Johnny Edwards	3	11	1	4	2	0	0	2	0	0	0	0	.364
Gene Freese	5	16	0	1	1	0	0	0	3	4	0	0	.063
Dick Gernert	4	4	0	0	0	0	0	0	0	1	0	0	.000
Joey Jay	2	4	0	0	0	0	0	0	0	2	0	0	.000
Darrell Johnson	2	4	0	2	0	0	0	0	0	0	0	0	.500
Eddie Kasko	5	22	1	7	0	0	0	1	0	2	0	0	.318
Jerry Lynch	4	3	0	0	0	0	0	0	1	1	0	0	.000
Jim O'Toole	2	3	0	0	0	0	0	0	0	1	0	0	.000
Vada Pinson	5	22	0	2	1	0	0	0	0	1	0	0	.091
Wally Post	5	18	3	6	1	0	1	2	0	1	0	0	.333
Bob Purkey	2	3	0	0	0	0	0	0	0	3	0	0	.000
Frank Robinson	5	15	3	3	2	0	1	4	3	4	0	0	.200
Totals	**5**	**170**	**13**	**35**	**8**	**0**	**3**	**11**	**8**	**27**	**0**	**0**	**.206**

PITCHING STATISTICS

New York	G	GS	CG	IP	H	ER	BB	SO	W-L	Sv	ERA
Luis Arroyo	2	0	0	4	4	1	2	3	1-0	0	2.25
Jim Coates	1	0	0	4	1	0	1	2	0-0	1	0.00
Bud Daley	2	0	0	7	5	0	0	3	1-0	0	0.00
Whitey Ford	2	2	1	14	6	0	1	7	2-0	0	0.00
Bill Stafford	1	1	0	6 2/3	7	2	2	5	0-0	0	2.70
Ralph Terry	2	2	0	9 1/3	12	5	2	7	0-1	0	4.82
Totals	**5**	**5**	**1**	**45**	**35**	**8**	**8**	**27**	**4-1**	**1**	**1.60**

Cincinnati	G	GS	CG	IP	H	ER	BB	SO	W-L	Sv	ERA
Jim Brosnan	3	0	0	6	9	5	4	5	0-0	0	7.50
Bill Henry	2	0	0	2 1/3	4	5	2	3	0-0	0	19.29
Ken Hunt	1	0	0	1	0	0	1	1	0-0	0	0.00
Joey Jay	2	2	1	9 2/3	8	6	6	6	1-1	0	5.59
Ken Johnson	1	0	0	0 2/3	0	0	0	0	0-0	0	0.00
Sherman Jones	1	0	0	0 2/3	0	0	0	0	0-0	0	0.00
Jim Maloney	1	0	0	0 2/3	4	2	1	0	0-0	0	27.00
Jim O'Toole	2	2	0	12	11	4	7	4	0-2	0	3.00
Bob Purkey	2	1	1	11	6	2	3	5	0-1	0	1.64
Totals	**5**	**5**	**2**	**44**	**42**	**24**	**24**	**25**	**1-4**	**0**	**4.91**

1962 World Series

NEW YORK YANKEES (4) VS. SAN FRANCISCO GIANTS (3)

GAME 1
Thursday, October 4
at Candlestick Park, San Francisco

	1	2	3	4	5	6	7	8	9	R	H	E
New York Yankees	2	0	0	0	0	1	2	1	6	11	0	
San Francisco Giants	0	1	1	0	0	0	0	0	0	2	10	0

HR - NY Clete Boyer

WP - Whitey Ford; LP - Billy O'Dell

GAME 2
Friday, October 5
at Candlestick Park, San Francisco

	1	2	3	4	5	6	7	8	9	R	H	E
New York Yankees	0	0	0	0	0	0	0	0	0	0	3	1
San Francisco Giants	1	0	0	0	0	1	0	x		2	6	0

HR - SF Willie McCovey

WP - Jack Sanford; LP - Ralph Terry

GAME 3
Sunday, October 7
at Yankee Stadium, New York

	1	2	3	4	5	6	7	8	9	R	H	E
San Francisco Giants	0	0	0	0	0	0	0	2	2	4	3	
New York Yankees	0	0	0	0	0	3	0	x		3	5	1

HR - SF Ed Bailey

WP - Bill Stafford; LP - Billy Pierce

GAME 4
Monday, October 8
at Yankee Stadium, New York

	1	2	3	4	5	6	7	8	9	R	H	E
San Francisco Giants	0	2	0	0	0	4	0	1		7	9	1
New York Yankees	0	0	0	0	2	0	0	1		3	9	1

HR - SF Tom Haller, Chuck Hiller

WP - Don Larsen; LP - Jim Coates; Sv - Billy O'Dell

GAME 5
Wednesday, October 10
at Yankee Stadium, New York

	1	2	3	4	5	6	7	8	9	R	H	E
San Francisco Giants	0	0	1	0	1	0	0	0	1	3	8	2
New York Yankees	0	0	0	1	0	1	0	1	3	x	5	6	0

HR - SF Jose Pagan; NY Tom Tresh

WP - Ralph Terry; **LP** - Jack Sanford

GAME 6
Monday, October 15
at Candlestick Park, San Francisco

	1	2	3	4	5	6	7	8	9	R	H	E
New York Yankees	0	0	0	0	1	0	0	1	0	2	3	2
San Francisco Giants	0	0	0	3	2	0	0	0	x	5	10	1

HR - NY Roger Maris

WP - Billy Pierce; **LP** - Whitey Ford

GAME 7
Tuesday, October 16
at Candlestick Park, San Francisco

	1	2	3	4	5	6	7	8	9	R	H	E
New York Yankees	0	0	0	0	1	0	0	0	0	1	7	0
San Francisco Giants	0	0	0	0	0	0	0	0	0	0	4	1

WP - Ralph Terry; **LP** - Jack Sanford

BATTING STATISTICS

New York	G	AB	R	H	2B	3B	HR	RBI	BB	SO	SB	CS	BA
Yogi Berra	2	2	0	0	0	0	0	0	2	0	0	0	.000
Johnny Blanchard	1	1	0	0	0	0	0	0	0	1	0	0	.000
Clete Boyer	7	22	2	7	1	0	1	4	1	3	0	0	.318
Whitey Ford	3	7	0	0	0	0	0	0	1	3	0	0	.000
Elston Howard	6	21	1	3	1	0	0	1	1	4	0	0	.143
Tony Kubek	7	29	2	8	1	0	0	1	1	3	0	1	.276
Dale Long	2	5	0	1	0	0	0	1	0	1	0	0	.200
Hector Lopez	2	2	0	0	0	0	0	0	0	0	0	0	.000
Mickey Mantle	7	25	2	3	1	0	0	0	4	5	2	0	.120
Roger Maris	7	23	4	4	1	0	1	5	5	2	0	0	.174
Bobby Richardson	7	27	3	4	0	0	0	0	3	1	0	0	.148
Bill Skowron	6	18	1	4	0	1	0	1	1	5	0	0	.222
Bill Stafford	1	3	0	0	0	0	0	0	0	1	0	0	.000
Ralph Terry	3	8	0	1	0	0	0	0	1	6	0	0	.125
Tom Tresh	7	28	5	9	1	0	1	4	1	4	2	0	.321
Totals	**7**	**221**	**20**	**44**	**6**	**1**	**3**	**17**	**21**	**39**	**4**	**1**	**.199**

San Francisco	G	AB	R	H	2B	3B	HR	RBI	BB	SO	SB	CS	BA
Felipe Alou	7	26	2	7	1	1	0	1	1	4	0	0	.269
Matty Alou	6	12	2	4	1	0	0	1	0	1	0	0	.333
Ed Bailey	6	14	1	1	0	0	1	2	0	3	0	0	.071
Ernie Bowman	2	1	1	0	0	0	0	0	0	0	0	0	.000
Orlando Cepeda	5	19	1	3	1	0	0	2	0	4	0	1	.158
Jim Davenport	7	22	3	3	1	0	0	1	4	7	0	0	.136
Tom Haller	4	14	1	4	1	0	1	3	0	2	0	1	.286
Chuck Hiller	7	26	4	7	3	0	1	5	3	4	0	0	.269
Harvey Kuenn	3	12	1	1	0	0	0	0	1	1	0	0	.083
Juan Marichal	1	2	0	0	0	0	0	0	0	1	0	0	.000
Willie Mays	7	28	3	7	2	0	0	1	1	5	1	0	.250
Willie McCovey	4	15	2	3	0	1	1	1	1	3	0	0	.200
Bob Nieman	1	0	0	0	0	0	0	0	1	0	0	0	—
Billy O'Dell	3	3	0	1	0	0	0	0	0	0	0	0	.333
John Orsino	1	1	0	0	0	0	0	0	0	0	0	0	.000
Jose Pagan	7	19	2	7	0	0	1	2	0	1	0	0	.368
Billy Pierce	2	5	0	0	0	0	0	0	0	1	0	0	.000
Jack Sanford	3	7	0	3	0	0	0	0	0	2	0	0	.429
Totals	**7**	**226**	**21**	**51**	**10**	**2**	**5**	**19**	**12**	**39**	**1**	**2**	**.226**

PITCHING STATISTICS

New York	G	GS	CG	IP	H	ER	BB	SO	W-L	Sv	ERA
Marshall Bridges	2	0	0	3 2/3	4	2	2	3	0-0	0	4.91
Jim Coates	2	0	0	2 2/3	1	2	1	3	0-1	0	6.75
Bud Daley	1	0	0	1	1	0	1	0	0-0	0	0.00
Whitey Ford	3	3	1	19 2/3	24	9	4	12	1-1	0	4.12
Bill Stafford	1	1	1	9	4	2	2	5	1-0	0	2.00
Ralph Terry	3	3	2	25	17	5	2	16	2-1	0	1.80
Totals	**7**	**7**	**4**	**61**	**51**	**20**	**12**	**39**	**4-3**	**0**	**2.95**

San Francisco	G	GS	CG	IP	H	ER	BB	SO	W-L	Sv	ERA
Bobby Bolin	2	0	0	2 2/3	4	2	2	2	0-0	0	6.75
Don Larsen	3	0	0	2 1/3	1	1	2	0	1-0	0	3.86
Juan Marichal	1	1	0	4	2	0	2	4	0-0	0	0.00
Stu Miller	2	0	0	1 1/3	1	0	2	0	0-0	0	0.00
Billy O'Dell	3	1	0	12 1/3	12	6	3	9	0-1	1	4.38
Billy Pierce	2	2	1	15	8	4	2	5	1-1	0	2.40
Jack Sanford	3	3	1	23 1/3	16	5	8	19	1-2	0	1.93
Totals	**7**	**7**	**2**	**61**	**44**	**18**	**21**	**39**	**3-4**	**1**	**2.66**

World Series 1963

LOS ANGELES DODGERS (4) VS. NEW YORK YANKEES (0)

GAME 1
Wednesday, October 2
at Yankee Stadium, New York

	1	2	3	4	5	6	7	8	9	R	H	E
Los Angeles Dodgers	0	4	1	0	0	0	0	0	0	5	9	0
New York Yankees	0	0	0	0	0	0	0	2	0	2	6	0

HR - LA John Roseboro; NY Tom Tresh

WP - Sandy Koufax; LP - Whitey Ford

GAME 2
Thursday, October 3
at Yankee Stadium, New York

	1	2	3	4	5	6	7	8	9	R	H	E
Los Angeles Dodgers	2	0	0	1	0	0	0	1	0	4	10	1
New York Yankees	0	0	0	0	0	0	0	1	1	1	7	0

HR - LA Bill Skowron

WP - Johnny Podres; LP - Al Downing; Sv - Ron Perranoski

GAME 3
Saturday, October 5
at Dodger Stadium, Los Angeles

	1	2	3	4	5	6	7	8	9	R	H	E
New York Yankees	0	0	0	0	0	0	0	0	0	0	3	0
Los Angeles Dodgers	1	0	0	0	0	0	0	0	x	1	4	1

WP - Don Drysdale; LP - Jim Bouton

GAME 4
Sunday, October 6
at Dodger Stadium, Los Angeles

	1	2	3	4	5	6	7	8	9	R	H	E
New York Yankees	0	0	0	0	0	0	1	0	0	1	6	1
Los Angeles Dodgers	0	0	0	1	0	1	0	x	2	2	1

HR - NY Mickey Mantle; LA Frank Howard

WP - Sandy Koufax; LP - Whitey Ford

BATTING STATISTICS

Los Angeles Dodgers	G	AB	R	H	2B	3B	HR	RBI	BB	SO	SB	CS	BA
Tommy Davis	4	15	0	6	0	2	0	2	0	2	1	0	.400
Willie Davis	4	12	2	2	0	0	0	3	0	6	0	0	.167
Don Drysdale	1	1	0	0	0	0	0	0	0	2	0	0	.000
Ron Fairly	4	1	0	0	0	0	0	0	3	0	0	0	.000
Jim Gilliam	4	13	3	2	0	0	0	0	3	1	0	1	.154
Frank Howard	3	10	2	3	1	0	1	1	0	2	0	0	.300
Sandy Koufax	2	6	0	0	0	0	0	0	0	2	0	0	.000
Johnny Podres	1	4	0	1	0	0	0	0	0	0	0	0	.250
John Roseboro	4	14	1	2	0	0	1	3	0	4	0	0	.143
Bill Skowron	4	13	2	5	0	0	1	3	1	3	0	0	.385
Dick Tracewski	4	13	1	2	0	0	0	0	1	2	0	0	.154
Maury Wills	4	15	1	2	0	0	0	0	1	3	1	0	.133
Totals	**4**	**117**	**12**	**25**	**3**	**2**	**3**	**12**	**11**	**25**	**2**	**1**	**.214**

New York Yankees	G	AB	R	H	2B	3B	HR	RBI	BB	SO	SB	CS	BA
Yogi Berra	1	1	0	0	0	0	0	0	0	0	0	0	.000
Johnny Blanchard	1	3	0	0	0	0	0	0	0	0	0	0	.000
Jim Bouton	1	2	0	0	0	0	0	0	0	0	0	0	.000
Clete Boyer	4	13	0	1	0	0	0	0	1	6	0	0	.077
Harry Bright	2	2	0	0	0	0	0	0	0	2	0	0	.000
Al Downing	1	1	0	0	0	0	0	0	0	1	0	0	.000
Whitey Ford	2	3	0	0	0	0	0	0	0	0	0	0	.000
Elston Howard	4	15	0	5	0	0	0	1	0	3	0	0	.333
Tony Kubek	4	16	1	3	0	0	0	0	0	3	0	1	.188
Phil Linz	3	3	0	1	0	0	0	0	0	1	0	0	.333
Hector Lopez	3	8	1	2	2	0	0	0	0	1	0	0	.250
Mickey Mantle	4	15	1	2	0	0	1	1	1	5	0	0	.133
Roger Maris	2	5	0	0	0	0	0	0	0	1	0	0	.000
Joe Pepitone	4	13	0	2	0	0	0	0	1	3	0	0	.154
Bobby Richardson	4	14	0	3	1	0	0	0	1	3	0	0	.214
Tom Tresh	4	15	1	3	0	0	1	2	1	6	0	0	.200
Totals	**4**	**129**	**4**	**22**	**3**	**0**	**2**	**4**	**5**	**37**	**0**	**1**	**.171**

PITCHING STATISTICS

Los Angeles Dodgers	G	GS	CG	IP	H	ER	BB	SO	W-L	Sv	ERA
Don Drysdale	1	1	1	9	3	0	1	9	1-0	0	0.00
Sandy Koufax	2	2	2	18	12	3	3	23	2-0	0	1.50
Ron Perranoski	1	0	0	0 2/3	1	0	0	1	0-0	1	0.00
Johnny Podres	1	1	0	8 1/3	6	1	1	4	1-0	0	1.08
Totals	**4**	**4**	**3**	**36**	**22**	**4**	**5**	**37**	**4-0**	**1**	**1.00**

New York Yankees	G	GS	CG	IP	H	ER	BB	SO	W-L	Sv	ERA
Jim Bouton	1	1	0	7	4	1	5	4	0-1	0	1.29
Al Downing	1	1	0	5	7	3	1	6	0-1	0	5.40
Whitey Ford	2	2	0	12	10	6	3	8	0-2	0	4.50
Steve Hamilton	1	0	0	1	0	0	0	1	0-0	0	0.00
Hal Reniff	3	0	0	3	0	0	1	1	0-0	0	0.00
Ralph Terry	1	0	0	3	3	1	1	0	0-0	0	3.00
Stan Williams	1	0	0	3	1	0	0	5	0-0	0	0.00
Totals	**4**	**4**	**0**	**34**	**25**	**11**	**11**	**25**	**0-4**	**0**	**2.91**

1964 World Series

ST. LOUIS CARDINALS (4) VS. NEW YORK YANKEES (3)

GAME 1
Wednesday, October 7
at Busch Stadium, St. Louis

	1	2	3	4	5	6	7	8	9	R	H	E
New York Yankees	0	3	0	0	1	0	0	1	0	5	12	2
St. Louis Cardinals	1	1	0	0	0	4	0	3	x	9	12	0

HR - NY Tom Tresh; STL Mike Shannon

WP - Ray Sadecki; LP - Whitey Ford; Sv - Barney Schultz

GAME 2
Thursday, October 8
at Busch Stadium, St. Louis

	1	2	3	4	5	6	7	8	9	R	H	E
New York Yankees	0	0	0	1	0	1	2	0	4	8	12	0
St. Louis Cardinals	0	0	1	0	0	0	0	1	1	3	7	0

HR - NY Phil Linz

WP - Mel Stottlemyre; LP - Bob Gibson

GAME 3
Saturday, October 10
at Yankee Stadium, New York

	1	2	3	4	5	6	7	8	9	R	H	E
St. Louis Cardinals	0	0	0	0	1	0	0	0	0	1	6	0
New York Yankees	0	1	0	0	0	0	0	0	1	2	5	2

HR - NY Mickey Mantle

WP - Jim Bouton; LP - Barney Schultz

GAME 4
Sunday, October 11
at Yankee Stadium, New York

	1	2	3	4	5	6	7	8	9	R	H	E
St. Louis Cardinals	0	0	0	0	0	4	0	0	0	4	6	1
New York Yankees	3	0	0	0	0	0	0	0	0	3	6	1

HR - STL Ken Boyer

WP - Roger Craig; LP - Al Downing; Sv - Ron Taylor

GAME 5
Monday, October 12
at Yankee Stadium, New York

	1	2	3	4	5	6	7	8	9	10	R	H	E
St. Louis Cardinals	0	0	0	0	2	0	0	0	0	3	5	10	1
New York Yankees	0	0	0	0	0	0	0	0	2	0	2	6	2

HR - STL Tim McCarver; NY Tom Tresh

WP - Bob Gibson; LP - Pete Mikkelsen

GAME 6
Wednesday, October 14
at Busch Stadium, St. Louis

	1	2	3	4	5	6	7	8	9	R	H	E
New York Yankees	0	0	0	0	1	2	0	5	0	8	10	0
St. Louis Cardinals	1	0	0	0	0	0	0	1	1	3	10	1

HR - NY Mickey Mantle, Roger Maris, Joe Pepitone

WP - Jim Bouton; LP - Curt Simmons; Sv - Steve Hamilton

GAME 7
Thursday, October 15
at Busch Stadium, St. Louis

	1	2	3	4	5	6	7	8	9	R	H	E
New York Yankees	0	0	0	0	0	3	0	0	0	3	9	2
St. Louis Cardinals	0	0	3	3	3	0	1	0	x	7	10	1

HR - NY Clete Boyer, Phil Linz, Mickey Mantle; STL Ken Boyer, Lou Brock

WP - Bob Gibson; LP - Mel Stottlemyre

BATTING STATISTICS

St. Louis Cardinals	G	AB	R	H	2B	3B	HR	RBI	BB	SO	SB	CS	BA
Ken Boyer	7	27	5	6	1	0	2	6	1	5	0	0	.222
Lou Brock	7	30	2	9	2	0	1	5	0	3	0	0	.300
Jerry Buchek	4	1	1	1	0	0	0	0	0	0	0	1	1.000
Roger Craig	2	1	0	0	0	0	0	0	0	0	0	0	.000
Curt Flood	7	30	5	6	0	1	0	3	3	1	0	0	.200
Bob Gibson	3	9	1	2	0	0	0	0	0	3	0	0	.222
Dick Groat	7	26	3	5	1	1	0	1	4	3	0	0	.192
Charlie James	3	3	0	0	0	0	0	0	0	1	0	0	.000
Julian Javier	1	0	1	0	0	0	0	0	0	0	0	0	—
Dal Maxvill	7	20	0	4	1	0	0	1	1	4	0	0	.200
Tim McCarver	7	23	4	11	1	1	1	5	5	1	1	0	.478
Ray Sadecki	2	2	0	1	0	0	0	0	1	0	1	0	.500
Barney Schultz	4	1	0	0	0	0	0	0	0	0	0	0	.000
Mike Shannon	7	28	6	6	0	0	1	2	0	9	1	0	.214
Curt Simmons	2	4	0	2	0	0	0	1	0	1	0	0	.500
Bob Skinner	4	3	0	2	1	0	0	1	1	0	0	0	.667
Ron Taylor	2	1	0	0	0	0	0	0	0	1	0	0	.000
Carl Warwick	5	4	2	3	0	0	0	1	1	0	0	0	.750
Bill White	7	27	2	3	1	0	0	2	2	6	1	0	.111
Totals	7	240	32	61	8	3	5	29	18	39	3	0	.254

New York Yankees	G	AB	R	H	2B	3B	HR	RBI	BB	SO	SB	CS	BA
Johnny Blanchard	4	4	0	1	1	0	0	0	0	1	0	0	.250
Jim Bouton	2	7	0	1	0	0	0	1	0	2	0	0	.143
Clete Boyer	7	24	2	5	1	0	1	3	1	5	1	0	.208
Al Downing	3	2	0	0	0	0	0	0	0	2	0	0	.000
Whitey Ford	1	1	0	1	0	0	0	1	2	0	0	0	1.000
Pedro Gonzalez	1	1	0	0	0	0	0	0	0	0	0	0	.000
Mike Hegan	3	1	0	0	0	0	0	0	1	1	0	0	.000
Elston Howard	7	24	5	7	1	0	0	2	4	6	0	0	.292
Phil Linz	7	31	5	7	1	0	2	2	2	5	0	1	.226
Hector Lopez	3	2	0	0	0	0	0	0	0	2	0	0	.000
Mickey Mantle	7	24	8	8	2	0	3	8	6	8	0	0	.333
Roger Maris	7	30	4	6	0	0	1	1	1	4	0	0	.200
Joe Pepitone	7	26	1	4	1	0	1	5	2	3	0	0	.154
Bobby Richardson	7	32	3	13	2	0	0	3	0	2	1	0	.406
Mel Stottlemyre	3	8	0	1	0	0	0	0	0	6	0	0	.125
Tom Tresh	7	22	4	6	2	0	2	7	6	7	0	0	.273
Totals	**7**	**239**	**33**	**60**	**11**	**0**	**10**	**33**	**27**	**54**	**2**	**1**	**.251**

PITCHING STATISTICS

St. Louis Cardinals	G	GS	CG	IP	H	ER	BB	SO	W-L	Sv	ERA
Roger Craig	2	0	0	5	2	0	3	9	1-0	0	0.00
Bob Gibson	3	3	2	27	23	9	8	31	2-1	0	3.00
Bob Humphreys	1	0	0	1	0	0	0	1	0-0	0	0.00
Gordie Richardson	2	0	0	0 2/3	3	3	2	0	0-0	0	40.50
Ray Sadecki	2	2	0	6 1/3	12	6	5	2	1-0	0	8.53
Barney Schultz	4	0	0	4	9	8	3	1	0-1	1	18.00
Curt Simmons	2	2	0	14 1/3	11	4	3	8	0-1	0	2.51
Ron Taylor	2	0	0	4 2/3	0	0	1	2	0-0	1	0.00
Totals	**7**	**7**	**2**	**63**	**60**	**30**	**25**	**54**	**4-3**	**2**	**4.29**

New York Yankees	G	GS	CG	IP	H	ER	BB	SO	W-L	Sv	ERA
Jim Bouton	2	2	1	17 1/3	15	3	5	7	2-0	0	1.56
Al Downing	3	1	0	7 2/3	9	7	2	5	0-1	0	8.22
Whitey Ford	1	1	0	5 1/3	8	5	1	4	0-1	0	8.44
Steve Hamilton	2	0	0	2	3	1	0	2	0-0	1	4.50
Pete Mikkelsen	4	0	0	4 2/3	4	3	2	4	0-1	0	5.79
Hal Reniff	1	0	0	0 1/3	2	0	0	0	0-0	0	0.00
Rollie Sheldon	2	0	0	2 2/3	0	0	2	2	0-0	0	0.00
Mel Stottlemyre	3	3	1	20	18	7	6	12	1-1	0	3.15
Ralph Terry	1	0	0	2	2	0	0	3	0-0	0	0.00
Totals	**7**	**7**	**2**	**62**	**61**	**26**	**18**	**39**	**3-4**	**1**	**3.77**

1976 League Championship Series
NEW YORK YANKEES (3) VS. KANSAS CITY ROYALS (2)

GAME 1
Saturday, October 9
at Royals Stadium, Kansas City

	1	2	3	4	5	6	7	8	9	R	H	E
New York Yankees	2	0	0	0	0	0	0	0	2	4	12	0
Kansas City Royals	0	0	0	0	0	0	0	1	0	1	5	2

WP - Jim "Catfish" Hunter; LP - Larry Gura

GAME 2
Sunday, October 10
at Royals Stadium, Kansas City

	1	2	3	4	5	6	7	8	9	R	H	E
New York Yankees	0	1	2	0	0	0	0	0	0	3	12	5
Kansas City Royals	2	0	0	0	0	2	0	3	x	7	9	0

WP - Paul Splittorff; LP - Ed Figueroa

GAME 3
Tuesday, October 12
at Yankee Stadium, New York

	1	2	3	4	5	6	7	8	9	R	H	E
Kansas City Royals	3	0	0	0	0	0	0	0	0	3	6	0
New York Yankees	0	0	0	2	0	3	0	0	x	5	9	0

HR - NY Chris Chambliss

WP - Dock Ellis; LP - Andy Hassler; Sv - Sparky Lyle

GAME 4
Wednesday, October 13
at Yankee Stadium, New York

	1	2	3	4	5	6	7	8	9	R	H	E
Kansas City Royals	0	3	0	2	0	1	0	1	0	7	9	1
New York Yankees	0	2	0	0	0	1	0	1	4	11	0

HR - NY Graig Nettles 2

WP - Doug Bird; LP - Jim "Catfish" Hunter; Sv - Steve Mingori

GAME 5
Thursday, October 14
at Yankee Stadium, New York

	1	2	3	4	5	6	7	8	9	R	H	E
Kansas City Royals	2	1	0	0	0	0	3	0	6	11	1
New York Yankees	2	0	2	0	0	2	0	0	1	7	11	1

HR - KC George Brett, John Mayberry; NY Chris Chambliss

WP - Dick Tidrow; LP - Mark Littell

BATTING STATISTICS

New York Yankees	G	AB	R	H	2B	3B	HR	RBI	BB	SO	SB	CS	Avg
Sandy Alomar	2	1	0	0	0	0	0	0	0	0	0	1	.000
Chris Chambliss	5	21	5	11	1	1	2	8	0	1	2	0	.524
Oscar Gamble	3	8	1	2	1	0	0	1	1	1	0	0	.250
Ron Guidry	1	0	0	0	0	0	0	0	0	0	0	0	—
Ellie Hendricks	1	1	0	1	0	0	0	0	0	0	0	1	1.000
Elliott Maddox	3	9	0	2	1	0	0	1	0	1	0	0	.222
Carlos May	3	10	1	2	1	0	0	1	4	0	0	.200
Thurman Munson	5	23	3	10	2	0	0	3	0	1	0	1	.435
Graig Nettles	5	17	2	4	1	0	2	4	3	3	0	0	.235
Lou Piniella	4	11	1	3	1	0	0	0	0	1	0	0	.273
Willie Randolph	5	17	3	2	0	0	0	1	3	1	1	0	.118
Mickey Rivers	5	23	5	8	0	1	0	0	1	1	0	1	.348
Fred Stanley	5	15	1	5	2	0	0	0	2	0	0	0	.333
Otto Velez	1	1	0	0	0	0	0	0	0	0	0	0	.000
Roy White	5	17	4	5	3	0	0	3	5	1	1	0	.294
Totals	5	174	23	55	13	2	4	21	16	15	4	3	.316

Kansas City Royals	G	AB	R	H	2B	3B	HR	RBI	BB	SO	SB	CS	Avg
George Brett	5	18	4	8	1	1	1	5	2	1	0	1	.444
Al Cowens	5	21	3	4	0	1	0	0	1	1	2	0	.190
Buck Martinez	5	15	0	5	0	0	0	4	1	3	0	0	.333
John Mayberry	5	18	4	4	0	0	1	3	1	0	0	0	.222
Hal McRae	5	17	2	2	1	1	0	1	1	4	0	1	.118
Dave Nelson	2	2	0	0	0	0	0	0	0	1	0	0	.000
Amos Otis	1	1	0	0	0	0	0	0	0	0	0	0	.000
Freddie Patek	5	18	2	7	2	0	0	4	0	1	0	3	.389
Tom Poquette	5	16	1	3	2	0	0	4	2	3	0	0	.188
Jamie Quirk	4	7	1	1	0	1	0	2	0	2	0	0	.143
Cookie Rojas	4	9	2	3	0	0	0	1	0	0	1	0	.333
Bob Stinson	2	1	0	0	0	0	0	0	0	0	0	0	.000
Frank White	4	8	2	1	0	0	0	0	0	1	0	0	.125
Jim Wohlford	5	11	3	2	0	0	0	0	3	1	2	0	.182
Totals	5	162	24	40	6	4	2	24	11	18	5	5	.247

PITCHING STATISTICS

New York Yankees	G	GS	CG	IP	H	ER	BB	SO	W-L	Sv	ERA
Dock Ellis	1	1	0	8	6	3	2	5	1-0	0	3.38
Ed Figueroa	2	2	0	12 1/3	14	8	2	5	0-1	0	5.84
Jim "Catfish" Hunter	2	2	1	12	10	6	1	5	1-1	0	4.50
Grant Jackson	2	0	0	3 1/3	4	3	1	3	0-0	0	8.10
Sparky Lyle	1	0	0	1	0	0	1	0	0-0	1	0.00
Dick Tidrow	3	0	0	7 1/3	6	3	4	0	1-0	0	3.68
Totals	5	5	1	44	40	23	11	18	3-2	1	4.70

Kansas City Royals	G	GS	CG	IP	H	ER	BB	SO	W-L	Sv	ERA
Doug Bird	1	0	0	4 2/3	4	1	0	1	1-0	0	1.93
Larry Gura	2	2	0	10 2/3	18	5	1	4	0-1	0	4.22
Tom Hall	1	0	0	0 1/3	1	0	0	0	0-0	0	0.00
Andy Hassler	2	1	0	7 1/3	8	5	6	4	0-1	0	6.14
Dennis Leonard	2	2	0	2 1/3	9	5	2	0	0-0	0	19.29
Mark Littell	3	0	0	4 2/3	4	1	1	3	0-1	0	1.93
Steve Mingori	3	0	0	3 1/3	4	1	0	1	0-0	1	2.70
Marty Pattin	2	0	0	0 1/3	0	1	1	0	0-0	0	27.00
Paul Splittorff	2	0	0	9 1/3	7	2	5	2	1-0	0	1.93
Totals	5	5	0	43	55	21	16	15	2-3	0	4.40

1976 World Series

CINCINNATI REDS (4) VS. NEW YORK YANKEES (0)

GAME 1

Saturday, October 16
at Riverfront Stadium, Cincinnati

	1	2	3	4	5	6	7	8	9	R	H	E
New York Yankees	0	1	0	0	0	0	0	0	0	1	5	1
Cincinnati Reds	1	0	1	0	0	1	2	0	x	5	10	1

HR - CIN Joe Morgan

WP - Don Gullett; LP - Doyle Alexander

GAME 2

Sunday, October 17
at Riverfront Stadium, Cincinnati

	1	2	3	4	5	6	7	8	9	R	H	E
New York Yankees	0	0	0	1	0	0	2	0	0	3	9	1
Cincinnati Reds	0	3	0	0	0	0	0	1		4	10	0

WP - Jack Billingham; LP - Jim "Catfish" Hunter

GAME 3

Tuesday, October 19
at Yankee Stadium, New York

	1	2	3	4	5	6	7	8	9	R	H	E
Cincinnati Reds	0	3	0	1	0	0	0	2	0	6	13	2
New York Yankees	0	0	0	1	0	0	1	0	0	2	8	0

HR - CIN Dan Driessen; NY Jim Mason

WP - Pat Zachry; LP - Dock Ellis; Sv - Will McEnaney

GAME 4

Thursday, October 21
at Yankee Stadium, New York

	1	2	3	4	5	6	7	8	9	R	H	E
Cincinnati Reds	0	0	0	3	0	0	0	4		7	9	2
New York Yankees	1	0	0	0	1	0	0	0		2	8	0

HR - CIN Johnny Bench 2

WP - Gary Nolan; LP - Ed Figueroa; Sv - Will McEnaney

BATTING STATISTICS

Cincinnati Reds	G	AB	R	H	2B	3B	HR	RBI	BB	SO	SB	CS	BA
Johnny Bench	4	15	4	8	1	1	2	6	0	1	0	1	.533
Dave Concepcion	4	14	1	5	1	1	0	3	1	3	1	1	.357
Dan Driessen	4	14	4	5	2	0	1	1	2	0	1	0	.357
George Foster	4	14	3	6	1	0	0	4	2	3	0	2	.429
Cesar Geronimo	4	13	3	4	2	0	0	1	2	2	2	0	.308
Ken Griffey Sr.	4	17	2	1	0	0	0	1	0	1	1	0	.059
Joe Morgan	4	15	3	5	1	1	1	2	2	2	2	0	.333
Tony Perez	4	16	1	5	1	0	0	2	1	2	0	1	.313
Pete Rose	4	16	1	3	1	0	0	1	2	2	0	0	.188
Totals	**4**	**134**	**22**	**42**	**10**	**3**	**4**	**21**	**12**	**16**	**7**	**5**	**.313**

New York Yankees	G	AB	R	H	2B	3B	HR	RBI	BB	SO	SB	CS	BA
Chris Chambliss	4	16	1	5	1	0	0	1	0	2	0	0	.313
Oscar Gamble	3	8	0	1	0	0	0	1	0	0	0	0	.125
Ellie Hendricks	2	2	0	0	0	0	0	0	0	0	0	0	.000
Elliott Maddox	2	5	0	1	0	1	0	0	1	2	0	0	.200
Jim Mason	3	1	1	1	0	0	1	1	0	0	0	0	1.000
Carlos May	4	9	0	0	0	0	0	0	0	1	0	0	.000
Thurman Munson	4	17	2	9	0	0	2	0	1	0	0	0	.529
Graig Nettles	4	12	0	3	0	0	0	2	3	1	0	1	.250
Lou Piniella	4	9	1	3	1	0	0	0	0	0	0	0	.333
Willie Randolph	4	14	1	1	0	0	0	0	1	3	0	0	.071
Mickey Rivers	4	18	1	3	0	0	0	0	1	2	1	1	.167
Fred Stanley	4	6	1	1	1	0	0	1	3	1	0	0	.167
Otto Velez	3	3	0	0	0	0	0	0	0	3	0	0	.000
Roy White	4	15	0	2	0	0	0	0	3	0	0	0	.133
Totals	**4**	**135**	**8**	**30**	**3**	**1**	**1**	**8**	**12**	**16**	**1**	**2**	**.222**

PITCHING STATISTICS

Cincinnati Reds	G	GS	CG	IP	H	ER	BB	SO	W-L	Sv	ERA
Jack Billingham	1	0	0	2 2/3	0	0	0	1	1-0	0	0.00
Pedro Borbon	1	0	0	1 2/3	0	0	0	0	0-0	0	0.00
Don Gullett	1	1	0	7 1/3	5	1	3	4	1-0	0	1.23
Will McEnaney	2	0	0	4 2/3	2	0	1	2	0-0	2	0.00
Gary Nolan	1	1	0	6 2/3	8	2	1	1	1-0	0	2.70
Fred Norman	1	1	0	6 1/3	9	3	2	2	0-0	0	4.26
Pat Zachry	1	1	0	6 2/3	6	2	5	6	1-0	0	2.70
Totals	**4**	**4**	**0**	**36**	**30**	**8**	**12**	**16**	**4-0**	**2**	**2.00**

New York Yankees	G	GS	CG	IP	H	ER	BB	SO	W-L	Sv	ERA
Doyle Alexander	1	1	0	6	9	5	2	1	0-1	0	7.50
Dock Ellis	1	1	0	3 1/3	7	4	0	1	0-1	0	10.80
Ed Figueroa	1	1	0	8	6	5	5	2	0-1	0	5.63
Jim "Catfish" Hunter	1	1	1	8 2/3	10	3	4	5	0-1	0	3.12
Grant Jackson	1	0	0	3 2/3	4	2	0	3	0-0	0	4.91
Sparky Lyle	2	0	0	2 2/3	1	0	0	3	0-0	0	0.00
Dick Tidrow	2	0	0	2 1/3	5	2	1	1	0-0	0	7.71
Totals	**4**	**4**	**1**	**34 2/3**	**42**	**21**	**12**	**16**	**0-4**	**0**	**5.45**

1977 League Championship Series
NEW YORK YANKEES (3) VS. KANSAS CITY ROYALS (2)

GAME 1
Wednesday, October 5
at Yankee Stadium, New York

	1	2	3	4	5	6	7	8	9	R	H	E
Kansas City Royals	2	2	2	0	0	0	0	1	0	7	9	0
New York Yankees	0	0	2	0	0	0	0	2		2	9	0

HR - KC Al Cowens, John Mayberry, Hal McRae; NY Thurman Munson

WP - Paul Splittorff; LP - Don Gullett

GAME 2
Thursday, October 6
at Yankee Stadium, New York

	1	2	3	4	5	6	7	8	9	R	H	E
Kansas City Royals	0	0	1	0	0	1	0	0	0	2	3	1
New York Yankees	0	0	0	0	2	3	0	1	x	6	10	1

HR - NY Cliff Johnson

WP - Ron Guidry; LP - Andy Hassler

GAME 3
Friday, October 7
at Royals Stadium, Kansas City

	1	2	3	4	5	6	7	8	9	R	H	E
New York Yankees	0	0	0	0	1	0	0	0	1	2	4	1
Kansas City Royals	0	1	1	0	1	2	1	0	x	6	12	1

WP - Dennis Leonard; LP - Mike Torrez

GAME 4
Saturday, October 8
at Royals Stadium, Kansas City

	1	2	3	4	5	6	7	8	9	R	H	E
New York Yankees	1	2	1	1	0	0	0	0	1	6	13	0
Kansas City Royals	0	0	2	2	0	0	0	0	0	4	8	2

WP - Sparky Lyle; LP - Larry Gura

GAME 5
Sunday, October 9
at Royals Stadium, Kansas City

	1	2	3	4	5	6	7	8	9	R	H	E
New York Yankees	0	0	1	0	0	0	0	1	3	5	10	0
Kansas City Royals	2	0	1	0	0	0	0	0	0	3	10	1

WP - Sparky Lyle; LP - Dennis Leonard

BATTING STATISTICS

New York Yankees	G	AB	R	H	2B	3B	HR	RBI	BB	SO	SB	CS	Avg
Paul Blair	3	5	1	2	0	0	0	0	0	0	0	0	.400
Chris Chambliss	5	17	0	1	0	0	0	0	3	4	0	0	.059
Bucky Dent	5	14	1	3	1	0	0	2	1	0	0	0	.214
Reggie Jackson	5	16	1	2	0	0	1	2	2	1	0	.125
Cliff Johnson	5	15	2	6	2	0	1	2	1	2	0	0	.400
Thurman Munson	5	21	3	6	1	0	1	5	0	2	0	0	.286
Graig Nettles	5	20	1	3	0	0	0	1	0	3	0	0	.150
Lou Piniella	5	21	1	7	3	0	0	2	0	1	0	0	.333
Willie Randolph	5	18	4	5	1	0	0	2	1	0	0	0	.278
Mickey Rivers	5	23	5	9	2	0	0	2	0	2	1	0	.391
Roy White	4	5	2	2	2	0	0	1	0	0	0	.400
Totals	**5**	**175**	**21**	**46**	**12**	**0**	**2**	**17**	**9**	**16**	**2**	**0**	**.263**

Kansas City Royals	G	AB	R	H	2B	3B	HR	RBI	BB	SO	SB	CS	Avg
George Brett	5	20	2	6	0	2	0	2	1	0	0	1	.300
Al Cowens	5	19	2	5	0	0	1	5	1	3	0	1	.263
Pete LaCock	1	1	0	0	0	0	0	0	1	1	0	0	.000
Joe Lahoud	1	1	2	0	0	0	0	0	2	0	0	0	.000
John Mayberry	4	12	1	2	1	0	1	3	1	2	0	0	.167
Hal McRae	5	18	6	8	3	0	1	2	3	1	0	1	.444
Amos Otis	5	16	1	2	1	0	0	2	2	3	2	0	.125
Freddie Patek	5	18	4	7	3	1	0	5	1	2	0	0	.389
Tom Poquette	2	6	0	1	0	0	0	0	0	0	0	0	.167
Darrell Porter	5	15	3	5	0	0	0	0	3	0	0	0	.333
Cookie Rojas	1	4	0	1	0	0	0	0	0	1	1	0	.250
John Wathan	4	6	0	0	0	0	0	0	0	3	0	0	.000
Frank White	5	18	1	5	1	0	0	2	0	4	1	1	.278
Joe Zdeb	4	9	0	0	0	0	0	0	0	2	1	0	.000
Totals	**5**	**163**	**22**	**42**	**9**	**3**	**3**	**21**	**15**	**22**	**5**	**4**	**.258**

PITCHING STATISTICS

New York Yankees	G	GS	CG	IP	H	ER	BB	SO	W-L	Sv	ERA
Ed Figueroa	1	1	0	3 1/3	5	4	2	3	0-0	0	10.80
Ron Guidry	2	2	1	11 1/3	9	5	3	8	1-0	0	3.97
Don Gullett	1	1	0	2	4	4	2	0	0-1	0	18.00
Sparky Lyle	4	0	0	9 1/3	7	1	0	3	2-0	0	0.96
Dick Tidrow	2	0	0	7	6	3	3	3	0-0	0	3.86
Mike Torrez	2	1	0	11	11	5	5	5	0-1	0	4.09
Totals	**5**	**5**	**1**	**44**	**42**	**22**	**15**	**22**	**3-2**	**0**	**4.50**

Kansas City Royals	G	GS	CG	IP	H	ER	BB	SO	W-L	Sv	ERA
Doug Bird	3	0	0	2	4	0	0	1	0-0	0	0.00
Larry Gura	2	1	0	2	7	4	1	2	0-1	0	18.00
Andy Hassler	1	1	0	5 2/3	5	3	0	3	0-1	0	4.76
Dennis Leonard	2	1	1	9	5	3	2	4	1-1	0	3.00
Mark Littell	2	0	0	3	5	1	3	1	0-0	0	3.00
Steve Mingori	3	0	0	1 1/3	0	0	0	1	0-0	0	0.00
Marty Pattin	1	0	0	6	6	1	0	0	0-0	0	1.50
Paul Splittorff	2	2	0	15	14	4	3	4	1-0	0	2.40
Totals	**5**	**5**	**1**	**44**	**46**	**16**	**9**	**16**	**2-3**	**0**	**3.27**

1977 World Series

NEW YORK YANKEES (4) VS. LOS ANGELES DODGERS (2)

GAME 1
Tuesday, October 11
at Yankee Stadium, New York

	1	2	3	4	5	6	7	8	9	10	11	12	R	H	E
Los Angeles Dodgers	2	0	0	0	0	0	0	1	0	0	0	0	3	6	0
New York Yankees	1	0	0	0	0	1	0	1	0	0	0	1	4	11	0

HR - NY Willie Randolph

WP - Sparky Lyle; **LP** - Rick Rhoden

GAME 2
Wednesday, October 12
at Yankee Stadium, New York

	1	2	3	4	5	6	7	8	9	R	H	E
Los Angeles Dodgers	2	1	2	0	0	0	0	1	0	6	9	0
New York Yankees	0	0	0	1	0	0	0	0	0	1	5	0

HR - LA Ron Cey, Steve Garvey, Reggie Smith, Steve Yeager

WP - Burt Hooton; **LP** - Jim "Catfish" Hunter

GAME 3
Friday, October 14
at Dodger Stadium, Los Angeles

	1	2	3	4	5	6	7	8	9	R	H	E
New York Yankees	3	0	0	1	1	0	0	0	0	5	10	0
Los Angeles Dodgers	0	0	3	0	0	0	0	0	0	3	7	1

HR - LA Dusty Baker

WP - Mike Torrez; **LP** - Tommy John

GAME 4
Saturday, October 15
at Dodger Stadium, Los Angeles

	1	2	3	4	5	6	7	8	9	R	H	E
New York Yankees	0	3	0	0	0	1	0	0	0	4	7	0
Los Angeles Dodgers	0	0	2	0	0	0	0	0	0	2	4	0

HR - NY Reggie Jackson; LA Davey Lopes

WP - Ron Guidry; **LP** - Doug Rau

GAME 5
Sunday, October 16
at Dodger Stadium, Los Angeles

	1	2	3	4	5	8	7	8	9	R	H	E
New York Yankees	0	0	0	0	0	2	2	0	4	9	2	
Los Angeles Dodgers	1	0	0	4	3	2	0	0	x	10	13	0

HR - NY Reggie Jackson, Thurman Munson; LA Reggie Smith, Steve Yeager

WP - Don Sutton; **LP** - Don Gullett

GAME 6
Tuesday, October 18
at Yankee Stadium, New York

	1	2	3	4	5	6	7	8	9	R	H	E
Los Angeles Dodgers	2	0	1	0	0	0	0	0	1	4	9	0
New York Yankees	0	2	0	3	2	0	0	1	x	8	8	1

HR - LA Reggie Smith; NY Chris Chambliss, Reggie Jackson 3

WP - Mike Torrez; LP - Burt Hooton

BATTING STATISTICS

New York Yankees	G	AB	R	H	2B	3B	HR	RBI	BB	SO	SB	CS	BA
Paul Blair	4	4	0	1	0	0	0	1	0	0	0	0	.250
Chris Chambliss	6	24	4	7	2	0	1	4	0	2	0	0	.292
Bucky Dent	6	19	0	5	0	0	0	2	2	1	0	0	.263
Ron Guidry	1	2	0	0	0	0	0	0	0	1	0	0	.000
Don Gullett	2	2	0	0	0	0	0	0	0	2	0	0	.000
Reggie Jackson	6	20	10	9	1	0	5	8	3	4	0	0	.450
Cliff Johnson	1	1	0	0	0	0	0	0	0	0	0	0	.000
Sparky Lyle	2	2	0	0	0	0	0	0	0	2	0	0	.000
Thurman Munson	6	25	4	8	2	0	1	3	2	8	0	0	.320
Graig Nettles	6	21	1	4	1	0	0	2	2	3	0	0	.190
Lou Piniella	6	22	1	6	0	0	0	3	0	3	0	0	.273
Willie Randolph	6	25	5	4	2	0	1	1	2	2	0	0	.160
Mickey Rivers	6	27	1	6	2	0	0	1	0	2	1	0	.222
Dick Tidrow	2	1	0	0	0	0	0	0	0	1	0	0	.000
Mike Torrez	2	6	0	0	0	0	0	0	0	4	0	0	.000
Roy White	2	2	0	0	0	0	0	0	0	0	0	0	.000
George Zeber	2	2	0	0	0	0	0	0	0	2	0	0	.000
Totals	**6**	**205**	**26**	**50**	**10**	**0**	**8**	**25**	**11**	**37**	**1**	**0**	**.244**

Los Angeles Dodgers	G	AB	R	H	2B	3B	HR	RBI	BB	SO	SB	CS	BA
Dusty Baker	6	24	4	7	0	0	1	5	0	2	0	0	.292
Glenn Burke	3	5	0	1	0	0	0	0	0	1	0	0	.200
Ron Cey	6	21	2	4	1	0	1	3	3	5	0	0	.190
Vic Davalillo	3	3	0	1	0	0	0	1	0	0	0	0	.333
Steve Garvey	6	24	5	9	1	1	1	3	1	4	0	1	.375
Ed Goodson	1	1	0	0	0	0	0	0	0	1	0	0	.000
Jerry Grote	1	1	0	0	0	0	0	0	0	0	0	0	.000
Burt Hooton	2	5	0	0	0	0	0	0	0	2	0	0	.000
Tommy John	1	2	0	0	0	0	0	0	0	2	0	0	.000
Lee Lacy	4	7	1	3	0	0	0	2	1	1	0	0	.429
Rafael Landestoy	1	0	0	0	0	0	0	0	0	0	0	0	—
Davey Lopes	6	24	3	4	0	1	1	2	4	3	2	1	.167
Rick Monday	4	12	0	2	0	0	0	0	0	3	0	1	.167
Manny Mota	3	3	0	0	0	0	0	0	0	1	0	0	.000
Johnny Oates	1	1	0	0	0	0	0	0	0	0	0	0	.000
Rick Rhoden	2	2	1	1	1	0	0	0	0	0	0	0	.500
Bill Russell	6	26	3	4	0	1	0	2	1	3	0	0	.154
Reggie Smith	6	22	7	6	1	0	3	5	4	3	0	1	.273
Don Sutton	2	6	0	0	0	0	0	0	1	4	0	0	.000
Steve Yeager	6	19	2	6	1	0	2	5	1	1	0	0	.316
Totals	**6**	**208**	**28**	**48**	**5**	**3**	**9**	**28**	**16**	**36**	**2**	**4**	**.231**

PITCHING STATISTICS

New York Yankees	G	GS	CG	IP	H	ER	BB	SO	W-L	Sv	ERA
Ken Clay	2	0	0	3 2/3	2	1	1	0	0-0	0	2.45
Ron Guidry	1	1	1	9	4	2	3	7	1-0	0	2.00
Don Gullett	2	2	0	12 2/3	13	9	7	10	0-1	0	6.39
Jim "Catfish" Hunter	2	1	0	4 1/3	6	5	0	1	0-1	0	10.38
Sparky Lyle	2	0	0	4 2/3	2	1	0	2	1-0	0	1.93
Dick Tidrow	2	0	0	3 2/3	5	2	0	1	0-0	0	4.91
Mike Torrez	2	2	2	18	16	5	5	15	2-0	0	2.50
Totals	**6**	**6**	**3**	**56**	**48**	**25**	**16**	**36**	**4-2**	**0**	**4.02**

Los Angeles Dodgers	G	GS	CG	IP	H	ER	BB	SO	W-L	Sv	ERA
Mike Garman	2	0	0	4	2	0	1	3	0-0	0	0.00
Burt Hooton	2	2	1	12	8	5	2	9	1-1	0	3.75
Charlie Hough	2	0	0	5	3	1	0	5	0-0	0	1.80
Tommy John	1	1	0	6	9	4	3	7	0-1	0	6.00
Doug Rau	2	1	0	2 1/3	4	3	0	1	0-1	0	11.57
Lance Rautzhan	1	0	0	0 1/3	0	0	2	0	0-0	0	0.00
Rick Rhoden	2	0	0	7	4	2	1	5	0-1	0	2.57
Elias Sosa	2	0	0	2 1/3	3	3	1	1	0-0	0	11.57
Don Sutton	2	2	1	16	17	7	1	6	1-0	0	3.94
Totals	**6**	**6**	**2**	**55**	**50**	**25**	**11**	**37**	**2-4**	**0**	**4.09**

1978 League Championship Series

NEW YORK YANKEES (3) VS. KANSAS CITY ROYALS (1)

GAME 1

Tuesday, October 3
at Royals Stadium, Kansas City

	1	2	3	4	5	6	7	8	9	R	H	E
New York Yankees	0	1	1	0	2	0	0	3	0	7	16	0
Kansas City Royals	0	0	0	0	1	0	0	0	1	2	2	2

HR - NY Reggie Jackson

WP - Jim Beattie; LP - Dennis Leonard; Sv - Ken Clay

GAME 2

Wednesday, October 4
at Royals Stadium, Kansas City

	1	2	3	4	5	6	7	8	9	R	H	E
New York Yankees	0	0	0	0	0	0	2	2	0	4	12	1
Kansas City Royals	1	4	0	0	0	0	3	2	x	10	16	1

HR - KC Freddie Patek

WP - Larry Gura; LP - Ed Figueroa

GAME 3

Friday, October 6
at Yankee Stadium, New York

	1	2	3	4	5	6	7	8	9	R	H	E
Kansas City Royals	1	0	1	0	1	0	0	2	0	5	10	1
New York Yankees	0	1	0	2	0	1	0	2	x	6	10	0

HR - KC George Brett 3; NY Reggie Jackson, Thurman Munson

WP - Rich "Goose" Gossage; LP - Doug Bird

GAME 4

Saturday, October 7
at Yankee Stadium, New York

	1	2	3	4	5	6	7	8	9	R	H	E
Kansas City Royals	1	0	0	0	0	0	0	0	0	1	7	0
New York Yankees	0	1	0	0	0	1	0	0	x	2	4	0

HR - NY Graig Nettles, Roy White

WP - Ron Guidry; LP - Dennis Leonard; Sv - Rich "Goose" Gossage

BATTING STATISTICS

New York Yankees	G	AB	R	H	2B	3B	HR	RBI	BB	SO	SB	CS	Avg
Paul Blair	4	6	1	0	0	0	0	0	0	1	0	0	.000
Chris Chambliss	4	15	1	6	0	0	0	2	0	4	0	0	.400
Bucky Dent	4	15	0	3	0	0	0	4	0	0	0	0	.200
Brian Doyle	3	7	0	2	0	0	0	1	1	1	0	0	.286
Reggie Jackson	4	13	5	6	1	0	2	6	3	4	0	0	.462
Cliff Johnson	1	1	0	0	0	0	0	0	0	0	0	0	.000
Thurman Munson	4	18	2	5	1	0	1	2	0	0	0	0	.278
Graig Nettles	4	15	3	5	0	1	1	2	0	1	0	0	.333
Lou Piniella	4	17	2	4	0	0	0	0	0	3	0	0	.235
Mickey Rivers	4	11	0	5	0	0	0	0	2	0	0	0	.455
Fred Stanley	2	5	0	1	0	0	0	0	0	2	0	0	.200
Gary Thomasson	3	1	0	0	0	0	0	0	0	0	0	0	.000
Roy White	4	16	5	5	1	0	1	1	1	2	0	0	.313
Totals	**4**	**140**	**19**	**42**	**3**	**1**	**5**	**18**	**7**	**18**	**0**	**0**	**.300**

Kansas City Royals	G	AB	R	H	2B	3B	HR	RBI	BB	SO	SB	CS	Avg
Steve Braun	2	5	0	0	0	0	0	0	1	1	0	0	.000
George Brett	4	16	7	7	1	1	3	3	0	1	0	0	.389
Al Cowens	4	15	2	2	0	0	0	1	0	2	0	0	.133
Clint Hurdle	4	8	1	3	0	1	0	1	2	3	0	0	.375
Pete LaCock	4	11	1	4	2	1	0	1	3	1	1	0	.364
Hal McRae	4	14	0	3	0	0	0	2	2	2	1	1	.214
Amos Otis	4	14	2	6	2	0	0	1	3	5	4	0	.429
Freddie Patek	4	13	2	1	0	0	1	2	1	4	0	1	.077
Tom Poquette	1	1	0	0	0	0	0	0	0	0	0	0	.000
Darrell Porter	4	14	1	5	1	0	0	3	2	0	0	0	.357
John Wathan	1	3	0	0	0	0	0	0	0	0	0	0	.000
Frank White	4	13	1	3	0	0	0	2	0	0	0	0	.231
Willie Wilson	3	4	0	1	0	0	0	0	0	2	0	1	.250
Totals	**4**	**133**	**17**	**35**	**6**	**3**	**4**	**16**	**14**	**21**	**6**	**3**	**.263**

PITCHING STATISTICS

New York Yankees	G	GS	CG	IP	H	ER	BB	SO	W-L	Sv	ERA
Jim Beattie	1	1	0	5 1/3	2	1	5	3	1-0	0	1.69
Ken Clay	1	0	0	3 2/3	0	0	3	2	0-0	1	0.00
Ed Figueroa	1	1	0	1	5	3	0	0	0-1	0	27.00
Rich "Goose" Gossage	2	0	0	4	3	2	0	3	1-0	1	4.50
Ron Guidry	1	1	0	8	7	1	1	7	1-0	0	1.13
Jim "Catfish" Hunter	1	1	0	6	7	3	3	5	0-0	0	4.50
Sparky Lyle	1	0	0	1 1/3	3	2	0	0	0-0	0	13.50
Dick Tidrow	1	0	0	5 2/3	8	3	2	1	0-0	0	4.76
Totals	**4**	**4**	**0**	**35**	**35**	**15**	**14**	**21**	**3-1**	**2**	**3.86**

Kansas City Royals	G	GS	CG	IP	H	ER	BB	SO	W-L	Sv	ERA
Doug Bird	2	0	0	1	2	1	0	1	0-1	0	9.00
Larry Gura	1	1	0	6 1/3	8	2	2	2	1-0	0	2.84
Al Hrabosky	3	0	0	3	3	1	0	2	0-0	0	3.00
Dennis Leonard	2	2	1	12	13	5	2	11	0-2	0	3.75
Steve Mingori	1	0	0	3 2/3	5	3	3	0	0-0	0	7.36
Marty Pattin	1	0	0	0 2/3	2	2	0	0	0-0	0	27.00
Paul Splittorff	1	1	0	7 1/3	9	4	0	2	0-0	0	4.91
Totals	**4**	**4**	**1**	**34**	**42**	**18**	**7**	**18**	**1-3**	**0**	**4.76**

1978 World Series

NEW YORK YANKEES (4) VS. LOS ANGELES DODGERS (2)

GAME 1

Tuesday, October 10
at Dodger Stadium, Los Angeles

	1	2	3	4	5	6	7	8	9	R	H	E
New York Yankees	0	0	0	0	0	0	3	2	0	5	9	1
Los Angeles Dodgers	0	3	0	3	1	0	3	1	x	11	15	2

HR - NY Reggie Jackson; LA Dusty Baker, Davey Lopes 2

WP - Tommy John; LP - Ed Figueroa

GAME 2

Wednesday, October 11
at Dodger Stadium, Los Angeles

	1	2	3	4	5	6	7	8	9	R	H	E
New York Yankees	0	0	2	0	0	0	1	0	0	3	11	0
Los Angeles Dodgers	0	0	0	1	0	3	0	0	x	4	7	0

HR - LA Ron Cey

WP - Burt Hooton; LP - Jim "Catfish" Hunter; Sv - Bob Welch

GAME 3

Friday, October 13
at Yankee Stadium, New York

	1	2	3	4	5	6	7	8	9	R	H	E
Los Angeles Dodgers	0	0	1	0	0	0	0	0	0	1	8	0
New York Yankees	1	1	0	0	0	0	3	0	x	5	10	1

HR - NY Roy White

WP - Ron Guidry; LP - Don Sutton

GAME 4

Saturday, October 14
at Yankee Stadium, New York

	1	2	3	4	5	6	7	8	9	10	R	H	E
Los Angeles Dodgers	0	0	0	0	3	0	0	0	0	0	3	6	1
New York Yankees	0	0	0	0	0	2	0	1	0	1	4	9	0

HR - LA Reggie Smith

WP - Rich "Goose" Gossage; LP - Bob Welch

GAME 5

Sunday, October 15
at Yankee Stadium, New York

	1	2	3	4	5	6	7	8	9	R	H	E
Los Angeles Dodgers	1	0	1	0	0	0	0	0	0	2	9	3
New York Yankees	0	0	4	3	0	0	4	1	x	12	18	0

WP - Jim Beattie; LP - Burt Hooton

GAME 6

Tuesday, October 17
at Dodger Stadium, Los Angeles

	1	2	3	4	5	6	7	8	9	R	H	E
New York Yankees	0	3	0	0	0	2	2	0	0	7	11	0
Los Angeles Dodgers	1	0	1	0	0	0	0	0	0	2	7	1

HR - NY Reggie Jackson; LA Davey Lopes

WP - Jim "Catfish" Hunter; LP - Don Sutton

BATTING STATISTICS

New York Yankees	G	AB	R	H	2B	3B	HR	RBI	BB	SO	SB	CS	BA
Paul Blair	6	8	2	3	1	0	0	0	1	4	0	0	.375
Chris Chambliss	3	11	1	2	0	0	0	0	1	1	0	0	.182
Bucky Dent	6	24	3	10	1	0	0	7	1	2	0	0	.417
Brian Doyle	6	16	4	7	1	0	0	2	0	0	0	0	.438
Reggie Jackson	6	23	2	9	1	0	2	8	3	7	0	0	.391
Cliff Johnson	2	2	0	0	0	0	0	0	0	1	0	0	.000
Thurman Munson	6	25	5	8	3	0	0	7	3	7	1	0	.320
Graig Nettles	6	25	2	4	0	0	0	1	0	6	0	0	.160
Lou Piniella	6	25	3	7	0	0	0	4	0	1	0	0	.280
Mickey Rivers	5	18	2	6	0	0	0	1	0	2	1	1	.333
Jim Spencer	4	12	3	2	0	0	0	0	2	4	0	0	.167
Fred Stanley	3	5	0	1	1	0	0	0	1	0	0	0	.200
Gary Thomasson	3	4	0	1	0	0	0	0	0	1	0	0	.250
Roy White	6	24	9	8	0	0	1	4	4	5	2	0	.333
Totals	**6**	**222**	**36**	**68**	**8**	**0**	**3**	**34**	**16**	**40**	**5**	**2**	**.306**

Los Angeles Dodgers	G	AB	R	H	2B	3B	HR	RBI	BB	SO	SB	CS	BA
Dusty Baker	6	21	2	5	0	0	1	1	1	3	0	0	.238
Ron Cey	6	21	2	6	0	0	1	4	3	3	0	0	.286
Vic Davalillo	2	3	0	1	0	0	0	0	0	0	0	0	.333
Joe Ferguson	2	4	1	2	2	0	0	0	0	1	0	0	.500
Steve Garvey	6	24	1	5	1	0	0	0	1	7	1	0	.208
Lee Lacy	4	14	0	2	0	0	0	1	1	3	0	0	.143
Davey Lopes	6	26	7	8	0	0	3	7	2	1	2	0	.308
Rick Monday	5	13	2	2	1	0	0	0	4	3	0	1	.154
Manny Mota	1	0	0	0	0	0	0	0	1	0	0	0	—
Bill North	4	8	2	1	1	0	0	2	1	0	1	0	.125
Johnny Oates	1	1	0	1	0	0	0	0	1	0	0	0	1.000
Bill Russell	6	26	1	11	2	0	0	2	2	2	1	2	.423
Reggie Smith	6	25	3	5	0	0	1	5	2	6	0	1	.200
Steve Yeager	5	13	2	3	1	0	0	0	1	2	0	0	.231
Totals	**6**	**199**	**23**	**52**	**8**	**0**	**6**	**22**	**20**	**31**	**5**	**4**	**.261**

PITCHING STATISTICS

New York Yankees	G	GS	CG	IP	H	ER	BB	SO	W-L	Sv	ERA
Jim Beattie	1	1	1	9	9	2	4	8	1-0	0	2.00
Ken Clay	1	0	0	2 1/3	4	3	2	2	0-0	0	11.57
Ed Figueroa	2	2	0	6 2/3	9	6	5	2	0-1	0	8.10
Rich "Goose" Gossage	3	0	0	6	1	0	1	4	1-0	0	0.00
Ron Guidry	1	1	1	9	8	1	7	4	1-0	0	1.00
Jim "Catfish" Hunter	2	2	0	13	13	6	1	5	1-1	0	4.15
Paul Lindblad	1	0	0	2 1/3	4	3	0	1	0-0	0	11.57
Dick Tidrow	2	0	0	4 2/3	4	1	0	5	0-0	0	1.93
Totals	6	6	2	53	52	22	20	31	4-2	0	3.74
Los Angeles Dodgers	G	GS	CG	IP	H	ER	BB	SO	W-L	Sv	ERA
Terry Forster	3	0	0	4	5	0	1	6	0-0	0	0.00
Burt Hooton	2	2	0	8 1/3	13	6	3	6	1-1	0	6.48
Charlie Hough	2	0	0	5 1/3	10	5	2	5	0-0	0	8.44
Tommy John	2	2	0	14 2/3	14	5	4	6	1-0	0	3.07
Doug Rau	1	0	0	2	1	0	0	3	0-0	0	0.00
Lance Rautzhan	2	0	0	2	4	3	0	0	0-0	0	13.50
Don Sutton	2	2	0	12	17	10	4	8	0-2	0	7.50
Bob Welch	3	0	0	4 1/3	4	3	2	6	0-1	1	6.23
Totals	6	6	0	52 2/3	68	32	16	40	2-4	1	5.47

1980 League Championship Series
KANSAS CITY ROYALS (3) VS. NEW YORK YANKEES

GAME 1
Wednesday, October 8
at Royals Stadium, Kansas City

	1	2	3	4	5	6	7	8	9	R	H	E
New York Yankees	0	2	0	0	0	0	0	0	0	2	10	1
Kansas City Royals	0	2	2	0	0	0	1	2	x	7	10	0

HR - NY Rick Cerone, Lou Piniella; KC George Brett

WP - Larry Gura; **LP** - Ron Guidry

GAME 2
Thursday, October 9
at Royals Stadium, Kansas City

	1	2	3	4	5	6	7	8	9	R	H	E
New York Yankees	0	0	0	0	2	0	0	0	0	2	8	0
Kansas City Royals	0	0	3	0	0	0	0	0	x	3	6	0

HR - NY Graig Nettles

WP - Dennis Leonard; **LP** - Rudy May; **Sv** - Dan Quisenberry

GAME 3
Friday, October 10
at Yankee Stadium, New York

	1	2	3	4	5	6	7	8	9	R	H	E
Kansas City Royals	0	0	0	0	1	0	3	0	0	4	12	1
New York Yankees	0	0	0	0	2	0	0	0	2	8	0

HR - KC George Brett, Roy White

WP - Dan Quisenberry; **LP** - Rich "Goose" Gossage

BATTING STATISTICS

Kansas City Royals	G	AB	R	H	2B	3B	HR	RBI	BB	SO	SB	CS	Avg
Willie Aikens	3	11	0	4	0	0	0	2	0	1	0	0	.364
George Brett	3	11	3	3	1	0	2	4	1	0	0	0	.273
Clint Hurdle	3	2	0	0	0	0	0	0	0	1	0	0	.000
Hal McRae	3	10	0	2	0	0	0	0	1	3	0	3	.200
Amos Otis	3	12	2	4	1	0	0	0	0	3	2	1	.333
Darrell Porter	3	10	2	1	0	0	0	0	1	0	0	0	.100
U.L. Washington	3	11	1	4	1	0	0	1	2	3	0	1	.364
John Wathan	3	6	1	0	0	0	0	0	3	1	0	0	.000
Frank White	3	11	3	6	1	0	1	3	0	1	1	0	.545
Willie Wilson	3	13	2	4	2	1	0	4	1	2	0	0	.308
Totals	3	97	14	28	6	1	3	14	9	15	3	5	.289

New York Yankees	G	AB	R	H	2B	3B	HR	RBI	BB	SO	SB	CS	Avg
Bobby Brown	3	10	1	0	0	0	0	0	1	2	0	0	.000
Rick Cerone	3	12	1	4	0	0	1	2	0	1	0	0	.333
Bucky Dent	3	11	0	2	0	0	0	0	0	1	0	0	.182
Oscar Gamble	2	5	1	1	0	0	0	0	1	1	0	0	.200
Reggie Jackson	3	11	1	3	1	0	0	0	1	4	0	0	.273
Bobby Murcer	1	4	0	0	0	0	0	0	0	2	0	0	.000
Graig Nettles	2	6	1	1	0	0	1	1	0	1	0	0	.167
Lou Piniella	2	5	1	1	0	0	1	1	2	1	0	0	.200
Willie Randolph	3	13	0	5	2	0	0	1	1	3	0	0	.385
Aurelio Rodriguez	2	6	0	2	1	0	0	0	0	0	0	0	.333
Eric Soderholm	2	6	0	1	0	0	0	0	0	0	0	0	.167
Jim Spencer	1	1	0	0	0	0	0	0	0	0	0	0	.000
Bob Watson	3	12	0	6	3	1	0	0	0	0	0	0	.500
Totals	**3**	**102**	**6**	**26**	**7**	**1**	**3**	**5**	**6**	**16**	**0**	**0**	**.255**

PITCHING STATISTICS

Kansas City Royals	G	GS	CG	IP	H	ER	BB	SO	W-L	Sv	ERA
Larry Gura	1	1	1	9	10	2	1	4	1-0	0	2.00
Dennis Leonard	1	1	0	8	7	2	1	8	1-0	0	2.25
Dan Quisenberry	2	0	0	4 2/3	4	0	2	1	1-0	1	0.00
Paul Splittorff	1	1	0	5 1/3	5	1	2	3	0-0	0	1.69
Totals	**3**	**3**	**1**	**27**	**26**	**6**	**6**	**16**	**3-0**	**1**	**1.67**

New York Yankees	G	GS	CG	IP	H	ER	BB	SO	W-L	Sv	ERA
Ron Davis	1	0	0	4	3	1	1	3	0-0	0	2.25
Rich "Goose" Gossage	1	0	0	0 1/3	3	2	0	0	0-1	0	54.00
Ron Guidry	1	1	0	3	5	4	4	2	0-1	0	12.00
Tommy John	1	1	0	6 2/3	8	2	1	3	0-0	0	2.70
Rudy May	1	1	1	8	6	3	3	4	0-1	0	3.38
Tom Underwood	2	0	0	3	3	0	0	3	0-0	0	0.00
Totals	**3**	**3**	**1**	**25**	**28**	**12**	**9**	**15**	**0-3**	**0**	**4.32**

1981 League Divisional Series
NEW YORK YANKEES (3) VS. MILWAUKEE BREWERS (2)

GAME 1
Wednesday, October 7
at County Stadium, Milwaukee

	1	2	3	4	5	6	7	8	9	R	H	E
New York Yankees	0	0	4	0	0	0	0	1		5	13	1
Milwaukee Brewers	0	1	1	0	1	0	0	0	0	3	8	3

HR - NY Oscar Gamble

WP - Ron Davis; **LP -** Moose Haas; **Sv -** Rich "Goose" Gossage

GAME 2
Thursday, October 8
at County Stadium, Milwaukee

	1	2	3	4	5	6	7	8	9	R	H	E
New York Yankees	0	0	0	1	0	0	0	0	2	3	7	0
Milwaukee Brewers	0	0	0	0	0	0	0	0	0	0	7	0

HR - NY Reggie Jackson, Lou Piniella

WP - Dave Righetti; **LP -** Mike Caldwell; **Sv -** Rich "Goose" Gossage

GAME 3
Friday, October 9
at Yankee Stadium, New York

	1	2	3	4	5	6	7	8	9	R	H	E
Milwaukee Brewers	0	0	0	0	0	3	2	0		5	9	0
New York Yankees	0	0	0	1	0	0	2	0	0	3	8	2

HR - MIL Paul Molitor, Ted Simmons

WP - Rollie Fingers; **LP -** Tommy John

GAME 4
Saturday, October 10
at Yankee Stadium, New York

	1	2	3	4	5	6	7	8	9	R	H	E
Milwaukee Brewers	0	0	0	2	0	0	0	0	0	2	4	2
New York Yankees	0	0	0	0	0	1	0	0	0	1	5	0

WP - Pete Vuckovich; **LP -** Rick Reuschel; **Sv -** Rollie Fingers

GAME 5
Sunday, October 11
at Yankee Stadium, New York

	1	2	3	4	5	6	7	8	9	R	H	E
Milwaukee Brewers	0	1	1	0	0	0	1	0	0	3	8	0
New York Yankees	0	0	0	4	0	0	1	2	x	7	13	0

HR - MIL Gorman Thomas; NY Rick Cerone, Oscar Gamble, Reggie Jackson

WP - Dave Righetti; **LP -** Moose Haas; **Sv -** Rich "Goose" Gossage

BATTING STATISTICS

New York Yankees	G	AB	R	H	2B	3B	HR	RBI	BB	SO	SB	CS	Avg
Bobby Brown	1	0	0	0	0	0	0	0	0	0	0	0	—
Rick Cerone	5	18	1	6	2	0	1	5	0	2	0	0	.333
Barry Foote	1	0	0	0	0	0	0	0	0	0	0	0	—
Oscar Gamble	4	9	2	5	1	0	2	3	1	2	0	0	.556
Reggie Jackson	5	20	4	6	0	0	2	4	1	5	0	0	.300
Larry Milbourne	5	19	4	6	1	0	0	0	0	1	0	0	.316
Jerry Mumphrey	5	21	2	2	0	0	0	0	0	1	1	1	.095
Bobby Murcer	2	1	0	0	0	0	0	0	1	0	0	0	.000
Graig Nettles	5	17	1	1	0	0	0	1	3	1	0	1	.059
Lou Piniella	4	10	1	2	1	0	1	3	0	0	0	0	.200
Willie Randolph	5	20	0	4	0	0	1	1	4	0	0	0	.200
Bob Watson	5	16	2	7	0	0	0	1	1	1	0	0	.438
Dave Winfield	5	20	2	7	3	0	0	0	1	5	0	0	.350
Totals	**5**	**171**	**19**	**46**	**8**	**0**	**6**	**18**	**9**	**22**	**1**	**2**	**.269**

Milwaukee Brewers	G	AB	R	H	2B	3B	HR	RBI	BB	SO	SB	CS	Avg
Sal Bando	5	17	1	5	3	0	0	1	2	3	0	1	.294
Thad Bosley	1	0	0	0	0	0	0	0	0	0	0	0	—
Cecil Cooper	5	18	1	4	0	0	0	3	1	3	0	0	.222
Marshall Edwards	2	1	0	0	0	0	0	0	0	1	0	0	.000
Jim Gantner	4	14	1	2	1	0	0	0	0	2	0	0	.143
Roy Howell	4	5	0	2	0	0	0	0	2	2	0	1	.400
Paul Molitor	5	20	2	5	0	0	1	1	2	5	0	0	.250
Don Money	2	3	0	0	0	0	0	0	0	0	0	0	.000
Charlie Moore	4	9	0	2	0	0	0	1	1	2	0	0	.222
Ben Oglivie	5	18	0	3	1	0	0	1	0	7	0	0	.167
Ed Romero	1	2	1	1	0	0	0	0	0	1	0	0	.500
Ted Simmons	5	18	1	4	1	0	1	4	2	2	0	0	.222
Gorman Thomas	5	18	2	2	0	0	0	1	1	9	0	0	.111
Robin Yount	5	19	4	6	0	1	0	1	2	2	1	0	.316
Totals	**5**	**162**	**13**	**36**	**6**	**1**	**3**	**13**	**13**	**39**	**1**	**2**	**.222**

PITCHING STATISTICS

New York Yankees	G	GS	CG	IP	H	ER	BB	SO	W-L	Sv	ERA
Ron Davis	3	0	0	6	1	0	2	6	1-0	0	0.00
Rich "Goose" Gossage	3	0	0	6 2/3	3	0	2	8	0-0	3	0.00
Ron Guidry	2	2	0	8 1/3	11	5	3	8	0-0	0	5.40
Tommy John	1	1	0	7	8	5	2	0	0-1	0	6.43
Rudy May	1	0	0	2	1	0	0	1	0-0	0	0.00
Rick Reuschel	1	1	0	6	4	2	1	3	0-1	0	3.00
Dave Righetti	2	1	0	9	8	1	3	13	2-0	0	1.00
Totals	**5**	**5**	**0**	**45**	**36**	**13**	**13**	**39**	**3-2**	**3**	**2.60**

Milwaukee Brewers	G	GS	CG	IP	H	ER	BB	SO	W-L	Sv	ERA
Dwight Bernard	2	0	0	2 1/3	0	0	0	0	0-0	0	0.00
Mike Caldwell	2	1	0	8 1/3	9	4	0	4	0-1	0	4.32
Jamie Easterly	2	0	0	1 1/3	2	1	0	1	0-0	0	6.75
Rollie Fingers	3	0	0	4 2/3	7	2	1	5	1-0	1	3.86
Moose Haas	2	2	0	6 2/3	13	7	1	1	0-2	0	9.45
Randy Lerch	1	1	0	6	3	1	4	3	0-0	0	1.50
Bob McClure	3	0	0	3 1/3	4	0	0	2	0-0	0	0.00
Jim Slaton	4	0	0	6	6	2	0	2	0-0	0	3.00
Pete Vuckovich	2	1	0	5 1/3	2	0	3	4	1-0	0	0.00
Totals	**5**	**5**	**0**	**44**	**46**	**17**	**9**	**22**	**2-3**	**1**	**3.48**

1981 League Championship Series

NEW YORK YANKEES (3) VS. OAKLAND A'S (0)

GAME 1
Tuesday, October 13
at Yankee Stadium, New York

	1	2	3	4	5	6	7	8	9	R	H	E
Oakland A's	0	0	0	0	1	0	0	0	0	1	6	1
New York Yankees	3	0	0	0	0	0	0	0	x	3	7	1

WP - Tommy John; LP - Mike Norris; Sv - Rich "Goose" Gossage

GAME 2
Wednesday, October 14
at Yankee Stadium, New York

	1	2	3	4	5	6	7	8	9	R	H	E
Oakland A's	0	0	1	2	0	0	0	0	0	3	11	1
New York Yankees	1	0	0	7	0	1	4	0	x	13	19	0

HR - NY Graig Nettles, Lou Piniella

WP - George Frazier; LP - Steve McCatty

GAME 3
Thursday, October 15
at Oakland-Alameda County Coliseum, Oakland

	1	2	3	4	5	6	7	8	9	R	H	E
New York Yankees	0	0	0	0	1	0	0	3	4	10	0	
Oakland A's	0	0	0	0	0	0	0	0	0	5	2	

HR - NY Willie Randolph

WP - Dave Righetti; LP - Matt Keough

BATTING STATISTICS

New York Yankees	G	AB	R	H	2B	3B	HR	RBI	BB	SO	SB	CS	Avg
Bobby Brown	3	1	2	1	0	0	0	0	0	0	0	0	1.000
Rick Cerone	3	10	1	1	0	0	0	0	0	0	0	0	.100
Barry Foote	2	1	0	1	0	0	0	0	0	0	0	0	1.000
Oscar Gamble	3	6	2	1	0	0	0	1	5	3	0	0	.167
Reggie Jackson	2	4	1	0	0	0	0	1	1	0	1	0	.000
Larry Milbourne	3	13	4	6	0	0	0	1	0	0	0	0	.462
Jerry Mumphrey	3	12	2	6	1	0	0	3	2	0	1	.500
Bobby Murcer	1	3	0	1	0	0	0	0	1	1	0	0	.333
Graig Nettles	3	12	2	6	2	0	1	9	1	0	0	0	.500
Lou Piniella	3	5	2	3	0	0	1	3	0	0	0	0	.600
Willie Randolph	3	12	2	4	0	0	1	2	0	1	0	0	.333
Dave Revering	2	2	0	1	0	0	0	0	0	0	0	0	.500
Andre Robertson	1	1	0	0	0	0	0	0	0	0	0	0	.000
Bob Watson	3	12	0	3	0	0	0	1	0	1	0	0	.250
Dave Winfield	3	13	2	2	1	0	0	2	2	2	1	0	.154
Totals	**3**	**107**	**20**	**36**	**4**	**0**	**3**	**20**	**13**	**10**	**2**	**1**	**.336**

Oakland A's	G	AB	R	H	2B	3B	HR	RBI	BB	SO	SB	CS	Avg
Tony Armas	3	12	0	2	0	0	0	0	0	5	0	0	.167
Rick Bosetti	2	4	1	1	1	0	0	0	0	1	0	0	.250
Mike Davis	1	1	0	1	0	0	0	0	0	0	0	0	1.000
Keith Drumright	3	4	0	0	0	0	0	0	1	0	0	0	.000
Wayne Gross	3	5	0	0	0	0	0	0	0	0	0	0	.000
Mike Heath	3	6	1	2	0	0	0	0	0	1	0	0	.333
Rickey Henderson	3	11	0	4	2	1	0	1	1	2	2	0	.364
Cliff Johnson	2	6	0	0	0	0	0	0	2	2	0	0	.000
Mickey Klutts	3	7	1	3	0	0	0	0	0	1	0	0	.429
Dave McKay	3	11	0	3	0	0	0	1	0	2	0	0	.273
Kelvin Moore	3	8	0	2	0	0	0	0	0	1	0	0	.250
Dwayne Murphy	3	8	0	2	1	0	0	1	2	3	0	0	.250
Jeff Newman	2	5	0	0	0	0	0	0	0	2	0	0	.000
Rob Picciolo	2	5	1	1	0	0	0	0	0	2	0	0	.200
Jim Spencer	2	3	0	0	0	0	0	0	0	0	0	0	.000
Fred Stanley	2	3	0	1	0	0	0	1	0	1	0	0	.333
Totals	**3**	**99**	**4**	**22**	**4**	**1**	**0**	**4**	**6**	**23**	**2**	**0**	**.222**

PITCHING STATISTICS

New York Yankees	G	GS	CG	IP	H	ER	BB	SO	W-L	Sv	ERA
Ron Davis	2	0	0	3 1/3	0	0	2	4	0-0	0	0.00
George Frazier	1	0	0	5 2/3	5	0	1	5	1-0	0	0.00
Rich "Goose" Gossage	2	0	0	2 2/3	1	0	0	2	0-0	1	0.00
Tommy John	1	1	0	6	6	1	1	3	1-0	0	1.50
Rudy May	1	0	0	3 1/3	6	3	0	5	0-0	0	8.10
Dave Righetti	1	1	0	6	4	0	2	4	1-0	0	0.00
Totals	**3**	**2**	**0**	**27**	**22**	**4**	**6**	**23**	**3-0**	**1**	**1.33**

Oakland A's	G	GS	CG	IP	H	ER	BB	SO	W-L	Sv	ERA
Dave Beard	1	0	0	0 2/3	5	3	0	0	0-0	0	40.50
Jeff Jones	1	0	0	2	2	1	1	0	0-0	0	4.50
Matt Keough	1	1	0	8 1/3	7	1	6	4	0-1	0	1.08
Brian Kingman	1	0	0	0 1/3	3	3	0	0	0-0	0	81.00
Steve McCatty	1	1	0	3 1/3	6	5	2	2	0-1	0	13.50
Mike Norris	1	1	0	7 1/3	6	3	2	4	0-1	0	3.68
Bob Owchinko	1	0	0	1 2/3	3	1	0	0	0-0	0	5.40
Tom Underwood	2	0	0	1 1/3	4	2	2	0	0-0	0	13.50
Totals	**3**	**3**	**0**	**25**	**36**	**19**	**13**	**10**	**0-3**	**0**	**6.84**

1981 World Series

LOS ANGELES DODGERS (4) VS. NEW YORK YANKEES (2)

GAME 1
Tuesday, October 20
at Yankee Stadium, New York

	1	2	3	4	5	6	7	8	9	R	H	E
Los Angeles Dodgers	0	0	0	0	1	0	0	2	0	3	5	0
New York Yankees	3	0	1	1	0	0	0	0	x	5	6	0

HR - LA Steve Yeager; NY Bob Watson

WP - Ron Guidry; LP - Jerry Reuss; Sv - Rich "Goose" Gossage

GAME 2
Wednesday, October 21
at Yankee Stadium, New York

	1	2	3	4	5	6	7	8	9	R	H	E
Los Angeles Dodgers	0	0	0	0	0	0	0	0	0	0	4	2
New York Yankees	0	0	0	0	1	0	0	2	x	3	6	1

WP - Tommy John; LP - Burt Hooton; Sv - Rich "Goose" Gossage

GAME 3
Friday, October 23
at Dodger Stadium, Los Angeles

	1	2	3	4	5	6	7	8	9	R	H	E
New York Yankees	0	2	2	0	0	0	0	0	0	4	9	0
Los Angeles Dodgers	3	0	0	0	2	0	0	0	x	5	11	1

HR - NY Rick Cerone, Bob Watson; LA Ron Cey

WP - Fernando Valenzuela; LP - George Frazier

GAME 4
Saturday, October 24
at Dodger Stadium, Los Angeles

	1	2	3	4	5	6	7	8	9	R	H	E
New York Yankees	2	1	1	0	0	2	0	1	0	7	13	1
Los Angeles Dodgers	0	0	2	0	1	3	2	0	x	8	14	2

HR - NY Reggie Jackson, Willie Randolph; LA Jay Johnstone

WP - Steve Howe; LP - George Frazier

GAME 5
Sunday, October 25
at Dodger Stadium, Los Angeles

	1	2	3	4	5	6	7	8	9	R	H	E
New York Yankees	0	1	0	0	0	0	0	0	0	1	5	0
Los Angeles Dodgers	0	0	0	0	0	0	2	0	x	2	4	3

HR - LA Pedro Guerrero, Steve Yeager

WP - Jerry Reuss; LP - Ron Guidry

GAME 6
Wednesday, October 28
at Yankee Stadium, New York

	1	2	3	4	5	6	7	8	9	R	H	E
Los Angeles Dodgers	0	0	0	1	3	4	0	1	0	9	13	1
New York Yankees	0	0	1	0	0	1	0	0	0	2	7	2

HR - LA Pedro Guerrero; NY Willie Randolph

WP - Burt Hooton; LP - George Frazier; Sv - Steve Howe

BATTING STATISTICS

Los Angeles Dodgers	G	AB	R	H	2B	3B	HR	RBI	BB	SO	SB	CS	BA
Dusty Baker	6	24	3	4	0	0	0	1	1	6	0	0	.167
Ron Cey	6	20	3	7	0	0	1	6	3	3	0	0	.350
Steve Garvey	6	24	3	10	1	0	0	0	2	5	0	0	.417
Pedro Guerrero	6	21	2	7	1	1	2	7	2	6	0	0	.333
Burt Hooton	2	4	1	0	0	0	0	0	1	3	0	0	.000
Steve Howe	3	2	0	0	0	0	0	0	0	2	0	0	.000
Jay Johnstone	3	3	1	2	0	0	1	3	0	0	0	0	.667
Ken Landreaux	5	6	1	1	1	0	0	0	0	2	1	0	.167
Davey Lopes	6	22	6	5	1	0	0	2	4	3	4	0	.227
Rick Monday	5	13	1	3	1	0	0	0	3	6	0	0	.231
Jerry Reuss	2	3	0	0	0	0	0	0	1	2	0	0	.000
Bill Russell	6	25	1	6	0	0	0	2	0	1	1	1	.240
Steve Sax	2	1	0	0	0	0	0	0	0	0	0	0	.000
Mike Scioscia	3	4	1	1	0	0	0	0	1	0	0	0	.250
Reggie Smith	2	2	0	1	0	0	0	0	0	1	0	0	.500
Derrel Thomas	5	7	2	0	0	0	0	1	1	2	0	0	.000
Fernando Valenzuela	1	3	0	0	0	0	0	0	0	1	0	0	.000
Steve Yeager	6	14	2	4	1	0	2	4	0	2	0	0	.286
Totals	**6**	**198**	**27**	**51**	**6**	**1**	**6**	**26**	**20**	**44**	**6**	**1**	**.258**

New York Yankees	G	AB	R	H	2B	3B	HR	RBI	BB	SO	SB	CS	BA
Bobby Brown	4	1	1	0	0	0	0	0	0	1	0	0	.000
Rick Cerone	6	21	2	4	1	0	1	3	4	2	0	0	.190
Barry Foote	1	1	0	0	0	0	0	0	0	1	0	0	.000
George Frazier	3	2	0	0	0	0	0	0	0	1	0	0	.000
Oscar Gamble	3	6	1	2	0	0	1	1	0	0	0	0	.333
Rich Gossage	3	1	0	0	0	0	0	0	0	1	0	0	.000
Ron Guidry	2	5	0	0	0	0	0	0	0	3	0	0	.000
Reggie Jackson	3	12	3	4	1	0	1	1	2	3	0	0	.333
Tommy John	3	2	0	0	0	0	0	0	0	0	0	0	.000
Rudy May	3	1	0	0	0	0	0	0	0	0	0	0	.000
Larry Milbourne	6	20	2	5	2	0	0	3	4	0	0	0	.250
Jerry Mumphrey	5	15	2	3	0	0	0	0	3	2	1	0	.200
Bobby Murcer	4	3	0	0	0	0	0	0	0	0	0	0	.000
Graig Nettles	3	10	1	4	1	0	0	0	1	1	0	0	.400
Lou Piniella	6	16	2	7	1	0	0	3	0	1	1	0	.438
Willie Randolph	6	18	5	4	1	1	2	3	9	0	1	1	.222
Rick Reuschel	2	2	0	0	0	0	0	0	0	1	0	0	.000
Dave Righetti	1	1	0	0	0	0	0	0	0	1	0	0	.000
Andre Robertson	1	0	0	0	0	0	0	0	0	0	0	0	—
Aurelio Rodriguez	4	12	1	5	0	0	0	0	1	2	0	0	.417
Bob Watson	6	22	2	7	1	0	2	7	3	0	0	0	.318
Dave Winfield	6	22	0	1	0	0	0	1	5	4	1	0	.045
Totals	**6**	**193**	**22**	**46**	**8**	**1**	**6**	**22**	**33**	**24**	**4**	**1**	**.238**

PITCHING STATISTICS

Los Angeles Dodgers	G	GS	CG	IP	H	ER	BB	SO	W-L	Sv	ERA
Bobby Castillo	1	0	0	1	0	1	5	0	0-0	0	9.00
Terry Forster	2	0	0	2	1	0	3	0	0-0	0	0.00
Dave Goltz	2	0	0	3 1/3	4	2	1	2	0-0	0	5.40
Burt Hooton	2	2	0	11 1/3	8	2	9	3	1-1	0	1.59
Steve Howe	3	0	0	7	7	3	1	4	1-0	1	3.86
Tom Niedenfuer	2	0	0	5	3	0	1	0	0-0	0	0.00
Jerry Reuss	2	2	1	11 2/3	10	5	3	8	1-1	0	3.86
Dave Stewart	2	0	0	1 2/3	1	0	2	1	0-0	0	0.00
Fernando Valenzuela	1	1	1	9	9	4	7	6	1-0	0	4.00
Bob Welch	1	1	0	0	3	2	1	0	0-0	0	∞
Totals	**6**	**6**	**2**	**52**	**46**	**19**	**33**	**24**	**4-2**	**1**	**3.29**

New York Yankees	G	GS	CG	IP	H	ER	BB	SO	W-L	Sv	ERA
Ron Davis	4	0	0	2 1/3	4	6	5	4	0-0	0	23.14
George Frazier	3	0	0	3 2/3	9	7	3	2	0-3	0	17.18
Rich "Goose" Gossage	3	0	0	5	2	0	2	5	0-0	2	0.00
Ron Guidry	2	2	0	14	8	3	4	15	1-1	0	1.93
Tommy John	3	2	0	13	11	1	0	8	1-0	0	0.69
Dave LaRoche	1	0	0	1	0	0	0	2	0-0	0	0.00
Rudy May	3	0	0	6 1/3	5	2	1	5	0-0	0	2.84
Rick Reuschel	2	1	0	3 2/3	7	2	3	2	0-0	0	4.91
Dave Righetti	1	1	0	2	5	3	2	1	0-0	0	13.50
Totals	**6**	**6**	**0**	**51**	**51**	**24**	**20**	**44**	**2-4**	**2**	**4.24**

1995 League Divisional Series

SEATTLE MARINERS (3) VS. NEW YORK YANKEES (2)

GAME 1

Tuesday, October 3
at Yankee Stadium, New York

	1	2	3	4	5	6	7	8	9	R	H	E
Seattle Mariners	0	0	0	1	0	1	2	0	2	6	9	0
New York Yankees	0	0	2	0	0	2	4	1	x	9	13	0

HR - SEA Ken Griffey Jr. 2; NY Wade Boggs, Ruben Sierra

WP - David Cone; LP - Jeff Nelson

GAME 2

Wednesday, October 4
at Yankee Stadium, New York

	1	2	3	4	5	6	7	8	9	10	11	12	13	R	H	E
Seattle Mariners	0	0	1	0	0	1	2	0	0	0	0	1	0	5	16	2
New York Yankees	0	0	0	0	1	2	1	0	0	0	0	1	0	7	11	0

HR - SEA Vince Coleman, Ken Griffey Jr.; NY Jim Leyritz, Don Mattingly, Paul O'Neill, Ruben Sierra

WP - Mariano Rivera; LP - Tim Belcher

GAME 3

Friday, October 6
at the Kingdome, Seattle

	1	2	3	4	5	6	7	8	9	R	H	E
New York Yankees	0	0	0	1	0	0	1	2	0	4	6	2
Seattle Mariners	0	0	0	0	2	4	1	0	x	7	7	0

HR - NY Mike Stanley, Bernie Williams 2; SEA Tino Martinez

WP - Randy Johnson; LP - Jack McDowell; Sv - Norm Charlton

GAME 4

Saturday, October 7
at the Kingdome, Seattle

	1	2	3	4	5	6	7	8	9	R	H	E
New York Yankees	3	0	2	0	0	0	0	1	2	8	14	1
Seattle Mariners	0	0	4	0	1	1	0	5	x	11	16	0

HR - NY Paul O'Neill; SEA Jay Buhner, Ken Griffey Jr., Edgar Martinez 2

WP - Norm Charlton; LP - John Wetteland; Sv - Bill Risley

GAME 5

Sunday, October 8
at the Kingdome, Seattle

	1	2	3	4	5	6	7	8	9	10	11	R	H	E
New York Yankees	0	0	0	2	0	2	0	0	0	0	1	5	6	0
Seattle Mariners	0	0	1	1	0	0	0	2	0	0	2	6	15	0

HR - NY Paul O'Neill; SEA Joey Cora, Ken Griffey Jr.

WP - Randy Johnson; LP - Jack McDowell

BATTING STATISTICS

Seattle Mariners	G	AB	R	H	2B	3B	HR	RBI	BB	SO	SB	CS	Avg
Mike Blowers	5	18	0	3	0	0	0	1	3	7	0	0	.167
Jay Buhner	5	24	2	11	1	0	1	3	2	4	0	1	.458
Vince Coleman	5	23	6	5	0	1	1	1	2	4	1	0	.217
Joey Cora	5	19	7	6	1	0	1	1	3	0	1	0	.316
Alex Diaz	2	3	0	1	0	0	0	0	1	1	0	0	.333
Felix Fermin	3	1	0	0	0	0	0	0	0	1	0	0	.000
Ken Griffey Jr.	5	23	9	9	0	0	5	7	2	4	1	0	.391
Edgar Martinez	5	21	6	12	3	0	2	10	6	2	0	0	.571
Tino Martinez	5	22	4	9	1	0	1	5	3	4	0	1	.409
Warren Newson	1	1	0	0	0	0	0	0	0	1	0	0	.000
Alex Rodriguez	1	1	1	0	0	0	0	0	0	0	0	0	.000
Luis Sojo	5	20	0	5	0	0	0	3	0	3	0	0	.250
Doug Strange	2	4	0	0	0	0	0	1	1	1	0	0	.000
Chris Widger	2	3	0	0	0	0	0	0	0	3	0	0	.000
Dan Wilson	5	17	0	2	0	0	0	1	2	6	0	0	.118
Totals	5	200	35	63	6	1	11	33	25	41	3	2	.315

New York Yankees	G	AB	R	H	2B	3B	HR	RBI	BB	SO	SB	CS	Avg
Wade Boggs	4	19	4	5	2	0	1	3	3	5	0	0	.263
Russ Davis	2	5	0	1	0	0	0	0	0	2	0	0	.200
Tony Fernandez	5	21	0	5	2	0	0	0	2	2	0	0	.238
Dion James	4	12	0	1	0	0	0	0	1	1	0	0	.083
Pat Kelly	5	3	3	0	0	0	0	1	3	0	0	0	.000
Jim Leyritz	2	7	1	1	0	0	1	2	0	1	0	0	.143
Don Mattingly	5	24	3	10	4	0	1	6	1	5	0	0	.417
Paul O'Neill	5	18	5	6	0	0	3	6	5	5	0	0	.333
Jorge Posada	1	0	1	0	0	0	0	0	0	0	0	0	—
Ruben Sierra	5	23	2	4	2	0	2	5	2	7	0	0	.174
Mike Stanley	4	16	2	5	0	0	1	3	2	1	0	0	.313
Darryl Strawberry	2	2	0	0	0	0	0	0	0	1	0	0	.000
Randy Velarde	5	17	3	3	0	0	0	1	6	4	0	1	.176
Bernie Williams	5	21	8	9	2	0	2	5	7	3	1	0	.429
Gerald Williams	5	5	1	0	0	0	0	0	2	3	0	0	.000
Totals	5	193	33	50	12	0	11	32	32	43	1	1	.259

PITCHING STATISTICS

Seattle Mariners	G	GS	CG	IP	H	ER	BB	SO	W-L	Sv	ERA
Bobby Ayala	2	0	0	0 2/3	6	4	1	0	0-0	0	54.00
Tim Belcher	2	0	0	4 1/3	4	3	5	0	0-1	0	6.23
Andy Benes	2	2	0	11 2/3	10	7	9	8	0-0	0	5.40
Chris Bosio	2	2	0	7 2/3	10	9	4	2	0-0	0	10.57
Norm Charlton	4	0	0	7 1/3	4	2	3	9	1-0	1	2.45
Randy Johnson	2	1	0	10	5	3	6	16	2-0	0	2.70
Jeff Nelson	3	0	0	5 2/3	7	2	3	7	0-1	0	3.18
Bill Risley	4	0	0	3	2	2	0	1	0-0	1	6.00
Bob Wells	1	0	0	1	2	1	1	0	0-0	0	9.00
Totals	5	5	0	51 1/3	50	33	32	43	3-2	2	5.79

New York Yankees	G	GS	CG	IP	H	ER	BB	SO	W-L	Sv	ERA
David Cone	2	2	0	15 2/3	15	8	9	14	1-0	0	4.60
Sterling Hitchcock	2	0	0	1 2/3	2	1	2	1	0-0	0	5.40
Steve Howe	2	0	0	1	4	2	0	0	0-0	0	18.00
Scott Kamieniecki	1	1	0	5	9	4	4	4	0-0	0	7.20
Jack McDowell	2	1	0	7	8	7	4	6	0-2	0	9.00
Andy Pettitte	1	1	0	7	9	4	3	0	0-0	0	5.14
Mariano Rivera	3	0	0	5 1/3	3	0	1	8	1-0	0	0.00
John Wetteland	3	0	0	4 1/3	8	7	2	5	0-1	0	14.54
Bob Wickman	3	0	0	3	5	0	0	3	0-0	0	0.00
Totals	5	5	0	50	63	33	25	41	2-3	0	5.94

1996 League Divisional Series

NEW YORK YANKES (3) VS. TEXAS RANGERS (1)

GAME 1

Tuesday, October 1
at Yankee Stadium, New York

	1	2	3	4	5	6	7	8	9	R	H	E
Texas Rangers	0	0	0	5	0	1	0	0	0	6	8	0
New York Yankees	1	0	0	1	0	0	0	0	0	2	19	0

HR - TEX Juan Gonzalez, Dean Palmer

WP - John Burkett; LP - David Cone

GAME 2

Wednesday, October 2
at Yankee Stadium, New York

	1	2	3	4	5	6	7	8	9	10	11	12	R	H	E
Texas Rangers	0	1	3	0	0	0	0	0	0	0	0	0	4	8	1
New York Yankees	0	1	0	1	0	0	1	1	0	0	0	1	5	8	0

HR - TEX Juan Gonzalez 2; NY Cecil Fielder

WP - Brian Boehringer; LP - Mike Stanton

GAME 3

Friday, October 4
at the Ballpark in Arlington

	1	2	3	4	5	6	7	8	9	R	H	E
New York Yankees	1	0	0	0	0	0	0	0	2	3	7	1
Texas Rangers	0	0	0	1	1	0	0	0	0	2	6	1

HR - NY Bernie Williams; TEX Juan Gonzalez

WP - Jeff Nelson; LP - Darren Oliver; Sv - John Wetteland

GAME 4

Saturday, October 5
at the Ballpark in Arlington

	1	2	3	4	5	6	7	8	9	R	H	E
New York Yankees	0	0	0	3	1	0	1	0	1	6	12	1
Texas Rangers	0	2	2	0	0	0	0	0	0	4	9	0

HR - NY Bernie Williams 2; TEX Juan Gonzalez

WP - Dave Weathers; LP - Roger Pavlik; Sv - Mariano Rivera

BATTING STATISTICS

New York Yankees	G	AB	R	H	2B	3B	HR	RBI	BB	SO	SB	CS	Avg
Wade Boggs	3	12	0	1	1	0	0	0	0	2	0	0	.083
Mariano Duncan	4	16	0	5	0	0	0	3	0	4	0	0	.313
Cecil Fielder	3	11	2	4	0	0	1	4	1	2	0	0	.364
Andy Fox	2	0	0	0	0	0	0	0	0	0	0	0	—
Joe Girardi	4	9	1	2	0	0	0	0	4	1	0	0	.222
Charlie Hayes	3	5	0	1	0	0	0	1	0	0	0	1	.200
Derek Jeter	4	17	2	7	1	0	0	1	0	2	0	0	.412
Jim Leyritz	2	3	0	0	0	0	0	0	1	0	0	0	.000
Tino Martinez	4	15	3	4	2	0	0	3	1	0	0	0	.267
Paul O'Neill	4	15	0	2	0	0	0	0	0	2	0	0	.133
Tim Raines	4	16	3	4	0	0	0	0	3	1	0	0	.250
Ruben Rivera	2	1	0	0	0	0	0	0	0	1	0	0	.000
Darryl Strawberry	2	5	0	0	0	0	0	0	0	2	0	0	.000
Bernie Williams	4	15	5	7	0	0	3	5	2	1	1	1	.467
Totals	4	140	16	37	4	0	4	15	13	20	1	2	.264

Texas Rangers	G	AB	R	H	2B	3B	HR	RBI	BB	SO	SB	CS	Avg
Damon Buford	2	0	0	0	0	0	0	0	0	0	0	0	—
Will Clark	4	16	1	2	0	0	0	0	3	2	0	0	.125
Kevin Elster	4	12	2	4	2	0	0	0	3	2	1	0	.333
Juan Gonzalez	4	16	5	7	0	0	5	9	3	2	0	0	.438
Rusty Greer	4	16	2	2	0	0	0	0	3	3	0	0	.125
Darryl Hamilton	4	19	0	3	0	0	0	0	0	2	0	0	.158
Mark McLemore	4	15	1	2	0	0	0	2	0	4	0	1	.133
Warren Newson	2	1	0	0	0	0	0	0	1	0	0	0	.000
Dean Palmer	4	19	3	4	1	0	1	2	0	5	0	0	.211
Ivan Rodriguez	4	16	1	6	1	0	0	0	2	3	0	0	.375
Mickey Tettleton	4	12	1	1	0	0	0	1	5	7	0	0	.083
Totals	4	142	16	31	4	0	6	16	20	30	1	1	.218

PITCHING STATISTICS

New York Yankees	G	GS	CG	IP	H	ER	BB	SO	W-L	Sv	ERA
Brian Boehringer	2	0	0	1 1/3	3	1	2	0	1-0	0	6.75
David Cone	1	1	0	6	8	6	2	8	0-1	0	9.00
Jimmy Key	1	1	0	5	5	2	1	3	0-0	0	3.60
Graeme Lloyd	2	0	0	1	0	0	0	0	0-0	0	0.00
Jeff Nelson	2	0	0	3 2/3	2	0	2	5	1-0	0	0.00
Andy Pettitte	1	1	0	6 1/3	4	4	6	3	0-0	0	5.68
Mariano Rivera	2	0	0	4 2/3	0	0	1	1	0-0	0	0.00
Kenny Rogers	2	1	0	2	5	2	2	1	0-0	0	9.00
Dave Weathers	2	0	0	5	1	0	0	5	1-0	0	0.00
John Wetteland	3	0	0	4	2	0	4	4	0-0	2	0.00
Totals	4	4	0	39	31	15	20	30	3-1	2	3.46

Texas Rangers	G	GS	CG	IP	H	ER	BB	SO	W-L	Sv	ERA
John Burkett	1	1	1	9	10	2	1	7	1-0	0	2.00
Dennis Cook	2	0	0	1 1/3	0	0	1	0	0-0	0	0.00
Mike Henneman	3	0	0	1	1	0	1	1	0-0	0	0.00
Ken Hill	1	1	0	6	5	3	3	1	0-0	0	4.50
Darren Oliver	1	1	0	8	6	3	2	3	0-1	0	3.38
Danny Patterson	1	0	0	0 1/3	1	0	0	0	0-0	0	0.00
Roger Pavlik	1	0	0	2 2/3	4	2	0	1	0-1	0	6.75
Jeff Russell	2	0	0	3	3	1	0	1	0-0	0	3.00
Mike Stanton	3	0	0	3 1/3	2	1	3	3	0-1	0	2.70
Ed Vosberg	1	0	0	0	1	0	0	0	0-0	0	∞
Bobby Witt	1	1	0	3 1/3	4	3	2	3	0-0	0	8.10
Totals	4	4	1	38	37	15	13	20	1-3	0	3.55

1996 League Championship Series

NEW YORK YANKEES (4) VS. BALTIMORE ORIOLES (1)

GAME 1
Wednesday, October 9
at Yankee Stadium, New York

	1	2	3	4	5	6	7	8	9	10	11	R	H	E
Baltimore Orioles	0	1	1	1	0	1	0	0	0	0	0	4	11	1
New York Yankees	1	1	0	0	0	0	1	1	0	0	1	5	11	0

HR - BAL Brady Anderson, Rafael Palmeiro; NY Derek Jeter, Bernie Williams

WP - Mariano Rivera; LP - Randy Myers

GAME 2
Thursday, October 10
at Yankee Stadium, New York

	1	2	3	4	5	6	7	8	9	R	H	E
Baltimore Orioles	0	0	2	0	0	0	2	1	0	5	10	0
New York Yankees	2	0	0	0	0	1	0	0	3	11	1

HR - BAL Rafael Palmeiro, Todd Zeile

WP - David Wells; LP - Jeff Nelson; Sv - Armando Benitez

GAME 3
Friday, October 11
at Oriole Park at Camden Yards, Baltimore

	1	2	3	4	5	6	7	8	9	R	H	E
New York Yankees	0	0	0	1	0	0	0	4	0	5	8	0
Baltimore Orioles	2	0	0	0	0	0	0	0	0	2	3	2

HR - NY Cecil Fielder; BAL Todd Zeile

WP - Jimmy Key; LP - Mike Mussina; Sv - John Wetteland

GAME 4
Saturday, October 12
at Oriole Park at Camden Yards, Baltimore

	1	2	3	4	5	6	7	8	9	R	H	E
New York Yankees	2	1	0	2	0	0	0	3	0	8	9	0
Baltimore Orioles	1	0	1	2	0	0	0	0	0	4	11	0

HR - NY Paul O'Neill, Darryl Strawberry 2, Bernie Williams; BAL Chris Hoiles

WP - Dave Weathers; LP - Rocky Coppinger

GAME 5
Sunday, October 13
at Oriole Park at Camden Yards, Baltimore

	1	2	3	4	5	6	7	8	9	R	H	E
New York Yankees	0	0	6	0	0	0	0	0	0	6	11	0
Baltimore Orioles	0	0	0	0	0	1	0	1	2	4	4	1

HR - NY Cecil Fielder, Jim Leyritz, Darryl Strawberry; BAL Bobby Bonilla, Eddie Murray, Todd Zeile

WP - Andy Pettitte; LP - Scott Erickson

BATTING STATISTICS

New York Yankees	G	AB	R	H	2B	3B	HR	RBI	BB	SO	SB	CS	Avg
Mike Aldrete	1	0	0	0	0	0	0	0	0	0	0	0	—
Wade Boggs	3	15	1	2	0	0	0	0	1	3	0	0	.133
Mariano Duncan	4	15	0	3	2	0	0	0	0	3	0	0	.200
Cecil Fielder	5	18	3	3	0	0	2	8	4	5	0	0	.167
Andy Fox	2	0	0	0	0	0	0	0	0	0	0	0	—
Joe Girardi	4	12	1	3	0	1	0	0	1	3	0	0	.250
Charlie Hayes	4	7	0	1	0	0	0	0	2	2	0	0	.143
Derek Jeter	5	24	5	10	2	0	1	1	0	5	2	0	.417
Jim Leyritz	3	8	1	2	0	0	1	2	1	4	0	0	.250
Tino Martinez	5	22	3	4	1	0	0	0	0	2	0	0	.182
Paul O'Neill	4	11	1	3	0	0	1	2	3	2	0	0	.273
Tim Raines	5	15	2	4	1	0	0	0	1	1	0	0	.267
Luis Sojo	3	5	0	1	0	0	0	0	0	1	0	0	.200
Darryl Strawberry	4	12	4	5	0	0	3	5	2	2	0	0	.417
Bernie Williams	5	19	6	9	3	0	2	6	5	4	1	0	.474
Totals	**5**	**183**	**27**	**50**	**9**	**1**	**10**	**24**	**20**	**37**	**3**	**0**	**.273**

Baltimore Orioles	G	AB	R	H	2B	3B	HR	RBI	BB	SO	SB	CS	Avg
Roberto Alomar	5	23	2	5	2	0	0	1	0	4	0	0	.217
Brady Anderson	5	21	5	4	1	0	1	1	3	5	0	0	.190
Bobby Bonilla	5	20	1	1	0	0	1	2	1	4	0	0	.050
Mike Devereaux	3	2	0	0	0	0	0	0	0	1	0	0	.000
Chris Hoiles	4	12	1	2	0	0	1	2	1	3	0	0	.167
Pete Incaviglia	1	2	1	1	0	0	0	0	0	0	0	0	.500
Eddie Murray	5	15	1	4	0	0	1	2	2	2	0	0	.267
Rafael Palmeiro	5	17	4	4	0	0	2	4	4	4	0	0	.235
Mark Parent	2	6	0	1	0	0	0	0	0	2	0	0	.167
Cal Ripken Jr.	5	20	1	5	1	0	0	0	1	4	0	0	.250
B.J. Surhoff	5	15	0	4	0	0	0	2	1	2	0	0	.267
Tony Tarasco	2	1	0	0	0	0	0	0	0	1	0	0	.000
Todd Zeile	5	22	3	8	0	0	3	5	2	1	0	0	.364
Totals	**5**	**176**	**19**	**39**	**4**	**0**	**9**	**19**	**15**	**33**	**0**	**0**	**.222**

PITCHING STATISTICS

New York Yankees	G	GS	CG	IP	H	ER	BB	SO	W-L	Sv	ERA
David Cone	1	1	0	6	5	2	5	5	0-0	0	3.00
Jimmy Key	1	1	0	8	3	2	1	5	1-0	0	2.25
Graeme Lloyd	2	0	0	1 2/3	0	0	0	1	0-0	0	0.00
Jeff Nelson	2	0	0	2 1/3	5	3	0	2	0-1	0	11.57
Andy Pettitte	2	2	0	15	10	6	5	7	1-0	0	3.60
Mariano Rivera	2	0	0	4	6	0	1	5	1-0	0	0.00
Kenny Rogers	1	1	0	3	5	4	2	3	0-0	0	12.00
Dave Weathers	2	0	0	3	3	0	0	0	1-0	0	0.00
John Wetteland	4	0	0	4	2	2	1	5	0-0	1	4.50
Totals	**5**	**5**	**0**	**47**	**39**	**19**	**15**	**33**	**4-1**	**1**	**3.64**

Baltimore Orioles	G	GS	CG	IP	H	ER	BB	SO	W-L	Sv	ERA
Armando Benitez	3	0	0	2 1/3	3	2	3	2	0-0	1	7.71
Rocky Coppinger	1	1	0	5 1/3	6	5	1	3	0-1	0	8.44
Scott Erickson	2	2	0	11 1/3	14	3	4	8	0-1	0	2.38
Terry Mathews	3	0	0	2 1/3	0	0	2	3	0-0	0	0.00
Alan Mills	3	0	0	2 1/3	3	1	1	3	0-0	0	3.86
Mike Mussina	1	1	0	7 2/3	8	5	2	6	0-1	0	5.87
Randy Myers	3	0	0	4	4	1	3	2	0-1	0	2.25
Jesse Orosco	4	0	0	2	1	1	2	0	0-0	0	4.50
Arthur Rhodes	3	0	0	2	2	0	0	2	0-0	0	0.00
David Wells	1	1	0	6 2/3	8	3	3	6	1-0	0	4.05
Totals	**5**	**5**	**0**	**46**	**50**	**21**	**20**	**37**	**1-4**	**1**	**4.11**

1996 World Series

NEW YORK YANKEES (4) VS. ATLANTA BRAVES (2)

GAME 1
Sunday, October 20
at Yankee Stadium, New York

	1	2	3	4	5	6	7	8	9	R	H	E
Atlanta Braves	0	2	6	0	1	3	0	0	0	12	13	0
New York Yankees	0	0	0	0	1	0	0	0	0	1	4	1

HR - ATL Andruw Jones 2, Fred McGriff

WP - John Smoltz; **LP** - Andy Pettitte

GAME 2
Monday, October 21
at Yankee Stadium, New York

	1	2	3	4	5	6	7	8	9	R	H	E
Atlanta Braves	1	0	1	0	1	1	0	0	0	4	10	0
New York Yankees	0	0	0	0	0	0	0	0	0	0	7	1

WP - Greg Maddux; **LP** - Jimmy Key

GAME 3
Tuesday, October 22
at Atlanta-Fulton County Stadium, Atlanta

	1	2	3	4	5	6	7	8	9	R	H	E
New York Yankees	1	0	0	1	0	0	0	3	0	5	8	1
Atlanta Braves	0	0	0	0	0	1	0	1	0	2	6	1

HR - NY Bernie Williams

WP - David Cone; **LP** - Tom Glavine; **Sv** - John Wetteland

GAME 4
Wednesday, October 23
at Atlanta-Fulton County Stadium, Atlanta

	1	2	3	4	5	6	7	8	9	10	R	H	E
New York Yankees	0	0	0	0	3	0	3	0	2	8	12	0
Atlanta Braves	0	4	1	0	1	0	0	0	0	0	6	9	2

HR - ATL Fred McGriff; NY Jim Leyritz

WP - Graeme Lloyd; **LP** - Steve Avery; **Sv** - John Wetteland

GAME 5
Thursday, October 24
at Atlanta-Fulton County Stadium, Atlanta

	1	2	3	4	5	6	7	8	9	R	H	E
New York Yankees	0	0	0	1	0	0	0	0	0	1	4	1
Atlanta Braves	0	0	0	0	0	0	0	0	0	0	5	1

WP - Andy Pettitte; **LP** - John Smoltz; **Sv** - John Wetteland

GAME 6
Saturday, October 26
at Yankee Stadium, New York

	1	2	3	4	5	6	7	8	9	R	H	E
Atlanta Braves	0	0	0	1	0	0	0	0	1	2	8	0
New York Yankees	0	0	3	0	0	0	0	0	x	3	8	1

WP - Jimmy Key; **LP** - Greg Maddux; **Sv** - John Wetteland

BATTING STATISTICS

New York Yankees	G	AB	R	H	2B	3B	HR	RBI	BB	SO	SB	CS	BA
Mike Aldrete	2	1	0	0	0	0	0	0	0	0	0	0	.000
Wade Boggs	4	11	0	3	1	0	0	2	1	0	0	0	.273
David Cone	1	2	0	0	0	0	0	0	0	1	0	0	.000
Mariano Duncan	6	19	1	1	0	0	0	0	0	4	1	0	.053
Cecil Fielder	6	23	1	9	2	0	0	2	2	2	0	0	.391
Andy Fox	4	0	1	0	0	0	0	0	0	0	0	0	—
Joe Girardi	4	10	1	2	0	1	0	1	1	2	0	0	.200
Charlie Hayes	5	16	2	3	0	0	0	1	1	5	0	0	.188
Derek Jeter	6	20	5	5	0	0	0	1	4	6	1	0	.250
Jim Leyritz	4	8	1	3	0	0	1	3	3	2	1	0	.375
Graeme Lloyd	4	1	0	0	0	0	0	0	0	0	0	0	.000
Tino Martinez	6	11	0	1	0	0	0	0	2	5	0	0	.091
Paul O'Neill	5	12	1	2	2	0	0	0	3	2	0	0	.167
Andy Pettitte	2	4	0	0	0	0	0	0	0	1	0	0	.000
Tim Raines	4	14	2	3	0	0	0	0	2	1	0	1	.214
Mariano Rivera	4	1	0	0	0	0	0	0	0	0	0	0	.000
Kenny Rogers	1	1	0	1	0	0	0	0	0	0	0	0	1.000
Luis Sojo	5	5	0	3	1	0	0	1	0	0	0	0	.600
Darryl Strawberry	5	16	0	3	0	0	0	1	4	6	0	0	.188
Bernie Williams	6	24	3	4	0	0	1	4	3	6	1	0	.167
Totals	**6**	**199**	**18**	**43**	**6**	**1**	**2**	**16**	**26**	**43**	**4**	**1**	**.216**

Atlanta Braves	G	AB	R	H	2B	3B	HR	RBI	BB	SO	SB	CS	BA
Mike Bielecki	2	1	0	0	0	0	0	0	0	1	0	0	.000
Jeff Blauser	6	18	2	3	1	0	0	1	1	4	0	0	.167
Jermaine Dye	5	17	0	2	0	0	0	1	1	1	0	0	.118
Tom Glavine	1	1	1	0	0	0	0	0	0	0	0	0	.000
Marquis Grissom	6	27	4	12	2	1	0	5	1	2	1	0	.444
Andruw Jones	6	20	4	8	1	0	2	6	3	6	1	2	.400
Chipper Jones	6	21	3	6	3	0	0	3	4	2	1	0	.286
Ryan Klesko	5	10	2	1	0	0	0	1	2	4	0	0	.100
Mark Lemke	6	26	2	6	1	0	0	2	0	3	0	0	.231
Javy Lopez	6	21	3	4	0	0	0	1	3	4	0	0	.190
Fred McGriff	6	20	4	6	0	0	2	6	5	4	0	0	.300
Mike Mordecai	1	1	0	0	0	0	0	0	0	0	0	0	.000
Denny Neagle	2	1	0	0	0	0	0	0	0	1	0	0	.000
Terry Pendleton	4	9	1	2	1	0	0	0	1	1	0	1	.222
Eddie Perez	2	1	0	0	0	0	0	0	0	0	0	0	.000
Luis Polonia	6	5	0	0	0	0	0	0	1	2	0	1	.000
John Smoltz	2	2	1	0	0	0	0	0	0	0	0	0	.500
Totals	**6**	**201**	**26**	**51**	**9**	**1**	**4**	**26**	**23**	**36**	**3**	**4**	**.254**

PITCHING STATISTICS

New York Yankees	G	GS	CG	IP	H	ER	BB	SO	W-L	Sv	ERA
Brian Boehringer	2	0	0	5	5	3	0	5	0-0	0	5.40
David Cone	1	1	0	6	4	1	4	3	1-0	0	1.50
Jimmy Key	2	2	0	11 1/3	15	5	5	1	1-1	0	3.97
Graeme Lloyd	4	0	0	2 2/3	0	0	0	4	1-0	0	0.00
Jeff Nelson	3	0	0	4 1/3	1	0	1	5	0-0	0	0.00
Andy Pettitte	2	2	0	10 2/3	11	7	4	5	1-1	0	5.91
Mariano Rivera	4	0	0	5 2/3	4	1	3	4	0-0	0	1.59
Kenny Rogers	1	1	0	2	5	5	2	0	0-0	0	22.50
Dave Weathers	3	0	0	3	2	1	3	3	0-0	0	3.00
John Wetteland	5	0	0	4 1/3	4	1	1	6	0-0	4	2.08
Totals	**6**	**6**	**0**	**55**	**51**	**24**	**23**	**36**	**4-2**	**4**	**3.93**

Atlanta Braves	G	GS	CG	IP	H	ER	BB	SO	W-L	Sv	ERA
Steve Avery	1	0	0	0 2/3	1	1	3	0	0-1	0	13.50
Mike Bielecki	2	0	0	3	0	0	3	6	0-0	0	0.00
Brad Clontz	3	0	0	1 2/3	1	0	1	2	0-0	0	0.00
Tom Glavine	1	1	0	7	4	1	3	8	0-1	0	1.29
Greg Maddux	2	2	0	15 2/3	14	3	1	5	1-1	0	1.72
Greg McMichael	2	0	0	1	5	3	0	1	0-0	0	27.00
Denny Neagle	2	1	0	6	5	2	4	3	0-0	0	3.00
John Smoltz	2	2	0	14	6	1	8	14	1-1	0	0.64
Terrell Wade	2	0	0	0 2/3	0	0	1	0	0-0	0	0.00
Mark Wohlers	4	0	0	4 1/3	7	3	2	4	0-0	0	6.23
Totals	**6**	**6**	**0**	**54**	**43**	**14**	**26**	**43**	**2-4**	**0**	**2.33**

1997 League Divisional Series
CLEVELAND INDIANS (3) VS. NEW YORK YANKEES (2)

GAME 1
Tuesday, September 30
at Yankee Stadium, New York

	1	2	3	4	5	6	7	8	9	R	H	E
Cleveland Indians	5	0	0	1	0	0	0	0	0	6	11	0
New York Yankees	0	1	0	1	1	5	0	0	x	8	11	0

HR - CLE Sandy Alomar Jr.; NY Derek Jeter, Tino Martinez, Paul O'Neill, Tim Raines

WP - Ramiro Mendoza; LP - Eric Plunk; Sv - Mariano Rivera

GAME 2
Thursday, October 2
at Yankee Stadium, New York

	1	2	3	4	5	6	7	8	9	R	H	E
Cleveland Indians	0	0	0	5	2	0	0	0	0	7	11	1
New York Yankees	3	0	0	0	0	0	0	1	1	5	7	2

HR - CLE Matt Williams; NY Derek Jeter

WP - Jaret Wright; LP - Andy Pettitte

GAME 3
Saturday, October 4
at Jacobs Field, Cleveland

	1	2	3	4	5	6	7	8	9	R	H	E
New York Yankees	1	0	1	4	0	0	0	0	0	6	4	1
Cleveland Indians	0	1	0	0	0	0	0	0	0	1	5	1

HR - NY Paul O'Neill

WP - David Wells; LP - Charles Nagy

GAME 4
Sunday, October 5
at Jacobs Field, Cleveland

	1	2	3	4	5	6	7	8	9	R	H	E
New York Yankees	2	0	0	0	0	0	0	0	0	2	9	1
Cleveland Indians	0	1	0	0	0	0	0	1	1	3	9	0

HR - CLE Sandy Alomar Jr., David Justice

WP - Mike Jackson; LP - Ramiro Mendoza

GAME 5
Monday, October 6
at Jacobs Field, Cleveland

	1	2	3	4	5	6	7	8	9	R	H	E
New York Yankees	0	0	0	0	2	1	0	0	0	3	12	0
Cleveland Indians	0	0	3	1	0	0	0	0	x	4	7	2

WP - Jaret Wright; LP - Andy Pettitte; Sv - Jose Mesa

BATTING STATISTICS

Cleveland Indians	G	AB	R	H	2B	3B	HR	RBI	BB	SO	SB	CS	Avg
Sandy Alomar Jr.	5	19	4	6	1	0	2	5	0	2	0	0	.316
Tony Fernandez	4	11	0	2	1	0	0	4	0	0	0	0	.182
Brian Giles	3	7	0	1	0	0	0	0	0	1	0	0	.143
Marquis Grissom	5	17	3	4	0	1	0	0	1	2	0	1	.235
David Justice	5	19	3	5	2	0	1	2	2	3	0	0	.263
Manny Ramirez	5	21	2	3	1	0	0	3	0	3	0	0	.143
Bip Roberts	5	19	1	6	0	0	0	1	2	2	2	1	.316
Kevin Seitzer	1	4	0	0	0	0	0	0	0	0	0	0	.000
Jim Thome	5	15	1	3	0	0	0	1	0	5	0	0	.200
Omar Vizquel	5	18	3	9	0	0	0	1	2	1	4	0	.500
Matt Williams	5	17	4	4	1	0	1	3	3	3	0	0	.235
Totals	**5**	**167**	**21**	**43**	**6**	**1**	**4**	**20**	**10**	**22**	**6**	**2**	**.257**

New York Yankees	G	AB	R	H	2B	3B	HR	RBI	BB	SO	SB	CS	Avg
Wade Boggs	3	7	1	3	0	0	0	2	0	0	0	0	.429
Chad Curtis	4	6	0	1	0	0	0	0	3	1	0	0	.167
Cecil Fielder	2	8	0	1	0	0	0	1	0	3	0	0	.125
Joe Girardi	5	15	2	2	0	0	0	0	1	3	0	0	.133
Charlie Hayes	5	15	0	5	0	0	0	1	0	2	0	0	.333
Derek Jeter	5	21	6	7	1	0	2	2	3	5	1	0	.333
Tino Martinez	5	18	1	4	1	0	1	4	2	4	0	0	.222
Paul O'Neill	5	19	5	8	2	0	2	7	3	0	0	0	.421
Jorge Posada	2	2	0	0	0	0	0	0	0	1	0	0	.000
Scott Pose	1	0	0	0	0	0	0	0	0	0	0	0	—
Tim Raines	5	19	4	4	0	0	1	3	3	1	2	0	.211
Rey Sanchez	5	15	1	3	1	0	0	1	1	2	0	0	.200
Mike Stanley	2	4	1	3	1	0	0	1	0	1	0	0	.750
Bernie Williams	5	17	3	2	1	0	0	1	4	3	0	0	.118
Totals	**5**	**166**	**24**	**43**	**7**	**0**	**6**	**23**	**20**	**26**	**3**	**0**	**.259**

PITCHING STATISTICS

Cleveland Indians	G	GS	CG	IP	H	ER	BB	SO	W-L	Sv	ERA
Paul Assenmacher	4	0	0	3 1/3	2	2	2	2	0-0	0	5.40
Orel Hershiser	2	2	0	11 1/3	14	5	2	4	0-0	0	3.97
Mike Jackson	4	0	0	4 1/3	3	0	1	5	1-0	0	0.00
Jose Mesa	2	0	0	3 1/3	5	1	1	2	0-0	1	2.70
Alvin Morman	1	0	0	0	0	0	1	0	0-0	0	—
Charles Nagy	1	1	0	3 2/3	2	4	6	1	0-1	0	9.82
Chad Ogea	1	0	0	5 1/3	2	1	0	1	0-0	0	1.69
Eric Plunk	1	0	0	1 1/3	4	4	0	1	0-1	0	27.00
Jaret Wright	2	2	0	11 1/3	11	5	7	10	2-0	0	3.97
Totals	**5**	**5**	**0**	**44**	**43**	**22**	**20**	**26**	**3-2**	**1**	**4.50**

New York Yankees	G	GS	CG	IP	H	ER	BB	SO	W-L	Sv	ERA
Brian Boehringer	1	0	0	1 2/3	1	0	1	2	0-0	0	0.00
David Cone	1	1	0	3 1/3	7	6	2	2	0-0	0	16.20
Dwight Gooden	1	1	0	5 2/3	5	1	3	5	0-0	0	1.59
Graeme Lloyd	2	0	0	1 1/3	0	0	1	0	0-0	0	0.00
Ramiro Mendoza	2	0	0	3 2/3	3	1	0	2	1-1	0	2.45
Jeff Nelson	4	0	0	4	4	0	2	0	0-0	0	0.00
Andy Pettitte	2	2	0	11 2/3	15	11	1	5	0-2	0	8.49
Mariano Rivera	2	0	0	2	2	1	0	1	0-0	1	4.50
Mike Stanton	3	0	0	1	1	0	1	3	0-0	0	0.00
David Wells	1	1	1	9	5	1	0	1	1-0	0	1.00
Totals	**5**	**5**	**1**	**43 1/3**	**43**	**21**	**10**	**22**	**2-3**	**1**	**4.36**

1998 League Divisional Series

NEW YORK YANKEES (3) VS. TEXAS RANGERS (0)

GAME 1
Tuesday, September 29
at Yankee Stadium, New York

	1	2	3	4	5	6	7	8	9	R	H	E
Texas Rangers	0	0	0	0	0	0	0	0	0	0	5	0
New York Yankees	0	2	0	0	0	0	0	0	x	2	6	0

WP - David Wells; **LP** - Todd Stottlemyre; **Sv** - Mariano Rivera

GAME 2
Wednesday, September 30
at Yankee Stadium, New York

	1	2	3	4	5	6	7	8	9	R	H	E
Texas Rangers	0	0	0	0	1	0	0	0	0	1	5	0
New York Yankees	0	1	0	2	0	0	0	0	x	3	8	0

HR - NY Scott Brosius, Shane Spencer

WP - Andy Pettitte; **LP** - Rick Helling; **Sv** - Mariano Rivera

GAME 3
Friday, October 2
at the Ballpark in Arlington

	1	2	3	4	5	6	7	8	9	R	H	E
New York Yankees	1	0	0	0	4	0	0	0	4	9	1	
Texas Rangers	0	0	0	0	0	0	0	0	0	3	1	

HR - NY Paul O'Neill, Shane Spencer

WP - David Cone; **LP** - Aaron Sele; **Sv** - Mariano Rivera

BATTING STATISTICS

New York Yankees	G	AB	R	H	2B	3B	HR	RBI	BB	SO	SB	CS	Avg
Scott Brosius	3	10	1	4	0	0	1	3	0	3	0	0	.400
Chad Curtis	3	3	1	2	1	0	0	0	1	1	1	0	1.000
Chili Davis	2	6	0	1	0	0	0	0	0	2	0	0	.167
Joe Girardi	2	7	0	3	0	0	0	0	0	1	0	0	.429
Derek Jeter	3	9	0	1	0	0	0	0	2	2	0	0	.111
Chuck Knoblauch	3	11	0	1	0	0	0	0	0	4	0	0	.091
Tino Martinez	3	11	1	3	2	0	0	0	0	2	0	0	.273
Paul O'Neill	3	11	1	4	2	0	1	1	1	1	0	0	.364
Jorge Posada	1	2	1	0	0	0	0	0	1	2	0	0	.000
Tim Raines	2	4	1	1	0	0	0	0	1	1	0	0	.250
Shane Spencer	2	6	3	3	0	0	2	4	0	1	0	0	.500
Bernie Williams	3	11	0	0	0	0	0	0	1	4	0	0	.000
Totals	**3**	**91**	**9**	**23**	**6**	**0**	**4**	**5**	**7**	**24**	**1**	**1**	**.247**

Texas Rangers	G	AB	R	H	2B	3B	HR	RBI	BB	SO	SB	CS	Avg
Luis Alicea	1	1	0	0	0	0	0	0	0	0	0	0	.000
Will Clark	3	11	0	1	0	0	0	0	1	2	0	0	.091
Royce Clayton	3	9	0	2	0	0	0	0	4	0	0	0	.222
Juan Gonzalez	3	12	1	1	1	0	0	0	0	3	0	0	.083
Tom Goodwin	2	4	0	1	0	0	0	0	0	1	0	0	.250
Rusty Greer	3	11	0	1	0	0	0	0	1	2	0	0	.091
Roberto Kelly	2	7	0	1	1	0	0	0	0	2	0	0	.143
Mark McLemore	3	10	0	1	1	0	0	0	2	3	0	0	.100
Ivan Rodriguez	3	10	0	1	0	0	0	1	0	5	0	0	.100
Mike Simms	2	5	0	1	0	0	0	0	0	2	0	0	.200
Lee Stevens	1	3	0	0	0	0	0	0	0	1	0	0	.000
Todd Zeile	3	9	0	3	0	0	0	0	0	2	0	0	.333
Total	**3**	**92**	**1**	**13**	**3**	**0**	**0**	**1**	**4**	**27**	**0**	**0**	**.141**

PITCHING STATISTICS

New York Yankees	G	GS	CG	IP	H	ER	BB	SO	W-L	Sv	ERA
David Cone	1	1	0	5 2/3	2	0	1	6	1-0	0	0.00
Graeme Lloyd	1	0	0	0 1/3	0	0	0	0	0-0	0	0.00
Jeff Nelson	2	0	0	2 2/3	2	0	1	2	0-0	0	0.00
Andy Pettitte	1	1	0	7	3	1	0	8	1-0	0	1.29
Mariano Rivera	3	0	0	3 1/3	1	0	1	2	0-0	2	0.00
David Wells	1	1	0	8	5	0	1	9	1-0	0	0.00
Total	**3**	**3**	**0**	**27**	**13**	**1**	**4**	**27**	**3-0**	**2**	**0.33**
Texas Rangers	G	GS	CG	IP	H	ER	BB	SO	W-L	Sv	ERA
Tim Crabtree	2	0	0	4	1	0	0	2	0-0	0	0.00
Rick Helling	1	1	0	6	8	3	1	9	0-1	0	4.50
Aaron Sele	1	1	0	6	8	4	1	4	0-1	0	6.00
Todd Stottlemyre	1	1	1	8	6	2	4	8	0-1	0	2.25
John Wetteland	1	0	0	1	0	0	1	1	0-0	0	0.00
Totals	**3**	**3**	**1**	**25**	**23**	**9**	**7**	**24**	**0-3**	**0**	**3.24**

1998 League Championship Series
NEW YORK YANKEES (4) VS. CLEVELAND INDIANS (2)

GAME 1
Tuesday, October 6
at Yankee Stadium, New York

	1	2	3	4	5	6	7	8	9	R	H	E
Cleveland Indians	0	0	0	0	0	0	0	2	2	5	0
New York Yankees	5	0	0	0	0	1	1	0	x	7	11	0

HR - CLE Manny Ramirez; NY Jorge Posada

WP - David Wells; LP - Jaret Wright

GAME 2
Wednesday, October 7
at Yankee Stadium, New York

	1	2	3	4	5	6	7	8	9	10	11	12	R	H	E
Cleveland Indians	0	0	0	1	0	0	0	0	0	0	0	3	4	8	1
New York Yankees	0	0	0	0	0	0	1	0	0	0	0	0	1	7	1

HR - CLE David Justice

WP - Dave Burba; LP - Jeff Nelson; Sv - Mike Jackson

GAME 3
Friday, October 9
at Jacobs Field, Cleveland

	1	2	3	4	5	6	7	8	9	R	H	E
New York Yankees	1	0	0	0	0	0	0	0	0	1	4	0
Cleveland Indians	0	2	0	0	4	0	0	0	x	6	12	0

HR - CLE Manny Ramirez, Jim Thome 2, Mark Whiten

WP - Bartolo Colon; LP - Andy Pettitte

GAME 4
Saturday, October 10
at Jacobs Field, Cleveland

	1	2	3	4	5	6	7	8	9	R	H	E
New York Yankees	1	0	0	2	0	0	0	0	1	4	4	0
Cleveland Indians	0	0	0	0	0	0	0	0	0	0	4	3

HR - NY Paul O'Neill

WP - Orlando Hernandez; LP - Dwight Gooden

GAME 5
Sunday, October 11
at Jacobs Field, Cleveland

	1	2	3	4	5	6	7	8	9	R	H	E
New York Yankees	3	1	0	1	0	0	0	0	0	5	6	0
Cleveland Indians	2	0	0	0	0	1	0	0	0	3	8	0

HR - NY Chili Davis; CLE Kenny Lofton, Jim Thome

WP - David Wells; **LP** - Chad Ogea; **Sv** - Mariano Rivera

GAME 6
Tuesday, October 13
at Yankee Stadium, New York

	1	2	3	4	5	6	7	8	9	R	H	E
Cleveland Indians	0	0	0	0	5	0	0	0	0	5	8	3
New York Yankees	2	1	3	0	0	3	0	0	x	9	11	1

HR - CLE Jim Thome; NY Scott Brosius

WP - David Cone; **LP** - Charles Nagy

BATTING STATISTICS

New York Yankees	G	AB	R	H	2B	3B	HR	RBI	BB	SO	SB	CS	Avg
Scott Brosius	6	20	2	6	1	0	1	6	2	4	0	0	.300
Homer Bush	2	0	1	0	0	0	0	0	0	0	1	0	.000
Chad Curtis	2	4	0	0	0	0	0	0	2	2	0	0	.000
Chili Davis	5	14	2	4	1	0	1	5	2	3	0	0	.286
Joe Girardi	3	8	2	2	0	0	0	0	1	0	0	0	.250
Derek Jeter	6	25	3	5	1	1	0	2	2	5	3	2	.200
Chuck Knoblauch	6	25	4	5	1	0	0	0	4	2	0	1	.200
Ricky Ledee	3	5	0	0	0	0	0	0	0	0	0	0	.000
Tino Martinez	6	19	1	2	1	0	0	1	6	8	2	0	.105
Paul O'Neill	6	25	6	7	2	0	1	3	3	4	2	0	.280
Jorge Posada	5	11	1	2	0	0	1	2	4	2	0	0	.182
Tim Raines	3	10	1	1	0	0	0	1	2	5	0	0	.100
Shane Spencer	3	10	1	1	0	0	0	0	1	3	0	0	.100
Bernie Williams	6	21	4	8	1	0	0	5	7	4	2	0	.381
Total	**6**	**197**	**27**	**43**	**8**	**1**	**4**	**25**	**35**	**42**	**9**	**3**	**.221**

Cleveland Indians	G	AB	R	H	2B	3B	HR	RBI	BB	SO	SB	CS	Avg
Sandy Alomar	5	16	1	1	0	0	0	0	0	2	0	0	.063
Jeff Branson	1	1	0	0	0	0	0	0	0	0	0	0	.000
Joey Cora	2	7	1	1	0	0	0	0	2	1	0	0	.143
Einar Diaz	5	4	0	0	0	0	0	0	0	1	0	0	.000
Travis Fryman	6	23	2	4	0	0	0	0	1	5	1	0	.174
Brian Giles	4	12	0	1	0	0	0	0	1	3	0	0	.083
David Justice	6	19	2	3	0	0	1	2	3	3	0	1	.158
Kenny Lofton	6	27	2	5	1	0	1	3	1	7	1	1	.185
Manny Ramirez	6	21	2	7	1	0	2	4	4	9	0	0	.333
Richie Sexson	3	6	0	0	0	0	0	0	0	3	0	0	.000
Jim Thome	6	23	4	7	0	0	4	8	1	8	0	0	.304
Omar Vizquel	6	25	2	11	0	1	0	0	1	3	4	0	.440
Mark Whiten	2	7	2	2	1	0	1	1	1	3	0	0	.286
Enrique Wilson	5	14	2	3	0	0	0	1	1	3	0	0	.214
Total	**6**	**205**	**20**	**45**	**3**	**1**	**9**	**19**	**16**	**51**	**6**	**2**	**.220**

PITCHING STATISTICS

New York Yankees	G	GS	CG	IP	H	ER	BB	SO	W-L	Sv	ERA
David Cone	2	2	0	13	12	6	6	13	1-0	0	4.15
Orlando Hernandez	1	1	0	7	3	0	2	6	1-0	0	0.00
Graeme Lloyd	1	0	0	0⅔	1	0	0	0	0-0	0	0.00
Ramiro Mendoza	2	0	0	4⅓	4	0	0	1	0-0	0	0.00
Jeff Nelson	3	0	0	1⅓	3	3	1	3	0-1	0	20.25
Andy Pettitte	1	1	0	4⅔	8	6	3	1	0-1	0	11.57
Mariano Rivera	4	0	0	5⅔	0	0	1	5	0-0	1	0.00
Mike Stanton	3	0	0	3⅔	2	0	1	4	0-0	0	0.00
David Wells	2	2	0	15⅔	12	5	2	18	2-0	0	2.87
Total	**6**	**6**	**0**	**56⅓**	**45**	**20**	**16**	**51**	**0-0**	**1**	**3.21**

Cleveland Indians	G	GS	CG	IP	H	ER	BB	SO	W-L	Sv	ERA
Paul Assenmacher	3	0	0	2	0	0	0	3	0-0	0	0.00
Dave Burba	3	0	0	6	3	2	5	8	1-0	0	3.00
Bartolo Colon	1	1	1	9	4	1	4	3	1-0	0	1.00
Dwight Gooden	1	1	0	4⅔	3	3	3	3	0-1	0	5.74
Mike Jackson	1	0	0	1	0	0	0	2	0-0	1	0.00
Charles Nagy	2	2	0	9⅔	13	4	1	6	0-1	0	3.72
Chad Ogea	2	1	0	6⅔	9	6	5	4	0-1	0	8.10
Jim Poole	4	0	0	1⅓	1	0	1	2	0-0	0	0.00
Steve Reed	3	0	0	1⅔	0	0	1	0	0-0	0	0.00
Paul Shuey	5	0	0	6⅓	4	0	7	7	0-0	0	0.00
Jaret Wright	2	1	0	6⅔	7	6	8	4	0-1	0	8.10
Total	**6**	**6**	**1**	**55⅓**	**43**	**22**	**35**	**42**	**2-4**	**1**	**3.60**

1998 World Series

NEW YORK YANKEES (4) VS. SAN DIEGO PADRES (0)

GAME 1
Saturday, October 17
at Yankee Stadium, New York

	1	2	3	4	5	6	7	8	9	R	H	E
San Diego Padres	0	0	2	0	3	0	0	1	0	6	8	1
New York Yankees	0	2	0	0	0	0	7	0	x	9	9	1

HR - SD Tony Gwynn, Greg Vaughn 2; NY Chuck Knoblauch, Tino Martinez

WP - David Wells; **LP** - Donne Wall; **Sv** - Mariano Rivera

GAME 2
Sunday, October 18
at Yankee Stadium, New York

	1	2	3	4	5	6	7	8	9	R	H	E
San Diego Padres	0	0	0	0	1	0	0	2	0	3	10	1
New York Yankees	3	3	1	0	2	0	0	0	x	9	16	0

HR - NY Jorge Posada, Bernie Williams

WP - Orlando Hernandez; **LP** - Andy Ashby

GAME 3
Tuesday, October 20
at Qualcomm Stadium, San Diego

	1	2	3	4	5	6	7	8	9	R	H	E
New York Yankees	0	0	0	0	0	0	2	3	0	5	9	1
San Diego Padres	0	0	0	0	0	3	0	1	0	4	7	1

HR - NY Scott Brosius 2

WP - Ramiro Mendoza; **LP** - Trevor Hoffman; **Sv** - Mariano Rivera

GAME 4
Wednesday, October 21
at Qualcomm Stadium, San Diego

	1	2	3	4	5	6	7	8	9	R	H	E
New York Yankees	0	0	0	0	0	1	0	2	0	3	9	0
San Diego Padres	0	0	0	0	0	0	0	0	0	0	7	0

WP - Andy Pettitte; **LP** - Kevin Brown; **Sv** - Mariano Rivera

BATTING STATISTICS

New York Yankees	G	AB	R	H	2B	3B	HR	RBI	BB	SO	SB	CS	BA
Scott Brosius	4	17	3	8	0	0	2	6	0	4	0	0	.471
Homer Bush	2	0	0	0	0	0	0	0	0	0	0	0	—
David Cone	1	2	0	1	0	0	0	0	0	0	0	0	.500
Chili Davis	3	7	3	2	0	0	0	2	3	2	0	0	.286
Joe Girardi	2	6	0	0	0	0	0	0	0	2	0	0	.000
Derek Jeter	4	17	4	6	0	0	0	1	3	3	0	0	.353
Chuck Knoblauch	4	16	3	6	0	0	1	3	3	2	1	0	.375
Ricky Ledee	4	10	1	6	3	0	0	4	2	1	0	1	.600
Graeme Lloyd	1	0	0	0	0	0	0	0	0	0	0	0	—
Tino Martinez	4	13	4	5	0	0	1	4	4	2	0	0	.385
Jeff Nelson	1	0	0	0	0	0	0	0	0	0	0	0	—
Ramiro Mendoza	1	1	0	0	0	0	0	0	0	0	0	0	.000
Paul O'Neill	4	19	3	4	1	0	0	0	1	2	0	0	.211
Andy Pettitte	1	2	0	0	0	0	0	0	0	2	0	0	.000
Jorge Posada	3	9	2	3	0	0	1	2	2	2	0	0	.333
Mariano Rivera	2	1	0	0	0	0	0	0	0	0	0	0	.000
Shane Spencer	1	3	1	1	0	0	0	0	0	2	0	0	.333
Bernie Williams	4	16	2	1	0	0	1	3	2	5	0	0	.063
Totals	**4**	**139**	**26**	**43**	**5**	**0**	**6**	**25**	**20**	**29**	**1**	**1**	**.309**

San Diego Padres	G	AB	R	H	2B	3B	HR	RBI	BB	SO	SB	CS	BA
Kevin Brown	1	2	0	1	0	0	0	0	0	0	0	0	.500
Ken Caminiti	4	14	1	2	1	0	0	1	2	7	0	0	.143
Steve Finley	3	12	0	1	1	0	0	0	0	2	1	0	.083
Chris Gomez	4	11	2	4	0	1	0	0	1	1	0	0	.364
Tony Gwynn	4	16	2	8	0	0	1	3	1	0	0	0	.500
Joey Hamilton	1	0	0	0	0	0	0	0	0	0	0	0	—
Carlos Hernandez	4	10	0	2	0	0	0	0	0	3	0	0	.200
Sterling Hitchcock	1	2	1	1	0	0	0	0	0	0	0	0	.500
Trevor Hoffman	1	0	0	0	0	0	0	0	0	0	0	0	—
Wally Joyner	3	8	0	0	0	0	0	0	3	1	0	0	.000
Jim Leyritz	4	10	0	0	0	0	0	0	1	4	0	0	.000
Dan Miceli	1	0	0	0	0	0	0	0	0	0	0	0	—
Greg Myers	2	4	0	0	0	0	0	0	0	2	0	0	.000
Randy Myers	2	0	0	0	0	0	0	0	0	0	0	0	—
Ruben Rivera	3	5	1	4	2	0	0	1	0	0	0	0	.800
Andy Sheets	2	2	0	0	0	0	0	0	0	1	0	0	.000
Mark Sweeney	3	3	0	2	0	0	0	1	0	0	0	0	.667
John Vander Wal	4	5	0	2	1	0	0	0	0	2	0	0	.400
Greg Vaughn	4	15	3	2	0	0	2	4	1	2	0	0	.133
Quilvio Veras	4	15	3	3	2	0	0	1	3	4	0	0	.200
Totals	**4**	**134**	**13**	**32**	**7**	**1**	**3**	**11**	**12**	**29**	**1**	**1**	**.239**

PITCHING STATISTICS

New York Yankees	G	GS	CG	IP	H	ER	BB	SO	W-L	Sv	ERA
David Cone	1	1	0	6	2	2	3	4	0-0	0	3.00
Orlando Hernandez	1	1	0	7	6	1	3	7	1-0	0	1.29
Graeme Lloyd	1	0	0	0 1/3	0	0	0	0	0-0	0	0.00
Ramiro Mendoza	1	0	0	1	2	1	0	1	1-0	0	9.00
Jeff Nelson	3	0	0	2 1/3	0	1	4	0	0-0	0	0.00
Andy Pettitte	1	1	0	7 1/3	5	0	3	4	1-0	0	0.00
Mariano Rivera	3	0	0	4 1/3	5	0	0	4	0-0	3	0.00
Mike Stanton	1	0	0	0 2/3	3	2	0	1	0-0	0	27.00
David Wells	1	1	0	7	7	5	2	4	1-0	0	6.43
Totals	**4**	**4**	**0**	**36**	**32**	**11**	**12**	**29**	**4-0**	**3**	**2.75**

San Diego Padres	G	GS	CG	IP	H	ER	BB	SO	W-L	Sv	ERA
Andy Ashby	1	1	0	2 2/3	10	4	1	1	0-1	0	13.50
Brian Boehringer	2	0	0	2	4	2	2	3	0-0	0	9.00
Kevin Brown	2	2	0	14 1/3	14	7	6	13	0-1	0	4.40
Joey Hamilton	1	0	0	1	0	0	1	1	0-0	0	0.00
Sterling Hitchcock	1	1	0	6	7	1	1	7	0-0	0	1.50
Trevor Hoffman	1	0	0	2	2	2	1	0	0-1	0	9.00
Mark Langston	1	0	0	0 2/3	1	3	2	0	0-0	0	40.50
Dan Miceli	2	0	0	1 2/3	2	0	2	1	0-0	0	0.00
Randy Myers	3	0	0	1	0	1	1	2	0-0	0	9.00
Donne Wall	2	0	0	2 2/3	3	2	3	1	0-1	0	6.75
Totals	**4**	**4**	**0**	**34**	**43**	**22**	**20**	**29**	**0-4**	**0**	**5.82**

1999 League Divisional Series

NEW YORK YANKEES (3) VS. TEXAS RANGERS (0)

GAME 1

Tuesday, October 5
at Yankee Stadium, New York

	1	2	3	4	5	6	7	8	9	R	H	E
Texas Rangers	0	0	0	0	0	0	0	0	0	0	2	1
New York Yankees	0	1	0	0	2	4	0	1	x	8	10	0

HR - NY Bernie Williams

WP - Orlando Hernandez; LP - Aaron Sele

GAME 2

Thursday, October 7
at Yankee Stadium, New York

	1	2	3	4	5	6	7	8	9	R	H	E
Texas Rangers	0	0	0	1	0	0	0	0	0	1	7	0
New York Yankees	0	0	0	0	1	0	1	1	x	3	7	2

HR - TEX Juan Gonzalez

WP - Andy Pettitte; LP - Rick Helling; Sv - Mariano Rivera

GAME 3

Saturday, October 9
at the Ballpark in Arlington

	1	2	3	4	5	6	7	8	9	R	H	E
New York Yankees	3	0	0	0	0	0	0	0	0	3	6	0
Texas Rangers	0	0	0	0	0	0	0	0	0	0	5	1

HR - NY Darryl Strawberry

WP - Roger Clemens; LP - Esteban Loaiza; Sv - Mariano Rivera

BATTING STATISTICS

New York Yankees	G	AB	R	H	2B	3B	HR	RBI	BB	SO	SB	CS	Avg
Clay Bellinger	1	0	0	0	0	0	0	0	0	0	0	0	.000
Scott Brosius	3	10	0	1	1	0	0	1	0	0	0	0	.100
Chad Curtis	3	3	1	0	0	0	0	0	0	0	0	0	.000
Chili Davis	1	3	0	1	0	0	0	0	0	2	0	0	.333
Joe Girardi	2	6	0	0	0	0	0	0	0	1	0	0	.000
Derek Jeter	3	11	3	5	1	1	0	0	2	3	0	0	.455
Chuck Knoblauch	3	12	1	2	0	0	0	0	1	3	0	0	.167
Ricky Ledee	3	11	1	3	2	0	0	2	1	5	0	0	.273
Jim Leyritz	2	2	0	0	0	0	0	1	1	0	0	0	.000
Tino Martinez	3	11	2	2	0	0	0	0	2	2	0	0	.182
Paul O'Neill	2	8	2	2	0	0	0	0	1	1	0	0	.250
Jorge Posada	1	4	0	1	1	0	0	0	0	0	0	0	.250
Darryl Strawberry	2	6	2	2	0	0	1	3	1	0	0	0	.333
Bernie Williams	3	11	2	4	1	0	1	6	1	2	0	0	.364
Totals	**3**	**98**	**14**	**23**	**6**	**1**	**2**	**13**	**10**	**19**	**0**	**0**	**.235**

Texas Rangers	G	AB	R	H	2B	3B	HR	RBI	BB	SO	SB	CS	Avg
Royce Clayton	3	10	0	0	0	0	0	0	0	1	0	0	.000
Juan Gonzalez	3	11	1	2	0	0	1	1	1	3	0	0	.182
Tom Goodwin	3	7	0	1	0	0	0	0	0	1	0	0	.143
Rusty Greer	3	9	0	1	0	0	0	0	3	1	0	0	.111
Roberto Kelly	1	3	0	1	0	0	0	0	0	2	0	0	.333
Mark McLemore	3	10	0	1	0	0	0	0	1	3	0	0	.100
Rafael Palmeiro	3	11	0	3	0	0	0	0	1	1	0	0	.273
Ivan Rodriguez	3	12	0	3	1	0	0	0	0	2	1	0	.250
Lee Stevens	3	9	0	1	1	0	0	0	1	2	0	0	.111
Todd Zeile	3	10	0	1	0	0	0	0	2	1	0	0	.100
Totals	**3**	**92**	**1**	**14**	**2**	**0**	**1**	**1**	**9**	**17**	**1**	**0**	**.152**

PITCHING STATISTICS

New York Yankees	G	GS	CG	IP	H	ER	BB	SO	W-L	Sv	ERA
Roger Clemens	1	1	0	7	3	0	2	2	1-0	0	0.00
Orlando Hernandez	1	1	0	8	2	0	6	4	1-0	0	0.00
Jeff Nelson	3	0	0	1 2/3	1	0	1	3	0-0	0	0.00
Andy Pettitte	1	1	0	7 1/3	7	1	0	5	1-0	0	1.23
Mariano Rivera	2	0	0	3	1	0	0	3	0-0	2	0.00
Totals	**3**	**3**	**0**	**27**	**14**	**1**	**9**	**17**	**3-0**	**2**	**0.33**

Texas Rangers	G	GS	CG	IP	H	ER	BB	SO	W-L	Sv	ERA
Tim Crabtree	2	0	0	1 2/3	1	1	1	1	0-0	0	5.40
Jeff Fassero	1	0	0	1	2	1	1	1	0-0	0	9.00
Rick Helling	1	1	0	6 1/3	5	2	1	8	0-1	0	2.84
Esteban Loaiza	1	1	0	7	5	3	1	4	0-1	0	3.86
Danny Patterson	1	0	0	1	1	0	0	0	0-0	0	0.00
Aaron Sele	1	1	0	5	6	3	5	3	0-1	0	5.40
Mike Venafro	2	0	0	1	2	0	1	0	0-0	0	0.00
John Wetteland	1	0	0	1	0	0	0	1	0-0	0	0.00
Jeff Zimmerman	1	0	0	1	1	0	0	1	0-0	0	0.00
Totals	**3**	**3**	**0**	**25**	**23**	**10**	**10**	**19**	**0-3**	**0**	**3.60**

1999 League Championship Series

NEW YORK YANKEES (4) VS. BOSTON RED SOX (1)

GAME 1
Wednesday, October 13
at Yankee Stadium, New York

	1	2	3	4	5	6	7	8	9	10	R	H	E
Boston Red Sox	2	1	0	0	0	0	0	0	0	0	3	8	3
New York Yankees	0	2	0	0	0	0	1	0	0	1	4	10	0

HR - NY Scott Brosius, Bernie Williams

WP - Mariano Rivera; LP - Rod Beck

GAME 2
Thursday, October 14
at Yankee Stadium, New York

	1	2	3	4	5	6	7	8	9	R	H	E
Boston Red Sox	0	0	0	0	2	0	0	0	0	2	10	0
New York Yankees	0	0	0	1	0	0	2	0	x	3	7	0

HR - NY Tino Martinez; BOS Nomar Garciaparra

WP - David Cone; LP - Ramon Martinez; Sv - Mariano Rivera

GAME 3
Saturday, October 16
at Fenway Park, Boston

	1	2	3	4	5	6	7	8	9	R	H	E
New York Yankees	0	0	0	0	0	0	0	1	0	1	3	3
Boston Red Sox	2	2	2	0	2	1	4	0	x	13	21	1

HR - NY Scott Brosius; BOS Brian Daubach, Nomar Garciaparra, Jose Valentin

WP - Pedro Martinez; LP - Roger Clemens

GAME 4
Sunday, October 17
at Fenway Park, Boston

	1	2	3	4	5	6	7	8	9	R	H	E
New York Yankees	0	1	0	2	0	0	0	6	9	11	0	
Boston Red Sox	0	1	1	0	0	0	0	0	2	10	4	

HR - NY Ricky Ledee, Darryl Strawberry

WP - Andy Pettitte; LP - Bret Saberhagen; Sv - Mariano Rivera

GAME 5
Tuesday, October 19
at Fenway Park, Boston

	1	2	3	4	5	6	7	8	9	R	H	E
New York Yankees	2	0	0	0	0	0	2	0	2	6	11	1
Boston Red Sox	0	0	0	0	0	0	0	1	0	1	5	2

HR - NY Derek Jeter, Jorge Posada; BOS Jason Varitek

WP - Orlando Hernandez; LP - Kent Mercker; Sv - Ramiro Mendoza

BATTING STATISTICS

New York Yankees	G	AB	R	H	2B	3B	HR	RBI	BB	SO	SB	CS	Avg
Clay Bellinger	3	1	0	0	0	0	0	0	0	1	0	0	.000
Scott Brosius	5	18	3	4	0	1	2	3	1	4	0	0	.222
Chad Curtis	3	6	1	0	0	0	0	0	0	2	1	0	.000
Chili Davis	5	11	0	1	0	0	0	1	3	4	0	0	.091
Joe Girardi	3	8	0	2	0	0	0	0	0	2	0	0	.250
Derek Jeter	5	20	3	7	1	0	1	3	2	3	0	0	.350
Chuck Knoblauch	5	18	3	6	1	0	0	1	3	0	1	0	.333
Ricky Ledee	3	8	2	2	0	0	1	4	1	4	0	1	.250
Tino Martinez	5	19	3	5	1	0	1	3	2	4	0	0	.263
Paul O'Neill	5	21	2	6	0	0	0	1	1	5	0	0	.286
Jorge Posada	3	10	1	1	0	0	1	2	1	2	0	0	.100
Luis Sojo	2	1	0	0	0	0	0	0	0	0	0	0	.000
Shane Spencer	3	9	1	1	0	0	0	0	1	6	0	0	.111
Darryl Strawberry	3	6	1	2	0	0	1	1	1	2	0	0	.333
Bernie Williams	5	20	3	5	1	0	1	2	2	5	1	0	.250
Totals	**5**	**176**	**23**	**42**	**4**	**1**	**8**	**21**	**18**	**44**	**3**	**1**	**.239**

Boston Red Sox	G	AB	R	H	2B	3B	HR	RBI	BB	SO	SB	CS	Avg
Damon Buford	4	5	1	2	0	0	0	0	0	2	1	0	.400
Brian Daubach	5	17	2	3	1	0	1	3	1	4	0	0	.176
Nomar Garciaparra	5	20	2	8	2	0	2	5	2	2	1	0	.400
Scott Hatteberg	3	1	0	0	0	0	0	0	0	1	0	0	.000
Butch Husky	4	5	1	1	0	0	0	0	0	1	0	0	.200
Darren Lewis	5	17	2	2	1	0	0	1	1	3	1	1	.118
Lou Merloni	1	0	0	0	0	0	0	0	1	0	0	0	.000
Trot Nixon	4	14	2	4	2	0	0	0	1	5	0	0	.286
Jose Offerman	5	24	4	11	0	1	0	2	1	3	1	0	.458
Troy O'Leary	5	20	2	7	3	0	0	1	2	5	0	0	.350
Donnie Sadler	2	0	0	0	0	0	0	0	0	0	0	0	.000
Mike Stanley	5	18	1	4	0	0	0	1	2	4	0	0	.222
Jose Valentin	5	23	3	8	2	0	1	5	2	4	0	0	.348
Jason Varitek	5	20	1	4	1	1	1	1	1	4	0	0	.200
Totals	**5**	**184**	**21**	**54**	**13**	**2**	**5**	**19**	**15**	**38**	**4**	**1**	**.293**

PITCHING STATISTICS

New York Yankees	G	GS	CG	IP	H	ER	BB	SO	W-L	Sv	ERA
Roger Clemens	1	1	0	2	6	5	2	2	0-1	0	22.50
David Cone	1	1	0	7	7	2	3	9	1-0	0	2.57
Orlando Hernandez	2	2	0	15	12	3	6	13	1-0	0	1.80
Hideki Irabu	1	0	0	4 2/3	13	7	0	3	0-0	0	13.50
Ramiro Mendoza	2	0	0	2 1/3	0	0	0	2	0-0	1	0.00
Jeff Nelson	2	0	0	0 2/3	0	0	0	0	0-0	0	0.00
Andy Pettitte	1	1	0	7 1/3	8	2	1	5	1-0	0	2.45
Mariano Rivera	3	0	0	4 2/3	5	0	0	3	1-0	2	0.00
Mike Stanton	3	0	0	0 1/3	1	0	1	0	0-0	0	0.00
Allen Watson	3	0	0	1	2	0	2	1	0-0	0	0.00
Totals	5	5	0	45	54	19	15	38	4-1	3	3.8

Boston Red Sox	G	GS	CG	IP	H	ER	BB	SO	W-L	Sv	ERA
Rod Beck	2	0	0	0 2/3	2	2	0	1	0-1	0	27.00
Rheal Cormier	4	0	0	3 2/3	3	0	3	4	0-0	0	0.00
Rich Garces	2	0	0	3	3	4	1	2	0-0	0	12.00
Tom Gordon	3	0	0	2	3	3	1	3	0-0	0	13.50
Derek Lowe	3	0	0	6 1/3	6	1	2	7	0-0	0	1.42
Pedro Martinez	1	1	0	7	2	0	2	12	1-0	0	0.00
Ramon Martinez	1	1	0	6 2/3	6	3	3	5	0-1	0	4.05
Kent Mercker	2	2	0	7 2/3	12	4	4	5	0-1	0	4.70
Pat Rapp	1	0	0	1	0	0	1	0	0-0	0	0.00
Bret Saberhagen	1	1	0	6	5	1	1	5	0-1	0	1.50
Totals	5	5	0	44	42	18	18	44	1-4	0	3.68

1999 World Series

NEW YORK YANKEES (4) VS. ATLANTA BRAVES (0)

GAME 1
Saturday, October 23
at Turner Field, Atlanta

	1	2	3	4	5	6	7	8	9	R	H	E
New York Yankees	0	0	0	0	0	0	4	0	4	6	0	
Atlanta Braves	0	0	0	1	0	0	0	0	0	1	2	2

HR - ATL Chipper Jones

WP - Orlando Hernandez; **LP** - Greg Maddux; **Sv** - Mariano Rivera

GAME 2
Sunday, October 24
at Turner Field, Atlanta

	1	2	3	4	5	6	7	8	9	R	H	E
New York Yankees	3	0	2	1	1	0	0	0	0	7	14	1
Atlanta Braves	0	0	0	0	0	0	0	2	2	5	1	

WP - David Cone; **LP** - Kevin Millwood

GAME 3
Tuesday, October 26
at Yankee Stadium, New York

	1	2	3	4	5	6	7	8	9	10	R	H	E
Atlanta Braves	1	0	3	1	0	0	0	0	0	0	5	14	1
New York Yankees	1	0	0	0	1	0	1	2	0	1	6	9	0

HR - NY Chad Curtis 2, Chuck Knoblauch, Tino Martinez

WP - Mariano Rivera; **LP** - Mike Remlinger

GAME 4
Wednesday, October 27
at Yankee Stadium, New York

	1	2	3	4	5	6	7	8	9	R	H	E
Atlanta Braves	0	0	0	0	0	0	1	0	1	5	0	
New York Yankees	0	0	3	0	0	0	1	x	4	8	0	

HR - NY Jim Leyritz

WP - Roger Clemens; **LP** - John Smoltz; **Sv** - Mariano Rivera

BATTING STATISTICS

New York Yankees	G	AB	R	H	2B	3B	HR	RBI	BB	SO	SB	CS	BA
Scott Brosius	4	16	2	6	1	0	0	1	0	5	0	0	.375
Roger Clemens	1	0	0	0	0	0	0	0	0	0	0	0	—
David Cone	1	4	0	0	0	0	0	0	0	0	0	0	.000
Chad Curtis	3	6	3	2	0	0	2	2	0	0	0	0	.333
Chili Davis	1	4	0	0	0	0	0	0	0	2	0	0	.000
Joe Girardi	2	7	1	2	0	0	0	0	0	1	0	0	.286
Jason Grimsley	1	0	0	0	0	0	0	0	0	0	0	0	—
Orlando Hernandez	1	1	0	0	0	0	0	0	0	0	0	0	.000
Derek Jeter	4	17	4	6	1	0	0	1	1	3	3	1	.353
Chuck Knoblauch	4	16	5	5	1	0	1	3	1	3	1	0	.313
Ricky Ledee	3	10	0	2	1	0	0	1	1	4	0	0	.200
Jim Leyritz	2	1	1	1	0	0	1	2	1	0	0	0	1.000
Tino Martinez	4	15	3	4	0	0	1	5	2	4	0	0	.267
Ramiro Mendoza	1	1	0	0	0	0	0	0	0	0	0	0	.000
Jeff Nelson	4	0	0	0	0	0	0	0	0	0	0	0	—
Paul O'Neill	4	15	0	3	0	0	0	4	2	2	0	0	.200
Andy Pettitte	1	0	0	0	0	0	0	0	0	0	0	0	—
Jorge Posada	2	8	0	2	1	0	0	1	0	3	0	0	.250
Mariano Rivera	3	0	0	0	0	0	0	0	0	0	0	0	—
Luis Sojo	1	0	0	0	0	0	0	0	0	0	0	0	—
Mike Stanton	1	0	0	0	0	0	0	0	0	0	0	0	—
Darryl Strawberry	2	3	0	1	0	0	0	0	1	2	0	0	.333
Bernie Williams	4	13	2	3	0	0	0	0	4	2	1	0	.231
Totals	**4**	**137**	**21**	**37**	**5**	**0**	**5**	**20**	**13**	**31**	**5**	**1**	**.270**

Atlanta Braves	G	AB	R	H	2B	3B	HR	RBI	BB	SO	SB	CS	BA
Howard Battle	1	0	0	0	0	0	0	0	0	0	0	0	—
Bret Boone	4	13	1	7	4	0	0	3	1	3	0	1	.538
Jorge Fabregas	1	1	0	0	0	0	0	0	0	1	0	0	.000
Tom Glavine	1	0	0	0	0	0	0	0	0	0	0	0	—
Ozzie Guillen	3	5	0	0	0	0	0	0	0	1	0	0	.000
Jose Hernandez	2	5	0	1	1	0	0	2	0	2	1	0	.200
Brian Hunter	2	4	0	1	0	0	0	0	0	1	0	0	.250
Andruw Jones	4	13	1	1	0	0	0	0	1	3	0	0	.077
Chipper Jones	4	13	2	3	0	0	1	2	4	2	0	1	.231
Brian Jordan	4	13	1	1	0	0	0	1	4	2	0	0	.077
Ryan Klesko	4	12	0	2	0	0	0	0	0	1	0	0	.167
Keith Lockhart	4	7	1	1	0	0	0	0	2	0	0	0	.143
Greg Maddux	1	2	0	0	0	0	0	0	0	2	0	0	.000
Kevin McGlinchy	1	0	0	0	0	0	0	0	0	0	0	0	—
Kevin Millwood	1	0	0	0	0	0	0	0	0	0	0	0	—
Terry Mulholland	2	0	0	0	0	0	0	0	1	0	0	0	.000
Greg Myers	4	6	0	2	0	0	0	1	1	0	0	0	.333
Otis Nixon	2	2	0	1	0	0	0	0	0	0	0	1	.500
Eddie Perez	3	8	0	1	0	0	0	0	1	3	0	0	.125
Mike Remlinger	2	0	0	0	0	0	0	0	0	0	0	0	—
John Rocker	2	0	0	0	0	0	0	0	0	0	0	0	—
John Smoltz	1	0	0	0	0	0	0	0	0	0	0	0	—
Russ Springer	2	0	0	0	0	0	0	0	0	0	0	0	—
Walt Weiss	3	9	1	2	0	0	0	0	0	1	0	0	.222
Gerald Williams	4	17	2	3	0	1	0	0	0	4	0	0	.176
Totals	**4**	**130**	**9**	**26**	**5**	**1**	**1**	**9**	**15**	**26**	**1**	**3**	**.200**

PITCHING STATISTICS

New York Yankees	G	GS	CG	IP	H	ER	BB	SO	W-L	Sv	ERA
Roger Clemens	1	1	0	7 2/3	4	1	2	4	1-0	0	1.17
David Cone	1	1	0	7	1	0	5	4	1-0	0	0.00
Jason Grimsley	1	0	0	2 1/3	2	0	2	0	0-0	0	0.00
Orlando Hernandez	1	1	0	7	1	1	2	10	1-0	0	1.29
Ramiro Mendoza	1	0	0	1 2/3	3	2	1	0	0-0	0	10.80
Jeff Nelson	4	0	0	2 2/3	2	0	1	3	0-0	0	0.00
Andy Pettitte	1	1	0	3 2/3	10	5	1	1	0-0	0	12.27
Mariano Rivera	3	0	0	4 2/3	3	0	1	3	1-0	2	0.00
Mike Stanton	1	0	0	0 1/3	0	0	0	1	0-0	0	0.00
Totals	**4**	**4**	**0**	**37**	**26**	**9**	**15**	**26**	**4-0**	**2**	**2.19**

Atlanta Braves	G	GS	CG	IP	H	ER	BB	SO	W-L	Sv	ERA
Tom Glavine	1	1	0	7	7	4	0	3	0-0	0	5.14
Greg Maddux	1	1	0	7	5	2	3	5	0-1	0	2.57
Kevin McGlinchy	1	0	0	2	2	0	1	2	0-0	0	0.00
Kevin Milwood	1	1	0	2	8	4	2	2	0-1	0	18.00
Terry Mulholland	2	0	0	3 2/3	5	3	1	3	0-0	0	7.36
Mike Remlinger	2	0	0	1	1	1	1	0	0-1	0	9.00
John Rocker	2	0	0	3	0	0	2	4	0-0	0	0.00
John Smoltz	1	1	0	7	6	3	3	11	0-1	0	3.86
Russ Springer	2	0	0	2 1/3	1	0	0	1	0-0	0	0.00
Totals	**4**	**4**	**0**	**35**	**37**	**17**	**13**	**31**	**0-4**	**0**	**4.37**

2000 League Division Series
NEW YORK YANKEES (3) VS. OAKLAND A'S (2)

GAME 1
Tuesday, October 3
at Network Associates Colisuem, Oakland

	1	2	3	4	5	6	7	8	9	R	H	E
New York Yankees	0	2	0	0	0	1	0	0	0	3	7	0
Oakland A's	0	0	0	0	3	1	0	1	x	5	10	2

WP - Gil Heredia; LP -Roger Clemens; Sv - Jason Isringhausen

GAME 2
Wednesday, October 4
at Network Associates Colisuem, Oakland

	1	2	3	4	5	6	7	8	9	R	H	E
New York Yankees	0	0	0	0	0	3	0	0	1	4	8	1
Oakland A's	0	0	0	0	0	0	0	0	0	0	6	1

WP - Andy Pettitte; LP - Kevin Appier; Sv - Mariano Rivera

GAME 3
Friday, October 6
at Yankee Stadium, New York

	1	2	3	4	5	6	7	8	9	R	H	E
Oakland A's	0	1	0	0	1	0	0	0	0	2	4	2
New York Yankees	0	2	0	1	0	0	0	1	x	4	6	1

WP - Orlando Hernandez; LP - Tim Hudson; Sv - Mariano Rivera

GAME 4
Saturday, October 7

	1	2	3	4	5	6	7	8	9	R	H	E
Oakland A's	3	0	0	0	0	3	0	1	4	11	11	0
New York Yankees	0	0	0	0	0	1	0	0	0	1	8	0

WP - Barry Zito; LP - Roger Clemens

GAME 5
Sunday, October 8
at Network Associates Colisuem, Oakland

	1	2	3	4	5	6	7	8	9	R	H	E
New York Yankees	6	0	0	1	0	0	0	0	0	7	12	0
Oakland A's	0	2	1	2	0	0	0	0	0	5	13	0

WP - Mike Stanton; LP - Gil Heredia; Sv - Mariano Rivera

BATTING STATISTICS

New York Yankees	G	AB	R	H	2B	3B	HR	RBI	BB	SO	SB	CS	Avg
Clay Bellinger	2	1	0	1	1	0	0	1	0	0	0	0	1.000
Scott Brosius	5	17	0	3	1	0	0	1	1	4	0	0	.176
Glenallen Hill	4	12	1	1	0	0	0	2	1	5	0	0	.083
Derek Jeter	5	19	1	4	0	0	0	2	2	3	0	1	.211
David Justice	5	18	2	4	0	0	1	3	4	0	0	0	.222
Chuck Knoblauch	3	9	1	3	0	0	0	1	0	2	1	0	.333
Tino Martinez	5	19	2	8	2	0	0	4	1	3	0	0	.421
Paul O'Neill	5	19	4	4	1	0	0	0	2	4	0	0	.211
Luis Polonia	1	1	0	1	0	0	0	0	0	0	0	0	1.000
Jorge Posada	5	17	2	4	2	0	0	1	3	5	0	0	.235
Luis Sojo	5	16	2	3	2	0	0	5	2	1	0	0	.188
Jose Vizcaino	1	0	1	0	0	0	0	0	0	0	0	0	.000
Bernie Williams	5	20	3	5	3	0	0	1	1	4	0	1	.250
Totals	**5**	**168**	**19**	**41**	**12**	**0**	**1**	**19**	**16**	**35**	**1**	**2**	**.244**

Oakland A's	G	AB	R	H	2B	3B	HR	RBI	BB	SO	SB	CS	Avg
Bo Porter	2	1	0	1	0	0	0	1	0	0	0	0	1.000
Eric Chavez	5	21	4	7	3	0	0	4	0	5	0	0	.333
Ryan Christenson	2	2	0	1	0	0	0	1	0	1	0	0	.500
Sal Fasano	1	0	0	0	0	0	0	0	0	0	0	0	.000
Jason Giambi	5	14	2	4	0	0	0	1	7	2	1	0	.286
Jeremy Giambi	4	9	1	3	0	0	0	1	2	2	0	0	.333
Ben Grieve	5	17	1	2	0	0	0	2	3	7	0	0	.118
Ramon Hernandez	5	16	3	6	2	0	0	3	0	3	0	0	.375
Terrence Long	5	19	2	3	0	0	1	1	3	2	0	0	.158
Frank Menechino	1	0	0	0	0	0	0	0	0	0	0	0	.000
Adam Piatt	3	6	2	1	0	0	0	0	0	1	0	0	.167
Olmedo Saenz	4	13	1	3	0	0	1	4	0	2	0	0	.231
Matt Stairs	3	9	0	1	1	0	0	0	0	1	0	0	.111
Miguel Tejada	5	20	5	7	2	0	0	1	2	2	1	0	.350
Randy Velarde	5	20	2	5	1	0	0	3	2	3	1	0	.250
Totals	**5**	**167**	**23**	**44**	**9**	**0**	**2**	**22**	**19**	**31**	**3**	**0**	**.263**

PITCHING STATISTICS

New York Yankees	G	GS	CG	IP	H	ER	BB	SO	W-L	Sv	ERA
Randy Choate	1	0	0	1 1/3	0	1	1	1	0-0	0	6.75
Roger Clemens	2	2	0	11	13	10	8	10	0-2	0	8.18
Dwight Gooden	1	0	0	1 2/3	4	4	1	1	0-0	0	21.60
Orlando Hernandez	2	1	0	7 1/3	5	2	5	5	1-0	0	2.45
Jeff Nelson	2	0	0	2	0	0	0	2	0-0	0	0.00
Andy Pettitte	2	2	0	11 1/3	15	5	3	7	1-0	0	3.97
Mariano Rivera	3	0	0	5	2	0	0	2	0-0	3	0.00
Mike Stanton	3	0	0	4 1/3	5	1	1	3	1-0	0	2.08
Totals	**5**	**5**	**0**	**44**	**44**	**23**	**19**	**31**	**3-2**	**3**	**4.70**

Oakland A's	G	GS	CG	IP	H	ER	BB	SO	W-L	Sv	ERA
Kevin Appier	2	1	0	10 1/3	10	4	6	13	0-1	0	3.48
Gil Heredia	2	2	0	6 1/3	11	9	3	3	1-1	0	12.79
Tim Hudson	1	1	1	8	6	3	4	5	0-1	0	3.38
Jason Isringhausen	2	0	0	2	1	0	0	3	0-0	1	0.00
Doug Jones	2	0	0	1 1/3	1	0	0	1	0-0	0	0.00
Mike Magnante	2	0	0	3	1	0	0	2	0-0	0	0.00
Jim Mecir	3	0	0	5 1/3	1	0	0	2	0-0	0	0.00
Jeff Tam	3	0	0	2	3	0	1	1	0-0	0	0.00
Barry Zito	1	1	0	5 2/3	7	1	2	5	1-0	0	1.59
Totals	**5**	**5**	**1**	**44**	**41**	**17**	**16**	**35**	**2-3**	**1**	**3.48**

2000 League Championship Series

NEW YORK YANKEES (4) VS. SEATTLE MARINERS

GAME 1
Tuesday, October 10
at Yankee Stadium, New York

	1	2	3	4	5	6	7	8	9	R	H	E
Seattle Mariners	0	0	0	0	1	1	0	0	0	2	5	0
New York Yankees	0	0	0	0	0	0	0	0	0	0	6	1

WP - Freddie Garcia; LP - Denny Neagle; Sv - Kazuhiro Sasaki

GAME 2
Wednesday, October 11
at Yankee Stadium, New York

	1	2	3	4	5	6	7	8	9	R	H	E
Seattle Mariners	0	0	1	0	0	0	0	0	0	1	7	1
New York Yankees	0	0	0	0	0	0	0	7	x	7	14	0

WP - Orlando Hernandez; LP - Arthur Rhodes

GAME 3
Friday, October 13
at Safeco Field, Seattle

	1	2	3	4	5	6	7	8	9	R	H	E
New York Yankees	0	2	1	0	0	1	0	0	4	8	13	0
Seattle Mariners	1	0	0	0	1	0	0	0	0	2	10	1

WP - Andy Pettitte; LP - Aaron Sele; Sv - Mariano Rivera

GAME 4
Saturday, October 14
at Safeco Field, Seattle

	1	2	3	4	5	6	7	8	9	R	H	E
New York Yankees	0	0	0	0	3	0	0	2	0	5	5	0
Seattle Mariners	0	0	0	0	0	0	0	0	0	1	0	

WP - Roger Clemens; LP - Paul Abbott

GAME 5
Sunday, October 15
at Safeco Field, Seattle

	1	2	3	4	5	6	7	8	9	R	H	E
New York Yankees	0	0	0	2	0	0	0	0	0	2	8	0
Seattle Mariners	1	0	0	0	5	0	0	0	x	6	8	0

WP - Freddie Garcia; LP - Denny Neagle

GAME 6
Tuesday, October 17
at Yankee Stadium, New York

	1	2	3	4	5	6	7	8	9	R	H	E
Seattle Mariners	2	0	0	2	0	0	0	3	0	7	10	0
New York Yankees	0	0	0	3	0	0	6	0	x	9	11	0

WP - Orlando Hernandez; LP - Jose Paniagua

BATTING STATISTICS

New York Yankees	G	AB	R	H	2B	3B	HR	RBI	BB	SO	SB	CS	Avg
Clay Bellinger	5	0	0	0	0	0	0	0	0	0	0	0	—
Scott Brosius	6	18	2	4	0	0	0	0	2	3	0	1	.222
Glenallen Hill	2	2	0	0	0	0	0	0	0	2	0	0	.000
Derek Jeter	6	22	6	7	0	0	2	5	6	7	1	0	.318
David Justice	6	26	4	6	2	0	2	8	2	7	0	0	.231
Chuck Knoblauch	6	23	3	6	2	0	0	2	3	4	0	0	.261
Tino Martinez	6	25	5	8	2	0	1	1	2	4	0	0	.320
Paul O'Neill	6	20	0	5	0	0	0	5	1	2	0	0	.250
Luis Polonia	1	1	0	0	0	0	0	0	0	1	0	0	.000
Jorge Posada	6	19	2	3	1	0	0	3	5	5	0	1	.158
Luis Sojo	6	23	1	6	1	0	0	2	0	2	3	0	.261
Jose Vizcaino	4	2	3	2	1	0	0	2	0	0	2	0	1.000
Bernie Williams	6	23	5	10	1	0	1	3	2	3	1	0	.435
Totals	**6**	**204**	**31**	**57**	**10**	**0**	**6**	**31**	**25**	**41**	**4**	**2**	**.279**

Seattle Mariners	G	AB	R	H	2B	3B	HR	RBI	BB	SO	SB	CS	Avg
David Bell	5	18	0	4	0	0	0	0	0	0	0	0	.222
Jay Buhner	4	11	0	2	0	0	0	0	1	6	0	0	.182
Mike Cameron	6	18	3	2	0	0	1	2	7	1	0	.111
Charles Gipson	2	0	0	0	0	0	0	0	0	0	0	0	—
Carlos Guillen	2	5	1	1	0	0	1	2	2	2	0	1	.200
Rickey Henderson	3	9	2	2	1	0	0	1	2	2	0	1	.222
Raul Ibanez	6	9	0	0	0	0	0	0	2	0	0	0	.000
Stan Javier	4	14	0	1	0	0	0	1	0	4	0	0	.071
Al Martin	4	11	1	2	2	0	0	0	2	3	0	0	.182
Edgar Martinez	6	21	2	5	1	0	1	4	3	5	0	0	.238
Mark McLemore	5	16	2	4	3	0	0	2	2	1	0	0	.250
John Olerud	6	20	3	7	3	0	1	2	2	2	1	0	.350
Joe Oliver	4	6	0	1	0	0	0	0	1	1	0	0	.167
Alex Rodriguez	6	22	4	9	2	0	2	5	3	8	1	0	.409
Dan Wilson	4	11	0	1	0	0	0	0	1	5	0	0	.091
Totals	**6**	**191**	**18**	**41**	**12**	**0**	**5**	**18**	**20**	**48**	**3**	**2**	**.215**

PITCHING STATISTICS

New York Yankees	G	GS	CG	IP	H	ER	BB	SO	W-L	Sv	ERA
Randy Choate	1	0	0	0 1/3	0	0	0	1	0-0	0	0.00
Roger Clemens	1	1	1	9	1	0	2	15	1-0	0	0.00
David Cone	1	0	0	1	0	0	0	0	0-0	0	0.00
Dwight Gooden	1	0	0	2 1/3	1	0	0	1	0-0	0	0.00
Jason Grimsley	2	0	0	1	2	0	3	1	0-0	0	0.00
Orlando Hernandez	2	2	0	15	13	7	8	14	2-0	0	4.20
Denny Neagle	2	2	0	10	6	5	7	7	0-2	0	4.50
Jeff Nelson	3	0	0	3	5	3	0	6	0-0	0	9.00
Andy Pettitte	1	1	0	6 2/3	9	2	1	2	1-0	0	2.70
Mariano Rivera	3	0	0	4 2/3	4	1	0	1	0-0	1	1.93
Totals	**6**	**6**	**1**	**53**	**41**	**18**	**21**	**48**	**4-2**	**1**	**3.06**
Seattle Mariners	**G**	**GS**	**CG**	**IP**	**H**	**ER**	**BB**	**SO**	**W-L**	**SV**	**ERA**
Paul Abbott	1	1	0	5	3	3	3	3	0-1	0	5.40
Freddy Garcia	2	2	0	11 2/3	10	2	4	11	2-0	0	1.54
John Halama	2	2	0	9 1/3	10	3	5	3	0-0	0	2.89
Jose Mesa	3	0	0	4 1/3	5	6	3	3	0-0	0	12.46
Jose Paniagua	5	0	0	4 1/3	4	2	1	4	0-1	0	4.15
Robert Ramsay	2	0	0	1 2/3	2	0	0	1	0-0	0	0.00
Arthur Rhodes	4	0	0	2	8	7	4	5	0-1	0	31.50
Kazuhiro Sasaki	2	0	0	2 2/3	3	0	1	3	0-0	1	0.00
Aaron Sele	1	1	0	6	9	4	0	4	0-1	0	6.00
Brett Tomko	2	0	0	5	3	4	4	4	0-0	0	7.20
Totals	**6**	**6**	**0**	**52**	**57**	**31**	**25**	**41**	**2-4**	**1**	**5.37**

2000 World Series

NEW YORK YANKEES (4) VS. NEW YORK METS (1)

GAME 1
Saturday, October 21
at Yankee Stadium, New York

	1	2	3	4	5	6	7	8	9	10	11	12	R	H	E
New York Mets	0	0	0	0	0	3	0	0	0	0	0	0	3	10	0
New York Yankees	0	0	0	0	2	0	0	1	0	0	1	4	12	0

WP - Mike Stanton; LP - Turk Wendell

GAME 2
Sunday, October 22
at Yankee Stadium, New York

	1	2	3	4	5	6	7	8	9	R	H	E
New York Mets	0	0	0	0	0	0	0	5	5	7	3
New York Yankees	2	1	0	0	1	0	1	1	x	6	12	1

HR - NYM Jay Payton, Mike Piazza; NYY Scott Brosius

WP - Roger Clemens; LP - Mike Hampton

GAME 3
Tuesday, October 24
at Shea Stadium, New York

	1	2	3	4	5	6	7	8	9	R	H	E
New York Yankees	0	0	1	1	0	0	0	0	0	2	8	0
New York Mets	0	1	0	0	0	1	0	2	x	4	9	0

HR - NYM Robin Ventura

WP - John Franco; LP - Orlando Hernandez; Sv - Armando Benitez

GAME 4
Wednesday, October 25
at Shea Stadium, New York

	1	2	3	4	5	6	7	8	9	R	H	E
New York Yankees	1	1	1	0	0	0	0	0	0	3	8	0
New York Mets	0	0	2	0	0	0	0	0	0	2	6	1

HR - NYY Derek Jeter; NYM Mike Piazza

WP - Jeff Nelson; LP - Bobby J. Jones; Sv - Mariano Rivera

GAME 5
Thursday, October 26
at Shea Stadium, New York

	1	2	3	4	5	6	7	8	9	R	H	E
New York Yankees	0	1	0	0	0	1	0	0	2	4	7	1
New York Mets	0	2	0	0	0	0	0	0	2	8	1

HR - NYY Derek Jeter, Bernie Williams

WP - Mike Stanton; LP - Al Leiter; Sv - Mariano Rivera

BATTING STATISTICS

New York Yankees	G	AB	R	H	2B	3B	HR	RBI	BB	SO	SB	CS	BA
Clay Bellinger	4	0	0	0	0	0	0	0	0	0	0	0	.000
Scott Brosius	5	13	2	4	0	0	1	3	2	2	0	0	.308
Jose Canseco	1	1	0	0	0	0	0	0	0	1	0	0	.000
David Cone	1	0	0	0	0	0	0	0	0	0	0	0	.000
Orlando Hernandez	1	2	0	0	0	0	0	0	0	2	0	0	.000
Glenallen Hill	3	3	0	0	0	0	0	0	0	0	0	0	.000
Derek Jeter	5	22	6	9	2	1	2	2	3	8	0	0	.409
David Justice	5	19	1	3	2	0	0	3	3	2	0	0	.158
Chuck Knoblauch	4	10	1	1	0	0	0	1	2	1	0	1	.100
Tino Martinez	5	22	3	8	1	0	0	2	1	4	0	0	.364
Denny Neagle	1	2	0	0	0	0	0	0	0	1	0	0	.000
Jeff Nelson	1	0	0	0	0	0	0	0	0	0	0	0	.000
Paul O'Neill	5	19	2	9	2	2	0	2	3	4	0	0	.474
Andy Pettitte	1	3	0	0	0	0	0	0	0	1	0	0	.000
Luis Polonia	2	2	0	1	0	0	0	0	0	0	0	0	.500
Jorge Posada	5	18	2	4	1	0	0	1	5	4	0	0	.222
Mariano Rivera	2	1	0	0	0	0	0	0	0	0	0	0	.000
Luis Sojo	4	7	0	2	0	0	0	2	1	0	1	0	.286
Mike Stanton	3	0	0	0	0	0	0	0	0	0	0	0	.000
Jose Vizcaino	4	17	0	4	0	0	0	1	0	5	0	1	.235
Bernie Williams	5	18	2	2	0	0	1	1	5	5	0	0	.111
Totals	**5**	**179**	**19**	**47**	**6**	**3**	**4**	**18**	**25**	**40**	**1**	**2**	**.263**

New York Mets	G	AB	R	H	2B	3B	HR	RBI	BB	SO	SB	CS	BA
Kurt Abbott	5	8	0	2	1	0	0	0	1	3	0	0	.250
Benny Agbayani	5	18	2	5	2	0	0	2	3	6	0	0	.278
Edgardo Alfonzo	5	21	1	3	0	0	0	1	1	5	0	0	.143
Armando Benitez	2	0	0	0	0	0	0	0	0	0	0	0	.000
Mike Bordick	4	8	0	1	0	0	0	0	0	3	0	0	.125
Dennis Cook	1	0	0	0	0	0	0	0	0	0	0	0	.000
John Franco	3	0	0	0	0	0	0	0	0	0	0	0	.000
Matt Franco	1	1	0	0	0	0	0	0	0	1	0	0	.000
Darryl Hamilton	4	3	0	0	0	0	0	0	0	2	0	0	.000
Lenny Harris	3	4	1	0	0	0	0	0	1	1	0	0	.000
Bobby J. Jones	1	2	0	0	0	0	0	0	0	1	0	0	.000
Al Leiter	1	2	0	0	0	0	0	0	0	0	0	0	.000
Joe McEwing	3	1	1	0	0	0	0	0	0	0	0	0	.000
Jay Payton	5	21	3	7	0	0	1	3	0	5	0	0	.333
Timo Perez	5	16	1	2	0	0	0	0	1	4	0	0	.125
Mike Piazza	5	22	3	6	2	0	2	4	0	4	0	1	.273
Todd Pratt	1	2	1	0	0	0	0	0	1	2	0	0	.000
Rick Reed	1	1	0	1	0	0	0	0	0	0	0	0	1.000
Glendon Rusch	1	0	0	0	0	0	0	0	0	0	0	0	.000
Bubba Trammell	4	5	1	2	0	0	0	3	1	1	0	0	.400
Robin Ventura	5	20	1	3	1	0	1	1	1	5	0	0	.150
Turk Wendell	1	0	0	0	0	0	0	0	0	0	0	0	.000
Todd Zeile	5	20	1	8	2	0	0	1	1	5	0	0	.400
Totals	**5**	**175**	**16**	**40**	**8**	**0**	**4**	**15**	**11**	**48**	**0**	**1**	**.229**

PITCHING STATISTICS

New York Yankees	G	GS	CG	IP	H	ER	BB	SO	W-L	Sv	ERA
Roger Clemens	1	1	0	8	2	0	0	9	1-0	0	0.00
David Cone	1	0	0	0 1/3	0	0	0	0	0-0	0	0.00
Orlando Hernandez	1	1	0	7 1/3	9	4	3	12	0-1	0	4.91
Denny Neagle	1	1	0	4 2/3	4	2	2	3	0-0	0	3.86
Jeff Nelson	3	0	0	2 2/3	5	3	1	1	1-0	0	10.13
Andy Pettitte	2	2	0	13 2/3	16	3	4	9	0-0	0	1.98
Mariano Rivera	4	0	0	6	4	2	1	7	0-0	2	3.00
Mike Stanton	4	0	0	4 1/3	0	0	0	7	2-0	0	0.00
Totals	**5**	**5**	**0**	**47**	**40**	**14**	**11**	**48**	**4-1**	**0**	**2.68**

New York Mets	G	GS	CG	IP	H	ER	BB	SO	W-L	Sv	ERA
Armando Benitez	3	0	0	3	3	1	2	2	0-0	1	3.00
Dennis Cook	3	0	0	0 2/3	1	0	3	1	0-0	0	0.00
John Franco	4	0	0	3 1/3	3	0	1	1	1-0	0	0.00
Mike Hampton	1	1	0	6	8	4	5	4	0-1	0	6.00
Bobby J. Jones	1	1	0	5	4	3	3	3	0-1	0	5.40
Al Leiter	2	2	0	15 2/3	12	5	6	16	0-1	0	2.87
Rick Reed	1	1	0	6	6	2	1	8	0-0	0	3.00
Glendon Rusch	3	0	0	4	6	1	2	2	0-0	0	2.25
Turk Wendell	2	0	0	1 2/3	3	1	2	2	0-1	0	5.40
Rick White	1	0	0	1 1/3	1	1	1	1	0-0	0	6.75
Totals	**5**	**5**	**0**	**46 2/3**	**47**	**18**	**25**	**40**	**1-4**	**1**	**3.47**

APPENDIX B:

New York Yankee Record Holders

Hitting categories

GAMES PLAYED

1 Mantle 2,401
2 Gehrig 2,164
3 Berra 2,116
4 Ruth 2,084
5 White 1,881
6 Dickey 1,789
7 Mattingly 1,785
8 DiMaggio 1,736
9 Randolph 1,694
10 Crosetti 1,682
11 Rizzuto 1,661
12 Lazzeri 1,659
13 Nettles 1,535
14 Howard 1,492
15 Pipp 1,488
16 Combs 1,455
17 Munson 1,423
18 Richardson 1,412
19 Bauer 1,406
20 McDougald 1,336

AT-BATS

1 Mantle 8,102
2 Gehrig 8,001
3 Berra 7,546
4 Ruth 7,217
5 Mattingly 7,003
6 DiMaggio 6,821
7 White 6,550
8 Randolph 6,303
9 Dickey 6,300
10 Crosetti 6,277
11 Lazzeri 6,094
12 Rizzuto 5,816
13 Combs 5,748
14 Pipp 5,594
15 Nettles 5,519
16 Richardson 5,386
17 Munson 5,344
18 Howard 5,044
19 Meusel 5,032
20 Rolfe 4,827

RUNS

1 Ruth 1,959
2 Gehrig 1,888
3 Mantle 1,677
4 DiMaggio 1,390

5 Combs 1,186
6 Berra 1,174
7 Randolph 1,027
8 Mattingly 1,007
9 Crosetti 1,006
10 White 964
11 Lazzeri 952
12 Rolfe 942
13 Dickey 930
14 Henrich 901
15 Rizzuto 877
16 B. Williams 862
17 Pipp 820
18 Bauer 792
19 Meusel 764.
20 Nettles 750

HITS

1 Gehrig 2,721
2 Ruth 2,518
3 Mantle 2,415
4 DiMaggio 2,214
5 Mattingly 2,153
6 Berra 2,148
7 Dickey 1,969
8 Combs 1,866
9 White 1,803
10 Lazzeri 1,784
11 Randolph 1,731
12 Rizzuto 1,588
13 Pipp 1,577
14 Meusel 1,565
15 Munson 1,558
16 Crosetti 1,541
17 B. Williams 1,463
18 Richardson 1,432
19 Howard 1,405
20 Nettles 1,396

DOUBLES

1 Gehrig 535
2 Mattingly 442
3 Ruth 424
4 DiMaggio 389
5 Mantle 344
6 Dickey 343
7 Meusel 338
8 Lazzeri 327
9 Berra 321
10 Combs 309
11 White 300
12 B. Williams 278
13 O'Neil 271

14 Henrich 269
15 Crosetti 260
16 Randolph 259
17 Pipp 259
18 Rolfe 257
19 Rizzuto 239
20 Winfield 236

TRIPLES

1 Gehrig 162
2 Combs 154
3 DiMaggio 131
4 Pipp 121
5 Lazzeri 115
6 Ruth 106
7 Meusel 87
8 Henrich 73
9 Dickey 72
9 Mantle 72
11 Keller 69
12 Rolfe 67
13 Stirnweiss 66
14 Crosetti 65
15 Chapman 64
16 Cree 62
16 Rizzuto 62
18 Conroy 59
19 Randolph 58
20 Bauer 56

HOME RUNS

1 Ruth 659
2 Mantle 536
3 Gehrig 493
4 DiMaggio 361
5 Berra 358
6 Nettles 250
7 Mattingly 222
8 Winfield 205
9 Maris 203
10 Dickey 202
11 Keller 184
12 Henrich 183
13 B Williams 181
14 Murcer 175
15 Lazzeri 169
16 Pepitone 166
17 Skowron 165
18 Howard 161
19 White 160
20 Bauer 158

RBI

1 Gehrig 1,991
2 Ruth 1,970
3 DiMaggio 1,537
4 Mantle 1,509
5 Berra 1,430
6 Dickey 1,209
7 Lazzeri 1,154
8 Mattingly 1,099
9 Meusel 1,005
10 Nettles 834
11 Pipp 825
12 Winfield 818
13 B. Williams 802
14 Henrich 795
15 O'Neill 788
16 White 758
17 Howard 732
18 Keller 723
19 Munson 701
20 Murcer 687

STOLEN BASES

1 Henderson 326
2 Randolph 251
3 Chase 248
4 White 233
5 Chapman 184
5 Conroy 184
7 Maisel 183
8 Mantle 153
9 Clarke 151
9 R. Kelly 151
11 Rizzuto 149
12 Lazzeri 147
13 Daniels 145
14 Peckinpaugh 143
15 Cree 132
16 Meusel 131
17 Stirnweiss 130
18 B. Williams 119
19 Keeler 118
20 Sax 117

BATTING AVERAGE
(500 games or more)

1 Ruth .349
2 Gehrig .340
3 Combs .325
3 DiMaggio .325
5 Jeter .322
6 Boggs .313
6 Dickey .313
8 Meusel .311
9 O'Neill .310
10 Mattingly .307
11 Chapman .305
12 B. Williams .304
13 Mantle .298
14 Schang .297
15 Piniella .295
16 Skowron .294
16 Keeler .294
16 Peckinpaugh .294
19 Lazzeri .293
20 Munson .294

Yankee Single-Season Leaders (by position):

HOME RUNS

Pitcher: Ruffing 5 (1936)
Catcher: Berra 30 (1952, 56)
1st base: Gehrig 49 (1934)
2nd base: Gordon 30 (1940)
3rd base: Nettles 37 (1977)
Shortstop: Smalley 24 (1999)
Outfield: Maris 61 (1961)

RBI

Pitcher: Ruffing 22 (1936,1941)
Catcher: Dickey 133 (1937)
1st base: Gehrig 184 (1931)
2nd base: Lazzeri 114 (1926)
3rd base: Nettles 107 (1977)
Dhortstop: Lary 107 (1931)
Outfield: Ruth 170 (1921)

BATTING AVERAGE

Pitcher: Ruffing .339 (1935)
Catcher: Dickey .362 (1936)
1st base: Gehrig .379 (1930)
2nd base: Lazzeri .354 (1929)
3rd base: Boggs .342 (1994)
Shortstop: Jeter .349 (1999)
Outfield: Ruth .393 (1923)

FIELDING PERCENTAGE

Pitcher: Mogridge 1.000 (1917) (*77 chances*); Bush 1.000 (1922) (*77 chances*)
Catcher: Howard .998 (1964)
Munson .998 (1971)
1st base: Mattingly .998 (1994)
2nd base: Stirnweiss .981 (1948)
3rd base: Boggs .981 (1995)
Shortstop: Stanley .983 (1976)
Outfield: White 1.000 (1971) (*314 chances*); O'Neill 1.000 (1996) (*300 chances*); B. Williams 1.000 (2000) (*355 chances*)

Pitching Leaders

GAMES PITCHED

1 Righetti 522
2 Ford, W. 498
3 Ruffing 426
4 Lyle 420
5 Shawkey 415
6 Murphy 383
7 Guidry 368
8 Gomez 367
9 Hoyt 365
10 Stottlemyre 360
11 Pennock 346
12 Gossage 319
13 Hamilton 311
14 Reynolds 295
15 Peterson 288
16 Page 278
17 Chesbro 269
18 Caldwell 248
19 Pipgras 247
19 Reniff 247

INNINGS

1 Ford, W. 3,170 $\frac{1}{3}$
2 Ruffing 3,168 $\frac{2}{3}$
3 Stottlemyre 2,661 $\frac{1}{3}$
4 Gomez 2,498 $\frac{1}{3}$
5 Shawkey 2,488 $\frac{2}{3}$
6 Guidry 2,392
7 Hoyt 2,272 $\frac{1}{3}$
8 Pennock 2,189 $\frac{2}{3}$
9 Chesbro 1,952

10	Peterson 1,857 ⅓
11	Caldwell 1,718 ⅓
12	Reynolds 1,700
13	Raschi 1,537
14	Lopat 1,497 ⅓
15	Chandler 1,485
16	Warhop 1,412 ⅔
17	Fisher 1,380 ⅓
18	John 1,367
19	Pipgras 1,351 ⅔
20	Quinn 1,270

WINS

1 Ford, W. 236
2 Ruffing 231
3 Gomez 189
4 Guidry 170
5 Shawkey 168
6 Stottlemyre 164
7 Pennock 162
8 Hoyt 157
9 Reynolds 131
10 Chesbro 128
11 Raschi 128
12 Lopat 113
13 Peterson 109
13 Chandler 109
15 Pettitte 100
16 Caldwell 96
17 Murphy 93
17 Pipgras 93
19 John 91
20 Turley 82

PERCENTAGE
(100 decisions or more)

1 Chandler .717
2 Raschi .706
3 Ford, W. .690
4 Reynolds .686
5 Mays .670
6 Lopat .657
7 Gomez .652
8 Guidry .651
8 Ruffing .651
10 Pettitte .645
11 Pennock .643
11 Byrne .643
13 Murphy .637
14 Hoyt .616
15 Bonham .612
15 Turley .612

17 John .603
18 Pipgras .592
19 Chesbro .579
20 Terry .569

STRIKEOUTS

1 Ford, W. 1,956
2 Guidry 1,778
3 Ruffing 1,526
4 Gomez 1,468
5 Stottlemyre 1,257
6 Shawkey 1,163
7 Downing 1,028
8 Reynolds 967
9 Raghetti 940
10 Chesbro 913
11 Turley 909
12 Peterson 893
13 Pettitte 834
14 Raschi 832
15 Caldwell 803
16 Cone 768
17 Hoyt 713
18 Pennock 700
19 Pipgras 656
20 Terry 615

SHUTOUTS

1 Ford, W. 45
2 Stottlemyre 40
2 Ruffing 40
4 Gomez 28
5 Reynolds 27
6 Chandler 26
6 Guidry 26
6 Shawkey 26
9 Raschi 24
10 Turley 21
11 Lopat 20
12 Pennock 19
13 Chesbro 18
13 Peterson 18
15 Bonham 17
16 Terry 16
17 Hoyt 15
18 Pipgras 14
19 Caldwell 13
20 Downing 12
20 John 12

COMPLETE GAMES

1 Ruffing 261
2 Gomez 173
3 Chesbro 168
4 Pennock 164
5 Shawkey 161
6 Ford, W. 156
6 Hoyt 156
8 Stottlemyre 152
9 Caldwell 151
10 Chandler 109
11 Warhop 105
12 Ford, R. 103
13 Orth 102
14 Raschi 99
15 Reynolds 96
16 Guidry 95
17 Bonham 91
17 Lopat 91
19 Pipgras 84
20 Quinn 82

ERA
(800 innings or more)

1 Ford, R. 2.54
2 Chesbro 2.58
3 Orth 2.72
4 Bonham 2.73
5 Ford, W. 2.75
6 Chandler 2.84
7 Fisher 2.91
8 Stottlemyre 2.97
9 Caldwell 3.00
10 Shawkey 3.10
10 Peterson 3.10
10 Bahnsen 3.10
13 Righetti 3.11
14 Warhop 3.12
15 Quinn 3.12
16 Lopat 3.25
16 Downing 3.25
16 Mays 3.25
19 Guidry 3.29
20 Reynolds 3.30

SAVES

1 Righetti 224
2 Rivera 165
3 Gossage 151
4 Lyle 141
5 Murphy 104
6 Farr 78
7 Page 76

8	Wetteland 74
9	McDaniel 58
10	Arroyo 43
10	Duren 43
12	Reniff 41
12	Reynolds 41
14	Sain 39
15	Hamilton 36
16	Aker 31
17	Howe 30
18	Grim 28
18	Hoyt 28
20	Morgan 26
20	Shawkey 26

Single-Season Club Records:

MOST WINS

Season: 114 (1998)
Home: 65 (1961)
Road: 54 (1939)
Month: 28 (August 1938)
Consecutive: 19 (1947)
Consecutive home: 18 (1942)
Consecutive road: 15 (1953)
Shutout: 24 (1951)

FEWEST WINS

Season: 50 (1912)
Home: 27 (1913)
Road: 19 (1912)

MOST LOSSES

Season: 103 (1908)
Home: 47 (1908, 1913)
Road: 58 (1912)
Month: 24 (July 1908)
Consecutive: 13 (1913)
Consecutive home: 17 (1913)
Consecutive road: 12 (1908)
Shutout: 27 (1914)

FEWEST LOSSES

Season: 44 (1927)
Home: 15 (1932)
Road: 20 (1939)
Most total players used: 50 (1989)

Fewest total players used: 25 (1923, 1927)
Most pitchers used: 24 (1996)
Fewest pitchers used: 8 (1922, 1923)

SINGLE-SEASON CLUB BATTING RECORDS

Most at-bats: 5,710 (1997)
Most runs: 1,067 (1931)
Fewest runs: 459 (1908)
Most hits: 1,683 (1930)
Fewest hits: 1,136 (1903)
Highest batting average: .309 (1930)
Lowest batting average: .214 (1968)
Most singles: 1,237 (1988)
Most doubles: 325 (1997)
Most triples: 110 (1930)
Most home runs: 240 (1961)
Most consecutive games with a home run: 25 (1941)
Most grand slams: 10 (1987)
Most pinch-hit home runs: 10 (1961)
Most total bases: 2,703 (1936)
Most bases on balls: 766 (1932)
Most hit by pitch: 57 (1998)
Fewest hit by pitch: 14 (1969)
Most stolen bases: 289 (1910)
Fewest stolen bases: 24 (1948)
Most caught stealing: 82 (1920)
Fewest caught stealing: 18 (1961, 1964)
Most strikeouts: 1,043 (1967)
Fewest strikeouts: 420 (1924)
Highest slugging percentage: .489 (1927)
Lowest slugging percentage: .287 (1914)
Most grounded into double plays: 153 (1996)
Fewest grounded into double plays: 91 (1963)
Most left on base: 1,258 (1996)
Fewest left on base: 1,010 (1920)
Most .300 hitters: 9 (1930)
Most hitters with 10 or more home runs: 10 (1998)

SINGLE-SEASON CLUB PITCHING RECORDS:

Lowest ERA: 2.57 (1904)
Highest ERA: 4.88 (1930)
Most innings pitched: 1,506.2 (1964)
Most complete games: 123 (1904)
Fewest complete games: 3 (1991)
Most shutouts: 24 (1951)
Most consecutive shutouts: 4 (1932)
Most consecutive shutout innings: 40 (1932)

Fewest shutouts: 2 (1994)
Most saves (since 1969): 58 (1986)
Fewest hits allowed: 1,143 (1919)
Most hits allowed: 1,566 (1930)
Fewest home runs allowed: 13 (1907)
Most home runs allowed: 179 (1987)
Fewest runs allowed: 507 (1942)
Most runs allowed: 898 (1930)
Fewest bases on balls: 245 (1903)
Most bases on balls: 812 (1949)
Fewest strikeouts: 431 (1927)
Most strikeouts: 1,165 (1997)

SINGLE-SEASON CLUB FIELDING RECORDS

Highest fielding percentage: .986 (1995)
Lowest fielding percentage: .939 (1912)
Fewest errors: 91 (1996)
Most errors: 386 (1912)
Most errorless games: 91 (1964)
Most consecutive errorless games 10 (1977, 1993, 1995)
Most double plays: 214 (1956)
Fewest double plays: 81 (1912)
Most consecutive games, double play turned: 19 (*27 DPs*) (1992)
Most passed balls: 32 (1913)
Fewest passed balls: 0 (1931)

Single Game/Inning Club Batting Records:

MOST RUNS

Game, 9 innings, home: 22 (7/26/31 vs. Chicago, Game 2)
Game, 9 innings, road: 25 (5/24/36 at Philadelphia)
Game, both teams, road: 33 (3 times; last 6/3/32 at Philadelphia, 20-13)
Game, both teams, home: 30 (4/10/98 vs. Oakland)
Game, opponent, home: 19 (6/17/25 vs. Detroit; 9/10/77 vs. Toronto)
Game, opponent, road: 24 (7/29/28 at Cleveland)
Shutout game: 21 (8/13/39 at Philadelphia)
Shutout game, opponent: 15 (7/15/07 at Chicago; 5/4/50 vs. Chicago)
Inning: 14 (7/6/20 at Washington, 5th inning)

BATTING

Most hits in one game, 9 innings:
30 (9/28/23 vs. Boston)
Most hits in one game, both teams:
45 (9/29/28 at Detroit)
Most singles: 22 (8/12/53 at Washington)
Most doubles: 10 (4/12/88 at Toronto)
Most triples: 5 (5/1/34 at Washington)
Most home runs, game: 8 (6/28/39 vs. Philadelphia, Game 1)
Most home runs, game, vs. one pitcher: 6 (Al Thomas, 6/27/36 vs. Philadelphia)
Most home runs, inning: 4 (6/30/77 at Toronto. Johnson (2), Piniella, Munson)
Most home runs, consecutive: 3 (9 times, last on 5/8/94 vs. Boston)
Most walks, game: 16 (6/23/15 at Philadelphia)
Most strikeouts, game: 17 (9/10/99 vs. Boston)
Most stolen bases, game: 15 (9/28/11 vs. St. Louis)
Most stolen bases, game, both teams: 15 (9/28/11 vs. St. Louis: NY 15, STL 0)
Most steals of home, game: 3 (4/17/15 vs. Philadelphia)
Most left on base, game, 9 innings: 20 (9/21/56 vs. Boston)
Most left on base, game, extra innings: 23 (9/5/27 at Boston, Game 1)

SINGLE-GAME/INNING CLUB PITCHING RECORDS

Most hits allowed, game: 28 (9/29/28 at Detroit)
Most runs allowed, game: 24 (7/29/28 at Cleveland)
Most runs allowed, inning: 13 (6/17/25 vs. Detroit)
Most home runs allowed, game: 6 (3 times, last on 5/30/97 at Boston)
Most home runs allowed, inning: 4 (5/2/92 vs. Minnesota)
Most strikeouts, game: 18 (6/17/78, vs. California)
Most bases on balls, game: 17 (9/11/49 vs. Washington)
Most bases on balls, inning: 11 (9/11/49 vs. Washington, 3rd inning)
Most wild pitches, game: 3 (many times)

SINGLE-GAME CLUB MISCELLANEOUS

Longest game, innings: 22 (6/24/62 at Detroit; NY 9, Det. 7)
Longest game time: 4:22 (9/5/97 vs. Baltimore)

INDIVIDUAL SINGLE-GAME PITCHING RECORDS

Most runs allowed, game: 13, Warhop (7/31/11 vs. Chicago), Caldwell (10/3/13 at Philadelphia), C. Mays (7/17/23 at Cleveland)
Most hits allowed, game: 21, Jack Quinn (6/29/12 at Boston)
Most home runs allowed, inning: 4, Catfish Hunter (6/17/77 at Boston 1st inning) Scott Sanderson
Most home runs allowed, game: 5 , John Cumberland (5/24/70 at Cleveland)
Most strikeouts, game, LHP: 18, Ron Guidry (6/17/78 vs. California)
Most strikeouts, game RHP: 16, David Cone (6/23/97 at Detroit)
Most strikeouts, relief: 8, Ron Davis (5/4/81 at California)
Most strikeouts, consecutive: 8, Ron Davis (5/4/81 at California)
Most bases on balls, game: 13, Tommy Byrne (6/8/49 at Detroit)
Most balks, game: 4, Vic Raschi (5/3/50 vs. Chicago)

INDIVIDUAL SINGLE-GAME BATTING RECORDS

Most at-bats: 11, Bobby Richardson (6/24/62 at Detroit)
Most runs: 5, 13 times by 10 players (last, Tino Martinez, 4/2/97 at Seattle)
Most hits: 6, Myril Hoag (6/6/34 at Boston)
Most hits, extra innings: 6, Gerald Williams (5/1/96 at Baltimore, 15 innings)
Most singles: 6, Myril Hoag (6/6/34 at Boston)
Most doubles: 4, J. Lindell (8/17/44 vs. Cleveland), J. Mason (7/8/74 at Texas)
Most triples: 3, H. Chase (8/30/06 vs. Washington), E. Combs (9/22/27 vs. Detroit), J. DiMaggio, (8/27/38 vs. Cleveland, Game 1)
Most home runs: 4, Lou Gehrig (6/3/32 at Philadelphia)

Most grand slams: 2, Tony Lazzeri (5/24/36 at Philadelphia)
Most total bases: 16, Lou Gehrig (6/3/32 at Philadelphia)
Most RBI: 11, Tony Lazzeri (5/24/36 at Philadelphia)
Most sacrifice flies: 3, B. Meusel (9/15/26 at Cleveland), D. Mattingly (5/3/86 vs. Texas)
Most stolen bases: 4, 16 times, last by Gerald Williams (6/2/96 at Detroit)
Most walks: 5, 6 times, last by Hersh Martin (9/1/45 at Washington)
Most strikeouts: 5, Johnny Broaca (6/25/34 vs. Chicago), Bernie Williams (8/1/91 vs. Minn.)

INDIVIDUAL SINGLE-SEASON PITCHING RECORDS

Most wins, RHP: 41, Jack Chesbro (1904)
Most wins, LHP: 26, Lefty Gomez (1934)
Most consecutive wins, RHP: 14, Jack Chesbro (1904)
Most consecutive wins, LHP: 14, Whitey Ford (1961)
Most shutouts: 9, Ron Guidry (1978)
Most shutouts lost: 7, Bill Zuber (1945)
Lowest ERA, RHP: 1.64, Spud Chandler (1943)
Lowest ERA, LHP: 1.74, Ron Guidry (1978)
Highest winning pct: .893, Ron Guidry (1978)
Most losses, RHP: 22, Joe Lake (1908)
Most losses, LHP: 17, Herb Pennock (1921)
Most consecutive losses, RHP: 9, Bill Hogg (1908), Thad Tillotson (1967)
Most consecutive losses, LFP: 11, George Mogridge (1916)
Most innings pitched, RHP: 454, Jack Chesbro (1904)
Most innings pitched, LHP: 286 1/3, Herb Pennock (1924)
Most saves, RHP: 45, Mariano Rivera (1999)
Most saves, LHP: 46, Dave Righetti (1986)
Most games, RHP: 77, Jeff Nelson (1997)
Most games, LHP: 74, Dave Righetti (1985, 1986)
Most games started: 51, Jack Chesbro (1904)
Most complete games: 48, Jack Chesbro (1904)

Most strikeouts, RHP: 239, Jack Chesbro
(1904)
Most strikeouts, LHP: 248, Ron Guidry
(1978)
Most walks, RHP: 177, Bob Turley (1955)
Most walks, LHP: 179, Tommy Byrne
(1949)
Most hits allowed: 337, Jack Chesbro
(1904)
Most runs allowed: 165, Russ Ford (1912)
Most earned runs allowed: 127, Sam Jones
(1925)
Most home runs allowed: 40, Ralph Terry
(1962)
Most wild pitches: 23, Tim Leary (1990)

INDIVIDUAL SINGLE-SEASON BATTING RECORDS

Most at-bats: 692, Bobby Richardson
(1962)
Highest batting average: .393, Babe Ruth
(1923)
Most hits: 238, Don Mattingly (1986)
Most consecutive games hitting safely:
56, Joe DiMaggio (1941)
Most runs: 177, Babe Ruth (1921)
Most singles: 171, Steve Sax (1989)
Most doubles: 53, Don Mattingly (1986)
Most triples: 23, Earle Combs (1927)
Most home runs, lefthander: 61, Roger
Maris (1961)
Most home runs, righthander: 46, Joe
DiMaggio (1937)
Most home runs, switch-hitter: 54, Mickey
Mantle (1961)
Most consecutive games, run scored:
18, Red Rolfe (1939)
Most home runs, home (Polo Grounds):
32, Babe Ruth (1921)
Most home runs, home (Yankee Stadium):
30, Lou Gehrig (1934); Roger Maris
(1961)
Most home runs, road: 32, Babe Ruth
(1927)
Most home runs, month: 17, Babe Ruth
(1927)
Most home runs, rookie: 29, Joe DiMaggio
(1936)
Most consecutive games, home run: 8,
Don Mattingly (1987)
Most grand slams: 6, Don Mattingly (1987)
Most RBI: 184, Lou Gehrig (1931)
Most consecutive games, RBI: 11, Babe
Ruth (1931)

Most extra-base hits: 119, Babe Ruth
(1921)
Most total bases: 457, Babe Ruth (1921)
Most strikeouts: 156, Danny Tartabull
(1993)
Most walks: 170, Babe Ruth (1923)
Most sacrifice hits: 42, Willie Keeler (1905)
Most sacrifice flies: 17, Roy White (1971)
Most stolen bases: 93, Rickey Henderson
(1988)
Most times, caught stealing: 23, Ben
Chapman (1931)
Most hit by pitch: 24, Don Baylor (1985)
Most grounded into double play: 30, Dave
Winfield (1983)
Fewest grounded into double play: 2,
Mickey Mantle (1961); Mickey Rivers
(1977)

YANKEE 20-GAME WINNERS

1903 Jack Chesbro, 21-15
1904 Jack Chesbro, 41-12; Jack Powell
23-19
1906 Al Orth, 27-17; Jack Chesbro, 24-16
1910 Russ Ford, 26-6
1911 Russ Ford, 22-11
1916 Bob Shawkey, 24-14
1919 Bob Shawkey, 20-11
1920 Carl Mays, 26-11; Bob Shawkey
20-13
1921 Carl Mays, 27-9
1922 Joe Bush, 26-7; Bob Shawkey
20-12
1923 Sam Jones, 21-8
1924 Herb Pennock, 21-9
1926 Herb Pennock, 23-11
1927 Waite Hoyt, 22-7
1928 George Pipgras, 24-13;
Waite Hoyt, 23-7
1931 Lefty Gomez, 21-9
1932 Lefty Gomez, 24-7
1934 Lefty Gomex, 26-5
1936 Red Ruffing, 20-12
1937 Lefty Gomez, 21-11;
Red Ruffing 20-7
1938 Red Ruffing, 21-7
1939 Red Ruffing, 21-7
1942 Tiny Bonham, 21-5
1943 Spud Chandler, 20-4
1946 Spud Chandler, 20-8
1949 Vic Raschi, 21-10
1950 Vic Raschi, 21-8
1951 Eddie Lopat, 21-9;
VicRaschi, 21-10

1952 Allie Reynolds, 20-8
1954 Bob Grim, 20-6
1958 Bob Turley, 21-7
1961 Whitey Ford, 25-4
1962 Ralph Terry, 23-12
1963 Whitey Ford, 24-7;
Jim Bouton, 21-7
1965 Mel Stottlemyre, 20-9
1968 Mel Stottlemyre, 21-12
1969 Mel Stottlemyre, 20-14
1970 Fritz Peterson, 20-11
1975 Catfish Hunter, 23-14
1978 Ron Guidry, 25-3;
Ed Figueroa, 20-9
1979 Tommy John, 21-9
1980 Tommy John, 22-9
1983 Ron Guidry, 21-9
1985 Ron Guidry, 22-6
1996 Andy Pettitte, 21-8
1998 David Cone, 20-7

Yankee Individual Champions

BATTING CHAMPIONS

1924 Babe Ruth, .378
1934 Lou Gehrig, .363
1939 Joe DiMaggio, .381
1940 Joe DiMaggio, .352
1945 Snuffy Stirnweiss, .309
1956 Mickey Mantle, .353
1984 Don Mattingly, .343
1994 Paul O'Neill, .359
1998 Bernie Williams, .339

HOME RUN CHAMPIONS

1916 Wally Pipp, 12
1917 Wally Pipp, 9
1920 Babe Ruth, 54
1921 Babe Ruth, 59
1923 Babe Ruth, 41
1924 Babe Ruth, 46
1925 Bob Meusel, 33
1926 Babe Ruth, 47
1927 Babe Ruth, 60
1928 Babe Ruth, 54
1929 Babe Ruth, 46
1930 Babe Ruth, 49
1931 Babe Ruth, 46

1931 Lou Gehrig, 46
1934 Lou Gehrig, 49
1936 Lou Gehrig, 49
1937 Joe DiMaggio, 46
1944 Nick Etten, 22
1948 Joe DiMaggio, 39
1955 Mickey Mantle, 37
1956 Mickey Mantle, 52
1958 Mickey Mantle, 42
1960 Mickey Mantle, 40
1961 Roger Maris, 61
1976 Graig Nettles, 32
1980 Reggie Jackson, 41

HITTING FOR THE CYCLE

(single, double, triple, home run in one game)

1912 Bert Daniels, of, vs. Chicago (July 25)
1921 Bob Meusel, of, at Washington (May 7)
1922 Bob Meusel, of, at Philadelphia (July 3)
1928 Bob Meusel, of, at Detroit (July 26)
1932 Tony Lazzeri, 2b, at Philadelphia (June 3)
1934 Lou Gehrig, 1b, vs. Chicago (June 25)
1937 Joe DiMaggio, of, vs. Washington (July 9)
1937 Lou Gehrig, 1b, vs. St. Louis (Aug 1)
1940 Buddy Rosar, c, vs. Cleveland (July 19)
1940 Joe Gordon, 2b, at Boston (Sept 8)
1948 Joe DiMaggio, of, at Chicago (May 20)
1957 Mickey Mantle, of, vs. Chicago (July 23)
1972 Bobby Murcer, of, vs. Texas (Aug 29, Game 1)
1995 Tony Fernandez, ss, vs. Oakland (Sept 3)

MVPs (MOST VALUABLE PLAYERS)

1923 Babe Ruth
1927 Lou Gehrig
1936 Lou Gehrig
1939 Joe DiMaggio
1941 Joe DiMaggio
1942 Joe Gordon

1943 Spud Chandler
1947 Joe DiMaggio
1950 Phil Rizzuto
1951 Yogi Berra
1954 Yogi Berra
1955 Yogi Berra
1956 Mickey Mantle
1957 Mickey Mantle
1960 Roger Maris
1961 Roger Maris
1962 Mickey Mantle
1963 Elston Howard
1976 Thurman Munson
1985 Don Mattingly

CY YOUNG AWARD WINNERS

1958 Bob Turley
1961 Whitey Ford
1977 Sparky Lyle
1978 Ron Guidry

AL CHAMPIONSHIP SERIES MVP

1981 Graig Nettles
1996 Bernie Williams
1998 David Wells

WORLD SERIES MVP

1949 Joe Page
1950 Jerry Coleman
1951 Phil Rizzuto
1952 Johnny Mize
1953 Billy Martin
1956 Don Larsen
1958 Elston Howard
1961 Whitey Ford
1962 Ralph Terry
1977 Reggie Jackson
1978 Bucky Dent
1996 Cecil Fielder
1998 Scott Brosius
1999 Mariano Rivera
2000 Derek Jeter

(Note: Beginning in 1955, *Sport* magazine also awarded a World Series MVP. *Sport's* MVP differed from the writers' MVP in the following seasons. 1958: Bob Turley and 1996: John Wetteland. In addition, in 1960, *Sport* awarded its MVP to Bobby Richardson. The baseball writers named Roberto Clemente of the Pirates.)

ROOKIE OF THE YEAR

1951 Gil McDougald, 3b
1954 Bob Grim, p
1957 Tony Kubek, inf-of
1962 Tom Tresh, ss-of
1968 Stan Bahnsen, p
1970 Thurman Munson, c
1981 Dave Righetti, p
1996 Derek Jeter, ss

GOLD GLOVE AWARD WINNERS

1957 Bobby Shantz, p
1958 Bobby Shantz, p; Norm Sieburn, of
1959 Bobby Shantz, p
1960 Bobby Shantz, p; Roger Maris, of
1961 Bobby Richardson, 2b
1962 Bobby Richardson, 2b; Mickey Mantle, of
1963 Elston Howard, c; Bobby Richardson, 2b
1964 Elston Howard, c; Bobby Richardson, 2b
1965 Joe Pepitone, 1b; Bobby Richardson, 2b; Tom Tresh, of
1966 Joe Pepitone, 1b
1969 Joe Pepitone, 1b
1972 Bobby Murcer, of
1973 Thurman Munson, c
1974 Thurman Munson, c
1975 Thurman Munson, c
1977 Graig Nettles, 3b
1978 Graig Nettles, 3b; Chris Chambliss, 1b
1982 Ron Guidry, p; Dave Winfield, of
1983 Ron Guidry, p; Dave Winfield, of
1984 Ron Guidry, p; Dave Winfield, of
1985 Ron Guidry, p; Dave Winfield, of; Don Mattingly, 1b
1986 Ron Guidry, p; Don Mattingly, 1b
1987 Dave Winfield, of; Don Mattingly, 1b
1988 Don Mattingly, 1b
1989 Don Mattingly, 1b
1991 Don Mattingly, 1b
1992 Don Mattingly, 1b
1993 Don Mattingly, 1b
1994 Don Mattingly, 1b; Wade Boggs, 3b
1995 Wade Boggs, 3b
1997 Bernie Williams, of
1998 Bernie Williams, of
1999 Bernie Williams, of; Scott Brosius, 3b
2000 Bernie Williams, of

Photo Credits

AP Photo/FILE: p. 425

AP/Lenny Ignelzi: p. 32

AP/Ron Frehm: p. 74

Baseball Hall of Fame
Library/Cooperstown, NY: pp. 10, 14, 24,
34, 40, 49, 52, 60, 62, 67, 70

Major League Baseball: pp. 20, 121, 149,
169, 201, 230, 233, 234, 236, 258, 264,
272, 273, 279, 282, 285, 295, 339, 341,
384, 402, 412, 418, 438, 449, 492, 502,
504, 506

Rich Pilling/Major League Baseball:
pp. 100, 119, 185, 198, 237

Steve Crandall Studio ©: p. 81

Transcendental Graphics: pp. 28, 31, 44,
57, 78, 92, 95, 109, 112, 122, 124, 126,
128, 130, 132, 138, 147, 154, 157, 174,
187, 193, 208, 210, 216, 220, 241, 247,
251, 255, 256, 268, 269, 284, 291, 301,
306, 312, 320, 328, 338, 434, 360, 377,
379, 410, 432, 434, 449, 454, 455, 462,
476, 485, 487, 489, 491, 494, 497, 499,
509, 516, 520, 525, 534